D0085037

The Duxbury Series
in Statistics and Decision Sciences

Applications, Basics, and Computing of Exploratory Data Analysis Velleman/Hoaglin

Applied Regression Analysis for Business and Economics Dielman

Elementary Statistics, Fifth Edition Johnson

Elementary Statistics for Business, Second Edition Johnson/Siskin

Essential Business Statistics: A Minitab Framework Bond/Scott

Fundamentals of Biostatistics, Third Edition Rosner

Fundamental Statistics for the Behavioral Sciences, Second Edition Howell

Introduction to Mathematical Programming: Applications and Algorithms Winston

Introduction to Probability and Statistics, Eighth Edition Mendenhall/Beaver

An Introduction to Statistical Methods and Data Analysis, Third Edition Ott

Introductory Business Statistics with Microcomputer Applications Shiffler/Adams

Introductory Statistical Methods: An Integrated Approach Using Minitab Groeneveld

Introductory Statistics for Management and Economics, Third Edition Kenkel

Making Hard Decisions: An Introduction to Decision Analysis Clemen

Mathematical Statistics with Applications, Fourth Edition Mendenhall/Wackerly/Scheaffer

Minitab Handbook, Second Edition Ryan/Joiner/Ryan

Minitab Handbook for Business and Economics Miller

Operations Research: Applications and Algorithms, Second Edition Winston

Probability and Statistics for Engineers, Third Edition Scheaffer/McClave

Probability and Statistics for Modern Engineering, Second Edition Lapin

SAS Applications Programming: A Gentle Introduction DiIorio

Statistical Methods for Psychology, Second Edition Howell

Statistical Thinking for Managers, Third Edition Hildebrand/Ott

Statistics: A Tool for the Social Sciences, Fourth Edition Ott/Larson/Mendenhall

Statistics for Business and Economics Bechtold/Johnson

Statistics for Business: Data Analysis and Modelling Cryer/Miller

Statistics for Management and Economics, Sixth Edition Mendenhall/Reinmuth/Beaver

Student Edition of Execustat the authors of Statgraphics

Understanding Statistics, Fifth Edition Ott/Mendenhall

The Duxbury Advanced Series
in Statistics and Decision Sciences

Applied Nonparametric Statistics, Second Edition Daniel

Applied Regression Analysis and Other Multivariate Methods, Second Edition Kleinbaum/Kupper/Muller

Classical and Modern Regression with Applications, Second Edition Myers

Elementary Survey Sampling, Fourth Edition Scheaffer/Mendenhall/Ott

A First Course in the Theory of Linear Statistical Models Myers/Milton

Introduction to Contemporary Statistical Methods, Second Edition Koopmans

Introduction to Probability and Its Applications Scheaffer

Introduction to Probability and Mathematical Statistics Bain/Engelhardt

Linear Statistical Models: An Applied Approach, Second Edition Bowerman/O'Connell

Probability Modeling and Computer Simulation Matloff

Quantitative Forecasting Methods Farnum/Stanton

Time Series Analysis Cryer

Time Series Forecasting: Unified Concepts and Computer Implementation, Second Edition Bowerman/O'Connell

Operations Research

Applications and Algorithms

EDITION 2

Operations Research
Applications and Algorithms

WAYNE L. WINSTON
Indiana University

PWS-KENT PUBLISHING COMPANY ◆ BOSTON

To my lovely and talented wife Vivian

 PWS–KENT
Publishing Company

Editor:	Michael Payne
Assistant Editor:	Marcia Cole
Production Editor:	Eve B. Mendelsohn
Manufacturing Coordinator:	Peter Leatherwood
Interior Designer:	Eve B. Mendelsohn
Production:	Hoyt Publishing Services
Cover Designer:	Eve B. Mendelsohn
Compositor:	The Alden Press
Cover Printer:	John P. Pow Company, Inc.
Text Printer and Binder:	R. R. Donnelley and Sons

Cover Art: MALEVICH, Kasimir. *Suprematist Composition: Airplane Flying*. (1915; dated 1914) Oil on canvas, $22\frac{7}{8}''$ × $19''$. Collection, The Museum of Modern Art, New York. Purchase. Photograph © 1990 The Museum of Modern Art, New York.

PWS-KENT Publishing Company is a division of Wadsworth, Inc.

Printed in the United States of America.
  2 3 4 5 6—94 93 92 91

Library of Congress Cataloging-in-Publication Data

Winston, Wayne L.
    Operations research: applications and algorithms / Wayne L.
  Winston.—2nd ed.
      p.   cm.
    Includes bibliographical references and index.
    ISBN 0-534-92495-6
    1. Operations research.   I. Title.
  T57.6W647   1991
  003—dc20   90-7817
                                                 CIP

International Student Edition ISBN: 0-534-98079-1

Contents

*Starred sections may be omitted with no loss of continuity.

4 THE SIMPLEX ALGORITHM *125*

5** SENSITIVITY ANALYSIS: AN APPLIED APPROACH *189*

6** SENSITIVITY ANALYSIS AND DUALITY *225*

** Note: Instructors should cover Chapter 5 or Chapter 6, but not both.

23   SIMULATION *1113*

24   FORECASTING MODELS *1163*

Preface

In recent years, operations research software for mainframes and microcomputers has become widely available. Like most tools, however, it is useless unless the user understands its application and purpose. Users must ensure that mathematical input accurately reflects the real-life problems to be solved and that the numerical results are correctly applied to solve them. With this in mind, this book emphasizes model-formulation and model-building skills as well as the interpretation of software output.

This book is intended to be used as an advanced beginning or an intermediate text in operations research or mathematical programming. The following groups of students can benefit from using it:

- Undergraduate majors in quantitative methods in business, operations research, management science, or industrial engineering.
- MBA students enrolled in applications-oriented operations research, management science, or mathematical programming courses.
- Graduate students who need an overview of the major topics in operations research and management science.

The book contains enough material for a three-semester course; this allows instructors ample flexibility in adapting the text to their individual course plans. For instance, courses in which certain chapters would be applicable include:

- Linear programming: Chapters 2–10 (omitting either Chapter 5 or Chapter 6).
- Deterministic models in operations research: Chapters 2–12, 15–16, and 20 (again omitting either Chapter 5 or Chapter 6).
- Probabilistic models in operations research: Chapters 13–15, 17–19, and 21–24.

The linear programming section of the book (Chapters 2–10) is completely self-contained, with all necessary mathematical background given in Chapter 2. Students who are familiar with matrix multiplication should have no problems with Chapters 2–10. Portions of the remaining chapters require a rudimentary knowledge of calculus and probability—equivalent to that obtained from a one-semester calculus course and a one-semester business statistics course. All topics in calculus and probability used in Chapters 12–24 are reviewed in Chapter 11.

The following features help to make this book reader-friendly:

- To provide immediate feedback to students, problems have been placed at the end of each section, and most chapters conclude with review problems. There are more than 1200 problems, grouped according to difficulty: Group A for practice of basic techniques, Group B for underlying concepts, and Group C for mastering the theory independently.

- The book avoids excessive theoretical formulas in favor of word problems and interesting problem applications. Many problems are based on published applications of operations research and management science. The exposition takes great pains, by means of several examples in each chapter, to guide the student step-by-step through even complex topics. Operations research algorithms still receive comprehensive treatment; for instance, Karmarkar's method for solving linear programming problems is explained in detail.

- To help students review for tests, each chapter has a summary of concepts and formulas. An instructor's manual with complete solutions to all problems and advice for instructors is available to adopters of the text.

- Each section is written to be as self-contained as possible. This allows the instructor to be extremely flexible in designing a course. The instructor's manual identifies which portions of the book must be covered as prerequisites to each section.

- The book includes guidance in using the popular LINDO and GINO software packages and interpreting their output. If desired, PC versions of LINDO and GINO may be purchased with the book. The LINDO and GINO sections are completely self-contained, however, and classes that do not use them can simply skip those sections. Starred (∗) sections cover less important topics and may be omitted with no loss of continuity.

Since not all students need a full-blown theoretical treatment of sensitivity analysis, there are two chapters on the topic. Chapter 5 (a new chapter) is an applied approach to sensitivity analysis, emphasizing the interpretation of computer output. Chapter 6 contains a full discussion of sensitivity analysis, duality, and the dual simplex method. The instructor should cover Chapter 5 *or* Chapter 6, but not both. Classes emphasizing model-building and model-formulation skills should cover Chapter 5. Those paying close attention to the algorithms of mathematical programming (particularly classes in which many students will go on to further operations research courses) should study Chapter 6. If Chapter 5 rather than Chapter 6 is covered, then Chapter 2 may be omitted.

Operations Research: Applications and Algorithms seeks to cover the important topics in operations research and management science at a beginning-to-intermediate level. It is hoped that after reading the book's discussions of particular topics, students will be able to (and will want to) delve into the more specialized references at the end of the chapters, which take up the topics in more detail.

◆ CHANGES IN THE SECOND EDITION

The favorable response to the first edition of this book has been truly gratifying. Many suggestions from users of the text have been incorporated into the second edition. There are several hundred new problems (mostly formulation and word problems) and minor changes in many sections of the book. Discussions of the following topics have been added:

1. Three-dimensional geometry of an LP's feasible region (in Section 4.2)

2. A discussion of matrix generators and scaling of LPs (in Section 4.8)

3. An "applied" sensitivity analysis chapter, emphasizing the graphical approach and interpretation of computer output (Chapter 5)

4. Rewrites of the discussion of the transshipment problem (Section 7.6) and the shortest path problem (Section 8.2), which make the approach more consistent with that of other books

5. A completely new section on Karmarkar's method for solving LPs (Section 10.6)

6. The network simplex method (Section 8.7)

7. Heuristic methods for the traveling salesperson problem (Section 9.6)

8. The cutting plane method for integer programming problems (Section 9.9)

9. The method of feasible directions for solving nonlinear programming problems (Section 12.11)

10. An introduction to the GINO software package for solving nonlinear programming problems (Section 12.12)

11. Bayesian inference with the normal distribution (Section 13.5)

12. Use of the analytical hierarchy principle (AHP) in decision-making problems involving multiple objectives (Section 14.3)

13. Extended coverage of inventory theory, including the (R, S) periodic review model (Section 17.8), the ABC classification method (Section 17.9), and recent advances in inventory theory such as MRP, just-in-time production, and exchange curves (Chapter 18)

14. First passage times in Markov chains (Section 19.5)

15. Average reward per period criterion in Markov decision processes (Section 21.5)

16. "Open" queuing networks (Section 22.10)

17. A new chapter on forecasting (Chapter 24), including comprehensive coverage of extrapolation and regression forecasting methods

◆ ACKNOWLEDGMENTS

Many people have played significant roles in the development of the second edition. My views on teaching operations research were greatly influenced by the many excellent teachers I have had, including Gordon Bradley, Eric Denardo, George Fishman, Richard Larson, John Little, Robert Mifflin, Matthew Sobel, Harvey Wagner, and Ward Whitt. In particular, I would like to acknowledge Professor Wagner's *Principles of Operations Research*, which taught me more about operations research than any other single book.

The LINDO and GINO printouts throughout the book appear courtesy of Professor Linus Schrage. I would also like to thank Professor Ashok Soni for his contributions to Chapter 23.

Kathy Wilson diligently proofread the manuscript, and Rob Easley, Avi Kreusch, and John Willems checked the page proofs. Nyla Fulk and Teena Albright did a great job of getting it ready for publication. Special thanks go to the helpful people at PWS-KENT: Senior Editor Michael Payne, Production Supervisor Eve Mendelsohn, and Assistant Editor Marcia Cole, as well as David Hoyt of Hoyt Publishing Services, who coordinated the production of the text.

Finally, I owe a great debt to the following reviewers of the second edition whose comments greatly improved the quality of the manuscript: Sant Arora, University of Minnesota; Harold Benson, University of Florida; Bruce Bowerman, Miami University (Oxford); Jerald Dauer, University of Tennessee; Yahya Fathi, North Carolina State University; Robert Freund, Massachusetts Institute of Technology; Irwin Greenberg, George Mason University; John Hooker, Carnegie-Mellon University; Patrick Lee, Pennsylvania State University; Sudhakar Pandit, Michigan Technological University; David Pentico, Duquesne University; Michael Richey, George Mason University; Lawrence Seiford, University of Massachusetts, Amherst; and Michael Stinchcomb, University of California at San Diego.

I retain responsibility for all errors and would greatly appreciate any comments on the book.

Wayne L. Winston

CHAPTER 1

Introduction to Operations Research

DURING WORLD WAR II, British military leaders asked scientists and engineers to analyze several military problems: the deployment of radar and the management of convoy, bombing, antisubmarine, and mining operations. The application of mathematics and the scientific method to military operations was called operations research. Today, the term *operations research* (or, often, *management science*) means a scientific approach to decision making, which seeks to determine how best to design and operate a system, usually under conditions requiring the allocation of scarce resources.

1-1   THE METHODOLOGY OF OPERATIONS RESEARCH

When operations research is used to solve a problem of an organization, the following seven-step procedure should be followed (Figure 1).

STEP 1. FORMULATE THE PROBLEM

The operations research (or OR) analyst first defines the organization's problem. Defining the problem includes specifying the organization's objectives and the parts of the organization (or system) that must be studied before the problem can be solved.

To illustrate the idea of problem formulation, suppose that a bank manager hires an operations research analyst to help the bank reduce expenditures on tellers' salaries while still maintaining an adequate level of customer service. After discussion with the manager of the bank, how might the analyst describe the bank's objectives? Here are three possibilities:

1. The bank may want to minimize the weekly salary cost needed to ensure that the average time a customer waits in line is at most 3 minutes.

2. The bank may wish to minimize the weekly salary cost required to ensure that only 5% of all customers wait in line more than 3 minutes for a teller.

3. The bank may be willing to spend up to $1000 per week on tellers' salaries and minimize the average time a customer must wait in line for a teller, given the salary constraint.

1

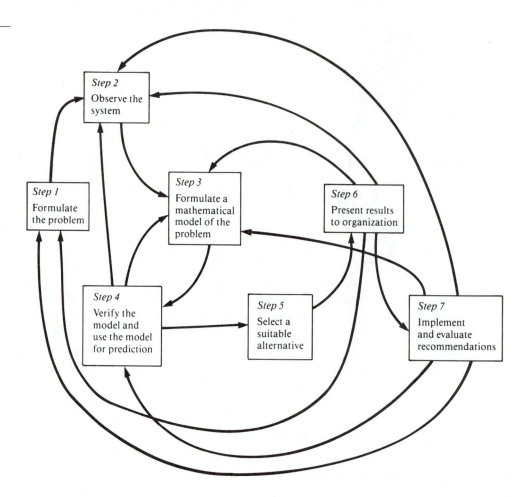

The analyst must also identify the aspects of the bank's operation that affect the achievement of the bank's objectives. For instance,

1. On the average, how many customers arrive at the bank each hour? The more customers, the more tellers will be needed to provide adequate service.

2. On the average, how many customers can a teller serve per hour?

3. How does having customers wait in a single line rather than in several tellers' lines affect the achievement of the bank's objectives?

4. If each teller has one line, will customers always join the shortest line? If one or another line becomes much longer, will customers jockey (or switch) between lines?

STEP 2. OBSERVE THE SYSTEM

Next, the analyst collects data to estimate the values of parameters that affect the organization's problem. These estimates are used to develop (in Step 3) and evaluate (in Step 4) a mathematical model of the organization's problem.

In our bank example, the analyst would collect data to estimate the following system parameters (among others):

1. On the average, how many customers arrive each hour? Does the arrival rate of customers depend on the time of day?

2. On the average, how many customers can a teller serve in one hour? Does the speed with which a teller serves customers depend on the number of customers waiting in line?

3. Do customers always join the shortest line? When at the end of a long line, do customers frequently switch to a shorter line?

STEP 3. FORMULATE A MATHEMATICAL MODEL OF THE PROBLEM

In this step, the analyst develops a mathematical model (or idealized representation) of the problem. In this book, we describe many mathematical techniques that can be used to model systems.

In our bank example, a mathematical model might be developed to predict the values of

W_q = average time customer waits in line

P = probability that a customer will spend at least 3 minutes waiting in line

based on knowing the following parameters:

λ = average number of customers arriving at the bank each hour

μ = average number of customers a teller can serve in an hour

s = number of bank tellers

Configuration of tellers and the manner in which customers join lines

A mathematical model that yields an equation relating these four parameters to W_q or P would be an example of an **analytic model**. (Analytic models of waiting-line problems are discussed in Chapter 22.) For instance, it can be shown that if there is only one teller, then under certain conditions

$$W_q = \frac{\lambda}{\mu(\mu - \lambda)} \tag{1}$$

Thus, the analyst knowing these parameters could use Eq. (1) to determine how well the system (the bank) is controlling W_q.

Many situations, however, are so complex that no analytic model exists. For example, if customers switch between lines, then in most situations there is no "tractable" mathematical equation that can be used to relate the four parameters to W_q or P. When no tractable analytic model exists, one must often develop a **simulation model**, which enables a computer to approximate the behavior of the actual system. (Simulation models are discussed in Chapter 23.)

STEP 4. VERIFY THE MODEL AND USE THE MODEL FOR PREDICTION

The analyst now tries to determine if the mathematical model developed in Step 3 is an accurate representation of reality. To determine how well the model fits reality, one determines how valid the model is for the current situation. For instance, in the bank example, suppose one believes the situation satisfies the conditions for which Eq. (1) is valid. Then current estimates of the parameters might be substituted into (1), and one would see how well (1) predicts the observed values of W_q. If the model's predictions of W_q and P are not close to the actual values (found by observing the bank), a new model is surely needed. In this case, one would return (note the feedback arrows in Figure 1) to either Step 2 or Step 3 and develop a new model that better describes the actual situation. Even if the first model does fit the current situation, one must beware of blindly applying it. For example, one might develop a model for the bank example that accurately predicts W_q and P when the bank is not crowded. If the bank attracts more customers and becomes more congested, however, the validity of the model under the new situation must be carefully checked.

STEP 5. SELECT A SUITABLE ALTERNATIVE

Given a model and a set of alternatives, the analyst now chooses the alternative (if there is one) that best meets the organization's objectives. For instance, in our bank example, one might determine the employment policy that minimizes the weekly salary cost needed to ensure that the average customer waits in line at most 3 minutes.

Sometimes the set of available alternatives is subject to certain restrictions or constraints. For example, suppose the bank can hire both full-time tellers and part-time tellers (who must work 4 consecutive hours per day). Assume that part-time tellers are less costly but work more slowly than full-time tellers. One might wish to minimize the average time a customer waits in line, subject to the following constraints:

1. At most $2000 per week can be spent on tellers' salaries.
2. Part-time tellers can work at most one quarter of all hours worked each week.

In many situations, the best alternative may be impossible or too costly to determine. For example, a firm considering purchasing a microcomputer might want to buy the one that best satisfies the following criteria:

1. Most economical computer
2. Ease of use
3. Most useful software available
4. Speed of operation

It is likely that no single computer will be the best with respect to all four criteria. Suppose three computers are under consideration. Computer A may be best with respect to criteria 1 and 3 and worst with respect to criteria 2 and 4; Computer B may be best on criteria 2 and 4 but less good for the others; and Computer C may be second best with respect to all the criteria. Which computer would best meet the firm's objectives? This is a difficult question that can be answered using the theory of multiattribute decision making (discussed in Chapter 14).

Even if a best alternative does exist, it may often be extremely costly to determine. Consider a food-processing company. Foodco, that produces canned foods and wants to minimize the cost of its warehousing and distribution operations. There are 200 sites under consideration for location of warehouses. Foodco's goal is to minimize the sum of warehousing costs (including costs of building and operating warehouses) plus the total cost of shipping the company's products from manufacturing plants to warehouses and from warehouses to customers. Clearly, Foodco would be interested in answers to the following questions:

1. How many warehouses should be built?
2. Where should the warehouses be built?
3. What should be the size (storage capacity) of each warehouse?
4. From which warehouse should a given customer receive shipments?

It is not difficult (see Chapter 9) to formulate a mathematical model of Foodco's problem, but an exact solution to this problem is beyond the capacity of today's computers. Solution methods do exist, however, to determine (at reasonable computational cost) a warehousing and distribution strategy that comes close (within 1–2%) to the minimum possible cost.

STEP 6. PRESENT THE RESULTS AND CONCLUSIONS OF THE STUDY TO THE ORGANIZATION

In this step, the analyst presents the model and recommendations from Step 5 to the decision-making individual or group. In some situations, one might present several alternatives and let the organization choose the alternative that best meets its needs.

After presenting the results of the operations research study to the organization, the analyst may find that the organization does not approve of the recommendations. This may result from incorrect definition of the organization's problems or from failure to involve the decision maker from the start of the project. In this case, the analyst should return to Step 1, 2, or 3 (see Figure 1).

STEP 7. IMPLEMENT AND EVALUATE RECOMMENDATIONS

If the organization has accepted the study, the analyst aids in implementing the recommendations. The system must be constantly monitored (and updated dynamically as the environment changes) to ensure that the recommendations are enabling the organization to meet its objectives. For instance, in the bank example, suppose the objective is to ensure that at most 5% of customers wait more than 3 minutes. Suppose that after the analyst's suggestions are implemented, 80% of customers spend more than 3 minutes in line. Then the bank's objective is clearly not being met, and the analyst should return to Step 1, 2, or 3 and re-examine the model (see Figure 1).

1-2   SUCCESSFUL APPLICATIONS OF OPERATIONS RESEARCH

In this section, we list several applications of operations research. In many of them, the business or government agency involved saved millions of dollars by successfully applying operations research models.

1. *Police Patrol Officer Scheduling in San Francisco.* Using linear programming (see Chapter 3), goal programming (see Chapter 14), and integer programming (see Chapter 9), Taylor and Huxley (1989) devised a method to schedule patrol officers for the San Francisco Police Department. By using their method, the department has saved $11 million per year, improved response times by 20%, and increased revenue from traffic citations by $3 million per year.

2. *Reducing Fuel Costs in the Electric Power Industry.* By using probabilistic dynamic programming (see Chapter 21) and a simulation model (see Chapter 23), Chao et al. (1989) saved 79 electric utilities over $125 million in purchasing, inventory, and shortage costs.

3. *Designing an Ingot Mold Stripping Facility at Bethlehem Steel.* Using integer programming (see Chapter 9), Vasko et al. (1989) helped Bethlehem Steel design an ingot mold stripping facility. The integer programming model has saved Bethlehem $8 million per year in operating costs.

4. *Gasoline Blending at Texaco.* Using the blending models discussed in Section 3.8 and nonlinear programming (discussed in Chapter 12), Dewitt et al. (1989) devised a model that is used by Texaco's refineries to determine how to blend incoming crude oils into leaded regular, unleaded regular, unleaded plus, and super unleaded gasolines. It is estimated that this model saves Texaco over $30 million annually. The model also allows Texaco to answer many what-if questions, such as what an increase of 0.01% in the sulfur content of regular gasoline will do to the cost of producing regular gasoline. The method used to answer such what-if questions is called **sensitivity analysis** and is discussed in Chapters 5 and 6.

5. *Scheduling Trucks at North American Van Lines.* Using network models (see Chapter 8) and dynamic programming (see Chapter 20), Powell et al. (1988) developed a model that is used to assign loads to North American Van Lines drivers. Use of this model has provided better service to customers and reduced costs by $2.5 million per year.

6. *Inventory Management at Blue Bell.* Blue Bell manufactures jeans, sportswear, and garments worn by white-collar workers. Using linear programming (see Chapter 3) and probabilistic inventory models (see Chapter 17), Edwards, Wagner, and Wood (1985) reduced Blue Bell's average inventory level by 31%.

7. *Using Linear Programming to Determine Bond Portfolios.* Linear programming (see Chapter 3) has been used by several people (see Chandy and Kharabe (1986)) to determine bond portfolios that maximize expected return subject to constraints on the level of risk and diversification in the portfolio.

8. *Using Linear Programming to Plan Creamery Production.* Sullivan and Secrest (1985) used linear programming (see Chapter 3) to determine how a creamery should process buttermilk, raw milk, sweet whey, and cream into cream cheese, cottage cheese, sour cream, and whey cream. Use of the model has increased the profitability of the creamery by $48,000 per year.

9. *Equipment Replacement at Phillips Petroleum.* How old should a car or truck be before a company should replace it? Phillips Petroleum (see Waddell (1983)) used equipment replacement models (discussed in Sections 8.2 and 20.5) to answer this question. These equipment replacement models are estimated to save Phillips $90,000 per year.

10. *Where Should a City Locate a New Airport?* Many objectives must be considered when determining the location of a new airport, including:

(a) Cost of building the airport
(b) Capacity it will provide
(c) Access time to the airport
(d) Safety of the system
(e) Social disruption caused in building it
(f) Noise pollution caused by airport operations

If no possible location site is best with regard to all objectives, where should the city choose to locate the new airport? Using the technique of multiattribute utility theory (discussed in Section 14.2), Keeney (1973) helped Mexico City determine where a new airport should be located.

1-3   WHERE TO READ MORE ABOUT OPERATIONS RESEARCH

Many journals publish articles involving the theory and applications of operations research: *Operations Research, Management Science, Interfaces, Mathematics of Operations Research, Marketing Science, AIIE Transactions, Decision Sciences, Mathematical Programming, European Journal of Operations Research, Production and Inventory Management, Omega,* and *Naval Research Logistics,* among others. For the reader who is particularly interested in present-day applications of OR, we heartily recommend *Interfaces.*

1-4   ABOUT THIS BOOK

In this book, we discuss many of the mathematical models commonly used by operations research analysts in modeling systems and organizations. In most chapters, we allocate at least as much space to the art of formulating mathematical models as to the solution of a mathematical model (selecting the best alternative). Even if the reader does not use most of the models discussed in this book, the emphasis on formulating mathematical models will be helpful in other quantitatively oriented courses and in any job in which quantitative reasoning ability is important.

We have tried to make this book as self-contained as possible. Certain chapters require a knowledge of basic differential and integral calculus and elementary probability theory, subjects reviewed in Chapter 11. Others require a knowledge of linear algebra, reviewed in Chapter 2.

Problems are given at the end of each section, with additional problems at the end of each chapter. We urge the reader to solve as many of the problems as possible. The best way to keep up with the material is to do some problems at the end of each section after attending a lecture. Remember that the only way to master the material covered in this book is by doing the problems!

◆ REFERENCES

CHANDY, P., and KHARABE, K. "Pricing in the Government Bond Market," *Interfaces* 16(1986, no. 1):65–71.

CHAO, H., ET AL. "EPRI Reduces Fuel Inventory Costs in the Electric Utility Industry," *Interfaces* 19(1989, no. 1):48–67.

DEWITT, C., ET AL. "OMEGA: An Improved Gasoline Blending System for Texaco," *Interfaces* 19(1989, no. 1):85–101.

EDWARDS, J., WAGNER, H., and WOOD, W. "Blue Bell Trims Its Inventory," *Interfaces* 15(1985, no. 1):34–53.

KEENEY, R. L. "A Decision Analysis with Multiple Objectives: The Mexico City Airport," *Bell Journal of Economics and Management Science* 4(1973):101–117.

POWELL, W., ET AL. "Maximizing Profits for North American Van Lines' Truckload Division: A New Framework for Pricing and Operations," *Interfaces* 18(1988, no. 1):21–41.

SULLIVAN, R., and SECREST, S. "A Simple Optimization DSS for Production Planning at Dairyman's Cooperative Creamery Association," *Interfaces* 15(1985, no. 5):46–53.

TAYLOR, P., and HUXLEY, S. "A Break from Tradition for the San Francisco Police: Patrol Officer Scheduling Using an Optimization-Based Decision Support System," *Interfaces* 19(1989, no. 1):4–24.

VASKO, F., ET AL. "Selecting Optimal Ingot Size for Bethlehem Steel," *Interfaces* 19(1989, no. 1):68–84.

WADDELL, R. "A Model for Equipment Replacement Decisions and Policies," *Interfaces* 13(1983, no. 4):1–7.

CHAPTER

2

Basic Linear Algebra

IN THIS CHAPTER, we study the topics in linear algebra that will be needed in the rest of the book. We begin by discussing the building blocks of linear algebra: matrices and vectors. Then we use our knowledge of matrices and vectors to develop a systematic procedure (the Gauss-Jordan method) for solving linear equations, which we then use to invert matrices. We close the chapter with an introduction to determinants.

The material covered in this chapter will be used in our study of linear programming, nonlinear programming, and Markov chains.

2-1 MATRICES AND VECTORS

MATRICES

DEFINITION A **matrix** is any rectangular array of numbers.

For example,

$$\begin{bmatrix} 1 & 2 \\ 3 & 4 \end{bmatrix}, \quad \begin{bmatrix} 1 & 2 & 3 \\ 4 & 5 & 6 \end{bmatrix}, \quad \begin{bmatrix} 1 \\ -2 \end{bmatrix}, \quad [2 \quad 1]$$

are all matrices.

If a matrix A has m rows and n columns, we call A an $m \times n$ matrix. We refer to $m \times n$ as the **order** of the matrix. A typical $m \times n$ matrix A may be written as

$$A = \begin{bmatrix} a_{11} & a_{12} & \cdots & a_{1n} \\ a_{21} & a_{22} & \cdots & a_{2n} \\ \vdots & \vdots & & \vdots \\ a_{m1} & a_{m2} & \cdots & a_{mn} \end{bmatrix}$$

DEFINITION The number in the ith row and jth column of A is called the **ijth element** of A and is written a_{ij}.

For example, if

$$A = \begin{bmatrix} 1 & 2 & 3 \\ 4 & 5 & 6 \\ 7 & 8 & 9 \end{bmatrix}$$

then $a_{11} = 1$, $a_{23} = 6$, and $a_{31} = 7$.

Sometimes we will use the notation $A = [a_{ij}]$ to indicate that A is the matrix whose ijth element is a_{ij}.

DEFINITION   Two matrices $A = [a_{ij}]$ and $B = [b_{ij}]$ are **equal** if and only if A and B are of the same order and for all i and j, $a_{ij} = b_{ij}$.

For example, if

$$A = \begin{bmatrix} 1 & 2 \\ 3 & 4 \end{bmatrix} \quad \text{and} \quad B = \begin{bmatrix} x & y \\ w & z \end{bmatrix}$$

then $A = B$ if and only if $x = 1$, $y = 2$, $w = 3$, and $z = 4$.

VECTORS

Any matrix with only one column (that is, any $m \times 1$ matrix) may be thought of as a **column vector**. The number of rows in a column vector is the **dimension** of the column vector. Thus,

$$\begin{bmatrix} 1 \\ 2 \end{bmatrix}$$

may be thought of as a 2×1 matrix or a two-dimensional column vector. R^m will denote the set of all m-dimensional column vectors.

In analogous fashion, we can think of any vector with only one row (a $1 \times n$ matrix) as a **row vector**. The dimension of a row vector is the number of columns in the vector. Thus, [9 2 3] may be viewed as a 1×3 matrix or a three-dimensional row vector. In this book, vectors appear in boldface type: for instance, vector **v**. An m-dimensional vector (either row or column) in which all elements equal zero is called a **zero vector** (written **0**). Thus,

$$[0 \quad 0] \quad \text{and} \quad \begin{bmatrix} 0 \\ 0 \end{bmatrix}$$

are two-dimensional zero vectors.

Any m-dimensional vector corresponds to a directed line segment in the m-dimensional plane. For example, in the two-dimensional plane, the vector

$$\mathbf{u} = \begin{bmatrix} 1 \\ 2 \end{bmatrix}$$

corresponds to the line segment joining the point

$$\begin{bmatrix} 0 \\ 0 \end{bmatrix}$$

to the point

$$\begin{bmatrix} 1 \\ 2 \end{bmatrix}$$

The directed line segments corresponding to

$$\mathbf{u} = \begin{bmatrix} 1 \\ 2 \end{bmatrix}, \qquad \mathbf{v} = \begin{bmatrix} 1 \\ -3 \end{bmatrix}, \qquad \mathbf{w} = \begin{bmatrix} -1 \\ -2 \end{bmatrix}$$

are drawn in Figure 1.

Figure 1
Vectors Are Directed
Line Segments

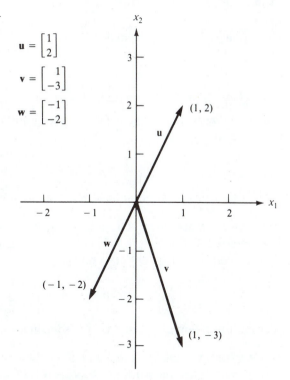

THE SCALAR PRODUCT OF TWO VECTORS

An important result of multiplying two vectors is the scalar product. To define the scalar product of two vectors, suppose we have a row vector $\mathbf{u} = [u_1 \quad u_2 \quad \cdots \quad u_n]$ and a column vector

$$\mathbf{v} = \begin{bmatrix} v_1 \\ v_2 \\ \vdots \\ v_n \end{bmatrix}$$

of the same dimension. The **scalar product** of $\mathbf{u}$ and $\mathbf{v}$ (written $\mathbf{u} \cdot \mathbf{v}$) is the number $u_1 v_1 + u_2 v_2 + \cdots + u_n v_n$.

For the scalar product of two vectors to be defined, the first vector must be a row vector and the second vector must be a column vector. For example, if

$$\mathbf{u} = [1 \quad 2 \quad 3] \quad \text{and} \quad \mathbf{v} = \begin{bmatrix} 2 \\ 1 \\ 2 \end{bmatrix}$$

then $\mathbf{u} \cdot \mathbf{v} = 1(2) + 2(1) + 3(2) = 10$. By these rules for computing a scalar product, if

$$\mathbf{u} = \begin{bmatrix} 1 \\ 2 \end{bmatrix} \quad \text{and} \quad \mathbf{v} = [2 \quad 3]$$

then $\mathbf{u} \cdot \mathbf{v}$ is not defined. Also, if

$$\mathbf{u} = [1 \quad 2 \quad 3] \quad \text{and} \quad \mathbf{v} = \begin{bmatrix} 3 \\ 4 \end{bmatrix}$$

then $\mathbf{u} \cdot \mathbf{v}$ is not defined.

It is useful to note that two vectors are perpendicular if and only if their scalar product equals 0. Thus, the vectors $[1 \quad -1]$ and $[1 \quad 1]$ are perpendicular.

We note that $\mathbf{u} \cdot \mathbf{v} = \|\mathbf{u}\| \, \|\mathbf{v}\| \cos \theta$, where $\|\mathbf{u}\|$ is the length of the vector $\mathbf{u}$ and θ is the angle between the vectors $\mathbf{u}$ and $\mathbf{v}$.

MATRIX OPERATIONS

We now describe the arithmetic operations on matrices that are used later in this book.

THE SCALAR MULTIPLE OF A MATRIX.   Given any matrix A and any number c (a number is sometimes referred to as a scalar), the matrix cA is obtained from the matrix A by multiplying each element of A by c. For example,

$$\text{if} \quad A = \begin{bmatrix} 1 & 2 \\ -1 & 0 \end{bmatrix}, \quad \text{then} \quad 3A = \begin{bmatrix} 3 & 6 \\ -3 & 0 \end{bmatrix}$$

For $c = -1$, scalar multiplication of the matrix A is sometimes written as $-A$.

ADDITION OF TWO MATRICES.   Let $A = [a_{ij}]$ and $B = [b_{ij}]$ be two matrices having the same order (say, $m \times n$). Then the matrix $C = A + B$ is defined to be the $m \times n$ matrix whose ijth element is $a_{ij} + b_{ij}$. Thus, to obtain the sum of two matrices A and B, we add the corresponding elements of A and B. For example, if

$$A = \begin{bmatrix} 1 & 2 & 3 \\ 0 & -1 & 1 \end{bmatrix} \quad \text{and} \quad B = \begin{bmatrix} -1 & -2 & -3 \\ 2 & 1 & -1 \end{bmatrix}$$

then

$$A + B = \begin{bmatrix} 1-1 & 2-2 & 3-3 \\ 0+2 & -1+1 & 1-1 \end{bmatrix} = \begin{bmatrix} 0 & 0 & 0 \\ 2 & 0 & 0 \end{bmatrix}$$

This rule for matrix addition may be used to add vectors of the same dimension. For example, if $\mathbf{u} = [1 \quad 2]$ and $\mathbf{v} = [2 \quad 1]$, then $\mathbf{u} + \mathbf{v} = [1 + 2 \quad 2 + 1] = [3 \quad 3]$. Vectors may be added geometrically by the parallelogram law (see Figure 2).

We can use scalar multiplication and the addition of matrices to define the concept of a line segment. A glance at Figure 1 should convince you that any point u in the m-dimensional plane corresponds to the m-dimensional vector $\mathbf{u}$ formed by joining the origin to the point u. For any two points u and v in the m-dimensional plane, the **line segment** joining u and v (called the line segment uv) is the set of all points in the m-dimensional plane that correspond to the vectors $c\mathbf{u} + (1 - c)\mathbf{v}$, where $0 \le c \le 1$ (Figure 3). For example, if $u = (1, 2)$ and $v = (2, 1)$, the line segment uv consists of the points corresponding to the vectors $c[1 \quad 2] + (1 - c)[2 \quad 1] = [2 - c \quad 1 + c]$, where $0 \le c \le 1$. For $c = 0$ and $c = 1$, we obtain the endpoints of the line segment uv; for $c = \frac{1}{2}$, we obtain the midpoint $(0.5\mathbf{u} + 0.5\mathbf{v})$ of the line segment uv.

Using the parallelogram law, the line segment uv may also be viewed as the points corresponding to the vectors $\mathbf{u} + c(\mathbf{v} - \mathbf{u})$, where $0 \le c \le 1$ (Figure 4). Observe that for $c = 0$, we obtain the vector $\mathbf{u}$ (corresponding to point u), and for $c = 1$, we obtain the vector $\mathbf{v}$ (corresponding to point v).

Figure 2
Addition of Vectors

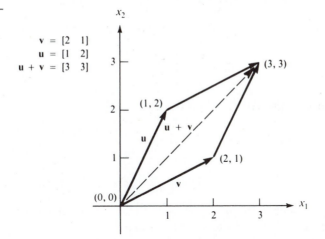

$$\mathbf{v} = [2 \quad 1]$$
$$\mathbf{u} = [1 \quad 2]$$
$$\mathbf{u} + \mathbf{v} = [3 \quad 3]$$

Figure 3
Line Segment
Joining $u = (1, 2)$
and $v = (2, 1)$

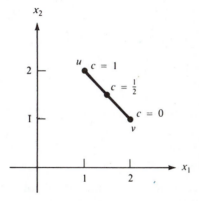

Figure 4
Representation of
Line Segment uv

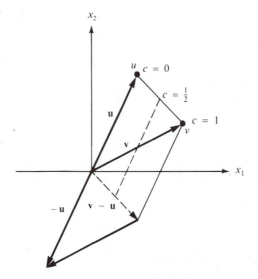

THE TRANSPOSE OF A MATRIX.   Given any $m \times n$ matrix

$$A = \begin{bmatrix} a_{11} & a_{12} & \cdots & a_{1n} \\ a_{21} & a_{22} & \cdots & a_{2n} \\ \vdots & \vdots & & \vdots \\ a_{m1} & a_{m2} & \cdots & a_{mn} \end{bmatrix}$$

the **transpose** of A (written A^T) is the $n \times m$ matrix

$$A^T = \begin{bmatrix} a_{11} & a_{21} & \cdots & a_{m1} \\ a_{12} & a_{22} & \cdots & a_{m2} \\ \vdots & \vdots & & \vdots \\ a_{1n} & a_{2n} & \cdots & a_{mn} \end{bmatrix}$$

Thus, A^T is obtained from A by letting row 1 of A be column 1 of A^T, letting row 2 of A be column 2 of A^T, and so on. For example,

$$\text{if} \quad A = \begin{bmatrix} 1 & 2 & 3 \\ 4 & 5 & 6 \end{bmatrix}, \quad \text{then} \quad A^T = \begin{bmatrix} 1 & 4 \\ 2 & 5 \\ 3 & 6 \end{bmatrix}$$

Observe that $(A^T)^T = A$. Let $B = [1 \quad 2]$; then

$$B^T = \begin{bmatrix} 1 \\ 2 \end{bmatrix} \quad \text{and} \quad (B^T)^T = [1 \quad 2] = B$$

As indicated by these two examples, for any matrix A, $(A^T)^T = A$.

MATRIX MULTIPLICATION.   Given two matrices A and B, the matrix product of A and B (written AB) is defined if and only if

$$\text{Number of columns in } A = \text{number of rows in } B \tag{1}$$

For the moment, assume that for some positive integer r, A has r columns and B has r rows. Then for some m and n, A is an $m \times r$ matrix and B is an $r \times n$ matrix.

DEFINITION	The **matrix product** $C = AB$ of A and B is the $m \times n$ matrix C whose ijth element is determined as follows:
	ijth element of C = scalar product of row i of A $\times$ column j of B (2)

If Eq. (1) is satisfied, then each row of A and each column of B will have the same number of elements. Also, if (1) is satisfied, the scalar product in Eq. (2) will be defined. The product matrix $C = AB$ will have the same number of rows as A and the same number of columns as B.

EXAMPLE 1

Compute $C = AB$ for

$$A = \begin{bmatrix} 1 & 1 & 2 \\ 2 & 1 & 3 \end{bmatrix} \quad \text{and} \quad B = \begin{bmatrix} 1 & 1 \\ 2 & 3 \\ 1 & 2 \end{bmatrix}$$

Solution

Since A is a 2×3 matrix and B is a 3×2 matrix, AB is defined, and C will be a 2×2 matrix. From Eq. (2),

$$c_{11} = [1 \quad 1 \quad 2] \begin{bmatrix} 1 \\ 2 \\ 1 \end{bmatrix} = 1(1) + 1(2) + 2(1) = 5$$

$$c_{12} = [1 \quad 1 \quad 2] \begin{bmatrix} 1 \\ 3 \\ 2 \end{bmatrix} = 1(1) + 1(3) + 2(2) = 8$$

$$c_{21} = [2 \quad 1 \quad 3] \begin{bmatrix} 1 \\ 2 \\ 1 \end{bmatrix} = 2(1) + 1(2) + 3(1) = 7$$

$$c_{22} = [2 \quad 1 \quad 3] \begin{bmatrix} 1 \\ 3 \\ 2 \end{bmatrix} = 2(1) + 1(3) + 3(2) = 11$$

$$C = AB = \begin{bmatrix} 5 & 8 \\ 7 & 11 \end{bmatrix}$$

EXAMPLE 2

Find AB for

$$A = \begin{bmatrix} 3 \\ 4 \end{bmatrix} \quad \text{and} \quad B = [1 \quad 2]$$

Solution

Since A has one column and B has one row, $C = AB$ will exist. From Eq. (2), we know that C is a 2×2 matrix with

$$c_{11} = 3(1) = 3 \qquad c_{21} = 4(1) = 4$$
$$c_{12} = 3(2) = 6 \qquad c_{22} = 4(2) = 8$$

Thus,

$$C = \begin{bmatrix} 3 & 6 \\ 4 & 8 \end{bmatrix}$$

E X A M P L E 3

Compute $D = BA$ for the A and B of Example 2.

Solution

In this case, D will be a 1×1 matrix (or a scalar). From Eq. (2),

$$d_{11} = \begin{bmatrix} 1 & 2 \end{bmatrix} \begin{bmatrix} 3 \\ 4 \end{bmatrix} = 1(3) + 2(4) = 11$$

Thus, $D = [11]$. In this example, matrix multiplication is equivalent to scalar multiplication of a row and column vector.

Recall that if you multiply together two real numbers a and b, then $ab = ba$. This is called the commutative property of multiplication. Examples 2 and 3 show that for matrix multiplication it may be that $AB \neq BA$. Matrix multiplication is not necessarily commutative. (In some cases, however, $AB = BA$ will hold.)

E X A M P L E 4

Show that AB is undefined if

$$A = \begin{bmatrix} 1 & 2 \\ 3 & 4 \end{bmatrix} \quad \text{and} \quad B = \begin{bmatrix} 1 & 1 \\ 0 & 1 \\ 1 & 2 \end{bmatrix}$$

Solution

This follows because A has two columns and B has three rows. Thus, Eq. (1) is not satisfied.

Many computations that commonly occur in operations research (and other branches of mathematics) can be concisely expressed by using matrix multiplication. To illustrate this, suppose an oil company manufactures three types of gasoline: premium unleaded, regular unleaded, and regular leaded. These gasolines are produced by mixing together two types of crude oil: crude oil 1 and crude oil 2. The number of gallons of crude oil required to manufacture 1 gallon of gasoline are given in Table 1.

Table 1		PREMIUM UNLEADED	REGULAR UNLEADED	REGULAR LEADED
Gallons of Crude Oil Required to Produce 1 Gallon of Gasoline	Crude 1	$\frac{3}{4}$	$\frac{2}{3}$	$\frac{1}{4}$
	Crude 2	$\frac{1}{4}$	$\frac{1}{3}$	$\frac{3}{4}$

From this information, we can find the amount of each type of crude oil needed to manufacture a given amount of gasoline. For example, if the company wants to produce 10 gallons of premium unleaded, 6 gallons of regular unleaded, and 5 gallons of regular leaded, the company's crude oil requirements would be

$$\text{Crude 1 required} = (\tfrac{3}{4})(10) + (\tfrac{2}{3})(6) + (\tfrac{1}{4})5 = 12.75 \text{ gallons}$$
$$\text{Crude 2 required} = (\tfrac{1}{4})(10) + (\tfrac{1}{3})(6) + (\tfrac{3}{4})5 = 8.25 \text{ gallons}$$

More generally, define

$$p_U = \text{gallons of premium unleaded produced}$$
$$r_U = \text{gallons of regular unleaded produced}$$
$$r_L = \text{gallons of regular leaded produced}$$
$$c_1 = \text{gallons of crude 1 required}$$
$$c_2 = \text{gallons of crude 2 required}$$

Then the relationship between these variables may be expressed by

$$c_1 = (\tfrac{3}{4})p_U + (\tfrac{2}{3})r_U + (\tfrac{1}{4})r_L$$
$$c_2 = (\tfrac{1}{4})p_U + (\tfrac{1}{3})r_U + (\tfrac{3}{4})r_L$$

Using matrix multiplication, these relationships may be expressed by

$$\begin{bmatrix} c_1 \\ c_2 \end{bmatrix} = \begin{bmatrix} \tfrac{3}{4} & \tfrac{2}{3} & \tfrac{1}{4} \\ \tfrac{1}{4} & \tfrac{1}{3} & \tfrac{3}{4} \end{bmatrix} \begin{bmatrix} p_U \\ r_U \\ r_L \end{bmatrix}$$

PROPERTIES OF MATRIX MULTIPLICATION

To close this section, we discuss some important properties of matrix multiplication. In what follows, we assume that all matrix products are defined.

1. Row i of AB = (row i of A)B. To illustrate this property, let

$$A = \begin{bmatrix} 1 & 1 & 2 \\ 2 & 1 & 3 \end{bmatrix} \quad \text{and} \quad B = \begin{bmatrix} 1 & 1 \\ 2 & 3 \\ 1 & 2 \end{bmatrix}$$

Then row 2 of the 2×2 matrix AB is equal to

$$[2 \quad 1 \quad 3] \begin{bmatrix} 1 & 1 \\ 2 & 3 \\ 1 & 2 \end{bmatrix} = [7 \quad 11]$$

This answer agrees with Example 1.

2. Column j of AB = A(column j of B). Thus, for A and B as given, the first column of AB is

$$\begin{bmatrix} 1 & 1 & 2 \\ 2 & 1 & 3 \end{bmatrix} \begin{bmatrix} 1 \\ 2 \\ 1 \end{bmatrix} = \begin{bmatrix} 5 \\ 7 \end{bmatrix}$$

Properties 1 and 2 are helpful when you need to compute only *part* of the matrix AB.

3. Matrix multiplication is associative. That is, $A(BC) = (AB)C$. To illustrate, let

$$A = [1 \quad 2], \qquad B = \begin{bmatrix} 2 & 3 \\ 4 & 5 \end{bmatrix}, \qquad C = \begin{bmatrix} 2 \\ 1 \end{bmatrix}$$

Then $AB = [10 \quad 13]$ and $(AB)C = 10(2) + 13(1) = [33]$.
On the other hand,

$$BC = \begin{bmatrix} 7 \\ 13 \end{bmatrix}$$

so $A(BC) = 1(7) + 2(13) = [33]$. In this case, $A(BC) = (AB)C$ does hold.

4. Matrix multiplication is distributive. That is, $A(B + C) = AB + AC$ and $(B + C)D = BD + CD$.

◆ PROBLEMS

GROUP A

1. For $A = \begin{bmatrix} 1 & 2 & 3 \\ 4 & 5 & 6 \\ 7 & 8 & 9 \end{bmatrix}$ and $B = \begin{bmatrix} 1 & 2 \\ 0 & -1 \\ 1 & 2 \end{bmatrix}$, find:

(a) $-A$ **(b)** $3A$ **(c)** $A + 2B$ **(d)** A^T **(e)** B^T
(f) AB **(g)** BA

2. Only three brands of beer (beer 1, beer 2, and beer 3) are available for sale in Metropolis. From time to time, people try one or another of these brands. Suppose that at the beginning of each month, people change the beer they are drinking according to the following rules:

30% of the people who prefer beer 1 switch to beer 2.

20% of the people who prefer beer 1 switch to beer 3.

30% of the people who prefer beer 2 switch to beer 3.

30% of the people who prefer beer 3 switch to beer 2.

10% of the people who prefer beer 3 switch to beer 1.

For $i = 1, 2, 3$, let x_i be the number who prefer beer i at the beginning of this month and y_i be the number who prefer beer i at the beginning of next month. Use matrix multiplication to relate the following:

$$\begin{bmatrix} y_1 \\ y_2 \\ y_3 \end{bmatrix}, \qquad \begin{bmatrix} x_1 \\ x_2 \\ x_3 \end{bmatrix}$$

GROUP B

3. Prove that matrix multiplication is associative.

4. Show that for any two matrices A and B, $(AB)^T = B^T A^T$.

2-2   MATRICES AND SYSTEMS OF LINEAR EQUATIONS

Consider a system of linear equations given by

$$\begin{aligned}
a_{11}x_1 + a_{12}x_2 + \cdots + a_{1n}x_n &= b_1 \\
a_{21}x_1 + a_{22}x_2 + \cdots + a_{2n}x_n &= b_2 \\
\vdots \qquad \vdots \qquad\quad \vdots \qquad \vdots \\
a_{m1}x_1 + a_{m2}x_2 + \cdots + a_{mn}x_n &= b_m
\end{aligned} \qquad (3)$$

In Eqs. (3), $x_1, x_2, \ldots, x_n$ are referred to as **variables**, or unknowns, and the a_{ij}'s and b_i's are **constants**. A set of equations like (3) is called a linear system of m equations in n variables.

| DEFINITION | A **solution** to a linear system of m equations in n unknowns is a set of values for the unknowns that satisfies each of the system's m equations. |

In order to understand linear programming, we need to know a great deal about the properties of solutions to linear equation systems. With this in mind, we will devote much effort to studying such systems.

We denote a possible solution to Eqs. (3) by an n-dimensional column vector $\mathbf{x}$, in which the ith element of $\mathbf{x}$ is the value of x_i. The following example illustrates the concept of a solution to a linear system.

E X A M P L E 5   Show that

$$\mathbf{x} = \begin{bmatrix} 1 \\ 2 \end{bmatrix}$$

is a solution to the linear system

$$\begin{aligned} x_1 + 2x_2 &= 5 \\ 2x_1 - x_2 &= 0 \end{aligned} \tag{4}$$

and that

$$\mathbf{x} = \begin{bmatrix} 3 \\ 1 \end{bmatrix}$$

is not a solution to linear system (4).

Solution   To show that

$$\mathbf{x} = \begin{bmatrix} 1 \\ 2 \end{bmatrix}$$

is a solution to Eqs. (4), we substitute $x_1 = 1$ and $x_2 = 2$ in both equations and check that they are satisfied: $1 + 2(2) = 5$ and $2(1) - 2 = 0$.

The vector

$$\mathbf{x} = \begin{bmatrix} 3 \\ 1 \end{bmatrix}$$

is not a solution to (4), because $x_1 = 3$ and $x_2 = 1$ fail to satisfy $2x_1 - x_2 = 0$. ◆

Using matrices can greatly simplify the statement and solution of a system of linear equations. To show how matrices can be used to compactly represent Eqs. (3), let

$$A = \begin{bmatrix} a_{11} & a_{12} & \cdots & a_{1n} \\ a_{21} & a_{22} & \cdots & a_{2n} \\ \vdots & \vdots & & \vdots \\ a_{m1} & a_{m2} & \cdots & a_{mn} \end{bmatrix}, \quad \mathbf{x} = \begin{bmatrix} x_1 \\ x_2 \\ \vdots \\ x_n \end{bmatrix}, \quad \mathbf{b} = \begin{bmatrix} b_1 \\ b_2 \\ \vdots \\ b_m \end{bmatrix}$$

Then (3) may be written as

$$A\mathbf{x} = \mathbf{b} \qquad (5)$$

Observe that both sides of Eq. (5) will be $m \times 1$ matrices (or $m \times 1$ column vectors). For the matrix $A\mathbf{x}$ to equal the matrix $\mathbf{b}$ (or for the vector $A\mathbf{x}$ to equal the vector $\mathbf{b}$), their corresponding elements must be equal. The first element of $A\mathbf{x}$ is the scalar product of row 1 of A with $\mathbf{x}$. This may be written as

$$[a_{11} \quad a_{12} \quad \cdots \quad a_{1n}] \begin{bmatrix} x_1 \\ x_2 \\ \vdots \\ x_n \end{bmatrix} = a_{11}x_1 + a_{12}x_2 + \cdots + a_{1n}x_n$$

This must equal the first element of $\mathbf{b}$ (which is b_1). Thus, Eq. (5) implies that $a_{11}x_1 + a_{12}x_2 + \cdots + a_{1n}x_n = b_1$. This is the first equation of Eqs. (3). Similarly, (5) implies that the scalar product of row i of A with $\mathbf{x}$ must equal b_i, and this is just the ith equation of (3). Our discussion shows that Eqs. (3) and (5) are two different ways of writing the same linear system. We call (5) the **matrix representation** of (3). For example, the matrix representation of Eqs. (4) is

$$\begin{bmatrix} 1 & 2 \\ 2 & -1 \end{bmatrix} \begin{bmatrix} x_1 \\ x_2 \end{bmatrix} = \begin{bmatrix} 5 \\ 0 \end{bmatrix}$$

Sometimes we abbreviate (5) by writing

$$A \mid \mathbf{b} \qquad (6)$$

If A is an $m \times n$ matrix, it is assumed that the variables in Eq. (6) are $x_1, x_2, \ldots, x_n$. Then (6) is still another representation of (3). For instance, the matrix

$$\begin{bmatrix} 1 & 2 & 3 & \mid & 2 \\ 0 & 1 & 2 & \mid & 3 \\ 1 & 1 & 1 & \mid & 1 \end{bmatrix}$$

represents the system of equations

$$\begin{aligned} x_1 + 2x_2 + 3x_3 &= 2 \\ x_2 + 2x_3 &= 3 \\ x_1 + x_2 + x_3 &= 1 \end{aligned}$$

◆ PROBLEM

GROUP A

1. Use matrices to represent the following system of equations in two different ways:

$$\begin{aligned} x_1 - x_2 &= 4 \\ 2x_1 + x_2 &= 6 \\ x_1 + 3x_2 &= 8 \end{aligned}$$

2-3   THE GAUSS-JORDAN METHOD FOR SOLVING SYSTEMS OF LINEAR EQUATIONS

We develop in this section an efficient method (the Gauss-Jordan method) for solving a system of linear equations. Using the Gauss-Jordan method, we show that any system of linear equations must satisfy one of the following three cases:

Case 1 The system has no solution.

Case 2 The system has a unique solution.

Case 3 The system has an infinite number of solutions.

The Gauss-Jordan method is also important because many of the manipulations used in this method are used when solving linear programming problems by the simplex algorithm (see Chapter 4).

ELEMENTARY ROW OPERATIONS

Before studying the Gauss-Jordan method, we need to define the concept of an **elementary row operation (ero)**. An ero transforms a given matrix A into a new matrix A' via one of the following operations.

Type 1 ero A' is obtained by multiplying any row of A by a nonzero scalar. For example, if

$$A = \begin{bmatrix} 1 & 2 & 3 & 4 \\ 1 & 3 & 5 & 6 \\ 0 & 1 & 2 & 3 \end{bmatrix}$$

then a Type 1 ero that multiplies row 2 of A by 3 would yield

$$A' = \begin{bmatrix} 1 & 2 & 3 & 4 \\ 3 & 9 & 15 & 18 \\ 0 & 1 & 2 & 3 \end{bmatrix}$$

Type 2 ero   Begin by multiplying any row of A (say, row i) by a nonzero scalar c. For some $j \neq i$, let row j of $A' = c(\text{row } i \text{ of } A) + \text{row } j$ of A, and let the other rows of A' be the same as the rows of A.

For example, we might multiply row 2 of A by 4 and replace row 3 of A by $4(\text{row } 2 \text{ of } A) + \text{row } 3$ of A. Then row 3 of A' becomes

$$4[1 \quad 3 \quad 5 \quad 6] + [0 \quad 1 \quad 2 \quad 3] = [4 \quad 13 \quad 22 \quad 27]$$

and

$$A' = \begin{bmatrix} 1 & 2 & 3 & 4 \\ 1 & 3 & 5 & 6 \\ 4 & 13 & 22 & 27 \end{bmatrix}$$

Type 3 ero Simply interchange any two rows of A. For instance, if we interchange rows 1 and 3 of A, we obtain

$$A' = \begin{bmatrix} 0 & 1 & 2 & 3 \\ 1 & 3 & 5 & 6 \\ 1 & 2 & 3 & 4 \end{bmatrix}$$

Type 1 and Type 2 ero's formalize the operations used to solve a linear equation system. To solve the system of equations

$$\begin{aligned} x_1 + x_2 &= 2 \\ 2x_1 + 4x_2 &= 7 \end{aligned} \tag{7}$$

we might proceed as follows. First replace the second equation in (7) by -2(first equation in (7)) + second equation in (7). This yields the following linear system:

$$\begin{aligned} x_1 + x_2 &= 2 \\ 2x_2 &= 3 \end{aligned} \tag{7.1}$$

Then multiply the second equation in (7.1) by $\frac{1}{2}$, yielding the system

$$\begin{aligned} x_1 + x_2 &= 2 \\ x_2 &= \tfrac{3}{2} \end{aligned} \tag{7.2}$$

Finally, replace the first equation in (7.2) by -1(second equation in (7.2)) + first equation in (7.2). This yields the system

$$\begin{aligned} x_1 &= \tfrac{1}{2} \\ x_2 &= \tfrac{3}{2} \end{aligned} \tag{7.3}$$

System (7.3) has the unique solution $x_1 = \frac{1}{2}$ and $x_2 = \frac{3}{2}$. The systems (7), (7.1), (7.2), and (7.3) are *equivalent* in that they have the same set of solutions. This means that $x_1 = \frac{1}{2}$ and $x_2 = \frac{3}{2}$ is also the unique solution to the original system, Eqs. (7).

If we view Eqs. (7) in the augmented matrix form $(A\,|\,\mathbf{b})$, we see that the steps used to solve (7) may be seen as Type 1 and Type 2 ero's applied to $A\,|\,\mathbf{b}$. Begin with the augmented matrix version of (7):

$$\begin{bmatrix} 1 & 1 & | & 2 \\ 2 & 4 & | & 7 \end{bmatrix} \tag{7'}$$

Now perform a Type 2 ero by replacing row 2 of (7′) by -2(row 1 of (7′)) + row 2 of (7′). The result is

$$\begin{bmatrix} 1 & 1 & | & 2 \\ 0 & 2 & | & 3 \end{bmatrix} \tag{7.1'}$$

which corresponds to (7.1). Next, we multiply row 2 of (7.1′) by $\frac{1}{2}$ (a Type 1 ero), resulting in

$$\begin{bmatrix} 1 & 1 & | & 2 \\ 0 & 1 & | & \tfrac{3}{2} \end{bmatrix} \tag{7.2'}$$

which corresponds to (7.2). Finally, perform a Type 2 ero by replacing row 1 of (7.2′) by -1(row 2 of (7.2′)) + row 1 of (7.2′). The result is

$$\begin{bmatrix} 1 & 0 & | & \frac{1}{2} \\ 0 & 1 & | & \frac{3}{2} \end{bmatrix} \tag{7.3′}$$

which corresponds to (7.3). Translating (7.3′) back into a linear system, we obtain the system $x_1 = \frac{1}{2}$ and $x_2 = \frac{3}{2}$, which is identical to (7.3).

FINDING A SOLUTION BY THE GAUSS-JORDAN METHOD

The discussion in the previous section indicates that if the matrix $A' \,|\, \mathbf{b}'$ is obtained from $A \,|\, \mathbf{b}$ via an ero, the systems $A\mathbf{x} = \mathbf{b}$ and $A'\mathbf{x} = \mathbf{b}'$ are equivalent. Thus, any sequence of ero's performed on the augmented matrix $A \,|\, \mathbf{b}$ corresponding to the system $A\mathbf{x} = \mathbf{b}$ will yield an equivalent linear system.

The Gauss-Jordan method solves a linear equation system by utilizing ero's in a systematic fashion. We illustrate the method by finding the solution to the following linear system:

$$\begin{aligned} 2x_1 + 2x_2 + x_3 &= 9 \\ 2x_1 - x_2 + 2x_3 &= 6 \\ x_1 - x_2 + 2x_3 &= 5 \end{aligned} \tag{8}$$

The augmented matrix representation is

$$A \,|\, \mathbf{b} = \begin{bmatrix} 2 & 2 & 1 & | & 9 \\ 2 & -1 & 2 & | & 6 \\ 1 & -1 & 2 & | & 5 \end{bmatrix} \tag{8′}$$

Suppose that by performing a sequence of ero's on (8′) we could transform (8′) into

$$\begin{bmatrix} 1 & 0 & 0 & | & 1 \\ 0 & 1 & 0 & | & 2 \\ 0 & 0 & 1 & | & 3 \end{bmatrix} \tag{9′}$$

We note that the result obtained by performing an ero on a system of equations can also be obtained by multiplying both sides of the matrix representation of the system of equations by a particular matrix. This explains why ero's do not change the set of solutions to a system of equations.

Matrix (9′) corresponds to the following linear system:

$$\begin{aligned} x_1 \phantom{{}+{}x_2+{}x_3} &= 1 \\ x_2 \phantom{{}+{}x_3} &= 2 \\ x_3 &= 3 \end{aligned} \tag{9}$$

System (9) has the unique solution $x_1 = 1$, $x_2 = 2$, $x_3 = 3$. Since (9′) was obtained from (8′) by a sequence of ero's, we know that (8) and (9) are equivalent linear systems. Thus, $x_1 = 1$, $x_2 = 2$, $x_3 = 3$ must also be the unique solution to (8). We now show how we can use ero's to transform a relatively complicated system like (8) into a relatively simple system like (9). This is the essence of the Gauss-Jordan method.

We begin by using ero's to transform the first column of (8') into

$$\begin{bmatrix} 1 \\ 0 \\ 0 \end{bmatrix}$$

Then we use ero's to transform the second column of the resulting matrix into

$$\begin{bmatrix} 0 \\ 1 \\ 0 \end{bmatrix}$$

Finally, we use ero's to transform the third column of the resulting matrix into

$$\begin{bmatrix} 0 \\ 0 \\ 1 \end{bmatrix}$$

As a final result, we will have obtained (9'). We now use the Gauss-Jordan method to solve (8). We begin by using a Type 1 ero to change the element of (8') in the first row and first column into a 1. Then we add multiples of row 1 to row 2 and then to row 3 (these are Type 2 ero's). The purpose of these Type 2 ero's is to put zeros in the rest of the first column. The following sequence of ero's will accomplish these goals.

Step 1 Multiply row 1 of (8') by $\frac{1}{2}$. This Type 1 ero yields

$$A_1 \mid \mathbf{b}_1 = \begin{bmatrix} 1 & 1 & \frac{1}{2} & \frac{9}{2} \\ 2 & -1 & 2 & 6 \\ 1 & -1 & 2 & 5 \end{bmatrix}$$

Step 2 Replace row 2 of $A_1 \mid \mathbf{b}_1$ by -2(row 1 of $A_1 \mid \mathbf{b}_1$) + row 2 of $A_1 \mid \mathbf{b}_1$. The result of this Type 2 ero is

$$A_2 \mid \mathbf{b}_2 = \begin{bmatrix} 1 & 1 & \frac{1}{2} & \frac{9}{2} \\ 0 & -3 & 1 & -3 \\ 1 & -1 & 2 & 5 \end{bmatrix}$$

Step 3 Replace row 3 of $A_2 \mid \mathbf{b}_2$ by -1(row 1 of $A_2 \mid \mathbf{b}_2$) + row 3 of $A_2 \mid \mathbf{b}_2$. The result of this Type 2 ero is

$$A_3 \mid \mathbf{b}_3 = \begin{bmatrix} 1 & 1 & \frac{1}{2} & \frac{9}{2} \\ 0 & -3 & 1 & -3 \\ 0 & -2 & \frac{3}{2} & \frac{1}{2} \end{bmatrix}$$

The first column of (8') has now been transformed into

$$\begin{bmatrix} 1 \\ 0 \\ 0 \end{bmatrix}$$

By our procedure, we have made sure that the variable x_1 occurs in only a single equation and in that equation has a coefficient of 1. We now transform the second column of $A_3 | \mathbf{b}_3$ into

$$\begin{bmatrix} 0 \\ 1 \\ 0 \end{bmatrix}$$

We begin by using a Type 1 ero to create a 1 in row 2 and column 2 of $A_3 | \mathbf{b}_3$. Then we use the resulting row 2 to perform the Type 2 ero's that are needed to put zeros in the rest of column 2. Steps 4–6 accomplish these goals.

Step 4 Multiply row 2 of $A_3 | \mathbf{b}_3$ by $-\frac{1}{3}$. The result of this Type 1 ero is

$$A_4 | \mathbf{b}_4 = \begin{bmatrix} 1 & 1 & \frac{1}{2} & | & \frac{9}{2} \\ 0 & 1 & -\frac{1}{3} & | & 1 \\ 0 & -2 & \frac{3}{2} & | & \frac{1}{2} \end{bmatrix}$$

Step 5 Replace row 1 of $A_4 | \mathbf{b}_4$ by -1(row 2 of $A_4 | \mathbf{b}_4$) + row 1 of $A_4 | \mathbf{b}_4$. The result of this Type 2 ero is

$$A_5 | \mathbf{b}_5 = \begin{bmatrix} 1 & 0 & \frac{5}{6} & | & \frac{7}{2} \\ 0 & 1 & -\frac{1}{3} & | & 1 \\ 0 & -2 & \frac{3}{2} & | & \frac{1}{2} \end{bmatrix}$$

Step 6 Replace row 3 of $A_5 | \mathbf{b}_5$ by 2(row 2 of $A_5 | \mathbf{b}_5$) + row 3 of $A_5 | \mathbf{b}_5$. The result of this Type 2 ero is

$$A_6 | \mathbf{b}_6 = \begin{bmatrix} 1 & 0 & \frac{5}{6} & | & \frac{7}{2} \\ 0 & 1 & -\frac{1}{3} & | & 1 \\ 0 & 0 & \frac{5}{6} & | & \frac{5}{2} \end{bmatrix}$$

Column 2 has now been transformed into

$$\begin{bmatrix} 0 \\ 1 \\ 0 \end{bmatrix}$$

Observe that our transformation of column 2 did not change column 1.

To complete the Gauss-Jordan procedure, we must transform the third column of $A_6 | \mathbf{b}_6$ into

$$\begin{bmatrix} 0 \\ 0 \\ 1 \end{bmatrix}$$

We first use a Type 1 ero to create a 1 in the third row and third column of $A_6 | \mathbf{b}_6$. Then we use Type 2 ero's to put zeros in the rest of column 3. Steps 7–9 accomplish these goals.

Step 7 Multiply row 3 of $A_6 | \mathbf{b}_6$ by $\frac{6}{5}$. The result of this Type 1 ero is

$$A_7 | \mathbf{b}_7 = \begin{bmatrix} 1 & 0 & \frac{5}{6} & \Big| & \frac{7}{2} \\ 0 & 1 & -\frac{1}{3} & \Big| & 1 \\ 0 & 0 & 1 & \Big| & 3 \end{bmatrix}$$

Step 8 Replace row 1 of $A_7 | \mathbf{b}_7$ by $-\frac{5}{6}$(row 3 of $A_7 | \mathbf{b}_7$) + row 1 of $A_7 | \mathbf{b}_7$. The result of this Type 2 ero is

$$A_8 | \mathbf{b}_8 = \begin{bmatrix} 1 & 0 & 0 & \Big| & 1 \\ 0 & 1 & -\frac{1}{3} & \Big| & 1 \\ 0 & 0 & 1 & \Big| & 3 \end{bmatrix}$$

Step 9 Replace row 2 of $A_8 | \mathbf{b}_8$ by $\frac{1}{3}$(row 3 of $A_8 | \mathbf{b}_8$) + row 2 of $A_8 | \mathbf{b}_8$. The result of this Type 2 ero is

$$A_9 | \mathbf{b}_9 = \begin{bmatrix} 1 & 0 & 0 & \Big| & 1 \\ 0 & 1 & 0 & \Big| & 2 \\ 0 & 0 & 1 & \Big| & 3 \end{bmatrix}$$

$A_9 | \mathbf{b}_9$ represents the system of equations

$$\begin{aligned} x_1 & & & = 1 \\ & x_2 & & = 2 \\ & & x_3 & = 3 \end{aligned} \qquad (9)$$

Thus, (9) has the unique solution $x_1 = 1$, $x_2 = 2$, $x_3 = 3$. Since (9) was obtained from (8) via ero's, the unique solution to (8) must also be $x_1 = 1$, $x_2 = 2$, $x_3 = 3$.

The reader might be wondering why we defined Type 3 ero's (interchanging of rows). To see why a Type 3 ero might be useful, suppose you want to solve

$$\begin{aligned} & & 2x_2 + x_3 & = 6 \\ x_1 & + x_2 & - x_3 & = 2 \\ 2x_1 & + x_2 & + x_3 & = 4 \end{aligned} \qquad (10)$$

To solve (10) by the Gauss-Jordan method, first form the augmented matrix

$$A | \mathbf{b} = \begin{bmatrix} 0 & 2 & 1 & \Big| & 6 \\ 1 & 1 & -1 & \Big| & 2 \\ 2 & 1 & 1 & \Big| & 4 \end{bmatrix}$$

The zero in row 1 and column 1 means that a Type 1 ero cannot be used to create a 1 in row 1 and column 1. If, however, we interchange rows 1 and 2 (a Type 3 ero), we obtain

$$\begin{bmatrix} 1 & 1 & -1 & \Big| & 2 \\ 0 & 2 & 1 & \Big| & 6 \\ 2 & 1 & 1 & \Big| & 4 \end{bmatrix} \qquad (10')$$

Now we may proceed as usual with the Gauss-Jordan method.

SPECIAL CASES: NO SOLUTION OR AN INFINITE NUMBER OF SOLUTIONS

Some linear systems have no solution, and some have an infinite number of solutions. The following two examples illustrate how the Gauss-Jordan method can be used to recognize these cases.

E X A M P L E 6

Find all solutions to the following linear system:

$$x_1 + 2x_2 = 3$$
$$2x_1 + 4x_2 = 4 \tag{11}$$

Solution

We apply the Gauss-Jordan method to the matrix

$$A \,|\, \mathbf{b} = \begin{bmatrix} 1 & 2 & | & 3 \\ 2 & 4 & | & 4 \end{bmatrix}$$

We begin by replacing row 2 of $A\,|\,\mathbf{b}$ by -2(row 1 of $A\,|\,\mathbf{b}$) + row 2 of $A\,|\,\mathbf{b}$. The result of this Type 2 ero is

$$\begin{bmatrix} 1 & 2 & | & 3 \\ 0 & 0 & | & -2 \end{bmatrix} \tag{12}$$

We would now like to transform the second column of (12) into

$$\begin{bmatrix} 0 \\ 1 \end{bmatrix}$$

but this is not possible. System (12) is equivalent to the following system of equations:

$$x_1 + 2x_2 = 3$$
$$0x_1 + 0x_2 = -2 \tag{12'}$$

Whatever values we give to x_1 and x_2, the second equation in (12') can never be satisfied. Thus, (12') has no solution. Since (12') was obtained from (11) by use of ero's, (11) also has no solution.

◆

Example 6 illustrates the following idea: *If you apply the Gauss-Jordan method to a linear system and obtain a row of the form* [0 0 ⋯ 0 | c] (c ≠ 0), *the original linear system has no solution.*

E X A M P L E 7

Apply the Gauss-Jordan method to the following linear system:

$$x_1 + x_2 \quad\;\;= 1$$
$$x_2 + x_3 = 3$$
$$x_1 + 2x_2 + x_3 = 4 \tag{13}$$

Solution   The augmented matrix form of (13) is

$$A \,|\, \mathbf{b} = \begin{bmatrix} 1 & 1 & 0 & | & 1 \\ 0 & 1 & 1 & | & 3 \\ 1 & 2 & 1 & | & 4 \end{bmatrix}$$

We begin by replacing row 3 of $A \,|\, \mathbf{b}$ by -1(row 1 of $A \,|\, \mathbf{b}$) + row 3 of $A \,|\, \mathbf{b}$. The result of this Type 2 ero is

$$A_1 \,|\, \mathbf{b}_1 = \begin{bmatrix} 1 & 1 & 0 & | & 1 \\ 0 & 1 & 1 & | & 3 \\ 0 & 1 & 1 & | & 3 \end{bmatrix} \tag{14}$$

Next we replace row 1 of $A_1 \,|\, \mathbf{b}_1$ by -1(row 2 of $A_1 \,|\, \mathbf{b}_1$) + row 1 of $A_1 \,|\, \mathbf{b}_1$. The result of this Type 2 ero is

$$A_2 \,|\, \mathbf{b}_2 = \begin{bmatrix} 1 & 0 & -1 & | & -2 \\ 0 & 1 & 1 & | & 3 \\ 0 & 1 & 1 & | & 3 \end{bmatrix}$$

Now we replace row 3 of $A_2 \,|\, \mathbf{b}_2$ by -1(row 2 of $A_2 \,|\, \mathbf{b}_2$) + row 3 of $A_2 \,|\, \mathbf{b}_2$. The result of this Type 2 ero is

$$A_3 \,|\, \mathbf{b}_3 = \begin{bmatrix} 1 & 0 & -1 & | & -2 \\ 0 & 1 & 1 & | & 3 \\ 0 & 0 & 0 & | & 0 \end{bmatrix}$$

We would now like to transform the third column of $A_3 \,|\, \mathbf{b}_3$ into

$$\begin{bmatrix} 0 \\ 0 \\ 1 \end{bmatrix}$$

but this is not possible. The linear system corresponding to $A_3 \,|\, \mathbf{b}_3$ is

$$x_1 \qquad\quad - \quad x_3 = -2 \tag{14.1}$$
$$x_2 + \quad x_3 = 3 \tag{14.2}$$
$$0x_1 + 0x_2 + 0x_3 = 0 \tag{14.3}$$

Suppose we assign an arbitrary value k to x_3. Then (14.1) will be satisfied if $x_1 - k = -2$, or $x_1 = k - 2$. Similarly, (14.2) will be satisfied if $x_2 + k = 3$, or $x_2 = 3 - k$. Of course, (14.3) will be satisfied for any values of x_1, x_2, and x_3. Thus, for any number k, $x_1 = k - 2$, $x_2 = 3 - k$, $x_3 = k$ is a solution to (14). Thus, (14) has an infinite number of solutions (one for each number k). Since (14) was obtained from (13) via ero's, (13) also has an infinite number of solutions. A more formal characterization of linear systems that have an infinite number of solutions will be given after the following summary of the Gauss-Jordan method.

SUMMARY OF THE GAUSS-JORDAN METHOD

Step 1 To solve $A\mathbf{x} = \mathbf{b}$, write down the augmented matrix $A\,|\,\mathbf{b}$.

Step 2a At any stage, define a current row, current column, and current entry (the entry in the current row and column). Begin with row 1 as the current row, column 1 as the current column, and a_{11} as the current entry. If a_{11} (the current entry) is nonzero, use ero's to transform column 1 (the current column) to

$$\begin{bmatrix} 1 \\ 0 \\ \vdots \\ 0 \end{bmatrix}$$

Then obtain the new current row, column, and entry by moving down one row and one column to the right, and go to Step 2b. If a_{11} (the current entry) equals 0, then determine whether, in the current column, there are any nonzero numbers in the rows below the current row. If so, do a Type 3 ero involving the current row and any such row and use ero's to transform column 1 to

$$\begin{bmatrix} 1 \\ 0 \\ \vdots \\ 0 \end{bmatrix}$$

Then obtain the new current row, column, and entry by moving one row down and one column to the right. Then go to Step 2b. In the current column, if there are no nonzero numbers in the rows below the current row, obtain a new current column and entry by moving one column to the right. Then go to Step 2b.

Step 2b If the current entry is nonzero, use ero's to transform the current entry to 1 and the rest of the current column's entries to 0. Obtain the new current row, column, and entry by moving down one row and over one column. If this is impossible, stop. Otherwise, repeat Step 2b. If the current entry is 0, determine whether, in the current column, there are any nonzero numbers below the current row. If so, do a Type 3 ero with the current row and any such row. Then use ero's to transform the current entry to 1 and the rest to the current column's entries to 0. Obtain the new current row, column, and entry by moving down one row and over one column. If this is impossible, stop. Otherwise, repeat Step 2b. If the current column has no nonzero numbers below the current row, obtain the new current column and entry by moving one column to the right (if possible), and repeat Step 2b. If it is impossible to move one column to the right, stop.

This procedure may require "passing over" one or more columns without transforming them (see Problem 8).

Step 3 Write down the system of equations $A'\mathbf{x} = \mathbf{b}'$ that corresponds to the matrix $A'\,|\,\mathbf{b}'$ obtained when Step 2 is completed. Then $A'\mathbf{x} = \mathbf{b}'$ will have the same set of solutions as $A\mathbf{x} = \mathbf{b}$.

BASIC VARIABLES AND SOLUTIONS TO LINEAR EQUATION SYSTEMS

To describe the set of solutions to $A'\mathbf{x} = \mathbf{b}'$ (and $A\mathbf{x} = \mathbf{b}$), we need to define the concepts of basic and nonbasic variables.

DEFINITION ■ For any linear system, a variable that appears with a coefficient of 1 in a single equation and a zero coefficient in all other equations is called a **basic variable**.

DEFINITION ■ Any variable that is not a basic variable is called a **nonbasic variable**.

Let BV be the set of basic variables for $A'\mathbf{x} = \mathbf{b}'$ and NBV be the set of nonbasic variables for $A'\mathbf{x} = \mathbf{b}'$. The character of the solutions to $A'\mathbf{x} = \mathbf{b}'$ depends on which of the following cases occurs.

Case 1 $A'\mathbf{x} = \mathbf{b}'$ has at least one row of form $[0 \quad 0 \quad \cdots \quad 0 \,|\, c]$ $(c \neq 0)$. Then $A\mathbf{x} = \mathbf{b}$ has no solution (recall Example 6). As an example of Case 1, suppose that when the Gauss-Jordan method is applied to the system $A\mathbf{x} = \mathbf{b}$, the following matrix is obtained:

$$A'\,|\,\mathbf{b}' = \begin{bmatrix} 1 & 0 & 0 & 1 & | & 1 \\ 0 & 1 & 0 & 2 & | & 1 \\ 0 & 0 & 1 & 3 & | & -1 \\ 0 & 0 & 0 & 0 & | & 0 \\ 0 & 0 & 0 & 0 & | & 2 \end{bmatrix}$$

In this case, $A'\mathbf{x} = \mathbf{b}'$ (and $A\mathbf{x} = \mathbf{b}$) has no solution.

Case 2 Suppose that Case 1 does not apply and NBV, the set of nonbasic variables, is empty. Then $A'\mathbf{x} = \mathbf{b}'$ (and $A\mathbf{x} = \mathbf{b}$) will have a unique solution. To illustrate this, we recall that in solving

$$\begin{aligned} 2x_1 + 2x_2 + x_3 &= 9 \\ 2x_1 - x_2 + 2x_3 &= 6 \\ x_1 - x_2 + 2x_3 &= 5 \end{aligned}$$

the Gauss-Jordan method yielded

$$A'\,|\,\mathbf{b}' = \begin{bmatrix} 1 & 0 & 0 & | & 1 \\ 0 & 1 & 0 & | & 2 \\ 0 & 0 & 1 & | & 3 \end{bmatrix}$$

In this case, $BV = \{x_1, x_2, x_3\}$ and NBV is empty. Then the unique solution to $A'\mathbf{x} = \mathbf{b}'$ (and $A\mathbf{x} = \mathbf{b}$) is $x_1 = 1$, $x_2 = 2$, $x_3 = 3$.

Case 3 Suppose that Case 1 does not apply and NBV is nonempty. Then $A'\mathbf{x} = \mathbf{b}'$ (and $A\mathbf{x} = \mathbf{b}$) will have an infinite number of solutions. To obtain these, first assign each nonbasic variable an arbitrary value. Then solve for the value of each basic variable in terms of the nonbasic variables. For example, suppose

$$A' \mid \mathbf{b}' = \begin{bmatrix} 1 & 0 & 0 & 1 & 1 & \bigm| & 3 \\ 0 & 1 & 0 & 2 & 0 & \bigm| & 2 \\ 0 & 0 & 1 & 0 & 1 & \bigm| & 1 \\ 0 & 0 & 0 & 0 & 0 & \bigm| & 0 \end{bmatrix} \tag{15}$$

Since Case 1 does not apply, and $BV = \{x_1, x_2, x_3\}$ and $NBV = \{x_4, x_5\}$, we have an example of Case 3: $A'\mathbf{x} = \mathbf{b}'$ (and $A\mathbf{x} = \mathbf{b}$) will have an infinite number of solutions. To see what these solutions look like, write down $A'\mathbf{x} = \mathbf{b}'$:

$$x_1 \qquad\qquad + x_4 + x_5 = 3 \tag{15.1}$$
$$x_2 \qquad + 2x_4 \qquad = 2 \tag{15.2}$$
$$x_3 \qquad + x_5 = 1 \tag{15.3}$$
$$0x_1 + 0x_2 + 0x_3 + 0x_4 + 0x_5 = 0 \tag{15.4}$$

Now assign the nonbasic variables (x_4 and x_5) arbitrary values c and k, with $x_4 = c$ and $x_5 = k$. From (15.1), we find that $x_1 = 3 - c - k$. From (15.2), we find that $x_2 = 2 - 2c$. From (15.3), we find that $x_3 = 1 - k$. Since (15.4) holds for all values of the variables, $x_1 = 3 - c - k$, $x_2 = 2 - 2c$, $x_3 = 1 - k$, $x_4 = c$, and $x_5 = k$ will, for any values of c and k, be a solution to $A'\mathbf{x} = \mathbf{b}'$ (and $A\mathbf{x} = \mathbf{b}$).

Our discussion of the Gauss-Jordan method is summarized in Figure 5. We have devoted so much time to the Gauss-Jordan method because in our study of linear programming, examples of Case 3 (linear systems with an infinite number of solutions) will occur repeatedly. Since the end result of the Gauss-Jordan method must always be one of Cases 1–3, we have shown that any linear system will have no solution, a unique solution, or an infinite number of solutions.

Figure 5
Description of
Gauss-Jordan
Method for Solving
Linear Equations

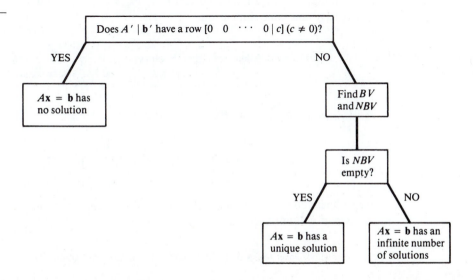

◆ PROBLEMS

GROUP A

Use the Gauss-Jordan method to determine whether each of the following linear systems has no solution, a unique solution, or an infinite number of solutions. Indicate the solutions (if any exist).

1.
$$\begin{aligned} x_1 + x_2 \quad\;\; + x_4 &= 3 \\ x_2 + x_3 \quad &= 4 \\ x_1 + 2x_2 + x_3 + x_4 &= 8 \end{aligned}$$

2.
$$\begin{aligned} x_1 + x_2 + x_3 &= 4 \\ x_1 + 2x_2 \quad &= 6 \end{aligned}$$

3.
$$\begin{aligned} x_1 + x_2 &= 1 \\ 2x_1 + x_2 &= 3 \\ 3x_1 + 2x_2 &= 4 \end{aligned}$$

4.
$$\begin{aligned} 2x_1 - x_2 + x_3 + x_4 &= 6 \\ x_1 + x_2 + x_3 \quad &= 4 \end{aligned}$$

5.
$$\begin{aligned} x_1 \quad\quad\;\; + x_4 &= 5 \\ x_2 \quad + 2x_4 &= 5 \\ x_3 + 0.5x_4 &= 1 \\ 2x_3 + \quad x_4 &= 3 \end{aligned}$$

6.
$$\begin{aligned} 2x_2 + 2x_3 &= 4 \\ x_1 + 2x_2 + x_3 &= 4 \\ x_2 - x_3 &= 0 \end{aligned}$$

7.
$$\begin{aligned} x_1 + x_2 \quad &= 2 \\ -x_2 + 2x_3 &= 3 \\ x_2 + x_3 &= 3 \end{aligned}$$

8.
$$\begin{aligned} x_1 + x_2 + x_3 \quad &= 1 \\ x_2 + 2x_3 + x_4 &= 2 \\ x_4 &= 3 \end{aligned}$$

GROUP B

9. Suppose that a linear system $A\mathbf{x} = \mathbf{b}$ has more variables than equations. Show that $A\mathbf{x} = \mathbf{b}$ cannot have a unique solution.

2-4

LINEAR INDEPENDENCE AND LINEAR DEPENDENCE*

In this section, we discuss the concepts of a linearly independent set of vectors, a linearly dependent set of vectors, and the rank of a matrix. These concepts will be useful in our study of matrix inverses.

Before defining a linearly independent set of vectors, we need to define a linear combination of a set of vectors. Let $V = \{\mathbf{v}_1, \mathbf{v}_2, \dots, \mathbf{v}_k\}$ be a set of row vectors all of which have the same dimension.

DEFINITION ■ A **linear combination** of the vectors in V is any vector of the form $c_1\mathbf{v}_1 + c_2\mathbf{v}_2 + \cdots + c_k\mathbf{v}_k$, where $c_1, c_2, \dots, c_k$ are arbitrary scalars. ■

For example, if $V = \{[1 \quad 2], [2 \quad 1]\}$, then

$$\begin{aligned} 2\mathbf{v}_1 - \mathbf{v}_2 &= 2([1 \quad 2]) - [2 \quad 1] = [0 \quad 3] \\ \mathbf{v}_1 + 3\mathbf{v}_2 &= [1 \quad 2] + 3([2 \quad 1]) = [7 \quad 5] \\ 0\mathbf{v}_1 + 3\mathbf{v}_2 &= [0 \quad 0] + 3([2 \quad 1]) = [6 \quad 3] \end{aligned}$$

are all linear combinations of vectors in V. The foregoing definition may also be applied to a set of column vectors.

---

*Starred sections cover topics that may be omitted with no loss of continuity.

Suppose we are given a set $V = \{\mathbf{v}_1, \mathbf{v}_2, \ldots, \mathbf{v}_k\}$ of m-dimensional row vectors. Let $\mathbf{0} = [0 \quad 0 \quad \cdots \quad 0]$ be the m-dimensional $\mathbf{0}$ vector. To determine whether V is a linearly independent set of vectors, we try to find a linear combination of the vectors in V that adds up to $\mathbf{0}$. Clearly, $0\mathbf{v}_1 + 0\mathbf{v}_2 + \cdots + 0\mathbf{v}_k$ is a linear combination of vectors in V that adds up to $\mathbf{0}$. We call the linear combination of vectors in V for which $c_1 = c_2 = \cdots = c_k = 0$ the trivial linear combination of vectors in V. We may now define linearly independent and linearly dependent sets of vectors.

DEFINITION   A set V of m-dimensional vectors is **linearly independent** if the only linear combination of vectors in V that equals $\mathbf{0}$ is the trivial linear combination.

DEFINITION   A set V of m-dimensional vectors is **linearly dependent** if there is a nontrivial linear combination of the vectors in V that adds up to $\mathbf{0}$.

The following examples should clarify these definitions.

E X A M P L E   8

Show that any set of vectors containing the $\mathbf{0}$ vector is a linearly dependent set.

Solution

To illustrate, we show that if $V = \{[0 \quad 0], [1 \quad 0], [0 \quad 1]\}$, then V is linearly dependent, because if, say, $c_1 \neq 0$, then $c_1([0 \quad 0]) + 0([1 \quad 0]) + 0([0 \quad 1]) = [0 \quad 0]$. Thus, there is a nontrivial linear combination of vectors in V that adds up to $\mathbf{0}$.

           ◆

E X A M P L E   9

Show that the set of vectors $V = \{[1 \quad 0], [0 \quad 1]\}$ is a linearly independent set of vectors.

Solution

We try to find a nontrivial linear combination of the vectors in V that yields $\mathbf{0}$. This requires that we find scalars c_1 and c_2 (at least one of which is nonzero) satisfying $c_1([1 \quad 0]) + c_2([0 \quad 1]) = [0 \quad 0]$. Thus, c_1 and c_2 must satisfy $[c_1 \quad c_2] = [0 \quad 0]$. This implies $c_1 = c_2 = 0$. The only linear combination of vectors in V that yields $\mathbf{0}$ is the trivial linear combination. Therefore, V is a linearly independent set of vectors.

           ◆

E X A M P L E   10

Show that $V = \{[1 \quad 2], [2 \quad 4]\}$ is a linearly dependent set of vectors.

Solution

Since $2([1 \quad 2]) - 1([2 \quad 4]) = [0 \quad 0]$, there is a nontrivial linear combination with $c_1 = 2$ and $c_2 = -1$ that yields $\mathbf{0}$. Thus, V is a linearly dependent set of vectors.

           ◆

Intuitively, what does it mean for a set of vectors to be linearly dependent? To understand the concept of linear dependence, observe that a set of vectors V is linearly dependent (as long as $\mathbf{0}$ is not in V) if and only if some vector in V can be written as a nontrivial linear combination of other vectors in V (see Problem 9 at the end of this section). For instance, in Example 10, [2 4] = 2([1 2]). Thus, if a set of vectors V is linearly dependent, the vectors in V are, in some way, not all "different" vectors. By "different" we mean that the direction specified by any vector in V cannot be expressed by adding together multiples of other vectors in V. For example, in two dimensions it can be shown that two vectors are linearly dependent if and only if they lie on the same line (see Figure 6).

Figure 6
(a) Two Linearly
Dependent Vectors
(b) Two Linearly
Independent Vectors

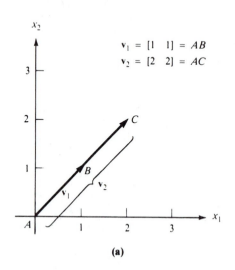

$\mathbf{v}_1 = [1 \quad 1] = AB$
$\mathbf{v}_2 = [2 \quad 2] = AC$

(a)

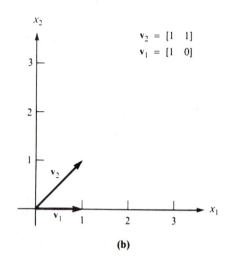

$\mathbf{v}_2 = [1 \quad 1]$
$\mathbf{v}_1 = [1 \quad 0]$

(b)

THE RANK OF A MATRIX

The Gauss-Jordan method can be used to determine whether a set of vectors is linearly independent or linearly dependent. Before describing how this is done, we define the concept of the rank of a matrix.

    Let A be any $m \times n$ matrix, and denote the rows of A by $\mathbf{r}_1, \mathbf{r}_2, \ldots, \mathbf{r}_m$. Also define $R = \{\mathbf{r}_1, \mathbf{r}_2, \ldots, \mathbf{r}_m\}$.

DEFINITION   The **rank** of A is the number of vectors in the largest linearly independent subset of R.

The following three examples illustrate the concept of rank.

E X A M P L E 11   Show that rank $A = 0$ for the following matrix:

$$A = \begin{bmatrix} 0 & 0 \\ 0 & 0 \end{bmatrix}$$

Solution   For the set of vectors $R = \{[0 \quad 0], [0 \quad 0]\}$, it is impossible to choose a subset of R that is linearly independent (recall Example 8).

EXAMPLE 12

Show that rank $A = 1$ for the following matrix:

$$A = \begin{bmatrix} 1 & 1 \\ 2 & 2 \end{bmatrix}$$

Solution

Here $R = \{[1 \quad 1], [2 \quad 2]\}$. The set $\{[1 \quad 1]\}$ is a linearly independent subset of R, so rank A must be at least 1. If we try to find two linearly independent vectors in R, we fail, because $2([1 \quad 1]) - [2 \quad 2] = [0 \quad 0]$. This means that rank A cannot be 2. Thus, rank A must equal 1.

EXAMPLE 13

Show that rank $A = 2$ for the following matrix:

$$A = \begin{bmatrix} 1 & 0 \\ 0 & 1 \end{bmatrix}$$

Solution

Here $R = \{[1 \quad 0], [0 \quad 1]\}$. From Example 9, we know that R is a linearly independent set of vectors. Thus, rank $A = 2$.

To find the rank of a given matrix A, simply apply the Gauss-Jordan method to the matrix A. Let the final result be the matrix $\bar{A}$. It can be shown that performing a sequence of ero's on a matrix does not change the rank of the matrix. This implies that rank A = rank $\bar{A}$. It is also apparent that the rank of $\bar{A}$ will be the number of nonzero rows in $\bar{A}$. Combining these facts, we find that rank A = rank $\bar{A}$ = number of nonzero rows in $\bar{A}$.

EXAMPLE 14

Find

$$\text{rank } A = \begin{bmatrix} 1 & 0 & 0 \\ 0 & 2 & 1 \\ 0 & 2 & 3 \end{bmatrix}$$

Solution

The Gauss-Jordan method yields the following sequence of matrices:

$$A = \begin{bmatrix} 1 & 0 & 0 \\ 0 & 2 & 1 \\ 0 & 2 & 3 \end{bmatrix} \rightarrow \begin{bmatrix} 1 & 0 & 0 \\ 0 & 1 & \frac{1}{2} \\ 0 & 2 & 3 \end{bmatrix} \rightarrow \begin{bmatrix} 1 & 0 & 0 \\ 0 & 1 & \frac{1}{2} \\ 0 & 0 & 2 \end{bmatrix} \rightarrow \begin{bmatrix} 1 & 0 & 0 \\ 0 & 1 & \frac{1}{2} \\ 0 & 0 & 1 \end{bmatrix} \rightarrow \begin{bmatrix} 1 & 0 & 0 \\ 0 & 1 & 0 \\ 0 & 0 & 1 \end{bmatrix}$$

$$= \bar{A}$$

Thus, rank A = rank $\bar{A}$ = 3.

HOW TO TELL WHETHER A SET OF VECTORS IS LINEARLY INDEPENDENT

We now describe a method for determining whether a set of vectors $V = \{\mathbf{v}_1, \mathbf{v}_2, \ldots, \mathbf{v}_m\}$ is linearly independent.

Form the matrix A whose ith row is $\mathbf{v}_i$. A will have m rows. If rank $A = m$, then V is a linearly independent set of vectors, while if rank $A < m$, then V is a linearly dependent set of vectors.

E X A M P L E
15

Determine whether $V = \{[1 \quad 0 \quad 0], [0 \quad 1 \quad 0], [1 \quad 1 \quad 0]\}$ is a linearly independent set of vectors.

Solution

The Gauss-Jordan method yields the following sequence of matrices:

$$A = \begin{bmatrix} 1 & 0 & 0 \\ 0 & 1 & 0 \\ 1 & 1 & 0 \end{bmatrix} \rightarrow \begin{bmatrix} 1 & 0 & 0 \\ 0 & 1 & 0 \\ 0 & 1 & 0 \end{bmatrix} \rightarrow \begin{bmatrix} 1 & 0 & 0 \\ 0 & 1 & 0 \\ 0 & 0 & 0 \end{bmatrix} = \bar{A}$$

Thus, rank A = rank $\bar{A}$ = 2 < 3. This shows that V is a linearly dependent set of vectors. In fact, the ero's used to transform A to $\bar{A}$ can be used to show that $[1 \quad 1 \quad 0] = [1 \quad 0 \quad 0] + [0 \quad 1 \quad 0]$. This equation also shows that V is a linearly dependent set of vectors.

◆

◆ PROBLEMS

GROUP A

Determine if each of the following sets of vectors is linearly independent or linearly dependent.

1. $V = \{[1 \quad 0 \quad 1], [1 \quad 2 \quad 1], [2 \quad 2 \quad 2]\}$

2. $V = \{[2 \quad 1 \quad 0], [1 \quad 2 \quad 0], [3 \quad 3 \quad 1]\}$

3. $V = \{[2 \quad 1], [1 \quad 2]\}$

4. $V = \{[2 \quad 0], [3 \quad 0]\}$

5. $V = \left\{ \begin{bmatrix} 1 \\ 2 \\ 3 \end{bmatrix}, \begin{bmatrix} 4 \\ 5 \\ 6 \end{bmatrix}, \begin{bmatrix} 5 \\ 7 \\ 9 \end{bmatrix} \right\}$

6. $V = \left\{ \begin{bmatrix} 1 \\ 0 \\ 0 \end{bmatrix}, \begin{bmatrix} 0 \\ 2 \\ 1 \end{bmatrix}, \begin{bmatrix} 1 \\ 0 \\ 1 \end{bmatrix} \right\}$

GROUP B

7. Show that the linear system $A\mathbf{x} = \mathbf{b}$ has a solution if and only if $\mathbf{b}$ can be written as a linear combination of the columns of A.

8. Suppose there is a collection of three or more two-dimensional vectors. Provide an argument showing that the collection must be linearly dependent.

9. Show that a set of vectors V (not containing the $\mathbf{0}$ vector) is linearly dependent if and only if there exists some vector in V that can be written as a nontrivial linear combination of other vectors in V.

2-5

THE INVERSE OF A MATRIX

To solve a single linear equation like $4x = 3$, we simply multiply both sides of the equation by the multiplicative inverse of 4, which is 4^{-1}, or $\frac{1}{4}$. This yields $4^{-1}(4x) = (4^{-1})3$, or $x = \frac{3}{4}$. (Of course, this method fails to work for the equation $0x = 3$, because zero has no multiplicative inverse.) In this section, we develop a generalization of this technique that can be used to solve "square" (number of equations = number of unknowns) linear systems. We begin with some preliminary definitions.

| DEFINITION | A **square matrix** is any matrix having an equal number of rows and columns. |

| DEFINITION | The **diagonal elements** of a square matrix are those elements a_{ij} such that $i = j$. |

| DEFINITION | A square matrix for which all diagonal elements are equal to 1 and all nondiagonal elements are equal to zero is called an **identity matrix**. |

The $m \times m$ identity matrix will be written as I_m. Thus,

$$I_2 = \begin{bmatrix} 1 & 0 \\ 0 & 1 \end{bmatrix}, \qquad I_3 = \begin{bmatrix} 1 & 0 & 0 \\ 0 & 1 & 0 \\ 0 & 0 & 1 \end{bmatrix}, \qquad \cdots$$

If the multiplications $I_m A$ and $A I_m$ are defined, it is easy to show that $I_m A = A I_m = A$. Thus, just as the number 1 serves as the unit element for multiplication of real numbers, I_m serves as the unit element for multiplication of matrices.

Recall that $\frac{1}{4}$ is the multiplicative inverse of 4. This is because $4(\frac{1}{4}) = (\frac{1}{4})4 = 1$. This motivates the following definition of the inverse of a matrix.

| DEFINITION | For a given $m \times m$ matrix A, the $m \times m$ matrix B is the **inverse** of A if $$BA = AB = I_m \qquad (16)$$ (It can be shown that if $BA = I_m$ or $AB = I_m$, then the other quantity will also equal I_m.) |

Some square matrices do not have inverses. If there does exist an $m \times m$ matrix B satisfying Eq. (16), we write $B = A^{-1}$. For example, if

$$A = \begin{bmatrix} 2 & 0 & -1 \\ 3 & 1 & 2 \\ -1 & 0 & 1 \end{bmatrix}$$

the reader can verify that

$$\begin{bmatrix} 2 & 0 & -1 \\ 3 & 1 & 2 \\ -1 & 0 & 1 \end{bmatrix} \begin{bmatrix} 1 & 0 & 1 \\ -5 & 1 & -7 \\ 1 & 0 & 2 \end{bmatrix} = \begin{bmatrix} 1 & 0 & 0 \\ 0 & 1 & 0 \\ 0 & 0 & 1 \end{bmatrix}$$

and

$$\begin{bmatrix} 1 & 0 & 1 \\ -5 & 1 & -7 \\ 1 & 0 & 2 \end{bmatrix} \begin{bmatrix} 2 & 0 & -1 \\ 3 & 1 & 2 \\ -1 & 0 & 1 \end{bmatrix} = \begin{bmatrix} 1 & 0 & 0 \\ 0 & 1 & 0 \\ 0 & 0 & 1 \end{bmatrix}$$

Thus,

$$A^{-1} = \begin{bmatrix} 1 & 0 & 1 \\ -5 & 1 & -7 \\ 1 & 0 & 2 \end{bmatrix}$$

To see why we are interested in the concept of a matrix inverse, suppose we wish to solve a linear system $A\mathbf{x} = \mathbf{b}$ that has m equations and m unknowns. Suppose that A^{-1} exists. Multiplying both sides of $A\mathbf{x} = \mathbf{b}$ by A^{-1}, we see that any solution of $A\mathbf{x} = \mathbf{b}$ must also satisfy $A^{-1}(A\mathbf{x}) = A^{-1}\mathbf{b}$. Using the associative law and the definition of a matrix inverse, we obtain

$$(A^{-1}A)\mathbf{x} = A^{-1}\mathbf{b}$$

or $\qquad I_m\mathbf{x} = A^{-1}\mathbf{b}$

or $\qquad \mathbf{x} = A^{-1}\mathbf{b}$

This shows that knowing A^{-1} enables us to find the unique solution to a square linear system. This is the analog of solving $4x = 3$ by multiplying both sides of the equation by 4^{-1}.

The Gauss-Jordan method may be used to find A^{-1} (or to show that A^{-1} does not exist). To illustrate how we can use the Gauss-Jordan method to invert a matrix, suppose we want to find A^{-1} for

$$A = \begin{bmatrix} 2 & 5 \\ 1 & 3 \end{bmatrix}$$

This requires that we find a matrix

$$\begin{bmatrix} a & b \\ c & d \end{bmatrix} = A^{-1}$$

satisfying

$$\begin{bmatrix} 2 & 5 \\ 1 & 3 \end{bmatrix}\begin{bmatrix} a & b \\ c & d \end{bmatrix} = \begin{bmatrix} 1 & 0 \\ 0 & 1 \end{bmatrix} \qquad (17)$$

From Eq. (17), we obtain the following pair of simultaneous equations that must be satisfied by a, b, c, and d:

$$\begin{bmatrix} 2 & 5 \\ 1 & 3 \end{bmatrix}\begin{bmatrix} a \\ c \end{bmatrix} = \begin{bmatrix} 1 \\ 0 \end{bmatrix}; \qquad \begin{bmatrix} 2 & 5 \\ 1 & 3 \end{bmatrix}\begin{bmatrix} b \\ d \end{bmatrix} = \begin{bmatrix} 0 \\ 1 \end{bmatrix}$$

Thus, to find

$$\begin{bmatrix} a \\ c \end{bmatrix}$$

(the first column of A^{-1}), we can apply the Gauss-Jordan method to the augmented matrix

$$\begin{bmatrix} 2 & 5 & | & 1 \\ 1 & 3 & | & 0 \end{bmatrix}$$

Once ero's have transformed

$$\begin{bmatrix} 2 & 5 \\ 1 & 3 \end{bmatrix}$$

to I_2,

$$\begin{bmatrix} 1 \\ 0 \end{bmatrix}$$

will have been transformed into the first column of A^{-1}. To determine

$$\begin{bmatrix} b \\ d \end{bmatrix}$$

(the second column of A^{-1}), we apply ero's to the augmented matrix

$$\begin{bmatrix} 2 & 5 & | & 0 \\ 1 & 3 & | & 1 \end{bmatrix}$$

When

$$\begin{bmatrix} 2 & 5 \\ 1 & 3 \end{bmatrix}$$

has been transformed into I_2,

$$\begin{bmatrix} 0 \\ 1 \end{bmatrix}$$

will have been transformed into the second column of A^{-1}. Thus, to find each column of A^{-1}, we must perform a sequence of ero's that transform

$$\begin{bmatrix} 2 & 5 \\ 1 & 3 \end{bmatrix}$$

into I_2. This suggests that we can find A^{-1} by applying ero's to the 2×4 matrix

$$A \,|\, I_2 = \begin{bmatrix} 2 & 5 & | & 1 & 0 \\ 1 & 3 & | & 0 & 1 \end{bmatrix}$$

When

$$\begin{bmatrix} 2 & 5 \\ 1 & 3 \end{bmatrix}$$

has been transformed to I_2,

$$\begin{bmatrix} 1 \\ 0 \end{bmatrix}$$

will have been transformed into the first column of A^{-1}, and

$$\begin{bmatrix} 0 \\ 1 \end{bmatrix}$$

will have been transformed into the second column of A^{-1}. Thus, *as A is transformed into* I_2, I_2 *is transformed into* A^{-1}. The computations to determine A^{-1} follow.

Step 1 Multiply row 1 of $A \mid I_2$ by $\frac{1}{2}$. This yields

$$A' \mid I_2' = \begin{bmatrix} 1 & \frac{5}{2} & \Big| & \frac{1}{2} & 0 \\ 1 & 3 & \Big| & 0 & 1 \end{bmatrix}$$

Step 2 Replace row 2 of $A' \mid I_2'$ by $-1(\text{row 1 of } A' \mid I_2') + \text{row 2 of } A' \mid I_2'$. This yields

$$A'' \mid I_2'' = \begin{bmatrix} 1 & \frac{5}{2} & \Big| & \frac{1}{2} & 0 \\ 0 & \frac{1}{2} & \Big| & -\frac{1}{2} & 1 \end{bmatrix}$$

Step 3 Multiply row 2 of $A'' \mid I_2''$ by 2. This yields

$$A''' \mid I_2''' = \begin{bmatrix} 1 & \frac{5}{2} & \Big| & \frac{1}{2} & 0 \\ 0 & 1 & \Big| & -1 & 2 \end{bmatrix}$$

Step 4 Replace row 1 of $A''' \mid I_2'''$ by $-\frac{5}{2}(\text{row 2 of } A''' \mid I_2''') + \text{row 1 of } A''' \mid I_2'''$. This yields

$$\begin{bmatrix} 1 & 0 & \Big| & 3 & -5 \\ 0 & 1 & \Big| & -1 & 2 \end{bmatrix}$$

Since A has been transformed into I_2, I_2 will have been transformed into A^{-1}. Hence,

$$A^{-1} = \begin{bmatrix} 3 & -5 \\ -1 & 2 \end{bmatrix}$$

The reader should verify that $AA^{-1} = A^{-1}A = I_2$.

A MATRIX MAY NOT HAVE AN INVERSE

Some matrices do not have inverses. To illustrate, let

$$A = \begin{bmatrix} 1 & 2 \\ 2 & 4 \end{bmatrix} \quad \text{and} \quad A^{-1} = \begin{bmatrix} e & f \\ g & h \end{bmatrix} \tag{18}$$

To find A^{-1} we must solve the following pair of simultaneous equations:

$$\begin{bmatrix} 1 & 2 \\ 2 & 4 \end{bmatrix} \begin{bmatrix} e \\ g \end{bmatrix} = \begin{bmatrix} 1 \\ 0 \end{bmatrix} \tag{18.1}$$

$$\begin{bmatrix} 1 & 2 \\ 2 & 4 \end{bmatrix} \begin{bmatrix} f \\ h \end{bmatrix} = \begin{bmatrix} 0 \\ 1 \end{bmatrix} \tag{18.2}$$

When we try to solve (18.1) by the Gauss-Jordan method, we find that

$$\begin{bmatrix} 1 & 2 & \Big| & 1 \\ 2 & 4 & \Big| & 0 \end{bmatrix}$$

is transformed into

$$\begin{bmatrix} 1 & 2 & | & 1 \\ 0 & 0 & | & -2 \end{bmatrix}$$

This indicates that (18.1) has no solution, and A^{-1} cannot exist.

Observe that (18.1) fails to have a solution, because the Gauss-Jordan method transforms A into a matrix with a row of zeros on the bottom. This can only happen if rank $A < 2$. If an $m \times m$ matrix A has rank $A < m$, then A^{-1} will not exist.

THE GAUSS-JORDAN METHOD FOR INVERTING AN $m \times m$ MATRIX A

Step 1 Write down the $m \times 2m$ matrix $A \,|\, I_m$.

Step 2 Use ero's to transform $A \,|\, I_m$ into $I_m \,|\, B$. This will only be possible if rank $A = m$. In this case, $B = A^{-1}$. If rank $A < m$, then A has no inverse.

USING MATRIX INVERSES TO SOLVE LINEAR SYSTEMS

As previously stated, matrix inverses can be used to solve a linear system $A\mathbf{x} = \mathbf{b}$ in which the number of variables and equations are equal. Simply multiply both sides of $A\mathbf{x} = \mathbf{b}$ by A^{-1} to obtain the solution $\mathbf{x} = A^{-1}\mathbf{b}$. For example, to solve

$$2x_1 + 5x_2 = 7$$
$$x_1 + 3x_2 = 4$$

(19)

write the matrix representation of (19):

$$\begin{bmatrix} 2 & 5 \\ 1 & 3 \end{bmatrix} \begin{bmatrix} x_1 \\ x_2 \end{bmatrix} = \begin{bmatrix} 7 \\ 4 \end{bmatrix}$$

(20)

Let

$$A = \begin{bmatrix} 2 & 5 \\ 1 & 3 \end{bmatrix}$$

We have already found that

$$A^{-1} = \begin{bmatrix} 3 & -5 \\ -1 & 2 \end{bmatrix}$$

Multiplying both sides of (20) by A^{-1}, we obtain

$$\begin{bmatrix} 3 & -5 \\ -1 & 2 \end{bmatrix} \begin{bmatrix} 2 & 5 \\ 1 & 3 \end{bmatrix} \begin{bmatrix} x_1 \\ x_2 \end{bmatrix} = \begin{bmatrix} 3 & -5 \\ -1 & 2 \end{bmatrix} \begin{bmatrix} 7 \\ 4 \end{bmatrix}$$

$$\begin{bmatrix} x_1 \\ x_2 \end{bmatrix} = \begin{bmatrix} 1 \\ 1 \end{bmatrix}$$

Thus, $x_1 = 1$, $x_2 = 1$ is the unique solution to system (19).

◆ PROBLEMS

GROUP A

Find A^{-1} (if it exists) for the following matrices:

1. $\begin{bmatrix} 1 & 3 \\ 2 & 5 \end{bmatrix}$ **2.** $\begin{bmatrix} 1 & 0 & 1 \\ 4 & 1 & -2 \\ 3 & 1 & -1 \end{bmatrix}$

3. $\begin{bmatrix} 1 & 0 & 1 \\ 1 & 1 & 1 \\ 2 & 1 & 2 \end{bmatrix}$ **4.** $\begin{bmatrix} 1 & 2 & 1 \\ 1 & 2 & 0 \\ 2 & 4 & 1 \end{bmatrix}$

5. Use the answer to Problem 1 to solve the following linear system:

$$x_1 + 3x_2 = 4$$
$$2x_1 + 5x_2 = 7$$

6. Use the answer to Problem 2 to solve the following linear system:

$$x_1 + \quad\quad x_3 = 4$$
$$4x_1 + x_2 - 2x_3 = 0$$
$$3x_1 + x_2 - \quad x_3 = 2$$

GROUP B

7. Show that a square matrix has an inverse if and only if its rows form a linearly independent set of vectors.

8. Consider a square matrix B whose inverse is given by B^{-1}.

(a) In terms of B^{-1}, what is the inverse of the matrix $100B$?

(b) Let B' be the matrix obtained from B by doubling every entry in row 1 of B. Explain how we could obtain the inverse of B' from B^{-1}.

(c) Let B' be the matrix obtained from B by doubling every entry in column 1 of B. Explain how we could obtain the inverse of B' from B^{-1}.

9. Suppose that A and B both have inverses. Find the inverse of the matrix AB.

10. Suppose A has an inverse. Show that $(A^T)^{-1} = (A^{-1})^T$. (*Hint*: Use the fact that $AA^{-1} = I$, and take the transpose of both sides.)

11. A square matrix A is *orthogonal* if $AA^T = I$. What properties must be possessed by the columns of an orthogonal matrix?

2-6   DETERMINANTS

Associated with any square matrix A is a number called the determinant of A (often abbreviated as $\det A$ or $|A|$). Knowing how to compute the determinant of a square matrix will be useful in our study of nonlinear programming.

For a 1×1 matrix $A = [a_{11}]$,

$$\det A = a_{11} \tag{21}$$

For a 2×2 matrix

$$A = \begin{bmatrix} a_{11} & a_{12} \\ a_{21} & a_{22} \end{bmatrix}$$

$$\det A = a_{11}a_{22} - a_{21}a_{12} \tag{22}$$

For example,

$$\det \begin{bmatrix} 2 & 4 \\ 3 & 5 \end{bmatrix} = 2(5) - 3(4) = -2$$

Before we learn how to compute $\det A$ for larger square matrices, we need to define the concept of the minor of a matrix.

DEFINITION	If A is an $m \times m$ matrix, then for any values of i and j, the ijth **minor** of A (written A_{ij}) is the $(m-1) \times (m-1)$ submatrix of A obtained by deleting row i and column j of A.

For example,

$$\text{if} \quad A = \begin{bmatrix} 1 & 2 & 3 \\ 4 & 5 & 6 \\ 7 & 8 & 9 \end{bmatrix}, \quad \text{then} \quad A_{12} = \begin{bmatrix} 4 & 6 \\ 7 & 9 \end{bmatrix} \quad \text{and} \quad A_{32} = \begin{bmatrix} 1 & 3 \\ 4 & 6 \end{bmatrix}$$

Let A be any $m \times m$ matrix. We may write A as

$$A = \begin{bmatrix} a_{11} & a_{12} & \cdots & a_{1m} \\ a_{21} & a_{22} & \cdots & a_{2m} \\ \vdots & \vdots & & \vdots \\ a_{m1} & a_{m2} & \cdots & a_{mm} \end{bmatrix}$$

To compute $\det A$, pick any value of i ($i = 1, 2, \ldots, m$) and compute $\det A$:

$$\det A = (-1)^{i+1} a_{i1}(\det A_{i1}) + (-1)^{i+2} a_{i2}(\det A_{i2}) + \cdots + (-1)^{i+m} a_{im}(\det A_{im}) \quad \textbf{(23)}$$

Formula (23) is called the expansion of $\det A$ by the cofactors of row i. The virtue of (23) is that is reduces the computation of $\det A$ for an $m \times m$ matrix to computations involving only $(m-1) \times (m-1)$ matrices. Apply (23) until $\det A$ can be expressed in terms of 2×2 matrices. Then use Eq. (22) to find the determinants of the relevant 2×2 matrices.

To illustrate the use of (23), we find $\det A$ for

$$A = \begin{bmatrix} 1 & 2 & 3 \\ 4 & 5 & 6 \\ 7 & 8 & 9 \end{bmatrix}$$

We expand $\det A$ by using row 1 cofactors. Notice that $a_{11} = 1$, $a_{12} = 2$, and $a_{13} = 3$. Also

$$A_{11} = \begin{bmatrix} 5 & 6 \\ 8 & 9 \end{bmatrix}$$

so by (22), $\det A_{11} = 5(9) - 8(6) = -3$;

$$A_{12} = \begin{bmatrix} 4 & 6 \\ 7 & 9 \end{bmatrix}$$

so by (22), $\det A_{12} = 4(9) - 7(6) = -6$; and

$$A_{13} = \begin{bmatrix} 4 & 5 \\ 7 & 8 \end{bmatrix}$$

so by (22), $\det A_{13} = 4(8) - 7(5) = -3$. Then by (23),

$$\det A = (-1)^{1+1} a_{11}(\det A_{11}) + (-1)^{1+2} a_{12}(\det A_{12}) + (-1)^{1+3} a_{13}(\det A_{13})$$
$$= (1)(1)(-3) + (-1)(2)(-6) + (1)(3)(-3) = -3 + 12 - 9 = 0$$

The interested reader may verify that expansion of det A by either row 2 or row 3 cofactors also yields det $A = 0$.

We close our discussion of determinants by noting that they can be used to invert square matrices and to solve linear equation systems. Since we already have learned to use the Gauss-Jordan method to invert matrices and to solve linear equation systems, we will not discuss these uses of determinants.

◆ **PROBLEMS**

GROUP A

1. Verify that $\det \begin{bmatrix} 1 & 2 & 3 \\ 4 & 5 & 6 \\ 7 & 8 & 9 \end{bmatrix} = 0$ by using expansions by row 2 and row 3 cofactors.

2. Find the determinant of the matrix $\begin{bmatrix} 1 & 0 & 0 & 0 \\ 0 & 2 & 0 & 0 \\ 0 & 0 & 3 & 0 \\ 0 & 0 & 0 & 5 \end{bmatrix}$

3. A matrix is said to be upper triangular if for $i > j$, $a_{ij} = 0$. Show that the determinant of any upper trian-gular 3×3 matrix is equal to the product of the matrix's diagonal elements. (This result is true for any upper trian-gular matrix.)

GROUP B

4. (a) Show that for any 1×1 and 3×3 matrix, $\det -A = -\det A$.

(b) Show that for any 2×2 and 4×4 matrix, $\det -A = \det A$.

(c) Generalize the results of parts (a) and (b).

◆ **SUMMARY**

MATRICES

A **matrix** is any rectangular array of numbers. For the matrix A, we let a_{ij} represent the element of A in row i and column j.

A matrix with only one row or one column may be thought of as a **vector**. Vectors appear in boldface type (**v**). Given a row vector $\mathbf{u} = [u_1 \quad u_2 \quad \cdots \quad u_n]$ and a column vector

$$\mathbf{v} = \begin{bmatrix} v_1 \\ v_2 \\ \vdots \\ v_n \end{bmatrix}$$

of the same dimension, the **scalar product** of **u** and **v** (written $\mathbf{u} \cdot \mathbf{v}$) is the number $u_1 v_1 + u_2 v_2 + \cdots + u_n v_n$.

Given two matrices A and B, the **matrix product** of A and B (written AB) is defined if and only if the number of columns in A = the number of rows in B. Suppose this is the case and A has m rows and B has n columns. Then the matrix product $C = AB$ of

A and B is the $m \times n$ matrix C whose ijth element is determined as follows: the ijth element of $C = $ the scalar product of row i of A with column j of B.

MATRICES AND LINEAR EQUATIONS

The **linear equation system**

$$a_{11}x_1 + a_{12}x_2 + \cdots + a_{1n}x_n = b_1$$
$$a_{21}x_1 + a_{22}x_2 + \cdots + a_{2n}x_n = b_2$$
$$\vdots \quad\quad \vdots \quad\quad\quad \vdots = \vdots$$
$$a_{m1}x_1 + a_{m2}x_2 + \cdots + a_{mn}x_n = b_m$$

may be written as $A\mathbf{x} = \mathbf{b}$ or $A \,|\, \mathbf{b}$, where

$$A = \begin{bmatrix} a_{11} & a_{12} & \cdots & a_{1n} \\ a_{21} & a_{22} & \cdots & a_{2n} \\ \vdots & \vdots & & \vdots \\ a_{m1} & a_{m2} & \cdots & a_{mn} \end{bmatrix}, \quad \mathbf{x} = \begin{bmatrix} x_1 \\ x_2 \\ \vdots \\ x_n \end{bmatrix}, \quad \mathbf{b} = \begin{bmatrix} b_1 \\ b_2 \\ \vdots \\ b_m \end{bmatrix}$$

THE GAUSS-JORDAN METHOD

Using **elementary row operations** (ero's), we may solve any linear equation system. From a matrix A, an ero yields a new matrix A' via one of the following three procedures.

Type 1 ero A' is obtained by multiplying any row of A by a nonzero scalar.

Type 2 ero Begin by multiplying any row of A (say, row i) by a nonzero scalar c. For some $j \neq i$, let row j of $A' = c(\text{row } i \text{ of } A) + \text{row } j$ of A, and let the other rows of A' be the same as the rows of A.

Type 3 ero Interchange any two rows of A.

The Gauss-Jordan method uses ero's to solve linear equation systems, as shown in the following steps.

Step 1 To solve $A\mathbf{x} = \mathbf{b}$, write down the augmented matrix $A \,|\, \mathbf{b}$.

Step 2a At any stage, define a current row, current column, and current entry (the entry in the current row and column). Begin with row 1 as the current row, column 1 as the current column, and a_{11} as the current entry. If a_{11} (the current entry) is nonzero, use ero's to transform column 1 (the current column) to

$$\begin{bmatrix} 1 \\ 0 \\ \vdots \\ 0 \end{bmatrix}$$

Then obtain the new current row, column, and entry by moving down one row and one column to the right, and go to Step 2b. If a_{11} (the current entry) equals 0, then determine whether, in the current column, there are any nonzero numbers in the rows below the current row. If so, do a Type 3 ero involving the current row and any such row and use ero's to transform column 1 to

$$\begin{bmatrix} 1 \\ 0 \\ \vdots \\ 0 \end{bmatrix}$$

These obtain the new current row, column, and entry by moving down one row and one column to the right. Then go to Step 2b. In the current column, if there are no nonzero numbers in the rows below the current row, obtain a new current column and entry by moving one column to the right. Then go to Step 2b.

Step 2b If the current entry is nonzero, use ero's to transform the current entry to 1 and the rest of the current column's entries to 0. Obtain the new current row, column, and entry by moving down one row and over one column. If this is impossible, stop. Otherwise, repeat Step 2b. If the current entry is 0, determine whether, in the current column, there are any nonzero numbers below the current row. If so, do a Type 3 ero with the current row and any such row. Then use ero's to transform the current entry to 1 and the rest to the current column's entries to 0. Obtain the new current row, column, and entry by moving down one row and over one column. If this is impossible, stop. Otherwise, repeat Step 2b. If the current column has no nonzero numbers below the current row, obtain the new current column and entry by moving one column to the right (if possible), and repeat Step 2b. If it is impossible to move one column to the right, stop.

This procedure may require "passing over" one or more columns without transforming them.

Step 3 Write down the system of equations $A'\mathbf{x} = \mathbf{b}'$ that corresponds to the matrix $A'|\mathbf{b}'$ obtained when Step 2 is completed. Then $A'\mathbf{x} = \mathbf{b}'$ will have the same set of solutions as $A\mathbf{x} = \mathbf{b}$.

To describe the set of solutions to $A'\mathbf{x} = \mathbf{b}'$ (and $A\mathbf{x} = \mathbf{b}$), we define the concepts of basic and nonbasic variables. For any linear system, a variable that appears with a coefficient of 1 in a single equation and a zero coefficient in all other equations is called a **basic variable**. Any variable that is not a basic variable is called a **nonbasic variable**.

Let BV be the set of basic variables for $A'\mathbf{x} = \mathbf{b}'$ and NBV be the set of nonbasic variables for $A'\mathbf{x} = \mathbf{b}'$. We can now characterize the solutions of $A\mathbf{x} = \mathbf{b}$. Their character depends on which of the following cases occurs.

Case 1 $A'\mathbf{x} = \mathbf{b}'$ contains at least one row of the form $[0 \quad 0 \quad \cdots \quad 0\,|\,c]\,(c \neq 0)$. In this case, $A\mathbf{x} = \mathbf{b}$ has no solution.

Case 2 If Case 1 does not apply and NBV, the set of nonbasic variables, is empty, $A\mathbf{x} = \mathbf{b}$ will have a unique solution.

Case 3 If Case 1 does not hold and NBV is nonempty, $A\mathbf{x} = \mathbf{b}$ will have an infinite number of solutions.

LINEAR INDEPENDENCE, LINEAR DEPENDENCE, AND THE RANK OF A MATRIX

A set V of m-dimensional vectors is **linearly independent** if the only linear combination of vectors in V that equals $\mathbf{0}$ is the trivial linear combination. A set V of m-dimensional vectors is **linearly dependent** if there is a nontrivial linear combination of the vectors in V that adds up to $\mathbf{0}$.

Let A be any $m \times n$ matrix, and denote the rows of A by $\mathbf{r}_1, \mathbf{r}_2, \ldots, \mathbf{r}_m$. Also define $R = \{\mathbf{r}_1, \mathbf{r}_2, \ldots, \mathbf{r}_m\}$. The **rank** of A is the number of vectors in the largest linearly independent subset of R. To find the rank of a given matrix A, apply the Gauss-Jordan method to the matrix A. Let the final result be the matrix $\bar{A}$. Then rank $A =$ rank $\bar{A} =$ number of nonzero rows in $\bar{A}$.

To determine if a set of vectors $V = \{\mathbf{v}_1, \mathbf{v}_2, \ldots, \mathbf{v}_m\}$ is linearly independent, form the matrix A whose ith row is $\mathbf{v}_i$. A will have m rows. If rank $A = m$, then V is a linearly independent set of vectors, while if rank $A < m$, then V is a linearly dependent set of vectors.

INVERSE OF A MATRIX

For a given square ($m \times m$) matrix A, if $AB = BA = I_m$, then B is the **inverse** of A (written $B = A^{-1}$). The Gauss-Jordan method for inverting an $m \times m$ matrix A to get A^{-1} is as follows:

Step 1 Write down the $m \times 2m$ matrix $A \,|\, I_m$.

Step 2 Use ero's to transform $A \,|\, I_m$ into $I_m \,|\, B$. This will only be possible if rank $A = m$. In this case, $B = A^{-1}$. If rank $A < m$, then A has no inverse.

DETERMINANTS

Associated with any square ($m \times m$) matrix A is a number called the **determinant** of A (written det A or $|A|$). For a 1×1 matrix, det $A = a_{11}$. For a 2×2 matrix, det $A = a_{11}a_{22} - a_{21}a_{12}$. For a general $m \times m$ matrix, we can find det A by repeated application of the following formula (valid for $i = 1, 2, \ldots, m$):

$$\det A = (-1)^{i+1}a_{i1}(\det A_{i1}) + (-1)^{i+2}a_{i2}(\det A_{i2}) + \cdots + (-1)^{i+m}a_{im}(\det A_{im})$$

Here A_{ij} is the ijth **minor** of A, which is the $(m-1) \times (m-1)$ matrix obtained from A after deleting the ith row and jth column of A.

◆ REVIEW PROBLEMS

GROUP A

1. Find all solutions to the following linear system:

$$
\begin{aligned}
x_1 + x_2 \qquad &= 2 \\
x_2 + x_3 &= 3 \\
x_1 + 2x_2 + x_3 &= 5
\end{aligned}
$$

2. Find the inverse of the matrix $\begin{bmatrix} 0 & 3 \\ 2 & 1 \end{bmatrix}$.

3. Each year, 20% of all untenured State University faculty become tenured, 5% quit, and 75% remain untenured. Each year, 90% of all tenured S.U. faculty remain tenured and 10% quit. Let U_t be the number of untenured S.U. faculty at the beginning of year t, and T_t be the number of tenured S.U. faculty at the beginning of year t. Use matrix multiplication to relate the vector $\begin{bmatrix} U_{t+1} \\ T_{t+1} \end{bmatrix}$ to the vector $\begin{bmatrix} U_t \\ T_t \end{bmatrix}$.

4. Use the Gauss-Jordan method to determine all solutions to the following linear system:

$$2x_1 + 3x_2 = 3$$
$$x_1 + x_2 = 1$$
$$x_1 + 2x_2 = 2$$

5. Find the inverse of the matrix $\begin{bmatrix} 0 & 2 \\ 1 & 3 \end{bmatrix}$.

6. The grades of two students during their last semester at S.U. are shown in Table 2.

Courses 1 and 2 are four-credit courses, and courses 3 and 4 are three-credit courses. Let GPA_i be the semester grade point average for student i. Use matrix multiplication to express the vector $\begin{bmatrix} GPA_1 \\ GPA_2 \end{bmatrix}$ in terms of the information given in the problem.

7. Use the Gauss-Jordan method to find all solutions to the following linear system:

$$2x_1 + x_2 = 3$$
$$3x_1 + x_2 = 4$$
$$x_1 - x_2 = 0$$

8. Find the inverse of the matrix $\begin{bmatrix} 2 & 3 \\ 3 & 5 \end{bmatrix}$.

9. Let C_t = number of children in Indiana at the beginning of year t, and A_t = number of adults in Indiana at the beginning of year t. During any given year, 5% of all children become adults, and 1% of all children die. Also, during any given year, 3% of all adults die. Use matrix multiplication to express the vector $\begin{bmatrix} C_{t+1} \\ A_{t+1} \end{bmatrix}$ in terms of $\begin{bmatrix} C_t \\ A_t \end{bmatrix}$.

10. Use the Gauss-Jordan method to find all solutions to the following linear equation system:

$$x_1 \qquad - x_3 = 4$$
$$x_2 + x_3 = 2$$
$$x_1 + x_2 \qquad = 5$$

11. Use the Gauss-Jordan method to find the inverse of the matrix $\begin{bmatrix} 1 & 0 & 2 \\ 0 & 1 & 0 \\ 0 & 1 & 1 \end{bmatrix}$.

12. During any given year, 10% of all rural residents move to the city, and 20% of all city residents move to a rural area (all other people stay put!). Let R_t be the number of rural residents at the beginning of year t, and C_t be the number of city residents at the beginning of year t. Use matrix multiplication to relate the vector $\begin{bmatrix} R_{t+1} \\ C_{t+1} \end{bmatrix}$ to the vector $\begin{bmatrix} R_t \\ C_t \end{bmatrix}$.

13. Determine whether the set $V = \{[1 \quad 2 \quad 1], [2 \quad 0 \quad 0]\}$ is a linearly independent set of vectors.

14. Determine whether the set $V = \{[1 \quad 0 \quad 0], [0 \quad 1 \quad 0], [-1 \quad -1 \quad 0]\}$ is a linearly independent set of vectors.

Table 2

	COURSE 1	COURSE 2	COURSE 3	COURSE 4
Student 1	3.6	3.8	2.6	3.4
Student 2	2.7	3.1	2.9	3.6

15. Let $A = \begin{bmatrix} a & 0 & 0 & 0 \\ 0 & b & 0 & 0 \\ 0 & 0 & c & 0 \\ 0 & 0 & 0 & d \end{bmatrix}$.

(a) For what values of a, b, c, and d will A^{-1} exist?

(b) If A^{-1} exists, find it.

16. Show that the following linear system has an infinite number of solutions:

$$\begin{bmatrix} 1 & 1 & 0 & 0 \\ 0 & 0 & 1 & 1 \\ 1 & 0 & 1 & 0 \\ 0 & 1 & 0 & 1 \end{bmatrix} \begin{bmatrix} x_1 \\ x_2 \\ x_3 \\ x_4 \end{bmatrix} = \begin{bmatrix} 2 \\ 3 \\ 4 \\ 1 \end{bmatrix}$$

17. Before paying employee bonuses and state and federal taxes, a company earns profits of $60,000. The company pays employees a bonus equal to 5% of after-tax profits. State tax is 5% of profits (after bonuses are paid). Finally, federal tax is 40% of profits (after bonuses and state tax are paid). Determine a linear equation system to find the amounts paid in bonuses, state tax, and federal tax.

18. Find the determinant of the matrix $A = \begin{bmatrix} 2 & 4 & 6 \\ 1 & 0 & 0 \\ 0 & 0 & 1 \end{bmatrix}$.

19. Show that any 2×2 matrix A that does not have an inverse will have $\det A = 0$.

GROUP B

20. Let A be an $m \times m$ matrix.

(a) Show that if rank $A = m$, then $A\mathbf{x} = \mathbf{0}$ has a unique solution. What is the unique solution?

(b) Show that if rank $A < m$, then $A\mathbf{x} = \mathbf{0}$ has an infinite number of solutions.

21. In our study of Markov chains (see Chapter 19), we will encounter the following linear system:

$$[x_1 \quad x_2 \quad \cdots \quad x_n] = [x_1 \quad x_2 \quad \cdots \quad x_n]P$$

where

$$P = \begin{bmatrix} p_{11} & p_{12} & \cdots & p_{1n} \\ p_{21} & p_{22} & \cdots & p_{2n} \\ \vdots & \vdots & & \vdots \\ p_{n1} & p_{n2} & \cdots & p_{nn} \end{bmatrix}$$

If the sum of each row of the P matrix equals 1, use Problem 20 to show that this linear system has an infinite number of solutions.

22.[†] The national economy of Seriland manufactures three products: steel, cars, and machines. (1) To produce a dollar's worth of steel requires 30 cents worth of steel, 15 cents worth of cars, and 40 cents worth of machines. (2) To produce a dollar's worth of cars requires 45 cents worth of steel, 20 cents worth of cars, and 10 cents worth of machines. (3) To produce a dollar's worth of machines requires 40 cents worth of steel, 10 cents worth of cars, and 45 cents worth of machines. During the coming year, Seriland wants to consume d_s dollars worth of steel, d_c dollars worth of cars, and d_m dollars worth of machinery.

For the coming year, let

$$s = \text{dollar value of steel produced}$$
$$c = \text{dollar value of cars produced}$$
$$m = \text{dollar value of machines produced}$$

Define A to be the 3×3 matrix whose ijth element is the dollar value of product i required to produce a dollar's worth of product j (steel = product 1, cars = product 2, machinery = product 3).

(a) Determine A.

(b) Show that

$$\begin{bmatrix} s \\ c \\ m \end{bmatrix} = A \begin{bmatrix} s \\ c \\ m \end{bmatrix} + \begin{bmatrix} d_s \\ d_c \\ d_m \end{bmatrix} \qquad (24)$$

(*Hint*: Observe that the value of next year's steel production = (next year's consumer steel demand) + (steel needed to make next year's steel) + (steel needed to make next year's cars) + (steel needed to make next year's machines). This should give you the general idea.)

(c) Show that Eq. (24) may be rewritten as

$$(I - A) \begin{bmatrix} s \\ c \\ m \end{bmatrix} = \begin{bmatrix} d_s \\ d_c \\ d_m \end{bmatrix}$$

(d) Given values for d_s, d_c, and d_m, describe how you can use $(I - A)^{-1}$ to determine if Seriland can meet next year's consumer demand.

(e) Suppose next year's demand for steel increases by $1. This will increase the value of the steel, cars, and machines that must be produced next year. In terms of $(I - A)^{-1}$, determine the change in next year's production requirements.

[†]Based on Leontief (1966). See references at end of chapter.

◆ REFERENCES

The following references contain more advanced discussions of linear algebra. To understand the theory of linear and nonlinear programming, master at least one of these books:

DANTZIG, G. *Linear Programming and Extensions*. Princeton, N.J.: Princeton University Press, 1963.

HADLEY, G. *Linear Algebra*. Reading, Mass.: Addison-Wesley, 1961.

STRANG, G. *Linear Algebra and Its Applications*, 2nd ed. Orlando, Fla.: Academic Press, 1980.

LEONTIEF, W. *Input–Output Economics*. New York: Oxford University Press, 1966.

TEICHROEW, D. *An Introduction to Management Science: Deterministic Models*. New York: Wiley, 1964. A more extensive discussion of linear algebra than this chapter gives (at a comparable level of difficulty).

CHAPTER 3

Introduction to Linear Programming

LINEAR PROGRAMMING (LP) is a tool for solving optimization problems. In 1947, George Dantzig developed an efficient method, the simplex algorithm, for solving linear programming problems (also called LP). Since the development of the simplex algorithm, LP has been used to solve optimization problems in industries as diverse as banking, education, forestry, petroleum, and trucking. In a survey of Fortune 500 firms, 85% of those responding said that they had used linear programming. As a measure of the importance of linear programming in operations research, approximately 40% of this book will be devoted to linear programming and related optimization techniques.

In Section 3.1, we begin our study of linear programming by describing the general characteristics shared by all linear programming problems. In Sections 3.2 and 3.3, we learn how to solve graphically those linear programming problems that involve only two variables. Solving these simple LPs will give us some useful insights for solving more complex LPs. The remainder of the chapter explains how to formulate linear programming models of real-life situations.

3-1   WHAT IS A LINEAR PROGRAMMING PROBLEM?

In this section, we introduce linear programming and define some important terms that are used to describe linear programming problems.

E X A M P L E 1

Giapetto's Woodcarving, Inc., manufactures two types of wooden toys: soldiers and trains. A soldier sells for $27 and uses $10 worth of raw materials. Each soldier that is manufactured increases Giapetto's variable labor and overhead costs by $14. A train sells for $21 and uses $9 worth of raw materials. Each train built increases Giapetto's variable labor and overhead costs by $10. The manufacture of wooden soldiers and trains requires two types of skilled labor: carpentry and finishing. A soldier requires 2 hours of finishing labor and 1 hour of carpentry labor. A train requires 1 hour of finishing labor and 1 hour of carpentry labor. Each week, Giapetto can obtain all the needed raw material but only 100 finishing hours and 80 carpentry hours. Demand for trains is unlimited, but at most 40 soldiers are bought each week. Giapetto wishes to maximize weekly profit (revenues − costs). Formulate a mathematical model of Giapetto's situation that can be used to maximize Giapetto's weekly profit.

Solution

In developing the Giapetto model, we explore characteristics shared by all linear programming problems.

Decision Variables. We begin by defining the relevant **decision variables**. In any linear programming model, the decision variables should completely describe the decisions to be made (in this case, by Giapetto). Clearly, Giapetto must decide how many soldiers and trains should be manufactured each week. With this in mind, we define

$$x_1 = \text{number of soldiers produced each week}$$
$$x_2 = \text{number of trains produced each week}$$

Objective Function. In any linear programming problem, the decision maker wants to maximize (usually revenue or profit) or minimize (usually costs) some function of the decision variables. The function to be maximized or minimized is called the **objective function**. For the Giapetto problem, we note that *fixed costs* (such as rent and insurance) do not depend on the values of x_1 and x_2. Thus, Giapetto can concentrate on maximizing (weekly revenues) − (raw material purchase costs) − (other variable costs).

Giapetto's weekly revenues and costs can be expressed in terms of the decision variables x_1 and x_2. It would be foolish for Giapetto to manufacture more soldiers than can be sold, so we assume that all toys produced will be sold. Then

$$
\begin{aligned}
\text{Weekly revenues} &= \text{weekly revenues from soldiers} \\
&\quad + \text{weekly revenues from trains} \\
&= \left(\frac{\text{dollars}}{\text{soldier}}\right)\left(\frac{\text{soldiers}}{\text{week}}\right) + \left(\frac{\text{dollars}}{\text{train}}\right)\left(\frac{\text{trains}}{\text{week}}\right) \\
&= 27x_1 + 21x_2
\end{aligned}
$$

Also,

$$\text{Weekly raw material costs} = 10x_1 + 9x_2$$
$$\text{Other weekly variable costs} = 14x_1 + 10x_2$$

Then Giapetto wishes to maximize

$$(27x_1 + 21x_2) - (10x_1 + 9x_2) - (14x_1 + 10x_2) = 3x_1 + 2x_2$$

Another way to see that Giapetto wishes to maximize $3x_1 + 2x_2$ is to note that

$$
\begin{aligned}
\text{Weekly revenues} \quad &= \text{weekly contribution to profit from soldiers} \\
- \text{weekly nonfixed costs} \quad &+ \text{weekly contribution to profit from trains} \\
&= \left(\frac{\text{contribution to profit}}{\text{soldier}}\right)\left(\frac{\text{soldiers}}{\text{week}}\right) \\
&+ \left(\frac{\text{contribution to profit}}{\text{train}}\right)\left(\frac{\text{trains}}{\text{week}}\right)
\end{aligned}
$$

Also,

$$\frac{\text{Contribution to profit}}{\text{Soldier}} = 27 - 10 - 14 = 3$$

$$\frac{\text{Contribution to profit}}{\text{Train}} = 21 - 9 - 10 = 2$$

Then, as before, we obtain

$$\text{Weekly revenues} - \text{weekly nonfixed costs} = 3x_1 + 2x_2$$

Thus, Giapetto's objective is to choose x_1 and x_2 to maximize $3x_1 + 2x_2$. We use the variable z to denote the objective function value of any LP. Giapetto's objective function is

$$\text{Maximize } z = 3x_1 + 2x_2 \tag{1}$$

(In the future, we abbreviate maximize by max and minimize by min.) The coefficient of a variable in the objective function is called the **objective function coefficient** of the variable. For example, the objective function coefficient for x_1 is 3, and the objective function coefficient for x_2 is 2. In this example (and in many other problems), the objective function coefficient for each variable is simply the contribution of the variable to the company's profit.

Constraints. As x_1 and x_2 increase, Giapetto's objective function grows larger. This means that if Giapetto were free to choose any values for x_1 and x_2, the company could make an arbitrarily large profit by choosing x_1 and x_2 to be very large. Unfortunately, the values of x_1 and x_2 are restricted by the following three restrictions (often called **constraints**):

Constraint 1 Each week, no more than 100 hours of finishing time may be used.

Constraint 2 Each week, no more than 80 hours of carpentry time may be used.

Constraint 3 Because of limited demand, at most 40 soldiers should be produced each week.

The amount of raw material available is assumed to be unlimited, so no restrictions have been placed on this.

The next step in formulating a mathematical model of the Giapetto problem is to express Constraints 1–3 in terms of the decision variables x_1 and x_2. To express Constraint 1 in terms of x_1 and x_2, note that

$$\frac{\text{Total finishing hrs.}}{\text{Week}} = \left(\frac{\text{finishing hrs.}}{\text{soldier}} \right) \left(\frac{\text{soldiers made}}{\text{week}} \right)$$

$$+ \left(\frac{\text{finishing hrs.}}{\text{train}} \right) \left(\frac{\text{trains made}}{\text{week}} \right)$$

$$= 2(x_1) + 1(x_2) = 2x_1 + x_2$$

Now Constraint 1 may be expressed by

$$2x_1 + x_2 \le 100 \tag{2}$$

Note that the units of each term in (2) are finishing hours per week. *For a constraint to be reasonable, all terms in the constraint must have the same units.* Otherwise one is adding apples and oranges, and the constraint won't have any meaning.

To express Constraint 2 in terms of x_1 and x_2, note that

$$\frac{\text{Total carpentry hrs.}}{\text{Week}} = \left(\frac{\text{carpentry hrs.}}{\text{soldier}}\right)\left(\frac{\text{soldiers}}{\text{week}}\right)$$
$$+ \left(\frac{\text{carpentry hrs.}}{\text{train}}\right)\left(\frac{\text{trains}}{\text{week}}\right)$$
$$= 1(x_1) + 1(x_2) = x_1 + x_2$$

Then Constraint 2 may be written as

$$x_1 + x_2 \le 80 \tag{3}$$

Again, note that the units of each term in (3) are the same (in this case, carpentry hours per week).

Finally, we express the fact that at most 40 soldiers per week can be sold by limiting the weekly production of soldiers to at most 40 soldiers. This yields the following constraint:

$$x_1 \le 40 \tag{4}$$

Thus, (2)–(4) express Constraints 1–3 in terms of the decision variables; they are called the **constraints** for the Giapetto linear programming problem. The coefficients of the decision variables in the constraints are called **technological coefficients**. This is because the technological coefficients often reflect the technology used to produce different products. For example, the technological coefficient of x_2 in (3) is 1, indicating that a soldier requires 1 carpentry hour. The number on the right-hand side of each constraint is called the constraint's **right-hand side** (or rhs). Often the rhs of a constraint represents the quantity of a resource that is available.

Sign Restrictions. To complete the formulation of a linear programming problem, the following question must be answered for each decision variable: Can the decision variable only assume nonnegative values, or is the decision variable allowed to assume both positive and negative values?

If a decision variable x_i can only assume nonnegative values, we add the **sign restriction** $x_i \ge 0$. If a variable x_i can assume both positive and negative (or zero) values, we say that x_i is **unrestricted in sign** (often abbreviated as urs). For the Giapetto problem, it is clear that $x_1 \ge 0$ and $x_2 \ge 0$. In other problems, however, some variables may be urs. For example, if x_i represented a firm's cash balance, x_i could be considered negative if the firm owed more money than it had on hand. In this case, it would be appropriate to classify x_i as urs. Other uses of urs variables are discussed in Section 4.12.

Combining the sign restrictions $x_1 \ge 0$ and $x_2 \ge 0$ with the objective function (1) and Constraints (2)–(4) yields the following optimization model:

$$\max z = 3x_1 + 2x_2 \qquad \text{(Objective function)} \tag{1}$$

subject to (s.t.)

$$2x_1 + x_2 \le 100 \qquad \text{(Finishing constraint)} \tag{2}$$
$$x_1 + x_2 \le 80 \qquad \text{(Carpentry constraint)} \tag{3}$$

$$x_1 \leq 40 \qquad \text{(Constraint on demand for soldiers)} \qquad (4)$$
$$x_1 \geq 0 \qquad \text{(Sign restriction)}^\dagger \qquad (5)$$
$$x_2 \geq 0 \qquad \text{(Sign restriction)} \qquad (6)$$

"Subject to" (s.t.) means that the values of the decision variables x_1 and x_2 must satisfy all the constraints and all the sign restrictions.

◆

Before formally defining a linear programming problem, we define the concepts of linear function and linear inequality.

DEFINITION ◆ A function $f(x_1, x_2, \ldots, x_n)$ of $x_1, x_2, \ldots, x_n$ is a **linear function** if and only if for some set of constants $c_1, c_2, \ldots, c_n$, $f(x_1, x_2, \ldots, x_n) = c_1 x_1 + c_2 x_2 + \cdots + c_n x_n$.

For example, $f(x_1, x_2) = 2x_1 + x_2$ is a linear function of x_1 and x_2, but $f(x_1, x_2) = x_1^2 x_2$ is not a linear function of x_1 and x_2.

DEFINITION ◆ For any linear function $f(x_1, x_2, \ldots, x_n)$ and any number b, the inequalities $f(x_1, x_2, \ldots, x_n) \leq b$ and $f(x_1, x_2, \ldots, x_n) \geq b$ are **linear inequalities**.

Thus, $2x_1 + 3x_2 \leq 3$ and $2x_1 + x_2 \geq 3$ are linear inequalities, but $x_1^2 x_2 \geq 3$ is not a linear inequality.

DEFINITION ◆ A **linear programming problem** (LP) is an optimization problem for which we do the following:

1. We attempt to maximize (or minimize) a *linear* function of the decision variables. The function that is to be maximized or minimized is called the *objective function*.

2. The values of the decision variables must satisfy a set of *constraints*. Each constraint must be a linear equation or linear inequality.

3. A *sign restriction* is associated with each variable. For any variable x_i, the sign restriction specifies either that x_i must be nonnegative ($x_i \geq 0$) or that x_i may be unrestricted in sign (urs).

Since Giapetto's objective function is a linear function of x_1 and x_2 and all of Giapetto's constraints are linear inequalities, the Giapetto problem is a linear programming problem. Note that the Giapetto problem is typical of a wide class of linear programming problems in which a decision maker's goal is to maximize profit subject to limited resources.

---

† The sign restrictions do constrain the values of the decision variables, but we choose to consider the sign restrictions as being separate from the constraints. The reason for this will become apparent when we study the simplex algorithm in Chapter 4.

THE PROPORTIONALITY AND ADDITIVITY ASSUMPTIONS

The fact that the objective function for an LP must be a linear function of the decision variables has two implications:

1. The contribution to the objective function from each decision variable is proportional to the value of the decision variable. For example, the contribution to the objective function from making four soldiers ($4 \times 3 = \$12$) is exactly four times the contribution to the objective function from making one soldier ($3).

2. The contribution to the objective function for any variable is independent of the values of the other decision variables. For example, no matter what the value of x_2, the manufacture of x_1 soldiers will always contribute $3x_1$ dollars to the objective function.

Analogously, the fact that each LP constraint must be a linear inequality or linear equation has two implications:

1. The contribution of each variable to the left-hand side of each constraint is proportional to the value of the variable. For example, it takes exactly three times as many finishing hours ($2 \times 3 = 6$ finishing hours) to manufacture three soldiers as it takes to manufacture one soldier (2 finishing hours).

2. The contribution of a variable to the left-hand side of each constraint is independent of the values of the other variables. For example, no matter what the value of x_1, the manufacture of x_2 trains uses x_2 finishing hours and x_2 carpentry hours.

The first implication given in each list is called the **Proportionality Assumption of Linear Programming**. Implication 2 of the first list implies that the value of the objective function is the sum of the contributions from individual variables, and implication 2 of the second list implies that the left-hand side of each constraint is the sum of the contributions from each variable. For this reason, the second implication in each list is called the **Additivity Assumption of Linear Programming**.

For an LP to be an appropriate representation of a real-life situation, the decision variables must satisfy both the Proportionality and Additivity Assumptions. Two other assumptions must also be satisfied before an LP can appropriately represent a real situation. These are the Divisibility and Certainty Assumptions.

THE DIVISIBILITY ASSUMPTION

The **Divisibility Assumption** requires that each decision variable be allowed to assume fractional values. For example, in the Giapetto problem, the Divisibility Assumption implies that it is acceptable to produce 1.5 soldiers or 1.63 trains. Since Giapetto cannot actually produce a fractional number of trains or soldiers, the Divisibility Assumption is not satisfied in the Giapetto problem. A linear programming problem in which some or all of the variables must be nonnegative integers is called an **integer programming problem**. The solution of integer programming problems is discussed in Chapter 9.

In many situations where divisibility is not present, rounding off each variable in the optimal LP solution to an integer may yield a reasonable solution. Suppose the optimal solution to an LP stated that an auto company should manufacture 150,000.4 compact cars during the current year. In this case, you could tell the auto company to manufacture 150,000 or 150,001 compact cars and be fairly confident that this would reasonably approximate an optimal production plan. On the other hand, if the number of missile sites that the U.S. should use were a variable in an LP and the optimal LP solution said that 0.4 missile sites should be built, it would make a big difference whether we rounded the number of missile sites down to zero or up to 1. In this situation, the integer programming methods of Chapter 9 would have to be used, because the number of missile sites is definitely not divisible.

THE CERTAINTY ASSUMPTION

The **Certainty Assumption** is that each parameter (objective function coefficient, right-hand side, and technological coefficient) is known with certainty. If we were unsure of the exact amount of carpentry and finishing hours required to build a train, the Certainty Assumption would be violated.

FEASIBLE REGION AND OPTIMAL SOLUTION

Two of the most basic concepts associated with a linear programming problem are feasible region and optimal solution. For defining these concepts, we use the term *point* to mean a specification of the value for each decision variable.

DEFINITION	The **feasible region** for an LP is the set of all points satisfying all the LP's constraints and all the LP's sign restrictions.

For example, in the Giapetto problem, the point $(x_1 = 40, x_2 = 20)$ is in the feasible region. Note that $x_1 = 40$ and $x_2 = 20$ satisfy the constraints (2)–(4) and the sign restrictions (5)–(6):

Constraint (2), $2x_1 + x_2 \leq 100$, is satisfied, because $2(40) + 20 \leq 100$.
Constraint (3), $x_1 + x_2 \leq 80$, is satisfied, because $40 + 20 \leq 80$.
Constraint (4), $x_1 \leq 40$, is satisfied, because $40 \leq 40$.
Restriction (5), $x_1 \geq 0$, is satisfied, because $40 \geq 0$.
Restriction (6), $x_2 \geq 0$, is satisfied, because $20 \geq 0$.

On the other hand, the point $(x_1 = 15, x_2 = 70)$ is not in the feasible region, because even though $x_1 = 15$ and $x_2 = 70$ satisfy (2), (4), (5), and (6), they fail to satisfy (3): $15 + 70$ is not less than or equal to 80. Any point that is not in an LP's feasible region is said to be an **infeasible point**. As another example of an infeasible point, consider $(x_1 = 40, x_2 = -20)$. Although this point satisfies all the constraints and the sign restriction (5), it is infeasible, because it fails to satisfy the sign restriction (6), $x_2 \geq 0$. The feasible region for the Giapetto problem is the set of possible production plans that Giapetto must consider in searching for the optimal production plan.

DEFINITION	For a maximization problem, an **optimal solution** to an LP is a point in the feasible region with the largest objective function value. Similarly, for a minimization problem, an optimal solution is a point in the feasible region with the smallest objective function value.

Most LPs have only one optimal solution. However, some LPs have no optimal solution, and some LPs have an infinite number of solutions (these situations are discussed in Section 3.3). In Section 3.2, we show that the unique optimal solution to the Giapetto problem is $(x_1 = 20, x_2 = 60)$. This solution yields an objective function value of

$$z = 3x_1 + 2x_2 = 3(20) + 2(60) = \$180$$

When we say that $(x_1 = 20, x_2 = 60)$ is the optimal solution to the Giapetto problem, we are saying that no point in the feasible region has an objective function value exceeding 180. Giapetto can maximize profit by building 20 soldiers and 60 trains each week. If Giapetto were to produce 20 soldiers and 60 trains each week, the weekly profit would be $180 less weekly fixed costs. For example, if Giapetto's only fixed cost were rent of $100 per week, weekly profit would be $180 - 100 = \$80$ per week.

◆ PROBLEMS

GROUP A

1. Farmer Jones must determine how many acres of corn and wheat to plant this year. An acre of wheat yields 25 bushels of wheat and requires 10 hours of labor per week. An acre of corn yields 10 bushels of corn and requires 4 hours of labor per week. All wheat can be sold at $4 a bushel, and all corn can be sold at $3 a bushel. Seven acres of land and 40 hours per week of labor are available. Government regulations require that at least 30 bushels of corn be produced during the current year. Let x_1 = number of acres of corn planted, and x_2 = number of acres of wheat planted. Using these decision variables, formulate an LP whose solution will tell farmer Jones how to maximize the total revenue from wheat and corn.

2. Answer these questions about Problem 1.
(a) Is $(x_1 = 2, x_2 = 3)$ in the feasible region?
(b) Is $(x_1 = 4, x_2 = 3)$ in the feasible region?
(c) Is $(x_1 = 2, x_2 = -1)$ in the feasible region?
(d) Is $(x_1 = 3, x_2 = 2)$ in the feasible region?

3. Using the variables x_1 = number of bushels of corn produced and x_2 = number of bushels of wheat produced, reformulate farmer Jones's LP.

4. Truckco manufactures two types of trucks: truck 1 and truck 2. Each truck must go through the painting shop and assembly shop. If the painting shop were completely devoted to painting type 1 trucks, 800 trucks per day could be painted, whereas if the painting shop were completely devoted to painting type 2 trucks, 700 trucks per day could be painted. If the assembly shop were completely devoted to assembling truck 1 engines, 1500 truck 1 engines per day could be assembled, and if the assembly shop were completely devoted to assembling truck 2 engines, 1200 truck 2 engines per day could be assembled. Each type 1 truck contributes $300 to profit, and each type 2 truck contributes $500 to profit. Formulate an LP that will maximize Truckco's profit.

GROUP B

5. Why don't we allow an LP to have < or > constraints?

<table>
<tr><td>3-2</td><td></td></tr>
</table>

THE GRAPHICAL SOLUTION OF TWO-VARIABLE LINEAR PROGRAMMING PROBLEMS

We now discuss how any LP with only two variables can be solved graphically. We always label the variables x_1 and x_2 and the coordinate axes the x_1 and x_2 axes. First, we need to show how to graph the set of points satisfying a linear inequality involving only two variables.

Suppose we wish to graph the set of points satisfying

$$2x_1 + 3x_2 \leq 6 \tag{7}$$

The set of points (x_1, x_2) satisfying the inequality (7) is the same as the set of points satisfying

$$3x_2 \leq 6 - 2x_1$$

The last inequality may be rewritten as

$$x_2 \leq \tfrac{1}{3}(6 - 2x_1) = 2 - \tfrac{2}{3}x_1 \tag{8}$$

Since moving downward on the graph decreases x_2 (see Figure 1), the set of points satisfying (8) and (7) is the set of points on or below the line $x_2 = 2 - \tfrac{2}{3}x_1$. This set of points is indicated by darker shading in Figure 1. Note, however, that the line $x_2 = 2 - \tfrac{2}{3}x_1$ is the same as the line $3x_2 = 6 - 2x_1$ and that this line is the same as $2x_1 + 3x_2 = 6$. This means that the set of points satisfying (7) is the set of points on or below the line $2x_1 + 3x_2 = 6$. Similar reasoning can be used to show that the set of points satisfying $2x_1 + 3x_2 \geq 6$ is the set of points on or above the line $2x_1 + 3x_2 = 6$. (These points are shown by lighter shading in Figure 1.)

Figure 1
Graphing a Linear
Inequality

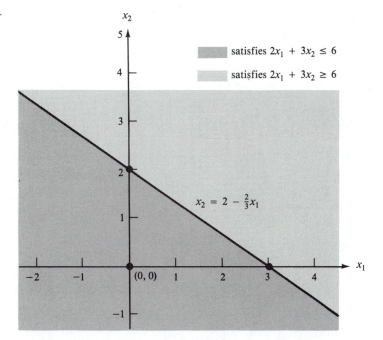

Consider a linear inequality constraint of the form $f(x_1, x_2) \geq b$ or $f(x_1, x_2) \leq b$. In general, it can be shown that in two dimensions, the set of points satisfying a linear inequality includes the points on the line $f(x_1, x_2) = b$ defining the inequality plus all points on one side of the line.

There is an easy way to determine the side of the line for which an inequality such as $f(x_1, x_2) \leq b$ or $f(x_1, x_2) \geq b$ is satisfied. Just choose any point P that does not satisfy the line $f(x_1, x_2) = b$. Determine whether P satisfies the inequality. If it does, then all points on the *same* side as P of $f(x_1, x_2) = b$ will satisfy the inequality. If P does not satisfy the inequality, then all points on the *other* side of $f(x_1, x_2) = b$, which does not contain P, will satisfy the inequality. For example, to determine whether $2x_1 + 3x_2 \geq 6$ is satisfied by points above or below the line $2x_1 + 3x_2 = 6$, we note that $(0, 0)$ does not satisfy $2x_1 + 3x_2 \geq 6$. Since $(0, 0)$ is *below* the line $2x_1 + 3x_2 = 6$, the set of points satisfying $2x_1 + 3x_2 \geq 6$ includes the line $2x_1 + 3x_2 = 6$ and the points *above* the line $2x_1 + 3x_2 = 6$. This agrees with Figure 1.

We illustrate how to solve two-variable LPs graphically by solving the Giapetto problem. To begin, we graphically determine the feasible region for Giapetto's problem. The feasible region for the Giapetto problem is the set of all points (x_1, x_2) satisfying

$$2x_1 + x_2 \leq 100 \qquad \text{(Constraints)} \qquad (2)$$

$$x_1 + x_2 \leq 80 \qquad\qquad\qquad (3)$$

$$x_1 \qquad \leq 40 \qquad\qquad\qquad (4)$$

$$x_1 \qquad \geq 0 \qquad \text{(Sign restrictions)} \qquad (5)$$

$$x_2 \geq 0 \qquad\qquad\qquad\qquad (6)$$

For a point (x_1, x_2) to be in the feasible region, (x_1, x_2) must satisfy *all* the inequalities (2)–(6). Note that the only points satisfying (5) and (6) are the points in the first quadrant of the x_1-x_2 plane. This is indicated in Figure 2 by the arrows pointing to the right from the x_2 axis and upward from the x_1 axis. Thus, any point that is outside the first quadrant cannot be in the feasible region. This means that the feasible region will be the

Figure 2
Graphical Solution
of Giapetto Problem

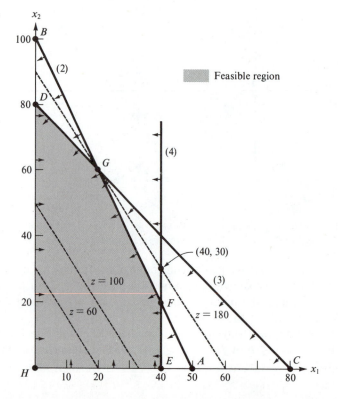

set of points in the first quadrant that satisfies (2)–(4). We now use our method for determining the set of points satisfying a linear inequality to determine the set of points satisfying (2)–(4). From Figure 2, we see that (2) is satisfied by all points below or on the line AB (AB is the line $2x_1 + x_2 = 100$). Inequality (3) is satisfied by all points on or below the line CD (CD is the line $x_1 + x_2 = 80$). Finally, (4) is satisfied by all points on or to the left of line EF (EF is the line $x_1 = 40$). The side of a line that satisfies an inequality is indicated by the direction of the arrows in Figure 2.

From Figure 2, we see that the set of points in the first quadrant that satisfies (2), (3), and (4) is bounded by the five-sided polygon $DGFEH$. Any point on this polygon or in its interior is in the feasible region. Any other point fails to satisfy at least one of the inequalities (2)–(6). For example, the point (40, 30) lies outside $DGFEH$ because it is above the line segment AB. Thus, (40, 30) is infeasible, because it fails to satisfy (2).

An easy way to find the feasible region is to determine the set of infeasible points. Note that all points above line AB in Figure 2 are infeasible, because they fail to satisfy (2). Similarly, all points above CD are infeasible, because they fail to satisfy (3). Also, all points to the right of the vertical line EF are infeasible, because they fail to satisfy (4). After these points are eliminated from consideration, we are left with the feasible region ($DGFEH$).

Having identified the feasible region for the Giapetto problem, we now search for the optimal solution, which will be the point in the feasible region with the largest value of $z = 3x_1 + 2x_2$. To find the optimal solution, we need to graph a line on which all points have the same z-value. In a max problem, such a line is called an **isoprofit line** (in a min problem, an **isocost line**). To draw an isoprofit line, choose any point in the feasible region and calculate its z-value. Let us choose (20, 0). For (20, 0), $z = 3(20) + 2(0) = 60$. Thus, (20, 0) lies on the isoprofit line $z = 3x_1 + 2x_2 = 60$. Rewriting $3x_1 + 2x_2 = 60$ as $x_2 = 30 - \frac{3}{2}x_1$, we see that the isoprofit line $3x_1 + 2x_2 = 60$ has a slope of $-\frac{3}{2}$. Since all isoprofit lines are of the form $3x_1 + 2x_2 = $ constant, all isoprofit lines have the same slope. *This means that once we have drawn one isoprofit line, we can find all other isoprofit lines by moving parallel to the isoprofit line we have drawn.*

It is now clear how to find the optimal solution to a two-variable LP. After you have drawn a single isoprofit line, generate other isoprofit lines by moving parallel to the drawn isoprofit line in a direction that increases z (for a max problem). After a while, the isoprofit lines will no longer intersect the feasible region. The last isoprofit line intersecting (touching) the feasible region defines the largest z-value of any point in the feasible region and indicates the optimal solution to the LP. In our problem, the objective function $z = 3x_1 + 2x_2$ will increase if we move in a direction for which both x_1 and x_2 increase. Thus, we construct additional isoprofit lines by moving parallel to $3x_1 + 2x_2 = 60$ in a northeast direction (upward and to the right). From Figure 2, we see that the isoprofit line passing through point G is the last isoprofit line to intersect the feasible region. Thus, point G is the point in the feasible region with the largest z-value and is therefore the optimal solution to the Giapetto problem. Note that point G is where the lines $2x_1 + x_2 = 100$ and $x_1 + x_2 = 80$ intersect. Solving these two equations simultaneously, we find that ($x_1 = 20, x_2 = 60$) is the optimal solution to the Giapetto problem. The optimal value of z may be found by substituting these values of x_1 and x_2 into the objective function. Thus, the optimal value of z is $z = 3(20) + 2(60) = 180$.

Once the optimal solution to an LP has been found, it is useful (see Chapters 5 and 6) to classify each constraint as being a binding constraint or a nonbinding constraint.

DEFINITION	A constraint is **binding** if the left-hand side and the right-hand side of the constraint are equal when the optimal values of the decision variables are substituted into the constraint.

Thus, (2) and (3) are binding constraints.

DEFINITION	A constraint is **nonbinding** if the left-hand side and the right-hand side of the constraint are unequal when the optimal values of the decision variables are substituted into the constraint.

Since $x_1 = 20$ is less than 40, (4) is a nonbinding constraint.

CONVEX SETS, EXTREME POINTS, AND LP

The feasible region for the Giapetto problem is an example of a convex set.

DEFINITION	A set of points S is a **convex set** if the line segment joining any pair of points in S is wholly contained in S.

Figure 3 gives four illustrations of this definition. In Figures 3a and 3b, each line segment joining two points in S contains only points in S. Thus, in both these figures, S is convex. In Figures 3c and 3d, S is not convex. In each figure, points A and B are in S, but there are points on the line segment AB that are not contained in S. In our study of linear programming, a certain type of point in a convex set (called an extreme point) is of great interest.

Figure 3
Examples of Convex
and Nonconvex Sets

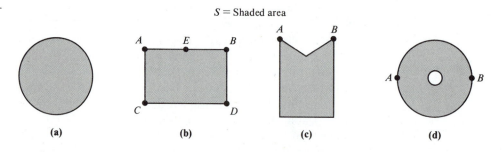

S = Shaded area

(a)   (b)   (c)   (d)

DEFINITION	For any convex set S, a point P in S is an **extreme point** if each line segment that lies completely in S and contains the point P has P as an endpoint of the line segment.

For example, in Figure 3a, each point on the circumference of the circle is an extreme point of the circle. In Figure 3b, points A, B, C, and D are extreme points of S. Although point E is on the boundary of S in Figure 3b, E is not an extreme point of S. This is because E lies on the line segment AB (AB lies completely in S), and E is not an endpoint of the line segment *AB*. Extreme points are sometimes called **corner points**, because if the set *S* is a polygon, the extreme points of *S* will be the vertices, or corners, of the polygon.

The feasible region for the Giapetto problem is a convex set. This is no accident: It can be shown that the feasible region for any LP will be a convex set. From Figure 2, we see that the extreme points of the feasible region are simply points *D*, *F*, *E*, *G*, and *H*. It can be shown that the feasible region for any LP has only a finite number of extreme points. Also note that the optimal solution to the Giapetto problem (point *G*) is an extreme point of the feasible region. It can be shown that *any LP that has an optimal solution has an extreme point that is optimal*. This result is very important, because it reduces the set of points yielding an optimal solution from the entire feasible region (which generally contains an *infinite* number of points) to the set of extreme points (a *finite* set).

For the Giapetto problem, it is easy to see why the optimal solution must be an extreme point of the feasible region. We note that *z* increases as we move isoprofit lines in a northeast direction, so the largest *z*-value in the feasible region must occur at some point *P* that has no points in the feasible region northeast of *P*. This means that the optimal solution must lie somewhere on the boundary of the feasible region *DGFEH*. The LP must have an extreme point that is optimal, because for any line segment on the boundary of the feasible region, the largest *z*-value on that line segment must be assumed at one of the endpoints of the line segment. To see this, look at the line segment *FG* in Figure 2. *FG* is part of the line $2x_1 + x_2 = 100$ and has a slope of -2. If we move along *FG* and decrease x_1 by 1, then x_2 will increase by 2. If we move along *FG* and decrease x_1 by 1, the value of *z* changes as follows: $3x_1$ goes down by $3(1) = 3$, and $2x_2$ goes up by $2(2) = 4$. Thus, in total, *z* increases by $4 - 3 = 1$. This means that moving along *FG* in a direction of decreasing x_1 increases *z*. Thus, the value of *z* at point *G* must exceed the value of *z* at any other point on the line segment *FG*. A similar argument shows that for any objective function, the maximum value of *z* on a given line segment must occur at an endpoint of the line segment. Therefore, for any LP, the largest *z*-value in the feasible region must be attained at an endpoint of one of the line segments forming the boundary of the feasible region. In short, one of the extreme points of the feasible region must be optimal. (To test understanding, the reader should show that if Giapetto's objective function were $z = 6x_1 + x_2$, point *F* would be optimal, whereas if Giapetto's objective function were $z = x_1 + 6x_2$, point *D* would be optimal.)

Our proof that an LP always has an optimal extreme point depended heavily on the fact that both the objective function and the constraints were linear functions. In Chapter 12, we show that for an optimization problem in which the objective function or some of the constraints are not linear, the optimal solution to the optimization problem may not occur at an extreme point.

THE GRAPHICAL SOLUTION OF MINIMIZATION PROBLEMS

E X A M P L E
2

Dorian Auto manufactures luxury cars and trucks. The company believes that its most likely customers are high-income women and high-income men. In order to reach these groups, Dorian Auto has embarked on an ambitious TV advertising campaign and has decided to purchase 1-minute commercial spots on two types of programs: comedy shows and football games. Each comedy commercial is seen by 7 million high-income women and 2 million high-income men. Each football commercial is seen by 2 million high-income women and 12 million high-income men. A 1-minute comedy ad costs $50,000, and a 1-minute football ad costs $100,000. Dorian would like the commercials to be seen by at least 28 million high-income women and at least 24 million high-income men. Use linear programming to determine how Dorian Auto can meet its advertising requirements at minimum cost.

Solution   Dorian must decide how many comedy and football ads should be purchased, so the decision variables are

$$x_1 = \text{number of 1-minute comedy ads purchased}$$
$$x_2 = \text{number of 1-minute football ads purchased}$$

Then Dorian wants to minimize total advertising cost (in thousands of dollars):

Total adv. cost = cost of comedy ads + cost of football ads

$$= \left(\frac{\text{cost}}{\text{comedy ad}}\right)\left(\begin{array}{c}\text{total}\\\text{comedy ads}\end{array}\right) + \left(\frac{\text{cost}}{\text{football ad}}\right)\left(\begin{array}{c}\text{total}\\\text{football ads}\end{array}\right)$$

$$= 50x_1 + 100x_2$$

Thus, Dorian's objective function is

$$\min z = 50x_1 + 100x_2 \tag{9}$$

Dorian faces the following constraints:

Constraint 1 Commercials must reach at least 28 million high-income women.
Constraint 2 Commercials must reach at least 24 million high-income men.

To express Constraints 1 and 2 in terms of x_1 and x_2, let HIW stand for high-income women viewers and HIM stand for high-income men viewers (in millions):

$$\text{HIW} = \left(\frac{\text{HIW}}{\text{comedy ad}}\right)\left(\begin{array}{c}\text{total}\\\text{comedy ads}\end{array}\right) + \left(\frac{\text{HIW}}{\text{football ad}}\right)\left(\begin{array}{c}\text{total}\\\text{football ads}\end{array}\right)$$

$$= 7x_1 + 2x_2$$

$$\text{HIM} = \left(\frac{\text{HIM}}{\text{comedy ad}}\right)\left(\begin{array}{c}\text{total}\\\text{comedy ads}\end{array}\right) + \left(\frac{\text{HIM}}{\text{football ad}}\right)\left(\begin{array}{c}\text{total}\\\text{football ads}\end{array}\right)$$

$$= 2x_1 + 12x_2$$

Constraint 1 may now be expressed as

$$7x_1 + 2x_2 \geq 28 \tag{10}$$

and Constraint 2 may be expressed as

$$2x_1 + 12x_2 \geq 24 \tag{11}$$

The sign restrictions $x_1 \geq 0$ and $x_2 \geq 0$ are necessary, so the Dorian LP is given by:

$$\min z = 50x_1 + 100x_2$$
$$\text{s.t.} \quad 7x_1 + 2x_2 \geq 28 \quad \text{(HIW)}$$
$$2x_1 + 12x_2 \geq 24 \quad \text{(HIM)}$$
$$x_1, x_2 \geq 0$$

This problem is typical of a wide range of LP applications in which a decision maker wants to minimize the cost of meeting a certain set of requirements. To solve this LP graphically, we begin by graphing the feasible region (Figure 4). Note that (10) is satisfied by points on or above the line AB (AB is part of the line $7x_1 + 2x_2 = 28$) and that (11) is satisfied by the points on or above the line CD (CD is part of the line $2x_1 + 12x_2 = 24$). From Figure 4, we see that the only first-quadrant points satisfying both (10) and (11) are the points in the shaded region bounded by the x_1 axis, CEB, and the x_2 axis.

Figure 4
Graphical Solution
of Dorian Problem

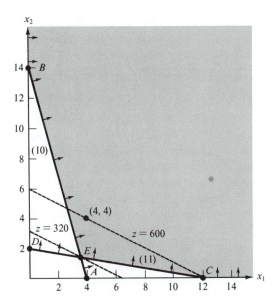

Like the Giapetto problem, the Dorian problem has a convex feasible region, but the feasible region for Dorian, unlike Giapetto's, contains points for which the value of at least one variable can assume arbitrarily large values. Such a feasible region is called an **unbounded feasible region**.

Since Dorian wishes to minimize total advertising cost, the optimal solution to the Dorian problem is the point in the feasible region with the smallest z-value. To find the optimal solution, we need to draw an *isocost line* that intersects the feasible region. An isocost line is any line on which all points have the same z-value (or same cost). We arbitrarily choose the isocost line passing through the point ($x_1 = 4$, $x_2 = 4$).

For this point, $z = 50(4) + 100(4) = 600$, and we graph the isocost line $z = 50x_1 + 100x_2 = 600$.

We consider lines parallel to the isocost line $50x_1 + 100x_2 = 600$ in the direction of decreasing z (southwest). The last point in the feasible region that intersects an isocost line will be the point in the feasible region having the *smallest* z-value. From Figure 4, we see that point E has the smallest z-value of any point in the feasible region. This means that point E is the optimal solution to the Dorian problem. Note that point E is where the lines $7x_1 + 2x_2 = 28$ and $2x_1 + 12x_2 = 24$ intersect. Simultaneously solving these equations yields the optimal solution ($x_1 = 3.6$, $x_2 = 1.4$). The optimal z-value can then be found by substituting these values of x_1 and x_2 into the objective function. Thus, the optimal z-value is $z = 50(3.6) + 100(1.4) = 320 = \$320,000$. Since at point E both the HIW and HIM constraints are satisfied with equality, both constraints are binding.

◆

Does the Dorian model meet the four assumptions of linear programming outlined in Section 3.1?

For the Proportionality Assumption to be valid, each extra comedy commercial must add exactly 7 million HIW and 2 million HIM. This contradicts empirical evidence, which indicates that after a certain point advertising yields diminishing returns. After, say, 500 auto commercials have been aired, most people have probably seen one, so it does little good to air more commercials. Thus, the Proportionality Assumption is violated.

We used the Additivity Assumption to justify writing (total HIW viewers) = (HIW viewers from comedy ads) + (HIW viewers from football ads). In reality, many of the same people will see a Dorian comedy commercial and a Dorian football commercial. We are double-counting such people, and this creates an inaccurate picture of the total number of people seeing Dorian commercials. The fact that the same person may see more than one type of commercial means that the effectiveness of, say, a comedy commercial depends on the number of football commercials. This violates the Additivity Assumption.

If only 1-minute commercials are available, it is unreasonable to say that Dorian should buy 3.6 comedy commercials and 1.4 football commercials, so the Divisibility Assumption is violated, and the Dorian problem should be considered an integer programming problem. In Section 9.3, we show that if the Dorian problem is solved as an integer programming problem, the minimum cost is attained by choosing ($x_1 = 6$, $x_2 = 1$) or ($x_1 = 4$, $x_2 = 2$). For either solution, the minimum cost is $400,000. This is 25% higher than the cost obtained from the optimal LP solution.

Since there is no way to know with certainty how many viewers are added by each type of commercial, the Certainty Assumption is also violated. Thus, all the assumptions of linear programming seem to be violated by the Dorian Auto problem. Despite these drawbacks, analysts have used similar models to help companies determine their optimal media mix.[†]

[†]Lilien and Kotler (1983).

◆ PROBLEMS

GROUP A

1. Graphically solve Problem 1 of Section 3.1.

2. Graphically solve Problem 4 of Section 3.1.

3. Leary Chemical manufactures three chemicals: chemical A, chemical B, and chemical C. These chemicals are produced via two production processes: process 1 and process 2. Running process 1 for an hour costs $4 and yields 3 units of chemical A, 1 unit of chemical B, and 1 unit of chemical C. Running process 2 for an hour costs $1 and produces 1 unit of chemical A and 1 unit of chemical B. To meet customer demands, at least 10 units of chemical A, 5 units of chemical B, and 3 units of chemical C must be produced daily. Graphically determine a daily production plan that minimizes the cost of meeting Leary Chemical's daily demands.

4. For each of the following objective functions, determine the direction in which the objective function increases:
(a) $z = 4x_1 - x_2$
(b) $z = -x_1 + 2x_2$
(c) $z = -x_1 - 3x_2$

5. Furnco manufactures desks and chairs. Each desk uses 4 units of wood, and each chair uses 3 units of wood. A desk contributes $40 to profit, and a chair contributes $25 to profit. Marketing restrictions require that the number of chairs produced be at least twice the number of desks produced. If 20 units of wood are available, formulate an LP to maximize Furnco's profit. Then graphically solve the LP.

3-3   SPECIAL CASES

The Giapetto and Dorian problems each had a unique optimal solution. In this section, we encounter three types of LPs that do not have unique optimal solutions:

    1. Some LPs have an infinite number of optimal solutions (*alternative* or *multiple optimal solutions*).

    2. Some LPs have no feasible solutions (*infeasible* LPs).

    3. Some LPs are *unbounded*: There are points in the feasible region with arbitrarily large (in a max problem) z-values.

ALTERNATIVE OR MULTIPLE OPTIMAL SOLUTIONS

E X A M P L E 3

An auto company manufactures cars and trucks. Each vehicle must be processed in the paint shop and body assembly shop. If the paint shop were only painting trucks, 40 trucks per day could be painted. If the paint shop were only painting cars, 60 cars per day could be painted. If the body shop were only producing cars, it could process 50 cars per day. If the body shop were only producing trucks, it could process 50 trucks per day. Each truck contributes $300 to profit, and each car contributes $200 to profit. Use linear programming to determine a daily production schedule that will maximize the company's profits.

Solution

The company must decide how many cars and trucks should be produced daily. This leads us to define the following decision variables:

$$x_1 = \text{number of trucks produced daily}$$
$$x_2 = \text{number of cars produced daily}$$

The company's daily profit (in hundreds of dollars) is $3x_1 + 2x_2$, so the company's objective function may be written as

$$\max z = 3x_1 + 2x_2 \tag{12}$$

The company's two constraints are the following:

Constraint 1 The fraction of the day during which the paint shop is busy is less than or equal to 1.

Constraint 2 The fraction of the day during which the body shop is busy is less than or equal to 1.

We have

$$\text{Fraction of day paint shop works on trucks} = \left(\frac{\text{fraction of day}}{\text{truck}} \right) \left(\frac{\text{trucks}}{\text{day}} \right)$$

$$= \tfrac{1}{40}x_1$$

$$\text{Fraction of day paint shop works on cars} = \tfrac{1}{60}x_2$$

$$\text{Fraction of day body shop works on trucks} = \tfrac{1}{50}x_1$$

$$\text{Fraction of day body shop works on cars} = \tfrac{1}{50}x_2$$

Thus, Constraint 1 may be expressed by

$$\tfrac{1}{40}x_1 + \tfrac{1}{60}x_2 \le 1 \quad \text{(Paint shop constraint)} \tag{13}$$

and Constraint 2 may be expressed by

$$\tfrac{1}{50}x_1 + \tfrac{1}{50}x_2 \le 1 \quad \text{(Body shop constraint)} \tag{14}$$

Figure 5
Graphical Solution
of Example 3

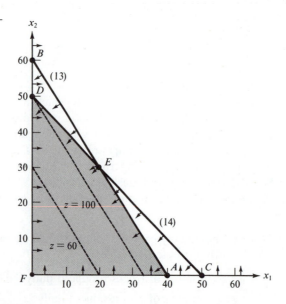

Since $x_1 \geq 0$ and $x_2 \geq 0$ must hold, the relevant LP is

$$\max z = 3x_1 + 2x_2 \tag{12}$$
$$\text{s.t.} \quad \tfrac{1}{40}x_1 + \tfrac{1}{60}x_2 \leq 1 \tag{13}$$
$$\tfrac{1}{50}x_1 + \tfrac{1}{50}x_2 \leq 1 \tag{14}$$
$$x_1, x_2 \geq 0$$

The feasible region for this LP is the shaded region in Figure 5 bounded by AEDF.[†]

For our isoprofit line, we choose the line passing through the point (20, 0). Since (20, 0) has a z-value of $3(20) + 2(0) = 60$, this yields the isoprofit line $z = 3x_1 + 2x_2 = 60$. Examining lines parallel to this isoprofit line in the direction of increasing z (northeast), we find that the last "point" in the feasible region to intersect an isoprofit line is the *entire* line segment AE. This means that any point on the line segment AE is optimal. We can use any point on AE to determine the optimal z-value. For example, point A, (40, 0), gives $z = 3(40) = 120$.   ◆

In summary, the auto company's LP has an infinite number of optimal solutions, or *multiple* or *alternative optimal solutions*. This is indicated by the fact that as an isoprofit line leaves the feasible region, it will intersect an entire line segment corresponding to the binding constraint (in this case, AE).

From our current example, it seems reasonable (and can be shown to be true) that if two points (A and E here) are optimal, then *any* point on the line segment joining these two points will also be optimal.

If an alternative optimum occurs, the decision maker can use a secondary criterion to choose between optimal solutions. The auto company's managers might prefer point A because it would simplify their business (and still allow them to maximize profits) by allowing them to produce only one type of product (trucks).

The technique of **goal programming** (see Section 14.1) is often used to choose among alternative optimal solutions.

INFEASIBLE LP

It is possible for an LP's feasible region to be empty (contain no points), resulting in an *infeasible* LP. Since the optimal solution to an LP is the best point in the feasible region, an infeasible LP has no optimal solution.

E X A M P L E 4

Suppose that auto dealers require that the auto company in Example 3 produce at least 30 trucks and 20 cars. Find the optimal solution to the new LP.

Solution

After adding the constraints $x_1 \geq 30$ and $x_2 \geq 20$ to the LP of Example 3, we obtain the following LP:

[†] The constraint (13) is satisfied by all points on or below AB (AB is $\tfrac{1}{40}x_1 + \tfrac{1}{60}x_2 \leq 1$), and (14) is satisfied by all points on or below CD (CD is the line $\tfrac{1}{50}x_1 + \tfrac{1}{50}x_2 \leq 1$).

$$\max z = 3x_1 + 2x_2$$

$$\text{s.t.} \quad \tfrac{1}{40}x_1 + \tfrac{1}{60}x_2 \le 1 \tag{15}$$

$$\tfrac{1}{50}x_1 + \tfrac{1}{50}x_2 \le 1 \tag{16}$$

$$x_1 \qquad\quad \ge 30 \tag{17}$$

$$x_2 \ge 20 \tag{18}$$

$$x_1, x_2 \ge 0$$

The graph of the feasible region for this LP is Figure 6.

Figure 6
An Empty Feasible Region (Infeasible LP)

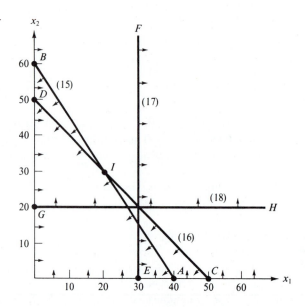

Constraint (15) is satisfied by all points on or below *AB* (*AB* is $\tfrac{1}{40}x_1 + \tfrac{1}{60}x_2 = 1$).
Constraint (16) is satisfied by all points on or below *CD* (*CD* is $\tfrac{1}{50}x_1 + \tfrac{1}{50}x_2 = 1$).
Constraint (17) is satisfied by all points on or to the right of *EF* (*EF* is $x_1 = 30$).
Constraint (18) is satisfied by all points on or above *GH* (*GH* is $x_2 = 20$).

From Figure 6, it is clear that no point satisfies all of (15)–(18). This means that Example 4 has an empty feasible region and is an infeasible LP.

◆

In Example 4, the LP is infeasible, because producing 30 trucks and 20 cars requires more paint shop time than is available.

UNBOUNDED LP

Our next special LP is an *unbounded* LP. For a max problem, an unbounded LP occurs if it is possible to find points in the feasible region with arbitrarily large z-values, corresponding to a decision maker earning arbitrarily large revenues or profits. This would indicate that an unbounded optimal solution should not occur in a correctly formulated LP. Thus, if the reader ever solves an LP on the computer and finds that the LP is unbounded, an error has probably been made in formulating the LP or in inputting the LP into the computer.

For a minimization problem, an LP is unbounded if there are points in the feasible region with arbitrarily small z-values. When graphically solving an LP, we can spot an unbounded LP as follows: A max problem is unbounded if, when we move parallel to our original isoprofit line in the direction of increasing z, we never entirely leave the feasible region. A minimization problem is unbounded if we never leave the feasible region when moving in the direction of decreasing z.

E X A M P L E
5

Graphically solve the following LP:

$$\max z = 2x_1 - x_2$$
$$\text{s.t.} \quad x_1 - x_2 \leq 1 \tag{19}$$
$$2x_1 + x_2 \geq 6 \tag{20}$$
$$x_1, x_2 \geq 0$$

Solution

From Figure 7, we see that (19) is satisfied by all points on or above AB (AB is the line $x_1 - x_2 = 1$). Also, (20) is satisfied by all points on or above CD (CD is $2x_1 + x_2 = 6$). Thus, the feasible region for Example 5 is the (shaded) unbounded region in Figure 7, which is bounded only by the x_2 axis, line segment DE, and the part of line AB beginning at E. To find the optimal solution, we draw the isoprofit line passing through $(2, 0)$. This isoprofit line has $z = 2x_1 - x_2 = 2(2) - 0 = 4$. The direction of increasing z is to the southeast (this makes x_1 larger and x_2 smaller). Moving parallel to $z = 2x_1 - x_2$ in a southeast direction, we see that any isoprofit line we draw will intersect the feasible region. (This is because any isoprofit line is steeper than the line $x_1 - x_2 = 1$.)

Figure 7
An Unbounded LP

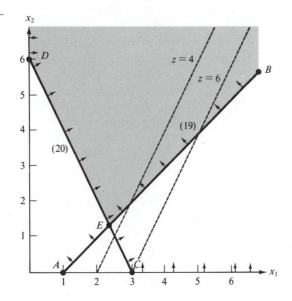

Thus, there are points in the feasible region that have arbitrarily large z-values. For example, if we wanted to find a point in the feasible region that had $z \geq 1,000,000$, we could choose any point in the feasible region that is southeast of the isoprofit line $z = 1,000,000$.

♦

From the discussion in the last two sections, we see that every LP with two variables must fall into one of the following four cases:

Case 1 The LP has a unique optimal solution.

Case 2 The LP has alternative or multiple optimal solutions: Two or more extreme points are optimal, and the LP will have an infinite number of optimal solutions.

Case 3 The LP is infeasible: The feasible region contains no points.

Case 4 The LP is unbounded: There are points in the feasible region with arbitrarily large z-values (max problem) or arbitrarily small z-values (min problem).

In Chapter 4, we show that every LP (not just LPs with two variables) must fall into one of Cases 1–4.

In the rest of this chapter, we lead the reader through the formulation of several more complicated linear programming models. The most important step in formulating an LP model is the proper choice of decision variables. If the decision variables have been properly chosen, the objective function and constraints should follow without much difficulty. Trouble in determining an LP's objective function and constraints is usually due to an incorrect choice of decision variables.

♦ PROBLEMS

GROUP A

Identify which of Cases 1–4 apply to each of the following LPs.

1. max $z = x_1 + x_2$
   s.t. $x_1 + x_2 \leq 4$
   $\quad\quad x_1 - x_2 \geq 5$
   $\quad\quad x_1, x_2 \geq 0$

2. max $z = 4x_1 + x_2$
   s.t. $8x_1 + 2x_2 \leq 16$
   $\quad\quad 5x_1 + 2x_2 \leq 12$
   $\quad\quad x_1, x_2 \geq 0$

3. max $z = -x_1 + 3x_2$
   s.t. $x_1 - \quad x_2 \leq 4$
   $\quad\quad x_1 + 2x_2 \geq 4$
   $\quad\quad x_1, x_2 \geq 0$

4. max $z = 3x_1 + x_2$
   s.t. $2x_1 + \quad x_2 \leq 6$
   $\quad\quad x_1 + 3x_2 \leq 9$
   $\quad\quad x_1, x_2 \geq 0$

5. True or false: For an LP to be unbounded, the LP's feasible region must be unbounded.

6. True or false: Every LP with an unbounded feasible region has an unbounded optimal solution.

7. If an LP's feasible region is not unbounded, we say the LP's feasible region is bounded. Suppose an LP has a bounded feasible region. Explain why you can find the optimal solution to the LP (without an isoprofit or isocost line) by simply checking the z-values at each of the feasible region's extreme points. Why might this method fail if the LP's feasible region is unbounded?

8. Graphically find all optimal solutions to the following LP:

$$\min z = x_1 - x_2$$
$$\text{s.t.} \quad x_1 + x_2 \leq 6$$
$$x_1 - x_2 \geq 0$$
$$x_2 - x_1 \geq 3$$
$$x_1, x_2 \geq 0$$

Combining the objective function, constraints (21)–(24), and the sign restrictions yields the following:

$$\min z = 50x_1 + 20x_2 + 30x_3 + 80x_4$$

$$\text{s.t.} \quad 400x_1 + 200x_2 + 150x_3 + 500x_4 \geq 500 \qquad \text{(Calorie constraint)} \qquad (21)$$

$$3x_1 + 2x_2 \qquad\qquad\qquad \geq 6 \qquad \text{(Chocolate constraint)} \qquad (22)$$

$$2x_1 + 2x_2 + 4x_3 + 4x_4 \geq 10 \qquad \text{(Sugar constraint)} \qquad (23)$$

$$2x_1 + 4x_2 + x_3 + 5x_4 \geq 8 \qquad \text{(Fat constraint)} \qquad (24)$$

$$x_i \geq 0 \quad (i = 1, 2, 3, 4) \qquad \text{(Sign restrictions)}$$

The optimal solution to this LP is $x_1 = x_4 = 0$, $x_2 = 3$, $x_3 = 1$, $z = 90$. Thus, the minimum-cost diet incurs a daily cost of 90¢ by eating three scoops of chocolate ice cream and drinking one bottle of cola. The optimal z-value may be obtained by substituting the optimal value of the decision variables into the objective function. This yields a total cost of $z = 3(20) + 1(30) = 90$¢. The optimal diet provides

$$200(3) + 150(1) = 750 \text{ calories}$$

$$2(3) = 6 \text{ oz of chocolate}$$

$$2(3) + 4(1) = 10 \text{ oz of sugar}$$

$$4(3) + 1(1) = 13 \text{ oz of fat}$$

Thus, the chocolate and sugar constraints are binding, but the calorie and fat constraints are nonbinding.

◆

A version of the diet problem with a more realistic list of foods and nutritional requirements was one of the first LPs to be solved by computer. Stigler (1945) proposed a diet problem in which 77 types of food were available and 10 nutritional requirements (vitamin A, vitamin C, etc.) had to be satisfied. When solved by computer, the optimal solution to Stigler's diet problem yielded a diet consisting of corn meal, wheat flour, evaporated milk, peanut butter, lard, beef, liver, potatoes, spinach, and cabbage. Although such a diet is clearly high in vital nutrients, few people would be satisfied with it, because it does not seem to meet a minimum standard of tastiness (and Stigler required that the same diet be eaten each day). The optimal solution to any LP model will reflect only those aspects of reality that are captured by the objective function and constraints. Stigler's (and our) formulation of the diet problem did not reflect people's desire for a tasty and varied diet. Integer programming has been used to plan institutional menus for a weekly or monthly period.[†] Menu planning models do contain constraints that reflect tastiness and variety requirements.

[†] Balintfy (1976).

♦ PROBLEMS

GROUP A

1. There are three factories on the Momiss River (factory 1, factory 2, and factory 3). Each factory emits two types of pollutants (pollutant 1 and pollutant 2) into the river. If the waste from each factory is processed, the pollution in the river can be reduced. It costs $15 to process a ton of factory 1 waste, and each ton of factory 1 waste processed will reduce the amount of pollutant 1 by 0.10 ton and the amount of pollutant 2 by 0.45 ton. It costs $10 to process a ton of factory 2 waste, and each ton of factory 2 waste processed will reduce the amount of pollutant 1 by 0.20 ton and the amount of pollutant 2 by 0.25 ton. It costs $20 to process a ton of factory 3 waste, and each ton of factory 3 waste processed reduces the amount of pollutant 1 by 0.40 ton and the amount of pollutant 2 by 0.30 ton. The state wishes to reduce the amount of pollutant 1 in the river by at least 30 tons and the amount of pollutant 2 in the river by at least 40 tons. Formulate an LP that will minimize the cost of reducing pollution by the desired amounts. Do you think that the LP assumptions (Proportionality, Additivity, Divisibility, and Certainty) are reasonable for this problem?

2.[†] U.S. Labs manufactures mechanical heart valves from the heart valves of pigs. Different heart operations require valves of different sizes. U.S. Labs purchases pig valves from three different suppliers. The cost and size mix of the valves purchased from each supplier are given in Table 2. Each month, U.S. Labs places one order with each supplier. At least 500 large, 300 medium, and 300 small valves must be purchased each month. Because of limited availability of pig valves, at most 500 valves per month can be pur-chased from each supplier. Formulate an LP that can be used to minimize the cost of acquiring the needed valves.

3. Peg and Al Fundy have a limited food budget, so Peg is trying to feed the family as cheaply as possible. However, she still wants to make sure her family members meet their daily nutritional requirements. Peg can buy two foods. Food 1 sells for $7 per pound, and each pound of food 1 contains 3 units of vitamin A and 1 unit of vitamin C. Food 2 sells for $1 per pound, and each pound of food 2 contains 1 unit of each vitamin. Each day, the family needs at least 12 units of vitamin A and 6 units of vitamin C.

(a) Verify that Peg should purchase 12 units of food 2 each day and thus oversatisfy the vitamin C requirement by 6 units.

(b) Al has put his foot down and demanded that Peg fulfill the family's daily nutritional requirement exactly by obtaining precisely 12 units of vitamin A and 6 units of vitamin C. The optimal solution to the new problem will involve ingesting less vitamin C, but it will be more expensive. Why?

4. Goldilocks needs to find at least 12 lb of gold and at least 18 lb of silver to pay the monthly rent. There are two mines in which Goldilocks can find gold and silver. Each day that Goldilocks spends in mine 1, she finds 2 lb of gold and 2 lb of silver. Each day that Goldilocks spends in mine 2, she finds 1 lb of gold and 3 lb of silver. Formulate an LP to help Goldilocks meet her requirements while spending as little time as possible in the mines. Graphically solve the LP.

Table 2

	COST PER VALVE	PERCENT LARGE	PERCENT MEDIUM	PERCENT SMALL
Supplier 1	$5	40	40	20
Supplier 2	$4	30	35	35
Supplier 3	$3	20	20	60

[†] Based on Hilal and Erickson (1981).

3-5 A WORK SCHEDULING PROBLEM

Many applications of linear programming involve determining the minimum-cost method for satisfying work force requirements. The following example illustrates the basic features common to many of these applications.

E X A M P L E A post office requires different numbers of full-time employees on different days of the
7 week. The number of full-time employees required on each day is given in Table 3. Union rules state that each full-time employee must work five consecutive days and then receive two days off. For example, an employee who works Monday to Friday must be off on Saturday and Sunday. The post office wants to meet its daily requirements using only full-time employees. Formulate an LP that the post office can use to minimize the number of full-time employees that must be hired.

Table 3
Employee
Requirements for
Post Office Example

	NUMBER OF FULL-TIME EMPLOYEES REQUIRED
Day 1 = Monday	17
Day 2 = Tuesday	13
Day 3 = Wednesday	15
Day 4 = Thursday	19
Day 5 = Friday	14
Day 6 = Saturday	16
Day 7 = Sunday	11

Solution Before giving the correct formulation of this problem, let's begin by discussing an *incorrect* solution. Many students begin by defining x_i to be the number of employees working on day i (day 1 = Monday, day 2 = Tuesday, etc.). Then they reason that (number of full-time employees) = (number of employees working on Monday) + (number of employees working on Tuesday) + $\cdots$ + (number of employees working on Sunday). This reasoning leads to the following objective function:

$$\min z = x_1 + x_2 + \cdots + x_6 + x_7$$

To ensure that the post office has enough full-time employees working on each day, simply add the constraints $x_i \geq$ (number of employees required on day i). For example, for Monday add the constraint $x_1 \geq 17$. Adding the sign restrictions $x_i \geq 0$ ($i = 1, 2, \ldots, 7$) yields the following LP:

$$\min z = x_1 + x_2 + x_3 + x_4 + x_5 + x_6 + x_7$$
$$\text{s.t.} \quad x_1 \qquad\qquad\qquad\qquad \geq 17$$
$$x_2 \qquad\qquad\qquad \geq 13$$
$$x_3 \qquad\qquad\qquad \geq 15$$
$$x_4 \qquad\qquad \geq 19$$
$$x_5 \qquad\quad \geq 14$$
$$x_6 \quad\; \geq 16$$
$$x_7 \geq 11$$
$$x_i \geq 0 \quad (i = 1, 2, \ldots, 7)$$

There are at least two flaws in this formulation. First, the objective function is *not* the number of full-time post office employees. The current objective function counts each employee five times, not once. For example, each employee who starts work on Monday works Monday to Friday and is included in x_1, x_2, x_3, x_4, and x_5. Second, the variables x_1, x_2, . . . , x_7 are interrelated, and the interrelation between the variables is not captured by the current set of constraints. For example, some of the people who are working on Monday (the x_1 people) will be working on Tuesday. This means that x_1 and x_2 are interrelated, but our constraints do not indicate that the value of x_1 has any effect on the value of x_2.

The key to correctly formulating this problem is to realize that the post office's primary decision is not how many people are working each day but rather how many people *begin* work on each day of the week. With this in mind, we define

$$x_i = \text{number of employees beginning work on day } i$$

For example, x_1 is the number of people beginning work on Monday (these people work Monday to Friday). With the variables properly defined, it is easy to determine the correct objective function and constraints. To determine the objective function, note that (number of full-time employees) = (number of employees who start work on Monday) + (number of employees who start work on Tuesday) + · · · + (number of employees who start work on Sunday). Since each employee begins work on exactly one day of the week, this expression does not double-count employees. Thus, when we correctly define the variables, the objective function is

$$\min z = x_1 + x_2 + x_3 + x_4 + x_5 + x_6 + x_7$$

The post office must ensure that enough employees are working on each day of the week. For example, at least 17 employees must be working on Monday. Who is working on Monday? Everybody except the employees who begin work on Tuesday or on Wednesday (they get, respectively, Sunday and Monday, and Monday and Tuesday off). This means that the number of employees working on Monday is $x_1 + x_4 + x_5 + x_6 + x_7$. To ensure that at least 17 employees are working on Monday, we require that the constraint

$$x_1 + x_4 + x_5 + x_6 + x_7 \geq 17$$

be satisfied. Adding similar constraints for the other six days of the week and the sign restrictions $x_i \geq 0$ ($i = 1, 2, \ldots, 7$) yields the following formulation of the post office's problem:

$$
\begin{aligned}
\min z = \ & x_1 + x_2 + x_3 + x_4 + x_5 + x_6 + x_7 \\
\text{s.t.} \quad & x_1 \ \ \ \ \ \ \ \ \ \ \ \ \ \ \ + x_4 + x_5 + x_6 + x_7 \geq 17 \quad &&\text{(Monday constraint)} \\
& x_1 + x_2 \ \ \ \ \ \ \ \ \ \ \ + x_5 + x_6 + x_7 \geq 13 \quad &&\text{(Tuesday constraint)} \\
& x_1 + x_2 + x_3 \ \ \ \ \ \ \ \ \ + x_6 + x_7 \geq 15 \quad &&\text{(Wednesday constraint)} \\
& x_1 + x_2 + x_3 + x_4 \ \ \ \ \ \ \ \ + x_7 \geq 19 \quad &&\text{(Thursday constraint)} \\
& x_1 + x_2 + x_3 + x_4 + x_5 \ \ \ \ \ \ \ \ \ \geq 14 \quad &&\text{(Friday constraint)} \\
& x_2 + x_3 + x_4 + x_5 + x_6 \ \ \ \ \ \geq 16 \quad &&\text{(Saturday constraint)} \\
& x_3 + x_4 + x_5 + x_6 + x_7 \geq 11 \quad &&\text{(Sunday constraint)} \\
& x_i \geq 0 \quad (i = 1, 2, \ldots, 7) \quad &&\text{(Sign restrictions)}
\end{aligned}
$$

The optimal solution to this LP is $z = \frac{67}{3}$, $x_1 = \frac{4}{3}$, $x_2 = \frac{10}{3}$, $x_3 = 2$, $x_4 = \frac{22}{3}$, $x_5 = 0$, $x_6 = \frac{10}{3}$, $x_7 = 5$. Since we are only allowing full-time employees, however, the variables must be integers, and the Divisibility Assumption is not satisfied. In an attempt to find a reasonable answer in which all variables are integers, we could try to round the fractional variables up, yielding the feasible solution $z = 25$, $x_1 = 2$, $x_2 = 4$, $x_3 = 2$, $x_4 = 8$, $x_5 = 0$, $x_6 = 4$, $x_7 = 5$. It turns out, however, that integer programming can be used to show that the optimal solution to the post office problem is $z = 23$, $x_1 = 4$, $x_2 = 4$, $x_3 = 2$, $x_4 = 6$, $x_5 = 0$, $x_6 = 4$, $x_7 = 3$. Notice that there is no way that the optimal linear programming solution could have been rounded to obtain the optimal all-integer solution.

◆

Baker (1974) has developed an efficient technique (which does not use linear programming) to determine the minimum number of employees required when each worker receives two consecutive days off.

◆ PROBLEMS

GROUP A

1. In the post office example, suppose that each full-time employee works 8 hours per day. Thus, Monday's requirement of 17 workers may be viewed as a requirement of $8(17) = 136$ hours. The post office may meet its daily labor requirements by using both full-time and part-time employees. During each week, a full-time employee works 8 hours a day for five consecutive days, and a part-time employee works 4 hours a day for five consecutive days. A full-time employee costs the post office $15 per hour, whereas a part-time employee (with reduced fringe benefits) costs the post office only $10 per hour. Union requirements limit part-time labor to 25% of weekly labor requirements. Formulate an LP to minimize the post office's weekly labor costs.

2. During each 4-hour period, the Smalltown police force requires the following number of on-duty police officers: 12 midnight to 4 A.M.—8; 4 to 8 A.M.—7; 8 A.M. to 12 noon—6; 12 noon to 4 P.M.—6; 4 to 8 P.M.—5; 8 P.M. to 12 midnight—4. Each police officer works two consecutive 4-hour shifts. Formulate an LP that can be used to minimize the number of police officers needed to meet Smalltown's daily requirements.

GROUP B

3. Suppose that the post office can force employees to work one day of overtime each week. For example, an employee whose regular shift is Monday to Friday can also be required to work on Saturday. Each employee is paid

$50 a day for each of the first five days worked during a week and $62 for the overtime day (if any). Formulate an LP whose solution will enable the post office to minimize the cost of meeting its weekly work requirements.

4. Suppose the post office had 25 full-time employees and was not allowed to hire or fire any employees. Formulate an LP that could be used to schedule the employees in order to maximize the number of weekend days off received by the employees.

5. Each day, workers at the Gotham City Police Department work two 6-hour shifts chosen from 12 A.M.–6 A.M., 6 A.M.–12 P.M., 12 P.M.–6 P.M., and 6 P.M.–12 A.M. The following number of workers are needed during each shift: 12 A.M.–6 A.M.—15 workers; 6 A.M.–12 P.M.—5 workers; 12 P.M.–6 P.M.—12 workers; 6 P.M.–12 A.M.—6 workers. Workers whose two shifts are consecutive are paid $12 per hour; workers whose shifts are not consecutive are paid $18 per hour. Formulate an LP that can be used to minimize the cost of meeting the daily work force demands of the Gotham City Police Department.

6. During each 6-hour period of the day, the Bloomington Police Department needs at least the number of policemen shown in Table 4. Policemen can be hired to work either 12 consecutive hours or 18 consecutive hours. Policemen are paid $4 per hour for each of the first 12 hours a day they work and are paid $6 per hour for each of the next 6 hours they work in a day. Formulate an LP that can be used to minimize the cost of meeting Bloomington's daily police requirements.

Table 4

TIME PERIOD	NUMBER OF POLICEMEN REQUIRED
12 A.M.–6 A.M.	12
6 A.M.–12 P.M.	8
12 P.M.–6 P.M.	6
6 P.M.–12 A.M.	15

3-6   A CAPITAL BUDGETING PROBLEM

In this section (and in Sections 3.7 and 3.11), we discuss how linear programming can be used to determine optimal financial decisions. This section considers a simple capital budgeting model.[†]

We first explain briefly the concept of net present value (NPV), which can be used to compare the desirability of different investments. Time 0 is the present.

Suppose investment 1 requires a cash outlay of $10,000 at time 0 and a cash outlay of $14,000 two years from now and yields a cash flow of $24,000 one year from now. Investment 2 requires a $6000 cash outlay at time 0 and a $1000 cash outlay two years from now and yields a cash flow of $8000 one year from now. Which investment would you prefer?

Investment 1 has a net cash flow of

$$-10,000 + 24,000 - 14,000 = \$0$$

and investment 2 has a net cash flow of

$$-6000 + 8000 - 1000 = \$1000$$

On the basis of net cash flow, investment 2 is superior to investment 1. When we compare investments on the basis of net cash flow, we are assuming that a dollar received at any point in time has the same value. This is not true! Suppose that there exists an investment (such as a money market fund) for which $1 invested at a given time will yield (with certainty) $(1 + r)$ one year later. We call r the annual interest rate. Since $1 at the present can be transformed into $(1 + r)$ one year from now, we may write

$$\$1 \text{ now} = \$(1 + r) \text{ one year from now}$$

Applying this reasoning to the $(1 + r)$ obtained one year from now shows that

$$\$1 \text{ now} = \$(1 + r) \text{ one year from now} = \$(1 + r)^2 \text{ two years from now}$$

and

$$\$1 \text{ now} = \$(1 + r)^k \text{ } k \text{ years from now}$$

Dividing both sides of this equality by $(1 + r)^k$ shows that

$$\$1 \text{ received } k \text{ years from now} = \$(1 + r)^{-k} \text{ now}$$

[†]This section is based on Weingartner (1963).

In other words, a dollar received k years from now is equivalent to receiving $\$(1 + r)^{-k}$ now.

We can use this idea to express all cash flows in terms of time 0 dollars (this process is called discounting cash flows to time 0). Using discounting, we can determine the total value (in time 0 dollars) of the cash flows for any investment. The total value (in time 0 dollars) of the cash flows for any investment is called the **net present value**, or NPV, of the investment. The NPV of an investment is the amount by which the investment will increase the firm's value (as expressed in time 0 dollars).

Assuming that $r = 0.20$, we can compute the NPV for investments 1 and 2:

$$\text{NPV of investment 1} = -10,000 + \frac{24,000}{1 + 0.20} - \frac{14,000}{(1 + 0.20)^2}$$
$$= \$277.78$$

This means that if a firm invested in investment 1, the value of the firm (in time 0 dollars) would increase by $277.78. For investment 2,

$$\text{NPV of investment 2} = -6000 + \frac{8000}{1 + 0.20} - \frac{1000}{(1 + 0.20)^2}$$
$$= -\$27.78$$

If a firm invested in investment 2, the value of the firm (in time 0 dollars) would be reduced by $27.78.

Thus, the NPV concept says that investment 1 is superior to investment 2. This conclusion is contrary to the conclusion reached by comparing the net cash flows of the two investments. Note that the comparison between investments often depends on the value of r. For example, the reader is asked to show in Problem 1 at the end of this section that for $r = 0.02$, investment 2 has a higher NPV than investment 1. Of course, our analysis assumes that the future cash flows of an investment are known with certainty.

With the above background information in hand, we are ready to explain how linear programming can be applied to problems in which limited investment funds must be allocated to investment projects. Such problems are called **capital budgeting problems**.

E X A M P L E 8 Star Oil Company is considering five different investment opportunities. The cash outflows and net present values (in millions of dollars) are given in Table 5. Star Oil has $40 million available for investment at the present time (time 0); it estimates that one year from now (time 1) $20 million will be available for investment. Star Oil may purchase

Table 5		INV.1	INV.2	INV.3	INV.4	INV.5
Cash Flows and Net Present Value for Investments in Capital Budgeting Example	Time 0 cash outflow	$11	$53	$5	$5	$29
	Time 1 cash outflow	$3	$6	$5	$1	$34
	NPV	$13	$16	$16	$14	$39

any fraction of each investment. In this case, the cash outflows and NPV are adjusted accordingly. For example, if Star Oil purchases one fifth of investment 3, then a cash outflow of $\frac{1}{5}(5) = \$1$ million would be required at time 0, and a cash outflow of $\frac{1}{5}(5) = \$1$ million would be required at time 1. The one-fifth share of investment 3 would yield an NPV of $\frac{1}{5}(16) = \$3.2$ million. Star Oil wishes to maximize the NPV that can be obtained by investing in investments 1–5. Formulate an LP that will help achieve this goal. Assume that any funds left over at time 0 cannot be used at time 1.

Solution

Star Oil must determine what fraction of each investment to purchase. We define

$$x_i = \text{fraction of investment } i \text{ purchased by Star Oil} \quad (i = 1, 2, 3, 4, 5)$$

Star's goal is to maximize the NPV earned from investments. Now, (total NPV) = (NPV earned from inv. 1) + (NPV earned from inv. 2) + $\cdots$ + (NPV earned from inv. 5). Note that

$$\text{NPV from inv. 1} = (\text{NPV from inv. 1})(\text{fraction of inv. 1 purchased})$$
$$= 13x_1$$

Applying analogous reasoning to investments 2–5 shows that Star Oil wishes to maximize

$$z = 13x_1 + 16x_2 + 16x_3 + 14x_4 + 39x_5 \tag{25}$$

Star Oil's constraints may be expressed as follows:

Constraint 1 Star cannot invest more than \$40 million at time 0.

Constraint 2 Star cannot invest more than \$20 million at time 1.

Constraints 3–7 Star cannot purchase more than 100% of investment i $(i = 1, 2, 3, 4, 5)$.

To express Constraint 1 mathematically, note that (dollars invested at time 0) = (dollars invested in inv. 1 at time 0) + (dollars invested in inv. 2 at time 0) + $\cdots$ + (dollars invested in inv. 5 at time 0). Also, in millions of dollars,

$$\begin{array}{l} \text{Dollars invested in inv. 1} \\ \text{at time 0} \end{array} = \left(\begin{array}{c} \text{dollars required for} \\ \text{inv. 1 at time 0} \end{array} \right) \left(\begin{array}{c} \text{fraction of} \\ \text{inv. 1 purchased} \end{array} \right)$$
$$= 11x_1$$

Similarly, for investments 2–5,

$$\text{Dollars invested at time 0} = 11x_1 + 53x_2 + 5x_3 + 5x_4 + 29x_5$$

Then Constraint 1 reduces to

$$11x_1 + 53x_2 + 5x_3 + 5x_4 + 29x_5 \le 40 \qquad \text{(Time 0 constraint)} \tag{26}$$

Constraint 2 reduces to

$$3x_1 + 6x_2 + 5x_3 + x_4 + 34x_5 \le 20 \qquad \text{(Time 1 constraint)} \tag{27}$$

Constraints 3–7 may be represented by

$$x_i \le 1 \quad (i = 1, 2, 3, 4, 5) \tag{28–32}$$

Combining (26)–(32) with the sign restrictions $x_i \geq 0$ ($i = 1, 2, 3, 4, 5$) yields the following LP:

$$\max z = 13x_1 + 16x_2 + 16x_3 + 14x_4 + 39x_5$$

$$\begin{aligned}
\text{s.t.} \quad 11x_1 + 53x_2 + 5x_3 + 5x_4 + 29x_5 &\leq 40 \quad &\text{(Time 0 constraint)} \\
3x_1 + 6x_2 + 5x_3 + x_4 + 34x_5 &\leq 20 \quad &\text{(Time 1 constraint)} \\
x_1 &\leq 1 \\
x_2 &\leq 1 \\
x_3 &\leq 1 \\
x_4 &\leq 1 \\
x_5 &\leq 1
\end{aligned}$$

$$x_i \geq 0 \quad (i = 1, 2, 3, 4, 5)$$

The optimal solution to this LP is $x_1 = x_3 = x_4 = 1$, $x_2 = 0.201$, $x_5 = 0.288$, $z = 57.449$. Star Oil should purchase 100% of investments 1, 3, and 4; 20.1% of investment 2; and 28.8% of investment 5. A total NPV of $57,449,000 will be obtained from these investments.

◆

It is often impossible to purchase only a fraction of an investment without sacrificing the investment's favorable cash flows. Suppose it costs $12 million to drill an oil well just deep enough to locate a $30-million gusher. If there were a sole investor in this project who invested $6 million to undertake half of the project, he or she would lose the entire investment and receive no positive cash flows. Since, in this example, reducing the money invested by 50% reduces the return by more than 50%, this situation would violate the Proportionality Assumption.

In many capital budgeting problems, it is unreasonable to allow the x_i to be fractions: Each x_i should be restricted to be zero (not investing at all in investment i) or 1 (purchasing all of investment i). Thus, many capital budgeting problems violate the Divisibility Assumption.

A capital budgeting model that allows each x_i to be only zero or 1 is discussed in Section 9.2.

◆ PROBLEMS

GROUP A

1. Show that if $r = 0.02$, investment 2 has a larger NPV than investment 1.

2. Two investments with varying cash flows (in thousands of dollars) are available, as shown in Table 6. At time 0, $10,000 is available for investment, and at time 1, $7000 is available for investment. Assuming that $r = 0.10$, set up an LP whose solution maximizes the NPV obtained from these investments. Graphically find the optimal solution to the LP. (Assume that any fraction of an investment may be purchased.)

Table 6

	CASH FLOW (IN THOUSANDS) AT TIME			
	0	*1*	*2*	*3*
Investment 1	− $6	− $5	$7	$9
Investment 2	− $8	− $3	$9	$7

3. Suppose that r, the annual interest rate, is 0.20, and that all money in the bank earns 20% interest each year (that is, after being in the bank for one year, $1 will increase to $1.20). If we place $100 in the bank for one year, what is the NPV of this transaction?

3-7   SHORT-TERM FINANCIAL PLANNING*

LP models can often be used to aid a firm in short- or long-term financial planning (also see Section 3.11). Here we consider a simple example that illustrates how linear programming can be used to aid a corporation's short-term financial planning.[†]

E X A M P L E
9

Semicond is a small electronics company that manufactures tape recorders and radios. The per-unit labor costs, raw material costs, and selling price of each product are given in Table 7. On December 1, 1991, Semicond has available raw material that is sufficient to manufacture 100 tape recorders and 100 radios. On the same date, the company's balance sheet is as shown in Table 8, and Semicond's asset/liability ratio (called the current ratio) is $20,000/10,000 = 2$.

Table 7
Cost Information for
Semicond Example

	TAPE RECORDER	RADIO
Selling price	$100	$90
Labor cost	$50	$35
Raw material cost	$30	$40

Table 8
Balance Sheet for
Semicond Example

	ASSETS	LIABILITIES
Cash	$10,000	
Accounts receivable[a]	$3,000	
Inventory outstanding[b]	$7,000	
Bank loan		$10,000

[a] Accounts receivable is money owed to Semicond by customers who have previously purchased Semicond products.
[b] Value of December 1, 1991 inventory $= 30(100) + 40(100) = \$7000$.

Semicond must determine how many tape recorders and radios should be produced during December. Demand is large enough to ensure that all goods produced will be sold. All sales are on credit, however, and payment for goods produced in December will not be received until February 1, 1992. During December, Semicond will collect $2000 in accounts receivable, and Semicond must pay off $1000 of the outstanding loan and a monthly rent of $1000. On January 1, 1992, Semicond will receive a shipment of raw material worth $2000, which will be paid for on February 1, 1992. Semicond's management has decided that the cash balance on January 1, 1992 must be at least $4000. Also,

*Starred sections cover material that may be omitted with no loss of continuity.
[†] This section is based on an example in Neave and Wiginton (1981).

Semicond's bank requires that the current ratio at the beginning of January be at least 2. In order to maximize the contribution to profit from December production, (revenues to be received) − (variable production costs), what should Semicond produce during December?

Solution   Semicond must determine how many tape recorders and radios should be produced during December. Thus, we define

$$x_1 = \text{number of tape recorders produced during December}$$
$$x_2 = \text{number of radios produced during December}$$

To express Semicond's objective function, note that

$$\frac{\text{Contribution to profit}}{\text{Tape recorder}} = 100 - 50 - 30 = \$20$$

$$\frac{\text{Contribution to profit}}{\text{Radio}} = 90 - 35 - 40 = \$15$$

As in the Giapetto example, this leads to the objective function

$$\max z = 20x_1 + 15x_2 \tag{33}$$

Semicond faces the following constraints:

Constraint 1 Because of limited availability of raw material, at most 100 tape recorders can be produced during December.

Constraint 2 Because of limited availability of raw material, at most 100 radios can be produced during December.

Constraint 3 Cash on hand on January 1, 1992 must be at least $4000.

Constraint 4 (Jan. 1 assets)/(Jan. 1 liabilities) ≥ 2 must hold.

Constraint 1 is described by

$$x_1 \leq 100 \tag{34}$$

Constraint 2 is described by

$$x_2 \leq 100 \tag{35}$$

To express Constraint 3, note that

$$
\begin{aligned}
\text{Jan. 1 cash on hand} = {} & \text{Dec. 1 cash on hand} \\
& + \text{ accounts receivable collected during Dec.} \\
& - \text{ portion of loan repaid during Dec.} \\
& - \text{ Dec. rent} - \text{ Dec. labor costs} \\
= {} & 10,000 + 2000 - 1000 - 1000 - 50x_1 - 35x_2 \\
= {} & 10,000 - 50x_1 - 35x_2
\end{aligned}
$$

Now Constraint 3 may be written as

$$10,000 - 50x_1 - 35x_2 \geq 4000 \tag{36'}$$

All computer codes require each LP constraint to be expressed in a form in which all variables are on the left-hand side of the constraint and the constant is on the right-hand side of the constraint. Thus, for computer solution, we should write (36′) as

$$50x_1 + 35x_2 \leq 6000 \qquad (36)$$

To express Constraint 4, we need to determine Semicond's January 1 cash position, accounts receivable, inventory position, and liabilities in terms of x_1 and x_2. We have already shown that

$$\text{Jan. 1 cash position} = 10{,}000 - 50x_1 - 35x_2$$

Then

$$\begin{aligned}
\text{Jan. 1 accounts receivable} &= \text{Dec. 1 accounts receivable} \\
&\quad + \text{accounts receivable from Dec. sales} \\
&\quad - \text{accounts receivable collected during Dec.} \\
&= 3000 + 100x_1 + 90x_2 - 2000 \\
&= 1000 + 100x_1 + 90x_2
\end{aligned}$$

It now follows that

$$\begin{aligned}
\text{Value of Jan. 1 inventory} &= \text{value of Dec. 1 inventory} \\
&\quad - \text{value of inventory used in Dec.} \\
&\quad + \text{value of inventory received on Jan. 1} \\
&= 7000 - (30x_1 + 40x_2) + 2000 \\
&= 9000 - 30x_1 - 40x_2
\end{aligned}$$

We can now compute the January 1 asset position:

$$\begin{aligned}
\text{Jan. 1 asset position} &= \text{Jan. 1 cash position} + \text{Jan. 1 accounts receivable} \\
&\quad + \text{Jan. 1 inventory position} \\
&= (10{,}000 - 50x_1 - 35x_2) + (1000 + 100x_1 + 90x_2) \\
&\quad + (9000 - 30x_1 - 40x_2) \\
&= 20{,}000 + 20x_1 + 15x_2
\end{aligned}$$

Finally,

$$\begin{aligned}
\text{Jan. 1 liabilities} &= \text{Dec. 1 liabilities} - \text{Dec. loan payment} \\
&\quad + \text{amount due on Jan. 1 inventory shipment} \\
&= 10{,}000 - 1000 + 2000 \\
&= \$11{,}000
\end{aligned}$$

Constraint 4 may now be written as

$$\frac{20{,}000 + 20x_1 + 15x_2}{11{,}000} \geq 2$$

Multiplying both sides of this inequality by 11,000 yields

$$20{,}000 + 20x_1 + 15x_2 \geq 22{,}000$$

Putting this in a form appropriate for computer input, we obtain

$$20x_1 + 15x_2 \geq 2000 \tag{37}$$

Combining (33)–(37) with the sign restrictions $x_1 \geq 0$ and $x_2 \geq 0$ yields the following LP:

$$\max z = 20x_1 + 15x_2$$

$$\begin{array}{llll}
\text{s.t.} & x_1 & \leq 100 & \text{(Tape recorder constraint)} \\
& x_2 \leq 100 & & \text{(Radio constraint)} \\
50x_1 & + 35x_2 \leq 6000 & & \text{(Cash position constraint)} \\
20x_1 & + 15x_2 \geq 2000 & & \text{(Current ratio constraint)} \\
& x_1, x_2 \geq 0 & & \text{(Sign restrictions)}
\end{array}$$

When solved graphically (or by computer), the following optimal solution is obtained: $z = 2500$, $x_1 = 50$, $x_2 = 100$. Thus, Semicond can maximize the contribution of December's production to profits by manufacturing 50 tape recorders and 100 radios during December. This will contribute $20(50) + 15(100) = \$2500$ to profits. ◆

◆ PROBLEMS

GROUP A

1. Graphically solve the Semicond problem.

2. Suppose that the January 1 inventory shipment had been valued at $7000. Show that Semicond's LP is now infeasible.

3-8   BLENDING PROBLEMS

Situations in which various inputs must be blended in some desired proportion to produce goods for sale are often amenable to linear programming analysis. Such problems are called **blending problems**. The following list gives some situations in which linear programming has been used to solve blending problems:

1. Blending together various types of crude oils to produce different types of gasoline and other outputs (such as heating oil)

2. Blending together various chemicals to produce other chemicals

3. Blending together various types of metal alloys to produce various types of steels

4. Blending together various livestock feeds in an attempt to produce a minimum-cost feed mixture for cattle

5. Mixing together various ores to obtain ore of a specified quality

6. Mixing together various ingredients (meat, filler, water, etc.) to produce a product like bologna

7. Mixing together various types of papers to produce recycled paper of varying quality

The following example illustrates the key ideas that are used in formulating LP models of blending problems.

E X A M P L E
10

Sunco Oil manufactures three types of gasoline (gas 1, gas 2, and gas 3). Each type of gasoline is produced by blending together three types of crude oil (crude 1, crude 2, and crude 3). The sales price per barrel of gasoline and the purchase price per barrel of crude oil are given in Table 9. Sunco can purchase up to 5000 barrels of each type of crude oil daily.

Table 9
Gas and Crude Oil
Prices for Blending
Example

	SALES PRICE PER BARREL		PURCHASE PRICE PER BARREL
Gas 1	$70	Crude 1	$45
Gas 2	$60	Crude 2	$35
Gas 3	$50	Crude 3	$25

The three types of gasoline differ in their octane rating and sulfur content. The crude oil blended to form gas 1 must have an average octane rating of at least 10 and contain at most 1% sulfur. The crude oil blended to form gas 2 must have an average octane rating of at least 8 and contain at most 2% sulfur. The crude oil blended to form gas 3 must have an octane rating of at least 6 and contain at most 1% sulfur. The octane rating and the sulfur content of the three types of oil are given in Table 10. It costs $4 to transform one barrel of oil into one barrel of gasoline, and Sunco's refinery can produce up to 14,000 barrels of gasoline daily.

Table 10
Octane Ratings and
Sulfur Requirements
for Blending
Example

	OCTANE RATING	SULFUR CONTENT
Crude 1	12	0.5%
Crude 2	6	2.0%
Crude 3	8	3.0%

Sunco's customers require the following amounts of each gasoline: gas 1—3000 barrels per day; gas 2—2000 barrels per day; gas 3—1000 barrels per day. The company considers it an obligation to meet these demands. Sunco also has the option of advertising to stimulate demand for its products. Each dollar spent daily in advertising a particular type of gas increases the daily demand for that type of gas by ten barrels. For example, if Sunco decides to spend $20 daily in advertising gas 2, the daily demand for gas 2 will increase by 20(10) = 200 barrels. Formulate an LP that will enable Sunco to maximize daily profits (profits = revenues − costs).

Solution

Sunco must make two types of decisions: first, how much money should be spent in advertising each type of gas, and second, how to blend each type of gasoline from the three types of crude oil available. For example, Sunco must decide how many barrels of crude 1 should be used to produce gas 1. We define the decision variables

a_i = dollars spent daily on advertising gas i ($i = 1, 2, 3$)

x_{ij} = barrels of crude oil i used daily to produce gas j ($i = 1, 2, 3; j = 1, 2, 3$)

For example, x_{21} is the number of barrels of crude 2 used each day to produce gas 1.

Knowledge of these variables is sufficient to determi
and constraints, but before we do this, we note that
variables implies that

$$x_{11} + x_{12} + x_{13} = \text{barrels of crude}$$
$$x_{21} + x_{22} + x_{23} = \text{barrels of crude}$$
$$x_{31} + x_{32} + x_{33} = \text{barrels of crud}$$

$$x_{11} + x_{21} + x_{31} = \text{barrels of gas 1 produced }$$
$$x_{12} + x_{22} + x_{32} = \text{barrels of gas 2 produced daily}$$
$$x_{13} + x_{23} + x_{33} = \text{barrels of gas 3 produced daily}$$

To simplify matters, let's assume that gasoline cannot be stored, so it must be sold on the day it is produced. This implies that for $i = 1, 2, 3$, the amount of gas i produced daily should equal the daily demand for gas i. Suppose that the amount of gas i produced daily exceeded the daily demand. Then we would have incurred unnecessary purchasing and production costs. On the other hand, if the amount of gas i produced daily is less than the daily demand for gas i, we are failing to meet mandatory demands or incurring unnecessary advertising costs.

We are now ready to determine Sunco's objective function and constraints. We begin with Sunco's objective function.

From (39),

$$\text{Daily revenues from gas sales} = 70(x_{11} + x_{21} + x_{31}) + 60(x_{12} + x_{22} + x_{32})$$
$$+ 50(x_{13} + x_{23} + x_{33})$$

From (38),

$$\text{Daily cost of purchasing crude oil} = 45(x_{11} + x_{12} + x_{13}) + 35(x_{21} + x_{22} + x_{23})$$
$$+ 25(x_{31} + x_{32} + x_{33})$$

Also,

$$\text{Daily advertising costs} = a_1 + a_2 + a_3$$
$$\text{Daily production costs} = 4(x_{11} + x_{12} + x_{13} + x_{21} + x_{22} + x_{23} + x_{31} + x_{32} + x_{33})$$

Then,

$$
\begin{aligned}
\text{Daily profit} = {} & \text{daily revenue from gas sales} \\
& - \text{daily cost of purchasing crude oil} \\
& - \text{daily advertising costs} - \text{daily production costs} \\
= {} & (70 - 45 - 4)x_{11} + (60 - 45 - 4)x_{12} + (50 - 45 - 4)x_{13} \\
& + (70 - 35 - 4)x_{21} + (60 - 35 - 4)x_{22} + (50 - 35 - 4)x_{23} \\
& + (70 - 25 - 4)x_{31} + (60 - 25 - 4)x_{32} \\
& + (50 - 25 - 4)x_{33} - a_1 - a_2 - a_3
\end{aligned}
$$

Thus, Sunco's goal is to maximize

$$z = 21x_{11} + 11x_{12} + x_{13} + 31x_{21} + 21x_{22} + 11x_{23}$$
$$+ 41x_{31} + 31x_{32} + 21x_{33} - a_1 - a_2 - a_3 \qquad \textbf{(40)}$$

Regarding Sunco's constraints, we see that the following 13 constraints must be satisfied:

Constraint 1 Gas 1 produced daily should equal daily demand for gas 1.

Constraint 2 Gas 2 produced daily should equal daily demand for gas 2.

Constraint 3 Gas 3 produced daily should equal daily demand for gas 3.

Constraint 4 At most 5000 barrels of crude 1 can be purchased daily.

Constraint 5 At most 5000 barrels of crude 2 can be purchased daily.

Constraint 6 At most 5000 barrels of crude 3 can be purchased daily.

Constraint 7 Because of limited refinery capacity, at most 14,000 barrels of gasoline can be produced daily.

Constraint 8 Crude oil blended to make gas 1 must have an average octane level of at least 10.

Constraint 9 Crude oil blended to make gas 2 must have an average octane level of at least 8.

Constraint 10 Crude oil blended to make gas 3 must have an average octane level of at least 6.

Constraint 11 Crude oil blended to make gas 1 must contain at most 1% sulfur.

Constraint 12 Crude oil blended to make gas 2 must contain at most 2% sulfur.

Constraint 13 Crude oil blended to make gas 3 must contain at most 1% sulfur.

To express Constraint 1 in terms of the decision variables, note that

$$\text{Daily demand for gas 1} = 3000 + \text{gas 1 demand generated by advertising}$$

$$\text{Gas 1 demand generated by advertising} = \left(\frac{\text{gas 1 demand}}{\text{dollar spent}}\right)\left(\frac{\text{dollars}}{\text{spent}}\right)$$

$$= 10a_1{}^{\dagger}$$

Thus, daily demand for gas 1 $= 3000 + 10a_1$. Constraint 1 may now be written as

$$x_{11} + x_{21} + x_{31} = 3000 + 10a_1 \tag{41'}$$

which we rewrite as

$$x_{11} + x_{21} + x_{31} - 10a_1 = 3000 \tag{41}$$

Constraint 2 is expressed by

$$x_{12} + x_{22} + x_{32} - 10a_2 = 2000 \tag{42}$$

Constraint 3 is expressed by

$$x_{13} + x_{23} + x_{33} - 10a_3 = 1000 \tag{43}$$

---

† Many students believe that gas 1 demand generated by advertising should be written as $\frac{1}{10}a_1$. Analyzing the units of this term will show that this is not correct. $\frac{1}{10}$ has units of dollars spent per barrel of demand, and a_1 has units of dollars spent. Thus, the term $\frac{1}{10}a_1$ would have units of (dollars spent)^2 per barrel of demand. This cannot be correct!

From (38), Constraint 4 reduces to

$$x_{11} + x_{12} + x_{13} \leq 5000 \tag{44}$$

Constraint 5 reduces to

$$x_{21} + x_{22} + x_{23} \leq 5000 \tag{45}$$

Constraint 6 reduces to

$$x_{31} + x_{32} + x_{33} \leq 5000 \tag{46}$$

Note that

Total gas produced = gas 1 produced + gas 2 produced + gas 3 produced

$$= (x_{11} + x_{21} + x_{31}) + (x_{12} + x_{22} + x_{32}) + (x_{13} + x_{23} + x_{33})$$

Then Constraint 7 becomes

$$x_{11} + x_{21} + x_{31} + x_{12} + x_{22} + x_{32} + x_{13} + x_{23} + x_{33} \leq 14{,}000 \tag{47}$$

To express Constraints 8–10, we must be able to determine the "average" octane level in a mixture of different types of crude oil. We assume that the octane levels of different crudes blend linearly. For example, if we blend two barrels of crude 1, three barrels of crude 2, and one barrel of crude 3, the average octane level in this mixture would be

$$\frac{\text{Total octane value in mixture}}{\text{Number of barrels in mixture}} = \frac{12(2) + 6(3) + 8(1)}{2 + 3 + 1} = \frac{50}{6} = 8\frac{1}{3}$$

Generalizing, we can express Constraint 8 by

$$\frac{\text{Total octane value in gas 1}}{\text{Gas 1 in mixture}} = \frac{12x_{11} + 6x_{21} + 8x_{31}}{x_{11} + x_{21} + x_{31}} \geq 10 \tag{48'}$$

Unfortunately, (48′) is not a linear inequality. To transform (48′) into a linear inequality, all we have to do is multiply both sides of (48′) by the denominator of the left-hand side of (48′). The resulting inequality is

$$12x_{11} + 6x_{21} + 8x_{31} \geq 10(x_{11} + x_{21} + x_{31})$$

which may be rewritten as

$$2x_{11} - 4x_{21} - 2x_{31} \geq 0 \tag{48}$$

Similarly, Constraint 9 yields

$$\frac{12x_{12} + 6x_{22} + 8x_{32}}{x_{12} + x_{22} + x_{32}} \geq 8$$

Multiplying both sides of this inequality by $x_{12} + x_{22} + x_{32}$ and simplifying yields

$$4x_{12} - 2x_{22} \geq 0 \tag{49}$$

Since each type of crude oil has an octane level of 6 or higher, whatever we blend to manufacture gas 3 will have an average octane level of at least 6. This means that any values of the variables will satisfy Constraint 10. To verify this, we may express

Constraint 10 by

$$\frac{12x_{13} + 6x_{23} + 8x_{33}}{x_{13} + x_{23} + x_{33}} \geq 6$$

Multiplying both sides of this inequality by $x_{13} + x_{23} + x_{33}$ and simplifying, we obtain

$$6x_{13} + 2x_{33} \geq 0 \tag{50}$$

Since $x_{13} \geq 0$ and $x_{33} \geq 0$ are always satisfied, (50) will automatically be satisfied and thus need not be included in the model. A constraint like (50) that is implied by other constraints in the model is said to be a **redundant constraint** and need not be included in the formulation. We choose to omit (50) from our final formulation. Constraint 11 may be written as

$$\frac{\text{Total sulfur in gas 1 mixture}}{\text{Number of barrels in gas 1 mixture}} \leq 0.01$$

Then, using the percentages of sulfur in each type of oil, we see that

$$\text{Total sulfur in gas 1 mixture} = \text{Sulfur in oil 1 used for gas 1}$$
$$+ \text{ sulfur in oil 2 used for gas 1}$$
$$+ \text{ sulfur in oil 3 used for gas 1}$$
$$= 0.005x_{11} + 0.02x_{21} + 0.03x_{31}$$

Constraint 11 may now be written as

$$\frac{0.005x_{11} + 0.02x_{21} + 0.03x_{31}}{x_{11} + x_{21} + x_{31}} \leq 0.01$$

Again, this is not a linear inequality, but we can multiply both sides of the inequality by $x_{11} + x_{21} + x_{31}$ and simplify, obtaining

$$-0.005x_{11} + 0.01x_{21} + 0.02x_{31} \leq 0 \tag{51}$$

Similarly, Constraint 12 is equivalent to

$$\frac{0.005x_{12} + 0.02x_{22} + 0.03x_{32}}{x_{12} + x_{22} + x_{32}} \leq 0.02$$

Multiplying both sides of this inequality by $x_{12} + x_{22} + x_{32}$ and simplifying yields

$$-0.015x_{12} + 0.01x_{32} \leq 0 \tag{52}$$

Finally, Constraint 13 is equivalent to

$$\frac{0.005x_{13} + 0.02x_{23} + 0.03x_{33}}{x_{13} + x_{23} + x_{33}} \leq 0.01$$

Multiplying both sides of this inequality by $x_{13} + x_{23} + x_{33}$ and simplifying yields the LP constraint

$$-0.005x_{13} + 0.01x_{23} + 0.02x_{33} \leq 0 \tag{53}$$

Combining (40)–(53), except the redundant constraint (50), with the sign restrictions $x_{ij} \geq 0$ and $a_i \geq 0$ yields an LP that may be expressed in tabular form (see Table 11).

	x_{11}	x_{12}	x_{13}	x_{21}	x_{22}	x_{23}	x_{31}	x_{32}	x_{33}	a_1	a_2	a_3	
Table 11	21	11	1	31	21	11	41	31	21	−1	−1	−1	(max)
Objective Function	1	0	0	1	0	0	1	0	0	−10	0	0	= 3000
and Constraints for	0	1	0	0	1	0	0	1	0	0	−10	0	= 2000
Blending Example	0	0	1	0	0	1	0	0	1	0	0	−10	= 1000
	1	1	1	0	0	0	0	0	0	0	0	0	≤ 5000
	0	0	0	1	1	1	0	0	0	0	0	0	≤ 5000
	0	0	0	0	0	0	1	1	1	0	0	0	≤ 5000
	1	1	1	1	1	1	1	1	1	0	0	0	≤ 14,000
	2	0	0	−4	0	0	−2	0	0	0	0	0	≥ 0
	0	4	0	0	−2	0	0	0	0	0	0	0	≥ 0
	−0.005	0	0	0.01	0	0	0.02	0	0	0	0	0	≤ 0
	0	−0.015	0	0	0	0	0	0.01	0	0	0	0	≤ 0
	0	0	−0.005	0	0	0.01	0	0	0.02	0	0	0	≤ 0

In Table 11, the first row (max) represents the objective function, the second row represents the first constraint, and so on. When solved on a computer, an optimal solution to Sunco's LP is found to be

$$z = 287,500$$

$$x_{11} = 2222.22 \qquad x_{12} = 2111.11 \qquad x_{13} = 666.67$$

$$x_{21} = 444.44 \qquad x_{22} = 4222.22 \qquad x_{23} = 333.34$$

$$x_{31} = 333.33 \qquad x_{32} = 3166.67 \qquad x_{33} = 0$$

$$a_1 = 0 \qquad a_2 = 750 \qquad a_3 = 0$$

Thus, Sunco should produce $x_{11} + x_{21} + x_{31} = 3000$ barrels of gas 1, using 2222.22 barrels of crude 1, 444.44 barrels of crude 2, and 333.33 barrels of crude 3. The firm should produce $x_{12} + x_{22} + x_{32} = 9500$ barrels of gas 2, using 2111.11 barrels of crude 1, 4222.22 barrels of crude 2, and 3166.67 barrels of crude 3. Sunco should also produce $x_{13} + x_{23} + x_{33} = 1000$ barrels of gas 3, using 666.67 barrels of crude 1 and 333.34 barrels of crude 2. The firm should also spend $750 on advertising gas 2. Sunco will earn a profit of $287,500. ◆

Observe that although gas 1 appears to be most profitable, we stimulate demand for gas 2, not gas 1. The reason for this is that given the quality (with respect to octane level and sulfur content) of the available crude, it is difficult to produce gas 1. Therefore, Sunco can make more money by producing more of the lower-quality gas 2 than by producing extra quantities of gas 1.

◆ PROBLEMS

GROUP A

1. You have decided to enter the candy business. You are considering producing two types of candies: Slugger Candy and Easy Out Candy, both of which consist solely of sugar, nuts, and chocolate. At present, you have in stock 100 oz of sugar, 20 oz of nuts, and 30 oz of chocolate. The mixture used to make Easy Out Candy must contain at least 20% nuts. The mixture used to make Slugger Candy must contain at least 10% nuts and at least 10% chocolate. Each ounce of Easy Out Candy can be sold for 25¢, and each ounce of Slugger Candy can be sold for 20¢. Formulate an LP that will enable you to maximize your revenue from candy sales.

2. O.J. Juice Company sells bags of oranges and cartons of orange juice. O.J. grades oranges on a scale of 1 (poor) to 10 (excellent). At present, O.J. has on hand 100,000 lb of grade 9 oranges and 120,000 lb of grade 6 oranges. The average quality of oranges sold in bags must be at least 7, and the average quality of the oranges used to produce orange juice must be at least 8. Each pound of oranges that is used for juice yields a revenue of $1.50 and incurs a variable cost (consisting of labor costs, variable overhead costs, inventory costs, etc.) of $1.05. Each pound of oranges sold in bags yields a revenue of 50¢ and incurs a variable cost of 20¢. Formulate an LP to help O.J. maximize profit.

3. A bank is attempting to determine where its assets should be invested during the current year. At present, $500,000 is available for investment in bonds, home loans, auto loans, and personal loans. The annual rate of return on each type of investment is known to be: bonds, 10%; home loans, 16%; auto loans, 13%; personal loans, 20%. In order to ensure that the bank's portfolio is not too risky, the bank's investment manager has placed the following three restrictions on the bank's portfolio:

    (1) The amount invested in personal loans cannot exceed the amount invested in bonds.
    (2) The amount invested in home loans cannot exceed the amount invested in auto loans.
    (3) No more than 25% of the total amount invested may be in personal loans.

The bank's objective is to maximize the annual return on its investment portfolio. Formulate an LP that will enable the bank to meet this goal.

4. Young MBA Erica Cudahy may invest up to $1000. She can invest her money in stocks and loans. Each dollar invested in stocks yields 10¢ profit, and each dollar invested in a loan yields 15¢ profit. At least 30% of all money invested must be invested in stocks, and at least $400 must be invested in loans. Formulate an LP that can be used to maximize total profit earned from Erica's investment. Then graphically solve the LP.

5. Chandler Oil Company has 5000 barrels of oil 1 and 10,000 barrels of oil 2. The company sells two products: gasoline and heating oil. Both products are produced by combining oil 1 and oil 2. The quality level of each oil is as follows: oil 1 : 10, and oil 2 : 5. Gasoline must have an average quality level of at least 8, and heating oil must have an average quality level of at least 6. Demand for each product must be created by advertising. Each dollar spent advertising gasoline creates 5 barrels of demand, and each dollar spent advertising heating oil creates 10 barrels of demand. Gasoline is sold for $25 per barrel; heating oil is sold for $20 per barrel. Formulate an LP to help Chandler maximize profit. Assume that no oil of either type can be purchased.

6. Bullco blends silicon and nitrogen to produce two types of fertilizers. Fertilizer 1 must be at least 40% nitrogen and sells for $70/lb. Fertilizer 2 must be at least 70% silicon and sells for $40/lb. Bullco can purchase up to 80 lb of nitrogen at $15/lb and up to 100 lb of silicon at $10/lb. Assuming that all fertilizer produced can be sold, formulate an LP to help Bullco maximize profits.

7. Eli Daisy uses chemicals 1 and 2 to produce two drugs. Drug 1 must be at least 70% chemical 1, and drug 2 must be at least 60% chemical 2. Up to 40 oz of drug 1 can be sold at $6 per oz; up to 30 oz of drug 2 can be sold at $5 per oz. Up to 45 oz of chemical 1 can be purchased at $6 per oz, and up to 40 oz of chemical 2 can be purchased at $4 per oz. Formulate an LP that can be used to maximize Daisy's profits.

8. Highland's TV-Radio Store must determine how many TVs and radios to keep in stock. A TV requires 10 sq ft of floor space, whereas a radio requires 4 sq ft; 200 sq ft of floor space is available. A TV will earn Highland $60 in profits, and a radio will earn $20 in profits. The store stocks only TVs and radios. Marketing requirements dictate that at least 60% of all appliances in stock be radios. Finally, a TV ties up $200 in capital, and a radio ties up $50. Highland wants to have at most $3000 worth of capital tied up at any time. Formulate an LP that can be used to maximize Highland's profit.

9. Linear programming models are used by many Wall Street firms in an attempt to select a desirable bond portfolio. The following is a simplified version of such a model. Solodrex is considering investing in four bonds; $1,000,000 is available for investment. The expected annual return, the worst-case annual return on each bond, and the "duration" of each bond are given in Table 12. The duration of a bond is a measure of the bond's sensitivity to interest rates. Solodrex wishes to maximize the expected return from its bond investments, subject to the three constraints shown at right.

1. The worst-case return of the bond portfolio must be at least 8%.

2. The average duration of the portfolio must be at most 6. For example, a portfolio that invested $600,000 in bond 1 and $400,000 in bond 4 would have an average duration of

$$\frac{600,000(3) + 400,000(9)}{1,000,000} = 5.4$$

3. Because of diversification requirements, at most 40% of the total amount invested can be invested in a single bond.

Formulate an LP that will enable Solodrex to maximize the expected return on its investment.

Table 12

	EXPECTED RETURN	WORST-CASE RETURN	DURATION
Bond 1	13%	6%	3
Bond 2	8%	8%	4
Bond 3	12%	10%	7
Bond 4	14%	9%	9

GROUP B

10. The owner of Sunco does not believe that our LP optimal solution will maximize daily profit. He reasons, "We have 14,000 barrels of daily refinery capacity, but your optimal solution produces only 13,500 barrels. Therefore, it cannot be maximizing profit." How would you respond?

3-9   PRODUCTION PROCESS MODELS

We now explain how to formulate an LP model of a simple production process.[†] The key step is to determine how the outputs from a later stage of the process are related to the outputs from an earlier stage.

E X A M P L E 11

Rylon Corporation manufactures Brute and Chanelle perfumes. The raw material needed to manufacture each type of perfume can be purchased for $3 a pound. Processing 1 lb of raw material requires 1 hour of laboratory time. Each pound of processed raw material yields 3 oz of Regular Brute Perfume and 4 oz of Regular Chanelle Perfume. Regular Brute can be sold for $7/oz and Regular Chanelle for $6/oz. Rylon also has the option of further processing Regular Brute and Regular Chanelle to produce Luxury Brute, sold at $18/oz, and Luxury Chanelle, sold at $14/oz. Each ounce of Regular Brute processed further requires an additional 3 hours of laboratory time and $4 processing cost and yields 1 oz of Luxury Brute. Each ounce of Regular Chanelle processed further requires an additional 2 hours of laboratory time and $4 processing cost and yields 1 oz of Luxury Chanelle. Each year, Rylon has 6000 hours of laboratory

[†] This section is based on Hartley (1971).

time available and can purchase up to 4000 lb of raw material. Formulate an LP that can be used to determine how Rylon·can maximize profits. Assume that the cost of the laboratory hours is a fixed cost.

Solution   Rylon must determine how much raw material to purchase and how much of each type of perfume should be produced. We therefore define our decision variables to be

$$x_1 = \text{number of ounces of Regular Brute sold annually}$$
$$x_2 = \text{number of ounces of Luxury Brute sold annually}$$
$$x_3 = \text{number of ounces of Regular Chanelle sold annually}$$
$$x_4 = \text{number of ounces of Luxury Chanelle sold annually}$$
$$x_5 = \text{number of pounds of raw material purchased annually}$$

Rylon wants to maximize

$$\text{Contribution to profit} = \text{revenues from perfume sales} - \text{processing costs}$$
$$- \text{costs of purchasing raw material}$$
$$= 7x_1 + 18x_2 + 6x_3 + 14x_4 - (4x_2 + 4x_4) - 3x_5$$
$$= 7x_1 + 14x_2 + 6x_3 + 10x_4 - 3x_5$$

Thus, Rylon's objective function may be written as

$$\max z = 7x_1 + 14x_2 + 6x_3 + 10x_4 - 3x_5 \tag{54}$$

Rylon faces the following constraints:

Constraint 1 No more than 4000 lb of raw material can be purchased annually.

Constraint 2 No more than 6000 hours of laboratory time can be used each year.

Constraint 1 is expressed by

$$x_5 \le 4000 \tag{55}$$

To express Constraint 2, note that

Total lab time used annually = time used annually to process raw material
+ time used annually to process Luxury Brute
+ time used annually to process Luxury Chanelle
$$= x_5 + 3x_2 + 2x_4$$

Then Constraint 2 becomes

$$3x_2 + 2x_4 + x_5 \le 6000 \tag{56}$$

After adding the sign restrictions $x_i \ge 0$ ($i = 1, 2, 3, 4, 5$), many students claim that Rylon should solve the following LP:

$$\max z = 7x_1 + 14x_2 + 6x_3 + 10x_4 - 3x_5$$
$$\text{s.t.} \qquad\qquad x_5 \le 4000$$
$$3x_2 + 2x_4 + x_5 \le 6000$$
$$x_i \ge 0 \quad (i = 1, 2, 3, 4, 5)$$

This formulation is incorrect. Observe that the variables x_1 and x_3 do not appear in any of the constraints. This means that any point with $x_2 = x_4 = x_5 = 0$ and x_1 and x_3 very large is in the feasible region. Points with x_1 and x_3 large can yield arbitrarily large profits. Thus, this LP is unbounded. Our mistake is that the current formulation does not indicate that the amount of raw material purchased determines the amount of Brute and Chanelle that is available for sale or further processing. More specifically, from Figure 8 (and the fact that 1 oz of processed Brute yields exactly 1 oz of Luxury Brute), it follows that

$$\begin{matrix} \text{Ounces of Regular Brute Sold} \\ \text{+ ounces of Luxury Brute sold} \end{matrix} = \left(\frac{\text{ounces of Brute produced}}{\text{pound of raw material}} \right) \left(\begin{matrix} \text{pounds of raw} \\ \text{material purchased} \end{matrix} \right)$$

$$= 3x_5$$

Figure 8
Production Process
for Brute-Chanelle
Example

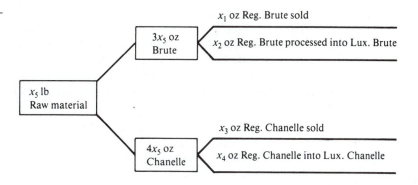

This relation is reflected in the constraint

$$x_1 + x_2 = 3x_5 \quad \text{or} \quad x_1 + x_2 - 3x_5 = 0 \tag{57}$$

Similarly, from Figure 8, it is clear that

Ounces of Regular Chanelle sold + ounces of Luxury Chanelle sold $= 4x_5$

This relation yields the constraint

$$x_3 + x_4 = 4x_5 \quad \text{or} \quad x_3 + x_4 - 4x_5 = 0 \tag{58}$$

Constraints (57) and (58) relate several decision variables. Students often omit constraints of this type. As this problem shows, leaving out even one constraint may very well lead to an unacceptable answer (such as an unbounded LP). If we combine (53)–(58) with the usual sign restrictions, we obtain the *correct* LP formulation:

$$\max z = 7x_1 + 14x_2 + 6x_3 + 10x_4 - 3x_5$$

$$\text{s.t.} \qquad\qquad\qquad\qquad\qquad\qquad\qquad\qquad x_5 \le 4000$$

$$3x_2 \qquad + 2x_4 + x_5 \le 6000$$

$$x_1 + x_2 \qquad\qquad - 3x_5 = 0$$

$$x_3 + x_4 - 4x_5 = 0$$

$$x_i \ge 0 \quad (i = 1, 2, 3, 4, 5)$$

The optimal solution is $z = 172,666.667$, $x_1 = 11,333.333$ oz, $x_2 = 666.667$ oz, $x_3 = 16,000$ oz, $x_4 = 0$, and $x_5 = 4000$ lb. Thus, Rylon should purchase all 4000 lb of available raw material and produce 11,333.333 oz of Regular Brute, 666.667 oz of Luxury Brute, and 16,000 oz of Regular Chanelle. This production plan will contribute $172,666.667 to Rylon's profits. In this problem, a fractional number of ounces seems reasonable, so the Divisibility Assumption holds.

We close our discussion of the Rylon problem by discussing an error that is made by many students. They reason that

$$1 \text{ lb raw material} = 3 \text{ oz Brute} + 4 \text{ oz Chanelle}$$

Since $x_1 + x_2 =$ total ounces of Brute produced, and $x_3 + x_4 =$ total ounces of Chanelle produced, students conclude that

$$x_5 = 3(x_1 + x_2) + 4(x_3 + x_4) \tag{59}$$

This equation might make sense as a statement for a computer program; in a sense, the variable x_5 is replaced by the right side of Eq. (59). As an LP constraint, however, (59) makes no sense. To see this, note that the left side of (59) has the units "pounds of raw material," and the term $3x_1$ on the right side of (59) has the units

$$\left(\frac{\text{Ounces of Brute}}{\text{Pounds of raw material}} \right) (\text{ounces of Brute})$$

Since some of the terms in (59) do not have the same units, (59) cannot be correct. *If there are doubts about a constraint, make sure that all terms in the constraint have the same units.* This will avoid many formulation errors. (Of course, even if the units on both sides of a constraint are the same, the constraint may still be wrong.)

♦ PROBLEMS

GROUP A

1. Sunco Oil has three different processes that can be used to manufacture various types of gasoline. Each process involves blending oils in the company's catalytic cracker. Running process 1 for an hour costs $5 and requires 2 barrels of crude oil 1 and 3 barrels of crude oil 2. The output from running process 1 for an hour is 2 barrels of gas 1 and 1 barrel of gas 2. Running process 2 for an hour costs $4 and requires 1 barrel of crude 1 and 3 barrels of crude 2. The output from running process 2 for an hour is 3 barrels of gas 2. Running process 3 for an hour costs $1 and requires 2 barrels of crude 2 and 3 barrels of gas 2. The output from running process 3 for an hour is 2 barrels of gas 3. Each week, 200 barrels of crude 1, at $2/barrel, and 300 barrels of crude 2, at $3/barrel, may be purchased. All gas produced can be sold at the following per-barrel prices: gas 1, $9; gas 2, $10; gas 3, $24. Formulate an LP whose solution will maximize revenues less costs. Assume that only 100 hours of time on the catalytic cracker are available each week.

2. Furnco manufactures tables and chairs. A table requires 40 board ft of wood, and a chair requires 30 board ft of wood. Wood may be purchased at a cost of $1 per board ft, and 40,000 board ft of wood are available for purchase. It takes 2 hours of skilled labor to manufacture an unfinished table or an unfinished chair. Three more hours of skilled labor will turn an unfinished table into a finished table, and 2 more hours of skilled labor will turn an unfinished chair into a finished chair. A total of 6000 hours of skilled labor are available (and have already been paid for). All furniture produced can be sold at the following unit prices: unfinished table, $70; finished table, $140; unfinished chair, $60; finished chair, $110. Formulate an LP that will maximize the contribution to profit from manufacturing tables and chairs.

3. Suppose that in Example 11, 1 lb of raw material could be used to produce either 3 oz of Brute *or* 4 oz of Chanelle. How would this change the formulation?

GROUP B

4. A company produces A, B, and C and can sell these products in unlimited quantities at the following unit prices: A, $10; B, $56; C, $100. Producing a unit of A requires 1 hour of labor; a unit of B, 2 hours of labor plus 2 units of A; and a unit of C, 3 hours of labor plus 1 unit of B. Any A that is used to produce B cannot be sold. Similarly, any B that is used to produce C cannot be sold. A total of 40 hours of labor are available. Formulate an LP to maximize the company's revenues.

5. Daisy Drugs manufactures two drugs: drug 1 and drug 2. The drugs are produced by blending together two chemicals: chemical 1 and chemical 2. By weight, drug 1 must contain at least 65% chemical 1, and drug 2 must contain at least 55% chemical 1. Drug 1 sells for $6/oz, and drug 2 sells for $4/oz. Chemicals 1 and 2 can be produced by one of two production processes. Running process 1 for an hour requires 3 oz of raw material and 2 hours skilled labor and yields 3 oz of each chemical. Running process 2 for an hour requires 2 oz of raw material and 3 hours of skilled labor and yields 3 oz of chemical 1 and 1 oz of chemical 2. A total of 120 hours of skilled labor and 100 oz of raw material are available. Formulate an LP that can be used to maximize Daisy's sales revenues.

6.[†] Lizzie's Dairy produces cream cheese and cottage cheese. Milk and cream are blended together to produce these two products. Both high-fat and low-fat milk can be used to produce cream cheese and cottage cheese. High-fat milk is 60% fat; low-fat milk is 30% fat. The milk used to produce cream cheese must average at least 50% fat, and the milk used to produce cottage cheese must average at least 35% fat. At least 40% (by weight) of the inputs to cream cheese must be cream. At least 20% (by weight) of the input to cottage cheese must be cream. Both cottage cheese and cream cheese are produced by putting milk and cream through the cheese machine. It costs 40¢ to process 1 lb of inputs into a pound of cream cheese. It costs 40¢ to produce 1 lb of cottage cheese, but every pound of input for cottage cheese yields 0.9 lb of cottage cheese and 0.1 lb of waste. Cream can be produced by evaporating high-fat and low-fat milk. It costs 40¢ to evaporate 1 lb of high-fat milk. Each pound of high-fat milk that is evaporated yields 0.6 lb of cream. It costs 40¢ to evaporate 1 lb of low-fat milk. Each pound of low-fat milk that is evaporated yields 0.3 lb of cream. Each day, up to 3000 lb of input may be sent through the cheese machine. Each day, at least 1000 lb of cottage cheese and at least 1000 lb of cream cheese must be produced. Up to 1500 lb of cream cheese and up to 2000 lb of cottage cheese can be sold each day. Cottage cheese is sold for $1.20/lb and cream cheese for $1.50/lb. High-fat milk is purchased for 80¢/lb and low-fat milk for 40¢/lb. The evaporator can process at most 2000 lb of milk daily. Formulate an LP that can be used to maximize Lizzie's daily profit.

7. A company produces six products in the following fashion. Each unit of raw material purchased yields four units of product 1, two units of product 2, and one unit of product 3. Up to 1200 units of product 1 can be sold, and up to 300 units of product 2 can be sold. Each unit of product 1 can be sold or processed further. Each unit of product 1 that is processed yields a unit of product 4. Demand for products 3 and 4 is unlimited. Each unit of product 2 can be sold or be processed further. Each unit of product 2 that is processed further yields 0.8 units of product 5 and 0.3 units of product 6. Up to 1000 units of product 5 can be sold, and up to 800 units of product 6 can be sold. Up to 3000 units of raw material can be purchased at $6 per unit. Leftover units of products 5 and 6 must be destroyed. It costs $4 to destroy each leftover unit of product 5 and $3 to destroy each leftover unit of product 6. Ignoring raw material purchase costs, the per-unit sales price and production costs for each product are shown in Table 13. Formulate an LP whose solution will yield a profit-maximizing production schedule.

Table 13

	SALES PRICE	PRODUCTION COST
Product 1	$7	$4
Product 2	$6	$4
Product 3	$4	$2
Product 4	$3	$1
Product 5	$20	$5
Product 6	$35	$5

[†] Based on Sullivan and Secrest (1985).

3-10   USING LINEAR PROGRAMMING TO SOLVE MULTIPERIOD DECISION PROBLEMS: AN INVENTORY MODEL

Up to this point, all the LP formulations we have discussed are examples of *static*, or *one-period, models*. In a static model, we assume that all decisions are made at a single point in time. The rest of the examples in this chapter show how linear programming can be used to determine optimal decisions in **multiperiod**, or **dynamic**, **models**. Dynamic models arise when the decision maker makes decisions at more than one point in time. In a dynamic model, decisions made during the current period influence decisions made during future periods. For example, consider a company that must determine how many units of a product should be produced during each month. If it produced a large number of units during the current month, this would reduce the number of units that should be produced during future months. The examples discussed in Sections 3.10–3.12 illustrate how earlier decisions affect later decisions. We will return to dynamic decision models when we study dynamic programming in Chapters 20 and 21.

E X A M P L E   **12**

Sailco Corporation must determine how many sailboats should be produced during each of the next four quarters (one quarter = three months). The demand during each of the next four quarters is as follows: first quarter, 40 sailboats; second quarter, 60 sailboats; third quarter, 75 sailboats; fourth quarter, 25 sailboats. Sailco must meet demands on time. At the beginning of the first quarter, Sailco has an inventory of 10 sailboats. At the beginning of each quarter, Sailco must decide how many sailboats should be produced during that quarter. For simplicity, we assume that sailboats manufactured during a quarter can be used to meet demand for that quarter. During each quarter, Sailco can produce up to 40 sailboats with regular-time labor at a total cost of $400 per sailboat. By having employees work overtime during a quarter, Sailco can produce additional sailboats with overtime labor at a total cost of $450 per sailboat.

At the end of each quarter (after production has occurred and the current quarter's demand has been satisfied), a carrying or holding cost of $20 per sailboat is incurred.[†] Use linear programming to determine a production schedule to minimize the sum of production and inventory costs during the next four quarters.

Solution

For each quarter, Sailco must determine the number of sailboats that should be produced by regular-time and by overtime labor. Thus, we define the following decision variables:

x_t = number of sailboats produced by regular-time labor (at $400/boat) during quarter t ($t = 1, 2, 3, 4$)

y_t = number of sailboats produced by overtime labor (at $450/boat) during quarter t ($t = 1, 2, 3, 4$)

It is convenient to define decision variables for the inventory (number of sailboats on hand) at the end of each quarter:

i_t = number of sailboats on hand at end of quarter t ($t = 1, 2, 3, 4$)

[†] We discuss the major components of holding costs in Chapter 16.

Sailco's total cost may be determined from

$$\begin{aligned}
\text{Total cost} &= \text{cost of producing regular-time boats} \\
&\quad + \text{ cost of producing overtime boats} + \text{inventory costs} \\
&= 400(x_1 + x_2 + x_3 + x_4) + 450(y_1 + y_2 + y_3 + y_4) \\
&\quad + 20(i_1 + i_2 + i_3 + i_4)
\end{aligned}$$

Thus, Sailco's objective function is

$$\begin{aligned}
\min z = {} &400x_1 + 400x_2 + 400x_3 + 400x_4 + 450y_1 + 450y_2 \\
&+ 450y_3 + 450y_4 + 20i_1 + 20i_2 + 20i_3 + 20i_4
\end{aligned} \tag{60}$$

Before determining Sailco's constraints, we make two observations that will aid in formulating multiperiod production scheduling models.

For quarter t,

$$\begin{aligned}
\text{Inventory at end of quarter } t = {} &\text{inventory at end of quarter } (t-1) \\
&+ \text{ quarter } t \text{ production} - \text{quarter } t \text{ demand}
\end{aligned}$$

This relation plays a key role in formulating almost all multiperiod production scheduling models. If we let d_t be the demand during period t (thus, $d_1 = 40, d_2 = 60, d_3 = 75$, and $d_4 = 25$), our observation may be expressed in the following compact form:

$$i_t = i_{t-1} + (x_t + y_t) - d_t \quad (t = 1, 2, 3, 4) \tag{61}$$

In (61), $i_0 = $ inventory at end of quarter $0 = $ inventory at beginning of quarter $1 = 10$. For example, if we had 20 sailboats on hand at the end of quarter 2 ($i_2 = 20$) and produced 65 sailboats during quarter 3 (this means $x_3 + y_3 = 65$), what would be our ending third-quarter inventory? Simply the number of sailboats on hand at the end of quarter 2 plus the sailboats produced during quarter 3, less quarter 3's demand of 75. In this case, $i_3 = 20 + 65 - 75 = 10$, which agrees with (61). Eq. (61) relates decision variables associated with different time periods. In formulating any multiperiod LP model, the hardest step is usually finding the relation (such as (61)) that relates decision variables from different periods.

We also note that quarter t's demand will be met on time if and only if (sometimes written iff) $i_t \geq 0$. To see this, observe that $i_{t-1} + (x_t + y_t)$ is available to meet period t's demand, so that period t's demand will be met if and only if

$$i_{t-1} + (x_t + y_t) \geq d_t \quad \text{or} \quad i_t = i_{t-1} + (x_t + y_t) - d_t \geq 0$$

This means that the sign restrictions $i_t \geq 0$ ($t = 1, 2, 3, 4$) will ensure that each quarter's demand will be met on time.

We can now determine Sailco's constraints. First, we use the following four constraints to ensure that each period's regular-time production will not exceed 40: $x_1, x_2, x_3, x_4 \leq 40$. Then we add constraints of the form (61) for each time period ($t = 1, 2, 3, 4$). This yields the following four constraints:

$$\begin{aligned}
i_1 &= 10 + x_1 + y_1 - 40 & i_2 &= i_1 + x_2 + y_2 - 60 \\
i_3 &= i_2 + x_3 + y_3 - 75 & i_4 &= i_3 + x_4 + y_4 - 25
\end{aligned}$$

Adding the sign restrictions $x_t \geq 0$ (to rule out negative production levels) and $i_t \geq 0$

(to ensure that each period's demand is met on time) yields the following formulation:

$$\min z = 400x_1 + 400x_2 + 400x_3 + 400x_4 + 450y_1 + 450y_2 + 450y_3 + 450y_4$$
$$+ 20i_1 + 20i_2 + 20i_3 + 20i_4$$
$$\text{s.t.} \quad x_1 \le 40, \qquad x_2 \le 40, \qquad x_3 \le 40, \qquad x_4 \le 40$$
$$i_1 = 10 + x_1 + y_1 - 40, \qquad i_2 = i_1 + x_2 + y_2 - 60$$
$$i_3 = i_2 + x_3 + y_3 - 75, \qquad i_4 = i_3 + x_4 + y_4 - 25$$
$$i_t \ge 0, \qquad y_t \ge 0, \qquad \text{and} \qquad x_t \ge 0 \quad (t = 1, 2, 3, 4)$$

The optimal solution to this problem is $z = 78{,}450$; $x_1 = x_2 = x_3 = 40$; $x_4 = 25$; $y_1 = 0$; $y_2 = 10$; $y_3 = 35$; $y_4 = 0$; $i_1 = 10$; $i_2 = i_3 = i_4 = 0$. Thus, the minimum total cost that Sailco can incur is \$78,450. To incur this cost, Sailco should produce 40 sailboats with regular-time labor during quarters 1–3 and 25 sailboats with regular-time labor during quarter 4. Sailco should also produce 10 sailboats with overtime labor during quarter 2 and 35 sailboats with overtime labor during quarter 3. Inventory costs will be incurred only during quarter 1.

◆

Some readers might worry that our formulation allows Sailco to use overtime production during quarter t even if period t's regular production is less than 40. It is true that our formulation does not make such a schedule infeasible. However, any production plan that had $y_t > 0$ and $x_t < 40$ could not be optimal. For example, consider the following two production schedules:

$$\text{Production schedule A} = x_1 = x_2 = x_3 = 40; \qquad x_4 = 25;$$
$$y_2 = 10; \qquad y_3 = 25; \qquad y_4 = 0$$
$$\text{Production schedule B} = x_1 = 40; \qquad x_2 = 30; \qquad x_3 = 30; \qquad x_4 = 25;$$
$$y_2 = 20; \qquad y_3 = 35; \qquad y_4 = 0$$

Schedules A and B both have the same production level during each period. This means that both schedules will have identical inventory costs. Also, both schedules are feasible, but schedule B incurs more overtime costs than schedule A. Thus, in minimizing costs, schedule B (or any schedule having $y_t > 0$ and $x_t < 40$) would never be chosen.

In reality, an LP such as Example 12 would be implemented by using a **rolling horizon**, which works in the following fashion. After solving Example 12, Sailco would implement only the quarter 1 production strategy (produce 40 boats with regular-time labor). Then the company would observe quarter 1's actual demand. Suppose quarter 1's actual demand is 35 boats. Then quarter 2 begins with an inventory of $10 + 40 - 35 = 15$ boats. We now make a forecast for quarter 5 demand (suppose the forecast is 36). Next determine production for quarter 2 by solving an LP in which quarter 2 is the first quarter, quarter 5 is the final quarter, and beginning inventory is 15 boats. Then quarter 2's production would be determined by solving the following LP:

$$\min z = 400(x_2 + x_3 + x_4 + x_5) + 450(y_2 + y_3 + y_4 + y_5) + 20(i_2 + i_3 + i_4 + i_5)$$
$$\text{s.t.} \quad x_2 \le 40, \qquad x_3 \le 40, \qquad x_4 \le 40, \qquad x_5 \le 40$$
$$i_2 = 15 + x_2 + y_2 - 60, \qquad i_3 = i_2 + x_3 + y_3 - 75$$
$$i_4 = i_3 + x_4 + y_4 - 25, \qquad i_5 = i_4 + x_5 + y_5 - 36$$
$$i_t \ge 0, \qquad y_t \ge 0 \qquad \text{and} \qquad x_t \ge 0 \quad (t = 2, 3, 4, 5)$$

Here, x_5 = quarter 5's regular-time production, y_5 = quarter 5's overtime production, and i_5 = quarter 5's ending inventory. The optimal values of x_2 and y_2 for this LP are then used to determine quarter 2's production. Thus, each quarter, an LP (with a planning horizon of four quarters) is solved to determine the current quarter's production. Then current demand is observed, and demand is forecasted for the next four quarters. Next another LP is solved to determine the next quarter's production, etc. This technique of "rolling planning horizon" is the method by which most dynamic or multiperiod LP models are implemented in real-world applications.

Our formulation of the Sailco problem has several other limitations.

1. Production cost may not be a linear function of the quantity produced. This would violate the Proportionality Assumption. We discuss how to deal with this problem in Chapters 9 and 20.

2. Future demands may not be known with certainty. In this situation, the Certainty Assumption is violated. In Chapter 21, we explain how the present model can be extended to allow for uncertain demands.

3. We have required Sailco to meet all demands on time. Often companies can meet demands during later periods but are assessed a penalty cost for demands that are not met on time. For example, if demand is not met on time, customer displeasure may result in a loss of future revenues. If demand can be met during later periods, we say that demand can be **backlogged**. Our present LP formulation can be modified to incorporate backlogging (see Problem 1 of Section 4.12).

4. We have ignored the fact that quarter-to-quarter variations in the quantity produced may result in extra costs (called **production smoothing costs**). For example, if we increase production a great deal from one quarter to the next, this will probably require the costly training of new workers. On the other hand, if production is greatly decreased from one quarter to the next, extra costs resulting from laying off workers may be incurred. In Section 4.12, we modify the present model to account for smoothing costs.

5. If any sailboats are left at the end of the last quarter, we have assigned them a value of zero. This is clearly unrealistic. In any inventory model with a finite horizon, the inventory left at the end of the last period should be assigned a **salvage value** that is indicative of the worth of the final period's inventory. For example, if Sailco feels that each sailboat left at the end of quarter 4 is worth \$400, a term $-400i_4$ (measuring the worth of quarter 4's inventory) should be added to the objective function.

◆ PROBLEMS

GROUP A

1. A customer requires during the next four months, respectively, 50, 65, 100, and 70 units of a commodity (no backlogging is allowed). Production costs are \$5, \$8, \$4, and \$7 per unit during these months. The storage cost from one month to the next is \$2 per unit (assessed on ending inventory). It is estimated that each unit on hand at the end of month 4 could be sold for \$6. Formulate an LP that will minimize the net cost incurred in meeting the demands of the next four months.

2. A company faces the following demands during the next three periods: period 1, 20 units; period 2, 10 units; period 3, 15 units. The unit production cost during each period is as follows: period 1, \$13; period 2, \$14; period 3, \$15. A holding cost of \$2 per unit is assessed against each period's ending inventory. At the beginning of period 1, the company has 5 units on hand.

Table 14

	MONTH 1		MONTH 2		MONTH 3	
	Demand	*Cost/Cake*	*Demand*	*Cost/Cake*	*Demand*	*Cost/Cake*
Cheesecake	40	$3.00	30	$3.40	20	$3.80
Black Forest	20	$2.50	30	$2.80	10	$3.40

In reality, not all goods produced during a month can be used to meet the current month's demand. To model this fact, we assume that only one half of the goods produced during a period can be used to meet the current period's demands. Formulate an LP to minimize the cost of meeting the demand for the next three periods. (*Hint:* Constraints such as $i_1 = x_1 + 5 - 20$ are certainly needed. Unlike our example, however, the constraint $i_1 \geq 0$ will not ensure that period 1's demand is met. For example, if $x_1 = 20$, then $i_1 \geq 0$ will hold, but since only $\frac{1}{2}(20) = 10$ units of period 1 production can be used to meet period 1's demand, $x_1 = 20$ would not be feasible. Try to think of a type of constraint that will ensure that what is available to meet each period's demand is at least as large as that period's demand.)

GROUP B

3. James Beerd bakes cheesecakes and Black Forest cakes. During any month, he can bake at most 60 cakes. The costs per cake and the demands for cakes, which must be met on time, are listed in Table 14. It costs 50¢ to hold a cheesecake, and 40¢ to hold a Black Forest cake, in inventory for a month. Formulate an LP to minimize the total cost of meeting the next three months' demands.

4. A manufacturing company produces two types of products: A and B. They have agreed to deliver the products on the schedule shown in Table 15. The company has two assembly lines, 1 and 2, with the available production hours shown in Table 16. The production rates for each assembly line and product combination, in terms of hours per product, are shown in Table 17. It takes 0.15 hours to manufacture 1 unit of product A on line 1, and so on. It costs $5 per hour of line time to produce any product. The inventory carrying cost per month for each product is 20¢

Table 15

	A	B
March 31	5000	2000
April 30	8000	4000

per unit (charged on each month's ending inventory). At present, there are 500 units of A and 750 units of B in inventory. Management would like at least 1000 units of each product in inventory at the end of April. Formulate an LP to determine the production schedule that minimizes the total cost incurred in meeting demands on time.

Table 16

	PRODUCTION HOURS AVAILABLE	
	Line 1	*Line 2*
March	800	2000
April	400	1200

Table 17

	PRODUCTION RATE	
	Line 1	*Line 2*
Product A	0.15	0.16
Product B	0.12	0.14

5. During the next two months, General Cars must meet (on time) the following demands for trucks and cars: month 1—400 trucks, 800 cars; month 2—300 trucks, 300 cars. During each month, at most 1000 vehicles can be produced. Each truck uses 2 tons of steel, and each car uses 1 ton of steel. During month 1, steel costs $400 per ton; during month 2, steel costs $600 per ton. At most 1500 tons of steel may be purchased each month (steel may only be used during the month in which it is purchased). At the beginning of month 1, 100 trucks and 200 cars are in inventory. At the end of each month, a holding cost of $150 per vehicle is assessed. Each car gets 20 mpg, and each truck gets 10 mpg. During each month, the vehicles produced by the company must average at least 16 mpg. Formulate an LP to meet the demand and mileage requirements at minimum cost (include steel costs and holding costs).

6. Gandhi Clothing Company produces shirts and pants. Each shirt requires 2 sq yd of cloth. Each pair of pants requires 3 sq yd of cloth. During the next two months, the following demands for shirts and pants must be met (on time): month 1 — 10 shirts, 15 pairs of pants; month 2 — 12 shirts, 14 pairs of pants. During each month, the following resources are available: month 1 — 90 sq yd of cloth; month 2 — 60 sq yd. (Cloth that is available during month 1 may, if unused during month 1, be used during month 2.)

During each month, it costs $4 to make an article of clothing with regular-time labor and $8 to make one with overtime labor. During each month, a total of at most 25 articles of clothing may be produced with regular-time labor, and an unlimited number of articles of clothing may be produced with overtime labor. At the end of each month, a holding cost of $3 per article of clothing is assessed. Formulate an LP that can be used to meet demands for the next two months (on time) at minimum cost. Assume that at the beginning of month 1, 1 shirt and 2 pairs of pants are available.

7. Each year, Paynothing Shoes faces demands (which must be met on time) for pairs of shoes as shown in Table 18. Workers work three consecutive quarters and then receive one quarter off. For example, a worker may work during quarters 3 and 4 of one year and quarter 1 of the next year. During a quarter in which a worker works, he or she can produce up to 50 pairs of shoes. Each worker is paid $500 per quarter. At the end of each quarter, a holding cost of $50 per pair of shoes is assessed. Formulate an LP that can be used to minimize the cost per year (labor + holding) of meeting the demands for shoes. To simplify matters, assume that at the end of each year, the ending inventory is zero. (*Hint:* It is allowable to assume that a given worker will get the same quarter off during each year.)

8. A company must meet (on time) the following demands: quarter 1 — 30 units; quarter 2 — 20 units; quarter 3 — 40 units. Each quarter, up to 27 units can be produced with regular-time labor, at a cost of $40 per unit. During each quarter, an unlimited number of units can be produced with overtime labor, at a cost of $60 per unit. Of all units produced, 20% are unsuitable and cannot be used to meet demand. Also, at the end of each quarter, 10% of all units on hand spoil and cannot be used to meet any future demands. After each quarter's demand is satisfied and spoilage is accounted for, a cost of $15 per unit is assessed against the quarter's ending inventory. Formulate an LP that can be used to minimize the total cost of meeting the next three quarters' demands. Assume that 20 usable units are available at the beginning of quarter 1.

9. Donovan Enterprises produces electric mixers. During the next four quarters, the following demands for mixers must be met on time: quarter 1 — 4000; quarter 2 — 2000; quarter 3 — 3000; quarter 4 — 10,000. Each of Donovan's workers works three quarters of the year and gets one quarter off. Thus, a worker may work during quarters 1, 2, and 4 and get quarter 3 off. Each worker is paid $30,000 per year and (if working) can produce up to 500 mixers during a quarter. At the end of each quarter, Donovan incurs a holding cost of $30 per mixer on each mixer in inventory. Formulate an LP to help Donovan minimize the cost (labor and inventory) of meeting the next year's demand (on time). 600 mixers are available at the beginning of quarter 1.

Table 18			
QUARTER 1	QUARTER 2	QUARTER 3	QUARTER 4
600	300	800	100

3-11   MULTIPERIOD FINANCIAL MODELS

The following example illustrates how linear programming can be used to model multiperiod cash management problems. The key is to determine the relations of cash on hand during different periods.

EXAMPLE 13

Finco Investment Corporation must determine investment strategy for the firm during the next three years. At present (time 0), $100,000 is available for investment. Investments A, B, C, D, and E are available. The cash flow associated with investing $1 in each investment is given in Table 19.

Table 19
Cash Flows for
Finco Example

	CASH FLOW AT TIME			
	0	*1*	*2*	*3*
From inv. A	− $1	+ $0.50	+ $1	$0
From inv. B	$0	− $1	+ $0.50	+ $1
From inv. C	− $1	+ $1.2	$0	$0
From inv. D	− $1	$0	$0	+ $1.9
From inv. E	$0	$0	− $1	+ $1.5

Note: Time 0 = present; time 1 = 1 year from now; time 2 = 2 years from now; time 3 = 3 years from now.

For example, $1 invested in investment B requires a $1 cash outflow at time 1 and returns 50¢ at time 2 and $1 at time 3. To ensure that the company's portfolio is diversified, Finco requires that at most $75,000 be placed in any single investment. In addition to investments A–E, Finco can earn interest at 8% per year by keeping uninvested cash in money market funds. Returns from investments may be immediately reinvested. For example, the positive cash flow received from investment C at time 1 may immediately be reinvested in investment B. Finco cannot borrow funds, so the cash available for investment at any time is limited to cash on hand. Formulate an LP that will maximize cash on hand at time 3.

Solution

Finco must decide how much money should be placed in each investment (including money market funds). Thus, we define the following decision variables:

A = dollars invested in investment A

B = dollars invested in investment B

C = dollars invested in investment C

D = dollars invested in investment D

E = dollars invested in investment E

S_t = dollars invested in money market funds at time t $(t = 0, 1, 2)$

Finco wants to maximize cash on hand at time 3. At time 3, Finco's cash on hand will be the sum of all cash inflows at time 3. From the description of investments A–E and the fact that from time 2 to time 3, S_2 will increase to $1.08S_2$,

$$\text{Time 3 cash on hand} = B + 1.9D + 1.5E + 1.08S_2$$

Thus, Finco's objective function is

$$\max z = B + 1.9D + 1.5E + 1.08S_2 \qquad (62)$$

In multiperiod financial models, the following type of constraint is usually used to relate decision variables from different periods:

Cash available at time t = cash invested at time t

$\qquad$ + uninvested cash at time t that is carried over to time $t + 1$

If we classify money market funds as investments, we see that

$$\text{Cash available at time } t = \text{cash invested at time } t \tag{63}$$

Since investments A, C, D, and S_0 are available at time 0, and $100,000 is available at time 0, (63) for time 0 becomes

$$100{,}000 = A + C + D + S_0 \tag{64}$$

At time 1, $0.5A + 1.2C + 1.08S_0$ is available for investment, and investments B and S_1 are available. Then for $t = 1$, (63) becomes

$$0.5A + 1.2C + 1.08S_0 = B + S_1 \tag{65}$$

At time 2, $A + 0.5B + 1.08S_1$ is available for investment, and investments E and S_2 are available. Thus, for $t = 2$, (63) reduces to

$$A + 0.5B + 1.08S_1 = E + S_2 \tag{66}$$

Let's not forget that at most $75,000 can be placed in any of investments A–E. To take care of this, we add the constraints

$$A \leq 75{,}000 \tag{67}$$
$$B \leq 75{,}000 \tag{68}$$
$$C \leq 75{,}000 \tag{69}$$
$$D \leq 75{,}000 \tag{70}$$
$$E \leq 75{,}000 \tag{71}$$

Combining (62) and (64)–(71) with the sign restrictions (all variables ≥ 0) yields the following LP:

$$\max z = B + 1.9D + 1.5E + 1.08S_2$$
$$\text{s.t.} \quad A + C + D + S_0 = 100{,}000$$
$$0.5A + 1.2C + 1.08S_0 = B + S_1$$
$$A + 0.5B + 1.08S_1 = E + S_2$$
$$A \leq 75{,}000$$
$$B \leq 75{,}000$$
$$C \leq 75{,}000$$
$$D \leq 75{,}000$$
$$E \leq 75{,}000$$
$$A, B, C, D, E, S_0, S_1, S_2 \geq 0$$

We find the optimal solution to be $z = 218{,}500$, $A = 60{,}000$, $B = 30{,}000$, $D = 40{,}000$, $E = 75{,}000$, $C = S_0 = S_1 = S_2 = 0$. Thus, Finco should not invest in money market funds. At time 0, Finco should invest $60,000 in A and $40,000 in D. Then, at time 1, the $30,000 cash inflow from A should be invested in B. Finally, at time 2, the $60,000 cash inflow from A and the $15,000 cash inflow from B should be invested in E. At time 3, Finco's $100,000 will have grown to $218,500.

♦

The reader might wonder how our formulation ensures that Finco never invests more money at any time than the firm has available. This is ensured by the fact that each variable S_i must be nonnegative. For example, $S_0 \geq 0$ is equivalent to $100,000 - A - C - D \geq 0$, which ensures that at most $100,000 will be invested at time 0.

♦ PROBLEMS

GROUP A

1. A consultant to Finco claims that Finco's cash on hand at time 3 is the sum of the cash inflows from all investments, not just those investments yielding a cash inflow at time 3. Thus, the consultant claims that Finco's objective function should be

$$\max z = 1.5A + 1.5B + 1.2C + 1.9D + 1.5E$$
$$+ 1.08S_0 + 1.08S_1 + 1.08S_2$$

Explain why the consultant is incorrect.

2. Show that Finco's objective function may also be written as

$$\max z = 100,000 + 0.5A + 0.5B + 0.2C + 0.9D$$
$$+ 0.5E + 0.08S_0 + 0.08S_1 + 0.08S_2$$

3. At time 0, we have $10,000. Investments A and B are available; their cash flows are shown in Table 20. Assume that any money not invested in A or B earns *no* interest. Formulate an LP that will maximize cash on hand at time 3. Can you guess the optimal solution to this problem?

Table 20

	A	B
Time 0	− $1	$0
Time 1	$0.2	− $1
Time 2	$1.5	$0
Time 3	$0	$1.9

GROUP B

4.[†] Broker Steve Johnson is currently trying to maximize his profit in the bond market. Four bonds are available for purchase and sale, with the bid and ask price of each bond as shown in Table 21. Steve can buy up to 1000 units of each bond at the ask price or sell up to 1000 units of each bond at the bid price. During each of the next three years, the person who sells a bond will pay the owner of the bond the cash payments shown in Table 22.

Table 21

	BID PRICE	ASK PRICE
Bond 1	980	990
Bond 2	970	985
Bond 3	960	972
Bond 4	940	954

Steve's goal is to maximize his revenue from selling bonds less his payment for buying bonds, subject to the constraint that after each year's payments are received, his current cash position (due only to cash payments from bonds and not purchases or sale of bonds) is nonnegative. Assume that cash payments are discounted, with a payment of $1 one year from now being equivalent to a payment of 90¢ now. Formulate an LP to maximize net profit from buying and selling bonds, subject to the arbitrage constraints previously described. Why do you think we limit the number of units of each bond that can be bought or sold?

[†] Based on Rohn (1987).

Table 22

YEAR	BOND 1	BOND 2	BOND 3	BOND 4
1	100	80	70	60
2	110	90	80	50
3	1100	1120	1090	1110

3-12   MULTIPERIOD WORK SCHEDULING

In Section 3.5, we saw that linear programming could be used to schedule employees in a static environment where demand did not change over time. The following example (a modified version of a problem from Wagner (1975)) shows how LP can be used to schedule employee training when a firm faces demand that changes over time.

E X A M P L E
14

CSL is a chain of computer service stores. The number of hours of skilled repair time that CSL requires during the next five months is as follows:

Month 1 (January): 6000 hours

Month 2 (February): 7000 hours

Month 3 (March): 8000 hours

Month 4 (April): 9500 hours

Month 5 (May): 11,000 hours

At the beginning of January, 50 skilled technicians work for CSL. Each skilled technician can work up to 160 hours per month. In order to meet future demands, new technicians must be trained. It takes one month to train a new technician. During the month of training, a trainee must be supervised for 50 hours by an experienced technician. Each experienced technician is paid $2000 a month (even if he or she does not work the full 160 hours). During the month of training, a trainee is paid $1000 a month. At the end of each month, 5% of CSL's experienced technicians quit to join Plum Computers. Formulate an LP whose solution will enable CSL to minimize the labor cost incurred in meeting the service requirements for the next five months.

Solution   CSL must determine the number of technicians that should be trained during month t ($t = 1, 2, 3, 4, 5$). Thus, we define

x_t = number of technicians trained during month t ($t = 1, 2, 3, 4, 5$)

CSL wants to minimize total labor cost during the next five months. Note that

Total labor cost = cost of paying trainees + cost of paying experienced technicians

To express the cost of paying experienced technicians, we need to define, for $t = 1, 2, 3, 4, 5$,

y_t = number of experienced technicians at the beginning of month t

Then

$$\text{Total labor cost} = (1000x_1 + 1000x_2 + 1000x_3 + 1000x_4 + 1000x_5)$$
$$+ (2000y_1 + 2000y_2 + 2000y_3 + 2000y_4 + 2000y_5)$$

Thus, CSL's objective function is

$$\min z = 1000x_1 + 1000x_2 + 1000x_3 + 1000x_4 + 1000x_5$$
$$+ 2000y_1 + 2000y_2 + 2000y_3 + 2000y_4 + 2000y_5$$

What constraints does CSL face? Note that we are given $y_1 = 50$, and that for $t = 1, 2, 3, 4, 5$, CSL must ensure that

Number of available technician hours during month t

$\geq$ Number of technician hours required during month t (72)

Since each trainee requires 50 hours of experienced technician time, and each skilled technician is available for 160 hours per month,

Number of available technician hours during month $t = 160y_t - 50x_t$

Now (72) yields the following five constraints:

$$160y_1 - 50x_1 \geq 6000 \qquad \text{(Month 1 constraint)}$$
$$160y_2 - 50x_2 \geq 7000 \qquad \text{(Month 2 constraint)}$$
$$160y_3 - 50x_3 \geq 8000 \qquad \text{(Month 3 constraint)}$$
$$160y_4 - 50x_4 \geq 9500 \qquad \text{(Month 4 constraint)}$$
$$160y_5 - 50x_5 \geq 11{,}000 \qquad \text{(Month 5 constraint)}$$

As in the other multiperiod formulations, we need constraints that relate variables from different periods. In the CSL problem, it is important to realize that the number of skilled technicians available at the beginning of any month is determined by the number of skilled technicians available during the previous month and the number of technicians trained during the previous month:

Experienced technicians available   experienced technicians available   (73)
at beginning of month t $=$ at beginning of month $(t - 1)$

+ technicians trained during month $(t - 1)$

− experienced technicians who quit during month $(t - 1)$

For example, for February, (73) yields

$$y_2 = y_1 + x_1 - 0.05y_1 \qquad \text{or} \qquad y_2 = 0.95y_1 + x_1$$

Similarly, for March, (73) yields

$$y_3 = 0.95y_2 + x_2$$

and for April,

$$y_4 = 0.95y_3 + x_3$$

and for May,

$$y_5 = 0.95y_4 + x_4$$

Adding the sign restrictions $x_t \geq 0$ and $y_t \geq 0$ ($t = 1, 2, 3, 4, 5$), we obtain the following LP:

$$\min z = 1000x_1 + 1000x_2 + 1000x_3 + 1000x_4 + 1000x_5$$
$$+ 2000y_1 + 2000y_2 + 2000y_3 + 2000y_4 + 2000y_5$$

s.t.
$$160y_1 - 50x_1 \geq 6000 \qquad\qquad y_1 = 50$$
$$160y_2 - 50x_2 \geq 7000 \qquad\quad 0.95y_1 + x_1 = y_2$$
$$160y_3 - 50x_3 \geq 8000 \qquad\quad 0.95y_2 + x_2 = y_3$$
$$160y_4 - 50x_4 \geq 9500 \qquad\quad 0.95y_3 + x_3 = y_4$$
$$160y_5 - 50x_5 \geq 11{,}000 \qquad 0.95y_4 + x_4 = y_5$$
$$x_t, y_t \geq 0 \quad (t = 1, 2, 3, 4, 5)$$

The optimal solution is $z = 593{,}777$; $x_1 = 0$; $x_2 = 8.45$; $x_3 = 11.45$; $x_4 = 9.52$; $x_5 = 0$; $y_1 = 50$; $y_2 = 47.5$; $y_3 = 53.58$; $y_4 = 62.34$; and $y_5 = 68.75$. In reality, the x_t's must be integers, so this solution is difficult to interpret. Of course, we could obtain a feasible integer solution by rounding x_2 up to 9, x_3 up to 12, and x_4 up to 10, but (as in the post office example) there is no guarantee that this solution is the optimal integer solution. We note that CSL's future service requirements may not be known with certainty, so the Certainty Assumption may be violated in this model. ◆

◆ PROBLEMS

GROUP A

1. If $y_1 = 38$, what would be the optimal solution to CSL's problem?

2. An insurance company believes that it will require the following numbers of personal computers during the next six months: January, 9; February, 5; March, 7; April, 9; May, 10; June, 5. Computers can be rented for a period of one, two, or three months at the following unit rates: one-month rate, $200; two-month rate, $350; three-month rate, $450. Formulate an LP that can be used to minimize the cost of renting the required computers. You may assume that if a machine is rented for a period of time extending beyond June, the cost of the rental should be prorated. For example, if a computer is rented for three months at the beginning of May, then a rental fee of $\frac{2}{3}(450) = \$300$, not $450, should be assessed in the objective function.

◆ SUMMARY

LINEAR PROGRAMMING DEFINITIONS

A **linear programming problem** (LP) consists of three parts:

1. A linear function (the **objective function**) of decision variables (say, $x_1, x_2, \ldots, x_n$) that is to be maximized or minimized.

2. A set of **constraints** (each of which must be a linear equality or linear inequality) that restrict the values that may be assumed by the decision variables.

3. The **sign restrictions**, which specify for each decision variable x_j either (1) variable x_j must be nonnegative—$x_j \geq 0$; or (2) variable x_j may be positive, zero, or negative —x_j is **unrestricted in sign** (urs).

The coefficient of a variable in the objective function is the variable's **objective function coefficient**. The coefficient of a variable in a constraint is a **technological coefficient**. The right-hand side of each constraint is (not surprisingly) a **right-hand side** (rhs).

A point is simply a specification of the values of each decision variable. The **feasible region** of an LP consists of all points satisfying the LP's constraints and sign restrictions. Any point in the feasible region that has the largest z-value of all points in the feasible region (for a max problem) is an **optimal solution** to the LP. An LP may have no optimal solution, one optimal solution, or an infinite number of optimal solutions.

A constraint in an LP is **binding** at an optimal solution if the left-hand side and the right-hand side are equal when the values of the variables in the optimal solution are substituted into the constraint.

GRAPHICAL SOLUTION OF LINEAR PROGRAMMING PROBLEMS

The feasible region for any LP is a **convex set**. If an LP has an optimal solution, there is an extreme (or corner) point of the feasible region that is an optimal solution to the LP.

We may graphically solve an LP (max problem) with two decision variables as follows:

Step 1 Graph the feasible region.

Step 2 Draw an isoprofit line.

Step 3 Move parallel to the isoprofit line in the direction of increasing z. The last point in the feasible region that contacts an isoprofit line is an optimal solution to the LP.

LP SOLUTIONS: FOUR CASES

When an LP is solved, one of the following four cases will occur:

Case 1 The LP has a unique solution.

Case 2 The LP has more than one (actually an infinite number of) optimal solutions. This is the case of **alternative optimal solutions**. Graphically, we recognize this case when the isoprofit line last hits an entire line segment before leaving the feasible region.

Case 3 The LP is **infeasible** (it has no feasible solution). This means that the feasible region contains no points.

Case 4 The LP is unbounded. This means (in a max problem) that there are points in the feasible region with arbitrarily large z-values. Graphically, we recognize this case by the fact that when we move parallel to an isoprofit line in the direction of increasing z, we never lose contact with the LP's feasible region.

FORMULATING LPs

The most important step in formulating most LPs is to determine the decision variables correctly.

In any constraint, the terms must have the same units. For example, one term cannot have the units "pounds of raw material" while another term has the units "ounces of raw material."

◆ REVIEW PROBLEMS

GROUP A

1. Bloomington Breweries produces beer and ale. Beer sells for $5 per barrel, and ale sells for $2 per barrel. Producing a barrel of beer requires 5 lb of corn and 2 lb of hops. Producing a barrel of ale requires 2 lb of corn and 1 lb of hops. Sixty pounds of corn and 25 lb of hops are available. Formulate an LP that can be used to maximize revenue. Solve the LP graphically.

2. Farmer Jones bakes two types of cake (chocolate and vanilla) to supplement his income. Each chocolate cake can be sold for $1, and each vanilla cake can be sold for 50¢. Each chocolate cake requires 20 minutes of baking time and uses 4 eggs. Each vanilla cake requires 40 minutes of baking time and uses 1 egg. Eight hours of baking time and 30 eggs are available. Formulate an LP to maximize farmer Jones's revenue. Then graphically solve the LP. (A fractional number of cakes is okay.)

3. I now have $100. The following investments are available during the next three years:

    Investment A Every dollar invested now yields $0.10 a year from now and $1.30 three years from now.

    Investment B Every dollar invested now yields $0.20 a year from now and $1.10 two years from now.

    Investment C Every dollar invested a year from now yields $1.50 three years from now.

During each year, uninvested cash can be placed in money market funds, which yield 6% interest per year. At most

$50 may be placed in each of investments A, B, and C. Formulate an LP to maximize my cash on hand three years from now.

4. Sunco processes oil into aviation fuel and heating oil. It costs $40 to purchase each 1000 barrels of oil, which is then distilled and yields 500 barrels of aviation fuel and 500 barrels of heating oil. Output from the distillation may be sold directly or processed in the catalytic cracker. If sold after distillation without further processing, aviation fuel sells for $60 per 1000 barrels. If sold after distillation without further processing, heating oil sells for $40 per 1000 barrels. It takes 1 hour to process 1000 barrels of aviation fuel in the catalytic cracker, and these 1000 barrels can be sold for $130. It takes 45 minutes to process 1000 barrels of heating oil in the cracker, and these 1000 barrels can be sold for $90. Each day, at most 20,000 barrels of oil can be purchased, and 8 hours of cracker time are available. Formulate an LP to maximize Sunco's profits.

5. Finco has the following investments available:

    Investment A For each dollar invested at time 0, we receive $0.10 at time 1 and $1.30 at time 2. (Time 0 = now; time 1 = one year from now; etc.)

    Investment B For each dollar invested at time 1, we receive $1.60 at time 2.

    Investment C For each dollar invested at time 2, we receive $1.20 at time 3.

At any time, leftover cash may be invested in T-bills, which pay 10% per year. At time 0, we have $100. At most $50 can be invested in each of investments A, B, and C. Formulate an LP that can be used to maximize Finco's cash on hand at time 3.

6. All steel manufactured by Steelco must meet the following requirements: 3.2–3.5% carbon; 1.8–2.5% silicon; 0.9–1.2% nickel; tensile strength of at least 45,000 pounds per square inch (psi). Steelco manufactures steel by combining two alloys. The cost and properties of each alloy are given in Table 23. Assume that the tensile strength of a mixture of the two alloys can be determined by averaging the tensile strength of the alloys that are mixed together. For example, a one-ton mixture that is 40% alloy 1 and 60% alloy 2 has a tensile strength of 0.4(42,000) + 0.6(50,000). Use linear programming to determine how to minimize the cost of producing a ton of steel.

Table 23

	ALLOY 1	ALLOY 2
Cost per ton	$190	$200
Percent silicon	2%	2.5%
Percent nickel	1%	1.5%
Percent carbon	3%	4%
Tensile strength	42,000 psi	50,000 psi

7. Steelco manufactures two types of steel at three different steel mills. During a given month, each steel mill has 200 hours of blast furnace time available. Because of differences in the furnaces at each mill, the time and cost to produce a ton of steel differs for each mill. The time and cost for each mill are shown in Table 24. Each month, Steelco must manufacture at least 500 tons of steel 1 and 600 tons of steel 2. Formulate an LP to minimize the cost of manufacturing the desired steel.

Table 24 Producing a Ton of Steel

	STEEL 1		STEEL 2	
	Cost	Time (*Minutes*)	Cost	Time (*Minutes*)
Mill 1	$10	20	$11	22
Mill 2	$12	24	$9	18
Mill 3	$14	28	$10	30

8.[†] Walnut Orchard has two farms that grow wheat and corn. Because of differing soil conditions, there are differences in the yields and costs of growing crops on the two farms. The yields and costs are shown in Table 25. Each farm has 100 acres available for cultivation; 11,000 bushels of wheat and 7000 bushels of corn must be grown. Determine a planting plan that will minimize the cost of meeting these demands. How could an extension of this model be used to allocate crop production efficiently throughout a nation?

Table 25

	FARM 1	FARM 2
Corn yield/acre	500 bushels	650 bushels
Cost/acre of corn	$100	$120
Wheat yield/acre	400 bushels	350 bushels
Cost/acre of wheat	$90	$80

9. Candy Kane Cosmetics (CKC) produces Leslie Perfume, which requires chemicals and labor. Two production processes are available: Process 1 transforms 1 unit of labor and 2 units of chemicals into 3 oz of perfume. Process 2 transforms 2 units of labor and 3 units of chemicals into 5 oz of perfume. It costs CKC $3 to purchase a unit of labor and $2 to purchase a unit of chemicals. Each year, up to 20,000 units of labor and 35,000 units of chemicals can be purchased. In the absence of advertising, CKC believes it can sell 1000 oz of perfume. To stimulate demand for Leslie, CKC can hire the lovely model Jenny Nelson. Jenny is paid $100/hour. Each hour Jenny works for the company is estimated to increase the demand for Leslie Perfume by 200 oz. Each ounce of Leslie Perfume sells for $5. Use linear programming to determine how CKC can maximize profits.

10. Carco has a $150,000 advertising budget. In order to increase automobile sales, the firm is considering advertising in newspapers and on television. The more Carco uses a particular medium, the less effective is each additional ad. Table 26 shows the number of new customers reached by each ad. Each newspaper ad costs $1000, and each television ad costs $10,000. At most 30 newspaper ads and at most 15 television ads can be placed. How can Cargo maximize the number of new customers created by advertising?

[†] Based on Heady and Egbert (1964).

Table 26

	NO. OF ADS	NEW CUSTOMERS
Newspaper	1–10	900
	11–20	600
	21–30	300
Television	1–5	10,000
	6–10	5,000
	11–15	2,000

Table 28

PERSON RESPONDING	PERCENT OF DAYTIME CALLS	PERCENT OF EVENING CALLS
Wife	30	30
Husband	10	30
Single male	10	15
Single female	10	20
None	40	5

11. Sunco Oil has refineries in Los Angeles and Chicago. The Los Angeles refinery can refine up to 2 million barrels of oil per year, and the Chicago refinery can refine up to 3 million barrels of oil per year. Once refined, oil is shipped to two distribution points: Houston and New York City. Sunco estimates that each distribution point can sell up to 5 million barrels of refined oil per year. Because of differences in shipping and refining costs, the profit earned (in dollars) per million barrels of oil shipped depends on where the oil was refined and on the point of distribution (see Table 27). Sunco is considering expanding the capacity of each refinery. Each million barrels of annual refining capacity that is added will cost $120,000 for the Los Angeles refinery and $150,000 for the Chicago refinery. Use linear programming to determine how Sunco can maximize its profits less expansion costs over a ten-year period.

Table 27

	PROFIT PER MILLION BARRELS	
	To Houston	*To New York*
From Los Angeles	$20,000	$15,000
From Chicago	$18,000	$17,000

12. For a telephone survey, a marketing research group needs to contact at least 150 wives, 120 husbands, 100 single adult males, and 110 single adult females. It costs $2 to make a daytime call and (because of higher labor costs) $5 to make an evening call. Table 28 lists the results. Because of limited staff, at most half of all phone calls can be evening calls. Formulate an LP to minimize the cost of completing the survey.

13. Feedco produces two types of cattle feed. Both feeds consist totally of wheat and alfalfa. Feed 1 must contain at least 80% wheat, and feed 2 must contain at least 60% alfalfa. Feed 1 sells for $1.50/lb, and feed 2 sells for $1.30/lb. Feedco can purchase up to 1000 lb of wheat at 50¢/lb and up to 800 lb of alfalfa at 40¢/lb. Demand for each type of feed is unlimited. Formulate an LP to maximize Feedco's profit.

14. Feedco (see Problem 13) has decided to give its customer (assume it has only one customer) a quantity discount. If the customer purchases over 300 lb of feed 1, each pound over the first 300 lb will sell for only $1.25/lb. Similarly, if the customer purchases more than 300 pounds of feed 2, each pound over the first 300 lb will sell for $1.00/lb. Modify the LP of Problem 13 to account for the presence of quantity discounts. (*Hint:* Define variables for the feed sold at each price.)

15. Chemco produces two chemicals: A and B. These chemicals are produced via two manufacturing processes. Process 1 requires 2 hours of labor and 1 lb of raw material to produce 2 oz of A and 1 oz of B. Process 2 requires 3 hours of labor and 2 lb of raw material to produce 3 oz of A and 2 oz of B. Sixty hours of labor and 40 lb of raw material are available. Demand for A is unlimited, but only 20 oz of B can be sold. A sells for $16/oz, and B sells for $14/oz. Any B that is unsold must be disposed of at a cost of $2/oz. Formulate an LP to maximize Chemco's revenue less disposal costs.

16. Suppose that in the CSL computer example of Section 3.12, it takes two months to train a technician and that during the second month of training, each trainee requires 10 hours of experienced technician time. Modify the formulation in the text to account for these changes.

17. Furnco manufactures tables and chairs. Each table and chair must be made entirely out of oak or entirely out of pine. A total of 150 board ft of oak and 210 board ft of pine are available. A table requires either 17 board ft of oak or 30 board ft of pine, and a chair requires either 5 board ft of oak or 13 board ft of pine. Each table can be sold for $40, and each chair can be sold for $15. Formulate an LP that can be used to maximize revenue.

18.[†] The city of Busville contains three school districts. The number of minority and nonminority students in each district is given in Table 29. Of all students, 25% ($\frac{200}{800}$) are minority students.

Table 29

DISTRICT	MINORITY STUDENTS	NONMINORITY STUDENTS
1	50	200
2	50	250
3	100	150

The local court has decided that each of the town's two high schools (Cooley High and Walt Whitman High) must have approximately the same percentage of minority students (within ± 5%) as the entire town. The distances (in miles) between the school districts and the high schools are given in Table 30. Each high school must have an enrollment of 300–500 students. Use linear programming to determine an assignment of students to schools that minimizes the total distance students must travel to school.

Table 30

DISTRICT	COOLEY HIGH	WALT WHITMAN HIGH
1	1	2
2	2	1
3	1	1

19.[‡] Brady Corporation produces cabinets. Each week, they require 90,000 cu ft of processed lumber. They may obtain processed lumber in two ways. First, they may purchase lumber from an outside supplier and then dry it at their kiln. Second, they may chop down logs on their land, cut them into lumber at their sawmill, and finally dry the lumber at their kiln. Brady can purchase grade 1 or grade 2 lumber. Grade 1 lumber costs $3 per cu ft and when dried yields 0.7 cu ft of useful lumber. Grade 2

lumber costs $7 per cubic foot and when dried yields ˙0.9 cu ft of useful lumber. It costs the company $3 to chop down a log. After being cut and dried, a log yields 0.8 cu ft of lumber. Brady incurs costs of $4 per cu ft of lumber dried. It costs $2.50 per cu ft of logs sent through the sawmill. Each week, the sawmill can process up to 35,000 cu ft of lumber. Each week, up to 40,000 cu ft of grade 1 lumber and up to 60,000 cu ft of grade 2 lumber can be purchased. Each week, 40 hours of time are available for drying lumber. The time it takes to dry 1 cu ft of grade 1 lumber, grade 2 lumber, or logs is as follows: grade 1—2 seconds; grade 2—0.8 seconds; log—1.3 seconds. Formulate an LP to help Brady minimize the weekly cost of meeting the demand for processed lumber.

20.[§] The Canadian Parks Commission controls two tracts of land. Tract 1 consists of 300 acres, and tract 2 consists of 100 acres. Each acre of tract 1 can be used for spruce trees, hunting, or both spruce trees and hunting. Each acre of tract 2 can be used for spruce trees, camping, or both spruce trees and camping. The capital (in hundreds of dollars) and labor (in man-days) required to maintain one acre of each tract, and the profit (in thousands of dollars) per acre for each possible use of land are given in Table 31. $150,000 of capital and 200 man-days of labor are available. How should the land be allocated to various uses in order to maximize profit received from the two tracts?

Table 31

	CAPITAL	LABOR	PROFIT
Tract 1 Spruce	3	0.1	0.2
Tract 1 Hunting	3	0.2	0.4
Tract 1 Both	4	0.2	0.5
Tract 2 Spruce	1	0.05	0.06
Tract 2 Camping	30	5	0.09
Tract 2 Both	10	1.01	1.1

21.[§§] Chandler Enterprises produces two competing products: A and B. The company wishes to sell these products to two groups of customers: group 1 and group 2. The value each customer places on a unit of A and B is as shown in Table 32. Each customer will buy either product A or product B, but not both. A customer is willing to buy product A if she believes that

Value of product A
− price of product A $\geq$ value of product B
− price of product B

[†] Based on Franklin and Koenigsberg (1973).
[‡] Based on Carino and Lenoir (1988).

[§] Based on Cheung and Auger (1976).
[§§] Based on Dobson and Kalish (1988).

and

Value of product A − price of product A ≥ 0

A customer is willing to buy product B if she believes that

Value of product B − price of product B ≥ value of product A − price of product A

and

Value of product B − price of product B ≥ 0

Group 1 has 1000 members, and group 2 has 1500 members. Chandler wants to set prices for each product so as to ensure that group 1 members purchase product A and group 2 members purchase product B. Formulate an LP that will help Chandler maximize revenues.

Table 32

	GROUP 1 CUSTOMER	GROUP 2 CUSTOMER
Value of A to	$10	$12
Value of B to	$8	$15

22.[†] Alden Enterprises produces two products. Each product can be produced on one of two machines. The length of time needed to produce each product (in hours) on each machine is as shown in Table 33. Each month, 500 hours of time are available on each machine. Each month, customers are willing to buy up to the quantities of each product at the prices given in Table 34. The company's goal is to maximize the revenue obtained from selling units during the next two months. Formulate an LP to help meet this goal.

Table 33

	MACHINE 1	MACHINE 2
Product 1	4	3
Product 2	7	4

23. Kiriakis Electronics produces three products. Each product must be processed on each of three types of machines. When a machine is in use, it must be manned by a worker. The time (in hours) required to process each product on each machine and the profit associated with each product are shown in Table 35. At present, 5 type 1 machines, 3 type 2 machines, and 4 type 3 machines are available. The company has 10 workers available and must determine how many workers to assign to each machine. The plant is open 40 hours per week, and each worker works 35 hours per week. Formulate an LP that will enable Kiriakis to assign workers to machines in a way that maximizes weekly profits. (*Note:* A worker need not spend the entire work week manning a single machine.)

GROUP B

24.[‡] Gotham City National Bank is open Monday–Friday from 9 A.M. to 5 P.M. From past experience, the bank knows that it needs the number of tellers shown in Table 36. The bank hires two types of tellers. Full-time tellers work 9–5 five days a week, except for 1 hour off for lunch. (The bank determines when a full-time employee takes lunch hour, but each teller must take lunch hour

Table 34

	DEMANDS		PRICES	
	Month 1	*Month 2*	*Month 1*	*Month 2*
Product 1	100	190	$55	$12
Product 2	140	130	$65	$32

Table 35

	PRODUCT 1	PRODUCT 2	PRODUCT 3
Machine 1	2	3	4
Machine 2	3	5	6
Machine 3	4	7	9
Profit	$6	$8	$10

[†] Based on Jain, Stott, and Vasold (1978). [‡] Based on Moondra (1976).

between noon and 1 P.M. or between 1 and 2 P.M.). Full-time employees are paid (including fringe benefits) $8/hour (this includes payment for lunch hour). The bank may also hire part-time tellers. Each part-time teller must work exactly 3 consecutive hours each day. A part-time teller is paid $5/hour (and receives no fringe benefits). In order to maintain adequate quality of service, the bank has decided that at most five part-time tellers can be hired. Formulate an LP to meet the teller requirements at minimum cost. Solve the LP on a computer. Fiddle around with the LP answer to determine an employment policy that comes close to minimizing labor cost.

Table 36

TIME PERIOD	TELLERS REQUIRED
9–10	4
10–11	3
11–Noon	4
Noon–1	6
1–2	5
2–3	6
3–4	8
4–5	8

25.[†] The Gotham City Police Department employs 30 police officers. Each officer works 5 days per week. The crime rate fluctuates with the day of the week, so the number of police officers required each day depends on which day of the week it is: Saturday, 28; Sunday, 18; Monday, 18; Tuesday, 24; Wednesday, 25; Thursday, 16; Friday, 21. The police department wishes to schedule police officers to minimize the number whose days off are not consecutive. Formulate an LP that will accomplish this goal. (*Hint:* Have a constraint for each day of the week that ensures that the proper number of officers are *not* working on the given day.)

26.[‡] Alexis Cornby makes her living buying and selling corn. On January 1, she has 50 tons of corn and $1000. On the first day of each month Alexis can buy corn at the following prices per ton: January, $300; February, $350; March, $400; April, $500. On the last day of each month Alexis can sell corn at the following prices per ton: January, $250; February, $400; March, $350; April, $550. Alexis stores her corn in a warehouse that can hold at most 100 tons of corn. She must be able to pay cash for all corn

at the time of purchase. Use linear programming to determine how Alexis can maximize her cash on hand at the end of April.

27.[§] At the beginning of month 1, Finco has $400 in cash. At the beginning of months 1, 2, 3, and 4, Finco receives certain revenues, after which it pays bills (see Table 37). Any money left over may be invested for one month at the interest rate of 0.1% per month; for two months at 0.5% per month; for three months at 1% per month; or for four months at 2% per month. Use linear programming to determine an investment strategy that maximizes cash on hand at the beginning of month 5.

Table 37

	REVENUES	BILLS
Month 1	$400	$600
Month 2	$800	$500
Month 3	$300	$500
Month 4	$300	$250

28. City 1 produces 500 tons of waste per day, and city 2 produces 400 tons of waste per day. Waste must be incinerated at incinerator 1 or incinerator 2, and each incinerator can process up to 500 tons of waste per day. The cost to incinerate waste is $40/ton at incinerator 1 and $30/ton at incinerator 2. Incineration reduces each ton of waste to 0.2 tons of debris, which must be dumped at one of two landfills. Each landfill can receive at most 200 tons of debris per day. It costs $3 per mile to transport a ton of material (either debris or waste). Distances (in miles) between locations are shown in Table 38. Formulate an LP that can be used to minimize the total cost of disposing of the waste of both cities.

Table 38

	INCIN. 1	INCIN. 2
City 1	30	5
City 2	36	42
	LANDFILL 1	LANDFILL 2
Incin. 1	5	8
Incin. 2	9	6

[†] Based on Rothstein (1973).
[‡] Based on Charnes and Cooper (1955).
[§] Based on Robichek, Teichroew, and Jones (1965).

29.[†] Silicon Valley Corporation (Silvco) manufactures transistors. An important aspect of the manufacture of transistors is the melting of the element germanium (a major component of a transistor) in a furnace. Unfortunately, the melting process yields germanium of highly variable quality.

There are two methods that can be used to melt germanium; method 1 costs $50 per transistor, and method 2 costs $70 per transistor. The qualities of germanium obtained by methods 1 and 2 are shown in Table 39. Silvco can refire melted germanium in an attempt to improve its quality. It costs $25 to refire the melted germanium for one transistor. The results of the refiring process are shown in Table 40. Silvco has sufficient furnace capacity to melt or refire germanium for at most 20,000 transistors per month. Silvco's monthly demands are for 1000 grade 4 transistors, 2000 grade 3 transistors, 3000 grade 2 transistors, 3000 grade 1 transistors. Use linear programming to minimize the cost of producing the needed transistors.

30.[‡] A paper recycling plant processes box board, tissue paper, newsprint, and book paper into pulp that can be used to produce three grades of recycled paper (grades 1, 2, and 3). The prices per ton and the pulp contents of the four inputs are shown in Table 41. Two methods, de-inking and asphalt dispersion, can be used to process the four inputs into pulp. It costs $20 to de-ink a ton of any input. The process of de-inking removes 10 percent of the input's pulp. It costs $15 to apply asphalt dispersion to a ton of material. The asphalt dispersion process removes 20% of the input's pulp. At most 3000 tons of input can be run through the asphalt dispersion process or the de-inking process. Grade 1 paper can only be produced with newsprint or book paper pulp; grade 2 paper, only with book paper, tissue paper, or box board pulp; and grade 3 paper, only with newsprint, tissue paper, or box board pulp. To meet its current demands, the company needs 500 tons of pulp for grade 1 paper, 500 tons of pulp for grade 2 paper, and 600 tons of pulp for grade 3 paper. Formulate an LP to minimize the cost of meeting the demands for pulp.

31. Turkeyco produces two types of turkey cutlets for sale to fast food restaurants. Each type of cutlet consists of white meat and dark meat. Cutlet 1 sells for $4/lb and must consist of at least 70% white meat. Cutlet 2 sells for $3/lb and must consist of at least 60% white meat. At most 50 lb of cutlet 1 and 30 lb of cutlet 2 can be sold. The two types of turkey used to manufacture the cutlets are purchased from the GobbleGobble Turkey Farm. Each type 1 turkey costs $10 and yields 5 lb of white meat and 2 lb of dark meat. Each type 2 turkey costs $8 and yields 3 lb of white meat and 3 lb of dark meat. Formulate an LP to maximize Turkeyco's profit.

Table 39

GRADE OF MELTED GERMANIUM	PERCENT YIELDED BY MELTING	
	Method 1	*Method 2*
Defective	30	20
Grade 1	30	20
Grade 2	20	25
Grade 3	15	20
Grade 4	5	15

Note: Grade 1 is poor; grade 4 is excellent. The quality of the germanium dictates the quality of the manufactured transistor.

Table 40

GRADE OF REFIRED GERMANIUM	PERCENT YIELDED BY REFIRING			
	Defective	*Grade 1*	*Grade 2*	*Grade 3*
Defective	30	0	0	0
Grade 1	25	30	0	0
Grade 2	15	30	40	0
Grade 3	20	20	30	50
Grade 4	10	20	30	50

[†] Based on Smith (1965).   [‡] Based on Glassey and Gupta (1975).

Table 41

	COST	PULP CONTENT
Box board	$5	15%
Tissue paper	$6	20%
Newsprint	$8	30%
Book paper	$10	40%

32. Priceler manufactures sedans and wagons. The number of vehicles that can be sold each of the next three months are listed in Table 42. Each sedan sells for $8000, and each wagon sells for $9000. It costs $6000 to produce a sedan and $7500 to produce a wagon. To hold a vehicle in inventory for one month costs $150 per sedan and $200 per wagon. During each month, at most 1500 vehicles can be produced. Production line restrictions dictate that during month 1, at least two thirds of all cars produced must be sedans. At the beginning of month 1, 200 sedans and 100 wagons are available. Formulate an LP that can be used to maximize Priceler's profit during the next three months.

Table 42

	SEDANS	WAGONS
Month 1	1100	600
Month 2	1500	700
Month 3	1200	500

33. The production-line employees at Grummins Engine work four days a week, 10 hours a day. Each day of the week, (at least) the following numbers of line employees are needed: Monday–Friday, 7 employees; Saturday and Sunday, 3 employees. Grummins has 11 production-line employees. Formulate an LP that can be used to maximize the number of consecutive days off received by the employees. For example, a worker who gets Sunday, Monday, and Wednesday off receives two consecutive days off.

34. Bank 24 is open 24 hours per day. Tellers work two consecutive 6-hour shifts and are paid $10 per hour. The possible shifts are as follows: midnight–6 A.M., 6 A.M.–noon, noon–6 P.M., 6 P.M.–midnight. During each shift, the following numbers of customers enter the bank: midnight–6 A.M. — 100; 6 A.M.–noon — 200; noon–6 P.M. — 300; and 6 P.M.–midnight — 200. Each teller can serve up to 50 customers per shift. To model a cost for customer impatience, we assume that any customer who is present at the end of a shift "costs" the bank $5. We assume that by midnight of each day, all customers must be served, so each day's midnight–6 A.M. shift begins with 0 customers in the bank. Formulate an LP that can be used to minimize the sum of the bank's labor and customer impatience costs.

35.[†] Transeast Airlines flies planes on the following route: L.A.–Houston–N.Y.–Miami–L.A. The length (in miles) of each segment of this trip is as follows: L.A.–Houston, 1500 miles; Houston–N.Y., 1700 miles; N.Y.–Miami, 1300 miles; Miami–L.A., 2700 miles. At each stop, the plane may purchase up to 10,000 gallons of fuel. The price of fuel at each city is as follows: L.A., 88¢; Houston, 15¢; N.Y., $1.05; Miami, 95¢. The plane's fuel tank can hold at most 12,000 gallons. To allow for the possibility of circling over a landing site, we require that the ending fuel level for each leg of the flight be at least 600 gallons. The number of gallons used per mile on each leg of the flight is

$$1 + (\text{average fuel level on leg of flight}/2000)$$

To simplify matters, assume that the average fuel level on any leg of the flight is

$$\frac{(\text{Fuel level at start of leg}) + (\text{fuel level at end of leg})}{2}$$

Formulate an LP that can be used to minimize the fuel cost incurred in completing the L.A.–Houston–N.Y.–Miami–L.A. schedule.

36.[‡] To process income tax forms, the IRS first sends each form through the data preparation (DP) department, where information is coded for computer entry. Then the form is sent to data entry (DE), where it is entered into the computer. During the next three weeks, the following number of forms will arrive: week 1, 40,000; week 2, 30,000; week 3, 60,000. The IRS meets the crunch by hiring employees who work 40 hours per week and are paid $200 per week. Data preparation of a form requires 15 minutes, and data entry of a form requires 10 minutes. Each week, an employee is assigned to either data entry or data preparation. The IRS must complete processing of all forms by the end of week 5 and wishes to minimize the cost of accomplishing this goal. Formulate an LP that will determine how many workers should be working each week and how the workers should be assigned over the next five weeks.

37. In the electrical circuit in Figure 9, I_t = current (in amperes) flowing through resistor t, V_t = voltage drop (in volts) across resistor t, and R_t = resistance (in ohms) of resistor t. Kirchoff's Voltage and Current Laws imply

† Based on Darnell and Loflin (1977).
‡ Based on Lanzenauer et al. (1987).

Figure 9

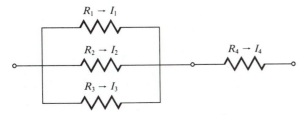

that $V_1 = V_2 = V_3$ and $I_1 + I_2 + I_3 = I_4$. The power dissipated by the current flowing through resistor t is $I_t^2 R_t$. Ohm's Law implies that $V_t = I_t R_t$. The two parts of this problem should be solved independently.

(a) Suppose you are told that $I_1 = 4$, $I_2 = 6$, $I_3 = 8$, and $I_4 = 18$ are required. Also, the voltage drop across each resistor must be between 2 and 10 volts. Your problem is to choose the R_t's to minimize the total dissipated power. Formulate an LP whose solution will solve your problem.

(b) Suppose you are told that $V_1 = 6$, $V_2 = 6$, $V_3 = 6$, and $V_4 = 4$ are required. Also, the current flowing through each resistor must be between 2 and 6 amperes. Your problem is to choose the R_t's to minimize the total dissipated power. Formulate an LP whose solution will solve your problem. (*Hint:* Let $\dfrac{1}{R_t}$ $(t = 1, 2, 3, 4)$ be your decision variables.)

GROUP C

38.[†] E.J. Korvair Department Store has $1000 in available cash at present. At the beginning of each of the next six months, E.J. will receive revenues and pay bills as shown in Table 43. It is clear that E.J. will have a short-term cash flow problem until the store receives revenues from the Christmas shopping season. To solve this problem, E.J. must borrow money.

Table 43

	REVENUES	BILLS
July	$1000	$5000
August	$2000	$5000
September	$2000	$6000
October	$4000	$2000
November	$7000	$2000
December	$9000	$1000

At the beginning of July, E.J. may take out a six-month loan. Any money borrowed for a six-month period must be paid back at the end of December along with 9% interest (early payback does not reduce the interest cost of the loan). E.J. may also meet cash needs through month-to-month borrowing. Any money borrowed for a one-month period incurs an interest cost of 4% per month. Use linear programming to determine how E.J. can minimize the cost of paying its bills on time.

39.[‡] Olé Oil produces three products: heating oil, gasoline, and jet fuel. The average octane levels must be at least 4.5 for heating oil, 8.5 for gas, and 7.0 for jet fuel. To produce these products Olé purchases two types of oil: crude 1 (at $12 per barrel) and crude 2 (at $10 per barrel). Each day, at most 10,000 barrels of each type of oil can be purchased.

Before crude can be used to produce products for sale, it must be distilled. Each day, at most 15,000 barrels of oil can be distilled. It costs 10¢ to distill a barrel of oil. The result of distillation is as follows. (1) Each barrel of crude 1 yields (after distillation) 0.6 barrel of naphtha, 0.3 barrel of distilled 1, and 0.1 barrel of distilled 2. (2) Each barrel of crude 2 yields (after distillation) 0.4 barrel of naphtha, 0.2 barrel of distilled 1, and 0.4 barrel of distilled 2. Distilled naphtha can be used only to produce gasoline or jet fuel. Distilled oil can be used to produce heating oil or it can be sent through the catalytic cracker (at a cost of 15¢ per barrel). Each day, at most 5000 barrels of distilled oil can be sent through the cracker. Each barrel of distilled 1 that is sent through the cracker yields 0.8 barrel of cracked 1 and 0.2 barrel of cracked 2. Each barrel of distilled 2 that is sent through the cracker yields 0.7 barrel of cracked 1 and 0.3 barrel of cracked 2. Cracked oil can be used to produce gasoline and jet fuel but not to produce heating oil.

The octane level of each type of oil is as follows: naphtha — 8; distilled 1 — 4; distilled 2 — 5; cracked 1 — 9; cracked 2 — 6.

All heating oil produced can be sold at $14 per barrel; all gasoline produced, $18 per barrel; and all jet fuel produced, $16 per barrel. Marketing considerations dictate that at least 3000 barrels of each product must be produced daily. Formulate an LP to maximize Olé's daily profit.

[†] Based on Robichek, Teichroew, and Jones (1965).

[‡] Based on Garvin et al. (1957).

◆ REFERENCES

Each of the following six books is a cornucopia of interesting LP formulations:

BRADLEY, S., A. HAX, and T. MAGNANTI. *Applied Mathematical Programming*. Reading, Mass.: Addison-Wesley, 1977.

LAWRENCE, K., and S. ZANAKIS. *Production Planning and Scheduling: Mathematical Programming Applications*. Atlanta, Ga.: Industrial Engineering and Management Press, 1984.

SCHRAGE, L. *Linear Integer and Quadratic Programming With LINDO*. Palo Alto, Calif.: Scientific Press, 1986.

SHAPIRO, J. *Optimization Models for Planning and Allocation: Text and Cases in Mathematical Programming*. New York: Wiley, 1984.

WAGNER, H. *Principles of Operations Research*, 2d ed. Englewood Cliffs, N.J.: Prentice-Hall, 1975.

WILLIAMS, H. *Model Building in Mathematical Programming*, 2d ed. New York: Wiley, 1985.

BAKER, K. "Scheduling a Full-Time Work Force to Meet Cyclic Staffing Requirements," *Management Science* 20(1974):1561–1568. Presents a method (other than LP) for scheduling personnel to meet cyclic work force requirements.

BALINTFY, J. "A Mathematical Programming System for Food Management Applications," *Interfaces* 6(no. 1, pt 2, 1976):13–31. Discusses menu planning models.

CARINO, H., and C. LENOIR. "Optimizing Wood Procurement in Cabinet Manufacturing," *Interfaces* 18(no. 2, 1988):11–19.

CHARNES, A., and W. COOPER. "Generalization of the Warehousing Model," *Operational Research Quarterly* 6(1955):131–172.

CHEUNG, H., and J. AUGER. "Linear Programming and Land Use Allocation," *Socio-Economic Planning Science* 10(1976):43–45.

DARNELL, W., and C. LOFLIN. "National Airlines Fuel Management and Allocation Model," *Interfaces* 7(no. 3, 1977):1–15.

DOBSON, G., and S. KALISH. "Positioning and Pricing a Product Line," *Marketing Science* 7(1988):107–126.

FORGIONNE, G. "Corporate MS Activities: An Update," *Interfaces* 13(1983):20–23. Concerns the fraction of large firms using linear programming (and other operations research techniques).

FRANKLIN, A., and E. KOENIGSBERG. "Computed School Assignments in a Large District," *Operations Research* 21(1973):413–426.

GARVIN, W., ET AL. "Applications of Linear Programming in the Oil Industry," *Management Science* 3(1957):407–430.

GLASSEY, R., and V. GUPTA. "An LP Analysis of Paper Recycling." In *Studies in Linear Programming*, ed. H. Salkin and J. Saha. New York: North-Holland, 1975.

HARTLEY, R. "Decision Making When Joint Products Are Involved," *Accounting Review* (1971):746–755.

HEADY, E., and A. EGBERT. "Regional Planning of Efficient Agricultural Patterns," *Econometrica* 32(1964):374–386.

HILAL, S., and W. ERICKSON. "Matching Supplies to Save Lives: Linear Programming the Production of Heart Valves," *Interfaces* 11(1981):48–56.

JAIN, S., K. STOTT, and E. VASOLD. "Orderbook Balancing Using a Combination of LP and Heuristic Techniques," *Interfaces* 9(no. 1, 1978):55–67.

LANZENAUER, C., ET AL. "RRSP Flood: LP to the Rescue," *Interfaces* 17(no. 4, 1987):27–41.

LILIEN, G., and P. KOTLER. *Marketing Decision Models*. New York: Harper and Row, 1983. Applications of linear (and nonlinear) programming to marketing problems.

MOONDRA, S. "An LP Model for Workforce Scheduling in Banks," *Journal of Bank Research* (1976).

NEAVE, E., and J. WIGINTON. *Financial Management: Theory and Strategies*. Englewood Cliffs, N.J.: Prentice-Hall, 1981.

ROBICHEK, A., D. TEICHROEW, and M. JONES. "Optimal Short-Term Financing Decisions," *Management Science* 12(1965):1–36.

ROHN, E. "A New LP Approach to Bond Portfolio Management," *Journal of Financial and Quantitative Analysis* 22(1987):439–467.

ROTHSTEIN, M. "Hospital Manpower Shift Scheduling by Mathematical Programming," *Health Services Research* (1973).

SMITH, S. "Planning Transistor Production by Linear Programming," *Operations Research* 13(1965):132–139.

STIGLER, G. "The Cost of Subsistence," *Journal of Farm Economics* 27(1945). Discusses the diet problem.

SULLIVAN, R., and S. SECREST. "A Simple Optimization DSS for Production Planning at Dairyman's Cooperative Creamery Association," *Interfaces* 15(no. 5, 1985):46–54.

WEINGARTNER, H. *Mathematical Programming and the Analysis of Capital Budgeting*. Englewood Cliffs, N.J.: Prentice-Hall, 1963.

4

The Simplex Algorithm

IN CHAPTER 3, we saw how to solve two-variable linear programming problems graphically. Unfortunately, most real-life LPs have many variables, so a method is needed to solve LPs with more than two variables. We devote most of this chapter to a discussion of the simplex algorithm, which is used to solve even very large LPs. (In many industrial applications, the simplex algorithm is used to solve LPs with thousands of constraints and thousands of variables.)

In this chapter, we explain how the simplex algorithm can be used to find optimal solutions to LPs. We close the chapter with a look at a recently developed method for solving LPs (Karmarkar's) and with a brief description of the widely used interactive computer package LINDO (Linear Interactive and Discrete Optimizer).

4-1 HOW TO CONVERT AN LP TO STANDARD FORM

We have seen that an LP can have both equality and inequality constraints. It can also have variables that are required to be nonnegative and variables that are allowed to be unrestricted in sign (urs). Before the simplex algorithm can be used to solve an LP, the LP must be converted into an equivalent problem in which all constraints are equations and all variables are nonnegative. An LP in this form is said to be in **standard form**.[†]

To convert an LP into standard form, each inequality constraint must be replaced by an equality constraint. We illustrate this procedure using the following problem.

E X A M P L E
1

Leather Limited manufactures two types of belts: the deluxe model and the regular model. Each type requires 1 sq yd of leather. A regular belt requires 1 hour of skilled labor, and a deluxe belt requires 2 hours of skilled labor. Each week, 40 sq yd of leather and 60 hours of skilled labor are available. Each regular belt contributes $3 to profit, and each deluxe belt contributes $4 to profit. If we define

$$x_1 = \text{number of deluxe belts produced weekly}$$
$$x_2 = \text{number of regular belts produced weekly}$$

[†]Throughout the first part of the chapter we assume that all variables must be nonnegative (≥ 0). The conversion of urs variables to nonnegative variables is discussed in Section 4.12.

the appropriate LP is

$$\max z = 4x_1' + 3x_2$$

$$\text{s.t.} \quad x_1 + x_2 \le 40 \quad \text{(Leather constraint)} \tag{1}$$

$$2x_1 + x_2 \le 60 \quad \text{(Labor constraint)} \tag{LP 1}$$

$$x_1, x_2 \ge 0 \tag{2}$$

◆

How can we convert (1) and (2) into equality constraints? We define for each $\le$ constraint a **slack variable** s_i (s_i = slack variable for ith constraint), which is the amount of the resource unused in the ith constraint. Since $x_1 + x_2$ sq yd of leather are being used, and 40 sq yd are available, we define s_1 by

$$s_1 = 40 - x_1 - x_2 \quad \text{or} \quad x_1 + x_2 + s_1 = 40$$

Similarly, we define s_2 by

$$s_2 = 60 - 2x_1 - x_2 \quad \text{or} \quad 2x_1 + x_2 + s_2 = 60$$

Observe that a point (x_1, x_2) satisfies the ith constraint if and only if $s_i \ge 0$. For example, $x_1 = 15$, $x_2 = 20$ satisfies (1) because $s_1 = 40 - 15 - 20 = 5 \ge 0$.

Intuitively, (1) is satisfied by the point $(15, 20)$, because $s_1 = 5$ sq yd of leather are unused. Similarly, $(15, 20)$ satisfies (2), because $s_2 = 60 - 2(15) - 20 = 10$ labor hours are unused. Finally, note that the point $x_1 = x_2 = 25$ fails to satisfy (1), because $s_1 = 40 - 25 - 25 = -10$. The point $(25, 25)$ also fails to satisfy (2), because $s_2 = 60 - 2(25) - 25 = -15$ indicates that $(25, 25)$ uses more labor than is available.

In summary, to convert (1) to an equality constraint, we replace (1) by $s_1 = 40 - x_1 - x_2$ (or $x_1 + x_2 + s_1 = 40$) and $s_1 \ge 0$. To convert (2) to an equality constraint, we replace (2) by $s_2 = 60 - 2x_1 - x_2$ (or $2x_1 + x_2 + s_2 = 60$) and $s_2 \ge 0$. This converts LP 1 to

$$\max z = 4x_1 + 3x_2$$

$$\text{s.t.} \quad x_1 + x_2 + s_1 \qquad = 40$$

$$2x_1 + x_2 \qquad + s_2 = 60 \tag{LP 1'}$$

$$x_1, x_2, s_1, s_2 \ge 0$$

Note that LP 1′ is in standard form. In summary, *if constraint i of an LP is a $\le$ constraint, we convert it to an equality constraint by adding a slack variable s_i to the ith constraint and adding the sign restriction $s_i \ge 0$.*

To illustrate how a $\ge$ constraint can be converted to an equality constraint, let's consider the diet problem of Section 3.4:

$$\min z = 50x_1 + 20x_2 + 30x_3 + 80x_4$$

$$\text{s.t.} \quad 400x_1 + 200x_2 + 150x_3 + 500x_4 \ge 500 \quad \text{(Calorie constraint)} \tag{3}$$

$$3x_1 + 2x_2 \qquad\qquad \ge 6 \quad \text{(Chocolate constraint)} \tag{4}$$

$$2x_1 + 2x_2 + 4x_3 + 4x_4 \ge 10 \quad \text{(Sugar constraint)} \tag{5}$$

$$2x_1 + 4x_2 + x_3 + 5x_4 \ge 8 \quad \text{(Fat constraint)} \tag{6}$$

$$x_1, x_2, x_3, x_4 \ge 0$$

To convert the ith $\geq$ constraint to an equality constraint, we define an **excess variable** (sometimes called a surplus variable) e_i. (e_i will always be the excess variable for the ith constraint.) We define e_i to be the amount by which the ith constraint is oversatisfied. Thus, for the diet problem,

$$e_1 = 400x_1 + 200x_2 + 150x_3 + 500x_4 - 500, \quad \text{or}$$
$$400x_1 + 200x_2 + 150x_3 + 500x_4 - e_1 = 500 \tag{3'}$$

$$e_2 = 3x_1 + 2x_2 - 6, \quad \text{or} \quad 3x_1 + 2x_2 - e_2 = 6 \tag{4'}$$

$$e_3 = 2x_1 + 2x_2 + 4x_3 + 4x_4 - 10, \quad \text{or} \quad 2x_1 + 2x_2 + 4x_3 + 4x_4 - e_3 = 10 \tag{5'}$$

$$e_4 = 2x_1 + 4x_2 + x_3 + 5x_4 - 8, \quad \text{or} \quad 2x_1 + 4x_2 + x_3 + 5x_4 - e_4 = 8 \tag{6'}$$

A point (x_1, x_2, x_3, x_4) satisfies the ith $\geq$ constraint if and only if e_i is nonnegative. For example, from (4'), $e_2 \geq 0$ if and only if $3x_1 + 2x_2 \geq 6$. For a numerical example, consider the point $x_1 = 2$, $x_3 = 4$, $x_2 = x_4 = 0$, which satisfies all four of the diet problem's constraints. For this point,

$$e_1 = 400(2) + 150(4) - 500 = 900 \geq 0$$
$$e_2 = 3(2) - 6 = 0 \geq 0$$
$$e_3 = 2(2) + 4(4) - 10 = 10 \geq 0$$
$$e_4 = 2(2) + 4 - 8 = 0 \geq 0$$

As another example, consider $x_1 = x_2 = 1$, $x_3 = x_4 = 0$. This point is infeasible; it violates the chocolate, sugar, and fat constraints. The infeasibility of this point is indicated by

$$e_2 = 3(1) + 2(1) - 6 = -1 < 0$$
$$e_3 = 2(1) + 2(1) - 10 = -6 < 0$$
$$e_4 = 2(1) + 4(1) - 8 = -2 < 0$$

Thus, to transform the diet problem into standard form, replace (3) by (3'); (4) by (4'); (5) by (5'); and (6) by (6'). We must also add the sign restrictions $e_i \geq 0$ ($i = 1, 2, 3, 4$). The resulting LP is in standard form and may be written as

$$\min z = 50x_1 + 20x_2 + 30x_3 + 80x_4$$
$$\text{s.t.} \quad 400x_1 + 200x_2 + 150x_3 + 500x_4 - e_1 \qquad\qquad = 500$$
$$3x_1 + 2x_2 \qquad\qquad\quad - e_2 \qquad\quad = 6$$
$$2x_1 + 2x_2 + 4x_3 + 4x_4 \qquad - e_3 \qquad = 10$$
$$2x_1 + 4x_2 + x_3 + 5x_4 \qquad\qquad - e_4 = 8$$
$$x_i, e_i \geq 0 \quad (i = 1, 2, 3, 4)$$

In summary, *if the ith constraint of an LP is a $\geq$ constraint, it can be converted to an equality constraint by subtracting an excess variable e_i from the ith constraint and adding the sign restriction $e_i \geq 0$.*

If an LP has both $\leq$ and $\geq$ constraints, simply apply the procedures we have described to each constraint. As an example, let's convert the short-term financial planning model of Section 3.7 into standard form. Recall that the original LP was

$$\max z = 20x_1 + 15x_2$$
$$\text{s.t.} \quad x_1 \qquad\qquad \leq 100$$
$$x_2 \leq 100$$
$$50x_1 + 35x_2 \leq 4000$$
$$20x_1 + 15x_2 \geq 2000$$
$$x_1, x_2 \geq 0$$

Following the procedures described previously, we transform this LP to standard form by adding slack variables s_1, s_2, and s_3, respectively, to the first three constraints and subtracting an excess variable e_4 from the fourth constraint. Then we add the sign restrictions $s_1 \geq 0$, $s_2 \geq 0$, $s_3 \geq 0$, and $e_4 \geq 0$. This yields the following LP in standard form:

$$\max z = 20x_1 + 15x_2$$
$$\text{s.t.} \quad x_1 \qquad + s_1 \qquad\qquad\qquad = 100$$
$$x_2 \qquad + s_2 \qquad\qquad = 100$$
$$50x_1 + 35x_2 \qquad\qquad + s_3 \qquad = 4000$$
$$20x_1 + 15x_2 \qquad\qquad\qquad - e_4 = 2000$$
$$x_i \geq 0 \quad (i = 1, 2); \quad s_i \geq 0 \quad (i = 1, 2, 3); \quad e_4 \geq 0$$

Of course, we could easily have labeled the excess variable for the fourth constraint e_1 (because it is the first excess variable). We chose to call it e_4 rather than e_1 to indicate that e_4 is the excess variable for the fourth constraint.

◆ PROBLEMS

GROUP A

1. Convert the Giapetto problem (Example 1 in Chapter 3) to standard form.

2. Convert the Dorian problem (Example 2 in Chapter 3) to standard form.

3. Convert the following LP to standard form:

$$\min z = 3x_1 + x_2$$
$$\text{s.t.} \quad x_1 \qquad \geq 3$$
$$x_1 + x_2 \leq 4$$
$$2x_1 - x_2 = 3$$
$$x_1, x_2 \geq 0$$

4-2   PREVIEW OF THE SIMPLEX ALGORITHM

Suppose we have converted an LP with m constraints into standard form. Assuming that the standard form contains n variables (labeled for convenience $x_1, x_2, \ldots, x_n$), the standard form for such an LP is

$$\max z = c_1 x_1 + c_2 x_2 + \cdots + c_n x_n$$
$$(\text{or min}) \cdot$$
$$\text{s.t.} \quad a_{11} x_1 + a_{12} x_2 + \cdots + a_{1n} x_n = b_1$$
$$a_{21} x_1 + a_{22} x_2 + \cdots + a_{2n} x_n = b_2$$
$$\vdots \qquad \vdots \qquad \qquad \vdots \qquad \vdots \qquad (7)$$
$$a_{m1} x_1 + a_{m2} x_2 + \cdots + a_{mn} x_n = b_m$$
$$x_i \geq 0 \quad (i = 1, 2, \ldots, n)$$

If we define

$$A = \begin{bmatrix} a_{11} & a_{12} & \cdots & a_{1n} \\ a_{21} & a_{22} & \cdots & a_{2n} \\ \vdots & \vdots & & \vdots \\ a_{m1} & a_{m2} & \cdots & a_{mn} \end{bmatrix}$$

and

$$\mathbf{x} = \begin{bmatrix} x_1 \\ x_2 \\ \vdots \\ x_n \end{bmatrix}, \quad \mathbf{b} = \begin{bmatrix} b_1 \\ b_2 \\ \vdots \\ b_m \end{bmatrix}$$

the constraints for (7) may be written as the system of equations $A\mathbf{x} = \mathbf{b}$. Before proceeding further with our discussion of the simplex algorithm, we must define the concept of a basic solution to a linear system.

Consider a system $A\mathbf{x} = \mathbf{b}$ of m linear equations in n variables (assume $n \geq m$).

DEFINITION ▪ A basic solution to $A\mathbf{x} = \mathbf{b}$ is obtained by setting $n - m$ variables equal to 0 and solving for the values of the remaining m variables. This assumes that setting the $n - m$ variables equal to 0 yields unique values for the remaining m variables or, equivalently, the columns for the remaining m variables are linearly independent.

To find a basic solution to $A\mathbf{x} = \mathbf{b}$, we choose a set of $n - m$ variables (the **nonbasic variables**, or NBV) and set each of these variables equal to zero. Then solve for the values of the remaining $n - (n - m) = m$ variables (the **basic variables**, or BV) that satisfy $A\mathbf{x} = \mathbf{b}$.

Of course, the different choices of nonbasic variables will lead to different basic solutions. To illustrate, we find all the basic solutions to the following system of two equations in three variables:

$$x_1 + x_2 \qquad = 3$$
$$- x_2 + x_3 = -1 \qquad (8)$$

We begin by choosing a set of $3 - 2 = 1$ nonbasic variables. For example, $NBV = \{x_3\}$. Then $BV = \{x_1, x_2\}$, and we obtain the values of the basic variables by setting $x_3 = 0$ and solving

$$x_1 + x_2 = 3$$
$$- x_2 = -1$$

We find that $x_1 = 2$, $x_2 = 1$. Thus, $x_1 = 2$, $x_2 = 1$, $x_3 = 0$ is a basic solution to (8). The reader should verify that if we choose $NBV = \{x_1\}$ and $BV = \{x_2, x_3\}$, we obtain the basic solution $x_1 = 0$, $x_2 = 3$, $x_3 = 2$. If we choose $NBV = \{x_2\}$, we obtain the basic solution $x_1 = 3$, $x_2 = 0$, $x_3 = -1$.

Some sets of m variables do not yield a basic solution. For example, consider the following linear system:

$$x_1 + 2x_2 + x_3 = 1$$
$$2x_1 + 4x_2 + x_3 = 3$$

If we choose $NBV = \{x_3\}$ and $BV = \{x_1, x_2\}$, the corresponding basic solution would be obtained by solving

$$x_1 + 2x_2 = 1$$
$$2x_1 + 4x_2 = 3$$

Since this system has no solution, there is no basic solution corresponding to $BV = \{x_1, x_2\}$.

A certain subset of the basic solutions to the constraints $A\mathbf{x} = \mathbf{b}$ of an LP plays an important role in the theory of linear programming.

DEFINITION ▪ Any basic solution to (7) in which all variables are nonnegative is a **basic feasible solution** (or bfs).

Thus, for an LP with the constraints given by (8), the basic solutions $x_1 = 2$, $x_2 = 1$, $x_3 = 0$, and $x_1 = 0$, $x_2 = 3$, $x_3 = 2$ are basic *feasible* solutions, but the basic solution $x_1 = 3$, $x_2 = 0$, $x_3 = -1$ fails to be a basic feasible solution (because $x_3 < 0$).

The following two theorems explain why the concept of a basic feasible solution is of great importance in linear programming (see Luenberger (1984) for more details).

THEOREM 1 ▪ The feasible region for any linear programming problem is a convex set. Also, if an LP has an optimal solution, there must be an extreme point of the feasible region that is optimal.

We understood Theorem 1 intuitively when we discussed solving LPs graphically in Section 3.2. Recall that if a two-variable LP has an optimal solution, it also has an optimal extreme point.

THEOREM 2 ▪ For any LP, there is a unique extreme point of the LP's feasible region corresponding to each basic feasible solution. Also, there is at least one bfs corresponding to each extreme point of the feasible region.

To illustrate the correspondence between extreme points and basic feasible solutions outlined in Theorem 2, let's look at the Leather Limited example of Section 4.1. Recall that the LP was

$$\max z = 4x_1 + 3x_2$$
$$\text{s.t.} \quad x_1 + x_2 \leq 40 \tag{1}$$
$$2x_1 + x_2 \leq 60 \tag{2}$$
$$x_1, x_2 \geq 0$$

(LP 1)

By adding slack variables s_1 and s_2, respectively, to (1) and (2), we obtain LP 1 in standard form:

$$\max z = 4x_1 + 3x_2$$
$$\text{s.t.} \quad x_1 + x_2 + s_1 \quad\quad = 40$$
$$2x_1 + x_2 \quad\quad + s_2 = 60$$
$$x_1, x_2, s_1, s_2 \geq 0$$

(LP 1′)

The feasible region for the Leather Limited problem is graphed in Figure 1. Inequality (1) is satisfied by all points below or on the line AB ($x_1 + x_2 = 40$), and (2) is satisfied by all points on or below the line CD ($2x_1 + x_2 = 60$). Thus, the feasible region for LP 1 is the shaded region bounded by the quadrilateral $BECF$. The extreme points of the feasible region are $B = (0, 40)$, $C = (30, 0)$, $E = (20, 20)$, and $F = (0, 0)$.

Table 1 shows the correspondence between the basic feasible solutions to LP 1′ and the extreme points of the feasible region for LP 1. This example should make it clear that the basic feasible solutions to the standard form of an LP correspond in a natural fashion to the LP's extreme points.

We can now explain the importance of Theorems 1 and 2. Theorem 1 tells us that when we search for the optimal solution to an LP with constraints $A\mathbf{x} = \mathbf{b}$, we need only search the extreme points of the LP's feasible region. Theorem 2 tells us that the extreme

Figure 1
Feasible Region for
Leather Limited
Example

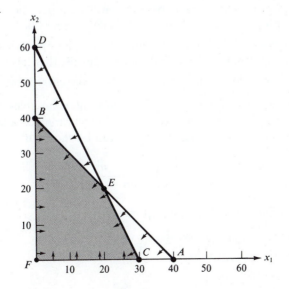

Table 1	BASIC VARIABLES	NONBASIC VARIABLES	BASIC FEASIBLE SOLUTION	CORRESPONDS TO CORNER POINT
Correspondence between Basic Feasible Solutions and Corner Points for Leather Limited Example	x_1, x_2	s_1, s_2	$s_1 = s_2 = 0, x_1 = x_2 = 20$	E
	x_1, s_1	x_2, s_2	$x_2 = s_2 = 0, x_1 = 30, s_1 = 10$	C
	x_1, s_2	x_2, s_1	$s_1 = x_2 = 0, x_1 = 40, s_2 = -20$	Not a bfs because $s_2 < 0$
	x_2, s_1	x_1, s_2	$s_2 = x_1 = 0, s_1 = -20, x_2 = 60$	Not a bfs because $s_1 < 0$
	x_2, s_2	x_1, s_1	$x_1 = s_1 = 0, x_2 = 40, s_2 = 20$	B
	s_1, s_2	x_1, x_2	$x_1 = x_2 = 0, s_1 = 40, s_2 = 60$	F

points of the LP's feasible region are (to all intents and purposes) the basic feasible solutions for the system $A\mathbf{x} = \mathbf{b}$. Putting these observations together, we see that *in searching for an optimal solution to an LP, we need only find the best basic feasible solution (largest z-value in a max problem or smallest z-value in a min problem) to $A\mathbf{x} = \mathbf{b}$.*

Before describing the simplex algorithm in general terms, we need to define the concept of an adjacent basic feasible solution.

DEFINITION   For any LP with m constraints, two basic feasible solutions are said to be **adjacent** if their sets of basic variables have $m - 1$ basic variables in common.

For example, in Figure 1, two basic feasible solutions will be adjacent if they have $2 - 1 = 1$ basic variable in common. Thus, the bfs corresponding to point E in Figure 1 is adjacent to the bfs corresponding to point C. Point E is not, however, adjacent to bfs F. Intuitively, two basic feasible solutions are adjacent if they both lie on the same edge of the boundary of the feasible region.

We are now ready to give a general description of how the simplex algorithm solves LPs. Assume that we are trying to solve a max problem.

Step 1 "Somehow" find a bfs to the LP. We call this bfs the initial basic feasible solution. In general, the most recent bfs will be called the current bfs, so at the beginning of the problem the initial bfs is the current bfs.

Step 2 "Somehow" find out if the current bfs is an optimal solution to the LP. If the current bfs is not optimal, find an adjacent bfs that has a larger z-value.

Step 3 Return to Step 2 using the new bfs as the current bfs.

If an LP in standard form has m constraints and n variables, there may be a basic solution for each choice of nonbasic variables. From n variables, a set of $n - m$ nonbasic variables (or equivalently, m basic variables) can be chosen in

$$\binom{n}{m} = \frac{n!}{(n-m)!m!}$$

different ways. Thus, an LP can have at most

$$\binom{n}{m}$$

basic solutions. Since some basic solutions may not be feasible, an LP can have at most

$$\binom{n}{m}$$

basic feasible solutions. If we were to proceed from the current bfs to a better bfs (without ever repeating a bfs), we would surely find the optimal bfs after examining at most

$$\binom{n}{m}$$

basic feasible solutions. This means (assuming that no bfs is repeated) that the simplex algorithm will find the optimal bfs after a finite number of calculations. We return to this discussion in Section 4.9.

In principle, we could enumerate all basic feasible solutions to an LP and find the bfs with the largest z-value. The problem with this approach is that even small LPs have a very large number of basic feasible solutions. For example, an LP in standard form that has 20 variables and 10 constraints might have (if each basic solution were feasible) up to

$$\binom{20}{10} = 184,756$$

basic feasible solutions. Fortunately, vast experience with the simplex algorithm indicates that when this algorithm is applied to an n-variable, m-constraint LP in standard form, an optimal solution is usually found after examining fewer than $3m$ basic feasible solutions. Thus, for a 20-variable, 10-constraint LP in standard form, the simplex will usually find the optimal solution after examining fewer than $3(10) = 30$ basic feasible solutions. Compared with the alternative of examining 184,756 basic solutions, the simplex is quite efficient![†]

GEOMETRY OF THREE-DIMENSIONAL LPs

Consider the following LP:

$$\max z = x_1 + 2x_2 + 2x_3$$
$$\text{s.t.} \quad 2x_1 + x_2 \quad\quad \leq 8$$
$$x_3 \leq 10$$
$$x_1, x_2, x_3 \geq 0$$

The set of points satisfying a linear inequality in three (or any number of) dimensions is a **half-space**. For example, the set of points in three dimensions satisfying $2x_1 + x_2 \leq 8$ is a half-space. Thus, the feasible region for our LP is the intersection of the following five half-spaces: $2x_1 + x_2 \leq 8$, $x_3 \leq 10$, $x_1 \geq 0$, $x_2 \geq 0$, and $x_3 \geq 0$. The intersection of half-spaces is called a **polyhedron**. The feasible region for our LP is the prism pictured in Figure 2.

[†]In solving many LPs with 50 variables and $m \leq 50$ constraints, Chvàtal (1983) found that the simplex algorithm examined an average of $2m$ basic feasible solutions before finding an LP's optimal solution.

Figure 2
Example of Feasible
Region in Three
Dimensions

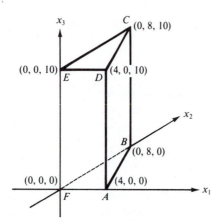

On each face (or facet) of the feasible region, there is one constraint (or sign restriction) that is binding for all points on that face. For example, the constraint $2x_1 + x_2 \leq 8$ is binding for all points on the face $ABCD$; $x_3 \geq 0$ is binding on face ABF; $x_3 \leq 10$ is binding on face DEC; $x_2 \geq 0$ is binding on face $ADEF$; $x_1 \geq 0$ is binding on face $CBEF$.

Clearly, the corner (or extreme) points of the LP's feasible region are A, B, C, D, E, and F. In this case, the correspondence between the bfs and corner points is as shown in Table 2.

To illustrate the concept of adjacent basic feasible solutions, note that corner points A, E, and B are adjacent to corner point F. Thus, if the simplex algorithm begins at F, we can be sure that the next bfs to be considered will be either A, E, or B.

Table 2
Correspondence
between bfs and
Corner Points

BASIC VARIABLES	BASIC FEASIBLE SOLUTION	CORRESPONDS TO CORNER POINT
x_1, x_3	$x_1 = 4, x_3 = 10, x_2 = s_1 = s_2 = 0$	D
s_1, s_2	$s_1 = 8, s_2 = 10, x_1 = x_2 = x_3 = 0$	F
s_1, x_3	$s_1 = 8, x_3 = 10, x_1 = x_2 = s_2 = 0$	E
x_2, x_3	$x_2 = 8, x_3 = 10, x_1 = s_1 = s_2 = 0$	C
x_2, s_2	$x_2 = 8, s_2 = 10, x_1 = x_3 = s_1 = 0$	B
x_1, s_2	$x_1 = 4, s_2 = 10, x_2 = x_3 = s_1 = 0$	A

◆ PROBLEMS

GROUP A

1. For the Giapetto problem (Example 1 in Chapter 3), show how the basic feasible solutions to the LP in standard form correspond to the extreme points of the feasible region.

2. For the Dorian problem (Equation 2 in Chapter 3), show how the basic feasible solutions to the LP in standard form correspond to the extreme points of the feasible region.

4-3 THE SIMPLEX ALGORITHM

We will now describe how the simplex algorithm can be used to solve LPs in which the goal is to maximize the objective function. The solution of minimization problems is discussed in Section 4.4.

The simplex algorithm proceeds as follows:

Step 1 Convert the LP to standard form (see Section 4.1).

Step 2 Obtain a bfs (if possible) from the standard form.

Step 3 Determine whether the current bfs is optimal.

Step 4 If the current bfs is not optimal, determine which nonbasic variable should become a basic variable and which basic variable should become a nonbasic variable in order to find a new bfs with a better objective function value.

Step 5 Use ero's to find the new bfs with the better objective function value and go to Step 3.

In performing the simplex algorithm, it is necessary to write an objective function

$$z = c_1 x_1 + c_2 x_2 + \cdots + c_n x_n$$

in the form

$$z - c_1 x_1 - c_2 x_2 - \cdots - c_n x_n = 0$$

We call this format the **row 0 version** of the objective function (row 0 for short).

E X A M P L E 2

The Dakota Furniture Company manufactures desks, tables, and chairs. The manufacture of each type of furniture requires lumber and two types of skilled labor: finishing labor and carpentry labor. The amount of each resource needed to make each type of furniture is given in Table 3.

Table 3
Resource
Requirements for
Dakota Furniture
Example

RESOURCE	DESK	TABLE	CHAIR
Lumber	8 board ft	6 board ft	1 board ft
Finishing hours	4 hours	2 hours	1.5 hours
Carpentry hours	2 hours	1.5 hours	0.5 hour

At present, 48 board ft of lumber, 20 finishing hours, and 8 carpentry hours are available. A desk sells for $60, a table for $30, and a chair for $20. Dakota believes that demand for desks and chairs is unlimited, but at most five tables can be sold. Since the available resources have already been purchased, Dakota wants to maximize total revenue. Defining the decision variables as

$$x_1 = \text{number of desks produced}$$
$$x_2 = \text{number of tables produced}$$
$$x_3 = \text{number of chairs produced}$$

it is easy to see that Dakota should solve the following LP:

$$\max z = 60x_1 + 30x_2 + 20x_3$$

$$
\begin{aligned}
\text{s.t.} \quad 8x_1 + 6x_2 + x_3 &\leq 48 && \text{(Lumber constraint)} \\
4x_1 + 2x_2 + 1.5x_3 &\leq 20 && \text{(Finishing constraint)} \\
2x_1 + 1.5x_2 + 0.5x_3 &\leq 8 && \text{(Carpentry constraint)} \\
x_2 &\leq 5 && \text{(Limitation on table demand)} \\
x_1, x_2, x_3 &\geq 0
\end{aligned}
$$

♦

CONVERT THE LP TO STANDARD FORM

We begin the simplex algorithm by converting the constraints of the LP to the standard form discussed in Section 4.1. Then we convert the LP's objective function to the row 0 format. To put the constraints in standard form, we simply add slack variables s_1, s_2, s_3, and s_4, respectively, to the four constraints. We label the constraints row 1, row 2, row 3, and row 4, and add the sign restrictions $s_i \geq 0$ ($i = 1, 2, 3, 4$). Note that the row 0 format for our objective function is

$$z - 60x_1 - 30x_2 - 20x_3 = 0$$

Putting rows 1–4 together with row 0 and the sign restrictions yields the equations and basic variables shown in Table 4. A system of linear equations (such as canonical form 0, shown in Table 4) in which each equation has a variable with a coefficient of 1 in that equation (and a zero coefficient in all other equations) is said to be in canonical form. We will soon see that if the right-hand side of each constraint in a canonical form is nonnegative, a basic feasible solution can be obtained by inspection.[†]

Table 4			BASIC VARIABLE
Canonical Form 0			
Row 0	$z - 60x_1 - 30x_2 - 20x_3$	$= 0$	$z = 0$
Row 1	$8x_1 + 6x_2 + x_3 + s_1$	$= 48$	$s_1 = 48$
Row 2	$4x_1 + 2x_2 + 1.5x_3 + s_2$	$= 20$	$s_2 = 20$
Row 3	$2x_1 + 1.5x_2 + 0.5x_3 + s_3$	$= 8$	$s_3 = 8$
Row 4	$x_2 + s_4$	$= 5$	$s_4 = 5$

From Section 4.2, we know that the simplex algorithm begins with a basic feasible solution and attempts to find better basic feasible solutions. After obtaining a canonical form, we therefore search for the initial bfs. By inspection, we see that if we set $x_1 = x_2 = x_3 = 0$, we can solve for the values of s_1, s_2, s_3, and s_4 by setting s_i equal to the right-hand side of row i. In this fashion, we can obtain a bfs with

$$BV = \{s_1, s_2, s_3, s_4\} \quad \text{and} \quad NBV = \{x_1, x_2, x_3\}$$

[†]If a canonical form with nonnegative right-hand sides is not readily available, however, the techniques described in Sections 4.10 and 4.11 can be used to find a canonical form and a basic feasible solution.

The basic feasible solution for this set of basic variables is $s_1 = 48$, $s_2 = 20$, $s_3 = 8$, $s_4 = 5$, $x_1 = x_2 = x_3 = 0$. It is important to observe that each basic variable may be associated with the row of the canonical form in which the basic variable has a coefficient of 1. Thus, for canonical form 0, s_1 may be thought of as the basic variable for row 1, s_2 as the basic variable for row 2, s_3 as the basic variable for row 3, and s_4 as the basic variable for row 4.

To perform the simplex algorithm, we also need a basic (although not necessarily nonnegative) variable for row 0. Since z appears in row 0 with a coefficient of 1, and z does not appear in any other row, we use z as the basic variable for row 0. With this convention, the basic feasible solution for our initial canonical form has

$$BV = \{z, s_1, s_2, s_3, s_4\} \quad \text{and} \quad NBV = \{x_1, x_2, x_3\}$$

For this basic feasible solution, $z = 0$, $s_1 = 48$, $s_2 = 20$, $s_3 = 8$, $s_4 = 5$, $x_1 = x_2 = x_3 = 0$.

As this example indicates, a slack variable can be used as a basic variable for an equation if the right-hand side of the constraint is nonnegative.

IS THE CURRENT BASIC FEASIBLE SOLUTION OPTIMAL?

Once we have obtained a basic feasible solution, we need to determine whether it is optimal; if the bfs is not optimal, we try to find a bfs adjacent to the initial bfs with a larger z-value than the initial bfs. To accomplish these goals, we try to determine whether there is any way that z can be increased by increasing some nonbasic variable from its current value of zero while holding all other nonbasic variables at their current values of zero. If we solve for z by rearranging row 0, we obtain

$$z = 60x_1 + 30x_2 + 20x_3 \tag{9}$$

For each nonbasic variable, we can use (9) to determine whether or not increasing a nonbasic variable (and holding all other nonbasic variables at zero) will increase z. For example, suppose we increase x_1 by 1 (holding the other nonbasic variables x_2 and x_3 at zero). Then (9) tells us that z will increase by 60. Similarly, if we choose to increase x_2 by 1 (holding x_1 and x_3 at zero), then (9) tells us that z will increase by 30. Finally, if we choose to increase x_3 by 1 (holding x_1 and x_2 at zero), then (9) tells us that z will increase by 20. Thus, increasing any of the nonbasic variables will increase z. Since a unit increase in x_1 causes the largest rate of increase in z, we choose to increase x_1 from its current value of zero. If x_1 is to increase from its current value of zero, it will have to enter the basis and become a basic variable. For this reason, we call x_1 the **entering variable**. Observe that x_1 has the most negative coefficient in row 0.

DETERMINE THE ENTERING VARIABLE

We choose the entering variable (in a max problem) to be the nonbasic variable with the most negative coefficient in row 0 (ties may be broken in an arbitrary fashion). Since each unit by which we increase x_1 increases z by 60, we would like to make x_1 as large as possible. What limits how large we can make x_1? To answer this question, note that as x_1 increases, the values of the current basic variables (s_1, s_2, s_3, and s_4) will change. This means that increasing x_1 may cause a basic variable to become negative. With this in mind, we look at how increasing x_1 (while holding $x_2 = x_3 = 0$) changes the values of the current set of basic variables. From row 1, we see that $s_1 = 48 - 8x_1$ (remember that $x_2 = x_3 = 0$). Since the sign restriction $s_1 \geq 0$ must be satisfied, we can only increase x_1 as long as $s_1 \geq 0$, or $48 - 8x_1 \geq 0$, or $x_1 \leq \frac{48}{8} = 6$. From row 2, we see that $s_2 = 20 - 4x_1$. Since we can only increase x_1 as long as $s_2 \geq 0$, this means that x_1 must satisfy $20 - 4x_1 \geq 0$ or $x_1 \leq \frac{20}{4} = 5$. From row 3, we see that $s_3 = 8 - 2x_1$. We can only increase x_1 as long as $8 - 2x_1 \geq 0$, or $x_1 \leq \frac{8}{2} = 4$. Similarly, we see from row 4 that $s_4 = 5$. Thus, whatever the value of x_1, s_4 will be nonnegative. Summarizing the above development, we see that

$$
\begin{array}{lll}
s_1 \geq 0 & \text{for} & x_1 \leq \frac{48}{8} = 6 \\
s_2 \geq 0 & \text{for} & x_1 \leq \frac{20}{4} = 5 \\
s_3 \geq 0 & \text{for} & x_1 \leq \frac{8}{2} = 4 \\
s_4 \geq 0 & \text{for all values of } x_1
\end{array}
$$

This means that to keep all the basic variables nonnegative, the largest that we can make x_1 is min $\left\{\frac{48}{8}, \frac{20}{4}, \frac{8}{2}\right\} = 4$. If we make $x_1 > 4$, then s_3 will become negative, and we will no longer have a basic feasible solution. Notice that each row in which the entering variable had a positive coefficient restricted how large the entering variable could become. Also, for any row in which the entering variable had a positive coefficient, the row's basic variable became negative when the entering variable exceeded

$$
\frac{\text{Right-hand side of row}}{\text{Coefficient of entering variable in row}} \tag{10}
$$

If the entering variable has a nonpositive coefficient in a row (such as x_1 in row 4), the row's basic variable will remain positive for all values of the entering variable. Using (10), we can quickly compute how large x_1 can become before a basic variable becomes negative:

Row 1 limit on $x_1 = \frac{48}{8} = 6$

Row 2 limit on $x_1 = \frac{20}{4} = 5$

Row 3 limit on $x_1 = \frac{8}{2} = 4$

Row 4 limit on $x_1 = $ no limit   (Because coefficient of x_1 in row 4 is nonpositive)

We can state the following rule for determining how large we can make an entering variable.

THE RATIO TEST.   When entering a variable into the basis, compute the ratio in (10) for every constraint in which the entering variable has a positive coefficient. The constraint with the smallest ratio is called the **winner of the ratio test**. The smallest ratio is the largest value of the entering variable that will keep all the current basic variables nonnegative. In our example, row 3 was the winner of the ratio test for entering x_1 into the basis.

**FIND A NEW BASIC FEASIBLE SOLUTION:
PIVOT IN THE ENTERING VARIABLE**

Returning to our example, we know that the largest we can make x_1 is 4. For x_1 to equal 4, it must become a basic variable. Looking at rows 1–4, we see that if we make x_1 a basic variable in row 1, x_1 will equal $\frac{48}{8} = 6$; if we make x_1 a basic variable in row 2, x_1 will equal $\frac{20}{4} = 5$; if we make x_1 a basic variable in row 3, x_1 will equal $\frac{8}{2} = 4$. Also, since x_1 does not appear in row 4, x_4 cannot be made a basic variable in row 4. Thus, if we want to make $x_1 = 4$, we have to make x_1 a basic variable in row 3. The fact that row 3 was the winner of the ratio test illustrates the following rule.

IN WHICH ROW DOES THE ENTERING VARIABLE BECOME BASIC? Always make the entering variable a basic variable in a row that wins the ratio test (ties may be broken arbitrarily).

To make x_1 a basic variable in row 3, we use elementary row operations to make x_1 have a coefficient of 1 in row 3 and a coefficient of zero in all other rows. This procedure is called **pivoting** on row 3, and row 3 is referred to as the **pivot row**. The final result is that x_1 replaces s_3 as the basic variable for row 3. The term in the pivot row that involves the entering basic variable is called the **pivot term**. Proceeding as we did when we studied the Gauss-Jordan method in Chapter 2, we make x_1 a basic variable in row 3 by performing the following ero's.

ero 1 Create a coefficient of 1 for x_1 in row 3 by multiplying row 3 by $\frac{1}{2}$. The resulting row (marked with a prime to show it is the first iteration) is

$$x_1 + 0.75x_2 + 0.25x_3 + 0.5s_3 = 4 \qquad \textbf{(row 3')}$$

ero 2 To create a zero coefficient for x_1 in row 0, replace row 0 by 60(row 3') + row 0. The resulting row is

$$z + 15x_2 - 5x_3 + 30s_3 = 240 \qquad \textbf{(row 0')}$$

ero 3 To create a zero coefficient for x_1 in row 1, replace row 1 by -8(row 3') + row 1. The resulting row is

$$-x_3 + s_1 - 4s_3 = 16 \qquad \textbf{(row 1')}$$

ero 4 To create a zero coefficient for x_1 in row 2, replace row 2 by -4(row 3') + row 2. The resulting row is

$$-x_2 + 0.5x_3 + s_2 - 2s_3 = 4 \qquad \textbf{(row 2')}$$

Since x_1 does not appear in row 4, we don't need to perform an ero to eliminate x_1 from row 4. Thus, we may write the "new" row 4 (call it row 4' to be consistent with other notation) as

$$x_2 + s_4 = 5 \qquad \textbf{(row 4')}$$

Putting rows 0'–4' together, we obtain the canonical form shown in Table 5.

Table 5
Canonical Form 1

			BASIC VARIABLE
Row 0'	$z + 15x_2 - 5x_3 + 30s_3$	$= 240$	$z = 240$
Row 1'	$- x_3 + s_1 - 4s_3$	$= 16$	$s_1 = 16$
Row 2'	$- x_2 + 0.5x_3 + s_2 - 2s_3$	$= 4$	$s_2 = 4$
Row 3'	$x_1 + 0.75x_2 + 0.25x_3 + 0.5s_3$	$= 4$	$x_1 = 4$
Row 4'	$x_2 + s_4$	$= 5$	$s_4 = 5$

Looking for a basic variable in each row of the current canonical form, we find that

$$BV = \{z, s_1, s_2, x_1, s_4\} \quad \text{and} \quad NBV = \{s_3, x_2, x_3\}$$

Thus, canonical form 1 yields the basic feasible solution $z = 240$, $s_1 = 16$, $s_2 = 4$, $x_1 = 4$, $s_4 = 5$, $x_2 = x_3 = s_3 = 0$. We could have predicted that the value of z in canonical form 1 would be 240 from the fact that each unit by which x_1 is increased increases z by 60. Since x_1 was increased by 4 units (from $x_1 = 0$ to $x_1 = 4$), we would expect that

$$\text{Canonical form 1 } z\text{-value} = \text{initial } z\text{-value} + 4(60)$$
$$= 0 + 240 = 240$$

In obtaining canonical form 1 from the initial canonical form, we have gone from one bfs to a better (larger z-value) bfs. Note that the bfs for the initial canonical form and the bfs for canonical form 1 are adjacent basic feasible solutions. This follows because the two basic feasible solutions have $4 - 1 = 3$ basic variables (s_1, s_2, and s_4) in common (excluding z, which is a basic variable in every canonical form). Thus, we see that in going from one canonical form to the next, we have proceeded from one bfs to a better adjacent bfs. The procedure used to go from one bfs to a better bfs is called an **iteration** (or sometimes, a pivot) of the simplex algorithm.

We now try to find a bfs that has a larger z-value than the bfs of canonical form 1. We begin by examining canonical form 1 to see if we can increase z by increasing the value of some nonbasic variable (while holding all other nonbasic variables equal to zero). Rearranging row 0′ to solve for z yields

$$z = 240 - 15x_2 + 5x_3 - 30s_3 \tag{11}$$

From (11), we see that increasing the nonbasic variable x_2 by 1 (while holding $x_3 = s_3 = 0$) will decrease z by 15. We don't want to do that! Increasing the nonbasic variable s_3 by 1 (holding $x_2 = x_3 = 0$) will decrease z by 30. Again, we don't want to do that. On the other hand, increasing x_3 by 1 (holding $x_2 = s_3 = 0$) will increase z by 5. Thus, we choose to enter x_3 into the basis. Recall that our rule for determining the entering variable was to choose the variable with the most negative coefficient in the current row 0. Since x_3 is the only variable with a negative coefficient in row 0′, our rule indicates that x_3 should be entered into the basis.

Since increasing x_3 by 1 will increase z by 5, it is to our advantage to make x_3 as large as possible. We can increase x_3 as long as the current basic variables (s_1, s_2, x_1, and s_4) remain nonnegative. To determine how large x_3 can be, we must solve for the values of the current basic variables in terms of x_3 (holding $x_2 = s_3 = 0$). We obtain

From row 1′: $s_1 = 16 + x_3$

From row 2′: $s_2 = 4 - 0.5x_3$

From row 3′: $x_1 = 4 - 0.25x_3$

From row 4′: $s_4 = 5$

These equations tell us that $s_1 \geq 0$ and $s_4 \geq 0$ will hold for all values of x_3. From row 2′, we see that $s_2 \geq 0$ will hold if $4 - 0.5x_3 \geq 0$, or $x_3 \leq \frac{4}{0.5} = 8$. From row 3′, we see that $x_1 \geq 0$ will hold if $4 - 0.25x_3 \geq 0$, or $x_3 \leq \frac{4}{0.25} = 16$. This shows that the largest we can make x_3 is min $\{\frac{4}{0.5}, \frac{4}{0.25}\} = 8$. This fact could also have been discovered by using (10) and the ratio test, as follows:

> Row 1': no ratio   (x_3 has negative coefficient in row 1)
>
> Row 2': $\frac{4}{0.5} = 8$
>
> Row 3': $\frac{4}{0.25} = 16$
>
> Row 4': no ratio   (x_3 has a nonpositive coefficient in row 4)

Thus, the smallest ratio occurs in row 2', and row 2' wins the ratio test. This means that we should use ero's to make x_3 a basic variable in row 2':

ero 1 Create a coefficient of 1 for x_3 in row 2' by replacing row 2' by 2(row 2'). The resulting row is

$$-2x_2 + x_3 + 2s_2 - 4s_3 = 8 \qquad \text{(row 2'')}$$

ero 2 Create a coefficient of zero for x_3 in row 0' by replacing row 0' by 5(row 2'') + row 0'. The resulting row is

$$z + 5x_2 + 10s_2 + 10s_3 = 280 \qquad \text{(row 0'')}$$

ero 3 Create a coefficient of zero for x_3 in row 1' by replacing row 1' with row 2'' + row 1'. The resulting row is

$$-2x_2 + s_1 + 2s_2 - 8s_3 = 24 \qquad \text{(row 1'')}$$

ero 4 Create a coefficient of zero for x_3 in row 3', by replacing row 3' with $-\frac{1}{4}$(row 2'') + row 3'. The resulting row is

$$x_1 + 1.25x_2 - 0.5s_2 + 1.5s_3 = 2 \qquad \text{(row 3'')}$$

Since x_3 already has a zero coefficient in row 4', we may write

$$x_2 + s_4 = 5 \qquad \text{(row 4'')}$$

Combining rows 0''–4'' gives the canonical form shown in Table 6.

Table 6 Canonical Form 2						BASIC VARIABLE
Row 0''	z	$+ \;\; 5x_2$		$+ \; 10s_2 + \; 10s_3$	$= 280$	$z = 280$
Row 1''		$- \;\; 2x_2$	$+ s_1 +$	$2s_2 - \;\; 8s_3$	$= 24$	$s_1 = 24$
Row 2''		$- \;\; 2x_2 + x_3$	$+$	$2s_2 - \;\; 4s_3$	$= 8$	$x_3 = 8$
Row 3''	$x_1 + 1.25x_2$			$- \; 0.5s_2 + 1.5s_3$	$= 2$	$x_1 = 2$
Row 4''		x_2		$+ s_4$	$= 5$	$s_4 = 5$

Looking for a basic variable in each row of canonical form 2, we find

$$BV = \{z, s_1, x_3, x_1, s_4\} \qquad \text{and} \qquad NBV = \{s_2, s_3, x_2\}$$

Canonical form 2 yields the following bfs: $z = 280$, $s_1 = 24$, $x_3 = 8$, $x_1 = 2$, $s_4 = 5$, $s_2 = s_3 = x_2 = 0$. We could have predicted that canonical form 2 would have $z = 280$ from the fact that each unit of the entering variable x_3 increased z by 5, and we have increased x_3 by 8 units. Thus,

Canonical form 2 z-value = canonical form 1 z-value + 8(5)

$$= 240 + 40 = 280$$

Since the basic feasible solutions for canonical forms 1 and 2 have (excluding z) $4 - 1 = 3$ basic variables in common (s_1, s_4, x_1), they are adjacent basic feasible solutions.

Now that the second iteration (or pivot) of the simplex algorithm has been completed, we examine canonical form 2 to see if we can find a better bfs than canonical form 2. If we rearrange row 0′ and solve for z, we obtain

$$z = 280 - 5x_2 - 10s_2 - 10s_3 \tag{12}$$

From (12), we see that increasing x_2 by 1 (while holding $s_2 = s_3 = 0$) will decrease z by 5; increasing s_2 by 1 (holding $s_3 = x_2 = 0$) will decrease z by 10; increasing s_3 by 1 (holding $x_2 = s_2 = 0$) will decrease z by 10. Thus, increasing any nonbasic variable will cause z to decrease. This might lead us to believe that our current bfs from canonical form 2 is an optimal solution. This is indeed correct! To see why our current bfs is optimal, look at (12). We know that any feasible solution to the Dakota Furniture problem must have $x_2 \geq 0$, $s_2 \geq 0$, and $s_3 \geq 0$, and $-5x_2 \leq 0$, $-10s_2 \leq 0$, and $-10s_3 \leq 0$. Combining these inequalities with (12), it is clear that any feasible solution must have $z = 280 +$ terms that are ≤ 0, and $z \leq 280$. Our current bfs from canonical form 2 has $z = 280$, so it must be optimal.

The argument that we just used to show that canonical form 2 is optimal revolved around the fact that in canonical form 2, each nonbasic variable had a nonnegative coefficient in row 0″. This means that we can determine whether a canonical form's bfs is optimal by applying the following simple rule.

IS A CANONICAL FORM OPTIMAL (MAX PROBLEM)?   A canonical form is optimal (for a max problem) if each nonbasic variable has a nonnegative coefficient in the canonical form's row 0.

REMARKS   **1.** The coefficient of a decision variable in row 0 is often referred to as the variable's **reduced cost**. Thus, in our optimal canonical form (canonical form 2), the reduced costs for x_1 and x_3 are zero, and the reduced cost for x_2 is 5. The reduced cost of a nonbasic variable is the amount by which the value of z will decrease if we increase the value of the nonbasic variable by 1 (while all the other nonbasic variables remain equal to zero). For example, the reduced cost for the variable "tables" (x_2) in canonical form 2 is 5. From (12), we see that increasing x_2 by 1 will reduce z by 5. Note that since all basic variables (except z, of course) must have zero coefficients in row 0, the reduced cost for a basic variable will always be zero. In Chapters 5 and 6, we discuss the concept of reduced costs in much greater detail.

The above comments are correct only if the values of all the basic variables remain nonnegative after the nonbasic variable is increased by 1. Since increasing x_2 to 1 leaves x_1, x_3, and s_1 all nonnegative, our comments are valid.

2. From canonical form 2, we see that the optimal solution to the Dakota Furniture problem is to manufacture 2 desks $(x_1 = 2)$ and 8 chairs $(x_3 = 8)$. Since $x_2 = 0$, no tables should be made. Also, $s_1 = 24$ is reasonable, because only $8 + 8(2) = 24$ board ft of lumber are being used. Thus, $48 - 24 = 24$ board ft of lumber are not being used. Similarly, $s_4 = 5$ makes sense, because although up to 5 tables could have been produced, 0 tables are actually being produced. Thus, the slack in constraint 4 is $5 - 0 = 5$. Since $s_2 = s_3 = 0$, all available finishing and carpentry hours are being utilized, so the finishing and carpentry constraints are binding.

3. We have chosen the entering variable to be the variable with the most negative coefficient in row 0, but this may not always lead us quickly to the optimal bfs (see Review Problem 11). Actually, even if we choose the entering variable to be the variable with the smallest (in absolute value) negative coefficient, the simplex algorithm will eventually find the LP's optimal solution.

4. Although any variable with a negative row 0 coefficient may be chosen to enter the basis, the pivot row *must* be chosen by the ratio test. To show this formally, suppose that we have chosen to enter x_i into the basis, and in the current tableau x_i is a basic variable in row k. Then row k may be written as

$$\bar{a}_{ki}x_i + \cdots = \bar{b}_k$$

Consider any other constraint (say, row j) in the canonical form. Row j in the current canonical form may be written as

$$\bar{a}_{ji}x_i + \cdots = \bar{b}_j$$

If we pivot on row k, row k becomes

$$x_i + \cdots \qquad = \frac{\bar{b}_k}{\bar{a}_{ki}}$$

The new row j after the pivot will be obtained by adding $-\bar{a}_{ji}$ times the last equation to row j of the current canonical form. This yields a new row j of

$$0x_i + \cdots \qquad = \bar{b}_j - \frac{\bar{b}_k \bar{a}_{ji}}{\bar{a}_{ki}}$$

We know that after the pivot, each constraint must have a nonnegative right-hand side. Thus, $\bar{a}_{ki} > 0$ must hold so as to ensure that row k has a nonnegative right-hand side after the pivot. Suppose $\bar{a}_{ji} > 0$. Then, to ensure that row j will have a nonnegative right-hand side after the pivot, we must have

$$\bar{b}_j - \frac{\bar{b}_k \bar{a}_{ji}}{\bar{a}_{ki}} \geq 0$$

or (since $\bar{a}_{ji} > 0$)

$$\frac{\bar{b}_j}{\bar{a}_{ji}} \geq \frac{\bar{b}_k}{\bar{a}_{ki}}$$

Thus, row k must be a "winner" of the ratio test to ensure that row j will have a nonnegative right-hand side after the pivot is completed.

If $\bar{a}_{ji} \leq 0$, then the right-hand side of row j will surely be nonnegative after the pivot. This follows because

$$-\frac{\bar{b}_k \bar{a}_{ji}}{\bar{a}_{ki}} \geq 0$$

will now hold.

As promised earlier, we have outlined an algorithm that proceeds from one bfs to a better bfs. The algorithm stops when an optimal solution has been found. The convergence of the simplex algorithm is discussed further in Section 4.9.

SUMMARY OF THE SIMPLEX ALGORITHM FOR A MAX PROBLEM

Step 1 Convert the LP to standard form.

Step 2 Find a basic feasible solution. This is easy if all the constraints are $\leq$ constraints with nonnegative right-hand sides. Then the slack variable s_i may be used as the basic variable for row i. If no bfs is readily apparent, use the techniques discussed in Sections 4.10 and 4.11 to find a bfs.

Step 3 If all nonbasic variables have nonnegative coefficients in row 0, the current bfs is optimal. If any variables in row 0 have negative coefficients, choose the variable with the most negative coefficient in row 0 to enter the basis. We call this variable the entering variable.

Step 4 Use ero's to make the entering variable the basic variable in any row that wins the ratio test (ties may be broken arbitrarily). After the ero's have been used to create a new canonical form, return to Step 3, using the current canonical form.

When using the simplex algorithm to solve problems, there should never be a constraint with a negative right-hand side (it is okay for row 0 to have a negative right-hand side; see Section 4.4). A constraint with a negative right-hand side is usually the result of an error in the ratio test or an error in performing one or more ero's. If one (or more) of the constraints has a negative right-hand side, there is no longer a bfs, and the rules of the simplex algorithm may not lead to a better bfs.

REPRESENTING SIMPLEX TABLEAUS

Rather than writing each variable in every constraint, we often used a shorthand display called a **simplex tableau**. For example, the canonical form

$$z + 3x_1 + x_2 \qquad\qquad = 6$$
$$x_1 \qquad + s_1 \qquad = 4$$
$$2x_1 + x_2 \qquad + s_2 = 3$$

would be written in abbreviated form as shown in Table 7 (rhs = right-hand side). This format makes it very easy to spot basic variables: Just look for columns having a single entry of 1 and all other entries equal to zero (for instance, s_1 and s_2 in Table 7). In our use of simplex tableaus, we will encircle the pivot term and denote the winner of the ratio test by *.

Table 7
Example of a
Simplex Tableau

z	x_1	x_2	s_1	s_2	rhs	BASIC VARIABLE
1	3	1	0	0	6	$z = 6$
0	1	0	1	0	4	$s_1 = 4$
0	2	1	0	1	3	$s_2 = 3$

◆ PROBLEMS

GROUP A

1. Use the simplex algorithm to solve the Giapetto problem.

2. Use the simplex algorithm to solve the following LP:

$$\max z = 2x_1 + 3x_2$$
$$\text{s.t.} \quad x_1 + 2x_2 \le 6$$
$$2x_1 + x_2 \le 8$$
$$x_1, x_2 \ge 0$$

3. Use the simplex algorithm to solve the following problem:

$$\max z = 2x_1 - x_2 + x_3$$
$$\text{s.t.} \quad 3x_1 + x_2 + x_3 \le 60$$
$$x_1 - x_2 + 2x_3 \le 10$$
$$x_1 + x_2 - x_3 \le 20$$
$$x_1, x_2, x_3 \ge 0$$

4. Suppose you want to solve the Dorian problem (Example 2 in Chapter 3) by the simplex algorithm. What difficulty would occur?

GROUP B

5. It has been suggested that at each iteration of the simplex algorithm, the entering variable should be chosen (in a maximization problem) to be the variable that would bring about the greatest increase in the objective function. Although this usually results in fewer pivots than the rule of entering the most negative row 0 entry, the greatest increase rule is hardly ever used. Why not?

4-4   USING THE SIMPLEX ALGORITHM TO SOLVE MINIMIZATION PROBLEMS

There are two different ways that the simplex algorithm can be used to solve minimization problems. We illustrate these methods by solving the following LP:

$$\min z = 2x_1 - 3x_2$$
$$\text{s.t.} \quad x_1 + x_2 \le 4$$
$$x_1 - x_2 \le 6 \qquad \textbf{(LP 2)}$$
$$x_1, x_2 \ge 0$$

METHOD 1

The optimal solution to LP 2 is the point (x_1, x_2) in the feasible region for LP 2 that makes $z = 2x_1 - 3x_2$ the smallest. Equivalently, we may say that the optimal solution to LP 2 is the point in the feasible region that makes $-z = -2x_1 + 3x_2$ the largest. This means that we can find the optimal solution to LP 2 by solving LP 2′:

$$\max -z = -2x_1 + 3x_2$$
$$\text{s.t.} \quad x_1 + x_2 \le 4$$
$$x_1 - x_2 \le 6 \qquad \textbf{(LP 2′)}$$
$$x_1, x_2 \ge 0$$

In solving LP 2′, we will use $-z$ as the basic variable for row 0. After adding slack variables s_1 and s_2 to the two constraints, we obtain the initial tableau in Table 8. Since x_2 is the only variable with a negative coefficient in row 0, we enter x_2 into the basis. The ratio test indicates that x_2 should enter the basis in the first constraint. The resulting

Table 8 Initial Tableau for LP 2—Method 1	$-z$	x_1	x_2	s_1	s_2	rhs	BASIC VARIABLE	RATIO
	1	2	-3	0	0	0	$-z = 0$	
	0	1	①	1	0	4	$s_1 = 4$	$\frac{4}{1} = 4*$
	0	1	-1	0	1	6	$s_2 = 6$	None

tableau is shown in Table 9. Since each variable in row 0 has a nonnegative coefficient, this is an optimal tableau. Thus, the optimal solution to LP 2′ is $-z = 12$, $x_2 = 4$, $s_2 = 10$, $x_1 = s_1 = 0$. Then the optimal solution to LP 2 is $z = -12$, $x_2 = 4$, $s_2 = 10$, $x_1 = s_1 = 0$. Substituting the values of x_1 and x_2 into LP 2's objective function, we obtain

$$z = 2x_1 - 3x_2 = 2(0) - 3(4) = -12$$

In summary, multiply the objective function for the min problem by -1 and solve the problem as a maximization problem with objective function $-z$. The optimal solution to the max problem will also be the optimal solution to the min problem. Remember that (optimal z-value for min problem) $= -$(optimal objective function value for max problem).

Table 9
Optimal Tableau for
LP 2—Method 1

$-z$	x_1	x_2	s_1	s_2	rhs	BASIC VARIABLE
1	5	0	3	0	12	$-z = 12$
0	1	1	1	0	4	$x_2 = 4$
0	2	0	1	1	10	$s_2 = 10$

METHOD 2

A simple modification of the simplex algorithm can be used to solve min problems directly. Modify Step 3 of the simplex as follows: If all nonbasic variables in row 0 have nonpositive coefficients, the current bfs is optimal. If any nonbasic variable in row 0 has a positive coefficient, choose the variable with the "most positive" coefficient in row 0 to enter the basis.

This modification of the simplex algorithm works because increasing a nonbasic variable with a positive cofficient in row 0 will *decrease z*. If we use this method to solve LP 2, our initial tableau will be as shown in Table 10. Since x_2 has the most positive coefficient in row 0, we enter x_2 into the basis. The ratio test says that x_2 should enter the basis in the first constraint. The resulting tableau is given in Table 11. Since each

Table 10
Initial Tableau for
LP 2—Method 2

z	x_1	x_2	s_1	s_2	rhs	BASIC VARIABLE	RATIO
1	-2	3	0	0	0	$z = 0$	
0	1	①	1	0	4	$s_1 = 4$	$\frac{4}{1} = 4*$
0	1	-1	0	1	6	$s_2 = 6$	None

Table 11
Optimal Tableau for
LP 2—Method 2

z	x_1	x_2	s_1	s_2	rhs	BASIC VARIABLE
1	-5	0	-3	0	-12	$z = -12$
0	1	1	1	0	4	$x_2 = 4$
0	2	0	1	1	10	$s_2 = 10$

variable in row 0 has a nonpositive coefficient, this is an optimal tableau.[†] Thus, the optimal solution to LP 2 is (as we have already seen) $z = -12$, $x_2 = 4$, $s_2 = 10$, $x_1 = s_1 = 0$.

◆ PROBLEMS

GROUP A

1. Use the simplex algorithm to find the optimal solution to the following LP:

$$\min z = 4x_1 - x_2$$
$$\text{s.t.} \quad 2x_1 + x_2 \le 8$$
$$x_2 \le 5$$
$$x_1 - x_2 \le 4$$
$$x_1, x_2 \ge 0$$

2. Use the simplex algorithm to find the optimal solution to the following LP:

$$\min z = -x_1 - x_2$$
$$\text{s.t.} \quad x_1 - x_2 \le 1$$
$$x_1 + x_2 \le 2$$
$$x_1, x_2 \ge 0$$

4-5   ALTERNATIVE OPTIMAL SOLUTIONS

Recall from Example 3 of Section 3.3 that for some LPs, more than one extreme point is optimal. If an LP has more than one optimal solution, we say that it has multiple or **alternative optimal solutions.** We show now how the simplex algorithm can be used to determine whether an LP has alternative optimal solutions.

Reconsider the Dakota Furniture example of Section 4.3, with the modification that tables sell for $35 instead of $30 (see Table 12). Since x_1 has the most negative coefficient in row 0, we enter x_1 into the basis. The ratio test indicates that x_1 should be entered in row 3 (see Table 13). Since only x_3 now has a negative coefficient in row 0, we enter x_3 into the basis. The ratio test indicates that x_3 should enter the basis in row 2. The resulting tableau is given in Table 14, an optimal tableau. As in Section 4.3, this tableau indicates that the optimal solution to the Dakota Furniture problem is $s_1 = 24$, $x_3 = 8$, $x_1 = 2$, $s_4 = 5$, and $x_2 = s_2 = s_3 = 0$.

Recall that all basic variables must have a zero coefficient in row 0 (or else they wouldn't be basic variables). However, in our optimal tableau, there is a nonbasic variable, x_2, which also has a zero coefficient in row 0. Let us see what happens if we enter

Table 12	z	x_1	x_2	x_3	s_1	s_2	s_3	s_4	rhs	BASIC VARIABLE	RATIO
Initial Tableau for Dakota Furniture Example ($35/Table)	1	-60	-35	-20	0	0	0	0	0	$z = 0$	
	0	8	6	1	1	0	0	0	48	$s_1 = 48$	$\frac{48}{8} = 6$
	0	4	2	1.5	0	1	0	0	20	$s_2 = 20$	$\frac{20}{4} = 5$
	0	②	1.5	0.5	0	0	1	0	8	$s_3 = 8$	$\frac{8}{2} = 4^*$
	0	0	1	0	0	0	0	1	5	$s_4 = 5$	None

[†]To see that this tableau is optimal, note that from row 0, $z = -12 + 5x_1 + 3s_1$. Since $x_1 \ge 0$ and $s_1 \ge 0$, this shows that $z \ge -12$. Thus, the current bfs (which has $z = -12$) must be optimal.

Table 13
First Tableau for
Dakota Furniture
Example ($35/Table)

z	x_1	x_2	x_3	s_1	s_2	s_3	s_4	rhs	BASIC VARIABLE	RATIO
1	0	10	-5	0	0	30	0	240	$z = 240$	
0	0	0	-1	1	0	-4	0	16	$s_1 = 16$	None
0	0	-1	(0.5)	0	1	-2	0	4	$s_2 = 4$	$\frac{4}{0.5} = 8^*$
0	1	0.75	0.25	0	0	0.5	0	4	$x_1 = 4$	$\frac{4}{0.25} = 16$
0	0	1	0	0	0	0	1	5	$s_4 = 5$	None

Table 14
Second (and
Optimal) Tableau for
Dakota Furniture
Example ($35/Table)

z	x_1	x_2	x_3	s_1	s_2	s_3	s_4	rhs	BASIC VARIABLE
1	0	0	0	0	10	10	0	280	$z = 280$
0	0	-2	0	1	2	-8	0	24	$s_1 = 24$
0	0	-2	1	0	2	-4	0	8	$x_3 = 8$
0	1	(1.25)	0	0	-0.5	1.5	0	2	$x_1 = 2^*$
0	0	1	0	0	0	0	1	5	$s_4 = 5$

x_2 into the basis. The ratio test indicates that x_2 should enter the basis in row 3 (check this). The resulting tableau is given in Table 15. The important thing to notice is that *because x_2 has a zero coefficient in the optimal tableau's row 0, the pivot that enters x_2 into the basis does not change row 0.* This means that all variables in our new row 0 will still have nonnegative coefficients. Thus, our new tableau (Table 15) is also an optimal tableau. Since the pivot has not changed the value of z, an alternative optimal solution for the Dakota example is $z = 280$, $s_1 = 27.2$, $x_3 = 11.2$, $x_2 = 1.6$, $s_4 = 3.4$, and $x_1 = s_3 = s_2 = 0$.

In summary, if tables sell for $35, Dakota can obtain $280 in sales revenue by manufacturing 2 desks and 8 chairs or by manufacturing 1.6 tables and 11.2 chairs. Thus, Dakota has multiple (or alternative) optimal extreme points.

As stated in Chapter 3, it can be shown that any point on the line segment joining two optimal extreme points will also be optimal. To illustrate this idea, let's write our two optimal extreme points:

$$\text{Optimal extreme point 1} = \begin{bmatrix} x_1 \\ x_2 \\ x_3 \end{bmatrix} = \begin{bmatrix} 2 \\ 0 \\ 8 \end{bmatrix}$$

$$\text{Optimal extreme point 2} = \begin{bmatrix} x_1 \\ x_2 \\ x_3 \end{bmatrix} = \begin{bmatrix} 0 \\ 1.6 \\ 11.2 \end{bmatrix}$$

Thus, for $0 \le c \le 1$,

$$\begin{bmatrix} x_1 \\ x_2 \\ x_3 \end{bmatrix} = c \begin{bmatrix} 2 \\ 0 \\ 8 \end{bmatrix} + (1 - c) \begin{bmatrix} 0 \\ 1.6 \\ 11.2 \end{bmatrix} = \begin{bmatrix} 2c \\ 1.6 - 1.6c \\ 11.2 - 3.2c \end{bmatrix}$$

Table 15
Another Optimal
Tableau for Dakota
Furniture Example
($35/Table)

z	x_1	x_2	x_3	s_1	s_2	s_3	s_4	rhs	BASIC VARIABLE
1	0	0	0	0	10	10	0	280	$z = 280$
0	1.6	0	0	1	1.2	−5.6	0	27.2	$s_1 = 27.2$
0	1.6	0	1	0	1.2	−1.6	0	11.2	$x_3 = 11.2$
0	0.8	1	0	0	−0.4	1.2	0	1.6	$x_2 = 1.6$
0	−0.8	0	0	0	0.4	−1.2	1	3.4	$s_4 = 3.4$

will be optimal. This shows that although the Dakota Furniture example has only two optimal extreme points, there are an infinite number of optimal solutions to the Dakota problem. For example, by choosing $c = 0.5$, we obtain the optimal solution $x_1 = 1$, $x_2 = 0.8$, $x_3 = 9.6$.

If there is no nonbasic variable with a zero coefficient in row 0 of the optimal tableau, the LP has a unique optimal solution (see Problem 3). Even if there is a nonbasic variable with a zero coefficient in row 0 of the optimal tableau, it is possible that the LP may not have alternative optimal solutions (see Review Problem 25).

♦ PROBLEMS

GROUP A

1. Show that if a toy soldier sold for $28, the Giapetto problem would have alternative optimal solutions.

2. Show that the following LP has alternative optimal solutions; find three of them.

$$\max z = -3x_1 + 6x_2$$
$$\text{s.t.} \quad 5x_1 + 7x_2 \le 35$$
$$-x_1 + 2x_2 \le 2$$
$$x_1, x_2 \ge 0$$

GROUP B

3. Suppose you have found this optimal tableau (Table 16) for a maximization problem. Use the fact that each nonbasic variable has a strictly positive coefficient in row 0 to show that $x_1 = 4$, $x_2 = 3$, $s_1 = s_2 = 0$ is the unique optimal solution to this LP. (*Hint:* Can any extreme point having $s_1 > 0$ or $s_2 > 0$ have $z = 10$?)

Table 16

z	x_1	x_2	s_1	s_2	rhs
1	0	0	2	3	10
0	1	0	3	2	4
0	0	1	1	1	3

4. Explain why the set of optimal solutions to an LP is a convex set.

5. Consider an LP with the optimal tableau shown in Table 17.

Table 17

z	x_1	x_2	x_3	x_4	rhs
1	0	0	0	2	2
0	1	0	−1	1	2
0	0	1	−2	3	3

(a) Does this LP have more than one bfs that is optimal?
(b) How many optimal solutions does this LP have? (*Hint:* If the value of x_3 is increased, how does this change the values of the basic variables and the z-value?)

4-6   UNBOUNDED LPs

Recall from Section 3.3 that for some LPs, there exist points in the feasible region for which z assumes arbitrarily large (in max problems) or arbitrarily small (in min problems) values. When this situation occurs, we say the LP is unbounded. In this section, we show how the simplex algorithm can be used to determine whether an LP is unbounded.

E X A M P L E 3

Breadco Bakeries bakes two kinds of bread: french bread and sourdough bread. Each loaf of french bread can be sold for 36¢, and each loaf of sourdough bread can be sold for 30¢. A loaf of french bread requires 1 yeast packet and 6 oz of flour, and a loaf of sourdough bread requires 1 yeast packet and 5 oz of flour. At present, Breadco has 5 yeast packets and 10 oz of flour. Additional yeast packets can be purchased at 3¢ each, and additional flour can be purchased at 4¢/oz. Formulate and solve an LP that can be used to maximize Breadco's profits (= revenues − costs).

Solution   Define

$$x_1 = \text{number of loaves of french bread baked}$$
$$x_2 = \text{number of loaves of sourdough bread baked}$$
$$x_3 = \text{number of yeast packets purchased}$$
$$x_4 = \text{number of ounces of flour purchased}$$

Then Breadco's objective is to maximize $z = $ revenues − costs, where

$$\text{Revenues} = 36x_1 + 30x_2 \quad \text{and} \quad \text{Costs} = 3x_3 + 4x_4$$

Thus, Breadco's objective function is

$$\max z = 36x_1 + 30x_2 - 3x_3 - 4x_4$$

Breadco faces the following two constraints:

Constraint 1 Number of yeast packages used to bake bread cannot exceed available yeast plus purchased yeast.

Constraint 2 Ounces of flour used to bake breads cannot exceed available flour plus purchased flour.

Since

$$\text{Available yeast} + \text{purchased yeast} = 5 + x_3$$
$$\text{Available flour} + \text{purchased flour} = 10 + x_4$$

Constraint 1 may be written as

$$x_1 + x_2 \le 5 + x_3 \quad \text{or} \quad x_1 + x_2 - x_3 \le 5$$

and Constraint 2 may be written as

$$6x_1 + 5x_2 \le 10 + x_4 \quad \text{or} \quad 6x_1 + 5x_2 - x_4 \le 10$$

Adding the sign restrictions $x_i \geq 0$ $(i = 1, 2, 3, 4)$ yields the following LP:

$$\max z = 36x_1 + 30x_2 - 3x_3 - 4x_4$$
$$\text{s.t.} \quad x_1 + x_2 - x_3 \qquad \leq 5 \qquad \text{(Yeast constraint)}$$
$$6x_1 + 5x_2 \qquad - x_4 \leq 10 \qquad \text{(Flour constraint)}$$
$$x_1, x_2, x_3, x_4 \geq 0$$

Adding slack variables s_1 and s_2 to the two constraints, we obtain the tableau in Table 18.

Table 18
Initial Tableau for Breadco Example

z	x_1	x_2	x_3	x_4	s_1	s_2	rhs	BASIC VARIABLE	RATIO
1	-36	-30	3	4	0	0	0	$z = 0$	
0	1	1	-1	0	1	0	5	$s_1 = 5$	$\frac{5}{1} = 5$
0	⑥	5	0	-1	0	1	10	$s_2 = 10$	$\frac{10}{6} = \frac{5}{3}*$

Since $-36 < -30$, we enter x_1 into the basis. The ratio test indicates that x_1 should enter the basis in row 2. Entering x_1 into the basis in row 2 yields the tableau in Table 19. Since x_4 has the only negative coefficient in row 0, we enter x_4 into the basis. The ratio test indicates that x_4 should enter the basis in row 1. The resulting tableau is given in Table 20. Since x_3 has the most negative coefficient in row 0, we would like to enter x_3 into the basis. The ratio test, however, fails to indicate the row in which x_3 should enter the basis. What is happening? Going back to the basic ideas that led us to the ratio test, we see that as x_3 is increased (holding the other nonbasic variables at zero), the current basic variables, x_4 and x_1, change as follows:

$$x_4 = 20 + 6x_3 \tag{13}$$
$$x_1 = 5 + x_3 \tag{14}$$

As x_3 is increased, both x_4 and x_1 increase. This means that no matter how large we make x_3, the inequalities $x_4 \geq 0$ and $x_1 \geq 0$ will still be true. Since each unit by which we increase x_3 will increase z by 9, we can find points in the feasible region for which z

Table 19
First Tableau for Breadco Example

z	x_1	x_2	x_3	x_4	s_1	s_2	rhs	BASIC VARIABLE	RATIO
1	0	0	3	-2	0	6	60	$z = 60$	
0	0	$\frac{1}{6}$	-1	⑥̄	1	$-\frac{1}{6}$	$\frac{10}{3}$	$s_1 = \frac{10}{3}$	$(\frac{10}{3})/(\frac{1}{6}) = 20*$
0	1	$\frac{5}{6}$	0	$-\frac{1}{6}$	0	$\frac{1}{6}$	$\frac{5}{3}$	$x_1 = \frac{5}{3}$	None

Table 20
Second Tableau for Breadco Example

z	x_1	x_2	x_3	x_4	s_1	s_2	rhs	BASIC VARIABLE	RATIO
1	0	2	-9	0	12	4	100	$z = 100$	
0	0	1	-6	1	6	-1	20	$x_4 = 20$	None
0	1	1	-1	0	1	0	5	$x_1 = 5$	None

assumes an arbitrarily large value. For example, can we find a feasible point with $z \geq 1000$? To do this, we need to increase z by $1000 - 100 = 900$. Since each unit by which x_3 is increased will increase z by 9, increasing x_3 by $\frac{900}{9} = 100$ should give us $z = 1000$. If we set $x_3 = 100$ (and hold the other nonbasic variables at zero), then (13) and (14) show that x_4 and x_1 must now equal

$$x_4 = 20 + 6(100) = 620$$
$$x_1 = 5 + 100 = 105$$

Thus, $x_1 = 105$, $x_3 = 100$, $x_4 = 620$, $x_2 = 0$ is a point in the feasible region with $z = 1000$. In a similar fashion, we can find points in the feasible region having arbitrarily large z-values. This means that Breadco problem is an unbounded LP.   ◆

From the Breadco example, we see that an unbounded LP occurs in a max problem if there is a nonbasic variable with a negative coefficient in row 0 and there is no constraint that limits how large we can make the nonbasic variable. This situation will occur if a nonbasic variable (such as x_3) has a negative coefficient in row 0 and nonpositive coefficients in each constraint. To summarize, *an unbounded LP for a max problem occurs when a variable with a negative coefficient in row 0 has a nonpositive coefficient in each constraint.*

If an LP is unbounded, one will eventually come to a tableau where one wants to enter a variable (such as x_3) into the basis, but the ratio test will fail. This is probably the easiest way to spot an unbounded LP.

As we noted in Chapter 3, an unbounded LP is usually caused by an incorrect formulation. In the Breadco example, we obtained an unbounded LP because we allowed Breadco to pay $3 + 6(4) = 27¢$ for the ingredients in a loaf of french bread and then sell a loaf of french bread for 36¢. Thus, each loaf of french bread earns a profit of 9¢. Since unlimited purchases of yeast and flour are allowed, it is clear that our model allows Breadco to manufacture as much french bread as it desires, thereby earning arbitrarily large profits. This is the cause of the unbounded LP.

Of course, our formulation of the Breadco example ignored several aspects of reality. First, we assumed that demand for Breadco's products is unlimited. Second, we ignored the fact that certain resources to make bread (such as ovens and labor) are in limited supply. Finally, we made the unrealistic assumption that unlimited quantities of yeast and flour could be purchased.

◆ PROBLEMS

GROUP A

1. Show that the following LP is unbounded:

$$\max z = 2x_2$$
$$\text{s.t.} \quad x_1 - x_2 \leq 4$$
$$-x_1 + x_2 \leq 1$$
$$x_1, x_2 \geq 0$$

Find a point in the feasible region with $z \geq 10{,}000$.

2. State a rule that can be used to determine if a min problem has an unbounded optimal solution (that is, z can be made arbitrarily small). Use the rule to show that

$$\min z = -2x_1 - 3x_2$$
$$\text{s.t.} \quad x_1 - x_2 \leq 1$$
$$x_1 - 2x_2 \leq 2$$
$$x_1, x_2 \geq 0$$

is an unbounded LP.

3. Suppose that in solving an LP, we obtain the tableau in Table 21. Although x_1 can enter the basis, this LP is unbounded. Why?

4. Use the simplex method to solve Problem 10 of Section 3.3.

Table 21

z	x_1	x_2	x_3	x_4	rhs
1	-3	-2	0	0	0
0	1	-1	1	0	3
0	2	0	0	1	4

4-7   THE LINDO COMPUTER PACKAGE

LINDO (Linear Interactive and Discrete Optimizer) was developed by Linus Schrage (1986). It is a user-friendly computer package that can be used to solve linear, integer, and quadratic programming problems.[†] The Appendix to this chapter gives a brief explanation of how LINDO can be used to solve LPs. In this section, we explain how the information on a LINDO printout is related to our discussion of the simplex algorithm.

We begin by discussing the LINDO output for the Dakota Furniture example (see Figure 3). We take advantage of the fact that LINDO allows the user to name the

Figure 3
LINDO Output for
Dakota Furniture
Example

```
MAX     60 DESKS + 30 TABLES + 20 CHAIRS
SUBJECT TO
     2)    8 DESKS + 6 TABLES + CHAIRS <=   48
     3)    4 DESKS + 2 TABLES + 1.5 CHAIRS <=   20
     4)    2 DESKS + 1.5 TABLES + 0.5 CHAIRS <=   8
     5)    TABLES <=   5
END

   LP OPTIMUM FOUND  AT STEP     2

       OBJECTIVE FUNCTION VALUE

  1)      280.000000

VARIABLE        VALUE         REDUCED COST
   DESKS        2.000000        0.000000
   TABLES       0.000000        5.000000
   CHAIRS       8.000000        0.000000

   ROW     SLACK OR SURPLUS     DUAL PRICES
    2)        24.000000          0.000000
    3)         0.000000         10.000000
    4)         0.000000         10.000000
    5)         5.000000          0.000000

NO. ITERATIONS=     2

RANGES IN WHICH THE BASIS IS UNCHANGED

                    OBJ COEFFICIENT RANGES
VARIABLE       CURRENT       ALLOWABLE      ALLOWABLE
                COEF         INCREASE       DECREASE
   DESKS      60.000000      20.000000      4.000000
   TABLES     30.000000       5.000000      INFINITY
   CHAIRS     20.000000       2.500000      5.000000

                    RIGHTHAND SIDE RANGES
   ROW         CURRENT       ALLOWABLE      ALLOWABLE
                RHS          INCREASE       DECREASE
    2         48.000000      INFINITY       24.000000
    3         20.000000       4.000000      4.000000
    4          8.000000       2.000000      1.333333
    5          5.000000      INFINITY       5.000000
```

[†]See Chapter 9 for a discussion of integer programming and Chapter 12 for a discussion of quadratic programming.

variables by defining

$$\text{DESKS} = \text{number of desks produced}$$
$$\text{TABLES} = \text{number of tables produced}$$
$$\text{CHAIRS} = \text{number of chairs produced}$$

Then the Dakota formulation in the first block of Figure 3 is

max	60 DESKS + 30 TABLES + 20 CHAIRS	(Row 1)	
s.t.	8 DESKS + 6 TABLES + CHAIRS ≤ 48	(Row 2)	(Lumber constraint)
	4 DESKS + 2 TABLES + 1.5 CHAIRS ≤ 20	(Row 3)	(Finishing constraint)
	2 DESKS + 1.5 TABLES + 0.5 CHAIRS ≤ 8	(Row 4)	(Carpentry constraint)
	TABLES ≤ 5	(Row 5)	

$$\text{DESKS, TABLES, CHAIRS} \geq 0$$

(LINDO assumes that all variables are nonnegative, so the nonnegativity constraints need not be inputted to the computer.) To be consistent with LINDO, we have labeled the objective function row 1 and the constraints rows 2–5.

Looking now at the LINDO output in the next two blocks of Figure 3, we see

LP OPTIMUM FOUND AT STEP 2

This indicates that LINDO found the optimal solution after two iterations (or pivots) of the simplex algorithm.

OBJECTIVE FUNCTION VALUE 280.000000

This indicates that the optimal z-value is 280.

VALUE

For each variable, the Value column gives the value of the variable in the optimal LP solution. Thus, the optimal solution calls for Dakota to produce 2 desks, 0 tables, and 8 chairs.

SLACK OR SURPLUS

For each constraint, the Slack or Surplus column gives the value of the slack or excess ("surplus variable" is another name for excess variable) in the optimal solution. Thus,

$$s_1 = \text{slack for row 2 on LINDO output} = 24$$
$$s_2 = \text{slack for row 3 on LINDO output} = 0$$
$$s_3 = \text{slack for row 4 on LINDO output} = 0$$
$$s_4 = \text{slack for row 5 on LINDO output} = 5$$

REDUCED COST

For each variable (in a max problem), this column gives the coefficient of the variable in row 0 of the optimal tableau. As discussed in Section 4.3, the reduced cost for each basic variable must be zero. For a nonbasic variable x_j, the reduced cost is the amount by which the optimal z-value is decreased if x_j is increased by 1 unit (and all other nonbasic variables remain equal to zero). In the LINDO output for the Dakota problem, the reduced cost is zero for each of the basic variables (DESKS and CHAIRS). Also, the reduced cost for TABLES is 5. This means that if Dakota were forced to produce a table, revenue would decrease by $5. The interpretation of DUAL PRICES, OBJ COEFFICIENT RANGES, and RIGHTHAND SIDE RANGES of the LINDO output are discussed in Chapters 5 and 6.

For a minimization problem, the LP Optimum, Objective Function Value, and Slack and Surplus columns are interpreted as described. In a minimization problem, the reduced cost for a variable is $-$(coefficient of variable in optimal row 0). Thus, in a min problem, the reduced cost for a basic variable will again be zero, but the reduced cost for a nonbasic variable x_j will be the amount by which the optimal z-value increases if x_j is increased by 1 unit (and all other nonbasic variables remain equal to zero).

To illustrate the interpretation of the LINDO output for a minimization problem, let's look at the LINDO output for the diet problem of Section 3.4 (see Figure 4). If we let

$$BR = \text{brownies eaten daily}$$
$$IC = \text{scoops of chocolate ice cream eaten daily}$$
$$COLA = \text{number of bottles of soda drunk daily}$$
$$PC = \text{pieces of pineapple cheesecake eaten daily}$$

Figure 4
LINDO Output for
Diet Example

```
MIN     50 BR + 20 IC + 30 COLA + 80 PC
SUBJECT TO
    2)    400 BR + 200 IC + 150 COLA + 500 PC >=    500
    3)    3 BR + 2 IC >=   6
    4)    2 BR + 2 IC + 4 COLA + 4 PC >=   10
    5)    2 BR + 4 IC +  COLA + 5 PC >=   8
END

    LP OPTIMUM FOUND  AT STEP    5

        OBJECTIVE FUNCTION VALUE

 1)      90.0000000

    VARIABLE        VALUE         REDUCED COST
          BR       0.000000         27.500000
          IC       3.000000          0.000000
        COLA       1.000000          0.000000
          PC       0.000000         50.000000

    ROW      SLACK OR SURPLUS    DUAL PRICES
     2)       250.000000          0.000000
     3)         0.000000         -2.500000
     4)         0.000000         -7.500000
     5)         5.000000          0.000000

NO. ITERATIONS=        5

    RANGES IN WHICH THE BASIS IS UNCHANGED

                        OBJ COEFFICIENT RANGES
    VARIABLE       CURRENT        ALLOWABLE        ALLOWABLE
                    COEF          INCREASE         DECREASE
          BR     50.000000        INFINITY        27.500000
          IC     20.000000       18.333334         5.000000
        COLA     30.000000       10.000000        30.000000
          PC     80.000000        INFINITY        50.000000

                        RIGHTHAND SIDE RANGES
    ROW          CURRENT        ALLOWABLE        ALLOWABLE
                   RHS          INCREASE         DECREASE
     2         500.000000      250.000000        INFINITY
     3           6.000000        4.000000         2.857143
     4          10.000000        INFINITY         4.000000
     5           8.000000        5.000000         INFINITY
```

then the diet problem may be formulated as

$$\min \quad 50\,BR + 20\,IC + 30\,COLA + 80\,PC$$

$$
\begin{array}{llll}
\text{s.t.} & 400\,BR + 200\,IC + 150\,COLA + 500\,PC \geq 500 & \text{(Calorie constraint)} \\
& 3\,BR + 2\,IC \qquad\qquad\qquad\qquad\qquad \geq 6 & \text{(Chocolate constraint)} \\
& 2\,BR + 2\,IC + 4\,COLA + 4\,PC \geq 10 & \text{(Sugar constraint)} \\
& 2\,BR + 4\,IC + COLA + 5\,PC \geq 8 & \text{(Fat constraint)} \\
& \quad BR,\ IC,\ COLA,\ PC \geq 0
\end{array}
$$

The Value column shows that the optimal solution is to eat three scoops of chocolate ice cream daily and drink 1 bottle of soda daily. The Objective Function Value on the LINDO output indicates that the cost of this diet is 90¢. The Slack or Surplus column shows that the first constraint (calories) has an excess of 250 calories and that the fourth constraint (fat) has an excess of 5 oz. Thus, the calorie and fat constraints are nonbinding. The chocolate and sugar constraints have no excess and are therefore binding constraints.

From the Reduced Cost column, we see that if we were forced to eat a brownie (while keeping $PC = 0$), the minimum cost of the daily diet would increase by 27.5¢, and if we were forced to eat a piece of pineapple cheesecake (while holding $BR = 0$), the minimum cost of the daily diet would increase by 50¢.

4-8　MATRIX GENERATORS AND SCALING OF LPs

Many LPs solved in practice contain thousands of constraints and thousands of decision variables. Very few users of linear programming would want to input the constraints and objective function each time such an LP is to be solved. For this reason, most actual applications of LP use a **matrix generator** to simplify the inputting of the LP. A matrix generator allows the user to input the relevant parameters that determine the LP's objective function and constraints; it then generates the LP formulation from that information. For example, let's consider the Sailco example from Section 3.10. If we were dealing with a planning horizon of 200 periods, this problem would involve 400 constraints and 600 decision variables—clearly too many for convenient input. A matrix generator for this problem would require the user to input only the following information: cost of producing a sailboat with regular time labor for each period, cost of producing a sailboat with overtime labor for each period, demand for each period, and holding cost for each period. From this information, the matrix generator would generate the LP's objective function and constraints. Then the matrix generator would call up an LP software package (such as LINDO) and solve the problem. Finally, an output analyzer would be written to display the output in a user-friendly format.

We close our discussion of computer packages by noting that an LP package may have trouble solving LPs in which there are nonzero coefficients that are either very small or very large in absolute value. If such coefficients are present, LINDO will respond with a message that the LP is poorly scaled. The LINDO manual recommends that the user define the units of the objective function, right-hand sides, and decision variables so that no nonzero coefficients have absolute values of more than 100,000 or less than 0.0001.

◆ PROBLEM

1. A company produces three products. The per-unit profit, labor usage, and pollution produced per unit are given in Table 22. At most 3 million labor hours can be used to produce the three products, and government regulations require that the company produce at most 2 lb of pollution. If we let x_i = units produced of product i, then the appropriate LP is

$$\max z = 6x_1 + 4x_2 + 3x_3$$

s.t.
$$4x_1 + 3x_2 + 2x_3 \leq 3,000,000$$
$$0.000003x_1 + 0.000002x_2 + 0.000001x_3 \leq 2$$
$$x_1, x_2, x_3 \geq 0$$

(a) Explain why this LP is poorly scaled.

(b) Eliminate the scaling problem by redefining the units of the objective function, decision variables, and right-hand sides.

Table 22

	PROFIT	LABOR USAGE	POLLUTION
Product 1	$6	4 hours	0.000003 lb
Product 2	$4	3 hours	0.000002 lb
Product 3	$3	2 hours	0.000001 lb

4-9

DEGENERACY AND THE CONVERGENCE OF THE SIMPLEX ALGORITHM

Theoretically, the simplex algorithm (as we have described it) can fail to find the optimal solution to an LP. However, LPs arising from actual applications seldom exhibit this unpleasant behavior. For the sake of completeness, however, we now discuss the type of situation in which the simplex can fail. Our discussion depends crucially on the following relationship (for a max problem) between the z-value for the current bfs and the z-value for the new bfs (that is, the bfs after the next pivot):

z-value for new bfs = z-value of current bfs

$\qquad$ − (value of entering variable in new bfs)(coefficient   **(15)**
$\qquad$ of entering variable in row 0 of current bfs)

Eq. (15) follows, because each unit by which the entering variable is increased will increase z by − (coefficient of entering variable in row 0 of current bfs). Recall that (coefficient of entering variable in row 0) < 0 and (value of entering variable in new bfs) ≥ 0. Combining these facts with (15), we can deduce the following facts:

1. If (value of entering variable in new bfs) > 0, then (z-value for new bfs) > (z-value of current bfs).

2. If (value of entering variable in new bfs) = 0, then (z-value for new bfs) = (z-value for current bfs).

For the moment, assume that the LP we are solving has the following property: In each of the LP's basic feasible solutions, all the basic variables are positive (positive means > 0). An LP with this property is a **nondegenerate LP**.

If we are using the simplex to solve a nondegenerate LP, fact 1 in the foregoing list tells us that each iteration of the simplex will *increase* z. This implies that when the simplex is used to solve a nondegenerate LP, it is impossible to encounter the same bfs twice. To see this, suppose that we are at a basic feasible solution (call it bfs 1) that has $z = 20$. Fact 1 shows that our next pivot will take us to a bfs (call it bfs 2) and has $z > 20$. Since no future pivot can decrease z, we can never return to a bfs having $z = 20$. Thus, we can never return to bfs 1. Now recall that every LP has only a finite number of basic feasible solutions. Since we can never repeat a bfs, this argument shows that when we use the simplex algorithm to solve a nondegenerate LP, we are guaranteed to find the optimal solution in a finite number of iterations. For example, suppose we are solving a nondegenerate LP with 10 variables and 5 constraints. Such an LP has at most

$$\binom{10}{5} = 252$$

basic feasible solutions. Since we will never repeat a bfs, we know that for this problem, the simplex is guaranteed to find an optimal solution after at most 252 pivots.

However, the simplex may fail for a degenerate LP.

DEFINITION ■ An LP is **degenerate** if it has at least one bfs in which a basic variable is equal to zero.

The following LP is degenerate:

$$\max z = 5x_1 + 2x_2$$
$$\text{s.t.} \quad x_1 + x_2 \le 6$$
$$x_1 - x_2 \le 0 \tag{16}$$
$$x_1, x_2 \ge 0$$

What happens when we use the simplex algorithm to solve (16)? After adding slack variables s_1 and s_2 to the two constraints, we obtain the initial tableau in Table 23. In this bfs, the basic variable $s_2 = 0$. Thus, (16) is a degenerate LP. Any bfs that has at least one basic variable equal to zero (or equivalently, at least one constraint with a zero right-hand side) is a **degenerate bfs**. Since $-5 < -2$, we enter x_1 into the basis. The winning ratio is zero. This means that after x_1 enters the basis, x_1 will equal zero in the new bfs. After doing the pivot, we obtain the tableau in Table 24. Our new bfs has the same z-value as the old bfs. This is consistent with fact 2. In the new bfs, all variables have exactly the same values as they had before the pivot! Thus, our new bfs is also degenerate. Continuing with the simplex, we enter x_2 in row 1. The resulting tableau is

Table 23
A Degenerate LP

z	x_1	x_2	s_1	s_2	rhs	BASIC VARIABLE	RATIO
1	-5	-2	0	0	0	$z = 0$	
0	1	1	1	0	6	$s_1 = 6$	6
0	①	-1	0	1	0	$s_2 = 0$	0*

Table 24
First Tableau for (16)

z	x_1	x_2	s_1	s_2	rhs	BASIC VARIABLE	RATIO
1	0	−7	0	5	0	$z = 0$	
0	0	②	1	−1	6	$s_1 = 6$	$\frac{6}{2} = 3^*$
0	1	−1	0	1	0	$x_1 = 0$	None

shown in Table 25. This is an optimal tableau, so the optimal solution to (16) is $z = 21$, $x_2 = 3$, $x_1 = 3$, $s_1 = s_2 = 0$.

We can now explain why the simplex may have problems in solving a degenerate LP. Suppose we are solving a degenerate LP for which the optimal z-value is $z = 30$. If we begin with a bfs that has, say, $z = 20$, we know (look at the LP we just solved) that it is possible for a pivot to leave the value of z unchanged. This means that it is possible for a sequence of pivots like the following to occur:

$$\text{Initial bfs (bfs 1): } z = 20$$
$$\text{After first pivot (bfs 2): } z = 20$$
$$\text{After second pivot (bfs 3): } z = 20$$
$$\text{After third pivot (bfs 4): } z = 20$$
$$\text{After fourth pivot (bfs 1): } z = 20$$

In this situation, we encounter the same bfs twice. This occurrence is called **cycling**. If cycling occurs, we will loop around forever, or cycle, among a set of basic feasible solutions and never get to the optimal solution ($z = 30$, in our example). Cycling can indeed occur (see Problem 3 at the end of this section). Fortunately, the simplex algorithm can be modified to ensure that cycling will never occur (see Bland (1977) or Dantzig (1963) for details).[†] In practice, however, cycling is an extremely rare occurrence.[‡] For this reason, most LP computer codes do not defend against the possibility of cycling.

If an LP has many degenerate basic feasible solutions (or a bfs with many basic variables equal to zero), the simplex algorithm is often very inefficient. To see why, look at the feasible region for (16) in Figure 5, which is the shaded triangle BCD. The extreme points of the feasible region in Figure 5 are B, C, and D. Following the procedure

Table 25
Optimal Tableau for (16)

z	x_1	x_2	s_1	s_2	rhs	BASIC VARIABLE
1	0	0	3.5	1.5	21	$z = 21$
0	0	1	0.5	−0.5	3	$x_2 = 3$
0	1	0	0.5	0.5	3	$x_1 = 3$

[†]Bland showed that cycling can be avoided by applying the following rules (assume that slack and excess variables are numbered $x_{n+1}, x_{n+2}, \ldots$):
  1. Choose as the entering variable (in a max problem) the variable with a negative coefficient in row 0 that has the smallest subscript.
  2. If there is a tie in the ratio test, break the tie by choosing the winner of the ratio test so that the variable leaving the basis has the smallest subscript.
[‡]For a practical example of cycling, see Kotiah and Slater (1973).

Figure 5
Feasible Region for
the LP (16)

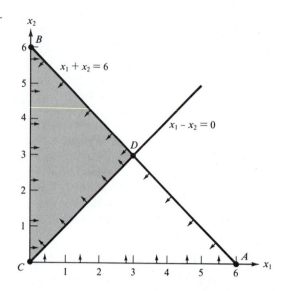

outlined in Section 4.2, let's look at the correspondence between the basic feasible solutions to (16) and the extreme points of its feasible region (see Table 26). Three sets of basic variables correspond to extreme point C. It can be shown that for an LP with n decision variables to be degenerate, $n + 1$ or more of the LP's constraints (including the sign restrictions $x_i \geq 0$ as constraints) must be binding at an extreme point.

Table 26
Three Sets of Basic
Variables
Correspond to
Corner Point C

BASIC VARIABLES	BASIC FEASIBLE SOLUTION	CORRESPONDS TO EXTREME POINT
x_1, x_2	$x_1 = x_2 = 3$, $s_1 = s_2 = 0$	D
x_1, s_1	$x_1 = 0$, $s_1 = 6$, $x_2 = s_2 = 0$	C
x_1, s_2	$x_1 = 6$, $s_2 = -6$, $x_2 = s_1 = 0$	Infeasible
x_2, s_1	$x_2 = 0$, $s_1 = 6$, $x_1 = s_2 = 0$	C
x_2, s_2	$x_2 = 6$, $s_2 = 6$, $s_1 = x_1 = 0$	B
s_1, s_2	$s_1 = 6$, $s_2 = 0$, $x_1 = x_2 = 0$	C

In (16), the constraints $x_1 - x_2 \leq 0$, $x_1 \geq 0$, and $x_2 \geq 0$ are all binding at point C. Each extreme point at which three or more constraints are binding will correspond to more than one set of basic variables. For example, at point C, s_1 must be one of the basic variables, but the other basic variable may be x_2, x_1, or s_2.

We can now discuss why the simplex algorithm often is an inefficient method for solving degenerate LPs. Suppose an LP is degenerate. Then there may be many sets (maybe hundreds) of basic variables corresponding to some nonoptimal extreme point. The simplex algorithm might encounter all these sets of basic variables before it finds that it was at a nonoptimal extreme point. This problem was illustrated (on a small scale) in solving (16): The simplex took two pivots before it found that point C was suboptimal. Fortunately, some degenerate LPs have a special structure that enables us to solve them by methods other than the simplex (see, for example, the discussion of the assignment problem in Chapter 7).

◆ PROBLEMS

1. Even if an LP's initial tableau is nondegenerate, later tableaus may exhibit degeneracy. Degenerate tableaus often occur in the tableau following a tie in the ratio test. To illustrate this, solve the following LP:

$$\max z = 5x_1 + 3x_2$$
$$\text{s.t.} \quad 4x_1 + 2x_2 \le 12$$
$$4x_1 + x_2 \le 10$$
$$x_1 + x_2 \le 4$$
$$x_1, x_2 \ge 0$$

Also graph the feasible region and show which extreme points correspond to more than one set of basic variables.

2. Find the optimal solution to the following LP:

$$\min z = -x_1 - x_2$$
$$\text{s.t.} \quad x_1 + x_2 \le 1$$
$$-x_1 + x_2 \le 0$$
$$x_1, x_2 \ge 0$$

GROUP B

3. Show that if ties in the ratio test are broken by favoring row 1 over row 2, cycling occurs when the following LP is solved by the simplex:

$$\max z = 2x_1 + 3x_2 - x_3 - 12x_4$$
$$\text{s.t.} \quad -2x_1 - 9x_2 + x_3 + 9x_4 \le 0$$
$$\frac{x_1}{3} + x_2 - \frac{x_3}{3} - 2x_4 \le 0$$
$$x_i \ge 0 \quad (i = 1, 2, 3, 4)$$

4-10   THE BIG M METHOD

Recall that the simplex algorithm requires a starting bfs. In all the problems we have solved so far, we found a starting bfs by using the slack variables as our basic variables. If an LP has any ≥ or equality constraints, however, a starting bfs may not be readily apparent. Example 4 will illustrate that a bfs may be hard to find. When a bfs is not readily apparent, the Big M method (or the two-phase simplex method of Section 4.11) may be used to solve the problem. In this section, we discuss the Big M method, a version of the simplex algorithm that first finds a bfs by adding "artificial" variables to the problem. The objective function of the original LP must, of course, be modified to ensure that the artificial variables are all equal to 0 at the conclusion of the simplex algorithm. The following example illustrates the Big M method.

E X A M P L E 4

Bevco manufactures an orange-flavored soft drink called Oranj by combining orange soda and orange juice. Each ounce of orange soda contains 0.5 oz of sugar and 1 mg of vitamin C. Each ounce of orange juice contains 0.25 oz of sugar and 3 mg of vitamin C. It costs Bevco 2¢ to produce an ounce of orange soda and 3¢ to produce an ounce of orange juice. Bevco's marketing department has decided that each 10-oz bottle of Oranj must contain at least 20 mg of vitamin C and at most 4 oz of sugar. Use linear programming to determine how Bevco can meet the marketing department's requirements at minimum cost.

Solution

Let

$$x_1 = \text{number of ounces of orange soda in a bottle or Oranj}$$
$$x_2 = \text{number of ounces of orange juice in a bottle of Oranj}$$

Then the appropriate LP is

$$\min z = 2x_1 + 3x_2$$

$$\text{s.t.} \quad \tfrac{1}{2}x_1 + \tfrac{1}{4}x_2 \leq 4 \qquad \text{(Sugar constraint)}$$

$$x_1 + 3x_2 \geq 20 \qquad \text{(Vitamin C constraint)} \qquad (18)$$

$$x_1 + x_2 = 10 \qquad \text{(10 oz in bottle of Oranj)}$$

$$x_1, x_2 \geq 0$$

(The solution will be continued later in this section.)

◆

To put (18) into standard form, we add a slack variable s_1 to the sugar constraint and subtract an excess variable e_2 from the vitamin C constraint. After writing the objective function as $z - 2x_1 - 3x_2 = 0$, we obtain the following standard form:

Row 0: $z - 2x_1 - 3x_2 \qquad\qquad = 0$

Row 1: $\tfrac{1}{2}x_1 + \tfrac{1}{4}x_2 + s_1 \qquad = 4$

Row 2: $x_1 + 3x_2 \qquad - e_2 = 20$

Row 3: $x_1 + x_2 \qquad\qquad = 10$

All variables nonnegative

In searching for a bfs, we see that $s_1 = 4$ could be used as a basic (and feasible) variable for row 1. If we multiply row 2 by -1, we see that $e_2 = -20$ could be used as a basic variable for row 2. Unfortunately, $e_2 = -20$ violates the sign restriction $e_2 \geq 0$. Finally, in row 3 there is no readily apparent basic variable. Thus, in order to use the simplex to solve (18), rows 2 and 3 each need a basic (and feasible) variable. To remedy this problem, we simply "invent" a basic feasible variable for each constraint that needs one. Since these variables are created by us and are not real variables, we call them **artificial variables**. If an artificial variable is added to row i, we label it a_i. In the current problem, we need to add an artificial variable a_2 to row 2 and an artificial variable a_3 to row 3. The resulting set of equations is

$$z - 2x_1 - 3x_2 \qquad\qquad\qquad = 0$$

$$\tfrac{1}{2}x_1 + \tfrac{1}{4}x_2 + s_1 \qquad\qquad = 4$$

$$x_1 + 3x_2 \qquad - e_2 + a_2 \qquad = 20 \qquad (19)$$

$$x_1 + x_2 \qquad\qquad + a_3 = 10$$

We now have a bfs: $z = 0$, $s_1 = 4$, $a_2 = 20$, $a_3 = 10$. Unfortunately, there is no guarantee that the optimal solution to (19) will be the same as the optimal solution to (18). In solving (19), we might obtain an optimal solution in which one or more artificial variables are positive. Such a solution may not be feasible in the original problem (18). For example, in solving (19), the optimal solution may easily be shown to be $z = 0$, $s_1 = 4, a_2 = 20, a_3 = 10, x_1 = x_2 = 0$. This "solution" contains no vitamin C and puts 0 ounces of soda in a bottle, so it cannot possibly solve our original problem! If the optimal solution to (19) is to solve (18), we must make sure that the optimal solution to (19) sets all artificial variables equal to zero. In a min problem, we can ensure that all the artificial variables will be zero by adding a term Ma_i to the objective function for each artificial variable a_i. (In a max problem, add a term $-Ma_i$ to the objective function.)

Here M represents a "very large" positive number. Thus, in (19), we would change our objective function to

$$\min z = 2x_1 + 3x_2 + Ma_2 + Ma_3$$

Then row 0 will change to

$$z - 2x_1 - 3x_2 - Ma_2 - Ma_3 = 0$$

Modifying the objective function in this way makes it extremely costly for an artificial variable to be positive. With this modified objective function, it seems reasonable that the optimal solution to (19) will have $a_2 = a_3 = 0$. In this case, the optimal solution to (19) will solve the original problem (18). It sometimes happens, however, that in solving the analog of (19), some of the artificial variables may assume positive values in the optimal solution. If this occurs, the original problem has no feasible solution.

For obvious reasons, the method we have just outlined is often called the Big M method. We now give a formal description of the Big M method.

DESCRIPTION OF BIG M METHOD

Step 1 Modify the constraints so that the right-hand side of each constraint is nonnegative. This requires that each constraint with a negative right-hand side be multiplied through by -1. Remember that if you multiply an inequality through by any negative number, the sense of the inequality is reversed. For example, our method would transform the inequality $x_1 + x_2 \geq -1$ into $-x_1 - x_2 \leq 1$. It would also transform $x_1 - x_2 \leq -2$ into $-x_1 + x_2 \geq 2$.

Step 1′ Identify each constraint that is now (after Step 1) an equality or $\geq$ constraint. In Step 3, we will add an artificial variable to each of these constraints.

Step 2 Convert each inequality constraint to standard form. This means that if constraint i is a $\leq$ constraint, we add a slack variable s_i, and if constraint i is a $\geq$ constraint, we subtract an excess variable e_i.

Step 3 If (after Step 1 has been completed) constraint i is a $\geq$ or equality constraint, add an artificial variable a_i to constraint i. Also add the sign restriction $a_i \geq 0$.

Step 4 Let M denote a very large positive number. If the LP is a min problem, add (for each artificial variable) Ma_i to the objective function. If the LP is a max problem, add (for each artificial variable) $-Ma_i$ to the objective function.

Step 5 Since each artificial variable will be in the starting basis, all artificial variables must be eliminated from row 0 before beginning the simplex. This ensures that we begin with a canonical form. In choosing the entering variable, remember that M is a very large positive number. For example, $4M - 2$ is more positive than $3M + 900$, and $-6M - 5$ is more negative than $-5M - 40$. Now solve the transformed problem by the simplex. If all artificial variables are equal to zero in the optimal solution, we have found the optimal solution to the original problem. If any artificial variables are positive in the optimal solution, the original problem is infeasible.[†]

[†]We have ignored the possibility that when the LP (with the artificial variables) is solved, the final tableau may indicate that the LP is unbounded. If the final tableau indicates the LP is unbounded and all artificial variables in this tableau equal zero, then the original LP is unbounded. If the final tableau indicates that the LP is unbounded and at least one artificial variable is positive, then the original LP is infeasible. See Bazaraa and Jarvis (1977) for details.

When an artificial variable leaves the basis, its column may be dropped from future tableaus. This is because the purpose of an artificial variable is only to get a starting basic feasible solution. Once an artificial variable leaves the basis, we no longer need it. Despite this fact, we often maintain the artificial variables in all tableaus. The reason for this will become apparent in Section 6.7.

Solution to Example 4 (continued)

Step 1 Since none of the constraints has a negative right-hand side, we don't have to multiply any constraint through by -1.

Step 1′ Constraints 2 and 3 will require artificial variables.

Step 2 Add a slack variable s_1 to row 1 and subtract an excess variable e_2 from row 2. The result is

$$\min z = 2x_1 + 3x_2$$

$$\text{Row 1:} \quad \tfrac{1}{2}x_1 + \tfrac{1}{4}x_2 + s_1 \qquad\qquad = 4$$

$$\text{Row 2:} \quad x_1 + 3x_2 \qquad - e_2 = 20$$

$$\text{Row 3:} \quad x_1 + x_2 \qquad\qquad = 10$$

Step 3 Add an artificial variable a_2 to row 2 and an artificial variable a_3 to row 3. The result is

$$\min z = 2x_1 + 3x_2$$

$$\text{Row 1:} \quad \tfrac{1}{2}x_1 + \tfrac{1}{4}x_2 + s_1 \qquad\qquad\qquad = 4$$

$$\text{Row 2:} \quad x_1 + 3x_2 \qquad - e_2 + a_2 \qquad = 20$$

$$\text{Row 3:} \quad x_1 + x_2 \qquad\qquad\quad + a_3 = 10$$

From this tableau, we see that our initial bfs will be $s_1 = 4$, $a_2 = 20$, and $a_3 = 10$.

Step 4 Since we are solving a min problem, we add $Ma_2 + Ma_3$ to the objective function (if we were solving a max problem, we would add $-Ma_2 - Ma_3$ to the objective function). This makes a_2 and a_3 very unattractive, and the act of minimizing z will cause a_2 and a_3 to be zero. The objective function is now

$$\min z = 2x_1 + 3x_2 + Ma_2 + Ma_3$$

Step 5 Row 0 is now

$$z - 2x_1 - 3x_2 - Ma_2 - Ma_3$$

Since a_2 and a_3 are in our starting bfs (that's why we introduced them), they must be eliminated from row 0. To eliminate a_2 and a_3 from row 0, simply replace row 0 by row 0 + M(row 2) + M(row 3). This yields

Row 0: $\quad z -$	$2x_1 -$	$3x_2$	$- Ma_2 - Ma_3 = 0$
M(row 2):	$Mx_1 +$	$3Mx_2 - Me_2 + Ma_2$	$= 20M$
M(row 3):	$Mx_1 +$	Mx_2	$+ Ma_3 = 10M$
New row 0: $\quad z + (2M - 2)x_1 + (4M - 3)x_2 - Me_2$			$= 30M$

Combining new row 0 with rows 1–3 yields the initial tableau shown in Table 27.

Since we are solving a min problem, the variable with the most positive coefficient in row 0 should enter the basis. Since $4M - 3 > 2M - 2$, variable x_2 should enter the

Table 27
Initial Tableau for
Bevco Example

z	x_1	x_2	s_1	e_2	a_2	a_3	rhs	BASIC VARIABLE	RATIO
1	$2M - 2$	$4M - 3$	0	$-M$	0	0	$30M$	$z = 30M$	
0	$\frac{1}{2}$	$\frac{1}{4}$	1	0	0	0	4	$s_1 = 4$	16
0	1	③	0	-1	1	0	20	$a_2 = 20$	$\frac{20}{3}*$
0	1	1	0	0	0	1	10	$a_3 = 10$	10

basis. The ratio test indicates that x_2 should enter the basis in row 2. Then the artificial variable a_2 will leave the basis. The most difficult part of doing the pivot is the elimination of x_2 from row 0. First replace row 2 by $\frac{1}{3}$ (row 2). Thus, new row 2 is

$$\tfrac{1}{3}x_1 + x_2 - \tfrac{1}{3}e_2 + \tfrac{1}{3}a_2 = \tfrac{20}{3}$$

We can now eliminate x_2 from row 0 by adding $-(4M - 3)$(new row 2) $= (3 - 4M)$ (new row 2) to row 0. Thus, new row 0 will be $(3 - 4M)$(new row 2) $+$ row 0. Now

$$(3 - 4M)(\text{new row 2}) =$$

$$\frac{(3 - 4M)x_1}{3} + (3 - 4M)x_2 - \frac{(3 - 4M)e_2}{3} + \frac{(3 - 4M)a_2}{3} = \frac{20(3 - 4M)}{3}$$

Row 0: $z + (2M - 2)x_1 + (4M - 3)x_2 - Me_2 = 30M$

New row 0: $z + \dfrac{(2M - 3)x_1}{3} + \dfrac{(M - 3)e_2}{3} + \dfrac{(3 - 4M)a_2}{3} = \dfrac{60 + 10M}{3}$

After using ero's to eliminate x_2 from row 1 and row 3, we obtain the tableau in Table 28. Since $\frac{2M-3}{3} > \frac{M-3}{3}$, we next enter x_1 into the basis. The ratio test indicates that x_1 should enter the basis in the third row of the current tableau. Then a_3 will leave the basis, and our next tableau will have $a_2 = a_3 = 0$. To enter x_1 into the basis in row 3, we first replace the row 3 by $\frac{3}{2}$(row 3). Thus, new row 3 will be

$$x_1 + \frac{e_2}{2} - \frac{a_2}{2} + \frac{3a_3}{2} = 5$$

Table 28
First Tableau for
Bevco Example

z	x_1	x_2	s_1	e_2	a_2	a_3	rhs	BASIC VARIABLE	RATIO
1	$\frac{2M-3}{3}$	0	0	$\frac{M-3}{3}$	$\frac{3-4M}{3}$	0	$\frac{60+10M}{3}$	$z = \frac{60+10M}{3}$	
0	$\frac{5}{12}$	0	1	$\frac{1}{12}$	$-\frac{1}{12}$	0	$\frac{7}{3}$	$s_1 = \frac{7}{3}$	$\frac{28}{5}$
0	$\frac{1}{3}$	1	0	$-\frac{1}{3}$	$\frac{1}{3}$	0	$\frac{20}{3}$	$x_2 = \frac{20}{3}$	20
0	②/③	0	0	$\frac{1}{3}$	$-\frac{1}{3}$	1	$\frac{10}{3}$	$a_3 = \frac{10}{3}$	$5*$

To eliminate x_1 from row 0, we replace row 0 by row 0 $+ (3 - 2M)$(new row 3)/3.

Row 0: $z + \dfrac{(2M - 3)x_1}{3} + \dfrac{(M - 3)e_2}{3} + \dfrac{(3 - 4M)a_2}{3} = \dfrac{60 + 10M}{3}$

$\dfrac{(3 - 2M)(\text{new row 3})}{3}:\dfrac{(3 - 2M)x_1}{3} + \dfrac{(3 - 2M)e_2}{6} + \dfrac{(2M - 3)a_2}{6} + \dfrac{(3 - 2M)a_3}{2} = \dfrac{15 - 10M}{3}$

New row 0: $z - \dfrac{e_2}{2} + \dfrac{(1 - 2M)a_2}{2} + \dfrac{(3 - 2M)a_3}{2} = 25$

New row 1 and new row 2 are computed as usual, yielding the tableau in Table 29. Since all variables in row 0 have nonpositive coefficients, this is an optimal tableau, and since all artificial variables are equal to zero in this tableau, we have found the optimal solution to the Bevco problem: $z = 25$, $x_1 = x_2 = 5$, $s_1 = \frac{1}{4}$, $e_2 = 0$. This means that Bevco can hold the cost of producing a 10-oz bottle of Oranj to 25¢ by mixing together 5 oz of orange soda and 5 oz of orange juice. Note that the a_2 column could have been dropped after a_2 left the basis (at the conclusion of the first pivot), and the a_3 column could have been dropped after a_3 left the basis (at the conclusion of the second pivot).

Table 29
Optimal Tableau for
Bevco Example

z	x_1	x_2	s_1	e_2	a_2	a_3	rhs	BASIC VARIABLE
1	0	0	0	$-\frac{1}{2}$	$\frac{1-2M}{2}$	$\frac{3-2M}{2}$	25	$z = 25$
0	0	0	1	$-\frac{1}{8}$	$\frac{1}{8}$	$-\frac{5}{8}$	$\frac{1}{4}$	$s_1 = \frac{1}{4}$
0	0	1	0	$-\frac{1}{2}$	$\frac{1}{2}$	$-\frac{1}{2}$	5	$x_2 = 5$
0	1	0	0	$\frac{1}{2}$	$-\frac{1}{2}$	$\frac{3}{2}$	5	$x_1 = 5$

HOW TO SPOT AN INFEASIBLE LP

We now modify the Bevco problem by requiring that a 10-oz bottle of Oranj contain at least 36 mg of vitamin C. Since even 10 oz of orange juice contain only $3(10) = 30$ mg of vitamin C, we know that Bevco cannot possibly meet the new vitamin C requirement. This means that Bevco's LP should now have no feasible solution. Let's see how the Big M method reveals the LP's infeasibility. We have changed Bevco's LP to

$$\min z = 2x_1 + 3x_2$$
$$\text{s.t.} \quad \tfrac{1}{2}x_1 + \tfrac{1}{4}x_2 \le 4 \qquad \text{(Sugar constraint)}$$
$$x_1 + 3x_2 \ge 36 \qquad \text{(Vitamin C constraint)} \qquad (20)$$
$$x_1 + x_2 = 10 \qquad \text{(10 oz constraint)}$$
$$x_1, x_2 \ge 0$$

After going through Steps 1–5 of the Big M method, we obtain the initial tableau in Table 30. Since $4M - 3 > 2M - 2$, we enter x_2 into the basis. The ratio test indicates that x_2 should be entered in row 3. This will cause a_3 to leave the basis. After entering x_2 into the basis, we obtain the tableau in Table 31. Since each variable has a nonpositive coefficient in row 0, this is an optimal tableau. The optimal solution indicated by this tableau is $z = 30 + 6M$, $s_1 = \frac{3}{2}$, $a_2 = 6$, $x_2 = 10$, $a_3 = e_2 = x_1 = 0$. Since an artificial variable (a_2) is positive in the optimal tableau, Step 5 shows that the original

Table 30
Initial Tableau for
Bevco (Infeasible)
Example

z	x_1	x_2	s_1	e_2	a_2	a_3	rhs	BASIC VARIABLE	RATIO
1	$2M - 2$	$4M - 3$	0	$-M$	0	0	$46M$	$z = 46M$	
0	$\frac{1}{2}$	$\frac{1}{4}$	1	0	0	0	4	$s_1 = 4$	16
0	1	3	0	-1	1	0	36	$a_2 = 36$	12
0	1	①	0	0	0	1	10	$a_3 = 10$	10*

Infeasible
$a_2 \neq ? 0$
3 -

Table 31
Tableau Indicating
Infeasibility for
Bevco (Infeasible)
Example

z	x_1	x_2	s_1	e_2	a_2	a_3	rhs	BASIC VARIABLE
1	$1 - 2M$	0	0	$-M$	0	$3 - 4M$	$30 + 6M$	$z = 6M + 30$
0	$\frac{1}{4}$	0	1	0	0	$-\frac{1}{4}$	$\frac{3}{2}$	$s_1 = \frac{3}{2}$
0	-2	0	0	-1	1	-3	6	$a_2 = 6$
0	1	1	0	0	0	1	10	$x_2 = 10$

LP has no feasible solution.[†] In summary, *if any artificial variable is positive in the optimal Big M tableau, the original LP has no feasible solution.*

Note that when the Big M method is used, it is difficult to determine how large M should be. Generally, M is chosen to be at least 100 times larger than the largest coefficient in the original objective function. The introduction of such large numbers into the problem can cause roundoff errors and other computational difficulties. For this reason, most computer codes solve LPs by using the two-phase simplex method (described in Section 4.11).

◆ PROBLEMS

GROUP A

Use the Big M method to solve the following LPs:

1.
$$\min z = 4x_1 + 4x_2 + x_3$$
$$\text{s.t.} \quad x_1 + x_2 + x_3 \leq 2$$
$$2x_1 + x_2 \quad\quad \leq 3$$
$$2x_1 + x_2 + 3x_3 \geq 3$$
$$x_1, x_2, x_3 \geq 0$$

2.
$$\min z = 2x_1 + 3x_2$$
$$\text{s.t.} \quad 2x_1 + x_2 \geq 4$$
$$x_1 - x_2 \geq -1$$
$$x_1, x_2 \geq 0$$

3.
$$\max z = 3x_1 + x_2$$
$$\text{s.t.} \quad x_1 + x_2 \geq 3$$
$$2x_1 + x_2 \leq 4$$
$$x_1 + x_2 = 3$$
$$x_1, x_2 \geq 0$$

4.
$$\min z = 3x_1$$
$$\text{s.t.} \quad 2x_1 + x_2 \geq 6$$
$$3x_1 + 2x_2 = 4$$
$$x_1, x_2 \geq 0$$

4-11   THE TWO-PHASE SIMPLEX METHOD*

When a basic feasible solution is not readily available, the two-phase simplex method may be used as an alternative to the Big M method. In the two-phase simplex method, we add artificial variables to the same constraints as we did in the Big M method. Then we find a bfs to the original LP by solving the Phase I LP. In the Phase I LP, the objective function is simply to minimize the sum of all artificial variables. At the completion of

[†]To explain why (20) can have no feasible solution, suppose that (20) had a feasible solution $(\bar{x}_1, \bar{x}_2)$. Clearly, if we set $a_3 = a_2 = 0$, $(\bar{x}_1, \bar{x}_2)$ will be feasible for our modified LP (the LP with artificial variables). If we substitute $(\bar{x}_1, \bar{x}_2)$ into the modified objective function ($z = 2\bar{x}_1 + 3\bar{x}_2 + Ma_2 + Ma_3$), we obtain $z = 2\bar{x}_1 + 3\bar{x}_2$ (this follows because $a_3 = a_2 = 0$). Since M is large, this z-value is certainly less than $6M + 30$. This contradicts the fact that the best z-value for our modified objective function is $6M + 30$. This means that our original LP (20) must have no feasible solution.

*This section covers topics that may be omitted with no loss of continuity.

Phase I, we reintroduce the original LP's objective function and determine the optimal solution to the original LP.

The following are the steps of the two-phase simplex method. Note that Steps 1–3 for the two-phase simplex are identical to Steps 1–3 for the Big M method.

Step 1 Modify the constraints so that the right-hand side of each constraint is nonnegative. This requires that each constraint with a negative right-hand side be multiplied through by -1.

Step 1′ Identify each constraint that is now (after Step 1) an equality or $\geq$ constraint. In Step 3, we will add an artificial variable to each of these constraints.

Step 2 Convert each inequality constraint to the standard form. If constraint i is a $\leq$ constraint, add a slack variable s_i. If constraint i is a $\geq$ constraint, subtract an excess variable e_i.

Step 3 If (after Step 1′) constraint i is a $\geq$ or equality constraint, add an artificial variable a_i to constraint i. Also add the sign restriction $a_i \geq 0$.

Step 4 For the time being, ignore the original LP's objective function. Instead solve an LP whose objective function is min w' = (sum of all the artificial variables). This is called the **Phase I LP**. The act of solving the Phase I LP will force the artificial variables to be zero.

Since each $a_i \geq 0$, solving the Phase I LP will result in one of the following three cases:

Case 1 The optimal value of w' is greater than zero. In this case, the original LP has no feasible solution.

Case 2 The optimal value of w' is equal to zero, and no artificial variables are in the optimal Phase I basis. In this case, we drop all columns in the optimal Phase I tableau that correspond to the artificial variables. We now combine the original objective function with the constraints from the optimal Phase I tableau. This yields the **Phase II LP**. The optimal solution to the Phase II LP is the optimal solution to the original LP.

Case 3 The optimal value of w' is equal to zero and at least one artificial variable is in the optimal Phase I basis. In this case, we can find the optimal solution to the original LP if at the end of Phase I we drop from the optimal Phase I tableau all nonbasic artificial variables and any variable from the original problem which has a negative coefficient in row 0 of the optimal Phase I tableau.

Before solving examples illustrating Cases 1 and 2, we briefly discuss why $w' > 0$ corresponds to the original LP having no feasible solution and $w' = 0$ corresponds to the original LP having at least one feasible solution.

Suppose the original LP is infeasible. Then the only way to obtain a feasible solution to the Phase I LP is to let at least one artificial variable be positive. In this situation, $w' > 0$ (Case 1) will result. On the other hand, if the original LP has a feasible solution, this feasible solution (with all $a_i = 0$) is feasible in the Phase I LP and yields $w' = 0$. This means that if the original LP has a feasible solution, the optimal Phase I solution will have $w' = 0$. We now work through examples of Cases 1 and 2 of the two-phase simplex method.

First we use the two-phase simplex to solve the Bevco problem of Section 4.10. Recall that the Bevco problem was

$$\min z = 2x_1 + 3x_2$$
$$\text{s.t.} \quad \tfrac{1}{2}x_1 + \tfrac{1}{4}x_2 \le 4$$
$$x_1 + 3x_2 \ge 20$$
$$x_1 + x_2 = 10$$
$$x_1, x_2 \ge 0$$

As in the Big M method, Steps 1–3 transform the constraints into

$$\tfrac{1}{2}x_1 + \tfrac{1}{4}x_2 + s_1 \qquad\qquad = 4$$
$$x_1 + 3x_2 \quad - e_2 + a_2 \qquad = 20$$
$$x_1 + x_2 \qquad\qquad + a_3 = 10$$

Step 4 yields the following Phase I LP:

$$\min w' = a_2 + a_3$$
$$\text{s.t.} \quad \tfrac{1}{2}x_1 + \tfrac{1}{4}x_2 + s_1 \qquad\qquad = 4$$
$$x_1 + 3x_2 \quad - e_2 + a_2 \qquad = 20$$
$$x_1 + x_2 \qquad\qquad + a_3 = 10$$

This set of equations yields a starting bfs for Phase I ($s_1 = 4$, $a_2 = 20$, $a_3 = 10$).

Note, however, that the row 0 for this tableau ($w' - a_2 - a_3 = 0$) contains the basic variables a_2 and a_3. As in the Big M method, a_2 and a_3 must be eliminated from row 0 before we can solve Phase I. To eliminate a_2 and a_3 from row 0, simply add row 2 and row 3 to row 0:

Row 0:	w' $\qquad\qquad\qquad\qquad - a_2 - a_3 = 0$	
+ Row 2:	$x_1 + 3x_2 - e_2 + a_2 \qquad\quad = 20$	
+ Row 3:	$x_1 + x_2 \qquad\quad + a_3 = 10$	
= New row 0:	$w' + 2x_1 + 4x_2 - e_2 \qquad\qquad = 30$	

Combining new row 0 with the Phase I constraints yields the initial Phase I tableau in Table 32. Since the Phase I problem is *always* a min problem (even if the original LP is a max problem), we enter x_2 into the basis. The ratio test indicates that x_2 will enter the basis in row 2. Then a_2 will exit from the basis. After performing the necessary ero's, we obtain the tableau in Table 33. Since $\tfrac{2}{3} > \tfrac{1}{3}$, x_1 enters the basis. The ratio test indicates that x_1 should enter the basis in row 3. Thus, a_3 will leave the basis. Since a_2 and a_3 will

Table 32 Initial Phase I Tableau for Bevco Example	w'	x_1	x_2	s_1	e_2	a_2	a_3	rhs	BASIC VARIABLE	RATIO
	1	2	4	0	−1	0	0	30	$w' = 30$	
	0	$\tfrac{1}{2}$	$\tfrac{1}{4}$	1	0	0	0	4	$s_1 = 4$	16
	0	1	③	0	−1	1	0	20	$a_2 = 20$	$\tfrac{20}{3}$*
	0	1	1	0	0	0	1	10	$a_3 = 10$	10

Table 33
Phase I Tableau for Bevco Example after One Iteration

w'	x_1	x_2	s_1	e_2	a_2	a_3	rhs	BASIC VARIABLE	RATIO
1	$\frac{2}{3}$	0	0	$\frac{1}{3}$	$-\frac{4}{3}$	0	$\frac{10}{3}$	$w' = \frac{10}{3}$	
0	$\frac{5}{12}$	0	1	$\frac{1}{12}$	$-\frac{1}{12}$	0	$\frac{7}{3}$	$s_1 = \frac{7}{3}$	$\frac{28}{5}$
0	$\frac{1}{3}$	1	0	$-\frac{1}{3}$	$\frac{1}{3}$	0	$\frac{20}{3}$	$x_2 = \frac{20}{3}$	20
0	$\boxed{\frac{2}{3}}$	0	0	$\frac{1}{3}$	$-\frac{1}{3}$	1	$\frac{10}{3}$	$a_3 = \frac{10}{3}$	5*

be nonbasic after the current pivot is completed, we already know that the next tableau will be of the optimal Phase I tableau. A glance at the tableau in Table 34 confirms this fact.

Since $w' = 0$, Phase I has been concluded. The basic feasible solution $s_1 = \frac{1}{4}$, $x_2 = 5$, $x_1 = 5$ has been found. Since no artificial variables are in the optimal Phase I basis, the problem is an example of Case 2. We now drop the columns for the artificial variables a_2 and a_3 (we no longer need them) and reintroduce the original objective function:

$$\min z = 2x_1 + 3x_2 \quad \text{or} \quad z - 2x_1 - 3x_2 = 0$$

Table 34
Optimal Phase I Tableau for Bevco Example

w'	x_1	x_2	s_1	e_2	a_2	a_3	rhs	BASIC VARIABLE
1	0	0	0	0	-1	-1	0	$w' = 0$
0	0	0	1	$-\frac{1}{8}$	$\frac{1}{8}$	$-\frac{5}{8}$	$\frac{1}{4}$	$s_1 = \frac{1}{4}$
0	0	1	0	$-\frac{1}{2}$	$\frac{1}{2}$	$-\frac{1}{2}$	5	$x_2 = 5$
0	1	0	0	$\frac{1}{2}$	$-\frac{1}{2}$	$\frac{3}{2}$	5	$x_1 = 5$

Since x_1 and x_2 are both in the optimal Phase I basis, they must be eliminated from the Phase II row 0. We add 3(row 2) + 2(row 3) of the optimal Phase I tableau to row 0:

$$
\begin{array}{lll}
\text{Phase II row 0:} & z - 2x_1 - 3x_2 & = 0 \\
+ \ 3(\text{row 2}): & 3x_2 - \frac{3}{2}e_2 & = 15 \\
+ \ 2(\text{row 3}): & 2x_1 \qquad + \ e_2 & = 10 \\
= \text{New Phase II row 0:} \ z & - \frac{1}{2}e_2 & = 25
\end{array}
$$

We now begin Phase II with the following set of equations:

$$
\begin{aligned}
\min z - \tfrac{1}{2}e_2 &= 25 \\
s_1 - \tfrac{1}{8}e_2 &= \tfrac{1}{4} \\
x_2 - \tfrac{1}{2}e_2 &= 5 \\
x_1 + \tfrac{1}{2}e_2 &= 5
\end{aligned}
$$

This is optimal. Thus, in this problem, Phase II requires no pivots to find an optimal solution. If the Phase II row 0 does not indicate an optimal tableau, simply continue with the simplex until an optimal row 0 is obtained. In summary, our optimal Phase II tableau shows that the optimal solution to the Bevco problem is $z = 25$, $x_1 = 5$, $x_2 = 5$, $s_1 = \frac{1}{4}$, and $e_2 = 0$. This agrees, of course, with the optimal solution found by the Big M method in Section 4.10.

To illustrate Case 2, we now modify Bevco's problem so that 36 mg of vitamin C are required. From Section 4.10, we know that this problem is infeasible. This means that the optimal Phase I solution should have $w' > 0$ (Case 1). To show that this is true, we begin with the original problem:

$$\min z = 2x_1 + 3x_2$$
$$\text{s.t.} \quad \tfrac{1}{2}x_1 + \tfrac{1}{4}x_2 \le 4$$
$$x_1 + 3x_2 \ge 36$$
$$x_1 + x_2 = 10$$
$$x_1, x_2 \ge 0$$

After completing Steps 1–4 of the two-phase simplex, we obtain the following Phase I problem:

$$\min w' = a_2 + a_3$$
$$\text{s.t.} \quad \tfrac{1}{2}x_1 + \tfrac{1}{4}x_2 + s_1 \qquad\qquad = 4$$
$$x_1 + 3x_2 \quad - e_2 + a_2 \qquad = 36$$
$$x_1 + x_2 \qquad\qquad + a_3 = 10$$

From this set of equations, we see that the initial Phase I bfs is $s_1 = 4$, $a_2 = 36$, and $a_3 = 10$. Since the basic variables a_2 and a_3 occur in the Phase I objective function, they must be eliminated from the Phase I row 0. To do this, we add rows 2 and 3 to row 0:

$$
\begin{aligned}
\text{Row 0:} \qquad & w' & - a_2 - a_3 & = 0 \\
+ \text{ Row 2:} \qquad & x_1 + 3x_2 - e_2 + a_2 & & = 36 \\
+ \text{ Row 3:} \qquad & x_1 + x_2 & + a_3 & = 10 \\
\hline
= \text{ New row 0:} \quad & w' + 2x_1 + 4x_2 - e_2 & & = 46
\end{aligned}
$$

With the new row 0, the initial Phase I tableau is as shown in Table 35. Since $4 > 2$, we should enter x_2 into the basis. The ratio test indicates that x_2 should enter the basis in row 3. This will force a_3 to leave the basis. The resulting tableau is shown in Table 36. Since no variable in row 0 has a positive coefficient, this is an optimal Phase I tableau,

Table 35
Initial Phase I Tableau for Bevco (Infeasible) Example

w'	x_1	x_2	s_1	e_2	a_2	a_3	rhs	BASIC VARIABLE	RATIO
1	2	4	0	-1	0	0	46	$w' = 46$	
0	$\tfrac{1}{2}$	$\tfrac{1}{4}$	1	0	0	0	4	$s_1 = 4$	16
0	1	3	0	-1	1	0	36	$a_2 = 36$	12
0	1	①	0	0	0	1	10	$a_3 = 0$	10*

Table 36
Tableau Indicating Infeasibility for Bevco (Infeasible) Example

w'	x_1	x_2	s_1	e_2	a_2	a_3	rhs	BASIC VARIABLE
1	-2	0	0	-1	0	-4	6	$w' = 6$
0	$\tfrac{1}{4}$	0	1	0	0	$-\tfrac{1}{4}$	$\tfrac{3}{2}$	$s_1 = \tfrac{3}{2}$
0	-2	0	0	-1	1	-3	6	$a_2 = 6$
0	1	1	0	0	0	1	10	$x_2 = 10$

and since the optimal value of w' is $6 > 0$, the original LP must have no feasible solution. This is reasonable, because if the original LP had a feasible solution, it would have been feasible in the Phase I LP (after setting $a_2 = a_3 = 0$). This feasible solution would have yielded $w' = 0$. Since the simplex could not find a Phase I solution with $w' = 0$, the original LP must have no feasible solution.

R E M A R K S   **1.** As with the Big M method, the column for any artificial variable may be dropped from future tableaus as soon as the artificial variable leaves the basis. Thus, when we solved the Bevco problem, a_2's column could have been dropped after the first Phase I pivot, and a_3's column could have been dropped after the second Phase I pivot.

2. It can be shown that (barring ties for the entering variable and in the ratio test) the Big M method and Phase I of the two-phase method make the same sequence of pivots. Despite this equivalence, most computer codes utilize the two-phase method to find a bfs. This is because M, being a large positive number, may cause roundoff errors and other computational difficulties. The two-phase method does not introduce any large numbers into the objective function, so it avoids this problem.

◆ PROBLEMS

GROUP A

1. Use the two-phase simplex method to solve the Section 4.10 problems.

2. Explain why the Phase I LP will usually have alternative optimal solutions.

4-12   UNRESTRICTED-IN-SIGN VARIABLES

In solving LPs with the simplex algorithm, we used the ratio test to determine the row in which the entering variable became a basic variable. Recall that the ratio test depended on the fact that any feasible point required all variables to be nonnegative. Thus, if some variables are allowed to be unrestricted in sign (urs), the ratio test and therefore the simplex algorithm are no longer valid. In this section, we show how an LP with unrestricted-in-sign variables can be transformed into an LP in which all variables are required to be nonnegative.

For each urs variable x_i, we begin by defining two new variables x_i' and x_i''. Then substitute $x_i' - x_i''$ for x_i in each constraint and in the objective function. Also add the sign restrictions $x_i' \geq 0$ and $x_i'' \geq 0$. The effect of this substitution is to express x_i as the difference of the two nonnegative variables x_i' and x_i''. Since all variables are now required to be nonnegative, we can proceed with the simplex. As we will soon see, no basic feasible solution can have both $x_i' > 0$ and $x_i'' > 0$. This means that for any basic feasible solution, each urs variable x_i must fall into one of the following three cases:

Case 1 $x_i' > 0$ and $x_i'' = 0$. This case occurs if a bfs has $x_i > 0$. In this case, $x_i = x_i' - x_i'' = x_i'$. Thus, $x_i = x_i'$. For example, if $x_i = 3$ in a bfs, this will be indicated by $x_i' = 3$ and $x_i'' = 0$.

Case 2 $x_i' = 0$ and $x_i'' > 0$. This case occurs if $x_i < 0$. Since $x_i = x_i' - x_i''$, we obtain $x_i = -x_i''$. For example, if $x_i = -5$ in a bfs, we will have $x_i' = 0$ and $x_i'' = 5$. Then $x_i = 0 - 5 = -5$.

Case 3 $x_i' = x_i'' = 0$. In this case, $x_i = 0 - 0 = 0$.

In solving the following example, we will learn why no bfs can ever have both $x_i' > 0$ and $x_i'' > 0$.

E X A M P L E 5

A baker has 30 oz of flour and 5 packages of yeast. Baking a loaf of bread requires 5 oz of flour and 1 package of yeast. Each loaf of bread can be sold for 30¢. The baker may purchase additional flour at 4¢/oz or sell leftover flour at the same price. Formulate and solve an LP to help the baker maximize profits (revenues − costs).

Solution

Define

x_1 = number of loaves of bread baked

x_2 = number of ounces by which flour supply is increased by cash transactions.

Therefore, $x_2 > 0$ means that x_2 oz of flour were purchased, and $x_2 < 0$ means that $-x_2$ ounces of flour were sold ($x_2 = 0$ means no flour was bought or sold). After noting that $x_1 \geq 0$ and x_2 is urs, the appropriate LP is

$$\max z = 30x_1 - 4x_2$$
$$\text{s.t.} \quad 5x_1 \leq 30 + x_2 \quad \text{(Flour constraint)}$$
$$x_1 \leq 5 \quad \text{(Yeast constraint)}$$
$$x_1 \geq 0, \ x_2 \text{ urs}$$

Since x_2 is urs, we substitute $x_2' - x_2''$ for x_2 in the objection function and constraints. This yields

$$\max z = 30x_1 - 4x_2' + 4x_2''$$
$$\text{s.t.} \quad 5x_1 \leq 30 + x_2' - x_2''$$
$$x_1 \leq 5$$
$$x_1, x_2', x_2'' \geq 0$$

After transforming the objective function to row 0 form and adding slack variables s_1 and s_2 to the two constraints, we obtain the initial tableau in Table 37. Notice that the x_2' column is simply the negative of the x_2'' column. We will see that *no matter how many pivots we make, the x_2' column will always be negative of the x_2'' column.*

Table 37
Initial Tableau for urs LP

z	x_1	x_2'	x_2''	s_1	s_2	rhs	BASIC VARIABLE	RATIO
1	−30	4	−4	0	0	0	$z = 0$	
0	5	−1	1	1	0	30	$s_1 = 30$	6
0	①	0	0	0	1	5	$s_2 = 5$	5*

Table 38	z	x_1	x_2'	x_2''	s_1	s_2	rhs	BASIC VARIABLE	RATIO
First Tableau for urs LP	1	0	4	-4	0	30	150	$z = 150$	
	0	0	-1	①	1	-5	5	$s_1 = 5$	5*
	0	1	0	0	0	1	5	$x_1 = 5$	None

Table 39	z	x_1	x_2'	x_2''	s_1	s_2	rhs	BASIC VARIABLE
Optimal Tableau for urs LP	1	0	0	0	4	10	170	$z = 170$
	0	0	-1	1	1	-5	5	$x_2'' = 5$
	0	1	0	0	0	1	5	$x_1 = 5$

Since x_1 has the most negative coefficient in row 0, x_1 enters the basis. The ratio test indicates that x_1 should enter the basis in row 2. The resulting tableau is shown in Table 38. Again note that the x_2' column is just the negative of the x_2'' column.

Since x_2'' has the most negative coefficient in row 0, we enter x_2'' into the basis. The ratio test indicates that x_2'' should enter the basis in row 1. The resulting tableau is shown in Table 39. Observe that the x_2' column is still the negative of the x_2'' column. This is an optimal tableau, so the optimal solution to the baker's problem is $z = 170$, $x_1 = 5$, $x_2'' = 5$, $x_2' = 0$, $s_1 = s_2 = 0$. Thus, the baker can earn a profit of 170¢ by baking 5 loaves of bread. Since $x_2 = x_2' - x_2'' = 0 - 5 = -5$, the baker should sell 5 oz of flour. It is optimal for the baker to sell flour, because having 5 packages of yeast limits the baker to manufacturing at most 5 loaves of bread. These 5 loaves of bread use $5(5) = 25$ oz of flour, so $30 - 25 = 5$ oz of flour are left to sell. ◆

The variables x_2' and x_2'' will never both be basic variables in the same tableau. To see why, suppose that x_2'' is basic (as it is in the optimal tableau). Then the x_2'' column will contain a single 1 and have every other entry equal to zero. Since the x_2' column is always the negative of the x_2'' column, the x_2' column will contain a single -1 and have all other entries equal to zero. Such a tableau cannot also have x_2' as a basic feasible variable. The same reasoning shows that if x_i is urs, then x_i' and x_i'' cannot both be basic variables in the same tableau. This means that in any tableau, x_i', x_i'', or both must equal zero and that one of Cases 1–3 must always occur.

The following example shows how urs variables can be used to model the production smoothing costs discussed in the Sailco example of Section 3.10.

E X A M P L E 6

Mondo Motorcycles is determining its production schedule for the next four quarters. Demand for motorcycles will be as follows: quarter 1—40; quarter 2—70; quarter 3 — 50; quarter 4—20. Mondo incurs four types of costs.

1. It costs Mondo $400 to manufacture each motorcycle.

2. At the end of each quarter, a holding cost of $100 per motorcycle is incurred.

3. Increasing production from one quarter to the next incurs costs for training employees. It is estimated that a cost of $700 per motorcycle is incurred if production is increased from one quarter to the next.

4. Decreasing production from one quarter to the next incurs costs for severance pay, decreasing morale, etc. It is estimated that a cost of $600 per motorcycle is incurred if production is decreased from one quarter to the next.

All demands must be met on time, and a quarter's production may be used to meet demand for the current quarter. During the quarter immediately preceding quarter 1, 50 Mondos were produced. Assume that at the beginning of quarter 1, zero Mondos are in inventory. Formulate an LP that minimizes Mondo's total cost during the next four quarters.

Solution

In order to express inventory and production costs, we need to define for $t = 1, 2, 3, 4,$

$$p_t = \text{number of motorcycles produced during quarter } t$$
$$i_t = \text{inventory at end of quarter } t$$

To determine smoothing costs (costs 3 and 4), we define

$$x_t = \text{amount by which quarter } t \text{ production exceeds quarter } t - 1 \text{ production}$$

Since x_t is unrestricted in sign, we may write $x_t = x_t' - x_t''$, where $x_t' \geq 0$ and $x_t'' \geq 0$. We know that if $x_t \geq 0$, then $x_t = x_t'$ and $x_t'' = 0$. Also, if $x_t \leq 0$, then $x_t = -x_t''$ and $x_t' = 0$. This means that

$$x_t' = \text{increase in quarter } t \text{ production over quarter } t - 1 \text{ production}$$
$$(x_t' = 0 \text{ if period } t \text{ production is less than period } t - 1 \text{ production})$$
$$x_t'' = \text{decrease in quarter } t \text{ production from quarter } t - 1 \text{ production}$$
$$(x_t'' = 0 \text{ if period } t \text{ production is more than period } t - 1 \text{ production})$$

For example, if $p_1 = 30$ and $p_2 = 50$, we have $x_2 = 50 - 30 = 20$, $x_2' = 20$, $x_2'' = 0$. Similarly, if $p_1 = 30$ and $p_2 = 15$, we have $x_2 = 15 - 30 = -15$, $x_2' = 0$, and $x_2'' = 15$. The variables x_t' and x_t'' can now be used to express the smoothing costs for quarter t.

We may now express Mondo's total cost as

Total cost = production cost + inventory cost

+ smoothing cost due to increasing production

+ smoothing cost due to decreasing production

$$= 400(p_1 + p_2 + p_3 + p_4) + 100(i_1 + i_2 + i_3 + i_4)$$
$$+ 700(x_1' + x_2' + x_3' + x_4') + 600(x_1'' + x_2'' + x_3'' + x_4'')$$

To complete the formulation, we add two types of constraints. First we need inventory constraints (as in the Sailco problem of Section 3.10) that relate the inventory from the current quarter to the past quarter's inventory and the current quarter's production. For quarter t, the inventory constraint takes the form

Quarter t inventory = (quarter $t - 1$ inventory) + (quarter t production)

− (quarter t demand)

For $t = 1, 2, 3, 4$, respectively, this yields the following four constraints:

$$i_1 = p_1 + 0 - 40 \qquad i_2 = i_1 + p_2 - 70$$
$$i_3 = i_2 + p_3 - 50 \qquad i_4 = i_3 + p_4 - 20$$

The sign restrictions $i_t \geq 0 \, (t = 1, 2, 3, 4)$ ensure that each quarter's demands will be met on time.

The second type of constraint reflects the fact that p_t, p_{t-1}, x_t', and x_t'' are related. This relationship is captured by

$$\text{(quarter } t \text{ production)} - \text{(quarter } t - 1 \text{ production)} = x_t = x_t' - x_t''$$

For $t = 1, 2, 3, 4$, this relation yields the following four constraints:

$$p_1 - 50 = x_1' - x_1'' \qquad p_2 - p_1 = x_2' - x_2''$$
$$p_3 - p_2 = x_3' - x_3'' \qquad p_4 - p_3 = x_4' - x_4''$$

Combining the objective function, the four inventory constraints, the last four constraints, and the sign restrictions ($i_t, p_t, x_t', x_t'' \geq 0$ for $t = 1, 2, 3, 4$), we obtain the following LP:

$$\min z = 400p_1 + 400p_2 + 400p_3 + 400p_4 + 100i_1 + 100i_2 + 100i_3 + 100i_4$$
$$+ 700x_1' + 700x_2' + 700x_3' + 700x_4' + 600x_1'' + 600x_2'' + 600x_3'' + 600x_4''$$

$$\text{s.t.} \quad i_1 = p_1 + 0 - 40$$
$$i_2 = i_1 + p_2 - 70$$
$$i_3 = i_2 + p_3 - 50$$
$$i_4 = i_3 + p_4 - 20$$
$$p_1 - 50 = x_1' - x_1''$$
$$p_2 - p_1 = x_2' - x_2''$$
$$p_3 - p_2 = x_3' - x_3''$$
$$p_4 - p_3 = x_4' - x_4''$$
$$i_t, p_t, x_t', x_t'' \geq 0 \qquad (t = 1, 2, 3, 4)$$

As in Example 5, the column for x_t' in the constraints is the negative of the x_t'' column. Thus, as in Example 5, no bfs to Mondo's LP can have both $x_t' > 0$ and $x_t'' > 0$. This means that x_t' actually is the increase in production during quarter t, and x_t'' actually is the amount by which production decreases during quarter t.

There is another way to show that the optimal solution will not have both $x_t' > 0$ and $x_t'' > 0$. Suppose, for example, that $p_2 = 70$ and $p_1 = 60$. Then the constraint

$$p_2 - p_1 = 70 - 60 = x_2' - x_2'' \tag{21}$$

can be satisfied by many combinations of x_2' and x_2''. For example, $x_2' = 10$ and $x_2'' = 0$ will satisfy (21); $x_2' = 20$, and $x_2'' = 10$ will satisfy (21); $x_2' = 40$ and $x_2'' = 30$ will also satisfy (21); and so on. If $p_2 - p_1 = 10$, the optimal LP solution will always choose $x_2' = 10$ and $x_2'' = 0$ over any other possibility. To see why, look at Mondo's objective function. If $x_2' = 10$ and $x_2'' = 0$, then x_2' and x_2'' contribute $10(700) = \$7000$ in smoothing costs. On the other hand, any other choice of x_2' and x_2'' satisfying (21) will contribute more than $\$7000$ in smoothing costs. For example, $x_2' = 20$ and $x_2'' = 10$

contributes $20(700) + 10(600) = \$20,000$ in smoothing costs. Since we are minimizing total cost, the simplex will never choose a solution where $x'_t > 0$ and $x''_t > 0$ both hold.

The optimal solution to Mondo's problem is $p_1 = 55, p_2 = 55, p_3 = 50, p_4 = 50$. This solution incurs a total cost of \$95,000. The optimal production schedule produces a total of 210 Mondos. Since total demand for the four quarters is only 180 Mondos, this means that Mondo will have an ending inventory of $210 - 180 = 30$ Mondos. Note that this is in contrast to the Sailco inventory model of Section 3.10, in which ending inventory was always zero. The optimal solution to the Mondo problem has a nonzero inventory in quarter 4, because for the quarter 4 inventory to be zero, quarter 4 production must be lower than quarter 3 production. Rather than incur the excessive smoothing costs associated with this strategy, the optimal solution opts for holding 30 Mondos in inventory at the end of quarter 4.

◆

◆ PROBLEMS

GROUP A

1. Suppose that Mondo no longer must meet demands on time. For each quarter that demand for a motorcycle is unmet, a penalty or shortage cost of \$110 per motorcycle short is assessed. Thus, demand can now be backlogged. All demands must be met, however, by the end of quarter 4. Modify the formulation of the Mondo problem to allow for backlogged demand. (*Hint:* Unmet demand corresponds to $i_t \leq 0$. Thus, i_t is now urs, and we must substitute $i_t = i'_t - i''_t$. Now i''_t will be the amount of demand that is unmet at the end of quarter t.)

2. Use the simplex algorithm to solve the following LP:

$$\max z = 2x_1 + x_2$$
$$\text{s.t.} \quad 3x_1 + x_2 \leq 6$$
$$x_1 + x_2 \leq 4$$
$$x_1 \geq 0, x_2 \text{ urs}$$

GROUP B

3. During the next three months, Steelco faces the following demands for steel: 100 tons (month 1); 200 tons (month 2); 50 tons (month 3). During any month, a worker can produce up to 15 tons of steel. Each worker is paid \$5000 per month. Workers can be hired or fired at a cost of \$3000 per worker fired and \$4000 per worker hired (it takes 0 time to hire a worker). The cost of holding a ton of steel in inventory for one month is \$100. Demand may be backlogged at a cost of \$70 per ton-month. That is, if 1 ton of month 1 demand is met during month 3, a backlogging cost of \$140 is incurred. At the beginning of month 1, Steelco has 8 workers. During any month, at most 2 workers can be hired. All demand must be met by the end of month 3. The raw material used to produce a ton of steel costs \$300. Formulate an LP to minimize Steelco's costs.

4. Show how you could use linear programming to solve the following problem:

$$\max z = |2x_1 - 3x_2|$$
$$\text{s.t.} \quad 4x_1 + x_2 \leq 4$$
$$2x_1 - x_2 \leq 0.5$$
$$x_1, x_2 \geq 0$$

5.[†] Steelco's main plant currently has a steel manufacturing area and shipping area located as shown in Figure 6. (Distances are in feet.) The company must determine where to locate a casting facility and an assembly and storage facility to minimize the daily cost of moving

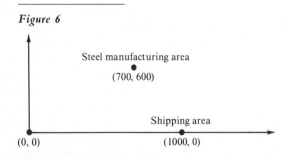

Figure 6

Steel manufacturing area
● (700, 600)

Shipping area

(0, 0)   (1000, 0)

[†]Based on Love and Yerex (1976).

material through the plant. Each day, the number of trips are made as shown in Table 40.

Assuming that all travel is in only an east–west or north–south direction, formulate an LP that can be used to determine where the casting and assembly and storage plants should be located in order to minimize daily transportation costs. (*Hint*: If the casting facility has co-ordinates $(c1, c2)$ how should the constraint $c1 - 700 = e_1 - w_1$ be interpreted?

Table 40

FROM	TO	DAILY NUMBER OF TRIPS	COST PER 100 FEET TRAVELED
Casting	Assembly and storage	40	10¢
Steel manufacturing	Casting	8	10¢
Steel manufacturing	Assembly and storage	8	10¢
Shipping	Assembly and storage	2	20¢

4-13   KARMARKAR'S METHOD FOR SOLVING LPs

We now give a brief description of Karmarkar's method for solving LPs. For a more detailed explanation, see Section 10.6. Karmarkar's method requires that the LP be placed in the following form:

$$\min z = \mathbf{cx}$$
$$\text{s.t.} \quad \mathbf{Kx} = 0$$
$$x_1 + x_2 + \cdots x_n = 1$$
$$x_i \geq 0$$

and that

1. The point $\mathbf{x}^0 = \begin{bmatrix} \frac{1}{n} & \frac{1}{n} & \cdots & \frac{1}{n} \end{bmatrix}$ be feasible for this LP.

2. The optimal z-value for the LP equals 0.

Surprisingly, any LP can be put in this form. Karmarkar's method uses a transformation from projective geometry to create a set of transformed variables $y_1, y_2, \ldots, y_n$. This transformation (call it f) will always transform the current point into the "center" of the feasible region in the space defined by the transformed variables. If the transformation takes the point $\mathbf{x}$ into the point $\mathbf{y}$, we write $f(\mathbf{x}) = \mathbf{y}$. The algorithm begins in the transformed space by moving from $f(\mathbf{x}^0)$ in the transformed space in a "good" direction (a direction that tends to improve z and maintains feasibility). This yields a point $\mathbf{y}^1$ in the transformed space which is close to the boundary of the feasible region. Our new point is the point $\mathbf{x}^1$, satisfying $f(\mathbf{x}^1) = \mathbf{y}^1$. The above procedure is repeated (this time $\mathbf{x}^1$ replaces $\mathbf{x}^0$), until the z-value for $\mathbf{x}^k$ is sufficiently close to 0.

If our current point is $\mathbf{x}^k$, the transformation will have the property that $f(\mathbf{x}^k) = \begin{bmatrix} \frac{1}{n} & \frac{1}{n} & \cdots & \frac{1}{n} \end{bmatrix}$. Thus, in transformed space, we are always moving away from the "center" of the feasible region.

Karmarkar's method has been shown to be a **polynomial time algorithm**. This implies that if an LP of size n is solved by Karmarkar's method, there exist positive numbers a and b such that for any n, an LP of size n can be solved in a time of at most an^b.[†]

In contrast to Karmarkar's method, the simplex algorithm is an **exponential time algorithm** for solving LPs. If an LP of size n is solved by the simplex, then there exists a positive number c such that for any n, the simplex algorithm will find the optimal solution in a time of at most $c2^n$. For large enough n (for positive a, b, and c), $c2^n > an^b$. This means that in theory, a polynomial time algorithm is superior to an exponential time algorithm. Preliminary testing of Karmarkar's method (by Karmarkar) has shown that for large LPs arising in actual application, Karmarkar's method may be up to 50 times as fast as the simplex algorithm. Hopefully, Karmarkar's method will enable researchers to solve many large LPs that currently require a prohibitively large amount of computer time when solved by the simplex. If Karmarkar's method lives up to its early promise, the ability to formulate LP models will be even more important in the near future than it is today.

Karmarkar's method has recently been utilized by the Military Airlift Command to determine how often to fly various routes, and which aircraft should be used. The resulting LP contained 150,000 variables and 12,000 constraints and was solved in one hour of computer time using Karmarkar's method. Using the simplex method, an LP with similar structure containing 36,000 variables and 10,000 constraints required four hours of computer time. Delta Airlines has recently begun using Karmarkar's method to develop a monthly schedule for 7000 pilots and more than 400 aircraft. When the project is completed, Delta expects to have saved millions of dollars.

◆ SUMMARY

PREPARING AN LP FOR SOLUTION BY THE SIMPLEX

An LP is in **standard form** if all constraints are equality constraints and all variables are nonnegative. To place an LP in standard form, we do the following:

Step 1 If the ith constraint is a $\leq$ constraint, we convert it to an equality constraint by adding a slack variable s_i and the sign restriction $s_i \geq 0$.

Step 2 If the ith constraint is a $\geq$ constraint, we convert it to an equality constraint by subtracting an excess variable e_i and adding the sign restriction $e_i \geq 0$.

Step 3 If the variable x_i is unrestricted in sign (urs), replace x_i in both the objective function and constraints by $x_i' - x_i''$, where $x_i' \geq 0$ and $x_i'' \geq 0$.

Suppose that once an LP is placed in standard form, it has m constraints and n variables.

A basic solution to $A\mathbf{x} = \mathbf{b}$ is obtained by setting $n - m$ variables equal to 0 and solving for the values of the remaining m variables. Any basic solution in which all variables are nonnegative is a **basic feasible solution** (bfs) to the LP.

[†]The size of an LP may be defined to be the number of symbols needed to represent the LP in decimal notation.

For any LP, there is a unique extreme point of the LP's feasible region corresponding to each bfs. Also, there is at least one bfs corresponding to each extreme point of the feasible region.

If an LP has an optimal solution, there is an extreme point that is optimal. Thus, in searching for an optimal solution to an LP, we may restrict our search to the LP's basic feasible solutions.

THE SIMPLEX ALGORITHM

If the LP is in standard form and a bfs is readily apparent, the simplex algorithm (for a max problem) proceeds as follows:

Step 1 If all nonbasic variables have nonnegative coefficients in row 0, the current bfs is optimal. If any variables in row 0 have negative coefficients, choose the variable with the most negative coefficient in row 0 to enter the basis.

Step 2 For each constraint in which the entering variable has a positive coefficient, compute the following ratio:

$$\frac{\text{Right-hand side of constraint}}{\text{Coefficient of entering variable in constraint}}$$

Any constraint attaining the smallest value of this ratio is the winner of the **ratio test**. Use ero's to make the entering variable a basic variable in any constraint that wins the ratio test. Return to Step 1.

If the LP (a max problem) is **unbounded**, then eventually we reach a tableau in which a nonbasic variable has a negative coefficient in row 0 and a nonpositive coefficient in each constraint. Otherwise (barring the extremely rare occurrence of *cycling*) the simplex algorithm will find an optimal solution to an LP.

If a bfs is not readily apparent, the Big M method or the two-phase simplex method must be used to obtain a bfs.

THE BIG M METHOD

Step 1 Modify the constraints so that the right-hand side of each constraint is nonnegative.

Step 1' Identify each constraint that is now (after Step 1) an equality or $\geq$ constraint. In Step 3, we will add an artificial variable to each of these constraints.

Step 2 Convert each inequality constraint to standard form.

Step 3 If (after Step 1 has been completed) constraint i is a $\geq$ or equality constraint, add an artificial variable a_i to constraint i. Also add the sign restriction $a_i \geq 0$.

Step 4 Let M denote a very large positive number. If the LP is a min problem, add (for each artificial variable) Ma_i to the objective function. If the LP is a max problem, add (for each artificial variable) $-Ma_i$ to the objective function.

Step 5 Since each artificial variable will be in the starting basis, all artificial variables must be eliminated from row 0 before beginning the simplex. If all artificial variables are equal to zero in the optimal solution, we have found the optimal solution to the original problem. If any artificial variables are positive in the optimal solution, the original problem is infeasible.

THE TWO-PHASE METHOD

Step 1 Modify the constraints so that the right-hand side of each constraint is nonnegative.

Step 1' Identify each constraint that is now (after Step 1) an equality or $\geq$ constraint. In Step 3, we will add an artificial variable to each of these constraints.

Step 2 Convert each inequality constraint to the standard form.

Step 3 If (after Step 1') constraint i is a $\geq$ or equality constraint, add an artificial variable a_i to constraint i. Also add the sign restriction $a_i \geq 0$.

Step 4 For the time being, ignore the original LP's objective function. Instead, solve an LP whose objective function is min $w' =$ (sum of all the artificial variables). This is called the **Phase I LP**.

Since each $a_i \geq 0$, solving the Phase I LP will result in one of the following three cases:

Case 1 The optimal value of w' is greater than zero. In this case, the original LP has no feasible solution.

Case 2 The optimal value of w' is equal to zero, and no artificial variables are in the optimal Phase I basis. In this case, we drop all columns in the optimal Phase I tableau that correspond to the artificial variables and combine the original objective function with the constraints from the optimal Phase I tableau. This yields the **Phase II LP**. The optimal solution to the Phase II LP is the optimal solution to the original LP.

Case 3 The optimal value of w' is equal to zero, and at least one artificial variable is in the optimal Phase I basis.

SOLVING MINIMIZATION PROBLEMS

To solve a minimization problem by the simplex, simply choose as the entering variable the nonbasic variable in row 0 with the most positive coefficient. A tableau or canonical form is optimal if each variable in row 0 has a nonpositive coefficient.

ALTERNATIVE OPTIMAL SOLUTIONS

If a nonbasic variable has a zero coefficient in row 0 of an optimal tableau and the nonbasic variable can be pivoted into the basis, the LP may have **alternative optimal solutions**. If two basic feasible solutions are optimal, any point on the line segment joining the two optimal basic feasible solutions is also an optimal solution to the LP.

UNRESTRICTED-IN-SIGN VARIABLES

If we replace a urs variable x_i by $x_i' - x_i''$, the LP's optimal solution will have x_i', x_i'' or both x_i' and x_i'' equal to zero.

◆ REVIEW PROBLEMS

GROUP A

1. Use the simplex algorithm to find *two* optimal solutions to the following LP:

$$\max z = 5x_1 + 3x_2 + x_3$$
$$\text{s.t.} \quad x_1 + x_2 + 3x_3 \le 6$$
$$5x_1 + 3x_2 + 6x_3 \le 15$$
$$x_3, x_1, x_2 \ge 0$$

2. Use the simplex algorithm to find the optimal solution to the following LP:

$$\min z = -4x_1 + x_2$$
$$\text{s.t.} \quad 3x_1 + x_2 \le 6$$
$$-x_1 + 2x_2 \le 0$$
$$x_1, x_2 \ge 0$$

3. Use the Big M method and the two-phase method to find the optimal solution to the following LP:

$$\max z = 5x_1 - x_2$$
$$\text{s.t.} \quad 2x_1 + x_2 = 6$$
$$x_1 + x_2 \le 4$$
$$x_1 + 2x_2 \le 5$$
$$x_1, x_2 \ge 0$$

4. Use the simplex algorithm to find the optimal solution to the following LP:

$$\max z = 5x_1 - x_2$$
$$\text{s.t.} \quad x_1 - 3x_2 \le 1$$
$$x_1 - 4x_2 \le 3$$
$$x_1, x_2 \ge 0$$

5. Use the simplex algorithm to find the optimal solution to the following LP:

$$\min z = -x_1 - 2x_2$$
$$\text{s.t.} \quad 2x_1 + x_2 \le 5$$
$$x_1 + x_2 \le 3$$
$$x_1, x_2 \ge 0$$

6. Use the Big M method and two-phase method to find the optimal solution to the following LP:

$$\max z = x_1 + x_2$$
$$\text{s.t.} \quad 2x_1 + x_2 \ge 3$$
$$3x_1 + x_2 \le 3.5$$
$$x_1 + x_2 \le 1$$
$$x_1, x_2 \ge 0$$

7. Use the simplex algorithm to find *two* optimal solutions to the following LP. How many optimal solutions does this LP have? Find a third optimal solution to this LP:

$$\max z = 4x_1 + x_2$$
$$\text{s.t.} \quad 2x_1 + 3x_2 \le 4$$
$$x_1 + x_2 \le 1$$
$$4x_1 + x_2 \le 2$$
$$x_1, x_2 \ge 0$$

8. Use the simplex method to find the optimal solution to the following LP:

$$\max z = 5x_1 + x_2$$
$$\text{s.t.} \quad 2x_1 + x_2 \le 6$$
$$x_1 - x_2 \le 0$$
$$x_1, x_2 \ge 0$$

9. Use the Big M method and the two-phase method to find the optimal solution to the following LP:

$$\min z = -3x_1 + x_2$$
$$\text{s.t.} \quad x_1 - 2x_2 \ge 2$$
$$-x_1 + x_2 \ge 3$$
$$x_1, x_2 \ge 0$$

10. Suppose that in the Dakota Furniture problem, there were ten types of furniture that could be manufactured. In order to obtain an optimal solution, how many types of furniture (at the most) would have to be manufactured?

11. Consider the following LP:

$$\max z = 10x_1 + x_2$$
$$\text{s.t.} \quad x_1 \le 1$$
$$20x_1 + x_2 \le 100$$
$$x_1, x_2 \ge 0$$

(a) Find all the basic feasible solutions for this LP.
(b) Show that when the simplex is used to solve this LP, every basic feasible solution must be examined before the optimal solution is found.

By generalizing this example, Klee and Minty (1972) constructed (for $n = 2, 3, \ldots$) an LP with n decision variables and n constraints for which the simplex algorithm examines $2^n - 1$ basic feasible solutions before the optimal solution is found. Thus, there exists an LP with 10 variables and 10 constraints for which the simplex requires $2^{10} - 1 = 1023$ pivots to find the optimal solution. Fortunately, such "pathological" LPs rarely occur in practical applications.

GROUP B

12. Consider a maximization problem with the optimal tableau in Table 41. The optimal solution to this LP is $z = 10$, $x_3 = 3$, $x_4 = 5$, $x_1 = x_2 = 0$. Determine the second-best bfs to this LP. (*Hint:* Show that the second-best solution must be a bfs that is one pivot away from the optimal solution.)

Table 41

z	x_1	x_2	x_3	x_4	rhs
1	2	1	0	0	10
0	3	2	1	0	3
0	4	3	0	1	5

13. A camper is considering taking two types of items on a camping trip. Item 1 weighs a_1 lb, and item 2 weighs a_2 lb. Each type 1 item earns the camper a benefit of c_1 units, and each type 2 item earns the camper a benefit of c_2 units. The knapsack can hold items weighing at most b lb.
(a) Assuming that the camper can carry a fractional number of items along on the trip, formulate an LP to maximize benefit.
(b) Show that if

$$\frac{c_2}{a_2} \geq \frac{c_1}{a_1}$$

then the camper can maximize benefit by filling a knapsack with $\frac{b}{a_2}$ type 2 items.
(c) Which of the linear programming assumptions are violated by this formulation of the camper's problem?

14. You are given the tableau shown in Table 42 for a maximization problem. Give conditions on the unknowns a_1, a_2, a_3, b, c that make the following statements true:
(a) The current solution is optimal.

all z values > 0

Table 42

z	x_1	x_2	x_3	x_4	x_5	rhs
1	$-c$	2	0	0	0	10
0	-1	a_1	1	0	0	4
0	a_2	-4	0	1	0	1
0	a_3	3	0	0	1	b

(b) The current solution is optimal, and there are alternative optimal solutions.
(c) The LP is unbounded (in this part, assume that $b \geq 0$).

15. Suppose we have obtained the tableau in Table 43 for a maximization problem. State conditions on a_1, a_2, a_3, b, c_1, and c_2 that are required to make the following statements true:
(a) The current solution is optimal, and there are alternative optimal solutions. *On nonbasic variable @ z row*
(b) The current basic solution is (not) a basic feasible solution. *(RHS < 0)*
(c) The current basic solution is a degenerate bfs.
(d) The current basic solution is feasible, but the LP is unbounded. *RATIO FAILS*
(e) The current basic solution is feasible, but the objective function value can be improved by replacing x_6 as a basic variable with x_1.

Table 43

z	x_1	x_2	x_3	x_4	x_5	x_6	rhs
1	c_1	c_2	0	0	0	0	10
0	4	a_1	1	0	a_2	0	b
0	-1	-5	0	1	-1	0	2
0	a_3	-3	0	0	-4	1	3

16. Suppose we are solving a maximization problem and the variable x_r is about to leave the basis.
(a) What is the coefficient of x_r in the current row 0?
(b) Show that after the current pivot is performed, the coefficient of x_r in row 0 cannot be less than zero.
(c) Explain why a variable that has left the basis on a given pivot cannot re-enter the basis on the next pivot.

17. A bus company believes that it will need the following number of bus drivers during each of the next five years: year 1, 60 drivers; year 2, 70 drivers; year 3, 50 drivers; year 4, 65 drivers; year 5, 75 drivers. At the beginning of each year, the bus company must decide how many drivers should be hired or fired. It costs $4000 to hire a driver and $2000 to fire a driver. A driver's salary is $10,000 per year. At the beginning of year 1, the company has 50 drivers. A driver hired at the beginning of a year may be used to meet the current year's requirements and is paid full salary for the current year. Formulate an LP to minimize the bus company's salary, hiring, and firing costs over the next five years.

18. Shoemakers of America forecasts the following demand for each of the next six months: month 1, 5000 pairs; month 2, 6000 pairs; month 3, 5000 pairs; month 4, 9000 pairs; month 5, 6000 pairs; month 6, 5000 pairs. It takes a shoemaker 15 minutes to produce a pair of shoes. Each shoemaker works 150 hours per month plus up to 40 hours per month of overtime. A shoemaker is paid a regular salary of $2000 per month plus $50 per hour for overtime. At the beginning of each month, Shoemakers can either hire or fire workers. It costs the company $1500 to hire a worker and $1900 to fire a worker. The monthly holding cost per pair of shoes is 3% of the cost of producing a pair of shoes with regular-time labor. (The raw materials in a pair of shoes cost $20). Formulate an LP that minimizes the cost of meeting (on time) the demands of the next six months. At the beginning of month 1, Shoemakers has 13 workers.

19. Monroe County is trying to determine where to place the county fire station. The locations of the county's four major towns are given in Figure 7. Town 1 is at $(10, 20)$; town 2 is at $(60, 20)$; town 3 is at $(40, 30)$; town 4 is at $(80, 60)$. Town 1 has an average of 20 fires per year, town 2 has an average of 30 fires per year, town 3 has an average of 40 fires per year, and town 4 has an average of 25 fires per year. The county wants to build the fire station in a location that minimizes the average distance that a fire engine must travel to respond to a fire. Since most roads run in either an east-west or a north-south direction, we assume that the fire engine must always be traveling in a north-south or east-west direction. Thus, if the fire station were located at $(30, 40)$ and a fire occurred at town 4, the fire engine would have to travel $(80 - 30) + (60 - 40) = 70$ miles to the fire. Use linear programming to determine where the fire station should be located. (*Hint*: If the fire station is to be located at the point (x, y) and there is a town at the point (a, b), define variables e, w, n, s (east, west, north, south) that satisfy the equations $x - a = w - e$ and $y - b = n - s$. It should now be easy to obtain the correct LP formulation.)

Figure 7

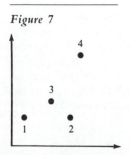

20.[†] During the 1972 football season, the games shown in Table 44 were played by the Miami Dolphins, the Buffalo Bills, and the New York Jets. Suppose that on the basis of these games, we want to rate these three teams. Let M = Miami rating, J = Jets rating, and B = Bills rating. Given values of M, J, and B, you would predict that when, say, the Bills play Miami, Miami is expected to win by $M - B$ points, etc. Thus, for the first Miami-Bills game, your prediction would have been in error by $|M - B - 1|$ points. Show how linear programming can be used to determine ratings for each team that minimize the sum of the prediction errors for all games.

At the conclusion of the season, this method has been used to determine ratings for college football and college basketball. What problems could be foreseen if this method were used to rate teams early in the season?

Table 44

MIAMI	BILLS	JETS
27	—	17
28	—	24
24	23	—
30	16	—
—	24	41
—	3	41

21. During the next four quarters, Dorian Auto must meet (on time) the following demands for cars: quarter 1, 4000; quarter 2, 2000; quarter 3, 5000; quarter 4, 1000. At the beginning of quarter 1, there are 300 autos in stock, and the company has the capacity to produce at most 3000 cars per quarter. At the beginning of each quarter, the company can change production capacity. It costs $100 to increase quarterly production capacity by one car. It costs $50 per quarter to maintain one car of production capacity (even if it is unused during the current quarter). The variable cost of producing a car is $2000. A holding cost of $150 per car is assessed against each quarter's ending inventory. It is required that at the end of quarter 4, plant capacity must be at least 4000 cars. Formulate an LP to minimize the total cost incurred during the next four quarters.

22. Ghostbusters, Inc. exorcises (gets rid of) ghosts. During each of the next three months, they will receive the following number of calls from people who want their ghosts exorcised: January, 100 calls; February, 300 calls; March, 200 calls. Ghostbusters is paid $800 for each ghost

---

[†]Based on Wagner (1954).

exorcised during the month in which the customer calls. Calls need not be responded to during the month they are made, but if a call is responded to one month after it is made, Ghostbusters loses $100 in future goodwill, and if a call is responded to two months after it is made, Ghostbusters loses $200 in goodwill. Each employee of Ghostbusters can exorcise 10 ghosts during a month. Each employee is paid a salary of $4000 per month. At the beginning of January, the company has 8 workers. Workers can be hired and trained (in 0 time) at a cost of $5000 per worker. Workers can be fired at a cost of $4000 per worker. Formulate an LP to maximize Ghostbusters' profit (revenue less costs) over the next three months. Assume that all calls must be handled by the end of March.

23. Carco uses robots to manufacture cars. The following demands for cars must be met (not necessarily on time, but all demands must be met by end of quarter 4): quarter 1, 600; quarter 2, 800; quarter 3, 500; quarter 4, 400. At the beginning of the quarter, Carco has two robots. Robots can be purchased at the beginning of each quarter. At most two robots can be purchased during any quarter. Each robot can build up to 200 cars per quarter. It costs $5000 to purchase a robot. Each quarter, a robot incurs $500 in maintenance costs (even if it is not used to build any cars). Robots can also be sold at the beginning of each quarter for $3000. At the end of each quarter, a holding cost of $200 per car is incurred. If any demand is backlogged, a cost of $300 per car is incurred for each quarter the demand is backlogged.

At the end of quarter 4, Carco must have at least two robots. Formulate an LP to minimize the total cost incurred in meeting the next four quarters' demands for cars.

24. Suppose we have found an optimal tableau for an LP, and the bfs for that tableau is nondegenerate. Also suppose that there is a nonbasic variable in row 0 with a zero coefficient. Prove that the LP has more than one optimal solution.

25. Suppose the bfs for an optimal tableau is degenerate, and a nonbasic variable in row 0 has a zero coefficient. Show by example that either of the following cases may hold:

Case 1 The LP has more than one optimal solution.

Case 2 The LP has a unique optimal solution.

◆ APPENDIX: HOW TO USE LINDO — AN INTRODUCTION

LINDO is a program that can be used to solve linear, integer, and quadratic programming problems. It is an interactive, user-friendly system. To illustrate the use of LINDO, we show how LINDO can be used to solve the Dakota Furniture problem. Since LINDO allows the user to name the variables, we write the Dakota problem as

$$
\begin{aligned}
\max \quad & 60 \text{ DESKS} + 30 \text{ TABLES} + 20 \text{ CHAIRS} \\
\text{s.t.} \quad & 8 \text{ DESKS} + 6 \text{ TABLES} + \text{CHAIRS} \leq 48 \\
& 4 \text{ DESKS} + 2 \text{ TABLES} + 1.5 \text{ CHAIRS} \leq 20 \\
& 2 \text{ DESKS} + 1.5 \text{ TABLES} + 0.5 \text{ CHAIRS} \leq 8 \\
& \phantom{2 \text{ DESKS} + 1.5} \text{TABLES} \phantom{+ 0.5 \text{ CHAIRS}} \leq 5 \\
& \text{DESKS, TABLES, CHAIRS} \geq 0
\end{aligned}
$$

Begin by logging on to your computer system. Then type LINDO followed by carriage return ([CR]). LINDO requires that all variables be non-negative, but the sign restrictions need not be input to the computer. As pointed out in Chapter 3, prior to computer input, each constraint must be rearranged so that *all terms involving variables are on the left side of the constraint and all constants are on the right side of the constraint.*

LINDO is easy to use, and for most purposes the following list of commands will suffice:

MAX. Start input of max problem.

MIN. Start input of min problem.

END. End problem input and get LINDO ready to accept other commands.

GO. Solve the current problem and display solution.

LOOK. Display selected portions of the current formulation.

ALTER. Alter an element of the current formulation.

EXT. Add one or more constraints to the current formulation.

DEL. Delete one or more constraints from the current formulation.

DIVERT. Divert output to a file so the output can be printed.

RVRT. Terminate the DIVERT command.

SAVE. Save an LP so it can be retrieved for later use.

RETRIEVE. Retrieve a previously saved LP file. (Allows you to resolve or change the LP.)

A complete list of commands may be obtained by typing COMMAND.

LINDO assumes that all variables must be nonnegative. Thus, when using LINDO, it is unnecessary to type in the nonnegativity constraints. To input a $\leq$ or $\geq$ constraint, type < or >, respectively. To input the Dakota problem, we would proceed as follows (# and : are user prompts):

```
#LINDO [CR]
LINDO (UC Dec 6 82)     (Response from LINDO)
:MAX 60DESKS + 30TABLES + 20CHAIRS [CR]
#ST [CR]     (ST means "subject to")
#8DESKS + 6TABLES + CHAIRS < 48 [CR]
#4DESKS + 2TABLES + 1.5CHAIRS < 20 [CR]
#2DESKS + 1.5TABLES + .5CHAIRS < 8 [CR]
#TABLES < 5 [CR]
#END
```

LINDO is now ready for any of the commands previously listed. For problems with many variables, the objective function or any of the constraints may be extended over more than one line. If an error is made at any stage of the input process, LINDO will respond with an easily understood error statement and corrective instructions.

Once the LP has been entered, it is advisable to check if this was done correctly. To display the formulation, use the command LOOK. The LOOK command asks for a row specification. Respond with either a single row number, e.g., 3, or a range, e.g., 1–3, or ALL. The command ALL will display all the rows entered, while the other responses will only display the specified rows. It is important to remember that LINDO considers the objective function to be row 1.

To change an aspect of the present formulation, use the ALTER command. After typing ALTER, LINDO will ask for a row number, variable name, and new coefficient, in sequence. For example, responding 2, CHAIRS, and 6, respectively, would change the coefficient of CHAIRS in the first constraint from 1 to 6. To change the right-hand side of a constraint, type RHS when asked for the variable. To change the kind of constraint (i.e., to change a $\leq$ constraint to a $\geq$ constraint, etc.), type DIR when prompted for the variable. Additional changes can be made to the input by using the EXT (for adding new rows), DEL (to delete a row) and APPC (to add a variable to a row or a number of rows).

Once you believe your problem has been correctly inputted, you should save the problem by using the SAVE command. After you type SAVE, LINDO will ask you for a file name. If you use LINDO at a later date, you can work on a previously saved problem by using the RETRIEVE command.

If you want to see the optimal solution to your LP on the terminal screen, simply type GO. To obtain a printed copy of the output, you must create an output file, and then print out this file. This is done by using the command DIVERT. After you type DIVERT, LINDO will ask for a file name (your instructor will tell you what types of file names are valid on your system). This creates an output file, and all output from this point will be diverted to the output file. At this point, it may be useful to type LOOK ALL so that your output file has the listing of the formulation. Next solve your LP by typing GO. On execution, only the optimal objective function value will appear on the screen, but the entire solution of the problem will be diverted to the output file. Next you will be asked if you require the sensitivity and range analysis (discussed in Chapters 5 and 6). Type YES or NO. Again, these analyses are diverted to your output file and will not appear on the screen. At this point, LINDO will prompt you with the colon sign :. If you have made no errors, you are done. To leave LINDO, type QUIT. LINDO will respond FORTRAN STOP. All files that you have created will be saved on your account. Any file that has been created by the DIVERT command may now be sent to the printer.

If you have problems with LINDO, you may type the command HELP or consult the LINDO user's guide (see Schrage (1986)). In closing, we observe that LINDO does not accept parentheses or commas. Thus, $400(X1 + X2)$ must be input as $400X1 + 400X2$ and 10,000 must be input as 10000. New versions of LINDO enable the user to designate variables as unrestricted in sign by using the FREE command.

◆ REFERENCES

There are many fine linear programming texts, for instance, any of the following books:

BAZARAA, M., and J. JARVIS. *Linear Programming and Network Flows*. New York: Wiley, 1977.

BRADLEY, S., A. HAX, and T. MAGNANTI. *Applied Mathematical Programming*. Reading, Mass.: Addison-Wesley, 1977.

CHVÀTAL, V. *Linear Programming*. San Francisco: Freeman, 1983.

DANTZIG, G. *Linear Programming and Extensions*. Princeton, N.J.: Princeton University Press, 1963.

GASS, S. *Linear Programming: Methods and Applications*, 5th ed. New York: McGraw-Hill, 1985.

LUENBERGER, D. *Linear and Nonlinear Programming*, 2nd ed. Reading, Mass.: Addison-Wesley, 1984.

MURTY, K. *Linear Programming*. New York: Wiley, 1983.

SIMMONS, D. *Linear Programming for Operations Research*. Englewood Cliffs, N.J.: Prentice-Hall, 1972.

SIMONNARD, M. *Linear Programming*. Englewood Cliffs, N.J.: Prentice-Hall, 1966.

WU, N., and R. COPPINS. *Linear Programming and Extensions*. New York: McGraw-Hill, 1981.

BLAND, R. "New Finite Pivoting Rules for the Simplex Method," *Mathematics of Operations Research* 2(1977):103–107. Describes simple, elegant approach to prevent cycling.

KARMARKAR, N. "A New Polynomial Time Algorithm for Linear Programming," *Combinatorica* 4(1984):373–395. Karmarkar's method for solving LPs.

KLEE, V., and G. MINTY. "How Good Is the Simplex Algorithm?" In *Inequalities—III*, ed. O. Shisha. New York: Academic Press, 1972. Describes LPs for which the simplex method examines every basic feasible solution before finding the optimal solution.

KOTIAH, T., and N. SLATER. "On Two-Server Poisson Queues with Two Types of Customers," *Operations Research* 21(1973):597–603. Describes an actual application that led to an LP in which cycling occurred.

LOVE, R., and L. YEREX. "An Application of a Facilities Location Model in the Prestressed Concrete Industry," *Interfaces* 6(no. 4, 1976):45–49.

PAPADIMITRIOU, C., and K. STEIGLITZ. *Combinatorial Optimization: Algorithms and Complexity*. Englewood Cliffs, N.J.: Prentice-Hall, 1982. More discussion of polynomial time and exponential time algorithms.

SCHRAGE, L. *User's Manual for LINDO*. Palo Alto, Calif.: Scientific Press, 1986. Gives complete details of LINDO.

WAGNER, H. "Linear Programming Techniques for Regression Analysis," *Journal of the American Statistical Association* 54(1954):206–212.

Sensitivity Analysis:
An Applied Approach

IN THIS CHAPTER, we discuss how changes in an LP's parameters affect the LP's optimal solution. This is called *sensitivity analysis*. We also explain how to use the LINDO output to answer questions of managerial interest such as "What is the most money a company would be willing to pay for an extra hour of labor?" We begin with a graphical explanation of sensitivity analysis.

5-1   A GRAPHICAL INTRODUCTION TO SENSITIVITY ANALYSIS

Sensitivity analysis is concerned with how changes in an LP's parameters affect the LP's optimal solution.

Reconsider the Giapetto problem of Section 3.1:

$$\max z = 3x_1 + 2x_2$$
$$\text{s.t.} \quad 2x_1 + x_2 \leq 100 \quad \text{(Finishing constraint)}$$
$$x_1 + x_2 \leq 80 \quad \text{(Carpentry constraint)}$$
$$x_1 \quad \leq 40 \quad \text{(Demand constraint)}$$
$$x_1, x_2 \geq 0$$

where

$$x_1 = \text{number of soldiers produced per week}$$
$$x_2 = \text{number of trains produced per week}$$

The optimal solution to this problem is $z = 180$, $x_1 = 20$, $x_2 = 60$ (point B in Figure 1), and it has x_1, x_2, and s_3 (the slack variable for the demand constraint) as basic variables. How would changes in the problem's objective function coefficients or right-hand sides change this optimal solution?

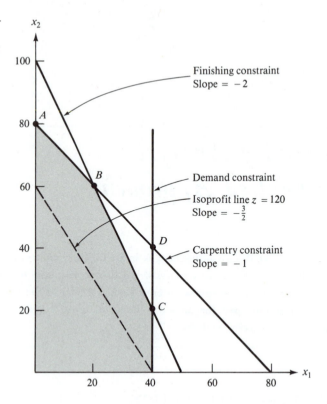

Figure 1
Analysis of Range of
Values for Which c_1
Remains Optimal in
Giapetto Problem

GRAPHICAL ANALYSIS OF THE EFFECT OF A CHANGE IN AN OBJECTIVE FUNCTION COEFFICIENT

If the contribution to profit of a soldier were to increase sufficiently, it seems reasonable that it would be optimal for Giapetto to produce more soldiers (i.e., s_3 would become nonbasic). Similarly, if the contribution to profit of a soldier were to decrease sufficiently, it seems reasonable that it would be optimal for Giapetto to produce only trains (i.e., x_1 would now be nonbasic). We now show how to determine the values of the contribution to profit for soldiers for which the current optimal basis will remain optimal.

Let c_1 be the contribution to profit by each soldier. For what values of c_1 does the current basis remain optimal?

At present, $c_1 = 3$ and each isoprofit line has the form $3x_1 + 2x_2 = $ constant, or

$$x_2 = -\frac{3x_1}{2} + \frac{\text{constant}}{2}$$

and each isoprofit line has a slope of $-\frac{3}{2}$. From Figure 1, we see that if a change in c_1 causes the isoprofit lines to be flatter than the carpentry constraint, the optimal solution will change from the current optimal solution (point B) to a new optimal solution (point A). If the profit for each soldier is c_1, the slope of each isoprofit line will be $-\frac{c_1}{2}$. Since the slope of the carpentry constraint is -1, the isoprofit lines will be flatter than the carpentry constraint if $-\frac{c_1}{2} > -1$, or $c_1 < 2$, and the current basis will no longer be optimal. The new optimal solution will be $(0, 80)$, point A in Figure 1.

If the isoprofit lines are steeper than the finishing constraint, the optimal solution will change from point B to point C. The slope of the finishing constraint is -2. If $-\frac{c_1}{2} < -2$, or $c_1 > 4$, the current basis is no longer optimal and point C, $(40, 20)$, will be optimal. In summary, we have shown that (if all other parameters remain unchanged) the current basis remains optimal for $2 \le c_1 \le 4$, and Giapetto should still manufacture 20 soldiers and 60 trains. Of course, even if $2 \le c_1 \le 4$, Giapetto's profit will change. For instance, if $c_1 = 4$, Giapetto's profit will now be $4(20) + 2(60) = \$200$ instead of $\$180$.

GRAPHICAL ANALYSIS OF THE EFFECT OF A CHANGE IN A RIGHT-HAND SIDE ON THE LP'S OPTIMAL SOLUTION

A graphical analysis can also be used to determine whether a change in the right-hand side of a constraint will make the current basis no longer optimal. Let b_1 be the number of available finishing hours. Currently $b_1 = 100$. For what values of b_1 does the current basis remain optimal? From Figure 2, we see that a change in b_1 shifts the finishing constraint parallel to its current position. The current optimal solution (point B in Figure 2) is where the carpentry and finishing constraints are binding. If we change the

Figure 2
Range of Values on Finishing Hours for Which Current Basis Remains Optimal in Giapetto Problem

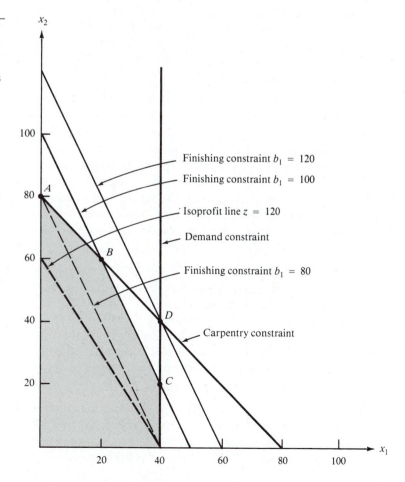

value of b_1, then *as long as the point where the finishing and carpentry constraints are binding remains feasible, the optimal solution will still occur where the finishing and carpentry constraints intersect.* From Figure 2, we see that if $b_1 > 120$, the point where the finishing and carpentry constraints are both binding will lie on the portion of the carpentry constraint below point *D*. In this region, $x_1 > 40$, and the demand constraint for soldiers is not satisfied. Thus, for $b_1 > 120$, the current basis will no longer be optimal. Similarly, if $b_1 < 80$, the carpentry and finishing constraints will be binding at an infeasible point having $x_1 < 0$, and the current basis will no longer be optimal. Thus (if all other parameters remain unchanged), the current basis remains optimal if $80 \leq b_1 \leq 120$.

Note that although for $80 \leq b_1 \leq 120$, the current basis remains optimal, *the values of the decision variables and the objective function value change.* For example, if $80 \leq b_1 \leq 100$, the optimal solution will change from point *B* to some other point on the line segment *AB*. Similarly, if $100 \leq b_1 \leq 120$, the optimal solution will change from point *B* to some other point on the line *BD*.

As long as the current basis remains optimal, it is a routine matter to determine how a change in the right-hand side of a constraint changes the values of the decision variables. To illustrate the idea, let b_1 = number of available finishing hours. If we change b_1 to $100 + \Delta$, we know that the current basis remains optimal for $-20 \leq \Delta \leq 20$. Note that as b_1 changes (as long as $-20 \leq \Delta \leq 20$), the optimal solution to the LP is still the point where the finishing-hour and carpentry-hour constraints are binding. Thus, if $b_1 = 100 + \Delta$, we can find the new values of the decision variables by solving

$$2x_1 + x_2 = 100 + \Delta \qquad \text{and} \qquad x_1 + x_2 = 80$$

This yields $x_1 = 20 + \Delta$ and $x_2 = 60 - \Delta$. Thus, an increase in the number of available finishing hours results in an increase in the number of soldiers produced and a decrease in the number of trains produced.

If b_2 (the number of available carpentry hours) equals $80 + \Delta$, it can be shown (see Problem 2) that the current basis remains optimal for $-20 \leq \Delta \leq 20$. If we change the value of b_2 (keeping $-20 \leq \Delta \leq 20$), the optimal solution to the LP is still the point where the finishing and carpentry constraints are binding. Thus, if $b_2 = 80 + \Delta$, the optimal solution to the LP is the solution to

$$2x_1 + x_2 = 100 \qquad \text{and} \qquad x_1 + x_2 = 80 + \Delta$$

This yields $x_1 = 20 - \Delta$ and $x_2 = 60 + 2\Delta$, which shows that an increase in the amount of available carpentry hours decreases the number of soldiers produced and increases the number of trains produced.

Suppose b_3, the demand for soldiers, is changed to $40 + \Delta$. Then it can be shown (see Problem 3) that the current basis remains optimal for $\Delta \geq -20$. For Δ in this range, the optimal solution to the LP will still occur where the finishing and carpentry constraints are binding. Thus, the optimal solution will be the solution to

$$2x_1 + x_2 = 100 \qquad \text{and} \qquad x_1 + x_2 = 80$$

Of course, this yields $x_1 = 20$ and $x_2 = 60$, which illustrates an important fact. Consider a constraint with positive slack (or positive excess) in an LP's optimal solution; if we change the right-hand side of this constraint in the range where the current basis remains optimal, the optimal solution to the LP is unchanged.

SHADOW PRICES

As we will see in Sections 5.2 and 5.3, it is often important for managers to determine how a change in a constraint's right-hand side changes the LP's optimal z-value. With this in mind, we define the **shadow price** for the ith constraint of an LP to be the amount by which the optimal z-value is improved—increased in a max problem and decreased in a min problem—if the right-hand side of the ith constraint is increased by 1. This definition applies only if the change in the right-hand side of Constraint i leaves the current basis optimal.

For any two-variable LP, it is a simple matter to determine each constraint's shadow price. For example, we know that if $100 + \Delta$ finishing hours are available (assuming the current basis remains optimal), then the LP's optimal solution is $x_1 = 20 + \Delta$ and $x_2 = 60 - \Delta$. Then the optimal z-value will equal $3x_1 + 2x_2 = 3(20 + \Delta) + 2(60 - \Delta) = 180 + \Delta$. Thus, as long as the current basis remains optimal, a unit increase in the number of available finishing hours will increase the optimal z-value by \$1. So the shadow price of the first (finishing hours) constraint is \$1.

For the second (carpentry hours) constraint, we know that if $80 + \Delta$ carpentry hours are available (and the current basis remains optimal), the optimal solution to the LP is $x_1 = 20 - \Delta$ and $x_2 = 60 + 2\Delta$. Then the new optimal z-value is $3x_1 + 2x_2 = 3(20 - \Delta) + 2(60 + 2\Delta) = 180 + \Delta$. So a unit increase in the number of finishing hours will increase the optimal z-value by \$1 (as long as the current basis remains optimal). Thus, the shadow price of the second (carpentry hour) constraint is \$1.

We now find the shadow price of the third (demand) constraint. If the right-hand side is $40 + \Delta$, then (as long as the current basis remains optimal) the optimal values of the decision variables remain unchanged. Then the optimal z-value will also remain unchanged, which shows that the shadow price of the third (demand) constraint is \$0. It turns out that whenever the slack variable or excess variable for a constraint is positive in an LP's optimal solution, the constraint will have a zero shadow price.

Suppose that the current basis remains optimal as we increase the right-hand side of the ith constraint of an LP by Δb_i. ($\Delta b_i < 0$ means that we are decreasing the right-hand side of the ith constraint.) Then each unit by which Constraint i's right-hand side is increased will increase the optimal z-value (for a max problem) by Constraint i's shadow price. Thus, the new optimal z-value is given by

$$\text{(New optimal } z\text{-value)} = \text{(old optimal } z\text{-value)} \\ + \text{(Constraint } i\text{'s shadow price) } \Delta b_i \tag{1}$$

For a minimization problem,

$$\text{(New optimal } z\text{-value)} = \text{(old optimal } z\text{-value)} \\ - \text{(Constraint } i\text{'s shadow price) } \Delta b_i \tag{2}$$

For example, if 95 carpentry hours are available, then $\Delta b_2 = 15$, and the new z-value is given by

$$\text{New optimal } z\text{-value} = 180 + 15(1) = \$195$$

We will continue our discussion of shadow prices in Sections 5.2 and 5.3.

IMPORTANCE OF SENSITIVITY ANALYSIS

Sensitivity analysis is important for several reasons. In many applications, the values of an LP's parameters may change. For example, the prices at which soldiers and trains are sold may change, or the availability of carpentry and finishing hours may change. If a parameter changes, sensitivity analysis often makes it unnecessary to solve the problem again. For example, if the profit contribution of a soldier increased to $3.50, we would not have to solve the Giapetto problem again, because the current solution remains optimal. Of course, solving the Giapetto problem again would not be much work, but solving an LP with thousands of variables and thousands of constraints again would be a chore. A knowledge of sensitivity analysis often enables the analyst to determine from the original solution how changes in an LP's parameters change an LP's optimal solution.

Recall that we may be uncertain about the values of parameters in an LP. For example, we might be uncertain about the weekly demand for soldiers. With the graphical method, it can be shown that if the weekly demand for soldiers is at least 20, the optimal solution to the Giapetto problem is still (20, 60) (see Problem 3 at the end of this section). Thus, even if Giapetto is uncertain about the demand for soldiers, the company can be fairly confident that it is still optimal to produce 20 soldiers and 60 trains.

◆ PROBLEMS

GROUP A

1. Show that if the contribution to profit for trains is between $1.50 and $3, the current basis remains optimal. If the contribution to profit for trains is $2.50, what would be the new optimal solution?

2. Show that if available carpentry hours remain between 60 and 100, the current basis remains optimal. If between 60 and 100 carpentry hours are available, would Giapetto still produce 20 soldiers and 60 trains?

3. Show that if the weekly demand for soldiers is at least 20, the current basis remains optimal, and Giapetto should still produce 20 soldiers and 60 trains.

4. For the Dorian Auto problem (Example 2 in Chapter 3),
(a) Find the range of values on the cost of a comedy ad for which the current basis remains optimal.
(b) Find the range of values on the cost of a football ad for which the current basis remains optimal.
(c) Find the range of values for required HIW exposures for which the current basis remains optimal. Determine the new optimal solution if $28 + \Delta$ million HIW exposures are required.
(d) Find the range of values for required HIM exposures for which the current basis remains optimal. Determine the new optimal solution if $24 + \Delta$ million HIM exposures are required.

(e) Find the shadow price of each constraint.
(f) If 26 million HIW exposures are required, determine the new optimal z-value.

5. Radioco manufactures two types of radios. The only scarce resource that is needed to produce radios is labor. At present, the company has two laborers. Laborer 1 is willing to work up to 40 hours per week and is paid $5 per hour. Laborer 2 is willing to work up to 50 hours per week and is paid $6 per hour. The price as well as the resources required to build each type of radio are given in Table 1.

Table 1

	RADIO 1		RADIO 2	
	Price	*Resource Required*	*Price*	*Resource Required*
	$25	Laborer 1: 1 hour	$22	Laborer 1: 2 hours
		Laborer 2: 2 hours		Laborer 2: 1 hour
		Raw material cost: $5		Raw material cost: $4

Letting x_i be the number of type i radios produced each week, Radioco should solve the following LP:

$$\max z = 3x_1 + 2x_2$$
$$\text{s.t.} \quad x_1 + 2x_2 \le 40$$
$$2x_1 + x_2 \le 50$$
$$x_1, x_2 \ge 0$$

(a) For what values of the price of a type 1 radio would the current basis remain optimal?

(b) For what values of the price of a type 2 radio would the current basis remain optimal?

(c) If laborer 1 were willing to work only 30 hours per week, would the current basis remain optimal? Find the new optimal solution to the LP.

(d) If laborer 2 were willing to work up to 60 hours per week, would the current basis remain optimal? Find the new optimal solution to the LP.

(e) Find the shadow price of each constraint.

5-2 THE COMPUTER AND SENSITIVITY ANALYSIS

If an LP has more than two decision variables, the range of values for a right-hand side (or objective function coefficient) for which the current basis remains optimal cannot be determined graphically. These ranges may be computed by hand calculations (see Section 6.3), but these are often tedious, so the range of values for a right-hand side or objective function coefficient in which the current basis remains optimal are usually determined by packaged computer programs. In this section, we discuss the interpretation of the sensitivity analysis information on the LINDO output. As an illustration of the LINDO output for a maximization problem, we will discuss the output for the following LP.

E X A M P L E 1

Winco sells four types of products. The resources needed to produce one unit of each product and the sales price for each product are given in Table 2. At present, 4600 units of raw material and 5000 labor hours are available. To meet customer demands, exactly 950 total units must be produced. Customers also demand that at least 400 units of product 4 be produced. Formulate an LP that can be used to maximize Winco's sales revenue.

Solution Let x_i = number of units of product i produced by Winco. Then the appropriate LP is

$$\max z = 4x_1 + 6x_2 + 7x_3 + 8x_4$$
$$\text{s.t.} \quad x_1 + x_2 + x_3 + x_4 = 950$$
$$x_4 \ge 400$$
$$2x_1 + 3x_2 + 4x_3 + 7x_4 \le 4600$$
$$3x_1 + 4x_2 + 5x_3 + 6x_4 \le 5000$$
$$x_1, x_2, x_3, x_4 \ge 0$$

Table 2		PRODUCT 1	PRODUCT 2	PRODUCT 3	PRODUCT 4
Costs and Resource Requirements for Winco Example	Raw material	2	3	4	7
	Hours of labor	3	4	5	6
	Sales price	$4	$6	$7	$8

Figure 3
LINDO Output for
Example 1

```
MAX      4 X1 + 6 X2 + 7 X3 + 8 X4
SUBJECT TO
       2)    X1 + X2 + X3 + X4 =      950
       3)    X4 >=    400
       4)    2 X1 + 3 X2 + 4 X3 + 7 X4 <=    4600
       5)    3 X1 + 4 X2 + 5 X3 + 6 X4 <=    5000
END

LP OPTIMUM FOUND AT STEP      4

       OBJECTIVE FUNCTION VALUE

       1)    6650.00000

   VARIABLE        VALUE          REDUCED COST
       X1          .000000          1.000000
       X2       400.000000           .000000
       X3       150.000000           .000000
       X4       400.000000           .000000


       ROW    SLACK OR SURPLUS     DUAL PRICES
       2)          .000000          3.000000
       3)          .000000         -2.000000
       4)          .000000          1.000000
       5)       250.000000           .000000

NO. ITERATIONS=        4

RANGES IN WHICH THE BASIS IS UNCHANGED:

                           OBJ COEFFICIENT RANGES
   VARIABLE       CURRENT       ALLOWABLE       ALLOWABLE
                   COEF         INCREASE        DECREASE
       X1        4.000000       1.000000        INFINITY
       X2        6.000000        .666667         .500000
       X3        7.000000       1.000000         .500000
       X4        8.000000       2.000000        INFINITY

                           RIGHTHAND SIDE RANGES
       ROW       CURRENT       ALLOWABLE       ALLOWABLE
                   RHS         INCREASE        DECREASE
        2       950.000000      50.000000      100.000000
        3       400.000000      37.500000      125.000000
        4      4600.000000     250.000000      150.000000
        5      5000.000000      INFINITY       250.000000
```

The LINDO output for this LP is given in Figure 3.

When we discuss the interpretation of the LINDO output for minimization problems, we will refer to the following example.

◆

E X A M P L E
2

Tucker Inc. must produce 1000 Tucker automobiles. The company has four production plants. The cost of producing a Tucker at each plant, along with the raw material and labor needed, are as shown in Table 3.

Table 3
Cost and
Requirements for
Producing a Tucker

PLANT	COST (in Thousands of Dollars)	LABOR	RAW MATERIAL
1	15	2	3
2	10	3	4
3	9	4	5
4	7	5	6

The auto workers' labor union requires that at least 400 cars be produced at plant 3; 3300 hours of labor and 4000 units of raw material are available for allocation to the four plants. Formulate an LP whose solution will enable Tucker Inc. to minimize the cost of producing 1000 cars.

Solution Let x_i = Number of cars produced at plant i. Then, expressing the objective function in thousands of dollars, the appropriate LP is

$$\min z = 15x_1 + 10x_2 + 9x_3 + 7x_4$$

$$\text{s.t.} \quad x_1 + x_2 + x_3 + x_4 = 1000$$

$$x_3 \geq 400$$

$$2x_1 + 3x_2 + 4x_3 + 5x_4 \leq 3300$$

$$3x_1 + 4x_2 + 5x_3 + 6x_4 \leq 4000$$

$$x_1, x_2, x_3 \geq 0$$

The LINDO output for this LP is given in Figure 4.

Figure 4
LINDO Output for
Example 2

```
MIN      15 X1 + 10 X2 + 9 X3 + 7 X4
SUBJECT TO
        2)    X1 + X2 + X3 + X4 =      1000
        3)    X3 >=    400
        4)    2 X1 + 3 X2 + 4 X3 + 5 X4 <=   3300
        5)    3 X1 + 4 X2 + 5 X3 + 6 X4 <=   4000
END

LP OPTIMUM FOUND AT STEP        3

        OBJECTIVE FUNCTION VALUE

    1)     11600.0000

   VARIABLE        VALUE          REDUCED COST
      X1        400.000000          .000000
      X2        200.000000          .000000
      X3        400.000000          .000000
      X4          .000000          7.000000


    ROW    SLACK OR SURPLUS      DUAL PRICES
    2)          .000000         -30.000000
    3)          .000000          -4.000000
    4)        300.000000          .000000
    5)          .000000          5.000000

NO. ITERATIONS=       3

RANGES IN WHICH THE BASIS IS UNCHANGED:

                         OBJ COEFFICIENT RANGES
VARIABLE        CURRENT       ALLOWABLE       ALLOWABLE
                 COEF         INCREASE        DECREASE
      X1      15.000000       INFINITY        3.500000
      X2      10.000000       2.000000        INFINITY
      X3       9.000000       INFINITY        4.000000
      X4       7.000000       INFINITY        7.000000

                         RIGHTHAND SIDE RANGES
    ROW         CURRENT       ALLOWABLE       ALLOWABLE
                 RHS          INCREASE        DECREASE
     2        1000.000000     66.666660       100.000000
     3         400.000000     100.000000      400.000000
     4        3300.000000     INFINITY        300.000000
     5        4000.000000     300.000000      200.000000
```

◆

OBJECTIVE FUNCTION COEFFICIENT RANGES

Recall from Section 5.1 that (at least in a two-variable problem) we could determine the range of values for an objective function coefficient for which the current basis remains optimal. For each objective function coefficient, this range is given in the OBJECTIVE COEFFICIENT RANGES portion of the LINDO output. The ALLOWABLE INCREASE (AI) section of the output indicates the amount by which an objective function coefficient can be increased with the current basis remaining optimal. Similarly, the ALLOWABLE DECREASE (AD) section of the output indicates the amount by which an objective function coefficient can be decreased with the current basis remaining optimal. To illustrate these ideas, let c_i be the objective function coefficient for x_i in Example 1. If c_1 is changed, then the current basis remains optimal if

$$-\infty = 4 - \infty \le c_1 \le 4 + 1 = 5$$

If c_2 is changed, the current basis remains optimal if

$$5.5 = 6 - 0.5 \le c_2 \le 6 + 0.666667 = 6.666667$$

We will refer to the range of values of c_i for which the current basis remains optimal as the **allowable range** for c_i. As discussed in Section 5.1, if c_i remains in its allowable range, the values of the decision variables remain unchanged, but the optimal z-value may change. The following examples illustrate these ideas.

E X A M P L E 3

a. Suppose Winco raises the price of product 2 by 50¢ per unit. What is the new optimal solution to the LP?

b. Suppose the sales price of product 1 is increased by 60¢ per unit. What is the new optimal solution to the LP?

c. Suppose the sales price of product 3 is decreased by 60¢. What is the new optimal solution to the LP?

Solution

a. Since the AI for c_2 is $0.666667, and we are increasing c_2 by only $0.5, the current basis remains optimal. The optimal values of the decision variables remain unchanged ($x_1 = 0$, $x_2 = 400$, $x_3 = 150$, and $x_4 = 400$ is still optimal). The new optimal z-value may be determined in two ways. First, we may simply substitute the optimal values of the decision variables into the new objective function, yielding

New optimal z-value $= 4(0) + 6.5(400) + 7(150) + 8(400) = \$6850$

Another way to see that the new optimal z-value is $6850 is to observe the only difference in sales revenue: Each unit of Product 2 brings in 50¢ more in revenue. Thus, total revenue should increase by $400(.50) = \$200$, so

New z-value $=$ original z-value $+ 200 = \$6850$

b. The AI for c_1 is 1, so the current basis remains optimal, and the optimal values of the decision variables remain unchanged. Since the value of x_1 in the optimal solution is 0, the change in the sales price for product 1 will not change the optimal z-value —it will remain $6650.

c. For c_3, AD $= .50$, so the current basis is no longer optimal. Without resolving the problem by hand or on the computer, we cannot determine the new optimal solution. ◆

REDUCED COSTS AND SENSITIVITY ANALYSIS

The REDUCED COST portion of the LINDO output gives us information about how changing the objective function coefficient for a nonbasic variable will change the LP's optimal solution. For simplicity, let's assume that the current optimal bfs is non-degenerate (that is, if the LP has m constraints, then the current optimal solution has m variables assuming positive values). For any nonbasic variable x_k, the reduced cost for x_k is the amount by which the objective function coefficient of x_k must be improved before the LP will have an optimal solution in which x_k is a basic variable. If the objective function coefficient of a nonbasic variable x_k is improved by its reduced cost, then the LP will have alternative optimal solutions—at least one in which x_k is a basic variable, and at least one in which x_k is not a basic variable. If the objective function coefficient of a nonbasic variable x_k is improved by more than its reduced cost, then (barring degeneracy) any optimal solution to the LP will have x_k as a basic variable and $x_k > 0$. To illustrate these ideas, note that in Example 1, the basic variables associated with the optimal solution are x_2, x_3, x_4, and s_4 (the slack for the labor constraint). The nonbasic variable x_1 has a reduced cost of \$1. This implies that if we increase x_1's objective function coefficient (in this case, the sales price per unit of x_1) by exactly \$1, there will be alternative optimal solutions, at least one of which will have x_1 as a basic variable. If we increase x_1's objective function coefficient by more than \$1, then (since the current optimal bfs is nondegenerate) any optimal solution to the LP will have x_1 as a basic variable (with $x_1 > 0$). Thus, the reduced cost for x_1 is the amount by which x_1 "misses the optimal basis." We must keep a close watch on x_1's sales price, because a slight increase will change the LP's optimal solution.

Let's now consider Example 2, a minimization problem. Here the basic variables associated with the optimal solution are x_1, x_2, x_3, and s_3 (the slack variable for the labor constraint). Again, the optimal bfs is nondegenerate. Since the nonbasic variable x_4 has a reduced cost of 7 (i.e., \$7000), we know that if the cost of producing x_4 is decreased by 7, there will be alternative optimal solutions, and in at least one of these optimal solutions, x_4 will be a basic variable. If the cost of producing x_4 is lowered by more than 7, then (since the current optimal solution is nondegenerate) any optimal solution to the LP will have x_4 as a basic variable (with $x_4 > 0$).

RIGHT-HAND SIDE RANGES

Recall from Section 5.1 that we could determine (at least for a two-variable problem) the range of values for a right-hand side within which the current basis remains optimal. This information is given in the RIGHTHAND SIDE RANGES section of the LINDO output. To illustrate, consider the first constraint in Example 1. Currently, the righthand side of this constraint (call it b_1) is 950. The current basis remains optimal if b_1 is decreased by up to 100 (the allowable decrease, or AD, for b_1) or increased by up to 50 (the allowable increase, or AI, for b_1). Thus, the current basis remains optimal if

$$850 = 950 - 100 \leq b_1 \leq 950 + 50 = 1000$$

We call this the allowable range for b_1. Even if a change in the right-hand side of a constraint leaves the current basis optimal, the LINDO output does not provide sufficient information to determine the new values of the decision variables. However, when the current basis remains optimal after the right-hand side of a constraint is changed, the LINDO output does allow us to determine the LP's new optimal z-value.

SHADOW PRICES AND DUAL PRICES

In Section 5.1, we defined the shadow price of an LP's ith constraint to be the amount by which the optimal z-value of the LP is improved if the right-hand side of Constraint i is increased by 1 unit (assuming this change leaves the current basis optimal). If, after a change in a constraint's right-hand side, the current basis is no longer optimal, the shadow prices of *all* constraints may change. We will discuss this further in Section 5.4. The shadow price for each constraint is found in the DUAL PRICES section of the LINDO output. If we increase the right-hand side of the ith constraint by an amount Δb_i—a decrease in b_i implies that $\Delta b_i < 0$—and the new right-hand side value for Constraint i remains within the allowable range for the right-hand side given in the RIGHTHAND SIDE RANGES section of the output, then formulas (1) and (2) may be used to determine the optimal z-value after a right-hand side is changed. The following example illustrates how shadow prices may be used to determine how a change in a right-hand side effects the optimal z-value.

E X A M P L E
4

a. In Example 1, suppose that a total of 980 units must be produced. Determine the new optimal z-value.

b. In Example 1, suppose that 4500 units of raw material are available. What is the new optimal z-value? Answer the same question if only 4400 units of raw material are available.

c. In Example 2, suppose that 4100 units of raw material are available. Find the new optimal z-value.

d. In Example 2, suppose that exactly 950 cars must be produced. What will be the new optimal z-value?

Solution

a. $\Delta b_1 = 30$. Since the allowable increase is 50, the current basis remains optimal, and the shadow price of $3 remains applicable. Then (1) yields

New optimal z-value $= 6650 + 30(3) = \$6740$

Here we see that (as long as the current basis remains optimal) each additional unit of demand increases revenues by $3.

b. $\Delta b_2 = -100$. Since the allowable decrease is 150, the shadow price of $1 remains valid. Then (1) yields

New optimal z-value $= 6650 - 100(1) = \$6550$

Thus (as long as the current basis remains optimal), a decrease in available raw material of 1 unit decreases revenue by $1. If only 4400 units of raw material are available, $\Delta b_2 = -200$. Since the allowable decrease is 150, we cannot determine the new optimal z-value.

c. $\Delta b_4 = 100$. The dual price is 5 (thousand). The current basis remains optimal, so (2) yields

New optimal z-value $= 11{,}600 - 100(5) = 11{,}100 \ (\$11{,}100{,}000)$

Thus, as long as the current basis remains optimal, each additional unit of raw material decreases costs by $5000.

d. $\Delta b_1 = -50$. Since the allowable decrease is 100, the shadow price of -30 (thousand) and (2) yield

New optimal z-value $= 11{,}600 - (-50)(-30) = 10{,}100 = \$10{,}100{,}000$

Thus, each unit by which demand is reduced (as long as the current basis remains optimal) decreases costs by $30,000.

Let's give an interpretation to the shadow price for each constraint in Examples 1 and 2. Again, all discussions are assuming that we are within the allowable range where the current basis remains optimal. The shadow price of $3 for Constraint 1 in Example 1 implies that each unit increase in total demand will increase sales revenues by $3. The shadow price of − $2 for Constraint 2 in Example 1 implies that each unit increase in the requirement for product 4 will decrease revenue by $2. The shadow price of $1 for Constraint 3 of Example 1 implies that an additional unit of raw material given to Winco (for no cost) increases total revenue by $1. Finally, the shadow price of $0 for Constraint 4 in Example 1 implies that an additional unit of labor given to Winco (at no cost) will not increase total revenue. This is reasonable; at present, 250 of the available 5000 labor hours are not being used, so why should we expect additional labor to raise revenues?

The shadow price of − $30 (thousand) for Constraint 1 of Example 2 means that each extra car that must be produced will decrease costs by − $30,000 (or increase costs by $30,000). The shadow price of − $4 (thousand) for Constraint 2 means that an extra car that the firm is forced to produce at plant 3 will decrease costs by − $4000 (or increase costs by $4000). The shadow price of $0 for the third constraint in Example 2 means that an extra hour of labor given to Tucker will decrease costs by $0. Thus, if Tucker is given an additional hour of labor, costs are unchanged. This is reasonable; at present, 300 hours of available labor are unused. The shadow price for Constraint 4 is $5 (thousand), which means that if Tucker were given an additional unit of raw material, costs would decrease by $5000.

SIGNS OF SHADOW PRICES

It turns out that a ≥ constraint will always have a nonpositive shadow price; a ≤ constraint will always have a nonnegative shadow price; and an equality constraint may have a positive, a negative, or a zero shadow price. To see why this is true, observe that adding points to an LP's feasible region can only improve the optimal z-value for the LP or leave it the same. Eliminating points from an LP's feasible region can only make the optimal z-value worse or leave it the same. For example, let's look at the shadow price of the raw-material constraint (a ≤ constraint) in Example 1. Why must this shadow price be nonnegative? The shadow price of the raw-material constraint represents the improvement in the optimal z-value if 4601 units (instead of 4600) of raw material are available. Since having an additional unit of raw material available adds points to the feasible region—points for which Winco uses > 4600 but ≤ 4601 units of raw material—we know that the optimal z-value must increase or stay the same. Thus, the shadow price of this ≤ constraint must be nonnegative. Similarly, let's consider the shadow price of the x_4 ≥ 400 constraint in Example 1. Increasing the right-hand side of this constraint to 401 eliminates points from the feasible region (points for which Winco produces ≥ 400 but < 401 units of product 4). Thus, the optimal z-value must decrease or stay the same, implying that the shadow price of this constraint must be nonpositive. Similar reasoning shows that for a minimization problem, a ≥ constraint will have a nonpositive shadow price, and a ≤ constraint will have a nonnegative shadow price. An equality constraint's shadow price may be positive, negative, or zero. To see why, consider the following two LPs:

$$\max z = x_1 + x_2$$
$$\text{s.t.} \quad x_1 + x_2 = 1 \qquad\qquad \textbf{(LP 1)}$$
$$x_1, x_2 \geq 0$$

$$\max z = x_1 + x_2$$
$$\text{s.t.} \quad -x_1 - x_2 = -1 \qquad\qquad \textbf{(LP 2)}$$
$$x_1, x_2 \geq 0$$

Both LPs have the same feasible region and set of optimal solutions (the portion of the line segment $x_1 + x_2 = 1$ in the first quadrant). However, LP 1's constraint has a shadow price of $+1$, whereas LP 2's constraint has a shadow price of -1. Thus, the sign of the shadow price for an equality constraint may either be positive, negative, or zero.

SENSITIVITY ANALYSIS AND SLACK AND EXCESS VARIABLES

It can be shown (see Section 6.10) that for any inequality constraint, the product of the values of the constraint's slack or excess variable and the constraint's shadow price must equal 0. This implies that any constraint whose slack or excess variable is > 0 will have a zero shadow price. It also implies that any constraint with a nonzero shadow price must be a binding constraint (have slack or excess equal to 0). To illustrate these ideas, consider the labor constraint in Example 1. This constraint has positive slack, so its shadow price must be 0. This is reasonable, because slack $= 250$ for this constraint indicates that 250 hours of currently available labor are unused at present. Thus, an extra hour of labor would not increase revenues. Now consider the raw material constraint of Example 1. Since this constraint has a nonzero shadow price, it must have slack $= 0$. This is reasonable; the nonzero shadow price means that additional raw material will increase revenue. This can be the case only if all presently available raw material is now being used.

For constraints with nonzero slack or excess, the value of the slack or excess variable is related to the ALLOWABLE INCREASE and ALLOWABLE DECREASE sections of the RIGHTHAND SIDE RANGES portion of the LINDO output. This relationship is detailed in Table 4.

Table 4
Allowable Increases and Decreases for Constraints with Nonzero Slack or Excess

TYPE OF CONSTRAINT	AI FOR rhs	AD FOR rhs
$\leq$	∞	$=$ Value for slack
$\geq$	$=$ Value of surplus	$= \infty$

For any constraint having positive slack or excess, the optimal z-value and values of the decision variables remain unchanged within the right-hand side's allowable range. To illustrate these ideas, consider the labor constraint in Example 1. Since slack $= 250$, we see from Table 4 that $AI = \infty$ and $AD = 250$. Thus, the current basis remains optimal for $4750 \leq$ available labor $\leq \infty$. Within this range, both the optimal z-value and values of the decision variables remain unchanged.

We close this section by noting that our discussions apply only if one objective function coefficient or one right-hand side is changed. If more than one objective function coefficient and/or right-hand side is changed, it is sometimes possible to use the LINDO output to determine whether the current basis remains optimal. See Section 6.4 for details.

◆ PROBLEMS

GROUP A

1. Farmer Leary grows wheat and corn on his 45-acre farm. He can sell at most 140 bushels of wheat and 120 bushels of corn. Each acre that is planted with wheat yields 5 bushels of wheat, and each acre that is planted with corn yields 4 bushels of corn. Wheat sells for $30 per bushel, and corn sells for $50 per bushel. To harvest an acre of wheat requires 6 hours of labor, and 10 hours of labor are needed to harvest an acre of corn. Up to 350 hours of labor can be purchased at $10 per hour. Let A1 = acres planted with wheat; A2 = acres planted with corn; and L = hours of labor that are purchased. In order to maximize profits, farmer Leary should solve the following LP:

$$\max z = 150A1 + 200A2 - 10L$$
$$\text{s.t.} \quad A1 + A2 \leq 45$$
$$6A1 + 10A2 - L \leq 0$$
$$L \leq 350$$
$$5A1 \leq 140$$
$$4A2 \leq 120$$
$$A1, A2, L \geq 0$$

Use the LINDO output in Figure 5 to answer the following questions:
(a) If only 40 acres of land were available, what would farmer Leary's profit be?
(b) If the price of wheat dropped to $26, what would be the new optimal solution to farmer Leary's problem?
(c) Use the SLACK portion of the output to determine the allowable increase and allowable decrease for the amount of wheat that can be sold. If only 130 bushels of wheat could be sold, would the answer to the problem change?

Figure 5 LINDO Output for Wheat/Corn in Problem 1

```
MAX      150 A1 + 200 A2 - 10 L
SUBJECT TO
      2)   A1 + A2 <=    45
      3)   6 A1 + 10 A2 - L <=   0
      4)   L <=    350
      5)   5 A1 <=    140
      6)   4 A2 <=    120
END

LP OPTIMUM FOUND AT STEP     4

        OBJECTIVE FUNCTION VALUE

     1)    4250.00000

VARIABLE        VALUE          REDUCED COST
    A1        25.000000           .000000
    A2        20.000000           .000000
    L        350.000000           .000000

   ROW     SLACK OR SURPLUS      DUAL PRICES
    2)          .000000          75.000000
    3)          .000000          12.500000
    4)          .000000           2.500000
    5)        15.000000           .000000
    6)        40.000000           .000000

NO. ITERATIONS=      4

RANGES IN WHICH THE BASIS IS UNCHANGED:

                        OBJ COEFFICIENT RANGES
VARIABLE        CURRENT      ALLOWABLE      ALLOWABLE
                 COEF        INCREASE       DECREASE
    A1        150.000000    10.000000      30.000000
    A2        200.000000    50.000000      10.000000
    L         -10.000000     INFINITY       2.500000

                       RIGHTHAND SIDE RANGES
   ROW        CURRENT      ALLOWABLE      ALLOWABLE
                RHS        INCREASE       DECREASE
    2        45.000000     1.200000       6.666667
    3         .000000     40.000000      12.000000
    4       350.000000    40.000000      12.000000
    5       140.000000     INFINITY      15.000000
    6       120.000000     INFINITY      40.000000
```

2. Carco manufactures cars and trucks. Each car contributes $300 to profit, and each truck contributes $400 to profit. The resources required to manufacture a car and a truck are shown in Table 5. Each day, Carco can rent up

Table 5

	DAYS ON TYPE 1 MACHINE	DAYS ON TYPE 2 MACHINE	TONS OF STEEL
Car	0.8	0.6	2
Truck	1	0.7	3

to 98 type 1 machines at a cost of $50 per machine. At present, the company has 73 type 2 machines and 260 tons of steel available. Marketing considerations dictate that at least 88 cars and at least 26 trucks be produced. Let x_1 = number of cars produced daily; x_2 = number of trucks produced daily; and m_1 = type 1 machines rented daily.

In order to maximize profit, Carco should solve the LP given in the LINDO output in Figure 6. Use the output to answer the following questions:

(a) If each car contributed $310 to profit, what would be the new optimal solution to the problem?

(b) If Carco were required to produce at least 86 cars, what would Carco's profit become?

Figure 6 LINDO Output for Carco in Problem 2

```
MAX     300 X1 + 400 X2 - 50 M1
SUBJECT TO
   2)     0.8 X1 + X2 - M1 <=    0
   3)     M1 <=    98
   4)     0.6 X1 + 0.7 X2 <=    73
   5)     2 X1 + 3 X2 <=   260
   6)     X1 >=    88
   7)     X2 >=    26
END

LP OPTIMUM FOUND AT STEP      4

       OBJECTIVE FUNCTION VALUE

    1)    32540.0000

   VARIABLE        VALUE          REDUCED COST
      X1         88.000000          .000000
      X2         27.600000          .000000
      M1         98.000000          .000000

    ROW   SLACK OR SURPLUS     DUAL PRICES
     2)         .000000         400.000000
     3)         .000000         350.000000
     4)         .879999            .000000
     5)        1.200003            .000000
     6)         .000000         -20.000000
     7)        1.599999            .000000

NO. ITERATIONS=      4

RANGES IN WHICH THE BASIS IS UNCHANGED:

                     OBJ COEFFICIENT RANGES
VARIABLE    CURRENT      ALLOWABLE      ALLOWABLE
            COEF         INCREASE       DECREASE
   X1.    300.000000     20.000000      INFINITY
   X2     400.000000      INFINITY     25.000000
   M1     -50.000000      INFINITY    350.000000

                     RIGHTHAND SIDE RANGES
ROW       CURRENT       ALLOWABLE      ALLOWABLE
          RHS           INCREASE       DECREASE
   2         .000000      .400001      1.599999
   3       98.000000      .400001      1.599999
   4       73.000000     INFINITY       .879999
   5      260.000000     INFINITY      1.200003
   6       88.000000     1.999999      3.000008
   7       26.000000     1.599999      INFINITY
```

3. Consider the diet problem discussed in Section 3.4. Use the LINDO output in Figure 7 to answer the following questions.

(a) If a Brownie costs 30¢, what would be the new optimal solution to the problem?

(b) If a bottle of cola cost 35¢, what would be the new optimal solution to the problem?

(c) If at least 8 oz of chocolate were required, what would be the cost of the optimal diet?

(d) If at least 600 calories were required, what would be the cost of the optimal diet?

(e) If at least 9 oz of sugar were required, what would be the cost of the optimal diet?

(f) What would the price of pineapple cheesecake have to be before it would be optimal to eat some cheesecake?

(g) What would the price of a brownie have to be before it would be optimal to eat a brownie?

(h) Use the SLACK or SURPLUS portion of the LINDO output to determine the allowable increase and allowable decrease for the fat constraint. If 10 oz of fat were required, would the optimal solution to the problem change?

Figure 7 LINDO Output for Diet Problem

```
MIN     50 BR + 20 IC + 30 COLA + 80 PC
SUBJECT TO
   2)    400 BR + 200 IC + 150 COLA + 500 PC >=    500
   3)      3 BR + 2 IC >=    6
   4)      2 BR + 2 IC + 4 COLA + 4 PC >=    10
   5)      2 BR + 4 IC + COLA + 5 PC >=    8
END

LP OPTIMUM FOUND AT STEP      2

       OBJECTIVE FUNCTION VALUE

    1)    90.0000000

   VARIABLE        VALUE          REDUCED COST
      BR          .000000         27.500000
      IC         3.000000          .000000
      COLA       1.000000          .000000
      PC          .000000         50.000000

    ROW   SLACK OR SURPLUS     DUAL PRICES
     2)      250.000000           .000000
     3)         .000000        -2.500000
     4)         .000000        -7.500000
     5)        5.000000           .000000

NO. ITERATIONS=      2

RANGES IN WHICH THE BASIS IS UNCHANGED:

                        OBJ COEFFICIENT RANGES
VARIABLE      CURRENT        ALLOWABLE       ALLOWABLE
              COEF           INCREASE        DECREASE
   BR        50.000000        INFINITY       27.500000
   IC        20.000000       18.333330        5.000000
   COLA      30.000000       10.000000       30.000000
   PC        80.000000        INFINITY       50.000000

                        RIGHTHAND SIDE RANGES
ROW         CURRENT         ALLOWABLE       ALLOWABLE
            RHS             INCREASE        DECREASE
   2       500.000000      250.000000       INFINITY
   3         6.000000        4.000000        2.857143
   4        10.000000        INFINITY        4.000000
   5         8.000000        5.000000        INFINITY
```

4. Gepbab Corporation produces three products at two different plants. The cost of producing a unit at each plant is shown in Table 6. Each plant can produce a total of 10,000 units. At least 6000 units of product 1, at least 8000 units of product 2, and at least 5000 units of product 3 must be produced. To minimize the cost of meeting these demands, the following LP should be solved:

$$\min z = 5x_{11} + 6x_{12} + 8x_{13} + 8x_{21} + 7x_{22} + 10x_{23}$$

$$\text{s.t.} \quad x_{11} + x_{12} + x_{13} \quad\quad\quad\quad \leq 10,000$$
$$x_{21} + x_{22} + x_{23} \leq 10,000$$
$$x_{11} \quad\quad\quad + x_{21} \quad\quad\quad \geq 6000$$
$$x_{12} \quad\quad\quad + x_{22} \quad\quad \geq 8000$$
$$x_{13} \quad\quad\quad + x_{23} \geq 5000$$
$$\text{All variables} \geq 0$$

Table 6

	PRODUCT 1	PRODUCT 2	PRODUCT 3
Plant 1	$5	$6	$8
Plant 2	$8	$7	$10

Here, x_{ij} = number of units of product j produced at plant i. Use the LINDO output in Figure 8 to answer the following questions:

(a) What would the cost of producing product 2 at plant 1 have to be in order for the firm to want to produce product 2 at plant 1?

(b) What would total cost be if plant 1 had 9000 units of capacity?

(c) If it cost $9 to produce a unit of product 3 at plant 1, what would be the new optimal solution?

Figure 8 LINDO Output for Problem 4

```
MIN    5 X11 + 6 X12 + 8 X13 + 8 X21 + 7 X22 + 10 X23
SUBJECT TO
        2)    X11 + X12 + X13 <=    10000
        3)    X21 + X22 + X23 <=    10000
        4)    X11 + X21 >=    6000
        5)    X12 + X22 >=    8000
        6)    X13 + X23 >=    5000
END

LP OPTIMUM FOUND AT STEP      5

        OBJECTIVE FUNCTION VALUE

        1)      128000.000

VARIABLE        VALUE           REDUCED COST
   X11        6000.000000         .000000
   X12          .000000         1.000000
   X13        4000.000000         .000000
   X21          .000000         1.000000
   X22        8000.000000         .000000
   X23        1000.000000         .000000

ROW      SLACK OR SURPLUS      DUAL PRICES
   2)          .000000          2.000000
   3)        1000.000000         .000000
   4)          .000000         -7.000000
   5)          .000000         -7.000000
   6)          .000000        -10.000000

NO. ITERATIONS=      5

RANGES IN WHICH THE BASIS IS UNCHANGED:

                        OBJ COEFFICIENT RANGES
VARIABLE      CURRENT      ALLOWABLE      ALLOWABLE
               COEF        INCREASE       DECREASE
   X11       5.000000     1.000000       7.000000
   X12       6.000000     INFINITY       1.000000
   X13       8.000000     1.000000       1.000000
   X21       8.000000     INFINITY       1.000000
   X22       7.000000     1.000000       7.000000
   X23      10.000000     1.000000       1.000000

                        RIGHTHAND SIDE RANGES
ROW          CURRENT      ALLOWABLE      ALLOWABLE
              RHS         INCREASE       DECREASE
   2      10000.000000   1000.000000   1000.000000
   3      10000.000000   INFINITY      1000.000000
   4       6000.000000   1000.000000   1000.000000
   5       8000.000000   1000.000000   8000.000000
   6       5000.000000   1000.000000   1000.000000
```

5. Mondo produces motorcycles at three plants. At each plant, the labor, raw material, and production costs (excluding labor cost) required to build a motorcycle are as shown in Table 7. Each plant has sufficient machine capacity to produce up to 750 motorcycles per week. Each of Mondo's workers can work up to 40 hours per week and is paid $12.50 per hour worked. Mondo has a total of 525 workers and now owns 9,400 units of raw material. Each week, at least 1400 Mondos must be produced. Let x_1 = motorcycles produced at plant 1; x_2 = motorcycles produced at plant 2; and x_3 = motorcycles produced at plant 3.

The LINDO output in Figure 9 enables Mondo to minimize the variable cost (labor + production) of meeting demand. Use the LINDO output to answer the following questions:

(a) What would be the new optimal solution to the problem if the production cost at plant 1 were only $40?
(b) How much money would Mondo save if the capacity of plant 3 were increased by 100 motorcycles?
(c) By how much would Mondo's cost increase if it had to produce one more motorcycle?

Table 7

PLANT	LABOR NEEDED	RAW MATERIAL NEEDED	PRODUCTION COST
1	20 hours	5 units	$50
2	16 hours	8 units	$80
3	10 hours	7 units	$100

Figure 9   LINDO Output for Problem 5

```
MIN      300 X1 + 280 X2 + 225 X3
SUBJECT TO
       2)   20 X1 + 16 X2 + 10 X3 <=    21000
       3)    5 X1 +  8 X2 +  7 X3 <=     9400
       4)   X1 <=    750
       5)   X2 <=    750
       6)   X3 <=    750
       7)   X1 + X2 + X3 >=    1400
END

LP OPTIMUM FOUND AT STEP        3

         OBJECTIVE FUNCTION VALUE

       1)    357750.000

    VARIABLE        VALUE        REDUCED COST
       X1       350.000000         .000000
       X2       300.000000         .000000
       X3       750.000000         .000000


       ROW    SLACK OR SURPLUS    DUAL PRICES
       2)      1700.000000         .000000
       3)          .000000        6.666668
       4)       400.000000         .000000
       5)       450.000000         .000000
       6)          .000000       61.666660
       7)          .000000     -333.333300

NO. ITERATIONS=        3

RANGES IN WHICH THE BASIS IS UNCHANGED:

                      OBJ COEFFICIENT RANGES
    VARIABLE      CURRENT      ALLOWABLE      ALLOWABLE
                   COEF        INCREASE       DECREASE
       X1       300.000000     INFINITY      20.000000
       X2       280.000000     20.000010     92.499990
       X3       225.000000     61.666660     INFINITY

                      RIGHTHAND SIDE RANGES
       ROW        CURRENT      ALLOWABLE      ALLOWABLE
                    RHS        INCREASE       DECREASE
        2       21000.000000    INFINITY     1700.000000
        3        9400.000000  1050.000000     900.000000
        4         750.000000    INFINITY      400.000000
        5         750.000000    INFINITY      450.000000
        6         750.000000   450.000000     231.818200
        7        1400.000000    63.750000     131.250000
```

6. Steelco uses coal, iron, and labor to produce three types of steel. The inputs (and sales price) for one ton of each type of steel are shown in Table 8. Up to 200 tons of coal can be purchased at a price of $10 per ton. Up to 60 tons of iron can be purchased at $8 per ton, and up to 100 labor hours can be purchased at $5 per hour. Let x_1 = tons of steel 1 produced; x_2 = tons of steel 2 produced; and x_3 = tons of steel 3 produced.

The LINDO output that yields a maximum profit for the company is given in Figure 10. Use the output to answer the following questions.

(a) What would profit be if only 40 tons of iron could be purchased?
(b) What is the smallest price per ton for steel 3 that would make it desirable to produce steel 3?
(c) Find the new optimal solution if steel 1 sold for $55 per ton.

Table 8

	COAL REQUIRED	IRON REQUIRED	LABOR REQUIRED	SALES PRICE
Steel 1	3 tons	1 ton	1 hour	$51
Steel 2	2 tons	0 ton	1 hour	$30
Steel 3	1 tons	1 ton	1 hour	$25

Figure 10   LINDO Output for Problem 6

```
MAX     8 X1 + 5 X2 + 2 X3
SUBJECT TO
        2)    3 X1 + 2 X2 + X3 <=    200
        3)    X1 + X3 <=    60
        4)    X1 + X2 + X3 <=    100
END

LP OPTIMUM FOUND AT STEP        2

        OBJECTIVE FUNCTION VALUE

        1)      530.000000

VARIABLE          VALUE          REDUCED COST
    X1          60.000000           .000000
    X2          10.000000           .000000
    X3           .000000           1.000000


    ROW     SLACK OR SURPLUS      DUAL PRICES
    2)          .000000           2.500000
    3)          .000000            .500000
    4)         30.000000           .000000

NO. ITERATIONS=        2

RANGES IN WHICH THE BASIS IS UNCHANGED:

                        OBJ COEFFICIENT RANGES
VARIABLE          CURRENT        ALLOWABLE       ALLOWABLE
                    COEF         INCREASE        DECREASE
    X1          8.000000         INFINITY         .500000
    X2          5.000000          .333333        5.000000
    X3          2.000000         1.000000        INFINITY

                        RIGHTHAND SIDE RANGES
    ROW             CURRENT        ALLOWABLE       ALLOWABLE
                      RHS          INCREASE        DECREASE
    2           200.000000        60.000000       20.000000
    3            60.000000         6.666667       60.000000
    4           100.000000        INFINITY        30.000000
```

GROUP B

7. Shoeco must meet (on time) the following demands for pairs of shoes: month 1 — 300; month 2 — 500; month 3 — 100; and month 4 — 100. At the beginning of month 1, 50 pairs of shoes are on hand, and Shoeco has three workers. A worker is paid $1500 per month. Each worker can work up to 160 hours per month before he receives overtime. During any month, each worker may be forced to work up to 20 hours of overtime; workers are paid $25 per hour for overtime labor. It takes 4 hours of labor and $5 of raw material to produce each pair of shoes. At the beginning of each month, workers can be hired or fired. Each hired worker costs $1600, and each fired worker costs $2000. At the end of each month, a holding cost of $30 per pair of shoes is assessed. Formulate an LP that can be used to minimize the total cost of meeting the next four months' demands. Then use LINDO to solve the LP. Finally, use the LINDO printout to answer the questions that follow these hints (which may help in the formulation). Let

x_t = Pairs of shoes produced during month t with nonovertime labor

o_t = Pairs of shoes produced during month t with overtime labor

i_t = Inventory of pairs of shoes at end of month t

h_t = Workers hired at beginning of month t

f_t = Workers fired at beginning of month t

w_t = Workers available for month t (after month t hiring and firing)

Four types of constraints will be needed:

Type 1 Inventory equations. For example, during month 1, $i_1 = 50 + x_1 + o_1 - 300$.

Type 2 Relate available workers to hiring and firing. For month 1, for example, the following constraint is needed: $w_1 = 3 + h_1 - f_1$.

Type 3 For each month, the amount of shoes made with nonovertime labor is limited by the number of workers. For example, for month 1, the following constraint is needed: $4x_1 \leq 160w_1$.

Type 4 For each month, the number of overtime labor hours used is limited by the number of workers. For example, for month 1, the following constraint is needed: $4(o_1) \leq 20w_1$.

For the objective function, the following costs must be considered:

1. Workers' salaries
2. Hiring costs
3. Firing costs
4. Holding costs
5. Overtime costs
6. Raw-material costs

(a) Describe the company's optimal production plan, hiring policy, and firing policy. Assume that it is acceptable to have a fractional number of workers, hirings, or firings.

(b) If overtime labor during month 1 costs $16 per hour, should any overtime labor be used during month 1?

(c) If the cost of firing workers during month 3 were $1800, what would be the new optimal solution to the problem?

(d) If the cost of hiring workers during month 1 were $1700, what would be the new optimal solution to the problem?

(e) By how much would total costs be reduced if demand in month 1 were 100 pairs of shoes?

(f) What would the total cost become if the company had 5 workers at the beginning of month 1 (before month 1's hiring or firing takes place)?

(g) By how much would costs increase if demand in month 2 were increased by 100 pairs of shoes?

5-3   MANAGERIAL USE OF SHADOW PRICES

In this section, we will discuss the managerial significance of shadow prices. In particular, we will learn how shadow prices can often be used to answer the following question: What is the maximum amount that a manager should be willing to pay for an additional unit of a resource? To answer this question, we usually focus our attention on the shadow price of the constraint that describes the availability of the resource. We now discuss four examples of the interpretation of shadow prices.

E X A M P L E
5

In Example 1, what is the most that Winco should be willing to pay for an additional unit of raw material? How about an extra hour of labor?

Solution

Since the shadow price of the raw-material-availability constraint is 1, an extra unit of raw material would increase total revenue by $1. Thus, Winco could pay up to $1 for an extra unit of raw material and be as well off as it is now. This means that Winco should be willing to pay up to $1 for an extra unit of raw material. The labor-availability constraint has a shadow price of 0. This means that an extra hour of labor will not increase revenues, so Winco should not be willing to pay anything for an extra hour of labor. (Note that this discussion is valid because the AIs for the labor and raw-material constraints both exceed 1). ◆

E X A M P L E
6

Let's reconsider Example 1 with the following changes. Suppose up to 4600 units of raw material are available, but they must be purchased at a cost of $4 per unit. Also suppose that up to 5000 hours of labor are available, but they must be purchased at a cost of $6 per hour. The per-unit sales price of each product is as follows: product 1—$30; product 2—$42; product 3—$53; product 4—$72. A total of 950 units must be produced, of which at least 400 must be product 4. Determine the maximum amount that the firm should be willing to pay for an extra unit of raw material and an extra hour of labor.

Solution

The contribution to profit from one unit of each product may be computed as follows:

$$\text{Product 1:} \quad 30 - 4(2) - 6(3) = \$4$$
$$\text{Product 2:} \quad 42 - 4(3) - 6(4) = \$6$$
$$\text{Product 3:} \quad 53 - 4(4) - 6(5) = \$7$$
$$\text{Product 4:} \quad 72 - 4(7) - 6(6) = \$8$$

Thus, Winco's profit is $4x_1 + 6x_2 + 7x_3 + 8x_4$. Then, to maximize Winco's profit, Winco should solve the same LP as in Example 1, and the relevant LINDO output is again Figure 3. To determine the most Winco should be willing to pay for an extra unit of raw material, note that the shadow price of the raw material constraint may be interpreted as follows. If Winco has the right to buy one more unit of raw material (at $4 per unit), then profits increase by $1. Thus, paying $4 + $1 = $5 for an extra unit of raw material will increase profits by $1 − $1 = $0. So Winco could pay up to $5 for an extra unit of raw material and still be better off. For the raw-material constraint, the shadow price of $1 represents a *premium* above and beyond the current price Winco is willing to pay for an extra unit of raw material.

The shadow price of the labor-availability constraint is $0, which means that the right to buy an extra hour of labor at $4 an hour will not increase profits. Unfortunately, all this tells us is that at the current price of $4 per hour, Winco should buy no more labor.

◆

E X A M P L E
7

Consider the farmer Leary problem (Problem 1 in Section 5.2).
a. What is the most that farmer Leary should be willing to pay for an additional hour of labor?
b. What is the most that farmer Leary should be willing to pay for an additional acre of land?

Solution

a. From the $L \leq 350$ constraint's shadow price of 2.5, we see that if 351 hours of labor are available, then (after paying $10 for another hour of labor) profits increase by $2.50. So if Leary pays $10 + $2.50 = $12.50 for an extra hour of labor, profits would increase by $2.50 − $2.50 = $0. This implies that farmer Leary should be willing to pay up to $12.50 for another hour of labor.

To look at it another way, the shadow price of the $6A1 + 10A2 − L \leq 0$ constraint is 12.5. This means that if the constraint $6A1 + 10A2 \leq L$ were replaced by the constraint $6A1 + 10A2 \leq L + 1$, profits would increase by $12.50. So if one extra hour of labor were "given" to Leary (at zero cost), profits would increase by $12.50. Thus, farmer Leary should be willing to pay up to $12.50 for an extra hour of labor.

b. If 46 acres of land were available, profits would increase by $75 (the shadow price of the $A1 + A2 \leq 45$ constraint). This includes the cost ($0) of purchasing an additional acre of land. Thus, farmer Leary should be willing to pay up to $75 for an extra acre of land.

◆

We now illustrate some of the managerial insights that can be gained by analyzing the shadow prices for a minimization problem.

E X A M P L E
8

The following questions refer to Example 2.
a. What is the most that Tucker should be willing to pay for an extra hour of labor?
b. What is the most that Tucker should be willing to pay for an extra unit of raw material?
c. A new customer is willing to purchase 20 cars at a price of $25,000 per vehicle. Should Tucker fill her order?

Solution

a. Since the shadow price of the labor-availability constraint (row 4) is 0, an extra hour of labor reduces costs by $0. Thus, Tucker should not pay anything for an extra hour of labor.

b. Since the shadow price of the raw-material-availability constraint (row 5) is 5 (thousand dollars), an additional unit of raw material reduces costs by $5000. Thus, Tucker should be willing to pay up to $5000 for an extra unit of raw material.

c. The allowable increase for the constraint $x_1 + x_2 + x_3 + x_4 = 1000$ is 66.666660. Since the shadow price of this constraint is -30 (thousand dollars), we know that if Tucker fills the order, its costs will increase by $-20(-30,000) = \$600,000$. So Tucker should not fill the order.

In Example 8, the astute reader may notice that each car costs at most \$15,000 to produce. How is it then possible that a unit increase in the number of cars that must be produced increases costs by \$30,000? To see why this is the case, we resolved Tucker's LP after increasing the number of cars that had to be produced to 1001. The new optimal solution has $z = 11,630$, $x_1 = 404$, $x_2 = 197$, $x_3 = 400$, $x_4 = 0$. We now see why increasing demand by one car raises costs by \$30,000. To produce one more car, Tucker must produce four more type 1 cars and 3 fewer type 2 cars. This ensures that Tucker still uses only 4400 units of raw material, but it increases total cost by $4(15,000) - 3(10,000) = \$30,000$!

♦ PROBLEMS

GROUP A

1. In Problem 2 of Section 5.2, what is the most that Carco should be willing to pay for an extra ton of steel?

2. In Problem 2 of Section 5.2, what is the most that Carco should be willing to pay to rent an additional type 1 machine for one day?

3. In Problem 3 of Section 5.2, what is the most that one should be willing to pay for an additional ounce of chocolate?

4. In Problem 4 of Section 5.2, how much should Gepbab be willing to pay for another unit of capacity at plant 1?

5. In Problem 5 of Section 5.2, suppose that Mondo could purchase an additional unit of raw material at a cost of \$6. Should the company do it? Explain.

6. In Problem 6 of Section 5.2, what is the most that Steelco should be willing to pay for an extra ton of coal?

7. In Problem 6 of Section 5.2, what is the most that Steelco should be willing to pay for an extra ton of iron?

8. In Problem 6 of Section 5.2, what is the most that Steelco should be willing to pay for an extra hour of labor?

9. In Problem 7 of Section 5.2, suppose that a new customer wishes to buy a pair of shoes during month 1 for \$70. Should Shoeco oblige him?

10. In Problem 7 of Section 5.2, what is the most the company would be willing to pay for having one more worker at the beginning of month 1?

5-4   WHAT HAPPENS TO THE OPTIMAL z-VALUE IF CURRENT BASIS IS NO LONGER OPTIMAL?

In Section 5.2, we used shadow prices to determine the new optimal z-value if the right-hand side of a constraint were changed and remained in the range where the current basis remains optimal. Suppose we change the right-hand side of a constraint to a value where the current basis is no longer optimal. In this situation, the LINDO PARA command enables us to determine how the shadow price of a constraint—and the optimal z-value—change.

We illustrate the use of the PARA command by varying the amount of raw material available in Example 1. Suppose we want to determine how the optimal z-value and shadow price change as the amount of available raw material varies between 0 and

10,000 units (recall that the current basis remains optimal only if available raw material is between 4450 and 4850). We now invoke the LINDO PARA command. We first tell LINDO to give us information on the change in z-value and shadow price as available raw material varies between its current value (4600) and 0. Then we use the PARA command to give us information on how the optimal z-value and shadow price change as available raw material varies between its current value (4600) and 10,000. It is important to point out that before each use of the PARA command, the analyst must resolve the LP (using the GO command). The resulting LINDO output contains the information shown in Figure 11.

Figure 11
Example of LINDO Output from PARA Command

VAR OUT	VAR IN	RHS VALUE	DUAL PRICE BEFORE PIVOT	OBJ VALUE
		10,000	0	6900
X3	S4	5250	0	6900
S5	S3	4850	1	6900
		4600	1	6650
X3	X1	4450	1	6500
X2	ART	3900	2	5400
		0	INFINITY	INFEASIBLE

Let rm be the amount of available raw material. Figure 11 tells us that if rm $<$ 3900, the LP is infeasible. If rm $=$ 3900, the optimal basis is obtained by pivoting in an artificial variable (at zero level) and letting x_2 leave the basis. The shadow price (or dual price) for raw material is now $2, and the optimal z-value is 5400. The current basis remains optimal until rm $=$ 4450. Between rm $=$ 3900 and rm $=$ 4450, each unit increase in rm will increase the optimal z-value by the shadow price of $2. Thus, when rm $=$ 4450, the optimal z-value will be

$$5400 + 2(4450 - 3900) = \$6500$$

From Figure 11, we see that when rm $=$ 4450, x_1 enters the basis, and x_3 exits. The shadow price of rm is now $1, and each additional unit of rm (up to the next change of basis) will increase the optimal z-value by $1. The next basis change occurs when rm $=$ 4850. At this point, the new optimal z-value may be computed as (optimal z-value for rm $=$ 4450) $+$ (4850 $-$ 4450)($1) $=$ $6900. When rm $=$ 4850, we pivot in SLACK3 (the slack variable for row 3 or Constraint 2), and SLACK5 exits. The new shadow price for rm is $0. Thus when rm $>$ 4850, we see that an additional unit of rm will not increase the optimal z-value. The above discussion is summarized in Figure 12, which shows the optimal z-value as a function of the amount of available raw material.

For any LP, a graph of the optimal objective function value as a function of a right-hand side will consist of several straight-line segments of possibly differing slopes. (Such a function is called a piecewise linear function.) The slope of each straight-line segment is just the constraint's shadow price. At points where the optimal basis changes (points B, C, and D in Figure 12), the slope of the graph may change. For a $\leq$ constraint in a maximization problem, the slope of each line segment must be nonnegative—more of a resource can't hurt. In a maximization problem, the slopes of successive line segments for a $\leq$ constraint will be nonincreasing. This is simply a consequence of diminishing returns; as we obtain more of a resource (and availability of other resources is held constant), the value of an additional unit of the resource cannot increase.

Figure 12
Optimal z-Value
versus Raw Material

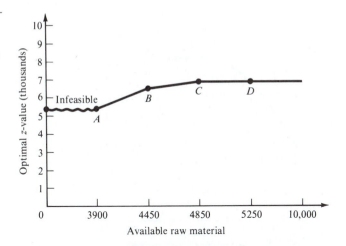

For a $\geq$ constraint in a maximization problem, the graph of optimal z-value as a function of the right-hand side will again be a piecewise linear function. The slope of each line segment will be nonpositive (corresponding to the fact that a $\geq$ constraint has a nonpositive shadow price). The slopes of successive line segments will be nonincreasing. For the $x_4 \geq 400$ constraint in Example 1, plotting the optimal z-value as a function of the constraint's right-hand side yields the graph in Figure 13.

Figure 13
Optimal z-Value
versus Product 4
Requirement

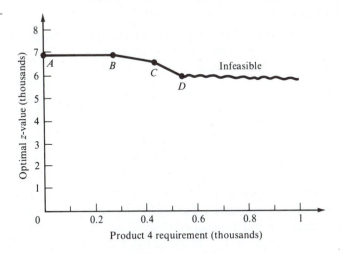

For an equality constraint in a maximization problem, the graph of optimal z-value as a function of right-hand side will again be piecewise linear. The slopes of each line segment may be positive or negative, but the slopes of successive line segments will again be nonincreasing. For the constraint $x_1 + x_2 + x_3 + x_4 = 950$ in Example 1, we obtain the graph in Figure 14.

For a minimization problem, the plot of optimal z-value against a constraint's right-hand side is again a piecewise linear function. For all minimization problems, the slopes of successive line segments will be nondecreasing. For a $\leq$ constraint, the slope

Figure 14
Optimal z-Value
versus Production
Requirement

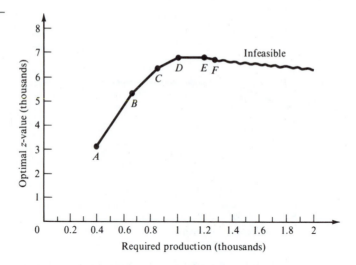

of each line segment is nonpositive; for a $\geq$ constraint, the slope of each line segment is nonnegative; and for an equality constraint, the slope of a line segment may be positive or negative.

EFFECT OF CHANGE IN OBJECTIVE FUNCTION COEFFICIENT ON OPTIMAL z-VALUE

We now discuss how to find the graph of the optimal objective function value as a function of a variable's objective function coefficient. To see how this works, let's reconsider the Giapetto problem.

$$\max z = 3x_1 + 2x_2$$
$$\text{s.t.} \quad 2x_1 + x_2 \leq 100$$
$$x_1 + x_2 \leq 80$$
$$x_1 \quad\quad \leq 40$$
$$x_1, x_2 \geq 0$$

Let c_1 = objective function coefficient for x_1. Currently, we have $c_1 = 3$. We want to determine how the optimal z-value depends on c_1. To determine this relationship, we must determine, for each value of c_1, the optimal values of the decision variables. Recall from Figure 1 that point $A = (0, 80)$ is optimal if the isoprofit line is flatter than the carpentry constraint. Also note that point $B = (20, 60)$ is optimal if the slope of the isoprofit line is steeper than the carpentry constraint and flatter than the finishing-hour constraint. Finally, point $C = (40, 20)$ is optimal if the slope of the isoprofit line is steeper than the slope of the finishing-hour constraint. Since a typical isoprofit line is $c_1 x_1 + 2x_2 = k$, we know that the slope of a typical isoprofit line is $-\frac{c_1}{2}$. This implies that point A is optimal if $-\frac{c_1}{2} \geq -1$ (or $c_1 \leq 2$). We also find that point B is optimal if $-2 \leq -\frac{c_1}{2} \leq -1$ (or $2 \leq c_1 \leq 4$). Finally, point C is optimal if $-\frac{c_1}{2} \leq -2$ (or $c_1 \geq 4$). By substituting the optimal values of the decision variables into the objective function ($c_1 x_1 + 2x_2$), we obtain the following information:

Value of c_1	Optimal z-value
$0 \le c_1 \le 2$	$c_1(0) + 2(80) = \$160$
$2 \le c_1 \le 4$	$c_1(20) + 2(60) = 120 + 20c_1$
$c_1 \ge 4$	$c_1(40) + 2(20) = 40 + 40c_1$

The relationship between c_1 and the optimal z-value is portrayed graphically in Figure 15. As seen in the figure, the graph of optimal z-value as a function of c_1 is a piecewise linear function. The slope of each line segment in the graph is equal to the value of x_1 in the optimal solution. In a maximization problem, it can be shown (see Problem 5) that as the value of an objective function coefficient increases, the value of the variable in the LP's optimal solution cannot decrease. Thus, the slope of the graph of the optimal z-value as a function of an objective function coefficient will be non-decreasing.

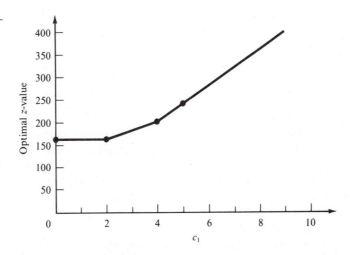

Figure 15
Optimal z-Value
versus c_1

Similarly, in a minimization problem, the graph of the optimal z-value as a function of a variable x_i's objective function coefficient c_i is a piecewise linear function. Again, the slope of each line segment is equal to the optimal value of x_i in the bfs corresponding to the line segment. It can be shown (see Problem 6) that the optimal x_i-value is a nonincreasing function of c_i. Thus, in a minimization problem, the graph of the optimal z-value as a function of c_i will be a piecewise linear function having a nonincreasing slope.

◆ PROBLEMS

GROUP A

In what follows, b_i represents the right-hand side of an LP's ith constraint.

1. Use the LINDO PARA command to graph the optimal z-value for Example 1 as a function of b_4.

2. Use the LINDO PARA command to graph the optimal z-value for Example 2 as a function of b_1. Then answer the same question for b_2, b_3, and b_4, respectively.

3. For the Giapetto example of Section 3.1, graph the optimal z-value as a function of x_2's objective function coefficient. Also graph the optimal z-value as a function of b_1, b_2, and b_3.

4. For the Dorian Auto example (Example 2 in Chapter 3), let c_1 be the objective function coefficient of x_1. Determine the optimal z-value as a function of c_1.

GROUP B

5. For Example 1, suppose that we increase the sales price of a product. Show that in the new optimal solution, the amount produced of that product cannot decrease.

6. For Example 2, suppose that we increase the cost of producing a type of car. Show that in the new optimal solution to the LP, the number of cars produced of that type cannot increase.

7. Consider the Sailco problem (Example 12 in Chapter 3). Suppose we want to consider how profit will be affected if we change the number of sailboats that can be produced each month with regular-time labor. How can we use the LINDO PARA command to answer this question? (*Hint:* Let c = change in number of sailboats that can be produced each month with regular-time labor. Change the right-hand side of some constraints to $40 + c$ and add a constraint to the problem.)

♦ SUMMARY

GRAPHICAL SENSITIVITY ANALYSIS

To determine whether the current basis remains optimal after changing an objective function coefficient, note that changing the objective function coefficient of a variable changes the slope of the isoprofit line. The current basis remains optimal as long as the current optimal solution is the last point in the feasible region to make contact with isoprofit lines as we move in the direction of increasing z (for a max problem). If the current basis remains optimal, the values of the decision variables remain unchanged, but the optimal z-value may change.

To determine if the current basis remains optimal after changing the right-hand side of a constraint, begin by finding the constraints (possibly including sign restrictions) that are binding for the current optimal solution. As we change the right-hand side of a constraint, the current basis remains optimal as long as the point where the constraints are binding remains feasible. Even if the current basis remains optimal, the values of the decision variables and the optimal z-value may change.

SHADOW PRICES

The **shadow price** of the ith constraint of a linear programming problem is the amount by which the optimal z-value is improved if the right-hand side of the ith constraint is increased by 1 (assuming that the current basis remains optimal). The shadow price of the ith constraint is the dual price for row $i + 1$ given on the LINDO output.

If the right-hand side of the ith constraint is increased by Δb_i, then (assuming the current basis remains optimal) the new optimal z-value for a maximization problem may be found as follows:

$$\text{(New optimal } z\text{-value)} = \text{(old optimal } z\text{-value)}$$
$$+ \text{(Constraint } i\text{'s shadow price)}\Delta b_i \tag{1}$$

For a minimization problem, the new optimal z-value may be found from

$$\text{(New optimal } z\text{-value)} = \text{(old optimal } z\text{-value)}$$
$$- \text{(Constraint } i\text{'s shadow price)}\Delta b_i \tag{2}$$

OBJECTIVE FUNCTION COEFFICIENT RANGE

The OBJ COEFFICIENT RANGES portion of the LINDO output gives the range of values for an objective function coefficient for which the current basis remains optimal. Within this range, the values of the decision variables remain unchanged, but the optimal z-value may or may not change.

REDUCED COST

For any nonbasic variable, the reduced cost for the variable is the amount by which the nonbasic variable's objective function coefficient must be improved before that variable will be a basic variable in some optimal solution to the LP.

RIGHT-HAND SIDE RANGE

If the right-hand side of a constraint remains within the RIGHTHAND SIDE RANGES value given on the LINDO printout, the current basis remains optimal, and the LINDO listing's value for that constraint's dual price may be used to determine how a change in the constraint's right-hand side changes the optimal z-value. Even if the right-hand side of a constraint remains within the RIGHTHAND SIDE RANGES value on the LINDO output, the values of the decision variables will probably change.

SIGNS OF SHADOW PRICES

A $\geq$ constraint will have a nonpositive shadow price; a $\leq$ constraint will have a non-negative shadow price; and an equality constraint may have a positive, negative, or zero shadow price.

OPTIMAL z-VALUE AS A FUNCTION OF A CONSTRAINT'S RIGHT-HAND SIDE

In all cases, the optimal z-value will be a piecewise linear function of a constraint's right-hand side. The exact form of the function is as shown in Table 9.

	TYPE OF LP	TYPE OF CONSTRAINT	SLOPES OF EACH PIECEWISE LINEAR SEGMENT ARE
Table 9	Maximization	$\leq$	Nonnegative and nonincreasing
	Maximization	$\geq$	Nonpositive and nonincreasing
	Maximization	$=$	Unrestricted in sign and nonincreasing
	Minimization	$\leq$	Nonpositive and nondecreasing
	Minimization	$\geq$	Nonnegative and nondecreasing
	Minimization	$=$	Unrestricted in sign and nondecreasing

OPTIMAL z-VALUE AS A FUNCTION OF AN OBJECTIVE FUNCTION COEFFICIENT

In a maximization problem, the optimal z-value will be a nondecreasing, piecewise linear function of an objective function coefficient. The slope of the function will be a nondecreasing function of the objective function coefficient.

In a minimization problem, the optimal z-value will be a nondecreasing, piecewise linear function of an objective function coefficient. The slope of the function will be a nonincreasing function of the objective function coefficient.

◆ REVIEW PROBLEMS

GROUP A

1. HAL produces two types of computers: PCs and VAXes. The computers are produced in two locations: New York and Los Angeles. New York can produce up to 800 computers, and Los Angeles can produce up to 1000 computers. HAL can sell up to 900 PCs and 900 VAXes. The profit associated with each production site and computer sale is as follows: New York—PC, $600; VAX, $800; Los Angeles—PC, $1000; VAX, $1300. The skilled labor required to build each computer at each location is as follows: New York—PC, 2 hours; VAX, 2 hours; Los Angeles—PC, 3 hours; VAX, 4 hours. A total of 4000 hours of labor are available. Labor is purchased at a cost of $20 per hour. Let

$$XNP = \text{PCs produced in New York}$$
$$XLP = \text{PCs produced in Los Angeles}$$
$$XNV = \text{VAXes produced in New York}$$
$$XLV = \text{VAXes produced in Los Angeles}$$

We then obtain the LINDO printout in Figure 16. Use this printout to answer the following questions.
(a) If 3000 hours of skilled labor were available, what would be HAL's profit?
(b) Suppose an outside contractor offers to increase the capacity of New York to 850 computers, at a cost of $5000. Should HAL hire the contractor?
(c) By how much would the profit for a VAX produced in Los Angeles have to increase before HAL would want to produce VAXes in Los Angeles?
(d) What is the most HAL should be willing to pay for an extra hour of labor?

2. Vivian's Gem Company produces two types of gems: type 1 and type 2. Each type 1 gem contains 2 rubies and 4 diamonds. A type 1 gem sells for $10 and costs $5 to produce. Each type 2 gem contains 1 ruby and 1 diamond. A type 2 gem sells for $6 and costs $4 to produce. 30 rubies and 50 diamonds are available. All gems that are produced can be sold, but marketing considerations dictate that at least 11 type 1 gems be produced. Let x_1 = number of type 1 gems produced and x_2 = number of type 2 gems produced. Assume that Vivian wants to maximize profit. Use the LINDO printout in Figure 17 to answer the following questions:
(a) What would Vivian's profit be if 46 diamonds were available?
(b) If type 2 gems sold for only $5.50, what would be the new optimal solution to the problem?
(c) What would Vivian's profit be if at least 12 type 1 gems had to be produced?

3. Wivco produces product 1 and product 2 by processing raw material. Up to 90 lb of raw material may be purchased at a cost of $10/lb. One pound of raw material can be used to produce either 1 lb of product 1 or 0.33 lb of product 2. Using a pound of raw material to produce a pound of product 1 requires 2 hours of labor. Using a pound of raw material to produce 0.33 lb of product 2 requires 3 hours of labor. 200 hours of labor are available, and at most 40 pounds of product 2 can be sold. Product 1 sells for $13/lb, and product 2 sells for $40/lb. Let

RM = pounds of raw material processed

$P1$ = pounds of raw material used to produce product 1

$P2$ = pounds of raw material used to produce product 2

In order to maximize profit, Wivco should solve the following LP:

$$\max z = 13P1 + 40(0.33)P2 - 10RM$$
$$\text{s.t.} \quad RM \geq P1 + P2$$
$$2P1 + 3P2 \leq 200$$
$$RM \leq 90$$
$$0.33P2 \leq 40$$
$$P1, P2, RM \geq 0$$

Use the LINDO output in Figure 18 to answer the following questions:

(**a**) If only 87 lb of raw material could be purchased, what
would be Wivco's profits?

(**b**) If product 2 sold for $39.50/lb, what would be the new
optimal solution to Wivco's problem?

(**c**) What is the most that Wivco should be willing to pay
for another pound of raw material?

(**d**) What is the most that Wivco should be willing to pay
for another hour of labor?

Figure 16   LINDO Output for Problem 1

```
MAX     600 XNP + 1000 XLP + 800 XNV + 1300 XLV - 20 L
SUBJECT TO
      2)     2 XNP + 3 XLP + 2 XNV + 4 XLV - L <=     0
      3)     XNP + XNV <=    800
      4)     XLP + XLV <=   1000
      5)     XNP + XLP <=    900
      6)     XNV + XLV <=    900
      7)     L <=    4000
END

LP OPTIMUM FOUND AT STEP      3

        OBJECTIVE FUNCTION VALUE

      1)     1360000.00

VARIABLE         VALUE          REDUCED COST
   XNP          .000000          200.000000
   XLP          800.000000          .000000
   XNV          800.000000          .000000
   XLV          .000000          33.333370
    L          4000.000000          .000000


   ROW     SLACK OR SURPLUS      DUAL PRICES
   2)          .000000          333.333300
   3)          .000000          133.333300
   4)          200.000000          .000000
   5)          100.000000          .000000
   6)          100.000000          .000000
   7)          .000000          313.333300

NO. ITERATIONS=      3

RANGES IN WHICH THE BASIS IS UNCHANGED:

                     OBJ COEFFICIENT RANGES
VARIABLE      CURRENT       ALLOWABLE       ALLOWABLE
              COEF          INCREASE        DECREASE
   XNP       600.000000     200.000000      INFINITY
   XLP      1000.000000     200.000000     25.000030
   XNV       800.000000      INFINITY      133.333300
   XLV      1300.000000     33.333370       INFINITY
    L        -20.000000      INFINITY      313.333300

                     RIGHTHAND SIDE RANGES
   ROW       CURRENT        ALLOWABLE       ALLOWABLE
             RHS            INCREASE        DECREASE
    2         .000000       300.000000     2400.000000
    3        800.000000     100.000000      150.000000
    4       1000.000000      INFINITY       200.000000
    5        900.000000      INFINITY       100.000000
    6        900.000000      INFINITY       100.000000
    7       4000.000000     300.000000     2400.000000
```

Figure 17   LINDO Output for Problem 2

```
MAX     5 X1 + 2 X2
SUBJECT TO
      2)     2 X1 + X2 <=    30
      3)     4 X1 + X2 <=    50
      4)     X1 >=    11
END

LP OPTIMUM FOUND AT STEP      2

        OBJECTIVE FUNCTION VALUE

      1)     67.0000000

VARIABLE         VALUE          REDUCED COST
   X1          11.000000          .000000
   X2          6.000000          .000000


   ROW     SLACK OR SURPLUS      DUAL PRICES
   2)         2.000000          .000000
   3)          .000000          2.000000
   4)          .000000         -3.000000

NO. ITERATIONS=      2

RANGES IN WHICH THE BASIS IS UNCHANGED:

                     OBJ COEFFICIENT RANGES
VARIABLE      CURRENT       ALLOWABLE       ALLOWABLE
              COEF          INCREASE        DECREASE
   X1        5.000000       3.000000        INFINITY
   X2        2.000000       INFINITY        .750000

                     RIGHTHAND SIDE RANGES
   ROW       CURRENT        ALLOWABLE       ALLOWABLE
             RHS            INCREASE        DECREASE
    2        30.000000      INFINITY        2.000000
    3        50.000000      2.000000        6.000000
    4        11.000000      1.500000        1.000000
```

Figure 18   LINDO Output for Problem 3

```
MAX     13 P1 + 13.2 P2 - 10 RM
SUBJECT TO
      2)   - P1 - P2 + RM >=     0
      3)     2 P1 + 3 P2 <=   200
      4)     RM <=    90
      5)     0.33 P2 <=    40
END

    LP OPTIMUM FOUND AT STEP      3

        OBJECTIVE FUNCTION VALUE

      1)     274.000000

VARIABLE         VALUE          REDUCED COST
   P1          70.000000          0.000000
   P2          20.000000          0.000000
   RM          90.000000          0.000000


   ROW     SLACK OR SURPLUS      DUAL PRICES
   2)         0.000000         -12.600000
   3)         0.000000          0.200000
   4)         0.000000          2.600000
   5)         33.400002          0.000000

NO. ITERATIONS=      3

RANGES IN WHICH THE BASIS IS UNCHANGED

                     OBJ COEFFICIENT RANGES
VARIABLE      CURRENT       ALLOWABLE       ALLOWABLE
              COEF          INCREASE        DECREASE
   P1        13.000000      0.200000        0.866667
   P2        13.200000      1.300000        0.200000
   RM        -10.000000     INFINITY        2.600000

                     RIGHTHAND SIDE RANGES
   ROW       CURRENT        ALLOWABLE       ALLOWABLE
             RHS            INCREASE        DECREASE
    2        0.000000       23.333334      10.000000
    3        200.000000     70.000000      20.000000
    4        90.000000      10.000000      23.333334
    5        40.000000      INFINITY       33.400002
```

4. Zales Jewelers uses rubies and sapphires to produce two types of rings. A type 1 ring requires 2 rubies, 3 sapphires, and 1 hour of jeweler's labor. A type 2 ring requires 3 rubies, 2 sapphires, and 2 hours of jeweler's labor. Each type 1 ring sells for $400, and each type 2 ring sells for $500. All rings produced by Zales can be sold. At present, Zales has 100 rubies, 120 sapphires, and 70 hours of jeweler's labor. Extra rubies can be purchased at a cost of $100 per ruby. Market demand requires that the company produce at least 20 type 1 rings and at least 25 type 2 rings. In order to maximize profit, Zales should solve the following LP:

$$X1 = \text{type 1 rings produced}$$
$$X2 = \text{type 2 rings produced}$$
$$R = \text{number of rubies purchased}$$
$$\max z = 400X1 + 500X2 - 100R$$
$$\text{s.t.} \quad 2X1 + 3X2 - R \le 100$$
$$3X1 + 2X2 \le 120$$
$$X1 + 2X2 \le 70$$
$$X1 \ge 20$$
$$X2 \ge 25$$
$$X1, X2 \ge 0$$

Use the LINDO output in Figure 19 to answer the following questions:

(a) Suppose that instead of costing $100, each ruby costs $190. Would Zales still purchase rubies? What would be the new optimal solution to the problem?

(b) Suppose that Zales were only required to produce at least 23 type 2 rings. What would Zales' profit now be?

(c) What is the most that Zales would be willing to pay for another hour of jeweler's labor?

(d) What is the most that Zales would be willing to pay for another sapphire?

5. Beerco manufactures ale and beer from corn, hops, and malt. At present, 40 lb of corn, 30 lb of hops, and 40 lb of malt are available. A barrel of ale sells for $40 and requires 1 lb of corn, 1 lb of hops, and 2 lb of malt. A barrel of beer sells for $50 and requires 2 lb of corn, 1 lb of hops, and 1 lb of malt. Beerco can sell all ale and beer that is produced. Assuming that Beerco's goal is to maximize total sales revenue, Beerco should solve the following LP:

$$\max z = 40ALE + 50BEER$$
$$\text{s.t.} \quad ALE + 2BEER \le 40 \quad \text{(Corn constraint)}$$
$$ALE + BEER \le 30 \quad \text{(Hops constraint)}$$
$$2ALE + BEER \le 40 \quad \text{(Malt constraint)}$$
$$ALE, BEER \ge 0$$

Figure 19 LINDO Output for Problem 4

```
MAX    400 X1 + 500 X2 - 100 R
SUBJECT TO
     2)    2 X1 + 3 X2 - R <=   100
     3)    3 X1 + 2 X2 <=   120
     4)    X1 + 2 X2 <=   70
     5)    X1 >=   20
     6)    X2 >=   25
END

LP OPTIMUM FOUND   AT STEP     2

           OBJECTIVE FUNCTION VALUE

   1)         19000.0000

VARIABLE         VALUE          REDUCED COST
    X1         20.000000          0.000000
    X2         25.000000          0.000000
    R          15.000000          0.000000

ROW       SLACK OR SURPLUS       DUAL PRICES
    2)         0.000000         100.000000
    3)        10.000000           0.000000
    4)         0.000000         200.000000
    5)         0.000000           0.000000
    6)         0.000000        -200.000000

NO. ITERATIONS=        2

RANGES IN WHICH THE BASIS IS UNCHANGED

                     OBJ COEFFICIENT RANGES
VARIABLE        CURRENT       ALLOWABLE      ALLOWABLE
                 COEF         INCREASE       DECREASE
    X1        400.000000      INFINITY      100.000000
    X2        500.000000     200.000000     INFINITY
    R        -100.000000     100.000000     100.000000

                     RIGHTHAND SIDE RANGES
ROW            CURRENT        ALLOWABLE      ALLOWABLE
                 RHS          INCREASE       DECREASE
    2         100.000000      15.000000     INFINITY
    3         120.000000      INFINITY      10.000000
    4          70.000000       3.333333      0.000000
    5          20.000000       0.000000     INFINITY
    6          25.000000       0.000000      2.500000
```

ALE = barrels of ale produced, and BEER = barrels of beer produced.

(a) Graphically find the range of values for the price of ale for which the current basis remains optimal.

(b) Graphically find the range of values for the price of beer for which the current basis remains optimal.

(c) Graphically find the range of values for the amount of available corn for which the current basis remains optimal. What is the shadow price of the corn constraint?

(d) Graphically find the range of values for the amount of available hops for which the current basis remains optimal. What is the shadow price of the hops constraint?

(e) Graphically find the range of values for the amount of available malt for which the current basis remains optimal. What is the shadow price of the malt constraint?

(f) Find the shadow price of each constraint if the constraints were expressed in ounces instead of pounds.

(g) Draw a graph of the optimal z-value as a function of the price of ale.

(h) Draw a graph of the optimal z-value as a function of the amount of available corn.

(i) Draw a graph of the optimal z-value as a function of the amount of available hops.

(j) Draw a graph of the optimal z-value as a function of the amount of available malt.

6. Gepbab Production Company uses labor and raw material to produce three products. The resource requirements and sales price for the three products are as shown in Table 10. At present, 60 units of raw material are available. Up to 90 hours of labor can be purchased at $1 per hour. In order to maximize profits, Gepbab should solve the following LP:

$$\max z = 6X1 + 8X2 + 13X3 - L$$

$$\text{s.t.} \quad 3X1 + 4X2 + 6X3 - L \leq 0$$

$$2X1 + 2X2 + 5X3 \qquad \leq 60$$

$$L \leq 90$$

$$X1, X2, X3, L \geq 0$$

Here, X_i = units of product i produced, and L = number of labor hours purchased. Use the LINDO output in Figure 20 to answer the following questions:

(a) What is the most the company would be willing to pay for another unit of raw material?

(b) What is the most the company would be willing to pay for another hour of labor?

(c) What would product 1 have to sell for to make it desirable for the company to produce it?

(d) If 100 hours of labor could be purchased, what would the company's profit be?

(e) Find the new optimal solution if product 3 sold for $15.

Table 10

	PRODUCT 1	PRODUCT 2	PRODUCT 3
Labor	3 hours	4 hours	6 hours
Raw material	2 units	2 units	5 units
Sales price	$6	$8	$13

Figure 20 LINDO Output for Problem 6

```
MAX      6 X1 + 8 X2 + 13 X3 - L
SUBJECT TO
      2)    3 X1 + 4 X2 + 6 X3 - L <=    0
      3)    2 X1 + 2 X2 + 5 X3 <=    60
      4)    L <=    90
END

LP OPTIMUM FOUND AT STEP       3

         OBJECTIVE FUNCTION VALUE

      1)     97.5000000

VARIABLE        VALUE          REDUCED COST
    X1          .000000          .250000
    X2        11.250000          .000000
    X3         7.500000          .000000
    L         90.000000          .000000


ROW     SLACK OR SURPLUS       DUAL PRICES
   2)          .000000          1.750000
   3)          .000000           .500000
   4)          .000000           .750000

NO. ITERATIONS=        3

RANGES IN WHICH THE BASIS IS UNCHANGED:

                       OBJ COEFFICIENT RANGES
VARIABLE        CURRENT        ALLOWABLE        ALLOWABLE
                 COEF          INCREASE         DECREASE
    X1         6.000000         .250000         INFINITY
    X2         8.000000         .666667          .666667
    X3        13.000000        3.000000         1.000000
    L         -1.000000        INFINITY          .750000

                       RIGHTHAND SIDE RANGES
ROW             CURRENT        ALLOWABLE        ALLOWABLE
                 RHS           INCREASE         DECREASE
   2             .000000       30.000000        18.000000
   3           60.000000       15.000000        15.000000
   4           90.000000       30.000000        18.000000
```

7. Giapetto, Inc., sells wooden soldiers and wooden trains. The resources used by Giapetto to produce a soldier and train are as shown in Table 11. 145,000 board ft of lumber and 90,000 hours of labor are available. Up to 50,000 soldiers and up to 50,000 trains can be sold, with trains selling for $55 and soldiers selling for $32. In addition to producing trains and soldiers itself, Giapetto can buy (from an outside supplier) extra soldiers at $27 per soldier and extra trains at $50 per train. Let

SM = thousands of soldiers manufactured

SB = thousands of soldiers bought at $27

TM = thousands of trains manufactured

TB = thousands of trains bought at $50

Table 11

	SOLDIER	TRAIN
Lumber	3 board ft	5 board ft
Labor	2 hours	4 hours

Then Giapetto can maximize profit by solving the LP in the LINDO printout in Figure 21. Use this printout to answer the following questions. (*Hint:* Think about the units of the constraints and objective function.)

(a) If Giapetto could purchase trains for $48 per train, what would be the new optimal solution to the LP? Explain.

(b) What is the most Giapetto would be willing to pay for another 100 board ft of lumber? What is the most Giapetto would be willing to pay for another 100 hours of labor?

(c) If 60,000 labor hours were available, what would Giapetto's profit be?

(d) If only 40,000 trains could be sold, what would Giapetto's profit be?

Figure 21   LINDO Output for Problem 7

```
MAX      32 SM + 55 TM + 5 SB + 5 TB
SUBJECT TO
    2)     3 SM + 5 TM <=    145
    3)     2 SM + 4 TM <=     90
    4)     SM + SB <=     50
    5)     TM + TB <=     50
END

LP OPTIMUM FOUND AT STEP       4

       OBJECTIVE FUNCTION VALUE

    1)      1715.00000

  VARIABLE        VALUE         REDUCED COST
     SM        45.000000           .000000
     TM          .000000          4.000000
     SB         5.000000           .000000
     TB        50.000000           .000000

    ROW    SLACK OR SURPLUS      DUAL PRICES
    2)         10.000000           .000000
    3)           .000000         13.500000
    4)           .000000          5.000000
    5)           .000000          5.000000

NO. ITERATIONS=       4

RANGES IN WHICH THE BASIS IS UNCHANGED:

                          OBJ COEFFICIENT RANGES
  VARIABLE      CURRENT       ALLOWABLE      ALLOWABLE
                 COEF         INCREASE       DECREASE
     SM       32.000000       INFINITY       2.000000
     TM       55.000000       4.000000       INFINITY
     SB        5.000000       2.000000       5.000000
     TB        5.000000       INFINITY       4.000000

                          RIGHTHAND SIDE RANGES
    ROW        CURRENT       ALLOWABLE      ALLOWABLE
                 RHS         INCREASE       DECREASE
     2       145.000000      INFINITY      10.000000
     3        90.000000      6.666667      90.000000
     4        50.000000      INFINITY       5.000000
     5        50.000000      INFINITY      50.000000
```

8. Wivco produces two products: product 1 and product 2. The relevant data are shown in Table 12. Each week, up to 400 units of raw material can be purchased at a cost of $1.50 per unit. The company employs four workers, who work 40 hours per week. (Their salaries are considered a fixed cost.) Workers can be asked to work overtime and are paid $6 per hour for overtime work. Each week, 320 hours of machine time are available.

In the absence of advertising, 50 units of product 1 will be demanded each week and 60 units of product 2 will be demanded each week. Advertising can be used to

Table 12

	PRODUCT 1	PRODUCT 2
Selling price	$15	$8
Labor required	0.75 hour	0.50 hour
Machine time required	1.5 hours	0.80 hour
Raw material required	2 units	1 unit

stimulate demand for each product. Each dollar spent on advertising product 1 increases the demand for product 1 by 10 units, and each dollar spent on advertising for product 2 increases the demand for product 2 by 15 units. At most $100 can be spent on advertising. Define

P1 = number of units of product 1 produced each week

P2 = number of units of product 2 produced each week

OT = number of hours of overtime labor used each week

RM = number of units of raw material purchased each week

A1 = dollars spent each week on advertising product 1

A2 = dollars spent each week on advertising product 2

Then Wivco should solve the following LP:

$$\max z = 15P1 + 8P2 - 6(OT) - 1.5RM - A1 - A2$$

$$
\begin{aligned}
\text{s.t.} \quad & P1 - 10A1 \le 50 && (1) \\
& P2 - 15A2 \le 60 && (2) \\
& 0.75P1 + 0.5P2 \le 160 + (OT) && (3) \\
& 2P1 + P2 \le RM && (4) \\
& RM \le 400 && (5) \\
& A1 + A2 \le 100 && (6) \\
& 1.5P1 + 0.8P2 \le 320 && (7)
\end{aligned}
$$

All variables nonnegative

Use LINDO to solve this LP. Then use the computer output to answer the following questions:

(a) If overtime were to cost only $4 per hour, would Wivco use overtime?

(b) If each unit of product 1 sold for $15.50, would the current basis remain optimal? What would be the new optimal solution?

(c) What is the most that Wivco should be willing to pay for another unit of raw material?

(d) How much would Wivco be willing to pay for another hour of machine time?

(e) If each worker were required (as part of the regular workweek) to work 45 hours per week, what would the company's profits now be?

(f) Explain why the shadow price of row (1) is 0.10. (*Hint:* If the right-hand side of (1) were increased from 50 to 51, then in the absence of advertising for product 1, 51 units of product 1 could now be sold each week.)

9. In this problem, we discuss how shadow prices can be interpreted for blending problems (see Section 3.8). To illustrate the ideas, we discuss Problem 2 of Section 3.8. If we define

$$x_{6J} = \text{pounds of grade 6 oranges in juice}$$
$$x_{9J} = \text{pounds of grade 9 oranges in juice}$$
$$x_{6B} = \text{pounds of grade 6 oranges in bags}$$
$$x_{9B} = \text{pounds of grade 9 oranges in bags}$$

then the appropriate formulation is

$$\max z = 0.45(x_{6J} + x_{9J}) + 0.30(x_{6B} + x_{9B})$$

$$
\begin{aligned}
\text{s.t.} \quad & x_{6J} + x_{6B} \le 120{,}000 && \text{(Grade 6 constraint)} \\
& x_{9J} + x_{9B} \le 100{,}000 && \text{(Grade 9 constraint)} \\
& \frac{6x_{6J} + 9x_{9J}}{x_{6J} + x_{9J}} \ge 8 && \text{(Orange juice constraint)} && (1) \\
& \frac{6x_{6B} + 9x_{9B}}{x_{6B} + x_{9B}} \ge 7 && \text{(Bags constraint)} && (2) \\
& x_{6J}, x_{9J}, x_{6B}, x_{9B} \ge 0
\end{aligned}
$$

Constraints (1) and (2) are examples of blending constraints, because they specify the proportion of grade 6 and grade 9 oranges that must be blended to manufacture orange juice and bags of oranges. It would be useful to determine how a slight change in the standards for orange juice and bags of oranges would affect profit. At the end of this problem, we explain how to use the shadow prices of Constraints (1) and (2) to answer the following questions:

(a) Suppose that the average grade for orange juice is increased to 8.1. Assuming the current basis remains optimal, by how much would profits change?

(b) Suppose the average grade requirements for bags of oranges is decreased to 6.9. Assuming the current basis remains optimal, by how much would profits change?

The shadow price for (1) is -0.15, and the shadow price for (2) is also -0.15. The optimal solution to the O.J. problem is $x_{6J} = 26{,}666.67$, $x_{9J} = 53{,}333.33$, $x_{6B} = 93{,}333.33$, $x_{9B} = 46{,}666.67$. To interpret the shadow prices of blending constraints (1) and (2), *we assume that a slight change in the quality standard for a product will not significantly change the quantity of the product that is produced.*

Now note that (1) may be written as

$$6x_{6J} + 9x_{9J} \ge 8(x_{6J} + x_{9J}) \quad \text{or} \quad -2x_{6J} + x_{9J} \ge 0$$

If the quality standard for orange juice is changed to $8 + \Delta$, then (1) can be written as

$$6x_{6J} + 9x_{9J} \geq (8 + \Delta)(x_{6J} + x_{9J})$$

or

$$-2x_{6J} + x_{9J} \geq \Delta(x_{6J} + x_{9J})$$

Since we are assuming that changing orange juice quality from 8 to $8 + \Delta$ does not change the amount of orange juice produced, $x_{6J} + x_{9J}$ will remain equal to 80,000, and (1) will become

$$-2x_{6J} + x_{9J} \geq 80{,}000\Delta$$

Using the definition of shadow price, answer parts (a) and (b).

10. Use LINDO to solve the Sailco problem of Section 3.10. Then use the LINDO output to answer the following questions:

(a) If month 1 demand decreased to 35 sailboats, what would be the total cost of satisfying the demands during the next four months?

(b) If the cost of producing a sailboat with regular-time labor during month 1 were $420, what would be the new optimal solution to the Sailco problem?

(c) Suppose a new customer is willing to pay $425 for a sailboat. If his demand must be met during month 1, should Sailco fill the order? How about if his demand must be met during month 4?

6

Sensitivity Analysis and Duality

Two of the most important topics in linear programming are sensitivity analysis and duality. After studying these important topics, the reader will have an appreciation of the beauty and logic of linear programming and be ready to study advanced linear programming topics like those discussed in Chapter 10.

In Section 6.1, we illustrate the concept of sensitivity analysis through a graphical example. In Section 6.2, we use our knowledge of matrices to develop some important formulas, which are used in Sections 6.3 and 6.4 to develop the mechanics of sensitivity analysis. The remainder of the chapter presents the important concept of duality. Duality provides many insights into the nature of linear programming, gives us the useful concept of shadow prices, and helps us to understand sensitivity analysis. It is a necessary basis for students planning to take advanced topics in linear and nonlinear programming.

6-1   A GRAPHICAL INTRODUCTION TO SENSITIVITY ANALYSIS

Sensitivity analysis is concerned with how changes in an LP's parameters affect the LP's optimal solution.

Reconsider the Giapetto problem of Section 3.1:

$$\max z = 3x_1 + 2x_2$$
$$\text{s.t.} \quad 2x_1 + x_2 \leq 100 \quad \text{(Finishing constraint)}$$
$$x_1 + x_2 \leq 80 \quad \text{(Carpentry constraint)}$$
$$x_1 \leq 40 \quad \text{(Demand constraint)}$$
$$x_1, x_2 \geq 0$$

where

$$x_1 = \text{number of soldiers produced per week}$$
$$x_2 = \text{number of trains produced per week}$$

The optimal solution to this problem is $z = 180$, $x_1 = 20$, $x_2 = 60$ (point B in Figure 1), and it has x_1, x_2, and s_3 (the slack variable for the demand constraint) as basic variables. How would changes in the problem's objective function coefficients or right-hand sides change this optimal solution?

GRAPHICAL ANALYSIS OF THE EFFECT OF A CHANGE IN AN OBJECTIVE FUNCTION COEFFICIENT

If the contribution to profit of a soldier were to increase sufficiently, it seems reasonable that it would be optimal for Giapetto to produce more soldiers (i.e., s_3 would become nonbasic). Similarly, if the contribution to profit of a soldier were to decrease sufficiently, it seems reasonable that it would be optimal for Giapetto to produce only trains (i.e., x_1 would now be nonbasic). We now show how to determine the values of the contribution to profit for soldiers for which the current optimal basis will remain optimal.

Let c_1 be the contribution to profit by each soldier. For what values of c_1 does the current basis remain optimal?

At present, $c_1 = 3$ and each isoprofit line has the form $3x_1 + 2x_2 = $ constant, or $x_2 = -\frac{3x_1}{2} + \frac{\text{constant}}{2}$, and each isoprofit line has a slope of $-\frac{3}{2}$. From Figure 1, we see that if a change in c_1 causes the isoprofit lines to be flatter than the carpentry constraint, the optimal solution will change from the current optimal solution (point B) to a new optimal solution (point A). If the profit for each soldier is c_1, the slope of each isoprofit line will be $-\frac{c_1}{2}$. Since the slope of the carpentry constraint is -1, the isoprofit lines will

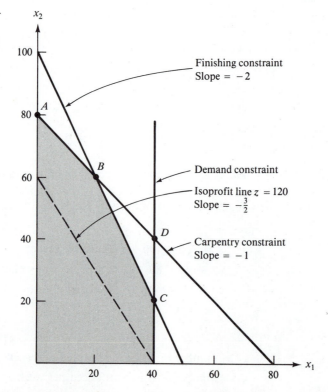

Figure 1
Analysis of Range of Values for Which c_1 Remains Optimal in Giapetto Problem

be flatter than the carpentry constraint if $-\frac{c_1}{2} > -1$, or $c_1 < 2$, and the current basis will no longer be optimal. The new optimal solution will be $(0, 80)$, point A in Figure 1.

If the isoprofit lines are steeper than the finishing constraint, the optimal solution will change from point B to point C. The slope of the finishing constraint is -2. If $-\frac{c_1}{2} < -2$, or $c_1 > 4$, the current basis is no longer optimal, and point C $(40, 20)$ will be optimal. In summary, we have shown that (if all other parameters remain unchanged) the current basis remains optimal for $2 \le c_1 \le 4$, and Giapetto should still manufacture 20 soldiers and 60 trains. Of course, even if $2 \le c_1 \le 4$, Giapetto's profit will change. For instance, if $c_1 = 4$, Giapetto's profit will now be $4(20) + 2(60) = \$200$ instead of $\$180$.

GRAPHICAL ANALYSIS OF THE EFFECT OF A CHANGE IN A RIGHT-HAND SIDE ON THE LP'S OPTIMAL SOLUTION

A graphical analysis can also be used to determine whether a change in the right-hand side of a constraint will make the current basis no longer optimal. Let b_1 be the number of available finishing hours. Currently, $b_1 = 100$. For what values of b_1 does the current basis remain optimal? From Figure 2, we see that a change in b_1 shifts the finishing

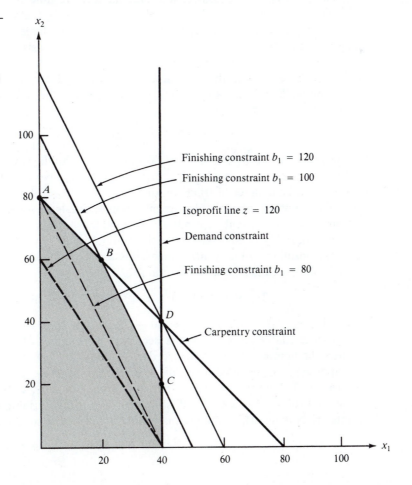

Figure 2
Range of Values on Finishing Hours for Which Current Basis Remains Optimal in Giapetto Problem

Finishing constraint $b_1 = 120$

Finishing constraint $b_1 = 100$

Isoprofit line $z = 120$

Demand constraint

Finishing constraint $b_1 = 80$

Carpentry constraint

constraint parallel to its current position. The current optimal solution (point B in Figure 2) is where the carpentry and finishing constraints are binding. If we change the value of b_1, then *as long as the point where the finishing and carpentry constraints are binding remains feasible, the optimal solution will still occur where the finishing and carpentry constraints intersect.* From Figure 2, we see that if $b_1 > 120$, the point where the finishing and carpentry constraints are both binding will lie on the portion of the carpentry constraint below point D. In this region, $x_1 > 40$, and the demand constraint for soldiers is not satisfied. Thus, for $b_1 > 120$, the current basis will no longer be optimal. Similarly, if $b_1 < 80$, the carpentry and finishing constraints will be binding at an infeasible point having $x_1 < 0$, and the current basis will no longer be optimal. Thus (if all other parameters remain unchanged), the current basis remains optimal if $80 \leq b_1 \leq 120$.

Note that although for $80 \leq b_1 \leq 120$, the current basis remains optimal, *the values of the decision variables and the objective function value change.* For example, if $80 \leq b_1 < 100$, the optimal solution will change from point B to some other point on the line segment AB. Similarly, if $100 < b_1 \leq 120$, the optimal solution will change from point B to some other point on the line BD.

As long as the current basis remains optimal, it is a routine matter to determine how a change in the right-hand side of a constraint changes the values of the decision variables. To illustrate the idea, let b_1 = number of available finishing hours. If we change b_1 to $100 + \Delta$, we know that the current basis remains optimal for $-20 \leq \Delta \leq 20$. Note that as b_1 changes (as long as $-20 \leq \Delta \leq 20$), the optimal solution to the LP is still the point where the finishing-hour and carpentry-hour constraints are binding. Thus, if $b_1 = 100 + \Delta$, we can find the new values of the decision variables by solving

$$2x_1 + x_2 = 100 + \Delta \qquad \text{and} \qquad x_1 + x_2 = 80$$

This yields $x_1 = 20 + \Delta$ and $x_2 = 60 - \Delta$. Thus, an increase in the number of available finishing hours results in an increase in the number of soldiers produced and a decrease in the number of trains produced.

If b_2 (the number of available carpentry hours) equals $80 + \Delta$, it can be shown (see Problem 2) that the current basis remains optimal for $-20 \leq \Delta \leq 20$. If we change the value of b_2 (keeping $-20 \leq \Delta \leq 20$), the optimal solution to the LP is still the point where the finishing and carpentry constraints are binding. Thus, if $b_2 = 80 + \Delta$, the optimal solution to the LP is the solution to

$$2x_1 + x_2 = 100 \qquad \text{and} \qquad x_1 + x_2 = 80 + \Delta$$

This yields $x_1 = 20 - \Delta$ and $x_2 = 60 + 2\Delta$, which shows that an increase in the amount of available carpentry hours decreases the number of soldiers produced and increases the number of trains produced.

Suppose b_3, the demand for soldiers, is changed to $40 + \Delta$. Then it can be shown (see Problem 3) that the current basis remains optimal for $\Delta \geq -20$. For Δ in this range, the optimal solution to the LP will still occur where the finishing and carpentry constraints are binding. Thus, the optimal solution will be the solution to

$$2x_1 + x_2 = 100 \qquad \text{and} \qquad x_1 + x_2 = 80$$

Of course, this yields $x_1 = 20$ and $x_2 = 60$, which illustrates an important point. In a constraint with positive slack (or positive excess) in an LP's optimal solution, if we change the right-hand side of the constraint in the range where the current basis remains optimal, the optimal solution to the LP is unchanged.

SHADOW PRICES

As we will see in Section 6.8, it is often important for managers to determine how a change in a constraint's right-hand side changes the LP's optimal z-value. With this in mind, we define the **shadow price** for the ith constraint of an LP to be the amount by which the optimal z-value is improved (improvement means increase in a max problem and decrease in a min problem) if the right-hand side of the ith constraint is increased by 1. This definition applies only if the change in the right-hand side of Constraint i leaves the current basis optimal.

For any two-variable LP, it is a simple matter to determine each constraint's shadow price. For example, we know that if $100 + \Delta$ finishing hours are available (assuming that the current basis remains optimal), then the LP's optimal solution is $x_1 = 20 + \Delta$ and $x_2 = 60 - \Delta$. Then the optimal z-value will equal $3x_1 + 2x_2 = 3(20 + \Delta) + 2(60 - \Delta) = 180 + \Delta$. Thus, as long as the current basis remains optimal, a unit increase in the number of available finishing hours will increase the optimal z-value by $1. So the shadow price of the first (finishing hour) constraint is $1.

For the second (carpentry hour) constraint, we know that if $80 + \Delta$ carpentry hours are available (and the current basis remains optimal), then the optimal solution to the LP is $x_1 = 20 - \Delta$ and $x_2 = 60 + 2\Delta$. Then the new optimal z-value is $3x_1 + 2x_2 = 3(20 - \Delta) + 2(60 + 2\Delta) = 180 + \Delta$. Thus, a unit increase in the number of carpentry hours will increase the optimal z-value by $1 (as long as the current basis remains optimal). So the shadow price of the second (carpentry hour) constraint is $1.

We now find the shadow price of the third (demand) constraint. If the right-hand side is $40 + \Delta$, then the optimal values of the decision variables remain unchanged, as long as the current basis remains optimal. Then the optimal z-value will also remain unchanged, which shows that the shadow price of the third (demand) constraint is $0. It turns out that whenever the slack variable or excess variable for a constraint is positive in an LP's optimal solution, the constraint will have a zero shadow price.

Suppose we increase the right-hand side of the ith constraint of an LP by Δb_i ($\Delta b_i < 0$ means that we are decreasing the right-hand side of the ith constraint), and the current basis remains optimal. Then each unit by which Constraint i's right-hand side is increased will increase the optimal z-value (for a max problem) by Constraint i's shadow price. Thus, the new optimal z-value is given by

$$\text{(New optimal } z\text{-value)} = \text{(old optimal } z\text{-value)}$$
$$+ \text{(Constraint } i\text{'s shadow price) } \Delta b_i$$

For a minimization problem,

$$\text{(New optimal } z\text{-value)} = \text{(old optimal } z\text{-value)}$$
$$- \text{(Constraint } i\text{'s shadow price) } \Delta b_i$$

For example, if 95 carpentry hours are available, then $\Delta b_2 = 15$, and the new z-value is given by

New optimal z-value $= 180 + 15(1) = \$195$

We will continue our discussion of shadow prices in Section 6.8.

IMPORTANCE OF SENSITIVITY ANALYSIS

Sensitivity analysis is important for several reasons. In many applications, the values of an LP's parameters may change. For example, the prices at which soldiers and trains are sold may change, as may the availability of carpentry and finishing hours. If a parameter changes, sensitivity analysis often makes it unnecessary to solve the problem again. For example, if the profit contribution of a soldier increased to $3.50, we would not have to solve the Giapetto problem again, because the current solution remains optimal. Of course, solving the Giapetto problem again would not be much work, but solving an LP with thousands of variables and thousands of constraints again would be a chore. A knowledge of sensitivity analysis often enables the analyst to determine from the original solution how changes in an LP's parameters change an LP's optimal solution.

Recall that we may be uncertain about the values of parameters in an LP. For example, we might be uncertain about the weekly demand for soldiers. With the graphical method, it can be shown that if the weekly demand for soldiers is at least 20, the optimal solution to the Giapetto problem is still (20, 60) (see Problem 3 at the end of this section). Thus, even if Giapetto is uncertain about the demand for soldiers, the company can still be fairly confident that it is optimal to produce 20 soldiers and 60 trains.

Of course, the graphical approach is not useful for sensitivity analysis on an LP with more than two variables. Before learning how to perform sensitivity analysis on an arbitrary LP, we need to use our knowledge of matrices to express simplex tableaus in matrix form. This is the subject of Section 6.2.

♦ PROBLEMS

GROUP A

1. Show that if the contribution to profit for trains is between $1.50 and $3, the current basis remains optimal. If the contribution to profit for trains is $2.50, what would be the new optimal solution?

2. Show that if available carpentry hours remain between 60 and 100, the current basis remains optimal. If between 60 and 100 carpentry hours are available, would Giapetto still produce 20 soldiers and 60 trains?

3. Show that if the weekly demand for soldiers is at least 20, the current basis remains optimal, and Giapetto should still produce 20 soldiers and 60 trains.

4. For the Dorian Auto problem (Example 2 in Chapter 3),
(a) Find the range of values on the cost of a comedy ad for which the current basis remains optimal.

(b) Find the range of values on the cost of a football ad for which the current basis remains optimal.
(c) Find the range of values for required HIW exposures for which the current basis remains optimal. Determine the new optimal solution if $28 + \Delta$ million HIW exposures are required.
(d) Find the range of values for required HIM exposures for which the current basis remains optimal. Determine the new optimal solution if $24 + \Delta$ million HIM exposures are required.
(e) Find the shadow price of each constraint.
(f) If 26 million HIW exposures are required, determine the new optimal z-value.

5. Radioco manufactures two types of radios. The only scarce resource that is needed to produce radios is labor. At present, the company has two laborers. Laborer 1 is willing to work up to 40 hours per week and is paid $5 per hour. Laborer 2 is willing to work up to 50 hours per week and is paid $6 per hour. The price as well as the resources required to build each type of radio are given in Table 1.

Table 1

	RADIO 1		RADIO 2	
Price	Resource Required	Price	Resource Required	
$25	Laborer 1: 1 hour Laborer 2: 2 hours Raw material cost: $5		$22	Laborer 1: 2 hours Laborer 2: 1 hour Raw material cost: $4

Letting x_i be the number of type i radios produced each week, show that Radioco should solve the following LP:

$$\max z = 3x_1 + 2x_2$$
$$\text{s.t.} \quad x_1 + 2x_2 \le 40$$
$$2x_1 + x_2 \le 50$$
$$x_1, x_2 \ge 0$$

(a) For what values of the price of a type 1 radio would the current basis remain optimal?
(b) For what values of the price of a type 2 radio would the current basis remain optimal?
(c) If laborer 1 were willing to work only 30 hours per week, would the current basis remain optimal? Find the new optimal solution to the LP.
(d) If laborer 2 were willing to work up to 60 hours per week, would the current basis remain optimal? Find the new optimal solution to the LP.
(e) Find the shadow price of each constraint.

6-2   SOME IMPORTANT FORMULAS

In this section, we use our knowledge of matrices to show how an LP's optimal tableau can be expressed in terms of the LP's parameters. The formulas developed in this section are used in our study of sensitivity analysis, duality, and advanced LP topics.

Assume that we are solving a max problem that has been prepared for solution by the Big M method and that at this point, the LP has m constraints and n variables. Although some of these variables may be slack, excess, or artificial ones, we choose to label them $x_1, x_2, \ldots, x_n$. Then the LP may be written as

$$\max z = c_1 x_1 + c_2 x_2 + \cdots + c_n x_n$$
$$\text{s.t.} \quad a_{11} x_1 + a_{12} x_2 + \cdots + a_{1n} x_n = b_1$$
$$a_{21} x_1 + a_{22} x_2 + \cdots + a_{2n} x_n = b_2$$
$$\vdots \qquad \vdots \qquad \qquad \vdots \qquad \vdots$$
$$a_{m1} x_1 + a_{m2} x_2 + \cdots + a_{mn} x_n = b_m$$
$$x_i \ge 0 \quad (i = 1, 2, \ldots, n)$$

$$(1)$$

Throughout this chapter, we use the Dakota Furniture problem of Section 4.3 (without the $x_2 \le 5$ constraint) as an example. For the Dakota problem, the analog of LP (1) is

$$\max z = 60x_1 + 30x_2 + 20x_3 + 0s_1 + 0s_2 + 0s_3$$
$$\text{s.t.} \quad 8x_1 + 6x_2 + x_3 + s_1 = 48$$
$$4x_1 + 2x_2 + 1.5x_3 + s_2 = 20$$
$$2x_1 + 1.5x_2 + 0.5x_3 + s_3 = 8$$
$$x_1, x_2, x_3, s_1, s_2, s_3 \ge 0$$

$$(1')$$

Suppose we have found the optimal solution to (1). Let BV_i be the basic variable for row i of the optimal tableau. Also define $BV = \{BV_1, BV_2, \ldots, BV_m\}$ to be the set of basic variables in the optimal tableau, and define the $m \times 1$ vector

$$\mathbf{x}_{BV} = \begin{bmatrix} x_{BV_1} \\ x_{BV_2} \\ \vdots \\ x_{BV_m} \end{bmatrix}$$

We also define

$NBV =$ the set of nonbasic variables in the optimal tableau

$\mathbf{x}_{NBV} = (n - m) \times 1$ vector listing the nonbasic variables (in any desired order)

To illustrate these definitions, we recall that the optimal tableau for the Dakota problem is

$$
\begin{array}{rrrrrrr}
z & + & 5x_2 & & + & 10s_2 + & 10s_3 = & 280 \\
 & - & 2x_2 & + s_1 + & & 2s_2 - & 8s_3 = & 24 \\
 & - & 2x_2 + x_3 & & + & 2s_2 - & 4s_3 = & 8 \\
 & & x_1 + 1.25x_2 & & & - 0.5s_2 + & 1.5s_3 = & 2
\end{array}
\tag{2}
$$

For this optimal tableau, $BV_1 = s_1$, $BV_2 = x_3$, and $BV_3 = x_1$. Then

$$\mathbf{x}_{BV} = \begin{bmatrix} s_1 \\ x_3 \\ x_1 \end{bmatrix}$$

We may choose $NBV = \{x_2, s_2, s_3\}$. Then

$$\mathbf{x}_{NBV} = \begin{bmatrix} x_2 \\ s_2 \\ s_3 \end{bmatrix}$$

Using our knowledge of matrix algebra, we can express the optimal tableau in terms of BV and the original LP (1). Recall that $c_1, c_2, \ldots, c_n$ are the objective function coefficients for the variables $x_1, x_2, \ldots, x_n$ (some of these may be slack, excess, or artificial variables).

DEFINITION ▪ $\mathbf{c}_{BV}$ is the $1 \times m$ row vector $[c_{BV_1} \quad c_{BV_2} \quad \cdots \quad c_{BV_m}]$.

Thus, the elements of $\mathbf{c}_{BV}$ are the objective function coefficients for the optimal tableau's basic variables. For the Dakota problem, $BV = \{s_1, x_3, x_1\}$. Then from (1′) we find that $\mathbf{c}_{BV} = [0 \quad 20 \quad 60]$.

DEFINITION ▪ $\mathbf{c}_{NBV}$ is the $1 \times (n - m)$ row vector whose elements are the coefficients of the nonbasic variables (in the order of NBV).

If we choose to list the nonbasic variables for the Dakota problem in the order $NBV = \{x_2, s_2, s_3\}$, then $\mathbf{c}_{NBV} = [30 \quad 0 \quad 0]$.

DEFINITION The $m \times m$ matrix B is the matrix whose jth column is the column for BV_j in (1).

For the Dakota problem, the first column of B is the s_1 column in (1′), the second column of B is the x_3 column in (1′), and the third column of B is the x_1 column in (1′). Thus,

$$B = \begin{bmatrix} 1 & 1 & 8 \\ 0 & 1.5 & 4 \\ 0 & 0.5 & 2 \end{bmatrix}$$

DEFINITION $\mathbf{a}_j$ is the column (in the constraints) for the variable x_j in (1).

For example, in the Dakota problem,

$$\mathbf{a}_2 = \begin{bmatrix} 6 \\ 2 \\ 1.5 \end{bmatrix} \quad \text{and} \quad \mathbf{a} \text{ (for } s_1) = \begin{bmatrix} 1 \\ 0 \\ 0 \end{bmatrix}$$

DEFINITION N is the $m \times (n - m)$ matrix whose columns are the columns for the nonbasic variables (in the NBV order) in (1).

If for the Dakota problem, we write $NBV = \{x_2, s_2, s_3\}$, then

$$N = \begin{bmatrix} 6 & 0 & 0 \\ 2 & 1 & 0 \\ 1.5 & 0 & 1 \end{bmatrix}$$

DEFINITION The $m \times 1$ column vector $\mathbf{b}$ is the right-hand side of the constraints in (1).

For the Dakota problem,

$$\mathbf{b} = \begin{bmatrix} 48 \\ 20 \\ 8 \end{bmatrix}$$

We write b_i for the right-hand side of the ith constraint in the original Dakota problem: $b_2 = 20$.

We can now use matrix algebra to determine how an LP's optimal tableau (with set of basic variables BV) is related to the original LP in the form (1).

**EXPRESSING THE CONSTRAINTS IN ANY TABLEAU
IN TERMS OF B^{-1} AND THE ORIGINAL LP**

We begin by observing that (1) may be written as

$$
\begin{aligned}
z &= \mathbf{c}_{BV}\mathbf{x}_{BV} + \mathbf{c}_{NBV}\mathbf{x}_{NBV} \\
\text{s.t.} \quad B\mathbf{x}_{BV} &+ N\mathbf{x}_{NBV} = \mathbf{b} \\
\mathbf{x}_{BV}, \mathbf{x}_{NBV} &\geq 0
\end{aligned}
\tag{3}
$$

Using the format of (3), the Dakota problem can be written as

$$
\max z = \begin{bmatrix} 0 & 20 & 60 \end{bmatrix}\begin{bmatrix} s_1 \\ x_3 \\ x_1 \end{bmatrix} + \begin{bmatrix} 30 & 0 & 0 \end{bmatrix}\begin{bmatrix} x_2 \\ s_2 \\ s_3 \end{bmatrix}
$$

$$
\text{s.t.} \quad \begin{bmatrix} 1 & 1 & 8 \\ 0 & 1.5 & 4 \\ 0 & 0.5 & 2 \end{bmatrix}\begin{bmatrix} s_1 \\ x_3 \\ x_1 \end{bmatrix} + \begin{bmatrix} 6 & 0 & 0 \\ 2 & 1 & 0 \\ 1.5 & 0 & 1 \end{bmatrix}\begin{bmatrix} x_2 \\ s_2 \\ s_3 \end{bmatrix} = \begin{bmatrix} 48 \\ 20 \\ 8 \end{bmatrix}
$$

$$
\begin{bmatrix} s_1 \\ x_3 \\ x_1 \end{bmatrix} \geq \begin{bmatrix} 0 \\ 0 \\ 0 \end{bmatrix}, \quad \begin{bmatrix} x_2 \\ s_2 \\ s_3 \end{bmatrix} \geq \begin{bmatrix} 0 \\ 0 \\ 0 \end{bmatrix}
$$

Multiplying the constraints in (3) through by B^{-1}, we obtain

$$
B^{-1}B\mathbf{x}_{BV} + B^{-1}N\mathbf{x}_{NBV} = B^{-1}\mathbf{b} \quad \text{or} \quad \mathbf{x}_{BV} + B^{-1}N\mathbf{x}_{NBV} = B^{-1}\mathbf{b}
\tag{4}
$$

In (4), BV_i occurs with a coefficient of 1 in the ith constraint and a zero coefficient in each other constraint. Thus, BV is the set of basic variables for (4), and (4) yields the constraints for the optimal tableau.

For the Dakota problem, the Gauss-Jordan method can be used to show that

$$
B^{-1} = \begin{bmatrix} 1 & 2 & -8 \\ 0 & 2 & -4 \\ 0 & -0.5 & 1.5 \end{bmatrix}
$$

Then (4) yields

$$
\begin{bmatrix} s_1 \\ x_3 \\ x_1 \end{bmatrix} + \begin{bmatrix} 1 & 2 & -8 \\ 0 & 2 & -4 \\ 0 & -0.5 & 1.5 \end{bmatrix}\begin{bmatrix} 6 & 0 & 0 \\ 2 & 1 & 0 \\ 1.5 & 0 & 1 \end{bmatrix}\begin{bmatrix} x_2 \\ s_2 \\ s_3 \end{bmatrix} = \begin{bmatrix} 1 & 2 & -8 \\ 0 & 2 & -4 \\ 0 & -0.5 & 1.5 \end{bmatrix}\begin{bmatrix} 48 \\ 20 \\ 8 \end{bmatrix}
$$

or

$$
\begin{bmatrix} s_1 \\ x_3 \\ x_1 \end{bmatrix} + \begin{bmatrix} -2 & 2 & -8 \\ -2 & 2 & -4 \\ 1.25 & -0.5 & 1.5 \end{bmatrix}\begin{bmatrix} x_2 \\ s_2 \\ s_3 \end{bmatrix} = \begin{bmatrix} 24 \\ 8 \\ 2 \end{bmatrix}
\tag{4'}
$$

Of course, these are the constraints for the Dakota optimal tableau, (2).

From (4), we see that the column of a nonbasic variable x_j in the constraints of the optimal tableau is given by $B^{-1}(\text{column for } x_j \text{ in (1)}) = B^{-1}\mathbf{a}_j$. For example, the x_2 column in the optimal tableau is $B^{-1}(\text{first column of } N) = B^{-1}\mathbf{a}_2$. From (4), we also find that the right-hand side of the optimal tableau's constraints is the vector $B^{-1}\mathbf{b}$. The following two equations summarize the preceding discussion:

$$\text{Column for } x_j \text{ in optimal tableau's constraints} = B^{-1}\mathbf{a}_j \qquad (5)$$

$$\text{Right-hand side of optimal tableau's constraints} = B^{-1}\mathbf{b} \qquad (6)$$

To illustrate (5), we find the column for x_2 in the Dakota optimal tableau:

$$\begin{array}{l}\text{Column for } x_2 \\ \text{in Dakota optimal tableau}\end{array} = B^{-1}\mathbf{a}_2$$

$$= \begin{bmatrix} 1 & 2 & -8 \\ 0 & 2 & -4 \\ 0 & -0.5 & 1.5 \end{bmatrix} \begin{bmatrix} 6 \\ 2 \\ 1.5 \end{bmatrix} = \begin{bmatrix} -2 \\ -2 \\ 1.25 \end{bmatrix}$$

To illustrate (6), we compute the right-hand side of the constraints in the Dakota optimal tableau:

$$\begin{array}{l}\text{Right-hand side of constraints} \\ \text{in Dakota optimal tableau}\end{array} = B^{-1}\mathbf{b}$$

$$= \begin{bmatrix} 1 & 2 & -8 \\ 0 & 2 & -4 \\ 0 & -0.5 & 1.5 \end{bmatrix} \begin{bmatrix} 48 \\ 20 \\ 8 \end{bmatrix} = \begin{bmatrix} 24 \\ 8 \\ 2 \end{bmatrix}$$

DETERMINING THE OPTIMAL TABLEAU'S ROW 0 IN TERMS OF THE INITIAL LP

We now show how to express row 0 of the optimal tableau in terms of BV and the original LP (1). To begin, we multiply the constraints (expressed in the form $B\mathbf{x}_{BV} + N\mathbf{x}_{NBV} = \mathbf{b}$) through by the vector $\mathbf{c}_{BV}B^{-1}$:

$$\mathbf{c}_{BV}\mathbf{x}_{BV} + \mathbf{c}_{BV}B^{-1}N\mathbf{x}_{NBV} = \mathbf{c}_{BV}B^{-1}\mathbf{b} \qquad (7)$$

and rewrite the original objective function, $z = \mathbf{c}_{BV}\mathbf{x}_{BV} + \mathbf{c}_{NBV}\mathbf{x}_{NBV}$, as

$$z - \mathbf{c}_{BV}\mathbf{x}_{BV} - \mathbf{c}_{NBV}\mathbf{x}_{NBV} = 0 \qquad (8)$$

By adding (7) to (8), we can eliminate the optimal tableau's basic variables and obtain the optimal tableau's row 0:

$$z + (\mathbf{c}_{BV}B^{-1}N - \mathbf{c}_{NBV})\mathbf{x}_{NBV} = \mathbf{c}_{BV}B^{-1}\mathbf{b} \qquad (9)$$

From (9), the coefficient of x_j in the optimal tableau's row 0 is

$$\mathbf{c}_{BV}B^{-1}(\text{column of } N \text{ for } x_j) - (\text{coefficient of } x_j \text{ in } \mathbf{c}_{NBV}) = \mathbf{c}_{BV}B^{-1}\mathbf{a}_j - c_j$$

and we learn that the right-hand side of the optimal tableau's row 0 is $\mathbf{c}_{BV}B^{-1}\mathbf{b}$.

To help summarize the preceding discussion, we let $\bar{c}_j$ be the coefficient of x_j in the optimal tableau's row 0. Then we have shown that

$$\bar{c}_j = \mathbf{c}_{BV} B^{-1} \mathbf{a}_j - c_j \tag{10}$$

and

$$\text{Right-hand side of optimal tableau's row } 0 = \mathbf{c}_{BV} B^{-1} \mathbf{b} \tag{11}$$

To illustrate the use of (10) and (11), we determine row 0 of the Dakota problem's optimal tableau. Recall that

$$\mathbf{c}_{BV} = [0 \quad 20 \quad 60] \quad \text{and} \quad B^{-1} = \begin{bmatrix} 1 & 2 & -8 \\ 0 & 2 & -4 \\ 0 & -0.5 & 1.5 \end{bmatrix}$$

Then $\mathbf{c}_{BV} B^{-1} = [0 \quad 10 \quad 10]$, and from (10) we find that the coefficients of the nonbasic variables in row 0 of the optimal tableau are

$$\bar{c}_2 = \mathbf{c}_{BV} B^{-1} \mathbf{a}_2 - c_2 = [0 \quad 10 \quad 10] \begin{bmatrix} 6 \\ 2 \\ 1.5 \end{bmatrix} - 30 = 20 + 15 - 30 = 5$$

and

$$\text{Coefficient of } s_2 \text{ in optimal row } 0 = \mathbf{c}_{BV} B^{-1} \begin{bmatrix} 0 \\ 1 \\ 0 \end{bmatrix} - 0 = 10$$

$$\text{Coefficient of } s_3 \text{ in optimal row } 0 = \mathbf{c}_{BV} B^{-1} \begin{bmatrix} 0 \\ 0 \\ 1 \end{bmatrix} - 0 = 10$$

Of course, the optimal tableau's basic variables (x_1, x_3, and s_1) will have zero coefficients in the optimal row 0.

From (11), the right-hand side of the optimal tableau's row 0 is

$$\mathbf{c}_{BV} B^{-1} \mathbf{b} = [0 \quad 10 \quad 10] \begin{bmatrix} 48 \\ 20 \\ 8 \end{bmatrix} = 280$$

Putting it all together, we see that row 0 of the optimal tableau is

$$z + 5x_2 + 10s_2 + 10s_3 = 280$$

Of course, this result agrees with (2).

SIMPLIFYING FORMULA (10) FOR SLACK, EXCESS, AND ARTIFICIAL VARIABLES

Formula (10) can be greatly simplified if x_j is a slack, excess, or artificial variable. For example, if x_j is the slack variable s_i, the coefficient of s_i in the objective function is zero, and the column for s_i in the original tableau has 1 in row i and zero in all other rows.

Then (10) yields

$$\text{Coefficient of } s_i \text{ in optimal row } 0 = i\text{th element of } \mathbf{c}_{BV}B^{-1} - 0$$
$$= i\text{th element of } \mathbf{c}_{BV}B^{-1} \tag{10'}$$

Similarly, if x_j is the excess variable e_i, the coefficient of e_i in the objective function is zero and the column for e_i in the original tableau has -1 in row i and zero in all other rows. Then (10) reduces to

$$\text{Coefficient of } e_i \text{ in optimal row } 0 = -(i\text{th element of } \mathbf{c}_{BV}B^{-1}) - 0$$
$$= -(i\text{th element of } \mathbf{c}_{BV}B^{-1}) \tag{10''}$$

Finally, if x_j is an artificial variable a_i, the objective function coefficient of a_i (for a max problem) is $-M$ and the original column for a_i has 1 in row i and zero in all other rows. Then (10) reduces to

$$\text{Coefficient of } a_i \text{ in optimal row } 0 = (i\text{th element of } \mathbf{c}_{BV}B^{-1}) - (-M)$$
$$= (i\text{th element of } \mathbf{c}_{BV}B^{-1}) + M \tag{10'''}$$

The derivations of this section have not been easy. Fortunately, use of (5), (6), (10), and (11) does not require a complete understanding of the derivations. A summary follows of the formulas derived in this section for computing an optimal tableau from the initial LP.

SUMMARY OF FORMULAS FOR COMPUTING THE OPTIMAL TABLEAU FROM THE INITIAL LP

$$x_j \text{ column in optimal tableau's constraints} = B^{-1}\mathbf{a}_j \tag{5}$$
$$\text{Right-hand side of optimal tableau's constraints} = B^{-1}\mathbf{b} \tag{6}$$
$$\bar{c}_j = \mathbf{c}_{BV}B^{-1}\mathbf{a}_j - c_j \tag{10}$$

Coefficient of slack variable s_i in optimal row 0
$$= i\text{th element of } \mathbf{c}_{BV}B^{-1} \tag{10'}$$

Coefficient of excess variable e_i in optimal row 0
$$= -(i\text{th element of } \mathbf{c}_{BV}B^{-1}) \tag{10''}$$

Coefficient of artificial variable a_i in optimal row 0
$$= (i\text{th element of } \mathbf{c}_{BV}B^{-1}) + M \quad \text{(max problem)} \tag{10'''}$$

$$\text{Right-hand side of optimal row } 0 = \mathbf{c}_{BV}B^{-1}\mathbf{b} \tag{11}$$

Knowing B^{-1} is necessary in order to compute all parts of the optimal tableau, so we must first find B^{-1}, and since knowing $\mathbf{c}_{BV}B^{-1}$ is also necessary in order to compute the optimal tableau's row 0, we must compute $\mathbf{c}_{BV}B^{-1}$.

The following example is another illustration of the use of the preceding formulas.

E X A M P L E
1

For the following LP, the optimal basis is $BV = \{x_2, s_2\}$. Compute the optimal tableau.

$$\max z = x_1 + 4x_2$$
$$\text{s.t.} \quad x_1 + 2x_2 \le 6$$
$$2x_1 + x_2 \le 8$$
$$x_1, x_2 \ge 0$$

Solution

After adding slack variables s_1 and s_2, we obtain the analog of (1):

$$\max z = x_1 + 4x_2$$
$$\text{s.t.} \quad x_1 + 2x_2 + s_1 \qquad = 6$$
$$2x_1 + x_2 \qquad + s_2 = 8$$

First we compute B^{-1}. Since

$$B = \begin{bmatrix} 2 & 0 \\ 1 & 1 \end{bmatrix}$$

we find B^{-1} by applying the Gauss-Jordan method to the following matrix:

$$B \,|\, I_2 = \begin{bmatrix} 2 & 0 & | & 1 & 0 \\ 1 & 1 & | & 0 & 1 \end{bmatrix}$$

The reader should verify that

$$B^{-1} = \begin{bmatrix} \frac{1}{2} & 0 \\ -\frac{1}{2} & 1 \end{bmatrix}$$

Use (5) and (6) to determine the optimal tableau's constraints. Since

$$\mathbf{a}_1 = \begin{bmatrix} 1 \\ 2 \end{bmatrix}$$

the column for x_1 in the optimal tableau is

$$B^{-1}\mathbf{a}_1 = \begin{bmatrix} \frac{1}{2} & 0 \\ -\frac{1}{2} & 1 \end{bmatrix} \begin{bmatrix} 1 \\ 2 \end{bmatrix} = \begin{bmatrix} \frac{1}{2} \\ \frac{3}{2} \end{bmatrix}$$

The other nonbasic variable is s_1. Since the column for s_1 in the original problem is

$$\begin{bmatrix} 1 \\ 0 \end{bmatrix}$$

(5) yields

$$\text{Column for } s_1 \text{ in optimal tableau} = \begin{bmatrix} \frac{1}{2} & 0 \\ -\frac{1}{2} & 1 \end{bmatrix} \begin{bmatrix} 1 \\ 0 \end{bmatrix} = \begin{bmatrix} \frac{1}{2} \\ -\frac{1}{2} \end{bmatrix}$$

Since

$$\mathbf{b} = \begin{bmatrix} 6 \\ 8 \end{bmatrix}$$

(6) yields

$$\text{Right-hand side of optimal tableau} = \begin{bmatrix} \frac{1}{2} & 0 \\ -\frac{1}{2} & 1 \end{bmatrix} \begin{bmatrix} 6 \\ 8 \end{bmatrix} = \begin{bmatrix} 3 \\ 5 \end{bmatrix}$$

Since BV is listed as $\{x_2, s_2\}$, x_2 is the basic variable for row 1, and s_2 is the basic variable for row 2. Thus, the constraints of the optimal tableau are

$$\begin{aligned} \tfrac{1}{2}x_1 + x_2 + \tfrac{1}{2}s_1 \quad &= 3 \\ \tfrac{3}{2}x_1 \quad - \tfrac{1}{2}s_2 + s_1 &= 5 \end{aligned}$$

Since $\mathbf{c}_{BV} = [4 \quad 0]$,

$$\mathbf{c}_{BV} B^{-1} = [4 \quad 0] \begin{bmatrix} \frac{1}{2} & 0 \\ -\frac{1}{2} & 1 \end{bmatrix} = [2 \quad 0]$$

Then (10) yields

$$\text{Coefficient of } x_1 \text{ in row 0 of optimal tableau} = \mathbf{c}_{BV} B^{-1} \mathbf{a}_1 - c_1$$

$$= [2 \quad 0] \begin{bmatrix} 1 \\ 2 \end{bmatrix} - 1 = 1$$

From (10′)

$$\text{Coefficient of } s_1 \text{ in optimal tableau} = \text{First element of } \mathbf{c}_{BV} B^{-1} = 2$$

Since

$$\mathbf{b} = \begin{bmatrix} 6 \\ 8 \end{bmatrix}$$

(11) shows that the right-hand side of the optimal tableau's row 0 is

$$\mathbf{c}_{BV} B^{-1} \mathbf{b} = [2 \quad 0] \begin{bmatrix} 6 \\ 8 \end{bmatrix} = 12$$

Of course, the basic variables x_2 and s_2 will have zero coefficients in row 0 of the optimal tableau. Thus, the optimal tableau's row 0 is $z + x_1 + 2s_1 = 12$, and the complete optimal tableau is

$$\begin{aligned} z + \; x_1 \quad\quad + 2s_1 \quad\quad &= 12 \\ \tfrac{1}{2}x_1 + x_2 + \tfrac{1}{2}s_1 \quad\quad &= 3 \\ \tfrac{3}{2}x_1 \quad\quad - \tfrac{1}{2}s_1 + s_2 &= 5 \end{aligned}$$

◆

We have used the formulas of this section to create an LP's optimal tableau, but they can also be used to create the tableau for *any* set of basic variables. This observation will be important when we study the revised simplex method in Section 10.1.

♦ PROBLEMS

GROUP A

1. For the following LP, x_1 and x_2 are basic variables in the optimal tableau. Use the formulas of this section to determine the optimal tableau.

$$\max z = 3x_1 + x_2$$
$$\text{s.t.} \quad 2x_1 - x_2 \leq 2$$
$$-x_1 + x_2 \leq 4$$
$$x_1, x_2 \geq 0$$

2. For the following LP, x_2 and s_1 are basic variables in the optimal tableau. Use the formulas of this section to determine the optimal tableau.

$$\max z = -x_1 + x_2$$
$$\text{s.t.} \quad 2x_1 + x_2 \leq 4$$
$$x_1 + x_2 \leq 2$$
$$x_1, x_2 \geq 0$$

6-3   SENSITIVITY ANALYSIS

We now explore how changes in an LP's parameters (objective function coefficients, right-hand sides, and technological coefficients) change the LP's optimal solution. As described in Section 6.1, the study of how an LP's optimal solution depends on its parameters is called sensitivity analysis. Our discussion focuses on maximization problems and relies heavily on the formulas of Section 6.2. (The modifications for min problems are straightforward; see Problem 8 at the end of this section.)

As in Section 6.2, we let BV be the set of basic variables in the optimal tableau. Given a change (or changes) in an LP, we want to determine whether BV remains optimal. The mechanics of sensitivity analysis hinge on the following important observation. *From Chapter 4, we know that a simplex tableau (for a max problem) for a set of basic variables BV is optimal if and only if each constraint has a nonnegative right-hand side and each variable has a nonnegative coefficient in row 0.* This follows, because if each constraint has a nonnegative right-hand side, BV's basic solution is feasible, and if each variable in row 0 has a nonnegative coefficient, we know that there can be no basic feasible solution with a higher z-value than BV. Our observation implies that whether or not a tableau is feasible and optimal depends only on the right-hand sides of the constraints and on the coefficients of each variable in row 0. For example, if an LP has variables $x_1, x_2, \ldots, x_6$, the following partial tableau would be optimal:

$$z + 2x_2 + x_4 + x_6 = 6$$
$$= 1$$
$$= 2$$
$$= 3$$

This tableau's being optimal does not depend on the parts of the tableau that are omitted.

Suppose we have solved an LP and have found that BV is an optimal basis. We can use the following procedure to determine if any change in the LP will cause BV to be no longer optimal.

Step 1 Using the formulas of Section 6.2, determine how changes in the LP's parameters change the right-hand side and row 0 of the optimal tableau (the tableau having BV as the set of basic variables).

Step 2 If each variable in row 0 has a nonnegative coefficient and each constraint has a nonnegative right-hand side, BV is still optimal. Otherwise, BV is no longer optimal.

If BV is no longer optimal, you can find the new optimal solution by using the Section 6.2 formulas to recreate the entire tableau for BV and then continuing the simplex algorithm with the BV tableau as your starting tableau.

There can be two reasons why a change in an LP's parameters causes BV to be no longer optimal. First, a variable (or variables) in row 0 may have a negative coefficient. In this case, a better (larger z-value) bfs can be obtained by pivoting in a nonbasic variable with a negative coefficient in row 0. If this occurs, we say that BV is now a **suboptimal basis**. Second, a constraint (or constraints) may now have a negative right-hand side. In this case, at least one member of BV will now be negative and BV will no longer yield a bfs. If this occurs, we say that BV is now an **infeasible basis**.

We illustrate the mechanics of sensitivity analysis on the Dakota Furniture example. Recall that

$$x_1 = \text{number of desks manufactured}$$
$$x_2 = \text{number of tables manufactured}$$
$$x_3 = \text{number of chairs manufactured}$$

The objective function for the Dakota problem was

$$\max z = 60x_1 + 30x_2 + 20x_3$$

and the initial tableau was

$$
\begin{aligned}
z - 60x_1 - 30x_2 - 20x_3 &= 0 \\
8x_1 + 6x_2 + x_3 + s_1 &= 48 \quad \text{(Lumber constraint)} \\
4x_1 + 2x_2 + 1.5x_3 + s_2 &= 20 \quad \text{(Finishing constraint)} \\
2x_1 + 1.5x_2 + 0.5x_3 + s_3 &= 8 \quad \text{(Carpentry constraint)}
\end{aligned}
\tag{12}
$$

The optimal tableau was

$$
\begin{aligned}
z + 5x_2 + 10s_2 + 10s_3 &= 280 \\
- 2x_2 + s_1 + 2s_2 - 8s_3 &= 24 \\
- 2x_2 + x_3 + 2s_2 - 4s_3 &= 8 \\
x_1 + 1.25x_2 - 0.5s_2 + 1.5s_3 &= 2
\end{aligned}
\tag{13}
$$

Note that $BV = \{s_1, x_3, x_1\}$ and $NBV = \{x_2, s_2, s_3\}$. The optimal bfs is $z = 280$, $s_1 = 24$, $x_3 = 8$, $x_1 = 2$, $x_2 = 0$, $s_2 = 0$, $s_3 = 0$.

We now discuss how six types of changes in an LP's parameters change the LP's optimal solution:

Change 1 Changing the objective function coefficient of a nonbasic variable

Change 2 Changing the objective function coefficient of a basic variable

Change 3 Changing the right-hand side of a constraint

Change 4 Changing the column for a nonbasic variable

Change 5 Adding a new variable or activity

Change 6 Adding a new constraint (see Section 6.11)

**CHANGING THE OBJECTIVE FUNCTION COEFFICIENT FOR
A NONBASIC VARIABLE**

In the Dakota problem, the only nonbasic decision variable is x_2 (tables). Currently, the objective function coefficient for x_2 is $c_2 = 30$. How would a change in c_2 affect the optimal solution to the Dakota problem? More specifically, for what values of c_2 would $BV = \{s_1, x_3, x_1\}$ remain optimal?

Suppose we change the objective function coefficient of x_2 from 30 to $30 + \Delta$. Then Δ represents the amount by which we have changed c_2 from its current value. For what values of Δ will the current set of basic variables (the current basis) remain optimal? We begin by determining how changing c_2 from 30 to $30 + \Delta$ will change the BV tableau. Note that B^{-1} and $\mathbf{b}$ are unchanged, and therefore, from (6), the right-hand side of BV's tableau $(B^{-1}\mathbf{b})$ has not changed, so BV is still feasible. Since x_2 is a nonbasic variable, $\mathbf{c}_{BV}$ has not changed. From (10), we can see that the only variable whose row 0 coefficient will be changed by a change in c_2 is x_2. Thus, BV will remain optimal if $\bar{c}_2 \geq 0$, and BV will be suboptimal if $\bar{c}_2 < 0$. In this case, z could be improved by entering x_2 into the basis.

We have

$$
\mathbf{a}_2 = \begin{bmatrix} 6 \\ 2 \\ 1.5 \end{bmatrix}
$$

and $c_2 = 30 + \Delta$. Also, from Section 6.2, we know that $\mathbf{c}_{BV}B^{-1} = [0 \quad 10 \quad 10]$. Now (10) shows that

$$
\bar{c}_2 = [0 \quad 10 \quad 10] \begin{bmatrix} 6 \\ 2 \\ 1.5 \end{bmatrix} - (30 + \Delta) = 35 - 30 - \Delta = 5 - \Delta
$$

Thus, $\bar{c}_2 \geq 0$ holds, and BV will remain optimal, if $5 - \Delta \geq 0$, or $\Delta \leq 5$. Similarly, $\bar{c}_2 < 0$ holds if $\Delta > 5$, but then BV is no longer optimal. This means that if the price of tables is decreased or increased by \$5 or less, BV remains optimal. Thus, for $c_2 \leq 30 + 5 = 35$, BV remains optimal.

If BV remains optimal after a change in a nonbasic variable's objective function coefficient, the values of the decision variables and the optimal z-value remain unchanged. This is because a change in the objective function coefficient for a nonbasic variable leaves the right-hand side of row 0 and the constraints unchanged. For example, if the price of tables increases to \$33 ($c_2 = 33$), the optimal solution to the Dakota problem remains unchanged (Dakota should still make 2 desks and 8 chairs, and $z = 280$). On the other hand, if $c_2 > 35$, BV will no longer be optimal, because $\bar{c}_2 < 0$. In this case, we can find the new optimal solution by recreating the BV tableau and then using the simplex algorithm. For example, if $c_2 = 40$, we know that the only part of the BV tableau that will change is the coefficient of x_2 in row 0. If $c_2 = 40$, then

$$
\bar{c}_2 = [0 \quad 10 \quad 10] \begin{bmatrix} 6 \\ 2 \\ 1.5 \end{bmatrix} - 40 = -5
$$

$z = 5 + \Delta$

$z - 5 - \Delta$

Now the BV "final" tableau is as shown in Table 2. This is not an optimal tableau (it is suboptimal), and we can increase z by making x_2 a basic variable in row 3. The resulting tableau is given in Table 3. This is an optimal tableau. Thus, if $c_2 = 40$, the optimal solution to the Dakota problem changes to $z = 288$, $s_1 = 27.2$, $x_3 = 11.2$, $x_2 = 1.6$, $x_1 = 0$, $s_2 = 0$, $s_3 = 0$. In this case, the increase in the price of tables has made tables sufficiently more attractive to induce us to manufacture them. Note that after changing a nonbasic variable's objective function coefficient, it may, in general, take more than one pivot to find the new optimal solution.

				BASIC VARIABLE	RATIO
Table 2					
"Final" (Suboptimal)	$z -\ 5x_2$	$+\ 10s_2 +\ 10s_3 = 280$		$z = 280$	
Dakota Tableau	$-\ 2x_2$	$+\ s_1 +\ 2s_2 -\ 8s_3 = 24$		$s_1 = 24$	None
($40/Table)	$-\ 2x_2 + x_3$	$+\ 2s_2 -\ 4s_3 = 8$		$x_3 = 8$	None
	$x_1 + 1.25x_2$	$-\ 0.5s_2 +\ 1.5s_3 = 2$		$x_1 = 2$	1.6*

				BASIC VARIABLE
Table 3				
Optimal Dakota	$z +\ 4x_1$	$+\ 8s_2 +\ 16s_3 = 288$		$z = 288$
Tableau ($40/Table)	$1.6x_1$	$+\ s_1 +\ 1.2s_2 -\ 5.6s_3 = 27.2$		$s_1 = 27.2$
	$1.6x_1$	$+ x_3 +\ 1.2s_2 -\ 1.6s_3 = 11.2$		$x_3 = 11.2$
	$0.8x_1 + x_2$	$-\ 0.4s_2 +\ 1.2s_3 = 1.6$		$x_2 = 1.6$

There is a more insightful way to show that the current basis in the Dakota problem remains optimal as long as the price of tables is decreased or increased by $5 or less. From the optimal row 0 in (13), we see that if $c_2 = 30$, then

$$z = 280 - 10s_2 - 10s_3 - 5x_2$$

This tells us that each table that Dakota decides to manufacture will decrease revenue by $5 (in other words, the reduced cost for tables is 5). If we increase the price of tables by more than $5, each table would now increase Dakota's revenue. For example, if $c_2 = 36$, each table would increase revenues by $6 - 5 = 1 and Dakota should manufacture tables. Thus, as before, we see that for $\Delta > 5$, the current basis is no longer optimal. This analysis yields another interpretation of the reduced cost of a nonbasic variable: *The reduced cost for a nonbasic variable (in a max problem) is the maximum amount by which the variable's objective function coefficient can be increased before the current basis becomes suboptimal and it becomes optimal for the nonbasic variable to enter the basis.*

In summary, if the objective function coefficient for a nonbasic variable x_j is changed, the current basis remains optimal if $\bar{c}_j \geq 0$. If $\bar{c}_j < 0$, the current basis is no longer optimal, and x_j will be a basic variable in the new optimal solution.

CHANGING THE OBJECTIVE FUNCTION COEFFICIENT
FOR A BASIC VARIABLE

In the Dakota problem, the decision variables x_1 (desks) and x_3 (chairs) are basic variables. We now explain how a change in the objective function coefficient for a basic variable will affect an LP's optimal solution. We begin by analyzing how a change in the objective function coefficient for a basic variable changes the BV tableau. Since we are not changing B (or therefore B^{-1}) or $\mathbf{b}$, (6) shows that the right-hand side of each constraint will remain unchanged, and BV will remain feasible. Since we are changing $\mathbf{c}_{BV}$, however, $\mathbf{c}_{BV}B^{-1}$ will change. From (10), we see that a change in $\mathbf{c}_{BV}B^{-1}$ may change more than one coefficient in row 0. To determine whether BV remains optimal after we have changed the objective function coefficient of a basic variable, we must use (10) to recompute row 0 for the BV tableau. If each variable in row 0 still has a nonnegative coefficient, BV remains optimal. Otherwise, BV is now suboptimal. To illustrate the preceding ideas, we analyze how a change in the objective function coefficient for x_1 (desks) from its current value of $c_1 = 60$ affects the optimal solution to the Dakota problem.

Suppose that c_1 is changed to $60 + \Delta$, changing $\mathbf{c}_{BV}$ to $\mathbf{c}_{BV} = [0 \quad 20 \quad 60 + \Delta]$. In order to compute the new row 0, we need to know B^{-1}. We could (as in Section 6.2) use the Gauss-Jordan method to compute B^{-1}. Recall that this method begins by writing down the 3×6 matrix $B|I_3$:

$$B|I_3 = \begin{bmatrix} 1 & 1 & 8 & 1 & 0 & 0 \\ 0 & 1.5 & 4 & 0 & 1 & 0 \\ 0 & 0.5 & 2 & 0 & 0 & 1 \end{bmatrix}$$

Then we use ero's to transform the first three columns of $B|I_3$ to I_3. At this point, the last three columns of the resulting matrix will be B^{-1}.

It turns out that when we solved the Dakota problem by the simplex algorithm, we (without realizing it) found B^{-1}. To see why this is the case, note that in going from the initial Dakota tableau (12) to the optimal Dakota tableau (13) we performed a series of ero's on the constraints. These ero's transformed the constraint columns corresponding to the initial basis (s_1, s_2, s_3)

$$\text{from} \quad \begin{array}{ccc} s_1 & s_2 & s_3 \end{array} \atop \begin{bmatrix} 1 & 0 & 0 \\ 0 & 1 & 0 \\ 0 & 0 & 1 \end{bmatrix} \quad \text{to} \quad \begin{array}{ccc} s_1 & s_2 & s_3 \end{array} \atop \begin{bmatrix} 1 & 2 & -8 \\ 0 & 2 & -4 \\ 0 & -0.5 & 1.5 \end{bmatrix}$$

These same ero's have transformed the columns corresponding to $BV = \{s_1, x_3, x_1\}$

$$\text{from} \quad B = \begin{array}{ccc} s_1 & x_3 & x_1 \end{array} \atop \begin{bmatrix} 1 & 1 & 8 \\ 0 & 1.5 & 4 \\ 0 & 0.5 & 2 \end{bmatrix} \quad \text{to} \quad \begin{array}{ccc} s_1 & x_3 & x_1 \end{array} \atop \begin{bmatrix} 1 & 0 & 0 \\ 0 & 1 & 0 \\ 0 & 0 & 1 \end{bmatrix}$$

This means that in solving the Dakota problem by the simplex algorithm, we have used ero's to transform B to I_3. These same ero's transformed I_3 into

$$\begin{bmatrix} 1 & 2 & -8 \\ 0 & 2 & -4 \\ 0 & -0.5 & 1.5 \end{bmatrix} = B^{-1}$$

We have discovered an extremely important fact: *For any simplex tableau, B^{-1} is the $m \times m$ matrix consisting of the columns in the current tableau that correspond to the initial tableau's set of basic variables* (*taken in the same order*). This means that if the starting basis for an LP consists entirely of slack variables, B^{-1} for the optimal tableau is simply the columns for the slack variables in the constraints of the optimal tableau. In general, if the starting basic variable for the ith constraint was the artificial variable a_i, the ith column of B^{-1} will be the column for a_i in the optimal tableau's constraints. In summary, we need not use the Gauss-Jordan method to find the optimal tableau's B^{-1}. We have already found B^{-1} by performing the simplex algorithm.

We can now compute what $\mathbf{c}_{BV} B^{-1}$ will be if $c_1 = 60 + \Delta$:

$$\mathbf{c}_{BV} B^{-1} = [0 \quad 20 \quad 60 + \Delta] \begin{bmatrix} 1 & 2 & -8 \\ 0 & 2 & -4 \\ 0 & -0.5 & 1.5 \end{bmatrix} \tag{14}$$

$$= [0 \quad 10 - 0.5\Delta \quad 10 + 1.5\Delta]$$

Observe that for $\Delta = 0$, (14) yields the original $\mathbf{c}_{BV} B^{-1}$. We can now compute the new row 0 corresponding to $c_1 = 60 + \Delta$. After noting that

$$\mathbf{a}_1 = \begin{bmatrix} 8 \\ 4 \\ 2 \end{bmatrix}, \quad \mathbf{a}_2 = \begin{bmatrix} 6 \\ 2 \\ 1.5 \end{bmatrix}, \quad \mathbf{a}_3 = \begin{bmatrix} 1 \\ 1.5 \\ 0.5 \end{bmatrix}, \quad c_1 = 60 + \Delta, \quad c_2 = 30, \quad c_3 = 20$$

we can use (10) to compute the new row 0. Since s_1, x_3, and x_1 are basic variables, their coefficients in row 0 must still be zero. The coefficient of each nonbasic variable in the new row 0 is as follows:

$$\bar{c}_2 = \mathbf{c}_{BV} B^{-1} \mathbf{a}_2 - c_2 = [0 \quad 10 - 0.5\Delta \quad 10 + 1.5\Delta] \begin{bmatrix} 6 \\ 2 \\ 1.5 \end{bmatrix} - 30 = 5 + 1.25\Delta$$

Coefficient of s_2 in row 0 = second element of $\mathbf{c}_{BV} B^{-1} = 10 - 0.5\Delta$

Coefficient of s_3 in row 0 = third element of $\mathbf{c}_{BV} B^{-1} = 10 + 1.5\Delta$

Thus, row 0 of the optimal tableau is now

$$z + (5 + 1.25\Delta)x_2 + (10 - 0.5\Delta)s_2 + (10 + 1.5\Delta)s_3 = ?$$

From the new row 0, we see that BV will remain optimal if and only if the following hold:

$$5 + 1.25\Delta \geq 0 \quad \text{(true iff } \Delta \geq -4)$$
$$10 - 0.5\Delta \geq 0 \quad \text{(true iff } \Delta \leq 20)$$
$$10 + 1.5\Delta \geq 0 \quad \text{(true iff } \Delta \geq -(20/3))$$

This means that the current basis remains optimal as long as $\Delta \geq -4$, $\Delta \leq 20$, and $\Delta \geq -\frac{20}{3}$. From Figure 3, we see that the current basis will remain optimal if and only if $-4 \leq \Delta \leq 20$: If c_1 is decreased by \$4 or less or increased by up to \$20, the current basis remains optimal. Thus, as long as $56 = 60 - 4 \leq c_1 \leq 60 + 20 = 80$, the current basis remains optimal. If $c_1 < 56$ or $c_1 > 80$, the current basis is no longer optimal.

Figure 3
Determination of
Range of Values on
c_1 for Which Current
Basis Remains
Optimal

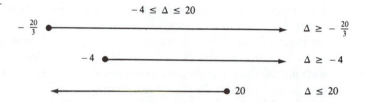

If the current basis remains optimal, the values of the decision variables don't change, because $B^{-1}\mathbf{b}$ remains unchanged. The optimal z-value does change, however. To illustrate this, suppose $c_1 = 70$. Since $56 \le 70 \le 80$, we know that the current basis remains optimal. Thus, Dakota should still manufacture 2 desks ($x_1 = 2$) and 8 chairs ($x_3 = 8$). However, changing c_1 to 70 changes z to $z = 70x_1 + 30x_2 + 20x_3$. This changes z to $70(2) + 20(8) = \$300$. Another way to see that z is now \$300 is to note that we have increased the revenue from each desk by $70 - 60 = \$10$. Since Dakota is making 2 desks, revenue should increase by $2(10) = \$20$, and new revenue $= 280 + 20 = \$300$.

Recall that if $c_1 < 56$ or $c_1 > 80$, the current basis is no longer optimal. Intuitively, if the price of desks is decreased sufficiently (with all other prices held constant), desks will no longer be worth making. Our analysis shows that this occurs if the price of desks is decreased by more than \$4. The reader should verify (see Problem 2 at the end of this section) that if $c_1 < 56$, x_1 is no longer a basic variable in the new optimal solution. On the other hand, if $c_1 > 80$, desks have become profitable enough to make the current basis suboptimal; desks are now so attractive that we want to make more of them. To do this, we must force another variable out of the basis. Suppose $c_1 = 100$. Since $100 > 80$, we know that the current basis is no longer optimal. How can we determine the new optimal solution? Simply create the optimal tableau for $c_1 = 100$ and proceed with the simplex. If $c_1 = 100$, then $\Delta = 100 - 60 = 40$, and the new row 0 will have

$$\bar{c}_1 = 0, \qquad \bar{c}_2 = 5 + 1.25\Delta = 55, \qquad \bar{c}_3 = 0$$

s_1 coefficient in row $0 = 0$

s_2 coefficient in row $0 = 10 - 0.5\Delta = -10$

s_3 coefficient in row $0 = 10 + 1.5\Delta = 70$

$$\text{Right-hand side of row } 0 = \mathbf{c}_{BV}B^{-1}\mathbf{b} = [0 \quad -10 \quad 70]\begin{bmatrix} 48 \\ 20 \\ 8 \end{bmatrix} = 360$$

From Eq. (6), changing c_1 does not change the constraints in the BV tableau. This means that if $c_1 = 100$, the BV tableau is as given in Table 4. $BV = \{s_1, x_3, x_1\}$ is now

Table 4				BASIC VARIABLE	RATIO
"Final" (Suboptimal)					
Tableau If $c_1 = 100$	$z + 55x_2 \qquad - 10s_2 + 70s_3 = 360$			$z = 360$	
	$- 2x_2 + s_1 + 2s_2 - 8s_3 = 24$			$s_1 = 24$	12
	$- 2x_2 + x_3 + 2s_2 - 4s_3 = 8$			$x_3 = 8$	4*
	$x_1 + 1.25x_2 \qquad - 0.5s_2 + 1.5s_3 = 2$			$x_1 = 2$	None

suboptimal. To find the new Dakota optimal solution, we enter s_2 into the basis in row 2 (Table 5). This is an optimal tableau. If $c_1 = 100$, the new optimal solution to the Dakota problem is $z = 400$, $s_1 = 16$, $s_2 = 4$, $x_1 = 4$, $x_2 = 0$, $x_3 = 0$. Notice that increasing the profitability of desks has caused Dakota to stop making chairs. The resources that were previously used to make the chairs are now used to make $4 - 2 = 2$ extra desks.

Table 5
Optimal Dakota
Tableau If $c_1 = 100$

	BASIC VARIABLE
$z + 45x_2 + 5x_3 \qquad + 50s_3 = 400$	$z = 400$
$- \quad x_3 + s_1 \quad - 4s_3 = 16$	$s_1 = 16$
$- \quad x_2 + 0.5x_3 \quad + s_2 - 2s_3 = 4$	$s_2 = 4$
$x_1 + 0.75x_2 + 0.25x_3 \qquad + 0.5s_3 = 4$	$x_1 = 4$

In summary, if the objective function coefficient for a basic variable x_j is changed, the current basis remains optimal if the coefficient of every variable in row 0 of the *BV* tableau remains nonnegative. If any variable in row 0 has a negative coefficient in the *BV* tableau, the current basis is no longer optimal.

INTERPRETATION OF THE OBJECTIVE COEFFICIENT RANGES BLOCK OF THE LINDO OUTPUT

In the OBJ COEFFICIENT RANGES block of the LINDO computer output, we see the amount by which each variable's objective function coefficient may be changed before the current basis becomes suboptimal (assuming all other LP parameters are held constant). Look at the LINDO output for the Dakota problem (Figure 4). For

Figure 4
LINDO Output for
Dakota Furniture
Problem

```
MAX     60 DESKS + 30 TABLES + 20 CHAIRS
SUBJECT TO
     2)    8 DESKS + 6 TABLES +   CHAIRS <=    48
     3)    4 DESKS + 2 TABLES + 1.5 CHAIRS <=   20
     4)    2 DESKS + 1.5 TABLES + 0.5 CHAIRS <=   8
END

     LP OPTIMUM FOUND  AT STEP    2

          OBJECTIVE FUNCTION VALUE

     1)       280.000000

VARIABLE        VALUE          REDUCED COST
     DESKS       2.000000         0.000000
     TABLES      0.000000         5.000000
     CHAIRS      8.000000         0.000000

     ROW      SLACK OR SURPLUS    DUAL PRICES
     2)          24.000000         0.000000
     3)           0.000000        10.000000
     4)           0.000000        10.000000

NO. ITERATIONS=     2

RANGES IN WHICH THE BASIS IS UNCHANGED

                    OBJ COEFFICIENT RANGES
VARIABLE        CURRENT       ALLOWABLE       ALLOWABLE
                 COEF         INCREASE        DECREASE
     DESKS      60.000000     20.000000       4.000000
     TABLES     30.000000      5.000000       INFINITY
     CHAIRS     20.000000      2.500000       5.000000

                    RIGHTHAND SIDE RANGES
     ROW         CURRENT      ALLOWABLE       ALLOWABLE
                  RHS         INCREASE        DECREASE
      2         48.000000     INFINITY       24.000000
      3         20.000000      4.000000       4.000000
      4          8.000000      2.000000       1.333333
```

each variable, the CURRENT COEF column gives the current value of the variable's objective function coefficient. For example, the objective function coefficient for DESKS is 60. For each variable, the ALLOWABLE INCREASE column gives the maximum amount by which the objective function coefficient of the variable can be increased with the current basis remaining optimal (assuming all other LP parameters stay constant). For example, if the objective function coefficient for DESKS is increased above $60 + 20 = 80$, the current basis is no longer optimal. Similarly, the ALLOWABLE DECREASE column gives the maximum amount by which the objective function coefficient of a variable can be decreased with the current basis remaining optimal (assuming all other LP parameters constant). For example, if the objective function coefficient for DESKS drops below $60 - 4 = 56$, the current basis is no longer optimal. In summary, we see from the LINDO output that if the objective function coefficient for DESKS is changed, the current basis remains optimal if

$$56 = 60 - 4 \leq \text{objective coefficient for DESKS} \leq 60 + 20 = 80$$

Of course, this agrees with our earlier computations.

CHANGING THE RIGHT-HAND SIDE OF A CONSTRAINT

In this section, we examine how the optimal solution to an LP changes if the right-hand side of a constraint is changed. Since **b** does not appear in (10), changing the right-hand side of a constraint will leave row 0 of the optimal tableau unchanged; changing a right-hand side cannot cause the current basis to become suboptimal. From (5) and (6), however, we see that a change in the right-hand side of a constraint will change the right-hand side of the constraints in the optimal tableau. *As long as the right-hand side of each constraint in the optimal tableau remains nonnegative, the current basis remains feasible and optimal. If at least one right-hand side in the optimal tableau becomes negative, the current basis is no longer feasible and therefore no longer optimal.*

Suppose we want to determine how changing the amount of finishing hours (b_2) affects the optimal solution to the Dakota problem. Currently, $b_2 = 20$. If we change b_2 to $20 + \Delta$, then from (6), the right-hand side of the constraints in the optimal tableau will become

$$B^{-1} \begin{bmatrix} 48 \\ 20 + \Delta \\ 8 \end{bmatrix} = \begin{bmatrix} 1 & 2 & -8 \\ 0 & 2 & -4 \\ 0 & -0.5 & 1.5 \end{bmatrix} \begin{bmatrix} 48 \\ 20 + \Delta \\ 8 \end{bmatrix}$$

$$= \begin{bmatrix} 24 + 2\Delta \\ 8 + 2\Delta \\ 2 - 0.5\Delta \end{bmatrix}$$

Of course, for $\Delta = 0$, the right-hand side reduces to the right-hand side of the original optimal tableau. If this does not happen, an error has been made.

It can be shown (see Problem 9) that if the right-hand side of the ith constraint is increased by Δ, then the right-hand side of the optimal tableau is given by (original right-hand side of the optimal tableau) $+ \Delta$(column i of B^{-1}). Since the second column of B^{-1} is

$$\begin{bmatrix} 2 \\ 2 \\ -0.5 \end{bmatrix} \quad \text{and the original right-hand side is} \quad \begin{bmatrix} 24 \\ 8 \\ 2 \end{bmatrix}$$

we again find that the right-hand side of the constraints in the optimal tableau is

$$\begin{bmatrix} 24 + 2\Delta \\ 8 + 2\Delta \\ 2 - 0.5\Delta \end{bmatrix}$$

For the current basis to remain optimal, we require that the right-hand side of each constraint in the optimal tableau remain nonnegative. This means that the current basis will remain optimal if and only if the following hold:

$$\begin{array}{ll} 24 + 2\Delta \geq 0 & \text{(true iff } \Delta \geq -12) \\ 8 + 2\Delta \geq 0 & \text{(true iff } \Delta \geq -4) \\ 2 - 0.5\Delta \geq 0 & \text{(true iff } \Delta \leq 4) \end{array}$$

As long as $\Delta \geq -12$, $\Delta \geq -4$, and $\Delta \leq 4$, the current basis remains feasible and therefore optimal. From Figure 5, we see that for $-4 \leq \Delta \leq 4$, the current basis remains feasible and therefore optimal. This means that for $20 - 4 \leq b_2 \leq 20 + 4$, or $16 \leq b_2 \leq 24$, the current basis remains optimal: If between 16 and 24 finishing hours are available, $BV = \{s_1, x_3, x_1\}$ remains optimal, and Dakota should still manufacture desks and chairs. If $b_2 > 24$ or if $b_2 < 16$, however, the current basis becomes infeasible and is no longer optimal.

Figure 5
Determination of
Range of Values on
b_2 for Which Current
Basis Remains
Optimal

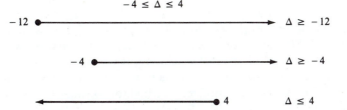

Even if the current basis remains optimal ($16 \leq b_2 \leq 24$), *the values of the decision variables and z change.* This was illustrated in our graphical discussion of sensitivity analysis in Section 6.1. To see how the values of the objective function and decision variables change, recall that the values of the basic variables in the optimal solution are given by $B^{-1}\mathbf{b}$ and the optimal z-value is given by $\mathbf{c}_{BV} B^{-1}\mathbf{b}$. Changing $\mathbf{b}$ will change the values of the basic variables and the optimal z-value. To illustrate this, suppose that 22 finishing hours are available. Since $16 \leq 22 \leq 24$, the current basis remains optimal and, from (6), the new values of the basic variables are as follows (since the same basis remains optimal, the nonbasic variables remain equal to zero):

$$\begin{bmatrix} s_1 \\ x_3 \\ x_1 \end{bmatrix} = B^{-1}\mathbf{b} = \begin{bmatrix} 1 & 2 & -8 \\ 0 & 2 & -4 \\ 0 & -0.5 & 1.5 \end{bmatrix} \begin{bmatrix} 48 \\ 22 \\ 8 \end{bmatrix} = \begin{bmatrix} 28 \\ 12 \\ 1 \end{bmatrix}$$

If 22 finishing hours were available, Dakota should manufacture 12 chairs and only 1 desk.

To determine how a change in a right-hand side affects the optimal z-value, we may use formula (11). If 22 finishing hours are available, we find that

$$\text{New } z\text{-value} = \mathbf{c}_{BV} B^{-1}(\text{new } \mathbf{b}) = [0 \quad 10 \quad 10] \begin{bmatrix} 48 \\ 22 \\ 8 \end{bmatrix} = 300$$

In Section 6.8, we explain how the important concept of shadow price can be used to determine how changes in a right-hand side change the optimal z-value.

If we change a right-hand side enough that the current basis is no longer optimal, how can we determine the new optimal basis? Suppose we change b_2 to 30. Since $b_2 > 24$, we know that the current basis is no longer optimal. If we recreate the optimal tableau, we see from the formulas of Section 6.2 that the only part of the optimal tableau that will change is the right-hand side of row 0 and the constraints. From (6), the right-hand side of the constraints in the tableau for $BV = \{s_1, x_3, x_1\}$ are

$$B^{-1}\mathbf{b} = \begin{bmatrix} 1 & 2 & -8 \\ 0 & 2 & -4 \\ 0 & -0.5 & 1.5 \end{bmatrix} \begin{bmatrix} 48 \\ 30 \\ 8 \end{bmatrix} = \begin{bmatrix} 44 \\ 28 \\ -3 \end{bmatrix}$$

From (11), the right-hand side of row 0 is now

$$\mathbf{c}_{BV} B^{-1}\mathbf{b} = [0 \quad 10 \quad 10] \begin{bmatrix} 48 \\ 30 \\ 8 \end{bmatrix} = 380$$

The tableau for the optimal basis, $BV = \{s_1, x_3, x_1\}$, is now as shown in Table 6. Since $x_1 = -3$, BV is no longer feasible or optimal. Unfortunately, this tableau does not yield a readily apparent basic feasible solution. If we use this as our initial tableau, we can't use the simplex algorithm to find the new optimal solution to the Dakota problem. In Section 6.11, we discuss a different method for solving LPs, the dual simplex algorithm, which can be used to solve LPs when the initial tableau has one or more negative right-hand sides and each variable in row 0 has a nonnegative coefficient. The dual simplex algorithm could easily be used to find the new optimal solution to the Dakota problem from Table 6.

In summary, if the right-hand side of a constraint is changed, the current basis remains optimal if the right-hand side of each constraint in the tableau of the current basis remains nonnegative. If the right-hand side of any constraint in the tableau of the

Table 6				BASIC VARIABLE
Final (Infeasible) Dakota Tableau If $b_2 = 30$	$z +\quad 5x_2 \qquad\qquad + 10s_2 + 10s_3 = 380$			$z = 380$
	$-\quad 2x_2 \quad + s_1 +\quad 2s_2 -\quad 8s_3 = 44$			$s_1 = 44$
	$-\quad 2x_2 + x_3 \qquad +\quad 2s_2 -\quad 4s_3 = 28$			$x_3 = 28$
	$x_1 + 1.25x_2 \qquad\qquad - 0.5s_2 + 1.5s_3 = -3$			$x_1 = -3$

current basis is negative, the current basis is infeasible, and a new optimal solution must be found.

INTERPRETATION OF THE RIGHTHAND SIDE RANGES BLOCK OF THE LINDO OUTPUT

The block of the LINDO output labeled RIGHTHAND SIDE RANGES (see Figure 4) gives information concerning the amount by which a right-hand side can be changed before the current basis becomes infeasible (all other LP parameters constant). For each constraint, the CURRENT RHS column gives the current right-hand side of each constraint. Thus, for row 3 (the second constraint), the current right-hand side is 20. For each constraint, the ALLOWABLE INCREASE column is the maximum amount by which the right-hand side of the constraint can be increased with the current basis remaining optimal (all other LP parameters constant). For example, if the amount of available finishing hours (second constraint) is increased by up to 4 hours, the current basis remains optimal. Similarly, for each constraint, the ALLOWABLE DECREASE column gives the maximum amount by which the right-hand side of a constraint can be decreased with the current basis remaining optimal (all other LP parameters constant). For example, if the amount of available finishing hours is decreased by more than 4 hours, the current basis is no longer optimal. In summary, if the number of finishing hours is changed (all other LP parameters constant), the current basis remains optimal if

$$16 = 20 - 4 \leq \text{available finishing hours} \leq 20 + 4 = 24$$

CHANGING THE COLUMN OF A NONBASIC VARIABLE

At present, 6 board ft of lumber, 2 finishing hours, and 1.5 carpentry hours are required to make a table that can be sold for $30. Also x_2 (the variable for tables) is a nonbasic variable in the optimal solution. This means that Dakota should not manufacture any tables at present. Suppose, however, that the price of tables increased to $43 and, because of changes in production technology, a table required 5 board ft of lumber, 2 finishing hours, and 2 carpentry hours. Would this change the optimal solution to the Dakota problem? Here we are changing elements of the column for x_2 in the original problem (including the objective function). Changing the column for a nonbasic variable like tables leaves B (and B^{-1}) and $\mathbf{b}$ unchanged. Thus, the right-hand side of the optimal tableau remains unchanged. A glance at (10) also shows that the only part of row 0 that is changed is $\bar{c}_2$; the current basis will remain optimal if and only if $\bar{c}_2 \geq 0$ holds. We now use (10) to compute the new coefficient of x_2 in row 0. This process is called **pricing out** x_2. From (10),

$$\bar{c}_2 = \mathbf{c}_{BV} B^{-1} \mathbf{a}_2 - c_2$$

Note that $\mathbf{c}_{BV} B^{-1}$ still equals [0 10 10], but $\mathbf{a}_2$ and c_2 have changed to

$$c_2 = 43 \quad \text{and} \quad \mathbf{a}_2 = \begin{bmatrix} 5 \\ 2 \\ 2 \end{bmatrix}$$

Now

$$\bar{c}_2 = [0 \quad 10 \quad 10] \begin{bmatrix} 5 \\ 2 \\ 2 \end{bmatrix} - 43 = -3 < 0$$

Since $\bar{c}_2 < 0$, the current basis is no longer optimal. The fact that $\bar{c}_2 = -3$ means that each table that Dakota manufactures now increases revenues by \$3. It is clearly to Dakota's advantage to enter x_2 into the basis. To find the new optimal solution to the Dakota problem, we recreate the tableau for $BV = \{s_1, x_3, x_1\}$ and then apply the simplex algorithm. From (5), the column for x_2 in the constraint portion of the BV tableau is now

$$B^{-1}\mathbf{a}_2 = \begin{bmatrix} 1 & 2 & -8 \\ 0 & 2 & -4 \\ 0 & -0.5 & 1.5 \end{bmatrix} \begin{bmatrix} 5 \\ 2 \\ 2 \end{bmatrix} = \begin{bmatrix} -7 \\ -4 \\ 2 \end{bmatrix}$$

and the tableau for $BV = \{s_1, x_3, x_1\}$ is now as shown in Table 7. To find the new optimal solution, we enter x_2 into the basis in row 3. This yields the optimal tableau in Table 8. Thus, the new optimal solution to the Dakota problem is $z = 283$, $s_1 = 31$, $x_3 = 12$, $x_2 = 1$, $x_1 = 0$, $s_2 = 0$, $s_3 = 0$. After the column for the nonbasic variable x_2 (tables) has been changed, Dakota should manufacture 12 chairs and 1 table.

Table 7		BASIC VARIABLE
"Final" (Suboptimal) Dakota Tableau for New Method of Making Tables	$z \quad - 3x_2 \qquad\qquad + 10s_2 + 10s_3 = 280$ $- 7x_2 \quad + s_1 + \quad 2s_2 - \quad 8s_3 = 24$ $- 4x_2 + x_3 \qquad + \quad 2s_2 - \quad 4s_3 = 8$ $x_1 + \boxed{2x_2} \qquad - 0.5s_2 + 1.5s_3 = 2$	$z = 280$ $s_1 = 24$ $x_3 = 8$ $x_1 = 2^*$

Table 8		BASIC VARIABLE
Optimal Dakota Tableau for New Method of Making Tables	$z + 1.5x_1 \qquad\qquad + 9.25s_2 + 12.25s_3 = 283$ $3.5x_1 \qquad + s_1 + 0.25s_2 - \quad 2.75s_3 = 31$ $2x_1 \quad + x_3 \qquad + \quad s_2 - \qquad s_3 = 12$ $0.5x_1 + x_2 \qquad - 0.25s_2 + \quad 0.75s_3 = 1$	$z = 283$ $s_1 = 31$ $x_3 = 12$ $x_2 = 1$

In summary, if the column of a nonbasic variable x_j is changed, the current basis remains optimal if $\bar{c}_j \geq 0$. If $\bar{c}_j < 0$, the current basis is no longer optimal and x_j will be a basic variable in the new optimal solution.

If the column for a basic variable is changed, it is usually difficult to determine whether the current basis remains optimal. This is because changing the column for a basic variable may change both B (and hence B^{-1}) and $\mathbf{c}_{BV}$ and thus the entire row 0 and the entire right-hand side of the optimal tableau. As always, the current basis would remain optimal if and only if each variable has a nonnegative coefficient in the optimal tableau's row 0 and each constraint in the optimal tableau has a nonnegative right-hand side.

ADDING A NEW ACTIVITY

In many situations, opportunities arise to undertake new activities. For example, in the Dakota problem, the company may be presented with the opportunity to manufacture additional types of furniture, such as footstools. If a new activity is available, we can determine whether it should be used by applying the method utilized to determine whether the current basis remains optimal after a change in the column of a nonbasic variable. The following example illustrates the approach.

Suppose that Dakota is considering making footstools. A stool sells for \$15 and requires 1 board ft of lumber, 1 finishing hour, and 1 carpentry hour. Should the company manufacture any stools?

To answer this question, define x_4 to be the number of footstools manufactured by Dakota. The initial tableau is now changed by the introduction of the x_4 column. Our new initial tableau is

$$
\begin{aligned}
z - 60x_1 - 30x_2 - 20x_3 - 15x_4 && = 0 \\
8x_1 + 6x_2 + x_3 + x_4 + s_1 && = 48 \\
4x_1 + 2x_2 + 1.5x_3 + x_4 + s_2 && = 20 \\
2x_1 + 1.5x_2 + 0.5x_3 + x_4 + s_3 &&= 8
\end{aligned}
\tag{15}
$$

We call the addition of the x_4 column to the problem **adding a new activity**. How will the addition of the new activity change the optimal $BV = \{s_1, x_3, x_1\}$ tableau? From (6), we see that the right-hand sides of all constraints in the optimal tableau will remain unchanged. From (10), we see that the coefficient of each of the old variables in row 0 will remain unchanged. We must of course, compute $\bar{c}_4$, the coefficient of the new activity in row 0 of the optimal tableau. Since the right-hand side of each constraint in the optimal tableau is unchanged and the only variable in row 0 that can have a negative coefficient is x_4, the current basis will remain optimal if $\bar{c}_4 \geq 0$, and the current basis will no longer be optimal if $\bar{c}_4 < 0$.

To determine whether a new activity causes the current basis to be no longer optimal, price out the new activity. Since

$$
c_4 = 15 \quad \text{and} \quad \mathbf{a}_4 = \begin{bmatrix} 1 \\ 1 \\ 1 \end{bmatrix}
$$

we may use (10) to price out x_4. The result is

$$
\bar{c}_4 = \begin{bmatrix} 0 & 10 & 10 \end{bmatrix} \begin{bmatrix} 1 \\ 1 \\ 1 \end{bmatrix} - 15 = 5
$$

Since $\bar{c}_4 \geq 0$, the current basis is still optimal. Equivalently, the reduced cost of footstools is \$5. This means that each stool manufactured will decrease revenues by \$5. For this reason, we choose not to manufacture any stools.

In summary, if a new column (corresponding to a variable x_j) is added to an LP, the current basis remains optimal if $\bar{c}_j \geq 0$. If $\bar{c}_j < 0$, the current basis is no longer optimal and x_j will be a basic variable in the new optimal solution. Table 9 presents a summary

Table 9	CHANGE IN INITIAL PROBLEM	EFFECT ON OPTIMAL TABLEAU	CURRENT BASIS IS STILL OPTIMAL IF:
Summary of Sensitivity Analysis (Max Problem)	Changing nonbasic objective function coefficient c_j	Coefficient of x_j in optimal row 0 is changed	Coefficient of x_j in row 0 for current basis is still nonnegative
	Changing basic objective function coefficient c_j	Entire row 0 may change	Each variable still has a nonnegative coefficient in row 0
	Changing right-hand side of a constraint	Right-hand side of constraints and row 0 are changed	Right-hand side of each constraint is still nonnegative
	Changing the column of a nonbasic variable x_j or adding a new variable x_j	Changes the coefficient for x_j in row 0 and x_j's constraint column in optimal tableau	The coefficient of x_j in row 0 is still nonnegative

of sensitivity analyses for a maximization problem. When applying the techniques of this section to a minimization problem, just remember that a tableau is optimal if and only if each variable has a *nonpositive* coefficient in row 0 and the right-hand side of each constraint is nonnegative.

◆ PROBLEMS

GROUP A

1. In the Dakota problem, show that the current basis remains optimal if c_3, the price of chairs, satisfies $15 \le c_3 \le 22.5$. If $c_3 = 21$, find the new optimal solution. Also, if $c_3 = 25$, find the new optimal solution.

2. If $c_1 = 55$ in the Dakota problem, show that the new optimal solution does not produce any desks.

3. In the Dakota problem, show that if the amount of lumber (board ft) available (b_1) satisfies $b_1 \ge 24$, the current basis remains optimal. If $b_1 = 30$, find the new optimal solution.

4. Show that if tables sell for $50 and use 1 board ft of lumber, 3 finishing hours, and 1.5 carpentry hours, the current basis for the Dakota problem will no longer be optimal. Find the new optimal solution.

5. Dakota Furniture is considering manufacturing home computer tables. A home computer table sells for $36 and uses 6 board ft of lumber, 2 finishing hours, and 2 carpentry hours. Should the company manufacture any home computer tables?

6. Sugarco can manufacture three types of candy bar. Each candy bar consists totally of sugar and chocolate. The compositions of each type of candy bar and the profit

earned from each candy bar are shown in Table 10. Fifty ounces of sugar and 100 ounces of chocolate are available. After defining x_i to be the number of type i candy bars manufactured, Sugarco should solve the following LP:

$$\max z = 3x_1 + 7x_2 + 5x_3$$
$$\text{s.t.} \quad x_1 + x_2 + x_3 \le 50 \quad \text{(Sugar constraint)}$$
$$2x_1 + 3x_2 + x_3 \le 100 \quad \text{(Chocolate constraint)}$$
$$x_1, x_2, x_3 \ge 0$$

After adding slack variables s_1 and s_2, the optimal tableau is as shown in Table 11. Using this optimal tableau answer the following questions:

(a) For what values of type 1 candy bar profit does the current basis remain optimal? If the profit for a

Table 10

	AMOUNT OF SUGAR (Ounces)	AMOUNT OF CHOCOLATE (Ounces)	PROFIT (Cents)
Bar 1	1	2	3
Bar 2	1	3	7
Bar 3	1	1	5

Table 11

z	x_1	x_2	x_3	s_1	s_2	rhs	BASIC VARIABLE
1	3	0	0	4	1	300	$z = 300$
0	$\frac{1}{2}$	0	1	$\frac{3}{2}$	$-\frac{1}{2}$	25	$x_3 = 25$
0	$\frac{1}{2}$	1	0	$-\frac{1}{2}$	$\frac{1}{2}$	25	$x_2 = 25$

type 1 candy bar were 7¢, what would be the new optimal solution to Sugarco's problem?

(b) For what values of type 2 candy bar profit would the current basis remain optimal? If the profit for a type 2 candy bar were 13¢, what would be the new optimal solution to Sugarco's problem?

(c) For what amount of available sugar would the current basis remain optimal?

(d) If 60 oz of sugar were available, what would be Sugarco's profit? How many of each candy bar should they make? Can these questions be answered if only 30 oz of sugar were available?

(e) Suppose a type 1 candy bar used only 0.5 oz of sugar and 0.5 oz of chocolate. Should Sugarco now make type 1 candy bars?

(f) Sugarco is considering making type 4 candy bars. A type 4 candy bar earns 17¢ profit and requires 3 oz of sugar and 4 oz of chocolate. Should Sugarco manufacture any type 4 candy bars?

7. The following questions refer to the Giapetto problem (Section 3.1). Giapetto's LP was

$$\max z = 3x_1 + 2x_2$$

s.t. $2x_1 + x_2 \leq 100$ (Finishing constraint)

 $x_1 + x_2 \leq 80$ (Carpentry constraint)

 $x_1 \leq 40$ (Limited demand for soldiers)

(x_1 = soldiers and x_2 = trains). After adding slack variables s_1, s_2, and s_3, the optimal tableau is as shown in Table 12. Use this optimal tableau to answer the following questions:

Table 12

z	x_1	x_2	s_1	s_2	s_3	rhs	BASIC VARIABLE
1	0	0	1	1	0	180	$z = 180$
0	1	0	1	-1	0	20	$x_1 = 20$
0	0	1	-1	2	0	60	$x_2 = 60$
0	0	0	-1	1	1	20	$s_3 = 20$

(a) Show that as long as soldiers (x_1) contribute between $2 and $4 to profit, the current basis remains optimal. If soldiers contribute $3.50 to profit, find the new optimal solution to the Giapetto problem.

(b) Show that as long as trains (x_2) contribute between $1.50 and $3.00 to profit, the current basis remains optimal.

(c) Show that if between 80 and 120 finishing hours are available, the current basis remains optimal. Find the new optimal solution to the Giapetto problem if 90 finishing hours are available.

(d) Show that as long as the demand for soldiers is at least 20, the current basis remains optimal.

(e) Giapetto is considering manufacturing toy boats. A toy boat uses 2 carpentry hours and 1 finishing hour. Demand for toy boats is unlimited. If a toy boat contributes $3.50 to profit, should Giapetto manufacture any toy boats?

GROUP B

8. Consider the Dorian problem (Example 2 of Chapter 3):

$$\min z = 50x_1 + 100x_2$$

s.t. $7x_1 + 2x_2 \geq 28$ (HIW)

 $2x_1 + 12x_2 \geq 24$ (HIM)

 $x_1, x_2 \geq 0$

(x_1 = number of comedy ads and x_2 = number of football ads). The optimal tableau is given in Table 13. Remember that for a min problem, a tableau is optimal if and only if each variable has a nonpositive coefficient in row 0 and the right-hand side of each constraint is nonnegative.

Table 13

z	x_1	x_2	e_1	e_2	a_1	a_2	rhs
1	0	0	-5	-7.5	$5 - M$	$7.5 - M$	320
0	1	0	$-\frac{3}{20}$	$\frac{1}{40}$	$\frac{3}{20}$	$-\frac{1}{40}$	3.6
0	0	1	$\frac{1}{40}$	$-\frac{7}{80}$	$-\frac{1}{40}$	$\frac{7}{80}$	1.4

(a) Find the range of values on the cost of a comedy ad (currently $50,000) for which the current basis remains optimal.

(b) Find the range of values on the number of required HIW exposures (currently 28 million) for which the current basis remains optimal. If 40 million HIW exposures were required, what would be the new optimal solution?

(c) Suppose an ad on a news program costs $110,000 and reaches 12 million HIW and 7 million HIM. Should Dorian advertise on the news program?

9. Show that if the right-hand side of the ith constraint is increased by Δ, then the right-hand side of the optimal tableau is given by (original right-hand side of the optimal tableau) + Δ(column i of B^{-1}).

6-4   SENSITIVITY ANALYSIS WHEN MORE THAN ONE PARAMETER IS CHANGED: THE 100% RULE*

In this section, we show how to use the LINDO output to determine whether the current basis remains optimal when more than one objective function coefficient or right-hand side is changed.

THE 100% RULE FOR CHANGING OBJECTIVE FUNCTION COEFFICIENTS

Depending on whether or not the objective function coefficient of any variable with a zero reduced cost in the optimal tableau is changed, there are two cases to consider:

Case 1 All variables whose objective function coefficients are changed have nonzero reduced costs in the optimal row 0.

Case 2 At least one variable whose objective function coefficient is changed has a reduced cost of zero.

In Case 1, the current basis remains optimal if and only if the objective function coefficient for each variable remains within the allowable range[†] given on the LINDO printout (see Problem 10 at the end of this section). If the current basis remains optimal, both the values of the decision variables and objective function remain unchanged. If the objective function coefficient for any variable is outside its allowable range, the current basis is no longer optimal.

The following two examples of Case 1 refer to the diet problem of Section 3.4. The LINDO printout for this problem is given in Figure 6.

E X A M P L E 2

Suppose the price of a brownie increases to 60¢ and the price of a piece of pineapple cheesecake decreases to 50¢. Does the current basis remain optimal? What would be the new optimal solution?

Solution

Since both brownies and pineapple cheesecake have nonzero reduced costs, we are in Case 1. From Figure 6 and the Case 1 discussion, we see that the current basis remains optimal if and only if

$$22.5 = 50 - 27.5 \le \text{cost of a brownie} \le 50 + \infty = \infty$$

$$30 = 80 - 50 \le \text{cost of a piece of cheesecake} \le 80 + \infty = \infty$$

Since the new prices satisfy both of these conditions, the current basis remains optimal. Also the optimal z-value and optimal value of the decision variables remain unchanged.

◆

---

*This section covers topics that may be omitted with no loss of continuity.
[†]The allowable range for c_j is the range of values for c_j for which the current basis remains optimal (assuming that only c_j is changed).

Figure 6
LINDO Output for
Diet Problem

```
MIN     50 BR + 20 IC + 30 COLA + 80 PC
SUBJECT TO
    2)    400 BR + 200 IC + 150 COLA + 500 PC >=   500
    3)    3 BR + 2 IC >=   6
    4)    2 BR + 2 IC + 4 COLA + 4 PC >=   10
    5)    2 BR + 4 IC +  COLA + 5 PC >=   8
END

    LP OPTIMUM FOUND  AT STEP     5

        OBJECTIVE FUNCTION VALUE

    1)        90.0000000

VARIABLE         VALUE        REDUCED COST
    BR         0.000000        27.500000
    IC         3.000000         0.000000
    COLA       1.000000         0.000000
    PC         0.000000        50.000000

    ROW     SLACK OR SURPLUS    DUAL PRICES
    2)       250.000000         0.000000
    3)         0.000000        -2.500000
    4)         0.000000        -7.500000
    5)         5.000000         0.000000

NO. ITERATIONS=     5

RANGES IN WHICH THE BASIS IS UNCHANGED

                      OBJ COEFFICIENT RANGES
VARIABLE      CURRENT       ALLOWABLE       ALLOWABLE
               COEF         INCREASE        DECREASE
    BR       50.000000      INFINITY        27.500000
    IC       20.000000      18.333334        5.000000
    COLA     30.000000      10.000000       30.000000
    PC       80.000000      INFINITY        50.000000

                      RIGHTHAND SIDE RANGES
    ROW       CURRENT       ALLOWABLE       ALLOWABLE
               RHS          INCREASE        DECREASE
    2        500.000000     250.000000      INFINITY
    3          6.000000       4.000000       2.857143
    4         10.000000      INFINITY        4.000000
    5          8.000000       5.000000      INFINITY
```

E X A M P L E
3

Solution

If the price of a brownie drops to 40¢ and the price of a piece of pineapple cheesecake drops to 25¢, is the current basis still optimal?

From Figure 6, we see that Case 1 again applies. Although the cost of a brownie remains in its allowable range, the price of a piece of pineapple cheesecake is no longer in its allowable range. Thus, the current basis is no longer optimal, and the problem must be solved again.

◆

In Case 2, we can often show that the current basis remains optimal by using the **100% Rule**. Let

c_j = original objective function coefficient for x_j

Δc_j = change in c_j

I_j = maximum allowable increase in c_j for which current basis remains optimal (from LINDO output)

D_j = maximum allowable decrease in c_j for which current basis remains optimal (from LINDO output)

For each variable x_j, we define the ratio r_j:

$$\text{If} \quad \Delta c_j \geq 0, \qquad r_j = \frac{\Delta c_j}{I_j}$$

$$\text{If} \quad \Delta c_j \leq 0, \qquad r_j = \frac{-\Delta c_j}{D_j}$$

If c_j is unchanged, $r_j = 0$. Thus, r_j measures the ratio of the actual change in c_j to the maximum allowable change in c_j that would keep the current basis optimal. If only one objective function coefficient were being changed, the current basis would remain optimal if $r_j \leq 1$ (or equivalently, if r_j, expressed as a percentage, were less than or equal to 100%). The 100% Rule for objective function coefficients is a generalization of this idea. It states that if $\sum r_j \leq 1$, we can be sure that the current basis remains optimal. If $\sum r_j > 1$, the current basis may or may not be optimal; we can't be sure. If the current basis does remain optimal, the values of the decision variables remain unchanged, but the optimal z-value may change. The reader is referred to Bradley, Hax, and Magnanti (1977) for a proof of the 100% Rule. We sketch the proof in Problem 11 at the end of this section.

The following two examples of Case 2 refer to the Dakota Furniture problem and illustrate the use of the 100% Rule.

E X A M P L E 4

Suppose the price of a desk increases to $70 and the price of a chair decreases to $18. Does the current basis remain optimal? What is the new optimal z-value?

Solution

Since both desks and chairs have zero reduced costs (because they are basic variables), we must apply the 100% Rule to determine whether the current basis remains optimal. Returning to the notation that $x_1 = $ desks, $x_2 = $ tables, and $x_3 = $ chairs, we may write

$$\Delta c_1 = 70 - 60 = 10, \qquad I_1 = 20, \qquad \text{so} \qquad r_1 = \tfrac{10}{20} = 0.5$$

$$\Delta c_3 = 18 - 20 = -2, \qquad D_3 = 5, \qquad \text{so} \qquad r_3 = \tfrac{2}{5} = 0.4$$

$$\Delta c_2 = 0, \qquad \text{so} \qquad r_2 = 0$$

Since $r_1 + r_2 + r_3 = 0.9 \leq 1$, the current basis remains optimal. Another way of looking at it: We changed c_1 50% of the amount it was "allowed" to change, and we changed c_3 40% of the amount it was "allowed" to change. Since 50% + 40% = 90% ≤ 100%, the current basis remains optimal.

Since the current basis remains optimal, the values of the decision variables do not change. Note that the revenue from each desk has increased by $10 and the revenue from each chair has decreased by $2. Dakota is still producing 2 desks and 8 chairs, so revenue increases by $2(10) - 8(2) = \$4$ and is now $280 + 4 = \$284$. ◆

E X A M P L E 5

Show that if the price of tables increases to $33 and the price of desks decreases to $58, the 100% Rule does not tell us whether or not the current basis is still optimal.

Solution

For this situation,

$$\Delta c_1 = 58 - 60 = -2, \qquad D_1 = 4, \qquad \text{so} \qquad r_1 = \tfrac{2}{4} = 0.5$$

$$\Delta c_2 = 33 - 30 = 3, \qquad I_2 = 5, \qquad \text{so} \qquad r_2 = \tfrac{3}{5} = 0.6$$

$$\Delta c_3 = 0, \qquad \text{so} \qquad r_3 = 0$$

Since $r_1 + r_2 + r_3 = 0.5 + 0.6 + 0 = 1.1 > 1$, the 100% Rule yields no information about whether or not the current basis is optimal. ◆

THE 100% RULE FOR CHANGING RIGHT-HAND SIDES

Depending on whether or not any of the constraints whose right-hand sides are being modified are binding constraints, there are two cases to consider:

Case 1 All constraints whose right-hand sides are being modified are nonbinding constraints.

Case 2 At least one of the constraints whose right-hand side is being modified is a binding constraint (that is, has zero slack or zero excess).

In Case 1, the current basis remains optimal if and only if each right-hand side remains within its allowable range.[†] Then the values of the decision variables and optimal objective function remain unchanged. If the right-hand side for any constraint is outside its allowable range, the current basis is no longer optimal (see Problem 12 at the end of this section). The following examples for the diet problem illustrate the application of Case 1.

E X A M P L E 6

Suppose the calorie requirement is decreased to 400 calories and the fat requirement is increased to 10 oz. Does the current basis remain optimal? What is the new optimal solution?

Solution

Since both the calorie and fat constraints are nonbinding, Case 1 applies. From Figure 6, we see that the allowable ranges for the calorie and fat constraints are

$$-\infty = 500 - \infty \leq \text{calorie requirement} \leq 500 + 250 = 750$$
$$-\infty = 8 - \infty \leq \text{fat requirement} \leq 8 + 5 = 13$$

The new calorie and fat requirements both remain within their allowable ranges, so the current basis remains optimal. The optimal z-value and the values of the decision variables remain unchanged. ◆

E X A M P L E 7

Suppose the calorie requirement is decreased to 400 calories and the fat requirement is increased to 15 oz. Is the current basis still optimal?

Solution

The fat requirement is no longer in its allowable range, so the current basis is no longer optimal. ◆

In Case 2, we can often show that the current basis remains optimal via another version of the 100% Rule. Let

b_j = current right-hand side of the jth constraint
(from row $j + 1$ on LINDO output)

Δb_j = change in b_j

[†]The allowable range for a right-hand side b_i is the range of values for b_i for which the current basis remains optimal (assuming the other LP parameters remain unchanged).

I_j = maximum allowable increase in b_j for which the current basis remains optimal (from LINDO output)

D_j = maximum allowable decrease in b_j for which the current basis remains optimal (from LINDO output)

For each constraint, compute the ratio r_j:

$$\text{If} \quad \Delta b_j \geq 0, \quad r_j = \frac{\Delta b_j}{I_j}$$

$$\text{If} \quad \Delta b_j \leq 0, \quad r_j = \frac{-\Delta b_j}{D_j}$$

If only the jth right-hand side is changed, the current basis remains optimal if $r_j \leq 1$. Also note that r_j is the fraction of the maximum allowable change (in the sense that the current basis remains optimal) in b_j that has occurred. The 100% Rule states that if $\sum r_j \leq 1$, the current basis remains optimal. If $\sum r_j > 1$, the current basis may or may not be optimal; we can't be sure (see Problem 13 at the end of this section for a sketch of the proof of this result). The following examples illustrate the use of the 100% Rule for right-hand sides.

E X A M P L E 8

In the Dakota problem, suppose 22 finishing hours and 9 carpentry hours are available. Does the current basis remain optimal?

Solution

Since the finishing and carpentry constraints are binding, we are in Case 2 and need to use the 100% Rule.

$$\Delta b_1 = 0, \quad \text{so} \quad r_1 = 0$$
$$\Delta b_2 = 22 - 20 = 2, \quad I_2 = 4, \quad \text{so} \quad r_2 = \tfrac{2}{4} = 0.5$$
$$\Delta b_3 = 9 - 8 = 1, \quad I_3 = 2, \quad \text{so} \quad r_3 = \tfrac{1}{2} = 0.5$$

Since $r_1 + r_2 + r_3 = 1$, the current basis remains optimal.

E X A M P L E 9

In the diet problem, suppose the chocolate requirement is increased to 8 oz and the sugar requirement is reduced to 7 oz. Does the current basis remain optimal?

Solution

Since the chocolate and sugar constraints are binding, we are in Case 2 and need to use the 100% Rule.

$$\Delta b_2 = 8 - 6 = 2, \quad I_2 = 4, \quad \text{so} \quad r_2 = \tfrac{2}{4} = 0.5$$
$$\Delta b_3 = 7 - 10 = -3, \quad D_3 = 4, \quad \text{so} \quad r_3 = \tfrac{3}{4} = 0.75$$
$$\Delta b_1 = \Delta b_4 = 0, \quad \text{so} \quad r_1 = r_4 = 0$$

Since $r_1 + r_2 + r_3 + r_4 = 1.25 > 1$, the 100% Rule yields no information about whether or not the current basis remains optimal.

◆ PROBLEMS

GROUP A

The following questions refer to the diet problem:

1. If the cost of a brownie is 70¢ and the cost of a piece of cheesecake is 60¢, does the current basis remain optimal?

2. If the cost of a brownie is 20¢ and the cost of a piece of cheesecake $1, does the current basis remain optimal?

3. If the fat requirement is reduced to 3 oz and the calorie requirement is increased to 800 calories, does the current basis remain optimal?

4. If the fat requirement is 6 oz and the calorie requirement is 600 calories, does the current basis remain optimal?

5. If the price of a bottle of soda is 15¢ and the price of a piece of cheesecake is 60¢, show that the current basis remains optimal. What will be the new optimal solution to the diet problem?

6. If 8 oz of chocolate and 60 calories are required, show that the current basis remains optimal.

The following questions refer to the Dakota problem.

7. Suppose that the price of a desk is $65, the price of a table is $25, and the price of a chair is $18. Show that the current basis remains optimal. What is the new optimal z-value?

8. Suppose that 60 board ft of lumber and 23 finishing hours are available. Show that the current basis remains optimal.

9. Suppose 40 board ft of lumber, 21 finishing hours, and 8.5 carpentry hours are available. Show that the current basis remains optimal.

GROUP B

10. Prove the Case 1 result for objective function coefficients.

11. To illustrate the validity of the 100% Rule for objective function coefficients, consider an LP with four decision variables ($x_1, x_2, x_3,$ and x_4) and two constraints in which x_1 and x_2 are basic variables in the optimal

basis. Suppose (if only a single objective function coefficient is changed) the current basis is known to be optimal for $L_1 \le c_1 \le U_1$ and $L_2 \le c_2 \le U_2$. Suppose we change c_1 to $c_1' = c_1 + \Delta c_1$ and change c_2 to $c_2' = c_2 + \Delta c_2$, where $\Delta c_1 > 0$ and $\Delta c_2 < 0$. Let

$$\frac{\Delta c_1}{U_1 - c_1} = r_1 \quad \text{and} \quad \frac{-\Delta c_2}{c_2 - L_2} = r_2$$

Show that if $r_1 + r_2 \le 1$, the current basis remains optimal. *Hint*: Any variable x_j prices out to $\mathbf{c}_{BV} B^{-1} \mathbf{a}_j - c_j$. To show that for the new values of c_1 and c_2, all variables still price out nonnegative, use the fact that

$$[c_1' c_2'] = r_1[U_1, c_2] + r_2[c_1, L_2] + (1 - r_1 - r_2)[c_1, c_2]$$

12. Prove the Case 1 result for right-hand sides. Use the fact that if a constraint is nonbinding in the optimal solution, its slack or excess variable is in the optimal basis, and the corresponding column of B^{-1} will have a single 1 and all other elements equal to zero.

13. In this problem, we sketch a proof of the 100% Rule for right-hand sides. Consider an LP with two constraints and right-hand sides b_1 and b_2. Suppose that if only one right-hand side is changed, the current basis remains optimal for $L_1 \le b_1 \le U_1$ and $L_2 \le b_2 \le U_2$. Suppose we change the right-hand sides to $b_1' = b_1 + \Delta b_1$ and $b_2' = b_2 + \Delta b_2$, where $\Delta b_1 > 0$ and $\Delta b_2 < 0$. Let

$$r_1 = \frac{\Delta b_1}{U_1 - b_1} \quad \text{and} \quad r_2 = \frac{-\Delta b_2}{b_2 - L_2}$$

Show that if $r_1 + r_2 \le 1$, the current basis remains optimal. (*Hint*: You must show that

$$B^{-1} \begin{bmatrix} b_1' \\ b_2' \end{bmatrix} \ge \begin{bmatrix} 0 \\ 0 \end{bmatrix}$$

Use the fact that

$$[b_1', b_2'] = r_1[U_1, b_2] + r_2[b_1, L_2]$$
$$+ (1 - r_1 - r_2)[b_1, b_2]$$

to show this.)

6-5 FINDING THE DUAL OF AN LP

Associated with any LP is another LP, called the **dual**. Knowing the relation between an LP and its dual is vital to understanding advanced topics in linear and nonlinear programming. This relation is important because it gives us interesting economic insights. Knowledge of duality will also provide additional insights into sensitivity analysis.

In this section, we explain how to find the dual of any LP; in Section 6.6, we discuss the economic interpretation of the dual; and in Sections 6.7–6.10, we discuss the relation that exists between an LP and its dual.

When taking the dual of a given LP, we refer to the given LP as the **primal**. If the primal is a max problem, the dual will be a min problem, and vice versa. This means that one of the LPs will be a min problem and the other will be a max problem. For convenience, we define the variables for the max problem to be z, x_1, x_2, . . . , x_n and the variables for the min problem to be w, y_1, y_2, . . . , y_m. We begin by explaining how to find the dual of a max problem in which all variables are required to be nonnegative and all constraints are $\leq$ constraints (called a **normal max problem**). A normal max problem may be written as

$$\max z = c_1 x_1 + c_2 x_2 + \cdots + c_n x_n$$
$$\text{s.t.} \quad a_{11} x_1 + a_{12} x_2 + \cdots + a_{1n} x_n \leq b_1$$
$$a_{21} x_1 + a_{22} x_2 + \cdots + a_{2n} x_n \leq b_2$$
$$\vdots \qquad \vdots \qquad \qquad \vdots$$
$$a_{m1} x_1 + a_{m2} x_2 + \cdots + a_{mn} x_n \leq b_m$$
$$x_j \geq 0 \quad (j = 1, 2, \ldots, n)$$

$$(16)$$

The dual of a normal max problem such as (16) is defined to be

$$\min w = b_1 y_1 + b_2 y_2 + \cdots + b_m y_m$$
$$\text{s.t.} \quad a_{11} y_1 + a_{21} y_2 + \cdots + a_{m1} y_m \geq c_1$$
$$a_{12} y_1 + a_{22} y_2 + \cdots + a_{m2} y_m \geq c_2$$
$$\vdots \qquad \vdots \qquad \qquad \vdots$$
$$a_{1n} y_1 + a_{2n} y_2 + \cdots + a_{mn} y_m \geq c_n$$
$$y_i \geq 0 \quad (i = 1, 2, \ldots, m)$$

$$(17)$$

A min problem like (17) that has all $\geq$ constraints and all variables nonnegative is called a **normal min problem**. If the primal is a normal min problem like (17), we define the dual of (17) to be (16).

FINDING THE DUAL OF A NORMAL MAX OR MIN PROBLEM

A tabular approach makes it easy to find the dual of an LP. If the primal is a normal max problem, it can be read across in Table 14; the dual is found by reading down in Table 14. Similarly, if the primal is a normal min problem, we find it by reading down in Table 14; the dual is found by reading across in the table. We illustrate the use of the table by finding the dual of the Dakota problem and the dual of the diet problem. The Dakota problem is

$$\max z = 60x_1 + 30x_2 + 20x_3$$
$$\text{s.t.} \quad 8x_1 + 6x_2 + x_3 \leq 48 \qquad \text{(Lumber constraint)}$$
$$4x_1 + 2x_2 + 1.5x_3 \leq 20 \qquad \text{(Finishing constraint)}$$
$$2x_1 + 1.5x_2 + 0.5x_3 \leq 8 \qquad \text{(Carpentry constraint)}$$
$$x_1, x_2, x_3 \geq 0$$

Table 14
Finding the Dual of
a Normal Max or
Min Problem

			max z				
min w		$(x_1 \geq 0)$	$(x_2 \geq 0)$	$\cdots$	$(x_n \geq 0)$		
		x_1	x_2		x_n		
$(y_1 \geq 0)$	y_1	a_{11}	a_{12}	$\cdots$	a_{1n}	$\leq b_1$	
$(y_2 \geq 0)$	y_2	a_{21}	a_{22}	$\cdots$	a_{2n}	$\leq b_2$	
$\vdots$	$\vdots$	$\vdots$	$\vdots$		$\vdots$	$\vdots$	
$(y_m \geq 0)$	y_m	a_{m1}	a_{m2}	$\cdots$	a_{mn}	$\leq b_m$	
		$\geq c_1$	$\geq c_2$		$\geq c_n$		

where

$$x_1 = \text{number of desks manufactured}$$
$$x_2 = \text{number of tables manufactured}$$
$$x_3 = \text{number of chairs manufactured}$$

Using the format of Table 14, we read the Dakota problem across in Table 15. Then, reading down in Table 15, we find the Dakota dual to be

$$\min w = 48y_1 + 20y_2 + 8y_3$$
$$\text{s.t.} \quad 8y_1 + 4y_2 + 2y_3 \geq 60$$
$$6y_1 + 2y_2 + 1.5y_3 \geq 30$$
$$y_1 + 1.5y_2 + 0.5y_3 \geq 20$$
$$y_1, y_2, y_3 \geq 0$$

Table 15
Finding the Dual of
the Dakota Problem

			max z		
min w		$(x_1 \geq 0)$	$(x_2 \geq 0)$	$(x_3 \geq 0)$	
		x_1	x_2	x_3	
$(y_1 \geq 0)$	y_1	8	6	1	≤ 48
$(y_2 \geq 0)$	y_2	4	2	1.5	≤ 20
$(y_3 \geq 0)$	y_3	2	1.5	0.5	≤ 8
		≥ 60	≥ 30	≥ 20	

The tabular method of finding the dual makes it clear that the ith dual constraint corresponds to the ith primal variable x_i. For example, the first dual constraint corresponds to x_1 (desks), because each number in the first dual constraint comes from the x_1 (desk) column of the primal. Similarly, the second dual constraint corresponds to x_2 (tables), and the third dual constraint corresponds to x_3 (chairs). In a similar fashion, dual variable y_i is associated with the ith primal constraint. For example, y_1 is associated with the first primal constraint (lumber constraint), because each coefficient of y_1 in the dual comes from the lumber constraint, or the availability of lumber. The importance of these correspondences between the primal and the dual will become clear in Section 6.6.

We now find the dual of the diet problem. Since the diet problem is a min problem, we follow the convention of using w to denote the objective function and y_1, y_2, y_3, and

y_4 for the variables. Then the diet problem may be written as

$$\min w = 50y_1 + 20y_2 + 30y_3 + 80y_4$$

$$\text{s.t.}\quad 400y_1 + 200y_2 + 150y_3 + 500y_4 \geq 500 \quad \text{(Calorie constraint)}$$
$$3y_1 + 2y_2 \qquad\qquad\qquad \geq 6 \quad \text{(Chocolate constraint)}$$
$$2y_1 + 2y_2 + 4y_3 + 4y_4 \geq 10 \quad \text{(Sugar constraint)}$$
$$2y_1 + 4y_2 + y_3 + 5y_4 \geq 8 \quad \text{(Fat constraint)}$$
$$y_1, y_2, y_3, y_4 \geq 0$$

where

y_1 = number of brownies eaten daily

y_2 = number of scoops of chocolate ice cream eaten daily

y_3 = bottles of soda drunk daily

y_4 = pieces of pineapple cheesecake eaten daily

Since the primal is a normal min problem, we can read it down, and read its dual across, in Table 16. We find that the dual of the diet problem is

$$\max z = 500x_1 + 6x_2 + 10x_3 + 8x_4$$

$$\text{s.t.}\quad 400x_1 + 3x_2 + 2x_3 + 2x_4 \leq 50$$
$$200x_1 + 2x_2 + 2x_3 + 4x_4 \leq 20$$
$$150x_1 \qquad\quad + 4x_3 + x_4 \leq 30$$
$$500x_1 \qquad\quad + 4x_3 + 5x_4 \leq 80$$
$$x_1, x_2, x_3, x_4 \geq 0$$

Table 16
Finding the Dual of the Diet Problem

min w		$(x_1 \geq 0)$ x_1	$(x_2 \geq 0)$ x_2	$(x_3 \geq 0)$ x_3	$(x_4 \geq 0)$ x_4	
$(y_1 \geq 0)$	y_1	400	3	2	2	≤ 50
$(y_2 \geq 0)$	y_2	200	2	2	4	≤ 20
$(y_3 \geq 0)$	y_3	150	0	4	1	≤ 30
$(y_4 \geq 0)$	y_4	500	0	4	5	≤ 80
		≥ 500	≥ 6	≥ 10	≥ 8	

(max z spans the x columns)

As in the Dakota problem, we see that the ith dual constraint corresponds to the ith primal variable. For example, the third dual constraint may be thought of as the soda constraint. Also, the ith dual variable corresponds to the ith primal constraint. For example, x_3 (the third dual variable) may be thought of as the dual sugar variable.

FINDING THE DUAL OF A NONNORMAL LP

Unfortunately, many LPs are not normal max problems or normal min problems. For example,

$$
\begin{aligned}
\max z = 2x_1 + x_2 \\
\text{s.t.} \quad x_1 + x_2 = 2 \\
2x_1 - x_2 \geq 3 \\
x_1 - x_2 \leq 1 \\
x_1 \geq 0, \; x_2 \text{ urs}
\end{aligned}
\tag{18}
$$

[handwritten notes: min w = 2y₁ +3y₂ + 1y₃ ; s.t. 1y₁ + 2y₃ -1y₃ ≥ 2 ; y₁ - y₂ - y₃ = 1 ; y₁ uri ; y₂ ≤ 0 ; y₃ ≥ 0]

is not a normal max problem, because it has a $\geq$ constraint, an equality constraint, and an unrestricted-in-sign variable. As another example of a nonnormal LP, consider

$$
\begin{aligned}
\min w = 2y_1 + 4y_2 + 6y_3 \\
\text{s.t.} \quad y_1 + 2y_2 + y_3 \geq 2 \\
y_1 \quad\quad - y_3 \geq 1 \\
y_2 + y_3 = 1 \\
2y_1 + \; y_2 \quad\quad \leq 3 \\
y_1 \text{ urs}, \; y_2, y_3 \geq 0
\end{aligned}
\tag{19}
$$

This LP is not a normal min problem, because it contains an equality constraint, a $\leq$ constraint, and an unrestricted-in-sign variable.

Fortunately, an LP can be transformed into normal form (either (16) or (17)). To place a max problem into normal form, we proceed as follows:

Step 1 Multiply each $\geq$ constraint by -1. This converts each $\geq$ constraint into a $\leq$ constraint. For example, in (18), $2x_1 - x_2 \geq 3$ would be transformed into $-2x_1 + x_2 \leq -3$.

Step 2 Replace each equality constraint by two inequality constraints (a $\leq$ constraint and a $\geq$ constraint). Then convert the $\geq$ constraint to a $\leq$ constraint. For example, in (18), we would replace $x_1 + x_2 = 2$ by the two inequalities $x_1 + x_2 \geq 2$ and $x_1 + x_2 \leq 2$. Then we would convert $x_1 + x_2 \geq 2$ to $-x_1 - x_2 \leq -2$. The net result is that $x_1 + x_2 = 2$ is replaced by the two inequalities $x_1 + x_2 \leq 2$ and $-x_1 - x_2 \leq -2$.

Step 3 As in Section 4.12, replace each urs variable x_i by $x_i = x_i' - x_i''$, where $x_i' \geq 0$ and $x_i'' \geq 0$. In (18), we would replace x_2 by $x_2' - x_2''$.

After these transformations are complete, (18) has been transformed into the following (equivalent) LP:

$$
\begin{aligned}
\max z = 2x_1 + x_2' - x_2'' \\
\text{s.t.} \quad x_1 + x_2' - x_2'' \leq 2 \\
-x_1 - x_2' + x_2'' \leq -2 \\
-2x_1 + x_2' - x_2'' \leq -3 \\
x_1 - x_2' + x_2'' \leq 1 \\
x_1, x_2', x_2'' \geq 0
\end{aligned}
\tag{18'}
$$

Since (18′) is a normal max problem, we could use (16) and (17) to find the dual of (18′).

If the primal is not a normal min problem, we can transform it into a normal min problem as follows:

Step 1 Change each $\leq$ constraint to a $\geq$ constraint by multiplying each $\leq$ constraint by -1. For example, in (19), $2y_1 + y_2 \leq 3$ is transformed into $-2y_1 - y_2 \geq -3$.

Step 2 Replace each equality constraint by a $\leq$ constraint and a $\geq$ constraint. Then transform the $\leq$ constraint into a $\geq$ constraint. For example, in (19), the constraint $y_2 + y_3 = 1$ is equivalent to $y_2 + y_3 \leq 1$ and $y_2 + y_3 \geq 1$. Transforming $y_2 + y_3 \leq 1$ into $-y_2 - y_3 \geq -1$, we see that we can replace the constraint $y_2 + y_3 = 1$ by the two constraints $y_2 + y_3 \geq 1$ and $-y_2 - y_3 \geq -1$.

Step 3 Replace any urs variable y_i by $y_i = y_i' - y_i''$, where $y_i' \geq 0$ and $y_i'' \geq 0$. Applying these steps to (19) yields the following standard min problem:

$$
\begin{aligned}
\min w = {}& 2y_1' - 2y_1'' + 4y_2 + 6y_3 \\
\text{s.t.} \quad & y_1' - y_1'' + 2y_2 + y_3 \geq 2 \\
& y_1' - y_1'' \quad\quad\;\; - y_3 \geq 1 \\
& \quad\quad\quad\quad\; y_2 + y_3 \geq 1 \\
& \quad\quad\quad\;\; - y_2 - y_3 \geq -1 \\
& -2y_1' + 2y_1'' - y_2 \quad\quad \geq -3 \\
& y_1', y_1'', y_2, y_3 \geq 0
\end{aligned}
\tag{19′}
$$

Since (19′) is a normal min problem in standard form, we may use (16) and (17) to find its dual.

It turns out that we can find the dual of a nonnormal LP without going through the transformations that we have described. All we have to do is use the following rules.[†]

FINDING THE DUAL OF A NONNORMAL MAX PROBLEM.

Step 1 Fill in Table 14 so that the primal can be read across.

Step 2 After making the following changes, the dual can be read down in the usual fashion: (a) If the ith primal constraint is a $\geq$ constraint, the corresponding dual variable y_i must satisfy $y_i \leq 0$. (b) If the ith primal constraint is an equality constraint, the dual variable y_i is now unrestricted in sign. (c) If the ith primal variable is urs, the ith dual constraint will be an equality constraint.

When this method is applied to (18), the Table 14 format yields Table 17. We note with an asterisk (*) the places where the rules must be used to determine part of the dual. For example, x_2 urs causes the second dual constraint to be an equality constraint. Also, the first primal constraint being an equality constraint makes y_1 urs, and the second primal constraint being a $\geq$ constraint makes $y_2 \leq 0$. Filling in the missing information across

---

[†] In Problems 5 and 6 at the end of this section, we show that these rules are consistent with taking the dual of the transformed LP via (16) and (17).

Table 17
Finding the Dual of LP (18)

min w		max z		
		$(x_1 \geq 0)$	$(x_2 \text{ urs})$*	
		x_1	x_2	
	y_1	1	1	$= 2$*
	y_2	2	-1	≥ 3*
$(y_3 \geq 0)$	y_3	1	-1	≤ 1
		≥ 2	1	

from the appropriate asterisk yields Table 18. Reading the dual down, we obtain

$$\begin{aligned} \min w &= 2y_1 + 3y_2 + y_3 \\ \text{s.t.} \quad y_1 + 2y_2 + y_3 &\geq 2 \\ y_1 - y_2 - y_3 &= 1 \\ y_1 \text{ urs}, \ y_2 \leq 0, \ y_3 &\geq 0 \end{aligned}$$

In Section 6.8, we give an intuitive explanation of why an equality constraint yields an unrestricted-in-sign dual variable and why a $\geq$ constraint yields a negative dual variable.

We can use the following rules to take the dual of a nonnormal min problem.

Table 18
Finding the Dual of LP (18) (Continued)

min w		max z		
		$(x_1 \geq 0)$	$(x_2 \text{ urs})$	
		x_1	x_2	
$(y_1 \text{ urs})$	y_1	1	1	$= 2$
$(y_2 \leq 0)$	y_2	2	-1	≥ 3
$(y_3 \geq 0)$	y_3	1	-1	≤ 1
		≥ 2	$= 1$	

FINDING THE DUAL OF A NONNORMAL MIN PROBLEM.

Step 1 Write out the primal so it can be read down in Table 14.

Step 2 Except for the following changes, the dual can be read across the table: (a) If the ith primal constraint is a $\leq$ constraint, the corresponding dual variable x_i must satisfy $x_i \leq 0$. (b) If the ith primal constraint is an equality constraint, the corresponding dual variable x_i will be urs. (c) If the ith primal variable y_i is urs, the ith dual constraint is an equality constraint.

When this method is applied to (19), we get Table 19. Asterisks (*) show where the new rules must be used to determine parts of the dual. Since y_1 is urs, the first dual constraint is an equality constraint. Since the third primal constraint is an equality constraint, the dual variable x_3 is urs. Finally, since the fourth primal constraint is a $\leq$ constraint, the fourth dual variable x_4 must satisfy $x_4 \leq 0$. We can now complete the table (see

Table 19
Finding the Dual of LP (19)

min w		max z				
		$(x_1 \geq 0)$	$(x_2 \geq 0)$			
		x_1	x_2	x_3	x_4	
$(y_1$ urs$)^*$	y_1	1	1	0	2	2
$(y_2 \geq 0)$	y_2	2	0	1	1	≤ 4
$(y_3 \geq 0)$	y_3	1	-1	1	0	≤ 6
		≥ 2	≥ 1	$= 1^*$	$\leq 3^*$	

Table 20). Reading the dual across, we obtain

$$\max z = 2x_1 + x_2 + x_3 + 3x_4$$
$$\text{s.t.} \quad x_1 + x_2 \qquad\quad + 2x_4 = 2$$
$$2x_1 \qquad + x_3 + x_4 \leq 4$$
$$x_1 - x_2 + x_3 \qquad\quad \leq 6$$
$$x_1, x_2 \geq 0, x_3 \text{ urs}, x_4 \leq 0$$

The reader may verify that with these rules, the dual of the dual is always the primal. This is easily seen from the Table 14 format, because when you take the dual of the dual you are changing the LP back to its original position.

Table 20
Finding the Dual of LP (19) (Continued)

min w		max z				
		$(x_1 \geq 0)$	$(x_2 \geq 0)$	$(x_3$ urs$)$	$(x_4 \leq 0)$	
		x_1	x_2	x_3	x_4	
$(y_1$ urs$)$	y_1	1	1	0	2	$= 2$
$(y_2 \geq 0)$	y_2	2	0	1	1	≤ 4
$(y_3 \geq 0)$	y_3	1	-1	1	0	≤ 6
		≥ 2	≥ 1	$= 1$	≤ 3	

◆ PROBLEMS

GROUP A

Find the duals of the following LPs:

1. $\max z = 2x_1 + x_2$

$$\text{s.t.} \quad -x_1 + x_2 \leq 1$$
$$x_1 + x_2 \leq 3$$
$$x_1 - 2x_2 \leq 4$$
$$x_1, x_2 \geq 0$$

2. $\min w = y_1 - y_2$

$$\text{s.t.} \quad 2y_1 + y_2 \geq 4$$
$$y_1 + y_2 \geq 1$$
$$y_1 + 2y_2 \geq 3$$
$$y_1, y_2 \geq 0$$

3. $\max z = 4x_1 - x_2 + 2x_3$ *min* $5y_1 + 7y_2 + 6y_3$

s.t. $x_1 + x_2 \quad \le 5$ *s.t.* $y_1 + 2y_2 + y_4 \ge 4$

$\quad 2x_1 + x_2 \quad \le 7$

$\qquad 2x_2 + x_3 \ge 6$ $y_1 + y_2 + 2y_3 = -1$

$\quad x_1 \qquad + x_3 = 4$

$\qquad \quad \frac{y_3 + y_4}{} = 2$

$x_1 \ge 0, x_2, x_3$ urs

$y_1 > 0$

4. $\min w = 4y_1 + 2y_2 - y_3$ $y_1 > 0$

s.t. $y_1 + 2y_2 \quad \le 6$ $y_2 > 0$

$\quad y_1 - y_2 + 2y_3 = 8$ $y_3 < 0$

$\quad y_1, y_2 \ge 0, y_3$ urs y_4 *urs*

GROUP B

5. This problem shows why the dual variable for an equality constraint should be urs.

(a) Use the rules given in the text to find the dual of

$$\max z = x_1 + 2x_2$$

s.t. $3x_1 + x_2 \le 6$

$\quad 2x_1 + x_2 = 5$

$\quad x_1, x_2 \ge 0$

(b) Now transform the LP in part (a) to the normal form. Using (16) and (17), take the dual of the transformed LP. Use y_2' and y_2'' as the dual variables for the two primal constraints derived from $2x_1 + x_2 = 5$.

(c) Make the substitution $y_2 = y_2' - y_2''$ in the part (b) answer. Now show that the two duals obtained in parts (a) and (b) are equivalent.

6. This problem shows why a dual variable y_i corresponding to a $\ge$ constraint in a max problem must satisfy $y_i \le 0$.

(a) Using the rules given in the text, find the dual of

$$\max z = 3x_1 + x_2$$

s.t. $x_1 + x_2 \le 1$

$\quad -x_1 + x_2 \ge 2$

$\quad x_1, x_2 \ge 0$

(b) Transform the LP of part (a) into a normal max problem. Now use (16) and (17) to find the dual of the transformed LP. Let $\bar{y}_2$ be the dual variable corresponding to the second primal constraint.

(c) Show that, defining $\bar{y}_2 = -y_2$, the dual in part (a) is equivalent to the dual in part (b).

6-6   ECONOMIC INTERPRETATION OF THE DUAL PROBLEM

INTERPRETING THE DUAL OF A MAX PROBLEM

The dual of the Dakota problem was

$$\min w = 48y_1 + 20y_2 + 8y_3$$

s.t. $8y_1 + 4y_2 + 2y_3 \ge 60$ (Desk constraint)

$\quad 6y_1 + 2y_2 + 1.5y_3 \ge 30$ (Table constraint)   (20)

$\quad y_1 + 1.5x_2 + 0.5y_3 \ge 20$ (Chair constraint)

$\quad y_1, y_2, y_3 \ge 0$

The first dual constraint is associated with desks, the second dual constraint with tables, and the third dual constraint with chairs. Also, y_1 is associated with lumber, y_2 with finishing hours, and y_3 with carpentry hours. The relevant information about the Dakota problem is shown in Table 21.

We are now ready to interpret the Dakota dual (20). Suppose an entrepreneur wants to purchase all of Dakota's resources. Then the entrepreneur must determine the price he or she is willing to pay for a unit of each of Dakota's resources. With this in mind,

	RESOURCE/PRODUCT			AMOUNT OF RESOURCE AVAILABLE
Resource	*Desk*	*Table*	*Chair*	
Lumber	8 board ft	6 board ft	1 board ft	48 board ft
Finishing	4 hours	2 hours	1.5 hours	20 hours
Carpentry	2 hours	1.5 hours	0.5 hour	8 hours
Selling price	$60	$30	$20	

Table 21
Relevant Information
for Dakota Problem

we define

$$y_1 = \text{price paid for 1 board ft of lumber}$$
$$y_2 = \text{price paid for 1 finishing hour}$$
$$y_3 = \text{price paid for 1 carpentry hour}$$

We now show that the resource prices y_1, y_2, and y_3 should be determined by solving the Dakota dual (20). The total price that should be paid for these resources is $48y_1 + 20y_2 + 8y_3$. Since the cost of purchasing the resources is to be minimized,

$$\min w = 48y_1 + 20y_2 + 8y_3$$

This is the objective function for the Dakota dual.

In setting resource prices, what constraints does the entrepreneur face? Resource prices must be set high enough to induce Dakota to sell its resources. For example, the entrepreneur must offer Dakota at least $60 for a combination of resources that includes 8 board ft of lumber, 4 finishing hours, and 2 carpentry hours, because Dakota could, if it desires, use these resources to produce a desk that can be sold for $60. Thus, the prospective buyer must pay at least $60 for the combination of resources required to produce a desk, or else Dakota would have no reason to sell these resources. Since the entrepreneur is offering $8y_1 + 4y_2 + 2y_3$ for the resources used to produce a desk, he or she must choose y_1, y_2, and y_3 to satisfy

$$8y_1 + 4y_2 + 2y_3 \geq 60$$

But this is just the first (or desk) constraint of the Dakota dual. Similar reasoning shows that at least $30 must be paid for the resources used to produce a table (6 board ft of lumber, 2 finishing hours, and 1.5 carpentry hours). This means that y_1, y_2 and y_3 must satisfy

$$6y_1 + 2y_2 + 1.5y_3 \geq 30$$

This is the second (or table) constraint of the Dakota dual.

Similarly, the third (or chair) dual constraint,

$$y_1 + 1.5y_2 + 0.5y_3 \geq 20$$

states that at least $20 (the price of a chair) must be paid for the resources needed to produce a chair (1 board ft of lumber, 1.5 finishing hours, and 0.5 carpentry hour). The sign restrictions $y_1 \geq 0$, $y_2 \geq 0$, and $y_3 \geq 0$ must also hold. Putting everything together, we see that the solution to the dual of the Dakota problem does yield prices for lumber, finishing hours, and carpentry hours. The preceding discussion also shows that the ith dual variable does indeed correspond in a natural way to the ith primal constraint.

In summary, when the primal is a normal max problem, the dual variables are related to the value of the resources available to the decision maker. For this reason, the dual variables are often referred to as **resource shadow prices**. A more thorough discussion of shadow prices is given in Section 6.8.

INTERPRETING THE DUAL OF A MIN PROBLEM

To interpret the dual of a min problem, we consider the dual of the diet problem of Section 3.4. In Section 6.5, we found that the diet problem dual was

$$\max z = 500x_1 + 6x_2 + 10x_3 + 8x_4$$

$$\begin{aligned}
\text{s.t.} \quad 400x_1 + 3x_2 + 2x_3 + 2x_4 &\leq 50 \quad &\text{(Brownie constraint)} \\
200x_1 + 2x_2 + 2x_3 + 4x_4 &\leq 20 \quad &\text{(Ice cream constraint)} \\
150x_1 \quad\quad + 4x_3 + \ x_4 &\leq 30 \quad &\text{(Soda constraint)} \\
500x_1 \quad\quad + 4x_3 + 5x_4 &\leq 80 \quad &\text{(Cheesecake constraint)}
\end{aligned}$$
$$x_1, x_2, x_3, x_4 \geq 0$$

(21)

The data for the diet problem are shown in Table 22. To interpret (21), suppose Candice is a "nutrient" salesperson who sells calories, chocolate, sugar, and fat. Candice wishes to ensure that a dieter will meet all of his or her daily requirements by purchasing calories, sugar, fat, and chocolate from Candice. Then Candice must determine

x_1 = price per calorie to charge dieter

x_2 = price per ounce of chocolate to charge dieter

x_3 = price per ounce of sugar to charge dieter

x_4 = price per ounce of fat to charge dieter

Table 22 Relevant Information for Diet Problem	CALORIES	CHOCOLATE (Ounces)	SUGAR (Ounces)	FAT (Ounces)	PRICE (Cents)
Brownie	400	3	2	2	50
Ice cream	200	2	2	4	20
Soda	150	0	4	1	30
Cheesecake	500	0	4	5	80
Requirements	500	6	10	8	

Candice wants to maximize her revenue from selling the dieter the daily ration of required nutrients. Since Candice will receive $500x_1 + 6x_2 + 10x_3 + 8x_4$ cents in revenue from the dieter, Candice's objective is to

$$\max z = 500x_1 + 6x_2 + 10x_3 + 8x_4$$

This is the objective function for the dual of the diet problem. But in setting nutrient prices, Candice must set prices low enough so that it will be in the dieter's economic interest to purchase all nutrients from her. For example, by purchasing a brownie for 50¢, the dieter can obtain 400 calories, 3 oz of chocolate, 2 oz of sugar, and 2 oz of fat. So Candice cannot charge more than 50¢ for this combination of nutrients. This leads to the following constraint (brownie constraint):

$$400x_1 + 3x_2 + 2x_3 + 2x_4 \leq 50$$

which is the first constraint in the diet problem dual. Similar reasoning yields the second dual constraint (ice cream constraint), the third dual constraint (soda constraint), and the fourth dual constraint (cheesecake constraint). Again, the sign restrictions $x_1 \geq 0$, $x_2 \geq 0$, $x_3 \geq 0$, and $x_4 \geq 0$ must be satisfied.

Our discussion shows that the optimal values of x_i may be interpreted as a price for 1 unit of the nutrient associated with the ith dual constraint. Thus, x_1 would be the price for 1 calorie, x_2 would be a price for 1 oz of chocolate, and so on. Again, we see that it is reasonable to associate the ith dual variable (x_i) and the ith primal constraint.

In summary, we have shown that when the primal is a normal max problem or a normal min problem, the dual problem has an intuitive economic interpretation. In Section 6.8, we explain more about the proper interpretation of the dual variables.

◆ PROBLEMS

GROUP A

1. Find the dual of Example 3 in Chapter 3 (an auto company) and give an economic interpretation for the dual problem.

2. Find the dual of Example 2 in Chapter 3 (Dorian Auto) and give an economic interpretation for the dual problem.

6-7   THE DUAL THEOREM AND ITS CONSEQUENCES

In this section, we discuss one of the most important results in linear programming: the Dual Theorem. In essence, the Dual Theorem states that the primal and dual have equal optimal objective function values (if the problems have optimal solutions). This result is interesting in its own right, but we will see that in proving the Dual Theorem, we gain many important insights into linear programming.

To simplify the exposition, we assume that the primal is a normal max problem with m constraints and n variables. Then the dual problem will be a normal min problem with m variables and n constraints. In this case, the primal and the dual may be written as follows:

$$\max z = c_1 x_1 + c_2 x_2 + \cdots + c_n x_n$$

$$\text{s.t.} \quad a_{11} x_1 + a_{12} x_2 + \cdots + a_{1n} x_n \leq b_1$$

$$a_{21} x_1 + a_{22} x_2 + \cdots + a_{2n} x_n \leq b_2$$

$$\vdots \qquad \vdots \qquad \qquad \vdots \quad \vdots$$

Primal Problem
$$a_{i1} x_1 + a_{i2} x_2 + \cdots + a_{in} x_n \leq b_i \qquad (22)$$

$$\vdots \qquad \vdots \qquad \qquad \vdots \quad \vdots$$

$$a_{m1} x_1 + a_{m2} x_2 + \cdots + a_{mn} x_n \leq b_m$$

$$x_j \geq 0 \quad (j = 1, 2, \ldots, n)$$

$$\min w = b_1 y_1 + b_2 y_2 + \cdots + b_m y_m$$

$$\text{s.t.} \quad a_{11} y_1 + a_{21} y_2 + \cdots + a_{m1} y_m \geq c_1$$

$$a_{12} y_1 + a_{22} y_2 + \cdots + a_{m2} y_m \geq c_2$$

$$\vdots \qquad \vdots \qquad \qquad \vdots \qquad \vdots$$

Dual Problem $\qquad a_{1j} y_1 + a_{2j} y_2 + \cdots + a_{mj} y_m \geq c_j$ $\qquad$ (23)

$$\vdots \qquad \vdots \qquad \qquad \vdots \qquad \vdots$$

$$a_{1n} y_1 + a_{2n} y_2 + \cdots + a_{mn} y_m \geq c_n$$

$$y_i \geq 0 \quad (i = 1, 2, \ldots, m)$$

WEAK DUALITY

If we choose any feasible solution to the primal and any feasible solution to the dual, the w-value for the feasible dual solution will be at least as large as the z-value for the feasible primal solution. This result is formally stated in Lemma 1.

LEMMA 1 (Weak Duality). Let

$$\mathbf{x} = \begin{bmatrix} x_1 \\ x_2 \\ \vdots \\ x_n \end{bmatrix}$$

be any feasible solution to the primal and $\mathbf{y} = [y_1 \quad y_2 \quad \cdots \quad y_m]$ be any feasible solution to the dual. Then (z-value for $\mathbf{x}$) $\leq$ (w-value for $\mathbf{y}$).

Proof Since $y_i \geq 0$, multiplying the ith primal constraint in (22) by y_i will yield the following valid inequality:

$$y_i a_{i1} x_1 + y_i a_{i2} x_2 + \cdots + y_i a_{in} x_n \leq b_i y_i \quad (i = 1, 2, \ldots, m) \qquad (24)$$

Adding up the m inequalities in (24), we find that

$$\sum_{i=1}^{i=m} \sum_{j=1}^{j=n} y_i a_{ij} x_j \leq \sum_{i=1}^{i=m} b_i y_i \qquad (25)$$

Since $x_j \geq 0$, multiplying the jth dual constraint in (23) by x_j yields the following valid inequality:

$$x_j a_{1j} y_1 + x_j a_{2j} y_2 + \cdots + x_j a_{mj} y_m \geq c_j x_j \quad (j = 1, 2, \ldots, n) \qquad (26)$$

Adding up the n inequalities in (26) yields

$$\sum_{i=1}^{i=m} \sum_{j=1}^{j=n} y_i a_{ij} x_j \geq \sum_{j=1}^{j=n} c_j x_j \qquad (27)$$

Combining (25) and (27), we obtain

$$\sum_{j=1}^{j=n} c_j x_j \leq \sum_{i=1}^{i=m} \sum_{j=1}^{j=n} y_i a_{ij} x_j \leq \sum_{i=1}^{i=m} b_i y_i$$

which is the desired result.

If a feasible solution to either the primal or the dual is readily available, weak duality can be used to obtain a bound on the optimal objective function value for the other problem. For example, in looking at the Dakota problem, it is easy to see that $x_1 = x_2 = x_3 = 1$ is primal feasible. This solution has a z-value of $60 + 30 + 20 = 110$. Weak duality now implies that any dual feasible solution (y_1, y_2, y_3) must satisfy

$$48y_1 + 20y_2 + 8y_3 \geq 110$$

Since the dual is a min problem, and any dual feasible solution must have $w \geq 110$, this means that the optimal w-value for the dual ≥ 110 (see Figure 7). This shows that weak duality enables us to use any primal feasible solution to bound the optimal value of the dual objective function.

Figure 7
Illustration of Weak Duality

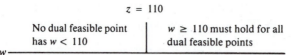

Analogously, we can use any feasible solution to the dual to develop a bound on the optimal value of the primal objective function. For example, looking at the Dakota dual, it can readily be verified that $y_1 = 10$, $y_2 = 10$, $y_3 = 0$ is dual feasible. This dual solution has a dual objective function value of $48(10) + 20(10) + 8(0) = 680$. From weak duality, we see that any primal feasible solution

$$\begin{bmatrix} x_1 \\ x_2 \\ x_3 \end{bmatrix}$$

must satisfy

$$60x_1 + 30x_2 + 20x_3 \leq 680$$

Since the primal is a max problem and every primal feasible solution has $z \leq 680$, we may conclude that the optimal primal objective function value ≤ 680 (see Figure 8).

Figure 8
Illustration of Weak Duality

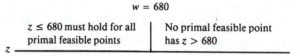

If we define

$$\mathbf{b} = \begin{bmatrix} b_1 \\ b_2 \\ \vdots \\ b_m \end{bmatrix} \quad \text{and} \quad \mathbf{c} = [c_1 \quad c_2 \quad \cdots \quad c_n]$$

then for a point

$$\mathbf{x} = \begin{bmatrix} x_1 \\ x_2 \\ \vdots \\ x_n \end{bmatrix}$$

the primal objective function value may be written as $\mathbf{cx}$, and for a point $\mathbf{y} = [y_1 \quad y_2 \quad \cdots \quad y_m]$ the dual objective function value may be written as $\mathbf{yb}$. We now use weak duality to prove the following important result.

LEMMA 2 Let

$$\mathbf{x} = \begin{bmatrix} \bar{x}_1 \\ \bar{x}_2 \\ \vdots \\ \bar{x}_n \end{bmatrix}$$

be a feasible solution to the primal and $\bar{\mathbf{y}} = [\bar{y}_1 \quad \bar{y}_2 \quad \cdots \quad \bar{y}_m]$ be a feasible solution to the dual. If $\mathbf{c\bar{x}} = \bar{\mathbf{y}}\mathbf{b}$, then $\bar{\mathbf{x}}$ is optimal for the primal and $\bar{\mathbf{y}}$ is optimal for the dual.

Proof From weak duality we know that for any primal feasible point $\mathbf{x}$,

$$\mathbf{cx} \leq \bar{\mathbf{y}}\mathbf{b}$$

Thus, any primal feasible point must yield a z-value that does not exceed $\bar{\mathbf{y}}\mathbf{b}$. Since $\bar{\mathbf{x}}$ is primal feasible and has a primal objective function value of $\mathbf{c\bar{x}} = \bar{\mathbf{y}}\mathbf{b}$, $\bar{\mathbf{x}}$ must be primal optimal. Similarly, since $\bar{\mathbf{x}}$ is primal feasible, weak duality implies that for any dual feasible point $\mathbf{y}$,

$$\mathbf{c\bar{x}} \leq \mathbf{yb}$$

Thus, any dual feasible point must yield an objective function value exceeding $\mathbf{c\bar{x}}$. Since $\bar{\mathbf{y}}$ is dual feasible and has a dual objective function value $\bar{\mathbf{y}}\mathbf{b} = \mathbf{c\bar{x}}$, $\bar{\mathbf{y}}$ must be an optimal solution for the dual. ◆

We use the Dakota problem to illustrate the use of Lemma 2. The reader may verify that

$$\bar{\mathbf{x}} = \begin{bmatrix} 2 \\ 0 \\ 8 \end{bmatrix}$$

is primal feasible and that $\bar{\mathbf{y}} = [0 \quad 10 \quad 10]$ is dual feasible. Since $\mathbf{c\bar{x}} = \bar{\mathbf{y}}\mathbf{b} = 280$, Lemma 2 implies that $\bar{\mathbf{x}}$ is optimal for the Dakota primal, and $\bar{\mathbf{y}}$ is optimal for the Dakota dual. Lemma 2 plays an important role in our proof of the Dual Theorem.

THE DUAL THEOREM

Before proceeding with our proof of the Dual Theorem, we note that weak duality can be used to prove the following results.

L E M M A   If the primal is unbounded, the dual problem is infeasible.
3

Proof   See Problem 7 at the end of this section.

◆

L E M M A   If the dual is unbounded, the primal is infeasible.
4

Proof   See Problem 8 at the end of this section.

◆

Lemmas 3 and 4 describe the relation between the primal and dual in two relatively unimportant cases.[†]

These cases are of limited interest. We are primarily interested in the relation between the primal and dual when the primal has an optimal solution. In what follows, we let $\bar{z}$ = optimal primal objective function value and $\bar{w}$ = optimal dual objective function value. If the primal has an optimal solution, the following important result (the Dual Theorem) describes the relation between the primal and the dual.

THEOREM 1   **THE DUAL THEOREM.** Suppose BV is an optimal basis for the primal. Then $\mathbf{c}_{BV}B^{-1}$ is an optimal solution to the dual. Also, $\bar{z} = \bar{w}$.

Proof   The argument used to prove the Dual Theorem includes the following steps:

1. Use the fact that BV is an optimal basis for the primal to show that $\mathbf{c}_{BV}B^{-1}$ is dual feasible.

2. Show that the optimal primal objective function value = the dual objective function for $\mathbf{c}_{BV}B^{-1}$.

3. We have found a primal feasible solution (from BV) and a dual feasible solution $(\mathbf{c}_{BV}B^{-1})$ that have equal objective function values. From Lemma 2, we can now conclude that $\mathbf{c}_{BV}B^{-1}$ is optimal for the dual and $\bar{z} = \bar{w}$.

We now verify Step 1 for the case where the primal is a normal maximization problem with n variables and m constraints.[‡] After adding slack variables $s_1, s_2, \ldots, s_m$ to the primal, we write the primal and dual problems as follows:

[†]It can happen that both the primal and dual can be infeasible, as in the following example:

	max $z = x_2$			min $w = -y_1 + y_2$	
	s.t. x_1	≤ -1		s.t. y_1	≥ 0
Primal			**Dual**		
	$-x_2 \leq 1$			$-y_2 \geq 1$	
	$x_1, x_2 \geq 0$			$y_1, y_2 \geq 0$	

[‡]Our proof can easily be modified to handle the situation where the primal is not a normal max problem.

$$\max z = c_1 x_1 + c_2 x_2 + \cdots + c_n x_n$$

Primal Problem

$$\text{s.t.} \quad \begin{array}{l} a_{11} x_1 + a_{12} x_2 + \cdots + a_{1n} x_n + s_1 \qquad\qquad = b_1 \\ a_{21} x_1 + a_{22} x_2 + \cdots + a_{2n} x_n \qquad + s_2 \qquad = b_2 \\ \quad\vdots \qquad\quad \vdots \qquad\qquad\quad \vdots \qquad\qquad\qquad\qquad \vdots \\ a_{m1} x_1 + a_{m2} x_2 + \cdots + a_{mn} x_n \qquad\qquad + s_m = b_m \end{array} \qquad (28)$$

$$x_j \geq 0 \quad (j = 1, 2, \ldots, n); \quad s_i \geq 0 \quad (i = 1, 2, \ldots, m)$$

$$\min w = b_1 y_1 + b_2 y_2 + \cdots + b_m y_m$$

Dual Problem

$$\text{s.t.} \quad \begin{array}{l} a_{11} y_1 + a_{21} y_2 + \cdots + a_{m1} y_m \geq c_1 \\ a_{12} y_1 + a_{22} y_2 + \cdots + a_{m2} y_m \geq c_2 \\ \quad\vdots \qquad\quad \vdots \qquad\qquad\quad \vdots \qquad\quad \vdots \\ a_{1n} y_1 + a_{2n} y_2 + \cdots + a_{mn} y_m \geq c_n \end{array} \qquad (29)$$

$$y_j \geq 0 \quad (j = 1, 2, \ldots, m)$$

Let BV be an optimal basis for the primal, and define $\mathbf{c}_{BV} B^{-1} = [y_1, y_2, \ldots, y_m]$. Thus, for the optimal basis BV, y_i is the ith element of $\mathbf{c}_{BV} B^{-1}$. We now use the fact that BV is optimal for the primal to show that $\mathbf{c}_{BV} B^{-1}$ is feasible for the dual. Since BV is optimal for the primal, the coefficient of each variable in row 0 of BV's primal tableau must be nonnegative. From (10), the coefficient of x_j in row 0 of the BV tableau ($\bar{c}_j$) is given by

$$\bar{c}_j = \mathbf{c}_{BV} B^{-1} \mathbf{a}_j - c_j$$

$$= [y_1 \quad y_2 \quad \cdots \quad y_m] \begin{bmatrix} a_{1j} \\ a_{2j} \\ \vdots \\ a_{mj} \end{bmatrix} - c_j$$

$$= y_1 a_{1j} + y_2 a_{2j} + \cdots + y_m a_{mj} - c_j$$

But we know that $\bar{c}_j \geq 0$, so for $j = 1, 2, \ldots, n$,

$$y_1 a_{1j} + y_2 a_{2j} + \cdots + y_m a_{mj} - c_j \geq 0$$

Thus, $\mathbf{c}_{BV} B^{-1}$ satisfies each of the n dual constraints.

Since BV is an optimal basis for the primal, we also know that each slack variable has a nonnegative coefficient in the BV primal tableau. From (10'), we find that the coefficient of s_i in BV's row 0 is y_i, the ith element of $\mathbf{c}_{BV} B^{-1}$. Thus, for $i = 1, 2, \ldots, m$, $y_i \geq 0$. We have shown that $\mathbf{c}_{BV} B^{-1}$ satisfies all n constraints in (29) and that all the elements of $\mathbf{c}_{BV} B^{-1}$ are nonnegative. Thus, $\mathbf{c}_{BV} B^{-1}$ is indeed dual feasible.

Step 2 of the Dual Theorem proof requires that we show

$$\begin{array}{c} \text{Dual objective function value for } \mathbf{c}_{BV} B^{-1} \\ = \text{primal objective function value for } BV \end{array} \qquad (30)$$

From (11), we know that the primal objective function value for BV is $\mathbf{c}_{BV} B^{-1} \mathbf{b}$. But the dual objective function value for the dual feasible solution $\mathbf{c}_{BV} B^{-1}$ is

$$b_1 y_1 + b_2 y_2 + \cdots + b_m y_m = [y_1 \quad y_2 \quad \cdots \quad y_m] \begin{bmatrix} b_1 \\ b_2 \\ \vdots \\ b_m \end{bmatrix} = \mathbf{c}_{BV} B^{-1} \mathbf{b}$$

Thus, (30) is valid.

We have shown that Steps 1 and 2 of the Dual Theorem proof are valid. Step 3 now completes our proof of the Dual Theorem.

R E M A R K S

1. In Step 1 of the Dual Theorem proof, we showed that a basis BV that is feasible for the primal is optimal if and only if $\mathbf{c}_{BV} B^{-1}$ is dual feasible. In Section 6.9, we use this result to gain useful insights into sensitivity analysis.

2. When we find the optimal solution to the primal by using the simplex algorithm, we have also found the optimal solution to the dual.

To see why Remark 2 is true, suppose that the primal is a normal max problem with m constraints. In order to use the simplex to solve this problem, we must add a slack variable s_i to the ith primal constraint. Suppose BV is an optimal basis for the primal. Then the Dual Theorem tells us that $\mathbf{c}_{BV} B^{-1} = [y_1 \quad y_2 \quad \cdots \quad y_m]$ is the optimal solution to the dual. Recall from (10′), however, that y_i is the coefficient of s_i in row 0 of the optimal (BV) primal tableau. Thus, we have shown that *if the primal is a normal max problem, the optimal value of the ith dual variable is the coefficient of s_i in row 0 of the optimal primal tableau.*

We use the Dakota problem to illustrate Remark 2. The optimal tableau for the Dakota problem is shown in Table 23. The optimal primal solution is $z = 280$, $s_1 = 24$, $x_3 = 8$, $x_1 = 2$, $x_2 = 0$, $s_2 = 0$, $s_3 = 0$. From the preceding discussion, the optimal dual solution is $y_1 = 0$, $y_2 = 10$, $y_3 = 10$, $w = 48(0) + 20(10) + 8(10) = 280$. Observe that the optimal primal and dual objective function values are equal, as required by the Dual Theorem.

Table 23
Optimal Solution to
the Dakota Problem

				BASIC VARIABLE
z +	$5x_2$	$+ 10s_2 + 10s_3 = 280$		$z = 280$
−	$2x_2$	$+ s_1 + 2s_2 - 8s_3 = 24$		$s_1 = 24$
−	$2x_2 + x_3$	$+ 2s_2 - 4s_3 = 8$		$x_3 = 8$
x_1 +	$1.25x_2$	$- 0.5s_2 + 1.5s_3 = 2$		$x_1 = 2$

Of course, we may always compute the optimal dual solution by directly computing

$$\mathbf{c}_{BV} B^{-1} = [0 \quad 20 \quad 60] \begin{bmatrix} 1 & 2 & -8 \\ 0 & 2 & -4 \\ 0 & -0.5 & 1.5 \end{bmatrix} = [0 \quad 10 \quad 10]$$

Of course, the two methods of obtaining the dual solution agree.

If the primal has $\geq$ or equality constraints, we can still find the optimal dual solution from the optimal primal tableau. To see how this is done, recall that the Dual Theorem tells us that the optimal value of the ith dual variable (y_i) is the ith element of $c_{BV}B^{-1}$. From (10″), we see that if the ith constraint of the primal is a $\geq$ constraint, then

Optimal value of ith dual variable $= y_i = -$(coefficient of e_i in the optimal row 0)

Since the coefficient of e_i in the optimal row 0 must be nonnegative, this shows that if the ith constraint in the primal is a $\geq$ constraint, then $y_i \leq 0$. This agrees with our previous convention (see Section 6.5) that a $\geq$ constraint must have a nonpositive dual variable. From (10‴), we see that if the ith primal constraint is an equality constraint, then

$$y_i = \text{(coefficient of } a_i \text{ in optimal row 0)} - M$$

Although the coefficient of a_i in the optimal row 0 must be nonnegative, the fact that M is a large positive number means that $y_i \geq 0$ or $y_i \leq 0$ is possible. This agrees with our previous convention, which stated that the dual variable for an equality constraint is urs.

HOW TO READ THE OPTIMAL DUAL SOLUTION FROM ROW 0 OF THE OPTIMAL TABLEAU IF PRIMAL IS A MAX PROBLEM

Optimal value of dual variable y_i if constraint i is a $\leq$ constraint $=$ coefficient of s_i in optimal row 0   (31)

Optimal value of dual variable y_i if constraint i is a $\geq$ constraint $= -$(coefficient of e_i in optimal row 0)   (31′)

Optimal value of dual variable y_i if constraint i is an equality constraint $=$ (coefficient of a_i in optimal row 0) $- M$ (31″)

The following example illustrates how to find the optimal dual solution to a problem with $\leq$, $\geq$, and equality constraints.

E X A M P L E 10   To solve the following LP,

$$\max z = 3x_1 + 2x_2 + 5x_3$$
$$\text{s.t.} \quad x_1 + 3x_2 + 2x_3 \leq 15$$
$$2x_2 - x_3 \geq 5 \quad (32)$$
$$2x_1 + x_2 - 5x_3 = 10$$
$$x_1, x_2, x_3 \geq 0$$

we add a slack variable s_1, subtract an excess variable e_2, and add two artificial variables a_2 and a_3. The optimal tableau for (32) is given in Table 24. From this tableau, the optimal solution to (32) is found to be $z = \frac{565}{23}$, $x_3 = \frac{15}{23}$, $x_2 = \frac{65}{23}$, $x_1 = \frac{120}{23}$, $s_1 = e_2 = a_2 = a_3 = 0$. Use this information to find the optimal solution to the dual of (32).

Table 24
Optimal Tableau for
LP (32)

z	x_1	x_2	x_3	s_1	e_2	a_2	a_3	rhs	BASIC VARIABLE
1	0	0	0	$\frac{51}{23}$	$\frac{58}{23}$	$M - \frac{58}{23}$	$M + \frac{9}{23}$	$\frac{565}{23}$	$z = \frac{565}{23}$
0	0	0	1	$\frac{4}{23}$	$\frac{5}{23}$	$-\frac{5}{23}$	$-\frac{2}{23}$	$\frac{15}{23}$	$x_3 = \frac{15}{23}$
0	0	1	0	$\frac{2}{23}$	$-\frac{9}{23}$	$\frac{9}{23}$	$-\frac{1}{23}$	$\frac{65}{23}$	$x_2 = \frac{65}{23}$
0	1	0	0	$\frac{9}{23}$	$\frac{17}{23}$	$-\frac{17}{23}$	$\frac{7}{23}$	$\frac{120}{23}$	$x_1 = \frac{120}{23}$

Solution

Following the steps in Section 6.5, we find the dual of (32) from the tableau in Table 25:

$$\min w = 15y_1 + 5y_2 + 10y_3$$
$$\text{s.t.} \quad y_1 \qquad\quad + 2y_3 \geq 3$$
$$3y_1 + 2y_2 + y_3 \geq 2 \tag{33}$$
$$2y_1 - y_2 - 5y_3 \geq 5$$
$$y_1 \geq 0,\, y_2 \leq 0,\, y_3 \text{ urs}$$

Table 25
Finding the Dual of
LP (32)

$\min w$		max z			
		$(x_1 \geq 0)$	$(x_2 \geq 0)$	$(x_3 \geq 0)$	
		x_1	x_2	x_3	
$(y_1 \geq 0)$	y_1	1	3	2	≤ 15
$(y_2 \leq 0)$	y_2	0	2	-1	$\geq 5^*$
$(y_3$ urs$)$	y_3	2	1	-5	$= 10^*$
		≥ 3	≥ 2	≥ 5	

From (31) and the optimal primal tableau, we can find the optimal solution to (33) as follows:

Since the first primal constraint is a $\leq$ constraint, we see from (31) that $y_1 =$ coefficient of s_1 in optimal row 0 $= \frac{51}{23}$. Since the second primal constraint is a $\geq$ constraint, we see from (31') that $y_2 = -$(coefficient of e_2 in optimal row 0) $= -\frac{58}{23}$. Since the third constraint is an equality constraint, we see from (31'') that $y_3 =$ (coefficient of a_3 in optimal row 0) $- M = \frac{9}{23}$.

By the Dual Theorem, the optimal dual objective function value w must equal $\frac{565}{23}$. In summary, the optimal dual solution is

$$\bar{w} = \frac{565}{23},\, y_1 = \frac{51}{23},\, y_2 = -\frac{58}{23},\, y_3 = \frac{9}{23}$$

The reader should check that this solution is indeed dual feasible (all dual constraints are satisfied with equality) and that

$$\bar{w} = 15(\tfrac{51}{23}) + 5(-\tfrac{58}{23}) + 10(\tfrac{9}{23}) = \tfrac{565}{23}$$

Even if the primal is a min problem, we may read the optimal dual solution from the optimal primal tableau.

**HOW TO READ THE OPTIMAL DUAL SOLUTION
FROM ROW 0 OF THE OPTIMAL TABLEAU
IF PRIMAL IS A MIN PROBLEM**

Optimal value of dual variable x_i
if constraint i is a $\leq$ constraint = coefficient of s_i in optimal row 0

Optimal value of dual variable x_i
if constraint i is a $\geq$ constraint = $-$(coefficient of e_i in optimal row 0)

Optimal value of dual variable x_i
if constraint i is an equality
constraint = (coefficient of a_i in optimal row 0) $+ M$

To illustrate how the optimal solution to the dual of a min problem may be read from
the optimal primal tableau, consider

$$\min w = 3y_1 + 2y_2 + y_3$$
$$\text{s.t.} \quad y_1 + y_2 + y_3 \geq 4$$
$$y_2 - y_3 \leq 2$$
$$y_1 + y_2 + 2y_3 = 6$$
$$y_1, y_2, y_3 \geq 0$$

The optimal tableau for this problem is given in Table 26. Thus, the optimal primal
solution is $w = 6$, $y_2 = y_3 = 2$, $y_1 = 0$. The dual of the preceding LP is

$$\max z = 4x_1 + 2x_2 + 6x_3$$
$$\text{s.t.} \quad x_1 \quad + x_3 \leq 3$$
$$x_1 + x_2 + x_3 \leq 2$$
$$x_1 - x_2 + 2x_3 \leq 1$$
$$x_1 \geq 0, x_2 \leq 0, x_3 \text{ urs}$$

From the optimal primal tableau, we find that the optimal dual solution is $z = 6$,
$x_1 = 3$, $x_2 = 0$, $x_3 = -1$.

	w	y_1	y_2	y_3	e_1	s_2	a_1	a_3	rhs
Table 26	1	-1	0	0	-3	0	$3 - M$	$-1 - M$	6
Finding the Optimal	0	1	1	0	-2	0	2	-1	2
Solution to the Dual	0	-1	0	0	3	1	-3	2	2
When Primal Is a	0	0	0	1	1	0	-1	1	2
Min Problem									

◆ PROBLEMS

GROUP A

1. The following questions refer to the Giapetto problem
(see Problem 7 of Section 6.3).
(a) Find the dual of the Giapetto problem.

(b) Use the optimal tableau of the Giapetto problem to
determine the optimal dual solution.
(c) Verify that the Dual Theorem holds in this instance.

2. Consider the following LP:

$$\max z = -2x_1 - x_2 + x_3$$
$$\text{s.t.} \quad x_1 + x_2 + x_3 \le 3$$
$$x_2 + x_3 \ge 2$$
$$x_1 \quad\quad + x_3 = 1$$
$$x_1, x_2, x_3 \ge 0$$

(a) Find the dual of this LP.
(b) After adding a slack variable s_1, subtracting an excess variable e_2, and adding artificial variables a_2 and a_3, row 0 of the LP's optimal tableau was found to be

$$z + 4x_1 + e_2 + (M - 1)a_2 + (M + 2)a_3 = 0$$

Find the optimal solution to the dual of this LP.

3. For the following LP,

$$\max z = -x_1 + 5x_2$$
$$\text{s.t.} \quad x_1 + 2x_2 \le 0.5$$
$$-x_1 + 3x_2 \le 0.5$$
$$x_1, x_2 \ge 0$$

row 0 of the optimal tableau was found to be $z + 0.4s_1 + 1.4s_2 = ?$. Determine the optimal z-value for the given LP.

4. The following questions refer to the Bevco problem of Section 4.10.
(a) Find the dual of the Bevco problem.
(b) Use the optimal tableau for the Bevco problem that is given in Section 4.10 to find the optimal solution to the Bevco dual. Verify that the Dual Theorem holds in this instance.

5. Consider the following linear programming problem:

$$\max z = 4x_1 + x_2$$
$$\text{s.t.} \quad 3x_1 + 2x_2 \le 6$$
$$6x_1 + 3x_2 \le 10$$
$$x_1, x_2 \ge 0$$

Suppose that in solving this problem, row 0 of the optimal tableau was found to be $z + 2x_2 + s_2 = \frac{20}{3}$. Use the Dual Theorem to prove that the computations must be incorrect.

6. Show that (for a max problem) if the ith primal constraint is a $\ge$ constraint, the optimal value of the ith dual variable may be written as (coefficient of a_i in optimal row 0) $- M$.

GROUP B

7. In this problem, we use weak duality to prove Lemma 3.
(a) Show that Lemma 3 is equivalent to the following: If the dual is feasible, then the primal is bounded. (*Hint*: Do you remember, from plane geometry, what the contrapositive is?)
(b) Use weak duality to show the validity of the form of Lemma 3 given in part (a). (*Hint*: If the dual is feasible, there must be a dual feasible point having a w-value of, say, w_0. Now use weak duality to show that the primal is bounded.)

8. Following along the lines of Problem 7, use weak duality to prove Lemma 4.

9. Use the information given in Problem 8 of Section 6.3 to determine the dual of the Dorian Auto problem and its optimal solution.

6-8   SHADOW PRICES

We now return to the concept of shadow price that was discussed in Section 6.1. A more formal definition follows.

DEFINITION	The **shadow price** of the ith constraint is the amount by which the optimal z-value is improved (increased in a max problem and decreased in a min problem) if we increase b_i by 1 (from b_i to $b_i + 1$).[†]

[†]This assumes that after the right-hand side of constraint i has been changed to $b_i + 1$, the current basis remains optimal.

By using the Dual Theorem, we can easily determine the shadow price of the ith constraint. To illustrate, we find the shadow price of the second constraint (finishing hours) of the Dakota problem. Let $\mathbf{c}_{BV} B^{-1} = [y_1 \quad y_2 \quad y_3] = [0 \quad 10 \quad 10]$ be the optimal solution to the dual of the max problem. From the Dual Theorem, we know that

$$\text{Optimal } z\text{-value when rhs of constraints are } (b_1 = 48, b_2 = 20, b_3 = 8)$$
$$= 48y_1 + 20y_2 + 8y_3 \tag{34}$$

What happens to the optimal z-value for the Dakota problem if b_2 (currently 20 finishing hours) is increased by 1 unit (to 21 hours)? We know that changing a right-hand side may cause the current basis to be no longer optimal (see Section 6.3). For the moment, however, we assume that the current basis remains optimal when we increase b_2 by 1. Then $\mathbf{c}_{BV}$ and B^{-1} remain unchanged, so the optimal solution to the dual of the Dakota problem remains unchanged.

We next find

$$\text{Optimal } z\text{-value when rhs of finishing constraint is } 21 = 48y_1 + 21y_2 + 8y_3 \tag{35}$$

Subtracting (34) from (35) yields

$$\text{Change in optimal } z\text{-value if finishing hours are increased by 1}$$
$$= \text{shadow price for finishing constraint 2} \tag{36}$$
$$= y_2 = 10$$

This example shows that *the shadow price of the ith constraint of a max problem is the optimal value of the ith dual variable*. Since the shadow prices are the dual variables, we know that the shadow price for a $\leq$ constraint will be nonnegative, the shadow price for a $\geq$ constraint will be nonpositive, and the shadow price for an equality constraint is unrestricted in sign. The examples discussed later in this section give intuitive justifications for these sign conventions.

Similar reasoning can be used to show that if (in a maximization problem) the right-hand side of the ith constraint is increased by an amount Δb_i, then (assuming the current basis remains optimal) the new optimal z-value may be found from

$$\text{New optimal } z\text{-value} = \text{old optimal } z\text{-value}$$
$$+ \Delta b_i \text{ (Constraint } i \text{ shadow price)} \tag{37}$$

For a minimization problem, the shadow price of the ith constraint is the amount by which a unit increase in the right-hand side of the ith constraint improves, or decreases, the optimal z-value (assuming that the current basis remains optimal after the right-hand side of the ith constraint has been increased by 1). It can be shown that the shadow price of the ith constraint of a min problem $= -$(optimal value of the ith dual variable). If the right-hand side of the ith constraint is increased by an amount Δb_i, then (assuming the current basis remains optimal) the new optimal z-value may be found from

$$\text{New optimal } z\text{-value} = \text{old optimal } z\text{-value}$$
$$- \Delta b_i \text{ (Constraint } i \text{ shadow price)} \tag{37'}$$

The following three examples should clarify the meaning of the shadow price concept.

E X A M P L E   For the Dakota problem:
11

    1. Find and interpret the shadow prices.

    2. If 18 finishing hours were available, what would be Dakota's revenue? (It can be shown by the methods of Section 6.3 that if $16 \leq$ finishing hours ≤ 24, the current basis remains optimal.)

    3. If 9 carpentry hours were available, what would be Dakota's revenue? (For $\frac{20}{3} \leq$ carpentry hours ≤ 10, the current basis remains optimal.)

    4. If 30 board ft of lumber were available, what would be Dakota's revenue? (For $24 \leq$ lumber $\leq \infty$, the current basis remains optimal.)

    5. If 30 carpentry hours were available, why couldn't the shadow price for the carpentry constraint be used to determine the new z-value?

Solution   **1.** In Section 6.7, we found the optimal solution to the Dakota dual to be $y_1 = 0$, $y_2 = 10$, $y_3 = 10$. Thus, the shadow price for the lumber constraint is zero, the shadow price for the finishing constraint is 10, and the shadow price for the carpentry constraint is 10. The fact that the lumber constraint has a shadow price of zero means that increasing the amount of available lumber by 1 board ft (or *any* amount) will not increase revenue. This is reasonable, because we are currently using only 24 of the available 48 board ft of lumber, so adding any amount of lumber will not do Dakota any good. The shadow price for the finishing constraint is $10; this is the amount by which Dakota's revenue would increase if 1 more finishing hour were available. Similarly, the fact that the carpentry constraint has a shadow price of 10 means that if 1 more carpentry hour were available, Dakota's revenue would increase by $10. In this problem, the shadow price of the ith constraint may be thought of as the maximum amount that the company would pay for an extra unit of the resource associated with the ith constraint. For example, an extra carpentry hour would raise revenue by $y_3 = \$10$ (see Example 12 for a max problem in which this interpretation is invalid). Thus, Dakota could pay up to $10 for an extra carpentry hour and still be better off. Similarly, the company would be willing to pay nothing ($0) for an extra board foot of lumber and up to $10 for an extra finishing hour. To answer questions 2–4, we apply (37), using the fact that the old z-value $= 280$.

    2. $y_2 = 10$, $\Delta b_2 = 18 - 20 = -2$. The current basis is still optimal, because $16 \leq 18 \leq 24$. Then (37) yields (new revenue) $= 280 + 10(-2) = \$260$.

    3. $y_3 = 10$, $\Delta b_3 = 9 - 8 = 1$. Since $\frac{20}{3} \leq 9 \leq 10$, the current basis remains optimal. Then (37) yields (new revenue) $= 280 + 10(1) = \$290$.

    4. $y_1 = 0$, $\Delta b_1 = 30 - 48 = -18$. Since $24 \leq 30 \leq \infty$, the current basis is still optimal. Then (37) yields (new revenue) $= 280 + 0(-18) = \$280$.

    5. If $b_3 = 30$, the current basis is no longer optimal, because $30 > 10$. This means that BV (and therefore $\mathbf{c}_{BV} B^{-1}$) changes, and we cannot use the current set of shadow prices to determine the new revenue level.

INTUITIVE EXPLANATION OF THE SIGN OF SHADOW PRICES

We can now give an intuitive explanation of why (in ↯ of a ≤ constraint will always be nonnegative. Consi↯ given two LP max problems (LP 1 and LP 2) that ↯ Suppose that every point that is feasible for LP 1 is als↯ that LP 2's feasible region contains all the points in LP 1's feasi↯ some other points. Then the optimal z-value for LP 2 must be at lea↯ the optimal z-value for LP 1. To see this, suppose that the point x' (with z-value ↯ optimal for LP 1. Since x' is also feasible for LP 2 (which has the same objective function as LP 1), LP 2 can attain a z-value of z' (by using the feasible point x'). It is also possible that by using one of the points feasible for only LP 2 (and not for LP 1), LP 2 might do better than z'. In short, *adding points to the feasible region of a max problem cannot decrease the optimal z-value.*

We can use this observation to show why a ≤ constraint must have a nonnegative shadow price. For the Dakota problem, if we increase the right-hand side of the carpentry constraint by 1 (from 8 to 9), we see that all points that were originally feasible remain feasible, and some new points (which use > 8 and ≤ 9 carpentry hours) may be feasible. Thus, the optimal z-value cannot decrease, and the shadow price for the carpentry constraint must be nonnegative.

The purpose of the following example is to show that (contrary to what many books say) the shadow price of a ≤ constraint is not always the maximum price you would be willing to pay for an additional unit of a resource.

E X A M P L E 12

Leatherco manufactures belts and shoes. A belt requires 2 sq yd of leather and 1 hour of skilled labor. A pair of shoes requires 3 sq yd of leather and 2 hours of skilled labor. Up to 25 sq yd of leather and 15 hours of skilled labor can be purchased at a price of $5/sq yd of leather and $10/hour of skilled labor. A belt sells for $23, and a pair of shoes sells for $40. Leatherco wishes to maximize profits (= revenues − costs). Formulate an LP that can be used to maximize Leatherco's profits. Then find and interpret the shadow prices for this LP.

Solution

Define

$$x_1 = \text{number of belts produced}$$
$$x_2 = \text{number of pairs of shoes produced}$$

After noting that

$$\text{Cost/belt} = 2(5) + 1(10) = \$20$$
$$\text{Cost/pair of shoes} = 3(5) + 2(10) = \$35$$

we find that Leatherco's objective function is

$$\max z = (23 - 20)x_1 + (40 - 35)x_2 = 3x_1 + 5x_2$$

Leatherco faces the following two constraints:

Constraint 1 Leatherco can use at most 25 sq yd of leather.

Constraint 2 Leatherco can use at most 15 hours of skilled labor.

Constraint 1 is expressed by

$$2x_1 + 3x_2 \leq 25 \qquad \text{(Leather constraint)}$$

while Constraint 2 is expressed by

$$x_1 + 2x_2 \leq 15 \qquad \text{(Skilled-labor constraint)}$$

After adding the sign restrictions $x_1 \geq 0$ and $x_2 \geq 0$, we obtain the following LP:

$$\max z = 3x_1 + 5x_2$$
$$\text{s.t.} \quad 2x_1 + 3x_2 \leq 25 \qquad \text{(Leather constraint)}$$
$$x_1 + 2x_2 \leq 15 \qquad \text{(Skilled-labor constraint)}$$
$$x_1, x_2 \geq 0$$

After adding slack variables s_1 and s_2 to the leather and skilled-labor constraints, respectively, we obtain the optimal tableau shown in Table 27. Thus, the optimal solution to Leatherco's problem is $z = 40$, $x_1 = 5$, $x_2 = 5$. The shadow prices are

y_1 = leather shadow price = coefficient of s_1 in optimal row 0 = 1

y_2 = skilled labor shadow price = coefficient of s_2 in optimal row 0 = 1

Table 27
Optimal Tableau for
Leatherco Example

	BASIC VARIABLE
$z \quad + \; s_1 + \; s_2 = 40$	$z = 40$
$x_1 \quad + 2s_1 - 3s_2 = 5$	$x_1 = 5$
$x_2 - \; s_1 + 2s_2 = 5$	$x_2 = 5$

The meaning of the leather shadow price is that if one more square yard of leather were available, Leatherco's objective function (profits) would increase by $1. Let's look further at what happens if an additional square yard of leather is available. Since s_1 is nonbasic, the extra square yard of leather will be purchased. Also, since s_2 is nonbasic, we will still use all available labor. This means that the $1 increase in profits includes the cost of purchasing an extra square yard of leather. If the availability of an extra square yard of leather increases profits by $1, it must be increasing revenue by $1 + 5 = $6. Thus, the maximum amount Leatherco would be willing to pay for an extra square yard of leather is $6 (not $1).

Another way to see this is as follows: If we purchase another square yard of leather at the current price of $5, profits increase by y_1 = $1. If we purchase another square yard of leather at a price of $6 = $5 + $1, profits increase by $1 − $1 = $0. Thus, the most Leatherco would be willing to pay for an extra square yard of leather is $6.

Similarly, the most Leatherco would be willing to pay for an extra hour of labor is y_2 + (cost of an extra hour of skilled labor) = $1 + 10 = $11. In this problem, we see that the shadow price for a resource represents the *premium* over and above the cost of the resource that Leatherco would be willing to pay for an extra unit of resource. ♦

The two preceding examples show that we must be careful when interpreting the shadow price of a ≤ constraint. Remember that the shadow price for a constraint in a max problem is the amount by which the objective function increases if the right-hand side of a constraint is increased by 1.

The following example illustrates the interpretation of the shadow prices of ≥ and equality constraints.

E X A M P L E
13

Steelco has received an order for 100 tons of steel. The order must contain at least 3.5 tons of nickel, at most 3 tons of carbon, and exactly 4 tons of manganese. Steelco receives $20/ton for the order. To fill the order, Steelco can combine four alloys, whose chemical composition is given in Table 28. Steelco wishes to maximize the profit (= revenues − costs) obtained from filling the order. Formulate the appropriate LP. Also find and interpret the shadow prices for each constraint.

Table 28
Relevant Information
for Steelco Example

	ALLOY 1	ALLOY 2	ALLOY 3	ALLOY 4
Nickel	6%	3%	2%	1%
Carbon	3%	2%	5%	6%
Manganese	8%	3%	2%	1%
Cost/ton	$12	$10	$8	$6

Solution

After we define x_i = number of tons of alloy i used to fill the order, Steelco's LP is seen to be

$$\max z = (20 - 12)x_1 + (20 - 10)x_2 + (20 - 8)x_3 + (20 - 6)x_4$$

$$\text{s.t.} \quad 0.06x_1 + 0.03x_2 + 0.02x_3 + 0.01x_4 \geq 3.5 \quad \text{(Nickel constraint)}$$

$$0.03x_1 + 0.02x_2 + 0.05x_3 + 0.06x_4 \leq 3 \quad \text{(Carbon constraint)}$$

$$0.08x_1 + 0.03x_2 + 0.02x_3 + 0.01x_4 = 4 \quad \text{(Manganese constraint)}$$

$$x_1 + x_2 + x_3 + x_4 = 100 \quad \text{(Order size = 100 tons)}$$

$$x_1, x_2, x_3, x_4 \geq 0$$

After adding a slack variable s_2, subtracting an excess variable e_1, and adding artificial variables a_1, a_3, and a_4, the following optimal solution is obtained: $z = 1000$, $s_2 = 0.25$, $x_1 = 25$, $x_2 = 62.5$, $x_4 = 12.5$, $e_1 = 0$, $x_3 = 0$. The optimal row 0 is

$$z + 400e_1 + (M - 400)a_1 + (M + 200)a_3 + (M + 16)a_4 = 1000$$

Using (31), (31′), and (31″), we obtain

Shadow price of nickel constraint = −(coefficient of e_1 in optimal row 0)

$$= -400$$

Shadow price of carbon constraint = coefficient of s_2 in optimal row 0

$$= 0$$

Shadow price of manganese constraint = (coefficient of a_3 in optimal row 0) − M

$$= 200$$

Shadow price of order size constraint = (coefficient of a_4 in optimal row 0) − M

$$= 16$$

By the sensitivity analysis procedures of Section 6.3, it can be shown that the current basis remains optimal if $3.46 \leq b_1 \leq 3.6$. As long as the nickel requirement is in this range, increasing the nickel requirement by an amount Δb_1 will increase Steelco's profits by $-400\Delta b_1$. For example, increasing the nickel requirement to 3.55 tons ($\Delta b_1 = 0.05$) would "increase" (actually decrease) profits by $-400(0.05) = -\$20$. The nickel constraint has a negative shadow price, because increasing the right-hand side of the nickel constraint makes it harder to satisfy the nickel constraint. In fact, it can be shown that an increase in the nickel requirement forces Steelco to use more of the expensive type 1 alloy. This raises costs and lowers profits. As we have already seen, the shadow price of a $\geq$ constraint (in a max problem) will always be nonpositive, because increasing the right-hand side of a $\geq$ constraint eliminates points from the feasible region. Thus, the optimal z-value must decrease or remain unchanged.

By the Section 6.3 sensitivity analysis procedures, it can be shown that for $2.75 \leq b_2 \leq \infty$, the current basis remains optimal. As stated before, the carbon constraint has a zero shadow price. This means that if we increase Steelco's carbon requirement, Steelco's profit will not change. Intuitively, this is because our present optimal solution contains only $2.75 < 3$ tons of carbon. Thus, relaxing the carbon requirement won't enable Steelco to reduce costs, so Steelco's profit will remain unchanged.

By the sensitivity analysis procedures, we can show that the current basis remains optimal if $3.83 \leq b_3 \leq 4.07$. Since the shadow price of the third (manganese) constraint is 200, we know that as long as the manganese requirement remains in the given range, increasing it by an amount of Δb_3 will increase profit by $200\Delta b_3$. For example, if the manganese requirement were 4.05 tons ($\Delta b_3 = 0.05$), profits would increase by $(0.05)200 = \$10$.

By the sensitivity analysis procedures, it can be shown that if $91.67 \leq b_4 \leq 103.12$, the current basis remains optimal. Since the shadow price of the fourth (order size) constraint is 16, increasing the order size by Δb_4 tons (with nickel, carbon, and manganese requirements unchanged) would increase profits by $16\Delta b_4$. For example, the profit from a 103-ton order that required ≥ 3.5 tons of nickel, ≤ 3 tons of carbon, and exactly 4 tons of manganese would be $1000 + 3(16) = \$1048$.

In this problem, both equality constraints had positive shadow prices. In general, we know that it is possible for an equality constraint's dual variable (and shadow price) to be negative. If this occurs, the equality constraint will have a negative shadow price. To illustrate this possibility, suppose that Steelco's customer required exactly 4.5 tons of manganese in the order. Since $4.5 > 4.07$, the current basis is no longer optimal. If we solve Steelco's LP again, it can be shown that the shadow price for the manganese constraint has changed to -54.55. This means that an increase in the manganese requirement will decrease Steelco's profits.

◆

INTERPRETATION OF THE DUAL PRICES COLUMN OF THE LINDO OUTPUT

For a max problem, LINDO gives the values of the shadow prices in the DUAL PRICES column of the output. The dual price for row $i + 1$ on the LINDO output is the shadow price for the ith constraint. The dual price for row $i + 1$ is also the optimal value for the ith dual variable. Thus, in Figure 4, we see that for the Dakota problem,

y_1 = shadow price for lumber constraint = row 2 dual price = 0

y_2 = shadow price for finishing constraint = row 3 dual price = 10

y_3 = shadow price for carpentry constraint = row 4 dual price = 10

For a maximization problem, the vector $c_{BV}B^{-1}$ (needed for pricing out new activities) is the same as the vector of dual prices given on the LINDO output. For the Dakota problem, we would price out new activities using $c_{BV}B^{-1} = [0 \quad 10 \quad 10]$.

For a minimization problem, the entry in the DUAL PRICE column for any constraint is the constraint's shadow price. Thus, from the LINDO printout in Figure 6, we find that the shadow prices for the constraints in the diet problem are as follows: calorie shadow price = 0; chocolate shadow price = $-2.5¢$; sugar shadow price = $-7.5¢$; and fat shadow price = 0. This implies that

1. Increasing the calorie requirement by 1 will leave the cost of the optimal diet unchanged.

2. Increasing the chocolate requirement by 1 oz will decrease the cost of the optimal diet by $-2.5¢$ (that is, increase the cost of the optimal diet by $2.5¢$).

3. Increasing the sugar requirement by 1 oz will decrease the cost of the optimal diet by $-7.5¢$ (that is, increase the cost of the optimal diet by $7.5¢$).

4. Increasing the fat requirement by 1 oz will leave the cost of the optimal diet unchanged.

The entry in the DUAL PRICE column for any constraint is, however, the negative of the constraint's dual variable. Thus, for the diet problem, we see from Figure 6 that the optimal dual solution to the diet problem is given by $c_{BV}B^{-1} = [0 \quad 2.5 \quad 7.5 \quad 0]$. When pricing out a new activity for a minimization problem, use the negative of each dual price as the corresponding element of $c_{BV}B^{-1}$.

Remember that for any LP, the dual prices remain valid only as long as the current basis remains optimal. As stated in Section 6.3, the range of right-hand side values for which the current basis remains optimal may be obtained from the RIGHTHAND SIDE RANGES block of the LINDO output.

◆ PROBLEMS

GROUP A

1. Use the Dual Theorem to prove (37).

2. The following questions refer to the Sugarco problem (Problem 6 of Section 6.3):
(a) Find the shadow prices for the Sugarco problem.
(b) If 60 oz of sugar were available, what would be Sugarco's profit?
(c) How about 40 oz of sugar?
(d) How about 30 oz of sugar?

3. Suppose we are working with a min problem and increase the right-hand side of a $\geq$ constraint. What can happen to the optimal z-value?

4. Suppose we are working with a min problem and increase the right-hand side of a $\leq$ constraint. What can happen to the optimal z-value?

5. A company manufactures two products (product 1 and product 2). Each unit of product 1 can be sold for $15, and each unit of product 2 can be sold for $25. Each product requires amounts of raw material and two types of labor (skilled and unskilled) (see Table 29). At present, the company has available 100 hours of skilled labor, 70 hours of unskilled labor, and 30 units of raw material. Because of marketing considerations at least 3 units of product 2 must be produced.

Table 29

	PRODUCT 1	PRODUCT 2
Skilled labor	3 hours	4 hours
Unskilled labor	2 hours	3 hours
Raw material	1 unit	2 units

(a) Explain why the company's goal is to maximize revenue.

(b) The relevant LP is

$$\max z = 15x_1 + 25x_2$$

$$\begin{aligned} \text{s.t.} \quad 3x_1 + 4x_2 &\leq 100 \quad \text{(Skilled labor constraint)} \\ 2x_1 + 3x_2 &\leq 70 \quad \text{(Unskilled labor constraint)} \\ x_1 + 2x_2 &\leq 30 \quad \text{(Raw material constraint)} \\ x_2 &\geq 3 \quad \text{(Product 2 constraint)} \\ x_1, x_2 &\geq 0 \end{aligned}$$

The optimal tableau for this problem has the following row 0:

$$z + 15s_3 + 5e_4 + (M - 5)a_4 = 435$$

The optimal solution to the LP is $z = 435$, $x_1 = 24$, $x_2 = 3$. Find and interpret the shadow price of each constraint. How much would the company be willing to pay for an additional unit of each type of labor? How much would it be willing to pay for an extra unit of raw material?

(c) Assuming the current basis remains optimal (it does), what would the company's revenue be if 35 units of raw material were available?

(d) With current basis optimal, what would the company's revenue be if 80 hours of skilled labor were available?

(e) With current basis optimal, what would the company's new revenue be if at least 5 units of product 2 were required? How about if at least 2 units of product 2 were required?

6. Suppose that the company in Problem 5 owns no labor and raw material but can purchase labor and raw material at the following prices: up to 100 hours of skilled labor can be purchased at $3/hour; up to 70 hours of unskilled labor can be purchased at $2/hour; up to 30 units of raw material can be purchased at $1 per unit of raw material. If the

company's goal is to maximize profit, show that the appropriate LP is

$$\max z = x_1 + 5x_2$$

$$\begin{aligned} \text{s.t.} \quad 3x_1 + 4x_2 &\leq 100 \\ 2x_1 + 3x_2 &\leq 70 \\ x_1 + 2x_2 &\leq 30 \\ x_2 &\geq 3 \\ x_1, x_2 &\geq 0 \end{aligned}$$

The optimal row 0 for this LP is

$$z + 1.5x_1 + 2.5s_3 + Ma_4 = 75$$

and the optimal solution is $z = 75$, $x_1 = 0$, $x_2 = 15$. In answering parts (a) and (b), assume that the current basis remains optimal.

(a) How much would the company be willing to pay for an extra unit of raw material?

(b) How much would the company be willing to pay for an extra hour of skilled labor? Unskilled labor? (Be careful here!)

7. For the Dorian problem (see Problem 8 of Section 6.3), answer the following questions:

(a) What would Dorian's cost be if 40 million HIW exposures were required?

(b) What would Dorian's cost be if only 20 million HIM exposures were required?

8. If it seems difficult to believe that the shadow price of an equality constraint should be urs, try this problem. Consider the following two LPs:

$$\max z = x_2 \qquad\qquad \max z = x_2$$

$$\text{(LP 1) s.t.} \quad x_1 + x_2 = 2 \quad \text{(LP 2) s.t.} \quad -x_1 - x_2 = -2$$

$$x_1, x_2 \geq 0 \qquad\qquad\qquad x_1, x_2 \geq 0$$

In which LP will the constraint have a positive shadow price? In which LP will the constraint have a negative shadow price?

GROUP B

9. For the Dakota problem, suppose that 22 finishing hours and 9 carpentry hours are available. What would be the new optimal z-value? (*Hint:* Use the 100% Rule to show that the current basis remains optimal, and mimic (34)–(36).)

10. For the diet problem, suppose at least 8 oz of chocolate and at least 9 oz of sugar are required (with other requirements remaining the same). What is the new optimal z-value?

6-9   DUALITY AND SENSITIVITY ANALYSIS

Our proof of the Dual Theorem demonstrated the following result: *Assuming that a set of basic variables BV is feasible, then BV is optimal* (*that is, each variable in row 0 has a nonnegative coefficient*) *if and only if the associated dual solution* ($\mathbf{c}_{BV}B^{-1}$) *is dual feasible.*

This result can be used for an alternative way of doing the following types of sensitivity analysis (see list of changes at the beginning of Section 6.3).

Change 1 Changing the objective function coefficient of a nonbasic variable

Change 4 Changing the column for a nonbasic variable

Change 5 Adding a new activity

In each case, the change leaves *BV* feasible. *BV* will remain optimal if the *BV* row 0 remains nonnegative. Since primal optimality and dual feasibility are equivalent, we see that *the above changes will leave the current basis optimal if and only if the current dual solution* $\mathbf{c}_{BV}B^{-1}$ *remains dual feasible.* If the current dual solution is no longer dual feasible, *BV* will be suboptimal, and a new optimal solution must be found.

We illustrate the duality-based approach to sensitivity analysis by reworking some of the Section 6.3 illustrations of sensitivity analysis. Recall that these illustrations dealt with the Dakota problem:

$$\max z = 60x_1 + 30x_2 + 20x_3$$

$$\begin{aligned}
\text{s.t.} \quad 8x_1 + 6x_2 + x_3 &\leq 48 && \text{(Lumber constraint)} \\
4x_1 + 2x_2 + 1.5x_3 &\leq 20 && \text{(Finishing constraint)} \\
2x_1 + 1.5x_2 + 0.5x_3 &\leq 8 && \text{(Carpentry constraint)} \\
x_1, x_2, x_3 &\geq 0
\end{aligned}$$

The optimal solution was $z = 280$, $s_1 = 24$, $x_3 = 8$, $x_1 = 2$, $x_2 = 0$, $s_2 = 0$, $s_3 = 0$. The only nonbasic decision variable in the optimal solution is x_2 (tables). The dual of the Dakota problem is

$$\min w = 48y_1 + 20y_2 + 8y_3$$

$$\begin{aligned}
\text{s.t.} \quad 8y_1 + 4y_2 + 2y_3 &\geq 60 && \text{(Desk constraint)} \\
6y_1 + 2y_2 + 1.5y_3 &\geq 30 && \text{(Table constraint)} \\
y_1 + 1.5y_2 + 0.5y_3 &\geq 20 && \text{(Chair constraint)} \\
y_1, y_2, y_3 &\geq 0
\end{aligned}$$

Recall that the optimal dual solution — and therefore the constraint shadow prices — are $y_1 = 0$, $y_2 = 10$, $y_3 = 10$. We now show how knowledge of duality can be applied to sensitivity analysis.

E X A M P L E 14

We wish to change the objective function coefficient of a nonbasic variable. Let c_2 be the coefficient of x_2 (tables) in the Dakota objective function. In other words, c_2 is the price at which a table is sold. For what values of c_2 will the current basis remain optimal?

Solution

If $y_1 = 0$, $y_2 = 10$, $y_3 = 10$ remains dual feasible, the current basis — and the values of all the variables — are unchanged. Note that if the objective function coefficient for x_2

is changed, the first and third dual constraints remain unchanged, but the second (table) dual constraint is changed to

$$6y_1 + 2y_2 + 1.5y_3 \geq c_2$$

If $y_1 = 0$, $y_2 = 10$, $y_3 = 10$ satisfies this inequality, dual feasibility (and therefore primal optimality) is maintained. Thus, the current basis remains optimal if c_2 satisfies $6(0) + 2(10) + 1.5(10) \geq c_2$, or $c_2 \leq 35$. This shows that for $c_2 \leq 35$, the current basis remains optimal. Conversely, if $c_2 > 35$, the current basis is no longer optimal. This agrees with the result obtained in Section 6.3.

◆

Using shadow prices, we may give an alternative interpretation of this result. We can use shadow prices to compute the implied value of the resources needed to construct a table (see Table 30). Since a table uses $35 worth of resources, the only way producing tables can increase Dakota's revenues is if a table sells for more than $35. Thus, the current basis fails to be optimal if $c_2 > 35$, and the current basis remains optimal if $c_2 \leq 35$.

Table 30	RESOURCE IN A TABLE	SHADOW PRICE OF RESOURCE	AMOUNT OF RESOURCE USED	VALUE OF RESOURCE USED
Why a Table Is Profitable at $> \$35$/Table	Lumber	$0	6 board ft	0(6) = \$0
	Finishing	$10	2 hours	10(2) = \$20
	Carpentry	$10	1.5 hours	10(1.5) = \$15
			Total:	= \$35

E X A M P L E 15

We wish to change the column for a nonbasic activity. Suppose a table sells for $43 and uses 5 board ft of lumber, 2 finishing hours, and 2 carpentry hours. Does the current basis remain optimal?

Solution

Changing the column for the nonbasic variable "tables" leaves the first and third dual constraints unchanged but changes the second dual constraint to

$$5y_1 + 2y_2 + 2y_3 \geq 43$$

Since $y_1 = 0$, $y_2 = 10$, $y_3 = 10$ does not satisfy the new second dual constraint, dual feasibility is not maintained, and the current basis is no longer optimal. In terms of shadow prices, this result is reasonable (see Table 31). Since each table uses $40 worth

Table 31	RESOURCE IN A TABLE	SHADOW PRICE OF RESOURCE	AMOUNT OF RESOURCE USED	VALUE OF RESOURCE USED
Shadow Price Interpretation of Table Production Decision ($40/Table)	Lumber	$0	5 board ft	0(5) = \$0
	Finishing	$10	2 hours	10(2) = \$20
	Carpentry	$10	2 hours	10(2) = \$20
			Total:	= \$40

of resources and sells for $43, Dakota can increase its revenue by 43 − 40 = $3 for each table that is produced. Thus, the current basis is no longer optimal, and x_2 (tables) will be basic in the new optimal solution.

◆

E X A M P L E 16

We wish to add a new activity. Suppose Dakota is considering manufacturing footstools (x_4). A footstool sells for $15 and uses 1 board ft of lumber, 1 finishing hour, and 1 carpentry hour. Does the current basis remain optimal?

Solution

Introducing the new activity (footstools) leaves the three dual constraints unchanged, but the new variable x_4 adds a new dual constraint (corresponding to footstools). The new dual constraint will be

$$y_1 + y_2 + y_3 \geq 15$$

The current basis remains optimal if $y_1 = 0$, $y_2 = 10$, $y_3 = 10$ satisfies the new dual constraint. Since $0 + 10 + 10 \geq 15$, the current basis remains optimal. In terms of shadow prices, a stool utilizes $1(0) = \$0$ worth of lumber, $1(10) = \$10$ worth of finishing hours, and $1(10) = \$10$ worth of carpentry time. Since a stool uses $0 + 10 + 10 = \$20$ worth of resources and sells for only $15, Dakota should not make footstools, and the current basis remains optimal.

◆

◆ PROBLEMS

GROUP A

1. For the Dakota problem, suppose computer tables sell for $35 and use 6 board ft of lumber, 2 hours of finishing time, and 1 hour of carpentry time. Is the current basis still optimal? Interpret this result in terms of shadow prices.

2. The following questions refer to the Sugarco problem (Problem 6 of Section 6.3):
(a) For what values of profit on a type 1 candy bar does the current basis remain optimal?
(b) If a type 1 candy bar used 0.5 oz of sugar and 0.75 oz of chocolate, would the current basis remain optimal?
(c) A type 4 candy bar is under consideration. A type 4 candy bar yields a 10¢ profit and uses 2 oz of sugar and 1 oz of chocolate. Does the current basis remain optimal?

3. Suppose, in the Dakota problem, a desk still sells for $60 but now uses 8 board ft of lumber, 4 finishing hours, and 15 carpentry hours. Determine whether the current basis remains optimal. What is wrong with the following reasoning?

The change in the column for desks leaves the second and third dual constraints unchanged and changes the first dual constraint to

$$8y_1 + 4y_2 + 15y_3 \geq 60$$

Since $y_1 = 0$, $y_2 = 10$, $y_3 = 10$ satisfies the new dual constraint, the current basis remains optimal.

6–10   COMPLEMENTARY SLACKNESS

The Theorem of Complementary Slackness is an important result that relates the optimal primal and dual solutions. To state this theorem, we assume that the primal is a normal max problem with variables $x_1, x_2, \ldots, x_n$ and $m \leq$ constraints. Let $s_1, s_2, \ldots, s_m$ be the slack variables for the primal. Then the dual is a normal min problem with variables $y_1, y_2, \ldots, y_m$ and $n \geq$ constraints. Let $e_1, e_2, \ldots, e_n$ be the excess variables for the dual. A statement of the Theorem of Complementary Slackness follows.

THEOREM 2   Let

$$\mathbf{x} = \begin{bmatrix} x_1 \\ x_2 \\ \vdots \\ x_n \end{bmatrix}$$

be a feasible primal solution and $\mathbf{y} = [\, y_1 \quad y_2 \quad \cdots \quad y_m \,]$ be a feasible dual solution. Then $\mathbf{x}$ is primal optimal and $\mathbf{y}$ is dual optimal if and only if

$$s_i y_i = 0 \qquad (i = 1, 2, \ldots, m) \tag{38}$$

$$e_j x_j = 0 \qquad (j = 1, 2, \ldots, n) \tag{39}$$

In Problem 4 at the end of this section, we sketch the proof of the Theorem of Complementary Slackness, but first we discuss the intuitive meaning of this theorem.

From (38), it follows that the optimal primal and dual solutions must satisfy

$$i\text{th primal slack} > 0 \text{ implies } i\text{th dual variable} = 0 \tag{40}$$

$$i\text{th dual variable} > 0 \text{ implies } i\text{th primal slack} = 0 \tag{41}$$

From (39), it follows that the optimal primal and dual solutions must satisfy

$$j\text{th dual excess} > 0 \text{ implies } j\text{th primal variable} = 0 \tag{42}$$

$$j\text{th primal variable} > 0 \text{ implies } j\text{th dual excess} = 0 \tag{43}$$

From (40) and (42), we see that if *a constraint in either the primal or dual is nonbinding* (*has either $s_i > 0$ or $e_j > 0$*), *then the corresponding variable in the other (or complementary) problem must equal zero.* Hence the name **complementary slackness**.

To illustrate the interpretation of the Theorem of Complementary Slackness, we return to the Dakota problem. Recall that the primal is

$$\max z = 60x_1 + 30x_2 + 20x_3$$

$$\begin{aligned}
\text{s.t.} \quad 8x_1 + \quad 6x_2 + \quad x_3 &\leq 48 \qquad \text{(Lumber constraint)} \\
4x_1 + \quad 2x_2 + 1.5x_3 &\leq 20 \qquad \text{(Finishing constraint)} \\
2x_1 + 1.5x_2 + 0.5x_3 &\leq 8 \qquad \text{(Carpentry constraint)} \\
x_1, x_2, x_3 &\geq 0
\end{aligned}$$

and the dual is

$$\min w = 48y_1 + 20y_2 + 8y_3$$

$$\begin{aligned}
\text{s.t.} \quad 8y_1 + \quad 4y_2 + \quad 2y_3 &\geq 60 \qquad \text{(Desk constraint)} \\
6y_1 + \quad 2y_2 + 1.5y_3 &\geq 30 \qquad \text{(Table constraint)} \\
y_1 + 1.5y_2 + 0.5y_3 &\geq 20 \qquad \text{(Chair constraint)} \\
y_1, y_2, y_3 &\geq 0
\end{aligned}$$

The optimal primal solution is

$$z = 280, \quad x_1 = 2, \quad x_2 = 0, \quad x_3 = 8$$
$$s_1 = 48 - (8(2) + 6(0) + 1(8)) = 24 \quad x_1 = 0$$
$$s_2 = 20 - (4(2) + 2(0) + 1.5(8)) = 0 \quad y_2$$
$$s_3 = 8 - (2(2) + 1.5(0) + 0.5(8)) = 0 \quad y_3$$

The optimal dual solution is

$$w = 280, \quad y_1 = 0, \quad y_2 = 10, \quad y_3 = 10$$
$$e_1 = (8(0) + 4(10) + 2(10)) - 60 = 0 \quad x_1$$
$$e_2 = (6(0) + 2(10) + 1.5(10)) - 30 = 5 \quad x_2 = 6$$
$$e_3 = (1(0) + 1.5(10) + 0.5(10)) - 20 = 0 \quad x_3$$

For the Dakota problem, (38) reduces to

$$s_1 y_1 = s_2 y_2 = s_3 y_3 = 0$$

which is indeed satisfied by the optimal primal and dual solutions. Also, (39) reduces to

$$e_1 x_1 = e_2 x_2 = e_3 x_3 = 0$$

which is also satisfied by the optimal primal and dual solutions.

We now illustrate the interpretation of (40)–(43). As an example of (40), note that (40) tells us that since the optimal primal solution has $s_1 > 0$, the optimal dual solution must have $y_1 = 0$. In the context of the Dakota problem, this means that positive slack in the lumber constraint implies that lumber must have a zero shadow price. Since slack in the lumber constraint means that extra lumber would not be used, an extra board foot of lumber should indeed be worthless.

As an example of (41), note that (41) tells us that since $y_2 > 0$ in the optimal dual solution, $s_2 = 0$ must hold in the optimal primal solution. This is reasonable, because $y_2 > 0$ means that an extra finishing hour has some value. This can only occur if we are at present using all available finishing hours (or equivalently, if $s_2 = 0$).

To illustrate (42), observe that (42) tells us that since $e_2 > 0$ in the optimal dual solution, $x_2 = 0$ must hold in the optimal primal solution. This is reasonable, because $e_2 = 6y_1 + 2y_2 + 1.5y_3 - 30$. Since y_1, y_2, and y_3 are resource shadow prices, e_2 may be written as

$$e_2 = \text{(value of resources used by a table)} - \text{(sales price of a table)}$$

Thus, if $e_2 > 0$, tables are selling for a price that is less than the value of the resources used to make 1 unit of x_2 (tables). This means that no tables should be made (or equivalently, that $x_2 = 0$). This shows that $e_2 > 0$ in the optimal dual solution implies that $x_2 = 0$ must hold in the optimal primal solution.

As an example of (43), note that for the Dakota problem, (43) tells us that $x_1 > 0$ for the optimal primal solution implies that $e_1 = 0$. This result simply reflects the following important fact. *For any variable x_j in the optimal primal basis, the marginal revenue obtained from producing a unit of x_j must equal the marginal cost of the resources used to produce a unit of x_j.* This is a consequence of the fact that each basic variable must have a zero coefficient in row 0 of the optimal primal tableau. In short, (43) is simply the LP version of the well-known economic maxim that an optimal production strategy must have marginal revenue equal marginal cost.

To be more specific, observe that $x_1 > 0$ means that desks are in the optimal basis. Then

$$\text{Marginal revenue obtained by manufacturing desk} = \$60$$

To compute the marginal cost of manufacturing a desk (in terms of shadow prices), note that

$$\text{Cost of lumber in desk} = 8(0) = \$0$$
$$\text{Cost of finishing hours used to make a desk} = 4(10) = \$40$$
$$\text{Cost of carpentry hours used to make a desk} = 2(10) = \$20$$
$$\text{Marginal cost of producing a desk} = 0 + 40 + 20 = \$60$$

Thus, for desks, marginal revenue is equal to marginal cost.

USING COMPLEMENTARY SLACKNESS TO SOLVE LPs

If the optimal solution to the primal or dual is known, complementary slackness can sometimes be used to determine the optimal solution to the complementary problem. For example, suppose we were told that the optimal solution to the Dakota problem was $z = 280$, $x_1 = 2$, $x_2 = 0$, $x_3 = 8$, $s_1 = 24$, $s_2 = 0$, $s_3 = 0$. Can we use Theorem 2 to help us find the optimal solution to the Dakota dual? Since $s_1 > 0$, (40) tells us that the optimal dual solution must have $y_1 = 0$. Since $x_1 > 0$ and $x_3 > 0$, (43) implies that the optimal dual solution must have $e_1 = 0$ and $e_3 = 0$. This means that for the optimal dual solution, the first and third constraints must be binding. Since we know that $y_1 = 0$, we know that the optimal values of y_2 and y_3 may be found by solving the first and third dual constraints as equalities (with $y_1 = 0$). Thus, the optimal values of y_2 and y_3 must satisfy

$$4y_2 + 2y_3 = 60 \quad \text{and} \quad 1.5y_2 + 0.5y_3 = 20$$

Solving these equations simultaneously shows that the optimal dual solution must have $y_2 = 10$ and $y_3 = 10$. Thus, complementary slackness has helped us find the optimal dual solution $y_1 = 0$, $y_2 = 10$, $y_3 = 10$. (From the Dual Theorem, we know, of course, that the optimal dual solution must have $\bar{w} = 280$.)

◆ PROBLEMS

GROUP A

1. Glassco manufactures wine glasses, beer glasses, champagne glasses, and whiskey glasses. Each type of glass uses time in the molding shop, time in the packaging shop, and a certain amount of glass. The resources required to make each type of glass are given in Table 32. At present, 600 minutes of molding time, 400 minutes of packaging time, and 500 oz of glass are available. Assuming that Glassco wants to maximize revenue, the following LP should be solved:

$$\max z = 6x_1 + 10x_2 + 9x_3 + 20x_4$$
$$\text{s.t.} \quad 4x_1 + 9x_2 + 7x_3 + 10x_4 \leq 600 \quad \text{(Molding constraint)}$$
$$x_1 + x_2 + 3x_3 + 40x_4 \leq 400 \quad \text{(Packaging constraint)}$$
$$3x_1 + 4x_2 + 2x_3 + x_4 \leq 500 \quad \text{(Glass constraint)}$$
$$x_1, x_2, x_3, x_4 \geq 0$$

It can be shown that the optimal solution to this LP is $z = \frac{2800}{3}$, $x_1 = \frac{400}{3}$, $x_4 = \frac{20}{3}$, $x_2 = 0$, $x_3 = 0$, $s_1 = 0$, $s_2 = 0$, $s_3 = \frac{280}{3}$.

(a) Find the dual of the Glassco problem.

(b) Using the given optimal primal solution and the Theorem of Complementary Slackness, find the optimal solution to the dual of the Glassco problem.

(c) Find an example of each of the complementary slackness conditions, (40)–(43). As in the text, interpret each of the examples in terms of shadow prices.

2. Use the Theorem of Complementary Slackness to show that in the LINDO output, the SLACK or SURPLUS and DUAL PRICE entries for any row cannot both be positive.

3. Consider the following LP:

$$\max z = 5x_1 + 3x_2 + x_3$$
$$\text{s.t.} \quad 2x_1 + x_2 + x_3 \leq 6$$
$$x_1 + 2x_2 + x_3 \leq 7$$
$$x_1, x_2, x_3 \geq 0$$

Graphically solve the dual of this LP. Then use complementary slackness to solve the max problem.

GROUP B

4. Let $\mathbf{x} = [x_1 \ x_2 \ x_3 \ s_1 \ s_2 \ s_3]$ be a primal feasible point for the Dakota problem and $\mathbf{y} = [y_1 \ y_2 \ y_3 \ e_1 \ e_2 \ e_3]$ be a dual feasible point.

(a) Multiply the ith constraint (in standard form) of the primal by y_i and add up the resulting constraints.

(b) Multiply the jth dual constraint (in standard form) by x_j and add them up.

(c) Compute: part (a) answer minus part (b) answer.

(d) Use the part (c) answer and the Dual Theorem to show that if $\mathbf{x}$ is primal optimal and $\mathbf{y}$ is dual optimal, then (38) and (39) hold.

(e) Use the part (c) answer to show that if (38) and (39) both hold, then $\mathbf{x}$ is primal optimal and $\mathbf{y}$ is dual optimal. (*Hint*: Look at Lemma 2).

Table 32

	x_1 WINE GLASS	x_2 BEER GLASS	x_3 CHAMPAGNE GLASS	x_4 WHISKEY GLASS
Molding time	4 minutes	9 minutes	7 minutes	10 minutes
Packaging time	1 minute	1 minute	3 minutes	40 minutes
Glass	3 oz	4 oz	2 oz	1 oz
Selling price	$6	$10	$9	$20

6-11 THE DUAL SIMPLEX METHOD

When we use the simplex method to solve a max problem (we will refer to the max problem as a primal), we begin with a primal feasible solution (because each constraint in the initial tableau has a nonnegative right-hand side). Since at least one variable in row 0 of the initial tableau has a negative coefficient, out initial primal solution is not dual feasible. Through a sequence of simplex pivots, we maintain primal feasibility and obtain an optimal solution when dual feasibility (a nonnegative row 0) is attained. In many situations, however, it is easier to solve an LP by beginning with a tableau in which each variable in row 0 has a nonnegative coefficient (so the tableau is dual feasible) and at least one constraint has a negative right-hand side (so the tableau is primal infeasible). The dual simplex method maintains a nonnegative row 0 (dual feasibility) and eventually obtains a tableau in which each right-hand side is nonnegative (primal feasibility). At this point, an optimal tableau has been obtained. Since this technique maintains dual feasibility, it is called the **dual simplex method**.

The dual simplex method can be applied (to a max problem) whenever there is a basic solution in which each variable has a nonnegative coefficient in row 0.

DUAL SIMPLEX METHOD FOR A MAX PROBLEM

Step 1 Is the right-hand side of each constraint nonnegative? If so, an optimal solution has been found; if not, at least one constraint has a negative right-hand side, and we go to Step 2.

Step 2 Choose the most negative basic variable as the variable to leave the basis. The row in which the variable is basic will be the pivot row. To select the variable that enters the basis, we compute the following ratio for each variable x_j that has a *negative* coefficient in the pivot row:

$$\frac{\text{Coefficient of } x_j \text{ in row 0}}{\text{Coefficient of } x_j \text{ in the pivot row}}$$

Choose the variable with the smallest ratio (in the sense of absolute value) as the entering variable. This form of the ratio test maintains a dual feasible tableau (all variables in row 0 have nonnegative coefficients). Now use ero's to make the entering variable a basic variable in the pivot row.

Step 3 If there is any constraint in which the right-hand side is negative and each variable has a nonnegative coefficient, the LP has no feasible solution. If no constraint indicating infeasibility is found, return to Step 1.

To illustrate the case of an infeasible LP, suppose the dual simplex method yielded a constraint such as $x_1 + 2x_2 + x_3 = -5$. Since $x_1 \geq 0$, $2x_2 \geq 0$, and $x_3 \geq 0$, $x_1 + 2x_2 + x_3 \geq 0$, and the constraint $x_1 + 2x_2 + x_3 = -5$ cannot be satisfied. In this case, the original LP must be infeasible.

We now discuss three uses of the dual simplex:

1. Finding the new optimal solution after a constraint is added to an LP
2. Finding the new optimal solution after changing a right-hand side of an LP
3. Solving a normal min problem

FINDING THE NEW OPTIMAL SOLUTION
AFTER A CONSTRAINT IS ADDED TO AN LP

The dual simplex method is often used to find the new optimal solution to an LP after a constraint is added. When a constraint is added, one of the following three cases will occur:

Case 1 The current optimal solution satisfies the new constraint.

Case 2 The current optimal solution does not satisfy the new constraint, but the LP still has a feasible solution.

Case 3 The additional constraint causes the LP to have no feasible solutions.

If Case 1 occurs, the current optimal solution satisfies the new constraint, and the current solution remains optimal. To illustrate why this is true, suppose we have added the constraint $x_1 + x_2 + x_3 \leq 11$ to the Dakota problem. The current optimal solution ($z = 280$, $x_1 = 2$, $x_2 = 0$, $x_3 = 8$) satisfies this constraint. To see why this solution remains optimal after the constraint $x_1 + x_2 + x_3 \leq 11$ is added, recall that adding a constraint to an LP either leaves the feasible region unchanged or eliminates points from the feasible region. In this case, the Section 6.8 discussion tells us that adding a constraint (to a max problem) either reduces the optimal z-value or leaves it unchanged. This means that if we add the constraint $x_1 + x_2 + x_3 \le 11$ to the Dakota problem, the new optimal z-value can be at most 280. Since the current solution is still feasible and has $z = 280$, it must still be optimal.

If Case 2 occurs, the current solution is no longer feasible, so it can no longer be optimal. The dual simplex method can be used to determine the new optimal solution. Suppose that in the Dakota problem, marketing considerations dictate that at least 1 table be manufactured. This adds the constraint $x_2 \ge 1$. Since the current optimal solution has $x_2 = 0$, it is no longer feasible and cannot be optimal. To find the new optimal solution, we subtract an excess variable e_4 from the constraint $x_2 \ge 1$. This yields the constraint $x_2 - e_4 = 1$. If we multiply this constraint through by -1, we obtain $-x_2 + e_4 = -1$, and we can use e_4 as a basic variable for this constraint. Appending this constraint to the optimal Dakota tableau yields Table 33.

Table 33 "Old" Optimal Dakota Tableau If $x_2 \ge 1$ Is Required		BASIC VARIABLE
$z \quad + 5x_2 \qquad\qquad + 10s_2 + 10s_3 \qquad\qquad = 280$		$z = 280$
$-\,2x_2 \qquad + s_1 + \quad 2s_2 - \quad 8s_3 \qquad\qquad = 24$		$s_1 = 24$
$-\,2x_2 + x_3 \qquad\quad + \quad 2s_2 - \quad 4s_3 \qquad\qquad = 8$		$x_3 = 8$
$x_1 + \tfrac{5}{4}x_2 \qquad\qquad - \tfrac{1}{2}s_2 + \tfrac{3}{2}s_3 \qquad\qquad = 2$		$x_1 = 2$
$-\;\boxed{x_2} \qquad\qquad\qquad\qquad\qquad + e_4 = -1$		$e_4 = -1$

Since we are using the row 0 from an optimal tableau, each variable has a non-negative coefficient in row 0, and we may proceed with the dual simplex method. The variable $e_4 = -1$ is the most negative basic variable, so e_4 will exit from the basis, and row 4 will be the pivot row. Since x_2 is the only variable with a negative coefficient in row 4, x_2 must enter into the basis (see Table 34).

Table 34 "New" Optimal Dakota Tableau If $x_2 \ge 1$ Is Required		BASIC VARIABLE
$z \qquad\qquad + 10s_2 + 10s_3 + 5e_4 = 275$		$z = 275$
$s_1 + \quad 2s_2 - \quad 8s_3 - 2e_4 = 26$		$s_1 = 26$
$x_3 + \quad 2s_2 - \quad 4s_3 - 2e_4 = 10$		$x_3 = 10$
$x_1 \qquad - \tfrac{1}{2}s_2 + \tfrac{3}{2}s_3 + \tfrac{5}{4}e_4 = \tfrac{3}{4}$		$x_1 = \tfrac{3}{4}$
$x_2 \qquad\qquad\qquad\qquad - e_4 = 1$		$x_2 = 1$

This is an optimal tableau. Thus, if the constraint $x_2 \ge 1$ is added to the Dakota problem, the optimal solution becomes $z = 275$, $s_1 = 26$, $x_3 = 10$, $x_1 = \tfrac{3}{4}$, $x_2 = 1$, which has reduced Dakota's objective function (revenue) by \$5 (the reduced cost for tables).

If we had wanted to, we could simply have added the constraint $x_2 \ge 1$ to the original Dakota initial tableau and used the regular simplex method to solve the problem. This would have entailed adding an artificial variable to the $x_2 \ge 1$ constraint and would probably have required many pivots. When we used the dual simplex to solve a problem again after a constraint has been added, we are taking advantage of the fact that we have already obtained a nonnegative row 0 and that most of our right-hand sides have nonnegative coefficients. This is why the dual simplex usually requires relatively few pivots to find a new optimal solution when a constraint is added to an LP.

If Case 3 occurs, Step 3 of the dual simplex method allows us to show that the LP is now infeasible. To illustrate the idea, suppose we add the constraint $x_1 + x_2 \geq 12$ to the Dakota problem. After subtracting an excess variable e_4 from this constraint, we obtain

$$x_1 + x_2 - e_4 = 12 \quad \text{or} \quad -x_1 - x_2 + e_4 = -12$$

Appending this constraint to the optimal Dakota tableau yields Table 35.

Table 35
"Old" Optimal Dakota Tableau If $x_1 + x_2 \geq 12$ Is Required

	BASIC VARIABLE
$z \quad + \quad 5x_2 \qquad\qquad + 10s_2 + 10s_3 \qquad = 280$	$z = 280$
$\quad - \quad 2x_2 \quad + s_1 + \quad 2s_2 - \quad 8s_3 \qquad = 24$	$s_1 = 24$
$\quad - \quad 2x_2 + x_3 \qquad + \quad 2s_2 - \quad 4s_3 \qquad = 8$	$x_3 = 8$
$x_1 + 1.25x_2 \qquad\qquad - 0.5s_2 + 1.5s_3 \qquad = 2$	$x_1 = 2$
$-x_1 - \qquad x_2 \qquad\qquad\qquad\qquad\qquad + e_4 = -12$	$e_4 = -12$

Since x_1 appears in the new constraint, it seems that x_1 can no longer be used as a basic variable for row 3. To remedy this problem, we eliminate x_1 (and in general all basic variables) from the new constraint by replacing row 4 by row 3 + row 4 (see Table 36). Since $e_4 = -10$ is the most negative basic variable, e_4 will leave the basis and row 4 will be the pivot row. The variable s_2 is the only one with a negative coefficient in row 4, so s_2 enters the basis and becomes a basic variable in row 4 (see Table 37). Now x_3 must leave the basis, and row 2 will be the pivot row. Since x_2 is the only variable in row 2 with a negative coefficient, x_2 now enters the basis (see Table 38). Since $x_1 \geq 0$, $x_3 \geq 0$, $2s_3 \geq 0$, and $3e_4 \geq 0$, the left side of row 3 must be nonnegative and cannot equal -20. Hence, the Dakota problem with the additional constraint $x_1 + x_2 \geq 12$ has no feasible solution.

Table 36
e_4 Is Now a Basic Variable in Row 4

	BASIC VARIABLE
$z \quad + \quad 5x_2 \qquad\qquad + 10s_2 + 10s_3 \qquad\quad = 280$	$z = 280$
$\quad - \quad 2x_2 \quad + s_1 + \quad 2s_2 - \quad 8s_3 \qquad\quad = 24$	$s_1 = 24$
$\quad - \quad 2x_2 + x_3 \qquad + \quad 2s_2 - \quad 4s_3 \qquad\quad = 8$	$x_3 = 8$
$x_1 + 1.25x_2 \qquad\qquad - 0.5s_2 + 1.5s_3 \qquad\quad = 2$	$x_1 = 2$
$0.25x_2 \qquad\qquad - 0.5s_2 + (1.5s_3) + e_4 = -10$	$e_4 = -10$

Table 37
s_2 Enters the Basis in Row 4

	BASIC VARIABLE
$z \quad + \quad 10x_2 \qquad\qquad + 40s_3 + 20e_4 = 80$	$z = 80$
$\quad - \quad x_2 \qquad + s_1 \qquad - \quad 2s_3 + \quad 4e_4 = -16$	$s_1 = -16$
$\quad - \quad (x_2) + x_3 \qquad + \quad 2s_3 + \quad 4e_4 = -32$	$x_3 = -32$
$x_1 + \quad x_2 \qquad\qquad\qquad\qquad - \quad e_4 = 12$	$x_2 = 12$
$\quad - 0.5x_2 \qquad\qquad + s_2 - \quad 3s_3 - \quad 2e_4 = 20$	$s_2 = 20$

Table 38		BASIC VARIABLE
Tableau Indicating Infeasibility of Dakota Example When $x_1 + x_2 \geq 12$ Is Required	$z + 10x_3 \quad\quad + 60s_3 + 60e_4 = -240$ $\quad - x_3 + s_1 \quad - 4s_3 \quad\quad = 16$ $x_2 - x_3 \quad\quad - 2s_3 - 4e_4 = 32$ $x_1 + x_3 \quad\quad + 2s_3 + 3e_4 = -20$ $\quad - 0.5x_3 \quad + s_2 - 4s_3 - 4e_4 = 36$	$z = -240$ $s_1 = 16$ $x_2 = 32$ $x_1 = -20$ $s_2 = 36$

FINDING THE NEW OPTIMAL SOLUTION AFTER CHANGING A RIGHT-HAND SIDE

If the right-hand side of a constraint is changed and the current basis becomes infeasible, the dual simplex can be used to find the new optimal solution. To illustrate, suppose that 30 finishing hours are now available. In Section 6.3, we showed that this changed the current optimal tableau to that shown in Table 39.

Table 39		BASIC VARIABLE
"Old" Optimal Dakota Tableau If 30 Finishing Hours Are Available	$z + 5x_2 \quad\quad + 10s_2 + 10s_3 = 380$ $\quad - 2x_2 \quad + s_1 + 2s_2 - 8s_3 = 44$ $\quad - 2x_2 + x_3 \quad + 2s_2 - 4s_3 = 28$ $x_1 + 1.25x_2 \quad - (0.5s_2) + 1.5s_3 = -3$	$z = 380$ $s_1 = 44$ $x_3 = 28$ $x_1 = -3$

Since each variable in row 0 has a nonnegative coefficient, the dual simplex method may be used to find the new optimal solution. The variable x_1 is the most negative one, so x_1 must leave the basis, and row 3 will be the pivot row. Since s_2 has the only negative coefficient in row 3, s_2 will enter the basis (see Table 40).

Table 40		BASIC VARIABLE
"New" Optimal Dakota Tableau If 30 Finishing Hours Are Available	$z + 20x_1 + 30x_2 \quad\quad + 40s_3 = 320$ $4x_1 + 3x_2 \quad + s_1 \quad - 2s_3 = 32$ $4x_1 + 3x_2 + x_3 \quad\quad + 2s_3 = 16$ $\quad - 2x_1 - 2.5x_2 \quad\quad + s_2 - 3s_3 = 6$	$z = 320$ $s_1 = 32$ $x_3 = 16$ $s_2 = 6$

This is an optimal tableau. If 30 finishing hours are available, the new optimal solution to the Dakota problem is to manufacture 16 chairs, 0 tables, and 0 desks. Of course, if we change the right-hand side of a constraint, it is possible that the LP will be infeasible. Step 3 of the dual simplex algorithm will indicate whether this is the case.

SOLVING A NORMAL MIN PROBLEM

To illustrate how the dual simplex can be used to solve a normal min problem, we solve the following LP:

$$\min z = x_1 + 2x_2$$
$$\text{s.t.} \quad x_1 - 2x_2 + x_3 \geq 4$$
$$2x_1 + x_2 - x_3 \geq 6$$
$$x_1, x_2, x_3 \geq 0$$

We begin by multiplying z by -1 to convert the LP to a max problem with objective function $z' = -x_1 - 2x_2$. After subtracting excess variables e_1 and e_2 from the two constraints, we obtain the initial tableau in Table 41. Since each variable has a non-negative coefficient in row 0, the dual simplex method can be applied. Before proceeding, we need to find the basic variables for the constraints. If we multiply each constraint through by -1, we can use e_1 and e_2 as basic variables. This yields the tableau in Table 42. At least one constraint has a negative right-hand side, so this is not an optimal tableau, and we proceed to Step 2.

Table 41
Initial Tableau for Solving Normal Min Problem

$$
\begin{aligned}
z' + x_1 + 2x_2 &= 0 \\
x_1 - 2x_2 + x_3 - e_1 &= 4 \\
2x_1 + x_2 - x_3 - e_2 &= 6
\end{aligned}
$$

Table 42
Initial Tableau in Canonical Form

		BASIC VARIABLE
$z' + x_1 + 2x_2 = 0$		$z' = 0$
$-x_1 + 2x_2 - x_3 + e_1 = -4$		$e_1 = -4$
$-\boxed{2x_1} - x_2 + x_3 + e_2 = -6$		$e_2 = -6$

We choose the most negative basic variable (e_2) to exit from the basis. Since e_2 is basic in row 2, row 2 will be the pivot row. To determine the entering variable, we find the following ratios:

$$x_1 \text{ ratio} = 1/-2 = -\tfrac{1}{2}$$
$$x_2 \text{ ratio} = 2/-1 = -2$$

The smaller ratio (in absolute value) is the x_1 ratio, so we use ero's to enter x_1 into the basis in row 2 (see Table 43).[†]

Table 43
First Dual Simplex Tableau

		BASIC VARIABLE
$z' + \tfrac{3}{2}x_2 + \tfrac{1}{2}x_3 + \tfrac{1}{2}e_2 = -3$		$z' = -3$
$\tfrac{5}{2}x_2 - \boxed{\tfrac{3}{2}x_3} + e_1 - \tfrac{1}{2}e_2 = -1$		$e_1 = -1$
$x_1 + \tfrac{1}{2}x_2 - \tfrac{1}{2}x_3 - \tfrac{1}{2}e_2 = 3$		$x_1 = 3$

Since there is no constraint indicating infeasibility (Step 3), we return to Step 1. The first constraint has a negative right-hand side, so the tableau is not optimal, and we go to Step 2. Since $e_1 = -1$ is the most negative basic variable, e_1 will exit from the basis, and row 1 will be the pivot row. The possible entering variables are x_3 and e_2. The relevant ratios are

$$x_3 \text{ ratio} = \tfrac{1}{2}/-\tfrac{3}{2} = -\tfrac{1}{3}$$
$$e_2 \text{ ratio} = \tfrac{1}{2}/-\tfrac{1}{2} = -1$$

[†]The interested reader may verify that if we had made an error in performing the ratio test and had chosen x_2 to enter the basis, a negative coefficient in row 0 would have resulted, and dual feasibility would have been destroyed.

The smallest ratio (in absolute value) is $-\frac{1}{3}$, so x_3 will enter the basis in row 1. After pivoting in x_3, the new tableau is as shown in Table 44.[†] Since each right-hand side is nonnegative, this is an optimal tableau. The original problem was a min problem, so the optimal solution to the original min problem is $z = \frac{10}{3}$, $x_1 = \frac{10}{3}$, $x_3 = \frac{2}{3}$, and $x_2 = 0$.

Observe that each dual simplex tableau (except the optimal dual simplex tableau) has a z'-value exceeding the optimal z'-value. For this reason, we say that the dual simplex tableaus are superoptimal. As the dual simplex proceeds, each pivot brings us closer to a primal feasible solution. Each pivot (barring degeneracy) decreases z', and we are "less superoptimal." Once primal feasibility is obtained, our solution is optimal.

Table 44
Optimal Tableau for
Dual Simplex
Example

	BASIC VARIABLE
$z' \quad + \frac{7}{3}x_2 \quad + \frac{1}{3}e_1 + \frac{1}{3}e_2 = -\frac{10}{3}$	$z' = -\frac{10}{3}$
$- \frac{5}{3}x_2 + x_3 - \frac{2}{3}e_1 + \frac{1}{3}e_2 = \frac{2}{3}$	$x_3 = \frac{2}{3}$
$x_1 - \frac{1}{3}x_2 \quad - \frac{1}{3}e_1 - \frac{1}{3}e_2 = \frac{10}{3}$	$x_1 = \frac{10}{3}$

◆ PROBLEMS

GROUP A

1. Use the dual simplex method to solve the following LP:

$$\max z = -2x_1 - x_3$$
$$\text{s.t.} \quad x_1 + x_2 - x_3 \geq 5$$
$$x_1 - 2x_2 + 4x_3 \geq 8$$
$$x_1, x_2, x_3 \geq 0$$

2. In solving the following LP, we obtain the optimal tableau shown in Table 45.

$$\max z = 6x_1 + x_2$$
$$\text{s.t.} \quad x_1 + x_2 \leq 5$$
$$2x_1 + x_2 \leq 6$$
$$x_1, x_2 \geq 0$$

Table 45

	BASIC VARIABLE
$z \quad + \quad 2x_2 \quad + \quad 3s_2 = 18$	$z = 18$
$0.5x_2 + s_1 - 0.5s_2 = 2$	$s_1 = 2$
$x_1 + 0.5x_2 \quad + 0.5s_2 = 3$	$x_1 = 3$

(a) Find the optimal solution to this LP if we add the constraint $3x_1 + x_2 \leq 10$.
(b) Find the optimal solution if we add the constraint $x_1 - x_2 \geq 6$.
(c) Find the optimal solution if we add the constraint $8x_1 + x_2 \leq 12$.

3. Find the new optimal solution to the Dakota problem if only 20 board ft of lumber are available.

4. Find the new optimal solution to the Dakota problem if 15 carpentry hours are available.

◆ SUMMARY

GRAPHICAL SENSITIVITY ANALYSIS

To determine whether the current basis remains optimal after changing an objective function coefficient, note that changing the objective function coefficient of a variable changes the slope of the isoprofit line. The current basis remains optimal as long as the

---

[†]If we had chosen to enter into the basis any variable with a positive coefficient in the pivot row, we would have ended up with some negative entries in row 0. This is why any variable that is entered into the basis must have a negative coefficient in the pivot row.

current optimal solution is the last point in the feasible region to make contact with isoprofit lines as we move in the direction of increasing z (for a max problem). If the current basis remains optimal, the values of the decision variables remain unchanged, but the optimal z-value may change.

To determine whether the current basis remains optimal after changing the right-hand side of a constraint, begin by finding the constraints (possibly including sign restrictions) that are binding for the current optimal solution. As we change the right-hand side of a constraint, the current basis remains optimal as long as the point where the constraints are binding remains feasible. Even if the current basis remains optimal, the values of the decision variables and the optimal z-value may change.

SHADOW PRICES

The **shadow price** of the ith constraint of a linear programming program problem is the amount by which the optimal z-value is improved if the right-hand side of the ith constraint is increased by 1. The shadow price of the ith constraint is the DUAL PRICE for row $i + 1$ given on the LINDO output.

NOTATION

BV_i = basic variable for ith constraint in the optimal tableau

$\mathbf{c}_{BV}$ = row vector whose ith element is the objective function coefficient for BV_i in the LP

$\mathbf{a}_j$ = column for variable x_j in constraints of original LP

$\mathbf{b}$ = right-hand side vector for original LP

$\bar{c}_j$ = coefficient of x_j in row 0 of the optimal tableau

HOW TO COMPUTE OPTIMAL TABLEAU FROM INITIAL LP

Column for x_j in optimal tableau's constraints = $B^{-1}\mathbf{a}_j$ (5)

Right-hand side of optimal tableau's constraints = $B^{-1}\mathbf{b}$ (6)

$\bar{c}_j = \mathbf{c}_{BV} B^{-1} \mathbf{a}_j - c_j$ (10)

Coefficient of slack variable s_i in optimal row 0

  = ith element of $\mathbf{c}_{BV} B^{-1}$ (10')

Coefficient of excess variable e_i in optimal row 0

  = $-(i$th element of $\mathbf{c}_{BV} B^{-1})$ (10'')

Coefficient of artificial variable a_i in optimal row 0

  = $(i$th element of $\mathbf{c}_{BV} B^{-1}) + M$ (10''')

Right-hand side of optimal row 0 = $\mathbf{c}_{BV} B^{-1} \mathbf{b}$ (11)

SENSITIVITY ANALYSIS

For a max problem, a tableau is optimal if and only if each variable has a nonnegative coefficient in row 0 and each constraint has a nonnegative right-hand side. For a min problem, a tableau is optimal if and only if each variable has a nonpositive coefficient in row 0 and each constraint has a nonnegative right-hand side.

If the current basis remains optimal after changing the objective function coefficient of a nonbasic variable, the values of the decision variables and the optimal z-value remain unchanged.

If the current basis remains optimal after changing the objective function coefficient of a basic variable, the values of the decision variables remain unchanged, but the optimal z-value may change.

If the current basis remains optimal after changing a right-hand side, the values of the decision variables and the optimal z-value may change. The new values of the decision variables may be found by computing B^{-1}(new right-hand side vector). The new optimal z-value may be determined by using shadow prices or Eq. (11).

OBJECTIVE FUNCTION COEFFICIENT RANGE

The OBJ COEFFICIENT RANGES section of the LINDO output gives the range of values for an objective function coefficient for which the current basis remains optimal. Within this range, the values of the decision variables remain unchanged, but the optimal z-value may or may not change.

REDUCED COST

For any nonbasic variable, the reduced cost for the variable is the amount by which the nonbasic variable's objective function coefficient must be improved before that variable will be a basic variable in some optimal solution to the LP.

RIGHT-HAND SIDE RANGE

If the right-hand side of a constraint remains within the right-hand side range given on the LINDO printout, the current basis remains optimal, and the LINDO listing for the constraint's dual price may be used to determine how a change in the constraint's right-hand side changes the optimal z-value. Even if the right-hand side of a constraint remains within the right-hand side range on the LINDO output, the values of the decision variables will probably change.

FINDING THE DUAL OF AN LP

For a normal (all $\leq$ constraints and all variables nonnegative) max problem or a normal min (all $\geq$ constraints and all variables nonnegative) problem, we find the dual as follows:

If we read the primal across in Table 14, we read the dual down. If we read the primal down in Table 14, we read the dual across. We use x_i's and z as variables for a maximization problem and y_j's and w as variables for a minimization problem.

To find the dual of a nonnormal max problem,

Step 1 Fill in Table 14 so that the primal can be read across.

Step 2 After making the following changes, the dual can be read down in the usual fashion: (a) If the ith primal constraint is a $\geq$ constraint, the corresponding dual variable y_i must satisfy $y_i \leq 0$. (b) If the ith primal constraint is an equality constraint, the dual variable y_i is now unrestricted in sign. (c) If the ith primal variable is urs, the ith dual constraint will be an equality constraint.

To find the dual of a nonnormal min problem,

Step 1 Write out the primal so it can be read down in Table 14.

Step 2 Except for the following changes, the dual can be read across the table: (a) If the ith primal constraint is a $\leq$ constraint, then the corresponding dual variable x_i must satisfy $x_i \leq 0$. (b) If the ith primal constraint is an equality constraint, then the corresponding dual variable x_i will be urs. (c) If the ith primal variable y_i is urs, then the ith dual constraint is an equality constraint.

THE DUAL THEOREM

Suppose BV is an optimal basis for the primal. Then $\mathbf{c}_{BV} B^{-1}$ is an optimal solution to the dual. Also, $\bar{z} = \bar{w}$.

FINDING THE OPTIMAL SOLUTION TO THE DUAL OF AN LP

If the primal is a max problem, then the optimal dual solution may be read from row 0 of the optimal tableau by using the following rules:

$$\begin{matrix} \text{Optimal value of dual variable } y_i \\ \text{if constraint } i \text{ is a } \leq \text{ constraint} \end{matrix} = \text{coefficient of } s_i \text{ in optimal row 0} \qquad (31)$$

$$\begin{matrix} \text{Optimal value of dual variable } y_i \\ \text{if constraint } i \text{ is a } \geq \text{ constraint} \end{matrix} = -(\text{coefficient of } e_i \text{ in optimal row 0}) \qquad (31')$$

$$\begin{matrix} \text{Optimal value of dual variable } y_i \\ \text{if constraint } i \text{ is an equality} \\ \text{constraint} \end{matrix} = (\text{coefficient of } a_i \text{ in optimal row 0}) - M \qquad (31'')$$

If the primal is a min problem, the optimal dual solution may be read from row 0 of the optimal tableau by using the following rules:

$$\begin{matrix} \text{Optimal value of dual variable } x_i \\ \text{if constraint } i \text{ is a } \leq \text{ constraint} \end{matrix} = \text{coefficient of } s_i \text{ in optimal row 0}$$

$$\begin{matrix} \text{Optimal value of dual variable } x_i \\ \text{if constraint } i \text{ is a } \geq \text{ constraint} \end{matrix} = -(\text{coefficient of } e_i \text{ in optimal row 0})$$

$$\begin{matrix} \text{Optimal value of dual variable } x_i \\ \text{if constraint } i \text{ is an equality} \\ \text{constraint} \end{matrix} = (\text{coefficient of } a_i \text{ in optimal row 0}) + M$$

SHADOW PRICES (AGAIN)

For a maximization LP, the shadow price of the ith constraint is the value of the ith dual variable in the optimal dual solution. For a minimization LP, the shadow price of the ith constraint $= -(i$th dual variable in the optimal dual solution). The shadow price of the ith constraint is found in row $i + 1$ of the DUAL PRICES portion of the LINDO printout.

New optimal z-value $= $ (old optimal z-value)

$$+ \text{(constraint } i\text{'s shadow price) } \Delta b_i \qquad \text{(max problem)} \qquad (37)$$

New optimal z-value $=$ (old optimal z-value)

$$- \text{(constraint } i\text{'s shadow price) } \Delta b_i \quad \text{(min problem)} \quad (37')$$

A $\geq$ constraint will have a nonpositive shadow price; a $\leq$ constraint will have a nonnegative shadow price; and an equality constraint may have a positive, negative, or zero shadow price.

DUALITY AND SENSITIVITY ANALYSIS

Our proof of the Dual Theorem showed that if a set of basic variables BV is feasible, then BV is optimal (that is, each variable in row 0 has a nonnegative coefficient) if and only if the associated dual solution, $\mathbf{c}_{BV}B^{-1}$, is dual feasible.

This result can be used to yield an alternative way of doing the following types of sensitivity analysis:

Change 1 Changing the objective function coefficient of a nonbasic variable

Change 4 Changing the column for a nonbasic variable

Change 5 Adding a new activity

In each case, simply determine whether a change in the original LP maintains dual feasibility. If dual feasibility is maintained, the current basis remains optimal. If dual feasibility is not maintained, then the current basis is no longer optimal.

COMPLEMENTARY SLACKNESS

THEOREM 2 Let

$$\mathbf{x} = \begin{bmatrix} x_1 \\ x_2 \\ \vdots \\ x_n \end{bmatrix}$$

be a feasible primal solution and $\mathbf{y} = [y_1 \quad y_2 \quad \cdots \quad y_m]$ be a feasible dual solution. Then $\mathbf{x}$ is primal optimal and $\mathbf{y}$ is dual optimal if and only if

$$s_i y_i = 0 \quad (i = 1, 2, \ldots, m) \tag{38}$$

$$e_j x_j = 0 \quad (j = 1, 2, \ldots, n) \tag{39}$$

THE DUAL SIMPLEX METHOD

The dual simplex method can be applied (to a max problem) whenever there is a basic solution in which each variable has a nonnegative coefficient in row 0. If we have found such a basic solution, the dual simplex method proceeds as follows:

Step 1 Is the right-hand side of each constraint nonnegative? If so, an optimal solution has been found; if not, at least one constraint has a negative right-hand side, and we go to Step 2.

Step 2 Choose the most negative basic variable as the variable to leave the basis. The row in which this variable is basic will be the pivot row. To select the variable that enters the basis, we compute the following ratio for each variable x_j that has a *negative* coefficient in the pivot row:

$$\frac{\text{Coefficient of } x_j \text{ in row } 0}{\text{Coefficient of } x_j \text{ in the pivot row}}$$

Choose the variable that has the smallest ratio (in the sense of absolute value) as the entering variable. Now use ero's to make the entering variable a basic variable in the pivot row.

Step 3 If there is any constraint in which the right-hand side is negative and each variable has a nonnegative coefficient, the LP has no feasible solution. The fact that the LP has no feasible solution would be indicated by the presence (after possibly several pivots) of a constraint such as $x_1 + 2x_2 + x_3 = -5$. If no constraint indicating infeasibility is found, return to Step 1.

The dual simplex method is often used in the following situations:

1. Finding the new optimal solution after a constraint is added to an LP

2. Finding the new optimal solution after changing an LP's right-hand side

3. Solving a normal min problem

◆ REVIEW PROBLEMS

All problems from Sections 5.2 and 5.3 are relevant, along with Chapter 5 Review Problems 1, 2, 6, and 7.

GROUP A

1. Consider the following LP and its optimal tableau (Table 46):

$$\max z = 4x_1 + x_2$$
$$\text{s.t.} \quad x_1 + 2x_2 = 6$$
$$\quad x_1 - x_2 \geq 3$$
$$\quad 2x_1 + x_2 \leq 10$$
$$\quad x_1, x_2 \geq 0$$

Table 46

z	x_1	x_2	e_2	s_3	a_1	a_2	rhs
1	0	0	0	$\frac{7}{3}$	$M - \frac{2}{3}$	M	$\frac{58}{3}$
0	0	1	0	$-\frac{1}{3}$	$\frac{2}{3}$	0	$\frac{2}{3}$
0	1	0	0	$\frac{2}{3}$	$-\frac{1}{3}$	0	$\frac{14}{3}$
0	0	0	1	1	-1	-1	1

(a) Find the dual of this LP and its optimal solution.
(b) Find the range of values on b_3 for which the current basis remains optimal. If $b_3 = 11$, what would be the new optimal solution?

2. For the LP in Problem 1, graphically determine the range of values on c_1 for which the current basis remains optimal. (*Hint*: The feasible region for the LP in Problem 1 is a line segment.)

3. Consider the following LP and its optimal tableau (Table 47):

$$\max z = 5x_1 + x_2 + 2x_3$$
$$\text{s.t.} \quad x_1 + x_2 + x_3 \leq 6$$
$$\quad 6x_1 \quad + x_3 \leq 8$$
$$\quad x_2 + x_3 \leq 2$$
$$\quad x_1, x_2, x_3 \geq 0$$

Table 47

z	x_1	x_2	x_3	s_1	s_2	s_3	rhs
1	0	$\frac{1}{6}$	0	0	$\frac{5}{6}$	$\frac{7}{6}$	9
0	0	$\frac{1}{6}$	0	1	$-\frac{1}{6}$	$-\frac{5}{6}$	3
0	1	$-\frac{1}{6}$	0	0	$\frac{1}{6}$	$-\frac{1}{6}$	1
0	0	1	1	0	0	1	2

(a) Find the dual to this LP and its optimal solution.
(b) Find the range of values on c_1 for which the current basis remains optimal.

(c) Find the range of values on c_2 for which the current basis remains optimal.

4. Carco manufactures cars and trucks. Each car contributes \$300 to profit, and each truck contributes \$400 to profit. The resources required to manufacture a car and a truck are shown in Table 48. Each day, Carco can rent up to 98 type 1 machines at a cost of \$50 per machine. At present, the company has 73 type 2 machines and 260 tons of steel available. Marketing considerations dictate that at least 88 cars and at least 26 trucks be produced. Let

$$X1 = \text{number of cars produced daily}$$

$$X2 = \text{number of trucks produced daily}$$

$$M1 = \text{type 1 machines rented daily}$$

Table 48

	DAYS ON TYPE 1 MACHINE	DAYS ON TYPE 2 MACHINE	TONS OF STEEL
Car	0.8	0.6	2
Truck	1	0.7	3

In order to maximize profit, Carco should solve the LP given in Figure 9. Use the LINDO output to answer the following questions:

(a) If cars contributed \$310 to profit, what would be the new optimal solution to the problem?

(b) What is the most that Carco should be willing to pay to rent an additional type 1 machine for 1 day?

(c) What is the most that Carco should be willing to pay for an extra ton of steel?

(d) If Carco were required to produce at least 86 cars, what would Carco's profit become?

(e) Carco is considering producing jeeps. A jeep contributes \$600 to profit and requires 1.2 days on machine 1, 2 days on machine 2, and 4 tons of steel. Should Carco produce any jeeps?

5. The following LP has the optimal tableau shown in Table 49:

$$\max z = 4x_1 + x_2$$

$$\text{s.t.} \quad 3x_1 + x_2 \geq 6$$

$$2x_1 + x_2 \geq 4$$

$$x_1 + x_2 = 3$$

$$x_1, x_2 \geq 0$$

(a) Find the dual of this LP and its optimal solution.

(b) Find the range of values on the objective function

Figure 9 LINDO Output for Carco (Problem 4)

```
MAX    300 X1 + 400 X2 - 50 M1
SUBJECT TO
      2)   0.8 X1 +  X2 - M1 <=    0
      3)      M1 <=   98
      4)   0.6 X1 + 0.7 X2 <=   73
      5)   2 X1 + 3 X2 <=   260
      6)      X1 >=   88
      7)      X2 >=   26
END

   LP OPTIMUM FOUND AT STEP     1

       OBJECTIVE FUNCTION VALUE

  1)        32540.0000

VARIABLE         VALUE          REDUCED COST
    X1        88.000000          0.000000
    X2        27.599998          0.000000
    M1        98.000000          0.000000

   ROW    SLACK OR SURPLUS      DUAL PRICES
    2)        0.000000         400.000000
    3)        0.000000         350.000000
    4)        0.879999           0.000000
    5)        1.200003           0.000000
    6)        0.000000         -20.000000
    7)        1.599999           0.000000

NO. ITERATIONS=      1

RANGES IN WHICH THE BASIS IS UNCHANGED

                      OBJ COEFFICIENT RANGES
VARIABLE       CURRENT      ALLOWABLE      ALLOWABLE
                COEF        INCREASE       DECREASE
    X1       300.000000     20.000000      INFINITY
    X2       400.000000     INFINITY       25.000000
    M1       -50.000000     INFINITY      350.000000

                      RIGHTHAND SIDE RANGES
   ROW         CURRENT      ALLOWABLE      ALLOWABLE
                RHS         INCREASE       DECREASE
    2          0.000000      0.400001       1.599999
    3         98.000000      0.400001       1.599999
    4         73.000000      INFINITY       0.879999
    5        260.000000      INFINITY       1.200003
    6         88.000000      1.999999       3.000008
    7         26.000000      1.599999       INFINITY
```

Table 49

z	x_1	x_2	e_1	e_2	a_1	a_2	a_3	rhs
1	0	3	0	0	M	M	M + 4	12
0	1	1	0	0	0	0	1	3
0	0	2	1	0	−1	0	3	3
0	0	1	0	1	0	−1	2	2

coefficient of x_2 for which the current basis remains optimal.

(c) Find the range of values for the objective function coefficient of x_1 for which the current basis remains optimal.

6. Consider the following LP and its optimal tableau (Table 50):

$$\max z = 3x_1 + x_2 - x_3$$

$$\text{s.t.} \quad 2x_1 + x_2 + x_3 \leq 8$$

$$4x_1 + x_2 - x_3 \leq 10$$

$$x_1, x_2, x_3 \geq 0$$

Table 50

z	x_1	x_2	x_3	s_1	s_2	rhs
1	0	0	1	$\frac{1}{2}$	$\frac{1}{2}$	9
0	0	1	3	2	-1	6
0	1	0	-1	$-\frac{1}{2}$	$\frac{1}{2}$	1

(a) Find the dual of this LP and its optimal solution.
(b) Find the range of values on b_2 for which the current basis remains optimal. If $b_2 = 12$, what is the new optimal solution?

7. Consider the following LP:

$$\max z = 3x_1 + 4x_2$$
$$\text{s.t.} \quad 2x_1 + x_2 \leq 8$$
$$4x_1 + x_2 \leq 10$$
$$x_1, x_2 \geq 0$$

The optimal solution to this LP is $z = 32$, $x_1 = 0$, $x_2 = 8$, $s_1 = 0$, $s_2 = 2$. Graphically find the range of values for c_1 for which the current basis remains optimal.

8. Wivco produces product 1 and product 2 by processing raw material. Up to 90 lb of raw material may be purchased at a cost of $10/lb. One pound of raw material can be used to produce either 1 lb of product 1 or 0.33 lb of product 2. Using a pound of raw material to produce a pound of product 1 requires 2 hours of labor. Using a pound of raw material to produce 0.33 lb of product 2 requires 3 hours of labor. 200 hours of labor are available, and at most 40 pounds of product 2 can be sold. Product 1 sells for $13/lb, and product 2 sells for $40/lb. Let

RM = pounds of raw material processed
P1 = pounds of raw material used to product produce 1
P2 = pounds of raw material used to produce product 2

In order to maximize profit, Wivco should solve the following LP:

$$\max z = 13\text{P1} + 40(0.33)\text{P2} - 10\text{RM}$$
$$\text{s.t.} \quad \text{RM} \geq \text{P1} + \text{P2}$$
$$2\text{P1} + 3\text{P2} \leq 200$$
$$\text{RM} \leq 90$$
$$0.33\text{P2} \leq 40$$
$$\text{P1, P2, RM} \geq 0$$

Use the LINDO output in Figure 10 to answer the following questions:
(a) If only 87 lb of raw material could be purchased, what would be Wivco's profits?
(b) If product 2 sold for $39.50/lb, what would be the new optimal solution to Wivco's problem?
(c) What is the most that Wivco should be willing to pay for another pound of raw material?
(d) What is the most that Wivco should be willing to pay for another hour of labor?
(e) Suppose that 1 lb of raw material could also be used to produce 0.8 lb of product 3. Product 3 sells for $24/lb, and processing 1 lb of raw material into 0.8 lb of product 3 requires 7 hours of labor. Should Wivco produce any of product 3?

Figure 10 LINDO Output for Wivco (Problem 8)

```
MAX     13 P1 + 13.2 P2 - 10 RM
SUBJECT TO
    2)  -  P1 -  P2 + RM >=    0
    3)    2 P1 + 3 P2 <=   200
    4)       RM <=    90
    5)    0.33 P2 <=    40
END

    LP OPTIMUM FOUND AT STEP    3

        OBJECTIVE FUNCTION VALUE

    1)      274.000000

VARIABLE        VALUE          REDUCED COST
    P1       70.000000          0.000000
    P2       20.000000          0.000000
    RM       90.000000          0.000000

ROW     SLACK OR SURPLUS       DUAL PRICES
    2)       0.000000         -12.600000
    3)       0.000000           0.200000
    4)       0.000000           2.600000
    5)      33.400002           0.000000

NO. ITERATIONS=    3

RANGES IN WHICH THE BASIS IS UNCHANGED

                  OBJ COEFFICIENT RANGES
VARIABLE    CURRENT     ALLOWABLE     ALLOWABLE
             COEF       INCREASE      DECREASE
    P1    13.000000     0.200000      0.866667
    P2    13.200000     1.300000      0.200000
    RM   -10.000000     INFINITY      2.600000

                   RIGHTHAND SIDE RANGES
ROW      CURRENT      ALLOWABLE     ALLOWABLE
          RHS         INCREASE      DECREASE
    2    0.000000     23.333334    10.000000
    3  200.000000     70.000000    20.000000
    4   90.000000     10.000000    23.333334
    5   40.000000     INFINITY     33.400002
```

9. Consider the following LP and its optimal tableau (Table 51):

$$\max z = 3x_1 + 4x_2 + x_3$$
$$\text{s.t.} \quad x_1 + x_2 + x_3 \leq 50$$
$$2x_1 - x_2 + x_3 \geq 15$$
$$x_1 + x_2 \quad\quad = 10$$
$$x_1, x_2, x_3 \geq 0$$

Table 51

z	x_1	x_2	x_3	s_1	e_2	a_2	a_3	rhs
1	1	0	0	1	0	M	$M+3$	80
0	-3	0	0	1	1	-1	-2	15
0	0	0	1	1	0	0	-1	40
0	1	1	0	0	0	0	1	10

(a) Find the dual of this LP and its optimal solution.
(b) Find the range of values on the objective function coefficient of x_1 for which the current basis remains optimal.
(c) Find the range of values on the objective function coefficient for x_2 for which the current basis remains optimal.

10. Consider the following LP and its optimal tableau (Table 52):

$$\max z = 3x_1 + 2x_2$$
$$\text{s.t.} \quad 2x_1 + 5x_2 \le 8$$
$$3x_1 + 7x_2 \le 10$$
$$x_1, x_2 \ge 0$$

Table 52

z	x_1	x_2	s_1	s_2	rhs
1	0	6	0	1	10
0	0	$\frac{1}{3}$	1	$-\frac{2}{3}$	$\frac{4}{3}$
0	1	$\frac{7}{3}$	0	$\frac{1}{3}$	$\frac{10}{3}$

(a) Find the dual of this LP and its optimal solution.
(b) Find the range of values for b_2 for which the current basis remains optimal. Also find the new optimal solution if $b_2 = 5$.

11. Consider the following LP:

$$\max z = 3x_1 + x_2$$
$$\text{s.t.} \quad 2x_1 + x_2 \le 8$$
$$4x_1 + x_2 \le 10$$
$$x_1, x_2 \ge 0$$

The optimal solution to this LP is $z = 9$, $x_1 = 1$, $x_2 = 6$. Graphically find the range of values on b_2 for which the current basis remains optimal.

12. Farmer Leary grows wheat and corn on his 45-acre farm. He can sell at most 140 bushels of wheat and 120 bushels of corn. Each planted acre yields either 5 bushels of wheat or 4 bushels of corn. Wheat sells for $30 per bushel, and corn sells for $50 per bushel. Six hours of labor are needed to harvest an acre of wheat, and 10 hours of labor are needed to harvest an acre of corn. Up to 350 hours of labor can be purchased at $10 per hour. Let

A1 = acres planted with wheat
A2 = acres planted with corn
L = hours of labor that are purchased

In order to maximize profits, farmer Leary should solve the following LP:

$$\max z = 150A1 + 200A2 - 10L$$
$$\text{s.t.} \quad A1 + A2 \le 45$$
$$6A1 + 10A2 - L \le 0$$
$$L \le 350$$
$$5A1 \le 140$$
$$4A2 \le 120$$
$$A1, A2, L \ge 0$$

Use the LINDO output in Figure 11 to answer the following questions:

Figure 11 LINDO Output for Wheat/Corn (Problem 12)

```
MAX       150 A1 + 200 A2 - 10 L
SUBJECT TO
        2)    A1 + A2 <=   45
        3)    6 A1 + 10 A2 - L <=   0
        4)    L <=   350
        5)    5 A1 <=   140
        6)    4 A2 <=   120
END

   LP OPTIMUM FOUND AT STEP     1

        OBJECTIVE FUNCTION VALUE

   1)        4250.00000

VARIABLE          VALUE          REDUCED COST
     A1        25.000000           0.000000
     A2        20.000000           0.000000
      L       350.000000           0.000000

   ROW     SLACK OR SURPLUS        DUAL PRICES
    2)        0.000000            75.000000
    3)        0.000000            12.500000
    4)        0.000000             2.500000
    5)       15.000002            0.000000
    6)       40.000000            0.000000

NO. ITERATIONS=       1

RANGES IN WHICH THE BASIS IS UNCHANGED

                          OBJ COEFFICIENT RANGES
VARIABLE      CURRENT        ALLOWABLE       ALLOWABLE
               COEF          INCREASE        DECREASE
     A1     150.000000      10.000000       30.000000
     A2     200.000000      50.000000       10.000000
      L     -10.000000       INFINITY        2.500000

                          RIGHTHAND SIDE RANGES
   ROW        CURRENT        ALLOWABLE       ALLOWABLE
                RHS          INCREASE        DECREASE
     2      45.000000        1.200000        6.666667
     3       0.000000       40.000000       12.000002
     4     350.000000       40.000000       12.000002
     5     140.000000        INFINITY       15.000002
     6     120.000000        INFINITY       40.000000
```

(a) What is the most that farmer Leary should be willing to pay for an additional hour of labor?

(b) What is the most that farmer Leary should be willing to pay for an additional acre of land?

(c) If only 40 acres of land were available, what would be farmer Leary's profit?

(d) If the price of wheat dropped to $26, what would be the new optimal solution to farmer Leary's problem?

(e) Farmer Leary is considering growing barley. Demand for barley is unlimited. An acre yields 4 bushels of barley and requires 3 hours of labor. If barley sells for $30 per bushel, should farmer Leary produce any barley?

13. Consider the following LP and its optimal tableau (Table 53):

$$\max z = 4x_1 + x_2 + 2x_3$$
$$\text{s.t.} \quad 8x_1 + 3x_2 + x_3 \le 2$$
$$6x_1 + x_2 + x_3 \le 8$$
$$x_1, x_2, x_3 \ge 0$$

Table 53

z	x_1	x_2	x_3	s_1	s_2	rhs
1	8	1	0	0	2	16
0	2	2	0	1	-1	4
0	6	1	1	0	1	8

(a) Find the dual to this LP and its optimal solution.

(b) Find the range of values for the objective function coefficient of x_3 for which the current basis remains optimal.

(c) Find the range of values for the objective function coefficient of x_1 for which the current basis remains optimal.

14. Consider the following LP and its optimal tableau (Table 54):

$$\max z = 3x_1 + x_2$$
$$\text{s.t.} \quad 2x_1 + x_2 \le 4$$
$$3x_1 + 2x_2 \ge 6$$
$$4x_1 + 2x_2 = 7$$
$$x_1 \ge 0, x_2 \ge 0$$

(a) Find the dual to this LP and its optimal solution.

(b) Find the range of values for the right-hand side of the third constraint for which the current basis remains optimal. Also find the new optimal solution if the right-hand side of the third constraint were $\frac{15}{2}$.

Table 54

z	x_1	x_2	s_1	e_2	a_2	a_3	rhs
1	0	0	0	1	$M-1$	$M+\frac{3}{2}$	$\frac{9}{2}$
0	0	0	1	0	0	$-\frac{1}{2}$	$\frac{1}{2}$
0	0	1	0	-2	2	$-\frac{3}{2}$	$\frac{3}{2}$
0	1	0	0	1	-1	1	1

15. Consider the following LP:

$$\max z = 3x_1 + x_2$$
$$\text{s.t.} \quad 4x_1 + x_2 \le 7$$
$$5x_1 + 2x_2 \le 10$$
$$x_1, x_2 \ge 0$$

The optimal solution to this LP is $z = \frac{17}{3}, x_1 = \frac{4}{3}, x_2 = \frac{5}{3}$. Use the graphical approach to determine the range of values for the right-hand side of the second constraint for which the current basis remains optimal.

16. Zales Jewelers uses rubies and sapphires to produce two types of rings. A type 1 ring requires 2 rubies, 3 sapphires, and 1 hour of jeweler's labor. A type 2 ring requires 3 rubies, 2 sapphires, and 2 hours of jeweler's labor. Each type 1 ring sells for $400, and each type 2 ring sells for $500. All rings produced by Zales can be sold. At present, Zales has 100 rubies, 120 sapphires, and 70 hours of jeweler's labor. Extra rubies can be purchased at a cost of $100 per ruby. Market demand requires that the company produce at least 20 type 1 rings and at least 25 type 2 rings. In order to maximize profit, Zales should solve the following LP:

$$X1 = \text{type 1 rings produced}$$
$$X2 = \text{type 2 rings produced}$$
$$R = \text{number of rubies purchased}$$
$$\max z = 400X1 + 500X2 - 100R$$
$$\text{s.t.} \quad 2X1 + 3X2 - R \le 100$$
$$3X1 + 2X2 \le 120$$
$$X1 + 2X2 \le 70$$
$$X1 \ge 20$$
$$X2 \ge 25$$
$$X1, X2 \ge 0$$

Use the LINDO output in Figure 12 to answer the following questions:

(a) Suppose that instead of costing $100, each ruby costs $190. Would Zales still purchase rubies? What would be the new optimal solution to the problem?

Figure 12 LINDO Output for Jewelry (Problem 16)

```
MAX     400 X1 + 500 X2 - 100 R
SUBJECT TO
     2)   2 X1 + 3 X2 -  R <=    100
     3)   3 X1 + 2 X2 <=    120
     4)    X1 + 2 X2 <=    70
     5)    X1 >=    20
     6)    X2 >=    25
END

    LP OPTIMUM FOUND  AT STEP    2

       OBJECTIVE FUNCTION VALUE

  1)      19000.0000

VARIABLE       VALUE        REDUCED COST
    X1      20.000000        0.000000
    X2      25.000000        0.000000
    R       15.000000        0.000000

 ROW    SLACK OR SURPLUS    DUAL PRICES
  2)      0.000000        100.000000
  3)     10.000000          0.000000
  4)      0.000000        200.000000
  5)      0.000000          0.000000
  6)      0.000000       -200.000000

NO. ITERATIONS=      2

  RANGES IN WHICH THE BASIS IS UNCHANGED

                    OBJ COEFFICIENT RANGES
VARIABLE     CURRENT      ALLOWABLE     ALLOWABLE
              COEF        INCREASE      DECREASE
    X1     400.000000     INFINITY     100.000000
    X2     500.000000    200.000000     INFINITY
    R     -100.000000    100.000000    100.000000

                    RIGHTHAND SIDE RANGES
 ROW     CURRENT       ALLOWABLE     ALLOWABLE
          RHS          INCREASE      DECREASE
  2     100.000000     15.000000     INFINITY
  3     120.000000     INFINITY      10.000000
  4      70.000000      3.333333      0.000000
  5      20.000000      0.000000     INFINITY
  6      25.000000      0.000000      2.500000
```

(b) Suppose that Zales were only required to produce at least 23 type 2 rings. What would Zales' profit now be?
(c) What is the most that Zales would be willing to pay for another hour of jeweler's labor?
(d) What is the most that Zales would be willing to pay for another sapphire?
(e) Zales is considering producing type 3 rings. Each type 3 ring can be sold for $550 and requires 4 rubies, 2 sapphires, and 1 hour of jeweler's labor. Should Zales produce any type 3 rings?

17. Use the dual simplex method to solve the following LP:

$$\max z = -2x_1 - x_2$$
$$\text{s.t.} \quad x_1 + x_2 \geq 5$$
$$x_1 - 2x_2 \geq 8$$
$$x_1, x_2 \geq 0$$

18. Consider the following LP:

$$\max z = -4x_1 - x_2$$
$$\text{s.t.} \quad 4x_1 + 3x_2 \geq 6$$
$$x_1 + 2x_2 \leq 3$$
$$3x_1 + x_2 = 3$$
$$x_1, x_2 \geq 0$$

After subtracting an excess variable e_1 from the first constraint, adding a slack variable s_2 to the second constraint, and adding artificial variables a_1 and a_3 to the first and third constraints, the optimal tableau for this LP is found to be as shown in Table 55.

Table 55

z	x_1	x_2	e_1	s_2	a_1	a_3	rhs
1	0	0	0	$\frac{1}{5}$	M	$M - \frac{7}{5}$	$-\frac{18}{5}$
0	0	1	0	$\frac{3}{5}$	0	$-\frac{1}{5}$	$\frac{6}{5}$
0	1	0	0	$-\frac{1}{5}$	0	$\frac{2}{5}$	$\frac{3}{5}$
0	0	0	1	1	-1	1	0

(a) Find the dual to this LP and its optimal solution.
(b) If we changed this LP to

$$\max z = -4x_1 - x_2 - x_3$$
$$\text{s.t.} \quad 4x_1 + 3x_2 + x_3 \geq 6$$
$$x_1 + 2x_2 + x_3 \leq 3$$
$$3x_1 + x_2 + x_3 = 3$$
$$x_1, x_2, x_3 \geq 0$$

would the current optimal solution remain optimal?

19. Consider the following LP:

$$\max z = -2x_1 + 6x_2$$
$$\text{s.t.} \quad x_1 + x_2 \geq 2$$
$$-x_1 + x_2 \leq 1$$
$$x_1, x_2 \geq 0$$

This LP is unbounded. Use this fact to show that the following LP has no feasible solution:

$$\min 2y_1 + y_2$$
$$\text{s.t.} \quad y_1 - y_2 \geq -2$$
$$y_1 + y_2 \geq 6$$
$$y_1 \leq 0, y_2 \geq 0$$

20. Use the Theorem of Complementary Slackness to find the optimal solution to the following LP and its dual:

$$\max z = 3x_1 + 4x_2 + x_3 + 5x_4$$
$$\text{s.t.} \quad x_1 + 2x_2 + x_3 + 2x_4 \le 5$$
$$2x_1 + 3x_2 + x_3 + 3x_4 \le 8$$
$$x_1, x_2, x_3, x_4 \ge 0$$

21. $z = 8$, $x_1 = 2$, $x_2 = 0$ is the optimal solution to the following LP:

$$\max z = 4x_1 + x_2$$
$$\text{s.t.} \quad 3x_1 + x_2 \le 6$$
$$5x_1 + 3x_2 \le 15$$
$$x_1, x_2 \ge 0$$

Use the graphical approach to answer the following questions:

(a) Determine the range of values for c_1 for which the current basis remains optimal.

(b) Determine the range of values for c_2 for which the current basis remains optimal.

(c) Determine the range of values for b_1 for which the current basis remains optimal.

(d) Determine the range of values for b_2 for which the current basis remains optimal.

22. Radioco manufactures two types of radios. The only scarce resource that is needed to produce radios is labor. At present, the company has two laborers. Laborer 1 is willing to work up to 40 hours per week and is paid $5 per hour. Laborer 2 is willing to work up to 50 hours per week and is paid $6 per hour. The price as well as the resources required to build each type of radio are given in Table 56.

(a) Letting x_i be the number of type i radios produced each week, show that Radioco should solve the following LP (its optimal tableau is given in Table 57):

Table 56

	RADIO 1		RADIO 2	
Price	Resource Required	Price	Resource Required	
$25	Laborer 1: 1 hour	$22	Laborer 1: 2 hours	
	Laborer 2: 2 hours		Laborer 2: 1 hour	
	Raw material cost: $5		Raw material cost: $4	

Table 57

z	x_1	x_2	s_1	s_2	rhs
1	0	0	$\frac{1}{3}$	$\frac{4}{3}$	80
0	1	0	$-\frac{1}{3}$	$\frac{2}{3}$	20
0	0	1	$\frac{2}{3}$	$-\frac{1}{3}$	10

$$\max z = 3x_1 + 2x_2$$
$$\text{s.t.} \quad x_1 + 2x_2 \le 40$$
$$2x_1 + x_2 \le 50$$
$$x_1, x_2 \ge 0$$

(b) For what values of the price of a type 1 radio would the current basis remain optimal?

(c) For what values of the price of a type 2 radio would the current basis remain optimal?

(d) If laborer 1 were willing to work only 30 hours per week, would the current basis remain optimal?

(e) If laborer 2 were willing to work up to 60 hours per week, would the current basis remain optimal?

(f) If laborer 1 were willing to work an additional hour, what is the most that Radioco should be willing to pay?

(g) If laborer 2 were willing to work only 48 hours, what would Radioco's profits be? Verify your answer by determining the number of radios of each type that would be produced if laborer 2 were willing to work only 48 hours.

(h) A type 3 radio is under consideration for production. The specifications of a type 3 radio are as follows: price, $30; 2 hours from laborer 1; 2 hours from laborer 2; cost of raw materials, $3. Should Radioco manufacture any type 3 radios?

23. Beerco manufactures ale and beer from corn, hops, and malt. At present, 40 lb of corn, 30 lb of hops, and 40 lb of malt are available. A barrel of ale sells for $40 and requires 1 lb of corn, 1 lb of hops, and 2 lb of malt. A barrel of beer sells for $50 and requires 2 lb of corn, 1 lb of hops, and 1 lb of malt. Beerco can sell all ale and beer that is produced. Assuming that Beerco's goal is to maximize total sales revenue, Beerco should solve the following LP:

$$\max z = 40\text{ALE} + 50\text{BEER}$$
$$\text{s.t.} \quad \text{ALE} + 2\text{BEER} \le 40 \quad \text{(Corn constraint)}$$
$$\text{ALE} + \text{BEER} \le 30 \quad \text{(Hops constraint)}$$
$$2\text{ALE} + \text{BEER} \le 40 \quad \text{(Malt constraint)}$$
$$\text{ALE, BEER} \ge 0$$

ALE = barrels of ale produced, and BEER = barrels of beer produced. An optimal tableau for this LP is shown in Table 58.

Table 58

z	ALE	BEER	s_1	s_2	s_3	rhs
1	0	0	20	0	10	1200
0	0	1	$\frac{2}{3}$	0	$-\frac{1}{3}$	$\frac{40}{3}$
0	0	0	$-\frac{1}{3}$	1	$-\frac{1}{3}$	$\frac{10}{3}$
0	1	0	$-\frac{1}{3}$	0	$\frac{2}{3}$	$\frac{40}{3}$

(a) Write down the dual to Beerco's LP and find its optimal solution.

(b) Find the range of values for the price of ale for which the current basis remains optimal.

(c) Find the range of values for the price of beer for which the current basis remains optimal.

(d) Find the range of values for the amount of available corn for which the current basis remains optimal.

(e) Find the range of values for the amount of available hops for which the current basis remains optimal.

(f) Find the range of values for the amount of available malt for which the current basis remains optimal.

(g) Suppose Beerco is considering manufacturing malt liquor. A barrel of malt liquor requires 0.5 lb of corn, 3 lb of hops, and 3 lb of malt and sells for \$50. Should Beerco manufacture any malt liquor?

(h) Suppose we express the Beerco constraints in ounces. Write down the new LP and its dual.

(i) What is the optimal solution to the dual of the new LP? (*Hint*: Think about what happens to $\mathbf{c}_{BV}B^{-1}$. Use the idea of shadow prices to explain why the dual to the original LP (pounds) and the dual to the new LP (ounces) should have different optimal solutions.)

GROUP B

24. Consider the following LP:

$$\max z = -3x_1 + x_2 + 2x_3$$
$$\text{s.t.} \quad x_2 + 2x_3 \leq 3$$
$$-x_1 \qquad + 3x_3 \leq -1$$
$$-2x_1 - 3x_2 \qquad \leq -2$$
$$x_1, x_2, x_3 \geq 0$$

(a) Find the dual to this LP and show that the dual has the same feasible region as the original LP.

(b) Use weak duality to show that the optimal objective function value for the LP (and its dual) must be zero.

25. Consider the following LP:

$$\max z = 2x_1 + x_2 + x_3$$
$$\text{s.t.} \quad x_1 \qquad + x_3 \leq 1$$
$$x_2 + x_3 \leq 2$$
$$x_1 + x_2 \qquad \leq 3$$
$$x_1, x_2, x_3 \geq 0$$

It is given that

$$\begin{bmatrix} 1 & 0 & 1 \\ 0 & 1 & 1 \\ 1 & 1 & 0 \end{bmatrix}^{-1} = \begin{bmatrix} \frac{1}{2} & -\frac{1}{2} & \frac{1}{2} \\ -\frac{1}{2} & \frac{1}{2} & \frac{1}{2} \\ \frac{1}{2} & \frac{1}{2} & -\frac{1}{2} \end{bmatrix}$$

(a) Show that the basic solution with basic variables x_1, x_2, and x_3 is optimal. Find the optimal solution.

(b) Write down the dual to this LP and find its optimal solution.

(c) Show that if we multiply the right-hand side of each constraint by a nonnegative constant k, the new optimal solution is obtained simply by multiplying the value of each variable in the original optimal solution by k.

26. Wivco produces two products: product 1 and product 2. The relevant data are shown in Table 59. Each week, up to 400 units of raw material can be purchased at a cost of \$1.50 per unit. The company employs four workers, who work 40 hours per week (their salaries are considered a fixed cost). Workers can be asked to work overtime and are paid \$6 per hour for overtime work. Each week 320 hours of machine time are available.

In the absence of advertising, 50 units of product 1 will be demanded each week, and 60 units of product 2 will be demanded each week. Advertising can be used to stimulate demand for each product. Each dollar spent on advertising product 1 increases the demand for product 1 by 10 units, whereas each dollar spent on advertising for product 2 increases the demand for product 2 by 15 units. At most \$100 can be spent on advertising. Define

P1 = number of units of product 1 produced each week

P2 = number of units of product 2 produced each week

OT = number of hours of overtime labor used each week

RM = number of units of raw material purchased each week

A1 = dollars spent each week on advertising product 1

A2 = dollars spent each week on advertising product 2

Table 59

	PRODUCT 1	PRODUCT 2
Selling price	$15	$8
Labor required	0.75 hour	0.50 hour
Machine time required	1.5 hours	0.80 hour
Raw material required	2 units	1 unit

Then Wivco should solve the following LP:

$$\max z = 15P1 + 8P2 - 6(OT) - 1.5RM$$
$$- A1 - A2$$

$$\text{s.t.} \quad P1 - 10A1 \leq 50 \tag{1}$$
$$P2 - 15A2 \leq 60 \tag{2}$$
$$0.75P1 + 0.5P2 \leq 160 + (OT) \tag{3}$$
$$2P1 + P2 \leq RM \tag{4}$$
$$RM \leq 400 \tag{5}$$
$$A1 + A2 \leq 100 \tag{6}$$
$$1.5P1 + 0.8P2 \leq 320 \tag{7}$$

All variables nonnegative

Use LINDO to solve this LP. Then use the computer output to answer the following questions:

(a) If overtime were to cost only $4 per hour, would Wivco use overtime?

(b) If each unit of product 1 sold for $15.50, would the current basis remain optimal? What would be the new optimal solution?

(c) What is the most that Wivco should be willing to pay for another unit of raw material?

(d) How much would Wivco be willing to pay for another hour of machine time?

(e) If each worker were required (as part of the regular workweek) to work 45 hours per week, what would the company's profits be?

(f) Explain why the shadow price of row (1) is 0.10. (*Hint*: If the right-hand side of (1) were increased from 50 to 51, then in the absence of advertising for product 1, 51 units of product 1 could now be sold each week.)

(g) Wivco is considering producing a new product (product 3). Each unit of product 3 sells for $17 and requires 2 hours of labor, 1 unit of raw material, and 2 hours of machine time. Should Wivco produce any of product 3?

(h) If each unit of product 2 sold for $10, would the current basis remain optimal?

27. The following question concerns the Rylon example discussed in Section 3.9. After defining

RB = ounces of Regular Brute produced annually

LB = ounces of Luxury Brute produced annually

RC = ounces of Regular Chanelle produced annually

LC = ounces of Luxury Chanelle produced annually

RM = pounds of raw material purchased annually

the LINDO output in Figure 13 was obtained for this problem. Use this output to answer the following questions:
(a) Interpret the shadow price of each constraint.
(b) If the price of RB were to increase by 50¢, what would be the new optimal solution to the Rylon problem?
(c) If 8000 laboratory hours were available each year, but only 2000 lb of raw material were available each year, would Rylon's profits increase or decrease? (*Hint*: Use the 100% Rule to show that the current basis remains optimal. Then use reasoning analogous to (34)–(37) to determine the new objective function value.)
(d) Rylon is considering expanding its laboratory capacity.

Figure 13 LINDO Output for Brute/Chanelle (Problem 27)

```
MAX    7 RB + 14 LB + 6 RC + 10 LC - 3 RM
SUBJECT TO
    2)     RM <=    4000
    3)     3 LB + 2 LC +  RM <=   6000
    4)     RB + LB - 3 RM =    0
    5)     RC + LC - 4 RM =    0
END
    LP OPTIMUM FOUND AT STEP     6

        OBJECTIVE FUNCTION VALUE

    1)      172666.672

VARIABLE        VALUE          REDUCED COST
    RB      11333.333008        0.000000
    LB        666.666687        0.000000
    RC      16000.000000        0.000000
    LC          0.000000        0.666667
    RM       4000.000000        0.000000

   ROW    SLACK OR SURPLUS     DUAL PRICES
    2)          0.000000       39.666668
    3)          0.000000        2.333333
    4)          0.000000        7.000000
    5)          0.000000        6.000000

NO. ITERATIONS=      6

RANGES IN WHICH THE BASIS IS UNCHANGED

                   OBJ COEFFICIENT RANGES
VARIABLE     CURRENT       ALLOWABLE       ALLOWABLE
              COEF         INCREASE        DECREASE
   RB       7.000000       1.000000       11.900001
   LB      14.000000     119.000000        1.000000
   RC       6.000000       INFINITY        0.666667
   LC      10.000000       0.666667        INFINITY
   RM      -3.000000       INFINITY       39.666668

                   RIGHTHAND SIDE RANGES
ROW         CURRENT        ALLOWABLE       ALLOWABLE
             RHS           INCREASE        DECREASE
   2      4000.000000     2000.000000     3400.000000
   3      6000.000000    33999.996094     2000.000000
   4         0.000000       INFINITY     11333.333008
   5         0.000000       INFINITY     16000.000000
```

Two options are under consideration:

Option 1 For a cost of $10,000 (incurred at the present time), annual laboratory capacity can be increased by 1000 hours.

Option 2 For a cost of $200,000 (incurred at the present time), annual laboratory capacity can be increased by 10,000 hours.

Suppose that all other aspects of the problem remain unchanged and that future profits are discounted, with the interest rate being $11\frac{1}{8}\%$ per year. Which option, if any, should Rylon choose?

(e) Rylon is considering purchasing a new type of raw material. Unlimited quantities of this raw material can be purchased at $8/lb. It requires 3 laboratory hours to process a pound of the new raw material. Each processed pound of the new raw material yields 2 oz of RB and 1 oz of RC. Should Rylon purchase any of the new material?

28. Consider the following two LPs:

$$\max z = c_1 x_1 + c_2 x_2$$
$$\text{s.t.} \quad a_{11} x_1 + a_{12} x_2 \le b_1$$
$$a_{21} x_1 + a_{22} x_2 \le b_2 \qquad \textbf{(LP 1)}$$
$$x_1, x_2 \ge 0$$

$$\max z = 100c_1 x_1 + 100c_2 x_2$$
$$\text{s.t.} \quad 100a_{11} x_1 + 100a_{12} x_2 \le b_1$$
$$100a_{21} x_1 + 100a_{22} x_2 \le b_2 \qquad \textbf{(LP 2)}$$
$$x_1, x_2 \ge 0$$

Suppose that $BV = \{x_1, x_2\}$ is an optimal basis for both LPs, and the optimal solution to LP 1 is $x_1 = 50$, $x_2 = 500$, $z = 550$. Also suppose that for LP 1, the shadow price of Constraint 1 $= \frac{100}{3}$, and the shadow price of Constraint 2 $= \frac{100}{3}$. Find the optimal solution to LP 2 and the optimal solution to the dual of LP 2. (*Hint:* If we multiply each number in a matrix by 100, what happens to B^{-1}?)

29. The following questions pertain to the Star Oil capital budgeting example of Section 3.6. The LINDO output for this problem is shown in Figure 14.

(a) Find and interpret the shadow price for each constraint.

(b) If the NPV of investment 1 were $5 million, would the optimal solution to the problem change?

(c) If the NPV of investment 2 and investment 4 were each decreased by 25%, would the optimal solution to the problem change? (This part requires knowledge of the 100% Rule.)

(d) Suppose that Star Oil's investment budget were

Figure 14 LINDO Output for Star Oil (Problem 29)

```
MAX     13 X1 + 16 X2 + 16 X3 + 14 X4 + 39 X5
SUBJECT TO
     2)    11 X1 + 53 X2 + 5 X3 + 5 X4 + 29 X5 <=    40
     3)     3 X1 + 6 X2 + 5 X3 +   X4 + 34 X5 <=    20
     4)    X1 <=   1
     5)    X2 <=   1
     6)    X3 <=   1
     7)    X4 <=   1
     8)    X5 <=   1
END

     LP OPTIMUM FOUND  AT STEP     5

          OBJECTIVE FUNCTION VALUE

     1)        57.4490166

VARIABLE          VALUE           REDUCED COST
    X1          1.000000            0.000000
    X2          0.200860            0.000000
    X3          1.000000            0.000000
    X4          1.000000            0.000000
    X5          0.288084            0.000000

    ROW     SLACK OR SURPLUS        DUAL PRICES
     2)        0.000000            0.190418
     3)        0.000000            0.984644
     4)        0.000000            7.951474
     5)        0.799140            0.000000
     6)        0.000000           10.124693
     7)        0.000000           12.063268
     8)        0.711916            0.000000

NO. ITERATIONS=        5

RANGES IN WHICH THE BASIS IS UNCHANGED

                        OBJ COEFFICIENT RANGES
VARIABLE      CURRENT        ALLOWABLE        ALLOWABLE
               COEF          INCREASE         DECREASE
    X1       13.000000       INFINITY         7.951474
    X2       16.000000      45.104530         9.117648
    X3       16.000000       INFINITY        10.124693
    X4       14.000000       INFINITY        12.063268
    X5       39.000000      51.666668        30.245283

                        RIGHTHAND SIDE RANGES
    ROW       CURRENT        ALLOWABLE        ALLOWABLE
               RHS           INCREASE         DECREASE
     2       40.000000      38.264709         9.617647
     3       20.000000      11.275863         8.849057
     4        1.000000       1.139373         1.000000
     5        1.000000       INFINITY         0.799140
     6        1.000000       1.995745         1.000000
     7        1.000000       2.319149         1.000000
     8        1.000000       INFINITY         0.711916
```

changed to $50 million at time 0 and $15 million at time 1. Would Star be better off? (This part requires knowledge of the 100% Rule.)

(e) Suppose a new investment (investment 6) is available. Investment 6 yields an NPV of $10 million and requires a cash outflow of $5 million at time 0 and a cash outflow of $10 million at time 1. Should Star Oil invest any money in investment 6?

30. The following questions pertain to the Finco investment example of Section 3.11. The LINDO output for this problem is shown in Figure 15.

(a) If Finco has $2000 more on hand at time 0, by how much would their time 3 cash increase?

(b) Observe that if Finco were given a dollar at time 1, the cash available for investment at time 1 would now be $0.5A + 1.2C + 1.08S_0 + 1$. Use this fact and the shadow

Figure 15   LINDO Output for Finco (Problem 30)

```
MAX     B + 1.9 D + 1.5 E + 1.08 S2
SUBJECT TO
      2)    D + A + C + SO =    100000
      3)  - B + 0.5 A + 1.2 C + 1.08 SO - S1 =    0
      4)    0.5 B - E - S2 + A + 1.08 S1 =   0
      5)    A <=    75000
      6)    B <=    75000
      7)    C <=    75000
      8)    D <=    75000
      9)    E <=    75000
END

     LP OPTIMUM FOUND  AT STEP      8

         OBJECTIVE FUNCTION VALUE

    1)      218500.000

  VARIABLE        VALUE         REDUCED COST
        B      30000.000000      0.000000
        D      40000.000000      0.000000
        E      75000.000000      0.000000
        S2         0.000000      0.040000
        A      60000.000000      0.000000
        C          0.000000      0.028000
        SO         0.000000      0.215200
        S1         0.000000      0.350400

     ROW    SLACK OR SURPLUS    DUAL PRICES
      2)        0.000000         1.900000
      3)        0.000000        -1.560000
      4)        0.000000        -1.120000
      5)    15000.000000         0.000000
      6)    45000.000000         0.000000
      7)    75000.000000         0.000000
      8)    35000.000000         0.000000
      9)        0.000000         0.380000

NO. ITERATIONS=      8

  RANGES IN WHICH THE BASIS IS UNCHANGED

                    OBJ COEFFICIENT RANGES
  VARIABLE    CURRENT      ALLOWABLE      ALLOWABLE
               COEF        INCREASE       DECREASE
        B    1.000000      0.029167       0.284416
        D    1.900000      0.475000       0.050000
        E    1.500000      INFINITY       0.380000
        S2   1.080000      0.040000       INFINITY
        A    0.000000      0.050000       0.058333
        C    0.000000      0.028000       INFINITY
        SO   0.000000      0.215200       INFINITY
        S1   0.000000      0.350400       INFINITY

                   RIGHTHAND SIDE RANGES
     ROW      CURRENT      ALLOWABLE      ALLOWABLE
               RHS         INCREASE       DECREASE
      2    100000.000000   35000.000000   40000.000000
      3         0.000000   37500.000000   56250.000000
      4         0.000000   18750.000000   43750.000000
      5     75000.000000   INFINITY       15000.000000
      6     75000.000000   INFINITY       45000.000000
      7     75000.000000   INFINITY       75000.000000
      8     75000.000000   INFINITY       35000.000000
      9     75000.000000   18750.000000   43750.000000
```

price of Constraint 2 to determine by how much Finco's time 3 cash position would increase if any extra dollar were available at time 1.

(c) By how much would Finco's time 3 cash on hand change if Finco were given an extra dollar at time 2?

(d) If investment D yielded $1.80 at time 3, would the current basis remain optimal?

(e) Suppose that a super money market fund yielded 25% for the period between time 0 and time 1. Should Finco invest in this fund at time 0?

(f) Show that if the investment limitations of $75,000 on investments A, B, C, and D were all eliminated, the current

basis would remain optimal. (Knowledge of the 100% Rule is requiured for this part.) What would be the new optimal z-value?

(g) A new investment (investment F) is under consideration. One dollar invested in investment F generates the following cash flows: time 0, $-\$1.00$; time 1, $+\$1.10$; time 2, $+\$0.20$; time 3, $+\$0.10$. Should Finco invest in investment F?

31. In this problem, we discuss how shadow prices can be interpreted for blending problems (see Section 3.8). To illustrate the ideas, we discuss Problem 2 of Section 3.8. If we define

$$x_{6J} = \text{pounds of grade 6 oranges in juice}$$
$$x_{9J} = \text{pounds of grade 9 oranges in juice}$$
$$x_{6B} = \text{pounds of grade 6 oranges in bags}$$
$$x_{9B} = \text{pounds of grade 9 oranges in bags}$$

then the appropriate formulation is

$$\max z = 0.45(x_{6J} + x_{9J}) + 0.30(x_{6B} + x_{9B})$$

s.t. $x_{6J} \qquad + x_{6B} \qquad \leq 120,000$ (Grade 6 constraint)

$\qquad\qquad x_{9J} \qquad + x_{9B} \leq 100,000$ (Grade 9 constraint)

(1) $\dfrac{6x_{6J} + 9x_{9J}}{x_{6J} + x_{9J}} \geq 8$ (Orange-juice constraint)

(2) $\dfrac{6x_{6B} + 9x_{9B}}{x_{6B} + x_{9B}} \geq 7$ (Bags constraint)

$$x_{6J}, x_{9J}, x_{6B}, x_{9B} \geq 0$$

Constraints (1) and (2) are examples of blending constraints, because they specify the proportion of grade 6 and grade 9 oranges that must be blended to manufacture orange juice and bags of oranges. It would be useful to determine how a slight change in the standards for orange juice and bags of oranges would affect profit. At the end of this problem, we explain how to use the shadow prices of Contraints (1) and (2) to answer the following questions:

(a) Suppose that the average grade for orange juice is increased to 8.1. Assuming the current basis remains optimal, by how much would profits change?

(b) Suppose the average grade requirement for bags of oranges is decreased to 6.9. Assuming the current basis remains optimal, by how much would profits change?

The shadow price for (1) is -0.15, and the shadow price for (2) is also -0.15. The optimal solution to the O.J. problem is $x_{6J} = 26,666.67$, $x_{9J} = 53,333.33$, $x_{6B} = 93,333.33$, $x_{9B} = 46,666.67$. To interpret the shadow prices of blending Constraints (1) and (2), *we assume that a slight change in the quality standard for a product will not significantly change the quantity of the product that is produced.*

Now note that (1) may be written as

$$6x_{6J} + 9x_{9J} \geq 8(x_{6J} + x_{9J}), \quad \text{or} \quad -2x_{6J} + x_{9J} \geq 0$$

If the quality standard for orange juice is changed to $8 + \Delta$, then (1) can be written as

$$6x_{6J} + 9x_{9J} \geq (8 + \Delta)(x_{6J} + x_{9J})$$

or

$$-2x_{6J} + x_{9J} \geq \Delta(x_{6J} + x_{9J})$$

Since we are assuming that changing orange juice quality from 8 to $8 + \Delta$ does not change the amount of orange juice produced, $x_{6J} + x_{9J}$ will remain equal to 80,000, and (1) will become

$$-2x_{6J} + x_{9J} \geq 80,000\Delta$$

Using the definition of shadow price, now answer parts (a) and (b).

32. Ballco manufactures large softballs, regular softballs, and hardballs. Each type of ball requires time in three departments: cutting, sewing, and packaging, as shown in Table 60 (in minutes). Because of marketing considerations, at least 1000 regular softballs must be produced. Each regular softball can be sold for $3, each large softball can be sold for $5, and each hardball can be sold for $4. 18,000 minutes of cutting time, 18,000 minutes of sewing time, and 9000 minutes of packaging time are available.

Ballco wishes to maximize sales revenue. If we define

RS = number of regular softballs produced
LS = number of large softballs produced
HB = number of hardballs produced

then the appropriate LP is

$$\max z = 3RS + 5LS + 4HB$$

s.t.
$$15RS + 10LS + 8HB \leq 18,000 \quad \text{(Cutting constraint)}$$
$$15RS + 15LS + 4HB \leq 18,000 \quad \text{(Sewing constraint)}$$
$$3RS + 4LS + 2HB \leq 9000 \quad \text{(Packaging constraint)}$$
$$RS \geq 1000 \quad \text{(Demand constraint)}$$

$$RS, LS, HB \geq 0$$

The optimal tableau for this LP is shown in Table 61.

(a) Find the dual of the Ballco problem and its optimal solution.

(b) Show that the Ballco problem has an alternative optimal solution. Find the alternative optimal solution. How many minutes of sewing time are used by the alternative optimal solution?

(c) By how much would an increase of 1 minute in the amount of available sewing time increase Ballco's revenue? How can this answer be reconciled with the fact that the sewing constraint is binding? (*Hint:* Look at the answer to part (b).)

Table 60

	CUTTING TIME	SEWING TIME	PACKAGING TIME
Regular softballs	15	15	3
Large softballs	10	15	4
Hardballs	8	4	2

Table 61

z	RS	LS	HB	s_1	s_2	s_3	e_4	a_4	rhs
1	0	0	0	0.5	0	0	4.5	$M - 4.5$	4500
0	0	0	1	0.19	-0.125	0	0.94	-0.94	187.5
0	0	1	0	-0.05	0.10	0	0.75	-0.75	150
0	0	0	0	-0.17	-0.15	1	-1.88	1.88	5025
0	1	0	0	0	0	0	-1	1	1000

(d) Assuming the current basis remains optimal, how would an increase of 100 in the regular softball requirement affect Ballco's revenue?

33. Consider the following LP:

$$\max z = c_1 x_1 + c_2 x_2$$
$$\text{s.t.} \quad 3x_1 + 4x_2 \le 6$$
$$2x_1 + 3x_2 \le 4$$
$$x_1, x_2 \ge 0$$

You are given that the optimal tableau for this LP is

$$z \quad + \ s_1 + 2s_2 = 14$$
$$x_1 \ + 3s_1 - 4s_2 = 2$$
$$x_2 - 2s_1 + 3s_2 = 0$$

Without doing any pivots, determine c_1 and c_2.

34. Consider the following LP and its partial optimal tableau (Table 62):

$$\max z = 20x_1 + 10x_2$$
$$\text{s.t.} \quad x_1 + x_2 = 150$$
$$x_1 \qquad \le 40$$
$$x_2 \ge 20$$
$$x_1, x_2 \ge 0$$

(a) Complete the optimal tableau.
(b) Find the dual to this LP and its optimal solution.

Table 62

z	x_1	x_2	s_2	e_3	a_1	a_3	rhs
1	0	0		0			1900
0	0	0	−1	1	1	−1	90
0	1	0	1	0	0	0	40
0	0	1	−1	0	1	0	110

35. Consider the following LP and its optimal tableau (Table 63):

$$\max z = c_1 x_1 + c_2 x_2$$
$$\text{s.t.} \quad a_{11} x_1 + a_{12} x_2 \le b_1$$
$$a_{21} x_1 + a_{22} x_2 \le b_2$$
$$x_1, x_2 \ge 0$$

Determine c_1, c_2, b_1, b_2, a_{11}, a_{12}, a_{21}, and a_{22}.

Table 63

z	x_1	x_2	s_1	s_2	b
1	0	0	2	3	$\frac{5}{2}$
0	1	0	3	2	$\frac{5}{2}$
0	0	1	1	1	1

36. Consider an LP with three $\le$ constraints. The right-hand sides of the three constraints are 10, 15, and 20, respectively. In the optimal tableau, s_2 is a basic variable in the second constraint, and the right-hand side of the second constraint in the optimal tableau is 12. Determine the range of values on b_2 for which the current basis remains optimal. (*Hint*: If rhs of Constraint 2 is $15 + \Delta$, this should help in finding the rhs of the optimal tableau.)

37. Use LINDO to solve the Sailco problem of Section 3.10. Then use the LINDO output to answer the following questions:
(a) If month 1 demand decreased to 35 sailboats, what would be the total cost of satisfying the demands during the next four months?
(b) If the cost of producing a sailboat with regular-time labor during month 1 were $420, what would be the new optimal solution to the Sailco problem?
(c) Suppose a new customer is willing to pay $425 for a sailboat. If his demand must be met during month 1, should you fill the order? How about if his demand must be met during month 4?

♦ REFERENCES

The following texts contain extensive discussions of sensitivity analysis and duality:

BAZARAA, M., and J. JARVIS, *Linear Programming and Network Flows*. New York: Wiley, 1977.
BRADLEY, S., A. HAX, and T. MAGNANTI. *Applied Mathematical Programming*. Reading, Mass.: Addison-Wesley, 1977.
DANTZIG, G. *Linear Programming and Extensions*. Princeton, N.J.: Princeton University Press, 1963.

GASS, S. *Linear Programming: Methods and Applications*, 5th ed. New York: McGraw-Hill, 1985.

LUENBERGER, D. *Linear and Nonlinear Programming*, 2d ed. Reading, Mass.: Addison-Wesley, 1984.

MURTY, K. *Linear Programming*. New York: Wiley, 1983.

SIMMONS, D. *Linear Programming for Operations Research*. Englewood Cliffs, N.J.: Prentice-Hall, 1972.

SIMONNARD, M. *Linear Programming*. Englewood Cliffs, N.J.: Prentice-Hall, 1966.

WU, N., and R. COPPINS. *Linear Programming and Extensions*. New York: McGraw-Hill, 1981.

C H A P T E R

7

Transportation, Assignment, and Transshipment Problems

In this chapter, we discuss three special types of linear programming problems: transportation problems, assignment problems, and transshipment problems. While each of these problems can be solved by the simplex algorithm, there are specialized algorithms for each type of problem that are much more efficient than the simplex algorithm.

7-1   **FORMULATING TRANSPORTATION PROBLEMS**

We begin our discussion of transportation problems by formulating a linear programming model of the following situation.

E X A M P L E
1

Powerco has three electric power plants that supply the power needs of four cities.[†] Each power plant can supply the following numbers of kilowatt-hours (kwh) of electricity: plant 1, 35 million; plant 2, 50 million; plant 3, 40 million (see Table 1). The peak power demands in these cities, which occur at the same time (2 P.M.), are as follows (in kwh): city 1, 45 million; city 2, 20 million; city 3, 30 million; city 4, 30 million (see Table 1). The costs of sending 1 million kwh of electricity from plant to city depend on the distance the electricity must travel (see Table 1). Formulate an LP to minimize the cost of meeting each city's peak power demand.

Solution   To formulate Powerco's problem as an LP, we begin by defining a variable for each decision that Powerco must make. Since Powerco must determine how much power is sent from each plant to each city, we define (for $i = 1, 2, 3$ and $j = 1, 2, 3, 4$)

$$x_{ij} = \text{number of (million) kwh produced at plant } i \text{ and sent to city } j$$

In terms of these variables, the total cost of supplying the peak power demands to cities 1–4 may be written as

[†]This example is based on Aarvik and Randolph (1975).

Table 1
Shipping Costs,
Supply, and Demand
for Powerco
Example

| | TO | | | | SUPPLY |
FROM	City 1	City 2	City 3	City 4	(Million kwh)
Plant 1	$8	$6	$10	$9	35
Plant 2	$9	$12	$13	$7	50
Plant 3	$14	$9	$16	$5	40
DEMAND (Million kwh)	45	20	30	30	

$$8x_{11} + 6x_{12} + 10x_{13} + 9x_{14} \quad \text{(Cost of shipping power from plant 1)}$$
$$+ \ 9x_{21} + 12x_{22} + 13x_{23} + 7x_{24} \quad \text{(Cost of shipping power from plant 2)}$$
$$+ \ 14x_{31} + 9x_{32} + 16x_{33} + 5x_{34} \quad \text{(Cost of shipping power from plant 3)}$$

Powerco faces two types of constraints. First, the total power supplied by each plant cannot exceed the plant's capacity. For example, the total amount of power sent from plant 1 to the four cities cannot exceed 35 million kwh. Each variable with first subscript 1 represents a shipment of power from plant 1, so we may express this restriction by the LP constraint

$$x_{11} + x_{12} + x_{13} + x_{14} \leq 35$$

In a similar fashion, we can find constraints that reflect plant 2's capacity and plant 3's capacity. Since power is supplied by the power plants, each power plant is a **supply point**. Analogously, a constraint that ensures that the total quantity shipped from a plant does not exceed plant capacity is a **supply constraint**. The LP formulation of Powerco's problem contains the following three supply constraints:

$$x_{11} + x_{12} + x_{13} + x_{14} \leq 35 \quad \text{(Plant 1 supply constraint)}$$
$$x_{21} + x_{22} + x_{23} + x_{24} \leq 50 \quad \text{(Plant 2 supply constraint)}$$
$$x_{31} + x_{32} + x_{33} + x_{34} \leq 40 \quad \text{(Plant 3 supply constraint)}$$

Second, we need constraints that ensure that each city will receive sufficient power to meet its peak demand. Since each city demands power, each city is a **demand point**. For example, city 1 must receive at least 45 million kwh. Each variable with second subscript 1 represents a shipment of power to city 1, so we obtain the following constraint:

$$x_{11} + x_{21} + x_{31} \geq 45$$

Similarly, we obtain a constraint for each of cities 2, 3, and 4. A constraint that ensures that a location receives its demand is a **demand constraint**. Powerco must satisfy the following four demand constraints:

$$x_{11} + x_{21} + x_{31} \geq 45 \quad \text{(City 1 demand constraint)}$$
$$x_{12} + x_{22} + x_{32} \geq 20 \quad \text{(City 2 demand constraint)}$$
$$x_{13} + x_{23} + x_{33} \geq 30 \quad \text{(City 3 demand constraint)}$$
$$x_{14} + x_{24} + x_{34} \geq 30 \quad \text{(City 4 demand constraint)}$$

Since all the x_{ij}'s must be nonnegative, we add the sign restrictions $x_{ij} \geq 0$ ($i = 1, 2, 3$; $j = 1, 2, 3, 4$).

Combining the objective function, supply constraints, demand constraints, and sign restrictions yields the following LP formulation of Powerco's problem:

$$\min z = 8x_{11} + 6x_{12} + 10x_{13} + 9x_{14} + 9x_{21} + 12x_{22} + 13x_{23} + 7x_{24}$$
$$+ 14x_{31} + 9x_{32} + 16x_{33} + 5x_{34}$$

$$\text{s.t.} \quad x_{11} + x_{12} + x_{13} + x_{14} \leq 35 \qquad \text{(Supply constraints)}$$
$$x_{21} + x_{22} + x_{23} + x_{24} \leq 50$$
$$x_{31} + x_{32} + x_{33} + x_{34} \leq 40$$
$$x_{11} + x_{21} + x_{31} \qquad \geq 45 \qquad \text{(Demand constraints)}$$
$$x_{12} + x_{22} + x_{32} \qquad \geq 20$$
$$x_{13} + x_{23} + x_{33} \qquad \geq 30$$
$$x_{14} + x_{24} + x_{34} \qquad \geq 30$$
$$x_{ij} \geq 0 \quad (i = 1, 2, 3; j = 1, 2, 3, 4)$$

In Section 7.3, we will find that the optimal solution to this LP is $z = 1020$, $x_{12} = 10$, $x_{13} = 25$, $x_{21} = 45$, $x_{23} = 5$, $x_{32} = 10$, $x_{34} = 30$. Figure 1 is a graphical representation of the Powerco problem and its optimal solution. The variable x_{ij} is represented by a line, or arc, joining the ith supply point (plant i) and the jth demand point (city j).

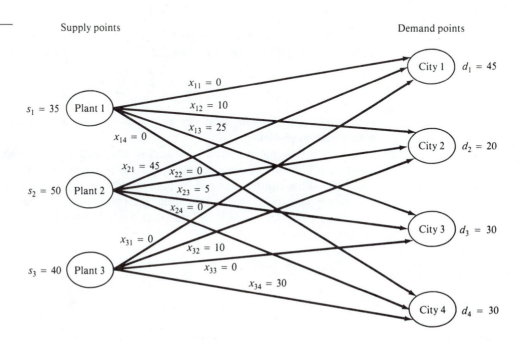

Figure 1
Graphical
Representation of
Powerco Problem
and Its Optimal
Solution

GENERAL DESCRIPTION OF A TRANSPORTATION PROBLEM

In general, a transportation problem is specified by the following information:

1. A set of m *supply points* from which a good is shipped. Supply point i can supply at most s_i units. In the Powerco example, $m = 3$, $s_1 = 35$, $s_2 = 50$, and $s_3 = 40$.

2. A set of n *demand points* to which the good is shipped. Demand point j must receive at least d_j units of the shipped good. In the Powerco example, $n = 4$, $d_1 = 45$, $d_2 = 20$, $d_3 = 30$, and $d_4 = 30$.

3. Each unit produced at supply point i and shipped to demand point j incurs a *variable cost* of c_{ij}. In the Powerco example, $c_{12} = 6$.

Let

$$x_{ij} = \text{number of units shipped from supply point } i \text{ to demand point } j$$

then the general formulation of a transportation problem is

$$\min \sum_{i=1}^{i=m} \sum_{j=1}^{j=n} c_{ij} x_{ij}$$

$$\text{s.t.} \quad \sum_{j=1}^{j=n} x_{ij} \leq s_i \quad (i = 1, 2, \ldots, m) \qquad \text{(Supply constraints)} \qquad (1)$$

$$\sum_{i=1}^{i=m} x_{ij} \geq d_j \quad (j = 1, 2, \ldots, n) \qquad \text{(Demand constraints)}$$

$$x_{ij} \geq 0 \quad (i = 1, 2, \ldots, m; j = 1, 2, \ldots, n)$$

If a problem has the constraints given in (1) and is a *maximization* problem, it is still a transportation problem (see Problem 7 at the end of this section). If

$$\sum_{i=1}^{i=m} s_i = \sum_{j=1}^{j=n} d_j$$

then total supply equals total demand, and the problem is said to be a **balanced transportation problem**.

For the Powerco problem, total supply and total demand both equal 125, so the Powerco problem is a balanced transportation problem. In a balanced transportation problem, all the constraints must be binding. For example, in the Powerco problem, if any supply constraint were nonbinding, the remaining available power would not be sufficient to meet the needs of all four cities. For a balanced transportation problem, (1) may be written as

$$\min \sum_{i=1}^{i=m} \sum_{j=1}^{j=n} c_{ij} x_{ij}$$

$$\text{s.t.} \quad \sum_{j=1}^{j=n} x_{ij} = s_i \quad (i = 1, 2, \ldots, m) \qquad \text{(Supply constraints)} \qquad (2)$$

$$\sum_{i=1}^{i=m} x_{ij} = d_j \quad (j = 1, 2, \ldots, n) \qquad \text{(Demand constraints)}$$

$$x_{ij} \geq 0 \quad (i = 1, 2, \ldots, m; j = 1, 2, \ldots, n)$$

Later in this chapter, we will see that it is relatively simple to find a basic feasible solution for a balanced transportation problem. Also, for a balanced transportation problem, simplex pivots do not involve multiplication and reduce to additions and subtractions. For these reasons, it is desirable to formulate a transportation problem as a balanced transportation problem.

BALANCING A TRANSPORTATION PROBLEM IF TOTAL SUPPLY EXCEEDS TOTAL DEMAND

If total supply exceeds total demand, we can balance a transportation problem by creating a **dummy demand point** that has a demand equal to the amount of excess supply. Since shipments to the dummy demand point are not real shipments, they are assigned a cost of zero. Shipments to the dummy demand point indicate unused supply capacity. To illustrate the use of a dummy demand point, suppose that in the Powerco problem, the demand for city 1 were reduced to 40 million kwh. To balance the Powerco problem, we would add a dummy demand point (point 5) with a demand of $125 - 120 = 5$ million kwh. From each plant, the cost of shipping 1 million kwh to the dummy is zero. The optimal solution to this balanced transportation problem is $z = 975$, $x_{13} = 20$, $x_{12} = 15$, $x_{21} = 40$, $x_{23} = 10$, $x_{32} = 5$, $x_{34} = 30$, and $x_{35} = 5$. Since $x_{35} = 5$, 5 million kwh of plant 3 capacity will be unused (see Figure 2).

A transportation problem is specified by the supply, the demand, and the shipping costs, so the relevant data for any transportation problem can be summarized in a

Figure 2
Graphical Representation of Unbalanced Powerco Problem and Its Optimal Solution (with Dummy Demand Point)

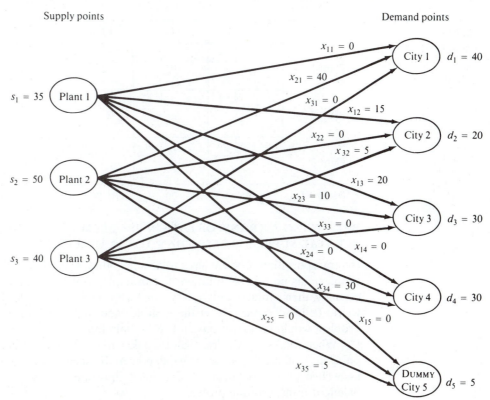

transportation tableau (see Table 2). The square, or **cell**, in row i and column j of a transportation tableau corresponds to the variable x_{ij}. If x_{ij} is a basic variable, its value is placed in the lower left-hand corner of the ijth cell of the tableau. For example, the balanced Powerco problem and its optimal solution could be displayed as shown in Table 3. The tableau format implicitly expresses the supply and demand constraints through the fact that the sum of the variables in row i must equal s_i and the sum of the variables in column j must equal d_j.

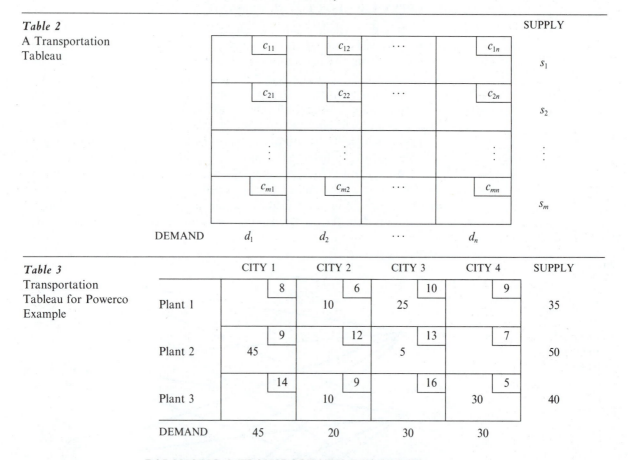

Table 2
A Transportation
Tableau

Table 3
Transportation
Tableau for Powerco
Example

BALANCING A TRANSPORTATION PROBLEM
IF TOTAL SUPPLY IS LESS THAN TOTAL DEMAND

If a transportation problem has a total supply that is strictly less than total demand, the problem has no feasible solution. For example, if plant 1 had only 30 million kwh of capacity, then a total of only 120 million kwh would be available. This amount of power would be insufficient to meet the total demand of 125 million kwh, and the Powerco problem would no longer have a feasible solution.

When total supply is less than total demand, it is sometimes desirable to allow the possibility of leaving some demand unmet. In such a situation, a penalty is often associated with unmet demand. Example 2 illustrates how such a situation can yield a balanced transportation problem.

E X A M P L E 2

Two reservoirs are available to supply the water needs of three cities. Each reservoir can supply up to 50 million gallons of water per day. Each city would like to receive 40 million gallons of water per day. For each million gallons per day of unmet demand, there is a penalty. At city 1, the penalty is $20; at city 2, the penalty is $22; and at city 3, the penalty is $23. The cost of transporting 1 million gallons of water from each reservoir to each city are shown in Table 4. Formulate a balanced transportation problem that can be used to minimize the sum of shortage and transport costs.

Table 4
Shipping Costs for
Reservoir Example

FROM	City 1	City 2	City 3
		TO	
Reservoir 1	$7	$8	$10
Reservoir 2	$9	$7	$8

Solution

In this problem,

Daily supply = 50 + 50 = 100 million gallons per day

Daily demand = 40 + 40 + 40 = 120 million gallons per day

To balance the problem, we add a dummy (or shortage) *supply point* having a supply of $120 - 100 = 20$ million gallons per day. The cost of shipping 1 million gallons from the dummy supply point to a city is just the shortage cost per million gallons for that city. Table 5 shows the balanced transportation problem and its optimal solution. Reservoir 1 should send 20 million gallons per day to city 1 and 30 million gallons per day to city 2, whereas reservoir 2 should send 10 million gallons per day to city 2 and 40 million gallons per day to city 3. Twenty million gallons per day of city 1's demand will be unsatisfied.

Table 5
Transportation
Tableau for
Reservoir Example

	CITY 1	CITY 2	CITY 3	SUPPLY
Reservoir 1	7 / 20	8 / 30	10	50
Reservoir 2	9	7 / 10	8 / 40	50
Dummy (shortage)	20 / 20	22	23	20
DEMAND	40	40	40	

MODELING INVENTORY PROBLEMS AS TRANSPORTATION PROBLEMS

Many inventory planning problems can be modeled as balanced transportation problems. To illustrate, we formulate a balanced transportation model of the Sailco problem of Section 3.10.

EXAMPLE
3

Sailco Corporation must determine how many sailboats should be produced during each of the next four quarters (one quarter is three months). Demand is as follows: first quarter, 40 sailboats; second quarter, 60 sailboats; third quarter, 75 sailboats; fourth quarter, 25 sailboats. Sailco must meet demand on time. At the beginning of the first quarter, Sailco has an inventory of 10 sailboats. At the beginning of each quarter, Sailco must decide how many sailboats should be produced during the current quarter. For simplicity, we assume that sailboats manufactured during a quarter can be used to meet demand for the current quarter. During each quarter, Sailco can produce up to 40 sailboats at a cost of $400 per sailboat. By having employees work overtime during a quarter, Sailco can produce additional sailboats at a cost of $450 per sailboat. At the end of each quarter (after production has occurred and the current quarter's demand has been satisfied), a carrying or holding cost of $20 per sailboat is incurred. Formulate a balanced transportation problem to minimize the sum of production and inventory costs during the next four quarters.

Solution

We define supply and demand points as follows:

$$\text{Point 1} = \text{initial inventory} \quad (s_1 = 10)$$
$$\text{Point 2} = \text{quarter 1 regular-time (RT) production} \quad (s_2 = 40)$$
$$\text{Point 3} = \text{quarter 1 overtime (OT) production} \quad (s_3 = 150)$$
$$\text{Point 4} = \text{quarter 2 RT production} \quad (s_4 = 40)$$

Supply Points $\quad \text{Point 5} = \text{quarter 2 OT production} \quad (s_5 = 150)$

$$\text{Point 6} = \text{quarter 3 RT production} \quad (s_6 = 40)$$
$$\text{Point 7} = \text{quarter 3 OT production} \quad (s_7 = 150)$$
$$\text{Point 8} = \text{quarter 4 RT production} \quad (s_8 = 40)$$
$$\text{Point 9} = \text{quarter 4 OT production} \quad (s_9 = 150)$$

There is a supply point corresponding to each source from which demand for sailboats can be met:

$$\text{Point 1} = \text{quarter 1 demand} \quad (d_1 = 40)$$
$$\text{Point 2} = \text{quarter 2 demand} \quad (d_2 = 60)$$

Demand Points $\quad \text{Point 3} = \text{quarter 3 demand} \quad (d_3 = 75)$

$$\text{Point 4} = \text{quarter 4 demand} \quad (d_4 = 25)$$
$$\text{Point 5} = \text{dummy demand point} \quad (d_5 = 770 - 200 = 570)$$

A shipment from, say, quarter 1 RT to quarter 3 demand means producing 1 unit on regular time during quarter 1 that is used to meet 1 unit of quarter 3's demand. To determine, say, c_{13}, observe that producing 1 unit during quarter 1 RT and using that unit to meet quarter 3 demand incurs a cost equal to the cost of producing 1 unit on quarter 1 RT plus the cost of holding a unit in inventory for $3 - 1 = 2$ quarters. Thus, $c_{13} = 400 + 2(20) = 440$.

Since there is no limit on the overtime production during any quarter, it is not clear what value should be chosen for the supply at each overtime production point. Since total demand $= 200$, at most $200 - 10 = 190$ (-10 is for initial inventory) units will be produced during any quarter. Since 40 units must be produced on regular time before any units are produced on overtime, overtime production during any quarter will never exceed $190 - 40 = 150$ units. Any unused overtime capacity will be "shipped" to the dummy demand point. To ensure that no sailboats are used to meet demand during a quarter prior to their production, a cost of M (M is a large positive number) is assigned to any cell that corresponds to using production to meet demand for an earlier quarter.

Total supply $= 770$ and total demand $= 200$, so we must add a dummy demand point with a demand of $770 - 200 = 570$ to balance the problem. The cost of shipping a unit from any supply point to the dummy demand point is zero.

Combining these observations yields the balanced transportation problem and its optimal solution shown in Table 6. Thus, Sailco should meet quarter 1 demand with 10 units of initial inventory and 30 units of quarter 1 RT production; quarter 2 demand with

Table 6
Transportation Tableau for Sailco Example

Each cell shows cost (top) and allocation.

	1	2	3	4	DUMMY	SUPPLY
Initial	0 [10]	20	40	60	0	10
Qtr 1 RT	400 [30]	420 [10]	440	460	0	40
Qtr 1 OT	450	470	490	510	0 [150]	150
Qtr 2 RT	M	400 [40]	420	440	0	40
Qtr 2 OT	M	450 [10]	470	490	0 [140]	150
Qtr 3 RT	M	M	400 [40]	420	0	40
Qtr 3 OT	M	M	450 [35]	470	0 [115]	150
Qtr 4 RT	M	M	M	400 [25]	0 [15]	40
Qtr 4 OT	M	M	M	450	0 [150]	150
DEMAND	40	60	75	25	570	

10 units of quarter 1 RT, 40 units of quarter 2 RT, and 10 units of quarter 2 OT production; quarter 3 demand with 40 units of quarter 3 RT and 35 units of quarter 3 OT production; and finally, quarter 4 demand with 25 units of quarter 4 RT production. ◆

In Problem 12 at the end of this section, we show how this formulation can be modified to incorporate other aspects of inventory problems (backlogged demand, perishable inventory, etc.).

◆ PROBLEMS

GROUP A

1. A company supplies goods to three customers, who each require 30 units. The company has two warehouses. Warehouse 1 has 40 units available and warehouse 2 has 30 units available. The costs of shipping 1 unit from warehouse to customer are shown in Table 7. There is a penalty for unmet demand. For each unit of customer 1's demand that is unmet, a penalty cost of $90 is incurred; for each unit of customer 2's unmet demand, a penalty cost of $80 is incurred; and for each unit of customer 3's unmet demand, a cost of $110 is incurred. Formulate a balanced transportation problem to minimize the sum of shortage and shipping costs.

2. Referring to Problem 1, suppose that extra units could be purchased and shipped to either warehouse for a total cost of $100 per unit and that all customer demand must be met. Formulate a balanced transportation problem to minimize the sum of purchasing and shipping costs.

3. A shoe company forecasts the following demands during the next six months: month 1, 200; month 2, 260; month 3, 240; month 4, 340; month 5, 190; month 6, 150. It costs $7 to produce a pair of shoes with regular-time labor (RT) and $11 with overtime labor (OT). During each month, regular production is limited to 200 pairs of shoes, and overtime production is limited to 100 pairs of shoes. It costs $1 per month to hold a pair of shoes in inventory.

Formulate a balanced transportation problem to minimize the total cost of meeting the next six months of demand on time.

4. Steelco manufactures three types of steel at different plants. The time required to manufacture 1 ton of steel (regardless of type) and the costs at each plant are shown in Table 8. Each week, 100 tons of each type of steel (steel 1, steel 2, and steel 3) must be produced. Each plant is open 40 hours per week.

(a) Formulate a balanced transportation problem to minimize the cost of meeting Steelco's weekly requirements.

(b) Suppose the time required to produce 1 ton of steel depends on the type of steel as well as on the plant at which the steel is produced (see Table 9). Could a transportation problem still be formulated?

Table 8

| | COST | | | |
	Steel 1	*Steel 2*	*Steel 3*	TIME (Minutes)
Plant 1	$60	$40	$28	20
Plant 2	$50	$30	$30	16
Plant 3	$43	$20	$20	15

Table 7

| | TO | | |
FROM	*Customer 1*	*Customer 2*	*Customer 3*
Warehouse 1	$15	$35	$25
Warehouse 2	$10	$50	$40

Table 9

	TIME (Minutes)		
	Steel 1	*Steel 2*	*Steel 3*
Plant 1	15	12	15
Plant 2	15	15	20
Plant 3	10	10	15

5. A hospital needs to purchase 3 gallons of a perishable medicine for use during the current month and 4 gallons of the medicine for use during the next month. Because the medicine is perishable, it can only be used during the month of purchase. Two companies (Daisy and Laroach) sell the medicine. The medicine is in short supply. Thus, during the next two months, the hospital is limited to buying at most 5 gallons from each company. The companies charge the prices shown in Table 10. Formulate a balanced transportation model to minimize the cost of purchasing the needed medicine.

6. A bank has two sites at which checks are processed. Site 1 can process 10,000 checks per day, and site 2 can process 6000 checks per day. The bank processes three types of checks: vendor checks, salary checks, and personal checks. The processing cost per check depends on the site at which the check is processed (see Table 11). Each day, 5000 checks of each type must be processed. Formulate a balanced transportation problem to minimize the daily cost of processing checks.

7.[†] The U.S. government is auctioning off oil leases at two sites: site 1 and site 2. At each site, 100,000 acres of land are to be auctioned. Cliff Ewing, Blake Barnes, and Alexis Pickens are bidding for the oil. Government rules state that no bidder can receive more than 40% of the land being auctioned. Cliff has bid $1000/acre for site 1 land and $2000/acre for site 2 land. Blake has bid $900/acre for site 1 land and $2200/acre for site 2 land. Alexis has bid

Table 11

	SITE 2	SITE 2
Vendor checks	5¢	3¢
Salary checks	4¢	4¢
Personal checks	2¢	5¢

Table 12

FROM	TO	
	England	*Japan*
Field 1	$1	$2
Field 2	$2	$1

$1100/acre for site 1 land and $1900/acre for site 2 land. Formulate a balanced transportation model to maximize the government's revenue.

8. The Ayatola Oil Company controls two oil fields. Field 1 can produce up to 40 million barrels of oil per day, and field 2 can produce up to 50 million barrels of oil per day. At field 1, it costs $3 to extract and refine a barrel of oil; at field 2, it costs $2 to extract and refine a barrel of oil. Ayatola sells oil to two countries: England and Japan. The shipping cost per barrel of oil is shown in Table 12. Each day, England is willing to buy up to 40 million barrels of oil (at $6 per barrel), and Japan is willing to buy up to 30 million barrels of oil (at $6.50 per barrel). Formulate a balanced transportation problem to maximize Ayatola's profits.

9. For the examples and problems of this section, discuss whether it is reasonable to assume that the proportionality assumption holds for the objective function.

10. Touche Young has three auditors. Each auditor can work up to 160 hours during the next month, during which time three projects must be completed. Project 1 will take

Table 10

	CURRENT MONTH'S PRICE PER GALLON	NEXT MONTH'S PRICE PER GALLON
Daisy	$800	$720
Laroach	$710	$750

[†] This problem is based on Jackson (1980).

130 hours, project 2 will take 140 hours, and project 3 will take 160 hours. The amount per hour that can be billed for assigning each auditor to each project is given in Table 13. Formulate a balanced transportation problem to maximize total billings during the next month.

Table 13

AUDITOR	PROJECT		
	1	*2*	*3*
1	$120	$150	$190
2	$140	$130	$120
3	$160	$140	$150

GROUP B

11.[†] Paperco recycles newsprint, uncoated paper, and coated paper into recycled newsprint, recycled uncoated paper, and recycled coated paper. Recycled newsprint can be produced by processing newsprint or uncoated paper. Recycled coated paper can be produced by recycling any type of paper. Recycled uncoated paper can be produced by processing uncoated paper or coated paper. The pro-

cess used to produce recycled newsprint removes 20% of the input's pulp. The process used to produce recycled coated paper removes 10% of the input's pulp. The process used to produce recycled uncoated paper removes 15% of the input's pulp. The purchasing costs, processing costs, and availability of each type of paper are shown in Table 14. To meet demand, Paperco must produce at least 250 tons of recycled newsprint pulp, at least 300 tons of recycled uncoated paper pulp, and at least 150 tons of recycled coated paper pulp. Formulate a balanced transportation problem that can be used to minimize the cost of meeting Paperco's demands.

12. Explain how each of the following would modify the formulation of the Sailco problem as a balanced transportation problem:
(a) Suppose demand could be backlogged at a cost of $30/sailboat/month. (*Hint:* Now it is permissible to ship from, say, month 2 production to month 1 demand.)
(b) If demand for a sailboat is not met on time, the sale is lost and an opportunity cost of $450 is incurred.
(c) Sailboats can be held in inventory for a maximum of two months.
(d) At a cost of $440/sailboat, Sailco can purchase up to 10 sailboats per month from a subcontractor.

Table 14

	PURCHASE COST PER TON OF PULP	PROCESSING COST PER TON OF INPUT	AVAILABILITY
Newsprint	$10		500
Coated paper	$9		300
Uncoated paper	$8		200
NP used for RNP		$3	
NP used for RCP		$4	
UCP used for RNP		$4	
UCP used for RUP		$1	
UCP used for RCP		$6	
CP used for RUP		$5	
CP used for RCP		$3	

[†]This problem is based on Glassey and Gupta (1974).

FINDING BASIC FEASIBLE SOLUTIONS
FOR TRANSPORTATION PROBLEMS

Consider a balanced transportation problem with m supply points and n demand points. From (2), we see that such a problem contains $m + n$ equality constraints. From our experience with the Big M method and the two-phase simplex method, we know it is difficult to find a bfs if all of an LP's constraints are equalities. Fortunately, the special structure of a balanced transportation problem makes it easy for us to find a bfs for any balanced transportation problem.

Before describing three methods commonly used to find a bfs to a balanced transportation problem, we need to make the following important observation. *If a set of values for the x_{ij}'s satisfies all but one of the constraints of a balanced transportation problem, the values for the x_{ij}'s will automatically satisfy the other constraint.* For example, in the Powerco problem, suppose a set of values for the x_{ij}'s is known to satisfy all the constraints with the exception of the first supply constraint. Then this set of x_{ij}'s must supply $d_1 + d_2 + d_3 + d_4 = 125$ million kwh to cities 1–4 and supply $s_2 + s_3 = 125 - s_1 = 90$ million kwh from plants 2 and 3. Thus, plant 1 must supply $125 - (125 - s_1) = 35$ million kwh, so the x_{ij}'s must also satisfy the first supply constraint.

The preceding discussion shows that when we solve a balanced transportation problem, we may omit from consideration any one of the problem's constraints and solve an LP having $m + n - 1$ constraints. We (arbitrarily) assume that the first supply constraint is omitted from consideration.

In trying to find a bfs to the remaining $m + n - 1$ constraints, you might think that any collection of $m + n - 1$ variables would yield a basic solution. Unfortunately, this is not the case. For example, consider (3), a balanced transportation problem. (We omit the costs, because they are not needed to find a bfs.)

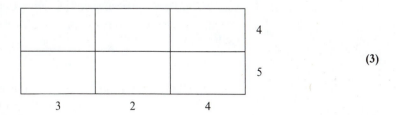

(3)

In matrix form, the constraints for this balanced transportation problem may be written as

$$\begin{bmatrix} 1 & 1 & 1 & 0 & 0 & 0 \\ 0 & 0 & 0 & 1 & 1 & 1 \\ 1 & 0 & 0 & 1 & 0 & 0 \\ 0 & 1 & 0 & 0 & 1 & 0 \\ 0 & 0 & 1 & 0 & 0 & 1 \end{bmatrix} \begin{bmatrix} x_{11} \\ x_{12} \\ x_{13} \\ x_{21} \\ x_{22} \\ x_{23} \end{bmatrix} = \begin{bmatrix} 4 \\ 5 \\ 3 \\ 2 \\ 4 \end{bmatrix}$$

(3′)

After dropping the first supply constraint, we obtain the following linear system:

$$\begin{bmatrix} 0 & 0 & 0 & 1 & 1 & 1 \\ 1 & 0 & 0 & 1 & 0 & 0 \\ 0 & 1 & 0 & 0 & 1 & 0 \\ 0 & 0 & 1 & 0 & 0 & 1 \end{bmatrix} \begin{bmatrix} x_{11} \\ x_{12} \\ x_{13} \\ x_{21} \\ x_{22} \\ x_{23} \end{bmatrix} = \begin{bmatrix} 5 \\ 3 \\ 2 \\ 4 \end{bmatrix} \qquad (3'')$$

A basic solution to (3″) must have four basic variables. Suppose we try $BV = \{x_{11}, x_{12}, x_{21}, x_{22}\}$. Then

$$B = \begin{bmatrix} 0 & 0 & 1 & 1 \\ 1 & 0 & 1 & 0 \\ 0 & 1 & 0 & 1 \\ 0 & 0 & 0 & 0 \end{bmatrix}$$

For $\{x_{11}, x_{12}, x_{21}, x_{22}\}$ to yield a basic solution, it must be possible to use ero's to transform B to I_4. Since rank $B = 3$ and ero's do not change the rank of a matrix, there is no way that ero's can be used to transform B into I_4. Thus, $BV = \{x_{11}, x_{12}, x_{21}, x_{22}\}$ cannot yield a basic solution to (3″). Fortunately, the simple concept of a loop may be used to determine whether an arbitrary set of $m + n - 1$ variables yields a basic solution to a balanced transportation problem.

DEFINITION   An ordered sequence of at least four different cells is called a **loop** if

     1. Any two consecutive cells lie in either the same row or same column

     2. No three consecutive cells lie in the same row or column

     3. The last cell in the sequence has a row or column in common with the first cell in the sequence

In the definition of a loop, the first cell is considered to follow the last cell, so the loop may be thought of as a closed path. Here are some examples of the preceding definition: Figure 3 represents the loop (2, 1)–(2, 4)–(4, 4)–(4, 1). Figure 4 represents the loop (1, 1)–(1, 2)–(2, 2)–(2, 3)–(4, 3)–(4, 5)–(3, 5)–(3, 1). In Figure 5, the path

Figure 3

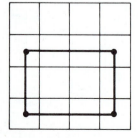

Figure 4

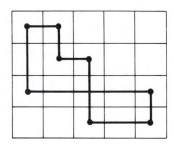

Figure 5

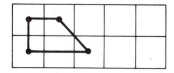

$(1, 1)$–$(1, 2)$–$(2, 3)$–$(2, 1)$ does not represent a loop, because $(1, 2)$ and $(2, 3)$ do not lie in the same row or column. In Figure 6, the path $(1, 2)$–$(1, 3)$–$(1, 4)$–$(2, 4)$–$(2, 2)$ does not represent a loop, because $(1, 2)$, $(1, 3)$, and $(1, 4)$ all lie in the same row.

Theorem 1 (which we state without proof) shows why the concept of a loop is important.

Figure 6

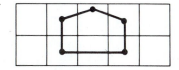

THEOREM 1	In a balanced transportation problem with m supply points and n demand points, the cells corresponding to a set of $m + n - 1$ variables contain no loop if and only if the $m + n - 1$ variables yield a basic solution.

Theorem 1 follows from the fact that a set of $m + n - 1$ cells contains no loop if and only if the $m + n - 1$ columns corresponding to these cells are linearly independent. Since $(1, 1)$–$(1, 2)$–$(2, 2)$–$(2, 1)$ is a loop, Theorem 1 tells us that $\{x_{11}, x_{12}, x_{22}, x_{21}\}$ cannot yield a basic solution for (3″). On the other hand, no loop can be formed with the cells $(1, 1)$–$(1, 2)$–$(1, 3)$–$(2, 1)$, so $\{x_{11}, x_{12}, x_{13}, x_{21}\}$ will yield a basic solution to (3″).

We are now ready to discuss three methods that can be used to find a basic feasible solution for a balanced transportation problem:

1. Northwest Corner method

2. Minimum cost method

3. Vogel's method

NORTHWEST CORNER METHOD
FOR FINDING A BASIC FEASIBLE SOLUTION

To find a bfs by the Northwest Corner method, we begin in the upper left (or northwest) corner of the transportation tableau and set x_{11} as large as possible. Clearly, x_{11} can be no larger than the smaller of s_1 and d_1. If $x_{11} = s_1$, cross out the first row of the transportation tableau; this indicates that no more basic variables will come from row 1 of the tableau. Also change d_1 to $d_1 - s_1$. If $x_{11} = d_1$, cross out the first column of the transportation tableau; this indicates that no more basic variables will come from the first column of the tableau. Also change s_1 to $s_1 - d_1$. If $x_{11} = s_1 = d_1$, cross out either row 1 or column 1 (but not both) of the transportation tableau. If you cross out row 1, change d_1 to 0; if you cross out column 1, change s_1 to 0.

Continue applying this procedure to the most northwest cell in the tableau that does not lie in a crossed-out row or column. Eventually, you will come to a point where there is only one cell that can be assigned a value. Assign this cell a value equal to its row or column demand, and cross out both the cell's row and column. A basic feasible solution has now been obtained.

We illustrate the use of the Northwest Corner method by finding a bfs for the balanced transportation problem in Table 15. (Since costs are not needed to apply the algorithm, we do not list the costs.) We indicate the crossing out of a row or column by placing an × by the row's supply or column's demand.

Table 15

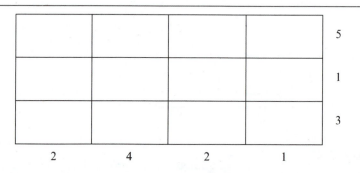

To begin, we set $x_{11} = \min\{5, 2\} = 2$. Then we cross out column 1 and change s_1 to $5 - 2 = 3$. This yields Table 16. The most northwest remaining variable is x_{12}. We set $x_{12} = \min\{3, 4\} = 3$. Then we cross out row 1 and change d_2 to $4 - 3 = 1$. This yields Table 17. The most northwest available variable is now x_{22}. We set

Table 16

Table 17

2	3			x
				1
				3
x	1	2	1	

$x_{22} = \min\{1, 1\} = 1$. Since both the supply and demand corresponding to the cell are equal, we may cross out either row 2 or column 2 (but not both). For no particular reason, we choose to cross out row 2. Then d_2 must be changed to $1 - 1 = 0$. The resulting tableau is Table 18. At the next step, this will lead to a *degenerate* bfs.

The most northwest available cell is now x_{32}, so we set $x_{32} = \min\{0, 3\} = 0$. Then we cross out column 2 and change s_3 to $3 - 0 = 3$. The resulting tableau is Table 19. We now set $x_{33} = \min\{3, 2\} = 2$. Then we cross out column 3 and reduce s_3 to $3 - 2 = 1$. The resulting tableau is Table 20. The only available cell is x_{34}. We set $x_{34} = \min\{1, 1\} = 1$. Then we cross out row 3 and column 4. Since no cells are available, we are finished. We have obtained the bfs $x_{11} = 2$, $x_{12} = 3$, $x_{22} = 1$, $x_{32} = 0$, $x_{33} = 2$, $x_{34} = 1$.

Why does the Northwest Corner method yield a bfs? The method ensures that no basic variable will be assigned a negative value (since no right-hand side ever becomes

Table 18

2	3			x
	1			x
				3
x	0	2	1	

Table 19

2	3			x
	1			x
	0			3
x	x	2	1	

Table 20

2	3			×
	1			×
	0	2		1
×	×	×	1	

negative) and also that each supply and demand constraint is satisfied (since every row and column is eventually crossed out). Thus, the Northwest Corner method yields a feasible solution. To complete the Northwest Corner method, $m + n$ rows and columns must be crossed out. Since the last variable assigned a value results in a row and column being crossed out, the Northwest Corner method will assign values to $m + n - 1$ variables. The variables chosen by the Northwest Corner method cannot form a loop, so Theorem 1 implies that the Northwest Corner method must yield a bfs.

MINIMUM COST METHOD FOR FINDING A BASIC FEASIBLE SOLUTION

The Northwest Corner method does not utilize shipping costs, so it can yield an initial bfs that has a very high shipping cost. Then determining an optimal solution may require very many pivots. The minimum cost method uses the shipping costs in an effort to produce a bfs that does not have an extremely high total cost. We hope that fewer pivots will then be required to find the problem's optimal solution.

To begin the minimum cost method, find the variable with the smallest shipping cost (call it x_{ij}). Then assign x_{ij} its largest possible value, $\min\{s_i, d_j\}$. As in the Northwest Corner method, cross out row i or column j and reduce the supply or demand of the non-crossed-out row or column by the value of x_{ij}. Then choose from the cells that do not lie in a crossed-out row or column the cell with the minimum shipping cost and repeat the procedure. Continue until there is only one cell that can be chosen. In this case, cross out both the cell's row and column. Remember that (with the exception of the last variable) if a variable satisfies both a supply and demand constraint, only cross out a row or column, not both.

To illustrate the minimum cost method, we find a bfs for the balanced transportation problem in Table 21. The variable with the minimum shipping cost is x_{22}. We set $x_{22} = \min\{10, 8\} = 8$. Then we cross out column 2 and reduce s_2 to $10 - 8 = 2$. The result is Table 22. We could now choose either x_{11} or x_{21} (both have shipping costs of 2). We arbitrarily choose x_{21} and set $x_{21} = \min\{2, 12\} = 2$. Then we cross out row 2 and change d_1 to $12 - 2 = 10$. The result is Table 23. Now we set $x_{11} = \min\{5, 10\} = 5$, cross out row 1, and change d_1 to $10 - 5 = 5$. The result is Table 24. The minimum cost that does not lie in a crossed-out row or column is x_{31}. We set $x_{31} = \min\{15, 5\} = 5$, cross out column 1, and reduce s_3 to $15 - 5 = 10$. The result is Table 25. Now we set $x_{33} = \min\{10, 4\} = 4$, cross out column 3, and reduce s_3 to $10 - 4 = 6$. The result is Table 26. The only cell that we can choose is x_{34}. We set $x_{34} = \min\{6, 6\}$ and cross out

Table 21

				Supply
2	3	5	6	5
2	1	3	5	10
3	8	4	6	15
12	8	4	6	

Table 22

				Supply
2	3	5	6	5
2	8 1	3	5	2
3	8	4	6	15
12	×	4	6	

Table 23

				Supply
2	3	5	6	5
2 2	8 1	3	5	×
3	8	4	6	15
10	×	4	6	

Table 24

				Supply
5 2	3	5	6	×
2 2	8 1	3	5	×
3	8	4	6	15
5	×	4	6	

Table 25

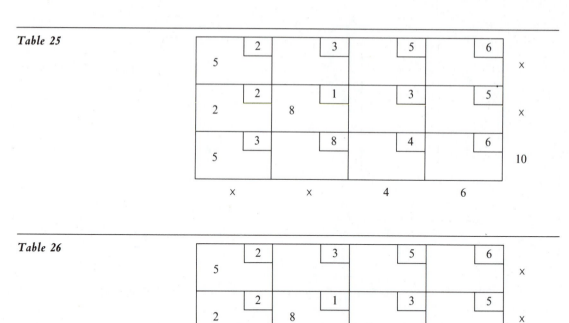

	Col 1	Col 2	Col 3	Col 4	Supply
Row 1	[2] 5	[3]	[5]	[6]	X
Row 2	[2] 2	[1] 8	[3]	[5]	X
Row 3	[3] 5	[8]	[4] 4	[6] 6	10
Demand	X	X	4	6	

Table 26

	Col 1	Col 2	Col 3	Col 4	Supply
Row 1	[2] 5	[3]	[5]	[6]	X
Row 2	[2] 2	[1] 8	[3]	[5]	X
Row 3	[3] 5	[8]	[4] 4	[6]	6
Demand	X	X	X	6	

both row 3 and column 4. We have now obtained the bfs: $x_{11} = 5$, $x_{21} = 2$, $x_{22} = 8$, $x_{31} = 5$, $x_{33} = 4$, and $x_{34} = 6$.

Since the minimum cost method chooses variables with small shipping costs to be basic variables, you might think that the minimum cost method would always yield a bfs with a relatively low total shipping cost. The following problem shows how the minimum cost method can be fooled into choosing a relatively high-cost bfs.

If we apply the minimum cost method to Table 27, we begin by setting $x_{11} = 10$ and crossing out row 1. This forces us to make x_{22} and x_{23} basic variables, thereby incurring the high shipping costs associated with x_{22} and x_{23}. Thus, for Table 27, the minimum cost method will yield a costly bfs. Vogel's method for finding a bfs usually avoids extremely high shipping costs.

Table 27

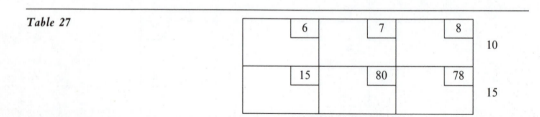

	Col 1	Col 2	Col 3	Supply
Row 1	[6]	[7]	[8]	10
Row 2	[15]	[80]	[78]	15
Demand	15	5	5	

VOGEL'S METHOD FOR FINDING
A BASIC FEASIBLE SOLUTION

Begin by computing for each row (and column) a "penalty" equal to the difference between the two smallest costs in the row (column). Next find the row or column with the largest penalty. Choose as the first basic variable the variable in this row or column that has the smallest shipping cost. As described in the Northwest Corner and minimum cost methods, make this variable as large as possible, cross out a row or column, and change the supply or demand associated with the basic variable. Now recompute new penalties (using only cells that do not lie in a crossed-out row or column) and repeat the procedure until only one uncrossed cell remains. Set this variable equal to the supply or demand associated with the variable, and cross out the variable's row and column. A bfs has now been obtained.

We illustrate Vogel's method by finding a bfs to Table 28. Column 2 has the largest penalty, so we set $x_{12} = \min\{5, 10\} = 5$. Then we cross out column 2 and reduce s_1 to $10 - 5 = 5$. After recomputing the new penalties (observe that after a column is crossed out, the column penalties will remain unchanged), we obtain Table 29. The largest penalty now occurs in column 3, so we set $x_{13} = \min\{5, 5\}$. We may cross out either row 1 or column 3. We arbitrarily choose to cross out column 3, and we reduce s_1 to $5 - 5 = 0$. Since each row has only one cell that is not crossed out, there are no row penalties. The resulting tableau is Table 30. Column 1 has the only (and, of course, the largest) penalty. We set $x_{11} = \min\{15, 0\} = 0$, cross out row 1, and change d_1 to $15 - 0 = 15$. The result is Table 31. No penalties can be computed, and the only cell

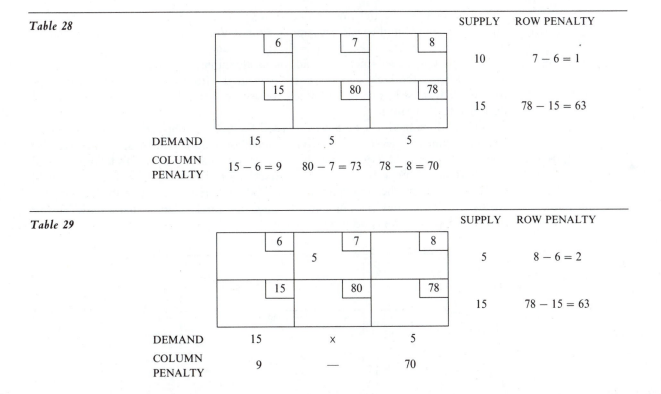

Table 28

	6	7	8	SUPPLY	ROW PENALTY
				10	$7 - 6 = 1$
	15	80	78	15	$78 - 15 = 63$
DEMAND	15	5	5		
COLUMN PENALTY	$15 - 6 = 9$	$80 - 7 = 73$	$78 - 8 = 70$		

Table 29

	6	7	8	SUPPLY	ROW PENALTY
	5			5	$8 - 6 = 2$
	15	80	78	15	$78 - 15 = 63$
DEMAND	15	x	5		
COLUMN PENALTY	9	—	70		

Table 30

			SUPPLY	ROW PENALTY
6 ⟶ 5	7 ⟶ 5	8	0	—
15	80	78	15	—
DEMAND 15	×	×		
COLUMN PENALTY 9	—	—		

Table 31

			SUPPLY	ROW PENALTY
0 6 ⟶ 5	7 ⟶ 5	8	×	—
15	80	78	15	—
DEMAND 15	×	×		
COLUMN PENALTY —	—	—		

that is not in a crossed-out row or column is x_{21}. Therefore, we set $x_{21} = 15$ and cross out both column 1 and row 2. Our application of Vogel's method is complete, and we have obtained the bfs: $x_{11} = 0$, $x_{12} = 5$, $x_{13} = 5$, and $x_{21} = 15$ (see Table 32).

Observe that Vogel's method avoids the costly shipments associated with x_{22} and x_{23}. This is because the high shipping costs associated with x_{22} and x_{23} resulted in large penalties that caused Vogel's method to choose other variables to satisfy the second and third demand constraints.

Of the three methods we have discussed for finding a bfs, the Northwest Corner method requires the least effort and Vogel's method requires the most effort. Extensive research (Glover et al. (1974)) has shown, however, that when Vogel's method is used to find an initial bfs, it usually takes substantially fewer pivots than if the Northwest Corner method or the minimum cost method had been used. For this reason, the Northwest Corner and minimum cost methods are rarely used to find a basic feasible solution to a large transportation problem.

Table 32

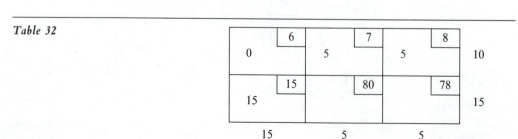

◆ PROBLEMS

GROUP A

1. Use the Northwest Corner method to find a bfs for Problems 1, 2, and 3 of Section 7.1.

2. Use the minimum cost method to find a bfs for Problems 4, 7, and 8 of Section 7.1. (*Hint:* For a maxi-

mization problem, call the minimum cost method the maximum profit method or the maximum revenue method.)

3. Use Vogel's method to find a bfs for Problems 5 and 6 of Section 7.1.

4. How should Vogel's method be modified to solve a maximization problem?

7–3   THE TRANSPORTATION SIMPLEX METHOD

In this section, we show how the simplex algorithm simplifies when a transportation problem is solved. We begin by discussing the pivoting procedure for a transportation problem.

Recall that when the pivot row was used to eliminate the entering basic variable from other constraints and row 0, many multiplications were usually required. In solving a transportation problem, however, *pivots require only additions and subtractions.*

HOW TO PIVOT IN A TRANSPORTATION PROBLEM

By using the following procedure, the pivots for a transportation problem may be performed within the confines of the transportation tableau:

Step 1 Determine (by a criterion to be developed shortly) the variable that should enter the basis.

Step 2 Find the loop (it can be shown that there is only one loop) involving the entering variable and some of the basic variables.

Step 3 Counting *only cells in the loop,* label the cells in the loop found in Step 2 that are an even number (0, 2, 4, etc.) of cells away from the entering variable as even cells. Also label those cells in the loop that are an odd number of cells away from the entering variable as odd cells.

Step 4 Find the odd cell whose variable assumes the smallest value. Call this value θ. The variable corresponding to this odd cell will leave the basis. To perform the pivot, decrease the value of each odd cell by θ and increase the value of each even cell by θ. The values of variables not in the loop remain unchanged. The pivot is now complete. If $\theta = 0$, the entering variable will equal zero, and an odd variable that has a current value of zero will leave the basis. In this case, a degenerate bfs existed before and will result after the pivot. If more than one odd cell in the loop equals θ, you may arbitrarily choose one of these odd cells to leave the basis; again a degenerate bfs will result.

We illustrate the pivoting procedure on the Powerco example. When the Northwest Corner method is applied to the Powerco example, the bfs in Table 33 is found. For this bfs, the basic variables are $x_{11} = 35$, $x_{21} = 10$, $x_{22} = 20$, $x_{23} = 20$, $x_{33} = 10$, and $x_{34} = 30$.

Table 33
Northwest Corner
Basic Feasible
Solution for Powerco
Example

35				35
10	20	20		50
		10	30	40
45	20	30	30	

Suppose we wish to find the bfs that would result if x_{14} were entered into the basis. The loop involving x_{14} and some of the basic variables is the loop

$$\text{E} \quad \text{O} \quad \text{E} \quad \text{O} \quad \text{E} \quad \text{O}$$
$$(1,4)-(3,4)-(3,3)-(2,3)-(2,1)-(1,1)$$

In this loop, $(1,4), (3,3)$, and $(2,1)$ are the even cells, and $(1,1), (3,4)$, and $(2,3)$ are the odd cells. The odd cell with the smallest value is $x_{23} = 20$. Thus, after the pivot, x_{23} will have left the basis. We now add 20 to each of the even cells and subtract 20 from each of the odd cells. The bfs in Table 34 results. Since each row and column has as many $+20$'s as -20's, the new solution will satisfy each supply and demand constraint. By choosing the smallest odd variable (x_{23}) to leave the basis, we have ensured that all variables will remain nonnegative. Thus, the new solution is feasible. Since there is no loop involving the cells $(1,1), (1,4), (2,1), (2,2), (3,3)$, and $(3,4)$, the new solution is a bfs. After the pivot, the new bfs is $x_{11} = 15, x_{14} = 20, x_{21} = 30, x_{22} = 20, x_{33} = 30$, and $x_{34} = 10$, and all other variables equal zero.

Table 34
New Basic Feasible
Solution After x_{14} Is
Pivoted into Basis

35 − 20			0 + 20	35
10 + 20	20	20 − 20 (nonbasic)		50
		10 + 20	30 − 20	40
45	20	30	30	

The preceding illustration of the pivoting procedure makes it clear that each pivot in a transportation problem involves only additions and subtractions. Using this fact, we can show that *if all the supplies and demands for a transportation problem are integers, then the transportation problem will have an optimal solution in which all the variables are integers.* Begin by observing that by the Northwest Corner method, we can find a bfs in which each variable is an integer. Since each pivot involves only additions and subtractions, each bfs obtained by performing the simplex algorithm (including the optimal solution) will assign all variables integer values. The fact that a transportation problem with integer supplies and demands has an optimal integer solution is useful, because it ensures that we need not worry about whether or not the Divisibility Assumption is justified.

PRICING OUT NONBASIC VARIABLES
(BASED ON CHAPTER 6)

To complete our discussion of the transportation simplex, we now show how to compute row 0 for any bfs. From Section 6.2, we know that for a bfs in which the set of basic variables is BV, the coefficient of the variable x_{ij} (call it $\bar{c}_{ij}$) in the tableau's row 0 is given by

$$\bar{c}_{ij} = \mathbf{c}_{BV}B^{-1}\mathbf{a}_{ij} - c_{ij}$$

where c_{ij} is the objective function coefficient for x_{ij} and $\mathbf{a}_{ij}$ is the column for x_{ij} in the original LP (we are assuming that the first supply constraint has been dropped).

Since we are solving a minimization problem, the current bfs will be optimal if all the $\bar{c}_{ij}$'s are nonpositive; otherwise, we enter into the basis the variable with the most positive $\bar{c}_{ij}$.

After determining $\mathbf{c}_{BV}B^{-1}$, we can easily determine $\bar{c}_{ij}$. Since the first constraint has been dropped, $\mathbf{c}_{BV}B^{-1}$ will have $m + n - 1$ elements. We write

$$\mathbf{c}_{BV}B^{-1} = \begin{bmatrix} u_2 & u_3 & \cdots & u_m & v_1 & v_2 & \cdots & v_n \end{bmatrix}$$

where $u_2, u_3, \ldots, u_m$ are the elements of $\mathbf{c}_{BV}B^{-1}$ corresponding to the $m - 1$ supply constraints, and $v_1, v_2, \ldots, v_n$ are the elements of $\mathbf{c}_{BV}B^{-1}$ corresponding to the n demand constraints.

To determine $\mathbf{c}_{BV}B^{-1}$, we use the fact that in any tableau, each basic variable x_{ij} must have $\bar{c}_{ij} = 0$. Thus, for each of the $m + n - 1$ variables in BV,

$$\mathbf{c}_{BV}B^{-1}\mathbf{a}_{ij} - c_{ij} = 0 \tag{4}$$

For a transportation problem, the equations in (4) are very easy to solve. To illustrate the solution of (4), we find $\mathbf{c}_{BV}B^{-1}$ for (5), the Northwest Corner method bfs to the Powerco problem.

	8		6		10		9	
35								35
	9		12		13		7	
10		20		20				50
	14		9		16		5	
				10		30		40
45		20		30		30		

(5)

For this bfs, $BV = \{x_{11}, x_{21}, x_{22}, x_{23}, x_{33}, x_{34}\}$. Applying (4), we obtain

$$\bar{c}_{11} = [u_2 \quad u_3 \quad v_1 \quad v_2 \quad v_3 \quad v_4] \begin{bmatrix} 0 \\ 0 \\ 1 \\ 0 \\ 0 \\ 0 \end{bmatrix} - 8 = v_1 - 8 = 0$$

$$\bar{c}_{21} = [u_2 \quad u_3 \quad v_1 \quad v_2 \quad v_3 \quad v_4] \begin{bmatrix} 1 \\ 0 \\ 1 \\ 0 \\ 0 \\ 0 \end{bmatrix} - 9 = u_2 + v_1 - 9 = 0$$

$$\bar{c}_{22} = [u_2 \quad u_3 \quad v_1 \quad v_2 \quad v_3 \quad v_4] \begin{bmatrix} 1 \\ 0 \\ 0 \\ 1 \\ 0 \\ 0 \end{bmatrix} - 12 = u_2 + v_2 - 12 = 0$$

$$\bar{c}_{23} = [u_2 \quad u_3 \quad v_1 \quad v_2 \quad v_3 \quad v_4] \begin{bmatrix} 1 \\ 0 \\ 0 \\ 0 \\ 1 \\ 0 \end{bmatrix} - 13 = u_2 + v_3 - 13 = 0$$

$$\bar{c}_{33} = [u_2 \quad u_3 \quad v_1 \quad v_2 \quad v_3 \quad v_4] \begin{bmatrix} 0 \\ 1 \\ 0 \\ 0 \\ 1 \\ 0 \end{bmatrix} - 16 = u_3 + v_3 - 16 = 0$$

$$\bar{c}_{34} = [u_2 \quad u_3 \quad v_1 \quad v_2 \quad v_3 \quad v_4] \begin{bmatrix} 0 \\ 1 \\ 0 \\ 0 \\ 0 \\ 0 \\ 1 \end{bmatrix} - 5 = u_3 + v_4 - 5 = 0$$

For each basic variable x_{ij} (except those having $i = 1$), we see that (4) reduces to $u_i + v_j = c_{ij}$. If we define $u_1 = 0$, we see that (4) reduces to $u_i + v_j = c_{ij}$ for all basic variables. Thus, to solve for $\mathbf{c}_{BV}B^{-1}$, we must solve the following system of $m + n$ equations: $u_1 = 0$, $u_i + v_j = c_{ij}$ for all basic variables.

For (5), we find $\mathbf{c}_{BV}B^{-1}$ by solving

$$u_1 = 0 \tag{6}$$
$$u_1 + v_1 = 8 \tag{7}$$
$$u_2 + v_1 = 9 \tag{8}$$
$$u_2 + v_2 = 12 \tag{9}$$
$$u_2 + v_3 = 13 \tag{10}$$
$$u_3 + v_3 = 16 \tag{11}$$
$$u_3 + v_4 = 5 \tag{12}$$

From (7), $v_1 = 8$. From (8), $u_2 = 1$. Then (9) yields $v_2 = 11$, and (10) yields $v_3 = 12$. From (11), $u_3 = 4$. Finally, (12) yields $v_4 = 1$. For each nonbasic variable, we now compute $\bar{c}_{ij} = u_i + v_j - c_{ij}$. We obtain

$$\bar{c}_{12} = 0 + 11 - 6 = 5 \qquad \bar{c}_{13} = 0 + 12 - 10 = 2$$
$$\bar{c}_{14} = 0 + 1 - 9 = -8 \qquad \bar{c}_{24} = 1 + 1 - 7 = -5$$
$$\bar{c}_{31} = 4 + 8 - 14 = -2 \qquad \bar{c}_{32} = 4 + 11 - 9 = 6$$

Since $\bar{c}_{32}$ is the most positive $\bar{c}_{ij}$, we would next enter x_{32} into the basis. Each unit of x_{32} that is entered into the basis will decrease Powerco's cost by $6.

HOW TO DETERMINE THE ENTERING NONBASIC VARIABLE (BASED ON CHAPTER 5)

For readers who have not covered Chapter 6, we now discuss how to determine whether a bfs is optimal and, if it is not, how to determine which nonbasic variable should enter the basis. Let $-u_i$ $(i = 1, 2, \ldots, m)$ be the shadow price of the ith supply constraint, and let $-v_j$ $(j = 1, 2, \ldots, n)$ be the shadow price of the jth demand constraint. We assume that the first supply constraint has been dropped, so we may set $-u_1 = 0$. From the definition of shadow price, if we were to increase the right-hand side of the ith supply and jth demand constraint by 1, the optimal z-value would decrease by $-u_i - v_j$. Equivalently, if we were to decrease the right-hand side of the ith supply and jth demand constraint by 1, the optimal z-value would increase by $-u_i - v_j$. Now suppose x_{ij} is a nonbasic variable. Should we enter x_{ij} into the basis? Observe that if we increase x_{ij} by

1, costs directly increase by c_{ij}. Also, increasing x_{ij} by 1 means that one less unit will be shipped from supply point i and one less unit will be shipped to demand point j. This is equivalent to reducing the right-hand sides of the ith supply constraint and jth demand constraint by 1. This will increase z by $-u_i - v_j$. Thus, increasing x_{ij} by 1 will increase z by a total of $c_{ij} - u_i - v_j$. So if $c_{ij} - u_i - v_j \geq 0$ (or $u_i + v_j - c_{ij} \leq 0$) for all nonbasic variables, the current bfs will be optimal. If, however, a nonbasic variable x_{ij} has $c_{ij} - u_i - v_j < 0$ (or $u_i + v_j - c_{ij} > 0$), then z can be decreased by $u_i + v_j - c_{ij}$ per unit of x_{ij} by entering x_{ij} into the basis. Thus, we may conclude that if $u_i + v_j - c_{ij} \leq 0$ for all nonbasic variables, then the current bfs is optimal. Otherwise, the nonbasic variable with the most positive value of $u_i + v_j - c_{ij}$ should enter the basis. How do we find the u_i's and v_j's? Since the coefficient of a nonbasic variable x_{ij} in row 0 of any tableau is the amount by which a unit increase in x_{ij} will decrease z, we can conclude that the coefficient of any nonbasic variable (and, it turns out, any basic variable) in row 0 is $u_i + v_j - c_{ij}$. So we may solve for the u_i's and v_j's by solving the following system of equations: $u_1 = 0$ and $u_i + v_j - c_{ij} = 0$ for all basic variables.

To illustrate the previous discussion, consider the bfs for the Powerco problem shown in (5).

	8	6	10	9	35
35					
	9	12	13	7	50
10	20	20			
	14	9	16	5	40
		10	30		
45	20	30	30		

(5)

We find the u_i's and v_j's by solving

$$u_1 = 0 \tag{6}$$
$$u_1 + v_1 = 8 \tag{7}$$
$$u_2 + v_1 = 9 \tag{8}$$
$$u_2 + v_2 = 12 \tag{9}$$
$$u_2 + v_3 = 13 \tag{10}$$
$$u_3 + v_3 = 16 \tag{11}$$
$$u_3 + v_4 = 5 \tag{12}$$

From (7), $v_1 = 8$. From (8), $u_2 = 1$. Then (9) yields $v_2 = 11$, and (10) yields $v_3 = 12$. From (11), $u_3 = 4$. Finally, (12) yields $v_4 = 1$. For each nonbasic variable, we now compute $\bar{c}_{ij} = u_i + v_j - c_{ij}$. We obtain

$$\bar{c}_{12} = 0 + 11 - 6 = 5 \qquad \bar{c}_{13} = 0 + 12 - 10 = 2$$
$$\bar{c}_{14} = 0 + 1 - 9 = -8 \qquad \bar{c}_{24} = 1 + 1 - 7 = -5$$
$$\bar{c}_{31} = 4 + 8 - 14 = -2 \qquad \bar{c}_{32} = 4 + 11 - 9 = 6$$

Since $\bar{c}_{32}$ is the most positive $\bar{c}_{ij}$, we would next enter x_{32} into the basis. Each unit of x_{32} that is entered into the basis will decrease Powerco's cost by \$6.

We can now summarize the procedure for using the transportation simplex to solve a transportation (min) problem.

SUMMARY AND ILLUSTRATION
OF THE TRANSPORTATION SIMPLEX METHOD

Step 1 If the problem is unbalanced, balance it.

Step 2 Use one of the methods described in Section 7.2 to find a bfs.

Step 3 Use the fact that $u_1 = 0$ and $u_i + v_j = c_{ij}$ for all basic variables to find the $[u_1\ u_2\ \ldots\ u_m\ v_1\ v_2\ \ldots\ v_n]$ for the current bfs.

Step 4 If $u_i + v_j - c_{ij} \leq 0$ for all nonbasic variables, then the current bfs is optimal. If this is not the case, we enter the variable with the most positive $u_i + v_j - c_{ij}$ into the basis using the pivoting procedure. This yields a new bfs.

Step 5 Using the new bfs, return to Steps 3 and 4.

For a maximization problem, proceed as stated, but replace Step 4 by Step 4′.

Step 4′ If $u_i + v_j - c_{ij} \geq 0$ for all nonbasic variables, the current bfs is optimal. Otherwise, enter the variable with the most negative $u_i + v_j - c_{ij}$ into the basis using the pivoting procedure described earlier.

We illustrate the procedure for solving a transportation problem by solving the Powerco problem. We begin with the bfs (5). We have already determined that x_{32} should enter the basis. As shown in Table 35, the loop involving x_{32} and some of the basic variables is (3, 2)–(3, 3)–(2, 3)–(2, 2). The odd cells in this loop are (3, 3) and (2, 2). Since $x_{33} = 10$ and $x_{22} = 20$, the pivot will decrease the value of x_{33} and x_{22} by 10 and increase the value of x_{32} and x_{23} by 10. The resulting bfs is shown in Table 36. The u_i's and v_j's for the new bfs were obtained by solving

$$
\begin{array}{ll}
u_1 = 0 & u_2 + v_3 = 13 \\
u_2 + v_2 = 12 & u_2 + v_1 = 9 \\
u_3 + v_4 = 5 & u_3 + v_2 = 9 \\
u_1 + v_1 = 8 &
\end{array}
$$

Table 35
Loop Involving
Entering Variable x_{32}

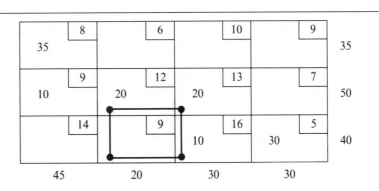

Table 36
x_{32} Has Entered the
Basis, and x_{12} Enters
Next

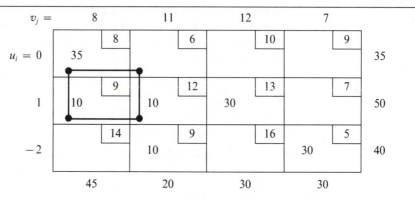

In computing $\bar{c}_{ij} = u_i + v_j - c_{ij}$ for each nonbasic variable, we find that $\bar{c}_{12} = 5$, $\bar{c}_{24} = 1$, and $\bar{c}_{13} = 2$ are the only positive $\bar{c}_{ij}$'s. Thus, we next enter x_{12} into the basis. The loop involving x_{12} and some of the basic variables is $(1,2)$–$(2,2)$–$(2,1)$–$(1,1)$. The odd cells are $(2,2)$ and $(1,1)$. Since $x_{22} = 10$ is the smallest entry in an odd cell, we decrease x_{22} and x_{11} by 10 and increase x_{12} and x_{21} by 10. The resulting bfs is shown in Table 37. For this bfs, the u_i's and v_j's were determined by solving

$$
\begin{aligned}
&u_1 = 0 &\quad &u_1 + v_2 = 6 \\
&u_2 + v_1 = 9 &\quad &u_3 + v_2 = 9 \\
&u_1 + v_1 = 8 &\quad &u_3 + v_4 = 5 \\
&u_2 + v_3 = 13
\end{aligned}
$$

Table 37
x_{12} Has Entered the
Basis, and x_{13} Enters
Next

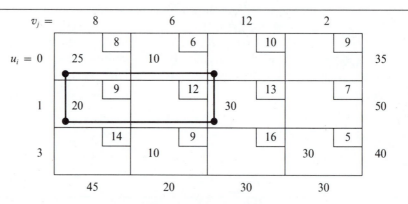

In computing $\bar{c}_{ij}$ for each nonbasic variable, we find that the only positive $\bar{c}_{ij}$ is $\bar{c}_{13} = 2$. Thus, x_{13} enters the basis. The loop involving x_{13} and some of the basic variables is $(1,3)$–$(2,3)$–$(2,1)$–$(1,1)$. The odd cells are x_{23} and x_{11}. Since $x_{11} = 25$ is the smallest entry in an odd cell, we decrease x_{23} and x_{11} by 25 and increase x_{13} and x_{21} by 25. The resulting bfs is shown in Table 38. For this bfs, the u_i's and v_j's were obtained by solving

$$
\begin{aligned}
&u_1 = 0 &\quad &u_2 + v_3 = 13 \\
&u_2 + v_1 = 9 &\quad &u_1 + v_3 = 10 \\
&u_3 + v_4 = 5 &\quad &u_3 + v_2 = 9 \\
&u_1 + v_2 = 6
\end{aligned}
$$

Table 38
Optimal Tableau for
Powerco Example

$u_i = 0$	$v_j = 6$	6	10	2	
$u_i = 0$	8	6 10	10 25	9	35
3	9 45	12	13 5	7	50
3	14	9 10	16	5 30	40
	45	20	30	30	

The reader should check that for this bfs, all $\bar{c}_{ij} \leq 0$, so an optimal solution has been obtained. Thus, the optimal solution to the Powerco problem is $x_{12} = 10$, $x_{13} = 25$, $x_{21} = 45$, $x_{23} = 5$, $x_{32} = 10$, $x_{34} = 30$, and

$$z = 6(10) + 10(25) + 9(45) + 13(5) + 9(10) + 5(30) = \$1020$$

◆ PROBLEMS

GROUP A

Use the transportation simplex to solve Problems 1–8 in Section 7.1. Begin with the bfs found in Section 7.2.

7-4   SENSITIVITY ANALYSIS FOR TRANSPORTATION PROBLEMS*

We have already seen that for a transportation problem, the determination of a bfs and of row 0 for a given set of basic variables, as well as the pivoting procedure, all simplify. It should therefore be no suprise that certain aspects of the sensitivity analysis discussed in Section 6.3 can be simplified. In this section, we discuss the following three aspects of sensitivity analysis for the transportation problem:

Change 1 Changing the objective function coefficient of a nonbasic variable.

Change 2 Changing the objective function coefficient of a basic variable.

Change 3 Increasing a single supply by Δ and a single demand by Δ.

We illustrate three changes on the Powerco problem. Recall from Section 7.3 that the optimal solution for the Powerco problem was $z = \$1020$ and the tableau in Table 39.

CHANGING THE OBJECTIVE FUNCTION COEFFICIENT OF A NONBASIC VARIABLE

As in Section 6.3, changing the objective function coefficient of a nonbasic variable x_{ij} will leave the right-hand side of the optimal tableau unchanged. Thus, the current basis

*This section covers topics that may be omitted with no loss of continuity.

Table 39
Optimal Tableau for Powerco Problem

		CITY 1	CITY 2	CITY 3	CITY 4	SUPPLY
$v_j =$		6	6	10	2	
Plant 1	$u_i = 0$	8	6 10	10 25	9	35
Plant 2	3	9 45	12	13 5	7	50
Plant 3	3	14	9 10	16	5 30	40
DEMAND		45	20	30	30	

will still be feasible. Since we are not changing $\mathbf{c}_{BV}B^{-1}$, the u_i's and v_j's remain unchanged. In row 0, only the coefficient of x_{ij} will change. Thus, as long as the coefficient of x_{ij} in the optimal row 0 is nonpositive, the current basis remains optimal.

To illustrate the method, we answer the following question: For what range of values of the cost of shipping 1 million kwh of electricity from plant 1 to city 1 will the current basis remain optimal? Suppose we change c_{11} from 8 to $8 + \Delta$. For what values of Δ will the current basis remain optimal? Now $\bar{c}_{11} = u_1 + v_1 - c_{11} = 0 + 6 - (8 + \Delta) = -2 - \Delta$. Thus, the current basis remains optimal for $-2 - \Delta \leq 0$, or $\Delta \geq -2$, and $c_{11} \geq 8 - 2 = 6$.

CHANGING THE OBJECTIVE FUNCTION COEFFICIENT OF A BASIC VARIABLE

Since we are changing $\mathbf{c}_{BV}B^{-1}$, the coefficient of each nonbasic variable in row 0 may change, and to determine whether the current basis remains optimal, we must find the new u_i's and v_j's and use these values to price out all nonbasic variables. The current basis remains optimal as long as all nonbasic variables price out nonpositive. To illustrate the idea, we determine for the Powerco problem the range of values of the cost of shipping 1 million kwh from plant 1 to city 3 for which the current basis remains optimal.

Suppose we change c_{13} from 10 to $10 + \Delta$. Then the equation $\bar{c}_{13} = 0$ changes from $u_1 + v_3 = 10$ to $u_1 + v_3 = 10 + \Delta$. Thus, to find the u_i's and v_j's, we must solve the following equations:

$$u_1 = 0 \qquad u_3 + v_2 = 9$$
$$u_2 + v_1 = 9 \qquad u_1 + v_3 = 10 + \Delta$$
$$u_1 + v_2 = 6 \qquad u_3 + v_4 = 5$$
$$u_2 + v_3 = 13$$

Solving these equations, we obtain $u_1 = 0$, $v_2 = 6$, $v_3 = 10 + \Delta$, $v_1 = 6 + \Delta$, $u_2 = 3 - \Delta$, $u_3 = 3$, and $v_4 = 2$.

We now price out each nonbasic variable. The current basis will remain optimal as long as each nonbasic variable has a nonpositive coefficient in row 0.

$$\bar{c}_{11} = u_1 + v_1 - 8 = \Delta - 2 \leq 0 \qquad \text{for } \Delta \leq 2$$
$$\bar{c}_{14} = u_1 + v_4 - 9 = -7$$

$$\bar{c}_{22} = u_2 + v_2 - 12 = -3 - \Delta \le 0 \qquad \text{for } \Delta \ge -3$$
$$\bar{c}_{24} = u_2 + v_4 - 7 = -2 - \Delta \le 0 \qquad \text{for } \Delta \ge -2$$
$$\bar{c}_{31} = u_3 + v_1 - 14 = -5 + \Delta \le 0 \qquad \text{for } \Delta \le 5$$
$$\bar{c}_{33} = u_3 + v_3 - 16 = \Delta - 3 \le 0 \qquad \text{for } \Delta \le 3$$

Thus, the current basis remains optimal for $-2 \le \Delta \le 2$, or $8 = 10 - 2 \le c_{13} \le 10 + 2 = 12$.

INCREASING BOTH SUPPLY s_i AND DEMAND d_j BY Δ

Observe that this change maintains a balanced transportation problem. Since the u_i's and v_j's may be thought of as the negative of each constraint's shadow prices, we know from Eq. (37') of Chapter 6 that if the current basis remains optimal,

$$\text{New } z\text{-value} = \text{old } z\text{-value} + \Delta u_i + \Delta v_j$$

For example, if we increase plant 1's supply and city 2's demand by 1 unit, then (new cost) $= 1020 + 1(0) + 1(6) = \$1026$.

We may also find the new values of the decision variables as follows:

1. If x_{ij} is a basic variable in the optimal solution, increase x_{ij} by Δ.

2. If x_{ij} is a nonbasic variable in the optimal solution, find the loop involving x_{ij} and some of the basic variables. Find an odd cell in the loop that is in row i. Increase the value of this odd cell by Δ and go around the loop, alternately increasing and then decreasing current basic variables in the loop by Δ.

To illustrate the first situation, suppose we increase s_1 and d_2 by 2. Since x_{12} is a basic variable in the optimal solution, the new optimal solution will be the one shown in Table 40. The new optimal z-value is $1020 + 2u_1 + 2v_2 = \$1032$. To illustrate the second situation, suppose we increase both s_1 and d_1 by 1. Since x_{11} is a nonbasic variable in the current optimal solution, we must find the loop involving x_{11} and some of the basic variables. The loop is $(1, 1)-(1, 3)-(2, 3)-(2, 1)$. The odd cell in the loop and row 1 is x_{13}. Thus, the new optimal solution will be obtained by increasing both x_{13} and x_{21} by 1 and decreasing x_{23} by 1. This yields the optimal solution shown in Table 41. The new optimal

Table 40
Optimal Tableau for Powerco Example If $s_1 = 35 + 2 = 37$ and $d_2 = 20 + 2 = 22$

		CITY 1	CITY 2	CITY 3	CITY 4	SUPPLY
	$v_j =$	6	6	10	2	
Plant 1	$u_i = 0$	8	6 12	10 25	9	37
Plant 2	3	9 45	12	13 5	7	50
Plant 3	3	14	9 10	16	5 30	40
DEMAND		45	22	30	30	

Table 41
Optimal Tableau for
Powerco Example If
$s_1 = 35 + 1 = 36$
and
$d_1 = 45 + 1 = 46$

		CITY 1	CITY 2	CITY 3	CITY 4	SUPPLY
	$v_j =$	6	6	10	2	
Plant 1	$u_i = 0$	8	6　10	10　26	9	36
Plant 2	3	9　46	12	13　4	7	50
Plant 3	3	14	9　10	16	5　30	40
DEMAND		46	20	30	30	

z-value is found from (new z-value) $= 1020 + u_1 + v_1 = \$1026$. Observe that if both s_1 and d_1 were increased by 6, the current basis would be infeasible. (Why?)

♦ PROBLEMS

GROUP A

The following problems refer to the Powerco example.

1. Determine the range of values on c_{14} for which the current basis remains optimal.

2. Determine the range of values on c_{34} for which the current basis remains optimal.

3. If s_2 and d_3 are both increased by 3, what is the new optimal solution to the Powerco problem?

4. If s_3 and d_3 are both decreased by 2, what is the new optimal solution to the Powrco problem?

7-5　ASSIGNMENT PROBLEMS

Although the transportation simplex appears to be very efficient, there is a certain class of transportation problems, called assignment problems, for which the transportation simplex is often very inefficient. In this section, we define assignment problems and discuss an efficient method that can be used to solve them.

E X A M P L E 4

Machineco has four machines and four jobs to be completed. Each machine must be assigned to complete one job. The time required to set up each machine for completing each job is shown in Table 42. Machineco wants to minimize the total setup time needed to complete the four jobs. Use linear programming to solve this problem.

Solution

Machineco must determine which machine should be assigned to each job. We define (for $i, j = 1, 2, 3, 4$)

$$x_{ij} = 1 \text{ if machine } i \text{ is assigned to meet the demands of job } j$$
$$x_{ij} = 0 \text{ if machine } i \text{ is not assigned to meet the demands of job } j$$

Table 42	TIME (Hours)			
Setup Times for Machineco Example	Job 1	Job 2	Job 3	Job 4
Machine 1	14	5	8	7
Machine 2	2	12	6	5
Machine 3	7	8	3	9
Machine 4	2	4	6	10

Then Machineco's problem may be formulated as

$$\min z = 14x_{11} + 5x_{12} + 8x_{13} + 7x_{14} + 2x_{21} + 12x_{22} + 6x_{23} + 5x_{24}$$
$$+ 7x_{31} + 8x_{32} + 3x_{33} + 9x_{34} + 2x_{41} + 4x_{42} + 6x_{43} + 10x_{44}$$

$$
\begin{aligned}
\text{s.t.} \quad & x_{11} + x_{12} + x_{13} + x_{14} = 1 && \text{(Machine constraints)} \\
& x_{21} + x_{22} + x_{23} + x_{24} = 1 \\
& x_{31} + x_{32} + x_{33} + x_{34} = 1 && \text{(13)} \\
& x_{41} + x_{42} + x_{43} + x_{44} = 1 \\
& x_{11} + x_{21} + x_{31} + x_{41} = 1 && \text{(Job constraints)} \\
& x_{12} + x_{22} + x_{32} + x_{42} = 1 \\
& x_{13} + x_{23} + x_{33} + x_{43} = 1 \\
& x_{14} + x_{24} + x_{34} + x_{44} = 1
\end{aligned}
$$

$$x_{ij} = 0 \quad \text{or} \quad x_{ij} = 1$$

The first four constraints in (13) ensure that each machine is assigned to a job, and the last four constraints in (13) ensure that each job is completed. If $x_{ij} = 1$, the objective function in (13) will pick up the time required to set up machine i for job j; if $x_{ij} = 0$, the objective function in (13) will not pick up the time required to set up machine i for job j.

Ignoring for the moment the $x_{ij} = 0$ or $x_{ij} = 1$ restrictions, we see that Machineco faces a balanced transportation problem in which each supply point has a supply of 1 and each demand point has a demand of 1. In general, an **assignment problem** is a balanced transportation problem in which all supplies and demands are equal to 1. Thus, an assignment problem is characterized by knowledge of the cost of assigning each supply point to each demand point. The assignment problem's matrix of costs is its **cost matrix**.

Since all the supplies and demands for the Machineco problem (and for any assignment problem) are integers, our discussion in Section 7.3 implies that all variables in Machineco's optimal solution must be integers. Since the right-hand side of each constraint is equal to 1, each x_{ij} must be a nonnegative integer that is no larger than 1, so each x_{ij} must equal 0 or 1. This means that we can ignore the restrictions that $x_{ij} = 0$ or 1 and solve (13) as a balanced transportation problem. By the minimum cost method, we obtain the bfs in Table 43. The current bfs is highly degenerate. (In any bfs to an $m \times m$ assignment problem, there will always be m basic variables that equal 1 and $m - 1$ basic variables that equal zero.)

We find that $\bar{c}_{43} = 1$ is the only positive $\bar{c}_{ij}$. We therefore enter x_{43} into the basis. The loop involving x_{43} and some of the basic variables is $(4, 3)$–$(1, 3)$–$(1, 2)$–$(4, 2)$. The odd

Table 43
Basic Feasible Solution for Machineco Example

		JOB 1	JOB 2	JOB 3	JOB 4	
	$v_j =$	3	5	8	7	
Machine 1	$u_i = 0$	14	5 1	8 0	7 0	1
Machine 2	-2	2	12	6	5 1	1
Machine 3	-5	7	8	3 1	9	1
Machine 4	-1	2 1	4 0	6	10	1
		1	1	1	1	

Table 44
x_{43} Has Entered the Basis

		JOB 1	JOB 2	JOB 3	JOB 4	
	$v_j =$	3	5	7	7	
Machine 1	$u_i = 0$	14	5 1	8	7 0	1
Machine 2	-2	2	12	6	5 1	1
Machine 3	-4	7	8	3 1	9	1
Machine 4	-1	2 1	4 0	6 0	10	1
		1	1	1	1	

variables in the loop are x_{13} and x_{42}. Since $x_{13} = x_{42} = 0$, either x_{13} or x_{42} will leave the basis. We arbitrarily choose x_{13} to leave the basis. After performing the pivot, we obtain the bfs in Table 44. All $\bar{c}_{ij}$'s are now nonpositive, so we have obtained an optimal assignment: $x_{12} = 1$, $x_{24} = 1$, $x_{33} = 1$, and $x_{41} = 1$. Thus, machine 1 is assigned to job 2, machine 2 is assigned to job 4, machine 3 is assigned to job 3, and machine 4 is assigned to job 1. A total setup time of $5 + 5 + 3 + 2 = 15$ hours is required.

♦

THE HUNGARIAN METHOD

Looking back at our initial bfs, we see that it was an optimal solution. We did not know that it was optimal, however, until performing one iteration of the transportation simplex. This suggests that the high degree of degeneracy in an assignment problem may cause the transportation simplex to be an inefficient way of solving assignment problems. For this reason (and the fact that the algorithm is even simpler than the transportation simplex), the Hungarian method is usually used to solve assignment (min) problems:

Step 1 Begin by finding the minimum element in each row of the $m \times m$ cost matrix. Construct a new matrix by subtracting from each cost the minimum cost in its row. For this new matrix, find the minimum cost in each column. Construct a new matrix (called the reduced cost matrix) by subtracting from each cost the minimum cost in its column.

Step 2 Draw the minimum number of lines (horizontal and/or vertical) that are needed to cover all the zeros in the reduced cost matrix. If m lines are required to cover all the zeros, an optimal solution is available among the covered zeros in the matrix. If fewer than m lines are needed to cover all the zeros, proceed to Step 3.

Step 3 Find the smallest nonzero element (call its value k) in the reduced cost matrix that is uncovered by the lines drawn in Step 2. Now subtract k from each uncovered element of the reduced cost matrix and add k to each element of the reduced cost matrix that is covered by two lines. Return to Step 2.

R E M A R K S   **1.** To solve an assignment problem in which the goal is to maximize the objective function, multiply the profits matrix through by -1 and solve the problem as a minimization problem.

2. If the number of rows and columns in the cost matrix are unequal, the assignment problem is **unbalanced**. The Hungarian method may yield an incorrect solution if the problem is unbalanced. Thus, any assignment problem should be balanced (by the addition of one or more dummy points) before it is solved by the Hungarian method.

3. In a large problem, it may not be easy to find the minimum number of lines needed to cover all zeros in the current cost matrix. For a discussion of how to find the minimum number of lines needed to cover all the zeros, see Gillett (1976). It can be shown that if j lines are required to cover all the zeros, then only j "jobs" can be assigned to zero costs in the current matrix. This explains why the algorithm terminates when m lines are required.

SOLUTION OF MACHINECO EXAMPLE BY THE HUNGARIAN METHOD.   We illustrate the Hungarian method by solving the Machineco problem (see Table 45).

Step 1 For each row, we subtract the row minimum from each element in the row, obtaining Table 46. We now subtract 2 from each cost in column 4, obtaining Table 47.

Step 2 As shown, lines through row 1, row 3, and column 1 cover all the zeros in the reduced cost matrix. From remark 3, it follows that only three jobs can be assigned to zero costs in the current cost matrix. Since fewer than four lines are required to cover all the zeros, we proceed to Step 3.

Step 3 The smallest uncovered element equals 1, so we now subtract 1 from each uncovered element in the reduced cost matrix and add 1 to each twice-covered element in the reduced cost matrix. The resulting matrix is Table 48. Four lines are now required to cover all the zeros. Thus, an optimal solution is available. To find an optimal assignment, observe that the only covered zero in column 3 is x_{33}, so we

Table 45
Cost Matrix for
Machineco Example

				ROW MINIMUM
14	5	8	7	5
2	12	6	5	2
7	8	3	9	3
2	4	6	10	2

Table 46
Cost Matrix After
Row Minimums Are
Subtracted

9	0	3	2
0	10	4	3
4	5	0	6
0	2	4	8

COLUMN MINIMUM   0   0   0   2

Table 47
Cost Matrix After
Column Minimums
Are Subtracted

~~9~~	~~0~~	~~3~~	~~0~~
0	10	4	1
~~4~~	~~5~~	~~0~~	~~4~~
0	2	4	6

must have $x_{33} = 1$. Also, the only available covered zero in column 2 is x_{12}, so we set $x_{12} = 1$ and observe that row 1 and column 2 cannot be used again. Now the only available covered zero in column 4 is x_{24}. Thus, we choose $x_{24} = 1$. Finally, we choose $x_{41} = 1$.

Thus, we have found the optimal assignment $x_{12} = 1$, $x_{24} = 1$, $x_{33} = 1$, and $x_{41} = 1$. Of course, this agrees with the result obtained by the transportation simplex.

Table 48
Four Lines
Required; Optimal
Solution Is Available

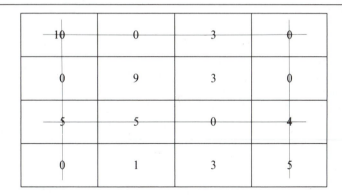

INTUITIVE JUSTIFICATION OF THE HUNGARIAN METHOD. To give an intuitive explanation of why the Hungarian algorithm works, we need to discuss the following result: *If a constant is added to each cost in a row (or column) of a balanced transportation problem, the optimal solution to the problem is unchanged.* To show why the result is true, suppose we add k to each cost in the first row of the Machineco problem. Then

New objective function = old objective function $+ k(x_{11} + x_{12} + x_{13} + x_{14})$

Since any feasible solution to the Machineco problem must have $x_{11} + x_{12} + x_{13} + x_{14} = 1$,

New objective function = old objective function $+ k$

Thus, the optimal solution to the Machineco problem remains unchanged if a constant k is added to each cost in the first row. A similar argument applies to any other row or column.

Step 1 of the Hungarian method consists (for each row and column) of subtracting a constant from each element in the row or column. Thus, Step 1 creates a new cost matrix having the same optimal solution as the original problem. Step 3 of the Hungarian method is equivalent (see Problem 6 at the end of this section) to adding k to each cost that lies in a covered row and subtracting k from each cost that lies in an uncovered column (or vice versa). Thus, Step 3 creates a new cost matrix with the same optimal solution as the initial assignment problem. Each time Step 3 is performed, at least one new zero is created in the cost matrix.

Steps 1 and 3 also ensure that all costs remain nonnegative. Thus, the net effect of Steps 1 and 3 of the Hungarian method is to create a sequence of assignment problems (with nonnegative costs) that all have the same optimal solution as the original assignment problem. Now consider an assignment problem in which all costs are nonnegative. Any feasible assignment in which all the x_{ij}'s that equal 1 have zero costs must be optimal for such an assignment problem. Thus, when Step 2 indicates that m lines are required to cover all the zeros in the cost matrix, an optimal solution to the original problem has been found.

◆ PROBLEMS

GROUP A

1. Five employees are available to perform four jobs. The time it takes each person to perform each job is given in Table 49. Determine the assignment of employees to jobs that minimizes the total time required to perform the four jobs.

Table 49

	TIME (Hours)			
	Job 1	*Job 2*	*Job 3*	*Job 4*
Person 1	22	18	30	18
Person 2	18	—	27	22
Person 3	26	20	28	28
Person 4	16	22	—	14
Person 5	21	—	25	28

Note: Dashes indicate person cannot do that particular job.

2.[†] Doc Councillman is putting together a relay team for the 400-meter relay. Each swimmer must swim 100 meters of breaststroke, backstroke, butterfly, or freestyle. Doc believes that each swimmer will attain the times given in Table 50. In order to minimize the team's time for the race, which swimmer should swim which stroke?

Table 50

	TIME (Seconds)			
	Free	*Breast*	*Fly*	*Back*
Gary Hall	54	54	51	53
Mark Spitz	51	57	52	52
Jim Montgomery	50	53	54	56
Chet Jastremski	56	54	55	53

3. Tom Selleck, Burt Reynolds, Tony Geary, and John Travolta are marooned on a desert island with Olivia Newton-John, Loni Anderson, Dolly Parton, and Genie Francis. The "compatibility measures" in Table 51 indicate how much happiness each couple would experience if they spent all their time together. The happiness earned by a couple is proportional to the fraction of time they spend

[†]This problem is based on Machol (1970).

Table 51

	ONJ	LA	DP	GF
TS	7	5	8	2
BR	7	8	9	4
TG	3	5	7	9
JT	5	5	6	7

together. For example, if Tony and Genie spend half their time together, they earn happiness of $\frac{1}{2}(9) = 4.5$.

(a) Let x_{ij} be the fraction of time that the ith man spends with the jth woman. The goal of the eight people is to maximize the total happiness of the people on the island. Formulate an LP whose optimal solution will yield the optimal values of the x_{ij}'s.

(b) Explain why the optimal solution in part (a) will have four $x_{ij} = 1$ and twelve $x_{ij} = 0$. Since the optimal solution requires that each person spend all his or her time with one person of the opposite sex, this result is often referred to as the Marriage Theorem.

(c) Determine the marriage partner for each person.

(d) Do you think the Proportionality Assumption of linear programming is valid in this situation?

GROUP B

4. Any transportation problem can be formulated as an assignment problem. To illustrate the idea, determine an assignment problem that could be used to find the optimal solution to the transportation problem in Table 52. (*Hint:* You will need five supply and five demand points.)

Table 52

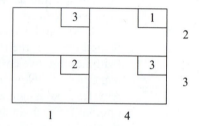

5. The Chicago Board of Education is taking bids on the city's four school bus routes. Four companies have made the bids in Table 53.

Table 53

	BIDS			
	Route 1	Route 2	Route 3	Route 4
Company 1	$4000	$5000	—	—
Company 2	—	$4000	—	$4000
Company 3	$3000	—	$2000	—
Company 4	—	—	$4000	$5000

(a) Suppose each bidder can be assigned only one route. Use the assignment method to minimize Chicago's cost of running the four bus routes.

(b) Suppose that each company can be assigned two routes. Use the assignment method to minimize Chicago's cost of running the four bus routes. (*Hint:* Two supply points will be needed for each company.)

6. Show that Step 3 of the Hungarian method is equivalent to performing the following operations: (1) Add k to each cost that lies in a covered row. (2) Subtract k from each cost that lies in an uncovered column.

7. Suppose c_{ij} is the smallest cost in row i and column j of an assignment problem. Must $x_{ij} = 1$ in any optimal assignment?

7-6   TRANSSHIPMENT PROBLEMS

A transportation problem allows only shipments that go directly from a supply point to a demand point. In many situations, shipments are allowed between supply points or between demand points. Sometimes there may also be points (called transshipment points) through which goods can be transshipped on their journey from a supply point to a demand point. Shipping problems with any or all of these characteristics are transshipment problems. Fortunately, the optimal solution to a transshipment problem can be found by solving a transportation problem.

In what follows, we define a **supply point** to be a point that can send goods to another point but cannot receive goods from any other point. Similarly, a **demand point** is a point that can receive goods from other points but cannot send goods to any other point. A **transshipment point** is a point that can both receive goods from other points and send goods to other points. The following example illustrates these definitions ("—"indicates that a shipment is impossible).

E X A M P L E 5

Widgetco manufactures widgets at two factories, one in Memphis and one in Denver. The Memphis factory can produce up to 150 widgets per day, and the Denver factory can produce up to 200 widgets per day. Widgets are shipped by air to customers in Los Angeles and Boston. The customers in each city require 130 widgets per day. Because of the deregulation of air fares, Widgetco believes that it may be cheaper to first fly some widgets to New York or Chicago and then fly the widgets to their final destinations. The costs of flying a widget are shown in Table 54. Widgetco wants to minimize the total cost of shipping the required widgets to its customers.

In this problem, Memphis and Denver are supply points, with supplies of 150 and 200 widgets per day, respectively. New York and Chicago are transshipment points. Los Angeles and Boston are demand points, each with a demand of 130 widgets per day. A graphical representation of possible shipments is given in Figure 7.

We now describe how the optimal solution to a transshipment problem can be found by solving a transportation problem. Given a transshipment problem, we create a

Table 54
Shipping Costs for
Transshipment
Example

FROM	TO					
	Memphis	*Denver*	*N.Y.*	*Chicago*	*L.A.*	*Boston*
Memphis	$0	—	$8	$13	$25	$28
Denver	—	$0	$15	$12	$26	$25
N.Y.	—	—	$0	$6	$16	$17
Chicago	—	—	$6	$0	$14	$16
L.A.	—	—	—	—	$0	—
Boston	—	—	—	—	—	$0

Figure 7
A Transshipment
Problem

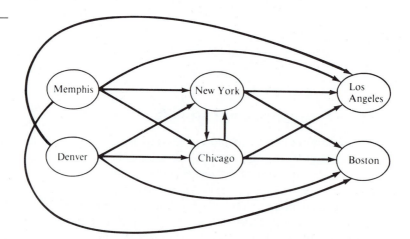

balanced transportation problem by the following procedure (assume that total supply exceeds total demand):

Step 1 If necessary, add a dummy demand point (with a supply of zero and a demand equal to the problem's excess supply) to balance the problem. Shipments to the dummy and from a point to itself will, of course, have a zero shipping cost. Let s = total available supply.

Step 2 Construct a transportation tableau as follows. A row in the tableau will be needed for each supply point and transshipment point, and a column will be needed for each demand point and transshipment point. Each supply point will have a supply equal to its original supply, and each demand point will have a demand equal to its original demand. Let s = total available supply. Then each transshipment point will have a supply equal to (point's original supply) + s and a demand equal to (point's original demand) + s. This ensures that any transshipment point that is a net supplier will have a net outflow equal to the point's original supply, and any transshipment point that is a net demander will have a net inflow equal to the point's original demand. Although we don't know how much will be shipped through each transshipment point, we can be sure that the total amount shipped through the point will not exceed s. This explains why we add s to the supply and demand at each transshipment point. By adding the same amounts to the supply and demand at each transshipment point, we ensure that the net outflow at each transshipment point will be correct, and we also maintain a balanced transportation tableau.

For the Widgetco example, this procedure yields the transportation tableau and its optimal solution given in Table 55. Since $s = $ (total supply) $= 150 + 200 = 350$ and (total demand) $= 130 + 130 = 260$, the dummy demand point has a demand of $350 - 260 = 90$. The other supplies and demands in the transportation tableau are obtained by adding $s = 350$ to each transshipment point's supply and demand.

Table 55		N.Y.		CHICAGO		L.A.		BOSTON		DUMMY	SUPPLY
Representation of Transshipment Problem as Balanced Transportation Problem	Memphis	130	8		13		25		28	20 0	150
	Denver		15		12		26	130	25	70 0	200
	N.Y.	220	0		6	130	16		17	0	350
	Chicago		6	350	0		14		16	0	350
	DEMAND	350		350		130		130		90	

In interpreting the solution to the transportation problem created from a transshipment problem, we simply ignore the shipments to the dummy and from a point to itself. From Table 55, we find that Widgetco should produce 130 widgets at Memphis, ship these widgets to New York, and transship these widgets from New York to Los Angeles. The 130 widgets produced at Denver should be shipped directly to Boston. The net flow out of each city is

Memphis: $130 + 20$ $= 150$
Denver: $130 + 70$ $= 200$
N.Y.: $220 + 130 - 130 - 220 = 0$
Chicago: $350 - 350 = 0$
L.A.: -130
Boston: -130
Dummy: $-20 - 70$ $= -90$

Of course, a negative net outflow represents an inflow. Observe that each transshipment point (New York and Chicago) has a net outflow of zero; whatever flows into the transshipment point must leave the transshipment point. A graphical representation of the optimal solution to the Wigetco example is given in Figure 8.

Suppose that we modify the Widgetco example and allow shipments between Memphis and Denver. This would make Memphis and Denver transshipment points, and would add columns for Memphis and Denver to the Table 55 tableau. The Memphis row in the tableau would now have a supply of $150 + 350 = 500$, and the Denver row would have a supply of $200 + 350 = 550$. The Memphis column would have a demand

Figure 8
Optimal Solution to
Widgetco Example

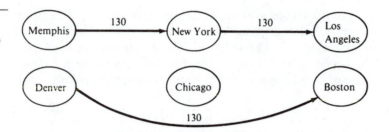

of $0 + 350 = 350$, and the Denver column would have a demand of $0 + 350 = 350$. Finally, suppose that shipments between demand points L.A. and Boston were allowed. This makes L.A. and Boston transshipment points, so we must add rows for L.A. and Boston to the Table 55 tableau. The supply for the L.A. row would be $0 + 350 = 350$, and the supply for the Boston row would also be $0 + 350 = 350$. The demand for the L.A. column would now be $130 + 350 = 480$, and the demand for the Boston column would also be $130 + 350 = 480$.

◆ PROBLEMS

GROUP A

1. General Ford produces cars at L.A. and Detroit and has a warehouse in Atlanta; the company supplies cars to customers in Houston and Tampa. The cost of shipping a car between points is given in Table 56 ("—" means that a shipment is not allowed). L.A. can produce up to 1100 cars, and Detroit can produce up to 2900 cars. Houston must receive 2400 cars, and Tampa must receive 1500 cars.
(a) Formulate a balanced transportation problem that can be used to minimize the shipping costs incurred in meeting demands at Houston and Tampa.
(b) Modify the answer to part (a) if shipments between L.A. and Detroit are not allowed.
(c) Modify the answer to part (a) if shipments between Houston and Tampa are allowed at a cost of $5.

2. Sunco Oil produces oil at two wells. Well 1 can produce up to 150,000 barrels per day, and well 2 can produce up to 200,000 barrels per day. Sunco must supply oil to customers in New York and Los Angeles. It is possible to ship oil directly from the wells to Los Angeles and New York. Alternatively, Sunco could transport oil to the ports of Mobile and Galveston and then ship it by tanker to New York or Los Angeles. Los Angeles requires 160,000 barrels of oil per day, and New York requires 140,000 barrels of oil per day. The costs of shipping 1000 barrels of oil between two points are shown in Table 57. Formulate a transshipment model (and equivalent transportation model) that could be used to minimize the transport costs in meeting the oil demands of Los Angeles and New York.

Table 56

			TO		
FROM	L.A.	Detroit	Atlanta	Houston	Tampa
L.A.	$0	$140	$100	$90	$225
Detroit	$145	$0	$111	$110	$119
Atlanta	$105	$115	$0	$113	$78
Houston	$89	$109	$121	$0	—
Tampa	$210	$117	$82	—	$0

Table 57

FROM	WELL 1	WELL 2	TO			
			Mobile	*Galveston*	*N.Y.*	*L.A.*
Well 1	$0	—	$10	$13	$25	$28
Well 2	—	$0	$15	$12	$26	$25
Mobile	—	—	$0	$6	$16	$17
Galveston	—	—	$6	$0	$14	$16
N.Y.	—	—	—	—	$0	$15
L.A.	—	—	—	—	$15	$0

Note: Dashes indicate shipments that are not allowed.

3. In Problem 2, assume that before being shipped to Los Angeles or New York, all oil produced at the wells must be refined at either Galveston or Mobile. It costs $12 to refine 1000 barrels of oil at Mobile and $10 to refine 1000 barrels of oil at Galveston. Assuming that both Mobile and Galveston have infinite refinery capacity, formulate a transshipment and balanced transportation model to minimize the daily cost of transporting and refining the oil requirements of Los Angeles and New York.

4. Rework Problem 3 under the assumption that Galveston has a refinery capacity of 150,000 barrels per day and Mobile has a refinery capacity of 180,000 barrels per day. (*Hint:* Modify the method used to determine the supply and demand at each transshipment point to incoporate the refinery capacity restrictions, but make sure to keep the problem balanced.)

GROUP B

5.[†] A company must meet the following demands for cash at the beginning of each of the next six months: month 1 —$200; month 2—$100; month 3—$50; month 4—$80; month 5—$160; month 6—$140. At the beginning of

month 1, the company has $150 in cash and $200 worth of bond 1, $100 worth of bond 2, and $400 worth of bond 3. Of course, the company will have to sell some bonds to meet demands, but a penalty will be charged for any bonds sold before the end of month 6. The penalties for selling $1 worth of each bond are as shown in Table 58.

(**a**) Assuming that all bills must be paid on time, formulate a balanced transportation problem that can be used to minimize the cost of meeting the cash demands for the next six months.

(**b**) Assume that payment of bills can be made after they are due, but a penalty of 5¢ per month is assessed for each dollar of cash demands that is postponed for one month. Assuming all bills must be paid by the end of month 6, develop a transhipment model that can be used to minimize the cost of paying the next six months' bills. (*Hint:* Transshipment points are needed, in the form Ct = cash available at beginning of month t after bonds for month t have been sold, but before month t demand is met. Shipments into Ct occur from bond sales and $Ct - 1$. Shipments out of Ct occur to $Ct + 1$ and demands for months 1, 2, . . . t.)

Table 58

BOND	MONTH OF SALE					
	1	*2*	*3*	*4*	*5*	*6*
1	$0.21	$0.19	$0.17	$0.13	$0.09	$0.05
2	$0.50	$0.50	$0.50	$0.33	$0	$0
3	$1.00	$1.00	$1.00	$1.00	$1.00	$0

[†] Based on Srinivasan (1974).

◆ SUMMARY

NOTATION

m = number of supply points

n = number of demand points

x_{ij} = number of units shipped from supply point i to demand point j

c_{ij} = cost of shipping 1 unit from supply point i to demand point j

s_i = supply at supply point i

d_j = demand at demand point j

$\bar{c}_{ij}$ = coefficient of x_{ij} in row 0 of a given tableau

$\mathbf{a}_{ij}$ = column for x_{ij} in transportation constraints

A transportation problem is **balanced** if total supply equals total demand. In order to use the methods of this chapter to solve a transportation problem, the problem must first be balanced by use of a dummy supply or a dummy demand point. A balanced transportation problem may be written as

$$\min \sum_{i=1}^{i=m} \sum_{j=1}^{j=n} c_{ij} x_{ij}$$

$$\text{s.t.} \quad \sum_{j=1}^{j=n} x_{ij} = s_i \quad (i = 1, 2, \ldots, m) \quad \text{(Supply constraints)}$$

$$\sum_{i=1}^{i=m} x_{ij} = d_j \quad (j = 1, 2, \ldots, n) \quad \text{(Demand constraints)}$$

$$x_{ij} \geq 0 \quad (i = 1, 2, \ldots, m; j = 1, 2, \ldots, n)$$

FINDING BASIC FEASIBLE SOLUTIONS
FOR BALANCED TRANSPORTATION PROBLEMS

We can find a bfs for a balanced transportation problem by the Northwest Corner method, the minimum cost method, or Vogel's method. To find a bfs by the Northwest Corner method, begin in the upper left-hand (or northwest) corner of the transportation tableau and set x_{11} as large as possible. Clearly, x_{11} can be no larger than the smaller of s_1 and d_1. If $x_{11} = s_1$, cross out the first row of the transportation tableau; this indicates that no more basic variables will come from row 1 of the tableau. Also change d_1 to $d_1 - s_1$. If $x_{11} = d_1$, cross out the first column of the transportation tableau and change s_1 to $s_1 - d_1$. If $x_{11} = s_1 = d_1$, cross out either row 1 or column 1 (but not both) of the transportation tableau. If you cross out row 1, change d_1 to 0; if you cross out column 1, change s_1 to 0. Continue applying this procedure to the most northwest cell in the tableau that does not lie in a crossed-out row or column. Eventually, you will come to a point where there is only one cell that can be assigned a value. Assign this cell a value equal to its row or column demand, and cross out both the cell's row and its column. A basic feasible solution has now been obtained.

FINDING THE OPTIMAL SOLUTION FOR A
TRANSPORTATION PROBLEM

Step 1 If the problem is unbalanced, balance it.

Step 2 Use one of the methods described in Section 7.2 to find a bfs.

Step 3 Use the fact that $u_1 = 0$ and $u_i + v_j = c_{ij}$ for all basic variables to find the $[u_1 \quad u_2 \quad \ldots \quad u_m \quad v_1 \quad v_2 \quad \ldots \quad v_n]$ for the current bfs.

Step 4 If $u_i + v_j - c_{ij} \leq 0$ for all nonbasic variables, then the current bfs is optimal. If this is not the case, we enter the variable with the most positive $u_i + v_j - c_{ij}$ into the basis. To do this, find the loop (it can be shown that there is only one loop) involving the entering variable and some of the basic variables. Then, *counting only cells in the loop*, label the cells in the loop that are an even number $(0, 2, 4,$ etc.) of cells away from the entering variable as even cells. Also label those cells in the loop that are an odd number of cells away from the entering variable as odd cells. Now find the odd cell whose variable assumes the smallest value. Call this value θ. The variable corresponding to this odd cell will leave the basis. To perform the pivot, decrease the value of each odd cell by θ and increase the value of each even cell by θ. The values of variables not in the loop remain unchanged. The pivot is now complete. If $\theta = 0$, the entering variable will equal zero, and an odd variable that has a current value of zero will leave the basis. In this case, a degenerate bfs will result. If more than one odd cell in the loop equals θ, you may arbitrarily choose one of these odd cells to leave the basis; again, a degenerate bfs will result. The pivoting yields a new bfs.

Step 5 Using the new bfs, return to Steps 3 and 4.

For a maximization problem, proceed as stated, but replace Step 4 by Step 4'.

Step 4' If $u_i + v_j - c_{ij} \geq 0$ for all nonbasic variables, the current bfs is optimal. Otherwise, enter the variable with the most negative $u_i + v_j - c_{ij}$ into the basis using the pivoting procedure.

ASSIGNMENT PROBLEMS

An **assignment problem** is a balanced transportation problem in which all supplies and demands equal 1. An $m \times m$ assignment problem may be efficiently solved by the Hungarian method:

Step 1 Begin by finding the minimum element in each row of the cost matrix. Construct a new matrix by subtracting from each cost the minimum cost in its row. For this new matrix, find the minimum cost in each column. Construct a new matrix (reduced cost matrix) by subtracting from each cost the minimum cost in its column.

Step 2 Draw the minimum number of lines (horizontal or vertical) that are needed to cover all the zeros in the reduced cost matrix. If m lines are required to cover all the zeros, an optimal solution is available among the covered zeros in the matrix. If fewer than m lines are needed to cover all the zeros, proceed to Step 3.

Step 3 Find the smallest nonzero element (call its value k) in the reduced cost matrix that is uncovered by the lines drawn in Step 2. Now subtract k from each uncovered element of the reduced cost matrix and add k to each element of the reduced cost matrix that is covered by two lines. Return to Step 2.

R E M A R K S   **1.** In solving an assignment problem in which the goal is to maximize the objective function, multiply the profits matrix through by -1 and solve the problem as a minimization problem.

2. If the number of rows and columns in the cost matrix are unequal, the problem is **unbalanced**. The Hungarian method may yield an incorrect solution if the problem is unbalanced. Thus, any assignment problem should be balanced (by the addition of one or more dummy points) before it is solved by the Hungarian method.

TRANSSHIPMENT PROBLEMS

A transshipment problem allows shipment between supply points and between demand points, and it may also contain transshipment points through which goods may be shipped on their way from a supply point to a demand point. Using the following method, a transshipment problem may be transformed into a balanced transportation problem.

Step 1 If necessary, add a dummy demand point (with a supply of zero and a demand equal to the problem's excess supply) to balance the problem. Shipments to the dummy and from a point to itself will, of course, have a zero shipping cost. Let s = total available supply.

Step 2 Construct a transportation tableau as follows. A row in the tableau will be needed for each supply point and transshipment point, and a column will be needed for each demand point and transshipment point. Each supply point will have a supply equal to its original supply, and each demand point will have a demand equal to its original demand. Let s = total available supply. Then each transshipment point will have a supply equal to (point's original supply) + s and a demand equal to (point's original demand) + s.

SENSITIVITY ANALYSIS FOR TRANSPORTATION PROBLEMS

Following the discussion of sensitivity analysis in Chapter 6, we can analyze how a change in a transportation problem changes the problem's optimal solution.

Change 1 Changing the objective function coefficient for a nonbasic variable. As long as the coefficient of x_{ij} in the optimal row 0 is nonpositive, the current basis remains optimal.

Change 2 Changing the objective function coefficient of a basic variable. To see whether the current basis remains optimal, we must find the new u_i's and v_j's and use these values to price out all nonbasic variables. The current basis remains optimal as long as all nonbasic variables have a nonpositive coefficient in row 0.

Change 3 Increasing both supply s_i and demand d_j by Δ.

$$\text{New } z\text{-value} = \text{old } z\text{-value} + \Delta u_i + \Delta v_j$$

We may find the new values of the decision variables as follows:

1. If x_{ij} is a basic variable in the optimal solution, increase x_{ij} by Δ.

2. If x_{ij} is a nonbasic variable in the optimal solution, find the loop involving x_{ij} and some of the basic variables. Find an odd cell in the loop that is in row i. Increase the value of this odd cell by Δ and go around the loop, alternately increasing and then decreasing current basic variables in the loop by Δ.

◆ REVIEW PROBLEMS

GROUP A

1. Televco produces TV picture tubes at three plants. Plant 1 can produce up to 50 tubes per week; plant 2 can produce up to 100 tubes per week; and plant 3 can produce up to 50 tubes per week. Tubes are shipped to three customers. The profit earned per tube depends on the site where the tube was produced and on the customer who purchases the tube (see Table 59). Customer 1 is willing to purchase up to 80 tubes per week; customer 2, up to 90 tubes per week; and customer 3, up to 100 tubes per week. Televco wants to find a shipping and production plan that will maximize profits.

Table 59

FROM	TO		
	Customer 1	Customer 2	Customer 3
Plant 1	$75	$60	$69
Plant 2	$79	$73	$68
Plant 3	$85	$76	$70

(a) Formulate a balanced transportation problem that can be used to maximize Televco's profits.
(b) Use the Northwest Corner method to find a bfs to the problem.
(c) Use the transportation simplex to find an optimal solution to the problem.

2. Five workers are available to perform four jobs. The time it takes each worker to perform each job is given in Table 60. The goal is to assign workers to jobs so as to minimize the total time required to perform the four jobs. Use the Hungarian method to solve the problem.

3. A company must meet the following demands for a product: January, 30 units; February, 30 units; March, 20 units. Demand may be backlogged at a cost of $5/unit/month. Of course, all demand must be met by the end of March. Thus, if 1 unit of January demand is met during March, a backlogging cost of $5(2) = $10 is incurred.

Table 60

	TIME (Hours)			
	Job 1	Job 2	Job 3	Job 4
Worker 1	10	15	10	15
Worker 2	12	8	20	16
Worker 3	12	9	12	18
Worker 4	6	12	15	18
Worker 5	16	12	8	12

Monthly production capacity and unit production cost during each month are given in Table 61. A holding cost of $20/unit is assessed on the inventory at the end of each month.
(a) Formulate a balanced transportation problem that could be used to determine how to minimize the total cost (including backlogging, holding, and production costs) of meeting demand.
(b) Use Vogel's method to find a basic feasible solution.
(c) Use the transportation simplex to determine how to meet each month's demand. Make sure to give an interpretation of your optimal solution. (For example, 20 units of month 2 demand is met from month 1 production, etc.)

Table 61

	PRODUCTION CAPACITY	UNIT PRODUCTION COST
January	35	$400
February	30	$420
March	35	$410

4. Appletree Cleaning has five maids. To complete cleaning my house, they must vacuum, clean the kitchen, clean the bathroom, and do general straightening up. The time it takes each maid to do each job is shown in Table 62. Each maid is assigned one job. Use the Hungarian method to determine assignments that minimize the total number of maid-hours needed to clean my house.

Table 62

| | TIME (Hours) | | | |
	Vacuum	Clean Kitchen	Clean Bathroom	Straighten Up
Maid 1	6	5	2	1
Maid 2	9	8	7	3
Maid 3	8	5	9	4
Maid 4	7	7	8	3
Maid 5	5	5	6	4

5.[†] Currently, State University can store 200 files on hard disk, 100 files in computer memory, and 300 files on tape. Users wish to store 300 word-processing files, 100 packaged-program files, and 100 data files. Each month a typical word-processing file is accessed eight times, a typical packaged-program file is accessed four times, and a typical data file is accessed two times. When a file is accessed, the time it takes for the file to be retrieved depends on the type of file and on the storage medium (see Table 63).

Table 63

| | TIME (Minutes) | | |
	Word Processing	Packaged Program	Data
Hard disk	5	4	4
Memory	2	1	1
Tape	10	8	6

(a) Assuming that the goal is to minimize the total time per month that users spend accessing their files, formulate a balanced transportation problem that can be used to determine where files should be stored.
(b) Use the minimum cost method to find a bfs.
(c) Use the transportation simplex to find an optimal solution.

6. The Gotham City Police have just received three calls for police. At present, five cars are available. The distance (in city blocks) of each car from each call is given in Table 64. Gotham City wants to minimize the total distance cars must travel to respond to the three police calls. Use the Hungarian method to determine which car should respond to which call.

Table 64

| | DISTANCE (Blocks) | | |
	Call 1	Call 2	Call 3
Car 1	10	11	18
Car 2	6	7	7
Car 3	7	8	5
Car 4	5	6	4
Car 5	9	4	7

7. There are three school districts in the town of Busville. The number of black and white students in each district are shown in Table 65. The Supreme Court requires the schools in Busville to be racially balanced. Thus, each school must have exactly 300 students, and each school must have the same number of black students. The distances between districts are shown in Table 65.

Formulate a balanced transportation problem that can be used to determine the minimum total distance that students must be bussed while still satisfying the Supreme Court's requirements. Assume that a student who remains in his or her own district will not be bussed.

8. Using the Northwest Corner method to find a bfs, find (via the transportation simplex) an optimal solution to the transportation (minimization) problem shown in Table 66.

9. Solve the following LP:

$$\min z = 2x_1 + 3x_2 + 4x_3 + 3x_4$$
$$\text{s.t.} \quad x_1 + x_2 \qquad\qquad \leq 4$$
$$x_3 + x_4 \leq 5$$
$$x_1 \qquad + x_3 \qquad \geq 3$$
$$x_2 \qquad + x_4 \geq 6$$
$$x_j \geq 0 \quad (j = 1, 2, 3, 4)$$

Table 65

	NO. OF STUDENTS		DISTANCE TO	
	Whites	*Blacks*	*District 2*	*District 3*
District 1	210	120	3 miles	5 miles
District 2	210	30	—	4 miles
District 3	180	150	—	—

Table 66

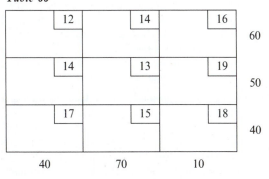

Table 67

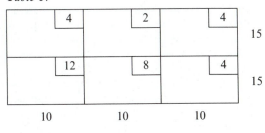

10. Find the optimal solution to the balanced transportation problem in Table 67 (minimization).

11. In Problem 10, suppose we increase s_1 to 16 and d_3 to 11. The problem is still balanced, and since 31 units (instead of 30 units) must be shipped, one would think that the total shipping cost would be increased. Show that the total shipping cost has actually decreased by $2, however. This is called the "more for less" paradox. Explain why increasing both the supply and the demand has decreased cost. Using the theory of shadow prices, explain how one could have predicted that increasing s_1 and d_3 by 1 would decrease total cost by $2.

12. Use the Northwest Corner method, the minimum cost method, and Vogel's method to find basic feasible solutions to the transportation problem in Table 68.

Table 68

13. Find the optimal solution to Problem 12.

14. Oilco has oil fields in San Diego and Los Angeles. The San Diego field can produce up to 500,000 barrels per day, and the Los Angeles field can produce up to 400,000 barrels per day. Oil is sent from the fields to a refinery, either in Dallas or in Houston (assume that each refinery has unlimited capacity). It costs $700 to refine 100,000 barrels of oil at Dallas and $900 to refine 100,000 barrels of oil at Houston. Refined oil is shipped to customers in Chicago and New York. Chicago customers require 400,000 barrels per day of refined oil, and New York customers require 300,000 barrels per day of refined oil. The costs of shipping 100,000 barrels of oil (refined or unrefined) between cities are given in Table 69. Formulate a balanced transportation model of this situation.

15. For the Powerco problem, find the range of values of c_{24} for which the current basis remains optimal.

16. For the Powerco problem, find the range of values of c_{23} for which the current basis remains optimal.

Table 69

FROM	TO			
	Dallas	Houston	N.Y.	Chicago
L.A.	$300	$110	—	—
San Diego	$420	$100	—	—
Dallas	—	—	$450	$550
Houston	—	—	$470	$530

GROUP B

17.[†] The Carter Caterer Company must have the following number of clean napkins available at the beginning of each of the next four days: day 1, 15; day 2, 12; day 3, 18; day 4, 6. After being used, a napkin can be cleaned by one of two methods: fast service or slow service. Fast service costs 10¢ per napkin, and a napkin cleaned via fast service is available for use the day after it was last used. Slow service costs 6¢ per napkin, and a napkin cleaned via slow service can be reused two days after the day it was last used. New napkins can be purchased for a cost of 20¢ per napkin. Formulate a balanced transportation problem to minimize the cost of meeting the demand for napkins during the next four days.

18. Braneast Airlines must staff the daily flights between New York and Chicago shown in Table 70. Each of Braneast's crews lives in either New York or Chicago. Each day a crew must fly one New York–Chicago and one Chicago–New York flight. A crew must have at least 1 hour of down time between flights. Braneast wishes to schedule the crews to minimize the total downtime. Set up an assignment problem that can be used to accomplish this goal. (*Hint:* Let $x_{ij} = 1$ if the crew that flies flight i also flies flight j, and $x_{ij} = 0$ otherwise. If $x_{ij} = 1$, a cost c_{ij} is incurred, corresponding to the down time associated with a crew flying flight i and flight j.) Of course, some assignments are not possible. Find the flight assignments that minimize the total down time. How many crews should be based in each city? Assume that at the end of the day, each crew must be in its home city.

19. A firm producing a single product has three plants and four customers. The three plants will produce 3000, 5000, and 5000 units, respectively, during the next time period. The firm has made a commitment to sell 4000 units to customer 1, 3000 units to customer 2, and at least 3000 units to customer 3. Both customers 3 and 4 also want to buy as many of the remaining units as possible. The profit associated with shipping a unit from plant i to customer j is given in Table 71.

Formulate a balanced transportation problem that can be used to maximize the company's profit.

20. A company can produce up to 35 units per month. The demands of its primary customers must be met on time each month; if it wishes, the company may also sell units to secondary customers each month. A $1/unit holding cost is assessed against each month's ending inventory. The relevant data are shown in Table 72. Formulate a balanced transportation problem that can be used to maximize profits earned during the next three months.

21. My home has four valuable paintings that are up for sale. Four customers are bidding for the paintings. Customer 1 is willing to buy two paintings, but each other customer is willing to purchase at most one painting. The prices that each customer is willing to pay for the paintings she is bidding on are given in Table 73. Use the Hungarian method to determine how to maximize the total revenue received from the sale of the paintings.

Table 70

FLIGHT	LEAVE CHICAGO	ARRIVE NEW YORK	FLIGHT	LEAVE NEW YORK	ARRIVE CHICAGO
1	6 A.M.	10 A.M.	1	7 A.M.	9 A.M.
2	9 A.M.	1 P.M.	2	8 A.M.	10 A.M.
3	12 noon	4 P.M.	3	10 A.M.	12 noon
4	3 P.M.	7 P.M.	4	12 noon	2 P.M.
5	5 P.M.	9 P.M.	5	2 P.M.	4 P.M.
6	7 P.M.	11 P.M.	6	4 P.M.	6 P.M.
7	8 P.M.	12 midnight	7	6 P.M.	8 P.M.

[†] This problem is based on Jacobs (1954).

Table 71

FROM	TO CUSTOMER			
	1	*2*	*3*	*4*
Plant 1	$65	$63	$62	$64
Plant 2	$68	$67	$65	$62
Plant 3	$63	$60	$59	$60

22. Powerhouse produces capacitors at three locations: Los Angeles, Chicago, and New York. Capacitors are shipped from these locations to public utilities in five regions of the country: northeast (NE), northwest (NW), midwest (MW), southeast (SE), and southwest (SW). The cost of producing and shipping a capacitor from each plant to each region of the country is given in Table 74. Each plant has an annual production capacity of 100,000 capaci-

tors. Each year, each region of the country must receive the following number of capacitors: NE, 55,000; NW, 50,000; MW, 60,000; SE, 60,000; SW, 45,000. Powerhouse feels shipping costs are too high, and the company is therefore considering building one or two more production plants. Possible sites are Atlanta and Houston. The costs of producing a capacitor and shipping it to each region of the country are given in Table 75. It costs $3 million (in current dollars) to build a new plant, and operating each plant incurs a fixed cost (in addition to variable shipping and production costs) of $50,000 per year. A plant at Atlanta or Houston will have the capacity to produce 100,000 capacitors per year.

Assume that future demand patterns and production costs will remain unchanged. If costs are discounted at a rate of $11\frac{1}{9}$ % per year, how can Powerhouse minimize the present value of all costs associated with meeting current and future demands?

Table 72

	PRODUCTION COST/UNIT	PRIMARY DEMAND	AVAILABLE FOR SECONDARY DEMAND	SALES PRICE/UNIT
Month 1	$13	20	15	$15
Month 2	$12	15	20	$14
Month 3	$13	25	15	$16

Table 73

	BID FOR			
	Painting 1	*Painting 2*	*Painting 3*	*Painting 4*
Customer 1	$8	$11	—	—
Customer 2	$9	$13	$12	$7
Customer 3	$9	—	$11	—
Customer 4	—	—	$12	$9

Table 74

FROM	TO				
	NE	*NW*	*MW*	*SE*	*SW*
L.A.	$27.86	$4.00	$20.54	$21.52	$13.87
Chicago	$8.02	$20.54	$2.00	$6.74	$10.67
N.Y.	$2.00	$27.86	$8.02	$8.41	$15.20

Table 75

			TO		
FROM	NE	NW	MW	SE	SW
Atlanta	$8.41	$21.52	$6.74	$3.00	$7.89
Houston	$15.20	$13.87	$10.67	$7.89	$3.00

23.[†] During the month of July, Pittsburgh resident B. Fly must make four round-trip flights between Pittsburgh and Chicago. The dates of the trips are as shown in Table 76. B. Fly must purchase four round-trip tickets. Without a discounted fare, a round-trip ticket between Pittsburgh and Chicago costs $500. If Fly's stay in a city includes a weekend, he gets a 20% discount on the round-trip fare. If his stay in a city is at least 21 days, he receives a 35% discount, and if his stay is more than 10 days, he receives a 30% discount. Of course, only one discount can be applied toward the purchase of any ticket. Formulate and solve an assignment problem that minimizes the total cost of purchasing the four round-trip tickets. (*Hint:* Let $x_{ij} = 1$ if a round-trip ticket is purchased for use on the ith flight out of Pittsburgh and the jth flight out of Chicago. Also think about where Fly should buy a ticket if, for example, $x_{21} = 1$.)

Table 76

LEAVE PITTSBURGH	LEAVE CHICAGO
Monday, July 1	Friday, July 5
Tuesday, July 9	Thursday, July 11
Monday, July 15	Friday, July 19
Wednesday, July 24	Thursday, July 25

24. Three professors must be assigned to teach six sections of finance. Each professor must teach two sections of finance, and each has ranked each of the six time periods during which finance is taught, as shown in Table 77. A ranking of 10 means that the professor wants to teach at that time, and a ranking of 1 means that he or she does not want to teach at that time. Determine an assignment of professors to sections so as to maximize the total satisfaction of the professors.

25.[‡] Three fires have just broken out in New York. Fires 1 and 2 each require two fire engines, and fire 3 requires three fire engines. The "cost" of responding to each fire depends on the time at which the fire engines arrive at the fire. Let t_{ij} be the time (in minutes) when the jth engine arrives at fire i. Then the cost of responding to each fire is as follows:

$$\text{Fire 1:} \quad 6t_{11} + 4t_{12}$$
$$\text{Fire 2:} \quad 7t_{21} + 3t_{22}$$
$$\text{Fire 3:} \quad 9t_{31} + 8t_{32} + 5t_{33}$$

There are three fire companies that can respond to the three fires. Company 1 has three engines available, and companies 2 and 3 each have two engines available. The time (in minutes) it takes an engine to travel from each company to each fire is shown in Table 78.

Table 78

	FIRE 1	FIRE 2	FIRE 3
Company 1	6	7	9
Company 2	5	8	11
Company 3	6	9	10

Table 77

	9 A.M.	10 A.M.	11 A.M.	1 P.M.	2 P.M.	3 P.M.
Professor 1	8	7	6	5	7	6
Professor 2	9	9	8	8	4	4
Professor 3	7	6	9	6	9	9

[†]Based on Hansen and Wendell (1982).

[‡]Based on Denardo, Rothblum, and Swersey (1988).

(a) Formulate and solve a transportation problem that can be used to minimize the cost associated with assigning the fire engines to fires. (*Hint:* Seven demand points will be needed.)

(b) Would the formulation in part (a) still be valid if the cost of fire 1 were $4t_{11} + 6t_{12}$?

◆ REFERENCES

The following six texts discuss transportation, assignment, and transshipment problems:

BAZARAA, M., and J. JARVIS. *Linear Programming and Network Flows.* New York: Wiley, 1977.

BRADLEY, S., A. HAX, and T. MAGNANTI. *Applied Mathematical Programming.* Reading, Mass.: Addison-Wesley, 1977.

DANTZIG, G. *Linear Programming and Extensions.* Princeton, N.J.: Princeton University Press, 1963.

GASS, S. *Linear Programming: Methods and Applications,* 5th ed. New York: McGraw-Hill, 1985.

MURTY, K. *Linear Programming.* New York: Wiley, 1983.

WU, N., and R. COPPINS. *Linear Programming and Extensions.* New York: McGraw-Hill, 1981.

AARVIK, O., and P. RANDOLPH. "The Application of Linear Programming to the Determination of Transmission Line Fees in an Electrical Power Network," *Interfaces* 6(1975):17–31.

DENARDO, E., U. ROTHBLUM, and A. SWERSEY. "Transportation Problem in Which Costs Depend on Order of Arrival," *Management Science* 34(1988):774–784.

EVANS, J. "The Factored Transportation Problem," *Management Science* 30(1984):1021–1024.

GILLETT, B. *Introduction to Operations Research: A Computer-Oriented Algorithmic Approach.* New York: McGraw-Hill, 1976.

GLASSEY, R., and V. GUPTA. "A Linear Programming Analysis of Paper Recycling," *Management Science* 21(1974):392–408.

GLOVER, F., ET AL. "A Computational Study on Starting Procedures, Basis Change Criteria, and Solution Algorithms for Transportation Problems," *Management Science* 20(1974):793–813. This article discusses the computational efficiency of various methods used to find basic feasible solutions for transportation problems.

HANSEN, P., and R. WENDELL. "A Note on Airline Commuting," *Interfaces* 11(no. 12, 1982):85–87.

JACKSON, B. "Using LP for Crude Oil Sales at Elk Hills: A Case Study," *Interfaces* 10(1980):65–70.

JACOBS, W. "The Caterer Problem," *Naval Logistics Research Quarterly* 1(1954):154–165.

MACHOL, R. "An Application of the Assignment Problem," *Operations Research* 18(1970):745–746.

SRINIVASAN, P. "A Transshipment Model for Cash Management Decisions," *Management Science* 20(1974):1364–1376.

8

Network Models

MANY IMPORTANT OPTIMIZATION problems can best be analyzed by means of a graphical or network representation. In this chapter, we consider four specific network models—shortest path problems, maximum flow problems, CPM-PERT project scheduling models, and minimum spanning tree problems—for which efficient solution procedures exist. We also discuss minimum cost network flow problems (MCNFPs), of which transportation, assignment, transshipment, shortest path, and maximum flow problems and the CPM project scheduling models are all special cases. Finally, we discuss a generalization of the transportation simplex, the network simplex, which can be used to solve MCNFPs. We begin the chapter with some basic terms used to describe graphs and networks.

8-1   BASIC DEFINITIONS

A **graph**, or **network**, is defined by two sets of symbols: nodes and arcs. First, we define a set (call it V) of points, or **vertices**. The vertices of a graph or network are also called **nodes**.

We also define a set of arcs A.

> **DEFINITION** ◾ An **arc** consists of an ordered pair of vertices and represents a possible direction of motion that may occur between vertices.

For our purposes, if a network contains an arc (j, k), motion is possible from node j to node k. Suppose nodes 1, 2, 3, and 4 of Figure 1 represent cities, and each arc represents a (one-way) road linking two cities. For this network, $V = \{1, 2, 3, 4\}$ and $A = \{(1, 2), (2, 3), (3, 4), (4, 3), (4, 1)\}$. For the arc (j, k), node j is the **initial node** of the arc, and node k is the **terminal node** of the arc. The arc (j, k) is said to go from node j to node k. Thus, the arc $(2, 3)$ has initial node 2 and terminal node 3, and it goes from node 2 to node 3. The arc $(2, 3)$ may be thought of as a (one-way) road on which we may travel from city 2 to city 3. In Figure 1, the arcs show that travel is allowed from city 3 to city 4, and from city 4 to city 3, but that travel between the other cities may be one way only.

Figure 1
Example of a
Network

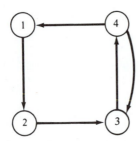

Later we often discuss a group or collection of arcs. The following definitions are convenient ways to describe certain groups or collections of arcs.

DEFINITION	A sequence of arcs such that every arc has exactly one vertex in common with the previous arc is called a **chain**.

DEFINITION	A **path** is a chain in which the terminal node of each arc is identical to the initial node of the next arc.

For example, in Figure 1, $(1, 2)$–$(2, 3)$–$(4, 3)$ is a chain but not a path; $(1, 2)$–$(2, 3)$–$(3, 4)$ is a chain *and* a path. The path $(1, 2)$–$(2, 3)$–$(3, 4)$ represents a way to travel from node 1 to node 4.

8-2   SHORTEST PATH PROBLEMS

In this section, we assume that each arc in the network has a length associated with it. Suppose we start at a particular node (say, node 1). The problem of finding the shortest path (path of minimum length) from node 1 to any other node in the network is called a **shortest path problem**. Examples 1 and 2 are shortest path problems.

E X A M P L E
1

Let us consider the Powerco example. Suppose that when power is sent from plant 1 (node 1 in Figure 2) to city 1 (node 6 in Figure 2), it must pass through relay substations (nodes 2–5 in Figure 2). For any pair of nodes between which power can be transported, Figure 2 gives the distance (in miles) between the nodes. Thus, substations 2 and 4 are

Figure 2
Network for
Powerco Example

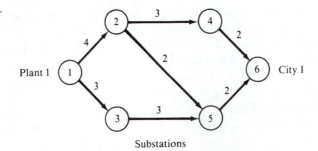

Substations

3 miles apart, and power cannot be sent between substations 4 and 5. Powerco wants the power sent from plant 1 to city 1 to travel the minimum possible distance, so it must find the shortest path in Figure 2 that joins node 1 to node 6.

If the cost of shipping power were proportional to the distance the power travels, then knowing the shortest path between plant 1 and city 1 in Figure 2 (and the shortest path between plant i and city j in similar diagrams) would be necessary in order to determine the shipping costs for the transportation version of the Powerco problem discussed in Chapter 7.

◆

E X A M P L E 2

I have just purchased (at time 0) a new car for $12,000. The cost of maintaining a car during a year depends on the age of the car at the beginning of the year, as given in Table 1. To avoid the high maintenance costs associated with an older car, I may trade in my car and purchase a new car. The price I receive on a trade-in depends on the age of the car at the time of trade-in (see Table 2). To simplify the computations, we assume that at any time, it costs $12,000 to purchase a new car. My goal is to minimize the net cost (purchasing costs + maintenance costs − money received in trade-ins) incurred during the next five years. Formulate this problem as a shortest path problem.

Table 1
Car Maintenance Costs

AGE OF CAR (Years)	ANNUAL MAINTENANCE COST
0	$2,000
1	$4,000
2	$5,000
3	$9,000
4	$12,000

Table 2
Car Trade-in Prices

AGE OF CAR (Years)	TRADE-IN PRICE
1	$7000
2	$6000
3	$2000
4	$1000
5	$0

Solution

Our network will have six nodes (1, 2, 3, 4, 5, and 6). Node i is the beginning of year i. For $i < j$, an arc (i, j) corresponds to purchasing a new car at the beginning of year i and keeping it until the beginning of year j. The length of arc (i, j) (call it c_{ij}) is the total net cost incurred in owning and operating a car from the beginning of year i to the beginning of year j if a new car is purchased at the beginning of year i and this car is traded in for a new car at the beginning of year j. Thus,

$$c_{ij} = \text{maintenance cost incurred during years } i, i + 1, \ldots, j - 1$$
$$+ \text{ cost of purchasing car at beginning of year } i$$
$$- \text{ trade-in value received at beginning of year } j$$

Figure 3
Network for
Minimizing Car
Costs

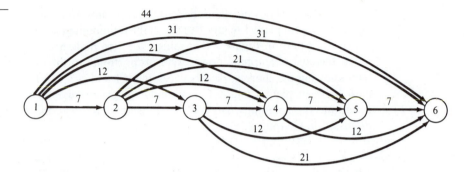

Applying this formula to the information in the problem yields (all costs are in thousands)

$c_{12} = 2 + 12 - 7 = 7$ $c_{26} = 2 + 4 + 5 + 9 + 12 - 1 = 31$

$c_{13} = 2 + 4 + 12 - 6 = 12$ $c_{34} = 2 + 12 - 7 = 7$

$c_{14} = 2 + 4 + 5 + 12 - 2 = 21$ $c_{35} = 2 + 4 + 12 - 6 = 12$

$c_{15} = 2 + 4 + 5 + 9 + 12 - 1 = 31$ $c_{36} = 2 + 4 + 5 + 12 - 2 = 21$

$c_{16} = 2 + 4 + 5 + 9 + 12 + 12 - 0 = 44$ $c_{45} = 2 + 12 - 7 = 7$

$c_{23} = 2 + 12 - 7 = 7$ $c_{46} = 2 + 4 + 12 - 6 = 12$

$c_{24} = 2 + 4 + 12 - 6 = 12$ $c_{56} = 2 + 12 - 7 = 7$

$c_{25} = 2 + 4 + 5 + 12 - 2 = 21$

We now see that the length of any path from node 1 to node 6 is the net cost incurred during the next five years corresponding to a particular trade-in strategy. For example, suppose I trade in the car at the beginning of year 3 and next trade in the car at the end of year 5 (the beginning of year 6). This strategy corresponds to the path 1–3–6 in Figure 3. The length of this path ($c_{13} + c_{36}$) is the total net cost incurred during the next five years if I trade in the car at the beginning of year 3 and at the beginning of year 6. Thus, the length of the shortest path from node 1 to node 6 in Figure 3 is the minimum net cost that can be incurred in operating a car during the next five years.   ◆

DIJKSTRA'S ALGORITHM

Assuming that all arc lengths are nonnegative, the following method, known as **Dijkstra's algorithm** can be used to find the shortest path from a node (say, node 1) to all other nodes. To begin, we label node 1 with a permanent label of 0. Then we label each node i that is connected to node 1 by a single arc with a "temporary" label equal to the length of the arc joining node 1 to node i. Each other node (except, of course, for node 1) will have a temporary label of ∞. Choose the node with the smallest temporary label and make this label permanent.

Now suppose that node i has just become the $(k + 1)$th node to be given a permanent label. Then node i is the kth closest node to node 1. At this point, the temporary label of any node (say, node i') is the length of the shortest path from node 1 to node i' that passes only through nodes contained in the $k - 1$ closest nodes to node 1. For each node j that now has a temporary label and is connected to node i by an arc, we replace node j's temporary label by

$$\text{min} \begin{cases} \text{node } j\text{'s current temporary label} \\ \text{node } i\text{'s permanent label} + \text{length of arc } (i,j) \end{cases}$$

(Here, min $\{a, b\}$ is the smaller of a and b.) The new temporary label for node j is the length of the shortest path from node 1 to node j that passes only through nodes contained in the k closest nodes to node 1. We now make the smallest temporary label a permanent label. The node with this new permanent label is the $(k + 1)$th closest node to node 1. Continue this process until all nodes have a permanent label. To find the shortest path from node 1 to node j, work backward from node j by finding nodes having labels differing by exactly the length of the connecting arc. Of course, if we want the shortest path from node 1 to node j, we can stop the labeling process as soon as node j receives a permanent label.

To illustrate Dijkstra's algorithm, we find the shortest path from node 1 to node 6 in Figure 2. We begin with the following labels (a * represents a permanent label, and the ith number is the label of node i); [0* 4 3 ∞ ∞ ∞]. Node 3 now has the smallest temporary label. We therefore make node 3's label permanent and obtain the following labels:

$$[0^*\ \ 4\ \ 3^*\ \ \infty\ \ \infty\ \ \infty]$$

We now know that node 3 is the closest node to node 1. We compute new temporary labels for all nodes that are connected to node 3 by a single arc. We only compute a new temporary label for node 5 as follows:

$$\text{New node 5 temporary label} = \text{min}\{\infty, 3 + 3\} = 6$$

Node 2 now has the smallest temporary label; we now make node 2's label permanent. We now know that node 2 is the second closest node to node 1. Our new set of labels is

$$[0^*\ \ 4^*\ \ 3^*\ \ \infty\ \ 6\ \ \infty]$$

Since nodes 4 and 5 are connected to the newly permanently labeled node 2, we must change the temporary labels of nodes 4 and 5. Node 4's new temporary label is min $\{\infty, 4 + 3\} = 7$, and node 5's new temporary label is min $\{6, 4 + 2\} = 6$. Node 5 now has the smallest temporary label, so we make node 5's label permanent. We now know that node 5 is the third closest node to node 1. Our new labels are

$$[0^*\ \ 4^*\ \ 3^*\ \ 7\ \ 6^*\ \ \infty]$$

Since only node 6 is connected to node 5, node 6's temporary label will change to min $\{\infty, 6 + 2\} = 8$. Node 4 now has the smallest temporary label, so we make node 4's label permanent. We now know that node 4 is the fourth closest node to node 1. Our new labels are

$$[0^*\ \ 4^*\ \ 3^*\ \ 7^*\ \ 6^*\ \ 8]$$

Since node 6 is connected to the newly permanently labeled node 4, we must change node 6's temporary label to min $\{8, 7 + 2\} = 8$. We can now make node 6's label permanent. Our final set of labels is [0* 4* 3* 7* 6* 8*]. We can now work backward and find the shortest path from node 1 to node 6. The difference between node 6's and node 5's permanent labels is 2 = length of arc $(5,6)$, so we go back to node 5. The difference between node 5's and node 2's permanent labels is 2 = length of arc $(2,5)$, so we may go back to node 2. Then, of course, we must go back to node 1. Thus, 1–2–5–6 is a shortest path (of length 8) from node 1 to node 6. Observe that when we were at node 5, we could also have worked backward to node 3 and obtained the shortest path 1–3–5–6.

THE SHORTEST PATH PROBLEM AS A TRANSSHIPMENT PROBLEM

Finding the shortest path between node i and node j in a network may be viewed as a transshipment problem. Simply try to minimize the cost of sending 1 unit from node i to node j (with all other nodes in the network being transshipment points), where the cost of sending 1 unit from node k to node k' is the length of arc (k, k') if such an arc exists and is M (a large positive number) if such an arc does not exist. As in Section 7.6, the cost of shipping 1 unit from a node to itself is zero. Following the method described in Section 7.6, this transshipment problem may be transformed into a balanced transportation problem.

To illustrate the preceding ideas, we formulate the balanced transportation problem associated with finding the shortest path from node 1 to node 6 in Figure 2. We wish to send 1 unit from node 1 to node 6. Node 1 is a supply point, node 6 is a demand point, and nodes 2, 3, 4 and 5 will be transshipment points. Using $s = 1$, we obtain the balanced transportation problem shown in Table 3. This transportation problem has two optimal solutions:

1. $z = 4 + 2 + 2 = 8$, $x_{12} = x_{25} = x_{56} = x_{33} = x_{44} = 1$ (all other variables equal zero). This solution corresponds to the path 1–2–5–6.

2. $z = 3 + 3 + 2 = 8$, $x_{13} = x_{35} = x_{56} = x_{22} = x_{44} = 1$ (all other variables equal zero). This solution corresponds to the path 1–3–5–6.

Table 3

Transshipment Representation of Shortest Path Problem and One Optimal Solution

NODE	2	3	4	5	6	SUPPLY
1	4 [1]	3	M	M	M	1
2	0	M	3	2 [1]	M	1
3	M	0 [1]	M	3	M	1
4	M	M	0 [1]	M	2	1
5	M	M	M	0	2 [1]	1
DEMAND	1	1	1	1	1	

◆ PROBLEMS

GROUP A

1. Find the shortest path from node 1 to node 6 in Figure 3.

2. Find the shortest path from node 1 to node 5 in Figure 4.

Figure 4 Network for Problem 2

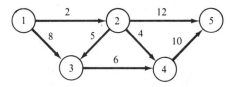

3. Formulate Problem 2 as a transshipment problem.

4. Use Dijkstra's algorithm to find the shortest path from node 1 to node 4 in Figure 5. Why does Dijkstra's algorithm fail to obtain the correct answer?

Figure 5 Network for Problem 4

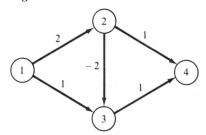

5. Suppose it costs $10,000 to purchase a new car. The annual operating cost and resale value of a used car is shown in Table 4. Assuming that one has a new car at present, determine a replacement policy that minimizes the net costs of owning and operating a car for the next six years.

6. It costs $40 to buy a telephone from the department store. Assume that I can keep a telephone for at most five years and that the estimated maintenance cost for each year of operation is as follows: year 1, $20; year 2, $30; year 3, $40; year 4, $60; year 5, $70. I have just purchased a new telephone. Assuming that a telephone has no salvage value, determine how to minimize the total cost of purchasing and operating a telephone for the next six years.

GROUP B

7.[†] A library must build shelving to shelve 200 4-inch high books, 100 8-inch high books, and 80 12-inch high books. Each book is 0.5 inch thick. The library has several ways to store the books. For example, an 8-inch high shelf may be built to store all books of height less than or equal to 8 inches, and a 12-inch high shelf may be built for the 12-inch books. Alternatively, a 12-inch high shelf might be built to store all books. The library believes it costs $2300 to build a shelf and that a cost of $5 per square inch is incurred for book storage. (Assume that the area required to store a book is given by height of storage area times book's thickness.)

Formulate and solve a shortest path problem that could be used to help the library determine how to shelve the books at minimum cost. (*Hint*: Have nodes 0, 4, 8, and 12, with c_{ij} being the total cost of shelving all books of height $> i$ and $\leq j$ on a single shelf.)

[†]Based on Ravindran (1971).

Table 4

AGE OF CAR (Years)	RESALE VALUE	OPERATING COST
1	$7000	$300 (year 1)
2	$6000	$500 (year 2)
3	$4000	$800 (year 3)
4	$3000	$1200 (year 4)
5	$2000	$1600 (year 5)
6	$1000	$2200 (year 6)

8-3   MAXIMUM FLOW PROBLEMS

Many situations can be modeled by a network in which the arcs may be thought of as having a capacity that limits the quantity of a product that may be shipped through the arc. In these situations, it is often desired to transport the maximum amount of flow from a starting point (called the **source**) to a terminal point (called the **sink**). Such problems are called **maximum flow problems**. Several specialized algorithms exist to solve maximum flow problems. In this section, we begin by showing how linear programming can be used to solve a maximum flow problem. Then we discuss the Ford-Fulkerson (1962) method for solving maximum flow problems.

LP SOLUTION OF MAXIMUM FLOW PROBLEMS

E X A M P L E 3

Sunco Oil wants to ship the maximum possible amount of oil (per hour) via pipeline from node *so* to node *si* in Figure 6. On its way from node *so* to node *si*, oil must pass through some or all of stations 1, 2, and 3. The various arcs in Figure 6 represent pipelines of different diameters. The maximum number of barrels of oil (millions of barrels per hour) that can be pumped through each arc is shown in Table 5. Each of these numbers is called an **arc capacity**. Formulate an LP that can be used to determine the maximum number of barrels of oil per hour that can be sent from *so* to *si*.

Figure 6
Network for Sunco
Oil Example

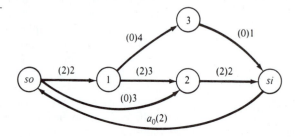

Table 5
Arc Capacities for
Sunco Oil

ARC	CAPACITY
(so, 1)	2
(so, 2)	3
(1, 2)	3
(1, 3)	4
(3, si)	1
(2, si)	2

Solution   Node *so* is called the source node because oil flows out of it but no oil flows into it. Analogously, node *si* is called the sink node because oil flows into it and no oil flows out of it. For reasons that will soon become clear, we have added an artificial arc a_0 from the sink to the source in Figure 6. The flow through a_0 is not actually oil; hence the term **artificial arc**.

To formulate an LP that will yield the maximum flow from node *so* to *si*, we observe that Sunco must determine how much oil (per hour) should be sent through arc (i, j). Thus, we define

x_{ij} = millions of barrels of oil per hour that will pass through arc (i,j) of pipeline

As an example of a possible flow (termed a feasible flow), consider the flow identified by the numbers in parentheses in Figure 6.

$$x_{so,1} = 2, \quad x_{13} = 0, \quad x_{12} = 2, \quad x_{3,si} = 0, \quad x_{2,si} = 2, \quad x_{si,so} = 2, \quad x_{so,2} = 0$$

For a flow to be feasible, it must have two characteristics:

$$0 \leq \text{flow through each arc} \leq \text{arc capacity} \tag{1}$$

and

$$\text{Flow into node } i = \text{flow out of node } i \tag{2}$$

We assume that no oil gets lost while being pumped through the network, so at each node, a feasible flow must satisfy (2), the *conservation-of-flow* constraint. The introduction of the artificial arc a_0 allows us to write the conservation-of-flow constraint for the source and sink.

If we let x_0 be the flow through the artificial arc, then conservation of flow implies that x_0 = total amount of oil entering the sink. Thus, Sunco's goal is to maximize x_0 subject to (1) and (2):

$$\max z = x_0$$

$$
\begin{array}{lll}
\text{s.t.} & x_{so,1} \leq 2 & \text{(Arc capacity constraints)} \\
& x_{so,2} \leq 3 & \\
& x_{12} \leq 3 & \\
& x_{2,si} \leq 2 & \\
& x_{13} \leq 4 & \\
& x_{3,si} \leq 1 & \\
& x_0 = x_{so,1} + x_{so,2} & \text{(Node } so \text{ flow constraint)} \\
& x_{so,1} = x_{12} + x_{13} & \text{(Node 1 flow constraint)} \\
& x_{so,2} + x_{12} = x_{2,si} & \text{(Node 2 flow constraint)} \\
& x_{13} = x_{3,si} & \text{(Node 3 flow constraint)} \\
& x_{3,si} + x_{2,si} = x_0 & \text{(Node } si \text{ flow constraint)} \\
& x_{ij} \geq 0 &
\end{array}
$$

One optimal solution to this LP is $z = 3$, $x_{so,1} = 2$, $x_{13} = 1$, $x_{12} = 1$, $x_{so,2} = 1$, $x_{3,si} = 1$, $x_{2,si} = 2$, $x_0 = 3$. Thus, the maximum possible flow of oil from node so to si is 3 million barrels per hour, with 1 million barrels per hour being sent via the path $so-1-2-si$, 1 million barrels per hour being sent via the path $so-1-3-si$, and 1 million barrels per hour being sent via the path $so-2-si$.

◆

The linear programming formulation of maximum flow problems is a special case of the minimum cost network flow problem (MCNFP) discussed in Section 8.5. A generalization of the transportation simplex (known as the network simplex) can be used to solve MCNFPs.

Before discussing the Ford-Fulkerson method for solving maximum flow problems, we give two examples of situations in which a maximum flow problem might arise.

E X A M P L E
4

Fly-by-Night Airlines must determine how many connecting flights daily can be arranged between Juneau, Alaska, and Dallas, Texas. Connecting flights must stop in Seattle and then stop in Los Angeles or Denver. Because of limited landing space, Fly-by-Night is limited to making the number of daily flights between pairs of cities shown in Table 6. Set up a maximum flow problem whose solution will tell the airline how to maximize the number of connecting flights daily from Juneau to Dallas.

Table 6
Arc Capacities for
Fly-by-Night Airlines

CITIES	MAXIMUM NUMBER OF DAILY FLIGHTS
Juneau–Seattle (J, S)	3
Seattle–L.A. (S, L)	2
Seattle–Denver (S, D)	3
L.A.–Dallas (L, D)	1
Denver–Dallas (D, D)	2

Solution

The appropriate network is given in Figure 7. Here the capacity of arc (i, j) is the maximum number of daily flights between city i and city j. The optimal solution to this maximum flow problem is $z = x_0 = 3$, $x_{J,S} = 3$, $x_{S,L} = 1$, $x_{S,D} = 2$, $x_{L,D} = 1$, $x_{D,D} = 2$. Thus, Fly-by-Night can send three flights daily connecting Juneau and Dallas. One flight connects via Juneau–Seattle–L.A.–Dallas and two flights connect via Juneau–Seattle–Denver–Dallas.

Figure 7
Network for Fly-by-Night Airlines Example

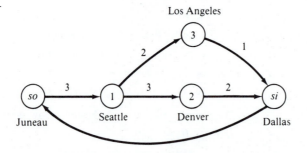

E X A M P L E
5

Five male and five female entertainers are at a dance. The goal of the matchmaker is to match each woman with a man in a way that maximizes the number of people who are matched with compatible mates. Table 7 describes the compatibility of the entertainers. Draw a network that makes it possible to represent the problem of maximizing the number of compatible pairings as a maximum flow problem.

Solution

Figure 8 is the appropriate network. In Figure 8, there is an arc with capacity 1 joining the source to each man, an arc with capacity 1 joining each pair of compatible mates,

Table 7
Compatabilities for
Matching Example

	LONI ANDERSON	MERYL STREEP	KATHARINE HEPBURN	LINDA EVANS	VICTORIA PRINCIPAL
Kevin Costner	—	C	—	—	—
Burt Reynolds	C	—	—	—	—
Tom Selleck	C	—	—	—	—
Michael Jackson	C	C	—	—	C
Tom Cruise	—	—	C	C	C

Note: C indicates compatibility.

Figure 8
Network for
Matchmaker
Problem

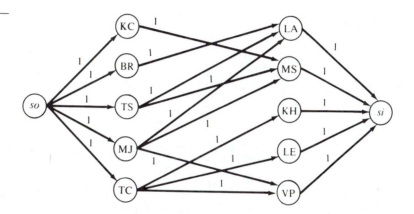

and an arc with capacity 1 joining each woman to the sink. The maximum flow in this network is the number of compatible couples that can be created by the matchmaker. For example, if the matchmaker pairs KC and MS, BR and LA, MJ and VP, and TC and KH, a flow of 4 from source to sink would be obtained. (This turns out to be a maximum flow for the network.)

To see why our network representation correctly models the matchmaker's problem, note that since the arc joining each woman to the sink has a capacity of 1, conservation of flow ensures that each woman will be matched with at most one man. Similarly, since each arc from the source to a man has a capacity of 1, each man can be paired with at most one woman. Since arcs do not exist joining noncompatible mates, we can be sure that a flow of k units from source to sink represents an assignment of men to women in which k compatible couples are created.

◆

THE FORD-FULKERSON METHOD FOR SOLVING MAXIMUM FLOW PROBLEMS

We assume that a feasible flow has been found (letting the flow in each arc equal zero gives a feasible flow), and we turn our attention to the following important questions:

Question 1 Given a feasible flow, how can we tell if it is an optimal flow (i.e., maximizes x_0)?

Question 2 If a feasible flow is nonoptimal, how can we modify the flow to obtain a new feasible flow that has a larger flow from a source to sink?

First, we answer question 2. We determine which of the following properties is possessed by each arc in the network:

Property 1 The flow through arc (i, j) is below the capacity of arc (i, j). In this case, the flow through arc (i, j) can be increased. For this reason, we let I represent the set of arcs with this property.

Property 2 The flow in arc (i, j) is positive. In this case, the flow through arc (i, j) can be reduced. For this reason, we let R be the set of arcs with this property.

As an illustration of the definitions of I and R, consider the network in Figure 9. The arcs in this figure may be classified as follows: $(so, 1)$ is in I and R; $(so, 2)$ is in I; $(1, si)$ is in R; $(2, si)$ is in I; and $(2, 1)$ is in I.

Figure 9
Illustration of I and R arcs

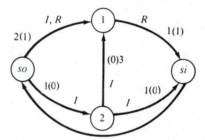

We can now describe the Ford-Fulkerson labeling procedure used to modify a feasible flow in an effort to increase the flow from the source to the sink.

Step 1 Label the source.

Step 2 Label nodes and arcs (except for arc a_0) according to the following rules: (1) If node x is labeled, node y is unlabeled and arc (x, y) is a member of I; then label node y and arc (x, y). In this case, arc (x, y) is called a **forward arc**. (2) If node y is unlabeled, node x is labeled and arc (y, x) is a member of R; label node y and arc (y, x). In this case, (y, x) is called a **backward arc**.

Step 3 Continue this labeling process until the sink has been labeled or until no more vertices can be labeled.

If the labeling process results in the sink being labeled, there will be a chain of labeled arcs (call it C) leading from the source to the sink. By adjusting the flow of the arcs in C, we can maintain a feasible flow and increase the total flow from source to sink. To see this, observe that C must consist of one of the following:

Case 1 C consists entirely of forward arcs.

Case 2 C contains both forward and backward arcs.[†]

In each case, we can obtain a new feasible flow that has a larger flow from source to sink than the current feasible flow. In Case 1, the chain C consists entirely of forward arcs. For each forward arc in C, let $i(x, y)$ be the amount by which the flow in arc (x, y) can be increased without violating the capacity constraint for arc (x, y). Let

---

[†]Since we exclude arc a_0 from the labeling procedure, no chain entirely of backward arcs can lead from source to sink.

$$k = \min_{(x,y) \in C} i(x, y)$$

Then $k > 0$. To create a new flow, increase the flow through each arc in C by k units. No capacity constraints are violated, and conservation of flow is still maintained. Thus, the new flow is feasible, and the new feasible flow will transport k more units from source to sink than does the current feasible flow.

We use Figure 10 to illustrate Case 1. Currently, 2 units are being transported from source to sink. The labeling procedure results in the sink being labeled by the chain $C = (so, 1)$–$(1, 2)$–$(2, si)$. Each of these arcs is in I, and $i(so, 1) = 5 - 2 = 3$; $i(1, 2) = 3 - 2 = 1$; and $i(2, si) = 4 - 2 = 2$. Hence, $k = \min(3, 1, 2) = 1$. Thus, an improved feasible flow can be obtained by increasing the flow on each arc in C by 1 unit. The resulting flow transports 3 units from source to sink (see Figure 11).

Figure 10
Illustration of Case 1
of Labeling Method

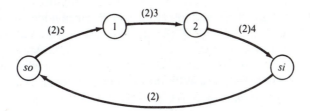

Flow from source to sink = 2
Chain is $(so, 1)$-$(1, 2)$-$(2, si)$

Figure 11
Improved Flow
from Source to Sink:
Case 1

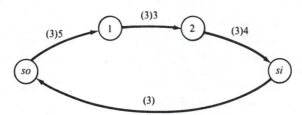

Flow from source to sink = 3

In Case 2, the chain C leading from the source to the sink contains both backward and forward arcs. For each backward arc in C, let $r(x, y)$ be the amount by which the flow through arc (x, y) can be reduced. Also define

$$k_1 = \min_{x,y \in C \cap R} r(x, y) \quad \text{and} \quad k_2 = \min_{x,y \in C \cap I} i(x, y)$$

Of course, both k_1 and k_2 and $\min(k_1, k_2)$ are > 0. To increase the flow from source to sink (while maintaining a feasible flow), decrease the flow in all of C's backward arcs by $\min(k_1, k_2)$ and increase the flow in all of C's forward arcs by $\min(k_1, k_2)$. This will maintain conservation of flow and ensure that no arc capacity constraints are violated. Since the last arc in C is a forward arc leading into the sink, we have found a new feasible flow and have increased the total flow into the sink by $\min(k_1, k_2)$. We now adjust the flow in the arc a_0 to maintain conservation of flow. To illustrate Case 2, suppose we have found the feasible flow in Figure 12. For this flow, $(so, 1) \in R$; $(so, 2) \in I$; $(1, 3) \in I$; $(1, 2) \in I$ and R; $(2, si) \in R$; and $(3, si) \in I$.

Figure 12
Illustration of Case 2
of Labeling Method

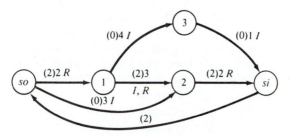

Flow from source to sink = 2

Chain is $(so, 2)$–$(1, 2)$–$(1, 3)$–$(3, si)$

We begin by labeling arc $(so, 2)$ and node 2 (thus $(so, 2)$ is a forward arc). Then we label arc $(1, 2)$ and node 1. Arc $(1, 2)$ is a backward arc, because node 1 was unlabeled before we labeled arc $(1, 2)$, and arc $(1, 2)$ is in R. Since nodes so, 1, and 2 are labeled, we can label arc $(1, 3)$ and node 3. (Arc $(1, 3)$ is a forward arc, because node 3 has not yet been labeled.) Finally we label arc $(3, si)$ and node si. Arc $(3, si)$ is a forward arc, because node si has not yet been labeled. We have now labeled the sink via the chain $C = (so, 2)$–$(1, 2)$–$(1, 3)$–$(3, si)$. With the exception of arc $(1, 2)$, all arcs in the chain are forward arcs. Since $i(so, 2) = 3$; $i(1, 3) = 4$; $i(3, si) = 1$; and $r(1, 2) = 2$, we have

$$\min_{(x,y) \in C \cap R} r(x, y) = 2 \quad \text{and} \quad \min_{(x,y) \in C \cap I} i(x, y) = 1$$

Thus, we can increase the flow on all forward arcs in C by 1 and decrease the flow in all backward arcs by 1. The new result, pictured in Figure 13, has increased the flow from source to sink by 1 unit (from 2 to 3). We accomplish this by diverting 1 unit that was transported through the arc $(1, 2)$ to the path 1–3–si. This enabled us to transport an extra unit from source to sink via the path so–2–si. Observe that the concept of a backward arc was needed to find this improved flow.

If the sink cannot be labeled, the current flow is optimal. The proof of this fact relies on the concept of a cut for a network.

Figure 13
Improved Flow
from Source to Sink:
Case 2

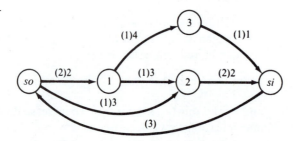

Flow from source to sink = 3

DEFINITION   Choose any set of nodes V' that contains the sink but does not contain the source. Then the set of arcs (i, j) with i not in V' and j a member of V' is a **cut** for the network.

DEFINITION	The **capacity** of a cut is the sum of the capacities of the arcs in the cut.

In short, a cut is a set of arcs whose removal from the network makes it impossible to travel from the source to the sink. A network may have many cuts. For example, in the network in Figure 14, $V' = \{1, si\}$ yields the cut containing the arcs $(so, 1)$ and $(2, si)$, which has capacity $2 + 1 = 3$. The set $V' = \{1, 2, si\}$ yields the cut containing the arcs $(so, 1)$ and $(so, 2)$, which has capacity $2 + 8 = 10$.

Lemma 1 and Lemma 2 indicate the connection between cuts and maximum flows.

Figure 14
Example of a Cut

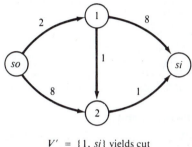

$V' = \{1, si\}$ yields cut
$\{(so, 1), (2, si)\}$

L E M M A **1**	The flow from source to sink for any feasible flow is less than or equal to the capacity of *any* cut.
Proof	Consider an arbitrary cut specified by a set of nodes V' that contains the sink but does not contain the source. Let V be all other nodes in the network. Also let x_{ij} be the flow in arc (i, j) for any feasible flow and f be the flow from source to sink for this feasible flow. Summing the flow balance equations (flow out of node i − flow into node $i = 0$) over all nodes i in V, we find that the terms involving arcs (i, j) having i and j both members of V will cancel, and we obtain

$$\sum_{\substack{i \in V; \\ j \in V'}} x_{ij} - \sum_{\substack{i \in V'; \\ j \in V}} x_{ij} = f \tag{3}$$

Now the first sum in (3) is less than or equal to the capacity of the cut. Since each x_{ij} is nonnegative, we see that $f \leq$ capacity of the cut, which is the desired result. ◆

Lemma 1 is analogous to the weak duality result discussed in Chapter 6. From Lemma 1, we see that the capacity of any cut is an upper bound for the maximum flow from source to sink. Thus, if we can find a feasible flow and a cut for which the flow from source to sink equals the capacity of the cut, we have found the maximum flow from source to sink.

Suppose that we find a feasible flow and cannot label the sink. Let CUT be the cut corresponding to the set of unlabeled nodes.

L E M M A   If the sink cannot be labeled, then
2

$$\text{Capacity of CUT} = \text{current flow from source to sink}$$

Proof   Let V' be the set of unlabeled nodes and V be the set of labeled nodes. Consider an arc (i, j) such that i is in V and j is in V'. Then we know that x_{ij} = capacity of arc (i, j) must hold; otherwise, we could label node j (via a forward arc) and node j would not be in V'. Now consider an arc (i, j) such that i is in V' and j is in V. Then $x_{ij} = 0$ must hold; otherwise, we could label node i (via a backward arc) and node i would not be in V'. Now (3) shows that the current flow must satisfy

$$\text{Capacity of CUT} = \text{current flow from source to sink}$$

which is the desired result.   ◆

From the remarks following Lemma 1, when the sink cannot be labeled, the maximum flow from source to sink has been obtained.

SUMMARY AND ILLUSTRATION OF THE FORD-FULKERSON METHOD

Step 1 Find a feasible flow (setting each arc's flow to zero will do).

Step 2 Using the labeling procedure, try to label the sink. If the sink cannot be labeled, the current feasible flow is a maximum flow; if the sink is labeled, go on to Step 3.

Step 3 Using the method previously described, adjust the feasible flow and increase the flow from the source to the sink. Return to Step 2.

To illustrate the Ford-Fulkerson method, we find the maximum flow from source to sink for Sunco Oil, Example 3 (see Figure 6). We begin by letting the flow in each arc equal zero. Then we try to label the sink: Label the source, and then label arc $(so, 1)$ and node 1; then label arc $(1, 2)$ and node 2; finally, label arc $(2, si)$ and node si. Thus, $C = (so, 1)-(1, 2)-(2, si)$. Each arc in C is a forward arc, so we can increase the flow through each arc in C by $\min(2, 3, 2) = 2$ units. The resulting flow is pictured in Figure 15.

As we saw previously (Figure 12), we can label the sink by using the chain $C = (so, 2)-(1, 2)-(1, 3)-(3, si)$. We can increase the flow through the forward arcs $(so, 2)$,

Figure 15
Network for Sunco
Oil Example
(Increased Flow)

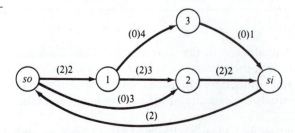

Flow from source to sink = 2
Label sink by $(so, 2)-(1, 2)-(1, 3)-(3, si)$

(1, 3), and (3, *si*) by 1 unit and decrease the flow through the backward arc (1, 2) by 1 unit. The resulting flow is pictured in Figure 16. It is now possible to label the sink: Any attempt to label the sink must begin by labeling arc (*so*, 2) and node 2; then we could label arc (1, 2) and arc (1, 3). But there is no way to label the sink.

Figure 16
Network for Sunco
Oil Example
(Optimal Flow)

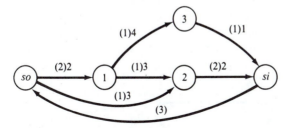

Flow from source to sink = 3
Since sink cannot be labeled, this is an optimal flow

We can verify that the current flow is maximal by finding the capacity of the cut corresponding to the set of unlabeled vertices (in this case, *si*). The cut corresponding to *si* is the set of arcs (2, *si*) and (3, *si*), with capacity 2 + 1 = 3. Thus, Lemma 1 implies that any feasible flow can transport at most 3 units from source to sink. Since our current flow transports 3 units from source to sink, it must be an optimal flow.

Another example of the Ford-Fulkerson method is given in Figure 17. Note that without the concept of a backward arc, we could not have obtained the maximum flow of 7 units from source to sink. The minimum cut (with capacity 7, of course) corresponds to nodes 1, 3, and *si* and consists of arcs (*so*, 1), (*so*, 3) and (2, 3).

Figure 17
Example of Ford–
Fulkerson Method

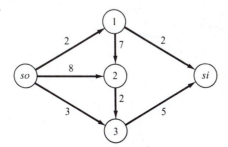

(a) Original network

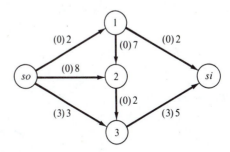

(b) Label sink by *so-3-si* (adds 3 units of flow using only forward arcs)

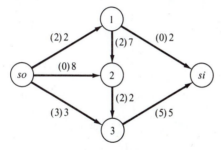

(c) Label sink by *so-1-2-3-si* (adds 2 units of flow using only forward arcs)

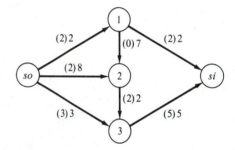

(d) Label sink by *so-2-1-si* (adds 2 units of flow by using backward arc (1, 2); maximum flow of 7 has been obtained)

◆ PROBLEMS

GROUP A

1–3. Figures 18–20 show the networks for Problems 1–3. Find the maximum flow from source to sink in each network. Find a cut in the network whose capacity equals the maximum flow in the network. Also, set up an LP that could be used to determine the maximum flow in the network.

4. For the network in Figure 21, find the maximum flow from source to sink. Also find a cut whose capacity equals the maximum flow in the network.

5. For the network in Figure 22, find the maximum flow from source to sink. Also find a cut whose capacity equals the maximum flow in the network.

Figure 18
Network for Problem 1

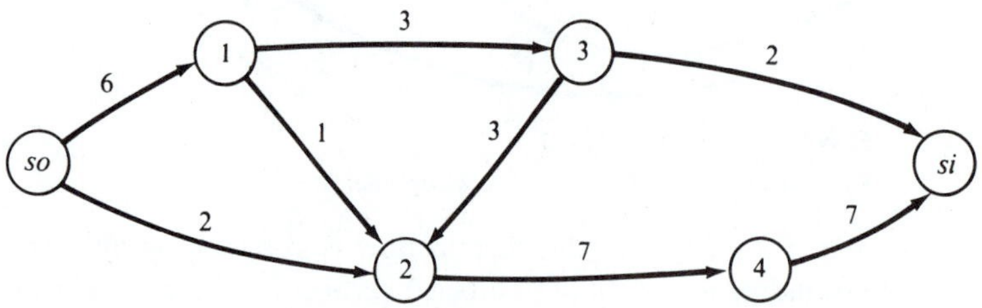

Figure 19
Network for Problem 2

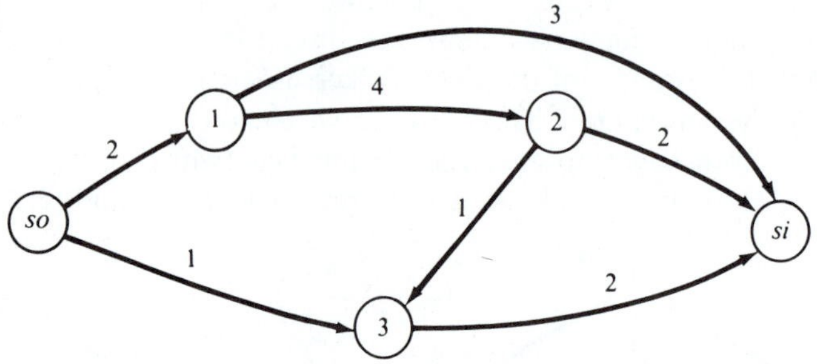

Figure 20
Network for Problem 3

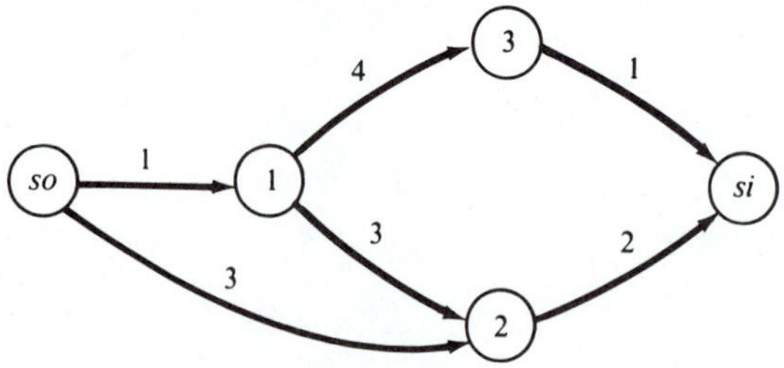

Figure 21
Network for Problem 4

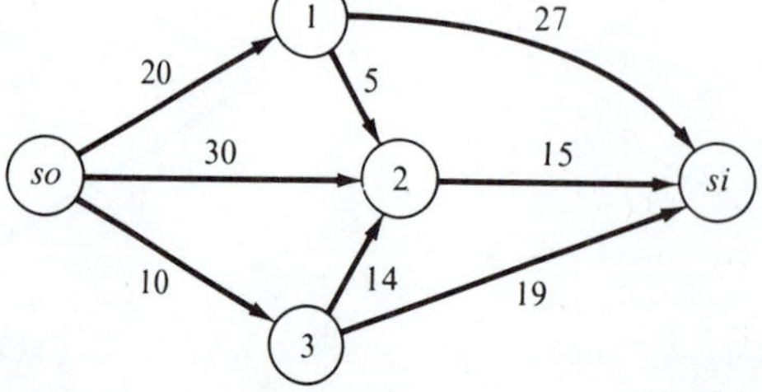

Figure 22 Network for Problem 5

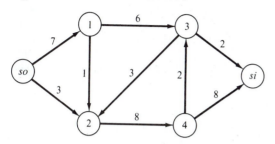

6. Seven types of packages are to be delivered by five trucks. There are three packages of each type, and the capacities of the five trucks are 6, 4, 5, 4, and 3 packages, respectively. Set up a maximum flow problem that can be used to determine whether the packages can be loaded so that no truck carries two packages of the same type.

7. Four workers are available to perform jobs 1–4. Unfortunately, three workers can do only certain jobs: worker 1, only job 1; worker 2, only jobs 1 and 2; worker 3, only job 2; worker 4, any job. Draw the network for the maximum flow problem that can be used to determine whether all jobs can be assigned to a suitable worker.

8. The Hatfields, Montagues, McCoys, and Capulets are going on their annual family picnic. Four cars are available to transport the families to the picnic. Car 1 can carry four people, car 2 can carry three people, car 3 can carry three people, and car 4 can carry four people. There are four people in each family, and it has been decreed that no car can carry more than two people from any one family. Formulate the problem of transporting the maximum possible number of people to the picnic as a maximum flow problem.

GROUP B

9. Suppose a network contains a finite number of arcs and the capacity of each arc is an integer. Explain why the Ford-Fulkerson method will find the maximum flow in a finite number of steps. Also show that the maximum flow from source to sink will be an integer.

10. Consider a network flow problem with several sources and several sinks in which the goal is to maximize the total flow into the sinks. Show how such a problem can be converted into a maximum flow problem having only a single source and a single sink.

11. Suppose the total flow into a node of a network is restricted to 10 units or less. How can we represent this restriction via an arc capacity constraint? (This still allows us to use the Ford-Fulkerson method to find the maximum flow.)

12. Suppose up to 300 cars per hour can travel between any two of the cities 1, 2, 3, and 4. Set up a maximum flow problem that can be used to determine how many cars can be sent in the next two hours from city 1 to city 4. (*Hint:* Have a portion of the network represent $t = 0$, a portion represent $t = 1$, and a portion represent $t = 2$.)

13. Fly-by-Night Airlines is considering flying three flights. The revenue from each flight and the airports used by each flight are shown in Table 8. When Fly-by-Night uses an airport, the company must pay the following landing fees (independent of the number of flights using the airport): airport 1, $300; airport 2, $700; airport 3, $500. Thus, if flights 1 and 3 are flown, a profit of $900 + 800 - 300 - 700 - 500 = \$200$ will be earned. Show that for the network in Figure 23 (maximum profit) = (total revenue from all flights) − capacity of minimal cut. Explain how this result can be used to help Fly-by-Night maximize profit (even if it has hundreds of possible flights). (*Hint:* Consider any set of flights F (say, flights 1 and 3). Consider the cut corresponding to the sink, the nodes associated with the flights not in F, and the

Table 8

FLIGHT	REVENUE	AIRPORTS USED
1	$900	Airports 1 and 2
2	$600	Airports 2
3	$800	Airports 2 and 3

Figure 23
Network for
Problem 13

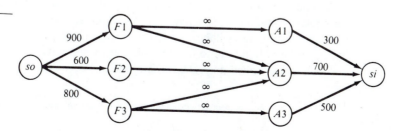

nodes associated with the airports not used by *F*. Show that (capacity of this cut) = (revenue from flights not in *F*) + (costs associated with airports used by *F*).)

14. During the next four months, a construction firm must complete three projects. Project 1 must be completed within three months and requires 8 man-months of labor. Project 2 must be completed within four months and requires 10 man-months of labor. Project 3 must be completed at the end of two months and requires 12 man-months of labor. Each month, 8 workers are available. During a given month, no more than 6 workers can work on a single job. Formulate a maximum flow problem that could be used to determine whether or not all three projects can be completed on time. (*Hint*: If the maximum flow in the network is 30, all projects can be completed on time.)

8-4   CPM AND PERT

Network models can be used as an aid in the scheduling of large complex projects that consist of many activities. If the duration of each activity is known with certainty, the critical path method (CPM) can be used to determine the length of time required to complete a project. CPM also can be used to determine how long each activity in the project can be delayed without delaying the completion of the project. CPM was developed in the late 1950s by researchers at du Pont and Sperry Rand.

If the duration of the activities is not known with certainty, the Program Evaluation and Review Technique (PERT) can be used to estimate the probability that the project will be completed by a given deadline. PERT was developed in the late 1950s by consultants working on the development of the Polaris missile. CPM and PERT were given a major share of the credit for the fact that the Polaris missile was operational two years ahead of schedule.

CPM and PERT have been successfully used in many applications, including

1. Scheduling construction projects such as office buildings, highways, and swimming pools

2. Scheduling the movement of a 400-bed hospital from Portland, Oregon, to a suburban location

3. Developing a countdown and "hold" procedure for the launching of space flights

4. Installing a new computer system

5. Designing and marketing a new product

6. Completing a corporate merger

7. Building a ship

To apply CPM and PERT, we need a list of the activities that make up the project. The project is considered to be completed when all the activities have been completed. For each activity, there is a set of activities (called the **predecessors** of the activity) that must be completed before the activity begins. A project network is used to represent the precedence relationships between activities. In our discussion, activities will be represented by directed arcs, and nodes will be used to represent the completion of a set of activities. (For this reason, we often refer to the nodes in our project network as **events**.) This type of project network is called an **AOA (activity on arc)** network.[†]

[†]In an AON (activity on node) project network, the nodes of the network are used to represent activities. See Wiest and Levy (1977) for details.

To understand how an AOA network represents precedence relationships, suppose that activity A is a predecessor of activity B. Each node in an AOA network represents the completion of one or more activities. Thus, node 2 in Figure 24 represents the completion of activity A and the beginning of activity B. Suppose activities A and B must be completed before activity C can begin. In Figure 25, node 3 represents the event that activities A and B are completed. Figure 26 shows activity A as a predecessor of both activities B and C.

Figure 24
Activity A Must Be
Completed Before
Activity B Can Begin

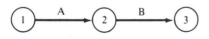

Figure 25
Activities A and B
Must Be Completed
Before Activity C
Can Begin

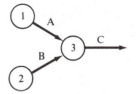

Figure 26
Activity A Must Be
Completed Before
Activities B and C
Can Begin

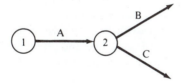

Given a list of activities and predecessors, an AOA representation of a project (called a **project network** or **project diagram**) can be constructed by using the following rules:

1. Node 1 represents the start of the project. An arc should lead from node 1 to represent each activity that has no predecessors.

2. A node (called the **finish node**) representing the completion of the project should be included in the network.

3. Number the nodes in the network so that the node representing the completion of an activity always has a larger number than the node representing the beginning of an activity (there may be more than one numbering scheme that satisfies rule 3).

4. An activity should not be represented by more than one arc in the network.

5. Two nodes can be connected by at most one arc.

To avoid violating rules 4 and 5, it is sometimes necessary to utilize a **dummy activity** that takes zero time. For example, suppose activities A and B are both predecessors of activity C and can begin at the same time. In the absence of rule 5, we could represent this by Figure 27. However, since nodes 1 and 2 are connected by more than one arc, Figure 27 violates rule 5. By using a dummy activity (indicated by a dotted arc), as in Figure 28, we may represent the fact that A and B are both predecessors of C. Figure 28 ensures

Figure 27
Violation of Rule 5

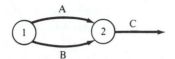

Figure 28
Use of Dummy
Activity

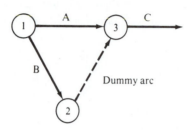

that activity C cannot begin until both activities A and B are completed, but Figure 28 does not violate rule 5. Problem 10 at the end of this section illustrates how dummy activities may be needed to avoid violating rule 4.

Example 6 illustrates a project network.

E X A M P L E
6

Widgetco is about to introduce a new product (product 3). One unit of product 3 is produced by assembling 1 unit of product 1 and 1 unit of product 2. Before production begins on either product 1 or product 2, raw materials must be purchased and workers must be trained. Before products 1 and 2 can be assembled into product 3, the finished product 2 must be inspected. A list of activities and their predecessors and of the duration of each activity is given in Table 9. Draw a project diagram for this project.

Table 9
Duration of Activities
and Predecessor
Relationships for
Widgetco Example

ACTIVITY	PREDECESSORS	DURATION (Days)
A = train workers	—	6
B = purchase raw materials	—	9
C = produce product 1	A, B	8
D = produce product 2	A, B	7
E = test product 2	D	10
F = assemble products 1 and 2	C, E	12

Figure 29
Project Diagram for
Widgetco Example

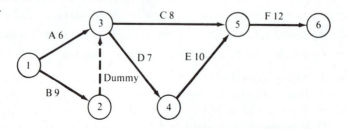

Node 1 = starting node
Node 6 = finish node

Solution

Observe that although we list only C and E as predecessors of F, it is actually true that activities A, B, and D must also be completed before F begins. Since C cannot begin until A and B are completed, and E cannot begin until D is completed, however, it is redundant to state that A, B, and D are predecessors of F. Thus, in drawing the project network, we need only be concerned with the immediate predecessors of each activity.

The AOA network for this project is given in Figure 29 (the numbers above each arc represents activity durations in days). Node 1 is the beginning of the project, and node 6 is the finish node representing completion of the project. The dummy arc (2, 3) is needed to ensure that rule 5 is not violated. ◆

The two key building blocks in CPM are the concepts of early event time (ET) and late event time (LT) for an event.

DEFINITION The **early event time** for node i, represented by $ET(i)$, is the earliest time at which the event corresponding to node i can occur.

DEFINITION The **late event time** for node i, represented by $LT(i)$, is the latest time at which the event corresponding to node i can occur without delaying the completion of the project.

COMPUTATION OF EARLY EVENT TIME

To find the early event time for each node in the project network, we begin by noting that since node 1 represents the start of the project, $ET(1) = 0$. Then we compute $ET(2)$, $ET(3)$, etc. and stop when ET(finish node) has been calculated. To illustrate how $ET(i)$ is calculated, suppose that for the segment of a project network in Figure 30, we have already determined that $ET(3) = 6$, $ET(4) = 8$, and $ET(5) = 10$. To determine $ET(6)$, observe that the earliest time that node 6 can occur is when the activities corresponding to arcs (3, 6), (4, 6), and (5, 6) have *all* been completed.

$$ET(6) = \max \begin{cases} ET(3) + 8 = 14 \\ ET(4) + 4 = 12 \\ ET(5) + 3 = 13 \end{cases}$$

Thus, the earliest time that node 6 can occur is 14, and $ET(6) = 14$.

Figure 30
Determination of
$ET(6)$

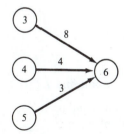

From this example, it is clear that computation of $ET(i)$ requires (for $j < i$) knowledge of one or more of the $ET(j)$'s. This explains why we begin by computing $ET(1)$, then $ET(2)$, etc. In general, if $ET(1)$, $ET(2)$, . . . , $ET(i - 1)$ have been determined, we compute $ET(i)$ as follows:

Step 1 Find each prior event to node i that is connected by an arc to node i. These events are the **immediate predecessors** of node i.

Step 2 To the ET for each immediate predecessor of node i add the duration of the activity connecting the immediate predecessor to node i.

Step 3 $ET(i)$ equals the maximum of the sums computed in Step 2.

We now compute the $ET(i)$'s for Example 6. We begin by observing that $ET(1) = 0$. Since node 1 is the only immediate predecessor of node 2, $ET(2) = ET(1) + 9 = 9$. The immediate predecessors of node 3 are nodes 1 and 2. Thus,

$$ET(3) = \max \begin{cases} ET(1) + 6 = 6 \\ ET(2) + 0 = 9 \end{cases} = 9$$

Node 4's only immediate predecessor is node 3. Thus, $ET(4) = ET(3) + 7 = 16$. Node 5's immediate predecessors are nodes 3 and 4. Thus,

$$ET(5) = \max \begin{cases} ET(3) + 8 = 17 \\ ET(4) + 10 = 26 \end{cases} = 26$$

Finally, node 5 is the only immediate predecessor of node 6. Thus, $ET(6) = ET(5) + 12 = 38$. Since node 6 represents the completion of the project, we see that the earliest time that product 3 can be assembled is 38 days from now.

It can be shown that $ET(i)$ is the length of the longest path in the project network from node 1 to node i.

COMPUTATION OF LATE EVENT TIME

To compute the $LT(i)$'s, we begin with the finish node and work backward (in descending numerical order) until we determine $LT(1)$. Since the project in Example 6 can be completed in 38 days, we know that $LT(6) = 38$. To illustrate how $LT(i)$ is computed for nodes other than the finish node, suppose we are working with a network for which we have already determined that $LT(5) = 24$, $LT(6) = 26$, and $LT(7) = 28$. In this situation, how can we compute $LT(4)$? If the event corresponding to node 4 occurs after $LT(5) - 3$, node 5 will occur after $LT(5)$, and the completion of the project will be delayed. Similarly, if node 4 occurs after $LT(6) - 4$, or if node 4 occurs after $LT(7) - 5$, the completion of the project will be delayed. Thus, in Figure 31,

$$LT(4) = \min \begin{cases} LT(5) - 3 = 21 \\ LT(6) - 4 = 22 = 21 \\ LT(7) - 5 = 23 \end{cases}$$

In general, if $LT(j)$ is known for $j > i$, we can find $LT(i)$ as follows:

Step 1 Find each node that occurs after node i and is connected to node i by an arc. These events are the **immediate successors** of node i.

Figure 31
Computation of
$LT(4)$

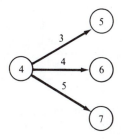

Step 2 From the LT for each immediate successor to node i subtract the duration of the activity joining the successor to node i.

Step 3 $LT(i)$ is the smallest of the differences determined in Step 2.

We now compute the $LT(i)$'s for Example 6. Recall that $LT(6) = 38$. Since node 6 is the only immediate successor of node 5, $LT(5) = LT(6) - 12 = 26$. Node 4's only immediate successor is node 5. Thus, $LT(4) = LT(5) - 10 = 16$. Nodes 4 and 5 are immediate successors of node 3. Thus,

$$LT(3) = \min \begin{cases} LT(4) - 7 = 9 \\ LT(5) - 8 = 18 \end{cases} = 9$$

Node 3 is the only immediate successor of node 2. Thus, $LT(2) = LT(3) - 0 = 9$. Finally, node 1 has nodes 2 and 3 as immediate successors. Thus,

$$LT(1) = \min \begin{cases} LT(3) - 6 = 3 \\ LT(2) - 9 = 0 \end{cases} = 0$$

Table 10 summarizes our computations for Example 6. If $LT(i) = ET(i)$, any delay in the occurrence of node i will delay the completion of the project. For example, since $LT(4) = ET(4)$, any delay in the occurrence of node 4 will delay the completion of the project.

Table 10
ET and *LT* for
Widgetco Example

NODE	$ET(i)$	$LT(i)$
1	0	0
2	9	9
3	9	9
4	16	16
5	26	26
6	38	38

TOTAL FLOAT

Before the project is begun, the duration of an activity is unknown, and the duration of each activity that is used to construct the project network is just an estimate of the activity's actual completion time. The concept of total float of an activity can be used as a measure of how important it is to keep each activity's duration from greatly exceeding our estimate of the activity's completion time.

DEFINITION   For an arbitrary arc representing activity (i, j), the **total float**, represented by $TF(i, j)$, of the activity represented by (i, j) is the amount by which the starting time of activity (i, j) could be delayed beyond its earliest possible starting time without delaying the completion of the project (assuming no other activities are delayed).

Equivalently, the total float of an activity is the amount by which the duration of the activity can be increased without delaying the completion of the project.

If we define t_{ij} to be the duration of activity (i, j), then $TF(i, j)$ can easily be expressed in terms of $LT(j)$ and $ET(i)$. Activity (i, j) begins at node i. If the occurrence of node i, or the duration of activity (i, j), is delayed by k time units, then activity (i, j) will be completed at time $ET(i) + k + t_{ij}$. Thus, the completion of the project will not be delayed if

$$ET(i) + k + t_{ij} \leq LT(j) \quad \text{or} \quad k \leq LT(j) - ET(i) - t_{ij}$$

Therefore,

$$TF(i, j) = LT(j) - ET(i) - t_{ij}$$

For Example 6, the $TF(i, j)$ are as follows:

$$
\begin{aligned}
\text{Activity B:} \quad & TF(1, 2) = LT(2) - ET(1) - 9 = 0 \\
\text{Activity A:} \quad & TF(1, 3) = LT(3) - ET(1) - 6 = 3 \\
\text{Activity D:} \quad & TF(3, 4) = LT(4) - ET(3) - 7 = 0 \\
\text{Activity C:} \quad & TF(3, 5) = LT(5) - ET(3) - 8 = 9 \\
\text{Activity E:} \quad & TF(4, 5) = LT(5) - ET(4) - 10 = 0 \\
\text{Activity F:} \quad & TF(5, 6) = LT(6) - ET(5) - 12 = 0 \\
\text{Dummy activity:} \quad & TF(2, 3) = LT(3) - ET(2) - 0 = 0
\end{aligned}
$$

FINDING A CRITICAL PATH

If an activity has a total float of zero, any delay in the start of the activity (or the duration of the activity) will delay the completion of the project. In fact, increasing the duration of an activity by Δ days will increase the length of the project by Δ days. Such an activity is critical to the completion of the project on time.

DEFINITION   Any activity with a total float of zero is a **critical activity**.

DEFINITION   A path from node 1 to the finish node that consists entirely of critical activities is called a **critical path**.

In Figure 29, activities B, D, E, F, and the dummy activity are critical activities and the path 1–2–3–4–5–6 is the critical path (it is possible for a network to have more than one critical path). A critical path in any project network is the longest path from the start node to the finish node (see Problem 2 in Section 8.5).

Since any delay in the duration of a critical activity will delay the completion of the project, it is advisable to monitor closely the completion of critical activities.

FREE FLOAT

As we have seen, the total float of an activity can be used as a measure of the flexibility in the duration of an activity. For example, activity A can take up to 3 days longer than its scheduled duration of 6 days without delaying the completion of the project. Another measure of the flexibility available in the duration of an activity is free float.

DEFINITION The **free float** of the activity corresponding to arc (i, j), denoted by $FF(i, j)$, is the amount by which the starting time of the activity corresponding to arc (i, j) (or the duration of the activity) can be delayed without delaying the start of any later activity beyond its earliest possible starting time.

Suppose the occurrence of node i, or the duration of activity (i, j), is delayed by k units. Then the earliest that node j can occur is $ET(i) + t_{ij} + k$. Thus, if $ET(i) + t_{ij} + k \leq ET(j)$, or $k \leq ET(j) - ET(i) - t_{ij}$, then node j will not be delayed. If node j is not delayed, no other activities will be delayed beyond their earliest possible starting times. Therefore,

$$FF(i, j) = ET(j) - ET(i) - t_{ij}$$

For Example 6, the $FF(i, j)$ are as follows:

Activity B: $FF(1, 2) = 9 - 0 - 9 = 0$

Activity A: $FF(1, 3) = 9 - 0 - 6 = 3$

Activity D: $FF(3, 4) = 16 - 9 - 7 = 0$

Activity C: $FF(3, 5) = 26 - 9 - 8 = 9$

Activity E: $FF(4, 5) = 26 - 16 - 10 = 0$

Activity F: $FF(5, 6) = 38 - 26 - 12 = 0$

For example, since the free float for activity C is 9 days, a delay in the start of activity C (or in the occurrence of node 3) or a delay in the duration of activity C of more than 9 days will delay the start of some later activity (in this case, activity F).

USING LINEAR PROGRAMMING TO FIND A CRITICAL PATH

Although the previously described method for finding a critical path in a project network is easily programmed on a computer, linear programming can also be used to determine the length of the critical path. Define

$$x_j = \text{the time that the event corresponding to node } j \text{ occurs}$$

For each activity (i, j), we know that before node j occurs, node i must occur and activity (i, j) must be completed. This implies that for each arc (i, j) in the project network, $x_j \geq x_i + t_{ij}$. Let F be the node that represents completion of the project. Since our goal is to minimize the time required to complete the project, we use an objective function of $z = x_F - x_1$.

To illustrate how linear programming can be used to find the length of the critical path, we apply the preceding approach to Example 6. The appropriate LP is

$$\min z = x_6 - x_1$$

$$\text{s.t.} \quad x_3 \geq x_1 + 6 \qquad \text{(Arc (1, 3) constraint)}$$
$$x_2 \geq x_1 + 9 \qquad \text{(Arc (1, 2) constraint)}$$
$$x_5 \geq x_3 + 8 \qquad \text{(Arc (3, 5) constraint)}$$
$$x_4 \geq x_3 + 7 \qquad \text{(Arc (3, 4) constraint)}$$
$$x_5 \geq x_4 + 10 \qquad \text{(Arc (4, 5) constraint)}$$
$$x_6 \geq x_5 + 12 \qquad \text{(Arc (5, 6) constraint)}$$
$$x_3 \geq x_2 \qquad \text{(Arc (2, 3) constraint)}$$

All variables urs

An optimal solution to this LP is $z = 38$, $x_1 = 0$, $x_2 = 9$, $x_3 = 9$, $x_4 = 16$, $x_5 = 26$, and $x_6 = 38$. This indicates that the project can be completed in 38 days.

This LP has many alternative optimal solutions. In general, the value of x_i in any optimal solution may assume any value between $ET(i)$ and $LT(i)$. All optimal solutions to this LP, however, will indicate that the length of any critical path is 38 days.

A critical path for this project network consists of a path from the start of the project to the finish in which each arc in the path corresponds to a constraint having a dual price of -1. From the LINDO output in Figure 32, we find, as before, that 1–2–3–4–5–6 is a critical path. For each constraint with a dual price of -1, increasing the duration of the activity corresponding to that constraint by Δ days will increase the duration of the project by Δ days. For example, an increase of Δ days in the duration of activity B will increase the duration of the project by Δ days. This assumes that the current basis remains optimal.

CRASHING THE PROJECT

In many situations, the project manager must complete the project in a time that is less than the length of the critical path. For instance, suppose Widgetco believes that in order to have any chance of being a success, product 3 must be available for sale before the competitor's product hits the market. Widgetco knows that the competitor's product is scheduled to hit the market 26 days from now, so Widgetco must introduce product 3 within 25 days. Since the critical path in Example 6 has a length of 38 days, Widgetco will have to expend additional resources to meet the 25-day project deadline. In such a situation, linear programming can often be used to determine the allocation of resources that minimizes the cost of meeting the project deadline.

Suppose that by allocating additional resources to an activity, Widgetco can reduce the duration of any activity by up to 5 days. The cost per day of reducing the duration of an activity is shown in Table 11. To find the minimum cost of completing the project by the 25-day deadline, define variables A, B, C, D, E, and F as follows:

Table 11	A	B	C	D	E	F
	$10	$20	$3	$30	$40	$50

Figure 32
LINDO Output for
Widgetco Example

```
MIN      X6 -  X1
SUBJECT TO
       2) -  X1 +  X3 >=    6
       3) -  X1 +  X2 >=    9
       4) -  X3 +  X5 >=    8
       5) -  X3 +  X4 >=    7
       6)    X5 -  X4 >=   10
       7)    X6 -  X5 >=   12
       8)    X3 -  X2 >=    0
END


    LP OPTIMUM FOUND  AT STEP       7

            OBJECTIVE FUNCTION VALUE

   1)        38.0000000

  VARIABLE         VALUE          REDUCED COST
      X6        38.000000          0.000000
      X1         0.000000          0.000000
      X3         9.000000          0.000000
      X2         9.000000          0.000000
      X5        26.000000          0.000000
      X4        16.000000          0.000000


     ROW    SLACK OR SURPLUS      DUAL PRICES
      2)         3.000000          0.000000
      3)         0.000000         -1.000000
      4)         9.000000          0.000000
      5)         0.000000         -1.000000
      6)         0.000000         -1.000000
      7)         0.000000         -1.000000
      8)         0.000000         -1.000000

  NO. ITERATIONS=        7


  RANGES IN WHICH THE BASIS IS UNCHANGED

                        OBJ COEFFICIENT RANGES
  VARIABLE       CURRENT       ALLOWABLE       ALLOWABLE
                  COEF         INCREASE        DECREASE
      X6        1.000000       INFINITY        0.000000
      X1       -1.000000       INFINITY        0.000000
      X3        0.000000       INFINITY        0.000000
      X2        0.000000       INFINITY        0.000000
      X5        0.000000       INFINITY        0.000000
      X4        0.000000       INFINITY        0.000000


                        RIGHTHAND SIDE RANGES
     ROW        CURRENT       ALLOWABLE       ALLOWABLE
                  RHS          INCREASE        DECREASE
      2        6.000000        3.000000        INFINITY
      3        9.000000        INFINITY        3.000000
      4        8.000000        9.000000        INFINITY
      5        7.000000        INFINITY        9.000000
      6       10.000000        INFINITY        9.000000
      7       12.000000        INFINITY       38.000000
      8        0.000000        INFINITY        3.000000
```

A = number of days by which duration of activity A is reduced

$\vdots \qquad\qquad\qquad \vdots$

F = number of days for which duration of activity F is reduced

x_j = time that the event corresponding to node j occurs

Then Widgeto should solve the following LP:

$$\min z = 10A + 20B + 3C + 30D + 40E + 50F$$

$$\text{s.t.} \quad A \leq 5$$

$$B \leq 5$$

$$C \leq 5$$

$$D \leq 5$$

$$E \leq 5$$

$$F \le 5$$

$x_2 \ge x_1 + 9 - B$	(Arc $(1, 2)$ constraint)
$x_3 \ge x_1 + 6 - A$	(Arc $(1, 3)$ constraint)
$x_5 \ge x_3 + 8 - C$	(Arc $(3, 5)$ constraint)
$x_4 \ge x_3 + 7 - D$	(Arc $(3, 4)$ constraint)
$x_5 \ge x_4 + 10 - E$	(Arc $(4, 5)$ constraint)
$x_6 \ge x_5 + 12 - F$	(Arc $(5, 6)$ constraint)
$x_3 \ge x_2 + 0$	(Arc $(2, 3)$ constraint)
$x_6 - x_1 \le 25$	

$$A, B, C, D, E, F \ge 0, \; x_j \text{ urs}$$

The first six constraints in the LP embody the fact that the duration of each activity can be reduced by at most 5 days. As before, the next seven constraints ensure that event j cannot occur until after node i occurs and activity (i, j) is completed. For example, activity B (arc $(1, 2)$) now has a duration of $9 - B$. Thus, we need the constraint $x_2 \ge x_1 + (9 - B)$. The constraint $x_6 - x_1 \le 25$ ensures that the project is completed within the 25-day deadline. The objective function is the total cost incurred in reducing the duration of the activities. An optimal solution to this LP is $z = \$390$, $x_1 = 0$, $x_2 = 4$, $x_3 = 4$, $x_4 = 6$, $x_5 = 13$, $x_6 = 25$, $A = 2$, $B = 5$, $C = 0$, $D = 5$, $E = 3$, $F = 0$. After reducing the durations of projects B, A, D, and E by the given amounts, we obtain the project network pictured in Figure 33. The reader should verify that A, B, D, E, and F are critical activities and that 1–2–3–4–5–6 and 1–3–4–5–6 are both critical paths (each having length 25). Thus, the project deadline of 25 days can be met for a cost of \$390.

Figure 33
Duration of
Activities After
Crashing

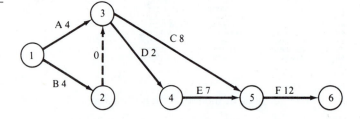

PERT: PROGRAM EVALUATION AND REVIEW TECHNIQUE

CPM assumes that the duration of each activity is known with certainty. For many projects, this is clearly not applicable. PERT is an attempt to correct this shortcoming of CPM by modeling the duration of each activity as a random variable.[†] For each activity, PERT requires that the project manager estimate the following three quantities:

$$a = \text{estimate of the activity's duration}$$
$$\text{under the most favorable conditions}$$

[†]The reader who does not have a strong background in probability may wish to review Sections 11.6 and 11.7 before continuing.

b = estimate of the activity's duration
under the least favorable conditions

m = most likely value for the activity's duration

Let $\mathbf{T}_{ij}$ (random variables are printed in boldface) be the duration of activity (i,j). PERT requires the assumption that $\mathbf{T}_{ij}$ follows a beta distribution. The specific definition of a beta distribution need not concern us, but it is important to realize that a beta distribution can approximate a wide range of random variables, including many positively skewed, negatively skewed, and symmetric random variables. If $\mathbf{T}_{ij}$ follows a beta distribution, it can be shown that the mean and variance of $\mathbf{T}_{ij}$ may be approximated by

$$E(\mathbf{T}_{ij}) = \frac{a + 4m + b}{6} \qquad (4)$$

$$\text{var}\,\mathbf{T}_{ij} = \frac{(b - a)^2}{36} \qquad (5)$$

PERT requires the assumption that the durations of all activities are independent. Then for any path in the project network, the mean and variance of the time required to complete the activities on the path are given by

$$\sum_{(i,j)\in \text{path}} E(\mathbf{T}_{ij}) = \text{expected duration of activities on any path} \qquad (6)$$

$$\sum_{(i,j)\in \text{path}} \text{var}\,\mathbf{T}_{ij} = \text{variance of duration of activities on any path} \qquad (7)$$

Let $\mathbf{CP}$ be the random variable denoting the total duration of the activities on a critical path found by CPM. PERT assumes that the critical path found by CPM contains enough activities to allow us to invoke the Central Limit Theorem (see Section 11.7) and conclude that

$$\mathbf{CP} = \sum_{(i,j)\in \text{critical path}} \mathbf{T}_{ij}$$

is normally distributed. With this assumption, Eqs. (4)–(7) can be used to answer questions concerning the probability that the project will be completed by a given date. For example, suppose that for Example 6, a, b, and m for each activity are shown in Table 12. Now Eqs. (4) and (5) yield

$$E(\mathbf{T}_{12}) = \frac{\{5 + 13 + 36\}}{6} = 9 \qquad \text{var}\,\mathbf{T}_{12} = \frac{(13 - 5)^2}{36} = 1.78$$

$$E(\mathbf{T}_{13}) = \frac{\{2 + 10 + 24\}}{6} = 6 \qquad \text{var}\,\mathbf{T}_{13} = \frac{(10 - 2)^2}{36} = 1.78$$

$$E(\mathbf{T}_{35}) = \frac{\{3 + 13 + 32\}}{6} = 8 \qquad \text{var}\,\mathbf{T}_{35} = \frac{(13 - 3)^2}{36} = 2.78$$

$$E(\mathbf{T}_{34}) = \frac{\{1 + 13 + 28\}}{6} = 7 \qquad \text{var}\,\mathbf{T}_{34} = \frac{(13 - 1)^2}{36} = 4$$

$$E(\mathbf{T}_{45}) = \frac{\{8 + 12 + 40\}}{6} = 10 \qquad \text{var}\,\mathbf{T}_{45} = \frac{(12 - 8)^2}{36} = 0.44$$

$$E(\mathbf{T}_{56}) = \frac{\{9 + 15 + 48\}}{6} = 12 \qquad \text{var}\,\mathbf{T}_{56} = \frac{(15 - 9)^2}{36} = 1$$

Table 12	ACTIVITY	*a*	*b*	*m*
a, b, and *m* for	(1, 2)	5	13	9
Activities in	(1, 3)	2	10	6
Widgetco Example	(3, 5)	3	13	8
	(3, 4)	1	13	7
	(4, 5)	8	12	10
	(5, 6)	9	15	12

Of course, the fact that arc (2, 3) is a dummy arc yields

$$E(\mathbf{T}_{23}) = \text{var } \mathbf{T}_{23} = 0$$

Recall that the critical path for Example 6 was 1–2–3–4–5–6. From Eqs. (6) and (7),

$$E(\mathbf{CP}) = 9 + 0 + 7 + 10 + 12 = 38$$
$$\text{var } \mathbf{CP} = 1.78 + 0 + 4 + 0.44 + 1 = 7.22$$

Then the standard deviation for **CP** is $(7.22)^{1/2} = 2.69$.

Applying the assumption that **CP** is normally distributed, we can answer questions such as the following: What is the probability that the project will be completed within 35 days? To answer this question, we must also make the following assumption: *No matter what the durations of the project's activities turn out to be, 1–2–3–4–5–6 will be a critical path.* This assumption implies that the probability that the project will be completed within 35 days is just $P(\mathbf{CP} \leq 35)$. Standardizing and applying the assumption that **CP** is normally distributed, we find that

$$P(\mathbf{CP} \leq 35) = P\left(\frac{\mathbf{CP} - 38}{2.69} \leq \frac{35 - 38}{2.69}\right) = P(\mathbf{Z} \leq -1.12) = .13$$

where $F(-1.12) = .13$ is obtained from Table 11.4. Thus, PERT would imply that there is a 13% chance that the project will be completed within 35 days.

DIFFICULTIES WITH PERT

There are several difficulties with PERT:

1. The assumption that the activity durations are independent is difficult to justify.

2. Activity durations may not follow a beta distribution.

3. The assumption that the critical path found by CPM will always be the critical path for the project may not be justified.

The last difficulty is the most serious. For example, in our analysis of Example 6, we assumed that 1–2–3–4–5–6 would always be the critical path. If, however, activity A were significantly delayed and activity B were completed ahead of schedule, the critical path might be 1–3–4–5–6.

Here is a more concrete example of the fact that (because of the uncertain duration of activities) the critical path found by CPM may not actually be the path that determines the completion date of the project. Consider the simple project network in Figure 34. Assume that for each activity in Table 13, *a, b,* and *m* each occur with

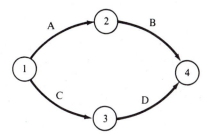

Figure 34
Project Network to
Illustrate Difficulties
with PERT

Table 13
a, *b*, and *m* for
Figure 4

ACTIVITY	a	b	m
A	1	9	5
B	6	14	10
C	5	7	6
D	7	9	8

probability $\frac{1}{3}$. If CPM were applied (using the expected duration of each activity as the duration of the activity), we would obtain the network in Figure 35. For this network, the critical path is 1–2–4. In actuality, however, the critical path could be 1–3–4. For example, if the optimistic duration of B (6 days) occurred and all other activities had a duration *m*, 1–3–4 would be the critical path in the network. If we assume that the durations of the four activities are independent random variables, then using elementary probability (see Problem 11 at the end of this section), it can be shown that there is a $\frac{10}{27}$ probability that 1–3–4 is the critical path, a $\frac{15}{27}$ chance that 1–2–4 is the critical path, and a $\frac{2}{27}$ chance that 1–2–4 and 1–3–4 will both be critical paths. This example shows that one must be cautious in designating an activity as critical. In this situation, the probability that each activity is actually a critical activity is shown in Table 14.

An alternative to PERT is to use Monte Carlo simulation (see Chapter 23) to determine the mean and variance of the critical path and the probability that a given activity is a critical activity.

Figure 35
Network to
Determine Critical
Path If Each
Activity's Duration
Equals *m*

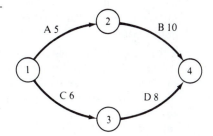

Table 14
Probability That
Each Arc Is on a
Critical Path

ACTIVITY	PROBABILITY
A	$\frac{17}{27}$
B	$\frac{17}{27}$
C	$\frac{12}{27}$
D	$\frac{12}{27}$

◆ PROBLEMS

GROUP A

1. What problem would arise if the network in Figure 36 were a portion of a project network?

Figure 36 Network for Problem 1

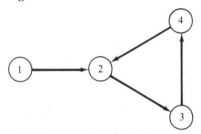

2. A company is planning to manufacture a product that consists of three parts (A, B, and C). The company anticipates that it will take 5 weeks to design the three parts and to determine the way in which these parts must be assembled to make the final product. Then the company estimates that it will take 4 weeks to make part A, 5 weeks to make part B, and 3 weeks to make part C. After part A is completed, the company must test part A (this takes 2 weeks). The assembly line process will then proceed as follows: assemble parts A and B (this takes 2 weeks) and then attach part C (this takes 1 week). Then the final product must undergo 1 week of testing. Draw the project network and find the critical path, total float, and free float for each activity. Also set up the LP that could be used to find the critical path.

When determining the critical path in Problems 3 and 4, assume that m = activity's duration.

3. Consider the project network in Figure 37. For each activity, you are given the estimates of a, b, and m in Table 15. Determine the critical path for this network, the total float for each activity, the free float for each activity, and the probability that the project is completed within 40 days. Also set up the LP that could be used to find the critical path.

4. The promoter of a rock concert in Indianapolis must perform the tasks shown in Table 16 before the concert can be held (all durations are in days).
(a) Draw the project network.
(b) Determine the critical path.
(c) If the advance promoter wants to have a 99% chance of completing all preparations by June 30, when should work begin on finding a concert site?

Table 15

ACTIVITY	a	b	m
(1, 2)	4	8	6
(1, 3)	2	8	4
(2, 4)	1	7	3
(3, 4)	6	12	9
(3, 5)	5	15	10
(3, 6)	7	18	12
(4, 7)	5	12	9
(5, 7)	1	3	2
(6, 8)	2	6	3
(7, 9)	10	20	15
(8, 9)	6	11	9

Figure 37 Network for Problem 3

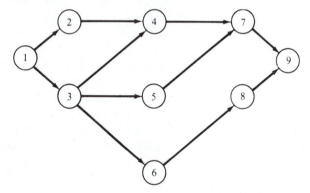

(d) Set up the LP that could be used to find the project's critical path.

5. Consider the (simplified) list of activities and predecessors that are involved in building a house (Table 17).
(a) Draw a project network, determine the critical path, find the total float for each activity, and find the free float for each activity.
(b) Suppose that by hiring additional workers, the duration of each activity can be reduced. The costs per day of reducing the duration of the activities are given in Table 18. Write down the LP to be solved in order to minimize the total cost of completing the project within 20 days.

Table 16

ACTIVITY	DESCRIPTION	IMMEDIATE PREDECESSORS	a	b	m
A	Find site	—	2	4	3
B	Find engineers	A	1	3	2
C	Hire opening act	A	2	10	6
D	Set radio and TV ads	C	1	3	2
E	Set up ticket agents	A	1	5	3
F	Prepare electronics	B	2	4	3
G	Print advertising	C	3	7	5
H	Set up transportation	C	0.5	1.5	1
I	Rehearsals	F, H	1	2	1.5
J	Last-minute details	I	1	3	2

Table 17

ACTIVITY	DESCRIPTION	IMMEDIATE PREDECESSORS	DURATION (Days)
A	Build foundation	—	5
B	Build walls and ceilings	A	8
C	Build roof	B	10
D	Do electrical wiring	B	5
E	Put in windows	B	4
F	Put on siding	E	6
G	Paint house	C, F	3

Table 18

ACTIVITY	COST PER DAY OF REDUCING DURATION OF ACTIVITY	MAXIMUM POSSIBLE REDUCTION IN DURATION OF ACTIVITY (Days)
Foundation	$30	2
Walls and ceiling	$15	3
Roof	$20	1
Electrical wiring	$40	2
Windows	$20	2
Siding	$30	3
Paint	$40	1

Table 19

ACTIVITY	DESCRIPTION	IMMEDIATE PREDECESSORS	DURATION (Weeks)
A	Choose stations	—	2
B	Get town council to approve expansion	A	4
C	Order converters needed to expand service	B	3
D	Install new dish to receive new stations	B	2
E	Install converters	C, D	10
F	Change billing system	B	4

6. Horizon Cable is about to expand its cable TV offerings in Smalltown by adding MTV and other exciting stations. The activities in Table 19 must be completed before the service expansion is completed.

(a) Draw the project network and determine the critical path for the network, the total float for each activity, and the free float for each activity.

(b) Set up the LP that can be used to find the project's critical path.

7. When an accounting firm audits a corporation, the first phase of the audit involves obtaining "knowledge of the business." This phase of the audit requires the activities in Table 20.

(a) Draw the project network and determine the critical path for the network, and total float for each activity, and the free float for each activity. Also set up the LP that can be used to find the project's critical path.

(b) Assume that the project must be completed in 30 days. The duration of each activity can be reduced by incurring the costs shown in Table 21. Formulate an LP that can be used to minimize the cost of meeting the project deadline.

8. The LINDO output in Figure 38 can be used to determine the critical path for Problem 5. Use this output to do the following:

(a) Draw the project diagram.

(b) Determine the length of the critical path and the critical activities for this project.

9. Explain why an activity's free float can never exceed the activity's total float.

10. A project is complete when activities A–E are completed. The predecessors of each activity are shown in Table 22. Draw the appropriate project diagram. (*Hint:* Don't violate rule 4.)

11. Determine the probabilities that 1–2–4 and 1–3–4 are critical paths for Figure 34.

12. Given the information in Table 23, **(a)** draw the appropriate project network, and **(b)** find the critical path.

Table 20

ACTIVITY	DESCRIPTION	IMMEDIATE PREDECESSORS	DURATION (Days)
A	Determining terms of engagement	—	3
B	Appraisal of auditability risk and materiality	A	6
C	Identification of types of transactions and possible errors	A	14
D	Systems description	C	8
E	Verification of systems description	D	4
F	Evaluation of internal controls	B, E	8
G	Design of audit approach	F	9

Table 21

ACTIVITY	COST PER DAY OF REDUCING DURATION OF ACTIVITY	MAXIMUM ALLOWABLE REDUCTION IN DURATION OF ACTIVITY (Days)
A	$100	3
B	$80	4
C	$60	5
D	$70	2
E	$30	4
F	$20	4
G	$50	4

Figure 38 LINDO Output for Problem 8

```
MIN      X6 -  X1
SUBJECT TO
     2) -  X1 +  X2 >=    5
     3) -  X2 +  X3 >=    8
     4) -  X3 +  X4 >=    4
     5) -  X3 +  X5 >=   10
     6) -  X4 +  X5 >=    6
     7)    X6 -  X3 >=    5
     8)    X6 -  X5 >=    3
END

     LP OPTIMUM FOUND AT STEP     6
          OBJECTIVE FUNCTION VALUE

     1)       26.0000000

VARIABLE        VALUE         REDUCED COST
     X6       26.000000         0.000000
     X1        0.000000         0.000000
     X2        5.000000         0.000000
     X3       13.000000         0.000000
     X4       17.000000         0.000000
     X5       23.000000         0.000000

     ROW    SLACK OR SURPLUS    DUAL PRICES
     2)        0.000000        -1.000000
     3)        0.000000        -1.000000
     4)        0.000000        -1.000000
     5)        0.000000         0.000000
     6)        0.000000        -1.000000
     7)        8.000000         0.000000
     8)        0.000000        -1.000000

     NO. ITERATIONS=     6

RANGES IN WHICH THE BASIS IS UNCHANGED
                OBJ COEFFICIENT RANGES
VARIABLE    CURRENT      ALLOWABLE     ALLOWABLE
            COEF         INCREASE      DECREASE
     X6     1.000000     INFINITY      0.000000
     X1    -1.000000     INFINITY      0.000000
     X2     0.000000     INFINITY      0.000000
     X3     0.000000     INFINITY      0.000000
     X4     0.000000     INFINITY      0.000000
     X5     0.000000     INFINITY      0.000000

                RIGHTHAND SIDE RANGES
ROW      CURRENT      ALLOWABLE     ALLOWABLE
         RHS          INCREASE      DECREASE
  2      5.000000     INFINITY      5.000000
  3      8.000000     INFINITY     13.000000
  4      4.000000     0.000000      8.000000
  5     10.000000     INFINITY      0.000000
  6      6.000000     0.000000      8.000000
  7      5.000000     8.000000     INFINITY
  8      3.000000     INFINITY      8.000000
```

Table 22

ACTIVITY	PREDECESSORS
A	—
B	A
C	A
D	B
E	B, C

Table 23

ACTIVITY	IMMEDIATE PREDECESSORS	DURATION (Days)
A	—	3
B	—	3
C	—	1
D	A, B	3
E	A, B	3
F	B, C	2
G	D, E	4
H	E	3

13. The government is going to build a high-speed computer in Austin, Texas. Once the computer is designed (D), we can select the exact site (S), the building contractor (C), and the operating personnel (P). Once the site is selected, we can begin erecting the building (B). We can start manufacturing the computer (COM) and prepare the operations manual (M) only after the contractor is selected. We can begin training the computer operators (T) when the operating manual and personnel selection are completed. When the computer and the building are both finished,

the computer may be installed (I). Then the computer is considered operational. Draw a project network that could be used to determine when the project is operational.

8-5   MINIMUM COST NETWORK FLOW PROBLEMS

The transportation, assignment, transshipment, shortest path, maximum flow, and CPM problems are all special cases of the minimum cost network flow problem (MCNFP). Any minimum cost network flow problem can be solved by a generalization of the transportation simplex called the **network simplex**.

To define an MCNFP, let

x_{ij} = number of units of flow sent from node i to node j through arc (i,j)

b_i = net supply (outflow–inflow) at node i

c_{ij} = cost of transporting 1 unit of flow from node i to node j via arc (i,j)

L_{ij} = lower bound on flow through arc (i,j)
(if there is no lower bound, let $L_{ij} = 0$)

U_{ij} = upper bound on flow through arc (i,j)
(if there is no upper bound, let $U_{ij} = \infty$)

Then the MCNFP may be written as

$$\min \sum_{\text{all arcs}} c_{ij} x_{ij}$$

$$\text{s.t.} \quad \sum_j x_{ij} - \sum_k x_{ki} = b_i \quad \text{(for each node } i \text{ in the network)} \qquad (8)$$

$$L_{ij} \leq x_{ij} \leq U_{ij} \quad \text{(for each arc in the network)} \qquad (9)$$

Constraints (8) express the fact that the net flow out of node i must equal b_i. Constraints (8) are referred to as the **flow balance equations** for the network. Constraints (9) ensure that the flow through each arc satisfies the arc capacity restrictions. In all our previous examples, we have set $L_{ij} = 0$.

Let us show that transportation and maximum flow problems are special cases of the minimum cost network flow problem.

FORMULATING A TRANSPORTATION PROBLEM AS AN MCNFP

Consider the transportation problem in Table 24. In this transportation problem, nodes 1 and 2 are the two supply points, and nodes 3 and 4 are the two demand points. Then $b_1 = 4$, $b_2 = 5$, $b_3 = -6$, and $b_4 = -3$. The network corresponding to this transportation problem contains arcs $(1,3)$, $(1,4)$, $(2,3)$, and $(2,4)$ (see Figure 39). The LP for this transportation problem may be written as shown in Table 25.

The first two constraints are the transportation problem's supply constraints, and the last two constraints are (after being multiplied by -1) the transportation problem's demand constraints. Since this transportation problem has no arc capacity restrictions, the flow balance equations are the only constraints. We note that if the problem had not been balanced, we could not have formulated the problem as an MCNFP. This is

Table 24

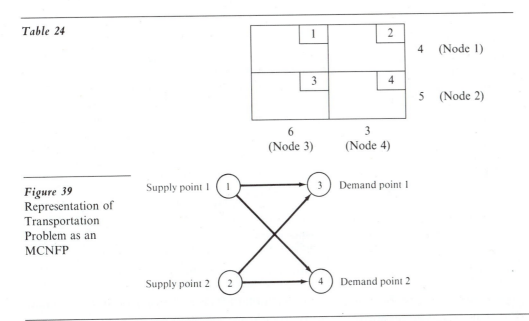

Figure 39
Representation of
Transportation
Problem as an
MCNFP

Table 25
MCNFP
Representation of
Transportation
Problem

$$\min z = x_{13} + 2x_{14} + 3x_{23} + 4x_{24}$$

x_{13}	x_{14}	x_{23}	x_{24}		rhs	Constraint
1	1	0	0	=	4	Node 1
0	0	1	1	=	5	Node 2
−1	0	−1	0	=	−6	Node 3
1	−1	0	−1	=	−3	Node 4

All variables nonnegative

because if total supply exceeded total demand, we would not know with certainty the net outflow at each supply point. Thus, to formulate a transportation (or a transshipment) problem as an MCNFP, it may be necessary to add a dummy point.

FORMULATING A MAXIMUM FLOW PROBLEM AS AN MCNFP

To see how a maximum flow problem fits into the minimum cost network flow context, consider the problem of finding the maximum flow from source to sink in the network of Figure 6. After creating an arc a_0 joining the sink to the source, we have $b_{so} = b_1 = b_2 = b_3 = b_{si} = 0$. Then the LP constraints for finding the maximum flow in Figure 6 may be written as shown in Table 26.

The first five constraints are the flow balance equations for the nodes of the network, and the last six constraints are the arc capacity constraints. Since there is no upper limit on the flow through the artificial arc, there is no arc capacity constraint for a_0.

The flow balance equations in any MCNFP have the following important property: *Each variable x_{ij} has a coefficient of +1 in the node i flow balance equation, a coefficient of −1 in the node j flow balance equation, and a coefficient of zero in all other flow balance equations.* For example, in a transportation problem, the variable x_{ij} will have a coeffi-

Table 26
MCNFP
Representation of
Maximum Flow
Problem

$$\min z = -x_0$$

$x_{so,1}$	$x_{so,2}$	x_{13}	x_{12}	$x_{3,si}$	$x_{2,si}$	x_0		rhs	Constraint
1	1	0	0	0	0	−1	=	0	Node so
−1	0	1	1	0	0	0	=	0	Node 1
0	−1	0	−1	0	1	0	=	0	Node 2
0	0	−1	0	1	0	0	=	0	Node 3
0	0	0	0	−1	−1	1	=	0	Node si
1	0	0	0	0	0	0	≤	2	Arc $(so, 1)$
0	1	0	0	0	0	0	≤	3	Arc $(so, 2)$
0	0	1	0	0	0	0	≤	4	Arc $(1, 3)$
0	0	0	1	0	0	0	≤	3	Arc $(1, 2)$
0	0	0	0	1	0	0	≤	1	Arc $(3, si)$
0	0	0	0	0	1	0	≤	2	Arc $(2, si)$

All variables nonnegative

cient of $+1$ in the flow balance equation for supply point i, a coefficient of -1 in the flow balance equation for demand point j, and a coefficient of zero in all other flow balance equations. Even if the constraints of an LP do not appear to contain the flow balance equations of a network, clever transformation of an LP's constraints can often show that an LP is equivalent to an MCNFP (see Problem 6 at the end of this section).

An MCNFP can be solved by a generalization of the transportation simplex known as the network simplex algorithm (see Section 8.7). As with the transportation simplex, the pivots in the network simplex involve only additions and subtractions. This fact can be used to prove that if all the b_i's and arc capacities are integers, then in the optimal solution to an MCNFP, all the variables will be integers. Computer codes that use the network simplex can quickly solve even extremely large network problems. For example, MCNFPs with 5000 nodes and 600,000 arcs have been solved in under 10 minutes. To use a network simplex computer code, the user need only input a list of the network's nodes and arcs, the c_{ij}'s and arc capacity for each arc, and the b_i's for each node. Since the network simplex is so efficient and easy to use, it is extremely important to formulate an LP, if at all possible, as an MCNFP.

To close this section, we formulate a simple traffic assignment problem as an MCNFP.

E X A M P L E
7

Each hour, an average of 900 cars enter the network in Figure 40 at node 1 and seek to travel to node 6. The time it takes a car to traverse each arc is shown in Table 27. In Figure 40, the number above each arc is the maximum number of cars that can pass

Figure 40
Representation of
Traffic Example as
MCNFP

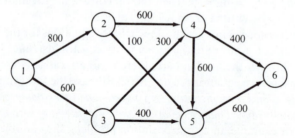

Table 27	ARC	TIME (Minutes)
Travel Times for Traffic Example	(1, 2)	10
	(1, 3)	50
	(2, 5)	70
	(2, 4)	30
	(5, 6)	30
	(4, 5)	30
	(4, 6)	60
	(3, 5)	60
	(3, 4)	10

	x_{12}	x_{13}	x_{24}	x_{25}	x_{34}	x_{35}	x_{45}	x_{46}	x_{56}		rhs	CONSTRAINT
Table 28	1	1	0	0	0	0	0	0	0	=	900	Node 1
MCNFP	−1	0	1	1	0	0	0	0	0	=	0	Node 2
Representation of	0	−1	0	0	1	1	0	0	0	=	0	Node 3
Traffic Example	0	0	−1	0	−1	0	1	1	0	=	0	Node 4
	0	0	0	−1	0	−1	−1	0	1	=	0	Node 5
	0	0	0	0	0	0	0	−1	−1	=	−900	Node 6
	1	0	0	0	0	0	0	0	0	≤	800	Arc (1, 2)
	0	1	0	0	0	0	0	0	0	≤	600	Arc (1, 3)
	0	0	1	0	0	0	0	0	0	≤	600	Arc (2, 4)
	0	0	0	1	0	0	0	0	0	≤	100	Arc (2, 5)
	0	0	0	0	1	0	0	0	0	≤	300	Arc (3, 4)
	0	0	0	0	0	1	0	0	0	≤	400	Arc (3, 5)
	0	0	0	0	0	0	1	0	0	≤	600	Arc (4, 5)
	0	0	0	0	0	0	0	1	0	≤	400	Arc (4, 6)
	0	0	0	0	0	0	0	0	1	≤	600	Arc (5, 6)

All variables nonnegative

by any point on the arc during a one-hour period. Formulate a minimum cost network flow problem that minimizes the total time required for all cars to travel from node 1 to node 6.

Solution   Let

$$x_{ij} = \text{number of cars per hour that traverse the arc from node } i \text{ to node } j$$

Then we wish to minimize

$$z = 10x_{12} + 50x_{13} + 70x_{25} + 30x_{24} + 30x_{56} + 30x_{45} + 60x_{46} + 60x_{35} + 10x_{34}$$

We are given that $b_1 = 900$, $b_2 = b_3 = b_4 = b_5 = 0$, and $b_6 = -900$ (we will not introduce the artificial arc connecting node 6 to node 1). The constraints for this minimum cost network flow problem are shown in Table 28.   ◆

◆ PROBLEMS

Note: To formulate a problem as an MCNFP, you should draw the appropriate network and determine the c_{ij}'s, the b_i's, and the arc capacities.

GROUP A

1. Formulate the problem of finding the shortest path from node 1 to node 6 in Figure 2 as a minimum cost network flow problem. (*Hint*: Think of the shortest path problem as the problem of minimizing the total cost of sending 1 unit of flow from node 1 to node 6.)

2. (a) Find the dual of the LP that was used to find the length of the critical path for Example 6 of Section 8.4.
(b) Show that the answer in part (a) is an MCNFP.
(c) Explain why the optimal objective function value for the LP found in part (a) is the longest path in the project network from node 1 to node 6. Why does this justify our earlier claim that the critical path in a project network is the longest path from the start node to the finish node?

3. Fordco produces cars in Detroit and Dallas. The Detroit plant can produce up to 6500 cars, and the Dallas plant can produce up to 6000 cars. It costs $2000 to produce a car in Detroit and $1800 to produce a car in Dallas. Cars must be shipped to three cities. City 1 must receive 5000 cars, city 2 must receive 4000 cars, and city 3 must receive 3000 cars. The cost of shipping a car from each plant to each city is given in Table 29. At most 2200 cars may be sent from a given plant to a given city. Formulate an MCNFP that can be used to minimize the cost of meeting demand.

Table 29

FROM	TO		
	City 1	City 2	City 3
Detroit	$800	$600	$300
Dallas	$500	$200	$200

4. Data Corporal produces computers in Boston and Raleigh. Boston can produce up to 400 computers per year, and Raleigh can produce up to 300 computers per year. Los Angeles customers must receive 400 computers per year, and 300 computers per year must be supplied to Austin customers. It costs $800 to produce a computer in Boston and $900 to produce a computer in Raleigh. Computers are transported by plane and may be sent through Chicago. The costs of sending a computer between pairs of cities are shown in Table 30.
(a) Formulate an MCNFP that can be used to minimize the total (production + distribution) cost of meeting Data Corporal's annual demand.
(b) How would you modify the part (a) formulation if at most 200 units could be shipped through Chicago? (*Hint*: Add an additional node and arc to this part (a) network.)

Table 30

FROM	TO		
	Chicago	Austin	Los Angeles
Boston	$80	$220	$280
Raleigh	$100	$140	$170
Chicago	—	$40	$50

5. Oilco has oil fields in San Diego and Los Angeles. The San Diego field can produce up to 500,000 barrels per day, and the Los Angeles field can produce up to 400,000 barrels per day. Oil is sent from the fields to a refinery, either in Dallas or in Houston (assume each refinery has unlimited capacity). It costs $700 to refine 100,000 barrels of oil at Dallas and $900 to refine 100,000 barrels of oil at Houston. Refined oil is shipped to customers in Chicago and New York. Chicago customers require 400,000 barrels per day of refined oil, and New York customers require 300,000 barrels per day of refined oil. The costs of shipping 100,000 barrels of oil (refined or unrefined) between cities are shown in Table 31.
(a) Formulate an MCNFP that can be used to determine how to minimize the total cost of meeting all demands.
(b) If each refinery had a capacity of 500,000 barrels per day, how would the part (a) answer be modified?

Table 31

FROM	TO			
	Dallas	Houston	New York	Chicago
Los Angeles	$300	$110	—	—
San Diego	$420	$100	—	—
Dallas	—	—	$450	$550
Houston	—	—	$470	$530

GROUP B

6. Workco must have the following number of workers available during the next three months: month 1, 20; month 2, 16; month 3, 25. At the beginning of month 1, Workco has no workers. It costs Workco $100 to hire a worker and $50 to fire a worker. Each worker is paid a salary of $140/month. We will show that the problem of determining a hiring and firing strategy that minimizes the total cost incurred during the next three (or in general, the next n) months can be formulated as an MCNFP.

(a) Let

x_{ij} = number of workers hired at beginning of month i and fired after working till end of month $j - 1$

(if $j = 4$, the worker is never fired). Explain why the following LP will yield a minimum cost hiring and firing strategy:

$$\min z = 50(x_{12} + x_{13} + x_{23})$$
$$+ 100(x_{12} + x_{13} + x_{14} + x_{23} + x_{24} + x_{34})$$
$$+ 140(x_{12} + x_{23} + x_{34})$$
$$+ 280(x_{13} + x_{24}) + 420x_{14}$$

s.t. (1) $x_{12} + x_{13} + x_{14} \quad - e_1 = 20$
(Month 1 constraint)

(2) $x_{13} + x_{14} + x_{23} + x_{24} - e_2 = 16$
(Month 2 constraint)

(3) $x_{14} + x_{24} + x_{34} \quad - e_3 = 25$
(Month 3 constraint)

$$x_{ij} \geq 0$$

(b) To obtain an MCNFP, replace the constraints in part (a) by
 (i) Constraint (1);
 (ii) Constraint (2)–Constraint (1);
(iii) Constraint (3)–Constraint (2);
(iv) −(Constraint (3)).
Explain why an LP with Constraints (i)–(iv) is an MCNFP.

(c) Draw the network corresponding to the MCNFP obtained in answering part (b).

7.[†] Braneast Airlines must determine how many airplanes should serve the Boston–New York–Washington air corridor and which flights to fly. Braneast may fly any of the daily flights shown in Table 32. The fixed cost of operating an airplane is $800/day. Formulate an MCNFP that can be used to maximize Braneast's daily profits. (*Hint*: Each node in the network represents a city and a time. In addition to arcs representing flights, we must allow for the possibility that an airplane will stay put for an hour or more. We must ensure that the model includes the fixed cost of operating a plane. To include this cost, the following three arcs might be included in the network: from Boston 7 P.M. to Boston 9 A.M.; from New York 7 P.M. to New York 9 A.M.; and from Washington 7 P.M. to Washington 9 A.M.)

8. Daisymay Van Line moves people between New York, Philadelphia, and Washington D.C. It takes a van one day to travel between any two of these cities. The company incurs costs of $1000 per day for a van that is fully loaded

[†]This problem is based on Glover et al. (1982).

Table 32

LEAVES		ARRIVES		FLIGHT REVENUE	VARIABLE COST OF FLIGHT
City	*Time*	*City*	*Time*		
NY	9 A.M.	Wash.	10 A.M.	$900	$400
NY	2 P.M.	Wash.	3 P.M.	$600	$350
NY	10 A.M.	Bos.	11 A.M.	$800	$400
NY	4 P.M.	Bos.	5 P.M.	$1200	$450
Wash.	9 A.M.	NY	10 A.M.	$1100	$400
Wash.	3 P.M.	NY	4 P.M.	$900	$350
Wash.	10 A.M.	Bos.	12 noon	$1500	$700
Wash.	5 P.M.	Bos.	7 P.M.	$1800	$900
Bos.	10 A.M.	NY	11 A.M.	$900	$500
Bos.	2 P.M.	NY	3 P.M.	$800	$450
Bos.	11 A.M.	Wash.	1 P.M.	$1100	$600
Bos.	3 P.M.	Wash.	5 P.M.	$1200	$650

Table 33

TRIP	MONDAY	TUESDAY	WEDNESDAY	THURSDAY	FRIDAY
Phil.–N.Y.	2			1	
Phil.–Wash.		2			2
N.Y.–Phil.	3	2			
N.Y.–Wash.			2	2	
N.Y.–Phil.	1				
Wash.–N.Y.			1		1

and traveling, $800 per day for an empty van that travels, $700 per day for a fully loaded van that stays in a city, and $400 per day for an empty van that remains in a city. Each day of the week, the loads described in Table 33 must be shipped. On Monday, for example, two trucks must be sent from Philadelphia to New York (arriving on Tuesday). Also, two trucks must be sent from Philadelphia to Washington on Friday (assume that Friday shipments must arrive on Monday). Formulate an MCNFP that can be used to minimize the cost of meeting weekly requirements. To simplify the formulation, assume that the requirements repeat each week. Then it seems plausible to assume that any of the company's trucks will begin each week in the same city in which it began the previous week.

8-6　MINIMUM SPANNING TREE PROBLEMS

Suppose that each arc (i, j) in a network has a length associated with it and that arc (i, j) represents a way of connecting node i to node j. For example, if each node in a network represents a computer at State University, arc (i, j) might represent an underground cable that connects computer i with computer j. In many applications, we wish to determine the set of arcs in a network that connect all nodes such that the sum of the length of the arcs is minimized. Clearly, such a group of arcs should contain no loop. (A loop is often called a closed path or cycle.) For example, in Figure 41, the sequence of arcs $(1, 2)$–$(2, 3)$–$(3, 1)$ is a loop.

Figure 41
Illustration of Loop
and Minimum
Spanning Tree

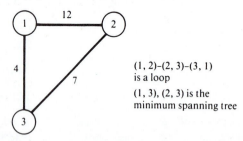

$(1, 2)$–$(2, 3)$–$(3, 1)$
is a loop

$(1, 3)$, $(2, 3)$ is the
minimum spanning tree

DEFINITION ▪ For a network with n nodes, a **spanning tree** is a group of $n - 1$ arcs that connects all nodes of the network and contains no loops.

In Figure 41, there are three spanning trees:

1. Arcs $(1, 2)$ and $(2, 3)$

2. Arcs $(1, 2)$ and $(1, 3)$

3. Arcs $(1, 3)$ and $(2, 3)$

A spanning tree of minimum length in a network is a **minimum spanning tree**. In Figure 41, the spanning tree consisting of arcs $(1, 3)$ and $(2, 3)$ is the unique minimum spanning tree.

The following method (M.S.T. algorithm) may be used to find a minimum spanning tree.

Step 1 Begin at any node i, and join node i to the node in the network (call it node j) that is closest to node i. The two nodes i and j now form a connected set of nodes $C = \{i, j\}$, and arc (i, j) will be in the minimum spanning tree. The remaining nodes in the network (call them C') are referred to as the unconnected set of nodes.

Step 2 Now choose a member of C' (call it n) that is closest to some node in C. Let m represent the node in C that is closest to n. Then the arc (m, n) will be in the minimum spanning tree. Now update C and C'. Since n is now connected to $\{i, j\}$, C now equals $\{i, j, n\}$ and we must eliminate node n from C'.

Step 3 Repeat this process until a minimum spanning tree is found. Ties for closest node and arc to be included in the minimum spanning tree may be broken arbitrarily.

Since at each step the algorithm chooses the shortest arc that can be used to expand C, the algorithm is often referred to as a "greedy" algorithm. It is remarkable that the act of being "greedy" at each step of the algorithm can never force us later to follow a "bad arc." A justification of the M.S.T. algorithm is given in Problem 3 at the end of this section. Example 8 illustrates the algorithm.

E X A M P L E 8

The State University campus has five minicomputers. The distance between each pair of computers (in city blocks) is given in Figure 42. The computers must be interconnected by underground cable. What is the minimum length of cable required? Note that if no arc is drawn connecting a pair of nodes, this means that (because of underground rock formations) no cable can be laid between these two computers.

Figure 42
Distances between
State University
Computers

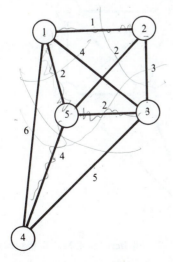

Solution   We want to find the minimum spanning tree for Figure 42.

Iteration 1 Following the M.S.T. algorithm, we arbitrarily choose to begin at node 1. The closest node to node 1 is node 2. Now $C = \{1, 2\}$, $C' = \{3, 4, 5\}$, and arc $(1, 2)$ will be in the minimum spanning tree (see Figure 43a).

Iteration 2 Node 5 is closest (two blocks distant) to C. Since node 5 is two blocks from node 1 and from node 2, we may include either arc $(2, 5)$ or arc $(1, 5)$ in the minimum spanning tree. We arbitrarily choose to include arc $(2, 5)$. Then $C = \{1, 2, 5\}$ and $C' = \{3, 4\}$ (see Figure 43b).

Figure 43   M.S.T. Algorithm for Computer Example

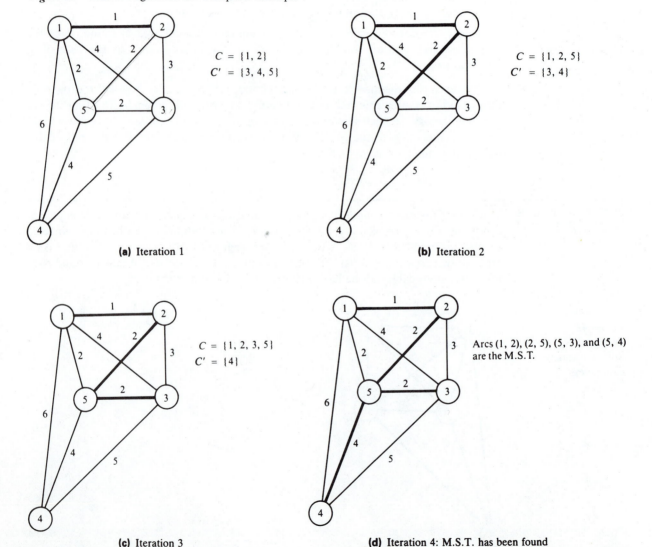

(a) Iteration 1

$C = \{1, 2\}$
$C' = \{3, 4, 5\}$

(b) Iteration 2

$C = \{1, 2, 5\}$
$C' = \{3, 4\}$

(c) Iteration 3

$C = \{1, 2, 3, 5\}$
$C' = \{4\}$

(d) Iteration 4: M.S.T. has been found

Arcs $(1, 2)$, $(2, 5)$, $(5, 3)$, and $(5, 4)$ are the M.S.T.

Iteration 3 Since node 3 is two blocks from node 5, we may include arc $(5, 3)$ in the minimum spanning tree. Now $C = \{1, 2, 3, 5\}$ and $C' = \{4\}$ (see Figure 43c).

Iteration 4 Node 5 is the closest node to node 4. Thus, we add arc $(5, 4)$ to the minimum spanning tree (see Figure 43d).

We have now obtained the minimum spanning tree consisting of arcs $(1, 2)$, $(2, 5)$, $(5, 3)$, and $(5, 4)$. The length of the minimum spanning tree is $1 + 2 + 2 + 4 = 9$ blocks.

◆

◆ PROBLEMS

GROUP A

1. The distances (in miles) between the Indiana cities of Gary, Fort Wayne, Evansville, Terre Haute, and South Bend are shown in Table 34. It is necessary to build a state road system that connects all these cities. Assume that for political reasons no road can be built connecting Gary and Fort Wayne, and no road can be built connecting South Bend and Evansville. What is the minimum length of road required?

2. The city of Smalltown consists of five subdivisions. Mayor John Lion wants to build telephone lines to ensure that all the subdivisions can communicate with each other. The distances between the subdivisions are given in Figure 44. What is the minimum length of telephone line required? Assume that no telephone line can be built between subdivisions 1 and 4.

GROUP B

3. In this problem, we explain why the M.S.T. algorithm works. Define

S = minimum spanning tree

C_t = nodes connected after iteration t
of M.S.T. algorithm has been completed

C_t' = nodes not connected after iteration t
of M.S.T. algorithm has been completed

Figure 44 Network for Problem 2

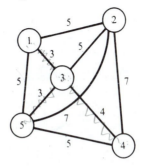

A_t = set of arcs in minimum spanning tree after t iterations of M.S.T. algorithm have been completed

Suppose the M.S.T. algorithm does not yield a minimum spanning tree. Then, for some t, it must be the case that all arcs in A_{t-1} are in S, but the arc chosen at iteration t (call it a_t) of the M.S.T. algorithm is not in S. Then S must contain some arc a_t' that leads from a node in C_{t-1} to a node in C_{t-1}'. Show that by replacing arc a_t' with arc a_t, we can obtain a shorter spanning tree than S. This contradiction proves that all arcs chosen by the M.S.T. algorithm must be in S. Thus, the M.S.T. algorithm does indeed find a minimum spanning tree.

Table 34

	GARY	FORT WAYNE	EVANSVILLE	TERRE HAUTE	SOUTH BEND
Gary	—	132	217	164	58
Fort Wayne	132	—	290	201	79
Evansville	217	290	—	113	303
Terre Haute	164	201	113	—	196
South Bend	58	79	303	196	—

8-7   THE NETWORK SIMPLEX METHOD*

In this section, we describe how the simplex algorithm simplifies for MCNFPs. To simplify our presentation, we assume that for each arc, $L_{ij} = 0$. Then the information needed to describe an MCNFP of the form (8)–(9) may be summarized graphically as in Figure 45. We will denote the c_{ij} for each arc by the symbol $\$$, and the other number on each arc will represent the arc's upper bound (U_{ij}). The b_i for any node with a nonzero outflow will be listed in parentheses. Thus, Figure 45 represents an MCNFP with $c_{12} = 5$, $c_{25} = 2$, $c_{13} = 4$, $c_{35} = 8$, $c_{14} = 7$, $c_{34} = 10$, $c_{45} = 5$, $b_1 = 10$, $b_2 = 4$, $b_3 = -3$, $b_4 = -4$, $b_5 = -7$, $U_{12} = 4$, $U_{25} = 10$, $U_{13} = 10$, $U_{35} = 5$, $U_{14} = 4$, $U_{34} = 5$, $U_{45} = 5$. For the network simplex to be used, we must have $\Sigma\, b_i = 0$; usually this can be ensured by adding a dummy node.

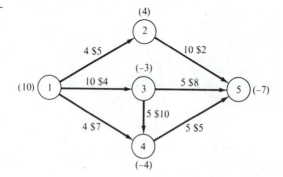

Figure 45
Graphical
Representation of an
MCNFP

Recall that when we used the simplex method to solve a transportation problem, the following aspects of the simplex algorithm simplified: finding a basic feasible solution, computing the coefficient of a nonbasic variable in row 0, and pivoting. We now describe how these aspects of the simplex algorithm simplify when we are solving an MCNFP.

BASIC FEASIBLE SOLUTIONS FOR MCNFPs

How can we determine whether a feasible solution to an MCNFP is a bfs? Begin by observing that any bfs to an MCNFP will contain three types of variables:

1. Basic variables: In the absence of degeneracy, each basic variable x_{ij} will satisfy $L_{ij} < x_{ij} < U_{ij}$; with degeneracy, it is possible for a basic variable x_{ij} to equal arc (i, j)'s upper or lower bound.

2. Nonbasic variables x_{ij}: These equal arc (i, j)'s upper bound U_{ij}.

3. Nonbasic variables x_{ij}: These equal arc (i, j)'s lower bound L_{ij}.

Suppose we are solving MCNFP with n nodes. In solving an MCNFP, we consider the n conservation-of-flow constraints and ignore the upper- and lower-bound constraints (for reasons that will soon become apparent). As in the transportation problem, any solution satisfying $n - 1$ of the conservation-of-flow constraints will automatically satisfy the last conservation-of-flow constraint, so we may drop one such constraint. This means that a bfs to an n-node MCNFP will have $n - 1$ basic variables. Suppose we

*This section covers topics that may be omitted with no loss of continuity.

choose a set of $n - 1$ variables (or arcs). How can we determine whether this set of $n - 1$ variables yields a basic feasible solution? It turns out that a set of $n - 1$ variables will yield a bfs if and only if the arcs corresponding to the basic variables form a spanning tree for the network. For example, consider the MCNFP in Figure 46. In Figure 47, we give a bfs for this MCNFP. The basic variables are x_{13}, x_{35}, x_{25}, and x_{45}. The variables $x_{12} = 5$ and $x_{14} = 4$ are nonbasic variables at their upper bound. (Such variables will be indicated by dashed arcs.) Since the arcs $(1, 3)$, $(3, 5)$, $(2, 5)$, and $(4, 5)$ form a spanning tree (because they connect all nodes of the graph and do not contain any cycles), we know that this is a bfs. As will soon become clear, a bfs for small problems can often be obtained by trial and error.

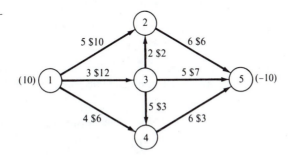

Figure 46
Example of an
MCNFP

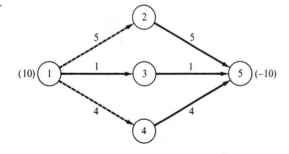

Figure 47
Example of a bfs for
an MCNFP

COMPUTING ROW 0 FOR ANY bfs

For any given bfs, how do we determine the objective function coefficient for a nonbasic variable? Suppose we arbitrarily choose to drop the conservation-of-flow constraint for node 1. For a given bfs, let $c_{BV} B^{-1} = [y_2 \quad y_3 \quad \cdots \quad y_n]$. Each variable x_{ij} will have a $+1$ coefficient in the node i flow constraint and a -1 coefficient to the node j constraint. If we define $y_1 = 0$, then the coefficient of x_{ij} in row 0 of a given tableau may be written as $\bar{c}_{ij} = y_i - y_j - c_{ij}$. Since each basic variable must have $\bar{c}_{ij} = 0$, we can find y_1, $y_2, \ldots, y_n$ by solving the following system of linear equations:

$$y_1 = 0, \qquad y_i - y_j = c_{ij} \qquad \text{for each basic variable}$$

The $y_1, y_2, \ldots, y_n$ corresponding to a bfs are often called the **simplex multipliers** for the bfs.

How can we determine whether a bfs is optimal? For a bfs to be optimal, it must be possible to improve (decrease) the value of z by changing the value of a nonbasic variable. Note that $\bar{c}_{ij} \leq 0$ if and only if increasing x_{ij} cannot decrease z. Also note that $\bar{c}_{ij} \geq 0$

if and only if decreasing x_{ij} cannot decrease z. These observations can be used to show that a bfs is optimal if and only if the following conditions are met:

1. If a variable $x_{ij} = L_{ij}$, then an increase in x_{ij} cannot result in a decrease in z. Thus, if $x_{ij} = L_{ij}$ and the bfs is optimal, then $\bar{c}_{ij} \leq 0$ must hold.

2. If a variable $x_{ij} = U_{ij}$, then a decrease in x_{ij} cannot result in a decrease in z. Thus, if $x_{ij} = U_{ij}$ and the bfs is optimal, then $\bar{c}_{ij} \geq 0$ must hold.

If conditions 1 and 2 are not met, z can be improved (barring degeneracy) by pivoting into the basis any nonbasic variable violating either condition. To illustrate, let's determine the objective function coefficient for each nonbasic variable in the simplex tableau corresponding to the bfs in Figure 47. To find y_1, y_2, y_3, y_4, and y_5, we solve the following set of equations:

$$y_1 = 0, \quad y_1 - y_3 = 12, \quad y_2 - y_5 = 6, \quad y_3 - y_5 = 7, \quad y_4 - y_5 = 3$$

The solutions to these equations are $y_1 = 0$, $y_2 = -13$, $y_3 = -12$, $y_4 = -16$, and $y_5 = -19$. We now "price out" each nonbasic variable and obtain

$\bar{c}_{12} = y_1 - y_2 - c_{12} = 0 - (-13) - 10 = 3$ (Satisfies optimality condition for nonbasic variable at upper bound)

$\bar{c}_{14} = y_1 - y_4 - c_{14} = 0 - (-16) - 6 = 10$ (Satisfies optimality condition for nonbasic variable at upper bound)

$\bar{c}_{32} = y_3 - y_2 - c_{32} = -12 - (-13) - 2 = -1$ (Satisfies optimality condition for nonbasic variable at lower bound)

$\bar{c}_{34} = y_3 - y_4 - c_{34} = -12 - (-16) - 3 = 1$ (Violates optimality condition for nonbasic variable at lower bound)

Since $\bar{c}_{34} = 1 > 0$, each unit by which we increase x_{34} (since x_{34} is at its lower bound, it's okay to increase it) will decrease z by one unit. Thus, we can improve z by entering x_{34} into the basis. Note that if a nonbasic variable x_{ij} at its upper bound had $\bar{c}_{ij} < 0$, we could decrease z by entering x_{ij} into the basis and decreasing x_{ij}. We now show that when solving an MCNFP, the pivot step may be performed almost by inspection.

PIVOTING IN THE NETWORK SIMPLEX

As we have just shown, for the bfs in Figure 47, we want to enter x_{34} into the basis. To do this, note that if we add the arc $(3, 4)$ to the set of arcs corresponding to the current set of basic variables, a cycle (or loop) will be formed. To enter x_{34} into the basis, note that since $x_{34} = 0$ is at its lower bound, we want to increase x_{34}. Suppose we try to increase x_{34} by θ. The values of all variables after x_{34} is entered into the basis may be found by invoking the conservation-of-flow constraints. In Figure 48, we find that arcs $(3, 4)$, $(4, 5)$, and $(3, 5)$ form a cycle. After the pivot, all variables corresponding to arcs not in the cycle will remain unchanged, but when we set $x_{34} = \theta$, the values of the variables corresponding to arcs in the cycle will change. Since setting $x_{34} = \theta$ increases the flow into node 4 by θ, the flow out of node 4 must increase by θ. This requires $x_{45} = 4 + \theta$. Since the flow into node 5 has now increased by θ, conservation of flow requires that $x_{35} = 1 - \theta$. The pivot leaves all other variables unchanged. To find the new values of the variables, observe that we want to increase x_{34} by as much as possible.

Figure 48
Cycle $(3, 4)$, $(4, 5)$,
$(3, 5)$ Helps Us Pivot
in x_{34}

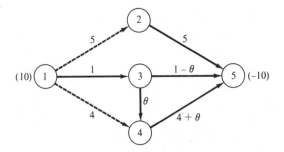

We can increase x_{34} to the point where a basic variable first attains its upper or lower bound. Thus, arc $(3, 4)$ implies that $\theta \le 5$; arc $(3, 5)$ requires $1 - \theta \ge 0$ or $\theta \le 1$; arc $(4, 5)$ requires $4 + \theta \le 6$ or $\theta \le 2$. So the best we can do is set $\theta = 1$. The basic variable that first hits its upper or lower bound as θ is increased is chosen to exit the basis (in case of a tie, we can choose the exiting variable arbitrarily). Now x_{35} exits the basis, and the new bfs is shown in Figure 49. The spanning tree corresponding to the current set of basic variables is $(1, 3)$, $(3, 4)$, $(4, 5)$, and $(2, 5)$. We now compute the coefficient of each nonbasic variable in row 0. To begin, we solve the following set of equations:

$$y_1 = 0, \quad y_1 - y_3 = 12, \quad y_3 - y_4 = 3, \quad y_2 - y_5 = 6, \quad y_4 - y_5 = 3$$

This yields $y_1 = 0$, $y_2 = -12$, $y_3 = -12$, $y_4 = -15$, and $y_5 = -18$.

Figure 49
New bfs ($\theta = 1$)
after x_{34} Enters and
x_{35} Exits

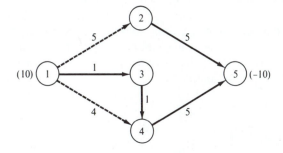

The nonbasic variables that currently equal their upper bounds will have row 0 coefficients of

$$\bar{c}_{12} = 0 - (-12) - 10 = 2 \quad \text{and} \quad \bar{c}_{14} = 0 - (-15) - 6 = 9$$

The nonbasic variables that currently equal their lower bounds will have row 0 coefficients of

$$\bar{c}_{32} = -12 - (-12) - 2 = -2 \quad \text{and} \quad \bar{c}_{35} = -12 - (-18) - 7 = -1$$

Since each nonbasic variable at its upper bound has $\bar{c}_{ij} \ge 0$, and each nonbasic variable at its lower bound has $\bar{c}_{ij} \le 0$, the current bfs is optimal. Thus, the optimal solution to the MCNFP in Figure 46 is

Upper bounded variables: $x_{12} = 5$, $\quad x_{14} = 4$

Lower bounded variables: $x_{32} = x_{35} = 0$

Basic variables: $x_{13} = 1$, $\quad x_{34} = 1$, $\quad x_{25} = 5$, $\quad x_{45} = 5$

SUMMARY OF THE NETWORK SIMPLEX METHOD

Step 1 Determine a starting bfs. The $n - 1$ basic variables will correspond to a spanning tree. Indicate nonbasic variables at their upper bound by dashed arcs.

Step 2 Compute $y_1, y_2, \ldots y_n$ (often called the simplex multipliers) by solving $y_1 = 0, y_i - y_j = c_{ij}$ for all basic variables x_{ij}. For all nonbasic variables, determine the row 0 coefficient $\bar{c}_{ij}$ from $\bar{c}_{ij} = y_i - y_j - c_{ij}$. The current bfs is optimal if $\bar{c}_{ij} \leq 0$ for all $x_{ij} = L_{ij}$ and $\bar{c}_{ij} \geq 0$ for all $x_{ij} = U_{ij}$. If the bfs is not optimal, choose the nonbasic variable that most violates the optimality conditions as the entering basic variable.

Step 3 Identify the cycle (there will be exactly one!) created by adding the arc corresponding to the entering variable to the current spanning tree of the current bfs. Use conservation of flow to determine the new values of the variables in the cycle. The variable that exits the basis will be the variable that first hits its upper or lower bound as the value of the entering basic variable is changed.

Step 4 Find the new bfs by changing the flows of the arcs in the cycle found in Step 3. Now go to step 2.

Example 9 illustrates the network simplex.

E X A M P L E 9

Use the network simplex to solve the MCNFP in Figure 50.

Solution

A bfs requires that we find a spanning tree (three arcs that connect nodes 1, 2, 3, and 4 and do not form a cycle). Any arcs not in the spanning tree may be set equal to their upper or lower bound. By trial and error, we find the bfs in Figure 51 involving the spanning tree $(1, 2)$, $(1, 3)$, and $(2, 4)$.

Figure 50
Example of Network Simplex

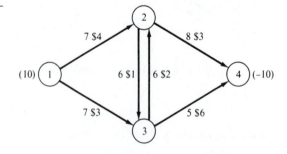

Figure 51
bfs for Example 9

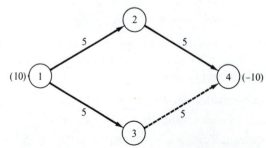

To find y_1, y_2, y_3, and y_4, we solve

$$y_1 = 0, \quad y_1 - y_2 = 4, \quad y_2 - y_4 = 3, \quad y_1 - y_3 = 3$$

This yields $y_1 = 0$, $y_2 = -4$, $y_3 = -3$, and $y_4 = -7$. The row 0 coefficients for each nonbasic variable are

$$\bar{c}_{34} = -3 - (-7) - 6 = -2 \quad \text{(Violates optimality condition)}$$
$$\bar{c}_{23} = -4 - (-3) - 1 = -2 \quad \text{(Satisfies optimality condition)}$$
$$\bar{c}_{32} = -3 - (-4) - 2 = -1 \quad \text{(Satisfies optimality condition)}$$

Thus, x_{34} enters the basis. We set $x_{34} = 5 - \theta$ and obtain the cycle in Figure 52. From arc $(1,2)$, we find $5 + \theta \leq 7$ or $\theta \leq 2$. From arc $(1,3)$, we find $5 - \theta \geq 0$ or $\theta \leq 5$. From arc $(2,4)$, we find $5 + \theta \leq 8$ or $\theta \leq 3$. From arc $(3,4)$, we find $5 - \theta \geq 0$ or $\theta \leq 5$. Thus, we can set $\theta = 2$. Now x_{12} exits the basis at its upper bound, and x_{34} enters, yielding the bfs in Figure 53.

Figure 52
Cycle Created When x_{34} Enters the Basis

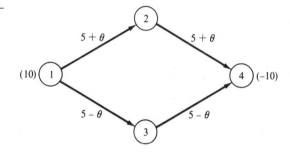

Figure 53
bfs After x_{12} Exits and x_{34} Enters

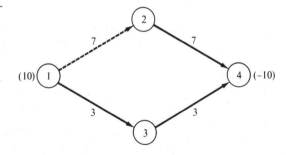

The new bfs is associated with the spanning tree $(1,3)$, $(2,4)$, and $(3,4)$. Solving for the new values of the simplex multipliers, we obtain

$$y_1 = 0, \quad y_1 - y_3 = 3, \quad y_3 - y_4 = 6, \quad y_2 - y_4 = 3$$

This yields $y_1 = 0$, $y_2 = -6$, $y_3 = -3$, $y_4 = -9$. The coefficient of each nonbasic variable in row 0 is given by

$$\bar{c}_{12} = 0 - (-6) - 4 = 2 \quad \text{(Satisfies optimality condition)}$$
$$\bar{c}_{23} = -6 - (-3) - 1 = -4 \quad \text{(Satisfies optimality condition)}$$
$$\bar{c}_{32} = -3 - (-6) - 2 = 1 \quad \text{(Violates optimality condition)}$$

Now x_{32} enters the basis, yielding the cycle in Figure 54. From arc $(2, 4)$, we find $7 + \theta \leq 8$ or $\theta \leq 1$; from arc $(3, 4)$, we find $3 - \theta \geq 0$ or $\theta \leq 3$. From arc $(3, 2)$, we find $\theta \leq 6$. So we now set $\theta = 1$ and have x_{24} exit from the basis at its upper bound. The new bfs is given in Figure 55.

Figure 54
Cycle Created When
x_{32} Enters Basis

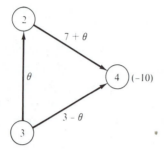

Figure 55
New bfs When x_{32}
Enters and x_{24} Exits

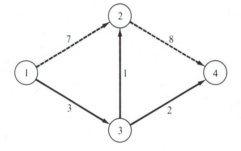

The current set of basic variables corresponds to the spanning tree $(1, 3)$, $(3, 2)$, and $(3, 4)$. The new values of the simplex multipliers are found by solving

$$y_1 = 0, \quad y_1 - y_3 = 3, \quad y_3 - y_2 = 2, \quad y_3 - y_4 = 6$$

which yields $y_1 = 0$, $y_2 = -5$, $y_3 = -3$, $y_4 = -9$. The coefficient of each nonbasic variable in row 0 is now

$$\bar{c}_{23} = -5 - (-3) - 1 = -3 \qquad \text{(Satisfies optimality condition)}$$
$$\bar{c}_{12} = 0 - (-5) - 4 = 1 \qquad \text{(Satisfies optimality condition)}$$
$$\bar{c}_{24} = -5 - (-9) - 3 = 1 \qquad \text{(Satisfies optimality condition)}$$

Thus, the current bfs is optimal. The optimal solution to the MCNFP is

Basic variables: $x_{13} = 3$, $x_{32} = 1$, $x_{34} = 2$

Nonbasic variables at their upper bound: $x_{12} = 7$, $x_{24} = 8$

Nonbasic variable at lower bound: $x_{23} = 0$

The optimal z-value is obtained from

$$z = 7(4) + 3(3) + 1(2) + 8(3) + 2(6) = \$75$$

◆ PROBLEMS

GROUP A

1. Consider the problem of finding the shortest path from node 1 to node 6 in Figure 2.
(a) Formulate this problem as an MCNFP.
(b) Find a bfs in which x_{12}, x_{24}, and x_{46} are positive. (*Hint*: A degenerate bfs will be obtained.)
(c) Use the network simplex to find the shortest path from node 1 to node 6.

2. For the MCNFP in Figure 56, find a bfs.

3. Find the optimal solution to the MCNFP in Figure 57, using the bfs in Figure 58 as a starting basis.

4. Find a bfs for the network in Figure 59.

5. Find the optimal solution to the MCNFP in Figure 60, using the bfs in Figure 61 as a starting basis.

Figure 56

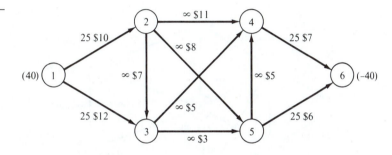

Figure 57

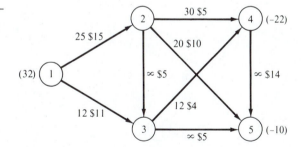

Figure 58

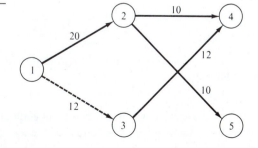

Figure 59

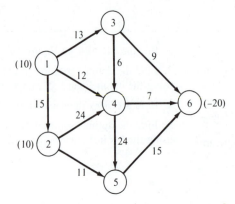

Figure 60

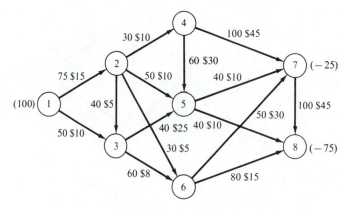

Figure 61

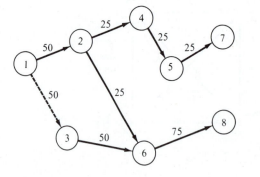

◆ SUMMARY

SHORTEST PATH PROBLEMS

Suppose we want to find the shortest path from node 1 to node j in a network in which all arcs have nonnegative lengths.

DIJKSTRA'S ALGORITHM.

1. Label node 1 with a permanent label of 0. Then label each arc that is connected to node 1 by a single arc with a "temporary" label equal to the length of the arc joining node 1 and node i. Each other node (except, of course, for node 1) will have a temporary label of ∞. Choose the node with the smallest temporary label and make this label permanent.

2. Suppose that node i is the $(k+1)$th node to be given a permanent label. For each node j that now has a temporary label and is connected to node i by an arc, we replace node j's temporary label by min {node j's current temporary label, (node i's permanent label) + length of arc (i, j)}. We now make the smallest temporary label a permanent label. Continue this process until all nodes have permanent labels. To find the shortest path from node 1 to node j, work backward from node j by finding nodes having labels differing by exactly the length of the connecting arc. If the shortest path from node 1 to node j is desired, stop the labeling process as soon as node j receives a permanent label.

THE SHORTEST PATH PROBLEM AS A TRANSSHIPMENT PROBLEM. To find the shortest path from node 1 to node j, simply try to minimize the cost of sending 1 unit from node 1 to node j (with all other nodes in the network being transshipment points), where the cost of sending 1 unit from node k to node k' is the length of arc (k, k') if such an arc exists and is M (a large positive number) if such an arc does not exist. As in Section 7.6, the cost of shipping 1 unit from a node to itself is zero.

MAXIMUM FLOW PROBLEMS

We can find the maximum flow from source to sink in a network by linear programming or by the Ford-Fulkerson method.

FINDING MAXIMUM FLOW BY LINEAR PROGRAMMING. Let

$$x_0 = \text{flow through artificial arc going from sink to source}$$

Then to find the maximum flow from source to sink, we maximize x_0 subject to the following two sets of constraints:

1. The flow through each arc must be nonnegative and cannot exceed the arc capacity.

2. Flow into node i = flow out of node i (Conservation of flow)

FINDING MAXIMUM FLOW BY THE FORD-FULKERSON METHOD. Let

$$I = \text{set of arcs in which flow may be increased}$$
$$R = \text{set of arcs in which flow may be reduced}$$

Step 1 Find a feasible flow (setting each arc's flow to zero will do).

Step 2 Using the following procedure, try to find a chain of labeled arcs and nodes that can be used to label the sink. Label the source. Then label vertices and arcs (except for arc a_0) according to the following rules: (1) If vertex x is labeled, vertex y is unlabeled and arc (x, y) is a member of I; then label vertex y and arc (x, y). In this case, arc (x, y) is called a **forward arc**. (2) If vertex y is unlabeled, vertex x is labeled and arc (y, x) is a member of R; then label vertex y and arc (y, x). In this case, (y, x) is called a **backward arc**.

If the sink cannot be labeled, the current feasible flow is a maximum flow; if the sink is labeled, go on to Step 3.

Step 3 If the chain used to label the sink consists entirely of forward arcs, the flow through each of the forward arcs in the chain may be increased, thereby increasing the flow from source to sink. If the chain used to label the sink consists of both forward and backward arcs, increase the flow in each forward arc in the chain and decrease the flow in each backward arc in the chain. Again, this will increase the flow from source to sink. Return to Step 2.

CRITICAL PATH METHOD

Assuming the duration of each activity is known, the critical path method (CPM) may be used to find the duration of a project.

RULES FOR CONSTRUCTING AN AOA PROJECT DIAGRAM.

1. Node 1 represents the start of the project. An arc should lead from node 1 to represent each activity that has no predecessors.

2. A node (called the finish node) representing the completion of the project should be included in the network.

3. Number the nodes in the network so that the node representing the completion of an activity always has a larger number than the node representing the beginning of an activity (there may be more than one numbering scheme that satisfies rule 3).

4. An activity should not be represented by more than one arc in the network.

5. Two nodes can be connected by at most one arc.

To avoid violating rules 4 and 5, it is sometimes necessary to utilize a **dummy activity** that takes zero time.

COMPUTATION OF EARLY EVENT TIME.   The early event time for node i, denoted $ET(i)$, is the earliest time at which the event corresponding to node i can occur. We compute $ET(i)$ as follows:

Step 1 Find each prior event to node i that is connected by an arc to node i. These events are the **immediate predecessors** of node i.

Step 2 To the ET for each immediate predecessor of node i, add the duration of the activity connecting the immediate predecessor to node i.

Step 3 $ET(i)$ equals the maximum of the sums computed in Step 2.

COMPUTATION OF LATE EVENT TIME.   The late event time for node i, denoted $LT(i)$, is the latest time at which the event corresponding to node i can occur without delaying the completion of the project. We compute $LT(i)$ as follows:

Step 1 Find each node that occurs after node i and is connected to node i by an arc. These events are the **immediate successors** of node i.

Step 2 From the LT for each immediate successor to node i, subtract the duration of the activity joining the successor to node i.

Step 3 $LT(i)$ is the smallest of the differences determined in Step 2.

TOTAL FLOAT.   For an arbitrary arc representing activity (i, j), the total float (denoted $TF(i, j)$ of the activity represented by (i, j) is the amount by which the starting time of activity (i,j) could be delayed beyond its earliest possible starting time without delaying the completion of the project (assuming no other activities are delayed):

$$TF(i,j) = LT(j) - ET(i) - t_{ij} \quad (t_{ij} = \text{duration of activity represented by arc } (i,j))$$

Any activity with a total float of zero is a **critical activity**. A path from node 1 to the finish node that consists entirely of critical activities is called a **critical path**. Any critical path (there may be more than one in a project network) is the longest path in the network from the start node (node 1) to the finish node. If the start of a critical activity is delayed, or if the duration of a critical activity is longer than expected, the completion of the project will be delayed.

FREE FLOAT. The free float of the activity corresponding to arc (i,j), denoted by $FF(i,j)$, is the amount by which the starting time of the activity corresponding to arc (i,j) (or the duration of the activity) can be delayed without delaying the start of any later activity beyond its earliest possible starting time:

$$FF(i,j) = ET(j) - ET(i) - t_{ij}$$

Linear programming can be used to find a critical path and the duration of the project. Let

$$x_j = \text{time at which node } j \text{ in project network occurs}$$
$$F = \text{node representing finish or completion of the project}$$

To find a critical path, minimize $z = x_F - x_1$ subject to

$$x_j \geq x_i + t_{ij} \quad \text{or} \quad x_j - x_i \geq t_{ij} \quad \text{for each arc}$$
$$x_j \text{ urs}$$

The optimal objective function value is the length of any critical path (or time to project completion). To find a critical path, simply find a path from node 1 to node F for which each arc in the path is represented by an arc (i,j) whose constraint $(x_j - x_i \geq t_{ij})$ has a dual price of -1.

Linear programming can also be used to determine the minimum cost method of reducing the duration of activities (crashing) in order to meet a project completion deadline.

PERT

If the durations of the project's activities are not known with certainty, PERT may be used to estimate the probability that the project will be completed in a specified amount of time. PERT requires that for each activity the following three numbers be specified:

$$a = \text{estimate of the activity's duration under the most favorable conditions}$$
$$b = \text{estimate of the activity's duration under the least favorable conditions}$$
$$m = \text{most likely value for the activity's duration}$$

If the estimates a, b, and m refer to the activity represented by arc (i,j), then $\mathbf{T}_{ij}$ is the random variable representing the duration of the activity represented by arc (i,j). $\mathbf{T}_{ij}$ has (approximately) the following properties:

$$E(\mathbf{T}_{ij}) = \frac{a + 4m + b}{6}$$

$$\operatorname{var} \mathbf{T}_{ij} = \frac{(b - a)^2}{36}$$

Then

$$\sum_{(i,j)\in\text{path}} E(\mathbf{T}_{ij}) = \text{expected duration of activities on any path}$$

$$\sum_{(i,j)\in\text{path}} \operatorname{var} \mathbf{T}_{ij} = \text{variance of duration of activities on any path}$$

Assuming (sometimes incorrectly) that the critical path found by CPM is the critical path, and assuming that the duration of the critical path is normally distributed, the preceding equations may be used to estimate the probability that the project will be completed within any specified length of time.

MINIMUM COST NETWORK FLOW PROBLEMS

The transportation, assignment, transshipment, shortest path, maximum flow, and critical path problems are all special cases of the minimum cost network flow problem (MCNFP).

x_{ij} = number of units of flow sent from node i to node j through arc (i,j)

b_i = net supply (outflow–inflow) at node i

c_{ij} = cost of transporting 1 unit of flow from node i to node j via arc (i,j)

L_{ij} = lower bound on flow through arc (i,j) (if there is no lower bound, let $L_{ij} = 0$)

U_{ij} = upper bound on flow through arc (i,j) (if there is no upper bound, let $U_{ij} = \infty$)

Then an MCNFP may be written as

$$\min \sum_{\text{all arcs}} c_{ij} x_{ij}$$

$$\text{s.t.} \quad \sum_j x_{ij} - \sum_k x_{ki} = b_i \quad \text{(for each node } i \text{ in the network)}$$

$$L_{ij} \le x_{ij} \le U_{ij} \quad \text{(for each arc in the network)}$$

The first set of constraints are the **flow balance equations**, and the second set of constraints express limitations on arc capacities.

Any MCNFP may be solved by a computer code using the **network simplex**. For a computer to solve an MCNFP, the user need only input the nodes and arcs in the network, the c_{ij}'s and arc capacity for each arc, and the b_i's for each node. Formulation of a problem of an MCNFP may require adding a dummy point to the problem.

MINIMUM SPANNING TREE PROBLEMS

The following method (M.S.T. algorithm) may be used to find a minimum spanning tree for a network:

Step 1 Begin at any node i, and join node i to the node in the network (call it node j) that is closest to node i. The two nodes i and j now form a connected set of nodes $C = \{i, j\}$, and arc (i, j) will be in the minimum spanning tree. The remaining nodes in the network (call them C') are referred to as the unconnected set of nodes.

Step 2 Now choose a member of C' (call it n) that is closest to some node in C. Let m represent the node in C that is closest to n. Then the arc (m, n) will be in the minimum spanning tree. Now update C and C'. Since n is now connected to $\{i, j\}$, C now equals $\{i, j, n\}$, and we must eliminate node n from C'.

Step 3 Repeat this process until a minimum spanning tree is found. Ties for closest node and arc to be included in the minimum spanning tree may be broken arbitrarily.

NETWORK SIMPLEX METHOD

Step 1 Determine a starting bfs. The $n - 1$ basic variables will correspond to a spanning tree. Indicate nonbasic variables at their upper bound by dashed arcs.

Step 2 Compute $y_1, y_2, \ldots y_n$ (often called the simplex multipliers) by solving $y_1 = 0, y_i - y_j = c_{ij}$ for all basic variables x_{ij}. For all nonbasic variables, determine the row 0 coefficient $\bar{c}_{ij}$ from $\bar{c}_{ij} = y_i - y_j - c_{ij}$. The current bfs is optimal if $\bar{c}_{ij} \leq 0$ for all $x_{ij} = L_{ij}$ and $\bar{c}_{ij} \geq 0$ for all $x_{ij} = U_{ij}$. If the bfs is not optimal, choose the nonbasic variable that most violates the optimality conditions as the entering basic variable.

Step 3 Identify the cycle (there will be exactly one!) created by adding the arc corresponding to the entering variable to the current spanning tree of the current bfs. Use conservation of flow to determine the new values of the variables in the cycle. The variable that exits the basis will be the variable that first hits its upper or lower bound as the value of the entering basic variable is changed.

Step 4 Find the new bfs by changing the flows of the arcs in the cycle found in Step 3. Now go to Step 2.

◆ REVIEW PROBLEMS

GROUP A

1. A truck must travel from New York to Los Angeles. As shown in Figure 62, a variety of routes are available. The number associated with each arc is the number of gallons of fuel required by the truck to traverse the arc.
(a) Use Dijkstra's algorithm to find the route from New York to Los Angeles that uses the minimum amount of gas.
(b) Formulate a balanced transportation problem that could be used to find the route from New York to Los Angeles that uses the minimum amount of gas.
(c) Formulate as an MCNFP the problem of finding the New York to Los Angeles route that uses the minimum amount of gas.

2. Telephone calls from New York to Los Angeles are transported as follows: First the call is sent to either Chicago or Memphis; then it is routed through either Denver or Dallas; and finally the call is sent to Los Angeles. The number of phone lines joining each pair of cities is shown in Table 35.
(a) Formulate an LP that can be used to determine the maximum number of calls that can be sent from New York to Los Angeles at any given time.
(b) Use the Ford-Fulkerson method to determine the maximum number of calls that can be sent from New York to Los Angeles at any given time.

3. Before a new product can be introduced, the activities in Table 36 must be completed (all times are in weeks).
(a) Draw the project diagram.
(b) Determine all critical paths and critical activities.
(c) Determine the total float and free float for each activity.

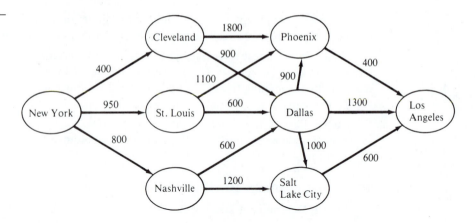

Figure 62
Network for
Problem 1

Table 35

CITIES	NO. OF TELEPHONE LINES
N.Y.–Chicago	500
N.Y.–Memphis	400
Chicago–Denver	300
Chicago–Dallas	250
Memphis–Denver	200
Memphis–Dallas	150
Denver–L.A.	400
Dallas–L.A.	350

(d) Set up an LP that could be used to determine the critical path.

(e) Formulate an MCNFP that could be used to find the critical path.

(f) It is now 12 weeks before Christmas. What is the probability that the product will be in the stores before Christmas?

(g) The duration of each activity can be reduced by up to 2 weeks at the following cost per week: A, $80; B, $60; C, $30; D, $60; E, $40; F, $30; G, $20. Assuming that the duration of each activity is known with certainty, formulate an LP that will minimize the cost of getting the product into the stores by Christmas.

4. During the next three months, Shoemakers, Inc. must meet (on time) the following demands for shoes: month 1, 1000 pairs; month 2, 1500 pairs; month 3, 1800 pairs. It takes 1 hour of labor to produce a pair of shoes. During each of the next three months, the following number of regular-time labor hours are available: month 1, 1000 hours; month 2, 1200 hours; month 3, 1200 hours. Each month, the company can require workers to put in up to 400 hours of overtime. Workers are only paid for the hours they work, and a worker receives $4 per hour for regular-time work and $6 per hour for overtime work. At the end of each month, a holding cost of $1.50 per pair of shoes is incurred. Formulate a MCNFP that can be used to minimize the total cost incurred in meeting the demands of the next three months. A formulation requires drawing the

Table 36

ACTIVITY	DESCRIPTION	PREDECESSORS	DURATION	a	b	m
A	Design the product	—	6	2	10	6
B	Survey the market	—	5	4	6	5
C	Place orders for raw materials	A	3	2	4	3
D	Receive raw materials	C	2	1	3	2
E	Build prototype of product	A, D	3	1	5	3
F	Develop ad campaign	B	2	3	5	4
G	Set up plant for mass production	E	4	2	6	4
H	Deliver product to stores	G, F	2	0	4	2

appropriate network and determining the c_{ij}'s, b_i's, and arc capacities. How would you modify your answer if demand could be backlogged (all demand must still be met by the end of month 3) at a cost of $20/pair/month?

5. Find a minimum spanning tree for the network in Figure 62.

6. A company produces a product at two plants: plant 1 and plant 2. The unit production cost and production capacity during each period are given in Table 37. The product is instantaneously shipped to the company's only customer according to the unit shipping costs given in Table 38. If a unit is produced and shipped during period 1, it can still be used to meet a period 2 demand, but a holding cost of $13 per unit in inventory is assessed. At the end of period 1, at most six units may be held in inventory. Demands are as follows: period 1–9; period 2–11. Formulate an MCNFP that can be used to minimize the cost of meeting all demands on time. Draw the network and determine the net outflow at each node, the arc capacities, and shipping costs.

Table 37

	UNIT PRODUCTION COST	CAPACITY
Plant 1 (period 1)	$33	7
Plant 1 (period 2)	$43	4
Plant 2 (period 1)	$30	9
Plant 2 (period 2)	$41	9

Table 38

	PERIOD 1	PERIOD 2
Plant 1 to customer	$51	$60
Plant 2 to customer	$42	$71

7. A project is considered completed when activities A–F have all been completed. The duration and predecessors of each activity are given in Table 39. The LINDO output in Figure 63 can be used to determine the critical path for this project.
(a) Use the LINDO output to draw the project network. Indicate the activity represented by each arc.
(b) Determine a critical path in the network. What is the earliest the project can be completed?

Table 39

ACTIVITY	DURATION	IMMEDIATE PREDECESSORS
A	2	—
B	3	—
C	1	A
D	5	A, B
E	7	B, C
F	5	D, E

Figure 63

```
MIN      X6 - X1
SUBJECT TO
     2)  - X1 + X3 >=    3
     3)    X4 - X2 >=    1
     4)  - X3 + X4 >=    0
     5)  - X4 + X5 >=    7
     6)  - X3 + X5 >=    5
     7)    X6 - X5 >=    5
     8)    X3 - X2 >=    0
     9)  - X1 + X2 >=    2
END

    LP OPTIMUM FOUND AT STEP    3

         OBJECTIVE FUNCTION VALUE

 1)        15.0000000

VARIABLE          VALUE          REDUCED COST
    X6         15.000000           0.000000
    X1          0.000000           0.000000
    X3          3.000000           0.000000
    X4          3.000000           0.000000
    X2          2.000000           0.000000
    X5         10.000000           0.000000

ROW        SLACK OR SURPLUS       DUAL PRICES
    2)          0.000000          -1.000000
    3)          0.000000           0.000000
    4)          0.000000          -1.000000
    5)          0.000000          -1.000000
    6)          2.000000           0.000000
    7)          0.000000          -1.000000
    8)          1.000000           0.000000
    9)          0.000000           0.000000

NO. ITERATIONS=        3
```

8.[†] State University has three professors who each teach four courses per year. Each year, four sections of Marketing, Finance, and Production must be offered. At least one section of each class must be offered during each semester (Fall and Spring). Each professor's time preference and preference for teaching various courses are given in Table 40.

The total satisfaction a professor earns teaching a class is the sum of the semester satisfaction and the course satisfaction. Thus, professor 1 derives a satisfaction of $3 + 6 = 9$ from teaching marketing during the fall

†Based on Mulvey (1979).

Table 40

	PROFESSOR 1	PROFESSOR 2	PROFESSOR 3
Fall preference	3	5	4
Spring preference	4	3	4
Marketing	6	4	5
Finance	5	6	4
Production	4	5	6

semester. Formulate an MCNFP that can be used to assign professors to courses so as to maximize the total satisfaction of the three professors.

GROUP B

9.[†] During the next two months, Machineco must meet (on time) the demands for three types of products shown in Table 41. Two machines are available to produce these products. Machine 1 can only produce products 1 and 2, and machine 2 can only produce products 2 and 3. Each machine can be used for up to 40 hours per month. Table 42 shows the time required to produce 1 unit of each product (independent of the type of machine); the cost of producing 1 unit of each product on each type of machine; and the cost of holding 1 unit of each product in inventory for one month. Formulate an MCNFP that could be used to minimize the total cost of meeting all demands on time.

Table 41

	PRODUCT 1	PRODUCT 2	PRODUCT 3
Month 1	50 units	70 units	80 units
Month 2	60 units	90 units	120 units

Table 42

	PRODUCTION TIME (Minutes)	PRODUCTION COST		HOLDING COST
		Machine 1	*Machine 2*	
Product 1	30	$40	—	$15
Product 2	20	$45	$60	$10
Product 3	15	—	$55	$5

◆ REFERENCES

BROWN, G., A. GEOFFRION, and G. BRADLEY. "Production and Sales Planning with Limited Shared Tooling at the Key Operation," *Management Science* 27(1981):247–259.

GLOVER, F., ET AL. "The Passenger-Mix Problem in the Scheduled Airlines," *Interfaces* 12(1982):73–80.

MULVEY, M. "Strategies in Modeling: A Personnel Example," *Interfaces* 9(no. 3, 1979):66–75.

RAVINDRAN, A. "On Compact Book Storage in Libraries," *Opsearch* 8(1971).

[†]This problem is based on Brown, Geoffrion, and Bradley (1981).

The following three texts contain an overview of networks at an elementary level:

CHACHRA, V., P. GHARE, and J. MOORE. *Applications of Graph Theory Algorithms*. New York: North-Holland, 1979.

MANDL, C. *Applied Network Optimization*. Orlando, Fla.: Academic Press, 1979.

PHILLIPS, D., and A. DIAZ. *Fundamentals of Network Analysis*. Engelwood Cliffs, N.J.: Prentice-Hall, 1981.

Detailed discussion of methods for solving shortest path problems can be found in the following three texts:

DENARDO, E. *Dynamic Programming: Theory and Applications*. Englewood Cliffs, N.J.: Prentice-Hall, 1982.

HU, T. *Combinatorial Algorithms*. Reading, Mass.: Addison-Wesley, 1982. Also discusses minimum spanning tree algorithms.

MINIEKA, E. *Optimization Algorithms for Networks and Graphs*. New York: Dekker, 1978. Also discusses minimum spanning tree algorithms.

Minieka (1978) and Hu (1982) discuss the maximum flow problem in detail, as do the following three texts:

FORD, L., and D. FULKERSON. *Flows in Networks*. Princeton, N.J.: Princeton University Press, 1962.

JENSEN, P., and W. BARNES. *Network Flow Programming*. New York: Wiley, 1980.

LAWLER, E. *Combinatorial Optimization: Networks and Matroids*. Chicago: Holt, Rinehart and Winston, 1976.

Excellent discussions of CPM and PERT are contained in:

HAX, A., and D. CANDEA. *Production and Inventory Management*. Englewood Cliffs, N.J.: Prentice-Hall, 1984.

WIEST, J., and F. LEVY. *A Management Guide to PERT/CPM*, 2nd ed. Englewood Cliffs, N.J.: Prentice-Hall, 1977.

Jensen and Barnes (1980) and the following references each contain a detailed discussion of the network simplex method used to solve an MCNFP.

CHVATAL, V. *Linear Programming*. San Francisco: Freeman, 1983.

SHAPIRO, J. *Mathematical Programming: Structures and Algorithms*. New York: Wiley, 1979.

WU, N., and R. COPPINS. *Linear Programming and Extensions*. New York: McGraw-Hill, 1981.

Integer Programming

THE READER MAY recall that we defined integer programming problems in our discussion of the Divisibility Assumption in Section 3.1. Simply stated, an *integer programming problem* (IP) is an LP in which some or all of the variables are required to be nonnegative integers.[†]

In this chapter (as for LPs in Chapter 3), we find that many real-life situations may be formulated as IPs. Unfortunately, we will also see that IPs are usually much harder to solve than LPs.

In Section 9.1, we begin with necessary definitions and some introductory comments about integer programming problems. In Section 9.2, we explain how to formulate integer programming models. In Sections 9.3–9.7, we discuss methods used to solve integer programming problems. Using LINDO[‡] to solve IPs is discussed in Section 9.8. In Section 9.9, we discuss the *cutting plane* method for solving integer programming problems.

9-1   INTRODUCTION TO INTEGER PROGRAMMING

An integer programming problem in which all variables are required to be integers is called a **pure integer programming problem.** For example,

$$\max z = 3x_1 + 2x_2$$
$$\text{s.t.} \quad x_1 + x_2 \leq 6 \tag{1}$$
$$x_1, x_2 \geq 0, \ x_1, x_2 \text{ integer}$$

is a pure integer programming problem.

[†]A nonlinear integer programming problem is an optimization problem in which either the objective function or the left-hand side of some of the constraints are nonlinear functions and some or all of the variables must be integers. Such problems are beyond the scope of this book.
[‡]Courtesy L. Schrage.

An integer programming problem in which only some of the variables are required to be integers is called a **mixed integer programming problem.** For example,

$$\max z = 3x_1 + 2x_2$$
$$\text{s.t.} \quad x_1 + x_2 \leq 6$$
$$x_1, x_2 \geq 0, \; x_1 \text{ integer}$$

is a mixed integer programming problem (x_2 is not required to be an integer).

An integer programming problem in which all the variables must equal 0 or 1 is called a 0–1 IP. In Section 9.2, we see that 0–1 IPs occur in surprisingly many situations.[†] The following is an example of a 0–1 IP:

$$\max z = x_1 - x_2$$
$$\text{s.t.} \quad x_1 + 2x_2 \leq 2 \qquad \qquad \text{(2)}$$
$$2x_1 - x_2 \leq 1$$
$$x_1, x_2 = 0 \text{ or } 1$$

Solution procedures especially designed for 0–1 IPs are discussed in Section 9.7.

The concept of the LP relaxation of an integer programming problem plays a key role in the solution of IPs.

DEFINITION	The LP obtained by omitting all integer or 0–1 constraints on variables is called the **LP relaxation** of the IP.

For example, the LP relaxation of (1) is

$$\max z = 3x_1 + 2x_2$$
$$\text{s.t.} \quad x_1 + x_2 \leq 6 \qquad \qquad \text{(1′)}$$
$$x_1, x_2 \geq 0$$

and the LP relaxation of (2) is

$$\max z = x_1 - x_2$$
$$\text{s.t.} \quad x_1 + 2x_2 \leq 2 \qquad \qquad \text{(2′)}$$
$$2x_1 - x_2 \leq 1$$
$$x_1, x_2 \geq 0$$

Any IP may be viewed as the LP relaxation plus some additional constraints (the constraints that state which variables must be integers or be 0 or 1). Hence, the LP relaxation is a less constrained, or more relaxed, version of the IP. This means that *the feasible region for any IP must be contained in the feasible region for the corresponding LP relaxation.* For any IP that is a max problem, this implies that

$$\text{Optimal } z\text{-value for LP relaxation} \geq \text{optimal } z\text{-value for IP} \qquad \text{(3)}$$

This result plays a key role when we discuss the solution of integer programming problems.

[†] Actually, any pure IP can be reformulated as an equivalent 0–1 IP (Section 9.7).

To shed more light on the properties of integer programming problems, we consider the following simple IP:

$$\max z = 21x_1 + 11x_2$$
$$\text{s.t.} \quad 7x_1 + 4x_2 \leq 13 \tag{4}$$
$$x_1, x_2 \geq 0; \; x_1, x_2 \text{ integer}$$

From Figure 1, we see that the feasible region for this problem consists of the following set of points: $S = \{(0,0), (0,1), (0,2), (0,3), (1,0), (1,1)\}$. Unlike the feasible region for any LP, the feasible region for (4) is not a convex set. By simply computing and comparing the z-values for each of the six points in the feasible region, we find the optimal solution to (4) is $z = 33$, $x_1 = 0$, $x_2 = 3$.

Figure 1
Feasible Region for
Simple IP (4)

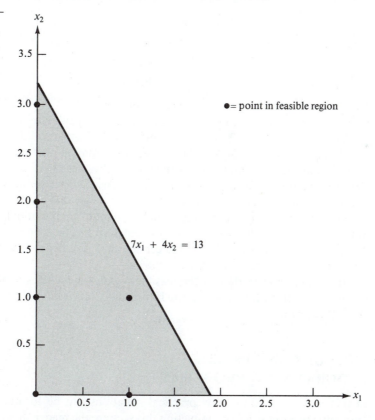

If the feasible region for a pure IP's LP relaxation is bounded, as in (4), the feasible region for the IP will consist of a finite number of points. In theory, such an IP could be solved (as described in the previous paragraph) by enumerating the z-values for each feasible point and determining the feasible point having the largest z-value. The problem with this approach is that (as Carl Sagan might say) most actual IPs have feasible regions consisting of billions and billions of feasible points. In such cases, a complete enumeration of all feasible points would require a large amount of computer time. As we explain in Section 9.3, IPs are often solved by cleverly enumerating all the points in the IP's feasible region.

Further study of (4) sheds light on some other interesting properties of IPs. Suppose that a naive analyst suggests the following approach for solving an IP: First solve the LP relaxation; then round off (to the nearest integer) each variable that is required to be an integer and that assumes a fractional value in the optimal solution to the LP relaxation.

Applying this approach to (4), we first find the optimal solution to the LP relaxation: $x_1 = \frac{13}{7}, x_2 = 0$. Rounding this solution yields the solution $x_1 = 2, x_2 = 0$ as a possible optimal solution to (4). But $x_1 = 2, x_2 = 0$ is infeasible for (4), so it cannot possibly be the optimal solution to (4). Even if we round x_1 downward (yielding the candidate solution $x_1 = 1, x_2 = 0$), we do not obtain the optimal solution ($x_1 = 0, x_2 = 3$ is the optimal solution).

For some IPs, it can even turn out that every roundoff of the optimal solution to the LP relaxation is infeasible for the IP. To see this, consider the following IP:

$$\max z = 4x_1 + x_2$$
$$\text{s.t.} \quad 2x_1 + x_2 \leq 5$$
$$2x_1 + 3x_2 = 5$$
$$x_1, x_2 \geq 0; \ x_1, x_2 \text{ integer}$$

The optimal solution to the LP relaxation for this IP is $z = 10$, $x_1 = \frac{5}{2}$, $x_2 = 0$. Rounding off this solution, we obtain either the candidate $x_1 = 2$, $x_2 = 0$ or the candidate $x_1 = 3$, $x_2 = 0$. Neither candidate is a feasible solution to the IP.

Recall from Chapter 4 that the simplex algorithm allowed us to solve LPs by going from one basic feasible solution to a better one. Also recall that in most cases, the simplex algorithm examines only a small fraction of all basic feasible solutions before the optimal solution is obtained. This property of the simplex algorithm enables us to solve relatively large LPs by expending a surprisingly small amount of computational effort. Analogously to the simplex algorithm, one would hope that an IP could be solved via an algorithm that proceeded from one feasible integer solution to a better feasible integer solution. Unfortunately, no such algorithm is known.

In summary, even though the feasible region for an IP is a subset of the feasible region for the IP's LP relaxation, the IP is usually much more difficult to solve than the IP's LP relaxation.

9-2 FORMULATING INTEGER PROGRAMMING PROBLEMS

In this section, we show how practical situations can be formulated as integer programming problems. After completing this section, the reader should have a good grasp of the art of developing integer programming formulations. We begin with some simple problems and gradually build up to more complicated formulations. Our first example is a capital budgeting problem reminiscent of the Star Oil problem of Section 3.6.

E X A M P L E   1   Stockco is considering four investments. Investment 1 will yield a net present value (NPV) of $16,000; investment 2, an NPV of $22,000; investment 3, an NPV of $12,000; and investment 4, an NPV of $8000. Each investment requires a certain cash outflow at the present time: investment 1, $5000; investment 2, $7000; investment 3, $4000; and investment 4, $3000. At present, $14,000 is available for investment. Formulate an IP whose solution will tell Stockco how to maximize the NPV obtained from investments 1–4.

Solution

As in LP formulations, we begin by defining a variable for each decision that Stockco must make. This leads us to define a 0–1 variable:

$$x_j \ (j = 1, 2, 3, 4) = \begin{cases} 1 & \text{if investment } j \text{ is made} \\ 0 & \text{otherwise} \end{cases}$$

For example, $x_2 = 1$ if investment 2 is made, and $x_2 = 0$ if investment 2 is not made. The NPV obtained by Stockco (in thousands of dollars) is

$$\text{Total NPV obtained by Stockco} = 16x_1 + 22x_2 + 12x_3 + 8x_4 \tag{5}$$

To see this, note that if $x_j = 1$, Eq. (5) includes the NPV of investment j, and if $x_j = 0$, Eq. (5) does not include the NPV of investment j. This means that whatever combination of investments is undertaken, (5) gives the NPV of that combination of projects. For example, if Stocko invests in investments 1 and 4, an NPV of $16,000 + 8000 = \$24,000$ is obtained. Since this combination of investments corresponds to $x_1 = x_4 = 1$, $x_2 = x_3 = 0$, Eq. (5) indicates that the NPV for this investment combination is $16(1) + 22(0) + 12(0) + 8(1) = \$24$ (thousand). This reasoning implies that Stockco's objective function is

$$\max z = 16x_1 + 22x_2 + 12x_3 + 8x_4 \tag{6}$$

Stockco faces the constraint that at most $14,000 can be invested. By the same reasoning used to develop (5), we can show that

$$\text{Total amount invested (in thousands of dollars)} = 5x_1 + 7x_2 + 4x_3 + 3x_4 \tag{7}$$

For example, if $x_1 = 0$, $x_2 = x_3 = x_4 = 1$, then Stockco makes investments 2, 3, and 4. In this case, Stockco must invest $7 + 4 + 3 = \$14$ (thousand). Eq. (7) yields a total amount invested of $5(0) + 7(1) + 4(1) + 3(1) = \$14$ (thousand). Since at most $14,000 can be invested, x_1, x_2, x_3, and x_4 must satisfy

$$5x_1 + 7x_2 + 4x_3 + 3x_4 \le 14 \tag{8}$$

Combining (6) and (8) with the constraints $x_j = 0$ or 1 ($j = 1, 2, 3, 4$) yields the following 0–1 integer programming problem:

$$\max z = 16x_1 + 22x_2 + 12x_3 + 8x_4$$
$$\text{s.t.} \quad 5x_1 + 7x_2 + 4x_3 + 3x_4 \le 14 \tag{9}$$
$$x_j = 0 \text{ or } 1 \quad (j = 1, 2, 3, 4)$$

◆

REMARKS

1. In Section 9.5, we show that the optimal solution to (9) is $x_1 = 0$, $x_2 = x_3 = x_4 = 1$, $z = \$42,000$. Hence, Stockco should invest in investments 2, 3, and 4 and not invest in investment 1. Since investment 1 yields a higher NPV per dollar invested than any of the other investments (investment 1 yields $3.20 per dollar invested, investment 2 yields $3.14 per dollar invested, investment 3 yields $3 per dollar invested, and investment 4 yields $2.67 per dollar invested), it may seem surprising that investment 1 is not undertaken. To see why the optimal solution to (9) does not involve making the "best" investment, note that any investment combination that includes investment 1 cannot use more than $12,000. This means that using investment 1 forces Stockco to forgo investing $2000. On the other hand, the optimal investment combination uses all $14,000 of the investment budget. This enables the optimal combination to obtain a higher NPV than any combination that includes investment 1. If, as in Chapter 3, fractional investments were allowed, the optimal solution to (9) would be $x_1 = x_2 = 1$, $x_3 = 0.50$, $x_4 = 0$, $z = \$44,000$, and investment 1 would be used. This simple example shows that the choice of modeling a capital budgeting problem as a linear programming or as an integer programming problem can significantly affect the optimal solution to the problem.

2. Any IP, such as (9), which has only one constraint is referred to as a **knapsack problem**. Suppose that Josie Camper is going on an overnight hike. There are four items Josie is considering taking along on the trip. The weight of each item and the benefit Josie feels she would obtain from each item are listed in Table 1.

Table 1
Weights and Benefits for Items in Josie's Knapsack

	WEIGHT (Pounds)	BENEFIT
Item 1	5	16
Item 2	7	22
Item 3	4	12
Item 4	3	8

Suppose Josie's knapsack can hold up to 14 lb of items. For $j = 1, 2, 3, 4$, define

$$x_j = \begin{cases} 1 & \text{if Josie takes item } j \text{ on the hike} \\ 0 & \text{otherwise} \end{cases}$$

Then Josie can maximize the total benefit by solving (9).

In the following example, we show how the Stockco formulation can be modified to handle additional constraints.

E X A M P L E   2

Modify the Stockco formulation to account for each of the following constraints:

1. Stockco can invest in at most two investments.

2. If Stockco invests in investment 2, they must also invest in investment 1.

3. If Stockco invests in investment 2, they cannot invest in investment 4.

Solution

1. Simply add the constraint

$$x_1 + x_2 + x_3 + x_4 \le 2 \tag{10}$$

to (9). Since any choice of three or four investments will have $x_1 + x_2 + x_3 + x_4 \ge 3$, constraint (10) excludes from consideration all investment combinations involving three or more investments. Thus, (10) eliminates from consideration exactly those combinations of investments that do not satisfy the first requirement.

2. In terms of x_1 and x_2, this requirement states that if $x_2 = 1$, then x_1 must also equal 1. If we add the constraint

$$x_2 \le x_1 \quad \text{or} \quad x_2 - x_1 \le 0 \tag{11}$$

to (9), we will have taken care of the second requirement. To show that (11) is equivalent to Constraint 2, we consider two possibilities: either $x_2 = 1$ or $x_2 = 0$.

Case 1 $x_2 = 1$. If $x_2 = 1$, then (11) implies that $x_1 \geq 1$. Since x_1 must equal 0 or 1, this implies that $x_1 = 1$, as required by Constraint 2.

Case 2 $x_2 = 0$. In this case, (11) reduces to $x_1 \geq 0$, which allows $x_1 = 0$ or $x_1 = 1$. In short, if $x_2 = 0$, Constraint (11) does not restrict the value of x_1. This is also consistent with Constraint 2.

In summary, for any value of x_2, (11) is equivalent to Constraint 2.

3. Simply add the constraint

$$x_2 + x_4 \leq 1 \tag{12}$$

to (9). We now show that for the two cases $x_2 = 1$ and $x_2 = 0$, Constraint (12) is equivalent to the third requirement.

Case 1 $x_2 = 1$. In this case, we are investing in investment 2, and Constraint 3 implies that Stockco cannot invest in investment 4 (that is, x_4 must equal 0). Note that if $x_2 = 1$, then (12) does imply $1 + x_4 \leq 1$, or $x_4 = 0$. Thus, if $x_2 = 1$, Constraint (12) is consistent with Constraint 3.

Case 2 $x_2 = 0$. In this case, Constraint 3 does not restrict the value of x_4. Note that if $x_2 = 0$, then (12) reduces to $x_4 \leq 1$, which also leaves x_4 free to equal 0 or 1.

◆

FIXED-CHARGE PROBLEMS

Example 3 illustrates an important trick that can be used to formulate many location and production problems as integer programming problems.

EXAMPLE 3

Gandhi Cloth Company is capable of manufacturing three types of clothing: shirts, shorts, and pants. The manufacture of each type of clothing requires that Gandhi have the appropriate type of machinery available. The machinery needed to manufacture each type of clothing must be rented at the following rates: shirt machinery, $200 per week; shorts machinery, $150 per week; pants machinery, $100 per week. The manufacture of each type of clothing also requires the amounts of cloth and labor given in Table 2. Each week 150 hours of labor and 160 sq yd of cloth are available. The variable unit cost and selling price for each type of clothing are shown in Table 3. Formulate an IP whose solution will maximize Gandhi's weekly profits.

Solution

As in LP formulations, we define a decision variable for each decision that Gandhi must make. Clearly, Gandhi must decide how many of each type of clothing should be manufactured each week, so we define

$$x_1 = \text{number of shirts produced each week}$$
$$x_2 = \text{number of shorts produced each week}$$
$$x_3 = \text{number of pants produced each week}$$

Note that the cost of renting machinery depends only on the types of clothing produced,

Constraints

Table 2		LABOR (Hours)	CLOTH (Square Yards)
Resource Requirements for Gandhi Example	Shirt	3	4
	Shorts	2	3
	Pants	6	4
		≤ 150	≤ 160

Table 3		SALES PRICE	VARIABLE COST
Revenue and Cost Information for Gandhi Example	Shirt	$12	$6
	Shorts	$8	$4
	Pants	$15	$8

not on the amount of each type of clothing. This enables us to express the cost of renting machinery by using the following variables:

$$y_1 = \begin{cases} 1 & \text{if any shirts are manufactured} \\ 0 & \text{otherwise} \end{cases}$$

$$y_2 = \begin{cases} 1 & \text{if any shorts are manufactured} \\ 0 & \text{otherwise} \end{cases}$$

$$y_3 = \begin{cases} 1 & \text{if any pants are manufactured} \\ 0 & \text{otherwise} \end{cases}$$

In short, if $x_j > 0$, then $y_j = 1$, and if $x_j = 0$, then $y_j = 0$. We can now express Gandhi's weekly profits: (weekly profits) = (weekly sales revenue) − (weekly variable costs) − (weekly costs of renting machinery).

Also,

$$\text{Weekly cost of renting machinery} = 200y_1 + 150y_2 + 100y_3 \qquad (13)$$

To justify (13), note that (13) picks up the rental costs only for the machines needed to manufacture those products that Gandhi is actually manufacturing. For example, suppose that shirts and pants are manufactured. Then $y_1 = y_3 = 1$ and $y_2 = 0$, and the total weekly rental cost will be $200 + 100 = \$300$, which agrees with (13).

Since the cost of renting, say, shirt machinery does not depend on the number of shirts produced, the cost of renting each type of machinery is called a **fixed charge**. A fixed charge for an activity is a cost that is assessed whenever the activity is undertaken at a nonzero level. The presence of fixed charges will make the formulation of the Gandhi problem much more difficult.

We can now express Gandhi's weekly profits as

$$\text{Weekly profit} = (12x_1 + 8x_2 + 15x_3) - (6x_1 + 4x_2 + 8x_3)$$
$$- (200y_1 + 150y_2 + 100y_3)$$
$$= 6x_1 + 4x_2 + 7x_3 - 200y_1 - 150y_2 - 100y_3$$

Thus, Gandhi wishes to maximize

$$z = 6x_1 + 4x_2 + 7x_3 - 200y_1 - 150y_2 - 100y_3$$

Since Gandhi's supply of labor and cloth is limited, Gandhi faces the following two constraints:

Constraint 1 At most 150 hours of labor can be used each week.

Constraint 2 At most 160 sq yd of cloth can be used each week.

Constraint 1 is expressed by

$$3x_1 + 2x_2 + 6x_3 \leq 150 \qquad \text{(Labor constraint)} \tag{14}$$

Constraint 2 is expressed by

$$4x_1 + 3x_2 + 4x_3 \leq 160 \qquad \text{(Cloth constraint)} \tag{15}$$

Observe that $x_j > 0$ and x_j integer ($j = 1, 2, 3$) must hold along with $y_j = 0$ or 1 ($j = 1, 2, 3$). Combining (14) and (15) with these restrictions and the objective function yields the following integer programming problem:

$$\max z = 6x_1 + 4x_2 + 7x_3 - 200y_1 - 150y_2 - 100y_3$$
$$\text{s.t.} \quad 3x_1 + 2x_2 + 6x_3 \leq 150$$
$$4x_1 + 3x_2 + 4x_3 \leq 160 \qquad \text{(IP 1)}$$
$$x_1, x_2, x_3 \geq 0; \; x_1, x_2, x_3 \text{ integer}$$
$$y_1, y_2, y_3 = 0 \text{ or } 1$$

The optimal solution to this problem is found to be $x_1 = 30$, $x_3 = 10$, $x_2 = y_1 = y_2 = y_3 = 0$. This cannot be the optimal solution to Gandhi's problem, because it indicates that Gandhi can manufacture shirts and pants without incurring the cost of renting the needed machinery. The current formulation is incorrect because the variables y_1, y_2, and y_3 are not present in the constraints. This means that there is nothing to stop us from setting $y_1 = y_2 = y_3 = 0$. Since setting $y_i = 0$ is certainly less costly than setting $y_i = 1$, a minimum cost solution to (IP 1) will always set $y_i = 0$. Somehow we must modify (IP 1) so that whenever $x_i > 0$, $y_i = 1$ must hold. The following trick will accomplish this goal. Let M_1, M_2, and M_3 be three large positive numbers, and add the following constraints to (IP 1):

$$x_1 \leq M_1 y_1 \tag{16}$$
$$x_2 \leq M_2 y_2 \tag{17}$$
$$x_3 \leq M_3 y_3 \tag{18}$$

Adding (16)–(18) to IP 1 will ensure that if $x_i > 0$, then $y_i = 1$. To illustrate the idea, let us show that (16) ensures that if $x_1 > 0$, then $y_1 = 1$. If $x_1 > 0$, then y_1 cannot be zero. For if $y_1 = 0$, then (16) would imply $x_1 \leq 0$ or $x_1 = 0$. Thus, if $x_1 > 0$, $y_1 = 1$ must hold. If any shirts are produced (i.e., $x_1 > 0$), (16) ensures that $y_1 = 1$, and the objective function will include the cost of the machinery needed to manufacture shirts. Note that if $y_1 = 1$, then (16) becomes $x_1 \leq M_1$, which does not unnecessarily restrict the value of x_1. If M_1 were not chosen large, however (say $M_1 = 10$), then (16) would unnecessarily restrict the value of x_1. In general, M_i should be set equal to the maximum value that x_i can attain. In the current problem, at most 40 shirts can be produced (if Gandhi produced more than 40 shirts, the company would run out of cloth), so we can safely choose $M_1 = 40$. The reader should verify that we can choose $M_2 = 53$ and $M_3 = 25$.

If $x_1 = 0$, (16) becomes $0 \leq M_1 y_1$. This allows either $y_1 = 0$ or $y_1 = 1$. Since $y_1 = 0$ is less costly than $y_1 = 1$, the optimal solution will choose $y_1 = 0$ if $x_1 = 0$. In summary, we have shown that if (16)–(18) are added to (IP 1), then $x_i > 0$ will imply $y_i = 1$, and $x_i = 0$ will imply $y_i = 0$.

The optimal solution to the Gandhi problem is $z = \$75$, $x_3 = 25$, $y_3 = 1$. Thus, Gandhi should produce 25 pants each week.

◆

The Gandhi problem is an example of a **fixed-charge problem**. In a fixed-charge problem, there is a cost associated with performing an activity at a nonzero level which does not depend on the level of the activity. Thus, in the Gandhi problem, if we make any shirts at all (no matter how many we make), we must pay the fixed charge of $200 to rent a shirt machine. Problems in which a decision maker must choose where to locate facilities are often fixed-charge problems. In such a problem, the decision maker must choose where to locate various facilities (such as plants, warehouses, or business offices), and a fixed charge is often associated with building or operating a facility. Example 4 is a typical location problem involving the idea of a fixed charge.

E X A M P L E
4

The Lockbox Problem J. C. Nickles receives credit card payments from four regions of the country (West, Midwest, East, and South). The average daily value of payments mailed by customers from each region is as follows: from the West, $70,000; from the Midwest, $50,000; from the East, $60,000; from the South, $40,000. Nickles must decide where customers should mail their payments. Since Nickles can earn 20% annual interest by investing these revenues, they would like to receive payments as quickly as possible. Nickles is considering setting up operations to process payments (often referred to as lockboxes) in four different cities: Los Angeles, New York, Chicago, and Atlanta. The average number of days (from time payment is sent) until a check clears and Nickles can deposit the money depends on the city to which the payment is mailed, as shown in Table 4. For example, if a check is mailed from the West to Atlanta, it would take an average of 8 days before Nickles could earn interest on the check. The annual cost of running a lockbox in any city is $50,000. Formulate an IP that Nickles can use to minimize the sum of costs due to lost interest and lockbox operations. Assume that each region must send all its money to a single city and that there is no limit on the amount of money that each lockbox can handle.

Solution

Nickles must make two types of decisions. First, Nickles must decide where to operate lockboxes. We define, for $j = 1, 2, 3, 4$,

$$y_j = \begin{cases} 1 & \text{if a lockbox is operated in city } j \\ 0 & \text{otherwise} \end{cases}$$

Thus, $y_2 = 1$ if a lockbox is operated in Chicago, and $y_3 = 0$ if no lockbox is operated in New York. Second, Nickles must determine where each region of the country should send payments. We define (for $i, j = 1, 2, 3, 4$)

$$x_{ij} = \begin{cases} 1 & \text{if region } i \text{ sends payments to city } j \\ 0 & \text{otherwise} \end{cases}$$

Table 4
Average Number of
Days from Mailing
of Payment Until
Payment Clears

FROM	TO			
	City 1 (*Los Angeles*)	City 2 (*Chicago*)	City 3 (*New York*)	City 4 (*Atlanta*)
Region 1 West	2	6	8	8
Region 2 Midwest	6	2	5	5
Region 3 East	8	5	2	5
Region 4 South	8	5	5	2

For example, $x_{12} = 1$ if the West sends payments to Chicago, and $x_{23} = 0$ if the Midwest does not send payments to New York.

Nickles wishes to minimize (total annual cost) = (annual cost of operating lockboxes) + (annual lost interest cost). To determine how much interest Nickles loses annually, we must determine how much revenue would be lost if payments from region i were sent to city j. For example, how much in annual interest would Nickles lose if customers from the West region sent payments to New York? On any given day, 8 days' worth, or $8(70,000) = \$560,000$ of West payments will be in the mail and will not be earning interest. Since Nickles can earn 20% annually, each year West funds will result in $0.20(560,000) = \$112,000$ in lost interest. Similar calculations for the annual cost of lost interest for each possible assignment of a region to a city yield the results shown in Table 5. Since the lost interest cost from sending region i's payments to city j is only incurred if $x_{ij} = 1$, Nickles' annual lost interest costs (in thousands) are

$$\begin{aligned}
\text{Annual lost interest costs} = {} & 28x_{11} + 84x_{12} + 112x_{13} + 112x_{14} \\
& + 60x_{21} + 20x_{22} + 50x_{23} + 50x_{24} \\
& + 96x_{31} + 60x_{32} + 24x_{33} + 60x_{34} \\
& + 64x_{41} + 40x_{42} + 40x_{43} + 16x_{44}
\end{aligned}$$

Table 5
Calculation of
Annual Lost Interest

ASSIGNMENT	ANNUAL LOST INTEREST COST
West to L.A.	$0.20(70,000)2 = \$28,000$
West to Chicago	$0.20(70,000)6 = \$84,000$
West to N.Y.	$0.20(70,000)8 = \$112,000$
West to Atlanta	$0.20(70,000)8 = \$112,000$
Midwest to L.A.	$0.20(50,000)6 = \$60,000$
Midwest to Chicago	$0.20(50,000)2 = \$20,000$
Midwest to N.Y.	$0.20(50,000)5 = \$50,000$
Midwest to Atlanta	$0.20(50,000)5 = \$50,000$
East to L.A.	$0.20(60,000)8 = \$96,000$
East to Chicago	$0.20(60,000)5 = \$60,000$
East to N.Y.	$0.20(60,000)2 = \$24,000$
East to Atlanta	$0.20(60,000)5 = \$60,000$
South to L.A.	$0.20(40,000)8 = \$64,000$
South to Chicago	$0.20(40,000)5 = \$40,000$
South to N.Y.	$0.20(40,000)5 = \$40,000$
South to Atlanta	$0.20(40,000)2 = \$16,000$

The cost of operating a lockbox in city i is incurred if and only if $y_i = 1$, so the annual lockbox operating costs (in thousands) are given by

Total annual lockbox operating cost $= 50y_1 + 50y_2 + 50y_3 + 50y_4$

Thus, Nickles' objective function may be written as

$$
\begin{aligned}
\min z = \;& 28x_{11} + 84x_{12} + 112x_{13} + 112x_{14} \\
&+ 60x_{21} + 20x_{22} + 50x_{23} + 50x_{24} \\
&+ 96x_{31} + 60x_{32} + 24x_{33} + 60x_{34} \\
&+ 64x_{41} + 40x_{42} + 40x_{43} + 16x_{44} \\
&+ 50y_1 + 50y_2 + 50y_3 + 50y_4
\end{aligned}
\tag{19}
$$

Nickles faces two types of constraints.

Type 1 Constraint Each region must send its payments to a single city.

Type 2 Constraint If a region is assigned to send its payments to a city, that city must have a lockbox.

The type 1 constraints state that for region i $(i = 1, 2, 3, 4)$ exactly one of x_{i1}, x_{i2}, x_{i3}, and x_{i4} must equal 1 and the others must equal 0. This can be accomplished by including the following four constraints:

$$
\begin{aligned}
x_{11} + x_{12} + x_{13} + x_{14} = 1 \quad &\text{(West region constraint)} &\tag{20}\\
x_{21} + x_{22} + x_{23} + x_{24} = 1 \quad &\text{(Midwest region constraint)} &\tag{21}\\
x_{31} + x_{32} + x_{33} + x_{34} = 1 \quad &\text{(East region constraint)} &\tag{22}\\
x_{41} + x_{42} + x_{43} + x_{44} = 1 \quad &\text{(South region constraint)} &\tag{23}
\end{aligned}
$$

The type 2 constraints state that if

$$
x_{ij} = 1 \quad \text{(that is, customers in region i send payments to city j)} \tag{24}
$$

then y_j must equal 1. For example, suppose $x_{12} = 1$. Then there must be a lockbox at city 2, so $y_2 = 1$ must hold. This can be ensured by adding 16 constraints of the form

$$
x_{ij} \le y_j \quad (i = 1, 2, 3, 4; j = 1, 2, 3, 4) \tag{25}
$$

If $x_{ij} = 1$, then (25) ensures that $y_j = 1$, as desired. Also, if $x_{1j} = x_{2j} = x_{3j} = x_{4j} = 0$, then (25) allows $y_j = 0$ or $y_j = 1$. As in the fixed-charge example, the act of minimizing costs will result in $y_j = 0$. In summary, the constraints in (25) ensure that Nickles pays for a lockbox at city i if and only if it uses a lockbox at city i.

Combining (19)–(23) with the $4(4) = 16$ constraints in (25) and the 0–1 restrictions on the variables yields the following formulation:

$$
\begin{aligned}
\min z = \;& 28x_{11} + 84x_{12} + 112x_{13} + 112x_{14} + 60x_{21} + 20x_{22} + 50x_{23} + 50x_{24} \\
&+ 96x_{31} + 60x_{32} + 24x_{33} + 60x_{34} + 64x_{41} + 40x_{42} + 40x_{43} + 16x_{44} \\
&+ 50y_1 + 50y_2 + 50y_3 + 50y_4
\end{aligned}
$$

$$
\begin{aligned}
\text{s.t.} \quad & x_{11} + x_{12} + x_{13} + x_{14} = 1 \quad &\text{(West region constraint)} \\
& x_{21} + x_{22} + x_{23} + x_{24} = 1 \quad &\text{(Midwest region constraint)} \\
& x_{31} + x_{32} + x_{33} + x_{34} = 1 \quad &\text{(East region constraint)}
\end{aligned}
$$

$$x_{41} + x_{42} + x_{43} + x_{44} = 1 \quad \text{(South region constraint)}$$

$$x_{11} \leq y_1, x_{21} \leq y_1, x_{31} \leq y_1, x_{41} \leq y_1, x_{12} \leq y_2, x_{22} \leq y_2, x_{32} \leq y_2, x_{42} \leq y_2,$$

$$x_{13} \leq y_3, x_{23} \leq y_3, x_{33} \leq y_3, x_{43} \leq y_3, x_{14} \leq y_4, x_{24} \leq y_4, x_{34} \leq y_4, x_{44} \leq y_4$$

$$\text{All } x_{ij} \text{ and } y_j = 0 \text{ or } 1$$

The optimal solution to this integer programming problem is $z = 242$, $y_1 = 1$, $y_3 = 1$, $x_{11} = 1$, $x_{23} = 1$, $x_{33} = 1$, $x_{43} = 1$. Thus, Nickles should have a lockbox operation in Los Angeles and New York. West customers should send payments to Los Angeles, and all other customers should send payments to New York.

There is an alternative way of modeling the type 2 constraints. Instead of the 16 constraints of the form $x_{ij} \leq y_j$, we may include the following four constraints:

$$x_{11} + x_{21} + x_{31} + x_{41} \leq 4y_1 \quad \text{(Los Angeles constraint)}$$
$$x_{12} + x_{22} + x_{32} + x_{42} \leq 4y_2 \quad \text{(Chicago constraint)}$$
$$x_{13} + x_{23} + x_{33} + x_{43} \leq 4y_3 \quad \text{(New York constraint)}$$
$$x_{14} + x_{24} + x_{34} + x_{44} \leq 4y_4 \quad \text{(Atlanta constraint)}$$

For the given city, each of these constraints ensures that if the lockbox in the given city is used, Nickles must pay for the lockbox. For example, consider $x_{14} + x_{24} + x_{34} + x_{44} \leq 4y_4$. The lockbox in Atlanta is used if $x_{14} = 1$, $x_{24} = 1$, $x_{34} = 1$, or $x_{44} = 1$. If any of these variables equals 1, then the Atlanta constraint ensures that $y_4 = 1$, and Nickles must pay for the lockbox. If all these variables are 0, the act of minimizing costs will cause $y_4 = 0$, and the cost of the Atlanta lockbox will not be incurred. Why does the right-hand side of each of these four constraints equal 4? This ensures that for each city, it is possible to send money from all four regions to the city. In Section 9.3, we discuss which of the two alternative formulations of the lockbox problem is easier for a computer to solve. The answer may surprise you! ◆

SET-COVERING PROBLEMS

The following example is typical of an important class of IPs known as set-covering problems.

E X A M P L E 5

There are six cities (cities 1–6) in Kilroy County. The county must determine where to build fire stations. The county wants to build the minimum number of fire stations needed to ensure that at least one fire station is within 15 minutes (driving time) of each city. The times (in minutes) required to drive between the cities in Kilroy County are shown in Table 6. Formulate an IP that will tell Kilroy how many fire stations should be built and where they should be located.

Solution

For each city, Kilroy must determine whether or not to build a fire station in that city. We define the 0–1 variables x_1, x_2, x_3, x_4, x_5, and x_6 by

$$x_i = \begin{cases} 1 & \text{if a fire station is built in city } i \\ 0 & \text{otherwise} \end{cases}$$

	TO					
FROM	*City 1*	*City 2*	*City 3*	*City 4*	*City 5*	*City 6*
City 1	0	10	20	30	30	20
City 2	10	0	25	35	20	10
City 3	20	25	0	15	30	20
City 4	30	35	15	0	15	25
City 5	30	20	30	15	0	14
City 6	20	10	20	25	14	0

Table 6
Time Required to
Travel between Cities
in Kilroy County

Then the total number of fire stations that are built is given by $x_1 + x_2 + x_3 + x_4 + x_5 + x_6$, and Kilroy's objective function is to minimize

$$z = x_1 + x_2 + x_3 + x_4 + x_5 + x_6$$

What are Kilroy's constraints? Kilroy must ensure that there is a fire station within 15 minutes of each city. Table 7 indicates which locations can reach the city in 15 minutes or less. To ensure that at least one fire station is within 15 minutes of city 1, we add the constraint

$$x_1 + x_2 \geq 1 \qquad \text{(City 1 constraint)}$$

Table 7
Cities within 15
Minutes of Given
City

City 1	1, 2
City 2	1, 2, 6
City 3	3, 4
City 4	3, 4, 5
City 5	4, 5, 6
City 6	2, 5, 6

This constraint ensures that $x_1 = x_2 = 0$ is impossible, so at least one fire station will be built within 15 minutes of city 1. Similarly the constraint

$$x_1 + x_2 + x_6 \geq 1 \qquad \text{(City 2 constraint)}$$

ensures that at least one fire station will be located within 15 minutes of city 2. In a similar fashion, we obtain constraints for cities 3–6. Combining these six constraints with the objective function (and with the fact that each variable must equal 0 or 1), we obtain the following 0–1 integer programming problem:

$$\min z = x_1 + x_2 + x_3 + x_4 + x_5 + x_6$$

$$
\begin{aligned}
\text{s.t.} \quad x_1 + x_2 & & \geq 1 & \quad \text{(City 1 constraint)} \\
x_1 + x_2 & + x_6 & \geq 1 & \quad \text{(City 2 constraint)} \\
x_3 + \cdot x_4 & & \geq 1 & \quad \text{(City 3 constraint)} \\
x_3 + x_4 + x_5 & & \geq 1 & \quad \text{(City 4 constraint)} \\
x_4 + x_5 + x_6 & \geq 1 & & \quad \text{(City 5 constraint)} \\
x_2 \qquad\quad + x_5 + x_6 & \geq 1 & & \quad \text{(City 6 constraint)}
\end{aligned}
$$

$$x_i = 0 \text{ or } 1 \quad (i = 1, 2, 3, 4, 5, 6)$$

One optimal solution to this IP is $z = 2$, $x_2 = x_4 = 1$, $x_1 = x_3 = x_5 = x_6 = 0$. Thus, Kilroy County can build two fire stations: one in city 2 and one in city 4. ◆

Example 5 represents a class of integer programming problems known as **set-covering problems**. In a set-covering problem, each member of a given set (call it Set 1) must be "covered" by an acceptable member of some set (call it Set 2). The objective in a set-covering problem is to minimize the number of elements in Set 2 that are required to cover all the elements in Set 1. In Example 5, Set 1 is the cities in Kilroy County, and Set 2 is the set of fire stations. The station in city 2 covers cities 1, 2, and 6, and the station in city 4 covers cities 3, 4, and 5. Set-covering problems have many applications in areas such as airline crew scheduling, political districting, airline scheduling, and truck routing.

EITHER–OR CONSTRAINTS

The following situation commonly occurs in mathematical programming problems. We are given two constraints of the form

$$f(x_1, x_2, \ldots, x_n) \leq 0 \qquad (26)$$

$$g(x_1, x_2, \ldots, x_n) \leq 0 \qquad (27)$$

We wish to ensure that at least one of (26) and (27) is satisfied, often called **either-or constraints**. Adding the two constraints (26′) and (27′) to the formulation will ensure that at least one of (26) and (27) is satisfied:

$$f(x_1, x_2, \ldots, x_n) \leq My \qquad (26')$$

$$g(x_1, x_2, \ldots, x_n) \leq M(1 - y) \qquad (27')$$

In (26′) and (27′), y is a 0–1 variable, and M is a number chosen large enough to ensure that $f(x_1, x_2, \ldots, x_n) \leq M$ and $g(x_1, x_2, \ldots, x_n) \leq M$ are satisfied for all values of $x_1, x_2, \ldots, x_n$ that satisfy the other constraints in the problem.

Let us show that the inclusion of constraints (26′) and (27′) is equivalent to at least one of (26) and (27) being satisfied. Either $y = 0$ or $y = 1$. If $y = 0$, then (26′) and (27′) become $f \leq 0$ and $g \leq M$. Thus, if $y = 0$, then (26) (and possibly (27)) must be satisfied. Similarly, if $y = 1$, then (26′) and (27′) become $f \leq M$ and $g \leq 0$. Thus, if $y = 1$, then (27) (and possibly (26)) must be satisfied. Therefore, whether $y = 0$ or $y = 1$, (26′) and (27′) ensure that at least one of (26) and (27) is satisfied.

The following example illustrates the use of either-or constraints.

E X A M P L E
6

Dorian Auto is considering manufacturing three types of autos: compact, midsize, and large. The resources required for, and the profits yielded by, each type of car are shown in Table 8. At present, 6000 tons of steel and 60,000 hours of labor are available. In order

Table 8
Resources and
Profits for Three
Types of Cars

	COMPACT	MIDSIZE	LARGE
Steel required	1.5 tons	3 tons	5 tons
Labor required	30 hours	25 hours	40 hours
Profit yielded	$2000	$3000	$4000

for production of a type of car to be economically feasible, at least 1000 cars of that type must be produced. Formulate an IP to maximize Dorian's profit.

Solution   Since Dorian must determine how many cars of each type should be built, we define

$$x_1 = \text{number of compact cars produced}$$
$$x_2 = \text{number of midsize cars produced}$$
$$x_3 = \text{number of large cars produced}$$

Then contribution to profit (in thousands of dollars) is $2x_1 + 3x_2 + 4x_3$, and Dorian's objective function is

$$\max z = 2x_1 + 3x_2 + 4x_3$$

We know that if any cars of a given type are produced, at least 1000 cars of that type must be produced. Thus, for $i = 1, 2, 3$, we must have $x_i \leq 0$ or $x_i \geq 1000$. Since steel and labor are limited, Dorian must satisfy the following five constraints:

Constraint 1 $x_1 \leq 0$ or $x_1 \geq 1000$.

Constraint 2 $x_2 \leq 0$ or $x_2 \geq 1000$.

Constraint 3 $x_3 \leq 0$ or $x_3 \geq 1000$.

Constraint 4   The cars produced can use at most 6000 tons of steel.

Constraint 5   The cars produced can use at most 60,000 hours of labor.

From our previous discussion, we see that if we define $f(x_1, x_2, x_3) = x_1$ and $g(x_1, x_2, x_3) = 1000 - x_1$, we can replace Constraint 1 by the following pair of constraints:

$$x_1 \leq M_1 y_1$$
$$1000 - x_1 \leq M_1(1 - y_1)$$
$$y_1 = 0 \text{ or } 1$$

To ensure that both x_1 and $1000 - x_1$ will never exceed M_1, it suffices to choose M_1 large enough so that M_1 exceeds 1000 and x_1 is always less than M_1. Since building $\frac{60,000}{30} = 2000$ compacts would use up all available labor (and still leave some steel), at most 2000 compacts can be built. Thus, we may choose $M_1 = 2000$. Similarly, Constraint 2 may be replaced by the following pair of constraints:

$$x_2 \leq M_2 y_2$$
$$1000 - x_2 \leq M_2(1 - y_2)$$
$$y_2 = 0 \text{ or } 1$$

The reader should verify that $M_2 = 2000$ is satisfactory. Similarly, Constraint 3 may be replaced by

$$x_3 \leq M_3 y_3$$
$$1000 - x_3 \leq M_3(1 - y_3)$$
$$y_3 = 0 \text{ or } 1$$

The reader should verify that $M_3 = 1200$ is satisfactory. Constraint 4 is a straightforward resource constraint that reduces to

$$1.5x_1 + 3x_2 + 5x_3 \leq 6000 \qquad \text{(Steel constraint)}$$

Constraint 5 is a straightforward resource usage constraint that reduces to

$$30x_1 + 25x_2 + 40x_3 \leq 60{,}000 \qquad \text{(Labor constraint)}$$

After noting that $x_i \geq 0$ and that x_i must be an integer, we obtain the following IP:

$$\max z = 2x_1 + 3x_2 + 4x_3$$
$$\text{s.t.} \qquad x_1 \leq 2000y_1$$
$$1000 - x_1 \leq 2000(1 - y_1)$$
$$x_2 \leq 2000y_2$$
$$1000 - x_2 \leq 2000(1 - y_2)$$
$$x_3 \leq 1200y_3$$
$$1000 - x_3 \leq 1200(1 - y_3)$$
$$1.5x_1 + 3x_2 + 5x_3 \leq 6000 \qquad \text{(Steel constraint)}$$
$$30x_1 + 25x_2 + 40x_3 \leq 60{,}000 \qquad \text{(Labor constraint)}$$
$$x_1, x_2, x_3 \geq 0; \; x_1, x_2, x_3 \text{ integer}$$
$$y_1, y_2, y_3 = 0 \text{ or } 1$$

The optimal solution to the IP is $z = 6000$, $x_2 = 2000$, $y_2 = 1$, $y_1 = y_3 = x_1 = x_3 = 0$. Thus, Dorian should produce 2000 midsize cars. If Dorian had not been required to manufacture at least 1000 cars of each type, the optimal solution would have been to produce 570 compacts and 1715 midsize cars. ◆

IF-THEN CONSTRAINTS

In many applications, the following situation occurs: We want to ensure that if a constraint $f(x_1, x_2, \ldots, x_n) > 0$ is satisfied, then the constraint $g(x_1, x_2, \ldots, x_n) \geq 0$ must be satisfied, while if $f(x_1, x_2, \ldots, x_n) > 0$ is not satisfied, then $g(x_1, x_2, \ldots, x_n) \geq 0$ may or may not be satisfied. In short, we wish to ensure that $f(x_1, x_2, \ldots, x_n) > 0$ implies $g(x_1, x_2, \ldots, x_n) \geq 0$.

To ensure this, we include the following constraints in the formulation:

$$-g(x_1, x_2, \ldots, x_n) \leq My \tag{28}$$
$$f(x_1, x_2, \ldots, x_n) \leq M(1 - y) \tag{29}$$
$$y = 0 \text{ or } 1$$

As usual, M is a large positive number. (M must be chosen large enough so that $f \leq M$ and $-g \leq M$ hold for all values of $x_1, x_2, \ldots, x_n$ that satisfy the other constraints in the problem.) Observe that if $f > 0$, then (29) can be satisfied only if $y = 0$. Then (28) implies $-g \leq 0$, or $g \geq 0$, which is the desired result. Thus, if $f > 0$, then (28) and (29) ensure that $g \geq 0$. Also, if $f > 0$ is not satisfied, then (29) allows $y = 0$ or $y = 1$. By choosing $y = 1$, (28) is automatically satisfied. Thus, if $f > 0$ is not satisfied, the values of $x_1, x_2, \ldots, x_n$ are unrestricted and $g < 0$ or $g \geq 0$ are both possible.

To illustrate the use of this idea, suppose we add the following constraint to the Nickles lockbox problem: If customers in region 1 send their payments to city 1, no other customers may send their payments to city 1. Mathematically, this restriction may be expressed by

$$\text{If } x_{11} = 1, \quad \text{then} \quad x_{21} = x_{31} = x_{41} = 0 \tag{30}$$

Since all x_{ij} must equal 0 or 1, (30) may be written as

$$\text{If } x_{11} > 0, \quad \text{then} \quad x_{21} + x_{31} + x_{41} \leq 0, \quad \text{or} \quad -x_{21} - x_{31} - x_{41} \geq 0 \tag{30'}$$

If we define $f = x_{11}$ and $g = -x_{21} - x_{31} - x_{41}$, we can use (28) and (29) to express (30') (and therefore (30)) by the following two constraints:

$$x_{21} + x_{31} + x_{41} \leq My$$
$$x_{11} \leq M(1 - y)$$
$$y = 0 \text{ or } 1$$

Since $-g$ and f can never exceed 3, we can choose $M = 3$ and add the following constraints to the original lockbox formulation:

$$x_{21} + x_{31} + x_{41} \leq 3y$$
$$x_{11} \leq 3(1 - y)$$
$$y = 0 \text{ or } 1$$

INTEGER PROGRAMMING AND PIECEWISE LINEAR FUNCTIONS

The next example shows how 0–1 variables can be used to model optimization problems involving piecewise linear functions. A **piecewise linear function** is a function that consists of several straight line segments. The piecewise linear function in Figure 2 is made up of four straight line segments. The points where the slope of the piecewise linear function changes (or the range of definition of the function ends) are called the **break points** of the function. Thus, 0, 10, 30, 40, and 50 are the break points of the function pictured in Figure 2.

To illustrate why piecewise linear functions can occur in applications, suppose we manufacture gasoline from oil. In purchasing oil from our supplier, we receive a quantity

Figure 2
A Piecewise Linear
Function

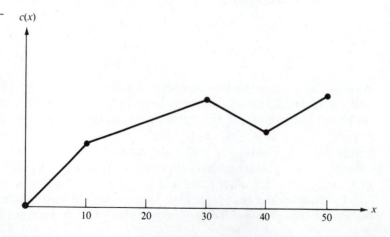

discount. The first 500 gallons of oil purchased cost 25¢ per gallon; the next 500 gallons cost 20¢ per gallon; and the next 500 gallons cost 15¢ per gallon. At most 1500 gallons of oil can be purchased. Let x be the number of gallons of oil purchased and $c(x)$ be the cost (in cents) of purchasing x gallons of oil. For $x \leq 0$, $c(x) = 0$. Then for $0 \leq x \leq 500$, $c(x) = 25x$. For $500 \leq x \leq 1000$, $c(x) =$ (cost of purchasing first 500 gallons at 25¢ per gallon) + (cost of purchasing next $x - 500$ gallons at 20¢ per gallon) $= 25(500) + 20(x - 500) = 20x + 2500$. For $1000 \leq x \leq 1500$, $c(x) =$ (cost of purchasing first 1000 gallons) + (cost of purchasing next $x - 1000$ gallons at 15¢ per gallon) $= c(1000) + 15(x - 1000) = 7500 + 15x$. Thus, $c(x)$ has break points 0, 500, 1000, and 1500 and is graphed in Figure 3.

Figure 3
Cost of Purchasing Oil

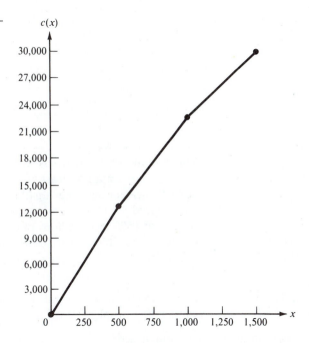

Since a piecewise linear function is not a linear function, one might think that linear programming could not be used to solve optimization problems involving piecewise linear functions. By using 0–1 variables, however, piecewise linear functions can be represented in linear form. Suppose that a piecewise linear function $f(x)$ has break points $b_1, b_2, \ldots, b_n$. For some k ($k = 1, 2, \ldots, n - 1$), $b_k \leq x \leq b_{k+1}$. Then, for some number z_k ($0 \leq z_k \leq 1$), x may be written as

$$x = z_k b_k + (1 - z_k)b_{k+1}$$

Since $f(x)$ is linear for $b_k \leq x \leq b_{k+1}$, we may write

$$f(x) = z_k f(b_k) + (1 - z_k)f(b_{k+1})$$

To illustrate the idea, take $x = 800$ in our oil example. Then we have $b_2 = 500 \leq 800 \leq 1000 = b_3$, and we may write

$$x = \tfrac{2}{5}(500) + \tfrac{3}{5}(1000)$$
$$f(x) = f(800) = \tfrac{2}{5}f(500) + \tfrac{3}{5}f(1000)$$
$$= \tfrac{2}{5}(12,500) + \tfrac{3}{5}(22,500) = 18,500$$

We are now ready to describe the method used to express a piecewise linear function via linear constraints and 0–1 variables:

Step 1 Wherever $f(x)$ occurs in the optimization problem, replace $f(x)$ by $z_1 f(b_1) + z_2 f(b_2) + \cdots + z_n f(b_n)$.

Step 2 Add the following constraints to the problem:

$$z_1 \leq y_1, z_2 \leq y_1 + y_2, z_3 \leq y_2 + y_3, \ldots, z_{n-1} \leq y_{n-2} + y_{n-1}, z_n \leq y_{n-1}$$
$$y_1 + y_2 + \cdots + y_{n-1} = 1$$
$$z_1 + z_2 + \cdots + z_n = 1$$
$$x = z_1 b_1 + z_2 b_2 + \cdots + z_n b_n$$
$$y_i = 0 \text{ or } 1 \quad (i = 1, 2, \ldots, n - 1); \qquad z_i \geq 0 \quad (i = 1, 2, \ldots, n)$$

E X A M P L E
7

Euing Gas produces two types of gasoline (gas 1 and gas 2) from two types of oil (oil 1 and oil 2). Each gallon of gas 1 must contain at least 50 percent oil 1, and each gallon of gas 2 must contain at least 60 percent oil 1. Each gallon of gas 1 can be sold for 12¢, and each gallon of gas 2 can be sold for 14¢. At present, 500 gallons of oil 1 and 1000 gallons of oil 2 are available. Up to 1500 more gallons of oil 1 can be purchased at the following prices: first 500 gallons, 25¢/gallon; next 500 gallons, 20¢/gallon; next 500 gallons, 15¢/gallon. Formulate an IP that will maximize Euing's profits (revenues − purchasing costs).

Solution

Except for the fact that the cost of purchasing additional oil 1 is a piecewise linear function, this is a straightforward blending problem. With this in mind, we define

$$x = \text{amount of oil 1 purchased}$$
$$x_{ij} = \text{amount of oil } i \text{ used to produce gas } j \qquad (i, j = 1, 2)$$

Then (in cents)

Total revenue − cost of purchasing oil $1 = 12(x_{11} + x_{21}) + 14(x_{12} + x_{22}) - c(x)$

As we have seen previously,

$$c(x) = \begin{cases} 25x & (0 \leq x \leq 500) \\ 20x + 2500 & (500 \leq x \leq 1000) \\ 15x + 7500 & (1000 \leq x \leq 1500) \end{cases}$$

Thus, Euing's objective function is to maximize

$$z = 12x_{11} + 12x_{21} + 14x_{12} + 14x_{22} - c(x)$$

Euing faces the following constraints:

Constraint 1 Euing can use at most $x + 500$ gallons of oil 1.

Constraint 2 Euing can use at most 1000 gallons of oil 2.

Constraint 3 The oil mixed to make gas 1 must be at least 50% oil 1.

Constraint 4 The oil mixed to make gas 2 must be at least 60% oil 1.

Constraint 1 yields

$$x_{11} + x_{12} \leq x + 500$$

Constraint 2 yields

$$x_{21} + x_{22} \leq 1000$$

Constraint 3 yields

$$\frac{x_{11}}{x_{11} + x_{21}} \geq 0.5 \quad \text{or} \quad 0.5x_{11} - 0.5x_{21} \geq 0$$

Constraint 4 yields

$$\frac{x_{12}}{x_{12} + x_{22}} \geq 0.6 \quad \text{or} \quad 0.4x_{12} - 0.6x_{22} \geq 0$$

Also all variables must be nonnegative. Thus, Euing Gas must solve the following optimization problem:

$$
\begin{aligned}
\max z = {}& 12x_{11} + 12x_{21} + 14x_{12} + 14x_{22} - c(x) \\
\text{s.t.} \quad & x_{11} \qquad\quad + \quad x_{12} \qquad\qquad \leq x + 500 \\
& \qquad\qquad x_{21} \qquad\quad + \quad x_{22} \leq 1000 \\
& 0.5x_{11} - 0.5x_{21} \qquad\qquad\qquad\quad \geq 0 \\
& \qquad\qquad\qquad 0.4x_{12} - 0.6x_{22} \geq 0 \\
& x_{ij} \geq 0, 0 \leq x \leq 1500
\end{aligned}
$$

Since $c(x)$ is a piecewise linear function, the objective function is not a linear function of x, and this optimization problem is not an LP. By using the method described earlier, however, we can transform this problem into an IP. After recalling that the break points for $c(x)$ are 0, 500, 1000, and 1500, we proceed as follows:

Step 1 Replace $c(x)$ by $c(x) = z_1 c(0) + z_2 c(500) + z_3 c(1000) + z_4 c(1500)$.

Step 2 Add the following constraints:

$$x = 0z_1 + 500z_2 + 1000z_3 + 1500z_4$$

$$z_1 \leq y_1, z_2 \leq y_1 + y_2, z_3 \leq y_2 + y_3, z_4 \leq y_3$$

$$z_1 + z_2 + z_3 + z_4 = 1, \qquad y_1 + y_2 + y_3 = 1$$

$$y_i = 0 \text{ or } 1 \ (i = 1, 2, 3); z_i \geq 0 \ (i = 1, 2, 3, 4)$$

Our new formulation is the following IP:

$$\max z = 12x_{11} + 12x_{21} + 14x_{12} + 14x_{22} - z_1 c(0) - z_2 c(500)$$
$$- z_3 c(1000) - z_4 c(1500)$$

$$\text{s.t.} \quad x_{11} \qquad + \quad x_{12} \qquad \qquad \leq x + 500$$

$$x_{21} \qquad + \quad x_{22} \leq 1000$$

$$0.5x_{11} - 0.5x_{21} \qquad \qquad \geq 0$$

$$0.4x_{12} - 0.6x_{22} \geq 0$$

$$x = 0z_1 + 500z_2 + 1000z_3 + 1500z_4 \tag{31}$$

$$z_1 \leq y_1 \tag{32}$$

$$z_2 \leq y_1 + y_2 \tag{33}$$

$$z_3 \leq y_2 + y_3 \tag{34}$$

$$z_4 \leq y_3 \tag{35}$$

$$y_1 + y_2 + y_3 = 1 \tag{36}$$

$$z_1 + z_2 + z_3 + z_4 = 1 \tag{37}$$

$$y_i = 0 \text{ or } 1 \quad (i = 1, 2, 3); \; z_i \geq 0 \; (i = 1, 2, 3, 4)$$

$$x_{ij} \geq 0$$

To see why this formulation works, observe that since $y_1 + y_2 + y_3 = 1$ and $y_i = 0$ or 1, exactly one of the y_i's will equal 1, and the others will equal 0. Now, (32)–(37) imply that if $y_i = 1$, then z_i and z_{i+1} may be positive, but all the other z_i's must equal zero. For instance, if $y_2 = 1$, then $y_1 = y_3 = 0$. Then (32)–(35) become $z_1 \leq 0$, $z_2 \leq 1$, $z_3 \leq 1$, and $z_4 \leq 0$. These constraints force $z_1 = z_4 = 0$ and allow z_2 and z_3 to be any nonnegative number less than or equal to 1. We can now show that (31)–(37) correctly represent the piecewise linear function $c(x)$. Choose any value of x, say $x = 800$. Note that $b_2 = 500 \leq 800 \leq 1000 = b_3$. For $x = 800$, what values do our constraints assign to y_1, y_2, and y_3? The value $y_1 = 1$ is impossible, because if $y_1 = 1$, then $y_2 = y_3 = 0$. Then (34)–(35) force $z_3 = z_4 = 0$. Then (31) reduces to $800 = x = 500z_2$, which cannot be satisfied by $z_2 \leq 1$. Similarly, $y_3 = 1$ is impossible. If we try $y_2 = 1$, (32) and (35) force $z_1 = z_4 = 0$. Then (33) and (34) imply $z_2 \leq 1$ and $z_3 \leq 1$. Now (31) becomes $800 = x = 500z_2 + 1000z_3$. Since $z_2 + z_3 = 1$, we obtain $z_2 = \frac{2}{5}$ and $z_3 = \frac{3}{5}$. Now the objective function reduces to

$$12x_{11} + 12x_{21} + 14x_{12} + 14x_{22} - \frac{2c(500)}{5} - \frac{3c(1000)}{5}$$

Since

$$c(800) = \frac{2c(500)}{5} + \frac{3c(1000)}{5}$$

our objective function yields the correct value of Euing's profits!

The optimal solution to Euing's problem is $z = 12{,}500$, $x = 1000$, $x_{12} = 1500$, $x_{22} = 1000$, $y_3 = z_3 = 1$. Thus, Euing should purchase 1000 gallons of oil 1 and produce 2500 gallons of gas 2.

◆

In general, constraints of the form (31)–(37) ensure that if $b_i \leq x \leq b_{i+1}$, then $y_i = 1$ and only z_i and z_{i+1} can be positive. Since $c(x)$ is linear for $b_i \leq x \leq b_{i+1}$, the objective function will assign the correct value to $c(x)$.

If a piecewise linear function $f(x)$ involved in a formulation has the property that the slope of $f(x)$ becomes less favorable to the decision maker as x increases, then the tedious IP formulation we have just described is unnecessary.

E X A M P L E 8

Dorian Auto has a $20,000 advertising budget. Dorian can purchase full-page ads in two magazines: *Inside Jocks* (IJ) and *Family Square* (FS). An exposure occurs when a person reads a Dorian Auto ad for the first time. The number of exposures generated by each ad in IJ is as follows: ads 1–6, 10,000 exposures; ads 7–10, 3000 exposures; ads 11–15, 2500 exposures; ads 16+, zero exposures. For example, 8 ads in IJ would generate $6(10,000) + 2(3000) = 66,000$ exposures. The number of exposures generated by each ad in FS is as follows: ads 1–4, 8000 exposures; ads 5–12, 6000 exposures; ads 13–15, 2000 exposures; ads 16+, zero exposures. Thus, 13 ads in FS would generate $4(8000) + 8(6000) + 1(2000) = 82,000$ exposures. Each full-page ad in either magazine costs $1000. Assume there is no overlap in the readership of the two magazines. Formulate an IP to maximize the number of exposures that Dorian can obtain with limited advertising funds.

Solution

If we define

$$x_1 = \text{number of IJ ads yielding 10,000 exposures}$$
$$x_2 = \text{number of IJ ads yielding 3000 exposures}$$
$$x_3 = \text{number of IJ ads yielding 2500 exposures}$$
$$y_1 = \text{number of FS ads yielding 8000 exposures}$$
$$y_2 = \text{number of FS ads yielding 6000 exposures}$$
$$y_3 = \text{number of FS ads yielding 2000 exposures}$$

the total number of exposures (in thousands) is given by

$$10x_1 + 3x_2 + 2.5x_3 + 8y_1 + 6y_2 + 2y_3$$

Thus, Dorian wishes to maximize

$$z = 10x_1 + 3x_2 + 2.5x_3 + 8y_1 + 6y_2 + 2y_3$$

Since the total amount spent by Dorian (in thousands) is just the total number of ads placed in both magazines, Dorian's budget constraint may be written as

$$x_1 + x_2 + x_3 + y_1 + y_2 + y_3 \leq 20$$

The statement of the problem implies that $x_1 \leq 6$, $x_2 \leq 4$, $x_3 \leq 5$, $y_1 \leq 4$, $y_2 \leq 8$, and $y_3 \leq 3$ all must hold. Adding the sign restrictions on each variable and noting that each variable must be an integer, we obtain the following IP:

$$\max z = 10x_1 + 3x_2 + 2.5x_3 + 8y_1 + 6y_2 + 2y_3$$
$$\text{s.t.} \quad x_1 + x_2 + x_3 + y_1 + y_2 + y_3 \leq 20$$
$$x_1 \qquad\qquad\qquad\qquad \leq 6$$
$$x_2 \qquad\qquad\qquad \leq 4$$

$$x_3 \qquad\qquad\qquad \le 5$$
$$y_1 \qquad\qquad \le 4$$
$$y_2 \qquad\quad \le 8$$
$$y_3 \le 3$$
$$x_i, y_i \text{ integer} \quad (i = 1, 2, 3)$$
$$x_i, y_i \ge 0 \quad (i = 1, 2, 3)$$

The reader might observe that the statement of the problem implies that x_2 cannot be positive unless x_1 assumes its maximum value of 6. Similarly, x_3 cannot be positive unless x_2 assumes its maximum value of 4. Since x_1 ads generate more exposures than x_2 ads, however, the act of maximizing ensures that x_2 will be positive only if x_1 has been made as large as possible. Similarly, since x_3 ads generate fewer exposures than x_2 ads, x_3 will be positive only if x_2 assumes its maximum value. (Also, y_2 will be positive only if $y_1 = 4$, and y_3 will be positive only if $y_2 = 8$.)

The optimal solution to Dorian's IP is $z = 146,000$, $x_1 = 6$, $x_2 = 2$, $y_1 = 4$, $y_2 = 8$, $x_3 = 0$, $y_3 = 0$. Thus, Dorian will place $x_1 + x_2 = 8$ ads in IJ and $y_1 + y_2 = 12$ ads in FS.

◆

In Example 8, additional advertising in a magazine yielded diminishing returns. This ensured that x_i (y_i) would be positive only if x_{i-1} (y_{i-1}) assumed its maximum value. If additional advertising generated increasing returns, this formulation would not yield the correct solution. For example, suppose that the number of exposures generated by each IJ ad was as follows: ads 1–6, 2500 exposures; ads 7–10, 3000 exposures; ads 11–15, 10,000 exposures; and that the number of exposures generated by each FS is as follows: ads 1–4, 2000 exposures; ads 5–12, 6000 exposures; ads 13–15, 8000 exposures.

If we define

$$x_1 = \text{number of IJ ads generating 2500 exposures}$$
$$x_2 = \text{number of IJ ads generating 3000 exposures}$$
$$x_3 = \text{number of IJ ads generating 10,000 exposures}$$
$$y_1 = \text{number of FS ads generating 2000 exposures}$$
$$y_2 = \text{number of FS ads generating 6000 exposures}$$
$$y_3 = \text{number of FS ads generating 8000 exposures}$$

the reasoning used in the previous example would lead to the following formulation:

$$\max z = 2.5x_1 + 3x_2 + 10x_3 + 2y_1 + 6y_2 + 8y_3$$
$$\text{s.t.} \quad x_1 + x_2 + x_3 + y_1 + y_2 + y_3 \le 20$$
$$x_1 \qquad\qquad\qquad\qquad \le 6$$
$$x_2 \qquad\qquad\qquad \le 4$$
$$x_3 \qquad\qquad\quad \le 5$$
$$y_1 \qquad\qquad \le 4$$
$$y_2 \qquad\quad \le 8$$
$$y_3 \le 3$$

$$x_i, y_i \text{ integer} \quad (i = 1, 2, 3)$$

$$x_i, y_i \geq 0 \quad (i = 1, 2, 3)$$

The optimal solution to this IP is $x_3 = 5$, $y_3 = 3$, $y_2 = 8$, $x_2 = 4$, $x_1 = 0$, $y_1 = 0$, which cannot be correct. According to this solution, $x_1 + x_2 + x_3 = 9$ ads should be placed in IJ. If 9 ads are placed in IJ, however, then it must be that $x_1 = 6$ and $x_2 = 3$. Therefore, we see that the type of formulation used in the Dorian Auto example is correct only if the piecewise linear objective function has a less favorable slope for larger values of x. In our second example, the effectiveness of an ad increased as the number of ads in a magazine increased, and the act of maximizing will not ensure that x_i can be positive only if x_{i-1} assumes its maximum value. In this case, the approach used in the Euing Gas example would yield a correct formulation (see Problem 8).

◆ PROBLEMS

GROUP A

1. Coach Night is trying to choose the starting lineup for the basketball team. The team consists of seven players who have been rated (on a scale of 1 = poor to 3 = excellent) according to their ball-handling, shooting, rebounding, and defensive abilities. The positions that each player is allowed to play and the player's abilities are listed in Table 9.

The five-player starting lineup must satisfy the following restrictions:

1. At least 4 members of the starting team must be able to play guard, at least 2 members must be able to play forward, and at least 1 member of the starting team must be able to play center.

2. The average ball-handling, shooting, and rebounding level of the starting lineup must be at least 2.

3. If player 3 starts, then player 6 cannot start.

4. If player 1 starts, then players 4 and 5 must both start.

5. Either player 2 or player 3 must start.

Given these constraints, coach Night wants to maximize the total defensive ability of the starting team. Formulate an IP that will help coach Night choose his starting team.

Table 9

PLAYER	POSITION	BALL-HANDLING	SHOOTING	REBOUNDING	DEFENSE
1	G	3	3	1	3
2	C	2	1	3	2
3	G-F	2	3	2	2
4	F-C	1	3	3	1
5	G-F	1	3	1	2
6	F-C	3	1	2	3
7	G-F	3	2	2	1

2. Because of excessive pollution on the Momiss River, the state of Momiss is going to build some pollution control stations. Three sites (sites 1, 2, and 3) are under consideration. Momiss is interested in controlling the pollution levels of two pollutants (pollutants 1 and 2). The state legislature requires that at least 80,000 tons of pollutant 1 and at least 50,000 tons of pollutant 2 be removed from the river. The relevant data for this problem are shown in Table 10. Formulate an IP to minimize the cost of meeting the state legislature's goals.

3. A manufacturer can sell product 1 at a profit of $2/unit and product 2 at a profit of $5/unit. Three units of raw material are needed to manufacture 1 unit of product 1, and 6 units of raw material are needed to manufacture 1 unit of product 2. A total of 120 units of raw material are available. If any of product 1 is produced, a setup cost of $10 is incurred, and if any of product 2 is produced, a setup cost of $20 is incurred. Formulate an IP to maximize profits.

4. Suppose we add the following restriction to Example 1 (Stockco): If investments 2 and 3 are chosen, then investment 4 must be chosen. What constraints would be added to the formulation given in the text?

5. How would the following restrictions modify the formulation of Example 6 (Dorian car sizes)? (Do each part separately.)
(a) If midsize cars are produced, compacts must also be produced.
(b) Either compacts or large cars must be manufactured.

6. In order to graduate from Basketweavers University with a major in operations research, a student must complete at least two math courses, at least two OR courses, and at least two computer courses. Some courses can be used to fulfill more than requirement: Calculus can fulfill

the math requirement; Operations Research, math and OR requirements; Data Structures, computer and math requirements; Business Statistics, math and OR requirements; Computer Simulation, OR and computer requirements; Introduction to Computer Programming, computer requirement; and Forecasting, OR and math requirements.

Some courses are prerequisites for others: Calculus is a prerequisite for Business Statistics; Introduction to Computer Programming is a prerequisite for Computer Simulation and for Data Structures; and Business Statistics is a prerequisite for Forecasting. Formulate an IP that minimizes the number of courses needed to satisfy the major requirements.

7. In Example 7 (Euing Gas), suppose that $x = 300$. What would be the values of y_1, y_2, y_3, z_1, z_2, z_3, and z_4? How about if $x = 1200$?

8. Formulate an IP to solve the Dorian Auto problem for the advertising data that exhibit increasing returns as more ads are placed in a magazine.

9. How can integer programming be used to ensure that the variable x can assume only the values 1, 2, 3, and 4?

10. If x and y are integers, how could you ensure that $x + y \le 3$, $2x + 5y \le 12$, or both are satisfied by x and y?

11. If x and y are both integers, how would you ensure that whenever $x \le 2$, then $y \le 3$?

12. A company is considering opening warehouses in four cities: New York, Los Angeles, Chicago, and Atlanta. Each warehouse can ship 100 units per week. The weekly fixed cost of keeping each warehouse open is $400 for New York, $500 for Los Angeles, $300 for Chicago, and $150 for Atlanta. Region 1 of the country requires 80 units per week, region 2 requires 70 units per week, and region

Table 10

	COST OF BUILDING STATION	COST OF TREATING 1 TON WATER	AMOUNT REMOVED PER TON OF WATER	
			Pollutant 1	*Pollutant 2*
Site 1	$100,000	$20	0.40 ton	0.30 ton
Site 2	$60,000	$30	0.25 ton	0.20 ton
Site 3	$40,000	$40	0.20 ton	0.25 ton

Table 11

FROM	TO		
	Region 1	*Region 2*	*Region 3*
New York	$20	$40	$50
Los Angeles	$48	$15	$26
Chicago	$26	$35	$18
Atlanta	$24	$50	$35

3 requires 40 units per week. The costs (including production and shipping costs) of sending 1 unit from a plant to a region are shown in Table 11. We wish to meet weekly demands at minimum cost, subject to the preceding information and the following restrictions:

1. If the New York warehouse is opened, then the Los Angeles warehouse must be opened.

2. At most two warehouses can be opened.

3. Either the Atlanta or the Los Angeles warehouse must be opened.

Formulate an IP that can be used to minimize the weekly costs of meeting demand.

13. Glueco produces three types of glue on two different production lines. Each line can be utilized by up to seven workers at a time. Workers on production line 1 are paid $500 per week, and workers on production line 2 are paid $900 per week. It costs $1000 to set up production line 1 for a week of production, and it costs $2000 to set up production line 2 for a week of production. During a week on a production line, each worker produces the number of units of glue shown in Table 12. Each week, at least 120 units of glue 1, at least 150 units of glue 2, and at least 200 units of glue 3 must be produced. Formulate an IP to minimize the total cost of meeting weekly demands.

Table 12

	GLUE 1	GLUE 2	GLUE 3
Production line 1	20	30	40
Production line 2	50	35	45

14.[†] The manager of State University's DED computer wants to be able to access five different files. These files are scattered on ten disks as shown in Table 13. The amount of storage required by each disk is as follows: disk 1, 3K;

[†] Based on Day (1965).

Table 13

	DISK									
	1	2	3	4	5	6	7	8	9	10
File 1	x	x		x	x			x	x	
File 2	x		x							
File 3		x			x		x			x
File 4			x			x		x		
File 5	x	x		x		x	x		x	x

disk 2, 5K; disk 3, 1K; disk 4, 2K; disk 5, 1K; disk 6, 4K; disk 7, 3K; disk 8, 1K; disk 9, 2K; disk 10, 2K.

(a) Formulate an IP that determines a set of disks requiring the minimum amount of storage such that each file is on at least one of the disks. For a given disk, we must either store the entire disk or store none of the disk; we cannot store part of a disk.

(b) Modify your formulation so that if disk 3 or disk 5 is used, then disk 2 must also be used.

15. Fruit Computer produces two types of computers: Pear computers and Apricot computers. Relevant data are given in Table 14. A total of 3000 chips and 1200 hours of labor are available. Formulate an IP to help Fruit maximize profits.

16. The Lotus Point Condo Project will contain both homes and apartments. The site can accommodate up to 10,000 dwelling units. The project must contain a recreation project: either a swimming-tennis complex or a sailboat marina, but not both. If a marina is built, the number of homes in the project must be at least triple the number of apartments in the project. A marina will cost $1.2 million, and a swimming-tennis complex will cost $2.8 million. The developers believe that each apartment will yield revenues with a net present value of $48,000, and each home will yield revenues with a net present value of $46,000. Each home (or apartment) costs $40,000 to build. Formulate an IP to help Lotus Point maximize profits.

Table 14

	LABOR	CHIPS	EQUIPMENT COSTS	SELLING PRICE
Pear	1 hour	2	$5000	$400
Apricot	2 hours	5	$7000	$900

Table 15

FROM	Customer 1	Customer 2	Customer 3
Evansville	16¢	34¢	26¢
Indianapolis	40¢	30¢	35¢
South Bend	45¢	45¢	23¢

GROUP B

17.[†] Breadco Bakeries is a new bakery chain that sells bread to customers throughout the state of Indiana. Breadco is considering building bakeries in three locations: Evansville, Indianapolis, and South Bend. Each bakery can bake up to 900,000 loaves of bread each year. The cost of building a bakery at each site is $5 million in Evansville, $4 million in Indianapolis, and $4.5 million in South Bend. To simplify the problem, we assume that Breadco has only three customers, whose demands each year are 700,000 loaves (customer 1); 400,000 loaves (customer 2); and 300,000 loaves (customer 3). The total cost of baking and shipping a loaf of bread to a customer is given in Table 15.

Assume that future shipping and production costs are discounted at a rate of $11\frac{1}{9}\%$ per year. Assume that once built, a bakery lasts forever. Formulate an IP to minimize Breadco's total cost of meeting demands (present and future). (*Hint:* You will need the fact that for $x < 1$, $a + ax + ax^2 + ax^3 + \cdots = a/(1 - x)$.) How would you modify the formulation if either Evansville or South Bend must produce at least 800,000 loaves per year?

18.[‡] Speaker's Clearinghouse must disburse sweepstakes checks to winners in four different regions of the country: Southeast (SE), Northeast (NE), Far West (FW), and Midwest (MW). The average daily amount of the checks written to winners in each region of the country is as follows: SE, $40,000; NE, $60,000; FW, $30,000; MW, $50,000. Speaker's must issue the checks the day they find

out a customer has won. They can delay winners from quickly cashing their checks by giving a winner a check drawn on an out-of-the-way bank (this will cause the check to clear slowly). Four bank sites are under consideration: Frosbite Falls, Montana (FF), Redville, South Carolina (R), Painted Forest, Arizona (PF), and Beanville, Maine (B). The annual cost of maintaining an account at each bank is as follows: FF, $50,000; R, $40,000; PF, $30,000; B, $20,000. Each bank has a requirement that the average daily amount of checks written cannot exceed $90,000. The average number of days is takes a check to clear is given in Table 16. Assuming that money invested by Speaker's earns 15% per year, where should the company have bank accounts, and from which bank should a given customer's check be written?

Table 16

	FF	R	PF	B
SE	7	2	6	5
NE	8	4	5	3
FW	4	8	2	11
MW	5	4	7	5

19.[§] Governor Blue of the state of Berry is attempting to get the state legislature to gerrymander Berry's congressional districts. The state consists of ten cities, and the numbers of registered Republicans and Democrats (in thousands) in each city are shown in Table 17. Berry has

---

[†]Based on Efroymson and Ray (1966).
[‡]Based on Shanker and Zoltners (1972).
[§]Based on Garfinkel and Nemhauser (1970).

Table 17

	REPUBLICANS	DEMOCRATS
City 1	80	34
City 2	60	44
City 3	40	44
City 4	20	24
City 5	40	114
City 6	40	64
City 7	70	14
City 8	50	44
City 9	70	54
City 10	70	64

five congressional representatives. To form congressional districts, cities must be grouped according to the following restrictions:

1. All voters in a city must be in the same district.

2. Each district must contain between 150,000 and 250,000 voters (there are no independent voters). Governor Blue is a Democrat. Assume that each voter always votes a straight party ticket. Formulate an IP to help Governor Blue maximize the number of Democrats who will win congressional seats.

20.[†] The Father Domino Company sells copying machines. A major factor in making a sale is Domino's quick service. Domino sells copiers in six cities: Boston, New York, Philadelphia, Washington, Providence, and Atlantic City. The annual sales of copiers are projected to depend on whether a service representative is within 150 miles of a city (see Table 18).

Each copier costs $500 to produce and sells for $1000. The annual cost per service representative is $80,000. Domino must determine in which of its markets to base a service representative. Only Boston, New York, Philadelphia, and Washington are under consideration as bases for service representatives. The distance (in miles) between the cities is shown in Table 19. Formulate an IP that will help Domino maximize annual profits.

Table 19

	BOSTON	N.Y.	PHILA.	WASH.
Boston	0	222	310	441
New York	222	0	89	241
Philadelphia	310	89	0	146
Washington	441	241	146	0
Providence	47	186	255	376
Atlantic City	350	123	82	178

21.[‡] Thailand inducts naval draftees at three drafting centers. Then the draftees must each be sent to one of three naval bases for training. The cost of transporting a draftee from a drafting center to a base is given in Table 20. Each year, 1000 men are inducted at center 1, 600 are inducted at center 2, and 700 are inducted at center 3. Base 1 can train 1000 men a year, base 2 can train 800 men per year, and base 3 can train 700 men per year. After the inductees are trained, they are sent to Thailand's main naval base (B). They may be transported on either a small ship or a large ship. It costs $5000 plus $2 per mile to use a small ship. A small ship can transport up to 200 men to the main base. A small ship may visit up to two bases on its way to the main base. Seven small and five large ships are available. It costs $10,000 plus $3 per mile to use a large ship. A large ship may visit up to three bases on its way to the main base and may transport up to 500 men. The possible "tours" for each type of ship are given in Table 21.

Table 20

FROM	TO		
	Base 1	*Base 2*	*Base 3*
Center 1	$200	$200	$300
Center 2	$300	$400	$220
Center 3	$300	$400	$250

Table 18

REPRESENTATIVE WITHIN 150 MILES?	SALES					
	Boston	*N.Y.*	*Phila.*	*Wash.*	*Prov.*	*Atl. City*
Yes	700	1000	900	800	400	450
No	500	750	700	450	200	300

[†] Based on Gelb and Khumawala (1984).   [‡] Based on Choypeng, Puakpong, and Rosenthal (1986).

Table 21

TOUR NUMBER	LOCATIONS VISITED	MILES TRAVELED
1	B–1–B	370
2	B–1–2–B	515
3	B–2–3–B	665
4	B–2–B	460
5	B–3–B	600
6	B–1–3–B	640
7	B–1–2–3–B	720

Table 22

SONG	TYPE	LENGTH (In Minutes)
1	Ballad	4
2	Hit	5
3	Ballad	3
4	Hit	2
5	Ballad	4
6	Hit	3
7		5
8	Ballad and hit	4

Assume that the assignment of draftees to training bases is done using the transportation method. Then formulate an IP that will minimize the total cost incurred in sending the men from the training bases to the main base. (*Hint:* Let y_{ij} = number of men sent by tour i from base j to main base (B) on a small ship, x_{ij} = number of men sent by tour i from base j to main base on a large ship, S_i = number of times tour i is used by a small ship, and L_i = number of times tour i is used by a large ship.)

22. You have been assigned to arrange the songs on the cassette version of Madonna's latest album. A cassette tape has two sides (side 1 and side 2). The songs on each side of the cassette must total between 14 and 16 minutes in length. The length and type of each song are given in Table 22. The assignment of songs to the tape must satisfy the following conditions:

1. Each side must have exactly two ballads.
2. Side 1 must have at least 3 hit songs.
3. Either song 5 or song 6 must be on side 1.
4. If songs 2 and 4 are on side 1, then song 5 must be on side 2.

Explain how you could use an integer programming formulation to determine whether there is an arrangement of songs satisfying these restrictions.

23. Cousin Bruzie of radio station WABC schedules radio commercials in 60-second blocks. This hour, they have sold commercial time for commercials of 15, 16, 20, 25, 30, 35, 40, and 50 seconds. Formulate an integer programming model that can be used to determine the minimum number of 60-second blocks of commercials that must be scheduled in order to fit in all of the current hour's commercials. (*Hint:* Certainly no more than eight blocks of time are needed. Let $y_i = 1$ if block i is used and $y_i = 0$ otherwise.)

24.[†] A Sunco oil delivery truck contains five compartments, holding up to 2700, 2800, 1100, 1800, and 3400 gallons of fuel, respectively. The company must deliver three types of fuel (super, regular, and unleaded) to a customer. The demands, penalty per gallon short, and the maximum allowed shortage are given in Table 23. Each compartment of the truck can carry only one type of gasoline. Formulate an integer programming problem whose solution will tell Sunco how to load the truck in a way that minimizes shortage costs.

25.[‡] Simon's Mall has 10,000 sq ft of space to rent and wants to determine the types of stores that should occupy the mall. The minimum number and maximum number of each type of store (along with the square footage of each

Table 23

TYPE OF GASOLINE	DEMAND	COST PER GALLON SHORT	MAXIMUM ALLOWED SHORTAGE
Super	2900	$10	500
Regular	4000	$8	500
Unleaded	4900	$6	500

[†] Based on Brown (1987).
[‡] Based on Bean et al. (1988).

Table 24

STORE TYPE	SQUARE FOOTAGE	MINIMUM	MAXIMUM
Jewelry	500	1	3
Shoe	600	1	3
Department	1500	1	3
Book	700	0	3
Clothing	900	1	3

type of store) is given in Table 24. The annual profit made by each type of store will, of course, depend on how many stores of that type are in the mall. This dependence is given in Table 25 (all profits are in units of $10,000). Thus, if there are two department stores in the mall, each department store earns $210,000 profit per year. Each store pays 5% of its annual profit as rent to Simon's. Formulate an integer programming problem whose solution will tell Simon's how to maximize rental income from the mall.

Table 25

TYPE OF STORE	NUMBER OF STORES		
	1	*2*	*3*
Jewelry	9	8	7
Shoe	10	9	5
Department	27	21	20
Book	16	9	7
Clothing	17	13	10

26.[†] Boris Milkem's financial firm owns six assets. The expected sales price (in millions of dollars) for each asset is given in Table 26. From the table, if asset 1 is sold in

Table 26

	SOLD IN		
	Year 1	*Year 2*	*Year 3*
Asset 1	15	20	24
Asset 2	16	18	21
Asset 3	22	30	36
Asset 4	10	20	30
Asset 5	17	19	22
Asset 6	19	25	29

year 2, the firm receives $20 million. In order to maintain a regular cash flow, Milkem must sell at least $20 million of assets during year 1, at least $30 million worth during year 2, and at least $35 million worth during year 3. Set up an integer programming problem that Milkem can use to determine how to maximize total revenue from assets sold during the next three years. In implementing this model, how could the idea of a rolling planning horizon be used?

27.[‡] The Smalltown Fire Department currently has seven conventional ladder companies and seven alarm boxes. The two closest ladder companies to each alarm box are given in Table 27. The city fathers want to maximize the number of conventional ladder companies that can be replaced with tower ladder companies. Unfortunately, political considerations dictate that a conventional company can be replaced only if, after replacement, at least one of the two closest companies to each alarm box is still a conventional company.

Table 27

ALARM BOX	TWO CLOSEST LADDER COMPANIES
1	2, 3
2	3, 4
3	1, 5
4	2, 6
5	3, 6
6	4, 7
7	5, 7

(**a**) Formulate an integer programming problem that can be used to maximize the number of conventional companies that can be replaced by tower companies.
(**b**) Suppose $y_k = 1$ if conventional company k is replaced. Show that if we let $z_k = 1 - y_k$, the answer in part (a) is equivalent to a set-covering problem.

[†]Based on Bean, Noon, and Salton (1987).

[‡]Based on Walker (1974).

28.[†] A power plant has three boilers. If a given boiler is operated, it can be used to produce a quantity of steam (in tons) between the minimum and maximum given in Table 28. The cost of producing a ton of steam on each boiler is also given in Table 28. Steam from the boilers is used to produce power on three turbines. If operated, each turbine can process an amount of steam (in tons) between the minimum and maximum given in Table 29. The cost of processing a ton of steam and the power produced by each turbine is also given in Table 29. Formulate an integer programming problem that can be used to minimize the cost of producing 8000 kwh of power.

29.[‡] An Ohio company, Clevcinn, consists of three subsidiaries. Each subsidiary has the respective average payroll, unemployment reserve fund, and estimated payroll given in Table 30. (All figures are in millions of dollars.) Any employer in the state of Ohio whose reserve/average payroll ratio is less than 1 must pay 20% of its estimated payroll in unemployment insurance premiums. Any employer whose reserve/average payroll ratio is at least 1 must pay only 10% of its estimated payroll in premiums. Clevcinn can aggregate its subsidiaries and label them as separate employers. For instance, if subsidiaries 2 and 3 are aggregated, these subsidiaries must pay 20% of their estimated payroll in unemployment insurance premiums. Formulate an integer programming problem that can be used to determine which subsidiaries should be aggregated.

Table 28

BOILER NUMBER	MINIMUM STEAM	MAXIMUM STEAM	COST/TON
1	500	1000	$10
2	300	900	$8
3	400	800	$6

Table 29

TURBINE NUMBER	MINIMUM	MAXIMUM	KWH PER TON OF STEAM	PROCESSING COST PER TON
1	300	600	4	$2
2	500	800	5	$3
3	600	900	6	$4

Table 30

SUBSIDIARY	AVERAGE PAYROLL	RESERVE	ESTIMATED PAYROLL
1	300	400	350
2	600	510	400
3	800	600	500

[†] Based on Cavalieri, Roversi, and Ruggeri (1971).   [‡] Based on Salkin (1979).

9–3   THE BRANCH-AND-BOUND METHOD FOR SOLVING PURE INTEGER PROGRAMMING PROBLEMS

In practice, most integer programming problems are solved by using the technique of branch-and-bound. Branch-and-bound methods find the optimal solution to an IP by efficiently enumerating the points in a subproblem's feasible region. Before explaining how branch-and-bound works, we need to make the following elementary but important observation: *If you solve the LP relaxation of a pure IP and obtain a solution in which all variables are integers, then the optimal solution to the LP relaxation is also the optimal solution to the IP.*

To see why this observation is true, consider the following IP:

$$\max z = 3x_1 + 2x_2$$
$$\text{s.t.} \quad 2x_1 + x_2 \leq 6$$
$$x_1, x_2 \geq 0; \; x_1, x_2 \text{ integer}$$

The optimal solution to the LP relaxation of this pure IP is $x_1 = 0$, $x_2 = 6$, $z = 12$. Since this solution gives integer values to all variables, the preceding observation implies that $x_1 = 0$, $x_2 = 6$, $z = 12$ is also the optimal solution to the IP. Observe that the feasible region for the IP is a subset of the points in the LP relaxation's feasible region (see Figure 4). Thus, the optimal z-value for the IP cannot be larger than the optimal z-value for the LP relaxation. This means that the optimal z-value for the IP must be ≤ 12. But the point $x_1 = 0$, $x_2 = 6$, $z = 12$ is feasible for the IP and has $z = 12$. Thus, $x_1 = 0$, $x_2 = 6$, $z = 12$ must be optimal for the IP.

Figure 4
Feasible Region for an IP and Its LP Relaxation

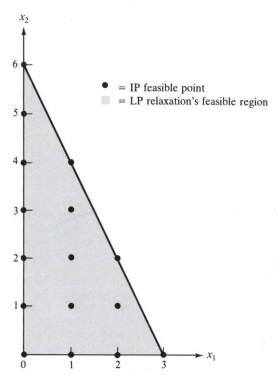

● = IP feasible point
▢ = LP relaxation's feasible region

E X A M P L E 9

The Telfa Corporation manufactures tables and chairs. A table requires 1 hour of labor and 9 sq bd ft of wood, and a chair requires 1 hour of labor and 5 sq bd ft of wood. Currently, 6 hours of labor and 45 sq bd ft of wood are available. Each table contributes $8 to profit, and each chair contributes $5 to profit. Formulate and solve an IP to maximize Telfa's profit.

Solution   Let

$$x_1 = \text{number of tables manufactured}$$

$$x_2 = \text{number of chairs manufactured}$$

Since x_1 and x_2 must be integers, Telfa wishes to solve the following IP:

$$\max z = 8x_1 + 5x_2$$

$$\text{s.t.} \quad x_1 + x_2 \leq 6 \qquad \text{(Labor constraint)}$$

$$9x_1 + 5x_2 \leq 45 \qquad \text{(Wood constraint)}$$

$$x_1, x_2 \geq 0; \; x_1, x_2 \text{ integer}$$

The branch-and-bound method begins by solving the LP relaxation of the IP. If all the decision variables assume integer values in the optimal solution to the LP relaxation, then the optimal solution to the LP relaxation will be the optimal solution to the IP. We call the LP relaxation subproblem 1. Unfortunately, the optimal solution to the LP relaxation is $z = \frac{165}{4}$, $x_1 = \frac{15}{4}$, $x_2 = \frac{9}{4}$ (see Figure 5). From Section 9.1, we know that (optimal z-value for IP) $\leq$ (optimal z-value for LP relaxation). This implies that the

Figure 5
Feasible Region for
Telfa Problem

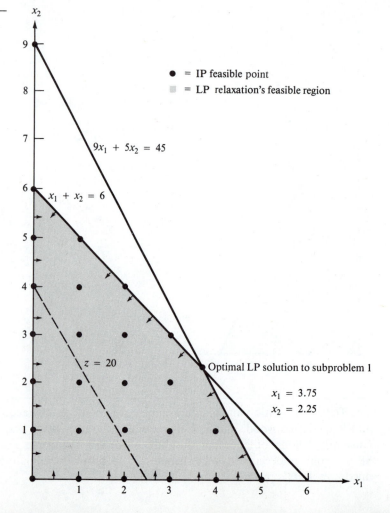

optimal z-value for the IP cannot exceed $\frac{165}{4}$. Thus, the optimal z-value for the LP relaxation is an **upper bound** for Telfa's profit.

Our next step is to partition the feasible region for the LP relaxation in an attempt to find out more about the location of the IP's optimal solution. We arbitrarily choose a variable that is fractional in the optimal solution to the LP relaxation—say, x_1. Now observe that every point in the feasible region for the IP must have either $x_1 \leq 3$ or $x_1 \geq 4$. (Why can't a feasible solution to the IP have $3 < x_1 < 4$?) With this in mind, we "branch" on the variable x_1 and create the following two additional subproblems:

Subproblem 2 Subproblem 1 + Constraint $x_1 \geq 4$.

Subproblem 3 Subproblem 1 + Constraint $x_1 \leq 3$.

Observe that neither subproblem 2 nor subproblem 3 includes any points with $x_1 = \frac{15}{4}$. This means that the optimal solution to the LP relaxation cannot recur when we solve subproblem 2 or subproblem 3.

From Figure 6, we see that every point in the feasible region for the Telfa IP is included in the feasible region for subproblem 2 or subproblem 3. Also, the feasible

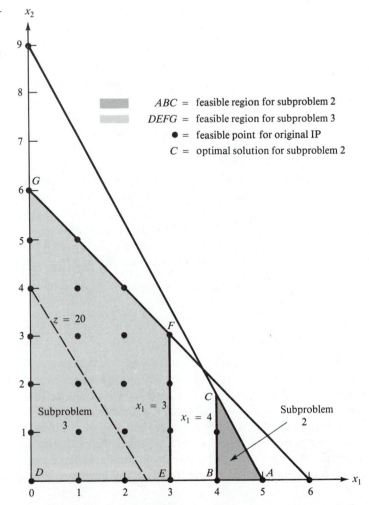

Figure 6
Feasible Region for
Subproblems 2 and 3
of Telfa Problem

regions for subproblems 2 and 3 have no points in common. Since subproblems 2 and 3 were created by adding constraints involving x_1, we say that subproblems 2 and 3 were created by **branching** on x_1.

We now choose any suproblem that has not yet been solved as an LP. We arbitrarily choose to solve subproblem 2. From Figure 6, we see that the optimal solution to subproblem 2 is $z = 41$, $x_1 = 4$, $x_2 = \frac{9}{5}$ (point C). Our accomplishments to date are summarized in Figure 7.

Figure 7
Telfa Subproblems 1
and 2 Solved

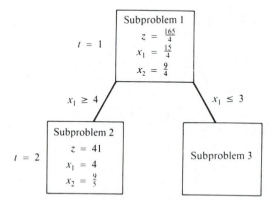

A display of all subproblems that have been created is called a **tree**. Each sub-problem is referred to as a **node** of the tree, and each line connecting two nodes of the tree is called an **arc**. The constraints associated with any node of the tree are the constraints for the LP relaxation plus the constraints associated with the arcs leading from subproblem 1 to the node. The label t indicates the chronological order in which the subproblems are solved.

Since the optimal solution to subproblem 2 did not yield an all-integer solution, we choose to use subproblem 2 to create two new subproblems. We choose a fractional-valued variable in the optimal solution to subproblem 2 and then branch on that variable. Since x_2 is the only fractional variable in the optimal solution to subproblem 2, we branch on x_2. We partition the feasible region for subproblem 2 into those points having $x_2 \geq 2$ and $x_2 \leq 1$. This creates the following two subproblems:

Subproblem 4 Subproblem 1 + Constraints $x_1 \geq 4$ and $x_2 \geq 2$ = subproblem 2 + Constraint $x_2 \geq 2$.

Subproblem 5 Subproblem 1 + Constraints $x_1 \geq 4$ and $x_2 \leq 1$ = subproblem 2 + Constraint $x_2 \leq 1$.

The feasible regions for subproblems 4 and 5 are displayed in Figure 8. The set of unsolved subproblems consists of subproblems 3, 4, and 5. We now choose a subproblem to solve. For reasons that are discussed later, we choose to solve the most recently created subproblem. (This is called the LIFO, or last-in-first-out, rule.) The LIFO rule implies that we should next solve subproblem 4 or subproblem 5. We arbitrarily choose to solve subproblem 4. From Figure 8, we see that subproblem 4 is infeasible. Thus, subproblem 4 cannot yield the optimal solution to the IP. To indicate this fact, we place an x by subproblem 4 (see Figure 9). Since any branches emanating from subproblem

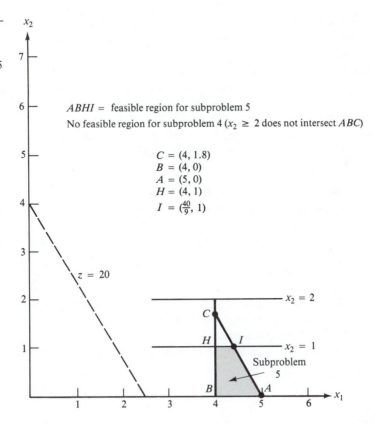

Figure 8
Feasible Regions for
Subproblems 4 and 5
of Telfa Problem

$ABHI =$ feasible region for subproblem 5

No feasible region for subproblem 4 ($x_2 \geq 2$ does not intersect ABC)

$C = (4, 1.8)$
$B = (4, 0)$
$A = (5, 0)$
$H = (4, 1)$
$I = (\frac{40}{9}, 1)$

$z = 20$

$x_2 = 2$

$x_2 = 1$

Subproblem 5

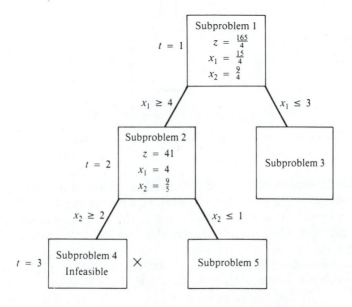

Figure 9
Telfa Subproblems 1,
2, and 4 Solved

Subproblem 1
$t = 1$ $z = \frac{165}{4}$
$x_1 = \frac{15}{4}$
$x_2 = \frac{9}{4}$

$x_1 \geq 4$ $x_1 \leq 3$

Subproblem 2
$t = 2$ $z = 41$
$x_1 = 4$
$x_2 = \frac{9}{5}$

Subproblem 3

$x_2 \geq 2$ $x_2 \leq 1$

$t = 3$ Subproblem 4
Infeasible $\times$ Subproblem 5

4 will yield no useful information, it is fruitless to create any branches emanating from subproblem 4. When further branching on a subproblem cannot yield any useful information, we say that the subproblem (or node) is **fathomed**. Our results to date are displayed in Figure 9.

Now the only unsolved subproblems are subproblems 3 and 5. The LIFO rule implies that subproblem 5 should be solved next. From Figure 8, we see that the optimal solution to subproblem 5 is point I in Figure 8: $z = \frac{365}{9}$, $x_1 = \frac{40}{9}$, $x_2 = 1$. This solution does not yield any immediately useful information, so we choose to partition subproblem 5's feasible region by branching on the fractional-valued variable x_1. This yields two new subproblems (see Figure 10):

Subproblem 6 Subproblem 5 + Constraint $x_1 \geq 5$.

Subproblem 7 Subproblem 5 + Constraint $x_1 \leq 4$.

Figure 10
Feasible Regions for
Subproblems 6 and 7
of Telfa Problem

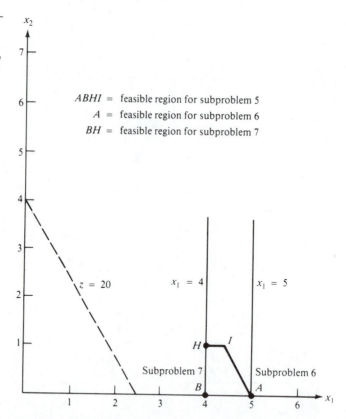

Together, subproblems 6 and 7 include all integer points that were included in the feasible region for subproblem 5. Also, no point having $x_1 = \frac{40}{9}$ can be in the feasible region for subproblem 6 or subproblem 7. Thus, the optimal solution to subproblem 5 will not recur when we solve subproblems 6 and 7. Our tree now looks as shown in Figure 11.

Subproblems 3, 6, and 7 are now unsolved. The LIFO rule implies that we next solve subproblem 6 or subproblem 7. We arbitrarily choose to solve subproblem 7. From

Figure 11
Telfa Subproblems 1,
2, 4, and 5 Solved

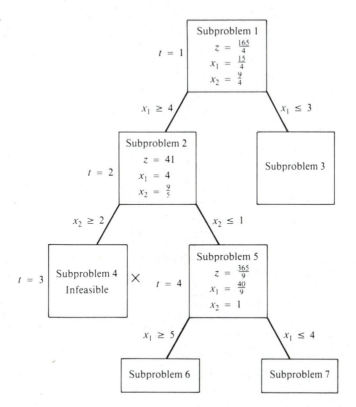

Figure 10, we see that the optimal solution to subproblem 7 is point H: $z = 37$, $x_1 = 4$, $x_2 = 1$. Since both x_1 and x_2 assume integer values, this solution is feasible for the original IP. A solution obtained by solving a subproblem in which all variables have integer values is a **candidate solution**. Since the candidate solution may be optimal, we must keep a candidate solution until a better feasible solution to the IP (if any exists) is found. We have a feasible solution to the original IP with $z = 37$, so we may conclude that the optimal z-value for the IP ≥ 37.

Thus, the z-value for the candidate solution is a **lower bound** on the optimal z-value for the original IP. We note this by placing the notation LB = 37 in the box corresponding to the *next* solved subproblem (see Figure 13). We now know that subproblem 7 yields a feasible integer solution with $z = 37$. We also know that subproblem 7 cannot yield a feasible integer solution having $z > 37$. Thus, further branching on subproblem 7 will yield no new information about the optimal solution to the IP, and subproblem 7 has been fathomed. The tree to date is pictured in Figure 12.

The only remaining unsolved subproblems are subproblems 6 and 3. Following the LIFO rule, we next solve subproblem 6. From Figure 10, we find that the optimal solution to subproblem 6 is point A: $z = 40$, $x_1 = 5$, $x_2 = 0$. Since all decision variables have integer values, the solution to subproblem 6 is a candidate solution. This candidate has a z-value of 40, which is larger than the z-value of the best previous candidate (candidate 7 with $z = 37$). Thus, subproblem 7 cannot yield the optimal solution of the IP (we denote this fact by placing an x by subproblem 7). We also update our LB to 40 (see Figure 14). Our progress to date is summarized in Figure 13.

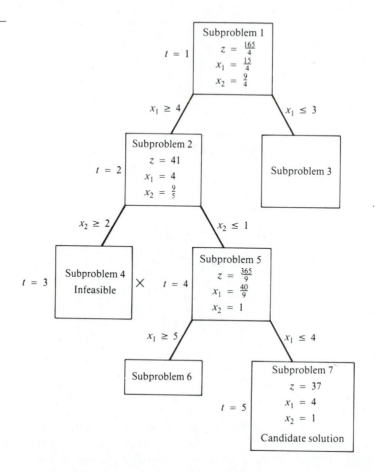

Subproblem 3 is the only remaining unsolved problem. From Figure 6, we find that the optimal solution to subproblem 3 is point F: $z = 39$, $x_1 = x_2 = 3$. Since subproblem 3 cannot yield a z-value exceeding the current lower bound of 40, subproblem 3 cannot yield the optimal solution to the original IP. Therefore, we place an × by subproblem 3 in Figure 14. From Figure 14, we see that there are no remaining unsolved subproblems and that only subproblem 6 can yield the optimal solution to the IP. Thus, the optimal solution to the IP is for Telfa to manufacture 5 tables and 0 chairs. This solution will contribute $40 to profits.

In using branch-and-bound to solve the Telfa problem, we have implicitly enumerated all points in the IP's feasible region. Eventually, all such points (except for the optimal solution) are eliminated from consideration, and the branch-and-bound procedure is complete. To show that the branch-and-bound procedure actually does consider all points in the IP's feasible region, we examine several possible solutions to the Telfa problem and show how the branch-and-bound procedure found these points to be nonoptimal. For example, how do we know that $x_1 = 2$, $x_2 = 3$ is not optimal?

Figure 13
Branch-and-Bound
Tree After Six
Subproblems Have
Been Solved

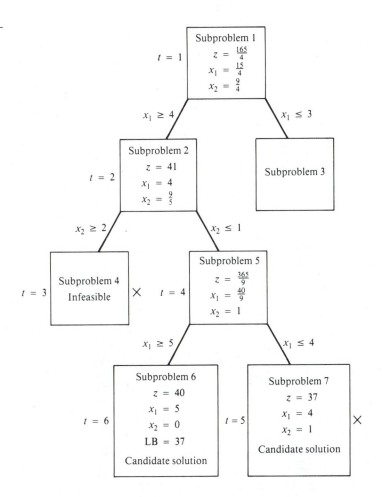

This point is in the feasible region for subproblem 3, and we know that all points in the feasible region for subproblem 3 have $z \leq 39$. Thus, our analysis of subproblem 3 shows that $x_1 = 2$, $x_2 = 3$ cannot beat $z = 40$ and cannot be optimal. As another example, why isn't $x_1 = 4$, $x_2 = 2$ optimal? Following the branches of the tree, we find that $x_1 = 4$, $x_2 = 2$ is associated with subproblem 4. Since no point associated with subproblem 4 is feasible, $x_1 = 4$, $x_2 = 2$ must fail to satisfy the constraints for the original IP and thus cannot be optimal for the Telfa problem. In a similar fashion, the branch-and-bound analysis has eliminated all points x_1, x_2 (except for the optimal solution) from consideration.

For the simple Telfa problem, the use of branch-and-bound may seem like using a cannon to kill a fly, but for an IP in which the feasible region contains a large number of integer points, branch-and-bound can be a very efficient method for eliminating nonoptimal points from consideration. For example, suppose we are applying branch-and-bound and our current LB = 42. Suppose we solve a subproblem that contains 1 million feasible points for the IP. If the optimal solution to this subproblem has $z < 42$, we have eliminated 1 million nonoptimal points by solving a single LP!

Figure 14
Final Branch-and-
Bound Tree for Telfa
Problem

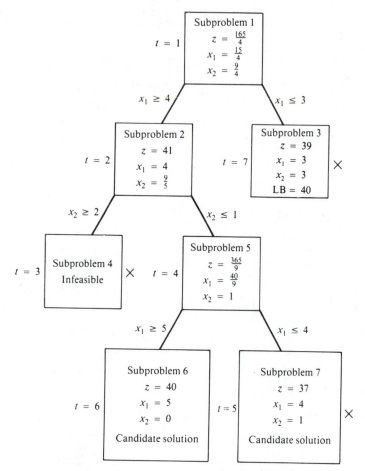

The key aspects of the branch-and-bound method for solving pure IPs (mixed IPs are considered in the next section) may be summarized as follows:

Step 1 If it is unnecessary to branch on a subproblem, it is fathomed. The following three situations result in a subproblem being fathomed: (1) The subproblem is infeasible. (2) The subproblem yields an optimal solution in which all variables have integer values. (3) The optimal z-value for the subproblem does not exceed (in a max problem) the current LB.

Step 2 A subproblem may be eliminated from consideration in the following situations: (1) The subproblem is infeasible. In the Telfa problem, subproblem 4 was eliminated from consideration for this reason. (2) LB (representing the z-value of the best candidate to date) is at least as large as the z-value for the subproblem. In the Telfa problem, subproblems 3 and 7 were eliminated for this reason.

Recall that in solving the Telfa problem by branch-and-bound, many seemingly arbitrary choices were made. For example, when x_1 and x_2 were both fractional in the optimal solution to subproblem 1, how did we determine the branching variable? Or how did we determine which subproblem should next be solved? The manner in which these questions are answered can result in trees that differ greatly in size and in the computer time required to find an optimal solution. Through experience and ingenuity, practitioners of branch-and-bound have developed some guidelines on how to make the necessary decisions.

Two general approaches are commonly used to determine which subproblem should be solved next. The most widely used is the LIFO rule, which chooses to solve the most recently created subproblem.[†] LIFO leads us down one side of the branch-and-bound tree (as in the Telfa problem) and quickly finds a candidate solution. Then we backtrack our way up to the top of the other side of the tree. For this reason, the LIFO approach is often called **backtracking**.

The second commonly used method to determine which subproblem should next be solved is **jumptracking**. When branching on a node, the jumptracking approach solves all the problems created by the branching. Then it branches again on the node with the best z-value. Jumptracking often jumps from one side of the tree to the other. It usually creates more subproblems and requires more computer storage than backtracking. The idea behind jumptracking is that moving toward the subproblems with good z-values should lead us more quickly to the best z-value.

If two or more variables are fractional in a subproblem's optimal solution, on which variable should we branch? Branching on the fractional-valued variable that has the greatest economic importance is often the best strategy. For example, in the Nickles example, suppose the optimal solution to a subproblem had y_1 and x_{12} fractional. Our rule would say to branch on y_1 because y_1 represents the decision to operate (or not operate) a lockbox in city 1, and this is presumably a more important decision than deciding whether or not region 1 payments should be sent to city 2. When more than one variable is fractional in a subproblem solution, many computer codes will branch on the lowest-numbered fractional variable. Thus, if an integer programming computer code requires that variables be numbered, they should be numbered in order of their economic importance (1 = most important, etc.).

R E M A R K S   **1.** For some IPs, the optimal solution to the LP relaxation will also be the optimal solution to the IP. Suppose the constraints of the IP are written as $A\mathbf{x} = \mathbf{b}$. If the determinant[‡] of every square submatrix of A is $+1$, -1, or 0, we say that the matrix A is **unimodular**. If A is unimodular and each element of $\mathbf{b}$ is an integer, the optimal solution to the LP relaxation will assign all variables integer values (see Shapiro (1979) for a proof) and will therefore be the optimal solution to the IP. It can be shown that the constraint matrix of any MCNFP is unimodular. Thus, as was discussed in Chapter 8, any MCNFP in which each node's net outflow and each arc's capacity are integers will have an integer-valued solution.

2. As a general rule, the more an IP looks like an MCNFP, the easier the problem is to solve by branch-and-bound methods. Thus, in formulating an IP, it is a good idea to try to choose a formulation in which as many variables as possible have coefficients of $+1$, -1, and 0. To illustrate this idea, recall that the formulation of the Nickles (lockbox) problem given in

---

[†]If two subproblems are created at the same time, many sophisticated methods have been developed to determine which subproblem should be solved first. See Taha (1975) for details.
[‡]The determinant of a matrix is defined in Section 2.6.

Section 9.2 contained 16 constraints of the following form:

Formulation 1 $x_{ij} \leq y_j$ $(i = 1, 2, 3, 4; j = 1, 2, 3, 4)$ **(25)**

As we have already seen in Section 9.2, if the 16 constraints in (25) are replaced by the following four constraints, an equivalent formulation results:

$$x_{11} + x_{21} + x_{31} + x_{41} \leq 4y_1$$

Formulation 2
$$x_{12} + x_{22} + x_{32} + x_{42} \leq 4y_2$$

$$x_{13} + x_{23} + x_{33} + x_{43} \leq 4y_3$$

$$x_{14} + x_{24} + x_{34} + x_{44} \leq 4y_4$$

Since formulation 2 has $16 - 4 = 12$ fewer constraints than formulation 1, one might think that formulation 2 would require less computer time than formulation 1 to find the optimal solution. This turns out to be untrue. To see why, recall that the branch-and-bound method begins by solving the LP relaxation of the IP. The feasible region of the LP relaxation of formulation 2 contains many more noninteger points than the feasible region of formulation 1. For example, the point $y_1 = y_2 = y_3 = y_4 = \frac{1}{4}$, $x_{11} = x_{22} = x_{33} = x_{44} = 1$ (all other x_{ij}'s equal zero) is in the feasible region for the LP relaxation of formulation 2 but is not in the feasible region for the LP relaxation of formulation 1. Since the branch-and-bound method must eliminate all noninteger points before obtaining the optimal solution to the IP, it seems reasonable that formulation 2 will require more computer time than formulation 1. Indeed, when the LINDO package was used to find the optimal solution to formulation 1, the LP relaxation yielded the optimal solution. When LINDO was used to find the optimal solution to formulation 2, 17 subproblems were solved before the optimal solution was found. Note that formulation 2 contains the terms $4y_1$, $4y_2$, $4y_3$, and $4y_4$. These terms "disturb" the network-like structure of the lockbox problem and cause branch-and-bound to be less efficient.

3. When solving an IP in the real world, we are usually happy with a near-optimal solution. For example, suppose that we are solving a lockbox problem and the LP relaxation yields a cost of $200,000. This means that the optimal solution to the lockbox IP will certainly have a cost of at least $200,000. If we find a candidate solution during the course of the branch-and-bound procedure that has a cost of, say, $205,000, why bother to continue with the branch-and-bound procedure? Even if we then found the optimal solution to the IP, it could not save more than $205,000 - 200,000 = \$5000$ in costs over the candidate solution with $z = 205,000$. It might even cost more than $5000 in computer time to find the optimal lockbox solution. For this reason, the branch-and-bound procedure is often terminated when a candidate solution is found with a z-value close to the z-value of the LP relaxation.

4. Subproblems for branch-and-bound problems are often solved using some variant of the dual simplex algorithm. To illustrate this, we return to the Telfa example. The optimal tableau for the LP relaxation of the Telfa problem is

$$z \quad + 1.25s_1 + 0.75s_2 = 41.25$$

$$x_2 + 2.25s_1 - 0.25s_2 = 2.25$$

$$x_1 \quad - 1.25s_1 + 0.25s_2 = 3.75$$

After solving the LP relaxation, we solved subproblem 2. Subproblem 2 is just subproblem 1 plus the constraint $x_1 \geq 4$. Recall that the dual simplex is an efficient method for finding the new optimal solution to an LP when we know the LP's optimal tableau and a new constraint is added to the LP. We have added the constraint $x_1 \geq 4$ (which may be written as $x_1 - e_3 = 4$). To utilize the dual simplex, we must eliminate the basic variable x_1 from this constraint and use e_3 as a basic variable for $x_1 - e_3 = 4$. Adding $-$(second row of optimal tableau) to the constraint $x_1 - e_3 = 4$, we obtain the constraint $1.25s_1 - 0.25s_2 - e_3 = 0.25$. Multiplying this constraint through by -1, we obtain $-1.25s_1 + 0.25s_2 + e_3 = -0.25$. After adding this constraint to subproblem 1's optimal tableau, we obtain the tableau in Table 31. The dual simplex method states that we should enter a variable from row 3 into the basis. Since s_1 is the only variable having

Table 31		BASIC VARIABLE
Initial Tableau for Solving Subproblem 2 by Dual Simplex	$z \quad + 1.25s_1 + 0.75s_2 \qquad\qquad = 41.25$ $x_2 + 2.25s_1 - 0.25s_2 \qquad\qquad = 2.25$ $x_1 \quad - 1.25s_1 + 0.25s_2 \qquad\qquad = 3.75$ $- 1.25s_1 + 0.25s_2 + e_3 = -0.25$	$z = 41.25$ $x_2 = 2.25$ $x_1 = 3.75$ $e_3 = -0.25$

Table 32		BASIC VARIABLE
Optimal Tableau for Solving Subproblem 2 by Dual Simplex	$z \qquad + \quad s_2 + \qquad e_3 = 41$ $x_2 \quad + 0.20s_2 + \quad 1.8e_3 = 1.8$ $x_1 \qquad\qquad - \quad e_3 = 4$ $s_1 - 0.20s_2 - 0.80e_3 = 0.20$	$z = 41$ $x_2 = 1.8$ $x_1 = 4$ $s_1 = 0.20$

a negative coefficient in row 3, s_1 will enter the basis in row 3. After the pivot, we obtain the (optimal) tableau in Table 32. Thus, the optimal solution to subproblem 2 is $z = 41$, $x_2 = 1.8$, $x_1 = 4$, $s_1 = 0.20$.

◆ PROBLEMS

GROUP A

Use branch-and-bound to solve the following IPs:

1. $\max z = 5x_1 + 2x_2$
  s.t. $3x_1 + x_2 \le 12$
  $x_1 + x_2 \le 5$
  $x_1, x_2 \ge 0$; x_1, x_2 integer

2. The Dorian Auto example of Section 3.2.

3. $\max z = 2x_1 + 3x_2$
  s.t. $x_1 + 2x_2 \le 10$
  $3x_1 + 4x_2 \le 25$
  $x_1, x_2 \ge 0$; x_1, x_2 integer

4. $\max z = 4x_1 + 3x_2$
  s.t. $4x_1 + 9x_2 \le 26$
  $8x_1 + 5x_2 \le 17$
  $x_1, x_2 \ge 0$; x_1, x_2 integer

5. $\min z = 4x_1 + 5x_2$
  s.t. $x_1 + 4x_2 \ge 5$
  $3x_1 + 2x_2 \ge 7$
  $x_1, x_2 \ge 0$; x_1, x_2 integer

6. $\max z = 4x_1 + 5x_2$
  s.t. $3x_1 + 2x_2 \le 10$
  $x_1 + 4x_2 \le 11$
  $3x_1 + 3x_2 \le 13$
  $x_1, x_2 \ge 0$; x_1, x_2 integer

7. Use the branch-and-bound method to find the optimal solution to the following IP:

$$\max z = 7x_1 + 3x_2$$
  s.t. $2x_1 + \quad x_2 \le 9$
  $3x_1 + 2x_2 \le 13$
  $x_1, x_2 \ge 0$; x_1, x_2 integer

GROUP B

8. Suppose we have branched on a subproblem (call it subproblem 0, having optimal solution SOL0) and have obtained the following two subproblems:

Subproblem 1 Subproblem 0 + Constraint $x_1 \le i$.

Subproblem 2 Subproblem 0 + Constraint $x_1 \ge i + 1$ (i is some integer).

Prove that there will exist at least one optimal solution to subproblem 1 having $x_1 = i$ and at least one optimal solution to subproblem 2 having $x_1 = i + 1$. (*Hint:* Suppose an optimal solution to subproblem 1 (call it SOL1) has $x_1 = \bar{x}_1$, where $\bar{x}_1 < i$. For some number c ($0 < c < 1$), $c(\text{SOL0}) + (1 - c)\text{SOL1}$ will have the following three properties:

1. The value of x_1 in $c(\text{SOL0}) + (1 - c)\text{SOL1}$ will equal i.

2. $c(\text{SOL0}) + (1 - c)\text{SOL1}$ will be feasible in subproblem 1.

3. The z-value for $c(\text{SOL0}) + (1 - c)\text{SOL1}$ will be at least as good as the z-value for SOL1.

Explain how this result can help when we graphically solve branch-and-bound problems.)

9-4   THE BRANCH-AND-BOUND METHOD FOR SOLVING MIXED INTEGER PROGRAMMING PROBLEMS

Recall that in a mixed IP, some variables are required to be integers and others are allowed to be either integers or nonintegers. To solve a mixed IP by branch-and-bound, modify the method described in Section 9.3 by branching only on variables that are required to be integers. Also, for a solution to a subproblem to be a candidate solution, it need only assign integer values to those variables that are required to be integers. To illustrate, let us solve the following mixed IP:

$$\max z = 2x_1 + x_2$$
$$\text{s.t.}\quad 5x_1 + 2x_2 \le 8$$
$$x_1 + x_2 \le 3$$
$$x_1, x_2 \ge 0;\ x_1 \text{ integer}$$

As before, we begin by solving the LP relaxation of the IP. The optimal solution of the LP relaxation is $z = \frac{11}{3}$, $x_1 = \frac{2}{3}$, $x_2 = \frac{7}{3}$. Since x_2 is allowed to be fractional, we do not branch on x_2; if we did so, we would be excluding points having x_2 values between 2 and 3, and we don't want to do that. Thus, we must branch on x_1. This yields subproblems 2 and 3 in Figure 15.

We next choose to solve subproblem 2. The optimal solution to subproblem 2 is the candidate solution $z = 3$, $x_1 = 0$, $x_2 = 3$. We now solve subproblem 3 and obtain the candidate solution $z = \frac{7}{2}$, $x_1 = 1$, $x_2 = \frac{3}{2}$. Since the z-value from the subproblem 3 candidate exceeds the z-value for the subproblem 2 candidate, subproblem 2 can be eliminated from consideration, and the subproblem 3 candidate ($z = \frac{7}{2}$, $x_1 = 1$, $x_2 = \frac{3}{2}$) is the optimal solution to the mixed IP.

Figure 15
Branch-and-Bound
Tree for Mixed IP

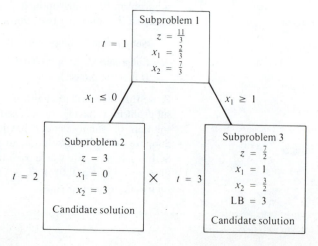

♦ PROBLEMS

GROUP A

Use the branch-and-bound method to solve the following IPs:

1. $\max z = 3x_1 + x_2$
s.t. $5x_1 + 2x_2 \leq 10$
$4x_1 + x_2 \leq 7$
$x_1, x_2 \geq 0, x_2$ integer

2. $\min z = 3x_1 + x_2$
s.t. $x_1 + 5x_2 \geq 8$
$x_1 + 2x_2 \geq 4$
$x_1, x_2 \geq 0, x_1$ integer

3. $\max z = 4x_1 + 3x_2 + x_3$
s.t. $3x_1 + 2x_2 + x_3 \leq 7$
$2x_1 + x_2 + 2x_3 \leq 11$
x_2, x_3 integer, $x_1, x_2, x_3 \geq 0$

9-5   SOLVING KNAPSACK PROBLEMS BY THE BRANCH-AND-BOUND METHOD

In Section 9.2, we learned that a knapsack problem is an IP with a single constraint. In this section, we discuss knapsack problems in which each variable must equal 0 or 1 (see Problem 1 at the end of this section for an explanation of how any knapsack problem can be reformulated as a knapsack problem in which each variable must equal 0 or 1). A knapsack problem in which each variable must equal 0 or 1 may be written as

$$\max z = c_1 x_1 + c_2 x_2 + \cdots + c_n x_n$$
$$\text{s.t. } a_1 x_1 + a_2 x_2 + \cdots + a_n x_n \leq b \tag{38}$$
$$x_i = 0 \text{ or } 1 \quad (i = 1, 2, \ldots, n)$$

Recall that c_i is the benefit obtained if item i is chosen, b is the amount of an available resource, and a_i is the amount of the available resource used by item i.

When knapsack problems are solved by branch-and-bound, two aspects of the branch-and-bound approach greatly simplify. Since each variable must equal 0 or 1, branching on x_i will yield an $x_i = 0$ and an $x_i = 1$ branch. Also, the LP relaxation (and other subproblems) may be solved by inspection. To see this, observe that $\frac{c_i}{a_i}$ may be interpreted as the benefit item i earns for each unit of the resource used by item i. Thus, the best items have the largest values of $\frac{c_i}{a_i}$ and the worst items have the smallest values of $\frac{c_i}{a_i}$. To solve any subproblem resulting from a knapsack problem, compute all the ratios $\frac{c_i}{a_i}$. Then put the best item in the knapsack. Then put the second-best item in the knapsack. Continue in this fashion until the best remaining item will overfill the knapsack. Then fill the knapsack with as much of this item as possible.

To illustrate, we solve the LP relaxation of

$$\max z = 40x_1 + 80x_2 + 10x_3 + 10x_4 + 4x_5 + 20x_6 + 60x_7$$
$$\text{s.t. } 40x_1 + 50x_2 + 30x_3 + 10x_4 + 10x_5 + 40x_6 + 30x_7 \leq 100 \tag{39}$$
$$x_i = 0 \text{ or } 1 \quad (i = 1, 2, \ldots, 7)$$

We begin by computing the $\frac{c_i}{a_i}$ ratios and ordering the variables from best to worst (see Table 33). To solve the LP relaxation of (39), we first choose item 7 ($x_7 = 1$). Then

	$\dfrac{c_i}{a_i}$	RANKING (1 = Best, 7 = Worst)
Item 1	1	3.5 (tie for third or fourth)
Item 2	$\frac{8}{5}$	2
Item 3	$\frac{1}{3}$	7
Item 4	1	3.5
Item 5	$\frac{4}{10}$	6
Item 6	$\frac{1}{2}$	5
Item 7	2	1

Table 33
Ordering Items From
Best to Worst in a
Knapsack Problem

$100 - 30 = 70$ units of the resource remain. Now we include the second-best item (item 2) in the knapsack by setting $x_2 = 1$. Now $70 - 50 = 20$ units of the resource remain. Since item 4 and item 1 have the same $\frac{c_i}{a_i}$ ratio, we can next choose either of these items. We arbitrarily choose to set $x_4 = 1$. Then $20 - 10 = 10$ units of the resource remain. The best remaining item is item 1. We now fill the knapsack with as much of item 1 as we can. Since only 10 units of the resource remain, we set $x_1 = \frac{10}{40} = \frac{1}{4}$. Thus an optimal solution to the LP relaxation of (39) is $z = 80 + 60 + 10 + (\frac{1}{4})(40) = 160$, $x_2 = x_7 = x_4 = 1$, $x_1 = \frac{1}{4}$, $x_3 = x_5 = x_6 = 0$.

To show how branch-and-bound can be used to solve a knapsack problem, let us find the optimal solution to the Stockco capital budgeting problem (Example 1). Recall that this problem was

$$\max z = 16x_1 + 22x_2 + 12x_3 + 8x_4$$
$$\text{s.t.} \quad 5x_1 + 7x_2 + 4x_3 + 3x_4 \leq 14$$
$$x_j = 0 \text{ or } 1$$

The branch-and-bound tree for this problem is shown in Figure 16. From the tree, we find that the optimal solution to Example 1 is $z = 42$, $x_1 = 0$, $x_2 = x_3 = x_4 = 1$. Thus, we should invest in investments 2, 3, and 4 and earn an NPV of $42,000. As discussed in Section 9.2, the "best" investment is not used.

REMARKS   The method we used in traversing the tree of Figure 16 is as follows:

1. We used the LIFO approach to determine which subproblem should be solved.

2. We arbitrarily chose to solve subproblem 3 before subproblem 2. To solve subproblem 3, we first set $x_3 = 1$ and then solved the resulting knapsack problem. After setting $x_3 = 1$, $14 - 4 = \$10$ million was still available for investment. Applying the technique used to solve the LP relaxation of a knapsack problem yielded the following optimal solution to subproblem 3: $x_3 = 1$, $x_1 = 1$, $x_2 = \frac{5}{7}$, $x_4 = 0$, $z = 16 + (\frac{5}{7})(22) + 12 = \frac{306}{7}$. Other subproblems were solved similarly; of course, if a subproblem specified $x_i = 0$, the optimal solution to that subproblem could not use investment i.

3. Subproblem 4 yielded the candidate solution $x_1 = x_3 = x_4 = 1$, $z = 36$. We then set LB = 36.

4. Subproblem 6 yielded a candidate solution with $z = 42$. Thus, subproblem 4 was eliminated from consideration, and LB was updated to 42.

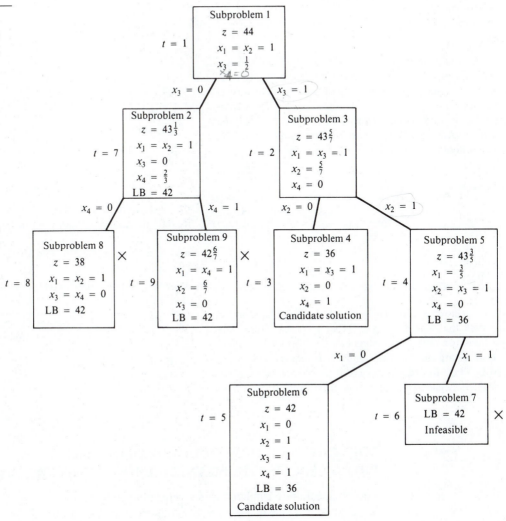

Figure 16
Branch-and-Bound
Tree for Knapsack
Problem

5. Subproblem 7 was infeasible because it required $x_1 = x_2 = x_3 = 1$, and such a solution requires at least $16 million.

6. Subproblem 8 was eliminated because its z-value ($z = 38$) did not exceed the current LB of 42.

7. Subproblem 9 had a z-value of $42\frac{6}{7}$. Since the z-value for any all-integer solution must also be an integer, this meant that branching on subproblem 9 could never yield a z-value larger than 42. Thus, further branching on subproblem 9 could not beat the current LB of 42, and subproblem 9 was eliminated from consideration.

In Chapter 20, we show how dynamic programming can be used to solve knapsack problems.

◆ PROBLEMS

GROUP A

1. Show how the following problem can be expressed as a knapsack problem in which all variables must equal 0 or 1. NASA is determining how many of three types of objects should be brought on board the space shuttle. The weight and benefit of each of the items are given in Table 34. If the space shuttle can carry up to 26 lb of items 1–3, which items should be taken on the space shuttle?

Table 34

	BENEFIT	WEIGHT (Pounds)
Item 1	10	3
Item 2	15	4
Item 3	17	5

2. I am moving from New Jersey to Indiana. I have rented a truck that can haul up to 1100 cu ft of furniture. The volume and value of each item I am considering moving on the truck are given in Table 35. Which items should I bring to Indiana? In order to solve this problem as a knapsack problem, what unrealistic assumptions must we make?

Table 35

ITEM	VALUE	VOLUME (Cubic Feet)
Bedroom set	$60	800
Dining room set	$48	600
Stereo	$14	300
Sofa	$31	400
TV set	$10	200

3. Four projects are available for investment. The projects require the cash flows and yield the net present values (in millions) shown in Table 36. If $6 million is available for investment at time 0, find the investment plan that maximizes NPV.

Table 36

	CASH OUTFLOW AT TIME 0	NPV
Project 1	$3	$5
Project 2	$5	$8
Project 3	$2	$3
Project 4	$4	$7

9-6   SOLVING COMBINATORIAL OPTIMIZATION PROBLEMS BY THE BRANCH-AND-BOUND METHOD

Loosely speaking, a **combinatorial optimization problem** is any optimization problem that has a finite number of feasible solutions. A branch-and-bound approach is often the most efficient way to solve a combinatorial optimization problem. Three examples of combinatorial optimization problems follow:

1. Ten jobs must be processed on a single machine. You know the time it takes to complete each job and the time at which each job must be completed (the job's due date). What ordering of the jobs minimizes the total delay of the ten jobs?

2. A salesperson must visit each of ten cities once before returning to his home. What order of visiting the cities minimizes the total distance the salesperson must travel before returning home? Not surprisingly, this problem is called the *traveling salesperson problem* (TSP).

3. Determine how to place eight queens on a chessboard so that no queen can capture any other queen (see Problem 6 at the end of this section).

In each of these problems, many possible solutions must be considered. For instance, in problem 1 the first job to be processed can be one of ten jobs, the next job to be processed can be one of nine jobs, etc. Thus, even for this relatively small problem there are $10(9)(8) \cdots (1) = 10! = 3{,}628{,}000$ possible ways to schedule the jobs. Since a combinatorial optimization problem may have many feasible solutions, it can require a great deal of computer time to enumerate all possible solutions explicitly. For this reason, branch-and-bound methods are often used for *implicit* enumeration of all possible solutions to a combinatorial optimization problem. As we will see, the branch-and-bound method should take advantage of the structure of the particular problem that is being solved.

To illustrate how branch-and-bound methods are used to solve combinatorial optimization problems, we show how a branch-and-bound approach can be used to solve problems 1 and 2 of the preceding list.

BRANCH-AND-BOUND APPROACH FOR MACHINE SCHEDULING PROBLEM

Example 10 illustrates how a branch-and-bound approach may be used to schedule jobs on a single machine. See Baker (1974) and Hax and Candea (1984) for a discussion of other branch-and-bound approaches to machine scheduling problems.

E X A M P L E
10

Four jobs must be processed on a single machine. The time required to process each job and the date the job is due are shown in Table 37. The delay of a job is the number of days after the due date that a job is completed (if a job is completed on time or early, the job's delay is zero). In what order should the jobs be processed to minimize the total delay of the four jobs?

Table 37
Durations and Due
Dates of Jobs

	TIME REQUIRED TO COMPLETE JOB (Days)	DUE DATE
Job 1	6	End of day 8
Job 2	4	End of day 4
Job 3	5	End of day 12
Job 4	8	End of day 16

Solution

Suppose the jobs are processed in the following order: job 1, job 2, job 3, and job 4. Then the delays shown in Table 38 would occur. For this sequence, total delay = $0 + 6 + 3 + 7 = 16$ days. We now describe a branch-and-bound approach for solving this type of machine scheduling problem.

Table 38
Delays Incurred If
Jobs Are Processed
in the Order 1–2–3–4

	COMPLETION TIME OF JOB	DELAY OF JOB
Job 1	6	0
Job 2	$6 + 4 = 10$	$10 - 4 = 6$
Job 3	$6 + 4 + 5 = 15$	$15 - 12 = 3$
Job 4	$6 + 4 + 5 + 8 = 23$	$23 - 16 = 7$

Since a possible solution to the problem must specify the order in which the jobs are processed, we define

$$x_{ij} = \begin{cases} 1 & \text{if job } i \text{ is the } j\text{th job to be processed} \\ 0 & \text{otherwise} \end{cases}$$

The branch-and-bound approach begins by partitioning all solutions according to the job that is *last* processed. Any sequence of jobs must process some job last, so each sequence of jobs must either have $x_{14} = 1$, $x_{24} = 1$, $x_{34} = 1$, or $x_{44} = 1$. This yields four branches with nodes 1–4 in Figure 17. After we create a node by branching, we obtain a lower bound on the total delay (D) associated with the node. For example, if $x_{44} = 1$, we know that job 4 is the last job to be processed. In this case, job 4 will be completed at the end of day $6 + 4 + 5 + 8 = 23$ and will be $23 - 16 = 7$ days late. Thus, any schedule having $x_{44} = 1$ must have $D \geq 7$. Thus, we write $D \geq 7$ inside node 4 of Figure 17. Similar reasoning shows that any sequence of jobs having $x_{34} = 1$ will have $D \geq 11$, any sequence having $x_{24} = 1$ will have $D \geq 19$, and any sequence of jobs having $x_{14} = 1$ will have $D \geq 15$. Since we have no reason to exclude any of nodes 1–4 from consideration as part of the optimal job sequence, we choose to branch on a node. We utilize the jumptracking approach and branch on the node that has the smallest bound on D: node 4. Any job sequence associated with node 4 must have $x_{13} = 1$, $x_{23} = 1$, or $x_{33} = 1$. Branching on node 4 yields nodes 5–7 in Figure 17. For each new node, we need a lower bound for the total delay. For example, at node 7, we know from our analysis of node 1 that job 4 will be processed last and will be delayed by 7 days. For node 7, we know that job 3 will be the third job processed. Thus, job 3 will be completed after $6 + 4 + 5 = 15$ days and will be $15 - 12 = 3$ days late. Any sequence associated with node 7 must have $D \geq 7 + 3 = 10$ days. Similar reasoning shows that node 5

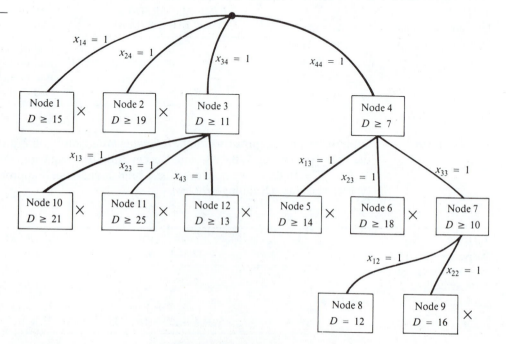

Figure 17
Branch-and-Bound
Tree for Machine
Scheduling Problem

must have $D \geq 14$, and node 6 must have $D \geq 18$. We still do not have any reason to eliminate any of nodes 1–7 from consideration, so we again branch on a node. The jumptracking approach directs us to branch on node 7. Any job sequence associated with node 7 must have either job 1 or job 2 as the second job processed. Thus, any job sequence associated with node 7 must have $x_{12} = 1$ or $x_{22} = 1$. Branching on node 7 yields nodes 8 and 9 in Figure 17.

Node 9 corresponds to processing the jobs in the order 1–2–3–4. This sequence yields a total delay of 7 (for job 4) + 3 (for job 3) + (6 + 4 − 4) (for job 2) + 0 (for job 1) = 16 days. Node 9 is a feasible sequence and may be considered a candidate solution having $D = 16$. We now know that any node that cannot have a total delay of less than 16 days can be eliminated.

Node 8 corresponds to the sequence 2–1–3–4. This sequence has a total delay of 7 (for job 4) + 3 (for job 3) + (4 + 6 − 8) (for job 1) + 0 (for job 2) = 12 days. Node 8 is a feasible sequence and may be viewed as a candidate solution with $D = 12$. Since node 8 is better than node 9, node 9 may be eliminated from consideration.

Similarly, node 5 (having $D \geq 14$), node 6 (having $D \geq 18$), node 1 (having $D \geq 15$), and node 2 (having $D \geq 19$) can be eliminated. Node 3 cannot yet be eliminated, because it is still possible for node 3 to yield a sequence having $D = 11$. Thus, we now branch on node 3. Since any job sequence associated with node 3 must have $x_{13} = 1$, $x_{23} = 1$, or $x_{43} = 1$, we obtain nodes 10–12.

For node 10, $D \geq$ (delay from processing job 3 last) + (delay from processing job 1 third) = 11 + (6 + 4 + 8 − 8) = 21. Since any sequence associated with node 10 must have $D \geq 21$ and we have a candidate with $D = 12$, node 10 may be eliminated.

For node 11, $D \geq$ (delay from processing job 3 last) + (delay from processing job 2 third) = 11 + (6 + 4 + 8 − 4) = 25. Any sequence associated with node 11 must have $D \geq 25$, and node 11 may be eliminated.

Finally, for node 12, $D \geq$ (delay from processing job 3 last) + (delay from processing job 4 third) = 11 + (6 + 4 + 8 − 16) = 13. Any sequence associated with node 12 must have $D \geq 13$, and node 12 may be eliminated.

With the exception of node 8, every node in Figure 17 has been eliminated from consideration. Node 8 yields the delay minimizing sequence $x_{44} = x_{33} = x_{12} = x_{21} = 1$. Thus, the jobs should be processed in the order 2–1–3–4 with a total delay of 12 days resulting. ◆

BRANCH-AND-BOUND APPROACH
FOR TRAVELING SALESPERSON PROBLEM

E X A M P L E 11   Joe State lives in Gary, Indiana. He owns insurance agencies in Gary, Fort Wayne, Evansville, Terre Haute, and South Bend. Each December, he visits each of his insurance agencies. The distance between each of his agencies (in miles) is shown in Table 39. What order of visiting his agencies will minimize the total distance traveled?

Solution   Joe must determine the order of visiting the five cities that minimizes the total distance traveled. For example, Joe could choose to visit the cities in the order 1–3–4–5–2–1. Then he would travel a total of 217 + 113 + 196 + 79 + 132 = 737 miles.

Table 39		FORT		TERRE	SOUTH
Distance between	GARY	WAYNE	EVANSVILLE	HAUTE	BEND
City 1 Gary	0	132	217	164	58
City 2 Fort Wayne	132	0	290	201	79
City 3 Evansville	217	290	0	113	303
City 4 Terre Haute	164	201	113	0	196
City 5 South Bend	58	79	303	196	0

Table 39
Distance between
Cities in Traveling
Salesperson Problem

To tackle the traveling salesperson problem, define

$$x_{ij} = \begin{cases} 1 & \text{if Joe leaves city } i \text{ and travels next to city } j \\ 0 & \text{otherwise} \end{cases}$$

Also, for $i \neq j$,

$$c_{ij} = \text{distance between cities } i \text{ and } j$$
$$c_{ii} = M, \text{ where } M \text{ is a large positive number}$$

It seems reasonable that we might be able to find the answer to Joe's problem by solving an assignment problem having a cost matrix whose ijth element is c_{ij}. For instance, suppose we solved this assignment problem and obtained the solution $x_{12} = x_{24} = x_{45} = x_{53} = x_{31} = 1$. Then Joe should go from Gary to Fort Wayne, from Fort Wayne to Terre Haute, from Terre Haute to South Bend, from South Bend to Evansville, and from Evansville to Gary. This solution can be written as 1–2–4–5–3–1. An itinerary that begins and ends at the same city and visits each city once is called a **tour**.

If the solution to the preceding assignment problem yields a tour, it is the optimal solution to the traveling salesperson problem. (Why?) Unfortunately, the optimal solution to the assignment problem need not be a tour. For example, the optimal solution to the assignment problem might be $x_{15} = x_{21} = x_{34} = x_{43} = x_{52} = 1$. This solution suggests going from Gary to South Bend, then to Fort Wayne, and then back to Gary. This solution also suggests that if Joe is in Evansville he should go to Terre Haute and then return to Evansville (see Figure 18). Of course, if Joe begins in Gary, this solution will never get him to Evansville or Terre Haute. This happens because the optimal solution to the assignment problem contains two **subtours**. A subtour is a round trip that does not pass through all cities. The present assignment contains the two subtours 1–5–2–1 and 3–4–3. If we could exclude all feasible solutions to the assignment problem that contain subtours and then solve the assignment problem, we would obtain

Figure 18
Example of Subtours
in Traveling
Salesperson Problem

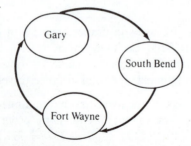
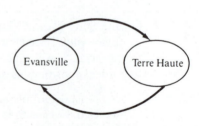

the optimal solution to the traveling salesperson problem. This is not easy to do, however. In most cases, a branch-and-bound approach is the most efficient approach for solving a traveling salesperson problem.

Several branch-and-bound approaches have been developed for solving traveling salesperson problems (see Wagner (1975)). We describe an approach here in which the subproblems reduce to assignment problems. To begin, we solve the preceding assignment problem, in which, for $i \neq j$, the cost c_{ij} is the distance between cities i and j and $c_{ii} = M$ (this prevents a person in a city from being assigned to visit that city itself). Since this assignment problem contains no provisions to prevent subtours, it is a relaxation (or less constrained problem) of the original traveling salesperson problem. Thus, if the optimal solution to the assignment problem is feasible for the traveling salesperson problem (i.e., if the assignment solution contains no subtours), the optimal solution to the assignment problem is also optimal for the traveling salesperson problem. The results of the branch-and-bound procedure are given in Figure 19.

We first solve the assignment problem in Table 40 (referred to as subproblem 1). The optimal solution is $x_{15} = x_{21} = x_{34} = x_{43} = x_{52} = 1$, $z = 495$. This solution con-

Figure 19
Branch-and-Bound
Tree for Traveling
Salesperson Problem

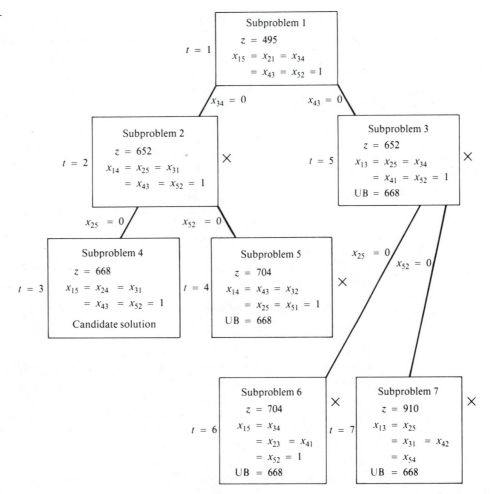

Table 40
Cost Matrix for
Subproblem 1

	CITY 1	CITY 2	CITY 3	CITY 4	CITY 5
City 1	M	132	217	164	58
City 2	132	M	290	201	79
City 3	217	290	M	113	303
City 4	164	201	113	M	196
City 5	58	79	303	196	M

tains two subtours (1–5–2–1 and 3–4–3) and cannot be the optimal solution to Joe's problem.

We now branch on subproblem 1 in a way that will prevent one of subproblem 1's subtours from recurring in solutions to subsequent subproblems. We choose to exclude the subtour 3–4–3. Observe that the optimal solution to Joe's problem must have either $x_{34} = 0$ or $x_{43} = 0$ (if $x_{34} = x_{43} = 1$, the optimal solution would have the subtour 3–4–3). Thus, we can branch on subproblem 1 by adding the following two subproblems:

Subproblem 2 Subproblem 1 + ($x_{34} = 0$, or $c_{34} = M$).

Subproblem 3 Subproblem 1 + ($x_{43} = 0$, or $c_{43} = M$).

We now choose a subproblem to solve. We arbitrarily choose to solve subproblem 2. We apply the Hungarian method to the cost matrix as shown in Table 41. The optimal solution to subproblem 2 is $z = 652$, $x_{14} = x_{25} = x_{31} = x_{43} = x_{52} = 1$. This solution includes the subtours 1–4–3–1 and 2–5–2, so this solution cannot be the optimal solution to Joe's problem.

Table 41
Cost Matrix for
Subproblem 2

	CITY 1	CITY 2	CITY 3	CITY 4	CITY 5
City 1	M	132	217	164	58
City 2	132	M	290	201	79
City 3	217	290	M	M	303
City 4	164	201	113	M	196
City 5	58	79	303	196	M

We now branch on subproblem 2 in an effort to exclude the subtour 2–5–2. We must ensure that either x_{25} or x_{52} equals zero. Thus, we add the following two subproblems:

Subproblem 4 Subproblem 2 + ($x_{25} = 0$, or $c_{25} = M$).

Subproblem 5 Subproblem 2 + ($x_{52} = 0$, or $c_{52} = M$).

Following the LIFO approach, we should next solve subproblem 4 or subproblem 5. We arbitrarily choose to solve subproblem 4. Applying the Hungarian method to the cost matrix shown in Table 42, we obtain the optimal solution $z = 668$, $x_{15} = x_{24} = x_{31} = x_{43} = x_{52} = 1$. This solution contains no subtours and yields the tour 1–5–2–4–3–1. Thus, subproblem 4 yields a candidate solution with $z = 668$. Any node that cannot yield a z-value < 668 may be eliminated from consideration.

Following the LIFO rule, we next solve subproblem 5. We apply the Hungarian method to the matrix in Table 43. The optimal solution to subproblem 5 is $z = 704$, $x_{14} = x_{43} = x_{32} = x_{25} = x_{51} = 1$. This solution is a tour, but $z = 704$ is not as good

Table 42
Cost Matrix for
Subproblem 4

	CITY 1	CITY 2	CITY 3	CITY 4	CITY 5
City 1	M	132	217	164	58
City 2	132	M	290	201	M
City 3	217	290	M	M	303
City 4	164	201	113	M	196
City 5	58	79	303	196	M

Table 43
Cost Matrix for
Subproblem 5

	CITY 1	CITY 2	CITY 3	CITY 4	CITY 5
City 1	M	132	217	164	58
City 2	132	M	290	201	79
City 3	217	290	M	M	303
City 4	164	201	113	M	196
City 5	58	M	303	196	M

as the subproblem 4 candidate's $z = 668$. Thus, subproblem 5 may be eliminated from consideration.

Only subproblem 3 remains. We find the optimal solution to the assignment problem in Table 44. $x_{13} = x_{25} = x_{34} = x_{41} = x_{52} = 1$, $z = 652$. This solution contains the subtours 1–3–4–1 and 2–5–2. Since $652 < 668$, however, it is still possible for subproblem 3 to yield a solution with no subtours that beats $z = 668$. Thus, we now branch on subproblem 3 in an effort to exclude the subtours. Any feasible solution to the traveling salesperson problem that emanates from subproblem 3 must have either $x_{25} = 0$ or $x_{52} = 0$ (why?), so we create subproblems 6 and 7:

Subproblem 6 Subproblem 3 + $(x_{25} = 0$, or $c_{25} = M)$.

Subproblem 7 Subproblem 3 + $(x_{52} = 0$, or $c_{52} = M)$.

Table 44
Cost Matrix for
Subproblem 3

	CITY 1	CITY 2	CITY 3	CITY 4	CITY 5
City 1	M	132	217	164	58
City 2	132	M	290	201	79
City 3	217	290	M	113	303
City 4	164	201	M	M	196
City 5	58	79	303	196	M

We next choose to solve subproblem 6. The optimal solution to subproblem 6 is $x_{15} = x_{34} = x_{23} = x_{41} = x_{52} = 1$, $z = 704$. This solution contains no subtours, but its z-value of 704 is inferior to the candidate solution from subproblem 4, so subproblem 6 cannot yield the optimal solution to the problem.

The only remaining subproblem is subproblem 7. The optimal solution to subproblem 7 is $x_{13} = x_{25} = x_{31} = x_{42} = x_{54} = 1$, $z = 910$. Again, $z = 910$ is inferior to $z = 668$, so subproblem 7 cannot yield the optimal solution.

Subproblem 4 thus yields the optimal solution: Joe should travel from Gary to South Bend, from South Bend to Fort Wayne, from Fort Wayne to Terre Haute, from Terre Haute to Evansville, and from Evansville to Gary. Joe will travel a total distance of 668 miles.

HEURISTICS FOR TSPs

When using branch-and-bound methods to solve traveling salesperson problems (TSPs) with many cities, large amounts of computer time may be required. For this reason, **heuristic methods**, or **heuristics**, which quickly lead to a good (but not necessarily optimal) solution to a TSP, are often used. A heuristic is a method used to solve a problem by trial and error when an algorithmic approach is impractical. Heuristics often have an intuitive justification. We now discuss two heuristics for the TSP: the nearest-neighbor and cheapest-insertion heuristics.

To apply the nearest-neighbor heuristic (NNH), we begin at any city and then "visit" the nearest city. Then we go to the unvisited city closest to the city we have most recently visited. Continue in this fashion until a tour is obtained. We now apply the NNH to Example 11. We arbitrarily choose to begin at city 1. City 5 is the closest city to city 1, so we have now generated the arc 1–5. Of cities 2, 3, and 4, city 2 is closest to city 5, so we have now generated the arcs 1–5–2. Of cities 3 and 4, city 4 is closest to city 2. We now have generated the arcs 1–5–2–4. Of course, we must next visit city 3 and then return to city 1; this yields the tour 1–5–2–4–3–1. In this case, the NNH yields an optimal tour. If we had begun at city 3, however, the reader should verify that the tour 3–4–1–5–2–3 would be obtained. This tour has length $113 + 164 + 58 + 79 + 290 = 704$ miles and is not optimal. Thus, the NNH need not yield an optimal tour. A popular heuristic is to apply the NNH beginning at each city and then take the best tour obtained.

In the cheapest-insertion heuristic (CIH), we begin at any city and find its closest neighbor. Then we create a subtour joining those two cities. Next, we replace an arc in the subtour (say, arc (i, j)) by the combination of two arcs—(i, k) and (k, j), where k is not in current subtour—that will increase the length of the subtour by the smallest (or cheapest) amount. Let c_{ij} be the length of arc (i, j). Note that if arc (i, j) is replaced by arcs (i, k) and (k, j), a length $c_{ik} + c_{kj} - c_{ij}$ is added to the subtour. Then we continue with this procedure until a tour is obtained. Suppose we begin the CIH at city 1. City 5 is closest to city 1, so we begin with the subtour $(1, 5)$–$(5, 1)$. Then we could replace $(1, 5)$ by $(1, 2)$–$(2, 5)$, $(1, 3)$–$(3, 5)$, or $(1, 4)$–$(4, 5)$. We could also replace arc $(5, 1)$ by $(5, 2)$–$(2, 1)$, $(5, 3)$–$(3, 1)$ or $(5, 4)$–$(4, 1)$. The calculations used to determine which arc of $(1, 5)$–$(5, 1)$ should be replaced are given in Table 45 (* indicates the correct replacement). As seen in the table, we may replace either $(1, 5)$ or $(5, 1)$. We arbitrarily choose to replace arc $(1, 5)$ by arcs $(1, 2)$ and $(2, 5)$. We currently have the subtour $(1, 2)$–$(2, 5)$–$(5, 1)$. We must now replace an arc (i, j) of this subtour by the arcs (i, k) and (k, j), where $k = 3$ or 4. The relevant computations are shown in Table 46.

Table 45	ARC REPLACED	ARCS ADDED TO SUBTOUR	ADDED LENGTH
Determining Which Arc of (1, 5)–(5, 1) Is Replaced	(1, 5)*	(1, 2)–(2, 5)	$c_{12} + c_{25} - c_{15} = 153$
	(1, 5)	(1, 3)–(3, 5)	$c_{13} + c_{35} - c_{15} = 462$
	(1, 5)	(1, 4)–(4, 5)	$c_{14} + c_{45} - c_{15} = 302$
	(5, 1)*	(5, 2)–(2, 1)	$c_{52} + c_{21} - c_{51} = 153$
	(5, 1)	(5, 3)–(3, 1)	$c_{53} + c_{31} - c_{51} = 462$
	(5, 1)	(5, 4)–(4, 1)	$c_{54} + c_{41} - c_{51} = 302$

Table 46	ARC REPLACED	ARCS ADDED	ADDED LENGTH
Determining Which	(1, 2)	(1, 3)–(3, 2)	$c_{13} + c_{32} - c_{12} = 375$
Arc of (1, 2)–(2, 5)–	(1, 2)*	(1, 4)–(4, 2)	$c_{14} + c_{42} - c_{12} = 233$
(5, 1) Is Replaced	(2, 5)	(2, 3)–(3, 5)	$c_{23} + c_{35} - c_{25} = 514$
	(2, 5)	(2, 4)–(4, 5)	$c_{24} + c_{45} - c_{25} = 318$
	(5, 1)	(5, 3)–(3, 1)	$c_{53} + c_{31} - c_{51} = 462$
	(5, 1)	(5, 4)–(4, 1)	$c_{54} + c_{41} - c_{51} = 302$

We now replace (1, 2) by arcs (1, 4) and (4, 2). This yields the subtour (1, 4)–(4, 2)–(2, 5)–(5, 1). An arc (i, j) in this subtour must now be replaced by arcs $(i, 3)$ and $(3, j)$. The relevant computations are shown in Table 47. We now replace arc (1, 4) by arcs (1, 3) and (3, 4). This yields the tour (1, 3)–(3, 4)–(4, 2)–(2, 5)–(5, 1). In this example, the CIH yields an optimal tour—but in general, the CIH does not necessarily do so.

Table 47	ARC REPLACED	ARCS ADDED	ADDED COST
Determining Which	(1, 4)*	(1, 3)–(3, 4)	$c_{13} + c_{34} - c_{14} = 166$
Arc of (1, 4)–(4, 2)–	(4, 2)	(4, 3)–(3, 2)	$c_{43} + c_{32} - c_{42} = 202$
(2, 5)–(5, 1) Is	(2, 5)	(2, 3)–(3, 5)	$c_{23} + c_{35} - c_{25} = 514$
Replaced	(5, 1)	(5, 3)–(3, 1)	$c_{53} + c_{31} - c_{51} = 462$

EVALUATION OF HEURISTICS

The following three methods have been suggested for evaluating heuristics:

1. Performance guarantees
2. Probabilistic analysis
3. Empirical analysis

A performance guarantee for a heuristic gives a worst-case bound on how far away from optimality a tour constructed by the heuristic can be. For the NNH, it can be shown that for any number r, a TSP can be constructed such that the NNH yields a tour that is r times as long as the optimal tour. Thus, in a worst-case scenario, the NNH fares poorly. For a symmetric TSP satisfying the triangle inequality (that is, for which $c_{ij} = c_{ji}$ and $c_{ik} \leq c_{ij} + c_{jk}$ for all i, j, and k), it has been shown that the length of the tour obtained by the CIH cannot exceed twice the length of the optimal tour.

In probabilistic analysis, a heuristic is evaluated by assuming that the location of cities follows some known probability distribution. For example, we might assume that the cities are independent random variables that are uniformly distributed on a cube of unit length, width, and height. Then for each heuristic, we would compute the following ratio:

$$\frac{\text{Expected length of the path found by the heuristic}}{\text{Expected length of an optimal tour}}$$

The closer the ratio is to 1, the better the heuristic.

For empirical analysis, heuristics are compared to the optimal solution for a number of problems for which the optimal tour is known. As an illustration, for five 100-city

TSPs, Golden, Bodin, Doyle, and Stewart (1980) found that the NNH—taking the best of all solutions found when the NNH was applied beginning at each city—produced tours that averaged 15% longer than the optimal tour. For the same set of problems, it was found that the CIH (again applying the best solution obtained by applying CIH to all cities) produced tours that also averaged 15% longer than the optimal tour.

R E M A R K S   **1.** Golden, Bodin, Doyle, and Stewart (1980) describe a heuristic that regularly comes within 2–3% of the optimal tour.

2. It is also important to compare heuristics with regard to computer running time and ease of implementation.

3. For an excellent discussion of heuristics, see Chapters 5–7 of Lawler (1985).

◆ PROBLEMS

GROUP A

1. Four jobs must be processed on a single machine. The time required to perform each job and the due date for each job are shown in Table 48. Use branch-and-bound to determine the order of performing the jobs that minimizes the total time the jobs are delayed.

Table 48

	TIME TO PERFORM JOB (Minutes)	DUE DATE OF JOB
Job 1	7	End of minute 14
Job 2	5	End of minute 13
Job 3	9	End of minute 18
Job 4	11	End of minute 15

2. Each day, Sunco manufactures four types of gasoline: lead-free premium, lead-free regular, leaded premium, and leaded regular. Because of cleaning and resetting of machinery, the time required to produce a batch of gasoline depends on the type of gasoline last produced. For example, it takes longer to switch between a lead-free gasoline and a leaded gasoline than it does to switch between two lead-free gasolines. The times (in minutes) required to manufacture each day's gasoline requirements are shown in Table 49. Use a branch-and-bound approach to determine the order in which the gasolines should be produced each day.

Table 49

LAST-PRODUCED GASOLINE	GAS TO BE NEXT PRODUCED			
	LFR	*LFP*	*LR*	*LP*
LFR	—	50	120	140
LFP	60	—	140	110
LR	90	130	—	60
LP	130	120	80	—

Note: Assume that the last gas produced yesterday precedes the first gas produced today.

3. A Hamiltonian path in a network is a closed path that passes exactly once through each node in the network before returning to its starting point. Taking a four-city TSP as an example, explain why solving a TSP is equivalent to finding the shortest Hamiltonian path in a network.

4. There are four pins on a printed circuit. The distance between each pair of pins (in inches) is given in Table 50. **(a)** Suppose we want to place three wires between the pins in a way that connects all the wires and uses the minimum

Table 50

	1	2	3	4
1	0	1	2	2
2	1	0	3	2.9
3	2	3	0	3
4	2	2.9	3	0

amount of wire. Solve this problem by using one of the techniques discussed in Chapter 8.

(b) Now suppose that we again want to place three wires between the pins in a way that connects all the wires and uses the minimum amount of wire. Also suppose that if more than two wires touch a pin, a short circuit will occur. Now set up a traveling-salesperson problem that can be used to solve this problem. (*Hint:* Add a pin 0 such that the distance between pin 0 and any other pin is 0.)

5. (a) Use the NNH to find a solution to the TSP in Problem 2. Begin with LFR.

(b) Use the CIH to find a solution to the TSP in Problem 2. Begin with the subtour LFR–LFP–LFR.

GROUP B

6. Use branch-and-bound to determine a way (if any exists) to place four queens on a 4 × 4 chessboard so that no queen can capture another queen. (*Hint:* Let $x_{ij} = 1$ if a queen is placed in row i and column j of the chessboard and $x_{ij} = 0$ otherwise. Then branch as in the machine-delay problem. Many nodes may be eliminated from consideration because they are infeasible. For example, the node associated with the arcs $x_{11} = x_{22} = 1$ is infeasible, because these two queens can capture each other.)

7. Although the Hungarian method is an efficient method for solving an assignment problem, branch-and-bound can also be used to solve an assignment problem. Suppose a company has five factories and five warehouses. Each factory's requirements must be met by a single warehouse, and each warehouse can be assigned to only one factory. The costs of assigning a warehouse to meet a factory's demand (in thousands) are shown in Table 51.

Table 51

	FACTORY				
	1	*2*	*3*	*4*	*5*
Warehouse 1	$5	$15	$20	$25	$10
Warehouse 2	$10	$12	$5	$15	$19
Warehouse 3	$5	$17	$18	$9	$11
Warehouse 4	$8	$9	$10	$5	$12
Warehouse 5	$9	$10	$5	$11	$7

Let $x_{ij} = 1$ if warehouse i is assigned to factory j and 0 otherwise. Begin by branching on the warehouse assigned to factory 1. This creates the following five branches: $x_{11} = 1, x_{21} = 1, x_{31} = 1, x_{41} = 1$, and $x_{51} = 1$. How can we obtain a lower bound on the total cost associated with a branch? Examine the branch $x_{21} = 1$. If $x_{21} = 1$, no further assignments can come from row 2 or column 1 of the cost matrix. In determining the factory to which each of the unassigned warehouses (1, 3, 4, and 5) are assigned, we cannot do better than to assign each of the unassigned warehouses to the smallest cost in the warehouse's row (excluding the factory 1 column). Thus, the minimum cost assignment having $x_{21} = 1$ must have a total cost of at least $10 + 10 + 9 + 5 + 5 = 39$.

Similarly, in determining the warehouse to which each of the unassigned factories (2, 3, 4, and 5) is assigned, we cannot do better than to assign each unassigned factory to the smallest cost in the factory's column (excluding the warehouse 2 row). Thus, the minimum cost assignment having $x_{21} = 1$ must have a total cost of at least $10 + 9 + 5 + 5 + 7 = 36$. Thus, the total cost of any assignment having $x_{21} = 1$ must be at least $\max(36, 39) = 39$. So if branching ever leads to a candidate solution having a total cost of 39 or less, the $x_{21} = 1$ branch may be eliminated from consideration. Use this idea to solve the problem by branch-and-bound.

8.[†] Consider a long roll of wallpaper that repeats its pattern every yard. Four sheets of wallpaper must be cut from the roll. With reference to the beginning (call it point 0) of the wallpaper, the beginning and end of each sheet are located as shown in Table 52. Thus, sheet 1 begins 0.3 yd from the beginning of the roll (and 1.3 yd from the beginning of the roll, etc.) and sheet 1 ends 0.7 yd from the beginning of the roll (and 1.7 yd from the beginning of the roll, etc.) Assume we are at the beginning of the roll. In what order should the sheets be cut so as to minimize the total amount of wasted paper? Assume that a final cut is made to bring the roll back to the beginning of the pattern.

Table 52

	BEGINNING (Yards)	END (Yards)
Sheet 1	0.3	0.7
Sheet 2	0.4	0.8
Sheet 3	0.2	0.5
Sheet 4	0.7	0.9

[†]Based on Garfinkel (1977).

9-7   IMPLICIT ENUMERATION

The method of implicit enumeration is often used to solve 0–1 IPs. Implicit enumeration uses the fact that each variable must equal 0 or 1 to simplify both the branching and bounding components of the branch-and-bound process and to determine efficiently when a node is infeasible.

Before discussing implicit enumeration, we show how any pure IP may be expressed as a 0–1 IP: Simply express each variable in the original IP as the sum of powers of 2. For example, suppose the variable x_i is required to be an integer. Let n be the smallest integer such that we can be sure that $x_i < 2^{n+1}$. Then x_i may be (uniquely) expressed as the sum of $2^0, 2^1, \ldots, 2^{n-1}, 2^n$, and

$$x_i = u_n 2^n + u_{n-1} 2^{n-1} + \cdots + u_2 2^2 + 2u_1 + u_0 \qquad (40)$$

where $u_i = 0$ or 1 $(i = 0, 1, \ldots, n)$.

To convert the original IP to a 0–1 IP, replace each occurrence of x_i by the right side of (40). For example, suppose we know that $x_i \le 100$. Then $x_i < 2^{6+1} = 128$. Then (40) yields

$$x_i = 64u_6 + 32u_5 + 16u_4 + 8u_3 + 4u_2 + 2u_1 + u_0 \qquad (41)$$

where $u_i = 0$ or 1 $(i = 0, 1, \ldots, 6)$. Then replace each occurrence of x_i by the right side of (41). How can we find the values of the u's corresponding to a given value of x_i? Suppose $x_i = 93$. Then u_6 will be the largest multiple of $2^6 = 64$ that is contained in 93. This yields $u_6 = 1$; then the rest of the right side of (41) must equal $93 - 64 = 29$. Then u_5 will be the largest multiple of $2^5 = 32$ that is contained in 29. This yields $u_5 = 0$. Then u_4 will be the largest multiple of $2^4 = 16$ that is contained in 29. This yields $u_4 = 1$. Continuing in this fashion, we obtain $u_3 = 1$, $u_2 = 1$, $u_1 = 0$, and $u_0 = 1$. Thus, $93 = 2^6 + 2^4 + 2^3 + 2^2 + 2^0$.

We will soon discover that 0–1 IPs are generally easier to solve than other pure IPs. Why, then, don't we transform every pure IP into a 0–1 IP? Simply because transforming a pure IP into a 0–1 IP greatly increases the number of variables. However, many situations (such as lockbox and knapsack problems) naturally yield 0–1 problems. Thus, it is certainly worthwhile to learn how to solve 0–1 IPs.

The tree used in the implicit enumeration method is similar to the trees that were used to solve 0–1 knapsack problems in Section 9.5. Each branch of the tree will specify, for some variable x_i, that $x_i = 0$ or $x_i = 1$. At each node, the values of some of the variables are specified. For instance, suppose a 0–1 problem has variables $x_1, x_2, x_3, x_4, x_5, x_6$, and part of the tree looks like Figure 20. At node 4, the values of x_3, x_4, and x_2 are specified. These variables are referred to as **fixed variables**. All variables whose values are unspecified at a node are called **free variables**. Thus, at node 4, x_1, x_5, and x_6 are free variables. For any node, a specification of the values of all the free variables is called a **completion** of the node. Thus, $x_1 = 1$, $x_5 = 1$, $x_6 = 0$ is a completion of node 4.

We are now ready to outline the three main ideas used in implicit enumeration:

1. Suppose we are at any node. Given the values of the fixed variables at that node, is there an easy way to find a good completion of the node that is feasible in the original 0–1 IP? To answer this question, we complete the node by setting each free variable equal to the value (0 or 1) that makes the objective function largest (in a max problem) or smallest (in a min problem). If this completion of the node is feasible, then it is certainly

Figure 20
Illustration of Free
and Fixed Variables

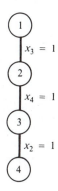

the best feasible completion of the node, and further branching of the node is unnecessary. Suppose we are solving

$$\max z = 4x_1 + 2x_2 - x_3 + 2x_4$$
$$\text{s.t.} \quad x_1 + 3x_2 - x_3 - 2x_4 \geq 1$$
$$x_i = 0 \text{ or } 1 \quad (i = 1, 2, 3, 4)$$

If we are at a node (call it node 4) where $x_1 = 0$ and $x_2 = 1$ are fixed, then the best we can do is set $x_3 = 0$ and $x_4 = 1$. Since $x_1 = 0$, $x_2 = 1$, $x_3 = 0$, and $x_4 = 1$ is feasible in the original problem, we have found the best feasible completion of node 4. Thus, node 4 is fathomed and $x_1 = 0$, $x_2 = 1$, $x_3 = 0$, $x_4 = 1$ (along with its z-value of 4) may be used as a candidate solution.

2. Even if the best completion of a node is not feasible, the best completion gives us a bound on the best objective function value that can be obtained via a feasible completion of the node. This bound can often be used to eliminate a node from consideration. For example, suppose we have previously found a candidate solution with $z = 6$, and our objective is to maximize

$$z = 4x_1 + 2x_2 + x_3 - x_4 + 2x_5$$

Also suppose that we are at a node where the fixed variables are $x_1 = 0$, $x_2 = 1$, and $x_3 = 1$. Then the best completion of this node is $x_4 = 0$ and $x_5 = 1$. This yields a z-value of $2 + 1 + 2 = 5$. Since $z = 5$ cannot beat the candidate with $z = 6$, we can immediately eliminate this node from consideration (whether or not the completion is feasible is irrelevant).

3. At any node, is there an easy way to determine if all completions of the node are infeasible? Suppose we are at node 4 of Figure 20 and one of the constraints is

$$-2x_1 + 3x_2 + 2x_3 - 3x_4 - x_5 + 2x_6 \leq -5 \tag{42}$$

Is there any completion of node 4 that can satisfy this constraint? We assign values to the free variables that make the left side of (42) as small as possible. If this completion of node 4 won't satisfy (42), then certainly no completion of node 4 can satisfy (42). Thus, we set $x_1 = 1$, $x_5 = 1$, and $x_6 = 0$. Substituting these values and the values of the fixed variables into (42), we obtain $-2 + 3 + 2 - 3 - 1 \leq -5$. Since this inequality does not hold, no completion of node 4 can satisfy (42). No completion of node 4 can be feasible for the original problem, and node 4 may be eliminated from consideration.

In general, we check whether a node has a feasible completion by looking at each constraint and assigning each free variable the best value (as described in Table 53 for satisfying the constraint.)[†] If even one constraint is not satisfied by its most feasible completion, we know that the node has no feasible completion. In this case, the node cannot yield the optimal solution to the original IP.

Table 53 How to Determine Whether a Node Has a Completion Satisfying a Given Constraint	TYPE OF CONSTRAINT	SIGN OF FREE VARIABLE'S COEFFICIENT IN CONSTRAINT	VALUE ASSIGNED TO FREE VARIABLE IN FEASIBILITY CHECK
	$\leq$	$+$	0
	$\leq$	$-$	1
	$\geq$	$+$	1
	$\geq$	$-$	0

We note, however, that even if a node has no feasible completion, our crude infeasibility check may not reveal that the node has no feasible completion until we have moved further down the tree to a node where there are more fixed variables. If we have failed to obtain any information about a node, we now branch on a free variable x_i and add two new nodes: one node with $x_i = 1$ and another node with $x_i = 0$.

E X A M P L E 12

Use implicit enumeration to solve the following 0–1 IP:

$$\max z = -7x_1 - 3x_2 - 2x_3 - x_4 - 2x_5$$
$$\text{s.t.} \quad -4x_1 - 2x_2 + x_3 - 2x_4 - x_5 \leq -3 \tag{43}$$
$$-4x_1 - 2x_2 - 4x_3 + x_4 + 2x_5 \leq -7 \tag{44}$$
$$x_i = 0 \text{ or } 1 \quad (i = 1, 2, 3, 4, 5)$$

Solution

At the beginning (node 1), all variables are free. We first check whether the best completion of node 1 is feasible. The best completion of node 1 is $x_1 = 0$, $x_2 = 0$, $x_3 = 0$, $x_4 = 0$, $x_5 = 0$, which is not feasible (it violates both constraints). We now check to see whether node 1 has no feasible completion. Checking (43) for feasibility, we set $x_1 = 1, x_2 = 1, x_3 = 0, x_4 = 1, x_5 = 1$. This satisfies (43) (it yields $-9 \leq -3$). We now check (44) for feasibility by setting $x_1 = 1$, $x_2 = 1$, $x_3 = 1$, $x_4 = 0$, $x_5 = 0$. This completion of node 1 satisfies (44) (it yields $-10 \leq -7$). Thus, node 1 has a feasible completion satisfying (44). Therefore, our infeasibility check does not allow us to classify node 1 as having no feasible completion. We now choose to branch on a free variable: arbitrarily, x_1. This yields two new nodes: node 2 with the constraint $x_1 = 1$ and node 3 with the constraint $x_1 = 0$ (see Figure 21).

We now choose to analyze node 2. The best completion of node 2 is $x_1 = 1$, $x_2 = 0$, $x_3 = 0, x_4 = 0$, and $x_5 = 0$. Unfortunately, this completion is not feasible. We now try to determine whether node 2 has a feasible completion. We check whether $x_1 = 1$, $x_2 = 1, x_3 = 0, x_4 = 1, x_5 = 1$ satisfies (43) (this yields $-9 \leq -3$). Then we check whether $x_1 = 1, x_2 = 1, x_3 = 1, x_4 = 0, x_5 = 0$ satisfies (44) (this yields $-10 \leq -7$).

[†]Each equality constraint should be replaced by a $\leq$ and a $\geq$ constraint.

Figure 21
Branching on Node 1

Figure 21
Branching on Node 1

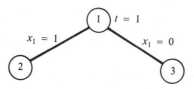

Thus, our infeasibility check has yielded no information about whether or not node 2 has a feasible completion.

We now choose to branch on node 2. We arbitrarily choose to branch on the free variable x_2. This yields nodes 4 and 5 in Figure 22. Using the LIFO rule, we choose to next analyze node 5. The best completion of node 5 is $x_1 = 1$, $x_2 = 0$, $x_3 = 0$, $x_4 = 0$, $x_5 = 0$. Again, this completion is infeasible. We now perform a feasibility check on node 5. We determine whether $x_1 = 1$, $x_2 = 0$, $x_3 = 0$, $x_4 = 1$, $x_5 = 1$ satisfies (43) (this yields $-7 \leq -3$). Then we check whether $x_1 = 1$, $x_2 = 0$, $x_3 = 1$, $x_4 = 0$, $x_5 = 0$ satisfies (44) (this yields $-8 \leq -7$). Again, our feasibility check has yielded no information. Thus, we branch on node 5 and arbitrarily choose to branch on the free variable x_3. This adds nodes 6 and 7 in Figure 23.

Figure 22
Branching on Node 2

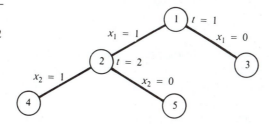

Figure 23
Branching on Node 5

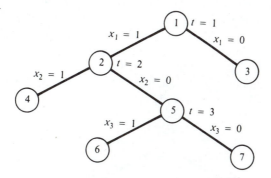

Applying the LIFO rule, we next choose to analyze node 6. The best completion of node 6 is $x_1 = 1$, $x_2 = 0$, $x_3 = 1$, $x_4 = 0$, $x_5 = 0$, $z = -9$. This point is feasible, so we have found a candidate solution with $z = -9$. Using the LIFO rule, we next analyze node 7. The best completion of node 7 is $x_1 = 1$, $x_2 = 0$, $x_3 = 0$, $x_4 = 0$, $x_5 = 0$, $z = -7$. Since $z = -7$ is better than $z = -9$, it is possible for node 7 to beat the current candidate. Thus, we must check node 7 to see whether it has any feasible completion. We see whether $x_1 = 1$, $x_2 = 0$, $x_3 = 0$, $x_4 = 1$, $x_5 = 1$ satisfies (43) (this yields $-7 \leq -3$). Then we see whether $x_1 = 1$, $x_2 = 0$, $x_3 = 0$, $x_4 = 0$, $x_5 = 0$ satisfies (44) (this yields $-4 \leq -7$). This means that no completion of node 7 can satisfy (44). Thus, node 7 has no feasible completion, and it may be eliminated from consideration (indicated by an × in Figure 24).

The LIFO rule now indicates that we should analyze node 4. The best completion of node 4 is $x_1 = 1$, $x_2 = 1$, $x_3 = 0$, $x_4 = 0$, $x_5 = 0$. This solution has $z = -10$. Thus, node 4 cannot beat the previous candidate solution from node 6 (having $z = -9$), and node 4 may be eliminated from consideration.

Figure 24
Node 6 Yields a
Candidate Solution,
and Node 7 Has No
Feasible Completion

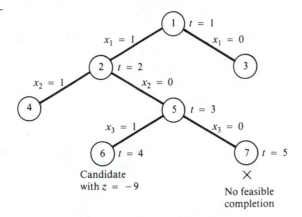

We are now facing the tree in Figure 25. Only node 3 remains to be analyzed. The best completion of node 3 is $x_1 = 0$, $x_2 = 0$, $x_3 = 0$, $x_4 = 0$, $x_5 = 0$. This point is infeasible. Since this point has $z = 0$, however, it is possible that node 3 can yield a feasible solution that is better than our current candidate (with $z = -9$). We now check whether node 3 has any feasible completion: Does $x_1 = 0$, $x_2 = 1$, $x_3 = 0$, $x_4 = 1$, $x_5 = 1$ satisfy (43)? This yields $-5 \le -3$, so node 3 does have a completion satisfying (43). Then we see whether node 3 has any completion satisfying (44): Does $x_1 = 0$, $x_2 = 1$, $x_3 = 1$, $x_4 = 0$, $x_5 = 0$ satisfy (44)? This yields $-6 \le -7$, which is untrue. Thus, node 3 has no completion satisfying (44), and node 3 may be eliminated from consideration. We now have the tree in Figure 26.

Since there are no nodes left to analyze, the node 6 candidate with $z = -9$ must be optimal. Thus, $x_1 = 1$, $x_2 = 0$, $x_3 = 1$, $x_4 = 0$, $x_5 = 0$, $z = -9$ is the optimal solution

Figure 25
Node 4 Cannot Beat
Node 6 Candidate

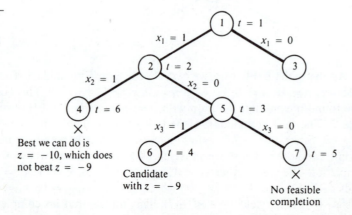

Figure 26
Node 3 Has No
Feasible Completion

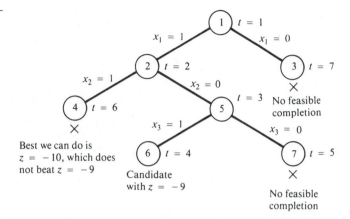

to the 0–1 IP. Note that every possible point $(x_1, x_2, x_3, x_4, x_5)$ where $x_i = 0$ or 1 has been implicitly considered, and all but the optimal solution have been eliminated. For example, for the point $x_1 = 1, x_2 = 1, x_3 = 1, x_4 = 1, x_5 = 0$, the analysis of node 4 shows that this point cannot be optimal because it cannot have a z-value better than -9. As another example, the point $x_1 = 0, x_2 = 1, x_3 = 1, x_4 = 1, x_5 = 1$ cannot be optimal, because our analysis of node 3 shows that no completion of node 3 can be feasible.

The use of subtler infeasibility tests (called **surrogate constraints**) can often reduce the number of nodes that must be examined before an optimal solution is found. For example, consider a 0–1 IP with the following constraints:

$$x_1 + x_2 + x_3 + x_4 + x_5 \leq 2 \tag{45}$$

$$x_1 - x_2 + x_3 - x_4 - x_5 \geq 1 \tag{46}$$

Suppose we are at a node where $x_1 = x_2 = 1$. To check whether this node has a feasible completion, we would first see whether $x_1 = 1, x_2 = 1, x_3 = 0, x_4 = 0, x_5 = 0$ satisfies (45) (it does). Then we would see whether $x_1 = 1, x_2 = 1, x_3 = 1, x_4 = 0, x_5 = 0$ satisfies (46) (it does). In this situation, our crude infeasibility tests do not yet indicate that this node is infeasible. Observe, however, that since $x_1 = x_2 = 1$, the only way to satisfy (45) is by choosing $x_3 = x_4 = x_5 = 0$. This completion of the $x_1 = x_2 = 1$ node fails to satisfy (46). Thus, the node with $x_1 = x_2 = 1$ will have no feasible completion. Eventually, our crude infeasibility test would have indicated this fact, but we might have been forced to examine several more nodes before we found that the node with $x_1 = x_2 = 1$ had no feasible completion. In a more complex problem, a subtler infeasibility test that combined information from both constraints might have enabled us to examine fewer nodes. Of course, a subtler infeasibility test would require more computation than our crude infeasibility test, so it might not be worth the effort. For a discussion of surrogate constraints, see Salkin (1975), Taha (1975), and Nemhauser and Wolsey (1988).

As with any branch-and-bound algorithm, there are many arbitrary choices that determine the efficiency of the implicit enumeration algorithm. See Salkin, Taha, and Nemhauser and Wolsey for further discussion of implicit enumeration techniques.

◆ PROBLEMS

GROUP A

Use implicit enumeration to solve the following 0–1 IPs:

1. $\max z = 3x_1 + x_2 + 2x_3 - x_4 + x_5$
s.t. $2x_1 + x_2 \qquad - 3x_4 \qquad \leq 1$
$\qquad x_1 + 2x_2 - 3x_3 - x_4 + 2x_5 \geq 2$
$\qquad\qquad\qquad x_i = 0 \text{ or } 1$

2. $\max z = 2x_1 - x_2 + x_3$
s.t. $x_1 + 2x_2 - x_3 \leq 1$
$\qquad x_1 + x_2 + x_3 \leq 2$
$\qquad\qquad x_i = 0 \text{ or } 1$

3. Finco is considering investing in five projects. Each project requires a cash outflow at time 0 and yields an NPV as described in Table 54 (all dollars in millions). At time 0, $10 million is available for investment. Projects 1 and 2 are mutually exclusive (that is, Finco cannot undertake both). Similarly, projects 3 and 4 are mutually exclusive. Also, project 2 cannot be undertaken unless project 5 is undertaken. Use implicit enumeration to determine which projects should be undertaken in order to maximize NPV.

Table 54

PROJECT	TIME 0 CASH OUTFLOW	NPV
1	$4	$5
2	$6	$9
3	$5	$6
4	$4	$3
5	$3	$2

4. Use implicit enumeration to find the optimal solution to Example 5 (the set-covering problem).

5. Use implicit enumeration to solve Problem 1 of Section 9.2.

GROUP B

6. Why are the values of $u_0, u_1, \ldots, u_n$ in (40) unique?

9-8   SOLVING INTEGER PROGRAMMING PROBLEMS WITH LINDO

LINDO can be used to solve pure or mixed IPs. In addition to the optimal solution, the LINDO output for an IP gives shadow prices and reduced costs. Unfortunately, the shadow prices and reduced costs refer to subproblems generated during the branch-and-bound solution process—*not* to the IP. Unlike linear programming, there is no well-developed theory of sensitivity analysis for integer programming. The reader interested in a discussion of sensitivity analysis for IPs should consult Williams (1985).

    To use LINDO to solve an IP, begin by entering the problem as if it were an LP. After typing the END statement (to designate the end of the LP constraints), type for each 0–1 variable x the following statement:

INTEGER x

Thus, for an IP in which x and y are 0–1 variables, the following statements would be typed after the END statement:

INTEGER x

INTEGER y

A variable (say, w) that can assume any nonnegative integer value is indicated by the GIN statement. Thus, if w may assume the values 0, 1, 2, . . . , we would type the following statement after the END statement:

GIN w

To tell LINDO that the first n variables appearing in the formulation must be 0–1 variables, use the command INT n.

To tell LINDO that the first n variables appearing in the formulation may assume any nonnegative integer value, use the command GIN n.

To view or print the solution to an IP, use the command SOLUTION.

9-9   THE CUTTING PLANE ALGORITHM*

In previous portions of this chapter, we have described in some detail how branch-and-bound methods can be used to solve integer programming problems. In this section, we discuss an alternative method, **the cutting plane algorithm,** which can be used to solve integer programming problems. We illustrate the cutting plane algorithm by solving the Telfa Corporation problem (Example 9). Recall from Section 9.3 that this problem was

$$\max z = 8x_1 + 5x_2$$
$$\text{s.t.} \quad x_1 + x_2 \leq 6$$
$$9x_1 + 5x_2 \leq 45 \tag{47}$$
$$x_1, x_2 > 0; \ x_1, x_2 \text{ integer}$$

After adding slack variables s_1 and s_2, we found the optimal tableau for the LP relaxation of the Telfa example to be as shown in Table 55.

Table 55
Optimal Tableau for
LP Relaxation of
Telfa Example

z	x_1	x_2	s_1	s_2	RHS
1	0	0	1.25	0.75	41.25
0	0	1	2.25	-0.25	2.25
0	1	0	-1.25	0.25	3.75

To apply the cutting plane method, we begin by choosing any constraint in the LP relaxation's optimal tableau in which a basic variable is fractional. We arbitrarily choose the second constraint, which is

$$x_1 - 1.25s_1 + 0.25s_2 = 3.75 \tag{48}$$

We now define $[x]$ to be the largest integer less than or equal to x. For example, $[3.75] = 3$ and $[-1.25] = -2$. Any number x can be written in the form $[x] + f$, where $0 \leq f < 1$. We call f the fractional part of x. For example, $3.75 = 3 + 0.75$, and $-1.25 = -2 + 0.75$. In (47)'s optimal tableau, we now write each variable's coefficient and the constraint's right-hand side in the form $[x] + f$, where $0 \leq f < 1$. Now (48) may be written as

$$x_1 - 2s_1 + 0.75s_1 + 0s_2 + 0.25s_2 = 3 + 0.75 \tag{49}$$

Putting all terms with integer coefficients on the left side and all terms with fractional coefficients on the right side yields

$$x_1 - 2s_1 + 0s_2 - 3 = 0.75 - 0.75s_1 - 0.25s_2 \tag{50}$$

*This section covers topics that may be omitted with no loss of continuity.

The cutting plane algorithm now suggests adding the following constraint to the LP relaxation's optimal tableau:

$$\text{Right-hand side of (50)} \leq 0$$

or

$$0.75 - 0.75s_1 - 0.25s_2 \leq 0 \tag{51}$$

This constraint is called (for reasons that will soon become apparent) a **cut**. We now show that a cut that is generated by the above method has two properties:

1. Any feasible point for the IP will satisfy the cut.

2. The current optimal solution to the LP relaxation will not satisfy the cut.

Thus, a cut "cuts off" the current optimal solution to the LP relaxation but does not cut off any feasible solutions to the IP. When the cut to the LP relaxation is added, we hope we will obtain a solution where all variables are integer-valued. If so, we have found the optimal solution to the original IP. If our new optimal solution (to the LP relaxation plus the cut) has some fractional-valued variables, we generate another cut and continue the process. Gomory (1958) showed that this process will yield an optimal solution to the IP after a finite number of cuts. Before finding the optimal solution to the IP (47), we show why the cut (51) satisfies properties 1 and 2.

We now show that any feasible solution to the IP (47) will satisfy the cut (51). Consider any point that is feasible for the IP. For such a point, x_1 and x_2 take on integer values, and the point must be feasible in the LP relaxation of (47). Since (50) is just a rearrangement of the optimal tableau's second constraint, any feasible point for the IP must satisfy (50). Any feasible solution to the IP must have $s_1 \geq 0$ and $s_2 \geq 0$. Since $0.75 < 1$, any feasible solution to the IP will make the right-hand side of (50) be less than 1. Also note that for any point that is feasible for the IP, the left-hand side of (50) will be an integer. Thus, for any feasible point to the IP, the right-hand side of (50) must be an integer that is less than 1. This implies that any point that is feasible for the IP satisfies (51), so our cut does not eliminate any feasible integer points from consideration!

We now show that the current optimal solution to the LP relaxation cannot satisfy the cut (51). The current optimal solution to the LP relaxation has $s_1 = s_2 = 0$. Thus, it cannot satisfy (51). This argument works because 0.75 (the fractional part of the right-hand side of the second constraint) is greater than 0. Thus, if we choose any constraint whose right-hand side in the optimal tableau is fractional, we can cut off the LP relaxation's optimal solution.

The effect of the cut (51) can be seen in Figure 27. From the figure, we see that all points feasible for the IP (47) satisfy the cut (51), but the current optimal solution to the LP relaxation ($x_1 = 3.75$ and $x_2 = 2.25$) does not satisfy the cut (51). To obtain the graph of the cut, we replaced s_1 by $6 - x_1 - x_2$ and s_2 by $45 - 9x_1 - 5x_2$. This enabled us to rewrite the cut (51) as $3x_1 + 2x_2 \leq 15$.

We now add (51) to the LP relaxation's optimal tableau and use the dual simplex to solve the resulting LP. Cut (51) may be rewritten as $-0.75s_1 - 0.25s_2 \leq -0.75$. After adding a slack variable s_3 to this constraint, we obtain the tableau shown in Table 56.

The dual simplex ratio test indicates that s_1 should enter the basis in the third constraint. The resulting tableau is given in Table 57, which yields the optimal solution $z = 40, x_1 = 5, x_2 = 0$.

Figure 27
Example of Cutting
Plane

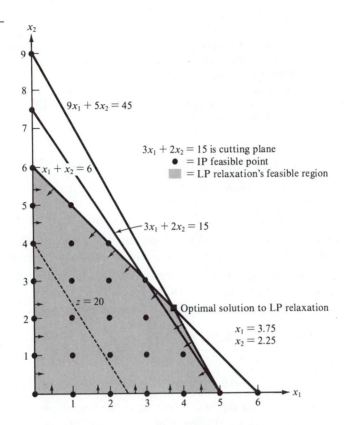

Table 56	z	x_1	x_2	s_1	s_2	s_3	RHS
Cutting Plane	1	0	0	1.25	0.75	0	41.25
Tableau After	0	0	1	2.25	−0.25	0	2.25
Adding Cut (51)	0	1	0	−1.25	0.25	0	3.75
	0	0	0	−0.75	−0.25	1	−0.75

Table 57	z	x_1	x_2	s_1	s_2	s_3	RHS
Optimal Tableau for	1	0	0	0	0.33	1.67	40
Cutting Plane	0	0	1	0	−1	3	0
Example	0	1	0	0	0.67	−1.67	5
	0	0	0	1	0.33	−1.33	1

Recall that a cut does not eliminate any points that are feasible for the IP. This means that whenever we solve the LP relaxation to an IP with several cuts as additional constraints and find an optimal solution in which all variables are integers, we have solved our original IP. Since x_1 and x_2 are integers in our current optimal solution, this point must be optimal for (47). Of course, if the first cut had not yielded the optimal solution to the IP, we would have kept adding cuts until we obtained an optimal tableau in which all variables were integers.

R E M A R K S   **1.** The algorithm requires that all coefficients of variables in the constraints and all right-hand sides of constraints be integers. This is to ensure that if the original decision variables are integers, the slack and excess variables will also be integers. Thus, a constraint such as $x_1 + 0.5x_2 \leq 3.6$ must be replaced by $10x_1 + 5x_2 \leq 36$.

2. If at any stage of the algorithm, two or more constraints have fractional right-hand sides, best results are often obtained if the next cut is generated by using the constraint whose right-hand side has the fractional part closest to $\frac{1}{2}$.

SUMMARY OF THE CUTTING PLANE ALGORITHM

Step 1 Find the optimal tableau for the IP's linear programming relaxation. If all variables in the optimal solution assume integer values, we have found an optimal solution to the IP; otherwise, we proceed to Step 2.

Step 2 Pick a constraint in the LP relaxation optimal tableau whose right-hand side has the fractional part closest to $\frac{1}{2}$. This constraint will be used to generate a cut.

Step 2a For the constraint identified in Step 2, write the constraint's right-hand side and each variable's coefficient in the form $[x] + f$, where $0 \leq f < 1$.

Step 2b Rewrite the constraint used to generate the cut as

All terms with integer coefficients = all terms with fractional coefficients

Then the cut is

All terms with fractional coefficients ≤ 0

Step 3 Use the dual simplex to find the optimal solution to the LP relaxation, with the cut as an additional constraint. If all variables assume integer values in the optimal solution, we have found an optimal solution to the IP. Otherwise, we pick the constraint with the most fractional right-hand side and use it to generate another cut, which is added to the tableau. We continue this process until a solution we obtain in which all variables are integers. This will be an optimal solution to the IP.

◆ PROBLEMS

GROUP A

1. Consider the following IP:

$$\max z = 14x_1 + 18x_2$$
$$\text{s.t.} \quad -x_1 + 3x_2 \leq 6$$
$$7x_1 + x_2 \leq 35$$
$$x_1, x_2 \geq 0; \; x_1, x_2 \text{ integer}$$

The optimal tableau for this IP's linear programming relaxation is given in Table 58. Use the cutting plane algorithm to solve this IP.

Table 58

z	x_1	x_2	s_1	s_2	RHS
1	0	0	$\frac{56}{11}$	$\frac{30}{11}$	126
0	0	1	$\frac{7}{22}$	$\frac{1}{22}$	$\frac{7}{2}$
0	1	0	$-\frac{1}{22}$	$\frac{3}{22}$	$\frac{9}{2}$

2. Consider the following IP:

$$\min z = 6x_1 + 8x_2$$
$$\text{s.t.} \quad 3x_1 + x_2 \geq 4$$
$$x_1 + 2x_2 \geq 4$$
$$x_1, x_2 \geq 0; \, x_1, x_2 \text{ integer}$$

The optimal tableau for this IP's linear programming relaxation is given in Table 59. Use the cutting plane algorithm to find the optimal solution to this IP.

Table 59

z	x_1	x_2	e_1	e_2	RHS
1	0	0	$-\frac{4}{5}$	$-\frac{18}{5}$	$\frac{88}{5}$
0	1	0	$-\frac{2}{5}$	$\frac{1}{5}$	$\frac{4}{5}$
0	0	1	$\frac{1}{5}$	$-\frac{3}{5}$	$\frac{8}{5}$

3. Consider the following IP:

$$\min z = 2x_1 - 4x_2$$
$$\text{s.t.} \quad 2x_1 + x_2 \leq 5$$
$$-4x_1 + 4x_2 \leq 5$$
$$x_1, x_2 \geq 0; \, x_1, x_2 \text{ integer}$$

The optimal tableau for this IP's linear programming relaxation is given in Table 60. Use the cutting plane algorithm to find the optimal solution to this IP.

Table 60

z	x_1	x_2	s_1	s_2	RHS
1	0	0	$-\frac{2}{3}$	$-\frac{5}{6}$	$-\frac{15}{2}$
0	1	0	$\frac{1}{3}$	$-\frac{1}{12}$	$\frac{5}{4}$
0	0	1	$\frac{1}{3}$	$\frac{1}{6}$	$\frac{5}{2}$

◆ SUMMARY

Integer programming problems (IPs) are usually much harder to solve than linear programming problems.

INTEGER PROGRAMMING FORMULATIONS

Most integer programming formulations involve **0–1 variables**.

FIXED-CHARGE PROBLEMS

Suppose activity i incurs a fixed charge if activity i is undertaken at any positive level. Let

$$x_i = \text{level of activity } i$$
$$y_i = \begin{cases} 1 & \text{if activity } i \text{ is undertaken at positive level } (x_i > 0) \\ 0 & \text{if } x_i = 0 \end{cases}$$

Then a constraint of the form $x_i \leq M_i y_i$ must be added to the formulation. Here, M_i must be large enough to ensure that x_i will be less than or equal to M_i.

EITHER-OR CONSTRAINTS

Suppose we wish to ensure that at least one of the following two constraints (and possibly both) are satisfied:

$$f(x_1, x_2, \ldots, x_n) \leq 0 \tag{26}$$
$$g(x_1, x_2, \ldots, x_n) \leq 0 \tag{27}$$

Adding the following two constraints to the formulation will ensure that at least one of

(26) and (27) is satisfied:

$$f(x_1, x_2, \ldots, x_n) \leq My \qquad (26')$$

$$g(x_1, x_2, \ldots, x_n) \leq M(1 - y) \qquad (27')$$

In (26′) and (27′), y is a 0–1 variable, and M is a number chosen large enough to ensure that $f(x_1, x_2, \ldots, x_n) \leq M$ and $g(x_1, x_2, \ldots, x_n) \leq M$ are satisfied for all values of $x_1, x_2, \ldots, x_n$ that satisfy the other constraints in the problem.

IF-THEN CONSTRAINTS

Suppose we wish to ensure that $f(x_1, x_2, \ldots, x_n) > 0$ implies $g(x_1, x_2, \ldots, x_n) \geq 0$. Then we include the following constraints in the formulation:

$$-g(x_1, x_2, \ldots, x_n) \leq My \qquad (28)$$

$$f(x_1, x_2, \ldots, x_n) \leq M(1 - y) \qquad (29)$$

$$y = 0 \text{ or } 1$$

Here, M is a large positive number, chosen large enough so that $f \leq M$ and $-g \leq M$ hold for all values of $x_1, x_2, \ldots, x_n$ that satisfy the other constraints in the problem.

HOW TO MODEL A PIECEWISE LINEAR FUNCTION $f(x)$ WITH 0–1 VARIABLES

Suppose the piecewise linear function $f(x)$ has break points $b_1, b_2, \ldots, b_n$.

Step 1 Wherever $f(x)$ occurs in the optimization problem, replace $f(x)$ by $z_1 f(b_1) + z_2 f(b_2) + \cdots + z_n f(b_n)$.

Step 2 Add the following constraints to the problem:

$$z_1 \leq y_1, z_2 \leq y_1 + y_2, z_3 \leq y_2 + y_3, \ldots, z_{n-1} \leq y_{n-2} + y_{n-1}, z_n \leq y_{n-1}$$

$$y_1 + y_2 + \cdots + y_{n-1} = 1$$

$$z_1 + z_2 + \cdots + z_n = 1$$

$$x = z_1 b_1 + z_2 b_2 + \cdots + z_n b_n$$

$$y_i = 0 \text{ or } 1 \ (i = 1, 2, \ldots, n - 1); z_i \geq 0 \ (i = 1, 2, \ldots, n)$$

BRANCH-AND-BOUND METHOD

Usually, IPs are solved by some version of the **branch-and-bound** procedure. Branch-and-bound methods implicitly enumerate all possible solutions to an IP. By solving a single **subproblem**, many possible solutions may be eliminated from consideration.

BRANCH-AND-BOUND FOR PURE IPs

Subproblems are generated by branching on an appropriately chosen fractional-valued variable x_i. Suppose that in a given subproblem (call it old subproblem), x_i assumes a fractional value between the integers i and $i + 1$. Then the two newly generated subproblems are

New Subproblem 1 Old subproblem + Constraint $x_i \leq i$.

New Subproblem 2 Old subproblem + Constraint $x_i \geq i + 1$.

If it is unnecessary to branch on a subproblem, we say that the subproblem is **fathomed**. The following three situations (for a max problem) result in a subproblem being fathomed: (1) The subproblem is infeasible. In this case, the subproblem cannot yield the optimal solution to the IP. (2) The subproblem yields an optimal solution in which all variables have integer values. Suppose this optimal solution has a better z-value than any previously obtained solution that is feasible in the IP. Then the subproblem's optimal solution becomes a **candidate solution**, and its z-value becomes the current lower bound (LB) on the optimal z-value for the IP. In this case, the current subproblem may yield the optimal solution to the IP. (3) The optimal z-value for the subproblem does not exceed (in a max problem) the current LB. In this case, the subproblem may be eliminated from consideration.

BRANCH-AND-BOUND FOR MIXED IPs

When branching on a fractional variable, only branch on variables that are required to be integers.

BRANCH-AND-BOUND FOR KNAPSACK PROBLEMS

Subproblems may easily be solved by first putting the best (in terms of benefit per unit weight) item in the knapsack, then the next best, etc., until a fraction of an item is used to completely fill the knapsack.

BRANCH-AND-BOUND TO MINIMIZE DELAY ON A SINGLE MACHINE

Begin the branching by determining which job should be processed last. Suppose there are n jobs. At a node where the jth job to be processed, $(j + 1)$th job to be processed, . . . , nth job to be processed are fixed, a lower bound on the total delay is given by (delay of jth job to be processed) + (delay of $(j + 1)$th job to be processed) + $\cdots$ + (delay of nth job to be processed).

BRANCH-AND-BOUND FOR TRAVELING SALESPERSON PROBLEM

Subproblems are assignment problems. If the optimal solution to a subproblem contains no subtours, it is a feasible solution to the traveling salesperson problem. Create new subproblems by branching to exclude a subtour. A subproblem can be eliminated if its optimal z-value is inferior to the best previously found feasible solution.

HEURISTICS FOR THE TSP

To apply the nearest-neighbor heuristic (NNH), we begin at any city and then "visit" the nearest city. Then we go to the unvisited city closest to the city we have most recently visited. We continue in this fashion until a tour is obtained. After applying this procedure beginning at each city, we take the best tour found.

In the cheapest-insertion heuristic (CIH), we begin at any city and find its closest neighbor. Then we create a subtour joining those two cities. Next, we replace an arc in the subtour (say, arc (i, j)) by the combination of two arcs—(i, k) and (k, j), where k is not in current subtour—that will increase the length of the subtour by the smallest (or cheapest) amount. Then we continue with this procedure until a tour is obtained. After applying this procedure beginning with each city, we take the best tour found.

IMPLICIT ENUMERATION

In a 0–1 IP, implicit enumeration may be used to find an optimal solution. When branching at a node, create two new subproblems by (for some free variable x_i) adding constraints $x_i = 0$ and $x_i = 1$. Suppose the best completion of a node is feasible. Then we need not branch on the node. If the best completion of a node is feasible and better than the current candidate solution, the current node yields a new LB (in a max problem) and may be optimal. If the best completion of the node is feasible and is not better than the current candidate solution, the current node may be eliminated from consideration. If at a given node, there is at least one constraint that is not satisfied by any completion of the node, then the node cannot yield a feasible solution to the IP, and the node cannot yield the optimal solution to the IP.

CUTTING PLANE ALGORITHM

Step 1 Find the optimal tableau for the IP's linear programming relaxation. If all variables in the optimal solution assume integer values, we have found an optimal solution to the IP; otherwise, we proceed to Step 2.

Step 2 Pick a constraint in the LP relaxation optimal tableau whose right-hand side has the fractional part closest to $\frac{1}{2}$. This constraint will be used to generate a cut.

Step 2a For the constraint identified in Step 2, write the constraint's right-hand side and each variable's coefficient in the form $[x] + f$, where $0 \leq f < 1$.

Step 2b Rewrite the constraint used to generate the cut as

All terms with integer coefficients = all terms with fractional coefficients

Then the cut is

All terms with fractional coefficients ≤ 0

Step 3 Use the dual simplex to find the optimal solution to the LP relaxation, with the cut as an additional constraint. If all variables assume integer values in the optimal solution, we have found an optimal solution to the IP. Otherwise, we pick the constraint with the most fractional right-hand side and use it to generate another cut, which is added to the tableau. We continue this process until we obtain a solution in which all variables are integers. This will be an optimal solution to the IP.

◆ REVIEW PROBLEMS

GROUP A

1. In the Sailco problem of Section 3.10, suppose that a fixed cost of $200 is incurred during each quarter that production takes place. Formulate an IP to minimize Sailco's total cost of meeting the demands for the four quarters.

2. Explain how you would use integer programming and piecewise linear functions to solve the following optimization problem. (*Hint:* Approximate x^2 and y^2 by piecewise linear functions.)

$$\max z = 3x^2 + y^2$$
$$\text{s.t.} \quad x + y \leq 1$$
$$x, y \geq 0$$

3.[†] The Transylvania Olympic Gymnastics Team consists of six people. Transylvania must choose three people to enter both the balance beam and floor exercises. They must also enter a total of four people in each event. The score that each individual gymnast can attain in each event is shown in Table 61. Formulate an IP to maximize the total score attained by the Transylvania gymnasts.

Table 61

	BALANCE BEAM	FLOOR EXERCISE
Gymnast 1	8.8	7.9
Gymnast 2	9.4	8.3
Gymnast 3	9.2	8.5
Gymnast 4	7.5	8.7
Gymnast 5	8.7	8.1
Gymnast 6	9.1	8.6

4.[‡] A court decision has stated that the enrollment of each high school in the city of Metropolis must be at least 20 percent black. The numbers of black and white high school students in each of the city's five school districts are shown in Table 62. The distance (in miles) that a student in each district must travel to each high school is shown in Table 63. School board policy requires that all the students in a given district attend the same school. Assuming that each school must have an enrollment of at least 150 students, formulate an IP that will minimize the total distance that Metropolis students must travel to high school.

[†]Based on Ellis and Corn (1984).
[‡]Based on Liggett (1973).

Table 62

	WHITES	BLACKS
District 1	80	30
District 2	70	5
District 3	90	10
District 4	50	40
District 5	60	30

Table 63

	HIGH SCHOOL 1	HIGH SCHOOL 2
District 1	1	2
District 2	0.5	1.7
District 3	0.8	0.8
District 4	1.3	0.4
District 5	1.5	0.6

5. The Cubs are trying to determine which of the following free agent pitchers should be signed: Rick Sutcliffe (RS), Bruce Sutter (BS), Dennis Eckersley (DE), Steve Trout (ST), Tim Stoddard (TS). The cost of signing each pitcher and the number of victories each pitcher will add to the Cubs are shown in Table 64. Subject to the following restrictions, the Cubs wish to sign the pitchers who will add the most victories to the team.

    1. At most $12 million can be spent.
    2. If DE and ST are signed, then BS cannot be signed.
    3. At most two right-handed pitchers can be signed.
    4. The Cubs cannot sign both BS and RS.

Formulate an IP to help the Cubs determine who they should sign.

Table 64

	COST OF SIGNING PITCHER (Millions)	VICTORIES ADDED TO CUBS
RS	$6	6 (righty)
BS	$4	5 (righty)
DE	$3	3 (righty)
ST	$2	3 (lefty)
TS	$2	2 (righty)

6. State University must purchase 1100 computers from three vendors. Vendor 1 charges $500 per computer plus a delivery charge of $5000. Vendor 2 charges $350 per computer plus a delivery charge of $4000. Vendor 3 charges $250 per computer plus a delivery charge of $6000. Vendor 1 will sell the university at most 500 computers, vendor 2 will sell the university at most 900 computers, and vendor 3 will sell the university at most 400 computers. Formulate an IP to minimize the cost of purchasing the needed computers.

7. Use the branch-and-bound method to solve the following IP:

$$\max z = 3x_1 + x_2$$
$$\text{s.t.} \quad 5x_1 + x_2 \le 12$$
$$2x_1 + x_2 \le 8$$
$$x_1, x_2 \ge 0; x_1, x_2 \text{ integer}$$

8. Use the branch-and-bound method to solve the following IP:

$$\min z = 3x_1 + x_2$$
$$\text{s.t.} \quad 2x_1 - x_2 \le 6$$
$$x_1 + x_2 \le 4$$
$$x_1, x_2 \ge 0; x_1 \text{ integer}$$

9. Use the branch-and-bound method to solve the following IP:

$$\max z = x_1 + 2x_2$$
$$\text{s.t.} \quad x_1 + x_2 \le 10$$
$$2x_1 + 5x_2 \le 30$$
$$x_1, x_2 \ge 0; x_1, x_2 \text{ integer}$$

10. Consider a country where there are 1¢, 5¢, 10¢, 20¢, 25¢, and 50¢ pieces. You work at the Two-Twelve Convenience Store and must give a customer 91¢ in change. Formulate an IP that can be used to minimize the number of coins needed to give the correct change. Use what you know about knapsack problems to solve the IP by branch-and-bound. (*Hint:* We need only solve a 90¢ problem.)

11. Use the brand-and-bound approach to find the optimal solution to the traveling salesperson problem shown in Table 65.

12. Use the implicit enumeration method to find the optimal solution to Problem 5.

Table 65

	CITY 1	CITY 2	CITY 3	CITY 4	CITY 5
City 1	—	3	1	7	2
City 2	3	—	4	4	2
City 3	1	4	—	4	2
City 4	7	4	4	—	7
City 5	2	2	2	7	—

13. Use the implicit enumeration method to find the optimal solution to the following 0–1 IP:

$$\max z = 5x_1 - 7x_2 + 10x_3 + 3x_4 - x_5$$
$$\text{s.t.} \quad -x_1 - 3x_2 + 3x_3 - x_4 - 2x_5 \le 0$$
$$2x_1 - 5x_2 + 3x_3 - 2x_4 - 2x_5 \le 3$$
$$- x_2 + x_3 + x_4 - x_5 \ge 2$$
$$\text{All variables 0 or 1}$$

14. A soda delivery truck starts at location 1 and must deliver soda to locations 2, 3, 4, and 5 before returning to location 1. The distance between these locations is given in Table 66. The soda truck wants to minimize the total distance traveled. In what order should the delivery truck make its deliveries?

Table 66

	1	2	3	4	5
Location 1	0	20	4	10	25
Location 2	20	0	5	30	10
Location 3	4	5	0	6	6
Location 4	10	25	6	0	20
Location 5	35	10	6	20	0

15. At Blair General Hospital, six types of surgical operations are performed. The types of operations each surgeon is qualified to perform (indicated by an X) are given in Table 67. Suppose that surgeon 1 and surgeon 2 dislike each other and cannot be on duty at the same time. Formulate an IP whose solution will determine the minimum number of surgeons required so that the hospital can perform all types of surgery.

GROUP B

16.[†] Gotham City has been divided into eight districts. The time (in minutes) it takes an ambulance to travel from one district to another is shown in Table 68. The popula-

[†]Based on Eaton et al. (1985).

Table 67

OPERATION NUMBER	1	2	3	4	5	6
Surgeon 1	×	×		×		
Surgeon 2			×		×	×
Surgeon 3			×		×	
Surgeon 4	×					×
Surgeon 5		×				
Surgeon 6					×	×

Table 68

DISTRICT	DISTRICT							
	1	*2*	*3*	*4*	*5*	*6*	*7*	*8*
1 40	0	3	4	6	8	9	8	10
2 30	3	0	5	4	8	6	12	9
3 35	4	5	0	2	2	3	5	7
4 20	6	4	2	0	3	2	5	4
5 15	8	8	2	3	0	2	2	4
6 50	9	6	3	2	2	0	3	2
7 45	8	12	5	5	2	3	0	2
8 60	10	9	7	4	4	2	2	0

tion of each district (in thousands) is as follows: district 1, 40; district 2, 30; district 3, 35; district 4, 20; district 5, 15; district 6, 50; district 7, 45; district 8, 60. The city has only two ambulances and wants to locate the ambulances so as to maximize the number of people who live within 2 minutes of an ambulance. Formulate an IP to accomplish this goal.

17. A company must complete three jobs. The amounts of processing time (in minutes) required to complete the jobs are shown in Table 69. A job cannot be processed on machine j unless for all $i < j$ the job has completed its processing on machine i. Once a job begins its processing on machine j, the job cannot be preempted on machine j.

Table 69

	MACHINE			
	1	*2*	*3*	*4*
Job 1	20	—	25	30
Job 2	15	20	—	18
Job 3	—	35	28	—

The flow time for a job is the difference between the job's completion time and the time at which the job begins its first stage of processing. Formulate an IP whose solution can be used to minimize the average flow time of the three jobs. (*Hint:* Two types of constraints will be needed: Constraint type 1 ensures that a job cannot begin to be processed on a machine until all earlier portions of the job are completed. You will need five constraints of this type. Constraint type 2 ensures that only one job will occupy a machine at any given time. For example, on machine 1 either job 1 is completed before job 2 begins on machine 1 or job 2 is completed on machine 1 before job 1 begins on machine 1.)

18. Arthur Ross, Inc., must complete many corporate tax returns during the period February 15–April 15. This year the company must begin and complete the five jobs shown in Table 70 during the eight-week period February 15–April 15. Arthur Ross employs four full-time accountants who normally work 40 hours per week. If necessary, however, they will work up to 20 hours of overtime per week and they are paid $100 per hour for overtime work. Use integer programming to determine how Arthur Ross can minimize the overtime cost incurred in completing all jobs by April 15.

Table 70

	DURATION (Weeks)	ACCOUNTANT HOURS NEEDED PER WEEK
Job 1	3	120
Job 2	4	160
Job 3	3	80
Job 4	2	80
Job 5	4	100

19.[†] PSI believes they will need the amounts of generating capacity shown in Table 71 during the next five years. The company has a choice of building (and then operating) power plants with the specifications shown in Table 72. Formulate an IP to minimize the total costs of meeting the generating capacity requirements of the next five years.

20.[†] Reconsider Problem 19. Suppose that at the beginning of year 1, power plants 1–4 have been constructed and are in operation. At the beginning of each year, PSI may shut down a plant that is operating or reopen a shut-down

[†]Based on Muckstadt and Wilson (1968).

Table 71

	GENERATING CAPACITY (Million kwh)
Year 1	80
Year 2	100
Year 3	120
Year 4	140
Year 5	160

Table 72

	GENERATING CAPACITY (Million kwh)	CONSTRUCTION COST (Millions)	ANNUAL OPERATING COST (Millions)
Plant 1	70	$20	$1.5
Plant 2	50	$16	$0.8
Plant 3	60	$18	$1.3
Plant 4	40	$14	$0.6

plant. The costs associated with reopening or shutting down a plant are shown in Table 73. Formulate an IP to minimize the total cost of meeting the demands of the next five years. (*Hint:* Let

$X_{it} = 1$ if plant i is operated during year t

$Y_{it} = 1$ if plant i is shut down at end of year t

$Z_{it} = 1$ if plant i is reopened at beginning of year t

You must ensure that if $X_{it} = 1$ and $X_{i,t+1} = 0$, then $Y_{it} = 1$. You must also ensure that if $X_{i,t-1} = 0$ and $X_{it} = 1$, then $Z_{it} = 1$.)

Table 73

	REOPENING COST (Millions)	SHUTDOWN COST (Millions)
Plant 1	$1.9	$1.7
Plant 2	$1.5	$1.2
Plant 3	$1.6	$1.3
Plant 4	$1.1	$0.8

21.[†] Houseco Developers is considering erecting three office buildings. The time required to complete each building and the number of workers required to be on the job at all times are shown in Table 74. Once a building is completed, the building brings in the following amount of rent per year: building 1, $50,000; building 2, $30,000; building 3, $40,000. Houseco faces the following constraints:

1. During each year 60 workers are available.
2. At most one building can be started during any year.
3. Building 2 must be completed by the end of year 4.

Formulate an IP that will maximize the total rent earned by Houseco through the end of year 4.

Table 74

	DURATION OF PROJECT (Years)	NUMBER OF WORKERS REQUIRED
Building 1	2	30
Building 2	2	20
Building 3	3	20

[†]Based on Peiser and Andrus (1983).

22. Four trucks are available to deliver milk to five groceries. The capacity and daily operating cost of each truck are shown in Table 75. The demand of each grocery can be supplied by only one truck, but a truck may deliver to more than one grocery. The daily demands of each grocery are as follows: grocery 1, 100 gallons: grocery 2, 200 gallons; grocery 3, 300 gallons; grocery 4, 500 gallons; grocery 5, 800 gallons. Formulate an IP that can be used to minimize the daily cost of meeting the demands of the four groceries.

Table 75

	CAPACITY (Gallons)	DAILY OPERATING COST
Truck 1	400	$45
Truck 2	500	$50
Truck 3	600	$55
Truck 4	1100	$60

23.[†] The State of Texas frequently does tax audits of companies doing business in Texas. Since these companies often have headquarters located outside the state, auditors must be sent to out-of-state locations. Each year, auditors must make 500 trips to cities in the northeast, 400 trips to cities in the midwest, 300 trips to cities in the west, and 400 trips to cities in the south. Texas is considering basing auditors in Chicago, New York, Atlanta, and Los Angeles. The annual cost of basing auditors in any city is $100,000. The cost of sending an auditor from any of these cities to a given region of the country is given in Table 76. Formulate an IP whose solution will minimize the annual cost of conducting out-of-state audits.

[†] Based on Fitzsimmons and Allen (1983).

Table 76

	NORTHEAST	MIDWEST	WEST	SOUTH
New York	$1100	$1400	$1900	$1400
Chicago	$1200	$1000	$1500	$1200
Los Angeles	$1900	$1700	$1100	$1400
Atlanta	$1300	$1400	$1500	$1050

◆ REFERENCES

The following six texts offer a more advanced discussion of integer programming:

GARFINKEL, R., and G. NEMHAUSER. *Integer Programming*. New York: Wiley, 1972.
NEMHAUSER, G., and L. WOLSEY. *Integer and Combinatorial Optimization*. New York: Wiley, 1988.
PARKER, G., and R. RARDIN. *Discrete Optimization*. San Diego: Academic Press, 1988.
SALKIN, H. *Integer Programming*. Reading, Mass.: Addison-Wesley, 1975.
SHAPIRO, J. *Mathematical Programming*: *Structures and Algorithms*. New York: Wiley, 1979.
TAHA, H. *Integer Programming*: *Theory, Applications, and Computations*. Orlando, Fla.: Academic Press, 1975. Also details branch-and-bound methods for traveling salesperson problem.

The following three texts contain extensive discussion of the art of formulating integer programming problems:

PLANE, D., and C. MCMILLAN. *Discrete Optimization: Integer Programming and Network Analysis for Management Decisions*. Englewood Cliffs, N.J.: Prentice-Hall, 1971.

WAGNER, H. *Principles of Operations Research*, 2d ed. Englewood Cliffs, N.J.: Prentice-Hall, 1975. Also details branch-and-bound methods for traveling salesperson problem.

WILLIAMS, H. *Model Building in Mathematical Programming*, 2d ed. New York: Wiley, 1985.

Recently, the techniques of Lagrangian Relaxation and Benders' Decomposition have been used to solve many large integer programming problems. Discussion of these techniques is beyond the scope of the text. The reader interested in Lagrangian Relaxation should read Shapiro (1979), Nemhauser and Wolsey (1988), or

FISHER, M. "An Applications-Oriented Guide to Lagrangian Relaxation," *Interfaces* 15(1985, no. 2):10–21.

GEOFFRION, A. "Lagrangian Relaxation for Integer Programming," in *Mathematical Programming Study 2: Approaches to Integer Programming*, ed. M. Balinski. New York: North-Holland, 1974, pp. 82–114.

The reader interested in Benders' Decomposition should read Shapiro (1979), Taha (1975), Nemhauser and Wolsey (1988), or the following reference:

GEOFFRION, A., and G. GRAVES. "Multicommodity Distribution System Design by Benders' Decomposition," *Management Science* 20(1974):822–844.

BAKER, K. *Introduction to Sequencing and Scheduling*. New York: Wiley, 1974. Discusses branch-and-bound methods for traveling salesperson and machine scheduling problems.

BEAN, J., C. NOON, and J. SALTON. "Asset Divestiture at Homart Development Company," *Interfaces* 17(no. 1, 1987):48–65.

BEAN, J., ET AL. "Selecting Tenants in a Shopping Mall," *Interfaces* 18(no. 2, 1988):1–10.

BROWN, G., ET AL. "Real-Time Wide Area Dispatch of Mobil Tank Trucks," *Interfaces* 17(no. 1, 1987):107–120.

CAVALIERI, F., A. ROVERSI, and R. RUGGERI. "Use of Mixed Integer Programming to Investigate Optimal Planning Policy for a Thermal Power Station and Extension to Capacity," *Operational Research Quarterly* 22(1971):221–236.

CHOYPENG, P., P. PUAKPONG, and R. ROSENTHAL. "Optimal Ship Routing and Personnel Assignment for Naval Recruitment in Thailand," *Interfaces* 16(no. 4, 1986):47–52.

DAY, R. "On Optimal Extracting from a Multiple File Data Storage System: An Application of Integer Programming," *Operations Research* 13(1965):482–494.

EATON, D., ET AL. "Determining Emergency Medical Service Vehicle Deployment in Austin, Texas," *Interfaces* 15(1985): 96–108.

EFROYMSON, M., and T. RAY. "A Branch-Bound Algorithm for Plant Location," *Operations Research* 14(1966): 361–368.

ELLIS, P., and R. CORN. "Using Bivalent Integer Programming to Select Teams for Intercollegiate Women's Gymnastics Competition," *Interfaces* 14(1984):41–46.

FITZSIMMONS, J., and L. ALLEN. "A Warehouse Location Model Helps Texas Comptroller Select Out-of-State Audit Offices," *Interfaces* 13(no. 5, 1983):40–46.

GARFINKEL, R. "Minimizing Wallpaper Waste. I: A Class of Traveling Salesman Problems," *Operations Research* 25(1977): 741–751.

GARFINKEL, R., and G. NEMHAUSER. "Optimal Political Districting by Implicit Enumeration Techniques," *Management Science* 16(1970):B495–B508.

GELB, B., and B. KHUMAWALA. "Reconfiguration of an Insurance Company's Sales Regions," *Interfaces* 14(1984):87–94.

GOLDEN, B., L. BODIN, T. DOYLE, and W. STEWART. "Approximate Traveling Salesmen

Algorithms," *Operations Research* 28(1980):694–712. Contains an excellent discussion of heuristics for the TSP.

GOMORY, R. "Outline of an Algorithm for Integer Solutions to Linear Programs," *Bulletin of the American Mathematical Society* 64(1958):275–278.

HAX, A., and D. CANDEA. *Production and Inventory Management*. Englewood Cliffs, N.J.: Prentice-Hall, 1984. Branch-and-bound methods for machine scheduling problems.

LAWLER, L., ET AL. *The Traveling Salesman Problem*. New York: Wiley, 1985. Everything you ever wanted to know about this problem.

LIGGETT, R. "The Application of an Implicit Enumeration Algorithm to the School Desegregation Problem," *Management Science* 20(1973):159–168.

MUCKSTADT, J., and R. WILSON. "An Application of Mixed Integer Programming Duality to Scheduling Thermal Generating Systems," *IEEE Transactions on Power Apparatus and Systems* (1968):1968–1978.

PEISER, R., and S. ANDRUS. "Phasing of Income-Producing Real Estate," *Interfaces* 13(1983): 1–11.

SALKIN, H., and C. LIN. "Aggregation of Subsidiary Firms for Minimal Unemployment Compensation Payments via Integer Programming," *Management Science* 25(1979):405–408.

SHANKER, R., and A. ZOLTNERS. "The Corporate Payments Problem," *Journal of Bank Research* (1972): 47–53.

WALKER, W. "Using the Set Covering Problem to Assign Fire Companies to Firehouses," *Operations Research* 22(1974):275–277.

10

*Advanced Topics in Linear Programming**

IN THIS CHAPTER, we discuss six advanced linear programming topics: the revised simplex method, the product form of the inverse, column generation, the Dantzig-Wolfe decomposition algorithm, the simplex method for upper-bounded variables, and Karmarkar's method for solving LPs. The techniques discussed are often utilized to solve large linear programming problems. The results of Section 6.2 play a key role throughout this chapter.

10-1   THE REVISED SIMPLEX ALGORITHM

In Section 6.2, we demonstrated how to create an optimal tableau from an initial tableau, given an optimal set of basic variables. Actually, the results of Section 6.2 can be used to create a tableau corresponding to *any set of basic variables*. To show how to create a tableau for any set of basic variables BV, we first describe the following notation (assume the LP has m constraints):

BV = any set of basic variables (the first element of BV is the basic variable in the first constraint, the second variable in BV is the basic variable in the second constraint, etc.; thus, BV_j is the basic variable for constraint j in the desired tableau)

$\mathbf{b}$ = right-hand side vector of the original tableau's constraints

$\mathbf{a}_j$ = column for x_j in the constraints of the original problem

B = $m \times m$ matrix whose jth column is the column for BV_j in the original constraints

c_j = coefficients of x_j in the objective function

$\mathbf{c}_{BV}$ = $1 \times m$ row vector whose jth element is the objective function coefficient for BV_j

$\mathbf{u}_i$ = $m \times 1$ column vector with ith element 1 and all other elements equal to zero

*This chapter covers topics that may be omitted with no loss of continuity.

Summarizing the formulas of Section 6.2, we write:

$$B^{-1}\mathbf{a}_j = \text{column for } x_j \text{ in } BV \text{ tableau} \qquad (1)$$

$$\mathbf{c}_{BV}B^{-1}\mathbf{a}_j - c_j = \text{coefficient of } x_j \text{ in row } 0 \qquad (2)$$

$$B^{-1}\mathbf{b} = \text{right-hand side of constraints in } BV \text{ tableau} \qquad (3)$$

$$\mathbf{c}_{BV}B^{-1}\mathbf{u}_i = \text{coefficient of slack variable } s_i \text{ in } BV \text{ in row } 0 \qquad (4)$$

$$\mathbf{c}_{BV}B^{-1}(-\mathbf{u}_i) = \text{coefficient of excess variable } e_i \text{ in } BV \text{ row } 0 \qquad (5)$$

$$M + \mathbf{c}_{BV}B^{-1}\mathbf{u}_i = \text{coefficient of artificial variable } a_i \text{ in } BV \text{ row } 0 \qquad (6)$$
$$\text{(in a max problem)}$$

$$\mathbf{c}_{BV}B^{-1}\mathbf{b} = \text{right-hand side of } BV \text{ row } 0 \qquad (7)$$

If we know BV, B^{-1}, and the original tableau, formulas (1)–(7) enable us to compute any part of the simplex tableau for any set of basic variables BV. This means that if a computer is programmed to perform the simplex algorithm, all the computer needs to store on any pivot is the current set of basic variables, B^{-1}, and the initial tableau. Then (1)–(7) can be used to generate any portion of the simplex tableau. This idea is the basis of the revised simplex algorithm.

We illustrate the revised simplex algorithm by using it to solve the Dakota problem of Chapter 6. Recall that after adding slack variables s_1, s_2, and s_3, the initial tableau (tableau 0) for the Dakota problem is

$$\max z = 60x_1 + 30x_2 + 20x_3$$
$$\begin{aligned}
\text{s.t.} \quad 8x_1 + 6x_2 + x_3 + s_1 &= 48 \\
4x_1 + 2x_2 + 1.5x_3 + s_2 &= 20 \\
2x_1 + 1.5x_2 + 0.5x_3 + s_3 &= 8
\end{aligned}$$

No matter how many pivots have been completed, B^{-1} for the current tableau will simply be the 3×3 matrix whose jth column is the column for s_j in the current tableau. Thus, for the original tableau $BV(0)$, the set of basic variables is given by

$$BV(0) = \{s_1, s_2, s_3\}$$
$$NBV(0) = \{x_1, x_2, x_3\}$$

We let B_i be the columns in the original LP that correspond to the basic variables for tableau i. Then

$$B_0^{-1} = B_0 = \begin{bmatrix} 1 & 0 & 0 \\ 0 & 1 & 0 \\ 0 & 0 & 1 \end{bmatrix}$$

We can now determine which nonbasic variable should enter the basis by computing the coefficient of each nonbasic variable in the current row 0. This procedure is often referred to as **pricing out** the nonbasic variable. From (2)–(5), we see that we can't price out the nonbasic variables until we have determined $\mathbf{c}_{BV}B_0^{-1}$. Since $\mathbf{c}_{BV} = [0 \quad 0 \quad 0]$, we have

$$\mathbf{c}_{BV}B_0^{-1} = [0 \quad 0 \quad 0] \begin{bmatrix} 1 & 0 & 0 \\ 0 & 1 & 0 \\ 0 & 0 & 1 \end{bmatrix} = [0 \quad 0 \quad 0]$$

We now use (2) to price out each nonbasic variable:

$$\bar{c}_1 = [0 \quad 0 \quad 0] \begin{bmatrix} 8 \\ 4 \\ 2 \end{bmatrix} - 60 = -60$$

$$\bar{c}_2 = [0 \quad 0 \quad 0] \begin{bmatrix} 6 \\ 2 \\ 1.5 \end{bmatrix} - 30 = -30$$

$$\bar{c}_3 = [0 \quad 0 \quad 0] \begin{bmatrix} 1 \\ 1.5 \\ 0.5 \end{bmatrix} - 20 = -20$$

Since x_1 has the most negative coefficient in the current row 0, x_1 should enter the basis. To continue the simplex, all we need to know about the new tableau is the new set of basic variables, $BV(1)$, and the corresponding B_1^{-1}. To determine $BV(1)$, we find the row in which x_1 enters the basis. We compute the column for x_1 in the current tableau and the right-hand side of the current tableau.

From (1),

$$\text{Column for } x_1 \text{ in current tableau} = \begin{bmatrix} 1 & 0 & 0 \\ 0 & 1 & 0 \\ 0 & 0 & 1 \end{bmatrix} \begin{bmatrix} 8 \\ 4 \\ 2 \end{bmatrix} = \begin{bmatrix} 8 \\ 4 \\ 2 \end{bmatrix}$$

From (3),

$$\text{Right-hand side of current tableau} = \begin{bmatrix} 1 & 0 & 0 \\ 0 & 1 & 0 \\ 0 & 0 & 1 \end{bmatrix} \begin{bmatrix} 48 \\ 20 \\ 8 \end{bmatrix} = \begin{bmatrix} 48 \\ 20 \\ 8 \end{bmatrix}$$

We now use the ratio test to determine the row in which x_1 should enter the basis. The appropriate ratios are row 1, $\frac{48}{8} = 6$; row 2, $\frac{20}{4} = 5$; and row 3, $\frac{8}{2} = 4$. Thus, x_1 should enter the basis in row 3. This means that our new tableau (tableau 1) will have $BV(1) = \{s_1, s_2, x_1\}$ and $NBV(1) = \{s_3, x_2, x_3\}$.

The new B^{-1} will be the columns of s_1, s_2, and s_3 in the new tableau. To determine the new B^{-1}, look at the column in tableau 0 for the entering variable x_1. From this column, we see that in going from tableau 0 to tableau 1, we must perform the following ero's:

1. Multiply row 3 of tableau 0 by $\frac{1}{2}$.
2. Replace row 1 of tableau 0 by -4(row 3 of tableau 0) + row 1 of tableau 0.
3. Replace row 2 of tableau 0 by -2(row 3 of tableau 0) + row 2 of tableau 0.

Applying these ero's to B_0^{-1} yields

$$B_1^{-1} = \begin{bmatrix} 1 & 0 & -4 \\ 0 & 1 & -2 \\ 0 & 0 & \frac{1}{2} \end{bmatrix}$$

We can now price out all the nonbasic variables for the new tableau. First we compute

$$\mathbf{c}_{BV}B_1^{-1} = [0 \quad 0 \quad 60]\begin{bmatrix} 1 & 0 & -4 \\ 0 & 1 & -2 \\ 0 & 0 & \frac{1}{2} \end{bmatrix} = [0 \quad 0 \quad 30]$$

Then use (2) and (4) to price out tableau 1's nonbasic variables:

$$\bar{c}_2 = [0 \quad 0 \quad 30]\begin{bmatrix} 6 \\ 2 \\ 1.5 \end{bmatrix} - 30 = 15$$

$$\bar{c}_3 = [0 \quad 0 \quad 30]\begin{bmatrix} 1 \\ 1.5 \\ 0.5 \end{bmatrix} - 20 = -5$$

$$\text{Coefficient of } s_3 \text{ in row } 0 = [0 \quad 0 \quad 30]\begin{bmatrix} 0 \\ 0 \\ 1 \end{bmatrix} - 0 = 30$$

Since x_3 is the only variable with a negative coefficient in row 0 of tableau 1, we enter x_3 into the basis. To determine the new set of basic variables, $BV(2)$, and the corresponding B_2^{-1}, we find the row in which x_3 enters the basis. We compute the column for x_3 in tableau 1 and the right-hand side of tableau 1:

$$x_3 \text{ column in tableau } 1 = B_1^{-1}\mathbf{a}_3 = \begin{bmatrix} 1 & 0 & -4 \\ 0 & 1 & -2 \\ 0 & 0 & 0.5 \end{bmatrix}\begin{bmatrix} 1 \\ 1.5 \\ 0.5 \end{bmatrix} = \begin{bmatrix} -1 \\ 0.5 \\ 0.25 \end{bmatrix}$$

$$\text{Right-hand side of tableau } 1 = B_1^{-1}\mathbf{b} = \begin{bmatrix} 1 & 0 & -4 \\ 0 & 1 & -2 \\ 0 & 0 & 0.5 \end{bmatrix}\begin{bmatrix} 48 \\ 20 \\ 8 \end{bmatrix} = \begin{bmatrix} 16 \\ 4 \\ 4 \end{bmatrix}$$

The appropriate ratios for determining where x_3 should enter the basis are row 1, none; row 2, $\frac{4}{0.5} = 8$; and row 3, $\frac{4}{0.25} = 16$. Hence, x_3 should enter the basis in row 2. Then tableau 2 will have $BV(2) = \{s_1, x_3, x_1\}$ and $NBV(2) = \{s_2, s_3, x_2\}$.

To compute B_2^{-1}, note that in order to make x_3 a basic variable in row 2, we must perform the following ero's on tableau 1:

1. Replace row 2 of tableau 1 by 2(row 2 of tableau 1).

2. Replace row 1 of tableau 1 by 2(row 2 of tableau 1) + row 1 of tableau 1.

3. Replace row 3 of tableau 1 by $-\frac{1}{2}$(row 2 of tableau 1) + row 3 of tableau 1.

Applying these ero's to B_1^{-1}, we obtain

$$B_2^{-1} = \begin{bmatrix} 1 & 2 & -8 \\ 0 & 2 & -4 \\ 0 & -0.5 & 1.5 \end{bmatrix}$$

We now price out the nonbasic variables in tableau 2. First we compute

$$\mathbf{c}_{BV}B_2^{-1} = \begin{bmatrix} 0 & 20 & 60 \end{bmatrix} \begin{bmatrix} 1 & 2 & -8 \\ 0 & 2 & -4 \\ 0 & -0.5 & 1.5 \end{bmatrix} = \begin{bmatrix} 0 & 10 & 10 \end{bmatrix}$$

Then we price out the nonbasic variables x_2, s_2, and s_3:

$$\bar{c}_2 = \begin{bmatrix} 0 & 10 & 10 \end{bmatrix} \begin{bmatrix} 6 \\ 2 \\ 1.5 \end{bmatrix} - 30 = 5$$

$$\text{Coefficient of } s_2 \text{ in row } 0 = \begin{bmatrix} 0 & 10 & 10 \end{bmatrix} \begin{bmatrix} 0 \\ 1 \\ 0 \end{bmatrix} - 0 = 10$$

$$\text{Coefficient of } s_3 \text{ in row } 0 = \begin{bmatrix} 0 & 10 & 10 \end{bmatrix} \begin{bmatrix} 0 \\ 0 \\ 1 \end{bmatrix} - 0 = 10$$

Since each nonbasic variable in tableau 2 has a nonnegative coefficient in row 0, tableau 2 is an optimal tableau. To find the optimal solution, we find the right-hand side of tableau 2. From (3), we obtain

$$\text{Right-hand side of tableau } 2 = \begin{bmatrix} 1 & 2 & -8 \\ 0 & 2 & -4 \\ 0 & -0.5 & 1.5 \end{bmatrix} \begin{bmatrix} 48 \\ 20 \\ 8 \end{bmatrix} = \begin{bmatrix} 24 \\ 8 \\ 2 \end{bmatrix}$$

Since $BV(2) = \{s_1, x_3, x_1\}$, the optimal solution to the Dakota problem is

$$\begin{bmatrix} s_1 \\ x_3 \\ x_1 \end{bmatrix} = \begin{bmatrix} 24 \\ 8 \\ 2 \end{bmatrix}$$

or $s_1 = 24$, $x_3 = 8$, $x_1 = 2$, $x_2 = s_2 = s_3 = 0$. The optimal z-value may be found from (7):

$$\mathbf{c}_{BV}B_2^{-1}\mathbf{b} = \begin{bmatrix} 0 & 10 & 10 \end{bmatrix} \begin{bmatrix} 48 \\ 20 \\ 8 \end{bmatrix} = 280$$

A summary of the revised simplex method (for a max problem) follows:

Step 0 Note the columns from which the current B^{-1} will be read. Initially, $B^{-1} = I$.

Step 1 For the current tableau, compute $\mathbf{c}_{BV}B^{-1}$.

Step 2 Price out all nonbasic variables in the current tableau. If each nonbasic variable prices out nonnegative, the current basis is optimal. If the current basis is not optimal, enter into the basis the nonbasic variable with the most negative coefficient in row 0. Call this variable x_k.

Step 3 To determine the row in which x_k enters the basis, compute x_k's column in the current tableau (it will be $B^{-1}\mathbf{a}_k$) and compute the right-hand side of the current tableau (it will be $B^{-1}\mathbf{b}$). Then use the ratio test to determine the row in which x_k should enter the basis. We now know the set of basic variables (BV) for the new tableau.

Step 4 Use the column for x_k in the current tableau to determine the ero's needed to enter x_k into the basis. Perform these ero's on the current B^{-1}. This will yield the new B^{-1}. Return to Step 1.

Most linear programming computer codes use some version of the revised simplex to solve LPs. Since knowing the current tableau's B^{-1} and the initial tableau is all that is needed to obtain the next tableau, the computational effort required to solve an LP by the revised simplex depends primarily on the size of B^{-1}. Suppose the LP being solved has m constraints and n variables. Then each B^{-1} will be an $m \times m$ matrix, and the effort required to solve an LP will depend primarily on the number of constraints (not the number of variables). This fact has important computational implications. For example, if we are solving an LP that has 500 constraints and 10 variables, the LP's dual will have 10 constraints and 500 variables. Then all the B^{-1}'s for the dual will be 10×10 matrices, and all the B^{-1}'s for the primal will be 500×500. Thus, it will be much easier to solve the dual than to solve the primal. In this situation, computation can be greatly reduced by solving the dual and reading the optimal primal solution from the SHADOW PRICE or DUAL VARIABLE section of a computer printout.

♦ PROBLEMS

GROUP A

Use the revised simplex method to solve the following LPs:

(Remember that B^{-1} is always found under the columns corresponding to the starting basis.)

1. $\max z = 3x_1 + x_2 + x_3$

s.t. $x_1 + x_2 + x_3 \le 6$

$2x_1 \qquad - x_3 \le 4$

$\qquad x_2 + x_3 \le 2$

$x_1, x_2, x_3 \ge 0$

2. $\max z = 4x_1 + x_2$

s.t. $x_1 + x_2 \le 4$

$2x_1 + x_2 \ge 6$

$3x_2 \ge 6$

$x_1, x_2, x_3 \ge 0$

3. $\min z = 3x_1 + x_2 - 3x_3$

s.t. $x_1 - x_2 + x_3 \le 4$

$x_1 \qquad + x_3 \le 6$

$\qquad 2x_2 - x_3 \le 5$

$x_1, x_2, x_3 \ge 0$

10-2   THE PRODUCT FORM OF THE INVERSE

Much of the computation in the revised simplex algorithm is concerned with updating B^{-1} from one tableau to the next. In this section, we develop an efficient method to update B^{-1}.

Suppose we are solving an LP with m constraints. Assume that we have found that x_k should enter the basis, and the ratio test indicates that x_k should enter the basis in row r. Let the column for x_k in the current tableau be

$$\begin{bmatrix} \bar{a}_{1k} \\ \bar{a}_{2k} \\ \vdots \\ \bar{a}_{mk} \end{bmatrix}$$

Define the $m \times m$ matrix E:

(column r)

$$E = \begin{bmatrix}
1 & 0 & \cdots & -\dfrac{\bar{a}_{1k}}{\bar{a}_{rk}} & \cdots & 0 & 0 \\
0 & 1 & \cdots & -\dfrac{\bar{a}_{2k}}{\bar{a}_{rk}} & \cdots & 0 & 0 \\
\vdots & \vdots & & \vdots & & \vdots & \vdots \\
0 & 0 & \cdots & \dfrac{1}{\bar{a}_{rk}} & \cdots & 0 & 0 \\
\vdots & \vdots & & \vdots & & \vdots & \vdots \\
0 & 0 & \cdots & -\dfrac{\bar{a}_{m-1,k}}{\bar{a}_{rk}} & \cdots & 1 & 0 \\
0 & 0 & \cdots & -\dfrac{\bar{a}_{mk}}{\bar{a}_{rk}} & \cdots & 0 & 1
\end{bmatrix} \text{(row } r)$$

In short, E is simply I_m with column r replaced by the column vector

$$\begin{bmatrix} -\dfrac{\bar{a}_{1k}}{\bar{a}_{rk}} \\ -\dfrac{\bar{a}_{2k}}{\bar{a}_{rk}} \\ \vdots \\ \dfrac{1}{\bar{a}_{rk}} \\ \vdots \\ -\dfrac{\bar{a}_{m-1,k}}{\bar{a}_{rk}} \\ -\dfrac{\bar{a}_{mk}}{\bar{a}_{rk}} \end{bmatrix}$$

DEFINITION   A matrix (like E) that differs from the identity matrix in only one column is called an **elementary matrix**.

We now show that

$$B^{-1} \text{ for new tableau} = E(B^{-1} \text{ for current tableau}) \tag{8}$$

To see why this is true, note that the ero's used to go from the current tableau to the new tableau boil down to

$$\text{Row } r \text{ of new } B^{-1} = \left(\frac{1}{\bar{a}_{rk}}\right)(\text{row } r \text{ of current } B^{-1}) \tag{9}$$

and for $i \neq r$,

$$\text{Row } i \text{ of new } B^{-1}$$
$$= (\text{row } i \text{ of current } B^{-1}) - \left(\frac{\bar{a}_{ik}}{\bar{a}_{rk}}\right)(\text{row } r \text{ of the current } B^{-1}) \tag{10}$$

Recall from Section 2.1 that

$$\text{Row } i \text{ of } E(\text{current } B^{-1}) = (\text{row } i \text{ of } E)(\text{current } B^{-1}) \tag{11}$$

Combining (11) with the definition of E, we find that

$$\text{Row } r \text{ of } E(\text{current } B^{-1}) = \left(\frac{1}{\bar{a}_{rk}}\right)(\text{row } r \text{ of current } B^{-1})$$

and for $i \neq r$,

$$\text{Row } i \text{ of } E(\text{current } B^{-1})$$
$$= (\text{row } i \text{ of current } B^{-1}) - \left(\frac{\bar{a}_{ik}}{\bar{a}_{rk}}\right)(\text{row } r \text{ of current } B^{-1})$$

Hence, (8) does agree with (9) and (10). Thus, we can use (8) to find the new B^{-1} from the current B^{-1}.

Define the initial tableau to be tableau 0, and let E_i be the elementary matrix E associated with the ith simplex tableau. Recall that $B_0^{-1} = I_m$. We now write

$$B_1^{-1} = E_0 B_0^{-1} = E_0$$

Then

$$B_2^{-1} = E_1 B_1^{-1} = E_1 E_0$$

and, in general,

$$B_k^{-1} = E_{k-1} E_{k-2} \cdots E_1 E_0 \tag{12}$$

Equation (12) is called the **product form of the inverse**. Most linear programming computer codes utilize the revised simplex method and compute successive B^{-1}'s by using the product form of the inverse.

E X A M P L E 1

Use the product form of the inverse to compute B_1^{-1} and B_2^{-1} for the Dakota problem that was solved by the revised simplex in Section 10.1.

Solution

Recall that in tableau 0, x_1 entered the basis in row 3. Hence, for tableau 0, $r = 3$ and $k = 1$. For tableau 0,

$$\begin{bmatrix} \bar{a}_{11} \\ \bar{a}_{21} \\ \bar{a}_{31} \end{bmatrix} = \begin{bmatrix} 8 \\ 4 \\ 2 \end{bmatrix}$$

Then

$$
E_0 = \begin{bmatrix} 1 & 0 & -\frac{8}{2} \\ 0 & 1 & -\frac{4}{2} \\ 0 & 0 & \frac{1}{2} \end{bmatrix} = \begin{bmatrix} 1 & 0 & -4 \\ 0 & 1 & -2 \\ 0 & 0 & \frac{1}{2} \end{bmatrix}
$$

$$
B_1^{-1} = \begin{bmatrix} 1 & 0 & -4 \\ 0 & 1 & -2 \\ 0 & 0 & \frac{1}{2} \end{bmatrix} \begin{bmatrix} 1 & 0 & 0 \\ 0 & 1 & 0 \\ 0 & 0 & 1 \end{bmatrix} = \begin{bmatrix} 1 & 0 & -4 \\ 0 & 1 & -2 \\ 0 & 0 & \frac{1}{2} \end{bmatrix}
$$

As we proceeded from tableau 1 to tableau 2, x_3 entered the basis in row 2. Hence, in computing E_1, we set $r = 2$ and $k = 3$. To compute E_1, we need to find the column for the entering variable (x_3) in tableau 1:

$$
\begin{bmatrix} \bar{a}_{13} \\ \bar{a}_{23} \\ \bar{a}_{33} \end{bmatrix} = B_1^{-1} \mathbf{a}_3 = \begin{bmatrix} 1 & 0 & -4 \\ 0 & 1 & -2 \\ 0 & 0 & 0.5 \end{bmatrix} \begin{bmatrix} 1 \\ 1.5 \\ 0.5 \end{bmatrix} = \begin{bmatrix} -1 \\ 0.5 \\ 0.25 \end{bmatrix}
$$

As before, x_3 enters the basis in row 2. Then

$$
E_1 = \begin{bmatrix} 1 & -(-\frac{1}{0.5}) & 0 \\ 0 & \frac{1}{0.5} & 0 \\ 0 & -\frac{0.25}{0.50} & 1 \end{bmatrix} = \begin{bmatrix} 1 & 2 & 0 \\ 0 & 2 & 0 \\ 0 & -0.5 & 1 \end{bmatrix}
$$

and (as before)

$$
B_2^{-1} = E_1 B_1^{-1} = \begin{bmatrix} 1 & 2 & 0 \\ 0 & 2 & 0 \\ 0 & -0.5 & 1 \end{bmatrix} \begin{bmatrix} 1 & 0 & -4 \\ 0 & 1 & -2 \\ 0 & 0 & 0.5 \end{bmatrix} = \begin{bmatrix} 1 & 2 & -8 \\ 0 & 2 & -4 \\ 0 & -0.5 & 1.5 \end{bmatrix} \quad \blacklozenge
$$

In the next two sections, we use the product form of the inverse in our study of column generation and of the Dantzig-Wolfe decomposition algorithm.

◆ PROBLEMS

GROUP A

For the problems of Section 10.1, use the product form of the inverse to perform the revised simplex method.

10-3   USING COLUMN GENERATION TO SOLVE LARGE-SCALE LPs

We have already seen that the revised simplex algorithm requires less computation than the simplex algorithm of Chapter 4. In this section, we discuss the method of column generation, devised by Gilmore and Gomory (1961). For LPs that have many variables, column generation can be used to increase the efficiency of the revised simplex algorithm. Column generation is also a very important component of the Dantzig-Wolfe decomposition algorithm, which is discussed in Section 10.4. To explain the idea of column generation, we solve a simple version of the classic *cutting stock problem*.

E X A M P L E 2

Woodco sells 3-ft, 5-ft, and 9-ft pieces of lumber. Woodco's customers demand 25 3-ft boards, 20 5-ft boards, and 15 9-ft boards. Woodco must meet its demands by cutting up 17-ft boards. Woodco wishes to minimize the waste incurred in meeting customer demands. Formulate an LP to help Woodco accomplish its goal, and solve the LP by column generation.

Solution

Woodco must decide how each 17-ft board should be cut. Hence, each of Woodco's decisions corresponds to a way in which a 17-ft board can be cut. For example, one decision variable would correspond to a board being cut into three 5-ft boards, which would incur waste of $17 - 15 = 2$ ft. Many possible ways of cutting a board need not be considered. For example, it would be foolish to cut a board into one 9-ft and one 5-ft piece; we could just as easily cut the board into a 9-ft piece, a 5-ft piece, *and* a 3-ft piece. In general, any cutting pattern that leaves 3 ft or more of waste need not be considered, because we could use the waste to obtain one or more 3-ft boards. Table 1 lists the sensible ways to cut a 17-ft board.

Table 1
Ways to Cut a Board in the Cutting Stock Problem

	NUMBER OF 3-FT BOARDS	NUMBER OF 5-FT BOARDS	NUMBER OF 9-FT BOARDS	WASTE (Feet)
Comb. 1	5	0	0	2
Comb. 2	4	1	0	0
Comb. 3	2	2	0	1
Comb. 4	2	0	1	2
Comb. 5	1	1	1	0
Comb. 6	0	3	0	2

We now define

$$x_i = \text{number of 17-ft boards cut according to combination } i$$

and formulate Woodco's LP:

$$\text{Woodco's waste} + \text{total customer demand} = \text{total length of board cut}$$

Since

$$\text{Total customer demand} = 25(3) + 20(5) + 15(9) = 310 \text{ ft}$$
$$\text{Total length of boards cut} = 17(x_1 + x_2 + x_3 + x_4 + x_5 + x_6)$$

we write

$$\text{Woodco's waste (in feet)} = 17x_1 + 17x_2 + 17x_3 + 17x_4 + 17x_5 + 17x_6 - 310$$

Then Woodco's objective function is to minimize

$$\min z = 17x_1 + 17x_2 + 17x_3 + 17x_4 + 17x_5 + 17x_6 - 310$$

This is equivalent to minimizing

$$17(x_1 + x_2 + x_3 + x_4 + x_5 + x_6)$$

which is equivalent to minimizing

$$x_1 + x_2 + x_3 + x_4 + x_5 + x_6$$

Hence, Woodco's objective function is

$$\min z = x_1 + x_2 + x_3 + x_4 + x_5 + x_6 \qquad (13)$$

This means that Woodco can minimize its total waste by minimizing the number of 17-ft boards that are cut.

Woodco faces the following three constraints:

Constraint 1 At least 25 3-ft boards may be cut.

Constraint 2 At least 20 5-ft boards must be cut.

Constraint 3 At least 15 9-ft boards must be cut.

Since the total number of 3-ft boards that are cut is given by $5x_1 + 4x_2 + 2x_3 + 2x_4 + x_5$, Constraint 1 becomes

$$5x_1 + 4x_2 + 2x_3 + 2x_4 + x_5 \geq 25 \qquad (14)$$

Similarly, Constraint 2 becomes

$$x_2 + 2x_3 + x_5 + 3x_6 \geq 20 \qquad (15)$$

and Constraint 3 becomes

$$x_4 + x_5 \geq 15 \qquad (16)$$

Note that the coefficient of x_i in the constraint for k-ft boards is just the number of k-ft boards yielded if a board is cut according to combination i.

It is clear that the x_i should be required to assume integer values. Despite this fact, in problems with large demands, a near-optimal solution can be obtained by solving the cutting stock problem as an LP and then rounding all fractional variables upward. This procedure may not yield the best possible integer solution, but it usually yields a near-optimal integer solution. For this reason, we concentrate on the LP version of the cutting stock problem. Combining the sign restrictions with (13)–(16), we obtain the following LP:

$$
\begin{aligned}
\min z = \ & x_1 + x_2 + x_3 + x_4 + x_5 + x_6 \\
\text{s.t.} \quad 5x_1 + 4x_2 + 2x_3 + 2x_4 + x_5 \ & \geq 25 \quad \text{(3-ft constraint)} \\
x_2 + 2x_3 \qquad + x_5 + 3x_6 \ & \geq 20 \quad \text{(5-ft constraint)} \qquad (17)\\
x_4 + x_5 \ & \geq 15 \quad \text{(9-ft constraint)} \\
x_1, x_2, x_3, x_4, x_5, x_6 \ & \geq 0
\end{aligned}
$$

Note that x_1 only occurs in the 3-ft constraint (because combination 1 yields only 3-ft boards), and x_6 only occurs in the 5-ft constraint (because combination 6 yields only 5-ft boards). This means that x_1 and x_6 can be used as starting basic variables for the 3-ft and 5-ft constraints. Unfortunately, none of combinations 1–6 yields only 9-ft boards, so the 9-ft constraint has no obvious basic variable. To avoid having to add an artificial variable to the 9-ft constraint, we define combination 7 to be the cutting combination that yields only one 9-ft board. Also, define x_7 to be the number of boards cut according to combination 7. Clearly, x_7 will be equal to zero in the optimal solution, but inserting x_7 in the starting basis allows us to avoid using the Big M or the two-phase simplex method. Note that the column for x_7 in the LP constraints will be

$$\begin{bmatrix} 0 \\ 0 \\ 1 \end{bmatrix}$$

and a term x_7 will be added to the objective function. We can now use $BV = \{x_1, x_6, x_7\}$ as a starting basis for LP (17). If we let the tableau for this basis be tableau 0, then we have

$$B_0 = \begin{bmatrix} 5 & 0 & 0 \\ 0 & 3 & 0 \\ 0 & 0 & 1 \end{bmatrix}$$

$$B_0^{-1} = \begin{bmatrix} \frac{1}{5} & 0 & 0 \\ 0 & \frac{1}{3} & 0 \\ 0 & 0 & 1 \end{bmatrix}$$

Then

$$\mathbf{c}_{BV} B_0^{-1} = \begin{bmatrix} 1 & 1 & 1 \end{bmatrix} \begin{bmatrix} \frac{1}{5} & 0 & 0 \\ 0 & \frac{1}{3} & 0 \\ 0 & 0 & 1 \end{bmatrix} = \begin{bmatrix} \frac{1}{5} & \frac{1}{3} & 1 \end{bmatrix}$$

We could now price out each nonbasic variable. This would tell us which variable should enter the basis. In a large-scale cutting stock problem, however, there may be thousands of variables, so pricing out each nonbasic variable would be an extremely tedious chore. This is the type of situation in which column generation comes into play. Since we are solving a minimization problem, we want to find a column that will price out positive (have a positive coefficient in row 0). In the cutting stock problem, each column, or variable, represents a combination for cutting up a board: A variable is specified by three numbers: a_3, a_5, and a_9, where a_i is the number of i-ft boards yielded by cutting one 17-ft board according to the given combination. For example, the variable x_2 is specified by $a_3 = 4$, $a_5 = 1$, and $a_9 = 0$. The idea of column generation is to search efficiently for a column that will price out favorably (positive in a min problem and negative in a max problem). For our current basis, a combination specified by a_3, a_5, and a_9 will price out as

$$\mathbf{c}_{BV} B_0^{-1} \begin{bmatrix} a_3 \\ a_5 \\ a_9 \end{bmatrix} - 1 = \frac{1}{5}a_3 + \frac{1}{3}a_5 + a_9 - 1$$

Note that a_3, a_5, and a_9 must be chosen so they don't use more than 17 ft of wood.

We also know that a_3, a_5, and a_9 must be nonnegative integers. In short, for any combination, a_3, a_5, and a_9 must satisfy

$$3a_3 + 5a_5 + 9a_9 \leq 17 \qquad (a_3 \geq 0, a_5 \geq 0, a_9 \geq 0; a_3, a_5, a_9 \text{ integer}) \qquad \textbf{(18)}$$

We can now find the combination that prices out most favorably by solving the following knapsack problem:

$$\max z = \tfrac{1}{5}a_3 + \tfrac{1}{3}a_5 + a_9 - 1$$
$$\text{s.t.} \quad 3a_3 + 5a_5 + 9a_9 \leq 17 \qquad \textbf{(19)}$$
$$a_3, a_5, a_9 \geq 0; a_3, a_5, a_9 \text{ integer}$$

Since (19) is a knapsack problem (without 0–1 restrictions on the variables), it can easily be solved by using the branch-and-bound procedure outlined in Section 9.5.

The resulting branch-and-bound tree is given in Figure 1. For example, to solve Problem 6 in Figure 1, we first set $a_5 = 1$ (because $a_5 \geq 1$ is necessary). Then we have 12 ft left in the knapsack, and we choose to make a_9 (the best item) as large as possible. Since $a_9 \leq 1$, we set $a_9 = 1$. This leaves 3 ft, so we set $a_3 = 1$ to fill the knapsack. From Figure 1, we find that the optimal solution to LP (19) is $z = \tfrac{8}{15}, a_3 = a_5 = a_9 = 1$. This corresponds to combination 5 and variable x_5. Hence, x_5 prices out to $\tfrac{8}{15}$, and entering

Figure 1
Branch-and-Bound
Tree for IP (19)

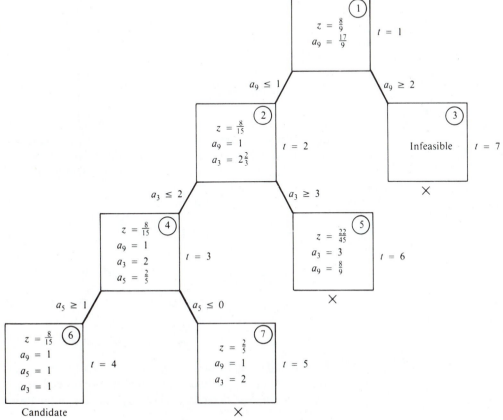

x_5 into the basis will decrease Woodco's waste. To enter x_5 into the basis, we create the right-hand side of the current tableau and the x_5 column of the current tableau.

$$x_5 \text{ column in current tableau} = B_0^{-1} \begin{bmatrix} 1 \\ 1 \\ 1 \end{bmatrix} = \begin{bmatrix} \frac{1}{5} & 0 & 0 \\ 0 & \frac{1}{3} & 0 \\ 0 & 0 & 1 \end{bmatrix} \begin{bmatrix} 1 \\ 1 \\ 1 \end{bmatrix} = \begin{bmatrix} \frac{1}{5} \\ \frac{1}{3} \\ 1 \end{bmatrix}$$

$$\text{Right-hand side of current tableau} = B_0^{-1}\mathbf{b} = \begin{bmatrix} \frac{1}{5} & 0 & 0 \\ 0 & \frac{1}{3} & 0 \\ 0 & 0 & 1 \end{bmatrix} \begin{bmatrix} 25 \\ 20 \\ 15 \end{bmatrix} = \begin{bmatrix} 5 \\ \frac{20}{3} \\ 15 \end{bmatrix}$$

The ratio test indicates that x_5 should enter the basis in row 3. This yields $BV(1) = \{x_1, x_6, x_5\}$. Using the product form of the inverse, we obtain

$$B_1^{-1} = E_0 B_0^{-1} = \begin{bmatrix} 1 & 0 & -\frac{1}{5} \\ 0 & 1 & -\frac{1}{3} \\ 0 & 0 & 1 \end{bmatrix} \begin{bmatrix} \frac{1}{5} & 0 & 0 \\ 0 & \frac{1}{3} & 0 \\ 0 & 0 & 1 \end{bmatrix}$$

$$= \begin{bmatrix} \frac{1}{5} & 0 & -\frac{1}{5} \\ 0 & \frac{1}{3} & -\frac{1}{3} \\ 0 & 0 & 1 \end{bmatrix}$$

Now

$$\mathbf{c}_{BV} B_1^{-1} = \begin{bmatrix} 1 & 1 & 1 \end{bmatrix} \begin{bmatrix} \frac{1}{5} & 0 & -\frac{1}{5} \\ 0 & \frac{1}{3} & -\frac{1}{3} \\ 0 & 0 & 1 \end{bmatrix} = \begin{bmatrix} \frac{1}{5} & \frac{1}{3} & \frac{7}{15} \end{bmatrix}$$

With our new set of shadow prices ($\mathbf{c}_{BV} B_1^{-1}$), we can again use column generation to determine whether there is any combination that should be entered into the basis. For the current set of shadow prices, a combination specified by a_3, a_5, and a_9 prices out to

$$\begin{bmatrix} \frac{1}{5} & \frac{1}{3} & \frac{7}{15} \end{bmatrix} \begin{bmatrix} a_3 \\ a_5 \\ a_9 \end{bmatrix} - 1 = \frac{1}{5}a_3 + \frac{1}{3}a_5 + \frac{7}{15}a_9 - 1$$

For the current tableau, the column generation procedure yields the following problem:

$$\max z = \frac{1}{5}a_3 + \frac{1}{3}a_5 + \frac{7}{15}a_9 - 1$$
$$\text{s.t.} \quad 3a_3 + 5a_5 + 9a_9 \le 17 \tag{20}$$
$$a_3, a_5, a_9 \ge 0; \ a_3, a_5, a_9 \text{ integer}$$

The branch-and-bound tree for (20) is given in Figure 2. We see that the combination with $a_3 = 4$, $a_5 = 1$, and $a_9 = 0$ (combination 2) will price out better than any other (it will have a row 0 coefficient of $\frac{2}{15}$). Since combination 2 prices out most

Figure 2
Branch-and-Bound
Tree for IP (20)

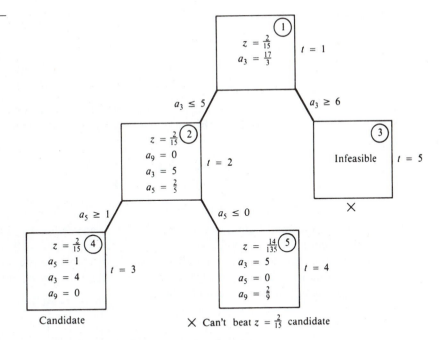

favorably, we now enter x_2 into the basis. The column for x_2 in the current tableau is

$$B_1^{-1}\begin{bmatrix} 4 \\ 1 \\ 0 \end{bmatrix} = \begin{bmatrix} \frac{1}{5} & 0 & -\frac{1}{5} \\ 0 & \frac{1}{3} & -\frac{1}{3} \\ 0 & 0 & 1 \end{bmatrix}\begin{bmatrix} 4 \\ 1 \\ 0 \end{bmatrix} = \begin{bmatrix} \frac{4}{5} \\ \frac{1}{3} \\ 0 \end{bmatrix}$$

The right-hand side of the current tableau is

$$B_1^{-1}\mathbf{b} = \begin{bmatrix} \frac{1}{5} & 0 & -\frac{1}{5} \\ 0 & \frac{1}{3} & -\frac{1}{3} \\ 0 & 0 & 1 \end{bmatrix}\begin{bmatrix} 25 \\ 20 \\ 15 \end{bmatrix} = \begin{bmatrix} 2 \\ \frac{5}{3} \\ 15 \end{bmatrix}$$

The ratio test indicates that x_2 should enter the basis in row 1. Hence, $BV(2) = \{x_2, x_6, x_5\}$. Using the product form of the inverse, we find that

$$E_1 = \begin{bmatrix} \frac{5}{4} & 0 & 0 \\ -\frac{5}{12} & 1 & 0 \\ 0 & 0 & 1 \end{bmatrix}$$

Then

$$B_2^{-1} = E_1 B_1^{-1} = \begin{bmatrix} \frac{5}{4} & 0 & 0 \\ -\frac{5}{12} & 1 & 0 \\ 0 & 0 & 1 \end{bmatrix}\begin{bmatrix} \frac{1}{5} & 0 & -\frac{1}{5} \\ 0 & \frac{1}{3} & -\frac{1}{3} \\ 0 & 0 & 1 \end{bmatrix} = \begin{bmatrix} \frac{1}{4} & 0 & -\frac{1}{4} \\ -\frac{1}{12} & \frac{1}{3} & -\frac{1}{4} \\ 0 & 0 & 1 \end{bmatrix}$$

The new set of shadow prices is given by

$$\mathbf{c}_{BV} B_2^{-1} = \begin{bmatrix} 1 & 1 & 1 \end{bmatrix} \begin{bmatrix} \frac{1}{4} & 0 & -\frac{1}{4} \\ -\frac{1}{12} & \frac{1}{3} & -\frac{1}{4} \\ 0 & 0 & 1 \end{bmatrix} = \begin{bmatrix} \frac{1}{6} & \frac{1}{3} & \frac{1}{2} \end{bmatrix}$$

For this set of shadow prices, a combination specified by a_3, a_5, and a_9 will price out to $\frac{1}{6}a_3 + \frac{1}{3}a_5 + \frac{1}{2}a_9 - 1$. Thus, the column generation procedure requires us to solve the following problem:

$$\max z = \tfrac{1}{6}a_3 + \tfrac{1}{3}a_5 + \tfrac{1}{2}a_9 - 1$$
$$\text{s.t.} \quad 3a_3 + 5a_5 + 9a_9 \leq 17 \tag{21}$$
$$a_3, a_5, a_9 \geq 0; \; a_3, a_5, a_9 \text{ integer}$$

The branch-and-bound tree for IP (21) is left as an exercise (see Problem 1 at the end of this section). The optimal z-value for (21) is found to be $z = 0$. This means that no combination can price out favorably. Hence, our current basic solution must be an optimal solution. To find the values of the basic variables in the optimal solution, we find the right-hand side of the current tableau:

$$B_2^{-1}\mathbf{b} = \begin{bmatrix} \frac{1}{4} & 0 & -\frac{1}{4} \\ -\frac{1}{12} & \frac{1}{3} & -\frac{1}{4} \\ 0 & 0 & 1 \end{bmatrix} \begin{bmatrix} 25 \\ 20 \\ 15 \end{bmatrix} = \begin{bmatrix} \frac{5}{2} \\ \frac{5}{6} \\ 15 \end{bmatrix}$$

Therefore, the optimal solution to Woodco's cutting stock problem is given by $x_2 = \frac{5}{2}$, $x_6 = \frac{5}{6}$, $x_5 = 15$. If desired, we could obtain a "reasonable" integer solution by rounding x_2 and x_6 upward. This yields the integer solution $x_2 = 3$, $x_6 = 1$, $x_5 = 15$. ♦

If we have a starting bfs for a cutting stock problem, we need not list all possible ways in which a board may be cut. At each iteration, a good combination (one that will improve the z-value when entered into the basis) is generated by solving a branch-and-bound problem. The fact that we don't have to list all the ways a board can be cut is very helpful; a cutting stock problem that was solved in Gilmore and Gomory (1961) for which customers demanded boards of 40 different lengths involved over 100 million possible ways a board could be cut. At the last stage of the column generation procedure for this problem, solving a single branch-and-bound problem indicated that none of the 100 million (nonbasic) ways would price out favorably. This method is certainly more pleasant than using $\mathbf{c}_{BV} B^{-1}$ to price out all 100 million variables!

♦ PROBLEMS

GROUP A

1. Show that the optimal solution to IP (21) has $z = 0$.

2. Use column generation to solve a cutting stock problem in which 15-ft boards are cut to satisfy the following requirements: 10 3-ft boards, 20 5-ft boards, and 15 8-ft boards.

3. Use column generation to solve a cutting stock problem in which 15-ft boards are cut to meet the following requirements: 80 4-ft boards, 50 6-ft boards, and 100 7-ft boards.

10-4   THE DANTZIG-WOLFE DECOMPOSITION ALGORITHM

In many LPs, the constraints and variables may be decomposed in the following manner:

Constraints in Set 1 only involve variables in Variable Set 1.

Constraints in Set 2 only involve variables in Variable Set 2.

$$\vdots$$

Constraints in Set k only involve variables in Variable Set k.

Constraints in Set $k + 1$ may involve any variable. The constraints in Set $k + 1$ are referred to as the **central constraints**. LPs that can be decomposed in this fashion can often be solved efficiently by the Dantzig-Wolfe decomposition algorithm.

E X A M P L E
3

Steelco manufactures two types of steel (steel 1 and steel 2) at two locations (plant 1 and plant 2). Three resources are needed to manufacture a ton of steel: iron, coal, and blast furnace time. The two plants have different types of furnaces, so the resources needed to manufacture a ton of steel depend on where the steel is manufactured (see Table 2). Each plant has its own coal mine. Each day, 12 tons of coal are available at plant 1 and 15 tons at plant 2. Coal cannot be shipped between plants. Each day, plant 1 has 10 hours of blast furnace time available, and plant 2 has 4 hours of blast furnace time available. Iron ore is mined in a mine that is located midway between the two plants; 80 tons of iron are available each day. Each ton of steel 1 can be sold for \$170/ton, and each ton of steel 2 can be sold for \$160/ton. All steel that is sold is shipped to a single customer. It costs \$80 to ship a ton of steel from plant 1, and \$100 a ton to ship a ton of steel from plant 2. Assuming that the only variable cost is the shipping cost, formulate and solve an LP to maximize Steelco's revenues less shipping costs.

Table 2 Resource Requirements for Steelco Problem	PRODUCT (1 Ton)	IRON REQUIRED (Tons)	COAL REQUIRED (Tons)	BLAST FURNACE TIME REQUIRED (Hours)
	Steel 1 at plant 1	8	3	2
	Steel 2 at plant 1	6	1	1
	Steel 1 at plant 2	7	3	1
	Steel 2 at plant 2	5	2	1

Solution

Define

$$x_1 = \text{tons of steel 1 produced daily at plant 1}$$
$$x_2 = \text{tons of steel 2 produced daily at plant 1}$$
$$x_3 = \text{tons of steel 1 produced daily at plant 2}$$
$$x_4 = \text{tons of steel 2 produced daily at plant 2}$$

Steelco's revenue is given by $170(x_1 + x_3) + 160(x_2 + x_4)$, and Steelco's shipping cost is $80(x_1 + x_2) + 100(x_3 + x_4)$. Therefore, Steelco wants to maximize

$$z = (170 - 80)x_1 + (160 - 80)x_2 + (170 - 100)x_3 + (160 - 100)x_4$$
$$= 90x_1 + 80x_2 + 70x_3 + 60x_4$$

Steelco faces the following five constraints:

Constraint 1 At plant 1, no more than 12 tons of coal can be used daily.

Constraint 2 At plant 1, no more than 10 hours of blast furnace time can be used daily.

Constraint 3 At plant 2, no more than 15 tons of coal can be used daily.

Constraint 4 At plant 2, no more than 4 hours of blast furnace time can be used daily.

Constraint 5 At most 80 tons of iron ore can be used daily.

Constraints 1–5 easily lead to the following five LP constraints:

$$3x_1 + x_2 \leq 12 \quad \text{(Plant 1 coal constraint)} \quad (22)$$
$$2x_1 + x_2 \leq 10 \quad \text{(Plant 1 furnace constraint)} \quad (23)$$
$$3x_3 + 2x_4 \leq 15 \quad \text{(Plant 2 coal constraint)} \quad (24)$$
$$x_3 + x_4 \leq 4 \quad \text{(Plant 2 furnace constraint)} \quad (25)$$
$$8x_1 + 6x_2 + 7x_3 + 5x_4 \leq 80 \quad \text{(Iron ore constraint)} \quad (26)$$

We also need the sign restrictions $x_i \geq 0$. Putting it all together, we write Steelco's LP as

$$\max z = 90x_1 + 80x_2 + 70x_3 + 60x_4$$
$$\text{s.t.} \quad 3x_1 + x_2 \qquad\qquad \leq 12 \quad \text{(Plant 1 coal constraint)} \quad (22)$$
$$2x_1 + x_2 \qquad\qquad \leq 10 \quad \text{(Plant 1 furnace constraint)} \quad (23)$$
$$3x_3 + 2x_4 \leq 15 \quad \text{(Plant 2 coal constraint)} \quad (24)$$
$$x_3 + x_4 \leq 4 \quad \text{(Plant 2 furnace constraint)} \quad (25)$$
$$8x_1 + 6x_2 + 7x_3 + 5x_4 \leq 80 \quad \text{(Iron ore constraint)} \quad (26)$$
$$x_1, x_2, x_3, x_4 \geq 0$$

Using our definition of decomposition, we may decompose the Steelco LP in the following manner:

Variable Set 1 x_1 and x_2 (plant 1 variables).

Variable Set 2 x_3 and x_4 (plant 2 variables).

Constraint Set 1 (22) and (23) (plant 1 constraints).

Constraint Set 2 (24) and (25) (plant 2 constraints).

Constraint Set 3 (26).

Constraint Set 1 and Variable Set 1 involve activities at plant 1 and do not involve x_3 and x_4 (which represent plant 2 activities). Constraint Set 2 and Variable Set 2 involve activities at plant 2 and do not involve x_1 and x_2 (plant 1 activities). Constraint Set 3 may be thought of as a centralized constraint that interrelates the two sets of variables. (Solution to be continued.)

The reader should see that problems in which several plants manufacture several products can easily be decomposed along the lines of Example 3.

In order to solve efficiently LPs that decompose along the lines of Example 3, Dantzig and Wolfe developed the Dantzig-Wolfe decomposition algorithm. To simplify our discussion of this algorithm, we assume we are solving an LP in which each subproblem has a bounded feasible region.[†] The decomposition algorithm depends on the results in Theorem 1.

THEOREM 1	Suppose the feasible region for an LP is bounded and the extreme points (or basic feasible solutions) of the LP's feasible region are $P_1, P_2, \ldots, P_k$. Then any point x in the LP's feasible region may be written as a linear combination of $P_1, P_2, \ldots, P_k$. In other words, there exist weights $\mu_1, \mu_2, \ldots, \mu_k$ satisfying

$$x = \mu_1 P_1 + \mu_2 P_2 + \cdots + \mu_k P_k \tag{27}$$

Moreover, the weights $\mu_1, \mu_2, \ldots, \mu_k$ in (27) may be chosen such that

$$\mu_1 + \mu_2 + \cdots + \mu_k = 1 \quad \text{and} \quad \mu_i \geq 0 \quad \text{for } i = 1, 2, \ldots, k \tag{28}$$

Any linear combination of vectors for which the weights satisfy (28) is called a **convex combination.** Thus, Theorem 1 states that if an LP's feasible region is bounded, any point in the LP's feasible region may be written as a convex combination of the extreme points of the LP's feasible region.

We illustrate Theorem 1 by showing how it applies to the LPs defined by Constraint Set 1 and Constraint Set 2 of Example 3. To begin, we look at the feasible region defined by the sign restrictions $x_1 \geq 0$ and $x_2 \geq 0$ and Constraint Set 1 (consisting of (22) and (23)). This feasible region is the interior and the boundary of the shaded quadrilateral $P_1 P_2 P_3 P_4$ in Figure 3. The extreme points of this feasible region are $P_1 = [0 \quad 0]$, $P_2 = [4 \quad 0]$, $P_3 = [2 \quad 6]$, and $P_4 = [0 \quad 10]$. For this feasible region, Theorem 1 states that any point

$$\begin{bmatrix} x_1 \\ x_2 \end{bmatrix}$$

in the feasible region for Constraint Set 1 may be written as

$$\begin{bmatrix} x_1 \\ x_2 \end{bmatrix} = \mu_1 \begin{bmatrix} 0 \\ 0 \end{bmatrix} + \mu_2 \begin{bmatrix} 4 \\ 0 \end{bmatrix} + \mu_3 \begin{bmatrix} 2 \\ 6 \end{bmatrix} + \mu_4 \begin{bmatrix} 0 \\ 10 \end{bmatrix} = \begin{bmatrix} 4\mu_2 + 2\mu_3 \\ 6\mu_3 + 10\mu_4 \end{bmatrix}$$

where $\mu_i \geq 0$ $(i = 1, 2, 3, 4)$ and $\mu_1 + \mu_2 + \mu_3 + \mu_4 = 1$. For example, the point

$$\begin{bmatrix} 2 \\ 2 \end{bmatrix}$$

is in the feasible region $P_1 P_2 P_3 P_4$. A glance at Figure 3 shows that

$$\begin{bmatrix} 2 \\ 2 \end{bmatrix}$$

[†]See Bradley, Hax, and Magnanti (1977) for a discussion of decomposition that includes the case where at least one subproblem has an unbounded feasible region.

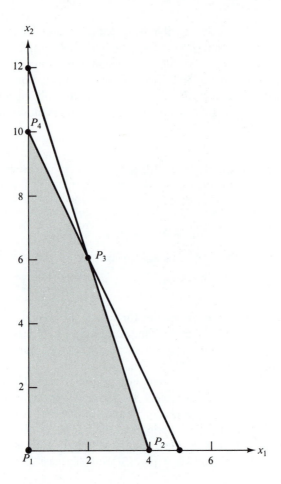

may be written as a linear combination of $\mathbf{P}_1$, $\mathbf{P}_2$, and $\mathbf{P}_3$. A little algebra shows that

$$\begin{bmatrix} 2 \\ 2 \end{bmatrix} = \frac{1}{3}\begin{bmatrix} 0 \\ 0 \end{bmatrix} + \frac{1}{3}\begin{bmatrix} 4 \\ 0 \end{bmatrix} + \frac{1}{3}\begin{bmatrix} 2 \\ 6 \end{bmatrix}$$

As another illustration of Theorem 1, consider the feasible region defined by the sign restrictions $x_3 \geq 0$ and $x_4 \geq 0$ and Constraint Set 2 ((24) and (25)). The feasible region for this LP is the shaded area $Q_1Q_2Q_3$ in Figure 4. The extreme points for this feasible region are $\mathbf{Q}_1 = (0, 0)$, $\mathbf{Q}_2 = (4, 0)$, and $\mathbf{Q}_3 = (0, 4)$. Theorem 1 tells us that any point

$$\begin{bmatrix} x_3 \\ x_4 \end{bmatrix}$$

that is in the feasible region for Constraint Set 2 may be written as

$$\begin{bmatrix} x_3 \\ x_4 \end{bmatrix} = \mu_1\begin{bmatrix} 0 \\ 0 \end{bmatrix} + \mu_2\begin{bmatrix} 4 \\ 0 \end{bmatrix} + \mu_3\begin{bmatrix} 0 \\ 4 \end{bmatrix}$$

where $\mu_i \geq 0$ and $\mu_1 + \mu_2 + \mu_3 = 1$. For example, the feasible point

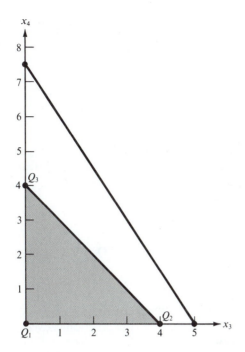

Figure 4
Feasible Region for
Constraint Set 2

$$\begin{bmatrix} 2 \\ 1 \end{bmatrix}$$

may be written as

$$\begin{bmatrix} 2 \\ 1 \end{bmatrix} = \frac{1}{4}\begin{bmatrix} 0 \\ 0 \end{bmatrix} + \frac{1}{2}\begin{bmatrix} 4 \\ 0 \end{bmatrix} + \frac{1}{4}\begin{bmatrix} 0 \\ 4 \end{bmatrix}$$

For our purposes, it is not important to know how to determine the set of weights corresponding to a particular feasible point. The decomposition algorithm does not require us to be able to find the weights for an arbitrary point.

To explain the basic ideas of the decomposition algorithm, we assume that the set of variables has been decomposed into Set 1 and Set 2. The reader should have no trouble generalizing to a situation where the set of variables is decomposed into more than two sets of variables.

The Dantzig-Wolfe decomposition algorithm proceeds as follows:

Step 1 Let the variables in Variable Set 1 be $x_1, x_2, \ldots, x_{n_1}$. Express the variables in Variable Set 1 as a convex combination (see Theorem 1) of the extreme points of the feasible region for Constraint Set 1 (the constraints that only involve the variables in Variable Set 1). If we let $\mathbf{P}_1, \mathbf{P}_2, \ldots, \mathbf{P}_k$ be the extreme points of this feasible region, then any point

$$\begin{bmatrix} x_1 \\ x_2 \\ \vdots \\ x_{n_1} \end{bmatrix}$$

in the feasible region for Constraint Set 1 may be written in the form

$$
\begin{bmatrix} x_1 \\ x_2 \\ \vdots \\ x_{n_1} \end{bmatrix} = \mu_1 \mathbf{P}_1 + \mu_2 \mathbf{P}_2 + \cdots + \mu_k \mathbf{P}_k \tag{29}
$$

where $\mu_1 + \mu_2 + \cdots + \mu_k = 1$ and $\mu_i \geq 0$ $(i = 1, 2, \ldots, k)$.

Step 2 Express the variables in Variable Set 2, $x_{n_1+1}, x_{n_1+2}, \ldots, x_n$, as a convex combination of the extreme points of Constraint Set 2's feasible region. If we let the extreme points of the feasible region be $\mathbf{Q}_1, \mathbf{Q}_2, \ldots, \mathbf{Q}_m$, then any point in Constraint Set 2's feasible region may be written as

$$
\begin{bmatrix} x_{n_1+1} \\ x_{n_1+2} \\ \vdots \\ x_n \end{bmatrix} = \lambda_1 \mathbf{Q} + \lambda_2 \mathbf{Q}_2 + \cdots + \lambda_m \mathbf{Q}_m \tag{30}
$$

where $\lambda_i \geq 0$ $(i = 1, 2, \ldots, m)$ and $\lambda_1 + \lambda_2 + \cdots + \lambda_m = 1$.

Step 3 Using (29) and (30), express the LP's objective function and centralized constraints in terms of the μ_i's and the λ_i's. After adding the constraints (called convexity constraints) $\mu_1 + \mu_2 + \cdots + \mu_k = 1$ and $\lambda_1 + \lambda_2 + \cdots + \lambda_m = 1$ and the sign restrictions $\mu_i \geq 0$ $(i = 1, 2, \ldots, k)$ and $\lambda_i \geq 0$ $(i = 1, 2, \ldots, m)$, we obtain the following LP, which is referred to as the **restricted master**:

$$
\text{max (or min) [objective function in terms of } \mu_i\text{'s and } \lambda_i\text{'s]}
$$

s.t. [central constraints in terms of μ_i's and λ_i's]

$$\mu_1 + \mu_2 + \cdots + \mu_k = 1 \quad \text{(Convexity constraints)}$$
$$\lambda_1 + \lambda_2 + \cdots + \lambda_m = 1$$
$$\mu_i \geq 0 \quad (i = 1, 2, \ldots, k) \quad \text{(Sign restrictions)}$$
$$\lambda_i \geq 0 \quad (i = 1, 2, \ldots, m)$$

In many large-scale LPs, the restricted master may have millions of variables (corresponding to the many basic feasible solutions of extreme points for each constraint set). Fortunately, however, we rarely have to write down the entire restricted master; all we need is to generate the column in the restricted master that corresponds to a specific μ_i or λ_i.

Step 4 Assume that a basic feasible solution for the restricted master is readily available.[†] Then use the column generation method of Section 10.3 to solve the restricted master.

Step 5 Substitute the optimal values of the μ_i's and λ_i's found in Step 4 into (29) and (30). This will yield the optimal values of $x_1, x_2, \ldots, x_n$.

[†]If this is not the case, the two-phase simplex method must be used. See Bradley, Hax, and Magnanti (1977) for details.

Continuation of Solution to Example 3 For Example 3, we have already seen that

$$\text{Variable Set } 1 = \{x_1, x_2\}$$

$$\text{Constraint Set } 1 = \begin{cases} 3x_1 + x_2 \le 12 & \text{(22)} \\ 2x_1 + x_2 \le 10 & \text{(23)} \end{cases}$$

We have also seen that the feasible region for Constraint Set 1 has four extreme points, and any feasible point

$$\begin{bmatrix} x_1 \\ x_2 \end{bmatrix}$$

for Constraint Set 1 may be written as

$$\begin{bmatrix} x_1 \\ x_2 \end{bmatrix} = \mu_1 \begin{bmatrix} 0 \\ 0 \end{bmatrix} + \mu_2 \begin{bmatrix} 4 \\ 0 \end{bmatrix} + \mu_3 \begin{bmatrix} 2 \\ 6 \end{bmatrix} + \mu_4 \begin{bmatrix} 0 \\ 10 \end{bmatrix} = \begin{bmatrix} 4\mu_2 + 2\mu_3 \\ 6\mu_3 + 10\mu_4 \end{bmatrix} \quad \text{(29')}$$

where $\mu_1 + \mu_2 + \mu_3 + \mu_4 = 1$ and $\mu_i \ge 0$.

$$\text{Variable Set } 2 = x_3 \text{ and } x_4$$

$$\text{Constraint Set } 2 = \begin{cases} 3x_3 + 2x_4 \le 15 & \text{(24)} \\ x_3 + x_4 \le 4 & \text{(25)} \end{cases}$$

Any point

$$\begin{bmatrix} x_3 \\ x_4 \end{bmatrix}$$

in the feasible region for Constraint Set 2 may be written as

$$\begin{bmatrix} x_3 \\ x_4 \end{bmatrix} = \lambda_1 \begin{bmatrix} 0 \\ 0 \end{bmatrix} + \lambda_2 \begin{bmatrix} 4 \\ 0 \end{bmatrix} + \lambda_3 \begin{bmatrix} 0 \\ 4 \end{bmatrix} = \begin{bmatrix} 4\lambda_2 \\ 4\lambda_3 \end{bmatrix} \quad \text{(30')}$$

where $\lambda_1 + \lambda_2 + \lambda_3 = 1$ and $\lambda_i \ge 0$ $(i = 1, 2, 3)$.

We now obtain the restricted master by substituting (29') and (30') into the objective function and the centralized constraint. The objective function (21) becomes

$$90x_1 + 80x_2 + 70x_3 + 60x_4 = 90(4\mu_2 + 2\mu_3) + 80(6\mu_3 + 10\mu_4) + 70(4\lambda_2) + 60(4\lambda_3)$$

$$= 360\mu_2 + 660\mu_3 + 800\mu_4 + 280\lambda_2 + 240\lambda_3$$

The centralized constraint becomes

$$8(4\mu_2 + 2\mu_3) + 6(6\mu_3 + 10\mu_4) + 7(4\lambda_2) + 5(4\lambda_3) \le 80$$

or

$$32\mu_2 + 52\mu_3 + 60\mu_4 + 28\lambda_2 + 20\lambda_3 \le 80$$

After adding a slack variable s_1 to this constraint and writing down the convexity constraints and the sign restrictions, we obtain the following restricted master program:

$$\max z = 360\mu_2 + 660\mu_3 + 800\mu_4 + 280\lambda_2 + 240\lambda_3$$
$$\text{s.t.} \quad 32\mu_2 + 52\mu_3 + 60\mu_4 \quad + 28\lambda_2 + 20\lambda_3 + s_1 = 80$$
$$\mu_1 + \quad \mu_2 + \quad \mu_3 + \quad \mu_4 \qquad\qquad\qquad = 1$$
$$\lambda_1 + \quad \lambda_2 + \quad \lambda_3 \qquad = 1$$
$$\mu_i, \lambda_i \geq 0$$

There is a more insightful way to obtain the column for a variable in the restricted master. Recall that each variable in the restricted master corresponds to an extreme point for the feasible region of Constraint Set 1 or Constraint Set 2. As an example, let's focus on how to find the column in the restricted master for a variable μ_i, which corresponds to an extreme point

$$\begin{bmatrix} x_1 \\ x_2 \end{bmatrix}$$

for Constraint Set 1. Since x_1 and x_2 correspond to activity at plant 1, we may consider any specification of x_1 and x_2 as a "proposal" from plant 1. For example, the point

$$\begin{bmatrix} 2 \\ 6 \end{bmatrix}$$

corresponds to plant 1 proposing to produce 2 tons of type 1 steel and 6 tons of type 2 steel. Then the weight μ_i may be thought of as a fraction of the proposal corresponding to extreme point $\mathbf{P}_i$ that is included in the actual production schedule. For example, since

$$\begin{bmatrix} 2 \\ 2 \end{bmatrix} = \tfrac{1}{3}\mathbf{P}_1 + \tfrac{1}{3}\mathbf{P}_2 + \tfrac{1}{3}\mathbf{P}_3$$

we may think of

$$\begin{bmatrix} 2 \\ 2 \end{bmatrix}$$

as consisting of one third of plant 1 proposal $\mathbf{P}_1$, one third of plant 1 proposal $\mathbf{P}_2$, and one third of plant 1 proposal $\mathbf{P}_3$.

We can now describe an easy method to determine the column for any variable in the restricted master. Suppose we want to determine the column for the extreme point

$$\begin{bmatrix} x_1 \\ x_2 \end{bmatrix}$$

corresponding to the weight μ_i. If we include a fraction μ_i of the extreme point

$$\begin{bmatrix} x_1 \\ x_2 \end{bmatrix}$$

what will this contribute to the objective function? If $\mu_i = 1$, then

$$\mu_i \begin{bmatrix} x_1 \\ x_2 \end{bmatrix}$$

will contribute $90x_1 + 80x_2$ to the objective function. By the Proportionality Assumption, if we use a fraction μ_i of the extreme point

$$\begin{bmatrix} x_1 \\ x_2 \end{bmatrix}$$

then it will contribute $\mu_i(90x_1 + 80x_2)$ to the objective function. Similarly, if $\mu_i = 1$, then

$$\mu_i \begin{bmatrix} x_1 \\ x_2 \end{bmatrix}$$

will contribute $8x_1 + 6x_2$ of iron usage. Thus, for an arbitrary value of μ_i,

$$\mu_i \begin{bmatrix} x_1 \\ x_2 \end{bmatrix}$$

will contribute an amount $\mu_i(8x_1 + 6x_2)$ to the left-hand side of the iron ore usage constraint.

To be more specific, let's use the reasoning we have just described to determine the column in the restricted master for the weight μ_3 corresponding to the extreme point

$$\begin{bmatrix} 2 \\ 6 \end{bmatrix}$$

Our logic shows that in this case the left-hand side of the objective function involving μ_3 is $\mu_3[90(2) + 80(6)] = 660\mu_3$. Similarly, the term involving μ_3 on the left-hand side of the iron ore constraint will be $\mu_3[8(2) + 6(6)] = 52\mu_3$. Also, μ_3 will have a coefficient of 1 in the first convexity constraint and a zero coefficient in the other convexity constraint. (If the reader understood how we obtained the μ_3 column, there should be little trouble with what follows; readers who are confused should reread the last two pages before continuing.)

We now solve the restricted master by using the revised simplex method and column generation. We refer to our initial tableau as tableau 0. Then $BV(0) = \{s_1, \mu_1, \lambda_1\}$. Also,

$$B_0 = \begin{bmatrix} 1 & 0 & 0 \\ 0 & 1 & 0 \\ 0 & 0 & 1 \end{bmatrix}, \quad \text{so} \quad B_0^{-1} = \begin{bmatrix} 1 & 0 & 0 \\ 0 & 1 & 0 \\ 0 & 0 & 1 \end{bmatrix}$$

Since s_1, μ_1, and λ_1 don't appear in the objective function of the restricted master, we have $\mathbf{c}_{BV} = [0 \ \ 0 \ \ 0]$, and the tableau 0 shadow prices are given by

$$\mathbf{c}_{BV} B_0^{-1} = [0 \ \ 0 \ \ 0] \begin{bmatrix} 1 & 0 & 0 \\ 0 & 1 & 0 \\ 0 & 0 & 1 \end{bmatrix} = [0 \ \ 0 \ \ 0]$$

We now apply the idea of column generation in two stages. We first determine whether there is any weight μ_i associated with Constraint Set 1 that prices out favorably (since we are solving a max problem, a negative coefficient in row 0 is favorable). A weight μ_i associated with an extreme point

$$\begin{bmatrix} x_1 \\ x_2 \end{bmatrix}$$

of Constraint Set 1 will have the following column in the restricted master:

$$\text{Objective function coefficient for } \mu_i = 90x_1 + 80x_2$$

$$\text{Column in constraints for } \mu_i = \begin{bmatrix} 8x_1 + 6x_2 \\ 1 \\ 0 \end{bmatrix}$$

From this information, we see that in tableau 0, the column for the weight μ_i corresponding to

$$\begin{bmatrix} x_1 \\ x_2 \end{bmatrix}$$

will price out to

$$\mathbf{c}_{BV} B_0^{-1} \begin{bmatrix} 8x_1 + 6x_2 \\ 1 \\ 0 \end{bmatrix} - (90x_1 + 80x_2) = -90x_1 - 80x_2$$

Since

$$\begin{bmatrix} x_1 \\ x_2 \end{bmatrix}$$

must satisfy Constraint Set 1 (or the plant 1 constraints), the weight μ_i that prices out most negatively will be the weight associated with the extreme point that is the optimal solution to the following LP:

Tableau 0
Plant 1 Subproblem

$$\min z = -90x_1 - 80x_2$$
$$\text{s.t.} \quad 3x_1 + x_2 \leq 12$$
$$2x_1 + x_2 \leq 10$$
$$x_1, x_2 \geq 0$$

Solving the plant 1 subproblem graphically, we obtain the solution $z = -800$, $x_1 = 0$, $x_2 = 10$. This means that the weight μ_i associated with the extreme point

$$\begin{bmatrix} 0 \\ 10 \end{bmatrix}$$

will price out most negatively. Recall that

$$\mathbf{P}_4 = \begin{bmatrix} 0 \\ 10 \end{bmatrix}$$

This means that μ_4 will price out with a coefficient of -800 in the restricted master.

We now look at the weights associated with Constraint Set 2 and try to determine the weight λ_i that will price out most negatively. The λ_i corresponding to an extreme point

$$\begin{bmatrix} x_3 \\ x_4 \end{bmatrix}$$

of Constraint Set 2 will have the following column in the restricted master:

Objective function coefficient for $\lambda_i = 70x_3 + 60x_4$

$$\text{Column in constraints for } \lambda_i = \begin{bmatrix} 7x_3 + 5x_4 \\ 0 \\ 1 \end{bmatrix}$$

This means that the λ_i corresponding to the extreme point

$$\begin{bmatrix} x_3 \\ x_4 \end{bmatrix}$$

will price out to

$$\mathbf{c}_{BV}\,B_0^{-1} \begin{bmatrix} 7x_3 + 5x_4 \\ 0 \\ 1 \end{bmatrix} - (70x_3 + 60x_4) = -70x_3 - 60x_4$$

Note that

$$\begin{bmatrix} x_3 \\ x_4 \end{bmatrix}$$

must satisfy Constraint Set 2. Thus, the extreme point whose weight λ_i prices out most favorably will be the solution to the following LP:

Tableau 0
Plant 2 Subproblem

$$\begin{aligned} \min z = &-70x_3 - 60x_4 \\ \text{s.t.} \quad 3x_3 + 2x_4 &\le 15 \\ x_3 + x_4 &\le 4 \\ x_3, x_4 &\ge 0 \end{aligned}$$

The optimal solution to this LP is $z = -280$, $x_3 = 4$, $x_4 = 0$. Since

$$\begin{bmatrix} 4 \\ 0 \end{bmatrix} = \mathbf{Q}_2$$

λ_2 prices out the most negatively of all the λ_i's. But μ_4 prices out more negatively than λ_2, so we enter μ_4 into the basis (by using the revised simplex procedure). To do this, we need to find the column for μ_4 in tableau 0 and also find the right-hand side of tableau 0. The column for μ_4 in tableau 0 is

$$B_0^{-1} \begin{bmatrix} 8(0) + 6(10) \\ 1 \\ 0 \end{bmatrix} = \begin{bmatrix} 60 \\ 1 \\ 0 \end{bmatrix}$$

and the right-hand side of tableau 0 is

$$B_0^{-1}\mathbf{b} = \begin{bmatrix} 1 & 0 & 0 \\ 0 & 1 & 0 \\ 0 & 0 & 1 \end{bmatrix} \begin{bmatrix} 80 \\ 1 \\ 1 \end{bmatrix} = \begin{bmatrix} 80 \\ 1 \\ 1 \end{bmatrix}$$

The ratio test now indicates that μ_4 should enter the basis in the second constraint. Then $BV(1) = \{s_1, \mu_4, \lambda_1\}$. Since

$$E_0 = \begin{bmatrix} 1 & -60 & 0 \\ 0 & 1 & 0 \\ 0 & 0 & 1 \end{bmatrix}$$

$$B_1^{-1} = E_0 B_0^{-1} = \begin{bmatrix} 1 & -60 & 0 \\ 0 & 1 & 0 \\ 0 & 0 & 1 \end{bmatrix}$$

The objective function coefficient for μ_4 is $90(0) + 80(10) = 800$, so the new set of shadow prices may be found from

$$\mathbf{c}_{BV} B_1^{-1} = [0 \quad 800 \quad 0] \begin{bmatrix} 1 & -60 & 0 \\ 0 & 1 & 0 \\ 0 & 0 & 1 \end{bmatrix} = [0 \quad 800 \quad 0]$$

We now try to find the weight that prices out most negatively in the current tableau. As before, we solve the current tableau's plant 1 and plant 2 subproblems. Also, as before, a weight μ_i that corresponds to a Constraint 1 extreme point

$$\begin{bmatrix} x_1 \\ x_2 \end{bmatrix}$$

will price out to

$$\mathbf{c}_{BV} B_1^{-1} \begin{bmatrix} 8x_1 + 6x_2 \\ 1 \\ 0 \end{bmatrix} - (90x_1 + 80x_2)$$

$$= [0 \quad 800 \quad 0] \begin{bmatrix} 8x_1 + 6x_2 \\ 1 \\ 0 \end{bmatrix} - (90x_1 + 80x_2) = 800 - 90x_1 - 80x_2$$

Since

$$\begin{bmatrix} x_1 \\ x_2 \end{bmatrix}$$

must satisfy the Constraint Set 1 constraints, the μ_i that prices out most favorably will correspond to the point

$$\begin{bmatrix} x_1 \\ x_2 \end{bmatrix}$$

that solves the following LP:

Tableau 1
Plant 1 Subproblem

$$\min z = 800 - 90x_1 - 80x_2$$
$$\text{s.t.} \quad 3x_1 + x_2 \leq 12$$
$$2x_1 + x_2 \leq 10$$
$$x_1, x_2 \geq 0$$

The optimal solution to this LP is $z = 0$, $x_1 = 0$, $x_2 = 10$. This means that no μ_i can price out favorably. We now solve the plant 2 subproblem in an effort to find a λ_i that prices out favorably. A λ_i corresponding to an extreme point

$$\begin{bmatrix} x_3 \\ x_4 \end{bmatrix}$$

of Constraint Set 2 will price out to

$$\mathbf{c}_{BV} B_1^{-1} \begin{bmatrix} 7x_3 + 5x_4 \\ 0 \\ 1 \end{bmatrix} - (70x_3 + 60x_4) = -70x_3 - 60x_4$$

Since

$$\begin{bmatrix} x_3 \\ x_4 \end{bmatrix}$$

must satisfy the plant 2 constraints, the λ_i that will price out most negatively will correspond to the extreme point

$$\begin{bmatrix} x_3 \\ x_4 \end{bmatrix}$$

that solves the plant 2 subproblem for tableau 1:

Tableau 1
Plant 2 Subproblem

$$\min z = -70x_3 - 60x_4$$
$$\text{s.t.} \quad 3x_3 + 2x_4 \leq 15$$
$$x_3 + x_4 \leq 4$$
$$x_3, x_4 \geq 0$$

The optimal solution to this LP is $x_3 = 4$, $x_4 = 0$, $z = -280$. This means that the λ_i corresponding to

$$\begin{bmatrix} 4 \\ 0 \end{bmatrix}$$

prices out to -280. Since

$$\begin{bmatrix} 4 \\ 0 \end{bmatrix} = \mathbf{Q}_2$$

λ_2 prices out to -280. No μ_i has priced out negatively, so the best we can do is to enter λ_2 into the basis. To enter λ_2 into the basis, we need the column for λ_2 in tableau 1 and the right-hand side for tableau 1. The column for λ_2 in tableau 1 is given by

$$B_1^{-1} \begin{bmatrix} 7(4) + 5(0) \\ 0 \\ 1 \end{bmatrix} = \begin{bmatrix} 1 & -60 & 0 \\ 0 & 1 & 0 \\ 0 & 0 & 1 \end{bmatrix} \begin{bmatrix} 28 \\ 0 \\ 1 \end{bmatrix} = \begin{bmatrix} 28 \\ 0 \\ 1 \end{bmatrix}$$

and the right-hand side of tableau 1 is

$$B_1^{-1}\mathbf{b} = \begin{bmatrix} 1 & -60 & 0 \\ 0 & 1 & 0 \\ 0 & 0 & 1 \end{bmatrix} \begin{bmatrix} 80 \\ 1 \\ 1 \end{bmatrix} = \begin{bmatrix} 20 \\ 1 \\ 1 \end{bmatrix}$$

The ratio test indicates that λ_2 should enter the basis in row 1. Thus, $BV(2) = \{\lambda_2, \mu_4, \lambda_1\}$. Since

$$E_1 = \begin{bmatrix} \frac{1}{28} & 0 & 0 \\ 0 & 1 & 0 \\ -\frac{1}{28} & 0 & 1 \end{bmatrix},$$

$$B_2^{-1} = E_1 B_1^{-1} = \begin{bmatrix} \frac{1}{28} & 0 & 0 \\ 0 & 1 & 0 \\ -\frac{1}{28} & 0 & 1 \end{bmatrix} \begin{bmatrix} 1 & -60 & 0 \\ 0 & 1 & 0 \\ 0 & 0 & 1 \end{bmatrix} = \begin{bmatrix} \frac{1}{28} & -\frac{60}{28} & 0 \\ 0 & 1 & 0 \\ -\frac{1}{28} & \frac{60}{28} & 1 \end{bmatrix}$$

To compute $\mathbf{c}_{BV} B_2^{-1}$, note that λ_2 has a coefficient of $70x_3 + 60x_4 = 70(4) + 60(0) = 280$ in the objective function of the restricted master. Recall that μ_4 has an objective coefficient of 800 in the restricted master objective function, and λ_1 has an objective function coefficient of zero in the restricted master. Then the new set of shadow prices is

$$\mathbf{c}_{BV} B_2^{-1} = [280 \quad 800 \quad 0] \begin{bmatrix} \frac{1}{28} & -\frac{60}{28} & 0 \\ 0 & 1 & 0 \\ -\frac{1}{28} & \frac{60}{28} & 1 \end{bmatrix} = [10 \quad 200 \quad 0]$$

By solving the plant 1 subproblem for tableau 2, we can determine whether any μ_i prices out favorably. The μ_i corresponding to

$$\begin{bmatrix} x_1 \\ x_2 \end{bmatrix}$$

prices out to

$$\mathbf{c}_{BV}B_2^{-1} \begin{bmatrix} 8x_1 + 6x_2 \\ 1 \\ 0 \end{bmatrix} - (90x_1 + 80x_2)$$

$$= \begin{bmatrix} 10 & 200 & 0 \end{bmatrix} \begin{bmatrix} 8x_1 + 6x_2 \\ 1 \\ 0 \end{bmatrix} - (90x_1 + 80x_2) = 200 - 10x_1 - 20x_2$$

Thus, we have

Tableau 2
Plant 1 Subproblem

$$\min z = 200 - 10x_1 - 20x_2$$
$$\text{s.t.} \quad 3x_1 + x_2 \le 12$$
$$2x_1 + x_2 \le 10$$
$$x_1, x_2 \ge 0$$

The optimal solution to this LP is $z = 0$, $x_1 = 0$, $x_2 = 10$. As before, this means that no μ_i can price out favorably.

To determine whether the λ_i corresponding to the extreme point

$$\begin{bmatrix} x_3 \\ x_4 \end{bmatrix}$$

should be entered into the basis, observe that the λ_i corresponding to

$$\begin{bmatrix} x_3 \\ x_4 \end{bmatrix}$$

prices out to

$$\begin{bmatrix} 10 & 200 & 0 \end{bmatrix} \begin{bmatrix} 7x_3 + 5x_4 \\ 0 \\ 1 \end{bmatrix} - (70x_3 + 60x_4) = -10x_4$$

Since

$$\begin{bmatrix} x_3 \\ x_4 \end{bmatrix}$$

must satisfy Constraint Set 2, the λ_i that prices out most favorably will be the λ_i associated with the point

$$\begin{bmatrix} x_3 \\ x_4 \end{bmatrix}$$

that solves the following LP:

Tableau 2
Plant 2 Subproblem

$$\min z = -10x_4$$
$$\text{s.t.} \quad 3x_3 + 2x_4 \le 15$$
$$x_3 + x_4 \le 4$$
$$x_3, x_4 \ge 0$$

This LP has the solution $z = -40$, $x_3 = 0$, $x_4 = 4$. Thus, the λ_i corresponding to

$$\begin{bmatrix} 0 \\ 4 \end{bmatrix} = \mathbf{Q}_3$$

should enter the basis, and λ_3 should be entered into the basis. The λ_3 column in tableau 2 is

$$B_2^{-1} \begin{bmatrix} 7(0) + 5(4) \\ 0 \\ 1 \end{bmatrix} = \begin{bmatrix} \frac{1}{28} & -\frac{60}{28} & 0 \\ 0 & 1 & 0 \\ -\frac{1}{28} & \frac{60}{28} & 1 \end{bmatrix} \begin{bmatrix} 20 \\ 0 \\ 1 \end{bmatrix} = \begin{bmatrix} \frac{20}{28} \\ 0 \\ \frac{8}{28} \end{bmatrix}$$

Tableau 2's right-hand side is

$$B_2^{-1} \mathbf{b} = \begin{bmatrix} \frac{1}{28} & -\frac{60}{28} & 0 \\ 0 & 1 & 0 \\ -\frac{1}{28} & \frac{60}{28} & 1 \end{bmatrix} \begin{bmatrix} 80 \\ 1 \\ 1 \end{bmatrix} = \begin{bmatrix} \frac{20}{28} \\ 1 \\ \frac{8}{28} \end{bmatrix}$$

The ratio test indicates that λ_3 should enter the basis in Constraint 1 or Constraint 3. We arbitrarily choose to enter λ_3 into the basis in Constraint 1. Thus, $BV(3) = \{\lambda_3, \mu_4, \lambda_1\}$. Since

$$E_2 = \begin{bmatrix} \frac{28}{20} & 0 & 0 \\ 0 & 1 & 0 \\ -\frac{2}{5} & 0 & 1 \end{bmatrix}$$

$$B_3^{-1} = E_2 B_2^{-1} = \begin{bmatrix} \frac{28}{20} & 0 & 0 \\ 0 & 1 & 0 \\ -\frac{2}{5} & 0 & 1 \end{bmatrix} \begin{bmatrix} \frac{1}{28} & -\frac{60}{28} & 0 \\ 0 & 1 & 0 \\ -\frac{1}{28} & \frac{60}{28} & 1 \end{bmatrix} = \begin{bmatrix} \frac{1}{20} & -3 & 0 \\ 0 & 1 & 0 \\ -\frac{1}{20} & 3 & 1 \end{bmatrix}.$$

λ_3 corresponds to

$$\begin{bmatrix} 0 \\ 4 \end{bmatrix}$$

so the coefficient of λ_3 in the objective function of the restricted master is $70x_3 + 60x_4 = 70(0) + 60(4) = 240$. Since the μ_4 coefficient in the objective function has already been found to be 800 and the λ_1 coefficient in the objective function has already been found to be zero, we have $\mathbf{c}_{BV} = [240 \quad 800 \quad 0]$, and the new set of shadow prices is given by

$$\mathbf{c}_{BV} B_3^{-1} = [240 \quad 800 \quad 0] \begin{bmatrix} \frac{1}{20} & -3 & 0 \\ 0 & 1 & 0 \\ -\frac{1}{20} & 3 & 1 \end{bmatrix} = [12 \quad 80 \quad 0]$$

With these shadow prices, the μ_i corresponding to the extreme point

$$\begin{bmatrix} x_1 \\ x_2 \end{bmatrix}$$

will price out to

$$[12 \quad 80 \quad 0]\begin{bmatrix} 8x_1 + 6x_2 \\ 1 \\ 0 \end{bmatrix} - (90x_1 + 80x_2) = 80 + 6x_1 - 8x_2$$

Then we have

Tableau 3
Plant 1 Subproblem

$$\min z = 80 + 6x_1 - 8x_2$$
$$\text{s.t.} \quad 3x_1 + x_2 \leq 12$$
$$2x_1 + x_2 \leq 10$$
$$x_1, x_2 \geq 0$$

The optimal solution to this LP is $z = 0$, $x_1 = 0$, $x_2 = 10$. Again, this means that no μ_i prices out favorably.

Using the new shadow prices, we now determine whether any λ_i will price out favorably. If no λ_i prices out favorably, we will have found an optimal tableau. The λ_i corresponding to

$$\begin{bmatrix} x_3 \\ x_4 \end{bmatrix}$$

will price out to

$$[12 \quad 80 \quad 0]\begin{bmatrix} 7x_3 + 5x_4 \\ 0 \\ 1 \end{bmatrix} - (70x_3 + 60x_4) = 14x_3$$

Then we have

Tableau 3
Plant 2 Subproblem

$$\min z = 14x_3$$
$$\text{s.t.} \quad 3x_3 + 2x_4 \leq 15$$
$$x_3 + x_4 \leq 4$$
$$x_3, x_4 \geq 0$$

The optimal solution to this LP is $z = 0$, $x_3 = x_4 = 0$. This means that no λ_i can price out favorably. Since no μ_i or λ_i prices out favorably for tableau 3, tableau 3 must be an optimal tableau for the restricted master. Recall that $BV(3) = \{\lambda_3, \mu_4, \lambda_1\}$. Thus,

$$\begin{bmatrix} \lambda_3 \\ \mu_4 \\ \lambda_1 \end{bmatrix} = B_3^{-1}\mathbf{b} = \begin{bmatrix} \frac{1}{20} & -3 & 0 \\ 0 & 1 & 0 \\ -\frac{1}{20} & 3 & 1 \end{bmatrix}\begin{bmatrix} 80 \\ 1 \\ 1 \end{bmatrix} = \begin{bmatrix} 1 \\ 1 \\ 0 \end{bmatrix}$$

Thus, the optimal solution to the restricted master is $\lambda_3 = 1$, $\mu_4 = 1$, $\lambda_1 = 0$, and all other weights equal zero.

We can now use the representation of the Constraint Set 1 feasible region as a convex combination of its extreme points to determine that the optimal value of

$$\begin{bmatrix} x_1 \\ x_2 \end{bmatrix}$$

is given by

$$\begin{bmatrix} x_1 \\ x_2 \end{bmatrix} = 0\mathbf{P}_1 + 0\mathbf{P}_2 + 0\mathbf{P}_3 + \mathbf{P}_4 = \begin{bmatrix} 0 \\ 10 \end{bmatrix}$$

Similarly, we can use the representation of the Constraint Set 2 feasible region as a convex combination of its extreme points to determine that the optimal value of

$$\begin{bmatrix} x_3 \\ x_4 \end{bmatrix}$$

is given by

$$\begin{bmatrix} x_3 \\ x_4 \end{bmatrix} = 0\mathbf{Q}_1 + 0\mathbf{Q}_2 + \mathbf{Q}_3 = \begin{bmatrix} 0 \\ 4 \end{bmatrix}$$

Then the optimal solution to Steelco's problem is $x_2 = 10$, $x_4 = 4$, $x_1 = x_3 = 0$, $z = 1040$. Thus, Steelco can maximize its net profit by manufacturing 10 tons of steel 2 at plant 1 and 4 tons of steel 2 at plant 2.

REMARKS   **1.** If there are k sets of variables, then the restricted master will contain the central constraints and k convexity constraints (one convexity constraint for each set of variables). For each tableau, there will also be k subproblems that must be solved (one for the weights associated with the extreme points of the constraint set corresponding to each set of variables). After solving these subproblems, use the revised simplex algorithm to enter into the basis the weight that prices out most favorably.

2. A major virtue of decomposition is that solving many relatively small LPs is often much easier than solving a large LP. For example, consider an analog of Example 3 in which there are five plants and each plant has 50 constraints. Also suppose that there are 40 central constraints. Then the master problem will involve a 45×45 B^{-1}, and each subproblem will involve a 50×50 B^{-1}. Solving the original LP would involve a 290×290 B^{-1}. Clearly, storing a 290×290 matrix requires more computer memory than storing five 50×50 matrices and a 45×45 matrix. This illustrates how decomposition greatly reduces storage requirements.

3. Decomposition has an interesting economic interpretation. What is the meaning of the shadow prices for the restricted master of Example 3? For each tableau, the shadow price for the central constraint (reflecting the limited amount of iron ore) is the amount by which an extra unit of iron would increase profits. It can be shown that for any tableau, the shadow price for the plant i ($i = 1, 2$) convexity constraint is the profit obtained from the current mix of extreme points being used at plant i less the value of the centralized resource (calculated via centralized shadow price) required by the current mix of extreme points that is being used at plant i. For example, in tableau 3, the shadow price for the plant 1 convexity constraint is 80. Currently, plant 1 is utilizing the mix $x_1 = 0$ and $x_2 = 10$. This mix yields a profit of $80(10) = \$800$. This mix also uses $6(10) = 60$ tons of iron worth $60(12) = \$720$. Thus, the plant 1 convexity constraint has a shadow price of $800 - 720 = \$80$. This means that if Δ of the plant 1 weight were taken away, profits would be reduced by 80Δ.

We can now give an economic interpretation of the pricing out procedure that we use to generate our subproblems. If we are at tableau 3, what are the benefits and costs if we try to introduce the μ_i associated with the extreme point

$$\begin{bmatrix} x_1 \\ x_2 \end{bmatrix}$$

into the basis? Recall that for tableau 3, the iron shadow price is 12 and the plant 1 convexity constraint has a shadow price of 80. In determining whether or not μ_i should enter the basis, we must balance

$$\text{Increased profits for } \mu_i = \text{profits earned by } \mu_i \begin{bmatrix} x_1 \\ x_2 \end{bmatrix}$$

$$= 90(\mu_i x_1) + 80(\mu_i x_2)$$

against the costs incurred if μ_i is entered into the basis.

If we enter μ_i into the basis, we incur two costs. First, we incur a cost of \$12 for each ton of iron used. This amounts to a cost of $12[8(\mu_i x_1) + 6(\mu_i x_2)]$. By entering μ_i into the basis, we are also diverting a fraction μ_i of the available plant 1 weights away from the current mix. This incurs an opportunity cost of $80\mu_i$. Hence,

$$\text{Increase in cost from entering } \mu_i \text{ into basis} = 96\mu_i x_1 + 72\mu_i x_2 + 80\mu_i$$

This means that entering μ_i into the basis can increase profits if and only if

$$90\mu_i x_1 + 80\mu_i x_2 > 96\mu_i x_1 + 72\mu_i x_2 + 80\mu_i$$

Canceling the μ_i's from both sides, we see that μ_i will price out favorably if

$$90x_1 + 80x_2 > 96x_1 + 72x_2 + 80 \quad \text{or} \quad 0 > 80 + 6x_1 - 8x_2$$

Thus, the best μ_i will be the μ_i associated with the extreme point

$$\begin{bmatrix} x_1 \\ x_2 \end{bmatrix}$$

that minimizes $80 + 6x_1 - 8x_2$. This is indeed the objective function for the plant 1 tableau 3 subproblem.

This discussion shows that the Dantzig-Wolfe decomposition algorithm combines centralized information (from the shadow prices of the centralized constraints) with local information (the shadow price of each plant's convexity constraint) in an effort to determine which weights should be entered into the basis (or equivalently, which extreme points from each plant should be used).

◆ PROBLEMS

GROUP A

Use the Dantzig-Wolfe decomposition algorithm to solve the following problems:

1. $\max z = 7x_1 + 5x_2 + 3x_3$

s.t. $x_1 + 2x_2 + x_3 \leq 10$

$x_2 + x_3 \leq 5$

$x_1 \leq 3$

$2x_2 + x_3 \leq 8$

$x_1, x_2, x_3 \geq 0$

2. $\max z = 4x_1 + 2x_2 + 3x_3 + 4x_4 + 2x_5$

s.t. $x_1 + 2x_2 + x_3 \leq 8$

$x_1 + 2x_2 + 2x_3 \leq 8$

$x_4 + x_5 \leq 3$

$x_1, x_2, x_3, x_4, x_5 \geq 0$

3. $\max z = 3x_1 + 6x_2 + 5x_3$

s.t. $x_1 + 2x_2 + x_3 \leq 4$

     $2x_1 + 3x_2 + 2x_3 \leq 6$

     $x_1 + x_2 \qquad \leq 2$

     $2x_1 + x_2 \qquad \leq 3$

     $x_1, x_2, x_3 \geq 0$

(*Hint*: There is no law against having only one set of variables and one subproblem.)

4. Give an economic interpretation to explain why λ_3 priced out favorably in the plant 2 tableau 2 subproblem.

5. Give an example to show why Theorem 1 does not hold for an LP with an unbounded feasible region.

10-5   THE SIMPLEX METHOD FOR UPPER-BOUNDED VARIABLES

Often, LPs contain many constraints of the form $x_i \leq u_i$ (where u_i is a constant). For example, in a production scheduling problem, there may be many constraints of the type $x_i \leq u_i$, where

$$x_i = \text{period } i \text{ production}$$

$$u_i = \text{period } i \text{ production capacity}$$

Since a constraint of the form $x_i \leq u_i$ provides an upper bound on x_i, it is called an **upper-bound constraint**. Since $x_i \leq u_i$ is a legal LP constraint, we can clearly use the ordinary simplex method to solve an LP that has upper-bound constraints. It turns out, however, that if an LP contains several upper-bound constraints, the procedure described in this section (called the simplex method for upper-bounded variables) is much more efficient than the ordinary simplex algorithm.

In order to solve efficiently an LP with upper-bound constraints, we allow the variable x_i to be nonbasic if $x_i = 0$ (the usual criterion for a nonbasic variable) or if $x_i = u_i$. To accomplish this, we use the following gimmick: For each variable x_i that has an upper-bound constraint $x_i \leq u_i$, we define a new variable x_i' by the relationship $x_i + x_i' = u_i$, or $x_i = u_i - x_i'$. Note that if $x_i = 0$, then $x_i' = u_i$, whereas if $x_i = u_i$, then $x_i' = 0$. Whenever we want x_i to equal its upper bound of u_i, we simply replace x_i by $u_i - x_i'$. This substitution is called an **upper-bound substitution**.

We are now ready to describe the simplex method for upper-bounded variables. We assume that a basic solution is available and that we are solving a max problem. As usual, at each iteration, we choose to increase the variable x_i with the most negative coefficient in row 0. There are three possible occurrences, or bottlenecks, that can restrict the amount by which we increase x_i:

Bottleneck 1 x_i cannot exceed its upper bound of u_i.

Bottleneck 2 x_i increases to a point where it causes one of the current basic variables to become negative. The smallest value of x_i that will cause one of the current basic variables to become negative may be found by expressing each basic variable in terms of x_i (recall that we used this idea in Chapter 4, in discussing the simplex algorithm).

Bottleneck 3 x_i increases to a point where it causes one of the current basic variables to exceed its upper bound. As in Bottleneck 2, the smallest value of x_i for which this bottleneck occurs can be found by expressing each basic variable in terms of x_i.

Let BN_k ($k = 1, 2, 3$) be the value of x_i where Bottleneck k occurs. Then x_i can be increased only to a value of min $\{BN_1, BN_2, BN_3\}$. The smallest of BN_1, BN_2, and BN_3 is called the winning bottleneck. If the winning bottleneck is BN_1, then we make an upper-bound substitution on x_i by replacing x_i by $u_i - x_i'$. If the winning bottleneck is BN_2, then we enter x_i into the basis in the row corresponding to the basic variable that caused BN_2 to occur. If the winning bottleneck is BN_3, then we make an upper-bound substitution on the variable x_j (by replacing x_j by $u_j - x_j'$) that reaches its upper bound when $x_i = BN_3$. Then we enter x_i into the basis in the row for which x_j was a basic variable.

After following this procedure, we examine the new row 0. If each variable has a nonnegative coefficient in row 0, we have obtained an optimal tableau. Otherwise, we try to increase the variable with the most negative coefficient in row 0. Our procedure ensures (through BN_1 and BN_3) that no upper-bound constraint is ever violated and (through BN_2) that all of the nonnegativity constraints are satisfied.

E X A M P L E 4

Solve the following LP:

$$\max z = 4x_1 + 2x_2 + 3x_3$$
$$\text{s.t.} \quad 2x_1 + x_2 + x_3 \leq 10$$
$$x_1 + \tfrac{1}{2}x_2 + \tfrac{1}{2}x_3 \leq 6$$
$$2x_1 + 2x_2 + 4x_3 \leq 20$$
$$x_1 \leq 4$$
$$x_2 \leq 3$$
$$x_3 \leq 1$$
$$x_1, x_2, x_3 \geq 0$$

Solution

The initial tableau for this problem is given in Table 3. Since x_1 has the most negative coefficient in row 0, we try to increase x_1 as much as we can. The three bottlenecks for x_1 are computed as follows: x_1 cannot exceed its upper bound of 4, so $BN_1 = 4$. To compute BN_2, we solve for the current set of basic variables in terms of x_1:

$$s_1 = 10 - 2x_1 \quad (s_1 \geq 0 \text{ iff } x_1 \leq 5)$$
$$s_2 = 6 - x_1 \quad (s_2 \geq 0 \text{ iff } x_1 \leq 6)$$
$$s_3 = 20 - 2x_1 \quad (s_3 \geq 0 \text{ iff } x_1 \leq 10)$$

Table 3
Initial Tableau for
Example 4

		BASIC VARIABLE
$z - 4x_1 - 2x_2 - 3x_3$	$= 0$	$z = 0$
$2x_1 + x_2 + x_3 + s_1$	$= 10$	$s_1 = 10$
$x_1 + \tfrac{1}{2}x_2 + \tfrac{1}{2}x_3 \quad + s_2$	$= 6$	$s_2 = 6$
$2x_1 + 2x_2 + 4x_3 \quad + s_3 = 20$		$s_3 = 20$

Hence, $BN_2 = \min\{5, 6, 10\} = 5$. Since the current basic variables ($\{s_1, s_2, s_3\}$) have no upper bounds, there is no value of BN_3. Then the winning bottleneck is $\min\{4, 5\} = 4 = BN_1$. Thus, we must make an upper-bound substitution on x_1 by replacing x_1 by $4 - x_1'$. The resulting tableau is Table 4.

Table 4
Replacing x_1 by
$4 - x_1'$

		BASIC VARIABLE
$z + 4x_1' - 2x_2 - 3x_3$ $= 16$		$z = 16$
$-2x_1' + x_2 + x_3 + s_1$ $= 2$		$s_1 = 2$
$-x_1' + \frac{1}{2}x_2 + \frac{1}{2}x_3 + s_2$ $= 2$		$s_2 = 2$
$-2x_1' + 2x_2 + 4x_3 + s_3 = 12$		$s_3 = 12$

Since x_3 has the most negative coefficient in row 0, we try to increase x_3 as much as possible. The x_3 bottlenecks are computed as follows: x_3 cannot exceed its upper bound of 1, so $BN_1 = 1$. For BN_2, we solve for the current set of basic variables in terms of x_3:

$$s_1 = 2 - x_3 \qquad (s_1 \geq 0 \text{ iff } x_3 \leq 2)$$
$$s_2 = 2 - \tfrac{1}{2}x_3 \qquad (s_2 \geq 0 \text{ iff } x_3 \leq 4)$$
$$s_3 = 12 - 4x_3 \qquad (s_3 \geq 0 \text{ iff } x_3 \leq 3)$$

Thus, $BN_2 = \min\{2, 4, 3\} = 2$. Since s_1, s_2, and s_3 do not have an upper bound, there is no BN_3. The winning bottleneck is $\min\{1, 2\} = BN_1 = 1$, so we make an upper-bound substitution on x_3 by replacing x_3 by $1 - x_3'$. The resulting tableau is Table 5.

Table 5
Replacing x_3 by
$1 - x_3'$

		BASIC VARIABLE
$z + 4x_1' - 2x_2 + 3x_3'$ $= 19$		$z = 19$
$-2x_1' + x_2 - x_3' + s_1$ $= 1$		$s_1 = 1$
$-x_1' + \frac{1}{2}x_2 - \frac{1}{2}x_3' + s_2$ $= \frac{3}{2}$		$s_2 = \frac{3}{2}$
$-2x_1' + 2x_2 - 4x_3' + s_3 = 8$		$s_3 = 8$

Since x_2 now has the most negative coefficient in row 0, we try to increase x_2. The computation of the bottlenecks follows: For BN_1, x_2 cannot exceed its upper bound of 3, so $BN_1 = 3$. For BN_2,

$$s_1 = 1 - x_2 \qquad (s_1 \geq 0 \text{ iff } x_2 \leq 1)$$
$$s_2 = \tfrac{3}{2} - \tfrac{1}{2}x_2 \qquad (s_2 \geq 0 \text{ iff } x_2 \leq 3)$$
$$s_3 = 8 - 2x_2 \qquad (s_3 \geq 0 \text{ iff } x_2 \leq 4)$$

Thus, $BN_2 = \min\{1, 3, 4\} = 1$. Note that BN_2 occurs because s_1 is forced to zero. Since none of the basic variables in the current set has an upper-bound constraint, there is no BN_3. The winning bottleneck is $\min\{3, 1\} = 1 = BN_2$, so x_2 will enter the basis in the row in which s_1 was a basic variable (row 1). After the pivot is performed, the new tableau is Table 6. Since each variable has a nonnegative coefficient in row 0, this is an optimal

			BASIC VARIABLE

Table 6
Optimal Tableau for
Example 4

$$z \quad\quad + \quad x_3' + 2s_1 \quad\quad\quad\quad = 21 \quad\quad\quad z = 21$$
$$-2x_1' + x_2 - \quad x_3' + \quad s_1 \quad\quad\quad\quad = 1 \quad\quad\quad x_2 = 1$$
$$-\tfrac{1}{2}s_1 + s_2 \quad\quad\quad = 1 \quad\quad\quad s_2 = 1$$
$$2x_1' \quad\quad - 2x_3' - 2s_1 \quad\quad + s_3 = 6 \quad\quad\quad s_3 = 6$$

tableau. Thus, the optimal solution to the LP is $z = 21$, $s_2 = 1$, $x_2 = 1$, $s_3 = 6$, $x_1' = 0$, $s_1 = 0$, $x_3' = 0$. Since $x_1' = 4 - x_1$ and $x_3' = 1 - x_3$, we also have $x_1 = 4$ and $x_3 = 1$. $\quad\blacklozenge$

E X A M P L E
5

Solve the following LP:

$$\max z = 6x_3$$
$$\text{s.t.} \quad x_1 \quad - \quad x_3 = 6$$
$$x_2 + 2x_3 = 8$$
$$x_1 \le 8, \; x_2 \le 10, \; x_3 \le 5; \; x_1, x_2, x_3 \ge 0$$

Solution

After putting the objective function in our standard row 0 format, we obtain the tableau in Table 7. Fortunately, the basic feasible solution $z = 0$, $x_1 = 6$, $x_2 = 8$, $x_3 = 0$ is readily apparent. We can now proceed with the simplex method for upper-bounded variables. Since x_3 has the most negative coefficient in row 0, we try to increase x_3. Since x_3 cannot exceed its upper bound of 5, $BN_1 = 5$. To compute BN_2,

$$x_1 = 6 + x_3 \quad\quad (x_1 \ge 0 \text{ iff } x_3 \ge -6)$$
$$x_2 = 8 - 2x_3 \quad\quad (x_2 \ge 0 \text{ iff } x_3 \le 4)$$

			BASIC VARIABLE

Table 7
Initial Tableau for
Example 5

$$z \quad\quad - 6x_3 = 0 \quad\quad\quad z = 0$$
$$x_1 \quad - \quad x_3 = 6 \quad\quad\quad x_1 = 6$$
$$x_2 + 2x_3 = 8 \quad\quad\quad x_2 = 8$$

Thus, all the current basic variables will remain nonnegative as long as $x_3 \le 4$. Hence, $BN_2 = 4$. For BN_3, note that $x_1 \le 8$ will hold iff $6 + x_3 \le 8$, or $x_3 \le 2$. Also, $x_2 \le 10$ will hold iff $8 - 2x_3 \le 10$, or $x_3 \ge -1$. Thus, for $x_3 \le 2$, each basic variable remains less than or equal to its upper bound, so $BN_3 = 2$. Note that BN_3 occurs when the basic variable x_1 attains its upper bound. The winning bottleneck is min $\{5, 4, 2\} = 2 = BN_3$, so the largest that we can make x_3 is 2, and the bottleneck occurs because x_1 attains its upper bound of 8. Thus, we make an upper-bound substitution on x_1 by replacing x_1 by $8 - x_1'$. The resulting tableau is

$$z \quad\quad\quad\quad\quad - 6x_3 = 0$$
$$-x_1' \quad\quad - \quad x_3 = -2$$
$$x_2 + 2x_3 = 8$$

After rewriting $-x_1' - x_3 = -2$ as $x_1' + x_3 = 2$, we obtain the tableau in Table 8.

Table 8
Replacing x_1 by
$8 - x_1'$

		BASIC VARIABLE
z	$- 6x_3 = 0$	$z = 0$
x_1'	$+ x_3 = 2$	$x_1' = 2$
	$x_2 + 2x_3 = 8$	$x_2 = 8$

Table 9
Optimal Tableau for
Example 5

		BASIC VARIABLE
$z + 6x_1'$	$= 12$	$z = 12$
x_1'	$+ x_3 = 2$	$x_3 = 2$
$- 2x_1' + x_2$	$= 4$	$x_2 = 4$

Since x_1, the variable that caused BN_3, was basic in row 1, we now make x_3 a basic variable in row 1. After the pivot, we obtain the tableau in Table 9. This is an optimal tableau. Thus, the optimal solution to the LP is $z = 12$, $x_3 = 2$, $x_2 = 4$, $x_1' = 0$. Since $x_1' = 0$, $x_1 = 8 - x_1' = 8$. ♦

To illustrate the efficiencies obtained by using the simplex algorithm with upper bounds, suppose we are solving an LP (call it LP 1) with 100 variables, each having an upper-bound constraint, with five other constraints. If we were to solve LP 1 by the revised simplex method, the B^{-1} for each tableau would be a 105×105 matrix. If we were to use the simplex method for upper-bounded variables, however, the B^{-1} for each tableau would be only a 5×5 matrix. Although the computation of the winning bottleneck in each iteration is more complicated than the ordinary ratio test, solving LP 1 by the simplex method for upper-bounded variables would still be much more efficient than solving LP 1 by the ordinary revised simplex.

♦ PROBLEMS

Use the upper-bounded simplex algorithm to solve the following LPs:

GROUP A

1. $\max z = 4x_1 + 3x_2 + 5x_3$
s.t. $2x_1 + 2x_2 + x_3 + x_4 \leq 9$
$4x_1 - x_2 - x_3 + x_5 \leq 6$
$2x_2 + x_3 \leq 5$
$x_1 \leq 2$
$x_2 \leq 3$
$x_3 \leq 4$
$x_4 \leq 5$
$x_5 \leq 7$
$x_1, x_2, x_3, x_4, x_5 \geq 0$

2. $\min z = -4x_1 - 9x_2$
s.t. $3x_1 + 5x_2 \leq 6$
$5x_1 + 6x_2 \leq 10$
$2x_1 - 3x_2 \leq 4$
$x_1 \leq 2$
$x_2 \leq 1$
$x_1, x_2 \geq 0$

3. $\max z = 4x_1 + 3x_2$

s.t. $\quad 2x_1 - x_2 \le 1$

$\qquad x_1 + 6x_2 \le 6$

$\qquad\qquad x_2 \le 5$

$\quad x_1, x_2 \ge 0$

4. Suppose an LP contained lower-bound constraints of the following form: $x_j \ge L_j$. Suggest an algorithm that could be used to solve such a problem efficiently.

10-6   KARMARKAR'S METHOD FOR SOLVING LPs

As discussed in Section 4.13, Karmarkar's method for solving LPs is a polynomial time algorithm. This is in contrast to the simplex algorithm, which is an exponential time algorithm. Unlike the ellipsoid method (another polynomial time algorithm), Karmarkar's method appears to solve many LPs faster than does the simplex algorithm. In this section, we give a description of the basic concepts underlying Karmarkar's method. Note that several versions of Karmarkar's method are computationally more efficient than the version we describe; our goal is simply to introduce the reader to the exciting ideas used in Karmarkar's method. For a more detailed description of Karmarkar's method, see Hooker (1986), Parker and Rardin (1988), and Murty (1989).

Karmarkar's method is applied to an LP in the following form:

$$\min z = \mathbf{c}\mathbf{x}$$
$$\text{s.t.} \quad A\mathbf{x} = \mathbf{0} \tag{31}$$
$$x_1 + x_2 + \cdots + x_n = 1$$
$$\mathbf{x} \ge \mathbf{0}$$

In (31), $\mathbf{x} = [x_1 \ x_2 \ \cdots \ x_n]^T$, A is an $m \times n$ matrix, $\mathbf{c} = [c_1 \ c_2 \ \cdots \ c_n]$ and $\mathbf{0}$ is an n-dimensional column vector of zeros. The LP must also satisfy

$$[\tfrac{1}{n} \ \tfrac{1}{n} \ \cdots \ \tfrac{1}{n}]^T \qquad \text{is feasible} \tag{32}$$
$$\text{Optimal } z\text{-value} = 0 \tag{33}$$

Although it may seem unlikely that an LP would have the form (31) and satisfy (32)–(33), it is easy to show that any LP may be put in a form such that (31)–(33) are satisfied. We omit the details and refer the reader to Parker and Rardin (1988).

The following three concepts play a key role in Karmarkar's method:

1. Projection of a vector onto the set of $\mathbf{x}$ satisfying $A\mathbf{x} = \mathbf{0}$

2. Karmarkar's centering transformation

3. Karmarkar's potential function

We now discuss the first two concepts, leaving a discussion of Karmarkar's potential function to the end of the section. Before discussing the ideas just listed, we need a definition.

DEFINITION ▪ The *n*-dimensional unit simplex S is the set of points $[x_1 \ x_2 \ \cdots \ x_n]^T$ satisfying $x_1 + x_2 + \cdots + x_n = 1$ and $x_j \ge 0, j = 1, 2, \ldots n$.

PROJECTION

Suppose we are given a point $\mathbf{x}^0$ that is feasible for (31), and we want to move from $\mathbf{x}^0$ to another feasible point (call it $\mathbf{x}^1$) that, for some fixed vector $\mathbf{v}$, will have a larger value of $\mathbf{vx}$. Suppose that we find $\mathbf{x}^1$ by moving away from $\mathbf{x}^0$ in a direction $\mathbf{d} = [d_1 \quad d_2 \quad \cdots \quad d_n]$. For $\mathbf{x}^1$ to be feasible, $\mathbf{d}$ must satisfy $A\mathbf{d} = \mathbf{0}$ and $d_1 + d_2 + \cdots + d_n = 0$. If we choose the direction $\mathbf{d}$ that solves the optimization problem

$$\max \mathbf{vd}$$

$$\text{s.t.} \quad A\mathbf{d} = \mathbf{0}$$

$$d_1 + d_2 + \cdots + d_n = 0$$

$$\|\mathbf{d}\| = 1$$

then we will be moving in the "feasible" direction that maximizes the increase in $\mathbf{vx}$ per unit of length moved. The direction $\mathbf{d}$ that solves this optimization problem is given by the **projection** of $\mathbf{v}$ onto the set of $\mathbf{x} = [x_1 \quad x_2 \quad \cdots \quad x_n]^T$ satisfying $A\mathbf{x} = \mathbf{0}$ and $x_1 + x_2 + \cdots + x_n = 0$. The projection of $\mathbf{v}$ onto the set of $\mathbf{x}$ satisfying $A\mathbf{x} = \mathbf{0}$ and $x_1 + x_2 + \cdots + x_n = 0$ is given by $[I - B^T(BB^T)^{-1})B]\mathbf{v}$, where B is the $(m + 1) \times n$ matrix whose first m rows are A and whose last row is a vector of 1's.

Geometrically, what does it mean to project a vector $\mathbf{v}$ onto the set of $\mathbf{x}$ satisfying $A\mathbf{x} = \mathbf{0}$? It can be shown that any vector $\mathbf{v}$ may be written (uniquely) in the form $\mathbf{v} = \mathbf{p} + \mathbf{w}$, where $\mathbf{p}$ satisfies $A\mathbf{p} = \mathbf{0}$ and $\mathbf{w}$ is perpendicular to all vectors $\mathbf{x}$ satisfying $A\mathbf{x} = \mathbf{0}$. Then $\mathbf{p}$ is the projection of $\mathbf{v}$ onto the set of $\mathbf{x}$ satisfying $A\mathbf{x} = \mathbf{0}$. An example of this idea is given in Figure 5, where $\mathbf{v} = [-2 \quad -1 \quad 7]$ is projected on the set of three-dimensional vectors satisfying $x_3 = 0$ (the x_1-x_2-plane). In this case, we decompose $\mathbf{v}$ as $\mathbf{v} = [-2 \quad -1 \quad 0] + [0 \quad 0 \quad 7]$. Thus, $\mathbf{p} = [-2 \quad -1 \quad 0]$. It is easy to show that $\mathbf{p}$ is the vector in the set of $\mathbf{x}$ satisfying $A\mathbf{x} = \mathbf{0}$ that is "closest" to $\mathbf{v}$. This is apparent from Figure 5.

Figure 5
Projection of
$[-2 \quad -1 \quad 7]$
on $x_3 = 0$

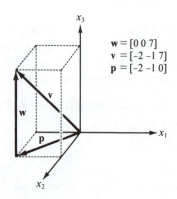

$\mathbf{w} = [0\ 0\ 7]$
$\mathbf{v} = [-2\ -1\ 7]$
$\mathbf{p} = [-2\ -1\ 0]$

KARMARKAR'S CENTERING TRANSFORMATION

Given a feasible point (in (31)) $\mathbf{x}^k = [x_1^k \quad x_2^k \quad \cdots \quad x_n^k]$ in S having $x_j^k > 0, j = 1, 2, \ldots, n$, we write the **centering transformation** associated with the point $\mathbf{x}^k$ as

$f([x_1 \quad x_2 \quad \cdots \quad x_n] \,|\, \mathbf{x}^k)$. If $\mathbf{x}^k$ is a point in S, then $f([x_1 \quad x_2 \quad \cdots \quad x_n] \,|\, \mathbf{x}^k)$ transforms a point $[x_1 \quad x_2 \quad \cdots \quad x_n]^T$ in S into a point $[y_1 \quad y_2 \quad \cdots \quad y_n]^T$ in S, where

$$y_j = \frac{\dfrac{x_j}{x_j^k}}{\displaystyle\sum_{r=1}^{r=n} \dfrac{x_r}{x_r^k}} \tag{34}$$

Let Diag $(\mathbf{x}^k)$ be the $n \times n$ matrix with all off-diagonal entries equal to 0 and Diag $(\mathbf{x}^k)_{ii} = x_i^k$. The centering transformation specified by (34) can be shown to have the properties listed in Lemma 1.

L E M M A 1   Karmarkar's centering transformation has the following properties:

$$f(\mathbf{x}^k \,|\, \mathbf{x}^k) = [\tfrac{1}{n} \quad \tfrac{1}{n} \quad \cdots \quad \tfrac{1}{n}]^T. \tag{35}$$

For $\mathbf{x} \neq \mathbf{x}'$, $\quad f(\mathbf{x} \,|\, \mathbf{x}^k) \neq f(\mathbf{x}' \,|\, \mathbf{x}^k)$ $\tag{36}$

$f(\mathbf{x} \,|\, \mathbf{x}^k) \in S$ $\tag{37}$

For any point $[y_1 \quad y_2 \quad \cdots \quad y_n]^T$ in S, there is a unique point $\tag{38}$
$[x_1 \quad x_2 \quad \cdots \quad x_n]^T$ in S satisfying

$$f([x_1 \quad x_2 \quad \cdots \quad x_n]^T \,|\, \mathbf{x}^k) = [y_1 \quad y_2 \quad \cdots \quad y_n]^T \tag{38'}$$

The point $[x_1 \quad x_2 \quad \cdots \quad x_n]^T$ is given by

$$x_j = \frac{x_j^k y_j}{\displaystyle\sum_{r=1}^{r=n} x_r^k y_r}$$

If $[x_1 \quad x_2 \quad \cdots \quad x_n]^T$ and $[y_1 \quad y_2 \quad \cdots \quad y_n]^T$ satisfy (38'), we write
$f^{-1}([y_1 \quad y_2 \quad \cdots \quad y_n]^T \,|\, \mathbf{x}^k) = [x_1 \quad x_2 \quad \cdots \quad x_n]^T$

A point $\mathbf{x}$ in S will satisfy $A\mathbf{x} = \mathbf{0}$ $\quad$ iff $\quad A[\text{Diag}(\mathbf{x}^k)]f(\mathbf{x} \,|\, \mathbf{x}^k) = \mathbf{0}$ $\tag{39}$ ◆

(See Problem 4 for a proof of Lemma 1.)
To illustrate the centering transformation, consider the following LP:

$$\min z = x_1 + 3x_2 - 3x_3$$
$$\text{s.t.} \quad x_2 - x_3 = 0$$
$$x_1 + x_2 + x_3 = 1 \tag{40}$$
$$x_i \geq 0$$

This LP is of the form (31); the point $[\tfrac{1}{3} \quad \tfrac{1}{3} \quad \tfrac{1}{3}]^T$ is feasible, and the LP's optimal z-value is 0. The feasible point $[\tfrac{1}{4} \quad \tfrac{3}{8} \quad \tfrac{3}{8}]$ yields the following centering transformation:

$$f([x_1 \quad x_2 \quad x_3] \,|\, [\tfrac{1}{4} \quad \tfrac{3}{8} \quad \tfrac{3}{8}]) = \begin{bmatrix} \dfrac{4x_1}{4x_1 + \dfrac{8x_2}{3} + \dfrac{8x_3}{3}} & \dfrac{\dfrac{8x_2}{3}}{4x_1 + \dfrac{8x_2}{3} + \dfrac{8x_3}{3}} & \dfrac{\dfrac{8x_3}{3}}{4x_1 + \dfrac{8x_2}{3} + \dfrac{8x_3}{3}} \end{bmatrix}$$

For example,

$$f([\tfrac{1}{3} \quad \tfrac{1}{3} \quad \tfrac{1}{3}]\,|\,[\tfrac{1}{4} \quad \tfrac{3}{8} \quad \tfrac{3}{8}]) = [\tfrac{12}{28} \quad \tfrac{8}{28} \quad \tfrac{8}{28}]$$

We now refer to the variables $x_1, x_2, \ldots x_n$ as being the *original* space and the variables $y_1, y_2, \ldots, y_n$ as being the *transformed* space. The unit simplex involving variables $y_1, y_2, \ldots y_n$ will be called the transformed unit simplex. We now discuss the intuitive meaning of (35)–(39). Equation (35) implies that $f(\cdot\,|\,\mathbf{x}^k)$ maps $\mathbf{x}^k$ into the "center" of the transformed unit simplex. Equations (36)–(37) imply that any point in S is transformed into a point in the transformed unit simplex, and no two points in S can yield the same point in the transformed unit simplex (that is, f is a one-to-one mapping). Equation (38) implies that for any point $\mathbf{y}$ in the transformed unit simplex, there is a point $\mathbf{x}$ in S that is transformed into $\mathbf{y}$. The formula for the $\mathbf{x}$ that is transformed into $\mathbf{y}$ is also given. Thus, (36)–(38) imply that f is a one-to-one and onto mapping from S to S. Finally, (39) states that feasible points in the original problem correspond to points $\mathbf{y}$ in the transformed unit simplex that satisfy $A[\mathrm{Diag}\,(\mathbf{x}^k)]\mathbf{y} = \mathbf{0}$.

DESCRIPTION AND EXAMPLE OF KARMARKAR'S METHOD

We assume that we will be satisfied with a feasible point having an optimal z-value $< \varepsilon$ (for some small ε). Karmarkar's method proceeds as follows:

Step 1 Begin at the feasible point $\mathbf{x}^0 = [\tfrac{1}{n} \quad \tfrac{1}{n} \quad \cdots \quad \tfrac{1}{n}]^T$ and set $k = 0$.

Step 2 Stop if $\mathbf{c}\mathbf{x}^k < \varepsilon$. If not, go to Step 3.

Step 3 Find the new point $\mathbf{y}^{k+1} = [y_1^{k+1} \quad y_2^{k+1} \quad \cdots \quad y_n^{k+1}]^T$ in the transformed unit simplex given by

$$\mathbf{y}^{k+1} = [\tfrac{1}{n} \quad \tfrac{1}{n} \quad \cdots \quad \tfrac{1}{n}]^T - \frac{\theta(I - P^T(PP^T)^{-1}P)[\mathrm{Diag}\,(\mathbf{x}^k)]\mathbf{c}^T}{\|\mathbf{c}\|\,\sqrt{n(n-1)}}$$

Here, $\|\mathbf{c}\| =$ the length of $(I - P^T(PP^T)^{-1}P)[\mathrm{Diag}\,(\mathbf{x}^k)]\mathbf{c}^T$, P is the $(m+1) \times n$ matrix whose first m rows are $A[\mathrm{Diag}\,(\mathbf{x}^k)]$ and whose last row is a vector of 1's, and $0 < \theta < 1$ is chosen to ensure convergence of the algorithm. $\theta = \tfrac{1}{4}$ is known to ensure convergence.

Now obtain a new point $\mathbf{x}^{k+1}$ in the original space by using the centering transformation to determine the point corresponding to y^{k+1}. That is, $\mathbf{x}^{k+1} = f^{-1}(\mathbf{y}^{k+1}\,|\,\mathbf{x}^k)$. Increase k by 1 and return to Step 2.

R E M A R K S   **1.** In Step 3, we move from the "center" of the transformed unit simplex in a direction opposite to the projection of $\mathrm{Diag}\,(\mathbf{x}^k)\mathbf{c}^T$ onto the transformation of the feasible region (the set of $\mathbf{y}$ satisfying $A[\mathrm{Diag}\,(\mathbf{x}^k)]\mathbf{y} = \mathbf{0}$). From our discussion of the projection, this ensures that we maintain feasibility (in the transformed space) and move in a direction that maximizes the rate of decrease of $[\mathrm{Diag}\,(\mathbf{x}^k)]\mathbf{c}^T$.

2. By moving a distance

$$\frac{\theta}{\sqrt{n(n-1)}}$$

from the center of the transformed unit simplex, we ensure that $\mathbf{y}^{k+1}$ will remain in the interior of the transformed unit simplex.

3. When we use the inverse of Karmarkar's centering transformation to transform $\mathbf{y}^{k+1}$ back into $\mathbf{x}^{k+1}$, the definition of projection and (39) imply that $\mathbf{x}^{k+1}$ will be feasible for the original LP (see Problem 5).

4. Why do we project $[\text{Diag}(\mathbf{x}^k)]\mathbf{c}^T$ rather than $\mathbf{c}^T$ onto the transformed feasible region? The answer to this question must await our discussion of Karmarkar's potential function. Problem 6 provides another explanation of why we project $[\text{Diag}(\mathbf{x}^k)]\mathbf{c}^T$ rather than $\mathbf{c}^T$.

We now work out the first iteration of Karmarkar's method when applied to (40). We choose $\varepsilon = 0.10$.

FIRST ITERATION OF KARMARKAR'S METHOD

Step 1 $\mathbf{x}^0 = [\frac{1}{3} \quad \frac{1}{3} \quad \frac{1}{3}]^T$ and $k = 0$.

Step 2 $\mathbf{x}^0$ yields $z = \frac{1}{3} > 0.10$, so we must proceed to Step 3.

Step 3

$$A = [0 \quad 1 \quad -1], \qquad \text{Diag}(\mathbf{x}^k) = \begin{bmatrix} \frac{1}{3} & 0 & 0 \\ 0 & \frac{1}{3} & 0 \\ 0 & 0 & \frac{1}{3} \end{bmatrix}$$

$$A[\text{Diag}(\mathbf{x}^k)] = [0 \quad \frac{1}{3} \quad -\frac{1}{3}], \qquad P = \begin{bmatrix} 0 & \frac{1}{3} & -\frac{1}{3} \\ 1 & 1 & 1 \end{bmatrix}$$

$$PP^T = \begin{bmatrix} \frac{2}{9} & 0 \\ 0 & 3 \end{bmatrix}, \qquad (PP^T)^{-1} = \begin{bmatrix} \frac{9}{2} & 0 \\ 0 & \frac{1}{3} \end{bmatrix}$$

$$(I - P^T(PP^T)^{-1}P) = \begin{bmatrix} \frac{2}{3} & -\frac{1}{3} & -\frac{1}{3} \\ -\frac{1}{3} & \frac{1}{6} & \frac{1}{6} \\ -\frac{1}{3} & \frac{1}{6} & \frac{1}{6} \end{bmatrix}, \qquad \mathbf{c} = [1 \quad 3 \quad -3]$$

$$[\text{Diag}\,\mathbf{x}^k]\mathbf{c}^T = \begin{bmatrix} \frac{1}{3} \\ 1 \\ -1 \end{bmatrix}$$

$$(I - P^T(PP^T)^{-1}P)[\text{Diag}\,\mathbf{x}^k]\mathbf{c}^T = [\frac{2}{9} \quad -\frac{1}{9} \quad -\frac{1}{9}]$$

Now, (using $\theta = 0.25$), we obtain

$$\mathbf{y}^1 = [\frac{1}{3} \quad \frac{1}{3} \quad \frac{1}{3}]^T - \frac{0.25[\frac{2}{9} \quad -\frac{1}{9} \quad -\frac{1}{9}]^T}{\sqrt{3(2)} \, \|[\frac{2}{9} \quad -\frac{1}{9} \quad -\frac{1}{9}]\|}$$

Since

$$\|[\frac{2}{9} \quad -\frac{1}{9} \quad -\frac{1}{9}]\|^T = \sqrt{(\frac{2}{9})^2 + (-\frac{1}{9})^2 + (-\frac{1}{9})^2}$$

$$= \frac{\sqrt{6}}{9}$$

we obtain

$$\mathbf{y}^1 = [\frac{1}{3} \quad \frac{1}{3} \quad \frac{1}{3}]^T - [\frac{6}{72} \quad -\frac{3}{72} \quad -\frac{3}{72}]^T = [\frac{1}{4} \quad \frac{3}{8} \quad \frac{3}{8}]^T$$

Using (38'), we now obtain $\mathbf{x}^1 = [x_1^1 \quad x_2^1 \quad x_3^1]^T$ from

$$x_1^1 = \frac{\frac{1}{3}(\frac{1}{4})}{\frac{1}{3}(\frac{1}{4}) + \frac{1}{3}(\frac{3}{8}) + \frac{1}{3}(\frac{3}{8})} = \frac{1}{4}$$

$$x_2^1 = \frac{\frac{1}{3}(\frac{3}{8})}{\frac{1}{3}(\frac{1}{4}) + \frac{1}{3}(\frac{3}{8}) + \frac{1}{3}(\frac{3}{8})} = \frac{3}{8}$$

$$x_3^1 = \frac{\frac{1}{3}(\frac{3}{8})}{\frac{1}{3}(\frac{1}{4}) + \frac{1}{3}(\frac{3}{8}) + \frac{1}{3}(\frac{3}{8})} = \frac{3}{8}$$

Thus, $\mathbf{x}^1 = [\frac{1}{4} \quad \frac{3}{8} \quad \frac{3}{8}]^T$. It will always be the case (see Problem 3) that $\mathbf{x}^1 = \mathbf{y}^1$, but for $k > 1$, $\mathbf{x}^k$ need not equal $\mathbf{y}^k$. Note that for $\mathbf{x}^1$, we have $z = \frac{1}{4} + 3(\frac{3}{8}) - 3(\frac{3}{8}) = \frac{1}{4} < \frac{1}{3}$ (the z-value for $\mathbf{x}^0$).

POTENTIAL FUNCTION

Since we are projecting $[\text{Diag}(\mathbf{x}^k)]\mathbf{c}^T$ rather than $\mathbf{c}^T$, we cannot be sure that each iteration of Karmarkar's method will decrease z. In fact, it is possible for $\mathbf{c}\mathbf{x}^{k+1} > \mathbf{c}\mathbf{x}^k$ to occur. To explain why Karmarkar projects $[\text{Diag}(\mathbf{x}^k)]\mathbf{c}^T$, we need to discuss Karmarkar's potential function. For $\mathbf{x} = [x_1 \quad x_2 \quad \cdots \quad x_n]^T$, we define the potential function $f(\mathbf{x})$ by

$$f(\mathbf{x}) = \sum_{j=1}^{j=n} \ln\left(\frac{\mathbf{c}\mathbf{x}^T}{x_j}\right)$$

Karmarkar showed that if we project $[\text{Diag}(\mathbf{x}^k)]\mathbf{c}^T$ (not $\mathbf{c}^T$) onto the feasible region in the transformed space, then for some $\delta > 0$, it will be true that for $k = 0, 1, 2, \ldots$,

$$f(\mathbf{x}^k) - f(\mathbf{x}^{k+1}) \geq \delta \tag{41}$$

Inequality (41) states that each iteration of Karmarkar's method decreases the potential function by an amount bounded away from 0. Karmarkar shows that if the potential function evaluated at $\mathbf{x}^k$ is small enough, then $\mathbf{z} = \mathbf{c}\mathbf{x}^k$ will be near 0. Since $f(\mathbf{x}^k)$ is decreased by at least δ per iteration, it follows that by choosing k sufficiently large, we can ensure that the z-value for $\mathbf{x}^k$ is less than ε.

◆ PROBLEMS

GROUP A

1. Perform one iteration of Karmarkar's method for the following LP:

$$\min z = x_1 + 2x_2 - x_3$$
$$\text{s.t.} \quad x_1 \qquad - x_3 = 0$$
$$x_1 + x_2 + x_3 = 1$$
$$x_1, x_2, x_3 \geq 0$$

2. Perform one iteration of Karmarkar's method for the following LP:

$$\min z = x_1 - x_2 + 6x_3$$
$$\text{s.t.} \quad x_1 - x_2 \qquad = 0$$
$$x_1 + x_2 + x_3 = 1$$
$$x_1, x_2, x_3 \geq 0$$

3. Prove that in Karmarkar's method, $\mathbf{x}^1 = \mathbf{y}^1$.

GROUP B

4. Prove Lemma 1.

5. Show that the point $\mathbf{x}^k$ in Karmarkar's method is feasible for the original LP.

6. Given a point $\mathbf{y}^k$ in Karmarkar's method, express the LP's original objective function as a function of $\mathbf{y}^k$. Use the answer to this question to give a reason why $[\text{Diag}(\mathbf{x}^k)]\mathbf{c}^T$ is projected, rather than $\mathbf{c}^T$.

◆ SUMMARY

THE REVISED SIMPLEX METHOD AND THE PRODUCT FORM OF THE INVERSE

Step 0 Note the columns from which the current B^{-1} will be read. Initially $B^{-1} = I$.

Step 1 For the current tableau, compute $\mathbf{c}_{BV}B^{-1}$.

Step 2 Price out all nonbasic variables in the current tableau. If (for a max problem) each nonbasic variable prices out nonnegative, the current basis is optimal. If the current basis is not optimal, enter into the basis the nonbasic variable with the most negative coefficient in row 0. Call this variable x_k.

Step 3 To determine the row in which x_k enters the basis, compute x_k's column in the current tableau (it will be $B^{-1}\mathbf{a}_k$) and compute the right-hand side of the current tableau (it will be $B^{-1}\mathbf{b}$). Then use the ratio test to determine the row in which x_k should enter the basis. We now know the set of basic variables (BV) for the new tableau.

Step 4 Use the column for x_k in the current tableau to determine the ero's needed to enter x_k into the basis. Perform these ero's on the current B^{-1}. This will yield the new B^{-1}. Return to Step 1.

Alternatively, we may use the product form of the inverse to update B^{-1}. Suppose we have found that x_k should enter the basis, and the ratio test indicates that x_k should enter the basis in row r. Let the column for x_k in the current tableau be

$$\begin{bmatrix} \bar{a}_{1k} \\ \bar{a}_{2k} \\ \vdots \\ \bar{a}_{mk} \end{bmatrix}$$

Define the $m \times m$ matrix E by

$$E = \begin{bmatrix} 1 & 0 & \cdots & -\dfrac{\bar{a}_{1k}}{\bar{a}_{rk}} & \cdots & 0 & 0 \\ 0 & 1 & \cdots & -\dfrac{\bar{a}_{2k}}{\bar{a}_{rk}} & \cdots & 0 & 0 \\ \vdots & \vdots & & \vdots & & \vdots & \vdots \\ 0 & 0 & \cdots & \dfrac{1}{\bar{a}_{rk}} & \cdots & 0 & 0 \\ \vdots & \vdots & & \vdots & & \vdots & \vdots \\ 0 & 0 & \cdots & -\dfrac{\bar{a}_{m-1,k}}{\bar{a}_{rk}} & \cdots & 1 & 0 \\ 0 & 0 & \cdots & -\dfrac{\bar{a}_{mk}}{\bar{a}_{rk}} & \cdots & 0 & 1 \end{bmatrix} \quad \text{(row } r\text{)}$$

$$\text{(column } r\text{)}$$

Then

$$B^{-1} \text{ for new tableau} = E(B^{-1} \text{ for current tableau})$$

Return to Step 1.

COLUMN GENERATION

When an LP has many variables, it is very time-consuming to price out each nonbasic variable individually. The column generation approach lets us determine the nonbasic variable that prices out most favorably by solving a subproblem (like the branch-and-bound problems in the cutting stock problem).

DANTZIG-WOLFE DECOMPOSITION METHOD

In many LPs, the constraints and variables may be decomposed in the following manner:

Constraints in Set 1 only involve variables in Variable Set 1

Constraints in Set 2 only involve variables in Variable Set 2.

$$\vdots$$

Constraints in Set k only involve variables in Variable Set k.

Constraints in Set $k + 1$ may involve any variable. The constraints in Set $k + 1$ are referred to as the **central constraints**.

LPs that can be decomposed in this fashion can often be efficiently solved by the Dantzig-Wolfe decomposition algorithm. The following explanation assumes that $k = 2$.

Step 1 Let the variables in Variable Set 1 be $x_1, x_2, \ldots, x_{n_1}$. Express the variables in Variable Set 1 as a convex combination of the extreme points of the feasible region for Constraint Set 1 (the constraints that involve only the variables in Variable Set 1). If we let $\mathbf{P}_1, \mathbf{P}_2, \ldots, \mathbf{P}_k$ be the extreme points of this feasible region, then any point

$$\begin{bmatrix} x_1 \\ x_2 \\ \vdots \\ x_{n_1} \end{bmatrix}$$

in the feasible region for Constraint Set 1 may be written in the form

$$\begin{bmatrix} x_1 \\ x_2 \\ \vdots \\ x_{n_1} \end{bmatrix} = \mu_1 \mathbf{P}_1 + \mu_2 \mathbf{P}_2 + \cdots + \mu_k \mathbf{P}_k \tag{29}$$

where $\mu_1 + \mu_2 + \cdots + \mu_k = 1$ and $\mu_i \geq 0 \; (i = 1, 2, \ldots, k)$.

Step 2 Express the variables in Variable Set 2, $x_{n_1+1}, x_{n_1+2}, \ldots, x_n$, as a convex combination of the extreme points of Constraint Set 2's feasible region. If we let the extreme points of the feasible region be $\mathbf{Q}_1, \mathbf{Q}_2, \ldots, \mathbf{Q}_m$, then any point in Constraint Set 2's feasible region may be written as

$$\begin{bmatrix} x_{n_1+1} \\ x_{n_1+2} \\ \vdots \\ x_n \end{bmatrix} = \lambda_1 \mathbf{Q}_1 + \lambda_2 \mathbf{Q}_2 + \cdots + \lambda_m \mathbf{Q}_m \tag{30}$$

where $\lambda_i \geq 0 \; (i = 1, 2, \ldots, m)$ and $\lambda_1 + \lambda_2 + \cdots + \lambda_m = 1$.

Step 3 Using (29) and (30), express the LPs objective function and centralized constraints in terms of the μ_i's and the λ_i's. After adding the constraints (called convexity constraints), $\mu_1 + \mu_2 + \cdots + \mu_k = 1$ and $\lambda_1 + \lambda_2 + \cdots + \lambda_m = 1$ and the sign restrictions $\mu_i \geq 0$ $(i = 1, 2, \ldots, k)$ and $\lambda_i \geq 0$ $(i = 1, 2, \ldots, m)$, we obtain the following LP, which is referred to as the **restricted master**:

$$\text{max (or min) [objective function in terms of } \mu_i\text{'s and } \lambda_i\text{'s]}$$

$$\text{s.t.} \quad \text{[central constraints in terms of } \mu_i\text{'s and } \lambda_i\text{'s]}$$

$$\mu_1 + \mu_2 + \cdots + \mu_k = 1 \qquad \text{(Convexity constraints)}$$

$$\lambda_1 + \lambda_2 + \cdots + \lambda_m = 1$$

$$\mu_i \geq 0 \quad (i = 1, 2, \ldots, k) \qquad \text{(Sign restrictions)}$$

$$\lambda_i \geq 0 \quad (i = 1, 2, \ldots, m)$$

Step 4 Assume that a basic feasible solution for the restricted master is readily available. Then use the column generation method of Section 10.3 to determine whether there is any μ_i or λ_i that can improve the z-value for the restricted master. If so, use the revised simplex method to enter that variable into the basis. Otherwise, the current tableau is optimal for the restricted master. If the current tableau is not optimal, continue with column generation until an optimal solution is found.

Step 5 Substitute the optimal values of the μ_i's and λ_i's found in Step 4 into (29) and (30). This will yield the optimal values of $x_1, x_2, \ldots, x_n$.

THE SIMPLEX METHOD FOR UPPER-BOUNDED VARIABLES

For each variable x_i that has an upper-bound constraint $x_i \leq u_i$, we define a new variable x_i' by the relationship $x_i + x_i' = u_i$, or $x_i = u_i - x_i'$.

At each iteration, we choose (for a max problem) to increase the variable x_i with the most negative coefficient in row 0. There are three possible occurrences, or bottlenecks, that can restrict the amount by which we increase x_i:

Bottleneck 1 x_i cannot exceed its upper bound of u_i.

Bottleneck 2 x_i increases to a point where it causes one of the current basic variables to become negative.

Bottleneck 3 x_i increases to a point where it causes one of the current basic variables to exceed its upper bound.

Let BN_k $(k = 1, 2, 3)$ be the value of x_i where Bottleneck k occurs. Then x_i can only be increased to a value of min $\{BN_1, BN_2, BN_3\}$. The smallest of BN_1, BN_2, and BN_3 is called the winning bottleneck. If the winning bottleneck is BN_1, we make an upper-bound substitution on x_i by replacing x_i by $u_i - x_i'$. If the winning bottleneck is BN_2, we enter x_i into the basis in the row corresponding to the basic variable that caused BN_2 to occur. If the winning bottleneck is BN_3, we make an upper-bound substitution on the variable x_j (by replacing x_j by $u_j - x_j'$) that reaches its upper bound when $x_i = BN_3$. Then enter x_i into the basis in the row for which x_j was a basic variable.

After following this procedure, examine the new row 0. If each variable has a nonnegative coefficient in row 0, we have obtained an optimal tableau. Otherwise, we try to increase the variable with the most negative coefficient in row 0.

KARMARKAR'S METHOD

Step 1 Begin at the feasible point $\mathbf{x}^0 = [\frac{1}{n} \quad \frac{1}{n} \quad \cdots \quad \frac{1}{n}]^T$ and set $k = 0$.

Step 2 Stop if $\mathbf{c}\mathbf{x}^k < \varepsilon$. If not, go to Step 3.

Step 3 Find the new point $\mathbf{y}^{k+1} = [y_1^{k+1} \quad y_2^{k+1} \quad \cdots \quad y_n^{k+1}]^T$ in the transformed unit simplex given by

$$\mathbf{y}^{k+1} = [\frac{1}{n} \quad \frac{1}{n} \quad \cdots \quad \frac{1}{n}]^T - \frac{\theta(I - P^T(PP^T)^{-1}P)[\text{Diag}(\mathbf{x}^k)]\mathbf{c}^T}{\|\mathbf{c}\|\sqrt{n(n-1)}}$$

Here, $\|\mathbf{c}\|$ = the length of $\mathbf{c}$, P is the $(m+1) \times n$ matrix whose first m rows are $A[\text{Diag}(\mathbf{x}^k)]$ and whose last row is a vector of 1's, and $0 < \theta < 1$ is chosen to ensure convergence of the algorithm. $\theta = \frac{1}{4}$ is known to ensure convergence.

Now obtain a new point $\mathbf{x}^{k+1}$ in the original space by using the centering transformation to determine the point corresponding to $\mathbf{y}^{k+1}$. That is, $\mathbf{x}^{k+1} = f^{-1}(\mathbf{y}^{k+1}|\mathbf{x}^k)$. Increase k by 1 and return to Step 2.

♦ REVIEW PROBLEMS

GROUP A

1. Use the revised simplex with the product form of the inverse to solve the following LP:

$$\max z = 4x_1 + 3x_2 + x_3$$
$$\text{s.t.} \quad 3x_1 + 2x_2 + x_3 \leq 6$$
$$x_2 + x_3 \leq 3$$
$$x_1 + x_3 \leq 2$$
$$x_1, x_2, x_3 \geq 0$$

2. Use the column generation technique to solve a cutting stock problem in which a customer demands 20 3-ft boards, 25 4-ft boards, and 30 5-ft boards, and demand is met by cutting up 14-ft boards.

3. Use the Dantzig-Wolfe decomposition method to solve the following LP:

$$\min z = 2x_1 - x_2 + x_3 - x_4$$
$$\text{s.t.} \quad x_1 + 2x_2 \leq 4$$
$$x_1 - x_2 \leq 1$$
$$x_3 - 3x_4 \leq 7$$
$$2x_3 + x_4 \leq 10$$
$$x_1 + 3x_2 - x_3 - 2x_4 \leq 10$$
$$x_i \geq 0 \ (i = 1, 2, 3, 4)$$

4. Consider the following situation:
(a) Two types of cars are produced at three production plants and are demanded by three customers.
(b) You are given the cost of producing each type of car at each plant and the cost of shipping each type of car from each plant to each customer.

(c) You are given the production capacity of each plant (for each type of car).
(d) You are also told that at most one half of the total number of cars demanded by customer 1 can be met from plant 1 production.

Explain how you would use decomposition to minimize the cost of meeting the customers' demands.

5. A company produces two products (product 1 and product 2) at two plants (plant 1 and plant 2). A total of 100 hours of production time is available at each plant. The times required to produce a unit of each product at each plant are shown in Table 10, and the profits earned for a unit of each product produced at each plant are shown in Table 11. At most 35 units of each product can be sold. Use decomposition to determine how the company can maximize profits.

Table 10

	PRODUCT 1	PRODUCT 2
Plant 1	2 hours	3 hours
Plant 2	3 hours	4 hours

Table 11

	PRODUCT 1	PRODUCT 2
Plant 1	$8	$6
Plant 2	$10	$8

◆ REFERENCES

The following three references are classic works that detail methods used to solve large LPs:

BEALE, E. *Mathematical Programming in Practice*. Pittman, 1968.

LASDON, L. *Optimization Theory for Large Systems*. New York: Macmillan, 1970.

ORCHARD-HAYS, W. *Advanced LP Computing Techniques*. New York: McGraw-Hill, 1968.

The following three references contain excellent discussions of Dantzig-Wolfe decomposition:

BRADLEY, S., A. HAX, and T. MAGNANTI. *Applied Mathematical Programming*. Reading, Mass.: Addison-Wesley, 1977.

CHVÀTAL, V. *Linear Programming*. San Francisco: Freeman, 1983.

SHAPIRO, J. *Mathematical Programming: Structures and Algorithms*. New York: Wiley, 1979.

The following two references discuss column generation and the cutting stock problem:

GILMORE, P., and R. GOMORY. "A Linear Programming Approach to the Cutting Stock Problem," *Operations Research* 9(1961):849–859.

——. "A Linear Programming Approach to the Cutting Stock Problem: Part II," *Operations Research* 11(1963):863–888.

The following three references contain lucid discussions of Karmarkar's method.

HOOKER, J. N. "Karmarkar's Linear Programming Algorithm," *Interfaces* 16(no. 4,1986):75–90.

MURTY, K. G. *Linear Complementarity, Linear and Nonlinear Programming*. Berlin, Germany: Heldermann Verlag, 1989.

PARKER, G., and R. RARDIN. *Discrete Optimization*. San Diego: Academic Press, 1988.

CHAPTER 11

Review of Calculus and Probability

WE REVIEW IN this chapter some basic topics in calculus and probability, which will be useful in later chapters.

11-1   REVIEW OF DIFFERENTIAL CALCULUS

LIMITS

The idea of a limit is one of the most basic ideas in calculus.

DEFINITION ■ The equation

$$\lim_{x \to a} f(x) = c$$

means that as x gets closer to a (but not equal to a), the value of $f(x)$ gets arbitrarily close to c.

It is also possible that $\lim_{x \to a} f(x)$ may not exist.

E X A M P L E 1

1. Show that $\lim_{x \to 2} x^2 - 2x = 2^2 - 2(2) = 0$.

2. Show that $\lim_{x \to 0} \frac{1}{x}$ does not exist.

Solution

1. To verify this result, evaluate $x^2 - 2x$ for values of x close to, but not equal to, 2.

2. To verify this result, observe that as x gets near zero, $\frac{1}{x}$ becomes either a very large positive number or a very large negative number. Thus, as x approaches zero, $\frac{1}{x}$ will not approach any single number. ◆

CONTINUITY

DEFINITION	A function $f(x)$ is **continuous** at a point a if
	$$\lim_{x \to a} f(x) = f(a)$$
	If $f(x)$ is not continuous at $x = a$, we say that $f(x)$ is **discontinuous** (or has a discontinuity) at a.

E X A M P L E 2

Bakeco orders sugar from Sugarco. The per-pound purchase price of the sugar depends on the size of the order (see Table 1). Let

$$x = \text{number of pounds of sugar purchased by Bakeco}$$
$$f(x) = \text{cost of ordering } x \text{ pounds of sugar}$$

Table 1
Price of Sugar Paid
by Bakeco

SIZE OF ORDER	PRICE PER POUND
$0 \le x < 100$	25¢
$100 \le x \le 200$	20¢
$x > 200$	15¢

Then

$$f(x) = 25x \text{ for } 0 \le x < 100$$
$$f(x) = 20x \text{ for } 100 \le x \le 200$$
$$f(x) = 15x \text{ for } x > 200$$

For all values of x, determine if x is continuous or discontinuous.

Solution

From Figure 1, it is clear that

$$\lim_{x \to 100} f(x) \quad \text{and} \quad \lim_{x \to 200} f(x)$$

Figure 1
Cost of Purchasing
Sugar in Bakeco
Example

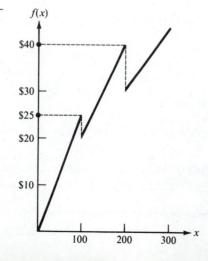

do not exist. Thus, $f(x)$ is discontinuous at $x = 100$ and $x = 200$ and is continuous for all other values of x satisfying $x \geq 0$. ◆

DIFFERENTIATION

DEFINITION	The **derivative** of a function $f(x)$ at $x = a$ (written $f'(a)$) is defined to be $$\lim_{\Delta x \to 0} \frac{f(a + \Delta x) - f(a)}{\Delta x}$$

If this limit does not exist, $f(x)$ has no derivative at $x = a$.

We may think of $f'(a)$ as the slope of $f(x)$ at $x = a$. Thus, if we begin at $x = a$ and increase x by a small amount Δ (Δ may be positive or negative), then $f(x)$ will increase by an amount approximately equal to $\Delta f'(a)$. If $f'(a) > 0$, $f(x)$ is increasing at $x = a$, whereas if $f'(a) < 0$, $f(x)$ is decreasing at $x = a$. The derivatives of many functions can be found via application of the rules in Table 2 (a represents an arbitrary constant). Example 3 illustrates the use and interpretation of the derivative.

Table 2
Rules for Finding
the Derivative of a
Function

FUNCTION	DERIVATIVE OF FUNCTION
a	0
x	1
$af(x)$	$af'(x)$
$f(x) + g(x)$	$f'(x) + g'(x)$
x^n	nx^{n-1}
e^x	e^x
a^x	$a^x \ln a$
$\ln x$	$\dfrac{1}{x}$
$[f(x)]^n$	$n[f(x)]^{n-1}f'(x)$
$e^{f(x)}$	$e^{f(x)}f'(x)$
$a^{f(x)}$	$a^{f(x)}f'(x)\ln a$
$\ln f(x)$	$\dfrac{f'(x)}{f(x)}$
$f(x)g(x)$	$f(x)g'(x) + f'(x)g(x)$
$\dfrac{f(x)}{g(x)}$	$\dfrac{g(x)f'(x) - f(x)g'(x)}{g(x)^2}$

EXAMPLE 3

If a company charges a price p for a product, it can sell $3e^{-p}$ thousand units of the product. Then, $f(p) = 3000pe^{-p}$ is the company's revenue if it charges a price p.

1. For what values of p is $f(p)$ decreasing? For what values of p is $f(p)$ increasing?

2. Suppose the current price is $4 and the company increases the price by 5¢. By approximately how much would the company's revenue change?

Solution   We have

$$f'(p) = -3000pe^{-p} + 3000e^{-p} = 3000e^{-p}(1 - p)$$

1. For $p < 1, f'(p) > 0$ and $f(p)$ is increasing, whereas for $p > 1, f'(p) < 0$ and $f(p)$ is decreasing.

2. Using the interpretation of $f'(4)$ as the slope of $f(p)$ at $p = 4$ (with $\Delta p = 0.05$), we see that the company's revenue would increase by approximately

$$0.05(3000e^{-4})(1 - 4) = -8.24$$

In actuality, of course, the company's revenue would increase by

$$f(4.05) - f(4) = 3000(4.05)e^{-4.05} - 3000(4)e^{-4}$$
$$= 211.68 - 219.79 = -8.11$$

HIGHER DERIVATIVES

We define $f^{(2)}(a) = f''(a)$ to be the derivative of the function $f'(x)$ at $x = a$. Similarly, we can define (if it exists) $f^{(n)}(a)$ to be the derivative of $f^{(n-1)}(x)$ at $x = a$. Thus, for Example 3,

$$f''(p) = 3000e^{-p}(-1) - 3000e^{-p}(1 - p)$$

TAYLOR SERIES EXPANSION

In our study of queuing theory (Chapter 22), we will need the Taylor series expansion of a function $f(x)$. Given that $f^{(n+1)}(x)$ exists for every point on the interval $[a, b]$, Taylor's theorem allows us to write for any h satisfying $0 \leq h \leq b - a$,

$$f(a + h) = f(a) + \sum_{i=1}^{i=n} \frac{f^{(i)}(a)}{i!} h^i + \frac{f^{(n+1)}(p)}{(n + 1)!} h^{n+1} \tag{1}$$

where (1) will hold for some number p between a and $a + h$. Eq. (1) is the **nth-order Taylor series expansion** of $f(x)$ about a.

E X A M P L E
4

Find the first-order Taylor series expansion of e^{-x} about $x = 0$.

Solution   Since $f'(x) = -e^{-x}$ and $f''(x) = e^{-x}$, we know that (1) will hold on any interval $[0, b]$. Also, $f(0) = 1, f'(0) = -1$, and $f''(x) = e^{-x}$. Then (1) yields the following first-order Taylor series expansion for e^{-x} about $x = 0$:

$$e^{-h} = f(h) = 1 - h + \frac{h^2 e^{-p}}{2}$$

This equation holds for some p between 0 and h.

PARTIAL DERIVATIVES

We now consider a function f of $n > 1$ variables $(x_1, x_2, \ldots, x_n)$, using the notation $f(x_1, x_2, \ldots, x_n)$ to denote such a function.

DEFINITION	The **partial derivative** of $f(x_1, x_2, \ldots, x_n)$ with respect to the variable x_i is written $\dfrac{\partial f}{\partial x_i}$, where

$$\frac{\partial f}{\partial x_i} = \lim_{\Delta x_i \to 0} \frac{f(x_1, \ldots, x_i + \Delta x_i, \ldots, x_n) - f(x_1, \ldots, x_i, \ldots, x_n)}{\Delta x_i}$$

Intuitively, if x_i is increased by Δ (and all other variables are held constant), then for small values of Δ, the value of $f(x_1, x_2, \ldots, x_n)$ will increase by approximately $\Delta \dfrac{\partial f}{\partial x_i}$. We find $\dfrac{\partial f}{\partial x_i}$ by treating all variables other than x_i as constants and finding the derivatives of $f(x_1, x_2, \ldots, x_n)$. More generally, suppose that for each i, we increase x_i by a small amount Δx_i. Then the value of f will increase by approximately

$$\sum_{i=1}^{i=n} \frac{\partial f}{\partial x_i} \Delta x_i$$

EXAMPLE 5

The demand $f(p, a) = 30{,}000 p^{-2} a^{1/6}$ for a product depends on $p = $ product price (in dollars) and $a = $ dollars spent advertising the product. Is demand an increasing or decreasing function of price? Is demand an increasing or decreasing function of advertising expenditure? If $p = 10$ and $a = 1{,}000{,}000$, by how much (approximately) will a \$1 cut in price increase demand?

Solution

$$\frac{\partial f}{\partial p} = 30{,}000(-2p^{-3})a^{1/6} = -60{,}000 p^{-3} a^{1/6} < 0$$

$$\frac{\partial f}{\partial a} = 30{,}000 p^{-2} \left(\frac{a^{-5/6}}{6} \right) = 5000 p^{-2} a^{-5/6} > 0$$

Thus, an increase in price (with advertising held constant) will decrease demand, while an increase in advertising (with price held constant) will increase demand. Since

$$\frac{\partial f}{\partial p}(10, \, 1{,}000{,}000) = -60{,}000 \left(\frac{1}{1000} \right)(1{,}000{,}000)^{1/6} = -600$$

a \$1 price cut will increase demand by approximately $(-1)(-600)$, or 600 units. ◆

We will also use *second-order partial derivatives* extensively. We use the notation $\dfrac{\partial^2}{\partial x_i \partial x_j}$ to denote a second-order partial derivative. To find $\dfrac{\partial^2}{\partial x_i \partial x_j}$, we first find $\dfrac{\partial f}{\partial x_i}$ and then take the partial derivative of $\dfrac{\partial f}{\partial x_i}$ with respect to x_j. If the second-order partials exist and are everywhere continuous, then

$$\frac{\partial^2 f}{\partial x_i \partial x_j} = \frac{\partial^2 f}{\partial x_j \partial x_i}$$

E X A M P L E
6

For $f(p, a) = 30,000p^{-2}a^{1/6}$, find all second-order partial derivatives.

Solution

$$\frac{\partial^2 f}{\partial p^2} = -60,000(-3p^{-4})a^{1/6} = \frac{180,000a^{1/6}}{p^4}$$

$$\frac{\partial^2 f}{\partial a^2} = 5000p^{-2}\left(\frac{-5a^{-11/6}}{6}\right) = -\frac{25,000p^{-2}a^{-11/6}}{6}$$

$$\frac{\partial^2 f}{\partial a \partial p} = 5000(-2p^{-3})a^{-5/6} = -10,000p^{-3}a^{-5/6}$$

$$\frac{\partial^2 f}{\partial p \partial a} = -60,000p^{-3}\left(\frac{a^{-5/6}}{6}\right) = -10,000p^{-3}a^{-5/6}$$

Observe that for $p \neq 0$,

$$\frac{\partial^2 f}{\partial a \partial p} = \frac{\partial^2 f}{\partial p \partial a}$$

◆ PROBLEMS

GROUP A

1. Find $\lim\limits_{h \to 0} \dfrac{3h + h^2}{h}$.

2. It costs Sugarco 25¢/lb to purchase the first 100 lb of sugar, 20¢/lb to purchase the next 100 lb of sugar, and 15¢ to buy each additional pound of sugar. Let $f(x)$ be the cost of purchasing x pounds of sugar. Is $f(x)$ continuous at all points? Are there any points where $f(x)$ has no derivative?

3. Find $f'(x)$ for each of the following functions:
(a) xe^{-x}
(b) $\dfrac{x^2}{x^2 + 1}$
(c) e^{3x}
(d) $(3x + 2)^{-2}$
(e) $\ln x^3$

4. Find all first- and second-order partial derivatives for $f(x_1, x_2) = x_1^2 e^{x_2}$.

5. Find the second-order Taylor series expansion of $\ln x$ about $x = 1$.

GROUP B

6. Let $q = f(p)$ be the demand for a product when the price of the product is p. For a given price p, the price elasticity E of the product is defined by

$$E = \frac{\text{percentage change in demand}}{\text{percentage change in price}}$$

If the change in price (Δp) is small, this formula reduces to

$$E = \frac{\frac{\Delta q}{q}}{\frac{\Delta p}{p}} = \left(\frac{p}{q}\right)\left(\frac{dq}{dp}\right)$$

(a) Would you expect $f(p)$ to be positive or negative?
(b) Show that if $E < -1$, a small decrease in price will increase the firm's total revenue (in this case, we say that demand is elastic).
(c) Show that if $-1 < E < 0$, a small price decrease will decrease total revenue (in this case, we say demand is inelastic).

7. Suppose that if x dollars are spent on advertising during a given year, $k(1 - e^{-cx})$ customers will purchase a product ($c > 0$).
(a) As x grows large, the number of customers purchasing the product approaches a limit. Find this limit.
(b) Can you give an interpretation for k?
(c) Show that the sales response from a dollar of advertising is proportional to the number of potential customers who are not purchasing the product at present.

8. Let the total cost of producing x units, $c(x)$, be given by $c(x) = kx^{1-b}$ ($0 < b < 1$). This cost curve is called the **learning**, or **experience cost curve**.
(a) Show that the cost of producing a unit is a decreasing function of the number of units that have been produced.
(b) Suppose that each time the number of units produced

is doubled, the per-unit product cost drops to $r\%$ of its previous value (because workers learn how to perform their jobs better). Show that $r = 100(2^{-b})$.

9. If a company has m hours of machine time and w hours of labor, it can produce $3m^{1/3}w^{2/3}$ units of a product. At present, the company has 216 hours of machine time and

1000 hours of labor. An extra hour of machine time costs $100 and an extra hour of labor costs $50. If the company had $100 to invest in purchasing additional labor and machine time, would it be better off buying 1 hour of machine time or 2 hours of labor?

11-2   REVIEW OF INTEGRAL CALCULUS

In our study of random variables, we often require a knowledge of the basics of integral calculus, which we briefly review in this section.

Consider two functions: $f(x)$ and $F(x)$. If $F'(x) = f(x)$, we say that $F(x)$ is the **indefinite integral** of $f(x)$. The fact that $F(x)$ is the indefinite integral of $f(x)$ is written

$$F(x) = \int f(x)\,dx$$

The following rules may be used to find the indefinite integrals of many functions (C is an arbitrary constant):

$$\int (1)\,dx = x + C$$

$$\int af(x)\,dx = a\int f(x)\,dx \qquad (a \text{ is any constant})$$

$$\int [f(x) + g(x)]\,dx = \int f(x)\,dx + \int g(x)\,dx$$

$$\int x^n\,dx = \frac{x^{n+1}}{n+1} + C \qquad (n \neq -1)$$

$$\int x^{-1}\,dx = \ln x + C$$

$$\int e^x\,dx = e^x + C$$

$$\int a^x\,dx = \frac{a^x}{\ln a} + C \qquad (a > 0, a \neq 1)$$

$$\int [f(x)]^n f'(x)\,dx = \frac{[f(x)]^{n+1}}{n+1} + C \qquad (n \neq -1)$$

$$\int f(x)^{-1} f'(x)\,dx = \ln f(x) + C$$

For two functions $u(x)$ and $v(x)$,

$$\int u(x)v'(x)\,dx = u(x)v(x) - \int v(x)u'(x)\,dx \qquad (\text{Integration by parts})$$

$$\int e^{f(x)} f'(x)\,dx = e^{f(x)} + C$$

$$\int a^{f(x)} f'(x)\,dx = \frac{a^{f(x)}}{\ln a} + C \qquad (a > 0, a \neq 1)$$

The concept of an integral is important for the following reason: Consider a function $f(x)$ that is continuous for all points satisfying $a \leq x \leq b$. Let $x_0 = a$, $x_1 = x_0 + \Delta$,

$x_2 = x_1 + \Delta, \ldots, x_i = x_{i-1} + \Delta, \quad x_n = x_{n-1} + \Delta = b,$ where $\Delta = \frac{b-a}{n}$. From Figure 2, we see that as Δ approaches zero (or equivalently, as n grows large),

$$\sum_{i=1}^{i=n} f(x_i)\Delta$$

Figure 2
Relation of Area and
Definite Integral

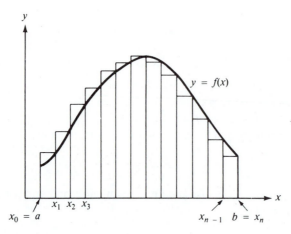

will closely approximate the area under the curve $y = f(x)$ between $x = a$ and $x = b$. If $f(x)$ is continuous for all x satisfying $a \leq x \leq b$, it can be shown that the area under the curve $y = f(x)$ between $x = a$ and $x = b$ is given by

$$\lim_{\Delta \to 0} \sum_{i=1}^{i=n} f(x_i)\Delta$$

which is written as

$$\int_a^b f(x)\, dx$$

or the **definite integral** of $f(x)$ from $x = a$ to $x = b$. The **Fundamental Theorem of Calculus** states that if $f(x)$ is continuous for all x satisfying $a \leq x \leq b$, then

$$\int_a^b f(x)\, dx = F(b) - F(a)$$

where $F(x)$ is any indefinite integral of $f(x)$. $F(b) - F(a)$ is often written as $[F(x)]_a^b$. Example 7 illustrates the use of the definite integral.

E X A M P L E
7

Suppose that at time t (t is measured in hours, and the present is $t = 0$), the rate $a(t)$ at which customers enter a bank is $a(t) = 100t$. During the next 2 hours, how many customers will enter the bank?

Solution

Let $t_0 = 0$, $t_1 = t_0 + \Delta$, $t_2 = t_1 + \Delta, \ldots, t_n = t_{n-1} + \Delta = 2$ (of course, $\Delta = \frac{2}{n}$). Between time t_{i-1} and time t_i, approximately $100t_i\Delta$ customers will arrive. Therefore, the total number of customers to arrive during the next 2 hours will equal

$$\lim_{\Delta \to 0} \sum_{i=1}^{i=n} 100t_i\Delta$$

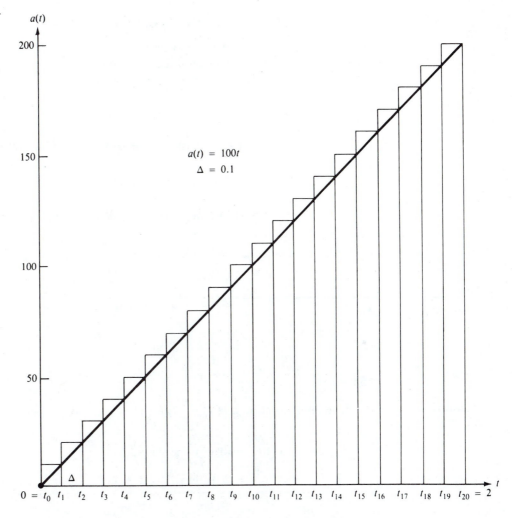

Figure 3
Relation of Total Arrivals in Next 2 Hours to Area under $a(t)$ Curve

$a(t) = 100t$
$\Delta = 0.1$

(see Figure 3). From the Fundamental Theorem of Calculus,

$$\lim_{\Delta \to 0} \sum_{i=1}^{i=n} 100t_i\Delta = \int_0^2 (100t)\, dt = [50t^2]_0^2 = 200 - 0 = 200$$

Thus, 200 customers will arrive during the next 2 hours.

◆

◆ PROBLEMS

GROUP A

1. The present is $t = 0$. At a time t years from now, I earn income at a rate e^{2t}. How much money do I earn during the next 5 years?

2. If money is continuously discounted at a rate of $r\%$ per year, then \$1 earned t years in the future is equivalent to e^{-rt} dollars earned at the present time. Use this fact to

determine the present value of the income earned in Problem 1.

3. At time 0, a company has I units of inventory in stock. Customers demand the product at a constant rate of d units per year (assume that $I \geq d$). The cost of holding 1 unit of stock in inventory for a time Δ is \$$h\Delta$. Determine the total holding cost incurred during the next year.

11-3   DIFFERENTIATION OF INTEGRALS

In our study of inventory theory in Chapter 17, we will have to differentiate a function whose value depends on an integral. Let $f(x, y)$ be a function of variables x and y, and let $g(y)$ and $h(y)$ be functions of y. Then

$$F(y) = \int_{g(y)}^{h(y)} f(x, y)\, dx$$

is a function only of y. **Leibniz's rule for differentiating an integral** states that

If $\quad F(y) = \int_{g(y)}^{h(y)} f(x, y)\, dx, \quad$ then

$$F'(y) = h'(y)f(h(y), y) - g'(y)f(g(y), y) + \int_{g(y)}^{h(y)} \frac{\partial f(x, y)}{\partial y}\, dx$$

Example 8 illustrates Leibniz's rule.

E X A M P L E 8   For

$$F(y) = \int_{1}^{y^2} \frac{y\, dx}{x}$$

find $F'(y)$.

Solution   We have that $f(x, y) = \frac{y}{x}$, $h(y) = y^2$, $h'(y) = 2y$, $\frac{\partial f}{\partial y} = \frac{1}{x}$, $g(y) = 1$, $g'(y) = 0$. Then

$$F'(y) = 2y\left(\frac{y}{y^2}\right) - 0\left(\frac{y}{1}\right) + \int_{1}^{y^2} \frac{dx}{x}$$

$$= 2 + [\ln x]_1^{y^2} = 2 + \ln y^2 - 0 = 2 + 2\ln y$$

◆

◆ PROBLEMS

GROUP A

For each of the following functions, use Leibniz's rule to find $F'(y)$:

1. $F(y) = \int_{y}^{y^2} (2y + x)\, dx$

2. $F(y) = \int_{0}^{y} yx^2\, dx$

3. $F(y) = \int_{0}^{y} 6(5 - x)f(x)\, dx + \int_{y}^{\infty} 4(x - 5)f(x)\, dx$

11-4   BASIC RULES OF PROBABILITY

In this section, we review some basic rules and definitions that you may have encountered during your previous study of probability.

DEFINITION	Any situation where the outcome is uncertain is called an **experiment**.

For example, drawing a card from a deck of cards would be an experiment.

DEFINITION	For any experiment, the **sample space** S of the experiment consists of all possible outcomes for the experiment.

For example, if we toss a die and are interested in the number of dots showing, then $S = \{1, 2, 3, 4, 5, 6\}$.

DEFINITION	An **event** E consists of any collection of points (set of outcomes) in the sample space.

DEFINITION	A collection of events $E_1, E_2, \ldots, E_n$ is said to be a **mutually exclusive** collection of events if for $i \neq j$ ($i = 1, 2, \ldots, n$ and $j = 1, 2, \ldots, n$), E_i and E_j have no points in common.

With each event E, we associate an event $\bar{E}$. $\bar{E}$ consists of the points in the sample space that are not in E. With each event E, we also associate a number $P(E)$, which is the probability that event E will occur when we perform the experiment. The probabilities of events must satisfy the following rules of probability:

Rule 1 For any event E, $P(E) \geq 0$.

Rule 2 If $E = S$ (that is, if E contains all points in the sample space), then $P(E) = 1$.

Rule 3 If $E_1, E_2, \ldots, E_n$ is a mutually exclusive collection of events, then

$$P(E_1 \cup E_2 \cup \cdots \cup E_n) = \sum_{k=1}^{k=n} P(E_k)$$

Rule 4 $P(\bar{E}) = 1 - P(E)$.

DEFINITION	For two events E_1 and E_2, $P(E_2 \mid E_1)$ (the **conditional probability** of E_2 given E_1) is the probability that the event E_2 will occur given that event E_1 has occurred. Then $$P(E_2 \mid E_1) = \frac{P(E_1 \cap E_2)}{P(E_1)} \qquad (2)$$

DEFINITION	Suppose events E_1 and E_2 both occur with positive probability. Events E_1 and E_2 are **independent** if and only if $P(E_2 \mid E_1) = P(E_2)$ (or equivalently, $P(E_1 \mid E_2) = P(E_1)$).

Thus, events E_1 and E_2 are independent if and only if knowledge that E_1 has occurred does not change the probability that E_2 has occurred, and vice versa. From (2), E_1 and E_2 are independent if and only if

$$\frac{P(E_1 \cap E_2)}{P(E_1)} = P(E_2) \quad \text{or} \quad P(E_1 \cap E_2) = P(E_1)P(E_2) \qquad (3)$$

E X A M P L E 9   Suppose we draw a single card from a deck of 52 cards.

1. What is the probability that a heart or spade is drawn?

2. What is the probability that the drawn card is not a 2?

3. Given that a red card has been drawn, what is probability that a diamond has been drawn? Are the events

$$E_1 = \text{red card is drawn}$$
$$E_2 = \text{diamond is drawn}$$

independent events?

4. Show that the events

$$E_1 = \text{spade is drawn}$$
$$E_2 = \text{2 is drawn}$$

are independent events.

Solution   **1.** Define the events

$$E_1 = \text{heart is drawn}$$
$$E_2 = \text{spade is drawn}$$

E_1 and E_2 are mutually exclusive events with $P(E_1) = P(E_2) = \frac{1}{4}$. We seek $P(E_1 \cup E_2)$. From probability rule 3,

$$P(E_1 \cup E_2) = P(E_1) + P(E_2) = (\tfrac{1}{4}) + (\tfrac{1}{4}) = \tfrac{1}{2}$$

2. Define event $E = $ a 2 is drawn. Then $P(E) = \frac{4}{52} = \frac{1}{13}$. We seek $P(\bar{E})$. From probability rule 4, $P(\bar{E}) = 1 - \frac{1}{13} = \frac{12}{13}$.

3. From (2),

$$P(E_2 \,|\, E_1) = \frac{P(E_1 \cap E_2)}{P(E_1)}$$
$$P(E_1 \cap E_2) = P(E_2) = \tfrac{13}{52} = \tfrac{1}{4}$$
$$P(E_1) = \tfrac{26}{52} = \tfrac{1}{2}$$

Thus,

$$P(E_2 \,|\, E_1) = \frac{\frac{1}{4}}{\frac{1}{2}} = \tfrac{1}{2}$$

Since $P(E_2) = \frac{1}{4}$, we see that $P(E_2 | E_1) \neq P(E_2)$. Thus, E_1 and E_2 are not independent events. (This is because knowing that a red card was drawn increases the probability that a diamond was drawn.)

4. $P(E_1) = \frac{13}{52} = \frac{1}{4}$, $P(E_2) = \frac{4}{52} = \frac{1}{13}$, and $P(E_1 \cap E_2) = \frac{1}{52}$. Since $P(E_1)P(E_2) = P(E_1 \cap E_2)$, E_1 and E_2 are independent events. Intuitively, since $\frac{1}{4}$ of all cards in the deck are spades and $\frac{1}{4}$ of all 2's in the deck are spades, knowing that a 2 has been drawn does not change the probability that the card drawn was a spade.

◆ **PROBLEMS**

GROUP A

1. Suppose two dice are tossed (for each die, it is equally likely that 1, 2, 3, 4, 5, or 6 dots will show).
(a) What is the probability that the total of the two dice will add up to 7 or 11?
(b) What is the probability that the total of the two dice will add up to a number other than 2 or 12?
(c) Are the events

$$E_1 = \text{first die shows a 3}$$
$$E_2 = \text{total of the two dice is 6}$$

independent events?

(d) Are the events

$$E_1 = \text{first die shows a 3}$$
$$E_2 = \text{total of the two dice is 7}$$

independent events?
(e) Given that the total of the two dice is 5, what is the probability that the first die showed 2 dots?
(f) Given that the first die shows a 5, what is the probability that the total of the two dice is even?

11-5   BAYES' RULE

An important decision often depends on the "state of the world." For example, we may want to know whether or not a person has tuberculosis. Then we would be concerned with the probability of the following states of the world:

$$S_1 = \text{person has tuberculosis}$$
$$S_2 = \text{person does not have tuberculosis}$$

More generally, n mutually exclusive states of the world $(S_1, S_2, \ldots, S_n)$ may occur. The states of the world are **collectively exhaustive**: $S_1, S_2, \ldots, S_n$ include all possibilities. Suppose a decision maker assigns a probability $P(S_i)$ to S_i. $P(S_i)$ is the **prior probability** of S_i. In order to obtain more information about the state of the world, the decision maker may observe the outcome of an experiment. Suppose that for each possible outcome O_j and each possible state of the world S_i, the decision maker knows $P(O_j | S_i)$, the **likelihood** of outcome O_j given state of the world S_i. Bayes' rule combines prior probabilities and likelihoods with the experimental outcomes to determine a post-experimental probability, or **posterior probability**, for each state of the world. To derive Bayes' rule, observe that (2) implies that

$$P(S_i | O_j) = \frac{P(S_i \cap O_j)}{P(O_j)} \qquad (4)$$

From (2), it also follows that

$$P(S_i \cap O_j) = P(O_j | S_i)P(S_i) \tag{5}$$

The states of the world $S_1, S_2, \ldots, S_n$ are collectively exhaustive, so the experimental outcome O_j (if it occurs) must occur with one of the S_i (see Figure 4). Since $S_1 \cap O_j$, $S_2 \cap O_j, \ldots, S_n \cap O_j$ are mutually exclusive events, probability rule 3 implies that

$$P(O_j) = P(S_1 \cap O_j) + P(S_2 \cap O_j) + \cdots + P(S_n \cap O_j) \tag{6}$$

Figure 4
Illustration of Eq. (6)

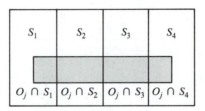

$$P(O_j) = P(O_j \cap S_1) + P(O_j \cap S_2)$$
$$+ P(O_j \cap S_3) + P(O_j \cap S_4)$$

Shaded area = outcome O_j

The probabilities of the form $P(S_i \cap O_j)$ are often referred to as **joint probabilities**, and the probabilities $P(O_j)$ are called **marginal probabilities**. Substituting (5) into (6), we obtain

$$P(O_j) = \sum_{k=1}^{k=n} P(O_j | S_k)P(S_k) \tag{7}$$

Substituting (5) and (7) into (4) yields **Bayes' rule**:

$$P(S_i | O_j) = \frac{P(O_j | S_i)P(S_i)}{\sum\limits_{k=1}^{k=n} P(O_j | S_k)P(S_k)} \tag{8}$$

The following example illustrates the use of Bayes' rule.

E X A M P L E
10

Suppose that 1% of all children have tuberculosis (TB). When a child who has TB is given the Mantoux test, a positive test result occurs 95% of the time. When a child who does not have TB is given the Mantoux test, a positive test result occurs 1% of the time. Given that a child is tested and a positive test result occurs, what is the probability that the child has TB?

Solution

The states of the world are

$$S_1 = \text{child has TB}$$
$$S_2 = \text{child does not have TB}$$

The possible experimental outcomes are

$$O_1 = \text{positive test result}$$
$$O_2 = \text{nonpositive test result}$$

We are given the prior probabilities $P(S_1) = .01$ and $P(S_2) = .99$ and the likelihoods $P(O_1 | S_1) = .95$, $P(O_1 | S_2) = .01$, $P(O_2 | S_1) = .05$, and $P(O_2 | S_2) = .99$. We seek $P(S_1 | O_1)$. From (8),

$$P(S_1 \mid O_1) = \frac{P(O_1 \mid S_1)P(S_1)}{P(O_1 \mid S_1)P(S_1) + P(O_1 \mid S_2)P(S_2)}$$

$$= \frac{.95(.01)}{.95(.01) + .01(.99)} = \frac{95}{194} = .49$$

◆

The reason a positive test result implies only a 49% chance that the child has TB is that many of the 99% of all children who do not have TB will test positive. For example, in a typical group of 10,000 children, 9900 will not have TB and .01(9900) = 99 children will yield a positive test result. In the same group of 10,000 children, .01(10,000) = 100 children will have TB and .95(100) = 95 children will yield a positive test result. Thus, the probability that a positive test result indicates TB is $\frac{95}{95+99} = \frac{95}{194}$.

◆ PROBLEMS

GROUP A

1. A desk contains three drawers. Drawer 1 contains two gold coins. Drawer 2 contains one gold coin and one silver coin. Drawer 3 contains two silver coins. I randomly choose a drawer and then randomly choose a coin. If a silver coin is chosen, what is the probability that I chose drawer 3?

2. Cliff Colby wants to determine whether or not his South Japan oil field will yield oil. He has hired geologist Digger Barnes to run tests on the field. If there is oil in the field, there is a 95% chance that Digger's tests will indicate that there is oil in the field. If the field contains no oil, there is a 5% chance that Digger's tests will indicate that there is oil in the field. If Digger's tests indicate that there is no oil

in the field, what is the probability that the field contains oil? Before Digger conducts the test, Cliff believes that there is a 10% chance that the field will yield oil.

3. A customer has approached a bank for a loan. Without further information, the bank believes there is a 4% chance that the customer will default on the loan. The bank can run a credit check on the customer. The check will yield either a favorable or an unfavorable report. From past experience, the bank believes that P (favorable report being received | customer will default) $= \frac{1}{40}$, and P (favorable report | customer will not default) $= \frac{99}{100}$. If a favorable report is received, what is the probability that the customer will default on the loan?

11-6   RANDOM VARIABLES, MEAN, VARIANCE, AND COVARIANCE

The concepts of random variables, mean, variance, and covariance are employed in several later chapters.

DEFINITION	A **random variable** is a function that associates a number with each point in an experiment's sample space. We denote random variables by boldface capital letters (usually **X**, **Y**, or **Z**).

DISCRETE RANDOM VARIABLES

DEFINITION	A random variable is **discrete** if it can assume only discrete values $x_1, x_2, \ldots$. A discrete random variable **X** is characterized by the fact that we know the probability that $\mathbf{X} = x_i$ (written $P(\mathbf{X} = x_i)$).

$P(\mathbf{X} = x_i)$ is the **probability mass function** (pmf) for the random variable **X**.

DEFINITION	The **cumulative distribution function** $F(x)$ for any random variable **X** is defined by $F(x) = P(\mathbf{X} \leq x)$. For a discrete random variable **X**,

$$F(x) = \sum_{\substack{\text{all } x \\ \text{having } x_k \leq x}} P(\mathbf{X} = x_k)$$

An example of a discrete random variable follows.

E X A M P L E
11

Let **X** be the number of dots that show when a die is tossed. Then for $i = 1, 2, 3, 4, 5, 6$, $P(\mathbf{X} = i) = \frac{1}{6}$. The cumulative distribution function (cdf) for **X** is shown in Figure 5.

Figure 5
Cumulative
Distribution
Function for
Example 11

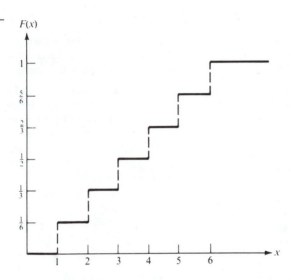

CONTINUOUS RANDOM VARIABLES

If, for some interval, the random variable **X** can assume all values on the interval, then **X** is a **continuous** random variable. Probability statements about a continuous random variable **X** require knowing **X**'s **probability density function** (pdf). The probability density function $f(x)$ for a random variable **X** may be interpreted as follows: For Δ small,

$$P(x \leq \mathbf{X} \leq x + \Delta) \cong \Delta f(x)$$

From Figure 6, we see that for a random variable **X** having density function $f(x)$,

$$\text{Area 1} = P(a \leq \mathbf{X} \leq a + \Delta) \cong \Delta f(a)$$

and

$$\text{Area 2} = P(b \leq \mathbf{X} \leq b + \Delta) \cong \Delta f(b)$$

Thus, for a random variable **X** with density function $f(x)$ as given in Figure 6, values of **X** near a are much more likely to occur than values of **X** near b.

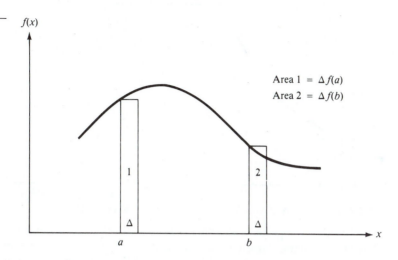

Figure 6
Illustration of
Probability Density
Function

From our previous discussion of the Fundamental Theorem of Calculus, it follows that

$$P(a \leq \mathbf{X} \leq b) = \int_a^b f(x) \, dx$$

Thus, for a continuous random variable, any area under the random variable's pdf corresponds to a probability. Using the concept of area as probability, we see that the cdf for a continuous random variable **X** with density $f(x)$ is given by

$$F(a) = P(\mathbf{X} \leq a) = \int_{-\infty}^a f(x) \, dx$$

E X A M P L E 12   Consider a continuous random variable **X** having a density function $f(x)$ given by

$$f(x) = \begin{cases} 2x & \text{if } 0 \leq x \leq 1 \\ 0 & \text{otherwise} \end{cases}$$

Find the cdf for **X**. Also find $P(\frac{1}{4} \leq \mathbf{X} \leq \frac{3}{4})$.

Solution   For $a \leq 0$, $F(a) = 0$. For $0 \leq a \leq 1$,

$$F(a) = \int_0^a 2x \, dx = a^2$$

For $a \geq 1$, $F(a) = 1$. $F(a)$ is graphed in Figure 7.

$$P(\tfrac{1}{4} \leq \mathbf{X} \leq \tfrac{3}{4}) = \int_{1/4}^{3/4} 2x \, dx = [x^2]_{1/4}^{3/4} = (\tfrac{9}{16}) - (\tfrac{1}{16}) = \tfrac{1}{2}$$

Figure 7
Cumulative
Distribution
Function for
Example 12

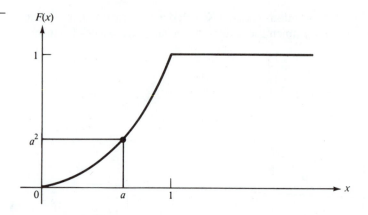

Figure 7
Cumulative
Distribution
Function for
Example 12

MEAN AND VARIANCE OF A RANDOM VARIABLE

The **mean** (or expected value) and **variance** are two important measures that are often used to summarize information contained in a random variable's probability distribution. The mean of a random variable $\mathbf{X}$ (written $E(\mathbf{X})$) is a measure of central location for the random variable.

MEAN OF A DISCRETE RANDOM VARIABLE.   For a discrete random variable $\mathbf{X}$,

$$E(\mathbf{X}) = \sum_{\text{all } k} x_k P(\mathbf{X} = x_k) \tag{9}$$

MEAN OF A CONTINUOUS RANDOM VARIABLE.   For a continuous random variable,

$$E(\mathbf{X}) = \int_{-\infty}^{\infty} xf(x)\, dx \tag{10}$$

Observe that in computing $E(\mathbf{X})$, each possible value of a random variable is weighted by its probability of occurring. Thus, the mean of a random variable is essentially the random variable's center of mass.

For a function $h(\mathbf{X})$ of a random variable $\mathbf{X}$ (such as $\mathbf{X}^2$ and $e^{\mathbf{X}}$), $E[h(\mathbf{X})]$ may be computed as follows. If $\mathbf{X}$ is a discrete random variable,

$$E[h(\mathbf{X})] = \sum_{\text{all } k} h(x_k)P(\mathbf{X} = x_k) \tag{9'}$$

If $\mathbf{X}$ is a continuous random variable,

$$E[h(\mathbf{X})] = \int_{-\infty}^{\infty} h(x)f(x)\, dx \tag{10'}$$

The variance of a random variable $\mathbf{X}$ (written as var $\mathbf{X}$) measures the dispersion or spread of $\mathbf{X}$ about $E(\mathbf{X})$. Then var $\mathbf{X}$ is defined to be $E[\mathbf{X} - E(\mathbf{X})]^2$.

VARIANCE OF A DISCRETE RANDOM VARIABLE.   For a discrete random variable $\mathbf{X}$, (9') yields

$$\text{var } \mathbf{X} = \sum_{\text{all } k} [x_k - E(\mathbf{X})]^2 P(\mathbf{X} = X_k) \tag{11}$$

VARIANCE OF A CONTINUOUS RANDOM VARIABLE. For a continuous random variable X, (10′) yields

$$\text{var } X = \int_{-\infty}^{\infty} [x - E(X)]^2 f(x) \, dx \tag{12}$$

Also, var X may be found from the relation

$$\text{var } X = E(X^2) - E(X)^2 \tag{13}$$

For any random variable X, $(\text{var } X)^{1/2}$ is the **standard deviation** of X (written σ_x).

Examples 13 and 14 illustrate the computation of mean and variance for a discrete and a continuous random variable.

E X A M P L E
13

Consider the discrete random variable X having $P(X = i) = \frac{1}{6}$ for $i = 1, 2, 3, 4, 5, 6.$ Find $E(X)$ and var X.

Solution

$$E(X) = (\tfrac{1}{6})(1 + 2 + 3 + 4 + 5 + 6) = \tfrac{21}{6} = \tfrac{7}{2}$$

$$\text{var } X = (\tfrac{1}{6})[(1 - 3.5)^2 + (2 - 3.5)^2 + (3 - 3.5)^2$$
$$+ (4 - 3.5)^2 + (5 - 3.5)^2 + (6 - 3.5)^2] = \tfrac{35}{12}$$

◆

E X A M P L E
14

Find the mean and variance for the continuous random variable X having the following density function:

$$f(x) = \begin{cases} 2x & \text{if } 0 \le x \le 1 \\ 0 & \text{otherwise} \end{cases}$$

Solution

$$E(X) = \int_0^1 x(2x) \, dx = \left[\frac{2x^3}{3}\right]_0^1 = \frac{2}{3}$$

$$\text{var } X = \int_0^1 \left(x - \frac{2}{3}\right)^2 2x \, dx = \int_0^1 \left(x^2 - \frac{4x}{3} + \frac{4}{9}\right) 2x \, dx$$

$$= \left[\frac{2x^4}{4} - \frac{8x^3}{9} + \frac{8x^2}{18}\right]_0^1 = \frac{1}{18}$$

◆

INDEPENDENT RANDOM VARIABLES

DEFINITION

Two random variables X and Y are **independent** if and only if for any two sets A and B,

$$P(X \in A \text{ and } Y \in B) = P(X \in A)P(Y \in B)$$

From this definition, it can be shown that X and Y are independent random variables if and only if knowledge about the value of Y does not change the probability of any event involving X. For example, suppose X and Y are independent random variables. This implies that where Y = 8, Y = 10, Y = 0, or Y = anything else,

$P(\mathbf{X} \geq 10)$ will be the same. If $\mathbf{X}$ and $\mathbf{Y}$ are independent, then $E(\mathbf{XY}) = E(\mathbf{X})E(\mathbf{Y})$ (the random variable $\mathbf{XY}$ has an expected value equal to the product of the expected value of $\mathbf{X}$ and the expected value of $\mathbf{Y}$).

The definition of independence generalizes to situations where more than two random variables are of interest. Loosely speaking, a group of n random variables is independent if knowlege of the values of any subset of the random variables does not change our view of the distribution of any of the other random variables (see Problem 5 at the end of this section).

COVARIANCE OF TWO RANDOM VARIABLES

An important concept in the study of financial models is covariance. For two random variables $\mathbf{X}$ and $\mathbf{Y}$, the **covariance** of $\mathbf{X}$ and $\mathbf{Y}$ (written cov $(\mathbf{X}, \mathbf{Y})$) is defined by

$$\text{cov}\,(\mathbf{X}, \mathbf{Y}) = E\{[\mathbf{X} - E(\mathbf{X})][\mathbf{Y} - E(\mathbf{Y})]\} \tag{14}$$

If $\mathbf{X} > E(\mathbf{X})$ tends to occur when $\mathbf{Y} > E(\mathbf{Y})$, and $\mathbf{X} < E(\mathbf{X})$ tends to occur when $\mathbf{Y} < E(\mathbf{Y})$, then cov $(\mathbf{X}, \mathbf{Y})$ will be positive. On the other hand, if $\mathbf{X} > E(\mathbf{X})$ tends to occur when $\mathbf{Y} < E(\mathbf{Y})$, and $\mathbf{X} < E(\mathbf{X})$ tends to occur when $\mathbf{Y} > E(\mathbf{Y})$, then cov $(\mathbf{X}, \mathbf{Y})$ will be negative. The value of cov $(\mathbf{X}, \mathbf{Y})$ measures the association (actually, linear association) between random variables $\mathbf{X}$ and $\mathbf{Y}$. It can be shown that if $\mathbf{X}$ and $\mathbf{Y}$ are independent random variables, then cov $(\mathbf{X}, \mathbf{Y}) = 0$. (However, cov $(\mathbf{X}, \mathbf{Y}) = 0$ can hold even if $\mathbf{X}$ and $\mathbf{Y}$ are not independent random variables. See Problem 6 at the end of this section for an example.)

E X A M P L E
15

Each summer in Gotham City is classified as being either a rainy summer or a sunny summer. The profits earned by Gotham City's two leading industries (the Gotham City Hotel and the Gotham City Umbrella Store) depend on the summer's weather, as shown in Table 3. Of all summers, 20% are rainy, and 80% are sunny. Let $\mathbf{H}$ and $\mathbf{U}$ be the following random variables:

$\mathbf{H}$ = profit earned by Gotham City Hotel during a summer

$\mathbf{U}$ = profit earned by Gotham City Umbrella Store during a summer

Find cov $(\mathbf{H}, \mathbf{U})$.

Table 3 Profits for Covariance Example	TYPE OF SUMMER	HOTEL PROFIT	UMBRELLA PROFIT
	Rainy	−$1000	$4500
	Sunny	$2000	−$500

Solution

We find that

$$E(\mathbf{H}) = .2(-1000) + .8(2000) = \$1400$$
$$E(\mathbf{U}) = .2(4500) + .8(-500) = \$500$$

With probability .20, Gotham City has a rainy summer. Then

$$[\mathbf{H} - E(\mathbf{H})][\mathbf{U} - E(\mathbf{U})] = (-1000 - 1400)(4500 - 500) = -9,600,000(\text{dollars})^2$$

With probability .80, Gotham City has a sunny summer. Then

$$[H - E(H)][U - E(U)] = (2000 - 1400)(-500 - 500) = -600,000(\text{dollars})^2$$

Thus,

$$\begin{aligned} \text{cov}(H, U) = E\{[H - E(H)][U - E(U)]\} &= .20(-9,600,000) + .80(-600,000) \\ &= -2,400,000 \ (\text{dollars})^2 \end{aligned}$$

The fact that cov (H, U) is negative indicates that when one industry does well, the other industry tends to do poorly.

◆

MEAN, VARIANCE, AND COVARIANCE FOR SUMS OF RANDOM VARIABLES

From given random variables X_1 and X_2, we often create new random variables (c is a constant): $cX_1, X_1 + c, X_1 + X_2$. The following rules can be used to express the mean, variance, and covariance of these random variables in terms of $E(X_1)$, $E(X_2)$, var X_1, var X_2, and cov (X_1, X_2). Examples 16 and 17 illustrate the use of these rules.

$$E(cX_1) = cE(X_1) \tag{15}$$

$$E(X_1 + c) = E(X_1) + c \tag{16}$$

$$E(X_1 + X_2) = E(X_1) + E(X_2) \tag{17}$$

$$\text{var } cX_1 = c^2 \text{var } X_1 \tag{18}$$

$$\text{var}(X_1 + c) = \text{var } X_1 \tag{19}$$

If X_1 and X_2 are independent random variables,

$$\text{var}(X_1 + X_2) = \text{var } X_1 + \text{var } X_2 \tag{20}$$

In general,

$$\text{var}(X_1 + X_2) = \text{var } X_1 + \text{var } X_2 + 2\text{cov}(X_1, X_2) \tag{21}$$

For random variables $X_1, X_2, \ldots, X_n$,

$$\text{var}(X_1 + X_2 + \cdots + X_n) = \text{var } X_1 + \text{var } X_2 + \cdots + \text{var } X_n + \sum_{i \neq j} \text{cov}(X_i, X_j) \tag{22}$$

Finally, for constants a and b,

$$\text{cov}(aX_1, bX_2) = ab \, \text{cov}(X_1, X_2) \tag{23}$$

E X A M P L E
16

Solution

I pay \$1 to play the following game: I toss a die and receive \$3 for each dot that shows. Determine the mean and variance of my profit.

Let X be the random variable representing the number of dots that show when the die is tossed. Then my profit is given by the value of the random variable $3X - 1$. From Example 13, we know that $E(X) = \frac{7}{2}$ and var $X = \frac{35}{12}$. In turn, Eqs. (16) and (15) yield

$$E(3X - 1) = E(3X) - 1 = 3E(X) - 1 = 3(\tfrac{7}{2}) - 1 = \tfrac{19}{2}$$

From Eqs. (19) and (18), respectively,

$$\text{var}(3\mathbf{X} - 1) = \text{var}(3\mathbf{X}) = 9(\text{var}\,\mathbf{X}) = 9(\tfrac{35}{12}) = \tfrac{315}{12}$$

◆

E X A M P L E 17

In Example 15, suppose I owned both the hotel and the umbrella store. Find the mean and variance of the total profit I would earn during a summer.

Solution

My total profits are given by the random variable $\mathbf{H} + \mathbf{U}$. From Eq. (17) and Example 15,

$$E(\mathbf{H} + \mathbf{U}) = E(\mathbf{H}) + E(\mathbf{U}) = 1400 + 500 = \$1900$$

Now

$$\text{var}\,\mathbf{H} = .2(-1000 - 1400)^2 + .8(2000 - 1400)^2 = 1,440,000 \text{ (dollars)}^2$$
$$\text{var}\,\mathbf{U} = .2(4500 - 500)^2 + .8(-500 - 500)^2 = 4,000,000 \text{ (dollars)}^2$$

From Example 15, $\text{cov}(\mathbf{H}, \mathbf{U}) = -2,400,000 \text{ (dollars)}^2$. Then Eq. (21) yields

$$\text{var}(\mathbf{H} + \mathbf{U}) = \text{var}\,\mathbf{H} + \text{var}\,\mathbf{U} + 2\,\text{cov}(\mathbf{H}, \mathbf{U})$$
$$= 1,440,000 \text{ (dollars)}^2 + 4,000,000 \text{ (dollars)}^2 - 2(2,400,000)(\text{dollars})^2$$
$$= 640,000 \text{ (dollars)}^2$$

◆

Thus, $\mathbf{H} + \mathbf{U}$ has a smaller variance than either $\mathbf{H}$ or $\mathbf{U}$. This is because by owning both the hotel and umbrella store, we will always have, regardless of the weather, one industry that does well and one that does poorly. This reduces the spread, or variability, of our profits.

◆ PROBLEMS

GROUP A

1. I have 100 items of a product in stock. The probability mass function for the product's demand $\mathbf{D}$ is $P(\mathbf{D} = 90) = P(\mathbf{D} = 100) = P(\mathbf{D} = 110) = \tfrac{1}{3}$.
(a) Find the mass function, mean, and variance of the number of items sold.
(b) Find the mass function, mean, and variance of the amount of demand that will be unfilled because of lack of stock.

2. I draw 5 cards from a deck (replacing each card immediately after it is drawn). I receive $4 for each heart that is drawn. Find the mean and variance of my total payoff.

3. Consider a continuous random variable $\mathbf{X}$ with the density function (called the exponential density)

$$f(x) = \begin{cases} e^{-x} & \text{if } x \geq 0 \\ 0 & \text{otherwise} \end{cases}$$

(a) Find and sketch the cdf for $\mathbf{X}$.
(b) Find the mean and variance of $\mathbf{X}$. (*Hint:* Use integration by parts.)
(c) Find $P(1 \leq \mathbf{X} \leq 2)$.

4. I have 100 units of a product in stock. The demand $\mathbf{D}$ for the item is a continuous random variable with the following density function:

$$f(d) = \begin{cases} \tfrac{1}{40} & \text{if } 80 \leq d \leq 120 \\ 0 & \text{otherwise} \end{cases}$$

(a) Find the probability that supply is insufficient to meet demand.
(b) What is the expected number of items sold? What is the variance of the number of items sold?

5. An urn contains 10 red balls and 30 blue balls.
(a) Suppose you draw 4 balls from the urn. Let $\mathbf{X}_i$ be the number of red balls drawn on the ith ball ($\mathbf{X}_i = 0$ or 1). After each ball is drawn, it is put back into the urn. Are the

random variables X_1, X_2, X_3, and X_4 independent random variables?

(b) Repeat part (a) for the case in which the balls are not put back into the urn after being drawn.

GROUP B

6. Let **X** be the following discrete random variable: $P(X = -1) = P(X = 0) = P(X = 1) = \frac{1}{3}$. Let $Y = X^2$. Show that $\text{cov}(X, Y) = 0$, but **X** and **Y** are not independent random variables.

11-7   THE NORMAL DISTRIBUTION

The most commonly used probability distribution in this book is the normal distribution. We discuss in this section some useful properties of the normal distribution.

DEFINITION A continuous random variable **X** has a normal distribution if for some μ and $\sigma > 0$, the random variable has the following density function:

$$f(x) = \frac{1}{\sigma(2\pi)^{1/2}} \exp\left[-\frac{(x - \mu)^2}{2\sigma^2} \right]$$

If a random variable **X** is normally distributed with a mean μ and variance σ^2, we write that **X** is $N(\mu, \sigma^2)$. It can be shown that for a normal random variable, $E(X) = \mu$ and $\text{var} X = \sigma^2$ (the standard deviation of **X** is σ). The normal density functions for several values of σ and a single value of μ are shown in Figure 8.

Figure 8
Some Examples of Normal Distributions

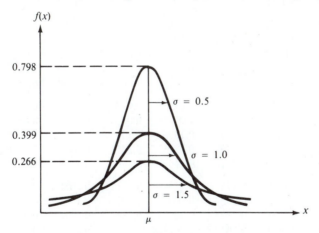

For any normal distribution, the normal density is symmetric about μ (that is, $f(\mu + a) = f(\mu - a)$). Also, as σ increases, the probability that the random variable assumes a value within c of μ (for any $c > 0$) decreases. Thus, as σ increases, the normal distribution becomes more spread out. These properties are illustrated in Figure 8.

USEFUL PROPERTIES OF THE NORMAL DISTRIBUTION

Property 1 If **X** is $N(\mu, \sigma^2)$, then $c\mathbf{X}$ is $N(c\mu, c^2\sigma^2)$.

Property 2 If **X** is $N(\mu, \sigma^2)$, then $\mathbf{X} + c$ (for any constant c) is $N(\mu + c, \sigma^2)$.

Property 3 If X_1 is $N(\mu_1, \sigma_1^2)$, X_2 is $N(\mu_2, \sigma_2^2)$, and X_1 and X_2 are independent, then $X_1 + X_2$ is $N(\mu_1 + \mu_2, \sigma_1^2 + \sigma_2^2)$.

Table 4†   Standard normal cumulative probabilities

z	0.00	0.01	0.02	0.03	0.04	0.05	0.06	0.07	0.08	0.09
−3.8	0.0001	0.0001	0.0001	0.0001	0.0001	0.0001	0.0001	0.0001	0.0001	0.0001
−3.7	0.0001	0.0001	0.0001	0.0001	0.0001	0.0001	0.0001	0.0001	0.0001	0.0001
−3.6	0.0002	0.0002	0.0001	0.0001	0.0001	0.0001	0.0001	0.0001	0.0001	0.0001
−3.5	0.0002	0.0002	0.0002	0.0002	0.0002	0.0002	0.0002	0.0002	0.0002	0.0002
−3.4	0.0003	0.0003	0.0003	0.0003	0.0003	0.0003	0.0003	0.0003	0.0003	0.0002
−3.3	0.0005	0.0005	0.0005	0.0004	0.0004	0.0004	0.0004	0.0004	0.0004	0.0003
−3.2	0.0007	0.0007	0.0006	0.0006	0.0006	0.0006	0.0006	0.0005	0.0005	0.0005
−3.1	0.0010	0.0009	0.0009	0.0009	0.0008	0.0008	0.0008	0.0008	0.0007	0.0007
−3.0	0.0014	0.0013	0.0013	0.0012	0.0012	0.0011	0.0011	0.0011	0.0010	0.0010
−2.9	0.0019	0.0018	0.0018	0.0017	0.0016	0.0016	0.0015	0.0015	0.0014	0.0014
−2.8	0.0026	0.0025	0.0024	0.0023	0.0023	0.0022	0.0021	0.0021	0.0020	0.0019
−2.7	0.0035	0.0034	0.0033	0.0032	0.0031	0.0030	0.0029	0.0028	0.0027	0.0026
−2.6	0.0047	0.0045	0.0044	0.0043	0.0041	0.0040	0.0039	0.0038	0.0037	0.0036
−2.5	0.0062	0.0060	0.0059	0.0057	0.0055	0.0054	0.0052	0.0051	0.0049	0.0048
−2.4	0.0082	0.0080	0.0078	0.0076	0.0073	0.0071	0.0069	0.0068	0.0066	0.0064
−2.3	0.0107	0.0104	0.0102	0.0099	0.0096	0.0094	0.0091	0.0089	0.0087	0.0084
−2.2	0.0139	0.0136	0.0132	0.0129	0.0125	0.0122	0.0119	0.0116	0.0113	0.0110
−2.1	0.0179	0.0174	0.0170	0.0166	0.0162	0.0158	0.0154	0.0150	0.0146	0.0143
−2.0	0.0228	0.0222	0.0217	0.0212	0.0207	0.0202	0.0197	0.0192	0.0188	0.0183
−1.9	0.0287	0.0281	0.0274	0.0268	0.0262	0.0256	0.0250	0.0244	0.0239	0.0233
−1.8	0.0359	0.0351	0.0344	0.0336	0.0329	0.0322	0.0314	0.0307	0.0301	0.0294
−1.7	0.0446	0.0436	0.0427	0.0418	0.0409	0.0401	0.0392	0.0384	0.0375	0.0367
−1.6	0.0548	0.0537	0.0526	0.0516	0.0505	0.0495	0.0485	0.0475	0.0465	0.0455
−1.5	0.0668	0.0655	0.0643	0.0630	0.0618	0.0606	0.0594	0.0582	0.0571	0.0559
−1.4	0.0808	0.0793	0.0778	0.0764	0.0749	0.0735	0.0721	0.0708	0.0694	0.0681
−1.3	0.0968	0.0951	0.0934	0.0918	0.0901	0.0885	0.0869	0.0853	0.0838	0.0823
−1.2	0.1151	0.1131	0.1112	0.1093	0.1075	0.1057	0.1038	0.1020	0.1003	0.0985
−1.1	0.1357	0.1335	0.1314	0.1292	0.1271	0.1251	0.1230	0.1210	0.1190	0.1170
−1.0	0.1587	0.1562	0.1539	0.1515	0.1492	0.1469	0.1446	0.1423	0.1401	0.1379
−0.9	0.1841	0.1814	0.1788	0.1762	0.1736	0.1711	0.1685	0.1660	0.1635	0.1611
−0.8	0.2119	0.2090	0.2061	0.2033	0.2005	0.1977	0.1949	0.1922	0.1894	0.1867
−0.7	0.2420	0.2389	0.2358	0.2327	0.2297	0.2266	0.2236	0.2206	0.2177	0.2148
−0.6	0.2743	0.2709	0.2676	0.2643	0.2611	0.2578	0.2546	0.2514	0.2483	0.2451
−0.5	0.3085	0.3050	0.3015	0.2981	0.2946	0.2912	0.2877	0.2843	0.2810	0.2776
−0.4	0.3446	0.3409	0.3372	0.3336	0.3300	0.3264	0.3228	0.3192	0.3156	0.3121
−0.3	0.3821	0.3783	0.3745	0.3707	0.3669	0.3632	0.3594	0.3557	0.3520	0.3483
−0.2	0.4207	0.4168	0.4129	0.4090	0.4052	0.4013	0.3974	0.3936	0.3897	0.3859
−0.1	0.4602	0.4562	0.4522	0.4483	0.4443	0.4404	0.4364	0.4325	0.4286	0.4247
−0.0	0.5000	0.4960	0.4920	0.4880	0.4840	0.4801	0.4761	0.4721	0.4681	0.4641

Note: Table entry is the area under the standard normal curve to the left of the indicated z-value, thus giving $P(Z \leq z)$.
†Reprinted by permission from Kleinbaum, Kupper, and Miller, *Applied Regression Analysis and Other Multivariable Methods*, 2nd edition. Copyright © PWS-KENT Publishing Company.

Table 4 Standard normal cumulative probabilities (*continued*)

z	0.00	0.01	0.02	0.03	0.04	0.05	0.06	0.07	0.08	0.09
0.0	0.5000	0.5040	0.5080	0.5120	0.5160	0.5199	0.5239	0.5279	0.5319	0.5359
0.1	0.5398	0.5438	0.5478	0.5517	0.5557	0.5596	0.5636	0.5675	0.5714	0.5753
0.2	0.5793	0.5832	0.5871	0.5910	0.5948	0.5987	0.6026	0.6064	0.6103	0.6141
0.3	0.6179	0.6217	0.6255	0.6293	0.6331	0.6368	0.6406	0.6443	0.6480	0.6517
0.4	0.6554	0.6591	0.6628	0.6664	0.6700	0.6736	0.6772	0.6808	0.6844	0.6879
0.5	0.6915	0.6950	0.6985	0.7019	0.7054	0.7088	0.7123	0.7157	0.7190	0.7224
0.6	0.7257	0.7291	0.7324	0.7357	0.7389	0.7422	0.7454	0.7486	0.7517	0.7549
0.7	0.7580	0.7611	0.7642	0.7673	0.7703	0.7734	0.7764	0.7794	0.7823	0.7852
0.8	0.7881	0.7910	0.7939	0.7967	0.7995	0.8023	0.8051	0.8078	0.8106	0.8133
0.9	0.8159	0.8186	0.8212	0.8238	0.8264	0.8289	0.8315	0.8340	0.8365	0.8389
1.0	0.8413	0.8438	0.8461	0.8485	0.8508	0.8531	0.8554	0.8577	0.8599	0.8621
1.1	0.8643	0.8665	0.8686	0.8708	0.8729	0.8749	0.8770	0.8790	0.8810	0.8830
1.2	0.8849	0.8869	0.8888	0.8907	0.8925	0.8943	0.8962	0.8980	0.8997	0.9015
1.3	0.9032	0.9049	0.9066	0.9082	0.9099	0.9115	0.9131	0.9147	0.9162	0.9177
1.4	0.9192	0.9207	0.9222	0.9236	0.9251	0.9265	0.9279	0.9292	0.9306	0.9319
1.5	0.9332	0.9345	0.9357	0.9370	0.9382	0.9394	0.9406	0.9418	0.9429	0.9441
1.6	0.9452	0.9463	0.9474	0.9484	0.9495	0.9505	0.9515	0.9525	0.9535	0.9545
1.7	0.9554	0.9564	0.9573	0.9582	0.9591	0.9599	0.9608	0.9616	0.9625	0.9633
1.8	0.9641	0.9649	0.9656	0.9664	0.9671	0.9678	0.9686	0.9693	0.9699	0.9706
1.9	0.9713	0.9719	0.9726	0.9732	0.9738	0.9744	0.9750	0.9756	0.9761	0.9767
2.0	0.9772	0.9778	0.9783	0.9788	0.9793	0.9798	0.9803	0.9808	0.9812	0.9817
2.1	0.9821	0.9826	0.9830	0.9834	0.9838	0.9842	0.9846	0.9850	0.9854	0.9857
2.2	0.9861	0.9864	0.9868	0.9871	0.9875	0.9878	0.9881	0.9884	0.9887	0.9890
2.3	0.9893	0.9896	0.9898	0.9901	0.9904	0.9906	0.9909	0.9911	0.9913	0.9916
2.4	0.9918	0.9920	0.9922	0.9924	0.9927	0.9929	0.9931	0.9932	0.9934	0.9936
2.5	0.9938	0.9940	0.9941	0.9943	0.9945	0.9946	0.9948	0.9949	0.9951	0.9952
2.6	0.9953	0.9955	0.9956	0.9957	0.9959	0.9960	0.9961	0.9962	0.9963	0.9964
2.7	0.9965	0.9966	0.9967	0.9968	0.9969	0.9970	0.9971	0.9972	0.9973	0.9974
2.8	0.9974	0.9975	0.9976	0.9977	0.9977	0.9978	0.9979	0.9979	0.9980	0.9981
2.9	0.9981	0.9982	0.9982	0.9983	0.9984	0.9984	0.9985	0.9985	0.9986	0.9986
3.0	0.9986	0.9987	0.9987	0.9988	0.9988	0.9989	0.9989	0.9989	0.9990	0.9990
3.1	0.9990	0.9991	0.9991	0.9991	0.9992	0.9992	0.9992	0.9992	0.9993	0.9993
3.2	0.9993	0.9993	0.9994	0.9994	0.9994	0.9994	0.9994	0.9995	0.9995	0.9995
3.3	0.9995	0.9995	0.9995	0.9996	0.9996	0.9996	0.9996	0.9996	0.9996	0.9997
3.4	0.9997	0.9997	0.9997	0.9997	0.9997	0.9997	0.9997	0.9997	0.9997	0.9998
3.5	0.9998	0.9998	0.9998	0.9998	0.9998	0.9998	0.9998	0.9998	0.9998	0.9998
3.6	0.9998	0.9998	0.9999	0.9999	0.9999	0.9999	0.9999	0.9999	0.9999	0.9999
3.7	0.9999	0.9999	0.9999	0.9999	0.9999	0.9999	0.9999	0.9999	0.9999	0.9999
3.8	0.9999	0.9999	0.9999	0.9999	0.9999	0.9999	0.9999	0.9999	0.9999	0.9999
3.9	1.0000									

FINDING NORMAL PROBABILITIES VIA STANDARDIZATION

If $\mathbf{Z}$ is a random variable that is $N(0, 1)$, then $\mathbf{Z}$ is said to be a standardized normal random variable. In Table 4, $F(z) = P(\mathbf{Z} \leq z)$ is tabulated. For example,

$$P(\mathbf{Z} \leq -1) = F(-1) = .1587$$

and

$$P(\mathbf{Z} \geq 2) = 1 - P(\mathbf{Z} \leq 2) = 1 - F(2) = 1 - .9772 = .0228.$$

If $\mathbf{X}$ is $N(\mu, \sigma^2)$, then $(\mathbf{X} - \mu)/\sigma$ is $N(0, 1)$. This follows, because by property 2 of the normal distribution, $\mathbf{X} - \mu$ is $N(\mu - \mu, \sigma^2) = N(0, \sigma^2)$. Then by property 1, $\frac{\mathbf{X}-\mu}{\sigma}$ is $N(\frac{0}{\sigma}, \frac{\sigma^2}{\sigma^2}) = N(0, 1)$. The last equality enables us to use Table 4 to find probabilities for any normal random variable, not just an $N(0, 1)$ random variable. Suppose $\mathbf{X}$ is $N(\mu, \sigma^2)$ and we want to find $P(a \leq \mathbf{X} \leq b)$. To find this probability from Table 4, we use the following relations (this procedure is called **standardization**):

$$P(a \leq \mathbf{X} \leq b) = P\left(\frac{a - \mu}{\sigma} \leq \frac{\mathbf{X} - \mu}{\sigma} \leq \frac{b - \mu}{\sigma}\right)$$

$$= P\left(\frac{a - \mu}{\sigma} \leq \mathbf{Z} \leq \frac{b - \mu}{\sigma}\right)$$

$$= F\left(\frac{b - \mu}{\sigma}\right) - F\left(\frac{a - \mu}{\sigma}\right)$$

THE CENTRAL LIMIT THEOREM. If $\mathbf{X}_1, \mathbf{X}_2, \ldots, \mathbf{X}_n$ are independent random variables, then for n sufficiently large (usually $n \geq 30$ will do, but the actual size of n depends on the distributions of $\mathbf{X}_1, \mathbf{X}_2, \ldots, \mathbf{X}_n$), the random variable $\mathbf{X} = \mathbf{X}_1 + \mathbf{X}_2 + \cdots + \mathbf{X}_n$ may be closely approximated by a normal random variable $\mathbf{X}'$ that has $E(\mathbf{X}') = E(\mathbf{X}_1) + E(\mathbf{X}_2) + \cdots + E(\mathbf{X}_n)$ and $\text{var } \mathbf{X}' = \text{var } \mathbf{X}_1 + \text{var } \mathbf{X}_2 + \cdots + \text{var } \mathbf{X}_n$. This result is known as the Central Limit Theorem. When we say that $\mathbf{X}'$ closely approximates $\mathbf{X}$, we mean that $P(a \leq \mathbf{X} \leq b)$ is close to $P(a \leq \mathbf{X}' \leq b)$.

EXAMPLE 18

Daily demand for chocolate bars at the Gillis Grocery has a mean of 100 chocolate bars and a variance of 3000 (chocolate bars)^2. At present, the store has 3500 chocolate bars in stock. What is the probability that the store will run out of chocolate bars during the next 30 days? Also, how many chocolate bars should Gillis have on hand at the beginning of a 30-day period if the store wants to have only a 1% chance of running out of chocolate bars during the 30-day period? Assume that the demands on different days are independent random variables.

Solution

Let

$$\mathbf{X}_i = \text{demand for chocolate bars on day } i \quad (i = 1, 2, \ldots, 30)$$
$$\mathbf{X} = \text{number of chocolate bars demanded in next 30 days}$$

Gillis will run out of stock during the next 30 days if $X \geq 3500$. The Central Limit Theorem implies that $X = X_1 + X_2 + \cdots + X_{30}$ can be closely approximated by a normal distribution X' with $E(X') = 30(100) = 3000$ and var $X' = 30(3000) = 90,000$ and $\sigma_{X'} = (90,000)^{1/2} = 300$. Then we approximate the probability that Gillis will run out of stock during the next 30 days by

$$P(X' \geq 3500) = P\left(\frac{X' - 3000}{300} \geq \frac{3500 - 3000}{300}\right)$$

$$= P(Z \geq 1.67) = 1 - P(Z \leq 1.67)$$

$$= 1 - F(1.67) = 1 - .9525 = .0475$$

Let c = number of chocolate bars that should be stocked in order to have a 1% chance of running out of chocolate bars within the next 30 days. We seek c satisfying $P(X' \geq c) = .01$, or

$$P\left(\frac{X' - 3000}{300} \geq \frac{c - 3000}{300}\right) = .01$$

This is equivalent to

$$P\left(Z \geq \frac{c - 3000}{300}\right) = .01$$

Since $F(2.33) = P(Z \leq 2.33) = .99$,

$$\frac{c - 3000}{300} = 2.33 \quad \text{or} \quad c = 3699$$

Thus if Gillis has 3699 chocolate bars in stock, there is a 1 percent probability that the store will run out of chocolate bars during the next 30 days. (We have defined running out of chocolate bars as having no chocolate bars left at the end of 30 days.) ◆

◆ PROBLEMS

GROUP A

1. The daily demand for milk (in gallons) at Gillis Grocery is $N(1000, 100)$. How many gallons of milk must be in stock at the beginning of the day if Gillis is to have only a 5% chance of running out of milk by the end of the day?

2. Before burning out, a light bulb gives X hours of light, where X is $N(500, 400)$. If we have 3 bulbs, what is the probability that they will give a total of at least 1460 hours of light?

GROUP B

3. The number of traffic accidents occurring in Bloomington in a single day has a mean and a variance of 3. What is the probability that during a given year (365-day period), there will be at least 1000 traffic accidents in Bloomington?

◆ SUMMARY

RULES FOR FINDING THE DERIVATIVE OF A FUNCTION

FUNCTION	DERIVATIVE OF FUNCTION
a	0
x	1
$af(x)$	$af'(x)$
$f(x) + g(x)$	$f'(x) + g'(x)$
x^n	nx^{n-1}
e^x	e^x
a^x	$a^x \ln a$
$\ln x$	$\dfrac{1}{x}$
$[f(x)]^n$	$n[f(x)]^{n-1}f'(x)$
$e^{f(x)}$	$e^{f(x)}f'(x)$
$a^{f(x)}$	$a^{f(x)}f'(x) \ln a$
$\ln f(x)$	$\dfrac{f'(x)}{f(x)}$
$f(x)g(x)$	$f(x)g'(x) + f'(x)g(x)$
$\dfrac{f(x)}{g(x)}$	$\dfrac{g(x)f'(x) - f(x)g'(x)}{g(x)^2}$

FORMULAS FOR DETERMINING INDEFINITE INTEGRALS

$$\int (1)\, dx = x + C$$

$$\int af(x)\, dx = a \int f(x)\, dx \qquad (a \text{ is any constant})$$

$$\int [f(x) + g(x)]\, dx = \int f(x)\, dx + \int g(x)\, dx$$

$$\int x^n\, dx = \frac{x^{n+1}}{n+1} + C \qquad (n \neq -1)$$

$$\int x^{-1}\, dx = \ln x + C$$

$$\int e^x\, dx = e^x + C$$

$$\int a^x\, dx = \frac{a^x}{\ln a} + C \qquad (a > 0, a \neq 1)$$

$$\int [f(x)]^n f'(x)\, dx = \frac{[f(x)]^{n+1}}{n+1} + C \qquad (n \neq -1)$$

$$\int f(x)^{-1} f'(x)\, dx = \ln f(x) + C$$

For two functions $u(x)$ and $v(x)$,

$$\int u(x)v'(x)\, dx = u(x)v(x) - \int v(x)u'(x)\, dx \qquad \text{(Integration by parts)}$$

$$\int e^{f(x)}f'(x)\, dx = e^{f(x)} + C$$

$$\int a^{f(x)}f'(x)\, dx = \frac{a^{f(x)}}{\ln a} + C \qquad (a > 0, a \neq 1)$$

LEIBNIZ'S RULE FOR DIFFERENTIATING AN INTEGRAL

$$\text{If} \qquad F(y) = \int_{g(y)}^{h(y)} f(x, y)\, dx, \qquad \text{then}$$

$$F'(y) = h'(y)f(h(y), y) - g'(y)f(g(y), y) + \int_{g(y)}^{h(y)} \frac{\partial f(x, y)}{\partial y}\, dx$$

PROBABILITY

BASIC RULES.

Rule 1 For any event E, $P(E) \geq 0$.

Rule 2 If $E = S$ (that is, if E contains all points in the sample space), then $P(E) = 1$.

Rule 3 If $E_1, E_2, \ldots, E_n$ is a mutually exclusive collection of events, then

$$P(E_1 \cup E_2 \cup \cdots \cup E_n) = \sum_{k=1}^{k=n} P(E_k)$$

Rule 4 $P(\bar{E}) = 1 - P(E)$.

FORMULA FOR CONDITIONAL PROBABILITY.

$$P(E_2 \mid E_1) = \frac{P(E_1 \cap E_2)}{P(E_1)} \tag{2}$$

BAYES' RULE

$$P(S_i \mid O_j) = \frac{P(O_j \mid S_i)P(S_i)}{\displaystyle\sum_{k=1}^{k=n} P(O_j \mid S_k)P(S_k)} \tag{8}$$

RANDOM VARIABLES, MEAN, VARIANCE, AND COVARIANCE

MEAN OF A DISCRETE RANDOM VARIABLE.

$$E(\mathbf{X}) = \sum_{\text{all } k} x_k P(\mathbf{X} = x_k) \tag{9}$$

MEAN OF A CONTINUOUS RANDOM VARIABLE.

$$E(\mathbf{X}) = \int_{-\infty}^{\infty} xf(x)\, dx \tag{10}$$

VARIANCE OF A DISCRETE RANDOM VARIABLE.

$$\operatorname{var} \mathbf{X} = \sum_{\text{all } k} [x_k - E(\mathbf{X})]^2 P(\mathbf{X} = x_k) \tag{11}$$

VARIANCE OF A CONTINUOUS RANDOM VARIABLE.

$$\operatorname{var} \mathbf{X} = \int_{-\infty}^{\infty} [x - E(\mathbf{X})]^2 f(x)\, dx \tag{12}$$

COVARIANCE OF TWO RANDOM VARIABLES.

$$\operatorname{cov}(\mathbf{X}, \mathbf{Y}) = E\{[\mathbf{X} - E(\mathbf{X})][\mathbf{Y} - E(\mathbf{Y})]\} \tag{14}$$

MEAN, VARIANCE, AND COVARIANCE FOR SUMS OF RANDOM VARIABLES.

$$E(c\mathbf{X}_1) = cE(\mathbf{X}_1) \tag{15}$$

$$E(\mathbf{X}_1 + c) = E(\mathbf{X}_1) + c \tag{16}$$

$$E(\mathbf{X}_1 + \mathbf{X}_2) = E(\mathbf{X}_1) + E(\mathbf{X}_2) \tag{17}$$

$$\operatorname{var} c\mathbf{X}_1 = c^2 \operatorname{var} \mathbf{X}_1 \tag{18}$$

$$\operatorname{var}(\mathbf{X}_1 + c) = \operatorname{var} \mathbf{X}_1 \tag{19}$$

If $\mathbf{X}_1$ and $\mathbf{X}_2$ are independent random variables,

$$\operatorname{var}(\mathbf{X}_1 + \mathbf{X}_2) = \operatorname{var} \mathbf{X}_1 + \operatorname{var} \mathbf{X}_2 \tag{20}$$

In general,

$$\operatorname{var}(\mathbf{X}_1 + \mathbf{X}_2) = \operatorname{var} \mathbf{X}_1 + \operatorname{var} \mathbf{X}_2 + 2\operatorname{cov}(\mathbf{X}_1, \mathbf{X}_2) \tag{21}$$

For random variables $\mathbf{X}_1, \mathbf{X}_2, \ldots, \mathbf{X}_n$,

$$\operatorname{var}(\mathbf{X}_1 + \mathbf{X}_2 + \cdots + \mathbf{X}_n) = \operatorname{var} \mathbf{X}_1 + \operatorname{var} \mathbf{X}_2 + \cdots \\ + \operatorname{var} \mathbf{X}_n + \sum_{i \neq j} \operatorname{cov}(\mathbf{X}_i, \mathbf{X}_j) \tag{22}$$

$$\operatorname{cov}(a\mathbf{X}_1, b\mathbf{X}_2) = ab\operatorname{cov}(\mathbf{X}_1, \mathbf{X}_2) \tag{23}$$

USEFUL PROPERTIES OF THE NORMAL DISTRIBUTION

Property 1 If $\mathbf{X}$ is $N(\mu, \sigma^2)$, then $c\mathbf{X}$ is $N(c\mu, c^2\sigma^2)$.

Property 2 If $\mathbf{X}$ is $N(\mu, \sigma^2)$, then $\mathbf{X} + c$ (for any constant c) is $N(\mu + c, \sigma^2)$.

Property 3 If $\mathbf{X}_1$ is $N(\mu_1, \sigma_1^2)$, $\mathbf{X}_2$ is $N(\mu_2, \sigma_2^2)$, and $\mathbf{X}_1$ and $\mathbf{X}_2$ are independent, then $\mathbf{X}_1 + \mathbf{X}_2$ is $N(\mu_1 + \mu_2, \sigma_1^2 + \sigma_2^2)$.

If $\mathbf{X}$ is $N(\mu, \sigma^2)$, then

$$P(a \leq \mathbf{X} \leq b) = F\left(\frac{b - \mu}{\sigma}\right) - F\left(\frac{a - \mu}{\sigma}\right)$$

where $F(x) = P(\mathbf{Z} \leq x)$ and $\mathbf{Z}$ is $N(0, 1)$.

◆ REVIEW PROBLEMS

GROUP A

1. Let $f(x) = xe^{-x}$.
(a) Find $f'(x)$ and $f''(x)$.
(b) For what values of x is $f(x)$ increasing? Decreasing?
(c) Find the first-order Taylor series expansion for $f(x)$ about $x = 1$.

2. Let $f(x_1, x_2) = x_1 \ln(x_2 - x_1)$. Determine all first-order and second-order partial derivatives.

3. Some t years from now, air conditioners are demanded at a rate of t air conditioners per year. How many air conditioners will be sold during the next 5 years?

4. Let **X** be a continuous random variable with density function

$$f(x) = \begin{cases} \frac{4-x}{k} & \text{if } 0 \le x \le 4 \\ 0 & \text{otherwise} \end{cases}$$

(a) What is k?
(b) Find the cdf for **X**.
(c) Find $E(\mathbf{X})$ and var **X**.
(d) Find $P(2 \le \mathbf{X} \le 5)$.

5. Let $\mathbf{X}_i$ be the price (in dollars) of stock i one year from now. Suppose that $\mathbf{X}_1$ is $N(15, 100)$ and $\mathbf{X}_2$ is $N(20, 2025)$. Today I buy three shares of stock 1 for \$12/share and two shares of stock 2 for \$17/share. Assume that $\mathbf{X}_1$ and $\mathbf{X}_2$ are independent random variables.
(a) Find the mean and variance of the value of my stocks one year from now.
(b) What is the probability that one year from now I will have earned at least a 30% return on my investment?
(c) If $\mathbf{X}_1$ and $\mathbf{X}_2$ were not independent, why would it be difficult to answer parts (a) and (b)?

GROUP B

6. An airplane has four engines. On a flight from New York to Paris, each engine has a 0.001 chance of failing. The plane will crash if at any time two or fewer engines are working properly. Assume that the failures of different engines are independent.
(a) What is the probability that the plane will crash?
(b) Given that engine 1 will not fail during the flight, what is the probability that the flight will crash?
(c) Given that engine 1 will fail during the flight, what is the probability that the plane will not crash?

7. Suppose that each engine can be inspected before the flight. After inspection, each engine is labeled as being in either good or bad condition. You are given that

$P(\text{inspection says engine is in good condition} \mid \text{engine will fail}) = .001$

$P(\text{inspection says engine is in bad condition} \mid \text{engine will fail}) = .999$

$P(\text{inspection says engine is in good condition} \mid \text{engine will not fail}) = .995$

$P(\text{inspection says engine is in bad condition} \mid \text{engine will not fail}) = .005$

(a) If the inspection indicates the engine is in bad condition, what is the probability that the engine will fail on the flight?
(b) If an inspector randomly inspects an engine (that is, with probability .001 she chooses an engine that is about to fail, and with probability .999 she chooses an engine that is not about to fail), what is the probability that she will make an error in her evaluation of the engine?

◆ REFERENCES

ALLEN, R. *Mathematical Analysis for Economists*. New York: St. Martin's Press, 1938. An advanced calculus review.

BYRKIT, D., and S. SHAMMA. *Calculus for Business and Economics*. New York: Van Nostrand, 1981. A review of calculus at a beginning level.

CHIANG, A. *Fundamental Methods of Mathematical Economics*. New York: McGraw-Hill, 1978. An advanced calculus review.

HARNETT, D. *Statistical Methods*. Reading, Mass.: Addison-Wesley, 1982. A review of probability.

WINKLER, R., and W. HAYS. *Statistics: Probability, Inference, and Decision*. Chicago: Holt, Rinehart and Winston, 1971. A review of probability.

CHAPTER 12

Nonlinear Programming

IN PREVIOUS CHAPTERS, we have studied linear programming problems. For a linear programming problem, our goal was to maximize or minimize a linear function subject to linear constraints. In many interesting maximization and minimization problems, the objective function may not be a linear function, or some of the constraints may not be linear constraints. Such an optimization problem is called a nonlinear programming problem (NLP). In this chapter, we discuss techniques used to solve NLPs.

12-1 INTRODUCTORY CONCEPTS

DEFINITION ◾ A general **nonlinear programming problem** (NLP) can be expressed as follows: Find the values of decision variables $x_1, x_2, \ldots, x_n$ that

$$\max \text{ (or min) } z = f(x_1, x_2, \ldots, x_n)$$
$$\text{s.t.} \quad g_1(x_1, x_2, \ldots, x_n) \ (\leq, =, \text{ or } \geq) \ b_1$$
$$g_2(x_1, x_2, \ldots, x_n) \ (\leq, =, \text{ or } \geq) \ b_2 \tag{1}$$
$$\vdots$$
$$g_m(x_1, x_2, \ldots, x_n) \ (\leq, =, \text{ or } \geq) \ b_m$$

As in linear programming, $f(x_1, x_2, \ldots, x_n)$ is the NLP's **objective function**, and $g_1(x_1, x_2, \ldots, x_n)$ ($\leq$, $=$, or $\geq$) b_1, $\ldots$, $g_m(x_1, x_2, \ldots, x_n)$ ($\leq$, $=$, or $\geq$) b_m are the NLP's **constraints**. An NLP with no constraints is an **unconstrained NLP**.

The set of all points $(x_1, x_2, \ldots, x_n)$ such that x_i is a real number is R^n. Thus, R^1 is the set of all real numbers. The following subsets of R^1 (called intervals) will be of particular interest:

$$[a, b] = \text{all } x \text{ satisfying } a \leq x \leq b$$
$$[a, b) = \text{all } x \text{ satisfying } a \leq x < b$$
$$(a, b] = \text{all } x \text{ satisfying } a < x \leq b$$
$$(a, b) = \text{all } x \text{ satisfying } a < x < b$$
$$[a, \infty) = \text{all } x \text{ satisfying } x \geq a$$
$$(-\infty, b] = \text{all } x \text{ satisfying } x \leq b$$

The following definitions are analogous to the corresponding definitions for LPs given in Section 3.1.

> **DEFINITION** ◆ The **feasible region** for NLP (1) is the set of points $(x_1, x_2, \ldots, x_n)$ that satisfy the m constraints in (1). A point in the feasible region is a feasible point, and a point that is not in the feasible region is an infeasible point.

Suppose (1) is a maximization problem.

> **DEFINITION** ◆ Any point $\bar{x}$ in the feasible region for which $f(\bar{x}) \geq f(x)$ holds for all points x in the feasible region is an **optimal solution** to the NLP. (For a minimization problem, $\bar{x}$ is the optimal solution if $f(\bar{x}) \leq f(x)$ for all feasible x.)

Of course, if f, g_1, g_2, . . . , g_m are all linear functions, then (1) is a linear programming problem and may be solved by the simplex algorithm.

EXAMPLES OF NLPs

E X A M P L E 1   It costs a company c dollars per unit to manufacture a product. If the company charges p dollars per unit for the product, customers demand $D(p)$ units. In order to maximize profits, what price should the firm charge?

Solution   The firm's decision variable is p. Since the firm's profit is $(p - c)D(p)$, the firm wishes to solve the following unconstrained maximation problem: $\max(p - c)D(p)$.

◆

E X A M P L E 2   If K units of capital and L units of labor are used, a company can produce KL units of a manufactured good. Capital can be purchased at \$4/unit and labor can be purchased at \$1/unit. A total of \$8 is available to purchase capital and labor. How can the firm maximize the quantity of the good that can be manufactured?

Solution   Let K = units of capital purchased and L = units of labor purchased. Then K and L must satisfy $4K + L \leq 8$, $K \geq 0$, and $L \geq 0$. Thus, the firm wishes to solve the following constrained maximization problem:

$$\max z = KL$$
$$\text{s.t.} \quad 4K + L \leq 8$$
$$K, L \geq 0$$

◆

DIFFERENCES BETWEEN NLPs AND LPs

Recall from Chapter 3 that the feasible region for any LP is a convex set (that is, if A and B are feasible for an LP, the entire line segment joining A and B is also feasible).

Also recall that if an LP has an optimal solution, there is an extreme point of the feasible region that is optimal. We will soon see, however, that even if the feasible region for an NLP is a convex set, the optimal solution for an NLP (unlike the optimal solution for an LP) need not be an extreme point of the NLP's feasible region. The previous example illustrates this idea. Figure 1 shows graphically the feasible region (bounded by triangle ABC) for the example and the isoprofit curves $KL = 1$, $KL = 2$, and $KL = 4$. We see that the optimal solution to the example occurs where an isoprofit curve is tangent to the boundary of the feasible region. Thus, the optimal solution to the example is $z = 4$, $K = 1$, $L = 4$ (point D). Of course, point D is not an extreme point of the NLP's feasible region. For this example (and many other NLPs with linear constraints), the optimal solution fails to be an extreme point of the feasible region, because the isoprofit curves are not straight lines. In fact, the optimal solution for an NLP may not be on the boundary of the feasible region. For example, consider the following NLP:

$$\max z = f(x)$$
$$\text{s.t.} \quad 0 \le x \le 1$$

Figure 1
An NLP Whose Optimal Solution Is Not an Extreme Point

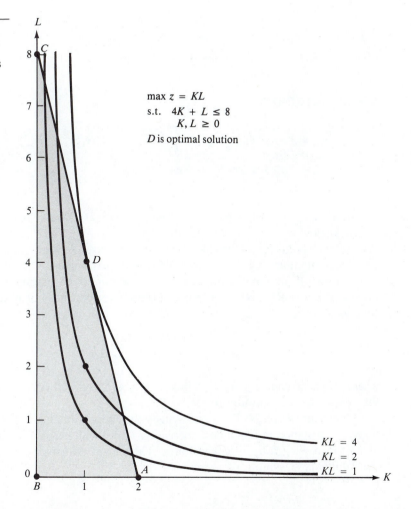

$\max z = KL$
s.t. $4K + L \le 8$
         $K, L \ge 0$
D is optimal solution

where $f(x)$ is pictured in Figure 2. The optimal solution for this NLP is $z = 1$, $x = \frac{1}{2}$. Of course, $x = \frac{1}{2}$ is not on the boundary of the feasible region.

Figure 2
An NLP Whose
Optimal Solution Is
Not on Boundary of
Feasible Region

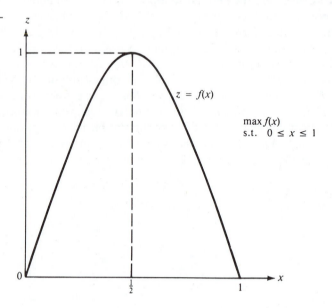

$z = f(x)$

$$\begin{aligned} \max & \ f(x) \\ \text{s.t.} & \ 0 \le x \le 1 \end{aligned}$$

LOCAL EXTREMUM

DEFINITION   For any NLP (maximization), a feasible point $x = (x_1, x_2, \ldots, x_n)$ is a **local maximum** if for sufficiently small ε, any feasible point $x' = (x_1', x_2', \ldots, x_n')$ having $|x_i - x_i'| < \varepsilon$ $(i = 1, 2, \ldots, n)$ satisfies $f(x) \ge f(x')$.

In short, a point x is a local maximum if $f(x) \ge f(x')$ for all feasible x' that are close to x. Analogously, for a minimization problem, a point x is a local minimum if $f(x) \le f(x')$ holds for all feasible x' that are close to x. A point that is a local maximum or a local minimum is called a **local**, or **relative**, **extremum**.

For an LP (max problem), any local maximum is an optimal solution to the LP. (Why?) For a general NLP, however, this may not be true. For example, consider the following NLP:

$$\max z = f(x)$$
$$\text{s.t.} \quad 0 \le x \le 10$$

where $f(x)$ is given in Figure 3. Points A, B, and C are all local maxima, but point C is the unique optimal solution to the NLP.

Unlike an LP, an NLP may not satisfy the Proportionality and Additivity assumptions. For instance, in Example 2, increasing L by 1 will increase z by K. Thus, the effect on z of increasing L by 1 depends on K. This means that the example does not satisfy the Additivity Assumption.

Figure 3
A Local Maximum
May Not Be the
Optimal Solution to
an NLP

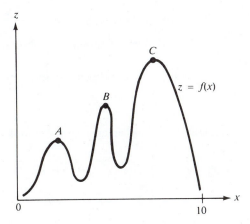

The NLP

$$\max z = x^{1/3} + y^{1/3}$$
$$\text{s.t.} \quad x + y = 1$$
$$x, y \geq 0$$

does not satisfy the Proportionality Assumption, because doubling the value of x does not double the contribution of x to the objective function.

◆ PROBLEMS

GROUP A

1. Q & H Company advertises on soap operas and football games. Each soap opera ad costs $50,000, and each football game ad costs $100,000. Giving all figures in millions of viewers, if S soap opera ads are bought, they will be seen by $5\sqrt{S}$ men and $20\sqrt{S}$ women. If F football ads are bought, they will be seen by $17\sqrt{F}$ men and $7\sqrt{F}$ women. Q & H wants at least 40 million men and at least 60 million women to see its ads.

(a) Formulate an NLP that will minimize Q & H's cost of reaching sufficient viewers.

(b) Does the NLP violate the Proportionality and Additivity Assumptions?

(c) Suppose that the number of women reached by F football ads and S soap opera ads is $7\sqrt{F} + 20\sqrt{S} - 0.2\sqrt{FS}$. Why might this be a more realistic representation of the number of women viewers seeing Q & H's ads?

2. The area of a triangle with sides of length a, b, and c is $\sqrt{s(s-a)(s-b)(s-c)}$, where s is half the perimeter of the triangle. We have 60 ft of fence and wish to fence a triangular-shaped area. Formulate an NLP that will enable us to maximize the fenced area.

3. The energy used in compressing a gas (in three stages) from an initial pressure I to a final pressure F is given by

$$K\left\{\sqrt{\frac{p_1}{I}} + \sqrt{\frac{p_2}{p_1}} + \sqrt{\frac{F}{p_2}} - 3\right\}$$

Formulate an NLP whose solution describes how to minimize the energy used in compressing the gas from I to F in three stages.

12-2   CONVEX AND CONCAVE FUNCTIONS

Convex and concave functions play an extremely important role in the study of nonlinear programming problems.

Let $f(x_1, x_2, \ldots, x_n)$ be a function that is defined for all points $(x_1, x_2, \ldots, x_n)$ in a convex set S.[†]

DEFINITION ■ A function $f(x_1, x_2, \ldots, x_n)$ is a **convex function** on a convex set S if for any $x' \in S$ and $x'' \in S$

$$f(cx' + (1 - c)x'') \leq cf(x') + (1 - c)f(x'') \tag{2}$$

holds for $0 \leq c \leq 1$.

DEFINITION ■ A function $f(x_1, x_2, \ldots, x_n)$ is a **concave function** on a convex set S if for any $x' \in S$ and $x'' \in S$

$$f(cx' + (1 - c)x'') \geq cf(x') + (1 - c)f(x'') \tag{3}$$

holds for $0 \leq c \leq 1$.

From (2) and (3), we see that $f(x_1, x_2, \ldots, x_n)$ is a convex function if and only if $-f(x_1, x_2, \ldots, x_n)$ is a concave function, and conversely.

To gain some insights into these definitions, let $f(x)$ be a function of a single variable. From Figure 4 and inequality (2), we find that $f(x)$ is convex if and only if the line segment joining any two points on the curve $y = f(x)$ is never below the curve $y = f(x)$. Similarly, Figure 5 and inequality (3) show that $f(x)$ is a concave function if and only if the straight line joining any two points on the curve $y = f(x)$ is never above the curve $y = f(x)$.

Figure 4
A Convex Function

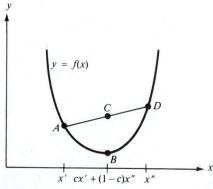

Point $A = (x', f(x'))$
Point $D = (x'', f(x''))$
Point $C = (cx' + (1 - c)x'', cf(x') + (1 - c)f(x''))$
Point $B = (cx' + (1 - c)x'', f(cx' + (1 - c)x''))$
From figure: $f(cx' + (1 - c)x'') \leq cf(x') + (1 - c)f(x'')$

[†] Recall from Chapter 3 that a set S is convex if $x' \in S$ and $x'' \in S$ imply that all points on the line segment joining x' and x'' are members of S. This ensures that $cx' + (1 - c)x''$ will be a member of S.

Figure 5
A Concave Function

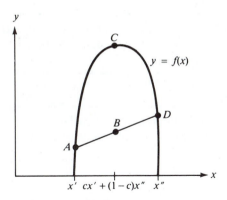

Point $A = (x', f(x'))$
Point $D = (x'', f(x''))$
Point $C = (cx' + (1 - c)x'', f(cx' + (1 - c)x''))$
Point $B = (cx' + (1 - c)x'', cf(x') + (1 - c)f(x''))$
From figure: $f(cx' + (1 - c)x'') \geq cf(x') + (1 - c)f(x'')$

E X A M P L E 3

For $x \geq 0, f(x) = x^2$ and $f(x) = e^x$ are convex functions and $f(x) = x^{1/2}$ is a concave function. These facts are evident from Figure 6.

Figure 6
Examples of Convex and Concave Functions

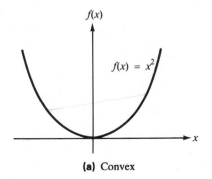

(a) Convex

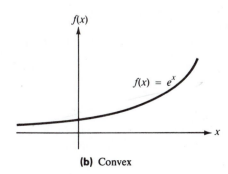

(b) Convex

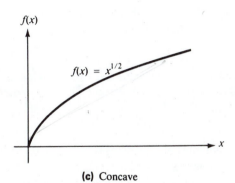

(c) Concave

E X A M P L E
4

It can be shown (see Problem 11 at the end of this section) that the sum of two convex functions is convex and the sum of two concave functions is concave. Thus, $f(x) = x^2 + e^x$ is a convex function.

E X A M P L E
5

Since the line segment AB lies below $y = f(x)$ and the line segment BC lies above $y = f(x)$, $f(x)$ as pictured in Figure 7 is not a convex or a concave function.

Figure 7
A Function That Is
Neither Convex Nor
Concave

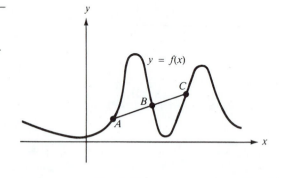

E X A M P L E
6

A linear function of the form $f(x) = ax + b$ is both a convex and a concave function. This follows from

$$f(cx' + (1 - c)x'') = a[cx' + (1 - c)x''] + b$$
$$= c(ax' + b) + (1 - c)(ax'' + b)$$
$$= cf(x') + (1 - c)f(x'')$$

Since both (2) and (3) hold with equality, $f(x) = ax + b$ is both a convex and a concave function.

Before discussing how to determine whether a given function is convex or concave, we prove a result that illustrates the importance of convex and concave functions.

THEOREM 1

Consider NLP (1) and assume it is a maximization problem. Suppose the feasible region S for NLP (1) is a convex set. If $f(x)$ is concave on S, then any local maximum for NLP (1) is an optimal solution to this NLP.

Proof

If the Theorem 1 is false, there must be a local maximum $\bar{x}$ that is not an optimal solution to NLP (1). Let S be the feasible region for NLP (1) (we have assumed that S is a convex set). Then, for some $x \in S$, $f(x) > f(\bar{x})$. Then inequality (3) implies that for any c satisfying $0 < c < 1$,

$$f(c\bar{x} + (1 - c)x) \geq cf(\bar{x}) + (1 - c)f(x)$$
$$> cf(\bar{x}) + (1 - c)f(\bar{x}) \quad \text{(from } f(x) > f(\bar{x}))$$
$$= f(\bar{x})$$

Now observe that for c arbitrarily near 1, $c\bar{x} + (1 - c)x$ is feasible (because S is convex) and is near $\bar{x}$. Thus, $\bar{x}$ cannot be a local maximum. This contradiction proves Theorem 1. ◆

Similar reasoning can be used to prove Theorem 1′ (See Problem 10 at the end of this section).

THEOREM 1′	Consider NLP (1) and assume it is a minimization problem. Suppose the feasible region S for NLP (1) is a convex set. If $f(x)$ is convex on S, then any local minimum for NLP (1) is an optimal solution to this NLP.

Theorems 1 and 1′ demonstrate that if we are maximizing a concave function (or minimizing a convex function) over a convex feasible region S, then any local maximum (or local minimum) will solve NLP (1). As we solve NLPs, we will repeatedly apply Theorems 1 and 1′.

We now explain how to determine if a function $f(x)$ of a single variable is convex or concave. Recall that if $f(x)$ is a convex function of a single variable, the line joining any two points on $y = f(x)$ is never below the curve $y = f(x)$. From Figures 4 and 6, we see that $f(x)$ convex implies that the slope of $f(x)$ must be nondecreasing for all values of x.

THEOREM 2	Suppose $f''(x)$ exists for all x in a convex set S. Then $f(x)$ is a convex function on S if and only if $f''(x) \geq 0$ for all x in S.

Since $f(x)$ is convex if and only if $-f(x)$ is concave, Theorem 2′ must also be true.

THEOREM 2′	Suppose $f''(x)$ exists for all x in a convex set S. Then $f(x)$ is a concave function on S if and only if $f''(x) \leq 0$ for all x in S.

E X A M P L E 7

1. Show that $f(x) = x^2$ is a convex function on $S = R^1$.
2. Show that $f(x) = e^x$ is a convex function on $S = R^1$.
3. Show that $f(x) = x^{1/2}$ is a concave function on $S = (0, \infty)$.
4. Show that $f(x) = ax + b$ is both a convex and a concave function on $S = R^1$.

Solution

1. $f''(x) = 2 \geq 0$, so $f(x)$ is convex on $S = R^1$.
2. $f''(x) = e^x \geq 0$, so $f(x)$ is convex on $S = R^1$.

3. $f''(x) = -x^{-3/2}/4 \le 0$, so $f(x)$ is a concave function on $S(0, \infty)$.

4. $f''(x) = 0$, so $f(x)$ is both convex and concave on $S = R^1$.

◆

How can we determine whether a function $f(x_1, x_2, \ldots, x_n)$ of n variables is convex or concave on a set $S \subset R^n$? We assume that $f(x_1, x_2, \ldots, x_n)$ has continuous second-order partial derivatives. Before stating the criterion used to determine whether $f(x_1, x_2, \ldots, x_n)$ is convex or concave, we require three definitions.

DEFINITION ▪ The **Hessian** of $f(x_1, x_2, \ldots, x_n)$ is the $n \times n$ matrix whose ijth entry is

$$\frac{\partial^2 f}{\partial x_i \partial x_j}$$

We let $H(x_1, x_2, \ldots, x_n)$ denote the value of the Hessian at $(x_1, x_2, \ldots, x_n)$. For example, if $f(x_1, x_2) = x_1^3 + 2x_1 x_2 + x_2^2$, then

$$H(x_1, x_2) = \begin{bmatrix} 6x_1 & 2 \\ 2 & 2 \end{bmatrix}$$

DEFINITION ▪ An **ith principal minor** of an $n \times n$ matrix is the determinant of any $i \times i$ matrix obtained by deleting $n - i$ rows and the corresponding $n - i$ columns of the matrix.

Thus, for the matrix

$$\begin{bmatrix} -2 & -1 \\ -1 & -4 \end{bmatrix}$$

the first principal minors are -2 and -4, and the second principal minor is $-2(-4) - (-1)(-1) = 7$. For any matrix, the first principal minors are just the diagonal entries of the matrix.

DEFINITION ▪ The **kth leading principal minor** of an $n \times n$ matrix is the determinant of the $k \times k$ matrix obtained by deleting the last $n - k$ rows and columns of the matrix.

We let $H_k(x_1, x_2, \ldots, x_n)$ be the kth leading principal minor of the Hessian matrix evaluated at the point $(x_1, x_2, \ldots, x_n)$. Thus, if $f(x_1, x_2) = x_1^3 + 2x_1 x_2 + x_2^2$, then $H_1(x_1, x_2) = 6x_1$, and $H_2(x_1, x_2) = 6x_1(2) - 2(2) = 12x_1 - 4$.

By applying Theorems 3 and 3′ (stated on the next page, without proof), the Hessian matrix can be used to determine whether $f(x_1, x_2, \ldots, x_n)$ is a convex or a concave (or neither) function on a convex set $S \subset R^n$. (See Bazaraa and Shetty (1979) for proof of Theorems 3 and 3′).

| THEOREM 3 | Suppose $f(x_1, x_2, \ldots, x_n)$ has continuous second-order partial derivatives for each point $x = (x_1, x_2, \ldots, x_n) \in S$. Then $f(x_1, x_2, \ldots, x_n)$ is a convex function on S if and only if for each $x \in S$, all principal minors of H are nonnegative. |

E X A M P L E
8

Show that $f(x_1, x_2) = x_1^2 + 2x_1 x_2 + x_2^2$ is a convex function on $S = R^2$.

Solution

We find that

$$H(x_1, x_2) = \begin{bmatrix} 2 & 2 \\ 2 & 2 \end{bmatrix}$$

The first principal minors of the Hessian are the diagonal entries (both equal $2 \geq 0$). The second principal minor is $2(2) - 2(2) = 0 \geq 0$. Since for any point, all principal minors of H are nonnegative, Theorem 3 shows that $f(x_1, x_2)$ is a convex function on R^2.

◆

| THEOREM 3' | Suppose $f(x_1, x_2, \ldots, x_n)$ has continuous second-order partial derivatives for each point $x = (x_1, x_2, \ldots, x_n) \in S$. Then $f(x_1, x_2, \ldots, x_n)$ is a concave function on S if and only if for each $x \in S$ and $k = 1, 2, \ldots n$, all nonzero principal minors have the same sign as $(-1)^k$. *(alternate start at negative)* |

E X A M P L E
9

Show that $f(x_1, x_2) = -x_1^2 - x_1 x_2 - 2x_2^2$ is a concave function on R^2.

Solution

We find that

$$H(x_1, x_2) = \begin{bmatrix} -2 & -1 \\ -1 & -4 \end{bmatrix}$$

The first principal minors are the diagonal entries of the Hessian (-2 and -4). These are both nonpositive. The second principal minor is the determinant of $H(x_1, x_2)$ and equals $-2(-4) - (-1)(-1) = 7 > 0$. Thus, $f(x_1, x_2)$ is a concave function on R^2.

◆

E X A M P L E
10

Show that for $S = R^2$, $f(x_1, x_2) = x_1^2 - 3x_1 x_2 + 2x_2^2$ is not a convex or a concave function.

Solution

We have

$$H(x_1, x_2) = \begin{bmatrix} 2 & -3 \\ -3 & 4 \end{bmatrix}$$

The first principal minors of the Hessian are 2 and 4. Since both the first principal minors are positive, $f(x_1, x_2)$ cannot be concave. The second principal minor is $2(4) - (-3)(-3) = -1 < 0$. Thus, $f(x_1, x_2)$ cannot be convex. Together, these facts show that $f(x_1, x_2)$ cannot be a convex or a concave function.

◆

◆ PROBLEMS

GROUP A

On the given set S, determine whether each function is convex, concave, or neither.

1. $f(x) = x^3$; $S = [0, \infty)$

2. $f(x) = x^3$; $S = R^1$

3. $f(x) = \frac{1}{x}$; $S = (0, \infty)$

4. $f(x) = x^a$ $(0 \le a \le 1)$; $S = (0, \infty)$

5. $f(x) = \ln x$; $S = (0, \infty)$

6. $f(x_1, x_2) = x_1^3 + 3x_1 x_2 + x_2^2$; $S = R^2$

7. $f(x_1, x_2) = x_1^2 + x_2^2$; $S = R^2$

8. $f(x_1, x_2) = -x_1^2 - x_1 x_2 - 2x_2^2$; $S = R^2$

9. For what values of a, b, and c will $ax_1^2 + bx_1 x_2 + cx_2^2$ be a convex function on R^2? A concave function on R^2?

GROUP B

10. Prove Theorem 1′.

11. Show that if $f(x_1, x_2, \ldots, x_n)$ and $g(x_1, x_2, \ldots, x_n)$ are convex functions on a convex set S, then $h(x_1, x_2, \ldots, x_n) = f(x_1, x_2, \ldots, x_n) + g(x_1, x_2, \ldots, x_n)$ is a convex function on S.

12. If $f(x_1, x_2, \ldots, x_n)$ is a convex function on a convex set S, show that for $c \ge 0$, $g(x_1, x_2, \ldots, x_n) = cf(x_1, x_2, \ldots, x_n)$ is a convex function on S, and for $c \le 0$, $g(x_1, x_2, \ldots, x_n) = cf(x_1, x_2, \ldots, x_n)$ is a concave function on S.

13. Show that if $y = f(x)$ is a concave function on R^1, then $z = \frac{1}{f(x)}$ is a convex function (assume that $f(x) > 0$).

14. A function $f(x_1, x_2, \ldots, x_n)$ is *quasiconcave* on a convex set $S \subset R^n$ if $x' \in S$, $x'' \in S$, and $0 \le c \le 1$ implies

$$f(cx' + (1 - c)x'') \ge \min\{f(x'), f(x'')\}$$

Show that if f is concave on R^1, then f is quasiconcave. Which of the functions in Figure 8 is quasiconcave? Is a quasiconcave function necessarily a concave function?

15. From Problem 11, it follows that the sum of concave functions is concave. Is the sum of quasiconcave functions necessarily quasiconcave?

16. Suppose a function's Hessian has both positive and negative entries on its diagonal. Show that the function is neither concave nor convex.

17. Show that if $f(x)$ is a nonnegative, increasing concave function, then $\ln(f(x))$ is also a concave function.

GROUP C

18. If $f(x_1, x_2)$ is a concave function on R^2, show that for any number a, the set of (x_1, x_2) satisfying $f(x_1, x_2) \ge a$ is a convex set.

19. Let $\mathbf{Z}$ be a $N(0, 1)$ random variable, and let $F(x)$ be the cumulative distribution function for $\mathbf{Z}$. Show that on $S = (-\infty, 0]$, $F(x)$ is an increasing convex function, and on $S = [0, \infty)$, $F(x)$ is an increasing concave function.

20. Recall the Dakota LP discussed in Chapter 6. Let $v(L, FH, CH)$ be the maximum revenue that can be earned when L sq board ft of lumber, FH finishing hours, and CH carpentry hours are available.
(a) Show that $v(L, FH, CH)$ is a concave function.
(b) Explain why this result shows that the value of each additional available unit of a resource must be a nonincreasing function of the amount of the resource that is available.

Figure 8

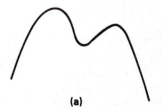

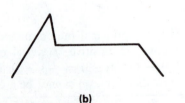

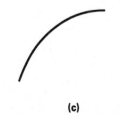

(a) (b) (c)

12-3   SOLVING NLPs WITH ONE VARIABLE

In this section, we explain how to solve the NLP

$$\max \text{ (or min) } f(x)$$
$$\text{s.t. } x \in [a, b] \tag{4}$$

(If $b = \infty$, the feasible region for NLP (4) is $x \geq a$, and if $a = -\infty$, the feasible region for (4) is $x \leq b$.)

To find the optimal solution to (4), we find all local maxima (or minima). A point that is a local maximum or a local minimum for (4) is called a local extremum. Then the optimal solution to (4) is the local maximum (or minimum) having the largest (or smallest) value of $f(x)$. Of course, if $a = -\infty$ or $b = \infty$, (4) may have no optimal solution (see Figure 9).

Figure 9
NLPs with No
Solution

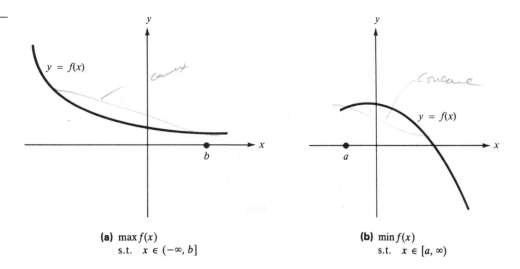

(a) $\max f(x)$
    s.t. $x \in (-\infty, b]$

(b) $\min f(x)$
    s.t. $x \in [a, \infty)$

There are three types of points for which (4) can have a local maximum or minimum (these points are often called extremum candidates):

Case 1 Points where $a < x < b$, and $f'(x) = 0$ (called a stationary point of $f(x)$).

Case 2 Points where $f''(x)$ does not exist.

Case 3 Endpoints a and b of the interval $[a, b]$.

CASE 1. POINTS WHERE $a < x < b$ AND $f'(x) = 0$

Suppose $a < x < b$, and $f'(x_0)$ exists. If x_0 is a local maximum or a local minimum, then $f'(x_0) = 0$. To see this, look at Figures 10a and 10b. From Figure 10a, we see that if $f'(x_0) > 0$, then there are points x_1 and x_2 near x_0 where $f(x_1) < f(x_0)$ and $f(x_2) > f(x_0)$. Thus, if $f'(x_0) > 0$, x_0 cannot be a local maximum or a local minimum. Similarly, Figure 10b shows that if $f'(x_0) < 0$, then x_0 cannot be a local maximum or a local minimum. From Figures 10c and 10d, however, we see that if $f'(x_0) = 0$, then x_0 may be a local maximum or a local minimum. Unfortunately, Figure 10e shows that

Figure 10
How to Determine
Whether x_0 Is a
Local Maximum or a
Local Minimum
When $f'(x_0)$ Exists

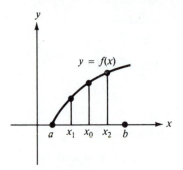

(a) $f'(x_0) > 0$
$f(x_1) < f(x_0)$
$f(x_2) > f(x_0)$
x_0 not a local extremum

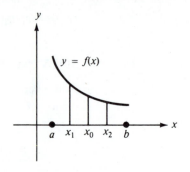

(b) $f'(x_0) < 0$
$f(x_1) > f(x_0)$
$f(x_2) < f(x_0)$
x_0 not a local extremum

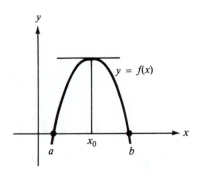

(c) $f'(x_0) = 0$
For $x < x_0, f'(x) > 0$
For $x > x_0, f'(x) < 0$
x_0 is a local maximum

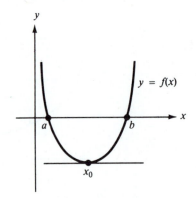

(d) $f'(x_0) = 0$
For $x < x_0, f'(x) < 0$
For $x > x_0, f'(x) > 0$
x_0 is a local minimum

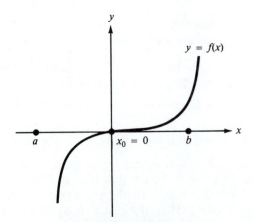

(e) $x_0 = 0$ not a local maximum
or a local minimum
but $f'(x_0) = 0$

$f'(x_0)$ can equal zero without x_0 being a local maximum or a local minimum. From Figure 10c, we see that if $f'(x)$ changes from positive to negative as we pass through x_0, then x_0 is a local maximum. Thus, if $f''(x_0) < 0$, x_0 is a local maximum. Similarly, from Figure 10d, we see that if $f'(x)$ changes from negative to positive as we pass through x_0, x_0 is a local minimum. Thus, if $f''(x_0) > 0$, x_0 is a local minimum.

THEOREM 4	If $f'(x_0) = 0$ and $f''(x_0) < 0$, then x_0 is a local maximum. If $f'(x_0) = 0$ and $f''(x_0) > 0$, then x_0 is a local minimum.

What happens if $f'(x_0) = 0$ and $f''(x_0) = 0$ (this is the case in Figure 10e)? In this case, we determine whether x_0 is a local maximum or a local minimum by applying Theorem 5.

THEOREM 5	If $f'(x_0) = 0$,
	1. If the first nonvanishing (nonzero) derivative at x_0 is an odd-order derivative ($f^{(3)}(x_0)$, $f^{(5)}(x_0)$, etc.), then x_0 is not a local maximum or a local minimum.
	2. If the first nonvanishing derivative at x_0 is positive and is an even-order derivative, then x_0 is a local minimum.
	3. If the first nonvanishing derivative at x_0 is negative and is an even-order derivative, then x_0 is a local maximum.

We omit the proofs of Theorems 4 and 5. (They follow in a straightforward fashion by applying the definition of a local maximum and a local minimum to the Taylor series expansion of $f(x)$ about x_0.) Theorem 4 is a special case of Theorem 5.

CASE 2. POINTS WHERE $f'(x)$ DOES NOT EXIST

If $f(x)$ does not have a derivative at x_0, x_0 may be a local maximum, a local minimum, or neither (see Figure 11). In this case, we determine whether x_0 is a local maximum or a local minimum by checking values of $f(x)$ at points $x_1 < x_0$ and $x_2 > x_0$ near x_0. The four possible cases that can occur are summarized in Table 1.

CASE 3. ENDPOINTS a AND b OF $[a, b]$

From Figure 12, we see that

If $f'(a) > 0$, then a is a local minimum.

If $f'(a) < 0$, then a is a local maximum.

If $f'(b) > 0$, then b is a local maximum.

If $f'(b) < 0$, then b is a local minimum.

If $f'(a) = 0$ or $f'(b) = 0$, draw a sketch like Figure 11 to determine whether a or b is a local extremum.

The following examples illustrate how these ideas can be applied to solve NLPs of the form (4).

Figure 11
How to Determine
Whether x_0 Is a
Local Maximum or a
Local Minimum
When $f'(x_0)$ Does
Not Exist

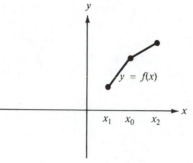

(a) x_0 not a local extremum

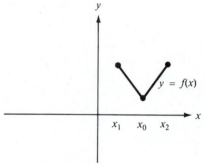

(b) x_0 not a local extremum

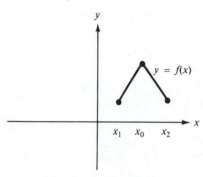

(c) x_0 is a local maximum

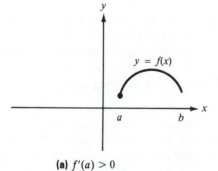

(d) x_0 is a local minimum

Figure 12
How to Determine
Whether x_0 Is a
Local Maximum or a
Local Minimum If x_0
Is an Endpoint

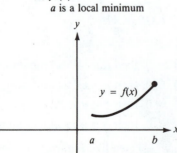

(a) $f'(a) > 0$
a is a local minimum

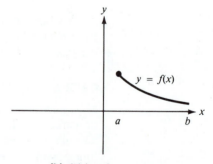

(b) $f'(a) < 0$
a is a local maximum

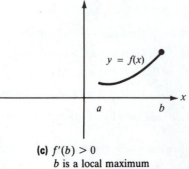

(c) $f'(b) > 0$
b is a local maximum

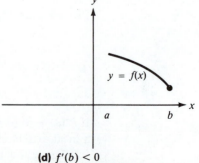

(d) $f'(b) < 0$
b is a local minimum

Table 1	RELATIONSHIP BETWEEN		
How to Determine Whether a Point Where $f'(x)$ Does Not Exist Is a Local Maximum or a Local Minimum	$f(x_0), f(x_1),$ AND $f(x_2)$	x_0	FIGURE
	$f(x_0) > f(x_1); f(x_0) < f(x_2)$	Not local extremum	11a
	$f(x_0) < f(x_1); f(x_0) > f(x_2)$	Not local extremum	11b
	$f(x_0) \geq f(x_1); f(x_0) \geq f(x_2)$	Local maximum	11c
	$f(x_0) \leq f(x_1); f(x_0) \leq f(x_2)$	Local minimum	11d

E X A M P L E 11

It costs a monopolist $5/unit to produce a product. If he produces x units of the product, each unit can be sold for $10 - x$ dollars $(0 \leq x \leq 10)$. In order to maximize profit, how much should the monopolist produce?

Solution

Let $P(x)$ be the monopolist's profit if he produces x units. Then

$$P(x) = x(10 - x) - 5x = 5x - x^2 \quad (0 \leq x \leq 10)$$

Thus, the monopolist wishes to solve the following NLP:

$$\max P(x)$$
$$\text{s.t.} \quad 0 \leq x \leq 10$$

We now classify all extremum candidates:

Case 1 $P'(x) = 5 - 2x$, so $P'(2.5) = 0$. Since $P''(x) = -2$, $x = 2.5$ is a local maximum yielding a profit of $P(2.5) = 6.25$.

Case 2 $P'(x)$ exists for all points in $[0, 10]$, so there are no Case 2 candidates.

Case 3 $a = 0$ has $P'(0) = 5 > 0$, so $a = 0$ is a local minimum; $b = 10$ has $P'(10) = -15 < 0$, so $b = 10$ is a local minimum.

Thus, $x = 2.5$ is the only local maximum. This means that the monopolist's profits are maximized by choosing $x = 2.5$.

Observe that $P''(x) = -2$ for all values of x. This shows that $P(x)$ is a concave function. Any local maximum for $P(x)$ must be the optimal solution to the NLP. Thus, Theorem 1 implies that once we have determined that $x = 2.5$ is a local maximum, we know that it is the optimal solution to the NLP.

◆

E X A M P L E 12

Let

$$f(x) = 2 - (x - 1)^2 \quad \text{for} \quad 0 \leq x < 3$$
$$f(x) = -3 + (x - 4)^2 \quad \text{for} \quad 3 \leq x \leq 6$$

Find

$$\max f(x)$$
$$\text{s.t.} \quad 0 \leq x \leq 6$$

Solution

Case 1 For $0 \leq x < 3$, $f'(x) = -2(x - 1)$ and $f''(x) = -2$. For $3 < x \leq 6$, $f'(x) = 2(x - 4)$ and $f''(x) = 2$. Thus, $f'(1) = f'(4) = 0$. Since $f''(1) < 0$, $x = 1$ is a local maximum. Since $f''(4) > 0$, $x = 4$ is a local minimum.

Figure 13
Graph for
Example 12

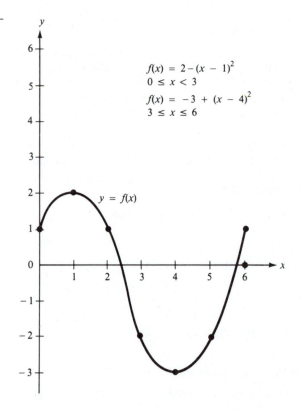

$$f(x) = 2 - (x - 1)^2$$
$$0 \le x < 3$$
$$f(x) = -3 + (x - 4)^2$$
$$3 \le x \le 6$$

$y = f(x)$

Case 2 From Figure 13, we see that $f(x)$ has no derivative at $x = 3$ (for x slightly less than 3, $f'(x)$ is near -4, and for x slightly bigger than 3, $f'(x)$ is near -2). Since $f(2.9) = -1.61, f(3) = -2$, and $f(3.1) = -2.19$, $x = 3$ is not a local extremum.

Case 3 Since $f'(0) = 2 > 0$, $x = 0$ is a local minimum. Since $f'(6) = 4 > 0$, $x = 6$ is a local maximum.

Thus, on $[0, 6]$, $f(x)$ has a local maximum for $x = 1$ and $x = 6$. Since $f(1) = 2$ and $f(6) = 1$, we find that the optimal solution to the NLP occurs for $x = 1$. ◆

If we are trying to maximize a function $f(x)$ that is a product of several functions, it is often easier to maximize $\ln(f(x))$. Since ln is an increasing function, we know that any x^* solving max $z' = \ln(f(x))$ subject to $x \in S$ will also solve max $z = f(x)$ over $x \in S$. See Problem 4 for an application of this idea.

◆ PROBLEMS

GROUP A

1. It costs a company $100 in variable costs to produce an air conditioner, plus a fixed cost of $5000 if any air conditioners are produced. If the company spends x dollars on advertising, it can sell $x^{1/2}$ air conditioners at $300 per air conditioner. How can the company maximize its profit? If the fixed cost of producing any air conditioners were $20,000, what should the company do?

2. If a monopolist produces q units, she can charge $100 - 4q$ dollars/unit. The fixed cost of production is $50 and the variable per-unit cost is $2. How can the monopolist maximize profits? If a sales tax of $2/unit must be paid by the monopolist, would she increase or decrease production?

3. Show that for all x, $e^x \geq x + 1$. (*Hint:* Let $f(x) = e^x - x - 1$. Show that

$$\min f(x)$$
$$\text{s.t.} \quad x \in R$$

occurs for $x = 0$.)

4. Suppose that in n "at bats," a baseball player gets x hits. Suppose we wish to estimate the player's probability (p) of getting a hit on each "at bat." The method of maximum likelihood estimates p by $\hat{p}$, where $\hat{p}$ maximizes the probability of observing x hits in n "at bats." Show that the method of maximum likelihood would choose $\hat{p} = \frac{x}{n}$.

5. Find the optimal solution to

$$\max x^3$$
$$\text{s.t.} \quad -1 \leq x \leq 1$$

6. Find the optimal solution to

$$\min x^3 - 3x^2 + 2x - 1.$$
$$\text{s.t.} \quad -2 \leq x \leq 4$$

GROUP B

7. It costs a company $c(x)$ dollars to produce x units. The curve $y = c'(x)$ is called the firm's marginal cost curve. (Why?) The firm's average cost curve is given by $z = \frac{c(x)}{x}$.

Let x^* be the production level that minimizes the company's average cost. Give conditions under which the marginal cost curve intersects the average cost curve at x^*.

8. When a machine is t years old, it earns revenue at a rate of e^{-t} dollars per year. After t years of use, the machine can be sold for $\frac{1}{t+1}$ dollars.

(a) In order to maximize total revenue, when should the machine be sold?

(b) If revenue is discounted continuously (so that $1 of revenue received t years from now is equivalent to e^{-rt} dollars of revenue received now), how would the answer in part (a) change?

9.[†] Suppose a company must service customers lying in an area of A sq mi with n warehouses. Kolesar and Blum have shown that the average distance between a warehouse and a customer is

$$\sqrt{\frac{A}{n}}$$

Assume that it costs the company $60,000 per year to maintain a warehouse and $400,000 to build a warehouse. (Assume that a $400,000 cost is equivalent to forever incurring a cost of $40,000 per year). The company fills 160,000 orders per year, and the shipping cost per order is $1 per mile. If the company serves an area of 100 sq mi, how many warehouses should it have?

[†] Based on Kolesar and Blum (1973).

GOLDEN SECTION SEARCH

Consider a function $f(x)$. (For some x, $f'(x)$ may not exist.) Suppose we want to solve the following NLP:

$$\max f(x)$$
$$\text{s.t.} \quad a \leq x \leq b \tag{5}$$

It may be that $f'(x)$ does not exist, or it may be difficult to solve the equation $f'(x) = 0$. In either case, it may be difficult to use the methods of the previous section to solve this NLP. In this section, we discuss how (5) can be solved if $f(x)$ is a special type of function (a unimodal function).

DEFINITION

A function $f(x)$ is **unimodal** on $[c, b]$ if for some point $\bar{x}$ on $[a, b]$, $f(x)$ is strictly increasing on $[a, \bar{x}]$ and strictly decreasing on $[\bar{x}, b]$.

If $f(x)$ is unimodal on $[a, b]$, then $f(x)$ will have only one local maximum ($\bar{x}$) on $[a, b]$ and that local maximum will solve (5) (see Figure 14). Let $\bar{x}$ denote the optimal solution to (5).

Figure 14
Definition of a
Unimodal Function

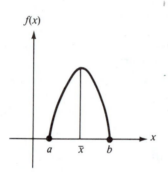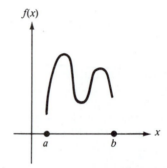

(a) A unimodal function on $[a, b]$
$\bar{x}$ = local maximum and solution to
$\max f(x)$
s.t. $a \le x \le b$

(b) A function that is not unimodal on $[a, b]$

Without any further information, all we can say is that the optimal solution to (5) is some point on the interval $[a, b]$. By evaluating $f(x)$ at two points x_1 and x_2 (assume $x_1 < x_2$) on $[a, b]$, we may reduce the size of the interval in which the solution to (5) must lie. After evaluating $f(x_1)$ and $f(x_2)$, one of three cases must occur. In each case, we can show that the optimal solution to (5) will lie in a subset of $[a, b]$.

Case 1 $f(x_1) < f(x_2)$. Since $f(x)$ is increasing for at least part of the interval $[x_1, x_2]$, the fact that $f(x)$ is unimodal shows that the optimal solution to (5) cannot occur on $[a, x_1]$. Thus, in Case 1, $\bar{x} \in (x_1, b]$ (see Figure 15).

Figure 15
If $f(x_1) < f(x_2)$,
$\bar{x} \in (x_1, b]$

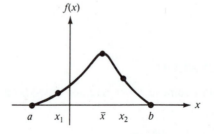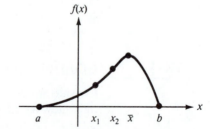

Case 2 $f(x_1) = f(x_2)$. For some part of the interval $[x_1, x_2]$, $f(x)$ must be decreasing, and the optimal solution to (5) must occur for some $\bar{x} < x_2$. Thus, in Case 2, $\bar{x} \in [a, x_2)$ (see Figure 16).

Case 3 $f(x_1) > f(x_2)$. In this case, $f(x)$ begins decreasing before x reaches x_2. Thus, $\bar{x} \in [a, x_2)$ (see Figure 17).

Figure 16
If $f(x_1) = f(x_2)$,
$\bar{x} \in [a, x_2)$

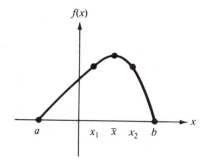

Figure 17
If $f(x_1) > f(x_2)$,
$\bar{x} \in [a, x_2)$

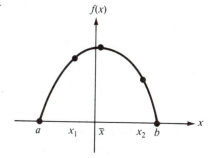
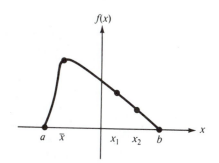

The interval in which $\bar{x}$ must lie—either $[a, x_2)$ or $(x_1, b]$—is called the **interval of uncertainty**.

Many search algorithms use these ideas to reduce the interval of uncertainty (see Bazaraa and Shetty (1979, Section 8.1)). Most of these algorithms proceed as follows:

Step 1 Begin with the region of uncertainty for x being $[a, b]$. Evaluate $f(x)$ at two judiciously chosen points x_1 and x_2.

Step 2 Determine which of Cases 1–3 holds, and find a reduced interval of uncertainty.

Step 3 Evaluate $f(x)$ at two new points (the algorithm specifies how the two new points are chosen). Return to Step 2 unless the length of the interval of uncertainty is sufficiently small.

We discuss in detail one such search algorithm: Golden Section Search. In using this algorithm to solve (5) for a unimodal function $f(x)$, we will see that when we choose two new points at Step 3, one of the new points will always coincide with a point at which we have previously evaluated $f(x)$.

Let r be the unique positive root of the quadratic equation $r^2 + r = 1$. Then the quadratic formula yields that

$$r = \frac{5^{1/2} - 1}{2} = 0.618$$

(See Problem 3 at the end of this section for an explanation of why r is referred to as the Golden Section.) Golden Section Search begins by evaluating $f(x)$ at points x_1 and x_2, where $x_1 = b - r(b - a)$, and $x_2 = a + r(b - a)$ (see Figure 18). From this figure, we see that to find x_1, we move a fraction r of the interval from the right endpoint of

Figure 18
Location of x_1 and
x_2 for Golden
Section Search

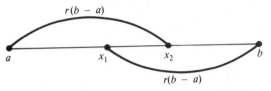

the interval, and to find x_2, we move a fraction r of the interval from the left endpoint of the interval. Then Golden Section Search generates two new points, at which $f(x)$ should again be evaluated with the following moves:

New Left-Hand Point Move a distance equal to a fraction r of the current interval of uncertainty from the right endpoint of the interval of uncertainty.

New Right-Hand Point Move a distance equal to a fraction r of the current interval of uncertainty from the left endpoint of the interval.

From our discussion of Cases 1–3, we know that if $f(x_1) < f(x_2)$, then $\bar{x} \in (x_1, b]$, whereas if $f(x_1) \geq f(x_2)$, then $\bar{x} \in [a, x_2)$. If $f(x_1) < f(x_2)$, the reduced interval of uncertainty has length $b - x_1 = r(b - a)$, and if $f(x_1) \geq f(x_2)$, the reduced interval of uncertainty has a length $x_2 - a = r(b - a)$. Thus, after evaluating $f(x_1)$ and $f(x_2)$, we have reduced the interval of uncertainty to a length $r(b - a)$.

Each time $f(x)$ is evaluated at two points and the interval of uncertainty is reduced, we say that an iteration of Golden Section Search has been completed. Define

$$L_k = \text{length of the interval of uncertainty}$$
$$\text{after } k \text{ iterations of the algorithm have been completed}$$

$$I_k = \text{interval of uncertainty}$$
$$\text{after } k \text{ iterations have been completed}$$

Then we see that $L_1 = r(b - a)$, and $I_1 = [a, x_2)$ or $I_1 = (x_1, b]$.

Following this procedure, we generate two new points, x_3 and x_4, at which $f(x)$ must be evaluated.

Case 1 $f(x_1) < f(x_2)$. The new interval of uncertainty, $(x_1, b]$, has length $b - x_1 = r(b - a)$. Then (see Figure 19a)

$$x_3 = \text{new left-hand point} = b - r(b - x_1) = b - r^2(b - a)$$
$$x_4 = \text{new right-hand point} = x_1 + r(b - x_1)$$

The new left-hand point, x_3, will equal the old right-hand point, x_2. To see this, use the fact that $r^2 = 1 - r$ to conclude that $x_3 = b - r^2(b - a) = b - (1 - r)(b - a) = a + r(b - a) = x_2$.

Case 2 $f(x_1) \geq f(x_2)$. The new interval of uncertainty, $[a, x_2)$, has length $x_2 - a = r(b - a)$. Then (see Figure 19b)

$$x_3 = \text{new left-hand point} = x_2 - r(x_2 - a)$$
$$x_4 = \text{new right-hand point} = a + r(x_2 - a) = a + r^2(b - a)$$

The new right-hand point, x_4, will equal the old left-hand point, x_1. To see this, use the fact that $r^2 = 1 - r$ to conclude that $x_4 = a + r^2(b - a) = a + (1 - r)(b - a) = b - r(b - a) = x_1$.

Figure 19
How to Generate
New Points in
Golden Section
Search

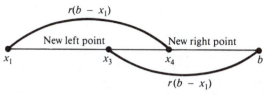

$r(b - x_1)$

New left point   New right point

x_1 x_3 x_4 b

$r(b - x_1)$

(a) If $f(x_1) < f(x_2)$, new interval of uncertainty is $(x_1, b]$

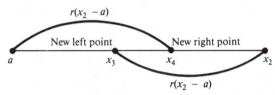

$r(x_2 - a)$

New left point   New right point

a x_3 x_4 x_2

$r(x_2 - a)$

(b) If $f(x_1) \geq f(x_2)$, new interval of uncertainty is $[a, x_2)$

Now the values of $f(x_3)$ and $f(x_4)$ can be used to reduce further the length of the interval of uncertainty. At this point, two iterations of Golden Section Search have been completed.

We have shown that at each iteration of Golden Section Search, $f(x)$ must be evaluated at only one of the new points. It is easy to see that $L_2 = rL_1 = r^2(b - a)$ and, in general, $L_k = rL_{k-1}$ yields that $L_k = r^k(b - a)$. Thus, if we want our final interval of uncertainty to have a length $< \varepsilon$, we must perform k iterations of Golden Section Search, where $r^k(b - a) < \varepsilon$.

**E X A M P L E
13**

Use Golden Section Search to find

$$\max -x^2 - 1$$

$$\text{s.t.} \quad -1 \leq x \leq 0.75$$

with the final interval of uncertainty having a length less than $\frac{1}{4}$.

Solution

Here $a = -1$, $b = 0.75$, and $b - a = 1.75$. To determine the number k of iterations of Golden Section Search that must be performed, we solve for k using $1.75(0.618^k) < 0.25$, or $0.618^k < \frac{1}{7}$. Taking logarithms to base e of both sides, we obtain

$$k \ln 0.618 < \ln \tfrac{1}{7}$$

$$k(-0.48) < -1.95$$

$$k > \tfrac{1.95}{0.48} = 4.06$$

Thus, five iterations of Golden Section Search must be performed. We first determine x_1 and x_2:

$$x_1 = 0.75 - (0.618)(1.75) = -0.3315$$

$$x_2 = -1 + (0.618)(1.75) = 0.0815$$

Then $f(x_1) = -1.1098$ and $f(x_2) = -1.0066$. Since $f(x_1) < f(x_2)$, the new interval of uncertainty is $I_1 = (x_1, b] = (-0.3315, 0.75]$, and we have that $x_3 = x_2$. Of course,

$L_1 = 0.75 + 0.3315 = 1.0815$. We now determine the two new points x_3 and x_4:

$$x_3 = x_2 = 0.0815$$
$$x_4 = -0.3315 + 0.618(1.0815) = 0.3369$$

Now $f(x_3) = f(x_2) = -1.0066$ and $f(x_4) = -1.1135$. Since $f(x_3) > f(x_4)$, the new interval of uncertainty is $I_2 = [-0.3315, x_4) = [-0.3315, 0.3369)$ and x_6 will equal x_3. Also, $L_2 = 0.3369 + 0.3315 = 0.6684$. Then

$$x_5 = 0.3369 - 0.618(0.6684) = -0.0762$$
$$x_6 = x_3 = 0.0815$$

Note that $f(x_5) = -1.0058$ and $f(x_6) = f(x_3) = -1.0066$. Since $f(x_5) > f(x_6)$, the new interval of uncertainty is $I_3 = [-0.3315, x_6) = [-0.3315, 0.0815)$ and $L_3 = 0.0815 + 0.3315 = 0.4130$. Since $f(x_6) < f(x_5)$, we have that $x_5 = x_8$ and $f(x_8) = -1.0058$. Now

$$x_7 = 0.0815 - 0.618(0.413) = -0.1737$$
$$x_8 = x_5 = -0.0762$$

and $f(x_7) = -1.0302$. Since $f(x_8) > f(x_7)$, the new interval of uncertainty is $I_4 = (x_7, 0.0815] = (-0.1737, 0.0815]$ and $L_4 = 0.0815 + 0.1737 = 0.2552$. Also, $x_9 = x_8$ will hold. Finally,

$$x_9 = x_8 = -0.0762$$
$$x_{10} = -0.1737 + 0.618(0.2552) = -0.016$$

Now $f(x_9) = f(x_8) = -1.0058$ and $f(x_{10}) = -1.0003$. Since $f(x_{10}) > f(x_9)$, the new interval of uncertainty is $I_5 = (x_9, 0.0815] = (-0.0762, 0.0815]$ and $L_5 = 0.0815 + 0.0762 = 0.1577 < 0.25$ (as desired).

Thus, we have determined that

$$\max -x^2 - 1$$
$$\text{s.t.} \quad -1 \le x \le 0.75$$

must lie within the interval $(-0.0762, 0.0815]$. (Of course, the actual maximum occurs for $\bar{x} = 0$.)

◆

Golden Section Search can be applied to a minimization problem by multiplying the objective function by -1. This assumes that the modified objective function is unimodal.

◆ PROBLEMS

GROUP A

1. Use Golden Section Search to determine (within an interval of 0.8) the optimal solution to

$$\max x^2 + 2x$$
$$\text{s.t.} \quad -3 \le x \le 5$$

2. Use Golden Section Search to determine (within an interval of 0.6) the optimal solution to

$$\max x - e^x$$
$$\text{s.t.} \quad -1 \le x \le 3$$

3. Consider a line segment $[0, 1]$ that is divided into two parts (Figure 20). The line segment is said to be divided into the **Golden Section** if

$$\frac{\text{Length of whole line}}{\text{Length of larger part of line}}$$
$$= \frac{\text{length of larger part of line}}{\text{length of smaller part of line}}$$

Figure 20

Show that for the line segment to be divided into the Golden Section,

$$r = \frac{5^{1/2} - 1}{2}$$

12-5   UNCONSTRAINED MAXIMIZATION AND MINIMIZATION WITH SEVERAL VARIABLES

We now discuss how to find an optimal solution (if it exists) or a local extremum for the following unconstrained NLP:

$$\max \text{ (or min) } f(x_1, x_2, \ldots, x_n)$$
$$\text{s.t.} \quad (x_1, x_2, \ldots, x_n) \in R^n \tag{6}$$

We assume that the first and second partial derivatives of $f(x_1, x_2, \ldots, x_n)$ exist and are continuous at all points. Let

$$\frac{\partial f(\bar{x})}{\partial x_i}$$

be the partial derivative of $f(x_1, x_2, \ldots, x_n)$ with respect to x_i, evaluated at $\bar{x}$. A necessary condition for $\bar{x} = (\bar{x}_1, \bar{x}_2, \ldots, \bar{x}_n)$ to be a local extremum for NLP (6) is given in Theorem 6.

THEOREM 6

If $\bar{x}$ is a local extremum for (6), then $\dfrac{\partial f(\bar{x})}{\partial x_i} = 0$.

To see why Theorem 6 holds, suppose $\bar{x}$ is a local extremum for (6)—say, a local maximum. If $\dfrac{\partial f(\bar{x})}{\partial x_i} > 0$ holds for any i, then by slightly increasing x_i (and holding all other variables constant), we can find a point x' near $\bar{x}$ with $f(x') > f(\bar{x})$. This would contradict the fact that $\bar{x}$ is a local maximum. Similarly, if $\bar{x}$ is a local maximum for (6) and $\dfrac{\partial f(\bar{x})}{\partial x_i} < 0$, then by slightly decreasing x_i (and holding all other variables constant), we can find a point x'' near $\bar{x}$ with $f(x'') > f(\bar{x})$. Thus, if $\bar{x}$ is a local maximum for (6), then $\dfrac{\partial f(\bar{x})}{\partial x_i} = 0$ must hold for $i = 1, 2, \ldots, n$. A similar argument shows that if $\bar{x}$ is a local minimum, then $\dfrac{\partial f(\bar{x})}{\partial x_i} = 0$ must hold for $i = 1, 2, \ldots, n$.

DEFINITION   A point $\bar{x}$ having $\dfrac{\partial f(\bar{x})}{\partial x_i} = 0$ for $i = 1, 2, \ldots, n$ is called a **stationary point** of f.

The following three theorems give conditions (involving the Hessian of f) under which a stationary point is a local minimum, a local maximum, or not a local extremum.

THEOREM 7   If $H_k(\bar{x}) > 0$, $k = 1, 2, \ldots, n$, then a stationary point $\bar{x}$ is a local minimum for NLP (6).

THEOREM 7'   If, for $k = 1, 2, \ldots, n$, $H_k(\bar{x})$ is nonzero and has the same sign as $(-1)^k$, a stationary point $\bar{x}$ is a local maximum for NLP (6).

THEOREM 7''   If $H_n(\bar{x}) \neq 0$ and the conditions of Theorems 7 and 7' do not hold, a stationary point $\bar{x}$ is not a local extremum.

If a stationary point $\bar{x}$ is not a local extremum, it is called a **saddle point**. If $H_n(\bar{x}) = 0$ for a stationary point $\bar{x}$, then $\bar{x}$ may be a local minimum, a local maximum, or a saddle point, and the preceding tests are inconclusive.

From Theorems 1 and 7', we know that if $f(x_1, x_2, \ldots, x_n)$ is a concave function (and NLP (6) is a max problem), then any stationary point for (6) is an optimal solution to (6). From Theorems 1' and 7, we know that if $f(x_1, x_2, \ldots, x_n)$ is a convex function (and NLP (6) is a min problem), then any stationary point for (6) is an optimal solution to (6).

E X A M P L E 14   A monopolist producing a single product has two types of customers. If q_1 units are produced for customer 1, then customer 1 is willing to pay a price of $70 - 4q_1$ dollars. If q_2 units are produced for customer 2, then customer 2 is willing to pay a price of $150 - 15q_2$ dollars. For $q > 0$, the cost of manufacturing q units is $100 + 15q$ dollars. In order to maximize profit, how much should the monopolist sell to each customer?

Solution   Let $f(q_1, q_2)$ be the monopolist's profit if she produces q_i units for customer i. Then (assuming some production takes place)

$$f(q_1, q_2) = q_1(70 - 4q_1) + q_2(150 - 15q_2) - 100 - 15q_1 - 15q_2$$

To find the stationary point(s) for $f(q_1, q_2)$, we set

$$\frac{\partial f}{\partial q_1} = 70 - 8q_1 - 15 = 0 \qquad \text{(for } q_1 = \tfrac{55}{8})$$

$$\frac{\partial f}{0q_2} = 150 - 30q_2 - 15 = 0 \qquad \text{(for } q_2 = \tfrac{9}{2})$$

Thus, the only stationary point of $f(q_1, q_2)$ is $(\frac{55}{8}, \frac{9}{2})$. Next we find the Hessian for $f(q_1, q_2)$.

$$H(q_1, q_2) = \begin{bmatrix} -8 & 0 \\ 0 & -30 \end{bmatrix}$$

Since the first leading principal minor of H is $-8 < 0$, and the second leading principal minor of H is $(-8)(-30) = 240 > 0$, Theorem 7' shows that $(\frac{55}{8}, \frac{9}{2})$ is a local maximum. Also, Theorem 3' implies that $f(q_1, q_2)$ is a concave function (on the set of points S of (q_1, q_2) satisfying $q_1 \geq 0$, $q_2 \geq 0$, and $q_1 + q_2 > 0$). Thus, Theorem 1 implies that $(\frac{55}{8}, \frac{9}{2})$ maximizes profit among all production possibilities (with the possible exception of no production). Then $(\frac{55}{8}, \frac{9}{2})$ yields a profit of

$$f(q_1, q_2) = \tfrac{55}{8}(70 - \tfrac{220}{8}) + \tfrac{9}{2}[150 - 15\,(\tfrac{9}{2})] - 100 - 15(\tfrac{55}{8} + \tfrac{9}{2}) = \$392.81$$

Since the profit from producing $(\frac{55}{8}, \frac{9}{2})$ exceeds the profit of \$0 that is obtained by producing nothing, $(\frac{55}{8}, \frac{9}{2})$ solves the NLP; the monopolist should sell $\frac{55}{8}$ units to customer 1 and $\frac{9}{2}$ units to customer 2.

♦

E X A M P L E 15

Suppose the grade point average (GPA) for a student can be accurately predicted from the student's GMAT (Graduate Management Admissions Test) score. More specifically, suppose that the ith student observed has a GPA of y_i and a GMAT score of x_i. How can we use the **least squares method** to estimate a hypothesized relation of the form $y_i = a + bx_i$?

Solution

Let $\hat{a}$ be our estimate of a and $\hat{b}$ our estimate of b. Given that for students $i = 1, 2, \ldots, n$ we have observed $(x_1, y_1), (x_2, y_2), \ldots, (x_n, y_n)$, $\hat{e}_i = y_i - (\hat{a} + \hat{b}x_i)$ is our error in estimating the GPA of student i. The least squares method chooses $\hat{a}$ and $\hat{b}$ to minimize

$$f(a, b) = \sum_{i=1}^{i=n} \hat{e}_i^2 = \sum_{i=1}^{i=n} (y_i - a - bx_i)^2$$

Since

$$\frac{\partial f}{\partial a} = -2 \sum_{i=1}^{i=n} (y_i - a - bx_i) \quad \text{and} \quad \frac{\partial f}{\partial b} = -2 \sum_{i=1}^{i=n} (y_i - a - bx_i)x_i$$

$\frac{\partial f}{\partial a} = \frac{\partial f}{\partial b} = 0$ will hold for the point $(\hat{a}, \hat{b})$ satisfying

$$\sum_{i=1}^{i=n} (y_i - a - bx_i) = 0 \quad \text{or} \quad \sum_{i=1}^{i=n} y_i = na + b \sum_{i=1}^{i=n} x_i$$

and

$$\sum_{i=1}^{i=n} x_i (y_i - a - bx_i) = 0 \quad \text{or} \quad \sum_{i=1}^{i=n} x_i y_i = a \sum_{i=1}^{i=n} x_i + b \sum_{i=1}^{i=n} x_i^2$$

These are the well-known **normal equations**. Does the solution $(\hat{a}, \hat{b})$ to the normal equations minimize $f(a, b)$? To answer this question, we must compute the Hessian for $f(a, b)$:

$$\frac{\partial^2 f}{\partial a^2} = 2n, \qquad \frac{\partial^2 f}{\partial b^2} = 2 \sum_{i=1}^{i=n} x_i^2, \qquad \frac{\partial^2 f}{\partial a \partial b} = \frac{\partial^2}{\partial b \partial a} = 2 \sum_{i=1}^{i=n} x_i$$

Thus,

$$H = \begin{bmatrix} 2n & 2 \sum_{i=1}^{i=n} x_i \\ 2 \sum_{i=1}^{i=n} x_i & 2 \sum_{i=1}^{i=n} x_i^2 \end{bmatrix}$$

Since $H_1(\hat{a}, \hat{b}) = 2n > 0$, $(\hat{a}, \hat{b})$ will be a local minimum if

$$H_2(\hat{a}, \hat{b}) = 4n \sum_{i=1}^{i=n} x_i^2 - 4 \left(\sum_{i=1}^{i=n} x_i \right)^2 > 0$$

In Example 19 of Section 7, we show that

$$n \sum_{i=1}^{i=n} x_i^2 \geq \left(\sum_{i=1}^{i=n} x_i \right)^2$$

with equality holding if and only if $x_1 = x_2 = \cdots = x_n$. Thus, if at least two of the x_i's are different, $(\hat{a}, \hat{b})$ will be a local minimum. Since $H(a, b)$ does not depend on the values of a and b, this reasoning (and Theorem 3) shows that if at least two of the x_i's are different, $f(a, b)$ is a convex function. If at least two of the x_i's are different, Theorem 1' shows that $(\hat{a}, \hat{b})$ minimizes $f(a, b)$.

◆

E X A M P L E 16

Find all local maxima, local minima, and saddle points for $f(x_1, x_2) = x_1^2 x_2 + x_2^3 x_1 - x_1 x_2$.

Solution

We have

$$\frac{\partial f}{\partial x_1} = 2x_1 x_2 + x_2^3 - x_2, \qquad \frac{\partial f}{\partial x_2} = x_1^2 + 3x_2^2 x_1 - x_1$$

Thus, $\dfrac{\partial f}{\partial x_1} = \dfrac{\partial f}{\partial x_2} = 0$ requires

$$2x_1 x_2 + x_2^3 - x_2 = 0 \qquad \text{or} \qquad x_2(2x_1 + x_2^2 - 1) = 0 \qquad (7)$$
$$x_1^2 + 3x_2^2 x_1 - x_1 = 0 \qquad \text{or} \qquad x_1(x_1 + 3x_2^2 - 1) = 0 \qquad (8)$$

For (7) to hold, either (i) $x_2 = 0$ or (ii) $2x_1 + x_2^2 - 1 = 0$ must hold. For (8) to hold, either (iii) $x_1 = 0$ or (iv) $x_1 + 3x_2^2 - 1 = 0$ must hold.

Thus, for (x_1, x_2) to be a stationary point, we must have

(i) and (iii) hold. This is only true at $(0, 0)$.

(i) and (iv) hold. This is only true at $(1, 0)$.

(ii) and (iii) hold. This is only true at $(0, 1)$ and $(0, -1)$.

(ii) and (iv) hold. This requires that $x_2^2 = 1 - 2x_1$ and $x_1 + 3(1 - 2x_1) - 1 = 0$ hold.

Then

$$x_1 = \frac{2}{5} \quad \text{and} \quad x_2 = \frac{5^{1/2}}{5} \quad \text{or} \quad -\frac{5^{1/2}}{5}$$

Thus, $f(x_1, x_2)$ has the following stationary points:

$$(0, 0), (1, 0), (0, 1), (0, -1), \left(\frac{2}{5}, \frac{5^{1/2}}{5}\right) \quad \text{and} \quad \left(\frac{2}{5}, -\frac{5^{1/2}}{5}\right)$$

Also,

$$H(x_1, x_2) = \begin{bmatrix} 2x_2 & 2x_1 + 3(x_2)^2 - 1 \\ 2x_1 + 3(x_2)^2 - 1 & 6x_1 x_2 \end{bmatrix}$$

$$H(0, 0) = \begin{bmatrix} 0 & -1 \\ -1 & 0 \end{bmatrix}$$

Since $H_1(0, 0) = 0$, the conditions of Theorems 7 and 7′ cannot be satisfied. Since $H_2(0, 1) = -4$ (so the hypotheses of Theorem 7 can't be satisfied). Since $H_2(0, 1) \neq 0$, because $f(0, 0) = 0$, and for h small and positive, $f(h, h) = h^3 + h^4 - h^2 < 0$ and $f(h, -h) = -h^3 - h^4 + h^2 > 0$. Thus, there are points near $(0, 0)$ where $f(x_1, x_2)$ is both positive and negative and $(0, 0)$ is a saddle point. We have

$$H(1, 0) = \begin{bmatrix} 0 & 1 \\ 1 & 0 \end{bmatrix}$$

Then $H_1(1, 0) = 0$ and $H_2(1, 0) = -1$, so $(1, 0)$ is also a saddle point. Since

$$H(0, 1) = \begin{bmatrix} 2 & 2 \\ 2 & 0 \end{bmatrix}$$

we have $H_1(0, 1) = 2 > 0$ (so the hypotheses of Theorem 7′ can't be satisfied) and $H_2(0, 1) = -4$ (so the hypotheses of Theorem 7 can't be satisfied). Since $H_2(0, 1) \neq 0$, $(0, 1)$ is a saddle point.

For $\left(\frac{2}{5}, -\frac{5^{1/2}}{5}\right)$, we have

$$H\left(\frac{2}{5}, -\frac{5^{1/2}}{5}\right) = \begin{bmatrix} -\dfrac{2}{5^{1/2}} & \dfrac{2}{5} \\ \dfrac{2}{5} & -\dfrac{12}{5(5)^{1/2}} \end{bmatrix}$$

Thus,

$$H_1\left(\frac{2}{5}, -\frac{5^{1/2}}{5}\right) = -\frac{2}{5^{1/2}} < 0 \quad \text{and} \quad H_2\left(\frac{2}{5}, -\frac{5^{1/2}}{5}\right) = \frac{20}{25} > 0$$

Thus, Theorem 7′ shows that $\left(\dfrac{2}{5}, -\dfrac{5^{1/2}}{5}\right)$ is a local maximum. Finally,

$$H\left(\frac{2}{5}, \frac{5^{1/2}}{5}\right) = \begin{bmatrix} \dfrac{2}{5^{1/2}} & \dfrac{2}{5} \\[2ex] \dfrac{2}{5} & \dfrac{12}{5(5)^{1/2}} \end{bmatrix}$$

Since $\det H_1\left(\dfrac{2}{5}, \dfrac{5^{1/2}}{5}\right) = \dfrac{2}{5^{1/2}} > 0$ and $H_2\left(\dfrac{2}{5}, \dfrac{5^{1/2}}{5}\right) = \dfrac{20}{25} > 0$, Theorem 7 shows that $\left(\dfrac{2}{5}, \dfrac{5^{1/2}}{5}\right)$ is a local minimum.

◆ PROBLEMS

GROUP A

1. A company has n factories. Factory i is located at point (x_i, y_i), in the x–y plane. The company wants to locate a warehouse at a point (x, y) that minimizes

$$\sum_{i=1}^{i=n} (\text{distance from factory } i \text{ to warehouse})^2$$

Where should the warehouse be located?

2. A company can sell all it produces of a given output for \$2/unit. The output is produced by combining two inputs. If q_1 units of input 1 and q_2 units of input 2 are used, the company can produce $q_1^{1/3} + q_2^{2/3}$ units of the output. If it costs \$1 to purchase a unit of input 1 and \$1.50 to purchase a unit of input 2, how can the company maximize its profit?

3. (Collusive Duopoly Model) There are two firms producing widgets. It costs the first firm q_1 dollars to produce q_1 widgets, and it costs the second firm $0.5q_2^2$ dollars to produce q_2 widgets. If a total of q widgets are produced, consumers will pay \$200 − q for each widget. If the two manufacturers want to collude in an attempt to maximize the sum of their profits, how many widgets should each company produce?

4. It costs a company \$6/unit to produce a product. If it charges a price p and spends a dollars on advertising, it can sell $10{,}000p^{-2}a^{1/6}$ units of the product. Find the price and advertising level that will maximize the company's profits.

5. A company manufactures two products. If it charges a price p_i for product i, it can sell q_i units of product i, where $q_1 = 60 - 3p_1 + p_2$ and $q_2 = 80 - 2p_2 + p_1$. It costs \$25 to produce a unit of product 1 and \$72 to produce a

unit of product 2. In order to maximize profits, how many units of each product should be produced?

6. Find all local maxima, local minima, and saddle points for $f(x_1, x_2) = x_1^3 - 3x_1x_2^2 + x_2^4$.

7. Find all local maxima, local minima, and saddle points for $f(x_1, x_2) = x_1x_2 + x_2x_3 + x_1x_3$.

GROUP B

8.[†] (Cournot Duopoly Model) Let's reconsider Problem 3. The Cournot solution to this situation is obtained as follows: Firm i will produce $\bar{q}_i$, where if firm 1 changes its production level from $\bar{q}_1$ (and firm 2 still produces $\bar{q}_2$), firm 1's profit will decrease. Also, if firm 2 changes its production level from $\bar{q}_2$ (and firm 1 still produces $\bar{q}_1$) firm 2's profit will decrease. If firm i produces $\bar{q}_i$, this solution is stable, because if either firm changes its production level it will do worse. Find $\bar{q}_1$ and $\bar{q}_2$.

9. In the Bloomington Girls Club Basketball League, the following games have been played: team A beat team B by 7 points, team C beat team A by 8 points, team B beat team C by 6 points, and team B beat team C by 9 points. Let A, B, and C represent "ratings" for each team in the sense that if, say, team A plays team B, we predict that team A will defeat team B by $A - B$ points. Determine values of A, B, and C that best fit (in the least-squares sense) the above results. In order to obtain a unique set of ratings, it may be helpful to add the constraint $A + B + C = 0$. This ensures that an "average" team will have a rating of 0.

[†] Based on Cournot (1897).

12-6   THE METHOD OF STEEPEST ASCENT

Suppose we wish to solve the following unconstrained NLP:

$$\max z = f(x_1, x_2, \ldots, x_n)$$
$$\text{s.t.} \quad (x_1, x_2, \ldots, x_n) \in R^n \tag{9}$$

Our discussion in Section 12.5 shows that if $f(x_1, x_2, \ldots, x_n)$ is a concave function, then the optimal solution to (9) (if there is one) will occur at a stationary point $\bar{x}$ having

$$\frac{\partial f(\bar{x})}{\partial x_1} = \frac{\partial f(\bar{x})}{\partial x_2} = \cdots = \frac{\partial f(\bar{x})}{\partial x_n} = 0$$

In Examples 14 and 15, it was easy to find a stationary point, but in many problems, it may be difficult. In this section, we discuss the method of steepest ascent, which can be used to approximate a function's satisfactory point.

DEFINITION   Given a vector $\mathbf{x} = (x_1, x_2, \ldots, x_n) \in R^n$, the **length** of $\mathbf{x}$ (written $\| \mathbf{x} \|$) is

$$\| \mathbf{x} \| = (x_1^2 + x_2^2 + \cdots + x_n^2)^{1/2}$$

Recall from Section 2.1 that any n-dimensional vector represents a direction in R^n. Unfortunately, for any direction, there are an infinite number of vectors representing that direction. For example, the vectors $(1, 1)$, $(2, 2)$, and $(3, 3)$ all represent the same direction (moving at a positive 45° angle) in R^2. For any vector $\mathbf{x}$, the vector $\mathbf{x}/ \| \mathbf{x} \|$ will have a length of 1 and will define the same direction as $\mathbf{x}$ (see Problem 1 at the end of this section). Thus, with any direction in R^n, we may associate a vector of length 1 (called a unit vector). For example, since $\mathbf{x} = (1, 1)$ has $\| \mathbf{x} \| = 2^{1/2}$, the direction defined by $\mathbf{x} = (1, 1)$ is associated with the unit vector $(1/2^{1/2}, 1/2^{1/2})$. For any vector $\mathbf{x}$, the unit vector $\mathbf{x}/\| \mathbf{x} \|$ is called the **normalized** version of $\mathbf{x}$. Henceforth, any direction in R^n will be described by the normalized vector defining that direction. Thus, the direction in R^2 defined by $(1, 1)$, $(2, 2)$, $(3, 3)$, . . . will be described by the normalized vector

$$\left(\frac{1}{2^{1/2}}, \frac{1}{2^{1/2}} \right)$$

Consider a function $f(x_1, x_2, \ldots, x_n)$, all of whose partial derivatives exist at every point.

DEFINITION   The **gradient vector** for $f(x_1, x_2, \ldots, x_n)$, written $\nabla f(\mathbf{x})$, is given by

$$\nabla f(\mathbf{x}) = \left[\frac{\partial f(\mathbf{x})}{\partial x_1}, \frac{\partial f(\mathbf{x})}{\partial x_2}, \ldots, \frac{\partial f(\mathbf{x})}{\partial x_n} \right]$$

$\nabla f(\mathbf{x})$ defines the direction

$$\frac{\nabla f(\mathbf{x})}{\| \nabla f(\mathbf{x}) \|}$$

For example, if $f(x_1, x_2) = x_1^2 + x_2^2$, then $\nabla f(x_1, x_2) = (2x_1, 2x_2)$. Thus, $\nabla f(3, 4) = (6, 8)$. Since $\| \nabla f(3, 4) \| = 10$, $\nabla f(3, 4)$ defines the direction $(\frac{6}{10}, \frac{8}{10}) = (0.6, 0.8)$.

At any point $\bar{x}$ that lies on the curve $f(x_1, x_2, \ldots, x_n) = f(\bar{x})$, the vector

$$\frac{\nabla f(\bar{x})}{\| \nabla f(\bar{x}) \|}$$

will be perpendicular to the curve $f(x_1, x_2, \ldots, x_n) = f(\bar{x})$ (see Problem 5 at the end of this section). For example, let $f(x_1, x_2) = x_1^2 + x_2^2$. Then at $(3, 4)$,

$$\frac{\nabla f(3, 4)}{\| \nabla f(3, 4) \|} = (0.6, 0.8)$$

is perpendicular to $x_1^2 + x_2^2 = 25$ (see Figure 21).

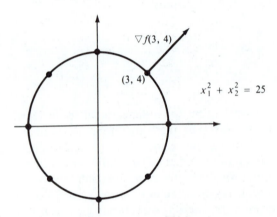

$f(x_1, x_2) = x_1^2 + x_2^2$

$\nabla f(3, 4)$

$(3, 4)$

$x_1^2 + x_2^2 = 25$

From the definition of $\dfrac{\partial f(x)}{\partial x_i}$, it follows that if the value of x_i is increased by a small amount δ, the value of $f(x)$ will increase by approximately $\delta \dfrac{\partial f(x)}{\partial x_i}$. Suppose we move from a point x a small length δ in a direction defined by a normalized column vector d. By how much does $f(x)$ increase? The answer is that $f(x)$ increases by δ times the scalar product of $\dfrac{\nabla f(x)}{\| \nabla f(x) \|}$ and d (written $\dfrac{\delta \nabla f(x) d}{\| \nabla f(x) \|}$). Thus, if $\dfrac{\nabla f(x) d}{\| \nabla f(x) \|} > 0$, moving in a direction d away from x will increase the value of $f(x)$, and if $\dfrac{\nabla f(x) d}{\| \nabla f(x) \|} < 0$, moving in a direction d away from x will decrease $f(x)$. For example, suppose $f(x_1, x_2) = x_1^2 + x_2^2$ and we move a length δ in a $45°$ direction away from the point $(3, 4)$. By how much will the value of $f(x_1, x_2)$ change? Since a $45°$ direction is represented by the vector $\left(\dfrac{1}{2^{1/2}}, \dfrac{1}{2^{1/2}} \right)$ and $\dfrac{\nabla f(3, 4)}{\| \nabla f(3, 4) \|} = (0.6, 0.8)$, the value of $f(x_1, x_2)$ will increase by approximately

$$\delta \begin{bmatrix} 0.6 & 0.8 \end{bmatrix} \begin{bmatrix} \dfrac{1}{2^{1/2}} \\ \dfrac{1}{2^{1/2}} \end{bmatrix} = 0.99\delta$$

Recall from Section 12.5 that the optimal solution $\bar{\mathbf{v}}$ to (9) must satisfy $\nabla f(\bar{\mathbf{v}}) = 0$. Now suppose that we are at a point $\mathbf{v}_0$ and want to find a point $\bar{\mathbf{v}}$ that solves (9). In an attempt to find $\bar{\mathbf{v}}$, it seems reasonable to move away from $\mathbf{v}_0$ in a direction that maximizes the rate (at least locally) at which $f(x_1, x_2, \ldots, x_n)$ increases. Lemma 1 proves useful here (see Review Problem 22).

L E M M A
1

Suppose we are at a point $\mathbf{v}$ and we move from $\mathbf{v}$ a small distance δ in a direction $\mathbf{d}$. Then for a given δ, the maximal increase in the value of $f(x_1, x_2, \ldots, x_n)$ will occur if we choose

$$\mathbf{d} = \frac{\nabla f(\mathbf{v})}{\|\nabla f(\mathbf{v})\|}$$

◆

In short, if we move a small distance away from $\mathbf{v}$ and we want $f(x_1, x_2, \ldots, x_n)$ to increase as quickly as possible, we should move in the direction of $\nabla f(\mathbf{v})$.

We are now ready to describe the method of steepest ascent. Begin at any point $\mathbf{v}_0$. Since moving in the direction of $\nabla f(\mathbf{v}_0)$ will result in a maximum rate of increase for f, we begin by moving away from $\mathbf{v}_0$ in the direction of $\nabla f(\mathbf{v}_0)$. For some nonnegative value of t, we move to a point $\mathbf{v}_1 = \mathbf{v}_0 + t\nabla f(\mathbf{v}_0)$. The maximum possible improvement in the value of f (for a max problem) that can be attained by moving away from $\mathbf{v}_0$ in the direction of $\nabla f(\mathbf{v}_0)$ results from moving to $\mathbf{v}_1 = \mathbf{v}_0 + t_0\nabla f(\mathbf{v}_0)$, where t_0 solves the following one-dimensional optimization problem:

$$\max f(\mathbf{v}_0 + t_0\nabla f(\mathbf{v}_0)) \tag{10}$$
$$\text{s.t.} \quad t_0 \geq 0$$

NLP (10) may be solved by the methods of Section 12.3 or, if necessary, by a search procedure like Golden Section Search.

If $\|\nabla f(\mathbf{v}_1)\|$ is small (say less than 0.01), we may terminate the algorithm with the knowledge that $\mathbf{v}_1$ is near a stationary point $\bar{\mathbf{v}}$ having $\nabla f(\bar{\mathbf{v}}) = 0$. If $\|\nabla f(\mathbf{v}_1)\|$ is not sufficiently small, we move away from $\mathbf{v}_1$ a distance t_1 in the direction of $\|\nabla f(\mathbf{v}_1)\|$. As before, we choose t_1 by solving

$$\max f(\mathbf{v}_1 + t_1\nabla f(\mathbf{v}_1))$$
$$\text{s.t.} \quad t_1 \geq 0$$

We are now at the point $\mathbf{v}_2 = \mathbf{v}_1 + t_1\nabla f(\mathbf{v}_1)$. If $\|\nabla f(\mathbf{v}_2)\|$ is sufficiently small, we terminate the algorithm and choose $\mathbf{v}_2$ as our approximation to a stationary point of $f(x_1, x_2, \ldots, x_n)$. Otherwise, we continue in this fashion until we reach a point $\mathbf{v}_n$ having $\|\nabla f(\mathbf{v}_n)\|$ sufficiently small. Then we choose $\mathbf{v}_n$ as our approximation to a stationary point of $f(x_1, x_2, \ldots, x_n)$.

This algorithm is called the method of steepest ascent because to generate points, we always move in the direction that maximizes that rate at which f increases (at least locally).

E X A M P L E
17

Use the method of steepest ascent to approximate the solution to

$$\max z = -(x_1 - 3)^2 - (x_2 - 2)^2 = f(x_1, x_2)$$
$$\text{s.t.} \quad (x_1, x_2) \in R^2$$

Solution

We arbitrarily choose to begin at the point $\mathbf{v}_0 = (1, 1)$. Since $\nabla f(\mathbf{x}_1, \mathbf{x}_2) = (-2(x_1 - 3), -2(x_2 - 2))$, we have $\nabla f(1, 1) = (4, 2)$. Thus, we must choose t_0 to maximize

$$f(t_0) = f((1, 1) + t_0(4, 2)) = f(1 + 4t_0, 1 + 2t_0) = -(-2 + 4t_0)^2 - (-1 + 2t_0)^2$$

Setting $f'(t_0) = 0$, we obtain

$$-8(-2 + 4t_0) - 4(-1 + 2t_0) = 0$$
$$20 - 40t_0 = 0$$
$$t_0 = 0.5$$

Our new point is $\mathbf{v}_1 = (1, 1) + 0.5(4, 2) = (3, 2)$. Now $\nabla f(3, 2) = (0, 0)$, and we terminate the algorithm. Since $f(x_1, x_2)$ is a concave function, we have found the optimal solution to the NLP.   ♦

♦ PROBLEMS

GROUP A

1. For any vector $\mathbf{x}$, show that the vector $\mathbf{x}/\|\mathbf{x}\|$ has unit length.

2. Use the method of steepest ascent to approximate the optimal solution to the following problem: $\max z = -(x_1 - 2)^2 - x_1 - x_2^2$. Begin at the point $(2.5, 1.5)$.

3. Use steepest ascent to approximate the optimal solution to the following problem: $\max z = 2x_1x_2 + 2x_2 - x_1^2 - 2x_2^2$. Begin at the point $(0.5, 0.5)$. Note that at later iterations, successive points are very close together. Variations of steepest ascent have been developed to deal with this problem (see·Bazaraa and Shetty (1979, Section 8.5)).

GROUP B

4. How would you modify the method of steepest ascent if each variable x_i were constrained to lie in an interval $[a_i, b_i]$?

GROUP C

5. Show that at any point $\bar{\mathbf{x}} = (\bar{x}_1, \bar{x}_2)$, $\nabla f(\bar{\mathbf{x}})$ is perpendicular to the curve $f(x_1, x_2) = f(\bar{x}_1, \bar{x}_2)$. (*Hint:* Two vectors are perpendicular if and only if their scalar product equals zero.)

12-7   LAGRANGE MULTIPLIERS

Lagrange multipliers can be used to solve NLPs in which all the constraints are equality constraints. We consider NLPs of the following type:

$$\max \text{ (or min) } z = f(x_1, x_2, \ldots, x_n)$$
$$\text{s.t.} \quad g_1(x_1, x_2, \ldots, x_n) = b_1$$
$$g_2(x_1, x_2, \ldots, x_n) = b_2 \qquad \textbf{(11)}$$
$$\vdots$$
$$g_m(x_1, x_2, \ldots, x_n) = b_m$$

To solve (11), we associate a **multiplier** λ_i with the ith constraint in (11) and form the **Lagrangian**

$$L(x_1, x_2, \ldots, x_n, \lambda_1, \lambda_2, \ldots, \lambda_m) = f(x_1, x_2, \ldots, x_n)$$
$$+ \sum_{i=1}^{i=m} \lambda_i[b_i - g_i(x_1, x_2, \ldots, x_n)] \qquad \textbf{(12)}$$

Then we attempt to find a point $(\bar{x}_1, \bar{x}_2, \ldots, \bar{x}_n, \bar{\lambda}_1, \bar{\lambda}_2, \ldots, \bar{\lambda}_m)$ that maximizes (or minimizes) $L(x_1, x_2, \ldots, x_n, \lambda_1, \lambda_2 \ldots, \lambda_m)$. In many situations, $(\bar{x}_1, \bar{x}_2, \ldots, \bar{x}_n)$ will solve (11). Suppose that (11) is a maximization problem. If $(\bar{x}_1, \bar{x}_2, \ldots, \bar{x}_n, \bar{\lambda}_1, \bar{\lambda}_2, \ldots, \bar{\lambda}_m)$ maximizes L, then at $(\bar{x}_1, \bar{x}_2, \ldots, \bar{x}_n, \bar{\lambda}_1, \bar{\lambda}_2, \ldots, \bar{\lambda}_n)$

$$\frac{\partial L}{\partial \lambda_i} = b_i - g_i(x_1, x_2, \ldots, x_n) = 0$$

Here $\dfrac{\partial L}{\partial \lambda_i}$ is the partial derivative of L with respect to λ_i. This shows that $(\bar{x}_1, \bar{x}_2, \ldots, \bar{x}_n)$ will satisfy the constraints in (11). To show that $(\bar{x}_1, \bar{x}_2, \ldots, \bar{x}_n)$ solves (11), let $(x'_1, x'_2, \ldots, x'_n)$ be any point that is in (11)'s feasible region. Since $(\bar{x}_1, \bar{x}_2, \ldots, \bar{x}_n, \bar{\lambda}_1, \bar{\lambda}_2, \ldots, \bar{\lambda}_m)$ maximizes L, for any numbers $\lambda'_1, \lambda'_2, \ldots, \lambda'_m$ we have

$$L(\bar{x}_1, \bar{x}_2, \ldots, \bar{x}_n, \bar{\lambda}_1, \bar{\lambda}_2, \ldots, \bar{\lambda}_m) \geq L(x'_1, x'_2, \ldots, x'_n, \lambda'_1, \lambda'_2, \ldots, \lambda'_m) \qquad \textbf{(13)}$$

Since $(\bar{x}_1, \bar{x}_2, \ldots, \bar{x}_n)$ and $(x'_1, x'_2, \ldots, x'_n)$ are both feasible in (11), the terms in (12) involving the λ's are all zero, and (13) becomes $f(\bar{x}_1, \bar{x}_2, \ldots, \bar{x}_n) \geq f(x'_1, x'_2, \ldots, x'_n)$. Thus, $(\bar{x}_1, \bar{x}_2, \ldots, \bar{x}_n)$ does solve (11). In short, if $(\bar{x}_1, \bar{x}_2, \ldots, \bar{x}_n, \bar{\lambda}_1, \bar{\lambda}_2, \ldots, \bar{\lambda}_m)$ solves the unconstrained maximization problem

$$\max L(x_1, x_2, \ldots, x_n, \lambda_1, \lambda_2, \ldots, \lambda_m) \qquad \textbf{(14)}$$

then $(\bar{x}_1, \bar{x}_2, \ldots, \bar{x}_n)$ solves (11).

From Section 12.5, we know that for $(\bar{x}_1, \bar{x}_2, \ldots, \bar{x}_n, \bar{\lambda}_1, \bar{\lambda}_2, \ldots, \bar{\lambda}_m)$ to solve (14), it is necessary that at $(\bar{x}_1, \bar{x}_2, \ldots, \bar{x}_n, \bar{\lambda}_1, \bar{\lambda}_2, \ldots, \bar{\lambda}_m)$,

$$\frac{\partial L}{\partial x_1} = \frac{\partial L}{\partial x_2} = \cdots = \frac{\partial L}{\partial x_n} = \frac{\partial L}{\partial \lambda_1} = \frac{\partial L}{\partial \lambda_2} = \cdots = \frac{\partial L}{\partial \lambda_m} = 0 \qquad \textbf{(15)}$$

Theorem 8 gives conditions implying that any point $(\bar{x}_1, \bar{x}_2, \ldots, \bar{x}_n, \bar{\lambda}_1, \bar{\lambda}_2, \ldots, \bar{\lambda}_m)$ that satisfies (15) will yield an optimal solution $(\bar{x}_1, \bar{x}_2, \ldots, \bar{x}_n)$ to (11).

THEOREM 8	Suppose (11) is a maximization problem. If $f(x_1, x_2, \ldots, x_n)$ is a concave function and each $g_i(x_1, x_2, \ldots, x_n)$ is a linear function, then any point $(\bar{x}_1, \bar{x}_2, \ldots, \bar{x}_n, \bar{\lambda}_1, \bar{\lambda}_2, \ldots, \bar{\lambda}_m)$ satisfying (15) will yield an optimal solution $(\bar{x}_1, \bar{x}_2, \ldots, \bar{x}_n)$ to (11).

THEOREM 8'	Suppose (11) is a minimization problem. If $f(x_1, x_2, \ldots, x_n)$ is a convex function and each $g_i(x_1, x_2, \ldots, x_n)$ is a linear function, then any point $(\bar{x}_1, \bar{x}_2, \ldots, \bar{x}_n, \bar{\lambda}_1, \bar{\lambda}_2, \ldots, \bar{\lambda}_m)$ satisfying (15) will yield an optimal solution $(\bar{x}_1, \bar{x}_2, \ldots, \bar{x}_n)$ to (11).

Even if the hypotheses of these theorems fail to hold, it is possible that any point satisfying (15) will solve (11). See the appendix of Henderson and Quandt (1980) for details.

The variables λ_i have an interpretation as the shadow price of the ith constraint. If the right-hand side of the ith constraint is increased by a small amount Δ (in either a max or a min problem), then the optimal objective function value for (11) will increase by approximately $\Delta \lambda_i$.

The two examples that follow illustrate the use of Lagrange multipliers. In most cases, the easiest way to find a point $(\bar{x}_1, \bar{x}_2, \ldots, \bar{x}_n, \bar{\lambda}_1, \bar{\lambda}_2, \ldots, \bar{\lambda}_m)$ satisfying (15) is first to solve for $\bar{x}_1, \bar{x}_2, \ldots, \bar{x}_n$ in terms of $\bar{\lambda}_1, \bar{\lambda}_2, \ldots, \bar{\lambda}_m$. Then determine the values of the $\bar{\lambda}_i$'s by substituting these relations into the constraints of (11). Finally, use the values of the $\bar{\lambda}_i$'s to determine $\bar{x}_1, \bar{x}_2, \ldots, \bar{x}_n$.

E X A M P L E 18

A company is planning to spend \$10,000 on advertising. It costs \$3000 per minute to advertise on television and \$1000 per minute to advertise on radio. If the firm buys x minutes of television advertising and y minutes of radio advertising, its revenue in thousands of dollars is given by $f(x, y) = -2x^2 - y^2 + xy + 8x + 3y$. How can the firm maximize its revenue?

Solution

We wish to solve the following NLP:

$$\max z = -2x^2 - y^2 + xy + 8x + 3y$$
$$\text{s.t.} \quad 3x + y = 10$$

Then $L(x, y, \lambda) = -2x^2 - y^2 + xy + 8x + 3y + \lambda(10 - 3x - y)$. We set

$$\frac{\partial L}{\partial x} = \frac{\partial L}{\partial y} = \frac{\partial L}{\partial \lambda} = 0$$

This yields

$$\frac{\partial L}{\partial x} = -4x + y + 8 - 3\lambda = 0 \tag{16}$$

$$\frac{\partial L}{\partial y} = -2y + x + 3 - \lambda = 0 \tag{17}$$

$$\frac{\partial L}{\partial x} = 10 - 3x - y = 0 \tag{18}$$

Observe that $10 - 3x - y = 0$ reduces to the constraint $3x + y = 10$. Eq. (16) yields $y = 3\lambda - 8 + 4x$, and Eq. (17) yields $x = \lambda - 3 + 2y$. Thus, $y = 3\lambda - 8 + 4(\lambda - 3 + 2y) = 7\lambda - 20 + 8y$, or

$$y = \tfrac{20}{7} - \lambda \tag{19}$$
$$x = \lambda - 3 + 2\left(\tfrac{20}{7} - \lambda\right) = \tfrac{19}{7} - \lambda \tag{20}$$

Substituting (19) and (20) in (18) yields $10 - 3\left(\tfrac{19}{7} - \lambda\right) - \left(\tfrac{20}{7} - \lambda\right) = 0$, or $4\lambda - 1 = 0$, or $\lambda = \tfrac{1}{4}$. Then (19) and (20) yield

$$\bar{y} = \tfrac{20}{7} - \tfrac{1}{4} = \tfrac{73}{28}$$
$$\bar{x} = \tfrac{19}{7} - \tfrac{1}{4} = \tfrac{69}{28}$$

The Hessian for $f(x, y)$ is

$$H(x, y) = \begin{bmatrix} -4 & 1 \\ 1 & -2 \end{bmatrix}$$

Since each first order principal minor is negative, and $H_2(x, y) = 7 > 0$, $f(x, y)$ is concave. The constraint is linear, so Theorem 8 shows that the Lagrange multiplier method does yield the optimal solution to the NLP.

Thus, the firm should purchase $\frac{69}{28}$ minutes of television time and $\frac{73}{28}$ minutes of radio time. Since $\lambda = \frac{1}{4}$, spending an extra Δ (thousands) (for small Δ) would increase the firm's revenues by approximately $\$0.25\Delta$ (thousands).

In general, if the firm had a dollars to spend on advertising, it could be shown that $\lambda = \frac{11-a}{4}$ (see Problem 1 at the end of this section). We see that as more money is spent on advertising, the increase to revenue for each additional advertising dollar becomes smaller.

◆

E X A M P L E
19

Given numbers $x_1, x_2, \ldots, x_n$, show that

$$n \sum_{i=1}^{i=n} x_i^2 \geq \left(\sum_{i=1}^{i=n} x_i \right)^2$$

with equality holding only if $x_1 = x_2 = \cdots = x_n$.

Solution

Suppose that $x_1 + x_2 + \cdots + x_n = c$. Consider the NLP

$$\min z = \sum_{i=1}^{i=n} x_i^2$$

$$\text{s.t.} \quad \sum_{i=1}^{i=n} x_i = c \tag{21}$$

To solve (21), we form

$$L(x_1, x_2, \ldots, x_n, \lambda) = x_1^2 + x_2^2 + \cdots + x_n^2 + \lambda(c - x_1 - x_2 - \cdots - x_n)$$

Then to solve (21), we need to find $(x_1, x_2, \ldots, x_n, \lambda)$ that satisfy

$$\frac{\partial L}{\partial x_i} = 2x_i - \lambda = 0 \qquad (i = 1, 2, \ldots, n) \qquad \text{and}$$

$$\frac{\partial L}{\partial \lambda} = c - x_1 - x_2 - \cdots - x_n = 0$$

From $\frac{\partial L}{\partial x_i} = 0$, we obtain $2\bar{x}_1 = 2\bar{x}_2 = \cdots = 2\bar{x}_n = \bar{\lambda}$, or $x_i = \frac{\bar{\lambda}}{2}$. From $\frac{\partial L}{\partial \lambda} = 0$, we obtain $c - \frac{n\bar{\lambda}}{2} = 0$, or $\bar{\lambda} = \frac{2c}{n}$. The objective function for (21) is convex (it is the sum of n convex functions), and the constraint is linear. Thus, Theorem 8′ shows that the Lagrange multiplier method does yield an optimal solution to (21). The optimal solution to (21) has

$$\bar{x}_i = \frac{\left(\dfrac{2c}{n}\right)}{2} = \frac{c}{n} \qquad \text{and} \qquad z = n\left(\frac{c^2}{n^2}\right) = \frac{c^2}{n}$$

Thus, if

$$\sum_{i=1}^{i=n} x_i = c$$

then

$$n \sum_{i=1}^{i=n} x_i^2 \geq n \left(\frac{c^2}{n} \right) = \left(\sum_{i=1}^{i=n} x_i \right)^2$$

with equality holding if and only if $x_1 = x_2 = \cdots = x_n$.

    ◆

If we are trying to maximize a function $f(x_1, x_2, \ldots, x_n)$ that is a product of several functions, it is often easier to maximize $\ln(f(x_1, x_2, \ldots, x_n))$. Since $\ln$ is an increasing function, we know that any x^* maximizing $\ln(f(x_1, x_2, \ldots, x_n))$ over any set of possible values for $(x_1, x_2, \ldots, x_n)$ will also maximize $f(x_1, x_2, \ldots, x_n)$ over the same set of possible values for $(x_1, x_2, \ldots, x_n)$. See Problem 2 for an application of this idea.

◆ PROBLEMS

GROUP A

1. For Example 18, show that if a dollars are available for advertising, an extra dollar spent on advertising will increase revenues by approximately $\frac{11 - a}{4}$.

2. It costs me $2 to purchase an hour of labor and $1 to purchase a unit of capital. If L hours of labor and K units of capital are available, then $L^{2/3}K^{1/3}$ machines can be produced. If I have $10 to purchase labor and capital, what is the maximum number of machines that can be produced?

3. In Problem 2, what is the minimum cost method of producing 6 machines?

4. A beer company has divided Bloomington into two territories. If x_1 dollars are spent on promotion in territory 1, then $6x_1^{1/2}$ cases of beer can be sold in territory 1, and if x_2 dollars are spent on promotion in territory 2, then $4x_2^{1/2}$ cases of beer can be sold in territory 2. Each case of beer sold in territory 1 sells for $10 and incurs $5 in shipping and production costs. Each case of beer sold in territory 2 sells for $9 and incurs $4 in shipping and production costs. A total of $100 is available for promotion. How can the beer company maximize profits? If an extra dollar could be spent on promotion, by approximately how much would profits increase? By how much would revenues increase?

GROUP B

5. We must invest all our money in two stocks: x and y. The variance of the annual return on one share of stock x is var x, and the variance of the annual return on one share of stock y is var y. Assume that the covariance between the annual return for one share of x and one share of y is $\text{cov}(x, y)$. If we invest $a\%$ of our money in stock x and $b\%$ in stock y, the variance of our return is given by a^2 var $x + b^2$ var $y + 2ab\,\text{cov}(x, y)$. We want to minimize the variance of the return on our invested money. What percentage of the money should be invested in each stock?

6. As in Problem 5, assume that we must determine the percentage of our money that is invested in stocks x and y. A choice of a and b is called a *portfolio*. A portfolio is efficient if there exists no other portfolio whose return has a higher mean return and lower variance, or a higher mean return and the same variance, or a lower variance with the same mean return. Let $\bar{x}$ be the mean return on stock x and $\bar{y}$ be the mean return on stock y. Consider the following NLP:

$$\begin{aligned} \max z = \; & c[a\bar{x} + b\bar{y}] \\ & - (1 - c)[a^2 \text{ var } x + b^2 \text{ var } y \\ & + 2ab \text{ cov}(x, y)] \\ \text{s.t.} \quad & a + b = 1 \\ & a, b \geq 0 \end{aligned}$$

Suppose that $1 > c > 0$. Show that any solution to the above NLP is an efficient portfolio.

7. Suppose product i $(i = 1, 2)$ costs c_i per unit. If x_i $(i = 1, 2)$ units of products 1 and 2 are purchased, a utility $x_1^a x_2^{1-a}$ $(0 < a < 1)$ is received.
(a) If $d are available to purchase products 1 and 2, how many of each type should be purchased?
(b) Show that an increase in the cost of product i decreases the number of units of product i that should be purchased.
(c) Show that an increase in the cost of product i does not change the number of units of the other product that should be purchased.

8. Suppose that a cylindrical soda can must have a volume of 26 cu in. If the soda company wants to minimize the surface area of the soda can, what should be the ratio of the height of the can to the radius of the can? (*Hint:* The volume of a right circular cylinder is $\pi r^2 h$, and the surface area of a right circular cylinder is $2\pi r^2 + 2\pi rh$, where r = the radius of the cylinder and h = the height of the cylinder.)

12-8   THE KUHN-TUCKER CONDITIONS

In this section, we discuss necessary and sufficient conditions for $\bar{x} = (\bar{x}_1, \bar{x}_2, \ldots, \bar{x}_n)$ to be an optimal solution for the following NLP:

$$\max \text{ (or min) } f(x_1, x_2, \ldots, x_n)$$
$$\text{s.t.} \quad g_1(x_2, x_2, \ldots, x_n) \leq b_1$$
$$g_2(x_1, x_2, \ldots, x_n) \leq b_2 \qquad (22)$$
$$\vdots$$
$$g_m(x_1, x_2, \ldots, x_n) \leq b_m$$

To apply the results of this section, all the NLP's constraints must be $\leq$ constraints. A constraint of the form $h(x_1, x_2, \ldots, x_n) \geq b$ must be rewritten as $-h(x_1, x_2, \ldots, x_n) \leq -b$. For example, the constraint $2x_1 + x_2 \geq 2$ should be rewritten as $-2x_1 - x_2 \leq -2$. A constraint of the form $h(x_1, x_2, \ldots, x_n) = b$ must be replaced by $h(x_1, x_2, \ldots, x_n) \leq b$ and $-h(x_1, x_2, \ldots, x_n) \leq -b$. For example, $2x_1 + x_2 = 2$ would be replaced by $2x_1 + x_2 \leq 2$ and $-2x_1 - x_2 \leq -2$.

Theorems 9 and 9′ give conditions (the **Kuhn-Tucker**, or K-T, **conditions**) that are necessary for a point $\bar{x} = (\bar{x}_1, \bar{x}_2, \ldots, \bar{x}_n)$ to solve (22). The partial derivative of a function f with respect to a variable x_j evaluated at $\bar{x}$ is written

$$\frac{\partial f(\bar{x})}{\partial x_j}$$

For the theorems to hold, the functions $g_1(x_1, x_2, \ldots, x_n), \ldots, g_m(x_1, x_2, \ldots, x_n)$ must satisfy certain **regularity conditions** (see Bazaraa and Shetty (1979, p. 137)).

When the constraints are linear, these regularity assumptions are always satisfied. In other situations (particularly when some of the constraints are equality constraints), the regularity conditions may not be satisfied. We assume that all problems we consider satisfy these regularity conditions.

THEOREM 9

Suppose (22) is a maximization problem. If $\bar{x} = (\bar{x}_1, \bar{x}_2, \ldots, \bar{x}_n)$ is an optimal solution to (22), then $\bar{x} = (\bar{x}_1, \bar{x}_2, \ldots, \bar{x}_n)$ must satisfy the m constraints in (22), and there must exist multipliers $\bar{\lambda}_1, \bar{\lambda}_2, \ldots, \bar{\lambda}_m$ satisfying

$$\frac{\partial f(\bar{x})}{\partial x_j} - \sum_{i=1}^{i=m} \bar{\lambda}_i \frac{\partial g_i(\bar{x})}{\partial x_j} = 0 \qquad (j = 1, 2, \ldots, n) \qquad (23)$$

$$\bar{\lambda}_i[b_i - g_i(\bar{x})] = 0 \qquad (i = 1, 2, \ldots, m) \qquad (24)$$

$$\bar{\lambda}_i \geq 0 \qquad (i = 1, 2, \ldots, m) \qquad (25)$$

THEOREM 9′

Suppose (22) is a minimization problem. If $\bar{x} = (\bar{x}_1, \bar{x}_2, \ldots, \bar{x}_n)$ is an optimal solution to (22), then $\bar{x} = (\bar{x}_1, \bar{x}_2, \ldots, \bar{x}_n)$ must satisfy the m constraints in (22), and there must exist multipliers $\bar{\lambda}_1, \bar{\lambda}_2, \ldots, \bar{\lambda}_m$ satisfying

$$\frac{\partial f(\bar{x})}{\partial x_j} + \sum_{i=1}^{i=m} \bar{\lambda}_i \frac{\partial g_i(\bar{x})}{\partial x_j} = 0 \qquad (j = 1, 2, \ldots, n)$$

$$\bar{\lambda}_i[b_i - g_i(\bar{x})] = 0 \qquad (i = 1, 2, \ldots, m)$$

$$\bar{\lambda}_i \geq 0 \qquad (i = 1, 2, \ldots, m)$$

Like the Lagrange multipliers of the preceding section, the multiplier $\bar{\lambda}_i$ associated with the K-T conditions may be thought of as the shadow price for the ith constraint in (22). Suppose (22) is a maximization problem. If the right-hand side of the ith constraint of (22) is increased from b_i to $b_i + \Delta$ (for Δ small), the optimal objective function value for (22) will increase by approximately $\Delta\bar{\lambda}_i$. Suppose (22) is a minimization problem. If the right-hand side of the ith constraint of (22) is increased from b_i to $b_i + \Delta$ (for Δ small), the optimal objective function value for (22) is decreased by $\Delta\bar{\lambda}_i$.

Bearing in mind this interpretation of the multipliers as shadow prices, we may interpret (23)–(25) for a max problem. Suppose we consider each constraint in (22) to be a resource-usage constraint. That is, at $\bar{x} = (\bar{x}_1, \bar{x}_2, \ldots, \bar{x}_n)$, we use $g_i(\bar{x}_1, \bar{x}_2, \ldots, \bar{x}_n)$ units of resource i, and b_i units of resource i are available. Suppose we increase the value of x_j by a small amount. Because of increasing x_j by Δ, the value of the objective function increases by

$$\frac{\partial f(\bar{x})}{\partial x_j} \Delta$$

Changing the value of x_j to $\bar{x}_j + \Delta$ also changes the ith constraint to

$$g_i(\bar{x}) + \frac{\partial g_i(\bar{x})}{\partial x_j} \Delta \leq b_i \qquad \text{or} \qquad g_i(\bar{x}) \leq b_i - \frac{\partial g_i(\bar{x})}{\partial x_j} \Delta$$

Thus, increasing x_j by Δ has the effect of increasing the right-hand side of the ith constraint by

$$- \frac{\partial g_i(\bar{x})}{\partial x_j} \Delta$$

These changes in the right-hand sides of the constraints will increase the value of z by approximately

$$-\Delta \sum_{i=1}^{i=m} \bar{\lambda}_i \frac{\partial g_i(\bar{x})}{\partial x_j}$$

In total, the approximate change in z due to increasing x_j by Δ is

$$\Delta \left[\frac{\partial f(\bar{x})}{\partial x_j} - \sum_{i=1}^{i=m} \bar{\lambda}_i \frac{\partial g_i(\bar{x})}{\partial x_j} \right]$$

If the term in brackets is larger than zero, we can increase f by choosing $\Delta > 0$. On the other hand, if this term is smaller than zero, we can increase f by choosing $\Delta < 0$. Thus, for $\bar{x}$ to be optimal, (23) must hold.

Condition (24) is a generalization of the complementary slackness conditions for LPs discussed in Section 6.10. Condition (24) implies that

$$\text{If } \bar{\lambda}_i > 0, \qquad \text{then} \qquad g_i(\bar{x}) = b_i \qquad (i\text{th constraint binding}) \qquad (24')$$

$$\text{If } g_i(\bar{x}) < b_i, \qquad \text{then} \qquad \bar{\lambda}_i = 0 \qquad (24'')$$

Suppose the constraint $g_i(x_1, x_2, \ldots, x_n) \leq b_i$ is a resource-usage constraint representing the fact that at most b_i units of the ith resource can be used. Then (24′) states that if an additional unit of the resource associated with the ith constraint is to have any value, the current optimal solution must use all b_i units of the ith resource currently available. On the other hand, (24″) states that if some of the ith resource currently available is unused, then additional amounts of the ith resource have no value.

If for $\Delta > 0$, we increase the right-hand side of the ith constraint from b_i to $b_i + \Delta$, the optimal objective function value must increase or stay the same, because the increase adds points to the problem's feasible region. Since increasing the right-hand side of the ith constraint by Δ increases the optimal objective function value by $\Delta\bar{\lambda}_i$, it must be that $\bar{\lambda}_i \geq 0$. This is why (25) is included in the K-T conditions.

In many situations, the K-T conditions are applied to NLPs in which the variables must be nonnegative. For example, we may wish to use the K-T conditions to find the optimal solution to

$$\max \text{ (or min) } z = f(x_1, x_2, \ldots, x_n)$$
$$\text{s.t.} \quad g_1(x_1, x_2, \ldots, x_n) \leq b_1$$
$$g_2(x_1, x_2, \ldots, x_n) \leq b_2$$
$$\vdots$$
$$g_m(x_1, x_2, \ldots, x_n) \leq b_m \qquad (26)$$
$$-x_1 \leq 0$$
$$-x_2 \leq 0$$
$$-x_n \leq 0$$

If we associate multipliers $\mu_1, \mu_2, \ldots, \mu_n$ with the nonnegativity constraints in (26), Theorems 9 and 9′ reduce to Theorems 10 and 10′.

THEOREM 10

Suppose (26) is a maximization problem. If $\bar{x} = (\bar{x}_1, \bar{x}_2, \ldots, \bar{x}_n)$ is an optimal solution to (26), then $\bar{x} = (\bar{x}_1, \bar{x}_2, \ldots, \bar{x}_n)$ must satisfy the constraints in (26), and there must exist multipliers $\bar{\lambda}_1, \bar{\lambda}_2, \ldots, \bar{\lambda}_m, \bar{\mu}_1, \bar{\mu}_2, \ldots, \bar{\mu}_n$ satisfying

$$\frac{\partial f(\bar{x})}{\partial x_j} - \sum_{i=1}^{i=m} \bar{\lambda}_i \frac{\partial g_i(\bar{x})}{\partial x_j} + \mu_j = 0 \qquad (j = 1, 2, \ldots, n) \qquad (27)$$

$$\bar{\lambda}_i[b_i - g_i(\bar{x})] = 0 \qquad (i = 1, 2, \ldots, m) \qquad (28)$$

$$\left[\frac{\partial f(\bar{x})}{\partial x_j} - \sum_{i=1}^{i=m} \bar{\lambda}_i \frac{\partial g_i(\bar{x})}{\partial x_j}\right] \bar{x}_j = 0 \qquad (j = 1, 2, \ldots, n) \qquad (29)$$

$$\bar{\lambda}_i \geq 0 \qquad (i = 1, 2, \ldots, m) \qquad (30)$$

$$\bar{\mu}_j \geq 0 \qquad (j = 1, 2, \ldots, n) \qquad (31)$$

Since $\bar{\mu}_j \geq 0$, (27) is equivalent to

$$\frac{\partial f(\bar{x})}{\partial x_j} - \sum_{i=1}^{i=m} \bar{\lambda}_i \frac{\partial g_i(\bar{x})}{\partial x_j} \leq 0 \quad (j = 1, 2, \ldots, n) \tag{27'}$$

Then (27)–(31), the K-T conditions for a maximization problem with nonnegativity constraints, may be rewritten as

$$\frac{\partial f(\bar{x})}{\partial x_j} - \sum_{i=1}^{i=m} \bar{\lambda}_i \frac{\partial g_i(\bar{x})}{\partial x_j} \leq 0 \quad (j = 1, 2, \ldots, n) \tag{27'}$$

$$\bar{\lambda}_i[b_i - g_i(\bar{x})] = 0 \quad (i = 1, 2, \ldots, m) \tag{28'}$$

$$\left[\frac{\partial f(\bar{x})}{\partial x_j} - \sum_{i=1}^{i=m} \bar{\lambda}_i \frac{\partial g_i(\bar{x})}{\partial x_j}\right] \bar{x}_j = 0 \quad (j = 1, 2, \ldots, n) \tag{29'}$$

$$\bar{\lambda}_i \geq 0 \quad (i = 1, 2, \ldots, m) \tag{30'}$$

THEOREM 10'   Suppose (26) is a minimization problem. If $\bar{x} = (\bar{x}_1, \bar{x}_2, \ldots, \bar{x}_n)$ is an optimal solution to (26), then $\bar{x} = (\bar{x}_1, \bar{x}_2, \ldots, \bar{x}_n)$ must satisfy the constraints in (26), and there must exist multipliers $\bar{\lambda}_1, \bar{\lambda}_2, \ldots, \bar{\lambda}_m, \bar{\mu}_1, \bar{\mu}_2, \ldots, \bar{\mu}_n$ satisfying

$$\frac{\partial f(\bar{x})}{\partial x_j} + \sum_{i=1}^{i=m} \bar{\lambda}_i \frac{\partial g_i(\bar{x})}{\partial x_j} - \mu_j = 0 \quad (j = 1, 2, \ldots, n) \tag{32}$$

$$\bar{\lambda}_i[b_i - g_i(\bar{x})] = 0 \quad (i = 1, 2, \ldots, m) \tag{33}$$

$$\left[\frac{\partial f(\bar{x})}{\partial x_j} + \sum_{i=1}^{i=m} \bar{\lambda}_i \frac{\partial g_i(\bar{x})}{\partial x_j}\right] \bar{x}_j = 0 \quad (j = 1, 2, \ldots, n) \tag{34}$$

$$\bar{\lambda}_i \geq 0 \quad (i = 1, 2, \ldots, m) \tag{35}$$

$$\bar{\mu}_j \geq 0 \quad (j = 1, 2, \ldots, n) \tag{36}$$

Since $\bar{\mu}_j \geq 0$, (32) may be written as

$$\frac{\partial f(\bar{x})}{\partial x_j} + \sum_{i=1}^{i=m} \bar{\lambda}_i \frac{\partial g_i(\bar{x})}{\partial x_j} \geq 0 \tag{32'}$$

Then (32)–(36), the K-T conditions for a minimization problem with nonnegativity constraints, may be rewritten as

$$\frac{\partial f(\bar{x})}{\partial x_j} + \sum_{i=1}^{i=m} \bar{\lambda}_i \frac{\partial g_i(\bar{x})}{\partial x_j} \geq 0 \quad (j = 1, 2, \ldots, n) \tag{32'}$$

$$\bar{\lambda}_i[b_i - g_i(\bar{x})] = 0 \quad (i = 1, 2, \ldots, m) \tag{33'}$$

$$\left[\frac{\partial f(\bar{x})}{\partial x_j} + \sum_{i=1}^{i=m} \bar{\lambda}_i \frac{\partial g_i(\bar{x})}{\partial x_j}\right] \bar{x}_j = 0 \quad (j = 1, 2, \ldots, n) \tag{34'}$$

$$\bar{\lambda}_i \geq 0 \quad (i = 1, 2, \ldots, m) \tag{35'}$$

Theorems 9, 9', 10, and 10' give conditions that are *necessary* for a point $\bar{x} = (\bar{x}_1, \bar{x}_2, \ldots, \bar{x}_n)$ to be an optimal solution to (22) or (26). The following two theorems give conditions that are *sufficient* for $\bar{x} = (\bar{x}_1, \bar{x}_2, \ldots, \bar{x}_n)$ to be an optimal solution to (22) or (26) (see Bazaraa and Shetty (1979)).

THEOREM 11	Suppose (22) is a maximization problem. If $f(x_1, x_2, \ldots, x_n)$ is a concave function and $g_1(x_1, x_2, \ldots, x_n), \ldots, g_m(x_1, x_2, \ldots, x_n)$ are convex functions, then any point $\bar{x} = (\bar{x}_1, \bar{x}_2, \ldots, \bar{x}_n)$ satisfying the hypotheses of Theorem 9 is an optimal solution to (22). Also, if (26) is a maximization problem, $f(x_1, x_2, \ldots, x_n)$ is a concave function, and $g_1(x_1, x_2, \ldots, x_n), \ldots, g_m(x_1, x_2, \ldots, x_n)$ are convex functions, then any point $\bar{x} = (\bar{x}_1, \bar{x}_2, \ldots, \bar{x}_n)$ satisfying the hypotheses of Theorem 10 is an optimal solution to (26).

THEOREM 11'	Suppose (22) is a minimization problem. If $f(x_1, x_2, \ldots, x_n)$ is a convex function and $g_1(x_1, x_2, \ldots, x_n), \ldots, g_m(x_1, x_2, \ldots, x_n)$ are convex functions, then any point $\bar{x} = (\bar{x}_1, \bar{x}_2, \ldots, \bar{x}_n)$ satisfying the hypotheses of Theorem 9' is an optimal solution to (22). Also, if (26) is a minimization problem, $f(x_1, x_2, \ldots, x_n)$ is a convex function, and $g_1(x_1, x_2, \ldots, x_n), \ldots, g_m(x_1, x_2, \ldots, x_n)$ are convex functions, then any point $\bar{x} = (\bar{x}_1, \bar{x}_2, \ldots, \bar{x}_n)$ satisfying the hypotheses of Theorem 10' is an optimal solution to (26).

The following two examples illustrate the use of the K-T conditions.

E X A M P L E 20

Describe the optimal solution to

$$\max f(x) \tag{37}$$
$$\text{s.t.} \quad a \le x \le b$$

Solution

From Section 12.3, we know (assuming that $f'(x)$ exists for all x on the interval $[a, b]$) that the optimal solution to this problem must occur at a (with $f'(a) \le 0$), at b (with $f'(b) \ge 0$), or at a point having $f'(x) = 0$. How do the K-T conditions yield these three cases?

We write (37) as

$$\max f(x)$$
$$\text{s.t.} \quad -x \le -a$$
$$x \le b$$

Then (23)–(25) yield

$$f'(x) + \lambda_1 - \lambda_2 = 0 \tag{38}$$
$$\lambda_1(-a + x) = 0 \tag{39}$$
$$\lambda_2(b - x) = 0 \tag{40}$$
$$\lambda_1 \ge 0 \tag{41}$$
$$\lambda_2 \ge 0 \tag{42}$$

In using the K-T conditions to solve NLPs, it is useful to note that each multiplier λ_i must satisfy $\lambda_i = 0$ or $\lambda_i > 0$. Thus, in attempting to find values of x, λ_1, and λ_2 that satisfy (38)–(42), we must consider the following four cases:

Case 1 $\lambda_1 = \lambda_2 = 0$. From (38), we obtain the case $f'(\bar{x}) = 0$.

Case 2 $\lambda_1 = 0$, $\lambda_2 > 0$. Since $\lambda_2 > 0$, (40) yields $\bar{x} = b$. Then (38) yields $f'(b) = \lambda_2$, and since $\lambda_2 > 0$, we obtain the case where $f'(b) > 0$.

Case 3 $\lambda_1 > 0$, $\lambda_2 = 0$. Since $\lambda_1 > 0$, (39) yields $\bar{x} = a$. Then (38) yields the case where $f'(a) = -\lambda_1 < 0$.

Case 4 $\lambda_1 > 0$, $\lambda_2 > 0$. From (39) and (40), we obtain $\bar{x} = a$ and $\bar{x} = b$. This contradiction indicates that Case 4 cannot occur.

Since the constraints are linear, Theorem 11 shows that if $f(x)$ is concave, then (38)–(42) yield the optimal solution to (34).

◆

E X A M P L E
21

A monopolist can purchase up to 17.25 oz of a chemical for \$10/oz. At a cost of \$3/oz, the chemical can be processed into an ounce of product 1, and at a cost of \$5/oz, the chemical can be processed into an ounce of product 2. If x_1 oz of product 1 are produced, product 1 sells for a price of $30 - x_1$ per ounce. If x_2 oz of product 2 are produced, product 2 sells for a price of $50 - 2x_2$ per ounce. Determine how the monopolist can maximize profits.

Solution   Let

$$x_1 = \text{ounces of product 1 produced}$$
$$x_2 = \text{ounces of product 2 produced}$$
$$x_3 = \text{ounces of chemical processed}$$

Then we wish to solve the following NLP:

$$\max z = x_1(30 - x_1) + x_2(50 - 2x_2) - 3x_1 - 5x_2 - 10x_3$$
$$\text{s.t.} \quad x_1 + x_2 \le x_3 \quad \text{or} \quad x_1 + x_2 - x_3 \le 0 \tag{43}$$
$$x_3 \le 17.25$$

Of course, we should add the constraints x_1, x_2, $x_3 \ge 0$. However, the optimal solution to (43) satisfies the nonnegativity constraints, so the optimal solution to (43) will be optimal for an NLP consisting of (43) with the nonnegativity constraints.

Observe that the objective function in (43) is the sum of concave functions (and is therefore concave), and the constraints in (43) are convex (because they are linear). Thus, Theorem 11 shows that the K-T conditions are necessary and sufficient for (x_1, x_2, x_3) to be an optimal solution to (43). From Theorem 9, the K-T conditions for (43) become

$$30 - 2x_1 - 3 - \lambda_1 = 0 \tag{44}$$
$$50 - 4x_2 - 5 - \lambda_1 = 0 \tag{45}$$
$$-10 + \lambda_1 - \lambda_2 = 0 \tag{46}$$
$$\lambda_1(-x_1 - x_2 + x_3) = 0 \tag{47}$$
$$\lambda_2(17.25 - x_3) = 0 \tag{48}$$
$$\lambda_1 \ge 0 \tag{49}$$
$$\lambda_2 \ge 0 \tag{50}$$

As in the previous example, there are four cases to consider:

Case 1 $\lambda_1 = \lambda_2 = 0$. This case cannot occur, because (46) would be violated.

Case 2 $\lambda_1 = 0$, $\lambda_2 > 0$. If $\lambda_1 = 0$, then (46) implies $\lambda_2 = -10$. This would violate (50).

Case 3 $\lambda_1 > 0$, $\lambda_2 = 0$. From (46), we obtain $\lambda_1 = 10$. Now (44) yields $x_1 = 8.5$, and (45) yields $x_2 = 8.75$. From (47), we obtain $x_1 + x_2 = x_3$, so $x_3 = 17.25$. Thus, $\bar{x}_1 = 8.5$, $\bar{x}_2 = 8.75$, $\bar{x}_3 = 17.25$, $\bar{\lambda}_1 = 10$, $\bar{\lambda}_2 = 0$ satisfies the K-T conditions.

Case 4 $\lambda_1 > 0$, $\lambda_2 > 0$. Since Case 3 yields an optimal solution, we need not consider Case 4.

Thus, the optimal solution to (43) is to buy 17.25 oz of the chemical and produce 8.5 oz of product 1 and 8.75 oz of product 2. For Δ small, $\bar{\lambda}_1 = 10$ indicates that if an extra Δ oz of the chemical were obtained at no cost, profits would increase by 10Δ. (Can you see why?) From (46), we find that $\bar{\lambda}_2 = 0$. This implies that the right to purchase an extra Δ oz of the chemical would not increase profits. (Can you see why?)

◆ PROBLEMS

GROUP A

1.[†] A power company faces demands during both peak and off-peak times. If a price of p_1 dollars per kilowatt-hour is charged during the peak time, customers will demand $60 - 0.5p_1$ kwh of power. If a price of p_2 dollars is charged during the off-peak time, customers will demand $40 - p_2$ kwh. The power company must have sufficient capacity to meet demand during both the peak and off-peak times. It costs \$10 per day to maintain each kilowatt-hour of capacity. Determine how the power company can maximize daily revenues less operating costs.

2. Use the K-T conditions to find the optimal solution to the following NLP:

$$\max z = x_1 - x_2$$
$$\text{s.t.} \quad x_1^2 + x_2^2 \leq 1$$

3. Consider the Giapetto problem of Section 3.1:

$$\max z = 3x_1 + 2x_2$$
$$\text{s.t.} \quad 2x_1 + x_2 \leq 100$$
$$x_1 + x_2 \leq 80$$
$$x_1 \leq 40$$
$$x_1 \geq 0$$
$$x_2 \geq 0$$

Find the K-T conditions for this problem and discuss their relation to the dual of the Giapetto LP and the complementary slackness conditions for the LP.

4. If the feasible region for (22) is bounded and contains its boundary points, it can be shown that (22) has an optimal solution. Suppose that the regularity conditions are valid but that the hypotheses of Theorems 11 and 11′ are not valid. If we can prove that only one point satisfies the K-T conditions, why must that point be the optimal solution to the NLP?

5. A total of 160 hours of labor are available each week at \$15/hour. Additional labor can be purchased at \$25/hour. Capital can be purchased in unlimited quantities at a cost of \$5/unit of capital. If K units of capital and L units of labor are available during a week, then $L^{1/2}K^{1/3}$ machines can be produced. Each machine sells for \$270. How can the firm maximize its weekly profits?

6. Use the K-T conditions to find the optimal solution to the following NLP:

$$\min z = (x_1 - 1)^2 + (x_2 - 2)^2$$
$$\text{s.t.} \quad -x_1 + x_2 = 1$$
$$x_1 + x_2 \leq 2$$
$$x_1, x_2 \geq 0$$

7. For Example 21, explain why $\bar{\lambda}_1 = 10$ and $\bar{\lambda}_2 = 0$. (*Hint:* Think about the economic principle that for each product produced, marginal revenue must equal marginal cost.)

[†]Based on Littlechild, "Peak Loads" (1970).

8. Use the K-T conditions to find the optimal solution to the following NLP:

$$\max z = -x_1^2 - x_2^2 + 4x_1 + 6x_2$$
$$\text{s.t.} \quad x_1 + x_2 \leq 6$$
$$x_1 \quad\quad \leq 3$$
$$x_2 \leq 4$$
$$x_1, x_2 \geq 0$$

9. Use the K-T conditions to find the optimal solution to the following NLP:

$$\min z = e^{-x_1} + e^{-2x_2}$$
$$\text{s.t.} \quad x_1 + x_2 \leq 1$$
$$x_1, x_2 \geq 0$$

10. Use the K-T conditions to find the optimal solution to the following NLP:

$$\min z = (x_1 - 3)^2 + (x_2 - 5)^2$$
$$\text{s.t.} \quad x_1 + x_2 \leq 7$$
$$x_1, x_2 \geq 0$$

GROUP B

11. We must determine the percentage of our money to be invested in stocks x and y. Let a = percentage of money invested in x and $b = 1 - a$ = percentage of money invested in y. A choice of a and b is called a *portfolio*. A portfolio is efficient if there exists no other portfolio whose return has a higher mean return and lower variance, or a higher mean return and the same variance, or a lower variance with the same mean return. Let $\bar{x}$ be the mean return on stock x and $\bar{y}$ be the mean return on stock y. The variance of the annual return on one share of stock x is var x, and the variance of the annual return on one share of stock y is var y. Assume that the covariance between the annual return for one share of x and one share of y is $\text{cov}(x, y)$. If we invest a% of our money in stock x and b% in stock y, the variance of the return is given by

$$a^2 \text{ var } x + b^2 \text{ var } y + 2ab \text{ cov}(x, y)$$

Consider the following NLP:

$$\max z = a\bar{x} + b\bar{y}$$
$$\text{s.t.} \quad a^2 \text{ var } x + b^2 \text{ var } y + 2ab \text{ cov}(x,y) \leq v^*,$$
$$a + b = 1$$

where v^* is a given nonnegative number.
(a) Show that any solution to this NLP is an efficient portfolio.
(b) Show that as v^* ranges over all nonnegative numbers, all efficient portfolios are obtained.

12-9   QUADRATIC PROGRAMMING

Consider an NLP whose objective function is the sum of terms of the form $x_1^{k_1} x_2^{k_2} \cdots x_n^{k_n}$. The degree of the term $x_1^{k_1} x_2^{k_2} \ldots x_n^{k_n}$ is $k_1 + k_2 + \cdots k_n$. Thus, the degree of the term $x_1^2 x_2$ is 3, and the degree of the term $x_1 x_2$ is 2. An NLP whose constraints are linear and whose objective is the sum of terms of the form $x_1^{k_1} x_2^{k_2} \cdots x_n^{k_n}$ (with each term having a degree of 2, 1, or 0) is a **quadratic programming problem** (QPP).

Several algorithms can be used to solve quadratic programming problems (see Bazaraa and Shetty (1979, Chapter 11)). We discuss here the application of quadratic programming to portfolio selection and show how LINDO can be used to solve quadratic programming problems. We also describe Wolfe's method for solving quadratic programming problems.

QUADRATIC PROGRAMMING AND PORTFOLIO SELECTION

Consider an investor who has a fixed amount of money that can be invested in several investments. It is often assumed that an investor wants to maximize the expected return from his investments (portfolio) while simultaneously ensuring that the risk of his portfolio is small (as measured by the variance of the return earned by the portfolio). Unfortunately, the return on stocks that yield a large expected return is usually highly variable. Thus, one often approaches the problem of selecting a portfolio by choosing an acceptable minimum expected return and finding the portfolio with the minimum variance that attains an acceptable expected return. For example, an investor may seek the minimum variance portfolio that yields a 12% expected return. By varying the minimum acceptable expected return, the investor may obtain and compare several desirable portfolios.

These ideas reduce the portfolio selection problem to a quadratic programming problem. To see this, we need to review the rules for finding means and variances of the sums of random variables that were discussed in Section 11.6. (The reader who is unfamiliar with the concept of covariance is urged to read Section 11.6.)

Recall that given random variables $\mathbf{X}_1, \mathbf{X}_2, \ldots, \mathbf{X}_n$ and constants a, b, and k,

$$E(\mathbf{X}_1 + \mathbf{X}_2 + \cdots + \mathbf{X}_n) = E(\mathbf{X}_1) + E(\mathbf{X}_2) + \cdots + E(\mathbf{X}_n) \tag{51}$$

$$\text{var}(\mathbf{X}_1 + \mathbf{X}_2 + \cdots + \mathbf{X}_n) = \text{var}\,\mathbf{X}_1 + \text{var}\,\mathbf{X}_2 + \cdots + \text{var}\,\mathbf{X}_n \tag{52}$$
$$+ \sum_{i \neq j} \text{cov}(\mathbf{X}_i, \mathbf{X}_j)$$

$$E(k\mathbf{X}_i) = kE(\mathbf{X}_i) \tag{53}$$

$$\text{var}(k\mathbf{X}_i) = k^2 \, \text{var}\,\mathbf{X}_i \tag{54}$$

$$\text{cov}(a\mathbf{X}_i, b\mathbf{X}_j) = ab\,\text{cov}(\mathbf{X}_i, \mathbf{X}_j) \tag{55}$$

In the following example, we show how the portfolio selection problem reduces to a quadratic programming problem.

E X A M P L E
22

I have \$1000 to invest in three stocks. Let $\mathbf{S}_i$ be the random variable representing the annual return on \$1 invested in stock i. Thus, if $\mathbf{S}_i = 0.12$, \$1 invested in stock i at the beginning of a year was worth \$1.12 at the end of the year. We are given the following information: $E(\mathbf{S}_1) = 0.14$, $E(\mathbf{S}_2) = 0.11$, $E(\mathbf{S}_3) = 0.10$, $\text{var}\,\mathbf{S}_1 = 0.20$, $\text{var}\,\mathbf{S}_2 = 0.08$, $\text{var}\,\mathbf{S}_3 = 0.18$, $\text{cov}(\mathbf{S}_1, \mathbf{S}_2) = 0.05$, $\text{cov}(\mathbf{S}_1, \mathbf{S}_3) = 0.02$, $\text{cov}(\mathbf{S}_2, \mathbf{S}_3) = 0.03$. Formulate a quadratic programming problem that can be used to find the minimum variance portfolio that attains an expected annual return of at least 12%.

Solution

Let x_j = number of dollars invested in stock j ($j = 1, 2, 3$). Then the annual return on the portfolio is $(x_1\mathbf{S}_1 + x_2\mathbf{S}_2 + x_3\mathbf{S}_3)/1000$ and the expected annual return on the portfolio is (by (51) and (53)),

$$\frac{x_1 E(\mathbf{S}_1) + x_2 E(\mathbf{S}_2) + x_3 E(\mathbf{S}_3)}{1000}$$

To ensure that the portfolio has an expected return of at least 12%, we must include the following constraint in the formulation:

$$\frac{0.14x_1 + 0.11x_2 + 0.10x_3}{1000} \geq 0.12 = 0.14x_1 + 0.11x_2 + 0.10x_2 \geq 0.12(1000) = 120$$

Of course, we must also include the constraint $x_1 + x_2 + x_3 = 1000$. We assume that the amount invested in a stock must be nonnegative (that is, no short sales of stock are allowed) and add the constraints $x_1, x_2, x_3 \geq 0$. Our objective is simply to minimize the variance of the portfolio's annual return. From (52), the variance of the portfolio is given by

$$\begin{aligned}
\text{var}(x_1 \mathbf{S}_1 + x_2 \mathbf{S}_2 + x_3 \mathbf{S}_3) &= \text{var}(x_1 \mathbf{S}_1) + \text{var}(x_2 \mathbf{S}_2) + \text{var}(\mathbf{x}_3 \mathbf{S}_3) \\
&\quad + 2\,\text{cov}(x_1 \mathbf{S}_1, x_2 \mathbf{S}_2) + 2\,\text{cov}(x_1 \mathbf{S}_1, x_3 \mathbf{S}_3) \\
&\quad + 2\,\text{cov}(x_2 \mathbf{S}_2, x_3 \mathbf{S}_3) \\
&= x_1^2 \,\text{var}\,\mathbf{S}_1 + x_2^2 \,\text{var}\,\mathbf{S}_2 + x_3^2 \,\text{var}\,\mathbf{S}_3 + 2x_1 x_2 \,\text{cov}(\mathbf{S}_1, \mathbf{S}_2) \\
&\quad + 2x_1 x_3 \,\text{cov}(\mathbf{S}_1, \mathbf{S}_3) + 2x_2 x_3 \,\text{cov}(\mathbf{S}_2, \mathbf{S}_3) \\
&\quad \text{(from Eqs. (54) and (55))} \\
&= 0.20x_1^2 + 0.08x_2^2 + 0.18x_3^2 + 0.10x_1 x_2 \\
&\quad + 0.04x_1 x_3 + 0.06x_2 x_3
\end{aligned}$$

Observe that each term in the last expression for the portfolio's variance is of degree 2. Thus, we have an NLP with linear constraints and an objective function consisting of terms of degree 2. To obtain the minimum variance portfolio yielding an expected return of at least 12%, we must solve the following QPP:

$$
\begin{aligned}
\min z = \;& 0.20x_1^2 + 0.08x_2^2 + 0.18x_3^2 + 0.10x_1 x_2 + 0.04x_1 x_3 + 0.06x_2 x_3 \\
\text{s.t.} \quad & 0.14x_1 + 0.11x_2 + 0.10x_3 \geq 120 \\
& x_1 + x_2 + x_3 = 1000 \\
& x_1, x_2, x_3 \geq 0
\end{aligned}
\tag{56}
$$

♦

USING LINDO TO SOLVE QUADRATIC PROGRAMMING PROBLEMS

To use LINDO to solve a QPP, we must formulate the problem as a minimization problem (if we are solving a maximization problem, we simply multiply the objective function by − 1). LINDO requires that all the variables be nonnegative. Then we must rewrite all the constraints as ≤ constraints and use the Section 12.8 techniques to determine the K-T conditions (32′) for the QPP. LINDO automatically includes all other aspects of the K-T conditions.

Thus, to solve Example 22 by LINDO, we rewrite QPP (56) as

$$
\begin{aligned}
\min z = \;& 0.20x_1^2 + 0.08x_2^2 + 0.18x_3^2 + 0.10x_1 x_2 + 0.04x_1 x_3 + 0.06x_2 x_3 \\
\text{s.t.} \quad & -0.14x_1 - 0.11x_2 - 0.10x_3 \leq -120 \\
& x_1 + x_2 + x_3 \leq 1000 \\
& -x_1 - x_2 - x_3 \leq -1000 \\
& x_1, x_2, x_3 \geq 0
\end{aligned}
\tag{57}
$$

Let LA1, LA2, and LA3 be the multipliers for the three constraints. Then (32′) yields the following three constraints:

$$0.40x_1 + 0.10x_2 + 0.04x_3 - 0.14\text{LA1} + \text{LA2} - \text{LA3} \geq 0$$
$$0.10x_1 + 0.16x_2 + 0.06x_3 - 0.11\text{LA1} + \text{LA2} - \text{LA3} \geq 0$$
$$0.04x_1 + 0.06x_2 + 0.36x_3 - 0.10\text{LA1} + \text{LA2} - \text{LA3} \geq 0$$

We then simply input these constraints followed by the actual constraints in (57) (excluding the nonnegativity constraints). The actual objective function of the QPP need not be entered; LINDO can infer the QPP's objective function from the K-T conditions (32′). The formal procedure for solving a QPP via LINDO is as follows:

Step 1 Access LINDO.

Step 2 Type MIN followed on the same line by a list of the variables (real variables first, then K-T multipliers) separated by + signs. Then hit [CR] (carriage return).

Step 3 Type ST (for subject to) followed by [CR].

Step 4 Type in the K-T conditions of the form (32′).

Step 5 Type in the problem's actual constraints (ignoring nonnegativity constraints).

Step 6 Type END followed by [CR].

Step 7 Type QCP followed by the row number in which the first actual constraint occurs (the list of variables is row 1). Then hit [CR] and GO.

Thus, to solve Example 22 via LINDO would require typing

$$
\begin{aligned}
&\text{MIN X1+X2+X3+LA1+LA2+LA3} \\
&\text{ST} \\
&\quad .40\text{X1}+.10\text{X2}+.04\text{X3}-.14\text{LA1}+\text{LA2}-\text{LA3} \ge 0 \\
&\quad .10\text{X1}+.16\text{X2}+.06\text{X3}-.11\text{LA1}+\text{LA2}-\text{LA3} \ge 0 \\
&\quad .04\text{X1}+.06\text{X2}+.36\text{X3}-.10\text{LA1}+\text{LA2}-\text{LA3} \ge 0 \\
&\quad -.14\text{X1}-.11\text{X2}-.10\text{X3} \le -120 \\
&\quad \text{X1}+\text{X2}+\text{X3} \le 1000 \\
&\quad -\text{X1}-\text{X2}-\text{X3} \le -1000 \\
&\text{END} \\
&\text{QCP 5} \\
&\text{GO}
\end{aligned}
$$

The optimal solution to this QPP is $z = 75{,}238$, X1 $= 380.95$, X2 $= 476.19$, X3 $= 142.86$, LA1 $= 2761.90$, LA2 $= 180.95$, LA3 $= 0$. Thus, the minimum variance portfolio having an expected return of at least 12% consists of placing \$380.95 in stock 1, \$476.19 in stock 2, and \$142.86 in stock 3. The variance of this portfolio is 75,238 (dollars)^2. This portfolio has a standard deviation of \$$(75{,}238)^{1/2}$ = \$274.30. The portfolio yields an expected return of $(0.14(380.95) + 0.11(476.19) + 0.10(142.86))/1000) = \$0.12$ per dollar invested (or 12%).

It is easy to verify that the objective function for Example 22 is convex (see Problem 2 at the end of this section). Since the constraints for (56) (and any QPP) are linear, the K-T conditions do yield the optimal solution to the example. In a more complex problem, however, it may be difficult to determine if the objective function is convex. If we type the command POSD, LINDO will tell us whether the objective function is convex, concave, or neither. If LINDO responds POSITIVE DEFINITE or POSITIVE SEMIDEFINITE, the objective function is convex. If LINDO responds NEGATIVE DEFINITE or NEGATIVE SEMIDEFINITE, the objective function is concave. If LINDO responds INDEFINITE, the objective function is neither convex nor concave.

WOLFE'S METHOD FOR SOLVING QUADRATIC PROGRAMMING PROBLEMS

Wolfe's method may be used to solve QPPs in which all variables must be nonnegative. We illustrate the method by solving the following QPP:

$$\min z = -x_1 - x_2 + (\tfrac{1}{2})x_1^2 + x_2^2 - x_1 x_2$$
$$\text{s.t.} \quad x_1 + x_2 \le 3$$
$$-2x_1 - 3x_2 \le -6$$
$$x_1, x_2 \ge 0$$

The objective function may be shown to be convex, so any point satisfying the Kuhn-Tucker conditions (32′)–(35′) will solve this QPP. After employing excess variables e_1 for the x_1 constraint in (32′), e_2 for the x_2 constraint in (32′), e_2' for the constraint $-2x_1 - 3x_2 \le -6$, and a slack variable s_1' for the constraint $x_1 + x_2 \le 3$, the K-T conditions may be written as

$$x_1 - 1 - x_2 + \lambda_1 - 2\lambda_2 - e_1 = 0 \qquad (x_1 \text{ constraint in (32′)})$$
$$2x_2 - 1 - x_1 + \lambda_1 - 3\lambda_2 - e_2 = 0 \qquad (x_2 \text{ constraint in (32′)})$$
$$x_1 + x_2 + s_1' = 3$$
$$2x_1 + 3x_2 - e_2' = 6$$

All variables nonnegative

$$\lambda_2 e_2' = 0, \qquad \lambda_1 s_1' = 0, \qquad e_1 x_1 = 0, \qquad e_2 x_2 = 0$$

Observe that with the exception of the last four equations, the K-T conditions are all linear or nonnegativity constraints. The last four equations are the complementary slackness conditions for this QPP. For a general QPP, the complementary slackness conditions may be verbally expressed by

e_i from x_i constraint in (32′) and x_i cannot both be positive

Slack or excess variable for ith constraint and λ_i cannot both be positive

$$(58)$$

To find a point satisfying the K-T conditions, Wolfe's method simply applies a modified version of Phase I of the two-phase simplex method to the K-T conditions (except for the complementary slackness conditions). We first add an artificial variable to each constraint in the K-T conditions that does not have an obvious basic variable, and then we attempt to minimize the sum of the artificial variables. To ensure that the final solution (with all artificial variables equal to zero) satisfies the complementary slackness conditions (58), Wolfe's method modifies the simplex's choice of the entering variable as follows:

1. Never perform a pivot that would make the e_i from the ith constraint in (32′) and x_i both basic variables.

2. Never perform a pivot that would make the slack (or excess) variable for the ith constraint and λ_i both basic variables.

To apply Wolfe's method to our example, we must solve the following LP:

$$\min w = a_1 + a_2 + a_2'$$
$$\text{s.t.} \quad x_1 - x_2 + \lambda_1 - 2\lambda_2 - e_1 + a_1 = 1$$
$$-x_1 + 2x_2 + \lambda_1 - 3\lambda_2 - e_2 + a_2 = 1$$
$$x_1 + x_2 + s_1' = 3$$
$$2x_1 + 3x_2 - e_2' + a_2' = 6$$
$$\text{All variables nonnegative}$$

After eliminating the artificial variables from row 0, we obtain the tableau in Table 2. The current basic feasible solution is $w = 8$, $a_1 = 1$, $a_2 = 1$, $s_1' = 3$, $a_2' = 6$. Since x_2 has the most positive coefficient in row 0, we choose to enter x_2 into the basis. The resulting tableau is Table 3. The current basic feasible solution is $w = 6$, $a_1 = \frac{3}{2}$, $x_2 = \frac{1}{2}$, $s_1' = \frac{5}{2}$, $a_2' = \frac{9}{2}$. Since x_1 has the most positive coefficient in row 0, we now enter x_1 into the basis. The resulting tableau is Table 4.

Table 2
Initial Tableau for Wolfe's Method

w	x_1	x_2	λ_1	λ_2	e_1	e_2	s_1'	e_2'	a_1	a_2	a_2'	rhs
1	2	4	2	-5	-1	-1	0	-1	0	0	0	8
0	1	-1	1	-2	-1	0	0	0	1	0	0	1
0	-1	②	1	-3	0	-1	0	0	0	1	0	1
0	1	1	0	0	0	0	1	0	0	0	0	3
0	2	3	0	0	0	0	0	-1	0	0	1	6

Table 3
First Tableau for Wolfe's Method

w	x_1	x_2	λ_1	λ_2	e_1	e_2	s_1'	e_2'	a_1	a_2	a_2'	rhs
1	4	0	0	1	-1	1	0	-1	0	-2	0	6
0	$\frac{1}{2}$	0	$\frac{3}{2}$	$-\frac{7}{2}$	-1	$-\frac{1}{2}$	0	0	1	$\frac{1}{2}$	0	$\frac{3}{2}$
0	$-\frac{1}{2}$	1	$\frac{1}{2}$	$-\frac{3}{2}$	0	$-\frac{1}{2}$	0	0	0	$\frac{1}{2}$	0	$\frac{1}{2}$
0	$\frac{3}{2}$	0	$-\frac{1}{2}$	$\frac{3}{2}$	0	$\frac{1}{2}$	1	0	0	$-\frac{1}{2}$	0	$\frac{5}{2}$
0	⑦⁄₂	0	$-\frac{3}{2}$	$\frac{9}{2}$	0	$\frac{3}{2}$	0	-1	0	$-\frac{3}{2}$	1	$\frac{9}{2}$

Table 4
Second Tableau for Wolfe's Method

w	x_1	x_2	λ_1	λ_2	e_1	e_2	s_1'	e_2'	a_1	a_2	a_2'	rhs
1	0	0	$\frac{12}{7}$	$-\frac{29}{7}$	-1	$-\frac{5}{7}$	0	$\frac{1}{7}$	0	$-\frac{2}{7}$	$-\frac{8}{7}$	$\frac{6}{7}$
0	0	0	$\frac{12}{7}$	$-\frac{29}{7}$	-1	$-\frac{5}{7}$	0	$\frac{1}{7}$	1	$\frac{5}{7}$	$-\frac{1}{7}$	$\frac{6}{7}$
0	0	1	$\frac{2}{7}$	$-\frac{6}{7}$	0	$-\frac{2}{7}$	0	$-\frac{1}{7}$	0	$\frac{2}{7}$	$\frac{1}{7}$	$\frac{8}{7}$
0	0	0	$\frac{1}{7}$	$-\frac{3}{7}$	0	$-\frac{1}{7}$	1	③⁄₇	0	$\frac{1}{7}$	$-\frac{3}{7}$	$\frac{4}{7}$
0	1	0	$-\frac{3}{7}$	$\frac{9}{7}$	0	$\frac{3}{7}$	0	$-\frac{2}{7}$	0	$-\frac{3}{7}$	$\frac{2}{7}$	$\frac{9}{7}$

The current basic feasible solution is $w = \frac{6}{7}$, $a_1 = \frac{6}{7}$, $x_2 = \frac{8}{7}$, $s_1' = \frac{4}{7}$, $x_1 = \frac{9}{7}$. The simplex method recommends that λ_1 should enter the basis. However, Wolfe's modification of the simplex method for selecting the entering variable does not allow λ_1 and s_1'

to both be basic variables. Thus, λ_1 cannot enter the basis. Since e_2' is the only other variable with a positive coefficient in row 0, we now enter e_2' into the basis. The resulting tableau is Table 5. The current basic feasible solution is $w = \frac{2}{3}$, $a_1 = \frac{2}{3}$, $x_2 = \frac{4}{3}$, $e_2' = \frac{4}{3}$, and $x_1 = \frac{5}{3}$. Since s_1' is now a nonbasic variable, we can now enter λ_1 into the basis. The resulting tableau is Table 6. This is (finally!) an optimal tableau. Since $w = 0$, we have found a solution that satisfies the Kuhn-Tucker conditions and is optimal for the QPP. Thus, the optimal solution to the QPP is $x_1 = \frac{9}{5}$, $x_2 = \frac{6}{5}$. From the optimal tableau, we also find that $\lambda_1 = \frac{2}{5}$ and $\lambda_2 = 0$ (since $e_2' = \frac{6}{5} > 0$, we know that $\lambda_2 = 0$ must hold).

Table 5
Third Tableau for Wolfe's Method

w	x_1	x_2	λ_1	λ_2	e_1	e_2	s_1'	e_2'	a_1	a_2	a_2'	rhs
1	0	0	$\frac{5}{3}$	-4	-1	$-\frac{2}{3}$	$-\frac{1}{3}$	0	0	$-\frac{1}{3}$	-1	$\frac{2}{3}$
0	0	0	$\textcircled{\frac{5}{3}}$	-4	-1	$-\frac{2}{3}$	$-\frac{1}{3}$	0	1	$\frac{2}{3}$	0	$\frac{2}{3}$
0	0	1	$\frac{1}{3}$	-1	0	$-\frac{1}{3}$	$\frac{1}{3}$	0	0	$\frac{1}{3}$	0	$\frac{4}{3}$
0	0	0	$\frac{1}{3}$	-1	0	$-\frac{1}{3}$	$\frac{7}{3}$	1	0	$\frac{1}{3}$	-1	$\frac{4}{3}$
0	1	0	$-\frac{1}{3}$	1	0	$\frac{1}{3}$	$\frac{2}{3}$	0	0	$-\frac{1}{3}$	0	$\frac{5}{3}$

Table 6
Optimal Tableau for Wolfe's Method

w	x_1	x_2	λ_1	λ_2	e_1	e_2	s_1'	e_2'	a_1	a_2	a_2'	rhs
1	0	0	0	0	0	0	0	0	-1	-1	-1	0
0	0	0	1	$-\frac{12}{5}$	$-\frac{3}{5}$	$-\frac{2}{5}$	$-\frac{1}{5}$	0	$\frac{3}{5}$	$\frac{2}{5}$	0	$\frac{2}{5}$
0	0	1	0	$-\frac{1}{5}$	$\frac{1}{5}$	$-\frac{1}{5}$	$\frac{2}{5}$	0	$-\frac{1}{5}$	$\frac{1}{5}$	0	$\frac{6}{5}$
0	0	0	0	$-\frac{1}{5}$	$\frac{1}{5}$	$-\frac{1}{5}$	$\frac{12}{5}$	1	$-\frac{1}{5}$	$\frac{1}{5}$	-1	$\frac{6}{5}$
0	1	0	0	$\frac{1}{5}$	$-\frac{1}{5}$	$\frac{1}{5}$	$\frac{3}{5}$	0	$\frac{1}{5}$	$-\frac{1}{5}$	0	$\frac{9}{5}$

Wolfe's method is guaranteed to obtain the optimal solution to a QPP if all leading principal minors of the objective function's Hessian are positive. Otherwise, Wolfe's method may not converge in a finite number of pivots. In practice, the method of **complementary pivoting** is most often used to solve QPPs. Unfortunately, space limitations preclude a discussion of complementary pivoting. The interested reader is referred to Shapiro (1979).

◆ PROBLEMS

GROUP A

1. We are considering investing in three stocks. The random variable S_i represents the value one year from now of \$1 invested in stock i. We are given that $E(S_1) = 1.15$, $E(S_2) = 1.21$, $E(S_3) = 1.09$, $\text{var}\,S_1 = 0.09$, $\text{var}\,S_2 = 0.04$, $\text{var}\,S_3 = 0.01$, $\text{cov}(S_1, S_2) = 0.006$, $\text{cov}(S_1, S_3) = -0.004$, and $\text{cov}(S_2, S_3) = 0.005$. We have \$100 to invest and wish to have an expected return of at least 15% during the next year. Formulate a QPP to find the portfolio of minimum variance that attains an expected return of at least 15%.

2. Show that the objective function for Example 22 is convex (it can be shown that the variance of any portfolio is a convex function of $(x_1, x_2, \ldots, x_n)$).

3. Interpret the multipliers LA1 and LA2 for Example 22.

4. Fruit Computer Company produces Pear and Apricot computers. If they charge a price p_1 for Pear computers and p_2 for Apricot computers, they can sell q_1 Pear and q_2 Apricot computers, where $q_1 = 4000 - 10p_1 + p_2$, and $q_2 = 2000 - 9p_2 + 0.8p_1$. Manufacturing a Pear computer requires 2 hours of labor and 3 computer chips. An Apricot computer uses 3 hours of labor and 1 computer chip. At present, 5000 hours of labor and 4500 chips are available. Formulate a QPP to maximize Fruit's revenue. Use the K-T conditions (or LINDO) to find Fruit's optimal pricing policy. What is the most that Fruit would be willing to pay for another hour of labor? What is the most that Fruit would be willing to pay for another computer chip?

5. Use Wolfe's method to solve the following QPP:

$$\min z = 2x_1^2 - x_2$$
$$\text{s.t.} \quad 2x_1 - x_2 \leq 1$$
$$x_1 + x_2 \leq 1$$
$$x_1, x_2 \geq 0$$

6. Use Wolfe's method to solve the following QPP:

$$\min x_1 + 2x_2^2$$
$$\text{s.t.} \quad x_1 + x_2 \leq 2$$
$$2x_1 + x_2 \leq 3$$
$$x_1, x_2 \geq 0$$

7. In an electrical network, the power loss incurred when a current of I amperes flows through a resistance of R ohms is $I^2 R$ watts. 710 amperes of current must be sent from node 1 to node 4 of Figure 22. The current flowing through each node must satisfy conservation of flow. For

Figure 22

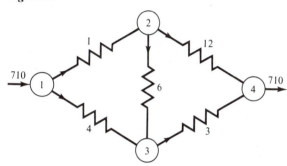

example, for node 1, 710 = flow through 1-ohm resistor + flow through 4-ohm resistor. Remarkably, nature determines the current flow through each resistor by minimizing the total power loss in the network.
(a) Formulate a QPP whose solution will yield the current flowing through each resistor.
(b) Use LINDO to determine the current flowing through each resistor.

8. Use Wolfe's method to find the optimal solution to the following QPP:

$$\min z = x_1^2 + x_2^2 - 2x_1 - 3x_2 + x_1 x_2$$
$$\text{s.t.} \quad x_1 + 2x_2 \leq 2$$
$$x_1, x_2 \geq 0$$

12-10   SEPARABLE PROGRAMMING*

Many NLPs are of the following form:

$$\max \text{ (or min) } z = \sum_{j=1}^{j=n} f_j(x_j)$$

$$\text{s.t.} \sum_{j=1}^{j=n} g_{ij}(x_j) \leq b_i \quad (i = 1, 2, \ldots, m)$$

Since the decision variables appear in separate terms of the objective function and the constraints, NLPs of this form are called **separable programming problems**. Separable programming problems are often solved by approximating each $f_j(x_j)$ and $g_{ij}(x_j)$ by a piecewise linear function (see Section 9.2). Before describing the separable programming technique, we give an example of a separable programming problem.

E X A M P L E
23

Oilco must determine how many barrels of oil to extract during each of the next two years. If Oilco extracts x_1 million barrels during year 1, each barrel can be sold for $30 - x_1$. If Oilco extracts x_2 million barrels during year 2, each barrel can be sold for

*This section covers topics that may be omitted with no loss of continuity.

$35 - x_2$. The cost of extracting x_1 million barrels of oil during year 1 is x_1^2 million dollars, and the cost of extracting x_2 million barrels of oil during year 2 is $2x_2^2$ million dollars. A total of 20 million barrels of oil are available, and at most \$250 million can be spent on extraction. Formulate an NLP to help Oilco maximize profits (revenues less costs) for the next two years.

Solution   Define

$$x_1 = \text{millions of barrels of oil extracted during year 1}$$
$$x_2 = \text{millions of barrels of oil extracted during year 2}$$

Then the appropriate NLP is

$$\max z = x_1(30 - x_1) + x_2(35 - x_2) - x_1^2 - 2x_2^2$$
$$= 30x_1 + 35x_2 - 2x_1^2 - 3x_2^2$$
$$\text{s.t.} \quad x_1^2 + 2x_2^2 \leq 250 \tag{59}$$
$$x_1 + x_2 \leq 20$$
$$x_1, x_2 \geq 0$$

This is a separable programming problem with $f_1(x_1) = 30x_1 - 2x_1^2, f_2(x_2) = 35x_2 - 3x_2^2, g_{11}(x_1) = x_1^2, g_{12}(x_2) = 2x_2^2, g_{21}(x_1) = x_1$, and $g_{22}(x_2) = x_2$. ◆

Before approximating the functions f_j and g_{ij} by piecewise linear functions, we must determine (for $j = 1, 2, \ldots, n$) numbers a_j and b_j such that we are sure that the value of x_j in the optimal solution will satisfy $a_j \leq x_j \leq b_j$. For the previous example, $a_1 = a_2 = 0$ and $b_1 = b_2 = 20$ will suffice. Next, for each variable x_j we choose grid points $p_{j1}, p_{j2}, \ldots, p_{jk}$ with $a_j = p_{j1} \leq p_{j2} \leq \cdots \leq p_{jk} = b_j$ (to simplify notation, we assume that each variable has the same number of grid points). For the previous example, we use five grid points for each variable: $p_{11} = p_{21} = 0$, $p_{12} = p_{22} = 5$, $p_{13} = p_{23} = 10$, $p_{14} = p_{24} = 15$, $p_{15} = p_{25} = 20$. The essence of the separable programming method is to approximate each function f_j and g_{ij} as if it were a linear function on each interval $[p_{j,r-1}, p_{j,r}]$.

More formally, suppose $p_{j,r} \leq x_j \leq p_{j,r+1}$. Then for some δ $(0 \leq \delta \leq 1)$, $x_j = \delta p_{j,r} + (1 - \delta)p_{j,r+1}$. We approximate $f_j(x_j)$ and $g_{ij}(x_j)$ (see Figure 23) by

$$\hat{f}_j(x_j) = \delta f_j(p_{j,r}) + (1 - \delta)f_j(p_{j,r+1})$$
$$\hat{g}_{ij}(x_j) = \delta g_{ij}(p_{j,r}) + (1 - \delta)g_{ij}(p_{j,r+1})$$

Figure 23
The Separable
Programming
Approximation of
$f_j(x_j)$

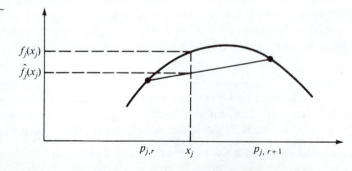

For example, how would we approximate $f_1(12)$? Since $f_1(10) = 30(10) - 2(10)^2 = 100$, $f_1(15) = 30(15) - 2(15)^2 = 0$, and $12 = 0.6(10) + 0.4(15)$, we approximate $f_1(12)$ by $\hat{f}_1(12) = 0.6(100) + 0.4(0) = 60$ (see Figure 24).

More formally, to approximate a separable programming problem, we add constraints of the form

$$\delta_{j1} + \delta_{j2} + \cdots + \delta_{j,k} = 1 \qquad (j = 1, 2, \ldots, n) \tag{60}$$

$$x_j = \delta_{j1} p_{j1} + \delta_{j2} p_{j2} + \cdots + \delta_{j,k} p_{j,k} \qquad (j = 1, 2, \ldots, n) \tag{61}$$

$$\delta_{j,r} \geq 0 \qquad (j = 1, 2, \ldots, n; \, r = 1, 2, \ldots, k) \tag{62}$$

Figure 24
Approximation of
$f_1(12)$

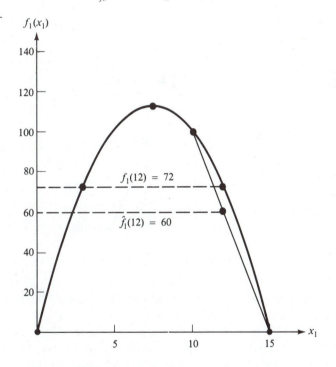

Then we replace $f_j(x_j)$ by

$$\hat{f}_j(x_j) = \delta_{j1} f_j(p_{j1}) + \delta_{j2} f_j(p_{j2}) + \cdots + \delta_{j,k} f_j(p_{j,k}) \tag{63}$$

and replace $g_{ij}(x_j)$ by

$$\hat{g}_{ij}(x_j) = \delta_{j1} g_{ij}(p_{j1}) + \delta_{j2} g_{ij}(p_{j2}) + \cdots + \delta_{j,k} g_{ij}(p_{j,k}) \tag{64}$$

To ensure that accuracy of the approximations in (63) and (64), we must be sure that for each j ($j = 1, 2, \ldots, n$) at most two of the $\delta_{j,k}$'s are positive. Also, for a given j, suppose that two $\delta_{j,k}$'s are positive. If $\delta_{j,k'}$ is positive, then the other positive $\delta_{j,k}$ must be either $\delta_{j,k'-1}$ or $\delta_{j,k'+1}$ (we say that $\delta_{j,k'}$ is adjacent to $\delta_{j,k'-1}$ and $\delta_{j,k'+1}$). To see the reason for these restrictions, suppose we want $x_1 = 12$. Then our approximations will be most accurate if $\delta_{13} = 0.6$ and $\delta_{14} = 0.4$. In this case, we approximate $f_1(12)$ by $0.6f_1(10) + 0.4f_1(15)$. We certainly don't want to have $\delta_{11} = 0.4$ and $\delta_{15} = 0.6$. This would yield $x_1 = 0.4(0) + 0.6(20) = 12$, but it would approximate $f_1(12)$ by $f_1(12) = 0.4f_1(0) + 0.6f_1(20)$, and in most cases this would be a poor approximation of $f_1(12)$ (see Figure 25). For the

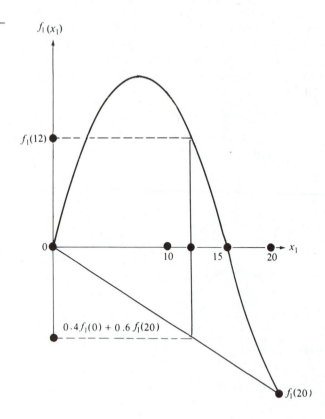

approximating problem to yield a good approximation to the functions f_j and $g_{j,k}$, we must add the following **adjacency assumption**: For $j = 1, 2, \ldots, n$, at most two $\delta_{j,k}$'s can be positive. If for a given j, two $\delta_{j,k}$'s are positive, they must be adjacent.

Thus, the approximating problem consists of an objective function obtained from (63) and constraints obtained from (60), (61), (62), and (64) and the adjacency assumption. Actually, the constraints (61) are only used to transform the values of the $\delta_{j,k}$'s into values for the original decision variables (the x_j's) and are not needed to determine the optimal values of the $\delta_{j,k}$'s. The constraints (61) need not be part of the approximating problem, and the **approximating problem** for a separable programming problem may be written as follows:

$$\text{max (or min) } \hat{z} = \sum_{j=1}^{j=n} [\delta_{j1}f_j(p_{j1}) + \delta_{j2}f_j(p_{j2}) + \cdots + \delta_{j,k}f_j(p_{j,k})]$$

$$\text{s.t.} \quad \sum_{j=1}^{j=n} [\delta_{j1}g_{ij}(p_{j1}) + \delta_{j2}g_{ij}(p_{j2}) + \cdots + \delta_{j,k}g_{ij}(p_{jk})] \le b_i \quad (i = 1, 2, \ldots, m)$$

$$\delta_{j1} + \delta_{j2} + \cdots + \delta_{j,k} = 1 \quad (j = 1, 2, \ldots, n)$$

$$\delta_{j,r} \ge 0 \quad (j = 1, 2, \ldots, n; r = 1, 2, \ldots, k)$$

Adjacency assumption

For the previous example, we have

$$f_1(0) = 0, \quad f_1(5) = 100, \quad f_1(10) = 100, \quad f_1(15) = 0, \quad f_1(20) = -200$$
$$f_2(0) = 0, \quad f_2(5) = 100, \quad f_2(10) = 50, \quad f_2(15) = -150, \quad f_2(20) = -500$$
$$g_{11}(0) = 0, \quad g_{11}(5) = 25, \quad g_{11}(10) = 100, \quad g_{11}(15) = 225, \quad g_{11}(20) = 400$$
$$g_{12}(0) = 0, \quad g_{12}(5) = 50, \quad g_{12}(10) = 200, \quad g_{12}(15) = 450, \quad g_{12}(20) = 800$$
$$g_{21}(0) = 0, \quad g_{21}(5) = 5, \quad g_{21}(10) = 10, \quad g_{21}(15) = 15, \quad g_{21}(20) = 20$$
$$g_{22}(0) = 0, \quad g_{22}(5) = 5, \quad g_{22}(10) = 10, \quad g_{22}(15) = 15, \quad g_{22}(20) = 20$$

Applying (63) to the objective function of (59) yields an approximating objective function of

$$\max \hat{z} = 100\delta_{12} + 100\delta_{13} - 200\delta_{15} + 100\delta_{22} + 50\delta_{23} - 150\delta_{24} - 500\delta_{25}$$

Constraint (60) yields the following two constraints:

$$\delta_{11} + \delta_{12} + \delta_{13} + \delta_{14} + \delta_{15} = 1$$
$$\delta_{21} + \delta_{22} + \delta_{23} + \delta_{24} + \delta_{25} = 1$$

Constraint (61) yields the following two constraints:

$$x_1 = 5\delta_{12} + 10\delta_{13} + 15\delta_{14} + 20\delta_{15}$$
$$x_2 = 5\delta_{22} + 10\delta_{23} + 15\delta_{24} + 20\delta_{25}$$

Applying (64) transforms the two constraints in (59) to

$$25\delta_{12} + 100\delta_{13} + 225\delta_{14} + 400\delta_{15} + 50\delta_{22} + 200\delta_{23} + 450\delta_{24} + 800\delta_{25} \leq 250$$
$$5\delta_{12} + 10\delta_{13} + 15\delta_{14} + 20\delta_{15} + 5\delta_{22} + 10\delta_{23} + 15\delta_{24} + 20\delta_{25} \leq 20$$

After adding the sign restrictions, (61), and the adjacency assumption, we obtain

$$\max \hat{z} = 100\delta_{12} + 100\delta_{13} - 200\delta_{15} + 100\delta_{22} + 50\delta_{23} - 150\delta_{24} - 500\delta_{25}$$
$$\text{s.t.} \quad \delta_{11} + \delta_{12} + \delta_{13} + \delta_{14} + \delta_{15} = 1$$
$$\delta_{21} + \delta_{22} + \delta_{23} + \delta_{24} + \delta_{25} = 1$$
$$25\delta_{12} + 100\delta_{13} + 225\delta_{14} + 400\delta_{15} + 50\delta_{22} + 200\delta_{23} + 450\delta_{24} + 800\delta_{25} \leq 250$$
$$5\delta_{12} + 10\delta_{13} + 15\delta_{14} + 20\delta_{15} + 5\delta_{22} + 10\delta_{23} + 15\delta_{24} + 20\delta_{25} \leq 20$$
$$\delta_{j,k} \geq 0 \ (j = 1, 2; \ k = 1, 2, 3, 4, 5)$$

Adjacency assumption

At first glance, the approximating problem may appear to be a linear programming problem. If we attempt to solve the approximating problem by the simplex, however, we may violate the adjacency assumption. To avoid this difficulty, we solve approximating problems via the simplex algorithm with the following restricted entry rule: If, for a given j all $\delta_{j,k} = 0$, any $\delta_{j,k}$ may enter the basis. If, for a given j, a single $\delta_{j,k}$ (say, $\delta_{j,k'}$) is positive, $\delta_{j,k'-1}$ or $\delta_{j,k'+1}$ may enter the basis, but no other $\delta_{j,k}$ may enter the basis. If, for a given j, two $\delta_{j,k}$'s are positive, no other $\delta_{j,k}$ can enter the basis.

There are two situations in which solving the approximating problem via the ordinary simplex will yield a solution that automatically satisfies the adjacency assumption. If the separable programming problem is a maximization problem, each $f_j(x_j)$ is concave, and each $g_{ij}(x_j)$ is convex, then any solution to the approximating problem obtained via the ordinary simplex will automatically satisfy the adjacency assumption. Also, if the separable programming problem is a minimization problem, each $f_j(x_j)$ is convex, and each $g_{ij}(x_j)$ is convex, then any solution to the approximating problem obtained via the ordinary simplex will automatically satisfy the adjacency assumption. Problem 3 at the end of this section indicates why this is the case.

In these two special cases, it can also be shown that as the maximum value of the distance between two adjacent grid points approaches zero, the optimal solution to the approximating problem approaches the optimal solution to the separable programming problem (see Bazaraa and Shetty (1979, p. 461)).

For the previous example, each $f_j(x_j)$ is concave and each $g_{ij}(x_j)$ is convex, so to find the optimal solution to the approximating problem, we may use the simplex and ignore the restricted entry rule. The optimal solution to the approximating problem for the previous example is $\delta_{12} = \delta_{22} = 1$. This yields $x_1 = 1(5) = 5, x_2 = 1(5) = 5, \hat{z} = 200$. Compare this with the actual optimal solution to the previous example, which is $x_1 = 7.5, x_2 = 5.83, z = 214.58$.

♦ PROBLEMS

GROUP A

Set up an approximating problem for the following separable programming problems:

1. $\min z = x_1^2 + x_2^2$
s.t. $x_1^2 + 2x_2^2 \le 4$
  $x_1^2 + x_2^2 \le 6$
  $x_1, x_2 \ge 0$

2. $\max z = x_1^2 - 5x_1 + x_2^2 - 5x_2 - x_3$
s.t. $x_1 + x_2 + x_3 \le 4$
  $x_1^2 - x_2 \le 3$
  $x_1, x_2, x_3 \ge 0$

GROUP B

3. This problem will give you an idea why the restricted entry rule is unnecessary when (for a maximization problem) each $f_j(x_j)$ is concave and each $g_{ij}(x_j)$ is convex. Consider the Oilco example. When we solve the approximating problem by the simplex, show that a solution that violates the adjacency assumption cannot be obtained. For example, why can the simplex not yield a solution (call

it x^*) havng $\delta_{11} = 0.4$ and $\delta_{15} = 0.6$? To show that $\delta_{11} = 0.4$ and $\delta_{15} = 0.6$ cannot occur, find a feasible solution to the approximating problem that has a larger $\hat{z}$-value than x^*. (*Hint:* Show that the solution that is identical to x^* with the exception that $\delta_{11} = 0$, $\delta_{15} = 0$, $\delta_{13} = 0.6$, and $\delta_{14} = 0.4$ is feasible for the approximating problem (use the convexity of $g_{ij}(x_j)$ for this part) and has a larger $\hat{z}$-value than x^* (use concavity of $f_j(x_j)$ for this part).)

4. Suppose an NLP appears to be separable except for the fact that a term of the form $x_i x_j$ appears in the objective function or constraints. Show that an NLP of this type can be made into a separable programming problem by defining two new variables y_i and y_j by $x_i = \frac{1}{2}(y_i + y_j)$ and $x_j = \frac{1}{2}(y_i - y_j)$. Use this technique to transform the following NLP into a separable programming problem:

$$\max z = x_1^2 + 3x_1 x_2 - x_2^2$$
$$\text{s.t.} x_1 x_2 \le 4$$
$$x_1^2 + x_2 \le 6$$
$$x_1, x_2 \ge 0$$

12-11   THE METHOD OF FEASIBLE DIRECTIONS*

In Section 12.6, we used the method of steepest ascent to solve an unconstrained NLP. We now describe a modification of that method—the feasible directions method, which can be used to solve NLPs with linear constraints. Suppose we want to solve

*This section covers topics that may be omitted with no loss of continuity.

$$\max z = f(\mathbf{x})$$
$$\text{s.t.} \quad A\mathbf{x} \le \mathbf{b} \tag{65}$$
$$\mathbf{x} \ge \mathbf{0}$$

where $\mathbf{x} = [x_1 x_2, \ldots, x_n]^T$, A is an $m \times n$ matrix, $\mathbf{0}$ is an n-dimensional column vector consisting entirely of zeros, $\mathbf{b}$ is an $m \times 1$ vector, and $f(\mathbf{x})$ is a concave function.

To begin, we must find (perhaps by using the Big M method or the two-phase simplex algorithm) a feasible solution $\mathbf{x}^0$ satisfying the constraints $A\mathbf{x} \le \mathbf{b}$. We now try to find a direction in which we can move away from $\mathbf{x}^0$. This direction should have two properties:

1. When we move away from $\mathbf{x}^0$, we remain feasible.

2. When we move away from $\mathbf{x}^0$, we increase the value of z.

From Section 12.6, we know that if $\nabla f(\mathbf{x}^0) \cdot \mathbf{d} > 0$ and we move a small distance away from $\mathbf{x}^0$ in a direction $\mathbf{d}$, then $f(\mathbf{x})$ will increase. We choose to move away from $\mathbf{x}^0$ in a direction $\mathbf{d}^0 - \mathbf{x}^0$, where $\mathbf{d}^0$ is an optimal solution to the following LP:

$$\max z = \nabla f(\mathbf{x}^0) \cdot \mathbf{d}$$
$$\text{s.t.} \quad A\mathbf{d} \le \mathbf{b} \tag{66}$$
$$\mathbf{d} \ge \mathbf{0}$$

Here $\mathbf{d} = [d_1 d_2 \ldots d_n]^T$. Observe that if $\mathbf{d}^0$ solves (66) (and $\mathbf{x}^0$ does not), then $\nabla f(\mathbf{x}^0) \cdot \mathbf{d}^0 > \nabla f(\mathbf{x}^0) \cdot \mathbf{x}^0$, or $\nabla f(\mathbf{x}^0) \cdot (\mathbf{d}^0 - \mathbf{x}^0) > 0$. This means that moving a small distance from $\mathbf{x}^0$ in a direction $\mathbf{d}^0 - \mathbf{x}^0$ will increase z.

We now choose our new point $\mathbf{x}^1$ to be $\mathbf{x}^1 = \mathbf{x}^0 + t_0(\mathbf{d}^0 - \mathbf{x}^0)$, where t_0 solves

$$\max f(\mathbf{x}^0 + t_0(\mathbf{d}^0 - \mathbf{x}^0))$$
$$0 \le t_0 \le 1$$

It can be shown that $f(\mathbf{x}^1) \ge f(\mathbf{x}^0)$ will hold, and that if $f(\mathbf{x}^1) = f(\mathbf{x}^0)$, then $\mathbf{x}^0$ is the optimal solution to (65). Thus, unless $\mathbf{x}^0$ is optimal, $\mathbf{x}^1$ will have a z-value larger than $\mathbf{x}^0$. It is easy to show that $\mathbf{x}^1$ is a feasible point. Observe that

$$A\mathbf{x}^1 = A[\mathbf{x}^0 + t_0(\mathbf{d}^0 - \mathbf{x}^0)] = (1 - t_0)A\mathbf{x}^0 + t_0 A\mathbf{d}^0 \le (1 - t_0)\mathbf{b} + t_0\mathbf{b} = \mathbf{b}$$

where the last inequality follows from the fact that both $\mathbf{x}^0$ and $\mathbf{d}^0$ satisfy the NLP's constraints and $0 \le t_0 \le 1$. $\mathbf{x}^1 \ge \mathbf{0}$ follows easily from $\mathbf{x}^0 \ge \mathbf{0}$, $\mathbf{d}^0 \ge \mathbf{0}$, and $0 \le t_0 \le 1$.

We now choose to move away from $\mathbf{x}^1$ in any direction $\mathbf{d}^1 - \mathbf{x}^1$, where $\mathbf{d}^1$ is an optimal solution to the following LP:

$$\max z = \nabla f(\mathbf{x}^1) \cdot \mathbf{d}$$
$$\text{s.t.} \quad A\mathbf{d} \le \mathbf{b}$$
$$\mathbf{d} \ge \mathbf{0}$$

Then we choose a new point $\mathbf{x}^2$ to be given by $\mathbf{x}^2 = \mathbf{x}^1 + t_1(\mathbf{d}^1 - \mathbf{x}^1)$, where t_1 solves

$$\max f(\mathbf{x}^1 + t_1(\mathbf{d}^1 - \mathbf{x}^1))$$
$$0 \le t_1 \le 1$$

Again, $\mathbf{x}^2$ will be feasible, and $f(\mathbf{x}^2) \geq f(\mathbf{x}^1)$ will hold. Also, if $f(\mathbf{x}^2) = f(\mathbf{x}^1)$, then $\mathbf{x}^1$ is the optimal solution to NLP (65).

We continue in this fashion and generate directions of movement $\mathbf{d}^2, \mathbf{d}^3, \ldots, \mathbf{d}^{n-1}$ and new points $\mathbf{x}^3, \mathbf{x}^4, \ldots \mathbf{x}^n$. We terminate the algorithm if $\mathbf{x}^k = \mathbf{x}^{k-1}$. This means that $\mathbf{x}^{k-1}$ is an optimal solution to NLP (65). If the values of f are strictly increasing at each iteration of the method, then (as with the method if steepest ascent) we terminate the method whenever two successive points are very close together.

After the point $\mathbf{x}^k$ has been determined, an upper bound on the optimal z-value for (65) is available. It can be shown that if $f(x_1, x_2, \ldots, x_n)$ is concave, then

$$\text{(Optimal } z\text{-value for (64))} \leq f(\mathbf{x}^k) + \nabla(\mathbf{x}^k) \cdot [\mathbf{d}^k - \mathbf{x}^k]^T \tag{67}$$

Thus, if $f(\mathbf{x}^k)$ is near the upper bound on the optimal z-value obtained from (67), we may terminate the algorithm.

The version of the feasible-directions method we have discussed was developed by Frank and Wolfe. For a discussion of other feasible-direction methods, we refer the reader to Chapter 11 of Bazaraa and Shetty (1979).

The following example illustrates the method of feasible directions.

E X A M P L E   24

Perform two iterations of the feasible-directions method on the following NLP:

$$\max z = f(x, y) = 2xy + 4x + 6y - 2x^2 - 2y^2$$
$$\text{s.t.} \quad x + y \leq 2$$
$$x, y \geq 0$$

Begin at the point $(0, 0)$.

Solution $\nabla f(x, y) = [2y - 4x + 4 \quad 6 + 2x - 4y]$, so $\nabla f(0, 0) = [4 \quad 6]$. We find a direction to move away from $[0 \quad 0]$ by solving the following LP:

$$\max z = 4d_1 + 6d_2$$
$$\text{s.t.} \quad d_1 + d_2 \leq 2$$
$$d_1, d_2 \geq 0$$

The optimal solution to this LP is $d_1 = 0$ and $d_2 = 2$. Thus, $\mathbf{d}^0 = [0 \quad 2]^T$. Since $\mathbf{d}^0 - \mathbf{x}^0 = [0 \quad 2]^T$, we now choose $\mathbf{x}^1 = [0 \quad 0]^T + t_0[0 \quad 2]^T = [0 \quad 2t_0]^T$, where t_0 solves

$$\max f(0, 2t) = 12t - 8t^2$$
$$0 \leq t \leq 1$$

Letting $g(t) = 12t - 8t^2$, we find $g'(t) = 12 - 16t = 0$ for $t = 0.75$. Since $g''(t) < 0$, we know that $t_0 = 0.75$. Thus, $\mathbf{x}^1 = [0, 1.5]^T$. At this point, $z = f(0, 1.5) = 4.5$. We now have (via (67) with $k = 0$) the following upper bound on the NLP's optimal z-value:

$$\text{(Optimal } z\text{-value)} \leq f(0, 0) + [4 \quad 6] \cdot [0 \quad 2]^T = 12$$

Now $\nabla(\mathbf{x}^1) = \nabla(0, 1.5) = [7 \quad 0]$. We now find the direction $\mathbf{d}^2$ to move away from $\mathbf{x}^1$ by solving

$$\max z = 7d_1$$
$$\text{s.t.} \quad d_1 + d_2 \leq 2$$
$$d_1, d_2 \geq 0$$

The optimal solution to this LP is $\mathbf{d}^1 = [2 \quad 0]^T$. Now we find $\mathbf{x}^2 = [0 \quad 1.5]^T + t_1\{[2 \quad 0]^T - [0 \quad 1.5]^T\} = [2t_1 \quad 1.5 - 1.5t_1]^T$, where t_1 is the optimal solution to

$$\max f(2t, 1.5 - 1.5t)$$
$$0 \leq t \leq 1$$

Now $f(2t, 1.5 - 1.5t) = 4.5 - 18.5t^2 + 14t$. Letting $g(t) = 4.5 - 18.5t^2 + 14t$, we find $g'(t) = 14 - 37t = 0$ for $t = \frac{14}{37}$. Since $g''(t) = -37 < 0$, we find that $t_1 = \frac{14}{37}$. Thus, $\mathbf{x}^2 = [\frac{28}{37} \quad \frac{69}{74}]^T = [0.76 \quad 0.93]^T$. Now we have $z = f(0.76, 0.93) = 7.15$. From (67) (with $k = 1$), we find

$$(\text{Optimal } z\text{-value}) \leq 4.5 + [7 \quad 0] \cdot \{[2 \quad 0]^T - [0 \quad 1.5]^T\} = 18.5$$

Since our first upper bound on the optimal z-value (12) is a better bound than 18.5, we ignore this bound.

Actually, the NLP's optimal solution is $z = 8.17$, $x = .83$, and $y = 1.17$. ◆

◆ PROBLEMS

GROUP A

Perform two iterations of the method of feasible directions for each of the following NLPs.

1. $\max z = 4x + 6y - 2x^2 - 2xy - 2y^2$
   s.t. $x + 2y \leq 2$
   $x, y \geq 0$
Begin at the point $(\frac{1}{2}, \frac{1}{2})$

2. $\max z = 3xy - x^2 - y^2$
   s.t. $3x + y \leq 4$
   $x, y \geq 0$
Begin at the point $(1, 0)$.

12-12   THE GINO SOFTWARE PACKAGE

GINO (General Interactive Nonlinear Optimizer) is an extremely user-friendly software package that can be used to solve NLPs, on both personal and mainframe computers. To illustrate the use of GINO, suppose we want to solve the following NLP:

$$\min z = x^2 + y^2$$
$$\text{s.t.} \quad x + y \leq 1$$
$$x, y \geq 0$$

After entering the GINO program (by typing "GINO"), we would type the following ("?" is the GINO prompt):

:Model
?min = x^2 + y^2;
? x + y < 1;
? x > 0;
? y > 0;
? End

A few comments on the input format might be helpful.

1. The objective function must come after the phrase "min=" or "max=".

2. A semicolon must occur at the end of the objective function and each constraint.

3. The ^ symbol is used for exponentiation, and * indicates multiplication (that is, $2x$ is written as $2*x$).

4. Type "End" to indicate the end of the problem.

5. Most LINDO commands (such as ALTER and DIVERT) can be used (with slight modifications). For details, consult the GINO manual (1986).

6. As with LINDO, a colon (:) indicates that GINO is ready to accept a command.

To solve the problem, simply type GO. GINO responds with the output shown in Figure 26. The output indicates that the NLP's optimal solution is $z = 0.5$, $x = 0.5$, $y = 0.5$. We omit discussion of the REDUCED COST column of the output. SLACK or SURPLUS has the same meaning as in the LINDO output. The PRICE column yields the rate of improvement in the objective function if the right-hand side of a constraint is increased by a small amount. Thus, we see that increasing the right-hand side of either nonnegativity constraint by a small amount will not change the optimal z-value. On the other hand, increasing the right-hand side of the $x + y = 1$ constraint by a small amount Δ will improve the optimal z-value by $-\Delta$ or increase the optimal z-value by Δ. This is reasonable, because if the constraint were written as $x + y = c$, we would find that the optimal z-value (as a function of c) would be $(\frac{c}{2})^2 + (\frac{c}{2})^2 = \frac{c^2}{2}$. At $c = 1$, the derivative of $\frac{c^2}{2}$ equals 1, as expected.

Figure 26
Example of GINO
Output

```
OBJECTIVE FUNCTION VALUE

1)  .50

VARIABLE        VALUE           REDUCED COST
X               .50             0
Y               .50             0

ROW         SLACK OR SURPLUS        PRICE
2)              0                   -1
3)              .5                   0
4)              .5                   0
```

We should caution the reader that for many NLPs, GINO may find a local extremum that does not solve the NLP. In such situations, the user may influence the solution found by GINO if starting values of the decision variables are inputted with the GUESS command. For example, if we direct GINO to solve

$$\min z = x \sin(\pi x)$$

$$\text{s.t.} \quad x \geq 0 \text{ and } x \leq 6$$

GINO may find the local minimum $x = 1.564$. A sketch of the function $x \sin(\pi x)$ reveals that another local minimum occurs for x between 5 and 6. By using the GUESS command, we may direct GINO to start with $x = 5$. Then GINO does indeed find the optimal solution to the NLP ($x = 5.52$).

◆ PROBLEMS

GROUP A

1. Use GINO to solve Problems 1–3 of Section 12.1. (In Problem 3, assume that $I = 64$ and $F = 1000$.)

◆ SUMMARY

CONVEX AND CONCAVE FUNCTIONS

A function $f(x_1, x_2, \ldots, x_n)$ is a **convex function** on a convex set S if for any $x' \in S$ and $x'' \in S$

$$f(cx' + (1 - c)x'') \leq cf(x') + (1 - c)f(x'') \tag{2}$$

holds for $0 \leq c \leq 1$.

A function $f(x_1, x_2, \ldots, x_n)$ is a **concave function** on a convex set S if for any $x' \in S$ and $x'' \in S$

$$f(cx' + (1 - c)x'') \geq cf(x') + (1 - c)f(x'') \tag{3}$$

holds for $0 \leq c \leq 1$.

Consider a general NLP. Suppose the feasible region S for an NLP is a convex set. If $f(x)$ is a concave (convex) function on S, then any local maximum (minimum) for the NLP is an optimal solution to the NLP.

Suppose $f''(x)$ exists for all x in a convex set S. Then $f(x)$ is a convex (concave) function on S if and only if $f''(x) \geq 0$ ($f''(x) \leq 0$) for all x in S.

Suppose $f(x_1, x_2, \ldots, x_n)$ has continuous second-order partial derivatives for each point $x = (x_1, x_2, \ldots, x_n) \in S$. Then $f(x_1, x_2, \ldots, x_n)$ is a convex function on S if and only if for each $x \in S$, all principal minors of H are nonnegative.

Suppose $f(x_1, x_2, \ldots, x_n)$ has continuous second-order partial derivatives for each point $x = (x_1, x_2, \ldots, x_n) \in S$. Then $f(x_1, x_2, \ldots, x_n)$ is a concave function on S if and only if for each $x \in S$ and $k = 1, 2, \ldots n$, all nonzero principal minors have the same sign as $(-1)^k$.

SOLVING ONE-VARIABLE NLPs

To find an optimal solution to

$$\max \text{ (or min) } f(x)$$
$$\text{s.t.} \quad x \in [a, b]$$

we must consider the following three types of points:

Case 1 Points where $f'(x) = 0$ (called a stationary point of $f(x)$).

Case 2 Points where $f'(x)$ does not exist.

Case 3 Endpoints a and b of the interval $[a, b]$.

If $f'(x_0) = 0$, $f''(x_0) < 0$, and $a < x_0 < b$, then x_0 is a local maximum. If $f'(x_0) = 0, f''(x_0) > 0$, and $a < x_0 < b$, then x_0 is a local minimum.

GOLDEN SECTION SEARCH

To determine (within ε) the optimal solution to

$$\max f(x)$$

$$\text{s.t.} \quad a \le x \le b$$

we can perform k iterations (where $r^k(b - a) < \varepsilon$) of Golden Section Search. New points are generated as follows:

New Left-Hand Point Move a distance equal to a fraction r of the current interval of uncertainty from the right endpoint of the interval of uncertainty.

New Right-Hand Point Move a distance equal to a fraction r of the current interval of uncertainty from the left endpoint of the interval.

At each iteration, one of the new points will equal an old point.

UNCONSTRAINED MAXIMIZATION AND MINIMIZATION PROBLEMS WITH SEVERAL VARIABLES

A local extremum $\bar{x}$ for

$$\max \text{ (or min) } f(x_1, x_2, \ldots, x_n)$$

$$\text{s.t.} \quad (x_1, x_2, \ldots, x_n) \in R^n \tag{6}$$

must satisfy $\dfrac{\partial f(\bar{x})}{\partial x_i} = 0$ for $i = 1, 2, \ldots, n$.

If $H_k(\bar{x}) > 0$ $(k = 1, 2, \ldots, n)$, a stationary point $\bar{x}$ is a local minimum for (6).

If, for $k = 1, 2, \ldots, n$, $H_k(\bar{x})$ has the same sign as $(-1)^k$, a stationary point $\bar{x}$ is a local maximum for (6).

If $H_n(\bar{x}) \ne 0$ and the conditions of Theorems 7 and 7' do not hold, then a stationary point $\bar{x}$ is not a local extremum.

METHOD OF STEEPEST ASCENT

The method of steepest ascent can be used to solve problems of the following type:

$$\max z = f(x_1, x_2, \ldots, x_n)$$

$$\text{s.t.} \quad (x_1, x_2, \ldots, x_n) \in R^n$$

To find a new point with a larger z-value, we move away from the current point (call it $\mathbf{v}$) in the direction of $\nabla f(\mathbf{v})$. The distance we move away from $\mathbf{v}$ is chosen to maximize the value of the function at the new point. We stop when $\| \nabla f(\mathbf{v}) \|$ is sufficiently close to zero.

LAGRANGE MULTIPLIERS

Lagrange multipliers are used to solve NLPs of the following type:

$$\max \text{ (or min) } z = f(x_1, x_2, \ldots, x_n)$$
$$\text{s.t.} \quad g_1(x_1, x_2, \ldots, x_n) = b_1$$
$$g_2(x_1, x_2, \ldots, x_n) = b_2$$
$$\vdots$$
$$g_m(x_1, x_2, \ldots, x_n) = b_m$$

(11)

To solve (11), form the Lagrangian

$$L(x_1, x_2, \ldots, x_n, \lambda_1, \lambda_2, \ldots, \lambda_m) = f(x_1, x_2, \ldots, x_n)$$
$$+ \sum_{i=1}^{i=m} \lambda_i [b_i - g_i(x_1, x_2, \ldots, x_n)]$$

and look for points $(\bar{x}_1, \bar{x}_2, \ldots, \bar{x}_n, \bar{\lambda}_1, \bar{\lambda}_2, \ldots, \bar{\lambda}_m)$ for which

$$\frac{\partial L}{\partial x_1} = \frac{\partial L}{\partial x_2} = \cdots = \frac{\partial L}{\partial x_n} = \frac{\partial L}{\partial \lambda_1} = \frac{\partial L}{\partial \lambda_2} = \cdots = \frac{\partial L}{\partial \lambda_m} = 0$$

THE KUHN-TUCKER CONDITIONS

The Kuhn-Tucker conditions are used to solve NLPs of the following type:

$$\max \text{ (or min) } f(x_1, x_2, \ldots, x_n)$$
$$\text{s.t.} \quad g_1(x_1, x_2, \ldots, x_n) \leq b_1$$
$$g_2(x_1, x_2, \ldots, x_n) \leq b_2$$
$$\vdots$$
$$g_m(x_1, x_2, \ldots, x_n) \leq b_m$$

(22)

Suppose (22) is a maximization problem. If $\bar{x} = (\bar{x}_1, \bar{x}_2, \ldots, \bar{x}_n)$ is an optimal solution to (22), then $\bar{x} = (\bar{x}_1, \bar{x}_2, \ldots, \bar{x}_n)$ must satisfy the m constraints in (22), and there must exist multipliers $\bar{\lambda}_1, \bar{\lambda}_2, \ldots, \bar{\lambda}_m$ satisfying

$$\frac{\partial f(\bar{x})}{\partial x_j} - \sum_{i=1}^{i=m} \bar{\lambda}_i \frac{\partial g_i(\bar{x})}{\partial x_j} = 0 \quad (j = 1, 2, \ldots, n)$$
$$\bar{\lambda}_i [b_i - g_i(\bar{x})] = 0 \quad (i = 1, 2, \ldots, m)$$
$$\bar{\lambda}_i \geq 0 \quad (i = 1, 2, \ldots, m)$$

Suppose (22) is a minimization problem. If $\bar{x} = (\bar{x}_1, \bar{x}_2, \ldots, \bar{x}_n)$ is an optimal solution to (22), then $\bar{x} = (\bar{x}_1, \bar{x}_2, \ldots, \bar{x}_n)$ must satisfy the m constraints in (22), and there must exist multipliers $\bar{\lambda}_1, \bar{\lambda}_2, \ldots, \bar{\lambda}_m$ satisfying

$$\frac{\partial f(\bar{x})}{\partial x_j} + \sum_{i=1}^{i=m} \bar{\lambda}_i \frac{\partial g_i(\bar{x})}{\partial x_j} = 0 \quad (j = 1, 2, \ldots, n)$$
$$\bar{\lambda}_i [b_i - g_i(\bar{x})] = 0 \quad (i = 1, 2, \ldots, m)$$
$$\bar{\lambda}_i \geq 0 \quad (i = 1, 2, \ldots, m)$$

The Kuhn-Tucker conditions are **necessary** conditions for a point to solve (22). If the $g_i(x_1, x_2, \ldots, x_n)$ are convex functions and the objective function $f(x_1, x_2, \ldots, x_n)$ is concave (convex), then for a maximization (minimization) problem, any point satisfying the Kuhn-Tucker conditions will yield an optimal solution to (22).

QUADRATIC PROGRAMMING

A quadratic programming problem (QPP) is an NLP in which each term in the objective function is of degree 2, 1, or 0 and all constraints are linear. LINDO solves QPPs when the Kuhn-Tucker conditions are input. Wolfe's method (a modified version of the two-phase simplex) may also be used to solve QPPs.

SEPARABLE PROGRAMMING

If an NLP can be written in the following form:

$$\max \text{ (or min) } z = \sum_{j=1}^{j=n} f_j(x_j)$$

$$\text{s.t. } \sum_{j=1}^{j=n} g_{ij}(x_j) \le b_i \quad (i = 1, 2, \ldots, m)$$

it is a **separable programming problem**. To approximate the optimal solution to a separable programming problem, we solve the following **approximating problem**:

$$\max \text{ (or min) } \hat{z} = \sum_{j=1}^{j=n} [\delta_{j1} f_j(p_{j1}) + \delta_{j2} f_j(p_{j2}) + \cdots + \delta_{jk} f_j(p_{jk})]$$

$$\text{s.t. } \sum_{j=1}^{j=n} [\delta_{j1} g_{ij}(p_{j1}) + \delta_{j2} g_{ij}(p_{j2}) + \cdots + \delta_{j,k} g_{ij}(p_{j,k})] \le b_i \quad (i = 1, 2, \ldots, m)$$

$$\delta_{j1} + \delta_{j2} + \cdots + \delta_{j,k} = 1 \quad (j = 1, 2, \ldots, n)$$

$$\delta_{j,r} \ge 0 \quad (j = 1, 2, \ldots, n; r = 1, 2, \ldots, k)$$

(For $j = 1, 2, \ldots, n$, at most two $\delta_{j,k}$'s can be positive. If for a given j, two $\delta_{j,k}$'s are positive, they must be adjacent.)

METHOD OF FEASIBLE DIRECTIONS

To solve

$$\max z = f(\mathbf{x})$$

$$\text{s.t. } A\mathbf{x} \le \mathbf{b}$$

$$\mathbf{x} \ge 0$$

we begin with a feasible solution $\mathbf{x}^0$. Let $\mathbf{d}^0$ be a solution to

$$\max z = \nabla f(\mathbf{x}^0) \cdot \mathbf{d}$$

$$\text{s.t. } A\mathbf{d} \le \mathbf{b}$$

$$\mathbf{d} \ge 0$$

Choose our new point $\mathbf{x}^1$ to be $\mathbf{x}^1 = \mathbf{x}^0 + t_0(\mathbf{d}^0 - \mathbf{x}^0)$, where t_0 solves

$$\max f(\mathbf{x}^0 + t_0(\mathbf{d}^0 - \mathbf{x}^0))$$

$$0 \le t_0 \le 1$$

Let $\mathbf{d}^1$ be a solution to

$$\max z = \nabla f(\mathbf{x}^1) \cdot \mathbf{d}$$
$$\text{s.t.} \quad A\mathbf{d} \leq \mathbf{b}$$
$$\mathbf{d} \geq \mathbf{0}$$

Choose our new point $\mathbf{x}^2$ to be $\mathbf{x}^2 = \mathbf{x}^1 + t_1(\mathbf{d}^1 - \mathbf{x}^1)$, where t_1 solves

$$\max f(\mathbf{x}^1 + t_1(\mathbf{d}^1 - \mathbf{x}^1))$$
$$0 \leq t_1 \leq 1$$

Continue generating points $\mathbf{x}^3, \ldots \mathbf{x}^k$ in this fashion until $\mathbf{x}^k = \mathbf{x}^{k-1}$ or successive points are sufficiently close together.

◆ REVIEW PROBLEMS

GROUP A

1. Show that $f(x) = e^{-x}$ is a convex function on R^1.

2. Five of a store's major customers are located as in Figure 27. Determine where the store should be located in order to minimize the sum of the squares of the distances that each customer would have to travel to the store. Can you generalize this result to the case of n customers located at points $x_1, x_2, \ldots, x_n$?

Figure 27

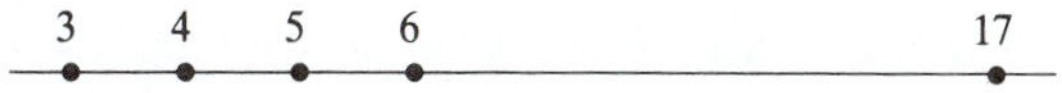

3. A company uses the raw material to produce two types of products. When processed, each unit of raw material yields 2 units of product 1 and 1 unit of product 2. If x_1 units of product 1 are produced, each unit can be sold for $\$49 - x_1$, and if x_2 units of product 2 are produced, each unit can be sold for $\$30 - 2x_2$. It costs $\$5$ to purchase and process each unit of raw material.
(**a**) Use the Kuhn-Tucker conditions to determine how the company can maximize profits.
(**b**) Use LINDO, GINO, or Wolfe's method to determine how the company can maximize profits.
(**c**) What is the most that the company would be willing to pay for an extra unit of raw material?

4. Show that $f(x) = |x|$ is a convex function on R^1.

5. Use Golden Section Search to locate, within 0.5, the optimal solution to

$$\max 3x - x^2$$
$$\text{s.t.} \quad 0 \leq x \leq 5$$

6. Perform two iterations of the method of steepest ascent in an attempt to maximize

$$f(x_1, x_2) = (x_1 + x_2)e^{-(x_1+x_2)} - x_1$$

Begin at the point $(0, 1)$.

7. The cost of producing x units of a product during a month is x^2 dollars. Find the minimum cost method of producing 60 units during the next three months. Can you generalize this result to the case where the cost of producing x units during a month is an increasing convex function?

8. Solve the following NLP:

$$\max z = xyw$$
$$\text{s.t.} \quad 2x + 3y + 4w = 36$$

9. Solve the following NLP:

$$\min z = \frac{50}{x} + \frac{20}{y} + xy$$
$$\text{s.t.} \quad x \geq 1, y \geq 1$$

10. If a company charges a price p for a product and spends $\$a$ on advertising, it can sell $10{,}000 + 5\sqrt{a} - 100p$ units of the product. If the product costs $\$10$ per unit to produce, how can the company maximize profits?

11. With L labor hours and M machine hours, a company can produce $L^{1/3}M^{2/3}$ computer disk drives. Each disk drive sells for $\$150$. If labor can be purchased at $\$50$ per hour and machine hours can be purchased at $\$100$ per hour, determine how the company can maximize profits.

GROUP B

12. In time t, a tree can grow to a size $F(t)$, where $F'(t) \geq 0$ and $F''(t) < 0$. Assume that for large t, $F'(t)$ is near 0. If the tree is cut at time t, then a revenue $F(t)$ is received. Assume that revenues are discounted continuously at a rate r, so \$1 received at time t is equivalent to $\$e^{-rt}$ received at time 0. The goal is to cut the tree at the time t^* that maximizes discounted revenue. Show that the tree should be cut at the time t^* satisfying the equation

$$r = \frac{F'(t^*)}{F(t^*)}$$

In the answer, explain why (if $\frac{F'(0)}{F(0)} > r$) this equation has a unique solution. Also show that the answer is a maximum, not a minimum. (*Hint:* Why is it sufficient to choose t^* to maximize $\ln(e^{-rt}F(t)?)$

13. Suppose we are hiring a weather forecaster to predict the probability that next summer will be rainy or sunny. The following suggests a method that can be used to ensure that the forecaster gives an accurate forecast. Suppose that the actual probability of rain next summer is q. For simplicity, we assume that the summer can only be rainy or sunny. If the forecaster announces a probability p that the summer will be rainy, he or she receives a payment of $1 - (1 - p)^2$ if the summer is rainy and a payment of $1 - p^2$ if the summer is sunny. Show that the forecaster will maximize expected profits by announcing that the probability of a rainy summer is q.

14. Show that if $b > a \geq e$, then $a^b > b^a$. Use this result to show that $e^\pi > \pi^e$. (*Hint:* Show that $\max\left(\frac{\ln x}{x}\right)$ over $x \geq a$ occurs for $x = a$.)

15. Consider the points $(0, 0)$, $(1, 1)$, and $(2, 3)$. Formulate an NLP whose solution will yield the circle of smallest radius enclosing these three points. Use GINO to solve the NLP.

16. The cost of producing x units of a product during a month is $x^{1/2}$ dollars. Show that the minimum cost method of producing 40 units during the next two months is to produce all 40 units during a single month. Is it possible to generalize this result to the case where the cost of producing x units during a month is an increasing concave function?

17. Consider the problem

$$\max z = f(x)$$
$$\text{s.t.} \quad a \leq x \leq b$$

(a) Suppose $f(x)$ is a convex function that has derivatives for all values of x. Show that $x = a$ or $x = b$ must be optimal for the NLP. (Draw a picture.)
(b) Suppose $f(x)$ is a convex function for which $f'(x)$ may not exist. Show that $x = a$ or $x = b$ must be optimal for the NLP. (Use the definition of a convex function.)

18. Reconsider Problem 2. Suppose that the store should now be located to minimize the total distance that customers must walk to the store. Where should the store be located? (*Hint:* Use Problem 4 and the fact that for any convex function a local minimum will solve the NLP; then show that locating the store where one of the customers lives yields a local minimum.) Can the result be generalized?

19.† A company uses raw material to produce two products. For c dollars, a unit of raw material can be purchased and processed into k_1 units of product 1 and k_2 units of product 2. If x_1 units of product 1 are produced, they can be sold at $p_1(x_1)$ dollars per unit. If x_2 units of product 2 are produced, they can be sold at $p_2(x_2)$ dollars per unit. Let z be the number of units of raw material that are purchased and processed. To maximize profits (ignoring nonnegativity constraints), the following NLP should be solved:

$$\max z = x_1 p_1(x_1) + x_2 p_2(x_2) - cz$$
$$\text{s.t.} \quad x_1 \leq k_1 z$$
$$x_2 \leq k_2 z$$

(a) Write down the Kuhn-Tucker conditions for this problem. Let $\bar{x}_1$, $\bar{x}_2$, $\bar{\lambda}_1$, $\bar{\lambda}_2$ represent the optimal solution to this problem.
(b) Consider a modified version of the problem. The company can now purchase each unit of product 1 for $\bar{\lambda}_1$ dollars and each unit of product 2 for $\bar{\lambda}_2$ dollars. Show that if the company tries to maximize profits in this situation, it will, as in part (a), produce $\bar{x}_1$ units of product 1 and $\bar{x}_2$ units of product 2. Also, show that profit and production costs will remain unchanged.
(c) Give an interpretation of $\bar{\lambda}_1$ and $\bar{\lambda}_2$ that might be useful to the company's accountant.

20. The area of a triangle with sides of length a, b, and c is $\sqrt{s(s - a)(s - b)(s - c)}$, where s is half the perimeter of the triangle. We have 60 ft of fence and wish to fence a triangular-shaped area. Determine how to maximize the fenced area.

21. The energy used in compressing a gas (in three stages) from an initial pressure I to a final pressure F is given by

$$K\left\{\sqrt{\frac{p_1}{I}} + \sqrt{\frac{p_2}{p_1}} + \sqrt{\frac{F}{p_2}} - 3\right\}$$

Determine how to minimize the energy used in compressing the gas from I to F in three stages.

22. Prove Lemma 1 (use Lagrange multipliers).

---

† Based on Littlechild, "Marginal Pricing" (1970).

◆ REFERENCES

The following books emphasize the theoretical aspects of nonlinear programming:

LUENBERGER, D. *Linear and Nonlinear Programming*. Reading, Mass.: Addison-Wesley, 1984.

MANGASARIAN, O. *Nonlinear Programming*. New York: McGraw-Hill, 1969.

MCCORMICK, G. *Nonlinear Programming: Theory, Algorithms, and Applications*. New York: Wiley, 1983.

SHAPIRO, J. *Mathematical Programming: Structures and Algorithms*. New York: Wiley, 1979.

ZANGWILL, W. *Nonlinear Programming*. Englewood Cliffs, N.J.: Prentice-Hall, 1969.

The following books emphasize various nonlinear programming algorithms:

RAO, S. *Optimization Theory and Applications*. New Delhi: Wiley Eastern Ltd., 1979.

WISMER, D., and R. CHATTERGY. *Introduction to Nonlinear Optimization: A Problem-Solving Approach*. New York: Elsevier North-Holland, 1978.

For some interesting applications of nonlinear programming, look at the next two books:

HENDERSON, R., and R. QUANDT. *Microeconomic Theory: A Mathematical Approach*. New York: McGraw-Hill, 1980.

LIEBMAN, J., ET AL. *Applications of Modeling and Optimization With GINO*. Palo Alto, Calif.: Scientific Press, 1986.

Bazaraa, M., and C. SHETTY. *Nonlinear Programming: Theory and Algorithms*. New York: Wiley, 1979. Excellent for both NLP theory and algorithms.

COURNOT, A. *Mathematical Principles of the Theory of Wealth*. New York: Macmillan, 1897.

KOLESAR, P., and E. BLUM. "Square Roots Laws for Fire Engine Response Distances," *Management Science* 19(1973):1368–1378.

LITTLECHILD, S. "Marginal Pricing With Joint Costs," *Economic Journal* 80(1970):323–334.

——. "Peak Loads and Efficient Pricing," *Bell Journal of Economics and Management Science* (Autumn 1970):191–210.

CHAPTER

13

Decision Making
Under Uncertainty

WE HAVE ALL had to make important decisions where we were uncertain about factors that were relevant to the decisions. In this chapter, we study situations in which decisions are made in an uncertain environment.

The following model encompasses several aspects of making a decision in the absence of certainty. The decision maker first chooses an action a_i from a set $A = \{a_1, a_2, \ldots, a_k\}$ of available actions. Then the state of the world is observed; with probability p_j, the state of the world is observed to be $s_j \in S = \{s_1, s_2, \ldots, s_n\}$. If action a_i is chosen and the state of the world is s_j, the decision maker receives a reward r_{ij}. We refer to this model as the *state-of-the-world decision-making model*.

This chapter presents the basic theory of decision making under uncertainty: four simple criteria for making decisions under uncertainty, the widely used Von Neumann–Morgenstern utility model, and the use of decision trees for making decisions at different points in time. We close by looking at Bayesian inference for continuous random variables.

13-1   DECISION CRITERIA

In this section, we consider four decision criteria that can be used to make decisions under uncertainty.

E X A M P L E
1

News vendor Phyllis Pauley sells newspapers at the corner of Kirkwood Avenue and Indiana Street, and each day she must determine how many newspapers to order. Phyllis pays the company 20¢ for each paper and sells the papers for 25¢ each. Newspapers that are unsold at the end of the day are worthless. Phyllis knows that each day she can sell between 6 and 10 papers, with each possibility being equally likely. Show how this problem fits into the state-of-the-world model.

Solution

In this example, the members of $S = \{6, 7, 8, 9, 10\}$ are the possible values of the daily demand for newspapers. We are given that $p_6 = p_7 = p_8 = p_9 = p_{10} = \frac{1}{5}$. Phyllis must choose an action (the number of papers to order each day) from $A = \{6, 7, 8, 9, 10\}$.

683

If Phyllis purchases i papers and j papers are demanded, then i papers are purchased at a cost of $20i¢$, and $\min(i,j)$ papers are sold for 25¢ each.[†] Thus, if Phyllis purchases i papers and j papers are demanded, she earns a net profit of r_{ij}, where

$$r_{ij} = 25i - 20i = 5i \qquad (i \leq j)$$
$$r_{ij} = 25j - 20i \qquad (i \geq j)$$

The values of r_{ij} are tabulated in Table 1.

Table 1
Rewards for News
Vendor Example

PAPERS ORDERED	PAPERS DEMANDED				
	6	7	8	9	10
6	30¢	30¢	30¢	30¢	30¢
7	10¢	35¢	35¢	35¢	35¢
8	− 10¢	15¢	40¢	40¢	40¢
9	− 30¢	− 5¢	20¢	45¢	45¢
10	− 50¢	− 25¢	0¢	25¢	50¢

DOMINATED ACTIONS

Why did we not consider the possibility that Phyllis would order 1, 2, 3, 4, 5, or more than 10 papers? Answering this question involves the idea of a dominated action.

DEFINITION   An action a_i is **dominated** by an action $a_{i'}$ if for all $s_j \in S$, $r_{ij} \leq r_{i'j}$, and for some state $s_{j'}$, $r_{ij'} < r_{i'j'}$.

If action a_i is dominated, then in no state of the world is a_i better than $a_{i'}$, and in at least one state of the world a_i is inferior to $a_{i'}$. Thus, if action a_i is dominated, there is no reason to choose a_i ($a_{i'}$ would be a better choice).

If Phyllis orders i papers ($i = 1, 2, 3, 4, 5$), she will earn (for all states of the world) a profit of $5i¢$. From the table of rewards, we see that, for $i = 1, 2, 3, 4, 5$, ordering 6 papers dominates ordering i papers ($j' = 6, 7, 8, 9,$ or 10 will do). Similarly, the reader should check that ordering i papers ($i > 11$) is dominated by ordering 10 papers (see Problem 3 at the end of this section). A quick check shows that none of the actions in $A = \{6, 7, 8, 9, 10\}$ are dominated. Thus, Phyllis should indeed choose her action from $A = \{6, 7, 8, 9, 10\}$.

We now discuss four criteria that can be used to choose an action.

THE MAXIMIN CRITERION

For each action, determine the worst outcome (smallest reward). The maximin criterion chooses the action with the "best" worst outcome.

[†]$\min(i,j)$ is the smaller of i and j.

DEFINITION	The **maximin criterion** chooses the action a_i with the largest value of $\min_{j \in S} r_{ij}$.

For Example 1, we obtain the results in Table 2. Thus, the maximin criterion recommends ordering 6 papers. This ensures that Phyllis will, no matter what the state of the world, earn a profit of at least 30¢. The maximin criterion is concerned with making the worst possible outcome as pleasant as possible. Unfortunately, choosing a decision to mitigate the worst case may prevent the decision maker from taking advantage of good fortune. For example, if Phyllis follows the maximin criterion, she will never make less than 30¢, but she will never make more than 30¢.

Table 2 Computation of Maximin Decision for News Vendor Example	PAPERS ORDERED	WORST STATE OF THE WORLD	REWARD IN WORST STATE OF THE WORLD
	6	6, 7, 8, 9, 10	30¢
	7	6	10¢
	8	6	−10¢
	9	6	−30¢
	10	6	−50¢

THE MAXIMAX CRITERION

For each action, determine the best outcome (largest reward). The maximax criterion chooses the action with the "best" best outcome.

DEFINITION	The **maximax criterion** chooses the action a_i with the largest value of $\max_{j \in S} r_{ij}$.

For Example 1, we obtain the results in Table 3. Thus, the maximax criterion would recommend ordering 10 papers. In the best state (when 10 papers are demanded), this yields a profit of 50¢. Of course, making a decision according to the maximax criterion leaves Phyllis open to the disastrous possibility that only 6 papers will be demanded, in which case she loses 50¢.

Table 3 Computation of Maximax Decision for News Vendor Example	PAPERS ORDERED	STATE YIELDING BEST OUTCOME	BEST OUTCOME
	6	6, 7, 8, 9, 10	30¢
	7	7, 8, 9, 10	35¢
	8	8, 9, 10	40¢
	9	9, 10	45¢
	10	10	50¢

MINIMAX REGRET

The minimax regret criterion (developed by L. J. Savage) uses the concept of opportunity cost to arrive at a decision. For each possible state of the world s_j, find an action $i^*(j)$ that maximizes r_{ij}. That is, $i^*(j)$ is the best possible action to choose if the state of the world is actually s_j. Then for any action a_i and state s_j, the opportunity loss or regret for a_i in s_j is $r_{i*(j),j} - r_{ij}$. For example, if $j = 7$ papers are demanded, the best decision is to order $i*(7) = 7$ papers, yielding a profit of $r_{77} = 7(25) - 7(20) = 35¢$. Suppose we chose to order $i = 6$ papers. Since $r_{67} = 6(25) - 6(20) = 30¢$, the opportunity loss or regret for $i = 6$ and $j = 7$ is $35 - 30 = 5¢$. Thus, if we order 6 papers and 7 papers are demanded, in hindsight we realize that by making the optimal choice (ordering 7 papers) for the actual state of the world (7 papers demanded), we would have done 5¢ better than we did by ordering 6 papers. Table 4 shows the opportunity cost or regret matrix for Example 1. The minimax regret criterion chooses an action by applying the minimax criterion to the regret matrix. In other words, the minimax regret criterion attempts to avoid disappointment over what might have been. From the regret matrix in Table 4, we obtain the minimax regret decision in Table 5. Thus, the minimax regret criterion recommends ordering 6 or 7 papers.

Table 4
Regret Matrix for
News Vendor
Example

PAPERS ORDERED	PAPERS DEMANDED				
	6	7	8	9	10
6	$30 - 30 = 0¢$	$35 - 30 = 5¢$	$40 - 30 = 10¢$	$45 - 30 = 15¢$	$50 - 30 = 20¢$
7	$30 - 10 = 20¢$	$35 - 35 = 0¢$	$40 - 35 = 5¢$	$45 - 35 = 10¢$	$50 - 35 = 15¢$
8	$30 + 10 = 40¢$	$35 - 15 = 20¢$	$40 - 40 = 0¢$	$45 - 40 = 5¢$	$50 - 40 = 10¢$
9	$30 + 30 = 60¢$	$35 + 5 = 40¢$	$40 - 20 = 20¢$	$45 - 45 = 0¢$	$50 - 45 = 5¢$
10	$30 + 50 = 80¢$	$35 + 25 = 60¢$	$40 - 0 = 40¢$	$45 - 25 = 20¢$	$50 - 50 = 0¢$

Table 5
Computation of
Minimax Regret
Decision for News
Vendor Example

PAPERS ORDERED	MAXIMUM REGRET
6	20¢
7	20¢
8	40¢
9	60¢
10	80¢

Table 6
Computation of
Expected Value
Decision for News
Vendor Example

PAPERS ORDERED	EXPECTED REWARD
6	$\frac{1}{5}(30 + 30 + 30 + 30 + 30) = 30¢$
7	$\frac{1}{5}(10 + 35 + 35 + 35 + 35) = 30¢$
8	$\frac{1}{5}(-10 + 15 + 40 + 40 + 40) = 25¢$
9	$\frac{1}{5}(-30 - 5 + 20 + 45 + 45) = 15¢$
10	$\frac{1}{5}(-50 - 25 + 0 + 25 + 50) = 0¢$

THE EXPECTED VALUE CRITERION

The expected value criterion chooses the action that yields the largest expected reward. For Example 1, the expected value criterion would recommend ordering 6 or 7 papers (see Table 6).

The decision-making criteria discussed in this section may seem reasonable, but many people make decisions without using any of them. A more comprehensive model of individual decision making, the Von Neumann-Morgenstern utility model, is discussed in Section 13.2.

◆ PROBLEMS

GROUP A

1. Pizza King and Noble Greek are two competing restaurants. Each must determine simultaneously whether to undertake small, medium, or large advertising campaigns. Pizza King believes that it is equally likely that Noble Greek will undertake a small, a medium, or a large advertising campaign. Given the actions chosen by Pizza King and Noble Greek, Pizza King's profits are as shown in Table 7. For the maximin, maximax, and minimax regret criteria, determine Pizza King's choice of advertising campaign.

Table 7

PIZZA KING CHOOSES	NOBLE GREEK CHOOSES		
	Small	*Medium*	*Large*
Small	$6000	$5000	$2000
Medium	$5000	$6000	$1000
Large	$9000	$6000	$0

2. Sodaco is considering producing a new product: Chocovan soda. Sodaco estimates that the annual demand for Chocovan, **D** (in thousands of cases), has the following mass function: $P(D = 30) = .30$, $P(D = 50) = .40$, $P(D = 80) = .30$. Each case of Chocovan sells for $5 and incurs a variable cost of $3. It costs $800,000 to build a plant to produce Chocovan. Assume that if $1 is received every year (forever), this is equivalent to receiving $10 at the present time. Considering the reward for each action and state of the world to be in terms of net present value, use each decision criterion of this section to determine whether or not Sodaco should build the plant.

3. For Example 1, show that ordering 11 or more papers is dominated by ordering 10 papers.

GROUP B

4. Suppose that Pizza King and Noble Greek stop advertising but must determine the price they will charge for each pizza sold. Pizza King believes that Noble Greek's price is a random variable **D** having the following mass function: $P(D = \$6) = .25$, $P(D = \$8) = .50$, $P(D = \$10) = .25$. If Pizza King charges a price p_1 and Noble Greek charges a price p_2, Pizza King will sell $100 + 25(p_2 - p_1)$ pizzas. It costs Pizza King $4 to make a pizza. Pizza King is considering charging $5, $6, $7, $8, or $9 for a pizza. Use each decision criterion of this section to determine the price that Pizza King should charge.

5. Alden Construction is bidding against Forbes Construction for a project. Alden believes that Forbes's bid is a random variable **B** with the following mass function: $P(B = \$6000) = .40$, $P(B = \$8000) = .30$, $P(B = \$11,000 = .30)$. It will cost Alden $6000 to complete the project. Use each of the decision criteria of this section to determine Alden's bid. Assume that in case of a tie, Alden wins the bidding. (*Hint:* Let p = Alden's bid. For $p \le 6000$, $6000 < p \le 8000$, $8000 < p \le 11,000$, and $p > 11,000$, determine Alden's profit in terms of Alden's bid and Forbes's bid.)

13-2 UTILITY THEORY

We now show how the Von Neumann-Morgenstern concept of a utility function can be used as an aid to decision making under uncertainty.

Consider a situation in which a person will receive, for $i = 1, 2, \ldots, n$, a reward r_i with probability p_i. This is denoted as the **lottery** $(p_1, r_1; p_2, r_2; \ldots; p_n, r_n)$. A lottery is often represented by a tree in which each branch stands for a possible outcome of the lottery, and the number on each branch represents the probability that the outcome will occur. Thus, the lottery $(\frac{1}{4}, \$500; \frac{3}{4}, \$0)$ could be denoted by

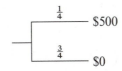

Suppose we are asked to choose between two lotteries (L_1 and L_2). With certainty, lottery L_1 yields $10,000:

$$L_1 \xrightarrow{\quad 1 \quad} \$10,000$$

Lottery L_2 consists of tossing a coin. If a head comes up, we receive $30,000, and if a tail comes up, we receive $0:

L_1 yields an expected reward of $10,000, and L_2 yields an expected reward of $(\frac{1}{2})(30,000) + (\frac{1}{2})(0) = \$15,000$. Although L_2 has a larger expected value than L_1, most people prefer L_1 to L_2, because L_1 offers the certainty of a relatively large payoff, whereas L_2 yields a substantial ($\frac{1}{2}$) chance of earning a reward of $0. In short, most people prefer L_1 to L_2 because L_1 involves less risk (or uncertainty) than L_2.

Our goal is to determine a method that a person can use to choose between lotteries. Suppose he or she must choose to play L_1 or L_2 but not both. We write $L_1 p L_2$ if the person prefers L_1. We write $L_1 i L_2$ if he or she is indifferent between choosing L_1 and L_2. If $L_1 i L_2$, we say that L_1 and L_2 are **equivalent lotteries**. Finally, we write $L_2 p L_1$ if the decision maker prefers L_2.

Suppose we ask a decision maker to rank the following lotteries:

The Von Neumann–Morgenstern approach to ranking these lotteries is as follows. Begin by identifying the most favorable ($30,000) and the least favorable ($-\$10,000$) outcomes that can occur. For all other possible outcomes ($r_1 = \$10,000$, $r_2 = \$500$, and $r_3 = \$0$), the decision maker is asked to determine a probability p_i such that he or she is indifferent between two lotteries:

Suppose that for $r_1 = \$10,000$, the decision maker is indifferent between

(1)

and for r_2 = \$500, indifferent between

$$\frac{1}{\quad\quad\quad}\text{\$500}\quad\text{and}\quad \begin{array}{c}\underset{.62}{\overline{\quad\quad\quad}}\;\text{\$30,000}\\ \underset{.38}{\overline{\quad\quad\quad}}\;-\text{\$10,000}\end{array}\qquad (2)$$

and for r_3 = \$0, indifferent between

$$\frac{1}{\quad\quad\quad}\text{\$0}\quad\text{and}\quad \begin{array}{c}\underset{.60}{\overline{\quad\quad\quad}}\;\text{\$30,000}\\ \underset{.40}{\overline{\quad\quad\quad}}\;-\text{\$10,000}\end{array}\qquad (3)$$

Using (1)–(3), the decision maker can construct lotteries L'_1, L'_2, L'_3, and L'_4 such that $L'_i i L_i$ and each L'_i involves only the best (\$30,000) and the worst (−\$10,000) possible outcomes. Thus, from (1), we find that $L_1 i L'_1$, where

$$L'_1 \begin{array}{c}\underset{.90}{\overline{\quad\quad\quad}}\;\text{\$30,000}\\ \underset{.10}{\overline{\quad\quad\quad}}\;-\text{\$10,000}\end{array}$$

From (3), we find that $L_2 i L''_2$, where

$$L''_2 \begin{array}{c}\underset{.50}{\overline{\quad\quad\quad}}\;\text{\$30,000}\\ \underset{.50}{\overline{\quad\quad\quad}}\;\begin{array}{c}\underset{.60}{\overline{\quad\quad}}\;\text{\$30,000}\\ \underset{.40}{\overline{\quad\quad}}\;-\text{\$10,000}\end{array}\end{array}$$

L''_2 is a compound lottery in which with probability .50 we receive \$30,000 and with probability .50 we play a lottery yielding a .60 chance at \$30,000 and a .40 chance at −\$10,000. More formally, a lottery L is a **compound lottery** if for some i, there is a probability p_i that the decision maker's reward is to play another lottery L'. The following is an example of a compound lottery:

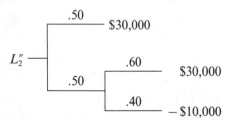

Thus, with probability .50, L yields a reward of −\$4, and with probability .50, L causes us to play L'. If a lottery is not a compound lottery, it is a **simple lottery**.

Returning to our discussion of L''_2, we observe that L''_2 is a lottery that yields a .50 + .50(.60) = .80 chance at \$30,000 and a .40(.50) = .20 chance at −\$10,000. Thus,

$L_2 i L_2'' i L_2'$, where

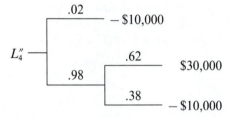

Similarly, using (3), we find that $L_3 i L_3'$, where

Using (2), we find that the decision maker is indifferent between L_4 and L_4'', where

In actuality, however, L_4'' yields a $.98(.62) = .6076$ chance at $30,000$ and a $.02 + .38(.98) = .3924$ chance at $-\$10,000$. Thus, $L_4 i L_4'' i L_4'$, where

Since $L_i i L_i'$, we may rank L_1, L_2, L_3, and L_4 by ranking L_1', L_2', L_3', and L_4'. Consider two lotteries whose only possible outcomes are $30,000 (the most favorable outcome) and $-\$10,000$ (the least favorable outcome). If he or she is given a choice between two lotteries of this type, the decision maker simply chooses the lottery with the larger chance of receiving the most favorable outcome. Applying this idea to L_1' through L_4' yields $L_1' p L_2' p L_4' p L_3'$. Since $L_i i L_i'$, we may conclude that $L_1 p L_2 p L_4 p L_3$.

We now give a more formal description of the process that we have used to rank L_1, L_2, L_3, and L_4. The **utility** of the reward r_i, written $u(r_i)$, is the number q_i such that the decision maker is indifferent between the following two lotteries:

This definition forces u(least favorable outcome) $= 0$ and u(most favorable outcome) $= 1$. For our possible payoffs of $30,000$, $-\$10,000$, 0, 500, and $10,000$, we first find that $u(\$30,000) = 1$ and $u(-\$10,000) = 0$. Then (1)–(3) yield $u(\$10,000) = .90$, $u(\$500) = .62$, and $u(\$0) = .60$. The specification of $u(r_i)$ for all rewards r_i is called the decision maker's **utility function**.

For a given lottery $L = (p_1, r_1; p_2, r_2; \ldots; p_n, r_n)$, define the expected utility of the lottery L, written $E(U$ for $L)$, by

$$E(U \text{ for } L) = \sum_{i=1}^{i=n} p_i u(r_i)$$

Thus, in our example

$$E(U \text{ for } L_1) = 1(.90) = .90$$
$$E(U \text{ for } L_2) = .50(1) + .50(.60) = .80$$
$$E(U \text{ for } L_3) = 1(.60) = .60$$
$$E(U \text{ for } L_4) = .02(0) + .98(.62) = .6076$$

Recall that we found that $L_i i L_i'$, where L_i' yielded an $E(U$ for $L_i)$ chance at \$30,000 and a $1 - E(U$ for $L_i)$ chance at $-\$10,000$. Thus, in choosing between lotteries L_1', L_2', L_3', and L_4' (or equivalently, L_1, L_2, L_3, and L_4), we simply chose the lottery with the largest expected utility. Given two lotteries L_1 and L_2, we may choose between them via the expected utility criteria:

$$L_1 p L_2 \quad \text{if and only if} \quad E(U \text{ for } L_1) > E(U \text{ for } L_2)$$
$$L_2 p L_1 \quad \text{if and only if} \quad E(U \text{ for } L_2) > E(U \text{ for } L_1)$$
$$L_1 i L_2 \quad \text{if and only if} \quad E(U \text{ for } L_2) = E(U \text{ for } L_1)$$

VON NEUMANN-MORGENSTERN AXIOMS

Von Neumann and Morgenstern proved that if a person's preferences satisfy the following axioms, then he or she should choose between lotteries by using the expected utility criterion.

AXIOM 1: COMPLETE ORDERING AXIOM. For any two rewards r_1 and r_2, one of the following must be true: The decision maker (1) prefers r_1 to r_2, (2) prefers r_2 to r_1, or (3) is indifferent between r_1 and r_2. Also, if the person prefers r_1 to r_2 and prefers r_2 to r_3, then he or she must prefer r_1 to r_3 (transitivity of preferences).

In our discussion, we used the Complete Ordering Axiom to determine the most and least favorable outcomes.

AXIOM 2: CONTINUITY AXIOM. If the decision maker prefers r_1 to r_2 and prefers r_2 to r_3, then for some c $(0 < c < 1)$, $L_1 i L_2$, where

In our informal discussion, we used the Continuity Axiom when we found, for example, that $L_3 i L_3'$, where

AXIOM 3: INDEPENDENCE AXIOM.   Suppose the decision maker is indifferent between rewards r_1 and r_2. Let r_3 be any other reward. Then for any c ($0 < c < 1$), $L_1 i L_2$, where

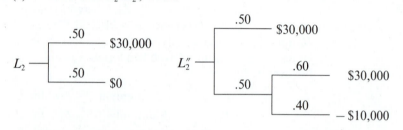

L_1 and L_2 differ only in that L_1 has a probability c of yielding a reward r_1, whereas L_2 has a probability c of yielding a reward r_2. Thus, the Independence Axiom implies that the decision maker views a chance c at r_1 and a chance c at r_2 to be of identical value, and this view holds for all values of c and r_3. We applied the Independence Axiom when we used (3) to claim that $L_2 i L_2''$, where

AXIOM 4: UNEQUAL PROBABILITY AXIOM.   Suppose the decision maker prefers reward r_1 to reward r_2. If two lotteries have only r_1 and r_2 as their possible outcomes, he or she will prefer the lottery with the higher probability of obtaining r_1.

We used the Unequal Probability Axiom when we concluded, for example, that L_1' was preferred to L_2' (because L_1' had a .90 chance at \$30,000 and L_2' had only a .80 chance at \$30,000).

AXIOM 5: COMPOUND LOTTERY AXIOM.   Suppose that when all possible outcomes are considered, a compound lottery L yields (for $i = 1, 2, \ldots, n$) a probability p_i of receiving a reward r_i. Then $L i L'$, where L' is the simple lottery $(p_1, r_1; p_2, r_2; \ldots; p_n, r_n)$.

For example, consider the following compound lottery:

L yields a $.50 + .50(.40) = .70$ chance at $-\$4$ and a $.50(.60) = .30$ chance at \$6. Thus, $L i L''$, where

In our informal discussion, we used the Compound Lottery Axiom when, for example, we stated that the compound equivalent of L_2 (L_2'')

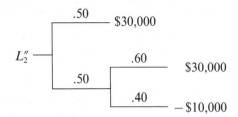

was equivalent to the following simple lottery:

$$.50 + .50(.60) = .80 \qquad \$30,000$$

$$.50(.40) = .20 \qquad -\$10,000$$

WHY WE MAY ASSUME u(WORST OUTCOME) = 0 AND u(BEST OUTCOME) = 1

Up to now, we have assumed that u(least favorable outcome) = 0 and u(most favorable outcome) = 1. Even if a decision maker's utility function does not have these values, we can transform his or her utility function (without changing the preferences among lotteries) into a utility function having u(least favorable outcome) = 0 and u(most favorable outcome) = 1.

L E M M A 1

Given a utility function $u(x)$, define for any $a > 0$ and any b the function $v(x) = au(x) + b$. Given any two lotteries L_1 and L_2, it will be the case that

1. A decision maker using $u(x)$ as his or her utility function will have $L_1 p L_2$ if and only if a decision maker using $v(x)$ as his or her utility function will have $L_1 p L_2$.

2. A decision maker using $u(x)$ as his or her utility function will have $L_1 i L_2$ if and only if a decision maker having $v(x)$ as his or her utility function will have $L_1 i L_2$.

Proof

Let

$$L_1 = (p_1, r_1; p_2, r_2; \ldots; p_n, r_n)$$
$$L_2 = (p_1', r_1'; p_2', r_2'; \ldots; p_m', r_m')$$

Suppose the decision maker using $u(x)$ prefers L_1 to L_2. Then by the expected utility criterion, we know that

$$\sum_{i=1}^{i=n} p_i u(r_i) > \sum_{i=1}^{i=m} p_i' u(r_i') \qquad (4)$$

Now the $v(x)$ decision maker will have $L_1 p L_2$ if

$$\sum_{i=1}^{i=n} p_i [au(r_i) + b] > \sum_{i=1}^{i=m} p_i' [au(r_i') + b] \qquad (5)$$

Since

$$\sum_{i=1}^{i=n} p_i = \sum_{i=1}^{i=m} p_i' = 1$$

(5) simplifies to

$$a \sum_{i=1}^{i=n} p_i u(r_i) + b > a \sum_{i=1}^{i=m} p_i' u(r_i') + b \qquad (6)$$

Since $a > 0$, (6) follows from (4). Thus, if the $u(x)$ decision maker has $L_1 p L_2$, the $v(x)$ decision maker has $L_1 p L_2$. Similarly, if (6) holds, then (4) will hold. Thus, if the $v(x)$ decision maker has $L_1 p L_2$, the $u(x)$ decision maker will also have $L_1 p L_2$. A similar argument can be used to prove part (3) of Lemma 1. ◆

Using Lemma 1, we can show that without changing how an individual ranks lotteries, we can transform the decision maker's utility function into a utility function having u(least favorable outcome) $= 0$ and u(most favorable outcome) $= 1$. To illustrate, let's reconsider ranking lotteries L_1–L_4. Suppose our decision maker's utility function had $u(-\$10,000) = -5$ and $u(\$30,000) = 10$. Define $v(x) = au(x) + b$. Choose a and b so that $v(\$30,000) = 10a + b = 1$ and $v(-\$10,000) = -5a + b = 0$. Then $a = \frac{1}{15}$ and $b = \frac{1}{3}$. Then by Lemma 1, the utility function $v(x) = \frac{u(x)}{15} + \frac{1}{3}$ will yield the same ranking of lotteries as does $u(x)$, and we will have constructed $v(x)$ so that $v(\$30,000) = 1$ and $v(-\$10,000) = 0$. Thus, we see that without loss of generality, we may assume that u(least favorable outcome) $= 0$ and u(most favorable outcome) $= 1$.

ESTIMATING AN INDIVIDUAL'S UTILITY FUNCTION

How might we estimate an individual's (call her Jill) utility function? We begin by assuming that the least favorable outcome (say, $-\$10,000$) has a utility of zero and that the most favorable outcome (say, $\$30,000$) has a utility of 1. Next we define a number $x_{1/2}$ having $u(x_{1/2}) = \frac{1}{2}$. To determine $x_{1/2}$, ask Jill for the number (call it $x_{1/2}$) that makes her indifferent between

Since Jill is indifferent between the two lotteries, they must have the same expected utility. Thus, $u(x_{1/2}) = (\frac{1}{2})(1) + (\frac{1}{2})(0) = \frac{1}{2}$.

This procedure yields a point $x_{1/2}$ having $u(x_{1/2}) = \frac{1}{2}$. Suppose Jill states that $x_{1/2} = -\$3400$. Using $x_{1/2}$ and the least favorable outcome ($-\$10,000$) as possible outcomes, we can construct a lottery that can be used to determine the point $x_{1/4}$ having a utility of $\frac{1}{4}$ (that is, $u(x_{1/4}) = \frac{1}{4}$). Point $x_{1/4}$ must be such that Jill is indifferent between

Then $u(x_{1/4}) = (\frac{1}{2})(\frac{1}{2}) + (\frac{1}{2})(0) = \frac{1}{4}$. Thus, $x_{1/4}$ will satisfy $u(x_{1/4}) = \frac{1}{4}$. Suppose Jill states that $x_{1/4} = -\$8000$. This gives us another point on Jill's utility function.

Jill can now use the $x_{1/2}$ and \$30,000 outcomes to construct a lottery that will yield a value $x_{3/4}$ satisfying $u(x_{3/4}) = \frac{3}{4}$. (How?) Suppose that $x_{3/4} = \$8000$. Similarly, outcomes of $x_{1/4}$ and $-\$10,000$ can be used to construct a lottery that will yield a value $x_{1/8}$ satisfying $u(x_{1/8}) = \frac{1}{8}$. Now Jill's utility function can be approximated by drawing a curve (smooth, we hope) joining the points

$$(-\$10,000, 0), (x_{1/8}, \tfrac{1}{8}), (x_{1/4}, \tfrac{1}{4}), \dots, (\$30,000, 1)$$

The result is shown in Figure 1. Unfortunately, if a decision maker's preferences violate any of the preceding axioms (such as transitivity), this procedure may not yield a smooth curve. If it does not yield a relatively smooth curve, more sophisticated procedures for assessing utility functions must be used (see Keeney and Raiffa (1976)).

Figure 1
Jill's Utility Function

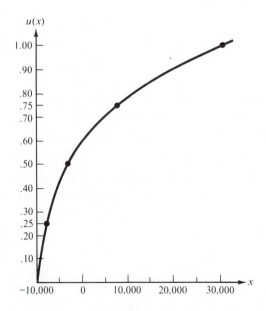

RELATION BETWEEN AN INDIVIDUAL'S UTILITY FUNCTION AND HIS OR HER ATTITUDE TOWARD RISK

A decision maker's utility function contains information about his or her attitude toward risk. To discuss this information, we need to define the concepts of a lottery's certainty equivalent and risk premium.

DEFINITION	The **certainty equivalent** of a lottery L, written $CE(L)$, is the number $CE(L)$ such that the decision maker is indifferent between the lottery L and receiving a certain payoff of $CE(L)$.

For example, we saw earlier that Jill was indifferent between

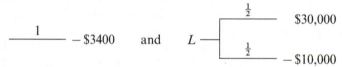

Thus, $CE(L) = -\$3400$.

For example, if

$$
L
\begin{cases}
\frac{1}{2} & \$30,000 \\
\frac{1}{2} & -\$10,000
\end{cases}
$$

then $EV(L) = (\frac{1}{2})(\$30,000) + (\frac{1}{2})(-\$10,000) = \$10,000$. We have already seen that $CE(L) = -\$3400$. Thus, $RP(L) = 10,000 - (-3400) = \$13,400$; Jill values L at $\$13,400$ less than its expected value, because she does not like the large degree of uncertainty that is associated with the reward yielded by L.

Let a **nondegenerate lottery** be any lottery in which more than one outcome can occur. With respect to attitude toward risk, a decision maker is

1. **Risk-averse** if and only if for any nondegenerate lottery L, $RP(L) > 0$
2. **Risk-neutral** if and only if for any nondegenerate lottery L, $RP(L) = 0$
3. **Risk-seeking** if and only if for any nondegenerate lottery L, $RP(L) < 0$

An individual's attitude toward risk depends on the concavity (or convexity) of his or her utility function.

If $u(x)$ is differentiable, then $u(x)$ will be strictly concave if and only if $u''(x) < 0$ for all x and $u(x)$ will be strictly convex if and only if $u''(x) > 0$ for all x. It can easily be shown that a decision maker with a utility function $u(x)$ is

1. Risk-averse if and only if $u(x)$ is strictly concave

2. Risk-neutral if and only if $u(x)$ is a linear function (if $u(x)$ is both convex and concave)

3. Risk-seeking if and only if $u(x)$ is strictly convex

To illustrate these definitions, we show that a decision maker with a concave utility function $u(x)$ exhibits risk-averse behavior (i.e., has $RP(L) > 0$). Consider a binary lottery L (a lottery with only two possible outcomes):

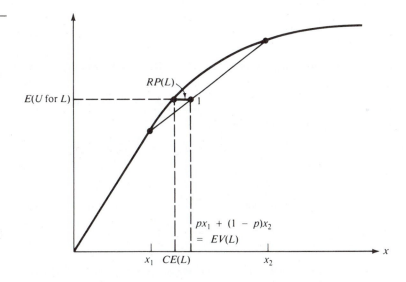

$$L \begin{cases} \overset{p}{} x_1 \\ \underset{1-p}{} x_2 \end{cases} \qquad (\text{Assume } x_1 < x_2)$$

Suppose $u(x)$ is strictly concave. Then, from Figure 2, we see that

$$E(U \text{ for } L) = p\,u(x_1) + (1-p)u(x_2) = y\text{-coordinate of point 1}$$

Since $CE(L)$ is the value x^* having $u(x^*) = E(U \text{ for } L)$, Figure 2 shows that $CE(L) < EV(L)$, so $RP(L) > 0$. This follows because the strict concavity of $u(x)$ implies that the line segment joining the points $(x_1, u(x_1))$ and $(x_2, u(x_2))$ lies below the curve $u(x)$.

Figure 2
Why a Concave
Utility Function
Implies Risk-Averse
Behavior

We can also give an algebraic proof that $u(x)$ strictly concave implies that $RP(L) = EV(L) - CE(L) > 0$. Recall that for

$$L \begin{cases} \overset{p}{} x_1 \\ \underset{1-p}{} x_2 \end{cases}$$

$EV(L) = px_1 + (1-p)x_2$. Now the strict concavity of $u(x)$ implies that $u[px_1 + (1-p)x_2] > pu(x_1) + (1-p)u(x_2) = E(U \text{ for } L)$. Thus, the decision maker prefers $px_1 + (1-p)x_2 = EV(L)$ with certainty to the prospect of playing L. The certainty equivalent of L must be less than $px_1 + (1-p)x_2 = EV(L)$. This implies that $RP(L) = EV(L) - CE(L) > 0$, and the decision maker exhibits risk-averse behavior. In Problem 4 at the end of this section, the reader will be asked to show that if $u(x)$ is strictly convex, the decision maker exhibits risk-seeking behavior.

If the decision maker is risk-neutral (that is, $u(x) = ax + b$), he or she chooses among lotteries via the expected reward criterion of Section 13.1 (see Problem 5 at the end of this section). Thus, when ranking lotteries, a risk-neutral decision maker considers only the expected value (and not the risk) of the lotteries.

Example 2 illustrates the concepts of risk premium, certainty equivalent, and risk aversion.

E X A M P L E 2

Joan's utility function for her asset position x is given by $u(x) = x^{1/2}$. Currently, Joan's assets consist of \$10,000 in cash and a \$90,000 home. During a given year, there is a .001 chance that Joan's home will be destroyed by fire or other causes. How much would Joan be willing to pay for an insurance policy that would replace her home if it were destroyed?

Solution

Let $x =$ annual insurance premium. Then Joan must choose between the following lotteries:

Asset Position

L_1: Buy insurance $\underset{\text{1}}{\quad\quad\quad}$ (\$100,000 $- x$)

L_2: Don't buy insurance
- .001 \$100,000 $-$ \$90,000 $=$ \$10,000
- .999 \$100,000

Joan will prefer L_1 to L_2 if L_1's expected utility exceeds L_2's expected utility. Thus, $L_1 \, \text{p} \, L_2$ if

$$(100,000 - x)^{1/2} > .001(10,000)^{1/2} + .999(100,000)^{1/2}$$
$$> .10 + 315.91$$
$$> 316.01$$

Squaring both sides of the last inequality we find that $L_1 \, \text{p} \, L_2$ if and only if

$$100,000 - x > (316.01)^2$$
$$x < \$137.68$$

Thus, Joan would pay up to \$137.68 for insurance. Of course, if $p = \$137.68$, $L_1 \, \text{i} \, L_2$. Let's compute the risk premium for L_2:

$$EV(L_2) = .001(10,000) + .999(100,000) = \$99,910$$

(an expected loss of $100,000 - 99,910 = \$90$). Since $E(U \text{ for } L_2) = 316.01$, we can find $CE(L_2)$ from the relation $u(CE(L_2)) = 316.01$, or $[CE(L_2)]^{1/2} = 316.01$. Thus, $CE(L_2) = (316.01)^2 = \$99,862.32$, and

$$RP(L_2) = EV(L_2) - CE(L_2) = 99,910 - 99,862.32 = \$47.68$$

Therefore, Joan is willing to pay for annual home insurance \$47.68 more than the expected loss of \$90. (Recall that Joan was willing to pay up to $90 + 47.68 = \$137.68$ to avoid the risk involved in her home being destroyed.) Joan exhibits risk-averse behavior ($RP(L_2) > 0$). Since

$$u''(x) = \frac{-x^{-3/2}}{4} < 0$$

$u(x)$ is strictly concave, and $RP(L) > 0$ would hold for any nondegenerate lottery. ◆

In reality, many people exhibit both risk-seeking behavior (they purchase lottery tickets, go to Las Vegas) and risk-averse behavior (they buy home insurance). A person whose utility function contains both convex and concave segments may exhibit both risk-averse and risk-seeking behavior. Consider a decision maker whose utility function $u(x)$ for change in current asset position is given in Figure 3. If forced to choose between

$$L_1 \overset{1}{\underline{\hspace{1cm}}} 0 \quad \text{and} \quad \begin{array}{l} \overset{.10}{\underline{\hspace{1cm}}} \$2500 \\ \overset{.90}{\underline{\hspace{1cm}}} -\$300 \end{array}$$

what would this person do?

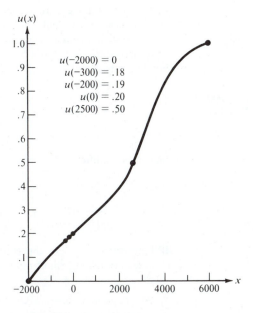

Figure 3
A Utility Function
That Exhibits Both
Risk-Seeking and
Risk-Averse
Behavior

$u(-2000) = 0$
$u(-300) = .18$
$u(-200) = .19$
$u(0) = .20$
$u(2500) = .50$

From Figure 3, we find that $u(0) = .20$, $u(2500) = .50$, and $u(-300) = .18$. Thus, $E(U \text{ for } L_1) = .20$ and $E(U \text{ for } L_2) = .10(.50) + .90(.18) = .212$. Thus, $L_2 p L_1$. This means that L_2 has a certainty equivalent of at least \$0. Since $EV(L_2) = -\$20$, this implies that $RP(L_2) = EV(L_2) - CE(L_2) < 0$. The decision maker exhibits risk-seeking behavior in this situation, because for changes in asset position between \$0 and \$2500, $u(x)$ is a convex function.

Now suppose the decision maker can, for \$200, insure himself against a loss of \$2000, which occurs with probability .08. Then he must choose between

$$L_3 \; \underline{\quad 1 \quad} \; -\$200 \quad \text{and} \quad L_4 \begin{cases} .08 & -\$2000 \\ .92 & \$0 \end{cases}$$

From Figure 3, $u(-200) = .19$, $u(0) = .20$, and $u(-2000) = 0$. Thus, $E(U$ for $L_3) = .19$ and $E(U$ for $L_4) = .08(0) + .92(.20) = .184$, and $L_3 p L_4$. This shows that $CE(L_4) < -\$200$. Since $EV(L_4) = .08(-2000) + .92(0) = -\$160$, $RP(L_4) = EV(L_4) - CE(L_4) > 0$, and the decision maker is exhibiting risk-averse behavior, because $u(x)$ is concave for $-2000 < x < 0$. Thus, if his utility function has both convex and concave segments, a person can exhibit both risk-seeking and risk-averse behavior.

◆ PROBLEMS

GROUP A

1. Suppose my utility function for asset position x is given by $u(x) = \ln x$.
(a) Am I risk-averse, risk-neutral, or risk-seeking?
(b) I now have $20,000 and am considering the following two lotteries:

  L_1: With probability 1, I lose $1000

  L: With probability $\frac{1}{3}$, he or she gains $80,000
  With probability $\frac{2}{3}$, he or she loses $10,000

Determine which lottery I prefer and the risk premium of L_2.

2. Answer Problem 1 for a utility function $u(x) = x^2$.

3. Answer Problem 1 for a utility function $u(x) = 2x + 1$.

4. Show that a decision maker who has a strictly convex utility function will exhibit risk-seeking behavior.

5. Show that if a decision maker who has a linear utility function will rank two lotteries according to their expected value.

6. A decision maker has a utility function for monetary gains x given by $u(x) = (x + 10,000)^{1/2}$.
(a) Show that the person is indifferent between the status quo and

  L: With probability $\frac{1}{3}$, he or she gains $80,000
  With probability $\frac{2}{3}$, he or she loses $10,000

(b) If there is a 10% chance that a painting valued at $10,000 will be stolen during the next year, what is the most (per year) that the decision maker would be willing to pay for insurance covering the loss of the painting?

7. Patty is trying to determine which of two courses to take. If she takes the operations research course, she believes that she has a 10% chance of receiving an A, a 40% chance for a B, and a 50% chance for a C. If Patty takes a statistics course, she has a 70% chance for a B, a 25% chance for a C, and a 5% chance for a D. Patty is indifferent between

$$L_1 \; \underline{\quad 1 \quad} \; C \quad \text{and} \quad L_2 \begin{cases} .25 & A \\ .75 & D \end{cases}$$

She is also indifferent between

$$L_3 \; \underline{\quad 1 \quad} \; B \quad \text{and} \quad L_4 \begin{cases} .70 & A \\ .30 & D \end{cases}$$

If Patty wants to take the course that maximizes the expected utility of her final grade, which course should she take?

8. We are going to invest $1000 for a period of 6 months. Two potential investments are available: T-bills and gold. If the $1000 is invested in T-bills, we are certain to end the 6-month period with $1296. If we invest in gold, there is a $\frac{3}{4}$ chance that we will end the 6-month period with $400 and a $\frac{1}{4}$ chance that we will end the 6-month period with $10,000. If we end up with x dollars, our utility function is given by $u(x) = x^{1/2}$. Should we invest in gold or T-bills?

9. We now have $5,000 in assets and are given a choice between investment 1 and investment 2. With investment

1, 80% of the time we increase our asset position by $295,000, and 20% of the time we increase our asset position by $95,000. With investment 2, 50% of the time we increase our asset position by $595,000, and 50% of the time we increase our asset position by $5000. Our utility function for final asset position x is $u(x)$. We are given the following values for $u(x)$: $u(0) = 0$, $u(640,000) = .80$, $u(810,000) = .90$, $u(0) = 0$, $u(90,000) = .30$, $u(1,000,000) = 1$, $u(490,000) = .7$.
(a) Are we risk-averse, risk-seeking, or risk-neutral? Explain.
(b) Will we prefer investment 1 or investment 2?

10. My current income is $40,000. I believe that I owe $8000 in taxes. For $500, I can hire a CPA to review my tax return; there is a 20% chance that she will save me $4000 in taxes. My utility function for (disposable income) = (current income) − (taxes) − (payment to accountant) is given by $\sqrt{x}$, where x is disposable income. Should I hire the CPA?

GROUP B

11.[†] (The Allais Paradox) Suppose we are offered a choice between the following two lotteries:

L_1: With probability 1, we receive $1 million

L_2: With probability .10, we receive $5 million
With probability .89, we receive $1 million
With probability .01, we receive $0

Which lottery do we prefer?
Now consider the following two lotteries:

L_3: With probability .11, we receive $1 million
With probability .89, we receive $0

L_4: With probability .10, we receive $5 million
With probability .90, we receive $0

Which lottery do we prefer? Suppose (like most people), we prefer L_1 to L_2. Show that L_3 must have a larger expected utility than L_4.

12. (The St. Petersburg Paradox) Let L represent the following lottery: I toss a coin until it comes up heads. If the first head is obtained on the nth toss of the coin, I receive a payoff of 2^n.
(a) If I were a risk-neutral decision maker, what would be the certainty equivalent of L? Is this reasonable?
(b) If a decision maker's utility function for increasing wealth by x dollars is given by $u(x) = \log_2(x)$, what would be the certainty equivalent of L?

13. Joe is a risk-averse decision maker. Which of the following lotteries will he prefer?

L_1: With probability .10, Joe loses $100
With probability .90, Joe receives $0

L_2: With probability .10, Joe loses $190
With probability .90, Joe receives $10

14.[‡] (The Ellsberg Paradox) An urn contains 90 balls. It is known that 30 of the balls are red and that each of the other 60 balls is either yellow or black. One ball will be drawn at random from the urn. Consider the following four options:

Option 1 We receive $1000 if a red ball is drawn.

Option 2 We receive $1000 if a yellow ball is drawn.

Option 3 We receive $1000 if a yellow or black ball is drawn.

Option 4 We receive $1000 if a red or black ball is drawn.

(a) Explain why most people prefer option 1 over option 2 and also prefer option 3 over option 4.
(b) If we prefer option 1 to option 2, explain why we should also prefer option 4 over option 3.

15. Although the Von Neumann-Morgenstern axioms seem plausible, there are many reasonable situations in which people appear to violate these axioms. For example, suppose a recent college graduate must choose between three job offers on the basis of starting salary, location of job, and opportunity for advancement. Given two job offers that are satisfactory with regard to all three attributes, the graduate will decide between two job offers by choosing the one that is superior on at least two of the three attributes. Suppose he or she has three job offers and has rated each one as shown in Table 8 (E = excellent, G = good, and S = satisfactory). Show that the graduate's preferences among these jobs violate the Complete Ordering Axiom.

GROUP C

16. Suppose my utility function for my asset position is $u(x) = x^{1/2}$. I have $10,000 at present. Consider the following lottery:

L: With probability $\frac{1}{2}$, L yields a payoff of $1025
With probability $\frac{1}{2}$, L yields a payoff of $-$199

(a) If I don't have the right to play L, find an equation that

Table 8

	STARTING SALARY	LOCATION	OPPORTUNITY FOR ADVANCEMENT
Job 1	E	S	G
Job 2	G	E	S
Job 3	S	G	E

when solved would yield the amount I would be willing to pay for the right to play L. This is called the **buying price** of lottery L.

(b) If I have the right to play L, what is the least I would accept from somebody who wanted to buy the right to play L? (After someone else buys L, I can't play L.) This is called the **selling price** of lottery L.

(c) Answer part (b) for the case that I have $1000.

(d) Suppose that my utility function for my asset position is $u(x) = 1 - e^{-x}$. Show that for all possible asset positions, the buying price of L and the selling price of L will remain the same. Show that for all asset positions the buying price of L will equal the selling price of L.

13-3   DECISION TREES

Often, people must make a series of decisions at different points in time. Then decision trees can often be used to determine optimal decisions. A decision tree enables a decision maker to decompose a large complex decision problem into several smaller problems.

E X A M P L E 3

Colaco currently has assets of $150,000 and wants to decide whether to market a new chocolate-flavored soda, Chocola. Colaco has three alternatives:

Alternative 1 Test market Chocola locally, then utilize the results of the market study to determine whether or not to market Chocola nationally.

Alternative 2 Immediately (without test marketing) market Chocola nationally.

Alternative 3 Immediately (without test marketing) decide not to market Chocola nationally.

In the absence of a market study, Colaco believes that Chocola has a 55% chance of being a national success and a 45% chance of being a national failure. If Chocola is a national success, Colaco's asset position will increase by $300,000, and if Chocola is a national failure, Colaco's asset position will decrease by $100,000.

If Colaco performs a market study (at a cost of $30,000), there is a 60% chance that the study will yield favorable results (referred to as a local success) and a 40% chance that the study will yield unfavorable results (referred to as a local failure). If a local success is observed, there is an 85% chance that Chocola will be a national success. If a local failure is observed, there is only a 10% chance that Chocola will be a national success. If Colaco is risk-neutral (wishes to maximize its expected final asset position), what strategy should the company follow?

Solution

To draw a decision tree that represents Colaco's problem, we begin at the present and proceed toward future events and decisions. The decision tree in Figure 4 is constructed with two kinds of forks: decision forks (denoted by □) and event forks (denoted by ○).

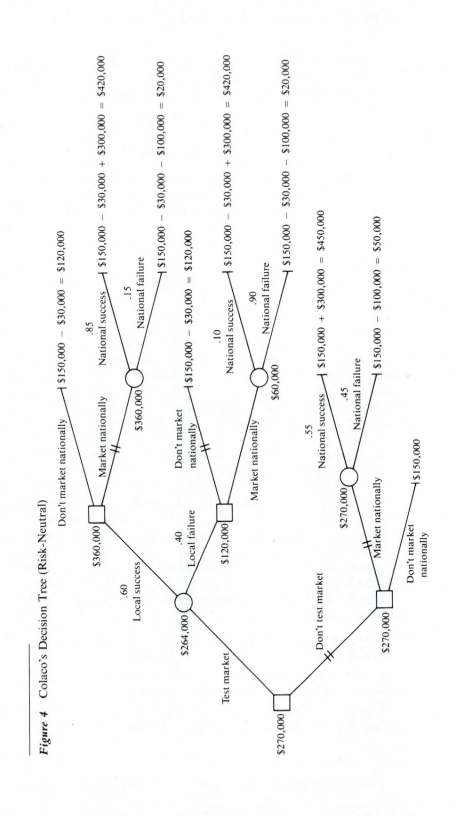

Figure 4 Colaco's Decision Tree (Risk-Neutral)

A **decision fork** represents a point in time when Colaco has to make a decision. Each branch emanating from a decision fork represents a possible decision. An example of a decision fork occurs when Colaco must determine whether or not to test market Chocola.

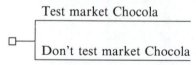

Test market Chocola

Don't test market Chocola

An **event fork** is drawn when outside forces determine which of several random events will occur. Each branch of an event fork represents a possible outcome, and the number on each branch represents the probability that the event will occur. For example, if Colaco decides to test market Chocola, Colaco faces the following event fork when observing the results of the test market study:

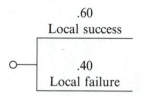

.60
Local success

.40
Local failure

A branch of a decision tree is a **terminal branch** if no forks emanate from the branch. Thus, the branches indicating National Success and National Failure are terminal branches of Colaco's decision tree. Since we are maximizing expected final asset position at each terminal branch, we must enter the final asset position that will result if the path leading to the given terminal branch occurs. For example, the terminal branch National Failure that follows Local Failure leads to a final asset position of 150,000 − 30,000 − 100,000 = \$20,000. If we were maximizing expected revenues, we would enter revenues on each terminal branch.

To determine the decisions that will maximize Colaco's expected final asset position, we work backward (sometimes called "folding back the tree") from right to left.[†] At each event fork, we calculate the expected final asset position and enter it in ○. At each decision fork, we denote by ‖ the decision that maximizes the expected final asset position and enter the expected final asset position associated with that decision in □. We continue working backward in this fashion until we reach the beginning of the tree. Then the optimal sequence of decisions can be obtained by following the ‖.

We begin by determining the expected final asset positions for the following three event forks:

1. Market Nationally after Local Success. Here we have an expected final asset position of .85(420,000) + .15(20,000) = \$360,000.

2. Market Nationally after Local Failure. Here we have an expected final asset position of .10(420,000) + .90(20,000) = \$60,000.

3. Market Nationally after Don't Test Market. Here we have an expected final asset position of .55(450,000) + .45(50,000) = \$270,000.

[†]See Chapters 20 and 21 for an explanation of working backward (often called dynamic programming).

We may now evaluate three decision forks:

1. Decision after Local Success. Market Nationally yields a larger expected final asset position than Don't Market Nationally, so we ‖ Market Nationally and enter an expected final asset position of $360,000.

2. Decision after Local Failure. Don't Market Nationally yields a larger expected final asset position than Market Nationally, so we ‖ Don't Market Nationally and enter an expected final asset position of $120,000.

3. Decision for Don't Test Market. Market Nationally yields a larger expected final asset position than Don't Market Nationally, so we ‖ Market Nationally and enter an expected final asset position of $270,000.

We now must evaluate the event fork emanating from the Test Market decision. This event fork yields an expected final asset position of .60(360,000) + .40(120,000) = $264,000, which is entered in ○.

All that remains is to determine the correct decision at the decision fork Test Market versus Don't Test Market. We have found that Test Market yields an expected final asset position of $264,000, and Don't Test Market yields an expected final asset position of $270,000. Thus, we ‖ Don't Test Market and enter $270,000 in □.

We have now reached the beginning of the tree and have found that Colaco's optimal decision is Don't Test Market and then Market Nationally. This strategy will yield an expected final asset position of $270,000. Observe that the decision tree also tells us that if we had test marketed and then acted optimally (Market Nationally after Local Success and Don't Market Nationally after Local Failure), we would have obtained an expected final asset position of $264,000.

◆

INCORPORATING RISK AVERSION INTO DECISION TREE ANALYSIS

Note that Colaco's optimal strategy yields a .45 chance that the company will end up with a relatively small final asset position of $50,000. On the other hand, the strategy of test marketing and acting optimally on the results of the test market study yields only a $(.60)(.15) = .09$ chance that Colaco's asset position will be below $100,000. (Why?) Thus, if Colaco is a risk-averse decision maker, the strategy of immediately marketing nationally may not reflect the company's preference.

To illustrate how risk aversion may be incorporated into decision tree analysis, suppose that Colaco has the risk-averse utility function $u(x)$ in Figure 5 (x = final asset position). (How do we know that this utility function exhibits risk aversion?) *To determine Colaco's optimal decisions (that is, the decisions that maximize expected utility), simply replace each final asset position x_0 by its utility $u(x_0)$. Then at each event fork, compute the expected utility of Colaco's final asset position, and at each decision fork, choose the branch having the largest expected utility.*

We find from Figure 5 that $u(\$450,000) = 1$, $u(\$420,000) = .99$, $u(\$150,000) = .48$, $u(\$120,000) = .40$, $u(\$50,000) = .19$, and $u(\$20,000) = 0$. Substituting these values in the decision tree of Figure 4 yields the decision tree in Figure 6.

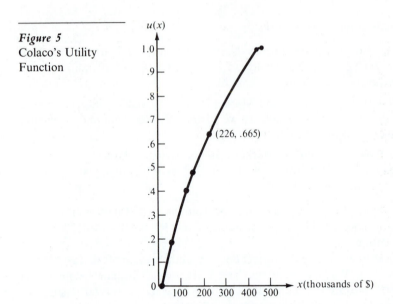

Figure 5
Colaco's Utility
Function

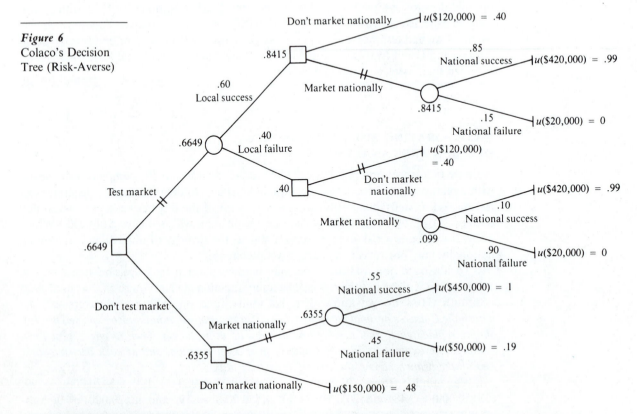

Figure 6
Colaco's Decision
Tree (Risk-Averse)

Don't market nationally ——| $u(\$120,000) = .40$

.85
National success ——| $u(\$420,000) = .99$

.8415

Market nationally

.8415

.15
National failure ——| $u(\$20,000) = 0$

.60
Local success

.6649

.40
Local failure

$u(\$120,000)$
$= .40$

Don't market
nationally

.40

| $u(\$420,000) = .99$

.10
National success

Market nationally

.099

.90
National failure ——| $u(\$20,000) = 0$

Test market

.55
National success ——| $u(\$450,000) = 1$

.6649

.6355

Market nationally

.6355

.45
National failure ——| $u(\$50,000) = .19$

Don't test market

Don't market nationally ——| $u(\$150,000) = .48$

$u(\$226,000) = .6649$, so this situation is
equivalent to a certain asset position of $226,000

706

We compute the expected utility at the following three event forks:

1. Market Nationally after Local Success. Here we have an expected utility of .85(.99) + .15(0) = .8415.

2. Market Nationally after Local Failure. Here we have an expected utility of .10(.99) + .90(0) = .099.

3. Marketing Nationally after Don't Test Market. Here we have an expected utility of .55(1) + .45(.19) = .6355.

We may now evaluate three decision forks:

1. Decision after Local Success. Market Nationally yields a larger expected utility than Don't Market Nationally, so for this fork we ‖ Market Nationally and enter an expected utility of .8415.

2. Decision after Local Failure. Don't Market Nationally yields a larger expected utility than Market Nationally, so for this fork we ‖ Don't Market Nationally and enter an expected utility of .40.

3. Decision for Don't Test Market. Market Nationally yields a larger expected utility than Don't Market Nationally, so for this fork we ‖ Market Nationally and enter an expected utility of .6355.

We now must evaluate the event fork emanating from the Test Market decision. This event fork yields an expected utility of .60(.8415) + .40(.40) = .6649, which is entered in ○. All that remains is to determine the correct decision at the decision fork Test Market versus Don't Test Market. We know that Test Market yields an expected utility of .6649, and Don't Test Market yields an expected utility of .6355, so we ‖ Test Market and enter an expected utility of .6649 in □.

We have now reached the beginning of the tree and have found that Colaco's optimal decision is to begin by test marketing. If a local success is observed, then Colaco should market Chocola nationally; if a local failure is observed, then Colaco should not market Chocola nationally. This optimal strategy yields only a .60(.15) = .09 chance that Colaco will have a final asset position of less than $100,000. This reflects the risk-averse nature of the utility function in Figure 5. Also, we see from Figure 5 that $u(\$226,000) = .665$. Since Colaco views the current situation as having an expected utility of .6649, this means that Colaco considers the current situation equivalent to a certain asset position of $226,000. Thus, if somebody offered to pay more than $226,000 - 150,000 = \$76,000$ to buy the rights to Chocola, Colaco should take the offer. This is because receiving more than $76,000 for the rights to Chocola would bring Colaco's asset position to more than $150,000 + 76,000 = \$226,000$, and this situation has a higher expected utility than .665.

EXPECTED VALUE OF SAMPLE INFORMATION

Decision trees can be used to measure the value of sample or test market information. To illustrate how this is done, we again assume that Colaco is risk-neutral. What is the value of the information that would be obtained by test marketing Chocola?

We begin by determining Colaco's expected final asset position if the company acts optimally and the test market study is costless. We call this expected final asset position Colaco's **expected value with sample information** (EVWSI). From Figure 4, we see that if we Test Market and then act optimally, we will now have an expected final asset position of $264,000 + 30,000 = \$294,000$. Since \$294,000 is larger than the expected asset position of the Don't Test Market branch (\$270,000), we find that EVWSI = \$294,000.

We next determine the largest expected final asset position that Colaco would obtain if the test market study were not available. We call this the **expected value with original information** (EVWOI). From the Don't Test Market branch of Figure 4, we find EVWOI = \$270,000. Now the expected value of the test market information, referred to as **expected value of sample information** (EVSI), is defined to be EVSI = EVWSI − EVWOI.

In the Colaco example, EVSI is the most that Colaco can pay for the test market information and still be at least as well off as without the test market information. Thus, for the Colaco example, EVSI = $294,000 - 270,000 = \$24,000$. Since the cost of the test market study (\$30,000) exceeds EVSI, Colaco should not (as we already know) conduct the test market study.

EXPECTED VALUE OF PERFECT INFORMATION

We can modify the analysis used to determine EVSI to find the value of perfect information. By **perfect information** we mean that all uncertain events that can affect Colaco's final asset position still occur with the given probabilities (so there is still a .55 chance of Chocola being a national success and a .45 chance that Chocola will be a national failure), but Colaco finds out whether or not Chocola is a national success or a national failure *before* making the decision to market Chocola nationally or not. This information can then be used to determine Colaco's optimal marketing strategy. Thus, **expected value with perfect information** (EVWPI) is found by drawing a decision tree in which the decision maker has perfect information about which state has occurred before making a decision. Then the **expected value of perfect information** (EVPI) is given by EVPI = EVWPI − EVWOI.

For the Colaco example, we find from Figure 7 that EVWPI = \$315,000. Then EVPI = $315,000 - 270,000 = \$45,000$. Thus, a perfect (one that was always correct) test marketing study would be worth \$45,000. EVPI is a useful upper bound on the value of sample or test market information; that is, no sample or test market information (no matter how good) can be worth more than \$45,000.

Figure 7
Expected Value With Perfect Information (EVWPI) for Colaco

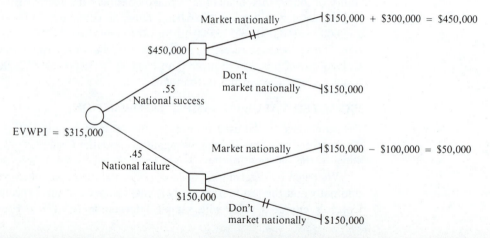

E X A M P L E
4

An art dealer's client is willing to buy the painting *Sunplant* at $50,000. The dealer can buy the painting today for $40,000 or can wait a day and buy the painting tomorrow (if it has not been sold) for $30,000. The dealer may also wait another day and buy the painting (if it is still available) for $26,000. At the end of the third day, the painting will no longer be available for sale. Each day, there is a .60 probability that the painting will be sold. What strategy maximizes the dealer's expected profit?

Solution

The decision tree for this example is given in Figure 8. The key to drawing this decision tree is that each day, the dealer must choose between buying the painting and waiting another day. Of course, waiting might mean that the dealer may never be able to buy the painting. As we see from the decision tree, the dealer should buy the painting on the first day.

Figure 8
Decision Tree for
Example 4

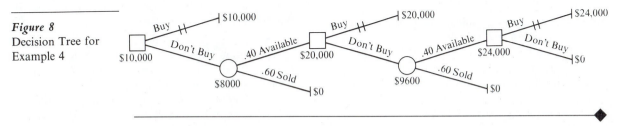

◆ PROBLEMS

GROUP A

1. Oilco must determine whether or not to drill for oil in the South China Sea. It costs $100,000 to drill for oil, and if oil is found, the value of the oil is estimated to be $600,000. At present, Oilco believes there is a 45% chance that the field contains oil. Before drilling for oil, Oilco can hire (for $10,000) a geologist to obtain more information about the likelihood that the field will contain oil. There is a 50% chance that the geologist will issue a favorable report and a 50% chance that the geologist will issue an unfavorable report. Given a favorable report, there is an 80% chance that the field contains oil. Given an unfavorable report, there is a 10% chance that the field contains oil. Determine Oilco's optimal course of action. Also determine EVSI and EVPI

2. The decision sciences department is trying to determine which of two copying machines to purchase. Both machines will satisfy the department's needs for the next ten years. Machine 1 costs $2000 and has a maintenance agreement which, for an annual fee of $150, covers all repairs. Machine 2 costs $3000, and its annual maintenance cost is a random variable. At present, the decision sciences department believes there is a 40% chance that the annual maintenance cost for machine 2 will be $0, a 40% chance that the annual maintenance cost will be $100, and a 20% chance that the annual maintenance cost will be $200.

Before the purchase decision is made, the department can have a trained repairperson evaluate the quality of machine 2. If the repairperson believes that machine 2 is satisfactory, there is a 60% chance that the annual maintenance cost for machine 2 will be $0 and a 40% chance that the annual maintenance cost will be $100. If the repairperson believes that machine 2 is unsatisfactory, there is 20% chance that the annual maintenance cost will be $0, a 40% chance that the annual maintenance cost will be $100, and a 40% chance that the annual maintenance cost will be $200. If there is a 50% chance that the repairperson will give a satisfactory report, what is EVSI? If the repairperson charges $40, what should the decision sciences department do? What is EVPI?

3. I am managing the Chicago Cubs. Suppose there is a runner on first base with nobody out and we want to determine whether or not we should bunt. Assume that a bunt will yield one or two results: (1) With probability .80, the bunt will be successful, in which case the batter is out and the runner on first base advances to second base. (2) With probability .20, the bunt is unsuccessful and the runner on first base is out trying to advance to second base and the batter is safe at first base.

The expected number of runs that the Cubs will score in an inning in various situations is given in Table 9.

(a) If our goal is to maximize the expected number of runs

Table 9

ON-BASE SITUATION	NUMBER OF OUTS	EXPECTED NUMBER OF RUNS
Runner on first	0	0.813
Runner on first	1	0.498
Runner on second	1	0.671
Runner on second	0	1.194
No base runners	1	0.243

scored in an inning, should we bunt? Despite this answer, why do you think teams bunt?

(b) If we are considering stealing second base with nobody out, what chance of success is needed for stealing second to be an optimal decision?

4. The Nitro Fertilizer Company is developing a new fertilizer. If Nitro markets the product and it is successful, the company will earn a $50,000 profit; if unsuccessful, the company will lose $35,000. In the past, similar products have been successful 60% of the time. At a cost of $5000, the effectiveness of the new fertilizer can be tested. If the test result is favorable, there is an 80% chance that the ferilizer will be successful. If the test result is unfavorable, there is only a 30% chance that the fertilizer will be successful. There is a 60% chance of a favorable test result and a 40% chance of an unfavorable test result. Determine Nitro's optimal strategy. Also find EVSI and EVPI.

5. During the summer, the Olympics swimmer Adam Johnson swims every day. On sunny summer days, he goes to an outdoor pool, where he may swim for no charge. On rainy days, he must go to a domed pool. At the beginning of the summer, he has the option of purchasing a $15 season pass to the domed pool, which enables him to use the domed pool for the entire summer. If he doesn't buy a season pass to the domed pool, he must pay $1 each time he goes there. Past meteorological records indicate that there is a 60% chance that the summer will be sunny (in which case there is an average of 6 rainy days during the summer) and a 40% chance that the summer will be rainy (in which case there is an average of 30 rainy days during the summer).

Before the summer begins, Adam has the option of purchasing a long-range weather forecast for $1. The forecast predicts a sunny summer 80% of the time and a rainy summer 20% of the time. If the forecast predicts a sunny summer, there is a 70% chance that the summer will actually be sunny. If the forecast predicts a rainy summer, there is an 80% chance that the summer will actually be rainy. Assuming that Adam's goal is to minimize his total

expected cost for the summer, what should he do? Also find EVSI and EVPI.

6. Pete is considering placing a bet on the NCAA playoff game between Indiana and Purdue. Without any further information, he believes that each team has an equal chance to win. If he wins the bet, he will win $10,000; if he loses, he will lose $11,000. Before betting, he may pay Bobby $1,000 for his inside prediction on the game; 60% of the time, Bobby will predict that Indiana will win, and 40% of the time, Bobby will predict that Purdue will win. When Bobby says that IU will win, IU has a 70% chance of winning, and when Bobby says that Purdue will win, IU has only a 20% chance of winning. Determine how Pete can maximize his total expected profit. What is EVSI? What is EVPI?

7. Erica is going to fly to London on August 5, 1991 and return home on August 20, 1991. It is now July 1, 1991. On July 1, 1991, she may buy a one-way ticket (for $350) or a round-trip ticket (for $660). She may also wait until August 1, 1991 to buy a ticket. On August 1, 1991, a one-way ticket will cost $370, and a round-trip ticket will cost $730. It is possible that between July 1 and August 1, her sister (who works for the airline) will be able to obtain a free one-way ticket for Erica. The probability that her sister will obtain the free ticket is .30. If Erica has bought a round-trip ticket on July 1 and her sister has obtained a free ticket, she may return "half" of her round-trip to the airline. In this case, her total cost will be $330 plus a $50 penalty. Use a decision tree approach to determine how to minimize Erica's expected cost of obtaining round-trip transportation to London.

8. I am a contestant on the TV show *Remote Jeopardy*, which works as follows. I am first asked a question about Stupid Videos. If I answer correctly, I earn $100. I believe that I have an 80% chance of answering such a question correctly. If I answer incorrectly, the game is over, and I win nothing. If I answer correctly, I may leave with $100 or go on and answer a question about Stupid TV Shows. If I answer this question correctly, I earn another $300, but if I answer it incorrectly, I lose all previous earnings and am sent home. My chance of answering this question correctly is .60. If I answer the Stupid TV Shows question correctly, I may leave with my "earnings" or go on and answer a question about Statistics. If I answer this question correctly, I earn another $500, but if I answer it incorrectly, I lose all previous earnings and am sent home. My chance of answering this question correctly is .40. Draw a decision tree that can be used to maximize my expected earnings. Then describe the strategy that maximizes my expected earnings. What are my expected earnings?

GROUP B

In many decision tree problems, the decision maker's goal is to maximize the probability of a favorable event occurring. To incorporate this goal into a decision tree, simply give a reward of 1 to any terminal branch that results in the favorable event occurring and a reward of zero to any terminal branch that results in the favorable event not occurring. Then maximizing expected reward is the same as maximizing the probability that the favorable event will occur. Use this idea to solve the next two problems.

9. The American chess master Jonathan Meller is playing the Soviet expert Yuri Gasparov in a two-game exhibition match. Each win earns a player one point, and each draw earns a player a half point. The player who has the most points after two games wins the match. If the players are tied after two games, they play until one wins a game; then the first player to win a game wins the match. During each game, Meller has two possible strategies: to play a daring strategy or to play a conservative strategy. His probabilities of winning, losing, and drawing when he follows each strategy are shown in Table 10. In order to maximize his probability of winning the match, what should the American do?

Table 10

STRATEGY	WIN	LOSS	DRAW
Daring	.45	.55	0
Conservative	0	.10	.90

10. Yvonne Delaney is playing Chris Becker a single point for the women's world tennis championship. She has won the coin toss and elected to serve. If she tries a hard serve, her probability of getting the serve into play is .60. Given that the hard serve is in play, she has a .60 chance of winning the point. If she tries a soft serve, her probability of getting the serve in play is .90, but if the soft serve is in play, her probability of winning the point is only .50. In order to maximize her probability of winning the point, what should Yvonne do?

11.[†] The Indiana Hoosiers trail the Purdue Boilermakers by a 14–0 score late in the fourth quarter of a football game. Indiana's guardian angel has informed Indiana that before the game ends they will have the ball two more times, and Indiana will score a touchdown each time they have the ball. The Indiana coach is indifferent between a tie and the following lottery: a 40% chance at beating Purdue

and a 60% chance at losing to Purdue. Indiana's kicker has never missed an extra point, and Indiana has been successful on 35% of all two-point conversion attempts. After each touchdown (worth six points), Indiana must decide whether or not to attempt a one-point or a two-point conversion. Help the Indiana coach maximize his expected utility.

12. Edwina, a commodities broker, has acquired an option to buy 1000 oz of gold from South Africa at \$50/oz. If she takes the option and if Congress relaxes import quotas, she can sell the gold for \$80/oz. If she takes the option and Congress does not relax the import quotas, however, the company will lose \$10/oz. Edwina believes that there is a 50% chance that the government will relax the quota. She also has the option of waiting until Congress decides whether or not to relax the import quota. If she adopts this strategy, however, there is a 70% chance that some other broker will have already taken the option.
(a) If Edwina is risk-neutral, what should she do?
(b) If Edwina's utility function for a change x in her asset position is given by $u(x) = (10,000 + x)^{1/2}$, what should she do?

13. We are going to see the movie *Fatal Repulsion*. There are three parking lots we may park in. One lot is one block east of the theater (call this lot -1); one lot is directly behind the theater (call this lot 0); and one lot is one block west of the theater (call this lot 1). We are approaching the theater from the east. There is an 80% chance that lot -1 will have a vacant space, a 60% chance that lot 0 will have a vacant space, and an 80% chance that lot 1 will have a vacant space. Once we pass a lot, we can't go back to it. Assume that when we are at a given parking lot, we can determine whether it has any vacant spaces, but we can't see any of the other lots. Our dates for the evening will assess us a penalty equal to the distance (in blocks) that we park from the theater. If we find no space, they will assess a penalty of 10 (and never go out with us again). What strategy minimizes our expected penalty? Answer the same question if there is a 70% chance that lot 0 has a vacant space.

14.[‡] A patient enters the hospital with severe abdominal pains. Based on past experience, Doctor Craig believes there is a 28% chance that the patient has appendicitis and a 72% chance that the patient has nonspecific abdominal pains. Dr. Craig may operate on the patient now or wait 12 hours in order to gain a more accurate diagnosis. In 12 hours, Dr. Craig will surely know whether the patient has appendicitis. The problem is that in the intervening 12 hours, the patient's appendix may perforate (if he has

†Based on Porter (1967).

‡Based on Clarke (1981).

appendicitis), thereby making the operation much more dangerous. Again based on past experience, Dr. Craig believes that if he waits 12 hours, there is a 6% chance that the patient will end up with a perforated appendix, a 22% chance the patient will end up with "normal" appendicitis, and a 72% chance that the patient will end up with nonspecific abdominable pain. From past experience, Dr. Craig assesses the probabilities shown in Table 11 of the patient dying. Assume that Dr. Craig's goal is to maximize the probability that the patient will survive. Use a decision tree to help Dr. Craig make the right decision.

Table 11

SITUATION	PROBABILITY THAT PATIENT WILL DIE
Operation on patient with appendicitis	.0009
Operation on patient with nonspecific abdominal pain	.0004
Operation on perforated appendix	.0064
No operation on patient with nonspecific abdominal pain	0

13-4 BAYES' RULE AND DECISION TREES

The Colaco example and many other decision tree problems share several common features.

There are several states of the world. Different states of the world result in different payoffs to the decision maker. In the Colaco example, the two states of the world were that Chocola is a national success (NS) and that Chocola is a national failure (NF). We are also given (before the test marketing, if any, is done) estimates of the probabilities of each state of the world. These are called **prior probabilities**. In the Colaco example, the prior probabilities are $p(NS) = .55$ and $p(NF) = .45$.

In different states of the world, different decisions may be optimal. In the Colaco example, the company should market nationally if the state of the world is NS and not market nationally if the state of the world is NF.

It may be desirable to purchase information that gives the decision maker more foreknowledge about the state of the world. This may enable the decision maker to make better decisions. For instance, in the Colaco example, the information obtained from test marketing might help Colaco decide whether or not Chocola should be marketed nationally.

The decision maker receives information by observing the outcomes of an experiment. Let $s_1, s_2, \ldots, s_n$ denote the possible states of the world, and let $o_1, o_2, \ldots, o_m$ be the possible outcomes of the experiment. Often, the decision maker is given the conditional probabilities $p(s_i | o_j)$ $(i = 1, 2, \ldots, n; j = 1, 2, \ldots, m)$. Given knowledge of the outcome of the experiment, these probabilities give new values for the probability of each state of the world. The probabilities $p(s_i | o_j)$ are called **posterior probabilities**.

In the Colaco example, the experiment was the test marketing procedure, and the two possible outcomes were LF = local failure and LS = local success. The posterior probabilities were given to be

$$p(NS|LS) = .85, \qquad p(NS|LF) = .10,$$
$$p(NF|LS) = .15, \qquad p(NF|LF) = .90$$

Thus, the knowledge of a local test market success would greatly increase Colaco's estimate of the probability of national success, and the knowledge of a local test market failure would greatly decrease Colaco's estimate of the probability of a national success. The posterior probabilities just listed were used to define the event forks in the decision tree that followed the action Test Market.

In many situations, however, we may be given the prior probabilities $p(s_i)$ for each state of the world, and instead of being given the posterior probabilities $p(s_i|o_j)$, we might be given the **likelihoods** $p(o_j|s_i)$. For each state of the world, the likelihoods give the probability of observing each experimental outcome. Thus, in the Colaco example, we might be given the prior probabilities $p(NS) = .55$ and $p(NF) = .45$ and the likelihoods $p(LS|NS) = \frac{51}{55}, p(LF|NS) = \frac{4}{55}, p(LS|NF) = \frac{9}{45}$, and $p(LF|NF) = \frac{36}{45}$.

To clarify the meaning of likelihoods, suppose that 55 products that have been national successes had previously been test marketed; of these 55 products, 51 were local successes and 4 were local failures. This would have led us to estimate $p(LS|NS)$ as $\frac{51}{55}$ and $p(LF|NS)$ as $\frac{4}{55}$.

To complete the decision tree in Figure 4, we still need to know the posterior probabilities $p(NS|LS)$, $p(NF|LS)$, $p(NS|LF)$, and $p(NF|LF)$. With the help of Bayes' rule (see Section 11.5), we can use the prior probabilities and likelihoods to determine the needed posterior probabilities. To begin the computation of the posterior probabilities, we need to determine the joint probabilities of each state of the world and experimental outcome (that is, we must determine $p(NS \cap LS)$, $p(NS \cap LF)$, $p(NF \cap LS)$, and $p(NF \cap LF)$). We obtain these joint probabilities by using the definition of conditional probability:

$$p(NS \cap LS) = p(NS)p(LS|NS) = .55(\tfrac{51}{55}) = .51$$
$$p(NS \cap LF) = p(NS)p(LF|NS) = .55(\tfrac{4}{55}) = .04$$
$$p(NF \cap LS) = p(NF)p(LS|NF) = .45(\tfrac{9}{45}) = .09$$
$$p(NF \cap LF) = p(NF)p(LF|NF) = .45(\tfrac{36}{45}) = .36$$

Next we compute the probability of each possible experimental outcome (often called a marginal probability) $p(LS)$ and $p(LF)$:

$$p(LS) = p(NS \cap LS) + p(NF \cap LS) = .51 + .09 = .60$$
$$p(LF) = p(NS \cap LF) + p(NF \cap LF) = .04 + .36 = .40$$

Now Bayes' rule can be applied to obtain the desired posterior probabilities:

$$p(NS|LS) = \frac{p(NS \cap LS)}{p(LS)} = \frac{.51}{.60} = .85$$

$$p(NF|LS) = \frac{p(NF \cap LS)}{p(LS)} = \frac{.09}{.60} = .15$$

$$p(NS|LF) = \frac{p(NS \cap LF)}{p(LF)} = \frac{.04}{.40} = .10$$

$$p(NF|LF) = \frac{p(NF \cap LF)}{p(LF)} = \frac{.36}{.40} = .90$$

These posterior probabilities can be used to complete the decision tree in Figure 4.

In summary, to find posterior probabilities, we go through the following three-step process:

Step 1 Determine the joint probabilities of the form $p(s_i \cap o_j)$ by multiplying the prior probability ($p(s_i)$) times the likelihood ($p(o_j | s_i)$).
Step 2 Determine the probabilities of each experimental outcome $p(o_j)$ by summing up all joint probabilities of the form $p(s_k \cap o_j)$.
Step 3 Determine each posterior probability ($p(s_i | o_j)$) by dividing the joint probability ($p(s_i \cap o_j)$) by the probability of the experimental outcome o_j ($p(o_j)$).

We now give a complete example of a decision tree analysis that requires use of Bayes' rule.

E X A M P L E 5

Fruit Computer Company manufactures memory chips in lots of ten chips. From past experience, Fruit knows that 80% of all lots contain 10% (1 out of 10) defective chips, and 20% of all lots contain 50% (5 out of 10) defective chips. If a good (that is, 10% defective) batch of chips is sent on to the next stage of production, processing costs of $1000 are incurred, and if a bad batch (50% defective) is sent on to the next stage of production, processing costs of $4000 are incurred. Fruit also has the alternative of reworking a batch at a cost of $1000. A reworked batch is sure to be a good batch. Alternatively, for a cost of $100, Fruit can test one chip from each batch in an attempt to determine whether the batch is defective. Determine how Fruit can minimize the expected total cost per batch. Also compute EVSI and EVPI.

Solution

We will multiply costs by -1 and work with maximizing $-$(total cost). This enables us to use the EVSI and EVPI formulas of Section 13.3. There are two states of the world:

$$G = \text{batch is good}$$
$$B = \text{batch is bad}$$

We are given the following prior probabilities:

$$p(G) = .80 \quad \text{and} \quad p(B) = .20$$

Fruit has the option of performing an experiment: inspecting one chip per batch. The possible outcomes of the experiment are

$$D = \text{defective chip is observed}$$
$$ND = \text{nondefective chip is observed}$$

We are given the following likelihoods:

$$p(D|G) = .10, \quad p(ND|G) = .90, \quad p(D|B) = .50, \quad P(ND|B) = .50$$

To complete the decision tree in Figure 9, we need to determine the posterior probabilities $p(B|D)$, $p(G|D)$, $p(B|ND)$, and $p(G|ND)$. We begin by computing joint probabilities:

$$p(D \cap G) = p(G)p(D|G) = .80(.10) = .08$$
$$p(D \cap B) = \cdot p(B)p(D|B) = .20(.50) = .10$$
$$p(ND \cap G) = p(G)p(ND|G) = .80(.90) = .72$$
$$p(ND \cap B) = p(B)p(ND|B) = .20(.50) = .10$$

Figure 9   Illustration of Use of Bayes' Rule in Decision Trees (Chip Example)

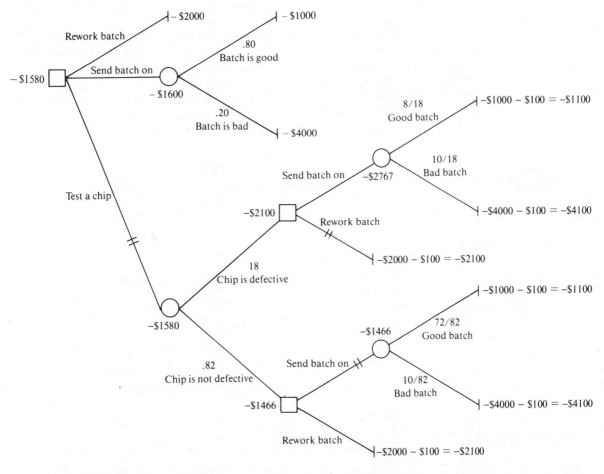

We then compute the probability of each experimental outcome:

$$p(D) = p(D \cap G) + p(D \cap B) = .08 + .10 = .18$$
$$p(ND) = p(ND \cap G) + p(ND \cap B) = .72 + .10 = .82$$

Then we use Bayes' rule to determine the required posterior probabilities:

$$p(B \mid D) = \frac{p(D \cap B)}{p(D)} = \frac{.10}{.18} = \frac{5}{9}$$

$$p(G \mid D) = \frac{p(D \cap G)}{p(D)} = \frac{.08}{.18} = \frac{4}{9}$$

$$p(B \mid ND) = \frac{p(ND \cap B)}{p(ND)} = \frac{.10}{.82} = \frac{10}{82}$$

$$p(G \mid ND) = \frac{p(ND \cap G)}{p(ND)} = \frac{.72}{.82} = \frac{72}{82}$$

These posterior probabilities are used to complete the tree in Figure 9. Straightforward computations show that the optimal strategy is to test a chip. If the chip is defective, rework the batch. If the chip is not defective, send the batch on. An expected cost of $1580 is incurred.

To find EVSI, suppose that testing one chip in a batch were costless. Then the Test Chip branch of the tree would have its expected value increased by $100 (to −$1480). Then we would have EVWSI = −$1480 and EVWOI = −$1600. Then EVSI = EVWSI − EVWOI = −$1480 − (−$1600) = $120.

To find EVPI, we use the tree in Figure 10. We find EVWPI = −$1200. Then EVPI = EVWPI − EVWOI = −$1200 − (−$1600) = $400.

Figure 10
Expected Value with Perfect Information (EVWPI) for Chip Example

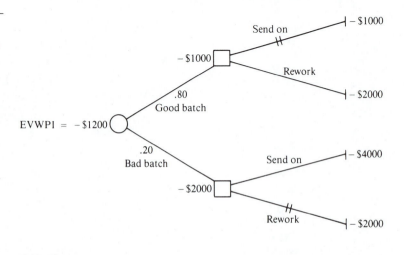

◆ PROBLEMS

GROUP A

1. A customer has approached a bank for a $50,000 one-year loan at 12% interest. If the bank does not approve the loan, the $50,000 will be invested in bonds that earn a 6% annual return. Without further information, the bank feels that there is a 4% chance that the customer will totally default on the loan. If the customer totally defaults, the bank loses $50,000. At a cost of $500, the bank can thoroughly investigate the customer's credit record and supply a favorable or unfavorable recommendation. Past experience indicates that

$$p(\text{favorable recommendation} \,|\,$$
$$\text{customer does not default}) = \tfrac{77}{96}$$

$$p(\text{favorable recommendation} \,|\,$$
$$\text{customer defaults}) = \tfrac{1}{4}$$

How can the bank maximize its expected profits? Also find EVSI and EVPI.

2. A nuclear power company is deciding whether or not to build a nuclear power plant at Diablo Canyon or at Roy Rogers City. The cost of building the power plant is $10 million at Diablo and $20 million at Roy Rogers City. If the company builds at Diablo, however, and an earthquake occurs at Diablo during the next five years, construction will be terminated and the company will lose $10 million (and will still have to build a power plant at Roy Rogers City). A priori, the company believes there is a 20% chance that an earthquake will occur at Diablo during the next five years. For $1 million, a geologist can be hired to analyze the fault structure at Diablo Canyon. He will either predict that an earthquake will occur or that an earthquake will not occur. The geologist's past record indicates that he will predict an earthquake on 95% of the occasions for which an earthquake will occur and no earthquake on 90% of the occasions for which an earthquake will not occur. Should the power company hire the geologist? Also find EVSI and EVPI.

3. Farmer Jones must determine whether to plant corn or wheat. If he plants corn and the weather is warm, he earns $8000; if he plants corn and the weather is cold, he earns $5000. If he plants wheat and the weather is warm, he earns $7000; if he plants wheat and the weather is cold, he earns $6500. In the past, 40% of all years have been cold and 60% have been warm. Before planting, farmer Jones can pay $600 for an expert weather forecast. If the year is actually cold, there is a 90% chance that the forecaster will predict a cold year. If the year is actually warm, there is an 80% chance that the forecaster will predict a warm year. How can farmer Jones maximize his expected profits? Also find EVSI and EVPI.

4. The NBS television network earns an average of $400,000 from a hit show and loses an average of $100,000 on a flop. Of all shows reviewed by the network, 25% turn out to be hits and 75% turn out to be flops. For $40,000, a market research firm will have an audience view a pilot of a prospective show and give its view about whether the show will be a hit or a flop. If a show is actually going to be a hit, there is a 90% chance that the market research firm will predict the show to be a hit. If the show is actually going to be a flop, there is an 80% chance that the market research firm will predict the show to be a flop. Determine how the network can maximize its expected profits. Also find EVSI and EVPI.

5. We are thinking of filming the Don Harnett story. We know that if the film is a flop, we will lose $4 million, and if the film is a success, we will earn $15 million. Beforehand, we believe that there is a 10% chance that the Don Harnett story will be a hit. Before filming, we have the option of paying the noted movie critic Paulane Keel $1 million for her view of the film. In the past, Keel has predicted 60% of all actual hits to be hits and has predicted 90% of all actual flops to be flops. We want to maximize our expected profits. Use a decision tree to determine our best strategy. What is EVSI? What is EVPI?

GROUP B

6. Abdul has one die in his left hand and one in his right hand. One die has six dots painted on each face, and the other has one dot painted on two of the faces and six dots painted on each of the other four faces. Greta is to pick one die (either "left" or "right") and will receive $10 for each

dot painted on the die that is picked. Before choosing, Greta may pay Abdul $15, and he will toss the die in his left hand and tell her how many dots are painted on the face that comes up. Use a decision tree to determine how to maximize Greta's profit. Also determine EVSI and EVPI.

7. Pat Sajork has two drawers. One drawer contains three gold coins, and the other contains one gold coin and two silver coins. We are allowed to choose one drawer, and we will be paid $500 for each gold coin in that drawer and $100 for each silver coin in that drawer. Before choosing a drawer, we may pay Pat $200, and he will draw a randomly selected coin (each of the six coins has an equal chance of being chosen) and tell us whether it is gold or silver. For instance, Pat may say that he drew a gold coin from drawer 1. Should we pay Pat $200? What is EVSI? What is EVPI?

8. Joe owns a coin that is either a fair coin or a two-headed coin. Imelda believes that there is a $\frac{1}{2}$ chance that the coin is two-headed. She must guess what kind of coin Joe has. If she guesses correctly, she pays Joe nothing, but if she guesses incorrectly, she must pay Joe $2. Before guessing, she may pay 30¢ to see the result of a single coin toss (heads or tails). Determine how Imelda should minimize her expected loss. Also determine EVSI and EVPI.

9. The government is attempting to determine whether or not immigrants should be tested for a contagious disease. Let's assume that the decision will be made on a financial basis. Assume that each immigrant who is allowed into the country and has the disease costs the United States $100,000, and each immigrant who enters and does not have the disease will contribute $10,000 to the national economy. Assume that 10% of all potential immigrants have the disease. The government may admit all immigrants, admit no immigrants, or test immigrants for the disease before determining whether or not they should be admitted. It costs $100 to test a person for the disease; the test result is either positive or negative. If the test result is positive, the person *definitely* has the disease. However, 20% of all people who *do* have the disease test negative. A person who does not have the disease always tests negative. The government's goal is to maximize (per potential immigrant) expected benefits minus expected costs. Use a decision tree to aid in this undertaking. Also determine EVSI and EVPI.

13-5   DECISION MAKING WITH THE NORMAL DISTRIBUTION*

In the previous sections of this chapter, we have dealt with decision making under uncertainty in situations involving discrete random variables. In many situations, uncertainty is better modeled by a continuous random variable. In this section, we discuss decision making under uncertainty in situations where uncertainty may be modeled by a random variable having a normal distribution. Throughout this section, we will assume that the decision maker is risk-neutral and wants either to maximize expected profit or to minimize expected cost.

The situation analyzed in this section may be described as follows. The decision maker must choose between two actions on the basis of maximizing expected profit (or reward) or minimizing expected cost. The expected profit (or expected cost) for each action is a linear function of the mean of a normally distributed random variable $\mathbf{X}$. $\mathbf{X}$ has a mean μ and variance σ^2. We assume that the decision maker knows σ^2 but does not know μ.

For example, Hole Cards, Inc. owns a chain of greeting card stores in malls throughout the country. The company is trying to determine whether a new greeting card, the Munster Card, should be sold. It now believes that the monthly sales (denoted by random variable $\mathbf{X}$) of the card at each store in the chain will be normally distributed with an unknown mean μ and a variance $\sigma^2 = 100$. Introducing the new card to each store will involve a fixed monthly cost of $57. Each card sells for 90¢ and carries a variable cost of 30¢. What should Hole Cards do if it wants to maximize expected profit? In this situation, the company must choose between two actions: Introduce the Card and Do Not Introduce the Card. The expected monthly per-store profit (in dollars) earned if the Munster card is introduced is given by $(.90 - .30)\mu - 57 = .60\mu - 57$. The expected monthly per-store profit will, of course, be $0 if the Munster card is not introduced.

THE PRIOR DISTRIBUTION FOR μ

We now assume that the decision maker has some opinion about the distribution of μ. For convenience, we assume that the decision maker believes that μ is $N(\mu_{\text{prior}}, \sigma^2_{\text{prior}})$. Before obtaining sample information about the value of μ, we refer to the decision maker's view of μ's distribution as the **prior distribution** of μ. σ^2_{prior} is the variance of μ's prior distribution, and μ_{prior} is the mean of μ's prior distribution.

To illustrate how we might estimate the mean and variance of a prior distribution, suppose that an experienced salesperson believes that expected monthly sales of the Munster card at each store is as likely to exceed 100 as to be below 100. By the symmetry of the normal distribution about its mean, this implies that $\mu_{\text{prior}} = 100$. To estimate σ^2_{prior}, we ask the salesperson to choose a number k such that he believes there is a 50% chance that expected monthly sales of the card in a store will be within k of 100. From Table 4 in Chapter 11, we find that a value within $.67\sigma$ of the mean of a normal distribution will occur half the time. If the salesperson chooses $k = 10$, this implies that $.67\sigma_{\text{prior}} = 10$ or $\sigma_{\text{prior}} = 14.93$. Thus, the prior distribution for μ (mean monthly sales of the Munster card at each store in the Hole Cards chain) is $N(100, 14.93^2)$.

*This section covers topics that may be omitted with no loss of continuity.

Using the prior distribution for μ, we can determine the action that maximizes expected profit (or minimizes expected cost). For the Hole Cards situation, the expected profit earned in each store if the Munster card is introduced is $.60E(\mu) - 57 = .60\mu_{\text{prior}} - 57 = .60(100) - 57 = \$3$. Since zero expected profit is earned if the Munster card is not introduced, Hole Cards should introduce the card.

EXPECTED VALUE OF PERFECT INFORMATION

For the problems being considered in this section, perfect information means that the decision maker is told the value of μ before making a decision. Then the decision maker can choose the decision that is "correct" for the actual value of μ. As in Sections 13.3 and 13.4, we define the expected value of perfect information (EVPI) to be the amount by which expected profit is increased if the decision maker learns the value of μ before making a decision. For the Hole Cards example, EVPI is computed as follows. We begin by determining the "correct" decision for each value of μ. The company should introduce the card if $.60\mu - 57 \geq 0$ or $\mu \geq \frac{57}{.60} = 95$. Also, Hole Cards should not introduce the Munster card if $.60\mu - 57 \leq 0$ or $\mu \leq \frac{57}{.60} = 95$. Thus, if $\mu \geq 95$, the company should introduce the Munster card, and if $\mu \leq 95$, it should not. We call 95 the *breakeven* point for the decision maker, because if $\mu = 95$, the two decisions yield identical expected profits, and the decision maker is indifferent between the two decisions. For each value of μ, we can now determine how much the decision maker is benefited by perfect information. If $\mu \leq 95$, the correct decision is not to introduce the card. This yields an expected profit of 0. Since without "perfect" information, the company would have marketed the card (earning an expected profit of $.60\mu - 57$), we see that if $\mu \leq 95$, perfect information benefits the decision maker by $0 - (.60\mu - 57) = 57 - .60\mu$. If $\mu > 95$ and the company is told the actual value of μ before making a decision, the optimal decision would be to introduce the Munster card. Since without "perfect" information, the decision would still have been to introduce the card, we find that the perfect information has left profits unchanged. Thus, if $\mu > 95$, perfect information benefits Hole Cards by 0. Assuming that the value of μ is governed by the prior distribution, we find that

$$\text{EVPI} = \int_{-\infty}^{95} (57 - .60\mu)f(\mu)d\mu \\ + \int_{95}^{\infty} 0(f(\mu))d\mu \tag{7}$$

where $f(\mu)$ is the prior density for μ. (In this case, $f(\mu)$ is the density function for an $N(100, 14.93^2)$ random variable.) To evaluate the first integral in (7), we need to use a table of the **normal loss function**. The normal loss function (*NL*) is tabulated in Table 12 of Chapter 17. For example, $NL(0.52) = 0.1917$. If μ is $N(m, \sigma^2)$, the normal loss function table can be used to evaluate the following integrals:

$$\text{For } k \leq m, \quad \int_{-\infty}^{k} (k - \mu)f(\mu)d\mu = \sigma NL\left(\frac{m - k}{\sigma}\right) \tag{8}$$

$$\text{For } k \geq m \quad \int_{k}^{\infty} (\mu - k)f(\mu)d\mu = \sigma NL\left(\frac{k - m}{\sigma}\right) \tag{9}$$

We can evaluate EVPI by using (8). Note that $NL(.33) = .2555$. Then

$$\text{EVPI} = \int_{-\infty}^{95} (57 - .60\mu)f(\mu)d\mu = .60 \int_{-\infty}^{95} (95 - \mu)f(\mu)d\mu$$

$$= .60(14.93)NL\left(\frac{100 - 95}{14.93}\right) = 8.96NL(.33) = 8.96(.2555)$$

$$= 2.29$$

We have used the parameters $m = 100$ and $\sigma = 14.93$ obtained from the prior distribution for μ. The EVPI of $2.29 means that Hole Cards would be willing to pay up to $2.29 for a forecast of μ that was guaranteed to be correct.

SAMPLE INFORMATION AND THE POSTERIOR DISTRIBUTION

In the hope of making a "better" decision, Hole Cards might test market the Munster card. The results of the test marketing can be combined with an analog of Bayes' Theorem for continuous random variables to obtain a **posterior distribution** for μ.

Again suppose that the prior distribution for μ is $N(\mu_{\text{prior}}, \sigma_{\text{prior}}^2)$ and the actual value of the random variable $\mathbf{X}$ is $N(\mu, \sigma^2)$. Suppose we observe n values of $\mathbf{X}$: $x_1, x_2, \ldots, x_n$, where all the observations are independent and each observation is $N(\mu, \sigma^2)$. Suppose we obtain a sample mean

$$\bar{x} = \frac{x_1 + x_2 + \cdots + x_n}{n}$$

It can be shown that after obtaining this sample information, μ will be $N(\mu_{\text{pos}}, \sigma_{\text{pos}}^2)$, where

$$\mu_{\text{pos}} = \frac{\left(\dfrac{1}{\sigma_{\text{prior}}^2}\right)\mu_{\text{prior}} + \left(\dfrac{n}{\sigma^2}\right)\bar{x}}{\dfrac{1}{\sigma_{\text{prior}}^2} + \dfrac{n}{\sigma^2}} \tag{10}$$

$$\sigma_{\text{pos}}^2 = \frac{\sigma_{\text{prior}}^2 \sigma^2}{\sigma^2 + n\sigma_{\text{prior}}^2} \tag{11}$$

We call $N(\mu_{\text{pos}}, \sigma_{\text{pos}}^2)$ the **posterior distribution** of μ. To illustrate the use of (10) and (11), suppose that a single store sells the Munster card for ten consecutive months, and that 900 Munster cards are sold. Then $\bar{x} = \frac{900}{10} = 90$. Also, $\mu_{\text{prior}} = 100$, $\sigma^2 = 100$, and $\sigma_{\text{prior}}^2 = 14.93^2 = 222.9$. The distribution of μ, the average monthly sales of Munster cards per store, is now $N(\mu_{\text{pos}}, \sigma_{\text{pos}}^2)$, where

$$\mu_{\text{pos}} = \frac{\left(\dfrac{1}{222.9}\right)100 + \left(\dfrac{10}{100}\right)90}{\dfrac{1}{222.9} + \dfrac{10}{100}} = 90.43$$

and

$$\sigma_{\text{pos}}^2 = \frac{222.9(100)}{100 + 10(222.9)} = 9.57$$

Thus, after observing ten months of sales data, we now believe that μ is $N(90.43, 9.57)$. Since the sample mean is less than μ_{prior}, our estimate of μ has decreased. Of course, obtaining sample information has reduced our estimate of the variance of μ (from 222.9 to 9.57).

After obtaining sample data, we may choose between two decisions by using the posterior distribution of μ. In the Hole Cards example, we have already shown that the Munster card should be marketed if and only if $\mu \geq 95$. Since $\mu_{pos} < 95$, this means that the correct decision now is not to market the Munster card. Thus, the sample information (indicating low sales for the Munster card) would change the optimal decision from introducing the Munster card to not introducing it.

REMARKS
1. μ_{pos} is a weighted average of μ_{prior} and the sample mean. Thus, μ_{pos} is always between the sample mean and μ_{prior}. An increase in σ_{prior}^2 decreases the weight given to μ_{prior}, so the less confident we are about our prior estimate of μ, the less weight we place on μ_{prior}. Also note that an increase in the sample size n increases the weight given to the sample mean in (10).

2. From (11), it easily follows that $\sigma_{pos}^2 < \sigma_{prior}^2$. It also follows that an increase in n will decrease σ_{pos}^2. Thus, an increase in the amount of available sample data decreases the variance of μ's posterior distribution.

◆ PROBLEMS

In all problems, assume that the decision maker is risk-neutral.

GROUP A

1. We have $10,000 available for investment. If we invest the money in bonds, we receive a certain return of 10% per year. We may also invest our money in an oil well. Investing in the oil well requires that we give the owner of the well $1000. Then we will receive an annual return of **X**% on the remaining $9000.

(a) If **X** is $N(23, 4)$, where should we invest our money?
(b) What is EVPI?
(c) Now suppose that the annual percentage return on the oil well is $N(\mu, 4)$, where μ is unknown and has a prior distribution given by $N(23, 9)$. A friend has invested in the oil well for the last five years and has received an average annual return of 16%. What is the posterior distribution of the mean return on money invested in the oil well?
(d) After receiving this sample information, should we invest in the oil well?

2. Wriggle, Inc. sells chewing gum. For a cost of $20,000 per year, Wriggle can rent a machine that will improve the packaging of the company's gum. Improved packaging will increase monthly gum sales by **X**. Each package of gum sells for 40¢ and incurs a variable cost of 30¢.

(a) Suppose **X** is $N(16,000, 4,000,000)$. Should the machine be rented?
(b) What is EVPI?
(c) Now suppose that **X** is $N(\mu, 4,000,000)$, where μ is unknown and has a prior distribution given by $N(16,000, 1,000,000)$. Wriggle has rented the machine for ten consecutive months and has found that sales averaged 20,000 per month higher than had been predicted in the absence of new packaging. Now find Wriggle's optimal decision.

3. A company is considering selling a new product. Each year, it costs $10,000 in fixed costs to produce the product. Each unit of the product is sold for $7 and involves variable costs of $5.

(a) If the company sells the product in 100 stores and mean annual sales per store are $N(52, 4)$, what is the optimal decision?
(b) What is EVPI?
(c) Now suppose that annual sales per store are $N(\mu, 9)$, where μ is unknown and has a prior distribution given by $N(52, 16)$. For a sample of ten stores, average sales were 35 units per year. Now determine the optimal decision.

◆ SUMMARY

CRITERIA FOR DECISION MAKING UNDER UNCERTAINTY

In the **state-of-the-world model**, the decision maker first chooses an action a_i from a set $A = \{a_1, a_2, \ldots, a_k\}$ of available actions. Then the state of the world is observed, and with probability p_j the state of the world is observed to be $s_j \in S = \{s_1, s_2, \ldots, s_n\}$. If action a_i is chosen and the state of the world is s_j, the decision maker receives a reward r_{ij}.

The **maximin criterion** chooses the action a_i with the largest value of $\min_{j \in S} r_{ij}$. The **maximax criterion** chooses the action a_i with the largest value of $\max_{j \in S} r_{ij}$. In each state, the **minimax regret criterion** chooses an action by applying the minimax criterion to the regret matrix. The **expected value criterion** chooses the decision that yields the largest expected reward.

UTILITY THEORY

A decision maker who subscribes to the Von Neumann-Morgenstern axioms, when facing a choice between several lotteries, should choose the lottery with the largest expected utility.

The **certainty equivalent** of a lottery L, written $CE(L)$, is the number $CE(L)$ such that the decision maker is indifferent between the lottery L and receiving a certain payoff of $CE(L)$. For a given lottery L, the **risk premium** of a lottery L, written $RP(L)$, is given by $RP(L) = EV(L) - CE(L)$.

A decision maker is **risk-averse** if and only if for any nondegenerate lottery L, $RP(L) > 0$. A risk-averse decision maker has a strictly concave utility function. A decision maker is **risk-neutral** if and only if for any nondegenerate lottery L, $RP(L) = 0$. A risk-neutral decision maker has a linear utility function. A decision maker is **risk-seeking** if and only for any nondegenerate lottery L, $RP(L) < 0$. A risk-seeking decision maker has a strictly convex utility function.

DECISION TREES

To determine the optimal decisions in a decision tree, we work backward (folding back the tree) from right to left. First assume that the decision maker is risk-neutral and wishes to maximize final asset position. At each event fork, we calculate the expected final asset position and enter it in ○. At each decision fork, we denote by ‖ the decision that maximizes the expected final asset position and enter the expected final asset position associated with that decision in □. We continue working backward in this fashion until we reach the beginning of the tree. Then the optimal sequence of decisions can be obtained by following the ‖.

To incorporate a decision maker's utility function into a decision tree analysis, simply replace each final asset position x_0 by its utility $u(x_0)$. Then at each event fork, compute expected utility, and at each decision fork, choose the branch having the largest expected utility.

The **expected value of sample information** (EVSI) measures the value associated with test or sample information: EVSI = EVWSI − EVWOI. **Expected value with perfect information** (EVWPI) is found by drawing a decision tree in which the decision maker has perfect information about which state has occurred before the decision must be made. Then the **expected value of perfect information** (EVPI) is given by

EVPI = EVWPI − EVWOI.

BAYES' RULE AND DECISION TREES

We use Bayes' rule in decision tree analysis when we are given prior probabilities and (for each state of the world) the likelihood that an experimental outcome will occur. Bayes' rule is then used to compute the probability that each experimental outcome will occur and (for each experimental outcome) the posterior probability of each state of the world. Then the decision tree analysis proceeds as already described.

DECISION MAKING WITH THE NORMAL DISTRIBUTION

The following formulas can be used to find EVPI:

$$\text{For } k \leq m, \qquad \int_{-\infty}^{k} (k - \mu)f(\mu)d\mu = \sigma NL\left(\frac{m - k}{\sigma}\right) \tag{8}$$

$$\text{For } k \geq m, \qquad \int_{k}^{\infty} (\mu - k)f(\mu)d\mu = \sigma NL\left(\frac{k - m}{\sigma}\right) \tag{9}$$

If we obtain a sample of n independent observations (each observation is $N(\mu, \sigma^2)$) with a sample mean of $\bar{x}$, then after obtaining this information, μ will be $N(\mu_{pos}, \sigma^2_{pos})$, where

$$\mu_{pos} = \frac{\left(\frac{1}{\sigma^2_{prior}}\right)\mu_{prior} + \left(\frac{n}{\sigma^2}\right)\bar{x}}{\frac{1}{\sigma^2_{prior}} + \frac{n}{\sigma^2}} \tag{10}$$

$$\sigma^2_{pos} = \frac{\sigma^2_{prior}\sigma^2}{\sigma^2 + n\sigma^2_{prior}} \tag{11}$$

◆ REVIEW PROBLEMS

GROUP A

1. We have $1000 to invest. All the money must be placed in one of three investments: gold, stock, or money market certificates. If $1000 is placed in an investment, the value of the investment one year from now depends on the state of the economy (see Table 12). Assume that each state of

the economy is equally likely. For each of the following decision criteria, determine the optimal decision:
(a) maximin
(b) maximax
(c) minimax regret
(d) expected value

2. In Problem 1, suppose that the utility function for the value of the investment (x) one year from now is given by $u(x) = \ln x$. Determine which investment we should choose. Could we have predicted this answer without a table of logarithms?

3. Consider the following four lotteries:

Table 12

	STATE 1	STATE 2	STATE 3
Value of $1000 (money market certificate)	$1100	$1100	$1100
Value of $1000 (stock)	$1000	$1100	$1200
Value of $1000 (gold)	$1600	$300	$1400

$$L_1 \underline{\quad 1 \quad} \$1,000,000$$

$$L_2 \begin{array}{c} \overline{\quad .50 \quad} \$3,000,000 \\ \underline{\quad .50 \quad} \$0 \end{array}$$

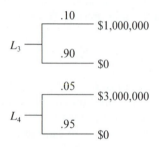

(a) Most people prefer L_1 to L_2 and prefer L_4 to L_3. Explain why.

(b) Suppose a decision maker subscribes to the Von Neumann-Morgenstern axioms and prefers L_1 to L_2. Show that he or she must also prefer L_3 to L_4.

4. Jay Boyville Corporation is being sued by Lark Dent. Lark can settle out of court and win $40,000, or Lark can go to court. If Lark goes to court, there is a 30% chance that she will win the case. If she wins, a small and a large settlement are equally likely (a small settlement nets Lark $50,000, and a large settlement nets Lark $300,000).

(a) If Lark is risk-neutral, what should she do? What should Lark do if her utility function for an increase x in her cash position is given by $u(x) = x^{1/2}$?

(b) For $10,000, Lark can hire a consultant who will predict who will win the trial. The consultant is correct 90% of the time. Should Lark hire the consultant? (Assume Lark is risk-neutral.) What is EVSI?

(c) If Lark is risk-neutral, what is EVPI?

5. Rollo Megabux has $1 million to invest in stocks or bonds. The percentage yield on each investment during the coming year depends on whether the economy has a good or a bad year (see Table 13). It is equally likely that the economy will have a good or a bad year.

Table 13

	ECONOMY HAS GOOD YEAR	ECONOMY HAS BAD YEAR
Yield on stocks	22%	10%
Yield on bonds	16%	14%

(a) If Rollo is risk-neutral, how should he invest his money?

(b) For $10,000, Rollo can hire a consulting firm to forecast the state of the economy. The consulting firm's forecasts have the following properties:

$$P(\text{good forecast} \mid \text{economy good}) = .80$$
$$P(\text{good forecast} \mid \text{economy bad}) = .20$$

Should Rollo hire the consulting firm? What are EVSI and EVPI?

GROUP B

6. In Problem 5, suppose Rollo cannot hire the consulting firm, and his utility function for ending cash position is $u(x) = \ln x$. How much money should he invest in stocks and bonds?

7. At present, littering is punished by a $50 fine, and there is a 10% chance that a litterer will be brought to justice. In order to cut down on littering, Gotham City is considering two alternatives:

> **Alternative 1** Raise the littering fine by 20% (to $60).
> **Alternative 2** Hire more police and increase by 20% the probability that a litterer will be brought to justice (to a 12% probability that a litterer will be caught).

Assuming that all Gotham City residents are risk-averse, which alternative will lead to a larger reduction in littering?

8. The Sono Corporation is considering making either minor or major repairs to a malfunctioning production process. When the process is malfunctioning, the percentage of defective items produced seems to be a constant, with either $p = .10$ or $p = .25$. Defective items are produced randomly, and there is no way Sono can tell for sure whether the machine needs minor or major repairs. If minor repairs are made when $p = .25$, the probability of a defective item is reduced to .05. If minor repairs are made when $p = .10$ or major repairs are made when $p = .10$ or $p = .25$, the proportion of defectives is reduced to zero. The company's prior probability that $p = .10$ is .70. Sono has recently received an order for 1000 items. This item yields Sono a profit of $0.50 per unit, except when the company has to pay a $2 penalty cost for each defective item. Major repairs to the process cost $100; minor repairs cost $60. The process cannot be adjusted once a production run has begun. Prior to starting a production run, however, Sono can sample (at a cost of $1 per item) items from a trial run.

(a) Find Sono's optimal course of action if the company is trying to decide between not sampling at all and sampling one item.

(b) Find the optimal action for Sono if it is willing to consider a sample of either one or two items.

GROUP C

9.[†] In Section 13.2, we discussed the concept of the risk premium of a lottery and a risk-averse decision maker. In many situations, we would like to measure the degree of risk aversion associated with a utility function, and how a decision maker's risk aversion depends on his or her wealth. In this problem, we develop **Pratt's measure of absolute risk aversion**. Consider Ivana, who has initial wealth W and utility function $u(w)$ for final wealth position w. She has placed money in a small investment. The investment will increase her wealth by a random amount $\mathbf{X}$, with $E(\mathbf{X}) = 0$. We wish to investigate how the risk premium of $\mathbf{X}$ depends on W. Let $RP(W, \mathbf{X})$ be the risk premium associated with investment $\mathbf{X}$ if the decision maker's wealth is W.

(a) Explain why $RP(W, \mathbf{X})$ satisfies the following equation:

$$E(\text{Utility for wealth level of } W + \mathbf{X})$$
$$= \text{utility of wealth level } [W - RP(W, \mathbf{X})]$$

(b) Perform a second-order Taylor series expansion on E(utility for wealth level of $W + \mathbf{X}$) about W.

(c) Perform a first-order Taylor series expansion on utility of wealth level $[W - RP(W, \mathbf{X})]$ about W.

[†]Based on Pratt (1964).

(d) Equating the answers in (b) and (c) (neglect the remainder terms), show that

$$RP(W, \mathbf{X}) = \frac{-\text{var}(\mathbf{X})u''(W)}{2u'(W)}$$

(e) Pratt's measure of absolute risk aversion at wealth level W, called $ARA(W)$, is defined to be twice the amount of risk premium per unit of variance when a decision maker is faced with a small lottery that has a zero expected value. Use your answer in part (d) to explain why

$$ARA(W) = \frac{-u''(W)}{u'(W)}$$

(f) If $ARA(W)$ is an increasing function of W, then $u(w)$ is said to exhibit increasing risk aversion, and if $ARA(W)$ is a decreasing function of W, then $u(w)$ exhibits decreasing risk aversion. Is increasing or decreasing risk aversion more consistent with most people's behavior?

Determine whether the following utility functions exhibit increasing or decreasing risk aversion:

(g) $u(w) = \ln w$

(h) $u(w) = w^{1/2}$

(i) $u(w) = aw - bw^2$, where $w < \frac{a}{2b}$. Explain how the answer indicates that a quadratic utility function probably is not an accurate representation of most people's preferences.

◆ REFERENCES

The following books discuss decision making under uncertainty at an intermediate level:

BUNN, D. *Applied Decision Analysis*. New York: McGraw-Hill, 1984.

VATTER, P., ET AL. *Quantitative Methods in Management: Text and Cases*. Homewood, Ill.: Irwin, 1978.

WINKLER, R. *Introduction to Bayesian Inference and Decision*. New York: Holt, Rinehart and Winston, 1972.

For discussion of decision making under uncertainty at a more advanced level, readers should consult the next five books:

FRENCH, S. *Decision Theory*. New York: Wiley, 1986.

KEENEY, R., and H. RAIFFA. *Decision Making With Multiple Objectives*. New York: Wiley, 1976.

RAIFFA, H. *Decision Analysis*. Reading, Mass.: Addison-Wesley, 1968.

WATSON, S., and D. BUEDE. *Decision Synthesis*. Cambridge, England: Cambridge Press, 1987.

WINTERFELDT, D. and W. EDWARDS. *Decision Analysis and Behavioral Research*. Cambridge, England: Cambridge Press, 1986.

ALLAIS, M. "Le comportement de l'homme rationnel devant le risque: Critique des postulats et axioms de l'école Americaine," *Econometrica* 21(1953):503–546.

CLARKE, J. "Application of Decision Analysis to Clinical Medicine," *Interfaces* 17(no.2,1981):27–34.

ELLSBERG, D. "Risk, Ambiguity, and the Savage Axioms," *Quarterly Journal of Economics* 75(1961):643–669.

PORTER, R. "Extra-Point Strategy in Football," *American Statistician* 21(1967):14–15.

PRATT, J. "Risk Aversion in the Small and the Large," *Econometrica* 32(1964):122–136.

14

Decision Making with Multiple Objectives

IN THE DECISION problems considered in Chapter 13, the decision maker made a choice based on how each possible action affected a single variable (or attribute). For example, in the news vendor problem, the number of papers ordered was determined by how this affected Phyllis's profits. Similarly, in the Colaco example, Colaco's decision depended on how each of Colaco's strategies affected Colaco's final asset position.

In many situations, however, the action chosen depends on how each possible action affects *more* than one attribute or variable. Four examples follow:

1. Suppose that Joe Bunker wants to buy a new car. In choosing which car to buy, Joe may consider the following attributes of each car:

Attribute 1 Size of car.

Attribute 2 Fuel economy of car (miles per gallon).

Attribute 3 Style of car.

Attribute 4 Price of car.

2. Suppose Joe Bunker has just graduated from the nation's top business school, Business School (B.S.) University, and has received five job offers. In choosing which job offer to accept, Joe will consider the following attributes of each job:

Attribute 1 Starting salary of job.

Attribute 2 Location of job.

Attribute 3 Degree of interest Joe has in doing the work involved in the particular job.

Attribute 4 Long-term opportunities associated with job.

3. Gotham City must determine where to locate a new jetport. In determining the site for the new jetport, three factors (or attributes) must be considered:

Attribute 1 Accessibility of jetport for residents of Gotham City.

Attribute 2 Degree of noise pollution caused by the jetport (if the jetport is placed in a densely populated area, noise pollution will be more serious than if the jetport is placed in a sparsely populated area).

Attribute 3 Size of the jetport (determined in part by the amount of land available at the jetport site).

4. Wivco Toy Corporation is introducing a new product (a globot). Wivco must determine the price to charge for each globot. Two factors (market share and profits) will affect the pricing decision.

In these four examples, the decision maker chooses an action by determining how each possible action affects the relevant attributes. Such problems are called *multiattribute decision problems.*

In Section 14.1, we consider multiattribute decision problems in which no uncertainty is present. Our primary emphasis in this section is on the widely used concept of goal programming. In Section 14.2, we discuss multiattribute decision problems in which uncertainty is present and briefly introduce multiattribute utility theory. Finally, in Section 14.3, we discuss the analytic hierarchy process (AHP) which can be used to determine optimal decisions in multiattribute decision problems.

14-1   MULTIATTRIBUTE DECISION MAKING IN THE ABSENCE OF UNCERTAINTY: GOAL PROGRAMMING

Suppose a woman believes that there are n attributes that will determine her decision. Let $x_i(a)$ be the value of the ith attribute associated with an alternative a. She associates a value $v(x_1(a), x_2(a), \ldots, x_n(a))$ with the alternative a. The function $v(x_1, x_2, \ldots, x_n)$ is the decision maker's **value function**. If A represents the decision maker's set of possible decisions, then she should choose the alternative a^* (with level x_i^* of attribute i) satisfying

$$\max_{a \in A} v(x_1(a), x_2(a), \ldots, x_n(a)) = v(x_1^*, x_2^*, \ldots, x_n^*)$$

Alternatively, the decision maker can associate a cost $c(x_1(a), x_2(a), \ldots, x_n(a))$ with the alternative a. The function $c(x_1, x_2, \ldots, x_n)$ is her **cost function**. If A represents the decision maker's set of possible decisions, then she should choose the alternative a^* (with level x_i^* of attribute i) satisfying

$$\min_{a \in A} c(x_1(a), x_2(a), \ldots, x_n(a)) = c(x_1^*, x_2^*, \ldots, x_n^*)$$

A particular form of the value or cost function is of special interest.

DEFINITION   A value function $v(x_1, x_2, \ldots, x_n)$ is an **additive value function** if there exist n functions $v_1(x_1), v_2(x_2), \ldots, v_n(x_n)$ satisfying

$$v(x_1, x_2, \ldots, x_n) = \sum_{i=1}^{i=n} v_i(x_i) \qquad (1)$$

| DEFINITION | A cost function $c(x_1, x_2, \ldots, x_n)$ is an **additive cost function** if there exist n functions $c_1(x_1), c_2(x_2), \ldots, c_n(x_n)$ satisfying |

$$c(x_1, x_2, \ldots, x_n) = \sum_{i=1}^{i=n} c_i(x_i) \qquad (1')$$

Under what conditions will a decision maker have an additive value (or cost) function? Before answering this question, we need some more definitions.

Mutual Independence

| DEFINITION | An attribute (call it attribute 1) is **preferentially independent (pi)** of another attribute (attribute 2) if preferences for values of attribute 1 do not depend on the value of attribute 2. |

To illustrate the concept of preferential independence, we consider Joe's search for a job following graduation. In this situation, attribute 1 would be preferentially independent of attribute 2 if, for any possible job location, a higher starting salary is preferred to a lower salary.

As another illustration of preferential independence, suppose that the Griswold family is trying to determine how to spend Sunday afternoon. Let the two relevant attributes be

Attribute 1 Choice of activity (either picnic or go to see movie *Antarctic Vacation*).

Attribute 2 Sunday afternoon's weather (either sunny or rainy).

Suppose that on a sunny day, the picnic is preferred to the movie, but on a rainy day, the movie is preferred to the picnic. Then attribute 1 is not preferentially independent of attribute 2.

| DEFINITION | If attribute 1 is pi of attribute 2, and attribute 2 is pi of attribute 1, then attribute 1 is **mutually preferentially independent** (mpi) of attribute 2. |

Again refer to Joe's search for a job. Suppose Joe's five job offers are located in Los Angeles, Chicago, Dallas, New York, and Indianapolis. If, for any given salary level, Joe prefers to work in Los Angeles rather than Chicago, etc., then attribute 2 is pi of attribute 1. If attribute 1 were also pi of attribute 2, then attributes 1 and 2 would be mpi.

The concept of mutual preferential independence can be generalized to sets of attributes.

| DEFINITION | A set of attributes S is **mutually preferentially independent** (mpi) of a set of attributes S' if (1) the values of the attributes in S' do not affect preferences for the values of attributes in S, and (2) the values of the attributes in S do not affect preferences for the values of attributes in S'. |

In the example of Joe's purchase of a new car, let S = attributes 1 and 2, and S' = attributes 3 and 4. Then for S to be mpi of S', it must be the case that (1) Joe's preferences for size and fuel economy are unaffected by a car's style and price, and (2) Joe's preferences for car style and price are unaffected by the car's size and fuel economy. Thus, if S and S' were mpi, we could conclude that if for a given style and price level, Joe preferred A_1 (a large car getting 15 mpg) to A_2 (a small car getting 25 mpg), then for any style and price level, Joe would prefer A_1 to A_2.

DEFINITION   A set of attributes $1, 2, \ldots, n$ is **mutually preferentially independent** (mpi) if for all subsets S of $\{1, 2, \ldots, n\}$, S is mpi of $\bar{S}$. ($\bar{S}$ is all members of $\{1, 2, \ldots, n\}$ that are not included in S.)

It is easy to see that if there are only two attributes (1 and 2), the attributes are mpi if and only if attribute 1 is mpi of attribute 2.

The following result gives a condition ensuring that the decision maker will have an additive value (or cost) function.

THEOREM 1   If the set of attributes $1, 2, \ldots, n$ is mpi, the decision maker's preferences can be represented by an additive value (or cost) function.

This is not an obvious result (for a proof, see Keeney and Raiffa (1976, Chapter 3)). To illustrate the result, suppose that the decision maker's value function for two attributes is given by

$$v(x_1, x_2) = x_1 + x_1 x_2 + x_2 \qquad (2)$$

(with handwritten note: "interaction term" pointing to $x_1 x_2$)

A decision maker with value function (2) would, for example, prefer $(6, 6)$ to $(4, 8)$ (because $v(6, 6) = 48$ and $v(4, 8) = 44$). The reader should verify that for (2), attribute 1 is pi of attribute 2, and attribute 2 is pi of attribute 1 (see Problem 3 at the end of this section). Thus, attributes 1 and 2 are mpi, and Theorem 1 implies that the decision maker's preferences can be represented by an additive function. To demonstrate this, define new attributes $1'$ and $2'$ by

$$\text{Value of attribute } 1' = x_1' = x_1 + x_2$$
$$\text{Value of attribute } 2' = x_2' = x_1 - x_2$$

Consider the additive value function

$$v'(x_1', x_2') = x_1' + \frac{(x_1')^2}{4} - \frac{(x_2')^2}{4}$$

It is easy to show that $v'(x_1', x_2') = v(x_1, x_2)$. Thus, $v'(x_1', x_2')$ represents the decision maker's preferences. For example, of the following two alternatives

$$\text{Alternative 1: } x_1 = 6, \ x_2 = 6$$
$$\text{Alternative 2: } x_1 = 4, \ x_2 = 8$$

we already know that the decision maker prefers alternative 1. In terms of the new attributes $1'$ and $2'$, we have

$$\text{Alternative 1: } x_1' = 12, x_2' = 0$$
$$\text{Alternative 2: } x_1' = 12, x_2' = -4$$

Then

$$v'(12, 0) = \text{value of alternative 1} = 12 + \frac{12^2}{4} = 48$$

$$v'(12, -4) = \text{value of alternative 2} = 12 + \frac{12^2}{4} - \frac{(-4)^2}{4} = 44$$

Therefore, in this example, the additive value function $v'(x_1', x_2')$ replicates the decision maker's preferences.

GOAL PROGRAMMING

Suppose a decision maker has an additive linear cost function of the form

$$c(x_1, x_2, \ldots, x_n) = c_1 x_1 + c_2 x_2 + \cdots + c_n x_n \tag{3}$$

A decision maker with this type of cost function can often use linear programming (or an extension of linear programming known as goal programming) to determine his best decision. Observe that a cost function of the form (3) defines (for all values of $x_1, x_2, \ldots, x_n$) the same tradeoff between each pair of attributes x_i and x_j. For example, for any values of the attributes and any value of k, if we increase the value of attribute i by k and decrease the value of attribute j by $\frac{kc_i}{c_j}$, then $c(x_1, x_2, \ldots, x_n)$ remains unchanged (check this). Thus, (3) implies that $\frac{c_i}{c_j}$ units of attribute j are equivalent to 1 unit of attribute i.

Even in situations when (3) is not an exact representation of the decision maker's preferences, it is often taken as an approximate representation. The following example shows how linear programming and goal programming can be used to determine optimal decisions for a decision maker whose cost function can be represented by (3).

EXAMPLE 1

The Leon Burnit Advertising Agency is trying to determine a TV advertising schedule for Priceler Auto Company. Priceler has three goals:

Goal 1 Its ads should be seen by at least 40 million high-income men (HIM).

Goal 2 Its ads should be seen by at least 60 million low-income people (LIP).

Goal 3 Its ads should be seen by at least 35 million high-income women (HIW).

Leon Burnit can purchase two types of ads: ads shown during football games and ads shown during soap operas; at most $600,000 can be spent on ads. The advertising costs and potential audiences of a one-minute ad of each type are shown in Table 1.

Table 1	HIM	LIP	HIW	COST
Football ad	7 million	10 million	5 million	$100,000
Soap opera ad	3 million	5 million	4 million	$60,000

Cost and Number of Viewers of Ads in Priceler Example

Leon Burnit must determine how many football ads and soap opera ads to purchase for Priceler.

Solution   Let

$$x_1 = \text{number of minutes of ads shown during football games}$$
$$x_2 = \text{number of minutes of ads shown during soap operas}$$

Then any feasible solution to the following LP would meet Priceler's goals:

$$\text{min (or max) } z = 0x_1 + 0x_2 \quad \text{(or any other objective function)}$$

s.t. $\quad 7x_1 + \;\; 3x_2 \geq 40 \qquad$ (HIM constraint)

$\qquad 10x_1 + \;\; 5x_2 \geq 60 \qquad$ (LIP constraint)

$\qquad\;\; 5x_1 + \;\; 4x_2 \geq 35 \qquad$ (HIW constraint) $\qquad$ **(4)**

$\qquad 100x_1 + 60x_2 \leq 600 \qquad$ (Budget constraint)

$\qquad x_1, x_2 \geq 0$

From Figure 1, we find that no point that satisfies the budget constraint meets all three of Priceler's goals. Thus, (4) has no feasible solution. Since it is impossible to meet all of Priceler's goals, Burnit might ask Priceler to identify, for each goal, a cost (per unit short of meeting each goal) that is incurred for failing to meet the goal. Suppose Priceler determines that

Each million exposures by which Priceler falls short of the HIM goal costs Priceler a $200,000 penalty because of lost sales.

Each million exposures by which Priceler falls short of the LIP goal costs Priceler a $100,000 penalty because of lost sales.

Each million exposures by which Priceler falls short of the HIW goal costs Priceler a $50,000 penalty because of lost sales.

Burnit can now formulate an LP that minimizes the cost incurred in deviating from Priceler's three goals. The trick is to transform each inequality constraint in (4) that represents one of Priceler's goals into an equality constraint. Since we don't know whether the cost-minimizing solution will undersatisfy or oversatisfy a given goal, we need to define the following variables:

$$s_i^+ = \text{amount by which we numerically exceed the } i\text{th goal}$$
$$s_i^- = \text{amount by which we are numerically under the } i\text{th goal}$$

The s_i^+ and s_i^- are referred to as **deviational variables**. For the Priceler problem, we assume that each s_i^+ and s_i^- is measured in millions of exposures. Using the deviational variables, we can rewrite the first three constraints in (4) as

$$7x_1 + 3x_2 + s_1^- - s_1^+ = 40 \qquad \text{(HIM constraint)}$$
$$10x_1 + 5x_2 + s_2^- - s_2^+ = 60 \qquad \text{(LIP constraint)}$$
$$5x_1 + 4x_2 + s_3^- - s_3^+ = 35 \qquad \text{(HIW constraint)}$$

Figure 1
Constraints for
Priceler Example

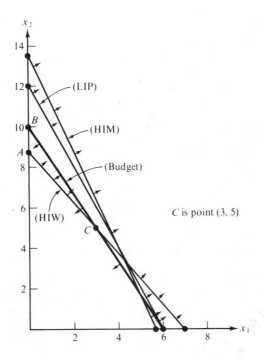

For example, suppose that $x_1 = 5$ and $x_2 = 2$. This advertising schedule yields $7(5) + 3(2) = 41$ million HIM exposures. Since this exceeds the HIM goal by $41 - 40 = 1$ million exposures, $s_1^- = 0$ and $s_1^+ = 1$. Also, this schedule yields $10(5) + 5(2) = 60$ million LIP exposures. This exactly meets the LIP requirement, and $s_2^- = s_2^+ = 0$. Finally, this schedule yields $5(5) + 4(2) = 33$ million HIW exposures. We are numerically under the HIW goal by $35 - 33 = 2$ million exposures, so $s_3^- = 2$ and $s_3^+ = 0$.

Suppose Priceler wants to minimize the total penalty from lost sales. In terms of the deviational variables, the total penalty from lost sales (in thousands of dollars) caused by deviation from the three goals is $200s_1^- + 100s_2^- + 50s_3^-$. The objective function coefficient for the variable associated with goal i is called the **weight** for goal i. The most important goal has the largest weight, and so on. Thus, in the Priceler example, goal 1 (HIM) is the most important goal, goal 2 (LIP) is the second most important goal, and goal 3 (HIW) is the least important goal.

Burnit can minimize the penalty from Priceler's lost sales by solving the following LP:

$$\min z = 200s_1^- + 100s_2^- + 50s_3^-$$

$$\text{s.t.} \quad 7x_1 + 3x_2 + s_1^- - s_1^+ = 40 \quad \text{(HIM constraint)}$$

$$10x_1 + 5x_2 + s_2^- - s_2^+ = 60 \quad \text{(LIP constraint)}$$

$$5x_1 + 4x_2 + s_3^- - s_3^+ = 35 \quad \text{(HIW constraint)}$$

$$100x_1 + 60x_2 \leq 600 \quad \text{(Budget constraint)}$$

$$\text{All variables nonnegative}$$

(5)

The optimal solution to this LP is $z = 250$, $x_1 = 6$, $x_2 = 0$, $s_1^+ = 2$, $s_2^+ = 0$, $s_3^+ = 0$, $s_1^- = 0$, $s_2^- = 0$, $s_3^- = 5$. This meets goal 1 and goal 2 (the goals with the highest costs, or weights, for each unit of deviation from the goal) but fails to meet the least important goal (goal 3).

◆

REMARKS   If failure to meet goal i occurs when the attained value of an attribute is numerically smaller than the desired value of goal i, a term involving s_i^- will appear in the objective function. If failure to meet goal i occurs when the attained value of an attribute is numerically larger than the desired value of goal i, a term involving s_i^+ will appear in the objective function. Also, if we wish to meet a goal exactly and a penalty is assessed for going both over and under a goal, terms involving both s_i^- and s_i^+ will occur in the objective function.

Suppose we modify the Priceler example by deciding that the budget restriction of $600,000 is a goal. If we decide that a $1 penalty is assessed for each dollar by which this goal is unmet, then the appropriate goal programming formulation would be

$$\min z = 200s_1^- + 100s_2^- + 50s_3^- + s_4^+$$

$$\text{s.t.} \quad 7x_1 + 3x_2 + s_1^- - s_1^+ = 40 \qquad \text{(HIM constraint)}$$

$$10x_1 + 5x_2 + s_2^- - s_2^+ = 60 \qquad \text{(LIP constraint)}$$

$$5x_1 + 4x_2 + s_3^- - s_3^+ = 35 \qquad \text{(HIW constraint)}$$

$$100x_1 + 60x_2 + s_4^- - s_4^+ = 600 \qquad \text{(Budget constraint)}$$

All variables nonnegative

In contrast to our previous optimal solution, the optimal solution to this LP is $z = 33\frac{1}{3}$, $x_1 = 4\frac{1}{3}$, $x_2 = 3\frac{1}{3}$, $s_1^- = \frac{1}{3}$, $s_2^+ = 0$, $s_3^+ = 0$, $s_4^+ = 33\frac{1}{3}$, $s_1^- = 0$, $s_2^- = 0$, $s_3^- = 0$, $s_4^- = 0$. Thus, when we define the budget restriction to be a goal, the optimal solution is to meet all three advertising goals by going $33\frac{1}{3}$ thousand over budget.

A method for determining weights for goals is given in Problem 18.

PRE-EMPTIVE GOAL PROGRAMMING

In our LP formulation of the Burnit example, we assumed that Priceler could exactly determine the relative importance of the three goals. For instance, Princeler determined that the HIM goal was $\frac{200}{100} = 2$ times as important as the LIP goal, and the LIP goal was $\frac{100}{50} = 2$ times as important as the HIW goal. In many situations, however, a decision maker may not be able to determine precisely the relative importance of the goals. When this is the case, *pre-emptive goal programming* may prove to be a useful tool. To apply pre-emptive goal programming, the decision maker must rank his or her goals from most important (goal 1) to least important (goal n). The objective function coefficient for the variable representing goal i will be P_i. We assume that

$$P_1 \ggg P_2 \ggg P_3 \ggg \cdots \ggg P_n$$

Thus, the weight for goal 1 is much larger than the weight for goal 2, the weight for goal 2 is much larger than the weight for goal 3, and so on. This definition of the $P_1, P_2, \ldots, P_n$ ensures that the decision maker first tries to satisfy the most important (goal 1) goal. Then, among all points that satisfy goal 1, the decision maker tries to come as close as possible to satisfying goal 2, and so forth. We continue in this fashion until the only way we can come closer to satisfying a goal is to increase the deviation from a higher-priority goal.

For the Priceler problem, the pre-emptive goal programming formulation is obtained from (5) by replacing (5)'s objective function by $P_1s_1^- + P_2s_2^- + P_3s_3^-$. Thus, the pre-emptive goal programming formulation of the Priceler problem is

$$\min z = P_1s_1^- + P_2s_2^- + P_3s_3^-$$

$$\text{s.t.} \quad 7x_1 + 3x_2 + s_1^- - s_1^+ = 40 \qquad \text{(HIM constraint)}$$

$$10x_1 + 5x_2 + s_2^- - s_2^+ = 60 \qquad \text{(LIP constraint)}$$

$$5x_1 + 4x_2 + s_3^- - s_3^+ = 35 \qquad \text{(HIW constraint)} \tag{6}$$

$$100x_1 + 60x_2 \qquad\qquad\quad \leq 600 \qquad \text{(Budget constraint)}$$

All variables nonnegative

Assume the decision maker has n goals. To apply pre-emptive goal programming, we must separate the objective function into n components, where component i consists of the objective function term involving goal i. We define

$$z_i = \text{objective function term involving goal } i$$

For the Priceler example, $z_1 = P_1s_1^-$, $z_2 = P_2s_2^-$, and $z_3 = P_3s_3^-$. Pre-emptive goal programming problems can be solved by an extension of the simplex known as the **goal programming simplex**. To prepare a problem for solution by the goal programming simplex, we must compute n row 0's, with the ith row 0 corresponding to goal i. Thus, for the Priceler problem, we have

$$\text{Row 0 (goal 1): } z_1 - P_1s_1^- = 0$$

$$\text{Row 0 (goal 2): } z_2 - P_2s_2^- = 0$$

$$\text{Row 0 (goal 3): } z_3 - P_3s_3^- = 0$$

From (6), we find that $BV = \{s_1^-, s_2^-, s_3^-, s_4\}$ ($s_4 =$ slack variable for fourth constraint) is a starting basic feasible solution that could be used to solve (6) via the simplex algorithm (or goal programming simplex algorithm). As with the regular simplex, we must first eliminate all variables in the starting basis from each row 0. Adding P_1 (HIM constraint) to row 0 (goal 1) yields

$$\text{Row 0 (goal 1): } z_1 + 7P_1x_1 + 3P_1x_2 - P_1s_1^+ = 40P_1 \qquad \text{(HIM)}$$

Adding P_2 (LIP constraint) to row 0 (goal 2) yields

$$\text{Row 0 (goal 2): } z_2 + 10P_2x_1 + 5P_2x_2 - P_2s_2^+ = 60P_2 \qquad \text{(LIP)}$$

Adding P_3 (HIW constraint) to row 0 (goal 3) yields

$$\text{Row 0 (goal 3): } z_3 + 5P_3x_1 + 4P_3x_2 - P_3s_3^+ = 35P_3 \qquad \text{(HIW)}$$

The Priceler problem can now be solved by the goal programming simplex.

The differences between the goal programming simplex and the ordinary simplex are as follows:

1. The ordinary simplex has a single row 0, whereas the goal programming simplex requires n row 0's (one for each goal).

2. In the goal programming simplex, the following method is used to determine the entering variable: Find the highest-priority goal (goal i') that has not been met (or find the highest-priority goal i' having $z_{i'} > 0$). Find the variable with the most positive coefficient in row 0 (goal i') and enter this variable (subject to the following restriction) into the basis. This will reduce $z_{i'}$ and ensure that we come closer to meeting goal i'. *If, however, a variable has a negative coefficient in row 0 associated with a goal having a higher priority than i', the variable cannot enter the basis.* Entering such a variable in the basis would increase the deviation from some higher-priority goal. If the variable with the most positive coefficient in row 0 (goal i') cannot be entered into the basis, try to find another variable with a positive coefficient in row 0 (goal i'). If no variable for row 0 (goal i') can enter the basis, there is no way to come closer to meeting goal i' without increasing the deviation from some higher-priority goal. In this case, move on to row 0 (goal $i' + 1$) in an attempt to come closer to meeting goal $i' + 1$.

3. When a pivot is performed, row 0 for each goal must be updated.

4. A tableau will yield the optimal solution if all goals are satisfied (that is, $z_1 = z_2 = \cdots = z_n = 0$), or if each variable that can enter the basis and reduce the value of z_i' for an unsatisfied goal i' will increase the deviation from some goal i having a higher priority than goal i'.

We now use the goal programming simplex to solve the Priceler example. In each tableau, the row 0's are listed in order of the goal's priorities (from highest priority to lowest priority). The initial tableau is Table 2. The current bfs is $s_1^- = 40$, $s_2^- = 60$, $s_3^- = 35$, $s_4 = 600$. Since $z_1 = 40P_1$, goal 1 is not satisfied. To reduce the penalty associated with not meeting goal 1, we enter the variable with the most positive coefficient (x_1) in row 0 (HIM). The ratio test indicates that x_1 should enter the basis in the HIM constraint.

Table 2	x_1	x_2	s_1^+	s_2^+	s_3^+	s_1^-	s_2^-	s_3^-	s_4	rhs
Initial Tableau for										
Pre-Emptive Goal Row 0 (HIM)	$7P_1$	$3P_1$	$-P_1$	0	0	0	0	0	0	$z_1 = 40P_1$
Programming Row 0 (LIP)	$10P_2$	$5P_2$	0	$-P_2$	0	0	0	0	0	$z_2 = 60P_2$
Example Row 0 (HIW)	$5P_3$	$4P_3$	0	0	$-P_3$	0	0	0	0	$z_3 = 35P_3$
HIM	⑦	3	-1	0	0	1	0	0	0	40
LIP	10	5	0	-1	0	0	1	0	0	60
HIW	5	4	0	0	-1	0	0	1	0	35
Budget	100	60	0	0	0	0	0	0	1	600

After entering x_1 into the basis, we obtain Table 3. The current basic solution is $x_1 = \frac{40}{7}$, $s_2^- = \frac{20}{7}$, $s_3^- = \frac{45}{7}$, $s_4 = \frac{200}{7}$. Since $s_1^- = 0$ and $z_1 = 0$, goal 1 is now satisfied. We now try to satisfy goal 2 (while ensuring that the higher-priority goal 1 is still satisfied). The variable with the most positive coefficient in row 0 (LIP) is s_1^+. Observe that entering s_1^+ into the basis will not increase z_1 (because the coefficient of s_1^+ in row 0 (HIM) is zero). Thus, after entering s_1^+ into the basis, goal 1 will still be satisfied. The ratio test indicates that s_1^+ could enter the basis in either the LIP or the budget constraint. We arbitrarily choose to enter s_1^+ into the basis in the budget constraint.

Table 3
First Tableau for Pre-Emptive Goal Programming Example

	x_1	x_2	s_1^+	s_2^+	s_3^+	s_1^-	s_2^-	s_3^-	s_4	rhs
Row 0 (HIM)	0	0	0	0	0	$-P_1$	0	0	0	$z_1 = 0$
Row 0 (LIP)	0	$\frac{5P_2}{7}$	$\frac{10P_2}{7}$	$-P_2$	0	$-\frac{10P_2}{7}$	0	0	0	$z_2 = \frac{20P_2}{7}$
Row 0 (HIW)	0	$\frac{13P_3}{7}$	$\frac{5P_3}{7}$	0	$-P_3$	$-\frac{5P_3}{7}$	0	0	0	$z_3 = \frac{45P_3}{7}$
HIM	1	$\frac{3}{7}$	$-\frac{1}{7}$	0	0	$\frac{1}{7}$	0	0	0	$\frac{40}{7}$
LIP	0	$\frac{5}{7}$	$\frac{10}{7}$	-1	0	$-\frac{10}{7}$	1	0	0	$\frac{20}{7}$
HIW	0	$\frac{13}{7}$	$\frac{5}{7}$	0	-1	$-\frac{5}{7}$	0	1	0	$\frac{45}{7}$
Budget	0	$\frac{120}{7}$	$\frac{100}{7}$	0	0	$-\frac{100}{7}$	0	0	1	$\frac{200}{7}$

After pivoting s_1^+ into the basis, we obtain Table 4. Since $z_1 = z_2 = 0$, goals 1 and 2 are met. Since $z_3 = 5P_3$, however, goal 3 is unmet. The current bfs is $x_1 = 6$, $s_2^- = 0$, $s_3^- = 5$, $s_1^+ = 2$. We now try to come closer to meeting goal 3 (without violating either goal 1 or goal 2). Since x_2 is the only variable with a positive coefficient in row 0 (HIW), the only way to come closer to meeting goal 3 (HIW) is to enter x_2 into the basis. Observe, however, that x_2 has a negative coefficient in row 0 for goal 2 (LIP). Thus, the only way we can come closer to meeting goal 3 (HIW) is to violate a higher-priority goal, goal 2 (LIP). This is therefore an optimal tableau. The pre-emptive goal programming solution is to purchase 6 minutes of football ads and no soap opera ads. Goals 1 and 2 (HIM and LIP) are met, and Priceler falls 5 million exposures short of meeting goal 3 (HIW).

Table 4
Optimal Tableau for Pre-Emptive Goal Programming Example

	x_1	x_2	s_1^+	s_2^+	s_3^+	s_1^-	s_2^-	s_3^-	s_4	rhs
Row 0 (HIM)	0	0	0	0	0	$-P_1$	0	0	0	$z_1 = 0$
Row 0 (LIP)	0	$-P_2$	0	$-P_2$	0	0	0	0	$-\frac{P_2}{10}$	$z_2 = 0$
Row 0 (HIW)	0	P_3	0	0	$-P_3$	0	0	0	$-\frac{P_3}{20}$	$z_3 = 5P_3$
HIM	1	$\frac{3}{5}$	0	0	0	0	0	0	$\frac{1}{100}$	6
LIP	0	-1	0	-1	0	0	1	0	$-\frac{1}{10}$	0
HIW	0	1	0	0	-1	0	0	1	$-\frac{1}{20}$	5
Budget	0	$\frac{6}{5}$	1	0	0	-1	0	0	$\frac{7}{100}$	2

If the analyst has access to a computerized goal programming code, then by reordering the priorities assigned to the goals, many solutions can be generated. From among these solutions, the decision maker can choose a solution that she feels best fits her preferences. Table 5 lists the solutions found by the pre-emptive goal programming method for each possible set of priorities. Thus, we see that different ordering of priorities can lead to different advertising strategies.

When a pre-emptive goal programming problem involves only two decision variables, the optimal solution can be found graphically. For example, suppose HIW is the

Table 5
Optimal Solutions to
Priceler Example
Found by Pre-
Emptive Goal
Programming

| PRIORITIES | | | OPTIMAL SOLUTION | | | | |
| Highest | *Second Highest* | Lowest | x_1 *Value* | x_2 *Value* | *Deviations from* | | |
					HIM	LIP	HIW
HIM	LIP	HIW	6	0	0	0	5
HIM	HIW	LIP	5	$\frac{5}{3}$	0	$\frac{5}{3}$	$\frac{10}{3}$
LIP	HIM	HIW	6	0	0	0	5
LIP	HIW	HIM	6	0	0	0	5
HIW	HIM	LIP	3	5	4	5	0
HIW	LIP	HIM	3	5	4	5	0

highest-priority goal, LIP is the second highest, and HIM is the lowest. From Figure 1, we find that the set of points satisfying the highest-priority goal (HIW) and the budget constraint is bounded by the triangle *ABC*. Among these points, we now try to come as close as we can to satisfying the second-highest-priority goal (LIP). Unfortunately, no point in triangle *ABC* satisfies the LIP goal. We see from the figure, however, that among all points satisfying the highest-priority goal, point *C* (*C* is where the HIW goal is exactly met and the budget constraint is binding) is the unique point that comes the closest to satsifying the LIP goal. Simultaneously solving the equations

$$5x_1 + 4x_2 = 35 \qquad \text{(HIW goal exactly met)}$$
$$100x_1 + 60x_2 = 600 \qquad \text{(Budget constraint binding)}$$

we find that point $C = (3, 5)$. Thus, for this set of priorities the pre-emptive goal programming solution is to purchase 3 football game ads and 5 soap opera ads.

Goal programming is not the only approach used to analyze multiple objective decision-making problems under certainty. See Steuer (1985) and Zionts and Wallenius (1976) for other approaches to multiple objective decision making under certainty.

USING LINDO TO SOLVE PRE-EMPTIVE GOAL PROGRAMMING PROBLEMS

Readers who do not have access to a computer program that will solve pre-emptive goal programming problems may still use LINDO (or any other LP package) to solve them. To illustrate how LINDO can be used to solve a pre-emptive goal programming problem, let's look at the Priceler example with our original set of priorities (HIM followed by LIP followed by HIW).

We begin by asking LINDO to minimize the deviation from the highest-priority (HIM) goal by solving the following LP:

$$\min z = s_1^-$$

$$\begin{aligned}
\text{s.t.} \quad & 7x_1 + 3x_2 + s_1^- - s_1^+ = 40 && \text{(HIM constraint)} \\
& 10x_1 + 5x_2 + s_2^- - s_2^+ = 60 && \text{(LIP constraint)} \\
& 5x_1 + 4x_2 + s_3^- - s_3^+ = 35 && \text{(HIW constraint)} \\
& 100x_1 + 60x_2 \leq 600 && \text{(Budget constraint)}
\end{aligned}$$

All variables nonnegative

Since goal 1 (HIM) can be met, LINDO reports an optimal z-value of zero. We now want to come as close as possible to meeting goal 2 while ensuring that goal 1 is still met. We use an objective function of s_2^- (to minimize goal 2) and add the constraint $s_1^- = 0$ (to ensure that goal 1 is still met). Now we ask LINDO to solve

$$\min z = s_2^-$$

$$
\begin{array}{llll}
\text{s.t.} & 7x_1 + 3x_2 + s_1^- - s_1^+ = 40 & \text{(HIM constraint)} \\
& 10x_1 + 5x_2 + s_2^- - s_2^+ = 60 & \text{(LIP constraint)} \\
& 5x_1 + 4x_2 + s_3^- - s_3^+ = 35 & \text{(HIW constraint)} \\
& 100x_1 + 60x_2 \leq 600 & \text{(Budget constraint)} \\
& s_1^- = 0 &
\end{array}
$$

All variables nonnegative

Since goals 1 and 2 can be simultaneously met, this LP will also yield an optimal z-value of zero. We now come as close as possible to meeting goal 3 (HIW) while keeping goals 1 and 2 satisfied. This requires LINDO to solve the following LP:

$$\min z = s_3^-$$

$$
\begin{array}{llll}
\text{s.t.} & 7x_1 + 3x_2 + s_1^- - s_1^+ = 40 & \text{(HIM constraint)} \\
& 10x_1 + 5x_2 + s_2^- - s_2^+ = 60 & \text{(LIP constraint)} \\
& 5x_1 + 4x_2 + s_3^- - s_3^+ = 35 & \text{(HIW constraint)} \\
& 100x_1 + 60x_2 \leq 600 & \text{(Budget constraint)} \\
& s_1^- = 0 & \\
& s_2^- = 0 &
\end{array}
$$

All variables nonnegative

REMARKS   **1.** The optimal solution to this LP is $z = 5$, $x_1 = 6$, $x_2 = 0$, $s_1^- = 0$, $s_2^- = 0$, $s_3^- = 5$, $s_1^+ = 2$, $s_2^+ = 0$, $s_3^+ = 0$, which agrees with the solution obtained by the pre-emptive goal programming method. The z-value of 5 indicates that if goals 1 and 2 are met, the best that Priceler can do is to come within 5 million exposures of meeting goal 3.

2. By the way, suppose we could only have come within two units of meeting goal 1. When solving our second LP, we would have added the constraint $s_1^- = 2$ (instead of $s_1^- = 0$).

◆ PROBLEMS

GROUP A

1. Wivco Toy Corporation is introducing a new product (a globot). Wivco must determine the price to charge for each globot. Two attributes (market share and profits) will affect Wivco's pricing decision. Do the two attributes exhibit mutual preferential independence? Why or why not?

2. Gotham City must determine how many ambulances should be allocated to various districts of the city. The following three attributes are important to the government of Gotham City:

Attribute 1 The average time (in minutes) it takes for an ambulance to respond to a call from the poor area of the city.

Attribute 2 The average time (in minutes) it takes for an ambulance to respond to a call from the rich area of the city.

Attribute 3 Money (in dollars) the city must spend on providing ambulance service.

(a) Do these attributes exhibit mpi? Why or why not?

(b) Suppose that the value function for the Gotham City government is $v(x_1, x_2, x_3) = -x_1 - 5000x_2 - 10,000x_3$. What attributes are represented by x_1, x_2, and x_3?

(c) What does the value function imply about the tradeoff between each pair of attributes?

3. Show that the value function $v(x_1, x_2) = x_1 + x_2 + x_1 x_2$ exhibits mpi.

4. Luigi is going out to eat at Lester's Italian Villa. The four attributes that will determine his satisfaction with dinner are as follows:

Attribute 1 Choice of appetizer.

Attribute 2 Choice of main course.

Attribute 3 Choice of wine.

Attribute 4 Quality of food.

Do you think that Luigi's value function will exhibit mpi? Why or why not?

5. Gotham City must determine how to allocate ambulances during the next year. It costs $5000 per year to run an ambulance. Each ambulance must be assigned to one of two districts. Let x_i = number of ambulances assigned to district i ($i = 1, 2$). The average time (in minutes) it takes for an ambulance to respond to a call from district i is, for district 1, $40 - 3x_1$, and for district 2, $50 - 4x_2$. Gotham City has three goals:

Goal 1 Average response time in district 1 should be at most 5 minutes.

Goal 2 Average response time in district 2 should be at most 5 minutes.

Goal 3 At most $100,000 per year should be spent on ambulance service.

Gotham City feels (for each district) that each minute by which average response time fails to meet the 5-minute goal is equivalent to a cost of $10,000, and each dollar by which the budget constraint is exceeded incurs a cost of $1.

(a) Set up and solve an LP model that can be used to determine how many ambulances should be assigned to each district.

(b) For each of the following ordering of priorities, use the goal programming simplex to determine an assignment of ambulances to districts (goal 1 > goal 2 indicates that goal 1 has higher priority than goal 2): goal 1 > goal 2 > goal 3; goal 2 > goal 1 > goal 3; goal 3 > goal 1 > goal 2.

6. Graphically determine the pre-emptive goal programming solution to the Priceler example for the following priorities:

(a) LIP is highest-priority goal, followed by HIW and then HIM.

(b) HIM is highest-priority goal, followed by LIP and then HIW.

(c) HIM is highest-priority goal, followed by HIW and then LIP.

(d) HIW is highest-priority goal, followed by HIM and then LIP.

7. Fruit Computer Company is ready to make its annual purchase of computer chips. Fruit can purchase chips (in lots of 100) from three suppliers. Each chip is rated as being of excellent, good, or mediocre quality. During the coming year, Fruit will need 5000 excellent chips, 3000 good chips, and 1000 mediocre chips. The characteristics of the chips purchased from each supplier are shown in Table 6. Each year, Fruit has budgeted $28,000 to spend on chips. If Fruit does not obtain enough chips of a given quality, the company may special-order additional chips at $10 per excellent chip, $6 per good chip, and $4 per mediocre chip. Fruit assesses a penalty of $1 for each dollar by which the amount paid to suppliers 1–3 exceeds the annual budget. Formulate and solve an LP to help Fruit minimize the penalty associated with meeting the annual chip requirements. Also use pre-emptive goal programming to determine a purchasing strategy. Let the budget constraint have the highest priority, followed in order by the restrictions on excellent, good, and mediocre chips.

Table 6

	CHARACTERISTICS OF A LOT OF 100 CHIPS			PRICE PER 100 CHIPS
	Excellent	Good	Mediocre	
Supplier 1	60	20	20	$400
Supplier 2	50	35	15	$300
Supplier 3	40	20	40	$250

8. Highland Appliance must determine how many color TVs and VCRs should be stocked. It costs Highland $300 to purchase a color TV and $200 to purchase a VCR. A color TV requires 3 sq yd of storage space, and a VCR requires 1 sq yd of storage space. The sale of a color TV earns Highland a profit of $150, and the sale of a VCR earns Highland a profit of $100. Highland has set the following goals (listed in order of importance):

    Goal 1 A maximum of $20,000 can be spent on purchasing color TVs and VCRs.

    Goal 2 Highland should earn at least $11,000 in profits from the sale of color TVs and VCRs.

    Goal 3 Color TVs and VCRs should not use up more than 200 sq yd of storage space.

Formulate a pre-emptive goal programming model that Highland could use to determine how many color TVs and VCRs to order. How would the pre-emptive goal formulation be modified if Highland's goal were to have a profit of exactly $11,000?

9. A company produces two products. Relevant information for each product is shown in Table 7. The company has a goal of $48 in profits and incurs a $1 penalty for each dollar it falls short of this goal. A total of 32 hours of labor are available. A $2 penalty is incurred for each hour of overtime (labor over 32 hours) used, and a $1 penalty is incurred for each hour of available labor that is unused. Marketing considerations require that at least 7 units of product 1 be produced and at least 10 units of product 2 be produced. For each unit (of either product) by which production falls short of demand, a penalty of $5 is assessed.

Table 7

	PRODUCT 1	PRODUCT 2
Labor required	4 hours	2 hours
Contribution to profit	$4	$2

(a) Formulate an LP that can be used to minimize the total penalty incurred by the company.
(b) Suppose the company sets (in order of importance) the following goals:

    Goal 1 Avoid underutilization of labor.

    Goal 2 Meet demand for product 1.

    Goal 3 Meet demand for product 2.

    Goal 4 Do not use any overtime.

Formulate and solve a pre-emptive goal programming model for this situation.

10.[†] Deancorp produces sausage by blending together beef head, pork chuck, mutton, and water. The cost per pound, fat per pound, and protein per pound for these ingredients is given in Table 8. Deancorp needs to produce 100 lb of sausage and has set the following goals, listed in order of priority:

    Goal 1 Sausage should consist of at least 15% protein.

    Goal 2 Sausage should consist of at most 8% fat.

    Goal 3 Cost per pound of sausage should not exceed 8¢.

Formulate a pre-emptive goal programming model for Deancorp.

11.[‡] The Touche Young accounting firm must complete three jobs during the next month. Job 1 will require 500 hours of work, job 2 will require 300 hours of work, and job 3 will require 100 hours of work. At present, the firm consists of 5 partners, 5 senior employees, and 5 junior employees, each of whom can work up to 40 hours per month. The dollar amount (per hour) that the company can bill depends on the type of accountant who is assigned to each job, as shown in Table 9. (The X indicates that a junior employee does not have enough experience to work on job 1.) All jobs must be completed. Touche Young has also set the following goals, listed in order of priority:

    Goal 1 Monthly billings should exceed $68,000.

    Goal 2 At most 1 partner should be hired.

    Goal 3 At most 3 senior employees should be hired.

    Goal 4 At most 5 junior employees should be hired.

Formulate a pre-emptive goal programming model for this situation.

[†]Based on Steuer (1984).
[‡]Based on Welling (1977).

Table 8

	HEAD	CHUCK	MUTTON	MOISTURE
Fat (per lb)	.05	.24	.11	0
Protein (per lb)	.20	.26	.08	0
Cost (in ¢)	12	9	8	0

Table 9

	JOB 1	JOB 2	JOB 3
Partner	160	120	110
Senior employee	120	90	70
Junior employee	X	50	40

12. There are four teachers in the Faber College Business School. Each semester, 200 students take each of the following courses: marketing, finance, production, and statistics. The "effectiveness" of each teacher in teaching each class is given in Table 10. Each teacher can teach a total of 200 students during the semester. The dean has set a goal of obtaining an average teaching effectiveness level of about 6 in each course. Deviations from this goal in any course are considered equally important. Formulate a goal programming model that can be used to determine the semester's teaching assignments.

GROUP B

13. Pinky Herman has $100 to spend at the clothing store. He wants to buy some red bow ties and some slippers. A bow tie costs $4, and a pair of slippers cost $10. Letting t = number of bow ties purchased and s = pairs of slippers purchased, Pinky has determined that his value function is $v(t, s) = t^{1/4} s^{3/4}$. How many bow ties and how many pairs of slippers should he purchase?

14. Suppose that Joe's value function is $v(x_1, x_2) = x_1^{2/3} x_2^{1/3}$. Show that Joe's value function exhibits mpi. Try to determine an additive value function (and a new set of attributes) that represents Joe's preferences.

15.[†] Faber College is admitting students for the class of 2001. It has set four goals for this class, listed in order of priority:

Goal 1 Entering class should be at least 5000 students.

Goal 2 Entering class should have an average SAT score of at least 640.

[†]Based on Lee and Moore, "University Admissions Planning" (1974).

Table 11

HOME STATE	SAT SCORE	NO. OF NERDS	NO. OF NON-NERDS
In-state	700	1500	400
In-state	600	1300	700
In-state	500	500	500
Out-of-state	700	350	50
Out-of-state	600	400	400
Out-of-state	500	400	600

Goal 3 Entering class should consist of at least 25 percent out-of-state students.

Goal 4 At least 2000 members of the entering class should not be nerds.

The applications received by Faber are categorized in Table 11. Formulate a pre-emptive goal programming model that could be used to determine how many applicants of each type should be admitted. Assume that all applicants who are admitted will decide to attend Faber.

16.[‡] During the next four quarters, Wivco faces the following demands for globots: quarter 1, 13 globots; quarter 2, 14 globots; quarter 3, 12 globots; quarter 4, 15 globots. Globots may be produced by regular-time labor or by overtime labor. Production capacity (number of globots) and production costs during the next four quarters are shown in Table 12. Wivco has set the following goals in order of importance:

Goal 1 Meet each quarter's demand on time.

Goal 2 Inventory at the end of each quarter cannot exceed 3 units.

Goal 3 Total production cost should be held below $250.

Formulate a pre-emptive goal programming model that could be used to determine Wivco's production schedule

[‡]Based on Lee and Moore, "Production Scheduling" (1974).

Table 10

	MARKETING	FINANCE	PRODUCTION	STATISTICS
Teacher 1	7	5	8	2
Teacher 2	7	8	9	4
Teacher 3	3	5	7	9
Teacher 4	5	5	6	7

during the next four quarters. Assume that at the beginning of the first quarter 1 globot is in inventory.

17. Ricky's Record Store at present employs five full-time employees and three part-time employees. The normal workload is 40 hours per week for full-time and 20 hours per week for part-time employees. Each full-time employee is paid $6 per hour for work up to 40 hours per week and can sell 5 records per hour. A full-time employee who works overtime is paid $10 per hour. Each part-time employee is paid $3 per hour and can sell 3 records per hour. It costs Ricky $6 to buy a record, and each record sells for $9. Ricky has weekly fixed expenses of $500. He has established the following weekly goals, listed in order of priority:

> **Goal 1** Sell at least 1600 records per week.
>
> **Goal 2** Earn a profit of at least $2200 per week.
>
> **Goal 3** Full-time employees should work at most 100 hours of overtime.
>
> **Goal 4** To increase their sense of job security, the number of hours by which each full-time employee fails to work 40 hours should be minimized.

Formulate a pre-emptive goal programming model that could be used to determine how many hours per week each employee should work.

18. The method outlined in this problem is often used to determine which variables are most important to a decision maker who has conflicting objectives. To illustrate the idea, suppose that a consumer has rated (on a scale of 1–10) five cereals with respect to five objectives or attributes: cost, nutritional content, sweetness, fiber content, and "prize" quality. These ratings are given in Table 13. (A score of 10 means low cost, lots of nutrition, very sweet, lots of fiber, or a great prize.)

Assume that our consumer has a weight for each objective which reflects the importance of the objective. Let

$$C = \text{weight for cost}$$
$$N = \text{weight for nutrition}$$
$$S = \text{weight for sweetness}$$
$$F = \text{weight for fiber}$$
$$P = \text{weight for prize}$$

Then the total score for a cereal is given by C (cost rating) $+ N$ (nutrition rating) $+ S$ (sweetness rating) $+ F$ (fiber rating) $+ P$ (prize rating). Suppose the consumer has expressed the following preferences: decision 1—cereal 2 over cereal 1; decision 2—cereal 3 over cereal 2; decision 3—cereal 3 over cereal 4; decision 4—cereal 5 over cereal 1; decision 5—cereal 5 over cereal 2. How can we determine a set of weights that best fits the consumer's announced preferences? We know that the consumer prefers cereal 2 to cereal 1. This provides evidence that

$$4C + 6N + 3S + 4F + 7P$$
$$\leq 2C + 2N + 10S + F + 10P$$

Table 12

	REGULAR-TIME		OVERTIME	
	Capacity	Cost/Unit	Capacity	Cost/Unit
Quarter 1	9	$4	5	$6
Quarter 2	10	$4	5	$7
Quarter 3	11	$5	5	$8
Quarter 4	12	$6	5	$9

Table 13

CEREAL	COST	NUTRITION	SWEETNESS	FIBER	PRIZE
1	4	6	3	4	7
2	2	2	10	1	10
3	4	10	5	5	4
4	4	7	1	10	3
5	1	7	6	5	8

For a given set of weights and an announced preference k, define a penalty $z_k = \max\{0, \text{(score of less preferred cereal in decision } k) - \text{(score of more preferred cereal in decision } k)\}$.

This implies that if a given set of weights results in a "preference reversal," a penalty equal to the amount of the preference reversal is charged. Formulate an LP that chooses the set of weights minimizing the sum of the penalties from all five decisions.[†] Assume that the weights must sum to 1. (This rules out the case where all weights equal 0.) (*Hint*: The constraint for decision 1 is $z_1 - 2C - 4N + 7S - 3F + 3P \geq 0$. Why will this constraint (together with the objective function) cause z_1 to assume the correct value?)

[†]Based on Srinivasan and Shocker (1973).

14-2   MULTIATTRIBUTE UTILITY FUNCTIONS

In Section 13.2, we described how the Von Neumann-Morgenstern utility theory could be used to make decisions under uncertainty when only one attribute affected the decision maker's preferences and attitude toward risk. In this section, we discuss the extension of utility theory to situations in which more than one attribute affects the decision maker's preferences and attitude toward risk. Even in this case, a decision maker who subscribes to the Von Neumann-Morgenstern axioms will still choose the lottery or the alternative that maximizes his or her expected utility. When more than one attribute affects a decision maker's preferences, the person's utility function is called a **multiattribute utility function**. We restrict ourselves here to explaining how to assess and use multiattribute utility functions when only two attributes are operative. The reader seeking a more detailed discussion of multiattribute utility functions is referred to Bunn (1984) and (at a more advanced level) the classic work by Keeney and Raiffa (1976).

Suppose a decision maker's preferences and attitude toward risk depend on two attributes. Let

x_i = level of attribute i

$u(x_1, x_2)$ = utility associated with level x_1 of attribute 1 and level x_2 of attribute 2

How can we find a utility function $u(x_1, x_2)$ such that choosing a lottery or alternative that maximizes the expected value of $u(x_1, x_2)$ will yield a decision consistent with the decision maker's preferences and attitude toward risk?

In general, determination of $u(x_1, x_2)$ (or, in the case of n attributes, determination of $u(x_1, x_2, \ldots, x_n)$) is a difficult matter. Under certain conditions, however, the assessment of a utility function $u(x_1, x_2)$ is greatly simplified.

PROPERTIES OF MULTIATTRIBUTE UTILITY FUNCTIONS

DEFINITION   Attribute 1 is **utility independent** (ui) of attribute 2 if preferences for lotteries involving different levels of attribute 1 do not depend on the level of attribute 2.

Let's reconsider the problem of Wivco Toy Corporation. Wivco is introducing a new product (a globot) and must determine the price to charge for each globot. Two factors (market share and profits) will affect Wivco's pricing decision. Let

x_1 = Wivco's market share

x_2 = Wivco's profits (millions of dollars)

Suppose that Wivco is indifferent between

$$L_1 \begin{cases} \frac{1}{2} & \text{—— 10\%, \$5} \\ \frac{1}{2} & \text{—— 30\%, \$5} \end{cases} \quad \text{and} \quad L_1' \overset{1}{\text{————}} 16\%, \$5$$

If attribute 1 (market share) is ui of attribute 2 (profit), Wivco would also be indifferent between

$$L_2 \begin{cases} \frac{1}{2} & \text{—— 10\%, \$20} \\ \frac{1}{2} & \text{—— 30\%, \$20} \end{cases} \quad \text{and} \quad L_2' \overset{1}{\text{————}} 16\%, \$20$$

In short, if market share is ui of profit, then for any level of profits, a $\frac{1}{2}$ chance at a 10% market share and a $\frac{1}{2}$ chance at a 30% market share has a certainty equivalent of a 16% market share.

DEFINITION	If attribute 1 is ui of attribute 2, and attribute 2 is ui of attribute 1, then attributes 1 and 2 are **mutually utility independent** (mui).

If attributes 1 and 2 are mui, it can be shown that the decision maker's utility function $u(x_1, x_2)$ must be of the following form:

$$u(x_1, x_2) = k_1 u_1(x_1) + k_2 u_2(x_2) + k_3 u_1(x_1) u_2(x_2) \tag{7}$$

In (7), k_1, k_2, and k_3 are constants, and $u_1(x_1)$ and $u_2(x_2)$ are functions of x_1 and x_2, respectively. Eq. (7) is often called a **multilinear utility function**.

To show that a multilinear utility function exhibits mui, we assume that Wivco's utility function is of the form (7) and that Wivco is indifferent between L_1 and L_1'. If Wivco exhibits mui, then Wivco should also be indifferent between L_2 and L_2'. Using (7), we can show that $L_1 \text{ i } L_1'$ implies $L_2 \text{ i } L_2'$. First, (7) and $L_1 \text{ i } L_1'$ imply

$$\frac{1}{2}[k_1 u_1(10) + k_2 u_2(5) + k_3 u_1(10)u_2(5)]$$
$$+ \frac{1}{2}[k_1 u_1(30) + k_2 u_2(5) + k_3 u_1(30)u_2(5)]$$
$$= k_1 u_1(16) + k_2 u_2(5) + k_3 u_1(16)u_2(5)$$

Simplifying this equation yields (if $k_1 \neq 0$)

$$\frac{1}{2}[u_1(10) + u_1(30)] = u_1(16) \tag{8}$$

Using (8), we find

$$E(U \text{ for } L_2) = \frac{1}{2}[k_1 u_1(10) + k_2 u_2(20) + k_3 u_1(10)u_2(20)]$$
$$+ \frac{1}{2}[k_1 u_1(30) + k_2 u_2(20) + k_3 u_1(30)u_2(20)]$$
$$= k_1 u_1(16) + k_2 u_2(20) + k_3 u_1(16)u_2(20)$$
$$= E(U \text{ for } L_2')$$

Thus, we see that a multilinear utility function of the form (7) implies that attribute 1 is ui of attribute 2. Similarly, it can be shown that (7) implies that attribute 2 is ui of attribute 1. Thus, (7) implies that attributes 1 and 2 are mui. It can also be shown that if x_1 and x_2 are mui, then $u(x_1, x_2)$ must be of the form (7) (see Keeney and Raiffa (1976)).

THEOREM 2	Attributes 1 and 2 are mui if and only if the decision maker's utility function $u(x_1, x_2)$ is a multilinear function of the form $$u(x_1, x_2) = k_1 u_1(x_1) + k_2 u_2(x_2) + k_3 u_1(x_1)u_2(x_2) \qquad (7)$$

The determination of a decision maker's utility function $u(x_1, x_2)$ can be further simplified if it exhibits **additive independence**. Before defining additive independence, we must define x_1(best) or x_2(best) to be the most favorable level of attribute 1 or 2 that can occur; also, x_1(worst) or x_2(worst) is the least favorable level of attribute 1 or 2 that can occur.

DEFINITION	A decision maker's utility function exhibits **additive independence** if the decision maker is indifferent between

Essentially, additive independence of attributes 1 and 2 implies that preferences over lotteries involving only attribute 1 (or only attribute 2) depend only on the marginal distribution for possible values of attribute 1 (or of attribute 2) and do not depend on the joint distribution of the possible values of attributes 1 and 2.

If attributes 1 and 2 are mui and the decision maker's utility function exhibits additive independence, it is easy to show that in Eq. (7), $k_3 = 0$ must hold. As in Section 13.2, simply scale $u_1(x_1)$ and $u_2(x_2)$ such that

$$u_1(x_1(\text{best})) = 1 \qquad u_1(x_1(\text{worst})) = 0$$
$$u_2(x_2(\text{best})) = 1 \qquad u_2(x_2(\text{worst})) = 0$$

Now (7) implies

$$u(x_1(\text{best}), x_2(\text{best})) = k_1 + k_2 + k_3 \qquad u(x_1(\text{worst}), x_2(\text{worst})) = 0$$
$$u(x_1(\text{best}), x_2(\text{worst})) = k_1 \qquad u(x_1(\text{worst}), x_2(\text{best})) = k_2$$

Then additive independence implies that

$$\tfrac{1}{2}(k_1 + k_2 + k_3) + \tfrac{1}{2}(0) = \tfrac{1}{2}(k_1) + \tfrac{1}{2}(k_2)$$
$$k_3 = 0$$

Thus, if attributes 1 and 2 àre mui and the decision maker's utility function exhibits additive independence, his or her utility function is of the following additive form:

$$u(x_1, x_2) = k_1 u_1(x_1) + k_2 u_2(x_2) \qquad (9)$$

ASSESSMENT OF MULTIATTRIBUTE UTILITY FUNCTIONS

If attributes 1 and 2 are mui, how can we determine $u_1(x_1)$, $u_2(x_2)$, k_1, k_2, and k_3? To determine $u_1(x_1)$ and $u_2(x_2)$, we apply the technique that was used to assess utility functions in Section 13.2. We illustrate by determining $u_1(x_1)$. Let $u_1(x_1(\text{best})) = 1$ and $u_1(x_1(\text{worst})) = 0$. Next determine a value of attribute 1 (call it $x_1(\frac{1}{2})$) having $u_1(x_1(\frac{1}{2})) = \frac{1}{2}$. By the definition of $u_1(x_1(\frac{1}{2}))$ and mui, the decision maker is (for any value of x_2) indifferent between

Thus, $x_1(\frac{1}{2})$ may be determined from the fact that the certainty equivalent of L is $(x_1(\frac{1}{2}), x_2)$. In a similar fashion, we can determine values $x_1(\frac{1}{4})$ and $x_1(\frac{3}{4})$ of the first attribute satisfying $u_1(x_1(\frac{1}{4})) = \frac{1}{4}$ and $u_1(x_1(\frac{3}{4})) = \frac{3}{4}$. Continuing in this fashion, we may approximate $u_1(x_1)$ and $u_2(x_2)$.

To find k_1, k_2, and k_3, we begin by rescaling $u_1(x_1)$, $u_2(x_2)$, and $u(x_1, x_2)$ such that

$$u(x_1(\text{best}), x_2(\text{best})) = 1, \qquad u(x_1(\text{worst}), x_2(\text{worst})) = 0,$$

$$u_1(x_1(\text{best})) = 1, \qquad u_1(x_1(\text{worst})) = 0, \qquad u_2(x_2(\text{best})) = 1, \qquad u_2(x_2(\text{worst})) = 0$$

Now (7) yields

$$u(x_1(\text{best}), x_2(\text{worst})) = k_1(1) + k_2(0) + k_3(0) = k_1$$

Thus, k_1 can be determined from the fact that the decision maker is indifferent between

Similarly (see Problem 3 at the end of this section), $u(x_1(\text{worst}), x_2(\text{best})) = k_2$ and k_2 can be determined from the fact that the decision maker is indifferent between

To determine k_3, observe that from (7) and

$$u(x_1(\text{best}), x_2(\text{best})) = u_1(x_1(\text{best})) = u_2(x_2(\text{best})) = 1$$

we find that

$$1 = u(x_1(\text{best}), x_2(\text{best})) = k_1(1) + k_2(1) + k_3(1) = k_1 + k_2 + k_3$$

Thus, $k_1 + k_2 + k_3 = 1$, or $k_3 = 1 - k_1 - k_2$. Of course, if the decision maker's utility function exhibits additive independence, then $k_3 = 0$.

The procedure to be used in assessing a multiattribute utility function (when there are two attributes) may be summarized as follows:

Step 1 Check whether attributes 1 and 2 are mui. If they are, go on to Step 2. If the attributes are not mui, the assessment of the multiattribute utility function is beyond the scope of our discussion. (See Keeney and Raiffa (1976, Section 5.7).)

Step 2 Check for additive independence.

Step 3 Assess $u_1(x_1)$ and $u_2(x_2)$.

Step 4 Determine k_1, k_2, and (if there is no additive independence) k_3.

Step 5 Check to see whether the assessed utility function is really consistent with the decision maker's preferences. To do this, set up several lotteries and use the expected utility of each lottery to rank the lotteries from most to least favorable. Then ask the decision maker to rank the lotteries from most to least favorable. If the assessed utility function is consistent with the decision maker's preferences, the ranking of the lotteries obtained from the assessed utility function should closely resemble the decision maker's ranking of the lotteries.

Example 2 illustrates the assessment and use of a multiattribute utility function.

E X A M P L E 2

Fruit Computer Company is certain that its market share during 1999 will be between 10% and 50% of the microcomputer market. Fruit is also sure that its profits during 1999 will be between \$5 million and \$30 million. Assess Fruit's multiattribute utility function $u(x_1, x_2)$, where

$$x_1 = \text{Fruit's market share during 1999}$$
$$x_2 = \text{Fruit's profit during 1999 (in millions of dollars)}$$

Solution

We begin by checking for mui. It is helpful to draw a diagram (see Figure 2) that displays various levels of each attribute. First, we check whether attribute 1 (market share) is ui of attribute 2 (profit). We ask Fruit for the certainty equivalent of a $\frac{1}{2}$ chance at the worst market share (10%) and a $\frac{1}{2}$ chance at the best market share (50%), with x_2 fixed at some level (say $x_2 = \$15$ million). Suppose the certainty equivalent of

is (30%, \$15). To determine whether attribute 1 is ui of attribute 2, we fix attribute 2 at some other level (say, $x_2 = \$20$ million) and find Fruit's certainty equivalent for the following lottery:

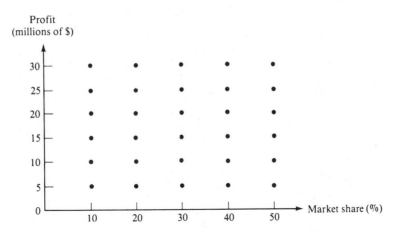

Figure 2
Possible Levels of
Each Attribute for
Fruit Computer
Company

If attribute 1 is ui of attribute 2, the certainty equivalent of this lottery should be close to (30%, $20). For other values of x_2 (say, $x_2 = $5, $10, $25,$ and 30), we check if the certainty equivalent of the lottery

$$\begin{array}{c}\frac{1}{2} \quad 10\%, x_2 \\ \frac{1}{2} \quad 50\%, x_2\end{array}$$

is close to $(30\%, x_2)$. Suppose this is the case. Then we repeat this procedure with other values of market share replacing 10% and 50%. If similar results ensue, then attribute 1 is ui of attribute 2. In analogous fashion, we can determine whether attribute 2 is ui of attribute 1. If attribute 1 is ui of attribute 2, and attribute 2 is ui of attribute 1, the two attributes are mui. Let's assume that attributes 1 and 2 are (at least approximately) mui and proceed to Step 2 (checking for additive independence).

To check for additive independence, we must determine whether Fruit is indifferent between

$$\begin{array}{c}\frac{1}{2} \quad 50\%, \$30 \\ \frac{1}{2} \quad 10\%, \$5\end{array} \quad \text{and} \quad \begin{array}{c}\frac{1}{2} \quad 50\%, \$5 \\ \frac{1}{2} \quad 10\%, \$30\end{array}$$

Suppose that Fruit is not indifferent between these lotteries. Then Fruit's utility function will not exhibit additive independence. We now know that $u(x_1, x_2)$ may be written as

$$u(x_1, x_2) = k_1 u_1(x_1) + k_2 u_2(x_2) + k_3 u_1(x_1) u_2(x_2)$$

We now proceed to Step 3 (assessing $u_1(x_1)$ and $u_2(x_2)$). Suppose we obtain the results shown in Figure 3. To complete the assessment of Fruit's multiattribute utility function, we must determine $k_1, k_2,$ and k_3 (Step 4). To find k_1, we ask Fruit to determine the number k_1 that makes Fruit indifferent between

$$\begin{array}{c} 1 \quad 50\%, \$5 \end{array} \quad \text{and} \quad \begin{array}{c} k_1 \quad 50\%, \$30 \\ 1 - k_1 \quad 10\%, \$5\end{array}$$

Figure 3
$u_1(x_1)$ and $u_2(x_2)$ for
Fruit Computer
Example

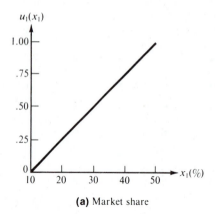

(a) Market share

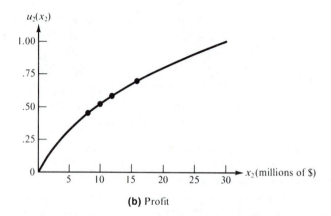

(b) Profit

Suppose that for $k_1 = 0.6$ Fruit is indifferent between these two lotteries. Similarly, k_2 is the number that makes Fruit indifferent between

$$\frac{1}{} 10\%, \$30 \qquad \text{and} \qquad \begin{array}{c} \overset{k_2}{\rule{1cm}{0.4pt}} 50\%, \$30 \\ \underset{1-k_2}{\rule{1cm}{0.4pt}} 10\%, \$5 \end{array}$$

Suppose that for $k_2 = 0.5$ Fruit is indifferent between these two lotteries. Now $k_3 = 1 - k_1 - k_2 = -0.1$, and Fruit's multiattribute utility function is

$$u(x_1, x_2) = 0.6u_1(x_1) + 0.5u_2(x_2) - 0.1u_1(x_1)u_2(x_2) \tag{10}$$

where $u_1(x_1)$ and $u_2(x_2)$ are sketched in Figure 3. Note that

$$\frac{\partial u(x_1, x_2)}{\partial x_1} = 0.6u_1'(x_1) - 0.1u_1'(x_1)u_2(x_2)$$

Thus, as Fruit's profit increases, we see that the utility gained from an additional point of market share decreases. Similarly, if $k_3 > 0$, then as profit increases, the benefit gained from an additional point of market share would increase. As outlined in Step 5, we should now check whether this multiattribute utility function is consistent with Fruit's preferences.

USE OF MULTIATTRIBUTE UTILITY FUNCTIONS

To illustrate how a multiattribute utility function might be used, suppose that Fruit must determine whether to mount a small or a large advertising campaign during the coming year. Fruit believes there is a $\frac{1}{2}$ probability that its main rival, CSL Computers, will mount a small TV ad campaign and a $\frac{1}{2}$ probability that CSL will mount a large TV ad campaign. At the end of the current year, Fruit's market share and profits (in millions of dollars) will be as shown in Table 14. Fruit must determine which of the following lotteries has the larger expected utility:

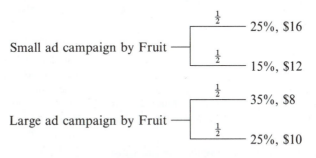

Table 14	CSL CHOOSES	
Effect of Advertising on Market Share and Profit		
FRUIT CHOOSES	*Small Ad Campaign*	*Large Ad Campaign*
Small ad campaign	25%, $16	15%, $12
Large ad campaign	35%, $8	25%, $10

From Figure 3, we find that $u_1(15) = 0.125$, $u_1(25) = 0.375$, $u_1(35) = 0.625$, $u_2(8) = 0.45$, $u_2(10) = 0.53$, $u_2(12) = 0.58$, and $u_2(16) = 0.70$. Then

$$u(25\%, \$16) = 0.6(.375) + 0.5(.7) - 0.1(.375)(.7) = .549$$
$$u(15\%, \$12) = 0.6(.125) + 0.5(.58) - 0.1(.125)(.58) = .358$$
$$u(35\%, \$8) = 0.6(.625) + 0.5(.45) - 0.1(.625)(.45) = .572$$
$$u(25\%, \$10) = 0.6(.375) + 0.5(.53) - 0.1(.375)(.53) = .470$$

Then

$$E(U \text{ for small ad campaign}) = (\tfrac{1}{2})(.549) + (\tfrac{1}{2})(.358) = .454$$
$$E(U \text{ for large ad campaign}) = (\tfrac{1}{2})(.572) + (\tfrac{1}{2})(.470) = .521$$

Thus, during the current year, Fruit should mount a large ad campaign.

◆ PROBLEMS

GROUP A

1. National Express Carriers is interested in two attributes:

Attribute 1 The average cost of delivering a letter (known to be between $1 and $5).

Attribute 2 Percentage of all letters reaching their destination on time (known to be between 70% and 100%).

(a) Would National's multiattribute utility function exhibit mui?

(b) Would National's utility function be additive?

(c) Assume that attributes 1 and 2 exhibit mui. Suppose National is indifferent between ($1, 70%) for certain and the following lottery:

Also assume that National is indifferent between ($5, 100%) for certain and

Find National's multiattribute utility function. Express National's multiattribute utility function in terms of $u_1(x_1)$ and $u_2(x_2)$.

2. Keeney and Raiffa (1976) discuss the assessment of a blood bank's multiattribute utility function. For simplicity, we assume that the blood bank must determine at the beginning of each week how many pints of blood should be ordered. Any blood that is left over at the end of the week spoils (it is outdated). For the blood bank, two attributes of interest are as follows:

Attribute 1 Number of pints of blood by which ordered blood falls short of the week's demand (the weekly shortage). The weekly shortage is known to be always between 0 and 10 pints.

Attribute 2 Number of pints of blood that are outdated (known to be always between 0 and 10 pints).

Assume that attributes 1 and 2 exhibit mui.

(a) Suppose the blood bank is indifferent between

and between

Let x_1 = value of attribute 1, and x_2 = value of attribute 2. Also suppose that

$$u_1(x_1) = .58 \exp\left(1 - \frac{x_1}{10}\right) - .58$$

and

$$u_2(x_2) = 1 - \frac{x_2^2}{100}$$

Determine the blood bank's multiattribute utility function.

(b) Suppose that each week there is a $\frac{1}{2}$ chance that the demand for blood will be 25 pints and a $\frac{1}{2}$ chance that the demand for blood will be 35 pints. Would the blood bank be better off ordering 28 pints, 30 pints, or 32 pints?

3. Show that the method for determining k_2 described in the text is valid.

4. Gotham City is trying to determine how many ambulances it should have and how to staff the ambulances. Each ambulance may be staffed with paramedics or emergency medical technicians. Paramedics are considered to provide better service than emergency medical technicians and are paid higher salaries. Budgetary limitations have forced the city to choose between the following two alternatives:

Alternative 1 Four ambulances, two staffed with emergency medical technicians and two staffed with paramedics.

Alternative 2 Three ambulances, all staffed with paramedics.

The city fathers believe that the following two attributes determine the city's satisfaction with ambulance service:

Attribute 1 Time until an ambulance reaches patient.

Attribute 2 Percentage of ambulance calls handled by paramedics. Assume that Gotham City's multiattribute utility function $u(x_1, x_2)$ exhibits mui and that

$$u_1(x_1) = 1 - \frac{x_1^2}{900} \quad \text{and} \quad u_2(x_2) = \frac{x_2^2}{10,000}$$

The time for an ambulance to reach a patient is always between 0 and 30 minutes. The city fathers are indifferent between

The city fathers are also indifferent between

Assume that if an ambulance is available when a call comes in, then the ambulance will arrive in 5 minutes; if an ambulance is not available when a call comes in, the ambulance will arrive in 20 minutes. With three ambulances, an ambulance will be immediately available 60% of the time, and with four ambulances, an ambulance will be immediately available 80% of the time.

(a) Determine the city fathers' multiattribute utility function.

(b) Which alternative should they choose?

5. Public Service Indiana (PSI) is considering two sites for a nuclear power plant. The following two attributes will influence its determination about where to build the plant:

> **Attribute 1** Cost of the plant (in millions of dollars).
>
> **Attribute 2** Acres of land damaged by building the plant.

Assume that PSI's multiattribute utility function is given by $u(x_1, x_2) = .70u_1(x_1) + .20u_2(x_2) + .10u_1(x_1)u_2(x_2)$, where $u_1(x_1) = .1 + \exp(-.1x_1)$ and $u_2(x_2) = 2.5 - 2.5\exp(.0006x_2 - .48)$.

Two locations for the power plant are under consideration. Location 1 is equivalent to the following lottery:

```
        .50
    ┌──────── (50, 300)
────┤
    │   .50
    └──────── (30, 400)
```

and location 2 is equivalent to the following lottery:

```
        .50
    ┌──────── (60, 200)
────┤
    │   .50
    └──────── (15, 600)
```

Which location should be chosen?

GROUP B

6. Consider the four points A, B, C, and D in Figure 4. Assume that more of each attribute is desirable and that a

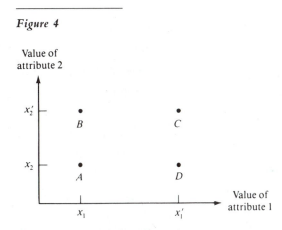

Figure 4

decision maker's utility function exhibits mui. Consider the following two lotteries:

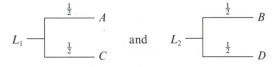

(a) Show that if $k_3 > 0$, then $L_1 \, \mathrm{p} \, L_2$.

(b) Show that if $k_3 < 0$, then $L_2 \, \mathrm{p} \, L_1$.

(c) Show that if the decision maker exhibits additive independence ($k_3 = 0$), then $L_1 \, \mathrm{i} \, L_2$.

(d) Let attribute 1 = performance of Germany on eastern front near end of World War II, and attribute 2 = performance of Germany on western front near end of World War II. A high level of an attribute means that Germany did well on the front, and a low level of an attribute means that Germany did poorly on a front. Suppose that Germany will suffer defeat if it performs poorly on either front. If these attributes exhibit mui, what would be the sign of k_3?

(e) General Motors has domestic and international divisions. Let attribute 1 = profits in the domestic division and attribute 2 = profits in the international division. Suppose General Motors is reasonably happy if at least one division has a good year but is very unhappy if both divisions have a bad year. If these attributes exhibit mui, what would be the sign of k_3?

14-3   THE ANALYTIC HIERARCHY PROCESS

In Section 14.1, we discussed situations in which a decision maker chooses between alternatives on the basis of how well the alternatives meet various objectives. For example, in determining which job offer to accept, a job seeker (call her Jane) might choose between the offers by determining how well each job offer meets the following four objectives:

Objective 1 High starting salary (SAL)
Objective 2 Quality of life in city where job is located (QL)
Objective 3 Interest of work (IW)
Objective 4 Job location near family and relatives (NF)

When multiple objectives are important to a decision maker, it may be difficult to choose between alternatives. For example, one job offer may offer the highest starting salary, but the job offer may score poorly on the other three objectives. Another job offer may meet objectives 2–4 but have a low starting salary. In such a case, it may be difficult for Jane to choose between the job offers. Thomas Saaty's **analytic hierarchy process** (AHP) provides a powerful tool that can be used to make decisions in situations involving multiple objectives.

To illustrate how the AHP works, let's suppose that Jane has three job offers and must determine which offer to accept. For the ith objective (in this example, $i = 1, 2, 3, 4$), the AHP generates (by a method to be described shortly) a weight w_i ($i = 1, 2, 3, 4$) for the ith objective. For convenience, the chosen weights always sum to 1. Suppose that for this example, we have found Jane's weights to be

$$w_1 = .5115, \qquad w_2 = .0986, \qquad w_3 = .2433, \qquad w_4 = .1467$$

(These weights fail to add up to 1 due to rounding.) The weights indicate that a high starting salary is the most important objective, followed by interest of work, nearness to family, and quality of life in the city where the job is located.

Next suppose (again by a method that is soon to be described) that Jane can determine how well each job "scores" on each objective. For example, suppose Jane determines that each job scores on each objective as shown in Table 15. For example, job 1 best meets the objective of a high starting salary but "scores" worst on all other objectives.

Table 15 Jane's "Score" for Each Job and Objective	OBJECTIVE	JOB 1	JOB 2	JOB 3
	Salary	.571	.286	.143
	Quality of life	.159	.252	.589
	Interest in work	.088	.669	.243
	Proximity to family	.069	.426	.506

Given Jane's weights and the score of each job on each objective, how can Jane determine which job offer to accept? For the jth job offer ($j = 1, 2, 3$), compute job offer j's overall score as follows:

$$\sum_{i=1}^{i=4} w_i \ (\text{job offer } j\text{'s score on objective } i)$$

Now choose the job offer with the highest overall score. Note that the overall score gives more weight to a job offer's score on the more important objectives. Computing each job's overall score, we obtain

Job 1 overall score $= .5115(.571) + .0986(.159) + .2433(.088)$
$$+ .1467(.069) = .339$$
Job 2 overall score $= .5115(.286) + .0986(.252) + .2433(.669)$
$$+ .1467(.426) = .396$$
Job 3 overall score $= .5115(.143) + .0986(.589) + .2433(.243)$
$$+ .1467(.506) = .264$$

Thus, the AHP would indicate that Jane should accept job 2.

OBTAINING WEIGHTS FOR EACH OBJECTIVE

Suppose there are n objectives. We begin by writing down an $n \times n$ matrix (known as the **pairwise comparison matrix**) A. The entry in row i and column j of A (call it a_{ij}) indicates how much more important objective i is than objective j. "Importance" is to be measured on an integer-valued 1–9 scale, with each number having the interpretation shown in Table 16. For all i, it is necessary that $a_{ii} = 1$. If, for example, $a_{13} = 3$, objective 1 is weakly more important than objective 3. If $a_{ij} = k$, then for consistency, it is necessary that $a_{ji} = \frac{1}{k}$. Thus, if $a_{13} = 3$, then $a_{31} = \frac{1}{3}$ must hold.

Table 16	VALUE OF a_{ij}	INTERPRETATION
Interpretation of Entries in a Pairwise Comparison Matrix	1	Objectives i and j are of equal importance
	3	Objective i is weakly more important than objective j
	5	Experience and judgment indicate that objective i is strongly more important than objective j
	7	Objective i is very strongly or demonstrably more important than objective j
	9	Objective i is absolutely more important than objective j
	2, 4, 6, 8	Intermediate values—for example, a value of 8 means that objective i is midway between strongly and absolutely more important than objective j

Suppose that Jane has identified the following pairwise comparison matrix for her four objectives (SAL = high salary; QL = high quality of life; IW = interesting work; NF = nearness to family):

$$
\begin{array}{c}
\quad\quad\text{SAL} \quad \text{QL} \quad \text{IW} \quad \text{NF} \\
\begin{array}{c} \text{SAL} \\ \text{QL} \\ \text{IW} \\ \text{NF} \end{array}
\begin{bmatrix}
1 & 5 & 2 & 4 \\
\frac{1}{5} & 1 & \frac{1}{2} & \frac{1}{2} \\
\frac{1}{2} & 2 & 1 & 2 \\
\frac{1}{4} & 2 & \frac{1}{2} & 1
\end{bmatrix}
\end{array}
$$

Unfortunately, some of Jane's pairwise comparisons are inconsistent. To illustrate the meaning of consistency, note that since $a_{13} = 2$, Jane feels SAL is twice as important as IW. Since $a_{32} = 2$, Jane also believes that IW is twice as important as QL. Consistency of preferences would imply that Jane should feel that SAL is $2(2) = 4$ times as important as QL. Since $a_{12} = 5$, however, Jane believes that SAL is 5 times as important as QL. This shows that Jane's pairwise comparisons exhibit a slight inconsistency. Slight inconsistencies are common and do not cause serious difficulties. An index that can be used to measure the consistency of Jane's preferences will be discussed later in this section.

Suppose there are n objectives. Let w_i = the weight given to objective i. To describe how the AHP determines the w_i's, let's suppose the decision maker is perfectly consistent. Then her pairwise comparison matrix should be of the following form:

$$A = \begin{bmatrix} \dfrac{w_1}{w_1} & \dfrac{w_1}{w_2} & \cdots & \dfrac{w_1}{w_n} \\[2mm] \dfrac{w_2}{w_1} & \dfrac{w_2}{w_2} & \cdots & \dfrac{w_2}{w_n} \\[2mm] \vdots & \vdots & & \vdots \\[2mm] \dfrac{w_n}{w_1} & \dfrac{w_n}{w_2} & \cdots & \dfrac{w_n}{w_n} \end{bmatrix} \tag{11}$$

For example, suppose that $w_1 = \frac{1}{2}$ and $w_2 = \frac{1}{6}$. Then objective 1 is three times as important as objective 2, so

$$a_{12} = \frac{w_1}{w_2} = 3$$

Now suppose that a consistent decision maker has a pairwise comparison matrix A of the form (11). How can we recover the vector $\mathbf{w} = [w_1 \quad w_2 \quad \cdots \quad w_n]$ from A? Consider the system of n equations

$$A\mathbf{w}^T = \Delta\mathbf{w}^T \tag{12}$$

where Δ is an unknown number and $\mathbf{w}^T$ is an unknown n-dimensional column vector. For any number Δ, Eq. (12) always has the trivial solution $\mathbf{w} = [0 \quad 0 \quad \cdots \quad 0]$. It can be shown that if A is the pairwise comparison matrix of a perfectly consistent decision maker (that is, if A is of the form (11)) and we do not allow $\Delta = 0$, then the only nontrivial solution to (12) is $\Delta = n$ and $\mathbf{w} = [w_1 \quad w_2 \quad \cdots \quad w_n]$. This shows that for a consistent decision maker, the weights w_i can be obtained from the only nontrivial solution to (12). Now suppose that the decision maker is not perfectly consistent. Let $\Delta_{\max}$ be the largest number for which (12) has a nontrivial solution (call this solution $\mathbf{w}_{\max}$). If the decision maker's comparisons do not deviate very much from perfect consistency, we would expect $\Delta_{\max}$ to be close to n and $\mathbf{w}_{\max}$ to be close to $\mathbf{w}$. Saaty verified that this intuition is indeed correct and suggested approximating $\mathbf{w}$ by $\mathbf{w}_{\max}$. Saaty also proposed measuring the decision maker's consistency by looking how close $\Delta_{\max}$ is to n. The software package *Expert Choice* gives (among other outputs) exact values of $\Delta_{\max}$ and $\mathbf{w}_{\max}$ and a measure of the decision maker's consistency. In what follows, we outline a simple method (easily implemented on any spreadsheet) that can be used to approximate $\Delta_{\max}$ and $\mathbf{w}_{\max}$ and an index of consistency.

To approximate $\mathbf{w}_{\max}$, we use the following two-step procedure:

Step 1 For each of A's columns, do the following. Divide each entry in column i of A by the sum of the entries in column i. This yields a new matrix (call it A_{norm}, for normalized) in which the sum of the entries in each column is 1. For Jane's pairwise comparison matrix, Step 1 yields

$$A_{\text{norm}} = \begin{bmatrix} .5128 & .5000 & .5000 & .5333 \\ .1026 & .1000 & .1250 & .0667 \\ .2564 & .2000 & .2500 & .2667 \\ .1282 & .2000 & .1250 & .1333 \end{bmatrix}$$

Step 2 To find an approximation to $\mathbf{w}_{\max}$ (to be used as our estimate of $\mathbf{w}$), proceed as follows. Estimate w_i as the average of the entries in row i of A_{norm}. This yields (as previously stated)

$$w_1 = \frac{.5128 + .5000 + .5000 + .5333}{4} = .5115$$

$$w_2 = \frac{.1026 + .1000 + .1250 + .0667}{4} = .0986$$

$$w_3 = \frac{.2564 + .2000 + .2500 + .2667}{4} = .2433$$

$$w_4 = \frac{.1282 + .2000 + .1250 + .1333}{4} = .1466$$

CHECKING FOR CONSISTENCY

We can now use the following four-step procedure to check for the consistency of the decision maker's comparisons. (From now on, $\mathbf{w}$ denotes our estimate of the decision maker's weights.)

Step 1 Compute $A\mathbf{w}^T$. For our example, we obtain

$$A\mathbf{w}^T = \begin{bmatrix} 1 & 5 & 2 & 4 \\ \frac{1}{5} & 1 & \frac{1}{2} & \frac{1}{2} \\ \frac{1}{2} & 2 & 1 & 2 \\ \frac{1}{4} & 2 & \frac{1}{2} & 1 \end{bmatrix} \begin{bmatrix} .5115 \\ .0986 \\ .2433 \\ .1466 \end{bmatrix} = \begin{bmatrix} 2.0775 \\ 0.3959 \\ 0.9894 \\ 0.5933 \end{bmatrix}$$

Step 2 Compute

$$\frac{1}{n} \sum_{i=1}^{i=n} \frac{i\text{th entry in } A\mathbf{w}^T}{i\text{th entry in } \mathbf{w}^T}$$

$$= \left(\frac{1}{4}\right) \left\{ \frac{2.0775}{.5115} + \frac{.3959}{.0986} + \frac{.9894}{.2433} + \frac{.5933}{.1466} \right\}$$

$$= 4.05$$

Step 3 Compute the **consistency index** (CI) as follows:

$$CI = \frac{(\text{Step 2 result}) - n}{n - 1} = \frac{4.05 - 4}{3} = .017$$

Step 4 Compare CI to the random index (RI) for the appropriate value of n, shown in Table 17.

For a perfectly consistent decision maker (see Problem 5), ith entry in $A\mathbf{w}^T = n$ (ith entry of $\mathbf{w}^T$). This implies that a perfectly consistent decision maker has CI $= 0$. The

	n	RI
Table 17	2	0
Values of the	3	.58
Random Index (RI)	4	.90
	5	1.12
	6	1.24
	7	1.32
	8	1.41
	9	1.45
	10	1.51

values of RI in Table 17 give the average value of CI if the entries in A were chosen at random, subject to the constraint that all diagonal entries must equal 1 and

$$a_{ij} = \frac{1}{a_{ji}}$$

If CI is sufficiently small, the decision maker's comparisons are probably consistent enough to give useful estimates of the weights for his or her objective function. If $\frac{CI}{RI} < .10$, the degree of consistency is satisfactory, but if $\frac{CI}{RI} > .10$, serious inconsistencies may exist, and the AHP may not yield meaningful results. In our example, $\frac{CI}{RI} = \frac{.017}{.90} = .019 < .10$, Thus, Jane's pairwise comparison matrix does not exhibit any serious inconsistencies.

FINDING THE SCORE OF AN ALTERNATIVE FOR AN OBJECTIVE

We have now described how to determine the objective function weights that we earlier used to help Jane determine which job offer to accept. We now determine how well each job "satisfies" or "scores" on each objective. To determine these scores, we construct for each objective a pairwise comparison matrix in which the rows and columns are Jane's possible decisions (in this case, job offers). For SAL, suppose we obtain the following pairwise comparison matrix:

$$
\begin{array}{cccc}
& \text{Job 1} & \text{Job 2} & \text{Job 3} \\
\begin{array}{c} \text{Job 1} \\ \text{Job 2} \\ \text{Job 3} \end{array} &
\left[\begin{array}{ccc}
1 & 2 & 4 \\
\frac{1}{2} & 1 & 2 \\
\frac{1}{4} & \frac{1}{2} & 1
\end{array} \right]
\end{array}
$$

Thus, for example, with respect to salary, job 1 is better (between weakly and strongly) than job 3. We can now apply our procedure for generating weights to the SAL pairwise comparison matrix. We obtain

$$
A_{\text{norm}} = \left[\begin{array}{ccc}
.571 & .571 & .571 \\
.286 & .286 & .286 \\
.143 & .143 & .143
\end{array} \right]
$$

This yields $\mathbf{w} = [.571 \quad .286 \quad .143]$. These weights indicate how well each job "scores" with respect to the SAL objective. As previously stated in Table 15, we obtain

$$\text{Job 1 salary score} = .571$$
$$\text{Job 2 salary score} = .286$$
$$\text{Job 3 salary score} = .143$$

By the way, since all three rows of the pairwise comparison matrix for salary are identical, Jane's pairwise comparisons for salary exhibit perfect consistency.

Suppose Jane's pairwise comparison matrix for quality of life (QL) is as follows:

$$
\begin{array}{c}
\\
\text{Job 1} \\
\text{Job 2} \\
\text{Job 3}
\end{array}
\begin{array}{ccc}
\text{Job 1} & \text{Job 2} & \text{Job 3}
\end{array}
\left[
\begin{array}{ccc}
1 & \frac{1}{2} & \frac{1}{3} \\
2 & 1 & \frac{1}{3} \\
3 & 3 & 1
\end{array}
\right]
$$

Then

$$
A_{\text{norm}} =
\left[
\begin{array}{ccc}
\frac{1}{6} & \frac{1}{9} & \frac{1}{5} \\
\frac{1}{3} & \frac{2}{9} & \frac{1}{5} \\
\frac{1}{2} & \frac{6}{9} & \frac{3}{5}
\end{array}
\right]
$$

and we obtain

$$\text{Job 1 quality of life score} = \frac{\frac{1}{6} + \frac{1}{9} + \frac{1}{5}}{3} = .159$$

$$\text{Job 2 quality of life score} = \frac{\frac{1}{3} + \frac{2}{9} + \frac{1}{5}}{3} = .252$$

$$\text{Job 3 quality of life score} = \frac{\frac{1}{2} + \frac{6}{9} + \frac{3}{5}}{3} = .589$$

For interest in work, suppose the pairwise comparison matrix is as follows:

$$
\begin{array}{c}
\\
\text{Job 1} \\
\text{Job 2} \\
\text{Job 3}
\end{array}
\begin{array}{ccc}
\text{Job 1} & \text{Job 2} & \text{Job 3}
\end{array}
\left[
\begin{array}{ccc}
1 & \frac{1}{7} & \frac{1}{3} \\
7 & 1 & 3 \\
3 & \frac{1}{3} & 1
\end{array}
\right]
$$

It can easily be shown that

$$\text{Job 1 interest in work score} = .088$$
$$\text{Job 2 interest in work score} = .669$$
$$\text{Job 3 interest in work score} = .243$$

Finally, for nearness to family, suppose the pairwise comparison matrix is as follows:

$$
\begin{array}{c}
\\
\text{Job 1} \\
\text{Job 2} \\
\text{Job 3}
\end{array}
\begin{array}{ccc}
\text{Job 1} & \text{Job 2} & \text{Job 3}
\end{array}
\left[
\begin{array}{ccc}
1 & \frac{1}{4} & \frac{1}{7} \\
4 & 1 & 2 \\
7 & 2 & 1
\end{array}
\right]
$$

Routine calculations yield

$$\text{Job 1 score for nearness to family} = .069$$
$$\text{Job 2 score for nearness to family} = .426$$
$$\text{Job 3 score for nearness to family} = .506$$

As described earlier, we can now "synthesize" the objective weights with the scores of each job on each objective to obtain an overall score for each alternative (in this case, each job offer). As before, we find that job offer 2 is the most preferred, followed by job offer 1, with job offer 3 the least preferred.

We close by noting that AHP has been applied by decision makers in countless areas, including accounting, finance, marketing, energy resource planning, microcomputer selection, sociology, architecture, and political science. See Zahedi (1986) and Saaty (1988) for a discussion of applications of AHP.

CRITICISMS OF AHP

Not all experts in decision making endorse the AHP as an acceptable tool for making decisions in multiple-objective problems. Some criticisms are as follows:

1. The method requires that the decision maker have an additive value function. Thus, before using the AHP, one should check that the decision maker believes that the objectives are mutually preferentially independent.

2. The use of a nine-point scale to measure preferences is arbitrary. For example, if $a_{13} = 7$ and $a_{34} = 8$, then a_{14} should equal 56, but it is impossible for a_{14} to exceed 9.

3. Adding another alternative may change the ranking of the original alternatives. (See Problem 4.)

Despite these criticisms, the AHP has proven to be a useful tool for making decisions in many complex situations.

◆ PROBLEMS

1. Each professor's annual salary increase is determined by performance in three areas: teaching, research, and service to the university. The administration has come up with the following pairwise comparison matrix for these objectives:

	Teaching	Research	Service
Teaching	1	$\frac{1}{3}$	5
Research	3	1	7
Service	$\frac{1}{5}$	$\frac{1}{7}$	1

The administration has compared two professors with regard to their teaching, research, and service over the past year. The pairwise comparison matrices are as follows. For teaching:

	Professor 1	Professor 2
Professor 1	1	4
Professor 2	$\frac{1}{4}$	1

For research:

	Professor 1	Professor 2
Professor 1	1	$\frac{1}{3}$
Professor 2	3	1

For service:

	Professor 1	Professor 2
Professor 1	1	6
Professor 2	$\frac{1}{6}$	1

(a) Which professor should receive a bigger raise?

(b) Does the AHP indicate how large a raise each professor should be given?

(c) Check the pairwise comparison matrix for consistency.

2. A business is about to purchase a new personal computer. Three objectives are important in determining which computer should be purchased: cost, user-friendliness, and software availability. The pairwise comparison matrix for these objectives is as follows:

	Cost	User-friendliness	Software availability
Cost	1	$\frac{1}{4}$	$\frac{1}{5}$
User-friendliness	4	1	$\frac{1}{2}$
Software availability	5	2	1

Three computers are being considered for purchase. The performance of each computer with regard to each objective is indicated by the following pairwise comparison matrices. For cost (low cost is good, high cost is bad!):

	Computer 1	Computer 2	Computer 3
Computer 1	1	3	5
Computer 2	$\frac{1}{3}$	1	2
Computer 3	$\frac{1}{5}$	$\frac{1}{2}$	1

For user-friendliness:

	Computer 1	Computer 2	Computer 3
Computer 1	1	$\frac{1}{3}$	$\frac{1}{2}$
Computer 2	3	1	5
Computer 3	2	$\frac{1}{5}$	1

For software availability:

	Computer 1	Computer 2	Computer 3
Computer 1	1	$\frac{1}{2}$	$\frac{1}{7}$
Computer 2	2	1	$\frac{1}{5}$
Computer 3	7	5	1

(a) Which computer should be purchased?

(b) Check the pairwise comparison matrices for consistency.

3. Woody is ready to select his mate for life and has determined that beauty, intelligence, and personality are the key factors in selecting a satisfactory mate. His pairwise comparison matrix for these objectives is as follows:

	Beauty	Intelligence	Personality
Beauty	1	3	5
Intelligence	$\frac{1}{3}$	1	3
Personality	$\frac{1}{5}$	$\frac{1}{3}$	1

Three women (Melanie Griffith, Meryl Streep, and Molly Ringwald) are begging to be Woody's mate. His views of these women's beauty, intelligence, and personality are given in the following pairwise comparison matrices. Beauty:

	Melanie	Meryl	Molly
Melanie	1	5	3
Meryl	$\frac{1}{5}$	1	$\frac{1}{2}$
Molly	$\frac{1}{3}$	2	1

Intelligence:

	Melanie	Meryl	Molly
Melanie	1	$\frac{1}{6}$	$\frac{1}{4}$
Meryl	6	1	2
Molly	4	$\frac{1}{2}$	1

Personality:

	Melanie	Meryl	Molly
Melanie	1	4	$\frac{1}{4}$
Meryl	$\frac{1}{4}$	1	$\frac{1}{9}$
Molly	4	9	1

(a) Whom should Woody choose as his lifetime mate?

(b) Evaluate all pairwise comparison matrices for consistency.

4. In determining where to invest my money, two objectives—expected rate of return and degree of risk—are considered equally important. Two investments (1 and 2) have the following pairwise comparison matrices: Expected return:

	Investment 1	Investment 2
Investment 1	1	$\frac{1}{2}$
Investment 2	2	1

Degree of risk:

	Investment 1	Investment 2
Investment 1	1	3
Investment 2	$\frac{1}{3}$	1

(a) How should I rank these investments?

(b) Now suppose another investment (investment 3) is available. Suppose the pairwise comparison matrices for these investments are as follows. Expected return:

	Investment 1	Investment 2	Investment 3
Investment 1	1	$\frac{1}{2}$	4
Investment 2	2	1	8
Investment 3	$\frac{1}{4}$	$\frac{1}{8}$	1

Degree of risk:

	Investment 1	Investment 2	Investment 3
Investment 1	1	3	$\frac{1}{2}$
Investment 2	$\frac{1}{3}$	1	$\frac{1}{6}$
Investment 3	2	6	1

(c) Observe that the entries in the comparison matrices for investments 1 and 2 have not changed. How should I now rank the investments? Contrast my ranking of investments 1 and 2 with the answer from part (a).

5. Show that for a perfectly consistent decision maker, ith entry in $A\mathbf{w}^T = n$ (ith entry of $\mathbf{w}^T$).

◆ SUMMARY

VALUE FUNCTIONS AND DECISION MAKING UNDER CERTAINTY

An attribute (call it attribute 1) is **preferentially independent** (pi) of another attribute (call it attribute 2) if preferences for values of attribute 1 do not depend on the value of attribute 2.

A set of attributes S is **mutually preferentially independent** (mpi) of a set of attributes S' if (1) the values of the attributes in S' do not affect preferences for the values of attributes in S; (2) the values of attributes in S do not affect preferences for the values of attributes in S'.

A set of attributes 1, 2, . . . , n is mutually preferentially independent (mpi) if for all subsets S of $\{1, 2, \ldots, n\}$, S is mpi of $\bar{S}$. ($\bar{S}$ is all members of $\{1, 2, \ldots, n\}$ that are not included in S.)

THEOREM 1   If the set of attributes 1, 2, . . . , n is mpi, the decision maker's preferences can be represented by an additive value (or cost) function.

GOAL PROGRAMMING

If a decision maker has a linear cost function, goal programming can be used in two different ways to represent tradeoffs between different goals (under certainty). In both methods, deviational variables are used to convert each goal into a constraint:

Method 1 Assign a penalty per unit deviation from each goal and use linear programming to minimize the total penalty incurred because of unmet goals.

Method 2 Rank goals in priority from highest (goal 1) to lowest (goal n) and use pre-emptive goal programming and the goal programming simplex.

Pre-emptive goal programming finds all points that come as close as possible to meeting goal 1. Then among these points, find the points that come as close as possible to meeting the second-highest-priority goal (goal 2). Continue in this fashion until any improvement in a goal can come only at the expense of a higher-priority goal.

The differences between the goal programming simplex and the ordinary simplex are as follows:

1. The ordinary simplex has a single row 0, whereas the goal programming simplex requires n row 0's (one for each goal).

2. In the goal programming simplex, the following method is used to determine the entering variable: Find the highest-priority goal (goal i') that has not been met (or find the highest-priority goal i' having $z_{i'} > 0$). Find the variable with the most positive coefficient in row 0 (goal i') and enter this variable (subject to the following restriction) into the basis. This will reduce $z_{i'}$ and ensure that we come closer to meeting goal i'. *If, however, a variable has a negative coefficient in a row 0 associated with a goal having a higher priority than i', the variable cannot enter the basis.* Entering such a variable in the basis would increase the deviation from goal i for some higher-priority goal. If the variable with the most positive coefficient in row 0 (goal i') cannot be entered into the basis, try to find another variable with a positive coefficient in row 0 (goal i'). If no variable for row 0 (goal i') can enter the basis, there is no way to come closer to meeting goal i' without increasing the deviation from goal i for some higher-priority goal. In this case, move on to row 0 (goal $i' + 1$) in an attempt to come closer to meeting goal $i' + 1$.

3. When a pivot is performed, row 0 for each goal must be updated.

4. A tableau will yield the optimal solution if all goals are satisfied (that is, $z_1 = z_2 = \cdots = z_n = 0$), or if each variable that can enter the basis and reduce the value of z_i' for an unsatisfied goal i' will increase the deviation from goal i for some goal i having a higher priority than goal i'.

MULTIATTRIBUTE UTILITY FUNCTIONS

Attribute 1 is **utility independent** (ui) of attribute 2 if preferences for lotteries involving different levels of attribute 1 do not depend on the level of attribute 2.

If attribute 1 is ui of attribute 2, and attribute 2 is ui of attribute 1, then attributes 1 and 2 are **mutually utility independent** (mui).

THEOREM 2	Attributes 1 and 2 are mui if and only if the decision maker's utility function $u(x_1, x_2)$ is a multilinear function of the form

$$u(x_1, x_2) = k_1 u_1(x_1) + k_2 u_2(x_2) + k_3 u_1(x_1) u_2(x_2) \qquad (7)$$

A decision maker's utility function exhibits **additive independence** if the decision maker is indifferent between

If attributes 1 and 2 are mpi and the decision maker's utility function exhibits additive independence, the decision maker's utility function is of the following additive form:

$$u(x_1, x_2) = k_1 u_1(x_1) + k_2 u_2(x_2) \qquad (9)$$

The following procedure is used to assess multiattribute utility functions:

Step 1 Check whether attributes 1 and 2 are mui. If they are, go on to Step 2. If the attributes are not mui, the assessment of the multiattribute utility function is beyond the scope of our discussion.

Step 2 Check for additive independence.

Step 3 Assess $u_1(x_1)$ and $u_2(x_2)$.

Step 4 Determine k_1, k_2, and (if there is no additive independence) k_3.

Step 5 Check to see whether the assessed utility function is really consistent with the decision maker's preferences. To do this, set up several lotteries and use the expected utility of each lottery to rank the lotteries from most to least favorable. Then ask the decision maker to rank the lotteries from most to least favorable. If the assessed utility function is consistent with the decision maker's preferences, the ranking of lotteries obtained from the assessed utility function should closely resemble the decision maker's ranking of the lotteries.

ANALYTIC HIERARCHY PROCESS (AHP)

The AHP is often used to make decisions in situations when there are multiple objectives. Given a pairwise comparison matrix A, we can approximate the weights for each attribute as follows:

Step 1 For each of A's columns, do the following. Divide each entry in column i of A by the sum of the entries in column i. This yields a new matrix (call it A_{norm}, for normalized), in which the sum of the entries in each column is 1.

Step 2 To find an approximation to $\mathbf{w}_{max}$, which will be used as our estimate of $\mathbf{w}$, proceed as follows. Estimate w_i as the average of the entries in row i of A_{norm}. To find the best decision, determine an overall score for a decision as follows:

$$\text{Decision Score} = \sum_i w_i \text{ (decision score on objective } i)$$

Now choose the decision with the largest score.

To check for consistency in pairwise comparison matrices, we use the following four-step process. ($\mathbf{w}$ denotes our estimate of the decision maker's weights.)

Step 1 Compute $A\mathbf{w}^T$.

Step 2 Compute

$$\frac{1}{n} \sum_{i=1}^{i=n} \frac{i\text{th entry in } A\mathbf{w}^T}{i\text{th entry in } \mathbf{w}^T}$$

Step 3 Compute the **consistency index** (CI) as follows:

$$\text{CI} = \frac{(\text{Step 2 result}) - n}{n - 1}$$

Step 4 Compare CI to the random index (RI) for the appropriate value of n. If $\frac{CI}{RI} < .10$, the degree of consistency is satisfactory, but if $\frac{CI}{RI} > .10$, serious inconsistencies may exist, and the AHP may not yield meaningful results.

◆ REVIEW PROBLEMS

GROUP A

1. The Pine Valley Board of Education must hire teachers for the coming school year. The types of teachers and the salaries they must be paid are given in Table 18. For example, 20 teachers who are qualified to teach history and science have applied for jobs, and each of these teachers must be paid an annual salary of $21,000. Each teacher who is hired teaches the two subjects he or she is qualified to teach. Pine Valley needs to hire 35 teachers who are qualified to teach history, 30 teachers who are qualified to teach science, 40 teachers who are qualified to teach math, and 32 teachers who are qualified to teach English.

The board has $1,400,000 to spend on teachers' salaries. A cost of $1 is incurred for each dollar the board goes over budget; for each teacher by which Pine Valley's goals are unmet, the following costs are incurred (because of the lower quality of education): science, $30,000; math, $28,000; history, $26,000; and English, $24,000. Formulate a goal programming model to help the board minimize its total cost due to unmet goals.

Table 18

CAN TEACH	NUMBER APPLYING FOR A JOB	ANNUAL SALARY EACH TEACHER IS PAID
History and science	20	$21,000
History and math	15	$22,000
English and science	12	$23,000
English and math	14	$24,000
English and history	13	$25,000
Science and math	12	$26,000

2. Let

x_1 = undergraduate grade point average (GPA) of a student applying to State U's MBA program

x_2 = GMAT score of the same student

Suppose that preference between applicants is based on the following value function:

$$v(x_1, x_2) = 200x_1 + x_2 - 0.1x_2(x_1)^2$$

(a) Would the MBA program prefer a student with a 3.8 GPA and a 500 GMAT score to a student with a 3.0 GPA and a 710 GMAT score?

(b) Does this value function exhibit mutual preferential independence?

3. Stockco fills orders for three products for a local warehouse. Stockco must determine how many of each product should be ordered at the beginning of the current month. This month, 400 units of product 1, 500 units of product 2, and 300 units of product 3 will be demanded. The cost and space taken up by 1 unit of each product are shown in Table 19. If Stockco runs out of stock before the end of the month, the stockout costs shown in Table 19 are incurred. Stockco has $17,000 to spend on ordering products and has 3700 sq ft of warehouse space. A $1

penalty is assessed for each dollar spent over the budget limit, and a $10 cost is assessed for every extra square foot of warehouse space that is needed.

(a) Formulate an LP that can be used to determine Stockco's optimal ordering policy.

(b) Suppose that Stockco has set the following goals, listed in order of priority:

Goal 1 Spend at most $17,000.

Goal 2 Use at most 3700 sq ft of warehouse space.

Goal 3 Meet demand for product 1.

Goal 4 Meet demand for product 2.

Goal 5 Meet demand for product 3.

Formulate a pre-emptive goal programming model for Stockco.

Table 19

	SPACE	COST	STOCKOUT COST
Product 1	6 sq ft	$20	$16
Product 2	5 sq ft	$18	$10
Product 3	4 sq ft	$16	$8

4. The Pine Valley Board of Education is trying to determine its multiattribute utility function with respect to the following attributes:

Attribute 1 Average score of students on an English achievement test.

Attribute 2 Average score of students on a mathematics achievement test.

The board believes that both attributes range between 70% and 90% correct answers. The board is indifferent between

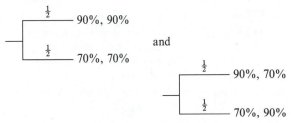

For any level x_2 of attribute 2, the Board is also indifferent between

For any level x_1 of attribute 1, the board is indifferent between

```
        .65
      ┌──── x_1, 90%
 ─────┤                    and    ──── 1 ──── x_1, 76%
      └──── x_1, 70%
        .35
```

The board is also indifferent between

```
                                      .40
 ──── 1 ──── 90%, 70%    and    ┌──────── 90%, 90%
                                │
                                └──────── 70%, 70%
                                  .60
```

Finally, the board is indifferent between

```
                                      .60
 ──── 1 ──── 70%, 90%    and    ┌──────── 90%, 90%
                                │
                                └──────── 70%, 70%
                                  .40
```

The board must decide which of two instructional techniques should be utilized in the Pine Valley schools. Technique 1 is equivalent to the following lottery:

```
        ½
      ┌──── 78%, 76%
 ─────┤
      └──── 70%, 90%
        ½
```

Technique 2 is equivalent to the following lottery:

```
        .60
      ┌──── 90%, 90%
 ─────┤
      └──── 70%, 70%
        .40
```

Would the board prefer technique 1 or technique 2?

GROUP B

5. At Lummins Engine Corporation, production employees work ten hours per day, four days per week. Each day of the week, at least the following number of employees must be working: Monday–Friday, 7 employees; Saturday and Sunday, 3 employees. Lummins has set the following goals, listed in order of priority:

Goal 1 Meet employee requirements with 11 workers.

Goal 2 The average number of weekend days off per employee should be at least 1.5 days.

Goal 3 The average number of consecutive days off an employee gets during the week should exceed 2.8 days.

Formulate a pre-emptive goal programming model that could be used to determine how to schedule Lummins employees.

GROUP C

6.[†] Wivco produces two products, which it sells on both a cash and credit basis. Revenues from credit sales will not have been received but are included in determining profit earned during the current six-month period. Sales during the next six months can be made either from units produced during the next six months or from beginning inventory. Relevant information about products 1 and 2 follows.

During the next six months, at most 150 units of product 1 can be sold on a cash basis, and at most 100 units of product 1 can be sold on a credit basis. It costs $35 to produce each unit of product 1, and each unit of product 1 sells for $40. A credit sale of a unit of product 1 yields $0.50 less profit than a cash sale of product 1 (because of delays in receiving payment). Two hours of production time are needed to produce each unit of product 1. At the beginning of the six-month period, 60 units of product 1 are in inventory.

During the next six months, at most 175 units of product 2 can be sold on a cash basis, and at most 250 units of product 2 can be sold on a credit basis. It costs $45 to produce each unit of product 2, and each unit of product 2 sells for $52.50. A credit sale of a unit of product 2 yields $1.00 less profit than a cash sale of product 2. Four hours of production time are needed to produce each unit of product 2. At the beginning of the six-month period, 30 units of product 2 are in inventory.

During the next six months, Wivco has available 1000 hours for production. At the end of the next six onths, Wivco incurs a 10% holding cost on the value of ending inventory (measured according to production cost). An opportunity cost of 5% is also assessed against any cash on hand at the end of the six-month period.

(a) Formulate and solve (via computer) an LP that yields Wivco's maximum profit during the next six months. What is Wivco's ending inventory position? Assuming an initial cash balance of zero, what is Wivco's ending cash balance?

(b) Since an ending inventory and cash position of zero is undesirable (why?), Wivco is considering other options. At the beginning of the six-month period, Wivco can obtain a loan (secured by ending inventory) that incurs an interest cost equal to 5% of the value of the loan. The maximum value of the loan is 75% of the value of the ending inven-

[†]Based on Sartoris and Spruill (1974).

tory. The loan will be repaid one year from now. Wivco has the following goals:

Goal 1 Make profit come as close as possible to the profit level obtained in part (a).

Goal 2 Make the ending cash balance of Wivco come as close as possible to $75.

Goal 3 At any time, Wivco's current ratio is defined to be (Wivco's assets)/(Wivco's liabilities). Assuming initially that liabilities equal $150, six months from now, Wivco's current ratio will equal

$$\frac{\text{Ending cash balance} + \text{value of accounts receivable} + \text{value of ending inventory}}{\$150 + \text{size of the loan}}$$

Six months from now, Wivco wants the current ratio to be as close as possible to 2. Given the following priorities, use pre-emptive goal programming to determine Wivco's production and financial strategy:

Set 1 Goal 2 has highest priority, goal 1 has second-highest priority, and goal 3 has lowest priority.

Set 2 Goal 3 has highest priority, goal 1 has second-highest priority, and goal 2 has lowest priority.

◆ REFERENCES

The following books give a more detailed explanation of goal programming:

IGNIZIO, J. *Goal Programming and Extensions*. Lexington, Mass.: Lexington Books, 1976.

LEE, S. *Goal Programming for Decision Analysis*. Philadelphia: Auerbach, 1972.

Alternative approaches to multiattribute decision making under certainty are discussed in the following:

STEUER, R. *Multiple Criteria Optimization*. New York: Wiley, 1985.

ZELENY, M. *Multiple Criteria Decision Making*. New York: McGraw-Hill, 1982.

ZIONTS, S., and J. WALLENIUS. "An Interactive Programming Method for Solving the Multiple Criteria Problem," *Management Science* 22(1976):652–663.

The following are recommended for elementary discussions of multiattribute utility theory:

BUNN, D. *Applied Decision Analysis*. New York: McGraw-Hill, 1984.

KENNEY, R. "An Illustrated Procedure for Accessing Multiattributed Utility Functions," *Sloan Management Review* 14(1972):37–50.

KEENEY, R., and H. RAIFFA. *Decision Making with Multiple Objectives*. New York: Wiley, 1976. This classic gives a comprehensive discussion of multiattribute utility theory.

LEE, S., and L. MOORE. "Optimizing University Admissions Planning," *Decision Sciences* 5(1974):405–414.

———. "A Practical Approach to Production Scheduling," *Production and Inventory Management* 15(1974):79–90.

SARTORIS, W., and M. SPRUILL. "Goal Programming and Working Capital Management," *Financial Management* 3(1974):67–74.

SRINIVASAN, S., and A. SHOCKER. "LP Techniques for Multidimensional Analysis of Preferences," *Psychometrika* 38(1973):337–369.

STEUER, R. "Sausage Blending Using Multiple Objective Programming," *Management Science* 30(1984):1376–1384.

WELLING, P. "A Goal Programming Model for Human Resource Allocation in a CPA Firm," *Accounting, Organizations and Society* 2(1977):307–316.

The following references discuss the AHP:

SAATY, T. *The Analytic Hierarchy Process*. Pittsburgh, Pa.: 1988.

ZAHEDI, F. "The Analytic Hierarchy Process—a Survey of the Method and Its Applications," *Interfaces* 16(no. 4,1986):96–108.

15

Game Theory

IN PREVIOUS CHAPTERS, we have encountered many situations in which a *single* decision maker chooses an optimal decision without reference to the effect that the decision has on other decision makers (and without reference to the effect that the decisions of others have on him or her). In many business situations, however, two or more decision makers simultaneously choose an action, and the action chosen by each player affects the rewards earned by the other players. For example, each fast food company must determine an advertising and pricing policy for its products, and each company's decision will affect the revenues and profits of other fast food companies.

Game theory is useful for making decisions in cases where two or more decision makers have conflicting interests. Most of our study of game theory deals with situations where there are only two decision makers (or players), but we briefly study *n*-person (where $n > 2$) game theory also. We begin our study of game theory with a discussion of two-player games in which the players have no common interest.

15-1   TWO-PERSON ZERO-SUM AND CONSTANT-SUM GAMES: SADDLE POINTS

CHARACTERISTICS OF TWO-PERSON ZERO-SUM GAMES

1. There are two players (called the row player and column player).

2. The row player must choose 1 of m strategies. Simultaneously, the column player must choose 1 of n strategies.

3. If the row player chooses her ith strategy and the column player chooses her jth strategy, the row player receives a reward of a_{ij} and the column player loses an amount a_{ij}. Thus, we may think of the row player's reward of a_{ij} as coming from the column player.

Such a game is called a **two-person zero-sum game**, which is represented by the matrix in Table 1 (the game's **reward matrix**). As previously stated, a_{ij} is the row player's reward (and the column player's loss) if the row player chooses her ith strategy and the column player chooses her jth column strategy.

Table 1 Example of Two-Person Zero-Sum Game	ROW PLAYER'S STRATEGY	COLUMN PLAYER'S STRATEGY			
		Column 1	Column 2	$\cdots$	Column n
	Row 1	a_{11}	a_{12}	$\cdots$	a_{1n}
	Row 2	a_{21}	a_{22}	$\cdots$	a_{2n}
	$\vdots$	$\vdots$	$\vdots$		$\vdots$
	Row m	a_{m1}	a_{m2}	$\cdots$	a_{mn}

For example, in the two-person zero-sum game in Table 2, the row player would receive 2 units (and the column player would lose 2 units) if the row player chose her second strategy and the column player chose her first strategy.

Table 2

$$\begin{array}{cccc} 1 & 2 & 3 & -1 \\ 2 & 1 & -2 & 0 \end{array}$$

A two-person zero-sum game has the property that for any choice of strategies, the sum of the rewards to the players is zero. In a zero-sum game, every dollar that one player wins comes out of the other player's pocket, so the two players have totally conflicting interests. Thus, cooperation between the two players would not occur.

John von Neumann and Oskar Morgenstern developed a theory of how two-person zero-sum games should be played, based on the following assumption.

BASIC ASSUMPTION OF TWO-PERSON ZERO-SUM GAME THEORY

Each player chooses a strategy that enables him to do the best he can, given that his opponent *knows the strategy he is following*. Let's use this assumption to determine how the row and column players should play the two-person zero-sum game in Table 3.

Table 3 A Game with a Saddle Point	ROW PLAYER'S STRATEGY	COLUMN PLAYER'S STRATEGY			ROW MINIMUM
		Column 1	Column 2	Column 3	
	Row 1	4	4	10	4
	Row 2	2	3	1	1
	Row 3	6	5	7	5
	COLUMN MAXIMUM	6	5	10	

How should the row player play this game? If he chooses row 1, the assumption implies that the column player will choose column 1 or column 2 and hold the row player to a reward of 4 units (the smallest number in row 1 of the game matrix). Similarly, if the row player chooses row 2, the assumption implies that the column player will choose column 3 and hold the row player's reward to 1 unit (the smallest or minimum number in the second row of the game matrix). If the row player chooses row 3, he will be held to the smallest number in the third row (5). Thus, the assumption implies that the row player should choose the row having the largest minimum. Since $\max(4, 1, 5) = 5$, the row player should choose row 3. By choosing row 3, the row player can ensure that he will win at least max (row minimum) = 5 units.

From the column player's viewpoint, if he chooses column 1, the row player will choose the strategy that makes the column player's losses as large as possible (and the row player's winnings as large as possible). Thus, if the column player chooses column 1, the row player will choose row 3 (because the largest number in the first column is the 6 in the third row). Similarly, if the column player chooses column 2, the row player will again choose row 3, because $5 = \max(4, 3, 5)$. Finally, if the column player chooses column 3, the row player will choose row 1, causing the column player to lose $10 = \max(10, 1, 7)$ units. Thus, the column player can hold his losses to min (column maximum) = $\min(6, 5, 10) = 5$ by choosing column 2.

We have shown that the row player can ensure that he will win at least 5 units and the column player can hold the row player's winnings to at most 5 units. Thus, the only rational outcome of this game is for the row player to win exactly 5 units; the row player cannot expect to win more than 5 units, because the column player (by choosing column 2) can hold the row player's winnings to 5 units.

The game matrix we have just analyzed has the property of satisfying the **saddle point condition**:

$$\max_{\substack{\text{all} \\ \text{rows}}} \text{(row minimum)} = \min_{\substack{\text{all} \\ \text{columns}}} \text{(column maximum)} \qquad (1)$$

Any two-person zero-sum game satisfying (1) is said to have a **saddle point**. If a two-person zero-sum game has a saddle point, the row player should choose any strategy (row) attaining the maximum on the left side of (1). The column player should choose any strategy (column) attaining the minimum on the right side of (1). Thus, for the game we have just analyzed, a saddle point occurred where the row player chose row 3 and the column player chose column 2. The row player could make sure of receiving a reward of at least 5 units (by choosing the optimal strategy of row 3), and the column player could ensure that the row player would receive a reward of at most 5 units (by choosing the optimal strategy of column 2). If a game has a saddle point, we call the common value of both sides of (1) the **value** (v) of the game to the row player. Thus, this game has a value of 5.

An easy way to spot a saddle point is to observe that the reward for a saddle point must be the smallest number in its row and the largest number in its column (see Problem 4 at the end of this section). Thus, like the center point of a horse's saddle, a saddle point for a two-person zero-sum game is a local minimum in one direction (looking across the row) and a local maximum in another direction (looking up and down the column).

A saddle point can also be thought of as an **equilibrium point** in that neither player can benefit from a unilateral change in strategy. For example, if the row player were to change from the optimal strategy of row 3 (to either row 1 or row 2), his reward would decrease, while if the column player changed from his optimal strategy of column 2 (to either column 1 or column 3), the row player's reward (and the column player's losses) would increase. Thus, a saddle point is stable in that neither player has an incentive to move away from it.

Many two-person zero-sum games do not have saddle points. For example, the game in Table 4 does not have a saddle point, because

$$\max(\text{row minimum}) = -1 < \min(\text{column maximum}) = +1$$

In Sections 15.2 and 15.3, we explain how to find the value and the optimal strategies for two-person zero-sum games that do not have saddle points.

Table 4 A Game with No Saddle Point	ROW PLAYER'S STRATEGY	COLUMN PLAYER'S STRATEGY		ROW MINIMUM
		Column 1	Column 2	
	Row 1	-1	$+1$	-1
	Row 2	$+1$	-1	-1
	COLUMN MAXIMUM	$+1$	$+1$	

TWO-PERSON CONSTANT-SUM GAMES

Even if a two-person game is not zero-sum, two players can still be in total conflict. To illustrate this, we now consider two-person constant-sum games.

DEFINITION	A **two-person constant-sum game** is a two-player game in which, for any choice of both players' strategies, the row player's reward and the column player's reward add up to a constant value c.

Of course, a two-person zero-sum game is just a two-person constant-sum game with $c = 0$. A two-person constant-sum game maintains the feature that the row and column players are in total conflict, because a unit increase in the row player's reward will always result in a unit decrease in the column player's reward. In general, the optimal strategies and value for a two-person constant-sum game may be found by the same methods used to find the optimal strategies and value for a two-person zero-sum game.

E X A M P L E
1

During the 8–9 P.M. time slot, two networks are vying for an audience of 100 million viewers. The networks must simultaneously announce the type of show they will air in that time slot. The possible choices for each network and the number of network 1 viewers (in millions) for each choice are shown in Table 5. For example, if both networks choose a western, the matrix indicates that 35 million people will watch network 1 and $100 - 35 = 65$ million people will watch network 2. Thus, we have a two-person constant-sum game with $c = 100$ (million). Does this game have a saddle point? What is the value of the game to network 1?

Solution

Looking at the row minima, we find that by choosing a soap opera, network 1 can be sure of at least $\max(15, 45, 14) = 45$ million viewers. Looking at the column

Table 5	NETWORK 1	NETWORK 2			ROW MINIMUM
A Constant-Sum Game		Western	Soap Opera	Comedy	
	Western	35	15	60	15
	Soap opera	45	58	50	45
	Comedy	38	14	70	14
	COLUMN MAXIMUM	45	58	70	

maxima, we find that by choosing a western, network 2 can hold network 1 to at most min $(45, 58, 70) = 45$ million viewers. Since

$$\max(\text{row minimum}) = \min(\text{column maximum}) = 45$$

we find that Eq. (1) is satisfied. Thus, network 1's choosing a soap opera and network 2's choosing a western yield a saddle point; neither side will do better if it unilaterally changes strategy (check this). Thus, the value of the game to network 1 is 45 million viewers, and the value of the game to network 2 is $100 - 45 = 55$ million viewers. The optimal strategy for network 1 is to choose a soap opera, and the optimal strategy for network 2 is to choose a western. ◆

◆ PROBLEMS

GROUP A

1. Find the value and optimal strategy for the game in Table 6.

Table 6

2	2
1	3

2. Find the value and the optimal strategies for the two-person zero-sum game in Table 7.

Table 7

4	5	5	8
6	7	6	9
5	7	5	4
6	6	5	5

GROUP B

3. Mad Max wants to travel from New York to Dallas by the shortest possible route. He may travel over the routes shown in Table 8. Unfortunately, the Wicked Witch can block one road leading out of Atlanta and one road leading out of Nashville. Mad Max will not know which roads have been blocked until he arrives at Atlanta or Nashville. Should Mad Max start toward Atlanta or Nashville? Which routes should the Wicked Witch block?

Table 8

ROUTE	LENGTH OF ROUTE (Miles)
New York–Atlanta	800
New York–Nashville	900
Nashville–St. Louis	400
Nashville–New Orleans	200
Atlanta–St. Louis	300
Atlanta–New Orleans	600
St. Louis–Dallas	500
New Orleans–Dallas	300

GROUP C

4. Explain why the reward for a saddle point must be the smallest number in its row and the largest number in its column. Suppose a reward is the smallest in its row and the largest in its column. Must that reward yield a saddle point? (*Hint*: Think about the idea of weak duality discussed in Chapter 6.)

15-2   TWO-PERSON ZERO-SUM GAMES: RANDOMIZED STRATEGIES, DOMINATION, AND GRAPHICAL SOLUTION

In the previous section, we found that not all two-person zero-sum games have saddle points. We now discuss how to find the value and optimal strategies for a two-person zero-sum game that does not have a saddle point. We begin with the simple game of Odds and Evens.

E X A M P L E 2

Odds and Evens   Two players (called Odd and Even) simultaneously choose the number of fingers (1 or 2) to put out. If the sum of the fingers put out by both players is odd, Odd wins $1 from Even. If the sum of the fingers put out by both players is even, Even wins $1 from Odd. We consider the row player to be Odd and the column player to be Even. Determine whether this game has a saddle point.

Table 9
Reward Matrix for Odds and Evens

ROW PLAYER (ODD)	COLUMN PLAYER (EVEN)		ROW MINIMUM
	1 Finger	2 Fingers	
1 Finger	-1	$+1$	-1
2 Fingers	$+1$	-1	-1
COLUMN MAXIMUM	$+1$	$+1$	

Solution   This is a zero-sum game, with the reward matrix shown in Table 9. Since max (row minimum) $= -1$ and min(column maximum) $= +1$, Eq. (1) is not satisfied, and this game has no saddle point. All we know is that Odd can be sure of a reward of at least -1, and Even can hold Odd to a reward of at most $+1$. Thus, it is unclear how to determine the value of the game and the optimal strategies. Observe that for any choice of strategies by both players, there is a player who can benefit by unilaterally changing her strategy. For example, if both players put out 1 finger, then Odd can increase her reward from -1 to $+1$ by putting out 2 fingers (instead of 1 finger). Thus, no choice of strategies by the player is stable. We now determine optimal strategies and the value for this game.   ◆

RANDOMIZED OR MIXED STRATEGIES

In order to make further progress with the analysis of Example 2 (and other games without saddle points), we must expand the set of allowable strategies for each player to include **randomized strategies**. Until now, we have assumed that each time a player plays a game, the player will choose the same strategy. Why not allow each player to select a probability of playing each strategy? For Example 2, we might define

$$x_1 = \text{probability that Odd puts out 1 finger}$$
$$x_2 = \text{probability that Odd puts out 2 fingers}$$
$$y_1 = \text{probability that Even puts out 1 finger}$$
$$y_2 = \text{probability that Even puts out 2 fingers}$$

If $x_1 \geq 0$, $x_2 \geq 0$, and $x_1 + x_2 = 1$, (x_1, x_2) is a randomized, or mixed, strategy for Odd. For example, the mixed strategy $(\frac{1}{2}, \frac{1}{2})$ could be realized by Odd if Odd tossed a coin before each play of the game and put out 1 finger for heads and 2 fingers for tails. Similarly, if $y_1 \geq 0$, $y_2 \geq 0$, and $y_1 + y_2 = 1$, (y_1, y_2) is a mixed strategy for Even.

Any mixed strategy $(x_1, x_2, \ldots, x_m)$ for the row player is a **pure strategy** if any of the x_i equals 1. Similarly, any mixed strategy $(y_1, y_2, \ldots, y_n)$ for the column player is a pure strategy if any of the y_i equals 1. A pure strategy is a special case of a mixed strategy in which a player always chooses the same action. Recall from Section 15.1 that the game in Table 10 had a value of 5 (corresponding to a saddle point), so the row player's optimal strategy could be represented as the pure strategy $(0, 0, 1)$, and the column player's optimal strategy could be represented as the pure strategy $(0, 1, 0)$.

Table 10

4	4	10
2	3	1
6	5	7

We continue to assume that both players will play two-person zero-sum games in accordance with the basic assumption of Section 15.1. In the context of randomized strategies, the assumption (from the standpoint of Odd) may be stated as follows: Odd should choose x_1 and x_2 to maximize her expected reward under the assumption that Even knows the value of x_1 and x_2.

It is important to realize that even though we assume that Even knows the values of x_1 and x_2, on a particular play of the game, Even is not assumed to know Odd's actual strategy choice until the instant the game is played.

GRAPHICAL SOLUTION OF ODDS AND EVENS

FINDING ODD'S OPTIMAL STRATEGY.   With this version of the basic assumption, we can determine the optimal strategy for Odd. Since $x_1 + x_2 = 1$, we know that $x_2 = 1 - x_1$. Thus, any mixed strategy may be written as $(x_1, 1 - x_1)$, and it suffices to determine the value of x_1. Suppose Odd chooses a particular mixed strategy $(x_1, 1 - x_1)$. What is Odd's expected reward against each of Even's strategies? If Even puts out 1 finger, Odd will receive a reward of -1 with probability x_1 and a reward of $+1$ with probability $x_2 = 1 - x_1$. Thus, if Even puts out 1 finger and Odd chooses the mixed strategy $(x_1, 1 - x_1)$, Odd's expected reward is

$$(-1)x_1 + (+1)(1 - x_1) = 1 - 2x_1$$

As a function of x_1, this expected reward is drawn as line segment AC in Figure 1.

Figure 1
Choosing Odd's
Strategy

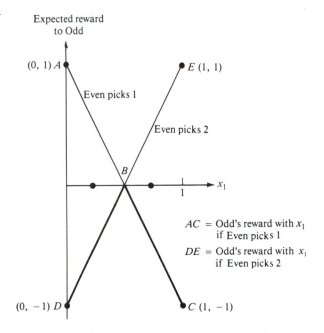

Similarly, if Even puts out 2 fingers and Odd chooses the mixed strategy $(x_1, 1 - x_1)$, Odd's expected reward is

$$(+1)(x_1) + (-1)(1 - x_1) = 2x_1 - 1$$

which is line segment DE in Figure 1.

Suppose Odd chooses the mixed strategy $(x_1, 1 - x_1)$. Since Even is assumed to know the value of x_1, for any value of x_1 Even will choose the strategy (putting out 1 or 2 fingers) that yields a smaller expected reward for Odd. From Figure 1, we see that as a function of x_1, Odd's expected reward will be given by the y coordinate in DBC. Since odd wishes to maximize her expected reward, Odd should choose the value of x_1 corresponding to point B. Point B occurs where the line segments AC and DE intersect, or where $1 - 2x_1 = 2x_1 - 1$. Solving this equation, we obtain $x_1 = \frac{1}{2}$. Thus, Odd should choose the mixed strategy $(\frac{1}{2}, \frac{1}{2})$. The reader should verify that against each of Even's strategies, $(\frac{1}{2}, \frac{1}{2})$ yields an expected reward of zero. Thus, zero is a **floor** on Odd's expected reward, because by choosing the mixed strategy $(\frac{1}{2}, \frac{1}{2})$, Odd can be sure that (for any choice of Even's strategy) her expected reward will always be at least zero.

FINDING EVEN'S OPTIMAL STRATEGY. We now consider how Even should choose a mixed strategy (y_1, y_2). Again, since $y_2 = 1 - y_1$, we may ask how Even should choose a mixed strategy $(y_1, 1 - y_1)$. The basic assumption implies that Even should choose y_1 to minimize her expected losses (or equivalently, minimize Odd's expected reward) under the assumption that Odd knows the value of y_1. Suppose Even chooses the mixed strategy $(y_1, 1 - y_1)$. What will Odd do? If Odd puts out 1 finger, Odd's expected reward is

$$(-1)y_1 + (+1)(1 - y_1) = 1 - 2y_1$$

which is line segment AC in Figure 2. If Odd puts out 2 fingers, Odd's expected

Figure 2
Choosing Even's
Strategy

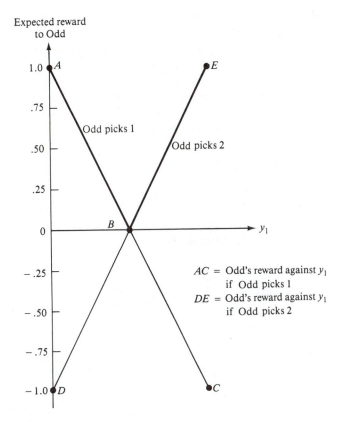

reward is

$$(+1)(y_1) + (-1)(1 - y_1) = 2y_1 - 1$$

which is line segment DE in Figure 2. Since Odd is assumed to know the value of y_1, Odd will put out the number of fingers corresponding to $\max(1 - 2y_1, 2y_1 - 1)$. Thus, for a given value of y_1, Odd's expected reward (and Even's expected loss) will be given by the y-coordinate on the piecewise linear curve ABE.

Now Even chooses the mixed strategy $(y_1, 1 - y_1)$ that will make Odd's expected reward as small as possible. Thus, Even should choose the value of y_1 corresponding to the lowest point on ABE (point B). Point B is where the line segments AC and DE intersect, or where $1 - 2y_1 = 2y_1 - 1$, or $y_1 = \frac{1}{2}$. The basic assumption implies that Even should choose the mixed strategy $(\frac{1}{2}, \frac{1}{2})$. For this mixed strategy, Even's expected loss (and Odd's expected reward) is zero. We say that zero is a **ceiling** on Even's expected loss (or Odd's expected reward), because by choosing the mixed strategy $(\frac{1}{2}, \frac{1}{2})$, Even can ensure that her expected loss (for any choice of strategies by Odd) will not exceed zero.

MORE ON THE IDEA OF VALUE AND
OPTIMAL STRATEGIES

For the game of Odds and Evens, the row player's floor and the column player's ceiling are equal. This is not a coincidence. When each player is allowed to choose mixed strategies, the row player's floor will always equal the column player's ceiling. In

Section 15.3, we use the Dual Theorem of Chapter 6 to prove this interesting result. We call the common value of the floor and ceiling the **value** of the game to the row player. Any mixed strategy for the row player that guarantees that the row player gets an expected reward at least equal to the value of the game is an **optimal strategy** for the row player. Similarly, any mixed strategy for the column player that guarantees that the column player's expected loss is no more than the value of the game is an optimal strategy for the column player. Thus, for Example 2, we have shown that the value of the game is zero, the row player's optimal strategy is $(\frac{1}{2}, \frac{1}{2})$, and the column player's optimal strategy is $(\frac{1}{2}, \frac{1}{2})$.

Example 2 illustrates that by allowing mixed strategies, we have enabled each player to find an optimal strategy in that *if the row player departs from her optimal strategy, the column player may have a strategy that reduces the row player's expected reward below the value of the game, and if the column player departs from her optimal strategy, the row player may have a strategy that increases row's expected reward above the value of the game.* Table 11 illustrates this idea for the game of Odds and Evens.

Table 11
How to Make a Nonoptimal Strategy Pay the Price

ODD'S MIXED STRATEGY	EVEN CAN CHOOSE	ODD'S EXPECTED REWARD (EVEN'S EXPECTED LOSSES)
$x_1 < \frac{1}{2}$	2 fingers	< 0 (on BD in Fig. 1)
$x_1 > \frac{1}{2}$	1 finger	< 0 (on BC in Fig. 1)

EVEN'S MIXED STRATEGY	ODD CAN CHOOSE	ODD'S EXPECTED REWARD (EVEN'S EXPECTED LOSSES)
$y_1 < \frac{1}{2}$	1 finger	> 0 (on AB in Fig. 2)
$y_1 > \frac{1}{2}$	2 fingers	> 0 (on BE in Fig. 2)

For example, suppose that Odd chooses a nonoptimal mixed strategy with $x_1 < \frac{1}{2}$. Then by choosing 2 fingers, Even ensures that Odd's expected reward can be read from BD in Figure 1. This means that if Odd chooses a mixed strategy having $x_1 < \frac{1}{2}$, her expected reward can be negative (less than the value of the game).

To close this section, we find the value and optimal strategies for a more complicated game.

E X A M P L E 3

A fair coin is tossed, and the result is shown to player 1. Player 1 must then decide whether to pass or bet. If player 1 passes, he must pay player 2 \$1. If player 1 bets, player 2 (who does not know the result of the coin toss) may either fold or call the bet. If player 2 folds, he pays player 1 \$1. If player 2 calls and the coin comes up heads, player 2 pays player 1 \$2; if player 2 calls and the coin comes up tails, player 1 must pay player 2 \$2. Formulate this as a two-person zero-sum game. Then graphically determine the value of the game and each player's optimal strategy.

Solution

Player 1's strategies may be represented as follows: PP, pass on heads and pass on tails; PB, pass on heads and bet on tails; BP, bet on heads and pass on tails; and BB, bet on heads and bet on tails. Player 2 simply has the two strategies call and fold. For each choice of strategies, player 1's expected reward is as shown in Table 12.

	PLAYER 1'S EXPECTED REWARD
Table 12 Computation of Reward Matrix for Example 3	
PP vs. call	$(\frac{1}{2})(-1) + (\frac{1}{2})(-1) = -\$1$
PP vs. fold	$(\frac{1}{2})(-1) + (\frac{1}{2})(-1) = -\$1$
PB vs. call	$(\frac{1}{2})(-1) + (\frac{1}{2})(-2) = -\$1.50$
PB vs. fold	$(\frac{1}{2})(-1) + (\frac{1}{2})(1) = \$0$
BP vs. call	$(\frac{1}{2})(2) + (\frac{1}{2})(-1) = \$0.50$
BP vs. fold	$(\frac{1}{2})(1) + (\frac{1}{2})(-1) = \$0$
BB vs. call	$(\frac{1}{2})(2) + (\frac{1}{2})(-2) = \$0$
BB vs. fold	$(\frac{1}{2})(1) + (\frac{1}{2})(1) = \$1$

To illustrate these computations, suppose player 1 chooses BP and player 2 calls. Then with probability $\frac{1}{2}$, heads is tossed. Then player 1 bets, is called, and wins \$2 from player 2. With probability $\frac{1}{2}$, tails is tossed. In this case, player 1 passes and pays player 2 \$1. Thus, if player 1 chooses BP and player 2 calls, player 1's expected reward is $(\frac{1}{2})(2) + (\frac{1}{2})(-1) = \$0.50$. For each line in Table 12, the first term in the expectation corresponds to heads being tossed, and the second term corresponds to tails being tossed.

Example 3 may be described as the two-person zero-sum game represented by the reward matrix in Table 13. Since max (row minimum) $= 0 <$ min (column maximum) $= \frac{1}{2}$, this game does not have a saddle point. Observe that player 1 would be unwise ever to choose the strategy PP, because (for each of player 2's strategies) player 1 could do better than PP by choosing either BP or BB. In general, a strategy i for a given player is **dominated** by a strategy i' if, for each of the other player's possible strategies, the given player does at least as well with strategy i' as she does with strategy i, and if for at least one of the other player's strategies, strategy i' is superior to strategy i. (This definition of a dominated strategy is similar to the definition of a dominated action given in Section 13.1). A player may eliminate all dominated strategies from consideration. We have just shown that for player 1, BP (or BB) dominates PP. Similarly, the reader should be able to show that player 1's PB strategy is dominated by BP (or BB). After eliminating the dominated strategies PP and PB, we are left with the game matrix shown in Table 14.

Table 13 Reward Matrix for Example 3	PLAYER 1	PLAYER 2		ROW MINIMUM
		Call	Fold	
	PP	-1	-1	-1
	PB	$-\frac{3}{2}$	0	$-\frac{3}{2}$
	BP	$\frac{1}{2}$	0	0
	BB	0	1	0
	COLUMN MAXIMUM	$\frac{1}{2}$	1	

As with Odds and Evens, this game has no saddle point, and we proceed with a graphical solution. Let

$$x_1 = \text{probability that player 1 chooses BP}$$
$$x_2 = 1 - x_1 = \text{probability that player 1 chooses BB}$$

Table 14	PLAYER 1	PLAYER 2		ROW MINIMUM
Reward Matrix for		Call	Fold	
Example 3 After	BP	$\frac{1}{2}$	0	0
Dominated Strategies	BB	0	1	0
Have Been				
Eliminated	COLUMN MAXIMUM	$\frac{1}{2}$	1	

$$y_1 = \text{probability that player 2 chooses call}$$

$$y_2 = 1 - y_1 = \text{probability that player 2 chooses fold}$$

To determine the optimal strategy for player 1, observe that for any value of x_1, player 1's expected reward against calling is

$$(\tfrac{1}{2})(x_1) + 0(1 - x_1) = \frac{x_1}{2}$$

which is line segment AB in Figure 3. Against folding, player 1's expected reward is

$$0(x_1) + 1(1 - x_1) = 1 - x_1$$

which is line segment CD in Figure 3. Since player 2 is assumed to know the value of x_1, player 1's expected reward (as a function of x_1) is given by the piecewise linear curve AED in Figure 3. Thus, to maximize her expected reward, player 1 should choose the value of x_1 corresponding to point E, which solves $x_1/2 = 1 - x_1$, or $x_1 = \frac{2}{3}$. Then $x_2 = 1 - \frac{2}{3} = \frac{1}{3}$, and player 1's expected reward against either of player 2's strategies is $\frac{x_1}{2}$ (or $1 - x_1$) = $\frac{1}{3}$.

How should player 2 choose y_1? (Remember, $y_2 = 1 - y_1$.) For a given value of y_1, suppose player 1 chooses BP. Then player 1's expected reward is

$$(\tfrac{1}{2})(y_1) + 0(1 - y_1) = \frac{y_1}{2}$$

Figure 3
How Player 1
Chooses Optimal
Strategy in
Example 3

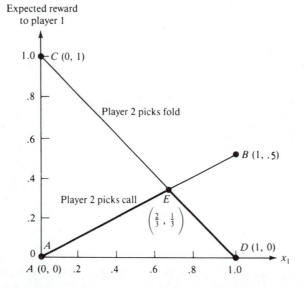

which is line segment AB in Figure 4. For a given value of y_1, suppose player 1 chooses BB. Then player 1's expected reward is

$$0(y_1) + 1(1 - y_1) = 1 - y_1$$

which is line segment CD in Figure 4. Thus, for a given value of y_1, player 1 will choose a strategy that causes player 1's expected reward to be given by the piecewise linear curve CEB in Figure 4. Knowing this, player 2 should choose the value of y_1 corresponding to point E in Figure 4. The value of y_1 at point E is the solution to $\frac{y_1}{2} = 1 - y_1$, or $y_1 = \frac{2}{3}$ (and $y_2 = \frac{1}{3}$). The reader should check that no matter what player 1 does, player 2's mixed strategy $(\frac{2}{3}, \frac{1}{3})$ ensures that player 1 earns an expected reward of $\frac{1}{3}$.

Figure 4
How Player 2
Chooses Optimal
Strategy in
Example 3

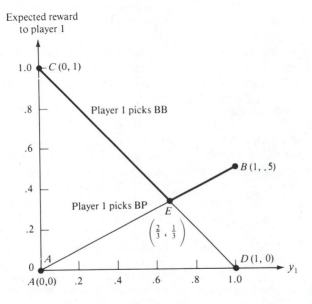

In summary, the value of the game is $\frac{1}{3}$ to player 1, the optimal mixed strategy for player 1 is $(\frac{2}{3}, \frac{1}{3})$, and the optimal strategy for player 2 is also $(\frac{2}{3}, \frac{1}{3})$. ◆

R E M A R K S

1. Observe that player 1 should bet $\frac{1}{3}$ of the time that she has a losing coin. Thus, our simple model indicates that player 1's optimal strategy includes bluffing.

2. In Problem 4 at the end of this section, it will be shown that if player 1 deviates from her optimal strategy, player 2 can hold player 1 to an expected reward that is less than the value ($\frac{1}{3}$) of the game. Similarly, Problem 5 will show that if player 2 deviates from her optimal strategy, player 1 can earn an expected reward in excess of the value ($\frac{1}{3}$) of the game.

3. Although we have only applied the graphical method to games in which each player (after dominated strategies have been eliminated) has only two strategies, the graphical approach can be used to solve two-person zero-sum games in which only one player has two strategies (games in which the reward matrix is $2 \times n$ or $m \times 2$). We choose, however, to solve all non-2×2 two-person games by the linear programming method outlined in the next section.

♦ PROBLEMS

GROUP A

1. Find the value and the optimal strategies for the two-person zero-sum game in Table 15.

Table 15

1	2	3
2	0	3

2. Player 1 writes an integer between 1 and 20 on a slip of paper. Without showing this slip of paper to player 2, player 1 tells player 2 what he has written. Player 1 may lie or tell the truth. Player 2 must then guess whether or not player 1 has told the truth. If caught in a lie, player 1 must pay player 2 $10; if falsely accused of lying, player 1 collects $5 from player 2. If player 1 tells the truth and player 2 guesses that player 1 has told the truth, then player 1 must pay $1 to player 2. If player 1 lies and player 2 does not guess that player 1 has lied, player 1 wins $5 from player 2. Determine the value of this game and each player's optimal strategy.

3. Find the value and optimal strategies for the two-person zero-sum game in Table 16.

Table 16

2	1	3
4	3	2

4. For Example 3, show that if player 1 deviates from her optimal strategy, then player 2 can ensure that player 1 earns an expected reward that is less than the value ($\frac{1}{3}$) of the game.

5. For Example 3, show that if player 2 deviates from her optimal strategy, then player 1 can ensure that player 1 earns an expected reward that is more than the value ($\frac{1}{3}$) of the game.

6. Two competing firms must simultaneously determine how much of a product to produce. The total profit earned by the two firms is always $1000. If firm 1's production level is low and firm 2's is also low, firm 1 earns a profit of $500; if firm 1's level is low and 2's is high, firm 1's profit is $400. If firm 1's production level is high and so is firm 2's, then firm 1's profit is $600, but if firm 1's level is high while firm 2's level is low, then firm 1's profit is only $300. Find the value and optimal strategies for this constant-sum game.

GROUP B

7. State University is about to play Ivy College for the state tennis championship. The State team has two players (A and B), and the Ivy team has three players (X, Y, and Z). The following facts are known about the players' relative abilities: X will always beat B; Y will always beat A; A will always beat Z. In any other match, each player has a $\frac{1}{2}$ chance of winning. Before State plays Ivy, the State coach must determine who will play first singles and who will play second singles. The Ivy coach (after choosing which two players will play singles) must also determine who will play first singles and second singles. Assume that each coach wants to maximize the expected number of singles matches won by the team. Use game theory to determine optimal strategies for each coach and the value of the game to each team.

15-3   LINEAR PROGRAMMING AND ZERO-SUM GAMES

Linear programming can be used to find the value and optimal strategies (for the row and column players) for any two-person zero-sum game. To illustrate the main ideas, we consider the well-known game Stone, Paper, Scissors.

E X A M P L E
4

Stone, Paper, Scissors Each of two players simultaneously utters one of the three words *stone*, *paper*, or *scissors*. If both players utter the same word, the game is a draw. Otherwise, one player wins $1 from the other player according to the following: Scissors defeats (cuts) paper, paper defeats (covers) stone, and stone defeats (breaks) scissors. Find the value and optimal strategies for this two-person zero-sum game. The solution is given later in this section.

◆

The reward matrix is shown in Table 17. Observe that no strategies are dominated and that the game does not have a saddle point. To determine optimal mixed strategies for the row and the column player, define

$$x_1 = \text{probability that row player chooses stone}$$
$$x_2 = \text{probability that row player chooses paper}$$
$$x_3 = \text{probability that row player chooses scissors}$$
$$y_1 = \text{probability that column player chooses stone}$$
$$y_2 = \text{probability that column player chooses paper}$$
$$y_3 = \text{probability that column player chooses scissors}$$

Table 17 Reward Matrix for Stone, Paper, Scissors	ROW PLAYER	COLUMN PLAYER			ROW MINIMUM
		Stone	Paper	Scissors	
	Stone	0	-1	$+1$	-1
	Paper	$+1$	0	-1	-1
	Scissors	-1	$+1$	0	-1
	COLUMN MAXIMUM	$+1$	$+1$	$+1$	

THE ROW PLAYER'S LP

If the row player chooses the mixed strategy (x_1, x_2, x_3), then her expected reward against each of the column player's strategies is as shown in Table 18. Suppose the row player chooses the mixed strategy (x_1, x_2, x_3). By the basic assumption, the column player will choose a strategy that makes the row player's expected reward equal to $\min(x_2 - x_3, -x_1 + x_3, x_1 - x_2)$. Then the row player should choose (x_1, x_2, x_3) to make $\min(x_2 - x_3, -x_1 + x_3, x_1 - x_2)$ as *large* as possible. To obtain an LP formulation (called the row player's LP) that will yield the row player's optimal strategy, observe that for any values of x_1, x_2, and x_3, $\min(x_2 - x_3, -x_1 + x_3, x_1 - x_2)$ is just the largest number (call it v) that is simultaneously less than or equal to $x_2 - x_3$, $-x_1 + x_3$, and $x_1 - x_2$. After noting that x_1, x_2, and x_3 must satisfy $x_1 \geq 0$, $x_2 \geq 0$, $x_3 \geq 0$, and $x_1 + x_2 + x_3 = 1$, we see that the row player's optimal strategy can be found by solving the following LP:

$$\max z = v$$
$$\text{s.t.} \quad v \leq x_2 - x_3 \qquad \text{(Stone constraint)}$$
$$v \leq -x_1 + x_3 \qquad \text{(Paper constraint)}$$
$$v \leq x_1 - x_2 \qquad \text{(Scissors constraint)}$$
$$x_1 + x_2 + x_3 = 1$$
$$x_1, x_2, x_3 \geq 0; \ v \text{ urs}$$

(2)

Table 18	COLUMN PLAYER CHOOSES	ROW PLAYER'S EXPECTED REWARD IF ROW PLAYER CHOOSES (x_1, x_2, x_3)
Expected Reward to Row Player in Stone, Paper, Scissors	Stone	$x_2 - x_3$
	Paper	$-x_1 + x_3$
	Scissors	$x_1 - x_2$

Note that there is a constraint in (2) for each of the column player's strategies. The value of v in the optimal solution to (2) is the row player's *floor*, because no matter what strategy (pure or mixed) is chosen by the column player, the row player is sure to receive an expected reward of at least v.

THE COLUMN PLAYER'S LP

How should the column player choose an optimal mixed strategy (y_1, y_2, y_3)? Suppose the column player has chosen the mixed strategy (y_1, y_2, y_3). For each of the row player's strategies, we may compute the row player's expected reward if the column player chooses (y_1, y_2, y_3) (see Table 19). Since the row player is assumed to know (y_1, y_2, y_3), the row player will choose a strategy to ensure that she obtains an expected reward of $\max(-y_2 + y_3, y_1 - y_3, -y_1 + y_2)$. Thus, the column player should choose (y_1, y_2, y_3) to make $\max(-y_2 + y_3, y_1 - y_3, -y_1 + y_2)$ as *small* as possible. To obtain an LP formulation that will yield the column player's optimal strategies, observe that for any choice of (y_1, y_2, y_3), $\max(-y_2 + y_3, y_1 - y_3, -y_1 + y_2)$ will equal the smallest number that is simultaneously greater than or equal to $-y_2 + y_3$, $y_1 - y_3$, and $-y_1 + y_2$ (call this number w). Also note that for (y_1, y_2, y_3) to be a mixed strategy, (y_1, y_2, y_3) must satisfy $y_1 + y_2 + y_3 = 1$, $y_1 \geq 0$, $y_2 \geq 0$, and $y_3 \geq 0$. Thus, the column player may find her optimal strategy by solving the following LP:

$$\min z = w$$
$$\text{s.t.} \quad w \geq -y_2 + y_3 \qquad \text{(Stone constraint)}$$
$$w \geq y_1 - y_3 \qquad \text{(Paper constraint)}$$
$$w \geq -y_1 + y_2 \qquad \text{(Scissors constraint)} \tag{3}$$
$$y_1 + y_2 + y_3 = 1$$
$$y_1, y_2, y_3 \geq 0; \ w \text{ urs}$$

Observe that (3) contains a constraint corresponding to each of the row player's strategies. Also, the optimal objective function w for (3) is a *ceiling* on the column player's expected losses (or the row player's expected reward), because by choosing a mixed strategy (y_1, y_2, y_3) that solves (3), the column player can ensure that her expected losses will be (against any of the row player's strategies) at most w.

Table 19	ROW PLAYER CHOOSES	ROW PLAYER'S EXPECTED REWARD IF COLUMN PLAYER CHOOSES (y_1, y_2, y_3)
Expected Reward to Row Player in Stone, Paper, Scissors	Stone	$-y_2 + y_3$
	Paper	$y_1 - y_3$
	Scissors	$-y_1 + y_2$

RELATION BETWEEN THE ROW AND THE COLUMN PLAYERS' LPs

It is easy to show that the column player's LP is the dual of the row player's LP. Begin by rewriting the row player's LP (2) as

$$
\begin{aligned}
\max z = v \\
\text{s.t.} \quad -x_2 + x_3 + v &\leq 0 \\
x_1 \quad\quad - x_3 + v &\leq 0 \\
-x_1 + x_2 \quad\quad + v &\leq 0 \\
x_1 + x_2 + x_3 \quad\quad &= 1 \\
x_1, x_2, x_3 \geq 0; \, v \text{ urs}
\end{aligned}
\tag{4}
$$

Let the dual variables for the constraints in (4) be y_1, y_2, y_3, and w, respectively. We can now show that the dual of the row player's LP is the column player's LP. As in Section 6.5, we read the row player's LP across in Table 20 and find the dual of the row player's LP by reading down. Recall that the dual constraint corresponding to the variable v will be an equality constraint (because v is urs), and the dual variable w corresponding to the primal constraint $x_1 + x_2 + x_3 = 1$ will be urs (because $x_1 + x_2 + x_3 = 1$ is an equality constraint). Reading down in Table 20, we find the dual of the row player's LP (4) to be

$$
\begin{aligned}
\min z = w \\
\text{s.t.} \quad y_2 - y_3 + w &\geq 0 \\
-y_1 \quad\quad + y_3 + w &\geq 0 \\
y_1 - y_2 \quad\quad + w &\geq 0 \\
y_1 + y_2 + y_3 \quad\quad &= 1 \\
y_1, y_2, y_3 \geq 0; \, w \text{ urs}
\end{aligned}
$$

After transposing all terms involving y_1, y_2, and y_3 in the first three constraints to the right-hand side, we see that the last LP is the same as the column player's LP (3). Thus, the dual of the row player's LP is the column player's LP. (Of course, the dual of the column player's LP would be the row player's LP.)

It is easy to show that both the row player's LP (2) and the column players LP (3) have an optimal solution (that is, neither LP can be infeasible or unbounded). Then the Dual Theorem of Section 6.7 implies that v, the optimal objective function value for the row player's LP, and w, the optimal objective function value for the column player's LP,

Table 20 Dual or Row Player's LP	MIN	MAX				
		x_1	x_2	x_3	v	
y_1	$(y_1 \geq 0)$	0	-1	1	1	≤ 0
y_2	$(y_2 \geq 0)$	1	0	-1	1	≤ 0
y_3	$(y_3 \geq 0)$	-1	1	0	1	≤ 0
w	(urs)	1	1	1	0	$= 1$
		≥ 0	≥ 0	≥ 0	$= 1$	

are equal. Thus, the row player's floor equals the column player's ceiling. This result is often known as the **Minimax Theorem**. We call the common value of v and w the **value** of the game to the row player. As in Sections 15.1 and 15.2, the row player can (by playing an optimal strategy) guarantee that her expected reward will at least equal the value of the game. Similarly, the column player can (by playing an optimal strategy) guarantee that her expected losses will not exceed the value of the game. It can also be shown (see Problem 6 at the end of this section) that the optimal strategies obtained via linear programming represent a stable equilibrium, because neither player can improve her situation by a unilateral change in strategy.

For the Stone, Paper, Scissors game, the optimal solution to the row player's LP (2) is $w = 0$, $x_1 = \frac{1}{3}$, $x_2 = \frac{1}{3}$, $x_3 = \frac{1}{3}$, and the optimal solution to the column player's LP (3) is $v = 0$, $y_1 = \frac{1}{3}$, $y_2 = \frac{1}{3}$, $y_3 = \frac{1}{3}$. Note that the first solution is feasible in (2), and the second solution is feasible in (3). Since each solution yields an objective function value of zero, Lemma 2 in Chapter 6 shows that $x_1 = \frac{1}{3}$, $x_2 = \frac{1}{3}$, $x_3 = \frac{1}{3}$ is optimal for the row player's LP, and $y_1 = \frac{1}{3}$, $y_2 = \frac{1}{3}$, $y_3 = \frac{1}{3}$ is optimal for the column player's LP.

The complementary slackness theory of linear programming (discussed in Section 6.10) could have been used to find the optimal strategies and value for Stone, Paper, Scissors (as well as other games). Before showing how, we state the row and the column players' LPs for a general two-person zero-sum game.

Consider a two-person zero-sum game with the reward matrix shown in Table 21. The reasoning used to derive (2) and (3) yields the following LPs:

$$\max z = v$$

Row Player's LP

$$
\begin{aligned}
\text{s.t.} \quad & v \le a_{11}x_1 + a_{21}x_2 + \cdots + a_{m1}x_m && \text{(Column 1 constraint)} \\
& v \le a_{12}x_1 + a_{22}x_2 + \cdots + a_{m2}x_m && \text{(Column 2 constraint)} \\
& \qquad\qquad\qquad \vdots \\
& v \le a_{1n}x_1 + a_{2n}x_2 + \cdots + a_{mn}x_m && \text{(Column } n \text{ constraint)} \\
& x_1 + x_2 + \cdots + x_m = 1 \\
& x_i \ge 0 \quad (i = 1, 2, \ldots, m); \ v \text{ urs}
\end{aligned}
$$

(5)

$$\min z = w$$

Column Player's LP

$$
\begin{aligned}
\text{s.t.} \quad & w \ge a_{11}y_1 + a_{12}y_2 + \cdots + a_{1n}y_n && \text{(Row 1 constraint)} \\
& w \ge a_{21}y_1 + a_{22}y_2 + \cdots + a_{2n}y_n && \text{(Row 2 constraint)} \\
& \qquad\qquad\qquad \vdots \\
& w \ge a_{m1}y_1 + a_{m2}y_2 + \cdots + a_{mn}y_n && \text{(Row } m \text{ constraint)} \\
& y_1 + y_2 + \cdots + y_n = 1 \\
& y_j \ge 0 \quad (j = 1, 2, \ldots, n); \ w \text{ urs}
\end{aligned}
$$

(6)

Table 21 A General Two-Person Zero-Sum Game	ROW PLAYER	COLUMN PLAYER		
		Strategy 1	Strategy 2 $\cdots$	Strategy n
	Strategy 1	a_{11}	a_{12} $\cdots$	a_{1n}
	Strategy 2	a_{21}	a_{22} $\cdots$	a_{2n}
	$\vdots$	$\vdots$	$\vdots$	$\vdots$
	Strategy m	a_{m1}	a_{m2} $\cdots$	a_{mn}

In (5), x_i = probability that the row player chooses row i, and in (6), y_j = probability that the column player chooses column j. The jth constraint ($j = 1, 2, \ldots, n$) in the row player's LP implies that the row player's expected reward against column j must at least equal v; otherwise, the column player could hold the row player's expected reward below v by choosing column j. Similarly, the ith ($i = 1, 2, \ldots, m$) constraint in the column player's LP implies that if the row player chooses row i, then the column player's expected losses cannot exceed w; if this were not the case, the row player could obtain an expected reward that exceeded w by choosing row i.

HOW TO SOLVE THE ROW AND THE COLUMN PLAYERS' LPs

It is easy to show (see Problem 9 at the end of this section) that if we add a constant c to each entry in a game's reward matrix, the optimal strategies for each player remain unchanged, but the optimal values of w and v (and thus the value of the game) are both increased by c. Let A be the original reward matrix. Suppose we add $c = $ |most negative entry in reward matrix| to each element of A. Call the new reward matrix A'. A' is a two-person constant-sum game. (Why?) Let $\bar{v}$ and $\bar{w}$ be the optimal objective function values for the row and the column players' LPs for A, and let $\bar{v}'$ and $\bar{w}'$ denote the same quantities for the game A'. Since A' will have no negative rewards, $\bar{v}' \geq 0$ and $\bar{w}' \geq 0$ must hold. Thus, when solving the row and the column players' LPs for A', we may assume that $v' \geq 0$ and $w' \geq 0$ and ignore v urs and w urs. Then the optimal strategies for A' will be identical to the optimal strategies for A, and the value of $A' = $ (value of A) + c, or value of $A = $ (value of A') − c.

In solving small games by hand, it is often helpful to use the constraint $x_1 + x_2 + \cdots + x_m = 1$ to eliminate one of the x_i's from the row player's LP and to use the constraint $y_1 + y_2 + \cdots + y_n = 1$ to eliminate one of the y_i's from the column player's LP. Then (as illustrated by Examples 5 and 6, which follow), the complementary slackness results of Section 6.10 can often be used to solve the row and the column players' LPs simultaneously.

Solution

Example 4—Stone, Paper, Scissors The most negative element in the Stone, Paper, Scissors reward matrix is -1. Therefore, we add $|-1| = 1$ to each element of the reward matrix. This yields the constant-sum game shown in Table 22. The row player's LP is as follows:

$$\max v'$$
$$\text{s.t.} \quad v' \leq x_1 + 2x_2$$
$$v' \leq x_2 + 2x_3$$
$$v' \leq 2x_1 + x_3$$
$$x_1 + x_2 + x_3 = 1$$
$$x_1, x_2, x_3, v' \geq 0$$

Table 22
Modified Reward
Matrix for Stone,
Paper, Scissors

ROW PLAYER	COLUMN PLAYER		
	Stone	Paper	Scissors
Stone	1	0	2
Paper	2	1	0
Scissors	0	2	1

Substituting $x_3 = 1 - x_1 - x_2$ transforms the row player's LP into the following LP:

$$\max v'$$

s.t. (a) $v' - x_1 - 2x_2 \leq 0$ (y_1, or column 1, constraint)

(b) $v' + 2x_1 + x_2 \leq 2$ (y_2, or column 2, constraint)   **(7)**

(c) $v' - x_1 + x_2 \leq 1$ (y_3, or column 3, constraint)

$x_1, x_2, v' \geq 0$

The column player's LP is as follows:

$$\min w'$$

s.t. $w' \geq y_1 + 2y_3$ (x_1, or row 1, constraint)

$w' \geq 2y_1 + y_2$ (x_2, or row 2, constraint)

$w' \geq 2y_2 + y_3$ (x_3, or row 3, constraint)

$y_1 + y_2 + y_3 = 1$

$y_1, y_2, y_3, w' \geq 0$

Substituting $y_3 = 1 - y_1 - y_2$ transforms the column player's LP into the following LP:

$$\min w'$$

s.t. (a) $w' + y_1 + 2y_2 \geq 2$ (x_1, or row 1, constraint)

(b) $w' - 2y_1 - y_2 \geq 0$ (x_2, or row 2, constraint)   **(8)**

(c) $w' + y_1 - y_2 \geq 1$ (x_3, or row 3, constraint)

$y_1, y_2, w' \geq 0$

Since Stone, Paper, Scissors appears to be a fair game, we might conjecture that $v = w = 0$. This would make $v' = w' = 0 + 1 = 1$. Let's try this and conjecture that constraints (7a) and (7b) are binding in the optimal solution to (7). If this is the case, solving (7a) and (7b) simultaneously (with $v' = 1$) yields $x_1 = x_2 = \frac{1}{3}$. Since $x_1 = \frac{1}{3}$, $x_2 = \frac{1}{3}$, $w' = 1$ satisfies (7c) with equality, we have obtained a feasible solution to the row player's LP. Suppose this solution is optimal for the row player's LP. Then by complementary slackness (see Section 6.10), $x_1 > 0$ and $x_2 > 0$ would imply that the first two dual constraints in (8) must be binding in the optimal solution to (8). Solving (8a) and (8b) simultaneously (using $w' = 1$) yields $y_1 = y_2 = \frac{1}{3}$, $w' = 1$. This solution is dual feasible. Thus, we have found a primal feasible and a dual feasible solution, both of which have the same objective function value and are optimal. Thus:

1. The value of Stone, Paper, Scissors is $v' - 1 = 0$.
2. The optimal strategy for the row player is $(\frac{1}{3}, \frac{1}{3}, \frac{1}{3})$.
3. The optimal strategy for the column player is $(\frac{1}{3}, \frac{1}{3}, \frac{1}{3})$.

◆

R E M A R K S   Suppose we have not been able to conjecture that $v' = w' = 1$. Then the row player's LP (7) would have had three unknowns (x_1, x_2, and v'), and we might have hoped that the optimal solution to (7) occurred where all three constraints (7a)–(7c) were binding. Solving (7a)–(7c) simultaneously yields $v' = 1$, $x_1 = x_2 = \frac{1}{3}$, $x_3 = 1 - \frac{2}{3} = \frac{1}{3}$. If this is the optimal solution to the row player's LP, then complementary slackness implies that constraints (8a)–(8c) must all be binding. Simultaneously solving (8a)–(8c) yields $w' = 1$, $y_1 = y_2 = \frac{1}{3}$, $y_3 = 1 - \frac{2}{3} = \frac{1}{3}$. Again we have obtained a primal feasible point and a dual feasible point having the same objective function value, and both solutions must be optimal.

E X A M P L E
5

Find the value and optimal strategies for the two-person zero-sum game in Table 23.

Table 23
Reward Matrix for
Example 5

	COLUMN PLAYER			ROW MINIMUM
ROW PLAYER	30	40	36	30
	60	10	36	10
COLUMN MAXIMUM	60	40	36	

Solution

The game has no saddle point and no dominated strategies, so we set up the row and the column players' LPs. Since all entries in the reward matrix are nonnegative, we are sure that the value of the game is nonnegative. The row and the column players' LPs for this game are as follows:

$$\max v$$
$$\text{s.t.} \quad v \leq 30x_1 + 60x_2$$
$$v \leq 40x_1 + 10x_2$$
$$v \leq 36x_1 + 36x_2 \tag{9}$$
$$x_1 + x_2 = 1$$
$$x_1, x_2, v \geq 0$$

Substituting $x_2 = 1 - x_1$ into the row player's LP yields

$$\max v$$
$$\text{s.t.} \quad \text{(a)} \quad v + 30x_1 \leq 60 \quad (y_1, \text{ or column 1, constraint})$$
$$\text{(b)} \quad v - 30x_1 \leq 10 \quad (y_2, \text{ or column 2, constraint}) \tag{9'}$$
$$\text{(c)} \quad v \qquad\quad \leq 36 \quad (y_3, \text{ or column 3, constraint})$$
$$x_1, v \geq 0$$

Similarly, we find

$$\min w$$
$$\text{s.t.} \quad \text{(a)} \quad w \geq 30y_1 + 40y_2 + 36y_3$$
$$\text{(b)} \quad w \geq 60y_1 + 10y_2 + 36y_3 \tag{10}$$
$$y_1 + y_2 + y_3 = 1$$
$$y_1, y_2, y_3, w \geq 0$$

and substituting $y_3 = 1 - y_1 - y_2$ into the column player's LP yields

$$\min w$$

s.t. (a) $w + 6y_1 - 4y_2 \geq 36$ (x_1, or row 1, constraint)

(b) $w - 24y_1 + 26y_2 \geq 36$ (x_2, or row 2, constraint) (10′)

$$y_1, y_2, w \geq 0$$

When using complementary slackness to solve an LP and its dual, it is usually easier to first examine the LP with the smaller number of variables. Thus, we first examine (9′). We assume that (9′a) and (9′b) are both binding in the optimal solution to the row player's LP. Then $v = 35$, $x_1 = \frac{5}{6}$, $x_2 = \frac{1}{6}$ would be the optimal solution to the row player's LP. This solution is feasible in the row player's LP and makes constraint (9′c) nonbinding. If this solution is optimal for the row player's LP, then complementary slackness implies that (10′a) and (10′b) must both be binding and $y_3 = 0$ must hold. This implies that $y_1 + y_2 = 1$, or $y_2 = 1 - y_1$. Trying $w = 35$ and substituting $y_2 = 1 - y_1$ in (10′a) and (10′b) yields $y_1 = y_2 = \frac{1}{2}$. Thus, we have found a feasible solution ($v = 35$, $x_1 = \frac{5}{6}$, $x_2 = \frac{1}{6}$) to the row player's LP and a feasible solution ($w = 35$, $y_1 = \frac{1}{2}$, $y_2 = \frac{1}{2}$, $y_3 = 0$) to the column player's LP, both of which have the same objective function value. We have therefore found the value of the game and the optimal strategy for each player.

In closing, we note that while the column player's third strategy is not dominated by column 1 or column 2, the column player should still never choose column 3. Why?

◆

In the following two-person zero-sum game, the complementary slackness method does not yield optimal strategies.

E X A M P L E 6

Two players in the game of Two-Finger Morra simultaneously put out either 1 or 2 fingers. Each player must also announce the number of fingers that he believes his opponent has put out. If neither or both players correctly guess the number of fingers put out by the opponent, the game is a draw. Otherwise, the player who guesses correctly wins (from the other player) the sum (in dollars) of the fingers put out by the two players. If we let (i, j) represent the strategy of putting out i fingers and guessing that the opponent has put out j fingers, the appropriate reward matrix is as shown in Table 24.

Solution

Again, this game has no saddle point and no dominated strategies. To ensure that the value of the game is nonnegative, we add 4 to each entry in the reward matrix. This yields

Table 24	ROW PLAYER	COLUMN PLAYER				ROW MINIMUM
Reward Matrix for		(1, 1)	(1, 2)	(2, 1)	(2, 2)	
Two-Finger Morra	(1, 1)	0	2	−3	0	−3
	(1, 2)	−2	0	0	3	−2
	(2, 1)	3	0	0	−4	−4
	(2, 2)	0	−3	4	0	−3
	COLUMN MAXIMUM	3	2	4	3	

the reward matrix in Table 25. For this game, the row player's and the column player's LPs are as follows (recall that the value for the original Two-Finger Morra game $= v' - 4$):

$$\max v'$$

Row Player's LP

$$\text{s.t.} \quad \text{(a)} \quad v' \le 4x_1 + 2x_2 + 7x_3 + 4(1 - x_1 - x_2 - x_3) \quad (y_1 \text{ constraint})$$
$$\text{(b)} \quad v' \le 6x_1 + 4x_2 + 4x_3 + (1 - x_1 - x_2 - x_3) \quad (y_2 \text{ constraint})$$
$$\text{(c)} \quad v' \le x_1 + 4x_2 + 4x_3 + 8(1 - x_1 - x_2 - x_3) \quad (y_3 \text{ constraint})$$
$$\text{(d)} \quad v' \le 4x_1 + 7x_2 + 4(1 - x_1 - x_2 - x_3) \quad (y_4 \text{ constraint})$$
$$x_1, x_2, x_3, v' \ge 0$$

$$\min w'$$

Column Player's LP

$$\text{s.t.} \quad \text{(a)} \quad w' \ge 4y_1 + 6y_2 + y_3 + 4(1 - y_1 - y_2 - y_3) \quad (x_1 \text{ constraint})$$
$$\text{(b)} \quad w' \ge 2y_1 + 4y_2 + 4y_3 + 7(1 - y_1 - y_2 - y_3) \quad (x_2 \text{ constraint})$$
$$\text{(c)} \quad w' \ge 7y_1 + 4y_2 + 4y_3 \quad (x_3 \text{ constraint})$$
$$\text{(d)} \quad w' \ge 4y_1 + y_2 + 8y_3 + 4(1 - y_1 - y_2 - y_3) \quad (x_4 \text{ constraint})$$
$$y_1, y_2, y_3, w' \ge 0$$

Table 25 Transformed Reward Matrix for Two-Finger Morra	ROW PLAYER	COLUMN PLAYER			
		(1, 1)	(1, 2)	(2, 1)	(2, 2)
	(1, 1)	4	6	1	4
	(1, 2)	2	4	4	7
	(2, 1)	7	4	4	0
	(2, 2)	4	1	8	4

An attempt to use complementary slackness to solve the row and the column players' LPs fails, because the optimal strategies for both players are degenerate. (Try complementary slackness and see what happens.) Using LINDO (or the simplex) to solve the LPs yields the following solutions: For the row player's problem, $v' = 4$, $x_1 = 0$, $x_2 = \frac{3}{5}$, $x_3 = \frac{2}{5}$, $x_4 = 0$ or $v' = 4$, $x_1 = 0$, $x_2 = \frac{4}{7}$, $x_3 = \frac{3}{7}$, $x_4 = 0$; for the column player's problem, $w' = 4$, $y_1 = 0$, $y_2 = \frac{3}{5}$, $y_3 = \frac{2}{5}$, $y_4 = 0$ or $w' = 4$, $y_1 = 0$, $y_2 = \frac{4}{7}$, $y_3 = \frac{3}{7}$, $y_4 = 0$. Since each player's LP has alternative optimal solutions, each player actually has an infinite number of optimal strategies. For example, for any c satisfying $0 \le c \le 1$, $x_1 = 0$, $x_2 = \frac{3c}{5} + \frac{4(1-c)}{7}$, $x_3 = \frac{2c}{5} + \frac{3(1-c)}{7}$, $x_4 = 0$ would be an optimal strategy for the row player. Of course, the value (to the row player) of the original Two-Finger Morra Game is $v' - 4 = 0$.

◆

R E M A R K S   **1.** Observe that both players have the same optimal strategies. (This is no accident; see Problem 5 at the end of this section.)

2. Also note that if each player utilizes her optimal strategy, neither player will ever lose or win any money. This illustrates the fact that if both players follow the basic assumption of two-person zero-sum game theory, conservative play will generally result, because the assumption is analogous to the minimax decision criterion of Section 13.1.

3. Finally, we see that if each player uses her optimal strategy, then a player never guesses the same number of fingers she puts out. This fact is explained in Table 26.

Now suppose the row player chooses the optimal strategy $(0, \frac{3}{5}, \frac{2}{5}, 0)$. Then the column player only breaks even by playing $(1, 1)$ and loses an average of $\frac{1}{5}$ per play when she plays $(2, 2)$. Similarly, if the row player chooses the optimal strategy $(0, \frac{4}{7}, \frac{3}{7}, 0)$, the column player breaks even with $(2, 2)$ and loses an average of $\frac{1}{7}$ per play when she plays $(1, 1)$. Thus, putting out the same number of fingers as you guess cannot have a positive expected reward against the other player's optimal strategy.

Table 26 Expected Reward to Row Player	ROW PLAYS OPTIMAL STRATEGY	EXPECTED REWARD TO ROW	
		Column plays $(1, 1)$	Column Plays $(2, 2)$
	$(0, \frac{3}{5}, \frac{2}{5}, 0)$	$-2(\frac{3}{5}) + 3(\frac{2}{5}) = 0$	$3(\frac{3}{5}) - 4(\frac{2}{5}) = \frac{1}{5}$
	$(0, \frac{4}{7}, \frac{3}{7}, 0)$	$-2(\frac{4}{7}) + 3(\frac{3}{7}) = \frac{1}{7}$	$3(\frac{4}{7}) - 4(\frac{3}{7}) = 0$

The preceding discussion explains why the seemingly reasonable strategy $(\frac{1}{4}, \frac{1}{4}, \frac{1}{4}, \frac{1}{4})$ is not optimal for either player. For instance, if the column player chooses the strategy $(\frac{1}{4}, \frac{1}{4}, \frac{1}{4}, \frac{1}{4})$ and the row player plays the optimal strategy $(0, \frac{3}{5}, \frac{2}{5}, 0)$, the row player's expected reward may be computed as in Table 27. In this situation, the expected reward received by the row player is $-2(\frac{3}{20}) + 0(\frac{3}{20}) + 0(\frac{3}{20}) + 3(\frac{3}{20}) + 3(\frac{2}{20}) + 0(\frac{2}{20}) + 0(\frac{2}{20}) - 4(\frac{2}{20}) = \frac{1}{20}$. Another way to see this: Each time the column player chooses $(1, 1)$, $(1, 2)$, or $(2, 1)$, the players break even, but on the plays for which the column player chooses $(2, 2)$ the row player wins an average of $\frac{1}{5}$ unit. Thus, the row player's expected reward is $(\frac{1}{4})(\frac{1}{5}) = \frac{1}{20}$ unit.

Table 27 Expected Reward to Row Player If Column Player Plays $(\frac{1}{4}, \frac{1}{4}, \frac{1}{4}, \frac{1}{4})$	ROW CHOOSES	COLUMN CHOOSES	REWARD TO ROW	PROBABILITY OF OCCURRENCE
	$(1, 2)$	$(1, 1)$	-2	$(\frac{3}{5})(\frac{1}{4}) = \frac{3}{20}$
	$(1, 2)$	$(1, 2)$	0	$(\frac{3}{5})(\frac{1}{4}) = \frac{3}{20}$
	$(1, 2)$	$(2, 1)$	0	$(\frac{3}{5})(\frac{1}{4}) = \frac{3}{20}$
	$(1, 2)$	$(2, 2)$	3	$(\frac{3}{5})(\frac{1}{4}) = \frac{3}{20}$
	$(2, 1)$	$(1, 1)$	3	$(\frac{2}{5})(\frac{1}{4}) = \frac{2}{20}$
	$(2, 1)$	$(1, 2)$	0	$(\frac{2}{5})(\frac{1}{4}) = \frac{2}{20}$
	$(2, 1)$	$(2, 1)$	0	$(\frac{2}{5})(\frac{1}{4}) = \frac{2}{20}$
	$(2, 1)$	$(2, 2)$	-4	$(\frac{2}{5})(\frac{1}{4}) = \frac{2}{20}$

4. In Odds and Evens and in Stone, Paper, Scissors, the optimal strategies may have been intuitively obvious, but the game of Two-Finger Morra shows that game theory can often yield subtle insights into how a two-person zero-sum game should be played.

SUMMARY OF HOW TO SOLVE A TWO-PERSON ZERO-SUM GAME

To close our discussion of two-person zero-sum games, we summarize a procedure that can be used to find the value and optimal strategies for any two-person zero-sum (or constant-sum) game.

Step 1 Check for a saddle point. If the game has no saddle point, go on to Step 2.

Step 2 Eliminate any of the row player's dominated strategies. Looking at the reduced matrix (dominated rows crossed out), eliminate any of the column player's dominated strategies. Now eliminate any of the row player's dominated strategies. Continue in this fashion until no more dominated strategies can be found. Now proceed to Step 3.

Step 3 If the game matrix is now 2×2, solve the game graphically. Otherwise, solve the game by using the linear programming methods of this section.

◆ PROBLEMS

GROUP A

1. A soldier can hide in one of five foxholes $(1, 2, 3, 4,$ or $5)$ (see Figure 5). A gunner has a single shot and may fire at any of the four spots A, B, C, or D. A shot will kill a soldier if the soldier is in a foxhole adjacent to the spot where the shot was fired. For example, a shot fired at spot B will kill the soldier if he is in foxhole 2 or 3, while a shot fired at spot D will kill the soldier if he is in foxhole 4 or 5. Suppose the gunner receives a reward of 1 if the soldier is killed and a reward of zero if the soldier survives the shot.

Figure 5

① A ② B ③ C ④ D ⑤

(a) Assuming this to be a zero-sum game, construct the reward matrix.

(b) Find and eliminate all dominated strategies.

(c) We are given that an optimal strategy for the soldier is to hide $\frac{1}{3}$ of the time in foxholes 1, 3, and 5. We are also told that for the gunner, an optimal strategy is to shoot $\frac{1}{3}$ of the time at A, $\frac{1}{3}$ of the time at D, and $\frac{1}{3}$ of the time at B or C. Determine the value of the game to the gunner.

(d) Suppose the soldier chooses the following nonoptimal strategy: $\frac{1}{2}$ of the time, hide in foxhole 1; $\frac{1}{4}$ of the time, hide in foxhole 3; and $\frac{1}{4}$ of the time, hide in foxhole 5. Find a strategy for the gunner that ensures that the gunner's expected reward will exceed the value of the game.

(e) Write down each player's LP and verify that the strategies given in part (c) are optimal strategies.

2. Find each player's optimal strategy and the value of the two-person zero-sum game in Table 28.

Table 28

4	5	1	4
2	1	6	3
1	0	0	2

3. Find each player's optimal strategy and the value of the two-person zero-sum game in Table 29.

Table 29

2	4	6
3	1	5

4. Two armies are advancing on two cities. The first army is commanded by General Custard and has four regiments; the second army is commanded by General Peabody and has three regiments. At each city, the army that sends more regiments to the city captures both the city and the opposing army's regiments. If both armies send the same number of regiments to a city, the battle at the city is a draw. Each army scores 1 point per city captured and 1 point per captured regiment. Assume that each army wishes to maximize the difference between its reward and its opponent's reward. Formulate this situation as a two-person zero-sum game and solve for the value of the game and each player's optimal strategies.

GROUP B

5. A two-person zero-sum game with an $n \times n$ reward matrix A is a **symmetric** game if $A = -A^T$.

(a) Explain why a game having $A = -A^T$ is called a symmetric game.

(b) Show that a symmetric game must have a value of zero.

(c) Show that if $(\bar{x}_1, \bar{x}_2, \ldots, \bar{x}_n)$ is an optimal strategy for the row player, then $(\bar{x}_1, \bar{x}_2, \ldots, \bar{x}_n)$ is also an optimal strategy for the column player.

(d) What examples discussed in this chapter are symmetric games? How could the results of this problem make it easier to solve for the value and optimal strategies of a symmetric game?

6. For a two-person zero-sum game with an $m \times n$ reward matrix, let $\bar{x} = (\bar{x}_1, \bar{x}_2, \ldots, \bar{x}_m)$ be a solution to the row player's LP and $\bar{y} = (\bar{y}_1, \bar{y}_2, \ldots, \bar{y}_n)$ be a solution to the column player's LP. Show that if the row player departs from his optimal strategy, he cannot increase his expected reward against $\bar{y}$.

7. Interpret the complementary slackness conditions for the row and the column players' LPs.

8. Wivco has observed the daily production and the daily variable production costs of widgets at the New York City plant. The data in Table 30 have been collected. Wivco believes that daily production and daily variable production costs are related as follows: For some numbers a and b,

Table 30

DAY	PRODUCTION	VARIABLE PRODUCTION COST
1	4000	$9,000
2	6000	$12,000
3	7000	$14,000
4	1000	$5,000
5	3000	$8,000

Daily production cost $= a + b$(daily production)

Wivco wants to find estimates of a and b ($\hat{a}$ and $\hat{b}$) that minimize the maximum error (in absolute value) incurred in estimating daily production costs. For example, if Wivco chooses $\hat{a} = 3$ and $\hat{b} = 2$, the predicted daily costs are as shown in Table 31. In this case, the maximum error would be $3000. Formulate an LP that can be used to find the optimal estimates $\hat{a}$ and $\hat{b}$.

Table 31

DAY	PREDICTED COST	ABSOLUTE ERROR
1	$11,000	$2000
2	$15,000	$3000
3	$17,000	$3000
4	$5,000	$0
5	$9,000	$1000

9. Suppose we add a constant c to every element in a reward matrix A. Call the new game matrix A'. Show that A and A' have the same optimal strategies and that value of $A' = $ (value of A) $+ c$.

15-4   TWO-PERSON NON-CONSTANT-SUM GAMES

Most game-theoretic models of business situations are not constant-sum games, because it is unusual for business competitors to be in total conflict.

In this section, we briefly discuss the analysis of two-person non-constant-sum games in which cooperation between the players is not allowed. We begin with a discussion of the famous Prisoner's Dilemma.

E X A M P L E **7**

Prisoner's Dilemma   Two prisoners who escaped and participated in a robbery have been recaptured and are awaiting trial for their new crime. Although they are both guilty, the Gotham City district attorney is not sure he has enough evidence to convict them. In order to entice them to testify against each other, the D.A. tells each prisoner the following: "If only one of you confesses and testifies against your partner, the person who confesses will go free while the person who does not confess will surely be convicted and given a 20-year jail sentence. If both of you confess, you will both be convicted and sent to prison for 5 years. Finally, if neither of you confesses, I can convict you both of a misdemeanor and you will each get 1 year in prison. What should each prisoner do?

Solution   If we assume that the prisoners cannot communicate with each other, the strategies and rewards for each are as shown in Table 32. The first number in each cell of this matrix

Table 32	PRISONER 1	PRISONER 2	
Reward Matrix for Prisoner's Dilemma		Confess	Don't confess
	Confess	$(-5, -5)$	$(0, -20)$
	Don't confess	$(-20, 0)$	$(-1, -1)$

is the reward (negative, since years in prison is undesirable) to prisoner 1, and the second matrix in each cell is the reward to prisoner 2. It is important to note that the sum of the rewards in each cell varies from a high of $-2 (-1 - 1)$ to a low of $-20 (-20 + 0)$. Thus, this is not a constant-sum two-player game.

Suppose each prisoner seeks to eliminate any dominated strategies from consideration. For each prisoner, the "confess" strategy dominates the "don't confess" strategy. If each prisoner follows his undominated ("confess") strategy, however, each prisoner will spend 5 years in jail. On the other hand, if each prisoner chooses the dominated "don't confess' strategy, each prisoner will spend only 1 year in prison. Thus, if each prisoner chooses his dominated strategy, both are better off than if each prisoner chooses his undominated strategy.

♦

> **DEFINITION**
>
> As in a two-person zero-sum game, a choice of strategy by each player (prisoner) is an **equilibrium point** if neither player can benefit from a unilateral change in strategy.

Thus, $(-5, -5)$ is an equilibrium point, because if either prisoner changes his strategy, his reward decreases (from -5 to -20). Clearly, however, each prisoner is better off at the point $(-1, -1)$. To see that the outcome $(-1, -1)$ may not occur, observe that $(-1, -1)$ is not an equilibrium point, because if we are currently at the outcome $(-1, -1)$, either prisoner can increase his reward (from -1 to 0) by changing his strategy from "don't confess" to "confess" (that is, each prisoner can benefit from double-crossing his opponent). This illustrates an important aspect of the Prisoner's Dilemma type of game: If the players are cooperating (if each prisoner chooses "don't confess"), each player can gain by double-crossing his opponent (assuming his opponent's strategy remains unchanged). If both players double-cross each other, however, they will both be worse off than if they had both chosen their cooperative strategy. This anomaly cannot occur in a two-person constant-sum game. (Why not?)

More formally, a Prisoner's Dilemma game may be described as in Table 33, where

NC = noncooperative action

C = cooperative action

P = punishment for not cooperating

S = payoff to person who is double-crossed

R = reward for cooperating if both players cooperate

T = temptation for double-crossing opponent

In a Prisoner's Dilemma game, (P, P) is an equilibrium point. This requires $P > S$. For (R, R) not to be an equilibrium point requires $T > R$. (This gives each player a

Table 33 A General Prisoner's Dilemma Reward Matrix	PLAYER 1	PLAYER 2	
		NC	*C*
	NC	(P, P)	(T, S)
	C	(S, T)	(R, R)

temptation to double-cross his opponent). The game is reasonable only if $R > P$. Thus, for Table 33 to represent a Prisoner's Dilemma game, we require that $T > R > P > S$. The Prisoner's Dilemma game is of interest because it explains why two adversaries often fail to cooperate with each other. This is illustrated by Examples 8 and 9.

E X A M P L E 8

Hot Dog King and Hot Dog Chef, competing restaurants, are attempting to determine their advertising budgets for next year. The two restaurants will have combined sales of $240 million and can spend either $6 million or $10 million on advertising. If one restaurant spends more money than the other, the restaurant that spends more money will have sales of $190 million. If both companies spend the same amount on advertising, they will have equal sales. Each dollar of sales yields 10¢ of profit. Suppose each restaurant is interested in maximizing (contribution of sales to profit) − (advertising costs). Find an equilibrium point for this game.

Table 34 Reward Matrix for Advertising Game	HOT DOG KING	HOT DOG CHEF	
		Spend $10 million	Spend $6 million
	Spend $10 million	$(2, 2)$	$(9, -1)$
	Spend $6 million	$(-1, 9)$	$(6, 6)$

Solution

The appropriate reward matrix is shown in Table 34. If we identify spending $10 million on advertising as the noncooperative action and spending $6 million as the cooperative action, then $(2, 2)$ (corresponding to heavy advertising by both restaurants) is an equilibrium point. Although both restaurants are better off at $(6, 6)$ than at $(2, 2)$, $(6, 6)$ is unstable because either restaurant may gain by changing its strategy. Thus, in order to protect its market share, each restaurant must spend heavily on advertising. ◆

E X A M P L E 9

The USA and the USSR are engaged in an arms race in which each nation is assumed to have two possible strategies: develop a new missile or maintain the status quo. The reward matrix is assumed to be as shown in Table 35. This reward matrix is based on the assumption that if only one nation develops a new missile, the nation with the new missile will conquer the other nation. In this case, the conquering nation earns a reward of 20 units and the conquered nation loses 100 units. It is also assumed that the cost of developing a new missile is 10 units. Identify an equilibrium point for this game.

Solution

Identifying "develop" as the noncooperative action and "maintain" as the cooperative action, we see that $(-10, -10)$ (both nations choosing their noncooperative action) is

Table 35	USA	USSR	
Reward Matrix for Arms Race Game		Develop new missile	Maintain status quo
	Develop new missile	$(-10, -10)$	$(10, -100)$
	Maintain status quo	$(-100, 10)$	$(0, 0)$

an equilibrium point. Although $(0, 0)$ leaves both nations better off than $(-10, -10)$, we see that in this situation, each nation can gain from a double-cross. Thus, $(0, 0)$ is not stable. This example shows how maintaining the balance of power may lead to an arms race.   ♦

The following two-person non-constant-sum game is not a Prisoner's Dilemma game.

E X A M P L E 10   Angry Max drives toward James Bound on a deserted road. Each person has two strategies: swerve or don't swerve. The reward matrix in Table 36 needs no explanation! Find the equilibrium point(s) for this game.

Table 36	ANGRY MAX	JAMES BOUND	
Reward Matrix for Swerve Game		Swerve	Don't swerve
	Swerve	$(0, 0)$	$(-5, 5)$
	Don't swerve	$(5, -5)$	$(-100, -100)$

Solution   For both $(5, -5)$ and $(-5, 5)$, neither player can gain by a unilateral change in strategy. Thus, $(5, -5)$ and $(-5, 5)$ are both equilibrium points.   ♦

Like constant-sum games, a non-constant-sum game may fail to have an equilibrium point in pure strategies. It can be shown that if mixed strategies are allowed, then in any two-person non-constant-sum game, each player has an equilibrium strategy (in that if one player plays her equilibrium strategy, the other player cannot benefit by deviating from her equilibrium strategy) (see Owen (1982, p. 127)). For example, consider the two-person non-constant-sum game in Table 37. For this game, the reader should verify that there is no equilibrium in pure strategies and also that each player's choosing the mixed strategy $(\frac{1}{2}, \frac{1}{2})$ is an equilibrium, because neither player can benefit from a

Table 37	PLAYER 1	PLAYER 2	
A Game with No Equilibrium in Pure Statistics		Strategy 1	Strategy 2
	Strategy 1	$(2, -1)$	$(-2, 1)$
	Strategy 2	$(-2, 1)$	$(2, -1)$

unilateral change in strategy (see Problem 4 at the end of this section). Owen (1982, Chapter 7) discusses two-person non-constant-sum games in which the players are allowed to cooperate.

◆ PROBLEMS

GROUP A

1. Find an equilibrium point (if one exists in pure strategies) for the two-person non-constant-sum game in Table 38.

Table 38

(9, −1)	(−2, −3)
(8, 7)	(−9, 11)

2. Find an equilibrium point in pure strategies (if any exists) for the two-person non-constant-sum game in Table 39.

Table 39

(9, 9)	(−10, 10)
(10, −10)	(−1, 1)

3. The New York City Council is ready to vote on two bills that authorize the construction of new roads in Manhattan and Brooklyn. If the two boroughs join forces, they can pass both bills, but neither borough by itself has enough power to pass a bill. If a bill is passed, it will cost the taxpayers of each borough $1 million, but if roads are built in a borough, the benefits to the borough are estimated to be $10 million. The council votes on both bills simultaneously, and each councilperson must vote on the bills without knowing how anybody else will vote. Assuming that each borough supports its own bill, determine whether this game has any equilibrium points. Is this game analogous to the Prisoner's Dilemma? Explain why or why not.

GROUP B

4. Given that each player's goal is to maximize her expected reward, show that for the game in Table 40, each player's choosing the mixed strategy $(\frac{1}{2}, \frac{1}{2})$ is an equilibrium point.

Table 40

PLAYER 1	PLAYER 2	
	Strategy 1	Strategy 2
Strategy 1	(2, −1)	(−2, 1)
Strategy 2	(−2, 1)	(2, −1)

5.[†] A Japanese electronics company and an American electronics company are both considering working on developing a superconductor. If both companies work on the superconductor, they will have to share the market, and each company will lose $10 billion. If only one company works on the superconductor, that company will earn $100 billion in profits. Of course, if neither company works on the superconductor, each company earns profits of $0.
(a) Formulate this situation as a two-person non-constant-sum game. Does the game have any equilibrium points?
(b) Now suppose the Japanese government offers the Japanese electronics company a $15 billion subsidy to work on the superconductor. Formulate the reward matrix for this game. Does this game have any equilibrium points?
(c) Businessmen have often said that a protectionist attitude toward trade can increase exports, but economists have usually argued that a protectionist attitude toward trade will reduce exports. Whose viewpoint does this problem support?

†Based on "Protectionism Gets Clever" (1988).

<u>**15-5**</u>   **INTRODUCTION TO *n*-PERSON GAME THEORY**

In many competitive situations, there are more than two competitors. With this in mind, we now turn our attention to games with three or more players. Let $N = \{1, 2, \ldots, n\}$ be the set of players. Any game with n players is an **n-person game**. For our purposes, an n-person game is specified by the game's characteristic function.

> **DEFINITION** ● For each subset S of N, the **characteristic function** v of a game gives the amount $v(S)$ that the members of S can be sure of receiving if they act together and form a coalition.

Thus, $v(S)$ can be determined by calculating the amount that members of S can get without any help from players who are not in S.

E X A M P L E
11

The Drug Game   Joe Willie has invented a new drug. Joe cannot manufacture the drug himself, but he can sell the drug's formula to company 2 or company 3. The lucky company will split a $1 million profit with Joe Willie. Find the characteristic function for this game.

Solution

Letting Joe Willie be player 1, company 2 be player 2, and company 3 be player 3, we find the characteristic function for this game to be:

$$v(\{\ \}) = v(\{1\}) = v(\{2\}) = v(\{3\}) = v(\{2,3\}) = 0$$
$$v(\{1,2\}) = v(\{1,3\}) = v(\{1,2,3\}) = \$1,000,000$$

E X A M P L E
12

The Garbage Game   Each of four property owners has one bag of garbage and must dump his or her bag of garbage on somebody's property. If b bags of garbage are dumped on the coalition of property owners, the coalition receives a reward of $-b$. Find the characteristic function for this game.

Solution

The best that the members of any coalition can do is to dump all their garbage on the property of owners who are not in S. Thus, the characteristic function for the garbage game ($|S|$ is the number of players in S) is given by

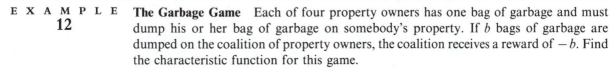

$$v(\{S\}) = -(4 - |S|) \qquad (\text{if } |S| < 4) \qquad \textbf{(11)}$$
$$v(\{1, 2, 3, 4\}) = -4 \qquad (\text{if } |S| = 4) \qquad \textbf{(11.1)}$$

Eq. (11.1) follows, because if all players are in S, they must dump their garbage on members of S.

E X A M P L E
13

The Land Development Game   Player 1 owns a piece of land and values the land at $10,000. Player 2 is a subdivider who can develop the land and increase its worth to $20,000. Player 3 is a subdivider who can develop the land and increase its worth to \$30,000. There are no other prospective buyers. Find the characteristic function for this game.

Solution   Note that any coalition that does not contain player 1 has a worth or value of \$0. Any other coalition has a value equal to the maximum value that a member of the coalition places on the piece of land. Thus, we obtain the following characteristic function:

$$v(\{1\}) = \$10,000, \qquad v(\{ \}) = v(\{2\}) = v(\{3\}) = \$0, \qquad v(\{1,2\}) = \$20,000,$$
$$v(\{1,3\}) = \$30,000, \qquad v(\{2,3\}) = \$0, \qquad v(\{1,2,3\}) = \$30,000$$

◆

Consider any two subsets of sets A and B such that A and B have no players in common ($A \cap B = \emptyset$). Then for each of our examples (and any n-person game), the characteristic function must satisfy the following inequality:

$$v(A \cup B) \geq v(A) + v(B) \tag{12}$$

This property of the characteristic function is called **superadditivity**. Eq. (12) is reasonable, because if the players in $A \cup B$ band together, one of their options (but not their only option) is to let the players in A fend for themselves and let the players in B fend for themselves. This would result in the coalition receiving an amount $v(A) + v(B)$. Thus, $v(A \cup B)$ must be at least as large as $v(A) + v(B)$.

There are many solution concepts for n-person games. A solution concept should indicate the reward that each player will receive. More formally, let $\mathbf{x} = \{x_1, x_2, \ldots, x_n\}$ be a vector such that player i receives a reward x_i. We call such a vector a **reward vector**. A reward vector $\mathbf{x} = (x_1, x_2, \ldots, x_n)$ is not a reasonable candidate for a solution unless $\mathbf{x}$ satisfies

$$v(N) = \sum_{i=1}^{i=n} x_i \qquad \text{(Group rationality)} \tag{13}$$

$$x_i \geq v(\{i\}) \qquad \text{(for each } i \in N) \qquad \text{(Individual rationality)} \tag{14}$$

If $\mathbf{x}$ satisfies both (13) and (14), we say that $\mathbf{x}$ is an **imputation**. Eq. (13) states that any reasonable reward vector must give all the players an amount that equals the amount that can be attained by the supercoalition consisting of all players. Eq. (14) implies that player i must receive a reward at least as large as what he can get for himself ($v\{i\}$).

To illustrate the idea of an imputation, consider the payoff vectors for Example 13, shown in Table 41. Any solution concept for n-person games chooses some subset of the set of imputations (possibly empty) as the solution to the n-person game. In Sections 15.6 and 15.7, we discuss two solution concepts, the core and the Shapley value. See Owen (1982) for a discussion of other solution concepts for n-person games. The problems involving n-person game theory are at the end of Section 15.7.

Table 41
Examples of
Imputation

$\mathbf{x}$	IS $\mathbf{x}$ AN IMPUTATION?
(\$10,000, \$10,000, \$10,000)	Yes
(\$5000, \$2000, \$5000)	No, $x_1 < v(\{1\})$, so (14) is violated
(\$12,000, \$19,000, $-$\$1000)	No, (14) is violated
(\$11,000, \$11,000, \$11,000)	No, (13) is violated

15-6   THE CORE OF AN n-PERSON GAME

An important solution concept for an n-person game is the core. Before defining this, we must define the concept of **domination**. Given an imputation $\mathbf{x} = (x_1, x_2, \ldots, x_n)$, we say that the imputation $\mathbf{y} = (y_1, y_2, \ldots, y_n)$ *dominates* $\mathbf{x}$ through a coalition S (written $\mathbf{y} > {}^S\mathbf{x}$) if

$$\sum_{i \in S} y_i \leq v(S) \qquad \text{and for all } i \in S, \quad y_i > x_i \tag{15}$$

If $\mathbf{y} > {}^S\mathbf{x}$, then both the following must be true:

1. Each member of S prefers $\mathbf{y}$ to $\mathbf{x}$.

2. Since $\sum_{i \in S} y_i \leq v(S)$, the members of S can attain the rewards given by $\mathbf{y}$.

Thus, if $\mathbf{y} > {}^S\mathbf{x}$, then $\mathbf{x}$ should not be considered a possible solution to the game, because the players in S can object to the rewards given by $\mathbf{x}$ and enforce their objection by banding together and thereby receiving the rewards given by $\mathbf{y}$ (since members of S can surely receive an amount equal to $v(S)$).

The founders of game theory, John von Neumann and Oskar Morgenstern, argued that a reasonable solution concept for an n-person game was the set of all undominated imputations.

| DEFINITION | The **core** of an n-person game is the set of all undominated imputations. |

Examples 14 and 15 illustrate the concept of domination.

E X A M P L E 14

Consider a three-person game with the following characteristic function:

$$v(\{\ \}) = v(\{1\}) = v(\{2\}) = v(\{3\}) = 0$$
$$v(\{1,2\}) = 0.1, \qquad v(\{1,3\}) = 0.2, \qquad v(\{2,3\}) = 0.2, \qquad v(\{1,2,3\}) = 1$$

Let $\mathbf{x} = (0.05, 0.90, 0.05)$ and $\mathbf{y} = (0.10, 0.80, 0.10)$. Show that $\mathbf{y} > {}^{\{1,3\}}\mathbf{x}$.

Solution

First note that both $\mathbf{x}$ and $\mathbf{y}$ are imputations. Next observe that with the imputation $\mathbf{y}$, players 1 and 3 both receive more than they receive with $\mathbf{x}$. Also, $\mathbf{y}$ gives the players in $\{1,3\}$ a total of $0.10 + 0.10 = 0.20$. Since 0.20 does not exceed $v(\{1,3\}) = 0.20$, it is reasonable to assume that players 1 and 3 can band together and receive a total reward of 0.20. Thus, players 1 and 3 will never allow the rewards given by $\mathbf{x}$ to occur.   ◆

E X A M P L E 15

For the land development game (Example 13), let $\mathbf{x} = (\$19{,}000, \$1000, \$10{,}000)$ and $\mathbf{y} = (\$19{,}800, \$100, \$10{,}100)$. Show that $\mathbf{y} > {}^{\{1,3\}}\mathbf{x}$.

Solution

We need only observe that players 1 and 3 both receive more from $\mathbf{y}$ than they receive from $\mathbf{x}$, and the total received by players 1 and 3 from $\mathbf{y}$ ($\$29{,}900$) does not exceed $v(\{1,3\})$. If $\mathbf{x}$ were proposed as a solution to the land development game, player 1 would sell the land to player 3 and **y** (or some other imputation that dominates **x**) would result. The important point is that **x** cannot occur, because players 1 and 3 will never allow **x** to occur.

◆

We are now ready to show how to determine the core of an *n*-person game, for which Theorem 1 is often useful.

THEOREM 1	An imputation $\mathbf{x} = \{x_1, x_2, \ldots, x_n)$ is in the core of an *n*-person game if and only if for each subset S of N, $$\sum_{i \in S} x_i \geq v(S)$$

Theorem 1 states that an imputation **x** is in the core (that **x** is dominated) if and only if for every coalition S, the total of the rewards received by the players in S (according to **x**) is at least as large as $v(S)$.

To illustrate the use of Theorem 1, we find the core of the three games discussed in Section 15.5.

EXAMPLE 11

The Drug Game (Continued)   Find the core of the drug game.

Solution   For this game, $\mathbf{x} = (x_1, x_2, x_3)$ will be an imputation if and only if

$$x_1 \geq 0 \tag{16}$$

$$x_2 \geq 0 \tag{17}$$

$$x_3 \geq 0 \tag{18}$$

$$x_1 + x_2 + x_3 = \$1,000,000 \tag{19}$$

Theorem 1 shows that $\mathbf{x} = (x_1, x_2, x_3)$ will be in the core if and only if x_1, x_2, and x_3 satisfy (16)–(19) and the following inequalities:

$$x_1 + x_2 \geq \$1,000,000 \tag{20}$$

$$x_1 + x_3 \geq \$1,000,000 \tag{21}$$

$$x_2 + x_3 \geq \$0 \tag{22}$$

$$x_1 + x_2 + x_3 \geq \$1,000,000 \tag{23}$$

To determine the core, note that if $\mathbf{x} = (x_1, x_2, x_3)$ is in the core, then x_1, x_2, and x_3 must satisfy the inequality generated by adding together inequalities (20)–(22). Adding together (20)–(22) yields $2(x_1 + x_2 + x_3) \geq \$2,000,000$, or

$$x_1 + x_2 + x_3 \geq \$1,000,000 \tag{24}$$

By (19), $x_1 + x_2 + x_3 = \$1,000,000$. Thus, (20)–(22) must all be binding.[†] Simultaneously solving (20)–(22) as equalities yields $x_1 = \$1,000,000$, $x_2 = \$0$, $x_3 = \$0$.

[†]If (20), (21), or (22) were nonbinding, then for any point in the core, the sum of (20)–(22) would also be nonbinding. Since we know that (24) must be binding, this implies that for any point in the core, (20), (21), and (22) must all be binding.

A quick check shows that ($1,000,000, $0, $0) does satisfy (16)–(23). In summary, the core of this game is the imputation ($1,000,000, $0, $0). Thus, the core emphasizes the importance of player 1.

◆

R E M A R K S   **1.** In Section 15.7, we show that for this game, an alternative solution concept, the Shapley value, gives player 1 less than $1,000,000 and gives both player 2 and player 3 some money.

2. For the drug game, if we choose an imputation that is not in the core, we can show how it is dominated. Consider the imputation $\mathbf{x}$ = ($900,000, $50,000, $50,000). If we let $\mathbf{y}$ = ($925,000, $75,000, $0), then $\mathbf{y} >$ [1,2]$\mathbf{x}$.

E X A M P L E   **The Garbage Game (Continued)**   Determine the core of the garbage game.
12

Solution   Note that $\mathbf{x} = (x_1, x_2, x_3, x_4)$ will be an imputation if and only if x_1, x_2, x_3, and x_4 satisfy the following inequalities:

$$x_1 \geq -3 \tag{25}$$
$$x_2 \geq -3 \tag{26}$$
$$x_3 \geq -3 \tag{27}$$
$$x_4 \geq -3 \tag{28}$$
$$x_1 + x_2 + x_3 + x_4 = -4 \tag{29}$$

Applying Theorem 1 to all three-player coalitions, we find that for $\mathbf{x} = \{x_1, x_2, x_3, x_4\}$ to be in the core, it is necessary that x_1, x_2, x_3, and x_4 satisfy the following inequalities:

$$x_1 + x_2 + x_3 \geq -1 \tag{30}$$
$$x_1 + x_2 + x_4 \geq -1 \tag{31}$$
$$x_1 + x_3 + x_4 \geq -1 \tag{32}$$
$$x_2 + x_3 + x_4 \geq -1 \tag{33}$$

We now show that no imputation $\mathbf{x} = (x_1, x_2, x_3, x_4)$ can satisfy (30)–(33) and that the garbage game has an empty core. Consider an imputation $\mathbf{x} = (x_1, x_2, x_3, x_4)$. If $\mathbf{x}$ is to be in the core of the garbage game, $\mathbf{x}$ must satisfy the inequality generated by adding together (30)–(33):

$$3(x_1 + x_2 + x_3 + x_4) \geq -4 \tag{34}$$

Eq. (29) implies that any imputation $\mathbf{x} = (x_1, x_2, x_3, x_4)$ must satisfy $x_1 + x_2 + x_3 + x_4 = -4$. Thus, (34) cannot hold. This means that no imputation $\mathbf{x} = (x_1, x_2, x_3, x_4)$ can satisfy (30)–(33) and the core of the garbage game is empty.

To understand why the garbage game has an empty core, consider the imputation $\mathbf{x} = (-2, -1, -1, 0)$, which treats players 1 and 2 unfairly. By joining together, players 1 and 2 could ensure that the imputation $\mathbf{y} = (-1.5, -0.5, -1, -1)$ occurred. Thus, $\mathbf{y} >$ [1,2]$\mathbf{x}$. In a similar fashion, any imputation can be dominated by another imputation. We note that for a two-player version of the garbage game, the core consists of the imputation $(-1, -1)$, and for $n > 2$, the n-player garbage game has an empty core (see Problems 4 and 5 at the end of Section 15.7).

◆

E X A M P L E
13

Solution

The Land Development Game (Continued)   Find the core of the land development game.

For the land development game, any imputation $\mathbf{x} = (x_1, x_2, x_3)$ must satisfy

$$x_1 \geq \$10,000 \tag{35}$$

$$x_2 \geq \$0 \tag{36}$$

$$x_3 \geq \$0 \tag{37}$$

$$x_1 + x_2 + x_3 = \$30,000 \tag{38}$$

An imputation $\mathbf{x} = (x_1, x_2, x_3)$ is in the core if and only if it satisfies the following inequalities:

$$x_1 + x_2 \geq \$20,000 \tag{39}$$

$$x_1 + x_3 \geq \$30,000 \tag{40}$$

$$x_2 + x_3 \geq \$0 \tag{41}$$

$$x_1 + x_2 + x_3 \geq \$30,000 \tag{42}$$

Adding together (36) and (40), we find that if $\mathbf{x} = (x_1, x_2, x_3)$ is in the core, then $x_1, x_2,$ and x_3 must satisfy $x_1 + x_2 + x_3 \geq \$30,000$. From (38), $x_1 + x_2 + x_3 = \$30,000$. Thus, (36) and (40) must be binding. This argument shows that for $\mathbf{x} = (x_1, x_2, x_3)$ to be in the core, x_1, x_2, and x_3 must satisfy

$$x_2 = \$0 \quad \text{and} \quad x_1 + x_3 = \$30,000 \tag{43}$$

Now (39) implies that

$$x_1 \geq \$20,000 \tag{44}$$

Thus, for $\mathbf{x} = (x_1, x_2, x_3)$ to be in the core, (43) and (44) must both be satisfied. Any vector in the core must also satisfy $x_3 \geq 0$ and $x_1 \leq \$30,000$, and any vector $\mathbf{x} = (x_1, x_2, x_3)$ satisfying (43), (44), $x_3 \geq \$0$, and $x_1 \leq \$30,000$ will be in the core of the land development game. Thus, if $\$20,000 \leq x_1 \leq \$30,000$, any vector of the form $(x_1, \$0, \$30,000 - x_1)$ will be in the core of the land development game. The interpretation of the core is as follows: Player 3 outbids player 2 and purchases the land from player 1 for a price x_1 ($\$20,000 \leq x_1 \leq \$30,000$). Then player 1 receives a reward of x_1 dollars, and player 3 receives a reward of $\$30,000 - x_1$. Player 2 is shut out and receives nothing. In this example, the core contains an infinite number of points.

The problems involving n-person game theory are at the end of Section 15.7.

15-7

THE SHAPLEY VALUE*

In Section 15.6, we found that the core of the drug game gave all benefits or rewards to the game's most important player (the inventor of the drug). Now we discuss an alternative solution concept for n-person games, the **Shapley value**, which in general gives more equitable solutions than the core does.[†]

*This section covers topics that can be omitted with no loss of continuity.
[†]See Owen (1982) for an excellent discussion of the Shapley value. See also Shapley (1953).

For any characteristic function, Lloyd Shapley showed there is a unique reward vector $\mathbf{x} = (x_1, x_2, \ldots, x_n)$ satisfying the following axioms:

Axiom 1 Relabeling of players interchanges the players' rewards. Suppose the Shapley value for a three-person game is $\mathbf{x} = (10, 15, 20)$. If we interchange the roles of player 1 and player 3 (for example, if originally $v(\{1\}) = 10$ and $v(\{3\}) = 15$, we would make $v(\{1\}) = 15$ and $v(\{3\}) = 10$), then the Shapley value for the new game would be $\mathbf{x} = (20, 15, 10)$.

Axiom 2 $\sum_{i=1}^{i=n} x_i = v(N)$. This is simply group rationality.

Axiom 3 If $v(S - \{i\}) = v(S)$ holds for all coalitions S, then the Shapley value has $x_i = 0$. If player i adds no value to any coalition, player i receives a reward of zero from the Shapley value.

Before stating Axiom 4, we define the sum of two n-person games. Let v and $\bar{v}$ be two characteristic functions for games with identical players. Define the game $(v + \bar{v})$ to be the game with the characteristic function $(v + \bar{v})$ given by $(v + \bar{v})(S) = v(S) + \bar{v}(S)$. For example, if $v(\{1, 2\}) = 10$ and $\bar{v}(\{1, 2\}) = -3$, then in the game $(v + \bar{v})$, the coalition $\{1, 2\}$ would have $(v + \bar{v})(\{1, 2\}) = 10 - 3 = 7$.

Axiom 4 Let $\mathbf{x}$ be the Shapley value vector for game v, and let $\mathbf{y}$ be the Shapley value vector for game $\bar{v}$. Then the Shapley value vector for the game $(v + \bar{v})$ is the vector $\mathbf{x} + \mathbf{y}$.

The validity of this axiom has often been questioned, because adding up rewards from two different games may be like adding up apples and oranges. If Axioms 1–4 are assumed to be valid, however, Shapley proved the remarkable result in Theorem 2.

THEOREM 2

Given any n-person game with characteristic function v, there is a unique reward vector $\mathbf{x} = (x_1, x_2, \ldots, x_n)$ satisfying Axioms 1–4. The reward of the ith player (x_i) is given by

$$x_i = \sum_{\substack{\text{all } S \text{ for which} \\ i \text{ is not in } S}} p_n(S)[v(S \cup \{i\}) - v(S)] \tag{45}$$

In (45),

$$p_n(S) = \frac{|S|!(n - |S| - 1)!}{n!} \tag{46}$$

where $|S|$ is the number of players in S, and for $n \geq 1$, $n! = n(n - 1) \cdots 2(1)$ $(0! = 1)$.

Although (45) seems complex, the equation has a simple interpretation. Suppose that players $1, 2, \ldots, n$ arrive in a random order. That is, any of the $n!$ permutations of $1, 2, \ldots, n$ has a $\frac{1}{n!}$ change of being the order in which the players arrive. For example, if $n = 3$, then there is a $\frac{1}{3}! = \frac{1}{6}$ probability that the players arrive in any one of the following sequences:

1, 2, 3	2, 3, 1
1, 3, 2	3, 1, 2
2, 1, 3	3, 2, 1

Suppose that when player i arrives, he finds that the players in the set S have already arrived. If player i forms a coalition with the players who are present when he arrives, player i adds $v(S \cup \{i\}) - v(S)$ to the coalition S. The probability that when player i arrives the players in the coalition S are present is $p_n(S)$. Then (45) implies that *player i's reward should be the expected amount that player i adds to the coalition made up of the players who are present when player i arrives.*

We now show that $p_n(S)$ (as given by (46)) is the probability that when player i arrives, the players in the subset S will be present. Observe that the number of permutations of $1, 2, \ldots, n$ that result in player i's arriving when the players in the coalition S are present is given by

$$\underbrace{|S|(|S| - 1)(|S| - 2) \cdots + (2)(1)}_{S \text{ arrives}} \quad \underbrace{(1)}_{i \text{ arrives}} \quad \underbrace{(n - |S| - 1)(n - |S| - 2) \cdots (2)(1)}_{\text{Players not in } S \cup \{i\} \text{ arrive}}$$

$$= |S|!(n - |S| - 1)!$$

Since there are a total of $n!$ permutations of $1, 2, \ldots, n$, the probability that player i will arrive and see the players in S is

$$\frac{|S|!(n - |S| - 1)!}{n!} = p_n(S)$$

We now compute the Shapley value for the drug game.

E X A M P L E 11

The Drug Game (Continued) Find the Shapley value for the drug game.

Solution To compute x_1, the reward that player 1 should receive, we list all coalitions S for which player 1 is not a member. For each of these coalitions we compute $v(S \cup \{i\}) - v(S)$ and $p_3(S)$ (see Table 42). Since player 1 adds (on the average)

$$(\tfrac{2}{6})(0) + (\tfrac{1}{6})(1,000,000) + (\tfrac{2}{6})(1,000,000) + (\tfrac{1}{6})(1,000,000) = \tfrac{\$4,000,000}{6}$$

the Shapley value concept recommends that player 1 receive a reward of $\frac{\$4,000,000}{6}$.

To compute the Shapley value for player 2, we require the information in Table 43.

Table 42	S	$p_3(S)$	$v(S \cup \{1\}) - v(S)$
Computation of Shapley Value for Player 1 (Joe Willie)	{ }	$\frac{2}{6}$	$0
	{2}	$\frac{1}{6}$	$1,000,000
	{2, 3}	$\frac{2}{6}$	$1,000,000
	{3}	$\frac{1}{6}$	$1,000,000

Table 43	S	$p_3(S)$	$v(S \cup \{2\}) - v(S)$
Computation of Shapley Value for Player 2	{ }	$\frac{2}{6}$	$0
	{1}	$\frac{1}{6}$	$1,000,000
	{3}	$\frac{1}{6}$	$0
	{1, 3}	$\frac{2}{6}$	$0

Thus, the Shapley value recommends a reward of

$$(\tfrac{1}{6})(1,000,000) = \tfrac{\$1,000,000}{6}$$

for player 2. Since the Shapley value must allocate a total of $v(\{1, 2, 3\}) = \$1,000,000$ to the players, the Shapley value will recommend that player 3 receive $\$1,000,000 - x_1 - x_2 = \tfrac{\$1,000,000}{6}$.

◆

R E M A R K S

1. Recall that the core of this game assigned \$1,000,000 to player 1 and no money to players 2 and 3. Thus, the Shapley value treats players 2 and 3 more fairly than the core. In general, the Shapley value provides more equitable solutions than the core.

2. For a game with few players, it may be easier to compute each player's Shapley value by using the fact that player i should receive the expected amount that she adds to the coalition present when she arrives. For Example 11, this method yields the computations in Table 44. Since each of the six orderings of the arrivals of the players is equally likely, we find that the Shapley value to each player is as follows:

$$x_1 = \frac{\$4,000,000}{6}, \qquad x_2 = \frac{\$1,000,000}{6}, \qquad x_3 = \frac{\$1,000,000}{6}$$

Table 44
Alternative Method for Determining Shapley Value

ORDER OF ARRIVAL	AMOUNT ADDED BY PLAYER'S ARRIVAL		
	Player 1	Player 2	Player 3
1, 2, 3	\$0	\$1,000,000	\$0
1, 3, 2	\$0	\$0	\$1,000,000
2, 1, 3	\$1,000,000	\$0	\$0
2, 3, 1	\$1,000,000	\$0	\$0
3, 1, 2	\$1,000,000	\$0	\$0
3, 2, 1	\$1,000,000	\$0	\$0

3. The Shapley value can be used as a measure of the power of individual members of a political or business organization. For example, the UN Security Council consists of five permanent members (who have veto power over any resolution) and ten nonpermanent members. For a resolution to pass the Security Council, it must receive at least nine votes, including the votes of all permanent members. Assigning a value of 1 to all coalitions that can pass a resolution and a value of zero to all coalitions that cannot pass a resolution defines a characteristic function. For this characteristic function, it can be shown that the Shapley value of each permanent member is 0.1963 and the Shapley value for each nonpermanent member is 0.001865, giving $5(0.1963) + 10(0.001865) = 1$. Thus, the Shapley value indicates that $5(0.1963) = 98.15\%$ of the power in the Security Council resides with the permanent members.

As a final application of the Shapley value, we discuss how it can be used to determine a pricing schedule for landing fees at an airport.

E X A M P L E 16

Suppose three types of planes (Piper Cubs, DC-10s, and 707s) use an airport. A Piper Cub requires a 100-yd runway, a DC-10 requires a 150-yd runway, and a 707 requires a 400-yd runway. Suppose the cost (in dollars) of maintaining a runway for one year is equal to the length of the runway. Since 707s land at the airport, the airport will have a 400-yd runway. For simplicity, suppose that each year only one plane of each type lands at the airport. How much of the $400 annual maintenance cost should be charged to each plane.

Solution

Let player 1 = Piper Cub, player 2 = DC-10, and player 3 = 707. We can now define a three player game in which the value to a coalition is the cost associated with the runway length needed to service the largest plane in the coalition. Thus, the characteristic function for this game (we list a cost as a negative revenue) would be

$$v(\{\ \}) = \$0, \qquad v(\{1\}) = -\$100, \qquad v(\{1,2\}) = v(\{2\}) = -\$150,$$
$$v(\{3\}) = v(\{2,3\}) = v(\{1,3\}) = v(\{1,2,3\}) = -\$400$$

To find the Shapley value (cost) to each player, we assume that the three planes land in a random order, and we determine how much cost (on the average) each plane adds to the cost incurred by the planes that are already present (see Table 45). The Shapley cost for each player is as follows:

$$\text{Player 1 cost} = (\tfrac{1}{6})(100 + 100) = \tfrac{\$200}{6}$$

$$\text{Player 2 cost} = (\tfrac{1}{6})(50 + 150 + 150) = \tfrac{\$350}{6}$$

$$\text{Player 3 cost} = (\tfrac{1}{6})(250 + 300 + 250 + 250 + 400 + 400) = \tfrac{\$1850}{6}$$

Table 45 Computation of Shapley Value for Airport Game	ORDER OF ARRIVAL	PROBABILITY OF ORDER	COST ADDED BY PLAYER'S ARRIVAL		
			Player 1	Player 2	Player 3
	1, 2, 3	$\frac{1}{6}$	$100	$50	$250
	1, 3, 2	$\frac{1}{6}$	$100	$0	$300
	2, 1, 3	$\frac{1}{6}$	$0	$150	$250
	2, 3, 1	$\frac{1}{6}$	$0	$150	$250
	3, 1, 2	$\frac{1}{6}$	$0	$0	$400
	3, 2, 1	$\frac{1}{6}$	$0	$0	$400

Thus, the Shapley value concept suggests that the Piper Cub pay $33.33, the DC-10 pay $58.33, and the 707 pay $308.33.

In general, even if more than one plane of each type lands, it has been shown that the Shapley value for the airport problem allocates runway operating cost as follows: All planes that use a portion of the runway should divide equally the cost of that portion of the runway (see Littlechild and Owen (1973)). Thus, all planes should cover the cost of the first 100 yd of runway, the DC-10s and 707s should pay for the next $150 - 100 = 50$ yd of runway, and the 707s should pay for the last $400 - 150 = 250$ yd of runway. If there were ten Piper Cub landings, five DC-10 landings, and two 707 landings, the Shapley value concept would recommend that each Piper Cub pay $\frac{100}{10+5+2} = \$5.88$ in landing fees, each DC-10 pay $\$5.88 + \frac{150-100}{5+2} = \$13.03$, and each 707 pay $\$13.03 + \frac{400-150}{2} = \$138.03$. ◆

◆ PROBLEMS

GROUP A

1. Consider the four-player game with the following characteristic function:

$$v(\{1,2,3\}) = v(\{1,2,4\}) = v(\{1,3,4\})$$
$$= v(\{2,3,4\}) = 75$$
$$v(\{1,2,3,4\}) = 100$$
$$v(\{3,4\}) = 60$$
$$v(S) = 0 \text{ for all other coalitions}$$

Show that this game has an empty core.

2. Show that if $v(\{3,4\})$ in Problem 1 were changed to 50, the game's core would consist of a single point.

3. The game of Odd Man Out is a three-player coin toss game in which each player must choose heads or tails. If all the players make the same choice, the house pays each player $1; otherwise, the odd man out pays each of the other players $1.
(a) Find the characteristic function for this game.
(b) Find the core of this game.
(c) Find the Shapley value for this game.

4. Show that for $n = 2$, the core of the garbage game is the imputation $(-1, -1)$.

5. Show that for $n > 2$, the n-player garbage game has an empty core.

6. For the four-player garbage game, find an imputation that dominates $(-1, -1, -1, -1)$.

7. The Gotham City Airport is 5000 ft long and costs $100,000 per year to maintain. Last year there were 2000 landings at the airport. Four types of planes landed. The length of runway required by each type of plane and the number of landings of each type are shown in Table 46. Assuming that the cost of operating a length of runway is proportional to the length of the runway, how much per landing should be paid by each type of plane?

Table 46

TYPE OF PLANE	NUMBER OF LANDINGS	LENGTH OF RUNWAY
Type 1	600	2000 ft
Type 2	700	3000 ft
Type 3	500	4000 ft
Type 4	200	5000 ft

8. Consider the following three-person game:

$$v(\{ \ \}) = 0, \qquad v(\{1\}) = 0.2,$$
$$v(\{2\}) = v(\{3\}) = 0, \qquad v(\{1,2\}) = 1.5,$$
$$v(\{1,3\}) = 1.6, \qquad v(\{2,3\}) = 1.8,$$
$$v(\{1,2,3\}) = 2$$

(a) Find the core of this game.
(b) Find the Shapley value for this game.
(c) Find an imputation dominating the imputation $(1, \frac{1}{2}, \frac{1}{2})$.

9. Howard Whose has left an estate of $200,000 to support his three ex-wives. Unfortunately, Howard's attorney has determined that each ex-wife needs the following amount of money to take care of Howard's children: wife 1—$100,000; wife 2—$200,000; wife 3—$300,000. Howard's attorney must determine how to divide the money among the three wives. He defines the value of a coalition S of ex-wives to be the maximum amount of money left for the ex-wives in S after all ex-wives not in S receive what they need. Using this definition, construct a characteristic function for this problem. Then determine the core and Shapley value for this game.

10. Indiana University leases WATTS lines and is charged according to the following rules: $400 per month for each of the first five lines; $300 per month for each of the next five lines; $100 per month for each additional line. The College of Arts and Sciences makes 150 calls per hour, the School of Business makes 120 calls per hour, and the rest of the university makes 30 calls per hour. Assume that each line can handle 30 calls per hour. Thus, the university will rent 10 WATTS lines. The university wants to determine how much each part of the university should pay for long-distance phone service.
(a) Set up a characteristic function representation of the problem.
(b) Use the Shapley value to allocate the university's long-distance phone costs.

11. Three doctors have banded together to form a joint practice: the Port Charles Trio. The overhead for the practice is $40,000 per year. Each doctor brings in annual revenues and incurs annual variable costs as follows: doctor 1—$155,000 in revenue, $40,000 in variable cost; doctor 2—$160,000 in revenue, $35,000 in variable cost; doctor 3—$140,000 in revenue, $38,000 in variable cost.

The Port Charles Trio wants to use game theory to determine how much each doctor should be paid. Determine the relevant characteristic function and show that the core of the game consists of an infinite number of points. Also determine the Shapley value of the game. Does the Shapley value give a reasonable division of the practice's profits?

12. Consider an *n*-person game in which the only winning coalitions are those coalitions containing player 1 and at least one other player. If a winning coalition receives a reward of $1, find the Shapley value to each player.

◆ SUMMARY

TWO-PERSON ZERO-SUM AND CONSTANT-SUM GAMES

John von Neumann and Oskar Morgenstern suggested that two-person zero-sum and constant-sum games be played according to the following basic assumption of two-person zero-sum game theory: Each player chooses a strategy that enables him to do the best he can, given that his opponent *knows the strategy he is following.*

A two-person zero-sum game has a saddle point if and only if

$$\max_{\substack{\text{all} \\ \text{rows}}} (\text{row minimum}) = \min_{\substack{\text{all} \\ \text{columns}}} (\text{column maximum}) \tag{1}$$

If a two-person zero-sum or constant-sum game has a saddle point, the row player should choose any strategy (row) attaining the maximum on the left side of (1). The column player should choose any strategy (column) attaining the minimum on the right side of (1).

In general, we may use the following method to find the optimal strategies and the value of a two-person zero-sum or constant-sum game:

Step 1 Check for a saddle point. If the game has no saddle point, go on to Step 2.

Step 2 Eliminate any of the row player's dominated strategies. Looking at the reduced matrix (dominated rows crossed out), eliminate any of the column player's dominated strategies. Now eliminate any of the row player's dominated strategies. Continue in this fashion until no more dominated strategies can be found. Now proceed to Step 3.

Step 3 If the game matrix is now 2×2, solve the game graphically. Otherwise, solve the game by using the linear programming method in Table 21.

The value of the game and the optimal strategies for the row player in the Table 21 reward matrix may be found by solving

$$\max z = v$$

Row Player's LP

$$
\begin{aligned}
\text{s.t.} \quad & v \leq a_{11}x_1 + a_{21}x_2 + \cdots + a_{m1}x_m && \text{(Column 1 constraint)} \\
& v \leq a_{12}x_1 + a_{22}x_2 + \cdots + a_{m2}x_m && \text{(Column 2 constraint)} \\
& \qquad\qquad\qquad\vdots \\
& v \leq a_{1n}x_1 + a_{2n}x_2 + \cdots + a_{mn}x_m && \text{(Column } n \text{ constraint)} \\
& x_1 + x_2 + \cdots + x_m = 1 \\
& x_i \geq 0 \quad (i = 1, 2, \ldots, m); \; v \text{ urs}
\end{aligned}
\tag{5}
$$

Table 21	ROW PLAYER	COLUMN PLAYER			
A General Two-Person Zero-Sum Game		Strategy 1	Strategy 2	$\cdots$	Strategy n
	Strategy 1	a_{11}	a_{12}	$\cdots$	a_{1n}
	Strategy 2	a_{21}	a_{22}	$\cdots$	a_{2n}
	$\vdots$	$\vdots$	$\vdots$		$\vdots$
	Strategy m	a_{m1}	a_{m2}	$\cdots$	a_{mn}

The value of the game and the optimal strategies for the column player may be found by solving

Column Player's LP

$$\min z = w$$
$$\text{s.t.} \quad w \geq a_{11}y_1 + a_{12}y_2 + \cdots + a_{1n}y_n \quad \text{(Row 1 constraint)}$$
$$w \geq a_{21}y_1 + a_{22}y_2 + \cdots + a_{2n}y_n \quad \text{(Row 2 constraint)}$$
$$\vdots$$
$$w \geq a_{m1}y_1 + a_{m2}y_2 + \cdots + a_{mn}y_n \quad \text{(Row } m \text{ constraint)} \tag{6}$$
$$y_1 + y_2 + \cdots + y_n = 1$$
$$y_j \geq 0 \quad (j = 1, 2, \ldots, n); \; w \text{ urs}$$

The dual of the row (column) player's LP is the column (row) player's LP. The optimal objective function value for either the row or the column player's LP is the value of the game to the row player. If the row player departs from her optimal strategy, she may receive an expected reward that is less than the value of the game. If the column player departs from his optimal strategy, he may incur an expected loss that exceeds the value of the game. Complementary slackness may be used to simultaneously solve the row and the column players' LPs.

TWO-PERSON NON-CONSTANT-SUM GAMES

As in a two-person zero-sum game, a choice of strategy by each player is an **equilibrium point** if neither player can benefit from a unilateral change in strategy.

A two-person non-constant-sum game of particular interest is Prisoner's Dilemma. If $T > R > P > S$, a reward matrix like the one in Table 33 will be a Prisoner's Dilemma game. For such a game, (NC, NC) (both players choosing a noncooperative action) is an equilibrium point.

n-PERSON GAMES

When more than two players are involved, the structure of a competitive situation may be summarized by the **characteristic function**. For each set of players S, the characteristic

Table 33	PLAYER 1	PLAYER 2	
A General Prisoner's Dilemma Reward Matrix		NC	C
	NC	(P, P)	(T, S)
	C	(S, T)	(R, R)

function v of a game gives the amount $v(S)$ that the members of S can be sure of receiving if they act together and form a coalition.

Let $\mathbf{x} = (x_1, x_2, \ldots, x_n)$ be a vector such that player i receives a reward x_i. We call such a vector a **reward vector**. A reward vector $\mathbf{x} = (x_1, x_2, \ldots, x_n)$ is an **imputation** if and only if

$$v(N) = \sum_{i=1}^{i=n} x_i \qquad \text{(Group rationality)} \qquad (13)$$

$$x_i \geq v(\{i\}) \quad \text{(for each } i \in N) \quad \text{(Individual rationality)} \qquad (14)$$

The imputation $\mathbf{y} = (y_1, y_2, \ldots, y_n)$ **dominates** $\mathbf{x}$ through a coalition S (written $\mathbf{y} >^S \mathbf{x}$) if

$$\sum_{i \in S} y_i \leq v(S) \qquad \text{and for all } i \in S, \quad y_i > x_i \qquad (15)$$

The **core** and the **Shapley value** are two alternative solution concepts for n-person games. The *core* of an n-person game is the set of all undominated imputations. An imputation $\mathbf{x} = (x_1, x_2, \ldots, x_n)$ is in the core of an n-person game if and only if for each subset S of $N = \{1, 2, \ldots, n\}$

$$\sum_{i \in S} x_i \geq v(S)$$

The Shapley value gives a reward x_i to the ith player, where x_i is given by

$$x_i = \sum_{\substack{\text{all } S \text{ for which} \\ i \text{ is not in } S}} p_n(S)[v(S \cup \{i\}) - v(S)] \qquad (45)$$

In (45),

$$p_n(S) = \frac{|S|!(n - |S| - 1)!}{n!} \qquad (46)$$

Eq. (45) implies that player i's reward should be the expected amount that player i adds to the coalition made up of the players who are present when player i arrives.

◆ REVIEW PROBLEMS

GROUP A

1. Two competing firms are deciding whether to locate a new store at point A, B, or C. There are 52 prospective customers for the two stores. Twenty customers live in village A, 20 customers live in village B, and 12 customers live in village C (see Figure 6). Each customer will shop at

Figure 6

20 customers   20 customers   12 customers

A B C

the nearer store. If a customer is equidistant from both stores, assume there is a $\frac{1}{2}$ chance that he or she will shop at either store. Each firm wishes to maximize the expected number of customers that will shop at its store. Where should each firm locate its store? ($AB = BC = 10$ miles.)

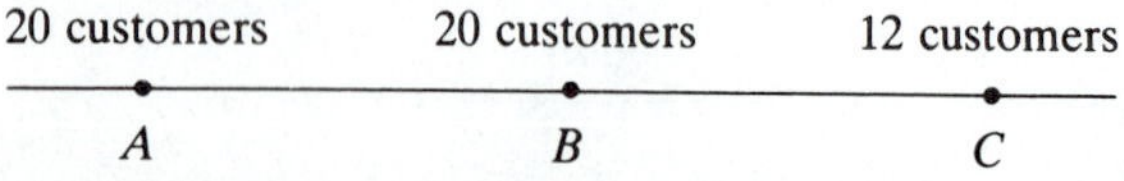

2. A total of 90,000 customers frequent the Ruby and the Swamp supermarkets. In order to induce customers to enter, each store gives away a free item. Each week, the giveaway item is announced in the Monday newspaper. Of course, neither store knows which item the other store will choose to give away this week. Ruby's is considering giving away a carton of soda or a half gallon of milk. Swamp's is considering giving away a pound of butter or a half gallon of orange juice. For each possible choice of items, the number of customers who will stop at Ruby's during the current week is shown in Table 47. Each store wants to maximize its expected number of customers during the current week. Use game theory to determine an optimal strategy for each store and the value of the game. Interpret the value of the game.

Table 47

RUBY CHOOSES	SWAMP CHOOSES	
	Butter	Orange juice
Soda	40,000	50,000
Milk	60,000	30,000

3. Consider the two-person zero-sum game in Table 48.

Table 48

$\frac{1}{2}$	-1	-1
-1	$\frac{1}{2}$	-1
-1	-1	1

(a) Write down each player's LP.
(b) We are told that player 1's optimal strategy has $x_1 > 0$, $x_2 > 0$, and $x_3 > 0$. Find the value of the game and each player's optimal strategies.
(c) Suppose the column player plays the nonoptimal strategy $(\frac{1}{2}, \frac{1}{2}, 0)$. Show how the row player can earn an expected reward that exceeds the value of the game.

4. Find optimal strategies for each player and the value of the two-person zero-sum game in Table 49.

Table 49

20	1	2
12	10	4
24	8	-2

5. Airway (a midwestern department store chain) and Corvett (an eastern department store chain) are determining whether or not to expand their geographical bases. The only viable manner by which expansion might be carried out is for a chain to open stores in the other's area. If neither chain expands, Airway's profits will be $3 million and Corvett's will be $2 million. If Airway expands and Corvett does not, Airway's profits will be $5 million, and Corvett will lose $2 million. If Airway does not expand and Corvett does, Airway will lose $1 million, and Corvett will earn $4 million. Finally, if both chains expand, Airway will earn $1 million and Corvett will earn $500,000 in profits. Determine the equilibrium points, if any, for this game.

6. The stock in Alden Corporation is held by three people. Person 1 owns 1% of the stock, person 2 owns 49% of the stock, and person 3 owns 50% of the stock. To pass a resolution at the annual stockholders' meeting, 51% of the stock is needed. A coalition receives a reward of 1 if it can pass a resolution and a reward of zero if it cannot pass a resolution.
(a) Find the characteristic function for this game.
(b) Find the core of this game.
(c) Find the Shapley value for this game.
(d) Since $(\frac{1}{3}, \frac{1}{3}, \frac{1}{3})$ is not in the core, there must be an imputation dominating $(\frac{1}{3}, \frac{1}{3}, \frac{1}{3})$. Find one.

GROUP B

7. In addition to the core and the Shapley value, the stable set is an alternative solution concept for n-person games. A set I of imputations is called a **stable set** if each imputation in I is undominated and every imputation that is not in I is dominated by some member of I. Consider the three-person game in which all zero- and 1-member coalitions have a characteristic function value of zero, and each two- and three-player coalition has a value of 1. Show that for this game $I = \{(\frac{1}{2}, \frac{1}{2}, 0), (0, \frac{1}{2}, \frac{1}{2}), (\frac{1}{2}, 0, \frac{1}{2})\}$ is a stable set.

◆ REFERENCES

The following books take an elementary, applications-oriented approach to game theory:

DAVIS, M. *Game Theory: An Introduction*. New York: Basic Books, 1983.

RAPOPORT, A. *Two-Person Game Theory*. Ann Arbor, Mich.: University of Michigan Press, 1973.

The following classics are still worth reading:

LUCE, R., and H. RAIFFA. *Games and Decisions*. New York: Wiley, 1957.

VON NEUMANN, J., and O. MORGENSTERN. *Theory of Games and Economic Behavior*. Princeton, N.J.: Princeton University Press, 1944.

For the more mathematically inclined reader, the next five books are recommended:

FRIEDMAN, J. *Game Theory with Applications to Economics*. New York: Oxford Press, 1986.

OWEN, G. *Game Theory*. Orlando, Fla.: Academic Press, 1982.

SHUBIK, M. *Game Theory in the Social Sciences: Concepts and Solutions*. Cambridge, Mass.: MIT Press, 1982.

——. *A Game-Theoretic Approach to Political Economy*. Cambridge, Mass.: MIT Press, 1984.

THOMAS, L. C. *Games, Theory and Applications*. Chichester, England: Ellis Horwood, 1986.

VOROBEV, N. *Game Theory Lectures for Economists and Social Sciences*. New York: Springer-Verlag, 1977.

LITTLECHILD, S., and G. OWEN. "A Simple Expression for the Shapley Value in a Special Case," *Management Science* 20(1973):370–372. Discusses applications of the Shapley value to airport landings.

"Protectionism Gets Clever," *The Economist* (November 21, 1988):78.

SHAPLEY, L. "Quota Solutions of *n*-Person Games." In *Contributions to the Theory of Games II*, ed. H. Kuhn and A. Tucker. Princeton, N.J.: Princeton University Press, 1953.

16

Deterministic EOQ Inventory Models

IN THIS CHAPTER, we begin our formal study of inventory modeling. We have already described how linear programming can be used to solve certain inventory problems (see Sections 3.10 and 4.12). Our study of inventory will continue in Chapters 17, 18, 20, and 21.

We begin by discussing some important concepts used to describe inventory models and then develop versions of the famous economic order quantity (EOQ) model that can be used to make optimal inventory decisions when demand is deterministic (known in advance). In Chapters 17 and 21, we discuss models in which demand is allowed to be random.

16-1   INTRODUCTION TO BASIC INVENTORY MODELS

In order to meet demand on time, companies often keep on hand stock that is awaiting sale. The purpose of inventory theory is to determine rules that management can use to minimize the costs associated with maintaining inventory and meeting customer demand. Inventory models answer the following questions: (1) When should an order be placed for a product? (2) How large should each order be?

COSTS INVOLVED IN INVENTORY MODELS

The inventory models considered in this book involve some or all of the following costs:

ORDERING AND SETUP COST.   Many costs associated with placing an order or producing a good internally do not depend on the size of the order or on the production run. Costs of this type are referred to as the ordering and setup cost. For example, ordering cost would include the cost of paperwork and billing associated with an order. If the product is made internally rather than ordered from an external source, the cost of labor (and idle time) for setting up and shutting down a machine for a production run would be included in the ordering and setup cost.

UNIT PURCHASING COST.   This is simply the variable cost associated with purchasing a single unit. Typically, the unit purchasing cost includes the variable labor cost, variable overhead cost, and raw material cost associated with purchasing or producing a single unit. If goods are ordered from an external source, the unit purchase cost must include shipping cost.

HOLDING OR CARRYING COST.   This is the cost of carrying one unit of inventory for one time period. If the time period is a year, the carrying cost will be expressed in dollars per unit per year. The holding cost usually includes storage cost, insurance cost, taxes on inventory, and a cost due to the possibility of spoilage, theft, or obsolescence. Usually, however, the most significant component of holding cost is the opportunity cost incurred by tying up capital in inventory. For example, suppose that one unit of a product costs $100 and the company can earn 15% annually on its investments. Then holding one unit in inventory for one year is costing the company $0.15(100) = \$15$. When interest rates are high, most firms assume that their annual holding cost is 20–40% of the unit purchase cost.

STOCKOUT OR SHORTAGE COST.   When a customer demands a product and the demand is not met on time, a stockout, or shortage, is said to occur. If customers will accept delivery at a later date (no matter how late that date may be), we say that demands may be **back-ordered**. The case in which back-ordering is allowed is often referred to as the **backlogged demand** case. If no customer will accept late delivery, we are in the **lost sales** case. Of course, reality lies between these two extremes, but by determining optimal inventory policies for both the backlogged demand and the lost sales cases, we can get a ballpark estimate of what the optimal inventory policy should be.

Many costs are associated with stockouts. If back-ordering is allowed, placement of back-orders usually results in an extra cost. Stockouts often cause customers to go elsewhere to meet current and future demands, resulting in lost sales and lost goodwill. Stockouts may also cause a company to fall behind in other aspects of its business and may force a plant to incur the higher cost of overtime production. Usually, the cost of a stockout is harder to measure than ordering, purchasing, or holding costs.

In this chapter, we study several versions of the classic economic order quantity (EOQ) model that was first developed in 1915 by F. W. Harris of Westinghouse Corporation. For the models in this chapter to be valid, certain assumptions must be satisfied.

ASSUMPTIONS OF EOQ MODELS

REPETITIVE ORDERING.   The ordering decision is repetitive in the sense that it is repeated in a regular fashion. For example, a company that is ordering bearing assemblies will place an order, then see its inventory depleted, then place another order, and so on. This contrasts with one-time orders. For example, when a news vendor decides how many Sunday newspapers to order, only one order (per Sunday) will be placed. Problems where an order is placed just once are referred to as single-period inventory problems; these are discussed in Chapter 17.

CONSTANT DEMAND.   Demand is assumed to occur at a known, constant rate. This implies, for example, that if demand occurs at a rate of 1000 units per year, the demand during any t-month period will be $\frac{1000t}{12}$.

CONSTANT LEAD TIME.   The lead time for each order is a known constant, L. By the **lead time** we mean the length of time between the instant when an order is placed and the instant at which the order arrives. For example, if $L = 3$ months, then each order will arrive exactly 3 months after the order is placed.

CONTINUOUS ORDERING.   An order may be placed at any time. Inventory models that allow this are called **continuous review models**. If the amount of on-hand inventory is reviewed periodically and orders may be placed only periodically, we are dealing with a **periodic review model**. For example, if a firm reviews its on-hand inventory only at the end of each month and decides at this time whether or not an order should be placed, we are dealing with a periodic review model. Periodic review models are discussed in Chapters 17, 19, and 20.

Although the Constant Demand and Constant Lead Time assumptions may seem overly restrictive and unrealistic, there are many situations in which the models of this chapter provide good approximations to reality. Models in which demand is not deterministic are discussed in Chapters 17 and 20. Models in which demand is determinstic but occurs at a nonconstant rate have already been reviewed in our discussion of LP inventory models (see Sections 3.10 and 4.12) and are examined further in Chapter 19.

16-2   THE BASIC ECONOMIC ORDER QUANTITY MODEL

ASSUMPTIONS OF THE BASIC EOQ MODEL

For the basic EOQ model to hold, certain assumptions are required (for the sake of definiteness, we assume that the unit of time is one year):

1. Demand is deterministic and occurs at a constant rate.

2. If an order of any size (say q units) is placed, an ordering and setup cost K is incurred.

3. The lead time for each order is zero.

4. No shortages are allowed.

5. The cost per unit year of holding inventory is h.

We define D to be the number of units demanded per year. Then assumption 1 implies that during any time interval of length t years, an amount Dt is demanded.

The setup cost K of assumption 2 is in addition to a cost pq of purchasing or producing the q units ordered. Note that we are assuming that the unit purchasing cost p does not depend on the size of the order. This excludes many interesting situations, such as quantity discounts for larger orders. In Section 16.3, we discuss a model that allows quantity discounts.

Assumption 3 implies that each order arrives as soon as it is placed. We relax this assumption later in this section.

Assumption 4 implies that all demands must be met on time; a negative inventory position is not allowed. We relax this assumption in Section 16.5.

Assumption 5 implies that a carrying cost of h dollars would be incurred if 1 unit is held for one year, if 2 units are held for half a year, or if $\frac{1}{4}$ unit is held for four years. In short, if I units are held for T years, a holding cost of ITh is incurred.

Given these five assumptions, the EOQ model determines an ordering policy that minimizes the yearly sum of ordering cost, purchasing cost, and holding cost.

DERIVATION OF BASIC EOQ MODEL

We begin our derivation of the optimal ordering policy by making some simple observations. Since orders arrive instantaneously, we should never place an order when I, the inventory level, is greater than zero; if we place an order when $I > 0$, we are incurring an unnecessary holding cost. On the other hand, if $I = 0$, we must place an order to prevent a shortage from occurring. Together, these observations show that the policy that minimizes yearly costs must place an order whenever $I = 0$. At all instants when an order is placed, we are facing the same situation ($I = 0$). This means that each time we place an order, we should order the same quantity. We let q be the quantity that is ordered each time $I = 0$.

We now determine the value of q that minimizes annual cost (call it q^*). Let $TC(q)$ be the total annual cost incurred if q units are ordered each time $I = 0$. Note that

$$TC(q) = \text{annual cost of placing orders} + \text{annual purchasing cost}$$
$$+ \text{annual holding cost}$$

Since each order is for q units, $\frac{D}{q}$ orders per year will have to be placed so that the annual demand of D units is met. Hence

$$\frac{\text{Ordering cost}}{\text{Year}} = \left(\frac{\text{ordering cost}}{\text{order}}\right)\left(\frac{\text{orders}}{\text{year}}\right) = \frac{KD}{q}$$

For all values of q, the per-unit purchasing cost is p. Since we always purchase D units per year,

$$\frac{\text{Purchasing cost}}{\text{Year}} = \left(\frac{\text{purchasing cost}}{\text{unit}}\right)\left(\frac{\text{units purchased}}{\text{year}}\right) = pD$$

To compute the annual holding cost, note that if we hold I units for a period of one year, we incur a holding cost of $(I \text{ units})(1 \text{ year})(h \text{ dollars/unit/year}) = hI$ dollars.

Suppose the inventory level is not constant and varies over time. If the average inventory level during a length of time T is $\bar{I}$, the holding cost for the time period will be $hT\bar{I}$. This idea is illustrated in Figure 1. If we define $I(t)$ to be the inventory level at time t, then during the interval $[0, T]$ the total inventory cost is given by

$$h(\text{area from zero to } T \text{ under the } I(t) \text{ curve}) = hT\bar{I}$$

The reader may verify that this result holds for the two cases graphed in Figure 1. More formally, $\bar{I}(T)$, the average inventory level from time 0 to time T, is given by

$$\bar{I}(t) = \frac{\int_0^T I(t)\, dt}{T}$$

and the total holding cost incurred between time 0 and time T is

$$\int_0^T hI(t)\, dt = hT\bar{I}(T)$$

Figure 1
Holding Cost and
Average Inventory
Level

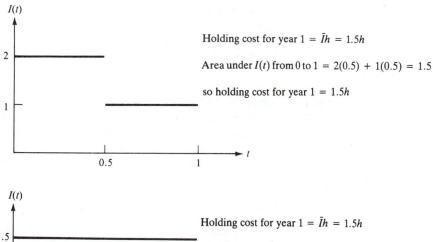

Holding cost for year 1 = $\bar{I}h$ = $1.5h$

Area under $I(t)$ from 0 to 1 = $2(0.5) + 1(0.5) = 1.5$

so holding cost for year 1 = $1.5h$

Holding cost for year 1 = $\bar{I}h$ = $1.5h$

Area under $I(t)$ from 0 to 1 = $1.5(1) = 1.5$

so holding cost for year 1 = $1.5h$

To determine the annual holding cost, we need to examine the behavior of I over time. Assume that an order of size q has just arrived at time 0. Since demand occurs at a rate of D per year, it will take $\frac{q}{D}$ years for inventory to reach zero again. Since demand during any period of length t is Dt, the inventory level over any time interval will decline along a straight line of slope $-D$. When inventory reaches zero, an order of size q is placed and arrives instantaneously, raising the inventory level back to q. Given these observations, Figure 2 describes the behavior of I over time.

A key concept in the study of EOQ models is the idea of a cycle.

Figure 2
Behavior of $I(t)$ in
Basic EOQ Model

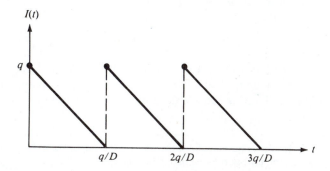

DEFINITION   Any interval of time that begins with the arrival of an order and ends the instant before the next order is received is called a **cycle**.

Observe that Figure 2 simply consists of repeated cycles of length $\frac{q}{D}$. Hence, each year will contain

$$\frac{1}{\frac{q}{D}} = \frac{D}{q}$$

cycles. The average inventory during any cycle is simply half of the maximum inventory level attained during the cycle. This result will hold in any model for which demand occurs at a constant rate and no shortages are allowed. Thus, for our model, the average inventory level during a cycle will be $\frac{q}{2}$ units.

We are now ready to determine the annual holding cost. We write

$$\frac{\text{Holding cost}}{\text{Year}} = \left(\frac{\text{holding cost}}{\text{cycle}}\right)\left(\frac{\text{cycles}}{\text{year}}\right)$$

Since the average inventory level during each cycle is $\frac{q}{2}$ and each cycle is of length $\frac{q}{D}$,

$$\frac{\text{Holding cost}}{\text{Cycle}} = \frac{q}{2}\left(\frac{q}{D}\right) h = \frac{q^2 h}{2D}$$

Then

$$\frac{\text{Holding cost}}{\text{Year}} = \frac{q^2 h}{2D}\left(\frac{D}{q}\right) = \frac{hq}{2}$$

Combining ordering cost, purchasing cost, and holding cost, we obtain

$$TC(q) = \frac{KD}{q} + pD + \frac{hq}{2}$$

To find the value of q that minimizes $TC(q)$, we set $TC'(q)$ equal to zero. This yields

$$TC'(q) = -\frac{KD}{q^2} + \frac{h}{2} = 0 \tag{1}$$

Eq. (1) is satisfied for $q = \pm(2KD/h)^{1/2}$. Since $q = -(2KD/h)^{1/2}$ makes no sense, let's hope that the **economic order quantity**, or EOQ,

$$q^* = \left(\frac{2KD}{h}\right)^{1/2} \tag{2}$$

minimizes $TC(q)$. Since $TC''(q) = 2KD/q^3 > 0$ for all q, we know that $TC(q)$ is a convex function. Then Theorem 1′ of Chapter 12 implies that any point where $TC'(q) = 0$ will minimize $TC(q)$. Thus, q^* does indeed minimize total annual cost.

R E M A R K S   **1.** The EOQ does not depend on the unit purchasing price p, because the size of each order does not change the unit purchase cost. Thus, the total annual purchasing cost is independent of q. In Section 16.3, we discuss models in which the size of the order changes the unit purchasing cost.

2. Since each order is for q^* units, a total of $\frac{D}{q^*}$ orders must be placed during each year.

3. To see whether the EOQ formula is reasonable, let's see how changes in certain parameters change q^*. For example, as K increases, we would expect the number of orders placed each year,

$\frac{D}{q*}$, to decrease. Equivalently, we would expect an increase in K to increase $q*$. A glance at Eq. (2) shows that this is indeed the case. Analogously, an increase in h makes it more costly to hold inventory, so we would expect an increase in h to reduce the average inventory level, $\frac{q*}{2}$. Eq. (2) shows that an increase in h does reduce $q*$; it also shows that the ratio of the ordering cost to the holding cost is the critical factor in determining $q*$. For example, if both K and h are doubled, $q*$ remains unchanged. Also note that $q*$ is proportional to $D^{1/2}$. Thus, quadrupling demand will only double $q*$.

4. It is not difficult to show that if the EOQ is ordered, then

$$\frac{\text{Holding cost}}{\text{Year}} = \frac{\text{ordering cost}}{\text{year}} \tag{3}$$

To prove this, note that

$$\frac{\text{Holding cost}}{\text{Year}} = \frac{hq*}{2} = \frac{h}{2}\left(\frac{2KD}{h}\right)^{1/2} = \left(\frac{KDh}{2}\right)^{1/2}$$

$$\frac{\text{Ordering cost}}{\text{Year}} = \frac{KD}{q*} = \frac{KD}{\left(\frac{2KD}{h}\right)^{1/2}} = \left(\frac{KDh}{2}\right)^{1/2}$$

Figure 3 illustrates the tradeoff between holding cost and ordering cost. The figure confirms the fact that at $q*$, the annual holding and ordering costs are the same.

Figure 3
Tradeoff between
Holding Cost and
Ordering Cost

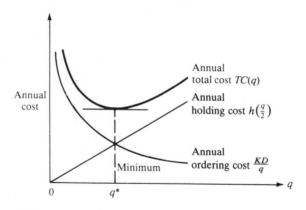

We illustrate the use of the EOQ formula with the following example.

E X A M P L E
1

Braneast Airlines uses 500 taillights per year. Each time an order for taillights is placed, an ordering cost of $5 is incurred. Each light costs 40¢, and the holding cost is 8¢/light/year. Assume that demand occurs at a constant rate and shortages are not allowed. What is the EOQ? How many orders will be placed each year? How much time will elapse between the placement of orders?

Solution   We are given that $K = \$5$, $h = \$0.08/\text{light/year}$, and $D = 500$ lights/year. The EOQ is

$$q* = \left(\frac{2(5)(500)}{0.08}\right)^{1/2} = 250$$

Hence, the airline should place an order for 250 taillights each time that inventory reaches zero.

$$\frac{\text{Orders}}{\text{Year}} = \frac{D}{q^*} = \frac{500}{250} = \frac{2 \text{ orders}}{\text{year}}$$

The time between placement (or arrival) of orders is simply the length of a cycle. Since the length of each cycle is $\frac{q^*}{D}$, the time between orders will be

$$\frac{q^*}{D} = \frac{250}{500} = \frac{1}{2} \text{ year}$$

◆

SENSITIVITY OF TOTAL COST TO SMALL VARIATIONS IN THE ORDER QUANTITY

In most situations, a slight deviation from the EOQ will result in only a slight increase in costs. For Example 1, let's see how deviations from the EOQ change the total annual cost. Since annual purchasing cost is unaffected by the order quantity, we focus our attention on how the annual holding and ordering costs are affected by changes in the order quantity. Let

$$HC(q) = \text{annual holding cost if the order quantity is } q$$
$$OC(q) = \text{annual ordering cost if the order quantity is } q$$

We find that

$$HC(q) = \tfrac{1}{2}(0.08q) = 0.04q \qquad OC(q) = 5\left(\frac{500}{q}\right) = \frac{2500}{q}$$

Using the information in Table 1, we obtain the sketch of $HC(q) + OC(q)$ given in Figure 4. The figure shows that $HC(q) + OC(q)$ is very flat near q^*. For example, ordering 20% more than the EOQ (i.e., $q = 300$) raises $HC(q) + OC(q)$ from 20 to 20.33 (an increase of under 2%).

The flatness of the $HC(q) + OC(q)$ curve is important, because it is often difficult to estimate h and K. Inaccurate estimation of h and K may result in a value of q that

	q	$HC(q)$	$OC(q)$	$HC(q) + OC(q)$
Table 1 Cost Calculations for Figure 4	50	2.0	50.00	52.00
	100	4.0	25.00	29.00
	150	6.0	16.67	22.67
	200	8.0	12.50	20.50
	220	8.8	11.36	20.16
	240	9.6	10.42	20.02
	250	10.0	10.00	20.00
	260	10.4	9.62	20.02
	280	11.2	8.93	20.13
	300	12.0	8.33	20.33
	350	14.0	7.14	21.14
	400	16.0	6.25	22.25

Figure 4
$OC(q) + HC(q)$ for
Braneast Example

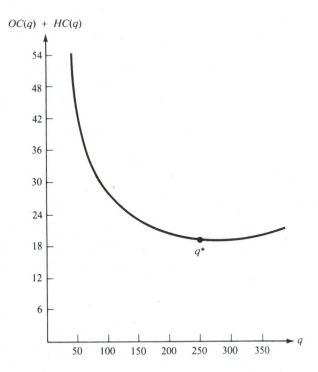

differs slightly from the actual EOQ. The flatness of the $HC(q) + OC(q)$ curve indicates that even a moderate error in the determination of the EOQ will only increase costs by a slight amount.

DETERMINATION OF EOQ WHEN HOLDING COST IS EXPRESSED IN TERMS OF DOLLAR VALUE OF INVENTORY

Often, the annual holding cost is expressed in terms of the cost of holding one dollar's worth of inventory for one year. Suppose that h_d = cost of holding one dollar in inventory for one year. Then the cost of holding one unit of inventory for one year will be ph_d and Eq. (2) may be written as

$$q^* = \left(\frac{2KD}{ph_d}\right)^{1/2} \tag{4}$$

E X A M P L E
2

A department store sells 10,000 cameras per year. The store orders cameras from a regional warehouse. Each time an order is placed, an ordering cost of $5 is incurred. The store pays $100 for each camera, and the cost of holding one dollar's worth of inventory for a year is estimated to be the annual capital opportunity cost of 20¢. Determine the EOQ.

Solution

We are given that $K = \$5$, $D = 10,000$ cameras per year, $h_d = 20¢/\text{dollar}/\text{year}$, and $p = \$100$ per camera. Then

$$q^* = \left(\frac{2(5)(10,000)}{(100)(0.20)} \right)^{1/2} = (5000)^{1/2} = 70.71 \text{ cameras}$$

Hence, the EOQ recommends that the camera store order 70.71 cameras each time the inventory level reaches zero. Of course, the number of cameras ordered must be an integer. Since $TC(q)$ is a convex function of q, either $q = 70$ or $q = 71$ must minimize $TC(q)$. (If this seems difficult to believe, look at Figure 4). Because of the flatness of the $HC(q) + OC(q)$ curve, it doesn't really matter whether the store chooses to order 70 or 71 cameras.

◆

THE EFFECT OF A NONZERO LEAD TIME

We now allow the lead time L to be greater than zero. The introduction of a nonzero lead time leaves the annual holding and ordering costs unchanged. Hence, the EOQ still minimizes total costs. To prevent shortages from occurring and to minimize holding cost, each order must be placed at an inventory level that ensures that when each order arrives, the inventory level will equal zero.

DEFINITION	The inventory level at which an order should be placed is the **reorder point**.

To determine the reorder point for the basic EOQ model, two cases must be considered:

Case 1 Demand during the lead time does not exceed the EOQ (this means that $LD \leq$ EOQ). In this case, the reorder point occurs when the inventory level equals LD. Then the order will arrive L time units later, and upon arrival of the order, the inventory level will equal $LD - LD = 0$. In Example 1, suppose that it takes one month for a shipment of taillights to arrive. Then $L = \frac{1}{12}$ year, and Braneast's reorder point will be $(\frac{1}{12})(500) = 41.67$ lights. Thus, whenever Braneast has 41.67 lights on hand, an order should be placed for more lights.

Case 2 Demand during the lead time exceeds the EOQ (this means that $LD >$ EOQ). In this case, the reorder point does not equal LD. Suppose that in Example 1, $L = 9$ months. Then $LD = (\frac{9}{12})(500) = 375$ lights. Why can't we place an order each time the inventory level reaches 375 lights? Since the EOQ = 250 lights, our inventory level will never reach 375 lights. To determine the correct reorder point, observe that orders are placed every six months. Suppose that an order has just arrived at time 0. Then an order must have been placed $L = 9$ months ago (at $T = -9$ months). Since orders arrive every six months, orders must be placed at $T = -3$ months, $T = 3$ months, and so on. At each of these points, the inventory level must equal the reorder point. Since at $T = 0$, an order for 250 lights has arrived, at $T = 3$ months, the inventory level will equal $250 - (\frac{3}{12})(500) = 125$ lights. Thus, the reorder point is 125 lights.

The determination of the reorder point becomes extremely important when demand is random and stockouts can occur. In Sections 17.6 and 17.7, we discuss the problem of determining the reorder point when demand is random.

We close this section by giving an example of a noninventory problem that can be solved by the reasoning that we used to develop the EOQ.

E X A M P L E 3

Each hour, D students want to ride a bus from the student union to Fraternity Row. The administration places a value of h dollars on each hour that a student is forced to wait for a bus. It costs the university K dollars to send a bus from the student union to Fraternity Row. Assuming that demand occurs at a constant rate, how many buses should be sent each hour from the student union to Fraternity Row?

Solution

Note that

$$\frac{\text{Total cost}}{\text{Hour}} = \frac{\text{cost of sending buses}}{\text{hour}} + \frac{\text{student waiting cost}}{\text{hour}}$$

Since demand occurs at a constant rate, buses should leave at regular time intervals. This means that each bus that arrives at the student union will find the same number of students waiting. Let q = number of students present when each bus arrives. Assuming that a bus has just arrived at time 0, "number of students waiting" displays the behavior shown in Figure 5. Then

$$\frac{\text{Cost of sending buses}}{\text{Hour}} = \left(\frac{K \text{ dollars}}{\text{bus}}\right)\left(\frac{\frac{D}{q} \text{ buses}}{\text{hour}}\right) = \frac{\frac{KD}{q} \text{ dollars}}{\text{hour}}$$

Figure 5
Evolution over Time
of Students Waiting
(Example 3)

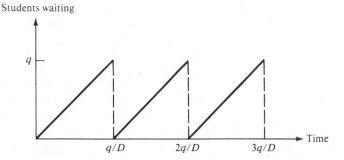

From Figure 5, the average number of students waiting is $\frac{q}{2}$. Then

$$\frac{\text{Student waiting cost}}{\text{Hour}} = \left(\frac{q}{2} \text{ students}\right)\left(\frac{h \text{ dollars/student}}{\text{hour}}\right) = \frac{\frac{hq}{2} \text{ dollars}}{\text{hour}}$$

These computations show that

$$\frac{\text{Total cost}}{\text{Hour}} = \frac{hq}{2} + \frac{KD}{q}$$

This is identical to $HC(q) + OC(q)$ for the basic EOQ model. Hence, the optimal value of q for our busing problem is simply the EOQ. This means that the optimal value of q is $q^* = \left(\frac{2KD}{h}\right)^{1/2}$. Since each bus picks up q^* students, $\frac{D}{q^*}$ buses should be sent each hour.

From Figure 5, we see that the time between buses will be $\frac{q^*}{D}$ hours. For example, if $h = \$5$/student/hour, $D = 100$ students/hour, and $K = \$10$/bus, we find that

$$q^* = \left(\frac{2(10)(100)}{5}\right)^{1/2} = 20$$

Then $\frac{100}{20} = 5$ buses/hour will leave the student union, and a bus will leave the student union every $\frac{1}{5}$ hour $= 12$ minutes.

◆

◆ PROBLEMS

GROUP A

1. Each month, a gas station sells 4000 gallons of gasoline. Each time the parent company refills the station's tanks, it charges the station $50 plus 70¢ per gallon. The annual cost of holding a gallon of gasoline is 30¢.
(a) How large should the station's orders be?
(b) How many orders per year will be placed?
(c) How long will it be between orders?
(d) Would the EOQ assumptions be satisfied in this situation? Why or why not?
(e) If the lead time is 2 weeks, what is the reorder point? If the lead time is 10 weeks, what is the reorder point? Assume 1 week $= \frac{1}{52}$ year.

2.[†] Money in my savings account earns interest at a 10% annual rate. Each time I go to the bank, I waste 15 minutes in line. My time is worth $10 per hour. During each year, I need to withdraw $10,000 to pay my bills.
(a) How often should I go to the bank?
(b) Each time I go to the bank, how much money should I withdraw?
(c) If my need for cash increases, will I go to the bank more often or less often?
(d) If interest rates rise, will I go to the bank more often or less often?
(e) If the bank adds more tellers, will I go to the bank more often or less often?

3.[‡] Father Dominic's Pizza Parlor receives 30 calls per hour for delivery of pizza. It costs Father Dominic's $10 to send out a truck to deliver pizzas. It is estimated that each minute a customer spends waiting for a pizza costs the pizza parlor 20¢ in lost future business.
(a) How often should Father Dominic's send out a truck?
(b) What would be the answer if a truck could only carry five pizzas?

†Based on Baumol (1952).
‡Based on Ignall and Kolesar (1972).

4. The efficiency of an inventory system is often measured by the **turnover ratio**. The turnover ratio (TR) is defined by

$$TR = \frac{\text{cost of goods sold during a year}}{\text{average value of on-hand inventory}}$$

(a) Does a high turnover ratio indicate an efficient inventory system?
(b) If the EOQ model is being used, determine TR in terms of K, D, h, and q.
(c) Suppose D is increased. Show that TR will also be increased.

GROUP B

5. Suppose that instead of ordering the EOQ q^*, we use the order quantity $0.8q^*$. Use Eq. (3) to show that $HC(q) + OC(q)$ will have increased by 2.50%.

6. In terms of K, D, and h, what is the average length of time that an item spends in inventory before being used to meet demand? Explain how this result can be used to characterize a fast- or a slow-moving item.

7. A drug store sells 30 bottles of antibiotics per week. Each time it orders antibiotics, there is a fixed ordering cost of $10 and a cost of $10/bottle. Assume that the annual holding cost is 20% of the cost of a bottle of antibiotics, and suppose antibiotics spoil and cannot be sold if they spend more than one week in inventory. When the drug store places an order, how many bottles of antibiotics should be ordered?

8. During each year, CSL Computer Company needs to train 27 service representatives. No matter how many students are trained, it costs $12,000 to run a training program. Since service reps earn a monthly salary of $1500, CSL does not want to train them before they are needed. Each training session takes one month.
(a) State the assumptions needed for the EOQ model to be applicable.

(b) How many service representatives should be in each training group?

(c) How many training programs should CSL undertake each year?

(d) How many trained service reps will be available when each training program begins?

9. A newspaper has 500,000 subscribers who pay $4 per month for the paper. It costs the company $200,000 to bill all its customers. Assume that the company can earn interest at a rate of 20% per year on all revenues. Determine how often the newspaper should bill its customers. (*Hint:* Look at unpaid subscriptions as the inventoried good.)

10. Consider a firm that knows that the price of the product it is ordering is going to increase permanently by $$X$. How much of the product should be ordered before the price increase goes into effect?

Here is one approach to this question: Suppose the firm orders Q units before the price increase goes into effect.

(a) What extra holding cost is incurred by ordering Q units now?

(b) How much in purchasing costs is saved by ordering Q units now?

(c) What value of Q maximizes purchasing cost savings less extra holding costs?

(d) Suppose that annual demand is 1000 units, holding cost per unit-year is $7.50, and the price of the item is going to increase by $10. How large an order should be placed before the price increase goes into effect?

16-3   COMPUTING THE OPTIMAL ORDER QUANTITY WHEN QUANTITY DISCOUNTS ARE ALLOWED

Up to now, we have assumed that the annual purchase cost does not depend on the order size. In Section 16.2, this assumption allowed us to ignore the annual purchasing cost when we computed the order quantity that minimizes total annual cost. In real life, however, suppliers often reduce the unit purchasing price for large orders. Such price reductions are referred to as *quantity discounts*. If a supplier gives quantity discounts, the annual purchasing cost will depend on the order size. If holding cost is expressed as a percentage of an item's purchasing cost, the annual holding cost will also depend on the order size. Since the annual purchasing cost now depends on the order size, we can no longer ignore purchasing cost while trading off holding cost against setup cost. Thus, the approach used in Section 16.2 to find the optimal order quantity is no longer valid, and a new approach is needed.

If we let q be the quantity ordered each time an order is placed, the general quantity discount model analyzed in this section may be described as follows:

$$\text{If } q < b_1, \text{ each item costs } p_1 \text{ dollars.}$$
$$\text{If } b_1 \leq q < b_2, \text{ each item costs } p_2 \text{ dollars.}$$
$$\text{If } b_{k-2} \leq q < b_{k-1}, \text{ each item costs } p_{k-1} \text{ dollars.}$$
$$\text{If } b_{k-1} \leq q < b_k = \infty, \text{ each item costs } p_k \text{ dollars.}$$

Since $b_1, b_2, \ldots, b_{k-1}$ are points where a price change (or break) occurs, we refer to $b_1, b_2, \ldots, b_{k-1}$ as **price break points**. Since larger order quantities should be associated with lower prices, we have $p_k < p_{k-1} < \cdots < p_2 < p_1$. The following example illustrates the quantity discount model.

E X A M P L E   4   **Buying Diskettes**   A local accounting firm in Smalltown orders boxes of floppy diskettes (10 diskettes to a box) from a store in Megalopolis. The per-box price charged by the store depends on the number of boxes purchased (see Table 2). The accounting firm uses

	NO. OF BOXES ORDERED (q)	PRICE PER BOX
Table 2 Purchase Costs for Diskettes	$0 \leq q < 100$	$50.00
	$100 \leq q < 300$	$49.00
	$q \geq 300$	$48.50

10,000 diskettes per year. The cost of placing an order is assumed to be $100. The only holding cost is the opportunity cost of capital, which is assumed to be 20% per year. For this example, $b_1 = 100$, $b_2 = 300$, $p_1 = \$50.00$, $p_2 = \$49.00$, and $p_3 = \$48.50$.

The example is continued later in this section. ◆

Before explaining how to find the order quantity minimizing total annual costs, we need the following definitions:

1. $TC_i(q) =$ total annual cost (including holding, purchasing, and ordering costs) if each order is for q units at a price p_i.

2. $EOQ_i =$ quantity that minimizes total annual cost if, for any order quantity, the purchasing cost of the item is p_i.

3. EOQ_i is *admissible* if $b_{i-1} \leq EOQ_i < b_i$.

4. $TC(q) =$ actual annual cost if q items are ordered each time an order is placed. (We determine $TC(q)$ by using price p_i if $b_{i-1} \leq q < b_i$.)

Our goal is to find the value of q minimizing $TC(q)$. Figures 6a and 6b illustrate these definitions. Observe that in Figure 6a, EOQ_2 is admissible because $b_1 < EOQ_2 < b_2$, but EOQ_1 and EOQ_3 are not admissible. In each figure, $TC(q)$ is the solid portion of the curve. The dashed portion of each curve represents unattainable costs. For instance, in Figure 6b, $TC_2(q)$ is dotted for $q < b_1$ because the price is not p_2 for $q < b_1$. In Figure 6b, for $q < b_1$, total annual cost is given by the solid portion of $TC_1(q)$ because for $q < b_1$, the price is p_1, and for $q \geq b_1$, total annual cost is given by the solid portion of $TC_2(q)$.

In general, the value of q minimizing $TC(q)$ can be either a break point (see Figure 6b) or some EOQ_i (see Figure 6a).

The following observations are helpful in determining the point (break point or EOQ_i) that minimizes $TC(q)$.

1. For any value of q,

$$TC_k(q) < TC_{k-1}(q) < \cdots < TC_2(q) < TC_1(q)$$

This observation is valid because for any order quantity q, $TC_k(q)$ will have the lowest holding and purchasing costs, since p_k is the lowest available price; $TC_1(q)$ will have the highest holding and purchasing costs, because p_1 is the highest available price. Thus, in Figure 6a, we find that $TC_3(q) < TC_2(q) < TC_1(q)$.

2. If EOQ_i is admissible, then minimum cost for $b_{i-1} \leq q < b_i$ occurs for $q = EOQ_i$ (see Figure 7a). If $EOQ_i < b_{i-1}$, the minimum cost for $b_{i-1} \leq q < b_i$ occurs for $q = b_{i-1}$ (see Figure 7b). This observation follows from the fact that $TC_i(q)$ decreases for $q < EOQ_i$ and increases for $q > EOQ_i$.

Figure 6
Illustrations of
Definitions of $TC_i(q)$
and EOQ_i

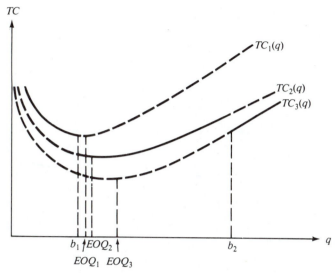

(a) EOQ_2 minimizes TC

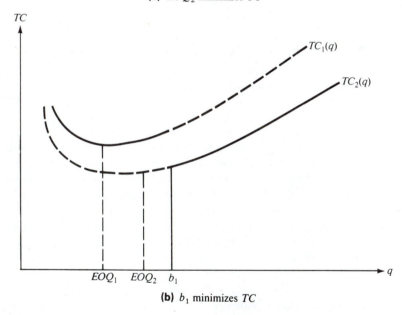

(b) b_1 minimizes TC

3. If EOQ_i is admissible, then $TC(q)$ cannot be minimized at an order quantity for which the purchasing price per item exceeds p_i. Thus, if EOQ_i is admissible, the optimal order quantity must occur for either price $p_i, p_{i+1}, \ldots,$ or p_k.

To see why observation 3 holds, suppose EOQ_i is admissible. Why can't an order quantity associated with a price $p_j > p_i$ have a lower cost than EOQ_i? Note that EOQ_i minimizes total annual cost if price is p_i and EOQ_j does not minimize total annual cost if price is p_i. Thus,

$$TC_i(EOQ_i) < TC_i(EOQ_j)$$

Figure 7
For $b_{i-1} \leq q < b_i$,
What Value of q
Minimizes $TC_i(q)$?

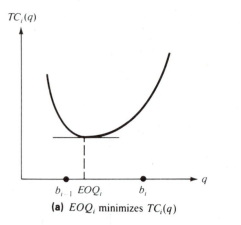

(a) EOQ_i minimizes $TC_i(q)$

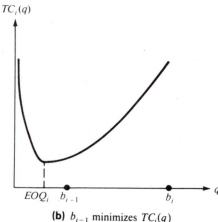

(b) b_{i-1} minimizes $TC_i(q)$

Since $p_j > p_i$,

$$TC_i(EOQ_j) < TC_j(EOQ_j)$$

The last two inequalities show that

$$TC_i(EOQ_i) < TC_j(EOQ_j)$$

By the definition of EOQ_j, we know that for all q,

$$TC_j(EOQ_j) \leq TC_j(q)$$

Thus,

$$TC_i(EOQ_i) < TC_j(EOQ_j) \leq TC_j(q)$$

and ordering EOQ_i at price p_i is superior to ordering any quantity at a higher price p_j.

These observations allow us to use the following method to determine the optimal order quantity when quantity discounts are allowed. Beginning with the lowest price, determine for each price the order quantity that minimizes total annual costs for $b_{i-1} \leq q < b_i$ (call this order quantity q_i^*). Continue determining $q_k^*, q_{k-1}^*, \ldots$ until one of the q_i^*'s (call it $q_{i'}^*$) is admissible; from observation 2, this will mean that $q_{i'}^* = EOQ_{i'}$. The optimal order quantity will be the member of $\{q_k^*, q_{k-1}^*, \ldots, q_{i'}^*\}$ with the smallest value of $TC(q)$.

E X A M P L E
4

Buying Diskettes (Continued)   Each time an order is placed for diskettes, how many boxes of diskettes should be ordered? How many orders will be placed annually? What is the total annual cost of meeting the accounting firm's diskette needs?

Solution

Note that $K = \$100$ and $D = 1000$ boxes per year. We first determine the best order quantity for $p_3 = \$48.50$ and $300 \leq q$. Then

$$EOQ_3 = \left(\frac{2(100)1000}{0.2(48.50)}\right)^{1/2} = 143.59$$

Since $EOQ_3 < 300$, EOQ_3 is not admissible. Therefore, Figure 7b is relevant, and for $q \geq 300$, $TC_3(q)$ is minimized by $q_3^* = 300$.

We next consider $p_2 = \$49.00$ and $100 \le q < 300$. Then

$$EOQ_2 = \left(\frac{2(100)(1000)}{9.8}\right)^{1/2} = 142.86$$

Since $100 \le EOQ_2 < 300$, EOQ_2 is admissible, and for a price $p_2 = \$49.00$, the best we can do is to choose $q_2^* = 142.86$; Figure 7a is relevant. Since q_2^* is admissible, $p_1 = \$50.00$ and $0 \le q < 100$ cannot yield the order quantity minimizing $TC(q)$ (see observation 3). Thus, either $q_2^* = 142.86$ or $q_3^* = 300$ will minimize $TC(q)$. To determine which of these order quantities minimizes $TC(q)$, we must find the smaller of $TC_3(300)$ and $TC_2(142.86)$. For $q_3^* = 300$, the annual holding cost/item/year is $0.20(48.50) = \$9.70$. Thus, for q_3^*,

$$\text{Annual ordering cost} = 100\left(\tfrac{1000}{300}\right) = \$333.33$$
$$\text{Annual purchasing cost} = 1000(48.50) = \$48,500$$
$$\text{Annual holding cost} = (\tfrac{1}{2})(300)(9.7) = \$1455$$
$$TC_3(300) = \$50,288.33$$

For $q_2^* = 142.86$, the annual holding cost/item/year is $0.20(49) = \$9.80$. Thus, for q_2^*,

$$\text{Annual ordering cost} = 100\left(\tfrac{1000}{142.86}\right) = \$699.99$$
$$\text{Annual purchasing cost} = 1000(49) = \$49,000$$
$$\text{Annual holding cost} = (\tfrac{1}{2})(142.86)(9.8) = \$700.01$$
$$TC_2(142.86) = \$50,400$$

Thus, $q_3^* = 300$ will minimize $TC(q)$.

Our analysis shows that each time an order is placed, 300 boxes of diskettes should be ordered. Then $\frac{1000}{300} = 3.33$ orders are placed each year. As we have already seen, the minimum total annual cost is \$50,288.33.   ◆

◆ PROBLEMS

GROUP A

1. A consulting firm is trying to determine how to minimize the annual costs associated with purchasing computer paper. Each time an order is placed for computer paper, an ordering cost of \$20 is incurred. The price per box of computer paper depends on q, the number of boxes ordered (see Table 3). The annual holding cost is 20% of

Table 3

NO. OF BOXES ORDERED	PRICE PER BOX
$q < 300$	\$10.00
$300 \le q < 500$	\$9.80
$q \ge 500$	\$9.70

the dollar value of inventory. During each month, the consulting firm uses 80 boxes of computer paper. Determine the optimal order quantity and the number of orders placed each year.

2. Each year, Shopalot Stores sells 10,000 cases of soda. The company is trying to determine how many cases of soda should be ordered each time an order is placed with the supplier. It costs \$5 to process each order, and the cost of carrying a case of soda in inventory for one year is 20% of the purchase price. The soda supplier offers Shopalot the schedule of quantity discounts shown in Table 4 (q = number of cases ordered per order). Each time an order is placed, how many cases of soda should the company order?

Table 4

NO. OF CASES ORDERED	PRICE PER CASE
$q < 200$	\$4.40
$200 \le q < 400$	\$4.20
$q \ge 400$	\$4.00

3. A firm buys a product using the price schedule given in Table 5. The company estimates holding costs at 10% of purchase price per year and ordering costs at \$40 per order. The firm's annual demand is 460 units.
(a) Determine how often the firm should order.
(b) Determine the size of each order.
(c) At what price should the firm order?

Table 5

ORDER SIZE	PRICE PER UNIT
0–99 units	\$20.00
100–199	\$19.50
200–499	\$19.00
500 or more	\$18.75

GROUP B

4. A hospital orders its thermometers from a hospital supply firm. The cost per thermometer depends on the order size q, as shown in Table 6. The annual holding cost is 25% of the purchasing cost. Let EOQ_{80} be the EOQ if the cost per thermometer is 80¢, and let EOQ_{79} be the EOQ if the cost per thermometer is 79¢.

Table 6

ORDER SIZE	PRICE PER THERMOMETER
$q < 100$	80¢
$q \ge 100$	79¢

(a) Explain why EOQ_{79} will be larger than EOQ_{80}.
(b) Explain why the optimal order quantity must be either EOQ_{79}, EOQ_{80}, or 100.
(c) If $EOQ_{80} > 100$, show that the optimal order quantity must be EOQ_{79}.
(d) If $EOQ_{80} < 100$ and $EOQ_{79} < 100$, show that the optimal order quantity must be either EOQ_{80} or 100.
(e) If $EOQ_{80} < 100$ and $EOQ_{79} > 100$, show that the optimal order quantity must be EOQ_{79}.

5. In Problem 4, suppose the cost per order is \$1 and the monthly demand is 50 thermometers. What is the optimal order quantity? How small a discount could the supplier offer and still have the hospital accept the discount?

16-4   THE CONTINUOUS-RATE EOQ MODEL

Many goods are produced internally rather than purchased from an outside supplier. In this situation, the EOQ assumption that each order arrives at the same instant seems unrealistic; it isn't possible to produce, say, 10,000 cars at the drop of a hard hat. If a company meets demand by making its own products, the continuous-rate EOQ model will be more realistic than the traditional EOQ model. Again, we assume that demand is deterministic and occurs at a constant rate; we also assume that shortages are not allowed.

The continuous-rate EOQ model assumes that a firm can produce a good at a rate of r units per time period (we again use one year as the time unit). This means that during any time period of length t, the firm can produce rt units. We define

q = number of units produced during each production run

K = cost of setting up a production run
(often due to idle time that occurs at the beginning or end of a production run)

h = cost of holding one unit in inventory for one year

D = annual demand for the product

Assuming that a production run begins at time 0, the variation of inventory over time is described by Figure 8. At the beginning of a production run, we are producing at a rate of r units per year, and demand is occurring at a rate of D units per year. Thus, until q units are produced, inventory increases at a rate of $r - D$ units per year. (Of course, $r \geq D$ must hold, or else demand could not be met.) At time $\frac{q}{r}$, q units will have been produced. At this time, the production run is complete, and inventory decreases at a rate of D units per year until a zero inventory position is reached. A zero inventory level will occur at time $\frac{q}{D}$. Then another production run begins.

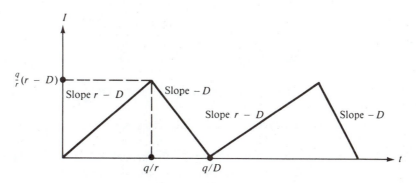

Figure 8
Variation of
Inventory for
Continuous-Rate
EOQ Model

Assuming that per-unit production costs are independent of run size, we must determine the value of q that minimizes

$$\frac{\text{Holding cost}}{\text{Year}} + \frac{\text{setup cost}}{\text{year}}$$

Since demand occurs at a constant rate, we know that (average inventory level) = ($\frac{1}{2}$)(maximum inventory level). From Figure 8, we see that the maximum inventory level occurs at time $\frac{q}{r}$. Since between zero and $\frac{q}{r}$, the inventory level is increasing at a rate of $r - D$ units per year, the inventory level at time $\frac{q}{r}$ will be $(\frac{q}{r})(r - D)$. Then (average inventory level) = $(\frac{1}{2})(\frac{q}{r})(r - D)$, and

$$\frac{\text{Holding cost}}{\text{Year}} = h(\text{average inventory})(1 \text{ year}) = \frac{h(r - D)q}{2r}$$

Observe that the annual holding cost for the continuous-rate EOQ model is the same as the annual holding cost for a conventional EOQ model in which the unit holding cost is $\frac{h(r-D)}{r}$. As usual,

$$\frac{\text{Ordering cost}}{\text{Year}} = \left(\frac{\text{ordering cost}}{\text{cycle}}\right)\left(\frac{\text{cycles}}{\text{year}}\right) = \frac{KD}{q}$$

The discussion shows that

$$\frac{\text{Holding cost}}{\text{Year}} + \frac{\text{ordering cost}}{\text{year}} = \frac{hq(r - D)}{2r} + \frac{KD}{q}$$

The last equation shows that the problem of minimizing the sum of annual holding and ordering costs for the continuous-rate model is equivalent to solving an EOQ model with holding cost $\frac{h(r-D)}{r}$, ordering cost K, and annual demand D. Using this observation and the economic order quantity (or lot size) formula (2), we may immediately deduce that for the continuous-rate EOQ model,

$$\text{Optimal run size} = \left(\frac{2KD}{\dfrac{h(r-D)}{r}}\right)^{1/2} = \left(\frac{2KDr}{h(r-D)}\right)^{1/2} \tag{5}$$

As usual, $\frac{D}{q}$ production runs must be made each year to meet the annual demand of D units. Using the fact that

$$\text{EOQ} = \left(\frac{2KD}{h}\right)^{1/2}$$

we may rewrite (5) as

$$\text{Optimal run size} = \text{EOQ}\left(\frac{r}{r-D}\right)^{1/2} \tag{6}$$

As r increases, production occurs at a more rapid rate. Hence, for large r, the rate model should approach the instantaneous-delivery situation of the EOQ model. To see that this is the case, note that for r large, $\frac{r}{(r-D)}$ approaches 1. Then (6) shows that as r increases toward infinity, the optimal run size for the continuous-rate model approaches the EOQ.

E X A M P L E
5

Macho Auto Company needs to produce 10,000 car chassis per year. Each car chassis is valued at $2000. The plant has the capacity to produce 25,000 chassis per year. It costs $200 to set up a production run, and the annual cost of holding inventory is 25¢ per dollar of inventory. Determine the optimal production run size. How many production runs should be made each year?

Solution We are given that

$$r = 25{,}000 \text{ chassis per year}$$
$$D = 10{,}000 \text{ chassis per year}$$
$$h = 0.25(\$2000)/\text{chassis/year} = \$500/\text{chassis/year}$$
$$K = \$200 \text{ per production run}$$

From Eq. (5),

$$\text{Optimal run size} = \left(\frac{2(200)(10{,}000)(25{,}000)}{500(25{,}000 - 10{,}000)}\right)^{1/2} = 115.47$$

Also, $\frac{10{,}000}{115.47} = 86.60$ production runs will be made each year.

◆

◆ PROBLEMS

GROUP A

1. Show that the optimal run size always exceeds the EOQ. Given an intuitive explanation for this result.

2. A company can produce 100 home computers per day. The setup cost for a production run is $1000. The cost of holding a computer in inventory for one year is $300. Customers demand 2000 home computers per month (assume that 1 month = 30 days and 360 days = 1 year). What is the optimal production run size? How many production runs must be made each year?

3. The production process at Father Dominic's Pizza can produce 400 pizza pies per day; the firm operates 250 days per year. Father Dominic's has a cost of $180 per production run and a holding cost of $5 per pizza-year. The pies are frozen immediately after they are produced and stored in a refrigerated warehouse with a current maximum capacity of 2000 pies.
(a) Annual demand is 37,500 pies per year. What production run size should be used?
(b) What is the total annual cost incurred in meeting demand?

(c) How many days per year will the company be producing pizza pies?

GROUP B

4. A company has the option of purchasing a good or manufacturing the item. If the item is purchased, the company will be charged $25 per unit plus a cost of $4 per order. If the company manufactures the item, it has a production capacity of 8000 units per year. It costs $50 to set up a production run, and annual demand is 3000 units per year. If the annual holding cost is 10% and the cost of manufacturing one unit is $23, determine whether the company should purchase or manufacture the item.

16-5   THE EOQ MODEL WITH BACK ORDERS ALLOWED

In many real-life situations, demand is not met on time, and shortages occur. When a shortage occurs, costs are incurred (because of lost business, the cost of placing special orders, loss of future goodwill, and so on). In this section, we modify the EOQ model of Section 16.2 to allow for the possibility of shortages. Let s be the cost of being short one unit for one year. The variables K, D, and h have their usual meanings. In most situations, s is very difficult to measure. We assume that all demand is backlogged and no sales are lost. In order to determine the order policy that minimizes annual costs, we define

$$q = \text{order quantity}$$

$$q - M = \text{maximum shortage that occurs under an ordering policy}$$

Equivalently (assuming a zero lead time), the firm will be $q - M$ units short each time an order is placed.

We assume that the lead time for each order is zero. Since an order is placed each time the firm is $q - M$ units short (or when the firm's inventory position is $M - q$), the firm's maximum inventory level will be $M - q + q = M$. For example, if $q = 500$ and $q - M = 100$, we know that an order for 500 units will be placed whenever the firm is 100 units short. Each order for 500 units will be used to satisfy the backlogged demand for 100 units and will result in an inventory level of $500 - 100 = 400$ units.

Assuming that an order is placed at time 0, the evolution of the inventory level over time is described by Figure 9. Since purchasing costs do not depend on q and M, we can minimize annual costs by determining the values of q and M that minimize

$$\frac{\text{Holding cost}}{\text{Year}} + \frac{\text{shortage cost}}{\text{year}} + \frac{\text{order cost}}{\text{year}} \tag{7}$$

Notice that what happens between time 0 and time B is identical to what happens between time B and time D. For this reason, we call the time periods $0B$ and BD **cycles**. A cycle may also be thought of as the time interval between placement of orders. To determine holding cost per year and shortage cost per year, we begin by finding holding cost per cycle and shortage cost per cycle. This requires that we find the length of line segments $0A$ and AB in Figure 9. Since a zero inventory level occurs after M units have been demanded, we conclude that $0A = \frac{M}{D}$. Since a cycle ends when q units have been demanded, we conclude that $0B = \frac{q}{D}$. Then

$$\text{Length of } AB = (\text{length of } 0B) - (\text{length of } 0A) = \frac{q - M}{D}$$

Figure 9
Evolution of
Inventory over Time
for EOQ Model with
Back Orders Allowed

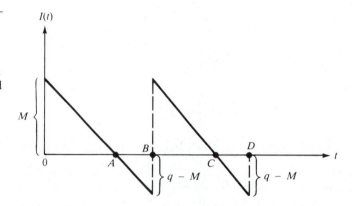

Also note that since q units are ordered during each cycle, $\frac{D}{q}$ cycles (and orders) must be placed during each year. We can now express the costs in (7). Recall that

$$\frac{\text{Holding cost}}{\text{Year}} = \left(\frac{\text{holding cost}}{\text{cycle}}\right)\left(\frac{\text{cycles}}{\text{year}}\right)$$

and

$$\frac{\text{Holding cost}}{\text{Cycle}} = \text{holding cost from time 0 to time } A$$

From Figure 9, the average inventory level between time 0 and time A is simply $\frac{M}{2}$. Since $0A$ is of length $\frac{M}{D}$,

$$\frac{\text{Holding cost}}{\text{Cycle}} = \left(\frac{M}{2}\right)\left(\frac{M}{D}\right)h = \frac{M^2 h}{2D}$$

Since there are $\frac{D}{q}$ cycles per year,

$$\frac{\text{Holding cost}}{\text{Year}} = \left(\frac{M^2 h}{2D}\right)\left(\frac{D}{q}\right) = \frac{M^2 h}{2q}$$

Similarly,

$$\frac{\text{Shortage cost}}{\text{Year}} = \left(\frac{\text{shortage cost}}{\text{cycle}}\right)\left(\frac{\text{cycles}}{\text{year}}\right)$$

Also observe that shortage cost per cycle = shortage cost incurred during time AB. Since demand occurs at a constant rate, the average shortage level during time AB is simply half of the maximum shortage. Thus, the average shortage level on the time interval AB is $\frac{q-M}{2}$. Since AB is a time interval of length $\frac{q-M}{D}$,

$$\frac{\text{Shortage cost}}{\text{Cycle}} = \frac{1}{2}(q - M)\left(\frac{q - M}{D}\right)s = \frac{(q - M)^2 s}{2D}$$

Since there are $\frac{D}{q}$ cycles per year,

$$\frac{\text{Shortage cost}}{\text{Year}} = \frac{(q - M)^2 s}{2D}\left(\frac{D}{q}\right) = \frac{(q - M)^2 s}{2q}$$

As usual, ordering cost per year $= \frac{KD}{q}$. Let $TC(q, M)$ be the total annual cost (excluding purchasing cost) if our order policy uses parameters q and M. From our discussion, we must choose q and M to minimize

$$TC(q, M) = \frac{M^2 h}{2q} + \frac{(q - M)^2 s}{2q} + \frac{KD}{q}$$

By using Theorem 3 of Chapter 12, we can show that $TC(q, M)$ is a convex function of q and M. From Theorem 1' and Theorem 7 of Chapter 12, the minimum value of $TC(q, M)$ will occur at the point where

$$\frac{\partial TC}{\partial q} = \frac{\partial TC}{\partial M} = 0$$

Some tedious algebra shows that $TC(q, M)$ is minimized for q^* and M^*:

$$q^* = \left[\frac{2KD(h + s)}{hs}\right]^{1/2} = \text{EOQ}\left(\frac{h + s}{s}\right)^{1/2}$$

$$M^* = \left[\frac{2KDs}{h(h + s)}\right]^{1/2} = \text{EOQ}\left(\frac{s}{h + s}\right)^{1/2}$$

$$\text{Maximum shortage} = q^* - M^*$$

As s approaches infinity, q^* and M^* both approach the EOQ, and the maximum shortage approaches zero. This is reasonable, because if s is large, the cost of a shortage is prohibitive, and we would expect the optimal ordering policy to incur very few, if any, shortages. In other words, if s is very large, we are facing (to all intents and purposes) the no-shortages-allowed situation of Section 16.2.

**E X A M P L E
6**

Each year, the Smalltown Optometry Clinic sells 10,000 frames for eyeglasses. The clinic orders frames from a regional supplier, who charges $15 per frame. Each order incurs an ordering cost of $50. Smalltown Optometry believes that the demand for frames can be backlogged and that the cost of being short one frame for one year is $15 (because of loss of future business). The annual holding cost for inventory is 30¢ per dollar value of inventory. What is the optimal order quantity? What is the maximum shortage that will occur? What is the maximum inventory level that will occur?

Solution

We are given that

$$K = \$50$$
$$D = 10{,}000 \text{ frames per year}$$

$$h = 0.3(15) = \$4.50/\text{frame}/\text{year}$$
$$s = \$15/\text{frame}/\text{year}$$

Our formulas for q^* and M^* now yield

$$q^* = \left(\frac{2(50)(10{,}000)(19.50)}{(4.50)(15)}\right)^{1/2} = 537.48$$

$$M^* = \left(\frac{2(50)(10{,}000)(15)}{(4.50)(19.50)}\right)^{1/2} = 413.45$$

Then the maximum shortage occurring will be $q^* - M^* = 124.03$ frames, and each order should be for 537 or 538 frames. A maximum inventory level of $M^* = 413.45$ frames will occur.

◆

As in Section 16.4, suppose that production is not instantaneous and we can produce at a rate of r units per year. If shortages are allowed, it can be shown that

$$q^* = \left(\frac{2KDr(h + s)}{h(r - D)s}\right)^{1/2}$$

$$M^* = \frac{q^*(r - D)}{r} - \left(\frac{2KD(r - D)h}{sr(h + s)}\right)^{1/2}$$

The maximum shortage occurring in this case (call it S^*) is given by

$$S^* = \left(\frac{2KD(r - D)h}{sr(h + s)}\right)^{1/2}$$

◆ PROBLEMS

GROUP A

1. Show that the optimal order quantity for the backlogged demand model is always at least as large as the EOQ but that the maximum inventory level for the backlogged demand model cannot exceed the EOQ.

2. A Mercedes dealer must pay $20,000 for each car purchased. The annual holding cost is estimated to be 25% of the dollar value of inventory. The dealer sells an average of 500 cars per year. He believes that demand is backlogged but estimates that if he is short one car for one year he will lose $20,000 worth of future profits. Each time the dealer places an order for cars, ordering cost amounts to $10,000. Determine the Mercedes dealer's optimal ordering policy. What is the maximum shortage that will occur?

GROUP B

3. Suppose that instead of measuring shortage in terms of cost per shortage year, a cost of S dollars is incurred for each unit the firm is short. This cost does not depend on the length of time before the backlogged demand is satisfied. Determine a new expression for $TC(q, M)$, and explain how to determine optimal values q^* and M^*.

4. For the model developed in this section, determine
(a) The average length of time it takes to meet demand for a unit
(b) The fraction of all demanded units that are backordered

16-6   WHEN TO USE EOQ MODELS

Demand is often irregular, or "lumpy." This may be caused by seasonality or other factors. If demand is irregular, the Constant Demand Assumption that was required for all the EOQ models will not be satisfied.

To determine whether the assumption of constant demand is reasonable, suppose that during n periods of time, demands $d_1, d_2, \ldots, d_n$ have been observed. Also, enough is known about future demands to make the assumption of deterministic demand a realistic one. To decide whether demand is sufficiently regular to justify use of EOQ models, Peterson and Silver (1985) recommend that the following computations be done:

1. Determine the estimate $\bar{d}$ of the average demand per period given by

$$\bar{d} = \frac{1}{n} \sum_{i=1}^{i=n} d_i$$

2. Determine an estimate of the variance of the per-period demand $\mathbf{D}$ from

$$\text{Est. var } \mathbf{D} = \frac{1}{n} \sum_{i=1}^{i=n} d_i^2 - \bar{d}^2$$

3. Determine an estimate of the relative variability of demand (called the **variability coefficient**). This quantity is labeled VC, where

$$VC = \frac{\text{est. var } \mathbf{D}}{\bar{d}^2}$$

Note that if all the d_i are equal, the estimate of the variance of $\mathbf{D}$ will equal zero. This will also make $VC = 0$. Hence, if VC is small, this indicates that the Constant Demand Assumption is reasonable. Research indicates that the EOQ should be used if $VC < 0.20$; otherwise, demand is too irregular to justify the use of an EOQ model (see Peterson and Silver (1985)).

If $VC > 0.20$, dynamic programming methods and the Silver-Meal heuristic, which are discussed in Chapter 20, may be used to determine optimal ordering policies. The lot-sizing methods described in Section 18.1 may also be used in the case of variable demand.

As an example of the use of the VC formula, suppose that demands during the four quarters of the past year have been as follows: 80 units, 100 units, 130 units, and 90 units. Assuming that future demand is known to follow a similar pattern, should an EOQ model be used in this situation?

Since $\bar{d} = \frac{400}{4} = 100$ and est. var $\mathbf{D} = (\frac{1}{4})(80^2 + 100^2 + 130^2 + 90^2) - 100^2 = 350$, we have $VC = \frac{350}{(100)^2} = 0.035$. Since VC is smaller than 0.20, an EOQ model can be used in this situation.

In closing, we note that the EOQ models of this chapter require the implicit assumption that demands during different periods of time are independent. In other words, the EOQ models require that any knowledge about demand during one period of time gives no information about demand at any other point in time. If a firm's inventory needs are met through internal production, this is often an unrealistic assumption. For example, suppose a company needs to produce 5 units of product A by December 11 and that each unit of product A requires 2 units of product B and 3 units of product C. Once product B and product C are available, it takes 10 days to assemble a unit of product A. Then the fact that there is a demand for 5 units of product A on December 11 *creates* a December 1 demand for 10 units of product B and 15 units of product C. Hence, the December 1 demand for products B and C *depends* on the December 11 product A demand. Our EOQ models do not take into account the dependence of demand that is present in many manufacturing situations. These can best be exploited by using material resource planning (MRP) systems (see Section 18.1 for details).

◆ PROBLEM

GROUP A

1. Observed demand for air conditioners during the last four quarters was as follows: fall, 100; winter, 50; spring, 150; summer, 300. Is it reasonable to use an EOQ model in this situation?

◆ SUMMARY

NOTATION

K = setup or ordering cost

h = cost of holding one unit in inventory for one unit of time

D = demand rate per unit time

r = rate at which firm can make product per unit time ($r > D$)

s = cost of being one unit short for one unit of time

BASIC EOQ MODEL

$$\text{Order quantity} = q^* = \left(\frac{2KD}{h}\right)^{1/2}$$

$\frac{D}{q^*}$ orders are placed each unit of time.

QUANTITY DISCOUNT MODEL

If $q < b_1$, each item costs p_1 dollars.

If $b_1 \leq q < b_2$, each item costs p_2 dollars.

If $b_{k-2} \leq q < b_{k-1}$, each item costs p_{k-1} dollars.

If $b_{k-1} \leq q < b_k = \infty$, each item costs p_k dollars.

Beginning with the lowest price, determine for each price the order quantity that minimizes total annual costs for $b_{i-1} \leq q < b_i$ (call this order quantity q_i^*). Continue determining $q_k^*, q_{k-1}^*, \ldots$ until one of the q_i^*'s (call it $q_{i'}^*$) is admissible; from observation 2, this will mean that $q_{i'}^* = EOQ_{i'}$. The optimal order quantity will be the member of $\{q_k^*, q_{k-1}^*, \ldots, q_{i'}^*\}$ with the smallest value of $TC(q)$.

If EOQ_i is admissible, then $q_i^* = EOQ_i$. If $EOQ_i < b_{i-1}$, then $q_i^* = b_{i-1}$.

CONTINUOUS-RATE MODEL

$$\text{Optimal run size} = \left[\frac{2KDr}{h(r - D)} \right]^{1/2}$$

EOQ WITH BACK ORDERS ALLOWED

q^* = optimal order quantity

M^* = maximum inventory level under optimal ordering policy

$q^* - M^*$ = maximum shortage occurring under optimal ordering policy

$$q^* = \left[\frac{2KD(h + s)}{hs} \right]^{1/2} = \text{EOQ} \left(\frac{h + s}{s} \right)^{1/2}$$

$$M^* = \left[\frac{2KDs}{h(h + s)} \right]^{1/2} = \text{EOQ} \left(\frac{s}{h + s} \right)^{1/2}$$

◆ REVIEW PROBLEMS

GROUP A

1. Customers at Joe's Office Supply Store demand an average of 6000 desks per year. Each time an order is placed for desks, an ordering cost of $300 is incurred. The annual holding cost for a single desk is 25% of the $200 cost of a desk. One week elapses between the placement of an order and the arrival of the order. In parts (a)–(d), assume that no shortages are allowed.

(a) Each time an order is placed, how many desks should be ordered?

(b) How many orders should be placed each year?

(c) Determine the total annual costs (excluding purchasing costs) of meeting the customers' demands for desks.

(d) Determine the reorder point. If the lead time were 5 weeks, what would be the reorder point? (52 weeks = 1 year.)

(e) How would the answers to parts (a) and (b) change if shortages were allowed and a cost of $80 is incurred if Joe's is short one desk for one year?

2. Suppose Joe's is considering manufacturing desks. It costs $250 to set up a production run, and Joe's has the capacity to manufacture up to 10,000 desks per year. What is the optimal production run size? How many production runs will be made each year?

3. A camera store sells an average of 100 cameras per month. The cost of holding a camera in inventory for a year is 30% of the price the camera shop pays for the camera. It costs $120 each time the camera store places an

Table 7

NO. OF CAMERAS ORDERED	PRICE PER CAMERA
1–10	$10.00
11–40	$9.00
41–100	$7.00
More than 100	$5.50

order with its supplier. The price charged per camera depends on the number of cameras ordered (see Table 7). Each time the camera store places an order, how many cameras should be ordered?

GROUP B

4. A company inventories two items. The relevant data for each item are shown in Table 8. Determine the optimal inventory policy if no shortages are allowed and if the average investment in inventory is not allowed to exceed $700. If this constraint could be relaxed by $1, by how much would the company's annual costs decrease? (This problem requires knowledge of Section 12.8.)

5. A company produces three types of items. A single machine is used to produce the three items on a cyclical basis. The company has the policy that every item is produced once during each cycle, and it wishes to determine the number of production cycles per year that will

Table 8

	ITEM 1	ITEM 2
Annual demand	6000	4000
Per-unit cost	$4.00	$3.50
Annual holding cost	30% per year	25% per year
Price per order	$35	$20

minimize the sum of holding and setup costs (no shortages are allowed). The following data are given:

P_i = number of units of product i that could be produced per year if the machine were entirely devoted to producing product i

D_i = annual demand for product i

K_i = cost of setting up production for product i

h_i = cost of holding one unit of product i in inventory for one year

(a) Suppose there are N cycles per year. Assuming that during each cycle, a fraction $\frac{1}{N}$ of all demand for each product is met, determine the annual holding cost and the annual setup cost.

(b) Let q_i^* be the number of units of product i produced during each cycle. Determine the optimal value of N (call it N^*) and q_i^*.

(c) Let $EROQ_i$ be the optimal production run size for product i if the cyclical nature of the problem is ignored. Suppose q_i^* is much smaller than $EROQ_i$. What conclusion could be drawn?

(d) Under certain circumstances, it might not be desirable to produce every item during each cycle. Which of the following factors would tend to make it undesirable to produce product i during each cycle: (1) Demand for product i is relatively low. (2) The setup cost for product i is relatively high. (3) The holding cost for product i is relatively high.

◆ REFERENCES

The following books emphasize applications over theory:

BROWN, R. *Decision Rules for Inventory Management.* New York: Holt, Rinehart and Winston, 1967.

MCLEAVEY, D., and S. NARASIMHAN. *Production Planning and Inventory Control.* Boston: Allyn and Bacon, 1985.

PETERSON, R., and E. SILVER. *Decision Systems for Inventory Management and Production Planning.* New York: Wiley, 1985.

TERSINE, R. *Principles of Inventory and Materials Management.* New York: North-Holland, 1982.

VOLLMAN, T., W. BERRY, and C. WHYBARK. *Manufacturing Planning and Control Systems.* Homewood, Ill.: Irwin, 1988.

The following three books contain extensive discussions of inventory theory as well as applications:

HADLEY, G., and T. WHITIN. *Analysis of Inventory Systems.* Englewood Cliffs, N.J.: Prentice-Hall, 1963.

HAX, A., and D. CANDEA. *Production and Inventory Management.* Englewood Cliffs, N.J.: Prentice-Hall, 1984.

JOHNSON, L., and D. MONTGOMERY. *Operations Research in Production, Planning, Scheduling, and Inventory Control.* New York: Wiley, 1974.

BAUMOL, W. "The Transactions Demand for Cash: An Inventory Theoretic Approach," *Quarterly Journal of Economics* 16(1952):545–556.

IGNALL, E., and P. KOLESAR. "Operating Characteristics of a Simple Shuttle under Local Dispatching Rules," *Operations Research* 20(1972):1077–1088.

CHAPTER 17

Probabilistic Inventory Models

ALL THE INVENTORY models discussed in Chapter 16 require that demand during any period of time be known with certainty. In this chapter, we consider inventory models in which demand over a given time period is uncertain, or random; single-period inventory models, where a problem is ended once a single ordering decision has been made; single-period bidding models; versions of the EOQ model for uncertain demand that incorporate the important concepts of safety stock and service level; the periodic review (R, S) model; and the ABC inventory classification system.

17-1 SINGLE-PERIOD DECISION MODELS

In many situations, a decision maker is faced with the problem of determining the value q for a variable (q may be the quantity ordered of an inventoried good, for example, or the bid on a contract). After q has been determined, the value d assumed by a random variable $\mathbf{D}$ is observed. Depending on the values of d and q, the decision maker incurs a cost $c(d, q)$. We assume that the person is risk-neutral and wishes to choose q to minimize his expected cost. Since the decision is made only once, we call a model of this type a *single-period decision model*.

17-2 THE CONCEPT OF MARGINAL ANALYSIS

For the single-period model described in Section 17.1, we now assume that $\mathbf{D}$ is an integer-valued discrete random variable with $P(\mathbf{D} = d) = p(d)$. Let $E(q)$ be the decision maker's expected cost if q is chosen. Then

$$E(q) = \sum_d p(d)c(d, q)$$

In most practical applications, $E(q)$ is a convex function of q. Let q^* be the value of q that minimizes $E(q)$. If $E(q)$ is a convex function, the graph of $E(q)$ must look something like Figure 1. From the figure, we see that q^* is the smallest value of q for which

Figure 1
Determination of q^*
by Marginal Analysis

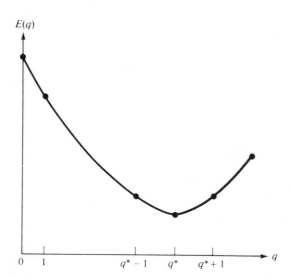

$$E(q^* + 1) - E(q^*) \geq 0 \tag{1}$$

Thus, if $E(q)$ is a convex function of q, we can find the value of q minimizing expected cost by finding the smallest value of q that satisfies inequality (1). Note that $E(q + 1) - E(q)$ is the change in expected cost that occurs if we increase the decision variable q to $q + 1$.

To determine q^*, we begin with $q = 0$. If $E(1) - E(0) \leq 0$, we can benefit by increasing q from 0 to 1. Now we check to see whether $E(2) - E(1) \leq 0$. If this is true, then increasing q from 1 to 2 will reduce expected cost. Continuing in this fashion, we see that increasing q by 1 will reduce expected costs up to the point where we try to increase q from q^* to $q^* + 1$. In this case, increasing q by 1 will increase expected cost. From Figure 1 (which is the appropriate picture if $E(q)$ is a convex function), we see that if $E(q^* + 1) - E(q^*) \geq 0$, then for $q \geq q^*$, $E(q + 1) - E(q) \geq 0$. Thus, q^* must be the value of q that minimizes $E(q)$. If $E(q)$ is not convex, this argument may not work (see Problem 1 at the end of this section).

Our approach determines q^* by repeatedly computing the effect of adding a marginal unit to the value of q. For this reason, it is often called **marginal analysis**. Marginal analysis is very useful if it is easy to determine a simple expression for $E(q + 1) - E(q)$. In the next section, we use marginal analysis to solve the classical news vendor problem.

◆ **PROBLEM**

GROUP A

1. Suppose $E(q)$ is $E(0) = 8$, $E(1) = 6$, $E(2) = 5$, $E(3) = 7$, $E(4) = 6$, $E(5) = 5.5$, $E(6) = 4.5$, and $E(7) = 5$.
(a) What value of q minimizes $E(q)$?

(b) If marginal analysis is used to determine the value of q that minimizes $E(q)$, what is the answer?
(c) Explain why marginal analysis fails to find the value of q that minimizes $E(q)$.

17-3   THE NEWS VENDOR PROBLEM: DISCRETE DEMAND

Organizations often face inventory problems where the following sequence of events occurs:

1. The organization decides how many units to order. We let q be the number of units ordered.

2. With probability $p(d)$, a demand of d units occurs. In this section, we assume that d must be a nonnegative integer. We let **D** be the random variable representing demand.

3. Depending on d and q, a cost $c(d, q)$ is incurred.

Problems that follow this sequence are often called **news vendor problems**. To see why, consider a vendor who must decide how many newspapers should be ordered each day from the newspaper plant. If the vendor orders too many papers, he or she will be left with many worthless newspapers at the end of the day. On the other hand, a vendor who orders too few newspapers will lose profit (and disappoint customers) that could have been earned if enough newspapers to meet customer demand had been ordered. The news vendor must order the number of papers that properly balances these two costs. We have already encountered a news vendor problem in the discussion of decision theory in Section 13.1.

In this section, we show how marginal analysis can be used to solve news vendor problems when demand is a discrete random variable and $c(d, q)$ has the following form:

$$c(d, q) = c_o q + \text{(terms not involving } q) \qquad (d \le q) \qquad \text{(2)}$$

$$c(d, q) = -c_u q + \text{(terms not involving } q) \qquad (d \ge q + 1) \qquad \text{(2.1)}$$

In (2), c_o is the per-unit cost of being overstocked. If $d \le q$, we have ordered more than was demanded—that is, overstocked. If the size of the order is increased from q to $q + 1$, then (2) shows that the cost increases by c_o. Hence, c_o is the cost due to being overstocked by 1 extra unit. We refer to c_o as the **overstocking cost**. Similarly, if $d \ge q + 1$, we have understocked (ordered an amount less than demand). If $d \ge q + 1$ and we increase the size of the order by 1 unit, we are understocked by 1 less unit. Then (2.1) implies that the cost is reduced by c_u, so c_u is the per-unit cost of being understocked. We call c_u the **understocking cost**.

To derive the optimal order quantity via marginal analysis, let $E(q)$ be the expected cost if an order is placed for q units. We assume that the decision maker's goal is to find the value q^* that minimizes $E(q)$. If $c(d, q)$ can be described by Eqs. (2) and (2.1), and $E(q)$ is a convex function of q, then marginal analysis can be used to determine q^*.

Following (1), we must determine the smallest value of q for which $E(q + 1) - E(q) \ge 0$. To calculate $E(q + 1) - E(q)$, we must consider two possibilities:

Case 1 $d \le q$. In this case, ordering $q + 1$ units instead of q units causes us to be overstocked by 1 more unit. This increases cost by c_o. The probability that Case 1 will occur is simply $P(\mathbf{D} \le q)$, where **D** is the random variable representing demand.

Case 2 $d \ge q + 1$. In this case, ordering $q + 1$ units instead of q units enables us to be short 1 less unit. This will decrease cost by c_u. The probability that Case 2 occurs is $P(\mathbf{D} \ge q + 1) = 1 - P(\mathbf{D} \le q)$.

In summary, a fraction $P(\mathbf{D} \leq q)$ of the time, ordering $q + 1$ units will cost c_o more than ordering q units; and a fraction $1 - P(\mathbf{D} \leq q)$ of the time, ordering $q + 1$ units costs c_u less than ordering q units. Thus, on the average, ordering $q + 1$ units costs

$$c_o P(\mathbf{D} \leq q) - c_u[1 - P(\mathbf{D} \leq q)]$$

more than ordering q units.

More formally, we have shown that

$$E(q + 1) - E(q) = c_o P(\mathbf{D} \leq q) - c_u[1 - P(\mathbf{D} \leq q)]$$
$$= (c_o + c_u)P(\mathbf{D} \leq q) - c_u{}^\dagger$$

Then $E(q + 1) - E(q) \geq 0$ will hold if

$$(c_o + c_u)P(\mathbf{D} \leq q) - c_u \geq 0 \quad \text{or} \quad P(\mathbf{D} \leq q) \geq \frac{c_u}{c_o + c_u}$$

Let $F(q) = P(\mathbf{D} \leq q)$ be the demand distribution function. Since marginal analysis is applicable, we have just shown that $E(q)$ will be minimized by the smallest value of q (call it q^*) satisfying

$$F(q^*) \geq \frac{c_u}{c_o + c_u} \tag{3}$$

The following example illustrates the use of (3).

E X A M P L E 1

In August, Walton Bookstore must decide how many of next year's nature calendars should be ordered. Each calendar costs the bookstore $2 and is sold for $4.50. After January 1, any unsold calendars are returned to the publisher for a refund of 75¢ per calendar. Walton believes that the number of calendars sold by January 1 follows the probability distribution shown in Table 1. Walton wishes to maximize the expected net profit from calendar sales. How many calendars should the bookstore order in August?[‡]

Table 1
Probability Mass
Function for
Calendar Sales

NO. OF CALENDARS SOLD	PROBABILITY
100	.30
150	.20
200	.30
250	.15
300	.05

Solution

Let

$$q = \text{number of calendars ordered in August}$$
$$d = \text{number of calendars demanded by January 1}$$

[†]Since $P(\mathbf{D} \leq q)$ increases as q increases, $E(q + 1) - E(q)$ will increase as q increases. Hence, if $c_o + c_u \geq 0$, $E(q)$ is a convex function of q, and our use of marginal analysis is justified.
[‡]Based on Barron (1985).

If $d \leq q$, the costs shown in Table 2 are incurred (revenue is negative cost). From (2), $c_o = 1.25$.

If $d \geq q + 1$, the costs shown in Table 3 are incurred. From (2), $-c_u = -2.5$, or $c_u = 2.5$. Then

$$\frac{c_u}{c_o + c_u} = \frac{2.5}{3.75} = \frac{2}{3}$$

From (3), Walton should order q^* calendars, where q^* is the smallest number for which $P(\mathbf{D} \leq q^*) \geq \frac{2}{3}$. As a function of q, $P(\mathbf{D} \leq q)$ increases only when $q = 100$, 150, 200, 250, or 300. Also note that $P(\mathbf{D} \leq 100) = .30$, $P(\mathbf{D} \leq 150) = .50$, $P(\mathbf{D} \leq 200) = .80$. Since $P(\mathbf{D} \leq 200)$ is greater than or equal to $\frac{2}{3}$, $q^* = 200$ calendars should be ordered.

Table 2 Computation of Total Cost If $d \leq q$		COST
	Buy q calendars at \$2/calendar	$2q$
	Sell d calendars at \$4.50/calendar	$-4.5d$
	Return $q - d$ calendars at 75¢/calendar	$-0.75(q - d)$
	Total cost	$1.25q - 3.75d$

Table 3 Computation of Total Cost If $d \geq q + 1$		COST
	Buy q calendars at \$2/calendar	$2q$
	Sell q calendars at \$4.50/calendar	$-4.50q$
	Total cost	$-2.5q$

◆

REMARKS   1. In terms of marginal analysis, the probability of selling the 200th calendar that is ordered is $P(\mathbf{D} \geq 200) = .50$. This implies that the 200th calendar has a $1 - .50 = .50$ chance of being unsold. Thus, the 200th calendar will increase Walton's expected costs by $.50(-2.50) + .50(1.25) = -\$0.625$. Hence, the 200th calendar should be ordered. On the other hand, the probability that the 201st calendar will be sold is $P(\mathbf{D} \geq 201) = .20$, and the probability that the 201st calendar will not be sold is $1 - .20 = .80$. Therefore, the 201st calendar will increase expected costs by $.20(-2.50) + .80(1.25) = \$0.50$. Thus, the 201st calendar will increase expected costs and should not be ordered.

2. In Example 1, c_o and c_u could easily have been determined without recourse to Eqs. (2) and (2.1). For example, being 1 more unit over actual demand increases Walton's costs by $2 - 0.75 = \$1.25$. Thus, $c_o = \$1.25$. Similarly, being 1 more unit under actual demand will cost Walton $4.50 - 2.00 = \$2.50$ in profit. Hence, $c_u = \$2.50$. If we are able to determine c_o and c_u without using (2) and (2.1), we should do so. In more difficult problems, however, they can be very useful (see Examples 2 and 3).

◆ PROBLEMS

GROUP A

1. In August 1991, a car dealer is trying to determine how many 1992 models should be ordered. Each car ordered in

August 1991 costs the dealer \$10,000. The demand for the dealer's 1992 models has the probability distribution shown in Table 4. Each car is sold for \$15,000. If the demand for 1992 cars exceeds the number of cars ordered in August, the dealer must reorder at a cost of $12,000 per car. If the demand for 1992 cars falls short, the dealer may dispose of excess cars in an end-of-model-year sale for $9000 per car. How many 1992 models should he order in August?

Table 4

NO. OF CARS DEMANDED	PROBABILITY
20	.30
25	.15
30	.15
35	.20
40	.20

2. Each day, a news vendor must determine how many *New York Herald Wonderfuls* to order. She pays 15¢ for each paper and sells each for 30¢. Any leftover papers are a total loss. From past experience, she believes that the number of papers she can sell each day is governed by the probability distribution shown in Table 5. How many papers should she order each day?

Table 5

NO. OF PAPERS DEMANDED	PROBABILITY
50	.30
70	.15
90	.25
110	.10
130	.20

3. If c_u is fixed, will an increase in c_o increase or decrease the optimal order quantity?

4. If c_o is fixed, will an increase in c_u increase or decrease the optimal order quantity?

5. The power at Ice Station Lion is supplied via solar cells. Once a year, a plane flies in and sells solar cells to the ice station at a price of $20 per cell. Because of uncertainty about future power needs, the ice station can only guess the number of cells that will be required during the coming year (see probability distribution in Table 6). If the ice station runs out of solar cells, a special order must be placed at a cost of $30 per cell.

(a) Assuming that the news vendor problem is relevant, how many cells should be ordered from the plane?
(b) In part (a), what type of cost is being ignored?

Table 6

NO. OF CELLS	PROBABILITY
50	.20
60	.15
70	.30
80	.10
90	.15
100	.10

GROUP B

6. Every four years, Blockbuster Publishers revises its textbooks. It has been three years since the best-selling book, *The Joy of OR*, has been revised. At present, 2000 copies of the book are in stock, and Blockbuster must determine how many copies of the book should be printed for the next year. The sales department believes that sales during the next year are governed by the distribution in Table 7. Each copy of *Joy* sold during the next year brings the publisher $35 in revenues. Any copies left at the end of the next year cannot be sold at full price but can be sold for $5 to Bonds Ennoble and Gitano's bookstores. The cost of a printing of the book is $50,000 plus $15 per book printed. How many copies of *Joy* should be printed? Would the answer change if 4000 copies of *Joy* were currently in stock?

Table 7

COPIES DEMANDED	PROBABILITY
5000	.30
6000	.20
7000	.40
8000	.10

7. Vivian and Wayne are planning on going to Lamaze natural childbirth classes. Lamaze classes meet once a week for five weeks. Each class gives 20% of the knowledge needed for "natural" childbirth. If Vivian and Wayne finish their classes before the birth of their child, they will forget during each week 5% of what they have learned in class. To maximize their expected knowledge at the time of childbirth, during which week of pregnancy should they begin classes? Assume that the number of weeks from conception to childbirth follows the probability distribution given in Table 8.

Table 8

Table 8

WEEK OF BIRTH	PROBABILITY
36	.05
37	.15
39	.20
40	.30
41	.15
42	.10
43	.05

8.[†] Some universities allow an employee to put an amount q into an account at the beginning of each year, to be used for child care expenses. The amount q put into the child care account is not subject to federal income tax. Assume that all other income is taxed by the federal government at a 40% rate. If child care expenses for the year (call them d) are less than q, the employee in effect loses $q - d$ dollars in before-tax income. If child care expenses exceed q, the employee must pay the excess child care expenses out of his or her own pocket but may credit 25% of the excess paid as a savings on his or her state income tax.

Suppose Professor Muffy Rabbit believes that there is an equal chance that her child care expenses for the coming year will be $3000, $4000, $5000, $6000, or $7000. At the beginning of the year, how much money should she place in the child care account?

[†] Based on Rosenfeld (1986).

17-4 THE NEWS VENDOR PROBLEM: CONTINUOUS DEMAND

We now consider the news vendor scenario of Section 17.3 when demand **D** is a continuous random variable having density function $f(d)$. By modifying our marginal analysis argument of Section 17.3 (or by using Leibniz's rule for differentiating an integral—see Problem 7 at the end of this section), it can be shown that the decision maker's expected cost is minimized by ordering q^* units, where q^* is the smallest number satisfying

$$P(\mathbf{D} \leq q^*) \geq \frac{c_u}{c_o + c_u} \tag{4}$$

Since demand is a continuous random variable, we can find a number q^* for which (4) holds with equality. Hence, in this case, the optimal order quantity can be determined by finding the value of q^* satisfying

$$P(\mathbf{D} \leq q^*) = \frac{c_u}{c_o + c_u} \quad \text{or} \quad P(\mathbf{D} \geq q^*) = \frac{c_o}{c_o + c_u} \tag{5}$$

From (5), we see that it is optimal to order units up to the point where the last unit ordered has a chance

$$\frac{c_o}{c_o + c_u}$$

of being sold. Examples 2 and 3 illustrate the use of Eq. (5).

E X A M P L E
2

The American Bar Association (ABA) is holding its annual convention in Las Vegas. Six months before the convention begins, the ABA must decide how many rooms should be reserved in the convention hotel. At this time, the ABA can reserve rooms at a cost of

$50 per room, but six months before the convention, the ABA does not know with certainty how many people will attend the convention. The ABA believes, however, that the number of rooms required is normally distributed with a mean of 5000 rooms and a standard deviation of 2000 rooms. If the number of rooms required exceeds the number of rooms reserved at the convention hotel, extra rooms will have to be found at neighboring hotels at a cost of $80 per room. It is inconvenient for convention participants to stay at neighboring hotels. We measure this inconvenience by assessing an additional cost of $10 for each room obtained at a neighboring hotel. If the goal is to minimize the expected cost to the ABA and its members, how many rooms should the ABA reserve at the convention hotel?

Solution   Define

$$q = \text{number of rooms reserved}$$

$$d = \text{number of rooms actually required}$$

If $d \leq q$, then the only cost incurred is the cost of the rooms reserved in advance, so if $d \leq q$, the total cost is $50q$. Thus, $c_o = 50$. If $d \geq q + 1$, the following costs are incurred:

Cost of reserving q rooms $= 50q$

Cost of renting $d - q$ rooms in neighboring hotels $= 80(d - q)$

Inconvenience cost to overflow participants $= 10(d - q)$

Total cost $= 90d - 40q$ and $c_u = 40$

Since $\dfrac{c_u}{c_o + c_u} = \frac{40}{90} = \frac{4}{9}$, we see from Eq. (5) that the optimal number of rooms to reserve is the number q^* satisfying

$$P(\mathbf{D} \leq q^*) = \tfrac{4}{9} \tag{6}$$

Since $\mathbf{D}$ is normally distributed with a mean of 5000 and a standard deviation of 2000, we can standardize Eq. (6) (see Section 11.7) with respect to the random variable $\mathbf{D}$ and obtain

$$P\left(\frac{\mathbf{D} - 5000}{2000} \leq \frac{q^* - 5000}{2000}\right) = .444$$

$$P\left(\mathbf{Z} \leq \frac{q^* - 5000}{2000}\right) = .444$$

From Figure 2, we see that $\frac{q^* - 5000}{2000}$ must equal the number in the standard normal tables that has an area .444 to the left of it. From the standard normal table (Table 4 of Chapter 11), we find that $P(\mathbf{Z} \leq -.14) = .4443$. Thus,

$$\frac{q^* - 5000}{2000} = -.14$$

$$q^* = 5000 - 2000(.14) = 4720$$

Therefore, the ABA should reserve 4720 rooms.

Figure 2
Determination of q^*
for Hotel Room
Reservation Example

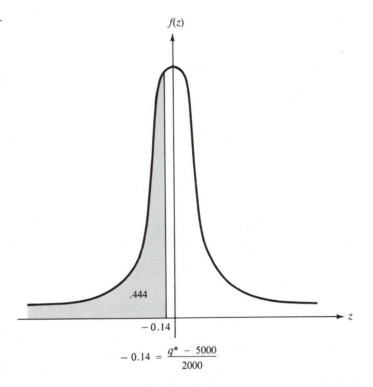

$$-0.14 = \frac{q^* - 5000}{2000}$$

**E X A M P L E
3**

The ticket price for a New York–Indianapolis flight is $200. Each plane can hold up to 100 passengers. Usually, some of the passengers who have purchased tickets for a flight fail to show up (no-shows). To protect against no-shows, the airline will try to sell more than 100 tickets for each flight. Federal law states that any ticketed customer who is unable to board the plane is entitled to compensation (say, $100). Past data indicate that the number of no-shows for each New York–Indianapolis flight is normally distributed with a mean of 20 and a standard deviation of 5. In order to maximize expected revenues less compensation costs, how many tickets should the airline sell for each flight? Assume that anybody who doesn't use a ticket receives a $200 refund.

Solution

Let

$$q = \text{number of tickets sold by airline}$$
$$d = \text{number of no-shows}$$

Observe that $q - d$ will be the number of customers actually showing up for the flight. If $q - d \le 100$, then all customers who show up will board the flight, and the cost to the airline is $-200(q - d) = 200d - 200q$. If $q - d \ge 100$, then 100 passengers will board the plane (paying the airline $200(100) = \$20,000$), and $q - d - 100$ customers will be turned away. These $q - d - 100$ customers will receive compensation of $100(q - d - 100)$. Hence, if $q - d \ge 100$, the total cost to the airline is given by $100(q - d - 100) - 200(100) = 100(q - 100) - 100d - 20,000$. In summary, the net cost to the airline may be expressed as shown in Table 9.

Table 9
Computation of
Total Cost If
$q - d \geq 100$

	TOTAL COST
$q - d \geq 100$ (or $d \leq q - 100$)	$100(q - 100) - 100d - 20{,}000$
$q - d \leq 100$ (or $d \geq q - 100$)	$200d - 200(q - 100) - 200(100)$

If $q - 100$ is considered as a decision variable, we have a news vendor problem with $-c_u = -200$ (or $c_u = 200$) and $c_o = 100$. From (5), we should choose $q - 100$ to satisfy

$$P(\mathbf{D} \leq q - 100) = \frac{c_u}{c_o + c_u} = \frac{2}{3} \tag{7}$$

Since **D** is normally distributed with a mean of 20 and standard deviation of 5, we may standardize (7) to obtain

$$P\left(\frac{\mathbf{D} - 20}{5} \leq \frac{q - 100 - 20}{5}\right) = .667$$

$$P\left(\mathbf{Z} \leq \frac{q - 120}{5}\right) = .667$$

From Figure 3, we see that $\frac{q - 120}{5}$ must be the number in the standarized normal tables that has an area .667 to the left of it. From Table 4 of Chapter 11, $P(\mathbf{Z} \leq .43) = .6664$. Therefore,

$$\frac{q - 120}{5} = .43$$

$$q = 120 + 5(.43) = 122.15$$

Figure 3
Determination of $q*$
for Airline
Reservation Example

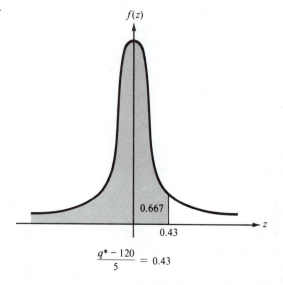

Therefore, we may conclude that the airline should attempt to sell 122 or 123 tickets. This means that once ticket sales have reached 122 (or 123), no more tickets should be sold for the flight. Of course, if fewer than 122 people want to purchase tickets for the flight, the airline should not refuse to sell anybody a ticket for the flight.

◆ PROBLEMS

GROUP A

1. (**a**) In Example 3, why is it unrealistic to assume that the distribution of the number of no-shows is independent of q?
(**b**) If the number of no-shows were normally distributed with a mean of $.05q$ and a standard deviation of $.05q$, would we still have a news vendor problem?

2. Condo Construction Company is going to First National Bank for a loan. At the present time, the bank is willing to lend Condo up to $1 million, with interest costs of 10%. Condo believes that the amount of borrowed funds needed during the current year is normally distributed with a mean of $700,000 and a standard deviation of $300,000. If Condo needs to borrow more money during the year, the company will have to go to Louie the Loan Shark. The cost per dollar borrowed from Louie is 25¢. In order to minimize expected interest costs for the year, how much money should Condo borrow from the bank?

3. Joe is selling Christmas trees to pay his college tuition. He purchases trees for $10 each and sells them for $25 each. The number of trees he can sell is normally distributed with a mean of 100 and standard deviation of 30. How many trees should Joe purchase?

4. A hot dog vendor at Wrigley Field sells hot dogs for $1.50 each. He buys them for $1.20 each. All the hot dogs he fails to sell at Wrigley Field during the afternoon can be sold that evening at Comiskey Park for $1 each. The daily demand for hot dogs at Wrigley Field is normally distributed with a mean of 40 and a standard deviation of 10.
(**a**) If the vendor buys hot dogs once a day, how many should he buy?
(**b**) If he buys 52 hot dogs, what is the probability that he will meet all of the day's demand for hot dogs at Wrigley?

GROUP B

5.[†] Motorama TV estimates the annual demand for its TVs is (and will be in the future) normally distributed with

a mean of 6000 and standard deviation of 2000. Motorama must determine how much production capacity it should have. The cost of building enough production capacity to make 1000 sets per year is $1,000,000 (equivalent in present-value terms to a cost of $100,000 per year forever). Exclusive of the cost of building capacity, each set sold contributes $250 to profits. How much production capacity should Motorama have?

6. I. L. Pea is a well-known mail order company. During the Christmas rush (from November 1 to December 15), the number of orders that I. L. Pea must fill each day (five days per week) is normally distributed with a mean of 2000 and a standard deviation of 500. I. L. Pea must determine how many employees should be working during the Christmas rush. Each employee works five days a week, eight hours a day, can process 50 orders per day, and is paid $10 per hour. If the full-time work force cannot handle the day's orders during regular hours, some employees will have to work overtime. Each employee is paid $15 per hour for overtime work. For example, if 300 orders are received in a day and there are four employees, then $300 - 4(50) = 100$ orders must be processed by employees who are working overtime. Since each employee can fill $\frac{50}{8} = 6.25$ orders per hour, I. L. Pea would need to pay workers $\frac{100}{6.25} = 16$ hours of overtime for that day. In order to minimize its expected labor costs, how many full-time employees should I. L. Pea employ during the Christmas rush?

7. Suppose demand is a continuous random variable having a probability density function $f(d)$, and $c(d, q)$ is given by Eq. (2). Show that if q units are ordered, the expected cost $E(q)$ may be written as

$$E(q) = \int_0^q c_o qf(t) \, dt + \int_q^\infty (-c_u)qf(t) \, dt$$
$$+ \text{ (terms not involving } q \text{ in integrand)}$$

Now use Leibniz's rule to derive (5).

[†] Based on Virts and Garrett (1970).

17–5   OTHER ONE-PERIOD MODELS

Many interesting single-period models in operations research cannot be easily handled by marginal analysis. In such situations, we express the decision maker's objective function (usually expected profit or expected cost) as a function $f(q)$ of the decision variable q. Then we find a maximum or minimum of $f(q)$ by setting $f'(q) = 0$. In this section, we illustrate this idea by a brief discussion of a bidding model.

E X A M P L E 4

Condo Construction Company is bidding on an important construction job. The job will cost $2 million to complete. One other company is bidding for the job. Condo believes that the opponent's bid is equally likely to be any amount between $2 million and $4 million. If Condo wants to maximize expected profit, what should its bid be?

Solution

Let

$$\mathbf{B} = \text{random variable representing bid of Condo's opponent}$$
$$b = \text{actual bid of Condo's opponent}$$

Then $f(b)$, the density function for $\mathbf{B}$, is given by

$$f(b) = \begin{cases} \dfrac{1}{2,000,000} & (2,000,000 \le b \le 4,000,000) \\ 0 & \text{otherwise} \end{cases}$$

Let q = Condo's bid. If $b > q$, Condo outbids the opponent and earns a profit of $q - 2,000,000$. On the other hand, if $b < q$, Condo is outbid by the opponent and earns nothing. The event $b = q$ has a zero probability of occurring and may be ignored. Let $E(q)$ be Condo's expected profit if it bids q. Then

$$E(q) = \int_{2,000,000}^{q} (0)f(b)\, db + \int_{q}^{4,000,000} (q - 2,000,000)f(b)\, db$$

Since $f(b) = \frac{1}{2,000,000}$ for $2,000,000 \le b \le 4,000,000$, we obtain

$$E(q) = \frac{(q - 2,000,000)(4,000,000 - q)}{2,000,000}$$

To find the value of q maximizing $E(q)$, we find

$$E'(q) = \frac{-(q - 2,000,000) + (4,000,000 - q)}{2,000,000} = \frac{6,000,000 - 2q}{2,000,000}$$

Hence, $E'(q) = 0$ for $q = 3,000,000$. Since $E''(q) = \frac{-2}{2,000,000} < 0$, we know that $E(q)$ is a concave function of q, and $q = 3,000,000$ does indeed maximize $E(q)$. Hence, Condo should bid $3 million. Condo's expected profit will be $E(3,000,000) = \$500,000$.

◆

◆ PROBLEMS

GROUP A

1. The City of Rulertown consists of the unit interval $[0, 1]$ (see Figure 4). Rulertown needs to determine where to build the city's only fire station. It knows that for small Δx, the probability that a given fire occurs at a location between x and $x + \Delta x$ is $2x(\Delta x)$. Rulertown wishes to minimize the average distance between the fire station and a fire. Where should the fire station be located?

Figure 4

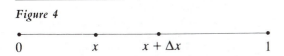

GROUP B

2. Assume that the Federal Reserve Board can control the growth rate of the U.S. money supply. Also assume that during a year in which the money supply grows by $x\%$, the Gross National Product (GNP) grows by $\mathbf{Z}x\%$, where $\mathbf{Z}$ is a known random variable. The government has decided it wants the GNP to grow by $k\%$ each year. (Too high a growth rate causes excessive inflation, and too low a growth rate causes high unemployment.) To model the government's view, the government assesses a cost of $(d - k)^2$ during a year in which the GNP grows by $d\%$.
(a) Determine the growth rate of the money supply that should be set by the Federal Reserve Board if the goal is to minimize the expected cost to the government.
(b) Show that for a given value of $E(\mathbf{Z})$, an increase in var $\mathbf{Z}$ will decrease the optimal growth rate of the money supply found in part (a). (*Hint:* Use the fact that var $\mathbf{Z} = E(\mathbf{Z}^2) - E(\mathbf{Z})^2$.)

17-6   THE EOQ WITH UNCERTAIN DEMAND: THE (r, q) AND (s, S) MODELS

In this section, we discuss a modification of the EOQ that is used when lead time is nonzero and the demand during each lead time is random. We begin by assuming that all demand can be backlogged. As in Chapter 16 we assume a continuous review model, so that orders may be placed at any time, and we define

$$K = \text{ordering cost}$$
$$h = \text{holding cost/unit/year}$$
$$L = \text{lead time for each order (assumed to be known with certainty)}$$
$$q = \text{quantity ordered each time an order takes place}$$

We also require the following definitions:

$\mathbf{D}$ = random variable (assumed continuous) representing annual demand with mean $E(\mathbf{D})$, variance var $\mathbf{D}$, and standard deviation $\sigma_\mathbf{D}$

c_B = cost incurred for each unit short, which does not depend on how long it takes to make up stockout

$OHI(t)$ = on-hand inventory (amount of stock on hand) at time t

From Figure 5, we can see that $OHI(1) = 100$, $OHI(0) = 200$, and $OHI(6) = OHI(7) = 0$.

$B(t)$ = number of outstanding back orders at time t

$I(t)$ = net inventory level at time $t = OHI(t) - B(t)$

r = inventory level at which order is placed (reorder point)

Figure 5
Evolution of
Inventory over Time
in Reorder Point
Model

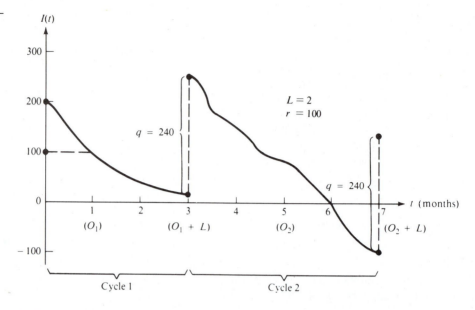

In Figure 5, $B(t) = 0$ for $0 \leq t \leq 6$ and $B(7) = 100$. $I(t)$ agrees with the inventory concept used in Chapter 16; in Figure 5, $I(0) = 200 - 0 = 200$, $I(3) = 260 - 0 = 260$, and $I(7) = 0 - 100 = -100$. In Figure 5, the reorder point $r = 100$; whenever the inventory level drops to r, an order is placed for q units.

$$\mathbf{X} = \text{random variable representing demand during lead time}$$

We assume that $\mathbf{X}$ is a continuous random variable having density function $f(x)$ and mean, variance, and standard deviation of $E(\mathbf{X})$, var $\mathbf{X}$, and $\sigma_{\mathbf{X}}$, respectively. If we assume that the demands at different points in time are independent, then it can be shown that the random lead time demand $\mathbf{X}$ satisfies

$$E(\mathbf{X}) = LE(\mathbf{D}), \qquad \text{var } \mathbf{X} = L(\text{var } \mathbf{D}), \qquad \sigma_{\mathbf{X}} = \sigma_{\mathbf{D}}\sqrt{L} \tag{8}$$

We assume that if $\mathbf{D}$ is normally distributed, then $\mathbf{X}$ will also be normally distributed.

Suppose we allow the lead time L to be a random variable (denoted by $\mathbf{L}$) with mean $E(\mathbf{L})$, variance var $\mathbf{L}$ and standard deviation $\sigma_{\mathbf{L}}$. If the length of the lead time is independent of the demand per unit time during the lead time, then

$$E(\mathbf{X}) = E(\mathbf{L})E(\mathbf{D}) \qquad \text{and} \qquad \text{var } \mathbf{X} = E(\mathbf{L})(\text{var } \mathbf{D}) + E(\mathbf{D})^2 (\text{var } \mathbf{L}) \tag{8'}$$

We wish to choose q and r to minimize the annual expected total cost (exclusive of purchasing cost). Before showing how optimal values of r and q can be found, we look at an illustration of how inventory evolves over time. Assume that an order of $q = 240$ units has just arrived at time 0. We also assume that $L = 2$. In Figure 5, orders of size q are placed at times $O_1 = 1$ and $O_2 = 5$. These orders are received at times $O_1 + L = 3$ and $O_2 + L = 7$, respectively. A **cycle** is defined to be the time interval between any two instants at which an order is received. Figure 5 contains two complete cycles: cycle 1, from arrival of order at time 0 to the instant before order arrives at time $O_1 + L = 3$; and cycle 2, from arrival of order at time $O_1 + L = 3$ to the instant before order arrives at time $O_2 + L = 7$.

During cycle 1, demand during lead time is less than r, so no shortage occurs. During cycle 2, however, demand during lead time exceeds r, so stockouts do occur between time 6 and time $O_2 + L = 7$. It should be clear that by increasing r, we can reduce the number of stockouts. Unfortunately, increasing r will force us to carry more inventory, thereby resulting in higher holding costs. Thus, an optimal value of r must represent some sort of tradeoff between holding and stockout costs.

We now show how the optimal values of q and r may be determined.

DETERMINATION OF REORDER POINT: BACK-ORDERED CASE

The situation in which all demand must eventually be met and no sales are lost is called the **back-ordered case**, for which we show how to determine the reorder point and order quantity that minimize annual expected cost.

We assume each unit is purchased for the same price, so purchasing costs are fixed. Define $TC(q, r) =$ expected annual cost (excluding purchasing cost) incurred if each order is for q units and is placed when the reorder point is r. Then $TC(q, r) =$ (expected annual holding cost) + (expected annual ordering cost) + (expected annual cost due to shortages). To determine the optimal reorder point and order quantity, we assume that the average number of back orders is small relative to the average on-hand inventory level. In most cases, this assumption is reasonable, because shortages (if they occur at all) usually occur during only a small portion of a cycle (see Problem 5 at the end of this section). Then $I(t) = OHI(t) - B(t)$ yields

$$\text{Expected value of } I(t) \cong \text{expected value of } OHI(t) \tag{9}$$

We can now approximate the expected annual holding cost. We know that expected annual holding cost $= h$(expected value of on-hand inventory level). Then from (9), we can approximate expected annual holding cost by h(expected value of $I(t)$). As in Chapter 16, the expected value of $I(t)$ will equal the expected value of $I(t)$ during a cycle. Since the mean rate at which demand occurs is constant, we may write

$$\text{Expected value of } I(t) \text{ during a cycle}$$
$$= \tfrac{1}{2}[(\text{expected value of } I(t) \text{ at beginning of cycle}) \tag{10}$$
$$+ (\text{expected value of } I(t) \text{ at end of a cycle})]$$

At the end of a cycle (the instant right before an order arrives), the inventory level will equal the inventory level at the reorder point (r) less the demand $\mathbf{X}$ during lead time. Thus, expected value of $I(t)$ at end of cycle $= r - E(\mathbf{X})$.

At the beginning of a cycle, the inventory level at the end of the cycle is augmented by the arrival of an order of size q. Thus, expected value of $I(t)$ at beginning of cycle $= r - E(\mathbf{X}) + q$. Now (10) yields

$$\text{Expected value of } I(t) \text{ during cycle} = \tfrac{1}{2}(r - E(\mathbf{X}) + r - E(\mathbf{X}) + q)$$
$$= \tfrac{q}{2} + r - E(\mathbf{X})$$

Thus, expected annual holding cost $\cong h(\tfrac{q}{2} + r - E(\mathbf{X}))$.

To determine the expected annual cost due to stockouts or back orders, we must define

$$\mathbf{B}_r = \text{random variable representing the number of stockouts}$$
$$\text{or back orders during a cycle if reorder point is } r$$

Now

$$\text{Expected annual shortage cost} = \left(\frac{\text{expected shortage cost}}{\text{cycle}}\right)\left(\frac{\text{expected cycles}}{\text{year}}\right)$$

By the definition of $\mathbf{B}_r$,

$$\frac{\text{Expected shortage cost}}{\text{Cycle}} = c_B E(\mathbf{B}_r)$$

Since all demand will eventually be met, an average of $\frac{E(\mathbf{D})}{q}$ orders will be placed each year. Then

$$\frac{\text{Expected shortage cost}}{\text{Year}} = \frac{c_B E(\mathbf{B}_r) E(\mathbf{D})}{q}$$

Finally,

$$\text{Expected annual order cost} = K\left(\frac{\text{expected orders}}{\text{year}}\right) = \frac{K E(\mathbf{D})}{q}$$

Putting together the expected annual holding, shortage, and ordering costs, we obtain

$$TC(q,r) = h\left(\frac{q}{2} + r - E(\mathbf{X})\right) + \frac{c_B E(\mathbf{B}_r) E(\mathbf{D})}{q} + \frac{K E(\mathbf{D})}{q} \tag{11}$$

Using the method described in Section 12.5, we could find the values of q and r that minimize (11) by determining values q^* and r^* of q and r satisfying

$$\frac{\partial TC(q^*, r^*)}{\partial q} = \frac{\partial TC(q^*, r^*)}{\partial r} = 0 \tag{12}$$

In most cases, however, the value of q^* satisfying (12) is very close to the EOQ[†] of $\left(\frac{2KE(\mathbf{D})}{h}\right)^{1/2}$. For this reason, we assume that the optimal order quantity q^* may be adequately approximated by the EOQ. Given a value q for the order quantity, we now show how marginal analysis can be used to determine a reorder point r^* that minimizes $TC(q,r)$.

If we assume a given value of q, the expected annual ordering cost is independent of r. Thus, in determining a value of r that minimizes $TC(q,r)$, we may concentrate on minimizing the sum of the expected annual holding and shortage costs. Following the marginal analysis approach of Sections 17.2–17.3, suppose we increase the reorder point (for Δ small) from r to $r + \Delta$ (with q fixed). Will this result in an increase or a decrease in $TC(q,r)$?

[†] Brown (1967) has shown that for approximating the optimal value of q, the EOQ is usually acceptable unless EOQ $\leq \sigma_{\mathbf{X}}$.

If we increase r to $r + \Delta$, the expected annual holding cost will increase by

$$h\left(\frac{q}{2} + r + \Delta - E(\mathbf{X})\right) - h\left(\frac{q}{2} + r - E(\mathbf{X})\right) = h\Delta$$

If we increase the reorder point from r to $r + \Delta$, expected annual stockout costs will be reduced, because of the fact that during any cycle in which lead time demand is at least r, the number of stockouts during the cycle will be reduced by Δ units. In other words, increasing the reorder point from r to $r + \Delta$ will reduce stockout costs by $c_B\Delta$ during a fraction $P(\mathbf{X} \geq r)$ of all cycles. Since there are an average of $\frac{E(\mathbf{D})}{q}$ cycles per year, increasing the reorder point from r to $r + \Delta$ will reduce expected annual stockout cost by

$$\frac{\Delta E(\mathbf{D})c_B P(\mathbf{X} \geq r)}{q}$$

Observe that as r increases, $P(\mathbf{X} \geq r)$ decreases, so as r increases, the expected reduction in expected annual shortage cost resulting from increasing the reorder point by Δ will decrease. This observation allows us to draw Figure 6.

Figure 6
Tradeoff between
Holding Cost and
Shortage Cost

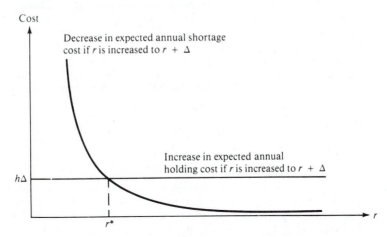

Let r^* be the value of r for which marginal benefit equals marginal cost, or

$$\frac{\Delta E(\mathbf{D})c_B P(\mathbf{X} \geq r^*)}{q} = h\Delta$$

$$P(\mathbf{X} \geq r^*) = \frac{hq}{c_B E(\mathbf{D})}$$

Suppose that $r < r^*$. Then Figure 6 shows that if we increase the reorder point from r to r^*, we can save more in shortage cost than we lose in holding cost. Now suppose that $r > r^*$. Figure 6 shows that by reducing the reorder point from r to r^*, we can save more in holding cost than we lose in increased shortage cost. Thus, r^* does attain the optimal tradeoff between shortage and holding costs. In summary, if we assume that the order quantity can be approximated by

$$\text{EOQ} = \left(\frac{2KE(\mathbf{D})}{h}\right)^{1/2}$$

then we have the reorder point r^* and the order quantity q^* for the back-ordered case:

$$q^* = \left(\frac{2KE(\mathbf{D})}{h} \right)^{1/2}$$

$$P(\mathbf{X} \geq r^*) = \frac{hq^*}{c_B E(\mathbf{D})}$$

(13)

If

$$\frac{hq^*}{c_B E(\mathbf{D})} > 1$$

then Eq. (13) will have no solution, and holding cost is prohibitively high relative to the stockout cost; then management should set the reorder point at the smallest acceptable level. If (13) yields a negative value of r^*, management should also set the reorder point at the smallest acceptable level.

R E M A R K S

1. $P(\mathbf{X} \geq r)$ is just the probability that a stockout occurs during a lead time. Also note that for h near zero, (13) yields a stockout probability near zero. For large c_B also, (13) yields a stockout probability near zero. Both of these results should be consistent with intuition.

2. After substituting the EOQ for q in (13), we may easily determine an approximately optimal value of r, the reorder point. Note that $r - E(\mathbf{X})$ is the amount in excess of expected lead time demand that is ordered to protect against the occurrence of stockouts during the lead time. For this reason, $r - E(\mathbf{X})$ is often referred to as **safety stock**.

3. From (11), we find that the expected annual cost of holding safety stock is $h(r - E(\mathbf{X})) = h$(safety stock level).

The following example illustrates the determination of the reorder point and safety stock level in the back-ordered demand case.

E X A M P L E 5

Each year, a computer store sells an average of 1000 boxes of diskettes. Annual demand for boxes of diskettes is normally distributed with a standard deviation of 40.8 boxes. The store orders diskettes from a regional distributor. Each order is filled in two weeks. The cost of placing each order is $50, and the annual cost of holding one box of diskettes in inventory is $10. The per-unit stockout cost (because of loss of goodwill and the cost of placing a special order) is assumed to be $20. The store is willing to assume that all demand is backlogged. Determine the proper order quantity, reorder point, and safety stock level for the computer store. Assume that annual demand is normally distributed. What is the probability that a stockout occurs during the lead time?

Solution

We begin by determining the EOQ. Since $h = \$10$/box/year, $K = \$50$, and $E(\mathbf{D}) = 1000$, we find that

$$\text{EOQ} = \left(\frac{2(50)(1000)}{10} \right)^{1/2} = 100$$

We now substitute $q^* = 100$ in (13) and use (13) to determine the reorder point. To do this, we need to determine the probability distribution of $\mathbf{X}$, the lead time demand. Since $L = 2$ weeks, $\mathbf{X}$ will be normally distributed with

$$E(\mathbf{X}) = \frac{E(\mathbf{D})}{26} = \frac{1000}{26} \doteq 38.46 \quad \text{and} \quad \sigma_x = \frac{\sigma_D}{\sqrt{26}} = \frac{40.8}{\sqrt{26}} = 8$$

Since $c_B = \$20$, (13) now yields

$$P(\mathbf{X} \geq r) = \frac{10(100)}{20(1000)} = .05 \tag{14}$$

Thus, the reorder point should be set so that the probability that a stockout occurs during a cycle equals .05. Standardizing (14) with respect to $\mathbf{X}$, we obtain

$$P\left(\frac{\mathbf{X} - 38.46}{8} \geq \frac{r - 38.46}{8}\right) = .05$$

$$P\left(\mathbf{Z} \geq \frac{r - 38.46}{8}\right) = .05$$

From Table 4 in Chapter 11, we find that $P(\mathbf{Z} \leq 1.65) = .9505$. Then $P(\mathbf{Z} \geq 1.65) = 1 - .9505 = .0495$ and

$$\frac{r - 38.46}{8} = 1.65$$

$$r = 38.46 + 8(1.65) = 51.66$$

Then the safety stock level is $r - E(\mathbf{X}) = 51.66 - 38.46 = 13.20$. ◆

To see how the reorder point and safety stock level would be affected by a variable lead time, suppose that the lead time still has a mean of two weeks but also has a standard deviation of one week ($\frac{1}{52}$ year). Then Eq. (8′) yields

$$\sigma_x^2 = (\tfrac{1}{26})(40.8)^2 + (1000)^2 (\tfrac{1}{52})^2 = 64.02 + 369.82 = 433.84$$

$$\sigma_x = \sqrt{433.84} = 20.83$$

Assuming that the lead time demand is normally distributed, we would find that $r = 38.46 + 1.65(20.83) = 72.83$, and the safety stock held is $1.65(20.83) = 34.37$. Thus, the variability of the lead time has more than doubled the required safety stock level!

DETERMINATION OF REORDER POINT: LOST SALES CASE

We now assume that all stockouts result in lost sales and that a cost of c_{LS} dollars is incurred for each lost sale. (In addition to penalties for loss of future goodwill, c_{LS} should include profit lost because of a lost sale.)

As in the back-ordered case, we assume that the optimal order quantity can be adequately approximated by the EOQ and attempt to use marginal analysis to determine the optimal reorder point r^* (see Problem 6 at the end of this section). The optimal order quantity q^* and the reorder point r^* for the lost sales case are

$$q^* = \left(\frac{2KE(\mathbf{D})}{h} \right)^{1/2}$$

$$P(\mathbf{X} \geq r^*) = \frac{hq^*}{hq^* + c_{LS}E(\mathbf{D})}$$

(15)

The key to the derivation of (15) is to realize that expected inventory in lost sales case = (expected inventory in back-ordered case) + (expected number of shortages per cycle). This equation follows because in the lost sales case, we find that during each cycle, an average of (expected shortages per cycle) fewer orders will be filled from inventory, thereby raising the average inventory level by an amount equal to expected shortages per cycle. Observe that the right-hand side of (15) is smaller than the right-hand side of (13). Thus, the lost sales assumption will yield a lower stockout probability (and a larger reorder point and safety stock level) than the back-ordered assumption.

To illustrate the use of (15), we continue our discussion of Example 5. Suppose that each box of diskettes sells for $50 and costs the store $30. Assuming that the stockout cost of $20 given in Example 5 represents lost goodwill, we obtain c_{LS} by adding the lost profit ($50 − $30) to the lost goodwill of $20. Thus, $c_{LS} = 20 + 20 = 40$. Recall from Example 5 that $E(\mathbf{D}) = 1000$ boxes per year, $h = \$10/box/year$, EOQ $= 100$ boxes, and $K = \$50$. Now (15) yields

$$P(\mathbf{X} \geq r^*) = \frac{10(100)}{10(100) + 40(1000)} = .024$$

Since $E(\mathbf{X}) = 38.46$ and $\sigma_\mathbf{X} = 8$, standardizing the last equation yields

$$P\left(\frac{\mathbf{X} - 38.46}{8} \geq \frac{r^* - 38.46}{8} \right) = .024$$

$$P\left(\mathbf{Z} \geq \frac{r^* - 38.46}{8} \right) = .024$$

From Table 4 of Chapter 11, $P(\mathbf{Z} \leq 1.98) = .9762$, so $P(\mathbf{Z} \geq 1.98) = 1 - .9762 = .0238$. Thus,

$$\frac{r - 38.46}{8} = 1.98$$

$$r = 38.46 + 8(1.98) = 54.30$$

Thus, in the lost sales case, the safety stock level is $54.30 - 38.46 = 15.84$.

CONTINUOUS REVIEW (r, q) POLICIES

A continuous review inventory policy, in which we order a quantity q whenever our inventory level reaches a reorder level r, is often called an (r, q) **policy**. An (r, q) policy is also called a **two-bin** policy, because it can easily be implemented by using two bins to store an item. For example, to implement a $(30, 500)$ policy, we fill orders from bin 1 as long as bin 1 contains any items. As soon as bin 1 becomes empty, we know that the reorder point $r = 30$ has been reached, and we place an order for $q = 500$ units. When the order arrives, we place $r = 30$ units in bin 2 and the remainder of the 500 units ordered in bin 1. Thus, whenever bin 1 has been emptied, we know that the reorder point has been reached.

CONTINUOUS REVIEW (s, S) POLICIES

In our derivation of the best (r, q) policy, we assumed that an order could be placed exactly at the point when the inventory level reached the reorder point r. We used this assumption to compute the expected inventory level at the beginning and end of a cycle. Suppose that a demand for more than one unit can arrive at a particular time. Then an order may be triggered when the inventory level is less than r, and our computation of expected inventory level at the end and beginning of a cycle is then incorrect. For example, suppose $r = 30$ and our current inventory level is 35. If an order for 10 units arrives, an order will be placed when the inventory level is 25 (not $r = 30$), and this invalidates the computations that led to (11). From this discussion, we see that it is possible for the inventory level to "undershoot" the reorder point. Note that this problem could not occur if all demands were for one unit, for then the inventory level would drop from (say) 32 to 31 and then to 30, and each order would be placed when the inventory level equaled the reorder point r. From this example, we see that if demands of size greater than one unit can occur at a point in time, then the (r, q) model may not yield a policy that minimizes expected annual cost. In such situations, it has been shown that an **(s, S) policy** is optimal. To implement an (s, S) policy, we place an order whenever the inventory level is less than or equal to s. The size of the order is sufficient to raise the inventory level to S (assuming zero lead time). For example, if we were implementing a $(5, 40)$ policy and the inventory level suddenly dropped from 7 to 3, we would immediately place an order for $40 - 3 = 37$ units. Exact computation of the optimal (s, S) policy is difficult. If we neglect the problem of the "undershoots," however, we may approximate the optimal (s, S) policy as follows. Set $S - s$ equal to the economic order quantity q. Then set s equal to the reorder point r obtained from (13) or (15). Finally, we obtain $S = r + q$. Thus, for Example 5 (with back orders allowed), we would set $s = 51.66$ and $S = 51.66 + 100 = 151.66$ and use (assuming that fractional demand is possible) a $(51.66, 151.66)$ policy.

◆ PROBLEMS

GROUP A

1. A hospital orders its blood from a regional blood bank. Each year, the hospital uses an average of 1040 pints of Type O blood. Each order placed with the regional blood bank incurs a cost of $20. The lead time for each order is one week. It costs the hospital $20 to hold 1 pint of blood in inventory for a year. The per-pint stockout cost is estimated to be $50. Annual demand for Type O blood is normally distributed with standard deviation of 43.26 pints. Determine the optimal order quantity, reorder point, and safety stock level. Assume that 52 weeks = 1 year and that all demand is backlogged. In order to use the techniques of this section, what unrealistic assumptions must be made? What (s, S) policy would be used in this situation?

2. Furnco sells secretarial chairs. Annual demand for secretarial chairs is normally distributed with mean of 1040 chairs and standard deviation of 50.99 chairs. Furnco orders its chairs from its flagship store. It costs $100 to place an order and the lead time on each order is two weeks. Furnco estimates that each stockout causes a loss of $50 in future goodwill. Furnco pays $60 for each chair and sells each chair for $100. The annual cost of holding a chair in inventory is 30% of the chair's purchase cost.

(a) Assuming that all demand is backlogged, what are the reorder point and the safety stock level?

(b) Assuming that all stockouts result in lost sales, determine the optimal reorder point and the safety stock level.

3. We are given the following information for a product:

> Order cost = $50
> Annual demand = N(960, 3,072.49)
> Annual holding cost = $6/item/year
> Shortage cost = $80 per unit
> Lead time = 1 month
> Sales price = $40 per unit
> Product cost = $30 per unit

(a) Determine the order quantity and the reorder point under the assumption that all demands are backordered.
(b) Determine the order quantity and the reorder point under the lost sales assumption.

4. The lead time demand for bathing suits is governed by the discrete random variable shown in Table 10. The company sells an average of 10,400 suits per year. The cost of placing an order for bathing suits is $30, and the cost of holding one bathing suit in inventory for a year is $3. The stockout cost is $3 per bathing suit. Use marginal analysis to determine the optimal order quantity and the reorder point.

Table 10

LEAD TIME DEMAND	PROBABILITY
180	.30
190	.30
200	.15
210	.10
220	.15

5. In Figure 5, assume that demand occurs at a constant rate during each cycle. Approximate the average level of on-hand inventory between $t = 0$ and $t = 7$. Also approximate the average number of shortages. Does the assumption that the average shortage level is small relative to the average level of on-hand inventory seem valid here?

GROUP B

6. In this problem, use marginal analysis to determine the optimal reorder point for the lost sales case.
(a) Show that the average inventory level for the lost sales case may be written as

$$\tfrac{1}{2}[(r - E(X) + E(B_r)) + (r - E(X) + E(B_r) + q)]$$
$$= r - E(X) + E(B_r) + \tfrac{q}{2}$$

(b) Although expected orders per year will no longer equal $\frac{E(D)}{q}$ (why?), we assume that the expected number of lost sales per year is relatively small. Thus, we may still assume that expected orders per year = $\frac{E(D)}{q}$. Now use marginal analysis to derive (15).

7. Suppose that a cost of S dollars (independent of the size of the stockout) is incurred whenever a stockout occurs during a cycle. Under the assumption of backlogged demand, use marginal analysis to determine the reorder point.

8. Explain the following statement: Faster-moving items require larger safety stocks than slower-moving items. (*Hint:* Does $\frac{q}{E(D)}$ large imply that an item is fast-moving or slow-moving?)

9. Suppose annual demand for a product is normally distributed with a mean of 600 and a variance of 300. Suppose that the lead time for an order is always one month. Show (without using Eq. (8)) that the lead time demand has mean 50, variance 25, and standard deviation 5. Assume that the demands during different one-month periods are independent, identically distributed random variables.

17-7 THE EOQ WITH UNCERTAIN DEMAND: THE SERVICE LEVEL APPROACH TO DETERMINING SAFETY STOCK LEVEL

As we have previously stated, it is usually very difficult to determine accurately the cost of being one unit short. For this reason, managers often decide to control shortages by meeting a specified service level. In this section, we discuss two measures of service level:

Service Level Measure 1 SLM_1, the expected fraction (usually expressed as a percentage) of all demand that is met on time.

Service Level Measure 2 SLM_2, the expected number of cycles per year during which a shortage occurs.

Throughout this section, we assume that all shortages are backlogged. The following example illustrates the meaning of the two service level measures.

<table>
<tr><td>E X A M P L E
6</td><td>Suppose that for a given inventory situation, average annual demand is 1000 and the EOQ is 100. Demand during a lead time is random and is described by the probability distribution in Table 11. For a reorder point of 30 units, determine SLM_1 and SLM_2.</td></tr>
</table>

Table 11
Mass Function for
Lead Time Demand

LEAD TIME DEMAND	PROBABILITY
20	$\frac{1}{5}$
30	$\frac{1}{5}$
40	$\frac{1}{5}$
50	$\frac{1}{5}$
60	$\frac{1}{5}$

Solution

The expected demand during a lead time is $\frac{1}{5}(20) + \frac{1}{5}(30) + \frac{1}{5}(40) + \frac{1}{5}(50) + \frac{1}{5}(60) = 40$ units. With a reorder point of 30 units, we will reorder during each cycle at the instant when the inventory level hits 30 units. If the lead time demand during a cycle is 20 or 30 units, we will experience no shortage. During a cycle in which lead time demand is 40, a shortage of 10 units will occur; if lead time demand is 50, a shortage of 20 units will occur; if lead time demand is 60, a shortage of 30 units will occur. Hence, the expected number of units short per cycle is given by $\frac{1}{5}(0) + \frac{1}{5}(0) + \frac{1}{5}(10) + \frac{1}{5}(20) + \frac{1}{5}(30) = 12$.

Since the EOQ = 100 and all demand must eventually be met, the average number of orders placed each year will be $\frac{E(\mathbf{D})}{q} = \frac{1000}{100} = 10$. Then the average number of shortages that occur during a year will equal $10(12) = 120$ units. Thus, each year, on the average, the demand for $1000 - 120 = 880$ units is met on time. In this case, the $SLM_1 = \frac{880}{1000} = 0.88$ or 88%. This shows that even if the reorder point is less than the mean lead time demand, a relatively high SLM_1 may result, because stockouts can only occur during the lead time, which is often a small portion of each cycle.

We now determine SLM_2 for a reorder point of 30. With a reorder point of 30, a stockout will occur during any cycle in which lead time demand exceeds 30 units. Thus, the probability of a stockout during a cycle = $P(\mathbf{X} = 40) + P(\mathbf{X} = 50) + P(\mathbf{X} = 60) = \frac{3}{5}$. Since there are an average of 10 cycles per year, the expected number of cycles per year that will result in shortages is $10(\frac{3}{5}) = 6$. Thus, a reorder point of 30 yields $SLM_2 = 6$ stockouts per year. ◆

**DETERMINATION OF REORDER POINT
AND SAFETY STOCK LEVEL FOR SLM_1**

Given a desired value of SLM_1, how do we determine a reorder point that provides the desired service level? Suppose we order the EOQ (q) and use a reorder point r. From Section 17.6,

$$\frac{\text{Expected shortages}}{\text{Cycle}} = E(\mathbf{B}_r)$$

$$\frac{\text{Expected shortages}}{\text{Year}} = \frac{E(\mathbf{B}_r)E(\mathbf{D})}{q}$$

Here, $E(\mathbf{D})$ is the average annual demand. Let SLM_1 be the percentage of all demand that is met on time. Then for given values q (for the order quantity) and r (for the reorder point), we have

$$1 - SLM_1 = \frac{\text{expected shortages per year}}{\text{expected demand per year}} = \frac{E(\mathbf{B}_r)E(\mathbf{D})/q}{E(\mathbf{D})} = \frac{E(\mathbf{B}_r)}{q} \tag{16}$$

Equation (16) can be used to determine the reorder point that yields a desired service level. We now assume that the lead time demand is normally distributed with mean $E(\mathbf{X})$ and standard deviation $\sigma_{\mathbf{X}}$. To use (16), we need to determine $E(\mathbf{B}_r)$. If $\mathbf{X}$ is normally distributed, the determination of $E(\mathbf{B}_r)$ requires a knowledge of the normal loss function.

DEFINITION   The **normal loss function**, $NL(y)$, is defined by the fact that $\sigma_{\mathbf{X}}NL(y)$ is the expected number of shortages that will occur during a lead time if (1) lead time demand is normally distributed with mean $E(\mathbf{X})$ and standard deviation $\sigma_{\mathbf{X}}$ and (2) the reorder point is $E(\mathbf{X}) + y\sigma_{\mathbf{X}}$.

In short, if we hold y standard deviations (in terms of lead time demand) of safety stock, then $NL(y)\sigma_{\mathbf{X}}$ is the expected number of shortages occurring during a lead time.

Since a larger reorder point leads to fewer shortages, we would expect $NL(y)$ to be a nonincreasing function of y. This is indeed the case. The function $NL(y)$ is tabulated in Table 12. For example, $NL(0) = 0.3989$ means that if the reorder point equals the expected lead time demand and the standard deviation of lead time demand is $\sigma_{\mathbf{X}}$, then an average of $0.3989\sigma_{\mathbf{X}}$ shortages will occur during a lead time. Similarly, $NL(2) = 0.0085$ means that if the reorder point exceeds the mean lead time demand by $2\sigma_{\mathbf{X}}$, then an average of $0.0085\sigma_{\mathbf{X}}$ shortages will occur during a given lead time. $NL(y)$ is not tabulated for negative values of y. This is because it can be shown that for $y \leq 0$, $NL(y) = NL(-y) - y$. For example, $NL(-2) = NL(2) + 2 = 2.0085$. This means that if the reorder point is $2\sigma_{\mathbf{X}}$ less than the mean lead time demand, an average of $2.0085\sigma_{\mathbf{X}}$ shortages will occur during each cycle.

Assuming normal lead time demand, we now determine the reorder point r that will yield a desired level of SLM_1 (expressed as a fraction). A reorder point of r corresponds to holding

$$y = \frac{r - E(\mathbf{X})}{\sigma_{\mathbf{X}}}$$

standard deviations of safety stock. Now the definition of the normal loss function implies that during a lead time a reorder point of r will yield an expected number of shortages $E(\mathbf{B}_r)$ given by

$$E(\mathbf{B}_r) = \sigma_{\mathbf{X}}NL\left(\frac{r - E(\mathbf{X})}{\sigma_{\mathbf{X}}}\right) \tag{17}$$

Table 12	x	$NL(x)$	x	$NL(x)$	x	$NL(x)$
The Normal Loss Function	0.00	0.3989	0.45	0.2137	0.90	0.1004
	0.01	0.3940	0.46	0.2104	0.91	0.09860
	0.02	0.3890	0.47	0.2072	0.92	0.09680
	0.03	0.3841	0.48	0.2040	0.93	0.09503
	0.04	0.3793	0.49	0.2009	0.94	0.09328
	0.05	0.3744	0.50	0.1978	0.95	0.09156
	0.06	0.3697	0.51	0.1947	0.96	0.08986
	0.07	0.3649	0.52	0.1917	0.97	0.08819
	0.08	0.3602	0.53	0.1887	0.98	0.08654
	0.09	0.3556	0.54	0.1857	0.99	0.08491
	0.10	0.3509	0.55	0.1828	1.00	0.08332
	0.11	0.3464	0.56	0.1799	1.01	0.08174
	0.12	0.3418	0.57	0.1771	1.02	0.08019
	0.13	0.3373	0.58	0.1742	1.03	0.07866
	0.14	0.3328	0.59	0.1714	1.04	0.07716
	0.15	0.3284	0.60	0.1687	1.05	0.07568
	0.16	0.3240	0.61	0.1659	1.06	0.07422
	0.17	0.3197	0.62	0.1633	1.07	0.07279
	0.18	0.3154	0.63	0.1606	1.08	0.07138
	0.19	0.3111	0.64	0.1580	1.09	0.06999
	0.20	0.3069	0.65	0.1554	1.10	0.06862
	0.21	0.3027	0.66	0.1528	1.11	0.06727
	0.22	0.2986	0.67	0.1503	1.12	0.06595
	0.23	0.2944	0.68	0.1478	1.13	0.06465
	0.24	0.2904	0.69	0.1453	1.14	0.02034
	0.25	0.2863	0.70	0.1429	1.15	0.06210
	0.26	0.2824	0.71	0.1405	1.16	0.06086
	0.27	0.2784	0.72	0.1381	1.17	0.05964
	0.28	0.2745	0.73	0.1358	1.18	0.05844
	0.29	0.2706	0.74	0.1334	1.19	0.05726
	0.30	0.2668	0.75	0.1312	1.20	0.05610
	0.31	0.2630	0.76	0.1289	1.21	0.05496
	0.32	0.2592	0.77	0.1267	1.22	0.05384
	0.33	0.2555	0.78	0.1245	1.23	0.05274
	0.34	0.2518	0.79	0.1223	1.24	0.05165
	0.35	0.2481	0.80	0.1202	1.25	0.05059
	0.36	0.2445	0.81	0.1181	1.26	0.04954
	0.37	0.2409	0.82	0.1160	1.27	0.04851
	0.38	0.2374	0.83	0.1140	1.28	0.04750
	0.39	0.2339	0.84	0.1120	1.29	0.04650
	0.40	0.2304	0.85	0.1100	1.30	0.04553
	0.41	0.2270	0.86	0.1080	1.31	0.04457
	0.42	0.2236	0.87	0.1061	1.32	0.04363
	0.43	0.2203	0.88	0.1042	1.33	0.04270
	0.44	0.2169	0.89	0.1023	1.34	0.04179

Table 12
Continued

x	NL(x)	x	NL(x)	x	NL(x)
1.35	0.04090	1.80	0.01428	2.25	0.004235
1.36	0.04002	1.81	0.01392	2.26	0.004114
1.37	0.03916	1.82	0.01357	2.27	0.003996
1.38	0.03831	1.83	0.01323	2.28	0.003882
1.39	0.03748	1.84	0.01290	2.29	0.003770
1.40	0.03667	1.85	0.01257	2.30	0.003662
1.41	0.03587	1.86	0.01226	2.31	0.003556
1.42	0.03508	1.87	0.01195	2.32	0.003453
1.43	0.03431	1.88	0.01164	2.33	0.003352
1.44	0.03356	1.89	0.01134	2.34	0.003255
1.45	0.03281	1.90	0.01105	2.35	0.003159
1.46	0.03208	1.91	0.01077	2.36	0.003067
1.47	0.03137	1.92	0.01049	2.37	0.002977
1.48	0.03067	1.93	0.01022	2.38	0.002889
1.49	0.02998	1.94	0.009957	2.39	0.002804
1.50	0.02931	1.95	0.009698	2.40	0.002720
1.51	0.02865	1.96	0.009445	2.41	0.002640
1.52	0.02800	1.97	0.009198	2.42	0.002561
1.53	0.02736	1.98	0.008957	2.43	0.002484
1.54	0.02674	1.99	0.008721	2.44	0.002410
1.55	0.02612	2.00	0.008491	2.45	0.002337
1.56	0.02552	2.01	0.008266	2.46	0.002267
1.57	0.02494	2.02	0.008046	2.47	0.002199
1.58	0.02436	2.03	0.007832	2.48	0.002132
1.59	0.02380	2.04	0.007623	2.49	0.002067
1.60	0.02324	2.05	0.007418	2.50	0.002004
1.61	0.02270	2.06	0.007219	2.51	0.001943
1.62	0.02217	2.07	0.007024	2.52	0.001883
1.63	0.02165	2.08	0.006835	2.53	0.001826
1.64	0.02114	2.09	0.006649	2.54	0.001769
1.65	0.02064	2.10	0.006468	2.55	0.001715
1.66	0.02015	2.11	0.006292	2.56	0.001662
1.67	0.01967	2.12	0.006120	2.57	0.001610
1.68	0.01920	2.13	0.005952	2.58	0.001560
1.69	0.01874	2.14	0.005788	2.59	0.001511
1.70	0.01829	2.15	0.005628	2.60	0.001464
1.71	0.01785	2.16	0.005472	2.61	0.001418
1.72	0.01742	2.17	0.005320	2.62	0.001373
1.73	0.01699	2.18	0.005172	2.63	0.001330
1.74	0.01658	2.19	0.005028	2.64	0.001288
1.75	0.01617	2.20	0.004887	2.65	0.001247
1.76	0.01578	2.21	0.004750	2.66	0.001207
1.77	0.01539	2.22	0.004616	2.67	0.001169
1.78	0.01501	2.23	0.004486	2.68	0.001132
1.79	0.01464	2.24	0.004358	2.69	0.001095

Table 12
Continued

x	NL(x)	x	NL(x)	x	NL(x)
2.70	0.001060	3.15	0.0002227	3.60	0.00003911
2.71	0.001026	3.16	0.0002147	3.61	0.00003755
2.72	0.0009928	3.17	0.0002070	3.62	0.00003605
2.73	0.0009607	3.18	0.0001995	3.63	0.00003460
2.74	0.0009295	3.19	0.0001922	3.64	0.00003321
2.75	0.0008992	3.20	0.0001852	3.65	0.00003188
2.76	0.0008699	3.21	0.0001785	3.66	0.00003059
2.77	0.0008414	3.22	0.0001720	3.67	0.00002935
2.78	0.0008138	3.23	0.0001657	3.68	0.00002816
2.79	0.0007870	3.24	0.0001596	3.69	0.00002702
2.80	0.0007611	3.25	0.0001537	3.70	0.00002592
2.81	0.0007359	3.26	0.0001480	3.71	0.00002486
2.82	0.0007115	3.27	0.0001426	3.72	0.00002385
2.83	0.0006879	3.28	0.0001373	3.73	0.00002287
2.84	0.0006650	3.29	0.0001322	3.74	0.00002193
2.85	0.0006428	3.30	0.0001273	3.75	0.00002103
2.86	0.0006213	3.31	0.0001225	3.76	0.00002016
2.87	0.0006004	3.32	0.0001179	3.77	0.00001933
2.88	0.0005802	3.33	0.0001135	3.78	0.00001853
2.89	0.0005606	3.34	0.0001093	3.79	0.00001776
2.90	0.0005417	3.35	0.0001051	3.80	0.00001702
2.91	0.0005233	3.36	0.0001012	3.81	0.00001632
2.92	0.0005055	3.37	0.00009734	3.82	0.00001563
2.93	0.0004883	3.38	0.00009365	3.83	0.00001498
2.94	0.0004716	3.39	0.00009009	3.84	0.00001435
2.95	0.0004555	3.40	0.00008666	3.85	0.00001375
2.96	0.0004398	3.41	0.00008335	3.86	0.00001317
2.97	0.0004247	3.42	0.00008016	3.87	0.00001262
2.98	0.0004101	3.43	0.00007709	3.88	0.00001208
2.99	0.0003959	3.44	0.00007413	3.89	0.00001157
3.00	0.0003822	3.45	0.00007127	3.90	0.00001108
3.01	0.0003689	3.46	0.00006852	3.91	0.00001061
3.02	0.0003560	3.47	0.00006587	3.92	0.00001016
3.03	0.0003436	3.48	0.00006331	3.93	0.00000972
3.04	0.0003316	3.49	0.00006085	3.94	0.000009307
3.05	0.0003199	3.50	0.00005848	3.95	0.000008908
3.06	0.0003087	3.51	0.00005620	3.96	0.000008525
3.07	0.0002978	3.52	0.00005400	3.97	0.000008158
3.08	0.0002873	3.53	0.00005188	3.98	0.000007806
3.09	0.0002771	3.54	0.00004984	3.99	0.000007469
3.10	0.0002672	3.55	0.00004788	4.00	0.000007145
3.11	0.0002577	3.56	0.00004599		
3.12	0.0002485	3.57	0.00004417		
3.13	0.0002396	3.58	0.00004242		
3.14	0.0002311	3.59	0.00004073		

From R. Peterson and E. Silver, *Decision Systems for Inventory and Production Planning*, © 1979, John Wiley & Sons, New York. Reprinted with permission.

Substituting (17) into (16), we obtain the reorder point for SLM_1 with normal lead time demand:

$$1 - SLM_1 = \frac{\sigma_X NL\left(\frac{r - E(X)}{\sigma_X}\right)}{q} \tag{18}$$

$$NL\left(\frac{r - E(X)}{\sigma_X}\right) = \frac{q(1 - SLM_1)}{\sigma_X}$$

With the exception of r, all quantities in (18) are known. Thus, (18) and Table 12 can be used to determine the reorder point corresponding to a given level of SLM_1.

E X A M P L E 7

Bads, Inc., sells an average of 1000 food processors each year. Each order for food processors that is placed by Bads costs $50. The lead time on each order is one month. It costs $10 to hold a food processor in inventory for one year. Annual demand for food processors is normally distributed with a standard deviation of 69.28. For each of the following values of SLM_1, determine the reorder point: 80%, 90%, 95%, 99%, 99.9%.

Solution

Note that $E(D) = 1000$, $K = \$50$, and $h = \$10$, so

$$q = \left[\frac{2(50)(1000)}{10}\right]^{1/2} = 100$$

Also,

$$E(X) = (\tfrac{1}{12})(1000) = 83.33 \quad \text{and} \quad \sigma_X = \frac{69.28}{\sqrt{12}} = 20$$

From (18), the reorder point for an 80% value of SLM_1 must satisfy

$$NL\left(\frac{r - 83.33}{20}\right) = \frac{100(1 - 0.80)}{20} = 1$$

From Table 12, we find that 1 exceeds any of the tabulated values of the normal loss function. Thus, the value of r must make $\frac{r - 83.33}{20}$ a negative number. A little trial and error reveals that $N(-0.9) = N(0.9) + 0.9 = 1.004$. Hence,

$$\frac{r - 83.33}{20} = -0.9$$

$$r = 83.33 - 20(0.9) = 65.33$$

For $SLM_1 = 0.90$, Eq. (18) shows that the reorder point must satisfy

$$NL\left(\frac{r - 83.33}{20}\right) = \frac{(1 - 0.90)100}{20} = 0.5$$

Again, 0.5 exceeds all tabulated values of the normal loss function. Hence, $\frac{r - 83.33}{20}$ must be a negative number. A little trial and error reveals that $N(-0.19) = N(0.19) + 0.19 = 0.5011$. Thus, the reorder point for a 90% service level must satisfy

$$\frac{r - 83.33}{20} = -0.19$$

$$r = 83.33 - 20(0.19) = 79.53$$

A 90% service level can be attained by a reorder point that is less than the expected lead time demand.

To attain a 95% service level, r must satisfy

$$NL\left(\frac{r - 83.33}{20}\right) = \frac{(1 - 0.95)100}{20} = 0.25$$

Since $NL(0.34) = 0.2518$,

$$\frac{r - 83.33}{20} = 0.34$$

$$r = 83.33 + 20(0.34) = 90.13$$

For a 99% service level,

$$NL\left(\frac{r - 83.33}{20}\right) = \frac{(1 - 0.99)100}{20} = 0.05$$

Since $NL(1.25) = 0.0506$, we see that

$$\frac{r - 8.33}{20} = 1.25$$

$$r = 83.33 + 20(1.25) = 108.33$$

Finally, for a 99.9% service level, r must satisfy

$$\frac{r - 83.33}{20} = \frac{(1 - 0.999)100}{20} = 0.005$$

Since $NL(2.19) = 0.005$,

$$\frac{r - 83.33}{20} = 2.19$$

$$r = 83.33 + 20(2.19) = 127.13$$

In summary, the reorder points corresponding to the various values of SLM_1 are given in Table 13. Notice that to go from an 80% to a 90% service level, we must increase the reorder point by 14.20, but to go from a 90% to a 99.9% service level, the reorder point

Table 13 Reorder Points for Various Service Levels	SLM_1	REORDER POINT
	80%	65.33
	90%	79.53
	95%	90.13
	99%	108.33
	99.9%	127.13

must be increased by 47.60. For higher service levels, a much greater increase in the reorder point is required in order to cause a commensurate increase in the service level. ◆

DETERMINATION OF REORDER POINT AND SAFETY STOCK LEVEL FOR SLM_2

Suppose that a manager wants to hold sufficient safety stock to ensure that an average of s_0 cycles per year will result in a stockout. Given a reorder point of r, a fraction $P(\mathbf{X} > r)$ of all cycles will lead to a stockout. Since an average of $\frac{E(\mathbf{D})}{q}$ cycles per year will occur (remember we are assuming backlogging), an average of $\frac{P(\mathbf{X} > r)E(\mathbf{D})}{q}$ cycles per year will result in a stockout. Thus, given s_0, the reorder point is the smallest value of r satisfying

$$\frac{P(\mathbf{X} > r)E(\mathbf{D})}{q} \le s_0 \quad \text{or} \quad P(\mathbf{X} > r) \le \frac{s_0 q}{E(\mathbf{D})}$$

If $\mathbf{X}$ is a continuous random variable, then $P(\mathbf{X} > r) = P(\mathbf{X} \ge r)$. Thus, we obtain the reorder point r for SLM_2 for continuous lead time demand,

$$P(\mathbf{X} \ge r) = \frac{s_0 q}{E(\mathbf{D})} \tag{19}$$

and the reorder point for SLM_2 for discrete lead time demand, by choosing the smallest value of r satisfying

$$P(\mathbf{X} > r) \le \frac{s_0 q}{E(\mathbf{D})} \tag{19'}$$

To illustrate the determination of the reorder point for SLM_2, we suppose that Bads, Inc., wants to ensure that stockouts occur during an average of two lead times per year. Recall from Example 7 that EOQ = 100, $E(\mathbf{D}) = 1000$ units per year, and $\mathbf{X}$ is $N(83.33, 400)$. Now (19) yields $P(\mathbf{X} \ge r) = \frac{2(100)}{1000} = .2$. Standardizing the last equation yields

$$P\left(\frac{\mathbf{X} - 83.33}{20} \ge \frac{r - 83.33}{20}\right) = .2$$

$$P\left(\mathbf{Z} \ge \frac{r - 83.33}{20}\right) = .2$$

From Table 4 of Chapter 11, $P(\mathbf{Z} \le .84) = .7995$ and $P(\mathbf{Z} \ge .84) = 1 - .7995 = .2005$. Then

$$\frac{r - 83.33}{20} = 0.84$$

$$r = 83.33 + 20(0.84) = 100.13$$

The safety stock level yielding an average of two stockouts per year would be $100.13 - E(\mathbf{X}) = 16.8$.

◆ PROBLEMS

GROUP A

1. For Problem 1 of Section 17.6, determine the reorder point that yields 80%, 90%, 95%, and 99% values of SLM_1. What reorder point would yield an average of 0.5 stockout per year?

2. For Problem 2 of Section 17.6, determine the reorder point that yields 80%, 90%, 95%, and 99% values of SLM_1. What reorder point would yield an average of 2 stockouts per year?

3. Suppose that the EOQ is 100, average annual demand is 1000 units, and the lead time demand is a random variable having the distribution shown in Table 14.
(a) What value of SLM_1 corresponds to a reorder point of 25?
(b) If we wanted to attain a 95 percent value of SLM_1, what reorder point should we choose?
(c) If we wanted an average of at most 2 stockouts per year, what reorder point should we choose?

Table 14

LEAD TIME DEMAND	PROBABILITY
10	$\frac{1}{6}$
15	$\frac{1}{4}$
20	$\frac{1}{4}$
25	$\frac{1}{12}$
30	$\frac{1}{4}$

4. A firm experiences demand with a mean of 100 units per day. Lead time demand is normally distributed with a mean of 1000 units and a standard deviation of 200 units. It costs $6 to hold one unit for one year. If the firm wants to meet 90% of all demand on time, what will be the annual cost of holding safety stock? (Assume that each order costs $50.)

17-8   (*R*, *S*) PERIODIC REVIEW POLICY*

In this section, we describe a widely used periodic review policy: the (*R*, *S*) policy. Before describing the operation of this policy, we need to define the concept of **on-order inventory level**. The on-order inventory level is simply the sum of on-hand inventory and inventory on order. Thus, if 30 units of a product are on hand and we order 70 units (with a lead time of, say, one month), our on-order inventory level is 100.

We can now describe the operation of the (*R*, *S*) inventory policy. Every *R* units of time (say, years), we review the on-hand inventory level and place an order to bring the on-order inventory level up to *S*. For example, if we were using a (.25, 100) policy, we would review the inventory level at the end of each quarter. If $i < 100$ units were on hand, an order for $100 - i$ units would be placed. In general, an (*R*, *S*) policy will incur higher holding costs than a cost-minimizing (*r*, *q*) policy, but an (*R*, *S*) policy is usually easier to administer than a continuous review policy. With an (*R*, *S*) policy (unlike a continuous review policy), we can predict with certainty the times when an order will be placed. An (*R*, *S*) policy also allows a company to coordinate replenishments. For example, a company could use $R = 1$ month for all products ordered from the same supplier and then order all products from that supplier on the first day of each month.

We now assume that the review interval *R* has been determined and focus on the determination of a value for *S* that will minimize expected annual costs. Later in this section, we will discuss how to determine an appropriate value for *R*. We now assume that all shortages are backlogged and demand is a continuous random variable whose distribution remains unchanged over time. Finally, we assume that the per-unit purchase

*This section covers topics that may be omitted with no loss of continuity.

price is constant. This implies that annual purchasing costs do not depend on our choice of R and S. We define

$$R = \text{time (in years) between reviews}$$
$$\mathbf{D} = \text{demand (random) during a one-year period}$$
$$E(\mathbf{D}) = \text{mean demand during a one-year period}$$
$$K = \text{cost of placing an order}$$
$$J = \text{cost of reviewing inventory level}$$
$$h = \text{cost of holding one item in inventory for one year}$$
$$c_B = \text{cost per unit short in the backlogged case (assumed to be}$$
$$\text{independent of the length of time until the order is filled)}$$
$$L = \text{lead time for each order (assumed constant)}$$
$$\mathbf{D}_{L+R} = \text{demand (random) during a time interval of length } L + R$$
$$E(\mathbf{D}_{L+R}) = \text{mean of } \mathbf{D}_{L+R}$$
$$\sigma_{\mathbf{D}_{L+R}} = \text{standard deviation of } \mathbf{D}_{L+R}$$

Given a value for R, we can now determine a value of S that minimizes expected annual costs. Our derivation mimics the derivation of (13). For a given choice of R and S, our expected annual costs are given by

(Annual expected purchase costs) + (annual review costs)
+ (annual ordering costs) + (annual expected holding costs)
+ (annual expected shortage costs)

Since $\frac{1}{R}$ reviews per year are placed, annual review costs are given by $\frac{J}{R}$. Also note that whenever an order is placed, the on-order inventory level will equal S. The only way that an order will not be placed at the next review point is if $\mathbf{D}_{L+R} = 0$. Since $\mathbf{D}_{L+R}$ is a continuous random variable, $\mathbf{D}_{L+R} = 0$ will occur with zero probability. Thus, an order is sure to be placed at the next review point (or any review point). This implies that annual order cost is given by $K(\frac{1}{R}) = \frac{K}{R}$. Observe that both the annual order cost and the review cost are independent of S. Thus, the value of S that minimizes annual expected costs will be the value of S that minimizes (annual expected holding costs) + (annual expected shortage costs).

To determine the annual expected holding cost for a given (R, S) policy, we first define a cycle to be the time interval between the arrival of orders. If we can determine the expected value of the average inventory level over a cycle, then expected annual holding cost is just h(expected value of on-hand inventory level over a cycle). As in our derivation of (11), we now assume that the average number of back orders is small relative to the average on-hand inventory level. Then, as in Section 17.6,

Expected value of $I(t) \cong$ expected value of $OHI(t)$

Then expected value of $I(t)$ over a cycle may be approximated by 0.5(expected value of $I(t)$ right before an order arrives) + 0.5(expected value of $I(t)$ right after an order arrives.)

Right before an order arrives, our maximum on-order inventory level (S) has been reduced by an average of $E(\mathbf{D}_{L+R})$. Thus, expected value of $I(t)$ right before an order arrives = $S - E(\mathbf{D}_{L+R})$.

Since $\frac{1}{R}$ orders are placed each year and an average of $E(\mathbf{D})$ units must be ordered each year, the average size of an order is $E(\mathbf{D})R$. Thus,

Expected value of $I(t)$ right after an order arrives $= S - E(\mathbf{D}_{L+R}) + E(\mathbf{D})R$

Then

$$\text{Expected value of } I(t) \text{ during a cycle } = S - E(\mathbf{D}_{L+R}) + \frac{E(\mathbf{D})R}{2}$$

Thus,

$$\text{Expected annual holding cost } = h\left[S - E(\mathbf{D}_{L+R}) + \frac{E(\mathbf{D})R}{2}\right]$$

From this expression, it follows that increasing S from S to $S + \Delta$ will increase expected annual holding costs by $h\Delta$.

We now focus on how an increase in S from S to $S + \Delta$ affects expected annual shortage costs. Then we can use marginal analysis to find the value of S that minimizes the sum of annual expected holding and shortage costs. Let's define the shortages "associated" with each order to be the shortages occurring in the time interval between the arrival of the order and the arrival of the next order. For example, an order placed at time 0 arrives at time L, and the next order will not arrive until time $R + L$. Thus, all shortages occurring between L and $R + L$ are associated with the time 0 order. Clearly, the sum of all shortages will equal the sum of the shortages associated with all orders. Let's again focus on the shortages associated with the time 0 order. Since the next order arrives at time $R + L$ and our time 0 order brought the on-order inventory level up to S, a shortage will be associated with the time 0 order if and only if the demand between time 0 and $R + L$ exceeds S. If a shortage occurs, the magnitude of the shortage will equal $\mathbf{D}_{L+R} - S$.

We can now use marginal analysis to determine (for a given R) the value of S that minimizes the sum of annual expected holding and shortage costs. If we increase S from S to $S + \Delta$, annual expected holding costs increase by $h\Delta$. Increasing S from S to $S + \Delta$ will decrease shortages associated with an order if $\mathbf{D}_{L+R} \geq S$. Thus, for a fraction $P(\mathbf{D}_{L+R} \geq S)$ of all orders, increasing S from S to $S + \Delta$ will save $c_B\Delta$ in shortage costs. Since $\frac{1}{R}$ orders are placed each year, increasing S from S to $S + \Delta$ will reduce expected annual shortage costs by $(\frac{1}{R})c_B\Delta P(\mathbf{D}_{L+R} \geq S)$. Marginal analysis then implies that the value of S minimizing the sum of annual expected holding and shortage costs will occur for the value of S satisfying

$$h\Delta = (\tfrac{1}{R})c_B\Delta P(\mathbf{D}_{L+R} \geq S)$$

or

$$P(\mathbf{D}_{L+R} \geq S) = \frac{Rh}{c_B} \tag{20}$$

Suppose that all shortages result in lost sales, and a cost of c_{LS} (including shortage cost plus lost profit) is incurred for each lost sale. Then the value of S minimizing the sum of annual expected holding and shortage costs is given by

$$P(\mathbf{D}_{L+R} \geq S) = \frac{Rh}{Rh + c_{LS}} \tag{21}$$

The following example illustrates the use of Eq. (20).

E X A M P L E
8

Lowland Appliance replenishes its stock of color TVs three times a year. Each order takes $\frac{1}{9}$ year to arrive. Annual demand for color TVs is $N(990, 1600)$. The cost of holding one color TV in inventory for one year is $100. Assume that all shortages are backlogged, with a shortage cost of $150 per TV. When Lowland places an order, what should the on-order inventory level be?

Solution

We are given that $R = \frac{1}{3}$ year, $L = \frac{1}{9}$ year, $R + L = \frac{4}{9}$ year, and $c_B = \$150$. $\mathbf{D}_{L+R}$ is normally distributed with $E(\mathbf{D}_{L+R}) = \frac{4}{9}(990) = 440$ and $\sigma_{\mathbf{D}_{L+R}} = \sqrt{\frac{4}{9}}\sqrt{1600} = 26.67$. From (20), S should be chosen to satisfy

$$P(\mathbf{D}_{L+R} \geq S) = \frac{(\frac{1}{3})100}{150} = .22$$

Standardizing the last inequality yields

$$P\left(\mathbf{Z} \geq \frac{S - 440}{26.67}\right) = .22$$

From Table 4 of Chapter 11, $F(.77) = .7794$. Thus, $\frac{S - 440}{26.67} = .77$, or $S = 460 + 26.67(.77) = 480.54$.

Thus, when Lowland places an order for TVs, it should order enough to bring the on-order inventory level up to 480.54 (or 481) TVs. For example, if 160 TVs are in stock when a review takes place, $481 - 160 = 321$ TVs should be ordered. ◆

DETERMINATION OF R. Often, the review interval R is set equal to $\frac{EOQ}{E(\mathbf{D})}$. This makes the number of orders placed per year equal the number recommended if a simple EOQ model were used to determine the size of orders. Since each order is accompanied by a review, however, we must set the cost per order to $K + J$. This yields

$$EOQ = \sqrt{\frac{2(K + J)E(\mathbf{D})}{h}}$$

To illustrate the idea, suppose that it costs $500 to review the inventory level and $5000 to place an order for TVs. Then

$$EOQ = \sqrt{\frac{2(5500)(990)}{100}} = 330$$

This implies a review interval $R = \frac{330}{990} = \frac{1}{3}$ year.

IMPLEMENTATION OF AN (R, S) SYSTEM

Retail stores (such as J. C. Penney's) often find an (R, S) policy easy to implement, because the quantity ordered equals the number of sales occurring during the period between reviews. For example, suppose a (1 month, 1000) policy is being used, and orders are placed on the first day of each month. If 800 items were sold during January, then an order of 800 items must be placed at the beginning of February to bring the on-order inventory level back up to 1000. By programming a computer to set monthly orders equal to monthly sales, such a policy can easily be implemented.

◆ PROBLEMS

GROUP A

1. A hospital must order the drug Porapill from Daisy Drug Company. It costs $500 to place an order and $30 to review the hospital's inventory of the drug. Annual demand for the drug is $N(10,000, 640,000)$, and it costs $5 to hold one unit of the drug in inventory for one year. Orders arrive one month after being placed. Assume that all shortages are backlogged.

(a) Estimate R and the number of orders per year that should be placed.

(b) Using the answer in part (a), determine the optimal (R, S) inventory policy. Assume that the shortage cost per unit of the drug is $100.

2. Chicago's Treadway Tires Dealer must order tires from its national warehouse. It costs $10,000 to place an order and $400 to review the inventory level. Annual tire sales are $N(20,000, 4,000,000)$. It costs $10 per year to hold a tire in inventory, and each order arrives two weeks after being placed (52 weeks = 1 year). Assume that all shortages are backlogged.

(a) Estimate R and the number of orders per year that should be placed.

(b) Using the answer in part (a), determine the optimal (R, S) inventory policy. Assume that the shortage cost is $100 per tire.

3. Suppose we have found the optimal (R, S) policy for the back-ordered case and have found that $S = 50$. Is the following true or false?

The optimal S for the lost sales case has $S > 50$.

<hr/>

17-9   THE ABC INVENTORY CLASSIFICATION SYSTEM

Many companies must develop inventory policies for thousands of items. In such a situation, a company cannot devote a great deal of attention to determining an "optimal" inventory policy for each item. The **ABC classification**, devised at General Electric during the 1950s, helps a company identify a small percentage of its items that account for a large percentage of the dollar value of annual sales. These items are called Type A items. Since most of the firm's inventory investment is in Type A items, concentrating effort on developing effective inventory control policies for these items should produce substantial savings.

Repeated studies have shown that in most companies, 5%–20% of all items stocked account for 55%–65% of sales; these are the Type A items. It has also been found that 20%–30% of all items account for 20%–40% of sales; these are called Type B items. Finally, it is often found that 50%–75% of all items account for only 5%–25% of sales; these are called Type C items. To illustrate how we determine which items are Type A, Type B, and Type C, consider a firm that stocks 100 items. We reorder the items as item 1, item 2, . . . , item 100, where item 1 generates the largest annual sales volume, item 2 generates the second largest annual sales volume, etc. Then we plot the points (k, percentage of annual sales due to top k% of all items). For example, the point (20, 60) indicates that the top 20 items (from the standpoint of dollar sales) generate 60% of all sales. We then obtain a graph like Figure 7, where items 1–20 are Type A items, items 21–40 are Type B items, and items 41–100 are Type C items.

Since most of our inventory investment is in Type A items, high service levels will result in huge investments in safety stocks. Therefore, Hax and Candea (1984) recommend that SLM_1 be set at only 80%–85% for Type A items. Tight management control of ordering procedures is essential for Type A items; individual demand forecasts should be made for each Type A item. Also, every effort should be made to lower the lead time needed to receive orders or produce the item. If an (R, S) policy is used, R should be small—perhaps one week. This enables us to keep a close watch on inventory

Figure 7
Example of ABC
Classification of
Inventory

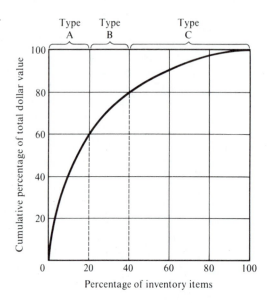

levels. Parameters such as estimates of annual mean demand, length of lead time, standard deviation of annual demand, and shortage costs should be reviewed fairly often.

For Type B items, Hax and Candea (1984) recommend that SLM_1 be set at 95%. Inventory policies for Type B items can generally be controlled by computer. Parameters for Type B items should be reviewed less often than for Type A items.

For Type C items, a simple two-bin system is usually adequate. Parameters may be reviewed once or twice a year. Demand for Type C items may be forecasted by simple extrapolation methods. A high value of SLM_1 (usually 98%–99%) is recommended. Little extra investment in safety stock will be required to maintain these high service levels.

DEVRO Incorporated, a producer of edible sausage casings, implemented an ABC analysis of its spare parts inventory and found that 2.5% of all items (the Type A items) accounted for 49% of all dollar usage, and 24.7% of all items (the Type B items) accounted for 38% of all dollar usage. By preparing requisition forms in advance for Type A and Type B items, DEVRO was able to substantially reduce the lead time needed to obtain those items. This helped DEVRO effect substantial savings in annual inventory costs. See Flowers and O'Neill (1978) for details.

◆ PROBLEM

GROUP A

1. Develop an ABC graph for the data in Table 15. Which items should be classified as A, B, and C?

Table 15

ITEM	ANNUAL USAGE	UNIT COST (in Dollars)
1	20,000	20
2	23,000	10
3	20,000	3
4	30,000	2
5	5,000	10
6	10,000	7
7	1,000	30
8	2,000	15
9	3,000	10
10	5,000	6

◆ SUMMARY

SINGLE-PERIOD DECISION MODELS

A decision maker begins by choosing a value q of a decision variable. Then a random variable $\mathbf{D}$ assumes a value d. Finally, a cost $c(d, q)$ is incurred. The decision maker's goal is to choose q to minimize expected cost.

NEWS VENDOR PROBLEM

If $c(d, q)$ has the structure

$$c(d, q) = c_o q + \text{(terms not involving } q) \qquad (d \le q) \tag{2}$$

$$c(d, q) = -c_u q + \text{(terms not involving } q) \qquad (d \ge q + 1) \tag{2.1}$$

the single-period decision model is a **news vendor problem**. Here

$$c_o = \text{per-unit overstocking cost}$$
$$c_u = \text{per-unit understocking cost}$$

If $\mathbf{D}$ is a discrete random variable, the optimal decision is given by the smallest value of q (call it q^*) satisfying

$$F(q^*) \ge \frac{c_u}{c_o + c_u} \tag{3}$$

If $\mathbf{D}$ is a continuous random variable, the optimal decision is the value of q (call it q^*) satisfying

$$P(\mathbf{D} \le q^*) = \frac{c_u}{c_o + c_u} \tag{5}$$

DETERMINATION OF REORDER POINT AND ORDER QUANTITY WITH UNCERTAIN DEMAND: MINIMIZING ANNUAL EXPECTED COST

Let

K = ordering cost

h = holding cost/unit/year

L = lead time for each order (assumed to be known with certainty)

q = order quantity

$\mathbf{D}$ = random variable representing annual demand
with mean $E(\mathbf{D})$, variance var $\mathbf{D}$, and standard deviation $\sigma_{\mathbf{D}}$

c_B = cost incurred for each unit short if shortages are backlogged

c_{LS} = cost (including lost profits, lost goodwill) incurred
for each lost sale if each shortage results in a lost sale

$\mathbf{X}$ = random variable representing lead time demand

Then

$$E(\mathbf{X}) = LE(\mathbf{D}), \qquad \text{var } \mathbf{X} = L \,(\text{var } \mathbf{D}), \qquad \sigma_{\mathbf{X}} = \sqrt{L}\,\sigma_{\mathbf{D}}$$

and r is the reorder point, or inventory level at which an order should be placed. Safety stock, $r - E(\mathbf{X})$, is the amount of inventory held in excess of lead time demand to meet shortages that may occur before an order arrives.

Assume that the optimal order quantity can be reasonably approximated by the EOQ, $\mathbf{D}$ is a continuous random variable, and all shortages are backlogged. Then annual expected cost is minimized by q^* and r^* given by

$$q^* = \left(\frac{2KE(\mathbf{D})}{h} \right)^{1/2}$$

$$P(\mathbf{X} \geq r^*) = \frac{hq^*}{c_B E(\mathbf{D})} \tag{13}$$

Assume that the optimal order quantity can be reasonably approximated by the EOQ, $\mathbf{D}$ is a continuous random variable, and all shortages result in lost sales. Then annual expected cost is minimized by q^* and r^* satisfying

$$q^* = \left(\frac{2KE(\mathbf{D})}{h} \right)^{1/2}$$

$$P(\mathbf{X} \geq r^*) = \frac{hq^*}{hq^* + c_{LS} E(\mathbf{D})} \tag{15}$$

DETERMINATION OF REORDER POINT: THE SERVICE LEVEL APPROACH

Since it may be difficult to determine the exact cost of a shortage or lost sale, it is often desirable to choose a reorder point that meets a desired service level. Two common measures of service level are

> **Service Level Measure 1** SLM_1, the expected fraction (usually expressed as a percentage) of all demand that is met on time.

> **Service Level Measure 2** SLM_2, the expected number of cycles per year during which a shortage occurs.

If lead time demand is normally distributed, then for a desired value SLM_1, the reorder point r is found from

$$NL\left(\frac{r - E(\mathbf{X})}{\sigma_{\mathbf{X}}}\right) = \frac{q(1 - SLM_1)}{\sigma_{\mathbf{X}}} \tag{18}$$

where $NL(y)$ is the **normal loss function**, tabulated in Table 12, and q is the EOQ.

If lead time demand is a continuous random variable, and we desire $SLM_2 = s_0$ shortages per year, the reorder point r is given by

$$P(\mathbf{X} \geq r) = \frac{s_0 q}{E(\mathbf{D})} \tag{19}$$

Again, q is the EOQ.

If lead time demand is a discrete random variable, and we desire $SLM_2 = s_0$ shortages per year, the reorder point is the smallest value of r satisfying

$$P(\mathbf{X} > r) \leq \frac{s_0 q}{E(\mathbf{D})} \tag{19'}$$

Again, q is the EOQ.

(R, S) PERIODIC REVIEW POLICY

Every R units of time, we review the inventory level and place an order to bring our on-hand inventory level up to S. Given a value of R, we determine the value of S from

$$P(\mathbf{D}_{L+R} \geq S) = \frac{Rh}{c_B}$$

ABC CLASSIFICATION

The 5%–20% of all items accounting for 55%–65% of sales are Type A items, the 20%–30% of all items accounting for 20%–40% of sales are Type B items, and the 50%–75% of all items that account for 5%–25% of all sales are Type C items. By concentrating effort on Type A (and possibly Type B) items, we can achieve substantial cost reductions.

◆ REVIEW PROBLEMS

GROUP A

1. The Chocochip Cookie Store bakes its cookies every morning before opening. It costs the store 15¢ to bake each cookie, and each cookie is sold for 35¢. At the end of the day, leftover cookies may be sold to a thrift bakery for 5¢ per cookie. The number of cookies sold each day is described by the discrete random variable in Table 16.

(a) How many dozen cookies should be baked before the store opens?
(b) If the daily demand (in dozens) for cookies is $N(50, 400)$, how many dozen cookies should be baked? A description of the $N(\mu, \sigma^2)$ notation can be found in Section 11.7.
(c) If the daily demand (in dozens) for cookies has a density function

$$f(d) = \frac{e^{-d/50}}{50} \qquad (d \geq 0)$$

how many dozen cookies should be baked?

Table 16

DEMAND (Dozens)	PROBABILITY
20	.30
30	.20
40	.20
50	.15
60	.15

2. An optometrist orders eyeglass frames at a cost of $40 per frame and sells each frame for $70. Annual holding cost for a frame is 20% of the optometrist's cost of purchasing a frame. Each time frames are ordered, a cost of $200 is incurred. Because of lost goodwill, a cost of $50 is incurred each time a customer wants a frame that is not in stock. Frames are delivered one week after an order is placed. Annual demand for frames is $N(1040, 15.73)$.
(a) Assuming all shortages are backlogged, determine the order quantity and reorder point.
(b) Assuming all shortages result in lost sales, determine the order quantity and reorder point.
(c) In order to meet 95% of all orders from stock, what should be the reorder point?
(d) In order to have shortages occur during an average of two lead times per year, what should be the reorder point?

3. We are given the following information about a product:

    Cost of placing an order = $100
    Cost per item = $5
    Sale price per item = $8
    Annual holding cost = 40% of cost of item
    Annual demand = 5000 units
    Lead time demand = $N(20, 900)$

(a) If the reorder point that minimizes expected cost is 80, what is the shortage cost? (Assume backlogging.)

(b) If the reorder point that minimizes expected cost is 80, what is the shortage cost? (Assume lost sales.)
(c) What reorder point would meet 90% of all demand on time?
(d) What reorder point would result in a stockout occurring during an average of 0.5 lead time per year?

GROUP B

4. A business believes that its needs for cash during the next month are described by the random variable shown in Table 17. At the beginning of the month, the business has $10,000 available, and the business manager must determine how much of the money should be placed in an account bearing 24% annual interest. If any money must be withdrawn before the end of the month, all interest on the withdrawn money is forfeited, and a penalty equal to 2% of the withdrawn money must be paid. How much money should be placed in the 24% annual interest account?

Table 17

CASH NEEDS	PROBABILITY
$4000	.30
$5000	.20
$6000	.10
$7000	.30
$8000	.10

5. A fur dealer buys fur coats for $100 each and sells them for $200 each. He believes that the demand for coats is $N(100, 100)$. Any coat not sold can be sold to a discount house for $100, but the fur dealer believes he must charge himself a cost of 10¢ per dollar invested in a fur coat that is sold at discount. How many coats should the dealer order? If the price at which the dealer sold his coats increased (assuming demand is unchanged), would he buy more or fewer coats?

6. A company currently has two warehouses. Each warehouse services half the company's demand, and the annual demand serviced by each warehouse is $N(10,000, 1,000,000)$. The lead time for meeting demand is $\frac{1}{10}$ year. The company wants to meet 95% of all demand on time. Assume that the EOQ at each warehouse is 2000.
(a) How much safety stock must be held?
(b) Show that if the company had only one warehouse, it would hold less safety stock than it does when it has two warehouses.

(c) A young MBA argues, "By having one central warehouse, I can reduce the total amount of safety stock needed to meet 95% of all customer demands on time. Therefore, we can save money by having only one central warehouse instead of several branch warehouses." How might this argument be rebutted?

◆ REFERENCES

The following references emphasize applications over theory:

BROWN, R. *Decision Rules for Inventory Management.* New York: Holt, Rinehart and Winston, 1967.

PETERSON, R., and E. SILVER. *Decision Systems for Inventory Management and Production Planning.* New York: Wiley, 1984.

TERSINE, R. *Principles of Inventory and Materials Management.* New York: North-Holland, 1982.

VOLLMAN, T., W. BERRY, and C. WHYBARK. *Manufacturing Planning and Control Systems.* Homewood, Ill.: Irwin, 1987.

The following references contain extensive theoretical discussions as well as applications:

HADLEY, G., and T. WHITIN. *Analysis of Inventory Systems.* Englewood Cliffs, N.J.: Prentice-Hall, 1963.

HAX, A., and D. CANDEA. *Production and Inventory Management.* Englewood Cliffs, N.J.: Prentice-Hall, 1984.

JOHNSON, L., and D. MONTGOMERY. *Operations Research in Production, Scheduling, and Inventory Control.* New York: Wiley, 1974.

BARRON, H. "Payoff Matrices Pay Off at Hallmark," *Interfaces* 15(no. 4, 1985):20–25.

FLOWERS, D., and J. O'NEILL. "An Application of Classical Inventory Analysis to a Spare Parts Inventory," *Interfaces* 8(no. 2, 1978):76–79.

ROSENFELD, D. "Optimal Management of Tax-Sheltered Employment Reimbursement Programs," *Interfaces* 16(no. 3, 1986): 68–72.

VIRTS, J., and R. GARRETT. "Weighting Risk in Capacity Expansion," *Harvard Business Review* 48 (1970).

CHAPTER 18

Recent Developments in Inventory Theory

IN THIS CHAPTER, we describe three recent developments in inventory theory: MRP (material requirements planning), JIT (just-in-time production, also known as zero inventories and stockless production), and exchange curves.

Consider a company that manufactures a final product—a personal computer, for example. Assembling the final product (let's call it a PC) requires that the company produce certain components, such as disk drives. Clearly, the demand for the component will depend on the demand for the final product. MRP uses the dependence between final product demand and demand for components, subcomponents, and assemblies to schedule production and control inventories. Section 18.1 discusses the basic concepts underlying MRP.

For years, Japanese businesses have operated under the assumption that high inventory levels indicate inefficiency. The Japanese believe that cutting inventory levels will increase efficiency. Perhaps the best way to reduce inventories is to schedule production of final products and components so that items are produced as closely as possible to the time they are needed for sale or for production. This "just-in-time" approach to production will be discussed in Section 18.2.

Most of the inventory models discussed in Chapters 16 and 17 require the decision maker to determine both the holding cost and the shortage cost, but these costs are usually very difficult to determine in real-life situations. In Section 18.3, we discuss exchange curves, which can be used to determine reasonable inventory policies when holding and shortage costs are unknown.

18-1 MATERIAL REQUIREMENTS PLANNING (MRP)

As pointed out in Section 16.6, EOQ models should not be used when demand is highly variable over time. The EOQ models discussed in Chapters 16 and 17 also ignore the fact that in a manufacturing environment, the demand for raw materials, components, and subassemblies used in making a final product is determined by the demand for the final product. **Material requirements planning** (MRP) recognizes the relationship between the demand for the final product and the components used to make it. This relationship is then used to determine the amount that should be produced of each final product, component, and subassembly during each period. In 1985, it was estimated that between 2000 and 5000 American companies (most with annual sales exceeding $20,000,000) used MRP to schedule production.

HOW DOES MRP REDUCE INVENTORIES?

We now illustrate how savings in inventory costs can result from recognizing that demand for components and subassemblies depends on final product demand. Consider a company that manufactures personal computers (PCs). For simplicity, let's assume that each PC has two disk drives, which the company produces rather than purchases. We make the following assumptions:

1. Annual demand for PCs is 2400.

2. Annual demand for disk drives is 2(2400) = 4800.

3. An EOQ model is being used to schedule production of the PCs, and the EOQ is 400 PCs.

4. Since PCs should be produced six times a year (or once every two months), we suppose that PC production is scheduled to begin at the beginning of months 1, 3, 5, 7, 9, and 11 of the current year.

5. The EOQ for disk drives is 1600.

6. Since disk drives should be produced $\frac{4800}{1600} = 3$ times per year, we choose to schedule disk drive production for the beginning of months 1, 5, and 9.

7. Month 1 production of PCs has exhausted disk drive inventory.

8. It takes one month to produce a batch of disk drives. Thus, for example, the batch of disks whose production begins in month 1 enters inventory during month 2.

9. During a month in which PCs are produced, disk drives are removed from inventory at the beginning of the month.

In this situation, the months during which disk drives are produced are chosen independently of the months during which PCs are produced. Let's determine the end-of-month inventory for disk drives (see Table 1).

Table 1	MONTH	INVENTORY	MONTH	INVENTORY
End-of-Month Disk Drive Inventory (Disk Drives Produced in Months 1, 5, 9; PCs Produced in Months 1, 3, 5, 7, 9, 11)	1	0	7	800
	2	1600	8	800
	3	800	9	0
	4	800	10	1600
	5	0	11	800
	6	1600	12	800

To illustrate the derivation of the inventory levels in Table 1, note that 1600 disk drives arrive at the beginning of month 2. At the beginning of month 3, 400 PCs are produced. This reduces the month 3 disk drive inventory to 1600 − (2(400)) = 800.

During month 4, no PCs or disk drives are produced, and disk drive inventory remains unchanged. During month 5, production of PCs uses the remaining 800 disk drives. This reduces month 5's disk drive inventory to 0. From Table 1, we see that the pattern of inventory (1600, 800, 800, 0) repeats every four months. Thus, the average end-of-month disk drive inventory is $\frac{1600 + 800 + 800 + 0}{4} = 800$ disk drives.

Now let's get smart and realize that the *demand for disk drives is determined by the PC demand*. Since PCs are to be produced during months 1, 3, 5, 7, 9, and 11, why not produce disk drives during months 2, 6, and 10? This will ensure that not all disk drives produced will "sit around" for a month before they are used. If we produce disk drives during months 2, 6, and 10, our end-of-month disk drive inventory is as shown in Table 2.

	MONTH	INVENTORY	MONTH	INVENTORY
Table 2	1	0	7	800
End-of-Month Disk	2	0	8	800
Drive Inventory	3	800	9	0
(Disk Drives	4	800	10	0
Produced in Months	5	0	11	800
2, 6, 10; PCs	6	0	12	800
Produced in Months				
1, 3, 5, 7, 9, 11)				

Since 1600 disk drives arrive at the beginning of month 3, and 800 disk drives are used to make PCs during month 3, 800 disk drives are in inventory at the end of month 3. Month 4's ending inventory of disk drives is still 800, but at the beginning of month 5, 800 more disk drives are used, so the month 5 ending inventory of disk drives is 0. Since the end-of-month inventory pattern of 800, 800, 0, and 0 repeats every four months, the average end-of-month inventory of disk drives is given by $\frac{800 + 800 + 0 + 0}{4} = 400$ disk drives.

This simple example shows that recognition of the fact that the demand for disk drives depends on the time PCs are produced can allow the average drive inventory to be cut by 50%. MRP uses the linkage between the demand for final products and components to cut inventory costs.

THE BILL OF MATERIAL AND THE MRP RECORD

To illustrate how MRP works, let's consider a company that produces two final products: *A* and *B*. Each unit of product *A* uses three units of component *C* (plus other subcomponents). Each unit of component *C* requires two units of subcomponent *D* (plus other subcomponents). Each unit of product *B* uses two components of component *C* (plus other subcomponents). These relationships are illustrated in the **bills of materials** for products *A* and *B*, displayed in Figure 1.

It takes two months to produce a unit of *C* and one month to produce a unit of *D*. These are the **lead times** for *C* and *D*.

To illustrate the logic underlying MRP computations, suppose that the demand for the final products *A* and *B* during each of the next 12 months is as given in Table 3. At the beginning of month 1, we have 150 units of *C* in stock; from previously planned manufacturing or purchasing orders, we are scheduled to receive 50 units of *C* at the

Figure 1
Bill of Materials for Product *A* and Product *B*

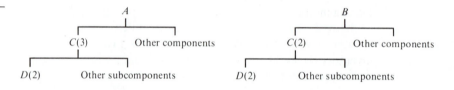

Table 3
Demands for Final Products *A* and *B*

PRODUCT	MONTH											
	1	*2*	*3*	*4*	*5*	*6*	*7*	*8*	*9*	*10*	*11*	*12*
A	0	0	80	0	0	80	0	0	80	0	0	80
B	0	50	0	50	0	50	0	50	0	50	0	50

beginning of month 2. To begin the MRP computations for component *C*, we determine the monthly **gross requirements** for component *C*. The month *t* gross requirement for component *C* ($GR_t(C)$) is the quantity of *C* needed at the beginning of month *t* to avoid shortages. If we assume (to simplify matters) that it takes zero time to assemble products *A* and *B* from their component parts, we find that

$$GR_t(C) = 3(\text{month } t \text{ demand for } A) + 2(\text{month } t \text{ demand for } B)$$

For example, $GR_6(C) = 3(80) + 2(50) = 340$. The gross requirements for *C* (and other important information) are given in Table 4, whose rows are enumerated and explained below.

Table 4
Computation of Net Requirements for Component *C*

	MONTH											
	1	*2*	*3*	*4*	*5*	*6*	*7*	*8*	*9*	*10*	*11*	*12*
Gross requirements	0	100	240	100	0	340	0	100	240	100	0	340
On-hand inventory (150)	150	100	0	0	0	0	0	0	0	0	0	0
Scheduled receipts	0	50	0	0	0	0	0	0	0	0	0	0
Net requirements	0	0	140	100	0	340	0	100	240	100	0	340
Planned production	?	?	?	?	?	?	?	?	?	?	?	?

1. *Gross requirements* gives the gross requirement for product *C* during each month—that is, the total amount of *C* needed at the beginning of month *t* if shortages are to be avoided. We let $GR_t(C)$ be the gross requirement for *C* during month *t*.

2. *Planned production* is the number of units of *C* that we should begin producing during a month (remember it takes two months to complete a unit of product *C*). We let $PP_t(C)$ be the planned production of *C* during month *t*.

3. *Scheduled receipts* is the number of units of *C* scheduled for delivery at the beginning of a month, including only orders that were placed before month 1. We let $SR_t(C)$ be the scheduled receipts during month *t*.

4. *On-hand inventory* measures how much of our beginning inventory (in this case, 150) and our scheduled receipts is left at the end of the month. We let $OHI_t(C)$ be our on-hand inventory of C at the end of month t. For the purpose of determining net requirements, on-hand inventory excludes receipts from planned production.

5. *Net requirements* for a month is the number of units of C needed during a month to meet gross requirements after on-hand inventory and scheduled receipts have been used to meet gross requirements. We let $NR_t(C)$ be the component C net requirement for month t.

What relationships exist among the quantities listed in Table 4? Let $[x]^+$ be the maximum of x and 0. Thus, $[3]^+ = 3$, but $[-3]^+ = 0$. Then

$$NR_t(C) = [GR_t(C) - SR_t(C) - OHI_{t-1}(C)]^+ \quad \text{and}$$
$$OHI_t(C) = [SR_t(C) + OHI_{t-1}(C) - GR_t(C)]^+$$

To illustrate,

$$OHI_1(C) = [0 + 150 - 0]^+ = 150$$
$$OHI_2(C) = [50 + 150 - 100]^+ = 100$$
$$OHI_3(C) = [0 + 100 - 240]^+ = 0$$
$$OHI_t(C) = 0 \quad \text{for } t = 4, 5, \dots, 12$$

Thus, once the beginning inventory and last scheduled receipts have been used to meet demands, the on-hand inventory for each month will be 0. We now find that

$$NR_1(C) = [0 - 0 - 150]^+ = 0$$
$$NR_2(C) = [100 - 50 - 150]^+ = 0$$
$$NR_3(C) = [240 - 0 - 100]^+ = 140$$

After month 3, no leftover beginning inventory or scheduled receipts are left to meet requirements, so we will have

$$NR_t(C) = GR_t(C), \quad \text{for } t = 4, 5, \dots, 12$$

$NR_t(C)$ is the number of units of C that must be delivered by the beginning of month t from planned production to ensure that no shortages of C occur during month t. There are many possible ways to meet the net requirements in Table 4. For example, since it takes two months to produce a unit of C, we could set month t's planned production equal to month $t + 2$'s net requirement. This would ensure that month $t + 2$'s net requirement is completely met from month t production. This approach to meeting net requirements is the **lot-for-lot approach**. The problem of determining how to meet net requirements is the **lot-sizing problem**. The lot-for-lot approach yields the **MRP record** for component C given in Table 5. Other lot-sizing methods will be discussed later in this section and in Section 20.7.

In Table 5, an X indicates that production for months 11 and 12 cannot be determined. In an MRP record, on-hand inventory includes inventory accumulated from planned production as well as from beginning inventory and receipts scheduled prior to month 1. Also, the Scheduled Receipts row now includes receipts from planned production. For example, month 4's scheduled receipts of 100 is simply month 2's planned production of 100. (Remember, however, in computing net requirements (as in Table 4), that inventories and scheduled receipts do not include any units from planned production during months 1–12.) With the new definition of scheduled receipts, our previous formula for on-hand inventory remains valid. For example,

$$OHI_3(C) = [100 + 140 - 240]^+ = 0$$

In Table 5, production was planned for each month. The length of a time period for which production is planned is called a **bucket**. Weekly time buckets are most common. The number of periods in an MRP record is called the **planning horizon**. Our example has a 12-month planning horizon.

Table 5		MONTH											
MRP Record for *C*: Lot-for-Lot Approach		*1*	*2*	*3*	*4*	*5*	*6*	*7*	*8*	*9*	*10*	*11*	*12*
	Gross requirements	0	100	240	100	0	340	0	100	240	100	0	340
	On-hand inventory (150)	150	100	0	0	0	0	0	0	0	0	0	0
	Scheduled receipts	0	50	140	100	0	340	0	100	240	100	0	340
	Net requirements	0	0	140	100	0	340	0	100	240	100	0	340
	Planned production	140	100	0	340	0	100	240	100	0	340	X	X

Before we discuss other lot-sizing methods, let's see if we can complete the MRP calculations needed to determine a lot-for-lot schedule for subcomponent *D*. Suppose that 600 units of *D* are in stock at the beginning of month 1, and previously scheduled production will cause 100 units to be received at the beginning of month 2. We assume that *C* is being produced according to the lot-for-lot method. To produce the required $PP_t(C)$ during month *t*, the bill of materials tells us that we will need $2PP_t(C)$ of *D*. Thus, $GR_t(D) = 2PP_t(C)$. Now we can obtain subcomponent *D*'s net requirements (as we did for *C*). Assuming that a lot-for-lot approach is used to schedule *D*'s production, we obtain the MRP record for *D* given in Table 6. Due to the one-month lead time for *D*,

Table 6		MONTH											
MRP Record for *D*: Lot-for-Lot Approach		*1*	*2*	*3*	*4*	*5*	*6*	*7*	*8*	*9*	*10*	*11*	*12*
	Gross requirements	280	200	0	680	0	200	480	200	0	680	X	X
	On-hand inventory (600)	320	220	220	0	0	0	0	0	0	0	0	0
	Scheduled receipts	0	100	0	460	0	200	480	200	0	680	X	X
	Net requirements	0	0	0	460	0	200	480	200	0	680	X	X
	Planned production	0	0	460	0	200	480	200	0	680	X	X	X

$PP_t(D) = NR_{t+1}(D)$. Some examples of the computations in Table 6 follow:

$$OHI_2(D) = [100 + 320 - 200]^+ = 220$$
$$NR_4(D) = [680 - 0 - 220]^+ = 460$$
$$PP_5(D) = NR_6(D)$$

Remember, when computing net requirements, the On-Hand Inventory and Scheduled Receipts rows do not include receipts from the Planned Production row. Once net requirements are determined, Planned Production may be determined, and the On-Hand Inventory and Scheduled Receipts rows will include Planned Production.

LOT-SIZING STRATEGIES

Several methods (called lot-sizing methods) are commonly used to determine the planned production for each month. We have already discussed the simple (and widely used) lot-for-lot method. We now discuss three other relatively simple lot-sizing methods: the period order quantity (POQ), the economic order quantity (EOQ), and the part-period balancing method. Two more complicated lot-sizing methods (the Wagner-Whitin method and Silver-Meal heuristic) are discussed in Section 20.7. Although the Wagner-Whitin and Silver-Meal methods yield lower (holding + setup) costs than the simpler lot-sizing methods, most companies using MRP utilize the simpler lot-sizing procedures. Lot-for-lot, POQ, and part-period balancing are the most widely used lot-sizing methods.

To illustrate various lot-sizing methods, we assume that the average demand for component C is 225 units per month, the setup cost of producing C during a month is $225, and the cost of holding one unit of C in inventory for one month is $0.50.

POQ METHOD. During a month in which production is scheduled, the **period order quantity method** (POQ) simply sets production equal to the sum of P months of positive net requirements (P is a fixed number). For example, if we set $P = 3$, planned production would be as shown in Table 7. Note that we must produce in month 1 in order to meet month 3's net requirement. Since $P = 3$, our month 1 production must meet demands for months 3, 4, and 6. (We meet month 6 demand because month 5 demand is 0.) Continuing in this fashion yields the results in Table 7. The POQ approach with $P = 3$ yields the MRP record shown in Table 8.

Table 7	MONTH	PRODUCED FOR MONTHS	QUANTITY PRODUCED
Planned Production for C (POQ; $P = 3$)	1	3, 4, 6	140 + 100 + 340 = 580
	6	8, 9, 10	100 + 240 + 100 = 440
	10	12	340

The total cost (holding + setup) incurred by this POQ lot-sizing method is determined as follows:

Holding cost = 0.5(150 + 100 + 440 + 340 + 340 + 340 + 100) = $905
Setup cost = 225(3) = $675
Total cost = $905 + $675 = $1580

Table 8								MONTH					
MRP Record for		*1*	*2*	*3*	*4*	*5*	*6*	*7*	*8*	*9*	*10*	*11*	*12*
C: (POQ Method;	Gross requirements	0	100	240	100	0	340	0	100	240	100	0	340
P = 3)	On-hand inventory (150)	150	100	440	340	340	0	0	340	100	0	0	0
	Scheduled receipts	0	50	580	0	0	0	0	440	0	0	0	340
	Net requirements	0	0	140	100	0	340	0	100	240	100	0	340
	Planned production	580	0	0	0	0	440	0	0	0	340	X	X

EOQ LOT-SIZING METHOD. In this method, the batch size is set equal to the EOQ. If this results in failure to meet any month's net requirement, we then produce the smallest multiple of the EOQ (2EOQ, 3EOQ, etc.) that will avoid a shortage. For the given data,

$$\text{EOQ} = \sqrt{\frac{2(225)225}{0.5}} = 450 \text{ units}$$

Thus, we begin by producing 450 units during month 1; this will arrive in time to meet month 3 requirements. These 450 units will enable us to meet all net requirements through month 5, so our next production of 450 units will be during month 4. In month 9, we will need more units of *C*, so we produce 450 units during month 7. Finally, we will need to produce 450 units during month 10. The EOQ lot-sizing method yields the MRP record shown in Table 9.

Table 9								MONTH					
MRP Record for		*1*	*2*	*3*	*4*	*5*	*6*	*7*	*8*	*9*	*10*	*11*	*12*
C: (EOQ Method)	Gross requirements	0	100	240	100	0	340	0	100	240	100	0	340
	On-hand inventory (150)	150	100	310	210	210	320	320	220	430	330	330	440
	Scheduled receipts	0	50	450	0	0	450	0	0	450	0	0	450
	Net requirements	0	0	140	100	0	340	0	100	240	100	0	340
	Planned production	450	0	0	450	0	0	450	0	0	450	X	X

The total cost incurred by the EOQ method is as follows:

Holding cost = $0.5(150 + 100 + \cdots + 440) = \$1685$

Setup cost = $4(225) = \$900$

Total cost = $\$1685 + \$900 = \$2585$

Many companies adopt a **fixed order quantity** lot-sizing approach. With this method, each production run is of the same size (not necessarily the EOQ).

PART-PERIOD BALANCING METHOD. In this method, we make each lot-sizing decision by producing for the number of months of net requirements that makes the holding cost associated with the production batch as close as possible to the setup cost for producing a batch. This idea is based on the fact that the EOQ minimizes costs at an order quantity for which setup and holding costs are equal. For our example, we begin by determining how much to produce during month 1. (This order will arrive in time to meet month 3's net requirements.) We may produce just for month 3, or for months 3 and 4, or for months 3, 4, and 5, and so on. The relevant computations are shown in Table 10.

Table 10	PRODUCED FOR MONTHS	SETUP COST	HOLDING COST
Part-Period	3	$225	$0
Balancing Method:	3, 4, 5	$225	$100(0.5) = $50*
Computations for	3, 4, 5, 6	$225	$(0.5)(340(3) + 100) = 560
Month 1 Production			
of C			

Note that since month 5 net requirements are 0, we do not consider meeting requirements for just months 3 and 4. The * indicates that costs balance most closely if we produce $140 + 100 + 0 = 240$ units during month 1. Next, we must produce during month 4 in order to meet demands for month 6 (and possibly some later months). The relevant computations are shown in Table 11.

Table 11	PRODUCED FOR MONTHS	SETUP COST	HOLDING COST
Part-Period	6	$225	$0
Balancing Method:	6, 7, 8	$225	$2(0.5)(100) = $100*$
Computations for	6, 7, 8, 9	$225	$2(0.5)(100) + 0.5(3)(240) = 460
Month 4 Production			
of C			

Thus, during month 4 we produce for the net requirements of months 6, 7, and 8 (a total of $340 + 0 + 100 = 440$ units). We now must produce in month 7 to meet requirements for month 9 (and possibly later months). The computations are shown in Table 12.

Table 12	PRODUCED FOR MONTHS	SETUP COST	HOLDING COST
Part-Period	9	$225	$0
Balancing Method:	9, 10, 11	$225	$(0.5)(100) = $50*$
Computations for	9, 10, 11, 12	$225	$(0.5)(100 + 3(340)) = 560
Month 7 Production			
of C			

Thus, during month 7, we should produce to meet requirements for months 9, 10, and 11 (a total of $240 + 100 + 0 = 340$ units). Finally, we must produce 340 units during month 10 to meet month 12's net requirements. The part-period balancing method yields the MRP record shown in Table 13. The total cost incurred by the part-period balancing method is as follows:

$$\text{Holding cost} = \$0.5(150 + 100 + 100 + 100 + 100 + 100) = \$325$$
$$\text{Setup cost} = \$225(4) = \$900$$
$$\text{Total cost} = \$900 + \$325 = \$1225$$

						MONTH						
Table 13	*1*	*2*	*3*	*4*	*5*	*6*	*7*	*8*	*9*	*10*	*11*	*12*
MRP Record for *C* (Part-Period Balancing Method)												
Gross requirements	0	100	240	100	0	340	0	100	240	100	0	340
On-hand inventory (150)	150	100	100	0	0	100	100	0	100	0	0	0
Scheduled receipts	0	50	240	0	0	440	0	0	340	0	0	340
Net requirements	0	0	140	100	0	340	0	100	240	100	0	340
Planned production	240	0	0	440	0	0	340	0	0	340	X	X

In this example, the part-period balancing method produced the lowest total cost. For other examples, however, POQ and EOQ might outperform the part-period balancing method. The only method guaranteed to yield a lot-sizing solution that minimizes total cost is the Wagner-Whitin method (described in Section 20.7). Unfortunately, the Wagner-Whitin method is more complex than most practitioners would like, so it is rarely used.

REMARKS   **1.** For a company producing many products, MRP requires considerable computer storage and computational requirements. This explains why MRP did not come into wide use until the 1970s.

2. Even a slight change in the requirements for an end product may cause substantial changes in the timing and lot sizes for components and subcomponents (see Problem 3 for an example of this). This phenomenon is known as the **nervousness** of the MRP system. Since frequent changes in timing and lot sizes are very disruptive, nervousness is very undesirable. See pages 515–518 of Vollman, Berry, and Whybark (1988) for a discussion of how to reduce nervousness in an MRP system.

3. Most MRP schedules involve planning horizons of one to two years. Clearly, if a product had many "levels" of subcomponents—for example, *D* is used in *C*, and *E* is used in *D*, etc.—the X's in the planned production row might take up most of the periods for some components. This is referred to as loss of low level visibility; it necessitates a long planning horizon.

4. An important decision is the frequency with which MRP records are updated. In a **regenerative** MRP system, the entire record for each final product, component, and subcomponent is updated periodically. In our example, each record might be updated each month: At the end of month 1, we would incorporate gross requirements for month 13 into our planning and update any changes in planned production, scheduled receipts, and gross requirements before recomputing our MRP records. This approach is analogous to the rolling planning horizon introduced in Section 3.10.

Alternatively, a company can update MRP records after each transaction occurs. This is called a *net change* system. As a general rule of thumb, a net change system is preferred in more volatile environments, because it keeps up with rapidly changing conditions better than a regenerative system does.

5. Assuming everything works as planned, MRP will result in no shortages or stockouts. Unfortunately, four types of uncertainty may cause shortages to occur:

a. *Lead time uncertainty.* Sometimes it will take more than two months to produce component C.

b. *Uncertainty about when orders are needed.* A customer may need an order a month earlier than planned.

c. *Uncertainty about size of orders.* Instead of needing 200 units this month, a customer may need 300.

d. *Uncertainty about production yield.* Even if we schedule to produce 300 units of C this month, machine breakdowns may reduce our output to 200 units.

Two approaches are used to avoid shortages caused by these four types of uncertainty.

1. Plan orders so they arrive earlier than needed (say, by one month). This called the safety lead time approach.

2. Increase the size of planned production over what is needed. This is the safety stock approach.

Research has shown that the safety lead time approach is better for dealing with uncertainty of types a and b, whereas the safety stock approach is better for dealing with uncertainty of types c and d.

◆ PROBLEMS

GROUP A

1. Table 14 gives the gross requirements for final products A and B during the next six weeks. Each unit of A uses two units of C, and each unit of B uses three units of C. Each unit of C uses four units of D. Assume that A and B can be produced in zero time once enough C is available. The lead time for C is one week, and the lead time for D is also one week. At the beginning of week 1, 120 units of C and 160 units of D are on hand. Fifty units of C and 80 units of D are scheduled to be received at the beginning of week 2. The average weekly demand is 100 units. The cost per production run is $200, and the cost of holding one unit in inventory for a week is $4.

(a) Using the lot-for-lot method, determine the MRP records for C and D.

(b) Determine the MRP record for C if POQ ($P = 2$) is used.

(c) Determine the MRP record for C if the EOQ lot-sizing method is used.

(d) Determine the MRP record for C if the part-period balancing lot-sizing method is used.

2. Table 15 gives the gross requirements for final product A. Each unit of A requires one unit of B. Each unit of B requires two units of C. Each unit of C requires three units of D. The lead time for items B and C is one week, and the lead time for item D is two weeks. At the beginning of week 1, we have 50 units of A, 20 units of B, 40 units of C, and

Table 14

	WEEK					
	1	2	3	4	5	6
A	20	0	30	10	20	0
B	10	30	0	10	5	10

Table 15

WEEK							
1	2	3	4	5	6	7	8
20	30	40	10	0	20	50	60

80 units of D. At the beginning of week 2, 40 units of B, C, and D are scheduled for receipt. Using the lot-for-lot method, determine the MRP record for each item.

3. We presently have 18 units of product A on hand. It takes two weeks to produce a unit of product A; POQ ($P = 4$ weeks) is being used to determine planned production. The gross requirements for product A for the next seven weeks are shown in Table 16.

(a) Determine planned production for each week.

(b) Suppose week 2's gross requirement is reduced by 1 (to 13 units). How does the planned production for each week change? How does this illustrate nervousness?

Table 16

WEEK						
1	*2*	*3*	*4*	*5*	*6*	*7*
2	14	3	6	2	1	45

4. Suppose a company manufactures bicycles. Each bicycle uses 40 screws. Should the company use MRP to monitor the purchasing and/or production of screws? If not, what would be a good inventory control approach to the ordering and/or production of screws?

18-2   THE JUST-IN-TIME (JIT) APPROACH TO PRODUCTION

Based on the example of many successful Japanese companies (most notably Toyota), many American companies (Xerox, GE, Whirlpool, and Hewlett Packard, to name a few) have recently attempted to reduce inventory levels by implementing a **Just-in-time** (JIT) approach to production and purchasing. The JIT approach consists of producing products or obtaining products from suppliers at the instant they are required. Since JIT strives to reduce inventory levels, many people refer to JIT as stockless production or zero inventories.

WHY JIT?

The primary motivation behind JIT (well explained by Hall (1983) and Schonberger (1982) and (1987)) is that inventory represents inefficiency. Just as high water levels in a river hide dangerous rocks, high inventory levels in a company hide sources of inefficiency and causes of poor product quality.

Advocates of JIT also believe that companies often underestimate the holding cost h used in the EOQ models of Chapters 16 and 17. The advocates of JIT argue that in the long run, the cost of a warehouse and the cost of shop storage should be considered as a variable cost and therefore included in the value of h used to compute the EOQ. Of course, an increase in h would lower the EOQ; thereby reducing the optimal lot size and the average inventory level.

An important determinant of the EOQ is the setup cost K. Often a major component of the setup cost is the time required to set up a machine for a production run. Since a reduction in K will reduce the EOQ and the average inventory level, it is clear that a reduction in K will make it easier to implement JIT. Much of the Japanese success in implementing JIT is due to their reduction in setup times. For example, workers at Toyota can set up an 800-ton punch press (used to produce hoods and fenders) in less than three minutes.

Another cause of high inventory levels in American companies is the belief that safety stocks must be held to reduce shortages caused by demand uncertainty and supply uncertainty (such as variability in lead times). JIT reduces the impact of demand uncertainty on inventory levels by "leveling" the production schedule. For example, if

3000 cars per month must be produced and a plant is open 20 days per month, the plant should aim for producing $\frac{3000}{20} = 150$ cars per day. For JIT to succeed, it is critical that the quantity of a product produced each day vary by at most $\pm 10\%$ from the average daily production level. By reducing safety stock levels, the causes of supply variability (such as unreliable suppliers and frequent machine breakdowns) are exposed. Then supply variability (and therefore safety stocks) can be reduced.

PUSH AND PULL SYSTEMS

To understand how JIT differs from the traditional American approach, we must define two types of production systems: **push and pull systems**. Let's consider a manufacturing process in which a product must pass through four work stations before being completed. First the product passes through work station 1, then work station 2, then work station 3, and finally work station 4. Think of the product as flowing down a river. Then work station 1, the first work station, is farthest upstream, and the final work station, work station 4, is the farthest downstream. In a "push" system, materials push their way through the system from work station 1 toward work station 4. Thus, if 100 units of the product are completed at work station 1, they are then pushed toward work station 2, causing work for the employees there. Once a unit of the product finishes at work station 2, it is pushed to work station 3, etc. Many American factories operate as a "push" system. This can cause huge work-in-process inventories to accumulate.

In contrast, JIT is a pull system, in which an upstream station does not produce anything unless production is authorized by the immediately succeeding downstream station. For example, work station 2 cannot work on any material unless authorized by work station 3. We now explain a commonly used implementation of a pull system: the **Kanban** system.

THE KANBAN SYSTEM

Probably the best-known method used to implement JIT is Toyota's Kanban system. The following three types of items are vital to implementing JIT through the Kanban system:

1. *Containers.* Each container contains a standard number of parts. Usually, the standard number of parts is less than 10% of the daily requirement for the part. This keeps lot sizes relatively small.

2. *Move cards* (also known as conveyance or withdrawal cards). Move cards are used to authorize movement of a container between two successive operations—for example, from operation 4 to operation 3 and back to operation 4. *A container cannot be moved unless a move card is attached to it.*

3. *Production cards.* A production card is used to authorize production of a container of parts. *Workers cannot produce the parts needed to fill a container unless authorized by a production card.*

There is a separate set of containers, move cards, and production cards for each possible flow of materials. For example, there is one set of containers, move cards, and production cards for movement between work stations 3 and 4, one set for movement between stations 2 and 3, and one set for movement between stations 1 and 2.

To illustrate how the Kanban system authorizes production and movement of containers, let's focus on the linkage between stations 3 and 4. Suppose we are working on a container of parts at station 4. This container will have a move card attached to it. Remove the move card from the container and place the move card on an empty container at station 4 (call this container 1). Now transport container 1 (with its move card) to station 3. At station 3, find a full container of parts (call it container 2). Container 2 will have a production card attached to it. Remove the production card from container 2 and put the production card in station 3's production card file box. Replace the production card on container 2 with a move card. This authorizes us to move container 2 to station 4 to replace parts being used at station 4. Periodically, workers at station 3 remove production cards from the production card file box. Each production card authorizes workers at station 3 to begin work on a container of parts. We can now see how the cards cause a pull system to govern operations. If station 4 employees don't go to station 3 and detach production cards from full containers, then station 3 can't produce anything. Also, if station 4 goes to station 3 to get parts, station 3 will eventually have to go to station 2 for parts, and eventually station 2 will have to go to station 1 for parts. This shows how station 4 "pulls" material downstream through the system. The beauty of the Kanban system is that, unlike MRP, no complicated paperwork or computer printouts are needed to keep track of the inventory status at each station. The cards do the job automatically! If we reduce the number of cards between two stations, we will automatically reduce the work-in-process inventory between the two stations. If we have too few cards, however, shortages may occur frequently. Only trial and error can determine the "right" number of cards. We summarize the rules of the Kanban system:

1. At all times, each container must have a card (either a move or a production card) attached to it.

2. Never move a container unless it has a move card attached to it.

3. Never begin producing a container without a production card.

4. A container should always contain a standard number of parts.

By the way, "cards" do not have to be used. Any type of signal (companies have used colored golf balls and empty spots on the shop floor) may be used to signal the start of production. What is important, of course, is that the signal to produce comes from a station that is downstream from the producing station.

Think of what happens to the system if station 4 breaks down. Eventually, this will result in production stopping at stations 1–3. At first glance, this might appear to reduce the plant's productivity. In reality, however, frequent plant shutdowns force workers to concentrate more on quality and plant efficiency. In the long run, the shutdowns will become less frequent, and a more efficient (and higher-quality) production process will result.

HOW MANY CARDS?

To understand the Kanban system better, let's try to figure out (in theory) how many move and production cards are needed to enable the plant to meet daily demand without holding unnecessary inventory. Let's focus on material being moved between stations 3 and 4. We define

c = number of parts in each container (less than 10% of daily requirement)

T_M = time (in days) for worker to go from station 4 to get a container at station 3 and return with it to station 4

T_P = time (in days) required to produce a container with c parts at station 3

D = daily demand for parts produced at station 3

M = number of move cards

P = number of production cards

How many move cards do we need? We can make $\frac{1}{T_M}$ trips per day to get containers, and on each trip we can get M containers with c parts per container. Since we need D parts per day, in theory we can meet daily requirements without accumulating excess inventory if

$$Mc\left(\frac{1}{T_M}\right) = D \qquad \text{or} \qquad M = \frac{DT_M}{c}$$

How many production cards do we need? With P cards, we can produce up to P containers (each with c parts) $\frac{1}{T_P}$ times per day. Since we must produce D units per day, we can (in theory) meet daily requirements without accumulating excess inventory if

$$Pc\left(\frac{1}{T_P}\right) = D \qquad \text{or} \qquad P = \frac{DT_P}{c}$$

For these formulas to be valid, we must assume that there is no variability in move and production times. The validity of the formulas also requires that containers will be ready for pickup whenever a worker from station 4 arrives at station 3. To allow for some slack in the system, the following formulas are often used to determine the required number of move and production cards:

$$M = \frac{DT_M(1 + k)}{c} \tag{1}$$

$$P = \frac{DT_P(1 + k)}{c} \tag{2}$$

In (1) and (2), k is a safety stock factor. If JIT is working well, k should be near 0. Toyota strives to keep k as close as possible to .10. In reality, a company may begin with k = .5. If shortages are infrequent, a card may be removed from the system. This will reduce inventory levels. If shortages are still rare, another card may be removed. This process continues until satisfactory results (infrequent shortages and low inventory levels) have been obtained.

Let's look at a numerical example of the application of (1) and (2). We assume that k = 0 and that station 4 must obtain 200 parts per day from station 3. Each container contains 10 parts, and it takes .10 day (T_P = .10) at station 3 to fill a container. Going from station 4 to station 3 to pick up a container and returning with it to station 4 takes a total of .05 day (T_M = .05). From (1) and (2), we find that

$$M = \frac{200(.05)(1 + 0)}{10} = 1 \text{ move card}$$

$$P = \frac{200(.10)(1 + 0)}{10} = 2 \text{ production cards}$$

are needed. Let's see how 1 move card and 2 production cards would enable the system to keep up with demand without accumulating excess inventories. Observe that station 4 will "use up" a container of parts in $\frac{10}{200} = .05$ days. Let's suppose that at time 0 (the beginning of a work day), station 4 has 1 full and 1 empty container, and station 3 has 2 full containers. At time 0, we begin using parts at station 4, so a worker takes the empty container (with a move card) to station 3. The worker arrives at station 3 at time $\frac{.05}{2} = .025$. There, the worker picks up a full container and removes the production card from it. At station 3, the detached production card causes production to begin at station 3. After attaching the move card to the full container at station 3, the worker heads back to station 4 and arrives at time .05, just in time for the full container of parts to be used when the full container at station 4 is used up at time .05. At time .05, another worker leaves station 4 and arrives at station 3 at time .075. Production begins at station 3 on another container. (This is okay, because we have two production cards.) We arrive back at station 4 with a full container (again, just in time) at time .10. At time .10, a worker again leaves for station 3, and at time .125, the worker picks up the full container whose production began at time .025. In summary, here's what happens:

1. At times 0, .05, .10, .15, . . . , a worker leaves station 4 for station 3.

2. At times .025, .075, .125, . . . , a worker arrives at station 3 and picks up a full container. Station 3 also begins producing a container of parts.

3. At times .05, .10, .15, . . . , a worker arrives at station 4 with a full container (just in time).

Observe that for our example, the maximum inventory level will be 30 parts. With more cards, the maximum possible inventory level would increase, but there would be slack in the system to handle unexpected shutdowns and shortages. Also note that a level production schedule (always producing 200 parts per day, for example) is critical to the success of JIT. If the production schedule were not level, we would have to adjust the number of cards daily in order to avoid shortages and/or excess inventory levels.

Experience with JIT and MRP has shown (not surprisingly) that MRP tends to outperform JIT when demand is highly variable and setup times are long. JIT tends to outperform MRP when demand is stable and setup times are brief.

Clearly, the smaller lot sizes associated with JIT will increase the number of setups required. Consider a company producing many different products. If such a company uses JIT, high setup costs will probably be incurred because it must frequently change from producing one product to another, due to the small lot sizes of JIT. This explains why JIT is most commonly used in a repetitive manufacturing environment where most setup times are small and very few products are made.

♦ PROBLEMS

GROUP A

1. Determine the number of move and production cards needed if 100 parts per day are required, five parts per container are used, and $T_M = T_P = .20$. Assume that material is being transported from station 1 to station 2.
(a) At what instants will a person arrive at station 2 with full containers?
(b) At what instants will production on containers begin at station 1?
(c) What is the maximum number of parts in inventory?

2. Determine the number of move and production cards required if 200 parts per day are needed, 20 parts per container are used, and $T_M = .10$ and $T_P = .30$. Assume that material is being transported from station 1 to station 2.

(a) At what instant will a person arrive at station 2 with full containers?
(b) At what instants will production on containers begin at station 1?
(c) What is the maximum number of parts in inventory?

3. Fill in the blanks: JIT may be thought of as MRP with _____ buckets and orders being filled according to the _____ lot-sizing method.

4. Supposedly, the Kanban version of a pull system was created after a Toyota employee observed an American supermarket. How is a supermarket a pull system? (Think about who does the pulling!) In a supermarket, what plays the role of the production card?

18-3

EXCHANGE CURVES

In many situations, it is difficult to estimate holding and shortage costs accurately. **Exchange curves** can be used in such situations to identify "reasonable" inventory policies. Consider a company that stocks two items (1 and 2). Many different ordering policies are possible. For example, the company may order item 1 five times a year and item 2 10 times a year (policy 1), or it may order each item once per year (policy 2). Clearly, policy 1 will result in higher ordering costs than policy 2, but policy 2 will result in higher holding costs and a higher average inventory level than policy 1. An exchange curve enables us to display graphically the tradeoff between annual order costs and average inventory investment.

To illustrate the construction of an exchange curve, suppose a company stocks two items (items 1 and 2), and suppose that

c_i = cost of purchasing each unit of product i

h = cost of holding \$1 worth of either product in inventory for one year

K_i = order cost for product i

q_i = EOQ for product i

D_i = annual demand for product i

Then

$$q_i = \sqrt{\frac{2K_i D_i}{hc_i}}$$

Suppose the company wishes to minimize the sum of annual order and holding costs. Then it should follow an EOQ policy for each product and order q_i of product $i \dfrac{D_i}{q_i}$ times per year. Two measures of effectiveness for this (or any other) ordering policy are

$$AII = \text{average dollar value of inventory}$$
$$AOC = \text{annual ordering cost}$$

If we follow the EOQ policy for each product, then

$$AII = \left(\frac{q_1}{2}\right)c_1 + \left(\frac{q_2}{2}\right)c_2$$

$$= \left(\frac{1}{2}\right)\left\{c_1\sqrt{\frac{2K_1D_1}{c_1h}} + c_2\sqrt{\frac{2K_2D_2}{c_2h}}\right\}$$

$$= \left(\frac{\sqrt{2}}{2\sqrt{h}}\right)\left\{\sqrt{K_1D_1c_1} + \sqrt{K_2D_2c_2}\right\}$$

$$AOC = K_1\left(\frac{D_1}{q_1}\right) + K_2\left(\frac{D_2}{q_2}\right)$$

$$= K_1D_1\sqrt{\frac{c_1h}{2K_1D_1}} + K_2D_2\sqrt{\frac{c_2h}{2K_2D_2}}$$

$$= \left(\frac{\sqrt{2h}}{2}\right)\left\{\sqrt{K_1D_1c_1} + \sqrt{K_2D_2c_2}\right\}$$

The expression for AII follows from the fact that the average inventory level of an item equals half the order quantity. The expression for AOC follows from the fact that $\dfrac{D_i}{q_i}$ orders per year are placed for item i.

Since h is often hard to estimate, let's suppose h is unknown and look at how a change in h affects AII and AOC. A plot of the points (AOC, AII) associated with each value of h is known as an **exchange curve**. For any point on the exchange curve, we see that

$$AII(AOC) = (\tfrac{1}{2})\{\sqrt{K_1D_1c_1} + \sqrt{K_2D_2c_2}\}^2 \tag{3}$$

This shows that the exchange curve is a hyperbola. Also, any point on the exchange curve satisfies $\frac{AII}{AOC} = \frac{1}{h}$ or $\frac{AOC}{AII} = h$. Thus, for any point on the exchange curve, the annual holding cost per dollar of inventory is the ratio of the x-coordinate to the y-coordinate. This shows how each point on the exchange curve can be identified with a value of h.

We now illustrate the computation of an exchange curve and show how the exchange curve can be used as an aid in decision making.

E X A M P L E
1

A company stocks two products. Relevant information is given in Table 17.

    a. Draw an exchange curve.

    b. Currently, the company is ordering each product ten times per year. Use the exchange curve to demonstrate to management that this is an unsatisfactory ordering policy.

    c. Suppose management limits the company's average inventory investment to $10,000. Use the exchange curve to determine an appropriate ordering policy.

Solution

    a. From (3), we find the equation of the exchange curve to be

$$(AII)(AOC) = (\tfrac{1}{2})\{\sqrt{50(10,000)(200)} + \sqrt{80(20,000)(2.5)}\}^2$$
$$= 72,000,000$$

	K_i	D_i	c_i
Product 1	$50	10,000	$200
Product 2	$80	20,000	$2.50

Table 17
Relevant
Information for
Example 1

AOC	AII	h
$2,000	$36,000	.06
$3,000	$24,000	.13
$4,000	$18,000	.22
$5,000	$14,400	.35
$6,000	$12,000	.50
$8,000	$9,000	.89

Table 18
Points on Exchange
Curve

Some representative points on the exchange curve, along with the associated value of h, are given in Table 18. The exchange curve is graphed in Figure 2.

b. If the company orders each product ten times per year,

$$\text{AOC} = 10(\$50) + 10(\$80) = \$1300$$

$$\text{AII} = \tfrac{1}{2}(1000)(\$200) + \tfrac{1}{2}(2000)(\$2.50) = \$102,500$$

Figure 2
Example of
Exchange Curve

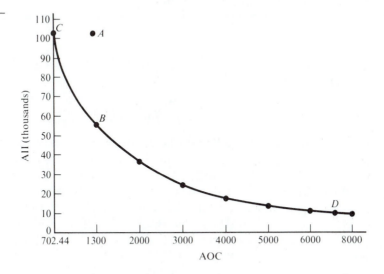

This is point A in Figure 2. Observe that point $B = (1300, 55,385)$, corresponding to $h = .02$, yields the same AOC as the current policy, but a much lower AII. Also, point $C = (702.44, 102,500)$, corresponding to $h = .01$, yields the same AII as the current policy, but a much lower AOC. Thus, we can use the exchange curve to show the manager how to improve on the current ordering policy.

c. From the exchange curve, we find that $D = (7200, 10,000)$ is on the exchange curve. Thus, for a $10,000 AII, the best we can do is to hold ordering costs to $7200. Of course, the manager could opt for AII = $9000 and AOC = $8000 or one of many other possibilities. The point is that the exchange curve clarifies many of the options available to management. ◆

EXCHANGE CURVES FOR STOCKOUTS

Exchange curves can also be used to assess the tradeoffs between average inventory investment (AII) and the expected number of lead times per year resulting in stockouts. To illustrate, consider a company stocking a single item for which

$$c = \text{purchase cost per unit}$$
$$K = \text{setup cost}$$
$$h = \text{annual cost of holding one unit in inventory}$$
$$c_B = \text{cost of a stockout (we assume all items are back-ordered)}$$
$$E(\mathbf{D}) = \text{mean annual demand}$$
$$q = \text{economic order quantity}$$
$$\mathbf{X} = \text{lead time demand}$$
$$E(\mathbf{X}) = \text{Mean lead time demand}$$
$$\sigma_X = \text{Standard deviation of lead time demand}$$
$$r = \text{reorder point (determined from Eq. (13) of Chapter 17)}$$

From Eq. (13) of Chapter 17, a fraction

$$\frac{qh}{c_B E(\mathbf{D})}$$

of all lead times will have a stockout. Since there are an average of $\frac{E(\mathbf{D})}{q}$ orders placed per year, an average of

$$\left(\frac{(E(\mathbf{D}))}{q}\right)\left(\frac{qh}{c_B E(\mathbf{D})}\right) = \frac{h}{c_B}$$

lead times per year will result in stockouts. We let SY = expected number of lead times per year resulting in stockouts. From (11) of Chapter 17, we know that the average inventory level is $(\frac{q}{2} + r - E(\mathbf{X}))$. Thus, we have AII = $c(\frac{q}{2} + r - E(\mathbf{X}))$.

An exchange curve for this situation is a graph of the points (AII, SY) corresponding to different values of c_B. To illustrate the construction of an exchange curve, let $E(\mathbf{X}) = 200, \sigma_X = 50, E(\mathbf{D}) = 100{,}000, K = \$12.50, h = \$10,$ and $c = \$100$. We will find four points on the exchange curve by setting $c_B = \$1, \$5, \$10,$ and $\$20$. First we find that

$$q = \sqrt{\frac{2(12.5)(100{,}000)}{10}} = 500$$

The stockout probabilities and SY are given in Table 19.

Using Table 4 in Chapter 11, we can calculate the reorder point r for each value of c_B. Then we determine the average inventory level and AII = average inventory investment. These calculations are given in Table 20.

The exchange curve (based on the four points we have computed) is graphed in Figure 3. For example, the exchange curve shows us that if current AII is $33,250, then

Table 19
Computation of SY

c_B	STOCKOUT PROBABILITY $= \dfrac{qh}{c_B E(\mathbf{D})}$	$SY = \dfrac{h}{c_B}$
$1	$\frac{500(10)}{1(100,000)} = .05$	$\frac{10}{1} = 10$
$5	$\frac{500(10)}{5(100,000)} = .01$	$\frac{10}{5} = 2$
$10	$\frac{500(10)}{10(100,000)} = .005$	$\frac{10}{10} = 1$
$20	$\frac{500(10)}{20(100,000)} = .0025$	$\frac{10}{20} = 0.50$

Table 20
Calculation of AII

c_B	REORDER POINT	AVERAGE INVENTORY LEVEL	AII
$1	$200 + 50(1.65) = 282.5$	$250 + 282.5 - 200 = 332.5$	$33,250
$5	$200 + 50(2.33) = 316.5$	$250 + 316.5 - 200 = 366.5$	$36,650
$10	$200 + 50(2.58) = 329$	$250 + 329 - 200 = 379$	$37,900
$20	$200 + 50(2.81) = 340.5$	$250 + 340.5 - 200 = 390.5$	$39,050

Figure 3
Exchange Curve for AII and SY

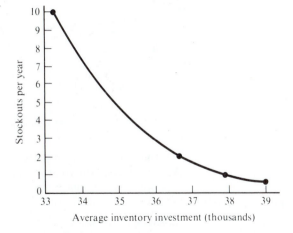

EXCHANGE SURFACES

for a $3400 increase in AII, we can reduce SY from 10 to 2, but an additional increase in AII of $3400 would decrease SY by less than 2.

Using more sophisticated techniques (see Gardner and Dannenbring (1979)), an **exchange surface** involving three or more quantities can be derived. The exchange surface in Figure 4 was derived from a sample of 500 items in a military distribution system. The x-coordinate is the annual number of orders placed, the y-coordinate is the average inventory investment (in thousands of dollars), and the z-coordinate is the percentage of requests that yield shortages. For example, suppose the military has fixed a $900,000 average inventory investment. By varying the number of orders per year between 1500 and 9042, the military can vary the percentage of requests that yield shortages between 6.31% and 3.42%. Also, if annual orders are fixed at 3000, then the percentage of requests yielding shortages can vary between 0.75% and 3.71%. An exchange surface makes it easy to identify the tradeoffs involved between improving service, increased inventory investment, and increased workload (orders per year).

Figure 4
Example of an exchange surface
(reprinted by permission of
E. Gardner and D. Dannenbring,
"Using Optimal Policy Surfaces to
Analyze Aggregate Inventory
Tradeoffs," *Management Science*,
Vol. 25, No. 8, August 1979. Copyright
1979, The Institute of Management
Sciences)

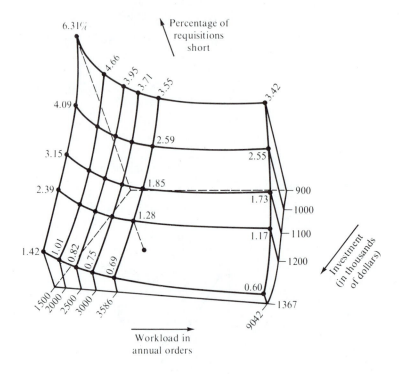

♦ PROBLEMS

GROUP A

1. Consider a two-item inventory system with the attributes given in Table 21.

(a) Draw an exchange curve for these products (use AOC and AII as the *x*- and *y*-coordinates).

(b) Currently, management is ordering each product twice a year. How can it improve on this strategy?

(c) The order costs correspond to machine setup times. Machine time is valued at $50 per hour. If management wants to limit machine setup time to 500 hours per year, what strategies are available?

2. Explain how to draw an exchange curve where the *x*-coordinate is AII and the *y*-coordinate is percentage of all requests for stock that result in shortages.

3. Consider the exchange surface in Figure 4. The current inventory policy has yielded 3586 orders per year, an AII of $1,367,000, and 0.89% shortages.

(a) Without changing orders per year and AII, by how much can shortages be improved?

(b) If AII and shortages are maintained at current levels, by how much can orders per year be reduced?

(c) If shortages and orders per year are maintained at current levels, by how much can AII be reduced?

Table 21

	K_i	D_i	c_i
Product 1	$500	10,000	$2000
Product 2	$800	20,000	$250

♦ SUMMARY

MATERIAL REQUIREMENTS PLANNING

MRP uses the relationship between the demand for the final product and the components used to make the final product to create a production schedule that leads to reduced inventories. An MRP record is used to determine net requirements for each period. Planned production for each period is usually met by one of the following lot-sizing methods: lot-for-lot, POQ, EOQ, fixed-order quantity, and part-period balancing.

THE JUST-IN-TIME APPROACH

The JIT approach consists of producing products or obtaining products from suppliers at the instant when the product is required. A successful implementation of JIT will lead to reduced inventories and increased product quality. A common method used to implement JIT is the Kanban system. It is a **pull** system, which is governed by the following rules:

1. At all times, each container must have a card (either a move card or a production card) attached to it.

2. Never move a container unless it has a move card attached to it.

3. Never begin producing a container without a production card.

4. A container should always contain a standard number of parts.

EXCHANGE CURVES

Exchange curves (and exchange surfaces) are used to display tradeoffs between various objectives. For example, an exchange curve may display the tradeoff between annual ordering costs and average dollar level of inventory. An exchange curve can be used to compare how various ordering policies compare with respect to several objectives.

◆ REFERENCES

The following references discuss MRP:

ORLICKY, J. *Materials Requirements Planning*: *The New Way of Life in Production and Inventory Management*. New York: McGraw-Hill, 1975.

PETERSON, R., and E. SILVER. *Decision Systems for Inventory Management and Production Planning*. New York: Wiley, 1984.

TERSINE, R. *Principles of Inventory and Materials Management*. New York: North-Holland, 1982. Explains MRP.

VOLLMAN, T., W. BERRY, and C. WHYBARK. *Manufacturing Planning and Control Systems*. Homewood, Ill.: Irwin, 1988.

The following references discuss JIT:

HALL, R. *Zero Inventories*. Homewood, Ill.: Dow-Jones-Irwin, 1983.

SCHONBERGER, R. *Japanese Manufacturing Techniques*: *Nine Hidden Lessons in Simplicity*. New York: Free Press, 1982.

—— *World Class Manufacturing*: *A Casebook*. New York: Free Press, 1987.

For a discussion of exchange curves and surfaces, see:

GARDNER, E., and D. DANNENBRING. "Using Optimal Policy Surfaces to Analyze Aggregate Inventory Tradeoffs," *Management Science* 25(1979):709–720.

HAX, A., and D. CANDEA. *Production and Inventory Management*. Englewood Cliffs, N.J.: Prentice-Hall, 1984.

CHAPTER 19

Markov Chains

SOMETIMES WE ARE interested in how a random variable changes over time. For example, we may want to know how the price of a share of stock or a firm's market share evolves over time. The study of how a random variable evolves over time includes stochastic processes. In this chapter, we explain stochastic processes—in particular, a type of stochastic process known as a Markov chain. Markov chains have been applied in areas such as education, marketing, health services, finance, accounting, and production. We begin by defining the concept of a stochastic process. In the rest of the chapter, we will discuss the basic ideas needed for an understanding of Markov chains.

19-1 WHAT IS A STOCHASTIC PROCESS?

Suppose we observe some characteristic of a system at discrete points in time (labeled $0, 1, 2, \ldots$). Let $\mathbf{X}_t$ be the value of the system characteristic at time t. In most situations, $\mathbf{X}_t$ is not known with certainty before time t and may be viewed as a random variable. A **discrete-time stochastic process** is simply a description of the relation between the random variables $\mathbf{X}_0, \mathbf{X}_1, \mathbf{X}_2, \ldots$. Some examples of discrete-time stochastic processes follow.

EXAMPLE 1

The Gambler's Ruin At time 0, I have \$2. At times $1, 2, \ldots$, I play a game in which I bet \$1. With probability p, I win the game, and with probability $1 - p$, I lose the game. My goal is to increase my capital to \$4, and as soon as I do, the game is over. The game is also over if my capital is reduced to \$0. If we define $\mathbf{X}_t$ to be my capital position after the time t game (if any) is played, then $\mathbf{X}_0, \mathbf{X}_1, \ldots, \mathbf{X}_t$ may be viewed as a discrete-time stochastic process. Note that $\mathbf{X}_0 = 2$ is a known constant, but $\mathbf{X}_1$ and later $\mathbf{X}_t$'s are random. For example, with probability p, $\mathbf{X}_1 = 3$, and with probability $1 - p$, $\mathbf{X}_1 = 1$. Note that if $\mathbf{X}_t = 4$, then $\mathbf{X}_{t+1}$ and all later $\mathbf{X}_t$'s will also equal 4. Similarly, if $\mathbf{X}_t = 0$, then $\mathbf{X}_{t+1}$ and all later $\mathbf{X}_t$'s will also equal zero. For obvious reasons, this type of situation is called a gambler's ruin problem.

E X A M P L E
2

An urn contains two unpainted balls at present. We choose a ball at random and flip a coin. If the chosen ball is unpainted and the coin comes up heads, we paint the chosen unpainted ball red; if the chosen ball is unpainted and the coin comes up tails, we paint the chosen unpainted ball black. If the ball has already been painted, then (whether head or tail has been tossed) we change the color of the ball (from red to black or from black to red). To model this situation as a stochastic process, we define time t to be the time after the coin has been flipped for the tth time and the chosen ball has been painted. The state at any time may be described by the vector $[u \quad r \quad b]$, where u is the number of unpainted balls in the urn, r is the number of red balls in the urn, and b is the number of black balls in the urn. We are given that $\mathbf{X}_0 = [2 \quad 0 \quad 0]$. After the first coin toss, one ball will have been painted either red or black, and the state will be either $[1 \quad 1 \quad 0]$ or $[1 \quad 0 \quad 1]$. Hence, we can be sure that $\mathbf{X}_1 = [1 \quad 1 \quad 0]$ or $\mathbf{X}_1 = [1 \quad 0 \quad 1]$. Clearly, there must be some sort of relation between the $\mathbf{X}_t$'s. For example, if $\mathbf{X}_t = [0 \quad 2 \quad 0]$, we can be sure that $\mathbf{X}_{t+1}$ will be $[0 \quad 1 \quad 1]$.

◆

E X A M P L E
3

Let $\mathbf{X}_0$ be the price of a share of CSL Computer stock at the beginning of the current trading day. Also, let $\mathbf{X}_t$ be the price of a share of CSL stock at the beginning of the tth trading day in the future. Clearly, knowing the values of $\mathbf{X}_0, \mathbf{X}_1, \ldots, \mathbf{X}_t$ tells us something about the probability distribution of $\mathbf{X}_{t+1}$; the question is, what does the past (stock prices up to time t) tell us about $\mathbf{X}_{t+1}$? The answer to this question is of critical importance in finance. (See Section 19.2 for more details.)

◆

We close this section with a brief discussion of continuous-time stochastic processes. A **continuous-time stochastic process** is simply a stochastic process in which the state of the system can be viewed at any time, not just at discrete instants in time. For example, the number of people in a supermarket t minutes after the store opens for business may be viewed as a continuous-time stochastic process. (Models involving continuous-time stochastic processes are studied in Chapter 22.) Since the price of a share of stock can be observed at any time (not just the beginning of each trading day), it may be viewed as a continuous-time stochastic process. Viewing the price of a share of stock as a continuous-time stochastic process has led to many important results in the theory of finance, including the famous Black-Scholes option pricing formula.

19-2   WHAT IS A MARKOV CHAIN?

One special type of discrete-time stochastic process is called a Markov chain. To simplify our exposition, we assume that at any time, the discrete-time stochastic process can be in one of a finite number of states labeled $1, 2, \ldots, s$.

DEFINITION ■ A discrete-time stochastic process is a **Markov chain** if, for $t = 0, 1, 2, \ldots$ and all states,

$$P(\mathbf{X}_{t+1} = i_{t+1} | \mathbf{X}_t = i_t, \mathbf{X}_{t-1} = i_{t-1}, \ldots, \mathbf{X}_1 = i_1, \mathbf{X}_0 = i_0)$$
$$= P(\mathbf{X}_{t+1} = i_{t+1} | \mathbf{X}_t = i_t)$$

(1)

Essentially, (1) says that the probability distribution of the state at time $t + 1$ depends on the state at time t (i_t) and does not depend on the states the chain passed through on the way to i_t at time t.

In our study of Markov chains, we make the further assumption that for all states i and j and all t, $P(\mathbf{X}_{t+1} = j \mid \mathbf{X}_t = i)$ is independent of t. This assumption allows us to write

$$P(\mathbf{X}_{t+1} = j \mid \mathbf{X}_t = i) = p_{ij} \tag{2}$$

where p_{ij} is the probability that given the system is in state i at time t, the system will be in a state j at time $t + 1$. If the system moves from state i during one period to state j during the next period, we say that a **transition** from i to j has occurred. The p_{ij}'s are often referred to as the **transition probabilities** for the Markov chain.

Eq. (2) implies that the probability law relating the next period's state to the current state does not change (or remains stationary) over time. For this reason, Eq. (2) is often called the **Stationarity Assumption**. Any Markov chain that satisfies (2) is called a **stationary Markov chain**.

Our study of Markov chains also requires us to define q_i to be the probability that the chain is in state i at time 0; in other words, $P(\mathbf{X}_0 = i) = q_i$. We call the vector $\mathbf{q} = [q_1 \quad q_2 \quad \cdots \quad q_s]$ the **initial probability distribution** for the Markov chain. In most applications, the transition probabilities are displayed as an $s \times s$ **transition probability matrix** P. The transition probability matrix P may be written as

$$P = \begin{bmatrix} p_{11} & p_{12} & \cdots & p_{1s} \\ p_{21} & p_{22} & \cdots & p_{2s} \\ \vdots & \vdots & & \vdots \\ p_{s1} & p_{s2} & \cdots & p_{ss} \end{bmatrix}$$

Given that the state at time t is i, the process must be somewhere at time $t + 1$. This means that for each i,

$$\sum_{j=1}^{j=s} P(\mathbf{X}_{t+1} = j \mid P(\mathbf{X}_t = i)) = 1$$

$$\sum_{j=1}^{j=s} p_{ij} = 1$$

We also know that each entry in the P matrix must be nonnegative. Hence, all entries in the transition probability matrix are nonnegative, and the entries in each row must sum to 1.

E X A M P L E
1

Solution

The Gambler's Ruin (Continued)   Find the transition matrix for Example 1.

Since the amount of money I have after $t + 1$ plays of the game depends on the past history of the game only through the amount of money I have after t plays, we definitely have a Markov chain. Since the rules of the game don't change over time, we also have a stationary Markov chain. The transition matrix is as follows (state i means that we have i dollars):

State

$$
P = \begin{array}{c} \\ 0 \\ 1 \\ 2 \\ 3 \\ 4 \end{array}
\begin{array}{ccccc}
\$0 & \$1 & \$2 & \$3 & \$4 \\
\begin{bmatrix} 1 & 0 & 0 & 0 & 0 \\ 1-p & 0 & p & 0 & 0 \\ 0 & 1-p & 0 & p & 0 \\ 0 & 0 & 1-p & 0 & p \\ 0 & 0 & 0 & 0 & 1 \end{bmatrix}
\end{array}
$$

If the state is $0 or $4, I don't play the game anymore, so the state cannot change; hence, $p_{00} = p_{44} = 1$. For all other states, we know that with probability p, the next period's state will exceed the current state by 1, and with probability $1 - p$, the next period's state will be 1 less than the current state.

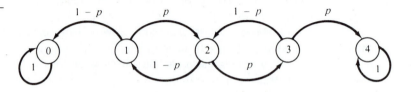

Figure 1
Graphical Representation of Transition Matrix for Gambler's Ruin Example

A transition matrix may be represented by a graph in which each node represents a state and arc (i, j) represents the transition probability p_{ij}. Figure 1 gives a graphical representation of Example 1's transition probability matrix.

◆

E X A M P L E 2

(Continued) Find the transition matrix for Example 2.

Solution

Since the state of the urn after the next coin toss only depends on the past history of the process through the state of the urn after the current coin toss, we have a Markov chain. Since the rules don't change over time, we have a stationary Markov chain. The transition matrix for Example 2 is as follows:

State

	[0 1 1]	[0 2 0]	[0 0 2]	[2 0 0]	[1 1 0]	[1 0 1]
[0 1 1]	0	$\frac{1}{2}$	$\frac{1}{2}$	0	0	0
[0 2 0]	1	0	0	0	0	0
[0 0 2]	1	0	0	0	0	0
[2 0 0]	0	0	0	0	$\frac{1}{2}$	$\frac{1}{2}$
[1 1 0]	$\frac{1}{4}$	$\frac{1}{4}$	0	0	0	$\frac{1}{2}$
[1 0 1]	$\frac{1}{4}$	0	$\frac{1}{4}$	0	$\frac{1}{2}$	0

$P =$

Table 1
Computations of
Transition
Probabilities If
Current State Is
[1 1 0]

EVENT	PROBABILITY	NEW STATE
Flip heads and choose unpainted ball	$\frac{1}{4}$	[0 2 0]
Choose red ball	$\frac{1}{2}$	[1 0 1]
Flip tails and choose unpainted ball	$\frac{1}{4}$	[0 1 1]

To illustrate the determination of the transition matrix, we determine the [1 1 0] row of this transition matrix. If the current state is [1 1 0], then one of the events shown in Table 1 must occur. Thus, the next state will be [1 0 1] with probability $\frac{1}{2}$, [0 2 0] with probability $\frac{1}{4}$, and [0 1 1] with probability $\frac{1}{4}$. Figure 2 gives a graphical representation of this transition matrix.

Figure 2
Graphical
Representation of
Transition Matrix
for Urn Example

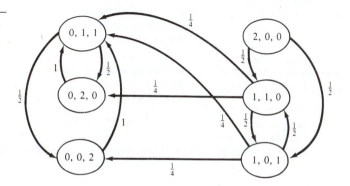

EXAMPLE
3

(Continued)   In recent years, students of finance have devoted much effort to answering the question of whether the daily price of a stock share can be described by a Markov chain. Suppose the daily price of a stock share (such as CSL Computer stock) can be described by a Markov chain. What does that tell us? Simply that the probability distribution of tomorrow's price for one share of CSL stock depends *only* on today's price of CSL stock, *not* on the past prices of CSL stock. If the price of a stock share can be described by a Markov chain, the "chartists" who attempt to predict future stock prices on the basis of the patterns followed by past stock prices are barking up the wrong tree. For example, suppose the daily price of a share of CSL stock follows a Markov chain, and today's price for a share of CSL stock is $50. Then to predict tomorrow's price of a share of CSL stock, it does not matter whether the price has increased or decreased during each of the last 30 days. In either situation (or any other situation that might have led to today's $50 price), a prediction of tomorrow's stock price should be based only on the fact that today's price of CSL stock is $50. At this time, the consensus is that for most stocks the daily price of the stock can be described as a Markov chain. This idea is often referred to as the **efficient market hypothesis**.

◆ PROBLEMS

GROUP A

1. In Smalltown, 90% of all sunny days are followed by sunny days and 80% of all cloudy days are followed by cloudy days. Use this information to model Smalltown's weather as a Markov chain.

2. Consider an inventory system in which the sequence of events during each period is as follows: (1) We observe the inventory level (call it i) at the beginning of the period. (2) If $i \leq 1$, $4 - i$ units are ordered. If $i \geq 2$, no units are ordered. Delivery of all ordered units is immediate. (3) With probability $\frac{1}{3}$, no units are demanded during the period; with probability $\frac{1}{3}$, 1 unit is demanded during the period; and with probability $\frac{1}{3}$, 2 units are demanded during the period. (4) We observe the inventory level at the beginning of the next period.

Define a period's state to be the period's beginning inventory level. Determine the transition matrix that could be used to model this inventory system as a Markov chain.

3. A company has two machines. During any day, each machine that is working at the beginning of the day has a $\frac{1}{3}$ chance of breaking down. If a machine breaks down during the day, it is sent to a repair facility and will be working two days after it breaks down. (Thus, if a machine breaks down during day 3, it will be working at the beginning of day 5.) Letting the state of the system be the number of machines working at the beginning of the day, formulate a transition probability matrix for this situation.

GROUP B

4. Referring to Problem 1, suppose that tomorrow's Smalltown weather depends on the last two days of Smalltown weather, as follows: (1) If the last two days have been sunny, then 95% of the time, tomorrow will be sunny. (2) If yesterday was cloudy and today is sunny, then 70% of the time, tomorrow will be sunny. (3) If yesterday was sunny and today is cloudy, then 60% of the time, tomorrow will be cloudy. (4) If the last two days have been cloudy, then 80% of the time, tomorrow will be cloudy.

Using this information, model Smalltown's weather as a Markov chain. If tomorrow's weather depended on the last three days of Smalltown weather, how many states will be needed to model Smalltown's weather as a Markov chain? (*Note*: The approach used in this problem can be used to model a discrete-time stochastic process as a Markov chain even if $\mathbf{X}_{t+1}$ depends on states prior to $\mathbf{X}_t$, such as $\mathbf{X}_{t-1}$ in the current example.)

5. Let $\mathbf{X}_t$ be the location of your token on the Monopoly board after t dice rolls. Can $\mathbf{X}_t$ be modeled as a Markov chain? If not, how can we modify the definition of the state at time t so that $\mathbf{X}_0, \mathbf{X}_1, \ldots, \mathbf{X}_t, \ldots$ would be a Markov chain? (*Hint*: How does a player go to Jail? In this problem, assume that players who are sent to Jail stay in Jail until they roll doubles or until they have spent three turns in Jail, whichever comes first.)

6. In Problem 3, suppose a machine that breaks down returns to service three days later (for instance, a machine that breaks down during day 3 would be back in working order at the beginning of day 6). Determine a transition probability matrix for this situation.

19-3 n-STEP TRANSITION PROBABILITIES

Suppose we are studying a Markov chain with a known transition probability matrix P. (Since all chains that we will deal with are stationary, we will not bother to label our Markov chains as stationary.) A question of interest is: If a Markov chain is in state i at time m, what is the probability that n periods later the Markov chain will be in state j? Since we are dealing with a stationary Markov chain, this probability will be independent of m, so we may write

$$P(\mathbf{X}_{m+n} = j \,|\, \mathbf{X}_m = i) = P(\mathbf{X}_n = j \,|\, \mathbf{X}_0 = i) = P_{ij}(n)$$

where $P_{ij}(n)$ is called the **n-step probability** of a transition from state i to state j.

Clearly, $P_{ij}(1) = p_{ij}$. To determine $P_{ij}(2)$, note that if the system is now in state i, then for the system to end up in state j 2 periods from now, we must go from state i to some state k and then go from state k to state j (see Figure 3). This reasoning allows us to write

$$P_{ij}(2) = \sum_{k=1}^{k=s} \text{(probability of transition from } i \text{ to } k)$$
$$\times \text{(probability of transition from } k \text{ to } j)$$

Using the definition of P, the transition probability matrix, we rewrite the last equation as

$$P_{ij}(2) = \sum_{k=1}^{k=s} p_{ik}p_{kj} \qquad (3)$$

The right-hand side of (3) is just the scalar product of row i of the P matrix with column j of the P matrix. Hence, $P_{ij}(2)$ is the ijth element of the matrix P^2. By extending this reasoning, it can be shown that for $n > 1$,

$$P_{ij}(n) = ij\text{th element of } P^n \qquad (4)$$

Of course, for $n = 0$, $P_{ij}(0) = P(\mathbf{X}_0 = j \mid \mathbf{X}_0 = i)$, so we must write

$$P_{ij}(0) = \begin{cases} 1 & \text{if } j = i \\ 0 & \text{if } j \neq i \end{cases}$$

We illustrate the use of Eq. (4) in Example 4.

Figure 3
$P_{ij}(2) = p_{i1}p_{1j} + p_{i2}p_{2j}$
$\quad + \cdots + p_{is}p_{sj}$

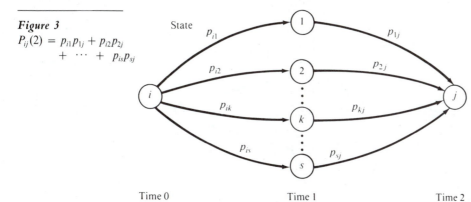

Time 0   Time 1   Time 2

E X A M P L E 4

The Cola Example Suppose the entire cola industry produces only two colas. Given that a person last purchased cola 1, there is a 90% chance that her next purchase will be cola 1. Given that a person last purchased cola 2, there is an 80% chance that her next purchase will be cola 2.

1. If a person is currently a cola 2 purchaser, what is the probability that she will purchase cola 1 two purchases from now?

2. If a person is currently a cola 1 purchaser, what is the probability that she will purchase cola 1 three purchases from now?

Solution

We view each person's purchases as a Markov chain with the state at any given time being the type of cola the person last purchased. Hence, each person's cola purchases may be represented by a two-state Markov chain, where

State 1 = person has last purchased cola 1

State 2 = person has last purchased cola 2

If we define X_n to be the type of cola purchased by a person on her nth future cola purchase (present cola purchase = X_0), then X_0, X_1, . . . may be described as the Markov chain with the following transition matrix:

$$P = \begin{array}{c} \\ \text{Cola 1} \\ \text{Cola 2} \end{array} \begin{array}{cc} \text{Cola 1} & \text{Cola 2} \\ \begin{bmatrix} .90 & .10 \\ .20 & .80 \end{bmatrix} \end{array}$$

We can now answer questions 1 and 2.

1. We seek $P(X_2 = 1 | X_0 = 2) = P_{21}(2) =$ element 21 of P^2:

$$P^2 = \begin{bmatrix} .90 & .10 \\ .20 & .80 \end{bmatrix} \begin{bmatrix} .90 & .10 \\ .20 & .80 \end{bmatrix} = \begin{bmatrix} .83 & .17 \\ .34 & .66 \end{bmatrix}$$

Hence, $P_{21}(2) = .34$. This means that the probability is .34 that two purchases in the future a cola 2 drinker will purchase cola 1. By using basic probability theory, we may obtain this answer in a different way (see Figure 4). Note that $P_{21}(2) =$ (probability that next purchase is cola 1 and second purchase is cola 1) + (probability that next purchase is cola 2 and second purchase is cola 1) $= p_{21}p_{11} + p_{22}p_{21} = (.20)(.90) + (.80)(.20) = .34$.

Figure 4
Probability That
Two Periods from
Now, a Cola 2
Purchaser Will
Purchase Cola 1
Is .20(.90) +
.80(.20) = .34

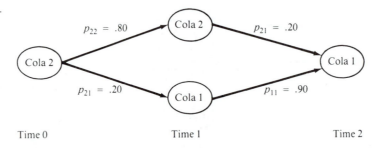

$p_{22} = .80$ Cola 2 $p_{21} = .20$

Cola 2

$p_{21} = .20$ Cola 1 $p_{11} = .90$

Cola 1

Time 0   Time 1   Time 2

2. We seek $P_{11}(3) =$ element 11 of P^3:

$$P^3 = P(P^2) = \begin{bmatrix} .90 & .10 \\ .20 & .80 \end{bmatrix} \begin{bmatrix} .83 & .17 \\ .34 & .66 \end{bmatrix} = \begin{bmatrix} .781 & .219 \\ .438 & .562 \end{bmatrix}$$

Therefore, $P_{11}(3) = .781$. ◆

In many situations, we do not know the state of the Markov chain at time 0. As defined in Section 19.2, let q_i be the probability that the chain is in state i at time 0. Then we can determine the probability that the system is in state i at time n by using the following reasoning (see Figure 5).

Figure 5
Determination of
Probability of Being
in State *j* at Time *n*
When Initial State Is
Unknown

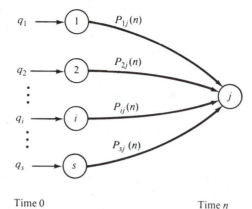

Time 0   Time *n*

Probability of being in state *j* at time *n*

$$= \sum_{i=1}^{i=s} (\text{probability that state is originally } i)$$

$$\times (\text{probability of going from } i \text{ to } j \text{ in } n \text{ transitions})$$

$$= \sum_{i=1}^{i=s} q_i P_{ij}(n) \tag{5}$$

$$= \mathbf{q}(\text{column } j \text{ of } P^n)$$

where $\mathbf{q} = [q_1 \quad q_2 \quad \cdots \quad q_s]$.

To illustrate the use of Eq. (5), we answer the following question: Suppose 60% of all people now drink cola 1, and 40% now drink cola 2. Three purchases from now, what fraction of all purchasers will be drinking cola 1? Since $\mathbf{q} = [.60 \quad .40]$ and

$\mathbf{q}(\text{column 1 of } P^3)$

= probability that three purchases from now a person drinks cola 1

the desired probability is

$$[.60 \quad .40] \begin{bmatrix} .781 \\ .438 \end{bmatrix} = .6438$$

Hence, three purchases from now, 64% of all purchasers will be purchasing cola 1.

To illustrate the behavior of the *n*-step transition probabilities for large values of *n*, we have computed several of the *n*-step transition probabilities for the Cola example in Table 2.

For large *n*, both $P_{11}(n)$ and $P_{21}(n)$ are nearly constant and approach .67. This means that for large *n*, no matter what the initial state, there is a .67 chance that a person will be a cola 1 purchaser. Similarly, we see that for large *n*, both $P_{12}(n)$ and $P_{22}(n)$ are nearly constant and approach .33. This means that for large *n*, no matter what the initial state, there is a .33 chance that a person will be a cola 2 purchaser. In Section 19.5, we make a thorough study of this settling down of the *n*-step transition probabilities.

Table 2	n	$P_{11}(n)$	$P_{12}(n)$	$P_{21}(n)$	$P_{22}(n)$
n-Step Transition	1	.90	.10	.20	.80
Probabilities for	2	.83	.17	.34	.66
Cola Example	3	.78	.22	.44	.56
	4	.75	.25	.51	.49
	5	.72	.28	.56	.44
	10	.68	.32	.65	.35
	20	.67	.33	.67	.33
	30	.67	.33	.67	.33
	40	.67	.33	.67	.33

◆ PROBLEMS

GROUP A

1. Each American family is classified as living in an urban, rural, or suburban location. During a given year, 15% of all urban families move to a suburban location, and 5% move to a rural location; also, 6% of all suburban families move to an urban location, and 4% move to a rural location; finally, 4% of all rural families move to an urban location, and 6% move to a suburban location.

(a) If a family now lives in an urban location, what is the probability that it will live in an urban area two years from now? A suburban area? A rural area?

(b) Suppose that at present, 40% of all families live in an urban area, 35% live in a suburban area, and 25% live in a rural area. Two years from now, what percentage of American families will live in an urban area?

(c) What problems might occur if this model were used to predict the future population distribution of the United States?

2. The following questions refer to Example 1.
(a) After playing the game twice, what is the probability that I will have $3? How about $2?
(b) After playing the game three times, what is the probability that I will have $2?

3. In Example 2, determine the following *n*-step transition probabilities:
(a) After two balls are painted, what is the probability that the state is [0 2 0]?
(b) After three balls are painted, what is the probability that the state is [0 1 1]? (Draw a diagram like Figure 4.)

19-4   CLASSIFICATION OF STATES IN A MARKOV CHAIN

In Section 19.3, we mentioned the fact that after many transitions, the *n*-step transition probabilities tend to settle down. Before we can discuss this in more detail, we need to study how mathematicians classify the states of a Markov chain. We use the following transition matrix to illustrate most of the following definitions (see Figure 6).

$$P = \begin{bmatrix} .4 & .6 & 0 & 0 & 0 \\ .5 & .5 & 0 & 0 & 0 \\ 0 & 0 & .3 & .7 & 0 \\ 0 & 0 & .5 & .4 & .1 \\ 0 & 0 & 0 & .8 & .2 \end{bmatrix}$$

DEFINITION ▪ Given two states i and j, a **path** from i to j is a sequence of transitions that begins in i and ends in j, such that each transition in the sequence has a positive probability of occurring.

Figure 6
Graphical
Representation of
Transition Matrix

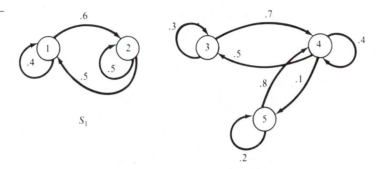

DEFINITION | A state j is **reachable** from a state i if there is a path leading from i to j.

DEFINITION | Two states i and j are said to **communicate** if j is reachable from i, and i is reachable from j.

For the transition probability matrix P represented in Figure 6, state 5 is reachable from state 3 (via the path 3–4–5), but state 5 is not reachable from state 1 (there is no path from 1 to 5 in Figure 6). Also, states 1 and 2 communicate (we can go from 1 to 2 and from 2 to 1).

DEFINITION | A set of states S in a Markov chain is a **closed set** if no state outside of S is reachable from any state in S.

From the Markov chain with transition matrix P in Figure 6, $S_1 = \{1, 2\}$ and $S_2 = \{3, 4, 5\}$ are both closed sets. Observe that once we enter a closed set, we can never leave the closed set (in Figure 6, no arc begins in S_1 and ends in S_2 or begins in S_2 and ends in S_1).

DEFINITION | A state i is an **absorbing state** if $p_{ii} = 1$.

Whenever we enter an absorbing state, we never leave the state. In Example 1, the gambler's ruin, states 0 and 4 are absorbing states. Of course, an absorbing state is a closed set containing only one state.

DEFINITION | A state i is a **transient state** if there exists a state j that is reachable from i, but the state i is not reachable from state j.

In other words, a state i is transient if there is a way to leave state i that never returns to state i. In the gambler's ruin example, states 1, 2, and 3 are transient states. For example (see Figure 1), from state 2, it is possible to go along the path 2–3–4, but there is no way to return to state 2 from state 4. Similarly, in Example 2, [2 0 0], [1 1 0], and [1 0 1] are all transient states (in Figure 2, there is a path from [1 0 1] to [0 0 2], but once both balls are painted, there is no way to return to [1 0 1]).

After a large number of periods, the probability of being in any transient state i is zero. Each time we enter a transient state i, there is a positive probability that we will leave i forever and end up in the state j described in the definition of a transient state. Thus, eventually we are sure to enter state j (and then we will never return to state i). To illustrate, in Example 2, suppose we are in the transient state [1 0 1]. With probability 1, the unpainted ball will eventually be painted, and we will never reenter state [1 0 1] (see Figure 2).

DEFINITION ■ If a state is not transient, it is called a **recurrent state**.

In Example 1, states 0 and 4 are recurrent states (and also absorbing states), and in Example 2, [0 2 0], [0 0 2], and [0 1 1] are recurrent states. For the transition matrix P in Figure 6, all states are recurrent.

DEFINITION ■ A state i is **periodic** with period $k > 1$ if k is the smallest number such that all paths leading from state i back to state i have a length that is a multiple of k. If a recurrent state is not periodic, it is referred to as **aperiodic**.

For the Markov chain with transition matrix

$$Q = \begin{bmatrix} 0 & 1 & 0 \\ 0 & 0 & 1 \\ 1 & 0 & 0 \end{bmatrix}$$

each state has period 3. For example, if we begin in state 1, the only way to return to state 1 is to follow the path 1–2–3–1 for some number of times (say, m) (see Figure 7). Hence, any return to state 1 will take $3m$ transitions, so state 1 has period 3. Wherever we are, we are sure to return three periods later.

Figure 7
A Periodic Markov
Chain $k = 3$

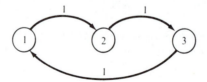

DEFINITION ■ If all states in a chain are recurrent, aperiodic, and communicate with each other, the chain is said to be **ergodic**.

The gambler's ruin example is not an ergodic chain, because (for example) states 3 and 4 do not communicate. Example 2 is also not an ergodic chain, because (for example) [2 0 0] and [0 1 1] do not communicate. Example 4, the Cola example, is an ergodic Markov chain. Of the following three Markov chains, P_1 and P_3 are ergodic, and P_2 is not ergodic.

$$P_1 = \begin{bmatrix} \frac{1}{3} & \frac{2}{3} & 0 \\ \frac{1}{2} & 0 & \frac{1}{2} \\ 0 & \frac{1}{4} & \frac{3}{4} \end{bmatrix} \quad \text{Ergodic}$$

$$P_2 = \begin{bmatrix} \frac{1}{2} & \frac{1}{2} & 0 & 0 \\ \frac{1}{2} & \frac{1}{2} & 0 & 0 \\ 0 & 0 & \frac{2}{3} & \frac{1}{3} \\ 0 & 0 & \frac{1}{4} & \frac{3}{4} \end{bmatrix} \quad \text{Nonergodic}$$

$$P_3 = \begin{bmatrix} \frac{1}{4} & \frac{1}{2} & \frac{1}{4} \\ \frac{2}{3} & \frac{1}{3} & 0 \\ 0 & \frac{2}{3} & \frac{1}{3} \end{bmatrix} \quad \text{Ergodic}$$

P_2 is not ergodic because there are two closed classes of states (class 1 $= \{1, 2\}$ and class 2 $= \{3, 4\}$, and the states in different classes do not communicate with each other.

After the next two sections, the importance of the concepts introduced in this section will become clear.

◆ PROBLEMS

GROUP A

1. In Example 1, what is the period of states 1 and 3?

2. Is the Markov chain of Section 19.3, Problem 1, an ergodic Markov chain?

3. Consider the following transition matrix:

$$P = \begin{bmatrix} 0 & 0 & 1 & 0 & 0 & 0 \\ 0 & 0 & 0 & 0 & 0 & 1 \\ 0 & 0 & 0 & 0 & 1 & 0 \\ \frac{1}{4} & \frac{1}{4} & 0 & \frac{1}{2} & 0 & 0 \\ 1 & 0 & 0 & 0 & 0 & 0 \\ 0 & \frac{1}{3} & 0 & 0 & 0 & \frac{2}{3} \end{bmatrix}$$

(a) Which states are transient?
(b) Which states are recurrent?
(c) Identify all closed sets of states.
(d) Is this chain ergodic?

4. For each of the following chains, determine whether the

Markov chain is ergodic. Also, for each chain, determine the recurrent, transient, and absorbing states.

$$P_1 = \begin{bmatrix} 0 & .8 & .2 \\ .3 & .7 & 0 \\ .4 & .5 & .1 \end{bmatrix} \quad P_2 = \begin{bmatrix} .2 & .8 & 0 & 0 \\ 0 & 0 & .9 & .1 \\ .4 & .5 & .1 & 0 \\ 0 & 0 & 0 & 1 \end{bmatrix}$$

5. Fifty-four players (including Gabe Kaplan and James Garner) participated in the 1980 World Series of Poker. Each player began with $10,000. Play continued until one player had won everybody else's money. If the World Series of Poker were to be modeled as a Markov chain, how many absorbing states would the chain have?

6. Which of the following chains is ergodic?

$$P_1 = \begin{bmatrix} .4 & 0 & .6 \\ .3 & .3 & .4 \\ 0 & .5 & .5 \end{bmatrix} \quad P_2 = \begin{bmatrix} .7 & 0 & 0 & .3 \\ .2 & .2 & .4 & .2 \\ .6 & .1 & .1 & .2 \\ .2 & 0 & 0 & .8 \end{bmatrix}$$

STEADY-STATE PROBABILITIES
AND MEAN FIRST PASSAGE TIMES

In our discussion of the Cola example (Example 4), we found that after a long time, the probability that a person's next cola purchase would be cola 1 approached .67, and the probability that a person's next cola purchase would be cola 2 approached .33 (see Table 2). These probabilities *did not* depend on whether or not the person was initially a cola 1 or a cola 2 drinker. In this section, we discuss the important concept of steady-state probabilities, which can be used to describe the long-run behavior of a Markov chain.

The following result is vital to an understanding of steady-state probabilities and the long-run behavior of Markov chains.

THEOREM 1   Let P be the transition matrix for an s-state ergodic chain.[†] Then there exists a vector $\pi = [\pi_1 \quad \pi_2 \quad \cdots \quad \pi_s]$ such that

$$\lim_{n \to \infty} P^n = \begin{bmatrix} \pi_1 & \pi_2 & \cdots & \pi_s \\ \pi_1 & \pi_2 & \cdots & \pi_s \\ \vdots & \vdots & & \vdots \\ \pi_1 & \pi_2 & \cdots & \pi_s \end{bmatrix}$$

Recall that the ijth element of P^n is $P_{ij}(n)$. Theorem 1 tells us that for any initial state i,

$$\lim_{n \to \infty} P_{ij}(n) = \pi_j$$

Observe that for large n, P^n approaches a matrix with identical rows. This means that after a long time, the Markov chain settles down, and (independent of the initial state i) there is a probability π_j that we are in state j.

The vector $\pi = [\pi_1 \quad \pi_2 \quad \cdots \quad \pi_s]$ is often called the **steady-state distribution**, or **equilibrium distribution**, for the Markov chain. For a given chain with transition matrix P, how can we find the steady-state probability distribution? From Theorem 1, observe that for large n and all i,

$$P_{ij}(n + 1) \cong P_{ij}(n) \cong \pi_j \tag{6}$$

Since $P_{ij}(n + 1) = (\text{row } i \text{ of } P^n)(\text{column } j \text{ of } P)$, we may write

$$P_{ij}(n + 1) = \sum_{k=1}^{k=s} P_{ik}(n)p_{kj} \tag{7}$$

If n is large, substituting (6) into (7) yields

$$\pi_j = \sum_{k=1}^{k=s} \pi_k p_{kj} \tag{8}$$

In matrix form, (8) may be written as

$$\pi = \pi P \tag{8'}$$

[†]To see why Theorem 1 fails to hold for a nonergodic chain, see Problems 9 and 10 at the end of this section. For a proof of this theorem, see Isaacson and Madsen (1976, Chapter 3).

Unfortunately, the system of equations specified in (8) has an infinite number of solutions, because the rank of the P matrix always turns out to be $\leq s - 1$ (see Chapter 2, Review Problem 21). To obtain unique values of the steady-state probabilities, note that for any n and any i

$$P_{i1}(n) + P_{i2}(n) + \cdots + P_{is}(n) = 1 \tag{9}$$

Letting n approach infinity in (9), we obtain

$$\pi_1 + \pi_2 + \cdots + \pi_s = 1 \tag{10}$$

Thus, after replacing any of the equations in (8) by (10), we may use (8) to solve for the steady-state probabilities.

To illustrate how to find the steady-state probabilities, we find the steady-state probabilities for Example 4, the Cola example. Recall that the transition matrix for Example 4 was

$$P = \begin{bmatrix} .90 & .10 \\ .20 & .80 \end{bmatrix}$$

Then (8) or (8′) yields

$$[\pi_1 \quad \pi_2] = [\pi_1 \quad \pi_2] \begin{bmatrix} .90 & .10 \\ .20 & .80 \end{bmatrix}$$

$$\pi_1 = .90\pi_1 + .20\pi_2$$
$$\pi_2 = .10\pi_1 + .80\pi_2$$

Replacing the second equation by the condition $\pi_1 + \pi_2 = 1$, we obtain the system

$$\pi_1 = .90\pi_1 + .20\pi_2$$
$$1 = \pi_1 + \pi_2$$

Solving for π_1 and π_2 we obtain $\pi_1 = \frac{2}{3}$ and $\pi_2 = \frac{1}{3}$. Hence, after a long time, there is a $\frac{2}{3}$ probability that a given person will purchase cola 1 and a $\frac{1}{3}$ probability that a given person will purchase cola 2.

TRANSIENT ANALYSIS

A glance at Table 2 shows that for Example 4, the steady state is reached (to two decimal places) after only ten transitions. No general rule can be given about how quickly a Markov chain reaches the steady state, but if P contains very few entries that are near 0 or near 1, the steady state is usually reached very quickly. The behavior of a Markov chain before the steady state is reached is often called **transient** (or short-run) **behavior**. To study the transient behavior of a Markov chain, one simply uses the formulas for $P_{ij}(n)$ given in Eqs. (4) and (5). It's nice to know, however, that for large n, the steady-state probabilities accurately describe the probability of being in any state.

INTUITIVE INTERPRETATION OF
STEADY-STATE PROBABILITIES

An intuitive interpretation can be given to the steady-state probability equations (8). By subtracting $\pi_j p_{jj}$ from both sides of (8), we obtain

$$\pi_j(1 - p_{jj}) = \sum_{k \neq j} \pi_k p_{kj} \tag{11}$$

Eq. (11) states that in the steady state,

> Probability that a particular transition leaves state j
> $=$ probability that a particular transition enters state j (12)

Recall that in the steady state, the probability that the system is in state j is π_j. From this observation, it follows that

> Probability that a particular transition leaves state j
> $=$ (probability that current period begins in j)
> $\times$ (probability that current transition leaves j)
> $= \pi_j(1 - p_{jj})$

and

> Probability that a particular transition enters state j
> $= \sum_k$ (probability that current period begins in $k \neq j$)
> $\times$ (probability that current transition enters j)
> $= \sum_{k \neq j} \pi_k p_{kj}$

Eq. (11) is reasonable; if (11) were violated for any state, then for some state j, the right-hand side of (11) would exceed the left-hand side of (11). This would result in probability "piling up" at state j, and a steady-state distribution would not exist. Eq. (11) may be viewed as saying that in the steady state, the "flow" of probability into each state must equal the flow of probability out of each state. This explains why steady-state probabilities are often called equilibrium probabilities.

USE OF STEADY-STATE PROBABILITIES IN DECISION MAKING

E X A M P L E 5   In Example 4, suppose that each customer makes one purchase of cola during any week (52 weeks = 1 year). Suppose there are 100 million cola customers. One selling unit of cola costs the company $1 to produce and is sold for $2. For $500 million per year, an advertising firm guarantees to decrease from 10% to 5% the fraction of cola 1 customers who switch to cola 2 after a purchase. Should the company that makes cola 1 hire the advertising firm?

Solution   At present, a fraction $\pi_1 = \frac{2}{3}$ of all purchases are cola 1 purchases. Each purchase of cola 1 earns the company a $1 profit. Since there are a total of 52(100,000,000), or 5.2 billion, cola purchases each year, the cola 1 company's current annual profit is

$$\tfrac{2}{3}(5,200,000,000) = \$3,466,666,667$$

The advertising firm is offering to change the P matrix to

$$P_1 = \begin{bmatrix} .95 & .05 \\ .20 & .80 \end{bmatrix}$$

For P_1, the steady-state equations become

$$\pi_1 = .95\pi_1 + .20\pi_2$$
$$\pi_2 = .05\pi_1 + .80\pi_2$$

Replacing the second equation by $\pi_1 + \pi_2 = 1$ and solving, we obtain $\pi_1 = .8$ and $\pi_2 = .2$. Now the cola 1 company's annual profit will be

$$(.80)(5,200,000,000) - 500,000,000 = \$3,660,000,000$$

Hence, the cola 1 company should hire the ad agency.

◆

EXAMPLE 6

With the assumption that each Monopoly player who goes to Jail stays until he or she rolls doubles or has spent three turns in Jail, the steady-state probability of a player landing on any Monopoly square has been determined by Ash and Bishop (1972) (see Table 3).[†] These steady-state probabilities can be used to measure the cost-effectiveness of various monopolies. For example, it costs $1500 to build hotels on the Orange monopoly. Each time a player lands on a Tennessee Ave. or a St. James Place hotel, the owner of the monopoly receives $950, and each time a player lands on a New York Ave. hotel, the owner receives $1000. From Table 3, we can compute the expected rent per dice roll earned by the Orange monopoly:

$$950(.0335) + 950(.0318) + 1000(.0334) = \$95.44$$

Thus, per dollar invested, the Orange monopoly yields $\frac{95.44}{1500} = \$0.064$ per dice roll.

Now let's consider the Green monopoly. To put hotels on the Green monopoly costs $3000. If a player lands on a North Carolina Ave. or a Pacific Ave. hotel, the owner receives $1275. If a player lands on a Pennsylvania Ave. hotel, the owner receives $1400. From Table 3, the average revenue per dice roll earned from hotels on the Green monopoly is

$$1275(.0294) + 1275(.0300) + 1400(.0279) = \$114.80$$

Thus, per dollar invested, the Green monopoly yields only $\frac{114.80}{3000} = \$0.038$ per dice roll.

This analysis shows that the Orange monopoly is superior to the Green monopoly. By the way, why does the Orange get landed on so often?

◆

MEAN FIRST PASSAGE TIMES

For an ergodic chain, let m_{ij} = expected number of transitions before we first reach state j, given that we are currently in state i. m_{ij} is called the **mean first passage time** from state i to state j. In Example 4, m_{12} would be the expected number of bottles of cola purchased by a person who just bought cola 1 before first buying a bottle of cola 2. Assume that we are currently in state i. Then with probability p_{ij}, it will take one transition to go from state i to state j. For $k \neq j$, we next go with probability p_{ik} to state

---

[†]This example is based on Ash and Bishop (1972).

Table 3
Steady-State
Probabilities for
Monopoly (reprinted
by permission from
R. Ash and R.
Bishop, "Monopoly
as a Markov
Process,"
*Mathematics
Magazine*
45(1972):26–29;
copyright 1972
Mathematical
Association of
America)

n POSITION	STEADY-STATE PROBABILITY
0 Go	.0346
1 Mediterranean Ave.	.0237
2 Community Chest 1	.0218
3 Baltic Ave.	.0241
4 Income tax	.0261
5 Reading RR	.0332
6 Oriental Ave.	.0253
7 Chance 1	.0096
8 Vermont Ave.	.0258
9 Connecticut Ave.	.0237
10 Visiting jail	.0254
11 St. Charles Place	.0304
12 Electric Co.	.0311
13 State Ave.	.0258
14 Virginia Ave.	.0288
15 Pennsylvania RR	.0313
16 St. James Place	.0318
17 Community Chest 2	.0272
18 Tennessee Ave.	.0335
19 New York Ave.	.0334
20 Free parking	.0336
21 Kentucky Ave.	.0310
22 Chance 2	.0125
23 Indiana Ave.	.0305
24 Illinois Ave.	.0355
25 B and O RR	.0344
26 Atlantic Ave.	.0301
27 Ventnor Ave.	.0299
28 Water works	.0315
29 Marvin Gardens	.0289
30 Jail	.1123
31 Pacific Ave.	.0300
32 North Carolina Ave.	.0294
33 Community Chest 3	.0263
34 Pennsylvania Ave.	.0279
35 Short Line RR	.0272
36 Chance 3	.0096
37 Park Place	.0245
38 Luxury tax	.0245
39 Boardwalk	.0295

k. In this case, it will take an average of $1 + m_{kj}$ transitions to go from i to j. This reasoning implies that

$$m_{ij} = p_{ij}(1) + \sum_{k \neq j} p_{ik}(1 + m_{kj})$$

Since

$$p_{ij} + \sum_{k \neq j} p_{ik} = 1$$

we may rewrite the last equation as

$$m_{ij} = 1 + \sum_{k \neq j} p_{ik} m_{kj} \tag{13}$$

By solving the linear equations given in (13), we may find all the mean first passage times. It can be shown that

$$m_{ii} = \frac{1}{\pi_i}$$

This can simplify the use of (13).

To illustrate the use of (13), let's solve for the mean first passage times in Example 4. Recall that $\pi_1 = \frac{2}{3}$ and $\pi_2 = \frac{1}{3}$. Then

$$m_{11} = \frac{1}{\frac{2}{3}} = 1.5 \quad \text{and} \quad m_{22} = \frac{1}{\frac{1}{3}} = 3$$

Now (13) yields the following two equations:

$$m_{12} = 1 + p_{11}m_{12} = 1 + 0.9m_{12}, \qquad m_{21} = 1 + p_{22}m_{21} = 1 + 0.8m_{21}$$

Solving these two equations, we find that $m_{12} = 10$ and $m_{21} = 5$. This means, for example, that a person who last drank cola 1 will drink an average of ten bottles of soda before switching to cola 2.

◆ PROBLEMS

GROUP A

1. Find the steady-state probabilities for Problem 1 of Section 19.3.

2. For the gambler's ruin problem (Example 1), why is it unreasonable to talk about steady-state probabilities?

3. For each of the following Markov chains, determine the long-run fraction of the time that each state will be occupied.

(a) $\begin{bmatrix} \frac{2}{3} & \frac{1}{3} \\ \frac{1}{2} & \frac{1}{2} \end{bmatrix}$ **(b)** $\begin{bmatrix} .8 & .2 & 0 \\ 0 & .2 & .8 \\ .8 & .2 & 0 \end{bmatrix}$

(c) Find all mean first passage times for part (b).

4. At the beginning of each year, my car is in good, fair, or broken-down condition. A good car will be good at the beginning of next year with probability .85; fair with probability .10; and broken-down with probability .05. A fair car will be a fair car at the beginning of the next year with probability .70 and broken-down with probability .30. It costs $6000 to purchase a good car; a fair car can be traded in for $2000; and a broken-down car has no trade-in value and must immediately be replaced by a good car.

It costs $1000 per year to operate a good car and $1500 to operate a fair car. Should I replace my car as soon as it becomes a fair car, or should I drive my car until it breaks down? Assume that the cost of operating a car during a year depends on the type of car on hand at the beginning of the year (after a new car, if any, arrives).

5. A square matrix is said to be doubly stochastic if its entries are all nonnegative and the entries in each row and each column sum to 1. For any ergodic, doubly stochastic matrix, show that all states have the same steady-state probability.

6. This problem will show why steady-state probabilities are sometimes referred to as stationary probabilities. Let $\pi_1, \pi_2, \ldots, \pi_s$ be the steady-state probabilities for an ergodic chain with transition matrix P. Also suppose that with probability π_i, the Markov chain begins in state i.

(a) What is the probability that after one transition, the system will be in state i? (*Hint*: Use Eq. (8).)

(b) For any value of n ($n = 1, 2, \ldots$), what is the probability that a Markov chain will be in state i after n transitions?

(c) Why are steady-state probabilities sometimes called stationary probabilities?

7. Consider two stocks. Stock 1 always sells for $10 or $20. If stock 1 is selling for $10 today, there is a .80 chance that stock 1 will sell for $10 tomorrow. If stock 1 is selling for $20 today, there is a .90 chance that stock 1 will sell for $20 tomorrow. Stock 2 always sells for $10 or $25. If stock 2 sells today for $10, there is a .90 chance that it will sell tomorrow for $10. If stock 2 sells today for $25, there is a .85 chance that it will sell tomorrow for $25. On the average, which stock will sell for a higher price? Find and interpret all mean first passage times.

GROUP B

8. Payoff Insurance Company charges a customer according to his or her accident history. A customer who has had no accident during the last two years is charged a $100 annual premium. Any customer who has had an accident during each of the last two years is charged a $400 annual premium. A customer who has had an accident during only one of the last two years is charged an annual premium of $300. A customer who has had an accident during the last year has a 10% chance of having an accident during the current year. If a customer has not had an accident during the last year, there is only a 3% chance that he or she will have an accident during the current year. During a given year, what is the average premium paid by a Payoff customer? (*Hint*: In case of difficulty, try a four-state Markov chain.)

9. Consider the following nonergodic chain:

$$P = \begin{bmatrix} \frac{1}{2} & \frac{1}{2} & 0 & 0 \\ \frac{1}{2} & \frac{1}{2} & 0 & 0 \\ 0 & 0 & \frac{1}{3} & \frac{2}{3} \\ 0 & 0 & \frac{2}{3} & \frac{1}{3} \end{bmatrix}$$

(a) Why is this chain nonergodic?
(b) Explain why Theorem 1 fails for this chain. *Hint*: Find out if the following equation is true:

$$\lim_{n \to \infty} P_{12}(n) = \lim_{n \to \infty} P_{32}(n)$$

(c) Despite the fact that Theorem 1 fails, determine

$$\lim_{n \to \infty} P_{13}(n), \qquad \lim_{n \to \infty} P_{21}(n),$$

$$\lim_{n \to \infty} P_{43}(n), \qquad \lim_{n \to \infty} P_{41}(n)$$

10. Consider the following nonergodic chain:

$$P = \begin{bmatrix} 0 & 1 & 0 \\ 0 & 0 & 1 \\ 1 & 0 & 0 \end{bmatrix}$$

(a) Why is this chain nonergodic?
(b) Explain why Theorem 1 fails for this chain. (*Hint*: Show that $\lim_{n \to \infty} P_{11}(n)$ does not exist by listing the pattern that $P_{11}(n)$ follows as n increases.)

19-6   ABSORBING CHAINS

Many interesting applications of Markov chains involve chains in which some of the states are absorbing and the rest of the states are transient states. Such a chain is called an **absorbing chain**. Consider an absorbing Markov chain: If we begin in a transient state, then eventually we are sure to leave the transient state and end up in one of the absorbing states. To see why we are interested in absorbing chains, we consider the following two absorbing chains.

E X A M P L E **Accounts Receivable**   The accounts receivable situation of a firm is often modeled as an
7   absorbing Markov chain.[†] Suppose a firm assumes that an account is uncollectable if the account is more than three months overdue. Then at the beginning of each month, each account may be classified into one of the following states:

[†]This example is based on Cyert, Davidson, and Thompson (1963).

State 1 New account.

State 2 Payment on account is one month overdue.

State 3 Payment on account is two months overdue.

State 4 Payment on account is three months overdue.

State 5 Account has been paid.

State 6 Account is written off as bad debt.

Suppose that past data indicate that the following Markov chain describes how the status of an account changes from one month to the next month:

	New	1 month	2 months	3 months	Paid	Bad debt
New	0	.6	0	0	.4	0
1 month	0	0	.5	0	.5	0
2 months	0	0	0	.4	.6	0
3 months	0	0	0	0	.7	.3
Paid	0	0	0	0	1	0
Bad debt	0	0	0	0	0	1

For example, if an account is two months overdue at the beginning of a month, there is a 40% chance that at the beginning of next month, the account will not be paid up (and therefore be three months overdue) and a 60% chance that the account will be paid up. To simplify our example, we assume that after three months, a debt is either collected or written off as a bad debt.

Once a debt is paid up or written off as a bad debt, the account is closed, and no further transitions occur. Hence, Paid and Bad Debt are absorbing states. Since every account will eventually be paid up or written off as a bad debt, New, 1 Month, 2 Months, and 3 Months are transient states. For example, a two-month overdue account can follow the path 2 Months—Collected, but there is no return path from Collected to 2 Months.

A typical new account will be absorbed as either a collected debt or a bad debt. A question of major interest is: What is the probability that a new account will eventually be collected? The answer is worked out later in this section.

E X A M P L E
8

Work Force Planning The law firm of Mason and Burger employs three types of lawyers: junior lawyers, senior lawyers, and partners. During a given year, there is a .15 probability that a junior lawyer will be promoted and become a senior lawyer and a .05 probability that he or she will leave the firm. Also, there is a .20 probability that a senior lawyer will be promoted to partner and a .10 probability that he or she will leave the firm. There is also a .05 probability that a partner will leave the firm. The firm never demotes a lawyer.

There are many interesting questions the law firm might want to answer. For example, what is the probability that a newly hired junior lawyer will leave the firm before becoming a partner? On the average, how long does a newly hired junior lawyer stay with the firm? The answers are worked out later in this section.   ◆

We model the career path of a lawyer through Mason and Burger as an absorbing Markov chain with the following transition probability matrix:

	Junior	Senior	Partner	Leave as NP	Leave as P
Junior	.80	.15	0	.05	0
Senior	0	.70	.20	.10	0
Partner	0	0	.95	0	.05
Leave as nonpartner	0	0	0	1	0
Leave as partner	0	0	0	0	1

The last two states are absorbing states, and all other states are transient. For example, Senior is a transient state, because there is a path from Senior to Leave as Nonpartner, but there is no path returning from Leave as Nonpartner to Senior (we assume that once a lawyer leaves the firm, he or she never returns).

For any absorbing chain, one might want to know: (1) If the chain begins in a given transient state, and before we reach an absorbing state, what is the expected number of times that each state will be entered? How many periods do we expect to spend in a given transient state before absorption takes place? (2) If a chain begins in a given transient state, what is the probability that we end up in each absorbing state?

To answer these questions, we need to write the transition matrix with the states listed in the following order: transient states first, then absorbing states. For the sake of definiteness, let's assume that there are $s - m$ transient states $(t_1, t_2, \ldots, t_{s-m})$ and m absorbing states $(a_1, a_2, \ldots, a_m)$. Then the transition matrix for the absorbing chain may be written as follows:

$$
P = \begin{array}{c} \\ s - m \text{ rows} \\ \\ m \text{ rows} \end{array}
\begin{array}{cc} s - m & m \\ \text{columns} & \text{columns} \end{array}
\left[\begin{array}{c|c} Q & R \\ \hline 0 & I \end{array} \right]
$$

In this format, the rows and columns of P correspond (in order) to the states t_1, $t_2, \ldots, t_{s-m}, a_1, a_2, \ldots, a_m$. Here, I is an $m \times m$ identity matrix reflecting the fact that we can never leave an absorbing state; Q is an $(s - m) \times (s - m)$ matrix that represents transitions between transient states; R is an $(s - m) \times m$ matrix representing transitions from transient states to absorbing states; 0 is an $m \times (s - m)$ matrix consisting entirely of zeros. This reflects the fact that it is impossible to go from an absorbing state to a transient state.

Applying this notation to Example 7, we let

$$t_1 = \text{New}$$
$$t_2 = 1 \text{ Month}$$
$$t_3 = 2 \text{ Months}$$
$$t_4 = 3 \text{ Months}$$
$$a_1 = \text{Paid}$$
$$a_2 = \text{Bad Debt}$$

Then for Example 7, the transition probability matrix may be written as

	New	1 month	2 months	3 months	Paid	Bad debt
New	0	.6	0	0	.4	0
1 month	0	0	.5	0	.5	0
2 months	0	0	0	.4	.6	0
3 months	0	0	0	0	.7	.3
Paid	0	0	0	0	1	0
Bad debt	0	0	0	0	0	1

Then $s = 6$, $m = 2$, and

$$Q = \begin{bmatrix} 0 & .6 & 0 & 0 \\ 0 & 0 & .5 & 0 \\ 0 & 0 & 0 & .4 \\ 0 & 0 & 0 & 0 \end{bmatrix}_{4 \times 4} \qquad R = \begin{bmatrix} .4 & 0 \\ .5 & 0 \\ .6 & 0 \\ .7 & .3 \end{bmatrix}_{4 \times 2}$$

For Example 8, we let

$$t_1 = \text{Junior}$$
$$t_2 = \text{Senior}$$
$$t_3 = \text{Partner}$$
$$a_1 = \text{Leave as nonpartner}$$
$$a_2 = \text{Leave as partner}$$

and we may write the transition probability matrix as

	Junior	Senior	Partner	Leave as NP	Leave as P
Junior	.80	.15	0	.05	0
Senior	0	.70	.20	.10	0
Partner	0	0	.95	0	.05
Leave as nonpartner	0	0	0	1	0
Leave as partner	0	0	0	0	1

Then $s = 5$, $m = 2$, and

$$Q = \begin{bmatrix} .80 & .15 & 0 \\ 0 & .70 & .20 \\ 0 & 0 & .95 \end{bmatrix}_{3 \times 3} \qquad R = \begin{bmatrix} .05 & 0 \\ .10 & 0 \\ 0 & .05 \end{bmatrix}_{3 \times 2}$$

We can now find out some facts about absorbing chains (see Kemeny and Snell (1960): (1) If the chain begins in a given transient state, and before we reach an absorbing state, what is the expected number of times that each state will be entered? How many periods do we expect to spend in a given transient state before absorption takes place? *Answer*: If we are at present in transient state t_i, the expected number of periods that will be spent in transient state t_j before absorption is the ijth element of the matrix $(I - Q)^{-1}$. (See Problem 8 at the end of this section for a proof.) (2) If a chain begins in a given transient state, what is the probability that we end up in each absorbing state? *Answer*: If we are at present in transient state t_i, the probability that we will eventually be absorbed in absorbing state a_j is the ijth element of the matrix $(I - Q)^{-1}R$. (See Problem 9 at the end of this section for a proof.)

The matrix $(I - Q)^{-1}$ is often referred to as the **Markov chain's fundamental matrix**. The reader interested in further study of absorbing chains is referred to Kemeny and Snell (1960).

E X A M P L E 7

Accounts Receivable (Continued)

1. What is the probability that a new account will eventually be collected?

2. What is the probability that a one-month overdue account will eventually become a bad debt?

3. If the firm's sales average $100,000 per month, how much money per year will go uncollected?

Solution

From our previous discussion, recall that

$$Q = \begin{bmatrix} 0 & .6 & 0 & 0 \\ 0 & 0 & .5 & 0 \\ 0 & 0 & 0 & .4 \\ 0 & 0 & 0 & 0 \end{bmatrix} \qquad R = \begin{bmatrix} .4 & 0 \\ .5 & 0 \\ .6 & 0 \\ .7 & .3 \end{bmatrix}$$

Then

$$I - Q = \begin{bmatrix} 1 & -.6 & 0 & 0 \\ 0 & 1 & -.5 & 0 \\ 0 & 0 & 1 & -.4 \\ 0 & 0 & 0 & 1 \end{bmatrix}$$

By using the Gauss-Jordan method of Chapter 2, we find that

$$(I - Q)^{-1} = \begin{array}{c} \\ t_1 \\ t_2 \\ t_3 \\ t_4 \end{array} \begin{array}{cccc} t_1 & t_2 & t_3 & t_4 \\ \left[\begin{array}{cccc} 1 & .60 & .30 & .12 \\ 0 & 1 & .50 & .20 \\ 0 & 0 & 1 & .40 \\ 0 & 0 & 0 & 1 \end{array}\right] \end{array}$$

To answer questions 1–3, we need to compute

$$(I - Q)^{-1}R = \begin{array}{c} \\ t_1 \\ t_2 \\ t_3 \\ t_4 \end{array} \begin{array}{cc} a_1 & a_2 \\ \left[\begin{array}{cc} .964 & .036 \\ .940 & .060 \\ .880 & .120 \\ .700 & .300 \end{array}\right] \end{array}$$

Then

1. t_1 = New, a_1 = Paid. Thus, the probability that a new account is eventually collected is element 11 of $(I - Q)^{-1}R$ = .964.

2. t_2 = 1 Month, a_2 = Bad Debt. Thus, the probability that a one-month overdue account turns into a bad debt is element 22 of $(I - Q)^{-1}R$ = .06.

3. From answer 1, only 3.6% of all debts are uncollected. Since yearly accounts payable are $1,200,000, on the average, $(.036)(1,200,000)$ = $43,200 per year will be uncollected.

◆

E X A M P L E 8

Work Force Planning (Continued)

1. What is the average length of time that a newly hired junior lawyer spends working for the firm?

2. What is the probability that a junior lawyer makes it to partner?

3. What is the average length of time that a partner spends with the firm (as a partner)?

Solution

Recall that for Example 8,

$$Q = \begin{bmatrix} .80 & .15 & 0 \\ 0 & .70 & .20 \\ 0 & 0 & .95 \end{bmatrix} \qquad R = \begin{bmatrix} .05 & 0 \\ .10 & 0 \\ 0 & .05 \end{bmatrix}$$

Then

$$I - Q = \begin{bmatrix} .20 & -.15 & 0 \\ 0 & .30 & -.20 \\ 0 & 0 & .05 \end{bmatrix}$$

By using the Gauss-Jordan method of Chapter 2, we find that

$$(I - Q)^{-1} = \begin{array}{c} \\ t_1 \\ t_2 \\ t_3 \end{array} \begin{array}{ccc} t_1 & t_2 & t_3 \\ \begin{bmatrix} 5 & 2.5 & 10 \\ 0 & \frac{10}{3} & \frac{40}{3} \\ 0 & 0 & 20 \end{bmatrix} \end{array}$$

Then

$$(I - Q)^{-1}R = \begin{array}{c} \\ t_1 \\ t_2 \\ t_3 \end{array} \begin{array}{cc} a_1 & a_2 \\ \begin{bmatrix} .50 & .50 \\ \frac{1}{3} & \frac{2}{3} \\ 0 & 1 \end{bmatrix} \end{array}$$

Then

1. Expected time junior lawyer stays with firm = (expected time junior lawyer stays with firm as junior) + (expected time junior lawyer stays with firm as senior) + (expected time junior lawyer stays with firm as partner). Now

$$\text{Expected time as junior} = (I - Q)_{11}^{-1} = 5$$
$$\text{Expected time as senior} = (I - Q)_{12}^{-1} = 2.5$$
$$\text{Expected time as partner} = (I - Q)_{13}^{-1} = 10$$

Hence, the total expected time that a junior lawyer spends with the firm is $5 + 2.5 + 10 = 17.5$ years.

2. The probability that a new junior lawyer makes it to partner is just the probability that he or she leaves the firm as a partner. Since $t_1 =$ Junior Lawyer and $a_2 =$ Leave as Partner, the answer is element 12 of $(I - Q)^{-1}R = .50$.

3. Since $t_3 =$ Partner, we seek the expected number of years that are spent in t_3, given that we begin in t_3. This is just element 33 of $(I - Q)^{-1} = 20$ years. This is reasonable, because during each year, there is 1 chance in 20 that a partner will leave the firm, so it should take an average of 20 years before a partner leaves the firm.

◆

◆ PROBLEMS

GROUP A

1.[†] The State College admissions office has modeled the path of a student through State College as a Markov chain:

	F.	So.	J.	Sen.	Q.	G.
Freshman	.10	.80	0	0	.10	0
Sophomore	0	.10	.85	0	.05	0
Junior	0	0	.15	.80	.05	0
Senior	0	0	0	.10	.05	.85
Quits	0	0	0	0	1	0
Graduates	0	0	0	0	0	1

[†]Based on Bessent and Bessent (1980).

Each student's state is observed at the beginning of each fall semester. For example, if a student is a junior at the beginning of the current fall semester, there is an 80% chance that he will be a senior at the beginning of the next fall semester, a 15% chance that he will still be a junior, and a 5% chance that he will have quit. (We assume that once a student quits, he never re-enrolls.)
(a) If a student enters State College as a freshman, how many years can he expect to spend as a student at State?
(b) What is the probability that a freshman graduates?

2.[‡] The *Herald Tribble* has obtained the following information about its subscribers: During the first year as

[‡]Based on Deming and Glasser (1968).

subscribers, 20% of all subscribers cancel their subscriptions. Of those subscribers who have subscribed for one year, 10% cancel during the second year. Of those who have been subscribing for more than two years, 4% will cancel during any given year. On the average, how long does a subscriber subscribe to the *Herald Tribble*?

3. A forest consists of two types of trees: those that are 0–5 ft tall and those that are taller than 5 ft. Each year, 40% of all 0–5-ft tall trees die, 10% are sold for $20 each, 30% stay between 0 and 5 ft, and 20% grow to be more than 5 ft tall. Each year, 50% of all trees taller than 5 ft are sold for $50, 20% are sold for $30, and 30% remain in the forest.

(a) What is the probability that a 0–5 ft-tall tree will die before being sold?

(b) If a tree (less than 5 ft tall) is planted, what is the expected revenue earned from that tree?

4.[†] Absorbing Markov chains are used in marketing to model the probability that a customer who is contacted by telephone will eventually buy a product. Consider a prospective customer who has never been called about purchasing a product. After one call, there is a 60% chance that the customer will express a low degree of interest in the product, a 30% chance the customer will express a high degree of interest in the product, and a 10% chance the customer will be deleted from the company's list of prospective customers. Consider a customer who currently expresses a low degree of interest in the product. After another call, there is a 30% chance that the customer will purchase the product, a 20% chance the person will be deleted from the list, a 30% chance that the customer will still possess a low degree of interest, and a 20% chance that the customer will express a high degree of interest. Consider a customer who currently expresses a high degree of interest in the product. After another call, there is a 50% chance that the customer will have purchased the product, a 40% chance that the customer will still have a high degree of interest, and a 10% chance that the customer will have a low degree of interest.

(a) What is the probability that a new prospective customer will eventually purchase the product?

(b) What is the probability that a low-interest prospective customer will ever be deleted from the list?

(c) On the average, how many times will a new prospective customer be called before either purchasing the product or being deleted from the list?

GROUP B

5. In the gambler's ruin problem (Example 1), assume $p = .60$.

[†]Based on Thompson and McNeal (1967).

(a) What is the probability that I reach $4?
(b) What is the probability that I am wiped out?
(c) What is the expected duration of the game?

6.[‡] In caring for elderly patients at a mental hospital, a major goal of the hospital is successful placement of the patients in boarding homes or nursing homes. The movement of patients between the hospital, outside homes, and the absorbing state (death) may be described by the following Markov chain (the unit of time is one month):

	Hospital	Homes	Death
Hospital	.991	.003	.006
Homes	.025	.969	.006
Death	0	0	1

Each month that a patient spends in the hospital costs the state $655, and each month that a patient spends in a home costs the state $226. To improve the success rate of the placement of patients in homes, the state has recently begun a "geriatric resocialization program" (GRP) to prepare the patients for functioning in the homes. Some patients are placed in the GRP and then released to homes. These patients presumably are less likely to fail to adjust in the homes. Other patients continue to go directly from hospital to homes without taking part in the GRP. The state pays $680 for each month that a patient spends in the GRP. The movement of the patients through various states is governed by the following Markov chain:

	GRP	Hos.	Homes (GRP)	Homes (Direct)	Dead
GRP	.854	.028	.112	0	.006
Hospital	.013	.978	0	.003	.006
Homes (GRP)	.025	0	.969	0	.006
Homes (Direct)	0	.025	0	.969	.006
Dead	0	0	0	0	1

(a) Does the GRP save the state money?
(b) Under the old system and under the GRP, compute the expected number of months that a patient spends in the hospital.

7. Freezco, Inc., sells refrigerators. The company has issued a warranty on all refrigerators that requires free replacement of any refrigerator that fails before it is three years old. We are given the following information: (1) 3% of all new refrigerators fail during their first year of operation; (2) 5% of all one-year-old refrigerators fail

[‡]Based on Meredith (1973).

during their second year of operation; and (3) 7% of all two-year old refrigerators fail during their third year of operation. A replacement refrigerator is not covered by the warranty.

(a) Use Markov chain theory to predict the fraction of all refrigerators that Freezco will have to replace.

(b) Suppose that it costs Freezco $500 to replace a refrigerator and that Freezco sells 10,000 refrigerators per year. If the company reduced the warranty period to two years, how much money in replacement costs would be saved?

8. For a Q matrix representing the transitions between transient states in an absorbing Markov chain, it can be shown that

$$(I - Q)^{-1} = I + Q + Q^2 + \cdots + Q^n + \cdots$$

(a) Explain why this expression for $(I - Q)^{-1}$ is plausible.

(b) Define m_{ij} = expected number of periods spent in transient state t_j before absorption, given that we begin in state t_i. (Assume that the initial period is spent in state t_i.) Explain why m_{ij} = (probability that we are in state t_j initially) + (probability that we are in state t_j after first transition) + (probability that we are in state t_j after second transition) + $\cdots$ + (probability that we are in state t_j after nth transition) + $\cdots$.

(c) Explain why the probability that we are in state t_j initially = ijth entry of the $(s - m) \times (s - m)$ identity matrix. Explain why the probability that we are in state t_j after nth transition = ijth entry of Q^n.

(d) Now explain why m_{ij} = ijth entry of $(I - Q)^{-1}$.

9. Define

b_{ij} = probability of ending up in absorbing state a_j given that we begin in transient state t_i

r_{ij} = ijth entry of R

q_{ik} = ikth entry of Q

$B = (s - m) \times m$ matrix whose ijth entry is b_{ij}

Suppose we begin in state t_i. On our first transition, three types of events may happen:

Event 1 We go to absorbing state a_j (with probability r_{ij}).

Event 2 We go to absorbing state other than a_j (with probability $\Sigma_{k \neq j} r_{ik}$).

Event 3 We go to transient state t_k (with probability q_{ik}).

(a) Explain why

$$b_{ij} = r_{ij} + \sum_{k=1}^{k=s-m} q_{ik} b_{kj}$$

(b) Now show that b_{ij} = ijth entry of $(R + QB)$ and that $B = R + QB$.

(c) Show that $B = (I - Q)^{-1} R$ and that b_{ij} = ijth entry of $B = (I - Q)^{-1} R$.

GROUP C

10. General Motors has three auto divisions (division 1, division 2, and division 3). It also has an accounting division and a management consulting division. The question is: What fraction of the cost of the accounting and management consulting divisions should be allocated to each auto division? We assume that the entire cost of the accounting and management consulting departments must be allocated to the three auto divisions. During a given year, the work of the accounting division and management consulting division is allocated as shown in Table 4.

For example, accounting spends 10% of its time on problems generated by the accounting department, 20% of its time on work generated by division 3, etc. Each year, it costs $63 million to run the accounting department and $210 million to run the management consulting department. What fraction of these costs should be allocated to each auto division? Think of $1 in costs incurred in accounting work. There is a .20 chance that this dollar in costs should be allocated to each auto division, a .30 chance the cost should be allocated to consulting, and a .10 chance the dollar should be allocated to accounting. If the dollar is allocated to an auto division, we know which division should be charged for that dollar. If the dollar is charged to consulting (for example), we repeat the process until the dollar is eventually charged to an auto division. Use knowledge of absorbing chains to figure out how to allocate the costs of running the accounting and management consulting departments among the three auto divisions.

Table 4

	ACCOUNTING	MANAGEMENT CONSULTING	DIVISION 1	DIVISION 2	DIVISION 3
Accounting	10%	30%	20%	20%	20%
Management	30%	20%	30%	0%	20%

19-7   WORK FORCE PLANNING MODELS*

Many organizations, like the Mason and Burger law firm of Example 8, employ several categories of workers. For long-term planning purposes, it is often useful to be able to predict the number of employees of each type who will (if present trends continue) be available in the steady state. Such predictions can be made via an analysis similar to the one in Section 19.5 of steady-state probabilities for Markov chains.

More formally, consider an organization whose members are classified at any point in time into one of s groups (labelled $1, 2, \ldots, s$). During every time period, a fraction p_{ij} of those who begin a time period in group i begin the next time period in group j. Also, during every time period, a fraction $p_{i,s+1}$ of all group i members leave the organization. Let P be the s $\times$ $(s + 1)$ matrix whose ijth entry is p_{ij}. At the beginning of each time period, the organization hires H_i group i members. Let $N_i(t)$ be the number of group i members at the beginning of period t. A question of natural interest is whether or not $N_i(t)$ approaches a limit as t grows large (call the limit, if it exists, N_i). If each $N_i(t)$ does approach a limit, we call $\mathbf{N} = (N_1, N_2, \ldots, N_s)$ the **steady-state census** of the organization.

If a steady-state census exists, we can find it by solving a system of s equations that is derived as follows: Simply note that for a steady-state census to exist, it must be true that in the steady state, for $i = 1, 2, \ldots, s$,

$$\text{Number of people entering group } i \text{ during each period}$$
$$= \text{number of people leaving group } i \text{ during each period} \tag{14}$$

After all, if (14) did not hold for all groups, then the number of people in at least one group would pile up as time progressed. We note that

$$\text{Number of people entering state } i \text{ during each period} = H_i + \sum_{k \neq i} N_k p_{ki}$$

$$\text{Number of people leaving state } i \text{ during each period} = N_i \sum_{k \neq i} p_{ik}$$

Then the equation used to compute the steady-state census is

$$H_i + \sum_{k \neq i} N_k p_{ki} = N_i \sum_{k \neq i} p_{ik} \quad (i = 1, 2, \ldots, s) \tag{14'}$$

Given the values of the p_{ij}'s and the H_i's (14') can be used to solve for the steady-state census. Conversely, given the p_{ij}'s and a desired steady-state census, (14') can be used to determine a hiring policy (specified by values of $H_1, H_2, \ldots, H_s$) that attains the desired steady-state census. Some steady-state censuses may be impossible to maintain unless some of the H_i's are negative (corresponding to firing employees).

The following two examples illustrate the use of the steady-state census equation.

E X A M P L E   Suppose that each American can be classified into one of three groups: children, working
9   adults, or retired people. During a one-year period, 0.959 of all children remain children, 0.04 of all children become working adults, and 0.001 of all children die. During any given year, 0.96 of all working adults remain working adults, 0.03 of all working adults

*This section covers topics that may be omitted with no loss of continuity.

retire, and 0.01 of all working adults die. Also, 0.95 of all retired people remain retired, and 0.05 of all retired people die. One thousand children are born each year.

1. Determine the steady-state census.

2. Each retired person receives a pension of $5000 per year. The pension fund is funded by payments from working adults. How much money must each working adult contribute annually to the pension fund?

Solution

1. Let

$$\text{Group 1} = \text{children}$$
$$\text{Group 2} = \text{working adults}$$
$$\text{Group 3} = \text{retired people}$$
$$\text{Group 4} = \text{died}$$

We are given that $H_1 = 1000$, $H_2 = H_3 = 0$, and

$$P = \begin{bmatrix} .959 & .040 & 0 & .001 \\ 0 & .960 & .030 & .010 \\ 0 & 0 & .950 & .050 \end{bmatrix}$$

Now (14) or (14′) yields

No. entering group i each year = no. leaving group i each year

$$1000 = (.04 + .001)N_1 \quad \text{(Children)}$$
$$.04N_1 = (.03 + .01)N_2 \quad \text{(Working adults)}$$
$$.03N_2 = .05N_3 \quad \text{(Retired people)}$$

Solving this system of equations, we find that $N_1 = 24,390.24$, $N_2 = 24,390.24$, and $N_3 = 14,634.14$.

2. Since in the steady state, there are 14,634.14 retired people, in the steady state they receive 14,634.14(5000) dollars per year. Hence, each working adult must pay

$$\frac{14,634.14(5000)}{24,390.24} = \$3000 \text{ per year}$$

This result is reasonable, because in the steady state, there are $\frac{5}{3}$ as many working adults as there are retired people. ◆

E X A M P L E 10

Let's return to the law firm of Mason and Burger (Example 8). Suppose the firm's long-term goal is to employ 50 junior lawyers, 30 senior lawyers, and 10 partners. To achieve this steady-state census, how many lawyers of each type should Mason and Burger hire each year?

Solution

Let

$$\text{Group 1} = \text{junior lawyers}$$
$$\text{Group 2} = \text{senior lawyers}$$
$$\text{Group 3} = \text{partners}$$
$$\text{Group 4} = \text{lawyers who have left firm}$$

Mason and Burger wish to obtain $N_1 = 50$, $N_2 = 30$, and $N_3 = 10$. Recall from Example 8 that

$$P = \begin{bmatrix} .80 & .15 & 0 & .05 \\ 0 & .70 & .20 & .10 \\ 0 & 0 & .95 & .05 \end{bmatrix}$$

Then (14) or (14′) yields

No. entering group i = no. leaving group i

$$H_1 = (.15 + .05)50 \qquad \text{(Junior lawyers)}$$
$$(.15)50 + H_2 = (.20 + .10)30 \qquad \text{(Senior lawyers)}$$
$$(.20)30 + H_3 = (.05)10 \qquad \text{(Partners)}$$

The unique solution to this system of equations is $H_1 = 10$, $H_2 = 1.5$, $H_3 = -5.5$. This means that to maintain the desired steady-state census, Mason and Burger would have to fire 5.5 partners each year. This is reasonable, because an average of $.20(30) = 6$ senior lawyers become partners every year, and once a senior lawyer becomes a partner, he or she stays a partner for an average of 20 years. This shows that to keep the number of partners down to 10, several partners must be released each year. An alternative solution might be to reduce (below its current value of .20) the fraction of senior lawyers who become partners during each year. ◆

For more information on work force planning models, the interested reader should consult the excellent book by Grinold and Marshall (1977).

◆ PROBLEMS

GROUP A

1. This problem refers to Problem 1 of Section 19.6. Suppose that each year, State College admits 7000 freshmen, 500 sophomore transfers, and 500 junior transfers. In the long run, what will be the composition of the State College student body?

2. In Example 9, suppose that advances in medical science have reduced the annual death rate for retired people from 5% to 3%. By how much would this increase the annual pension contribution that a working adult would have to make to the pension fund?

3. New York City produces 1000 tons of pollution per day, Jersey City produces 100 tons of pollution per day, and Newark produces 50 tons of pollution per day. Each day, $\frac{1}{3}$ of New York's pollution is blown to Newark, $\frac{1}{3}$ dissipates, and $\frac{1}{3}$ remains in New York. Each day, $\frac{1}{3}$ of Jersey City's pollution is blown to New York, $\frac{1}{3}$ stays in Jersey City, and $\frac{1}{3}$ is blown to Newark. Each day, $\frac{1}{3}$ of Newark's pollution stays in Newark, and the rest is blown

to Jersey City. On a typical day, which city will be the most polluted?

4. Money circulates among the Federation's three "capital" planets: Vulcan, Romulanville, and Klingonville. Ideally, the Federation would like to have $5 billion in circulation at each planet. Each month, $\frac{1}{3}$ of all the money at Vulcan leaves circulation, $\frac{1}{3}$ stays at Vulcan, and $\frac{1}{3}$ ends up in Klingonville. Each month, $\frac{1}{3}$ of the money at Romulanville remains in Romulanville, $\frac{1}{3}$ ends up in Klingonville, and $\frac{1}{3}$ ends up at Vulcan. Each month, $\frac{2}{3}$ of the money in Klingonville ends up in Romulanville, and $\frac{1}{3}$ stays in Klingonville. The Federation introduces money into the system at Vulcan. Is there any way to have a steady-state level of $5 billion in circulation at each planet?

GROUP B

5. All State University Business School faculty members are classified as tenured or untenured. Each year, 10% of the untenured faculty are granted tenure and 10% leave State University; 95% of the tenured faculty remain and

5% percent leave. The business school wants to maintain a faculty with 100 members, of which x% are untenured. Determine a hiring policy that will achieve this goal. For what values of x does this goal require firing tenured faculty members? Describe a hiring policy that maintains a faculty that is 10% untenured. Describe a hiring policy that maintains a faculty that is 40% untenured.

GROUP C

6.[†] For simplicity, suppose that fresh blood obtained by a hospital will spoil if it is not transfused within 5 days. The hospital receives 100 pints of fresh blood daily from a local blood bank. Two policies are possible for determining the order in which blood is transfused (see Table 5). For example, under policy 1, blood has a 10% chance of being transfused during its first day at the hospital. Under policy 2, four-day-old blood has a 10% chance of being transfused.

[†]Based on Pegels and Jelmert (1970).

Table 5

	AGE OF BLOOD (beginning of day)				
Chance of transfusion	0	1	2	3	4
Policy 1	.10	.20	.30	.40	.50
Policy 2	.50	.40	.30	.20	.10

(a) A FIFO (first in, first out) blood-issuing policy issues "old" blood first, whereas a LIFO (last in, first out) policy issues "young" blood first. Which policy represents a LIFO policy, and which represents a FIFO policy?
(b) For each policy, determine the probability that a new pint of blood will spoil.
(c) For each policy, determine the average number of pints of blood in inventory.
(d) For each policy, find the average age of transfused blood.
(e) Comment on the relative merits of a FIFO policy and a LIFO policy.

◆ SUMMARY

Let $\mathbf{X}_t$ be the value of a system's characteristic at time t. A **discrete-time stochastic process** is simply a description of the relation between the random variables $\mathbf{X}_0, \mathbf{X}_1, \mathbf{X}_2, \ldots$. A discrete-time stochastic process is a **Markov chain** if, for $t = 0, 1, 2, \ldots$ and all states,

$$P(\mathbf{X}_{t+1} = i_{t+1} | \mathbf{X}_t = i_t, \mathbf{X}_{t-1} = i_{t-1}, \ldots, \mathbf{X}_1 = i_1, \mathbf{X}_0 = i_0)$$
$$= P(\mathbf{X}_{t+1} = i_{t+1} | \mathbf{X}_t = i_t)$$

For a stationary Markov chain, the **transition probability** p_{ij} is the probability that given the system is in state i at time t, the system will be in state j at time $t + 1$.

The vector $\mathbf{q} = [q_1 \quad q_2 \quad \cdots \quad q_s]$ is the **initial probability distribution** for the Markov chain. $P(\mathbf{X}_0 = i)$ is given by q_i.

n-STEP TRANSITION PROBABILITIES

The **n-step transition probability**, $P_{ij}(n)$, is the probability that n periods from now, the state will be j, given that the current state is i. $P_{ij}(n) = ij$th element of P^n.

Given the initial probability vector $\mathbf{q}$, the probability of being in state j at time n is given by $\mathbf{q}$(column j of P^n).

CLASSIFICATION OF STATES IN A MARKOV CHAIN

Given two states i and j, a **path** from i to j is a sequence of transitions that begins in i and ends in j, such that each transition in the sequence has a positive probability of occurring. A state j is **reachable** from a state i if there is a path leading from i to j. Two states i and j are said to **communicate** if j is reachable from i, and i is reachable from j.

A set of states S in a Markov chain is a **closed set** if no state outside of S is reachable from any state in S.

A state i is an **absorbing state** if $p_{ii} = 1$. A state i is a **transient state** if there exists a state j that is reachable from i, but the state i is not reachable from state j.

If a state is not transient, it is a **recurrent state**. A state i is **periodic** with period $k > 1$ if all paths leading from state i back to state i have a length that is a multiple of k. If a recurrent state is not periodic, it is **aperiodic**. If all states in a chain are recurrent, aperiodic, and communicate with each other, the chain is said to be **ergodic**.

STEADY-STATE PROBABILITIES

Let P be the transition probability matrix for an ergodic Markov chain with states $1, 2, \ldots, s$ (with ijth element p_{ij}). After a large number of periods have elapsed, the probability (call it π_j) that the Markov chain is in state j is independent of the initial state. The long-run or **steady-state**, probability π_j may be found by solving the following set of linear equations:

$$\pi_j = \sum_{k=1}^{k=s} \pi_k p_{kj} \quad (j = 1, 2, \ldots, s; \text{ omit one of these equations})$$

$$\pi_1 + \pi_2 + \cdots + \pi_s = 1$$

ABSORBING CHAINS

A Markov chain in which one or more states is an absorbing state is an **absorbing Markov chain**. To answer important questions about an absorbing Markov chain, we list the states in the following order: transient states first, then absorbing states. Assume there are $s - m$ transient states $(t_1, t_2, \ldots, t_{s-m})$ and m absorbing states $(a_1, a_2, \ldots, a_m)$. Write the transition probability matrix P as follows:

$$
P = \begin{array}{c} \\ s - m \text{ rows} \\ m \text{ rows} \end{array}
\begin{bmatrix} Q & R \\ \hline 0 & I \end{bmatrix}
$$

with $s - m$ columns and m columns.

The following questions may now be answered: (1) If the chain begins in a given transient state, and before we reach an absorbing state, what is the expected number of times that each state will be entered? How many periods do we expect to spend in a given transient state before absorption takes place? *Answer*: If we are at present in transient state t_i, the expected number of periods that will be spent in transient state t_j before absorption is the ijth element of the matrix $(I - Q)^{-1}$. (2) If a chain begins in a given transient state, what is the probability that we end up in each absorbing state? *Answer*: If we are at present in transient state t_i, the probability that we will eventually be absorbed in absorbing state a_j is the ijth element of the matrix $(I - Q)^{-1}R$.

WORK FORCE PLANNING MODELS

For an organization in which each member is classified into one of s groups,

p_{ij} = fraction of members beginning a time period in group i who begin the next time period in group j

$$p_{i,s+1} = \text{fraction of all group } i \text{ members}$$
$$\text{who leave the organization during a period}$$
$$P = s \times (s+1) \text{ matrix whose } ij\text{th entry is } p_{ij}$$
$$H_i = \text{number of group } i \text{ members}$$
$$\text{hired at the beginning of each period}$$
$$N_i = \text{limiting number (if it exists) of group } i \text{ members}$$

N_i may be found by equating the number of people per period who enter group i with the number of people per period who leave group i. Thus, $(N_1, N_2, \ldots, N_s)$ may be found by solving

$$H_i + \sum_{k \neq i} N_k p_{ki} = N_i \sum_{k \neq i} p_{ik} \quad (i = 1, 2, \ldots, s)$$

◆ REVIEW PROBLEMS

GROUP A

1. A machine is used to produce precision tools. If the machine is in good condition today, then 90% of the time, it will be in good condition tomorrow. If the machine is in bad condition today, then 80% of the time, it will be in bad condition tomorrow. If the machine is in good condition, it produces 100 tools per day. If the machine is in bad condition, it produces 60 tools per day. On the average, how many tools per day are produced?

2. Customers buy cars from three auto companies. Given the company from which a customer last bought a car, the probability that she will buy her next car from each company is as follows:

	Will Buy Next From		
Last bought from	Co. 1	Co. 2	Co. 3
Co. 1	.80	.10	.10
Co. 2	.05	.85	.10
Co. 3	.10	.20	.70

(a) If someone currently owns a company 1 car, what is the probability that at least one of the next two cars she buys will be a company 1 car?

(b) At present, it costs company 1 an average of $5000 to produce a car, and the average price a customer pays for a company 1 car is $8000. Company 1 is considering instituting a five-year warranty. It estimates that this will increase the cost per car by $300, but a market research survey indicates that the probabilities will change as follows:

	Will Buy Next From		
Last bought from	Co. 1	Co. 2	Co. 3
Co. 1	.85	.10	.05
Co. 2	.10	.80	.10
Co. 3	.15	.10	.75

Should company 1 institute the five-year warranty?

3.[†] A baseball team consists of 2 stars, 13 starters, and 10 substitutes. For tax purposes, the team owner must value the players. The value of each player is defined to be the total value of the salary he will earn until retirement. At the beginning of each season, the players are classified into one of four categories:

Category 1 Star (a star earns $1 million per year).
Category 2 Starter (a starter earns $400,000 per year).
Category 3 Substitute (a substitute earns $100,000 per year).
Category 4 Retired (earns no more salary).

Given that a player is a star, starter, or substitute at the beginning of the current season, the probabilities that he will be a star, starter, substitute, or retired at the beginning

[†]Based on Flamholtz, Geis, and Perle (1984).

of the next season are as follows:

Next Season

This Season	Star	Starter	Substitute	Retired
Star	.50	.30	.15	.05
Starter	.20	.50	.20	.10
Substitute	.05	.15	.50	.30
Retired	0	0	0	1

Determine the value of the team's players.

4. The best-selling college statistics text, *The Thrill of Statistics*, sells 5 million copies every fall. Some users of the book keep the book, and some sell the book back to the bookstore. Suppose that 90% of all students who buy a new book sell it back, 80% of all students who buy a once-used book sell it back, and 60% of all students who buy a twice-used book sell it back. If a book has been used four or more times, the cover falls off, and it cannot be sold back.

(a) In the steady state, how many new copies of the book will the publisher be able to sell each year?

(b) Suppose that a bookstore's profit on each type of book is as follows:

New book: $6.00

Once-used book: $3.00

Twice-used book: $2.00

Thrice-used book: $1.00

If the steady-state census is representative of the bookstore's sales, what will be the bookstore's average profit per book?

5. Hearts Dog Food and Corporal Dog Food are battling tooth and nail for the nation's dog biscuit market. A dog owner buys one box of dog biscuits per month. If a dog owner's last purchase was a Hearts box of biscuits, there is a .8 chance that his next purchase will also be a Hearts box of biscuits. If a dog owner's last purchase was a Corporal box of biscuits, there is a .9 chance that his next purchase will also be a Corporal box of biscuits. It costs Hearts 80¢ to produce a box of biscuits, and Hearts currently sells biscuits for $1.00.

(a) If there are 40 million dog owners in the United States, what is Hearts' annual expected profit?

(b) If Hearts sells each box of biscuits for $100 - x$ cents ($0 \le x \le 20$), then a fraction $.8 + \frac{x}{100}$ of all dog owners whose last purchase was from Hearts will purchase their next box of biscuits from Hearts. How can Hearts maximize expected annual profit?

GROUP B

6. At the beginning of a period, a company observes its inventory level. Then an order may be placed (and is instantaneously received). Finally, the period's demand is observed. We are given the following information: (1) A $2 cost is assessed against each unit of inventory on hand at the end of a period. (2) A $3 penalty is assessed against each unit of demand that is not met on time. Assume that all shortages result in lost sales. (3) Placing an order costs 50¢ per unit plus a $5 ordering cost. (4) During each period, demand is equally likely to equal 1, 2, or 3 units.

The company is considering the following ordering policy: At the end of any period, if the on-hand inventory is 1 unit or less, order sufficient units to bring the on-hand inventory level at the beginning of the next period up to 4 units.

(a) What fraction of the time will the on-hand inventory level at the end of each period be 0 units? 1 unit? 2 units? 3 units? 4 units?

(b) Determine the average cost per period incurred by this ordering policy.

(c) Answer parts (a) and (b) if all shortages are backlogged. Assume that the cost for each unit backlogged is $3.

7.[†] In problem 3, suppose that in evaluating a player's value, the owner must discount future salaries. Assume that $1 paid out in salary during the next season is equivalent to 90¢ paid out during the current season. Can you still determine the value of the team's players? (*Hint*: Modify the probabilities in the transition probability matrix to account for the discounting of future salaries, or look at Problem 8 of Section 19.6.)

8.[‡] During any month, Cashco has a .5 chance of receiving a $1000 cash inflow and a .5 chance that there will be a $1000 cash outflow. For every $1000 in cash on hand at the end of a month, Cashco incurs a $15 cost (due to lost interest). At the beginning of each month, Cashco can adjust its on-hand cash balance upward or downward with the cost per transaction being $20. Cashco can never let the on-hand cash balance become negative. The company is considering the following two cash management policies:

Policy 1 At the beginning of a month in which the on-hand cash balance is $3000, immediately reduce the cash balance to $1000. At the beginning of a month in which the on-hand cash balance is $0,

---

†Based on Flamholtz, Geis, and Perle (1984).

‡Based on Eppen and Fama (1970).

immediately bring the on-hand cash balance up to $1000.

Policy 2 At the beginning of a month in which the on-hand cash balance is $4000, immediately reduce the cash balance to $2000. At the beginning of a month in which the on-hand cash balance is $0, immediately bring the on-hand cash balance up to $2000.

Which policy will incur a smaller expected monthly cost (opportunity plus transaction)? The sequence of events during each month is as follows:

1. Observe beginning cash balance

2. Adjust (if desired) cash balance

3. Cash balance changes

4. Opportunity cost is assessed

9. In the game of craps, we roll a pair of six-sided dice. On the first throw, if we roll a 7 or an 11, we win right away. If we roll a 2, a 3, or a 12, we lose right away. If we first roll a total of 4, 5, 6, 8, 9, or 10, we keep rolling the dice until we get either a 7 or the total rolled on the first throw. If we get a 7, we lose. If we roll the same total as the first throw, we win. Use knowledge of Markov chains to determine our probability of winning at craps.

◆ REFERENCES

GRINOLD, R., and K. MARSHALL. *Manpower Planning Models*. New York: North-Holland, 1977. Contains an extensive discussion of manpower planning models.

The following two references are the sources for two applications of Markov chains discussed in the chapter:
MEREDITH, J. "A Markovian Analysis of a Geriatric Ward," *Management Science* 19(1973):604–612.
WALKER, J., and J. LEHMANN. *100 Ways to Win at Monopoly*. New York: Dell, 1975.

The following books give both the theoretical aspects and many interesting applications of Markov chains:
BHAT, N. *Elements of Applied Stochastic Processes*, 2d ed. New York: Wiley, 1985.
ISAACSON, D., and R. MADSEN. *Markov Chains: Theory and Applications*. New York: Wiley, 1976.
KARLIN, S., and H. TAYLOR. *A First Course in Stochastic Processes*, 2d ed. Orlando, Fla.: Academic Press, 1975.
KEMENY, J., and L. SNELL. *Finite Markov Chains*. Princeton, N.J.: Van Nostrand, 1960.

ASH, R., and R. BISHOP. "Monopoly as a Markov Process," *Mathematics Magazine* 45(1972):26–29.
BESSENT, W., and A. BESSENT. "Student Education Flow in a University Department: Results of a Markov Analysis," *Interfaces* 10(1980):52–59.
CYERT, R., M. DAVISON, and G. THOMPSON. "Estimation of the Allowance for Doubtful Accounts by Markov Chains," *Management Science* 8(1963):287–303.
DEMING, E., and G. GLASSER. "A Markovian Analysis of the Life of Newspaper Subscriptions," *Management Science* 14(1968):B283–B294.
EPPEN, G., and E. FAMA. "Three Asset Cash Balance and Dynamic Portfolio Problems," *Management Science* 17(1970):311–319.
FLAMHOLTZ, E., G. GEIS, and R. PERLE. "A Markovian Model for the Valuation of Human Assets Acquired by an Organizational Purchase," *Interfaces* 14(1984):11–15.
PEGELS, C., and A. JELMERT. "An Evaluation of Blood-Inventory Policies: A Markov Chain Application," *Operations Research* 18(1970):1097–1098.
THOMPSON, W., and J. McNEAL. "Sales Planning and Control Using Absorbing Markov Chains," *Journal of Marketing Research* 4(1967):62–66.

CHAPTER 20

Deterministic Dynamic Programming

DYNAMIC PROGRAMMING is a technique that can be used to solve many optimization problems. In most applications, dynamic programming obtains solutions by working backward from the end of a problem toward the beginning, thus breaking up a large unwieldy problem into a series of smaller, more tractable problems.

We introduce the idea of working backward by solving two well-known puzzles and then show how dynamic programming can be used to solve network, inventory, and resource allocation problems. A more detailed discussion of the use of dynamic programming to solve inventory problems then follows. Finally, we show how dynamic programming can be viewed as "building up," or working forward.

20-1

TWO PUZZLES*

In this section, we show how working backward can make a seemingly difficult problem almost trivial to solve.

E X A M P L E
1

Suppose there are 30 matches on a table. I begin by picking up 1, 2, or 3 matches. Then my opponent must pick up 1, 2, or 3 matches. We continue in this fashion until the last match is picked up. The player who picks up the last match is the loser. How can I (the first player) be sure of winning the game?

Solution

If I can ensure that it will be my opponent's turn when 1 match remains, I will certainly win. Working backward one step, if I can ensure that it will be my opponent's turn when 5 matches remain, I will win. The reason for this is that no matter what he does when 5 matches remain, I can make sure that when he has his next turn, only 1 match will remain. For example, suppose it is my opponent's turn when 5 matches remain. If my opponent picks up 2 matches, I will pick up 2 matches, leaving him with 1 match and sure defeat. Similarly, if I can force my opponent to play when 5, 9, 13, 17, 21, 25, or

*This section covers topics that may be omitted with no loss of continuity.

29 matches remain, I am sure of victory. Thus, I cannot lose if I pick up 30 − 29 = 1 match on my first turn. Then I simply make sure that my opponent will always be left with 29, 25, 21, 17, 13, 9, or 5 matches on his turn. Notice that we have solved this puzzle by working backward from the end of the problem toward the beginning. Try solving this problem without working backward!

◆

E X A M P L E 2

I have a 9-oz cup and a 4-oz cup. My mother has ordered me to bring home exactly 6 oz of milk. How can I accomplish this goal?

Solution

By starting near the end of the problem, I cleverly realize that the problem can easily be solved if I can somehow get 1 oz of milk into the 4-oz cup. Then I can fill the 9-oz cup and empty 3 oz from the 9-oz cup into the partially filled 4-oz cup. At this point, I will be left with 6 oz of milk. After I have this flash of insight, the solution to the problem may easily be described as in Table 1 (the initial situation is written last, and the final situation is written first).

Table 1
Moves in the Cup-
and-Milk Problem

NO. OF OUNCES IN 9-OZ CUP	NO. OF OUNCES IN 4-OZ CUP
6	0
6	4
9	1
0	1
1	0
1	4
5	0
5	4
9	0
0	0

◆

◆ PROBLEMS

GROUP A

1. Suppose there are 40 matches on a table. I begin by picking up 1, 2, 3, or 4 matches. Then my opponent must pick up 1, 2, 3, or 4 matches. We continue until the last match is picked up. The player who picks up the last match is the loser. Can I be sure of victory? If so, how?

2. Three players have played three rounds of a gambling game. Each round has one loser and two winners. The losing player must pay each winner the amount of money that the winning player had at the beginning of the round. At the end of the three rounds each player has $10. You are told that each player has won one round. By working backward, determine the original stakes of the three players. (*Note:* If the answer turns out to be (for example) 5, 15, 10,

don't worry about which player had which stake; we can't really tell which player ends up with how much, but we can determine the numerical values of the original stakes.)

GROUP B

3. We have 21 coins and are told that one of the coins is heavier than any of the other coins. How many weighings on a balance will it take to find the heaviest coin? (*Hint:* If the heaviest coin is in a group of three coins, we can find the heaviest coin in one weighing. Then work backward to two weighings, and so on.)

4. Given a 7-oz cup and a 3-oz cup, explain how we can return from a well with 5 oz of water.

20-2   A NETWORK PROBLEM

Many applications of dynamic programming reduce to finding the shortest (or longest) path joining two points in a given network. The following example illustrates how dynamic programming (working backward) can be used to find the shortest path in a network.

E X A M P L E
3

Joe Cougar lives in New York City, but he plans to drive to Los Angeles in order to seek fame and fortune. Joe's funds are limited, so he has decided to spend each night on his trip at a friend's house. Joe has friends in Columbus, Nashville, Louisville, Kansas City, Omaha, Dallas, San Antonio, and Denver. Joe knows tht after one day's drive he can reach Columbus, Nashville, or Louisville. After two days of driving, he can reach Kansas City, Omaha, or Dallas. After three days of driving, he can reach San Antonio or Denver. Finally, after four days of driving, he can reach Los Angeles. In order to minimize the number of miles traveled, where should Joe spend each night of the trip? The actual road mileages between cities are given in Figure 1.

Figure 1
Joe's Trip across the
United States

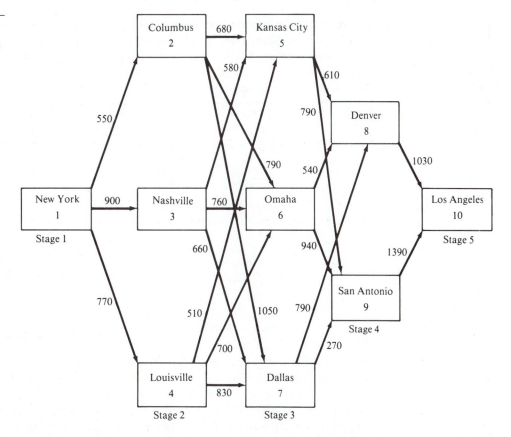

Solution

Joe needs to know the shortest path between New York and Los Angeles in Figure 1. We will find the shortest path from New York to Los Angeles by working backward. In Figure 1, we have classified all the cities that Joe can be in at the beginning of the *n*th day of his trip as stage n cities. For example, since Joe can only be in San Antonio or Denver at the beginning of the fourth day (day 1 begins when Joe leaves New York), we classify San Antonio and Denver as stage 4 cities. The reason for classifying cities according to stages will become apparent later.

The idea of working backward implies that we should begin by solving an easy problem that will eventually help us to solve a complex problem. Hence, we begin by finding the shortest path to Los Angeles from each city in which there is only one day of driving left (stage 4 cities). Then we use this information to find the shortest path to Los Angeles from each city for which only two days of driving remain (stage 3 cities). With this information in hand, we are able to find the shortest path to Los Angeles from each city that is three days distant (stage 2 cities). Finally, we find the shortest path to Los Angeles from each city (there is only one: New York) that is four days away.

To simplify the exposition, we use the numbers 1, 2, ... , 10 given in Figure 1 to label the ten cities. We also define c_{ij} to be the road mileage between city i and city j. For example, $c_{35} = 580$ is the road mileage between Nashville and Kansas City. We let $f_t(i)$ be the length of the shortest path from city i to Los Angeles, given that city i is a stage t city.[†]

STAGE 4 COMPUTATIONS.   We first determine the shortest path to Los Angeles from each stage 4 city. Since there is only one path from each stage 4 city to Los Angeles, we immediately see that $f_4(8) = 1030$, the shortest path from Denver to Los Angeles simply being the *only* path from Denver to Los Angeles. Similarly, $f_4(9) = 1390$, the shortest (and only) path from San Antonio to Los Angeles.

STAGE 3 COMPUTATIONS.   We now work backward one stage (to stage 3 cities) and find the shortest path to Los Angeles from each stage 3 city. For example, to determine $f_3(5)$, we note that the shortest path from city 5 to Los Angeles must be one of the following:

Path 1 Go from city 5 to city 8 and then take the shortest path from city 8 to city 10.

Path 2 Go from city 5 to city 9 and then take the shortest path from city 9 to city 10.

The length of path 1 may be written as $c_{58} + f_4(8)$, and the length of path 2 may be written as $c_{59} + f_4(9)$. Hence, the shortest distance from city 5 to city 10 may be written as

$$f_3(5) = \min \begin{cases} c_{58} + f_4(8) = 610 + 1030 = 1640^* \\ c_{59} + f_4(9) = 790 + 1390 = 2180 \end{cases}$$

(the * indicates the choice of arc that attains the $f_3(5)$). Thus, we have shown that the shortest path from city 5 to city 10 is the path 5–8–10. Note that in order to obtain this result, we made use of our knowledge of $f_4(8)$ and $f_4(9)$.

Similarly, to find $f_3(6)$, we note that the shortest path to Los Angeles from city 6 must begin by going to city 8 or to city 9. This leads us to the following equation:

[†]In this example, keeping track of the stages is unnecessary, but to be consistent with later examples, we keep track of the stages.

$$f_3(6) = \min \begin{cases} c_{68} + f_4(8) = 540 + 1030 = 1570^* \\ c_{69} + f_4(9) = 940 + 1390 = 2330 \end{cases}$$

Thus, $f_3(6) = 1570$, and the shortest path from city 6 to city 10 is the path 6–8–10.
    To find $f_3(7)$, we note that

$$f_3(7) = \min \begin{cases} c_{78} + f_4(8) = 790 + 1030 = 1820 \\ c_{79} + f_4(9) = 270 + 1390 = 1660^* \end{cases}$$

Therefore, $f_3(7) = 1660$, and the shortest path from city 7 to city 10 is the path 7–9–10.

STAGE 2 COMPUTATIONS.   Given our knowledge of $f_3(5), f_3(6)$, and $f_3(7)$, it is now easy to work backward one more stage and compute $f_2(2), f_2(3)$, and $f_2(4)$ and thus the shortest paths to Los Angeles from city 2, city 3, and city 4. To illustrate how this is done, we find the shortest path (and its length) from city 2 to city 10. The shortest path from city 2 to city 10 must begin by going from city 2 to city 5, city 6, or city 7. Once this shortest path gets to city 5, city 6, or city 7, it must follow a shortest path from that city to Los Angeles. This reasoning shows that the shortest path from city 2 to city 10 must be one of the following:

Path 1 Go from city 2 to city 5. Then follow a shortest path from city 5 to city 10. A path of this type has a total length of $c_{25} + f_3(5)$.

Path 2 Go from city 2 to city 6. Then follow a shortest path from city 6 to city 10. A path of this type has a total length of $c_{26} + f_3(6)$.

Path 3 Go from city 2 to city 7. Then follow a shortest path from city 7 to city 10. This path has a total length of $c_{27} + f_3(7)$. We may now conclude that

$$f_2(2) = \min \begin{cases} c_{25} + f_3(5) = 680 + 1640 = 2320^* \\ c_{26} + f_3(6) = 790 + 1570 = 2360 \\ c_{27} + f_3(7) = 1050 + 1660 = 2710 \end{cases}$$

Thus, $f_2(2) = 2320$, and the shortest path from city 2 to city 10 is to go from city 2 to city 5 and then follow the shortest path from city 5 to city 10 (5–8–10).
    Similarly,

$$f_2(3) = \min \begin{cases} c_{35} + f_3(5) = 580 + 1640 = 2220^* \\ c_{36} + f_3(6) = 760 + 1570 = 2330 \\ c_{37} + f_3(7) = 660 + 1660 = 2320 \end{cases}$$

Thus, $f_2(3) = 2220$, and the shortest path from city 3 to city 10 consists of arc 3–5 and the shortest path from city 5 to city 10 (5–8–10).
    In a similar fashion,

$$f_2(4) = \min \begin{cases} c_{45} + f_3(5) = 510 + 1640 = 2150^* \\ c_{46} + f_3(6) = 700 + 1570 = 2270 \\ c_{47} + f_3(7) = 830 + 1660 = 2490 \end{cases}$$

Thus, $f_2(4) = 2150$, and the shortest path from city 4 to city 10 consists of arc 4–5 and the shortest path from city 5 to city 10 (5–8–10).

STAGE 1 COMPUTATIONS.   We can now use our knowledge of $f_2(2)$, $f_2(3)$, and $f_2(4)$ to work backward one more stage to find $f_1(1)$ and the shortest path from city 1 to city 10. Note that the shortest path from city 1 to city 10 must begin by going to city 2, city 3, or city 4. This means that the shortest path from city 1 to city 10 must be one of the following:

Path 1 Go from city 1 to city 2 and then follow a shortest path from city 2 to city 10. The length of such a path is $c_{12} + f_2(2)$.

Path 2 Go from city 1 to city 3 and then follow a shortest path from city 3 to city 10. The length of such a path is $c_{13} + f_2(3)$.

Path 3 Go from city 1 to city 4 and then follow a shortest path from city 4 to city 10. The length of such a path is $c_{14} + f_2(4)$. It now follows that

$$f_1(1) = \min \begin{cases} c_{12} + f_2(2) = 550 + 2320 = 2870* \\ c_{13} + f_2(3) = 900 + 2220 = 3120 \\ c_{14} + f_2(4) = 770 + 2150 = 2920 \end{cases}$$

DETERMINATION OF THE OPTIMAL PATH.   Thus, $f_1(1) = 2870$, and the shortest path from city 1 to city 10 goes from city 1 to city 2 and then follows the shortest path from city 2 to city 10. Checking back to the $f_2(2)$ calculations, we see that the shortest path from city 2 to city 10 is 2–5–8–10. Translating the numerical labels into real cities, we see that the shortest path from New York to Los Angeles passes through New York, Columbus, Kansas City, Denver, and Los Angeles. This path has a length of $f_1(1) = 2870$ miles.

◆

COMPUTATIONAL EFFICIENCY OF DYNAMIC PROGRAMMING

For Example 3, it would have been an easy matter to determine the shortest path from New York to Los Angeles by enumerating all the possible paths (after all, there are only $3(3)(2) = 18$ paths). Thus, in this problem, the use of dynamic programming did not really serve much purpose. For larger networks, however, dynamic programming is much more efficient for determining a shortest path than the explicit enumeration of all paths. To see this, consider the network in Figure 2. In this network, it is possible to travel from any node in stage k to any node in stage $k + 1$. Let the distance between node i and node j be c_{ij}. Suppose we want to determine the shortest path from node 1 to node 27. One way to solve this problem is explicit enumeration of all paths. There are 5^5 possible paths from node 1 to node 27. It takes five additions to determine the length of each path. Thus, explicitly enumerating the length of all paths requires $5^5(5) = 5^6 = 15,625$ additions.

Suppose we use dynamic programming to determine the shortest path from node 1 to node 27. Let $f_t(i)$ be the length of the shortest path from node i to node 27, given that node i is in stage t. To determine the shortest path from node 1 to node 27, we begin by finding $f_6(22)$, $f_6(23)$, $f_6(24)$, $f_6(25)$, and $f_6(26)$. This does not require any additions. Then we find $f_5(17)$, $f_5(18)$, $f_5(19)$, $f_5(20)$, $f_5(21)$. For example, to find $f_5(21)$ we use the following equation:

Figure 2
Illustration of
Computational
Efficiency of
Dynamic
Programming

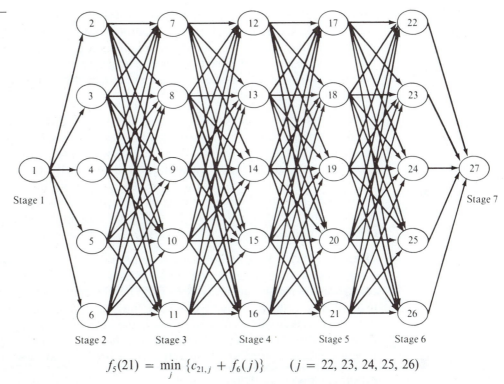

$$f_5(21) = \min_{j} \{c_{21,j} + f_6(j)\} \qquad (j = 22, 23, 24, 25, 26)$$

Determining $f_5(21)$ in this manner requires five additions. Thus, the calculation of all the $f_5(\cdot)$'s requires $5(5) = 25$ additions. Similarly, the calculation of all the $f_4(\cdot)$'s requires 25 additions, and the calculation of all the $f_3(\cdot)$'s requires 25 additions. The determination of all the $f_2(\cdot)$'s also requires 25 additions, and the determination of $f_1(1)$ requires 5 additions. Thus, in total, dynamic programming requires $4(25) + 5 = 105$ additions to find the shortest path from node 1 to node 27. Since explicit enumeration requires 15,625 additions, we see that dynamic programming requires only 0.007 times as many additions as explicit enumeration. For larger networks, the computational savings effected by dynamic programming are even more dramatic.

Besides additions, determination of the shortest path in a network requires comparisons between the lengths of paths. If explicit enumeration is used, $5^5 - 1 = 3124$ comparisons must be made (that is, compare the length of the first two paths, then compare the length of the third path with the shortest of the first two paths, and so on). If dynamic programming is used, then for $t = 2, 3, 4, 5$, determination of each $f_t(i)$ requires $5 - 1 = 4$ comparisons. Then to compute $f_1(1)$, $5 - 1 = 4$ comparisons are required. Thus, to find the shortest path from node 1 to node 27, dynamic programming requires a total of $20(5 - 1) + 4 = 84$ comparisons. Again, dynamic programming comes out far superior to explicit enumeration.

CHARACTERISTICS OF DYNAMIC
PROGRAMMING APPLICATIONS

We close this section with a discussion of the characteristics of Example 3 that are common to most applications of dynamic programming.

CHARACTERISTIC 1.   *The problem can be divided into stages with a decision required at each stage.* In Example 3, stage t consisted of those cities where Joe could be at the beginning of day t of his trip. As we will see, in many dynamic programming problems, the stage is the amount of time that has elapsed since the beginning of the problem. We note that in some situations, decisions are not required at every stage (see Sections 20.5 and 20.7).

CHARACTERISTIC 2.   *Each stage has a number of states associated with it.* By a **state** we mean the information that is needed at any stage to make an optimal decision. In Example 3, the state at stage t is simply the city where Joe is at the beginning of day t. For example, in stage 3, the possible states are Kansas City, Omaha, and Dallas. Note that in order to make the correct decision at any stage, Joe doesn't need to know how he got to his present location. For example, if Joe is in Kansas City, then his remaining decisions don't depend on how he got to Kansas City; his future decisions just depend on the fact that he is now in Kansas City.

CHARACTERISTIC 3.   *The decision chosen at any stage describes how the state at the current stage is transformed into the state at the next stage.* In Example 3, Joe's decision at any stage is simply the next city to visit. This determines the state at the next stage in an obvious fashion. In many problems, however, a decision does not determine the next stage's state with certainty; instead, the current decision only determines the probability distribution of the state at the next stage. In Chapter 21, we discuss dynamic programming models in which the future states are not known with certainty.

CHARACTERISTIC 4.   *Given the current state, the optimal decision for each of the remaining stages must not depend on previously reached states or previously chosen decisions.* This idea is known as the **principle of optimality**. In the context of Example 3, the principle of optimality reduces to the following: Suppose the shortest path (call it R) from city 1 to city 10 is known to pass through city i. Then the portion of R that goes from city i to city 10 must be a shortest path from city i to city 10. If this were not the case, we could create a path from city 1 to city 10 that was shorter than R by appending a shortest path from city i to city 10 to the portion of R leading from city 1 to city i. This would create a path from city 1 to city 10 that is shorter than R, thereby contradicting the fact that R is a shortest path from city 1 to city 10. For example, if the shortest path from city 1 to city 10 is known to pass through city 2, then the shortest path from city 1 to city 10 must include a shortest path from city 2 to city 10 (2–5–8–10). This follows because any path from city 1 to city 10 that passes through city 2 and does not contain a shortest path from city 2 to city 10 will have a length of c_{12} + (something bigger than $f_2(2)$). Of course, such a path cannot be a shortest path from city 1 to city 10.

CHARACTERISTIC 5.   *If the states for the problem have been classified into one of T stages, there must be a recursion that relates the cost or reward earned during stages t, $t + 1, \ldots, T$ to the cost or reward earned from stages $t + 1, t + 2, \ldots, T$.* In essence, the recursion formalizes the working-backward procedure. In Example 3, our recursion could have been written as

$$f_t(i) = \min_j \{c_{ij} + f_{t+1}(j)\}$$

where j must be a stage $t + 1$ city and $f_5(10) = 0$.

We can now describe how to make optimal decisions. Let's assume that the initial state during stage 1 is i_1. To use the recursion, we begin by finding the optimal decision for each state associated with the last stage. Then we use the recursion described in characteristic 5 to determine $f_{T-1}(\cdot)$ (along with the optimal decision) for every stage $T-1$ state. Then we use the recursion to determine $f_{T-2}(\cdot)$ (along with the optimal decision) for every stage $T-2$ state. We continue in this fashion until we have computed $f_1(i_1)$ and the optimal decision when we are in stage 1 and state i_1. Then our optimal decision in stage 1 is chosen from the set of decisions attaining $f_1(i_1)$. Choosing this decision at stage 1 will lead us to some stage 2 state (call it state i_2) at stage 2. Then at stage 2, we choose any decision attaining $f_2(i_2)$. We continue in this fashion until a decision has been chosen for each stage. An alternative method of developing a recursion (working forward) is discussed in Section 20.8.

In the rest of this chapter, we discuss many applications of dynamic programming. The presentation will seem easier if the reader attempts to determine how each problem fits into the network context introduced in Example 3. In the next section, we begin by studying how dynamic programming can be used to solve inventory problems.

◆ PROBLEMS

GROUP A

1. Find the shortest path from node 1 to node 10 in the network shown in Figure 3. Also, find the shortest path from node 3 to node 10.

2. A sales representative lives in Bloomington and must be in Indianapolis next Thursday. On each of the days Monday, Tuesday, and Wednesday, he can sell his wares in Indianapolis, Bloomington, or Chicago. From past experience, he believes that he can earn $12 from spending a day in Indianapolis, $16 from spending a day in Bloomington, and $17 from spending a day in Chicago. In order to maximize his sales income less travel costs, where should he spend the first three days and nights of the week? Travel costs are shown in Table 2.

Figure 3

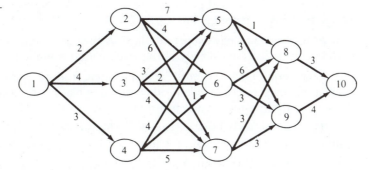

Table 2

| FROM | TO | | |
	INDIANAPOLIS	BLOOMINGTON	CHICAGO
Indianapolis	—	5	2
Bloomington	5	—	7
Chicago	2	7	—

3. I must drive from Bloomington to Cleveland. Several paths are available (see Figure 4). The number on each arc is the length of time it takes to drive between the two cities. For example, it takes 3 hours to drive from Bloomington to Cincinnati. By working backward, determine the shortest path (in terms of time) from Bloomington to Cleveland. (*Hint:* Work backward and don't worry about stages—only about states.)

Figure 4

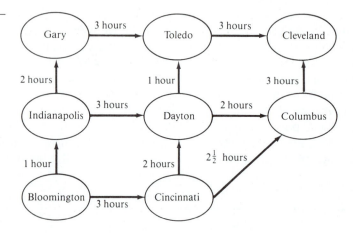

20-3 AN INVENTORY PROBLEM

In this section, we illustrate how dynamic programming can be used to solve an inventory problem with the following characteristics:

1. Time is broken up into periods, the present period being period 1, the next period being period 2, and the final period being period T. At the beginning of period 1, the demand during each period is known.

2. At the beginning of each period, the firm must determine how many units should be produced. Production capacity during each period is limited.

3. Each period's demand must be met on time from inventory or current production. During any period in which production takes place, a fixed cost of production as well as a variable per-unit cost is incurred.

4. The firm has limited storage capacity. This is reflected by a limit on end-of-period inventory. A per-unit holding cost is incurred on each period's ending inventory.

5. The firm's goal is to minimize the total cost of meeting on time the demands for periods 1, 2, . . . , T.

In this model, the firm's inventory position is reviewed at the end of each period (say, at the end of each month), and then the production decision is made. Such a model is called a **periodic review model**. This model is in contrast to the continuous review models discussed in Chapters 16 and 17. In continuous review models, the firm knows its inventory position at all times and may place an order or begin production at any time.

If we exclude the setup cost for producing any units, the inventory problem just described is similar to the Sailco inventory problem that we solved by linear programming in Section 3.10. Here, we illustrate how dynamic programming can be used to determine a production schedule that minimizes the total cost incurred in an inventory problem that meets the preceding description.

E X A M P L E
4

A company knows that the demand for its product during each of the next four months will be as follows: month 1, 1 unit; month 2, 3 units; month 3, 2 units; month 4, 4 units. At the beginning of each month, the company must determine how many units should be produced during the current month. During a month in which any units are produced, a setup cost of $3 is incurred. In addition, there is a variable cost of $1 for every unit produced. At the end of each month, a holding cost of 50¢ per unit on hand is incurred. Capacity limitations allow a maximum of 5 units to be produced during each month. The size of the company's warehouse restricts the ending inventory for each month to at most 4 units. The company wants to determine a production schedule that will meet all demands on time and will minimize the sum of production and holding costs during the four months. Assume that zero units are on hand at the beginning of the first month.

Solution

We recall from Section 3.10 that we can ensure that all demands are met on time by restricting each month's ending inventory to be nonnegative. In order to use dynamic programming to solve this problem, we need to identify the appropriate state, stage, and decision. The stage should be defined so that when one stage remains, the problem will be trivial to solve. If we are at the beginning of month 4, the firm would meet demand at minimum cost by simply producing just enough units to ensure that (month 4 production) + (month 3 ending inventory) = (month 4 demand). Thus, when one month remains, the firm's problem is easy to solve. Hence, we let time represent the stage. In most dynamic programming problems, the stage has something to do with time.

At each stage (or month), the company must decide how many units to produce. In order to make this decision, the company need only know the inventory level at the beginning of the current month (or the end of the previous month). Therefore, we let the state at any stage be the beginning inventory level.

Before writing a recursive relation that can be used to "build up" the optimal production schedule, we must define $f_t(i)$ to be the minimum cost of meeting demands for months $t, t + 1, \ldots, 4$ if i units are on hand at the beginning of month t. We define $c(x)$ to be the cost of producing x units during a period. Then $c(0) = 0$, and for $x > 0$, $c(x) = 3 + x$. Because of the limited storage capacity and the fact that all demand must be met on time, the possible states during each period are 0, 1, 2, 3, and 4. Thus, we begin by determining $f_4(0)$, $f_4(1)$, $f_4(2)$, $f_4(3)$, and $f_4(4)$. Then we use this information to determine $f_3(0)$, $f_3(1)$, $f_3(2)$, $f_3(3)$, and $f_3(4)$. Then we determine $f_2(0)$, $f_2(1)$, $f_2(2)$, $f_2(3)$, and $f_2(4)$. Finally, we determine $f_1(0)$. Then we determine an optimal production level for each month. We define $x_t(i)$ to be a production level during month t that minimizes the total cost during months $t, t + 1, \ldots, 4$ if i units are on hand at the beginning of month t. We now begin to work backward.

MONTH 4 COMPUTATIONS. · During month 4, the firm will produce just enough units to ensure that the month 4 demand of 4 units is met. This yields

$f_4(0)$ = cost of producing $4 - 0$ units = $c(4) = 3 + 4 = \$7$ and $x_4(0) = 4 - 0 = 4$

$f_4(1)$ = cost of producing $4 - 1$ units = $c(3) = 3 + 3 = \$6$ and $x_4(1) = 4 - 1 = 3$

$f_4(2) = $ cost of producing $4 - 2$ units $= c(2) = 3 + 2 = \$5$ and $x_4(2) = 4 - 2 = 2$

$f_4(3) = $ cost of producing $4 - 3$ units $= c(1) = 3 + 1 = \$4$ and $x_4(3) = 4 - 3 = 1$

$f_4(4) = $ cost of producing $4 - 4$ units $= c(0) = \$0$ and $x_4(4) = 4 - 4 = 0$

MONTH 3 COMPUTATIONS. How can we now determine $f_3(i)$ for $i = 0, 1, 2, 3, 4$? The cost $f_3(i)$ is the minimum cost incurred during months 3 and 4 if the inventory at the beginning of month 3 is i. For each possible production level x during month 3, the total cost during months 3 and 4 is

$$(\tfrac{1}{2})(i + x - 2) + c(x) + f_4(i + x - 2) \tag{1}$$

This follows because if x units are produced during month 3, the ending inventory for month 3 will be $i + x - 2$. Then the month 3 holding cost will be $(\tfrac{1}{2})(i + x - 2)$, and the month 3 production cost will be $c(x)$. Then we enter month 4 with $i + x - 2$ units on hand. Since we proceed optimally from this point onward (remember the principle of optimality), the cost for month 4 will be $f_4(i + x - 2)$. Since we wish to choose the month 3 production level to minimize Eq. (1), we write

$$f_3(i) = \min_x \{(\tfrac{1}{2})(i + x - 2) + c(x) + f_4(i + x - 2)\} \tag{2}$$

In Eq. (2), x must be a member of $\{0, 1, 2, 3, 4, 5\}$, and x must satisfy $4 \geq i + x - 2 \geq 0$. This reflects the fact that the current month's demand must be met ($i + x - 2 \geq 0$), and ending inventory cannot exceed the capacity of 4 ($i + x - 2 \leq 4$). Recall that $x_3(i)$ is any value of x attaining $f_3(i)$. The computations for $f_3(0), f_3(1), f_3(2), f_3(3)$, and $f_3(4)$ are given in Table 3.

				TOTAL COST	$f_3(i)$
i	x	$(\tfrac{1}{2})(i + x - 2) + c(x)$	$f_4(i + x - 2)$	MONTHS 3, 4	$x_3(i)$
0	2	$0 + 5 = 5$	7	$5 + 7 = 12^*$	$f_3(0) = 12$
0	3	$\tfrac{1}{2} + 6 = \tfrac{13}{2}$	6	$\tfrac{13}{2} + 6 = \tfrac{25}{2}$	$x_3(0) = 2$
0	4	$1 + 7 = 8$	5	$8 + 5 = 13$	
0	5	$\tfrac{3}{2} + 8 = \tfrac{19}{2}$	4	$\tfrac{19}{2} + 4 = \tfrac{27}{2}$	
1	1	$0 + 4 = 4$	7	$4 + 7 = 11$	$f_3(1) = 10$
1	2	$\tfrac{1}{2} + 5 = \tfrac{11}{2}$	6	$\tfrac{11}{2} + 6 = \tfrac{23}{2}$	$x_3(1) = 5$
1	3	$1 + 6 = 7$	5	$7 + 5 = 12$	
1	4	$\tfrac{3}{2} + 7 = \tfrac{17}{2}$	4	$\tfrac{17}{2} + 4 = \tfrac{25}{2}$	
1	5	$2 + 8 = 10$	0	$10 + 0 = 10^*$	
2	0	$0 + 0 = 0$	7	$0 + 7 = 7^*$	$f_3(2) = 7$
2	1	$\tfrac{1}{2} + 4 = \tfrac{9}{2}$	6	$\tfrac{9}{2} + 6 = \tfrac{21}{2}$	$x_3(2) = 0$
2	2	$1 + 5 = 6$	5	$6 + 5 = 11$	
2	3	$\tfrac{3}{2} + 6 = \tfrac{15}{2}$	4	$\tfrac{15}{2} + 4 = \tfrac{23}{2}$	
2	4	$2 + 7 = 9$	0	$9 + 0 = 9$	
3	0	$\tfrac{1}{2} + 0 = \tfrac{1}{2}$	6	$\tfrac{1}{2} + 6 = \tfrac{13}{2}^*$	$f_3(3) = \tfrac{13}{2}$
3	1	$1 + 4 = 5$	5	$5 + 5 = 10$	$x_3(3) = 0$
3	2	$\tfrac{3}{2} + 5 = \tfrac{13}{2}$	4	$\tfrac{13}{2} + 4 = \tfrac{21}{2}$	
3	3	$2 + 6 = 8$	0	$8 + 0 = 8$	
4	0	$1 + 0 = 1$	5	$1 + 5 = 6^*$	$f_3(4) = 6$
4	1	$\tfrac{3}{2} + 4 = \tfrac{11}{2}$	4	$\tfrac{11}{2} + 4 = \tfrac{19}{2}$	$x_3(4) = 0$
4	2	$2 + 5 = 7$	0	$7 + 0 = 7$	

Table 3 Computations for $f_3(i)$

MONTH 2 COMPUTATIONS. We can now determine $f_2(i)$, the minimum cost incurred during months 2, 3, and 4 given that at the beginning of month 2, the on-hand inventory is i units. Suppose that month 2 production $= x$. Since month 2 demand is 3 units, a holding cost of $(\frac{1}{2})(i + x - 3)$ is incurred at the end of month 2. Thus, the total cost incurred during month 2 is $(\frac{1}{2})(i + x - 3) + c(x)$. During months 3 and 4, we follow an optimal policy. Since month 3 begins with an inventory of $i + x - 3$, the cost incurred during months 3 and 4 is $f_3(i + x - 3)$. In analogy to Eq. (2), we now write

$$f_2(i) = \min_x \{(\tfrac{1}{2})(i + x - 3) + c(x) + f_3(i + x - 3)\} \tag{3}$$

where x must be a member of $\{0, 1, 2, 3, 4, 5\}$ and x must also satisfy $0 \le i + x - 3 \le 4$. The computations for $f_2(0)$, $f_2(1)$, $f_2(2)$, $f_2(3)$, and $f_2(4)$ are given in Table 4.

Table 4
Computations for $f_2(i)$

i	x	$(\tfrac{1}{2})(i + x - 3) + c(x)$	$f_3(i + x - 3)$	TOTAL COST MONTHS 2–4	$f_2(i)$ $x_2(i)$
0	3	$0 + 6 = 6$	12	$6 + 12 = 18$	$f_2(0) = 16$
0	4	$\frac{1}{2} + 7 = \frac{15}{2}$	10	$\frac{15}{2} + 10 = \frac{35}{2}$	$x_2(0) = 5$
0	5	$1 + 8 = 9$	7	$9 + 7 = 16*$	
1	2	$0 + 5 = 5$	12	$5 + 12 = 17$	$f_2(1) = 15$
1	3	$\frac{1}{2} + 6 = \frac{13}{2}$	10	$\frac{13}{2} + 10 = \frac{33}{2}$	$x_2(1) = 4$
1	4	$1 + 7 = 8$	7	$8 + 7 = 15*$	
1	5	$\frac{3}{2} + 8 = \frac{19}{2}$	$\frac{13}{2}$	$\frac{19}{2} + \frac{13}{2} = 16$	
2	1	$0 + 4 = 4$	12	$4 + 12 = 16$	$f_2(2) = 14$
2	2	$\frac{1}{2} + 5 = \frac{11}{2}$	10	$\frac{11}{2} + 10 = \frac{31}{2}$	$x_2(2) = 3$
2	3	$1 + 6 = 7$	7	$7 + 7 = 14*$	
2	4	$\frac{3}{2} + 7 = \frac{17}{2}$	$\frac{13}{2}$	$\frac{17}{2} + \frac{13}{2} = 15$	
2	5	$2 + 8 = 10$	6	$10 + 6 = 16$	
3	0	$0 + 0 = 0$	12	$0 + 12 = 12$	$f_2(3) = 13$
3	1	$\frac{1}{2} + 4 = \frac{9}{2}$	10	$\frac{9}{2} + 10 = \frac{29}{2}$	$x_2(3) = 2$
3	2	$1 + 5 = 6$	7	$6 + 7 = 13*$	
3	3	$\frac{3}{2} + 6 = \frac{15}{2}$	$\frac{13}{2}$	$\frac{15}{2} + \frac{13}{2} = 14$	
3	4	$2 + 7 = 9$	6	$9 + 6 = 15$	
4	0	$\frac{1}{2} + 0 = \frac{1}{2}$	10	$\frac{1}{2} + 10 = \frac{21}{2}*$	$f_2(4) = \frac{21}{2}$
4	1	$1 + 4 = 5$	7	$5 + 7 = 12$	$x_2(4) = 0$
4	2	$\frac{3}{2} + 5 = \frac{13}{2}$	$\frac{13}{2}$	$\frac{13}{2} + \frac{13}{2} = 13$	
4	3	$2 + 6 = 8$	6	$8 + 6 = 14$	

MONTH 1 COMPUTATIONS. The reader should now be able to show that the $f_1(i)$'s can be determined via the following recursive relation:

$$f_1(i) = \min_x \{(\tfrac{1}{2})(i + x - 1) + c(x) + f_2(i + x - 1)\} \tag{4}$$

where x must be a member of $\{0, 1, 2, 3, 4, 5\}$ and x must satisfy $0 \le i + x - 1 \le 4$. Since the inventory at the beginning of month 1 is zero, we actually need only determine $f_1(0)$ and $x_1(0)$. To give the reader more practice, however, the computations for $f_1(1)$, $f_1(2)$, $f_1(3)$, and $f_1(4)$ are given in Table 5.

DETERMINATION OF THE OPTIMAL PRODUCTION SCHEDULE. We can now determine a production schedule that minimizes the total cost of meeting the demand for all four

Table 5
Computations for
$f_1(i)$

i	x	$(\tfrac{1}{2})(i + x - 1) + c(x)$	$f_2(i + x - 1)$	TOTAL COST	$f_1(i)$ $x_1(i)$
0	1	$0 + 4 = 4$	16	$4 + 16 = 20*$	$f_1(0) = 20$
0	2	$\tfrac{1}{2} + 5 = \tfrac{11}{2}$	15	$\tfrac{11}{2} + 15 = \tfrac{41}{2}$	$x_1(0) = 1$
0	3	$1 + 6 = 7$	14	$7 + 14 = 21$	
0	4	$\tfrac{3}{2} + 7 = \tfrac{17}{2}$	13	$\tfrac{17}{2} + 13 = \tfrac{43}{2}$	
0	5	$2 + 8 = 10$	$\tfrac{21}{2}$	$10 + \tfrac{21}{2} = \tfrac{41}{2}$	
1	0	$0 + 0 = 0$	16	$0 + 16 = 16*$	$f_1(1) = 16$
1	1	$\tfrac{1}{2} + 4 = \tfrac{9}{2}$	15	$\tfrac{9}{2} + 15 = \tfrac{39}{2}$	$x_1(1) = 0$
1	2	$1 + 5 = 6$	14	20	
1	3	$\tfrac{3}{2} + 6 = \tfrac{15}{2}$	13	$\tfrac{15}{2} + 13 = \tfrac{41}{2}$	
1	4	$2 + 7 = 9$	$\tfrac{21}{2}$	$9 + \tfrac{21}{2} = \tfrac{39}{2}$	
2	0	$\tfrac{1}{2} + 0 = \tfrac{1}{2}$	15	$\tfrac{1}{2} + 15 = \tfrac{31}{2}*$	$f_1(2) = \tfrac{31}{2}$
2	1	$1 + 4 = 5$	14	$5 + 14 = 19$	$x_1(2) = 0$
2	2	$\tfrac{3}{2} + 5 = \tfrac{13}{2}$	13	$\tfrac{13}{2} + 13 = \tfrac{39}{2}$	
2	3	$2 + 6 = 8$	$\tfrac{21}{2}$	$8 + \tfrac{21}{2} = \tfrac{37}{2}$	
3	0	$1 + 0 = 1$	14	$1 + 14 = 15*$	$f_1(3) = 15$
3	1	$\tfrac{3}{2} + 4 = \tfrac{11}{2}$	13	$\tfrac{11}{2} + 13 = \tfrac{37}{2}$	$x_1(3) = 0$
3	2	$2 + 5 = 7$	$\tfrac{21}{2}$	$7 + \tfrac{21}{2} = \tfrac{35}{2}$	
4	0	$\tfrac{3}{2} + 0 = \tfrac{3}{2}$	13	$\tfrac{3}{2} + 13 = \tfrac{29}{2}*$	$f_1(4) = \tfrac{29}{2}$
4	1	$2 + 4 = 6$	$\tfrac{21}{2}$	$6 + \tfrac{21}{2} = \tfrac{33}{2}$	$x_1(4) = 0$

months on time. Since our initial inventory is zero, the minimum cost for the four months will be $f_1(0) = \$20$. To attain $f_1(0)$, we must produce $x_1(0) = 1$ unit during month 1. Then the inventory at the beginning of month 2 will be $0 + 1 - 1 = 0$. Thus, in month 2, we should produce $x(0) = 5$ units. Then at the beginning of month 3, our beginning inventory will be $0 + 5 - 3 = 2$. Hence, during month 3, we need to produce $x_3(2) = 0$ units. Then month 4 will begin with $2 - 2 + 0 = 0$ units on hand. Thus, $x_4(0) = 4$ units should be produced during month 4. In summary, the optimal production schedule incurs a total cost of $20 and produces 1 unit during month 1, 5 units during month 2, 0 units during month 3, and 4 units during month 4.

◆

Note that finding the solution to Example 4 is equivalent to finding the shortest route joining the node $(1, 0)$ to the node $(5, 0)$ in Figure 5. Each node in Figure 5 corresponds to a state, and each column of nodes corresponds to all the possible states associated with a given stage. For example, if we are at node $(2, 3)$, we are at the beginning of month 2, and the inventory at the beginning of month 2 is 3 units. Each arc in the network represents the way in which a decision (i.e., how much to produce during the current month) transforms the current state into next month's state. For example, the arc joining nodes $(1, 0)$ and $(2, 2)$ (call it arc 1) corresponds to producing 3 units during month 1. To see this, note that if 3 units are produced during month 1, then we begin month 2 with $0 + 3 - 1 = 2$ units. The length of each arc is simply the sum of production and inventory costs during the current period, given the current state and the decision associated with the chosen arc. For example, the cost associated with arc 1 would be $6 + (\tfrac{1}{2})2 = 7$. Note that some nodes in adjacent stages are not joined by an arc. For example, node $(2, 4)$ is not joined to node $(3, 0)$. The reason for this is that if we begin

Figure 5
Network
Representation of
Inventory Example

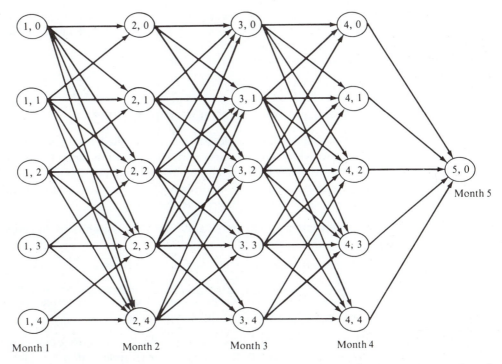

Month 1   Month 2   Month 3   Month 4

month 2 with 4 units, then at the beginning of month 3, we will have at least $4 - 3 = 1$ unit on hand. Also note that we have drawn arcs joining all month 4 states to the node $(5, 0)$, since having a positive inventory at the end of month 4 would clearly be suboptimal.

Returning to Example 4, the minimum-cost production schedule corresponds to the shortest path joining $(1, 0)$ and $(5, 0)$. As we have already seen, this would be the path corresponding to production levels of 1, 5, 0, and 4. In Figure 5, this would correspond to the path beginning at $(1, 0)$, then going to $(2, 0 + 1 - 1) = (2, 0)$, then to $(3, 0 + 5 - 3) = (3, 2)$, then to $(4, 2 + 0 - 2) = (4, 0)$, and finally to $(5, 0 + 4 - 4) = (5, 0)$. Thus, our optimal production schedule corresponds to the path $(1, 0)–(2, 0)–(3, 2)–(4, 0)–(5, 0)$ in Figure 5.

In Section 20.7, we discuss a more efficient approach that can be used to solve periodic review inventory problems. In Chapter 21, we explain how to use dynamic programming to solve periodic review inventory problems when each period's demand is uncertain.

◆ PROBLEMS

GROUP A

1. In Example 4, determine the optimal production schedule if the initial inventory is 3 units.

2. An electronics firm has a contract to deliver the following number of radios during the next three months: month 1, 200 radios; month 2, 300 radios; month 3, 300

radios. For each radio produced during months 1 and 2, a $10 variable cost is incurred; for each radio produced during month 3, a $12 variable cost is incurred. The inventory cost is $1.50 for each radio in stock at the end of a month. The cost of setting up for production during a month is $250. Radios made during a month may be used to meet demand for that month or any future month. Assume that production during each month must be a multiple of 100. Given that the initial inventory level is zero, use dynamic programming to determine an optimal production schedule.

3. In Figure 5, determine the production level and cost associated with each of the following arcs:
(a) $(2, 3)$–$(3, 1)$
(b) $(4, 2)$–$(5, 0)$

20-4   RESOURCE ALLOCATION PROBLEMS

Resource allocation problems, in which limited resources must be allocated among several activities, are often solved by dynamic programming. Recall that we have solved such problems by linear programming (for instance, the Giapetto problem and many of the Chapter 3 formulation problems). To use linear programming to do resource allocation, three assumptions must be made:

Assumption 1 The amount of a resource assigned to an activity may be any nonnegative number.

Assumption 2 The benefit obtained from each activity is proportional to the amount of the resource assigned to the activity.

Assumption 3 The benefit obtained from more than one activity is the sum of the benefits obtained from the individual activities.

Even if assumptions 1 and 2 do not hold, dynamic programming can be used to solve resource allocation problems efficiently when assumption 3 is valid and when the amount of the resource allocated to each activity is a member of a finite set.

E X A M P L E
5

Finco has $6000 to invest, and three investments are available. If d_j dollars (in thousands) are invested in investment j, then a net present value (in thousands) of $r_j(d_j)$ is obtained, where the $r_j(d_j)$'s are as follows:

$$r_1(d_1) = 7d_1 + 2 \quad (d_1 > 0)$$
$$r_2(d_2) = 3d_2 + 7 \quad (d_2 > 0)$$
$$r_3(d_3) = 4d_3 + 5 \quad (d_3 > 0)$$
$$r_1(0) = r_2(0) = r_3(0) = 0$$

The amount placed in each investment must be an exact multiple of $1000. In order to maximize the net present value obtained from the investments, how should Finco allocate the $6000?

Solution

The return on each investment is not proportional to the amount invested in it (for example, $16 = r_1(2) \neq 2r_1(1) = 18$). Thus, linear programming cannot be used to find an optimal solution to this problem.[†]

Mathematically, Finco's problem may be expressed as

$$\max \{r_1(d_1) + r_2(d_2) + r_3(d_3)\}$$
$$\text{s.t.} \quad d_1 + d_2 + d_3 = 6$$
$$d_j \text{ nonnegative integer } (j = 1, 2, 3)$$

[†]The fixed-charge approach described in Section 9.2 could be used to solve this problem.

Of course, if the $r_j(d_j)$'s were linear, we would have a knapsack problem like those we studied in Section 9.5.

To formulate Finco's problem as a dynamic programming problem, we begin by identifying the stage. As in the inventory and shortest-route examples, the stage should be chosen so that when one stage remains the problem is easy to solve. Then, given that the problem has been solved for the case where one stage remains, it should be easy to solve the problem where two stages remain, etc. Clearly, it would be easy to solve a problem in which only one investment was available, so we define stage t to represent a case where funds must be allocated to investments $t, t + 1, \ldots, 3$.

For a given stage, what must we know to determine the optimal investment amount? Simply how much money is available for investments $t, t + 1, \ldots, 3$. Thus, we define the state at any stage to be the amount of money (in thousands) available for investments $t, t + 1, \ldots, 3$. Since we can never have more than \$6000 available, the possible states at any stage are 0, 1, 2, 3, 4, 5, and 6. We define $f_t(d_t)$ to be the maximum net present value (NPV) that can be obtained by investing d_t thousand dollars in investments t, $t + 1, \ldots, 3$. Also define $x_t(d_t)$ to be the amount that should be invested in investment t in order to attain $f_t(d_t)$. We start to work backward by computing $f_3(0)$, $f_3(1)$, $\ldots, f_3(6)$ and then determine $f_2(0), f_2(1), \ldots, f_2(6)$. Since \$6000 is available for investment in investments 1, 2, and 3, we terminate our computations by computing $f_1(6)$. Then we retrace our steps and determine the amount that should be allocated to each investment (just as we retraced our steps to determine the optimal production level for each month in Example 4).

STAGE 3 COMPUTATIONS. We first determine $f_3(0), f_3(1), \ldots, f_3(6)$. We see that $f_3(d_3)$ is attained by investing all available money (d_3) in investment 3. Thus,

$$
\begin{aligned}
f_3(0) &= 0 & x_3(0) &= 0 \\
f_3(1) &= 9 & x_3(1) &= 1 \\
f_3(2) &= 13 & x_3(2) &= 2 \\
f_3(3) &= 17 & x_3(3) &= 3 \\
f_3(4) &= 21 & x_3(4) &= 4 \\
f_3(5) &= 25 & x_3(5) &= 5 \\
f_3(6) &= 29 & x_3(6) &= 6
\end{aligned}
$$

STAGE 2 COMPUTATIONS. To determine $f_2(0), f_2(1), \ldots, f_2(6)$, we look at all possible amounts that can be placed in investment 2. To find $f_2(d_2)$, let x_2 be the amount invested in investment 2. Then an NPV of $r_2(x_2)$ will be obtained from investment 2, and an NPV of $f_3(d_2 - x_2)$ will be obtained from investment 3 (remember the principle of optimality). Since x_2 should be chosen to maximize the net present value earned from investments 2 and 3, we write

$$f_2(d_2) = \max_{x_2} \{r_2(x_2) + f_3(d_2 - x_2)\} \tag{5}$$

where x_2 must be a member of $\{0, 1, \ldots, d_2\}$. The computations for $f_2(0), f_2(1), \ldots, f_2(6)$ and $x_2(0), x_2(1), \ldots, x_2(6)$ are given in Table 6.

Table 6
Computations for $f_2(0)$, $f_2(1), \ldots, f_2(6)$

d_2	x_2	$r_2(x_2)$	$f_3(d_2 - x_2)$	NPV FROM INVESTMENTS 2, 3	$f_2(d_2)$ $x_2(d_2)$
0	0	0	0	0*	$f_2(0) = 0$ $x_2(0) = 0$
1	0	0	9	9	$f_2(1) = 10$
1	1	10	0	10*	$x_2(1) = 1$
2	0	0	13	13	$f_2(2) = 19$
2	1	10	9	19*	$x_2(2) = 1$
2	2	13	0	13	
3	0	0	17	17	$f_2(3) = 23$
3	1	10	13	23*	$x_2(3) = 1$
3	2	13	9	22	
3	3	16	0	16	
4	0	0	21	21	$f_2(4) = 27$
4	1	10	17	27*	$x_2(4) = 1$
4	2	13	13	26	
4	3	16	9	25	
4	4	19	0	19	
5	0	0	25	25	$f_2(5) = 31$
5	1	10	21	31*	$x_2(5) = 1$
5	2	13	17	30	
5	3	16	13	29	
5	4	19	9	28	
5	5	22	0	22	
6	0	0	29	29	$f_2(6) = 35$
6	1	10	25	35*	$x_2(6) = 1$
6	2	13	21	34	
6	3	16	17	33	
6	4	19	13	32	
6	5	22	9	31	
6	6	25	0	25	

STAGE 1 COMPUTATIONS. Following Eq. (5), we write

$$f_1(6) = \max_{x_1} \{r_1(x_1) + f_2(6 - x_1)\}$$

where x_1 must be a member of $\{0, 1, 2, 3, 4, 5, 6\}$. The computations for $f_1(6)$ are given in Table 7.

Table 7
Computations for $f_1(6)$

d_1	x_1	$r_1(x_1)$	$f_2(6 - x_1)$	NPV FROM INVESTMENTS 1–3	$f_1(6)$ $x_1(6)$
6	0	0	35	35	$f_1(6) = 49$
6	1	9	31	40	$x_1(6) = 4$
6	2	16	27	43	
6	3	23	23	46	
6	4	30	19	49*	
6	5	37	10	47	
6	6	44	0	44	

DETERMINATION OF OPTIMAL RESOURCE ALLOCATION. Since $x_1(6) = 4$, Finco invests \$4000 in investment 1. This leaves $6000 - 4000 = \$2000$ for investments 2 and 3. Hence, Finco should invest $x_2(2) = \$1000$ in investment 2. Then \$1000 is left for investment 3, so Finco chooses to invest $x_3(1) = \$1000$ in investment 3. Therefore, Finco can attain a maximum net present value of $f_1(6) = \$49,000$ by investing \$4000 in investment 1, \$1000 in investment 2, and \$1000 in investment 3. ◆

NETWORK REPRESENTATION OF RESOURCE EXAMPLE

As with the inventory example of Section 20.3, Finco's problem has a network representation, equivalent to finding the *longest route* from $(1, 6)$ to $(4, 0)$ in Figure 6. In the figure, the node (t, d) represents the situation in which d thousand dollars is available for investments $t, t + 1, \ldots, 3$. The arc joining the nodes (t, d) and $(t + 1, d - x)$ has a length $r_t(x)$ corresponding to the net present value obtained by investing x thousand dollars in investment t. For example, the arc joining nodes $(2, 4)$ and $(3, 1)$ has a length $r_2(3) = \$16,000$, corresponding to the \$16,000 net present value that can be obtained by investing \$3000 in investment 2. Note that not all pairs of nodes in adjacent stages are joined by arcs. For example, there is no arc joining the nodes $(2, 4)$ and $(3, 5)$; after all, if you have only \$4000 available for investments 2 and 3, how can you have \$5000 available for investment 3? From our computations, we see that the longest path from $(1, 6)$ to $(4, 0)$ is the path $(1, 6)$–$(2, 2)$–$(3, 1)$–$(4, 0)$.

Figure 6
Network
Representation of
Finco Problem

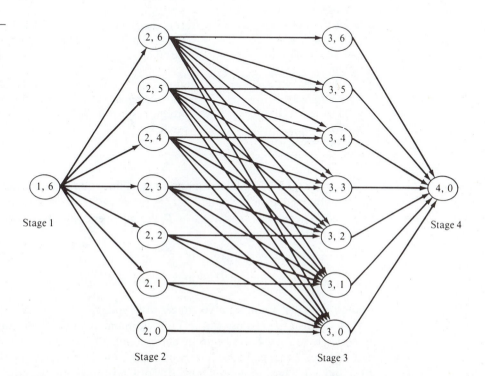

GENERALIZED RESOURCE ALLOCATION PROBLEM

We now consider a generalized version of Example 5. Suppose we have w units of a resource available and T activities to which the resource can be allocated. If activity t is implemented at a level x_t (we assume x_t must be a nonnegative integer), then $g_t(x_t)$ units of the resource are used by activity t, and a benefit $r_t(x_t)$ is obtained. The problem of determining the allocation of resources that maximizes total benefit subject to the limited resource availability may be written as

$$\max \sum_{t=1}^{t=T} r_t(x_t)$$

$$\text{s.t.} \quad \sum_{t=1}^{t=T} g_t(x_t) \leq w \tag{6}$$

where x_t must be a member of $\{0, 1, 2, \ldots\}$. Some possible intepretations of $r_t(x_t)$, $g_t(x_t)$, and w are given in Table 8.

Table 8	INTERPRETATION OF $r_t(x_t)$	INTERPRETATION OF $g_t(x_t)$	INTERPRETATION OF w
Examples of a Generalized Resource Allocation Problem	Benefit from placing x_t type t items in a knapsack	Weight of x_t type t items	Maximum weight that knapsack can hold
	Grade obtained in course t if we study course t for x_t hours per week	No. of hours per week x_t spent studying course t	Total no. of study hours available each week
	Sales of a product in region t if x_t sales reps are assigned to region t	Cost of assigning x_t sales reps to region t	Total sales force budget
	No. of fire alarms per week responded to within 1 minute if precinct t is assigned x_t engines	Cost per week of maintaining x_t fire engines in precinct t	Total weekly budget for maintaining fire engines

To solve (6) by dynamic programming, define $f_t(d)$ to be the maximum benefit that can be obtained from activities $t, t + 1, \ldots, T$ if d units of the resource may be allocated to activities $t, t + 1, \ldots, T$. We may generalize the recursions of Example 5 to this situation by writing

$$f_{T+1}(d) = 0 \quad \text{for all } d$$
$$f_t(d) = \max_{x_t} \{r_t(x_t) + f_{t+1}(d - g_t(x_t))\} \tag{7}$$

where x_t must be a nonnegative integer satisfying $g_t(x_t) \leq d$. Let $x_t(d)$ be any value of x_t that attains $f_t(d)$. To use Eqs. (7) to determine an optimal allocation of resources to activities 1, 2, . . . , T, we begin by determining all $f_T(\cdot)$ and $x_T(\cdot)$. Then we use (7) to determine all $f_{T-1}(\cdot)$ and $x_{T-1}(\cdot)$, continuing to work backward in this fashion until all $f_2(\cdot)$ and $x_2(\cdot)$ have been determined. To wind things up, we now calculate $f_1(w)$ and

$x_1(w)$. Then we implement activity 1 at a level $x_1(w)$. At this point, we have $w - g_1(x_1(w))$ units of the resource available for activities 2, 3, . . . , T. Then activity 2 should be implemented at a level of $x_2[w - g_1(x_1(w))]$. We continue in this fashion until we have determined the level at which all activities should be implemented.

SOLUTION OF KNAPSACK PROBLEMS BY DYNAMIC PROGRAMMING

We illustrate the use of Eqs. (7) by solving a simple knapsack problem (see Section 9.5). Then we develop an alternative recursion that can be used to solve knapsack problems.

E X A M P L E 6

Suppose a 10-lb knapsack is to be filled with the items listed in Table 9. In order to maximize total benefit, how should the knapsack be filled?

Table 9
Weights and Benefits for Knapsack Problem

	WEIGHT	BENEFIT
Item 1	4 lb	11
Item 2	3 lb	7
Item 3	5 lb	12

Solution

We have $r_1(x_1) = 11x_1$, $r_2(x_2) = 7x_2$, $r_3(x_3) = 12x_3$, $g_1(x_1) = 4x_1$, $g_2(x_2) = 3x_2$, and $g_3(x_3) = 5x_3$. Define $f_t(d)$ to be the maximum benefit that can be earned from a d-pound knapsack that is filled with items of type t, $t + 1$, . . . , 3.

STAGE 3 COMPUTATIONS. Now (7) yields

$$f_3(d) = \max_{x_3} \{12x_3\}$$

where $5x_3 \leq d$ and x_3 is a nonnegative integer. This yields

$$f_3(10) = 24$$
$$f_3(5) = f_3(6) = f_3(7) = f_3(8) = f_3(9) = 12$$
$$f_3(0) = f_3(1) = f_3(2) = f_3(3) = f_4(4) = 0$$
$$x_3(10) = 2$$
$$x_3(9) = x_3(8) = x_3(7) = x_3(6) = x_3(5) = 1$$
$$x_3(0) = x_3(1) = x_3(2) = x_3(3) = x_3(4) = 0$$

STAGE 2 COMPUTATIONS. Now (7) yields

$$f_2(d) = \max_{x_2} \{7x_2 + f_3(d - 3x_2)\}$$

where x_2 must be a nonnegative integer satisfying $3x_2 \leq d$. We now obtain

$$f_2(10) = \max \begin{cases} 7(0) + f_3(10) = 24^* & x_2 = 0 \\ 7(1) + f_3(7) = 19 & x_2 = 1 \\ 7(2) + f_3(4) = 14 & x_2 = 2 \\ 7(3) + f_3(1) = 21 & x_2 = 3 \end{cases}$$

Thus, $f_2(10) = 24$ and $x_2(10) = 0$.

$$f_2(9) = \max \begin{cases} 7(0) + f_3(9) = 12 & x_2 = 0 \\ 7(1) + f_3(6) = 19 & x_2 = 1 \\ 7(2) + f_3(3) = 14 & x_2 = 2 \\ 7(3) + f_3(0) = 21^* & x_2 = 3 \end{cases}$$

Thus, $f_2(9) = 21$ and $x_2(9) = 3$.

$$f_2(8) = \max \begin{cases} 7(0) + f_3(8) = 12 & x_2 = 0 \\ 7(1) + f_3(5) = 19^* & x_2 = 1 \\ 7(2) + f_3(2) = 14 & x_2 = 2 \end{cases}$$

Thus, $f_2(8) = 19$ and $x_2(8) = 1$.

$$f_2(7) = \max \begin{cases} 7(0) + f_3(7) = 12 & x_2 = 0 \\ 7(1) + f_3(4) = 7 & x_2 = ! \\ 7(2) + f_3(1) = 14^* & x_2 = 2 \end{cases}$$

Thus, $f_2(7) = 14$ and $x_2(7) = 2$.

$$f_2(6) = \max \begin{cases} 7(0) + f_3(6) = 12 & x_2 = 0 \\ 7(1) + f_3(3) = 7 & x_2 = 1 \\ 7(2) + f_3(0) = 14^* & x_2 = 2 \end{cases}$$

Thus, $f_2(6) = 14$ and $x_2(6) = 2$.

$$f_2(5) = \max \begin{cases} 7(0) + f_3(5) = 12^* & x_2 = 0 \\ 7(1) + f_3(2) = 7 & x_2 = 1 \end{cases}$$

Thus, $f_2(5) = 12$ and $x_2(5) = 0$.

$$f_2(4) = \max \begin{cases} 7(0) + f_3(4) = 0 & x_2 = 0 \\ 7(1) + f_3(1) = 7^* & x_2 = 1 \end{cases}$$

Thus, $f_2(4) = 7$ and $x_2(4) = 1$.

$$f_2(3) = \max \begin{cases} 7(0) + f_3(3) = 0 & x_2 = 0 \\ 7(1) + f_3(0) = 7^* & x_2 = 1 \end{cases}$$

Thus, $f_2(3) = 7$ and $x_2(3) = 1$.

$$f_2(2) = 7(0) + f_3(2) = 0 \quad x_2 = 0$$

Thus, $f_2(0)$ and $x_2(2) = 0$.

$$f_2(1) = 7(0) + f_3(1) = 0 \quad x_2 = 0$$

Thus, $f_2(1) = 0$ and $x_2(1) = 0$.

$$f_2(0) = 7(0) + f_3(0) = 0 \quad x_2 = 0$$

Thus $f_2(0) = 0$ and $x_2(0) = 0$.

STAGE 1 COMPUTATIONS.   Finally, we determine $f_1(10)$ from

$$f_1(10) = \max \begin{cases} 11(0) + f_2(10) = 24 & x_1 = 0 \\ 11(1) + f_2(6) = 25^* & x_1 = 1 \\ 11(2) + f_2(2) = 22 & x_1 = 2 \end{cases}$$

DETERMINATION OF THE OPTIMAL SOLUTION TO KNAPSACK PROBLEM.   We have $f_1(10) = 25$ and $x_1(10) = 1$. Hence, we should include one type 1 item in the knapsack. Then we have $10 - 4 = 6\,\text{lb}$ left for type 2 and type 3 items, so we should include $x_2(6) = 2$ type 2 items. Finally, we have $6 - 2(3) = 0\,\text{lb}$ left for type 3 items, and we include $x_3(0) = 0$ type 3 items. In summary, the maximum benefit that can be gained from a 10-lb knapsack is $f_3(10) = 25$. To obtain a benefit of 25, one type 1 and two type 2 items should be included.

♦

NETWORK REPRESENTATION OF KNAPSACK PROBLEM

Finding the optimal solution to Example 6 is equivalent to finding the longest path in Figure 7 from node $(10, 1)$ to some stage 4 node. In Figure 7, for $t \le 3$, the node (d, t) represents a situation in which d pounds of space may be allocated to items of type t, $t + 1, \dots, 3$. The node $(d, 4)$ represents d pounds of unused space. Each arc from a stage t node to a stage $t + 1$ node represents a decision of how many type t items are placed in the knapsack. For example, the arc from $(10, 1)$ to $(6, 2)$ represents placing one type 1 item in the knapsack. This leaves $10 - 4 = 6\,\text{lb}$ for items of types 2 and 3. This arc has a length of 11, representing the benefit obtained by placing one type 1 item in the knapsack. Our solution to Example 6 shows that the longest path in Figure 7 from node $(10, 1)$ to a stage 4 node is the path $(10, 1)$–$(6, 2)$–$(0, 3)$–$(0, 4)$. We note that the optimal solution to a knapsack problem does not always use all the available weight. For example, the reader should verify that if a type 1 item earned 16 units of benefit, the optimal solution would be to include two type 1 items, corresponding to the path $(10, 1)$–$(2, 2)$–$(2, 3)$–$(2, 4)$. This solution leaves $2\,\text{lb}$ of space unused.

AN ALTERNATIVE RECURSION FOR KNAPSACK PROBLEMS

Other approaches can be used to solve knapsack problems by dynamic programming. The approach we now discuss builds up the optimal knapsack by first determining how to fill a small knapsack optimally and then, using this information, how to fill a larger knapsack optimally. We define $g(w)$ to be the maximum benefit that can be gained from a w-pound knapsack. In what follows, b_j is the benefit earned from a single type j item, and w_j is the weight of a single type j item. Clearly, $g(0) = 0$, and for $w > 0$,

$$g(w) = \max_j \{b_j + g(w - w_j)\} \tag{8}$$

where j must be a member of $\{1, 2, 3\}$, and j must satisfy $w_j \le w$. The reasoning behind Eq. (8) is as follows: To fill a w-pound knapsack optimally, we must begin by putting some type of item into the knapsack. If we begin by putting a type j item into a w-pound knapsack, the best we can do is earn b_j + (best we can do from a $(w - w_j)$-pound knapsack). After noting that a type j item can be placed into a w-pound knapsack only

Figure 7
Network
Representation of
Knapsack Problem

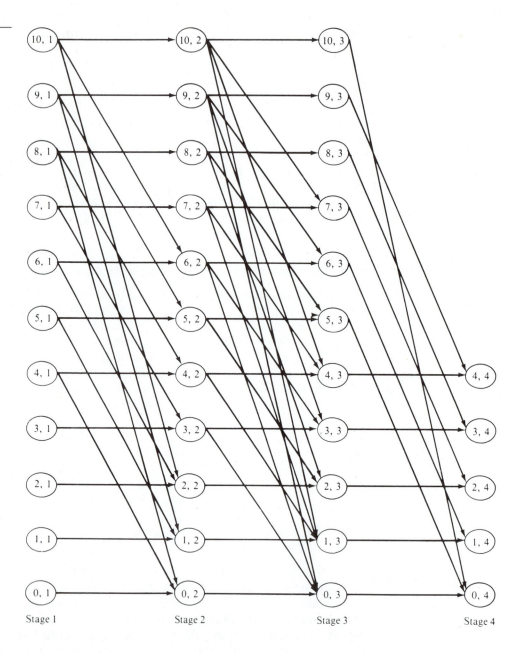

Stage 1   Stage 2   Stage 3   Stage 4

if $w_j \leq w$, we obtain (8). We define $x(w)$ to be any type of item that attains the maximum in (8) and $x(w) = 0$ to mean that no item can fit into a w-pound knapsack.

To illustrate the use of Eq. (8), we re-solve Example 6. Since no item can fit in a 0-, 1-, or 2-lb knapsack, we have $g(0) = g(1) = g(2) = 0$ and $x(0) = x(1) = x(2) = 0$. Since only a type 2 item fits into a 3-lb knapsack, we have that $g(3) = 7$ and $x(3) = 2$. Continuing, we find that

$$g(4) = \max \begin{cases} 11 + g(0) = 11^* & \text{(Type 1 item)} \\ 7 + g(1) = 7 & \text{(Type 2 item)} \end{cases}$$

Thus, $g(4) = 11$ and $x(4) = 1$.

$$g(5) = \max \begin{cases} 11 + g(1) = 11 & \text{(Type 1 item)} \\ 7 + g(2) = 7 & \text{(Type 2 item)} \\ 12 + g(0) = 12^* & \text{(Type 3 item)} \end{cases}$$

Thus, $g(5) = 12$ and $x(5) = 3$.

$$g(6) = \max \begin{cases} 11 + g(2) = 11 & \text{(Type 1 item)} \\ 7 + g(3) = 14^* & \text{(Type 2 item)} \\ 12 + g(1) = 12 & \text{(Type 3 item)} \end{cases}$$

Thus, $g(6) = 14$ and $x(6) = 2$.

$$g(7) = \max \begin{cases} 11 + g(3) = 18^* & \text{(Type 1 item)} \\ 7 + g(4) = 18^* & \text{(Type 2 item)} \\ 12 + g(2) = 12 & \text{(Type 3 item)} \end{cases}$$

Thus, $g(7) = 18$ and $x(7) = 1$ or $x(7) = 2$.

$$g(8) = \max \begin{cases} 11 + g(4) = 22^* & \text{(Type 1 item)} \\ 7 + g(5) = 19 & \text{(Type 2 item)} \\ 12 + g(3) = 19 & \text{(Type 3 item)} \end{cases}$$

Thus, $g(8) = 22$ and $x(8) = 1$.

$$g(9) = \max \begin{cases} 11 + g(5) = 23^* & \text{(Type 1 item)} \\ 7 + g(6) = 21 & \text{(Type 2 item)} \\ 12 + g(4) = 23^* & \text{(Type 3 item)} \end{cases}$$

Thus, $g(9) = 23$ and $x(9) = 1$ or $x(9) = 3$.

$$g(10) = \max \begin{cases} 11 + g(6) = 25^* & \text{(Type 1 item)} \\ 7 + g(7) = 25^* & \text{(Type 2 item)} \\ 12 + g(5) = 24 & \text{(Type 3 item)} \end{cases}$$

Thus, $g(10) = 25$ and $x(10) = 1$ or $x(10) = 2$. To fill the knapsack optimally, we begin by putting any $x(10)$ item in the knapsack. Let's arbitrarily choose a type 1 item. This leaves us with $10 - 4 = 6\,\text{lb}$ to fill, so we now put an $x(10 - 4) = 2$ (type 2) item in the knapsack. This leaves us with $6 - 3 = 3\,\text{lb}$ to fill, which we do with an $x(6 - 3) = 2$ (type 2) item. Hence, we may attain the maximum benefit of $g(10) = 25$ by filling the knapsack with two type 2 items and one type 1 item.

A TURNPIKE THEOREM

For a knapsack problem, let

$$c_j = \text{benefit obtained from each type } j \text{ item}$$
$$w_j = \text{weight of each type } j \text{ item}$$

In terms of benefit per unit weight, the best item is the item with the largest value of $\frac{c_j}{w_j}$. Assume there are n types of items that have been ordered, so that

$$\frac{c_1}{w_1} \geq \frac{c_2}{w_2} \geq \cdots \geq \frac{c_n}{w_n}$$

Thus, type 1 items are the best, type 2 items are the second best, and so on. Recall from Section 9.5 that it is possible for the optimal solution to a knapsack problem to use none of the best item. For example, the optimal solution to the knapsack problem

$$\max z = 16x_1 + 22x_2 + 12x_3 + 8x_4$$
$$\text{s.t.} \quad 5x_1 + 7x_2 + 5x_3 + 4x_4 \leq 14$$
$$x_i \text{ nonnegative integer}$$

is $z = 44$, $x_2 = 2$, $x_1 = x_3 = x_4 = 0$, and this solution does not use any of the best (type 1) item. Assume that

$$\frac{c_1}{w_1} > \frac{c_2}{w_2}$$

Thus, there is a unique best item type. It can be shown that for some number w^*, it is optimal to use at least one type 1 item if the knapsack is allowed to hold w pounds, where $w \geq w^*$. In Problem 6 at the end of this section, you will show that this result holds for

$$w^* = \frac{c_1 w_1}{c_1 - w_1 \left(\dfrac{c_2}{w_2}\right)}$$

Thus, for the knapsack problem

$$\max z = 16x_1 + 22x_2 + 12x_3 + 8x_4$$
$$\text{s.t.} \quad 5x_1 + 7x_2 + 5x_3 + 4x_4 \leq w$$
$$x_i \text{ nonnegative integer}$$

at least one type 1 item will be used if

$$w \geq \frac{16(5)}{16 - 5(\frac{22}{7})} = 280$$

This result can greatly reduce the computation needed to solve a knapsack problem. For example, suppose that $w = 4000$. Since we know that for $w \geq 280$, the optimal solution will use at least one type 1 item, we can conclude that the optimal way to fill a 4000-lb knapsack will consist of one type 1 item plus the optimal way to fill a knapsack of $4000 - 5 = 3995$ lb. Repeating this reasoning shows that the optimal way to fill a 4000-lb knapsack will consist of $\frac{4000 - 280}{5} = 744$ type 1 items plus the optimal way to fill a knapsack of 280 lb. This reasoning substantially reduces the computation needed to determine how to fill a 4000-lb knapsack. (Actually, the 280-lb knapsack will use at least one type 1 item, so we know that to fill a 4000-lb knapsack optimally, we can use 745 type 1 items and then optimally fill a 275-lb knapsack.)

Why is this result referred to as a **turnpike theorem**? Think about taking an automobile trip in which our goal is to minimize the time needed to complete the trip. For a long enough trip, it may be advantageous to go slightly out of our way so that most of the trip will be spent on a turnpike, on which we can travel at the greatest speed. For a short trip, it may not be worth our while to go out of our way to get on the turnpike.

Similarly, in a long (large weight) knapsack problem, it is always optimal to use some of the best item, but this may not be the case in a short knapsack problem. Turnpike results abound in the dynamic programming literature (see Morton (1979)).

◆ PROBLEMS

GROUP A

1. J. R. Carrington has $4 million to invest in three oil well sites. The amount of revenue earned from site i ($i = 1, 2, 3$) depends on the amount of money invested in site i (see Table 10). Assuming that the amount invested in a site must be an exact multiple of $1 million, use dynamic programming to determine an investment policy that will maximize the revenue J. R. will earn from his three oil wells.

Table 10

AMOUNT INVESTED (millions)	REVENUE (millions)		
	Site 1	*Site 2*	*Site 3*
$0	$4	$3	$3
$1	$7	$6	$7
$2	$8	$10	$8
$3	$9	$12	$13
$4	$11	$14	$15

2. Use either of the approaches outlined in this section to solve the following knapsack problem:

$$\max z = 5x_1 + 4x_2 + 2x_3$$
$$\text{s.t.} \quad 4x_1 + 3x_2 + 2x_3 \le 8$$
$$x_1, x_2, x_3 \ge 0; \ x_1, x_2, x_3 \text{ integer}$$

3. The knapsack problem of Problem 2 can be viewed as finding the longest route in a particular network.
(a) Draw the network corresponding to the recursion derived from Eqs. (7).
(b) Draw the network corresponding to the recursion derived from Eq. (8).

4. The number of crimes in each of a city's three police precincts depends on the number of patrol cars assigned to each precinct (see Table 11). A total of five patrol cars are available. Use dynamic programming to determine how many patrol cars should be assigned to each precinct.

Table 11

	NO. OF PATROL CARS ASSIGNED TO PRECINCT					
	0	*1*	*2*	*3*	*4*	*5*
Precinct 1	14	10	7	4	1	0
Precinct 2	25	19	16	14	12	11
Precinct 3	20	14	11	8	6	5

5. Use dynamic programming to solve a knapsack problem in which the knapsack can hold up to 13 lb (see Table 12).

Table 12

	WEIGHT	BENEFIT
Item 1	3 lb	12
Item 2	5 lb	25
Item 3	7 lb	50

6. Consider a knapsack problem for which

$$\frac{c_1}{w_1} > \frac{c_2}{w_2}$$

Show that if the knapsack can hold w pounds, and $w \geq w^*$, where

$$w^* = \frac{c_1 w_1}{c_1 - w_1 \left(\dfrac{c_2}{w_2} \right)}$$

then the optimal solution to the knapsack problem must use at least one type 1 item.

20-5   EQUIPMENT REPLACEMENT PROBLEMS

Many companies and customers face the problem of determining how long a machine should be utilized before it should be traded in for a new one. Problems of this type are called **equipment replacement problems** and can often be solved by dynamic programming.

E X A M P L E
7

An auto repair shop always needs to have an engine analyzer available. A new engine analyzer costs $1000. The cost m_i of maintaining an engine analyzer during its ith year of operation is as follows: $m_1 = \$60$, $m_2 = \$80$, $m_3 = \$120$. An analyzer may be kept for 1, 2, or 3 years, and after i years of use ($i = 1, 2, 3$) it may be traded in for a new one. If an i-year-old engine analyzer is traded in, a salvage value s_i is obtained, where $s_1 = \$800$, $s_2 = \$600$, and $s_3 = \$500$. Given that a new machine must be purchased at the present time (time 0; see Figure 8), the shop wishes to determine a replacement and trade-in policy that minimizes net costs = (maintenance costs) + (replacement costs) − (salvage value received) during the next 5 years.

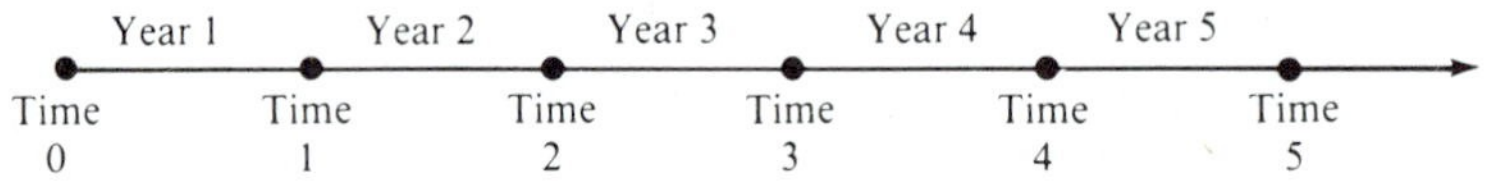

Figure 8
Time Horizon for
Equipment
Replacement
Problem

Year 1	Year 2	Year 3	Year 4	Year 5
Time 0	Time 1	Time 2	Time 3	Time 4	Time 5

Solution

We note that after a new machine is purchased, the firm must decide when the newly purchased machine should be traded in for a new one. With this in mind, we define $g(t)$ to be the minimum net cost incurred from time t until time 5 (including the purchase cost and salvage value for the newly purchased machine) given that a new machine has been purchased at time t. We also define c_{tx} to be the net cost (including purchase cost and salvage value) of purchasing a machine at time t and operating it until time x. Then the appropriate recursion is

$$g(t) = \min_{x} \{c_{tx} + g(x)\} \quad (t = 0, 1, 2, 3, 4) \tag{9}$$

where x must satisfy the inequalities $t + 1 \leq x \leq t + 3$ and $x \leq 5$. Since the problem is over at time 5, no cost is incurred from time 5 onward, so we may write $g(5) = 0$.

To justify (9), note that after a new machine is purchased at time t, we must decide when to replace the machine. Let x be the time at which the replacement occurs. The replacement must be after time t but within 3 years of time t. This explains the restriction that $t + 1 \leq x \leq t + 3$. Since the problem ends at time 5, we must also have $x \leq 5$.

If we choose to replace the machine at time x, what will be the cost from time t to time 5? Simply the sum of the cost incurred from the purchase of the machine to the sale of the machine at time x (which is by definition c_{tx}) and the total cost incurred from time x to time 5 (given that a new machine has just been purchased at time x). By the principle of optimality, the latter cost is, of course, $g(x)$. Hence, if we keep the machine that was purchased at time t until time x, then from time t to time 5, we incur a cost of $c_{tx} + g(x)$. Thus, x should be chosen to minimize this sum, and this is exactly what Eq. (9) does. Since we have assumed that maintenance costs, salvage value, and purchase price remain unchanged over time, each c_{tx} will depend only on how long the machine is kept; that is, each c_{tx} depends only on $x - t$. More specifically,

$$c_{tx} = \$1000 + m_1 + \cdots + m_{x-t} - s_{x-t}$$

This yields

$$c_{01} = c_{12} = c_{23} = c_{34} = c_{45} = 1000 + 60 - 800 = \$260$$
$$c_{02} = c_{13} = c_{24} = c_{35} = 1000 + 60 + 80 - 600 = \$540$$
$$c_{03} = c_{14} = c_{25} = 1000 + 60 + 80 + 120 - 500 = \$760$$

We begin by computing $g(4)$ and work backward until we have computed $g(0)$. Then we use our knowledge of the values of x attaining $g(0), g(1), g(2), g(3)$, and $g(4)$ to determine the optimal replacement strategy. The calculations follow.

At time 4, there is only one sensible decision (keep the machine until time 5 and sell it for its salvage value), so we find

$$g(4) = c_{45} + g(5) = 260 + 0 = \$260*$$

Thus, if a new machine is purchased at time 4, it should be traded in at time 5.

If a new machine is purchased at time 3, we keep it until time 4 or time 5. Hence,

$$g(3) = \min \begin{cases} c_{34} + g(4) = 260 + 260 = \$520* & \text{(Trade at time 4)} \\ c_{35} + g(5) = 540 + 0 = \$540 & \text{(Trade at time 5)} \end{cases}$$

Thus, if a new machine is purchased at time 3, we should trade it in at time 4.

If a new machine is purchased at time 2, we trade it in at time 3, time 4, or time 5. This yields

$$g(2) = \min \begin{cases} c_{23} + g(3) = 260 + 520 = \$780 & \text{(Trade at time 3)} \\ c_{24} + g(4) = 540 + 260 = \$800 & \text{(Trade at time 4)} \\ c_{25} + g(5) = \$760* & \text{(Trade at time 5)} \end{cases}$$

Thus, if we purchase a new machine at time 2, we should keep it until time 5 and then trade it in.

If a new machine is purchased at time 1, we trade it in at time 2, time 3, or time 4. Then

$$g(1) = \min \begin{cases} c_{12} + g(2) = 260 + 760 = \$1020* & \text{(Trade at time 2)} \\ c_{13} + g(3) = 540 + 520 = \$1060 & \text{(Trade at time 3)} \\ c_{14} + g(4) = 760 + 260 = \$1020* & \text{(Trade at time 4)} \end{cases}$$

Thus, if a new machine is purchased at time 1, it should be traded in at time 2 or time 4.

The new machine that was purchased at time 0 may be traded in at time 1, time 2, or time 3. Thus,

$$g(0) = \min \begin{cases} c_{01} + g(1) = 260 + 1020 = \$1280^* & \text{(Trade at time 1)} \\ c_{02} + g(2) = 540 + 760 = \$1300 & \text{(Trade at time 2)} \\ c_{03} + g(3) = 760 + 520 = \$1280^* & \text{(Trade at time 3)} \end{cases}$$

Thus, the new machine purchased at time 0 should be replaced at time 1 or time 3. Let's arbitrarily choose to replace the time 0 machine at time 1. Then the new time 1 machine may be traded in at time 2 or time 4. Again we make an arbitrary choice and replace the time 1 machine at time 2. Then the time 2 machine should be kept until time 5, when it is sold for salvage value. With this replacement policy, we will incur a net cost of $g(0) = \$1280$. The reader should verify that the following replacement policies are also optimal: (1) trading in at times 1, 4, and 5 and (2) trading in at times 3, 4, and 5.

We have assumed that all costs remain stationary over time. This assumption was made solely to simplify the computation of the c_{tx}'s. If we had relaxed the assumption of stationary costs, the only complication would have been that the c_{tx}'s would have been messier to compute. We also note that if a short planning horizon is used, the optimal replacement policy may be extremely sensitive to the length of the planning horizon. Thus, more meaningful results can be obtained by using a longer planning horizon. ◆

An equipment replacement model was actually used by Phillips Petroleum to reduce costs associated with maintaining the company's stock of trucks (see Waddell (1983)).

NETWORK REPRESENTATION OF EQUIPMENT REPLACEMENT PROBLEM

The reader should verify that our solution to Example 7 was equivalent to finding the shortest path from node 0 to node 5 in the network in Figure 9. The length of the arc joining nodes i and j is c_{ij}.

Figure 9
Network Representation of Equipment Replacement Problem

Time
0   1   2   3   4   5

AN ALTERNATIVE RECURSION

There is another dynamic-programming formulation of the equipment replacement model. If we define the stage to be the time t and the state at any stage to be the age of the engine analyzer at time t, then an alternative dynamic-programming recursion can be developed. Define $f_t(x)$ to be the minimum cost incurred from time t to time 5, given that at time t the shop has an x-year-old analyzer. Since the problem is over at time 5, we sell the machine at time 5 and receive $-s_x$. Then $f_5(x) = -s_x$, and for $t = 0, 1, 2, 3, 4,$

$$f_t(3) = -500 + 1000 + 60 + f_{t+1}(1) \qquad \text{(Trade)} \qquad \textbf{(10)}$$

$$f_t(2) = \min \begin{cases} -600 + 1000 + 60 + f_{t+1}(1) & \text{(Trade)} \\ 120 + f_{t+1}(3) & \text{(Keep)} \end{cases} \qquad \textbf{(10.1)}$$

$$f_t(1) = \min \begin{cases} -800 + 1000 + 60 + f_{t+1}(1) & \text{(Trade)} \\ 80 + f_{t+1}(2) & \text{(Keep)} \end{cases} \qquad \textbf{(10.2)}$$

$$f_0(0) = 1000 + 60 + f_1(1) \qquad \text{(Keep)} \qquad \textbf{(10.3)}$$

The rationale behind Eqs. (10)–(10.3) is that if we have a 1- or 2-year-old analyzer, we must decide between replacing the machine or keeping it another year. In (10.1) and (10.2), we compare the costs of these two options. For any option, the total cost from t until time 5 is the sum of the cost during the current year plus costs from time $t + 1$ to time 5. If we have a 3-year-old analyzer, we must replace it, so there is no choice. The way we have defined the state means that it is only possible to be in state 0 at time 0. In this case, we must keep the analyzer for the first year (incurring a cost of $1060). From this point on, a total cost of $f_1(1)$ is incurred. Thus, (10.3) follows. Since we know that $f_5(1) = -800, f_5(2) = -600$, and $f_5(3) = -500$, we can immediately compute all the $f_4(\cdot)$'s. Then we can compute the $f_3(\cdot)$'s. We continue in this fashion until $f_0(0)$ is determined (remember that we begin with a new machine). Then we follow our usual method for determining an optimal policy. That is, if $f_0(0)$ is attained by keeping the machine, we keep the machine for a year and then, during year 1, we choose the action that attains $f_1(1)$. Continuing in this fashion, we can determine for each time whether or not the machine should be replaced. (See Problem 1 at the end of this section.)

◆ PROBLEMS

GROUP A

1. Use Eqs. (10)–(10.3) to determine an optimal replacement policy for the engine analyzer example.

2. Suppose that a new car costs $10,000 and that the annual operating cost and resale value of the car are as shown in Table 13. If I have a new car now, determine a replacement policy that minimizes the net cost of owning and operating a car for the next six years.

3. It costs $40 to buy a telephone from a department store. The estimated maintenance cost for each year of operation is shown in Table 14. (I can keep a telephone for at most five years.) I have just purchased a new telephone, and my old telephone has no salvage value. Determine how to minimize the total cost of purchasing and operating a telephone for the next six years.

Table 13

AGE OF CAR (Years)	RESALE VALUE	OPERATING COST	
1	$7000	$300	(year 1)
2	$6000	$500	(year 2)
3	$4000	$800	(year 3)
4	$3000	$1200	(year 4)
5	$2000	$1600	(year 5)
6	$1000	$2200	(year 6)

Table 14

YEAR	MAINTENANCE COST
1	$20
2	$30
3	$40
4	$60
5	$70

FORMULATING DYNAMIC PROGRAMMING RECURSIONS

In many dynamic programming problems (such as the inventory and shortest path examples), a given stage simply consists of all the possible states that the system can occupy at that stage. If this is the case, the dynamic programming recursion (for a min problem) can often be written in the following form:

$$f_t(i) = \min \{(\text{cost during stage } t) + f_{t+1} (\text{new state at stage } t + 1)\} \qquad (11)$$

where the minimum in (11) is over all decisions that are allowable, or feasible, when the state at stage t is i. In (11), $f_t(i)$ is the minimum cost incurred from stage t to the end of the problem (say, the problem ends after stage T), given that at stage t the state is i.

Eq. (11) reflects the fact that the minimum cost incurred from stage t to the end of the problem must be attained by choosing at stage t an allowable decision that minimizes the sum of the costs incurred during the current stage (stage t) plus the minimum cost that can be incurred from stage $t + 1$ to the end of the problem. Correct formulation of a recursion of the form (11) requires that we identify three important aspects of the problem:

Aspect 1 *The set of decisions that is allowable, or feasible, for the given state and stage.* Often, the set of feasible decisions depends on both t and i. For instance, in the inventory example of Section 20.3, let

$$d_t = \text{demand during month } t$$

$$i_t = \text{inventory at beginning of month } t$$

In this case, the set of allowable month t decisions (let x_t represent an allowable production level) consists of the members of $\{0, 1, 2, 3, 4, 5\}$ that satisfy $0 \leq (i_t + x_t - d_t) \leq 4$. Note how the set of allowable decisions at time t depends on the stage t and the state at time t, which is i_t.

Aspect 2 *We must specify how the cost during the current time period (stage t) depends on the value of t, the current state, and the decision chosen at stage t.* For instance, in the inventory example of Section 20.3, suppose a production level x_t is chosen during month t. Then the cost during month t is given by $c(x_t) + (\frac{1}{2})(i_t + x_t - d_t)$.

Aspect 3 *We must specify how the state at stage $t + 1$ depends on the value of t, the state at stage t, and the decision chosen at stage t.* Again referring to the inventory example, the month $t + 1$ state is $i_t + x_t - d_t$.

If one has properly identified the state, stage, and decision, then aspects 1–3 shouldn't be too hard to handle. A word of caution, however: Not all recursions are of the form (11). For instance, our first equipment replacement recursion skipped over time $t + 1$. This often occurs when the stage alone supplies sufficient information to make an optimal decision. We now work through several examples that illustrate the art of formulating dynamic programming recursions.

E X A M P L E
8

The owner of a lake must decide how many bass to catch and sell each year. If she sells x bass during year t, a revenue $r(x)$ is earned. The cost of catching x bass during a year is a function $c(x, b)$ of the number of bass caught during the year and of b, the number of bass in the lake at the beginning of the year. Of course, bass do reproduce. To model this, we assume that the number of bass in the lake at the beginning of a year is 20% more than the number of bass left in the lake at the end of the previous year. Assume that there are 10,000 bass in the lake at the beginning of the first year. Develop a dynamic programming recursion that can be used to maximize the owner's net profits over a T-year horizon.

Solution　　In problems where decisions must be made at several points in time, there is often a tradeoff of current benefits against future benefits. For example, we could catch many bass early in the problem, but then the lake would be depleted in later years, and there would be very few bass to catch. On the other hand, if we catch very few bass now, we won't make much money early, but we can make a lot of money near the end of the horizon. In intertemporal optimization problems, dynamic programming is often used to analyze these complex tradeoffs.

At the beginning of year T, the owner of the lake need not worry about the effect that the capture of bass will have on the future population of the lake. (At time T, there is no future!) So at the beginning of year T, the problem is relatively easy to solve. For this reason, we let time be the stage. At each stage, the owner of the lake must decide how many bass to catch. We define x_t to be the number of bass caught during year t. To determine an optimal value of x_t, the owner of the lake need only know the number of bass (call it b_t) in the lake at the beginning of year t. Therefore, the state at the beginning of year t is b_t.

We define $f_t(b_t)$ to be the maximum net profit that can be earned from bass caught during years $t, t + 1, \ldots, T$ given that b_t bass are in the lake at the beginning of year t. We may now dispose of aspects 1–3 of the recursion.

Aspect 1 What are the allowable decisions? During any year, we can't catch more bass than there are in the lake. Thus, in each state and for all t, $0 \leq x_t \leq b_t$ must hold.

Aspect 2 What is the net profit earned during year t? If x_t bass are caught during a year that begins with b_t bass in the lake, the net profit is $r(x_t) - c(x_t, b_t)$.

Aspect 3 What will be the state during year $t + 1$? At the end of year t, there will be $b_t - x_t$ bass in the lake. By the beginning of year $t + 1$, these bass will have multiplied by 20%. This implies that at the beginning of year $t + 1$, $1.2(b_t - x_t)$ bass will be in the lake. Thus, the year $t + 1$ state will be $1.2(b_t - x_t)$.

We can now use (11) to develop the appropriate recursion. After year T, there are no future profits to consider, so

$$f_T(b_T) = \max_{x_T} \{r_T(x_T) - c(x_T, b_T)\}$$

where $0 \leq x_T \leq b_T$. Applying (11), we obtain

$$f_t(b_t) = \max \{r(x_t) - c(x_t, b_t) + f_{t+1}(1.2(b_t - x_t))\} \tag{12}$$

where $0 \leq x_t \leq b_t$. To begin the computations, we first determine $f_T(b_T)$ for all values of b_T that might occur. (b_T could be up to $10,000(1.2)^{T-1}$. Why?) Then we use (12) to work backward until $f_1(10,000)$ has been computed. Then, to determine an optimal fishing policy, we begin by choosing x_1 to be any value attaining the maximum in the (12) equation for $f_1(10,000)$. Then year 2 will begin with $1.2(10,000 - x_1)$ bass in the lake.

This means that x_2 should be chosen to be any value attaining the maximum in the (12) equation for $f_2(1.2(10{,}000 - x_1))$. Continue in this fashion until the optimal values of $x_3, x_4, \ldots, x_T$ have been determined.

◆

INCORPORATING THE TIME VALUE OF MONEY
INTO DYNAMIC PROGRAMMING FORMULATIONS

A weakness of the present formulation is that profits received during later years are weighted the same as profits received during earlier years. As mentioned in the Chapter 3 discussion of discounting, later profits should be weighted less than earlier profits. Suppose that for some $\beta < 1$, \$1 received at the beginning of year $t + 1$ is equivalent to β dollars received at the beginning of year t. We can incorporate this idea into the dynamic programming recursion by replacing (12) with

$$f_t(b_t) = \max_{x_t} \{r(x_t) - c(x_t, b_t) + \beta f_{t+1}(1.2(b_t - x_t))\} \tag{12'}$$

where $0 \leq x_t \leq b_t$. Then we redefine $f_t(b_t)$ to be the maximum net profit (*in year t dollars*) that can be earned during years $t, t + 1, \ldots, T$. Since f_{t+1} is measured in year $t + 1$ dollars, multiplying it by β converts $f_{t+1}(\cdot)$ to year t dollars, which is just what we want. In Example 8, once we have worked backward and determined $f_1(10{,}000)$, an optimal fishing policy is found by using the same method that was previously described. This approach can be used to account for the time value of money in any dynamic-programming formulation.

E X A M P L E
9

An electric power utility forecasts that r_t kilowatt-hours (kwh) of generating capacity will be needed during year t (the present year is year 1). Each year, the utility must decide by how much generating capacity should be expanded. It costs $c_t(x)$ dollars to increase generating capacity by x kwh during year t. Since it may be desirable to reduce capacity, x need not be nonnegative. During each year, 10% of the old generating capacity becomes obsolete and unusable (capacity does not become obsolete during its first year of operation). It costs the utility $m_t(i)$ dollars to maintain i units of capacity during year t. At the beginning of year 1, 100,000 kwh of generating capacity are available. Formulate a dynamic-programming recursion that will enable the utility to minimize the total cost of meeting power requirements for the next T years.

Solution

Again, we let time be the stage. At the beginning of year t, the utility must determine the amount of capacity (call it x_t) to add during year t. To choose x_t properly, all the utility needs to know is the amount of available capacity at the beginning of year t (call it i_t). Hence, we define the state at the beginning of year t to be the current capacity level. We may now dispose of aspects 1–3 of the formulation.

> **Aspect 1** What values of x_t are feasible? In order to meet year t's requirement of r_t, we must have $i_t + x_t \geq r_t$, or $x_t \geq r_t - i_t$. So the feasible x_t's are those values of x_t satisfying $x_t \geq r_t - i_t$.

> **Aspect 2** What cost is incurred during year t? If x_t kwh are added during a year that begins with i_t kwh of available capacity, then during year t, a cost $c_t(x_t) + m_t(i_t + x_t)$ is incurred.

Aspect 3 What will be the state at the beginning of year $t + 1$? At the beginning of year $t + 1$, the utility will have $0.9i_t$ kwh of old capacity plus the x_t kwh that have been added during year t. Thus, the state at the beginning of year $t + 1$ will be $0.9i_t + x_t$.

We can now use (11) to develop the appropriate recursion. Define $f_t(i_t)$ to be the minimum cost incurred by the utility during years $t, t + 1, \ldots, T$, given that i_t kwh of capacity are available at the beginning of year t. At the beginning of year T, there are no future costs to consider, so

$$f_T(i_T) = \min_{x_T} \{c_T(x_T) + m_T(i_T + x_T)\} \tag{13}$$

where x_T must satisfy $x_T \geq r_T - i_T$. For $t < T$,

$$f_t(i_t) = \min_{x_t} \{c_t(x_t) + m_t(i_t + x_t) + f_{t+1}(0.9i_t + x_t)\} \tag{14}$$

where x_t must satisfy $x_t \geq r_t - i_t$. If the utility does not start with any excess capacity, we can safely assume that the capacity level would never exceed $r_{\text{MAX}} = \max_{t=1,2,\ldots,T} \{r_t\}$. This means that we need consider only states $0, 1, 2, \ldots, r_{\text{MAX}}$. To begin computations, we use (13) to compute $f_T(0), f_T(1), \ldots, f_T(r_{\text{MAX}})$. Then we use (14) to work backward until $f_1(100,000)$ has been determined. To determine the optimal amount of capacity that should be added during each year, proceed as follows. During year 1, add an amount of capacity x_1 that attains the minimum in the (14) equation for $f_1(100,000)$. Then the utility will begin year 2 with $90,000 + x_1$ kwh of capacity. Then, during year 2, x_2 kwh of capacity should be added, where x_2 attains the minimum in the (14) equation for $f_2(90,000 + x_1)$. Continue in this fashion until the optimal value of x_T has been determined. ♦

E X A M P L E
10

Farmer Jones now possesses $5000 in cash and 1000 bushels of wheat. During month t, the price of wheat is p_t. During each month, he must decide how many bushels of wheat to buy (or sell). There are three restrictions on each month's wheat transactions. (1) During any month, the amount of money spent on wheat cannot exceed the cash on hand at the beginning of the month. (2) During any month, he cannot sell more wheat than he has at the beginning of the month. (3) Because of limited warehouse capacity, the ending inventory of wheat for each month cannot exceed 1000 bushels.

Show how dynamic programming can be used to maximize the amount of cash that farmer Jones has on hand at the end of six months.

Solution

Again, we let time be the stage. At the beginning of month t (the present is the beginning of month 1), farmer Jones must decide by how much to change the amount of wheat on hand. We define Δw_t to be the change in farmer Jones's wheat position during month t: $\Delta w_t \geq 0$ corresponds to a month t wheat purchase, and $\Delta w_t \leq 0$ corresponds to a month t sale of wheat. To determine an optimal value for Δw_t, we must know two things: the amount of wheat on hand at the beginning of month t (call it w_t) and the cash on hand at the beginning of month t (call this c_t). We define $f_t(c_t, w_t)$ to be the maximum cash that farmer Jones can obtain at the end of month 6, given that farmer Jones has c_t dollars and w_t bushels of wheat at the beginning of month t. We now discuss aspects 1–3 of the formulation.

Aspect 1 What are the allowable decisions? If the state at time t is (c_t, w_t), then restrictions 1–3 restrict Δw_t in the following manner:

$$p_t(\Delta w_t) \leq c_t \quad \text{or} \quad \Delta w_t \leq \frac{c_t}{p_t}$$

ensures that we won't run out of money at the end of month t. The inequality $\Delta w_t \geq -w_t$ ensures that during month t, we will not sell more wheat than we had at the beginning of month t, and $w_t + \Delta w_t \leq 1000$, or $\Delta w_t \leq 1000 - w_t$, ensures that we will end month t with at most 1000 bushels of wheat. Putting these three restrictions together, we see that

$$-w_t \leq \Delta w_t \leq \min \left\{ \frac{c_t}{p_t}, 1000 - w_t \right\}$$

will ensure that restrictions 1–3 are satisfied during month t.

Aspect 2 Since farmer Jones wants to maximize his cash on hand at the end of month 6, no benefit is earned during months 1 through 5. In effect, during months 1–5, we are doing bookkeeping to keep track of farmer Jones's position. Then, during month 6, we turn all of farmer Jones's assets into cash.

Aspect 3 If the current state is (c_t, w_t) and farmer Jones changes his month t wheat position by an amount Δw_t, what will be the new state at the beginning of month $t + 1$? Cash on hand will increase by $-(\Delta w_t)p_t$, and farmer Jones's wheat position will increase by Δw_t. Hence, the month $t + 1$ state will be $(c_t - (\Delta w_t)p_t, w_t + \Delta w_t)$.

We may now use (11) to develop the appropriate recursion. To maximize his cash position at the end of month 6, farmer Jones should convert his month 6 wheat into cash by selling all of it. This means that $\Delta w_6 = -w_6$. This leads to the following relation:

$$f_6(c_6, w_6) = c_6 + w_6 p_6 \tag{15}$$

Using (11), we obtain for $t < 6$

$$f_t(c_t, w_t) = \max_{\Delta w_t} \{ 0 + f_{t+1}(c_t - (\Delta w_t)p_t, w_t + \Delta w_t) \} \tag{16}$$

where Δw_t must satisfy

$$-w_t \leq \Delta w_t \leq \min \left\{ \frac{c_t}{p_t}, 1000 - w_t \right\}$$

We begin our calculations by determining $f_6(c_6, w_6)$ for all states that can possibly occur during month 6. Then we use (16) to work backward until $f_1(5000, 1000)$ has been computed. Next, farmer Jones should choose Δw_1 to attain the maximum value in the (16) equation for $f_1(5000, 1000)$, and a month 2 state of $(5000 - p_1(\Delta w_1), 1000 + \Delta w_1)$ will ensue. Farmer Jones should next choose Δw_2 to attain the maximum value in the (16) equation for $f_2(5000 - p_1(\Delta w_1), 1000 + \Delta w_1)$. We continue in this manner until the optimal value of Δw_6 has been determined. ◆

E X A M P L E
11

Sunco Oil needs to build enough refinery capacity to refine 5000 barrels of oil per day and 10,000 barrels of gasoline per day. Sunco can build refinery capacity at four locations. The cost of building a refinery at site t that has the capacity to refine x barrels of oil per day and y barrels of gasoline per day is $c_t(x, y)$. Use dynamic programming to determine how much capacity should be located at each site.

Solution

If Sunco had only one possible refinery site, the problem would be easy to solve. Then Sunco could solve a problem in which there were two possible refinery sites, and finally, a problem in which there were four refinery sites. For this reason, we let the stage represent the number of available oil sites. At any stage, Sunco must determine how much oil and gas capacity should be built at the given site. To do this, the company must know how much refinery capacity of each type must be built at the available sites. We now define $f_t(o_t, g_t)$ to be the minimum cost of building o_t barrels per day of oil refinery capacity and g_t barrels per day of gasoline refinery capacity at sites $t, t + 1, \ldots, 4$.

To determine $f_4(o_4, g_4)$, note that if only site 4 is available, Sunco must build a refinery at site 4 with o_4 barrels of oil capacity and g_4 barrels of gasoline capacity. This implies that $f_4(o_4, g_4) = c_4(o_4, g_4)$. For $t = 1, 2, 3$, we can determine $f_t(o_t, g_t)$ by noting that if we build a refinery at site t that can refine x_t barrels of oil per day and y_t barrels of gasoline per day, we incur a cost of $c_t(x_t, y_t)$ at site t. Then we will need to build a total oil refinery capacity of $o_t - x_t$ and a gas refinery capacity of $g_t - y_t$ at sites $t + 1$, $t + 2, \ldots, 4$. By the principle of optimality, the cost of doing this will be $f_{t+1}(o_t - x_t, g_t - y_t)$. Since $0 \le x_t \le o_t$ and $0 \le y_t \le g_t$ must hold, we obtain the following recursion:

$$f_t(o_t, g_t) = \min \{c_t(o_t, g_t) + f_{t+1}(o_t - x_t, g_t - y_t)\} \tag{17}$$

where $0 \le x_t \le o_t$ and $0 \le y_t \le g_t$. As usual, we work backward until $f_1(5000, 10,000)$ has been determined. Then Sunco chooses x_1 and y_1 to attain the minimum in the (17) equation for $f_1(5000, 10,000)$. Then Sunco should choose x_2 and y_2 that attain the minimum in the (17) equation for $f_2(5000 - x_1, 10,000 - y_1)$. Sunco continues in this fashion until optimal values of x_4 and y_4 are determined.

◆

**E X A M P L E
12**

The traveling salesperson problem (see Section 9.6) can be solved by using dynamic programming. As an example, we solve the following traveling salesperson problem: It's the last weekend of the 1992 election campaign, and candidate Walter Glenn is in New York City. Before election day, Walter must visit Miami, Dallas, and Chicago and then return to his New York City headquarters. Walter wants to minimize the total distance he must travel. In what order should he visit the cities? The distances in miles between the four cities are given in Table 15.

Table 15
Distances for a
Traveling
Salesperson Problem

	NEW YORK	MIAMI	DALLAS	CHICAGO
City 1 New York	—	1334	1559	809
City 2 Miami	1334	—	1343	1397
City 3 Dallas	1559	1343	—	921
City 4 Chicago	809	1397	921	—

Solution

We know that Walter must visit each city exactly once, the last city he visits must be New York, and his tour originates in New York. When Walter has only one city left to visit, his problem is trivial: simply go from his current location to New York. Then we can work backward to a problem in which he is in some city and has only two cities left to visit, and finally we can find the shortest tour that originates in New York and has four cities left to visit. We therefore let the stage be indexed by the number of cities that Walter has already visited. At any stage, to determine which city should next be visited, we need to know two things: Walter's current location and the cities he has already visited. The state at any stage consists of the last city visited and the set of cities that have already been visited. We define $f_t(i, S)$ to be the minimum distance that must be traveled to complete a tour if the $t - 1$ cities in the set S have been visited and city i was the last city visited. We let c_{ij} be the distance between cities i and j.

STAGE 4 COMPUTATIONS. We note that at stage 4, it must be the case that $S = \{2, 3, 4\}$ (why?), and the only possible states are $(2, \{2, 3, 4\})$, $(3, \{2, 3, 4\})$, and $(4, \{2, 3, 4\})$. In stage 4, we must go from the current location to New York. This observation yields

$$f_4(2, \{2, 3, 4\}) = c_{21} = 1334^* \qquad \text{(Go from city 2 to city 1)}$$
$$f_4(3, \{2, 3, 4\}) = c_{31} = 1559^* \qquad \text{(Go from city 3 to city 1)}$$
$$f_4(4, \{2, 3, 4\}) = c_{41} = 809^* \qquad \text{(Go from city 4 to city 1)}$$

STAGE 3 COMPUTATIONS. Working backward to stage 3, we write

$$f_3(i, S) = \min_{\substack{j \notin S \\ \text{and } j \neq 1}} \{c_{ij} + f_4(j, S \cup \{j\})\} \tag{18}$$

This result follows, because if Walter is now at city i and he travels to city j, he travels a distance c_{ij}. Then he is at stage 4, has last visited city j, and has visited the cities in $S \cup \{j\}$. Hence, the length of the rest of his tour must be $f_4(j, S \cup \{j\})$. In order to use (18), note that at stage 3, Walter must have visited $\{2, 3\}$, $\{2, 4\}$, or $\{3, 4\}$ and must next visit the nonmember of S that is not equal to 1. We can use (18) to determine $f_3(\cdot)$ for all possible states:

$$f_3(2, \{2, 3\}) = c_{24} + f_4(4, \{2, 3, 4\}) = 1397 + 809 = 2206^* \qquad \text{(Go from 2 to 4)}$$
$$f_3(3, \{2, 3\}) = c_{34} + f_4(4, \{2, 3, 4\}) = 921 + 809 = 1730^* \qquad \text{(Go from 3 to 4)}$$
$$f_3(2, \{2, 4\}) = c_{23} + f_4(3, \{2, 3, 4\}) = 1343 + 1559 = 2902^* \qquad \text{(Go from 2 to 3)}$$
$$f_3(4, \{2, 4\}) = c_{43} + f_4(3, \{2, 3, 4\}) = 921 + 1559 = 2480^* \qquad \text{(Go from 4 to 3)}$$
$$f_3(3, \{3, 4\}) = c_{32} + f_4(2, \{2, 3, 4\}) = 1343 + 1334 = 2677^* \qquad \text{(Go from 3 to 2)}$$
$$f_3(4, \{3, 4\}) = c_{42} + f_4(2, \{2, 3, 4\}) = 1397 + 1334 = 2731^* \qquad \text{(Go from 4 to 2)}$$

In general, we write, for $t = 1, 2, 3$,

$$f_t(i, S) = \min_{\substack{j \notin S \\ \text{and } j \neq 1}} \{c_{ij} + f_{t+1}(j, S \cup \{j\})\} \tag{19}$$

This result follows, because if Walter is at present in city i and he next visits city j, he travels a distance c_{ij}. The remainder of his tour will originate from city j, and he will have visited the cities in $S \cup \{j\}$. Hence, the length of the remainder of his tour must be $f_{t+1}(j, S \cup \{j\})$. Eq. (19) now follows.

STAGE 2 COMPUTATIONS. At stage 2, Walter has visited only one city, so the only possible states are $(2, \{2\})$, $(3, \{3\})$, and $(4, \{4\})$. Applying (19), we obtain

$$f_2(2, \{2\}) = \min \begin{cases} c_{23} + f_3(3, \{2,3\}) = 1343 + 1730 = 3073^* \\ \text{(Go from 2 to 3)} \\ c_{24} + f_3(4, \{2,4\}) = 1397 + 2480 = 3877 \\ \text{(Go from 2 to 4)} \end{cases}$$

$$f_2(3, \{3\}) = \min \begin{cases} c_{34} + f_3(4, \{3,4\}) = 921 + 2731 = 3652 \\ \text{(Go from 3 to 4)} \\ c_{32} + f_3(2, \{2,3\}) = 1343 + 2206 = 3549^* \\ \text{(Go from 3 to 2)} \end{cases}$$

$$f_2(4, \{4\}) = \min \begin{cases} c_{42} + f_3(2, \{2,4\}) = 1397 + 2902 = 4299 \\ \text{(Go from 4 to 2)} \\ c_{43} + f_3(3, \{3,4\}) = 921 + 2677 = 3598^* \\ \text{(Go from 4 to 3)} \end{cases}$$

STAGE 1 COMPUTATIONS. Finally, we are back to stage 1 (where no cities have been visited). Since Walter is currently in New York and has visited no cities, the stage 1 state must be $f_1(1, \{\cdot\})$. Applying (19),

$$f_1(1, \{\cdot\}) = \min \begin{cases} c_{12} + f_2(2, \{2\}) = 1334 + 3073 = 4407^* \\ \text{(Go from 1 to 2)} \\ c_{13} + f_2(3, \{3\}) = 1559 + 3549 = 5108 \\ \text{(Go from 1 to 3)} \\ c_{14} + f_2(4, \{4\}) = 809 + 3598 = 4407^* \\ \text{(Go from 1 to 4)} \end{cases}$$

So from city 1 (New York), Walter may go to city 2 (Miami) or city 4 (Chicago). We arbitrarily have him choose to go to city 4. Then he must choose to visit the city that attains $f_2(4, \{4\})$, which requires that he next visit city 3 (Dallas). Then he must visit the city attaining $f_3(3, \{3,4\})$, which requires that he next visit city 2 (Miami). Then Walter must visit the city attaining $f_4(2, \{2,3,4\})$, which means, of course, that he must next visit city 1 (New York). The optimal tour (1–4–3–2–1, or New York–Chicago–Dallas–Miami–New York) is now complete. The length of this tour is $f_1(1, \{\cdot\}) = 4407$. As a check, note that

New York to Chicago distance = 809 miles

Chicago to Dallas distance = 921 miles

Dallas to Miami distance = 1343 miles

Miami to New York distance = 1334 miles

so the total distance that Walter travels is $809 + 921 + 1343 + 1334 = 4407$ miles. Of course, if we had first sent him to city 2, we would have obtained another optimal tour (1–2–3–4–1) that would simply be a reversal of the original optimal tour. ◆

COMPUTATIONAL DIFFICULTIES IN USING DYNAMIC PROGRAMMING

For large traveling salesperson problems, the state space becomes very large, and the branch-and-bound approach outlined in Chapter 9 (along with other branch-and-bound approaches) is much more efficient than the dynamic-programming approach outlined here. For example, for a 30-city problem, suppose we are at stage 16 (this means that 15 cities have been visited). Then it can be shown that there are over 1 billion possible states. This brings up a problem that limits the practical application of dynamic programming. In many problems, *the state space becomes so large that excessive computational time is required to solve the problem by dynamic programming.* For instance, in Example 8, suppose that $T = 20$. It is possible that if no bass were caught during the first 20 years, the lake might contain $10,000(1.2)^{20} = 383,376$ bass at the beginning of year 21. If we view this example as a network in which we need to find the longest route from the node (1, 10,000) (representing year 1 and 10,000 bass in the lake) to some stage 21 node, then stage 21 would have 383,377 nodes. Even a powerful computer would have difficulty solving this problem. Techniques to make problems with large state spaces computationally tractable are discussed in Bersetkas (1976) and Dernardo (1982).

NONADDITIVE RECURSIONS

The last two examples in this section differ from the previous ones in that the recursion does not represent $f_t(i)$ as the sum of the cost (or reward) incurred during the current period and future costs (or rewards) incurred during future periods.

E X A M P L E
13

Joe Cougar needs to drive from city 1 to city 10. He is no longer interested in minimizing the length of his trip, but he is interested in minimizing the maximum altitude above sea level that he will encounter during his drive. To get from city 1 to city 10, he must follow a path in Figure 10. The length c_{ij} of the arc connecting city i and city j represents the maximum altitude (in thousands of feet above sea level) encountered when driving from city i to city j. Use dynamic programming to determine how Joe should proceed from city 1 to city 10.

Figure 10
Joe's Trip (Altitudes Given)

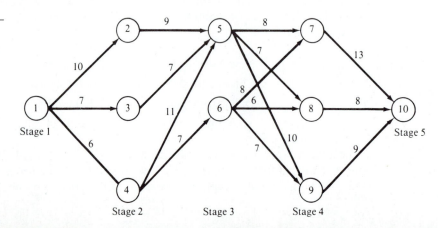

Solution

To solve this problem by dynamic programming, note that for a trip that begins in city i and goes through stages $t, t + 1, \ldots, 5$, the maximum altitude that Joe encounters will be the maximum of the following two quantities: (1) the maximum altitude encountered on stages $t + 1, t + 2, \ldots, 5$ or (2) the altitude encountered when traversing the arc that begins in stage t. Of course, if we are in a stage 4 state, quantity 1 does not exist.

After defining $f_t(i)$ as the smallest maximum altitude that Joe can encounter in a trip from city i in stage t to city 10, this reasoning leads us to the following recursion:

$$f_4(i) = c_{i,10}$$
$$f_t(i) = \min_j \{\max(c_{ij}, f_{t+1}(j))\} \quad (t = 1, 2, 3) \tag{20}$$

where j may be any city such that there is an arc connecting city i and city j.

We first compute $f_4(7), f_4(8),$ and $f_4(9)$ and then use (20) to work backward until $f_1(1)$ has been computed. We obtain the following results:

$$f_4(7) = 13^* \qquad \text{(Go from 7 to 10)}$$
$$f_4(8) = 8^* \qquad \text{(Go from 8 to 10)}$$
$$f_4(9) = 9^* \qquad \text{(Go from 9 to 10)}$$

$$f_3(5) = \min \begin{cases} \max(c_{57}, f_4(7)) = 13 & \text{(Go from 5 to 7)} \\ \max(c_{58}, f_4(8)) = 8^* & \text{(Go from 5 to 8)} \\ \max(c_{59}, f_4(9)) = 10 & \text{(Go from 5 to 9)} \end{cases}$$

$$f_3(6) = \min \begin{cases} \max(c_{67}, f_4(7)) = 13 & \text{(Go from 6 to 7)} \\ \max(c_{68}, f_4(8)) = 8^* & \text{(Go from 6 to 8)} \\ \max(c_{69}, f_4(9)) = 9 & \text{(Go from 6 to 9)} \end{cases}$$

$$f_2(2) = \max(c_{25}, f_3(5)) = 9^* \qquad \text{(Go from 2 to 5)}$$
$$f_2(3) = \max(c_{35}, f_3(5)) = 8^* \qquad \text{(Go from 3 to 5)}$$

$$f_2(4) = \min \begin{cases} \max(c_{45}, f_3(5)) = 11 & \text{(Go from 4 to 5)} \\ \max(c_{46}, f_3(6)) = 8^* & \text{(Go from 4 to 6)} \end{cases}$$

$$f_1(1) = \min \begin{cases} \max(c_{12}, f_2(2)) = 10 & \text{(Go from 1 to 2)} \\ \max(c_{13}, f_2(3)) = 8^* & \text{(Go from 1 to 3)} \\ \max(c_{14}, f_2(4)) = 8^* & \text{(Go from 1 to 4)} \end{cases}$$

To determine the optimal strategy, note that Joe can begin by going from city 1 to city 3 or from city 1 to city 4. Suppose Joe begins by traveling to city 3. Then he should choose the arc attaining $f_2(3)$, which means he should next travel to city 5. Then Joe must choose the arc that attains $f_3(5)$, driving next to city 8. Then, of course, he must drive to city 10. Thus, the path 1–3–5–8–10 is optimal, and Joe will encounter a maximum altitude equal to $f_1(1) = 8000$ ft. The reader should verify that the path 1–4–6–8–10 is also optimal. ◆

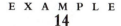

Glueco is planning to introduce a new product in three different regions. Present estimates are that the product will sell well in each region with respective probabilities .6, .5, and .3. The firm has available two top sales representatives that it can send to any of the three regions. The estimated probabilities that the product will sell well in each region when 0, 1, or 2 additional sales reps are sent to a region are given in Table 16. If Glueco wants to maximize the probability that its new product will sell well in all three regions, where should the company assign its sales representatives? You may assume that sales in the three regions are independent.

Table 16 Relation between Regional Sales and Sales Representatives	NO. OF ADDITIONAL SALES REPRESENTATIVES	PROBABILITY OF SELLING WELL		
		Region 1	*Region 2*	*Region 3*
	0	.6	.5	.3
	1	.8	.7	.55
	2	.85	.85	.7

Solution

If Glueco had just one region to worry about and wanted to maximize the probability that the new product would sell well in that region, the proper strategy would be clear: Assign both sales reps to the region. We could then work back and solve a problem in which Glueco's goal is to maximize the probability that the product will sell in two regions. Finally, we could work back and solve a problem with three regions. We define $f_t(s)$ as the probability that the new product will sell well in regions $t, t + 1, \ldots, 3$ if s sales reps are optimally assigned to these regions. Then

$$f_3(2) = .7 \quad \text{(Assign 2 sales reps to region 3)}$$
$$f_3(1) = .55 \quad \text{(Assign 1 sales rep to region 3)}$$
$$f_3(0) = .3 \quad \text{(Assign 0 sales reps to region 3)}$$

Also, $f_1(2)$ will be the maximum probability that the product will sell well in all three regions. To develop a recursion for $f_2(\cdot)$ and $f_1(\cdot)$, we define p_{tx} to be the probability that the new product sells well in region t if x sales reps are assigned to region t. For example, $p_{21} = .7$. For $t = 1$ and $t = 2$, we then write

$$f_t(s) = \max_x \{ p_{tx} f_{t+1}(s - x) \} \tag{21}$$

where x must be a member of $\{0, 1, \ldots, s\}$. To justify (21), observe that if s sales reps are available for regions $t, t + 1, \ldots, 3$ and x sales reps are assigned to region t, then

$$p_{tx} = \text{probability that product sells in region } t$$
$$f_{t+1}(s - x) = \text{probability that product sells well in regions } t + 1, \ldots, 3$$

Note that the sales in each region are independent. This implies that if x sales reps are assigned to region t, then the probability that the new product sells well in regions $t, t + 1, \ldots, 3$ is $p_{tx} f_{t+1}(s - x)$. We want to maximize this probability, so we obtain (21). Applying (21) yields the following results:

$$f_2(2) = \max \begin{cases} (.5)f_3(2 - 0) = .35 \\ \text{(Assign 0 sales reps to region 2)} \\ (.7)f_3(2 - 1) = .385^* \\ \text{(Assign 1 sales rep to region 2)} \\ (.85)f_3(2 - 2) = .255 \\ \text{(Assign 2 sales reps to region 2)} \end{cases}$$

Thus, $f_2(2) = .385$, and 1 sales rep should be assigned to region 2.

$$f_2(1) = \max \begin{cases} (.5)f_3(1 - 0) = .275^* \\ (\text{Assign 0 sales reps to region 2}) \\ (.7)f_3(1 - 1) = .21 \\ (\text{Assign 1 sales rep to region 2}) \end{cases}$$

Thus, $f_2(1) = .275$, and no sales reps should be assigned to region 2.

$$f_2(0) = (.5)f_3(0 - 0) = .15^*$$
$$(\text{Assign 0 sales reps to region 2})$$

Finally, we are back to the original problem, which is to find $f_1(2)$. Eq. (21) yields

$$f_1(2) = \max \begin{cases} (.6)f_2(2 - 0) = .231^* \\ (\text{Assign 0 sales reps to region 1}) \\ (.8)f_2(2 - 1) = .220 \\ (\text{Assign 1 sales rep to region 1}) \\ (.85)f_2(2 - 2) = .1275 \\ (\text{Assign 2 sales reps to region 1}) \end{cases}$$

Thus, $f_1(2) = .231$, and no sales reps should be assigned to region 1. Then Glueco needs to attain $f_2(2 - 0)$, which requires that 1 sales rep be assigned to region 2. Glueco must next attain $f_3(2 - 1)$, which requires that 1 sales rep be assigned to region 3. In summary, Glueco can obtain a .231 probability of the new product selling well in all three regions by assigning 1 sales rep to region 2 and 1 sales rep to region 3.   ◆

◆ PROBLEMS

GROUP A

1. At the beginning of year 1, Sunco Oil owns i_0 barrels of oil reserves. During year t ($t = 1, 2, \ldots, 10$), the following events occur in the order listed: (1) Sunco extracts and refines x barrels of oil reserves and incurs a cost $c(x)$; (2) Sunco sells year t's extracted and refined oil at a price of p_t dollars per barrel; and (3) exploration for new reserves results in a discovery of b_t barrels of new reserves.

Sunco wants to maximize sales revenues less costs over the next ten years. Formulate a dynamic programming recursion that will help Sunco accomplish its goal. If Sunco felt that cash flows in later years should be discounted, how should the formulation be modified?

2. At the beginning of year 1, Julie Ripe has D dollars (this includes year 1 income). During each year, Julie earns i dollars and must determine how much money she should consume and how much she should invest in Treasury bills. During a year in which Julie consumes d dollars, she earns a utility of $\ln d$. Each dollar invested in Treasury bills

yields $1.10 in cash at the beginning of the next year. Julie's goal is to maximize the total utility she earns during the next ten years.

(a) Why might $\ln d$ be a better indicator of Julie's utility than a function like d^2?

(b) Formulate a dynamic programming recursion that will enable Julie to maximize the total utility she receives during the next ten years. Assume that year t revenue is received at the beginning of year t.

3. Assume that during minute t (the present minute is minute 1), the following sequence of events occurs: (1) At the beginning of the minute, x_t customers arrive at the cash register; (2) the store manager decides how many cash registers should be operated during the current minute; (3) if s cash registers are operated and i customers are present (including the current minute's arrivals), $c(s, i)$ customers complete service; and (4) the next minute begins.

A cost of 10¢ is assessed for each minute a customer spends waiting to check out (this time includes checkout time). Assume that it costs $c(s)$ cents to operate s cash registers for 1 minute. Formulate a dynamic programming recursion that minimizes the sum of holding and service costs during the next 60 minutes. Assume that before the first minute's arrivals, no customers are present and that holding cost is assessed at the end of each minute.

4. Develop a dynamic programming formulation of the CSL Computer problem of Section 3.12.

5. In order to graduate from State University, Angie Warner needs to pass at least one of the three subjects she is taking this semester. She is now enrolled in French, German, and statistics. Angie's busy schedule of extracurricular activities allows her to spend only 4 hours per week on studying. Angie's probability of passing each course depends on the number of hours she spends studying for the course (see Table 17). Use dynamic programming to determine how many hours per week Angie should spend studying each subject. (*Hint:* Explain why maximizing the probability of passing at least one course is equivalent to minimizing the probability of failing all three courses.)

Table 17

HOURS OF STUDY PER WEEK	PROBABILITY OF PASSING COURSE		
	French	*German*	*Statistics*
0	.20	.25	.10
1	.30	.30	.30
2	.35	.33	.40
3	.38	.35	.45
4	.40	.38	.50

6. E.T. is about to fly home. For the trip to be successful, the ship's solar relay, warp drive, and candy maker must all function properly. E.T. has found three unemployed actors who are willing to help get the ship ready for takeoff. Table 18 gives, as a function of the number of

Table 18

COMPONENT	NO. OF ACTORS ASSIGNED TO COMPONENT			
	0	*1*	*2*	*3*
Warp drive	.30	.55	.65	.95
Solar relay	.40	.50	.70	.90
Candy maker	.45	.55	.80	.98

actors assigned to repair each component, the probability that each component will function properly during the trip home. Use dynamic programming to help E.T. maximize the probability of having a successful trip home.

7. Farmer Jones is trying to raise a prize steer for the Bloomington 4-H show. At present, the steer weights w_0 pounds. Each week, farmer Jones must determine how much food to feed the steer. If the steer weighs w pounds at the beginning of a week and is fed p pounds of food during a week, then at the beginning of the next week, the steer will weigh $g(w, p)$ pounds. It costs farmer Jones $c(p)$ dollars to feed the steer p pounds of food during a week. At the end of the tenth week (or equivalently, the beginning of the eleventh week), the steer may be sold for $10/lb. Formulate a dynamic programming recursion that can be used to determine how farmer Jones can maximize profit from the steer.

GROUP B

8. MacBurger has just opened a fast food restaurant in Bloomington. At present, i_0 customers frequent MacBurger (we call these loyal customers), and $N - i_0$ customers frequent other fast food establishments (we call these nonloyal customers). At the beginning of each month, MacBurger must decide how much money to spend on advertising. At the end of a month in which MacBurger spends d dollars on advertising, a fraction $p(d)$ of the loyal customers become nonloyal customers, and a fraction $q(d)$ of the nonloyal customers become loyal customers. During the next 12 months, MacBurger wishes to spend D dollars on advertising. Develop a dynamic programming recursion that will enable MacBurger to maximize the number of loyal customers the company will have at the end of month 12. (Ignore the possibility of a fractional number of loyal customers.)

9. Public Service Indiana (PSI) is considering five possible locations to build power plants during the next 20 years. It will cost c_i dollars to build a plant at site i and h_i dollars to operate a site i plant for a year. A plant at site i can supply k_i kilowatt-hours (kwh) of generating capacity. During year t, d_t kwh of generating capacity are required. Suppose that at most one plant can be built during a year, and if it is decided to build a plant at site i during year t, then the site i plant can be used to meet the year t (and later) generating requirements. Initially, PSI has 500,000 kwh of generating capacity available. Formulate a recursion that PSI could use to minimize the sum of building and operating costs during the next 20 years.

10. During month t, a firm faces a demand for d_t units of a product. The firm's production cost during month t

consists of two components. First, for each unit produced during month t, the firm incurs a variable production cost of c_t. Second, if the firm's production level during month $t - 1$ is x_{t-1} and the firm's production level during month t is x_t, then during month t, a smoothing cost of $5|x_t - x_{t-1}|$ will be incurred (see Section 4.12 for an explanation of smoothing costs). At the end of each month, a holding cost of h_t per unit is incurred. Formulate a recursion that will enable the firm to meet (on time) its demands over the next 12 months. Assume that at the beginning of the first month, 20 units are in inventory and that last month's production was 20 units. (*Hint:* The state during each month must consist of two quantities.)

11. The state of Transylvania consists of three cities with the following populations: city 1, 1.2 million people; city 2, 1.4 million people; city 3, 400,000 people. The Transylvania House of Representatives consists of three representatives. Given proportional representation, city 1 should have $d_1 = (\frac{1.2}{3}) = 1.2$ representatives; city 2 should have $d_2 = 1.4$ representatives; and city 3 should have $d_3 = 0.40$ representative. Since each city must receive an integral number of representatives, this is impossible. Transylvania has therefore decided to allocate x_i representatives to city i, where the allocation x_1, x_2, x_3 minimizes the maximum discrepancy between the desired and actual number of representatives received by a city. In short, Transylvania must determine x_1, x_2, and x_3 to minimize the largest of the following three numbers: $|x_1 - d_1|$, $|x_2 - d_2|$, $|x_3 - d_3|$. Use dynamic programming to solve Transylvania's problem.

12. A job shop has four jobs that must be processed on a single machine. The due date and processing time for each job are given in Table 19. Use dynamic programming to determine the order in which the jobs should be done so as to minimize the total lateness of the jobs. (The lateness of a job is simply how long after the job's due date the job is completed; for example, if the jobs are processed in the given order, job 3 will be 2 days late, job 4 will be 4 days late, and jobs 1 and 2 will not be late.)

Table 19

	PROCESSING TIME (Days)	DUE DATE (Days from now)
Job 1	2	4
Job 2	4	14
Job 3	6	10
Job 4	8	16

20-7   THE WAGNER-WHITIN ALGORITHM AND THE SILVER-MEAL HEURISTIC*

The inventory example of Section 20.3 is a special case of the *dynamic lot-size model*.

DESCRIPTION OF DYNAMIC LOT-SIZE MODEL

1. Demand d_t during period t ($t = 1, 2, \ldots, T$) is known at the beginning of period 1.

2. Demand for period t must be met on time from inventory or from period t production. The cost $c(x)$ of producing x units during any period is given by $c(0) = 0$, and for $x > 0$, $c(x) = K + cx$, where K is a fixed cost for setting up production during a period, and c is the variable per-unit cost of production.

3. At the end of period t, the inventory level i_t is observed, and a holding cost hi_t is incurred. We let i_0 denote the inventory level before period 1 production occurs.

4. The goal is to determine a production level x_i for each period t that minimizes the total cost of meeting (on time) the demands for periods 1, 2, . . . , T.

---

*This section covers topics that may be omitted with no loss of continuity.

5. There is a limit c_t placed on period t's ending inventory.

6. There is a limit r_t placed on period t's production.

In this section, we consider the first four points above. We let x_t = period t production. Period t production can be used to meet period t demand.

**E X A M P L E
15**

We now determine an optimal production schedule for a five-period dynamic lot-size model with $K = \$250$, $c = \$2$, $h = \$1$, $d_1 = 220$, $d_2 = 280$, $d_3 = 360$, $d_4 = 140$, and $d_5 = 270$. We assume that the initial inventory level is zero. The solution to this example is given later in this section. ♦

DISCUSSION OF THE WAGNER-WHITIN ALGORITHM

If the dynamic programming approach outlined in Section 20.3 were used to find an optimal production policy for Example 15, we would have to consider the possibility of producing any amount between zero and $d_1 + d_2 + d_3 + d_4 + d_5 = 1270$ units during period 1. Thus, it would be possible for the period 2 state (period 2's entering inventory) to be 0, 1, . . . , $1270 - d_1 = 1050$, and we would have to determine $f_2(0)$, $f_2(1)$, . . . , $f_2(1050)$. Using the dynamic programming approach of Section 20.3 to find an optimal production schedule for Example 15 would therefore require a great deal of computational effort. Fortunately, however, Wagner and Whitin (1958) have developed a method that greatly simplifies the computation of optimal production schedules for dynamic lot-size models. Lemmas 1 and 2 are necessary for the development of the Wagner-Whitin algorithm.

**L E M M A
1**

Suppose it is optimal to produce a positive quantity during period t. Then for some $j = 0, 1, . . . , T - t$, the amount produced during period t must be such that after period t's production, a quantity $d_t + d_{t+1} + \cdots + d_{t+j}$ will be in stock. In other words, if production occurs during period t, we must (for some j) produce an amount that exactly suffices to meet the demands for periods $t, t + 1, . . . , t + j$.

Proof

If the lemma is false, then for some t, some $j = 0, 1, . . . , T - t - 1$, and some x satisfying $0 < x < d_{t+j+1}$, period t production must bring the stock level to $d_t + d_{t+1} + \cdots + d_{t+j} + x$, and at the beginning of period $t + j + 1$, our inventory level would be $x < d_{t+j+1}$. Thus, production must occur during period $t + j + 1$. By deferring production of x units from period t to period $t + j + 1$ (with all other production levels unchanged), we save $h(j + 1)x$ in holding costs while incurring no additional setup costs (because production is already occurring during period $t + j + 1$). Thus, it cannot have been optimal to bring our period t stock level to $d_t + d_{t+1} + \cdots + d_{t+j} + x$. This contradiction proves the lemma. ♦

**L E M M A
2**

If it is optimal to produce anything during period t, then $i_{t-1} < d_t$. In other words, production cannot occur during period t unless there is insufficient stock to meet period t demand.

Proof   If the lemma is false, there must be an optimal policy that (for some t) has $x_t > 0$ and $i_{t-1} \geq d_t$. If this is the case, then by deferring the period t production of x_t units to period $t + 1$, we save hx_t in holding costs and possibly K (if the optimal policy produces during period $t + 1$) in setup costs. Thus, any production schedule having $x_t > 0$ and $i_{t-1} \geq d_t$ cannot be optimal.

♦

Lemma 2 shows that no production will occur until the first period t for which $i_{t-1} < d_t$, so production must occur during period t (or else period t's demand would not be met on time). Lemma 1 now implies that for some $j = 0, 1, \ldots, T - t$, period t production will be such that after period t's production, on-hand stock will equal $d_t + d_{t+1} + \cdots + d_{t+j}$. Then Lemma 2 implies that no production can occur until period $t + j + 1$. Since the entering inventory level for period $t + j + 1$ will equal zero, production must occur during period $t + j + 1$. During period $t + j + 1$, Lemma 1 implies that period $t + j + 1$ production will (for some k) equal $d_{t+j+1} + d_{t+j+2} + \cdots + d_{t+j+k}$ units. Then period $t + j + k + 1$ will begin with zero inventory, and production again occurs, and so on. *With the possible exception of the first period, production will occur only during periods in which beginning inventory is zero, and during each period in which beginning inventory is zero (and $d_t \neq 0$), production must occur.*

Using this insight, Wagner and Whitin developed a recursion that can be used to determine an optimal production policy. We assume that the initial inventory level is zero. (See Problem 1 at the end of this section if this is not the case.) Define f_t as the minimum cost incurred during periods $t, t + 1, \ldots, T$, given that at the beginning of period t, the inventory level is zero. Then $f_1, f_2, \ldots, f_T$ must satisfy

$$f_t = \min_{j = 0, 1, 2, \ldots, T-t} (c_{tj} + f_{t+j+1}) \tag{22}$$

where $f_{T+1} = 0$ and c_{tj} is the total cost incurred during periods $t, t + 1, \ldots, t + j$ if production during period t is exactly sufficient to meet demands for periods t, $t + 1, \ldots, t + j$. Thus,

$$c_{tj} = K + c(d_t + d_{t+1} + \cdots + d_{t+j}) + h[jd_{t+j} + (j - 1)d_{t+j-1} + \cdots + d_{t+1}]$$

where K is the setup cost incurred during period t, $c(d_t + d_{t+1} + \cdots + d_{t+j})$ is the variable production cost incurred during period t, and $h[jd_{t+j} + (j - 1)d_{t+j-1} + \cdots + d_{t+1}]$ is the holding cost incurred during periods $t, t + 1, \ldots, t + j$. For example, an amount d_{t+j} of period t production will be held in inventory for j periods (during periods $t, t + 1, \ldots, t + j - 1$), thereby incurring a holding cost of hjd_{t+j}.

To find an optimal production schedule by the Wagner-Whitin algorithm, begin by using (22) to find f_T. Then use (22) to compute $f_{T-1}, f_{T-2}, \ldots, f_1$. Once f_1 has been determined, an optimal production schedule may be easily obtained.

Solution   **Example 15**   To illustrate the Wagner-Whitin algorithm, we find an optimal production schedule for Example 15. The computations follow.

$$f_6 = 0$$
$$f_5 = 250 + 2(270) + f_6 = 790^* \qquad \text{(Produce for period 5)}$$

If we begin period 5 with zero inventory, we should produce enough during period 5 to meet period 5 demand.

$$f_4 = \min \begin{cases} 250 + 2(140) + f_5 = 1320^* \\ (\text{Produce for period 4}) \\ 250 + 2(140 + 270) + 270 + f_6 = 1340 \\ (\text{Produce for periods } 4, 5) \end{cases}$$

If we begin period 4 with zero inventory, we should produce enough during period 4 to meet the demand for period 4.

$$f_3 = \min \begin{cases} 250 + 2(360) + f_4 = 2290 \\ (\text{Produce for period 3}) \\ 250 + 2(360 + 140) + 140 + f_5 = 2180^* \\ (\text{Produce for periods } 3, 4) \\ 250 + 2(360 + 140 + 270) + 140 + 2(270) + f_6 = 2470 \\ (\text{Produce for periods } 3, 4, 5) \end{cases}$$

If we begin period 3 with zero inventory, we should produce enough during period 3 to meet the demand for periods 3 and 4.

$$f_2 = \min \begin{cases} 250 + 2(280) + f_3 = 2990^* \\ (\text{Produce for period 2}) \\ 250 + 2(280 + 360) + 360 + f_4 = 3210 \\ (\text{Produce for periods } 2, 3) \\ 250 + 2(280 + 360 + 140) + 360 + 2(140) + f_5 = 3240 \\ (\text{Produce for periods } 2, 3, 4) \\ 250 + 2(280 + 360 + 140 + 270) + 360 + 2(140) + 3(270) + f_6 = 3800 \\ (\text{Produce for periods } 2, 3, 4, 5) \end{cases}$$

If we begin period 2 with zero inventory, we should produce enough during period 2 to meet the demand for period 2.

$$f_1 = \min \begin{cases} 250 + 2(220) + f_2 = 3680^* \\ (\text{Produce for period 1}) \\ 250 + 2(220 + 280) + 280 + f_3 = 3710 \\ (\text{Produce for periods } 1, 2) \\ 250 + 2(220 + 280 + 360) + 280 + 2(360) + f_4 = 4290 \\ (\text{Produce for periods } 1, 2, 3) \\ 250 + 2(220 + 280 + 360 + 140) + 280 + 2(360) + 3(140) + f_5 = 4460 \\ (\text{Produce for periods } 1, 2, 3, 4) \\ 250 + 2(220 + 280 + 360 + 140 + 270) + 280 \\ \qquad + 2(360) + 3(140) + 4(270) + f_6 = 5290 \\ (\text{Produce for periods } 1, 2, 3, 4, 5) \end{cases}$$

If we begin period 1 with zero inventory, it is optimal to produce $d_1 = 220$ units during period 1; then we begin period 2 with zero inventory. Since f_2 is attained by producing period 2's demand, we should produce $d_2 = 280$ units during period 2; then we enter period 3 with zero inventory. Since f_3 is attained by meeting the demands for periods 3 and 4, we produce $d_3 + d_4 = 500$ units during period 3; then we enter period 5 with zero inventory and produce $d_5 = 270$ units during period 5. The optimal production schedule will incur at total cost of $f_1 = \$3680$.

◆

For Example 15, any optimal production schedule must produce exactly $d_1 + d_2 + d_3 + d_4 + d_5 = 1270$ units, incurring variable production costs of $2(1270) = \$2540$. Thus, in computing the optimal production schedule, we may always ignore the variable production costs. This substantially simplifies the calculations.

THE SILVER-MEAL HEURISTIC

The Silver-Meal (S-M) heuristic involves less work than the Wagner-Whitin algorithm and can be used to find a near-optimal production schedule. The S-M heuristic is based on the fact that our goal is to minimize average cost per period (for the reasons stated, variable production costs may be ignored). Suppose we are at the beginning of period 1 and are trying to determine how many periods of demand should be satisfied by period 1's production. During period 1, if we produce an amount sufficient to meet demand for the next t periods, then a cost of $TC(t) = K + HC(t)$ will be incurred (ignoring variable production costs). Here, $HC(t)$ is the holding cost incurred during the next t periods (including the current period) if production during the current period is sufficient to meet demand for the next t periods.

Let $AC(t) = \frac{TC(t)}{t}$ be the average per-period cost incurred during the next t periods. Since $\frac{1}{t}$ is a decreasing convex function of t, as t increases, $\frac{K}{t}$ decreases at a decreasing rate. In most cases, $\frac{HC(t)}{t}$ tends to be an increasing function of t (see Problem 4 at the end of this section). Thus, in most situations, an integer t^* can be found such that for $t < t^*$, $AC(t + 1) \leq AC(t)$ and $AC(t^* + 1) \geq AC(t^*)$. The S-M heuristic recommends that period 1's production be sufficient to meet the demands for periods $1, 2, \ldots, t^*$ (if no t^* exists, period 1 production should satisfy the demand for periods $1, 2, \ldots, T$). Since t^* is a local (and perhaps a global) minimum for $AC(t)$, it seems reasonable that producing $d_1 + d_2 + \cdots + d_{t^*}$ units during period 1 will come close to minimizing the average per-period cost incurred during periods $1, 2, \ldots, t^*$. Next we apply the S-M heuristic while considering period $t^* + 1$ as the initial period. We find that during period $t^* + 1$, the demand for the next t_1^* periods should be produced. Continue in this fashion until the demand for period T has been produced.

To illustrate, we apply the S-M heuristic to Example 15. We have

$$TC(1) = 250 \qquad\qquad AC(1) = \frac{250}{1} = 250$$

$$TC(2) = 250 + 280 = 530 \qquad AC(2) = \frac{530}{2} = 265$$

Since $AC(2) \geq AC(1)$, $t^* = 1$, and the S-M heuristic dictates that we produce $d_1 = 220$ units during period 1. Then

$$TC(1) = 250 \qquad\qquad AC(1) = \frac{250}{1} = 250$$

$$TC(2) = 250 + 360 = 610 \qquad AC(2) = \frac{610}{2} = 305$$

Since $AC(2) \geq AC(1)$, the S-M heuristic recommends producing $d_2 = 280$ units during period 2. Then

$$TC(1) = 250 \qquad\qquad AC(1) = \frac{250}{1} = 250$$

$$TC(2) = 250 + 140 = 390 \qquad\qquad AC(2) = \frac{390}{2} = 195$$

$$TC(3) = 250 + 2(270) + 140 = 930 \qquad AC(3) = \frac{930}{3} = 310$$

Since $AC(3) \geq AC(2)$, period 3 production should meet the demand for the next two periods (periods 3 and 4). During period 3, we should produce $d_3 + d_4 = 500$ units. This brings us to period 5. Period 5 is the final period, so $d_5 = 270$ units should be produced during period 5.

For Example 15 (and many other dynamic lot-size problems), the S-M heuristic yields an optimal production schedule. In extensive testing, the S-M heuristic usually yielded a production schedule costing less than 1% above the optimal policy obtained by the Wagner-Whitin algorithm (see Peterson and Silver (1985)).

Other lot-sizing methods are described in Section 18.1.

◆ **PROBLEMS**

GROUP A

1. For Example 15, suppose we had an initial inventory of 200 units. What would be the optimal production schedule? What if the initial inventory were 400 units?

2. Use the Wagner-Whitin and Silver-Meal methods to find production schedules for the following dynamic lot-size problem: $K = \$50$, $h = \$0.40$, $d_1 = 10$, $d_2 = 60$, $d_3 = 20$, $d_4 = 140$, $d_5 = 90$.

3. Use the Wagner-Whitin and Silver-Meal methods to find production schedules for the following dynamic lot-size problem: $K = \$30$, $h = \$1$, $d_1 = 40$, $d_2 = 60$, $d_3 = 10$, $d_4 = 70$, $d_5 = 20$.

GROUP B

4. Explain why $HC(t)/t$ tends to be an increasing function of t.

_____
20-8   **FORWARD RECURSIONS***

For our previous (minimization) examples of dynamic programming, we defined $f_t(i)$ to be the minimum cost incurred during stages $t, t + 1, \ldots, T$ given that the state is i at the beginning of stage t. Then we worked backward: We began by computing all the $f_T(i)$, then the $f_{T-1}(i), \ldots$, and finally $f_1(i_1)$, where i_1 is the initial state. Then we determined the optimal stage 1 decision, the optimal stage 2 decision, and so on, up to the optimal stage T decision.

*This section covers topics that may be omitted with no loss of continuity.

Often, dynamic programming problems can also be solved by working forward. We assume that there is a desired state in which we want the system to be at the end of stage T. To work forward, define $f_t(i)$ as the minimum cost incurred during stages $1, 2, \ldots, t$, given that the state is i at the end of stage t.

We first compute $f_1(i)$ for all possible states that can occur at the end of stage 1. Then we develop a recursion for the $f_2(i)$'s in terms of the $f_1(i)$'s and calculate $f_2(i)$ for all possible ending stage 2 states. We continue in this fashion until f_T (the desired ending stage t state) has been determined. Next, we determine a stage T decision that attains f_T (the desired ending stage T state). Knowledge of the stage T decision enables us to determine the state at the end of stage $T - 1$, and then the stage $T - 1$ decision may be determined. We continue in this fashion until the optimal stage 1 decision has been found.

To illustrate the forward recursion technique, we solve the Section 20.3 inventory example (Example 4). Begin by defining $f_t(i_t)$ as the minimum cost incurred during months $1, 2, \ldots, t$, given that month t's ending inventory is i_t; and $x_t(i_t)$ as a month t production level attaining $f_t(i_t)$. Limited storage capacity requires that ending inventory must equal 0, 1, 2, 3, or 4 units at the end of months 1, 2, and 3. To minimize total cost, month 4's ending inventory must equal zero. (Why?)

Next, we compute $f_1(i_1)$. Since month 1's demand is 1 unit and initial inventory is zero, we will end month 1 with i_1 units if $i_1 + 1$ units are produced during month 1. As in Section 20.3, we let $c(x)$ be the cost of producing x units during a month. Thus, $c(0) = 0$, $c(1) = 4$, $c(2) = 5$, $c(3) = 6$, $c(4) = 7$, and $c(5) = 8$. Since the holding cost is \$0.50/unit/month, we obtain $f_1(i_1) = c(i_1 + 1) + 0.5i_1$. Simple computations yield

$$f_1(0) = c(1) = \$4.00 \qquad\qquad x_1(0) = 1$$
$$f_1(1) = c(2) + 0.5 = \$5.50 \qquad x_1(1) = 2$$
$$f_1(2) = c(3) + 1 = \$7.00 \qquad\quad x_1(2) = 3$$
$$f_1(3) = c(4) + 1.5 = \$8.50 \qquad x_1(3) = 4$$
$$f_1(4) = c(5) + 2 = \$10.00 \qquad\; x_1(4) = 5$$

We must now develop a recursion that can be used to compute the $f_2(\cdot)$'s from the $f_1(\cdot)$'s. If x_2 units are produced during month 2, then to end month 2 with i_2 units, we must have had i_1 units at the end of month 1, where $i_1 + x_2 - 3 = i_2$, or $i_1 = 3 + i_2 - x_2$ (recall that month 2 demand $= 3$ units). Then for a given level of production x_2 during month 2 and a given ending month 2 inventory i_2, the month 2 cost will equal $c(x_2) + 0.5i_2$, and the month 1 cost will be $f_1(3 + i_2 - x_2)$. This yields the following recursion:

$$f_2(i_2) = \min_{x_2}\ (c(x_2) + 0.5i_2 + f_1(3 + i_2 - x_2))$$

where x_2 must satisfy $0 \le x_2 \le 5$ and $4 \ge 3 + i_2 - x_2 \ge 0$. This recursion yields

$$f_2(0) = \min \begin{cases} c(0) + f_1(3) = 0 + 8.5 = \$8.50^* & x_2 = 0 \\ c(1) + f_1(2) = 4 + 7 = \$11.00 & x_2 = 1 \\ c(2) + f_1(1) = 5 + 5.5 = \$10.50 & x_2 = 2 \\ c(3) + f_1(0) = 6 + 4 = \$10.00 & x_2 = 3 \end{cases}$$

Thus, $f_2(0) = \$8.50$ and $x_2(0) = 0$.

$$f_2(1) = \min \begin{cases} c(0) + 0.5 + f_1(4) = 0 + 0.5 + 10 = \$10.50^* & x_2 = 0 \\ c(1) + 0.5 + f_1(3) = 4 + 0.5 + 8.5 = \$13.00 & x_2 = 1 \\ c(2) + 0.5 + f_1(2) = 5 + 0.5 + 7 = \$12.50 & x_2 = 2 \\ c(3) + 0.5 + f_1(1) = 6 + 0.5 + 5.5 = \$12.00 & x_2 = 3 \\ c(4) + 0.5 + f_1(0) = 7 + 0.5 + 4 = \$11.50 & x_2 = 4 \end{cases}$$

Thus, $f_2(1) = \$10.50$ and $x_2(1) = 0$.

$$f_2(2) = \min \begin{cases} c(1) + 1 + f_1(4) = 4 + 1 + 10 = \$15.00 & x_2 = 1 \\ c(2) + 1 + f_1(3) = 5 + 1 + 8.5 = \$14.50 & x_2 = 2 \\ c(3) + 1 + f_1(2) = 6 + 1 + 7 = \$14.00 & x_2 = 3 \\ c(4) + 1 + f_1(1) = 7 + 1 + 5.5 = \$13.50 & x_2 = 4 \\ c(5) + 1 + f_1(0) = 8 + 1 + 4 = \$13.00^* & x_2 = 5 \end{cases}$$

Thus, $f_2(2) = \$13.00$ and $x_2(2) = 5$.

$$f_2(3) = \min \begin{cases} c(2) + 1.5 + f_1(4) = 5 + 1.5 + 10 = \$16.50 & x_2 = 2 \\ c(3) + 1.5 + f_1(3) = 6 + 1.5 + 8.5 = \$16.00 & x_2 = 3 \\ c(4) + 1.5 + f_1(2) = 7 + 1.5 + 7 = \$15.50 & x_2 = 4 \\ c(5) + 1.5 + f_1(1) = 8 + 1.5 + 5.5 = \$15.00^* & x_2 = 5 \end{cases}$$

Thus, $f_2(3) = \$15.00$ and $x_2(3) = 5$.

$$f_2(4) = \min \begin{cases} c(3) + 2 + f_1(4) = 6 + 2 + 10 = \$18.00 & x_2 = 3 \\ c(4) + 2 + f_1(3) = 7 + 2 + 8.5 = \$17.50 & x_2 = 4 \\ c(5) + 2 + f_1(2) = 8 + 2 + 7 = \$17.00^* & x_2 = 5 \end{cases}$$

Thus, $f_2(4) = \$17.00$ and $x_2(4) = 5$.

To determine $f_3(i_3)$ in terms of the $f_2(i_2)$, let x_3 be the month 3 production level. Since month 3's demand is 2 units, $i_3 = i_2 + x_3 - 2$, or $i_2 = i_3 - x_3 + 2$. This implies that if x_3 units are produced during month 3, and month 3 is to end with i_3 units, then month 2 must have ended with $i_3 - x_3 + 2$ units. We obtain the following recursion:

$$f_3(i_3) = \min_{x_3} \{c(x_3) + 0.5i_3 + f_2(i_3 - x_3 + 2)\}$$

where x_3 satisfies $0 \le x_3 \le 5$ and $0 \le i_3 - x_3 + 2 \le 4$. This recursion yields

$$f_3(0) = \min \begin{cases} 0 + f_2(2) = \$13.00^* & x_3 = 0 \\ 4 + f_2(1) = \$14.50 & x_2 = 1 \\ 5 + f_2(0) = \$13.50 & x_2 = 2 \end{cases}$$

Thus, $f_3(0) = \$13.00$ and $x_3(0) = 0$.

$$f_3(1) = \min \begin{cases} 0 + 0.5 + f_2(3) = \$15.50 & x_3 = 0 \\ 4 + 0.5 + f_2(2) = \$17.50 & x_3 = 1 \\ 5 + 0.5 + f_2(1) = \$16.00 & x_3 = 2 \\ 6 + 0.5 + f_2(0) = \$15.00^* & x_3 = 3 \end{cases}$$

Thus, $f_3(1) = \$15.00$ and $x_3(1) = 3$.

$$f_3(2) = \min \begin{cases} 0 + 1 + f_2(4) = \$18.00 & x_3 = 0 \\ 4 + 1 + f_2(3) = \$20.00 & x_3 = 1 \\ 5 + 1 + f_2(2) = \$19.00 & x_3 = 2 \\ 6 + 1 + f_2(1) = \$17.50 & x_3 = 3 \\ 7 + 1 + f_2(0) = \$16.50* & x_3 = 4 \end{cases}$$

Thus, $f_3(2) = \$16.50$ and $x_3(2) = 4$.

$$f_3(3) = \min \begin{cases} 4 + 1.5 + f_2(4) = \$22.50 & x_3 = 1 \\ 5 + 1.5 + f_2(3) = \$21.50 & x_3 = 2 \\ 6 + 1.5 + f_2(2) = \$20.50 & x_3 = 3 \\ 7 + 1.5 + f_2(1) = \$19.00 & x_3 = 4 \\ 8 + 1.5 + f_2(0) = \$18.00* & x_3 = 5 \end{cases}$$

Thus, $f_3(3) = \$18.00$ and $x_3(3) = 5$.

$$f_3(4) = \min \begin{cases} 5 + 2 + f_2(4) = \$24.00 & x_3 = 2 \\ 6 + 2 + f_2(3) = \$23.00 & x_3 = 3 \\ 7 + 2 + f_2(2) = \$22.00 & x_3 = 4 \\ 8 + 2 + f_2(1) = \$20.50* & x_3 = 5 \end{cases}$$

Thus, $f_3(4) = \$20.50$ and $x_3(4) = 5$.

In a similar fashion, $f_4(i_4)$ can be determined from

$$f_4(i_4) = \min_{x_4} \{c(x_4) + 0.5i_4 + f_3(i_4 - x_4 + 4)\}$$

where x_4 must satisfy $0 \leq x_4 \leq 5$ and $0 \leq i_4 - x_4 + 4 \leq 4$. Since we know that it is optimal to have $i_4 = 0$, we need only determine $f_4(0)$:

$$f_4(0) = \min \begin{cases} 0 + f_3(4) = \$20.50 & x_4 = 0 \\ 4 + f_3(3) = \$22.00 & x_4 = 1 \\ 5 + f_3(2) = \$21.50 & x_4 = 2 \\ 6 + f_3(1) = \$21.00 & x_4 = 3 \\ 7 + f_3(0) = \$20.00* & x_4 = 4 \end{cases}$$

Thus, $f_4(0) = \$20.00$ and $x_4(0) = 4$.

We can now determine an optimal production schedule. Since $x_4(0) = 4$, we produce 4 units during month 4. This leaves us with $i_3 = i_4 - x_4 + 4 = 0$ units at the end of month 3, and $x_3(0) = 0$ units should be produced during month 3. This leaves us with $i_2 = i_3 - x_3 + 2 = 2$ units at the end of month 2, and $x_2(2) = 5$ units should be produced during month 2. Finally, at the end of month 1, we have $i_1 = i_2 - x_2 + 3 = 0$ units, so $x_1(0) = 1$ unit should be produced during month 1. This is, of course, the same production schedule that we found in Section 20.3 via a backward recursion.

◆ PROBLEMS

GROUP A

1. Use a forward recursion to find the optimal solution to the Finco example (Example 5 of Section 20.4).

2. Use a forward recursion to solve Problem 2 of Section 20.3.

3. Suppose we did not know the desired ending state for stage T. How would we modify the forward recursion procedure?

4. Formulate a forward recursion for Problem 1 of Section 20.6.

5. Formulate a forward recusion for Problem 7 of Section 20.6.

◆ SUMMARY

Dynamic programming solves a relatively complex problem by decomposing the problem into a series of simpler problems. First we solve a one-stage problem, then a two-stage problem, and finally a T-stage problem (T = total number of stages in the original problem).

In most applications, a decision is made at each stage (t = current stage), a reward is earned (or a cost is incurred) at each stage, and we go on to the stage $t + 1$ state.

WORKING BACKWARD

In formulating dynamic programming recursions by working backward, it is helpful to remember that in most cases:

1. The **stage** is the mechanism by which we build up the problem.

2. The **state** at any stage gives the information needed to make the correct decision at the current stage.

3. In most cases, we must determine how the reward received (or cost incurred) during the current stage depends on the stage t decision, the stage t state, and the value of t.

4. We must also determine how the stage $t + 1$ state depends on the stage t decision, the stage t state, and the value of t.

5. If we define (for a minimization problem) $f_t(i)$ as the minimum cost incurred during stages $t, t + 1, \ldots, T$, given that the stage t state is i, then (in many cases) we may write $f_t(i) = \min\{(\text{cost during stage } t) + f_{t+1}(\text{new state at stage } t + 1)\}$, where the minimum is over all decisions allowable in state i during stage t.

6. We begin by determining all the $f_T(\cdot)$'s, then all the $f_{T-1}(\cdot)$'s, and finally f_1 (the initial state).

7. We then determine the optimal stage 1 decision. This leads us to a stage 2 state, at which we determine the optimal stage 2 decision. We continue in this fashion until the optimal stage T decision is found.

FORWARD RECURSIONS

In a minimization problem, define $f_t(i)$ as the minimum cost incurred during stages $1, 2, \ldots, t$, given that the state is i at the end of stage t. We begin by computing $f_1(i)$ for all possible states at the end of stage 1. Then we compute the $f_2(i)$ in terms of the

$f_1(\cdot)$, and so on. Once f_T (the desired ending state) is determined, we may determine the optimal stage T decision, then the optimal stage $T - 1$ decision, etc., and finally the optimal stage 1 decision.

WAGNER-WHITIN ALGORITHM AND SILVER-MEAL HEURISTIC FOR DYNAMIC LOT-SIZE MODEL

A periodic review inventory model in which each period's demand is known at the beginning of the problem is a **dynamic lot-size model**. A cost-minimizing production or ordering policy may be found via a backward recursion, a forward recursion, the Wagner-Whitin algorithm, or the Silver-Meal heuristic.

The Wagner-Whitin algorithm uses the fact that production occurs during a period if and only if the period's beginning inventory is zero. The decision during such a period is the number of consecutive periods of demand that production should meet.

During a period in which beginning inventory is zero, the Silver-Meal heuristic computes the average cost per period (setup plus holding) incurred in meeting the demand during the next k periods. If k^* minimizes this average cost, then the next k^* periods of demand should be met by the current period's production.

COMPUTATIONAL CONSIDERATIONS

Dynamic programming is much more efficient than explicit enumeration of the total cost associated with each possible set of decisions that may be chosen during the T stages. Unfortunately, however, many practical applications of dynamic programming involve very large state spaces, and in these situations, considerable computational effort is required to determine optimal decisions.

◆ REVIEW PROBLEMS

GROUP A

1. In the network in Figure 11, find the shortest path from node 1 to node 10 and the shortest path from node 2 to node 10.

2. A company must meet the following demands on time: month 1, 1 unit; month 2, 1 unit; month 3, 2 units; month 4, 2 units. It costs $4 to place an order, and a $2 per-unit holding cost is assessed against each month's ending inventory. At the beginning of month 1, 1 unit is available. Orders are delivered instantaneously.

(a) Use a backward recursion to determine an optimal ordering policy.

(b) Use a forward recursion to determine an optimal ordering policy.

(c) Use the Wagner-Whitin method to determine an optimal ordering policy.

(d) Use the Silver-Meal heuristic to determine an ordering policy.

Figure 11

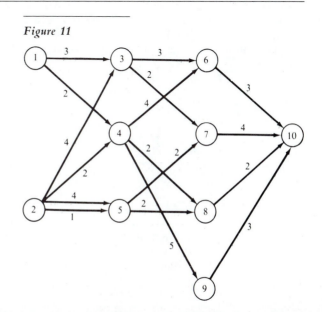

Table 20

DESTINATION	NUMBER OF PLANES					
	1	*2*	*3*	*4*	*5*	*6*
New York	$80	$150	$210	$250	$270	$280
Los Angeles	$100	$195	$275	$325	$300	$250
Miami	$90	$180	$265	$310	$350	$320

3. Reconsider Problem 2, but now suppose that demands need not be met on time. Assume that all lost demand is backlogged and that a $1 per-unit shortage cost is assessed against the number of shortages incurred during each month. All demand must be met by the end of month 4. Use dynamic programming to determine an ordering policy that minimizes total cost.

4. Indianapolis Airlines has been told that it may schedule six flights per day departing from Indianapolis. The destination of each flight may be New York, Los Angeles, or Miami. Table 20 shows the contribution to the company's profit from any given number of daily flights from Indianapolis to each possible destination. Find the optimal number of flights that should depart Indianapolis for each destination. How would the answer change if the airline were restricted to only four daily flights?

5. I am working as a cashier at the local convenience store. A customer's bill is $1.09, and he gives me $2.00. I wish to give him change using the smallest possible number of coins. Use dynamic programming to determine how to give the customer his change. Does the answer suggest a general result about giving change? Resolve the problem if a 20¢ piece (in addition to other United States coins) were available.

6. A company needs to have a working machine during each of the next six years. At present, it has a new machine. At the beginning of each year, the company may keep the machine or sell it and buy a new one. A machine cannot be kept for more than three years. A new machine costs $5000. The revenues earned by a machine, the cost of maintaining it, and the salvage value that can be obtained by selling it at the end of a year depend on the age of the machine (see Table 21). Use dynamic programming to maximize the net profit earned during the next six years.

7. A company needs the following number of workers during each of the next five years: year 1, 15; year 2, 30; year 3, 10; year 4, 30; year 5, 20. At present, the company has 20 workers. Each worker is paid $30,000 per year. At the beginning of each year, workers may be hired or fired. It costs $10,000 to hire a worker and $20,000 to fire a worker. A newly hired worker can be used to meet the current year's worker requirement. During each year, 10% of all workers quit (workers who quit do not incur any firing cost).

(a) With dynamic programming, formulate a recursion that can be used to minimize the total cost incurred in meeting the worker requirements of the next five years.

(b) How would the recursion be modified if hired workers cannot be used to meet worker requirements until the year following the year in which they are hired?

Table 21

	AGE OF MACHINE AT BEGINNING OF YEAR		
	0 years	*1 year*	*2 years*
Revenues	$4500	$3000	$1500
Operating costs	$500	$700	$1100
Salvage value at end of year	$3000	$1800	$500

8. At the beginning of each year, Barnes Carr Oil sets the world oil price. If a price p is set, then $D(p)$ barrels of oil will be demanded by world customers. We assume that during any year, each oil company sells the same number of barrels of oil. It costs Barnes Carr Oil c dollars to extract and refine each barrel of oil. Barnes Carr cannot set too high a price, however, because if a price p is set and there are currently N oil companies, then $g(p, N)$ oil companies will enter the oil business ($g(p, N)$ could be negative). Setting too high a price will dilute future profits because of the entrance of new companies. Barnes Carr wishes to maximize the discounted profit the company will earn over the next 20 years. Formulate a recursion that will aid Barnes Carr in meeting its goal. Initially, there are ten oil companies.

9. For a computer to work properly, three subsystems of the computer must all function properly. To increase the reliability of the computer, spare units may be added to each system. It costs $100 to add a spare unit to system 1, $300 to add a spare unit to system 2, and $200 to add a spare unit to system 3. As a function of the number of added spares (a maximum of two spares may be added to each system), the probability that each system will work is given in Table 22. Use dynamic programming to maximize the probability that the computer will work properly, given that $600 is available for spare units.

Table 22

	PROBABILITY THAT A SYSTEM WORKS		
NO. OF SPARES	*System 1*	*System 2*	*System 3*
0	.85	.60	.70
1	.90	.85	.90
2	.95	.95	.98

GROUP B

10. During any year, I can consume any amount that does not exceed my current wealth. If I consume c dollars during a year, I earn c^a units of happiness. By the beginning of the next year, the previous year's ending wealth grows by a factor k.
(a) Formulate a recursion that can be used to maximize total utility earned during the next T years. Assume I originally have w_0 dollars.
(b) Let $f_t(w)$ be the maximum utility earned during years, $t, t + 1, \ldots, T$, given that I have w dollars at the beginning of year t; and $c_t(w)$ be the amount that should be consumed during year t to attain $f_t(w)$. By working backward, show that for appropriately chosen constants a_t and b_t,

$$f_t(w) = b_t w^a \quad \text{and} \quad c_t(w) = a_t w$$

Interpret these results.

11. At the beginning of month t, farmer Smith has x_t bushels of wheat in his warehouse. He has the opportunity to sell wheat at a price s_t dollars per bushel and can buy wheat at p_t dollars per bushel. Farmer Smith's warehouse can hold at most C units at the end of each month.
(a) Formulate a recursion that can be used to maximize the total profit earned during the next T months.
(b) Let $f_t(x_t)$ be the maximum profit that can be earned during months $t, t + 1, \ldots, T$, given that x_t bushels of wheat are in the warehouse at the beginning of month t. By working backward, show that for appropriately chosen constants a_t and b_t,

$$f_t(x_t) = a_t + b_t x_t$$

(c) During any given month, show that the profit-maximizing policy has the following properties: (1) The amount sold during month t will equal either x_t or zero. (2) The amount purchased during a given month will be either zero or sufficient to bring the month's ending stock to C bushels.

◆ REFERENCES

The following references are oriented toward applications and are written at an intermediate level:
DREYFUS, S., and A. LAW. *The Art and Theory of Dynamic Programming*. Orlando, Fla.: Academic Press, 1977.
NEMHAUSER, G. *Introduction to Dynamic Programming*. New York: Wiley, 1966.
WAGNER, H. *Principles of Operations Research*, 2d ed. Englewood Cliffs, N.J.: Prentice-Hall, 1975.

The following five references are oriented toward theory and are written at a more advanced level:

BELLMAN, R. *Dynamic Programming*. Princeton, N.J.: Princeton University Press, 1957.

BELLMAN, R., and S. DREYFUS. *Applied Dynamic Programming*. Princeton, N.J.: Princeton University Press, 1962.

BERSETKAS, D. *Dynamic Programming and Stochastic Control*. Orlando, Fla.: Academic Press, 1976.

DENARDO, E. *Dynamic Programming: Theory and Applications*. Englewood Cliffs, N.J.: Prentice-Hall, 1982.

WHITTLE, P. *Optimization Over Time: Dynamic Programming and Stochastic Control*, vol. 1. New York: Wiley, 1982.

MORTON, T. "Planning Horizons for Dynamic Programs", *Operations Research* 27(1979):730–743. A discussion of turnpike theorems.

PETERSON, R., and E. SILVER. *Decision Systems for Inventory Management and Production Planning*. New York: Wiley, 1985. Discusses the Silver-Meal method.

WADDELL, R. "A Model for Equipment Replacement Decisions and Policies," *Interfaces* 13(1983): 1–8. An application of the equipment replacement model.

WAGNER, H., and T. WHITIN. "Dynamic Version of the Economic Lot Size Model," *Management Science* 5(1958):89–96. Discusses Wagner-Whitin method.

CHAPTER 21

Probabilistic Dynamic Programming

RECALL FROM OUR study of deterministic dynamic programming that many recursions were of the following form:

$$f_t(\text{current state}) = \min_{\substack{\text{all feasible} \\ \text{decisions}}} (\text{or max})\{\text{costs during current stage} + f_{t+1}(\text{new state})\}$$

For all the examples in Chapter 20, a specification of the current state and current decision was enough to tell us *with certainty* the new state and the costs during the current stage. In many practical problems, the current period's costs or the next period's state may not be known with certainty, even if the current state and decision are known. For example, in the inventory model of Section 20.3, we assumed that each period's demand was known at the beginning of the problem. In most situations, it would be more realistic to assume that period t's demand is a random variable whose value is not known until after period t's production decision is made. Even if we know the current period's state (beginning inventory level) and decision (production during the current period), the next period's state and the current period's cost will be random variables whose values are not known until the value of period t's demand is known. The Chapter 20 discussion simply does not apply to this type of problem.

   In this chapter, we explain how to use dynamic programming to solve problems in which the current period's cost or the next period's state are random. We call these problems *probabilistic dynamic programming problems* (or PDPs). In a PDP, the decision maker's goal is usually to minimize expected (or expected discounted) cost incurred or to maximize expected (or expected discounted) reward earned over a given time horizon. Chapter 21 concludes with a brief study of *Markov decision processes*. A Markov decision process is just a probabilistic dynamic programming problem in which the decision maker faces an infinite horizon.

AN EXAMPLE IN WHICH COSTS DURING THE CURRENT STAGE ARE UNCERTAIN, BUT THE NEXT PERIOD'S STATE IS CERTAIN

For problems in this section, the next period's state is known with certainty, but the reward earned during the current stage is not known with certainty (given the current state and decision).

E X A M P L E
1

For a price of $1/gallon, the Safeco Supermarket chain has purchased 6 gallons of milk from a local dairy. Each gallon is sold in the chain's three stores for $2/gallon. The dairy must buy back for 50¢/gallon any milk that is left at the end of the day. Unfortunately for Safeco, demand for each of the chain's three stores is uncertain. Past data indicate that the daily demand at each store is as shown in Table 1. Safeco wants to allocate the 6 gallons of milk to the three stores so as to maximize the expected net daily profit (revenues less costs) earned from milk. Use dynamic programming to determine how Safeco should allocate the 6 gallons of milk among the three stores.

Table 1
Probability
Distributions for
Daily Milk Demand

	DAILY DEMAND (Gallons)	PROBABILITY
Store 1	1	.60
	2	0
	3	.40
Store 2	1	.50
	2	.10
	3	.40
Store 3	1	.40
	2	.30
	3	.30

Solution

With the exception of the fact that demand (and therefore revenue) is uncertain, this problem is very similar to the resource allocation problems studied in Section 20.4.

Observe that since Safeco's daily purchase costs are always $6, we may concentrate our attention on the problem of allocating the milk to maximize daily expected revenue earned from the 6 gallons.

Define

$r_t(g_t)$ = expected revenue earned from g_t gallons assigned to store t

$f_t(x)$ = maximum expected revenue earned from x gallons assigned to stores $t, t + 1, \ldots, 3$

Since $f_3(x)$ must by definition be the expected revenue earned from assigning x gallons of milk to store 3, we see that $f_3(x) = r_3(x)$. For $t = 1, 2$, we may write

$$f_t(x) = \max_{g_t} \{r_t(g_t) + f_{t+1}(x - g_t)\} \tag{1}$$

where g_t must be a member of $\{0, 1, \ldots, x\}$. Eq. (1) follows, because for any choice of g_t (the number of gallons assigned to store t), the expected revenue earned from store t,

$t + 1, \ldots, 3$ will be the sum of the expected revenue earned from store t if g_t gallons are assigned to store t plus the maximum expected revenue that can be earned from stores $t + 1, t + 2, \ldots, 3$ when $x - g_t$ gallons are assigned to these stores. To compute the optimal allocation of milk to stores, we begin by computing $f_3(0), f_3(1), \ldots, f_3(6)$. Then we use Eq. (1) to compute $f_2(0), f_2(1), \ldots, f_2(6)$. Finally we determine $f_1(6)$.

We begin by computing the $r_t(g_t)$'s. Note that it would be foolish to assign more than 3 gallons to any store. For this reason, we compute the $r_t(g_t)$'s only for $x = 0, 1, 2,$ or 3. As an example, we compute $r_3(2)$, the expected revenue earned if 2 gallons are assigned to store 3. If the demand at store 3 is for 2 or more gallons, both gallons assigned to store 3 will be sold, and \$4 in revenue will be earned. If the demand at store 3 is 1 gallon, 1 gallon will be sold for \$2, and 1 gallon will be returned for 50¢. Hence, if demand at store 3 is for 1 gallon, a revenue of \$2.50 will be earned. Since there is a .60 chance that demand at store 3 will be for 2 or more gallons and a .40 chance that store 3 demand will be for 1 gallon, it follows that $r_3(2) = (.30 + .30)(4.00) + .40(2.50) = \$3.40$. Similar computations yield the following results:

$$
\begin{array}{lll}
r_3(0) = \$0 & r_2(0) = \$0 & r_1(0) = \$0 \\
r_3(1) = \$2.00 & r_2(1) = \$2.00 & r_1(1) = \$2.00 \\
r_3(2) = \$3.40 & r_2(2) = \$3.25 & r_1(2) = \$3.10 \\
r_3(3) = \$4.35 & r_2(3) = \$4.35 & r_1(3) = \$4.20
\end{array}
$$

We now use (1) to determine an optimal allocation of milk to stores. Let $g_t(x)$ be an allocation of milk to store t that attains $f_t(x)$. Then

$$
\begin{array}{ll}
f_3(0) = r_3(0) = 0 & g_3(0) = 0 \\
f_3(1) = r_3(1) = 2.00 & g_3(1) = 1 \\
f_3(2) = r_3(2) = 3.40 & g_3(2) = 2 \\
f_3(3) = r_3(3) = 4.35 & g_3(3) = 3
\end{array}
$$

We need not compute $f_3(4), f_3(5),$ and $f_3(6)$, because an optimal allocation will never have more than 3 gallons to allocate to a single store (demand at any store is never more than 3 gallons).

Using (1) to work backward, we obtain

$$
f_2(0) = r_2(0) + f_3(0 - 0) = 0 \qquad g_2(0) = 0
$$

$$
f_2(1) = \max \begin{cases} r_2(0) + f_3(1 - 0) = 2.00^* \\ r_2(1) + f_3(1 - 1) = 2.00^* \end{cases} \qquad g_2(1) = 0 \text{ or } 1
$$

$$
f_2(2) = \max \begin{cases} r_2(0) + f_3(2 - 0) = 0 + 3.40 = 3.40 \\ r_2(1) + f_3(2 - 1) = 2.00 + 2.00 = 4.00^* \\ r_2(2) + f_3(2 - 2) = 3.25 + 0 = 3.25 \end{cases} \qquad g_2(2) = 1
$$

$$
f_2(3) = \max \begin{cases} r_2(0) + f_3(3 - 0) = 0 + 4.35 = 4.35 \\ r_2(1) + f_3(3 - 1) = 2.00 + 3.40 = 5.40^* \\ r_2(2) + f_3(3 - 2) = 3.25 + 2.00 = 5.25 \\ r_2(3) + f_3(3 - 3) = 4.35 + 0 = 4.35 \end{cases} \qquad g_2(3) = 1
$$

Note that in computing $f_2(4)$, $f_2(5)$, and $f_2(6)$, we need not consider any allocation for more than 3 gallons to store 2 or any that leaves more than 3 gallons for store 3.

$$f_2(4) = \max \begin{cases} r_2(1) + f_3(4 - 1) = 2.00 + 4.35 = 6.35 \\ r_2(2) + f_3(4 - 2) = 3.25 + 3.40 = 6.65^* \\ r_2(3) + f_3(4 - 3) = 4.35 + 2.00 = 6.35 \end{cases} \quad g_2(4) = 2$$

$$f_2(5) = \max \begin{cases} r_2(2) + f_3(5 - 2) = 3.25 + 4.35 = 7.60 \\ r_2(3) + f_3(5 - 3) = 4.35 + 3.40 = 7.75^* \end{cases} \quad g_2(5) = 3$$

$$f_2(6) = r_2(3) + f_3(6 - 3) = 4.35 + 4.35 = 8.70^* \quad g_2(6) = 3$$

Finally,

$$f_1(6) = \max \begin{cases} r_1(0) + f_2(6 - 0) = 0 + 8.70 \\ r_1(1) + f_2(6 - 1) = 2.00 + 7.75 = 9.75^* \\ r_1(2) + f_2(6 - 2) = 3.10 + 6.65 = 9.75^* \\ r_1(3) + f_2(6 - 3) = 4.20 + 5.40 = 9.60 \end{cases} \quad g_1(6) = 1 \text{ or } 2$$

Thus, we can either assign 1 or 2 gallons to store 1. Suppose we arbitrarily choose to assign 1 gallon to store 1. Then we have $6 - 1 = 5$ gallons for stores 2 and 3. Since $f_2(5)$ is attained by $g_2(5) = 3$, we assign 3 gallons to store 2. Then $5 - 3 = 2$ gallons are available for store 3. Since $g_3(2) = 2$, we assign 2 gallons to store 3. Note that although this policy obtains the maximum expected revenue, $f_1(6) = \$9.75$, the total revenue actually received on a given day may be more or less than \$9.75. For example, if demand at each store were 1 gallon, total revenue would be $3(2.00) + 3(0.50) = \$7.50$, whereas if demand at each store were 3 gallons, all milk would be sold at \$2/gallon, and total revenue would be $6(2.00) = \$12.00$.

◆

Table 2   Investment Probability for Problem 2

	INVESTMENT (Millions)	PROBABILITY		
Project 1	$1	$P(I_1 = 2) = .6$	$P(I_1 = 4) = .3$	$P(I_1 = 5) = .1$
	$2	$P(I_1 = 4) = .5$	$P(I_1 = 6) = .3$	$P(I_1 = 8) = .2$
	$3	$P(I_1 = 6) = .4$	$P(I_1 = 7) = .5$	$P(I_1 = 10) = .1$
	$4	$P(I_1 = 7) = .2$	$P(I_1 = 9) = .4$	$P(I_1 = 10) = .4$
Project 2	$1	$P(I_2 = 1) = .5$	$P(I_2 = 2) = .4$	$P(I_2 = 4) = .1$
	$2	$P(I_2 = 3) = .4$	$P(I_2 = 5) = .4$	$P(I_2 = 6) = .2$
	$3	$P(I_2 = 4) = .3$	$P(I_2 = 6) = .3$	$P(I_2 = 8) = .4$
	$4	$P(I_2 = 3) = .4$	$P(I_2 = 8) = .3$	$P(I_2 = 9) = .3$
Project 3	$1	$P(I_3 = 0) = .2$	$P(I_3 = 4) = .6$	$P(I_3 = 5) = .2$
	$2	$P(I_3 = 4) = .4$	$P(I_3 = 6) = .4$	$P(I_3 = 7) = .2$
	$3	$P(I_3 = 5) = .3$	$P(I_3 = 7) = .4$	$P(I_3 = 8) = .3$
	$4	$P(I_3 = 6) = .1$	$P(I_3 = 8) = .5$	$P(I_3 = 9) = .4$

◆ PROBLEMS

GROUP A

1. In Example 1, find another allocation of milk that maximizes expected daily revenue.

2. Suppose that $4 million is available for investment in three projects. The probability distribution of the net present value earned from each project depends on how much is invested in each project. Let $\mathbf{I}_t$ be the random variable denoting the net present value earned by project t. The distribution of $\mathbf{I}_t$ depends on the amount of money invested in project t, as shown in Table 2 (a zero investment in a project always earns a zero NPV). Use dynamic programming to determine an investment allocation that maximizes the expected NPV obtained from the three investments.

<hr>

| 21-2 | **A PROBABILISTIC INVENTORY MODEL** |

In this section, we modify the inventory model of Section 20.3 to allow for uncertain demand. This will illustrate the difficulties involved in solving a PDP for which the state during the next period is uncertain (given the current state and current decision).

<hr>

E X A M P L E
2

Consider the following three-period inventory problem. At the beginning of each period, a firm must determine how many units should be produced during the current period. During a period in which x units are produced, a production cost $c(x)$ is incurred, where $c(0) = 0$, and for $x > 0$, $c(x) = 3 + 2x$. Production during each period is limited to at most 4 units. After production occurs, the period's random demand is observed. Each period's demand is equally likely to be 1 or 2 units. After meeting the current period's demand out of current production and inventory, the firm's end-of-period inventory is evaluated, and a holding cost of $1 per unit is assessed. Because of limited capacity, the inventory at the end of each period cannot exceed 3 units. It is required that all demand be met on time. Any inventory on hand at the end of period 3 can be sold at $2 per unit. At the beginning of period 1, the firm has 1 unit of inventory. Use dynamic programming to determine a production policy that minimizes the expected net cost incurred during the three periods.

Solution

Define $f_t(i)$ to be the minimum expected net cost incurred during periods t, $t + 1, \ldots, 3$ when the inventory at the beginning of period t is i units. Then

$$f_3(i) = \min_x \{c(x) + (\tfrac{1}{2})(i + x - 1) + (\tfrac{1}{2})(i + x - 2)$$
$$- (\tfrac{1}{2})2(i + x - 1) - (\tfrac{1}{2})2(i + x - 2)\} \tag{2}$$

where x must be a member of $\{0, 1, 2, 3, 4\}$ and x must satisfy $(2 - i) \leq x \leq (4 - i)$.

Eq. (2) follows, because if x units are produced during period 3, the net cost during period 3 is (expected production cost) + (expected holding cost) − (expected salvage value). If x units are produced, the expected production cost is $c(x)$, and there is a $\tfrac{1}{2}$ chance that the period 3 holding cost will be $i + x - 1$ and a $\tfrac{1}{2}$ chance that the period 3 holding cost will be $i + x - 2$. Hence, the period 3 expected holding cost will be $(\tfrac{1}{2})(i + x - 1) + (\tfrac{1}{2})(i + x - 2) = i + x - \tfrac{3}{2}$. Similar reasoning shows that the expected salvage value (a negative cost) at the end of period 3 will be $(\tfrac{1}{2})2(i + x - 1) + (\tfrac{1}{2})2(i + x - 2) = 2i + 2x - 3$. To ensure that the period 3 demand is met, we must have $i + x \geq 2$, or $x \geq 2 - i$. Similarly, to ensure that ending period 3 inventory does not exceed 3 units, we must have $i + x - 1 \leq 3$, or $x \leq 4 - i$.

For $t = 1, 2$, we can derive a recursive relation for $f_t(i)$ by noting that for any month t production level x, the expected costs incurred during periods $t, t + 1, \ldots, 3$ are the sum of the expected costs incurred during period t and the expected costs incurred during periods $t + 1, t + 2, \ldots, 3$. As before, if x units are produced during month t, the expected cost during month t will be $c(x) + (\frac{1}{2})(i + x - 1) + (\frac{1}{2})(i + x - 2)$. (Note that during periods 1 and 2, no salvage value is received.) If x units are produced during month t, the expected cost during periods $t + 1, t + 2, \ldots, 3$ is computed as follows. Half of the time, the demand during period t will be 1 unit, and the inventory at the beginning of period $t + 1$ will be $i + x - 1$. In this situation, the expected costs incurred during periods $t + 1, t + 2, \ldots, 3$ (assuming we act optimally during these periods) is $f_{t+1}(i + x - 1)$. Similarly, there is a $\frac{1}{2}$ chance that the inventory at the beginning of period $t + 1$ will be $i + x - 2$. In this case, the expected cost incurred during periods $t + 1, t + 2, \ldots, 3$ will be $f_{t+1}(i + x - 2)$. In summary, the expected cost during periods $t + 1, t + 2, \ldots, 3$ will be $(\frac{1}{2})f_{t+1}(i + x - 1) + (\frac{1}{2})f_{t+1}(i + x - 2)$. With this in mind, we may write for $t = 1, 2$,

$$f_t(i) = \min_x [c(x) + (\tfrac{1}{2})(i + x - 1) + (\tfrac{1}{2})(i + x - 2)$$
$$+ (\tfrac{1}{2})f_{t+1}(i + x - 1) + (\tfrac{1}{2})f_{t+1}(i + x - 2)] \tag{3}$$

where x must be a member of $\{0, 1, 2, 3, 4\}$ and x must satisfy $(2 - i) \leq x \leq (4 - i)$.

Generalizing the reasoning that led to Eq. (3) yields the following important observation concerning the formulation of PDPs. Suppose the possible states during period $t + 1$ are $s_1, s_2, \ldots, s_n$ and the probability that the period $t + 1$ state will be s_i is p_i. Then the minimum expected cost incurred during periods $t + 1, t + 2, \ldots,$ end of the problem is

$$\sum_{i=1}^{i=n} p_i f_{t+1}(s_i)$$

Table 3 Computations for $f_3(i)$			EXPECTED HOLDING COST	EXPECTED SALVAGE VALUE	TOTAL EXPECTED	$f_3(i)$
i	x	$c(x)$	$(i + x - \frac{3}{2})$	$(2i + 2x - 3)$	COST	$x_3(i)$
3	0	0	$\frac{3}{2}$	3	$-\frac{3}{2}$*	$f_3(3) = -\frac{3}{2}$
3	1	5	$\frac{5}{2}$	5	$\frac{5}{2}$	$x_3(3) = 0$
2	0	0	$\frac{1}{2}$	1	$-\frac{1}{2}$*	$f_3(2) = -\frac{1}{2}$
2	1	5	$\frac{3}{2}$	3	$\frac{7}{2}$	$x_3(2) = 0$
2	2	7	$\frac{5}{2}$	5	$\frac{9}{2}$	
1	1	5	$\frac{1}{2}$	1	$\frac{9}{2}$*	$f_3(1) = \frac{9}{2}$
1	2	7	$\frac{3}{2}$	3	$\frac{11}{2}$	$x_3(1) = 1$
1	3	9	$\frac{5}{2}$	5	$\frac{13}{2}$	
0	2	7	$\frac{1}{2}$	1	$\frac{13}{2}$*	$f_3(0) = \frac{13}{2}$
0	3	9	$\frac{3}{2}$	3	$\frac{15}{2}$	$x_3(0) = 2$
0	4	11	$\frac{5}{2}$	5	$\frac{17}{2}$	

where $f_{t+1}(s_i)$ is the minimum expected cost incurred from period $t + 1$ to the end of the problem, given that the state during period $t + 1$ is s_i.

We define $x_t(i)$ to be a period t production level attaining the minimum in Eq. (3) for $f_t(i)$. We now work backward until $f_1(1)$ is determined. The relevant computations are summarized in Tables 3, 4, and 5. Since each period's ending inventory must be nonnegative and cannot exceed 3 units, the state during each period must be 0, 1, 2, or 3.

Table 4
Computations for $f_2(i)$

i	x	$c(x)$	EXPECTED HOLDING COST $(i + x - \frac{3}{2})$	EXPECTED FUTURE COST $((\frac{1}{2})f_3(i + x - 1) + (\frac{1}{2})f_3(i + x - 2))$	TOTAL EXPECTED COST PERIODS 2,3	$f_2(i)$ $x_2(i)$
3	0	0	$\frac{3}{2}$	2	$\frac{7}{2}$*	$f_2(3) = \frac{7}{2}$
3	1	5	$\frac{5}{2}$	-1	$\frac{13}{2}$	$x_2(3) = 0$
2	0	0	$\frac{1}{2}$	$\frac{11}{2}$	6*	$f_2(2) = 6$
2	1	5	$\frac{3}{2}$	2	$\frac{17}{2}$	$x_2(2) = 0$
2	2	7	$\frac{5}{2}$	-1	$\frac{17}{2}$	
1	1	5	$\frac{1}{2}$	$\frac{11}{2}$	11	$f_2(1) = \frac{21}{2}$
1	2	7	$\frac{3}{2}$	2	$\frac{21}{2}$*	$x_2(1) = 2$ or 3
1	3	9	$\frac{5}{2}$	-1	$\frac{21}{2}$*	
0	2	7	$\frac{1}{2}$	$\frac{11}{2}$	13	$f_2(0) = \frac{25}{2}$
0	3	9	$\frac{3}{2}$	2	$\frac{25}{2}$*	$x_2(0) = 3$ or 4
0	4	11	$\frac{5}{2}$	-1	$\frac{25}{2}$*	

Table 5
Computations for $f_1(1)$

x	$c(x)$	EXPECTED HOLDING COST $(i + x - \frac{3}{2})$	EXPECTED FUTURE COST $((\frac{1}{2})f_2(i + x - 1) + (\frac{1}{2})f_2(i + x - 2))$	TOTAL EXPECTED COST PERIODS 1–3	$f_1(1)$ $x_1(1)$
1	5	$\frac{1}{2}$	$\frac{23}{2}$	17	$f_1(1) = \frac{65}{4}$
2	7	$\frac{3}{2}$	$\frac{33}{4}$	$\frac{67}{4}$	$x_1(1) = 3$
3	9	$\frac{5}{2}$	$\frac{19}{4}$	$\frac{65}{4}$*	

As in Section 20.3, we begin by producing $x_1(1) = 3$ units during period 1. We cannot, however, determine period 2's production level until period 1's demand is observed. Also, period 3's production level cannot be determined until period 2's demand is observed. To illustrate the idea, we determine the optimal production schedule if the period 1 and period 2 demands are both 2 units. Since $x_1(1) = 3$, 3 units will be produced during period 1. Then period 2 will begin with an inventory of $1 + 3 - 2 = 2$ units, so $x_2(2) = 0$ units should be produced. After period 2's demand of 2 units is met, period 3 will begin with $2 - 2 = 0$ units on hand. Thus, $x_3(0) = 2$ units will be produced during period 3.

◆

In contrast, suppose that period 1 and period 2 demands are both 1 unit. As before, $x_1(1) = 3$ units will be produced during period 1. Then period 2 will begin with $1 + 3 - 1 = 3$ units, and $x_2(3) = 0$ units will be produced during period 2. Then period 3 will begin with $3 - 1 = 2$ units on hand, and $x_3(2) = 0$ units will be produced during period 3. Note that the optimal production policy has adapted to the low demand by reducing period 3 production. This example illustrates an important aspect of dynamic programming solutions for problems in which future states are not known with certainty at the beginning of the problem: *If a random factor (like random demand) influences transitions from the period t state to the period $t + 1$ state, the optimal action for period t cannot be determined until period t's state is known.*

(s, S) POLICIES

Consider the following modification of the dynamic lot-size model of Section 20.7, for which there exists an optimal production policy called an (s, S) inventory policy:

1. The cost of producing $x > 0$ units during a period consists of a fixed cost K and a per-unit variable production cost c.

2. With probability $p(x)$, the demand during a given period will be x.

3. A holding cost of h per unit is assessed on each period's ending inventory. If we are short, a per-unit shortage cost of d is incurred. (The case where no shortages are allowed may be obtained by letting d be very large.)

4. The goal is to minimize the total expected cost incurred during periods $1, 2, \ldots, T$.

5. All demands must be met by the end of period t.

For such an inventory problem, Scarf (1960) used dynamic programming to prove that there exists an optimal production policy of the following form: For each t $(t = 1, 2, \ldots, T)$ there exists a pair of numbers (s_t, S_t) such that if i_{t-1}, the entering inventory for period t, is less than s_t, then an amount $S_t - i_{t-1}$ is produced; if $i_{t-1} \geq s_t$, then it is optimal not to produce during period t. Such a policy is called an **(s, S) policy**.

For Example 2, our calculations show that $s_2 = 2, S_2 = 3$ or $4, s_3 = 2$, and $S_3 = 2$. Thus, if we enter period 2 with 1 or 0 units, we produce enough to bring our stock level (before meeting period 2 demand) to 3 or 4 units. If we enter period 2 with more than 1 unit, then no production should take place during period 2.

♦ PROBLEMS

GROUP A

1. For Example 2, suppose that the period 1 demand is 1 unit, and the period 2 demand is 2 units. What would be the optimal production schedule?

2. Re-solve Example 2 if the end-of-period holding cost is $2 per unit.

3. In Example 2, suppose that shortages are allowed, and each shortage results in a lost sale and a cost incurred of $3. Now resolve Example 2.

GROUP B

4. Chip Bilton sells sweatshirts at State U football games. He is equally likely to sell 200 or 400 sweatshirts at each game. Each time Chip places an order, he pays $500 plus $5 for each sweatshirt he orders. Each sweatshirt sells for $8. A holding cost of $2 per shirt (because of the opportunity cost for capital tied up in sweatshirts as well as storage costs) is assessed against each shirt left at the end of a game. Chip can store at most 400 shirts after each game. Assuming that the number of shirts ordered by Chip must be a multiple of 100, determine an ordering policy that maximizes expected profits earned during the first three games of the season. Assume that any leftover sweatshirts have a value of $6.

21-3   HOW TO MAXIMIZE THE PROBABILITY OF A FAVORABLE EVENT OCCURRING*

There are many occasions on which the decision maker's goal is to maximize the probability of a favorable event occurring. For instance, a company may want to maximize its probability of reaching a specified level of annual profits. To solve such a problem, we assign a reward of 1 if the favorable event occurs and a reward of 0 if the favorable event does not occur. Then maximization of expected reward will be equivalent to maximizing the probability that the favorable event will occur. Also, the maximum expected reward will equal the maximum probability of the favorable event occurring. The following two examples illustrate how this idea may be used to solve some fairly complex problems.

E X A M P L E 3

A gambler has $2. She is allowed to play a game of chance four times, and her goal is to maximize her probability of ending up with at least $6. If the gambler bets b dollars on a play of the game, then with probability .40, she wins the game and increases her capital position by b dollars; with probability .60, she loses the game and decreases her capital by b dollars. On any play of the game, the gambler may not bet more money than she has available. Determine a betting strategy that will maximize the gambler's probability of attaining a wealth of at least $6 by the end of the fourth game. We assume that bets of zero dollars (that is, not betting) are permissible.

Solution

Define $f_t(d)$ to be the probability that by the end of game 4, the gambler will have at least $6, given that she acts optimally and has d dollars immediately before the game is played for the tth time. If we give the gambler a reward of 1 when her ending wealth is at least $6 and a reward of 0 if her ending wealth is less than $6, then $f_t(d)$ will equal the maximum expected reward that can be earned during games $t, t + 1, \ldots, 4$ if the gambler has d dollars immediately before the tth play of the game. As usual, we define $b_t(d)$ dollars to be a bet size that attains $f_t(d)$.

If the gambler is playing the game for the fourth and final time, her optimal strategy is clear: If she has $6 or more, don't bet anything, but if she has less than $6, bet enough money to ensure (if possible) that she will have $6 if she wins the last game. Note that if she begins game 4 with $0, $1, or $2, there is no way to win (i.e., no way to earn a reward of 1). This reasoning yields the following results:

$$f_4(0) = 0 \qquad b_4(0) = \$0$$
$$f_4(1) = 0 \qquad b_4(1) = \$0 \text{ or } \$1$$
$$f_4(2) = 0 \qquad b_4(2) = \$0, \$1, \text{ or } \$2$$
$$f_4(3) = .40 \qquad b_4(3) = \$3$$
$$f_4(4) = .40 \qquad b_4(4) = \$2, \$3, \text{ or } \$4$$
$$f_4(5) = .40 \qquad b_4(5) = \$1, \$2, \$3, \$4, \text{ or } \$5$$

For $d \geq 6$,

$$f_4(d) = 1 \qquad b_4(d) = \$0, \$1, \ldots, \$(d - 6)$$

*This section covers topics that may be omitted with no loss of continuity.

For $t \leq 3$, we can find a recursion for $f_t(d)$ by noting that if the gambler has d dollars, is about to play the game for the tth time, and bets b dollars, then the following diagram summarizes what can occur:

Thus, if the gambler has d dollars at the beginning of game t and bets b dollars, the expected reward (or expected probability of reaching \$6) will be $.4f_{t+1}(d + b) + .6f_{t+1}(d - b)$. This leads to the following recursion:

$$f_t(d) = \max_b (.4f_{t+1}(d + b) + .6f_{t+1}(d - b)) \tag{4}$$

where b must be a member of $\{0, 1, \ldots, d\}$. Then $b_t(d)$ is any bet size that attains the maximum in Eq. (4) for $f_t(d)$. Using Eq. (4), we work backward until $f_1(2)$ has been determined.

STAGE 3 COMPUTATIONS.

$$f_3(0) = 0 \qquad b_3(0) = \$0$$

$$f_3(1) = \max \begin{cases} .4f_4(1) + .6f_4(1) = 0^* & \text{(Bet \$0)} \\ .4f_4(2) + .6f_4(0) = 0^* & \text{(Bet \$1)} \end{cases}$$

Thus, $f_3(1) = 0$, and $b_3(1) = \$0$ or \$1.

$$f_3(2) = \max \begin{cases} .4f_4(2) + .6f_4(2) = 0 & \text{(Bet \$0)} \\ .4f_4(3) + .6f_4(1) = .16^* & \text{(Bet \$1)} \\ .4f_4(4) + .6f_4(0) = .16^* & \text{(Bet \$2)} \end{cases}$$

Thus, $f_3(2) = .16$, and $b_3(2) = \$1$ or \$2.

$$f_3(3) = \max \begin{cases} .4f_4(3) + .6f_4(3) = .40^* & \text{(Bet \$0)} \\ .4f_4(4) + .6f_4(2) = .16 & \text{(Bet \$1)} \\ .4f_4(5) + .6f_4(1) = .16 & \text{(Bet \$2)} \\ .4f_4(6) + .6f_4(0) = .40^* & \text{(Bet \$3)} \end{cases}$$

Thus, $f_3(3) = .40$, and $b_3(3) = \$0$ or \$3.

$$f_3(4) = \max \begin{cases} .4f_4(4) + .6f_4(4) = .40^* & \text{(Bet \$0)} \\ .4f_4(5) + .6f_4(3) = .40^* & \text{(Bet \$1)} \\ .4f_4(6) + .6f_4(2) = .40^* & \text{(Bet \$2)} \\ .4f_4(7) + .6f_4(1) = .40^* & \text{(Bet \$3)} \\ .4f_4(8) + .6f_4(0) = .40^* & \text{(Bet \$4)} \end{cases}$$

Thus, $f_3(4) = .40$, and $b_3(4) = \$0, \$1, \$2, \$3,$ or \$4.

$$f_3(5) = \max \begin{cases} .4f_4(5) + .6f_4(5) = .40 & \text{(Bet \$0)} \\ .4f_4(6) + .6f_4(4) = .64^* & \text{(Bet \$1)} \\ .4f_4(7) + .6f_4(3) = .64^* & \text{(Bet \$2)} \\ .4f_4(8) + .6f_4(2) = .40 & \text{(Bet \$3)} \\ .4f_4(9) + .6f_4(1) = .40 & \text{(Bet \$4)} \\ .4f_4(10) + .6f_4(0) = .40 & \text{(Bet \$5)} \end{cases}$$

Thus, $f_3(5) = .64$, and $b_3(5) = \$1$ or $\$2$. For $d \geq 6$, $f_3(d) = 1$, and $b_3(d) = \$0$, $\$1, \ldots, \$(d - 6)$.

STAGE 2 COMPUTATIONS.

$$f_2(0) = 0 \qquad b_2(0) = 0$$

$$f_2(1) = \max \begin{cases} .4f_3(1) + .6f_3(1) = 0 & \text{(Bet \$0)} \\ .4f_3(2) + .6f_3(0) = .064^* & \text{(Bet \$1)} \end{cases}$$

Thus, $f_2(1) = .064$, and $b_2(1) = \$1$.

$$f_2(2) = \max \begin{cases} .4f_3(2) + .6f_3(2) = .16^* & \text{(Bet \$0)} \\ .4f_3(3) + .6f_3(1) = .16^* & \text{(Bet \$1)} \\ .4f_3(4) + .6f_3(0) = .16^* & \text{(Bet \$2)} \end{cases}$$

Thus, $f_2(2) = .16$, and $b_2(2) = \$0$, $\$1$, or $\$2$.

$$f_2(3) = \max \begin{cases} .4f_3(3) + .6f_3(3) = .40^* & \text{(Bet \$0)} \\ .4f_3(4) + .6f_3(2) = .256 & \text{(Bet \$1)} \\ .4f_3(5) + .6f_3(1) = .256 & \text{(Bet \$2)} \\ .4f_3(6) + .6f_3(0) = .40^* & \text{(Bet \$3)} \end{cases}$$

Thus, $f_2(3) = .40$, and $b_2(3) = \$0$ or $\$3$.

$$f_2(4) = \max \begin{cases} .4f_3(4) + .6f_3(4) = .40 & \text{(Bet \$0)} \\ .4f_3(5) + .6f_3(3) = .496^* & \text{(Bet \$1)} \\ .4f_3(6) + .6f_3(2) = .496^* & \text{(Bet \$2)} \\ .4f_3(7) + .6f_3(1) = .40 & \text{(Bet \$3)} \\ .4f_3(8) + .6f_3(0) = .40 & \text{(Bet \$4)} \end{cases}$$

Thus, $f_2(4) = .496$, and $b_2(4) = \$1$ or $\$2$.

$$f_2(5) = \max \begin{cases} .4f_3(5) + .6f_3(5) = .64^* & \text{(Bet \$0)} \\ .4f_3(6) + .6f_3(4) = .64^* & \text{(Bet \$1)} \\ .4f_3(7) + .6f_3(3) = .64^* & \text{(Bet \$2)} \\ .4f_3(8) + .6f_3(2) = .496 & \text{(Bet \$3)} \\ .4f_3(9) + .6f_3(1) = .40 & \text{(Bet \$4)} \\ .4f_3(10) + .6f_3(0) = .40 & \text{(Bet \$5)} \end{cases}$$

Thus, $f_2(5) = .64$, and $b_2(5) = $0, $1,$ or 2. For $d \geq 6$, $f_2(d) = 1$ and $b_2(d) = $0, $1, \ldots $(d - 6)$.

STAGE 1 COMPUTATIONS.

$$f_1(2) = \max \begin{cases} .4f_2(2) + .6f_2(2) = .16 & \text{(Bet \$0)} \\ .4f_2(3) + .6f_2(1) = .1984^* & \text{(Bet \$1)} \\ .4f_2(4) + .6f_2(0) = .1984^* & \text{(Bet \$2)} \end{cases}$$

Thus, $f_1(2) = .1984$, and $b_1(2) = $1 or 2. Hence, the gambler has a $.1984$ chance of reaching \$6. Suppose the gambler begins by betting $b_1(2) = $1. Then Figure 1 indicates the various possibilities that can occur. By following the strategy outlined in the figure, the gambler can reach her goal of \$6 in two different ways. First, she can win game 1 and game 3. This will occur with probability $(.4)^2 = .16$. Second, the gambler can win if she loses the first game but wins the next three games. This will occur with proability $.6(.4)^3 = .0384$. Hence, the gambler's probability of reaching \$6 is $.16 + .0384 = .1984 = f_1(2)$.

Figure 1
Ways Gambler Can
Reach \$6

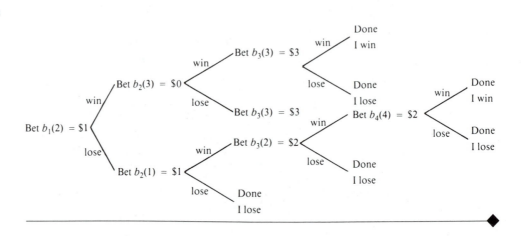

E X A M P L E
4

Martina McEnroe has two types of serves: a hard serve (H) and a soft serve (S).[†] The probability that Martina's hard serve will land in bounds is p_H, and the probability that her soft serve will land in bounds is p_S. If Martina's hard serve lands in bounds, there is a probability w_H that Martina will win the point. If Martina's soft serve lands in bounds, there is a probability w_S that Martina will win the point. We assume that $p_H < p_S$ and $w_H > w_S$. Martina's goal is to maximize the probability of winning a point on which she serves. Use dynamic programming to help Martina select an optimal serving strategy. Remember that if both serves are out of bounds, Martina loses the point.

[†]Based on material by E. V. Denardo, personal communication.

Solution

To maximize Martina's probability of winning the point, we give her a reward of 1 if she wins the point and a reward of 0 if she loses the point. We also define f_t ($t = 1, 2$) to be the probability that Martina wins a point if she plays optimally and is about to take her tth serve. To determine the optimal serving strategy, we work backward, beginning with f_2. If Martina serves hard on the second serve, she will win the point (and earn a reward of 1) with probability $p_H w_H$. Similarly, if she serves soft on the second serve, her expected reward is $p_S w_S$. Thus, we have

$$f_2 = \max \begin{cases} p_H w_H & \text{(Serve hard)} \\ p_S w_S & \text{(Serve soft)} \end{cases}$$

For the moment, let's assume that

$$p_S w_S > p_H w_H \tag{5}$$

If (5) holds, then Martina should serve soft on the second serve. In this situation, $f_2 = p_S w_S$.

To determine f_1, we need to look at what happens on the first serve. If Martina serves hard on the first serve, the events in Table 6 can occur, and Martina earns an expected reward of $p_H w_H + (1 - p_H)f_2$. If Martina serves soft on the first serve, then the events in Table 7 can occur, and Martina's expected reward is $p_S w_S + (1 - p_S)f_2$. We now write the following recursion for f_1:

$$f_1 = \max \begin{cases} p_H w_H + (1 - p_H)f_2 & \text{(Serve hard)} \\ p_S w_S + (1 - p_S)f_2 & \text{(Serve soft)} \end{cases}$$

Table 6
Computation of Expected Reward If First Serve Is Hard

EVENT	PROBABILITY OF EVENT	EXPECTED REWARD FOR GIVEN EVENT
First serve in and Martina wins point	$p_H w_H$	1
First serve in and Martina loses point	$p_H(1 - w_H)$	0
First serve out of bounds	$1 - p_H$	f_2

Table 7
Computation of Expected Reward If First Serve Is Soft

EVENT	PROBABILITY OF EVENT	EXPECTED REWARD FOR GIVEN EVENT
First serve in and Martina wins point	$p_S w_S$	1
First serve in and Martina loses point	$p_S(1 - w_S)$	0
First serve out of bounds	$1 - p_S$	f_2

From this equation, we see that Martina should serve hard on the first serve if

$$p_H w_H + (1 - p_H)f_2 \geq p_S w_S + (1 - p_S)f_2 \tag{6}$$

(If Eq. (6) is not satisfied, Martina should serve soft on the first serve.)

Continuing with the assumption that $p_S w_S > w_H p_H$ (which implies that $f_2 = p_S w_S$), we may substitute $f_2 = p_S w_S$ in (6) to obtain the result that Martina should serve hard on the first serve if

$$p_H w_H + (1 - p_H)p_S w_S \geq p_S w_S + (1 - p_S)p_S w_S$$

or

$$p_H w_H \geq p_S w_S(1 + p_H - p_S) \tag{7}$$

For example, if $p_H = .60$, $p_S = .90$, $w_H = .55$, and $w_S = .50$, then Eqs. (5) and (7) are both satisfied, and Martina should serve hard on her first serve and soft on her second serve. On the other hand, if $p_H = .25$, $p_S = .80$, $w_H = .60$, and $w_S = .45$, then both serves should be soft. The reason for this is that in this case, the hard serve's advantage from the fact that w_H exceeds w_S is outweighed by the fact that a hard serve on the first serve greatly increases the chances of a double fault.

To complete our analysis, we must consider the situation where (5) does not hold. We now show that if

$$p_H w_H \geq p_S w_S \tag{8}$$

Martina should serve hard on both serves. Note that if Eq. (8) holds, then $f_2 = \max \{p_H w_H, p_S w_S\} = p_H w_H$, and Martina should serve hard on the second serve. Now (6) implies that Martina should serve hard on the first serve if

$$p_H w_H + (1 - p_H)p_H w_H \geq p_S w_S + (1 - p_S)p_H w_H$$

Upon rearrangement, the last inequality becomes

$$p_H w_H(1 + p_S - p_H) \geq p_S w_S$$

Dividing both sides of the last inequality by $p_S w_S$ shows that Martina should serve hard on the first serve if

$$\frac{p_H w_H}{p_S w_S}(1 + p_S - p_H) \geq 1$$

After noting that $p_H w_H \geq p_S w_S$ and $(1 + p_S - p_H) > 1$ (because $p_S > p_H$), we see that the last inequality holds. Thus, we have shown that if $p_H w_H \geq p_S w_S$, Martina should serve hard on both serves. This is reasonable, because if it is optimal to serve hard on the second serve (and this requires $p_H w_H \geq p_S w_S$), then it should be optimal to serve hard on the first serve, because the danger of double-faulting (which is the drawback to the hard serve) is less immediate on the first serve. Of course, Example 4 could have been solved using a decision tree; see Problem 10 of Section 13.3.

In our solution to Example 4, we have shown how Martina's optimal strategy depends on the values of the parameters defining the problem. This is a kind of sensitivity analysis reminiscent of the sensitivity analysis that we applied to linear programming problems in Chapters 5 and 6.

◆ PROBLEMS

GROUP A

1. Vladimir Ulanowsky is playing Keith Smithson a two-game chess match. Winning a game scores 1 match point, and drawing a game scores $\frac{1}{2}$ match point. After the two games are played, the player with more match points is declared the champion. If the two players are tied after two games, they continue playing until somebody wins a game (the winner of that game will be the champion). During each game, Ulanowsky can play one of two ways: boldly or conservatively. If he plays boldly, he has a 45% chance of winning the game and a 55% chance of losing the game. If he plays conservatively, he has a 90% chance of drawing the game and a 10% chance of losing the game. Ulanowsky's goal is to maximize his probability of winning the match. Use dynamic programming to help him accomplish this goal. If this problem is solved correctly, even though Ulanowsky is the inferior player, his chance of winning the match is over $\frac{1}{2}$. Explain this anomalous result.

2. Dickie Hustler has $2 and is going to toss an unfair coin (probability .4 of heads) three times. Before each toss, he can bet any amount of money (up to what he now has). If heads comes up, Dickie wins the number of dollars he bets; if tails comes up, he loses the number of dollars he bets. Use dynamic programming to determine a strategy that maximizes Dickie's probability of having at least $5 after the third coin toss.

GROUP B

3. Suppose that Army trails by 14 points late in the Army-Navy football game. Army's guardian angel has assured the Army coach that his team will have the ball two more times during the game and will score a touchdown (worth 6 points) each time it has the ball. The Army coach has also been assured that Navy will not score any more points. Suppose a win is assigned a value of 1, a tie is assigned a vaue of .3, and a loss is assigned a value of 0. Army's problem is to determine whether to go for 1 point or 2 points after each touchdown. A 1-point conversion is always successful, and a 2-point conversion is successful only 40% of the time. The Army coach wishes to maximize the expected reward earned from the outcome of the game. Use dynamic programming to determine an optimal strategy. Then prove the following result: *No matter what value is assigned to a tie, it is never optimal to use the following strategy: Go for a 1-point conversion after the first touchdown and go for a 2-point conversion after the second touchdown.* Note that this (suboptimal) strategy is the one most coaches follow!

21-4

FURTHER EXAMPLES OF PROBABILISTIC DYNAMIC PROGRAMMING FORMULATIONS

Many probabilistic dynamic programming problems can be solved using recursions of the following form (for max problems):

$$f_t(i) = \max_a \left\{ (\text{expected reward earned during stage } t \mid i, a) + \sum_j p(j \mid i, a, t) f_{t+1}(j) \right\} \quad (9)$$

In Eq. (9), $f_t(i)$ is the maximum expected reward that can be earned during stages t, $t + 1, \ldots$ end of the problem, given that the state at the beginning of stage t is i. The max in (9) is taken over all actions a that are feasible when the state at the beginning of stage t is i. In (9), $p(j \mid i, a, t)$ is the probability that the next period's state will be j, given that the current (stage t) state is i and action a is chosen. Hence, the summation in Eq. (9) represents the expected reward earned from stage $t + 1$ to the end of the problem. By choosing a to maximize the right-hand side of (9), we are choosing a to maximize the expected reward earned from stage t to the end of the problem, and this is what we want to do. The following are six examples of probabilistic dynamic programming formulations.

E X A M P L E
5

Sunco Oil has D dollars to allocate for drilling at sites $1, 2, \ldots, T$. If x dollars are allocated to site t, the probability is $q_t(x)$ that oil will be found on site t. Sunco estimates that if site t has any oil, the oil on site t is worth r_t dollars. Formulate a recursion that could be used to enable Sunco to maximize the expected value of all oil found on sites $1, 2, \ldots, T$.

Solution

This is a typical resource allocation problem (see Example 1). Therefore, the stage should represent the number of sites, the decision for site t is how many dollars to allocate to site t, and the state is the number of dollars available to allocate to sites $t, t + 1, \ldots, T$. We therefore define $f_t(d)$ to be the maximum expected value of the oil that can be found on sites $t, t + 1, \ldots, T$ if d dollars are available to allocate to sites $t, t + 1, \ldots, T$.

We make the reasonable assumption that $q_T(x)$ is a nondecreasing function of x. If this is the case, then at stage T, all money should be allocated to site T. This yields

$$f_T(d) = r_T q_T(d) + (1 - q_T(d))0 = r_T q_T(d)$$

For $t < T$,

$$f_t(d) = \max_x \{r_t q_t(x) + f_{t+1}(d - x)\}$$

where x must satisfy $0 \leq x \leq d$. The last recursion follows, because $r_t q_t(x)$ is the expected value of the reward for stage t, and since Sunco will have $d - x$ dollars available for sites $t + 1, t + 2, \ldots, T, f_{t+1}(d - x)$ is the expected value of the oil that can be found by optimally drilling at sites $t + 1, t + 2, \ldots, T$. To solve the problem, we would work backward until $f_1(D)$ had been determined.   ◆

E X A M P L E
6

Each year, the owner of a lake must determine how many bass to capture and sell. During year t, a price p_t will be received for each bass that is caught. If the lake contains b bass at the beginning of year t, the cost of capturing x bass is $c_t(x \,|\, b)$. Between the time that year t's bass are caught and year $t + 1$ begins, the bass in the lake multiply by a random factor $\mathbf{D}$, where $P(\mathbf{D} = d) = q(d)$.

Formulate a dynamic programming recursion that can be used to determine a bass-catching strategy that will maximize the owner's net profit over the next ten years. At present, the lake contains 10,000 bass.

Solution

As in Example 8 of Chapter 20, the stage is the year, the state is the number of bass in the lake at the beginning of the year, and the decision is how many bass to catch during each year. We define $f_t(b)$ to be the maximum expected net profit that can be earned during years $t, t + 1, \ldots, 10$ if the lake contains b bass at the beginning of year t. Then

$$f_{10}(b) = \max_x \{xp_{10} - c_{10}(x \,|\, b)\}$$

where $0 \leq x \leq b$, and for $t < 10$

$$f_t(b) = \max_x \left\{xp_t - c_t(x \,|\, b) + \sum_d q(d) f_{t+1}(d(b - x))\right\}$$

In this recursion, x must satisfy $0 \leq x \leq b$. To justify the recursion for $t < 10$, first note that the profits during year t are (with certainty) $xp_t - c_t(x \,|\, b)$. Then with probability

$q(d)$, year $t + 1$'s state will be $d(b - x)$. It then follows that if x bass are caught during year t, the maximum expected net profit that can be earned during years $t + 1$, $t + 2, \ldots, 10$ will be

$$\sum_d q(d)f_{t+1}(d(b - x))$$

Hence, the recursion chooses the number of bass caught during year t to maximize the sum of year t profits and future profits. To use this recursion, we work backward until $f_1(10{,}000)$ is computed. Then, after the number of bass in the lake at the beginning of year t is observed, we use the recursion to determine the number of bass that should be caught during year t. ◆

E X A M P L E
7

When Sally Mutton arrives at the bank, 30 minutes remain on her lunch break. If Sally makes it to the head of the line and gets served before the end of her lunch break, she earns a reward r. However, Sally does not enjoy waiting in lines, so to reflect her dislike for waiting in line, she incurs a cost c for each minute she waits. During a minute in which n people are ahead of Sally, there is a probability $p(x \mid n)$ that x people will complete their transactions. Suppose that when Sally arrives, 20 people are ahead of her in line. Use dynamic programming to determine a strategy for Sally that will maximize her expected net revenue (reward − waiting costs).

Solution

When Sally arrives at the bank, she must decide whether to join the line or to give up and leave. At any later time, she may also decide to leave if it is unlikely that she will be served by the end of her lunch break. If 1 minute remained, Sally's decision would be simple: She should stay in line if and only if her expected reward exceeds the cost of waiting for 1 minute (c). Then we can work backward to a problem with 2 minutes left, etc. We define $f_t(n)$ to be the maximum expected net reward that Sally can receive from time t to the end of her lunch break if at time t, n people are ahead of her. We let $t = 0$ be the present and $t = 30$ be the end of the problem. Since $t = 29$ is the beginning of the last minute of the problem, we write

$$f_{29}(n) = \max \begin{cases} 0 & \text{(Leave)} \\ rp(n \mid n) - c & \text{(Stay)} \end{cases}$$

This follows because if Sally chooses to leave at time 29, she earns no reward and incurs no more costs. On the other hand, if she stays at time 29, she will incur a waiting cost of c (a revenue of $-c$) and with probability $p(n \mid n)$ will enter service and receive a reward r. Thus, if Sally stays, her expected net reward is $rp(n \mid n) - c$.

For $t < 29$, we write

$$f_t(n) = \max \begin{cases} 0 & \text{(Leave)} \\ rp(n \mid n) - c + \sum_{k < n} p(k \mid n)f_{t+1}(n - k) & \text{(Stay)} \end{cases}$$

The last recursion follows, because if Sally stays, she will earn an expected reward (as in the $t = 29$ case) of $rp(n \mid n) - c$ during the current minute, and with probability $p(k \mid n)$, there will be $n - k$ people ahead of her; in this case, her expected net reward from time $t + 1$ to time 30 will be $f_{t+1}(n - k)$. If Sally stays, her overall expected reward received from time $t + 1, t + 2, \ldots, 30$ will be

$$\sum_{k<n} p(k \mid n) f_{t+1}(n - k)$$

Of course, if n people complete their transactions during the current minute, the problem ends, and Sally's future net revenue will be zero.

To determine Sally's optimal waiting policy, we work backward until $f_0(20)$ is computed. If $f_0(20)$ is attained by "stay," Sally stays and sees how many people are ahead of her at time 1. She continues to stay until a situation arises for which the optimal action is "leave" or she begins to be served. In either case, the problem terminates.

Problems in which the decision maker can terminate the problem by choosing a particular action are known as **stopping rule problems**; they often have a special structure that simplifies the determination of optimal policies. See Ross (1983) for more information on stopping rule problems.

◆

E X A M P L E
8

E. J. Korvair Department Store is trying to determine an optimal cash management policy. During each day, the demand for cash may be described by a random variable **D**, where $P(\mathbf{D} = d) = p(d)$. At the beginning of each day, the store sends an employee to the bank to deposit or withdraw funds. Each bank transaction costs K dollars. Then E.J.'s demand for cash is met by cash left from the previous day plus money withdrawn (or minus money deposited). At the end of the day, the store determines its cash balance at the store. If the cash balance is negative, a shortage cost of s dollars per dollar short is incurred. If the ending balance is positive, a cost of i dollars per dollar held is incurred (because of loss of interest that could have been earned by depositing cash in the bank). At the beginning of day 1, the store has $10,000 cash on hand an a bank balance of $100,000. Formulate a dynamic programming model that can be used to minimize the expected cost of filling the store's cash needs for the next 30 days.

Solution

To determine how much money should be withdrawn or deposited, E.J. needs to know its cash on hand and bank balance at the beginning of the day. As usual, we let time be the stage. At the beginning of each stage (or day), E.J. must decide how much to withdraw from or deposit in the bank. We let $f_t(c, b)$ be the minimum expected cost incurred by the store during days $t, t + 1, \ldots, 30$, given that at the beginning of day t, the store has c dollars cash at the store and b dollars in the bank.

We observe that

$$f_{30}(c, b) = \min_x \left\{ K\delta(x) + \sum_{d \le c+x} p(d)(c + x - d)i + \sum_{d \ge c+x} p(d)(d - c - x)s \right\} \quad \textbf{(10)}$$

Here, x is the amount of money transferred from the bank to the store (if $x < 0$ money is transferred from the store to the bank). Since the store cannot withdraw more than b dollars from the bank or deposit more than c dollars in the bank, x must satisfy $b \ge x \ge -c$. Also, in Eq. (10), $\delta(0) = 0$ and $\delta(x) = 1$ for $x \ne 0$. In short, $K\delta(x)$ picks up the transaction cost (if there is a transaction). If $d \le c + x$, the store will end the day with $c + x - d$ dollars, so a cost of $i(c + x - d)$ is incurred (because of lost interest). Since this occurs with probability $p(d)$, the first sum in Eq. (10) represents the expected interest costs incurred during day 30. Also note that if $d \geq c + x$, the store will be $d - c - x$ dollars short, and a shortage cost of $s(d - c - x)$ will be incurred. Again, this cost is incurred with probability $p(d)$. Hence, the second sum in (10) is the expected shortage cost incured during day 30.

For $t < 30$, we write

$$f_t(c, b) = \min_x \left\{ K\delta(x) + \sum_{d \leq c+x} p(d)(c + x - d)i \right.$$

$$\left. + \sum_{d \geq c+x} p(d)(d - c - x)s + \sum_d p(d)f_{t+1}(c + x - d, b - x) \right\} \quad (11)$$

.

As in (10), x must satisfy $b \geq x \geq -c$. Also, the term $K\delta(x)$ and the first two summations yield the expected cost incurred during day t. If day t demand is d, then at the beginning of day $t + 1$, the store will have $c + x - d$ dollars cash on hand and a bank balance of $b - x$. Thus, with probability $p(d)$, the store's expected cost during days $t + 1, t + 2, \ldots, 30$ will be $f_{t+1}(c + x - d, b - x)$. Weighting $f_{t+1}(c + x - d, b - x)$ by the probability that day t demand will be d, we see that he last sum in Eq. (11) is the expected cost incurred during days $t + 1, t + 2, \ldots, 30$. Hence, (11) is correct. To determine the optimal cash management policy, we would use (10) and (11) to work backward until $f_1(10{,}000, 100{,}000)$ has been computed.   ◆

**E X A M P L E
9**

Robert Blue is trying to find a parking place near his favorite restaurant. He is approaching the restaurant from the west, and his goal is to park as close as possible to the restaurant. The available parking places are pictured in Figure 2. Robert is nearsighted and cannot see ahead; he can only see whether or not the space he is at now is empty. When Robert arrives at an empty space, he must decide whether to park in the empty space or to continue to look for a closer space. Once he passes a space, he cannot return to the space. Robert estimates that the probability that space t is empty is p_t. If he does not end up with a parking space, he is embarrassed and incurs a cost M (M is a big positive number). If he does park in space t, he incurs a cost $|t|$. Show how Robert can use dynamic programming to develop a parking strategy that minimizes his expected cost.

Figure 2
Location of Parking
Places

$\rightarrow$ $\boxed{-T}$ $\boxed{1 - T}$ $\boxed{2 - T}$ $\cdots$ $\boxed{-1}$ $\boxed{-2}$ $\boxed{0}$ $\boxed{1}$ $\boxed{2}$ $\cdots$ $\boxed{T}$

Solution

If Robert is at space T, his problem is easy to solve: park in space T if it is empty; otherwise, incur a cost of M. Then Robert can work backward until he determines what to do at space $-T$. For this reason, we let the space Robert is at represent the stage. In order to make a decision at any stage, all Robert must know is whether or not the space is empty (if a space is not empty, he must continue). Thus, the state at any stage is whether or not the space is empty. Of course, if the space is empty, Robert's decision is whether to take the space or to continue.

We define

$f_t(o)$ = minimum expected cost if Robert is at space t and space t is occupied

$f_t(e)$ = minimum expected cost if Robert is at space t and space t is empty

If Robert is at space T, he will park in the space if it is empty (incurring a cost T) or incur a cost M if the space is occupied. Thus, we have $f_T(o) = M$ and $f_T(e) = T$.

For $t < T$, we write

$$f_t(o) = p_{t+1}f_{t+1}(e) + (1 - p_{t+1})f_{t+1}(o) \tag{12}$$

$$f_t(e) = \min \begin{cases} |t| & \text{(Take space } t\text{)} \\ p_{t+1}f_{t+1}(e) + (1 - p_{t+1})f_{t+1}(o) & \text{(Don't take space } t\text{)} \end{cases} \tag{13}$$

To justify (12), note that if space t is occupied, Robert must next look at space $t + 1$. With probability p_{t+1}, space $t + 1$ will be empty; in this case, Robert's expected cost will be $f_{t+1}(e)$. Similarly, with probability $(1 - p_{t+1})$, space $t + 1$ will be occupied, and Robert will incur an expected cost of $f_{t+1}(o)$. Thus, Robert's expected cost is

$$p_{t+1}f_{t+1}(e) + (1 - p_{t+1})f_{t+1}(o)$$

To justify (13), note that Robert can either take space t (incurring a cost of $|t|$) or continue. Thus, if Robert continues, his expected cost will be

$$p_{t+1}f_{t+1}(e) + (1 - p_{t+1})f_{t+1}(o)$$

Since Robert wishes to minimize his expected cost, (13) follows. By using (12) and (13), Robert can work backward to compute $f_{-T}(e)$ and $f_{-T}(o)$. Then he will continue until he reaches an empty space at some location t for which the minimum in (13) is attained by taking space t. If no such empty space is reached, Robert will not find a space, and he will incur a cost M.

♦

E X A M P L E
10

During month t ($t = 1, 2, \ldots, 60$), expert safecracker Dirk Stack knows that he will be offered a role in a bank job that will pay him d_t dollars. There is, however, a probability p_t that month t's job will result in his capture. If Dirk is captured, all his money will be lost. Dirk's goal is to maximize his expected asset position at the end of month 60. Formulate a dynamic programming recursion that will help Dirk accomplish his goal. At the beginning of month 1, Dirk has \$50,000.

Solution

At the beginning of month 60, Dirk has no future to consider and his problem is easy to solve, so we let time represent the stage. At the beginning of each month, Dirk must decide whether or not to take the current month's job offer. In order to make this decision, Dirk must know how much money he has at the beginning of the month. We define $f_t(d)$ to be Dirk's maximum expected asset position at the end of month 60, given that at the beginning of month t, Dirk has d dollars. Then

$$f_{60}(d) = \max \begin{cases} p_{60}(0) + (1 - p_{60})(d + d_{60}) & \text{(Accept month 60 job)} \\ d & \text{(Reject month 60 job)} \end{cases}$$

This result follows, because if Dirk takes the job during month 60, there is a probability p_{60} that he will be caught and end up with zero dollars and a probability $(1 - p_{60})$ that he will not be caught and end up with $d + d_{60}$ dollars. Of course, if Dirk does not take the month 60 job, he ends month 60 with d dollars.

Extending this reasoning yields, for $t < 60$,

$$f_t(d) = \max \begin{cases} p_t(0) + (1 - p_t)f_{t+1}(d + d_t) & \text{(Accept month } t \text{ job)} \\ f_{t+1}(d) & \text{(Reject month } t \text{ job)} \end{cases}$$

Note that if Dirk accepts month t's job, there is a probability p_t that he will be caught (and end up with zero) and a probability $(1 - p_t)$ that he will successfully complete month t's job and earn d_t dollars. In this case, Dirk will begin month $t + 1$ with $d + d_t$ dollars, and his expected final cash position will be $f_{t+1}(d + d_t)$. Of course, if Dirk rejects the month t job, he begins month $t + 1$ with d dollars, and his expected final cash position will be $f_{t+1}(d)$. Since Dirk wants to maximize his expected cash position at the end of month 60, the recursion follows. By using the recursion, Dirk can work backward to compute $f_1(50,000)$. Then he can decide whether or not to accept the month 1 job. Assuming he has not been caught, he can then determine whether or not to accept the month 2 job, etc.

◆

◆ PROBLEMS

GROUP A

1. The space shuttle is about to go up on another flight. With probability $p_t(z)$, it will use z type t fuel cells during the flight. The shuttle has room for at most W fuel cells. If at any time during the flight, all the type t fuel cells burn out, a cost c_t will be incurred. Assuming the goal is to minimize the expected cost due to fuel cell shortages, set up a dynamic programming model that could be used to determine how to stock the space shuttle with fuel cells. There are T different types of fuel cells.

2. At the beginning of each year, a firm observes its asset position (call it d) and may invest any amount x $(0 \le x \le d)$ in a risky investment. During each year, the money invested doubles with probability p and is completely lost with probability $1 - p$. Independently of this investment, the firm's asset position increases by an amount y with probability q_y (y may be negative). If the firm's asset position is negative at the beginning of a year, it cannot invest any money during that year. The firm initially has $10,000 in assets and wants to maximize its expected asset position ten years from now. Formulate a dynamic programming recursion that will help accomplish this goal.

3. Consider a machine that may be in any one of the states 0, 1, 2, ... At the beginning of each month, the state of the machine is observed, and it is decided whether to replace or keep the machine. If the machine is replaced, a new state 0 machine arrives instantaneously. It costs R dollars to replace a machine. Each month that a state i machine is in operation, a maintenance cost of $c(i)$ is incurred. If a machine is in state i at the beginning of a month, then with probability p_{ij}, the machine will begin the next month in state j. At the beginning of the first month, we own a state i_0 machine. Assuming that the interest rate is 12% per year, formulate a dynamic programming recursion that could be used to minimize the expected discounted cost incurred during the next T months. Note that if we replace a machine at the beginning of a month, we incur a maintenance cost of $c(0)$ during the month, and with probability p_{0i}, we begin the next month with a state i machine.

4. In the time interval between t and $t - 1$ seconds before the departure of Braneast Airlines Flight 313, there is a probability p_t that the airline will receive a reservation for the flight and a probability $1 - p_t$ that the airline will receive no reservation. The flight can seat up to 100 passengers. At departure time, if r reservations have been accepted by the airline, there is a probability $q(y|r)$ that y passengers will actually show up for the flight. Each passenger who boards the flight adds $500 to Braneast's revenues, but each passenger who shows up for the flight and cannot be seated receives $200 in compensation. Formulate a dynamic programming recursion to enable the airline to maximize its expected revenue from Flight 313. Assume that no reservations are received more than 100,000 seconds before flight time.

5. At the beginning of each week, a machine is either running or is broken down. If the machine runs throughout a week, it earns revenues of $100. If the machine breaks down during a week, the machine earns no revenue for that week. If the machine is running at the beginning of a week, we may perform maintenance on the machine in order to lessen the chance of a breakdown. If maintenance is performed, a running machine has a .4 chance of breaking down during the week; if maintenance is not performed, a running machine has a .7 chance of breaking down during the week. Maintenance costs $20 per week. If the machine is broken down at the beginning of the week, it must be replaced or repaired. Both repair and replacement occur instantaneously. Repairing a broken-down machine costs $40, and there is a .4 chance that the repaired machine will break down during the week. Replacing a broken-down machine costs $90, but the machine is guaranteed to run throughout the next week of operation. Use dynamic programming to determine a repair, replacement, and maintenance policy that maximizes the expected net profit earned over a four-week period. Assume that the machine is running at the beginning of the first week.

6. I own a single share of Wivco stock. I must sell my share of stock at the beginning of one of the next 30 days. Each day, the price of the stock changes. With probability $q(x)$, the price of the stock tomorrow will increase by $x\%$ over today's stock price (x can be negative). For example, with probability $q(5)$, tomorrow's stock price will be 5% higher than today's stock price. Show how dynamic programming can be used to determine a strategy that maximizes the expected revenue earned from selling the share of Wivco stock. Assume that at the beginning of the first day, the stock sells for $10 per share.

GROUP B

7. The National Cat Foundling Home encourages people to adopt its cats, but (because of limited funds) it allows each prospective owner to inspect only four cats before choosing one of them to take home. Ten-year-old Sara is eager to adopt a cat and agrees to abide by the following rules. A randomly selected cat is brought for Sara to see, and then Sara must either choose the cat or reject it. If the first cat is rejected, Sara sees another randomly selected cat and must accept or reject it. This procedure continues until Sara has selected her cat. Once Sara rejects a cat, she cannot go back later and choose it as her pet. Determine a strategy for Sara that will maximize her probability of ending up with the cat she actually prefers.

8. Consider the following probabilistic inventory model:

1. At the beginning of each period, a firm observes its inventory position.

2. Then the firm decides how many units to produce during the current period. It costs the firm $c(x)$ dollars to produce x units during a period.

3. With probability $q(d)$, d units are demanded during the period. From units on hand (including the current period's production), the firm satisfies as much of the demand as possible. The firm receives r dollars for each unit sold. For each unit of demand that is unsatisfied, a penalty cost p is incurred. All unsatisfied demand is assumed to be lost. For example, if the firm has 20 units available and current demand is 30, a revenue of $20r$ would be received, and a penalty of $10p$ would be incurred.

4. If ending inventory is positive, a holding cost of $1 per unit is incurred.

5. The next period now begins.

The firm's initial inventory is zero, and the firm's goal is to minimize the expected cost over a 100-period horizon. Formulate a dynamic programming recursion that will help the firm accomplish its goal.

9. Martha and Ken Allen want to sell their house. At the beginning of each day, they receive an offer. We assume that from day to day, the size of the offers are independent random variables and that the probability that a given day's offer is for j dollars is p_j. An offer may be accepted during the day it is made or at any later date. For each day that the house remains unsold, a maintenance cost of c dollars is incurred. The house must be sold within 30 days. Formulate a dynamic programming recursion that Martha and Ken can use to maximize their expected net profit (selling price − maintenance cost). Assume that the maintenance cost for a day is incurred before the current day's offer is received and that each offer is for an integral number of dollars.

10. An advertising firm has D dollars to spend on reaching customers in T separate markets. Market t consists of k_t people. If x dollars are spent on advertising in market t, the probability that a given person in market t will be reached is $p_t(x)$. Each person in market t who is reached will buy c_t units of the product. A person who is not reached will not buy any of the product. Formulate a dynamic programming recursion that could be used to maximize the expected number of units sold in T markets.

11. Georgia Stein is the new owner of the New York Yankees. Each season, Georgia must decide how much money to spend on the free agent draft. During each season, Georgia can spend any amount of money on free agents up to the team's capital position at the beginning of the season. If the Yankees finish in ith place during a season, their capital position increases by $R(i)$ dollars less the amount of money spent in the free agent draft. If the Yankees finished in ith place during the last season and spend d dollars on free agents during the off-season, the probability that the Yankees will finish in place j during the next season is $p_{ij}(d)$ $(j = 1, 2, \ldots, 7)$. Last season, the Yankees finished in first place, and at the end of the season, they had a capital position of D dollars. Formulate a dynamic programming recursion that will enable the Yankees to maximize their expected cash position at the end of T seasons.

12. Bailey Bliss is the campaign manager for Walter Glenn's presidential campaign. He has D dollars to allocate to T winner-take-all primaries. If x_t dollars are allocated to primary t, then with probability $p_t(x_t)$, Glenn will win primary t and obtain v_t delegates. With probability $1 - p_t(x_t)$, Glenn loses primary t and obtains no delegates from primary t. Glenn needs K delegates to be nominated. Use dynamic programming to help Bliss maximize Glenn's probability of being nominated. What aspect of a real campaign does the present formulation ignore?

13. At 7 A.M., eight people leave their cars for repair at Harry's Auto Repair Shop. If person i's car is ready by time t (7 A.M. = time 0, etc.), he will pay Harry $r_i(t)$ dollars. For example, if person 2's car must be ready by 2 P.M., we may have $r_2(8) = 0$. Harry estimates that with probability $p_i(t)$, it will take t hours to repair person i's car. Formulate a dynamic programming recursion that will enable Harry to maximize his expected revenue for the day. His workday ends at 5 P.M. = time 10.

21-5 MARKOV DECISION PROCESSES*

To use dynamic programming in a problem for which the stage is represented by time, one must determine the value of T, the number of time periods over which expected revenue or expected profit is maximized (or expected costs are minimzed). T is referred to as the **horizon length**. For instance, in the equipment replacement problem of Section 20.5, if our goal is to minimize costs over a 30-year period, then $T = 30$. Of course, it may be difficult for a decision maker to determine exactly the most suitable horizon length. In fact, when a decision maker is facing a long horizon and is not sure of the horizon length, it is more convenient to assume that the horizon length is infinite.

Suppose a decision maker's goal is to maximize the expected reward earned over an infinite horizon. In many situations, the expected reward earned over an infinite horizon may be unbounded. For example, if for any state and decision, the reward earned during a period is at least \$3, then the expected reward earned during an infinite number of periods will, no matter what decisions are chosen, be unbounded. In this situation, it is not clear how a decision maker should choose a decision. Two approaches are commonly used to resolve the problem of unbounded expected rewards over an infinite horizon:

1. We can discount rewards (or costs) by assuming that a \$1 reward received during the next period will have the same value as a reward of β dollars ($0 < \beta < 1$) received during the current period. This is equivalent to assuming that the decision maker wishes to maximize expected discounted reward. Let M be the maximum reward (over all possible states and choices of decisions) that can be received during a single period. Then the maximum expected discounted reward (measured in terms of current period dollars) that can be received over an infinite period horizon is

$$M + M\beta + M\beta^2 + \cdots = \frac{M}{1 - \beta} < \infty$$

Thus, discounting rewards (or costs) resolves the problem of an infinite expected reward.

*This section covers topics that may be omitted with no loss of continuity.

2. The decision maker can choose to maximize the expected reward earned per period. Then he or she would choose a decision during each period in an attempt to maximize the average reward per period as given by

$$E \left(\lim_{n \to \infty} \frac{\text{reward earned during periods } 1, 2, \ldots, n}{n} \right)$$

Thus, if a $3 reward were earned each period, the total reward earned during an infinite number of periods would be unbounded, but the average reward per period would equal $3.

In our discussion of infinite horizon problems, we choose to resolve the problem of unbounded expected rewards by discounting rewards by a factor β per period. A brief discussion of the criterion of average reward per period is also included. Infinite horizon probabilistic dynamic programming problems are called **Markov decision processes** (or M.D.P.s).

DESCRIPTION OF AN M.D.P.

An M.D.P. is described by four types of information:

1. State space
2. Decision set
3. Transition probabilities
4. Expected rewards

STATE SPACE. At the beginning of each period, the M.D.P. is in some state i, where i is a member of $S = \{1, 2, \ldots, N\}$. S is referred to as the M.D.P.'s **state space**.

DECISION SET. For each state i, there is a finite set of allowable decisions, $D(i)$.

TRANSITION PROBABILITIES. Suppose a period begins in state i, and a decision $d \in D(i)$ is chosen. Then with probability $p(j \mid i, d)$, the next period's state will be j. The next period's state depends only on the current period's state and on the decision chosen during the current period (not on previous states and decisions). This is why we use the term *Markov* decision process.

EXPECTED REWARDS. During a period in which the state is i and a decision $d \in D(i)$ is chosen, an expected reward of r_{id} is received.

E X A M P L E
11

Machine Replacement   At the beginning of each week, a machine is in one of four conditions (states): excellent (E), good (G), average (A), or bad (B). The weekly revenue earned by a machine in each type of condition is as follows: excellent, $100; good, $80; average, $50; bad, $10. After observing the condition of a machine at the beginning of the week, we have the option of instantaneously replacing it with an excellent machine, which costs $200. The quality of a machine deteriorates over time, as shown in Table 8. For this situation, determine the state space, decision sets, transition probabilities, and expected rewards.

	PROBABILITY THAT MACHINE BEGINS NEXT WEEK AS			
Table 8 Next Period's States of Machines	**PRESENT STATE OF MACHINE**	*Excellent*	*Good*	*Average*	*Bad*
	Excellent	.7	.3	—	—
	Good	—	.7	.3	—
	Average	—	—	.6	.4
	Bad	—	—	—	1.0 until replaced

Solution

The set of possible states is $S = \{E, G, A, B\}$. Let

$$R = \text{replace at beginning of current period}$$
$$NR = \text{do not replace during current period}$$

Since it is absurd to replace an excellent machine, we write

$$D(E) = \{NR\} \qquad D(G) = D(A) = D(B) = \{R, NR\}$$

We are given the following transition probabilities:

$$p(E\,|\,NR, E) = .7 \quad p(G\,|\,NR, E) = .3 \quad p(A\,|\,NR, E) = 0 \quad p(B\,|\,NR, E) = 0$$
$$p(E\,|\,NR, G) = 0 \quad p(G\,|\,NR, G) = .7 \quad p(A\,|\,NR, G) = .3 \quad p(B\,|\,NR, G) = 0$$
$$p(E\,|\,NR, A) = 0 \quad p(G\,|\,NR, A) = 0 \quad p(A\,|\,NR, A) = .6 \quad p(B\,|\,NR, A) = .4$$
$$p(E\,|\,NR, B) = 0 \quad p(G\,|\,NR, B) = 0 \quad p(A\,|\,NR, B) = 0 \quad p(B\,|\,NR, B) = 1$$

If we replace a machine with an excellent machine, the transition probabilities will be the same as if we had begun the week with an excellent machine. Thus,

$$p(E\,|\,G, R) = p(E\,|\,A, R) = p(E\,|\,B, R) = .7$$
$$p(G\,|\,G, R) = p(G\,|\,A, R) = p(G\,|\,B, R) = .3$$
$$p(A\,|\,G, R) = p(A\,|\,A, R) = p(A\,|\,B, R) = 0$$
$$p(B\,|\,G, R) = p(B\,|\,A, R) = p(B\,|\,B, R) = 0$$

If a machine is not replaced, then during the week, we receive the revenues given in the problem. Therefore, $r_{E,NR} = \$100$, $r_{G,NR} = \$80$, $r_{A,NR} = \$50$, and $r_{B,NR} = \$10$. If we replace a machine with an excellent machine, then no matter what type of machine we had at the beginning of the week, we receive $100 and pay a cost of $200. Thus, $r_{E,R} = r_{G,R} = r_{A,R} = r_{B,R} = -\$100$. ♦

In an M.D.P., what criterion should be used to determine the correct decision? Answering this question requires that we discuss the idea of an **optimal policy** for an M.D.P.

DEFINITION	A **policy** is a rule that specifies how each period's decision is chosen.

Period t's decision may depend on the prior history of the process. Thus, period t's decision can depend on the state during periods $1, 2, \ldots, t$ and the decisions chosen during periods $1, 2, \ldots, t - 1$.

DEFINITION ◆ A policy δ is a **stationary policy** if whenever the state is i, the policy δ chooses (independently of the period) the same decision (call this decision $\delta(i)$).

We let δ represent an arbitrary policy and Δ represent the set of all policies. Then

$\mathbf{X}_t$ = random variable for state of M.D.P. at beginning of period t (e.g., $\mathbf{X}_2, \mathbf{X}_3, \ldots, \mathbf{X}_n$)

X_1 = given state of process at beginning of period 1 (initial state)

d_t = decision chosen during period t

$V_\delta(i)$ = expected discounted reward earned during an infinite number of periods, given that at beginning of period 1, state is i and stationary policy will be δ

Then

$$V_\delta(i) = E_\delta \left(\sum_{t=1}^{t=\infty} \beta^{t-1} r_{\mathbf{X}_t d_t} \mid X_1 = i \right)$$

where $E_\delta(\beta^{t-1} r_{\mathbf{X}_t d_t} \mid X_1 = i)$ is the expected discounted reward earned during period t, given that at the beginning of period 1, the state is i and stationary policy δ is followed.

In a maximization problem, we define

$$V(i) = \max_{\delta \in \Delta} V_\delta(i) \tag{14}$$

In a minimization problem, we define

$$V(i) = \min_{\delta \in \Delta} V_\delta(i)$$

DEFINITION ◆ If a policy δ^* has the property that for all $i \in S$

$$V(i) = V_{\delta^*}(i)$$

then δ^* is an **optimal policy**.

The existence of a single policy δ^* that simultaneously attains all N maxima in Eq. (14) is not obvious. If the r_{id}'s are bounded, Blackwell (1962) has shown that an optimal policy exists, and there is always a stationary policy that is optimal. (Even if the r_{id}'s are not bounded, an optimal policy may exist.)

We now consider three methods that can be used to determine an optimal stationary policy:

1. Policy iteration

2. Linear programming

3. Value iteration, or successive approximations

POLICY ITERATION

VALUE DETERMINATION EQUATIONS.   Before we can explain the policy iteration method, we need to determine a system of linear equations that can be used to find $V_\delta(i)$ for $i \in S$ and any stationary policy δ. Let $\delta(i)$ be the decision chosen by the stationary policy δ whenever the process begins a period in state i. Then $V_\delta(i)$ can be found by solving the following system of N linear equations, the value determination equations:

$$V_\delta(i) = r_{i,\delta(i)} + \beta \sum_{j=1}^{j=N} p(j \mid i, \delta(i)) V_\delta(j) \qquad (i = 1, 2, \ldots, N) \qquad (15)$$

To justify Eq. (15), suppose we are in state i and we follow a stationary policy δ. The current period is period 1. Then the expected discounted reward earned during an infinite number of periods consists of $r_{i,\delta(i)}$ (the expected reward received during the current period) plus β (expected discounted reward, to beginning of period 2, earned from period 2 onward). But with probability $p(j \mid i, \delta(i))$, we will begin period 2 in state j and earn an expected discounted reward, back to period 2, of $V_\delta(j)$. Thus, the expected discounted reward, discounted back to the beginning of period 2 and earned from the beginning of period 2 onward, is given by

$$\sum_{j=1}^{j=N} p(j \mid i, \delta(i)) V_\delta(j)$$

Eq. (15) now follows.

   To illustrate the use of the value determination equations, we consider the following stationary policy for the machine replacement example:

$$\delta(E) = \delta(G) = NR \qquad \delta(A) = \delta(B) = R$$

This policy replaces a bad or average machine and does not replace a good or excellent machine. For this policy, Eq. (15) yields the following four equations:

$$V_\delta(E) = 100 + .9(.7V_\delta(E) + .3V_\delta(G))$$
$$V_\delta(G) = 80 + .9(.7V_\delta(G) + .3V_\delta(A))$$
$$V_\delta(A) = -100 + .9(.7V_\delta(E) + .3V_\delta(G))$$
$$V_\delta(B) = -100 + .9(.7V_\delta(E) + .3V_\delta(G))$$

Solving these equations yields $V_\delta(E) = 687.81$, $V_\delta(G) = 572.19$, $V_\delta(A) = 487.81$, and $V_\delta(B) = 487.81$.

HOWARD'S POLICY ITERATION METHOD.   We now describe Howard's (1960) policy iteration method for finding an optimal stationary policy for an M.D.P. (max problem).

   Step 1 Policy evaluation—Choose a stationary policy δ and use the value determination equations to find $V_\delta(i)$ $(i = 1, 2, \ldots, N)$.

   Step 2 Policy improvement—For all states $i = 1, 2, \ldots, N$, compute

$$T_\delta(i) = \max_{d \in D(i)} \left(r_{id} + \beta \sum_{j=1}^{j=N} p(j \mid i, d) V_\delta(j) \right) \qquad (16)$$

Since we can choose $d = \delta(i)$ for $i = 1, 2, \ldots, n$, $T_\delta(i) \geq V_\delta(i)$. If $T_\delta(i) = V_\delta(i)$ for $i = 1, 2, \ldots, N$, then δ is an optimal policy. If $T_\delta(i) > V_\delta(i)$ for at least one state, then δ is not an optimal policy. In this case, modify δ so that the decision in each state i is the decision attaining the maximum in Eq. (16) for $T_\delta(i)$. This yields a new stationary policy δ' for which $V_{\delta'}(i) \geq V_\delta(i)$ for $i = 1, 2, \ldots, N$, and for at least one state i', $V_{\delta'}(i') > V_\delta(i')$. Return to Step 1, with policy δ' replacing policy δ.

In a minimization problem, we replace max in Eq. (16) by min. If $T_\delta(i) = V_\delta(i)$ for $i = 1, 2, \ldots, N$, then δ is an optimal policy. If $T_\delta(i) < V_\delta(i)$ for at least one state, then δ is not an optimal policy. In this case, modify δ so that the decision in each state i is the decision attaining the minimum in Eq. (16) for $T_\delta(i)$. This yields a new stationary policy δ' for which $V_{\delta'}(i) \leq V_\delta(i)$ for $i = 1, 2, \ldots, N$, and for at least one state i', $V_{\delta'}(i') < V_\delta(i')$. Return to Step 1, with policy δ' replacing policy δ.

The policy iteration method is guaranteed to find an optimal policy after evaluating a finite number of policies. We now use the policy iteration method to find an optimal stationary policy for the machine replacement example. We begin with the following stationary policy:

$$\delta(E) = \delta(G) = NR \qquad \delta(A) = \delta(B) = R$$

For this policy, we have already found that $V_\delta(E) = 687.81$, $V_\delta(G) = 572.19$, $V_\delta(A) = 487.81$, and $V_\delta(B) = 487.81$. We now compute $T_\delta(E)$, $T_\delta(G)$, $T_\delta(A)$, and $T_\delta(B)$. Since NR is the only possible decision in E,

$$T_\delta(E) = V_\delta(E) = 687.81$$

and $T_\delta(E)$ is attained by the decision NR.

$$T_\delta(G) = \max \begin{cases} -100 + .9(.7V_\delta(E) + .3V_\delta(G)) = 487.81 & (R) \\ 80 + .9(.7V_\delta(G) + .3V_\delta(A)) = V_\delta(G) = 572.19^* & (NR) \end{cases}$$

Thus, $T_\delta(G) = 572.19$ is attained by the decision NR.

$$T_\delta(A) = \max \begin{cases} -100 + .9(.7V_\delta(E) + .3V_\delta(G)) = 487.81 & (R) \\ 50 + .9(.6V_\delta(A) + .4V_\delta(B)) = 489.03^* & (NR) \end{cases}$$

Thus, $T_\delta(A) = 489.03$ is attained by the decision NR.

$$T_\delta(B) = \max \begin{cases} -100 + .9(.7V_\delta(E) + .3V_\delta(G)) = V_\delta(B) = 487.81^* & (R) \\ 10 + .9V_\delta(B) = 449.03 & (NR) \end{cases}$$

Thus, $T_\delta(B) = V_\delta(B) = 487.81$. We have found that $T_\delta(E) = V_\delta(E)$, $T_\delta(G) = V_\delta(G)$, $T_\delta(B) = V_\delta(B)$, and $T_\delta(A) > V_\delta(A)$. Thus, the policy δ is not optimal, and the policy δ' given by $\delta'(E) = \delta'(G) = \delta'(A) = NR, \delta'(B) = R$, is an improvement over δ. We now return to Step 1 and solve the value determination equations for δ'. From Eq. (15), the value determination equations for δ' are

$$V_{\delta'}(E) = 100 + .9(.7V_{\delta'}(E) + .3V_{\delta'}(G))$$
$$V_{\delta'}(G) = 80 + .9(.7V_{\delta'}(G) + .3V_{\delta'}(A))$$
$$V_{\delta'}(A) = 50 + .9(.6V_{\delta'}(A) + .4V_{\delta'}(B))$$
$$V_{\delta'}(B) = -100 + .9(.7V_{\delta'}(E) + .3V_{\delta'}(G))$$

Solving these equations, we obtain $V_{\delta'}(E) = 690.23$, $V_{\delta'}(G) = 575.50$, $V_{\delta'}(A) = 492.35$, and $V_{\delta'}(B) = 490.23$. Observe that in each state i, $V_{\delta'}(i) > V_{\delta}(i)$. We now apply the policy iteration procedure to δ'. We compute

$$T_{\delta'}(E) = V_{\delta'}(E) = 690.23$$

$$T_{\delta'}(G) = \max \begin{cases} -100 + .9(.7V_{\delta'}(E) + .3V_{\delta'}(G)) = 490.23 & (R) \\ 80 + .9(.7V_{\delta'}(G) + .3V_{\delta'}(A)) = V_{\delta'}(G) = 575.50^* & (NR) \end{cases}$$

Thus, $T_{\delta'}(G) = V_{\delta'}(G) = 575.50$ is attained by NR.

$$T_{\delta'}(A) = \max \begin{cases} -100 + .9(.7V_{\delta'}(E) + .3V_{\delta'}(G)) = 490.23 & (R) \\ 50 + .9(.6V_{\delta'}(A) + .4V_{\delta'}(B)) = V_{\delta'}(A) = 492.35^* & (NR) \end{cases}$$

Thus, $T_{\delta'}(A) = V_{\delta'}(A) = 492.35$ is attained by NR.

$$T_{\delta'}(B) = \max \begin{cases} -100 + .9(.7V_{\delta'}(E) + .3V_{\delta'}(G)) = V_{\delta'}(B) = 490.23^* & (R) \\ 10 + .9V_{\delta'}(B) = 451.21 & (NR) \end{cases}$$

Thus, $T_{\delta'}(B) = V_{\delta'}(B) = 490.23$ is attained by R.

For each state i, $T_{\delta'}(i) = V_{\delta'}(i)$. Thus, δ' is an optimal stationary policy. In order to maximize expected discounted rewards (profits), a bad machine should be replaced, but an excellent, good, or average machine should not be replaced. If we began period 1 with an excellent machine, an expected discounted reward of \$690.23 could be earned.

LINEAR PROGRAMMING

It can be shown (see Ross (1983)) that an optimal stationary policy for a maximization problem can be found by solving the following LP:

$$\min z = V_1 + V_2 + \cdots + V_N$$

$$\text{s.t.} \quad V_i - \beta \sum_{j=1}^{j=N} p(j \mid i, d)V_j \geq r_{id} \qquad \text{(For each state } i \text{ and each } d \in d(i))$$

All variables urs

For a minimization problem, we solve the following LP:

$$\max z = V_1 + V_2 + \cdots + V_N$$

$$\text{s.t.} \quad V_i - \beta \sum_{j=1}^{j=N} p(j \mid i, d)V_j \leq r_{id} \qquad \text{(For each state } i \text{ and each } d \in d(i))$$

All variables urs

The optimal solution to these LPs will have $V_i = V(i)$. Also, if a constraint for state i and decision d is binding (has no slack or excess), then decision d is optimal in state i.

R E M A R K S   **1.** In the objective function, the coefficient of each V_i may be any positive number.

2. If all the V_i's are nonnegative (this will surely be the case if all the r_{id}'s are nonnegative), we may assume that all variables are nonnegative. If it is possible for some state to have $V(i)$ negative, then we must replace each variable V_i by $V_i' - V_i''$, where both V_i' and V_i'' are nonnegative.

Our machine replacement example yields the following LP:

$$\min z = V_E + V_G + V_A + V_B$$

$$
\begin{array}{llll}
\text{s.t.} & V_E \geq 100 + .9(.7V_E + .3V_G) & & (NR \text{ in } E)\\
& V_G \geq 80 + .9(.7V_G + .3V_A) & & (NR \text{ in } G)\\
& V_G \geq -100 + .9(.7V_E + .3V_G) & & (R \text{ in } G)\\
& V_A \geq 50 + .9(.6V_A + .4V_B) & & (NR \text{ in } A)\\
& V_A \geq -100 + .9(.7V_E + .3V_G) & & (R \text{ in } A)\\
& V_B \geq 10 + .9V_B & & (NR \text{ in } B)\\
& V_B \geq -100 + .9(.7V_E + .3V_G) & & (R \text{ in } B)
\end{array}
$$

All variables urs

The LINDO output for this LP yields $V_E = 690.23$, $V_G = 575.50$, $V_A = 492.35$, and $V_B = 490.23$. These values agree with those found via the policy iteration method. The LINDO output also indicates that the first, second, fourth, and seventh constraints have no slack. Thus, the optimal policy is to replace a bad machine and not to replace an excellent, good, or average machine.

VALUE ITERATION

There are several versions of value iteration (see Denardo (1982)). We discuss for a maximization problem the simplest value iteration scheme, also known as successive approximations. Let $V_t(i)$ be the maximum expected discounted reward that can be earned during t periods if the state at the beginning of the current period is i. Then

$$V_t(i) = \max_{d \in D(i)} \left\{ r_{id} + \beta \sum_{j=1}^{j=N} p(j|i,d)V_{t-1}(j) \right\} \qquad (t \geq 1)$$

$$V_0(i) = 0$$

This result follows, because during the current period, we earn an expected reward (in current period dollars) of r_{id}, and during the next $t - 1$ periods, our expected discounted reward (in terms of period 2 dollars) is

$$\sum_{j=1}^{j=N} p(j|i,d)V_{t-1}(j)$$

Let $d_t(i)$ be the decision that must be chosen during period 1 in state i to attain $V_t(i)$. For an M.D.P. with a finite state space and each $D(i)$ containing a finite number of elements, the most basic result in successive approximations states that for $i = 1, 2, \ldots, N$,

$$|V_t(i) - V(i)| \leq \frac{\beta^t}{1 - \beta} \max_{i,d} |r_{id}|$$

Recall that $V(i)$ is the maximum expected discounted reward earned during an infinite number of periods if the state is i at the beginning of the current period. Then

$$\lim_{t \to \infty} d_t(i) = \delta^*(i)$$

where $\delta^*(i)$ defines an optimal stationary policy. Since $\beta < 1$, for t sufficiently large, $V_t(i)$ will come arbitrarily close to $V(i)$. For instance, in the machine replacement example, $\beta = .9$ and $\max |r_{id}| = 100$. Thus, for all states, $V_{50}(i)$ would differ by at most $(.9)^{50} \left(\frac{100}{.10}\right) = \$5.15$ from $V(i)$. The equation

$$\lim_{t \to \infty} d_t(i) = \delta^*(i)$$

implies that for t sufficiently large, the decision that is optimal in state i for a t-period problem is also optimal in state i for an infinite horizon problem. This result is reminiscent of the turnpike theorem result for the knapsack problem that was discussed in Chapter 20.

Unfortunately, there is usually no easy way to determine a t^* such that for all i and $t \geq t^*$, $d_t(i) = \delta^*(i)$. (See Denardo (1982) for a partial result in this direction.) Despite this fact, value iteration methods usually obtain a satisfactory approximation to the $V(i)$ and $\delta^*(i)$ with less computational effort than is needed by the policy iteration method or by linear programming. Again, see Denardo (1982) for a discussion of this matter.

We illustrate the computation of V_1 and V_2 for the machine replacement example:

$$V_1(E) = 100 \qquad (NR)$$

$$V_1(G) = \max \begin{cases} 80^* & (NR) \\ -100 & (R) \end{cases} = 80$$

$$V_1(A) = \max \begin{cases} 50^* & (NR) \\ -100 & (R) \end{cases} = 50$$

$$V_1(B) = \max \begin{cases} 10^* & (NR) \\ -100 & (R) \end{cases} = 10$$

The * indicates the action attaining $V_1(i)$. Then

$$V_2(E) = 100 + .9(.7V_1(E) + .3V_1(G)) = 184.6 \qquad (NR)$$

$$V_2(G) = \max \begin{cases} 80 + .9(.7V_1(G) + .3V_1(A)) = 143.9^* & (NR) \\ -100 + .9(.7V_1(E) + .3V_1(G)) = -15.4 & (R) \end{cases}$$

$$V_2(A) = \max \begin{cases} 50 + .9(.6V_1(A) + .4V_1(B)) = 80.6^* & (NR) \\ -100 + .9(.7V_1(E) + .3V_1(G)) = -15.4 & (R) \end{cases}$$

$$V_2(B) = \max \begin{cases} 10 + .9(V_1(B)) = 19^* & (NR) \\ -100 + .9(.7V_1(E) + .3V_1(G)) = -15.4 & (R) \end{cases}$$

The * now indicates the decision $d_2(i)$ attaining $V_2(i)$. Observe that after two iterations of successive approximations, we have not yet come close to the actual values of $V(i)$ and have not found it optimal to replace even a bad machine.

In general, if we wish to ensure that all the $V_t(i)$'s are within ε of the corresponding $V(i)$, we would perform t^* iterations of successive approximations, where

$$\frac{\beta^{t^*}}{1 - \beta} \max_{i,d} |r_{i,d}| < \varepsilon$$

There is no guarantee, however, that after t^* iterations of successive approximations, the optimal stationary policy will have been found.

MAXIMIZING AVERAGE REWARD PER PERIOD

We now briefly discuss how linear programming can be used to find a stationary policy that maximizes the expected per-period reward earned over an infinite horizon. Consider a decision rule or policy Q that chooses decision $d \in D(i)$ with probability $q_i(d)$ during a period in which the state is i. A policy Q will be a stationary policy if each $q_i(d)$ equals 0 or 1. To find a policy that maximizes expected reward per period over an infinite horizon, let π_{id} be the fraction of all periods in which the state is i and decision $d \in D(i)$ is chosen. Then the expected reward per period may be written as

$$\sum_{i=1}^{i=N} \sum_{d \in D(i)} \pi_{id} r_{id} \tag{17}$$

What constraints must be satisfied by the π_{id}? First, all π_{id}'s must be nonnegative. Second,

$$\sum_{i=1}^{i=N} \sum_{d \in D(i)} \pi_{id} = 1$$

must hold. Finally, the fraction of all periods during which a transition occurs out of state j must equal the fraction of all periods during which a transition occurs into state j. This is identical to the restriction on steady-state probabilities for Markov chains discussed in Section 19.5. This yields (for $j = 1, 2, \ldots, n$),

$$\sum_{d \in D(j)} \pi_{jd}(1 - p(j|j,d)) = \sum_{d \in D(i)} \sum_{i \neq j} \pi_{id} p(j|i,d)$$

Rearranging the last equality yields (for $j = 1, 2, \ldots, N$)

$$\sum_{d \in D(j)} \pi_{jd} = \sum_{d \in D(i)} \sum_{i=1}^{i=N} \pi_{id} p(j|i,d)$$

Putting together our objective function (17) and all the constraints yields the following LP:

$$\max z = \sum_{i=1}^{i=N} \sum_{d \in D(i)} \pi_{id} r_{id}$$

$$\text{s.t.} \sum_{i=1}^{i=N} \sum_{d \in D(i)} \pi_{id} = 1$$

$$\sum_{d \in D(j);} \pi_{jd} = \sum_{d \in D(i)} \sum_{i=1}^{i=N} \pi_{id} p(j|i,d) \tag{18}$$

$$(j = 1, 2, \ldots, N)$$

$$\text{All } \pi_{id}\text{'s} \geq 0$$

It can be shown that this LP has an optimal solution in which for each i, at most one $\pi_{id} > 0$. This optimal solution implies that expected reward per period is maximized by a solution in which each $q_i(d)$ equals 0 or 1. Thus, the optimal solution to (18) will occur for a stationary policy. For states having $\pi_{id} = 0$, any decision may be chosen without affecting the expected reward per period.

We illustrate the use of (18) for Example 11 (machine replacement). For this example, (18) yields

$$\max z = 100\pi_{ENR} + 80\pi_{GNR} + 50\pi_{ANR} + 10\pi_{BNR} - 100(\pi_{GR} + \pi_{AR} + \pi_{BR})$$

s.t.
$$\pi_{ENR} + \pi_{GNR} + \pi_{ANR} + \pi_{BNR} + \pi_{GR} + \pi_{AR} + \pi_{BR} = 1$$
$$\pi_{ENR} = .7(\pi_{ENR} + \pi_{GR} + \pi_{AR} + \pi_{BR})$$
$$\pi_{GNR} + \pi_{GR} = .3(\pi_{GR} + \pi_{AR} + \pi_{BR} + \pi_{ENR}) + .7\pi_{GNR}$$
$$\pi_{AR} + \pi_{ANR} = .3\pi_{GNR} + .6\pi_{ANR}$$
$$\pi_{BR} + \pi_{BNR} = \pi_{BNR} + .4\pi_{ANR}$$

Using LINDO, we find the optimal objective function value for this LP to be $z = 60$. The only nonzero decision variables are $\pi_{ENR} = .35$, $\pi_{GNR} = .50$, $\pi_{AR} = .15$. Thus, an average of $60 profit per period can be earned by not replacing an excellent or good machine but replacing an average machine. Since we are replacing an average machine, the action chosen during a period in which a machine is in bad condition is of no importance.

◆ PROBLEMS

GROUP A

1. A warehouse has an end-of-period capacity of 3 units. During a period in which production takes place, a setup cost of $4 is incurred. A $1 holding cost is assessed against each unit of a period's ending inventory. Also, a variable production cost of $1 per unit is incurred. During each period, demand is equally likely to be 1 or 2 units. All demand must be met on time, and $\beta = .8$. The goal is to minimize expected discounted costs over an infinite horizon.
(a) Use the policy iteration method to determine an optimal stationary policy.
(b) Use linear programming to determine an optimal stationary policy.
(c) Perform two iterations of value iteration.

2. Priceler Auto Corporation must determine whether or not to give consumers 8% or 11% financing on new cars. If Priceler gives 8% financing during the current month, the probability distribution of sales during the current month will be as shown in Table 9. If Priceler gives 11% financing during the current month, the probability distribution of sales during the current month will be as shown in Table 10. "Good sales" represents 400,000 sales per month, "bad sales" represents 300,000 sales per month. For example, if last month's sales were bad and Priceler gives 8% financing during the current month, there is a .40 chance that sales will be good during the current month. At 11% financing rates, Priceler earns $1000 per car, and at 8% financing, Priceler earns $800 per

car. Priceler's goal is to maximize expected discounted profit over an infinte horizon (use $\beta = .98$).
(a) Use the policy iteration method to determine an optimal stationary policy.
(b) Use linear programming to determine an optimal stationary policy.
(c) Perform two iterations of value iteration.
(d) Find a policy that maximizes average profit per month.

Table 9

LAST MONTH'S SALES	CURRENT MONTH'S SALES	
	Good	Bad
Good	.95	.05
Bad	.40	.60

Table 10

LAST MONTH'S SALES	CURRENT MONTH'S SALES	
	Good	Bad
Good	.80	.20
Bad	.20	.80

3. Suppose you are using the policy iteration method to determine an optimal policy for an M.D.P. How might you use LINDO to solve the value determination equations?

GROUP B

4. During any day, I may own either 0 or 1 share of a stock. The price of the stock is governed by the Markov chain shown in Table 11. At the beginning of a day in which I own a share of stock, I may either sell the stock at today's price or keep the stock. At the beginning of a day in which I don't own a share of stock, I may either buy a share of stock at today's price or not buy a share of stock. My goal is to maximize my expected discounted profit over an infinite horizon (use $\beta = .95$).

Table 11

TODAY'S PRICE	TOMORROW'S PRICE			
	$0	$1	$2	$3
$0	.5	.3	.1	.1
$1	.1	.5	.2	.2
$2	.2	.1	.5	.2
$3	.1	.1	.3	.5

(a) Use the policy iteration method to determine an optimal stationary policy.
(b) Use linear programming to determine an optimal stationary policy.
(c) Perform two iterations of value iteration.
(d) Find a policy that maximizes average daily profit.

5. Ethan Sherwood owns two printing presses, on which he prints two types of jobs. At the beginning of each day, there is a .5 probability that a type 1 job will arrive, a .1 probability that a type 2 job will arrive, and a .4 probability that no job will arrive. Ethan receives $400 for completing a type 1 job and $200 for completing a type 2 job. (Payment for a job is received in advance). Each type of job takes an average of three days to complete. To model this, we assume that each day a job is in press there is a $\frac{1}{3}$ probability that its printing will be completed at the end of the day. If both presses are busy at the beginning of the day, any arriving job is lost to the system. The crucial decision is when (if ever) Ethan should accept the less profitable type 2 job. Ethan's goal is to maximize expected discounted profit (use $\beta = .90$).
(a) Use the policy iteration method to determine an optimal stationary policy.
(b) Use linear programming to determine an optimal stationary policy.
(c) Perform two iterations of value iteration.

◆ SUMMARY

KEY TO FORMULATING PROBABILISTIC DYNAMIC PROGRAMMING PROBLEMS (PDPs)

Suppose the possible states during period $t + 1$ are $s_1, s_2, \ldots, s_n$, and the probability that the period $t + 1$ state will be s_i is p_i. Then the minimum expected cost incurred during periods $t + 1, t + 2, \ldots$, end of the problem is

$$\sum_{i=1}^{i=n} p_i f_{t+1}(s_i)$$

where $f_{t+1}(s_i)$ is the minimum expected cost incurred from period $t + 1$ to the end of the problem, given that the state during period $t + 1$ is s_i.

MAXIMIZING THE PROBABILITY OF A FAVORABLE EVENT OCCURRING

To maximize the probability that a favorable event will occur, assign a reward of 1 if the favorable event occurs and a reward of 0 if the favorable event does not occur.

MARKOV DECISION PROCESSES

A **Markov decision process** (M.D.P.) is simply an infinite horizon PDP. Let $V_\delta(i)$ be the expected discounted reward earned during an infinite number of periods, given that at the beginning of period 1, the state is i and stationary policy δ is followed.

For a maximization problem, we define

$$V(i) = \max_{\delta \in \Delta} V_\delta(i)$$

For a minimization problem, we define

$$V(i) = \min_{\delta \in \Delta} V_\delta(i)$$

If a policy δ^* has the property that for all $i \in S$,

$$V(i) = V_{\delta^*}(i)$$

then δ^* is an **optimal policy**. We can use the **value determination equations** to determine $V_\delta(i)$:

$$V_\delta(i) = r_{i,\delta(i)} + \beta \sum_{j=1}^{j=N} p(j \,|\, i, \delta(i)) V_\delta(j) \qquad (i = 1, 2, \ldots, N) \tag{15}$$

An optimal policy for an M.D.P. may be determined by one of three methods:

1. Policy iteration

2. Linear programming

3. Value iteration, or successive approximations

POLICY ITERATION

A summary of Howard's policy iteration method for a maximization problem follows:

Step 1 Policy evaluation — Choose a stationary policy δ and use the value determination equations to find $V_\delta(i)$ ($i = 1, 2, \ldots, N$).

Step 2 Policy improvement — For all states $i = 1, 2, \ldots, N$, compute

$$T_\delta(i) = \max_{d \in D(i)} \left\{ r_{id} + \beta \sum_{j=1}^{j=N} p(j \,|\, i, d) V_\delta(j) \right\} \tag{16}$$

Since we can choose $d = \delta(i)$ for $i = 1, 2, \ldots, n$, $T_\delta(i) \geq V_\delta(i)$. If $T_\delta(i) = V_\delta(i)$ for $i = 1, 2, \ldots, N$, then δ is an optimal policy. If $T_\delta(i) > V_\delta(i)$ for at least one state, then δ is not an optimal policy. In this case, modify δ so that the decision in each state i is the decision attaining the maximum in Eq. (16) for $T_\delta(i)$. This yields a new stationary policy δ' for which $V_{\delta'}(i) \geq V_\delta(i)$ for $i = 1, 2, \ldots, N$, and for at least one state i', $V_{\delta'}(i') > V_\delta(i')$. Return to Step 1, with policy δ' replacing policy δ.

LINEAR PROGRAMMING

In a maximization problem, $V(i)$ for each state may be determined by solving the following LP:

$$\min z = V_1 + V_2 + \cdots + V_N$$

s.t. $V_i - \beta \sum_{j=1}^{j=N} p(j \mid i, d)V_j \geq r_{id}$ (For each state i and each $d \in D(i)$)

All variables urs

If the constraint for state i and decision d has no slack, then decision d is optimal in state i.

VALUE ITERATION, OR SUCCESSIVE APPROXIMATIONS

Let $V_t(i)$ be the maximum expected discounted reward that can be earned during t periods if the state at the beginning of the current period is i. Then

$$V_t(i) = \max_{d \in D(i)} \left\{ r_{id} + \beta \sum_{j=1}^{j=N} p(j \mid i, d)V_{t-1}(j) \right\}   (t \geq 1)$$

$$V_0(i) = 0$$

As t grows large, $V_t(i)$ will approach $V(i)$. For t sufficiently large, the decision that is optimal in state i for a t-period problem is also optimal in state i for an infinite horizon problem.

◆ REVIEW PROBLEMS

GROUP A

1. A company has five sales representatives available for assignment to three sales districts. The sales in each district during the current year depend on the number of sales representatives assigned to the district and on whether the national economy has a bad or good year (see Table 12). In the Sales column for each district, the first number represents sales if the national economy had a bad year, and the second number represents sales if the economy had a good year. There is a .3 chance that the national economy will have a good year and a .7 chance that the national economy will have a bad year. Use dynamic programming to determine an assignment of sales representatives to districts that maximizes the company's expected sales.

Table 12

NO. OF SALES REPS ASSIGNED TO DISTRICT	SALES (Millions)		
	District 1	District 2	District 3
0	$1, $4	$2, $5	$3, $4
1	$2, $6	$4, $6	$5, $5
2	$3, $7	$5, $6	$6, $7
3	$4, $8	$6, $6	$7, $7

2. At the beginning of each period, a company must determine how many units to produce. A setup cost of $5 is incurred during each period in which production takes place. The production of each unit also incurs a $2 variable cost. All demand must be met on time, and there is a $1 per-unit holding cost on each period's ending inventory. During each period, it is equally likely that demand will equal 0 or 1 unit. Assume that each period's ending inventory cannot exceed 2 units.

(a) Use dynamic programming to minimize the expected cost incurred during three periods. Assume initial inventory is zero.

(b) Now suppose that each unit demanded can be sold for $4. If demand is not met on time, the sale is lost. Use dynamic programming to maximize the expected profit earned during three periods. Assume that the initial inventory is zero.

(c) In parts (a) and (b), is an (s, S) policy optimal?

3. At Hot Dog Queen Restaurant, the following sequence of events occurs during each minute:

   1. With probability p, a customer arrives and waits in line.

   2. Hot Dog Queen determines the rate s at which customers are served. If any customers are in the restaurant, then with probability s, one customer completes service and leaves the restaurant. It costs $c(s)$ dollars per period to serve customers at a rate s. Each customer spends R dollars, and the customer's food costs Hot Dog Queen $R - 1$ dollars to prepare.

    3. For each customer in line at the end of the minute, a cost of h dollars is assessed (because of customer inconvenience).

    4. The next minute begins.

Formulate a recursion that could be used to maximize expected revenues less costs (including customer inconvenience costs) incurred during the next T minutes. Assume that initially no customers are present.

4. At the beginning of 1990, the United States has B barrels of oil. If x barrels of oil are consumed during a year, then consumers earn a benefit (measured in dollars) of $u(x)$. The United States may spend money on oil exploration. If d dollars are spent during a year on oil exploration, then there is a probability $p(d)$ that an oil field (containing 500,000 barrels of oil) will be found. Formulate a recursion that can be used to maximize the expected discounted value of benefits less exploration expenditures earned from the beginning of 1990 to the end of the year 2525.

5. I am a contestant on the popular TV game show *Tired of Fortune*. During the bonus round, I will be asked up to four questions. For each question that is correctly answered, I win a certain amount of money; one incorrect answer, however, means that I lose all the money I have previously won, and the game is over. If I elect to pass, or not answer a question, the game is over, but I may keep what I have already won. The amount of money I win for each correct question and the probability that I will answer each question correctly are shown in Table 13.
(a) My goal is to maximize the expected amount of money won. Use dynamic programming to accomplish this goal.
(b) Suppose that I am allowed to pass, or not answer a question, and still go on to the next question. Now determine how to maximize the expected amount of money won.

Table 13

QUESTION	PROBABILITY OF CORRECT ANSWER	MONEY WON
1	.6	$10,000
2	.5	$20,000
3	.4	$30,000
4	.3	$40,000

6. A machine in excellent condition earns $100 profit per week, a machine in good condition earns $70 per week, and a machine in bad condition earns $20 per week. At the beginning of any week, a machine may be sent out for repairs at a cost of $90. A machine that is sent out for repairs returns in excellent condition at the beginning of the next week. If a machine is not repaired, the condition of the machine evolves in accordance with the Markov chain shown in Table 14. The company wishes to maximize its expected discounted profit over an infinite horizon ($\beta = .9$).
(a) Use policy iteration to determine an optimal stationary policy.
(b) Use linear programming to determine an optimal stationary policy.
(c) Perform two iterations of value iteration.

Table 14

THIS WEEK	NEXT WEEK		
	Excellent	*Good*	*Bad*
Excellent	.7	.2	.1
Good	0	.7	.3
Bad	0	.1	.9

GROUP B

7. A syndicate of college students spends weekends gambling in Las Vegas. They begin week 1 with W dollars. At the beginning of each week, they may wager any amount of their money at the gambling tables. If they wager d dollars, then with probability p, their wealth increases by d dollars, and with probability $1 - p$, their wealth decreases by d dollars. Their goal is to maximize their expected wealth at the end of T weeks.
(a) Show that if $p \geq \frac{1}{2}$, the students should bet all their money.
(b) Show that if $p < \frac{1}{2}$, the students should bet no money. (*Hint:* Define $f_t(w)$ as the maximum expected wealth at the end of week T, given that wealth is w dollars at beginning of week t; by working backward, find an expression for $f_t(w)$.)

◆ REFERENCES

The following books contain elementary discussions of Markov decision processes and probabilistic dynamic programming:

HOWARD, R. *Dynamic Programming and Markov Processes*. Cambridge, Mass.: MIT Press, 1960.

WAGNER, H. *Principles of Operations Research*, 2d ed. Englewood Cliffs, N.J.: Prentice-Hall, 1975.

The following books treat Markov decision processes and probabilistic dynamic programming at a more advanced level:

BERSETKAS, D. *Dynamic Programming*. Englewood Cliffs, N.J.: Prentice-Hall, 1987.

HEYMAN, D., and M. SOBEL. *Stochastic Models in Operations Research*, vol. 2, New York: McGraw-Hill, 1984.

KOHLAS, S. *Stochastic Methods of Operations Research*. Cambridge: Cambridge University Press, 1982.

ROSS, S. *Introduction to Stochastic Dynamic Programming*. Orlando, Fla.: Academic Press, 1983.

WHITTLE, P. *Optimization Over Time: Dynamic Programming and Stochastic Control*. New York: Wiley, 1982.

Excellent one-chapter introductions to Markov decision processes are given in the following two books:

DENARDO, E. *Dynamic Programming Theory and Applications*. Englewood Cliffs, N.J.: Prentice-Hall, 1982.

SHAPIRO, J. *Mathematical Programming: Structures and Algorithms*. New York: Wiley, 1979.

BLACKWELL, D. "Discrete Dynamic Programming," *Annals of Mathematical Statistics* 33(1962):719–726. Indicates how one proves that a stationary policy is optimal for a Markov decision process.

SCARF, H. "The Optimality of (s, S) Policies for the Dynamic Inventory Problem," *Proceedings of the First Stanford Symposium on Mathematical Methods in the Social Sciences*. Stanford, Calif.: Stanford University Press, 1960. A proof of the optimality of (s, S) policies.

22

Queuing Theory

EACH OF US has spent a great deal of time waiting in lines. In this chapter, we develop mathematical models for waiting lines, or queues. In Section 22.1, we begin by discussing some terminology that is often used to describe queues. In Section 22.2, we look at some distributions (the exponential and the Erlang distributions) that are needed to describe queuing models. In Section 22.3, we introduce the idea of a birth–death process, which is basic to many queuing models involving the exponential distribution. The remainder of the chapter examines several models of queuing systems that can be used to answer questions like the following:

1. What fraction of the time is each server idle?

2. What is the expected number of customers present in the queue?

3. What is the expected time that a customer spends in the queue?

4. What is the probability distribution of the number of customers present in the queue?

5. What is the probability distribution of a customer's waiting time?

6. If a bank manager wants to ensure that only 1% of all customers will have to wait more than 5 minutes for a teller, how many tellers should be employed?

22-1   SOME QUEUING TERMINOLOGY

To describe a queuing system, an input process and an output process must be specified. Some examples of input and output processes are given in Table 1.

THE INPUT OR ARRIVAL PROCESS

The input process is usually called the **arrival process**. Arrivals are called **customers**. In all models that we will discuss, we assume that no more than one arrival can occur at a given instant. For a case like a restaurant, this is a very unrealistic assumption. If more than one arrival can occur at a given instant, we say that **bulk arrivals** are allowed.

Usually, we assume that the arrival process is unaffected by the number of customers present in the system. In the context of a bank, this would imply that whether there are 500 or 5 people at the bank, the process governing arrivals remains unchanged.

Table 1	SITUATION	INPUT PROCESS	OUTPUT PROCESS
Examples of Queuing Systems	Bank	Customers arrive at bank	Tellers serve the customers
	Pizza parlor	Requests for pizza delivery are received	Pizza parlor sends out truck to deliver pizzas
	Hospital blood bank	Pints of blood arrive	Patients use up pints of blood
	Naval shipyard	Ships at sea break down and are sent to shipyard for repairs	Ships are repaired and return to sea

There are two common situations in which the arrival process may depend on the number of customers present. The first occurs when arrivals are drawn from a small population. Suppose that there are only four ships in a naval shipyard. If all four ships are being repaired, then no ship can break down in the near future. On the other hand, if all four ships are at sea, a breakdown has a relatively high probability of occurring in the near future. Models in which arrivals are drawn from a small population are called **finite source models**. Another situation in which the arrival process depends on the number of customers present occurs when the rate at which customers arrive at the facility decreases when the facility becomes too crowded. For example, if you see that the bank parking lot is full, you might pass by and come another day. If a customer arrives but fails to enter the system, we say that the customer has **balked**. The phenomenon of balking was described by Yogi Berra when he said, "Nobody goes to that restaurant anymore; it's too crowded."

If the arrival process is unaffected by the number of customers present, we usually describe it by specifying a probability distribution that governs the time between successive arrivals.

THE OUTPUT OR SERVICE PROCESS

To describe the output process (often called the service process) of a queuing system, we usually specify a probability distribution — the **service time distribution** — which governs a customer's service time. In most cases, we assume that the service time distribution is independent of the number of customers present. This implies, for example, that the server does not work faster when more customers are present.

In this chapter, we study two arrangements of servers: **servers in parallel** and **servers in series**. Servers are in parallel if all servers provide the same type of service and a customer need only pass through one server to complete service. For example, the tellers in a bank are usually arranged in parallel; any customer need only be serviced by one teller, and any teller can perform the desired service. Servers are in series if a customer must pass through several servers before completing service. An assembly line is an example of a series queuing system.

QUEUE DISCIPLINE

In order to describe a queuing system completely, we must also describe the queue discipline and the manner in which customers join lines.

The **queue discipline** describes the method used to determine the order in which customers are served. The most common queue discipline is the **FCFS discipline** (first come, first served), in which customers are served in the order of their arrival. Under the **LCFS discipline** (last come, first served), the most recent arrivals are the first to enter service. If we consider exiting from an elevator to be service, then a crowded elevator illustrates an LCFS discipline. Sometimes the order in which customers arrive has no effect on the order in which they are served. This would be the case if the next customer to enter service is randomly chosen from those customers waiting for service. Such a situation is referred to as the **SIRO discipline** (service in random order). When callers to an airline are put on hold, the luck of the draw often determines the next caller serviced by an operator.

Finally, we consider **priority queuing disciplines**. A priority discipline classifies each arrival into one of several categories. Each category is then given a priority level, and within each priority level, customers enter service on an FCFS basis. Priority disciplines are often used in emergency rooms to determine the order in which customers receive treatment, and in copying and computer time-sharing facilities, where priority is usually given to jobs with shorter processing times.

METHOD USED BY ARRIVALS TO JOIN QUEUE

Another factor that has an important effect on the behavior of a queuing system is the method that customers use to determine which line to join. For example, in some banks, customers must join a single line, but in other banks, customer's may choose the line they wish to join. When there are several lines, customers often join the shortest line. Unfortunately, in many situations (such as a supermarket), it is difficult to define the shortest line. If there are several lines at a queuing facility, it is important to know whether or not customers are allowed to switch, or jockey, between lines. In most queuing systems with multiple lines, jockeying is permitted, but jockeying at a toll booth plaza is not recommended.

22-2   MODELING ARRIVAL AND SERVICE PROCESSES

MODELING THE ARRIVAL PROCESS

As previously mentioned, we assume that at most one arrival can occur at a given instant of time. We define t_i to be the time at which the ith customer arrives. To illustrate this, consider Figure 1. For $i \geq 1$, we define $T_i = t_{i+1} - t_i$ to be the ith interarrival time. Thus, in the figure, $T_1 = 8 - 3 = 5$, and $T_2 = 15 - 8 = 7$. In modeling the arrival process, we assume that the T_i's are independent, continuous random variables described by the random variable **A**. The independence assumption means, for example, that the value of T_2 has no effect on the value of T_3, T_4, or any later T_i. The assumption that each T_i is continuous is usually a good approximation of reality. After all, an interarrival time need not be exactly 1 minute or 2 minutes; it could just as easily be, say, 1.55892 minutes. The assumption that each interarrival time is governed by the same random variable implies that the distribution of arrivals is independent of the time of day or the day of the week. This is the assumption of stationary interarrival times. Because of phenomena such as rush hours, the assumption of stationary interarrival times is often unrealistic, but we may often approximate reality by breaking the time of day into segments. For example, if we were modeling traffic flow, we might break the day up into three segments:

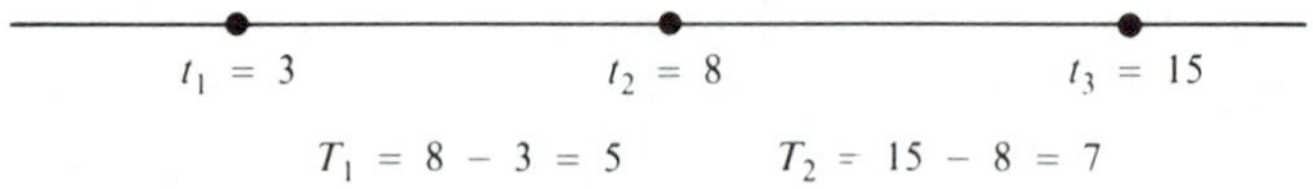

Figure 1
Definition of
Interarrival Times

$$t_1 = 3 \qquad t_2 = 8 \qquad t_3 = 15$$

$$T_1 = 8 - 3 = 5 \qquad T_2 = 15 - 8 = 7$$

a morning rush hour segment, a midday segment, and an afternoon rush hour segment. During each of these segments, interarrival times may be stationary.

We assume that **A** has a density function $a(t)$. Recall from Section 11.6 that for small Δt, $P(t \le \mathbf{A} \le t + \Delta t)$ is approximately $\Delta t a(t)$. Of course, a negative interarrival time is impossible. This allows us to write

$$P(\mathbf{A} \le c) = \int_0^c a(t)\, dt \qquad \text{and} \qquad P(\mathbf{A} > c) = \int_c^\infty a(t)\, dt \tag{1}$$

We define $\frac{1}{\lambda}$ to be the mean or average interarrival time. Without loss of generality, we assume that time is measured in units of hours. Then $\frac{1}{\lambda}$ will have units of hours per arrival. From Section 11.6, we may compute $\frac{1}{\lambda}$ from $a(t)$ by using the following equation:

$$\frac{1}{\lambda} = \int_0^\infty t a(t)\, dt \tag{2}$$

We define λ to be the **arrival rate**, which will have units of arrivals per hour.

In most applications of queuing, an important question is how to choose **A** to reflect reality and still be computationally tractable. The most common choice for **A** is the **exponential distribution**. An exponential distribution with parameter λ has a density $a(t) = \lambda e^{-\lambda t}$. Figure 2 shows the density function for an exponential distribution. We see that $a(t)$ decreases very rapidly for t small. This indicates that very long interarrival times are unlikely. Using Eq. (2) and integration by parts, we can show that the average or mean interarrival time (call it $E(\mathbf{A})$) is given by

$$E(\mathbf{A}) = \frac{1}{\lambda} \tag{3}$$

Using the fact that $\operatorname{var} \mathbf{A} = E(\mathbf{A}^2) - E(\mathbf{A})^2$, we can show that

$$\operatorname{var} \mathbf{A} = \frac{1}{\lambda^2} \tag{4}$$

Figure 2
Density Function for
Exponential
Distribution

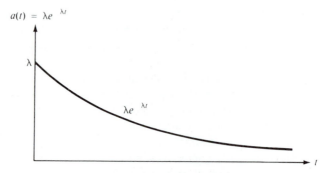

NO-MEMORY PROPERTY OF THE EXPONENTIAL DISTRIBUTION. The reason the exponential distribution is often used to model interarrival times is embodied in the following lemma.

L E M M A   **If A** has an exponential distribution, then for all nonnegative values of t and h,
1

$$P(\mathbf{A} > t + h \,|\, \mathbf{A} \geq t) = P(\mathbf{A} > h) \qquad (5)$$

Proof   First note that from Eq. (1), we have

$$P(\mathbf{A} > h) = \int_{h}^{\infty} \lambda e^{-\lambda t} = [-e^{-\lambda t}]_{h}^{\infty} = e^{-\lambda h} \qquad (6)$$

Then

$$P(\mathbf{A} > t + h \,|\, \mathbf{A} \geq t) = \frac{P(\mathbf{A} > t + h \cap \mathbf{A} \geq t)}{P(\mathbf{A} \geq t)}$$

From (6),

$$P(\mathbf{A} > t + h \cap \mathbf{A} \geq t) = e^{-\lambda(t+h)} \qquad \text{and} \qquad P(\mathbf{A} \geq t) = e^{-\lambda t}$$

Thus,

$$P(\mathbf{A} > t + h \,|\, \mathbf{A} \geq t) = \frac{e^{-\lambda(t+h)}}{e^{-\lambda t}} = e^{-\lambda h} = P(\mathbf{A} > h)$$

◆

It can be shown that no other density function can satisfy Eq. (5) (see Feller (1957)). For reasons that become apparent, a density that satisfies (5) is said to have the **no-memory property**. Suppose we are told that there has been no arrival for the last t hours (this is equivalent to being told that $\mathbf{A} \geq t$) and are asked what the probability is that there will be no arrival during the next h hours (i.e., $\mathbf{A} > t + h$). Then (5) implies that this probability *does not depend on the value of t*, and for all values of t, this probability equals $P(\mathbf{A} > h)$. In short, if we know that at least t time units have elapsed since the last arrival occurred, then the distribution of the remaining time until the next arrival (h) does not depend on t. For example, if $h = 4$, then (5) yields, for $t = 5, t = 3$, $t = 2$, and $t = 0$,

$$P(\mathbf{A} > 9 \,|\, \mathbf{A} \geq 5) = P(\mathbf{A} > 7 \,|\, \mathbf{A} \geq 3) = P(\mathbf{A} > 6 \,|\, \mathbf{A} \geq 2)$$
$$= P(\mathbf{A} > 4 \,|\, \mathbf{A} \geq 0) = e^{-4\lambda}$$

The no-memory property of the exponential distribution is important because it implies that if we want to know the probability distribution of the time until the next arrival, then *it does not matter how long it has been since the last arrival*. To put it in concrete terms, suppose interarrival times are exponentially distributed with $\lambda = 6$. Then the no-memory property implies that no matter how long it has been since the last arrival, the probability distribution governing the time until the next arrival has the density function $6e^{-6t}$. This means that in order to predict future arrival patterns, we need not keep track of how long it has been since the last arrival. This observation can appreciably simplify analysis of a queuing system.

To see that knowledge of the time since the last arrival does affect the distribution of time until the next arrival in most situations, suppose that $\mathbf{A}$ is discrete with $P(\mathbf{A} = 5) = P(\mathbf{A} = 100) = \frac{1}{2}$. If we are told that there has been no arrival during the last 6 time units, we *know with certainty* that it will be $100 - 6 = 94$ time units until the next arrival. On the other hand, if we are told that no arrival has occurred during the last time unit, then there is some chance that the time until the next arrival will be $5 - 1 = 4$ time units and some chance that it will be $100 - 1 = 99$ time units. Hence, in this situation, the distribution of the next interarrival time cannot be predicted with knowledge of the time that has elapsed since the last arrival.

RELATION BETWEEN POISSON DISTRIBUTION AND EXPONENTIAL DISTRIBUTION. If interarrival times are exponential, the probability distribution of the number of arrivals occurring in any time interval of length t is given by the following important theorem.

THEOREM 1   Interarrival times are exponential with parameter λ if and only if the number of arrivals to occur in an interval of length t follows a Poisson distribution with parameter λt.

A discrete random variable $\mathbf{N}$ has a Poisson distribution with parameter λ if, for $n = 0, 1, 2, \ldots$,

$$P(\mathbf{N} = n) = \frac{e^{-\lambda}\lambda^n}{n!} \qquad (n = 0, 1, 2, \ldots) \qquad (7)$$

If $\mathbf{N}$ is a Poisson random variable, it can be shown that $E(\mathbf{N}) = \text{var}\,\mathbf{N} = \lambda$. If we define $\mathbf{N}_t$ to be the number of arrivals to occur during any time interval of length t, Theorem 1 states that

$$P(\mathbf{N}_t = n) = \frac{e^{-\lambda t}(\lambda t)^n}{n!} \qquad (n = 0, 1, 2, \ldots)$$

Since $\mathbf{N}_t$ is Poisson with parameter λt, $E(\mathbf{N}_t) = \text{var}\,\mathbf{N}_t = \lambda t$. An average of λt arrivals occur during a time interval of length t, so λ may be thought of as the average number of arrivals per unit time, or the arrival rate.

What assumptions are required for interarrival times to be exponential? Theorem 2 provides a partial answer. Consider the following two assumptions:

1. Arrivals defined on nonoverlapping time intervals are independent (for example, the number of arrivals occurring between times 1 and 10 does not give us any information about the number of arrivals occurring between times 30 and 50).

2. For small Δt (and any value of t), the probability of one arrival occurring between times t and $t + \Delta t$ is $\lambda\Delta t + o(\Delta t)$, where $o(\Delta t)$ refers to any quantity satisfying

$$\lim_{\Delta t \to 0} \frac{o(\Delta t)}{\Delta t} = 0$$

Also, the probability of no arrival during the interval between t and $t + \Delta t$ is $1 - \lambda\Delta t + o(\Delta t)$, and the probability of more than one arrival occurring between t and $t + \Delta t$ is $o(\Delta t)$.

THEOREM 2   If assumptions 1 and 2 hold, then $\mathbf{N}_t$ follows a Poisson distribution with parameter λt, and interarrival times are exponential with parameter λ. That is, $a(t) = \lambda e^{-\lambda t}$.

In essence, Theorem 2 states that if the arrival rate is stationary, if bulk arrivals cannot occur, and if past arrivals do not affect future arrivals, then interarrival times will follow an exponential distribution with parameter λ, and the number of arrivals in any interval of length t is Poisson with parameter λt. The assumptions of Theorem 2 may appear to be very restrictive, but interarrival times are often exponential even if the assumptions of Theorem 2 are not satisfied (see Denardo (1982)). In Section 22.12, we discuss how to use data to test whether or not the hypothesis of exponential interarrival times is reasonable. In many applications, the assumption of exponential interarrival times turns out to be a fairly good approximation of reality.

Example 1 illustrates the relation between the exponential and Poisson distributions.

E X A M P L E
1

The number of glasses of beer ordered per hour at Dick's Pub follows a Poisson distribution, with an average of 30 beers per hour being ordered.

1. Find the probability that exactly 60 beers are ordered between 10 P.M. and 12 midnight.

2. Find the mean and standard deviation of the number of beers ordered between 9 P.M. and 1 A.M.

3. Find the probability that the time between two consecutive orders is between 1 and 3 minutes.

Solution

1. The number of beers ordered between 10 P.M. and 12 midnight will follow a Poisson distribution with parameter $2(30) = 60$. From Eq. (7), the probability that 60 beers are ordered between 10 P.M. and 12 midnight is

$$\frac{e^{-60}60^{60}}{60!}$$

2. $\lambda = 30$ beers per hour; $t = 4$ hours. Thus, the mean number of beers ordered between 9 P.M. and 1 A.M. is $4(30) = 120$ beers. The standard deviation of the number of beers ordered between 10 P.M. and 1 A.M. is $(120)^{1/2} = 10.95$.

3. Let **X** be the time (in minutes) between successive beer orders. The mean number of orders per minute is exponential with parameter or rate $\frac{30}{60} = 0.5$ beer per minute. Thus, the probability density function of the time between beer orders is $0.5e^{-0.5t}$. Then

$$P(1 \leq \mathbf{X} \leq 3) = \int_1^3 (0.5e^{-0.5t})\,dt = e^{-0.5} - e^{-1.5} = .38$$

◆

THE ERLANG DISTRIBUTION.   If interarrival times do not appear to be exponential, they are often modeled by an Erlang distribution. An Erlang distribution is a continuous random variable (call it **T**) whose density function $f(t)$ is specified by two parameters: a rate parameter R and a shape parameter k (k must be a positive integer). Given values of R and k, the Erlang density has the following probability density function:

$$f(t) = \frac{R(Rt)^{k-1}e^{-Rt}}{(k-1)!} \qquad (t \geq 0) \tag{8}$$

Using integration by parts, we can show that if $\mathbf{T}$ is an Erlang distribution with rate parameter R and shape parameter k, then

$$E(\mathbf{T}) = \frac{k}{R} \quad \text{and} \quad \text{var } \mathbf{T} = \frac{k}{R^2} \qquad (9)$$

To see how varying the shape parameter changes the shape of the Erlang distribution, we consider for a given value of λ, a family of Erlang distributions with rate parameter $k\lambda$ and shape parameter k. By Eq. (9), each of these Erlangs has a mean of $\frac{1}{\lambda}$. As k varies, the Erlang distribution takes on many shapes. For example, Figure 3 shows, for a given value of λ, the density functions for Erlang distributions having shape parameters 1, 2, 4, 6, and 20. For $k = 1$, the Erlang density looks similar to an exponential distribution; in fact, if we set $k = 1$ in Eq. (8), we find that for $k = 1$, the Erlang distribution is an exponential distribution with parameter R. As k increases, the Erlang distribution behaves more and more like a normal distribution. For extremely large values of k, the Erlang distribution approaches a random variable with zero variance (i.e., a constant interarrival time). Thus, by varying k, we may approximate both skewed and symmetric distributions.

Figure 3
Density Functions
for Erlang
Distributions

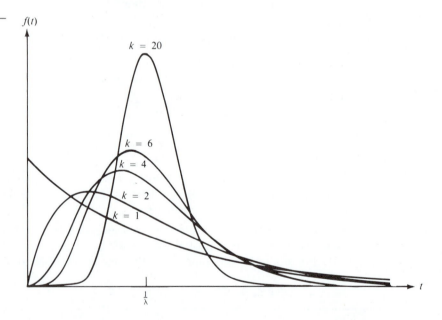

It can be shown that an Erlang distribution with shape parameter k and rate parameter $k\lambda$ has the same distribution as the random variable $\mathbf{A}_1 + \mathbf{A}_2 + \cdots + \mathbf{A}_k$, where each $\mathbf{A}_i$ is an exponential random variable with parameter $k\lambda$, and the $\mathbf{A}_i$'s are independent random variables.

If we model interarrival times as an Erlang distribution with shape parameter k, we are really saying that the interarrival process is equivalent to a customer going through k phases (each of which has the no-memory property) before arriving. For this reason, the shape parameter is often referred to as the number of phases of the Erlang distribution.

MODELING THE SERVICE PROCESS

We now turn our attention to modeling the service process. We assume that the service times of different customers are independent random variables and that each customer's service time is governed by a random variable **S** having a density function $s(t)$. We let $\frac{1}{\mu}$ be the mean service time for a customer. Of course,

$$\frac{1}{\mu} = \int_0^\infty ts(t)\,dt$$

The variable $\frac{1}{\mu}$ will have units of hours per customer, so μ has units of customers per hour. For this reason, we call μ the service rate. For example, $\mu = 5$ means that if customers were always present, the server could serve an average of 5 customers per hour, and the average service time of each customer would be $\frac{1}{5}$ hour. As with interarrival times, we hope that service times can be accurately modeled as exponential random variables. If we can model a customer's service time as an exponential random variable, we can determine the distribution of a customer's remaining service time without having to keep track of how long the customer has been in service. Also note that if service times follow an exponential density $s(t) = \mu e^{-\mu t}$, then a customer's mean service time will be $\frac{1}{\mu}$.

As an example of how the assumption of exponential service times can simplify computations, consider a three-server system in which each customer's service time is governed by an exponential distribution $s(t) = \mu e^{-\mu t}$. Suppose all three servers are busy, and a customer is waiting (see Figure 4). What is the probability that the customer who is waiting will be the last of the four customers to complete service? From Figure 4, it is clear that the following will occur. One of customers 1–3 (say, customer 3) will be the first to complete service. Then customer 4 will enter service. By the no-memory property, customer 4's service time has the same distribution as the remaining service times of customers 1 and 2. Thus, by symmetry, customers 4, 1, and 2 will have the same chance of being the last customer to complete service. This implies that customer 4 has a $\frac{1}{3}$ chance of being the last customer to complete service. Without the no-memory property, this problem would be hard to solve, because it would be very difficult to determine the probability distribution of the remaining service time (after customer 3 completes service) of customers 1 and 2.

Figure 4
Example of
Usefulness of
Exponential
Distribution

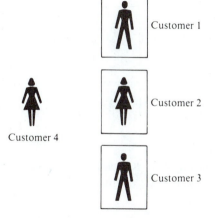

Customer 1

Customer 2

Customer 4

Customer 3

Unfortunately, actual service times may not be consistent with the no-memory property. For this reason, we often assume that $s(t)$ is an Erlang distribution with shape parameter k and rate parameter $k\mu$. From Eq. (9), this yields a mean service time of $\frac{1}{\mu}$. Modeling service times as an Erlang distribution with shape parameter k also implies that a customer's service time may be considered to consist of passage through k phases of service, in which the time to complete each phase has the no-memory property, and the time to complete each phase has a mean of $\frac{1}{k\mu}$ (see Figure 5). In many situations, an Erlang distribution can be closely fitted to observed service times (see Section 22.13).

Figure 5
Representation of
Erlang Service Time

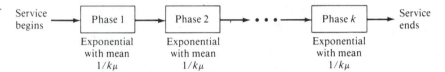

In certain situations, interarrival or service times may be modeled as having zero variance; in this case, interarrival or service times are considered to be **deterministic**. For example, if interarrival times are deterministic, then each interarrival time will be exactly $\frac{1}{\lambda}$, and if service times are deterministic, each customer's service time will be exactly $\frac{1}{\mu}$.

THE KENDALL-LEE NOTATION FOR QUEUING SYSTEMS

We have now developed enough terminology to describe the standard notation used to describe many queuing systems. The notation that we discuss in this section is used to describe a queuing system in which all arrivals wait in a single line until one of s identical parallel servers is free. Then the first customer in line enters service, and so on (see Figure 6). If, for example, the customer in server 3 is the next customer to complete service, then (assuming an FCFS discipline) the first customer in line would enter server 3. The next customer in line would enter service after the next service completion, and so on.

Figure 6
Single-Line Queuing
System with Parallel
Servers

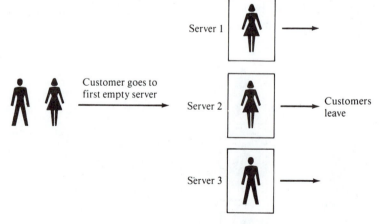

To describe such a queuing system, Kendall (1951) devised the following notation. Each queuing system is described by six characteristics:

$$1/2/3/4/5/6$$

The first characteristic specifies the nature of the arrival process. The following standard abbreviations are used:

M = Interarrival times are independent, identically distributed (iid) random variables having an exponential distribution.

D = Interarrival times are iid and deterministic.

E_k = Interarrival times are iid Erlangs with shape parameter k.

GI = Interarrival times are iid and governed by some general distribution.

The second characteristic specifies the nature of the service times:

M = Service times are iid and exponentially distributed.

D = Service times are iid and deterministic.

E_k = Service times are iid Erlangs with shape parameter k.

G = Service times are iid and follow some general distribution.

The third characteristic is the number of parallel servers. The fourth characteristic describes the queue discipline:

FCFS = First come, first served

LCFS = Last come, first served

SIRO = Service in random order

GD = General queue discipline.

The fifth characteristic specifies the maximum allowable number of customers in the system (including customers who are waiting and customers who are in service). The sixth characteristic gives the size of the population from which customers are drawn. Unless the number of potential customers is of the same order of magnitude as the number of servers, the population size is considered to be infinite. In many important models 4/5/6 is $GD/\infty/\infty$. If this is the case, then 4/5/6 is often omitted.

As an illustration of this notation, $M/E_2/8/FCFS/10/\infty$ might represent a health clinic with 8 doctors, exponential interarrival times, two-phase Erlang service times, an FCFS queue discipline, and a total capacity of 10 patients.

THE WAITING TIME PARADOX

We close this section with a brief discussion of an interesting paradox known as the waiting time paradox.

Suppose the time between the arrival of buses at the student center is exponentially distributed with a mean of 60 minutes. If we arrive at the student center at a randomly chosen instant, what is the average amount of time that we will have to wait for a bus?

The no-memory property of the exponential distribution implies that no matter how long it has been since the last bus arrived, we would still expect to wait an average of 60 minutes until the next bus arrived. This answer is indeed correct, but it appears to be contradicted by the following argument. On the average, somebody who arrives at a random time should arrive in the middle of a typical interval between arrivals of successive buses. If we arrive at the midpoint of a typical interval, and the average time between buses is 60 minutes, then we should have to wait, on the average, $(\frac{1}{2})60 = 30$

minutes for the next bus. Why is this argument incorrect? Simply because the typical interval between buses is *longer* than 60 minutes. The reason for this anomaly is that we are more likely to arrive during a longer interval than a shorter interval. Let's simplify the situation by assuming that half of all buses run 30 minutes apart and half of all buses run 90 minutes apart. One might think that since the average time between buses is 60 minutes, the average wait for a bus would be $(\frac{1}{2})60 = 30$ minutes, but this is incorrect. Look at a typical sequence of bus interarrival times (see Figure 7). Half of the interarrival times are 30 minutes, and half are 90 minutes. Clearly, there is a $\frac{90}{30+90} = \frac{3}{4}$ chance that one will arrive during a 90-minute interarrival time and a $\frac{30}{30+90} = \frac{1}{4}$ chance that one will arrive during a 30-minute interarrival time. Thus, the average-size interarrival time into which a customer arrives is $(\frac{3}{4})(90) + (\frac{1}{4})(30) = 75$ minutes. Since we do arrive, on the average, in the middle of an interarrival time, our average wait will be $(\frac{3}{4})(\frac{1}{2})90 + (\frac{1}{4})(\frac{1}{2})30 = 37.5$ minutes, which is longer than 30 minutes.

● Arrival of a bus

Figure 7
The Waiting Time
Paradox

Returning to the case where interarrival times are exponential with mean 60 minutes, the average size of a typical interarrival time turns out to be 120 minutes. Thus, the average time that we will have to wait for a bus is $(\frac{1}{2})(120) = 60$ minutes. Note that if buses *always* arrived 60 minutes apart, then the average time a person would have to wait for a bus would be $(\frac{1}{2})(60) = 30$ minutes. In general, it can be shown that if **A** is the random variable for the time between buses, then the average time until the next bus (as seen by an arrival who is equally likely to come at any time) is given by

$$\frac{1}{2}\left(E(\mathbf{A}) + \frac{\text{var } \mathbf{A}}{E(\mathbf{A})} \right)$$

For our bus example, $\lambda = \frac{1}{60}$, so Eqs. (3) and (4) show that $E(\mathbf{A}) = 60$ minutes and var $\mathbf{A} = 3600$ minutes^2. Substituting into this formula yields

$$\text{Expected waiting time} = \frac{1}{2}(60 + \tfrac{3600}{60}) = 60 \text{ minutes}$$

♦ PROBLEMS

GROUP A

1. Suppose I arrive at an $M/M/7/FCFS/8/\infty$ queuing system when all servers are busy. What is the probability that I will complete service before at least one of the seven customers in service?

2. The time between buses follows the mass function shown in Table 2. What is the average length of time one must wait for a bus?

Table 2

TIME BETWEEN BUSES	PROBABILITY
30 minutes	$\frac{1}{4}$
1 hour	$\frac{1}{4}$
2 hours	$\frac{1}{2}$

3. There are four sections of the third grade at Jefferson Elementary School. The number of students in each section is as follows: section 1, 20 students; section 2, 25 students; section 3, 35 students; section 4, 40 students. What is the average size of a third-grade section? Suppose the board of education randomly selects a Jefferson third-grader. On the average, how many students will be in her class?

4. The time between arrivals of buses follows an exponential distribution with a mean of 60 minutes.

(a) What is the probability that exactly four buses will arrive during the next 2 hours?

(b) That at least two buses will arrive during the next 2 hours?

(c) That no buses will arrive during the next 2 hours?

(d) A bus has just arrived. What is the probability that it will be between 30 and 90 minutes before the next bus arrives.

22-3   BIRTH–DEATH PROCESSES

In this section, we discuss the important idea of a birth–death process. We subsequently use birth–death processes to answer questions about several different types of queuing systems.

We define the number of people present in any queuing system at time t to be the **state** of the queuing system at time t. For $t = 0$, the state of the system will equal the number of people initially present in the system. Of great interest to us is the quantity $P_{ij}(t)$ which is defined as the probability that j people will be present in the queuing system at time t, given that at time 0, i people are present. Note that $P_{ij}(t)$ is analogous to the n-step transition probability $P_{ij}(n)$ (the probability that after n transitions, a Markov chain will be in state j, given that the chain began in state i), discussed in Chapter 19. Recall that for most Markov chains, the $P_{ij}(n)$ approached a limit π_j, which was independent of the initial state i. Similarly, it turns out that for many queuing systems, $P_{ij}(t)$ will, for large t, approach a limit π_j, which is independent of the initial state i. We call π_j the **steady state**, or equilibrium probability, of state j.

For the queuing systems that we will discuss, π_j may be thought of as the probability that at an instant in the distant future, j customers will be present. Alternatively, π_j may be thought of (for time in the distant future) as the fraction of the time that j customers are present. In most queuing systems, the value of $P_{ij}(t)$ for small t will critically depend on i, the number of customers initially present. For example, if t is small, then we would expect that $P_{50,1}(t)$ and $P_{1,1}(t)$ would differ substantially. However, if steady-state probabilities exist, then for large t, both $P_{50,1}(t)$ and $P_{1,1}(t)$ will be near π_1. The question of how large t must be before the steady state is approximately reached is difficult to answer. The behavior of $P_{ij}(t)$ before the steady state is reached is called the **transient behavior** of the queuing system. For all but the simplest queuing systems, analysis of the system's transient behavior is extremely difficult. For this reason, when we analyze the behavior of a queuing system, we assume that the steady state has been reached. This allows us to work with the π_j's instead of the $P_{ij}(t)$'s.

We now discuss a certain class of continuous-time stochastic processes, called birth–death processes, which includes many interesting queuing systems. For a birth–death process, it is easy to determine the steady-state probabilities (if they exist).

A **birth–death process** is a continuous-time stochastic process for which the system's state at any time is a nonnegative integer (see Section 19.1 for a definition of a continuous-time stochastic process). If a birth–death process is in state j at time t, then the motion of the process is governed by the following laws.

LAWS OF MOTION FOR BIRTH–DEATH PROCESSES

Law 1 With probability $\lambda_j \Delta t + o(\Delta t)$, a birth occurs between time t and time $t + \Delta t$.[†] A birth increases the system state by 1, to $j + 1$. The variable λ_j is called the **birth rate** in state j. In most queuing systems, a birth is simply an arrival.

Law 2 With probability $\mu_j \Delta t + o(\Delta t)$, a death occurs between time t and time $t + \Delta t$. A death decreases the system state by 1, to $j - 1$. The variable μ_j is the **death rate** in state j. In most queuing systems, a death is a service completion. Note that $\mu_0 = 0$ must hold, or a negative state could occur.

Law 3 Births and deaths are independent of each other.

Laws 1–3 can be used to show that the probability that more than one event (birth or death) occurs between t and $t + \Delta t$ is $o(\Delta t)$. Note that any birth–death process is completely specified by knowledge of the birth rates λ_j and the death rates μ_j. Since a negative state cannot occur, any birth–death process must have $\mu_0 = 0$.

RELATION OF EXPONENTIAL DISTRIBUTION TO BIRTH–DEATH PROCESSES

Most queuing systems with exponential interarrival times and exponential service times may be modeled as birth–death processes. To illustrate why this is so, consider an $M/M/1/FCFS/\infty/\infty$ queuing system in which interarrival times are exponential with parameter λ and service times are exponentially distributed with parameter μ. If the state (number of people present at time t) at time t is j, then the no-memory property of the exponential distribution implies that the probability of a birth during the time interval $[t, t + \Delta t]$ will not depend on how long the system has been in state j. This means that the probability of a birth occurring during $[t, t + \Delta t]$ will not depend on how long the system has been in state j and thus may be determined as if an arrival had just occurred at time t. Then the probability of a birth occurring during $[t, t + \Delta t]$ is

$$\int_0^{\Delta t} \lambda e^{-\lambda t} \, dt = 1 - e^{-\lambda \Delta t}$$

By the Taylor series expansion given in Section 11.1,

$$e^{-\lambda \Delta t} = 1 - \lambda \Delta t + o(\Delta t)$$

This means that the probability of a birth occurring during $[t, t + \Delta t]$ is $\lambda \Delta t + o(\Delta t)$. From this we may conclude that the birth rate in state j is simply the arrival rate λ.

To determine the death rate at time t, note that if the state is zero at time t, then nobody is in service, so no service completion can occur between t and $t + \Delta t$. Thus, $\mu_0 = 0$. If the state at time t is $j \geq 1$, then we know (since there is only one server) that exactly one customer will be in service. The no-memory property of the exponential distribution then implies that the probability that a customer will complete service between t and $t + \Delta t$ is given by

$$\int_0^{\Delta t} \mu e^{-\mu t} \, dt = 1 - e^{-\mu \Delta t} = \mu \Delta t + o(\Delta t)$$

[†]Recall from Section 22.2 that $o(\Delta t)$ means that

$$\lim_{\Delta t \to 0} \frac{o(\Delta t)}{\Delta t} = 0$$

Thus, for $j \geq 1$, $\mu_j = \mu$. In summary, if we assume that service completions and arrivals occur independently, then an $M/M/1/FCFS/\infty/\infty$ queuing system is a birth–death process. The birth and death rates for the $M/M/1/FCFS/\infty/\infty$ queuing system may be represented in a rate diagram (see Figure 8).

Figure 8
Rate Diagram for
$M/M/1/FCFS/\infty/\infty$
Queuing System

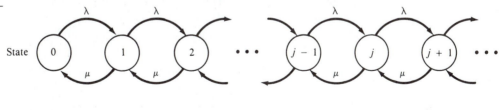

State

Represents a "death" (service completion)
Represents a "birth" (arrival)

More complicated queuing systems with exponential interarrival times and exponential service times may often be modeled as birth–death processes by adding the service rates for occupied servers and adding the arrival rates for different arrival streams. For example, consider an $M/M/3/FCFS/\infty/\infty$ queuing system in which interarrival times are exponential with $\lambda = 4$ and service times are exponential with $\mu = 5$. To model this system as a birth–death process, we would use the following parameters (see Figure 9):

$$\lambda_j = 4 \quad (j = 0, 1, 2, \ldots)$$
$$\mu_0 = 0, \quad \mu_1 = 5, \quad \mu_2 = 5 + 5 = 10, \quad \mu_j = 5 + 5 + 5 = 15 \quad (j = 3, 4, 5, \ldots)$$

$$\lambda = 4 \qquad \mu = 5$$

Figure 9
Rate Diagram for
M/M/3/FCFS/∞/∞
Queuing System

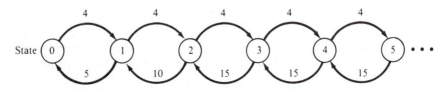

State

If either interarrival times or service times are nonexponential, then the birth–death process model is not appropriate.[†] Suppose, for example, that service times are not exponential and we are considering an $M/G/1/FCFS/\infty/\infty$ queuing system. Since the service times for an $M/G/1/FCFS/\infty/\infty$ system may be nonexponential, the probability that a death (service completion) occurs between t and $t + \Delta t$ will depend on the time since the last service completion. This violates law 2, so we cannot model an $M/G/1/FCFS/\infty/\infty$ system as a birth–death process.

DERIVATION OF STEADY-STATE PROBABILITIES FOR BIRTH–DEATH PROCESSES

We now show how the π_j's may be determined for an arbitrary birth–death process. The key is to relate (for small Δt) $P_{ij}(t + \Delta t)$ to $P_{ij}(t)$. The way to do this is to note that there are four ways for the state at time $t + \Delta t$ to be j. For $j \geq 1$, the four ways are shown

[†]A modified birth–death model can be developed if service times and interarrival times are Erlang distributions.

in Table 3. For $j \geq 1$, the probability that the state of the system will be $j - 1$ at time t and j at time $t + \Delta t$ is (see Figure 10)

$$P_{i,j-1}(t)(\lambda_{j-1}\Delta t + o(\Delta t))$$

Similar arguments yield (II) and (III). (IV) follows, because if the system is in a state other than $j, j - 1$, or $j + 1$ at time t, then to end up in state j at time $t + \Delta t$, more than one event (birth or death) must occur between t and $t + \Delta t$. By law 3, this has probability $o(\Delta t)$. Thus,

$$P_{ij}(t + \Delta t) = (I) + (II) + (III) + (IV)$$

Table 3	STATE AT TIME t	STATE AT TIME $t + \Delta t$	PROBABILITY OF THIS SEQUENCE OF EVENTS
Computations of Probability That State at Time $t + \Delta t$ Is j	$j - 1$	j	$P_{i,j-1}(t)(\lambda_{j-1}\Delta t + o(\Delta t)) = $ (I)
	$j + 1$	j	$P_{i,j+1}(t)(\mu_{j+1}\Delta t + o(\Delta t)) = $ (II)
	j	j	$P_{i,j}(t)(1 - \mu_j\Delta t - \lambda_j\Delta t - 2o(\Delta t)) = $ (III)
	Any other state	j	$o(\Delta t) = $ (IV)

Figure 10
Probability That
State Is $j - 1$
at Time t and j at
Time $t + \Delta t$ Is
$P_{i,j-1}(t)(\lambda_{j-1}(\Delta t) + o(\Delta t))$

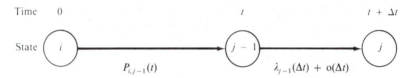

After regrouping terms in this equation, we obtain

$$\begin{aligned} P_{ij}(t + \Delta t) = P_{ij}(t) \\ + \Delta t(\lambda_{j-1}P_{i,j-1}(t) + \mu_{j+1}P_{i,j+1}(t) - P_{ij}(t)\mu_j - P_{ij}(t)\lambda_j) \quad \text{(10)} \\ + o(\Delta t)(P_{i,j-1}(t) + P_{i,j+1}(t) + 1 - 2P_{ij}(t)) \end{aligned}$$

Since the underlined term may be written as $o(\Delta t)$, we rewrite (10) as

$$P_{ij}(t + \Delta t) - P_{ij}(t) = \Delta t(\lambda_{j-1}P_{i,j-1}(t) + \mu_{j+1}P_{i,j+1}(t) - P_{ij}(t)\mu_j - P_{ij}(t)\lambda_j) + o(\Delta t)$$

Dividing both sides of this equation by Δt and letting Δt approach zero, we see that for all i and $j \geq 1$,

$$P'_{ij}(t) = \lambda_{j-1}P_{i,j-1}(t) + \mu_{j+1}P_{i,j+1}(t) - P_{ij}(t)\mu_j - P_{ij}(t)\lambda_j \quad \text{(10')}$$

Since for $j = 0$, $P_{i,j-1}(t) = 0$ and $\mu_j = 0$, we obtain, for $j = 0$,

$$P'_{i,0}(t) = \mu_1 P_{i,1}(t) - \lambda_0 P_{i,0}(t)$$

This is an infinite system of differential equations. (A differential equation is simply an equation in which a derivative appears.) In theory, these equations may be solved for the $P_{ij}(t)$. In reality, however, this system of equations is usually extremely difficult to solve. All is not lost, however. We can use (10') to obtain the steady-state probabilities π_j ($j = 0, 1, 2, \ldots$). As with Markov chains, we define the steady-state probability π_j to be

$$\lim_{t \to \infty} P_{ij}(t)$$

Then for large t and any initial state i, $P_{ij}(t)$ will not change very much and may be thought of as a constant. Thus, in the steady state (t large), $P'_{ij}(t) = 0$. In the steady state, also, $P_{i,j-1}(t) = \pi_{j-1}$, $P_{i,j+1}(t) = \pi_{j+1}$, and $P_{ij}(t) = \pi_j$ will all hold. Substituting these relations into (10′), we obtain, for $j \geq 1$,

$$\lambda_{j-1}\pi_{j-1} + \mu_{j+1}\pi_{j+1} - \pi_j\mu_j - \pi_j\lambda_j = 0$$

$$\lambda_{j-1}\pi_{j-1} + \mu_{j+1}\pi_{j+1} = \pi_j(\lambda_j + \mu_j) \qquad (j = 1, 2, \ldots) \tag{10″}$$

For $j = 0$, we obtain

$$\mu_1 \pi_1 = \pi_0 \lambda_0$$

Eqs. (10″) are an infinite system of *linear* equations that can be easily solved for the π_j's. Before discussing how to solve (10″), we give an intuitive derivation of (10″), based on the following observation: *At any time t that we observe a birth–death process, it must be true that for each state j, the number of times we have entered state j differs by at most 1 from the number of times we have left state j.*

Suppose that by time t, we have entered state 6 three times. Then one of the cases in Table 4 must have occurred. For example, if Case 2 occurs, we begin in state 6 and end up in some state other than 6. Since we have observed three transitions into state 6 by time t, the following events (among others) must have occurred:

Start in state 6	Enter state 6 (second time)
Leave state 6 (first time)	Leave state 6 (third time)
Enter state 6 (first time)	Enter state 6 (third time)
Leave state 6 (second time)	Leave state 6 (fourth time)

Hence, if Case 2 occurs, then by time t, we must have left state 6 four times.

Table 4			NUMBER OF TRANSITIONS
Relation between	INITIAL STATE	STATE AT TIME t	OUT OF STATE 6 BY TIME t
Number of	Case 1: state 6	State 6	3
Transitions into and	Case 2: state 6	Any state except 6	4
out of a State by	Case 3: any state		
Time t	except state 6	State 6	2
	Case 4: any state		
	except state 6	Any state except 6	3

This observation suggests that for large t and for $j = 0, 1, 2, \ldots$ (and for any initial conditions), it will be true that

$$\frac{\text{Expected no. of departures from state } j}{\text{Unit time}}$$

$$= \frac{\text{expected no. of entrances into state } j}{\text{unit time}} \tag{11}$$

Assuming the system has settled down into the steady state, we know that the system spends a fraction π_j of its time in state j. We can now use Eq. (11) to determine the steady-state probabilities π_j. For $j \geq 1$, we can only leave state j by going to state $j + 1$ or state $j - 1$, so for $j \geq 1$ we obtain

$$\frac{\text{Expected no. of departures from state } j}{\text{Unit time}} = \pi_j(\lambda_j + \mu_j) \qquad (12)$$

Since for $j \geq 1$ we can only enter state j from state $j - 1$ or state $j + 1$,

$$\frac{\text{Expected no. of entrances into state } j}{\text{Unit time}} = \pi_{j-1}\lambda_{j-1} + \pi_{j+1}\mu_{j+1} \qquad (13)$$

Substituting (12) and (13) into (11) yields

$$\pi_{j-1}\lambda_{j-1} + \pi_{j+1}\mu_{j+1} = \pi_j(\lambda_j + \mu_j) \qquad (j = 1, 2, \ldots) \qquad (14)$$

For $j = 0$, we know that $\mu_0 = \pi_{-1} = 0$, so we also have

$$\pi_1\mu_1 = \pi_0\lambda_0 \qquad (14')$$

Eqs. (14) and (14′) are often called the **flow balance equations**, or **conservation of flow equations**, for a birth–death process. Note that (14) expresses the fact that in the steady state, the rate at which transitions occur into any state i must equal the rate at which transitions occur out of state i. If (14) did not hold for all states, then probability would "pile up" at some state, and a steady state would not exist.

Writing out the equations for (14) and (14′), we obtain the flow balance equations for a birth–death process:

$$
\begin{array}{lll}
(j = 0) & \pi_0\lambda_0 = \pi_1\mu_1 & \\
(j = 1) & (\lambda_1 + \mu_1)\pi_1 = \lambda_0\pi_0 + \mu_2\pi_2 & \\
(j = 2) & (\lambda_2 + \mu_2)\pi_2 = \lambda_1\pi_1 + \mu_3\pi_3 & (15) \\
& \;\;\vdots & \\
(j\text{th equation}) & (\lambda_j + \mu_j)\pi_j = \lambda_{j-1}\pi_{j-1} + \mu_{j+1}\pi_{j+1} &
\end{array}
$$

SOLUTION OF BIRTH–DEATH FLOW BALANCE EQUATIONS

To solve (15), we begin by expressing all the π_j's in terms of π_0. From the ($j = 0$) equation, we obtain

$$\pi_1 = \frac{\pi_0\lambda_0}{\mu_1}$$

Substituting this result into the ($j = 1$) equation yields

$$\lambda_0\pi_0 + \mu_2\pi_2 = \frac{(\lambda_1 + \mu_1)\pi_0\lambda_0}{\mu_1}$$

$$\mu_2\pi_2 = \frac{\pi_0(\lambda_0\lambda_1)}{\mu_1}$$

Thus,

$$\pi_2 = \frac{\pi_0(\lambda_0\lambda_1)}{\mu_1\mu_2}$$

We could now use the ($j = 3$) equation to solve for π_3 in terms of π_0, etc. If we define

$$c_j = \frac{\lambda_0 \lambda_1 \cdots \lambda_{j-1}}{\mu_1 \mu_2 \cdots \mu_j}$$

then it can be shown that

$$\pi_j = \pi_0 c_j \tag{16}$$

(See Problem 1 at the end of this section.) Since at any given time, we must be in some state, the steady-state probabilities must sum to 1:

$$\sum_{j=0}^{j=\infty} \pi_j = 1 \tag{17}$$

Substituting (16) into (17) yields

$$\pi_0 \left(1 + \sum_{j=1}^{j=\infty} c_j \right) = 1 \tag{18}$$

If $\sum_{j=1}^{j=\infty} c_j$ is finite, we can use (18) to solve for π_0:

$$\pi_0 = \frac{1}{1 + \sum_{j=1}^{j=\infty} c_j} \tag{19}$$

Then (16) can be used to determine $\pi_1, \pi_2, \ldots$. It can be shown that if $\sum_{j=1}^{j=\infty} c_j$ is infinite, then no steady-state distribution exists. The most common reason for a steady state failing to exist is that the arrival rate is at least as large as the maximum rate in which customers can be served.

In Sections 22.4–22.6 and 22.9–22.10, we apply the theory of birth–death processes to determine the steady-state probability distributions for a variety of queuing systems. Then we use the steady-state probability distributions to determine other quantities of interest (such as expected waiting time and expected number of customers in the system).

Birth–death models have been used to model phenomena other than queuing systems. For example, the number of firms in an industry can be modeled as a birth–death process: The state of the industry at any given time is the number of firms that are in business; a birth corresponds to a firm entering the industry; and a death corresponds to a firm going out of business.

◆ PROBLEMS

GROUP A

1. Show that the values of the π_j's given in Eq. (16) do indeed satisfy the flow balance equations (14) and (14′).

2. My home uses two light bulbs. On average, a light bulb lasts for 22 days (exponentially distributed). When a light bulb is replaced, it takes me an average of 2 days (exponentially distributed) before I replace the bulb.

(a) Formulate a three-state birth–death model of this situation.

(b) Determine the fraction of the time that both light bulbs are working.

(c) Determine the fraction of the time that no light bulbs are working.

22-4   THE $M/M/1/GD/\infty/\infty$ QUEUING SYSTEM AND THE QUEUING FORMULA $L = \lambda W$

We now use the birth–death methodology explained in the previous section to analyze the properties of the $M/M/1/GD/\infty/\infty$ queuing system. Recall that the $M/M/1/GD/\infty/\infty$ queuing system has exponential interarrival times (we assume the arrival rate per unit time is λ) and a single server with exponential service times (we assume each customer's service time is exponential with rate μ). In Section 22.3, we showed that an $M/M/1/GD/\infty/\infty$ queuing system may be modeled as a birth–death process with the following parameters:

$$\lambda_j = \lambda \qquad (j = 0, 1, 2, \dots)$$
$$\mu_0 = 0 \tag{20}$$
$$\mu_j = \mu \qquad (j = 1, 2, 3, \dots)$$

DERIVATION OF STEADY-STATE PROBABILITIES

We can use Eqs. (15)–(19) to solve for π_j, the steady-state probability that j customers will be present. Substituting (20) into (16) yields

$$\pi_1 = \frac{\lambda \pi_0}{\mu}, \qquad \pi_2 = \frac{\lambda^2 \pi_0}{\mu^2}, \qquad \dots, \qquad \pi_j = \frac{\lambda^j \pi_0}{\mu^j} \tag{21}$$

We define $\rho = \frac{\lambda}{\mu}$. For reasons that will become apparent later, we call ρ the **traffic intensity** of the queuing system. Substituting (21) into (17) yields

$$\pi_0(1 + \rho + \rho^2 + \cdots) = 1 \tag{22}$$

We now assume that $0 \le \rho < 1$. Then we evaluate the sum $S = 1 + \rho + \rho^2 + \cdots$ as follows: Multiplying S by ρ yields $\rho S = \rho + \rho^2 + \rho^3 + \cdots$. Then $S - \rho S = 1$, and

$$S = \frac{1}{1 - \rho} \tag{23}$$

Substituting (23) into (22) yields

$$\pi_0 = 1 - \rho \qquad (0 \le \rho < 1) \tag{24}$$

Substituting (24) into (21) yields

$$\pi_j = \rho^j(1 - \rho) \qquad (0 \le \rho < 1) \tag{25}$$

If $\rho \ge 1$, however, the infinite sum in (22) "blows up" (try $\rho = 1$, for example, and you get $1 + 1 + 1 + \cdots$). Thus, if $\rho \ge 1$, no steady-state distribution exists. Since $\rho = \frac{\lambda}{\mu}$, we see that if $\lambda \ge \mu$ (that is, the arrival rate is at least as large as the service rate), then no steady-state distribution exists.

If $\rho > 1$, it is easy to see why no steady-state distribution can exist. Suppose $\lambda = 6$ customers per hour and $\mu = 4$ customers per hour. Even if the server were working all the time, she could only serve an average of 4 people per hour. Thus, the average number of customers in the system would grow by at least $6 - 4 = 2$ customers per hour. This means that after a long time, the number of customers present would "blow up," and no steady-state distribution could exist. If $\rho = 1$, the nonexistence of a steady state is not quite so obvious, but our analysis does indicate that no steady state exists.

DERIVATION OF L

Throughout the rest of this section, we assume that $\rho < 1$, ensuring that a steady-state probability distribution, as given in (25), does exist. We now use the steady-state probability distribution in (25) to determine several quantities of interest. For example, assuming that the steady state has been reached, the average number of customers present in the queuing system (call it L) is given by

$$L = \sum_{j=0}^{j=\infty} j\pi_j = \sum_{j=0}^{j=\infty} j\rho^j(1 - \rho)$$
$$= (1 - \rho) \sum_{j=0}^{j=\infty} j\rho^j$$

Defining

$$S' = \sum_{j=0}^{j=\infty} j\rho^j = \rho + 2\rho^2 + 3\rho^3 + \cdots$$

we see that $\rho S' = \rho^2 + 2\rho^3 + 3\rho^4 + \cdots$. Subtracting yields

$$S' - \rho S' = \rho + \rho^2 + \cdots = \frac{\rho}{1 - \rho}$$

Thus,

$$S' = \frac{\rho}{(1 - \rho)^2}$$

and

$$L = (1 - \rho) \frac{\rho}{(1 - \rho)^2} = \frac{\rho}{1 - \rho} = \frac{\lambda}{\mu - \lambda} \qquad (26)$$

DERIVATION OF L_q

In some circumstances, we are interested in the expected number of people waiting in line (or in the queue). We denote this number by L_q. Note that if 0 or 1 customer is present in the system, then nobody is waiting in line, but if j people are present ($j \geq 1$), there will be $j - 1$ people waiting in line. Thus, if we are in the steady state,

$$L_q = \sum_{j=1}^{j=\infty} (j - 1)\pi_j = \sum_{j=1}^{j=\infty} j\pi_j - \sum_{j=1}^{j=\infty} \pi_j$$
$$= L - (1 - \pi_0) = L - \rho$$

where the last equation follows from (24). Since $L = \frac{\rho}{1-\rho}$, we write

$$L_q = \frac{\rho}{1 - \rho} - \rho = \frac{\rho^2}{1 - \rho} = \frac{\lambda^2}{\mu(\mu - \lambda)} \qquad (27)$$

DERIVATION OF L_s

Also of interest is L_s, the expected number of customers in service. For an $M/M/1/GD/\infty/\infty$ queuing system,

$$L_s = 0\pi_0 + 1(\pi_1 + \pi_2 + \cdots) = 1 - \pi_0 = 1 - (1 - \rho) = \rho$$

Since every customer who is present is either in line or in service, it follows that for any queuing system (not just an $M/M/1/GD/\infty/\infty$ system), $L = L_s + L_q$. Thus, using our formula for L and L_s, we could have determined L_q from

$$L_q = L - L_s = \frac{\rho}{1 - \rho} - \rho = \frac{\rho^2}{1 - \rho}$$

THE QUEUING FORMULA $L = \lambda W$

Often, we are interested in the amount of time that a typical customer spends in a queuing system. We define W as the expected time a customer spends in the queuing system, including time in line plus time in service, and W_q as the expected time a customer spends waiting in line. Both W and W_q are computed under the assumption that the steady state has been reached. By using a powerful result known as **Little's queuing formula**, W and W_q may be easily computed from L and L_q. We first define (for any queuing system or any subset of a queuing system) the following quantities:

λ = average number of arrivals *entering* the system per unit time

L = average number of customers present in the queuing system

L_q = average number of customers waiting in line

L_s = average number of customers in service

W = average time a customer spends in the system

W_q = average time a customer spends in line

W_s = average time a customer spends in service

In these definitions, all averages are steady-state averages. For most queuing systems, Little's queuing formula may be summarized as in Theorem 3.

THEOREM 3	For *any* queuing system in which a steady-state distribution exists, the following relations hold:

$$L = \lambda W \qquad (28)$$
$$L_q = \lambda W_q \qquad (29)$$
$$L_s = \lambda W_s \qquad (30)$$

Before using these important results, we present an intuitive justification of (28). First note that both sides of (28) have the same units (we assume the unit of time is hours). This follows, because L is expressed in terms of number of customers, λ is expressed in terms of customers per hour, and W is expressed in hours. Thus, λW has the same units (customers) as L. For a rigorous proof of Little's theorem, see Ross (1970). We content ourselves with the following heuristic discussion.

Consider a queuing system in which customers are served on a first come, first served basis. An arbitrary arrival enters the system (assume the steady state has been reached). This customer stays in the system until he completes service, and upon his departure, there will be (on the average) L customers present in the system. But when this customer leaves, who will be left in the system? Only those customers who arrive during the time the initial customer spends in the system. Since the initial customer spends an average of W hours in the system, an average of λW customers will arrive during his stay in the system. Hence, $L = \lambda W$. The "real" proof of $L = \lambda W$ is virtually independent of the number of servers, the interarrival time distribution, the service discipline, and the service time distribution. Thus, as long as a steady state exists, we may apply Eqs. (28)–(30) to any queuing system.

To illustrate the use of (28) and (29), we determine W and W_q for an $M/M/1/GD/\infty/\infty$ queuing system. From (26),

$$L = \frac{\rho}{1 - \rho}$$

Then (28) yields

$$W = \frac{L}{\lambda} = \frac{\rho}{\lambda(1 - \rho)} = \frac{1}{\mu - \lambda} \tag{31}$$

From (27), we obtain

$$L_q = \frac{\lambda^2}{\mu(\mu - \lambda)}$$

and (29) implies

$$W_q = \frac{L_q}{\lambda} = \frac{\lambda}{\mu(\mu - \lambda)} \tag{32}$$

Notice that (as expected) as ρ approaches 1, both W and W_q become very large. For ρ near zero, W_q approaches zero, but for small ρ, W approaches $\frac{1}{\mu}$, the mean service time.

The following three examples show applications of the formulas we have developed.

E X A M P L E 2

An average of 10 cars per hour arrive at a single-server drive-in teller. Assume the average service time for each customer is 4 minutes, and both interarrival times and service times are exponential. Answer the following questions:

1. What is the probability that the teller is idle?

2. What is the average number of cars waiting in line for the teller? (A car that is being served is not considered to be waiting in line.)

3. What is the average amount of time a drive-in customer spends in the bank parking lot (including time in service)?

4. On the average, how many customers per hour will be served by the teller?

Solution

By assumption, we are dealing with an $M/M/1/GD/\infty/\infty$ queuing system for which $\lambda = 10$ cars per hour and $\mu = 15$ cars per hour. Thus, $\rho = \frac{10}{15} = \frac{2}{3}$.

1. From (24), $\pi_0 = 1 - \rho = 1 - \frac{2}{3} = \frac{1}{3}$. Thus, the teller will be idle an average of one third of the time.

2. We seek L_q. From (27),

$$L_q = \frac{\rho^2}{1-\rho} = \frac{(\frac{2}{3})^2}{1-\frac{2}{3}} = \frac{4}{3} \text{ customers}$$

3. We seek W. From (28), $W = \frac{L}{\lambda}$. Then from (26),

$$L = \frac{\rho}{1-\rho} = \frac{\frac{2}{3}}{1-\frac{2}{3}} = 2 \text{ customers}$$

Thus, $W = \frac{2}{10} = \frac{1}{5}$ hour $= 12$ minutes (W will have the same units as λ).

4. If the teller were always busy, he would serve an average of $\mu = 15$ customers per hour. From part (1), we know that the teller is only busy two thirds of the time. Thus, during each hour, the teller will serve an average of $(\frac{2}{3})(15) = 10$ customers. This must be the case, because in the steady state, 10 customers are arriving each hour, so each hour, 10 customers must leave the system.

E X A M P L E 3

Suppose that all car owners fill up when their tanks are exactly half full.[†] At the present time, an average of 7.5 customers per hour arrive at a single-pump gas station. It takes an average of 4 minutes to service a car. Assume that interarrival times and service times are both exponential.

1. For the present situation, compute L and W.

2. Suppose that a gas shortage occurs and panic buying takes place. To model this phenomenon, suppose that all car owners now purchase gas when their tanks are exactly three quarters full. Since each car owner is now putting less gas into the tank during each visit to the station, we assume that the average service time has been reduced to $3\frac{1}{3}$ minutes. How has panic buying affected L and W?

Solution

1. We have an $M/M/1/GD/\infty/\infty$ system with $\lambda = 7.5$ cars per hour and $\mu = 15$ cars per hour. Thus, $\rho = \frac{7.5}{15} = .50$. From (26), $L = \frac{.50}{1-.50} = 1$, and from (28), $W = \frac{L}{\lambda} = \frac{1}{7.5} = 0.13$ hour. Hence, in this situation, everything is under control, and long lines appear to be unlikely.

2. We now have an $M/M/1/GD/\infty/\infty$ system with $\lambda = 2(7.5) = 15$ cars per hour. (This follows because each car owner will fill up twice as often.) Now $\mu = \frac{60}{3.333} = 18$ cars per hour, and $\rho = \frac{15}{18} = \frac{5}{6}$. Then

$$L = \frac{\frac{5}{6}}{1-\frac{5}{6}} = 5 \text{ cars} \quad \text{and} \quad W = \frac{L}{\lambda} = \frac{5}{15} = \frac{1}{3} \text{ hours} = 20 \text{ minutes}$$

Thus, panic buying has caused long lines.

Example 3 illustrates the fact that as ρ approaches 1, L and therefore W increase rapidly. Table 5 illustrates this fact.

[†]This example is based on Erickson (1973).

ρ	L FOR AN $M/M/1/GD/\infty/\infty$ SYSTEM
0.30	0.43
0.40	0.67
0.50	1.00
0.60	1.50
0.70	2.33
0.80	4.00
0.90	9.00
0.95	19.00
0.99	99.00

Table 5
Relation between ρ and L for an $M/M/1/GD/\infty/\infty$ System

A QUEUING OPTIMIZATION MODEL

Example 4 shows how queuing theory can be used as an aid in decision making.

E X A M P L E 4

Machinists who work at a tool-and-die plant must check out tools from a tool center.[†] An average of ten machinists per hour arrive seeking parts. At present, the tool center is staffed by a clerk who is paid $6 per hour and who takes an average of 5 minutes to handle each request for tools. Since machinists are paid $10 per hour, each hour that a machinist spends at the tool center costs the company $10. The company is deciding whether or not it is worthwhile to hire (at $4 per hour) a helper for the clerk. If the helper is hired, the clerk will take an average of only 4 minutes to process requests for tools. Assume that service and interarrival times are exponential. Should the helper be hired?

Solution

Problems in which a decision maker must choose between alternative queuing systems are called **queuing optimization problems**. In the current problem, the company's goal is to minimize the sum of the hourly service cost and the expected hourly cost due to the idle times of machinists. In queuing optimization problems, the component of cost due to customers waiting in line is referred to as the delay cost. Thus, the firm wants to minimize

$$\frac{\text{Expected cost}}{\text{Hour}} = \frac{\text{service cost}}{\text{hour}} + \frac{\text{expected delay cost}}{\text{hour}}$$

The computation of the hourly service cost is usually simple. The easiest way to compute the hourly delay cost is to note that

$$\frac{\text{Expected delay cost}}{\text{Hour}} = \left(\frac{\text{expected delay cost}}{\text{customer}}\right)\left(\frac{\text{expected customers}}{\text{hour}}\right)$$

In our problem,

$$\frac{\text{Expected delay cost}}{\text{Customer}} = \left(\frac{\$10}{\text{machinist-hour}}\right)\left(\begin{array}{c}\text{average hours machinist}\\\text{spends in system}\end{array}\right)$$

Thus,

[†]This example is based on Brigham (1955).

$$\frac{\text{Expected delay cost}}{\text{Customer}} = 10W \quad \text{and} \quad \frac{\text{expected delay cost}}{\text{hour}} = 10W\lambda$$

We can now compare the expected cost per hour if the helper is not hired to the expected cost per hour if the helper is hired. If the helper is not hired, $\lambda = 10$ machinists per hour and $\mu = 12$ machinists per hour. From (31), $W = \frac{1}{12-10} = \frac{1}{2}$ hour. Since the clerk is paid $6 per hour, we have that

$$\frac{\text{Service cost}}{\text{Hour}} = \$6 \quad \text{and} \quad \frac{\text{expected delay cost}}{\text{hour}} = 10(\tfrac{1}{2})10 = \$50$$

Thus, without the helper, the expected hourly cost is $6 + 50 = \$56$. With the helper, $\mu = 15$ customers per hour. Then $W = \frac{1}{15-10} = \frac{1}{5}$ hour and

$$\frac{\text{Expected delay cost}}{\text{Hour}} = 10(\tfrac{1}{5})(10) = \$20$$

Since the hourly service cost is now $6 + 4 = \$10$ per hour, the expected hourly cost with the helper is $20 + 10 = \$30$. Thus, the helper should be hired, because he saves $50 - 20 = \$30$ per hour in delay costs, which more than makes up for his $4-per-hour salary.

◆ PROBLEMS

GROUP A

1.[†] Each airline passenger and his or her luggage must be checked to determine whether he or she is carrying weapons onto the airplane. Suppose that at Gotham City Airport, an average of 10 passengers per minute arrive (interarrival times are exponential). To check passengers for weapons, the airport must have a checkpoint consisting of a metal detector and baggage X-ray machine. Whenever a checkpoint is in operation, two employees are required. A checkpoint can check an average of 12 passengers per minute (the time to check a passenger is exponential). Under the assumption that the airport has only one checkpoint, answer the following questions:
(a) What is the probability that a passenger will have to wait before being checked for weapons?
(b) On the average, how many passengers are waiting in line to enter the checkpoint?
(c) On the average, how long will a passenger spend at the checkpoint?

2. The Decision Sciences Department is trying to determine whether to rent a slow or a fast copier. The department believes that an employee's time is worth $15 per hour. The slow copier rents for $4 per hour, and it takes an employee an average of 10 minutes to complete copying

(exponentially distributed). The fast copier rents for $15 per hour, and it takes an employee an average of 6 minutes to complete copying. An average of 4 employees per hour need to use the copying machine (interarrival times are exponential). Which machine should the department rent?

3. For an $M/M/1/GD/\infty/\infty$ queuing system, suppose that both λ and μ are doubled.
(a) How is L changed?
(b) How is W changed?
(c) How is the steady-state probability distribution changed?

GROUP B

4.[‡] Referring to Problem 1, suppose the airline wants to determine how many checkpoints to operate in order to minimize operating costs and delay costs over a ten-year period. Assume that the cost of delaying a passenger for 1 hour is $10 and that the airport is open every day for 16 hours per day. It costs $1 million to purchase, staff, and maintain a metal detector and baggage X-ray machine for a ten-year period. Finally, assume that each passenger is equally likely to enter a given checkpoint.

[†]Based on Gilliam (1979).

[‡]Based on Gilliam (1979).

5.[†] Each machine on Widgetco's assembly line gets out of whack an average of once a minute. Laborers are assigned to reset a machine that gets out of whack. The company pays each laborer c_s dollars per hour and estimates that each hour of idle machine time costs the company c_m dollars in lost production. Data indicate that the time between successive breakdowns of a machine and the time to reset a machine are exponential. Widgetco plans to assign each worker a certain number of machines to watch over and repair. Let M = total number of Widgetco machines, w = number of laborers hired by Widgetco, and $R = \frac{M}{w}$ = machines assigned to each laborer.

(a) Express Widgetco's hourly cost in terms of R and M.

(b) Show that the optimal value of R does not depend on the value of M.

(c) Use calculus to show that costs are minimized by choosing

$$R = \frac{\dfrac{\mu}{60}}{1 + \left(\dfrac{c_m}{c_s}\right)^{1/2}}$$

(d) Suppose c_m = 78¢ and c_s = $2.75. Widgetco has 200 machines, and a laborer can reset a machine in an average of 7.8 seconds. How can Widgetco minimize costs?

(e) In parts (a)–(d), we have tacitly assumed that at any point in time, the rate at which the machines assigned to a worker break down does not depend on the number of his or her assigned machines that are currently working properly. Does this assumption seem reasonable?

6. Consider an airport where taxis and customers arrive (exponential interarrival times) with respective rates of 1 and 2 per minute. No matter how many other taxis are present, a taxi will wait. If an arriving customer does not find a taxi, the customer immediately leaves.

(a) Model this system as a birth–death process (*Hint*: Determine what the state of the system is at any given time and draw a rate diagram.)

(b) Find the average number of taxis that are waiting for a customer.

(c) Suppose all customers who use a taxi pay a $2 fare. During a typical hour, how much revenue will the taxis receive?

7. A bank is trying to determine which of two machines should be rented to process checks. Machine 1 rents for $10,000 per year and processes 1000 checks per hour. Machine 2 rents for $15,000 per year and processes 1600 checks per hour. Assume that machines work 8 hours a day, 5 days a week, 50 weeks a year. The bank must process an average of 800 checks per hour, and the average check processed is for $100. Assume an annual interest rate of 20%. Then determine the cost to the bank (in lost interest) for each hour that a check spends waiting for and undergoing processing. Assuming that interarrival times and service times are exponential, which machine should the bank rent?

8.[‡] A tire plant must produce an average of 100 tires per day. The plant produces tires in a batch of size x. The plant manager must determine the batch size x that minimizes the time a batch spends in the plant. From the time a batch of tires arrives, it takes an average of $\frac{1}{20}$ of a day to set up the plant for production of tires. Once the plant is set up, it takes an average of $\frac{1}{150}$ day to produce each tire. Assume that the time to produce a batch of tires is exponentially distributed and that the time for a batch of tires to "arrive" is also exponentially distributed. Determine the batch size that minimizes the expected time a batch spends in the plant (from arrival of batch to time production of batch is completed).

[†]Based on Vogel (1979).

[‡]Based on Karmarkar (1985).

22-5   The $M/M/1/GD/c/\infty$ QUEUING SYSTEM

In this section, we analyze the $M/M/1/GD/c/\infty$ queuing system. Recall that this queuing system is an $M/M/1/GD/\infty/\infty$ system with a total capacity of c customers. The $M/M/1/GD/c/\infty$ system is identical to the $M/M/1/GD/\infty/\infty$ system except for the fact that when c customers are present, all arrivals are turned away and are forever lost to the system. As in Section 22.4, we assume that interarrival times are exponential with rate λ, and service times are exponential with rate μ. Then the $M/M/1/GD/c/\infty$ system may be modeled (see Figure 11) as a birth–death process with the following parameters:

Figure 11
Rate Diagram for
$M/M/1/GD/c/\infty$
Queuing System

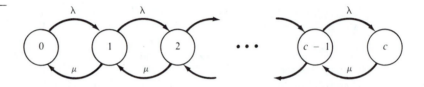

$$\lambda_j = \lambda \quad (j = 0, 1, \ldots, c - 1)$$
$$\lambda_c = 0$$
$$\mu_0 = 0 \tag{33}$$
$$\mu_j = \mu \quad (j = 1, 2, \ldots, c)$$

Since $\lambda_c = 0$, the system will never reach state $c + 1$ (or any higher-numbered state). As in Section 22.4, it is convenient to define $\rho = \frac{\lambda}{\mu}$. Then we can apply Eqs. (16)–(19) to find that if $\lambda \neq \mu$, the steady-state probabilities for the $M/M/1/GD/c/\infty$ model are given by

$$\pi_0 = \frac{1 - \rho}{1 - \rho^{c+1}}$$
$$\pi_j = \rho^j \pi_0 \quad (j = 1, 2, \ldots, c) \tag{34}$$
$$\pi_j = 0 \quad\quad (j = c + 1, c + 2, \ldots)$$

Combining (34) with the fact that $L = \sum_{j=0}^{j=c} j\pi_j$, we can show that when $\lambda \neq \mu$,

$$L = \frac{\rho[1 - (c + 1)\rho^c + c\rho^{c+1}]}{(1 - \rho^{c+1})(1 - \rho)} \tag{35}$$

If $\lambda = \mu$, then all the c_j's in (16) equal 1, and all the π_j's must be equal. Hence, if $\lambda = \mu$, the steady-state probabilities for the $M/M/1/GD/c/\infty$ system are

$$\pi_j = \frac{1}{c + 1} \quad (j = 0, 1, \ldots, c)$$
$$L = \frac{c}{2} \tag{36}$$

As with the $M/M/1/GD/\infty/\infty$ system, $L_s = 0\pi_0 + 1(\pi_1 + \pi_2 + \cdots) = 1 - \pi_0$. As before, we may determine L_q from $L_q = L - L_s$.

Determination of W and W_q from (28) and (29) is a tricky matter. Recall that in (28) and (29), λ represents the average number of customers per unit time who *actually enter* the system. In our finite capacity model, an average of λ arrivals per unit time arrive, but $\lambda\pi_c$ of these arrivals find the system filled to capacity and leave. Thus, an average of $\lambda - \lambda\pi_c = \lambda(1 - \pi_c)$ arrivals per unit time will actually enter the system. Combining this fact with (28) and (29) yields

$$W = \frac{L}{\lambda(1 - \pi_c)} \quad \text{and} \quad W_q = \frac{L_q}{\lambda(1 - \pi_c)} \tag{37}$$

For an $M/M/1/GD/c/\infty$ system, a steady state will exist even if $\lambda \geq \mu$. This is because, even if $\lambda \geq \mu$, the finite capacity of the system prevents the number of people in the system from "blowing up."

E X A M P L E
5

A one-man barber shop has a total of 10 seats. Interarrival times are exponentially distributed, and an average of 20 prospective customers arrive each hour at the shop. Those customers who find the shop full do not enter. The barber takes an average of 12 minutes to cut each customer's hair. Haircut times are exponentially distributed.

1. On the average, how many haircuts per hour will the barber complete?

2. On the average, how much time will be spent in the shop by a customer who enters?

Solution

1. A fraction π_{10} of all arrivals will find the shop full. Thus, an average of $\lambda(1 - \pi_{10})$ will enter the shop each hour. All entering customers will receive a haircut, so the barber will give an average of $\lambda(1 - \pi_{10})$ haircuts per hour. From our problem, $c = 10$, $\lambda = 20$ customers per hour, and $\mu = 5$ customers per hour. Then $\rho = \frac{20}{5} = 4$, and Eq. (34) yields

$$\pi_0 = \frac{1 - 4}{1 - 4^{11}}$$

and

$$\pi_{10} = 4^{10}\left(\frac{1 - 4}{1 - 4^{11}}\right) = \frac{-3(4^{10})}{1 - 4^{11}} = .75$$

Thus, an average of $20(1 - \frac{3}{4}) = 5$ customers per hour will receive haircuts. This means that an average of $20 - 5 = 15$ prospective customers per hour will not enter the shop.

2. To determine W, we use (35) and (37). From (35),

$$L = \frac{4[1 - 11(4^{10}) + 10(4^{11})]}{(1 - 4^{11})(1 - 4)} = 9.67 \text{ customers}$$

Then (37) yields

$$W = \frac{9.67}{20(1 - \frac{3}{4})} = 1.93 \text{ hours}$$

This barber shop is crowded, and the barber would be well advised to hire at least one more barber!

◆ PROBLEMS

GROUP A

1. A service facility consists of one server who can serve an average of 2 customers per hour (service times are exponential). An average of 3 customers per hour arrive at the facility (interarrival times are assumed exponential). The system capacity is 3 customers.

(a) On the average, how many potential customers enter the system each hour?

(b) What is the probability that the server will be busy?

2. An average of 40 cars per hour (interarrival times are exponentially distributed) are tempted to use the drive-in window at the Hot Dog King Restaurant. If a total of more than 4 cars are in line (including the car at the window) a car will not enter the line. It takes an average of 4 minutes (exponentially distributed) to serve a car.

(a) What is the average number of cars waiting for the drive-in window (not including a car at the window)?

(b) On the average, how many cars will be served per hour?

(c) I have just joined the line at the drive-in window. On the average, how long will it be before I have received my food?

GROUP B

3. Show that if $\rho \neq 1$

$$1 + \rho + \rho^2 + \cdots + \rho^c = \frac{1 - \rho^{c+1}}{1 - \rho}$$

(*Hint*: Recall how we evaluated $1 + \rho + \rho^2 + \cdots$.)

4. Use the answer to Problem 3 to derive the steady-state probabilities for the $M/M/1/GD/c/\infty$ system given in Eq. (34).

5. There are two one-man barber shops side by side in Dunkirk Square. Each barber shop can hold a maximum of 4 people, and any potential customer who finds a shop full will not wait for a haircut. Barber 1 charges $11 per haircut and takes an average of 12 minutes to complete a haircut. Barber 2 charges $5 per haircut and takes an average of 6 minutes to complete a haircut. An average of 10 potential customers per hour arrive at each barber shop. Of course, a potential customer becomes an actual customer only if the customer finds that the shop is not full. Assuming that interarrival times and haircut times are exponential, which barber will earn more money?

22-6   THE $M/M/s/GD/\infty/\infty$ QUEUING SYSTEM

We now consider the $M/M/s/GD/\infty/\infty$ system. We assume that interarrival times are exponential (with rate λ), service times are exponential (with rate μ), and there is a single line of customers waiting to be served at one of s parallel servers. If $j \leq s$ customers are present, then all j customers are in service; if $j > s$ customers are present, then all s servers are occupied, and $j - s$ customers are waiting in line. Any arrival who finds an idle server enters service immediately, but an arrival who does not find an idle server joins the queue of customers awaiting service. Banks and post office branches in which all customers wait in a single line for service can often be modeled as $M/M/s/GD/\infty/\infty$ queuing systems.

To describe the $M/M/s/GD/\infty/\infty$ system as a birth–death model, note that (as in the $M/M/1/GD/\infty/\infty$ model) $\lambda_j = \lambda$ ($j = 0, 1, 2, \ldots$). If j servers are occupied, then service completions occur at a rate

$$\underbrace{\mu + \mu + \cdots}_{j\mu\text{'s}} = j\mu$$

Whenever j customers are present, $\min(j, s)$ servers will be occupied. Thus, $\mu_j = \min(j, s)\mu$. Summarizing, we find that the $M/M/s/GD/\infty/\infty$ system can be modeled as a birth–death process (see Figure 12) with parameters

$$\begin{aligned}
\lambda_j &= \lambda & (j = 0, 1, \ldots) \\
\mu_j &= j\mu & (j = 0, 1, \ldots, s) \\
\mu_j &= s\mu & (j = s + 1, s + 2, \ldots)
\end{aligned} \qquad (38)$$

Figure 12
Rate Diagram for
$M/M/s/GD/\infty/\infty$
Queuing System

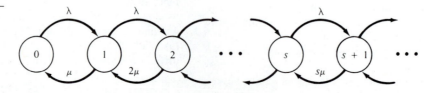

We define $\rho = \frac{\lambda}{s\mu}$. For $\rho < 1$, substituting (38) into (16)–(19) yields the following steady-state probabilities:

$$\pi_0 = \cfrac{1}{\displaystyle\sum_{i=0}^{i=(s-1)} \frac{(s\rho)^i}{i!} + \frac{(s\rho)^s}{s!(1 - \rho)}} \tag{39}$$

$$\pi_j = \frac{(s\rho)^j \pi_0}{j!} \qquad (j = 1, 2, \ldots, s) \tag{39.1}$$

$$\pi_j = \frac{(s\rho)^j \pi_0}{s! s^{j-s}} \qquad (j = s, s + 1, s + 2, \ldots) \tag{39.2}$$

If $\rho \geq 1$, no steady state exists. In other words, if the arrival rate is at least as large as the maximum possible service rate ($\lambda \geq s\mu$), the system "blows up."

From (39.2) it can be shown that the steady-state probability that all servers are busy is given by

$$P(j \geq s) = \frac{(s\rho)^s \pi_0}{s!(1 - \rho)} \tag{40}$$

Table 6 tabulates $P(j \geq s)$ for a variety of situations. It can also be shown that

$$L_q = \frac{P(j \geq s)\rho}{1 - \rho} \tag{41}$$

	ρ	$s = 2$	$s = 3$	$s = 4$	$s = 5$	$s = 6$	$s = 7$
Table 6 $P(j \geq s)$ for the $M/M/s/GD/\infty/\infty$ Queuing System	.10	.02	.00	.00	.00	.00	.00
	.20	.07	.02	.00	.00	.00	.00
	.30	.14	.07	.04	.02	.01	.00
	.40	.23	.14	.09	.06	.04	.03
	.50	.33	.24	.17	.13	.10	.08
	.55	.39	.29	.23	.18	.14	.11
	.60	.45	.35	.29	.24	.20	.17
	.65	.51	.42	.35	.30	.26	.21
	.70	.57	.51	.43	.38	.34	.30
	.75	.64	.57	.51	.46	.42	.39
	.80	.71	.65	.60	.55	.52	.49
	.85	.78	.73	.69	.65	.62	.60
	.90	.85	.83	.79	.76	.74	.72
	.95	.92	.91	.89	.88	.87	.85

Then (28) yields

$$W_q = \frac{L_q}{\lambda} = \frac{P(j \geq s)}{s\mu - \lambda} \tag{42}$$

To determine L (and then W), we use the fact that $L = L_q + L_s$. Since $W_s = \frac{1}{\mu}$, Eq. (30) shows that $L_s = \frac{\lambda}{\mu}$. Then

$$L = L_q + \frac{\lambda}{\mu} \tag{43}$$

Also,

$$
\begin{aligned}
W &= \frac{L}{\lambda} \\
&= \frac{L_q}{\lambda} + \frac{1}{\mu} \\
&= W_q + \frac{1}{\mu} \\
&= \frac{P(j \geq s)}{s\mu - \lambda} + \frac{1}{\mu}
\end{aligned}
\tag{44}
$$

When we need to determine L, L_q, W, or W_q, we begin by looking up $P(j \geq s)$ in Table 6. Then we use (41)–(44) to calculate the quantity we want. If we are interested in the steady-state probability distribution, we find $P(j \geq s)$ in Table 6 and then use (40) to obtain π_0. Then (39.1) and (39.2) yield the entire steady-state distribution. The following two examples illustrate the use of the preceding formulas.

E X A M P L E 6

Consider a bank with two tellers. An average of 80 customers per hour arrive at the bank and wait in a single line for an idle teller. The average time it takes to serve a customer is 1.2 minutes. Assume that interarrival times and service times are exponential. Determine

1. The expected number of customers present in the bank
2. The expected length of time a customer spends in the bank
3. The fraction of the time that a particular teller is idle

Solution

1. We have an $M/M/2/GD/\infty/\infty$ system with $\lambda = 80$ customers per hour and $\mu = 50$ customers per hour. Thus, $\rho = \frac{80}{2(50)} = 0.80 < 1$, so a steady state does exist. (For $\lambda \geq 100$, no steady state would exist.) From Table 6, $P(j \geq 2) = .71$. Then (41) yields

$$L_q = \frac{.80(.71)}{1 - .80} = 2.84 \text{ customers}$$

and from (43), $L = 2.84 + \frac{80}{50} = 4.44$ customers.

2. Since $W = \frac{L}{\lambda}$, $W = \frac{4.44}{80} = 0.055$ hour $= 3.3$ minutes.

3. To determine the fraction of time that a particular server is idle, note that he or she is idle during the entire time that $j = 0$ and half the time (by symmetry) that $j = 1$. The probability that a server is idle is given by $\pi_0 + 0.5\pi_1$. Using the fact that $P(j \geq 2) = .71$, we obtain π_0 from (40):

$$\pi_0 = \frac{s!P(j \geq s)(1 - \rho)}{(s\rho)^2} = \frac{2!(.71)(1 - .80)}{(1.6)^2} = .11$$

Now (39.1) yields

$$\pi_1 = \frac{(1.6)^1 \pi_0}{1!} = .176$$

Thus, the probability that a particular teller is idle is $\pi_0 + 0.5\pi_1 = .11 + 0.5(.176) = .198$. We could have determined π_0 directly from (39):

$$\pi_0 = \frac{1}{1 + \dfrac{[2(.80)]^1}{1!} + \dfrac{[2(.80)]^2}{2!(1 - .80)}} = \frac{1}{1 + 1.6 + 6.4} = \frac{1}{9}$$

This is consistent with our computation of $\pi_0 = .11$.

◆

E X A M P L E 7

The manager of a bank must determine how many tellers should work on Fridays. For every minute a customer stands in line, the manager believes that a delay cost of 5¢ is incurred. An average of 2 customers per minute arrive at the bank. On the average, it takes a teller 2 minutes to complete a customer's transaction. It costs the bank $9 per hour to hire a teller. Interarrival times and service times are exponential. In order to minimize the sum of service costs and delay costs, how many tellers should the bank have working on Fridays?

Solution

Since $\lambda = 2$ customers per minute and $\mu = 0.5$ customer per minute, $\frac{\lambda}{s\mu} < 1$ requires that $\frac{4}{s} < 1$, or $s \geq 5$. Thus, there must be at least 5 tellers or the number of customers present will "blow up." We now compute, for $s = 5, 6, \ldots ,$

$$\frac{\text{Expected service cost}}{\text{Minute}} + \frac{\text{expected delay cost}}{\text{minute}}$$

Since each teller is paid $\frac{9}{60} = \$0.15$ per minute,

$$\frac{\text{Expected service cost}}{\text{Minute}} = \$0.15s$$

As in Example 4,

$$\frac{\text{Expected delay cost}}{\text{Minute}} = \left(\frac{\text{expected customers}}{\text{minute}}\right)\left(\frac{\text{expected delay cost}}{\text{customer}}\right)$$

But

$$\frac{\text{Expected delay cost}}{\text{Customer}} = \$0.05W_q$$

Since an average of 2 customers arrive per minute,

$$\frac{\text{Expected delay cost}}{\text{Minute}} = 2(0.05W_q) = \$0.10W_q$$

For $s = 5$, $\rho = \frac{2}{.5(5)} = .80$ and $P(j \geq 5) = .55$. From (42),

$$W_q = \frac{.55}{5(.5) - 2} = 1.1 \text{ minutes}$$

Thus, for $s = 5$,

$$\frac{\text{Expected delay cost}}{\text{Minute}} = 0.10(1.1) = \$0.11$$

and, for $s = 5$,

$$\frac{\text{Total expected cost}}{\text{Minute}} = 0.15(5) + 0.11 = \$0.86$$

Since $s = 6$ has a service cost per minute of $6(0.15) = \$0.90$, 6 tellers cannot have a lower total cost than 5 tellers. Hence, having 5 tellers serve is optimal. Putting it another way, adding an additional teller can save the bank at most $\$0.11$ per minute in delay costs. Since an additional teller costs $\$0.15$ per minute, it cannot be optimal to hire more than 5 tellers.

◆

In addition to a customer's expected time in the system, the distribution of a customer's waiting time is of interest. For example, if all customers who have to wait more than 5 minutes at a supermarket checkout counter decide to switch to another store, the probability that a given customer will switch to another store equals $P(\mathbf{W} > 5)$. To determine this probability, we need to know the distribution of a customer's waiting time. For an $M/M/s/\text{FCFS}/\infty/\infty$ queuing system, it can be shown that

$$P(\mathbf{W} > t) = e^{-\mu t} \left\{ 1 + P(j \geq s) \frac{1 - \exp\left[-\mu t(s - 1 - s\rho)\right]}{s - 1 - s\rho} \right\}^\dagger \tag{45}$$

$$P(\mathbf{W}_q > t) = P(j \geq s) \exp\left[-s\mu(1 - \rho)t\right] \tag{46}$$

To illustrate the use of (45) and (46), suppose that in Example 7 (for $s = 5$), the bank manager wants to know the probability that a customer will have to wait in line for more than 10 minutes. For $s = 5$, $\rho = .80$, $P(j \geq 5) = .55$, and $\mu = 0.5$ customer per minute, Eq. (46) yields

$$P(\mathbf{W}_q > 10) = .55 \exp\left[-5(0.5)(1 - .80)(10)\right] = .55e^{-5} = .004$$

Thus, the bank manager can be sure that the chance of a customer's having a wait of more than 10 minutes is quite small.

$\dagger$If $s - 1 = s\rho$, then $P(\mathbf{W} > t) = e^{-\mu t}(1 + P(j \geq s)\mu t)$.

◆ PROBLEMS

GROUP A

1. A supermarket is trying to decide how many cash registers to keep open. Suppose an average of 18 customers arrive each hour, and the average checkout time for a customer is 4 minutes. Interarrival times and service times are exponential, and the system may be modeled as an $M/M/s/GD/\infty/\infty$ queuing system. It costs $\$20$ per hour to operate a cash register, and a cost of 25¢ is assessed for each minute the customer spends in the cash register area. How many registers should the store open?

2. A small bank is trying to determine how many tellers to employ. The total cost of employing a teller is $\$100$ per day, and a teller can serve an average of 60 customers per day. An average of 50 customers per day arrive at the bank, and both service times and interarrival times are exponential. If the delay cost per customer day is $\$100$, how many tellers should the bank hire?

3. In this problem, all interarrival and service times are exponential.

(a) At present, the finance department and the marketing department each have their own typists. Each typist can type 25 letters per day. Finance requires that an average of 20 letters per day be typed, and marketing requires that an average of 15 letters per day be typed. For each department, determine the average length of time elapsing between a request for a letter and completion of the letter.

(b) Suppose that the two typists were grouped into a typing pool; that is, each typist would be available to type letters for either department. For this arrangement, calculate the average length of time between a request for a letter and completion of the letter.

(c) Comment on the results of parts (a) and (b).

(d) Under the pooled arrangement, what is the probability that more than 0.20 day will elapse between a request for a letter and completion of the letter?

4. MacBurger's is attempting to determine how many servers (or lines) should be available during the breakfast shift. During each hour, an average of 100 customers arrive at the restaurant. Each line or server can handle an average of 50 customers per hour. A server costs $5 per hour, and the cost of a customer waiting in line for 1 hour is $20. Assuming that an $M/M/s/GD/\infty/\infty$ model is applicable, determine the number of lines that minimizes the sum of delay and service costs.

5. An average of 100 customers arrive each hour at the Gotham City Bank. The average service time for each customer is 1 minute. Service times and interarrival times are exponential. The manager wants to ensure that no more than 1% of all customers will have to wait in line for more than 5 minutes. If the bank follows the policy of having all customers join a single line, how many tellers must the bank hire?

GROUP B

6. An average of 100 customers per hour arrive at Gotham City Bank. It takes a teller an average of 2 minutes to serve a customer. Interarrival and service times are exponential. The bank currently has four tellers working. The bank manager wishes to compare the following two systems with regard to average number of customers present in the bank and the probability that a customer will spend more than 8 minutes in the bank:

System 1 Each teller has her own line, and no jockeying between lines is permitted.

System 2 All customers wait in a single line for the first available teller.

If you were the bank manager, which system would you prefer?

7. A muffler shop has three mechanics. Each mechanic takes an average of 45 minutes to install a new muffler. Suppose an average of 1 customer per hour arrives. What is the expected number of mechanics that are busy at any given time? Answer this question without assuming that service times and interarrival times are exponential.

8. Consider the following two queuing systems:

System 1 An $M/M/1$ system with arrival rate λ and service rate 3μ.

System 2 An $M/M/3$ system with arrival rate λ and each server working at rate μ.

Without doing extensive calculations, which system will have the smaller W and L? (*Hint:* Write down the birth–death parameters for each system. Then determine which system is more efficient.)

22-7   THE $M/G/\infty/GD/\infty/\infty$ AND $GI/G/\infty/GD/\infty/\infty$ MODELS

There are many examples of systems in which a customer never has to wait for service to begin. In such a system, the customer's entire stay in the system may be thought of as his or her service time. Since a customer never has to wait for service, there is, in essence, a server available for each arrival, and we may think of such a system as an infinite-server (or self-service) system. Two examples of an infinite-server system are given in Table 7.

Using the Kendall-Lee notation, an infinite-server system in which interarrival and service times may follow arbitrary probability distributions may be written as $GI/G/\infty/GD/\infty/\infty$ queuing system. Such a system operates as follows:

		SERVICE TIME	
SITUATION	ARRIVAL	(TIME IN SYSTEM)	STATE OF SYSTEM
Industry	Firm enters industry	Time until firm leaves industry	Number of firms in industry
College program	Student enters program	Time student remains in program	Number of students in program

Table 7
Examples of Infinite-Server Queuing Systems

1. Interarrival times are iid with common distribution **A**. Define $E(A) = \frac{1}{\lambda}$. Thus, λ is the arrival rate.

2. When a customer arrives, he or she immediately enters service. Each customer's time in the system is governed by a distribution **S** having $E(S) = \frac{1}{\mu}$.

Let L be the expected number of customers in the system in the steady state, and W be the expected time that a customer spends in the system. By definition, $W = \frac{1}{\mu}$. Then Eq. (30) implies that

$$L = \frac{\lambda}{\mu} \tag{47}$$

Eq. (47) does not require any assumptions of exponentiality. If interarrival times are exponential, it can be shown (even for an arbitrary service time distribution) that the steady-state probability that j customers are present (call it π_j) follows a Poisson distribution with mean $\frac{\lambda}{\mu}$. This implies that

$$\pi_j = \frac{(\frac{\lambda}{\mu})^j e^{-\lambda/\mu}}{j!}$$

The following example is a typical application of a $GI/G/\infty/GD/\infty/\infty$ system.

E X A M P L E 8

During each year, an average of 3 ice cream shops open up in Smalltown. The average time that an ice cream shop stays in business is 10 years. On January 1, 2525, what is the average number of ice cream shops that you would find in Smalltown? If the time between the opening of ice cream shops is exponential, what is the probability that on January 1, 2525, there will be 25 ice cream shops in Smalltown?

Solution

We are given that $\lambda = 3$ shops per year and $\frac{1}{\mu} = 10$ years per shop. Assuming that the steady state has been reached, there will be an average of $L = \lambda(\frac{1}{\mu}) = 3(10) = 30$ shops in Smalltown. If interarrivals of ice cream shops are exponential, then

$$\pi_{25} = \frac{(30)^{25} e^{-30}}{25!} = .05$$

◆

◆ PROBLEMS

GROUP A

1. Each week, the Columbus Record Club attracts 100 new members. Members remain members for an average of one year (1 year = 52 weeks). On the average, how many members will the record club have?

2. The state U doctoral program in business admits an average of 25 doctoral students each year. If a doctoral student spends an average of 4 years in residence at State U, how many doctoral students would one expect to find at State U?

3. There are at present 40 solar energy construction firms in the state of Indiana. An average of 20 solar energy construction firms open each year in the state. The average firm stays in business for 10 years. If present trends continue, what is the expected number of solar energy construction firms that will be found in Indiana? If the time between the entries of firms into the industry is exponentially distributed, what is the probability that (in the steady state) there will be more than 300 solar energy firms in business? (*Hint*: For large λ, the Poisson distribution can be approximated by a normal distribution.)

22-8   THE $M/G/1/GD/\infty/\infty$ QUEUING SYSTEM

In this section, we consider a single-server queuing system in which interarrival times are exponential, but the service time distribution (**S**) need not be exponential. Let λ be the arrival rate (assumed to be measured in arrivals per hour). Also define $\frac{1}{\mu} = E(\mathbf{S})$ and $\sigma^2 = \text{var } \mathbf{S}$.

In Kendall's notation, such a queuing system is described as an $M/G/1/GD/\infty/\infty$ queuing system. An $M/G/1/GD/\infty/\infty$ system is *not* a birth–death process, because the probability that a service completion occurs between t and $t + \Delta t$ when the state of the system at time t is j depends on the length of time since the last service completion (because service times no longer have the no-memory property). Thus, we cannot write the probability of a service completion between t and $t + \Delta t$ in the form $\mu \Delta t$, and a birth–death model is not appropriate.

Determination of the steady-state probabilities for an $M/G/1/GD/\infty/\infty$ queuing system is a difficult matter. Since the birth–death steady-state equations are no longer valid, a different approach must be taken. Markov chain theory is used to determine π_i', the probability that after the system has operated for a long time, i customers will be present at the instant immediately after a service completion occurs (see Problem 4 at the end of this section). It can be shown that $\pi_i' = \pi_i$, where π_i is the fraction of the time after the system has operated for a long time that i customers are present (see Kleinrock (1975)).

Fortunately, however, utilizing the results of Pollaczek and Khinchin, we may determine L_q, L, L_s, W_q, W, and W_s. Pollaczek and Khinchin showed that for the $M/G/1/GD/\infty/\infty$ queuing system,

$$L_q = \frac{\lambda^2 \sigma^2 + \rho^2}{2(1 - \rho)} \tag{48}$$

where $\rho = \frac{\lambda}{\mu}$. Since $W_s = \frac{1}{\mu}$, Eq. (30) implies that $L_s = \lambda(\frac{1}{\mu}) = \rho$. Since $L = L_s + L_q$, we obtain

$$L = L_q + \rho \tag{49}$$

Then (29) and (28) imply that

$$W_q = \frac{L_q}{\lambda} \tag{50}$$

$$W = W_q + \frac{1}{\mu} \tag{51}$$

It can also be shown that π_0, the fraction of the time that the server is idle, is $1 - \rho$. (See Problem 2 at the end of this section.) This result is similar to the one for the $M/M/1/GD/\infty/\infty$ system.

To illustrate the use of (48)–(51), consider an $M/M/1/GD/\infty/\infty$ system with $\lambda = 5$ customers per hour and $\mu = 8$ customers per hour. From our study of the $M/M/1/GD/\infty/\infty$ model, we know that

$$L = \frac{\lambda}{\mu - \lambda} = \frac{5}{8 - 5} = \frac{5}{3} \text{ customers}$$

$$L_q = L - \rho = \frac{5}{3} - \frac{5}{8} = \frac{25}{24} \text{ customers}$$

$$W = \frac{L}{\lambda} = \frac{\frac{5}{3}}{5} = \frac{1}{3} \text{ hour}$$

$$W_q = \frac{L_q}{\lambda} = \frac{\frac{25}{24}}{5} = \frac{5}{24} \text{ hour}$$

From (3) and (4), we know that $E(\mathbf{S}) = \frac{1}{8}$ hour and $\text{var}\,\mathbf{S} = \frac{1}{64}$ hour^2. Then (48) yields

$$L_q = \frac{\frac{(5)^2}{64} + \left(\frac{5}{8}\right)^2}{2\left(1 - \frac{5}{8}\right)} = \frac{25}{24} \text{ customers}$$

$$L = L_q + \rho = \frac{25}{24} + \frac{5}{8} = \frac{40}{24} = \frac{5}{3} \text{ customers}$$

$$W_q = \frac{L_q}{\lambda} = \frac{\frac{25}{24}}{5} = \frac{5}{24} \text{ hour}$$

$$W = \frac{L}{\lambda} = \frac{\frac{5}{3}}{5} = \frac{1}{3} \text{ hour}$$

To demonstrate how the variance of the service time can significantly affect the efficiency of a queuing system, we consider an $M/D/1/GD/\infty/\infty$ queuing system having λ and μ identical to the $M/M/1/GD/\infty/\infty$ system that we have just analyzed. For this $M/D/1/GD/\infty/\infty$ model, $E(\mathbf{S}) = \frac{1}{8}$ hour and $\text{var}\,\mathbf{S} = 0$. Then

$$L_q = \frac{\left(\frac{5}{8}\right)^2}{2\left(1 - \frac{5}{8}\right)} = \frac{25}{48} \text{ customer}$$

$$W_q = \frac{L_q}{\lambda} = \frac{\frac{25}{48}}{5} = \frac{5}{48} \text{ hour}$$

In this $M/D/1/GD/\infty/\infty$ system, a typical customer will spend only half as much time in line as in an $M/M/1/GD/\infty/\infty$ queuing system with identical arrival and service rates.

As this example shows, even if mean service times are not decreased, a decrease in the variability of service times can substantially reduce queue size and customer waiting time.

◆ PROBLEMS

GROUP A

1. An average of 20 cars per hour arrive at the drive-in window of a fast food restaurant. If each car's service time is 2 minutes, how many cars (on the average) will be waiting in line? Assume exponential interarrival times.

2. Using the fact that $L_s = \frac{\lambda}{\mu}$, demonstrate that for an $M/G/1/GD/\infty/\infty$ queuing system, the probability that the server is busy is $\rho = \frac{\lambda}{\mu}$.

GROUP B

3. Consider an $M/G/1/GD/\infty/\infty$ queuing system in which an average of 10 arrivals occur each hour. Suppose that each customer's service time follows an Erlang distribution with rate parameter 1 customer per minute and shape parameter 4.
(a) Find the expected number of customers waiting in line.
(b) Find the expected time that a customer will spend in the system.
(c) What fraction of the time will the server be idle?

4. Consider an $M/G/1/GD/\infty/\infty$ queuing system in which interarrival times are exponentially distributed with par-

ameter λ and service times have a probability density function $s(t)$. Let X_i be the number of customers present an instant after the ith customer completes service.
(a) Explain why $X_1, X_2, \ldots, X_k, \ldots$ is a Markov chain.
(b) Explain why $P_{ij} = P(X_{k+1} = j \mid X_k = i)$ is zero for $j < i - 1$.
(c) Explain why for $i > 0$, $P_{i,i-1} =$ (probability that no arrival occurs during a service time); $P_{ii} =$ (probability that one arrival occurs during a service time); and for $j \geq i$, $P_{ij} =$ (probability that $j - i + 1$ arrivals occur during a service time).
(d) Explain why, for $j \geq i - 1$ and $i > 0$,

$$P_{ij} = \int_0^\infty \frac{s(x)e^{-\lambda x}(\lambda x)^{j-i+1}}{(j-i+1)!} \, dx$$

Hint: The probability that a service time is between x and $x + \Delta x$ is $\Delta x s(x)$. Given that the service time equals x, the probability that $j - i + 1$ arrivals will occur during the service time is

$$\frac{e^{-\lambda x}(\lambda x)^{j-i+1}}{(j-i+1)!}$$

22-9

FINITE SOURCE MODELS: THE MACHINE REPAIR MODEL

With the exception of the $M/M/1/GD/c/\infty$ model, all the models we have studied have displayed arrival rates that were independent of the state of the system. As discussed previously, there are two situations where the assumption of state-independent arrival rates may be invalid:

1. If customers do not wish to buck long lines, the arrival rate may be a decreasing function of the number of people present in the queuing system. For an illustration of this situation, see Problems 4 and 5 at the end of this section.

2. If arrivals to a system are drawn from a small population, the arrival rate may greatly depend on the state of the system. For example, if a bank has only 10 depositors, then at an instant when all depositors are in the bank, the arrival rate must be zero, while if fewer than 10 people are in the bank, the arrival rate will be positive.

Models in which arrivals are drawn from a small population are called **finite source models**. We now analyze an important finite source model known as the machine repair (or machine interference) model.

In the machine repair problem, the system consists of K machines and R repair people. At any instant in time, a particular machine is in either good or bad condition. The length of time that a machine remains in good condition follows an exponential distribution with rate λ. Whenever a machine breaks down, the machine is sent to a repair center consisting of R repair people. The repair center services the broken-down machines as if they were arriving at an $M/M/R/GD/\infty/\infty$ system.

Thus, if $j \leq R$ machines are in bad condition, a machine that has just broken down will immediately be assigned for repair; if $j > R$ machines are broken down, $j - R$ machines will be waiting in a single line for a repair worker to become idle. The time it takes to complete repairs on a broken-down machine is assumed exponential with rate μ (or mean repair time is $\frac{1}{\mu}$). Once a machine is repaired, it returns to good condition and is again susceptible to breakdown. The machine repair model may be modeled as a birth–death process, where the state j at any time is the number of machines in bad condition. Using the Kendall-Lee notation, the model just described may be expressed as an $M/M/R/GD/K/K$ model. The first K indicates that at any time no more than K customers (or machines) may be present, and the second K indicates that arrivals are drawn from a finite source of size K.

Table 8 exhibits the interpretation of each state for a machine repair model having $K = 5$ and $R = 2$ (G = machine in good condition; B = broken-down machine). To find the birth–death parameters for the machine repair model (see Figure 13), note that a birth corresponds to a machine breaking down and a death corresponds to a machine having just been repaired. To figure out the birth rate in state j, we must determine the rate at which machines break down when the state of the system is j. When the state is j, there are $K - j$ machines in good condition. Since each machine breaks down at rate λ, the total rate at which breakdowns occur when the state is j is

$$\lambda_j = \underbrace{\lambda + \lambda + \cdots + \lambda}_{(K - j)\lambda\text{'s}} = (K - j)\lambda$$

To determine the death rate for the machine repair model, we proceed as we did in our discussion of the $M/M/s/GD/\infty/\infty$ queuing model. When the state is j, $\min(j, R)$ repair people will be busy. Since each occupied repair worker completes repairs at rate μ, the death rate μ_j is given by

Table 8	STATE	NO. OF GOOD MACHINES					REPAIR QUEUE			NO. OF REPAIR WORKERS BUSY
Possible States in a Machine Repair Problem When $K = 5$ and $R = 2$	0	G	G	G	G	G				0
	1	G	G	G	G					1
	2	G	G	G						2
	3	G	G				B			2
	4	G					B	B		2
	5						B	B	B	2

Figure 13
Rate Diagram for $M/M/R/GD/K/K$ Queuing System When $R = 2$, $K = 5$

State is number of machines in bad condition

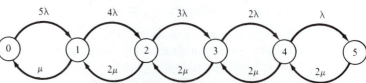

$$\mu_j = j\mu \qquad (j = 0, 1, \ldots, R)$$
$$\mu_j = R\mu \qquad (j = R + 1, R + 2, \ldots, K)$$

If we define $\rho = \frac{\lambda}{\mu}$, an application of (16)–(18) yields the following steady-state probability distribution:

$$\pi_j = \binom{K}{j} \rho^j \pi_0 \qquad (j = 0, 1, \ldots, R)$$

$$= \frac{\binom{K}{j} \rho^j j! \pi_0}{R! R^{j-R}} \qquad (j = R + 1, R + 2, \ldots, K) \tag{52}$$

In (52),

$$\binom{K}{j} = \frac{K!}{j!(K - j)!}$$

where $0! = 1$, and for $n \geq 1$, $n! = n(n - 1) \cdots (2)(1)$. To use (52), begin by finding π_0 from the fact that $\pi_0 + \pi_1 + \cdots + \pi_K = 1$. Using the steady-state probabilities in (52), we can determine the following quantities of interest:

L = expected number of broken-down machines

L_q = expected number of machines waiting for service

W = average time a machine spends broken down (down time)

W_q = average time a machine spends waiting for service

Unfortunately, there are no simple formulas for L, L_q, W, and W_q. The best we can do is express these quantities in terms of the π_j's:

$$L = \sum_{j=0}^{j=K} j\pi_j \tag{53}$$

$$L_q = \sum_{j=R}^{j=K} (j - R)\pi_j \tag{54}$$

We can now use (28) and (29) to obtain W and W_q. Since the arrival rate is state-dependent, the average number of arrivals per unit time is given by $\bar{\lambda}$, where

$$\bar{\lambda} = \sum_{j=0}^{j=K} \pi_j \lambda_j = \sum_{j=0}^{j=k} \lambda(K - j)\pi_j = \lambda(K - L) \tag{55}$$

If (28) is applied to the machines being repaired and to those machines awaiting repairs, we obtain

$$W = \frac{L}{\bar{\lambda}} \tag{56}$$

Applying (29) to the machines awaiting repair, we obtain

$$W_q = \frac{L_q}{\bar{\lambda}} \tag{57}$$

The following example illustrates the use of these formulas.

E X A M P L E
9

The Gotham Township Police Department has 5 patrol cars. A patrol car breaks down and requires service once every 30 days. The police department has two repair workers, each of whom takes an average of 3 days to repair a car. Breakdown times and repair times are exponential.

1. Determine the average number of police cars in good condition.
2. Find average down time for a police car that needs repairs.
3. Find the fraction of the time a particular repair worker is idle.

Solution

This is a machine repair problem with $K = 5$, $R = 2$, $\lambda = \frac{1}{30}$ car per day, and $\mu = \frac{1}{3}$ car per day. Then

$$\rho = \frac{\frac{1}{30}}{\frac{1}{3}} = \frac{1}{10}$$

From (52),

$$\pi_1 = \binom{5}{1}\left(\frac{1}{10}\right)\pi_0 = .5\pi_0$$

$$\pi_2 = \binom{5}{2}\left(\frac{1}{10}\right)^2\pi_0 = .1\pi_0$$

$$\pi_3 = \binom{5}{3}\left(\frac{1}{10}\right)^3\frac{3!}{2!2}\pi_0 = .015\pi_0 \qquad\qquad (58)$$

$$\pi_4 = \binom{5}{4}\left(\frac{1}{10}\right)^4\frac{4!}{2!(2)^2}\pi_0 = .0015\pi_0$$

$$\pi_5 = \binom{5}{5}\left(\frac{1}{10}\right)^5\frac{5!}{2!(2)^3}\pi_0 = .000075\pi_0$$

Then $\pi_0(1 + .5 + .1 + .015 + .0015 + .000075) = 1$, or $\pi_0 = .619$. Now (58) yields $\pi_1 = .310$, $\pi_2 = .062$, $\pi_3 = .009$, $\pi_4 = .001$, and $\pi_5 = 0$.

1. The expected number of cars in good condition is $K - L$, which is given by

$$K - \sum_{j=0}^{j=5} j\pi_j = 5 - [0(.619) + 1(.310) + 2(.062) + 3(.009) + 4(.001) + 5(0)]$$

$$= 5 - .465 = 4.535 \text{ cars in good condition}$$

2. We seek $W = \frac{L}{\lambda}$. From (55),

$$\bar{\lambda} = \sum_{j=0}^{j=5} \lambda(5 - j)\pi_j = \frac{1}{30}(5\pi_0 + 4\pi_1 + 3\pi_2 + 2\pi_3 + \pi_4 + 0\pi_5)$$

$$= \frac{1}{30}[5(.619) + 4(.310) + 3(.062) + 2(.009) + 1(.001) + 0(0)]$$

$$= 0.151 \text{ car per day}$$

or

$$\bar{\lambda} = \lambda(K - L) = \frac{4.535}{30} = 0.151 \text{ car per day}$$

Since $L = 0.465$ car, we find that $W = \frac{0.465}{0.151} = 3.08$ days.

3. The fraction of the time that a particular repair worker will be idle is $\pi_0 + 0.5\pi_1 = .619 + .5(.310) = .774$.

If there were three repair people, the fraction of the time that a particular server would be idle would be $\pi_0 + (\frac{2}{3})\pi_1 + (\frac{1}{3})\pi_2$, and for a repair staff of R people, the probability that a particular server would be idle is given by

$$\pi_0 + \frac{(R - 1)\pi_1}{R} + \frac{(R - 2)\pi_2}{R} + \cdots + \frac{\pi_{R-1}}{R}$$

◆ PROBLEMS

GROUP A

1. A laundromat has five washing machines. A typical machine breaks down once every 5 days. A repair worker can repair a machine in an average of 2.5 days. Currently, three workers are on duty. The owner of the laundromat has the option of replacing them with a superworker, who can repair a machine in an average of $\frac{5}{6}$ day. The salary of the superworker equals the pay of the three regular employees. Breakdown and service times are exponential. Should the laundromat replace the three repair workers with the superworker?

2. My dog just had three puppies. The puppies are frisky and jump in and out of their whelping box. A puppy spends an average of 10 minutes (exponentially distributed) in the whelping box before jumping out of the box. Once out of the box, a puppy spends an average of 15 minutes (exponentially distributed) before jumping back into the box.
(a) At any given time, what is the probability that more puppies will be out of the box than will be in the box?
(b) On the average, how many puppies will be in the box?

GROUP B

3.[†] Gotham City has 10,000 streetlights. City investigators have determined that at any given time, an average of 1000 lights are burned out. A streetlight burns out after an average of 100 days of use. The city has hired Mafia, Inc., to replace burned-out lamps. Mafia, Inc.'s contract states that they are supposed to replace a burned-out street lamp in an average of 7 days. Do you think that Mafia, Inc., is living up to the contract?

[†]Based on Kolesar (1979).

4. This problem illustrates balking. The Oryo Cookie Ice Cream Shop in Dunkirk Square has three competitors. Since people don't like to wait in long lines for ice cream, the arrival rate to the Oryo Cookie Ice Cream Shop depends on the number of people in the shop. More specifically, while $j \leq 4$ customers are present in the Oryo shop, customers arrive at a rate of $(20 - 5j)$ customers per hour. If more than 4 people are in the Oryo shop, the arrival rate is zero. For each customer, revenues less raw material costs are 50¢. Each server is paid $3 per hour. A server can serve an average of 10 customers per hour. In order to maximize expected profits (revenues less raw material and labor costs), how many servers should Oryo hire? Assume that interarrival and service times are exponential.

5. Suppose that interarrival times to a single-server system are exponential, but when n customers are present, there is a probability $\frac{n}{n+1}$ that an arrival will balk and leave the system before entering service. Also assume exponential service times.
(a) Find the probability distribution of the number of people present in the steady state.
(b) Find the expected number of people present in the steady state. (*Hint*: The fact that

$$e^x = 1 + x + \frac{x^2}{2!} + \frac{x^3}{3!} + \cdots$$

may be useful.)

GROUP C

6. Bectol, Inc. is building a dam. A total of 10,000,000 cu ft of dirt is needed to construct the dam. A bulldozer is used to collect dirt for the dam. Then the dirt is moved via dumpers to the dam site. Only one bulldozer is available, and it rents for $100 per hour. Bectol can rent, at $40 per hour, as many dumpers as desired. Each dumper can hold 1000 cu ft of dirt. It takes an average of 12 minutes for the bulldozer to load a dumper with dirt, and takes each dumper an average of five minutes to deliver the dirt to the dam and return to the bulldozer. Making appropriate assumptions about exponentiality, determine how Bectol can minimize the total expected cost of moving the dirt needed to build the dam. (*Hint*: There is a machine repair problem somewhere!)

22-10   EXPONENTIAL QUEUES IN SERIES AND OPEN QUEUING NETWORKS

In the queuing models that we have studied so far, a customer's entire service time is spent with a single server. In many situations (such as the production of an item on an assembly line), the customer's service is not complete until the customer has been served by more than one server (see, for example, Figure 14).

Upon entering the system in Figure 14, the arrival undergoes stage 1 service (after waiting in line if all stage 1 servers are busy on arrival). After completing stage 1 service, the customer waits for and undergoes stage 2 service. This process continues until the customer completes stage k service. A system like Figure 14 is called a **k-stage series** (or tandem) **queuing system**. A remarkable theorem due to Jackson (1957) is as follows (see Heyman and Sobel (1984) for a proof).

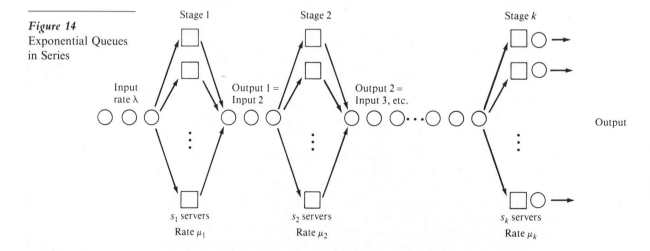

Figure 14
Exponential Queues in Series

| THEOREM 4 | If (1) interarrival times for a series queuing system are exponential with rate λ, (2) service times for each stage i server are exponential, and (3) each stage has an infinite-capacity waiting room, then interarrival times for arrivals to each stage of the queuing system are exponential with rate λ. |

For this result to be valid, each stage must have sufficient capacity to service a stream of arrivals that arrives at rate λ; otherwise, the queue will "blow up" at the stage with insufficient capacity. From our discussion of the $M/M/s/GD/\infty/\infty$ queuing system in Section 22.6, we see that each stage will have sufficient capacity to handle an arrival stream of rate λ if and only if, for $j = 1, 2, \ldots, k$, $\lambda < s_j \mu_j$. If $\lambda < s_j \mu_j$, Jackson's result implies that stage j of the system in Figure 14 may be analyzed as an $M/M/s_j/GD/\infty/\infty$ system with exponential interarrival times having rate λ and exponential service times with a mean service time of $\frac{1}{\mu_j}$. The usefulness of Jackson's result is illustrated by the following example.

E X A M P L E
10

The last two things that are done to a car before its manufacture is complete are installing the engine and putting on the tires. An average of 54 cars per hour arrive requiring these two tasks. One worker is available to install the engine and can service an average of 60 cars per hour. After the engine is installed, the car goes to the tire station and waits for its tires to be attached. Three workers serve at the tire station. Each works on one car at a time and can put tires on a car in an average of 3 minutes. Both interarrival times and service times are exponential.

1. Determine the mean queue length at each work station.

2. Determine the total expected time that a car spends waiting for service.

Solution

This is a series queuing system with $\lambda = 54$ cars per hour, $s_1 = 1$, $\mu_1 = 60$ cars per hour, $s_2 = 3$, and $\mu_2 = 20$ cars per hour (see Figure 15). Since $\lambda < \mu_1$ and $\lambda < 3\mu_2$, neither queue will "blow up," and Jackson's theorem is applicable. For stage 1 (engine), $\rho = \frac{54}{60} = .90$. Then (27) yields

$$L_q \text{ (for engine)} = \left(\frac{\rho^2}{1 - \rho} \right) = \left[\frac{(.90)^2}{1 - .90} \right] = 8.1 \text{ cars}$$

Figure 15
Series Queuing
System for
Automobile Example

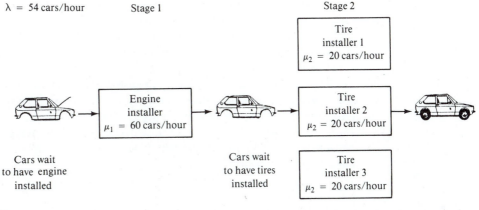

Now (32) yields

$$W_q \text{ (for engine)} = \frac{L_q}{\lambda} = \frac{8.1}{54} = 0.15 \text{ hour}$$

For stage 2 (tires), $\rho = \frac{54}{3(20)} = .90$. Table 6 yields $P(j \geq 3) = .83$. Now (41) yields

$$L_q \text{ (for tires)} = \frac{.83(.90)}{1 - .90} = 7.47 \text{ cars}$$

Then

$$W_q \text{ (for tires)} = \frac{L_q}{\lambda} = \frac{7.47}{54} = 0.138 \text{ hours}$$

Thus, the total expected time a car spends waiting for engine installation and tires is $0.15 + 0.138 = 0.288$ hour.

♦

OPEN QUEUING NETWORKS

We now describe **open queuing networks**, a generalization of queues in series. As in Figure 14, assume that station j consists of s_j exponential servers, each operating at rate μ_j. Customers are assumed to arrive at station j from outside the queuing system at rate r_j. These interarrival times are assumed to be exponentially distributed. Once completing service at station i, a customer joins the queue at station j with probability p_{ij} and completes service with probability

$$1 - \sum_{j=1}^{j=k} p_{ij}$$

Define λ_j, the rate at which customers arrive at station j (this includes arrivals at station j from outside the system *and* from other stations). $\lambda_1, \lambda_2, \ldots, \lambda_k$ can be found by solving the following system of linear equations:

$$\lambda_j = r_j + \sum_{i=1}^{i=k} p_{ij} \lambda_i \qquad (j = 1, 2, \ldots, k)$$

This follows, because a fraction p_{ij} of the λ_i arrivals to station i will next go to station j. Suppose $s_j \mu_j > \lambda_j$ holds for all stations. Then it can be shown that the probability distribution of the number of customers present at station j and the expected number of customers present at station j can be found by treating station j as an $M/M/s_j/GD/\infty/\infty$ system with arrival rate λ_j and service rate μ_j. If for some j, $s_j \mu_j \leq \lambda_j$, then no steady-state distribution of customers exists.

To find L, the expected number of customers in the queuing system, simply add up the expected number of customers present at each station. To find W, the average time a customer spends in the system, simply apply the formula $L = \lambda W$ to the entire system. Here, $\lambda = r_1 + r_2 + \cdots + r_k$, because this represents the average number of customers per unit time arriving at the system. The following example illustrates the analysis of open queuing networks.

E X A M P L E
11

Consider two servers. An average of 8 customers per hour arrive from outside at server 1, and an average of 17 customers per hour arrive from outside at server 2. Interarrival times are exponential. Server 1 can serve at an exponential rate of 20 customers per hour, and server 2 can serve at an exponential rate of 30 customers per hour. After completing service at server 1, half of the customers leave the system, and half go to server 2. After completing service at server 2, $\frac{3}{4}$ of the customers complete service, and $\frac{1}{4}$ return to server 1.

1. What fraction of the time is server 1 idle?

2. Find the expected number of customers at each server.

3. Find the average time a customer spends in the system.

4. How would the answers to parts (1)–(3) change if server 2 could serve only an average of 20 customers per hour?

Solution   We have an open queuing network with $r_1 = 8$ customers/hour and $r_2 = 17$ customers per hour. Also, $p_{12} = .5$, $p_{21} = .25$, and $p_{11} = p_{22} = 0$. We can find λ_1 and λ_2 by solving $\lambda_1 = 8 + .25\lambda_2$ and $\lambda_2 = 17 + .5\lambda_1$. This yields $\lambda_1 = 14$ customers/hour and $\lambda_2 = 24$ customers/hour.

1. Server 1 may be treated as an $M/M/1/GD/\infty/\infty$ system with $\lambda = 14$ customers/hour and $\mu = 20$ customers/hour. Then $\pi_0 = 1 - \rho = 1 - .7 = .3$. Thus, server 1 is idle 30% of the time.

2. From (26), we find L at server $1 = \frac{14}{20-14} = \frac{7}{3}$ and L at server $2 = \frac{24}{30-24} = 4$. Thus, an average of $4 + \frac{7}{3} = \frac{19}{3}$ customers will be present in the system.

3. $W = \frac{L}{\lambda}$, where $\lambda = 8 + 17 = 25$ customers/hour. Thus,

$$W = \frac{\left(\dfrac{19}{3}\right)}{25} = \frac{19}{75} \text{ hours}$$

4. In this case, $s_2\mu_2 = 20 < \lambda_2$, so no steady state exists.

◆ PROBLEMS

GROUP A

1. A Social Security Administration branch is considering the following two options for processing applications for social security cards:

Option 1 Three clerks process applications in parallel from a single queue. Each clerk fills out the form for the application in the presence of the applicant. Processing time is exponential with a mean of 15 minutes. Interarrival times are exponential.

Option 2 Each applicant first fills out an application without the clerk's help. The time to accomplish this is exponentially distributed with a mean of 65 minutes. When the applicant has filled out the form, he or she joins a single line to wait for one of the three clerks to check the form. It takes a clerk an average of 4 minutes (exponentially distributed) to review an application.

The interarrival time of applicants is exponential, and an average of 4.8 applicants arrive each hour. Which option will get applicants out of the office more quickly?

2. Consider an automobile assembly line in which each car undergoes two types of service: painting, then engine installation. Each hour, an average of 22.4 unpainted chassis arrive at the assembly line. It takes an average of 2.4 minutes to paint a car and an average of 3.75 minutes to install an engine. The assembly line has one painter and two engine installers. Assume that interarrival times and service times are exponential.

(a) On the average, how many painted cars without completely installed engines will be in the facility?

(b) On the average, how long will a painted car have to wait before installation of its engine begins?

3. Consider the following two queuing systems:

System 1 An average of 40 customers arrive each hour; interarrival times are exponential. Customers must complete two types of service before leaving the system. The first server takes an average of 30 seconds (exponentially distributed) to perform type 1 service. After waiting in line, each customer obtains type 2 service (exponentially distributed with a mean of 1 minute) from a single server. After completing type 2 service, a customer leaves the system.

System 2 The arrival process for system 2 is identical to the interarrival process for system 1. In system 2, a customer must complete only one type of service. Service time averages 1.5 minutes and is exponentially distributed. Two servers are available.

In which system does a typical customer spend less time?

4. An average of 120 students arrive each hour (interarrival times are exponential) at State College's Registrar's Office to change their course registrations. To complete this process, a person must pass through three stations. Each station consists of a single server. Service times at each station are exponential with the following mean times: station 1, 20 seconds; station 2, 15 seconds; station 3, 12 seconds. On the average, how many students will be present in the registrar's office for changing courses?

5. An average of 10 jobs per hour arrive at a job shop. Interarrival times of jobs are exponentially distributed. It takes an average of $\frac{10}{3}$ minutes (exponentially distributed) to complete a job. Unfortunately, $\frac{1}{3}$ of all completed jobs

need to be reworked. Thus, with probability $\frac{1}{3}$, a completed job must wait in line to be reworked. In the steady state, how many jobs would one expect to find in the job shop? What would the answer be if it took an average of 5 minutes to finish a job?

6. Consider a queuing system consisting of three stations in series. Each station consists of a single server, who can process an average of 20 jobs per hour (processing times at each station are exponential). An average of ten jobs per hour arrive (interarrival times are exponential) at station 1. When a job completes service at station 2, there is a .1 chance that it will return to station 1 and a .9 chance that it will move on to station 3. When a job completes service at station 3, there is a .2 chance that it will return to station 2 and a .8 chance that it will leave the system. All jobs completing service at station 1 immediately move on to station 2.

(a) Determine the fraction of the time each server is busy.
(b) Determine the expected number of jobs in the system.
(c) Determine the average time a job spends in the system.

22-11   THE $M/G/s/GD/s/\infty$ SYSTEM (BLOCKED CUSTOMERS CLEARED)

In many queuing systems, an arrival who finds all servers occupied is, for all practical purposes, lost to the system. For example, a person who calls an airline for a reservation and gets a busy signal will probably call another airline. Or suppose that someone calls in a fire alarm and no engines are available; the fire will then burn out of control. Thus, in some sense, a request for a fire engine that occurs when no engines are available may be considered lost to the system. If arrivals who find all servers occupied leave the system, we call the system a blocked customers cleared, or BCC, system. Assuming that interarrival times are exponential, such a system may be modeled as an $M/G/s/GD/s/\infty$ system.

For an $M/G/s/GD/s/\infty$ system, L, W, L_q, and W_q are of limited interest. For example, since a queue can never occur, $L_q = W_q = 0$. If we let $\frac{1}{\mu}$ be the mean service time and λ be the arrival rate, then $W = W_s = \frac{1}{\mu}$.

In most BCC systems, primary interest is focused on the fraction of all arrivals who are turned away. Since arrivals are turned away only when s customers are present, a fraction π_s of all arrivals will be turned away. Hence, an average of $\lambda\pi_s$ arrivals per unit time will be lost to the system. Since an average of $\lambda(1 - \pi_s)$ arrivals per unit time will actually enter the system, we may conclude that

$$L = L_s = \frac{\lambda(1 - \pi_s)}{\mu}$$

For an $M/G/s/GD/s/\infty$ system, it can be shown that π_s depends on the service time distribution only through its mean ($\frac{1}{\mu}$). This fact is known as **Erlang's loss formula**. In other words, any $M/G/s/GD/s/\infty$ system with an arrival rate λ and mean service time of

$\frac{1}{\mu}$ will have the same value of π_s. If we define $\rho = \frac{\lambda}{\mu}$, then for a given value of s, the value of π_s can be found from Figure 16. Simply read the value of ρ on the x-axis. Then the y-value on the s server curve that corresponds to ρ will equal π_s. The following example illustrates the use of Figure 16.

E X A M P L E
12

An average of 20 ambulance calls per hour are received by Gotham City Hospital. An ambulance requires an average of 20 minutes to pick up a patient and take the patient to the hospital. The ambulance is then available to pick up another patient. How many ambulances should the hospital have in order to ensure that there is at most a 1% probability of not being able to respond immediately to an ambulance call? Assume that interarrival times are exponentially distributed.

Solution

We are given that $\lambda = 20$ calls per hour, and $\frac{1}{\mu} = \frac{1}{3}$ hour. Thus, $\rho = \frac{\lambda}{\mu} = \frac{20}{3} = 6.67$. For $\rho = 6.67$, we seek the smallest value of s for which π_s is .01 or smaller. From Figure 16, we see that for $s = 13$, $\pi_s = .011$; and for $s = 14$, $\pi_s = .005$. Thus, the hospital needs 14 ambulances to meet its desired service standards.   ◆

◆ PROBLEMS

GROUP A

1. Suppose that a fire department receives an average of 24 requests for fire engines each hour. Each request for a fire engine causes a fire engine to be unavailable for an average of 20 minutes. In order to have at most a 1% chance of being unable to respond to a request for a fire engine, how many fire engines should the fire department have?

2. A telephone order sales company must determine how many telephone operators are needed to staff the phones during the 9-to-5 shift. It is estimated that an average of 480 calls are received during this time period and that the average call lasts for 6 minutes. If the company wants to have at most 1 chance in 100 of a caller receiving a busy signal, how many operators should be hired for the 9-to-5 shift? What assumption does the answer require?

3. In Example 12, suppose the hospital had 10 ambulances. On the average, how many ambulances would be en route or returning from a call?

GROUP B

4. On the average, 26 patrons per year come to the I.U. library to borrow the *I Ching* (assume that interarrival times are exponential). Borrowers who find the book unavailable leave and never return. A borrower keeps a copy of the *I Ching* for an average of 4 weeks.

(a) If the library has only one copy of the *I Ching*, what is the expected number of borrowers who will come to borrow the *I Ching* each year and find that the book is not available?

(b) Suppose that each person who comes to borrow the *I Ching* and is unable to borrow a copy is considered to cost the library $1 in goodwill. A copy of the *I Ching* lasts two years and costs $11. A thief has just stolen the library's only copy. In order to minimize the sum of purchasing and goodwill costs over the next two years, how many copies of the *I Ching* should be purchased?

5.† A company's warehouse can store up to four units of a good. Each month, an average of ten orders for the good are received. The times between the receipt of successive orders are exponentially distributed. When an item is used to fill an order, a replacement item is immediately ordered, and it takes an average of one month for a replacement item to arrive. If no items are on hand when an order is received, the order is lost. What fraction of all orders will be lost due to shortages? (*Hint*: Let the storage space for each item be a server and think about what it means for a server to be busy. Then come up with an appropriate definition of "service" time.)

†Based on Karush (1957).

Figure 16 Loss Probabilities for $M/G/s/GD/s/\infty$ Queuing System. Reprinted by permission of the publisher from *Introduction to Queuing Theory* by Robert Cooper, p. 316. Copyright © 1980 by Elsevier Science Publishing Co., Inc.

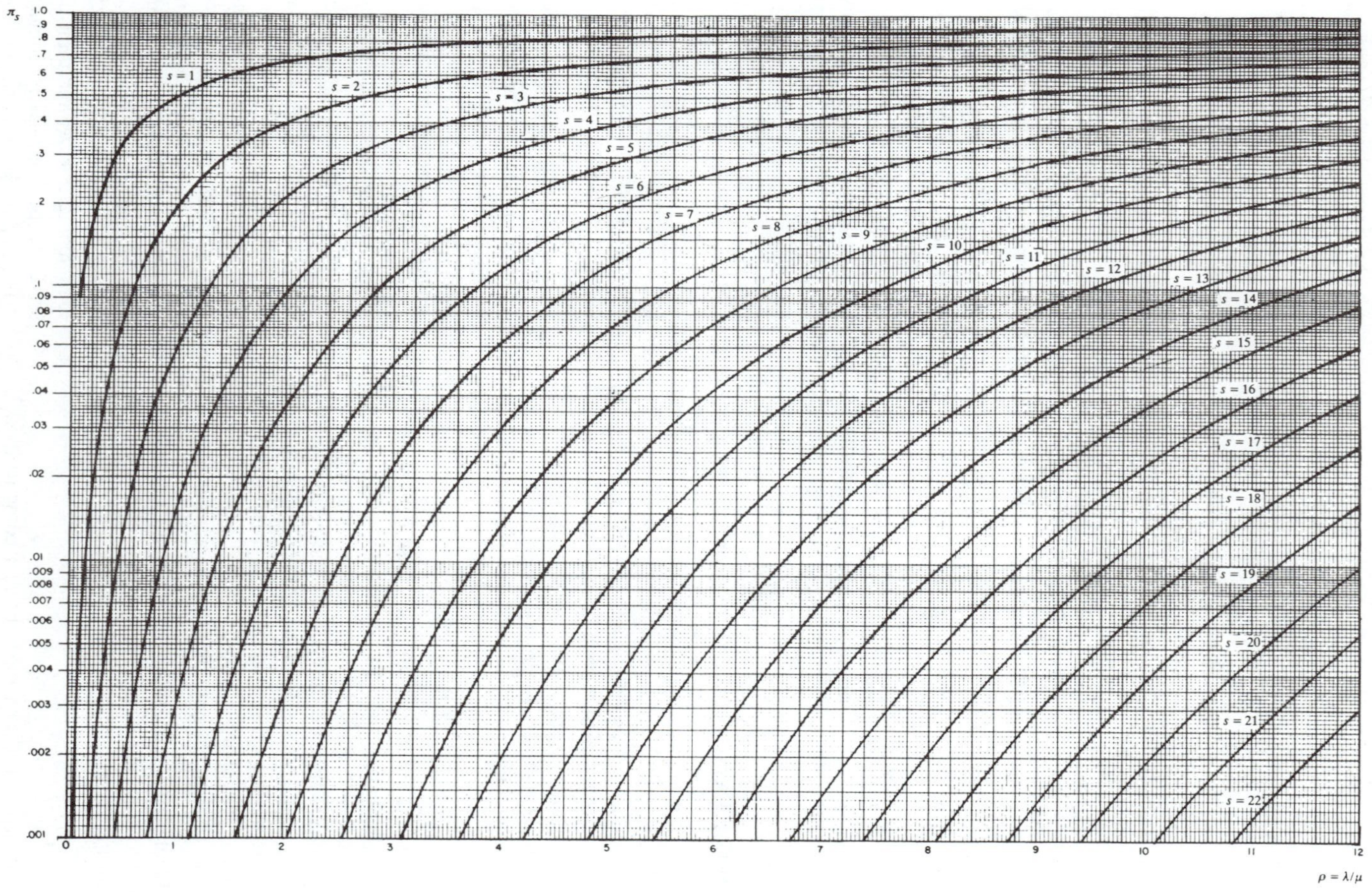

22-12 HOW TO TELL WHETHER INTERARRIVAL TIMES AND SERVICE TIMES ARE EXPONENTIAL*

How can we determine whether the actual data are consistent with the assumption of exponential interarrival times and service times? Suppose, for example, that interarrival times of $t_1, t_2, \ldots, t_n$ have been observed. It can be shown that a reasonable estimate of the arrival rate λ is given by

$$\hat{\lambda} = \frac{n}{\displaystyle\sum_{i=1}^{i=n} t_i}$$

For example, if $t_1 = 20$, $t_2 = 30$, $t_3 = 40$, and $t_4 = 50$, we have seen 4 arrivals in 140 time units, or an average of 1 arrival per 35 time units. In this case, our estimate of the arrival rate $\hat{\lambda}$ is given by

$$\hat{\lambda} = \frac{4}{20 + 30 + 40 + 50} = \frac{1}{35}$$

customer per unit time. Given $\hat{\lambda}$, we can try to determine whether $t_1, t_2, \ldots, t_n$ are consistent with the assumption that interarrival times are governed by an exponential distribution with rate $\hat{\lambda}$ and density $\hat{\lambda}e^{-\hat{\lambda}t}$. The easiest way to test this conjecture is by using a chi-square goodness-of-fit test to determine whether it is reasonable to conclude that $t_1, t_2, \ldots, t_n$ represent a random sample from a random variable with a given density function $f(t)$. A Kolmogorov-Smirnov test may also be used (see Law and Kelton (1982)).

To begin, we break up the set of possible interarrival times into k categories. Under the assumption that $f(t)$ does govern interarrival times, we determine the number of the t_i's that we would expect to fall into category i. We call this number e_i. Then we count up how many of the observed t_i's actually were in category i. We call this number o_i. Next we use the following formula to compute the observed value of the chi-square statistic, written $\chi^2(obs)$:

$$\chi^2(obs) = \sum_{i=1}^{i=k} \frac{(o_i - e_i)^2}{e_i}$$

The value of $\chi^2(obs)$ follows a chi-square distribution, with $k - 2$ degrees of freedom. Important percentile points of the chi-square distribution are tabulated in Table 9.

If $\chi^2(obs)$ is small, it is reasonable to assume that the t_i's are samples from a random variable with density function $f(t)$. (After all, a perfect fit would have $o_i = e_i$ for $i = 1, 2, \ldots, k$, resulting in a χ^2 value of zero.) If $\chi^2(obs)$ is large, it is reasonable to assume that the t_i's do not represent a random sample from a random variable with density $f(t)$.

More formally, we are interested in testing the following hypotheses:

H_0: $t_1, t_2, \ldots, t_n$ is a random sample from a random variable with density $f(t)$

H_a: $t_1, t_2, \ldots, t_n$ is not a random sample from a random variable with density function $f(t)$

*This section covers topics that may be omitted with no loss of continuity.

Table 9
Percentiles of
Chi-Square
Distribution

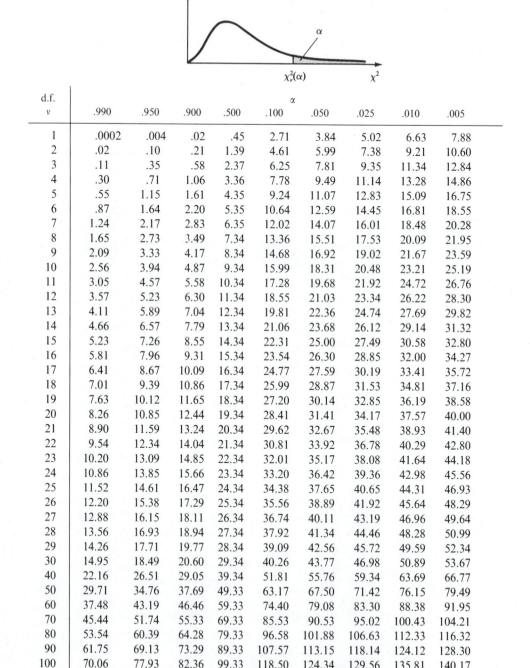

d.f. v	.990	.950	.900	.500	α .100	.050	.025	.010	.005
1	.0002	.004	.02	.45	2.71	3.84	5.02	6.63	7.88
2	.02	.10	.21	1.39	4.61	5.99	7.38	9.21	10.60
3	.11	.35	.58	2.37	6.25	7.81	9.35	11.34	12.84
4	.30	.71	1.06	3.36	7.78	9.49	11.14	13.28	14.86
5	.55	1.15	1.61	4.35	9.24	11.07	12.83	15.09	16.75
6	.87	1.64	2.20	5.35	10.64	12.59	14.45	16.81	18.55
7	1.24	2.17	2.83	6.35	12.02	14.07	16.01	18.48	20.28
8	1.65	2.73	3.49	7.34	13.36	15.51	17.53	20.09	21.95
9	2.09	3.33	4.17	8.34	14.68	16.92	19.02	21.67	23.59
10	2.56	3.94	4.87	9.34	15.99	18.31	20.48	23.21	25.19
11	3.05	4.57	5.58	10.34	17.28	19.68	21.92	24.72	26.76
12	3.57	5.23	6.30	11.34	18.55	21.03	23.34	26.22	28.30
13	4.11	5.89	7.04	12.34	19.81	22.36	24.74	27.69	29.82
14	4.66	6.57	7.79	13.34	21.06	23.68	26.12	29.14	31.32
15	5.23	7.26	8.55	14.34	22.31	25.00	27.49	30.58	32.80
16	5.81	7.96	9.31	15.34	23.54	26.30	28.85	32.00	34.27
17	6.41	8.67	10.09	16.34	24.77	27.59	30.19	33.41	35.72
18	7.01	9.39	10.86	17.34	25.99	28.87	31.53	34.81	37.16
19	7.63	10.12	11.65	18.34	27.20	30.14	32.85	36.19	38.58
20	8.26	10.85	12.44	19.34	28.41	31.41	34.17	37.57	40.00
21	8.90	11.59	13.24	20.34	29.62	32.67	35.48	38.93	41.40
22	9.54	12.34	14.04	21.34	30.81	33.92	36.78	40.29	42.80
23	10.20	13.09	14.85	22.34	32.01	35.17	38.08	41.64	44.18
24	10.86	13.85	15.66	23.34	33.20	36.42	39.36	42.98	45.56
25	11.52	14.61	16.47	24.34	34.38	37.65	40.65	44.31	46.93
26	12.20	15.38	17.29	25.34	35.56	38.89	41.92	45.64	48.29
27	12.88	16.15	18.11	26.34	36.74	40.11	43.19	46.96	49.64
28	13.56	16.93	18.94	27.34	37.92	41.34	44.46	48.28	50.99
29	14.26	17.71	19.77	28.34	39.09	42.56	45.72	49.59	52.34
30	14.95	18.49	20.60	29.34	40.26	43.77	46.98	50.89	53.67
40	22.16	26.51	29.05	39.34	51.81	55.76	59.34	63.69	66.77
50	29.71	34.76	37.69	49.33	63.17	67.50	71.42	76.15	79.49
60	37.48	43.19	46.46	59.33	74.40	79.08	83.30	88.38	91.95
70	45.44	51.74	55.33	69.33	85.53	90.53	95.02	100.43	104.21
80	53.54	60.39	64.28	79.33	96.58	101.88	106.63	112.33	116.32
90	61.75	69.13	73.29	89.33	107.57	113.15	118.14	124.12	128.30
100	70.06	77.93	82.36	99.33	118.50	124.34	129.56	135.81	140.17

Note: For example, $P(\chi_4^2 > 7.78) = .10$.

Given a value of α (the desired Type I error), we accept H_0 if $\chi^2(\text{obs}) \leq \chi^2_{k-r-1}(\alpha)$ and accept H_a if $\chi^2(\text{obs}) > \chi^2_{k-r-1}(\alpha)$. From Table 9, we obtain $\chi^2_{k-r-1}(\alpha)$, which represents the point in the χ^2_{k-r-1} table that has an area α to the right of it. Here, r is the number of parameters that must be estimated to specify the interarrival time distribution. Thus, if interarrival times are exponential, $r = 1$, and if interarrival times follow a normal distribution or an Erlang distribution, $r = 2$. When choosing the boundaries for the k categories, it is desirable to ensure that each e_i is at least 5, $k \leq 30$, and the e_i's be kept as equal as possible. Example 13 illustrates the use of the chi-square test.

E X A M P L E 13

The following interarrival times (in minutes) have been observed: 0.01, 0.07, 0.03, 0.08, 0.04, 0.10, 0.05, 0.10, 0.11, 1.17, 1.50, 0.93, 0.54, 0.19, 0.22, 0.36, 0.27, 0.46, 0.51, 0.11, 0.56, 0.72, 0.29, 0.04, 0.73. Does it seem reasonable to conclude that these observations come from an exponential distribution?

Solution

There are 25 observations with $\sum_{i=1}^{i=25} t_i = 9.19$. Thus, $\bar{\lambda} = \frac{25}{9.19} = 2.72$ arrivals per minute. We now test whether or not our data are consistent with an exponential random variable (call it **A**) having a density $f(t) = 2.72e^{-2.72t}$. We choose five categories so as to ensure that the probability that an observation from **A** falls into each of the five categories is .20. This yields $e_i = 25(.20) = 5$ for each category. To set the category boundaries, we need to determine the cumulative distribution function, $F(t)$, for **A**:

$$F(t) = P(\mathbf{A} \leq t) = \int_0^t 2.72e^{-2.72s}\, ds = 1 - e^{-2.72t}$$

Then we choose the categories to be as follows:

Category 1 $0 \leq t < m_1$ minutes
Category 2 $m_1 \leq t < m_2$ minutes
Category 3 $m_2 \leq t < m_3$ minutes
Category 4 $m_3 \leq t < m_4$ minutes
Category 5 $m_4 \leq t$ minutes

where $F(m_1) = .20$, $F(m_2) = .40$, $F(m_3) = .60$, and $F(m_4) = .80$.

Since $F(t) = 1 - e^{-2.72t}$, we see that for any number p, the value of t satisfying $F(t) = p$ may be found as follows:

$$1 - e^{-2.72t} = p$$
$$1 - p = e^{-2.72t}$$

Taking logarithms (to base e) of both sides yields

$$t = \frac{\ln(1-p)}{-2.72}$$

$$m_1 = \frac{\ln .80}{-2.72} = 0.08$$

$$m_2 = \frac{\ln .60}{-2.72} = 0.19$$

$$m_3 = \frac{\ln .40}{-2.72} = 0.34$$

$$m_4 = \frac{\ln .20}{-2.72} = 0.59$$

Hence, our categories are as follows:

Category 1 $0 \leq t < 0.08$ minute

Category 2 $0.08 \leq t < 0.19$ minute

Category 3 $0.19 \leq t < 0.34$ minute

Category 4 $0.34 \leq t < 0.59$ minute

Category 5 $0.59 \leq t$

After classifying the data into these categories, we find that $o_1 = 6$, $o_2 = 5$, $o_3 = 4$, $o_4 = 5$, and $o_5 = 5$. By the construction of our categories, $e_1 = e_2 = e_3 = e_4 = e_5 = .20(25) = 5$. We now compute $\chi^2(\text{obs})$:

$$\chi^2(\text{obs}) = \frac{(6-5)^2}{5} + \frac{(5-5)^2}{5} + \frac{(4-5)^2}{5} + \frac{(5-5)^2}{5} + \frac{(5-5)^2}{5}$$

$$= .20 + 0 + .20 + 0 + 0 = .40$$

We arbitrarily choose $\alpha = .05$. Since we are trying to fit an exponential distribution to interarrival times, $r = 1$. Then $\chi_3^2(.05) = 7.81$, and we see that for $\alpha = .05$, we can accept the hypothesis that the observed interarrival times come from an exponential distribution with $\lambda = 2.72$ arrivals per minute.

♦

To test whether service times are exponentially distributed, simply apply the preceding approach to observed service times $s_1, s_2, \ldots, s_n$. Begin by obtaining an estimate (call it $\hat{\mu}$) of the actual service rate μ from

$$\hat{\mu} = \frac{n}{s_1 + s_2 + \cdots + s_n}$$

Then use the chi-square test to test whether or not it is reasonable to assume that the observed service times are observations from an exponential distribution with density $\hat{\mu}e^{-\hat{\mu}t}$.

In the next section, we explain how to use Erlang distributions to model many situations in which the hypothesis of exponential interarrival or service times is unreasonable.

♦ PROBLEM

GROUP A

1. A travel agency wishes to determine if the length of customers' phone calls can be adequately modeled by an exponential distribution. Last week, the agency recorded the length of all phone calls and obtained the following results (in seconds): 4, 6, 5, 8, 9, 10, 12, 8, 16, 20, 24, 27, 33, 37, 43, 50, 58, 68, 70, 78, 88, 100, 120, 130. Do these data indicate that the length of phone calls to the travel agency is governed by an exponential distribution?

<table>
<tr><td>**22-13**</td></tr>
</table>

WHAT TO DO IF INTERARRIVAL OR SERVICE TIMES ARE NOT EXPONENTIAL*

Suppose that the chi-square test has indicated that interarrival or service times are not exponential. The nonexponential distribution can often be well approximated by an Erlang distribution. We illustrate this with an example in which service times are not exponential.

Recall from Section 22.2 that if $\mathbf{T}$ is an Erlang distribution with rate parameter $k\mu$ and shape parameter k, then

$$E(\mathbf{T}) = \frac{1}{\mu} \quad \text{and} \quad \text{var}\,\mathbf{T} = \frac{1}{k\mu^2}$$

For $k > 1$, we see that for any Erlang distribution, $\text{var}\,\mathbf{T} < E(\mathbf{T})^2$. If the sample data indicate that $\text{var}\,\mathbf{T} < E(\mathbf{T})^2$, an Erlang distribution can be fitted to observed service times (or observed interarrival times) by using the following procedure:

Step 1 Service times of $t_1, t_2, \ldots, t_n$ have been observed. Estimate $E(\mathbf{T})$ by

$$\bar{t} = \frac{t_1 + t_2 + \cdots + t_n}{n}$$

and estimate $\text{var}\,\mathbf{T}$ by

$$s^2 = \left(\frac{1}{n-1}\right)\left[\sum_{i=1}^{i=n}(t_i - \bar{t})^2\right]$$

Step 2 Choose μ so that $E(\mathbf{T}) = \bar{t}$. This forces $\frac{1}{\mu} = \bar{t}$, or $\mu = \frac{1}{\bar{t}}$.

Step 3 Under the assumption that $\mu = \frac{1}{\bar{t}}$, find the value of the shape parameter k (k must be a positive integer) that makes $\text{var}\,\mathbf{T}$ come closest to s^2. Then your fitted Erlang distribution will have rate parameter of $k\mu$ and shape parameter k.

**E X A M P L E
14**

For a sample of 100 hospital patients, the average length of stay was 7 days with a variance of 16 days. Fit an Erlang distribution to these data.

Solution From Step 2, we find μ from $\frac{1}{\mu} = 7$, or $\mu = \frac{1}{7}$. To find k, note that if k could be nonintegral, we would choose k to satisfy

$$\frac{1}{k(\frac{1}{7})^2} = 16$$

This equation is satisfied by $k = \frac{49}{16}$. Hence, $k = 3$ or 4 will be the integer that makes the variance of the fitted Erlang distribution come closest to 16. For $k = 3$ and $k = 4$, the variance of the fitted Erlang is as follows: $k = 3$, $\text{var}\,\mathbf{S} = 16.33$; $k = 4$, $\text{var}\,\mathbf{S} = 12.25$. Thus, $k = 3$ comes closest to making $\text{var}\,\mathbf{S} = 16$. In summary, we would fit a patient's length of stay in the hospital by an Erlang distribution with rate parameter $\frac{3}{7}$ and shape parameter 3.

◆

If interarrival times and service times of queuing systems are Erlang distributions, the computation of steady-state probabilities is very difficult. Fortunately, Hillier and Yu (1981) have tabulated the steady-state probabilities for a variety of queuing systems.

*This section covers topics that may be omitted with no loss of continuity.

Table 10	STATE			STATE		
CDF of Number in	i	$P(N = i)$	$P(N \leq i)$	i	$P(N = i)$	$P(N \leq i)$
$M/E_3/4$ System	0	.363253E-01	.036325	14	.287754E-02	.994514
$\left(\rho = \dfrac{\lambda}{s\mu} = .75 \right)$	1	.110735	.147060	15	.188758E-02	.996401
	2	.170922	.317982	16	.123818E-02	.997639
	3	.180650	.498632	17	.812189E-03	.998452
	4	.151531	.650163	18	.532760E-03	.998984
	5	.112893	.763056	19	.349466E-03	.999334
	6	.790289E-01	.842085	20	.229235E-03	.999563
	7	.535434E-01	.895629	21	.150368E-03	.999713
	8	.356720E-01	.931300	22	.986346E-04	.999812
	9	.235679E-01	.954868	23	.646999E-04	.999876
	10	.155088E-01	.970377	24	.424403E-04	.999919
	11	.101869E-01	.980564	25	.278390E-04	.999947
	12	.668577E-02	.987250	26	.182611E-04	.999965
	13	.438647E-02	.991636	30	.338086E-05	.999993

Reprinted by permission of the publisher from *Queuing Tables and Graphs* by Frederick Hillier and Oliver Yu, p. 76, Copyright © 1981 by Elsevier Science Publishing Co., Inc.

An excerpt from one of their tables is given in Table 10. In this table, $\rho = \frac{\lambda}{s\mu}$, where s is the number of servers and μ is the average number of service completions per unit time. The following example illustrates how the Hillier and Yu tables can be used to determine operating characteristics of queuing systems in which interarrival or service times follow an Erlang distribution.

E X A M P L E 15

Suppose that a walk-in hospital clinic with four doctors can be modeled as an $M/E_3/4/$ FCFS/∞/∞ queuing system. An average of 12 patients arrive each hour. Each doctor can see an average of 4 patients per hour.

1. What is the probability that a patient will have to wait to see a doctor?

2. What is the average time a patient spends waiting for a doctor?

3. What is the average number of patients present in the clinic?

Solution

We are given that $\lambda = 12$ patients per hour and $\mu = 4$ patients per hour. Then $\rho = \frac{12}{4(4)} = .75$.

1. Let π_j be the steady-state probability that j patients are in the clinic. We seek

$$\pi_5 + \pi_6 + \pi_7 + \cdots = 1 - \pi_0 - \pi_1 - \pi_2 - \pi_3 - \pi_4$$
$$= 1 - (.036 + .110 + .171 + .181 + .152) = .350$$

Thus, there is a 35% chance that a patient will have to wait for a doctor.

2. First we find

$$L_q = (5 - 4)\pi_5 + (6 - 4)\pi_6 + (7 - 4)\pi_7 + \cdots$$
$$= .113 + 2(.079) + 3(.054) + \cdots = 0.96$$

Then

$$W_q = \frac{L_q}{\lambda} = \frac{0.96}{12} \text{ hours} = 0.08 \text{ hour} = 4.8 \text{ minutes}$$

3. We know that $L = L_q + L_s$. We also know that $L_s = \lambda W_s$, $W_s = \frac{1}{4}$ hour, and $\lambda = 12$ patients per hour. Then $L_s = 12(\frac{1}{4}) = 3$ patients. Since we already know that $L_q = 0.96$ patient, we obtain $L = 0.96 + 3 = 3.96$ patients.

◆

We close by noting that in many actual queuing situations, there may be no analytical model that yields values for quantities of interest such as W and L. In these situations, one must utilize tables like the Hillier and Yu tables or resort to simulation (see Chapter 23).

◆ PROBLEM

GROUP A

1. A survey of a single-pump gas station has yielded the following information:

Average number of arrivals per hour = 40

Standard deviation of interarrival times = 1.4 minutes

Average service time = 1 minute

Standard deviation of service time = 30 seconds

(a) What queuing model should be used in this situation?

Explain how the Hillier and Yu tables could be used to answer the following questions:

(b) What is the expected number of cars present at the gas station?

(c) What is the probability that at most 2 cars are present at the gas station?

(d) How long does the average car spend at the gas station?

22-14   PRIORITY QUEUING MODELS*

There are many situations in which customers are not served on a first come, first served (FCFS) basis. In Section 22.1, we also discussed the service in random order (SIRO) and last come, first served (LCFS) queue disciplines. Let $\mathbf{W}_{\text{FCFS}}$, $\mathbf{W}_{\text{SIRO}}$, and $\mathbf{W}_{\text{LCFS}}$ be the random variables representing a customer's waiting time in queuing systems under the disciplines FCFS, SIRO, and LCFS, respectively. It can be shown that

$$E(\mathbf{W}_{\text{FCFS}}) = E(\mathbf{W}_{\text{SIRO}}) = E(\mathbf{W}_{\text{LCFS}})$$

Thus, the average time (steady-state) that a customer spends in the system does not depend on which of these three queue disciplines is chosen. It can also be shown that

$$\text{var } \mathbf{W}_{\text{FCFS}} < \text{var } \mathbf{W}_{\text{SIRO}} < \text{var } \mathbf{W}_{\text{LCFS}} \tag{59}$$

Since a large variance is usually associated with a random variable that has a relatively large chance of assuming extreme values, (59) indicates that relatively large waiting times are most likely to occur with an LCFS discipline and least likely to occur with an FCFS discipline. This is reasonable, because in an LCFS system, a customer can get lucky and immediately enter service but can also be bumped to the end of a long line. In FCFS, however, the customer cannot be bumped to the end of a long line, so a very long wait is relatively unlikely.

*This section covers topics that may be omitted with no loss of continuity.

In many organizations, the order in which customers are served depends on the customer's "type." For example, hospital emergency rooms usually serve seriously ill patients before they serve nonemergency patients. Also, in many computer systems, longer jobs do not enter service until all shorter jobs in the queue have been completed. Models in which a customer's type determines the order in which customers undergo service are called **priority queuing models**.

The following scenario encompasses many priority queuing models (including all the models discussed in this section). Assume there are n types of customers (labeled type 1, type 2, . . . , type n). The interarrival times of type i customers are exponentially distributed with rate λ_i. Interarrival times of different customer types are assumed to be independent. The service time of a type i customer is described by a random variable $\mathbf{S}_i$ (not necessarily exponential). We assume that lower-numbered customer types have priority over higher-numbered customer types.

NONPREEMPTIVE PRIORITY MODELS

We begin by considering nonpreemptive priority models. In a nonpreemptive model, a customer's service cannot be interrupted. After each service completion, the next customer to enter service is chosen by giving priority to lower-numbered customer types (with ties broken on an FCFS basis). For example, if $n = 3$ and three type 2 and four type 3 customers are present, the next customer to enter service would be the type 2 customer who was the first of that type to arrive.

In the Kendall-Lee notation, a nonpreemptive priority model is indicated by labeling the fourth characteristic as NPRP. To indicate multiple customer types, we subscript the first two characteristics with i's. Thus, $M_i/G_i/\cdots$ would represent a situation in which the interarrival times for the ith customer type are exponential and the service times for the ith customer type have a general distribution. In what follows, we let

$$W_{qk} = \text{expected steady-state waiting time in line spent by a type } k \text{ customer}$$
$$W_k = \text{expected steady-state time in the system spent by a type } k \text{ customer}$$
$$L_{qk} = \text{expected steady-state number of type } k \text{ customers waiting in line}$$
$$L_k = \text{expected steady-state number of type } k \text{ customers in the system}$$

THE $M_i/G_i/1/\text{NPRP}/\infty/\infty$ MODEL

Our first results concern the single-server, nonpreemptive $M_i/G_i/1/\text{NPRP}/\infty/\infty$ system. Define $\rho_i = \frac{\lambda_i}{\mu_i}$, $a_0 = 0$, and $a_k = \sum_{i=1}^{i=k} \rho_i$. We assume[†] that

$$\sum_{i=1}^{i=n} \frac{\lambda_i}{\mu_i} < 1$$

Then

[†]If this condition does not hold, then for one or more customer types, no steady-state waiting time will exist.

$$W_{qk} = \frac{\sum\limits_{k=1}^{k=n} \lambda_k E(S_k^2)/2}{(1 - a_{k-1})(1 - a_k)}$$

$$L_{qk} = \lambda_k W_{qk}$$

$$W_k = W_{qk} + \frac{1}{\mu_k}$$ (60)

$$L_k = \lambda_k W_k$$

The following example illustrates the use of (60).

E X A M P L E
16

A copying facility gives shorter jobs priority over long jobs. Interarrival times for each type of job are exponential, and an average of 12 short jobs and 6 long jobs arrive each hour. Let type 1 job = short job and type 2 job = long job. Then we are given that

$$E(S_1) = 2 \text{ minutes} \qquad E(S_1^2) = 6 \text{ minutes}^2 = \frac{1}{600} \text{ hours}^2$$

$$E(S_2) = 4 \text{ minutes} \qquad E(S_2^2) = 18 \text{ minutes}^2 = \frac{1}{200} \text{ hours}^2$$

Determine the average length of time each type of job spends in the copying facility.

Solution

We are given that $\lambda_1 = 12$ jobs per hour, $\lambda_2 = 6$ jobs per hour, and $\mu_1 = 30$ jobs per hour, and $\mu_2 = 15$ jobs per hour. Then $\rho_1 = \frac{12}{30} = .4$ and $\rho_2 = \frac{6}{15} = .4$. Since $\rho_1 + \rho_2 < 1$, a steady state will exist. Now $a_0 = 0$, $a_1 = .4$, and $a_2 = .4 + .4 = .8$. Eqs. (60) now yield

$$W_{q1} = \frac{\dfrac{12\left(\dfrac{1}{600}\right)}{2} + \dfrac{6\left(\dfrac{1}{200}\right)}{2}}{(1 - 0)(1 - .4)} = \frac{\dfrac{30}{1200}}{.6} = 0.042 \text{ hour}$$

$$W_{q2} = \frac{\dfrac{12\left(\dfrac{1}{600}\right)}{2} + \dfrac{6\left(\dfrac{1}{200}\right)}{2}}{(1 - .4)(1 - .8)} = \frac{\dfrac{30}{1200}}{.12} = 0.208 \text{ hour}$$

Also,

$$W_1 = W_{q1} + \frac{1}{\mu_1} = 0.042 + 0.033 = 0.075 \text{ hour}$$

$$W_2 = W_{q2} + \frac{1}{\mu_2} = 0.208 + 0.067 = 0.275 \text{ hour}$$

Thus, as expected, the long jobs spend much more time in the copying facility than the short jobs do.

THE $M_i/G_i/1/\text{NPRP}/\infty/\infty$ MODEL
WITH CUSTOMER-DEPENDENT WAITING COSTS

Consider a single-server, nonpreemptive priority system in which a cost c_k is charged for each unit of time that a type k customer spends in the system. If we wish to minimize the expected cost incurred per unit time (in the steady state), what priority ordering should be placed on the customer types? Suppose the n customer types are numbered such that

$$c_1 \mu_1 \geq c_2 \mu_2 \geq \cdots \geq c_n \mu_n \tag{61}$$

Then expected cost is minimized by giving the highest priority to type 1 customers, the second-highest priority to type 2 customers, etc., and the lowest priority to type n customers. To see why this priority ordering is reasonable, observe that when a type k customer is being served, cost leaves the system at a rate $c_k \mu_k$. Thus, cost can be minimized by giving the highest priority to customer types with the largest values of $c_k \mu_k$.

As a special case of this result, suppose we want to minimize L, the expected number of jobs in the system. Let $c_1 = c_2 = \cdots = c_n = 1$. Then at any time, the cost per unit time is equal to the number of customers in the system. Thus, the expected cost per unit time will equal L. Now (61) becomes

$$\mu_1 \geq \mu_2 \geq \cdots \geq \mu_n \quad \text{or} \quad \frac{1}{\mu_1} \leq \frac{1}{\mu_2} \leq \cdots \leq \frac{1}{\mu_n}$$

Thus, we may conclude that the expected number of jobs in the system will be minimized if the highest priority is given to the customer types with the shortest mean service time. This priority discipline is known as the shortest processing time (SPT) discipline.

THE $M_i/M/s/\text{NPRP}/\infty/\infty$ MODEL

To obtain tractable analytic results for multiserver priority systems, we must assume that each customer type has exponentially distributed service times with a mean of $\frac{1}{\mu}$, and that type i customers have interarrival times that are exponentially distributed with rate λ_i. Such a system with s servers is denoted by the notation $M_i/M/s/\text{NPRP}/\infty/\infty$. For this model,

$$W_{qk} = \frac{P(j \geq s)}{s\mu(1 - a_{k-1})(1 - a_k)} \tag{62}$$

In (62),

$$a_k = \sum_{i=1}^{i=k} \frac{\lambda_i}{s\mu} \quad (k \geq 1)$$

$a_0 = 0$, and $P(j \geq s)$ is obtained from Table 6 for an s-server system having

$$\rho = \frac{\lambda_1 + \lambda_2 + \cdots + \lambda_n}{s\mu}$$

Example 17 illustrates the use of (62).

EXAMPLE
17

Gotham Township has 5 police cars. The police department receives two types of calls: emergency (type 1) and nonemergency (type 2) calls. Interarrival times for each type of call are exponentially distributed, with an average of 10 emergency and 20 nonemergency calls being received each hour. Each type of call has an exponential service time, with a mean of 8 minutes (assume that, on the average, 6 of the 8 minutes is the travel time from the police station to the call and back to the station). Emergency calls are given priority over nonemergency calls. On the average, how much time will elapse between the placement of a nonemergency call and the arrival of a police car?

Solution

We are given that $s = 5$, $\lambda_1 = 10$ calls per hour, $\lambda_2 = 20$ calls per hour, $\mu = 7.5$ calls per hour, $\rho = \frac{10+20}{5(7.5)} = .80$, $a_0 = 0$, $a_1 = \frac{10}{37.5} = .267$, and $a_2 = \frac{10+20}{37.5} = .80$. From Table 6, with $s = 5$ and $\rho = .80$, $P(j \geq 5) = .55$. Then (62) yields

$$W_{q2} = \frac{.55}{5(7.5)(1 - .267)(1 - .80)} = \frac{.55}{5.50} = 0.10 \text{ hour} = 6 \text{ minutes}$$

The average time between the placement of a nonemergency call and the arrival of the car is $W_{q2} + (\frac{1}{2})$ (total travel time per call) $= 6 + 3 = 9$ minutes.

PREEMPTIVE PRIORITIES

We close our discussion of priority queuing systems by discussing a single-server **preemptive queuing system**. In a preemptive queuing system, a lower-priority customer (say a type i customer) can be bumped from service whenever a higher-priority customer arrives. Once no higher-priority customers are present, the bumped type i customer re-enters service. In a **preemptive resume model**, a customer's service continues from the point at which it was interrupted. In a **preemptive repeat model**, a customer begins service anew each time he or she re-enters service. Of course, if service times are exponentially distributed, the resume and repeat disciplines are identical. (Why?) In the Kendall-Lee notation, we denote a preemptive queuing system by labeling the fourth characteristic PRP. We now consider a single-server $M_i/M/1/PRP/\infty/\infty$ system in which the service time of each customer is exponential with mean $\frac{1}{\mu}$ and the interarrival times for the ith customer type are exponentially distributed with rate λ_i. Then

$$W_k = \frac{\frac{1}{\mu}}{(1 - a_{k-1})(1 - a_k)} \tag{63}$$

where $a_0 = 0$ and

$$a_k = \sum_{i=1}^{i=k} \frac{\lambda_i}{\mu}$$

For obvious reasons, preemptive disciplines are rarely used if the customers are people. Preemptive disciplines are sometimes used, however, for "customers" like computer jobs. The following example illustrates the use of (63).

E X A M P L E
18

On the Podunk U computer system, faculty jobs (type 1) always preempt student jobs (type 2). The length of each type of job follows an exponential distribution with mean 30 seconds. Each hour, an average of 10 faculty and 50 student jobs are submitted. What is the average length of time between the submission and completion of a student's computer job? Assume that interarrival times are exponential.

Solution

We are given that $\mu = 2$ jobs per minute, $\lambda_1 = \frac{1}{6}$ job per minute, and $\lambda_2 = \frac{5}{6}$ job per minute. Then

$$a_0 = 0, \qquad a_1 = \frac{\frac{1}{6}}{2} = \frac{1}{12}, \qquad a_2 = \frac{1}{12} + \frac{\frac{5}{6}}{2} = \frac{1}{2}$$

Eq. (63) yields

$$W_2 = \frac{\frac{1}{2}}{\left(1 - \frac{1}{12}\right)\left(1 - \frac{1}{2}\right)} = \frac{12}{11} \text{ minutes} = 1.09 \text{ minutes}$$

An average of 1.09 minutes will elapse between the time a student submits a job and the time the job is completed.

◆

◆ PROBLEMS

GROUP A

1. English professor Jacob Bright has one typist, who types for 8 hours per day. He submits three types of jobs to the typist: tests, research papers, and class handouts. The information in Table 11 is available. Professor Bright has told the typist that tests have priority over research papers, and research papers have priority over class handouts. Assuming a nonpreemptive system, determine the expected time that Professor Bright will have to wait before each type of job is completed.

Table 11

TYPE OF JOB	FREQUENCY (Number per day)	$E(S_i)$ (Hours)	$E(S_i^2)$ (Hours²)
Test	2	1	2
Research paper	0.5	4	20
Class handout	5	0.5	0.50

2. Suppose a supermarket uses a system in which all customers wait in a single line for the first available cashier. Assume that the service time for a customer who purchases

k items is exponentially distributed with mean k seconds. Also, a customer who purchases k items feels that the cost of waiting in line for 1 minute is $\frac{\$1}{k}$. If customers can be assigned priorities, what priority assignment will minimize the expected waiting cost incurred by the supermarket's customers? Why would a customer's waiting cost per minute be a decreasing function of k?

3. Four doctors work in a hospital emergency room that handles three types of patients. The time a doctor spends with each type of patient is exponentially distributed with a mean of 15 minutes. Interarrival times for each customer type are exponential, with the average number of arrivals per hour for each patient type being as follows: type 1, three patients; type 2, five patients; type 3, three patients. Assume that type 1 patients have the highest priority, and type 3 patients have the lowest priority (no preemption is allowed). What is the average length of time that each type of patient must wait before seeing a doctor?

4. Consider a computer system to which two types of computer jobs are submitted. The mean time to run each type of job is $\frac{1}{\mu}$. The interarrival times for each type of job are exponential, with an average of λ_i type i jobs arriving each hour. Consider the following three situations.

1. Type 1 jobs have priority over type 2 jobs, and preemption is allowed.

2. Type 1 jobs have priority over type 2 jobs, and no preemption is allowed.

3. All jobs are serviced on a FCFS basis.

Under which system are type 1 jobs best off? Worst off? Answer the same questions for type 2 jobs.

◆ SUMMARY

EXPONENTIAL DISTRIBUTION

A random variable $\mathbf{X}$ has an exponential distribution with parameter λ if the density of $\mathbf{X}$ is given by

$$f(t) = \lambda e^{-\lambda t} \qquad (t \geq 0)$$

Then

$$E(\mathbf{X}) = \frac{1}{\lambda} \qquad \text{and} \qquad \text{var}\,\mathbf{X} = \frac{1}{\lambda^2}$$

The exponential distribution has the no-memory property. This means, for instance, that if interarrival times are exponentially distributed with rate or parameter λ, then no matter how long it has been since the last arrival, there is a probability $\lambda \Delta t$ that an arrival will occur during the next Δt time units.

Interarrival times are exponential with parameter λ if and only if the number of arrivals to occur in an interval of length t follows a Poisson distribution with parameter λt. The mass function for a Poisson distribution with parameter λ is given by

$$P(\mathbf{N} = n) = \frac{e^{-\lambda} \lambda^n}{n!} \qquad (n = 0, 1, 2, \ldots)$$

ERLANG DISTRIBUTION

If interarrival or service times are not exponential, an Erlang random variable can often be used to model them. If $\mathbf{T}$ is an Erlang random variable with rate parameter R and shape parameter k, the density of $\mathbf{T}$ is given by

$$f(t) = \frac{R(Rt)^{k-1} e^{-Rt}}{(k-1)!} \qquad (t \geq 0)$$

and

$$E(\mathbf{T}) = \frac{k}{R} \qquad \text{and} \qquad \text{var}\,\mathbf{T} = \frac{k}{R^2}$$

BIRTH–DEATH PROCESSES

For a birth–death process, the steady-state probability (π_j) or fraction of the time that the process spends in state j can be found from the following flow balance equations:

$$
\begin{aligned}
(j = 0) && \pi_0 \lambda_0 &= \pi_1 \mu_1 \\
(j = 1) && (\lambda_1 + \mu_1)\pi_1 &= \lambda_0 \pi_0 + \mu_2 \pi_2 \\
(j = 2) && (\lambda_2 + \mu_2)\pi_2 &= \lambda_1 \pi_1 + \mu_3 \pi_3 \\
& \vdots & \\
(j\text{th equation}) && (\lambda_j + \mu_j)\pi_j &= \lambda_{j-1}\pi_{j-1} + \mu_{j+1}\pi_{j+1}
\end{aligned}
$$

The jth flow balance equation states that the expected number of transitions per unit time out of state j = (expected number of transitions per unit time into state j). The solution to the balance equations is found from

$$
\pi_j = \pi_0 \frac{\lambda_0 \lambda_1 \cdots \lambda_{j-1}}{\mu_1 \mu_2 \cdots \mu_j} \qquad (j = 1, 2, \ldots)
$$

and the fact that $\pi_0 + \pi_1 + \cdots = 1$.

NOTATION FOR CHARACTERISTICS OF QUEUING SYSTEMS

π_j = steady-state probability that j customers are in system

L = expected number of customers in system

L_q = expected number of customers in line (queue)

L_s = expected number of customers in service

W = expected time a customer spends in system

W_q = expected time a customer spends waiting in line

W_s = expected time a customer spends in service

λ = average number of customers per unit time

μ = average number of service completions per unit time (service rate)

$\rho = \dfrac{\lambda}{s\mu}$ = traffic intensity

THE $M/M/1/GD/\infty/\infty$ MODEL

If $\rho \geq 1$, no steady state exists. For $\rho < 1$,

$$
\pi_j = \rho^j(1 - \rho) \qquad (j = 0, 1, 2, \ldots)
$$

$$
L = \frac{\lambda}{\mu - \lambda}
$$

$$
L_q = \frac{\lambda^2}{\mu(\mu - \lambda)}
$$

$$
L_s = \rho
$$

$$
W = \frac{1}{\mu - \lambda}
$$

$$
W_q = \frac{\lambda}{\mu(\mu - \lambda)}
$$

$$W_s = \frac{1}{\mu}$$

(The last three formulas were obtained from the L, L_q, and L_s formulas via the relation $L = \lambda W$.)

THE $M/M/1/GD/c/\infty$ MODEL

If $\lambda \neq \mu$,

$$\pi_0 = \frac{1 - \rho}{1 - \rho^{c+1}}$$

$$\pi_j = \rho^j \pi_0 \quad (j = 1, 2, \ldots, c)$$

$$\pi_j = 0 \quad (j = c + 1, c + 2, \ldots)$$

$$L = \frac{\rho[1 - (c + 1)\rho^c + c\rho^{c+1}]}{(1 - \rho^{c+1})(1 - \rho)}$$

If $\lambda = \mu$,

$$\pi_j = \frac{1}{c + 1} \quad (j = 0, 1, \ldots, c)$$

$$L = \frac{c}{2}$$

For all values of λ and μ,

$$L_s = 1 - \pi_0$$

$$L_q = L - L_s$$

$$W = \frac{L}{\lambda(1 - \pi_c)}$$

$$W_q = \frac{L_q}{\lambda(1 - \pi_c)}$$

$$W_s = \frac{1}{\mu}$$

THE $M/M/s/GD/\infty/\infty$ MODEL

For $\rho \geq 1$, no steady state exists. For $\rho < 1$,

$$\pi_0 = \frac{1}{\displaystyle\sum_{i=0}^{i=s-1} \frac{(s\rho)^i}{i!} + \frac{(s\rho)^s}{s!(1 - \rho)}}$$

$$\pi_j = \frac{(s\rho)^j \pi_0}{j!} \quad (j = 1, 2, \ldots, s)$$

$$\pi_j = \frac{(s\rho)^j \pi_0}{s! s^{j-s}} \quad (j = s, s + 1, s + 2, \ldots)$$

$$P(j \geq s) = \frac{(s\rho)^s \pi_0}{s!(1 - \rho)} \qquad \text{(tabulated in Table 6)}$$

$$L_q = \frac{P(j \geq s)\rho}{1 - \rho}$$

$$W_q = \frac{P(j \geq s)}{s\mu - \lambda}$$

$$L_s = \frac{\lambda}{\mu}$$

$$W_s = \frac{1}{\mu}$$

$$L = L_q + \frac{\lambda}{\mu}$$

$$W = \frac{L}{\lambda}$$

THE $M/G/\infty/GD/\infty/\infty$ MODEL

$$L = L_s = \frac{\lambda}{\mu}$$

$$W = W_s = \frac{1}{\mu}$$

$$W_q = L_q = 0$$

THE $M/G/1/GD/\infty/\infty$ MODEL

$$\sigma^2 = \text{variance of service time distribution}$$

$$L_q = \frac{\lambda^2 \sigma^2 + \rho^2}{2(1 - \rho)}$$

$$L = L_q + \rho$$

$$L_s = \lambda \left(\frac{1}{\mu}\right)$$

$$W_q = \frac{L_q}{\lambda}$$

$$W = W_q + \frac{1}{\mu}$$

$$W_s = \frac{1}{\mu}$$

$$\pi_0 = 1 - \rho$$

MACHINE REPAIR ($M/M/R/GD/K/K$) MODEL

$$\rho = \frac{\lambda}{\mu}$$

L = expected number of broken-down machines

L_q = expected number of machines waiting for service

W = average time a machine spends broken down

W_q = average time a machine spends waiting for service

π_j = steady-state probability that j machines are broken down

λ = rate at which machine breaks down

μ = rate at which machine is repaired

Also,

$$\pi_j = \binom{K}{j} \rho^j \pi_0 \qquad (j = 0, 1, \ldots, R)$$

$$= \frac{\binom{K}{j} \rho^j j! \pi_0}{R! R^{j-R}} \qquad (j = R + 1, R + 2, \ldots, K)$$

$$L = \sum_{j=0}^{j=K} j\pi_j$$

$$L_q = \sum_{j=R}^{j=K} (j - R)\pi_j$$

$$\bar{\lambda} = \sum_{j=0}^{j=K} \pi_j \lambda_j = \sum_{j=0}^{j=K} \lambda(K - j)\pi_j = \lambda(K - L)$$

$$W = \frac{L}{\bar{\lambda}}$$

$$W_q = \frac{L_q}{\bar{\lambda}}$$

EXPONENTIAL QUEUES IN SERIES

If a steady state exists and if (1) interarrival times for a series queuing system are exponential with rate λ; (2) service times for each stage i server are exponential; and (3) each stage has an infinite-capacity waiting room, then interarrival times for arrivals to each stage of the queuing system are exponential with rate λ.

THE $M/G/s/GD/s/\infty$ MODEL

A fraction π_s of all customers are lost to the system, and π_s depends only on the arrival rate λ and on the mean $\frac{1}{\mu}$ of the service time. Figure 16 can be used to find π_s.

WHAT TO DO IF INTERARRIVAL OR SERVICE TIMES ARE NOT EXPONENTIAL

A chi-square test may be used to determine if the actual data indicate that interarrival or service times are exponential. If interarrival or service times are not exponential, they can often be approximated by an Erlang distribution. In this case, steady-state probabilities, L, L_q, W, and W_q may be found from tables like those prepared by Hillier and Yu (1981).

For many queuing systems, there is no formula or table that can be used to compute the system's operating characteristics. In this case, we must resort to simulation (see Chapter 23).

◆ REVIEW PROBLEMS

GROUP A

1. Buses arrive at the downtown bus stop and leave for the mall stop. Past experience indicates that 20% of the time, the interval between buses is 20 minutes; 40% of the time, the interval is 40 minutes; and 40% of the time, the interval is 2 hours. If I have just arrived at the downtown bus stop, how long, on the average, should I expect to wait for a bus?

2. Registration at State University proceeds as follows: Upon entering the registration hall, the students first wait in line to register for classes. A single clerk handles registration for classes, and it takes the clerk an average of 2 minutes to handle a student's registration. Next, the student must wait in line to pay fees. A single clerk handles the payment of fees. The clerk takes an average of 2 minutes to process a student's fees. Then the student leaves the registration building. An average of 15 students per hour arrive at the registration hall.
(a) If interarrival and service times are exponential, what is the expected time a student spends in the registration hall?
(b) What is the probability that during the next 5 minutes, exactly two students will enter the registration hall?
(c) Without any further information, what is the probability that during the next 3 minutes, no student will arrive at the fee clerk's desk?
(d) Suppose the registration system is changed so that a student can register for classes and pay fees at the same station. If the service time at this single station follows an Erlang distribution with rate parameter 1.5 per minute and shape parameter 2, what is the expected time a student spends waiting in line?

3. At the Smalltown post office, patrons wait in a single line for the first open window. An average of 100 patrons per hour enter the post office, and each window can serve an average of 45 patrons per hour. The post office estimates a cost of 10¢ for each minute a patron waits in line and believes that it costs $20 per hour to keep a window open. Interarrival times and service times are exponential.
(a) In order to minimize the total expected hourly cost, how many windows should be open?
(b) If the post office's goal is to ensure that at most 5% of all patrons will spend more than 5 minutes in line, how many windows should be open?

4. Each year, an average of 500 people pass the New York state bar exam and enter the legal profession. On the average, a lawyer practices law in New York State for 35 years. Twenty years from now, how many lawyers would you expect there to be in New York State?

5. There are 5 students and one keg of beer at a wild and crazy campus party. The time to draw a glass of beer follows an exponential distribution, with an average time of 2 minutes. The time to drink a beer also follows an exponential distribution, with a mean of 18 minutes. After finishing a beer, each student immediately goes back to get another beer.
(a) On the average, how long does a student wait in line for a beer?
(b) What fraction of the time is the keg not in use?
(c) If the keg holds 500 glasses of beer, how long, on the average, will it take to finish the keg?

6. The manager of a large group of employees must decide if she needs another photocopying machine. The cost of a machine is $40 per 8-hour day whether or not the machine is in use. An average of 4 people per hour need to use the copying machine. Each person uses the copier for an average of 10 minutes. Interarrival times and copying times are exponentially distributed. Employees are paid $8 per hour, and we assume that a waiting cost is incurred when a worker is waiting in line or is using the copying machine. How many copying machines should be rented?

7. An automated car wash will wash a car in 10 minutes. Arrivals occur an average of 15 minutes apart (exponentially distributed).

(a) On the average, how many cars are waiting in line for a wash?

(b) If the car wash could be speeded up, what wash time would reduce the average waiting time to 5 minutes?

8. The Newcoat Painting Company has for some time been experiencing high demand for its automobile repainting service. Since it has had to turn away business, management is concerned that the limited space available to store cars awaiting painting has cost lost revenue. A small vacant lot next to the painting facility has recently been made available for rental on a long-term basis at a cost of $10 per day. Management believes that each lost customer costs $20 in profit. Current demand is estimated to be 21 cars per day with exponential interarrival times (including those turned away), and the facility can service at an exponential rate of 24 cars per day. Cars are processed on an FCFS basis. Waiting space is now limited to 9 cars but can be increased to 20 cars with the lease of the vacant lot. Newcoat wants to determine whether or not the vacant lot should be leased. Management also wants to know the expected daily lost profit due to turning away customers if the lot is leased. Only one car can be painted at a time.

9. At an exclusive restaurant, there is only one table and waiting space for only one other group; others that arrive when the waiting space is filled are turned away. The arrival rate follows an exponential distribution with a rate of one group per hour. It takes the average group 1 hour (exponentially distributed) to be served and eat the meal. What is the average time that a group spends waiting for a table?

10. The owner of an exclusive restaurant has two tables but only one waiter. If the second table is occupied, the owner waits on that table himself. Service times are exponentially distributed with mean 1 hour, and the time between arrivals is exponentially distributed with mean 1.5 hours. When the restaurant is full, people must wait outside in line.

(a) What percentage of the time is the owner waiting on a table?

(b) If the owner wants to spend at most 10% of his time waiting on tables, what is the maximum arrival rate that can be tolerated?

11. Ships arrive at a port facility at an average rate of two ships every 3 days. On the average, it takes a single crew 1 day to unload a ship. Assume that interarrival and service times are exponential. The shipping company owns the port facility as well as the ships using that facility. It is estimated to cost the company $1000 per day that each ship spends in port. The crew servicing the ships consists of 100 workers, who are each paid an average of $30 per day. A consultant has recommended that the shipping company hire an additional 40 workers and split the employees into two equal-sized crews of 70 each. This would give each crew an unloading or loading time averaging $\frac{3}{2}$ days. Which crew arrangement would you recommend to the company?

GROUP B

12. The mail order firm of L. L. Pea receives an average of 200 calls per hour (times between calls are exponentially distributed). It takes an L. L. Pea operator an average of 3 minutes to handle a call. If a caller gets a busy signal, L. L. Pea assumes that he or she will call Seas Beginning (a competing mail order house), and L. L. Pea will lose an average of $30 in profit. The cost of keeping a phone line open is $9 per hour. How many operators should L. L. Pea have on duty?

13. Each hour, an average of three type 1 and three type 2 customers arrive at a single-server station. Interarrival times for each customer type are exponential and independent. The average service time for a type 1 customer is 6 minutes, and the average service time for a type 2 customer is 3 minutes (all service times are exponentially distributed). Consider the following three service arrangements:

> **Arrangement 1** All customers wait in a single line and are served on an FCFS basis.
>
> **Arrangement 2** Type 1 customers are given non-preemptive priority over type 2 customers.
>
> **Arrangement 3** Type 2 customers are given non-preemptive priority over type 1 customers.

Which arrangement will result in the smallest average per-customer waiting time? Which arrangement will result in the largest average per-customer waiting time?

14. The Podunk University Operations Research Department has two phone lines. An average of 30 people per hour try to call the OR Department, and the average length of a phone call is 1 minute. If a person attempts to call when both lines are busy, he or she hangs up and is lost to the system. Assume that the time between people attempting to call and service times are exponential.

(a) What fraction of the time will both lines be free? What fraction of the time will both lines be busy? What fraction of the time will exactly one line be free?

(b) On the average, how many lines will be busy?

(c) On the average, how many callers will hang up each hour?

15[†] Smalltown has two ambulances. Ambulance 1 is based at the local college, and ambulance 2 is based downtown. If a request for an ambulance comes from the local college, the college-based ambulance is sent if it is available. Otherwise, the downtown-based ambulance is sent (if available). If no ambulance is available, the call is assumed to be lost to the system. If a request for an ambulance comes from anywhere else in the town, the downtown-based ambulance is sent if it is available. Otherwise, the college-based ambulance is sent if available. If no ambulance is available, the call is considered lost to the system. The time between calls is exponentially distributed. An average of 3 calls per hour are received from the college, and an average of 4 calls per hour are received from the rest of the town. The average time (exponentially distributed) it takes an ambulance to respond to a call and be ready to respond to another call is shown in Table 12.

Table 12

AMBULANCE COMES FROM	AMBULANCE GOES TO	
	College	*Noncollege*
College	4 minutes	7 minutes
Downtown	5 minutes	4 minutes

[†]Based on Carter (1972).

(a) What fraction of the time is the downtown ambulance busy?

(b) What fraction of the time is the college ambulance busy?

(c) What fraction of all calls will be lost to the system?

(d) On the average, who waits longer for an ambulance, a college student or a town person?

16. An average of 10 people per hour arrive (interarrival times are exponential) intending to swim laps at the local YMCA. Each swimmer intends to swim an average of 30 minutes. The YMCA has three lanes open for lap swimming. If one swimmer is in a lane, he or she swims up and down the right side of the lane. If two swimmers are in a lane, each swimmer swims up and down one side of the lane. Swimmers always join the lane with the fewest number of swimmers. If all three lanes are occupied by two swimmers, a prospective swimmer becomes disgusted and goes running.

(a) What fraction of the time will 3 people be swimming laps?

(b) On the average, how many people are swimming laps in the pool?

(c) How many lanes does the YMCA need to allot to lap swimming to ensure that at most 5% of all prospective swimmers will become disgusted and go running?

◆ REFERENCES

The following books contain excellent discussions of queuing theory at an intermediate level:

COOPER, R. *Introduction to Queuing Theory*, 2d ed. New York: North-Holland, 1981.

GROSS, D., and C. HARRIS. *Fundamentals of Queuing Theory*, 2d ed. New York: Wiley, 1985.

KARLIN, S., and H. TAYLOR. *A First Course in Stochastic Processes*, 2d ed. Orlando, Fla.: Academic Press, 1975.

LEE, A. *Applied Queuing Theory*. New York: St. Martin's Press, 1966.

The following four books contain excellent discussions of queuing theory at a more advanced level:

HEYMAN, D., and M. SOBEL. *Stochastic Models in Operations Research*, vol. 1. New York: McGraw-Hill, 1984.

KLEINROCK, L. *Queuing Systems*, vols. 1 and 2. New York: Wiley, 1975.

Ross, S. *Applied Probability Models with Optimization Applications.* San Francisco, Calif.: Holden-Day, 1970.

Saaty, T. *Elements of Queuing Theory with Applications.* New York: Dover, 1983.

Brigham, G. "On a Congestion Problem in an Aircraft Factory," *Operations Research* 3(1955):412–428.

Carter, G., J. Chaiken, and E. Ignall. "Response Areas for Two Emergency Units," *Operations Research* 20(1972):571–594.

Denardo, E. *Dynamic Programming: Theory and Applications.* Englewood Cliffs, N.J.: Prentice-Hall, 1982. Explains why interarrival times are often exponential.

Erickson, W. "Management Science and the Gas Shortage," *Interfaces* 4(1973):47–51.

Feller, W. *An Introduction to Probability Theory and Its Applications,* 2d ed., vol. 1. New York: Wiley, 1957. Proves that the exponential distribution is the only continuous random variable with the no-memory property.

Gilliam, R. "An Application of Queuing Theory to Airport Passenger Security Screening," *Interfaces* 9(1979):117–123.

Hillier, F., and O. Yu. *Queuing Tables and Graphs.* New York: North-Holland, 1981.

Jackson, J. "Networks of Waiting Lines," *Operations Research* 5(1957):518–521.

Karmarker, U. "Lot-Sizing and Lead-Time Performance in a Manufacturing Cell," *Interfaces* 15(no.2.1985):1–9.

Karush, W. "A Queuing Model for an Inventory Problem," *Operations Research* 5(1957):693–703.

Kendall, D. "Some Problems in the Theory of Queues," *Journal of the Royal Statistical Society,* Series B, 13(1951):151–185.

Kolesar, P. "A Quick and Dirty Response to the Quick and Dirty Crowd: Particularly to Jack Byrd's 'The Value of Queuing Theory,'" *Interfaces* 9(1979):77–82.

Law, A., and W. Kelton. *Simulation Modeling and Analysis.* New York: McGraw-Hill, 1982. Discusses simulation of queuing systems and fitting random variables to actual interarrival and service time data.

Vogel, M. "Queuing Theory Applied to Machine Manning," *Interfaces* 9(1979):1–8.

CHAPTER 23

Simulation

SIMULATION IS A **very powerful and widely used management science technique for the analysis and study of complex systems. In previous chapters, we were concerned with the formulation of models that could be solved analytically. In almost all of those models, our goal was to determine optimal solutions. However, because of complexity, stochastic relations, and so on, not all real-world problems can be represented adequately in the model forms of the previous chapters. Attempts to use analytical models for such systems usually require so many simplifying assumptions that the solutions are likely to be inferior or inadequate for implementation. Often, in such instances, the only alternative form of modeling and analysis available to the decision maker is simulation.**

**   *Simulation* may be defined as a technique that imitates the operation of a real-world system as it evolves over time. This is normally done by developing a simulation model. A *simulation model* usually takes the form of a set of assumptions about the operation of the system, expressed as mathematical or logical relations between the objects of interest in the system. In contrast to the exact mathematical solutions available with most analytical models, the simulation process involves executing or running the model through time, usually on a computer, to generate representative samples of the measures of performance. In this respect, simulation may be seen as a sampling experiment on the real system, with the results being sample points. For example, to obtain the best estimate of the mean of the measure of performance, we average the sample results. Clearly, the more sample points we generate, the better our estimate will be. However, other factors, such as the starting conditions of the simulation, the length of the period being simulated, and the accuracy of the model itself, all have a bearing on how good our final estimate will be. We discuss such issues later in the chapter.**

**   As with most other techniques, simulation has its advantages and disadvantages. The major advantage of simulation is that simulation theory is relatively straightforward. In general, simulation methods are easier to apply than analytical methods. Whereas analytical models may require us to make many simplifying assumptions, simulation models have few such restrictions, thereby allowing much greater flexibility in representing the real system. Once a model is built, it can be used repeatedly to analyze different policies, parameters, or designs. For example, if a business firm has a simulation model of its inventory system, various inventory policies can be tried on the model rather than taking the chance of experimenting on the real-world system. However, it must be**

emphasized that simulation is not an optimizing technique. It is most often used to analyze "what if" types of questions. Optimization with simulation is possible, but it is usually a slow process. Simulation can also be costly. However, with the development of special-purpose simulation languages, decreasing computational cost, and advances in simulation methodologies, the problem of cost is becoming less important.

In this chapter, we focus our attention on simulation models and the simulation technique. We present several examples of simulation models and explore such concepts as random numbers, time flow mechanisms, Monte Carlo sampling, simulation languages, and statistical issues in simulation.

23-1   BASIC TERMINOLOGY

We begin our discussion by presenting some of the terminology used in simulation. In most simulation studies, we are concerned with the simulation of some system. Thus, in order to model a system, we must understand the concept of a system. Among the many different ways of defining a system, the most appropriate definition for simulation problems is the one proposed by Schmidt and Taylor (1970).

DEFINITION   A **system** is a collection of entities that act and interact toward the accomplishment of some logical end.

In practice, however, this definition generally tends to be more flexible. The exact description of the system usually depends on the objectives of the simulation study. For example, what may be a system for a particular study may be only a subset of the overall system for another.

Systems generally tend to be dynamic — their status changes over time. To describe this status, we use the concept of the state of a system.

DEFINITION   The **state** of a system is the collection of variables necessary to describe the status of the system at any given time.

As an example of a system, let us consider a bank. Here, the system consists of the servers and the customers waiting in line or being served. As customers arrive or depart, the status of the system changes. To describe these changes in status, we require a set of variables called the **state variables**. For example, the number of busy servers, the number of customers in the bank, the arrival time of the next customer, and the departure time of the customers in service together describe every possible change in the status of the bank. Thus, these variables could be used as the state variables for this system. In a system, an object of interest is called an **entity**, and any properties of an entity are called **attributes**. For example, the bank's customers may be described as the entities, and the characteristics of the customers (such as the occupation of a customer) may be defined as the attributes.

Systems may be classified as discrete or continuous.

| DEFINITION | A **discrete system** is one in which the state variables change only at discrete or countable points in time. |

A bank is an example of a discrete system, since the state variables change only when a customer arrives or when a customer finishes being served and departs. These changes take place at discrete points in time.

| DEFINITION | A **continuous system** is one in which the state variables change continuously over time. |

A chemical process is an example of a continuous system. Here, the status of the system is changing continuously over time. Such systems are usually modeled using differential equations. We do not discuss any continuous systems in this chapter.

There are two types of simulation models, static and dynamic.

| DEFINITION | A **static simulation model** is a representation of a system at a particular point in time. |

We usually refer to a static simulation as a **Monte Carlo simulation**.

| DEFINITION | A **dynamic simulation** is a representation of a system as it evolves over time. |

Within these two classifications, a simulation may be deterministic or stochastic. A **deterministic simulation model** is one that contains no random variables; a **stochastic simulation model** contains one or more random variables. Discrete and continuous simulation models are similar to discrete and continuous systems. In this chapter, we concentrate mainly on discrete stochastic models. Such models are called discrete-event simulation models; discrete-event simulation concerns the modeling of a stochastic system as it evolves over time by a representation in which state variables change only at discrete points in time.

23-2   AN EXAMPLE OF A DISCRETE-EVENT SIMULATION

Before we proceed to the details of simulation modeling, it will be useful to work through a simple simulation example in order to illustrate some of the basic concepts in discrete-event simulation. The model we have chosen as our initial example is a single-server queuing system. Customers arrive into this system from some population and either go into service immediately if the server is idle or join a waiting line (queue) if the server is busy. Examples of this kind of a system are a one-person barber shop, a small grocery store with only one checkout counter, and a single ticket counter at an airline terminal.

The same model was studied in Chapter 22 in connection with queuing theory. In that chapter, we used an analytical model to determine the various operating characteristics of the system. However, we had to make several restrictive assumptions in order to use queuing theory. In particular, when we studied an $M/M/1$ system, we had to assume that both interarrival times and service times were exponentially distributed. In many situations, these assumptions may not be appropriate. For example, arrivals at an airline counter generally tend to occur in bunches, because of such factors as arrivals of shuttle buses and connecting flights. For such a system, an empirical distribution of arrival times must be used, which implies that the analytical model from queuing theory is no longer feasible. With simulation, any distribution of interarrival times and service times may be used, thereby giving much more flexibility to the solution process.

To simulate a queuing system, we first have to describe it. For this single-server system, we assume arrivals are drawn from an infinite calling population. There is unlimited waiting room capacity, and customers will be served in the order of their arrival—that is, on a first come, first served (FCFS) basis. We further assume that arrivals occur one at a time in a random fashion, with the distribution of interarrival times as specified in Table 1. All arrivals are eventually served with the distribution of service times shown in Table 2. Service times are also assumed to be random. After service, all customers return to the calling population. This queuing system can be represented as shown in Figure 1.

Table 1 Interarrival Time Distribution	INTERARRIVAL TIME (Minutes)	PROBABILITY
	1	.20
	2	.30
	3	.35
	4	.15

Table 2 Service Time Distribution	SERVICE TIME (Minutes)	PROBABILITY
	1	.35
	2	.40
	3	.25

Figure 1
Single-Server
Queuing System

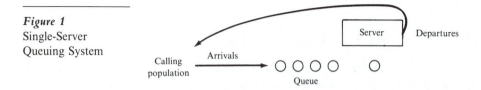

Before dealing with the details of the simulation itself, we must define the state of this system and understand the concepts of events and clock time within a simulation. For this example, we use the following variables to define the state of the system: (1) the number of customers in the system; (2) the status of the server—that is, whether the server is busy or idle; and (3) the time of the next arrival.

Closely associated with the state of the system is the concept of an event. An **event** is defined as a situation that causes the state of the system to change instantaneously. In the single-server queuing model, there are only two possible events that can change the state of the system: an arrival into the system and a departure from the system at the completion of service. In the simulation, these events will be scheduled to take place at certain points in time. All the information about them is maintained in a list called the **event list**. Within this list, we keep track of the type of events scheduled and, more important, the time at which these events are scheduled to take place. Time in a simulation is maintained using a variable called the **clock time**. The concept of clock time will become clearer as we work through the example.

We begin this simulation with an empty system and arbitrarily assume that our first event, an arrival, takes place at clock time 0. This arrival finds the server idle and enters service immediately. Arrivals at other points in time may find the server either idle or busy. If the server is idle, the customer enters service. If the server is busy, the customer joins the waiting line. These actions can be summarized as shown in Figure 2.

Figure 2
Flowchart for an Arrival

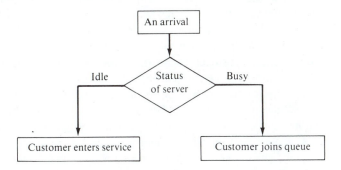

Next, we schedule the departure time of the first customer. This is done by randomly generating a service time from the service time distribution (described later in the chapter) and setting the departure time as

$$\text{Departure time} = \text{clock time now} + \text{generated service time} \qquad (1)$$

Also, we now schedule the next arrival into the system by randomly generating an interarrival time from the interarrival time distribution and setting the arrival time as

$$\text{Arrival time} = \text{clock time now} + \text{generated interarrival time} \qquad (2)$$

If, for example, we have generated a service time of 2 minutes, then the departure time for the first customer will be set at clock time 2. Similarly, if we have generated an interarrival time of 1 minute, the next arrival will be scheduled for clock time 1.

Both these events and their scheduled times are maintained on the event list. Once we have completed all the necessary actions for the first arrival, we scan the event list to determine the next scheduled event and its time. If the next event is determined to be an arrival, we move the clock time to the scheduled time of the arrival and go through the preceding sequence of actions for an arrival. If the next event is a departure, we move the clock time to the time of the departure and process a departure. For a departure, we check whether the length of the waiting line is greater than zero. If it is, we remove the first customer from the queue and begin service on this customer by setting a departure time using Eq. (1). If no one is waiting, we set the status of the system to idle. These departure actions are summarized in Figure 3.

Figure 3
Flowchart for a
Departure

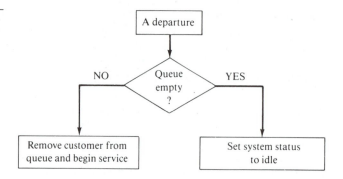

This approach of simulation is called the **next-event time-advance mechanism**, because of the way the clock time is updated. We advance the simulation clock to the time of the most imminent event — that is, the first event in the event list. Since the state variables change only at event times, we skip over the periods of inactivity between the events by jumping from event to event. As we move from event to event, we carry out the appropriate actions for each event, including any scheduling of future events. We continue in this manner until some prespecified stopping condition is satisfied. However, the procedure requires that at any point in the simulation, we have an arrival and a departure scheduled for the future. Thus, a future arrival is always scheduled when processing a new arrival into the system. A departure time, on the other hand, can only be scheduled when a customer is brought into service. Thus, if the system is idle, no departures can be scheduled. In such instances, the usual practice is to schedule a dummy departure by setting the departure time equal to a very large number — say, 9999 (or larger if the clock time is likely to exceed 9999). This way our two events will consist of a real arrival and a dummy departure.

The jump to the next event in the next-event mechanism may be a large one or a small one; that is, the jumps in this method are variable in size. We contrast this approach with the **fixed-increment time-advance method**. With this method, we advance the simulation clock in increments of Δt time units, where Δt is some appropriate time unit, usually 1 time unit. After each update of the clock, we check to determine whether any event is scheduled to take place at the current clock time. If an event is scheduled, we carry out the appropriate actions for the event. If none is scheduled, or if we have completed all the required actions for the current time, we update the simulation clock by Δt units and repeat the process. As with the next-event approach, we continue in this manner until the prespecified stopping condition is reached. The fixed-increment time-advance mechanism is often simpler to comprehend, because of its fixed steps in time. For most models, however, the next event mechanism tends to be more efficient computationally. Consequently, we use only the next-event approach for the development of the models for the rest of the chapter.

We now illustrate the mechanics of the single-server queuing system simulation, using a numerical example. In particular, we want to show how the simulation model is represented in the computer as the simulation progresses through time. The entire simulation process for the single-server queuing model is presented in the flowchart in Figure 4. All the blocks in this flowchart are numbered for easy reference. For simplicity, we assume that both the interarrival times (*IT*s) and the service times (*ST*s) have already

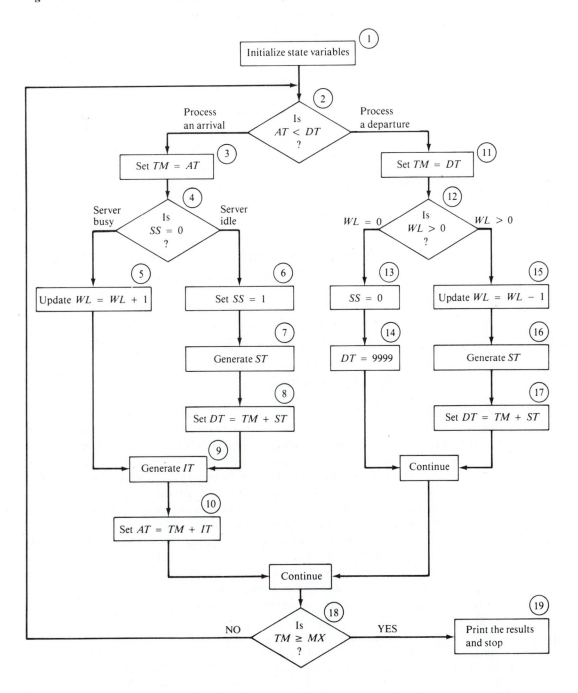

Figure 4 Flowchart for Simulation Model for Single-Server Queuing System

1119

been generated for the first few customers from the given probability distributions in Tables 1 and 2. These times are shown in Table 3, from which we can see that the time between the first and the second arrival is 2 time units, the time between the second and the third arrival is also 2 time units, and so on. Similarly, the service time for the first customer is 3 time units, ST for the second customer is also 3 time units, and so on.

Table 3	CUSTOMER NUMBER	INTERARRIVAL TIME (IT)	SERVICE TIME (ST)
Generated	1	—	3
Interarrival and	2	2	3
Service Times	3	2	2
	4	3	1
	5	4	1
	6	2	2
	7	1	1
	8	3	2
	9	3	—

To demonstrate the simulation model, we need to define several variables:

$$TM = \text{clock time of the simulation}$$
$$AT = \text{scheduled time of the next arrival}$$
$$DT = \text{scheduled time of the next departure}$$
$$SS = \text{status of the server } (1 = \text{busy}, 0 = \text{idle})$$
$$WL = \text{length of the waiting line}$$
$$MX = \text{length (in time units) of a simulation run}$$

Having taken care of these preliminaries, we now begin the simulation by initializing all the variables (block 1 in Figure 4). Since the first arrival is assumed to take place at time 0, we set $AT = 0$. We also assume that the system is empty at time 0, so we set $SS = 0$, $WL = 0$, and $DT = 9999$. (Note that DT must be greater than MX). This implies that our list of events now consists of two scheduled events: an arrival at time 0 and a dummy departure at time 9999. This completes the initialization process and gives us the computer representation of the simulation shown in Table 4.

We are now ready for our first action in the simulation: searching through the event list to determine the first event (block 2). Since our simulation consists of only two events, we simply determine the next event by comparing AT and DT. (In other simulations, we might have more than two events, so we would have to have an efficient system of searching through the event list.) An arrival is indicated by $AT < DT$, a departure by $DT < AT$. At this point, $AT = 0$ is less than $DT = 9999$, indicating that an arrival will take place next. We label this event 1 and update the clock time, TM, to the time of event 1 (block 3). That is, we set $TM = 0$.

The arrival at time 0 finds the system empty, indicated by the fact that $SS = 0$ (block 4). Consequently, the customer enters service immediately. For this part of the simulation, we first set $SS = 1$ to signify that the server is now busy (block 6). We next generate a service time (block 7) and set the departure time for this customer (block 8).

Table 4

Computer
Representation of
the Simulation

END OF EVENT	TYPE OF EVENT	CUSTOMER NUMBER	SYSTEM VARIABLES			EVENT LIST	
			TM	SS	WL	AT	DT
0	Initialization	—	0	0	0	0	9999
1	Arrival	1	0	1	0	2	3
2	Arrival	2	2	1	1	4	3
3	Departure	1	3	1	0	4	6
4	Arrival	3	4	1	1	7	6
5	Departure	2	6	1	0	7	8
6	Arrival	4	7	1	1	11	8
7	Departure	3	8	1	0	11	9
8	Departure	4	9	0	0	11	9999
9	Arrival	5	11	1	0	13	12
10	Departure	5	12	0	0	13	9999
11	Arrival	6	13	1	0	14	15
12	Arrival	7	14	1	1	17	15
13	Departure	6	15	1	0	17	16
14	Departure	7	16	0	0	17	9999
15	Arrival	8	17	1	0	20	19

From Table 3, we see that ST for customer 1 is 3. Since $TM = 0$ at this point, we set $DT = 3$ for the first customer. In other words, customer 1 will depart from the system at clock time 3. Finally, in order to complete all the actions of processing an arrival, we schedule the next arrival into the system by generating an interarrival time, IT (block 9), and setting the time of this arrival using the equation $AT = TM + IT$ (block 10). Since $IT = 2$, we set $AT = 2$. That is, the second arrival will take place at clock time 2. At the end of event 1, our computer representation of the simulation will be as shown in Table 4.

At this stage of the simulation, we proceed to block 18 to determine whether the clock time, TM, has exceeded the specified time length of the simulation, MX. If it has, we print out the results (block 19) and stop the execution of the simulation model. If it has not, we continue with the simulation. We call this the termination process. We execute this process at the end of each event. However, for this example, we assume that MX is a large number. Consequently, from here on, we will not discuss the termination process.

At this point, we loop back to block 2 to determine the next event. Since $AT = 2$ and $DT = 3$, the next event, event 2, will be an arrival at time 2. Having determined the next event, we now advance the simulation to the time of this arrival by updating TM to 2.

The arrival at time 2 finds the server busy, so we put this customer in the waiting line by updating WL from 0 to 1 (block 5). Since the present event is an arrival, we now schedule the next arrival into the system. Given that $IT = 2$ for arrival 3, the next arrival takes place at clock time 4. This completes all the necessary actions for event 2. We again loop back to block 2 to determine the next event. From the computer representation of the system in Table 4, we see that at this point (end of event 2), $DT = 3$ is less that $AT = 4$. This implies that the next event, event 3, will be a departure at clock time 3. We advance the clock to the time of this departure; that is, we update *TM* to 3 (block 11).

At time 3, we process the first departure from the system. With the departure, the server now becomes idle. We check the status of the waiting line to see whether there are any customers waiting for service (block 12). Since $WL = 1$, we have one customer waiting. We remove this customer from the waiting line, set $WL = 0$ (block 15), and bring this customer into service by generating a service time, *ST* (block 16), and setting the departure time using the relation $DT = TM + ST$ (block 17). From Table 3, we see that for customer 2, $ST = 3$. Since $TM = 3$, we set $DT = 6$. We have now completed all the actions for event 3, giving us the computer representation shown in Table 4.

From here on, we leave it to the reader to work through the logic of the simulation for the rest of the events in this example. Table 4 shows the status of the simulation at the end of each of these events. Note that at the end of events 8, 10, and 14 (all departures), the system becomes idle. During the sequence of actions for these events, we set $SS = 0$ (block 13) and $DT = 9999$ (block 14). In each case, the system stays idle until an arrival takes place. This simulation is summarized in the time continuum diagram in Figure 5. Here, the *A*'s represent the arrivals and the *D*'s the departures. Note that the hatched areas, such as the one between times 9 and 11, signify that the system is idle.

Figure 5
Time Continuum
Representation of
Single-Server
Simulation

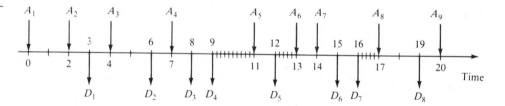

This simple example illustrates some of the basic concepts in simulation and the way in which simulation can be used to analyze a particular problem. Although this model is not likely to be used to evaluate many situations of importance, it has provided us with a specific example and, more important, has introduced a variety of key simulation concepts. In the rest of the chapter, we analyze some of these simulation concepts in more detail. No mention was made in the example of the collection of statistics, but procedures can be easily incorporated into the model to determine the measures of performance of this system. For example, we could expand the flowchart to calculate and print the mean waiting time, the mean number in the waiting line, and the proportion of idle time. We discuss statistical issues in detail later in the chapter.

23-3   RANDOM NUMBERS AND MONTE CARLO SIMULATION

In our queuing simulation example, we saw that the underlying movement through time is achieved in the simulation by generating the interarrival and the service times from the specified probability distributions. In fact, all event times are determined either directly or indirectly by these generated service and interarrival times. The procedure of generating these times from the given probability distributions is known as sampling from probability distributions, or random variate generation, or **Monte Carlo sampling**. In this section, we present and discuss several different methods of sampling from discrete distributions. We initially demonstrate the technique using a roulette wheel and then expand it by carrying out the sampling using random numbers.

The principle of sampling from discrete distributions is based on the frequency interpretation of probability. That is, in the long run, we would like the outcomes to occur with the frequencies specified by the probabilities in the distribution. For example, if we consider the service time distribution in Table 2, we would like, in the long run, to generate a service time of 1 minute 35% the time, a service time of 2 minutes 40% of the time, and a service time of 3 minutes 25% of the time. In addition to obtaining the right frequencies, the sampling procedure should be independent; that is, each generated service time should be independent of the service times that precede it and follow it.

To achieve these two properties using a roulette wheel, we first partition the wheel into three segments, each proportional in area to a probability in the distribution (see Figure 6). For example, the first segment, say S_1, is allocated 35% of the area of the roulette wheel. This area corresponds to the probability of .35 and the service time of 1 minute. The second segment, S_2, covers 40% of the area and corresponds to the probability of .40 and the service time of 2 minutes. Finally, the third segment, S_3, is allocated the remaining 25% of the area, corresponding to the probability .25 and the service time of 3 minutes. If we now spin the roulette wheel and the pointer falls in segment S_1, it means that we have generated a service time of 1 minute. If the pointer falls in segment S_2, we allocate a service time of 2 minutes. If it falls in segment S_3, we have generated a service time of 3 minutes. If the roulette wheel is fair, as we assume, then in the long run, (1) we will generate the service times with approximately the same frequency as specified in the distribution, and (2) the results of each spin will be independent of the results that precede and follow it.

We now expand on this technique by using numbers for segmentation instead of areas. We assume that the roulette wheel has 100 numbers on it, ranging from 00 to 99,

Figure 6
Segmentation of
Roulette Wheel

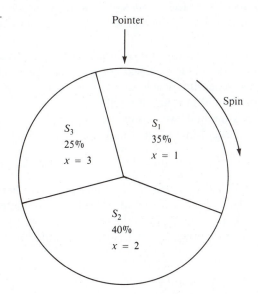

inclusive. We further assume that the segmentation is such that each number has the same probability, .01, of showing up. Using this method of segmentation, we allocate 35 numbers, say from 00 to 34, to the service time of 1 minute. Since each number has a probability .01 of showing up, the 35 numbers together are equivalent to a probability of .35. Similarly, if we allocate the numbers from 35 to 74 to the service time of 2 minutes, and the numbers from 75 to 99 to the service time of 3 minutes, we achieve the desired probabilities. As before, we spin the roulette wheel to generate the service times, but with this method, the numbers directly determine the service times. In other words, if we generate a number between 00 and 34, we set the service time equal to 1 minute; if the number is between 35 and 74, we set the service time equal to 2 minutes; and if the number is between 75 and 99, we set the service time equal to 3 minutes.

This procedure of segmentation and using a roulette wheel is equivalent to generating integer random numbers between 00 and 99. This follows from the fact that a sequence of integer random numbers is such that each random number in the sequence (in this case from 00 to 99) has an equal probability (in this case, .01) of showing up, and each random number is independent of the numbers that precede and follow it. If we now had a procedure for generating the 100 random numbers between 00 and 99, then instead of spinning a roulette wheel to obtain a service time, we could use a generated random number. Technically, a random number, R_i, is defined as an independent random sample drawn from a continuous uniform distribution whose probability density function (pdf) is given by

$$f(x) = \begin{cases} 1 & 0 \leq x \leq 1 \\ 0 & \text{otherwise} \end{cases}$$

Thus, each random number will be uniformly distributed over the range between 0 and 1. Because of this, these random numbers are usually referred to as $U(0, 1)$ random numbers, or simply as uniform random numbers.

Uniform random numbers can be generated in many different ways. Since our interest in random numbers is for use within simulations, we need to be able to generate them on a computer. This is done using mathematical functions called **random number generators**.

Most random number generators use some form of a congruential relationship. Examples of such generators include the linear congruential generator, the multiplicative generator, and the mixed generator. The linear congruential generator is by far the most widely used. In fact, most built-in random number functions on computer systems use this generator. With this method, we produce a sequence of integers $x_1, x_2, x_3, \ldots$ between zero and $m - 1$ according to the following recursive relation:

$$x_{i+1} = (ax_i + c) \text{ modulo } m \qquad (i = 0, 1, 2, \ldots)$$

The initial value of x_0 is called the seed, a is the constant multiplier, c is the increment, and m is the modulus. These four variables are called the parameters of the generator. Using this relation, the value of x_{i+1} equals the remainder from the division of $ax_i + c$ by m. The random number between 0 and 1 is then generated using the equation

$$R_i = \frac{x_i}{m} \qquad (i = 1, 2, 3, \ldots)$$

For example, if $x_0 = 35, a = 13, c = 65$, and $m = 100$, the algorithm works as follows:

Iteration 0 Set $x_0 = 35, a = 13, c = 65$, and $m = 100$.

Iteration 1 Compute

$$x_1 = (ax_0 + c) \text{ modulo } m$$
$$= [13(35) + 65] \text{ modulo } 100$$
$$= 20$$

Deliver

$$R_1 = \frac{x_1}{m}$$
$$= \frac{20}{100}$$
$$= 0.20$$

Iteration 2 Compute

$$x_2 = (ax_1 + c) \text{ modulo } m$$
$$= [13(20) + 65] \text{ modulo } 100$$
$$= 25$$

Deliver

$$R_2 = \frac{x_2}{m}$$
$$= \frac{25}{100}$$
$$= 0.25$$

Iteration 3 Compute

$$x_3 = (ax_2 + c) \text{ modulo } m$$
$$\vdots$$

and so on.

Each random number generated using this method will be a decimal number between 0 and 1. Note that although it is possible to generate a zero, a random number cannot equal 1. Random numbers generated using congruential methods are called **pseudorandom numbers**. They are not true random numbers in the technical sense, since they are completely determined once the recurrence relation is defined and the parameters of the generator are specified. However, by carefully selecting the values of a, c, m, and x_0, the pseudorandom numbers can be made to meet all the statistical properties of true random numbers. In addition to the statistical properties, random number generators must have several other important characteristics if they are to be used efficiently within computer simulations. Some of these characteristics are (1) the routine must be fast; (2) the routine should not require a lot of core storage; (3) the random numbers should be replicable; and (4) the routine should have a sufficiently long cycle — that is, we should be able to generate a long sequence without repetition of the random numbers.

There is one important point worth mentioning at this stage: Most programming languages have built-in library functions that provide random (or pseudorandom) numbers directly. Therefore, most users need only know the library function for a particular system. In some systems, a user may have to specify a value for the seed, x_0, but it is unlikely that a user would have to develop or design a random number generator. However, for more information on random numbers and random number generators, the interested reader may consult Banks and Carson (1984), Knuth (1969), or Law and Kelton (1982).

We now take the method of Monte Carlo sampling a stage further and develop a procedure using random numbers generated on a computer. The idea is to transform the $U(0, 1)$ random numbers into integer random numbers between 00 and 99 and then to use these integer random numbers to achieve the segmentation by numbers. The transformation is a relatively straightforward procedure. If the $(0, 1)$ random numbers are multiplied by 100, they will be uniformly distributed over the range from 0 to 100. Then, if the fractional part of the number is dropped, the result will be integers from 00 to 99, all equally likely. For example, if we had generated the random number 0.72365, multiplying it by 100 gives us 72.365. Truncating the decimal portion of the number will leave us with the integer random number 72. On the computer, we achieve this transformation by first generating a $U(0, 1)$ random number. Next, we multiply it by 100. Finally, we store the product using an integer variable; this final stage will truncate the decimal portion of the number. This procedure will give us integer random numbers between 00 and 99. Table 5 lists some integer pseudorandom numbers obtained using this procedure. (These random numbers will be used in several examples later in the chapter.)

We now formalize this procedure and use it to generate random variates for a discrete random variable. The procedure consists of two steps: (1) We develop the cumulative probability distribution (cdf) for the given random variable, and (2) we use the cdf to allocate the integer random numbers directly to the various values of the random variable. To illustrate this procedure, we use the distribution of interarrival times from the queuing example of Section 23.2 (see Table 1). If we develop the cdf for this distribution, we get the probabilities shown in Table 6. The first interarrival time of 1 minute occurs with a probability of .20. Thus, we need to allocate 20 random numbers to this outcome. If we assign the 20 numbers from 00 to 19, we utilize the decimal random number range from 0 to 0.19999. Note that the upper end of this range lies just below the cumulative probability of .20. For the interarrival time of 2 minutes, we allocate 30 random numbers. If we assign the integer numbers from 20 to 49, we notice that this covers the decimal random number range from 0.20 to 0.49999. As before, the upper end of this range lies just below the cumulative probability of .50, but the lower end coincides with the previous cumulative probability of .20. If we now allocate the integer random numbers from 50 to 84 to the interarrival time of 3 minutes, we notice that these numbers are obtained from the decimal random number range from 0.50 (the same as the cumulative probability associated with an interarrival time of 2 minutes) to 0.84999, which is a fraction smaller than .85. Finally, the same analyses apply to the interarrival time of 4 minutes. In other words, the cumulative probability distribution enables us to allocate the integer random number ranges directly. Once these ranges have been specified for a given distribution, all we must do to obtain the value of a random variable is generate an integer random number and match it against the random number allocations. For example, if the random number had turned out to be 35, this would translate

Table 5
Two-Digit Integer
Random Numbers

69	56	30	32	66	79	55	24	80	35	10	98
92	92	88	82	13	04	86	31	13	23	44	93
13	42	51	16	17	29	62	08	59	41	47	72
25	96	58	14	68	15	18	99	13	05	03	83
34	78	50	89	98	93	70	11	49	01	79	35
64	43	71	48	36	78	53	67	37	57	25	17
84	59	68	45	12	53	68	38	18	60	02	82
31	28	52	89	27	35	34	74	96	93	45	63
21	17	71	55	32	74	20	68	44	34	53	68
91	84	39	25	20	83	60	62	99	61	32	98
55	86	18	93	51	77	68	37	69	02	85	60
43	16	20	42	82	17	41	50	54	21	25	43
40	98	71	03	68	05	37	02	86	17	38	99
42	37	72	33	72	43	51	60	17	94	51	39
18	06	28	75	69	80	33	69	12	25	53	36
13	20	42	92	57	08	24	06	41	12	89	95
58	18	98	89	08	60	89	93	58	13	29	34
63	68	69	62	07	49	95	48	20	03	71	90
92	54	29	31	80	28	48	45	92	71	31	33
84	11	57	64	93	69	86	22	23	84	38	60
33	24	65	76	87	95	98	47	00	71	31	97
53	08	80	85	73	13	25	35	22	82	26	43
02	19	61	38	00	21	42	79	31	70	00	17
22	81	43	44	78	88	30	31	15	63	09	99
38	25	32	92	11	55	18	52	47	30	43	87
04	61	82	18	82	75	12	19	44	87	77	93
06	54	51	64	81	98	63	47	57	52	74	56
51	51	00	41	78	84	42	79	06	82	58	53
99	93	87	86	83	79	16	33	53	34	40	32
29	12	64	73	38	08	49	32	53	33	91	90
31	78	93	25	37	51	68	40	34	47	83	76
81	69	27	35	71	12	69	78	96	93	35	96
26	73	28	81	38	09	55	10	27	29	52	46
92	29	08	15	73	26	33	05	89	08	26	99
00	86	32	46	80	22	97	19	99	95	53	20
39	25	07	41	74	71	01	64	23	69	74	95
38	86	41	38	71	91	75	54	65	73	47	86
41	74	68	21	74	89	43	19	98	74	09	50
63	53	45	07	47	15	58	75	88	51	88	99
00	54	86	59	77	09	54	55	99	15	67	63
01	38	88	03	71	88	72	39	76	45	11	07
38	05	53	31	18	11	26	65	61	77	19	03
34	43	19	12	35	02	09	86	69	90	53	50
23	41	56	34	77	30	50	02	34	68	49	16
57	24	80	69	51	81	83	05	19	45	30	20
93	86	08	08	99	62	75	97	29	51	68	96
16	10	38	33	32	25	34	66	72	17	51	97
75	28	35	14	01	00	98	51	74	10	79	30
53	38	65	32	78	77	64	11	31	06	73	47
91	90	95	95	66	80	10	90	51	24	81	06

Table 6	INTERARRIVAL TIME (Minutes)	PROBABILITY	CUMULATIVE PROBABILITY	RANDOM NUMBER RANGES
Cumulative Distribution Function and Random Number Ranges for Interarrival Times	1	.20	.20	00–19
	2	.30	.50	20–49
	3	.35	.85	50–84
	4	.15	1.00	85–99

to an interarrival time of 2 minutes. Similarly, the random number 67 would translate to an interarrival time of 3 minutes, and so on. We now demonstrate these concepts in an example of a Monte Carlo simulation.

23-4   AN EXAMPLE OF MONTE CARLO SIMULATION

In this section, we use a Monte Carlo simulation to simulate a news vendor problem (see Chapter 17).

E X A M P L E
1

Pierre's Bakery bakes and sells french bread. Each morning, the bakery satisfies the demand for the day using freshly baked bread. Pierre's can bake the bread only in batches of a dozen loaves each. Each loaf costs 25¢ to make. For simplicity, we assume that the total daily demand for bread also occurs in multiples of 12. Past data have shown that this demand ranges from 36 to 96 loaves per day. A loaf sells for 40¢, and any bread left over at the end of the day is sold to a charitable kitchen for a salvage price of 10¢/loaf. If demand exceeds supply, we assume that there is a lost-profit cost of 15¢/loaf (because of loss of goodwill, loss of customers to competitors, and so on). The bakery records show that the daily demand can be categorized into three types: high, average, and low. These demands occur with probabilities of .30, .45, and .25, respectively. The distribution of the demand by categories is given in Table 7. Pierre's would like to determine the optimal number of loaves to bake each day in order to maximize profit (revenues + salvage revenues − cost of bread − cost of lost profits).

Table 7		DEMAND PROBABILITY DISTRIBUTION		
Demand Distribution by Demand Categories	DEMAND	*High*	*Average*	*Low*
	36	.05	.10	.15
	48	.10	.20	.25
	60	.25	.30	.35
	72	.30	.25	.15
	84	.20	.10	.05
	96	.10	.05	.05

Solution

To solve this problem by simulation, we require a number of different policies to evaluate. Here, we define a policy as the number of loaves to bake each day. Each given policy is then evaluated over a fixed period of time to determine its profit margin. The policy that gives the highest profit is selected as the best policy.

In the simulation process, we first develop a procedure for generating the demand for the day:

Step 1 Determine the type of demand — that is, whether the demand for the day is high, average, or low. To do this, calculate the cdf for this distribution and set up the random number assignments (see Table 8). Then, to determine the type of demand, all we have to do is to generate a two-digit random number and match it against the random number allocations in this table.

	TYPE OF DEMAND	PROBABILITY	CUMULATIVE DISTRIBUTION	RANDOM NUMBER RANGES
Table 8 Distribution of Demand Type	High	.30	.30	00–29
	Average	.45	.75	30–74
	Low	.25	1.00	75–99

Step 2 Generate the actual demand for the day from the appropriate demand distribution. The cdf and the random number allocations for the distribution of each of the three demand types are presented in Table 9. Then, to generate a demand, we simply generate an integer random number and match it against the appropriate random number assignments.

	DEMAND	CUMULATIVE DISTRIBUTION			RANDOM NUMBER RANGES		
		High	Average	Low	High	Average	Low
Table 9 Distribution by Demand Type	36	.05	.10	.15	00–04	00–09	00–14
	48	.15	.30	.40	05–14	10–29	15–39
	60	.40	.60	.75	15–39	30–59	40–74
	72	.70	.85	.90	40–69	60–84	75–89
	84	.90	.95	.95	70–89	85–94	90–94
	96	1.00	1.00	1.00	90–99	95–99	95–99

For example, if our demand type was "average" in Step 1, the random number 80 would translate into a demand of 72. Similarly, if the type of demand was "high" in Step 1, the random number 9 would translate into a demand of 48.

The simulation process for this problem is relatively simple. For each day, we generate a demand for the day. Then we evaluate the various costs for a given policy. Suppose, for example, that the policy is to bake 60 loaves each day. If the demand for a particular day turns out to be 72, we have $60(0.40) = \$24.00$ in revenues, $60(0.25) = \$15.00$ in production costs, and $12(0.15) = \$1.80$ in lost-profit costs (because of the shortfall of 12 loaves). This gives us a net profit of $24.00 - 15.00 - 1.80 = \$7.20$ for that day.

Using this procedure, we calculate a profit margin for each day in the simulation. To evaluate a policy, we run the simulation for a fixed number of days for the given policy. At the end of the simulation, we average the profit margins over the set number of days to obtain the expected profit margin per day for the policy. Note that the procedure in this simulation is different from the queuing simulation, in that the present simulation does not evolve over time in the same way. Here, each day is an independent simulation. Such simulations are commonly referred to as **Monte Carlo simulations**.

To illustrate this procedure, we present in Table 10 a manual simulation for the first 15 days for a policy where we bake 60 loaves per day. From this table, the demand for both day 1 and day 2 turns out to be 60 loaves. (Random numbers used in this example were obtained from Table 5.) This demand generates a revenue of $24.00 for each of these days. Since the 60 loaves cost $15.00 to bake, our profit margin for each of the first 2 days is $9.00. On day 3, the demand is 72, giving us a shortfall of 12 loaves. As shown in the table, the profit margin for day 3 is $7.20 (24.00 − 15.00 − 1.80). On day 4, we generate a demand of 48. Since our policy is to bake 60 loaves, we will have 12 loaves left over. The 48 loaves sold give us revenues of only $19.20. However, the 12 loaves left over provide an additional $1.20 in salvage revenue, yielding a profit of $5.40 (19.20 + 1.20 − 15.00) for day 4.

Table 10   Simulation Table for Baking 60 Loaves per Day

DAY	RANDOM NO. FOR DEMAND TYPE	TYPE OF DEMAND	RANDOM NO. FOR DEMAND	DEMAND	REVENUE	LOST PROFIT	SALVAGE REVENUE	PROFIT
1	69	Average	56	60	$24.00	—	—	$9.00
2	30	Average	32	60	$24.00	—	—	$9.00
3	66	Average	79	72	$24.00	$1.80	—	$7.20
4	55	Average	24	48	$19.20	—	$1.20	$5.40
5	80	Low	35	48	$19.20	—	$1.20	$5.40
6	10	High	98	96	$24.00	$5.40	—	$3.60
7	92	Low	88	72	$24.00	$1.80	—	$7.20
8	82	Low	17	48	$19.20	—	$1.20	$5.40
9	04	High	86	84	$24.00	$3.60	—	$5.40
10	31	Average	13	48	$19.20	—	$1.20	$3.00
11	23	High	44	72	$24.00	$1.80	—	$7.20
12	93	Low	13	36	$14.40	—	$2.40	$1.80
13	42	Average	51	60	$24.00	—	—	$9.00
14	16	High	17	60	$24.00	—	—	$9.00
15	29	High	62	72	$24.00	$1.80	—	$7.20

If we now complete the manual simulation for the period of 15 days, the total profit earned during this time comes to $94.80. This gives us an average daily profit figure of $\frac{94.80}{15}$ = $6.32. However, this cannot be accepted as the final profit margin for this policy. The simulation results over this short a period are likely to be highly dependent on the sequence of random numbers generated, so they cannot be accepted as statistically valid. The simulation would have to be carried out over a long period of time before the profit margin is accepted as truly representative. These statistical issues are discussed later. In the meantime, we have evaluated several different policies for this problem using a simulation model on a computer. The results of these policies are presented in Table 11. We see that the best policy for Pierre's Bakery is to bake 72 loaves each day. This table also compares the results from the simulation with the exact solution for each policy. We

Table 11 Evaluation of Policies	POLICY	NO. OF LOAVES BAKED DAILY	AVERAGE DAILY PROFIT Exact	AVERAGE DAILY PROFIT Simulation
	A	36	$1.273	$1.273
	B	48	$4.347	$4.349
	C	60	$6.435	$6.436
	D	72	$6.917	$6.915
	E	84	$6.102	$6.104
	F	96	$4.653	$4.642

can see that simulation does a remarkable job of converging to the right solution. The closeness of the two solutions is not totally unexpected, since we ran the simulation model for 10,000 days for each policy.

◆ PROBLEMS

GROUP A

Use the random numbers in Table 5 to solve the following problems.

1. Simulate the single-server queuing system described in Section 23.2 for the first 25 departures from the system to develop an estimate for the expected time in the waiting line. Is this a reasonable estimate? Explain.

2. Perform the simulation for Pierre's Bakery for 25 more days (days 16 through 40) for policy C in Table 11. Compare the answer with the results in the table.

GROUP B

3. Consider the simplest form of craps. In this game, we roll a pair of dice. If we roll a 7 or an 11 on the first throw, we win right away. If we roll a 2 or a 3 or a 12, we lose right away. Any other total (that is, 4, 5, 6, 8, 9, or 10) gives us a second chance. In this part of the game, we keep rolling the dice until we get either a 7 or the total rolled on the first throw. If we get a 7, we lose. If we roll the same total as on the first throw, we win. Assuming that the dice are fair, develop a simulation experiment to determine the percentage of time we win.

4. Tankers arrive at an oil port with the distribution of interarrival times shown in Table 12. The port has two terminals, terminal A and terminal B. Terminal B is newer and therefore more efficient than terminal A. The time it takes to unload a tanker depends on the tanker's size. A supertanker takes 4 days to unload at terminal A and 3 days at terminal B. A midsize tanker takes 3 days at terminal A and 2 days at terminal B. The small tankers

Table 12

INTERARRIVAL TIMES (Days)	PROBABILITY
1	.20
2	.25
3	.35
4	.15
5	.05

take 2 days at terminal A and 1 day at terminal B. Arriving tankers form a single waiting line in the port area until a terminal becomes available for service. Service is given on an FCFS basis. The type of tankers and the frequency with which they visit this port is given by the distribution in Table 13. Develop a simulation model for this port. Compute such statistics as the average number of tankers in port, the average number of days in port for a tanker, and the percentage of idle time for each of the terminals. (*Hint*: Use the flowchart in Figure 4 and modify it for a multi-server queuing system.

Table 13

TYPE OF TANKER	PROBABILITY
Supertanker	.40
Midsize tanker	.35
Small tanker	.25

SIMULATIONS WITH CONTINUOUS RANDOM VARIABLES

The simulation examples presented thus far used only discrete probability distributions for the random variables. However, in many simulations, it is more realistic and practical to use continuous random variables. In this section, we present and discuss several procedures for generating random variates from continuous distributions. The basic principle is very similar to the discrete case. As in the discrete method, we first generate a $U(0, 1)$ random number and then transform it into a random variate from the specified distribution. The process for carrying out the transformation, however, is quite different from the discrete case.

There are many different methods for generating continuous random variates. The selection of a particular algorithm will depend on the distribution from which we wish to generate, taking into account such factors as the exactness of the random variables, the computational and storage efficiencies, and the complexity of the algorithm. The two most commonly used algorithms are the inverse transformation method (ITM) and the acceptance-rejection method (ARM). Between these two methods, it is possible to generate random variables from almost all of the most frequently used distributions. We present a detailed description of both these algorithms, along with several examples for each method. In addition to this, we present two methods for generating random variables from the normal distribution.

INVERSE TRANSFORMATION METHOD

The inverse transformation method is generally used for distributions whose cumulative distribution function can be obtained in closed form. Examples include the exponential, the uniform, the triangular, and the Weibull distributions. For distributions whose cdf does not exist in closed form, it may be possible to use some numerical method, such as a power-series expansion, within the algorithm to evaluate the cdf. However, this is likely to complicate the procedure to such an extent that it may be more efficient to use a different algorithm to generate the random variates. The ITM is relatively easy to describe and execute. It consists of the following three steps:

Step 1 Given a probability density function $f(x)$ for a random variable **X**, obtain the cumulative distribution function $F(x)$ as

$$F(x) = \int_{-\infty}^{x} f(t)\, dt$$

Step 2 Generate a random number r.

Step 3 Set $F(x) = r$ and solve for x. The variable x is then a random variate from the distribution whose pdf is given by $f(x)$.

We now describe the mechanics of the algorithm using an example. For this, we consider the distribution given by the function

$$f(x) = \begin{cases} \dfrac{x}{2} & 0 \leq x \leq 2 \\ 0 & \text{otherwise} \end{cases}$$

A function of this type is called a **ramp function**. It can be represented graphically as shown in Figure 7. The area under the curve, $f(x) = \frac{x}{2}$, represents the probability of the occurrence of the random variable **X**. We assume that in this case, **X** represents the service times of a bank teller. To obtain random variates from this distribution using the inverse transformation method, we first compute the cdf as

$$F(x) = \int_0^x \frac{t}{2} dt$$

$$= \frac{x^2}{4}$$

Figure 7
The pdf of a Ramp
Function

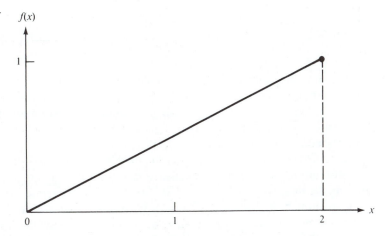

This cdf is represented formally by the function

$$F(x) = \begin{cases} 0 & x < 0 \\ \dfrac{x^2}{4} & 0 \le x \le 2 \\ 1 & x \ge 2 \end{cases}$$

Next, in Step 2, we generate a random number r. Finally, in Step 3, we set $F(x) = r$ and solve for x.

$$\frac{x^2}{4} = r$$

$$x = \pm 2\sqrt{r}$$

Since the service times are defined only for positive values of x, a service time of $x = -2\sqrt{r}$ is not feasible. This leaves us with $x = 2\sqrt{r}$ as the solution for x. This equation is called a **random variate generator** or a **process generator**. Thus, to obtain a service time, we first generate a random number and then transform it using the preceding equation. Each execution of the equation will give us one service time from the given distribution. For instance, if a random number $r = 0.64$ is obtained, a service time of $x = 2\sqrt{0.64} = 1.6$ will be generated.

Graphically, the inverse transformation method can be represented as shown in Figure 8. We see from this graph that the range of values for the random variable (that

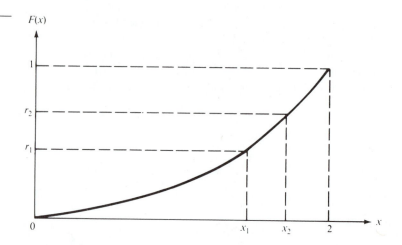

is, $0 \le x \le 2$) coincides with the cumulative probabilities, $0 \le F(x) \le 1.0$. In other words, for any value of $F(x)$ over the interval $[0, 1]$, there exists a corresponding value of the random variable, given by x. Since a random number is also defined in the range between 0 and 1, this implies that a random number can be translated directly into a corresponding value of x using the relation $r = F(x)$. The solution for x in terms of r is known as taking the inverse of $F(x)$, denoted by $x = F^{-1}(r)$—hence the name inverse transformation. Note that if r is equal to zero, we will generate a random variate equal to zero, the smallest possible value of x. Similarly, if we generate a random number equal to 1, it will be transformed to 2, the largest possible value of x.

To show that the ITM generates numbers with the same distribution as x, consider the fact that for any two numbers x_1 and x_2, the probability $P(x_1 \le X \le x_2) = F(x_2) - F(x_1)$. Then what we have to show is that the probability that the generated value of X lies between x_1 and x_2 is also the same. From Figure 8, we see that the generated value of X will be between x_1 and x_2 if and only if the chosen random number is between $r_1 = F(x_1)$ and $r_2 = F(x_2)$. Thus, the probability that the generated value of X is between x_1 and x_2 is also $F(x_2) - F(x_1)$. This shows that the ITM does indeed generate numbers with the same distribution as X.

As this example shows, the major advantage of the inverse transformation method is its simplicity and ease of application. However, as mentioned earlier, we must be able to determine $F(x)$ in closed form for the desired distribution before we can use the method efficiently. Also, in this example, we see that we need exactly one random number to produce one random variable. Other methods, such as the acceptance-rejection method, may require several random numbers to generate a single value of X. The following three examples illustrate the application of the ITM.

E X A M P L E
2

The Exponential Distribution   As mentioned in Chapter 22, the exponential distribution has important applications in the mathematical representation of queuing systems. The pdf of the exponential distribution is given by

$$f(x) = \begin{cases} \lambda e^{-\lambda x} & x \ge 0, \lambda > 0 \\ 0 & \text{otherwise} \end{cases}$$

Use the inverse transformation method to generate observations from an exponential distribution.

Solution   In Step 1, we compute the cdf. This is given by

$$F(x) = \begin{cases} 0 & x < 0 \\ 1 - e^{-\lambda x} & x \geq 0 \end{cases}$$

Next, we generate a random number r and set $F(x) = r$ to solve for x. This gives us

$$1 - e^{-\lambda x} = r$$

Rearranging to

$$e^{-\lambda x} = 1 - r$$

and taking the natural logarithm of both sides, we have

$$-\lambda x = \ln(1 - r)$$

Finally, solving for x gives the solution

$$x = -\frac{1}{\lambda}\ln(1 - r)$$

To simplify our computations, we can replace $(1 - r)$ by r. Since r is a random number, $(1 - r)$ will also be a random number. This means that we have not changed anything except the way we are writing the $U(0, 1)$ random number. Thus, our process generator for the exponential distribution will now be

$$x = -\frac{1}{\lambda}\ln r$$

For instance, $r = \frac{1}{e}$ yields $x = \frac{1}{\lambda}$, and $r = 1$ yields $x = 0$.

◆

EXAMPLE 3   **The Uniform Distribution**   Consider a random variable **X** that is uniformly distributed on the interval $[a, b]$. The pdf of this distribution is given by the function

$$f(x) = \begin{cases} \dfrac{1}{b - a} & a \leq x \leq b \\ 0 & \text{otherwise} \end{cases}$$

Use the ITM to generate observations from this random variable.

Solution   The cdf of this distribution is given by

$$F(x) = \begin{cases} 0 & x < a \\ \dfrac{x - a}{b - a} & a \leq x \leq b \\ 1 & x > b \end{cases}$$

To use the ITM to generate observations from a uniform distribution, we first generate a random number r and then set $F(x) = r$ to solve for x. This gives

$$\frac{x - a}{b - a} = r$$

Solving for x yields

$$x = a + (b - a)r$$

as the process generator for the uniform distribution. For example, $r = \frac{1}{2}$ yields $x = \frac{a+b}{2}$, $r = 1$ yields $x = b$, $r = 0$ yields $x = a$, and so on.

◆

E X A M P L E 4

The Triangular Distribution   Consider a random variable **X** whose pdf is given by

$$f(x) = \begin{cases} \frac{1}{2}(x - 2) & 2 \le x \le 3 \\ \frac{1}{2}(2 - \frac{x}{3}) & 3 \le x \le 6 \\ 0 & \text{otherwise.} \end{cases}$$

Use the ITM to generate observations from the distribution. This distribution, called a triangular distribution, is represented graphically in Figure 9. It has the endpoints [2, 6], and its mode is at 3. We can see that 25% of the area under the curve lies in the range of x from 2 to 3, and the other 75% lies in the range from 3 to 6. In other words, 25% of the values of the random variable **X** lie between 2 and 3, and the other 75% fall between 3 and 6. The triangular distribution has important applications in simulation. It is often used to represent activities for which there are few or no data. (For a detailed account of this distribution, see Banks and Carson (1984) or Law and Kelton (1982).)

Figure 9
Density Function for
a Triangular
Distribution

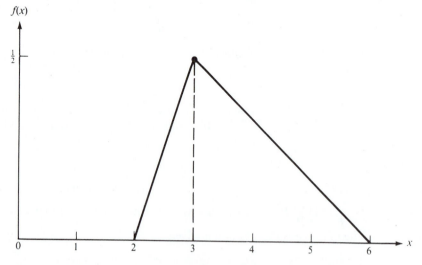

Solution   The cdf of this triangular distribution is given by the function

$$F(x) = \begin{cases} 0 & x < 2 \\ \frac{1}{4}(x - 2)^2 & 2 \le x \le 3 \\ -\frac{1}{12}(x^2 - 12x + 24) & 3 \le x \le 6 \\ 1 & \text{otherwise} \end{cases}$$

For simplicity, we redefine $F(x) = (\frac{1}{4})(x - 2)^2$, for $2 \leq x \leq 3$, as $F_1(x)$, and $F(x) = (-\frac{1}{12})(x^2 - 12x + 24)$, for $3 \leq x \leq 6$, as $F_2(x)$.

This cdf can be represented graphically as shown in Figure 10. Note that at $x = 3$, $F(3) = 0.25$. This implies that the function $F_1(x)$ covers the first 25% of the range of the cdf, and $F_2(x)$ applies over the remaining 75% of the range. Since we now have two separate functions representing the cdf, the ITM has to be modified to account for these two functions, their ranges, and the distribution of the ranges. As far as the ITM goes, the distribution of the ranges is the most important. This distribution is achieved by using the random number from Step 2. In other words, if $r < 0.25$, we use the function $F_1(x) = (\frac{1}{4})(x - 2)^2$ in Step 3. Otherwise, we use $F_2(x) = (-\frac{1}{12})(x^2 - 12x + 24)$. Since $r < 0.25$ for 25% of the time and $r \geq 0.25$ for the other 75%, we achieve the desired distribution. In either case, we set the function $F_1(x)$ or $F_2(x)$ equal to r and solve for x. That is, we solve one of the following equations:

$$(\tfrac{1}{4})(x - 2)^2 = r \qquad \text{for } 0 \leq r < 0.25$$
$$(-\tfrac{1}{12})(x^2 - 12x + 24) = r \qquad \text{for } 0.25 \leq r \leq 1.0$$

x will then be our random variate of interest.

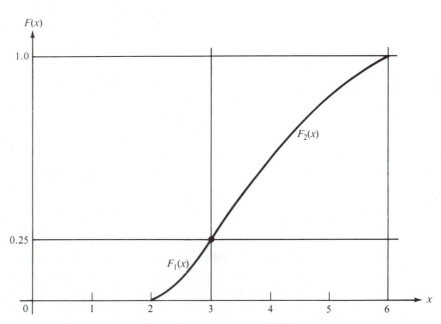

As the graph in Figure 10 shows, a random number between 0 and 0.25 will be transformed into a value of x between 2 and 3. Similarly, if $r \geq 0.25$, it will be transformed into a value of x between 3 and 6.

To solve the first equation, $(\frac{1}{4})(x - 2)^2 = r$, we multiply the equation by 4 and then take the square root of both sides. This gives us

$$x - 2 = \pm\sqrt{4r}$$
$$x = 2 \pm 2\sqrt{r}$$

Since x is defined only for values greater than 2, $x = 2 - 2\sqrt{r}$ is infeasible, leaving

$$x = 2 + 2\sqrt{r}$$

as the process generator for a random number in the range from 0 to 0.25. Note that when $r = 0$, $x = 2$, the smallest possible value for this range. Similarly, when we generate $r = 0.25$, it will be transformed to $x = 3$.

To solve the second equation, $(-\frac{1}{12})(x^2 - 12x + 24) = r$, we can use one of two methods: (1) employing the quadratic formula or (2) completing the square. (See Banks and Carson (1984) for details of the quadratic formula method.) Here, we use the method of completing the square. We multiply the equation by -12 and rearrange the terms to get

$$x^2 - 12x = -24 - 12r$$

To complete the square, we first divide the x term's coefficient by 2. This gives us -6. Next, we square this value to get 36. Finally, we add this resultant to both sides of the equation. This leaves us with the equation

$$x^2 - 12x + 36 = 12 - 12r$$
$$(x - 6)^2 = 12 - 12r$$

Writing the equation in this form enables us to take the square root of both sides. That is,

$$x - 6 = \pm\sqrt{12 - 12r}$$
$$x = 6 \pm 2\sqrt{3 - 3r}$$

As before, part of the solution is infeasible. In this case, x is feasible only for values less than 6. Thus, we use only the equation $x = 6 - 2\sqrt{3 - 3r}$ as our process generator. Note that when $r = 0.25$, our random variate is equal to 3. Similarly, when $r = 1$, we generate a random variate equal to 6.

◆

ACCEPTANCE-REJECTION METHOD

There are several important distributions, including the Erlang (used in queuing models) and the beta (used in PERT), whose cumulative distribution functions do not exist in closed form. For these distributions, we must resort to other methods of generating random variates, one of which is the acceptance-rejection method (ARM). This method is generally used for distribution whose domains are defined over finite intervals. Thus, given a distribution whose pdf, $f(x)$, is defined over the interval $a \leq x \leq b$, the algorithm consists of the following steps:

Step 1 Select a constant M such that M is the largest value of $f(x)$ over the interval $[a, b]$.

Step 2 Generate two random numbers, r_1 and r_2.

Step 3 Compute $x^* = a + (b - a)r_1$. (This ensures that each member of $[a, b]$ has an equal chance to be chosen as x^*.)

Step 4 Evaluate the function $f(x)$ at the point x^*. Let this be $f(x^*)$.

Step 5 If

$$r_2 \leq \frac{f(x^*)}{M}$$

deliver x^* as a random variate from the distribution whose pdf is $f(x)$. Otherwise, reject x^* and go back to Step 2.

Note that the algorithm continues looping back to Step 2 until a random variate is accepted. This may take several iterations. For this reason, the algorithm can be relatively inefficient. The efficiency, however, is highly dependent on the shape of the distribution. There are several ways by which the method can be made more efficient. One of these is to use a function in Step 1 instead of a constant. See Fishman (1978) or Law and Kelton (1982) for details of the algorithm.

We now illustrate the details of the algorithm using a ramp function. Consider a random variable **X** whose pdf is given by the function

$$f(x) = \begin{cases} 2x & 0 \leq x \leq 1 \\ 0 & \text{otherwise} \end{cases}$$

In Step 1 of the ARM, it is generally useful to graph the pdf. Since our objective is to obtain the largest value of $f(x)$ over the domain of the function, graphing will enable us to determine the value of M simply by inspection. The graph of the pdf is shown in Figure 11. We see that the largest value of $f(x)$ occurs at $x = 1$ and is equal to 2. In other words, we set $M = 2$ in Step 1. Next, we generate two random numbers, r_1 and r_2. In Step 3, we transform the first random number, r_1, into an **X** value, x^*, using the relationship $x^* = a + (b - a)r_1$. This step is simply a procedure for randomly generating a value of the random variable **X**. Given that we are using a random number r_1 to determine x^*, every value over the interval $[a, b]$ has an equal probability of showing up. Note that if $r_1 = 0$, x^* will be equal to a, the left endpoint of the domain. Similarly, if $r_1 = 1$, x^* will be equal to b, the right endpoint of the domain. Since $a = 0$ and $b = 1$ for this distribution, it follows that $x^* = r_1$. This value of x^* now becomes our potential random variate for the current iteration. In Steps 4 and 5, we have to determine whether to accept or reject x^*. We first evaluate the function $f(x)$ at $x = x^*$ to obtain $f(x^*)$ and then compute $\frac{f(x^*)}{M}$. If $r_2 \leq \frac{f(x^*)}{M}$, we accept x^*. Otherwise, we reject x^*. Substituting $x^* = r_1$ in $f(x)$ gives us $f(x^*) = 2r_1$. Since $M = 2$, the term $\frac{f(x^*)}{M}$ reduces to r_1. Given

Figure 11
The pdf of a Ramp Function

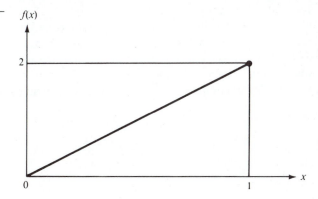

this, our decision rule (in Step 5) for accepting x^* simplifies to a comparison of r_2 and r_1. If $r_2 \leq r_1$, we accept x^* as our random variate. Otherwise, we go back to Step 2 and repeat the process until we obtain an acceptance. For example, if $r_1 = 0.7$ and $r_2 = 0.6$, we choose $x = 0.7$, and if $r_1 = 0.7$ and $r_2 = 0.8$, no value of the random variable is generated. For this problem, exactly half the random variates generated in Step 3 will be rejected in Step 5.

E X A M P L E 5

Use the acceptance-rejection method to generate random variates from a triangular distribution whose pdf is given by

$$f(x) = \begin{cases} -\frac{1}{6} + \frac{x}{12} & 2 \leq x \leq 6 \\ \frac{4}{3} - \frac{x}{6} & 6 \leq x \leq 8 \end{cases}$$

Solution

For simplicity, we redefine $f(x) = -\frac{1}{6} + \frac{x}{12}$ as $f_1(x)$, and $f(x) = \frac{4}{3} - \frac{x}{6}$ as $f_2(x)$. This distribution is represented graphically in Figure 12.

Since this distribution is defined over two intervals, we must modify Steps 4 and 5 of the acceptance-rejection method to account for these ranges. The first three steps of the algorithm, however, stay the same as before. That is, Step 1 determines M, Step 2 generates r_1 and r_2, and Step 3 transforms r_1 into a value x^* of **X**.

Figure 12
The pdf of Triangular Distribution of Example 5

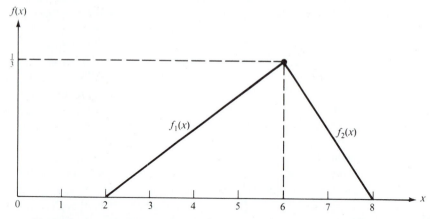

From the graph of the pdf in Figure 12, it is clear that $M = \frac{1}{3}$. This distribution has the endpoints [2, 8], which implies that $a = 2$ and $b = 8$. If we now substitute these endpoints in Step 3, the x^*-values are generated by the equation $x^* = 2 + 6r_1$. Then we see that if r_1 is between 0 and $\frac{2}{3}$, x^* will lie in the range from 2 to 6. If $r_1 > \frac{2}{3}$, x^* will lie in the interval [6, 8]. To account for this, we make our first modification in Step 4. If x^* lies between 2 and 6, then in Step 4, we use the function $f_1(x)$ to evaluate $f(x^*)$. Otherwise, we use $f_2(x)$ to compute $f(x^*)$. Step 4 now can be summarized as follows: If $2 \leq x^* \leq 6$,

$$f(x^*) = f_1(x^*)$$

$$= -\frac{1}{6} + \frac{x^*}{12}$$

$$= \frac{r_1}{2}$$

If $6 \leq x^* \leq 8$,

$$f(x^*) = f_2(x^*)$$
$$= \frac{4}{3} - \frac{x^*}{6}$$
$$= 1 - r_1$$

The next step in the algorithm is either to accept or to reject the current value of x^*. We accept x^* if the condition $r_2 \leq \frac{f(x^*)}{M}$ is satisfied. However, following Step 4, we need to evaluate this condition over the two intervals by substituting the appropriate function, $f(x^*)$, into the relation. In other words, Step 5 for this distribution will now be as follows: For $2 \leq x^* \leq 6$, we accept x^* if $r_2 \leq \frac{f_1(x^*)}{M}$—that is, if $r_2 \leq \frac{3r_1}{2}$. For $6 \leq x^* \leq 8$, we accept x^* if $r_2 \leq \frac{f_2(x^*)}{M}$—that is, if $r_2 \leq 3(1 - r_1)$. If x^* is rejected, we go back to Step 2 and repeat the process.

As before, some of the x^*-values will be rejected. In this case, also, the probability of accepting a random variate is .5. That is, one half of all random variates generated in Step 3 will, in the long run, be rejected in Step 5.

◆

We now give an intuitive justification of the validity of the ARM. In particular, we want to show that the ARM does generate observations from the given random variable **X**. To illustrate the main idea, suppose that **X** has a density function $f(x)$, where $f(x_1) = 2$ and $f(x_2) = 4$. Then the ARM should (for small Δ) result in $P(x_2 \leq \mathbf{X} \leq x_2 + \Delta)$ being twice as large as $P(x_1 \leq \mathbf{X} \leq x_1 + \Delta)$. On any given step, the probability that a point between x_1 and $x_1 + \Delta$ is generated on an iteration of the ARM is equal to the probability that Step 3 yields x^* between x_1 and $x_1 + \Delta$ times the probability that $r_2 \leq \frac{f(x_1)}{M}$; that is,

$$\left(\frac{\Delta}{b - a}\right)\left(\frac{f(x_1)}{M}\right) = \frac{2\Delta}{M(b - a)}$$

Similar reasoning shows that the probability that a point between x_2 and $x_2 + \Delta$ is generated on an iteration of the ARM is given by $\frac{4\Delta}{M(b-a)}$. Thus, the ARM ensures that

$$2P(x_1 \leq \mathbf{X} \leq x_1 + \Delta) = P(x_2 \leq \mathbf{X} \leq x_2 + \Delta)$$

We also note that on any ARM iteration, there is a probability of $\frac{1}{M(b-a)}$ that a value of the random variable will be generated (see Problem 6 at the end of this section).

DIRECT AND CONVOLUTION METHODS FOR THE NORMAL DISTRIBUTION

Because of the importance of the normal distribution, considerable attention has been paid to generating normal random variates. This has resulted in many different algorithms for the normal distribution. Both the inverse transformation method and the acceptance-rejection method are inappropriate for the normal distribution, because (1) the cdf does not exist in closed form and (2) the distribution is not defined over a finite interval. Although it is possible to use numerical methods within the ITM and to truncate the distribution for the acceptance-rejection method, other methods tend to be much more efficient. In this section, we describe two such methods—first, an algorithm based on convolution techniques, and then a direct transformation algorithm that produces two standard normal variates with mean 0 and variance 1.

In the convolution algorithm, we make direct use of the Central Limit Theorem. The Central Limit Theorem states that the sum $\mathbf{Y}$ of n independent and identically distributed random variables (say, $\mathbf{Y}_1, \mathbf{Y}_2, \ldots, \mathbf{Y}_n$, each with mean μ and finite variance σ^2) is approximately normally distributed with mean $n\mu$ and variance $n\sigma^2$. If we now apply this to $U(0, 1)$ random variables, $\mathbf{R}_1, \mathbf{R}_2, \ldots, \mathbf{R}_n$, with mean $\mu = 0.5$ and $\sigma^2 = \frac{1}{12}$, it follows that

$$\mathbf{Z} = \frac{\sum\limits_{i=1}^{n} \mathbf{R}_i - 0.5n}{\left(\frac{n}{12}\right)^{1/2}}$$

is approximately normal with mean 0 and variance 1. We would expect this approximation to work better as the value of n increases. However, most simulation literature suggests using a value of $n = 12$. Using 12 not only seems adequate but, more important, has the advantage that it simplifies the computational procedure. If we now substitute $n = 12$ into the preceding equation, the process generator simplifies to

$$\mathbf{Z} = \sum\limits_{i=1}^{12} \mathbf{R}_i - 6$$

This equation avoids a square root and a division, both of which are relatively time-consuming routines on a computer.

If we wish to generate a normal variate $\mathbf{X}$ with mean μ and variance σ^2, we first generate $\mathbf{Z}$ using this process generator and then transform it using the relation $\mathbf{X} = \mu + \sigma\mathbf{Z}$. Note that this convolution is unique to the normal distribution and cannot be extended to other distributions. Several other distributions do, of course, lend themselves to convolution methods. For example, we can generate random variates from an Erlang distribution with shape parameter k and rate parameter $k\lambda$, using the fact that an Erlang random variable can be obtained by the sum of k iid exponential random variables, each with parameter $k\lambda$.

The direct method for the normal distribution was developed by Box and Muller (1958). Although it is not as efficient as some of the newer techniques, it is easy to apply and execute. The algorithm generates two $U(0, 1)$ random numbers, r_1 and r_2, and then transforms them into two normal random variates, each with mean 0 and variance 1, using the direct transformations

$$\mathbf{Z}_1 = (-2 \ln r_1)^{1/2} \sin 2\pi r_2$$
$$\mathbf{Z}_2 = (-2 \ln r_1)^{1/2} \cos 2\pi r_2$$

As in the convolution method, it is easy to transform these standardized normal variates into normal variates $\mathbf{X}_1$ and $\mathbf{X}_2$ from the distribution with mean μ and variance σ^2, using the equations

$$\mathbf{X}_1 = \mu + \sigma\mathbf{Z}_1$$
$$\mathbf{X}_2 = \mu + \sigma\mathbf{Z}_2$$

The direct method produces exact normal random variates, whereas the convolution method gives us only approximate normal random variates. For this reason, the direct method is much more commonly used. For details of these and other normal algorithms, see Fishman (1978) or Law and Kelton (1982).

◆ PROBLEMS

GROUP A

1. Consider a continuous random variable with the following pdf:

$$f(x) = \begin{cases} \frac{1}{2} & 0 \leq x \leq 1 \\ \frac{3}{4} - \frac{x}{4} & 1 \leq x \leq 3 \end{cases}$$

Develop a process generator for these breakdown times using the inverse transformation method and the acceptance-rejection method.

2. A job shop manager wishes to develop a simulation model in order to help schedule jobs through the shop. He has evaluated the completion times for all the different types of jobs. For one particular job, the times to completion can be represented by the following triangular distribution:

$$f(x) = \begin{cases} \frac{x}{8} - \frac{1}{4} & 2 \leq x \leq 4 \\ \frac{10}{24} - \frac{x}{24} & 4 \leq x \leq 10 \end{cases}$$

Develop a process generator for this distribution using the inverse transformation method.

3. Given the continuous triangular distribution in Figure 13, develop a process generator using the inverse transformation method.

_____

Figure 13

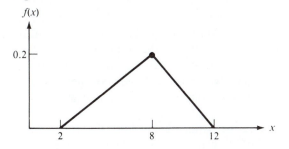

GROUP B

4. For Problem 2, develop a computer program for the process generator. Generate 100 random variates and compare the mean and variance of this sample against the theoretical mean and variance of this distribution. Now repeat the experiment for 250 random variates, 500 random variates, 1000 random variates, and 5000 random variates. From these experiments, what can be said about the process generator?

5. A machine operator processes two types of jobs, type A and type B, during the course of the day. Analyses of past data show that 40% of all jobs are type A jobs, and 60% of all jobs are type B jobs. Type A jobs have completion times that can be represented by an Erlang distribution with rate parameter 5 and shape parameter 2. Completion times of type B jobs can be represented by the following triangular distribution:

$$f(x) = \begin{cases} \dfrac{x - 1}{12} & 1 \leq x \leq 4 \\ \dfrac{9 - x}{20} & 4 \leq x \leq 9 \end{cases}$$

If jobs arrive at an exponential rate of 10 per hour, develop a simulation model to calculate the percentage of idle time of the operator and the average number of jobs in the line waiting to be processed.

6. Show that on any iteration of the acceptance-rejection method, there is a probability $\dfrac{1}{M(b-a)}$ that a value of the random variable is generated.

23-6   **AN EXAMPLE OF A STOCHASTIC SIMULATION**

We now present an example of a simulation using some of the concepts covered in Section 23.5. We consider the case of Cabot, Inc., a large mail order firm in Chicago. Orders arrive into the warehouse via telephones. At present, Cabot maintains 10 operators on-line 24 hours a day. The operators take the orders and feed them directly into a central computer, using terminals. Each operator has one terminal. At present, the company has a total of 11 terminals. That is, if all terminals are working, there will be 1 spare terminal.

A terminal on-line may break down. If that happens, the terminal is removed from the workstation and is replaced with a spare, if one is available. If none is available, the operator must wait until one becomes available. During this time, this operator does not take any orders. The broken terminal is sent to the workshop, where the company has one repair channel allocated to repairing terminals. At the completion of a repair, the terminal either acts as a spare or goes directly into service if an operator is waiting for a terminal. The flow of terminals in the system is shown in Figure 14.

Figure 14
Flow of Terminals

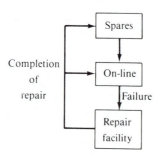

The Cabot managers believe that the terminal system needs evaluation, because the down time of operators due to broken-down terminals has been excessive. They feel that the problem can be solved by the purchase of some additional terminals for the spares pool. Their accountants have determined that a new terminal will cost a total of $75 per week in such costs as investment cost, capital cost, maintenance, and insurance. It has also been estimated that the cost of terminal down time, in terms of delays, lost orders, and so on, is $1000 per week. Given this information, the Cabot managers would like to determine how many additional terminals they should purchase.

This model is a version of the machine repair problem (see Section 22.9). In such models, if both the breakdown and the repair times can be represented by the exponential distribution, it is easy to find an analytical solution to the problem using birth–death processes. However, in analyzing the historical data for the terminals, it has been determined that although the breakdown times can be represented by the exponential distribution, the repair times can be adequately represented only by the triangular distribution. This implies that analytical methods cannot be used and that we must use simulation.

To simulate this system, we first require the parameters of both the distributions. For the breakdown time distribution, the data show that the breakdown rate is exponential and equal to 1 per week per terminal. In other words, the time between breakdowns for a terminal is exponential with a mean equal to 1 week. Analysis for the repair times (measured in weeks) show that this distribution can be represented by the triangular distribution

$$f(x) = \begin{cases} -10 + 400x & 0.025 \le x \le 0.075 \\ 50 - 400x & 0.075 \le x \le 0.125 \end{cases}$$

which has a mean of 0.075 week. That is, the repair staff can, on the average, repair 13.33 terminals per week. We represent the repair time distribution graphically in Figure 15.

In order to find the optimum number of terminals for the system, we must balance the cost of the additional terminals against the increased revenues (because of reduced down time costs) generated as a result of the increase in the number of terminals. In the simulation, we increase the number of terminals in the system, n, from the present total of 11 in increments of 1. For this fixed value of n, we then run our simulation model to estimate the net revenue. Net revenue here is defined as the difference between the increase in revenues due to the additional terminals and the cost of these additional terminals. We keep on adding terminals until the net revenue position reaches a peak. Thus, our primary objective in the simulation is to determine the net revenue for a fixed number of terminals.

Figure 15
The pdf of the Repair Times

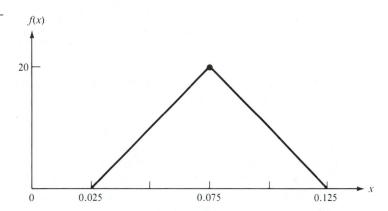

To calculate the net revenue, we first compute the average number of on-line terminals, EL_n (or equivalently, the average number of down time terminals, ED_n) for a fixed number of terminals in the system, n. In fact, ED_n is simply equal to $n - EL_n$. Once we have a value for EL_n, we can compute the expected weekly down time costs, given by $1000(10 - EL_n)$. Then the increase in revenues as a result of increasing the number of terminals from 11 to n is $1000(EL_n - EL_{11})$.

Mathematically, we compute EL_n as

$$EL_n = \frac{\int_0^T N(t)\,dt}{T} = \frac{\sum_{i=1}^m A_i}{T}$$

where

$T =$ length of the simulation

$N(t) =$ number of terminals on-line at time t $(0 \le t \le T)$

$A_i =$ area of rectangle under $N(t)$ between e_{i-1} and e_i (where e_i is the time of ith event)

$m =$ number of events that occur in the interval $[0, T]$

This computation is illustrated in Figure 16 for $n = 10$. In this example, we start with 10 terminals on-line at time 0. Between time 0 and time e_1, the time of the first event, the

Figure 16
Computation of EL_{10}

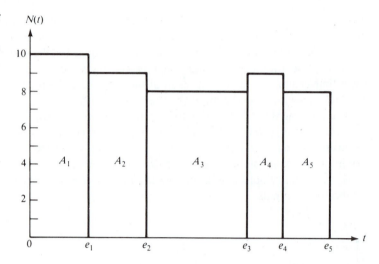

total on-line time for all the terminals is given by $10e_1$, since each terminal is on-line for a period of e_1 time units. Similarly, the total on-line time between events 1 and 2 is $9(e_2 - e_1)$, given that the breakdown at time e_1 leaves us with only 9 working terminals between time e_1 and time e_2. If we now run this simulation over T time units and sum up the areas $A_1, A_2, A_3, \ldots$, we can get an estimate for EL_{10} by dividing this sum by T. This statistic is called a **time-average statistic**. As long as the simulation is run for a sufficiently long period of time, our estimate for EL_{10} should be fairly close to the actual.

In this simulation, we would like to set up the process in such a way that it will be possible to collect the statistics to compute the areas $A_1, A_2, A_3, \ldots$. That is, as we move from event to event, we would like to keep track of at least the number of terminals on-line between the events and the time between events. To do this, we first define the state of the system as the number of terminals in the repair facility. From this definition, it follows that the only time the state of the system will change is when there is either a breakdown or a completion of a repair. This implies that there are two events in this simulation: breakdown and completion of repairs.

To set up the simulation, our first task is to determine the process generators for both the breakdown and the repair times. Since both these distributions have cdf's in closed form, we use the ITM to develop the process generators. For the exponential distribution, the process generator is simply

$$x = -\log r$$

In the case of the repair times, applying the ITM gives us

$$x = 0.025 + \sqrt{0.005r} \qquad (0 \le r \le 0.5)$$

and

$$x = 0.125 - \sqrt{0.005(1 - r)} \qquad (0.5 \le r \le 1.0)$$

as the process generators.

Within this experiment, we run several different simulations, one for each different value of n. Since n at present equals 11, we begin the experiment with this number and increase n until the net revenues reach a peak. For each n, we start the simulation in the state where there are no terminals in the repair facility. In this state, all 10 operators are on-line and any remaining terminals are in the spares pool.

Our first action in the simulation is to schedule the first series of events, the breakdown times for the terminals presently on-line. We do this in the usual way, by generating an exponential random variate for each on-line terminal from the breakdown distribution and setting the time of breakdown by adding this generated time to the current clock time, which is zero. Having scheduled these events, we next determine the first event, the first breakdown, by searching through the current event list. We then move the simulation clock to the time of this event and process this breakdown.

To process a breakdown, we take two separate series of actions: (1) Determine whether a spare is available. If one is available, bring the spare into service and schedule the breakdown time for this terminal. If none is available, update the back-order position. (2) Determine whether the repair staff is idle. If so, start the repair on the broken terminal by generating a random variate from the service times distribution and scheduling the completion time of the repair. If the repair staff is busy, place the broken terminal in the repair queue. Having completed these two series of actions, we now update all the statistical counters. These actions are summarized in the system flow diagram in Figure 17. We proceed with the simulation by determining the next event and moving the clock to the time of this event. If the next event is another breakdown, we repeat the preceding series of actions. Otherwise, we process a completion of a repair.

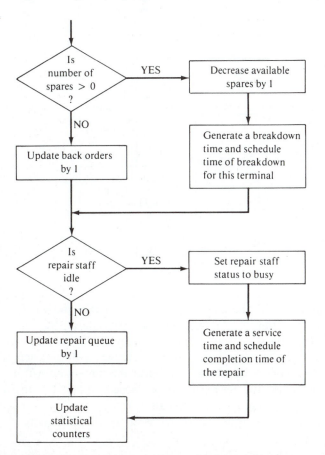

Figure 17
Flowchart for a Breakdown

To process the completion of a repair, we also undertake two series of actions. (1) At the completion of a repair, we have an additional working terminal, so we determine whether the terminal goes directly to an operator or to the spares pool. If a back order exists, we bring the terminal directly into service and schedule the time of breakdown for this terminal in the usual manner. If no operator is waiting for a terminal, the terminal goes into the spares pool. (2) We check the repair queue to see whether any terminals are waiting to be repaired. If the queue is greater than zero, we bring the first terminal from the queue into repair and schedule the time of the completion of this repair. Otherwise, we set the status of the repair staff to idle. Finally, at the completion of these actions, we update all the statistical counters. This part of the simulation is summarized in Figure 18.

Figure 18
Flowchart for
Completion of a
Repair

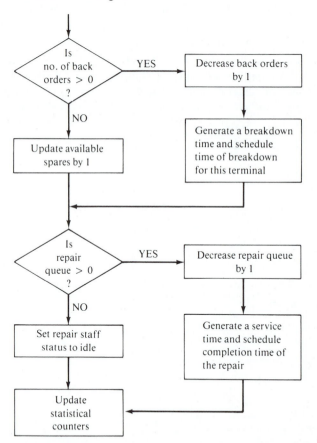

We proceed with the simulation (for a given n) by moving from event to event until the termination time T. At this time, we calculate all the relevant measures of performance from the statistical counters. Our key measure is the net revenue for the current value of n. If this revenue is greater than the revenue for a system with $n - 1$ terminals, we increase the value of n by 1 and repeat the simulation with $n + 1$ terminals in the system. Otherwise, the net revenue has reached a peak. If this is the case, we stop the experiment and accept $n - 1$ terminals as the optimal number of terminals to have in the system. This simulation experiment is summarized in Figure 19. For this experiment,

Figure 19
Flowchart for
Terminal Simulation

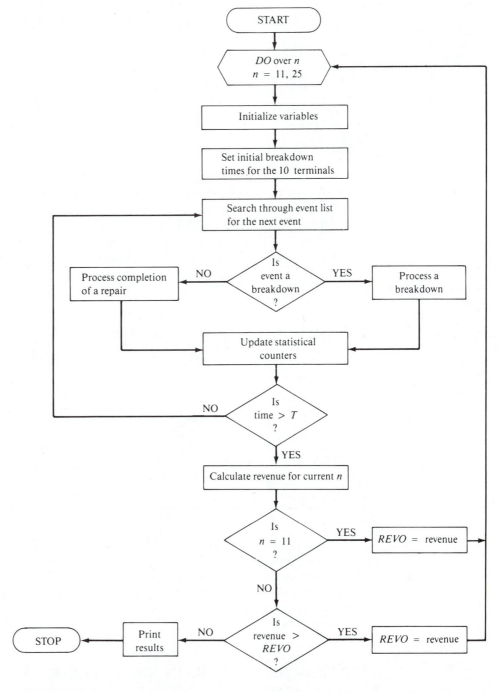

we assume that the maximum number of terminals we can have is 25. (Note that the variable *REVO* in the flowchart is revenue for the system with $n - 1$ terminals.)

For this problem, we ran a complete experiment, whose results are summarized in Table 14. In this table, we show the overall effect on the net revenues as we increase the

Table 14
Simulation Results
for the Terminal
System

	NO. OF TERMINALS (n)				
	11	*12*	*13*	*14*	*15*
EL_n	9.362	9.641	9.801	9.878	9.931
ED_n	0.638	0.359	0.199	0.122	0.069
$EL_n - EL_{11}$	—	0.279	0.439	0.516	0.569
Increase in revenue	—	$279	$439	$516	$569
Cost of terminals	—	$75	$150	$225	$300
Net revenue	—	$204	$289	$291	$269

number of terminals from 11. For example, when we increase n from 11 to 12, the expected number of on-line terminals increases from 9.362 to 9.641, for a net increase of 0.279. This results in an increase of $279 in revenues per week at a cost of $75, giving us a net revenue increase of $204 per week. Similarly, if we increase the number of terminals from 11 to 13, we have a net increase of $289. The net increase peaks with 14 terminals in the system. This is further highlighted by the graph in Figure 20.

Figure 20
Revenue and Costs
for Terminal System

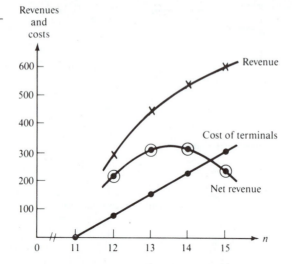

The simulation outlined in this example can be used to analyze other policy options that management may have. For example, instead of purchasing additional terminals, Cabot could hire a second repair worker or choose a preventive maintenance program for the terminals. Alternatively, the company might prefer a combination of these policies. The simulation model provides a very flexible mechanism for evaluating alternative policies.

23-7   STATISTICAL ANALYSIS IN SIMULATIONS

As previously mentioned, output data from simulation always exhibit random variability, since random variables are input to the simulation model. For example, if we run the same simulation twice, each with a different sequence of random numbers, the statistics generated for the two simulations will almost certainly have different values. Because of this, we must utilize statistical methods to analyze output from simulations. If the performance of the system is measured by a parameter (say, θ), then our objective in the simulation will be to develop an estimate $\hat{\theta}$ of θ, and determine the accuracy of the estimator $\hat{\theta}$. We measure this accuracy by the standard deviation (also called the standard error) of $\hat{\theta}$. The overall measure of variability is generally stated in the form of a confidence interval at a given level of confidence. Thus, the purpose of the statistical analysis is to estimate this confidence interval.

Determination of the confidence intervals in simulation is complicated by the fact that output data are rarely, if ever, independent. That is, the data are autocorrelated. For example, in a queuing simulation, the waiting time of a customer often depends on the prior customers. Similarly, in an inventory simulation, the models are usually set up such that the beginning inventory on a given day is the ending inventory from the previous day, thereby creating a correlation. This means that the classical methods of statistics, which assume independence are not directly applicable to the analysis of simulation output data. Thus, we must modify the statistical methods in order to make proper inferences from simulation data.

In addition to the problem of autocorrelation, we may have a second problem, in that the specification of the initial conditions of the system at time 0 may influence the output data. For example, suppose that in the queuing simulation from Section 23.2, the arrival and the service distribution are such that the average waiting time per customer exceeds 15 minutes. In other words, the system is heavily congested. If we were to begin this simulation with no one in the system, the first few customers would have either zero or very small waiting times. These initial waiting times are highly dependent on the starting conditions and may therefore not be representative of the steady-state behavior of the system. This initial period of time before a simulation reaches steady state is called the **transient period** or **warmup period**.

There are two ways of overcoming the problems associated with the transient period. The first approach is to use a set of initial conditions that are representative of the system in steady state. However, in many simulations, it may be difficult to set such initial conditions. This is particularly true of queuing simulations. The alternative approach is to let the simulation run for a while and discard the initial part of the simulation. With this approach, we are assuming that the initial part of the simulation warms the model up to an equilibrium state. Since we do not collect any statistics during the warmup stage, we can reduce much of the initialization bias. Unfortunately, there are no easy ways to assess how much initial data to delete in order to reduce the initialization bias to negligible levels. Since each simulation model is different, it is up to the analyst to determine when the transient period ends. Although this is a difficult process, there are some general guidelines one can use. For these and other details of this topic, see Law and Kelton (1982).

For the purpose of analyzing output data, we generally categorize simulations into one of two types: terminating simulations and steady-state simulations. A **terminating simulation** is one that runs for a duration of time T_E, where E is a specified event (or events) that stops the simulation. The event E may be a specified time, in which case the simulation runs for a fixed amount of time. Or, if it is a specified condition, the length of the simulation will be a random variable. A **steady-state simulation** is one that runs over a long period of time; that is, the length of the simulation goes to "infinity."

Often, the type of model determines which type of output analysis is appropriate for a particular simulation. For example, in the simulation of a bank, we would most likely use a terminating simulation, since the bank physically closes every evening, giving us an appropriate terminating event. When simulating a computer system, a steady-state simulation may be more appropriate, since most large computer systems do not shut down except in cases of breakdowns or maintenance. However, the system or model may not always be the best indicator of which simulation would be the most appropriate. It is quite possible to use the terminating simulation approach for systems more suited to steady-state simulations, and vice versa. In this section, we provide a detailed description of the statistical analysis associated with terminating simulations. The analysis for steady-state simulations is much more involved. For details of the latter, see Banks and Carson (1984) or Law and Kelton (1982).

Suppose we make n independent replications using a terminating simulation approach. If each of the n simulations is started with the same initial conditions and is executed using a different sequence of random numbers, then each simulation can be treated as an independent replication. For simplicity, we assume that there is only a single measure of performance, represented by the variable X. Thus, X_j is the estimator of the measure of performance from the jth replication. Then, given the conditions of the replications, the sequence $X_1, X_2, \ldots, X_n$ will be iid random variables. With these iid random variables, we can use classical statistical analysis to construct a $100(1 - \alpha)\%$ confidence interval for $\theta = E(X)$ as follows:

$$\bar{X}(n) \pm t_{(\alpha/2, n-1)} \sqrt{\frac{S^2(n)}{n}}$$

where

$$\bar{X}(n) = \sum_{i=1}^{n} \frac{X_i}{n}$$

$$S^2(n) = \sum_{i=1}^{n} \frac{(X_i - \bar{X}(n))^2}{n - 1}$$

and $t_{(\alpha, n-1)}$ is the number such that for a t-distribution with $n - 1$ degrees of freedom,

$$P(t_{n-1} \geq t_{(\alpha, n-1)}) = \alpha$$

(see Table 13 in Chapter 24). The overall mean $\bar{X}(n)$ is simply the average of the X-values computed over the n samples and can be used as the best estimate of the measure of performance. The quantity $S^2(n)$ is the sample variance.

To illustrate the terminating simulation approach, we use an example from the Cabot, Inc., case. For this illustration, we assume there are 11 terminals in the system, and we perform only 10 independent terminating runs of the simulation model. The terminating event, E, is a fixed time. That is, all 10 simulations are run for the same length of time. The results from these runs are shown in Table 15. The overall average for these 10 runs for the expected number of terminals on-line turns out to be 9.331. (Compare this average with the result in Table 14 of 9.362, which was obtained using the

RUN NUMBER	x_j
1	9.252
2	9.273
3	9.413
4	9.198
5	9.532
6	9.355
7	9.155
8	9.558
9	9.310
10	9.269

Table 15
Sample Averages of
Number of On-Line
Terminals from Ten
Replications

steady-state approach.) If we now calculate the sample variance, we find $S^2(10) = 0.018$. Since $t_{(.025,9)} = 2.26$, we obtain

$$9.331 \pm 2.26 \sqrt{\frac{0.0180}{10}} = 9.331 \pm 0.096$$

as the 95% confidence interval for this sample.

The length of the confidence interval will, of course, depend on how good our sample results are. If this confidence interval is unacceptable, we can reduce the length of the confidence interval by either increasing the number of terminating replications or increasing the length of each simulation. For example, if we increase the number of runs from 10 to 20, we improve the results on two fronts. First, the overall average (9.359) approaches the result from the steady-state simulation; second, the confidence interval length decreases from 0.192 to 0.058. As we saw in this example, the terminating simulation approach offers a relatively easy method for analyzing output data. However, it must be emphasized that other methods for analyzing simulation data may be more efficient for a given problem. For a detailed treatment of this topic, see Banks and Carson (1984) or Law and Kelton (1982).

23-8   SIMULATION LANGUAGES

One of the most important aspects of a simulation study is the computer programming. Writing the computer code for a complex simulation model is often a difficult and arduous task. Because of this, several special-purpose computer simulation languages have been developed to simplify the programming. In this section, we describe several of the best-known and most readily available simulation languages, including GPSS, GASP IV, and SLAM.

Most simulation languages use one of two different modeling approaches or orientations: event scheduling or process interaction. As we have seen, in the event-scheduling approach, we model the system by identifying its characteristic events and writing routines to describe the state changes that take place at the time of each event. The simulation evolves over time by updating the clock to the next scheduled event and making whatever changes are necessary to the system and the statistics by executing the routines. In the process-interaction approach, we model the system as a series of activities that an entity (or a customer) must undertake as it passes through the system. For example, in a queuing simulation, the activities for an entity consist of arriving, waiting in line, getting service, and departing from the system. Thus, using the process-interaction approach, we model these activities instead of events. When programming in a general-purpose language such as FORTRAN or BASIC, we generally use the event-scheduling approach. GPSS uses the process-interaction approach. SLAM allows the modeler to use either approach or even a mixture of the two, whichever is the most appropriate for the model being analyzed.

Of the general-purpose languages, FORTRAN is the most commonly used in simulation. In fact, several simulation languages, including GASP IV and SLAM, use a FORTRAN base. Generally, simulation programs in FORTRAN are written as a series of subroutines, one for each major function of the simulation process. This is particularly true of the FORTRAN-based simulation languages. For example, in GASP IV, there are approximately 30 FORTRAN subroutines and functions. These include a time-advance routine, random variate generation routines, routines to manage the future events list, routines to collect statistics, and so on. In order to use GASP IV, we must provide a main program, an initialization routine, and the event routines. For the rest of the program, we use the GASP routines. Because of these prewritten routines, GASP IV provides a great deal of programming flexibility. For more details of this language, see Pritsker (1974).

GPSS, in contrast to GASP, is a highly structured special-purpose language. It was developed by IBM. GPSS does not require writing a program in the usual sense. The language is made up of about 40 standard statements or blocks. Building a GPSS model then consists of combining these sets of blocks into a flow diagram so that it represents the path an entity takes as it passes through the system. For example, for a single-server queuing system, the statements are of the form GENERATE (arrive in the system), QUEUE (join the waiting line), DEPART (leave the queue to enter service), ADVANCE (advance the clock to account for the service time), RELEASE (release the service facility at the end of service), and TERMINATE (leave the system). The simulation program is then compiled from these statements of the flow diagram. GPSS was designed for relatively easy simulation of queuing systems. However, because of its structure, it is not as flexible as GASP IV, especially for the nonqueuing type of simulations. For a more detailed description of GPSS, see Schriber (1974).

SLAM was developed by Pritsker and Pegden (1979). It allows us to develop simulation models as network models, discrete-event models, continuous models, or any combination of these. The discrete-event orientation is an extension of GASP IV. The network representation can be thought of as a pictorial representation of a system through which entities flow. In this respect, the structure of SLAM is similar to that of GPSS. Once the network model of the system has been developed, it is translated into a set of SLAM program statements for execution on the computer.

The decision of which language to use is one of the most important that a modeler or an analyst must make in performing a simulation study. The simulation languages offer several advantages. The most important of these is that the special-purpose languages provide a natural framework for simulation modeling and most of the features needed in programming a simulation model. However, this must be balanced against the fact that the general-purpose languages allow greater programming flexibility, and that languages like FORTRAN and BASIC are much more widely used and available.

23-9   THE SIMULATION PROCESS

In this chapter, we have considered several simulation models and presented a number of key simulation concepts. We now discuss the process for a complete simulation study and present a systematic approach of carrying out a simulation. A simulation study normally consists of several distinct stages. These are presented in Figure 21. However, not all simulation studies consist of all these stages or follow the order stated here. On the other hand, there may even be considerable overlap between some of these stages.

The initial stage of any scientific study, including a simulation project, requires an explicit statement of the objectives of the study. This should include the questions to be

Figure 21
Steps in a Simulation Study

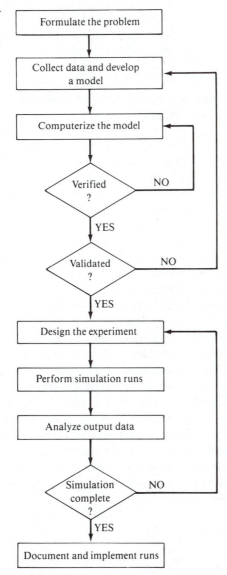

answered, the hypothesis to be tested, and the alternatives to be considered. Without a clear understanding and description of the problem, the chances of successful completion and implementation are greatly diminished. Also in this step, we address issues such as the performance criteria, the model parameters, and the identification and definition of the state variables. It is, of course, very likely that the initial formulation of the problem will undergo many modifications as the study proceeds and as we learn more about the situation being studied. Nevertheless, a clear initial statement of the objectives is essential.

The next stage is the development of the model and the collection of data. The development of the model is probably the most difficult and critical part of a simulation study. Here, we try to represent the essential features of the systems under study by mathematical or logical relations. There are few firm rules to guide an analyst on how to go about this process. In many ways, this is as much an art as a science. However, most experts agree that the best approach is to start with a simple model and make it more detailed and complex as one learns more about the system.

Having developed the model, we next put it into a form in which it can be analyzed on the computer. This usually involves developing a computer program for the model. One of the key decisions here is the choice of the language. As noted earlier, the special-purpose languages require less programming than the general-purpose languages but are less flexible and tend to require longer computer running times. In either case, the programming part of the study is likely to be a time-consuming process, since simulation programs tend to be long and complex. Once the program has been developed and debugged, we determine whether the program is working properly. In other words, is the program doing what it is supposed to do? This process is called the verification step and is usually difficult, since for most simulations, we will not have any results with which to compare the computer output.

If we are satisfied with the program, we now move to the validation stage. This is another critical part of a simulation study. In this step, we validate the model to determine whether it realistically represents the system being analyzed and whether the results from the model will be reliable. As with the verification stage, this is generally a difficult process. Each model presents a different challenge. However, there are some general guidelines that one can follow. For more on these procedures, see Law and Kelton (1982) or Shannon (1979). If we are satisfied at this stage with the performance of the model, we can use the model to conduct the experiments to answer the questions at hand. The data generated by the simulation experiments must be collected, processed, and analyzed. The results are analyzed not only as the solution to the model but also in terms of statistical reliability and validity. Finally, after the results are processed and analyzed, a decision must be made whether to perform any additional experiments.

The primary emphasis in this chapter has been on sampling procedures and model construction. As a result, many topics of the simulation process are either not covered or treated only briefly. However, these are important issues in simulation, and the reader interested in using simulation should consult Law and Kelton (1982), Shannon (1979), or Banks and Carson (1984).

◆ SUMMARY

INTRODUCTION TO SIMULATION

Simulation may be defined as a technique that imitates the operation of a real-world system as it evolves over a period of time. There are two types of simulation models: static and dynamic. A **static simulation model** represents a system at a particular point in time. A **dynamic simulation model** represents a system as it evolves over time. Simulations can be deterministic or stochastic. A **deterministic simulation** contains no random variables, whereas a **stochastic simulation** contains one or more random variables. Finally, simulations may be represented by either discrete or continuous models. A **discrete simulation** is one in which the state variables change only at discrete points in time. In a **continuous simulation**, the state variables change continuously over time. In this chapter, we have dealt only with discrete stochastic models. Such models are called **discrete-event simulation models**.

THE SIMULATION PROCESS

The simulation process consists of several distinct stages. Each study may be somewhat different, but in general, we use the following framework:

1. Formulate the problem.
2. Collect data and develop a model.
3. Computerize the model.
4. Verify the computer model.
5. Validate the simulation model.
6. Design the experiment.
7. Perform the simulation runs.
8. Document and implement.

GENERATING RANDOM VARIABLES

Random variables are represented using probability distributions. The procedure for generating random variables from given probability distributions is known as random variate generation or **Monte Carlo sampling**. The principle of sampling is based on the frequency interpretation of probability and requires a steady stream of random numbers. We generate random numbers for this procedure using congruential methods. The most commonly used of the congruential methods is the **linear congruential method**. Random numbers generated from a linear congruential generator use the following relation:

$$x_{i+1} = (ax_i + c) \text{ modulo } m \qquad (i = 0, 1, 2, \ldots)$$

This gives us the remainder from the division of $(ax_i + c)$ by m. The random numbers are delivered using the relation

$$R_i = \frac{x_i}{m} \qquad (i = 1, 2, 3, \ldots)$$

For discrete distributions, Monte Carlo sampling is achieved by allocating ranges of random numbers according to the probabilities in the distribution. For continuous distributions, we generate random variates using one of several algorithms, including the **inverse transformation method** and the **acceptance-rejection method**. The inverse transformation method requires a cdf in closed form and consists of the following steps:

Step 1 Given a probability density function $f(x)$, develop the cumulative distribution function as

$$F(x) = \int_{-\infty}^{x} f(t)\,dt$$

Step 2 Generate a random number r.

Step 3 Set $F(x) = r$ and solve for x. The variable x is then a random variate from the distribution whose pdf is given by $f(x)$.

The acceptance-rejection method requires the pdf to be defined over a finite interval. Thus, given a probability density function $f(x)$ over the interval $a \leq x \leq b$, we execute the acceptance-rejection algorithm as follows:

Step 1 Select a constant M such that M is the largest value of $f(x)$ over the interval $[a, b]$.

Step 2 Generate two random numbers, r_1 and r_2.

Step 3 Compute $x^* = a + (b - a)r_1$.

Step 4 Evaluate the function $f(x)$ at the point x^*. Let this be $f(x^*)$.

Step 5 If $r_2 < \frac{f(x^*)}{M}$, deliver x^* as a random variate. Otherwise, reject x^* and go back to Step 2.

Between these two methods, it is possible to generate random variates from almost all of the commonly used distributions. The one exception is the normal distribution. For the normal distribution, we generate random variates directly by transforming the random numbers r_1 and r_2 into standardized normal variates, $\mathbf{Z}_1$ and $\mathbf{Z}_2$, using the relations

$$\mathbf{Z}_1 = (-2\ln r_1)^{1/2} \sin 2\pi r_2$$
$$\mathbf{Z}_2 = (-2\ln r_1)^{1/2} \cos 2\pi r_2$$

TYPES OF SIMULATIONS

In discrete-event simulations, we generally simulate using the next-event time-advance approach. In this procedure, the simulation evolves over time by updating the clock to the next scheduled event and taking whatever actions are necessary for each event. The events are scheduled by generating random variates from probability distributions. Data from a simulation can be analyzed using either a terminating simulation approach or a steady-state simulation approach. In terminating simulations, we make n independent replications of the model, using the same initial conditions but running each replication with a different sequence of random numbers. If the measure of performance is represented by the variable X, this approach gives us the estimators $X_1, X_2, \ldots, X_n$ from the n replications. These estimators are used to develop a $100(1 - \alpha)\%$ confidence interval as

$$\bar{X}(n) \pm t_{(\alpha/2, n-1)} \sqrt{\frac{S^2(n)}{n}}$$

for a fixed value of n.

Simulation gives us the flexibility to study systems that are too complex for analytical methods. However, it must be put into proper perspective. Simulation models are time-consuming and costly to construct and run. Additionally, the results may not be very precise and are often hard to validate. Simulation can be a powerful tool, but only if it is used properly.

♦ REVIEW PROBLEMS

GROUP A

1. Use the linear congruential generator to obtain a sequence of 10 random numbers, given that $a = 17$, $c = 43$, $m = 100$, and $x_0 = 31$.

2. A news vendor sells newspapers and tries to maximize profits. The number of papers sold each day is a random variable. However, analysis of the past month's data shows the distribution of daily demand in Table 16. A paper costs the vendor 20¢. The vendor sells the paper for 30¢. Any unsold papers are returned to the publisher for a credit of 10¢. Any unsatisfied demand is estimated to cost 10¢ in goodwill and lost profit. If the policy is to order a quantity equal to the preceding day's demand, determine the average daily profit of the news vendor by simulating this system. Assume that the demand for day 0 is equal to 32.

Table 16

DEMAND PER DAY	PROBABILITY
30	.05
31	.15
32	.22
33	.38
34	.14
35	.06

3. An airport hotel has 100 rooms. On any given night, it takes up to 105 reservations, because of the possibility of no-shows. Past records indicate that the number of daily reservations is uniformly distributed over the integer range [96, 105]. That is, each integer number in this range has an equal probability, .1, of showing up. The no-shows are represented by the distribution in Table 17. Develop a simulation model to find the following measures of per-

Table 17

NUMBER OF NO-SHOWS	PROBABILITY
0	.10
1	.20
2	.25
3	.30
4	.10
5	.05

formance of this booking system: the expected number of rooms used per night and the percentage of nights when more than 100 rooms are claimed.

4. The university library has one copying machine for the students to use. Students arrive at the machine with the distribution of interarrival times shown in Table 18. The time to make a copy is uniformly distributed over the range [16, 25] seconds. Analysis of past data has shown that the number of copies a student makes during a visit has the distribution in Table 19. The librarian feels that under the present system, the lines in front of the copying

Table 18

INTERARRIVAL TIME (Minutes)	PROBABILITY
1	.20
2	.25
3	.40
4	.10
5	.05

Table 19

NUMBER OF COPIES	PROBABILITY
6	.20
7	.25
8	.35
9	.15
10	.05

machine are too long and that the time a student spends in the system (waiting time + service time) is excessive. Develop a simulation model to estimate the average length of the waiting line and the expected waiting time in the system.

5. A salesperson in a large bicycle shop is paid a bonus if he sells more than 4 bicycles a day. The probability of selling more than 4 bicycles a day is only .40. If the number of bicycles sold is greater than 4, the distribution of sales is as shown in Table 20. The shop has four different models of bicycles. The amount of the bonus paid out varies by type. The bonus for model A is $10; 40% of the bicycles sold are of this type. Model B accounts for 35% of the sales and pays a bonus of $15. Model C has a bonus rating of $20 and makes up 20% of the sales. Finally, model D pays a bonus of $25 for each sale but accounts for only 5% of the sales. Develop a simulation model to calculate the bonus a salesperson can expect in a day.

Table 20

NO. OF BICYCLES SOLD	PROBABILITY
5	.35
6	.45
7	.15
8	.05

6. A heart specialist schedules 16 patients each day, 1 every 30 minutes, starting at 9 A.M. Patients are expected to arrive for their appointments at the scheduled times. However, past experience shows that 10% of all patients arrive 15 minutes early, 25% arrive 5 minutes early, 50% arrive exactly on time, 10% arrive 10 minutes late, and 5% arrive 15 minutes late. The time the specialist spends with a patient varies, depending on the type of problem. Analysis of past data shows that the length of appointment has the distribution in Table 21. Develop a simulation model to calculate the average length of the doctor's day.

Table 21

LENGTH OF APPOINTMENT (Minutes)	PROBABILITY
24	.10
27	.20
30	.40
33	.15
36	.10
39	.05

GROUP B

7. Suppose we are considering the selection of the reorder point, R, of a (Q, R) inventory policy. With this policy, we order up to Q when the inventory level falls to R or less. The probability distribution of daily demand is given in Table 22. The lead time is also a random variable and has the distribution in Table 23. We assume that the "order up to" quantity for each order stays the same at 100. Our interest here is to determine the value of the reorder point, R, that minimizes the total variable inventory cost. This variable cost is the sum of the expected inventory carrying cost, the expected ordering cost, and the expected stockout cost. All stockouts are backlogged. That is, a customer waits until an item is available. Inventory carrying cost is

Table 22

DAILY DEMAND (Units)	PROBABILITY
12	.05
13	.15
14	.25
15	.35
16	.15
17	.05

Table 23

LEAD TIME (Days)	PROBABILITY
1	.20
2	.30
3	.35
4	.15

estimated to be \$0.20/unit/day and is charged on the units in inventory at the end of a day. A stockout costs \$1 for every unit short. The cost of ordering is \$10 per order. Orders arrive at the beginning of a day. Develop a simulation model to simulate this inventory system to find the best value of R.

8. A large car dealership in Bloomington, Indiana, employs 5 salespeople. All salespeople work on commission. That is, they are paid a percentage of the profits from the cars they sell. The dealership has 3 types of cars: luxury, midsize, and subcompact. Data from the past few years show that the car sales per week per salesperson have the distribution in Table 24. If the car sold is a subcompact, a salesperson is given a commission of \$250. For a midsize car, a salesperson makes a commission of either \$400 or \$500, depending on the model sold. On the midsize cars, a commission of \$400 is paid out 40% of the time and \$500 is paid out the other 60% of the time. For a luxury car, commission is paid out according to three separate rates: \$1000 with a probability of 35%, \$1500 with a probability of 40%, and \$2000 with a probability of 25%. If the distribution of type of cars sold is as shown in Table 25, what is the average commission for a salesperson in a week?

Table 24

NO. OF CARS SOLD	PROBABILITY
0	.10
1	.15
2	.20
3	.25
4	.20
5	.10

Table 25

TYPE OF CAR SOLD	PROBABILITY
Subcompact	.40
Midsize	.35
Luxury	.25

9. Consider a bank with 4 tellers. Customers arrive at an exponential rate of 60 per hour. A customer goes directly into service if a teller is idle. Otherwise, the arrival joins a waiting line. There is only one waiting line for all the tellers. If an arrival finds the line too long, he or she may decide to leave immediately (reneging). The probability of a customer reneging is shown in Table 26. If a customer joins the waiting line, we assume that he or she will stay in the system until served. Each teller serves at the same service rate. Service times are uniformly distributed over the range [3, 5]. Develop a simulation model to find the following measues of performance for this system: (1) the expected time a customer spends in the system, (2) the percentage of customers who renege, and (3) the percentage of idle time for each teller.

Table 26

LENGTH OF QUEUE (q)	PROBABILITY OF RENEGING
$6 \leq q \leq 8$	.20
$9 \leq q \leq 10$	.40
$11 \leq q \leq 14$	.60
$q > 14$	.80

10. Jobs arrive at a workshop, which has two work centers (A and B) in series, at an exponential rate of 5 per hour. Each job requires processing at both these work centers, first on A and then on B. Jobs waiting to be processed at each center can wait in line; the line in front of work center A has unlimited space, and the line in front of center B has space for only 4 jobs at a time. If this space reaches its capacity, jobs cannot leave center A. In other words, center A stops processing until space becomes available in front of B. The processing time for a job at center A is uniformly distributed over the range [6, 10]. The processing time for a job at center B is represented by the following triangular distribution:

$$f(x) = \begin{cases} \frac{1}{4}(x - 1) & 1 \leq x \leq 3 \\ \frac{1}{4}(5 - x) & 3 \leq x \leq 5 \end{cases}$$

Develop a simulation model of this system to determine the following measures of performance: (1) the expected number of jobs in the workshop at any given time, (2) the percentage of time center A is shut down because of shortage of queuing space in front of center B, and (3) the expected completion time of a job.

◆ REFERENCES

There are several outstanding books on simulation. For a beginning book, we recommend Watson (1981); for an intermediate approach, Banks and Carson (1984); and for a more advanced treatment, Law and Kelton (1982).

BANKS, J., and J. CARSON. *Discrete-Event System Simulation.* Englewood Cliffs, N.J.: Prentice-Hall, 1984.

BOX, G., and M. MULLER. "A Note on the Generation of Random Normal Deviates," *Annals of Mathematical Statistics* 29(1958):610–611.

FISHMAN, G. *Principles of Discrete Event Simulation.* New York: Wiley, 1978.

KNUTH, D.W. *The Art of Computer Programming. II. Seminumerical Algorithms.* Reading, Mass.: Addison-Wesley, 1969.

LAW, A.M., and W. KELTON. *Simulation Modeling and Analysis.* New York: McGraw-Hill, 1982.

PRITSKER, A. *The GASP IV Simulation Language.* New York: Wiley, 1974.

PRITSKER, A., and C. PEGDEN. *Introduction to Simulation and SLAM.* New York: Wiley, 1979.

SCHMIDT, J.W., and R.E. TAYLOR. *Simulation and Analysis of Industrial Systems.* Homewood, Ill.: Irwin, 1970.

SCHRIBER, T. *Simulation Using GPSS.* New York: Wiley, 1974.

SHANNON, R. E. *Systems Simulation: The Art and Science.* Englewood Cliffs, N.J.: Prentice-Hall, 1979.

WATSON, H. *Computer Simulation in Business.* New York: Wiley, 1981.

24

Forecasting Models

IN PREVIOUS CHAPTERS, we have often blindly substituted numbers into problems without considering where the numbers came from. For example, in the Giapetto LP (Example 1 in Chapter 3), we assumed that the variable cost of producing a train was $21. In reality, we would have to estimate the cost of producing a train. This can be done using the method of *simple linear regression*, explained in Section 24.6.

In Chapters 16–18 we used inventory theory to determine production quantities and reorder points. To use the models of Chapters 16–18, we need to be able to forecast the demand for a product. In Sections 24.1–24.5, we discuss extrapolation and smoothing methods that can be used to forecast future demand for a product.

As another example of how we can use "good forecasts," suppose that we want to use the queuing models of Chapter 22 to determine how the number of tellers at a bank should vary with the day of the week and the time of day. To tackle this problem, we need to determine how the rate at which customers enter the bank depends on the time of day and the day of the week. For example, if we knew that over half the bank's customers arrived during the lunch hour (noon to 1 P.M.), that would have a significant effect on the optimal staffing policy.

In this chapter, we discuss two important types of forecasting methods: extrapolation methods and causal forecasting methods. In Sections 24.1–24.5, we discuss *extrapolation methods*, which are used to forecast future values of a time series from past values of a time series. To illustrate, consider Lowland Appliance Company's monthly sales of TVs, compact disc players (CDs), and air conditioners (ACs) for the last 24 months, given in Table 1. In an extrapolation forecasting method, it is assumed that past patterns and trends in sales will continue in future months. Thus, past data on appliance sales (and no other information) are used to generate forecasts for appliance sales during future months. Extrapolation methods (unlike the causal forecasting methods described in Sections 24.6–24.8) don't take into account what "caused" past data; they simply assume that past trends and patterns will continue in the future.

Causal forecasting methods attempt to forecast future values of a variable (called the dependent variable) by using past data to estimate the relationship between the dependent variable and one or more independent variables. For example, Lowland might try to forecast future monthly sales of air conditioners by using past data to

1163

Table 1   Lowland Appliance Sales

MONTH	TV SALES	CD SALES	AC SALES	MONTH	TV SALES	CD SALES	AC SALES
1	30	40	13	13	38	79	36
2	32	47	7	14	30	82	21
3	30	50	23	15	35	80	47
4	39	49	32	16	30	85	81
5	33	56	58	17	34	94	112
6	34	53	60	18	40	89	139
7	34	55	90	19	36	96	230
8	38	63	93	20	32	100	201
9	36	68	63	21	40	100	122
10	39	65	39	22	36	105	84
11	30	72	37	23	40	108	74
12	36	69	29	24	34	110	62

determine how air conditioner sales are related to independent variables such as price, advertising, and the month of the year. Causal forecasting methods will be discussed in Sections 24.6–24.8.

24-1   MOVING-AVERAGE FORECASTING METHODS

Let $x_1, x_2, \ldots, x_t, \ldots$ be observed values of a time series, where x_t is the value of the time series observed during period t. One of the most commonly used forecasting methods is the moving-average method. We define $f_{t,1}$ to be the forecast for period $t + 1$ made after observing x_t. For the moving-average method,

$$f_{t,1} = \text{average of the last } N \text{ observations}$$
$$= \text{average of } x_t, x_{t-1}, x_{t-2}, \ldots, x_{t-N+1}$$

where N is a given parameter.

To illustrate the use of the moving-average method, we choose $N = 3$ and use the moving-average method to forecast TV sales for the first six months of data in Table 1. The resulting computations are given in Table 2. For months 1–3, we have not yet observed three months of data, so (for $N = 3$) we cannot develop a moving-average fore-

Table 2	MONTH	ACTUAL SALES	PREDICTED SALES
Moving-Average Forecasts ($N = 3$) for TV Sales	1	30	—
	2	32	—
	3	30	—
	4	39	$\frac{30 + 32 + 30}{3}$
	5	33	$\frac{32 + 30 + 39}{3}$
	6	34	$\frac{30 + 39 + 33}{3}$

cast for sales for these months. For month 4, we find our forecast, $f_{3,1} = \frac{30 + 32 + 30}{3} = 30.67$. For month 5, our forecast is $f_{4,1} = \frac{32 + 30 + 39}{3} = 33.67$. For month 6, our forecast is $f_{5,1} = \frac{30 + 39 + 33}{3} = 34$.

Note that from one period to the next, our forecast "moves" by replacing the "oldest" observation in the average by the most recent observation.

CHOICE OF N

How should we choose N, the number of periods used to compute the moving average? To answer this question, we need to define a measure of forecast accuracy. We will use the **mean absolute deviation** (MAD) as our measure of forecast accuracy. Before defining the MAD, we need to define the concept of a **forecast error**. Given a forecast for x_t, we define e_t to be the error in our forecast for x_t, to be given by

$$e_t = x_t - (\text{forecast for } x_t)$$

From Table 2, we find $e_4 = 39 - 30.67 = 8.33$, $e_5 = 33 - 33.67 = -0.67$, and $e_6 = 34 - 34 = 0$. The MAD is simply the average of the absolute values of all the e_t's. Thus, for periods 1–6, our moving-average forecast yields a MAD given by

$$\text{MAD} = \frac{|e_4| + |e_5| + |e_6|}{3} = \frac{8.33 + 0.67 + 0}{3} = 3$$

Thus, on the average, our forecasts for TV sales are off by 3 TVs per month.

It seems reasonable to choose a value of N that minimizes the MAD. If we apply the moving-average technique to all 24 months of TV sales from Table 1, we find the MADs in Table 3. Thus, a 3- or 4-period moving average appears to yield the best forecasts for TV sales.

Table 3
MADs for Moving-Average Forecasts of TV Sales

N	MAD
2	3.21
3	2.78
4	2.79
5	2.99
6	3.27

Moving-average forecasts perform well for a time series that fluctuates about a constant **base level**. From Figure 1, it appears that monthly TV sales fluctuate about a base level of 35. More formally, moving-average forecasts work well if

$$x_t = b + \varepsilon_t \tag{1}$$

where b is the base level for the series and ε_t is the random fluctuation in period t about the base level.

From Figures 2 and 3, we see that sales of CDs and air conditioners are not well described in Eq. (1). From Figure 2, we see that there is an upward **trend** in CD sales, so CD sales do not fluctuate about a base level. From Figure 3, we find that air conditioner sales exhibit **seasonality**: The peaks and valleys of the series repeat at regular 12-month intervals. Figure 3 also shows that air conditioner sales exhibit an upward

Figure 1
TV Sales

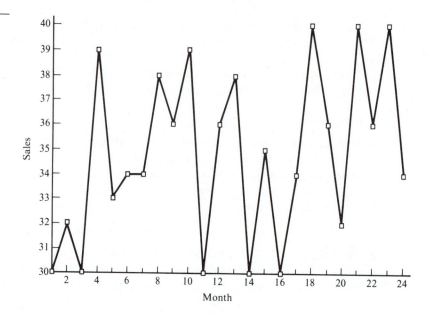

Figure 2
CD Sales

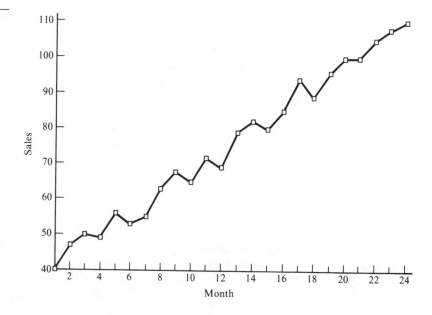

trend. In situations where trend and/or seasonality are present, the moving-average method usually yields poor forecasts. To close this section, we note that in addition to trend and seasonality, a time series may exhibit **cyclic behavior**. For example, auto sales often follow the business cycle of the national economy. Cyclic behavior is much more irregular than a seasonal pattern and is often hard to detect.

Figure 3
Air Conditioner
Sales

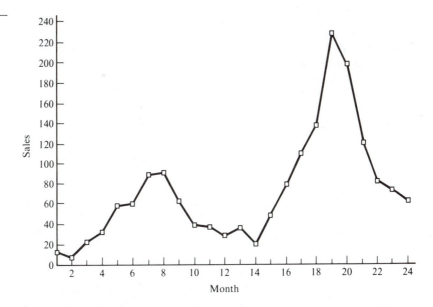

SIMPLE EXPONENTIAL SMOOTHING

If a time series fluctuates about a base level, **simple exponential smoothing** may be used to obtain good forecasts for future values of the series. To describe simple exponential smoothing, let A_t = smoothed average of a time series after observing x_t. After observing x_t, A_t is the forecast for the value of the time series during any future period. The key equation in simple exponential smoothing is

$$A_t = \alpha x_t + (1 - \alpha)A_{t-1} \tag{2}$$

In (2), α is a **smoothing constant** that satisfies $0 < \alpha < 1$. To initialize the forecasting procedure, we must have (before observing x_1) a value for A_0. Usually, we let A_0 be the observed value for the period immediately preceding period 1. As with moving-average forecasts, we let $f_{t,k}$ be the forecast for x_{t+k} made at the end of period t. Then

$$A_t = f_{t,k} \tag{3}$$

Assuming that we are trying to forecast one period ahead, our error for predicting x_t (written again as e_t) is given by

$$e_t = x_t - f_{t-1,1} = x_t - A_{t-1} \tag{4}$$

To understand (2) better, we use (4) to rewrite (2) as

$$A_t = A_{t-1} + \alpha(x_t - A_{t-1}) = A_{t-1} + \alpha e_t$$

Thus, our new forecast $A_t = f_{t,1}$ is equal to our old forecast (A_{t-1}) plus a fraction of our period t error (e_t). This implies that if we "overpredict" x_t, we lower our forecast, and if we "underpredict" x_t, we raise our forecast. For larger values of the smoothing constant α, more weight is given to the most recent observation (see Remark (3) at the end of the section).

We illustrate simple exponential smoothing (with $\alpha = 0.1$) for the first six months of TV sales. The results are given in Table 4. We assume that 32 TVs were sold last month, so we initialize the procedure with $A_0 = 32$. Here are some illustrations of the computations:

$$A_1 = 0.1x_1 + 0.9A_0 = 0.1(30) + 0.9(32) = 31.8$$
$$f_{0,1} = A_0 = 32$$
$$e_1 = x_1 - A_0 = 30 - 32 = -2$$
$$f_{1,1} = A_1 = 31.8$$
$$e_2 = x_2 - A_1 = 32 - 31.8 = 0.2$$
$$A_2 = 0.1x_2 + 0.9A_1 = 0.1(32) + 0.9(31.8) = 31.82.$$

For months 1–6, the MAD of our forecast is given by

$$\text{MAD} = \frac{|-2| + |0.2| + |-1.82| + |7.36| + |0.63| + |1.56|}{6}$$

$$= 2.26$$

For the entire 24-month period, we can determine (using a spreadsheet) the value of α yielding the lowest MAD. The results are given in Table 5. It appears that a value of α between 0.20 and 0.25 yields the lowest MAD.

	MONTH	ACTUAL SALES	FORECAST	A_t	e_t
Table 4 Simple Exponential Smoothing for TV Sales ($\alpha = .1$)	1	30	32	31.8	−2.00
	2	32	31.8	31.82	0.20
	3	30	31.82	31.64	−1.82
	4	39	31.64	32.37	7.36
	5	33	32.37	32.44	0.63
	6	34	32.44	32.60	1.56

	α	MAD
Table 5 MAD for TV Sales	0.05	3.20
	0.10	3.04
	0.15	2.94
	0.20	2.89
	0.25	2.88
	0.30	2.90
	0.35	2.94
	0.40	2.98
	0.45	3.05
	0.50	3.13

REMARKS   1. Since $\alpha < 1$, exponential smoothing "smooths out" variations in a time series by not giving total weight to the last observation.

2. If $\alpha = \frac{2}{N+1}$, simple exponential smoothing (with smoothing parameter α) and an N-period moving-average forecast will both yield similar forecasts. For example, $\alpha = 0.33$ is roughly equivalent to a five-period moving average.

3. To see why we call the method *exponential* smoothing, consider (2) for $t - 1$:

$$A_{t-1} = \alpha x_{t-1} + (1 - \alpha)A_{t-2} \qquad (5)$$

Substituting (5) into (2) yields

$$\begin{aligned} A_t &= \alpha x_t + (1 - \alpha)[\alpha x_{t-1} + (1 - \alpha)A_{t-2}] \\ &= \alpha x_t + \alpha(1 - \alpha)x_{t-1} + (1 - \alpha)^2 A_{t-2} \end{aligned} \qquad (6)$$

Note that

$$A_{t-2} = \alpha x_{t-2} + (1 - \alpha)A_{t-3} \qquad (7)$$

Substituting (7) into (6) yields

$$A_t = \alpha x_t + \alpha(1 - \alpha)x_{t-1} + \alpha(1 - \alpha)^2 x_{t-2} + (1 - \alpha)^3 A_{t-3}$$

Repeating this process yields

$$A_t = \alpha x_t + \alpha(1 - \alpha)x_{t-1} + \alpha(1 - \alpha)^2 x_{t-2} + \cdots + \alpha(1 - \alpha)^k x_{t-k} + \cdots \qquad (8)$$

Since $\alpha + \alpha(1 - \alpha) + \alpha(1 - \alpha)^2 + \cdots = 1$, Eq. (8) shows that if we go back an "infinite" number of periods, our current smoothed average is a weighted average of all past observations. The weight given to the observation from k periods in the past declines exponentially (by a factor of $1 - \alpha$). The larger the value of α, the more weight is given to the most recent observations. For example, for $\alpha = 0.2$, the three most recent observations have 49% of the weight (20%, 16%, and 13%), whereas for $\alpha = 0.5$, the three most recent observations have 88% of the weight (50%, 25%, and 13%).

4. In practice, α is usually chosen to equal 0.10, 0.30, or 0.50. If the value of α that minimizes the MAD exceeds 0.5, then trend, seasonality, or cyclical variation is probably present, and simple exponential smoothing is not a recommended forecast technique. In such cases, better forecasts will probably be provided by either Holt's method (exponential smoothing with trend, discussed in Section 24.3) or Winter's method (exponential smoothing with trend and seasonality, discussed in Section 24.4).

5. Even if a time series is not fluctuating about a constant base level, simple exponential smoothing may still provide good forecasts. If $x_t = m_t + \varepsilon_t$ and $m_t = m_{t-1} + \delta_t$, where ε_t and δ_t are independent error terms each having mean 0, then simple exponential smoothing will provide good forecasts. This implies that if the mean demand (m_t) for a product is randomly shifting over time, simple exponential smoothing will still provide good forecasts of product demand.

24-3 HOLT'S METHOD: EXPONENTIAL SMOOTHING WITH TREND

If we believe that a time series exhibits a linear trend (and no seasonality), **Holt's method** often yields good forecasts. At the end of the tth period, Holt's method yields an estimate of the base level (L_t) and the per-period trend (T_t) of the series. For example, suppose that $L_{20} = 20$ and $T_{20} = 2$. This means that after observing x_{20}, we believe that the base level of the series is 20 and that the base level is increasing by two units per period. Thus, five periods from now, we estimate that the base level of the series will equal 30.

After observing x_t, equations (9) and (10) are used to update the base and trend estimates. α and β are smoothing constants, each between 0 and 1.

$$L_t = \alpha x_t + (1 - \alpha)(L_{t-1} + T_{t-1}) \qquad (9)$$

$$T_t = \beta(L_t - L_{t-1}) + (1 - \beta)T_{t-1} \qquad (10)$$

To compute L_t, we take a weighted average of the following two quantities:

1. x_t, which is an estimate of the period t base level from the current period.

2. $L_{t-1} + T_{t-1}$, which is an estimate of the period t base level based on previous data

To compute T_t, we take a weighted average of the following two quantities:

1. An estimate of trend from the current period given by the increase in the smoothed base from period $t - 1$ to period t

2. T_{t-1}, which is our previous estimate of the trend

As before, we define $f_{t,k}$ to be the forecast for x_{t+k} made at the end of period t. Then

$$f_{t,k} = L_t + kT_t \qquad (11)$$

To initialize Holt's method, we need an initial estimate (call it L_0) of the base and an initial estimate (call it T_0) of the trend. We might set T_0 equal to the average monthly increase in the time series during the previous year, and we might set L_0 equal to last month's observation.

From Figure 2, it is clear that CD sales exhibit an upward trend, but no obvious seasonal pattern is present. Therefore, Holt's method should yield good forecasts. Let's assume that CD sales during each of the last twelve months are given by 4, 6, 8, 10, 14, 18, 20, 22, 24, 28, 31, and 34. Then

$$T_0 = \frac{(6 - 4) + (8 - 6) + (10 - 8) + \cdots + (34 - 31)}{11}$$

$$= \frac{34 - 4}{11} = 2.73$$

We then estimate $L_0 = 34$.

Applying the Holt method to the first six months of CD sales (using $\alpha = 0.30$ and $\beta = 0.10$) we obtain the results shown in Table 6. Here are some illustrations of the calculations:

$$L_1 = 0.30x_1 + 0.70(L_0 + T_0) = 0.3(40) + 0.7(34 + 2.73) = 37.71$$
$$T_1 = 0.1(L_1 - L_0) + 0.9T_0 = 0.1(37.71 - 34) + 0.9(2.73) = 2.83$$
$$f_{1,1} = L_1 + T_1 = 37.71 + 2.83 = 40.54$$
$$e_2 = x_2 - f_{1,1} = 47 - 40.54 = 6.46$$

For the first six months of CD sales, we find

Table 6
Holt's Method for CD Sales ($\alpha = 0.30$, $\beta = 0.10$)

MONTH	SALES	L_t	T_t	$f_{t-1,1}$ $(L_{t-1} + T_{t-1})$	e_t $(x_t - f_{t-1,1})$
1	40	37.71	2.83	36.73	3.27
2	47	42.48	3.02	40.54	6.46
3	50	46.85	3.16	45.50	4.50
4	49	49.70	3.13	50.01	−1.01
5	56	53.78	3.22	52.83	3.17
6	53	55.80	3.10	57.00	−4.00

$$\text{MAD} = \frac{3.27 + 6.46 + 4.5 + 1.01 + 3.17 + 4.00}{6} = 3.74$$

For the entire 24-month period, we find MAD = 2.85.

As one more illustration of Eq. (11), suppose that we want to make a forecast at the end of month 6 for month 10 CD sales. From (11), we find that $f_{6,4} = L_6 + 4T_6 = 55.80 + 4(3.10) = 68.2$. By trying various combinations of α and β, we could find the values of α and β that minimize the MAD. If these values of α and β are not both less than 0.5, then seasonality or cyclical behavior is probably present, and another forecasting method should be used.

In summary, Holt's method will provide good forecasts for a series with a linear trend. Such a series may be modeled as $x_t = a + bt + \varepsilon_t$, where

$$a = \text{base level at beginning of period 1}$$
$$b = \text{per-period trend}$$
$$\varepsilon_t = \text{error term for period } t$$

A multiplicative version of Holt's method (see Problem 15) can be used to generate good forecasts for a series of the form $x_t = ab^t\varepsilon_t$. Here, the value of b represents the percentage growth in the base level of the series during each period. Thus, $b = 1.1$ implies that the base level of the series is increasing by 10% per period. In this model, ε_t is a random error factor with a mean of 1.

24-4   WINTER'S METHOD: EXPONENTIAL SMOOTHING WITH SEASONALITY

The appropriately named **Winter's method** is used to forecast time series for which trend and seasonality are present. As previously mentioned, Figure 3 shows that air conditioner sales exhibit an upward trend and seasonality, so Winter's method is a logical candidate for forecasting these sales.

To describe Winter's method, we require two definitions. Let $c = $ the number of periods in the length of the seasonal pattern ($c = 4$ for quarterly data, and $c = 12$ for monthly data). Let s_t be an estimate of a seasonal multiplicative factor for month t, obtained after observing x_t. For instance, suppose month 7 is July and $s_7 = 2$. Then after observing month 7's air conditioner sales, we believe that July air conditioner sales will (all other things being equal) equal twice the sales expected during an average month. If month 24 is December, and $s_{24} = 0.4$, then after observing month 24 sales, we predict that December air conditioner sales will be 40% of the expected sales during an average month. In what follows, L_t and T_t have the same meaning as they did in Holt's method. Each period, L_t, T_t, and s_t are updated (in that order) by using the equations (12)–(14). Again, α, β, and γ are smoothing constants, each of which is between 0 and 1.

$$L_t = \alpha \frac{x_t}{s_{t-c}} + (1 - \alpha)(L_{t-1} + T_{t-1}) \tag{12}$$

$$T_t = \beta(L_t - L_{t-1}) + (1 - \beta)T_{t-1} \tag{13}$$

$$s_t = \gamma \frac{x_t}{L_t} + (1 - \gamma)s_{t-c} \tag{14}$$

Equation (12) updates the estimate of the series base by taking a weighted average of the following two quantities:

1. $L_{t-1} + T_{t-1}$, which is our base level estimate before observing x_t

2. The deseasonalized observation $\dfrac{x_t}{s_{t-c}}$, which is an estimate of the base obtained from the current period

Equation (13) is identical to the T_t equation (10) used to update trend in the Holt method.

Equation (14) updates the estimate of month t's seasonality by taking a weighted average of the following two quantities:

1. Our most recent estimate of month t's seasonality (s_{t-c})

2. $\dfrac{x_t}{L_t}$, which is an estimate of month t's seasonality, obtained from the current month

At the end of period t, the forecast ($f_{t,k}$) for month $t + k$ is given by

$$f_{t,k} = (L_t + kT_t)s_{t+k-c} \tag{15}$$

Thus, to forecast the value of the series during period $t + k$, we multiply our estimate of the period $t + k$ base ($L_t + kT_t$) by our most recent estimate of month ($t + k$)'s seasonality factor (s_{t+k-c}).

INITIALIZATION OF WINTER'S METHOD

To obtain good forecasts with Winter's method, we must obtain good initial estimates of base, trend, and all seasonal factors. Let

$$
\begin{aligned}
L_0 &= \text{estimate of base at beginning of month 1} \\
T_0 &= \text{estimate of trend at beginning of month 1} \\
s_{-11} &= \text{estimate of January seasonal factor at beginning of month 1} \\
s_{-10} &= \text{estimate of February seasonal factor at beginning of month 1} \\
&\vdots \\
s_0 &= \text{estimate of December seasonal factor at beginning of month 1}
\end{aligned}
\tag{16}
$$

A variety of methods are available to estimate the parameters in (16). We choose a simple method that requires two years of data. Suppose that the last two years of sales (by month) were as follows:

$$
\begin{aligned}
&\text{Year } -2: \quad 4, 3, 10, 14, 25, 26, 38, 40, 28, 17, 16, 13 \\
&\text{Year } -1: \quad 9, 6, 18, 27, 48, 50, 75, 77, 52, 33, 31, 24 \\
&\text{Total sales during year } -2 = 234 \\
&\text{Total sales during year } -1 = 450
\end{aligned}
$$

We estimate T_0 by

$$T_0 = \frac{(\text{Average monthly sales during year} - 1) - (\text{Average monthly sales during year} - 2)}{12}$$

or

$$T_0 = \frac{\frac{450}{12} - \frac{234}{12}}{12} = 1.5$$

To estimate L_0, we first determine the average monthly demand during year -1 ($\frac{450}{12}$). This estimates the base at the middle of year -1 (month 6.5 of year -1). To bring this estimate to the end of month 12 of year -1, we add $(12 - 6.5)T_0 = 5.5T_0$. Thus, our estimate of $L_0 = 37.5 + 5.5(1.5) = 45.75$.

To estimate the seasonality factor for a given month (say, January $= s_{-11}$), we take an estimate of January seasonality for year -2 and year -1 and average them. In year -2, average monthly demand was $\frac{234}{12} = 19.5$; in January of year -2, 4 air conditioners were sold. Therefore,

$$\text{Year} -2 \text{ estimate of January seasonality} = \frac{4}{19.5} = 0.205$$

Similarly,

$$\text{Year} -1 \text{ estimate of January seasonality} = \frac{9}{37.5} = 0.240$$

Finally, we obtain $s_{-11} = \frac{0.205 + 0.24}{2} = 0.22$. In similar fashion, we obtain

$$s_{-10} = 0.16, \quad s_{-9} = 0.50, \quad s_{-8} = 0.72, \quad s_{-7} = 1.28, \quad s_{-6} = 1.33,$$

$$s_{-5} = 1.97, \quad s_{-4} = 2.05, \quad s_{-3} = 1.41, \quad s_{-2} = 0.88, \quad s_{-1} = 0.82, \quad s_0 = 0.65$$

As a check, initial seasonal factor estimates should average to 1.

Before showing how (12)–(14) are used, we demonstrate how to use (15) for forecasting. At the beginning of month 1, our forecast for month 1 air conditioner sales is

$$f_{0,1} = (L_0 + T_0)s_{0+1-12} = (45.75 + 1.5)0.22 = 10.40$$

At the beginning of month 1, our forecast for month 7 air conditioner sales is

$$f_{0,7} = (L_0 + 7T_0)s_{0+7-12} = (45.75 + 7(1.5))1.97 = 110.81$$

For $\alpha = 0.5, \beta = 0.4, \gamma = 0.6$, applying Winter's method to the first twelve months of air conditioner sales data yields the results in Table 7.

Table 7	MONTH	SALES	L_t	T_t	s_t	$f_{t-1,1}$	ERROR
Winter's Method for	1	13	53.17	3.87	0.23	10.40	2.60
Air Conditioners	2	7	50.39	1.21	0.15	9.13	−2.13
($\alpha = 0.5, \beta = 0.4,$	3	23	48.80	0.09	0.48	25.80	−2.80
$\gamma = 0.6$)	4	32	46.67	−0.80	0.70	35.20	−3.20
	5	58	45.59	−0.91	1.28	58.71	−0.71
	6	60	44.90	−0.82	1.33	59.42	0.58
	7	90	44.88	−0.50	1.99	86.82	3.18
	8	93	44.87	−0.30	2.06	90.97	2.03
	9	63	44.62	−0.28	1.41	62.84	0.16
	10	39	44.33	−0.29	0.88	39.02	−0.02
	11	37	44.58	−0.07	0.83	36.12	0.88
	12	29	44.56	−0.05	0.65	28.93	0.07

We illustrate the computations by computing L_1, T_1, and s_1.

$$L_1 = 0.5\left(\frac{x_1}{s_{-11}}\right) + 0.5(L_0 + T_0) = 0.5\left(\frac{13}{0.22}\right) + 0.5(45.75 + 1.5) = 53.17$$

$$T_1 = 0.4(L_1 - L_0) + 0.6T_0 = 0.4(53.17 - 45.75) + 0.6(1.5) = 3.87$$

$$s_1 = 0.6\left(\frac{x_1}{L_1}\right) + 0.4s_{-11} = 0.6\left(\frac{13}{53.17}\right) + 0.4(0.22) = 0.23$$

Thus, at the end of month 1, our forecast for (say) month 7 air conditioner sales is $f_{1,6} = (L_1 + 6T_1)s_{1+6-12} = (53.17 + 6(3.87))1.97 = 150.49$. Our forecast for month 7 at the end of month 1 exceeds the forecast for month 7 made at the beginning of month 1, because month 1 sales were higher than predicted.

For all 24 months of data, spreadsheet calculations show that MAD $= 10.48$.

R E M A R K S   **1.** Since Winter's method uses three smoothing constants, it is quite a chore to find the combination of α, β, and γ values that yields the smallest MAD.

2. Although the values of α and β that minimize MAD should not exceed 0.5 (as in the Holt method), it is not uncommon for the best value of γ to exceed 0.5. This is because for monthly data, each monthly seasonal factor is updated during only $\frac{1}{12}$ of all periods. Since the seasonality factors are updated so infrequently, we may need to give more weight to each observation, so $\gamma > 0.5$ is not out of the question.

3. Figure 4 shows how well forecasts of air conditioner sales (for $\alpha = 0.5$, $\beta = 0.4$, and $\gamma = 0.6$) compare to actual air conditioner sales. The agreement between predicted and actual sales is quite good except during months 15 and 17. During these months, our forecasts are much too high. Perhaps new salesmen were hired during these two months, causing sales to be less than anticipated.

Figure 4
Air Conditioner
Sales Predictions

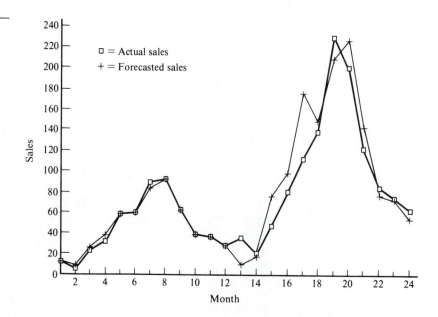

FORECASTING ACCURACY

For any forecasting model in which forecast errors are normally distributed, we may use MAD to estimate s_e = standard deviation of our forecast errors. The relationship between MAD and s_e is given in formula (17).

$$s_e = 1.25 \text{ MAD} \tag{17}$$

Assuming that errors are normally distributed, we know that approximately 68% of our predictions should be within s_e of the actual value, and approximately 95% of our predictions should be within $2s_e$ of the actual value. Thus, for our air conditioner sales predictions, we find that $s_e = 1.25(10.48) = 13.10$. So we would expect that for about $0.68(24) = 16$ of 24 months, our predictions for sales would be off by at most 13.10 air conditioners, and for $0.95(24) = 23$ of 24 months, our predictions would be off by at most $2(13.10) = 26.2$ air conditioners. Actually, our predictions for air conditioner sales are accurate within 13.10 during 17 months and accurate within 26.2 during 22 months.

We note that in most situations where a forecast is required, knowing something about the probable accuracy of the forecast is almost as important as the actual forecast. Thus, this short subsection is very important!

◆ PROBLEMS

GROUP A

1. Simple exponential smoothing (with $\alpha = 0.2$) is being used to forecast monthly beer sales at Gordon's liquor store. After observing April's demand, the predicted demand for May is 4000 cans of beer.

(a) At the beginning of May, what is the prediction for July's beer sales?

(b) Actual demand during May and June is as follows: May—4500 cans of beer; June—3500 cans of beer. After observing June's demand, what is the forecast for July's demand?

(c) The demand during May and June averages out to $\frac{4500 + 3500}{2} = 4000$ cans per month. This is the same as the forecast for monthly sales before we observed the May and June data. Yet after observing the May and June demands for beer, our forecast for July demand has decreased from what it was at the end of April. Why?

2. We are predicting quarterly sales for soda at Gordon's Liquor Store using Winter's method. We are given the following information:

Seasonality factors: fall = 0.8   spring = 1.2

winter = 0.7   summer = 1.3

Current base estimate = 400 cases per quarter

Current trend estimate = 40 cases per quarter

$\alpha = 0.2$ $\beta = 0.3$ $\gamma = 0.5$

Now sales of 650 cases during the summer quarter are observed.

(a) Use this information to update the estimates of base, trend, and seasonality.

(b) After observing the summer demand, forecast demand for the fall quarter and the winter quarter.

3. We are using Winter's method and monthly data to forecast the GNP. (All numbers are in billions of dollars.) At the end of January, 1992, $L_t = 600$ and $T_t = 5$. We are given the following seasonalities: January—0.80, February—0.85, December—1.2. During February, 1992, the GNP is at a level of 630. At the end of February, 1992, what is the forecast for the December, 1992 level of the GNP? Use $\alpha = \beta = \gamma = 0.5$.

4. We are using the Holt method to predict monthly VCR sales at Highland Appliance. At the end of October, 1992, $L_t = 200$ and $T_t = 10$. During November, 1992, 230 VCRs are sold. At the end of November, 1992, MAD = 25. At the end of November, 1992, we are 95% sure that VCR sales for December, 1992 will be between ____ and ____. Use $\alpha = \beta = 0.5$.

5. We are using simple exponential smoothing to predict monthly electric shaver sales at Hook's Drug Store. At the end of October, 1992, our forecast for December, 1992 sales was 40. In November, 1992, 50 shavers were sold, and during December, 1992, 45 shavers were sold. Suppose

$\alpha = 0.50$. At the end of December, 1992, what is our prediction for the total number of shavers that will be sold during March and April of 1993?

6. We are using simple exponential smoothing to predict monthly auto sales at Bloomington Ford. The company believes that sales do not exhibit trend or seasonality, so simple exponential smoothing has yielded satisfactory forecasts for the most part. Each March, however, Bloomington Ford has observed that sales tend to exceed the simple exponential smoothing forecast (A_{Feb}) by 200. Suppose that at the end of February, 1993, $A_t = 600$. During March, 1993, 900 cars are sold.
(a) Using $\alpha = 0.3$, determine (at the end of March, 1993) a forecast for April, 1993 car sales.
(b) Assume that at the end of March, MAD $= 60$. We are 95% sure that April sales will be between ____ and ____.

7. The University Credit Union is open Monday through Saturday. Winter's method is being used (with $\alpha = \beta = \gamma = 0.5$) to predict the number of customers entering the bank each day. After incorporating the arrivals of October 16, 1993, $L_t = 200$ customers, $T_t = 1$ customer, and the seasonalities are as follows: Monday—0.90; Tuesday—0.70; Wednesday—0.80; Thursday—1.1; Friday—1.2; Saturday—1.3. For example, this means that on a typical Monday, the number of customers is 90% of the number of customers entering the bank on an average day. On Tuesday, October 17, 1993, 182 customers enter the bank. At the close of business on October 17, 1993, make a prediction for the number of customers to enter the bank on October 25, 1993.

8. The Holt method (exponential smoothing with trend and without seasonality) is being used to forecast weekly car sales at TOD Ford. Currently, the base is estimated to be 50 cars per week, and the trend is estimated to be 6 cars per week. During the current week, 30 cars are sold. After observing the current week's sales, forecast the number of cars to be sold during the week that begins three weeks after the conclusion of the current week. Use $\alpha = \beta = 0.3$.

9. Winter's method (with $\alpha = 0.2$, $\beta = 0.1$ and $\gamma = 0.5$) is being used to forecast the number of customers served each day by Last National Bank. The bank is open Monday through Friday. At present, the following seasonalities have been estimated: Monday—0.80; Tuesday—0.90; Wednesday—0.95; Thursday—1.10; Friday—1.25. A seasonality of 0.80 for Monday means that on a Monday, the number of customers served by the bank tends to be 80% of average. Currently, the base is estimated to be 20 customers, and the trend is estimated to equal 1 customer. After observing that on Monday, 30 customers are served

by the bank, predict the number of customers to be served by the bank on Wednesday.

10. We have been assigned to forecast the number of aircraft engines ordered each month by Engine Company. At the end of February, the forecast is that 100 engines will be ordered during April. During March, 120 engines are ordered.
(a) Using $\alpha = 0.3$, determine (at the end of March) a forecast for the number of orders placed during April. Answer the same question for May.
(b) Suppose at the end of March, MAD $= 16$. At the end of March, we are 68% sure that April orders will be between ____ and ____.

11. Winter's method is being used to forecast quarterly U.S. retail sales (in billions of dollars). At the end of the first quarter of 1992, $L_t = 300$, $T_t = 30$, and the seasonal indexes are as follows: quarter 1—0.90; quarter 2—0.95; quarter 3—0.95; quarter 4—1.20. During the second quarter of 1992, retail sales are \$360 billion. Assume $\alpha = 0.2$, $\beta = 0.4$, and $\gamma = 0.5$.
(a) At the end of the second quarter of 1992, develop a forecast for retail sales during the fourth quarter of 1992.
(b) At the end of the second quarter of 1992, develop a forecast for the second quarter of 1993.

GROUP B

12. Simple exponential smoothing with $\alpha = 0.3$ is being used to predict sales of radios at Lowland Appliance. Predictions are made on a monthly basis. After observing August radio sales, the forecast for September is 100 radios.
(a) During September, 120 radios are sold. After observing September sales, what is the prediction for October radio sales? For November radio sales?
(b) It turns out that June sales were recorded as 10 radios. Actually, however, 100 radios were sold in June. After correcting for this error, what would be the prediction for October radio sales?

13. In our discussion of Winter's method, a monthly seasonality of (say) 0.80 for January means that during January, air conditioner sales are expected to be 80% of the sales during an average month. An alternative approach to modeling seasonality is to let the seasonality factor for each month represent how far above average air conditioner sales will be during the current month. For instance, if $s_{\text{Jan}} = -50$, then air conditioner sales during January are expected to be 50 less than air conditioner sales during an average month. If $s_{\text{July}} = 90$, then air conditioner sales during July are expected to be 90 more than air conditioner sales during an average month. Let

s_t = the seasonality for month t after month t demand is observed

L_t = estimate of base after month t demand is observed

T_t = estimate of trend after month t demand is observed

Then the Winter's method equations given in the text are modified to be as follows (* indicates multiplication):

$$L_t = \alpha * (I) + (1 - \alpha) * (L_{t-1} + T_{t-1})$$

$$T_t = \beta * (L_t - L_{t-1}) + (1 - \beta) * T_{t-1}$$

$$s_t = \gamma * (II) + (1 - \gamma) * s_{t-12}$$

(a) What should I and II be?

(b) Suppose that month 13 is a January, $L_{12} = 30$, $T_{12} = -3$, $s_1 = -50$, and $s_2 = -20$. Let $\alpha = \gamma = \beta = 0.5$. Suppose 12 air conditioners are sold during month 13. At the end of month 13, what is the prediction for air conditioner sales during month 14?

14. Winter's method assumes a multiplicative seasonality but an additive trend. For example, a trend of 5 means that the base will increase by 5 units per period. Suppose there is actually a multiplicative trend. Then (ignoring seasonality) if the current estimate of the base is 50 and the current estimate of the trend is 1.2, we would predict demand to increase by 20% per period. Ignoring seasonality, we would thus forecast the next period's demand to be 50(1.2) and forecast the demand two periods in the future to be $50(1.2)^2$. If we want to use a multiplicative trend in Winter's method, we should use the following equations:

$$L_t = \alpha * \left(\frac{x_t}{s_{t-c}}\right) + (1 - \alpha) * (I)$$

$$T_t = \beta * (II) + (1 - \beta) * T_{t-1}$$

$$s_t = \gamma * \left(\frac{x_t}{L_t}\right) + (1 - \gamma) * s_{t-12}$$

(a) Determine what I and II should be.

(b) Suppose we are working with monthly data and month 12 is a December, month 13 a January, etc. Also suppose that $L_{12} = 100$, $T_{12} = 1.2$, $s_1 = 0.90$, $s_2 = 0.70$, and $s_3 = 0.95$. Suppose $x_{13} = 200$. At the end of month 13, what is the prediction for x_{15}? Assume $\alpha = \beta = \gamma = 0.5$.

15. Holt's method assumes an additive trend. For example, a trend of 5 means that the base will increase by 5 units per period. Suppose there is actually a multiplicative trend.

Thus, if the current estimate of the base is 50 and the current estimate of the trend is 1.2, we would predict demand to increase by 20% per period. So we would forecast the next period's demand to be 50(1.2) and forecast the demand two periods in the future to be $50(1.2)^2$. If we want to use a multiplicative trend in Holt's method, we should use the following equations:

$$L_t = \alpha * (x_t) + (1 - \alpha) * (I)$$

$$T_t = \beta * (II) + (1 - \beta) * T_{t-1}$$

(a) Determine what I and II should be.

(b) Suppose we are working with monthly data and month 12 is a December, month 13 a January, etc. Also suppose that $L_{12} = 100$ and $T_{12} = 1.2$. Suppose $x_{13} = 200$. At the end of month 13, what is the prediction for x_{15}? Assume $\alpha = \beta = 0.5$.

16. A version of simple exponential smoothing can be used to predict the outcome of sporting events. To illustrate, consider pro football. We first assume that all games are played on a neutral field. Before each day of play, we assume that each team has a rating. For example, if the Bears' rating is $+10$ and the Bengals' rating is $+6$, we would predict the Bears to beat the Bengals by $10 - 6 = 4$ points. Suppose the Bears play the Bengals and win by 20 points. For this observation, we "underpredicted" the Bears' performance by $20 - 4 = 16$ points. The best α for pro football is 0.10. After the game, we therefore increase the Bears' rating by $16(0.1) = 1.6$ and decrease the Bengals' rating by 1.6 points. In a rematch, the Bears would be favored by $(10 + 1.6) - (6 - 1.6) = 7.2$ points.

(a) How does this approach relate to the equation $A_t = A_{t-1} + \alpha(e_t)$?

(b) Suppose the home-field advantage in pro football is 3 points; that is, home teams tend to outscore visiting teams by an average of 3 points a game. How could the home-field advantage be incorporated into this system?

(c) How could we determine the best α for pro football?

(d) How might we determine ratings for each team at the beginning of the season?

(e) Suppose we tried to apply the above method to predict pro football (16-game schedule), college football (11-game schedule), college basketball (30-game schedule), and pro basketball (82-game schedule). Which sport would have the smallest optimal α? Which sport would have the largest optimal α?

(f) Why would this approach probably yield poor forecasts for major-league baseball?

24-5   AD HOC FORECASTING

Suppose we want to determine how many tellers a bank must have working each day to provide adequate service. In order to use the queuing models of Chapter 22 to answer this question, we need to be able to predict the number of customers who will enter the bank each day. The bank manager believes that the month of the year and the day of the week influence the number of customers entering the bank. (The bank is open Monday through Saturday, except for holidays.) Can we develop a simple forecasting model to help the bank predict the number of customers who will enter each day?

The number of customers entering the bank each day during the last year is given in Table 8. We have used 1 = Monday, 2 = Tuesday, . . . , 6 = Saturday, and 7 = Sunday to denote the days of the week. A "Y" in the AH column means that the day is the day after the bank was closed for a holiday.

Table 8 Arrivals to Bank	MONTH	DAY M	DAY W	CUST	AH	FORECAST
	1	1	1			
	1	2	2	431	Y	399.13
	1	3	3	271		415.88
	1	4	4	362		416.51
	1	5	5	696		560.10
	1	6	6	315		356.32
	1	7	7			
	1	8	1	330		493.98
	1	9	2	352		399.13
	1	10	3	606		415.88
	1	11	4	550		416.51
	1	12	5	626		560.10
	1	13	6	392		356.32
	1	14	7			
	1	15	1	540		493.98
	1	16	2	474		399.13
	1	17	3	457		415.88
	1	18	4	401		416.51
	1	19	5	691		560.10
	1	20	6	388		356.32
	1	21	7			
	1	22	1	533		493.98
	1	23	2	384		399.13
	1	24	3	360		415.88
	1	25	4	515		416.51
	1	26	5	325		560.10
	1	27	6	412		356.32
	1	28	7			
	1	29	1	592		493.98
	1	30	2	366		399.13
	1	31	3	512		415.88
	2	1	4	476		425.33
	2	2	5	531		571.97
	2	3	6	303		363.87

	MONTH	DAY M	DAY W	CUST	AH	FORECAST
Table 8	2	4	7			
Continued	2	5	1	474		504.45
	2	6	2	255		407.58
	2	7	3	282		424.69
	2	8	4	321		425.33
	2	9	5	416		571.97
	2	10	6	257		363.87
	2	11	7			
	2	12	1	638		504.45
	2	13	2	506		407.58
	2	14	3	420		424.69
	2	15	4	459		425.33
	2	16	5	515		571.97
	2	17	6	501		363.87
	2	18	7			
	2	19	1	556		504.45
	2	20	2	510		407.58
	2	21	3	436		424.69
	2	22	4	512		425.33
	2	23	5	547		571.97
	2	24	6	319		363.87
	2	25	7			
	2	26	1	637		504.45
	2	27	2	474		407.58
	2	28	3	487		424.69
	2	29	4	402		425.33
	3	1	5	778		574.26
	3	2	6	374		365.32
	3	3	7			
	3	4	1	544		506.46
	3	5	2	485		409.21
	3	6	3	361		426.39
	3	7	4	315		427.03
	3	8	5	423		574.26
	3	9	6	357		365.32
	3	10	7			
	3	11	1	649		506.46
	3	12	2	351		409.21
	3	13	3	405		426.39
	3	14	4	404		427.03
	3	15	5	483		574.26
	3	16	6	411		365.32
	3	17	7			
	3	18	1	309		506.46
	3	19	2	453		409.21
	3	20	3	515		426.39
	3	21	4	380		427.03

(continues)

Table 8	MONTH	DAY M	DAY W	CUST	AH	FORECAST
Continued	3	22	5	426		574.26
	3	23	6	427		365.32
	3	24	7			
	3	25	1	489		506.46
	3	26	2	341		409.21
	3	27	3	471		426.39
	3	28	4	517		427.03
	3	29	5	647		574.26
	3	30	6	415		365.32
	3	31	7			
	4	1	1	363		483.02
	4	2	2	337		390.27
	4	3	3	314		406.65
	4	4	4	465		407.26
	4	5	5	584		547.67
	4	6	6	313		348.41
	4	7	7			
	4	8	1	376		483.02
	4	9	2	292		390.27
	4	10	3	484		406.65
	4	11	4	227		407.26
	4	12	5	496		547.67
	4	13	6	395		348.41
	4	14	7			
	4	15	1	625		483.02
	4	16	2	430		390.27
	4	17	3	454		406.65
	4	18	4	372		407.26
	4	19	5	455		547.67
	4	20	6	253		348.41
	4	21	7			
	4	22	1	432		483.02
	4	23	2	469		390.27
	4	24	3	392		406.65
	4	25	4	467		407.26
	4	26	5	684		547.67
	4	27	6	349		348.41
	4	28	7			
	4	29	1	750		483.02
	4	30	2	409		390.27
	5	1	3	348		373.31
	5	2	4	230		373.88
	5	3	5	630		502.78
	5	4	6	358		319.85
	5	5	7			
	5	6	1	269		443.43
	5	7	2	107		358.27
	5	8	3	360		373.31
	5	9	4	208		373.88

	MONTH	DAY M	DAY W	CUST	AH	FORECAST
Table 8	5	10	5	547		502.78
Continued	5	11	6	325		319.85
	5	12	7			
	5	13	1	473		443.43
	5	14	2	337		358.27
	5	15	3	317		373.31
	5	16	4	341		373.88
	5	17	5	338		502.78
	5	18	6	369		319.85
	5	19	7			
	5	20	1	618		443.43
	5	21	2	458		358.27
	5	22	3	457		373.31
	5	23	4	572		373.88
	5	24	5	668		502.78
	5	25	6	318		319.85
	5	26	7			
	5	27	1	300		443.43
	5	28	2	469		358.27
	5	29	3	434		373.31
	5	30	4	419		373.88
	5	31	5			
	6	1	6	432	Y	354.08
	6	2	7			
	6	3	1	463		490.89
	6	4	2	457		396.62
	6	5	3	273		413.27
	6	6	4	327		413.90
	6	7	5	554		556.60
	6	8	6	256		354.08
	6	9	7			
	6	10	1	465		490.89
	6	11	2	479		396.62
	6	12	3	437		413.27
	6	13	4	585		413.90
	6	14	5	616		556.60
	6	15	6	318		354.08
	6	16	7			
	6	17	1	724		490.89
	6	18	2	390		396.62
	6	19	3	550		413.27
	6	20	4	266		413.90
	6	21	5	410		556.60
	6	22	6	303		354.08
	6	23	7			
	6	24	1	514		490.89
	6	25	2	353		396.62

(continues)

	MONTH	DAY M	DAY W	CUST	AH	FORECAST
Table 8 Continued	6	26	3	397		413.27
	6	27	4	539		413.90
	6	28	5	411		556.60
	6	29	6	413		354.08
	6	30	7			
	7	1	1	583		484.44
	7	2	2	477		391.42
	7	3	3	410		407.85
	7	4	4			
	7	5	5	615	Y	549.29
	7	6	6	288		349.44
	7	7	7			
	7	8	1	478		484.44
	7	9	2	298		391.42
	7	10	3	253		407.85
	7	11	4	366		408.46
	7	12	5	410		549.29
	7	13	6	270		349.44
	7	14	7			
	7	15	1	541		484.44
	7	16	2	331		391.42
	7	17	3	318		407.85
	7	18	4	441		408.46
	7	19	5	651		549.29
	7	20	6	300		349.44
	7	21	7			
	7	22	1	608		484.44
	7	23	2	401		391.42
	7	24	3	390		407.85
	7	25	4	391		408.46
	7	26	5	619		549.29
	7	27	6	391		349.44
	7	28	7			
	7	29	1	413		484.44
	7	30	2	474		391.42
	7	31	3	503		407.85
	8	1	4	267		418.33
	8	2	5	619		562.56
	8	3	6	370		357.88
	8	4	7			
	8	5	1	406		496.15
	8	6	2	432		400.87
	8	7	3	333		417.70
	8	8	4	327		418.33
	8	9	5	647		562.56
	8	10	6	407		357.88
	8	11	7			
	8	12	1	396		496.15
	8	13	2	664		400.87

	MONTH	DAY M	DAY W	CUST	AH	FORECAST
Table 8	8	14	3	508		417.70
Continued	8	15	4	519		418.33
	8	16	5	555		562.56
	8	17	6	365		357.88
	8	18	7			
	8	19	1	492		496.15
	8	20	2	420		400.87
	8	21	3	360		417.70
	8	22	4	469		418.33
	8	23	5	488		562.56
	8	24	6	326		357.88
	8	25	7			
	8	26	1	465		496.15
	8	27	2	384		400.87
	8	28	3	280		417.70
	8	29	4	292		418.33
	8	30	5	649		562.56
	8	31	6	493		357.88
	9	1	7			
	9	2	1			
	9	3	2	459	Y	391.76
	9	4	3	353		408.21
	9	5	4	287		408.82
	9	6	5	471		549.77
	9	7	6	266		349.74
	9	8	7			
	9	9	1	505		484.87
	9	10	2	528		391.76
	9	11	3	342		408.21
	9	12	4	551		408.82
	9	13	5	525		549.77
	9	14	6	304		349.74
	9	15	7			
	9	16	1	479		484.87
	9	17	2	258		391.76
	9	18	3	263		408.21
	9	19	4	450		408.82
	9	20	5	540		549.77
	9	21	6	297		349.74
	9	22	7			
	9	23	1	399		484.87
	9	24	2	264		391.76
	9	25	3	479		408.21
	9	26	4	459		408.82
	9	27	5	915		549.77
	9	28	6	247		349.74
	9	29	7			

(continues)

	MONTH	DAY M	DAY W	CUST	AH	FORECAST
Table 8 Continued	9	30	1	725		484.87
	10	1	2	197		390.39
	10	2	3	326		406.78
	10	3	4	374		407.39
	10	4	5	477		547.85
	10	5	6	367		348.52
	10	6	7			
	10	7	1	317		483.17
	10	8	2	205		390.39
	10	9	3	519		406.78
	10	10	4	483		407.39
	10	11	5	489		547.85
	10	12	6	345		348.52
	10	13	7			
	10	14	1	660		483.17
	10	15	2	262		390.39
	10	16	3	395		406.78
	10	17	4	522		407.39
	10	18	5	582		547.85
	10	19	6	335		348.52
	10	20	7			
	10	21	1	503		483.17
	10	22	2	396		390.39
	10	23	3	548		406.78
	10	24	4	471		407.39
	10	25	5	528		547.85
	10	26	6	344		348.52
	10	27	7			
	10	28	1	419		483.17
	10	29	2	429		390.39
	10	30	3	609		406.78
	10	31	4	519		407.39
	11	1	5	674		596.31
	11	2	6	352		379.35
	11	3	7			
	11	4	1	360		525.91
	11	5	2	500		424.92
	11	6	3	339		442.76
	11	7	4	326		443.43
	11	8	5	459		596.31
	11	9	6	255		379.35
	11	10	7			
	11	11	1	432		525.91
	11	12	2	527		424.92
	11	13	3	394		442.76
	11	14	4	424		443.43
	11	15	5	388		596.31
	11	16	6	356		379.35
	11	17	7			

	MONTH	DAY M	DAY W	CUST	AH	FORECAST
Table 8	11	18	1	635		525.91
Continued	11	19	2	309		424.92
	11	20	3	613		442.76
	11	21	4	580		443.43
	11	22	5	627		596.31
	11	23	6	514		379.35
	11	24	7			
	11	25	1	686		525.91
	11	26	2	452		424.92
	11	27	3	384		442.76
	11	28	4			
	11	29	5	701	Y	596.31
	11	30	6	425		379.35
	12	1	7			
	12	2	1	291		510.06
	12	3	2	407		412.12
	12	4	3	458		429.42
	12	5	4	243		430.06
	12	6	5	449		578.34
	12	7	6	315		367.91
	12	8	7			
	12	9	1	633		510.06
	12	10	2	429		412.12
	12	11	3	375		429.42
	12	12	4	540		430.06
	12	13	5	615		578.34
	12	14	6	455		367.91
	12	15	7			
	12	16	1	385		510.06
	12	17	2	472		412.12
	12	18	3	576		429.42
	12	19	4	321		430.06
	12	20	5	679		578.34
	12	21	6	430		367.91
	12	22	7			
	12	23	1	407		510.06
	12	24	2	328		412.12
	12	25	3			
	12	26	4	491	Y	430.06
	12	27	5	586		578.34
	12	28	6	367		367.91
	12	29	7			
	12	30	1	707		510.06
	12	31	2	400		412.12

Let x_t = number of customers entering the bank on day t. We postulate that $x_t = B \times DW_t \times M_t \times \varepsilon_t$, where

B = base level of customer traffic corresponding to an average day

DW_t = day of the week factor corresponding to day of the week on which day t falls

M_t = Monthly factor corresponding to month during which day t occurs

ε_t = random error term whose average value equals 1

To begin, we estimate B = average number of arrivals per day the bank is open = 438.33. We illustrate the estimation of the DW_t by estimating

$$DW_t \text{ for Monday} = \frac{\text{average number of arrivals on Mondays bank is open}}{B}$$

$$= \frac{492.07}{438.33} = 1.122$$

Similarly, we find

$$DW_t \text{ for Tuesday} = 0.907$$
$$DW_t \text{ for Wednesday} = 0.945$$
$$DW_t \text{ for Thursday} = 0.947$$
$$DW_t \text{ for Friday} = 1.273$$
$$DW_t \text{ for Saturday} = 0.809$$

To estimate M_t (say, for May), we write

$$M_t \text{ for May} = \frac{\text{average number of arrivals on May day for which bank is open}}{B}$$

$$= \frac{395}{438.33} = 0.901$$

In a similar fashion, we find the M_t for the remaining months:

$$M_t \text{ for January} = 1.004$$
$$M_t \text{ for February} = 1.025$$
$$M_t \text{ for March} = 1.029$$
$$M_t \text{ for April} = 0.982$$
$$M_t \text{ for June} = 0.998$$
$$M_t \text{ for July} = 0.984$$
$$M_t \text{ for August} = 1.008$$
$$M_t \text{ for September} = 0.985$$
$$M_t \text{ for October} = 0.982$$
$$M_t \text{ for November} = 1.069$$
$$M_t \text{ for December} = 1.037$$

To illustrate how the forecasts in Table 8 were generated, consider how we would generate a forecast for the number of customers to enter the bank on Thursday,

February 1, of the current year. Assuming ε_t equals its average value of 1, we would forecast $B \times (DW_t$ for Thursday) $\times (M_t$ for February) = 438.33(0.947)(1.025) = 425.48 customers would enter. (The difference from the printout value shown in the table is due to rounding of DW_t and M_t values.) To forecast customer arrivals for a future day (say, Saturday, February 8, of next year), we would obtain $B \times (DW_t$ for Saturday) $\times (M_t$ for February) = 438.33 (0.809)(1.025) = 363.47 customers.

For the data given in Table 8, our simple model yielded a MAD of 79.1. If this method were used to generate forecasts for the coming year, however, the MAD would probably exceed 79.1. This is because we have fit our parameters to past data; there is no guarantee that future data will "know" that they should follow the same pattern as past data. We have also neglected to consider whether or not an upward trend in the data is present (see Problem 3).

Suppose the bank manager observes that on the day after a holiday, bank traffic is much higher than the model predicts. The data in Table 9 indicate that this is indeed the case. How can we use this information to obtain more accurate customer forecasts for days after holidays? From Table 9, we find that the average value of Actual/Forecasted for days after a holiday is 1.15. Thus, for any day after a holiday, we obtain a new forecast simply by multiplying our previous forecast by 1.15.

Table 9 Bank Traffic on Day after Holiday	DAY AFTER HOLIDAY	ACTUAL	FORECASTED (Rounded)	ACTUAL/FORECASTED
	January 2	431	399	1.08
	June 1	432	354	1.22
	July 5	615	549	1.12
	September 3	459	392	1.17
	November 29	701	596	1.18
	December 26	491	430	1.14

◆ PROBLEMS

GROUP A

1. Suppose the bank is a college credit union and that on days when the college's professors get paid, bank traffic is much higher than usual. Assuming that college professors are paid on the first weekday of each month, how could we incorporate this fact into the forecasting procedure described in this section?

2. Suppose again that the bank is a college credit union, but now the staff gets paid every other Friday. Again, bank traffic is much higher than usual on staff paydays. How could we incorporate this fact into the forecasting procedure described in this section?

3. Suppose that the number of customers entering the bank is growing at around 20% per year. How could we incorporate this fact into the forecasting procedure described in this section?

24-6   SIMPLE LINEAR REGRESSION

Often, we try to predict the value of one variable (called the **dependent variable**) from the value of another variable (the **independent variable**). Some examples follow:

Dependent Variable	Independent Variable
Sales of product	Price of product
Automobile sales	Interest rate
Total production cost	Units produced

If the dependent variable and the independent variable are related in a linear fashion, simple linear regression can be used to estimate this relationship. In Section 24.7, we will discuss how to estimate nonlinear relationships.

To illustrate simple linear regression, let's recall the Giapetto problem (Example 1 of Chapter 3). To set up this problem, we need to determine the cost of producing a soldier and the cost of producing a train. Let's suppose that we want to determine the cost of producing a train. To estimate this cost, we have observed for ten weeks the number of trains produced each week and the total cost of producing those trains. This information is given in Table 10.

Table 10
Weekly Cost Data
on Trains

WEEK	TRAINS PRODUCED	COST OF PRODUCING TRAINS
1	10	$257.40
2	20	$601.60
3	30	$782.00
4	40	$765.40
5	45	$895.50
6	50	$1133.00
7	60	$1152.80
8	55	$1132.70
9	70	$1459.20
10	40	$970.10

The data from Table 10 are plotted in Figure 5. Observe that there appears to be a strong linear relationship between x_i (number of trains produced during week i) and y_i (cost of producing trains made during week i). The line plotted in Figure 5 appears, in a way to be made precise later, to come close to capturing the linear relationship between units produced and production cost. We will soon see how this line was chosen.

To begin, we model the linear relationship between x_i and y_i by the following equation:

$$y_i = \beta_0 + \beta_1 x_i + \varepsilon_i$$

where ε_i is an error term representing the fact that during a week during which x_i trains are produced, the production cost might not always equal $\beta_0 + \beta_1 x_i$. If $\varepsilon_i > 0$, the cost of producing x_i trains during week i will exceed $\beta_0 + \beta_1 x_i$, whereas if $\varepsilon_i < 0$, the cost of producing x_i trains during week i will be less than $\beta_0 + \beta_1 x_i$. However, we expect ε_i to average out to 0, so the expected cost during a week in which x_i trains are produced is $\beta_0 + \beta_1 x_i$.

Figure 5
Scatterplot of Cost
of Producing Trains

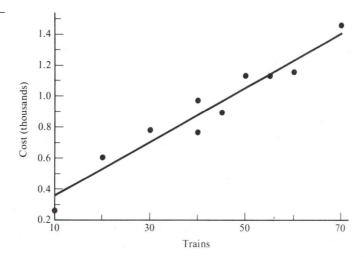

The true values of β_0 and β_1 are unknown. Suppose we estimate β_0 by $\hat{\beta}_0$ and estimate β_1 by $\hat{\beta}_1$. Then our prediction for y_i (since the average value of $\varepsilon_i = 0$) is given by $\hat{y}_i = \hat{\beta}_0 + \hat{\beta}_1 x_i$.

Suppose we have data points of the form $(x_1, y_1), (x_2, y_2), \ldots, (x_n, y_n)$. How should we choose values of $\hat{\beta}_0$ and $\hat{\beta}_1$ that yield good estimates of β_0 and β_1? We select values of $\hat{\beta}_0$ and $\hat{\beta}_1$ that make our predictions $\hat{y}_i = \hat{\beta}_0 + \hat{\beta}_1 x_i$ close to the actual data points (x_i, y_i). To formalize this idea, define e_i = error or residual for data point i = (actual cost y_i) − (predicted cost $\hat{y}_i$) = $y_i - \hat{\beta}_0 - \hat{\beta}_1 x_i$. We now choose $\hat{\beta}_0$ and $\hat{\beta}_1$ to minimize

$$F(\hat{\beta}_0, \hat{\beta}_1) = \sum e_i^2 = \sum (y_i - \hat{\beta}_0 - \hat{\beta}_1 x_i)^2$$

The values $\hat{\beta}_0$ and $\hat{\beta}_1$ minimizing $F(\hat{\beta}_0, \hat{\beta}_1)$ are called the **least squares estimates** of β_0 and β_1. As described in Example 15 of Chapter 12, we find $\hat{\beta}_0$ and $\hat{\beta}_1$ by setting

$$\frac{\partial F}{\partial \hat{\beta}_0} = \frac{\partial F}{\partial \hat{\beta}_1} = 0$$

The resulting values of $\hat{\beta}_0$ and $\hat{\beta}_1$ are given by

$$\hat{\beta}_1 = \frac{\sum (x_i - \bar{x})(y_i - \bar{y})}{\sum (x_i - \bar{x})^2} \qquad \hat{\beta}_0 = \bar{y} - \hat{\beta}_1 \bar{x} \tag{18}$$

where $\bar{x}$ = average value of all x_i's and $\bar{y}$ = average value of all y_i's.

We call $\hat{y}_i = \hat{\beta}_0 + \hat{\beta}_1 x_i$ the **least squares regression line**. Essentially, if the least squares line fits the points well (in a sense to be made more precise later), we will use $\hat{\beta}_0 + \hat{\beta}_1 x_i$ as our prediction for y_i.

Usually, the least squares line is determined by computer. Lotus, STORM, Minitab, and many other popular packages will provide $\hat{\beta}_0$ and $\hat{\beta}_1$. For the sake of completeness, however, the computations needed to determine $\hat{\beta}_0$ and $\hat{\beta}_1$ for the data in Table 10 are given in Table 11, where we have used

$$\bar{x} = \frac{\sum x_i}{10} = 42 \qquad \text{and} \qquad \bar{y} = \frac{\sum y_i}{10} = 914.97$$

	x_i	y_i	$x_i - \bar{x}$	$y_i - \bar{y}$	$(x_i - \bar{x})(y_i - \bar{y})$	$(x_i - \bar{x})^2$
Table 11	10	257.4	-32	-657.57	21,042.24	1024
Computation of $\hat{\beta}_0$	20	601.6	-22	-313.37	6894.14	484
and $\hat{\beta}_1$ for Train	30	782.0	-12	-132.97	1595.64	144
Cost Data	40	765.4	-2	-149.57	299.14	4
	45	895.5	3	-19.47	-58.41	9
	50	1133.0	8	218.03	1744.24	64
	60	1152.8	18	237.83	4280.94	324
	55	1132.7	13	217.73	2830.49	169
	70	1459.2	28	544.23	15,238.44	784
	40	970.1	-2	55.13	-110.26	4

From Table 11, we find that $\sum (x_i - \bar{x})(y_i - \bar{y}) = 53{,}756.6$ and $\sum (x_i - \bar{x})^2 = 3010$. From (18), we now find that

$$\hat{\beta}_1 = \frac{53{,}756.6}{3010} = 17.86 \quad \text{and} \quad \hat{\beta}_0 = 914.97 - (17.86)42 = 164.88$$

Our least squares line is $\hat{y} = 164.88 + 17.86x$. Thus, we estimate that each extra train incurs a variable cost of $\hat{\beta}_1 = \$17.86$.

Our predictions and errors for all ten weeks are given in Table 12. To illustrate the computations, consider the first point $(10, 257.4)$. The predicted cost is $\hat{y}_1 = 164.88 + 17.86(10) = 343.5$, and the error is given by $e_1 = 257.4 - 343.5 = -86.1$.

	x_i	y_i	$\hat{y}_i$	e_i
Table 12	10	257.4	343.5	-86.1
Computations of	20	601.6	522.1	79.5
Errors	30	782.0	700.7	81.3
	40	765.4	879.3	-113.9
	45	895.5	968.5	-73.0
	50	1133.0	1057.8	75.2
	60	1152.8	1236.4	-83.6
	55	1132.7	1147.1	-14.4
	70	1459.2	1415	44.2
	40	970.1	879.3	90.8

Every least squares line has two properties:

1. It passes through the point $(\bar{x}, \bar{y})$. Thus, during a week in which Giapetto produced $\bar{x} = 42$ trains, we would predict that these trains would cost \$914.97 to produce.

2. $\sum e_i = 0$. The least squares line "splits" the data points, in the sense that the sum of the vertical distances from points above the least squares line to the least squares line equals the sum of the vertical distances from points below the least squares line to the least squares line.

HOW GOOD A FIT?

How do we determine how well the least squares line fits our data points? To answer this question, we need to discuss three components of variation: **sum of squares total** (SST), **sum of squares error** (SSE), and **sum of squares regression** (SSR). Sum of squares total is given by $SST = \sum(y_i - \bar{y})^2$. SST measures the total variation of y_i about its mean $\bar{y}$. Sum of squares error is given by $SSE = \sum(y_i - \hat{y}_i)^2 = \sum e_i^2$. If the least squares line passes through all the data points, $SSE = 0$. Thus, SSE small would indicate that the least squares line fits the data well. We define sum of squares regression to be $SSR = \sum(\hat{y}_i - \bar{y})^2$. It can be shown that

$$SST = SSR + SSE \tag{19}$$

Note that SST is a function only of the values of y. For a good fit, SSE will be small, so (19) shows that SSR will be large for a good fit. More formally, we may define the **coefficient of determination** (R^2) for y by

$$R^2 = \frac{SSR}{SST} = \text{percentage of variation in } y \text{ explained by } x$$

Equivalently, (19) allows us to write

$$1 - R^2 = \frac{SSE}{SST} = \text{percentage of variation in } y \text{ not explained by } x$$

From computer output, we find that $SST = 1{,}021{,}762$ and $SSE = 61{,}705$. Then (19) yields $SSR = SST - SSE = 960{,}057$. Thus, we find that $R^2 = \frac{960{,}057}{1{,}021{,}762} = 0.94$. This means that the number of trains produced during a week explains 94% of the variation in weekly cost of producing trains. All other factors combined can explain at most 6% of the variation in weekly cost, so we can be quite sure that the linear relationship between x and y is strong.

A measure of the linear association between x and y is the **sample linear correlation** r_{xy}. A sample correlation near $+1$ indicates a strong positive linear relationship between x and y; a sample correlation near -1 indicates a strong negative linear relationship between x and y; and a sample correlation near 0 indicates a weak linear relationship between x and y.

By the way, if $\hat{\beta}_1 \geq 0$, then r_{xy} equals $+\sqrt{R^2}$, whereas if $\hat{\beta}_1 \leq 0$, the sample correlation between x and y is given by $-\sqrt{R^2}$. Thus, in our cost example, $r_{xy} = \sqrt{0.94} = 0.97$, indicating a strong linear relationship between x and y.

FORECASTING ACCURACY

A measure of the accuracy of predictions derived from regression is given by the **standard error of the estimate** (s_e). If we let $n = $ number of observations, s_e is given by

$$s_e = \sqrt{\frac{SSE}{n - 2}}$$

For our example,

$$s_e = \sqrt{\frac{61{,}705}{10 - 2}} = 87.8$$

It is usually true[†] that approximately 68% of the values of y will be within s_e of the predicted value $\hat{y}$, and 95% of the values of y will be within $2s_e$ of the predicted value $\hat{y}$. In the current example, we expect that 68% of our cost estimates will be within \$87.80 of the true cost, and 95% of our cost estimates will be within \$175.60 of the true cost. In actuality, for 80% of our data points, actual cost is within s_e of the predicted cost, and for 100% of our data points, actual cost is within $2s_e$ of the predicted cost.

Any observation for which y is not within $2s_e$ of $\hat{y}$ is called an **outlier**. Outliers represent unusual data points and should be carefully examined. Of course, if an outlier is the result of a data entry error, it should be corrected. If an outlier is in some way uncharacteristic of the remaining data points, it may be better to omit the outlier and re-estimate the least squares line. Since all the errors are smaller than $2s_e$ in absolute value, there are no outliers in our cost example.

t-TESTS IN REGRESSION

Using a **t-test**, we can test the significance of a linear relationship. To test $H_0: \beta_1 = 0$ (no significant linear relationship between x and y) against $H_a: \beta_1 \neq 0$ (significant linear relationship between x and y) at a level of significance α, we compute the t-statistic given by

$$ t = \frac{\hat{\beta}_1}{\text{StdErr}(\hat{\beta}_1)} $$

$\text{StdErr}(\hat{\beta}_1)$ measures the uncertainty in our estimate of β_1; it can usually be found on a computer printout. We reject H_0 if $|t| \geq t_{(\alpha/2, n-2)}$, where $t_{(\alpha/2, n-2)}$ is obtained from Table 13. For our cost example, $\text{StdErr}(\hat{\beta}_1) = 1.6$ (found from a computer printout), so $t = \frac{17.86}{1.6} = 11.16$. Using $\alpha = 0.05$, we find $t_{(.025, 8)} = 2.306$, so we reject H_0 and again conclude that there is a strong linear relationship between x and y.

ASSUMPTIONS UNDERLYING THE SIMPLE LINEAR REGRESSION MODEL

Statistical analysis of the simple linear regression model requires that the following assumptions hold.

ASSUMPTION 1. The variance of the error term should not depend on the value of the independent variable x. This assumption is called **homoscedasticity**. If the variance of the error term depends on x, then we say that **heteroscedasticity** is present. To see whether the homoscedasticity assumption is satisfied, we plot the errors on the y-axis and the value of x on the x-axis. Figure 6 illustrates a situation where the homoscedasticity

[†]Actually, approximately 68% of the points should be within

$$ s_e \sqrt{1 + \frac{1}{n} + \frac{(x - \bar{x})^2}{\sum (x_i - \bar{x})^2}} $$

of $\hat{y}$, and 95% of the points should be within

$$ 2s_e \sqrt{1 + \frac{1}{n} + \frac{(x - \bar{x})^2}{\sum (x_i - \bar{x})^2}} $$

of $\hat{y}$.

Table 13
Percentage Points of
the *t*-Distribution

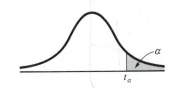

df	$a = 0.1$	$a = 0.05$	$a = 0.025$	$a = 0.01$	$a = 0.005$
1	3.078	6.314	12.706	31.821	63.657
2	1.886	2.920	4.303	6.965	9.925
3	1.638	2.353	3.182	4.541	5.841
4	1.533	2.132	2.776	3.747	4.604
5	1.476	2.015	2.571	3.365	4.032
6	1.440	1.943	2.447	3.143	3.707
7	1.415	1.895	2.365	2.998	3.499
8	1.397	1.860	2.306	2.896	3.355
9	1.383	1.833	2.262	2.821	3.250
10	1.372	1.812	2.228	2.764	3.169
11	1.363	1.796	2.201	2.718	3.106
12	1.356	1.782	2.179	2.681	3.055
13	1.350	1.771	2.160	2.650	3.012
14	1.345	1.761	2.145	2.624	2.977
15	1.341	1.753	2.131	2.602	2.947
16	1.337	1.746	2.120	2.583	2.921
17	1.333	1.740	2.110	2.567	2.898
18	1.330	1.734	2.101	2.552	2.878
19	1.328	1.729	2.093	2.539	2.861
20	1.325	1.725	2.086	2.528	2.845
21	1.323	1.721	2.080	2.518	2.831
22	1.321	1.717	2.074	2.508	2.819
23	1.319	1.714	2.069	2.500	2.807
24	1.318	1.711	2.064	2.492	2.797
25	1.316	1.708	2.060	2.485	2.787
26	1.315	1.706	2.056	2.479	2.779
27	1.314	1.703	2.052	2.473	2.771
28	1.313	1.701	2.048	2.467	2.763
29	1.311	1.699	2.045	2.462	2.756
30	1.310	1.697	2.042	2.457	2.750
40	1.303	1.684	2.021	2.423	2.704
60	1.296	1.671	2.000	2.390	2.660
120	1.289	1.658	1.980	2.358	2.617
240	1.285	1.651	1.970	2.342	2.596
inf.	1.282	1.645	1.960	2.326	2.576

Computed by P. J. Hildebrand. Reprinted with permission of PWS-KENT Publishing Company.

Figure 6
Homoscedasticity

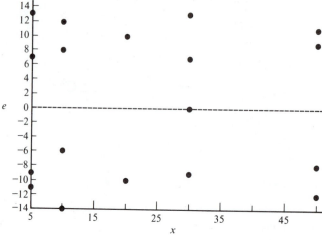

Figure 7
Heteroscedasticity

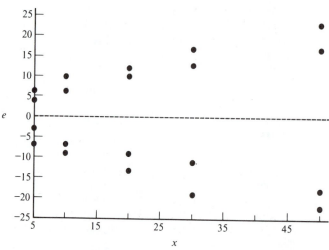

Check for autocorrelation

errors

time series

assumption is satisfied; the figure indicates no tendency for the size of the errors to depend on x. In Figure 7, however, the magnitude of the errors tends to increase as x increases. This is an example of heteroscedasticity.

ASSUMPTION 2. Errors are normally distributed. This assumption is not of vital importance, so we will not discuss it further.

ASSUMPTION 3. The errors should be independent. This assumption is often violated when data is collected (as in our example) over time. Independence of the errors implies that knowing the value of one error should tell us nothing about the value of the next (or any other) error. The validity of this assumption can be checked by plotting the errors in time series sequence. In Figure 8, we find that the errors had the following signs: + + + + + + − − − − − −. This sequence of errors exhibits the following pattern: a positive error (corresponding to underprediction of the actual value of y) is usually followed by another positive error, and a negative error (corresponding to overprediction of the actual value of y) is usually followed by another negative error. This pattern indicates that successive errors are not independent; it is referred to as

Figure 8
Positive
Autocorrelation

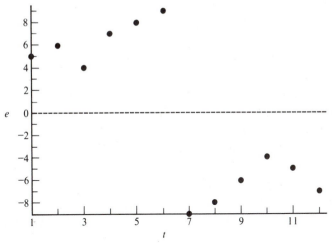

Figure 9
Negative
Autocorrelation

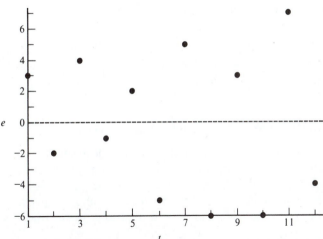

positive autocorrelation. In other words, positive autocorrelation indicates that successive errors have a positive linear relationship and are not linearly independent. If the sequence of errors in time sequence resembles Figure 9, we have **negative autocorrelation**. Here, the sequence of errors is $+ - + - + - + - + - + -$. This indicates that a positive error tends to be followed by a negative error, and vice versa. This indicates that successive errors have a negative linear relationship and are not independent. In Figure 10, we have the following sequence of errors: $+ + - + + - + - + + + -$. Here, no obvious pattern is present, and the independence assumption appears to be satisfied. Observe that the errors "average out" to 0, so we would expect about half our errors to be positive and half to be negative. Thus, if there is no pattern in the errors, we would expect the errors to change sign about half the time. This observation enables us to formalize the above discussion as follows:

  1. If the errors change sign very rarely (much less than half the time), they probably violate the independence assumption, and positive autocorrelation is probably present.

  2. If the errors change sign very often (much more than half the time), they probably violate the independence assumption, and negative autocorrelation is probably present.

Figure 10
No Autocorrelation

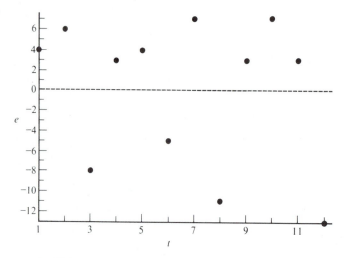

3. If the errors change sign about half the time, they probably satisfy the independence assumption.

If positive or negative autocorrelation is present, correcting for the autocorrelation will often result in much more accurate forecasts. See pages 215–221 of Pindyck and Rubinfeld (1981) for details.

24-7   FITTING NONLINEAR RELATIONSHIPS

Often, a plot of points of the form (x_i, y_i) indicates that y is not a linear function of x. In such cases, however, the plot may indicate that there is a nonlinear relationship between x and y. For example, if the plot of the (x_i, y_i) looks like any of parts (a)–(i) of Figure 11, a nonlinear relationship between x and y is indicated.

The following procedure may be used to estimate a nonlinear relationship:

Step 1 Plot the points and find which part of Figure 11 best fits the data. For illustrative purposes, suppose the data look like part (c).

Step 2 The second column of Table 14 gives the functional relationship between x and y. For part (c), this would be $y = \beta_0 \exp(\beta_1 x)$.

Step 3 Transform each data point according to the rules in the third column of Table 14. Thus, if part (c) of the figure is relevant, we transform each value of y into $\ln y$ and transform each value of x into x. Given the relationship in the second column of Table 14, the transformed data in Table 14 should, if plotted, indicate a straight-line relationship. For part (c), for example, if $y = \beta_0 \exp(\beta_1 x)$, then taking natural logarithms of both sides yields $\ln y = \ln(\beta_0) + \beta_1 x$, so there is indeed a linear relationship between x and $\ln y$.

Step 4 Estimate the least squares regression line for the transformed data. If $\hat{\beta}_0$ is the intercept of the least squares line (for transformed data) and $\hat{\beta}_1$ is the slope of the least squares line (for transformed data), then we read the estimated relationship from the final column of Table 14. Thus, if part (c) were relevant, we would estimate that $\hat{y} = \exp(\hat{\beta}_0 + \hat{\beta}_1 x)$.

Figure 11
Graphs of
Linearizable
Functions (reprinted
by permission from
C. Daniel and F.
Wood, *Fitting
Functions to Data*;
copyright 1980 John
Wiley and Sons)

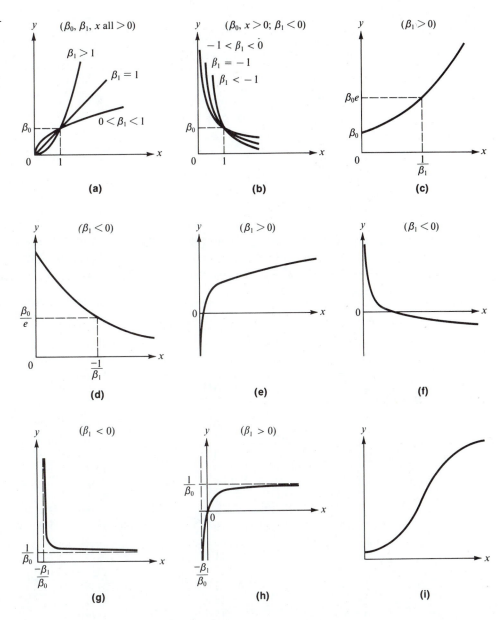

To illustrate the idea, suppose we want to predict future VCR sales for an appliance store. Sales for the last 24 months are given in Table 15 and are plotted in Figure 12 (where ☐ means actual sales). We will use x = number of the month as the independent variable. Figure 12 indicates an S-shaped relationship between x = number of the month and y = sales during the month (like part (i) of Figure 11). So according to Table 14,

$$y = \exp\left(\beta_0 + \frac{\beta_1}{x}\right)$$

Table 14 How to Fit a Nonlinear Relationship	IF GRAPH LOOKS LIKE FIGURE 11, PART	WE HAVE THE FUNCTIONAL RELATIONSHIP	TRANSFORM (x_i, y_i) INTO	ESTIMATE OF FUNCTIONAL RELATIONSHIP
	(a) or (b)	$y = \beta_0 x^{\beta_1}$	$(\ln x_i, \ln y_i)$	$\hat{y} = \exp(\hat{\beta}_0) x^{\beta_1}$
	(c) or (d)	$y = \beta_0 \exp(\beta_1 x)$	$(x_i, \ln y_i)$	$\hat{y} = \exp(\hat{\beta}_0 + \hat{\beta}_1 x)$
	(e) or (f)	$y = \beta_0 + \beta_1 (\ln x)$	$(\ln x_i, y_i)$	$\hat{y} = \hat{\beta}_0 + \hat{\beta}_1 (\ln x)$
	(g) or (h)	$y = \dfrac{x}{\beta_0 x + \beta_1}$	$\left(\dfrac{1}{x_i}, \dfrac{1}{y_i}\right)$	$\hat{y} = \dfrac{x}{\hat{\beta}_0 x + \hat{\beta}_1}$
	(i)	$y = \exp\left(\beta_0 + \dfrac{\beta_1}{x}\right)$	$\left(\dfrac{1}{x_i}, \ln y_i\right)$	$\hat{y} = \exp\left(\hat{\beta}_0 + \dfrac{\hat{\beta}_1}{x}\right)$

Following the third column of Table 14, we now estimate the least squares regression line for the points $(\frac{1}{1}, \ln 23)$, $(\frac{1}{2}, \ln 156)$, ..., $(\frac{1}{24}, \ln 3495)$. We find $\hat{\beta}_0 = 8.387$ and $\hat{\beta}_1 = -5.788$. From the last column of Table 14, we obtain the estimated relationship between x and y:

$$\hat{y} = \exp\left(8.387 - \frac{5.788}{x}\right)$$

Table 15 VCR Sales	MONTH	SALES OF VCRs
	1	23
	2	156
	3	330
	4	482
	5	1209
	6	1756
	7	2000
	8	2512
	9	2366
	10	2942
	11	2872
	12	2937
	13	3136
	14	3241
	15	3149
	16	3524
	17	3542
	18	3312
	19	3547
	20	3376
	21	3375
	22	3403
	23	3697
	24	3495

Figure 12
VCR Sales

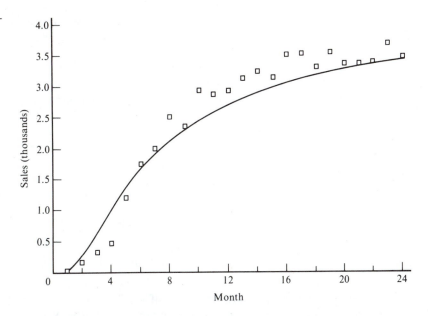

To illustrate how this formula could be used to predict future sales, suppose we want to predict VCR sales during month 26. For $x = 26$, we would forecast that $\hat{y} = \exp\left(8.387 - \frac{5.788}{26}\right) = 3512.8$ or 3513 VCRs would be sold.

REMARKS   **1.** For the regression on the points $(\frac{1}{1}, \ln 23)$, $(\frac{1}{2}, \ln 156)$, ..., $R^2 = 0.95$. This means that 95% of the variation in $\ln y$ is explained by variation in $\frac{1}{x}$. Unfortunately, this does not tell us anything about how accurate our predictions of actual sales (y) are likely to be. For this, we compute the predicted sales for each month, and $e_i = $ (actual month i sales) $-$ (predicted month i sales). By averaging $|e_i|$ for the 24 months, we find the MAD of our predictions to be 223.7. By applying (17), we may estimate the standard deviation of our forecasts to be 1.25(223.7) = 279.6. Thus, 95% of the time, we would expect our predictions for VCR sales to be accurate within 2(279.6) = 559.2 VCRs.

2. If we had mistakenly tried to fit a straight line to this data, we would have obtained $s_e = 546$, so fitting the S-shaped curve has greatly improved our forecasts.

24-8   MULTIPLE REGRESSION

In many situations, more than one independent variable may be useful in predicting the value of a dependent variable. We then use **multiple regression**. For example, if we are trying to predict the monthly sales for a national fast food chicken chain, we might consider using the following independent variables: national income, price of chicken, dollars spent on advertising during the current month, and dollars spent on advertising during the previous month.

Suppose we are using k independent variables to predict the dependent variable y and we have n data points of the form $(y_i, x_{1i}, x_{2i}, \ldots, x_{ki})$, where $x_{ji} = $ value of jth independent variable for ith data point and $y_i = $ value of dependent variable for ith data point. In multiple regression, we model the relationship between y and the k independent variables by

$$y_i = \beta_0 + \beta_1 x_{1i} + \beta_2 x_{2i} + \cdots + \beta_k x_{ki} + \varepsilon_i$$

where ε_i is an error term with mean 0, representing the fact that the actual value of y_i may not equal $\beta_0 + \beta_1 x_{1i} + \beta_2 x_{2i} + \cdots + \beta_k x_{ki}$. β_i may be thought of as the increase in y if the value of the ith independent variable is increased by 1 and all other independent variables are held constant. Thus, β_i is analogous to $\dfrac{\partial y}{\partial x_i}$, where x_i is the ith independent variable.

ESTIMATION OF THE β_i's

Suppose we estimate β_i $(i = 0, 1, 2, \ldots, k)$ by $\hat{\beta}_i$. Then our prediction or estimate for y_j is given by

$$\hat{y}_i = \hat{\beta}_0 + \hat{\beta}_1 x_{1i} + \hat{\beta}_2 x_{2i} + \cdots + \hat{\beta}_k x_{ki}$$

As in Section 24.6, we define $e_i = y_i - \hat{y}_i$ and choose $\hat{\beta}_0, \hat{\beta}_1, \ldots, \hat{\beta}_k$ to minimize $\sum e_i^2$. Usually, these least squares estimates of $\beta_0, \beta_1, \ldots, \beta_k$ will be obtained from a computer package such as Lotus 123, Minitab, or STORM. We call

$$\hat{y}_i = \hat{\beta}_0 + \hat{\beta}_1 x_{1i} + \hat{\beta}_2 x_{2i} + \cdots + \hat{\beta}_k x_{ki}$$

the **least squares regression equation**.

E X A M P L E 1

We want to predict maintenance expense (y) for a truck during the current year, from the independent variables $x_1 =$ miles driven (in thousands) during the current year and $x_2 =$ age of the truck (in years) at the beginning of the current year. We are given the information in Table 16.

Table 16
Truck Maintenance
Data

y	x_1	x_2
$832	6	8
$733	7	7
$647	9	6
$553	11	5
$467	13	4
$373	15	3
$283	17	2
$189	18	1
$96	19	0

Solution

Computer output for this example is given in Table 17. Reading down the Coefficient column and rounding to two decimal places, we obtain $\hat{\beta}_0 = 17.74$, $\hat{\beta}_1 = 4.06$, and $\hat{\beta}_2 = 98.51$. Thus, we would predict annual maintenance cost for a truck from

$$\hat{y} = 17.74 + 4.06x_1 + 98.51x_2 \tag{20}$$

Table 17
Computer Output
for Example 1

VARIABLE	COEFFICIENT	STANDARD ERROR	t-VALUE
Constant	17.73846	31.0271	0.57171
x_1	4.061538	1.56742	2.59123
x_2	98.50769	2.756428	35.73744

Standard error of estimate = 2.106157

For a five-year-old truck that is driven 10,000 miles during a year, we predict annual maintenance costs by $17.74 + 4.06(10) + 98.51(5) = \$550.89$.

From (20), we conclude that (holding the age of the truck constant) driving an extra thousand miles during a year increases annual maintenance costs by $\hat{\beta}_1 = \$4.06$, and that an increase of one year in the age of the truck (holding miles driven constant) increases annual maintenance costs by $\hat{\beta}_2 = \$98.51$. ◆

GOODNESS OF FIT REVISITED

For multiple regression, we define SSR, SSE, and SST as we did in Section 24.6. We also find that $R^2 = \frac{SSR}{SST}$ = percentage of variation in y explained by the k independent variables and $1 - R^2$ = percentage of variation in y not explained by the k independent variables. If we define the standard error of the estimate as

$$s_e = \sqrt{\frac{SSE}{(n - k - 1)}}$$

then (as in Section 24.6) we expect approximately 68% of the y-values to be within s_e of $\hat{y}$ and approximately 95% of the y-values to be within $2s_e$ of $\hat{y}$. We have already seen from Table 17 that $s_e = 2.106$. Thus, 95% of the time, we expect our predictions for annual maintenance expenditures to be accurate within \$4.21.

HYPOTHESIS TESTING

If we have included independent variables $x_1, x_2, \ldots, x_k$ in a multiple regression, we often wish to test

$\quad H_0: \beta_i = 0 \quad$ (x_i does not have a significant effect on y when the other independent variables are included in the regression equation)

against

$\quad H_a: \beta_i \neq 0 \quad$ (x_i does have a significant effect on y when the other independent variables are included in the regression equation)

To test these hypotheses, we compute

$$t = \frac{\hat{\beta}_i}{\text{StdErr}(\hat{\beta}_i)}$$

where $\text{StdErr}(\hat{\beta}_i)$ measures the amount of uncertainty present in our estimate of β_i. $\text{StdErr}(\hat{\beta}_i)$ (and often the t-statistic) is read from computer output. At a level of significance α, we reject H_0 if $|t| > t_{(\alpha/2, n-k-1)}$. From Table 17, we find that (t for

x_1) = 2.59 and (t for x_2) = 35.74. Suppose α = 0.05. Since $t_{(.025, 9-2-1)}$ = 2.447, we reject H_0 for each independent variable and conclude that both miles driven and age of the truck have a significant effect on annual maintenance cost.

Usually, variables included in a regression equation should have significant t-statistics. (α = 0.10 or α = 0.05 are commonly used levels of significance in regression analysis.) If an independent variable has an insignificant t-statistic, we usually remove the independent variable from the equation and obtain new least squares estimates. To illustrate this idea, suppose we have the data shown in Table 18 on sales at the Bloomington Happy Chicken Restaurant during the last 20 years. (POP = population within 10 miles of Happy Chicken Restaurant, AD = thousands of dollars spent on advertising during the current year, LAGAD = thousands of dollars spent on advertising during the previous year, SALES = sales in thousands of dollars.)

	YEAR	POP	AD	LAGAD	SALES
Table 18	1	96,020	30	—	13,000
Happy Chicken	2	102,558	20	30	15,713
Sales Data	3	101,792	15	20	12,937
	4	104,347	25	15	12,872
	5	106,180	30	25	16,227
	6	106,562	15	30	15,388
	7	105,209	25	15	13,180
	8	109,185	35	25	17,199
	9	109,976	40	35	20,674
	10	110,659	20	40	20,350
	11	111,844	25	20	14,444
	12	111,576	35	25	17,530
	13	113,784	5	35	16,711
	14	112,482	12	5	9,715
	15	116,487	16	12	12,248
	16	117,316	21	16	13,856
	17	117,830	22	21	15,285
	18	118,148	24	22	15,620
	19	118,481	26	24	17,158
	20	121,069	28	26	17,800

We attempt to estimate the model

$$\text{SALES} = \beta_0 + \beta_1 \text{YEAR} + \beta_2 \text{POP} + \beta_3 \text{AD} + \beta_4 \text{LAGAD} + \varepsilon$$

We are using YEAR as an independent variable in the hopes of picking up a possible upward trend in sales. LAGAD is used as an independent variable because we believe that last year's advertising might affect this year's sales. We obtain the following estimated regression equation (t-statistics for each independent variable are in parentheses):

$$\widehat{\text{SALES}} = 109.42 + 1.69\,\text{YEAR} - 0.59\,\text{POP} + 1.22\,\text{AD} + 2.77\,\text{LAGAD}$$
$$\quad\quad\quad\quad\quad (1.91) \quad\quad (-0.70) \quad\quad (13.90) \quad\quad (29.16)$$

(21)

We cannot use the first year of data, since LAGAD is undefined. Since $t_{(.05, 19-4-1)} = 1.761$, we find that all independent variables except for POP are significant for $\alpha = 0.10$. Thus, YEAR, AD, and LAGAD appear to have a significant effect on sales. After dropping the insignificant variable POP from the equation, we obtain the following estimated regression equation:

$$\text{SALES} = 99.06 + 1.09\,\text{YEAR} + 1.22\,\text{AD} + 2.74\,\text{LAGAD}$$
$$\qquad\qquad (8.3)\qquad\quad (14.14)\qquad\quad (31.8)$$

All independent variables are significant. Also, we find $R^2 = 0.99$ and $s_e = 3.1$. Thus, we are reasonably satisfied with this equation and expect that 95% of the time, our prediction for sales will be within $6200 of actual sales.

CHOOSING THE BEST REGRESSION EQUATION

How can we choose between several regression equations having different sets of independent variables? We usually want to choose the equation with the lowest value of s_e, since that will yield the most accurate forecasts. We also want the t-statistics for all variables in the equation to be significant. These two objectives may conflict, in which case it is difficult to determine the "best" equation. If the available computer printout contains the C_p statistic, then the regression chosen should have a C_p value close to (number of independent variables in equation) + 1. For example, if a regression with three independent variables has $C_p = 80$, we can be sure that it is not a "good" regression. Actually, if a regression has C_p much larger than p, it means that at least one important variable has been omitted from the regression. (See Daniel and Wood (1980) for a discussion of the C_p statistic.) _ ? ?

MULTICOLLINEARITY

If an estimated regression equation contains two or more independent variables that exhibit a strong linear relationship, we say that **multicollinearity** is present. A strong linear relationship between some of the independent variables may make the computer's estimates of the β_i's unreliable. In certain circumstances, multicollinearity can even cause a variable that should have β_i positive to have $\hat{\beta}_i$ substantially less than 0. The Happy Chicken example illustrates multicollinearity: We began with both YEAR and POP as independent variables, and as POP and YEAR both increase over time, we would expect a strong positive linear relationship to exist between them. Indeed, the correlation between YEAR and POP is 0.98. To see that the estimates of β_{YEAR} and β_{POP} are unreliable, note that in (21), $\hat{\beta}_{\text{POP}} < 0$, indicating that an increase in the number of customers near Happy Chicken decreases sales. This anomaly is due to multicollinearity. The strong linear relationship between YEAR and POP makes it difficult for the computer to estimate β_{POP} and β_{YEAR} accurately. After we drop POP from the estimated equation, the multicollinearity problem disappears, because there is no strong linear relationship between the remaining independent variables.

By the way, if an *exact* linear relationship exists between two or more independent variables, there are an infinite number of combinations of the $\hat{\beta}_i$'s which will minimize the sum of the squared errors, and most computer packages will print an error message. For example, if we let $x_1 =$ U.S. consumer expenditure during a year, $x_2 =$ U.S. investment during a year, $x_3 =$ U.S. government expenditure during a year, and

x_4 = U.S. national income during a year, it is well known that $x_4 = x_1 + x_2 + x_3$. In this case, we cannot use x_1, x_2, x_3, and x_4 as independent variables; at least one of the independent variables should be dropped from the equation.

DUMMY VARIABLES

Often, a nonquantitative or qualitative independent variable may influence the dependent variable. Some examples are as follows:

Dependent Variable	Categorical Independent Variable
Salary of employee	Race of employee
Consumer expenditures during year	Whether it is a wartime or a peacetime year
Customers entering bank on a given day	Day of the week
Air conditioner sales during a given month	Month of the year

In each of these situations, the independent variable does not assume a numerical value, but it may be classified into one of c categories. To illustrate, for monthly air conditioner sales, $c = 12$, and for the consumer expenditure example, $c = 2$.

Let the possible values of the categorical variable be listed as value 1, value 2, . . . , value c. To model the effect of a categorical variable on a dependent variable, we define $c - 1$ **dummy variables** as follows:

$x_1 = 1$ if observation takes on value 1 of categorical variable

$x_1 = 0$ otherwise

$x_2 = 1$ if observation takes on value 2 of categorical variable

$x_2 = 0$ otherwise

$\vdots$

$x_{c-1} = 1$ if observation takes on value $c - 1$ of categorical variable

$x_{c-1} = 0$ otherwise

We now include $x_1, x_2, \ldots, x_{c-1}$ (along with any other relevant independent variables) in the estimated regression equation.

To illustrate the use of dummy variables, suppose we are trying to predict the number of customers to enter the University Credit Union each day. The bank manager believes that bank traffic is influenced by the day of the week (the credit union is open Monday through Friday) and by whether or not the day is a payday for university employees. We are given the number of people to enter the bank during 18 randomly chosen days. (Day 1 is the present, day 6 is a week from now, etc.) The relevant information is given in Table 19.

In this situation, there are two categorical variables of interest: the day of the week ($c = 5$) and whether or not a day is a payday ($c = 2$). For the day of the week, we define value 1 = Monday, value 2 = Tuesday, value 3 = Wednesday, value 4 = Thursday, and value 5 = Friday. Then we let

$x_1 = 1$ if day is a Monday $x_1 = 0$ otherwise

$x_2 = 1$ if day is a Tuesday $x_2 = 0$ otherwise

$x_3 = 1$ if day is a Wednesday $x_3 = 0$ otherwise

$x_4 = 1$ if day is a Thursday $x_4 = 0$ otherwise

Table 19 Customer Traffic at University Credit Union	DAY NUMBER	DAY OF WEEK	UNIVERSITY PAYDAY?	CUSTOMERS ENTERING CREDIT UNION
	1	Monday	No	515
	12	Tuesday	No	360
	18	Wednesday	Yes	548
	23	Wednesday	No	386
	24	Thursday	No	440
	46	Monday	Yes	687
	48	Wednesday	No	350
	52	Tuesday	No	430
	54	Thursday	No	370
	55	Friday	No	496
	70	Friday	No	506
	81	Monday	No	509
	89	Thursday	Yes	508
	104	Thursday	No	396
	106	Monday	No	600
	108	Wednesday	No	266
	122	Tuesday	No	360
	130	Friday	Yes	521
	152	Tuesday	No	398

For whether or not a day is a payday, we define $c - 1 = 1$ dummy variables. Letting value 1 = payday and value 2 = not a payday, we define

$$x_5 = 1 \quad \text{if day is a payday} \quad x_5 = 0 \quad \text{otherwise}$$

To account for a possible trend in the number of customers, we include T = number of the day as an independent variable. To illustrate how this information would be coded on the computer, we "code" the last two observations:

T	x_1	x_2	x_3	x_4	x_5	Customers
130	0	0	0	0	1	521
152	0	1	0	0	0	398

We obtain the following estimated regression equation (t-statistics in parentheses):

$$\hat{y} = 496.1 - 0.36T + 71.1x_1 - 78.5x_2 - 122.5x_3 - 74.8x_4 + 127.1x_5$$
$$\quad\quad (-1.29) \quad (1.87) \quad (-2.04) \quad (-3.17) \quad (-1.99) \quad (4.43)$$

For $\alpha = 0.10$, we find that all independent variables except T are significant. After eliminating T from the estimated equation, we obtain the following equation:

$$\hat{y} = 466.2 + 80.4x_1 - 79.2x_2 - 109.8x_3 - 68.8x_4 + 124.3x_5$$
$$\quad (2.1) \quad (-2.0) \quad -(2.86) \quad (-1.79) \quad (4.24)$$

(22)

For $\alpha = 0.10$, all independent variables are significant, so this equation appears satisfactory. We also find that $R^2 = 0.85$ and $s_e = 48.8$. Thus, on 95% of all days, our prediction for the number of customers entering the credit union should be accurate within $2(48.8) = 97.6$ customers.

INTERPRETATION OF COEFFICIENTS OF DUMMY VARIABLES

How do we interpret the coefficients of dummy variables? To illustrate, let's determine how whether or not a day is a payday affects credit union traffic. On a payday, $x_5 = 1$, and we predict that $466.2 + 80.4x_1 - 79.2x_2 - 109.8x_3 - 68.8x_4 + 124.3$ customers will enter the credit union. On a day that is not a payday, $x_5 = 0$, and we predict that $466.2 + 80.4x_1 - 79.2x_2 - 109.8x_3 - 68.8x_4$ customers will enter the credit union. Subtracting, we find that on a payday, we predict (all other things being equal) that $\hat{\beta}_5 = 124.3$ more customers will enter the credit union than on a day that is not a payday.

To see how the day of the week influences credit union traffic, we note that (22) yields a different prediction for each day of the week. For Monday, $x_1 = 1$, $x_2 = x_3 = x_4 = 0$, and we obtain $\hat{y} = 466.2 + 80.4 + 124.3x_5 = 546.6 + 124.3x_5$. For Tuesday, $x_2 = 1$, $x_1 = x_3 = x_4 = 0$, and we obtain $\hat{y} = 466.2 - 79.2 + 124.3x_5 = 387 + 124.3x_5$. For Wednesday, $x_3 = 1$, $x_2 = x_1 = x_4 = 0$, and we obtain $\hat{y} = 466.2 - 109.8 + 124.3x_5 = 356.4 + 124.3x_5$. For Thursday, $x_4 = 1$, $x_1 = x_3 = x_2 = 0$, and we obtain $\hat{y} = 466.2 - 68.8 + 124.3x_5 = 397.4 + 124.3x_5$. For Friday, $x_1 = x_2 = x_3 = x_4 = 0$, and we obtain $\hat{y} = 466.2 + 124.3x_5$. Thus, we find that (all other things being equal) credit union traffic is heaviest on Mondays, next heaviest on Fridays, third heaviest on Thursdays, fourth heaviest on Tuesdays, and lightest on Wednesdays.

MULTIPLICATIVE MODELS

Often, we believe that there is a relationship of the following form:

$$Y = \beta_0 x_1^{\beta_1} x_2^{\beta_2} \cdots x_k^{\beta_k} \tag{23}$$

To estimate such a relationship, simply take logarithms of both sides of (23). This yields

$$\ln Y = \ln \beta_0 + \beta_1 (\ln x_1) + \beta_2 (\ln x_2) + \cdots + \beta_k (\ln x_k)$$

Thus, to estimate (23), we run a multiple regression with the dependent variable being $\ln Y$ and the independent variables being $\ln x_1, \ln x_2, \ldots, \ln x_k$. To illustrate the idea, suppose we want to determine how the annual operating costs of an insurance company depend on the number of home insurance and car insurance policies that have been written. Table 20 gives relevant information for ten branches of the insurance company.

To fit the model $Y = \beta_0 x_1^{\beta_1} x_2^{\beta_2}$, where $Y =$ annual operating cost, $x_1 =$ home insurance policies, and $x_2 =$ car insurance policies, we would input points of the form $(\ln 124{,}000, \ln 400, \ln 1200)$, etc. into the computer. The least squares estimates obtained are

$$\text{Constant term estimate} = 5.339$$
$$\text{Estimate for } \beta_1 = 0.583$$
$$\text{Estimate for } \beta_2 = 0.409$$

This regression yields an R^2 of 0.998, indicating a very good fit. The constant term estimate is an estimate of $\ln \beta_0$, so our actual estimate of β_0 is $e^{5.339} = 208.3$, and we estimate that $Y = 208.3 x_1^{0.583} x_2^{0.409}$. To illustrate the use of this equation, we predict annual operating cost for an insurance branch writing 500 home policies and 1200 car policies. For this branch, we obtain $Y = 208.3(500)^{0.583}(1200)^{0.409} = \$141{,}767$.

Table 20 Insurance Company Branch Data	BRANCH	ANNUAL OPERATING COST	NUMBER OF HOME INSURANCE POLICIES	NUMBER OF CAR INSURANCE POLICIES
	1	$124,000	400	1200
	2	$71,000	350	360
	3	$136,000	600	800
	4	$219,000	800	1800
	5	$230,000	900	1600
	6	$75,000	200	1000
	7	$56,000	120	900
	8	$110,000	340	1100
	9	$120,000	490	900
	10	$144,000	700	800

HETEROSCEDASTICITY AND AUTOCORRELATION IN MULTIPLE REGRESSION

By plotting the errors in time series sequence, we may check, (as described in Section 24.6) to see whether the errors from a multiple regression are independent. If autocorrelation is present and the errors do not appear to be independent, then correcting for autocorrelation will usually yield better forecasts.

By plotting the errors (on the y-axis) against the predicted value of y (on the x-axis), we can determine whether homoscedasticity or heteroscedasticity is present. If homoscedasticity is present, the plot should show no obvious pattern (that is, the plot should resemble Figure 6), whereas if heteroscedasticity is present, the plot should show an obvious pattern indicating that the errors somehow depend on the predicted value of y (perhaps as in Figure 7). If heteroscedasticity is present, the t-tests described in this section are invalid.

◆ PROBLEMS

GROUP A

1. For the years 1961–1970, the annual return on General Motors stock and the return on the Standard and Poor's market index were as given in Table 21.

(a) Let Y = return on General Motors stock during a year and X = return on Standard and Poor's index during a year. Financial theory suggests that $Y = \beta_0 + \beta_1 X + \varepsilon$, where β_1 is called the **beta** for General Motors. Give an interpretation for the beta of a stock (in this case, General Motors), and use the data in Table 21 to estimate the beta for General Motors.

(b) Does the Standard and Poor's index appear to have a significant effect (for $\alpha = 0.05$) on the return on General Motors stock?

(c) What percentage of the variation in the return on General Motors stock is explained by variation in the Standard and Poor's index?

Table 21		
YEAR	RETURN ON GENERAL MOTORS STOCK	RETURN ON STANDARD AND POOR'S INDEX
1961	12%	21%
1962	2%	−3%
1963	38%	15%
1964	26%	20%
1965	18%	12%
1966	−10%	0%
1967	0%	10%
1968	9%	10%
1969	−2%	2%
1970	−1%	−15%

(d) What percentage of the variation in the return on General Motors stock is unexplained by variation in Standard and Poor's index?
(e) During a year in which the Standard and Poor's index increased by 15%, what would we predict for the return on General Motors stock?

2. We are trying to determine the number of labor hours required to produce a unit of a product. We are given the information in Table 22. For example, the second unit produced required 517 labor hours, and the 600th unit produced required 34 labor hours.

Table 22

CUMULATIVE PRODUCTION	LABOR HOURS NEEDED FOR LAST UNIT
1	715
2	517
10	239
20	174
40	126
60	104
100	82
150	68
200	59
300	47
500	37
600	34

(a) Try to determine a relationship between the number of units already produced and the labor hours needed to produce the next unit. Why is this relationship called the **learning curve**?
(b) How many labor hours would be needed to produce the 800th unit?
(c) We are 95% sure that the prediction in part (b) is accurate within ____ hours.

3. Quarterly sales for a department store over a six-year period are given in Table 23.
(a) Use multiple regression to develop a model that can be used to predict future quarterly sales. (*Hint:* Use dummy variables and an independent variable for the number of the quarter (quarter 1, quarter 2, . . . , quarter 24).)
(b) Letting Y_t = sales during quarter number t, discuss how to fit the following model to the data in Table 23:

$$Y_t = \beta_0 \beta_1^t \beta_2^{x_2} \beta_3^{x_3} \beta_4^{x_4}$$

where $x_2 = 1$ if t is a first quarter, $x_3 = 1$ if t is a second quarter, and $x_4 = 1$ if t is a fourth quarter. (*Hint:* Take logarithms of both sides.)

Table 23

YEAR	QUARTER	SALES (Millions)
1984	1	$50,147
1984	2	$49,325
1984	3	$57,048
1984	4	$76,781
1985	1	$48,617
1985	2	$50,898
1985	3	$58,517
1985	4	$77,691
1986	1	$50,862
1986	2	$53,028
1986	3	$58,849
1986	4	$79,660
1987	1	$51,640
1987	2	$54,119
1987	3	$65,681
1987	4	$85,175
1988	1	$56,405
1988	2	$60,031
1988	3	$71,486
1988	4	$92,183
1989	1	$60,800
1989	2	$64,900
1989	3	$76,997
1989	4	$103,337

(c) Interpret the answer to part (b).
(d) Which model appears to yield better predictions for sales?

4. To determine how price influences sales, a company changed the price of a product over a 20-week period. The price charged each week and the number of units sold are given in Table 24. Develop a model to relate sales to price.

5. Confederate Express Service is attempting to determine how its shipping costs for a month depend on the number of units shipped during a month. For the last 15 months, the number of units shipped and total shipping cost are given in Table 25.
(a) Determine a relationship between units shipped and monthly shipping cost.
(b) Plot the errors for the predictions in order of time sequence. Is there any unusual pattern?
(c) We have been told that there was a trucking strike during months 11–15, and we believe that this may have influenced shipping costs. How could the answer to part (a) be modified to account for the effects of the strike?

Table 24

PRICE	UNITS SOLD
$1	1145
$2	788
$3	617
$4	394
$5	275
$6	319
$7	289
$8	241
$9	259
$10	176
$11	179
$12	232
$13	183
$14	181
$15	222
$16	212
$17	186
$18	110
$19	183
$20	172

Table 25

MONTH	UNITS SHIPPED	TOTAL SHIPPING COST
1	300	$1060
2	400	$1380
3	500	$1640
4	200	$740
5	300	$1060
6	350	$1190
7	460	$1520
8	480	$1580
9	120	$540
10	760	$2420
11	580	$2200
12	340	$1470
13	120	$790
14	100	$720
15	500	$1960

After accounting for the effects of the strike, does the unusual pattern in part (b) disappear?

GROUP B

6. In Example 1, we ran a regression with only x_1 (miles driven) as an independent variable. We found the coefficient of x_1 in this regression to be -51.68. This appears to indicate (contrary to what we would expect) that increasing the miles driven will lead to decreased maintenance costs. Explain this result. (*Hint:* Estimate the correlation between x_1 and x_2.)

7. Suppose we are trying to fit a curve to data, and part (i) of Figure 11 is relevant. Explain why the points of the form $\left(\dfrac{1}{x_i}, \ln y_i \right)$ should, when plotted, indicate a straight-line relationship.

8. Consider the regression in which we estimated cost of running an insurance company as a function of the number of home and car insurance policies. If there were a 1% increase in the number of car insurance policies, by what percentage would we predict that total costs would increase?

9. In the example in which we predicted the number of customers to enter the credit union, suppose that we have used five (instead of four) dummy variables to represent the days of the week. What problem would have arisen?

◆ SUMMARY

MOVING-AVERAGE FORECASTS

$$f_{t,1} = \text{average of last } N \text{ observations}$$

$$e_t = x_t - (\text{prediction for } x_t)$$

$$\text{MAD} = \text{average value of } |e_t|$$

Choose N to minimize MAD.

SIMPLE EXPONENTIAL SMOOTHING

$$A_t = \text{smoothed average at end of period } t$$
$$= f_{t,k} = \text{forecast for period } t + k \text{ made at end of period } t$$
$$A_t = \alpha x_t + (1 - \alpha)A_{t-1}$$

Choose α to minimize MAD.

HOLT'S METHOD

Holt's method is used when trend is present, but there is no seasonality.

$$L_t = \text{estimate of base at end of period } t$$
$$T_t = \text{estimate of per-period trend at end of period } t$$
$$L_t = \alpha x_t + (1 - \alpha)(L_{t-1} + T_{t-1})$$
$$T_t = \beta(L_t - L_{t-1}) + (1 - \beta)T_{t-1}$$
$$f_{t,k} = L_t + kT_t$$

WINTER'S METHOD

Winter's method is used when we believe that trend and seasonality may be present.

$$s_t = \text{estimate for month } t \text{ seasonal factor at the end of month } t$$
$$L_t = \frac{\alpha x_t}{s_{t-c}} + (1 - \alpha)(L_{t-1} + T_{t-1})$$
$$T_t = \beta(L_t - L_{t-1}) + (1 - \beta)T_{t-1}$$
$$s_t = \frac{\gamma x_t}{L_t} + (1 - \gamma)s_{t-c}$$
$$f_{t,k} = (L_t + kT_t)s_{t+k-c}$$

For all extrapolation methods, we expect 68% of our predictions to be within $s_e = 1.25$ MAD of the actual value and 95% of our predictions to be within $2s_e$ of the actual value.

SIMPLE LINEAR REGRESSION

Given data points $(x_1, y_1), \ldots, (x_n, y_n)$, we estimate a linear relationship between x and y by $\hat{y} = \hat{\beta}_0 + \hat{\beta}_1 x$, where

$$\hat{\beta}_1 = \frac{\sum (x_i - \bar{x})(y_i - \bar{y})}{\sum (x_i - \bar{x})^2} \quad \text{and} \quad \hat{\beta}_0 = \bar{y} - \hat{\beta}_1 \bar{x}$$

$$R^2 = \frac{\text{SSR}}{\text{SST}} = \text{percentage of variation in } y \text{ explained by } x$$

$$r_{xy} = \text{sample linear correlation between } x \text{ and } y$$

$$(r_{xy} \text{ indicates the strength of the linear relationship between } x \text{ and } y)$$

$$s_e = \sqrt{\frac{\text{SSE}}{n - 2}}$$

We expect 68% of our predictions to be within s_e of the actual value and 95% of our predictions to be within $2s_e$ of the actual value.

A t-statistic exceeding $t_{(\alpha/2, n-2)}$ in absolute value is evidence (at level of significance α) that there is a significant linear relationship between x and y.

FITTING A NONLINEAR RELATIONSHIP

Step 1 Plot the points and find the part of Figure 11 that best fits the data.

Step 2 The second column of Table 14 gives the functional relationship between x and y.

Step 3 Transform each data point according to the rules in the third column of Table 14.

Step 4 Estimate the least squares regression line for the transformed data. If $\hat{\beta}_0$ is the intercept of the least squares line (for transformed data) and $\hat{\beta}_1$ is the slope of the least squares line (for transformed data), then we read the estimated relationship from the final column of Table 14.

MULTIPLE REGRESSION

Multiple regression is used when more than one independent variable is needed to predict y.

R^2 = percentage of variation in y explained by the independent variables

Reject $H_0: \beta_i = 0$ at a level of significance α if $(t$ for $x_i) \geq t_{(\alpha/2, n-k-1)}$, where k is the number of independent variables being used to predict y.

If there is a strong linear relationship between two or more independent variables, then $\hat{\beta}_i$ may be an unreliable estimate of β_i. In such cases, we say that **multicollinearity** is present.

If a nonquantitative or qualitative independent variable (such as the day of the week or the month of the year) is believed to influence a dependent variable, **dummy variables** may be used to model the effect of the qualitative independent variable on the dependent variable. If the qualitative variable can assume c values, use only $c - 1$ dummy variables.

◆ REVIEW PROBLEMS

GROUP A

1. Table 26 gives data concerning pork sales. (Price is in dollars per hundred lb sold, quantity sold is in billions of pounds, per-capita income is in dollars, U.S. population is in millions, and GNP is in billions of dollars.)

(a) Use this data to develop a regression equation that could be used to predict the quantity of pork sold during future periods. Is autocorrelation, heteroscedasticity, or multicollinearity a problem?

(b) Suppose that during each of the next two quarters, price = \$45, U.S. population = 240, GNP = 2620, and per-capita income = \$10,000. Predict the quantity of pork sold during each of the next two quarters.

(c) 68% of the time, we expect our prediction for pork sales to be accurate within ____.

(d) Use Winter's method to develop a forecast for pork sales during the next two quarters. (Use the first two years to initialize.)

2. We are to predict sales for a motel chain based on the information in Table 27.

(a) Use this data and multiple regression to make predictions for the motel chain's sales during the next four

Table 26

QUARTER	YEAR	PRICE OF PORK	QUANTITY SOLD	PER-CAPITA INCOME	U.S. POPULATION	GNP
1	1975	39.35	30.44	8255	212	1549
2	1975	46.11	29.23	8671	213	1589
3	1975	58.83	25.12	8583	214	1629
4	1975	52.2	28.35	8649	215	1669
1	1976	47.99	28.95	8775	216	1718
2	1976	49.19	27.83	8812	217	1768
3	1976	43.88	29.53	8884	218	1818
4	1976	34.25	35.9	8967	219	1868
1	1977	39.08	32.94	9036	220	1918
2	1977	40.87	31.86	9125	221	1978
3	1977	43.85	30.74	9280	222	2038
4	1977	41.38	34.99	9399	223	2098
1	1978	47.44	32.43	9487	224	2148
2	1978	47.84	32.65	9530	225	2218
3	1978	48.52	31.58	9622	226	2288
4	1978	50.05	35.40	9732	227	2338
1	1979	51.98	33.98	9813	228	2398
2	1979	48.04	37.58	9778	229	2448
3	1979	38.52	38.59	9809	230	2478
4	1979	36.39	43.47	9867	231	2508
1	1980	36.31	41.24	9958	232	2539
2	1980	31.18	43.00	9805	235	2598
3	1980	46.23	37.57	9882	235	2598

quarters. Assume that advertising during each of the next four quarters is $50,000.

(b) Use the Holt method to make forecasts for the motel chain's sales during the next four quarters.

(c) Use simple exponential smoothing to make predictions for the motel chain's sales during the next four quarters.

(d) Use Winter's method to determine predictions for the motel chain's sales during the next four quarters.

(e) Which forecasts would be expected to be the most reliable? (*Hint:* Use advertising, lagged by one period, as an independent variable.)

3. Table 28 gives the following data for monthly U.S. housing sales (in thousands of houses) for 1965–1972.

(a) Use the years 1965–1966 to initialize the parameters for Winter's method. Then find values of α, β, and γ that yield a MAD (for 1967–1972) of less than 3.5. (*Hint:* It may be necessary to use $\alpha > 0.5$.)

(b) We would expect 68% of our forecasts to be accurate within ____ and 95% of our forecasts to be accurate within ____.

(c) Check to see whether the data is consistent with the answer to part (b).

(d) Although we have not discussed autocorrelation for smoothing methods, good forecasts derived from smoothing methods should exhibit no autocorrelation. Do the forecast errors for this problem exhibit autocorrelation?

(e) It has been stated that if only trend and seasonality are important factors, then α should be at most 0.5. Explain why this problem required $\alpha > 0.5$.

(f) At the end of December 1972, what is the forecast for housing sales during the first three months of 1973?

Note: This assignment is a snap on a spreadsheet such as Lotus 1–2–3. The Spreadsheet might be set up as in Table 29. In B14, enter +A$3*A14/D2+ (1-A$3)*(B13+C13). Do C14, D14, E14 yourself. Remember that the forecast must be made before "seeing" A14. In F14, enter +A14-E14. In G14, enter @ABS(F14). Copy from B14..G14 to ??. To compute MAD, average the absolute errors for each month (rows 14–85).

Table 27

QUARTER	POTENTIAL CUSTOMERS (Thousands)	ADVERTISING (Thousands of dollars)	SEASON	SALES (Millions)
1	100	30	Winter	1200
2	105	20	Spring	880
3	111	15	Summer	1800
4	117	40	Fall	1050
5	122	10	Winter	1700
6	128	50	Spring	350
7	135	5	Summer	2500
8	142	40	Fall	760
9	149	20	Winter	2300
10	156	10	Spring	1000
11	164	60	Summer	1570
12	172	5	Fall	2430
13	181	35	Winter	1320
14	190	15	Spring	1400
15	200	70	Summer	1890
16	210	25	Fall	3200
17	221	30	Winter	2200
18	232	60	Spring	1440
19	243	80	Summer	4000
20	264	60	Fall	4100

Table 28

YEAR	JAN	FEB	MAR	AP	MAY	JUNE	JULY	AUG	SEPT	OCT	NOV	DEC
1965	38	44	53	49	54	57	51	58	48	44	42	37
1966	42	43	53	49	49	40	40	36	29	31	26	23
1967	29	32	41	44	49	47	46	47	43	45	34	31
1968	35	43	46	46	43	41	44	47	41	40	32	32
1969	34	40	43	42	43	44	39	40	33	32	31	28
1970	34	29	36	42	43	44	44	48	45	44	40	37
1971	45	49	62	62	58	59	64	62	50	52	50	44
1972	51	56	60	65	64	63	63	72	61	65	51	47

4. Using x as the independent variable and y as the dependent variable, find the least squares line for the following three data points:

x	y
1	2
4	5
7	2

5. We are trying to predict the number of uses of automatic bank teller machines as a function of time. The data are given in Table 30. Here, x = number of years after 1980 and y = number of monthly uses of ATMs (in millions) during the given year. The estimated regression equation is $\hat{y} = 102.3 + 34.8x$. We are given that SST = 74,100 and SSE = 1298. We are given that StdErr $(\hat{\beta}_1) = 1.76$.

Table 29

ROW	A	B	C	D	E	F	G
1	SALES	BASE	TREND	SEASON	FORE	ERR	ABSERR
2	ALPHA	BETA	GAMMA	S-11			
3	.1	.2	.3	S-10			
.							
.							
.							
13		LO	TO	SO			
14	29						
15	32						
.							
.							
85	47						

Table 30

x	y
0	100
1	130
2	170
3	200
4	260
5	300
6	305
7	330
8	380

(a) Test H_0: $\beta_1 = 0$ against H_a: $\beta_1 \neq 0$ for $\alpha = 0.05$. Interpret the result.

(b) Find the correlation between x and y.

(c) Is the 1987 data an outlier?

(d) If present trends continue, what is the approximate probability that during 1990, more than 470 million ATM transactions per month will occur? (*Hint:* Use the fact that the errors are normally distributed.)

6. Carboco puts metal coatings on jet propeller blades. The harder the coating, the higher the quality of the coating. The coating is shot onto the blade using pressurized gas contained in an F-Gun. Carboco can control the temperature and gas pressure in the F-gun and can also control the room humidity. To see how gas pressure, temperature, and humidity influence hardness, Carboco engineers have run a regression for which the dependent variable is

HARD = hardness of a coating

and the independent variables are

HUMIDI = room humidity

TEMP = 1   if temperature level is high

= 0   if temperature level is low

PRESS = 1   if gas pressure is high

= 0   if gas pressure is low

T*P = product of TEMP and PRESS

We assume that temperature and gas pressure have only two possible levels, low and high. The relevant data are given in Table 31.

(a) Ignoring considerations of heteroscedasticity, multicollinearity, and autocorrelation, which equation should be used to predict hardness? Explain.

(b) What combination of gas pressure and temperature setting will maximize hardness?

(c) Explain how changing temperature from a low level to a high level affects hardness. Be specific!

7. We have been assigned to determine how the total weekly production cost for Widgetco depends on the number of widgets produced during the week. The following model has been proposed:

$$\mu_Y = \beta_0 + \beta_1 X + \beta_2 X^2 + \beta_3 X^3 + \varepsilon$$

where X = number of widgets produced during the week and Y = total production cost for the week. For 15 weeks of data, we found that SSR = 215,475 and SST = 229,228. For this model, we obtain the following estimated regression equation:

Table 31

HUMIDI	TEMP	PRESS	HARD
40	1	0	148
60	1	0	209
50	1	0	177
70	1	0	208
80	1	0	262
60	1	1	248
65	1	1	253
70	1	1	263
35	1	1	184
45	1	1	220
70	0	0	129
28	0	0	53
49	0	0	98
89	0	0	170
90	0	0	172
34	0	1	80
56	0	1	90
77	0	1	151
23	0	1	58
56	0	1	107

Table 32

MONTH	SALES .	PRICE
1	400	5
2	1042	4
3	1129	8
4	1110	6
5	1336	6
6	1363	10
7	1177	9
8	603	8
9	582	12
10	697	9
11	586	8
12	673	9
13	546	10
14	334	11
15	27	8
16	76	9
17	298	10
18	746	6
19	962	7
20	907	8

$$\hat{y} = -29.7 + 19.8X - 0.39X^2 + 0.005X^3$$
$$\quad\quad\quad (0.78)\quad\quad (0.62)\quad\quad (1.25)$$

(t-statistics for each coefficient are in parentheses.)

(a) For $\alpha = 0.10$, test H_0: $\beta_i = 0$ against H_a: $\beta_i \neq 0$ ($i = 1, 2, 3$).

(b) Determine R^2 for this model. How can the high R^2 value be reconciled with the answer to part (a)?

8. Let Y_t = sales during month t (in thousands of dollars) for a photography studio (SALES in Table 32) and P_t = price charged for portraits during month t (PRICE in Table 32). Use a computer to fit the following model to the data in Table 32:

$$Y_t = \beta_0 + \beta_1 Y_{t-1} + \beta_2 P_t + \varepsilon_t$$

Thus, last month's sales and the current month's price are independent variables.

(a) If the price of a portrait during month 21 is $10, what would we predict for month 21's sales?

(b) Does there appear to be a problem with autocorrelation, heteroscedasticity, or multicollinearity?

9. The U.S. GNP during the years 1975–1984 is given in Table 33 (in billions of dollars).

(a) Plot x = years after 1974 against GNP, and use the plot to describe how to fit a curve that could be used to predict GNP during future years.

Table 33

YEAR	GNP
1975	1060
1976	1170
1977	1305
1978	1455
1979	1630
1980	1800
1981	2000
1982	2220
1983	2450
1984	2730

(b) When the regression on transformed data is done, we find that $\hat{\beta}_0 = 6.86$ and $\hat{\beta}_1 = 0.105$. What is the prediction for 1985 GNP?

GROUP B

10. Suppose the true relationship between Y and time t is given by

$$Y = \beta_0 e^{\beta_1 t} + \varepsilon$$

where $\beta_1 > 0$. If we try to fit our usual linear model $Y = \beta_0 + \beta_1 t + \varepsilon$ to the data, are we likely to encounter autocorrelation? Heteroscedasticity? Multicollinearity?

◆ REFERENCES

For further information on extrapolation methods, we recommend:

HAX, A., and D. CANDEA. *Production and Inventory Management*. Englewood Cliffs, N.J.: Prentice-Hall, 1984.

MAKRIDAKIS, S., and S. WHEELWRIGHT. *Forecasting: Methods and Applications*. New York: Wiley, 1986.

For further information on regression, we recommend:

CHATTERJEE, S., and B. PRICE. *Regression Analysis by Example*. New York: Wiley, 1977.

DANIEL, C., and F. WOOD. *Fitting Equations to Data*. New York: Wiley, 1980.

MONTGOMERY, D., and E. PECK. *Introduction to Linear Regression Analysis*. New York: Wiley, 1982.

PINDYCK, R., and D. RUBINFELD. *Econometric Models and Economic Forecasts*. New York: McGraw-Hill, 1981.

Answers to Selected Problems

◆ CHAPTER 2

SECTION 2.1

1a. $-A = \begin{bmatrix} -1 & -2 & -3 \\ -4 & -5 & -6 \\ -7 & -8 & -9 \end{bmatrix}$

b. $3A = \begin{bmatrix} 3 & 6 & 9 \\ 12 & 15 & 18 \\ 21 & 24 & 27 \end{bmatrix}$

c. $A + 2B$ is undefined.

d. $A^T = \begin{bmatrix} 1 & 4 & 7 \\ 2 & 5 & 8 \\ 3 & 6 & 9 \end{bmatrix}$

e. $B^T = \begin{bmatrix} 1 & 0 & 1 \\ 2 & -1 & 2 \end{bmatrix}$

f. $AB = \begin{bmatrix} 4 & 6 \\ 10 & 15 \\ 16 & 24 \end{bmatrix}$

g. BA is undefined.

2. $\begin{bmatrix} y_1 \\ y_2 \\ y_3 \end{bmatrix} = \begin{bmatrix} 0.50 & 0 & 0.10 \\ 0.30 & 0.70 & 0.30 \\ 0.20 & 0.30 & 0.60 \end{bmatrix} \begin{bmatrix} x_1 \\ x_2 \\ x_3 \end{bmatrix}$

SECTION 2.2

1. $\begin{bmatrix} 1 & -1 \\ 2 & 1 \\ 1 & 3 \end{bmatrix} \begin{bmatrix} x_1 \\ x_2 \end{bmatrix} = \begin{bmatrix} 4 \\ 6 \\ 8 \end{bmatrix}$ or $\begin{bmatrix} 1 & -1 & | & 4 \\ 2 & 1 & | & 6 \\ 1 & 3 & | & 8 \end{bmatrix}$

SECTION 2.3

1. No solution.

2. Infinite number of solutions of the form $x_1 = 2 - 2k$, $x_2 = 2 + k$, $x_3 = k$.

3. $x_1 = 2, x_2 = -1$.

SECTION 2.4

1. Linearly dependent.

2. Linearly independent.

SECTION 2.5

2. $A^{-1} = \begin{bmatrix} \frac{1}{2} & \frac{1}{2} & -\frac{1}{2} \\ -1 & -2 & 3 \\ \frac{1}{2} & -\frac{1}{2} & \frac{1}{2} \end{bmatrix}$

3. A^{-1} does not exist.

8a. $\frac{1}{100}B^{-1}$.

SECTION 2.6

2. 30.

REVIEW PROBLEMS

1. Infinite number of solutions of the form $x_1 = k - 1$, $x_2 = 3 - k, x_3 = k$.

3. $\begin{bmatrix} U_{t+1} \\ T_{t+1} \end{bmatrix} = \begin{bmatrix} 0.75 & 0 \\ 0.20 & 0.90 \end{bmatrix} \begin{bmatrix} U_t \\ T_t \end{bmatrix}$

4. $x_1 = 0, x_2 = 1$.

13. Linearly independent.

14. Linearly dependent.

15a. Only if a, b, c, and d are all nonzero will rank $A = 4$. Thus, A^{-1} exists if and only if all of a, b, c, and d are nonzero.
(b) Applying the Gauss-Jordan method, we find if a, b, c, and d are all nonzero,

$$A^{-1} = \begin{bmatrix} \frac{1}{a} & 0 & 0 & 0 \\ 0 & \frac{1}{b} & 0 & 0 \\ 0 & 0 & \frac{1}{c} & 0 \\ 0 & 0 & 0 & \frac{1}{d} \end{bmatrix}$$

18. -4.

◆ CHAPTER 3

SECTION 3.1

1. $\max z = 30x_1 + 100x_2$

s.t. $x_1 + x_2 \leq 7$ (Land constraint)
  $4x_1 + 10x_2 \leq 40$ (Labor constraint)
  $10x_1 \geq 30$ (Government constraint)
  $x_1, x_2 \geq 0$

2. No, the government constraint is not satisfied.
b. No, the labor constraint is not satisfied.
c. No, $x_2 \geq 0$ is not satisfied.

SECTION 3.2

1. $z = \$370$, $x_1 = 3$, $x_2 = 2.8$.
3. $z = \$14$, $x_1 = 3$, $x_2 = 2$.
4a. We want to make x_1 larger and x_2 smaller, so we move down and to the right.
b. We want to make x_1 smaller and x_2 larger, so we move up and to the left.
c. We want to make both x_1 and x_2 smaller, so we move down and to the left.

SECTION 3.3

1. No feasible solution.
2. Alternative optimal solutions.
3. Unbounded LP.

SECTION 3.4

1. For $i = 1, 2, 3$, let x_i = tons of processed factory i waste. Then the appropriate LP is

$\min z = 15x_1 + 10x_2 + 20x_3$

s.t. $0.10x_1 + 0.20x_2 + 0.40x_3 \geq 30$ (Pollutant 1)
  $0.45x_1 + 0.25x_2 + 0.30x_3 \geq 40$ (Pollutant 2)
    $x_1, x_2, x_3 \geq 0$

It is doubtful that the processing cost is proportional to the amount of waste processed. For example, processing 10 tons of waste is probably not 10 times as costly as processing 1 ton of waste. The Divisibility and Certainty Assumptions seem reasonable.

SECTION 3.5

1. Let x_1 = number of full-time employees (FTE) who start work on Sunday, x_2 = number of FTE who start work on Monday, $\ldots$, x_7 = number of FTE who start work on Saturday; x_8 = number of part-time employees (PTE) who start work on Sunday, $\ldots$, x_{14} = number of PTE who start work on Saturday. Then the appropriate LP is

$\min z = 15(8)(5)(x_1 + x_2 + \cdots + x_7)$
    $+ 10(4)(5)(x_8 + x_9 + \cdots + x_{14})$

s.t. $8(x_1 + x_4 + x_5 + x_6 + x_7) + 4(x_8 + x_{11} + x_{12}$
    $+ x_{13} + x_{14}) \geq 88$ (Sunday)
  $8(x_1 + x_2 + x_5 + x_6 + x_7) + 4(x_8 + x_9 + x_{12}$
    $+ x_{13} + x_{14}) \geq 136$ (Monday)
  $8(x_1 + x_2 + x_3 + x_6 + x_7) + 4(x_8 + x_9 + x_{10}$
    $+ x_{13} + x_{14}) \geq 104$ (Tuesday)
  $8(x_1 + x_2 + x_3 + x_4 + x_7) + 4(x_8 + x_9 + x_{10}$
    $+ x_{11} + x_{14}) \geq 120$ (Wednesday)
  $8(x_1 + x_2 + x_3 + x_4 + x_5) + 4(x_8 + x_9 + x_{10}$
    $+ x_{11} + x_{12}) \geq 152$ (Thursday)
  $8(x_2 + x_3 + x_4 + x_5 + x_6) + 4(x_9 + x_{10} + x_{11}$
    $+ x_{12} + x_{13}) \geq 112$ (Friday)
  $8(x_3 + x_4 + x_5 + x_6 + x_7) + 4(x_{10} + x_{11} + x_{12}$
    $+ x_{13} + x_{14}) \geq 128$ (Saturday)
  $20(x_8 + x_9 + x_{10} + x_{11} + x_{12} + x_{13} + x_{14})$
    $\leq 0.25(136 + 104 + 120 + 152 + 112 + 128 + 88)$

(The last constraint ensures that part-time labor will fulfill at most 25% of all labor requirements)

All variables ≥ 0

3. Let x_1 = number of employees who start work on Sunday and work five days, x_2 = number of employees who start work on Monday and work five days, ..., x_7 = number of employees who start work on Saturday and work five days. Also let o_1 = number of employees who start work on Sunday and work six days, ..., o_7 = number of employees who start work on Saturday and work six days. Then the appropriate LP is

$$\min z = 250(x_1 + x_2 + \cdots + x_7) \\ + 312(o_1 + o_2 + \cdots + o_7)$$

s.t. $x_1 + x_4 + x_5 + x_6 + x_7 + o_1 + o_3 + o_4$
$$+ o_5 + o_6 + o_7 \geq 11 \qquad \text{(Sunday)}$$

$x_1 + x_2 + x_5 + x_6 + x_7 + o_1 + o_2 + o_4$
$$+ o_5 + o_6 + o_7 \geq 17 \qquad \text{(Monday)}$$

$x_1 + x_2 + x_3 + x_6 + x_7 + o_1 + o_2 + o_3$
$$+ o_5 + o_6 + o_7 \geq 13 \qquad \text{(Tuesday)}$$

$x_1 + x_2 + x_3 + x_4 + x_7 + o_1 + o_2 + o_3$
$$+ o_4 + o_6 + o_7 \geq 15 \qquad \text{(Wednesday)}$$

$x_1 + x_2 + x_3 + x_4 + x_5 + o_1 + o_2 + o_3$
$$+ o_4 + o_5 + o_7 \geq 19 \qquad \text{(Thursday)}$$

$x_2 + x_3 + x_4 + x_5 + x_6 + o_1 + o_2 + o_3$
$$+ o_4 + o_5 + o_6 \geq 14 \qquad \text{(Friday)}$$

$x_3 + x_4 + x_5 + x_6 + x_7 + o_2 + o_3 + o_4$
$$+ o_5 + o_6 + o_7 \geq 16 \qquad \text{(Saturday)}$$

$$\text{All variables} \geq 0$$

SECTION 3.6

2. NPV of investment $1 = -6 - \dfrac{5}{1.1} + \dfrac{7}{(1.1)^2} +$

$\dfrac{9}{(1.1)^3} = \$2.00.$

NPV of investment $2 = -8 - \dfrac{3}{1.1} + \dfrac{9}{(1.1)^2} +$

$\dfrac{7}{(1.1)^3} = \$1.97.$

Let x_1 = fraction of investment 1 that is undertaken and x_2 = fraction of investment 2 that is undertaken. If we measure NPV in thousands of dollars, we wish to solve the following LP:

$$\max z = 2x_1 + 1.97x_2$$

s.t. $6x_1 + 8x_2 \leq 10$
$$5x_1 + 3x_2 \leq 7$$
$$x_1 \qquad\quad \leq 1$$
$$\qquad x_2 \leq 1$$

$$\text{All variables} \geq 0$$

The optimal solution to this LP is $x_1 = 1$, $x_2 = 0.5$, $z = \$2985$.

SECTION 3.7

1. $z = \$2500$, $x_1 = 50$, $x_2 = 100$.

SECTION 3.8

1. Let ingredient 1 = sugar, ingredient 2 = nuts, ingredient 3 = chocolate, candy 1 = Slugger, and candy 2 = Easy Out. Let x_{ij} = ounces of ingredient i used to make candy j. (All variables are in ounces.) The appropriate LP is

$$\max z = 25(x_{12} + x_{22} + x_{32}) + 20(x_{11} + x_{21} + x_{31})$$

s.t. $x_{11} + x_{12} \leq 100 \qquad \text{(Sugar constraint)}$
$$x_{21} + x_{22} \leq 20 \qquad \text{(Nuts constraint)}$$
$$x_{31} + x_{32} \leq 30 \qquad \text{(Chocolate constraint)}$$
$$x_{22} \geq 0.2(x_{12} + x_{22} + x_{32})$$
$$x_{21} \geq 0.1(x_{11} + x_{21} + x_{31})$$
$$x_{31} \geq 0.1(x_{11} + x_{21} + x_{31})$$
$$\text{All variables} \geq 0$$

SECTION 3.9

1. Let x_1 = hours of process 1 run per week
x_2 = hours of process 2 run per week
x_3 = hours of process 3 run per week
g_2 = barrels of gas 2 sold per week
o_1 = barrels of oil 1 purchased per week
o_2 = barrels of oil 2 purchased per week

$$\max z = 9(2x_1) + 10g_2 + 24(2x_3) - 5x_1 - 4x_2 \\ - x_3 - 2o_1 - 3o_2$$

s.t. $o_1 = 2x_1 + x_2$
$$o_2 = 3x_1 + 3x_2 + 2x_3$$
$$o_1 \leq 200$$
$$o_2 \leq 300$$
$$g_2 + 3x_3 = x_1 + 3x_2 \qquad \text{(Gas 2 production)}$$
$$x_1 + x_2 + x_3 \leq 100 \qquad \text{(100 hours per week} \\ \text{of cracker time)}$$

$$\text{All variables} \geq 0$$

4. Let A = total number of units of A produced
B = total number of units of B produced
CS = total number of units of C produced (and sold)
AS = units of A sold

BS = units of B sold

$$\max z = 10AS + 56BS + 100CS$$
$$\text{s.t.} \quad A + 2B + 3C \leq 40$$
$$A = AS + 2B$$
$$B = BS + CS$$
$$\text{All variables} \geq 0$$

SECTION 3.10

1. Let x_t = production during month t and i_t = inventory at end of month t.

$$\min z = 5x_1 + 8x_2 + 4x_3 + 7x_4$$
$$+ 2i_1 + 2i_2 + 2i_3 + 2i_4 - 6i_4$$
$$\text{s.t.} \quad i_1 = x_1 - 50$$
$$i_2 = i_1 + x_2 - 65$$
$$i_3 = i_2 + x_3 - 100$$
$$i_4 = i_3 + x_4 - 70$$
$$\text{All variables} \geq 0$$

SECTION 3.11

3. Let A = dollars invested in A, B = dollars invested in B, c_0 = leftover cash at time 0, c_1 = leftover cash at time 1, and c_2 = leftover cash at time 2. Then a correct formulation is

$$\max z = c_2 + 1.9B$$
$$\text{s.t.} \quad A + c_0 = 10{,}000$$
$$\text{(Time 0 available} = \text{time 0 invested)}$$
$$0.2A + c_0 = B + c_1$$
$$\text{(Time 1 available} = \text{time 1 invested)}$$
$$1.5A + c_1 = c_2$$
$$\text{(Time 2 available} = \text{time 2 invested)}$$
$$\text{All variables} \geq 0$$

The optimal solution to this LP is $B = c_0 = \$10{,}000$, $A = c_1 = c_2 = 0$, and $z = \$19{,}000$. Notice that it is optimal to wait for the "good" investment (B) even though leftover cash earns no interest.

SECTION 3.12

2. Let JAN1 = number of computers rented at beginning of January for one month, etc. Also define IJAN = number of computers available to meet January demand, etc. The appropriate LP is

$$\min z = 200(\text{JAN1} + \text{FEB1} + \text{MAR1} + \text{APR1}$$
$$+ \text{MAY1} + \text{JUN1}) + 350(\text{JAN2} + \text{FEB2}$$
$$+ \text{MAR2} + \text{APR2} + \text{MAY2} + \text{JUN2})$$

$$+ 450(\text{JAN3} + \text{FEB3} + \text{MAR3} + \text{APR3})$$
$$+ \text{MAY3} + \text{JUN3}) - 150\text{MAY3}$$
$$- 300\ \text{JUN3} - 175\text{JUN2}$$
$$\text{s.t.} \quad \text{IJAN} = \text{JAN1} + \text{JAN2} + \text{JAN3}$$
$$\text{IFEB} = \text{IJAN} - \text{JAN1} + \text{FEB1} + \text{FEB2}$$
$$+ \text{FEB3}$$
$$\text{IMAR} = \text{IFEB} - \text{JAN2} - \text{FEB1} + \text{MAR1}$$
$$+ \text{MAR2} + \text{MAR3}$$
$$\text{IAPR} = \text{IMAR} - \text{FEB2} - \text{MAR1} - \text{JAN3}$$
$$+ \text{APR1} + \text{APR2} + \text{APR3}$$
$$\text{IMAY} = \text{IAPR} - \text{FEB3} - \text{MAR2} - \text{APR1}$$
$$+ \text{MAY1} + \text{MAY2} + \text{MAY3}$$
$$\text{IJUN} = \text{IMAY} - \text{MAR3} - \text{APR2} - \text{MAY1}$$
$$+ \text{JUN1} + \text{JUN2} + \text{JUN3}$$
$$\text{IJAN} \geq 9$$
$$\text{IFEB} \geq 5$$
$$\text{IMAR} \geq 7$$
$$\text{IAPR} \geq 9$$
$$\text{IMAY} \geq 10$$
$$\text{IJUN} \geq 5$$
$$\text{All variables} \geq 0$$

REVIEW PROBLEMS

2. Let x_1 = number of chocolate cakes baked and x_2 = number of vanilla cakes baked. Then we must solve

$$\max z = x_1 + \tfrac{1}{2}x_2$$
$$\text{s.t.} \quad \tfrac{1}{3}x_1 + \tfrac{2}{3}x_2 \leq 8$$
$$4x_1 + x_2 \leq 30$$
$$x_1, x_2 \geq 0$$

The optimal solution is $z = \frac{\$69}{7}$, $x_1 = \frac{36}{7}$, $x_2 = \frac{66}{7}$.

8. Let x_1 = acres of farm 1 devoted to corn, x_2 = acres of farm 1 devoted to wheat, x_3 = acres of farm 2 devoted to corn, x_4 = acres of farm 2 devoted to wheat. Then a correct formulation is

$$\min z = 100x_1 + 90x_2 + 120x_3 + 80x_4$$
$$\text{s.t.} \quad x_1 + x_2 \leq 100$$
$$\text{(Farm 1 land)}$$
$$x_3 + x_4 \leq 100$$
$$\text{(Farm 2 land)}$$
$$500x_1 + 650x_3 \geq 7000$$
$$\text{(Corn requirement)}$$
$$400x_2 + 350x_4 \geq 11{,}000$$
$$\text{(Wheat requirement)}$$
$$x_1, x_2, x_3, x_4 \geq 0$$

9. Let x_1 = units of process 1, x_2 = units of process 2, and x_3 = modeling hours hired. Then a correct formulation is

$$\max z = 5(3x_1 + 5x_2) - 3(x_1 + 2x_2)$$
$$- 2(2x_1 + 3x_2) - 100x_3$$

s.t. $x_1 + 2x_2 \leq 20{,}000$ (Limited labor)

$2x_1 + 3x_2 \leq 35{,}000$ (Limited chemicals)

$3x_1 + 5x_2 = 1000 + 200x_3$

(Perfume production = perfume demands)

$x_1, x_2, x_3 \geq 0$

17. Let OT = number of tables made of oak, OC = number of chairs made of oak, PT = number of tables made of pine, and PC = number of chairs made of pine. Then the correct formulation is

$$\max z = 40(OT + PT) + 15(OC + PC)$$

s.t. $17(OT) + 5(OC) \leq 150$

(Use at most 150 board ft of oak)

$30PT + 13PC \leq 210$

(Use at most 210 board ft of pine)

$OT, OC, PT, PC \geq 0$

18. Let school 1 = Cooley High, and school 2 = Walt Whitman High. Let M_{ij} = number of minority students who live in district i who will attend school j, and let NM_{ij} = number of nonminority students who live in district i who will attend school j. Then the correct LP is

$$\min z = (M_{11} + NM_{11}) + 2(M_{12} + NM_{12})$$
$$+ 2(M_{21} + NM_{21}) + (M_{22} + NM_{22})$$
$$+ (M_{31} + NM_{31}) + (M_{32} + NM_{32})$$

s.t. $M_{11} + M_{12} = 50$

$M_{21} + M_{22} = 50$

$M_{31} + M_{32} = 100$

$NM_{11} + NM_{12} = 200$

$NM_{21} + NM_{22} = 250$

$NM_{31} + NM_{32} = 150$

For school 1, we obtain the following blending constraints:

$$0.20 \leq \frac{M_{11} + M_{21} + M_{31}}{M_{11} + M_{21} + M_{31} + NM_{11} + NM_{21} + NM_{31}}$$
$$\leq 0.30$$

This yields the following two LP constraints:

$0.8M_{11} + 0.8M_{21} + 0.8M_{31} - 0.2NM_{11}$
$$- 0.2NM_{21} - 0.2NM_{31} \geq 0$$

$0.7M_{11} + 0.7M_{21} + 0.7M_{32} - 0.3NM_{11}$
$$- 0.3NM_{21} - 0.3NM_{31} \leq 0$$

For school 2, we obtain the following blending constraints:

$$0.20 \leq \frac{M_{12} + M_{22} + M_{32}}{M_{12} + M_{22} + M_{32} + NM_{12} + NM_{22} + NM_{32}}$$
$$\leq 0.30$$

This yields the following two LP constraints:

$0.8M_{12} + 0.8M_{22} + 0.8M_{32} - 0.20NM_{12}$
$$- 0.20NM_{22} - 0.20NM_{32} \geq 0$$

$0.7M_{12} + 0.7M_{22} + 0.7M_{32} - 0.30NM_{12}$
$$- 0.30NM_{22} - 0.30NM_{32} \leq 0$$

We must also ensure that each school has between 300 and 500 students. Thus, we also need the following constraints:

$$300 \leq M_{11} + NM_{11} + M_{21} + NM_{21} + M_{31} + NM_{31}$$
$$\leq 500$$

$$300 \leq M_{12} + NM_{12} + M_{22} + NM_{22} + M_{32} + NM_{32}$$
$$\leq 500$$

To complete the formulation, add the sign restrictions that all variables are ≥ 0.

25. For $i < j$, let X_{ij} = number of workers who get off days i and j of week (day 1 = Sunday, day 2 = Monday, . . . , day 7 = Saturday).

$$\max z = X_{12} + X_{17} + X_{23} + X_{34} + X_{45} + X_{56} + X_{67}$$

s.t. $X_{17} + X_{27} + X_{37} + X_{47} + X_{57} + X_{67} = 2$

(Saturday constraint)

$X_{12} + X_{13} + X_{14} + X_{15} + X_{16} + X_{17} = 12$

(Sunday constraint)

$X_{12} + X_{23} + X_{24} + X_{25} + X_{26} + X_{27} = 12$

(Monday constraint)

$X_{13} + X_{23} + X_{34} + X_{35} + X_{36} + X_{37} = 6$

(Tuesday constraint)

$X_{14} + X_{24} + X_{34} + X_{45} + X_{46} + X_{47} = 5$

(Wednesday constraint)

$X_{15} + X_{25} + X_{35} + X_{45} + X_{56} + X_{57} = 14$

(Thursday constraint)

$X_{16} + X_{26} + X_{36} + X_{46} + X_{56} + X_{67} = 9$

(Friday constraint)

All variables ≥ 0

27. Let X_{ij} = money invested at beginning of month i for a period of j months. After noting that for each month (money invested) + (bills paid) = (money available), we obtain the following formulation:

$$\max z = 1.08X_{14} + 1.03X_{23} + 1.01X_{32} + 1.001X_{41}$$

s.t. $X_{11} + X_{12} + X_{13} + X_{14} + 600 = 400 + 400$

(Month 1)

$$X_{21} + X_{22} + X_{23} + 500 = 1.001X_{11} + 800$$
$$\text{(Month 2)}$$

$$X_{31} + X_{32} + 500 = 1.01X_{12} + 1.001X_{21} + 300$$
$$\text{(Month 3)}$$

$$X_{41} + 250 = 1.03X_{13} + 1.01X_{22} + 1.001X_{31} + 300$$
$$\text{(Month 4)}$$

$$\text{All variables} \geq 0$$

31. Let T_1 = number of type 1 turkeys purchased

T_2 = number of type 2 turkeys purchased

D_1 = pounds of dark meat used in cutlet 1

W_1 = pounds of white meat used in cutlet 1

D_2 = pounds of dark meat used in cutlet 2

W_2 = pounds of white meat in cutlet 2

Then the appropriate formulation is

$$\max z = 4(W_1 + D_1) + 3(W_2 + D_2) - 10T_1 - 8T_2$$

$$\text{s.t.} \quad W_1 + D_1 \leq 50 \quad \text{(Cutlet 1 demand)}$$

$$W_2 + D_2 \leq 30 \quad \text{(Cutlet 2 demand)}$$

$$W_1 + W_2 \leq 5T_1 + 3T_2 \quad \begin{array}{l}\text{(Don't use more white} \\ \text{meat than you have)}\end{array}$$

$$D_1 + D_2 \leq 2T_1 + 3T_2 \quad \begin{array}{l}\text{(Don't use more dark} \\ \text{meat than you have)}\end{array}$$

$$W_1/(W_1 + D_1) \geq 0.7 \text{ or } 0.3W_1 \geq 0.7D_1$$

$$W_2/(W_2 + D_2) \geq 0.6 \text{ or } 0.4W_2 \geq 0.6D_2$$

$$T_1, T_2, D_1, W_1, D_2, W_2 \geq 0$$

◆ CHAPTER 4

SECTION 4.1

1. $\max z = 3x_1 + 2x_2$

$$\text{s.t.} \quad 2x_1 + x_2 + s_1 \qquad\qquad = 100$$

$$x_1 + x_2 \qquad + s_2 \qquad = 80$$

$$x_1 \qquad\qquad + s_3 = 40$$

3. $\min z = 3x_1 + x_2$

$$\text{s.t.} \quad x_1 \qquad - e_1 \qquad = 3$$

$$x_1 + x_2 \qquad + s_2 = 4$$

$$2x_1 - x_2 \qquad\qquad = 3$$

SECTION 4.2

1. From Figure 2 of Chapter 3, we find the extreme points of the feasible region.

POINT	BASIC VARIABLES
$H = (0,0)$	$s_1 = 100,\ s_2 = 80,\ s_3 = 40$
$E = (40,0)$	$x_1 = 40,\ s_1 = 20,\ s_2 = 40$
$F = (40,20)$	$x_1 = 40,\ x_2 = 20,\ s_2 = 20$
$G = (20,60)$	$x_1 = 20,\ x_2 = 60,\ s_3 = 20$
$D = (0,80)$	$x_2 = 80,\ s_1 = 20,\ s_3 = 40$

SECTION 4.3

1. $z = 180$, $x_1 = 20$, $x_2 = 60$.

2. $z = \frac{32}{3}$, $x_1 = \frac{10}{3}$, $x_2 = \frac{4}{3}$.

SECTION 4.4

1. $z = -5$, $x_1 = 0$, $x_2 = 5$.

SECTION 4.5

2. Solution 1: $z = 6$, $x_1 = 0$, $x_2 = 1$; solution 2: $z = 6$, $x_1 = \frac{56}{17}$, $x_2 = \frac{45}{17}$. By averaging these two solutions we obtain solution 3: $z = 6$, $x_1 = \frac{28}{17}$, $x_2 = \frac{31}{17}$.

SECTION 4.6

1. $x_1 = 4999$, $x_2 = 5000$ has $z = 10,000$.

SECTION 4.8

1a. Both very small numbers (e.g., 0.000003) and large numbers (e.g., 3,000,000) appear in the problem.

b. Let x_i = units of product i produced (in millions). If we measure our profit in millions of dollars, the LP becomes

$$\max = 6x_1 + 4x_2 + 3x_3$$

$$\text{s.t.} \quad 4x_1 + 3x_2 + 2x_3 \leq 3 \quad \text{(Million labor hours)}$$

$$3x_1 + 2x_2 + x_3 \leq 2 \quad \text{(lb of pollution)}$$

$$x_1, x_2, x_3 \geq 0$$

SECTION 4.9

1. $z = 16$, $x_1 = x_2 = 2$. The point where all three constraints are binding ($x_1 = x_2 = 2$) corresponds to the following three sets of basic variables:

$$\text{Set 1} = \{x_1, x_2, s_1\}$$

$$\text{Set 2} = \{x_1, x_2, s_2\}$$

$$\text{Set 3} = \{x_1, x_2, s_3\}$$

SECTIONS 4.10 AND 4.11

1. $z = 1, x_1 = x_2 = 0, x_3 = 1$.

4. Infeasible LP.

SECTION 4.12

1. Let $i_t = i'_t - i''_t$ be the inventory position at the end of month t. For each constraint in the original problem, replace i_t by $i'_t - i''_t$. Also add the sign restrictions $i'_t \geq 0$ and $i''_t \geq 0$. To ensure that demand is met by end of quarter 4, add constraint $i''_4 = 0$. Replace the terms involving i_t in the objective function by

$$(100i'_1 + 110i''_1 + 100i'_2 + 110i''_2 + 100i'_3$$
$$+ 110i''_3 + 100i'_4 + 110i''_4)$$

2. $z = 5, x_1 = 1, x_2 = 3$.

REVIEW PROBLEMS

4. Unbounded LP.

5. $z = -6, x_1 = 0, x_2 = 3$.

6. Infeasible LP.

8. $z = 12, x_1 = x_2 = 2$.

10. Four types of furniture.

12. $z = \frac{17}{2}, x_2 = \frac{3}{2}, x_4 = \frac{1}{2}$.

14a. $-c \geq 0$ and $b \geq 0$.

b. $b \geq 0$ and $c = 0$. Also need $a_2 > 0$ and/or $a_3 > 0$ to ensure that when x_1 is pivoted in, a feasible solution results. If only $a_3 > 0$, then we need b to be strictly positive.

c. $-c < 0, a_2 \leq 0, a_3 \leq 0$ ensures that x_1 can be made arbitrarily large and z will become arbitrarily large.

17. Let c_t = net number of drivers hired at beginning of year t. Then $c_t = h_t - f_t$, where h_t = number of drivers hired at beginning of year t, and f_t = number of drivers fired at beginning of year t. Also let d_t = number of drivers after drivers have been hired or fired at beginning of year t. Then a correct formulation is (cost in thousands of dollars)

$$\min z = 10(d_1 + d_2 + d_3 + d_4 + d_5)$$
$$+ 2(f_1 + f_2 + f_3 + f_4 + f_5)$$
$$+ 4(h_1 + h_2 + h_3 + h_4 + h_5)$$

s.t.
$$d_1 = 50 + h_1 - f_1$$
$$d_2 = d_1 + h_2 - f_2$$
$$d_3 = d_2 + h_3 - f_3$$
$$d_4 = d_3 + h_4 - f_4$$
$$d_5 = d_4 + h_5 - f_5$$
$$d_1 \geq 60, d_2 \geq 70, d_3 \geq 50, d_4 \geq 65, d_5 \geq 75$$

All variables ≥ 0

23. Let

R_t = robots available during quarter t (after robots are bought or sold for the quarter)

B_t = robots bought during quarter t

S_t = robots sold during quarter t

I'_t = cars in inventory at end of quarter t

C_t = cars produced during quarter t

I''_t = backlogged demand for cars at the end of quarter t

Then a correct formulation is

$$\min z = 500(R_1 + R_2 + R_3 + R_4)$$
$$+ 200(I'_1 + I'_2 + I'_3 + I'_4)$$
$$+ 5000(B_1 + B_2 + B_3 + B_4)$$
$$- 3000(S_1 + S_2 + S_3 + S_4)$$
$$+ 300(I''_1 + I''_2 + I''_3 + I''_4)$$

s.t.
$$R_1 = 2 + B_1 - S_1$$
$$R_2 = R_1 + B_2 - S_2$$
$$R_3 = R_2 + B_3 - S_3$$
$$R_4 = R_3 + B_4 - S_4$$
$$I'_1 - I''_1 = C_1 - 600$$
$$I'_2 - I''_2 = I'_1 - I''_1 + C_2 - 800$$
$$I'_3 - I''_3 = I'_2 - I''_2 + C_3 - 500$$
$$I'_4 - I''_4 = I'_3 - I''_3 + C_4 - 400$$
$$R_4 \geq 2$$
$$C_1 \leq 200R_1$$
$$C_2 \leq 200R_2$$
$$C_3 \leq 200R_3$$
$$C_4 \leq 200R_4, I''_4 = 0$$
$$B_1, B_2, B_3, B_4 \leq 2$$

All variables ≥ 0

◆ CHAPTER 5

SECTION 5.1

1. Decision variables remain the same. New z-value is $210.

4a. $\frac{50}{3} \le c_1 \le 350$.
c. $4{,}000{,}000 \le \text{HIW} \le 84{,}000{,}000$; $x_1 = 3.6 + 0.15\Delta$, $x_2 = 1.4 - 0.025\Delta$.
f. $310,000.

SECTION 5.2

1a. $3875.
b. Decision variables remain the same. New z-value is $3750.
c. Solution remains the same.

3a. Still 90¢.
b. 95¢.
c. 95¢.
d. Still 90¢.
e. 82.5¢.
f. 30¢ or less.
g. 22.5¢ or less.

SECTION 5.3

3. 2.5¢
4. $2.
5. Buy raw material, because it will reduce cost by $6.67.

SECTION 5.4

3. See Figures 1–4.

Figure 1

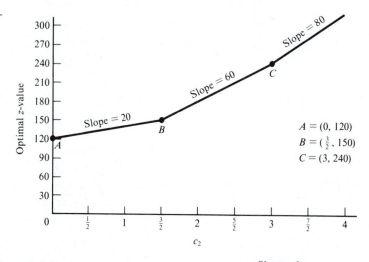

$A = (0, 120)$
$B = (\frac{3}{2}, 150)$
$C = (3, 240)$

Figure 2

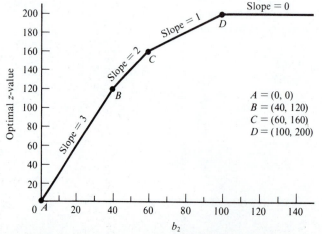

$A = (0, 0)$
$B = (40, 120)$
$C = (60, 160)$
$D = (100, 200)$

Figure 3

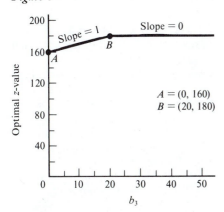

$A = (0, 160)$
$B = (20, 180)$

Figure 4

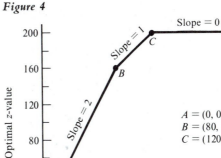

$A = (0, 0)$
$B = (80, 160)$
$C = (120, 200)$

REVIEW PROBLEMS

1a. $1,046,667.

b. Yes.

c. $33.33.

d. $333.33.

7a. Decision variables remain unchanged. New z-value is $1,815,000.

b. Pay $0 for an additional 100 board ft of lumber. Pay $1350 for an additional 100 hours of labor.

c. $1,310,000.

d. $1,665,000.

◆ CHAPTER 6

SECTION 6.1

1. Decision variables remain the same. New z-value is $210.

SECTION 6.2

1.
$$z \quad + 4s_1 + 5s_2 = 28$$
$$x_1 \; + \; s_1 \; + \; s_2 = 6$$
$$x_2 + \; s_1 + 2s_2 = 10$$

SECTION 6.3

3. $x_1 = 2$, $x_2 = 0$, $x_3 = 8$, $z = 280$ (same as original solution).

5. Home computer tables should not be produced.

6a. Profit for candy bar $1 \leq 6$¢. If type 1 candy bar earns 7¢ profit, new optimal solution is $z = 3.50$, $x_1 = 50$, $x_2 = x_3 = 0$.

b. 5¢ $\leq$ candy bar 2 profit ≤ 15¢. If candy bar 2 profit is 13¢, decision variables remain the same, but profit is now $4.50.

c. $\frac{100}{3} \leq$ sugar ≤ 100.

d. $z = 3.40$, $x_1 = 0$, $x_2 = 20$, $x_3 = 40$. If 30 oz of sugar is available, current basis is no longer optimal, and problem must be solved again.

e. Make type 1 candy bars.

f. Make type 4 candy bars.

8a. $16,666.67 $\leq$ comedy cost $\leq 350,000.

b. 4 million $\leq$ HIW $\leq$ 84 million. For 40 million HIW exposures, new optimal solution is $x_1 = 5.4$, $x_2 = 1.1$, $z = 380,000.

c. Advertise on news program.

SECTION 6.4

1. Yes.

2. No.

4. Yes.

SECTION 6.5

1. min $w = y_1 + 3y_2 + 4y_3$

s.t. $-y_1 + y_2 + y_3 \geq 2$

$y_1 + y_2 - 2y_3 \geq 1$

$y_1, y_2, y_3 \geq 0$

2. max $z = 4x_1 + x_2 + 3x_3$

s.t. $2x_1 + x_2 + x_3 \le 1$

$x_1 + x_2 + 2x_3 \le -1$

$x_1, x_2, x_3 \ge 0$

3. min $w = 5y_1 + 7y_2 + 6y_3 + 4y_4$

s.t. $y_1 + 2y_2 \qquad + y_4 \ge 4$

$y_1 + \quad y_2 + 2y_3 \qquad = -1$

$y_3 + y_4 = 2$

$y_1, y_2 \ge 0; y_3 \le 0; y_4 \text{ urs}$

4. max $z = 6x_1 + 8x_2$

s.t. $x_1 + x_2 \le 4$

$2x_1 - x_2 \le 2$

$2x_2 = -1$

$x_1 \le 0; x_2 \text{ urs}$

SECTION 6.7

1a. min $w = 100y_1 + 80y_2 + 40y_3$

s.t. $2y_1 + y_2 + y_3 \ge 3$

$y_1 + y_2 \ge 2$

$y_1, y_2, y_3 \ge 0$

b. and c. $y_1 = 1, y_2 = 1, y_3 = 0, w = 180$. Observe that this solution has a w-value that equals the optimal primal z-value. Since this solution is dual feasible, it must be optimal (by Lemma 2) for the dual.

2a. min $w = 3y_1 + 2y_2 + y_3$

s.t. $y_1 + \qquad y_3 \ge -2$

$y_1 + y_2 \ge -1$

$y_1 + y_2 + y_3 \ge 1$

$y_1 \ge 0; y_2 \le 0; y_3 \text{ urs}$

b. $y_1 = $ coefficient of s_1 in optimal row $0 = 0$

$y_2 = -(\text{coefficient of } e_2 \text{ in optimal row } 0) = -1$

$y_3 = $ coefficient of a_3 in optimal row $0 - M = 2$

Optimal w-value $= 0$.

9. Dual is max $w = 28y_1 + 24y_2$

s.t. $7y_1 + 2y_2 \le 50$

$2y_1 + 12y_2 \le 100$

$y_1, y_2 \ge 0$

Optimal dual solution is $w = \$320{,}000, y_1 = 5, y_2 = 7.5$.

SECTION 6.8

2b. New z-value $= \$3.40$.

c. New z-value $= \$2.60$.

d. Since current basis is no longer optimal, the current shadow prices cannot be used to determine the new z-value.

5b. Skilled labor shadow price $= 0$, unskilled labor shadow price $= 0$, raw material shadow price $= 15$, and product 2 constraint shadow price $= -5$.

We would be willing to pay $0 for an additional hour of either type of labor. We would pay up to $15 for an extra unit of raw material. Reducing the product 2 marketing requirement by 1 unit will save the company $5.

c. $\Delta b_3 = 5$, so new z-value $= 435 + 5(15) = \$510$.

d. Since shadow price of each labor constraint is zero, the optimal z-value remains unchanged.

e. For a 5-unit requirement, $\Delta b_4 = 2$. Thus, new z-value $= 435 + 2(-5) = \$425$. For a 2-unit requirement, $\Delta b_4 = -1$. Thus, new z-value $= 435 + (-1)(-5) = \$440$.

6a. If purchased at the given price of $1, an extra unit of raw material increases profits by $2.50. Thus, the firm would be willing to pay up to $1 + 2.5 = \$3.50$ for an extra unit of raw material.

b. Both labor constraints are nonbinding. All we can say is that if an additional hour of skilled labor were available at $3/hour, we would not buy it, and if an additional hour of unskilled labor were available at $2/hour, we would not buy it.

7a. New z-value $= \$380{,}000$.

b. New z-value $= \$290{,}000$.

SECTION 6.9

1. The current basis is no longer optimal. We should make computer tables, because they sell for $35 each and use only $30 worth of resources.

2a. Current basis remains optimal if type 1 profit $\le 6¢$.

SECTION 6.10

1a. min $w = 600y_1 + 400y_2 + 500y_3$

s.t. $4y_1 + \quad y_2 + 3y_3 \ge 6$

$9y_1 + \quad y_2 + 4y_3 \ge 10$

$7y_1 + 3y_2 + 2y_3 \ge 9$

$10y_1 + 40y_2 + \quad y_3 \ge 20$

$y_1, y_2, y_3, y_4 \ge 0$

b. $w = \frac{2800}{3}, y_1 = \frac{22}{5}, y_2 = \frac{2}{15}, y_3 = 0$.

SECTION 6.11

1. $z = -9, x_1 = 0, x_2 = 14, x_3 = 9$.

2a. The current solution is still optimal.

b. The LP is now infeasible.

c. The new optimal solution is $z = 10, x_1 = 1, x_2 = 4$.

REVIEW PROBLEMS

1a. $\min w = 6y_1 + 3y_2 + 10y_3$

s.t. $y_1 + y_2 + 2y_3 \geq 4$

$2y_1 - y_2 + y_3 \geq 1$

y_1 urs; $y_2 \leq 0$; $y_3 \geq 0$

Optimal dual solution is $w = \frac{58}{3}$, $y_1 = -\frac{2}{3}$, $y_2 = 0$, $y_3 = \frac{7}{3}$.

b. $9 \leq b_3 \leq 12$. If $b_3 = 11$, the new optimal solution is $z = \frac{65}{3}$, $x_1 = \frac{16}{3}$, $x_2 = \frac{1}{3}$.

2. $c_1 \geq \frac{1}{2}$.

3a. $\min w = 6y_1 + 8y_2 + 2y_3$

s.t. $y_1 + 6y_2 \qquad \geq 5$

$y_1 + \qquad y_3 \geq 1$

$y_1 + y_2 + y_3 \geq 2$

$y_1, y_2, y_3 \geq 0$

Optimal dual solution is $w = 9$, $y_1 = 0$, $y_2 = \frac{5}{6}$, $y_3 = \frac{7}{6}$.

b. $0 \leq c_1 \leq 6$.

c. $c_2 \leq \frac{7}{6}$.

4a. New z-value $= 32,540 + 10(88) = \$33,420$. Decision variables remain the same.

b. Can't tell, since allowable increase is < 1.

c. $\$0$.

d. $32,540 + (-2)(-20) = \$32,580$.

e. Produce jeeps.

8a. New z-value $= \$266.20$.

b. New z-value $= \$270.70$. Decision variables remain the same.

c. $\$12.60$.

d. $20\cent$.

e. Produce product 3.

17. $z = -16$, $x_1 = 8$, $x_2 = 0$.

20. Optimal primal solution: $z = 13$, $x_1 = 1$, $x_2 = x_3 = 0$, $x_4 = 2$. Optimal dual solution: $w = 13$, $y_1 = 1$, $y_2 = 1$.

21a. $c_1 \geq 3$.

b. $c_2 \leq \frac{4}{3}$.

c. $0 \leq b_1 \leq 9$.

d. $b_2 \geq 10$.

28. LP 2 optimal solution: $z = 550$, $x_1 = 0.5$, $x_2 = 5$. Optimal solution to dual of LP 2: $w = 550$, $y_1 = y_2 = \frac{100}{3}$.

36. $b_2 \geq 3$.

◆ CHAPTER 7

SECTION 7.1

1.

	CUSTOMER 1	CUSTOMER 2	CUSTOMER 3	SUPPLY
Warehouse 1	15	35	25	40
Warehouse 2	10	50	40	30
Shortage	90	80	110	20
DEMAND	30	30	30	

3.

	200	260	240	340	190	150	420	
1-RT	7	8	9	10	11	12	0	200
1-OT	11	12	13	14	15	16	0	100
2-RT	M	7	8	9	10	11	0	200
2-OT	M	11	12	13	14	15	0	100
3-RT	M	M	7	8	9	10	0	200
3-OT	M	M	11	12	13	14	0	100
4-RT	M	M	M	7	8	9	0	200
4-OT	M	M	M	11	12	13	0	100
5-RT	M	M	M	M	7	8	0	200
5-OT	M	M	M	M	11	12	0	100
6-RT	M	M	M	M	M	7	0	200
6-OT	M	M	M	M	M	11	0	100

5.

	MONTH 1	MONTH 2	DUMMY	SUPPLY
Daisy	800	720	0	5
Laroach	710	750	0	5
DEMAND	3	4	3	

7. This is a maximization problem, so number in each cell is a revenue, not a cost.

	CLIFF	BLAKE	ALEXIS	SUPPLY
Site 1	1000	900	1100	100,000
Site 2	2000	2200	1900	100,000
Dummy	0	0	0	40,000
DEMAND	80,000	80,000	80,000	

12a. Replace the M's by incorporating a backlogging cost. For example, month 3 regular production can be used to meet month 1 demand at a cost of $400 + 2(30) = \$460$. **b.** Add a supply point called "lost sales," with cost of shipping a unit to any month's demand being $450. Supply of "lost sales" supply point should equal total demand. Then adjust dummy demand point's demand to rebalance the problem. **c.** A shipment from month 1 production to month 4 demand should have a cost of M. **d.** For each month, add a month i subcontracting supply point, with a supply of 10 and a cost that is $40 more than the cost for the corresponding month i regular supply point. Then adjust the demand at the dummy demand point so that the problem is balanced.

SECTIONS 7.2 AND 7.3

The optimal solution to Problem 1 of Section 7.1 is to ship 10 units from warehouse 1 to customer 2, 30 units from warehouse 1 to customer 3, and 30 units from warehouse 2 to customer 1.

The optimal solution to Problem 5 of Section 7.1 to buy 4 gallons from Daisy in month 2 and 3 gallons from Laroach in month 1.

In Problem 7 of Section 7.1, Cliff gets 20,000 acres at site 1 and 20,000 acres at site 2. Blake gets 80,000 acres at site 2. Alexis gets 80,000 acres at site 1.

SECTION 7.4

2. Current basis remains optimal if $c_{34} \le 7$.
4. New optimal solution is $x_{12} = 12$, $x_{13} = 23$, $x_{21} = 45$, $x_{23} = 5$, $x_{32} = 8$, $x_{34} = 30$, and $z = 1020 - 2(3) - 2(10) = 994$.

SECTION 7.5

1. Person 1 does job 2, person 2 does job 1, person 3 does no job, person 4 does job 4, and person 5 does job 3.
5a. Company 1 does route 1, company 2 does route 2, company 3 does route 3, and company 4 does route 4.
b. Company 3 does routes 3 and 1, company 2 does routes 2 and 4.

SECTION 7.6

1a.

	L.A.	DETROIT	ATLANTA	HOUSTON	TAMPA	DUMMY	
L.A.	0	140	100	90	225	0	5100
Detroit	145	0	111	110	119	0	6900
Atlanta	105	115	0	113	78	0	4000
Houston	89	109	121	0	M	0	4000
Tampa	210	117	82	M	0	0	4000
	4000	4000	4000	6400	5500	100	

b.

	L.A.	DETROIT	ATLANTA	HOUSTON	TAMPA	DUMMY	
L.A.	0	M	100	90	225	0	5100
Detroit	M	0	111	110	119	0	6900
Atlanta	105	115	0	113	78	0	4000
Houston	89	109	121	0	M	0	4000
Tampa	210	117	82	M	0	0	4000
	4000	4000	4000	6400	5500	100	

c.

	L.A.	DETROIT	ATLANTA	HOUSTON	TAMPA	DUMMY	
L.A.	0	140	100	90	225	0	5100
Detroit	145	0	111	110	119	0	6900
Atlanta	105	115	0	113	78	0	4000
Houston	89	109	121	0	5	0	4000
Tampa	210	117	82	5	0	0	4000
	4000	4000	4000	6400	5500	100	

REVIEW PROBLEMS

3. Meet January demand with 30 units of January production. Meet February demand with 5 units of January production, 10 units of February production, and 15 units of March production. Meet March demand with 20 units of March production.

4. Maid 1 does the bathroom, maid 2 straightens up, maid 3 does the kitchen, maid 4 gets the day off, and maid 5 vacuums.

7. Shipping 1 unit from W_i to W_j means one white student from district i goes to school in district j. Shipping 1 unit from B_i to B_j means one black student from district i goes to school in district j. The costs of M ensure that shipments from W_i to B_j or B_i to W_j cannot occur. See table below.

8. Optimal solution is $z = 1580$, $x_{11} = 40$, $x_{12} = 10$, $x_{13} = 10$, $x_{22} = 50$, $x_{32} = 10$, $x_{34} = 30$.

13. Optimal solution is $z = 98$, $x_{13} = 5$, $x_{21} = 3$, $x_{24} = 7$, $x_{32} = 3$, $x_{33} = 7$, $x_{34} = 5$.

21. Sell painting 1 to customer 1, painting 2 to customer 2, painting 3 to customer 3, and painting 4 to customer 4.

	W_1	B_1	W_2	B_2	W_3	B_3	SUPPLY
W_1	0	M	3	M	5	M	210
B_1	M	0	M	3	M	5	120
W_2	3	M	0	M	4	M	210
B_2	M	3	M	0	M	4	30
W_3	5	M	4	M	0	M	180
B_3	M	5	M	4	M	0	150
DEMAND	200	100	200	100	200	100	

◆ CHAPTER 8

SECTION 8.2

2. 1–2–5 (length 14).

3.

	NODE 2	NODE 3	NODE 4	NODE 5	SUPPLY
Node 1	2	8	M	M	1
Node 2	0	5	4	12	1
Node 3	M	0	6	M	1
Node 4	M	M	0	10	1
DEMAND	1	1	1	1	

M = large number to prevent shipping a unit through a nonexistent arc.

5. Replace the car at times 2, 4, and 6. Total cost = $14,400.

SECTION 8.3

1. max $z = x_0$

s.t. $x_{so,1} \leq 6$, $x_{so,2} \leq 2$, $x_{12} \leq 1$, $x_{32} \leq 3$,

$x_{13} \leq 3$, $x_{3,si} \leq 2$, $x_{24} \leq 7$, $x_{4,si} \leq 7$

$x_0 = x_{so,1} + x_{so,2}$ (Node so)

$x_{so,1} = x_{13} + x_{12}$ (Node 1)

$x_{12} + x_{32} + x_{so,2} = x_{24}$ (Node 2)

$x_{13} = x_{32} + x_{3,si}$ (Node 3)

$x_{24} = x_{4,si}$ (Node 4)

$x_{3,si} + x_{4,si} = x_0$ (Node si)

All variables ≥ 0

Maximum flow = 6. Cut associated with $V' = \{2, 3, 4, si\}$ has capacity 6.

2. max $z = x_0$

s.t. $x_{so,1} \leq 2$, $x_{12} \leq 4$, $x_{1,si} \leq 3$, $x_{2,si} \leq 2$,

$x_{23} \leq 1$, $x_{3,si} \leq 2$, $x_{so,3} \leq 1$

$x_0 = x_{so,1} + x_{so,3}$ (Node so)

$x_{so,1} = x_{1,si} + x_{12}$ (Node 1)

$x_{12} = x_{23} + x_{2,si}$ (Node 2)

$x_{23} + x_{so,3} = x_{3,si}$ (Node 3)

$x_{1,si} + x_{2,si} + x_{3,si} = x_0$ (Node si)

All variables ≥ 0

Maximum flow = 3. Cut associated with $V' = \{1, 2, 3, si\}$ has capacity 3.

6. See Figure 5. An arc of capacity 1 goes from each package type node to each truck node. If maximum flow = 21, all packages can be delivered.

7. See Figure 6. If maximum flow = 4, then all jobs can be completed.

SECTION 8.4

4a. See Figure 7.

b. Critical path is A–C–G (project duration is 14 days).

c. Start project by June 13.

Figure 5

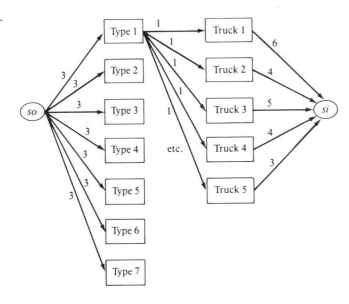

Figure 6

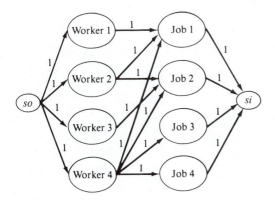

Figure 7

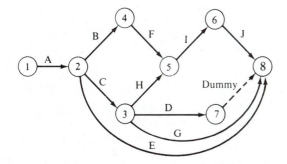

d. $\min z = x_8 - x_1$

s.t. $x_2 \geq x_1 + 3$

$x_3 \geq x_2 + 6$

$x_4 \geq x_2 + 2$

$x_5 \geq x_4 + 3$

$x_5 \geq x_3 + 1$

$x_6 \geq x_5 + 1.5$

$x_8 \geq x_6 + 2$

$x_8 \geq x_7$ $(x_7 \geq x_3 + 2)$

$x_8 \geq x_2 + 3$

$x_8 \geq x_3 + 5$

All variables urs

5a. See Figure 8. A–B–E–F–G and A–B–C–G are critical paths. Duration of project is 26 days.

Figure 8

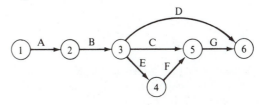

ACTIVITY	TOTAL FLOAT	FREE FLOAT
A	0	0
B	0	0
C	0	0
D	8	8
E	0	0
F	0	0
G	0	0

b. $\min z = 30A + 15B + 20C + 40D$
$$+ 20E + 30F + 40G$$

s.t. $x_2 \geq x_1 + 5 - A$

$x_3 \geq x_2 + 8 - B$

$x_4 \geq x_3 + 4 - E$

$x_5 \geq x_3 + 10 - C$

$x_5 \geq x_4 + 6 - F$

$x_6 \geq x_3 + 5 - D$

$x_6 \geq x_5 + 3 - G$

$x_6 - x_1 \leq 20$

$A \leq 2, B \leq 3, C \leq 1, D \leq 2, E \leq 2,$

$F \leq 3, G \leq 1$

$A, B, C, D, E, F, G \geq 0$

All other variables urs

8b. From the LP output, we find the critical path 1–2–3–4–5–6. This implies that activities A, B, E, F, and G are critical. (Since 1–2–3–5–6 is also a critical path, activity C is also a critical activity, but the LP does not give us this information.)

SECTION 8.5

1. $\min z = 4x_{12} + 3x_{24} + 2x_{46} + 3x_{13}$
$$+ 3x_{35} + 2x_{25} + 2x_{56}$$

s.t. $x_{12} + x_{13} = 1$ (Node 1)

$x_{12} = x_{24} + x_{25}$ (Node 2)

$x_{13} = x_{35}$ (Node 3)

$x_{24} = x_{46}$ (Node 4)

$x_{25} = x_{56}$ (Node 5)

$x_{46} + x_{56} = 1$ (Node 6)

$x_{ij} \geq 0$

If $x_{ij} = 1$, the shortest path from node 1 to node 6 contains arc (i, j); if $x_{ij} = 0$, the shortest path from node 1 to node 6 does not contain arc (i, j).

4a. See Figure 9. All arcs have infinite capacity.

Figure 9

ARC	SHIPPING COST
Bos.–Chic.	$800 + 80 = \$880$
Bos.–Aus.	$800 + 220 = \$1020$
Bos.–L.A.	$800 + 280 = \$1080$
Ral.–Chic.	$900 + 100 = \$1000$
Ral.–Aus.	$900 + 140 = \$1040$
Ral.–L.A.	$900 + 170 = \$1070$
Chic.–Aus.	$\$40$
Chic.–L.A.	$\$50$

Problem is balanced, so no dummy point is needed.

CITY	NET OUTFLOW
Boston	400
Raleigh	300
Chicago	0
L.A.	−400
Austin	−300

5.

ARC	UNIT COST
S.D.–Dal.	$\$420$
S.D.–Hous.	$\$100$
L.A.–Dal.	$\$300$
L.A.–Hous.	$\$110$
S.D.–Dummy	$\$0$
L.A.–Dummy	$\$0$
Dal.–Chic.	$700 + 550 = \$1250$
Dal.–N.Y.	$700 + 450 = \$1150$
Hous.–Chic.	$900 + 530 = \$1430$
Hous.–N.Y.	$900 + 470 = \$1370$

CITY	NET OUTFLOW (100,000 barrels/day)
San Diego	5
L.A.	4
Dallas	0
Houston	0
Chicago	−4
N.Y.	−3
Dummy	−2

SECTION 8.6

2. The M.S.T. consists of the arcs $(1, 3)$, $(3, 5)$, $(3, 4)$, and $(3, 2)$. Total length of M.S.T. is 15.

SECTION 8.7

1c. $z = 8$, $\ x_{12} = x_{25} = x_{56} = 1$, $\quad x_{13} = x_{24} = x_{35} = x_{46} = 0$.

3. $z = 590$, $\ x_{12} = 20$, $\ x_{24} = 20$, $\ x_{34} = 2$, $\ x_{35} = 10$, $x_{13} = 12$, $x_{23} = 0$, $x_{25} = 0$, $x_{45} = 0$.

REVIEW PROBLEMS

1a. N.Y.–St. Louis–Phoenix–L.A. uses 2450 gallons of fuel.

2a. See Figure 10.

Figure 10

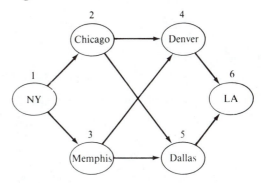

$$\max z = x_0$$
$$\text{s.t.} \quad x_{12} + x_{13} = x_0 \qquad \text{(Node 1)}$$
$$x_{12} = x_{24} + x_{25} \qquad \text{(Node 2)}$$
$$x_{13} = x_{34} + x_{35} \qquad \text{(Node 3)}$$
$$x_{24} + x_{34} = x_{46} \qquad \text{(Node 4)}$$
$$x_{25} + x_{35} = x_{56} \qquad \text{(Node 5)}$$
$$x_{46} + x_{56} = x_0 \qquad \text{(Node 6)}$$
$$x_{12} \leq 500, \ x_{13} \leq 400, \ x_{24} \leq 300,$$
$$x_{25} \leq 250, \ x_{34} \leq 200, \ x_{35} \leq 150,$$
$$x_{46} \leq 400, \ x_{56} \leq 350$$
$$\text{All variables} \geq 0$$

5. The M.S.T. consists of the following arcs: N.Y.–Clev., N.Y.–Nash., Nash.–Dal., Dal.–St.L., Dal.–Pho., Pho.–L.A., and S.L.C.–L.A. Total length of the M.S.T. is 4300.

◆ CHAPTER 9

SECTION 9.2

1. Let $x_i = \begin{cases} 1 & \text{if player } i \text{ starts} \\ 0 & \text{otherwise} \end{cases}$

Then the appropriate IP is

$$\max z = 3x_1 + 2x_2 + 2x_3 + x_4 + 2x_5 + 3x_6 + x_7$$
$$\text{s.t.} \quad x_1 + x_3 + x_5 + x_7 \geq 4 \qquad \text{(Guards)}$$
$$x_3 + x_4 + x_5 + x_6 + x_7 \geq 2 \qquad \text{(Forwards)}$$
$$x_2 + x_4 + x_6 \geq 1 \qquad \text{(Center)}$$
$$x_1 + x_2 + x_3 + x_4 + x_5 + x_6 + x_7 = 5$$
$$3x_1 + 2x_2 + 2x_3 + x_4 + x_5 + 3x_6 + 3x_7 \geq 10 \qquad \text{(Ballhandling)}$$
$$3x_1 + x_2 + 3x_3 + 3x_4 + 3x_5 + x_6 + 2x_7 \geq 10 \qquad \text{(Shooting)}$$
$$x_1 + 3x_2 + 2x_3 + 3x_4 + x_5 + 2x_6 + 2x_7 \geq 10 \qquad \text{(Rebounding)}$$
$$x_6 + x_3 \leq 1$$
$$-x_4 - x_5 + 2 \leq 2y$$
$$\text{(If } x_1 > 0, \text{ then } x_4 + x_5 \geq 2)$$
$$x_1 \leq 2(1 - y)$$
$$x_2 + x_3 \geq 1$$
$$x_1, x_2, \ldots, x_7, y \text{ all 0–1 variables}$$

3. Let x_1 = units of product 1 produced

x_2 = units of product 2 produced

$$y_i = \begin{cases} 1 & \text{if any product } i \text{ is produced} \\ 0 & \text{otherwise} \end{cases}$$

Then the appropriate IP is

$$\max z = 2x_1 + 5x_2 - 10y_1 - 20y_2$$

s.t. $3x_1 + 6x_2 \leq 120$

$x_1 \leq 40y_1$

$x_2 \leq 20y_2$

$x_1, x_2 \geq 0;\ y_1, y_2 = 0 \text{ or } 1$

6. $y_1 = \begin{cases} 1 & \text{if calculus is taken} \\ 0 & \text{otherwise} \end{cases}$

$y_2 = \begin{cases} 1 & \text{if operations research is taken} \\ 0 & \text{otherwise} \end{cases}$

$y_3 = \begin{cases} 1 & \text{if data structure is taken} \\ 0 & \text{otherwise} \end{cases}$

$y_4 = \begin{cases} 1 & \text{if business statistics is taken} \\ 0 & \text{otherwise} \end{cases}$

$y_5 = \begin{cases} 1 & \text{if computer simulation is taken} \\ 0 & \text{otherwise} \end{cases}$

$y_6 = \begin{cases} 1 & \text{if introduction to computer programming} \\ & \text{is taken} \\ 0 & \text{otherwise} \end{cases}$

$y_7 = \begin{cases} 1 & \text{if forecasting is taken} \\ 0 & \text{otherwise} \end{cases}$

Then the appropriate IP is

$$\min z = y_1 + y_2 + y_3 + y_4 + y_5 + y_6 + y_7$$

s.t. $y_1 + y_2 + y_3 + y_4 + y_7 \geq 2$ (Math)

$y_2 + y_4 + y_5 + y_7 \geq 2$ (OR)

$y_3 + y_5 + y_6 \geq 2$ (Computers)

$y_4 \leq y_1$

$y_5 \leq y_6$

$y_3 \leq y_6$

$y_7 \leq y_4$

$y_1, y_2, \ldots, y_7 = 0 \text{ or } 1$

10. Add the constraints $x + y - 3 \leq Mz$, $2x + 5y - 12 \leq M(1 - z)$, $z = 0$ or 1, where M is a large positive number.

11. Add the constraints $y - 3 \leq Mz$, $3 - x \leq (1 - z)M$, $z = 0$ or 1, where M is a large positive number.

13. Let x_i = number of workers employed on line i

$$y_i = \begin{cases} 1 & \text{if line } i \text{ is used} \\ 0 & \text{otherwise} \end{cases}$$

Then the appropriate IP is

$$\min z = 1000y_1 + 2000y_2 + 500x_1 + 900x_2$$

s.t. $20x_1 + 50x_2 \geq 120$

$30x_1 + 35x_2 \geq 150$

$40x_1 + 45x_2 \geq 200$

$x_1 \leq 7y_1$

$x_2 \leq 7y_2$

$x_1, x_2 \geq 0;\ y_1, y_2 = 0 \text{ or } 1$

14a. Let $x_i = \begin{cases} 1 & \text{if disk } i \text{ is used} \\ 0 & \text{otherwise} \end{cases}$

Then the appropriate IP is

$$\min z = 3x_1 + 5x_2 + x_3 + 2x_4 + x_5 + 4x_6$$
$$+ 3x_7 + x_8 + 2x_9 + 2x_{10}$$

s.t. $x_1 + x_2 + x_4 + x_5 + x_8 + x_9 \geq 1$ (File 1)

$x_1 + x_3 \geq 1$ (File 2)

$x_2 + x_5 + x_7 + x_{10} \geq 1$ (File 3)

$x_3 + x_6 + x_8 \geq 1$ (File 4)

$x_1 + x_2 + x_4 + x_6 + x_7 + x_9 + x_{10} \geq 1$ (File 5)

$x_i = 0 \text{ or } 1 \quad (i = 1, 2, \ldots, 10)$

b. Add the constraints $1 - x_2 \leq 2y$, $x_3 + x_5 \leq 2(1 - y)$, $y = 0$ or 1 (need $M = 2$, because $x_3 + x_5 = 2$ is possible). We could also have added the constraints $x_2 \geq x_3$ and $x_2 \geq x_5$.

SECTION 9.3

1. $z = 20$, $x_1 = 4$, $x_2 = 0$.

2. $z = \$400,000$. $(x_1 = 6, x_2 = 1)$ and $(x_1 = 4, x_2 = 2)$ are both optimal solutions.

4. $z = 8$, $x_1 = 2$, $x_2 = 0$.

SECTION 9.4

1. $z = 5.6$, $x_1 = 1.2$, $x_2 = 2$.

SECTION 9.5

2. $\max z = 60x_1 + 48x_2 + 14x_3 + 31x_4 + 10x_5$

s.t. $800x_1 + 600x_2 + 300x_3 + 400x_4 + 200x_5 \leq 1100$

$x_i = 0 \text{ or } 1$

Optimal solution is $z = 79$, $x_2 = x_4 = 1$, $x_1 = x_3 = x_5 = 0$.

SECTION 9.6

1. Do jobs in following order: job 2, job 1, job 3, and job 4. Total delay is 20 minutes.

2. LFR–LFP–LP–LR–LFR has a total cost of $330.

7. Warehouse 1 to factory 1, warehouse 2 to factory 3, warehouse 3 to factory 4, warehouse 4 to factory 2, warehouse 5 to factory 5 has a total cost of $35,000.

SECTION 9.7

1. $z = 4, x_1 = x_2 = x_4 = x_5 = 1, x_3 = 0$.

2. $z = 3, x_1 = x_3 = 1, x_2 = 0$.

SECTION 9.9

1. $z = 110, x_1 = 4, x_2 = 3$.

REVIEW PROBLEMS

3. Let $z_i = \begin{cases} 1 & \text{if gymnast } i \text{ enters both events} \\ 0 & \text{otherwise} \end{cases}$

$x_i = \begin{cases} 1 & \text{if gymnast } i \text{ enters only balance beam} \\ 0 & \text{otherwise} \end{cases}$

$y_i = \begin{cases} 1 & \text{if gymnast } i \text{ enters only floor exercises} \\ 0 & \text{otherwise} \end{cases}$

Then the appropriate IP is

$$\max z = 16.7z_1 + 17.7z_2 + \cdots + 17.7z_6 + 8.8x_1$$
$$+ 9.4x_2 + \cdots + 9.1x_6 + 7.9y_1$$
$$+ 8.3y_2 + \cdots + 8.6y_6$$

s.t. $z_1 + z_2 + \cdots + z_6 = 3$

$x_1 + x_2 + \cdots + x_6 = 1$

$y_1 + y_2 + \cdots + y_6 = 1$

$x_1 + y_1 + z_1 \leq 1$

$x_2 + y_2 + z_2 \leq 1$

$x_3 + y_3 + z_3 \leq 1$

$x_4 + y_4 + z_4 \leq 1$

$x_5 + y_5 + z_5 \leq 1$

$x_6 + y_6 + z_6 \leq 1$

All variables 0 or 1

4. Let $x_{ij} = \begin{cases} 1 & \text{if students from district } i \\ & \text{are sent to school } j \\ 0 & \text{otherwise} \end{cases}$

Then the appropriate IP is

$$\min z = 110x_{11} + 220x_{12} + 37.5x_{21} + 127.5x_{22}$$
$$+ 80x_{31} + 80x_{32} + 117x_{41} + 36x_{42}$$
$$+ 135x_{51} + 54x_{52}$$

s.t. $110x_{11} + 75x_{21} + 100x_{31} + 90x_{41} + 90x_{51} \geq 150$
(School 1 $\geq$ 150 students)

$110x_{12} + 75x_{22} + 100x_{32} + 90x_{42} + 90x_{52} \geq 150$
(School 2 $\geq$ 150 students)

$0.20 \leq \dfrac{30x_{11} + 5x_{21} + 10x_{31} + 40x_{41} + 30x_{51}}{110x_{11} + 75x_{21} + 100x_{31} + 90x_{41} + 90x_{51}},$

or $0 \leq 8x_{11} - 10x_{21} - 10x_{31} + 22x_{41} + 12x_{51}$

$0.20 \leq \dfrac{30x_{12} + 5x_{22} + 10x_{32} + 40x_{42} + 30x_{52}}{110x_{12} + 75x_{22} + 100x_{32} + 90x_{42} + 90x_{52}},$

or $0 \leq 8x_{12} - 10x_{22} - 10x_{32} + 22x_{42} + 12x_{52}$

$x_{11} + x_{12} = 1$

$x_{21} + x_{22} = 1$

$x_{31} + x_{32} = 1$

$x_{41} + x_{42} = 1$

$x_{51} + x_{52} = 1$

All variables 0 or 1

5. Let $x_1 = \begin{cases} 1 & \text{if RS is signed} \\ 0 & \text{otherwise} \end{cases}$

$x_2 = \begin{cases} 1 & \text{if BS is signed} \\ 0 & \text{otherwise} \end{cases}$

$x_3 = \begin{cases} 1 & \text{if DE is signed} \\ 0 & \text{otherwise} \end{cases}$

$x_4 = \begin{cases} 1 & \text{if ST is signed} \\ 0 & \text{otherwise} \end{cases}$

$x_5 = \begin{cases} 1 & \text{if TS is signed} \\ 0 & \text{otherwise} \end{cases}$

Then the appropriate IP is

$$\max z = 6x_1 + 5x_2 + 3x_3 + 3x_4 + 2x_5$$

s.t. $6x_1 + 4x_2 + 3x_3 + 2x_4 + 2x_5 \leq 12$

$x_2 + x_3 + x_4 \leq 2$

$x_1 + x_2 + x_3 + x_5 \leq 2$

$x_1 + x_2 \leq 1$

All variables 0 or 1

10. Use two 20¢ coins, one 50¢ coin, and one 1¢ coin.

13. Infeasible.

21. Let $x_{it} = \begin{cases} 1 & \text{if building } i \text{ is started during year } t \\ 0 & \text{otherwise} \end{cases}$

Then the appropriate IP (in thousands) is

$$\max z = 100x_{11} + 50x_{12} + 60x_{21} + 30x_{22} + 40x_{31}$$

s.t. $30x_{11} + 20x_{21} + 20x_{31} \leq 60$ (Year 1 workers)

$30(x_{11} + x_{12}) + 20(x_{21} + x_{22})$
$+ 20(x_{31} + x_{32}) \leq 60$ (Year 2 workers)

$30(x_{12} + x_{13}) + 20(x_{22} + x_{23})$
$+ 20(x_{31} + x_{32} + x_{33}) \leq 60$ (Year 3 workers)

$30(x_{13} + x_{14}) + 20(x_{23} + x_{24})$
$+ 20(x_{32} + x_{33} + x_{34}) \leq 60$ (Year 4 workers)

$\left.\begin{array}{l} x_{11} + x_{21} + x_{31} \leq 1 \\ x_{12} + x_{22} + x_{32} \leq 1 \\ x_{13} + x_{23} + x_{33} \leq 1 \end{array}\right\}$ (No more than one building begins during each year)

$\left.\begin{array}{l} x_{11} + x_{12} + x_{13} + x_{14} \leq 1 \\ x_{21} + x_{22} + x_{23} + x_{24} \leq 1 \\ x_{31} + x_{32} + x_{33} + x_{34} \leq 1 \end{array}\right\}$ (Each building is started at most once)

$x_{21} + x_{22} + x_{23} = 1$ (Building 2 is finished by end of year 4)

All variables 0 or 1

22. Let $y_i = \begin{cases} 1 & \text{if truck } i \text{ is used} \\ 0 & \text{otherwise} \end{cases}$

$x_{ij} = \begin{cases} 1 & \text{if truck } i \text{ is used to deliver to grocer } j \\ 0 & \text{otherwise} \end{cases}$

Then the appropriate IP is

$$\min z = 45y_1 + 50y_2 + 55y_3 + 60y_4$$

s.t. $100x_{11} + 200x_{12} + 300x_{13} + 500x_{14} + 800x_{15}$
$\leq 400y_1$

$100x_{21} + 200x_{22} + 300x_{23} + 500x_{24} + 800x_{25}$
$\leq 500y_2$

$100x_{31} + 200x_{32} + 300x_{33} + 500x_{34} + 800x_{35}$
$\leq 600y_3$

$100x_{41} + 200x_{42} + 300x_{43} + 500x_{44} + 800x_{45}$
$\leq 1100y_4$

$x_{11} + x_{21} + x_{31} + x_{41} = 1$
$x_{12} + x_{22} + x_{32} + x_{42} = 1$
$x_{13} + x_{23} + x_{33} + x_{43} = 1$
$x_{14} + x_{24} + x_{34} + x_{44} = 1$
$x_{15} + x_{25} + x_{35} + x_{45} = 1$

All variables 0 or 1

◆ CHAPTER 10

SECTIONS 10.1 AND 10.2

1. $z = 11$, $x_1 = 3$, $x_2 = 0$, $x_3 = 2$.

2. $z = 10$, $x_1 = 2$, $x_2 = 2$.

SECTION 10.3

2. Let x_i = number of 15-ft boards cut according to combination i, where

COMBINATION	3-FT BOARDS	5-FT BOARDS	8-FT BOARDS
1	0	1	1
2	2	0	1
3	0	3	0
4	1	2	0
5	3	1	0
6	5	0	0

Then we wish to solve

$$\min z = x_1 + x_2 + x_3 + x_4 + x_5 + x_6$$

s.t. $2x_2 + x_4 + 3x_5 + 5x_6 \geq 10$
$x_1 + 3x_3 + 2x_4 + x_5 \geq 20$
$x_1 + x_2 \geq 15$
$x_i \geq 0$

The optimal solution is $z = \frac{55}{3}$, $x_1 = 10$, $x_2 = 5$, $x_3 = \frac{10}{3}$.

SECTION 10.4

1. $z = 40$, $x_1 = 3$, $x_2 = 2$, $x_3 = 3$.

3. $z = 15$, $x_1 = 0$, $x_2 = 0$, $x_3 = 3$.

SECTION 10.5

1. $z = 29.5$, $x_1 = 2$, $x_2 = 0.5$, $x_3 = 4$, $x_4 = x_5 = 0$.

3. $z = \frac{81}{13}$, $x_1 = \frac{12}{13}$, $x_2 = \frac{11}{13}$.

SECTION 10.6

1. $\mathbf{y}^1 = \mathbf{x}^1 = [\frac{3}{8} \quad \frac{1}{4} \quad \frac{3}{8}]$.

REVIEW PROBLEMS

1. $z = 9$, $x_1 = x_3 = 0$, $x_2 = 3$.

3. $z = -12$, $x_2 = 2$, $x_4 = 10$, $x_1 = x_3 = 0$.

5. Maximum profit is $540. Optimal production levels are

Product 1 at plant 1 $= \frac{5}{3}$ units

Product 1 at plant 2 $= \frac{100}{3}$ units

Product 2 at plant 1 $= \frac{200}{9}$ units

Product 2 at plant 2 $= 0$ units

♦ CHAPTER 11

SECTION 11.1

1. 3.

3a. $-xe^{-x} + e^{-x}$.

e. $\dfrac{3}{x}$.

5. $\ln(1 + x) = x - \dfrac{x^2}{2} + \dfrac{x^3}{3p^3}$ for some p between 1 and $1 + x$.

7a. k.

b. The maximim size of the market (as measured in sales per year).

9. The machine time is the better buy.

SECTION 11.2

1. $\dfrac{e^{10} - 1}{2}$.

3. $Ih - \dfrac{dh}{2}$.

SECTION 11.3

1. $2y(2y + y^2) - 3y + 2(y^2 - y)$.

SECTION 11.4

1a. $\frac{2}{9}$.

c. No.

e. $\frac{1}{4}$.

SECTION 11.5

1. $\frac{2}{3}$.

3. .001.

SECTION 11.6

1a. Let S = number sold. Then $E(S) = \frac{200}{3}$, and $\operatorname{var} S = \frac{200}{9}$.

3a. $F(a) = 0$ for $a \leq 0$, $F(a) = 1 - e^{-a}$ for $a \geq 0$.

b. $E(X) = 1 \operatorname{var} X = 1$.

c. $e^{-1} - e^{-2}$.

SECTION 11.7

2. .8749.

REVIEW PROBLEMS

3. $\frac{25}{2}$.

5a. $E(X) = 85$; $\operatorname{var} X = 9000$.

b. $P\left(Z \geq \dfrac{91 - 85}{(9000)^{1/2}}\right) = .476$.

7a. $\frac{1}{6}$.

b. .004996.

♦ CHAPTER 12

SECTION 12.1

1a. Let S = soap opera ads and F = football ads. Then we wish to solve the following LP:

$$\min z = 50S + 100F$$
$$\text{s.t.} \quad 5S^{1/2} + 17F^{1/2} \geq 40 \quad \text{(Men)}$$
$$20S^{1/2} + 7F^{1/2} \geq 60 \quad \text{(Women)}$$
$$S, F \geq 0$$

b. Since doubling S does not double the contribution of S to the constraints, we are violating the Proportionality Assumption. Additivity is not violated.

SECTION 12.2

1. Convex.

2. Neither convex nor concave.

5. Concave.

8. Concave.

SECTION 12.3

1. If fixed cost is $5000, spend $10,000 on advertising. If fixed cost is $20,000, don't spend any money on advertising.

2. Without tax, produce 12.25 units; with tax, produce 12 units.

5. $z = 1$, $x = 1$.

SECTION 12.4

2. After four iterations, the interval of uncertainty is $[-0.42, \ 0.17)$.

SECTION 12.5

1. $x = \dfrac{x_1 + x_2 + \cdots + x_n}{n}$,

$y = \dfrac{y_1 + y_2 + \cdots + y_n}{n}$.

3. $q_1 = 98.5$, $q_2 = 1$.

6. $(0,0)$ is a saddle point. $(\frac{3}{2}, \frac{3}{2})$ and $(\frac{3}{2}, -\frac{3}{2})$ are each a local minimum.

SECTION 12.6

3. Successive points are $(\frac{1}{2}, \frac{3}{4})$, $(\frac{3}{4}, \frac{3}{4})$, $(\frac{3}{4}, \frac{7}{8})$.

SECTION 12.7

2. $L = K = \frac{10}{3}$; produce 10 machines.

4. $x_1 = \dfrac{900}{13}$, $x_2 = \dfrac{400}{13}$, $\lambda = \dfrac{13^{1/2}}{2} - 1$. An extra dollar spent on promotion would increase profit by approximately $\$\left(\dfrac{13^{1/2}}{2} - 1\right)$.

SECTION 12.8

1. Capacity $= 27.5\,$kwh. Peak price $= \$65$. Off-peak price $= \$20$.

2. $z = 2^{1/2}$, $x_1 = \dfrac{2^{1/2}}{2}$, $x_2 = -\dfrac{2^{1/2}}{2}$.

6. $z = \frac{1}{2}$, $x_1 = \frac{1}{2}$, $x_2 = \frac{3}{2}$.

SECTION 12.9

1. min $z = 0.09x_1^2 + 0.04x_2^2 + 0.01x_3^2$
$+ 0.012x_1x_2 - 0.008x_1x_3 + 0.010x_2x_3$

s.t. $x_2 - x_3 \geq 0$

$x_1 + x_2 + x_3 = 100$

$x_1, \ x_2, \ x_3 \geq 0$

4. $p_1 = \$292.81$, $p_2 = \$158.33$. Pay no money for an additional hour of labor. Pay up to (approximately) $\$53.81$ for another chip.

SECTION 12.10

1. Using grid points 0, 0.5, 1, 1.5, and 2 for x_1 and grid points 0, 0.5, 1, 1.5, 2, and 2.5 for x_2, we obtain the following approximating problem:

min $z = 0.25\delta_{12} + \delta_{13} + 2.25\delta_{14} + 4\delta_{15} + 0.25\delta_{22}$
$+ \delta_{23} + 2.25\delta_{24} + 4\delta_{25} + 6.25\delta_{26}$

s.t. $0.25\delta_{12} + \delta_{13} + 2.25\delta_{14} + 4\delta_{15} + 2(0.25\delta_{22}$
$+ \delta_{23} + 2.25\delta_{24} + 4\delta_{25} + 6.25\delta_{26}) \leq 4$

$0.25\delta_{12} + \delta_{13} + 2.25\delta_{14} + 4\delta_{15} + 0.25\delta_{22} + \delta_{23}$
$+ 2.25\delta_{24} + 4\delta_{25} + 6.25\delta_{26} \leq 6$

$\delta_{11} + \delta_{12} + \delta_{13} + \delta_{14} + \delta_{15} = 1$

$\delta_{21} + \delta_{22} + \delta_{23} + \delta_{24} + \delta_{25} + \delta_{26} = 1$

All variables nonnegative

Adjacency Assumption

SECTION 12.11

1. $\mathbf{x}^1 = [0 \quad 1]$ and $\mathbf{x}^2 = [\frac{1}{3} \quad \frac{5}{6}]$.

SECTION 12.12

2. $a = b = c = 20$ yields the maximum area of $(30{,}000)^{1/2}$.

REVIEW PROBLEMS

2. Locate the store at point 7. In general, locate store at arithmetic mean of the location of all customers.

3a. Use $\frac{93}{8}$ units of raw material, sell $\frac{93}{4}$ units of product 1, and sell $\frac{15}{2}$ units of product 2.

c. Pay slightly less than $5 for an extra unit of raw material.

5. $[1.18, 1.63)$.

7. Produce 20 units during each of the three months.

18. Locate the store at point 5; in general, locate store at the median of the customer's locations.

♦ CHAPTER 13

SECTION 13.1

1. Maximin decision: small campaign. Maximax decision: large campaign. Minimax regret decision: large campaign.

2. Maximin decision: don't build. Maximax decision: build. Maximax regret decision: build. Expected value decision: build.

5. Maximin decision: $6000, $8000, or $11,000 bid. Maximax decision: $11,000 bid. Minimax regret decision: $11,000 bid. Expected value decision: $11,000 bid.

SECTION 13.2

1a. Risk-averse.

b. Prefer L_1; risk premium for $L_2 = \$339$.

2a. Risk-seeking.

b. Prefer L_2; risk premium for $L_2 = -\$235$.

6b. $1900.

7. Take statistics course.

13. L_1 is preferred.

SECTION 13.3

1. Hire the geologist. If she gives a favorable report, drill; if she gives an unfavorable report, don't drill. Expected profit is $180,000; EVSI = $20,000; EVPI = $55,000.

4. Market without testing. Expected profit = $16,000; EVSI = $3800; EVPI = $14,000.

9. Play daringly during the first game. If he wins the first game, play conservatively during the second game. If he loses the first game, play daringly during the second game. If tied after two games, play daringly during the third game.

12a. Buy the gold now.

b. Wait for Congress and (if possible) buy the gold later.

SECTION 13.4

2. Hire the geologist. If he predicts an earthquake, build at Roy Rogers; if he predicts no earthquake, build at Diablo. Expected total cost = $13,900,000. EVSI = $1,100,000; EVPI = $2,000,000.

4. Hire the firm. If it predicts a hit, air the show. If it predicts a flop, don't air the show. Expected profit = $35,000; EVSI = $50,000; EVPI = $75,000.

SECTION 13.5

1a. Invest in the oil well.

b. EVPI = $42.10.

c. $N(16.6, \frac{36}{49})$.

d. Invest in bonds.

REVIEW PROBLEMS

1a. Invest in money market fund.

b. Invest in gold.

c. Money market fund has a maximum regret of $500.

d. All investments have the same expected return.

2. Because of the risk-averse nature of the utility function, invest in the least risky investment (the money market fund).

5a. Invest all money in stocks.

b. Indifferent between hiring and not hiring forecaster. Expected final asset position = $1,160,000; EVSI = $10,000; EVPI = $20,000.

7. If all potential litterers are risk-averse, then raising the fine will result in the larger decrease in littering.

8a. Sample one item. If the item is good, do minor repairs; if the item is bad, do major repairs.

♦ CHAPTER 14

SECTION 14.1

2b. It would seem that $x_1 = $ attribute 3, $x_2 = $ attribute 1, and $x_3 = $ attribute 2.

c. $10,000 is equivalent to a 1-minute reduction in rich area response time or a 2-min reduction in poor area response time. A 2-minute reduction in poor area response time is equivalent to a 1-minute reduction in rich area response time.

4. Probably not. Whether one prefers red wine or white wine probably depends on one's choice of appetizer and main course.

5a. $\min z = 10,000s_1^+ + 10,000s_2^+ + s_3^+$

$$\text{s.t.} \quad 40 - 3x_1 + s_1^- - s_1^+ = 5$$
$$50 - 4x_2 + s_2^- - s_2^+ = 5$$
$$5000x_1 + 5000x_2 + s_3^- - s_3^+ = 100,000$$
$$\text{All variables} \geq 0$$

b. If $P_1 \gg P_2 \gg P_3$, then optimal solution is $x_1 = \frac{35}{3}$, $x_2 = \frac{45}{4}$. If $P_2 \gg P_1 \gg P_3$, then optimal solution is $x_1 = \frac{35}{3}$, $x_2 = \frac{45}{4}$. If $P_3 \gg P_1 \gg P_2$, then optimal solution is $x_1 = \frac{35}{3}$, $x_2 = \frac{25}{3}$.

7. Let $x_i =$ number of lots purchased from supplier i. The appropriate LP is

$$\min z = 10s_1^- + 6s_2^- + 4s_3^- + s_4^+$$

s.t. $\quad 60x_1 + 50x_2 + 40x_3 + s_1^- - s_1^+ = 5000$
$$\text{(Excellent chips)}$$
$$20x_1 + 35x_2 + 20x_3 + s_2^- - s_2^+ = 3000$$
$$\text{(Good chips)}$$
$$20x_1 + 15x_2 + 40x_3 + s_3^- - s_3^+ = 1000$$
$$\text{(Mediocre chips)}$$
$$400x_1 + 300x_2 + 250x_3 + s_4^- - s_4^+ = 28,000$$
$$\text{(Budget constraint)}$$

All variables ≥ 0

13. Buy 6.25 ties and 7.5 pairs of slippers.

SECTION 14.2

1c. National's utility function is of the form $.3u_1(x_1) + .5u_2(x_2) + .2u_1(x_1)u_2(x_2)$.

6d. $k_3 > 0$.

SECTION 14.3

1a. Professor 2 should receive the bigger raise.
c. Pairwise comparison matrix is consistent.

REVIEW PROBLEMS

1. Let

$x_1 =$ number of history and science teachers hired

$x_2 =$ number of history and math teachers hired

$x_3 =$ number of English and science teachers hired

$x_4 =$ number of English and math teachers hired

$x_5 =$ number of English and history teachers hired

$x_6 =$ number of science and math teachers hired

$$\min z = 1000s_1^+ + 26{,}000s_2^- + 30{,}000s_3^-$$
$$+ 28{,}000s_4^- + 24{,}000s_5^-$$

s.t. $\quad 21x_1 + 22x_2 + 23x_3 + 24x_4 + 25x_5 + 26x_6$
$$+ s_1^- - s_1^+ = 1400$$
$$\text{(Budget constant in thousands of dollars)}$$
$$x_1 + x_2 + x_5 + s_2^- - s_2^+ = 35 \quad \text{(History)}$$
$$x_1 + x_3 + x_6 + s_3^- - s_3^+ = 30 \quad \text{(Science)}$$
$$x_2 + x_4 + x_6 + s_4^- - s_4^+ = 40 \quad \text{(Math)}$$
$$x_3 + x_4 + x_5 + s_5^- - s_5^+ = 32 \quad \text{(English)}$$
$$x_1 \leq 20, \ x_2 \leq 15, \ x_3 \leq 12, \ x_4 \leq 14, \ x_5 \leq 13, \ x_6 \leq 12$$

All variables ≥ 0

4. Choose technique 2 (with expected utility .60) over technique 1 (with expected utility of .595).

◆ CHAPTER 15

SECTION 15.1

1. Value to row player $= 2$. Row player plays row 1, and column player plays column 1.

2. Value to row player $= 6$. Row player plays row 2, and column player plays column 1 or column 3.

SECTION 15.2

1. Value to row player $= \frac{4}{3}$. Row player's optimal strategy is $(\frac{2}{3}, \frac{1}{3})$ and column player's optimal strategy is $(\frac{2}{3}, \frac{1}{3}, 0)$.

7. State's optimal strategy is, with probability $\frac{1}{2}$, play A first and B second; with probability $\frac{1}{2}$, play B first and A second. Ivy's optimal strategy is, with probability $\frac{1}{2}$, play X first and Y second; with probability $\frac{1}{2}$, play X second and Y first. Value of game to State $= \frac{1}{2}$.

SECTION 15.3

1a.

GUNNER	SOLDIER				
	1	2	3	4	5
Spot A	1	1	0	0	0
Spot B	0	1	1	0	0
Spot C	0	0	1	1	0
Spot D	0	0	0	1	1

b. Columns 2 and 4 are dominated.
c. Expected value to the gunner $= \frac{1}{3}$.
d. Always firing at A.
e. Gunner's LP is

$$\max z = v$$

$$\text{s.t.} \quad v \le x_1$$
$$v \le x_1 + x_2$$
$$v \le x_2 + x_3$$
$$v \le x_3 + x_4$$
$$v \le x_4$$
$$x_1 + x_2 + x_3 + x_4 = 1$$
$$x_1, x_2, x_3, x_4 \ge 0; v \text{ urs}$$

Soldier's LP is

$$\min w$$

$$\text{s.t.} \quad w \ge y_1 + y_2$$
$$w \ge y_2 + y_3$$
$$w \ge y_3 + y_4$$
$$w \ge y_4 + y_5$$
$$y_1 + y_2 + y_3 + y_4 + y_5 = 1$$
$$y_1, y_2, y_3, y_4, y_5 \ge 0; w \text{ urs}$$

3. Value to row player $= \frac{5}{2}$. Row player's optimal strategy is $(\frac{1}{2}, \frac{1}{2})$, and column player's optimal strategy is $(\frac{3}{4}, \frac{1}{4}, 0)$.

SECTION 15.4

1. $(9, -1)$ is an equilibrium point.

3. This is a Prisoner's Dilemma game, with the equilibrium point occurring where each borough opposes the other borough's bond issues. Reward is \$0 to each borough.

SECTION 15.7

2. Core consists of the point $(25, 25, 25, 25)$.

3a. $v(\{ \ \}) = \$0; \quad v(\{1\}) = v(\{2\}) = v(\{3\}) = -\$2;$ $v(\{1,2\}) = v(\{2,3\}) = v(\{1,3\}) = \$2; v(\{1,2,3\}) = \$3.$
b. and **c.** The Shapley value gives \$1 to each player. The core is $(\$1, \$1, \$1)$.

7. Assuming that the runway costs \$1/ft, the Shapley value recommends the following fees per landing: type 1, \$20; type 2, $\$\frac{240}{7}$; type 3, $\$\frac{440}{7}$; type 4, $\$\frac{1140}{7}$.

REVIEW PROBLEMS

1. Both stores will be located at point B, and the two firms will each have 26 customers.

3b. Value to row player $= -\frac{5}{11}$. For each player, the optimal strategy is $(\frac{4}{11}, \frac{4}{11}, \frac{3}{11})$.

6a. $v(\{ \ \}) = v(\{49\}) = v(\{50\}) = v(\{1\}) = v(\{1,49\}) = 0; v(\{1,50\}) = v(\{49,50\}) = v(\{1,49,50\}) = 1.$
b. Core consists of point $(0, 0, 1)$.
c. Shapley value gives $\frac{1}{6}$ to player 1, $\frac{1}{6}$ to player 2, and $\frac{2}{3}$ to player 3.

◆ CHAPTER 16

SECTION 16.2

1a. 4000 gallons.
b. 12 orders per year.
c. One month.
e. For a 2-week lead time, reorder point $= \frac{48,000}{26} = 1846.15$ gallons. For 10-week lead time, reorder point $= 1230.77$ gallons.
3a. Send out $\frac{30}{7.07} = 4.24$ trucks per hour.
b. Send out $\frac{30}{5} = 6$ trucks per hour.
8b. Six trainees in each program.
c. Run 4.5 programs per year.
d. 2.25 trainees.

SECTION 16.3

1. Order 300 boxes per year. Place 3.2 orders per year.
5. Order 100 thermometers.

SECTION 16.4

2. Optimal run size $= 692.82$. Place 34.64 orders per year.

SECTION 16.5

2. Whenever dealer is 10 cars short, an order for 50 cars should be placed. Maximum shortage will be 10 cars.

SECTION 16.6

1. Demand is too lumpy to justify using EOQ.

REVIEW PROBLEMS

1a. 268.33 desks.
b. 22.36 orders per year.
c. $2(22.36)(300) = \$13,416$.
d. For 1-week lead time, reorder point $= 115.38$ desks; for 5-week lead time, reorder point $= 40.93$ desks.
e. Order 342.05 desks 17.54 times per year.

3. The EOQ for the lowest price is optimal. Thus, 417.79 cameras should be ordered.

◆ CHAPTER 17

SECTION 17.2

1a. $q = 6$.
b. $q = 2$.
c. $E(q)$ is not a convex function of q.

SECTION 17.3

1. Order 35 cars.
3. q^* will decrease.
5a. Order 60 cells.

SECTION 17.4

2. $775,000, using $F(.25) = .60$.
3. 107.5 trees, using $F(.25) = .60$.

SECTION 17.5

1. Locate at $\dfrac{2^{1/2}}{2}$.

SECTION 17.6

1. Order quantity $= 45.61$, reorder point $= 32.6$, safety stock $= 12.6$.
2a. Reorder point $= 57.9$, safety stock $= 17.9$.
b. Reorder point $= 60.60$, safety stock $= 20.60$.

SECTION 17.7

1.

SLM_1	REORDER POINT
80%	11.06
90%	16.46
95%	20.24
99%	26.30

For $SLM_2 = 0.5$ stockout per year, the reorder point is 32.06.

3a. $SLM_1 = 98.75\%$.
b. $r = 20$ is the smallest reorder point with SLM_1 exceeding 95%.
c. Need a reorder point of at least 30 units.

SECTION 17.8

1. $R = 0.23$ years and $S = 3241$.

SECTION 17.9

1. Type A items: 1 and 2; type B items: 3 through 6; type C items: 7 through 10. See Figure 11.

REVIEW PROBLEMS

1a. Bake 40 dozen cookies.
b. Bake 58.6 dozen cookies.
c. Bake 55 dozen cookies.

3a. Order quantity $= 707.11$, shortage cost $= \$12.41$.
b. Order quantity $= 707.11$. Assuming a penalty for lost sales of $8 - 5 = \$3$, shortage cost $= \$9.12$.
c. Reorder point of zero will do the job.

Figure 11

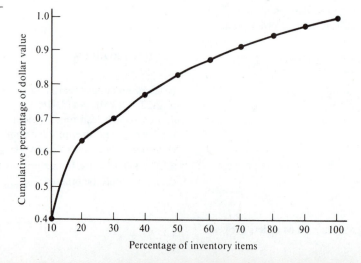

♦ CHAPTER 18

SECTION 18.1

1a. Using the lot-for-lot method, we obtain the following MRP record for C:

Week	1	2	3	4	5	6
Gross requirements	70	90	60	50	55	30
Onhand inventory (120)	50	10	0	0	0	0
Scheduled receipts	0	50	50	50	55	30
Net requirements	0	0	50	50	55	30
Planned production	0	50	50	55	30	X

Now the lot-for-lot method yields the following record for D:

Week	1	2	3	4	5	6
Gross requirements	0	200	200	220	120	X
Onhand inventory (160)	160	40	0	0	0	0
Scheduled receipts	0	80	160	220	120	X
Net requirements	0	0	160	220	120	X
Planned production	0	160	220	120	X	X

1b.

Week	1	2	3	4	5	6
Gross requirements	70	90	60	50	55	30
Onhand inventory (120)	50	10	50	0	30	0
Scheduled receipts	0	50	100	0	85	0
Net requirements	0	0	50	50	55	30
Planned production	0	100	0	85	0	0

SECTION 18.2

1. $M = \frac{100(.2)}{5} = 4$, $P = \frac{100(.2)}{5} = 4$.

a. Arrive at 0.20, 0.25, 0.30, 0.35, etc.

b. Begin production at 0.10, 0.15, 0.20, 0.25, etc.

c. Begin with 4 full containers at each station. Maximum inventory of $8(5) = 40$ items.

SECTION 18.3

1a. See Figure 12.

Figure 12

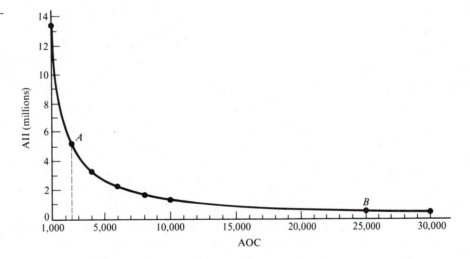

♦ CHAPTER 19

SECTION 19.2

1.

	Sunny	Cloudy
Sunny	.90	.10
Cloudy	.20	.80

2.

State

	0	1	2	3	4
0	0	0	$\frac{1}{3}$	$\frac{1}{3}$	$\frac{1}{3}$
1	0	0	$\frac{1}{3}$	$\frac{1}{3}$	$\frac{1}{3}$
2	$\frac{1}{3}$	$\frac{1}{3}$	$\frac{1}{3}$	0	0
3	0	$\frac{1}{3}$	$\frac{1}{3}$	$\frac{1}{3}$	0
4	0	0	$\frac{1}{3}$	$\frac{1}{3}$	$\frac{1}{3}$

4. Let *SC* denote that yesterday was sunny and today is cloudy, etc.

$$\begin{array}{c} \\ SS \\ SC \\ CS \\ CC \end{array} \begin{array}{cccc} SS & SC & CS & CC \end{array} \\ \begin{bmatrix} .95 & .05 & 0 & 0 \\ 0 & 0 & .40 & .60 \\ .70 & .30 & 0 & 0 \\ 0 & 0 & .20 & .80 \end{bmatrix}$$

SECTION 19.3

1a. Urban, .651; suburban, .258; rural, .091.
b. 31.5%.

SECTION 19.4

1. 2.
2. Yes.
3a. State 4.
b. States 1, 2, 3, 5, and 6.
c. $\{1, 3, 5\}$ and $\{2, 6\}$.
4. P_1 is ergodic; P_2 is not ergodic.

SECTION 19.5

1. Urban, $\frac{38}{183}$; suburban, $\frac{90}{183}$; rural, $\frac{55}{183}$.
3a. State 1, $\frac{3}{5}$; state 2, $\frac{2}{5}$.
4. Replace a fair car.
7. Expected price of stock 1 = $16.67; expected price of stock 2 = $16.00.

SECTION 19.6

1a. $1.11 + 0.99 + 0.99 + 0.88 = 3.97$.
b. .748.
2. $1 + 0.80 + 18 = 19.80$ years.
7a. 14.3%.
b. Reducing warranty period will save $715,000 − $392,500 = $322,500.

SECTION 19.7

1. 7778 freshmen, 7469 sophomores, 8057 juniors, and 7162 seniors.
2. Each working adult must contribute $2000 more.

REVIEW PROBLEMS

1. An average of $\frac{260}{3}$ tools per day will be produced.
2a. .815.
b. Annual profit without warranty = (3000)(total market size)($\frac{1}{4}$). Annual profit with warranty = (2700)(total market size)($\frac{4}{9}$). Profit with warranty is larger.
3. Value of star = $4,400,000; value of starter = $3,199,000; value of substitute = $1,600,000.
4a. Each year, 1,638,270 new books, 1,474,443 once-used books, 1,179,554 twice-used books, and 707,733 thrice-used books will be sold.

◆ CHAPTER 20

SECTION 20.1

1. Begin by picking up 4 matches. On each successive turn, pick up 5 − (number of matches picked up by opponent on last turn).
2. The players began with $16.25, $8.75, and $5.00.

SECTION 20.2

1. 1–3–5–8–10, 1–4–6–9–10, and 1–4–5–8–10 are all shortest paths from node 1 to node 10 (each has length 11). The path 3–5–8–10 is the shortest path from node 3 to node 10 (this path has length 7).
3. Bloomington–Indianapolis–Dayton–Toledo–Cleveland takes 8 hours.

SECTION 20.3

1. Produce no units during month 1, 3 units during month 2, no units during month 3, and 4 units during month 4. Total cost is $15.00.
2. Month 1, 200 radios; month 2, 600 radios; month 3, no radios. Total cost is $8950.
3a. Produce 1 unit. Cost associated with arc is $4.50.

SECTION 20.4

1. Site 1, $1 million; site 2, $2 million; site 3, $1 million. Total revenue is $24 million.
2. Obtain a benefit of 10 with two type 1 items or two type 2 and one type 3 item.
3a. See Figure 13.

Figure 13

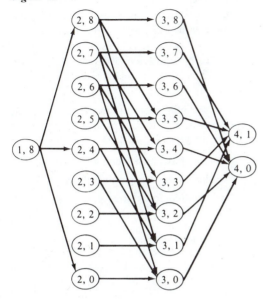

5. One type 2 item and one type 3 item yield a benefit of 75.

SECTION 20.5

2. Trade in car whenever it is two years old (at times 2, 4, and 6). Net cost is $14,400.

SECTION 20.6

1. Let $f_t(i)$ be the maximum expected net profit earned during years $t, t + 1, \ldots, 10$, given that Sunco has i barrels of reserves at the beginning of year t. Then

$$f_{10}(i) = \max_x \{xp_{10} - c(x)\}$$

where x must satisfy $0 \le x \le i$. For $t \le 9$,

$$f_t(i) = \max_x \{xp_t - c(x) + f_{t+1}(i + b_t - x)\} \quad \textbf{(1)}$$

where $0 \le x \le i$. We use Eq. (1) to work backward until $f_1(i_0)$ is determined. If discounting is allowed, let $\beta =$ the discount factor. Then we redefine $f_t(i)$ to be measured in terms of year t dollars. Then we replace Eq. (1) by Eq. (1'):

$$f_t(i) = \max_x \{xp_t - c(x) + \beta f_{t+1}(i + b_t - x)\} \quad \textbf{(1')}$$

where $0 \le x \le b$.

2b. Let $f_t(d)$ be the maximum utility that can be earned during years $t, t + 1, \ldots, 10$, given that d dollars are available at the beginning of year t (including year t income). During year 10, it makes sense to consume all

available money (after all, there is no future). Thus, $f_{10}(d) = \ln d$. For $t \le 9$,

$$f_t(d) = \max_c \{\ln c + f_{t+1}(1.1(d - c) + i)\}$$

where $0 \le c \le d$. We work backward from the $f_{10}(\cdot)$'s to $f_1(D)$.

5. French, 1 hour; English, no hours; statistics, 3 hours. There is a .711 chance of passing at least one course.

7. Define $f_t(w)$ to be the maximum net profit (revenues less costs) obtained from the steer during weeks $t, t + 1, \ldots, 10$, given that the steer weighs w pounds at the beginning of week t. Now

$$f_{10}(w) = \max_p \{10g(w, p) - c(p)\}$$

where $0 \le p$. Then for $t \le 9$,

$$f_t(w) = \max_p \{-c(p) + f_{t+1}(g(w, p))\}$$

Farmer Jones should work backward until $f_1(w_0)$ has been computed.

8. Define $f_t(i, d)$ to be the maximum number of loyal customers at the end of month 12, given that there are i loyal customers at the beginning of month t and d dollars available to spend on advertising during months $t, t + 1, \ldots, 12$. If there is only one month left, all available funds should be spent during that month. This yields

$$f_{12}(i, d) = (1 - p(d))i + (N - i)q(d)$$

For $t \le 11$,

$$f_t(i, d) = \max_x \{f_{t+1}[(1 - p(x))i + (N - i)q(x), d - x]\}$$

where $0 \le x \le d$. We work backward until $f_1(i_0, D)$ has been determined.

10. Let $f_t(i_t, x_{t-1})$ be the minimum cost incurred during months $t, t + 1, \ldots, 12$, given that inventory at the beginning of month t is i_t and production during month $t - 1$ was x_{t-1}. Then

$$f_{12}(i_{12}, x_{11}) = \min_{x_{12}} \{c_{12}x_{12} + 5|x_{12} - x_{11}| + h_{12}(i_{12} + x_{12} - d_{12})\}$$

where x_{12} must satisfy $x_{12} \ge 0$ and $i + x_{12} \ge d_{12}$. For $t \le 11$,

$$f_t(i_t, x_{t-1}) = \min_{x_t} \{c_t x_t + 5|x_t - x_{t-1}| + h_t(i + x_t - d_t) + f_{t+1}(i_t + x_t - d_t, x_t)\}$$

where x_t must satisfy $x_t \ge 0$ and $i_t + x_t \ge d_t$. We work backward until $f_1(20, 20)$ has been computed.

SECTION 20.7

1. If initial inventory is 200 units, only modification is to produce 200 fewer units during period 1.

2. The Wagner–Whitin and Silver-Meal methods both yield the following production schedule: period 1, 90 units; period 4, 230 units. Total cost is $176.

SECTION 20.8

2. Month 1, 200 radios; month 2, 600 radios; month 3, no radios.

4. Let $f_t(i)$ be the maximum profit earned during years $1, 2, \ldots, t$, given that at the end of year t, i barrels of oil are available. Then

$$f_t(i) = \max\{-c(x) + p_t x + f_{t-1}(i + x - b_t)\}$$
$$\text{s.t.} \quad 0 \le x \quad \text{and} \quad x \ge b_t - i$$

We begin by computing all $f_1(\cdot)$, and we stop when $f_{10}(0)$ has been determined; this assumes that by the end of the problem, all oil will be extracted.

REVIEW PROBLEMS

1. Shortest path from node 1 to node 10 is 1–4–8–10. Shortest path from node 2 to node 10 is 2–5–8–10.

2. Month 2, 1 unit; month 3, 4 units. Total cost is $12.

4. For 6 flights, the airline earns $540 with 3 Miami, 2 L.A. and 1 N.Y. flight; or 3 Miami and 3 L.A. flights. For four flights, the airline earns $375 with 2 Miami and 2 L.A. flights.

5. Without the 20¢ piece, use one 50¢, one 25¢, one 10¢, one 5¢, and one 1¢ piece. With the 20¢ piece, use one 50¢, two 20¢, and one 1¢ piece.

7a. Let $f_t(w)$ be the minimum cost incurred in meeting demands for years $t, t + 1, \ldots, 5$, given that (before hiring and firing for year t) w workers are available.

$$h_t = \text{workers hired at beginning of year } t$$
$$d_t = \text{workers fired at beginning of year } t$$
$$w_t = \text{workers required during year } t$$

Then

$$f_t(w) = \min_{h_t, d_t} \{10{,}000h_t + 20{,}000d_t$$
$$+ 30{,}000(w + h_t - d_t) + f_{t+1}(h_t + .9(w - d_t))\}$$

where h_t and d_t must satisfy $0 \le h_t$, $0 \le d_t \le w$, and $w + h_t - d_t \ge w_t$.

♦ CHAPTER 21

SECTION 21.1

1. Two gallons of milk to each store.

2. $2 million to investment 1, $0 to investment 2, and $2 million to investment 3.

SECTION 21.2

1. Produce 3 units during period 1, no units during period 2, and 1 unit during period 3.

2. At any time, produce the number of units needed to bring the period's stock level (before the period's demand is met) to 2 units.

SECTION 21.3

1. Ulanowsky should play boldly during the first game. If he wins the first game, then he should play conservatively in the second game. If he loses the first game, then he should play boldly in the second game. If there is a tie-breaking game, Ulanowsky should play boldly. His chance of winning the match is .537.

2. On the first toss, Dickie should bet $2. If he loses, he is wiped out, but if he wins, he bets $1 on the second toss. If he wins on the second toss, he stops. If he loses on the second toss, he bets $2 on the third toss.

SECTION 21.4

2. Let $f_t(d)$ be the maximum expected asset position of the firm at the end of year 10, given that at the beginning of year t, the firm has d dollars in assets. Then

$$f_{10}(d) = \max_i \left\{ p \sum_y q_y(d + i + y) + (1 - p) \sum_y q_y(d - i + y) \right\}$$

where $0 \le i \le d$. For $t \le 9$,

$$f_t(d) = \max_i \left\{ p \sum_y q_y f_{t+1}(d + i + y) + (1 - p) \sum_y q_y f_{t+1}(d - i + y) \right\}$$

We work backward until $f_1(10{,}000)$ has been computed.

5. We should always do maintenance on a running machine and always repair a broken-down machine.

6. Let $f_t(p)$ be the maximum expected revenue earned from selling a share of Wivco stock during days t, $t + 1, \ldots, 30$, given that the price of a share at the beginning of day t is p dollars. Then

$$f_{30}(p) = p \quad \text{(Sell stock)}$$

and for $t \leq 29$,

$$f_t(p) = \max \begin{cases} p & \text{(Sell stock)} \\ \sum_x q(x) f_{t+1}((1 + x/100)p) & \text{(Keep stock)} \end{cases}$$

We work backward until $f_1(10)$ has been determined, and we continue until the optimal action is to sell the stock.

7. Sara should not accept the first cat, but any later cat that is the best Sara has seen so far should be accepted. The probability that Sara will get her preferred cat is $\frac{11}{24}$.

8. Define $f_t(i)$ to be the minimum net expected cost incurred during periods $t, t + 1, \ldots, 100$, given that the inventory level is i at the beginning of period t. Then

$$f_{100}(i) = \min_x \left\{ \sum_{d \leq i+x} q_d(i + x - d - rd) + \sum_{d > i+x} q_d(p(d - i - x) - r(i + x)) + c(x) \right\}$$

where $x \geq 0$. For $t \leq 99$,

$$f_t(i) = \min_x \left\{ \sum_{d \leq i+x} q_d(i + x - d - rd) + \sum_{d > i+x} (p(d - i - x) - r(i + x))q_d + c(x) + \sum_{d \leq i+x} q_d f_{t+1}(i + x - d) + \sum_{d > i+x} q_d f_{t+1}(0) \right\}$$

where $x \geq 0$. We work backward until $f_1(0)$ has been determined.

10. Define $f_t(d)$ to be the maximum expected number of units sold in markets $t, t + 1, \ldots, T$, given that d dollars are available to spend on these markets. Then

$$f_T(d) = c_T k_T p_T(d)$$

and for $t \leq T - 1$,

$$f_t(d) = \max_x \{c_t k_t p_t(x) + f_{t+1}(d - x)\}$$

where $0 \leq x \leq d$. We work backward until $f_1(D)$ has been computed.

SECTION 21.5

1a.

PERIOD'S BEGINNING INVENTORY	PERIOD'S PRODUCTION LEVEL
0	4
1	3
2	0
3	0

2a. Always charge 11% interest rate on loans.

REVIEW PROBLEMS

1. Assign 2 sales reps to district 1, 1 sales rep to district 2, and 2 sales reps to district 3.

2a. Produce 2 units during period 1. During period 2, produce 1 or 2 units if beginning inventory is zero; if beginning inventory for period 2 is 1 or 2 units, produce no units during period 2. During period 3, produce 1 unit if beginning inventory is zero; otherwise, produce no units during period 3.

4. Let $f_t(b)$ be the maximum discounted net benefit earned during years $t, t + 1, \ldots, 2025$, given that b barrels of oil are available at the beginning of year t. Then

$$f_t(b) = \max_{d,x} \{u(x) - d + \beta p(d) f_{t+1}(b - x + 500,000) + \beta(1 - p(d)) f_{t+1}(b - x)\}$$

where $0 \leq d$ and $0 \leq x \leq b$. We work backward until $f_{1990}(B)$ is determined and then compute the optimal consumption strategy.

5a. Try to answer the first two questions and then stop. The expected amount of money won is $9000.

◆ CHAPTER 22

SECTION 22.2

1. $\dfrac{6}{7}$.

2. $\dfrac{555}{11}$ minutes.

4a. $\dfrac{2e^{-2}}{3} = .09$.

b. $1 - e^{-2} - 2e^{-2} = .594$.

SECTION 22.3

2b. $\dfrac{121}{144}$.

c. $\dfrac{1}{144}$.

SECTION 22.4

1a. $\frac{5}{6}$.

b. $\frac{25}{6}$ passengers.

c. $\frac{1}{2}$ minute.

3a. Unchanged.

b. Cut in half.

c. Unchanged.

4. Two checkpoints.

6b. 1 taxi.

c. $120 per hour.

SECTION 22.5

1a. 1.75 customers per hour.

b. $\frac{114}{130}$.

5. Barber 1's average hourly revenue = $53.23. Barber 2's average hourly revenue = $40.00.

SECTION 22.6

1. Two registers.

3a. Finance, $\frac{1}{5}$ day; Marketing, $\frac{1}{10}$ day.

b. 0.078 day.

d. .07.

4. 4 servers.

7. $\frac{3}{4}$ mechanic.

8. System 1 is more efficient.

SECTION 22.7

1. 5200 members.

3. 200 firms. The probability that there are at least 300 firms is zero.

SECTION 22.8

1. $\frac{2}{3}$ car.

3a. $\frac{5}{6}$ customer.

b. 9 minutes.

c. $\frac{1}{3}$.

SECTION 22.9

1. Superworker is better.

2a. $\frac{81}{125}$.

b. $\frac{6}{5}$ puppies.

SECTION 22.10

2a. 2.73 cars.

b. 0.06 hour.

4. $\frac{11}{3}$ students.

SECTION 22.11

1. 15 fire engines.

4b. 2 copies.

SECTION 22.12

1. Using four categories (each having $e_i = 6$), we accept the hypothesis that the length of a telephone call is exponential with mean $\frac{1024}{24}$ seconds.

SECTION 22.13

1a. $M/E_4/1$ system with arrival rate of $\frac{2}{3}$ customer per minute and mean service time of 1 minute.

c. Add up the steady state probabilities $\pi_0 + \pi_1 + \pi_2$ (use a table with $\rho = \frac{2}{3}$).

SECTION 22.14

1. Tests spend an average of $\frac{19}{8}$ hours in the system, research papers spend an average of $\frac{27}{4}$ hours in the system, and class handouts spend an average of $\frac{23}{2}$ hours in the system.

2. Highest priority to $k = 1$ customers, next highest priority to $k = 2$ customers, etc.

REVIEW PROBLEMS

2a. 8 minutes.

b. $\dfrac{(1.25)^2 e^{-1.25}}{2!} = .22$.

c. $e^{-0.75} = .47$.

3a. 3 windows.

b. 3 windows.

6. 2 copiers.

7a. $\frac{2}{3}$ car.

b. 8.2 minutes.

8. Rent the vacant lot. Then expected daily lost profit is $21(20)(0.008) = \$3.36$.

9. $\frac{1}{2}$ hour.

11. Have one crew of 100 workers.

14a. Both lines are free $\frac{8}{13}$ of time, one line is free $\frac{4}{13}$ of the time, and both lines are busy $\frac{1}{13}$ of the time.

b. $\frac{6}{13}$ line.

c. $30(\frac{1}{13}) = \frac{30}{13}$ callers per hour.

◆ CHAPTER 23

SECTION 23.4

1. Approximately 0.76 minute. The answer may vary according to the random numbers used in the computations.

3. See Figure 14. Variables used in the model:

VALUE = face value from the roll of the dice

WINS = total number of wins up to current simulation

LOSSES = total number of losses up to current simulation

POINT = face value from the first roll

PWON = proportion of wins

SECTION 23.5

1. ITM: Generate a random number r.

If $(r \leq 0.5)$ then

$x = 2r$

else

$x = 3 - 2\sqrt{2 - 2r}$

endif

ARM: Generate two random numbers, r_1 and r_2.

Set $x^* = 3r_1$

If $(x^* \leq 1)$ then

Accept x^* as the random variate

else

If $(r_2 \leq \frac{3}{2}(1 - r_1))$ then

Accept x^* as the random variate

else

Reject x^* and repeat the process

endif

endif

2. Generate a random number r.

If $(r \leq 0.25)$ then

$x = 2 + 4\sqrt{r}$

else

$x = 10 - 4\sqrt{3 - 3r}$

endif

4.

	$E(x)$	var x
After 250 variates	5.274	2.823
After 500 variates	5.318	2.755
After 1000 variates	5.364	2.856
After 5000 variates	5.344	2.887
Theoretical values	5.333	2.889

REVIEW PROBLEMS

1. 0.70, 0.33, 0.04, 0.11, 0.30, 0.53, 0.44, 0.91, 0.90, 0.73.

3. See Figure 15. Variables used in the model:

DAY = current day in the simulation

EXC = total number of days with net demand greater than 100

NRES = number of rooms reserved for the current day in simulation

NNSH = number of no-shows for the current day in simulation

NUSD = number of rooms used on the current day in simulation

PERCENT = percentage of days when net demand exceeded 100

Figure 14

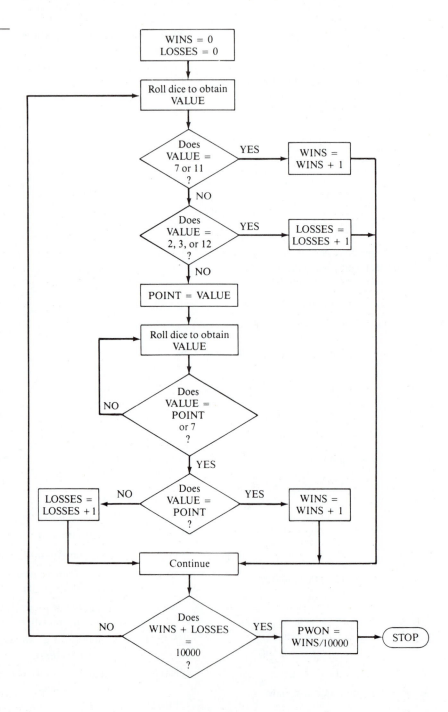

Figure 15

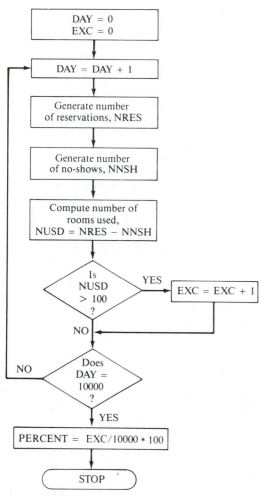

Figure 16

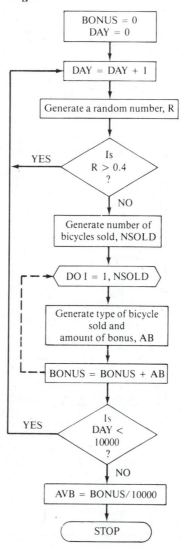

5. See Figure 16. Variables used in the model:

DAY = current day in simulation

BONUS = total amount of bonus up to current day

NSOLD = number of bicycles sold on current day

AB = amount of bonus for a bicycle

AVB = average bonus per day

9. See Figure 17. Variables used in the model:

TIME = clock time of simulation

MAX = length of simulation in time units

AT = clock time of next arrival

DT(NEXT) = clock time of next departure from system

NRENG = total number of customers who have reneged up to current simulated time

Figure 17

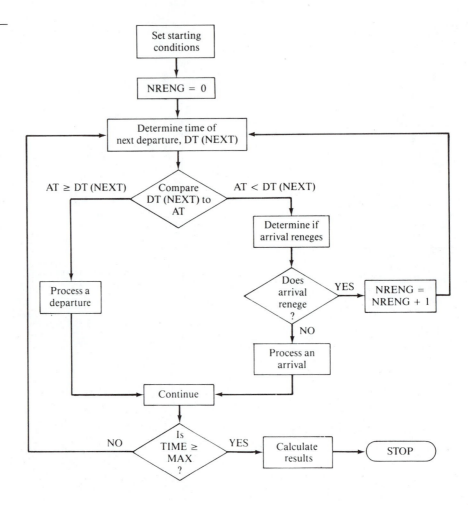

◆ CHAPTER 24

SECTION 24.4

1a. 4000 cases.

b. 3980 cases.

2a. New base = 452; new trend = 43.6; new summer seasonality = 1.37.

b. Forecast for winter quarter = 377.44.

4. 95% sure that December sales will be between 172.5 and 297.5.

12a. 106.

b. 115.26.

SECTION 24.5

1. For each professor's payday, compute

$$\frac{\text{Actual customers}}{\text{Forecasted customers}}$$

Average these ratios. Suppose we obtain 1.3. Then to obtain forecast for a day on which professors are paid, compute a forecast by our basic method and multiply this forecast by 1.3.

SECTION 24.8

1a. Estimate beta $= 0.88$.

b. Yes.

c. 45%.

e. 16.1%

3a. $\widehat{\text{SALES}} = 52{,}900 + 912.5T - 9859Q_1 - 8467Q_2 + 20{,}129Q_4$, where $T =$ quarter number and $Q_i =$ dummy variable for quarter i.

d. The part (b) model has smaller standard error than the part (a) model. Thus, the part (b) model will yield a better forecast.

4. $\widehat{\text{SALES}} = e^{6.98}\text{PRICE}^{-0.67}$.

5b. Indicates positive autocorrelation.

Index